The Heads of Religious Houses
England and Wales
1216–1377

This book is the long-awaited continuation of *The Heads of Religious Houses: England and Wales 940–1216*, edited by David Knowles, C. N. L. Brooke, and Vera London, which itself is now reissued with substantial addenda by Professor Brooke.

This present volume continues the lists from 1216 to 1377. In this period further record sources have been provided by episcopal registers, governmental enrolments, court records, and so on. Full references are given for establishing the dates and outline of the career of each abbot or prior, abbess or prioress, when known, although the information varies considerably from the richly documented lists of the great Benedictine houses to the small cells where perhaps only a single name or date may be recorded in a chance archival survival.

The lists are arranged by order: the Benedictine houses (independent, dependencies, and alien priories); the Cluniacs; the Grandmontines; the Cistercians; the Carthusians; the Augustinian canons; the Premonstratensians; the Gilbertine order; the Trinitarian houses; the Bonhommes; and the nuns. An introduction discusses the nature, use, and history of the lists and examines critically the sources on which they are based.

DAVID M. SMITH is Professor and Director of the Borthwick Institute of Historical Research, University of York.

VERA C. M. LONDON is co-editor, with David Knowles and Christopher Brooke, of *The Heads of Religious Houses: England and Wales 940–1216* (1972).

THE
HEADS OF RELIGIOUS HOUSES
ENGLAND AND WALES
II
1216–1377

Edited by

PROFESSOR DAVID M. SMITH
Director, Borthwick Institute, University of York

VERA C. M. LONDON

CAMBRIDGE
UNIVERSITY PRESS

CAMBRIDGE UNIVERSITY PRESS
Cambridge, New York, Melbourne, Madrid, Cape Town, Singapore, São Paulo

Cambridge University Press
The Edinburgh Building, Cambridge CB2 2RU, UK

Published in the United States of America by Cambridge University Press, New York

www.cambridge.org
Information on this title: www.cambridge.org/9780521802710

First published 2001
This digitally printed first paperback version 2006

A catalogue record for this publication is available from the British Library

Library of Congress Cataloguing in Publication data

The heads of religious houses: England and Wales, 1216–1377 / edited by David M.
Smith and Vera C. M. London.
p. cm.
Includes bibliographical references and indexes.
ISBN 0 521 80271 7 (hardback)
1. Monasticism and religious orders – England – History – Middle Ages,
600–1500 – Sources. 2. Superiors, Religious – England – Registers. 3. Monasticism and
religious orders – Wales – History – Middle Ages, 600–1500 – Sources. 4. Superiors,
Religious – Wales – Registers. I. Smith, David M. (David Michael) II. London, Vera C. M.

BX2592.H43 ·2001
271′.00942 – dc21 00–050240

ISBN-13 978-0-521-80271-0 hardback
ISBN-10 0-521-80271-7 hardback

ISBN-13 978-0-521-02848-6 paperback
ISBN-10 0-521-02848-5 paperback

CONTENTS

Preface		*page* vii
Manuscript sources cited		ix
Printed books and articles cited, with abbreviated references		xix
Other abbreviations		lxv

INTRODUCTION

I	*The purpose and scope*		1
II	*The materials*		1
III	*The arrangement of the lists*		9

HEADS OF RELIGIOUS HOUSES: ENGLAND AND WALES 1216–1377

THE BENEDICTINE HOUSES	15
INDEPENDENT HOUSES	15
DEPENDENCIES	89
ALIEN PRIORIES	138
THE CLUNIAC HOUSES	219
THE GRANDMONTINE HOUSES	255
THE CISTERCIAN HOUSES	258
THE CARTHUSIAN MONKS	325
THE AUGUSTINIAN CANONS	327
THE PREMONSTRATENSIAN CANONS	491
THE GILBERTINE CANONS AND NUNS	519
THE TRINITARIAN HOUSES	532
MONASTERIES OF BONHOMMES	535
UNIDENTIFIED ORDER AND UNCERTAIN STATUS	536
THE NUNS	537

Index of heads	627
Index of religious houses	722

PREFACE

As the authors of the first volume wrote of it in 1972, this book has been long in the making. Soon after the publication of the 940–1216 volume, Miss Vera London went on to make notes from printed sources for a second volume continuing the lists up to 1377. This work progressed slowly but surely, when periodic access to Cambridge University Library allowed, on her regular visits from Shropshire. In 1985, following discussions with Professor Christopher Brooke, I became involved in the project with the prime responsibility for checking through the manuscript sources. The activity has continued from then until the present time. With such collecting work there is always the temptation not to finish – there is always just another cache of documents to check, just another plea roll to consult – but it is in the nature of such fasti lists that they can never attain to anything approaching completeness. To search systematically through the hundreds of unpublished plea rolls for the period is beyond one individual's efforts and one can only aim to improve on existing lists and provide a good basis for lists not produced before. That we have achieved such a limited aim is in no small part due to the unstinting help generously given by friends and colleagues over these fifteen years. Chief among them is Professor Christopher Brooke, who has meticulously checked and commented upon all our drafts, urged us on when the task seemed endless, and has always been ready to scour Cambridge libraries and archives and further afield 'in the cause'. That the volume is now ready for publication is largely due to his continued interest and encouragement. Many others have given generous help. Some have let us have access to their notes on archives, editions and research projects before publication; others have always been on the look-out for new finds in our 'head-hunting', or have volunteered to check collections. To all of them we express our profound thanks for their generosity and kindness. Particular attention must be drawn to the great help received from the following (in alphabetical sequence): Dr John Alban, Miss Cressida Annesley, Mr Michael Ashcroft, Miss Melanie Barber, Mr Bernard Barr, Dr Julia Barrow, Dr Nicholas Bennett, Miss S. J. Berry, Dr Claire Breay, Dr Martin Brett, Mr Tim Bridges, Dr Janet Burton, Mrs Christine Butterill, Mr Trevor Chalmers, M. Robert Chanaud, the late Professor Christopher Cheney, Mrs Mary Cheney, Mr W. J. Connor, Fr Richard Copsey, Dr David Crook, Dr Christopher de Hamel, Professor Barrie Dobson, Dr Gwilym Dodd, Dr Robert Dunning, Dr Charles Fonge, Dr Trevor Foulds, Mrs Margaret Goodrich, Professor Joan Greatrex, Professor Diana Greenway, Miss Ruth Harman, Professor

Christopher Harper-Bill, Dr Kate Harris, Mr Julian Harrison, Miss Barbara Harvey, Dr Rosemary Hayes, Dr Roger Highfield, the late Professor Rosalind Hill, Mr Steven Hobbs, Professor Christopher Holdsworth, Dr Philippa Hoskin, Dr Richard Huscroft, Professor Dominique Iogna-Prat, Mr Hugh Jaques, Dr David Johnson, Mr Nicholas Karn, Professor Brian Kemp, Dr Berenice Kerr, Dr Christian Liddy, Mrs Lisa Liddy, Professor Donald Logan, Dr Catherine Macdonald, Dr Peter Mackie, Miss Alison Maddock, Dr Alison McHardy, Miss Mary McKenzie, Dr Philip Morgan, Dr Richard Mortimer, Mr John Nightingale, Dr Pamela Nightingale, Fr Robert Ombres, Professor Nicholas Orme, Mr Arthur Owen, Dr Dorothy Owen, Dr Oliver Padel, Miss Christine Penney, Mr Alan Piper, Dr Huw Pryce, Dr Nigel Ramsay, Mrs Una Rees, Dr Michael Robson, Dr Michael Rogers, Mr Nicholas Rogers, Professor Richard Sharpe, Miss Eileen Simpson, Mr Brian Smith, Dr Michael Stansfield, Professor Philip Stell, Mr James Stevenson, Professor Robin Storey, Mr Malcolm Underwood, Professor Nicholas Vincent, Mr Robin Whittaker, Mr Christopher Whittick, Mr J. S. Williams, Dr Chris Woolgar, Mr Geoffrey Yeo. If I have unintentionally omitted anyone (and the memory grows dim after fifteen years!) I can only apologise. Particular thanks must go to the British Academy and the Wolfson Foundation for grants to assist the searching of the feet of fines undertaken on our behalf by Mr Trevor Chalmers, and for travel expenses. Our thanks also go to the many archivists and librarians who have given unstinting help and advice over the years and have alerted us to more obscure archives and collections that might otherwise have been missed. Finally, special tribute must be paid to Vera London, who embarked on this second volume alone in the early 1970s, and who now at ninety-six has happily lived to see it completed.

DMS
April 2000

MANUSCRIPT SOURCES CITED

Aberystwyth, National Library of Wales:
  Badminton archives
Alençon, Archives départementales de l'Orne: H.928, 930
Alnwick, Duke of Northumberland's archives:
  Ctl. Tynemouth
Althorp, Spencer muniments (NRA list)
Angers, Archives départementales de Maine et Loire:
  243 H1
  244 H1
  246 H2
Aylesbury, Buckinghamshire Records and Local Studies Service: D42/B1/2
Baildon's ms. notes: *see* Leeds, Yorkshire Archaeological Society
Belvoir Castle: ms. 71
Birmingham City Library and Archives, Central Library: Hampton archives
Bodleian Library, *see under* Oxford
Borthwick Institute, *see under* York
Bristol Record Office:
  5139(77)
  P/StJ/D/1/4
British Library, *see under* London
Buckinghamshire Records and Local Studies Service, *see* Aylesbury
Burghley House, Stamford: Exeter mss.
Bury St Edmunds branch, Suffolk Record Office:
  449/2/688 Hengrave estate records
Cambridge:
  Christ's College muniments
  Corpus Christi College mss. 59, 281
  Emmanuel College muniments
  Fitzwilliam Museum: McLean ms. 45
  Jesus College muniments
  King's College muniments
  St John's College muniments
  Trinity College muniments
    mss.: o. 9. 25
Cambridge University Library:
  Add. mss. 2950, 2957, 3020–1, 3824, 4020
  EDC. 1A/3
  EDR. G3/28; 5/4/19; 7/7/2; *and see under* Ely, Registers of the Bishops of
  mss. Bb. 8. 92; Dd. 3. 87(20); Dd. 8.2; Ee. 5. 31; Gg. 3. 21; Gg. 3. 28; Kk. 1. 22; Mm. 2. 20
  Peterborough cathedral manuscripts: mss. 1, 5
Canterbury Cathedral Archives:
  Ch. Ant.: Chartae Antiquae series
  Eastry correspondence
  Registers A, E, G

SVSB: Sede Vacante Scrapbooks
   mss.: Litt. D. 4, D. 12
Carlisle, DRC/1/2 Reg. Appleby register of Bishop Thomas Appleby (1363–95) (at Cumbria
   Record Office, Carlisle)
Chatsworth, Duke of Devonshire's archives
Chester, Cheshire Record Office (incorporating the Chester City Archives):

CHB.2	Chester Pentice ctl.
DCH.	Cholmondeley archives: Ctl. Scrope of Bolton DCH/X/15/1
DCR.	Crewe archives
DLT.	Leicester-Warren archives
MR.	

Cobham mss.
Cornwall Record Office, *see* Truro
Coughton Court, Throckmorton muniments
Ctl. Beauchief, *see* Sheffield Archives
Ctl. Flamstead, *see* Hertford, Hertfordshire Archives and Local Studies
Ctl. Marham, *see* Norwich, Norfolk Record Office
Ctl. Newhouse, *see* Lincoln, Lincolnshire Archives Office
Ctl. Scrope of Bolton, *see* Chester, Cheshire Record Office
Ctl. Tynemouth, *see* Alnwick
Denbighshire Record Office, *see* Ruthin
Devon Record Office, *see* Exeter
Dublin, Trinity College Library:
   ms. 516
   ms. 524
Durham, Archives and Special Collections (Dean and Chapter archives, 5 The College)
   Reg. Hatfield (register of Bishop Thomas Hatfield (1345–81)
   DCD (Dean and Chapter archives):
      Accounts: Bursar's; Cellarer's; Farne; Holy Island; Jarrow; Lytham; Norham; Wearmouth;
         Westoe
      Cartularies (Cart.)
      Charters: series Archd. Dun.; Archiep.; Ebor.; Finc. Loc.; Pont.; Spec.
      Miscellaneous Charters (Misc. Cht.)
      Registers (Reg.)
      Status: Holy Island; Jarrow; Lytham
Durham Cathedral Library: ms. B. II. 1
East Sussex Record Office, *see* Lewes
Eaton Hall, Cheshire (Duke of Westminster): charters
Elveden Hall, Suffolk, Lord Iveagh's archives
Ely, Registers of the Bishops of (in Cambridge University Library):
   G/1/2 registers of Bishops Simon Montacute (1337–45) and Thomas de Lisle (1345–61)
   G/1/2 register of Bishop Thomas Arundel (1374–88)
   G/1/3 register of Bishop John Fordham (1388–1425)
Essex Record Office, Chelmsford:
   T/B.3 Tilty abbey register
Eton College records (ECR):
   charters
   Ctl. Modbury

Evreux, Arch. dép. de l'Eure:
    H1453 Wootton Wawen ctl.
Exeter, Devon Record Office:
    Exeter city records (ED)
    Hole of Parke archives (312M)
    Magee catalogue no. 416
    Petre archives (123M)
    Tavistock archives (W1258M)
    TD.42 Ctl. Otterton
Exeter Cathedral, Dean and Chapter archives:
    Vicars' choral records
Glasgow University Library:
    Hunterian ms. U2.6
Gloucester Cathedral, Dean and Chapter archives:
    Registers A and B
    Seals and Documents series
Guildhall Library, *see under* London
Hampshire Record Office, *see under* Winchester
Hereford Cathedral, Dean and Chapter muniments
Hertford, Hertfordshire Archives and Local Studies:
    Ctl. Flamstead – ms. 17465
    Panshanger papers
    Potternewton deeds
Holkham, Coke muniments
Hull, University Archives:
    DDCA (Carlton Towers)
    DDEV (Constable of Everingham archives)
Ipswich branch, Suffolk Record Office
    HA3
    HD226
    HD533
    HD1538 (Phillipps Suffolk collection)
Isle of Wight County Record Office, *see* Newport
Lambeth (Lambeth Palace Library, London)
    Chartae Antiquae (Ch. Ant.)
    mss. 20; 241; 368; 585; 1106; 1212

Reg. Arundel I–II	registers of Archbishop Thomas Arundel of Canterbury (1396–7; 1399–1414)
Reg. Courtenay	register of Archbishop William Courtenay of Canterbury (1381–96)
Reg. Islip	register of Archbishop Simon Islip of Canterbury (1349–66)
Reg. Reynolds	register of Archbishop Walter Reynolds of Canterbury (1313–27)
Reg. Sudbury	register of Archbishop Simon Sudbury of Canterbury (1375–81)
Reg. Wareham	register of Archbishop William Wareham of Canterbury (1503–32)
Reg. Whittlesey	register of Archbishop William Whittlesey of Canterbury (1368–74)

Lancashire Record Office, *see* Preston

Leeds, West Yorkshire Archives:
 Newby Hall archives (NH)
 Nostell archives (NP)
 Stansfield archives (ST)
Leeds, Yorkshire Archaeological Society:
 Baildon's mss. notes
 Grantley mss.
Lennoxlove, Duke of Hamilton's archives: bundle 3020
Lewes, East Sussex Record Office:
 Hastings charters (T466)
Lichfield, Registers of the Bishops of (at Lichfield Record Office):
 B/A/1/1   register of Bishop Walter Langton (1296–1321)
 B/A/1/2–3   registers of Bishop Roger Northburgh (1322–58)
 B/A/1/6   register of Bishops Walter Skirlaw (1386) and Richard Scrope (1386–98)
 B/A/1/7   register of Bishop John Burghill (1398–1414)
Limoges, Archives départementales de la Haute Vienne:
 5HH25/16
Lincoln, Lincolnshire Archives Office:
 Archives of the Earl of Ancaster (Anc)
 Lincoln Dean and Chapter archives (Dij)
 Archives of the Earl of Yarborough: Ctl. Newhouse (Yarb.3/3/1/1)
Lincoln, Registers of the Bishops of (at Lincolnshire Archives Office):
 Ep. Reg. II–III   registers of Bishop John Dalderby (1300–20)
 Ep. Reg. IV–V   registers of Bishop Henry Burghersh (1320–40)
 Ep. Reg. VI–VII, VIIB   registers of Bishop Thomas Bek (1342–7)
 Ep. Reg. VIII–IX, IXC   registers of Bishop John Gynwell (1347–62)
 Ep. Reg. X–XII   registers of Bishop John Buckingham (1363–98)
 Ep. Reg. XIII   register of Bishop Henry Beaufort (1398–1404)
 Ep. Reg. XIV   register of Bishop Philip Repingdon (1405–19)
London, British Library, Manuscripts Collections:
 Add. Chts.:   Additional Charters series
 Add. mss.:   4535, 4934, 4936, 5819, 5823, 5827, 5829, 5843, 6041, 6060, 6118, 6159,
                6160, 6165, 6275, 6343, 6671, 8157, 8172, 9822, 10013, 15668, 18641, 19082,
                19090, 19096, 19111, 25288, 26736, 28550, 29436, 33381, 34560, 35295,
                35296, 36872, 37503, 37640, 38816, 39977, 41612, 43972, 46353, 47677,
                47784, 70506
 Arundel mss: 2, 17, 68
 Campbell Chts.: Campbell Charters series
 Cotton Chts.: Cotton Charters series
 Cotton mss.:   Caligula A VIII, Caligula A XII, Caligula A XIII, Claudius B III, Claudius
                D III, Claudius D VIII, Claudius D XI, Claudius D XIII, Claudius E IV,
                Cleopatra C III, Cleopatra C VII, Cleopatra D III, Domitian A III,
                Domitian A XI, Domitian A XIV, Faustina A IV, Faustina A VI, Faustina
                A VIII, Faustina B I, Faustina B VI, Faustina C I, Faustina C V, Galba E II,
                Galba E IV, Julius A I, Julius D V, Julius D X, Nero A XII, Nero C IX, Nero
                D III, Nero D VII, Nero D VIII, Nero E VI, Otho B XIV, Tiberius A X,
                Tiberius B II, Tiberius C IX, Tiberius D VI, Tiberius E V, Tiberius E VI,
                Titus A I, Titus C VIII, Titus D XX, Titus F III, Vespasian A V, Vespasian
                A VI, Vespasian A IX, Vespasian A XXII, Vespasian B XI, Vespasian C XV,

Vespasian E XVIII, Vespasian E XIX, Vespasian E XX, Vespasian E XXII, Vespasian E XXIII, Vitellius A I, Vitellius D IX, Vitellius E XVI, Vitellius F XVII

Cotton Rolls series

Egerton Chts.: Egerton Charters series

Egerton mss.: 2104A, 2823, 2827, 2849, 3033, 3047, 3088, 3137, 3140, 3316

Harl. Chts.: Harley Charters series

Harl. mss.: Harley mss. 61, 112, 280, 391, 544, 639, 662, 797, 838, 1761, 1804, 2063, 2071, 2072, 2101, 2110, 2162, 2272, 3586, 3640, 3658, 3697, 3725, 3776, 3868, 3897, 3950, 4015, 4664, 4714, 6203, 6959, 6972, 6974, 7568

Harl. Rolls: Harley Rolls series

Lansdowne Chts.: Lansdowne Charters series

Lansdowne mss.: 207A, 207B, 207C, 326, 375, 402, 415, 436, 860A

Royal mss.: 8 C VII, 12 E XIV

Sloane Chts.: Sloane Charters series

Stowe Chts.: Stowe Charters series

Stowe mss.: 882, 935, 937, 1083

Topham Chts.: Topham Charters series

Woolley Chts.: Woolley Charters series

London, College of Arms: mss. 5, 6, 8, 15, 65, 113/3

London, Guildhall Library:

Dean and Chapter of St Paul's archives

Diocesan records (*see also* London, Registers of the Bishops)

ms. 9171/1

London, Lambeth, *see under* Lambeth

London Metropolitan Archives

Acc. 76 court rolls of Harrow

London, Public Record Office, Kew:

Chancery records: C47; C67; C81; C84; C85; C106; C115; C143; C146; C202; C241; C260; C269; C270; C279

Chester Palatinate records: Ches. 29

Common Pleas records: CP25; CP40

Duchy of Lancaster records: DL25; DL27; DL34; DL36; DL41; DL42

Exchequer records: E36; E40; E41; E42; E43; E101; E106; E135; E159; E164; E179; E210; E211; E212; E213; E315; E326; E328; E329; E371; E372; E401; LR14

Justices Itinerant, Assize and gaol Delivery records: Just.1

King's Bench records: KB27

PRO Collections of Transcripts: PRO31

Principality of Wales records: Wales 29

Special Collections: SC1; SC2; SC6; SC8; SC10; SC11/75

Wards and Liveries records: Wards 2

London, Registers of the Bishops of (at Guildhall Library):

Reg. Braybrooke ms. 9531/3 register of Bishop Braybrooke (1382–1404)

Reg. Gilbert ms. 9531/6 register of Bishop Gilbert (1436–48)

Reg. Stokesley ms. 9531/11 register of Bishop Stokesley (1530–9)

London, Society of Antiquaries:

mss. 38, 60

Longleat, muniments of the Marquess of Bath

Maidstone, Centre for Kentish Studies
   DRc/BZ1
   see also Rochester, Registers of the Bishops
Manchester, John Rylands University Library:
   Arley charters
   Latin ms. 215
Newport, Isle of Wight County Record Office:
   St Helen's charters (STH)
Norfolk Record Office, *see* Norwich
Northallerton, North Yorkshire County Record Office:
   Bellerby charters (ZDX)
   Ingleby Arncliffe deeds (ZFL)
   Clervaux ctl. (ZQH)
   ZRL.3/77
Norwich, Norfolk Record Office:
   Consistory Court probate registers (Heydon)
   Dean and Chapter of Norwich Cathedral archives (DCN)
   Priory registers (Reg.)
   DCN. charters
   Diocesan records: DN/SUN.8; *and see* Norwich, Registers of the Bishops of
   Blickling/Lothian records
   Flitcham estate records
   Hare archives: incl. 1/232X Ctl. Marham
   Holkham misc. deeds
   ms. Fel. 30
   ms. 3794
   ms. 3812
   ms. 21509/60
   NRS. 18199
   NRS. 24077
   NRS. 27204
   Phillipps ms. (Phi)
   Tanner, Norwich mss.
Norwich, Registers of the Bishops of (at Norfolk Record Office):
   Reg/1/1   register of Bishop John Salmon (1299–1325)
   Reg/1/2   registers of Bishop-elect Baldock and Bishop Walter Ayremine (1325–36)
   Reg/1/3   register of Bishop Antony Bek (1337–43)
   Reg/2/4   register of Bishop William Bateman (1344–55)
   Reg/2/5   register of Bishop Thomas Percy (1356–69)
   Reg/3/6   register of Bishop Henry Dispenser (1370–1406)
   Reg/3/7   registers of Bishops Alexander Tottington (1407–13) and Richard
                Courtenay (1413–15)
Nottingham, University Library, Department of Manuscripts:
   Clifton of Clifton Hall archives (Cl.)
   Middleton mss. (Mi)
Oxford, All Souls College:
   college charters
Oxford, Balliol College:
   ms. 35a
   ms. 271

Oxford, Bodleian Library:
    Ashmole mss.:   794, 801
    Berks Chts.:   Berkshire Charters series
    Bodl. ms.:   242
    Digby mss.:   20, 81, 227
    Dodsworth mss.: 7, 63, 74, 75, 76, 90, 91, 94, 95, 107, 135, 144
    Douce Chts.:   Douce Charters series
    Douce ms.:   136
    Essex Chts.:   Essex Charters series
    Essex Rolls: Essex Rolls series
    Fairfax mss.:   7, 9
    Gough mss.:   Essex 1, Kent 18, Norfolk 18
    Jesus Coll. ms.:   131
    Kent Chts.:   Kent Charters series
    Kent Rolls: Kent Rolls series
    Lat. Liturg. ms.: e 6
    Laud misc. mss.: 625, 642
    Norfolk Chts.:   Norfolk Charters series
    Norfolk Rolls: Norfolk Rolls series
    Oxford Chts.:   Oxford Charters series
    Phillipps Robinson ms.: e 77
    Rawlinson mss.: B.177, B.329, B.336, B.444, B.461, D.318
    Shropshire Rolls: Shropshire Rolls series
    Staffs Chts.:   Staffordshire Charters series
    Suffolk Chts.:   Suffolk Charters series
    Sussex Chts.:   Sussex Charters series
    Tanner mss.:   166, 342, 425
    ms. Top.:   Topographical mss. Devon d 5, Glos. c 5, Lincs d 1, Northants c 5, Yorks c
    72, Yorks d 2, Yorks e 7, Yorks e 8, Yorks e 9
    Wood ms.:   D. 18
Oxford, Brasenose College:
    college deeds
Oxford, Magdalen College:
    college charters
    ms. 53
Oxford, Merton College muniments
Oxford, New College muniments
    college charters
    Liber Niger
    Registrum Secundum
Oxford, Oriel College: charters
Oxford, Queen's College: charters
Paris, Bibliothèque Nationale: ms. Lat. 13905
Preston, Lancashire Record Office:
    DDTO Lord O'Hagan's archives (Towneley)
Public Record Office, *see under* London
Rochester, Registers of the Bishops (at Maidstone, Centre for Kentish Studies)
    Drb/Ar.
    Reg. Sheppey   register of Bishop John Sheppey (1353–60)

Reg. Trillek   register of Bishop Thomas Trillek (1364–72)

Reg. Whittlesey   register of Bishop William Whittlesey (1362–4)

Rome, Vatican Library, Barberini ms. xliii

Romsey parish church: Winchester psalter

Ruthin, Denbighshire Record Office: DD/WY/1591

S.Omer, public library: ms. 746, part II

Salisbury, Registers of the Bishops of (at Wiltshire and Swindon Record Office, Trowbridge)

     Reg. Erghum   register of Bishop Ralph Erghum (1375–88)

     Reg. Mitford   register of Bishop Richard Mitford (1395–1407)

     Reg. Neville   register of Bishop Robert Neville (1427–38)

     Reg. Wyvill I–II   registers of Bishop Robert Wyvill (1330–75)

Salisbury Cathedral, dean and chapter archives

San Marino, California, Henry Huntington Library:

     Battle Abbey mss. (HEH/BA)

Sheffield Archives:

     Beauchief ctl. (MD.3414)

     Wentworth Woodhouse muniments

Shrewsbury, Shropshire Records and Research Centre: mss.

     20

     327

     356

     972

     1514

     3365

     6000

Somerset Archive and Record Service, *see* Taunton

Southampton University Library: ms. 28/9

Southwell Minster: ms. 1

Stafford, Staffordshire Record Office:

     Acc. 938

     B/1/20/1/5

     D593

     D798

     D(W)1721

     D1790

     D3764

Stratford, Shakespeare Birthplace Trust:

     DR18

Suffolk Record Office, *see under* Bury St Edmunds; Ipswich

Surrey History Centre, *see* Woking

Taunton, Somerset Archive and Record Service

     Ctl. Hungerford

     DD/LP/37

     DD/L/P

     Reg. Droxford   register of Bishop John Droxford (1309–29)

Trowbridge, Wiltshire and Swindon Record Office:

     Acc. 192/54

     Ailesbury (Brudenell-Bruce) archives (9/15)

     1332

     see also Salisbury, Registers of the Bishops of

Truro, Cornwall Record Office:
    Arundell of Wardour archives
West Yorkshire Archives, *see* Leeds
Westminster Abbey muniments:
    charters (mun. + number)
    Domesday (mun. bk. 11)
Wiltshire and Swindon Record Office, *see* Trowbridge
Winchester, Hampshire Record Office:
    5M53 Wriothesley deeds
    13M/63/2
    46M48/109
    M69/C257
Winchester, Registers of the Bishops of (at Hampshire Record Office)

Reg. Beaufort	register of Bishop Henry Beaufort (1405–47)
Reg. Orleton I–II	registers of Bishop Adam Orleton (1333–45)
Reg. Stratford	register of Bishop John Stratford (1323–33)
Reg. Wykeham	register of Bishop William Wykeham (1367–1404)

Winchester Cathedral Library:
    Allchin Scrapbook
    Ellingham Priory transcripts
Winchester College muniments
Windsor, Dean and Chapter of St George's Chapel:
    Arundel White Book
    I.C. 1–4
Woking, Surrey History Centre
    Loseley mss.
Worcester, Registers of the Bishops of (at Worcestershire Record Office, City Centre branch, St Helen's):

Reg. Barnet	register of Bishop John Barnet (1362–3)
Reg. Brian I	register of Bishop Reginald Brian (1353–61)
Reg. Lenn	register of Bishop William Lenn (1369–73)
Reg. Maidstone	register of Bishop Walter Maidstone (1313–17)
Reg. Morgan	register of Bishop Philip Morgan (1419–26)
Reg. Poulton	register of Bishop Thomas Poulton (1426–33)
Reg. Thoresby	register of Bishop John Thoresby (1350–2)
Reg. Whittlesey	register of Bishop William Whittlesey (1364–8)
Reg. Winchcombe	register of Bishop Tideman of Winchcombe (1395–1401)

Worcester Cathedral Library muniments
    charters (B/C + number)
    Liber Albus
    Liber Pensionum
York, Borthwick Institute, University of York
    CP. E. cause papers, 14th century
    Ph. photocopy collection
    PR. Sel. parish records of Selby abbey
    Prob. Reg. probate registers from 1389

York, Reg.	Registers of the Archbishops of York (at the Borthwick Institute, University of York):
Reg. 5A	Sede Vacante Register 1299–1554
Reg. 8	William Greenfield (1306–15)

Reg. 9A–B   William Melton (1317–40)
Reg. 10   William Zouche (1342–52)
Reg. 11   John Thoresby (1353–73)
Reg. 12   Alexander Neville (1374–88)
Reg. 14   Thomas Arundel (1388–96)
Reg. 18   Henry Bowet (1407–23)
Reg. 20   William Booth (1452–64)
York, York Minster Archives:
    Chapter act books (H1/1–3, H2/1)
    Consistory court records (M2/1c, g, h)
    ms. XVI.A.1
    Probate register (L2/4)
    Torre's mss. (L1/7–10)
Yorke family records (at Halton Place, Hellifield, Skipton)
Yorkshire Archaeological Society, *see* Leeds

PRINTED BOOKS AND ARTICLES
CITED, WITH ABBREVIATED
REFERENCES

Most annals, chronicles, cartularies, and registers have references starting *Ann.*, *Ch.*, *Ctl.*, and *Reg.*; most collections of fines, etc., are under the headings FINES.

AASRP: *Associated Architectural Societies Reports and Papers*.
'Abbot Newland's Roll': 'Abbot Newland's Roll of the Abbots of St Augustine's, Bristol', ed. I. H. Jeayes, *BGAS*, XIV (1889–90), 117–30.
Abbrev. Rot. Orig.: *Rotulorum Originalium in curia scaccarii abbreviatio*, ed. H. Playford and J. Caley (2 vols., Record Commission, 1805–10).
Abrams, L. and Carley, J. P. eds., *The Archaeology and History of Glastonbury Abbey: essays in honour of the ninetieth birthday of C. R. Ralegh Radford* (Woodbridge, 1991).
Accts of Papal Collectors: *Accounts rendered by Papal Collectors in England 1317–1378*, ed. W. E. Lunt and E. B. Graves (Philadelphia, 1968).
Acta Langton: *Acta Stephani Langton, Cantuariensis archiepiscopi, A.D. 1207–1228*, ed. Kathleen Major (Canterbury and York Society 50, 1950).
Acta Wells: *The Acta of Hugh of Wells, Bishop of Lincoln 1209–1235*, ed. D. M. Smith (Lincoln Record Society 88, 2000).
Ad. Dom.: *Adami de Domerham, Historia de rebus gestis Glastoniensibus*, ed. T. Hearne (2 vols., London, 1727).
Addy, *Beauchief Abbey*: S. O. Addy, *Historical Memorials of Beauchief Abbey* (Oxford, London, and Sheffield, 1878).
Addy, S. O., *XVI Charters of Roche Abbey, now first published* (Sheffield, 1878).
An. Sac. Ord. Cist: *Analecta Sacri Ordinis Cisterciensis*.
Andrews, H. C., 'Cathale priory, Herts: its history and site', *Trans. East Herts Arch. Soc.*, VI (1915), 90–7.
'Rowney Priory', *Trans. East Herts Arch. Soc.*, VI (1915), 1–29.
Ang. Sac.: *Anglia sacra sive collectio historiarum de archiepiscopis et episcopis Angliae ad annum 1540*, ed. H. Wharton (2 vols., London, 1691).
Anglesey Chts.: I. H. Jeayes, *Descriptive catalogue of the charters and muniments of the Marquis of Anglesey, sometime preserved at Beaudesert but now at Plas Newydd, Isle of Anglesey* (*SHC*, 1937).
Ann. Bermondsey, in *Ann. Mon.*, III.
Ann. Burton, in *Ann. Mon.*, I.
Ann. Camb.: *Annales Cambriae*, ed. Rev. J. Williams ab Ithel (RS, 1860).
Ann. Chester: *Annales Cestrienses: or, the chronicle of the abbey of St Werburg at Chester*, ed. R. C. Christie (Lancashire and Cheshire Record Society 14, 1887).
Ann. Dunstable, in *Ann. Mon.*, III.
Ann. Durham: *Durham Annals and Documents of the Thirteenth Century*, ed. F. Barlow (Surtees Society 155, 1945).

Ann. Margam, in *Ann. Mon.,* I.

Ann. Mon.: Annales Monastici, ed. H. R. Luard (5 vols., RS, 1864–9).

Ann. Osney, in *Ann. Mon.,* IV.

Ann. Rad.: C. W. Previté-Orton, 'Annales Radingenses posteriores, 1135–1264', *EHR,* XXXVII (1922), 400–3.

Ann. Southwark: M. Tyson, ed., 'The Annals of Southwark and Merton', *Surrey Arch. Coll.,* XXXVI (1925), 24–57.

Ann. Tewkesbury, in *Ann. Mon.,* I.

Ann. Thorney: C. Hart, ed., 'The Thorney Annals', *Peterborough's Past: the Journal of the Peterborough Museum Society* 1 (1982–3), 15–34.

Ann. Waverley, in *Ann. Mon.,* II.

Ann. Winchester, in *Ann. Mon.,* II.

Ann. Worcs, in *Ann. Mon.,* IV.

Anon.: Anonimalle Chronicle, 1333 to 1381, The, ed. V. H. Galbraith (Manchester, 1927).

Antiquities of Sunderland.

Arch. Aeliana: Archaeologia Aeliana.

Arch. Camb.: Archaeologia Cambrensis.

Arch. Cant.: Archaeologia Cantiana.

Arch. J.: Archaeological Journal.

Arley Chts.: W. Beamont, *Arley Charters: a calendar of ancient family charters preserved at Arley Hall, Cheshire,* . . . (London, 1866).

Assize of Nuisance: London Assize of Nuisance 1301–1431, ed. H. M. Chew and W. Kellaway (London Record Society 10, 1973).

Atkinson, J. C., *History of Cleveland Ancient and Modern, vol. I* (Barrow in Furness, 1874).

Backmund, N., O. Praem., *Monasticon Praemonstratense* (3 vols., Straubing, 1949–56).

Baildon: *Notes on the religious and secular houses of Yorkshire.* Extracted from the public records by W. P. Baildon (2 vols., Yorkshire Archaeological Society, record series XVII, LXXXI, 1895, 1931).

Baker, *Northants:* G. Baker, *The History and Antiquities of the County of Northampton* (2 vols., London, 1822–30).

Bannister, A. T., 'A note on an obscure episode in the history of St Guthlac's priory, Hereford', *Trans. Woolhope Nat. Field Club* (1908–11), 20–4.

Bannister, *Ewyas:* A. T. Bannister, *The History of Ewyas Harrold, its castle, priory and church* (Hereford, 1902).

BAR: British Archaeological Reports.

Barnes, G. D., *Kirkstall Abbey 1147–1539* (Thoresby Society 58, 1984).

Baronia de Kemeys: Baronia de Kemeys from the original documents at Bronwydd (London, n.d.).

Barrell, A. D. M., *The Papacy, Scotland and Northern England 1342–78* (Cambridge, 1995).

Bart. Cotton: Bartholomaei de Cotton, monachi Norwicensis, historia Anglicana (A.D. 449–1298) . . ., ed. H. R. Luard (RS, 1859).

Basset Chts.: Basset Charters c. 1120 to 1250, ed. W. T. Reedy (PRS, new ser. 50, 1995).

Bate, G. E., *A history of the priory and church of Holy Trinity, Hounslow* (Hounslow, 1924).

Bates, E. H., 'Stavordale priory', *Proc. Soms ANHS* 50 (1904), 94–103. *See also* Harbin.

Battiscombe, C. F., 'Note on a copy of the seal matrix of Henry of Stamford, prior of Finchale, A.D. 1312,' *Trans. AAS Durham & Northumberland,* VIII (1937), 106–9.

Beauchamp Reg.: Two registers formerly belonging to the family of Beauchamp of Hatch, ed. H. C. Maxwell Lyte (Somerset Record Society 35, 1920).

Bec Documents: Select Documents of the English Lands of the Abbey of Bec, ed. M. Chibnall (Camden 3rd ser., LXXIII, 1951).

Bede and his World II: The Jarrow Lectures 1979–1993 (Aldershot, 1994).

Beds Eyre: Roll of the justices in eyre at Bedford, 1227, ed. G. H. Fowler (BHRS, III, 1916), 1–206.

Beds Eyre Roll 1247: Calendar of the roll of the justices on eyre, 1247, ed. G. H. Fowler (BHRS, XXI, 1939).

Beds F., *see under* FINES

Beds Sessions of the Peace: Sessions of the Peace for Bedfordshire 1355–1359, 1363–1364, ed. E. G. Kimball (BHRS, XLVIII, and *HMC* joint publication 16, 1969).

Bennett, 'Lancs and Cheshire clergy': M. J. Bennett, 'The Lancashire and Cheshire clergy, 1379', *Trans. Lancs and Ches. Hist. Soc.*, 124 (1973 for 1972), 1–30.

Bentham, *Ely*: James Bentham, *The history and antiquities of the Conventual and Cathedral Church of Ely* (2 vols., Cambridge, 1771; 2nd edn 1 vol., Norwich, 1812). Supplement by W. Stevenson (Norwich, 1817).

Berkeley Chts.: *Descriptive catalogue of charters and muniments in the possession of the Right Hon. Lord FitzHardinge at Berkeley Castle*, ed. I. H. Jeayes (Bristol, 1892).

Berks Eyre: The Roll and Writ File of the Berkshire Eyre of 1248, ed. M. T. Clanchy (Selden Society 90, 1973).

BGAS: *Transactions of the Bristol and Gloucestershire Archaeological Society.*

BHRS: Bedfordshire Historical Record Society.

BIB: *Borthwick Institute Bulletin.*

BIHR: *Bulletin of the Institute of Historical Research.*

Binns: A. Binns, *Dedications of Monastic Houses in England and Wales, 1066–1216* (Studies in the History of Medieval Religion 1, Woodbridge, 1989).

Birch, *Bristol Original Docts*: W. de G. Birch, 'Original documents relating to Bristol and the neighbourhood', *JBAA*, 31 (1875), 289–305.

Birch, W. de G., *A History of Margam Abbey* (London, 1897).

A History of Neath Abbey (Neath, 1902).

BJRL: *Bulletin of the John Rylands Library.*

Blaauw, W. H., 'On the early history of Lewes Priory and its Seals', *Sussex Arch. Coll.*, II (1849), 7–37.

'Episcopal visitations of the Benedictine nunnery of Easebourne', *Sussex Arch. Coll.*, IX (1857), 1–32.

Black Book: The register of St Augustine's abbey, Canterbury, commonly called the Black Book, ed. G. J. Turner and H. E. Salter (2 vols., British Academy, records of social and economic history II, III, 1915–24).

Blair, C. H., 'Some medieval seal matrices', *Antiquaries Journal*, 4 (1924), 242–8.

Blair, J., 'The foundation of Goring priory', *Oxoniensia*, LI (1986), 194–7.

Blair, J. and Steane, J. N., 'Investigations at Cogges, Oxfordshire 1978–81: the priory and the parish church', *Oxoniensia*, XLVIII (1982), 37–125.

Blomefield, *Norfolk*: Blomefield, F., *An essay towards a topographical history of the county of Norfolk* (2nd edn, 11 vols., London, 1805–10).

Blount, M. N., 'A critical edition of the Annals of Hailes (MS. Cotton Cleopatra D III, ff. 33–59v), with an examination of their sources' (unpublished MA. thesis, University of Manchester, 1974).

BM Seals: W. de G. Birch, *Catalogue of Seals in the department of manuscripts in the British Museum* (6 vols., London, 1887–1900).

Bolton Priory: A. H. Thompson, *History and architectural description of the priory of St Mary, Bolton-in-Wharfedale, with some account of the canons regular of the order of St Augustine and their houses in Yorkshire* (Thoresby Society XXX, 1928).

Bostock, T. and Hogg, S., *Vale Royal Abbey and the Cistercians 1277–1538* (Northwich, 1998).

Bourne, *Hist. Newcastle*: H. Bourne, *The History of Newcastle upon Tyne; or The Ancient and Present State of that Town* (Newcastle, 1736).

Bowers and Clough, *Hist. of Parish and Parish Church of Stone*: W. H. Bowers and J. W. Clough, *Researches into the history of the Parish and Parish Church of Stone, Staffordshire* (Birmingham, 1929).

Bowles, *Ann. Lacock*: W. L. Bowles, *Annals and Antiquities of Lacock Abbey* (London, 1835).

Boyle, L. E., *A Survey of the Vatican Archives and of its medieval holdings* (Toronto, 1972).

Bracton's Note Book, ed. F. W. Maitland (3 vols., London, 1887).

Brakspear, H., 'Corsham', *Wilts AM*, XLIII (1925–7), 511–39.

  'Wigmore Abbey', *Arch. J.*, XC (1933), 26–51.

Brand, *Hist. Newcastle*: J. Brand, *The History and Antiquities of the Town and County of the Town of Newcastle upon Tyne* (2 vols., London, 1789).

Brett, M., 'The annals of Bermondsey, Southwark, and Merton' in D. Abulafia, M. Franklin and M. Rubin, eds., *Church and City 1000–1500: essays in honour of Christopher Brooke* (Cambridge, 1992), pp. 279–310.

Brewood Chts.: G. P. Mander, ed., *The Priory of the Black Ladies of Brewood: some charters, records etc.* in *SHC* 1939, pp. 177–220.

Bridges, J., *The History and Antiquities of Northamptonshire* (2 vols., Oxford, 1791).

Bristol F., see under FINES.

Brown, W., 'The nunnery of St Stephen's of Thimbleby', *YAJ*, IX (1886), 334–7.

Bruel, *Cluny Chts.*: *Recueil des chartes de l'abbaye de Cluny, vol. VI 1211–1300*, ed. A. Bruel (Paris, 1903).

Brut Peniarth: *Brut y Tywysogion, or the Chronicle of the Princes (Peniarth MS. 20 Version)*, ed. T. Jones (Board of Celtic Studies, University of Wales, History and Law ser., VI, 1941, XI, 1952 (references are to pages of vol. XI, translation)).

Brut Red Book: *Brut y Tywysogion, or the Chronicle of the Princes (Red book of Hergest Version)*, ed. and trans. T. Jones (Board of Celtic Studies, University of Wales, History and Law ser. XVI, 1955).

Buckingham Writ Register: *Royal Writs addressed to John Buckingham, Bishop of Lincoln 1363–1398*, ed. A. K. McHardy (Lincoln Record Society 86 and Canterbury and York Society 86, 1997).

Bucks Eyre: *Calendar of the roll of the justices on eyre, 1227*, ed. J. G. Jenkins (Buckinghamshire Record Society 6, 1945).

Bucks F., see under FINES.

Bucks Inquests and Indictments: *Inquests and Indictments from late fourteenth century Buckinghamshire: the superior eyre of 1389 at High Wycombe*, ed. L. Boatwright (Buckinghamshire Record Society 29, 1994).

Burton, J. E., 'The election of Joan Fletcher as prioress of Baysdale, 1524', *BIB*, I (1975–8), 145–53.

Burton, *Mon. Ebor.*: J. Burton, *Monasticon Eboracense* (York, 1758).

Burton Chts.: *Descriptive catalogue of the charters and muniments belonging to the Marquis of Anglesey . . .*, ed. I. H. Jeayes (*SHC*, 3rd ser., 1937).

Butler, R. F., 'Brimpsfield church history, part IV: the priory', *BGAS*, 82 (1963), 127–42.

Butley Chts.: *Leiston Abbey Cartulary and Butley Priory Charters*, ed. R. Mortimer (Suffolk Charters ser. I, 1979).

Butterill, C. A., 'The Cartulary of Flamstead Priory – St Giles in the Wood' (unpublished MA thesis, University of Manitoba, 1988).

Caen Chts.: *Charters and Custumals of the abbey of Holy Trinity, Caen*, ed. M. Chibnall (British Academy, records of social and economic history, new ser. V, 1982).

Caernarvon Court Rolls, 1361–1402, ed. G. P. Jones and H. Owen (Caernarvonshire Historical Record Ser. 1, 1951).

Cal. Anc. Corr. Wales: Calendar of Ancient Correspondence concerning Wales, ed. J. G. Edwards (Cardiff, 1935).

Cal. Anc. Pet. Wales: Calendar of Ancient Petitions relating to Wales (thirteenth to sixteenth century), ed. W. Rees (Board of Celtic Studies, University of Wales, History and Law ser., XXVIII, 1975).

Cal. Bodl. Chts.: Calendar of Charters and Rolls preserved in the Bodleian Library (Oxford), ed. W. H. Turner and H. O. Coxe (Oxford, 1878).

Cal. Chanc. Warr.: Calendar of Chancery Warrants preserved in the Public Record Office, AD. 1244–1326 (PRO, 1927).

Cal. Chancery Rolls: Calendar of various Chancery Rolls preserved in the Public Record Office, AD 1277–1326 (PRO, 1912).

Cal. Docs. Ireland: Calendar of Documents relating to Ireland . . ., I, 1171–1251, ed. H. S. Sweetman (London, 1875).

Cal. Docs. Scotland: Calendar of Documents relating to Scotland, ed. J. Bain (4 vols., 1881–8).

Cal. Early Mayors' Court Rolls, 1298–1307: Calendar of Early Mayors' Court Rolls of the City of London 1298–1307, ed. A. H. Thomas (Cambridge, 1924).

Cal. Inq. PM: Calendar of Inquisitions post mortem and other analogous documents preserved in the Public Record Office (PRO, 1904–in progress).

Cal. London Letter Books A: Calendar of Letter-Books of the City of London: Letter-Book A, c. A.D. 1275–1298, ed. R. R. Sharpe (London, 1899).

Cal. London Letter Books B: Calendar of Letter-Books of the City of London: Letter-Book B, c. A.D. 1275–1312, ed. R. R. Sharpe (London, 1900).

Cal. London Letter Books F: Calendar of Letter-Books of the City of London: Letter-Book F, c. A.D. 1337–1352, ed. R. R. Sharpe (London, 1904).

Cal. London Letter Books G: Calendar of Letter-Books of the City of London: Letter-Book G, ed. R. R. Sharpe (London, 1905).

Cal. Misc. Inq.: Calendar of Inquisitions miscellaneous (Chancery) preserved in the Public Record Office (7 vols., PRO, 1916–69).

Cal. Plea Rolls 1364–81: Calendar of Plea and Memoranda Rolls of the City of London 1364–1381 (Cambridge, 1929).

Calverley Chts.: The Calverley Charters presented to the British Museum by Sir Walter Calverley Trevelyan, baronet, ed. W. P. Baildon and S. Margerison (Thoresby Society 6, 1904).

Calvert, W. K. and Peck, H., 'Calder Abbey', *Trans. CWAAS*, new ser. 53 (1953), 81–97.

Cameron, H. K., '14th-century Flemish brasses to ecclesiastics in English churches', *TMBS*, XIII (1) (1980), 3–24.

Canivez: Statuta Capitulorum Generalium Ordinis Cisterciensis ab anno 1116 ad annum 1786, Bibliothèque de la Revue d'Histoire Ecclésiastique, ed. J.-M. Canivez, vols. I–III (1116–1400), (Louvain, 1933–5).

Canterbury Sede Vacante Institutions: Calendar of institutions by the chapter of Canterbury sede vacante, ed. C. E. Woodruff and I. J. Churchill (Kent Archaeological Society, records branch 8, 1923).

CAP: Collectanea Anglo-Praemonstratensia, arranged and ed. F. A. Gasquet (3 vols., Camden 3rd Series, VI, X, XI, 1904–6).

Cart. de la Couture: Cartulaire des Abbayes de Saint-Pierre de la Couture et de Saint-Pierre de Solesmes (Le Mans, 1889).

Cartae Antiquae 11–20: The Cartae Antiquae rolls 11–20, ed. J. Conway Davies (PRS, new ser. 33, 1960).

CAS: Cambridge Antiquarian Society.

Casus Placitorum: *Casus Placitorum and Reports of Cases in the King's Courts, 1272–1278*, ed. W. H. Dunham (Selden Society 69, 1952).

Cat. Lyttelton Papers: *Catalogue of the Lyttelton Papers: the property of the Viscount Cobham* (Sotheby's, 1978).

CChR: *Calendar of the Charter Rolls preserved in the Public Record Office* (6 vols., PRO, 1903–27).

CCR: *Calendar of the Close Rolls preserved in the Public Record Office* (PRO, 1896–in progress).

CDF: *Calendar of Documents preserved in France illustrative of the History of Great Britain and Ireland, I, A.D. 918–1206*, ed. J. H. Round (PRO, 1899).

CFR: *Calendar of Fine Rolls preserved in the Public Record Office* (22 vols., PRO, 1911–63).

Ch. Abingdon: *Chronicon monasterii de Abingdon*, ed. J. Stevenson (2 vols., RS, 1858).

Ch. Alnwick: W. Dickson, ed.,'Cronica monasterii de Alnewyke ex quodam libro cronicorum in libraria Collegii Regalis Cantabrigiae de dono Regis Henrici VI fundatoris', *Arch. Aeliana*, 1st ser., III (1844), 33–45.

Ch. Amundesham: *Annales monasterii S. Albani a Johanne Amundesham, monacho, ut videtur, conscripti A.D. 1421–1440 . . .*, ed. H. T. Riley (2 vols., RS, 1871–2).

Ch. Angl. Pet.: *Chronicon Angliae Petriburgense*, ed. J. A. Giles (Caxton Society II, 1845).

Ch. Barnwell: *Liber memorandorum ecclesie de Bernewelle*, ed. J. W. Clark (Cambridge, 1907).

Ch. Bristol: *see* 'Abbot Newland's Roll'.

Ch. Bury: *The Chronicle of Bury St Edmunds 1212–1301*, ed. A. Gransden (OMT, 1964).

Ch. Dale: W. H. St John Hope, ed., 'Chronicle of the Abbey of St Mary de Parco Stanley, or Dale, Derbyshire', *Journal of the Derbyshire Archaeological and Nat. Hist. Society*, v (1883), 1–29, also medieval list, 'The Abbots of the Monastery of . . . Dale, Derbyshire', *ibid.*, 81–100; new edition by A. Saltman, *see* Saltman.

Ch. Evesham: *Chronicon abbatiae de Evesham . . .*, ed. W. D. Macray (RS, 1863).

Ch. Knighton: *Knighton's Chronicle, 1337–1396*, ed. G. H. Martin (OMT, 1995).

Ch. Lanercost: *Chronicon de Lanercost*, ed. J. Stevenson (Bannatyne Club, Edinburgh, 1839).

Ch. Lewes: W. H. Blaauw, 'On the early history of Lewes Priory, and its seals, with extracts from a MS. Chronicle', *Sussex Arch. Soc.*, II (1849), 7–37.

Ch. Louth Park: *Chronicon abbatie de Parco Lude*, ed. E. Venables (Lincolnshire Record Society I, 1891).

Ch. Meaux: *Chronica monasterii de Melsa a fundatione usque ad annum 1396 . . .*, ed. E. A. Bond (3 vols., RS, 1866–8).

Ch. Melrose: *The Chronicle of Melrose*, facsimile ed. A. O. and M. O. Anderson (London, 1936).

Ch. Oxenedes: *Chronica Johannis de Oxenedes*, ed. H. Ellis (RS, 1859).

Ch. Peterborough: *Chronicon Petroburgense*, ed. T. Stapleton (Camden, old ser. XLVII, 1849).

Ch. Ramsey: *Chronicon abbatiae Rameseiensis . . .*, ed. W. D. Macray (RS, 1886).

Ch. Walden: 'The Book of the Foundation of Walden Abbey', translated H. Collar, *Essex Review*, XLV (1936), 73–236 *passim*, XLVI (1937), 12–234 *passim*, XLVII (1938), 36–220 *passim*.

Ch. Walt. of Guisborough: *The Chronicle of Walter of Guisborough, previously edited as the Chronicle of Walter of Hemmingford or Hemingburgh*, ed. H. Rothwell (Camden, 3rd ser. LXXXIX, 1957).

Ch. Wigmore: J. Taylor, ed., 'A Wigmore Chronicle, 1355–77', *Proceedings of the Leeds Philosophical and Literary Society, literary and historical section*, vol. XI, part V (1964), 81–94.

Ch. Witham: E. M. Thompson, 'A fragment of a Witham Charterhouse Chronicle and Adam of Dryburgh, Premonstratensian, and Carthusian of Witham', *BJRL*, XVI (1932), 482–506; *see also* Wilmart.

Ch. York: *The Chronicle of St Mary's abbey, York*, ed. H. H. E. Craster and M. E. Thornton, (Surtees Society 148, 1934).

Chap. Aug. Cans.: *Chapters of the Augustinian Canons*, ed. H. E. Salter (Canterbury and York Society 29, 1922).

Chaplais, P., *Diplomatic Documents I: 1101–1272* (London, 1964).

Chapters of English Black Monks: Documents illustrating the activities of the general and provincial chapters of the English Black Monks, 1215–1540, ed. W. A. Pantin (3 vols., Camden 3rd ser.,XLV, XLVII, LIV, 1931–7).

Charlton, L., *The History of Whitby and of Whitby Abbey* (York, 1779).

Chartes de Cluny: Recueil des chartes de l'abbaye de Cluny, ed. A. Bernard and A. Bruel (Collection de documents inédits sur l'histoire de France) (6 vols., Paris, 1876–1903).

Chartes de S. Bertin: Les Chartes de Saint-Bertin, ed. D. Haigneré (4 vols., Société des Antiquaires de la Morinie, Saint-Omer, 1886–99).

Charvin: G. Charvin, *Statuts, Chapitres Généraux et Visites de l'Ordre de Cluny, I–IV* (to 1408) (Paris, 1965–9).

Cheney, C. R., 'A visitation of St Peter's priory, Ipswich', *EHR*, 47 (1932), 268–72.

'Notes on the making of the Dunstable annals, A.D. 33–1242' in T. A. Sandquist and M. R. Powicke, eds., *Essays in Medieval History presented to Bertie Wilkinson* (Toronto, 1969), pp. 79–98, repd in *Medieval Texts and Studies* (Oxford, 1973), pp. 209–30.

Cheney, *Inn. III: The Letters of Pope Innocent III (1198–1216) concerning England and Wales*, ed. C. R. and M. G. Cheney (Oxford, 1967).

Cheney, *Innocent III and England*: C. R. Cheney, *Pope Innocent III and England* (Päpste und Papsttum 9, Stuttgart, 1976).

Cheney, M. G., *Roger, Bishop of Worcester 1164–1179* (Oxford, 1980).

Cheshire Chts.: *Facsimiles of early Cheshire charters*, ed. G. Barraclough (Lancashire and Cheshire Record Society, 1957).

Chester City Courts: Selected Rolls of the Chester City Courts, late thirteenth and early fourteenth centuries, ed. A. Hopkins (Chetham Society, 3rd ser., 2, 1950).

Chettle, H. F., 'The *Boni Homines* of Ashridge and Edington', *Downside Review*, 62 (1944), 40–55.

'The English houses of the Order of Fontevrauld', *Downside Review*, 60 (1942), 33–55.

'The Trinitarian friars and Easton Royal', *Wilts AM*, 51 (1945–7), 365–77.

Chicksands Chts.: 'Early charters of the priory of Chicksands', ed. G. H. Fowler (BHRS, I (1913), 101–28).

Chope, R. Pearse, 'Frithelstock Priory', *TDA*, 61 (1929), 167–91.

Chron. SHR: Chronicles of the Reigns of Stephen, Henry II and Richard I, ed. R. Howlett (4 vols., RS, 1884–9).

Chronicles, see Ch.

Chronology: The Handbook of British Chronology, 3rd edn, ed. E. B. Fryde, D. E. Greenway, S. Porter, and I. Roy (Royal Historical Society, Guides and Handbooks 2, London, 1986).

Chs. Peterborough: *see* Sparke.

Church in Chester 1300–1540, The: D. Jones (Chetham Soc., 3rd ser., VII, 1957).

Cist. Devon: J. Brooking Rowe, *Contributions to a history of the Cistercian houses of Devon* (Plymouth, 1878).

Clarke, K. M., ed., 'Records of St Nicholas' priory, Exeter', *TDA*, 44 (1912), 192–205.

Clarkson, *Hist. of Richmond*: C. Clarkson, *The History of Richmond in the county of York* (Richmond, 1821).

Clay, Sir Charles T., *Early Abbots*: 'The early abbots of the Yorkshire Cistercian houses', *YAJ*, XXXVIII (1952–5), 8–43.

'The early priors and abbots of Warter', *EYC*, X, 140–2.

'The early priors of Pontefract', *YAJ*, XXXVIII (1952–5), 456–64.

Seals: 'The seals of the religious houses of Yorkshire', *Archaeologia*, LXXVIII (1928), 1–36.

Fasti: *York Minster Fasti* (2 vols., Yorkshire Archaeological Society, Record Series, CXXIII–IV, 1958–9).

Clay, *Hist. of Landbeach*: W. K. Clay, *A History of the parish of Landbeach in the county of Cambridge* (Cambridge, 1861).

Cleeve Chts.: T. Hugo, 'On the charters and other archives of Cleeve Abbey', *Proc. Soms ANHS* VI (1855), 17–73.

Clerical Poll-Taxes: *Clerical Poll-Taxes of the diocese of Lincoln 1377–1381*, ed. A. K. McHardy (Lincoln Record Society 81, 1992).

Cluniac Visitations: *Visitations of English Cluniac Foundations in 47 Hen. III (1262), 3 and 4 Edw. I (1275–6) & 7 Edw. I (1279)*, ed. G. F. Duckett (London, 1890).

Cluny Chts.: *Charters and Records illustrative of the English foundations of the Ancient Abbey of Cluni*, ed. G. F. Duckett (2 vols., London, 1888).

Colchester Leger Book: J. L. Fisher, ed., 'The Leger Book of St John's Abbey, Colchester', *TEAS*, new ser. XXIV (1951), 77–127.

Coldicott, D. K., *Hampshire Nunneries* (Chichester, 1989).

Cole, R. E. G., 'The priory, or house of nuns of St Mary of Brodholme, of the order of Prémontré', *AASRP*, XXVIII (1905), 48–86.

Collectanea III, ed. M. Burrows (Oxford Historical Soc. XXXII, 1896).

Collinson, *Hist. Soms*: J. Collinson, *The History and Antiquities of the County of Somerset...* (3 vols., Bath, 1791).

Collinson, P., Ramsay, N., and Sparks, M., eds., *A History of Canterbury Cathedral* (Oxford, 1995).

Colvin: H. M. Colvin, *The White Canons in England* (Oxford, 1951).

Communar Rolls: *The early communar and pittancer rolls of Norwich cathedral priory, with an account of the building of the cloister*, ed. F. C. Fernie and A. B. Whittingham (Norfolk Record Society XLI, 1972).

Complete Peerage: *The Complete Peerage* by G. E. C., revised edn V. Gibbs, H. A. Doubleday, D. Warrand, Lord Howard de Walden, G. H. White, R. S. Lea, and P. W. Hammond (13 vols. in 14, London, 1910–98).

Cooper, G. M., 'The Premonstratensian Abbey of Bayham', *Sussex Arch. Coll.*, IX (1857), 145–80.

Cooper, W., *Wootton Wawen, its history and records* (Leeds, 1936).

Cooper, W. D., 'Proofs of age of Sussex families *temp.* Edward II to Edward IV', *Sussex Arch. Coll.*, XII (1860), 23–44.

Coram Rege Roll: *Placita coram domino rege apud Westmonasterium de termino Sancte Trinitatis anno regni regis Edwardi filii regis Henrici vicesimo quinto: The pleas of the Court of King's Bench, Trinity term, 25 Edward I, 1297*, ed. W. P. W. Phillimore and E. A. Fry (British Record Society, Index Library 19, 1898).

Cornwall F. see under FINES.

Court Rolls Colchester: *Court Rolls of the Borough of Colchester 1310–1367*, ed. I. H. Jeayes (2 vols., Colchester, 1921–38).

Cowdray Archives: *The Cowdray Archives*, ed. A. A. Dibben (2 vols., Chichester, 1960–4).

Cowley, *Monastic Order in South Wales*: F. G. Cowley, *The Monastic Order in South Wales 1066–1349* (Studies in Welsh History 1, Cardiff, 1977).

Cox, *Mag. Brit.*: T. Cox, *Magna Britannia et Hibernia, antiqua et nova...* (6 vols., London, 1720–31).

Coxe, *see Cal. Bodl. Chts.*

CPL: *Calendar of entries in the papal registers relating to Great Britain and Ireland: papal letters*, ed. W. H. Bliss, C. Johnson, J. A. Twemlow, M. J. Haren *et al.* (PRO and Irish Manuscripts Commission, Dublin, 1893–in progress).

CPP: *Calendar of entries in the Papal Registers relating to Great Britain and Ireland: petitions to the pope, vol. I, A.D. 1342–1419*, ed. W. H. Bliss (PRO, 1896).

CPR: *Calendar of the Patent Rolls preserved in the Public Record Office* (PRO, 1891–in progress).

CPR Supplement: *Calendar of the General and Special Assize and General Gaol Delivery Commissions on the dorses of the Patent Rolls: Richard II (1377–1399)* (Nendeln, Liechtenstein, 1977).

CR: *Close Rolls of the Reign of Henry III preserved in the Public Record Office* (14 vols., PRO Calendars, 1902–38).

Crittall, E., ed., 'Fragment of an account of the cellaress of Wilton Abbey, 1299' in *Collectanea* (Wiltshire Record Society XII, 1956), pp. 142–56.

Crouch, D. and Thomas, G., 'Three Goldcliff Charters', *Nat. Lib. Wales Jnl.*, 24 (1985), 153–63.

CRR: *Curia Regis Rolls* (PRO, 1922 – in progress).

CS: *Councils and Synods, with other documents relating to the English Church, II, 1205–1313*, ed. F. M. Powicke and C. R. Cheney (2 parts, Oxford, 1964).

CTG: *Collectanea topographica et genealogica*, ed. J. G. Nichols (8 vols., London, 1834–43).

Ctl. Abingdon: *Two Cartularies of Abingdon Abbey*, ed. C. F. Slade and G. Lambrick (Oxford Historical Society, new ser. XXXII, XXXIII, 1990–2).

Ctl. Athelney: *Two cartularies of the Benedictine abbeys of Muchelney and Athelney in the county of Somerset*, ed. E. H. Bates (Somerset Record Society 14, 1899).

Ctl. Bath: *Two Chartularies of the Priory of St Peter at Bath*, ed. W. Hunt (Somerset Record Society 7, 1893).

Ctl. Beaulieu: *The Beaulieu Cartulary*, ed. S. F. Hockey with an introduction by P. D. A. Harvey and S. F. Hockey (Southampton Records Ser. XVII, 1974).

Ctl. Bilsington: *The Cartulary and Terrier of the Priory of Bilsington, Kent*, ed. N. Neilson (British Academy, records of social and economic history VII, 1928).

Ctl. Blyth: *The Cartulary of Blyth Priory*, ed. R. M. Timson (Thoroton Record Society XXVI and *HMC* joint publication 17, 1973).

Ctl. Blythburgh: *Blythburgh Priory Cartulary*, ed. C. Harper-Bill (2 vols., Suffolk Charters ser. II, III, 1980–1).

Ctl. Boarstall: *The Boarstall Cartulary*, ed. H. E. Salter and A. H. Cooke (Oxford Historical Society LXXXVIII, 1930).

Ctl. Boxgrove: *The Cartulary of Boxgrove Priory*, ed. L. Fleming (Sussex Record Society, lix, 1960).

Ctl. Bradenstoke: *The Cartulary of Bradenstoke Priory*, ed. V. C. M. London (Wiltshire Record Society XXXV, 1979).

Ctl. Brecon: 'Cartularium Prioratus S. Johannis Evang. de Brecon', ed. R. W. Banks, *Archaeologia Cambrensis*, 4th ser., XIII (1882), 275–308; XIV (1883), 18–311.

'Ctl. Breedon': 'The Cartulary of Breedon Priory', ed. R. A. McKinley (unpublished MA thesis, Manchester University, 1950).

Ctl. Bridlington: *Abstract of the Charters and other documents contained in the Chartulary of the Priory of Bridlington*, ed. W. T. Lancaster (Leeds, 1912).

Ctl. Brinkburn: *The Chartulary of Brinkburn priory*, ed. W. Page (Surtees Society 90, 1893 for 1892).

Ctl. Bristol, St Mark: *The Cartulary of St Mark's Hospital, Bristol*, ed. C. D. Ross (Bristol Record Society XXI, 1959).

Ctl. Bruton: *Two Cartularies of the Augustinian Priory of Bruton and the Cluniac Priory of Montacute in the county of Somerset* (Somerset Record Society 8, 1894).

Ctl. Buckfast: *Register of John de Grandisson, Bishop of Exeter*, ed. F. C. Hingeston-Randolph, vol. III (1899), 1563–610.

Ctl. Buckland: *A Cartulary of Buckland Priory in the county of Somerset*, ed. F. W. Weaver (Somerset Record Society 25, 1909).

Ctl. Burscough: *An edition of the Cartulary of Burscough Priory*, ed. A. N. Webb (Chetham Society, 3rd ser., 18, 1970).

Ctl. Burton: G. Wrottesley, ed.,'The Burton Chartulary', *SHC*, V(i) (1884), 1–104.

Ctl. Burton Lazars: *The Burton Lazars Cartulary: a medieval Leicestershire estate*, ed. T. Bourne and D. Marcombe (Nottingham University, Centre for Local History record ser. 6, 1987).

Ctl. Bushmead: *The cartulary of Bushmead priory*, ed. G. H. Fowler and J. Godber (BHRS, XXII, 1945).

Ctl. Canonsleigh: *The cartulary of Canonsleigh Abbey (Harleian Ms. no. 3660): a calendar*, ed. V. C. M. London (Devon and Cornwall Record Society, new ser. 8, 1965 for 1962).

Ctl. Carisbrooke: *The Cartulary of Carisbrooke Priory*, ed. S. F. Hockey (Isle of Wight Records ser. 2, 1981).

Ctl. Carmarthen: *Cartularium S. Johannis Baptiste de Caermarthen . . .*, ed. Sir T. Phillipps (Cheltenham, 1865).

Ctl. Cerne: B. F. Lock, ed., 'The Cartulary of Cerne Abbey', *Proc. Dorset Nat. Hist. and Antiq. Field Club*, XXVIII (1907), 65–95; XXIX (1908), 195–223.

Ctl. Chatteris: *The Cartulary of Chatteris Abbey*, ed. C. Breay (Woodbridge, 1999).

Ctl. Chertsey: *Chertsey (Abbey) Cartularies*, vols. I, II, (Surrey Record Society, XII, 1915–63).

Ctl. Chester: *The Chartulary or Register of the Abbey of St Werburgh, Chester*, ed. J. Tait (2 vols., Chetham Society, new ser. LXXIX, LXXXII, 1920–3).

Ctl. Chetwynd: 'The Chetwynd Chartulary', ed. G. Wrottesley, *SHC*, XII (1891), 241–336.

Ctl. Chichester: *The Chartulary of the High Church of Chichester*, ed. W. D. Peckham (Sussex Record Society, XLVI, 1946, for 1942–3).

Ctl. Cirencester: *The Cartulary of Cirencester Abbey, Gloucestershire*, ed. C. D. Ross and M. Devine (3 vols., London, 1964 (I, II); Oxford, 1977 (III)).

Ctl. Clerkenwell: *The Cartulary of St Mary, Clerkenwell*, ed. W. O. Hassall (Camden 3rd ser. LXXI, 1949).

Ctl. Cockersand: *The Chartulary of Cockersand Abbey*, ed. W. Farrer (3 vols. in 7 parts, Chetham Society, new ser. XXXVIII–XL, XLIII, LVI, LVII, LXIV, 1898–1909).

Ctl. Colchester: *Cartularium monasterii S. Johannis Baptiste de Colecestria*, ed. S. A. Moore (2 vols., Roxburghe Club, 1897).

Ctl. Colne: *Cartularium Prioratus de Colne*, ed. J. L. Fisher (Essex Archaeological Society, Occasional Publications I, 1946).

Ctl. Coxford: H. W. Saunders. ed., 'A history of Coxford Priory', *Norfolk Archaeology*, XVII (1910), 284–370 (extracts, pp. 330ff.; calendar, pp. 355ff.).

Ctl. Crabhouse: Mary Bateson, ed., 'The Register of Crabhouse Nunnery', *Norfolk Archaeology*, XI (1892), 1–71.

Ctl. Creake: *A Cartulary of Creake Abbey*, ed. A. L. Bedingfeld (Norfolk Record Society XXXV, 1966).

Ctl. Crich: *Two Cartularies of the Wakebridge Chantries at Crich*, ed. A. Saltman (Derbyshire Archaeological Society, record ser. 6, 1976).

Ctl. Dale: *The Cartulary of Dale Abbey*, ed. A. Saltman (Derbyshire Archaeological Society, record ser. 2, 1967 for 1966).

Ctl. Darley: *The Cartulary of Darley Abbey*, ed. R. R. Darlington (2 vols., Kendal for the Derbyshire Archaeological Society, 1945).

Ctl. Daventry: *The Cartulary of Daventry Priory*, ed. M. J. Franklin (Northamptonshire Record Society 35, 1988).

Ctl. Dieulacres: G. Wrottesley, ed., 'Chartulary of Dieulacres Abbey', *SHC,* new ser. IX (1906), 293–365.

Ctl. Dryburgh: *Liber S. Marie de Dryburgh*, ed. J. Spottiswoode (Bannatyne Club, 1847).

Ctl. Dunstable: *A digest of the Charters preserved in the Cartulary of the Priory of Dunstable*, ed. G. H. Fowler (BHRS, X, 1926).

Ctl. Edington: *The Edington Cartulary*, ed. J. H. Stevenson (Wiltshire Record Society XLII, 1987).

Ctl. Exeter: 'List of charters in the cartulary of St Nicholas Priory at Exeter', in *CTG*, vol. I (1834), 60–5, 184–9, 250–4, 374–88.

Ctl. Eye: *Eye Priory Cartulary and Charters*, ed. V. Brown (2 vols., Suffolk Charters ser. XII, XIII, 1992–4).

Ctl. Eynsham: *Eynsham Cartulary*, ed. H. E. Salter (2 vols., Oxford Historical Society, XLIX, LI, 1907–8).

Ctl. Flaxley: *The Cartulary and Historical Notes of the Cistercian Abbey of Flaxley . . .*, ed. A. W. Crawley-Boevey (Exeter, 1887).

Ctl. Forde: *The Cartulary of Forde Abbey*, ed. S. Hobbs (Somerset Record Society 85, 1998).

Ctl. Fountains: *Abstracts of the charters and other documents contained in the chartulary of the Cistercian abbey of Fountains*, ed. W. T. Lancaster (2 vols., Leeds, 1915).

Ctl. Furness: *The Coucher Book of Furness Abbey*, ed. J. C. Atkinson and J. Brownbill (2 vols. in 6 parts, Chetham Society, new ser. IX, XI, XIV, LXXIV, LXXVI, LXXVIII, 1886–1919).

Ctl. Glastonbury: *The Great Chartulary of Glastonbury*, ed. Dom Aelred Watkin (3 vols., Somerset Record Society 59, 63, 64, 1947–56).

Ctl. Gloucester: *Historia et Cartularium monasterii sancti Petri Gloucestriae*, ed. W. H. Hart (3 vols., RS, 1863–7).

Ctl. God's House: *The Cartulary of God's House, Southampton*, ed. J. M. Kaye (2 vols., Southampton Records Ser. XIX, XX, 1976).

Ctl. Godstow: *The English Register of Godstow Nunnery*, ed. A. Clark (3 vols., EETS, original ser. CXXIX, CXXX, CXLII, 1905–11).

Ctl. Guisborough: *Cartularium Prioratus de Gyseburne,* ed. W. Brown (2 vols., Surtees Society 86, 89, 1889, 1894 for 1891).

Ctl. Harrold: *Records of Harrold Priory*, ed. G. H. Fowler (BHRS, XVII, 1935).

Ctl. Haughmond: *The Cartulary of Haughmond Abbey*, ed. U. Rees (Cardiff, 1985).

Ctl. Healaugh Park: *The Chartulary of the Augustinian Priory of St John the Evangelist of the Park of Healaugh*, ed. J. S. Purvis (Yorkshire Archaeological Society, Record Series, 92, 1936 for 1935).

Ctl. Holm Cultram: *The Register and Records of Holm Cultram*, ed. F. Grainger and W. G. Collingwood (Cumberland and Westmorland Antiquarian and Archaeological Society, Record Ser. VII, 1929).

Ctl. Holy Trinity, Aldgate: *The Cartulary of Holy Trinity Aldgate*, ed. G. A. J. Hodgett (London Record Society 7, 1971).

Ctl. Hospitallers: *The Cartulary of the Knights of St John of Jerusalem in England, Secunda Camera Essex; Prima Camera Essex*, ed. M. Gervers (2 vols., British Academy, records of social and economic history, new ser. VI, XXIII, 1982–96).

Ctl. Hulme: *St Benet of Holme, 1020–1210*, ed. J. R. West (2 vols., Norfolk Record Society II, III, 1932).

Ctl. Hungerford: *The Hungerford Cartulary: a calendar of the Earl of Radnor's Cartulary of the Hungerford Family*, ed. J. L. Kirby (Wiltshire Record Society 49, 1994).

Ctl. Huntingdon: W. M. Noble, ed., 'The cartulary of the priory of St Mary, Huntingdon', *Trans. of the Cambridgeshire and Huntingdonshire Archaeological Society*, IV (1930), 89–280 *passim*.

Ctl. Kirkstall: *Coucher Book of the Cistercian abbey of Kirkstall*, ed. W. T. Lancaster and W. P. Baildon (Thoresby Society VIII, 1904).

Ctl. Lanercost: *The Lanercost Cartulary*, ed. J. M. Todd (Surtees Society 203, and Cumberland and Westmorland Antiquarian and Archaeological Society record ser. 11, 1997).

Ctl. Launceston: *The Cartulary of Launceston Priory (Lambeth Palace ms. 719): a calendar*, ed. P. L. Hull (Devon and Cornwall Record Society, new ser. 30, 1987).

Ctl. Leiston: *Leiston Abbey Cartulary and Butley Priory Charters*, ed. R. Mortimer (Suffolk Charters ser. I, 1979).

Ctl. Lewes: *The chartulary of the priory of St Pancras of Lewes*, ed. L. F. Salzman (2 vols., Sussex Record Society, XXXVIII, XL, 1933–5).

Ctl. Lewes, Norfolk: *The Norfolk portion of the Chartulary of the priory of St Pancras of Lewes*, ed. J. H. Bullock (Norfolk Record Society, XII, 1939).

Ctl. Lewes, Wilts etc.: W. Budgen and L. F. Salzman, eds., 'The Wiltshire, Devonshire and Dorset portion of the Lewes chartulary, with London and Essex documents from the Surrey portion', *The chartulary of Lewes priory. The portions relating to counties other than Sussex* (Sussex Record Society, Additional volume, 1943).

Ctl. Lilleshall: *The Cartulary of Lilleshall Abbey*, ed. U. Rees (Shropshire Archaeological and History Society, 1997).

Ctl. Llanthony (Irish): *The Irish Cartularies of Llanthony Prima and Secunda*, ed. E. St J. Brooks (Irish Manuscripts Commission, 1953).

Ctl. Loders: *Cartulaire de Loders: prieuré dépendant de l'abbaye de Montebourg*, ed. L. Guilloreau (Evreux, 1905).

Ctl. Malmesbury: *Registrum Malmesburiense*, ed. J. S. Brewer and C. T. Martin (2 vols., RS, 1879–80).

'*Ctl. Meaux*': G. V. Orange, 'The Cartulary of Meaux: a critical edition' (unpublished Ph.D. thesis, University of Hull, 1966).

Ctl. Missenden: *The Cartulary of Missenden Abbey*, ed. J. G. Jenkins (3 vols., Buckinghamshire Record Society, 2, 10, 12, 1938–62).

Ctl. Monk Bretton: *Abstracts of the Chartularies of the Priory of Monkbretton*, ed. J. W. Walker (Yorkshire Archaeological Society, Record Series LXVI, 1924).

Ctl. Montacute: *Two Cartularies of the Augustinian Priory of Bruton and the Cluniac Priory of Montacute in the county of Somerset* (Somerset Record Society 8, 1894).

Ctl. Muchelney: *Two Cartularies of the Benedictine Abbeys of Muchelney and Athelney in the county of Somerset*, ed. E. H. Bates (Somerset Record Society 14, 1890).

Ctl. Newminster: *Chartularium abbathiae de Novo Monasterio*, ed. J. T. Fowler (Surtees Society 66, 1878 for 1876).

Ctl. Newnham: *The Cartulary of Newnham Priory*, ed. Joyce Godber (1 vol. in 2, BHRS, XLIII, 1964).

Ctl. Oseney: *Cartulary of Oseney Abbey*, ed. H. E. Salter (6 vols., Oxford Historical Society, LXXXIX–XCI, XCVII–XCVIII, CI, 1929–36).

Ctl. Pontefract: *Chartulary of St John of Pontefract*, ed. R. Holmes (2 vols., Yorkshire Archaeological Society, Record Series, XXV, XXX, 1899–1902).

Ctl. Pyel: *A Calendar of the Cartularies of John Pyel and Adam Fraunceys*, ed. S. J. O'Connor (Camden, 5th ser., 2, 1993).

Ctl. Ramsey: *Cartularium monasterii de Rameseia*, ed. W. H. Hart and P. A. Lyons (3 vols., RS, 1884–93).

Ctl. Ranton: G. Wrottesley, ed., 'The Chartulary of Ronton Priory', *SHC*, IV (i) (1883), 264–95.

Ctl. Reading: *Reading Abbey Cartularies*, ed. B. R. Kemp (2 vols, Camden 4th ser. 31, 33, 1986–7).

Ctl. Rievaulx: *Cartularium abbathiae de Rievalle*, ed. J. C. Atkinson (Surtees Society 83, 1889 for 1887).

Ctl. Rydeware: 'The Rydeware Chartulary', ed. I. H. Jeayes and G. Wrottesley, *SHC*, XVI (1895), 229–302.

Ctl. St Bartholomew's, London: *Cartulary of St Bartholomew's Hospital: a calendar*, ed. N. J. M. Kerling (London, 1973).

Ctl. St Bees: *The Register of the Priory of St Bees*, ed. J. Wilson (Surtees Society 126, 1915).

Ctl. St Denys: *The Cartulary of the Priory of St Denys near Southampton*, ed. E. O. Blake (2 vols., Southampton Records Ser. XXIV, XXV, 1981).

Ctl. St Frideswide: *The Cartulary of the monastery of St Frideswide at Oxford*, ed. S. R. Wigram (2 vols., Oxford Historical Society, XXVIII, XXXI, 1895–6).

Ctl. St Gregory, Canterbury: *Cartulary of the Priory of St Gregory, Canterbury*, ed. Audrey M. Woodcock (Camden, 3rd ser., LXXXVIII, 1956).

Ctl. St John the Baptist, Oxford: *A Cartulary of the Hospital of St John the Baptist*, ed. H. E. Salter (3 vols., Oxford Historical Society LXVI, LXVIII, LXIX, 1914–17).

Ctl. St Michael's Mount: *The Cartulary of St Michael's Mount (Hatfield House MS. no. 315)*, ed. P. L. Hull (Devon and Cornwall Record Society, new ser., 5, 1962 for 1958).

Ctl. St Nicholas, Salisbury: *The fifteenth century Cartulary of St Nicholas's Hospital, Salisbury, with other records*, ed. C. Wordsworth (Wilts Record Society, 1902).

Ctl. Sallay: *The Chartulary of the Cistercian Abbey of St Mary of Sallay in Craven*, ed. J. McNulty (2 vols., Yorkshire Archaeological Society, Record Series, LXXXVII, XC, 1933–4).

Ctl. Sandford: *The Sandford Cartulary*, ed. A. M. Leys (2 vols., Oxfordshire Record Society 19, 22, 1938–41).

Ctl. Selby: *The Coucher Book of Selby*, ed. J. T. Fowler (2 vols., Yorkshire Archaeological Society, Record Series, X, XIII, 1891–3).

Ctl. Sele: *Chartulary of the priory of St Peter at Sele*, ed. L. F. Salzman (Cambridge, 1923).

Ctl. Shrewsbury: *The Cartulary of Shrewsbury Abbey*, ed. U. Rees (2 vols., Aberystwyth, 1975).

Ctl. Sibton: *Sibton Abbey Cartularies and Charters*, ed. P. Brown (4 vols., Suffolk Charters ser. VII–X, 1985–8).

Ctl. Snelshall: *The Cartulary of Snelshall Priory*, ed. J. G. Jenkins (Buckinghamshire Record Society 9, 1952).

Ctl. Southwick: *The Cartularies of Southwick Priory*, ed. K. A. Hanna (2 vols., Hampshire Record Ser. IX, X, 1988–9).

Ctl. Stafford: F. Parker, ed., 'A Chartulary of the Priory of St Thomas the Martyr, near Stafford', *SHC*, VIII (1887), 125–201.

Ctl. Staffs: G. Wrottesley, ed., 'The Staffordshire Chartulary, series I–II', *SHC*, II (1881), 178–276.

Ctl. Staffs 2: G. Wrottesley, ed., 'The Staffordshire Chartulary, series III', *SHC*, III (i) (1882), 178–231.

Ctl. Staffs 3: J. C. Wedgewood, ed., 'Staffordshire Cartulary, 1200–1237', *SHC* (1911), 415–48.

Ctl. Stoke by Clare: *Stoke by Clare Cartulary*, ed. C. Harper-Bill and R. Mortimer (3 vols., Suffolk Charters ser. IV–VI, 1982–4).

Ctl. Stone: G. Wrottesley, ed., 'The Stone Chartulary', *SHC*, VI (i) (1885), 1–28.

Ctl. Stoneleigh: *The Stoneleigh Leger Book*, ed. R. H. Hilton (Dugdale Society XXIV, 1960).

Ctl. Thame: *The Thame Cartulary*, ed. H. E. Salter (2 vols., Oxfordshire Record Society 25–6, 1947–8).

Ctl. Thurgarton: *The Thurgarton Cartulary*, ed. T. Foulds (Stamford, 1994).

Ctl. Tockwith: *The Chartulary of Tockwith alias Scokirk, a cell to the Priory of Nostell*, ed. G. C. Ransome, in *Miscellanea III* (Yorkshire Archaeological Society, Record Series LXXX, 1931), pp. 149–206.

Ctl. Trentham: F. Parker, ed., 'A Chartulary of the Augustine Priory of Trentham', *SHC*, XI, (1890), 295–336.

Ctl. Tropenell: *The Tropenell Cartulary*, ed. J. S. Davies (2 vols., Wiltshire Historical Society, Devizes, 1908).

Ctl. Tutbury: *The Cartulary of Tutbury Priory*, ed. A. Saltman (*SHC*, 4th ser. IV, 1962 and *HMC* joint publication 2).

Ctl. Walsall: *Walsall Records: translations of ancient documents in the Walsall Chartulary at the British Museum* (Walsall, 1914).

Ctl. Wardon: *Cartulary of the Abbey of Old Wardon*, ed. G. H. Fowler (BHRS, XIII, 1930).

Ctl. Wetheral: *The Register of the Priory of Wetherhal*, ed. J. E. Prescott (Cumberland and Westmorland Antiquarian and Archaeological Society, Record Series, I, 1897).

Ctl. Whalley: *The Coucher Book . . . of Whalley Abbey*, ed. W. A. Hulton (4 vols., Chetham Society, X–XI, XVI, XX, 1847–9).

Ctl. Whitby: *Cartularium abbathiae de Whiteby*, ed. J. C. Atkinson (2 vols., Surtees Society 69, 72, 1879–81).

Ctl. Wilton: *Registrum Wiltunense*, ed. R. C. Hoare *et al.* (London, 1827).

Ctl. Winchcombe: *Landboc sive Registrum monasterii B. M. Virginis et Sancti Cenhelmi de Winchelcumba . . .*, ed. D. Royce (2 vols., Exeter, 1892–1903).

Ctl. Winchester: *Chartulary of Winchester Cathedral*, ed. A. W. Goodman (Winchester, 1927).

Ctl. Wombridge: G. Morris, ed., 'Abstracts of . . . the Chartulary of Wombridge', *Trans. Shrops ANHS*, 1st ser. IX, 305ff.; xi, 325ff.; 2nd ser. I, 294ff.; IX, 96ff.; X, 180ff.; XI, 331ff.; XII, 205ff., 1886–1900.

Ctl. Worcester: *The Cartulary of Worcester Cathedral Priory*, ed. R. R. Darlington (PRS, LXXVI, 1968 for 1962–3).

Cumbd F., *see under* FINES.

DAJ: *Derbyshire Archaeological Journal*.

Dashwood, G. H., 'Notes of deeds and survey of Crabhouse nunnery, Norfolk', *Norfolk Archaeology*, V (1859), 257–62.

Davidson, *History of Newenham Abbey*: J. Davidson, *The History of Newenham Abbey in the county of Devon* (London, 1843).

Davies, J. Conway, 'Strata Marcella documents', *Montgomeryshire Coll.*, 51 (1949–50), 164–87.

Davis: G. R. C. Davis, *Medieval Cartularies of Great Britain: a Short Catalogue* (London, 1958).

Davis, R. G., 'The Oratory at Barton', *Hants Field Club*, 2 (1890–3), 295–307.

DC: *Documents illustrative of the Social and Economic History of the Danelaw from various collections*, ed. F. M. Stenton (British Academy, records of social and economic history V, 1920).

DCNQ: *Devon and Cornwall Notes and Queries*.

Dell, R., *The records of Rye Corporation: a catalogue* (Lewes, 1962).

Demay: G. Demay, *Inventaire des sceaux de la Normandie recueillis dans les dépôts d'archives, musées et collections particulières des départements de la Seine-Inférieure, du Calvados, de l'Eure, de la Manche, et de l'Orne* (Paris, 1881).

Denton, J. H., *English Royal Free Chapels 1100–1300: a constitutional history* (Manchester, 1970).

Derbys Arch. and Nat. Hist. Soc.: *Derbyshire Archaeological and Natural History Society*.

Derbys Chts.: *Descriptive catalogue of Derbyshire charters in public and private libraries and muniment rooms*, ed. I. H. Jeayes (London and Derby, 1906).

Derbys F., *see under* FINES.

Devon F., *see under* FINES.

Devon Gaol Delivery: Medieval Gaol Delivery Rolls for the county of Devon, ed. A. J. Howard (Pinner, 1986).

Diceto: Radulfi de Diceto decani Londoniensis opera historica..., ed. W. Stubbs (2 vols., RS, 1876).

Dickinson: J. C. Dickinson, *The Priory of Cartmel* (Milnthorpe, 1991).

The Shrine of Our Lady at Walsingham (Cambridge, 1956).

Dict. Welsh Biography: The Dictionary of Welsh Biography down to 1940 (Honourable Society of Cymmrodorion, 1959).

DKR (+ number of report): Reports of the Deputy Keeper of the Public Records.

DNB: Dictionary of National Biography, ed. L. Stephen and S. Lee (66 vols., London, 1885–1901, repr. 22 vols., Oxford, 1921–2).

Dobson, R. B. and Donaghey, S., *The History of Clementhorpe Nunnery, York* (York Archaeological Trust, 1984).

Dodds, M. Hope, 'The Prioresses of St Bartholomew's nunnery, supplementary note', *Proc. Soc. Ant. Newcastle*, 4th ser., 6 (1933–5), 122.

Dodnash Chts.: Dodnash Priory Charters, ed. C. Harper-Bill (Suffolk Charters ser. XVI, 1998).

Dodwell, B., 'A papal bull for Torksey priory', *BIHR*, 52 (1979), 87–90.

Dore Abbey: R. Shoesmith and R. Richardson, eds., *A definitive history of Dore Abbey* (Logaston, Herefordshire, 1997).

Dorset F., see under FINES.

Dorset IPM: Dorset Inquisitiones post mortem from Henry III to Richard III, A.D. 1216 to 1485, vol. I, A–C, ed. E. A. Fry (1916).

Douglass, S. P., 'Langley Priory', *Trans. Leics AHS*, 62 (1988), 16–30.

Drury, G. Dru, 'The Abbots of Bindon', *Proc. Dorset NHAS*, 55 (1934), 1–19.

'Catalogue of seal casts in the Dorset County Museum, 1944', *Proc. Dorset NHAS*, 66 (1944), 84–126.

Dugdale, *Baronage*: W. Dugdale, *Baronage of England* (2 vols., London, 1675–6).

Dugdale, W., *The Antiquities of Warwickshire illustrated* (London, 1656, repd Coventry, 1765; 2nd edn. by W. Thomas, 2 vols., London, 1730).

Dunkin, *History of Bicester*: J. Dunkin, *The History and Antiquities of Bicester* (London, 1816).

Dunn, F. I., 'The priory of Mobberley and its charters', *Cheshire History*, 8 (1981), 73–88.

Dunning, R.W., 'Somerset parochial clergy, 1373–1404', *Proc. Soms ANHS*, 114 (1970), 91–5.

Durham Account Rolls: Extracts from the Account Rolls of the Abbey of Durham, ed. J. T. Fowler (3 vols., Surtees Society 99, 100, 103, 1898–1901).

Durham Assize Rolls: 'Two thirteenth-century assize rolls for the county of Durham', ed. K. C. Bayley, in *Miscellanea II* (Surtees Society 128, 1916), pp. 1–105.

Durham Seals: Catalogue of the Seals in the Treasury of the Dean and Chapter of Durham, ed. W. Greenwell and C. H. Hunter Blair (2 vols., Society of Antiquaries of Newcastle upon Tyne, 1911–21).

Earldom of Cornwall Accounts: Ministers' accounts for the Earldom of Cornwall, 1296–1297, ed. L. M. Midgley (2 vols., Camden 3rd ser. LXVI, LXVIII, 1942–5).

Earliest English Brasses: J. Coales, *The Earliest English Brasses: patronage, style and workshops, 1270–1350* (London, Monumental Brass Society, 1987).

Earliest English Law Reports, The, ed. P. A. Brand (2 vols., Selden Society 111–12, 1996).

Early Newcastle Deeds: Early Deeds relating to Newcastle upon Tyne, ed. A. M. Oliver (Surtees Society 137, 1924).

East Herts Arch. Soc. Trans.: East Herts Archaeological Society Transactions.

Easterling, R. C., 'List of Civic Officials of Exeter in the 12th and 13th centuries', *TDA*, 70 (1938), 455–94.

Eastwood, J., *History of the parish of Ecclesfield in the county of York* (London, 1862).

ECSP: *Early Charters of the Cathedral Church of St Paul, London*, ed. M. Gibbs (Camden 3rd Series, LVIII, 1939).

EEA: *English Episcopal Acta* (British Academy 1980–in progress).

EETS: Early English Text Society.

EHD: *English Historical Documents, II, 1042–1189*, ed. D. C. Douglas and G. W. Greenaway (London, 1968).

EHR: *English Historical Review*.

Elmham, E: Thomas of Elmham, *Historia monasterii S. Augustini Cantuariensis*, ed. C. Hardwick, (RS, 1858).

Elvins, M. T., *Arundel Priory 1380–1980: The College of the Holy Trinity* (Chichester, 1981).

Emden, *BRUC*: A. B. Emden, *A Biographical Register of the University of Cambridge to 1500* (Cambridge, 1963).

Emden, *BRUO*: A. B. Emden, *A Biographical Register of the University of Oxford to 1500* (3 vols., Oxford, 1957–9).

English Baronies: I. J. Sanders, *English Baronies: a study of their origin and descent, 1086–1327* (Oxford, 1960).

Epp. Cant.: *Epistolae Cantuarienses*, ed. W. Stubbs (RS, 1865).

Essays in Medieval History presented to Bertie Wilkinson, ed. T. A. Sandquist and M. R. Powicke, (Toronto, 1969).

Essex F., see under FINES.

Eubel: C. Eubel *et al.*, *Hierarchia Catholica Medii Aevi* (7 vols., Munster, 1913–68).

Eulog. Hist.: *Eulogium historiarum sive temporis . . .*, ed. F. S. Haydon (3 vols., RS, 1858).

Evans, D. H., *Valle Crucis Abbey* (CADW, revised edn, 1995).

Excerpta e Rot. Fin.: *Excerpta e Rotulis finium in turri Londinensi asservatis, Henrico tertio rege, A.D. 1216–1272*, ed. C. Roberts (2 vols., Record Commission, 1835–6).

EYC: *Early Yorkshire Charters*, I–III, ed. W. Farrer (Edinburgh, 1914–16); IV–XII, ed. C. T. Clay, (Yorkshire Archaeological Society, Record Series, Extra Series, I–III, V–X, 1935–65 (Extra Series vol. IV is Index to *EYC*, I–III, ed. C. T. and E. M. Clay, 1947)).

Eyre Roll 1221–2: *Rolls of the justices in Eyre, being the rolls of pleas and assizes for Gloucestershire, Warwickshire and Staffordshire (recte Shropshire) 1221, 1222*, ed. D. M. Stenton (Selden Society 69, 1940).

Eyton, *Salop*: R.W. Eyton, *Antiquities of Shropshire* (12 vols., London and Shifnal, 1854–60).

F, FF: *see* FINES.

FA: *Feudal Aids: Inquisitions and assessments relating to feudal aids, with other analogous documents preserved in the Public Record Office, A.D. 1284–1431* (6 vols., PRO, 1899–1920).

Fairweather, J. H., 'The Augustinian priory of Weybourne', *Norfolk Archaeology*, XXIV (1932), 201–28.

Fairweather, J. H. and Bradfer-Lawrence, H. I., 'The priory of St Mary and All Saints, Westacre, and excavations upon its site', *Norfolk Archaeology*, XXIII (1929), 359–94.

Farnham, *Charnwood Forest*: G. F. Farnham, 'Charnwood Forest: the Charnwood Manors', *Trans. Leics AHS*, XV (1927–8), 139–181; *Charnwood Forest and its historians and the Charnwood Manors* (Leicestershire Archaeological Society, 1930).

Farnham, *Leics Notes*: G. F. Farnham, *Leicestershire Medieval Village Notes* (6 vols., Leicester, 1929–33).

Farrer, E., 'The seal of a prior of Stoke-by-Clare', *Proc. Suffolk Inst.*, XX (1930), 265–9.

Farrer, *Honors and Knights' Fees*: W. Farrer, *Honors and Knights' Fees: an attempt to identify the component parts of certain honors and to trace the descent of the tenants of the same who hold of knight's service or serjeanty from the eleventh to the fourteenth century* (3 vols., Manchester, 1923–5).

Fasti Cistercienses Cambrenses: D. H. Williams, 'Fasti Cistercienses Cambrenses', *Bulletin of the Board of Celtic Studies*, XXIV (1971), 181–229; XXV (1973), 156–7.

Fasti Ecclesiae Scoticanae: *Fasti Ecclesiae Scoticanae Medii Aevi ad annum 1638*, ed. D. E. R. Watt (Scottish Record Society, new ser. 1, 1969).

Fasti Parochiales: *Fasti Parochiales* ed. A. H. Thompson, C. T. Clay, N. A. H. Lawrence, N. K. M. Gurney and D. M. Smith (5 vols., Yorkshire Archaeological Society, Record Series LXXXV, CVII, CXXIX, CXXXIII, CXLIII, 1933–85).

Feltoe, C. L., *Three Canterbury Kalendars*, London, n.d. [1922].

Feodarium prioratus Dun.: *Feodarium prioratus Dunelmensis: A survey of the estates of the prior and convent of Durham compiled in the fifteenth century, illustrated by the original grants and other evidences*, ed. W. Greenwell (Surtees Society 68, 1872).

FF: *Feet of Fines of the reign of Henry II and of the first seven years of the reign of Richard I, A.D. 1182–A.D. 1196* (PRS, XVII, 1894).

FF 7–8 Richard I: *Feet of Fines of the seventh and eighth years of the reign of Richard I, A.D. 1196 to A.D. 1197* (PRS, 20, 1896).

Finberg, H. P. R., 'Abbots of Tavistock', *Devon and Cornwall Notes and Queries*, XXII (1942–6), 159–62, 174–5, 186–8, 194–7.

    Tavistock Abbey: a study in the social and economic history of Devon (Cambridge, 1951, repr Newton Abbot, 1969).

    'The tragi-comedy of Abbot Bonus', in W. G. Hoskins and H. P. R. Finberg, *Devonshire Studies* (London, 1952), pp. 198–211.

    West-Country Historical Studies (Newton Abbot, 1969).

Finchale Priory: *The charters of endowment, inventories and account rolls of the priory of Finchale in the county of Durham*, ed. J. Raine (Surtees Society, vi, 1837).

FINES:

Beds F. I: *A calendar of the feet of fines for Bedfordshire preserved in the Public Record Office, of the reigns of Richard I, John and Henry III*, ed. G. H. Fowler, *BHRS*, VI (1919).

Beds F. II: *A calendar of the feet of fines, part III, for the reign of Edward I, with some additions*, ed. G. H. Fowler, *BHRS*, XII (1928), 3–82.

Bristol F.: E. W. W. Veale, ed., *The Great Red Book of Bristol, part I* (Bristol Record Society II, 1931), app. 1: Calendar of the Feet of Fines 8 Richard I to 47 Edward III, pp. 180–247.

Bucks F. I: *A calendar of the feet of fines for the county of Buckingham, 7 Richard I – 44 Henry III*, ed. M. W. Hughes (Buckinghamshire Record Society, 4, 1942 for 1940).

Bucks F. II: *A calendar of the feet of fines for Buckinghamshire 1259–1307, with an appendix 1179–1259*, ed. A. Travers (Buckinghamshire Record Society 25, 1989).

Cambs. F.: *Pedes finium . . . relating to the county of Cambridge* (calendar 7 Richard I – 1485), ed. W. Rye (Cambridge Antiquarian Society, Octavo Series, XXVI, 1891).

Cornwall F.: *Cornwall feet of fines, Richard I – Edward III, 1195–1377*, ed. J. H. Rowe (Devon and Cornwall Record Society, 1914).

Cumbd F.: F. H. M. Parker, ed., ' A calendar of the feet of fines for Cumberland from their commencement to the accession of Henry VII', *Trans. CWAAS*, new ser. 7 (1907), 215–61.

Derbys F.: W. H. Hart and C. Kerry, eds., 'A calendar of the fines in the county of Derby (1196–1324)', ed. *Derbyshire Archaeological and Nat. Hist. Society Journal*:

    Derbys F. (1885): VII (1885), 195–217.

    Derbys F. (1886): VIII (1886), 15–64.

    Derbys F. (1887): IX (1887), 84–93.

    Derbys F. (1888): X (1888), 151–8.

    Derbys F. (1889): XI (1889), 93–106.

    Derbys F. (1890): XII (1890), 23–42.

    Derbys F. (1891): XIII (1891), 9–31.

Devon F. I: Devon feet of fines, I (Richard I – Henry III), 1196–1272, ed. O. J. Reichel (Devon and Cornwall Record Society, 1912).

Devon F. II: Devon feet of fines, II (1 Edward I – 43 Edward III), 1272–1369, ed. O. J. Reichel, F. B. Prideaux and H. Tapley-Soper (Devon and Cornwall Record Society, 1939).

Dorset F.: Full abstracts of the Feet of Fines relating to the county of Dorset . . ., 1195–1485, ed. E. A. Fry and G. S. Fry (2 vols., Dorset Record Society, V, X (1896–1910)).

Essex F. I: Feet of fines for Essex vol. I (A.D., 1182–1272), ed. R. E. G. Kirk and E. F. Kirk, (Essex Archaeological Society, Colchester, 1899–1910).

Essex F. II: Feet of fines for Essex vol. II (A.D. 1272–1326), ed. R. E. G. Kirk and E. F. Kirk, (Essex Archaeological Society, Colchester, 1913–28).

Essex F. III: Feet of fines for Essex vol. III (A.D. 1327–1422), ed. R. E. G. Kirk and E. F. Kirk, (Essex Archaeological Society, Colchester, 1929–49).

Glos F.: J. Maclean, ed., 'Pedes finium . . . or excerpts from the feet of fines for the county of Gloucester, 7 John – 57 Henry III', ed. *BGAS*, xvi (1892), 183–95.

Hunts F.: A calendar of the feet of fines relating to the county of Huntingdon, 1194–1603, ed. G. J. Turner (Cambridge Antiquarian Society, Octavo Series, XXXVII, 1913).

Kent F.: Calendar of Kent feet of fines to the end of Henry III's reign. Prepared in collaboration by I. J. Churchill, R. Griffin, F. W. Hardman, with introduction by F. W. Jessup (Kent Archaeological Society, XV, 1956).

Lancs F. I: Final Concords of the county of Lancaster from the original chirographs, or feet of fines, preserved in the Public Record Office, London, part I, 7 Richard I – 35 Edward I, A.D. 1196 – A.D. 1307. Transcribed, translated and annotated by W. Farrer (Lancashire and Cheshire Record Society 39, 1899).

Lancs F. II: Final Concords of the county of Lancaster, part II (Edward II and Edward III), A.D. 1307 to A.D. 1377, ed. W. Farrer (Lancashire and Cheshire Record Society 46, 1903).

Lincs F., I: Abstracts of Final Concords, temp. Richard I, John and Henry III (1193–1244), ed. W. K. Boyd and W. O. Massingberd, I (in 2 parts), (1896).

Lincs F., II: Final concords of the county of Lincoln from the feet of fines preserved in the Public Record Office, A.D. 1244–1272, with additions from various sources, A.D. 1176–1250, ed. C. W. Foster (Lincoln Record Society 17, 1920).

Lincs F. 1199–1216: Feet of fines for the county of Lincoln for the reign of King John, 1199–1216, ed. M. S. Walker (PRS, new ser. 29, 1953).

London and Middlesex F.: A calendar of the feet of fines for London and Middlesex, Richard I – Elizabeth, ed. W. J. Hardy and W. Page (2 vols., London, 1892–3).

Norfolk F. 1198–1202: Feet of fines for the county of Norfolk for the tenth year of the reign of King Richard the First, 1198–1199, and for the first four years of the reign of King John, 1199–1202, ed. B. Dodwell (PRS, LXV, 1952).

Norfolk F. 1201–1215: Feet of fines for the county of Norfolk for the reign of King John, 1201–15 . . ., ed. B. Dodwell (PRS, LXX, 1959 for 1956).

Norfolk F. (Rye): A short calendar of the feet of fines for Norfolk (Richard I – Richard III), ed. Walter Rye (2 parts, Norwich, 1885–6).

Northumberland and Durham F. I: Feet of fines, Northumberland and Durham (abstracts 1196–1228), ed. A. M. Oliver and C. Johnson from transcripts by P. Oliver (Newcastle upon Tyne Record Ser. X, 1931 (1933)).

Northumberland and Durham F. II: Feet of Fines, Northumberland A.D. 1273 – A.D. 1346 (Newcastle upon Tyne Record Ser. XI, 1932).

Oxford F.: The Feet of Fines for Oxfordshire, 1195–1291. Transcribed and calendared by H. E. Salter (Oxfordshire Record Society XII, 1930).

Soms F. I: Pedes finium, commonly called feet of fines, for the county of Somerset, Richard I – Edward I, A.D. 1196 – A.D. 1307, ed. E. Green (Somerset Record Society 6, 1892).

Soms F. II: Pedes finium, commonly called feet of fines, for the county of Somerset, 1 Edward I to 20 Edward III, ed. E. Green (Somerset Record Society 12, 1898).

Soms F. III: Pedes finium, commonly called feet of fines, for the county of Somerset, 21 Edward III to 20 Richard II, ed. E. Green (Somerset Record Society 17, 1902).

Staffs F. 1: G . Wrottesley, ed., 'Calendar of final concords or pedes finium, Staffordshire, temp. Richard I – Henry III', *SHC*, III(i), 165–77; IV(i), 217–63, 1882–3.

Staffs F. 2: G . Wrottesley, ed., 'Final concords, or pedes finium, Staffordshire temp. Henry III', *SHC* IV(i) (1883), 217–63.

Staffs F. 3: 'Final concords, Edward I and Edward II', *SHC* (1911), 27–111.

Suffolk F. 1199–1214: Feet of fines . . . for the county of Suffolk, 1199–1214, ed. B. Dodwell (PRS, LXX, 1959 for 1956), nos. 280–565.

Suffolk F. (Rye): A calendar of the feet of fines for Suffolk (1 Richard I – 3 Richard III), ed. W. Rye (Suffolk Institute of Archaeology and Natural History, 1900).

Surrey F.: (Calendar of) Pedes Finium, or fines relating to . . . Surrey (Richard I – Henry VII), ed. F. B. Lewis (Surrey Archaeological Collections, Extra vol. 1, 1894).

Sussex F. I: An abstract of feet of fines relating to the county of Sussex, from Richard I to 33 Henry III, compiled L. F. Salzman (Sussex Record Society II, 1903).

Sussex F. II: An abstract of feet of fines relating to the county of Sussex, from 34 Henry III to 35 Edward I, compiled L. F. Salzman (Sussex Record Society VII, 1908).

Sussex F. III: An abstract of feet of fines relating to the county of Sussex, from 1 Edward II to 24 Henry VII, compiled L. F. Salzman (Sussex Record Society XXIII, 1916).

Warws F. I: Warwickshire feet of fines, 7 Richard I (1195) – 12 Edward I (1284). Abstracted by E. Stokes and ed. F. C. Wellstood, with introduction and indexes by F. T. S. Houghton (Dugdale Society XI, 1932).

Warws F. II: Warwickshire feet of fines, vol. II: 13 Edward I (1284) – 18 Edward III (1345). Abstracted by E. Stokes and L. Drucker, with introduction and indexes by F. T. S. Houghton (Dugdale Society XV, 1939).

Wilts F. I: A calendar of the feet of fines relating to the county of Wiltshire, remaining in the Public Record Office, London. From their commencement in the reign of Richard I (1195) to the end of Henry III (1272), compiled by E. A. Fry (Wiltshire Archaeological and Natural History Society, 1930).

Wilts F. II: Abstracts of feet of fines relating to Wiltshire for the reigns of Edward I and Edward II, ed. R. B. Pugh (Wiltshire Archaeological and Natural History Society, 1939).

Wilts F. III: Abstracts of feet of fines relating to Wiltshire for the reign of Edward III, ed. C. R. Elrington (Wiltshire Record Society XXIX, 1974).

Yorks F., John: Pedes finium Ebor., regnante Johanne, A.D. MCXCIX – A.D. MCCXIV, ed. W. Brown (Surtees Society 94, 1897).

Yorks F., 1218–31: Feet of Fines for the county of York from 1218 to 1231, ed. J. Parker (Yorkshire Archaeological Society, Record Series LXII, 1921).

Yorks F., 1232–46: Feet of Fines for the county of York from 1232 to 1246, ed. J. Parker (Yorkshire Archaeological Society, Record Series LXVII, 1925).

Yorks F. 1246–72: Feet of Fines for the county of York from 1246 to 1272, ed. J. Parker (Yorkshire Archaeological Society, Record Series, LXXXII, 1932).

Yorks F. 1272–1300: Feet of Fines for the county of York from 1272 to 1300, ed. F. H. Slingsby (Yorkshire Archaeological Society, Record Series, CCXXI, 1956).

Yorks F. 1300–1314: Feet of Fines for the county of York from 1300 to 1314, ed. M. Roper (Yorkshire Archaeological Society, Record Series, CXXVII, 1965).

Yorks F. 1347–1377: *Feet of Fines for the county of York from 1347 to 1377*, ed. W. P. Baildon (Yorkshire Archaeological Society, Record Series, LII, 1915).

First Reg. Norwich: *The First Register of Norwich cathedral priory*, ed. H. W. Saunders (Norfolk Record Society XI, 1939).

Fishwick, H., *The history of the parish of Lytham in the county of Lancaster* (Chetham Soc., new ser. 60, 1907).

Flete: *Flete's History of Westminster Abbey*, ed. J. Armitage Robinson (Cambridge, 1909).

Flight, C., *The Bishops and Monks of Rochester 1076–1214* (Kent Archaeological Society, Maidstone, 1997).

Flor. Hist.: (Matthew Paris) *Flores Historiarum per Mattheum Westmonasteriensem collecti*, ed. H. R. Luard (3 vols., RS, 1890).

Florence: Florence of Worcester, *Chronica ex chronicis*, ed. B. Thorpe (2 vols., English Historical Society, London, 1848–9).

Floyer and Hamilton: *Catalogue of MSS. preserved in the Chapter Library of Worcester Cathedral*, ed. J. K. Floyer and S. G. Hamilton (Worcestershire Historical Society, 1906).

Foreville & Keir, *Book of St Gilbert*: *The Book of St Gilbert*, ed. R. Foreville and G. Keir (OMT, 1987).

Foster, M. R., 'Durham monks at Oxford *c.* 1286–1381: a house of studies and its inmates', *Oxoniensia*, LV (1990), 99–114.

Foster, *Visitations of Yorkshire*: *The Visitations of Yorkshire made in the years 1584/5 by Robert Glover, Somerset Herald, to which is added the subsequent Visitation made in 1612 by Richard St George, Norroy King of Arms* ed. J. Foster (London, 1875).

Foulds, T. 'The history of Thurgarton priory before 1316', *Trans. Thoroton Soc.*, LXXXIV (1980), 21–32.

'Lenton priory: a reconstruction of the lost cartulary, with charters illustrative of the endowment', microfiche appendix to his article, 'The foundation of Lenton priory and a reconstruction of its lost cartulary', *Trans. Thoroton Soc.*, XCII (1988), 34–42.

Fowler, R., 'Tiptree Priory and the Coronation', *TEAS*, new ser. VIII (1901), 334–5.

Fowler, R. C., 'An abbot and seal of Tiltey', *TEAS*, new ser. XVI (1921), 57.

Fowler, R. C. and Clapham, A. W., *Beeleigh Abbey* (London, 1922).

Fraser, C. M., *A history of Antony Bek, bishop of Durham 1283–1311* (Oxford, 1957).

Fulman: 'Historiae Croylandensis continuatio' in *Rerum Anglicarum Scriptores*, I, ed. W. Fulman (Oxford, 1684).

Fundacio: 'Fundacio Abbathiae de Kyrkestall', ed. and translated E. K. Clark, 'The Foundation of Kirkstall Abbey', *Miscellanea* (Thoresby Society), IV (1895), 169–208.

Gallia Christiana (16 vols., Paris, 1715–1865).

GASA: *Gesta Abbatum S. Albani*, ed. H. T. Riley (3 vols., RS, 1867–9).

Gervase: *The Historical Works of Gervase of Canterbury*, ed. W. Stubbs (2 vols., RS, 1879–80).

Gesta Henrici II: *Gesta regis Henrici secundi Benedicti abbatis. The chronicle of the reigns of Henry II and Richard I, A.D. 1169–1192, known commonly under the name of Benedict of Peterborough*, ed. W. Stubbs (2 vols., RS, 1867).

GFL: *The Letters and Charters of Gilbert Foliot*, ed. A. Morey and C. N. L. Brooke (Cambridge, 1967).

Gibson, M., *Churches of Door, Home Lacy and Hempsted* (1727).

Gibson, *Tynemouth*: W. S. Gibson, *The History of the Monastery founded at Tynemouth* (2 vols., London, 1846).

Gilbertine Chts.: *Transcripts of charters relating to the Gilbertine houses of Sixle, Ormsby, Catley, Bullington and Alvingham*, ed. with a translation, from the King's Remembrancer

Memoranda rolls nos. 183, 185, and 187, by F. M. Stenton (Lincoln Record Society 18, 1922).

Gilyard-Beer: R. Gilyard-Beer, 'The graves of the abbots of Fountains', *YAJ*, 59 (1987), 45–50.

Gir. Camb.: Giraldi Cambrensis Opera, ed. J. S. Brewer, J. F. Dimock, and G. F. Warner (8 vols., RS, 1861–91).

Glam. Chts.: Cartae et alia munimenta quae ad Dominium de Glamorgan pertinent, ed. G. T. Clark (2nd edn, 6 vols., Cardiff, 1910).

Glapwell Chts.: The Glapwell Charters, ed. R. R. Darlington (Derbyshire Archaeological and Nat. Hist. Society, 1957–9).

Glos IPM 1236–1300: Abstracts of inquisitiones post mortem for Gloucestershire returned into the court of chancery during the Plantagenet period, part IV: 20 Henry III to 29 Edward I, 1236–1300, ed. S. J. Madge (British Record Society, Index Library 30, 1903).

Glos IPM 1359–1413: Abstracts of inquisitiones post mortem for Gloucestershire returned into the court of chancery during the Plantagenet period, part VI: 33 Edward III to 14 Henry IV, 1359–1413, ed. E. Stokes (British Record Society, Index Library 47, 1914).

Gloucestershire Peace Rolls 1361–98: Rolls of the Gloucestershire Sessions of the Peace 1361–1398, ed. E. G. Kimball (*BGAS*, 62, 1942 for 1940).

Goddard, *Ickleton Church and Priory*: A. R. Goddard, 'Ickleton Church and Priory', *Proc. Cambs. Ant. Soc.*, XI (1903–6), 181–95.

Godfrey, J. T., *The History of the Parish and Priory of Lenton in the County of Nottingham* (London and Derby, 1884).

Golding, B., *Gilbert of Sempringham and the Gilbertine Order c. 1130 – c. 1300* (Oxford, 1995).

Goodrich, M., 'Westwood: a rural English nunnery with its local and French connections' in J. Greatrex, ed., *The Vocation of Service to God and Neighbour: essays on the interests, involvements and problems of religious communities and their members in medieval society* (International Medieval Research 5, Brepols, 1998), pp. 43–57.

'The White Ladies of Worcester: their place in contemporary medieval life', *Trans. Worcs. Archaeol. Soc.*, 3rd ser. 14 (1994), 129–47.

Goring Chts.: A collection of charters relating to Goring, Streatley and the neighbourhood, 1181–1546, preserved in the Bodleian Library, with a supplement, ed. T. R. Gambier- Parry, (2 vols., Oxfordshire Record Society, xiii, xiv, 1931–2).

Graham, 'Bermondsey': Rose Graham, 'The priory of La Charité-sur-Loire and the monastery of Bermondsey', *JBAA*, 32 (1926), 157–91.

Graham, Rose, 'Alberbury Priory', *Trans. Shrops ANHS*, 44 (1928), 257–303.

'The Cluniac priory of St Martin des Champs, Paris, and its dependent priories in England', *JBAA*, 3rd ser., 11 (1948), 36–59.

English Ecclesiastical Studies: being some essays in research in medieval history (London, 1929).

'Four alien priories in Monmouthshire', *JBAA*, new ser. 35 (1929), 102–21.

The history of the alien priory of Wenlock (HMSO, 1965), also in *JBAA*, 3rd ser. 4 (1939), 117–40.

'Richard de Maners, abbot of Bindon', *JBAA*, new ser. 39 (1934), 186.

'The seals of the Cluniac monastery of Bermondsey', *Surrey Arch. Coll.*, XXXIX (1931), 78–9.

(with C. A. Ralegh Radford) 'The Cluniac priory of St Mary, Carswell', *TDA*, 84 (1952), 115–21.

Gray, A., *List of Obiits of Carthusians of the English Houses from the earliest times to the present day* (typescript at Parkminster).

Gray, J. M., 'The Barnwell canons and the Papal Court at Avignon', *Proc. Cambs. Ant. Soc.*, XXXIII (1933), 98–107.

Gray, M., *The Trinitarian Order in England: excavations at Thelsford priory*, ed. L. Watts and P. Rahtz (BAR, British ser. 226, 1993).

Gray, *St Radegund*: Gray, A., *Priory of St Radegund, Cambridge* (CAS, octavo ser. XXXI, 1898).

Great Red Book of Bristol, The, ed. E. W. W. Veale (5 vols., Bristol Record Society I, IV, VIII, XVI, XVIII, 1931–53).

Greatrex, *Biog. Reg.*: J. Greatrex, *Biographical Register of the English Cathedral Priories of the Province of Canterbury c. 1066–1540* (Oxford, 1997).

Greatrex, J., 'Prior John de Evesham of Worcester: one of St Benedict's worthy stewards?' in V. King and A. Horton, eds., *From Buckfast to Borneo: essays presented to Father Robert Nicholl on the 85th anniversary of his birth, 27 March 1995* (Hull, 1995).

Greene, J. P., 'The elevation of Norton priory, Cheshire, to the status of mitred abbey', *Trans. Lancs and Ches. Hist. Soc.*, 128 (1979), 97–122.

Greenhill: F. A. Greenhill, *Monumental incised slabs in the county of Lincoln* (Newport Pagnall, 1986).

Gresley Chts: I. H. Jeayes, *Descriptive Catalogue of the Charters and Muniments of the Gresley family in the possession of Sir Robert Gresley, bart., at Drakelowe* (London, 1895).

Grosjean, P., 'De S. Iohanne Bridlingtoniensi collectanea', *Analecta Bollandiana*, 53 (1935), 101–29.

Guala Letters: The Letters and Charters of Cardinal Guala Bicchieri, papal legate in England 1216–1218, ed. N. Vincent (Canterbury and York Society 83, 1996).

Guéry, *Hist. Lyre*: C. Guéry, *Histoire de l'Abbaye de Lyre* (Evreux, 1917).

Guildford Obits: J. S. Purvis, ed., 'Obituary kalendar of the Dominican Friary of Guildford', *Surrey Arch. Coll.*, XLII (1934), 90–9.

Guilloreau, L., *Les Prieurés anglais de l'ordre de Cluny* (Macon, 1910).

 Prieurés Anglais de la dépendence de Saint-Serge d'Angers: Totnes, Tywardreath, Minster (Ligugé, 1909).

Hackett, M. B., *The original Statutes of Cambridge University* (Cambridge, 1970).

Hadley, A., *Register of Conway* (London, 1900).

Hailstone, *History of Bottisham*: E. Hailstone, *The History and Antiquities of the parish of Bottisham and the priory of Anglesey in Cambridgeshire* (CAS, XIV, XVI, 1873–8).

Haines, *Dover Priory*: C. R. Haines, *Dover Priory* (Cambridge, 1930).

Haines, R. M., *The administration of the diocese of Worcester in the first half of the fourteenth century* (London, 1965).

 'The election of an abbot of Tewkesbury in 1347' in R. M. Haines, *Ecclesia Anglicana: studies in the English Church of the later middle ages* (Toronto, 1989), 15–25.

Hall, H., *A formula book of English official historical documents, part I: Diplomatic documents* (Cambridge, 1908).

Hall, J., *Book of the Abbey of Combermere: The Book of the Abbey of Combermere 1289 to 1529* in *Miscellanies relating to Lancashire and Cheshire II* (Lancashire and Cheshire Record Society 31, 1896).

Hall, K. G., 'A note on the Benedictine nunnery at Holystone', *Proc. Soc. Ant. Newcastle*, 4th ser. 6 (1933–5), 155–8.

Hampshire Notes and Queries.

Hancock, *Dunster Church and Priory*: F. Hancock, *Dunster Church and Priory: their history and architectural features* (Taunton, 1905).

Hants Field Club: Hampshire Field Club and Archaeological Society.

Harbin, E. H. Bates, 'Two deeds relating to Stavordale priory and the family of Sanzaver', *Proc. Soms ANHS*, 61 (1916 for 1915), 105–14. *See also* Bates.

 'The priory of St Michael on the Steep Holme', *Proc. Soms ANHS*, 62 (1917 for 1916), 26–45. *See also* Bates.

Harbottle, B., 'Bishop Hatfield's visitation of Durham Priory in 1354', *Arch. Aeliana*, 4th ser. XXXVI (1958), 81–100.

Harland, *Hist. Acct of Sallay Abbey*: J. Harland, *Historical Account of the Cistercian Abbey of Sallay in Craven, Yorkshire* (London, 1853).

Harrison, J., 'The troubled foundation of Grace Dieu abbey', *Monmouthshire Antiquary*, 14 (1998), 25–9.

Harvey, B. F., ed., *Documents illustrating the rule of Walter de Wenlok, abbot of Westminster* (Camden 4th ser. 2, 1965).

Haslop, G. S., 'The creation of brother John Sherburn as abbot of Selby', *YAJ*, XLII (1967), 25–30.

Hasted, *Hist. of Kent*: E. Hasted, *The History and Topographical Survey of Kent* (2nd edn, 12 vols., 1797–1801).

Hatton Wood MSS.: F. Taylor, 'Hatton Wood Manuscripts in the John Rylands Library', *BJRL*, 24 (1940).

Hatton's Book of Seals: Sir Christopher Hatton's Book of Seals, ed. L. C. Loyd and D. M. Stenton (Oxford, and Northamptonshire Record Society XV, 1950)

Hays, R. W., *History of the Abbey of Aberconway, 1186–1537* (Cardiff, 1963).

Heads, I: D. Knowles, C. N. L. Brooke, and V. C. M. London, *The Heads of Religious Houses: England and Wales 940–1216* (Cambridge, 1972).

Heales: Heales, A. C., *Records of Merton Priory* (London, 1898).

Heales, *Tandridge Priory*: A. Heales, 'Tanridge priory and the Austin canons', *Surrey Arch. Coll.*, IX (1888), 19–156.

Hearne's Coll.: *Remarks and Collections of Thomas Hearne*, ed. C. E. Doble, D. W. Rannie, H. E. Salter *et al.* (11 vols., Oxford Historical Society II, VII, XIII, XXXIV, XLII, XLIII, XLVIII, L, LXV, LXVII, LXXII, 1885–1921).

Hemingby's Reg.: *Hemingby's Register*, ed. H. M. Chew (Wiltshire Record Society 18, 1963).

Henwood, G., *Abbot Richard Wallingford, a fourteenth-century astronomer and instrument-maker* (Wallingford, 1988).

Hereford Seals: F. C. Morgan and P. E. Morgan, *A Concise List of Seals belonging to the Dean and Chapter of Hereford Cathedral, with a preliminary note* (Hereford, Woolhope Naturalists' Field Club, 1966).

HF: *Recueil des historiens des Gaules et de la France*, ed. M. Bouquet *et al.*, new edn, ed. Delisle (24 vols., Paris, 1869–1904).

Hicks, F. W. Potto, 'Original documents relating to Bristol', *BGAS*, 56 (1934), 165–77.
'Original documents of the thirteenth century relating to Bristol', *BGAS*, 58 (1936), 219–42.

Highworth Hundred Rolls: *The Rolls of Highworth Hundred, 1275–1287*, ed. B. Farr (2 vols., Wiltshire Record Society 21–2, 1966–8).

Hill, *Eccles. Letter-Books*: R. M. T. Hill, *Ecclesiastical Letter-Books of the thirteenth century* (priv. pd, n.d.).

Hill, R. M. T., 'Bishop Sutton and the institutions of heads of religious houses in the diocese of Lincoln', *EHR*, LVIII (1943), 201–9.

Hillen, H. J., *History of the Borough of King's Lynn* (2 vols., Norwich, [1907]).

Hist. Northumberland: *A History of Northumberland*. Issued under the direction of the Northumberland County History Committee, vols. I– , (Newcastle upon Tyne, 1893–).

Hist. Shulbrede: A. Ponsonby, *The Priory and Manor of Lynchmere and Shulbrede* (Taunton, 1920).

HMC: *Royal Commission on Historical Manuscripts*. Appendices to Reports and Calendars (London, 1870–).

HMC Abergavenny: *Report on the manuscripts of the Marquess of Abergavenny, Lord Braye, G. F. Luttrell esq., etc.* (1887).

HMC Ancaster: *Report on the manuscripts of the Earl of Ancaster preserved at Grimsthorpe* (1907).

HMC De L'Isle and Dudley: *Report on the manuscripts of Lord De L'Isle and Dudley, preserved at Penshurst Place* (4 vols., 1925–42).

HMC Duke of Leeds etc.: *Report on the manuscripts of the Duke of Leeds, the Bridgewater Trust, Reading Corporation, the Inner Temple etc.* (1888).

HMC Lothian: *Report on the manuscripts of the Marquess of Lothian (formerly) preserved at Blickling Hall, Norfolk* (1905).

HMC Middleton: *Report on the manuscripts of Lord Middleton (formerly) preserved at Wollaton Hall, Nottinghamshire* (1911).

HMC R. R. Hastings: *Report on the manuscripts of the late Reginald Rawdon Hastings, Esq., of the Manor House, Ashby de la Zouche* (4 vols., 1928–47).

HMC Rutland: *Report on the manuscripts of his Grace the Duke of Rutland, G.C.B., preserved at Belvoir Castle* (4 vols., 1888–1905).

HMC Rye and Hereford: *Report on the manuscripts of Rye and Hereford Corporations, Capt. Loder-Symonds, Mr. E. R. Wodehouse, MP, and others* (1892).

HMC Var. Coll.: *Report on manuscripts in various collections* (8 vols., 1901–14).

HMC Wells: *Calendar of the manuscripts of the Dean and Chapter of Wells* (2 vols., 1907–14).

HMC Westmorland etc.: *Report on the manuscripts of the Earl of Westmorland, Captain Stewart, Lord Stafford, Lord Muncaster, and others* (1906).

Hockey, S. F., 'Llangua, alien priory of Lyre', *JHSCW*, XXII (1990), 8–13.

Quarr Abbey and its Lands, 1132–1631 (Leicester, 1970).

Hodgson, *Northumberland*: J. Hodgson, *A History of Northumberland* (7 vols., Newcastle, 1820–58).

Hogg, *Priors*: J. Hogg, 'The pre-reformation priors of the *Provincia Angliae*', *Analecta Cartusiana*, 1, no. 1 (1989), 25–59.

Hope, *History of London Charterhouse*: W. St J. Hope, *The History of the London Charterhouse from its foundation until the suppression of the monastery* (London, 1925).

Hope, T. M., *The Township of Hatfield Peverel: its history, natural history and inhabitants* (Chelmsford, 1930).

Hope Dodds, *see* Dodds.

Hornchurch Priory: H. F. Westlake, ed., *Hornchurch Priory: a kalendar of documents in the possession of the warden and fellows of New College, Oxford* (London, 1923).

Howden: *Chronica Rogeri de Houedene*, ed. W. Stubbs (4 vols., RS, 1868–71).

Hughes, A., 'The manor of Tooting Bec and its reputed priory', *Surrey Arch. Coll.*, 59 (1962), 1–14.

Hugo, *Nunneries*: T. Hugo, *The Medieval Nunneries of the county of Somerset and diocese of Bath and Wells* (London, 1867).

Hull, M. R., 'Fourteenth-century seal of Simon de Blyton, abbot of Colchester', *TEAS*, new ser. XXIV (1951), 69–96.

Hundred Rolls: *Rotuli Hundredorum temp. Henrici III et Edwardi I in turr' Lond' et in curia receptae scaccarii West. asservati*, ed. W. Illingworth (2 vols., RC, 1812–18).

Hunt, R. W., *The Schools and the Cloister: the life and writings of Alexander Nequam (1157–1217)*, ed. M. T. Gibson (Oxford, 1984).

Hunter, J., *South Yorkshire: the history and topography of the deanery of Doncaster* (2 vols., London, 1828–31).

Hunts F., *see under* FINES.

Hustings Wills: *Calendar of Wills proved and enrolled in the Court of Husting, London, A.D. 1258 – A.D. 1688*, ed. R. R. Sharpe (2 vols., London, 1890).

Hutchins: J. Hutchins, *The history and antiquities of the county of Dorset* (2 vols., London, 1774; 3rd edn by W. Shipp and J. W. Hodson, 4 vols., Westminster, 1861–70).

Hutchinson, *Archdeaconry of Stoke*: S. W. Hutchinson, *The Archdeaconry of Stoke-on-Trent: historical notes on the North Staffordshire Abbeys, Churches, Chapels and Parishes from the earliest times* (London, 1893).

Hutchison, C. A., *The Hermit Monks of Grandmont* (Cistercian Studies ser. 118, Kalamazoo, 1989).

Hyde Breviary: *The Monastic Breviary of Hyde Abbey, Winchester, vol. V*, ed. J. B. L. Tolhurst (Henry Bradshaw Society LXXI, 1934).

Hylle Ctl.: *The Hylle Cartulary*, ed. R. W. Dunning (Somerset Record Society 68, 1968).

Index to Placita de Banco 1327–28 (2 parts, PRO List and Index XXXII, 1910).

Irwin, C. R. and Irwin, M., *The Gilbertines and Ravenstonedale* (Kirkby Stephen, 1990).

Jackson, J. E., 'Kington St Michael', *Wilts AM*, 4 (1858), 36–124.

James, J. M., 'The Norman Benedictine alien priory of St George, Modbury, A.D. *c.* 1135–1480', *TDA*, 131 (1999), 81–103.

Jarrow and Wearmouth: *The inventories and account rolls of the Benedictine houses or cells of Jarrow and Monk-Wearmouth in the county of Durham*, ed. J. Raine (Surtees Society 29, 1854).

JBAA: *Journal of the British Archaeological Association.*

JEH: *Journal of Ecclesiastical History.*

Jenkins, 'Lost cartulary': J. G. Jenkins, 'The Lost Cartulary of Nutley Abbey', *Huntington Library Quarterly*, XVII (1953–4), 379–96.

JHSCW: *Journal of the Historical Society of the Church in Wales.*

John of Glastonbury: *John of Glastonbury: Cronica sive Antiquitates Glastoniensis Ecclesie*, ed. J. P. Carley (2 parts, BAR 47, 1978).

Jones, A., 'Basingwerk Abbey' in J. G. Edwards, V. H. Galbraith, and E. F. Jacob, eds., *Historical Essays in honour of James Tait* (Manchester, 1933), pp. 169–78.

Jones, D. Daven, *A History of Kidwelly* (Carmarthen, 1908).

JRIC: *Journal of the Royal Institution of Cornwall.*

JSA: *Journal of the Society of Archivists.*

Keil, I., 'Profiles of some abbots of Glastonbury', *Downside Review*, 81 (1963), 355–70.
'The abbots of Glastonbury in the early fourteenth century', *Downside Review*, 82 (1964), 327–48.

Kemp, B. R., 'The monastic dean of Leominster', *EHR*, LXXXIII (1968), 505–15.

Kemp, R. L. and Graves, C. P., *The Church and Gilbertine Priory of St Andrew, Fishergate* (York Archaeological Trust, 1996).

Kennett, *Parochial Antiquities*: White Kennett, *Parochial antiquities . . . in the counties of Oxford and Buckingham* (Oxford, 1695; new edn, 2 vols., 1818).

Kent, E. A., 'St Olave's priory', *JBAA*, new ser. 31 (1925), 110–13.

Kent F., see under FINES.

Kentish Ctl.: *A Kentish Cartulary of the Order of St John of Jerusalem*, ed. C. Cotton (Kent Archaeological Society, records branch XI, 1930).

Kerr, B., *Religious life for Women*: *Religious life for Women c. 1100 – c. 1350: Fontevraud in England* (Oxford, 1999).

Kershaw, I., *Bolton Priory: the economy of a northern monastery 1286–1325* (Oxford, 1973).

KH: Knowles, D. and Hadcock, R. N., *Medieval Religious Houses: England and Wales* (London, 1st edn, 1953, 2nd edn, 1971 (all refs. to 2nd edn)).

King, E., *Estate Records of the Hotot Family* in E. King, ed., *A Northamptonshire Miscellany*, (Northamptonshire Record Society XXXII, 1983).

King's Bench, Edward I: *Select Cases in the Court of King's Bench under Edward I*, ed. G. O. Sayles (3 vols., Selden Society 55, 57, 58, 1936–9).

King's Bench, Edward III: *Select Cases in the Court of King's Bench, Edward III, vols. V–VI*, ed. G. O. Sayles (2 vols., Selden Society 76, 82, 1958–65).

Kingsford, *Grey Friars of London*: C. L. Kingsford, *The Grey Friars of London: their history, with the register of their convent and an appendix of documents* (British Society of Franciscan Studies 6, Aberdeen, 1915, repd 1965).

Kirby, 'Clerical poll-taxes': J. L. Kirby ed., 'Clerical Poll-taxes in the diocese of Salisbury, 1377–81' in N. J. Williams, ed., *Collectanea* (Wiltshire Archaeological and Natural History Society, records branch XII, 1956), 157–67.

Kirby, R. L. *et al.*, eds., *The Rural Deanery of Cartmel in the Diocese of Carlisle, its churches and endowments* (Ulverston, 1892).

Kirby, T. F., 'The alien priory of St Andrew, Hamble, and its transfer to Winchester College in 1391', *Archaeologia*, L (1887), 251–62.

Kirkby, A. E. and Tailby, A. R., *The Abbey of St Mary and St Peter, Humberston, Lincolnshire* (Waltham, 1974).

Kissack, K. E., *Medieval Monmouth* (Monmouth, 1974).

Kniveton Leiger, The, ed. A. Saltman (Derbyshire Archaeological Society, record ser. 7, and *HMC* joint publication 24, 1977).

Knowles, D., *The Historian and Character and other Essays* (Cambridge, 1963).

Knowles, *Mon. Order*: D. Knowles, *The Monastic Order in England* (Cambridge, 1940; 2nd edn 1963, pagination unaltered).

Knowles, *Religious Orders*: D. Knowles, *The Religious Orders in England* (3 vols., Cambridge, 1948–59).

Kuttner, S. and Rathbone, E., 'Anglo-Norman canonists of the twelfth century', *Traditio*, VII (1949–51), 279–358.

Lackner, B. K., ed., *Stephen of Sawley: Treatises* (Cistercian Fathers 36, Kalamazoo, 1984).

Lacock Chts.: *Lacock Abbey Charters*, ed. K. H. Rogers (Wiltshire Record Society XXXIV, 1974).

Lancaster Hist.: *Materials for the History of the church of Lancaster*, ed. W. O. Roper (4 vols., Chetham Society, new ser. XXVI, XXXI, LVIII, LIX, 1892–1906).

Lancs Assize Rolls: *Lancashire Assize Rolls I*, ed. J. Parker (Lancashire and Cheshire Record Society 47, 1904).

Lancs F., see under FINES.

Langley, *Hist. of Desborough Hundred*: T. Langley, *The History and Antiquities of the Hundred of Desborough and Deanery of Wycombe in Buckinghamshire* (London, 1797).

Langston, J. N., 'The Priors of Lanthony by Gloucester', *BGAS*, 63 (1942), 1–144.

Lawrence, *St Edmund of Abingdon*: C. H. Lawrence, *St Edmund of Abingdon: a study of hagiography and history* (Oxford, 1960, repd 2000).

Laws, E., 'Notes on the alien Benedictine priory of St Nicholas and St John the Evangelist in Monkton, Pembrokeshire', *Arch. Camb.* 6th ser. IX (1909), 165–202.

Le Faye, D., 'Selborne Priory, 1233–1486', *Hants Field Club*, 30 (1975), 47–71.

Le Livere de Reis de Brittanie e le livere de Reis de Engleterre, ed. J. Glover (RS, 1865).

Le Neve 1066–1300: John Le Neve, *Fasti Ecclesiae Anglicanae, 1066–1300*, ed. D. E. Greenway (revised edn, 6 vols. – in progress – London, 1968–99).

Le Neve 1300–1541: John Le Neve, *Fasti Ecclesiae Anglicanae, 1300–1541*, ed. H. P. F. King, J. M. Horn, and B. Jones (revised edn, 12 vols., London, 1962–7).

Lega-Weekes, E., 'Pre-Reformation history of the priory of St Katherine, Polsloe, Exeter, part 1', *TDA* 66 (1934), 181–99.

Legge, M. D., *Anglo-Norman Literature and its background* (Oxford, 1963).

Leland, *Coll.*: J. Leland, *Collectanea*, ed. T. Hearne (2nd edn, 6 vols., London, 1770).

Leland, *Iter.*: *The Itinerary of J. Leland*, ed. L. T. Smith (5 vols., Oxford, 1907–10).

Lenton Chts.: J. E. Burton, ed., 'A roll of charters for Lenton Priory', *BIB*, 2 (1979–82), 13–26.

Les Registres, see under Registres.

Letter-book of William of Hoo: The Letter-book of William of Hoo, sacrist of Bury St Edmunds, *1280–1294*, ed. A. Gransden (Suffolk Records Society 5, 1963).

Letters from Northern Registers, ed. J. Raine (RS, 1873).

Lewis and Davies, *Records of Court of Augmentations*: Records of the Court of Augmentations relating to Wales and Monmouthshire, ed. E. A. Lewis and J. Conway Davies (Board of Celtic Studies, University of Wales, History and Law ser. 13, Cardiff, 1954).

Lib. Rolls: Calendar of Liberate Rolls (6 vols., PRO, 1917–64).

Liber Elemosinarii: Liber Elemosinarii: the almoner's book of the priory of Worcester, ed. J. H. Bloom (Worcestershire Historical Society, 1911).

Liber Landav.: The Text of the Book of Llan Dâv, ed. J. G. Evans and J. Rhys (Oxford, 1893; revised edn, Aberystwyth, 1979).

Liber Luciani: Liber Luciani de laude Cestrie, ed. M. V. Taylor (Lancashire and Cheshire Record Society, LXIV, 1912).

Liber Pensionum Prioratus Wigorn.: Liber Pensionum Prioratus Wigorn.: being a collection of documents relating to pensions from appropriated churches and other payments receivable by the prior and convent of Worcester and to the privileges of the monastery, ed. C. Price (Worcestershire Historical Society, 1925).

Lincoln Sessions 1351–54: Records of some sessions of the peace in the city of Lincoln, *1351–1354*, and the borough of Stamford, *1351*, ed. E. G. Kimball (Lincoln Record Society 65, 1971).

Lincoln Visitations: Visitations of Religious Houses in the Diocese of Lincoln, vol. I: Injunctions and other documents from the registers of Richard Fleming and William Gray, Bishops of Lincoln, A.D. *1420–1436*; vols. II–III: Records of visitations held by William Alnwick, Bishop of Lincoln, A.D. *1436–1449*, ed. A. H. Thompson (Lincoln Record Society 7, 14, 21, 1914–29, and Canterbury and York Society 17, 24, 33, 1915–27).

Lincs Assize Roll: The earliest Lincolnshire assize rolls, A.D. *1202–1209*, ed. D. M. Stenton (Lincoln Record Society 22, 1926).

Lincs F., see under FINES.

Lincs N. & Q.: Lincolnshire Notes and Queries.

Lincs Sessions of the Peace 1360–75: Records of some sessions of the peace in Lincolnshire, *1360–1375*, ed. R. Sillem (Lincoln Record Society 30, 1936).

Lincs Sessions of the Peace 1381–96: Records of some sessions of the peace in Lincolnshire, *1381–1396*, ed. E. G. Kimball (2 vols., Lincoln Record Society 49, 56, 1955–62).

Lindley, E. S., 'Kingswood Abbey: its land and mills', *BGAS*, LXXIII (1954), 115–91.

List of Sheriffs: List of Sheriffs for England and Wales from the earliest times to A.D. *1831* (PRO List and Index IX, 1898).

Lit. Cant.: Literae Cantuarienses, The letter books of the monastery of Christ Church, Canterbury, ed. J. B. Sheppard (3 vols., RS, 1887–9).

Litt. Wallie: Littere Wallie preserved in Liber A in the Public Record Office, ed. J. G. Edwards (Board of Celtic Studies, University of Wales, History and Law ser. V, 1940).

Little, A. G. ed., *Fratris Thomae vulgo dicti de Eccleston Tractatus: De Adventu Fratrum Minorum in Angliam* (Manchester, 1951).

Liveing, *Records of Romsey*: H. G. D. Liveing, *Records of Romsey Abbey* (Winchester, 1906).

Llandaff Episcopal Acta: Llandaff Episcopal Acta *1140–1287*, ed. D. Crouch (South Wales Record Society 5, 1988).

Logan, *Runaway Religious*: F. D. Logan, *Runaway Religious in Medieval England c. 1240 – 1540* (Cambridge, 1996).

London and Middlesex F., see under FINES.

London IPM (Fry): G. S. Fry, *Abstracts of Inquisitiones post mortem relating to the city of London, part 1: 1 Henry VII to 3 Elizabeth, 1485–1561* (London and Middlesex Archaeological Society, 1896).

Lordship and Landscape: *Lordship and Landscape in Norfolk 1250–1350: the early records of Holkham*, ed. W. Hassall and J. Beauroy (British Academy, records of social and economic history, new ser. XX, 1993).

Lowndes, G. A., 'History of the priory at Hatfield Regis *alias* Hatfield Broad Oak', *TEAS* new ser. II (1884), 117–52.

Luffield Chts.: *Luffield Priory Charters*, ed. G. R. Elvey (2 vols., Buckinghamshire Record Society XV, XVIII; Northamptonshire Record Society XXII, XXVI, 1968–75).

Lugard, *Trailbaston*: *Trailbaston: Derbyshire*, ed. C. E. Lugard (2 vols., priv. pd, Ashover, 1933–5).

LV Durham, 1st edn: *Liber vitae ecclesiae Dunelmensis; nec non obituaria duo ejusdem ecclesiae*, ed. J. Stevenson (Surtees Society 13, 1841).

Macdonald, A. C., 'Women and the monastic life in late medieval Yorkshire' (unpublished D.Phil. thesis, University of Oxford, 1997).

Mackie, F. P., 'The clerical population of the province of York: an edition of the clerical poll-tax enrolments 1377–81' (unpublished D.Phil. thesis, University of York, 1998).

Macray, W. D., *Notes from the Muniments of St Mary Magdalen College, Oxford . . .* (Oxford and London, 1882).

Madox, *Form.*: *Formulare Anglicanum*, ed. T. Madox (London, 1702).

Mag. Vit.: *Magna Vita S. Hugonis*, ed. and translated D. L. Douie and E. Farmer (2 vols., NMT, 1961–2; 2nd edn OMT, 1985).

Magnum Reg. Album Lichfield: *The Great Register of Lichfield Cathedral known as Magnum Registrum Album*, ed. H. E. Savage (*SHC*, 1924).

Marchegay, P., 'Les prieurés anglais de Saint-Florent près Saumur: notice et documents inédits', *Bibliothèque de l'École des Chartes*, XL (1879), 154–94; published separately as *Les prieurés anglais de Saint-Florent près Saumur* (Les Roches-Baritaud, 1879).

Martène, *Marmoutier*: E. Martène, *Histoire de l'Abbaye de Marmoutier . . .* (2 vols., Tours, 1874–5).

Martin, *Hist. Thetford*: T. Martin, *The history of the town of Thetford in the counties of Norfolk and Suffolk from the earliest accounts to the present time* (London, 1779).

Matthew, *Norman Monasteries*: D. J. A. Matthew, *The Norman Monasteries and their English Possessions* (Oxford, 1962).

Maund, K., ed., *Handlist of the Acts of the Native Welsh Rulers 1132–1283* (Cardiff, 1996).

Maxwell-Lyte, *History of Dunster*: H. C. Maxwell-Lyte, *A History of Dunster and of the Families of Mohun and Luttrell* (London, 1909).

McHardy, *Church in London*: *The Church in London 1375–1392*, ed. A. K. McHardy (London Record Society 13, 1977).

'Effects of war on the Church: the case of the alien priories in the fourteenth century' in M. Jones and M. Vale, eds., *England and her Neighbours, 1066–1453: essays in honour of Pierre Chaplais* (London, 1989), pp. 277–95.

McNulty, J., 'Stephen of Eston, abbot of Sallay', *YAJ*, XXXI (1934), 49–64.

ed., 'Thomas Sotheron v. Cockersand Abbey: a suit as to the advowson of Mitton church 1369–70' in *Chetham Miscellanies, new ser. vol. VII* (Chetham Soc., new ser. 100, 1939).

Med. Deeds of Bath: *Medieval Deeds of Bath and District*, ed. B. R. Kemp and D. M. M. Shorrocks (Somerset Record Society 73, 1974).

Medieval Archives of Christ Church: *Cartulary of the Medieval Archives of Christ Church*, ed. N. Denholm-Young (Oxford Historical Society XCII, 1931).

Medieval Lindsey Marsh: *The Medieval Lindsey Marsh: select documents*, ed. A. E. B. Owen (Lincoln Record Society 85, 1996).

Mem. Bury: *Memorials of St Edmund's Abbey*, ed. T. Arnold (RS, 3 vols., 1890–6).

Mem. Fountains: *Memorials of the abbey of St Mary of Fountains*, ed. J. R. Walbran and J. T. Fowler (3 vols., Surtees Society 42, 67, 130, 1863–1918).

Memo. Roll 1326–7: *Calendar of Memoranda Rolls (Exchequer) preserved in the Public Record Office, Michaelmas 1326 – Michaelmas 1327* (PRO, 1969).

Michelmore, D. J. H., 'A monastic cell at Holbeck' in M. L. Faull and S. A. Moorhouse, *West Yorkshire Archaeological Survey to A.D. 1500* (3 vols., Wakefield, 1981), III, 798.

Misc. D. M. Stenton: *A Medieval Miscellany for Doris Mary Stenton*, ed. P. M. Barnes and C. F. Slade (PRS, LXXVI, 1962).

Moir, A. L., *Bromfield Priory and Church in Shropshire* (Chester, 1947).

Mon. Angl.: W. Dugdale, *Monasticon Anglicanum*, rev. edn J. Caley, H. Ellis, and B. Bandinel (6 vols in 8, London, 1817–30, repr. 1846).

Mon. Seals: R. H. Ellis, *Catalogue of Seals in the Public Record Office: Monastic Seals, vol. I* (London, 1986).

Money, *Newbury*: W. Money, *The History of the Ancient Town and Borough of Newbury in the county of Berks* (Oxford and London, 1887).

Monmouthshire Antiquary.

Montgomeryshire Coll.: *Montgomeryshire Collections*.

Moorman, J. R. H., *Lanercost Priory* (Brampton, 1945).

Morant, *Essex*: P. Morant, *The History and Antiquities of the County of Essex* (2 vols., London, 1768).

Morgan, M., *English Lands of Bec*: M. Morgan, *The English Lands of the Abbey of Bec* (Oxford, 1946, repd 1968).

Morris, M. C. F., *Nunburnholme and its history and antiquities* (London, 1907).

Mountain, J., *The History of Selby* (York, 1800).

MPCM: *Matthei Parisiensis Chronica Majora*, ed. H. R. Luard (7 vols., RS, 1872–84).

MRB: *Monastic Research Bulletin* (Borthwick Institute, York, 1995–in progress).

Mumford, W. F., 'Monks of Wenlock priory', *Trans. Shrops. ANHS*, LX (1975–6), 97–111.

Muniments of Wallingford: J. G. Milne, 'Muniments of Holy Trinity priory, Wallingford', *Oxoniensia* V (1940), 50–77.

Mynors, R. A. B., *Catalogue of the Manuscripts of Balliol College, Oxford* (Oxford, 1963).

Myres, J. N. L., 'Butley priory, Suffolk', *Arch. J.*, XC (1933), 177–281.

'Notes on the history of Butley priory, Suffolk', in *Salter Essays*, pp. 190–206.

Nash, *Worcs*: T. R. Nash, *Collections for the history of Worcestershire* (2 vols., London, 1781–2; 2nd edn with supplement, 1799).

Nat. Lib. Wales Jnl.: *National Library of Wales Journal*.

Nelson, P., 'Some British medieval seal-matrices', *Arch. J.*, XCIII (1936), 13–44.

Newburgh, William of Newburgh: *Stephen*, etc., I, II; also *Guilielmi Newbrigensis Historia sive Chronica Rerum Anglicarum*, ed. T. Hearne (3 vols., Oxford, 1719).

Newcourt, *Repertorium*: Newcourt, R., *Repertorium ecclesiasticum parochiale Londinense* (2 vols., London, 1708–10).

Newington Longeville Chts.: *Newington Longeville Charters*, ed. H. E. Salter (Oxfordshire Record Society 3, 1921).

Nicholls and Taylor, *Bristol Past and Present*: J. F. Nicholls and J. Taylor, *Bristol past and present* (3 vols., Bristol, 1881–2).

Nichols, A., 'The history and cartulary of the Cistercian nuns of Marham Abbey, 1249–1536', (unpublished Ph.D. thesis, Kent State University, 1974).

Nichols, *Leics*: J. Nichols, *The history and antiquities of the county of Leicester* (4 vols. in 8, London, 1795–1815).

Nicholson, H. J., 'Margaret de Lacy and the hospital of St John at Aconbury, Herefordshire', *JEH*, 50 (1999), 629–51.

Nicholson and Burn, *History of Westmorland*: J. Nicholson and R. Burn, *The History and Antiquities of the Counties of Westmorland and Cumberland* (2 vols., London, 1777).

Nightingale, J. E., *Memorials of Wilton . . .* (Devizes, 1906).

NMT: Nelson Medieval Texts (later Oxford Medieval Texts).

Norfolk Ant. Misc.: *The Norfolk Antiquarian Miscellany*, II (1883).

Norfolk F., see under FINES.

Northumberland and Durham Deeds: *Northumberland and Durham Deeds from the Dodsworth MSS. in Bodley's Library, Oxford* (Newcastle upon Tyne Record Ser. VII, 1929).

Northumberland and Durham Seals: C. H. Hunter Blair, 'Seals of Northumberland and Durham', *Arch. Aeliana*, 3rd ser. XX (1923), 69–186; XXI (1924), 38–120b (part II cited).

Northumberland Assize Roll: *Three early assize rolls for the county of Northumberland, saec. XIII*, ed. W. Page (Surtees Society 88, 1891).

Northumberland De Banco Rolls: F. W. Dendy, 'Extracts from the De Banco rolls relating to Northumberland 1308–1558', *Arch. Aeliana*, 3rd ser. VI (1910), 41–88.

Northumberland Pleas: *Northumberland pleas from the curia regis and assize rolls, 1198–1272*, ed. A. H. Thompson (Newcastle upon Tyne Records Ser. II, 1922).

Norwich Cath. Chts.: *The Charters of Norwich Cathedral Priory*, ed. B. Dodwell (2 vols., PRS, new ser. 40, 46, 1974–85).

Norwich Customary: *The customary of the cathedral priory church of Norwich*, ed. J. B. L. Tolhurst (Henry Bradshaw Society LXXXII, 1948).

Nottingham Borough Records: *Records of the Borough of Nottingham*, ed. W. H. Stevenson (5 vols., London etc., 1882–1900).

NRA: National Register of Archives

Obit roll of W. Ebchester and J. Burnby: *The obituary roll of William Ebchester and John Burnby, Priors of Durham, with notices of similar records preserved at Durham, from the year 1233 downwards, letters of fraternity etc.*, ed. J. Raine (Surtees Society 31, 1856).

Oliver: G. Oliver, *Monasticon Diocesis Exoniensis* (Exeter, 1846).

Oliver, A. M., 'A list of the abbots of Alnwick', *Proc. Soc. Ant. Newcastle*, 3rd ser. LX (1919–20), 42–4.

'A list of the abbots of Newminster', *Archaeologia Aeliana*, 3rd ser. XII (1915), 206–25.

'List of the prioresses of the Benedictine nunnery of St Bartholomew of Newcastle', *Proc. Soc. Ant. Newcastle*, 4th ser. VI (1933–5), 65–6.

Oliver, *Supplement*: G. Oliver, *Supplement to Monasticon Diocesis Exoniensis* (Exeter, 1854).

OMT: Oxford Medieval Texts.

Orig. Papal Letters: *Original Papal Letters in England 1305–1415*, ed. P. N. R. Zutshi (Rome, Vatican, 1990, Index Actorum Romanorum Pontificum V).

Ormerod, *Cheshire*: G. Ormerod, *The History of the county Palatine and city of Chester* (2nd edn, ed. T. Helsby, 3 vols., 1875–82).

Owen, D. M., *Church and Society in Medieval Lincolnshire* (History of Lincolnshire V, Lincolnshire Local History Society, 1971).

Owen, *King's Lynn*: *The Making of King's Lynn: a documentary survey*, ed. D. M. Owen (British Academy, records of social and economic history, 2nd ser. IX, 1984).

Owen, E., *A Catalogue of the Manuscripts relating to Wales in the British Museum* (4 vols., London 1910–22).

Oxford F., see under FINES.

Padel, O. J., 'Glastonbury's Cornish connections' in L. Abrams and J. P. Carley, eds., *The Archaeology and History of Glastonbury Abbey: essays in honour of the ninetieth birthday of C. R. Ralegh Radford* (Woodbridge, 1991), pp. 245–56.

Page, F. M., *Estates of Crowland Abbey: a study in manorial organisation* (Cambridge, 1934).

Palmer, W. M., 'The Benedictine nunnery of Swaffham Bulbeck', *Proc. Cambs. Ant. Soc.*, XXXI (1931), 30–65.

Swavesey Priory: W. M. Palmer and C. Parsons, 'Swavesey Priory', *Trans. of the Cambridgeshire and Huntingdonshire Archaeological Society*, I (1) (1901), 29–48.

Pantin, W. A., 'Gloucester College', *Oxoniensia*, XI–XII (1946–7), 65–74.

'Notley Abbey', *Oxoniensia*, VI (1941), 22–43.

Parlty Writs: F. Palgrave, ed., *Parliamentary Writs II* (Record Commission, 1834).

Pearce, E. H., *Walter de Wenlok, Abbot of Westminster* (London, 1920).

Ped. Fin.: *Fines sive Pedes Finium sive Finales Concordiae in Curia Domini Regis, 7 Richard I – 16 John, 1195–1214*, ed. J. Hunter (2 vols., Record Commission, 1835–44).

Pedigrees from the Plea Rolls: G. Wrottesley, *Pedigrees from the Plea Rolls collected from the pleadings in the various courts of law A.D. 1200 to 1500* (London, ?1905).

Pegge, *Beauchief*: S. Pegge, *An historical account of Beauchief Abbey in the county of Derby, from its first foundation to its final dissolution* (London, 1901).

Penrice and Margam MSS: *A descriptive catalogue of the Penrice and Margam Abbey manuscripts in the possession of Miss Talbot of Margam*, ed. W. de G. Birch, Series 1–4 (London, 1893–1904).

Penwortham Docts.: *Documents relating to the priory of Penwortham and other possessions in Lancashire of the abbey of Evesham*, ed. W. A. Hulton (Chetham Society, old ser. XXX, 1853).

Perceval, C. S., 'Remarks on some charters and other documents relating to the abbey of Robertsbridge in the county of Sussex . . .', *Archaeologia*, XLV (1880), 427–61.

Percy Ctl.: *The Percy Chartulary*, ed. M. T. Martin (Surtees Society 117, 1911).

Perkins, V. R., 'Documents relating to the Cistercian monastery of St Mary, Kingswood', *BGAS*, 22 (1899), 179–256.

Piper, A. J., *The Durham Monks at Jarrow* (Jarrow Lecture, 1986).

'St Leonard's Priory, Stamford', *Stamford Historian*, 5 (1980), 5–25; 6 (1982), 1–23.

PL: *Patrologiae Cursus completus, series Latina*, ed. J. P. Migne (221 vols., Paris, 1844–64).

Placita de Quo Warranto, ed. W. Illingworth (Record Commission, 1818).

Plantagenet-Harrison, *Gilling West*: G. H. de S. N. Plantagenet-Harrison, *The History of Yorkshire I; Wapentake of Gilling* (London and Aylesbury, 1879).

Pollard, H. P., 'The alien Benedictine priory at Ware', *East Herts Arch. Soc. Trans.* 3 (1905–7), 119–32.

Powicke, *Studies*: R. W. Hunt, W. A. Pantin, R. W. Southern, eds., *Studies in Medieval History presented to Frederick Maurice Powicke* (Oxford, 1948, repd 1969).

The Thirteenth Century (2nd edn, Oxford, 1962).

Powys Fadog: J. Y. W. Lloyd, *The History of the Princes, the Lords Marcher, and the ancient nobility of Powys Fadog, and the ancient Lords of Arwystli, Cedewen, and Meirionydd* (6 vols., London, 1881–7).

PR: Pipe Rolls, cited by the regnal year, ed. in PRS.

Preest, D. and Still, M., *Hugh of Eversden, Abbot of St Albans* (Fraternity of the Friends of St Albans Abbey, occasional paper 2, 1998).

Price, G. V., *Valle Crucis Abbey* (Liverpool, 1952).

Priory of Coldingham: *The Priory of Coldingham: the correspondence, inventories, account rolls, and law proceedings, of the priory of Coldingham*, ed. J. Raine (Surtees Society 12, 1841).

Pritchard, E. M., *Cardigan Priory in the olden days* (London, 1904).

    The history of St Dogmaels Abbey, together with her cells, Pill, Caldy and Glascareg, and the mother abbey of Tiron (London, 1907).

Privy Council: *Proceedings and Ordinances of the Privy Council of England vol. I, 10 Richard II to 11 Henry IV*, ed. H. Nicolas (Record Commission, 1834).

Proc. Cambs. Ant. Soc.: *Proceedings of the Cambridge Antiquarian Society.*

Proc. Dorset NHAS: *Proceedings of the Dorset Natural History and Archaeological Society.*

Proc. Soc. Ant. Newcastle: *Proceedings of the Society of Antiquaries of Newcastle upon Tyne.*

Proc. Soc. Antiq.: *Proceedings of the Society of Antiquaries of London.*

Proc. Soms ANHS.: *Proceedings of the Somerset Archaeological and Natural History Society.*

Proc. Suffolk Inst.: *Proceedings of the Suffolk Institute of Archaeology and History.*

PRS: Pipe Roll Society.

Prynne, *Records*: Prynne, W., *An exact Chronological vindication of our kings' supreme ecclesiastical jurisdiction over all religious affairs . . .* (3 vols. in 6, London, 1666–8).

Pudsay Deeds, The, ed. R. P. Littledale (Yorkshire Archaeological Society, Record Series LVI, 1916).

PUE: W. Holtzmann, *Papsturkunden in England*, (3 vols., Abhandlungen der Gesellschaft der Wissenschaften in Göttingen, phil.-hist. Klasse, Berlin, Göttingen; I = neue Folge XXV (1930–1), II = 3 Folge XIV–XV (1935–6), III = 3 Folge XXXIII (1952)).

Purvis, J. S., *St John of Bridlington* (Journal of the Bridlington Augustinian Society 2, Bridlington, 1924).

Putnam, *Justices*: *Proceedings before the Justices of the Peace in the fourteenth and fifteenth centuries*, ed. B. H. Putnam (Ames Foundation, London, 1938).

Quarr Chts.: *The Charters of Quarr Abbey*, ed. S. F. Hockey (Isle of Wight Record Ser. 3, 1991).

Radford, C. A. R., *Margam Museum, Glamorgan* (London, 1949).

Raine, *Hexham Priory*: *The Priory of Hexham*, ed. J. Raine (2 vols., Surtees Society 44, 46, 1864–5).

Raine, *Hist. Blyth*: J. Raine, *The History and Antiquities of the Parish of Blyth* (Westminster, 1860).

Raine, *North Durham*: J. Raine, *The History and Antiquities of North Durham* (London, 1852).

Ralph Coggeshall: *Chronicon Anglicanum Radulphi de Coggeshall*, ed. J. Stevenson (RS, 1875).

Record Evidences of Cluny: *Record evidences among the archives of the ancient Abbey of Cluni from 1077 to 1534*, ed. G. F. Duckett (Lewes, 1886).

Records of Turvey: *Early Records of Turvey and its neighbourhood: part 1, A. The Drayton Charters; B. The Halstead Charters*, ed. G. H. Fowler (BHRS XI, 1927).

Records of Wroxall: J. W. Ryland, *Records of Wroxall Abbey and manor, Warwickshire* (London, 1903).

Recs. A. Bek: *Records of Antony Bek, Bishop and Patriarch, 1283–1311*, ed. C. M. Fraser (Surtees Society 162, 1953).

Reg. Ant. Lincoln: *The Registrum Antiquissimum of the Cathedral Church of Lincoln*, ed. C. W. Foster and K. Major (10 vols. and 2 vols. of facsimiles, Lincoln Record Society 27–9, 32, 34, 41–2, 46, 51, 62, 67–8, 1931–73).

Reg. Archdny Richmond: A. H. Thompson, ed., 'The Registers of the Archdeaconry of Richmond, 1361–1442', *YAJ*, XXV (1920), 129–268; 'The Register of the Archdeacons of Richmond, 1442–1477', *YAJ*, XXX (1931), 1–134; XXXII (1936), 111–45.

Reg. Asserio: *The Registers of John of Sandale and Rigaud de Asserio, Bishops of Winchester (A.D. 1316–1323) with an appendix of contemporaneous and other illustrative documents*, ed. F. J. Baigent (Hampshire Record Society, 1897).

1

Reg. Baldock: *Registrum Radulphi Baldock, Gilberti Segrave, Ricardi Newport, et Stephani Gravesend, episcoporum Londoniensium, A.D. MCCCIV–MCCCXXXVIII*, ed. R. C. Fowler (Canterbury and York Society 7, 1911).

Reg. Bateman: *The Register of William Bateman, Bishop of Norwich 1344–1355, vol. I*, ed. P. E. Pobst (Canterbury and York Society 84, 1996).

Reg. Berkeley: *The Register of John de Grandisson, Bishop of Exeter (A.D. 1327–1369), part I, 1327–1330, with some account of the episcopate of James de Berkeley (A.D. 1327)*, ed. F. C. Hingeston-Randolph (London and Exeter, 1894).

Reg. Black Prince: *Register of Edward the Black Prince preserved in the Public Record Office* (4 vols., PRO, 1930–3).

Reg. Bowet: *The Registers of Walter Giffard, Bishop of Bath and Wells, 1265–6, and of Henry Bowett, Bishop of Bath and Wells, 1401–7*, ed. T. S. Holmes (Somerset Record Society 13, 1899), pp. 14–96.

Reg. Bransford: *A calendar of the Register of Wolstan de Bransford, Bishop of Worcester 1339–1349*, ed. R. M. Haines (Worcestershire Historical Society new ser. 4 and *HMC* joint publication 9, 1966).

Reg. Brantingham: *The Register of Thomas de Brantyngham, Bishop of Exeter (A.D. 1370–1394)*, ed. F. C. Hingeston-Randolph (2 vols., London and Exeter, 1901–6).

Reg. Bronescombe: *The Registers of Walter Bronescombe (A.D. 1257–1280), and Peter Quivil (A.D. 1280–1291), Bishops of Exeter, with some records of the episcopate of Bishop Thomas de Bytton (A.D. 1292–1307)*, ed. F. C. Hingeston-Randolph (London and Exeter, 1889).

Reg. Burghersh: *The Registers of Bishop Henry Burghersh 1320–1342, vol. I*, ed. N. Bennett (Lincoln Record Society 87, 1999).

Reg. Bury: *Richard d'Aungerville of Bury: fragments of his register and other documents*, ed. G. W. Kitchin (Surtees Society 119, 1910).

Reg. Bytton: *The Registers of Walter Bronescombe (A.D. 1257–1280), and Peter Quivil (A.D. 1280–1291), Bishops of Exeter, with some records of the episcopate of Bishop Thomas de Bytton (A.D. 1292–1307)*, ed. F. C. Hingeston-Randolph (London and Exeter, 1889).

Reg. Cantilupe: *Registrum Thome de Cantilupe, episcopi Herefordensis (A.D. 1275–1282)*, ed. R. G. Griffiths and W. W. Capes (Cantilupe Society 1906, and Canterbury and York Society 2, 1907).

Reg. Chichele: *The Register of Henry Chichele, Archbishop of Canterbury, 1414–1443*, ed. E. F. Jacob (4 vols., Oxford, and Canterbury and York Society 42, 45–7, 1937–47).

Reg. Cobham: *The Register of Thomas de Cobham, Bishop of Worcester, 1317–1327*, ed. E. H. Pearce (Worcestershire Historical Society 40, 1930).

Reg. Corbridge: *The Register of Thomas of Corbridge, Lord Archbishop of York, 1300–1304*, ed. W. Brown and A. H. Thompson (2 vols., Surtees Society 138, 141, 1925–8).

Reg. Courtenay: *Registrum Willelmi de Courtenay, episcopi Herefordensis, A.D. MCCCLXX–MCCCLXXV*, ed. W. W. Capes (Cantilupe Society 1913, and Canterbury and York Society 15, 1914).

Reg. Droxford: *Calendar of the Register of John de Drokensford, Bishop of Bath and Wells (A.D. 1309–1329)*, ed. E. Hobhouse (Somerset Record Society 1, 1887).

Reg. Edington: *The Register of William Edington, Bishop of Winchester 1346–1366*, ed. S. F. Hockey (2 vols., Hampshire Record Ser. VII, VIII, 1986–7).

Reg. Fleming: *The Register of Richard Fleming, Bishop of Lincoln, 1420–31, vol. I*, ed. N. H. Bennett (Canterbury and York Society 73, 1984).

Reg. G. Giffard: *Episcopal registers, diocese of Worcester. Register of Bishop Godfrey Giffard, September 23rd 1268 to August 15th 1301*, ed. J. W. Willis Bund (2 vols., Worcestershire Historical Society 15, 1898–1902).

Reg. Gainsborough: *The Register of William de Geynesburgh, Bishop of Worcester, 1302–1307*, ed. J. W. Willis Bund with an introduction by R.A. Wilson (Worcestershire Historical Society 22, 1907–29).

Reg. Gandavo: *Registrum Simonis de Gandavo diocesis Saresbiriensis A.D. 1297–1315*, ed. C. T. Flower and M. C. B. Dawes (2 vols., Canterbury and York Society 40–1, 1934).

Reg. Gloucester: 'Register pertaining to the churches of the monastery of St Peter's, Gloucester', ed. D. Walker, in *An Ecclesiastical Miscellany* (Bristol and Gloucestershire Archaeological Society, records section XI, 1976), pp. 1–58.

Reg. Grandisson: *The Register of John de Grandisson, Bishop of Exeter (A.D. 1327–1369)*, ed. F. C. Hingeston-Randolph (3 vols., London and Exeter, 1894–9).

Reg. Gray: *The register, or rolls, of Walter Gray, lord archbishop of York*, ed. J. Raine (Surtees Society 56, 1872).

Reg. Greenfield: *The register of William Greenfield, lord archbishop of York, 1306–15*, ed. W. Brown and A. H. Thompson (5 vols., Surtees Society 145, 149, 151–3, 1931–40).

Reg. Grosseteste: *Rotuli Roberti Grosseteste, episcopi Lincolniensis A.D. MCCXXXV–MCCLIII*, ed. F. N. Davis (Canterbury and York Society 10, 1913, and Lincoln Record Society 11, 1914), pp. 1–502.

Reg. Hallum: *The Register of Robert Hallum, Bishop of Salisbury, 1407–17*, ed. J. M. Horn (Canterbury and York Society 72, 1982).

Reg. Halton: *The Register of John de Halton, Bishop of Carlisle A.D. 1292–1324*, ed. W. N. Thompson (2 vols., Canterbury and York Society 12–13, and Cumberland and Westmorland Antiquarian and Archaeological Society, record or chartulary ser. 2, 1913).

Reg. Hethe: *Registrum Hamonis Hethe, diocesis Roffensis, A.D. 1319–1352*, transcribed and ed. C. Johnson (2 vols., Canterbury and York Society 48–9, 1948).

Reg. J. Gilbert: *Registrum Johannis Gilbert, episcopi Herefordensis, A.D. MCCCLXXV–MCCCLXXXIX*, ed. J. H. Parry (Cantilupe Society, 1913, and Canterbury and York Society 18, 1915).

Reg. John of Gaunt 1371–5: *John of Gaunt's Register*, ed. S. Armitage-Smith (2 vols., Camden, 3rd ser. 20–1, 1911).

Reg, John of Gaunt 1379–83: *John of Gaunt's Register, 1379–1383*, ed. E. C. Lodge and R. Somerville (2 vols., Camden, 3rd ser. 56–7, 1937).

Reg. Kirkby: *The Register of John Kirkby, Bishop of Carlisle, 1332–1352, and the Register of John Ross, Bishop of Carlisle, 1325–32*, ed. R. L. Storey (2 vols., Canterbury and York Society 79, 81, 1993–5).

Reg. L. Charlton: *Registrum Ludowici de Charltone, episcopi Herefordensis, A.D. MCCCLXI–MCCCLXX*, ed. J. H. Parry (Cantilupe Society 1913, and Canterbury and York Society 14, 1914).

Reg. Langham: *Registrum Simonis de Langham, Cantuariensis archiepiscopi*, ed. A. C. Wood (Canterbury and York Society 53, 1956).

Reg. Langley: *The Register of Thomas Langley, Bishop of Durham, 1406–1437*, ed. R. L. Storey (6 vols., Surtees Society 164, 166, 169–70, 177, 182, 1956–70).

Reg. Lexington: *Rotuli Roberti Grosseteste, episcopi Lincolniensis A.D. MCCXXXV–MCCLIII*, ed. F. N. Davis (Canterbury and York Society 10, 1913, and Lincoln Record Society 11, 1914), pp. 508–14.

Reg. Martival: *The Registers of Roger Martival, Bishop of Salisbury, 1315–1330*, ed. K. Edwards, C. R. Elrington, S. Reynolds and D. M. Owen (5 vols., Canterbury and York Society 55–9, 68, 1959–75).

Reg. Melton: *The Register of William Melton, Archbishop of York, 1317–1340*, ed. R. M. T. Hill, D. B. Robinson, and R. Brocklesby (4 vols., Canterbury and York Society 70–1, 76, 85, 1977–97, in progress).

Reg. Montacute: *Calendar of the Register of Simon Montacute, Bishop of Worcester, 1334–1337*, ed. R. M. Haines (Worcestershire Historical Society, new ser. 15, 1996).

Reg. Newark: *The Registers of John le Romeyn, Lord Archbishop of York, 1286–1296, part II, and of Henry of Newark, Lord Archbishop of York, 1296–1299*, ed. W. Brown (Surtees Society 128, 1917), pp. 205–317.

Reg. Orleton (Hereford): *Registrum Ade de Orleton, episcopi Herefordensis, A.D. MCCCXVII–MCCCXXVII*, ed. A. T. Bannister (Cantilupe Society 1907, and Canterbury and York Society 5, 1908).

Reg. Orleton (Worc.): *Calendar of the Register of Adam de Orleton, Bishop of Worcester 1327–1333*, ed. R. M. Haines (Worcestershire Historical Society, new ser. 10, and *HMC* joint publication 27, 1980).

Reg. Pal. Dun.: *Registrum Palatinum Dunelmense*, ed. T. D. Hardy (4 vols., RS, 1873–8).

Reg. Pecham: *The Register of John Pecham, Archbishop of Canterbury, 1279–1292*, ed. F. N. Davis, D. L. Douie, and others (Canterbury and York Society 64, 65, 1908–69).

Reg. Peckham: *Registrum Epistolarum Fratris Johannis Peckham, Archiepiscopi Cantuariensis*, ed. C. T. Martin (3 vols., RS, 1882–5).

Reg. Pinchbeck: *The Pinchbeck Register*, ed. Lord Francis Hervey (2 vols., Brighton, 1925).

Reg. Pontissara: *Registrum Johannis de Pontissara, episcopi Wyntoniensis A.D. MCCLXXXII–MCCCIV*, translated and ed. C. Deedes (2 vols., Canterbury and York Society 19, 30, 1915–24).

Reg. Quivil: *The Registers of Walter Bronescombe (A.D. 1257–1280), and Peter Quivil (A.D. 1280–1291), Bishops of Exeter, with some records of the episcopate of Bishop Thomas de Bytton (A.D. 1292–1307)*, ed. F. C. Hingeston-Randolph (London and Exeter, 1889).

Reg. R. Gravesend: *Rotuli Ricardi Gravesend, diocesis Lincolniensis*, ed. F. N. Davis, additions by C. W. Foster and A. H. Thompson (Lincoln Record Society 20 and Canterbury and York Society 31, 1925).

Reg. R. Mascall: *Registrum Roberti Mascall, episcopi Herefordensis, A.D. MCCCCIV–MCCCCXVI*, ed. J. H. Parry and C. Johnson (Cantilupe Society 1916, and Canterbury and York Society 21, 1917).

Reg. R. Shrewsbury: *The Register of Ralph of Shrewsbury, Bishop of Bath and Wells, 1329–1363*, ed. T. S. Holmes (2 vols., Somerset Record Society 9, 10, 1896).

Reg. Rede: *The Episcopal Register of Robert Rede, ordinis predicatorum, lord bishop of Chichester, 1397–1415*, ed. C. Deedes (2 vols., Sussex Record Society 8, 10, 1908–10).

Reg. Repingdon: *The Register of Bishop Philip Repingdon*, ed. M. Archer (3 vols., Lincoln Record Society 57–8, 74, 1963–82).

Reg. Reynolds: *The Register of Walter Reynolds, Bishop of Worcester, 1308–1313*, ed. R. A. Wilson (Worcestershire Historical Society 39, 1927, and Dugdale Society 9, 1928).

Reg. Roff.: *Registrum Roffense...*, ed. J. Thorpe (London, 1769).

Reg. Romeyn: *The Register of John le Romeyn, Lord Archbishop of York, 1286–1296*, ed. W. Brown (2 vols., Surtees Society 123, 128, 1913–17).

Reg. Rotherham: *The Register of Thomas Rotherham, Archbishop of York, 1480–1500, vol. I*, ed. E. E. Barker (Canterbury and York Society 69, 1976).

Reg. S. Gravesend: *Registrum Radulphi Baldock, Gilberti Segrave, Ricardi Newport, et Stephani Gravesend, episcoporum Londoniensium, A.D. MCCCIV–MCCCXXXVIII*, ed. R. C. Fowler (Canterbury and York Society 7, 1911).

Reg. Sandale: *The Registers of John of Sandale and Rigaud de Asserio, Bishops of Winchester (A.D. 1316–1323) with an appendix of contemporaneous and other illustrative documents*, ed. F. J. Baigent (Hampshire Record Society, 1897).

Reg. Scrope: *A Calendar of the Register of Richard Scrope, Archbishop of York, 1398–1405*, ed. R. N. Swanson (Borthwick Texts and Calendars 8, 11, 1981–5).

Reg. Spofford: Registrum Thome Spofford, episcopi Herefordensis, A.D. MCCCCXXII–MCCC-CXLVIII, ed. A. T. Bannister (Cantilupe Society 1917, and Canterbury and York Society 23, 1919).

Reg. St Osmund: Vetus registrum Sarisberiense alias dictum registrum S. Osmundi episcopi . . ., ed. W. H. R. Jones (2 vols., RS, 1883–4).

Reg. Stafford: The Register of Edmund Stafford (A.D. 1395–1419): an index and abstract of its contents, ed. F. C. Hingeston-Randolph (London and Exeter, 1886).

Reg. Stapeldon: The Register of Walter de Stapeldon, Bishop of Exeter (A.D. 1307–1326), ed. F. C. Hingeston-Randolph (London and Exeter, 1892).

Reg. Stretton I: The registers or act books of the bishops of Coventry and Lichfield. Book 4, being the register of the guardian of the spiritualities during the vacancy of the see, and the first register of Bishop Robert de Stretton, 1358–1385: an abstract of the contents, ed. R. A. Wilson (William Salt Archaeological Society, new ser. 10, part 2, 1907).

Reg. Stretton II: The registers or act books of the bishops of Coventry and Lichfield. Book 5, being the second register of Bishop Robert de Stretton, 1360–1385: an abstract of the contents, ed. R. A. Wilson (William Salt Archaeological Society, new ser. 8, 1905).

Reg. Sudbury: Registrum Simonis de Sudbiria, episcopi Londoniensis, A.D. 1362–1375, ed. R. C. Fowler and C. Jenkins (Canterbury and York Society 34, 38, 1927–38).

Reg. Sutton: The rolls and register of Bishop Oliver Sutton, 1280–1299, ed. R. M. T. Hill (8 vols., Lincoln Record Society 39, 43, 48, 52, 60, 64, 69, 76, 1948–86).

Reg. Swinfield: Registrum Ricardi Swinfield, episcopi Herefordensis, A.D. MCCLXXXII–MCC-CXVII, ed. W. W. Capes (Cantilupe Society and Canterbury and York Society 6, 1909).

Reg. T. Charlton: Registrum Thome Charlton, episcopi Herefordensis, A.D. MCCCXXVII–MCC-CXLIV, ed. W. W. Capes (Cantilupe Society 1912, and Canterbury and York Society 9, 1913).

Reg. Trefnant: Registrum Johannis Trefnant, episcopi Herefordensis, A.D. MCCCLXXXIX–MCCCCIV, ed. W. W. Capes (Cantilupe Society 1914, and Canterbury and York Society 20, 1916).

Reg. Trillek: Registrum Johannis de Trillek, episcopi Herefordensis, A.D. MCCCXLIV–MCCCLXI, ed. J. H. Parry (Cantilupe Society 1910, and Canterbury and York Society 8, 1912).

Reg. W. Bronescombe: The Register of Walter Bronescombe, Bishop of Exeter 1258–1280, vols. I–II, ed. O. F. Robinson (Canterbury and York Society 82, 87, 1995–9).

Reg. W. Giffard: The register of Walter Giffard, lord archbishop of York, 1266–1279, ed. W. Brown (Surtees Society 109, 1904).

Reg. W. Giffard (Bath): The Registers of Walter Giffard, Bishop of Bath and Wells, 1265–6, and of Henry Bowett, Bishop of Bath and Wells, 1401–7, ed. T. S. Holmes (Somerset Record Society 13, 1899), pp. 1–11.

Reg. Wakefield: A calendar of the Register of Henry Wakefield, Bishop of Worcester 1375–1395, ed. W. P. Marett (Worcestershire Historical Society, new ser. 7, 1972).

Reg. Waldby: A calendar of the register of Robert Waldby, archbishop of York, 1397, ed. D. M. Smith (Borthwick Texts and Calendars 2, 1974).

Reg. Waltham: The Register of John Waltham, Bishop of Salisbury 1388–1395, ed. T. C. B. Timmins (Canterbury and York Society 80, 1994).

Reg. Wells: Rotuli Hugonis de Welles, episcopi Lincolniensis A.D. MCCIX–MCCXXXV, ed. W. P. W. Phillimore and F. N. Davis (3 vols., Canterbury and York Society 1, 3, 4, 1907–9; Lincoln Record Society 3, 6, 9, 1912–14).

Reg. Welton: The Register of Gilbert Welton, Bishop of Carlisle 1353–1362, ed. R. L. Storey (Canterbury and York Society 88, 1999).

Reg. Whethamstede: Registra quorundam abbatum monasterii S. Albani, qui saeculo XV^{mo} floruere, ed. H. T. Riley (2 vols., RS, 1872–3).

Reg. Wickwane: The Register of William Wickwane, Lord Archbishop of York, 1279–1285, ed. W. Brown (Surtees Society 114, 1907).

Reg. Winchelsey: Registrum Roberti Winchelsey Cantuariensis Archiepiscopi, ed. R. Graham (2 vols., Canterbury and York Society 51–2, 1952–6).

Reg. Woodlock: Registrum Henrici Woodlock, diocesis Wintoniensis, A.D. 1305–1316, ed. A. W. Goodman (2 vols., Canterbury and York Society 43–4, 1940–1).

Reg. Wykeham: Wykeham's Register, ed. T. F. Kirby (2 vols., Hampshire Record Society, 1896–9).

Registres d'Alexandre IV, Les, ed. B. de la Roncière *et al.* (3 vols., Bibliothèque des Ecoles Françaises d'Athènes et de Rome, 2nd ser. XV, Paris, 1895–1959).

Registres de Boniface VIII, Les, ed. G. Digard *et al.* (4 vols., Bibliothèque des Ecoles Françaises d'Athènes et de Rome, 2nd ser. IV, Paris, 1907–39).

Registres de Grégoire IX, Les, ed. L. Auvray (4 vols., Bibliothèque des Ecoles Françaises d'Athènes et de Rome, 2nd ser. IX, Paris, 1890–1955).

Registres d'Honorius IV, Les, ed. M. Prou (Bibliothèque des Ecoles Françaises d'Athènes et de Rome, 2nd ser. VII, Paris, 1886–8).

Registres de Nicolas III, Les, ed. J. Gay and S. Vitte (Bibliothèque des Ecoles Françaises d'Athènes et de Rome, 2nd ser. XIV, Paris, 1898–1938).

Regs. St Davids: The Episcopal Registers of the Diocese of St David's, 1397 to 1518, ed. R. F. Isaacson, with a study of the registers by A. Roberts (3 vols., Cymmrodorion Record Series 6, 1917–20).

Richardson, R. K., 'Gesta Dunelmensia A.D. MCCC' in *Camden Miscellany XIII* (Camden, 3rd ser. 34, 1924).

Ridley Chts.: E. M. Halcrow, 'Ridley Charters', *Arch. Aeliana*, 4th ser. XXXIV (1956), 57–76.

Robertsbridge Chts.: Calendar of charters and documents relating to the abbey of Robertsbridge, co. Sussex, preserved at Penshurst among the muniments of Lord De Lisle and Dudley (London, 1873).

Robinson, C. B., *History of the priory and peculiar of Snaith in the county of York* (London, 1861).

Robinson, J. A., 'The foundation charter of Witham charterhouse', *Proc. Soms ANHS*, LXIV (1919 for 1918), 1–28.

Rogers, N., 'The earliest known description of the de la Mare brass at St Albans abbey', *TMBS*, XIV(2), (1987), 154–7.

Rolls of Lincolnshire Justices: Rolls of the justices in eyre, being the rolls of pleas and assizes for Lincolnshire, 1218–19, and Worcestershire, 1221, ed. D. M. Stenton (Selden Society 53, 1934).

Rot. Chart.: Rotuli Chartarum in Turri Londinensi asservati, 1199–1216, ed. T. D. Hardy (Record Commission, 1837).

Rot. Cur. Reg.: Rotuli Curiae Regis: Rolls and Records of the Court held before the King's Justiciars or Justices, 6 Richard I – I John, ed. F. Palgrave (2 vols., Record Commission, 1835).

Rot. de Finibus: Rotuli de Oblatis et Finibus in Turri Londinensi asservati temp. Regis Iohannis, ed. T. D. Hardy (Record Commission, 1835).

Rot. Lit. Claus.: Rotuli Litterarum Clausarum in Turri Londinensi asservati, ed. T. D. Hardy (2 vols., Record Commission, 1833–4).

Rot. Lit. Pat.: Rotuli Litterarum Patentium in Turri Londinensi asservati, 1201–16, ed. T. D. Hardy (Record Commission, 1835).

Rot. Parl.: Rotuli Parliamentorum; ut et petitiones, et placita in parliamento (6 vols., Record Commission, 1783–1832).

Rowntree, A., *The history of Scarborough* (London, 1931).

Rowntree, C., 'Studies in Carthusian history in later medieval England with special reference to the Order's relations with secular society' (unpublished D.Phil. thesis, University of York, 1981).

Royal Inquest 1341: *The 1341 Royal Inquest in Lincolnshire*, ed. B. W. McLane (Lincoln Record Society 78, 1988).

RS: Rolls Series.

Rufford Chts.: *Rufford Charters*, ed. C. J. Holdsworth (4 vols., Thoroton Society XXIX, XXX, XXXII, XXXIV, 1972–81).

Rye, W., *Carrow Abbey* (Norwich, 1889).

Rymer, *Foedera*: *Foedera, conventiones* . . . Accurante Thoma Rymer (2nd edn. 20 vols., London, 1727–35).

Sacrist Rolls of Ely, ed. F. R. Chapman (2 vols., Cambridge, 1907).

St Davids Acta: *St Davids Episcopal Acta 1085–1280*, ed. J. Barrow (South Wales Record Society 13, 1998).

St Nicholas, Abingdon: *The church and parish of St Nicholas, Abingdon* . . ., ed. A. E. Preston (Oxford Historical Society XCIX, 1935).

St Richard of Chichester: D. Jones ed., *St Richard of Chichester: the sources for his life* (Sussex Record Society 79, 1995).

Salt MSS.: M. E. Cornford and E. B. Miller, *Calendar of the Salt MSS. in SHC* 1921, 1–39.

Salter, H. E., 'A chronicle roll of the abbots of Abingdon', *EHR*, 26 (1911), 727–38.

Salter, 'Priory': H. E. Salter, 'The priory of Poughley', *Berks, Bucks and Oxon. Arch. Jnl*, 13 (1907–8), 107–9.

Salter Essays: *Oxford Essays in Medieval History presented to Herbert Edward Salter* (Oxford, 1934).

Saltman, A., 'The History of the Foundation of Dale Abbey, or the so-called Chronicle of Dale', *Derbyshire Archaeological Journal*, 87 (1967), 18–38.

Salzmann, *Hailsham*: L. F. Salzmann, *The history of the parish of Hailsham, the abbey of Otham, and the priory of Michelham* (Lewes, 1901).

Sarum Chts.: *Charters and Documents illustrating the history of the cathedral, city and diocese of Salisbury in the twelfth and thirteenth centuries*, ed. W. (H.) R. Jones and W. D. Macray (RS, 1891).

Sayers: *Original Papal Documents in England and Wales from the accession of Pope Innocent III to the death of Pope Benedict XI (1198–1304)*, ed. J. E. Sayers (Oxford, 1999).

Sayers, *Honorius III*: J. E. Sayers, *Papal Government and England during the pontificate of Honorius III (1216–1227)* (Cambridge, 1984).

Scarisbrick Chts.: E. Powell, ed., 'Ancient charters preserved at Scarisbrick Hall in the county of Lancaster', *Trans. Lancs and Ches. Hist. Soc.*, 48 (1897), 259–94; 49 (1898), 185–230.

Scriptores Tres: *Historiae Dunelmensis scriptores tres: Gaufridus de Coldingham, Robertus de Graystanes et Willelmus de Chambre*, ed. J. Raine (Surtees Society 9, 1839).

Scrope-Grosvenor: N. H. Nicolas, ed., *The Controversy between Sir Richard Scrope and Sir Robert Grosvenor in the Court of Chivalry* (2 vols., London, 1832).

SDNQ: *Somerset and Dorset Notes and Queries*.

Selborne Chts.: *Calendar of Charters and Documents relating to possessions of Selborne and its priory preserved in the muniment room of Magdalen College, Oxford*, ed. W. D. Macray (2 vols., Hampshire Record Society 1894–6).

Select Bills in Eyre, A.D. 1292–1333, ed. W. C. Bolland (Selden Society 30, 1914).

Select Canterbury Cases: *Select Cases from the Ecclesiastical Courts of the Province of Canterbury C, 1200–1301*, ed. N. Adams and C. Donahue (Selden Society 95, 1981).

Select Cases, Law Merchant: *Select Cases concerning the Law Merchant, A.D. 1270–1638*, ed. C. Gross (Selden Society 23, 1908).

Select Cases in the Exchequer of Pleas, ed. H. Jenkinson and B. E. R. Formoy (Selden Society 48, 1932).

Select Cases of Procedure: Select Cases of procedure without writ under Henry III, ed. H. G. Richardson and G. O. Sayles (Selden Society 60, 1941).

Select Cases of Trespass: Select Cases of Trespass from the King's Courts 1307–1399, ed. M. S. Arnold (2 vols., Selden Society 100, 103, 1985–7).

Sempringham Chts.: E. M. Poynton, ed., 'Charters relating to the Priory of Sempringham', *Genealogist*, new ser. 15 (1899), 158–61, 221–7; 16 (1900), 30–5, 76–83, 153–8, 223–8; 17 (1901), 29–35, 164–8, 232–9.

Serjeantson, R. M., 'The priory of St Andrew, Northampton', *Northants Nat. Hist. Society and Field Club*, XIII (1905).

Seymour, *Torre Abbey*: D. Seymour, *Torre Abbey: an account of its history, buildings, cartularies and lands* (Exeter, 1977).

Sharpe, *Latin Writers*: R. Sharpe, *A Handlist of Latin Writers of Great Britain and Ireland before 1540* (Publications of the Journal of Medieval Latin 1, Turnhout, 1997).

Shaw, *Hist. of Staffs*: S. Shaw, *The History and Antiquities of Staffordshire* (2 vols., London, 1798–1801).

SHC: *Staffordshire Historical Collections*, William Salt Archaeological Society, now Staffs. Record Society.

Shenstone Chts.: *The Shenstone Charters, copied from the chartulary or great coucher book of the Duchy of Lancaster*, ed. G. and H. S. Grazebrook, *SHC*, XVII (1896), 237–98.

Sheppard, *The Buildwas Books*: J. M. Sheppard, *The Buildwas Books: book production, acquisition and use at an English Cistercian monastery, 1165 – c. 1400* (Oxford Bibliographical Society, 3rd ser. II, 1997).

Shropshire Eyre: The Roll of the Shropshire Eyre of 1256, ed. A. Harding (Selden Society 96, 1981).

Sibton Abbey Estates: The Sibton Abbey Estates: select documents 1325–1509, ed. A. H. Denney (Suffolk Records Society II, 1960).

Signet Letters: Calendar of Signet Letters of Henry IV and Henry V (1399–1422), ed. J. L. Kirby (London, 1978).

Simeon of Durham: Symeonis monachi opera omnia, ed. T. Arnold (2 vols., RS, 1882–5).

Sleigh, *Leek*: J. Sleigh, *A history of the ancient parish of Leek in Staffordshire* (2nd edn, London, 1883).

Smith, D. M., *Guide to Bishops' Registers of England and Wales: a survey from the Middle Ages to the abolition of Episcopacy in 1646* (Royal Historical Society guide and handbook 11, 1981). 'The rolls of Hugh of Wells, Bishop of Lincoln, 1209–35', *BIHR*, XLV (1972), 155–95.

Smith, *Canterbury Cathedral Priory*: R. A. L. Smith, *Canterbury Cathedral Priory: a study in monastic administration* (Cambridge, 1943).

Smith, *Court of York 1301–1399*: D. M. Smith, *Ecclesiastical Cause Papers at York: The Court of York 1301–1399* (Borthwick Texts and Calendars 14, 1988).

Smith, W., 'A Register from Reading Abbey', *JSA*, 7, no. 8 (1985), 513–25.

Snape, M. G., 'A letter from a Yorkshire prioress to Archbishop Thoresby, c. 1356', *BIHR*, XXVII (1954), 190–2.

Snappe's Formulary and other records, ed. H. E. Salter (Oxford Historical Society LXXX, 1924).

Solloway, J., *The Alien Benedictines of York: being a complete history of Holy Trinity Priory, York* (Leeds, 1910).

Somerset Pleas: Somersetshire Pleas, civil and criminal, from the rolls of the itinerant justices, ed. T. S. Holmes and L. Landon (4 vols., Somerset Record Society 11, 36, 41, 44, 1897–1929).

Soms F., see under FINES.

South Wales and Mon. Rec. Soc.: South Wales and Monmouth Record Society publications.

Sparke: *Historiae Coenobii Burgensis Scriptores varii* (Chs. Peterborough), ed. J. Sparke in *Historiae Anglicanae Scriptores Varii* (2 vols. in 3, London, 1723).

Sparrow, *History of Church Preen*: A. Sparrow, *The History of Church Preen in the County of Salop*, ed. E. A. Ebblewhite (London, 1898).

Speight, H., *Lower Wharfedale* (London, 1902).

Stacpoole, A., ed., *The Noble City of York* (York, 1972).

Staffs F., *Staffs F. 2*, *Staffs F. 3*, *see under* FINES.

Staffs Forest Pleas: G. Wrottesley, ed., 'The Pleas of the Forest, Staffordshire, temp. Henry III and Edward I', *SHC*, V(i), 123–80.

Staffs Plea Rolls, Henry III: G. Wrottesley ed., 'Plea Rolls temp. Henry III. Suits affecting Staffordshire tenants, taken from the plea rolls of the reign of Henry III', *SHC*, IV (i) (1883), 1–215.

Staffs Plea Rolls 1272–94: G. Wrottesley, ed., 'Extract from the Plea Rolls A.D. 1272 to A.D. 1294, taken from the original rolls in the Public Record Office', *SHC*, VI (i), (1885), 37–300.

Staffs Plea Rolls 1294–1307: G. Wrottesley, ed., 'Extracts from the Plea Rolls, A.D. 1294 to A.D. 1307', *SHC*, VII (1886), 1–191.

Staffs Plea Rolls 1307–27: G. Wrottesley, ed., 'Extracts from the Assize Rolls and De Banco Rolls of the reign of Edward II, A.D. 1307 to A.D. 1327', *SHC*, IX (1888), 1–118.

Staffs Plea Rolls 1–15 Edward III: G. Wrottesley, ed., 'Extracts from the Plea Rolls, 1 to 15 Edward III', *SHC*, XI (1890), 1–123.

Staffs Plea Rolls 16–33 Edward III: G. Wrottesley, ed., 'Extracts from the Plea Rolls, 16 to 33 Edward III', *SHC*, XIII (1891), 1–173.

Staffs Plea Rolls 1360–87: G. Wrottesley, ed., 'Extracts from the Plea Rolls of Edward III and Richard II, A.D. 1360 to A.D. 1387', *SHC*, XIII (1892), 1–204.

Staffs Plea Rolls 1387–1405: G. Wrottesley, ed., 'Extracts from the Plea Rolls of the reigns of Richard II and Henry IV, A.D. 1387 to A.D. 1405', *SHC*, XV (1894), 1–126.

Staffs Studies: *Staffordshire Studies*.

Stansfield, J., 'A rent roll of Kirkstall Abbey' in *Miscellanea I* (Thoresby Soc. 2, 1891), 1– 21.

Starrs and Jewish Chts.: *Starrs and Jewish Charters preserved in the British Museum*, ed. H. Loewe (3 vols., Jewish Historical Society of England, 1930–2).

State Trials: *State Trials of the Reign of Edward the First 1289–1293*, ed. T. F. Tout and H. Johnstone (Camden, 3rd ser. IX, 1906).

Stenton, *Eyre 1221–2*: *Rolls of the justices in eyre, being the rolls of pleas and assizes for Gloucestershire, Warwickshire and Staffordshire [recte Shropshire], 1221, 1222*, ed. D. M. Stenton (Selden Society 59, 1940).

Stenton, *Yorkshire Eyre*: *Rolls of the justices in eyre, being the rolls of pleas and assizes for Yorkshire in 3 Henry III (1218–19)*, ed. D. M. Stenton (Selden Society 56, 1937).

Stephan, Dom J., *Buckfast Abbey* (Buckfast, 1962).

Stewart-Brown, R., *Birkenhead Priory and the Mersey Ferry* (Liverpool, 1925).

Stockdale, J., *Annales Caermoelenses* (1872, repd Whitehaven, 1978).

Stogursey Chts.: *Stogursey Charters*, ed. T. D. Tremlett and N. Blakiston (Somerset Record Society 61, 1949 for 1946).

Storey, R. L., 'Papal provisions to English monasteries', *Nottingham Medieval Studies*, XXXV (1991), 77–91.

Suckling, *Suffolk*: A. Suckling, *The History and Antiquities of the County of Suffolk* (2 vols., London, 1846–8).

Sudbury Chts.: *Charters of St Bartholomew's Priory, Sudbury*, ed. R. Mortimer (Suffolk Charters ser. XV, 1996).

Suffolk F., see under FINES.

Surrey Arch. Coll.: *Surrey Archaeological Collections.*

Surrey F., see under FINES.

Sussex Arch. Coll.: *Sussex Archaeological Collections.*

Sussex F., see under FINES.

Swynnerton, C., 'The priory of Leonard Stanley, co. Gloucester, in the light of recent discoveries documentary and structural', *Archaeologia*, LXXI (1921), 199–226.

Talbot, C. H., 'Cadogan of Bangor', *Cîteaux*, 9 (1958), 18–40.

'Cîteaux and Scarborough', *Studia Monastica*, II, (1960), 95–158.

Talbot, C. H. and Hammond, E. A., *The Medical Practitioners in Medieval England: a biographical register* (London, 1965).

Talbot, H., 'Richard Straddell, abbot of Dore 1305–46', *Downside Review*, 61 (1943), 11–20.

Tanner, *Notitia Monastica*: T. Tanner, *Notitia Monastica: an account of all abbeys etc., in England and Wales* (London, 1744, repd with additions by J. Nasmyth, Cambridge, 1787).

Tate, *Hist. of Alnwick*: G. Tate, *The History of the Borough, Castle and Barony of Alnwick* (2 vols., Alnwick, 1866–9).

Taylor, A. J., 'The alien priory of Minster Lovell', *Oxoniensia*, 2 (1937), 103–17.

TDA: *Transactions of the Devonshire Association for the Advancement of Science, Literature and the Arts.*

TEAS: *Transactions of the Essex Archaeological Society.*

Test. Ebor.: *Testamenta Eboracensia*, ed. J. Raine senior, J. Raine junior, and J. W. Clay (6 vols., Surtees Society 4, 30, 45, 53, 79, 106, 1836–1902).

Thomas, S. P., 'Limebrook priory', *Trans. Radnorshire Soc.*, 56 (1986), 23–5.

Thompson, A. H., *The Abbey of St Mary of the Meadows* (Leicester, 1949).

'The jurisdiction of the Archbishops of York in Gloucestershire', *BGAS*, XLIII (1922), 85–180.

The Premonstratensian Abbey of Welbeck (London, 1938).

Thompson, *Carthusian Order*: E. M. Thompson, *The Carthusian Order in England* (London, 1930).

Thompson, *Somerset Carthusians*: E. M. Thompson, *A History of the Somerset Carthusians* (London, 1895).

Thompson, *Women Religious*: S. Thompson, *Women Religious: The Founding of English Nunneries after the Norman Conquest* (Oxford, 1991).

Thomson, R. M., ed., *The Chronicle of the Election of Hugh, Abbot of Bury St Edmunds, and later Bishop of Ely* (OMT, 1974).

Thomson, R. M., *MSS. from St Albans*: *Manuscripts from St Albans Abbey 1066–1235*, ed. R. M. Thomson (2 vols., Woodbridge, 1982).

Thorne: William Thorne, *Chronica de rebus gestis abbatum sancti Augustini Cantuariae*, ed. R. Twysden, *Historiae Anglicanae Scriptores* x (London, 1652), cols. 1753–2202 (also translation by A. H. Davis, *William Thorne's Chronicle...* (Oxford, 1934), with pages of Twysden noted).

Thoroton, *Notts*: R. Thoroton, *The Antiquities of Nottinghamshire*, with additions by J. Throsby, (3 vols., Nottingham, 1797).

Tillmann: H. Tillmann, *Die päpstlichen Legaten in England bis zur Beendigung der Legation Gualas (1218)* (Bonn, 1926).

TMBS: *Transactions of the Monumental Brass Society.*

'Tolleshunt Major and Coggeshall abbey', *TEAS*, IX (1903), 181.

Tomkinson, J. T., 'The documentation of Hulton abbey: two cases of forgery', *Staffs Studies*, 6 (1994), 73–99.

Tonkin, J. W., 'The nunnery of Limebrook and its property', *Trans. Woolhope Nat. Field Club* 41 part 1 (1974), 149–64.

Trabut-Cussac, J. F., *Les possessions Anglaises de l'abbaye de la Sauve-Majeure. Le prieuré de Burwell, Lincolnshire* (Paris, 1958).

Trans. AAS Durham & Northumberland: *Transactions of the Architectural and Archaeological Society of Durham and Northumberland.*

Trans. Carmarthenshire Antiq. Soc. & Field Club: *Transactions of the Carmarthenshire Antiquarian Society and Field Club.*

Trans. CWAAS: *Transactions of the Cumberland and Westmorland Antiquarian and Archaeological Society.*

Trans. East Herts Arch. Soc.: *Transactions of the East Hertfordshire Archaeological Society.*

Trans. Lancs and Ches. Hist. Soc.: *Transactions of the Historic Society of Lancashire and Cheshire.*

Trans. Leics AHS: *Transactions of the Leicestershire Archaeological and Historical Society.*

Trans. Radnorshire Soc.: *Transactions of the Radnorshire Society.*

Trans. Shrops ANHS: *Transactions of the Shropshire Archaeological and Natural History Society.*

Trans. St Albans and Herts AAS: *Transactions of the St Albans and Hertfordshire Architectural and Archaeological Society.*

Trans. Thoroton Soc.: *Transactions of the Thoroton Society of Nottinghamshire.*

Trans. Woolhope Nat. Field Club: *Transactions of the Woolhope Naturalists' Field Club, Herefordshire.*

Trans. Worcs Archaeol. Soc.: *Transactions of the Worcestershire Archaeological Society.*

Traskey, J. P., *Milton Abbey: a Dorset monastery in the middle ages* (Tisbury, 1978).

TRHS: *Transactions of the Royal Historical Society.*

Trokelowe, ed. Hearne: *Johannis de Trokelowe, Annales Edwardi II*, etc., ed. T. Hearne (Oxford, 1729).

Turner, 'Ankerwyke': F. Turner, 'The Benedictine priory of St Mary Magdalene, Ankerwyke, Bucks', *Berks, Bucks and Oxon Arch. Jnl.*, 29 (1925), 50–74.

Turner, 'Broomhall': F. Turner, 'The Benedictine priory of Broomhall, Berks.', *Berks, Bucks and Oxon Arch. Jnl.*, 27 (1922), 90–5, 183–9.

Turner, H. H., Wigram, W. A., Garrod, H. W. and Gunther, R. T., 'Richard of Wallingford, abbot of St Albans 1326–1335', *Trans. St Albans and Herts AAS*, 1926, 221–39.

Tyson, *Rylands Chts.*: M. Tyson, *Hand-list of charters, deeds, and similar documents in the possession of the John Rylands Library, part II* (Manchester, 1935).

Urry: W. Urry, *Canterbury under the Angevin Kings* (London, 1967).

Vale Royal Ledger: *The Ledger-Book of Vale Royal Abbey*, ed. J. Brownbill (Lancashire and Cheshire Record Society 68, 1914).

Valor: *Valor Ecclesiasticus temp. Henrici VIII*, ed. J. Caley and J. Hunter (6 vols., Record Commission, 1810–34).

Vaughan, R., 'The election of abbots at St Albans in the thirteenth and fourteenth centuries', *Proc. Cambs AS*, XLVII (1954), 1–12.

VCH: *Victoria History of the Counties of England.*

Vickers, N., 'Grosmont priory', *YAJ*, 56 (1984), 45–9.

Vincent, N., 'The early years of Keynsham abbey', *BGAS*, CXI (1994 for 1993), 95–113.

'The foundation of Westacre priory 1102 x 1126', *Norfolk Archaeology* 41(4) (1993), 490–4.

'The foundation of Wormegay priory', *Norfolk Archaeology*, 43(2) (1999), 307–12.

Wakefield Court Rolls: *The Court Rolls of the Manor of Wakefield from September 1348 to September 1350*, ed. H. M. Jewell (Yorkshire Archaeological Society, Wakefield court rolls ser. 2, 1981).

Walker, *Monk Bretton Priory*: J. W. Walker, *An historical and architectural description of the priory of St Mary Magdalene of Monk Bretton in the West Riding of the county of Yorkshire* (Yorkshire Archaeological Society, Extra Series, 1926).

Walsingham: Chronica monasterii S. Albani: Thomae Walsingham quondam monachi S. Albani Historia Anglicana, ed. H.T. Riley (2 vols., RS, 1863–4).

Walt. Cov.: Memoriale fratris Walteri de Coventria. The historical collections of Walter of Coventry, ed. W. Stubbs (2 vols., RS, 1872–3).

Waltham Chts.: The Early Charters of Waltham Abbey, 1062–1230, ed. R. Ransford (Studies in the History of Medieval Religion 2, Woodbridge, 1989).

Warren, R. H., 'St Augustine's abbey, Bristol: the work of Abbot Knowle 1298–1332', *Proc. Clifton Antiquarian Club*, 5 (1904), 162–9.

Warws F., see under FINES.

Watkin, A., 'The correspondence of Walter de Monyton, abbot of Glastonbury', *Proc. Dorset NHAS*, 85 (1964), 135–40.

Watkin, *Totnes Priory*: H. R. Watkin, *The History of Totnes Priory and Medieval Town, Devonshire, together with the sister priory of Tywardreath . . .* (3 vols., Torquay, 1914– 19).

Welford, R., *History of Newcastle and Gateshead in the 14th and 15th centuries* (London, n.d.).

Welsh Assize Roll 1277–84: The Welsh Assize Rolls 1277–1284, ed. J. Conway Davies (Board of Celtic Studies, University of Wales, History and Law ser. VII, Cardiff, 1940).

Welsh Episcopal Acts: Episcopal Acts and cognate documents relating to Welsh dioceses, 1066–1272, ed. J. Conway Davies (Historical Society of the Church in Wales, 1, 3–4, 2 vols., Cardiff, 1946–8).

Welsh Memoranda: List of Welsh entries in the Memoranda Rolls 1282–1343, ed. N. Fryde (Cardiff, University of Wales, 1974).

West Wales Ministers' Accounts: Ministers' Accounts for West Wales 1277 to 1306, part 1, ed. M. Rhys (Cymmrodorion Record Series XIII, 1936).

Wethered, F. T., *Corrections and amendments to St Mary's Hurley in the middle ages* (London, 1903).

'Hurley Church and Priory', *Berks, Bucks and Oxon Arch. Jnl.* 23 (1917), 94–104.

Hurley Church and Priory (Reading, 1917).

St Mary's Hurley in the middle ages, based on Hurley charters and deeds (London, 1898).

Wheater, W., *Knaresburgh and its rulers* (Leeds, 1907).

Whitaker, *Craven*: T. D. Whitaker, *History and antiquities of the Deanery of Craven* (3rd edn, Leeds, 1878).

Whitaker, *Whalley*: T. D. Whitaker, *An History of the original parish of Whalley and Honor of Clitheroe in the counties of Lancaster and York to which is subjoined an account of the parish of Cartmell* (3rd edn, London, 1818).

White, R., *The Dukery Records* (Worksop, 1904).

Whitehead, J. L., 'The priory and manor of Appuldurcombe, Isle of Wight', *Hants Field Club*, 5 (1904–6), 185–95.

Williams, D., 'Basingwerk abbey', *Cîteaux*, 32 (1981), 87–113.

Williams, D. H., *Catalogue of Seals in the National Museum of Wales, I: Seal Dies, Welsh Seals, Papal Bullae* (Cardiff, 1993).

Williams, G., *The Welsh Church from Conquest to Reformation* (Cardiff, 1962).

Williams, *Hist. of Radnor*: J. Williams, *A General History of the County of Radnor*, ed. E. Davies (Brecknock, 1905).

Williams, *Strata Florida*: Williams, S. W., *The Cistercian Abbey of Strata Florida: its history, and an account of the recent excavations made on its site* (London, 1889).

Willis: Browne Willis, *An History of the Mitred Parliamentary Abbies . . .* (2 vols., London, 1718–19).

Willis, *Hist. Buckingham*: B. Willis, *The History and Antiquities of the Town Hundred, and Deanry of Buckingham* . . . (London, 1755).

Wilmart, A., 'Maître Adam chanoine Prémontré devenu Chartreux à Witham', *Analecta Premonstratensia* IX (1933), 209–32.

Wilts AM: Wiltshire Archaeological and Natural History Magazine.

Wilts Civil Pleas: Civil Pleas of the Wiltshire Eyre, 1249, ed. M. T. Clanchy (Wiltshire Record Society XXVI, 1971).

Wilts Crown Pleas: Crown Pleas of the Wiltshire Eyre, 1249, ed. C. A. F. Meekings (Wiltshire Archaeological and Natural History Society records branch XVI, 1961).

Wilts F., see under FINES.

Wilts Gaol Deliveries: Wiltshire Gaol Delivery and Trailbaston Trials 1275–1306, ed. R. B. Pugh (Wiltshire Record Society XXXIII, 1976).

Wilts IPM 1242–1326: Abstracts of Wiltshire inquisitiones post mortem . . . *1242–1326*, ed. E. A. Fry (British Record Society, Index Library 37, and Wiltshire Archaeological and Natural History Society, 1908).

Winchester Common Seal Reg.: The Register of the Common Seal of the Priory of St Swithun, Winchester 1345–1497, ed. J. Greatrex (Hampshire Record Series 2, 1978).

Wood, *City of Oxford:* Anthony Wood, 'Survey of the antiquities of the city of Oxford, composed in 1661–6', ed. A. Clark (3 vols., Oxford Historical Society XV, XVII, XXXVII, 1889–99).

Wood, *Letters of . . . Royal Ladies*: M. A. E. Wood ed., *Letters of Royal and Illustrious Ladies of Great Britain* (3 vols., London, 1846).

Woodruff, C. E., 'Some early professions of canonical obedience to the see of Canterbury by heads of religious houses', *Arch. Cant.*, XXXVII (1925), 53–72.

Woolley, E., 'A study of the character of Abbot Thomas de la Mare', *Trans. St Albans and Herts AAS*, 1928, 163–71.

'The brass of Thomas de la Mare, St Albans abbey church', *Trans. St Albans and Herts AAS*, 1928, 172–5.

Worcester Liber Albus: The Liber Albus of the priory of Worcester, parts 1 and 2, priors John de Wyke, 1301–1317, and Wulstan de Bransford, 1317–1339, folios 1–162, ed. J. M. Wilson (Worcestershire Historical Society, 1919).

Worcester Liber Albus (1920): J. M. Wilson, *The Worcester Liber Albus: glimpses of life in a great Benedictine monastery in the fourteenth century* (London, 1920).

Worcestre: William Worcestre: Itineraries, ed. J. H. Harvey (OMT, 1969).

Worcs Reg. Sede Vacante: The Register of the diocese of Worcester during the vacancy of the see, usually called registrum sede vacante 1301–1435, ed. J. W. Willis Bund (Worcestershire Historical Society, 1897).

Wordsworth, C., 'I: A Kalendar or Directory of Lincoln Use; and II: Kalendarium e Consuetudinario monasterii de Burgo sancti Petri', *Archaeologia*, LI (1888), 1–40.

YAJ: Yorkshire Archaeological Journal.

YB I: Year Books of Edward II, vol. I, 1–2 Edward II, A.D. 1307–1309, ed. F. W. Maitland (Selden Society 17, 1903).

YB II: Year Books of Edward II, vol. II, 2–3 Edward II, A.D. 1308–9 and 1309–10, ed. F. W. Maitland (Selden Society 19, 1904).

YB III: Year Books of Edward II, vol. III, 3 Edward II, A.D. 1309–10, ed. F. W. Maitland (Selden Society 20, 1905).

YB IV: Year Books of Edward II, vol. IV, 3–4 Edward II, A.D. 1309–1311, ed. F. W. Maitland and G. J. Turner (Selden Society 22, 1907).

YB VIII: Year Books of Edward II, vol. VIII, The eyre of Kent, 6 and 7 Edward II, A.D. 1313–1314, vol. III, ed. W. C. Bolland (Selden Society 29, 1913).

YB IX: Year Books of Edward II, vol. IX, 4 Edward II, A.D. 1311, ed. G. J. Turner (Selden Society 42, 1926).

YB XI: Year Books of Edward II, vol. XI, 5 Edward II, A.D. 1311–1312, ed. W. C. Bolland (Selden Society 31, 1915).

YB XII: Year Books of Edward II, vol. XII, 5 Edward II, A.D. 1312, ed. W. C. Bolland (Selden Society 33, 1916).

YB XIII: Year Books of Edward II, vol. XIII, 6 Edward II, A.D. 1312–1313, ed. P. Vinogradoff and L. Ehrlich (Selden Society 34, 1918).

YB XIV(i): Year Books of Edward II, vol. XIV, part I, 6 Edward II, A.D. 1312–1313, ed. P. Vinogradoff and L. Ehrlich (Selden Society 38, 1921).

YB XIV(ii): Year Books of Edward II, vol. XIV, part II, 6 Edward II, A.D. 1313, ed. W. C. Bolland (Selden Society 43, 1927).

YB XV: Year Books of Edward II, vol. XV, 7 Edward II, A.D. 1313–1314, ed. W. C. Bolland (Selden Society 39, 1922).

YB XVI: Year Books of Edward II, vol. XVI, 7 Edward II, A.D. 1313–1314, ed. W. C. Bolland (Selden Society 39, 1922).

YB XVIII: Year Books of Edward II, vol. XVIII, 8 Edward II, A.D. 1315, ed. W. C. Bolland (Selden Society 37, 1920).

YB XX: Year Books of Edward II, vol. XX, 10 Edward II, A.D. 1316–1317, ed. M. D. Legge and W. Holdsworth (Selden Society 52, 1934).

YB XXI: Year Books of Edward II, vol. XXI, 10 Edward II, A.D. 1316–1317, ed. M. D. Legge and W. Holdsworth (Selden Society 54, 1935).

YB XXII: Year Books of Edward II, vol. XXII, 11 Edward II, A.D. 1317–1318, ed. J. P. Collas and W. S. Holdsworth (Selden Society 61, 1942).

YB XXIII: Year Books of Edward II, vol. XXIII, 12 Edward II, Michaelmas A.D. 1318, ed. J. P. Collas and T. F. T. Plucknett (Selden Society 65, 1950).

YB XXIV: Year Books of Edward II, vol. XXIV, 12 Edward II, Hilary and part of Easter 1319, ed. J. P. Collas and T. F. T. Plucknett (Selden Society 70, 1953).

YB XXVI: Year Books of Edward II, vol. XXVI, part I: The eyre of London, 14 Edward II, A.D. 1321, ed. H. M. Cam (Selden Society 85, 1968).

YB 20–1 Edward I: Year Books of the Reign of King Edward the First, years XX and XXI, ed. A. J. Horwood (RS, 1866).

YB 21–2 Edward I: Year Books of the Reign of King Edward the First, years XXI and XXII, ed. A. J. Horwood (RS, 1873).

YB 30–1 Edward I: Year Books of the Reign of King Edward the First, 30–31 Edward I, ed. A. J. Horwood (RS, 1863).

YB 33–35 Edward I: Year Books of the Reign of King Edward the First, years XXXIII and XXXV, ed. A. J. Horwood (RS, 1879).

YB 11–12 Edward III: Year Books of the Reign of King Edward the Third, years XI and XII, ed. A. J. Horwood (RS, 1883).

YB 15 Edward III: Year Books of the Reign of King Edward the Third, year XV, ed. L. O. Pike (RS, 1891).

YB 16 Edward III: Year Books of the Reign of King Edward the Third, year XVI, part I, ed. L. O. Pike (RS, 1897).

YB 16 Edward III part 2: Year Books of the Reign of King Edward the Third, year XVI, part II, ed. L. O. Pike (RS, 1900).

YB 17 Edward III: Year Books of the Reign of King Edward the Third, year XVII, ed. L. O. Pike (RS, 1901).

YB 17–18 Edward III: Year Books of the Reign of King Edward the Third, years XVII and XVIII, ed. L. O. Pike (RS, 1903).

YB 18 Edward III: *Year Books of the Reign of King Edward the Third, year XVIII*, ed. L. O. Pike (RS, 1904).

YB 19 Edward III: *Year Books of the Reign of King Edward the Third, year XIX*, ed. L. O. Pike (RS, 1906).

YB 20 Edward III part 1: *Year Books of the Reign of King Edward the Third, year XX, part I*, ed. L. O. Pike (RS, 1908).

YB 20 Edward III part 2: *Year Books of the Reign of King Edward the Third, year XX, part II*, ed. L. O. Pike (RS, 1911).

YB 6 Richard II: *Year Books of Richard II: 6 Richard II 1382–1383*, ed. S. E. Thorne, M. E. Hager, and M. M. Thorne (Ames Foundation, 1996).

YB 7 Richard II: *Year Books of Richard II: 7 Richard II 1383–1384*, ed. M. J. Holland (Ames Foundation, 1989).

YB 8–10 Richard II: *Year Books of Richard II: 8–10 Richard II 1385–1387*, ed. L. C. Hector and M. E. Hager (Ames Foundation, 1987).

YB 12 Richard II: *Year Books of Richard II: 12 Richard II, AD. 1388–1389*, ed. G. F. Deiser (Ames Foundation, 1914).

YB 13 Richard II: *Year Books of Richard II: 13 Richard II, 1389–1390*, ed. T. F. T. Plucknett (Ames Foundation, 1929).

Yeo, G., *The Monks of Cowick* (Cowick, 1987).

York Memo. Bk: *York Memorandum Book*, ed. M. Sellers and J. W. Percy (3 vols., Surtees Society 120, 125, 186, 1912–73).

York Sede Vacante Reg. 1352–3: D. M. Smith, 'A reconstruction of the York *sede vacante* register 1352–1353', *BIB*, 1 (1975–8), 75–90.

York Vicars Choral Chts.: *Charters of the Vicars Choral of York Minster: city of York and its suburbs to 1546*, ed. N. J. Tringham (Yorkshire Archaeological Society, Record Series CXLVIII, 1993).

Yorks Assize Rolls: *Three Yorkshire Assize Rolls for the reigns of King John and King Henry III*, ed. C. T. Clay (Yorkshire Archaeological Society, Record Series XLIV, 1911).

Yorks Chantry Surveys: *The Certificates of the Commissioners appointed to survey the Chantries, Guilds, Hospitals, etc., in the county of York*, ed. W. Page (2 vols., Surtees Society 91–2, 1894–5).

Yorks Deeds: *Yorkshire Deeds*, ed. W. Brown, C. T. Clay, M. J. Hebditch (Mrs Stanley Price) (10 vols., Yorkshire Archaeological Society, Record Series XXXIX, L, LXIII, LXV, LXIX, LXXVI, LXXXIII, CII, CXI, CXX, 1909–55).

Yorks F., see under FINES.

Yorks Inq.: *Yorkshire Inquisitions of the reigns of Henry III and Edward I*, ed. W. Brown (4 vols., Yorkshire Archaeological Society, Record Series XII, XXIII, XXXI, XXXVII, 1892–1906).

Yorks Sessions of the Peace 1361–64: *Yorkshire Sessions of the Peace 1361–1364*, ed. B. H. Putnam (Yorkshire Archaeological Society Record Series C, 1939).

Young, *Hist. of Whitby*: G. Young, *A History of Whitby and Streoneshalh Abbey* (2 vols., Whitby, 1817).

Ystrad Marchell Chts.: *The Charters of the Abbey of Ystrad Marchell*, ed. G. C. G. Thomas (Aberystwyth, 1997).

OTHER ABBREVIATIONS

abb.	abbot
abbs	abbess
Ac.	Account roll (Durham)
acc.	accepted
acct	account
add.	additional
adm.	admitted, admission
ann.	annals
app.	appendix
appt	appointment
apptd	appointed
Arch.	Archaeological
archbp	archbishop
archdn	archdeacon
ass.	assent
Aug.	Augustinian
bach. theol.	bachelor of theology
Ben.	Benedictine
BI	Borthwick Institute, York
bl.	blessed, blessing
BL	British Library
Bodl.	Bodleian Library, Oxford
bp	bishop
bur.	buried, burial
cath.	cathedral
cent.	century
cert.	certified, certificate
cess.	cession
ch.	chronicle
chap.	chapter
cht(s).	charter(s)
Cist.	Cistercian
Clun.	Cluniac
Coll.	College, collection
commem.	commemorated, commemoration
commn	commission

conf.	confirmed, confirmation
consec.	consecrated
conv.	convent
ctl.	cartulary
CUL	Cambridge University Library
d./D.	died, dead, death
D. & C.	Dean and Chapter
DCD	Dean and Chapter of Durham muniments
DCN	Dean and Chapter of Norwich muniments
dep.	deposed
depr.	deprived
desc.	described
doct	document
East.	Easter
ECR	Eton College Records
ed.	edited (by)
edn	edition
el.	elected
eln	election
ESRO	East Sussex Record Office, Lewes
f	founded, foundation
F	Fine(s)
fig.	figure
Gilb.	Gilbertine
gt	grant
gtd	granted
Hil.	Hilary
inf.	information
inq.	inquisition, inquiry
inst.	instituted
instn	institution
IOW	Isle of Wight Record Office
j.d.	judge delegate
JRL	John Rylands Library, University of Manchester
LAO	Lincolnshire Archives Office
lic.	licence
m.	membrane
mag.	*magister*
mand.	mandate
ment.	mention

mentd	mentioned
Mich.	Michaelmas
misc.	miscellaneous, miscellanea
mon.	monument, monumental
ms.	manuscript
mun(s).	muniment(s)
n.	note; nun
n.d.	no date
notif.	notification
occ.	occurs, occurrence
pa.	parish (of)
pal.	palaeography
pd	printed
p.j.d.	papal judge(s) delegate
poss.	possibly
postn	postulation
pr.	prior
Prem.	Premonstratensian
pres.	presented, presentation
presum.	presumably
PRO	Public Record Office
prob.	probable, probably
Proc.	Proceedings (of)
prof. obed.	profession of obedience
prov.	provision
prs	prioress
re-el.	re-elected
ref.	refounded, refoundation; reference
Reg.	Register (of)
repd	reprint(ed)
Rept	Report
res.	resigned, resignation
RO	Record Office
rot.	rotulus, rotulet, roll
s. a.	*sub anno*
SBT	Shakespeare Birthplace Trust, Stratford on Avon
s.d.	same date
ser.	series
Soc.	Society
sub-pr.	sub-prior

sub-prs	sub-prioress
succ.	succeeded, succession
TCD	Trinity College, Dublin
temp.	*tempore*
temps	temporalities
Trans.	Transactions (of)
Trin.	Trinity/Trinitarian
UL	University Library
Univ.	University
unpd	unprinted
vac.	vacant, vacated
WAM	Westminster Abbey muniments
WCM	Winchester College muniments
YMA	York Minster Archives

INTRODUCTION

I. *The purpose and scope*

This book aims at providing lists of all known superiors of the religious houses in England and Wales between 1216 and 1377. Like the previous volume, covering the years 940–1216,[1] we have restricted our interpretation of religious house to cover all establishments of monks, regular canons, and nuns, whether of abbatial or lower rank and whether autonomous or dependent. These lists are based on houses in existence between 1216 and 1377 as recorded in the relevant sections of *Medieval Religious Houses, England and Wales*. A few small houses have failed to reveal the names of any heads and we have intentionally omitted hospitals, colleges,[2] the military orders, and for this period the mendicant orders who arrived in England in the thirteenth century. The decision to omit the last-mentioned was taken partly because of the work that is presently being done on biographical registers of the mendicant friars by such scholars as Dr Michael Robson (Franciscans in England and Wales)[3] and Fr Richard Copsey (Carmelites in England, Scotland and Wales)[4] and the as yet unused research material left by the late Dr A. B. Emden (in the Modern Papers Department of the Bodleian Library, Oxford).

II. *The materials*

The one great advantage for compilers of the 1216–1377 volume over the earlier volume, which is at the same time daunting and overwhelming, is the development of record-keeping in the thirteenth century and the consequent great growth of surviving material – both the new series of records and the bulkier continuations of earlier extant series. Much of the material described in the 940–1216 volume has of course been used in this second volume – chronicles and annals; charters, cartularies, and registers; obituaries and calendars (and antiquarian copies of lost records) have all been consulted. To these are added the documentary results of further developments in record-keeping at

---

[1] D. Knowles, C. N. L. Brooke and V. C. M. London, *Heads of Religious Houses: England and Wales I: 940–1216* (Cambridge, 1972; 2nd edn. 2001).
[2] The only exceptions being Gloucester abbey's cell at Oxford *c.* 1283–91, before it was reconstituted as Gloucester College to become the general house of studies under the abbots-president of the English Benedictine province; and Durham's affiliated house at Oxford, until it was endowed as Durham College in 1380–1 (*KH*, pp. 56, 72; W. A. Pantin, 'Gloucester College', *Oxoniensia*, XI–XII (1946–7), 65–74; M. R. Foster, 'Durham monks at Oxford *c.* 1286–1381: a house of studies and its inmates', *Oxoniensia*, LV (1990), 99–114). [3] See *MRB*, 1 (1995), 19–22. [4] See *MRB*, 2 (1996), 21–2.

governmental and ecclesiastical level. Of considerable importance for our research are the bishops' rolls or registers which seem to have developed from the early years of the thirteenth century onwards and provide an enormous source of information on religious houses in most dioceses.[5] They are supplemented by other and subsidiary diocesan and peculiar series – court books (instance, office, and visitation) and related case files, probate registers and original testamentary records. At a wider ecclesiastical level the series of papal registers provide another important research source. Amongst the English royal governmental archives, as well as the formidable series of enrolments begun in the late twelfth or early thirteenth centuries (patent, close, charter, and fine rolls), are the records of the royal courts, itinerant justices and assizes, and the overwhelming bulk of the records of Common Pleas and of the King's Bench; the archives of clergy taxation (clerical subsidies E179); the new series of ecclesiastical petitions (C84); significations of excommunication (C85); returns of aliens (E106); 'ancient' correspondence (SC1); and warrants for the Great Seal (C81). The vast series of feet of fines was systematically searched till the end of the thirteenth century when the religious seem not to make so much use of this form of transaction, an action presumably linked with recent mortmain legislation. In the case of the governmental court records with 236 Curia Regis Rolls up to the end of Henry III's reign, let alone the accumulation of assize records for the whole period, and 466 rolls each for Common Pleas and King's Bench from 1272 to 1377 – the roll for each term in the fourteenth century often extending to several hundred membranes – it is clear that sampling is the only feasible way to approach these records, even over a fifteen-year research period, and that is what has had to be done. The series of pipe rolls has also been only sporadically searched, partly again because of bulk, but also because this particular record, as Professor Brooke found in the twelfth century, can be misleading and provide traps for the historian. Just as Walter, abbot of Tavistock (c. 1154–1168) was a regular feature in later twelfth-century pipe rolls,[6] so you find mention of heads in later pipe rolls in respect to debts incurred much earlier, and still mentioned as though head rather than former head when a successor is known from other sources to be in office. Because of these problems and pitfalls this source needs to be used warily.

Annals and chronicles can also be a source of confusion, not just because of the obvious errors, miscopyings, or misunderstandings.[7] Sir Charles Clay and

---

[5] Listed in D. M. Smith, *Guide to Bishops' Registers of England and Wales: a survey from the Middle Ages to the abolition of Episcopacy in 1646* (Royal Historical Society guide and handbook 11, 1981).

[6] *Heads*, I, 12.

[7] For a good example of the problems of unreliable annals or chronicles see M. Brett, 'The annals of Bermondsey, Southwark, and Merton' in D. Abulafia, M. Franklin, and M. Rubin, eds., *Church and City 1000–1500: essays in honour of Christopher Brooke* (Cambridge, 1992), pp. 279–310.

others have noted in the case of a chronicle of Fountains abbey, for example, that in the calculations of length of abbatial rule no details of vacancy periods are given, some abbots are omitted from the numbering scheme adopted by the chronicler, and, most importantly, that the calculations of the abbot's rule are based on the lunar month of twenty-eight days not the calendar month. At Furness, the annals numbered abbots who had ruled for more than ten years and thereby merited an entry in the abbey *mortuarium*, omitting those who were abbots for a shorter period; evidence from other houses possibly points to an omission of abbots from the numbering sequence for more personal reasons, reflecting dissatisfaction with their rule and a desire to gloss over their maladministration.

Moving on from a cursory review of the primary sources which provide us with evidence, it will be useful to consider what sort of information typically survives for the appointment to and vacation of office of religious heads in the period, and how the particular religious order, patronage, exempt status, etc., could considerably affect the extent and survival of such records. The three main forms of election laid down by the Fourth Lateran Council of 1215 were by scrutiny, compromise, or inspiration: *per viam scrutinii*, the formal ballot of members of the community; *per viam compromissi*, the appointment of a small group (committee) within the religious house delegated with the responsibility for choosing the new superior; and *per viam inspirationis*, the spontaneous choice of a new head by general agreement within the community. On occasion the community voluntarily ceded its rights to the diocesan to choose a new head (and the bishop could also exercise his right of appointment if the office had been vacant for six months (*per lapsum temporis*) or if the form of election had been contrary to canon law and required to be quashed). Sometimes the election procedure in a particular instance was regulated by composition or settlement, usually after disputes had arisen. The Benedictine cathedral priory of Worcester was just such a case where a composition between Bishop William of Blois and the convent in 1224 regulated the choice of the prior, an arrangement which remained in force until the dissolution. By the terms of this composition the convent chose seven candidates to be presented to the bishop of Worcester, who having examined them chose one to be prior and admitted him.[8]

Exemption of a house or order from diocesan control meant of course that in most cases the election of superiors does not feature at all in our main source for such evidence, the episcopal registers. The Carthusians, the Trinitarians, the Grandmontines only feature when they receive a commission or some other

[8] *Acta Langton*, pp. 160–3; *EEA*, 13, app. II, no. 2; Greatrex, *Biog. Reg.*, p. 755; R. M. Haines, *The administration of the diocese of Worcester in the first half of the fourteenth century* (London, 1965), pp. 220–1.

ad hoc occurrence, but are never found at the time of appointment or vacation of office, an internal matter for the order.[9] There are isolated exceptions. In the Gilbertine order, for example, the prior of an individual house was appointed by the master of the order, who also possessed the power to remove him. The choice of prioresses was rather more unusual in that the order devised an arrangement whereby three prioresses were chosen, elected by the nuns, and exercised authority in turn, each ruling for a week.[10] The names of the three prioresses of Sempringham in 1366 have come down to us by chance, but usually the male and female superiors do not feature in the extant records, except as one-off occurrences. The master of the order was a different matter. He was elected by the general chapter of the order and his election was regularly presented to the bishop of Lincoln for confirmation as part of the procedural sequence surrounding the appointment. A similar situation arises in respect of the exempt Cistercians and Premonstratensians. The formal election process was conducted internally within the order without diocesan involvement – the system of filiation meant the supervision of the election process by the father-abbot of the house from whom it had been established and colonised.[11] Only after the formal election procedure was complete did the diocesan bishop become involved when the new abbot was required to be blessed. Quite often the episcopal benediction and profession of obedience of the newly elected abbot are recorded in the bishop's registers – the frequency and occurrence of such entries, I suspect, being more a matter of changing registrational practice, diocese by diocese, than of fluctuating episcopal involvement. The highly centralised Order of Fontevraud controlled the appointments to its three English houses (Amesbury, Nuneaton, and Westwood): the abbess of Fontevraud chose the prioress and the prior of each house. Of course there was occasional resistance. In the 1290s at Amesbury there was contention between the convent and a French nun sent as prioress by the abbess of Fontevraud, and in a dispute at Nuneaton in the 1320s an interloper supported by the earl of Lancaster and the bishop of Coventry and Lichfield succeeded in holding out for some time against successive nominees of the abbess.[12]

What documentary evidence survives for the election process varies of course according to the record-keeping practices of individual diocesan

---

[9] See E. M. Thompson, *The Carthusian Order in England* (London, 1930); C. Rowntree, 'Studies in Carthusian history in later medieval England with special reference to the Order's relations with secular society', unpublished D. Phil. thesis, University of York, 1981; M. Gray, *The Trinitarian Order in England* (BAR, 1993); and C. A. Hutchison, *The Hermit Monks of Grandmont* (Kalamazoo, 1989).

[10] B. Golding, *Gilbert of Sempringham and the Gilbertine Order c. 1130 –c. 1300* (Oxford, 1995), pp. 106–7.

[11] Canivez, I, xxvi–xxxi; *EHD*, 687–91; Colvin, pp. 236, 239–55.

[12] Kerr, *Religious life for Women*, pp. 132–4, 138–9.

chanceries, and the other bodies involved. Some are very full; others confine the election and confirmation to a brief summary entry in the episcopal register. Very occasionally a cache of documents survives by chance which gives considerable detail of the stages of the choice and confirmation of a new superior, and very rarely the actual number of votes cast in an election is recorded.[13] As a general rule, not too much survives from the monastic archives, and only occasional references in the archives of non-royal patrons (the initial notification of the vacancy and the seeking of permission to elect). Whenever the Crown is involved, the series of ecclesiastical petitions (C84) and the patent and close rolls shed considerable light on the process and are usefully supplemented by the relevant diocesan archives. If we take the Yorkshire Benedictine abbey of Selby as an example, the reader will discover the sort of range of information on the stages of the process that the royal and archiepiscopal archives of York contain. The first document is an ecclesiastical petition of 27 December 1321 in the Public Record Office notifying the king of the death of Simon of Scarborough the late abbot of Selby and requesting licence to elect (on occasion these petitions give the exact date of death of the predecessor). Royal licence to elect was granted on 3 January 1322. The election took place soon afterwards (though no precise details have survived in this instance) and the election of John of Wistow, monk of Selby, was presented to the king for royal assent in a further petition of 15 January. Royal assent to the election was granted on 20 January, and notification of this royal assent was sent by the king to the archbishop of York on the same day. On 28 January Archbishop Melton issued a proclamation *si quis* relating to the election (asking anyone who wished to oppose John's election to appear on 9 February) and subsequently confirmed the election on 9 February, at which time the archbishop sent a mandate to the convent ordering them to obey the new abbot. Notification of the confirmation was sent to the king on the same day, asking for the release of temporalities, and these were duly restored to the new abbot on 23 February. The abbot made his profession of obedience to the archbishop and received benediction from him on 15 March, and next day the archbishop issued a mandate to the Official of York to install the new abbot. Among the royal records, two other documents issued at the time of the restitution of the temporalities are also found. The writ of restitution is normally addressed to the local escheator(s) or sheriff(s) and is often accompanied on the patent rolls by the record of the issue of a writ *de intendendo* to the tenants of the house ordering them to be obedient to the new

---

[13] For details about elections at Tewkesbury and Baysdale, see R. M. Haines, 'The appointment of a prelate: A. The election of an abbot of Tewkesbury in 1347' in his *Ecclesia Anglicana: studies in the English Church of the later middle ages* (Toronto, 1989), pp. 15–25; J. E. Burton, 'The election of Joan Fletcher as prioress of Baysdale, 1524' in *BIB*, I (1975–8), 145–53. For details of votes cast, see, for example, the entries relating to the nunneries of Goring 1301 and Legbourne 1309.

superior, while the close roll occasionally includes a related mandate to give seisin.[14] At all stages of the diocesan's involvement he could of course depute some or all of his functions, hence the regular occurrence of commissions to subordinates to examine and confirm elections, and even commissions to other diocesans to give benediction. Certain major Benedictine houses, immediately subject to the papal see (such as Bury St Edmunds, St Augustine's Canterbury, Evesham, St Albans, and Westminster), obtained papal confirmation of their elections.[15]

There was often a problem with the dependent cells of English abbeys and those alien priories and cells subservient to foreign religious houses, mostly in the former Norman and Angevin domains. To take the English dependencies first, in 1219, for instance, a dispute between Hugh of Wells, bishop of Lincoln, and the abbot of St Albans was finally settled by papal judges delegate. Priors of the dependent St Albans' cells within the diocese – Beadlow, Belvoir, and Hertford – were to be presented to the diocesan bishop by the abbot and convent of St Albans to receive administration of the spiritualities and be admitted. The abbot was to have cure of the souls of monks dwelling at the cells within the Lincoln diocese, and the power of placing monks in them and correcting them. The abbot was also permitted to recall priors of cells who had been admitted by the bishop.[16] The abbot thus retained great control over the affairs of his dependent priories: soon after this composition Roger of Wendover, the famous chronicler and prior of Belvoir, having effectively shown that his literary talents far outweighed his administrative abilities, was recalled to St Albans in disgrace in 1226. Needless to say, both diocesan and abbey were anxious to abide by the composition without jeopardising any of the rights which they possessed by virtue of its provisions. It made for recurrent prickly situations and a degree of wariness that comes out even in what it might be assumed were relatively formal documents. The letters of presentation to these Lincoln diocesan dependencies are regularly copied in full in the episcopal enrolments. They are couched in near-identical terms. Having given the reason for the vacancy, the abbot proceeds to nominate a successor to the former prior, taking care to mention the 1219 award: '. . . providimus in priorem eiusdem domus eidem Willelmo substituendum. Ipsum igitur sanctitati vestre presentamus humiliter et devote supplicantes quatinus secundum formam compositionis inter ecclesiam vestram et nostram facte et firmate, ipsum sine mora,

---

[14] For the Latin form of some of these documents (petition for licence to elect, royal licence to elect, presentation of election for royal assent, the royal assent, certificate of episcopal confirmation of the election, restitution of temporalities), see H. Hall, *A formula book of English official historical documents, part I: Diplomatic documents* (Cambridge, 1908), nos. 88–93.

[15] For the question of papal provisions to monasteries, see R. L. Storey, 'Papal provisions to English monasteries', *Nottingham Medieval Studies*, XXXV (1991), 77–91.   [16] *Reg. Ant. Lincoln*, III, no. 653.

dispendio et difficultate velitis admittere'.[17] The bishop admits and institutes the presentee *per librum* and exacts an oath of canonical obedience. An indication of the care that was taken by the diocesan occurs in the 1233 admission of Prior John of Hertford. John's letters of presentation only bore the seal of the abbot of St Albans, William of Trumpington, and not that of the convent. The bishop was uncertain whether the convent had assented to John's nomination and the new prior had to swear that the letters were issued by both the abbot and the convent. After his admission '*salvo tamen iure conventus sancti Albani*', he was enjoined to obtain additional letters from the convent assenting to the presentation.[18]

Not all the monastic cells or priories or bailiwicks dependent upon foreign monasteries resembled the cells of English mother-houses as regards the appointment of superiors or in respect of their actual status. Professor Matthew and others have ably surveyed the conditions that gave rise to the establishment of these various types of 'priory', ranging from the small monastic community to the solitary monk-bailiff administering the English possessions of the French mother-house.[19] The distinction between the dative and the conventual types of alien priory hinges primarily upon the difference in relationship between the priory and the parent-abbey. The dative priories were in a greater degree of subjection to their mother-houses. Their priors were appointed by the abbot and were removable at will; the houses had no real corporate existence and the priors were content to act as general proctors of the French abbeys in England. Indeed one of the major problems in providing lists of alien priors in this period is the elasticity over the use of titles to describe them. AB, described as the prior of X in one source, can equally well be described in another contemporary document as AB, general proctor in England of the abbey of Y. The conventual alien priories on the other hand enjoyed legal rights as owners of property and patrons of churches, and shared a fully corporate life. Their degree of dependence upon the foreign mother-house varied considerably. Most houses were in the position of St Neots which had its priors sent by the abbots of Bec, and the English convent had no say in the choice of a new superior. A few priories possessed the right of electing their own prior, but whatever the method of selection or nomination employed, a most important distinction between the position of conventual and dative priors is discernible in the fact that the former had security of tenure, until they died or resigned or were canonically removed for maladministration or other offences — they were 'perpetual priors' and could not be recalled at the whim

---

[17] *Reg. Wells*, III, 44.   [18] ibid., III, 44–5.
[19] See D. Matthew, *The Norman Monasteries and their English possessions* (Oxford, 1962).

of an abbot living the other side of the English Channel. The procedure for the institution of priors presented by these French abbeys did not differ from that adopted for admission of heads of dependent cells of English houses – the candidate was presented to the diocesan bishop for admission and institution, and after this ceremony had taken place, professed canonical obedience to him. Subsequently he was inducted into corporal possession by the local archdeacon or his deputy. It has to be said that the evidence from English episcopal registers suggests that more attention was paid by bishops to the technicalities of the admission of new priors to these alien cells than is ever usually found in entries relating to English establishments. There was sometimes a relatively high turnover rate of alien priors in dative priories – (between 1250 and 1300 there were twelve priors of Wilsford and at least eleven priors of Weedon Lois) – and extra care seems to have been taken over the language of the documents and the examination of the candidates and causes of vacancy. It was by no means unknown for dative priors to be recalled or return to their French mother-house without informing the English diocesan or without formally resigning. This blatant disregard of episcopal jurisdiction normally did not go unheeded and great care was taken to determine whether the priors had in fact canonically resigned. The bishop of Coutances was prompted on one such occasion to inform his counterpart at Lincoln that the former prior of Haugham had resigned his office into the hands of the abbot of St Sever in the episcopal presence.[20] Richard de Capella, prior of Hinckley, then at Lire abbey in Normandy, submitted his resignation by letter to the bishop '*et impotentia sua revertendi ad partes istas ob id tam per litteras ipsas quam per testes idoneos sufficienter probata*'. For added measure the prior procured the seals of the bishop of Evreux and the abbot of Bec to be appended to his resignation deed.[21] Such care with respect to alien priors was not just taken by diocesan bishops. In 1376 at Stoke by Clare the patron, the earl of March, was the recipient of successive letters of presentation from the abbot of Bec and his proctor, with apologies for certain faults found in the initial document, before he would accept the presentation and write to the bishop of Norwich asking for the presentee's admission.[22]

Mention has already been made, in respect of non-exempt houses, of the diocesan bishop's careful scrutiny to check if the election procedures had been carried out in accordance with canon law. If he or his deputed commissaries found any such irregularities, regardless of the calibre or suitability of the candidate, they would quash the election and assume the right to appoint by episcopal authority. A scrutiny of episcopal registers suggests that while this

---

[20] *Reg. Wells*, III, 158.   [21] ibid., II, 315–16.   [22] BL., Add. ms. 6041, f. 63r–v.

practice was universal, some bishops were more assiduous than others. The late Professor Rosalind Hill called attention long ago to the activities of Bishop Oliver Sutton of Lincoln (1280–99) in this regard.[23] Of 105 elections to abbeys and priories in his diocese during his episcopate, Sutton confirmed 52 but quashed 53 on account of canonical and procedural irregularity. In almost all of these 53 cases he deprived the electors of their power to choose for this particular occasion and then having examined the candidates previously chosen, appointed them to office himself.

Internal disputes, quarrels between rival candidates for election, problems with patrons or superior religious authorities (father-abbots, general chapters of certain orders, diocesan bishops and provincial archbishops, the pope, etc.) all contributed to the occasional disturbances which have gained notoriety because of the plentiful documentary sources extant for these disputes – often a welter of accusations, excommunications, physical attacks, imprisonments, exile. The famous problems of Tavistock abbey in the fourteenth century, starting with a disputed double election, the involvement of the bishop of Exeter, king, and pope, and the papal intrusion of Abbot Bonus who was subsequently deposed by the bishop, are a well-known example – as is the Exeter episcopal register's marginal comment on this abbot: '*Iste abbas qui dicebatur bonus erat pessimus quasi hereticus.*'[24] The long-running dispute at Bardney between 1303 and 1318 after Bishop Dalderby's attempts to remove Abbot Robert of Wainfleet,[25] and the Durham cathedral priory dispute involving Bishop Anthony Bek and Prior Richard de Hoton, are equally *causes célèbres*.[26]

III. *The arrangement of the lists*

We can only reiterate what the editors of the first volume were at pains to point out: complete consistency in the layout of entries in each list has proved neither desirable nor possible. Within each list the heads are in chronological order, wherever this is known; within each entry the occurrences are, usually, in chronological order. Some selection had to be made with regard to the entries on account of the often voluminous record of occurrences of heads of the larger or more well-documented houses. Where precise dates of appointment and of vacation are known, then this is normally the only information noted. Where evidence comprises a series of occurrences then some pruning has often been done, with the earliest and latest occurrence being noted and, where possible,

---

[23] R. M. T. Hill, 'Bishop Sutton and the institutions of heads of religious houses in the diocese of Lincoln', *EHR*, LVIII (1943), 201–9. See also *Reg. Sutton*, I, xxiii–xxvii.   [24] *Reg. Grandisson*, I, 395.
[25] See *AASRP*, XXXII (1914), 362–71.
[26] See C. M. Fraser, *A history of Antony Bek, bishop of Durham 1283–1311* (Oxford, 1957), pp. 123–75.

a few select references inserted in between. Where possible, each list has the following items.

1. *Name, county and dedication.* The names of pre-1974 English and Welsh counties are used. The dedications are based mainly on documentary evidence and the work of Alison Binns, *Dedications of Monastic Houses in England and Wales 1066–1216* (Studies in the History of Medieval Religion 1, Woodbridge, 1989). For Cistercians and dependencies we give also the name of the mother-house. Variant names for the house are also noted.

2. *Date of foundation.* This is generally taken from *KH*, but supplemented where possible by more recent work on particular houses or orders, e.g. appendix A on foundation dates in Sally Thompson's *Women Religious: the Founding of English Nunneries after the Norman Conquest* (Oxford, 1991), pp. 217–31. If a house was dissolved in this period or shortly afterwards this is also noted, as is the issue of letters of denization to alien houses.

3. *A note of former lists.* We include a *VCH* list where one exists, and, in general, more recent lists backed by archival references. As in the case of the 940–1216 volume, we have normally omitted antiquarian lists when they are not based on given references or are uncritical in their treatment of the information. References to medieval manuscript lists (e.g. in annals, chronicles, cartularies, etc.) and obits are noted.

4. *An entry for each known head.* An entry for each head known, in chronological order wherever possible (chance survivals of references in undated thirteenth-century material often make the precise sequence of heads uncertain at this date). Each list ends, in principle, with the first vacation of office, or the first occurrence of a successor where such precise information is unknown, after 1377. No systematic attempt has been made to note all 'ghost' heads (that is, names in old lists that are unsourced and for which no evidence has since been found). Where errors are likely (e.g. Roger de Berton, said to be Cluniac prior of Thetford in the *VCH* list, is likely to have been prior of the Dominican friary there) or when cited documentary evidence can no longer be found, they are noted in a footnote. If a head resigned, details of pension provision, if recorded, and later occurrences, where found, are noted. Each entry may consist of the following: name and outside dates, and surnames when known (variant spellings are included in brackets). Dates of election, confirmation, and blessing (in the case of royal involvement a note of the royal assent, restitution of temporalities, or issue of writ *de intendendo* and related matters), where known, are recorded; as are also length of tenure if specified in the sources, and reason for the vacation of office (death, resignation, deprivation). On the other hand, where further details of reason for vacation survive (e.g. Abbot Philip of Jervaulx being murdered by one of his monks; Abbot Richard

of Abingdon drowning while trying to cross the Thames in flood; Prior Guy de Marchant of Montacute removed and sent to the Tower for clipping coin; the Premonstratensian Abbot of Barlings, Richard of Hanworth, resigning to become a Franciscan; Prior Robert of Hornby being killed when his horse collided at speed with a stone cross), these are noted. If known, monumental inscriptions and grave-slabs of heads are also noted, and if a description of a personal (as opposed to institutional) seal survives, this is recorded. Where the record of the appointment of a new head does not note the reason for the vacancy this is stated. Occurrences are only very selectively noted if the full tenure of office of a head can be established from the sources – e.g. to help establish that a long tenure was indeed continuous. In other cases where precise dates of appointment and vacation are unknown a selection of occurrences (pruned in the case of well-documented heads) is provided. Grouping of dates by source has often been done. If it is known that a head became incapacitated or a coadjutor was appointed this is noted. The use of an initial before a date indicates that the head is identified by an initial only in that specific instance; in all others the full Christian name is given. The dating of undated documents remains of course a major problem, often based on the tenure of other ecclesiastics and secular officers or nobles, and in such cases notes have been appended to indicate either the reason for the approximate dating or the modern printed source where the arguments for the dating have been rehearsed. Much use has been made of the *Handbook of British Chronology*, the *Complete Peerage*, and the Le Neve *Fasti Ecclesiae Anglicanae* revised for 1066–1300 and 1300–1541.

'+' attached to a date means in or after; '−' means in or before; 'x' links the limiting dates of an undated charter or the like.

References in nearly all cases are given to all essential primary sources; those to secondary literature are much more selective. Little Marlow appears under L; West Ravendale under W; but cross-references are given in such cases to reduce any inconvenience. The order of the lists follows the earlier volume, which itself was based on *KH*. The Benedictines are divided into three sections: the independent houses; their dependencies; the alien priories. The nuns, except for the Gilbertines, have been gathered together into a single alphabetical sequence.

HEADS OF RELIGIOUS HOUSES
ENGLAND AND WALES
II
1216–1377

THE BENEDICTINE HOUSES:
INDEPENDENT HOUSES

ABBOTSBURY (Dorset), St Peter f. *c*.1044
Lists in *VCH Dorset*, II, 53; *Heads*, I, 23.
Abbey vacant 15 July 1213 when ordered to send candidates for the king's choice (*Rot. Lit. Claus.*, I, 150).

Hugh II –?**1246** Occ. 1216 x 1220 (*Ctl. Loders*, pp. 62–4). Occ. 1227 (*Dorset F.*, p. 33); Aug. 1238 (*Sarum Chts.*, p. 246, no. ccxvii). Lic to el. (no reason given for vacancy) 16 Jan. 1246 (*CPR 1232–47*, p. 470).

Roger de Brideton 1246–?1258 Sacrist of Abbotsbury, royal ass. 3 Feb. 1246, writ *de intendendo* 11 Feb. 1246 (*CPR 1232–47*, p. 473). Cert. conf. eln by bp of Salisbury 10 Feb. 1246 (PRO, C84/1/52). Bl. at Woodford 21 Feb. 1246 (*Sarum Chts.*, pp. 291–2, no. ccl). Lic to el. (no reason given for vacancy) 17 Oct. 1258 (*CPR 1247–58*, p. 653).

Joan of Hilton (Helton) **1258–1284** Pr. of Abbotsbury, royal ass. 28 Oct. 1258, temps. (no name), the eln having been conf. by bp of Salisbury 31 Oct. 1258 (ibid., p. 654; *CPR 1258–66*, p. 1). D. by 28 Apr. 1284 (PRO, C84/8/22). D., lic. to el. 5 May 1284 (*CPR 1281–92*, p. 120).

Philip of Sherborne (Shireburn) **1284–1296** Chamberlain of Abbotsbury, royal ass. 27 May 1284 (*CPR 1281–92*, p. 121). By reason of his debility attorneys apptd for 2 years 15 Sept. 1293 (*CPR 1292–1301*, p. 36.). D., lic. to el. 26 Dec. 1296 (*CPR 1292–1301*, p. 225).

[William of Kingston (Kingeston, Kyngeston) Pr. of Abbotsbury, royal ass. 14 Jan. 1297 (ibid., p. 228). Eln quashed by Bp N[icholas] of Salisbury by 2 Mar. (presumably by 22 Feb.) 1297 (ibid., p. 239, cf. p. 264.).]

Benedict of Loders (Lodres) **1297–1320** M. of Abbotsbury, royal protection for abb.-el. 22 Feb. 1297 (ibid., p. 264). Temps. 2 Mar. 1297 (ibid., p. 239). D. by 17 June 1320 (PRO, C84/19/51). D., lic. to el. 25 June 1320 (*CPR 1317–21*, p. 456).

Ralph of Sherborne (Schirborn, Shirborne, Shirburn) **1320–1321** Pr. of Abbotsbury, royal ass. 6 July 1320, temps. 4 Aug. 1320 (ibid., pp. 458, 494); eln pres. to bp 11 July 1320, conf. 26 July, bl. 10 Aug. 1320 (*Reg. Martival*, I, 416; PRO, C84/19/52). D. by 2 Feb. 1321 (PRO, C84/20/3). D., lic. to el. 7 Feb. 1321 (*CPR 1317–21*, p. 559).

Peter of Sherborne (Schirborn, Shirborne, Shireborn) **1321–1324** M. of Abbotsbury, eln pres. to king for royal ass. 16 Feb. 1321 (PRO, C84/20/4); royal ass. 21 Feb. 1321, temps. 12 Mar. 1321 (*CPR 1317–21*, pp. 564, 570). Eln pres. to bp 24 Feb. 1321, conf. 10 Mar. 1321, bl. 22 Mar. 1321 (*Reg. Martival*, I, 416–17). D., lic. to el. 9 Jan. 1324 (*CPR 1321–24*, p. 360, cf. *Cal. Chanc. Warr.*, p. 550).

William le Fauconer 1324–1343 M. of Abbotsbury, eln reported to king and royal ass. sought 20 Jan. 1324 (*Cal. Chanc. Warr.*, p. 550); royal ass. 29 Jan. 1324, temps. 23 Feb. 1324 (*CPR 1321–24*, pp. 365, 367). D., lic. to el. 2 Dec. 1343 (*CPR 1343–45*, p. 144).

Walter de Saunford (Samford) **1343–1348** M. of Abbotsbury, royal ass. 19 Dec. 1343, temps. 26 Jan. 1344 (ibid., pp. 155, 188). Lic. of Chapter of Salisbury for Walter de Samford, abb.-el. of Abbotsbury to receive blessing elsewhere than in Salisbury Cathedral, 23 Jan. 1344 (*Hemingby's Reg.*, p. 116, no. 186). House void 30 Oct. 1348 (*CPR 1348–50*, p. 198). D., lic. to el. 22 Nov. 1348 (ibid., p. 208).

Walter de Stokes (Stoke) **1348–1354** M. of Abbotsbury, royal ass. 22 Dec. 1348, temps. 17 Jan. 1349 (ibid., pp. 220, 226). Cert. conf. eln by bp of Salisbury 10 Jan. 1349 (PRO, C84/25/49). Commn to enquire into the wastage of the abbey's goods 28 Jan. 1354 (*Cal. Misc. Inq.*, III, 67). D. 13 June 1354 (PRO, C84/27/12). Lic. to el. 18 June 1354 (*CPR 1354–58*, p. 73, cf. *CFR 1347–56*, p. 398). Seal (*BM Seals*, no. 2540).

Henry (of) Toller (Tolre) **1354–1376** M. of Abbotsbury, eln pres. to king for royal ass. 27 June 1354 (PRO, C84/27/17); royal ass. 2 July 1354, temps. 16 July 1354 (*CPR 1354–58*, pp. 77, 91). Cert. conf. eln. by bp of Salisbury 13 July 1354 (PRO, C84/27/18). Occ 7 June 1376 (Salisbury, Reg. Erghum, f. 111v). D. 11 Aug. 1376 (*Dorset IPMs*, no. 150). D., lic. to el. 25 Aug. 1376 (*CPR 1374–77*, p. 335; cf. *CCR 1374–77*, p. 384).

William Cerne 1376–1401 M. of Abbotsbury, eln pres. to king for royal ass. 2 Sept. 1376 (PRO, C84/31/41); royal ass. 5 Sept. 1376. temps. 22 Sept. 1376 (*CPR 1374–77*, pp. 336, 343). Eln conf. 20 Sept. 1376 (Salisbury, Reg. Erghum, f. 20v). D. 18 Nov. 1401 (*Dorset IPMs*, no. 151). D., lic. to el. 26 Nov. 1401 (*CPR 1401–05*, p. 24).

ABINGDON (Berks), St Mary ref. *c.* 954

Lists in *VCH Berks*, II, 61–2; *Heads*, I, 23–5. Obits in CUL., ms. Kk. I. 22, ff. 1v (obit 1); Bodl., Digby ms. 227 (obit 2); H.E. Salter, 'A chronicle roll of the abbots of Abingdon', *EHR* 26 (1911), 727–38.

Hugh 1189/90–1221 M. of Abingdon, el. 1189/90 (*Ch. Abingdon*, II, 245, 293). D. 14 July (obits 1, 2); d. 14 July 1220 (sic) (*Ann. Osney*, p. 62). D., lic. to el. 24 July 1221 (*CPR 1216–25*, p. 297).

Robert of Hendred (Henreth) **1221–1234** Chamberlain of Abingdon, royal ass. 29 July 1221 (ibid., p. 298). Succ. 24 Aug. 1220 (sic) (*Ann. Osney*, p. 62). D. 1234 (*Ann. Osney*, p. 81; cf. *Ann Dunstable*, p. 139). D. (R.), lic. to el. 10 Sept. 1234 (*CPR 1232–47*, p. 68; cf. PRO, C84/4/4). Seal (*Mon. Seals*, p. 2; *BM Seals*, no. 2543).

Luke 1234–?1241 Succ. Robert 1234, chamberlain of Abingdon (*Ann. Osney*, p. 81). Occ. 13 May 1235 (PRO, Glos.F., CP25/1/73/9, no. 143); 3 May 1237 (*Beds F.*, I, p. 106, no. 396). Lic. to el. (no reason given for vacancy) 3 Feb. 1241 (*CPR 1232–47*, p. 244).

John de Blosmeville (Blomesvyle, Blostmevile) **1241–1256** M. of Abingdon, royal ass. 28 Feb. 1241, writ *de intendendo* 7 Mar. 1241 (ibid., pp. 246–7). Gt to the pr. and convent for a fine that they should have the future keeping of the abbey when it shall be void by the d. or cess. of abb. John 25 May 1256 (*CPR 1247–58*, p. 476). D. 11 June 1256 (*Ann. Osney*, p. 113). Lic. to el. (no reason given for vacancy) 11 June 1256 (*CPR 1247–58*, p. 480).

William of Newbury (Neuberi, Neubiry, Neubyri) **1256–1260** M. of Abingdon, royal ass. 24 July 1256, writ *de intendendo* 19 Sept. 1256 (ibid., pp. 489, 501); cert. conf. eln by the officials of Bp Giles of Salisbury 13 Sept. 1256 (PRO, C84/1/43); installed 11 Nov. 1256 (*Ann. Osney*, p. 113). Envoy of Richard, king of the Romans 1259 (*CPR 1258–66*, p. 45). Dep. *c.* 29 Aug. 1260 (*Ann. Osney*, p. 127; cf. Hill, *Eccles. Letter-Books*, p. 73). Cess., lic. to el. 8 Aug. 1260 (*CPR 1258–66*, p. 87).

Henry of Frilford (Frilleford, Fryleford) **1260–1261** Chamberlain of Abingdon, succ. 1260 (*Ann. Osney*, p. 129). Royal ass. 15 Aug. 1260, writ *de intendendo*, 20 Aug. 1260, his eln having been conf. by Bp Giles of Salisbury (*CPR 1258–66*, pp. 89–90). D. 19 June 1261 (*Ann. Osney*, p. 130; PRO, C84/2/30).

Richard of Hendred (Hanrade, Hanreth, Hariel, Henreth) **1261–1289** Sacrist of Abingdon, succ. 1261 (*Ann. Osney*, p. 130). Eln conf. by bp of Salisbury 1262 (PRO, SC1/5/104). Royal ass. 14 June 1262 (*CPR 1258–66*, p. 216, cf. *DKR 5*, app. II, p. 67, no. 519). D. by 30 Aug. 1289 (PRO, C84/9/37). D., lic. to el. 31 Aug. 1289 (*CPR 1281–92*, p. 321).

Nicholas of Culham (Coleham, Culeham) **1289–1306** Pr. of Abingdon, eln pres. to king for royal ass. 8 Sept. 1289 (PRO, C84/9/38); royal ass. 10 Sept. 1289, temps. 29 Sept. 1289 (*CPR 1281–92*, pp. 322, 324). Cert. conf. eln by bp of Salisbury 22 Sept. 1289 (PRO, C84/9/39). D. 1306 (*Ann. Worcs.*, p. 559). D., lic. to el. 16 Feb. 1306 (*CPR 1301–07*, p. 415).

Richard of Bishops Cleeve (Cliva Episcopi, Clive, Clyve) **1306–1315** M. of Abingdon, bach. theol., succ. 1306 (*Ann. Worcs.*, p. 559). Appt of abbey's proctor to pres. the eln 10 Mar. 1306; pres. to bp 26 Mar. 1306; eln conf. 28 Mar., bl. 3 Apr., notif. to king 5 Apr. (*Reg. Gandavo*, II, 668–74). Temps. 31 Mar. 1306 (*CPR 1301–07*, p. 421). Drowned, with various companions, while crossing the Thames in flood 1316 (*sic*) (Salter, 'Chronicle roll', p. 730). House void by 28 July 1315 (*CFR 1307–19*, p. 257). Lic. to el. 1 Aug. 1315 (*CPR 1313–17*, p. 338). See Sharpe, *Latin Writers*, p. 465.

John of Sutton (Suttone) **1315–1322** M. of Abingdon, report of eln to king 14 Aug. 1315, royal ass. 21 Aug. 1315, notif. by Roger, bp-el. of Salisbury of his conf. 17 Sept., mand. to receive fealty 21 Sept. 1315 (*Cal. Chanc. Warr.*, pp. 420–1, 423). Eln pres. to bp 21 Aug. 1315, conf. by bp's commissaries 25 Sept.; bl. 19 Oct. 1315 (*Reg. Martival*, I, 411–12). Mandate citing opposers 23 Aug., commn to examine eln 5 Sept. 1315, conf. by bp n. d. (*Reg. Martival*, II, 32–5). Temps. 21 Sept. 1315 (*CPR 1313–17*, p. 352). King gtd royal protection and apptd custodian of the abbey during pleasure, on account of its debts 14 Aug. 1318 (*CPR 1317–21*, pp. 199, 205). Suspension by the Pope of abb. John on the complaints of the pr. and conv. of his misappropriation of goods, removal of muniments, and imprisonment of the pr. and some monks 3 Feb. 1322 (*Reg. Martival*, II ii, 385–6; *CPL*, II, 218). D. 28 Apr. 1322 (Salter, 'Chronicle roll', p. 737). D., lic. to el. 12 May 1322 (*CPR 1321–24*, p. 105).

John de Canyng (Canynges, Canyngg, Canyngges) **1322–1328** Order to sub-pr. and convent to admit John de Canyng, their pr., when he comes to the monastery, as eln of an abb. is in the offing. Pr. had absented himself for some time for certain reasons 13 May 1322 (*CCR 1318–23*, p. 556). Eln pres. to bp 5 June 1322, eln quashed but John apptd by bp of Salisbury 19 June 1322; bl. 4 July 1322 (*Reg. Martival*, I, 417–19). Royal ass. 1 May 1322, temps. 25 June 1322 (*CPR 1321–24*, pp. 123, 140). Appt of Gilbert de Ellesfeld and Thomas de Coudray to custody of abbey, devastated by rioters and abandoned by the monks 20 Aug. 1327 (*CPR 1327–30*, p. 159). House void by 9 Dec. 1328 (*CFR 1327–37*, p. 115). D., lic. to el. 13 Dec. 1328 (*CPR 1327–30*, p. 339).

Robert of Garford (Gareford, Gereford) **1328–1332** M. of Abingdon, eln pres. to king for royal ass. 14 Dec. 1328 (PRO, C84/22/14); royal ass. 16 Dec. 1328, temps. 18 Jan. 1329 (*CPR 1327–30*, pp. 339, 344). Cert. conf. eln by bp of Salisbury 2 Jan. 1329 (PRO, C84/22/15). Occ. 1 Aug. 1332 (PRO, C270/7/2). House void by 16 Aug. 1332 (*CFR 1327–37*, p. 322). D., lic. to el. 20 Aug. 1332 (*CPR 1330–34*, p.324). Obit (*Ctl. Abingdon*, II, pp. 60–1, no. C33). Seal (*Mon. Seals*, p. 2).

William (of) Cumnor (Comenor, Comenore) **1332–1335** M. of Abingdon, royal ass. 23 Aug. 1332. temps. 11 Sept. 1332 (*CPR 1330–34*, pp. 324, 327). Bl. 4 Oct. 1332 (Salisbury, Reg. Wyvil, II, f. 17r). Occ. 24 Dec. 1332 (Lincoln, Ep. Reg., IV, f. 265v); 13 June 1334 (*Cal. Misc. Inq.*, II, 356). D. by 25 Nov. 1335 (PRO, C84/23/22). Obit (*Ctl. Abingdon*, II, pp. 60–1, no. C33).

Roger of Thame (Tame) **1335–1361** M. of Abingdon, royal ass. 1 Dec. 1334, temps. 23 Jan. 1335 (*CPR 1334–38*, pp. 53, 57). Eln conf. 3 Jan. 1335, no reason given for vacancy, bl. 22 Feb. 1335 (Salisbury, Reg. Wyvil, II, f. 35v.). D. 1361, probably of plague (*St Nicholas, Abingdon*, p. 26).[1] D. by 12 July 1361 (PRO, C84/28/5). D., lic. to el. 14 July 1361 (*CPR 1361–64*, p. 41).

---

[1] On 30 June 1361 an unnamed abb. of Abingdon, acting as collector for the General Chapter of Black monks, issued a document which has a round seal attached to it on which the name of Walter can be apparently deciphered (*Durham Seals*, no. 3398, cf. pd document *Chapters of English Black Monks*, III, no. 290, cf. no. 289).

Peter of Hanney (Hanneye) **1361–1399** M. of Abingdon, royal ass. 24 July 1361, temps. 2 Aug. 1361 (ibid., pp. 41, 44). Eln conf. 31 July 1361, bl. 1 Aug. 1361 (Salisbury, Reg. Wyvil, II, f. 294r). D. by 5 Feb. 1399 (PRO, C84/37/35). D., lic. to el. 20 Feb. 1399 (*CPR 1396–99*, p. 483).

ALCESTER (De Insula, Oversley) (Warws), St Mary and St John the Baptist (Binns). f. 1140

Lists in *VCH Warws*, II, 60–1; *Heads*, I, 25–6.

[**William** Sub-pr. of Worcester, el. 1216, but refused office (*Ann. Worcs.*, p. 407). Lic. to el. (no name or reason given) 14 Nov. 1216 (*CPR 1216–25*, pp. 2–3)]

Matthew 1216–1232 (M.) Sacrist of Alcester, el. 1216 (*Ann. Worcs.*, p. 407). Royal ass. (M.) 1 Jan. 1217 (*CPR 1216–25*, p. 18). D. *c.* 4 Oct. 1232 (*Ann. Tewkesbury*, p. 89 – Maurice; *Ann. Worcs.*, p. 424 – M.). D., lic. to el. 8 Oct. 1232 (*CPR 1225–32*, p. 505).

Bartholomew 1232–1252 Cellarer of Alcester, succ. (B.), bl. at Worcester 28 Feb. 1233 (*Ann. Worcs.*, p. 424). Mand. for seisin (B.) 27 Oct. 1232 (*CR 1231–34*, p. 124). Cess. by 14 Nov. 1252 (PRO, C84/1/31). Lic. to el. (no reason given for vacancy) 22 Nov. 1252 (*CPR 1247–58*, p. 165).

Hugh 1252– Sacrist of Alcester, eln pres. to king for royal ass. 3 Dec. 1252 (PRO, C84/2/2); royal ass. 10 Dec. 1252 (*CPR 1247–58*, p. 166, cf. *DKR 5*, app. II, p. 67, no. 524).

William of Whitchurch (Witchirche, Wytchirche) **1254–1266** Cellarer of Pershore, royal ass. 29 Dec. 1253, temps. 28 Jan. 1254 (*CPR 1247–58*, p. 362). Res. (W.) to be abb. of Evesham by 15 Sept. 1266 (*CPR 1258–66*, p. 638). Pr. and convent seek lic. to el. on translation of abb. William 23 Feb. 1266 (*DKR 5th Rept*, app. II, p. 67, no. 522).

Hugh 1266–1275[2] Pr. of Alcester, eln pres. to king n.d. [1266] (ibid., no. 523). D. by [10] Aug. 1275 (PRO, C84/5/39). D., lic. to el. 12 Aug. (*CPR 1272–81*, p. 102). Letter of bp to pr. and convent exhorting them to el. a new abb. 15 Aug. 1275 (*Reg. G. Giffard*, pp. 83–4).

William of Elmdon (Ilmedon, Ylmedon) **1275–1276** Sacrist of Alcester, eln pres. to king for royal ass. 16 Aug. 1275 (PRO, C84/5/41); royal ass. 17 Aug. 1275, writ *de intendendo* 21 Aug. 1275 (*CPR 1272–81*, p. 102); bp's conf. 19 Aug. 1275 (*Reg. G. Giffard*, p. 84; PRO, C84/5/42). D. by 20 July 1276 (PRO, C84/5/55). D. (W.), lic. to el. 23 July 1276 (*CPR 1272–81*, p. 153).

John of Ipsley (Ippeleye, Ippesleya) **1276–1279** Pr. of Alcester, royal ass. 6 Aug. 1276, temps. 14 Aug. 1276 (ibid., pp. 158–9). Cert. conf. eln by bp of Worcester 12 Aug. 1276 (PRO, C84/5/56). Cess. by 10 Oct. 1279 (PRO, C84/6/27; cf. *CFR 1272–1307*, p. 118), but cf. following entry. D., lic to el. 17 Oct. 1279 (*CPR 1272–81*, p. 327).

Walter of Worcester (Wygornia) **1279–1300** M. of Great Malvern, pr. of Alvecote, eln pres. to king for royal ass. 22 Oct. 1279 (PRO, C84/14/2); royal ass. (William) 24 Oct. 1279, writ *de intendendo* (Walter) 28 Oct. 1279 (*CPR 1272–81*, p. 329). Cert. conf eln by bp of Worcester 30 Oct. 1279 (PRO, C84/6/30). D. 18 Dec. 1300 (*Ann. Worcs.*, p. 548). D., lic. to el. 22 Dec. 1300 (*CPR 1292–1301*, p. 559; cf. PRO, C84/14/2).

Robert de Oudeby (Oudebi) **1301–1334** M. of Alcester, abb.'s chaplain (*Ann. Worcs.*, p. 548). Eln pres. to king for royal ass. 25 Dec. 1300 (PRO, C84/13/51); royal ass. 8 Jan. 1301 (*CPR 1292–1301*, p. 561). Letter to king from bp requesting temps. for Robert de Oudeby who had been el. 17 Jan. 1301. Commn to bp of Hereford to bl. abb.–el. (John (*sic*) de Oudeby) (*Reg. G. Giffard*, p. 540; cf. PRO, C84/14/4, 6). Temps. 25 Jan. 1301 (*CPR 1292–1301*, p. 562). Correction of abb. Robert for incontinence with Agnes la Couppestre of Alcester 1325

---

[2] *VCH* gives his eln as 1266 and cites Patent Roll 50 Henry III, m. 4 (i.e. *CPR 1258–66*, p. 638). Actually his eln is not recorded there, only the eln of abb. William to be abb. of Evesham, and the gt, during pleasure, of the abbey of Alcester to William de Clifford, the king's escheator.

(*Reg. Cobham*, pp. 191–2). D. by 28 Dec. 1334 (PRO, C84/23/28). D., lic. to el. 4 Jan. 1335 (*CPR 1334–38*, p. 56).

Robert of Albrighton (Abryton, Adbrigton, Adbriton, Adbrygham, Adbryton) **1335–1361** M. of Alcester, eln quashed but apptd by bp 4 Mar. 1335; prof. obed. 5 Mar. (*Reg. Montacute*, no. 228). Temps. 14 Mar. 1335 (*CPR 1334–38*, p. 83). D., lic. to el. 5 Oct. 1361 (*CPR 1361–64*, p. 79).

Maurice of Minsterworth (Munstreworth, Mynstreworth) **1362–1369** M. of St Peter's, Gloucester, royal ass. 22 Jan. 1362 (ibid., p. 145) having been sought by pr. of Worcester 14, 19 Jan. 1362 (*Worcs. Reg. Sede Vacante*, p. 210). Eln pres. to king for royal ass. 14 Jan. 1362; subsequent cert. by pr. of Worcester *sede vacante* that he had apptd Maurice *per lapsum temporis* 31 Jan. 1362 (PRO, C84/28/35, 37). Temps. 6 Feb. 1362 (*CPR 1361–64*, p. 160). Accused of theft but acquitted Mich. 1364 (*Gloucestershire Peace Rolls 1361–98*, p. 67, no. 16 & n. 192). D. by 2 Aug. 1369 (PRO, C84/30/6). D., lic. to el. 4 Aug. 1369 (*CPR 1367–70*, p. 294). Also pr. of Leonard Stanley to 1362 (q.v.).

John (de) Bradeweye 1369–1390 M. of Alcester, eln pres. to king for royal ass. 9 Oct. 1369 (PRO, C84/30/13); royal ass. 15 Oct. 1369, temps. 28 Jan. 1370 (*CPR 1367–70*, pp. 308, 358). Eln quashed but apptd by bp of Worcester 14 Dec. 1369; bl. 23 Dec. 1369 (Worcester, Reg. Lenn, p. 45). Abbey vac. by 16 Apr. 1390 (PRO, C84/34/39). D., lic. to el. 22 Apr. 1390 (*CPR 1388–92*, p. 232).

ATHELNEY (Soms), (St Saviour) St Peter, St Paul and St Ethelwin. ref. *c.* 960
Lists in *VCH Soms*, II, 102; *Ctl. Athelney*, pp. 116–17; *Heads*, I, 26–7.

Benedict II –?1227 Occ. 1197 x 1205 (*HMC Wells*, I, 57); 1200 x 1205 (*CDF*, no. 770); 1213 x 1214 (*Ctl. Athelney*, no. 99); 25 Nov. 1220 (ibid., no. 7); 1225 (ibid., no. 84). Lic. to el. (no reason given for vacancy) 26 Feb. 1227 (*CPR 1225–32*, p. 111).

Roger 1227–?1245 Pr. of Athelney, royal ass. 6 May 1227 (ibid., p. 123). Occ. 18 Nov. 1227 (*Devon F.*, I, p. 88, no. 174); 16 June 1242 (*Soms. F.*, I, 108; *Ctl. Athelney*, no. 118). Lic. to el. (no reason given for vacancy) 15 July 1245 (*CPR 1232–47*, p. 457).

Robert 1245–?1267 Pr. of Athelney, royal ass. 24 July 1245; temps. 28 July 1245 (ibid., p. 458). Occ. 1263 (*Ctl. Athelney*, nos. 24, 135). Prob. the unnamed abb. who had res. by 16 Oct. 1267 due to old age and illness (PRO, C84/3/32). Fine paid by pr. and convent for keeping of the priory when vacant 27 Oct. 1267 (*CPR 1266–72*, p. 124; *CCR 1261–72*, p. 124).

Richard de Derham 1267– M. of Athelney, temps. 27 Nov. 1267 (*CPR 1266–72*, p. 169). Occ. 1276, 1279 (*Ctl. Athelney*, nos. 9, 173).

Andrew de Sacro Fonte 1280–1300 M. of Athelney, royal ass. 14 Mar. 1280, temps. 29 Apr. 1280 (*CPR 1272–81*, pp. 366, 368). D., lic. to el. 5 Apr. 1300 (*CPR 1292–1301*, p. 503).

Osmund 1300–1325 M. of Athelney, royal ass. 19 Apr. 1300, temps. 13 May 1300 (ibid., pp. 510, 513). D., lic. to el. 19 Jan. 1325 (*CPR 1324–27*, p. 86). Called de Sowi in *Ctl.* list, but name does not occ. in ctl. Poss. also the abb. Osmund Regney said to be abb. *temp.* Henry III, see *Ctl. Athelney*, no. 241.

Robert de Ile (Ele) 1325–1341 Pr. of Athelney, royal ass. 13 Feb. 1325, temps. 16 Mar. 1325 (*CPR 1324–27*, pp. 88, 109). Bl. & prof. obed. 25 Mar. 1325 (*Reg. Droxford*, p. 243). D. by 26 July 1341 (PRO, C84/24/20). D., lic. to el. 19 Jan. 1341 (*CPR 1340–43*, p. 86).

Richard of Goathurst (Gothurst) **1341–1349** M. of Athelney, royal ass. 20 Aug. 1341, temps. 4 Sept. 1341 (ibid., pp. 278, 282). D. 15 Sept. 1349 (*Cal. Misc. Inq.*, III, 15). D., lic. to el. 23 Sept. 1349 (*CPR 1348–50*, p. 376; cf. PRO, C84/26/22).

John of Stour (Stoure) **1349** Pr. of Athelney, el. but d. while on way to king, d. by 8 Oct. 1349 (PRO, C84/26/28); lic. to el. 10 Oct. 1349 (*CPR 1348–50*, p. 395).

Robert of Hatch (Hacche, Hache) **1349–1390** M. of Athelney, royal ass. 22 Oct. 1349, temps. 5 Nov. 1349 (ibid., pp. 410, 419). D. by 5 Oct. 1390 (PRO, C84/34/66). D., lic. to el. 7 Oct. 1390 (*CPR 1388–92*, p. 307).

BARDNEY (Lincs), St Peter, St Paul and St Oswald f. –697; 1087 (dependent on Charroux); 1115 x 1116 (independent abbey; cf. Cheney, *Inn. III*, no. 891).
  Lists in *VCH Lincs*, II, 103; *Heads*, I, 27.

Peter of Lenton 1214– Pr. of Lenton, temps. 26 June 1214 (*Rot. Lit. Claus.*, I, 207b; cf. *Walt. Cov.*, II, 217; *Ann. Dunstable*, p. 40, s.a. 1213; *Ch. Ramsey*, p. 342 (not named). Occ. j.d. +27 Apr. 1217 (PRO, E326/8548).

Matthew –1223 Occ. 4 Mar. 1218 (BL, Cotton ms. Vespasian E XX, ff. 33v–34r); n.d. (1215 x 1223 (*Reg. Ant. Lincoln*, IV, no. 1202). An abb. (not named) d. 1223 (*Ann. Dunstable*, p. 79). Custody given to pr. and convent 28 July 1223, lic. to el. (no reason given for vacancy) (*CPR 1216–25*, p. 379). Seal (*BM Seals*, no. 2581).

Adam of Aswardby (Asewardeby) **1223–** Sacrist of Bardney, royal ass. 16 Aug. 1223 (*CPR 1216–25*, p. 381). Eln conf. & bl. 8 Sept. 1223 (*Reg. Wells*, III, 127). Occ. 1226, 1231 (*Lincs F.*, I, 183, 241); Mich. term 1230 (*CRR*, XIV, no. 509); 16 Aug. 1240 (BL, Cotton ms. Vespasian E XX, f. 47r; *Lincs F.*, I, 334).

Walter of Benniworth (Benigworth, Benigwurth) **1241–1243/4** M. of Bardney, royal ass. 25 Sept. 1241 (*CPR 1232–47*, p. 259); writ *de intendendo* 29 Oct. 1241 (ibid., p. 265). El. & adm. June 1241 x June 1242, no reason given for vacancy (*Reg. Grosseteste*, pp. 64–5). Mentioned 29 Oct. 1243 as former abb. (*CR 1242–47*, p. 131), but cf. occ. Easter 1244 (*CRR*, XVIII, no. 916). House void by 22 Apr. 1244 (*CR 1242–47*, pp. 178–9). Res., lic. to el. 5 June 1244 (*CPR 1232–47*, p. 427).

William of Hatton 1244–?1258 M. of Bardney, royal ass. 28 June 1244, writ *de intendendo* 16 July 1244 (ibid., pp. 430, 432). Occ. 26 May 1245, 1 July 1249, 19 June 1250, 12 Nov. 1256 (*Lincs F.*, II, 17, 50, 87, 133, 158). Lic. to el. (no reason given for vacancy) 11 July 1258 (*CPR 1247–58*, p. 641).

William of Torksey (Thorkeseye, Torkes') **1258–1267** M. of Bardney, royal ass. 30 July 1258, temps. 16 Aug. 1258 (ibid., pp. 643, 650). D., lic. to el. 12 Jan. 1267 (*CPR 1266–72*, p. 25).

Peter of Barton 1267–1280 M. and cellarer of Bardney, el. 26 Feb. 1267, eln quashed but apptd by bp of Lincoln. Lic. to seek bl. from any Catholic bp (*Reg. R. Gravesend*, pp. 23, 271). Prof. obed. 9 Jan. 1268 (ibid., p. 23). Temps. 4 March 1267, having been conf. by mag. John de Lindsey, Official of Lincoln and vicegerent of absent bp (*CPR 1266–72*, p. 44). House vacant 4 Feb. 1276, 13 May 1276 (*CPR 1272–81*, pp. 135, 140). Writ *de intendendo* 10 Dec. 1276 for Peter who had been unjustly removed by Bp Gravesend and restored on appeal by the archbp of Canterbury (ibid., p. 185, cf. *CPL*, I, 452). Cess. by 8 Apr. 1280 (PRO, C84/6/35). Cess., lic. to el. 10 Apr. 1280 (*CPR 1272–81*, p. 367; cf. *Reg. Sutton*, I, 2).

Robert of Wainfleet (Waynflet(e), Wainflet, Wayinflette, Waynflet, Weinflet, Weynflet) **1280–1318** [Robert was one of the monks sent away by Archbp Kilwardby after his visitation; to return to Bardney 12 Aug. 1279; ordered by Archbp Pecham to be received back Mar. 1280 (*Reg. Peckham*, I, 24, 41, 102); alleged to have been excommunicated by his abb. on his return 18 Nov. 1279 (ibid., 55)]. M. of Bardney, royal ass. 1 May 1280, temps. 9 May 1280 (*CPR 1272–81*, p. 369). El. 23 Apr. 1280, eln conf. 6 May 1280 (*Reg. Sutton*, I, 2–3). Bl. 10 June 1280 (ibid., 3). 3 Sept. 1303 letter to king from Bp Dalderby informing him of the deposition of Robert (Lincoln, Ep. Reg., III, f. 60r). Ref. to him as former abb. 28 Jan. 1304 (ibid., f. 63r–v). 10 Feb. 1304 house void by the deposition of Robert of Wainfleet and royal custodian apptd (*CPR 1301–07*, p. 210). 10 May 1304 keeper of Bardney ordered to allow Abb. Robert full administration. The order by Bp Dalderby to remove him has been reversed on appeal to the Court of Canterbury and Robert restored by the presidents of that Court (ibid., p. 222; for case see *Reg. Winchelsey*, I, 472, 474–5, 477; *CCR 1302–07*, p. 111). Robert absolved by pope from excommunication 1306 (*CPL*, II, 20). 23 July 1307 the king is informed that the Roman Curia has confirmed the deposition and requests the king to treat the abbey as vacant (Lincoln, Ep. Reg., III, f. 119r). From 1305 Robert was several times abroad and visited Rome in 1310 (*CPR 1301–7*, pp. 382, 519; *1307–13*, p. 277). Temps. restored 20 May 1311 in compliance with papal request (*CPR 1307–13*, p. 349). 20 Dec. 1314 excommunication of Robert by bp of Lincoln (Lincoln, Ep. Reg., III, f. 310v). 9 Sept. 1316 abbey granted to the king's cousin for keeping in the absence of the abb. abroad at the Roman Curia (*Cal. Chanc. Warr.*, I, 445, cf. *CPR 1313–17*, p. 542). 3 Nov. 1317 Robert in dispute with the bp of Lincoln is ready to renounce his status before the bp and provision is to be made for him (*CPR 1313–17*, pp. 41–2). 11 Jan. 1318 Robert appeared before the bp and withdrew his action and at the same time ceded the abbey, which cession the bp accepted (Lincoln, Ep. Reg., III, f. 377v). Notification of vacancy to the king 13 Jan. 1318 (ibid., ff. 378v–379r; PRO, C84/19/20; cf. C84/19/23); 15 Jan. 1318 provision made for abb. (Lincoln, Ep. Reg., III, f. 378r–v). 12 Feb. 1318 royal conf. of episcopal provision (*CPR 1317–21*, p. 109). Cess., lic. to el. 26 Jan. 1318 (ibid., p. 74).

Richard of Gainsborough (Gaynesburgh, Geyneshburgh) **1318–1342** Submission of the abbey 29 Mar. 1318. The pr. and convent ask the bp to provide them with an abb. in place of Robert de Wainfleet who had res. On 13 Apr. the bp announced that he had found Richard de Gaynesburgh, m. of Spalding, and his nomination was accepted by the pr. and convent (Lincoln, Ep. Reg., II, f. 72r; Lincoln, Ep. Reg., III, f. 387v). M. of Spalding, royal ass. (m. of Bardney) 14 May 1318, temps. (m. of Spalding) 8 June 1318 (*CPR 1317–21*, pp. 140, 151). 26 Apr. 1318 king informed that Richard had been nominated by bp and king's ass. requested (Lincoln, Ep. Reg., III, f. 387r). 28 May 1318 bl. by the ex-archbp of Armagh and prof. obed. (ibid., f. 389r). Royal commn to take fealty 4 June 1318 (PRO, C84/19/1938). D., lic to el. 14 Oct. 1342 (*CPR 1340–43*, p. 530).

Roger (of) Barrow (Barou, Barowe) **1342–1355** M. of Bardney, royal ass. 4 Nov. 1342, temps. 8 Dec. 1342 (ibid., pp. 561, 574). El. 27 Nov. 1342, eln conf. by bp 28 Nov. 1342 (Lincoln, Ep. Reg., VI, f. 2r). D., lic. to el. 6 Sept. 1355 (*CPR 1354–58*, p. 279). Grave slab, n.d. (Greenhill, p. 6).

Thomas of Stapelton (Stapilton, Stapulton) **1355–1379** M. of Bardney, eln pres. to king for royal ass. 17 Sept. 1355 (PRO, C84/27/28); royal ass. 20 Sept. 1355, temps. 4 Oct. 1355 (*CPR 1354–60*, pp. 280, 286). El. appeared before bp of Lincoln 21 Sept., eln examined 30 Sept., eln conf. 20 Oct. 1355 (Lincoln, Ep. Reg., IX, f. 117r–v). D., lic. to el. 11 Sept. 1379 (*CPR 1377–81*, p. 382).

BATH (Soms), St Peter ref. *c.* 963 (abbey); 1090 (cathedral priory)
Lists in *VCH Soms*, II, 80; *Ctl. Bath*, pp. lxxviii–lix; *Heads*, I, 27–9. Biographical details in Greatrex, *Biog. Reg.*, pp. 1–49.

Robert of Bath **–1223** Occ. *c.* 1198 (*Ctl. Bath*, II, no. 22; cf. *EEA*, 10, nos. 192, 203, 214); 1204 (*Rot. Chart.*, p. 136b; *Ctl. Bath*, II, no. 63); 10 May 1223 (*Ctl. Bath*, II, no. 115). El. abb. of Glastonbury 1223 (q.v.) (*Ad. Dom.*, II, 478; *Ann. Waverley*, p. 299) See Greatrex, *Biog. Reg.* pp. 12–13.

Thomas de Stocton **1223–1261** Occ. 13 Oct. 1224 (PRO, Glos. F., CP25/1/73/6, no. 71). Surname (*Cal. Misc. Inq.*, II, 337). D. 23 June 1261 (*Ctl. Bath*, II, no. 253). Seal (*BM Seals*, no. 2609). See Greatrex, p. 44.

Walter de Anno (Dune) **1261–1290** Eln announced 27 June 1261 (*Ctl. Bath*, II, nos. 256–7). D. by 14 Jan. 1290 (ibid., no. 394). See Greatrex, p. 11.

Thomas of Winchester (Winton) **1290–1301** El. soon after 14 Jan. 1290 (ibid.). Eln conf. by bp of Bath and Wells 27 Jan. 1290 (see Greatrex, *Biog. Reg.*, p. 48, citing unpd part of priory reg.). Occ. 10 Mar. 1290 (*CPR 1281–92*, p. 348). Archbp Winchelsey orders the bp of Bath and Wells to punish pr. Thomas, whose offences were manifest when the bp visited the priory 31 Jan. 1301 (*Reg. Winchelsey*, II, 726–7). Res. 10 Apr. 1301 and gtd a pension (*Ctl. Bath*, II, no. 578). See Greatrex, p. 48. Previously sacrist of Bath.

Robert de Clopcote (Cloppecote) **1301–1332** El. 14 Apr. 1301 (*Ctl. Bath*, II, no. 580). Occ. 11 June 1301 (*HMC Wells*, I, 397). Commn to hold enquiry into evil reports against the pr. 5 Nov. 1321 (*Reg. Droxford*, p. 195). Request for lic. to el. to replace pr. Robert, who is dead, 26 Feb. 1332 (*Reg. R. Shrewsbury*, I, no. 356). However, he had previously sent in his res. to the pope with recommendation in favour of Thomas Crist (*Ctl. Bath*, II, no. 710; and see below). See Greatrex, pp. 19–20.

Robert of Sutton 1332 El. 6 Mar. 1332; installed 14 Mar. (*Ctl. Bath*, II, no. 704). Commn to confirm eln 11 Mar. 1332 (*Reg. R. Shrewsbury*, I, no. 363, cf. no. 409). Occ. 15 June 1332 (ibid., no. 633). 30 Sept. 1332 apptd as pr. of Dunster (q.v.) to make way for Thomas Crist as papal nominee (ibid., nos. 697, 486). See Greatrex, pp. 42–3.

Thomas Crist (Christi, Cristi) **1332–1340** Papal provision on res. of Robert de Clopcote 14 July 1332 (*CPL*, II, 357). Adm. by virtue of papal mand. 24 Sept. 1332 (*Reg. R. Shrewsbury*, no. 449). Cess., lic. to el. sought 12 Aug. 1340 (ibid., no. 1397). Provision made for maintenance of former pr. 27 Aug. 1340 (ibid., no. 1400). See Greatrex, p. 21.

John of Iford (Iforde) **1340–** Sacrist of Bath from 6 Feb. 1329 (*Reg. R. Shrewsbury*, I, nos. 117–18). El. *c.* 12 Aug. 1340 (ibid., no. 1397). In his 9th year as pr. 1348/49 (*Ctl. Bath*, II, no. 40). Occ. 16 Aug. 1357 (*CPR 1354–58*, p. 597). Poss. vacated priory by 31 July 1359 when sub-pr. presents to a Bath vicarage (*Ctl. Bath*, II, no. 917). See Greatrex, pp. 29–30.

John (de) Berewyk Occ. 20 June 1362 (*CPR 1361–64*, p. 225); Jan. 1370 x Jan. 1371 (*Bristol F.*, p. 245); 1371 (Lincoln, Ep. Reg., X, f. 353v); 1377 (PRO, E179/4/2, m. 1); 11 Oct. 1379 (BL, Egerton ms. 3316, f. 99v). See Greatrex, pp. 14–15.

Pr. **John** occ. 29 June 1386 (Lambeth, Reg. Courtenay, f. 218v), 23 Jan. 1388 (*Reg. Wakefield*, no. 423) and 6 Jan. 1392 (*CPR 1391–96*, p. 50), but it is uncertain whether he is Berewyk or Dunster.

The next recorded pr., **John of Dunster** (Dunsterre), occ. 3 May 1397 (*CPL*, V, 50); 1 June 1398 (*Cal. Misc. Inq.*, VI, no. 185). See Greatrex, p. 22.

BATTLE (Sussex), St Martin (and Holy Trinity and St Mary) f. 1067.

Lists in *VCH Sussex*, Ii, 55; *Heads*, I, 29–30.

Richard 1215–1235 M. of Battle, royal ass. 22 Jan. 1215 (*Rot. Lit. Pat.*, p. 126; see *Heads*, I, corrigenda). El. 1215 (*Gervase*, II, 109). Occ (R.) 1218 (*CPR 1216–25*, p. 177); 23 Mar. 1219 (*Devon F.*, I, p. 44, no. 75); 1222, 1232 (*Kent F.*, pp. 77, 118); 20 Jan. 1235 (*Essex F.*, I, p. 99). D. 30 July 1235 (*Ann. Tewkesbury*, p. 99). Lic. to el. 14 Aug. 1235, no reason given for vacancy (*CPR 1232–47*, p. 115). Seal (*BM Seals*, nos. 2612–13).

Ralph of Coventry (Covintre) **1235–1260** Cellarer of Battle, royal ass. 29 Aug. 1235, writ *de intendendo* 6 Nov. 1235 (*CPR 1232–47*, pp. 117, 130). Occ. Oct. 1259 x Oct. 1260 (*Surrey F.*, p. 39). Lic. to el. 28 Oct. 1260, no reason given for vacancy (*CPR 1258–66*, p. 124), but d. of Ralph conf. by petition of 29 Oct. 1260 (PRO, C84/2/18). Seal (*BM Seals*, no. 2614).

Reginald 1260–1281 M. of Battle, pr. of Brecon, royal ass. 27 Nov. 1260 (*CPR 1258–66*, p. 130). Res. by 18 Apr. 1281 (PRO, C84/7/20). Lic. to el. 9 May 1281 (*CPR 1272–81*, p. 431). Seal (*BM Seals*, nos. 2615–16).

Henry of Aylesford 1281–1297 Pr. of Battle, eln pres. to king for royal ass. 14 May 1281 (PRO, C84/7/26); royal ass. 20 May 1281, writ *de intendendo* 28 May 1281 (*CPR 1272–81*, pp. 426, 440). D., lic. to el. 3 Dec. 1297 (*CPR 1292–1301*, p. 323).

John of Thanet (Taneto) **1297–1308** M. of Battle, eln pres. to king for royal ass. 13 Dec. 1297 (PRO, C84/13/8); royal ass. 3 Jan. 1298, temps. 30 Jan. 1298 (*CPR 1292–1301*, pp. 326, 328). Cert. conf. eln by bp of Chichester 25 Jan. 1298 (PRO, C84/13/10). Res. 16 Feb. 1308 (PRO, C84/4/36). Res., lic. to el. 23 Feb. 1308 (*CPR 1307–13*, p. 45).

John of Whatlington (Whatlinton, Whatlyngtone) **1308–1311** Sacrist of Battle, eln pres. to king for royal ass. 9 Mar. 1308 (PRO, C84/4/37); royal ass. 10 Mar. 1308, writ *de intendendo* 24 Mar. 1308 (*CPR 1307–13*, pp. 50, 57). Cert. conf. eln by bp of Chichester 23 Mar. 1308 (PRO, C84/16/7). D., lic. to el. 27 Apr. 1311 (*CPR 1307–13*, p. 336).

John de Northburne (Nortburne) **1311–1318** Royal ass. 25 May 1311, writ *de intendendo* 15 June 1311 (ibid., pp. 348, 355). Res. by 18 Feb. 1318 (PRO, C84/19/29). Cess., lic. to el. 26 Feb. 1318 (*CPR 1317–21*, p. 109).

Roger of Pevensey (Pevenese, Pevense) **1318–1324** M. of Battle, pr. of St Nicholas, Exeter (*Reg. Stapeldon*, p. 214). Eln pres. to king for royal ass. 16 Mar. 1318 (PRO, C84/19/9); royal ass. (John) 19 Mar. 1318, writ *de intendendo* (Roger) 6 May 1318 (*CPR 1317–21*, pp. 120, 140). Cert. conf. eln by bp of Chichester 25 Apr. 1318 (PRO, C84/19/33). D. 17 Jan. 1324 (PRO, C84/20/21). D., lic. to el. 31 Jan. 1324 (*CPR 1321–24*, p. 363).

Alan de Retlyng (Rotlyng) **1324–1351** M. of Battle, eln pres. to king for royal ass. 26 Feb. 1324 (PRO, C84/20/22); royal ass. 7 Mar. 1324, writ *de intendendo* 28 Mar. 1324 (*CPR 1321–24*, pp. 395, 399). Occ. 1328 to 1334 (Norwich, Reg/1/2, ff. 19v, 63v); 12 Oct. 1344, 13 June 1345 (*CPL*, III, 158, 211). D. (no name), lic. to el. 1 Feb. 1351 (*CPR 1350–54*, p. 34; cf. PRO, C84/26/40), but clearly d. by 28 Jan. 1351 (BL, Harl. ms. 3586, ff. 16v–17r).

Robert of Battle (Bello) **1351–1364** Eln set for 2 Mar. 1351 (ibid., f. 18r). Sub-pr. of Battle, royal ass. 7 Mar. 1351, writ *de intendendo* 23 Mar. 1351 (*CPR 1350–54*, pp. 50, 53). D. by 31 Oct. 1364 (PRO, C84/29/12). Lic. to el. 1 Nov. 1364 (*CPR 1364–67*, p. 22).

Hamo of Offington (Offyn(g)ton) **1364–1383** M. of Battle, royal ass. 27 Nov. 1364; temps. 29 Dec. 1364 (ibid., pp. 43, 56; cf. royal ass. 13 Dec. 1364 – Lambeth, Reg. Islip, f. 305v); cert. of his eln having been conf. by the vicar-general of the bp of Chichester 21 Dec. 1364 (PRO, C84/29/16). Lic. to receive bl. from any Catholic bp 20 Dec. 1364; bl. by archbp of Canterbury 29 Dec. 1364 (Lambeth, Reg. Islip, ff. 305v, 346v). D. by 15 Feb. 1383 (PRO, C84/33/11). D., lic. to el. 18 Feb. 1383 (*CPR 1381–85*, p. 225).

BIRKENHEAD (Ches.), St Mary and St James f. *c.* 1150 (priory)
Lists in *VCH Ches.*, III, 131–2; Stewart-Brown, *Birkenhead Priory*, pp. 84–5; *Heads*, I, 30.

Oliver Occ. *temp.* John (Stewart-Brown in *Cheshire Sheaf*, XX (1923), pp. 60–1); mentd in 1357 as having been pr. *c.* 1216 (Stewart-Brown, p. 85).

Robert Occ. 14 July 1282 (*Chester City Court*, p. 46); 29 Sept. 1283 (*CCR 1279–88*, p. 241).

William of Whaley (Waley) Occ. early 14th cent. (according to Stewart-Brown, p. 85, citing inf. on Poulton chts. by W. F. Irvine). However, Irvine himself in *Cheshire Sheaf*, XLIV (1949), p. 26 dates a cht. naming William to *c.* 1280 and ascribes to him a possible priorate of *c.* 1250 to *c.* 1283, so he could come before Robert in the sequence of priors.

Robert de Bechington (Becheton) **–1339** Occ. July 1320 x July 1322 (Stewart-Brown, pp. 85–6). D. by 25 Apr. 1339 (Lichfield, B/A/1/2, f. 113r).

[**James of Neston** M. of Birkenhead, el. 1339 and immediately renounced eln (ibid.).]

Henry de Bechington (Becheton) **1339–** Right of appt transferred to bp and he apptd Henry 25 Apr. 1339 (ibid.). Occ. 3 Aug. 1339 (BL, Harl. ms. 2072, f. 76v), Jan. 1341 x Jan. 1342 (*DKR 28*, app. 6, p. 40); and until July 1348 (Stewart-Brown, p. 86, citing eyre roll).

Thomas de Tyddesbury Occ. from 6 Nov. 1350 to 1357 (Stewart-Brown, p. 86, citing Cheshire plea and forest rolls, PRO, Ches.29/62, m. 23).

Roger de Tyddesbury Occ. from 1362 to 1400 (Stewart-Brown, p. 86, citing Cheshire plea rolls). Occ. 1 Dec. 1361 (*Reg. Black Prince*, III, 434); 9 Oct. 1370, 6 Mar. 1371 (*Reg. Stretton*, II, 139, 140). 1379 (Bennett, 'Lancs & Ches. Clergy', p. 22); 27 Aug. 1389 (*DKR 36*, app. II, no. 1, p. 37).

BRADWELL (Bucks), St Mary f. ?–1136
  Lists in *VCH Bucks*, I, 351–2; *Heads*, I, 30
Richard Latest recorded occ. 12 Nov. 1201 (*Bucks F.*, I, 21).
John Occ. 25 Nov. 1218, 23 June 1219 (ibid., 39); Dec. 1218 x Dec. 1219 (*Reg. Wells*, II, 48); (J.) 22 Sept. 1220 (*Ctl. St Denys*, II, no. 432).[3]
Richard –1236/7 Occ. 1220 x *c.* 1225 (*Luffield Chts.*, I, no. 15). Unnamed pr. deposed at Bp Grosseteste's visitation 1236 (*Ann. Dunstable*, p. 143). Res. June 1236 x June 1237 (*Reg. Grosseteste*, p. 344).
Simon of Kent (Kantia) 1236/7– Sacrist of Peterborough, apptd by bp, the canons having made an eln against the form of the Lateran Council, June 1236 x June 1237 (ibid.). Occ. (S.) 8 Nov. 1242 (*Luffield Chts.*, I, no. 42).
John Occ. 5 May 1253 (*Bucks F.*, I, 99).
Bartholomew Occ. 6 Oct. 1272 (*Bucks F.*, II, 27); n.d. (PRO, SC.11/75 nos. 47, 72, 78).
Robert of Ramsey (Ramesia, Rammeseye) 1280/1– El. during Bp Sutton's first pontifical year (19 May 1280 x 18 May 1281), lic. to el. obtained from Anthony Bek, custodian of John FitzAlan, a minor, patron (Bodl., Dodsworth ms. 107, f. 140v). Ref. in 1362 to his having been pr. before the publication of the Statute of Mortmain (1279) (*Cal. Misc. Inq.*, III, 188).
John –1320 Occ. 24 Jan. 1309 (PRO, SC.11/75 no. 26); 9 May 1313 (ibid., no. 52). D. by 4 Dec. 1320 (Lincoln, Ep. Reg., IV, f. 325r). Indulgence for soul of pr. John, bur. in the conventual church (Lincoln, Ep. Reg., V, f. 323v).
Robert of Rowsham (Rolesham) 1320– M. of Bradwell, eln pres. to bp 4 Dec. 1320, eln quashed but apptd by bp 9 Dec. 1320 (Lincoln, Ep. Reg., IV, f. 325r). Lic. to visit Rome 1324 (Lincoln, Ep. Reg., V, f. 361v). Occ. 1329 (*CCR 1327–30*, p. 575; *Luffield Chts.*, I, nos. 78, 18a); 25 Apr. 1331 (*CCR 1330–33*, p. 302).
Robert Folyot –1331 Cess. by 23 June 1331 (Lincoln, Ep. Reg., IV, f. 338r–v). Poss. the same as Robert above. If not, some of the above occurrences of pr. Robert could be to this pr.
Simon of Elstow (Elnestowe) 1331–1336 M. of Bradwell, eln quashed but apptd by bp 23 June 1331 (ibid.). Cess. by 29 June 1336 (ibid., f. 349r).
William of Loughton 1336–1349 M. of Bradwell, apptd by bp 1 July 1336 (ibid.). D. by 25 July 1349 (Lincoln, Ep. Reg., IX, f. 287v).
John of Billing (Billyng, Byllyng) 1349– M. of Bradwell, eln quashed and apptd by bp 25 July 1349 (ibid.). Commn dated 22 June 1361 to the rector of Horwode to sequestrate the goods of the priory and appt custodians, as John de Billyng, the pr., is old and in ill health. If John wishes to res., his cess. is to be accepted (Lincoln, Ep. Reg., VIII, f. 161v).
Commn dated 30 Sept. 1367 to appt Thomas de Benestede, m. of Bradwell, to administer custody and administration of priory. Oath of Thomas dated 20 Oct. 1367 (Lincoln, Ep. Reg., XII, f. 42v).
Commn dated 18 Aug. 1375 to administer goods of priory in vacancy (ibid., f. 128v).
Commn dated 18 Apr. 1382 to the sequestrator in the archdeaconries of Northampton and Buckingham, the rector of Cogenhoe and John of Chalfont, m. of Bradwell, to administer spiritual and temporal goods of the priory (ibid., f. 237r).

---

[3] PRO, SC.11/75 nos. 24, 72 are undated charters of John le (de) Legath, pr. of Bradwell. He is prob. to be identified with one of the two 13th-cent. pr. Johns.

John of Horwood (Horwod(e)) **–1410** Occ. 29 Apr. 1388 (*CPR 1385–89*, p. 419). D. by 13 Feb. 1410 (Lincoln, Ep. Reg., XIV, f. 444r).

BURTON (Staffs), St Mary and St Modwenna f. 1004 (so *Ann. Burton*, p. 183).
Lists in *VCH Staffs*, III, 213; *Heads*, I, 30–1.

Nicholas of Wallingford 1216–1222 Pr. of Burton, el. 1216 (*Ann. Burton*, p. 224). D. 1222 (ibid., p. 225); D. Tues. 29 July 1222 according to unreliable 15th-cent. Ann. – 29 fell on Fri., and see below (*Mon. Angl.*, III, 48).

Richard de Insula 1222–1229 Pr. of Bury, succ. 1222 (*Ann. Burton*, p. 225; *Ann. Dunstable*, p. 76). Royal ass. to R., pr. of Bury 10 July 1222 (*CPR 1216–25*, p. 333). Abb. of Bury St Edmunds 1229 (q.v.). Lic. to el. 13 July 1229 (*CPR 1225–32*, p. 256). See Sharpe, *Latin Writers*, p. 484.

Laurence of St Edward (de Sancto Edwardo) **1229–1260** M. of Burton, royal ass. 25 July 1229, writ *de intendendo* 6 Aug. 1229 (*CPR 1225–32*, pp. 258, 261). 15th-cent Ann. state he was kitchener (*Mon. Angl.*, III, 48). Installed 9 Nov. 1229 – 'in secunda festivitate sancte Modvenne' (*Ann. Burton*, p. 245). D. 1259 (ibid., p. 491). D. Wed. 2 July 1260 according to 15th-cent. Ann. – 2 fell on Fri. (*Mon. Angl.*, III, 48). D. *c.* 20 July 1260, but see date of lic. to el. (*Ann. Dunstable*, p. 216). D. (L.) by 3 July [1260] (PRO, C84/2/11). D. (L.), lic. to el. 6 July 1260 (*CPR 1258–66*, p. 80). Seal (*BM Seals*, nos. 2784–6).

John of Stafford 1260–1281 Pr. of Burton, el. 12 July 1260 (PRO, C84/2/13); royal ass. 15 July 1260, writ *de intendendo* 26 July 1260 (*CPR 1258–66*, pp. 82–3). Res. Sat. 14 Jan. 1261 according to 15th-cent Ann. – 14 fell on Tues. (*Mon. Angl.*, III, 48; PRO, C84/7/12, but bp's notif. of res. 13 Jan. 1281 (PRO, C84/7/14)). Res., lic. to el. 18 Jan. 1281 (*CPR 1272–81*, p. 423). Seal (*BM Seals*, no. 2787).

Thomas of Packington (Pakinton) **1281–1305** Pr. of Burton, eln pres. to king for royal ass. 3 Feb. 1281 (PRO, C84/7/17); royal ass. 8 Feb. 1281, temps. 20 Feb. 1281 (*CPR 1272–81*, pp. 424–5). Cert. conf. eln by bp of Coventry and Lichfield 15 Feb. 1281 (PRO, C84/7/19). D. Thurs. 1 Oct. 1305, according to 15th-cent Ann. – but 1 fell on Fri. (*Mon. Angl.*, III, 48). D., lic. to el. 7 Oct. 1305 (*CPR 1301–07*, p. 380). Seal (*BM Seals*, no. 2788).

John of Burton (*alias* **Fisher** *alias* **Stapenhulle**) **1305–1316** Pr. of Burton, eln conf. 30 Oct. 1305 (Lichfield, B/A/1/1, f. 16r; PRO, C84/15/36). Temps. 1 Nov. 1305 (*CPR 1301–07*, p. 392). D. Thurs. 24 June 1316, according to 15th-cent Ann., but see following. D. by 28 May 1316 (PRO, C84/18/29). D. (J.), lic. to el. 30 May 1316 (*CPR 1313–17*, p. 463; cf. *CFR 1307–19*, p. 283).

William of Bromley (Bromlegh, Bromleye) **1316–1329** M. of Burton, eln pres. to king for royal ass. 11 June 1316 (PRO, C84/18/32–3); royal ass. 15 June 1316, temps. 12 July 1316 (*CPR 1313–17*, pp. 472, 508). 15th-cent. Ann. states he was cellarer (*Mon. Angl.*, III, 49). Eln conf. 1 July 1316, bl. and prof. obed. 5 Aug. 1316 (Lichfield, B/A/1/1, f. 48v; PRO, C84/18/37). D. Wed. 21 June 1329 according to 15th-cent. Ann. (*Mon. Angl.*, III, 49); certainly d. by 24 June (PRO, C84/22/26). D., lic. to el. 28 June 1329 (*CPR 1327–30*, p. 402).

Robert of Langdon (Langedon, Longdon, Longedon) **1329–1340** Pr. of Tutbury. Bp writes to the king 3 Sept. 1329 about the disputed eln of Robert of Longdon, pr. of Tutbury, and **Roger de Bylyngton**, m. of Burton. The bp had quashed the elns and apptd Robert as abb. Letter of appt dated 4 Sept. 1329 (Lichfield, B/A/1/2, ff. 144v–145v). 10 Sept. 1329 order to restore temps. to Robert of Langdon, apptd by bp of Lichfield to whom king had referred the double eln of Robert, pr. of Tutbury and of Roger of Bilyngton, m. of Burton (*CPR 1327–30*, p. 442). Warrant for the issue of writs 12 Sept. (PRO, SC1/38/185). D. Wed. 28 Feb. 1340 according to 15th-cent. Ann. – 28 fell on Mon. (*Mon. Angl.*, III, 49). D., lic. to el. 5 Mar. 1340 (*CPR 1338–40*, p. 432).

Robert de Brykhull (Brikhull) **1340–1347** Pr. of Burton, royal ass. 27 Mar. 1340, temps. 5 Apr. 1340 (ibid., pp. 443, 448). D. 13 Aug. 1347 according to 15th-cent. Ann. (*Mon. Angl.*, III, 49)., but see following entries D. by 5 Aug. 1347 (*CFR 1347–56*, p. 42). D., lic. to el. 6 Aug. 1347 (*CPR 1345–48*, p. 360).

John of Ibstock (Ibbestoke, Ibestok(e), Ibstoke) **1347–1366** M. and almoner of Burton, eln pres. to king for royal ass. 17 Aug. 1347 (PRO, C84/25/15–16); royal ass. 22 Aug. 1347, temps. 5 Sept. 1347 (*CPR 1345–48*, pp. 370, 403). Eln conf. 30 Aug. 1347 (Lichfield, B/A/1/2, f. 179r). D. Mon. 27 Sept. 1366 according to 15th-cent. Ann. – 27 fell on Mon. (*Mon. Angl.*, III, 49) and see following entries. D., lic. to el. 18 Sept. 1366 (*CPR 1364–67*, p. 308).

Thomas (of) Southam 1366–1400 M. of Burton, eln pres. to king for royal ass. 25 Sept. 1366 (PRO, C84/29/35); royal ass. 10 (*sic*) Sept. 1366, temps. 20 Oct. 1366 (*CPR 1364–67*, pp. 308, 321). 15th-cent Ann. states he was abb.'s chaplain (*Mon. Angl.*, III, 49). Cert. conf. eln by bp of Coventry and Lichfield 19 Oct. 1366 (PRO, C84/29/37). Cess. by 31 Oct. 1400 (PRO, C84/38/16). Cess. before 1 Nov. 1400 according to 15th-cent. Ann. (*Mon. Angl.*, III, 49; cf. *Burton Chts.*, p. 153, no. 606). Cess., lic. to el. 5 Nov. 1400 (*CPR 1399–1401*, p. 369).

BURY ST EDMUNDS (Suffolk), St Edmund f. 1020
Lists in *VCH Suffolk*, II, 72; *Heads*, I, 31–3.

Hugh (II) of Northwold 1213–1229 M. of Bury. El. 7 Aug. 1213, bl. 1215 after conf. by judges-delegate on 11 Mar. (*The Chronicle of the Election of Hugh, Abbot of Bury St Edmunds*, ed. R. M. Thomson (OMT, 1974), *passim; Mem. Bury*, II, 33 etc.; III, 9–11; *Gervase*, III, 109). El. bp of Ely *ante* 3 Feb. 1229, consec. 10 June 1229; d. 6 Aug. 1254. Benefactor of Cambridge University (M. B. Hackett, *The Original Statutes of Cambridge University* (Cambridge, 1970), pp. 38–9).

Richard de Insula 1229–1233 Pr. of Bury, abb. of Burton, el. 5 June 1229 (*Ch. Bury*, p. 7); royal ass. 20 June 1229 (*CPR 1225–32*, pp. 253–4); 12 Oct. 1229 royal ass. to papal conf. (ibid., p. 275); installed 20 Nov. 1229 (*Ann. Burton*, p. 245). D. 29 Aug. 1233 at Ponthieu (*Ch. Bury*, p . 8); 1233 (*Ann. Dunstable*, p. 134; *Ann. Worcs.*, p. 425). Lic. to el. 17 Sept. 1233 (*CPR 1232–47*, p. 26). Seal (*BM Seals*, no. 2803). See Sharpe, *Latin Writers*, p. 484.

Henry of Rushbrooke 1233–1248 Pr. of Bury, el. 27 Sept. 1233, bl. by bp of Ely 2 Feb. 1234 (*Ch. Bury*, p. 8); royal ass. (no name) 10 Oct. 1233 (*CPR 1232–47*, p. 27); lic. to bp of Ely to bl. abb.-el. 16 Dec. 1233 (*CPL*, I, 137). Succ. 1233 (*Ann. Dunstable*, p. 134). Mand. for seisin 1 Feb. 1234 (*CR 1231–34*, p. 373). D. 19 June 1248 (*Ch. Bury*, p. 15).

Edmund of Walpole (Walpol) **1248–1256** M. of Bury, royal ass. 14 July 1248 (*CPR 1247–58*, p. 21). Mand. for seisin 17 Sept. 1248 (*CR 1247–51*, p. 87). El. 7 July 1248, bl. by bp of Ely 27 Sept. 1248 (*Ch. Bury*, p. 15). D. 31 Dec. 1256 (ibid., p. 21). Lic. to el. 8 Jan. 1257 (*CPR 1247–58*, p. 536).

Simon of Luton *alias* **of Hoo** (Del Ho, Hou) **1257–1279** Pr. of Bury, el. 14 Jan. 1257, set out for Rome 30 July, and bl. at Viterbo by pope 22 Oct. 1257 (*Ch. Bury*, p. 21). Royal ass. 16 July 1257; writ *de intendendo* 12 Jan. 1258 (*CPR 1247–58*, pp. 538, 612). D. 9 Apr. 1279 and bur. 5 May (*Ch. Bury*, p. 68; PRO, C84/6/18). D., lic. to el. 20 Apr. 1279 (*CPR 1272–81*, p. 307). Seal (*BM Seals*, no. 2804; *Mon. Seals*, p. 16).

John of Northwold (Norwold) **1279–1301** Guest-master of Bury (*Ch. Bury*, p. 68). Eln pres. to king for royal ass. 5 May 1279 (PRO, C84/6/20); royal ass. 8 May 1279, writ *de intendendo* 5 Nov. 1279 (*CPR 1272–81*, pp. 314, 331). Papal conf. of eln 18 Sept. 1279 (*CPL*, I, 460). Adm. to abbey after bl. and temps. 28 Dec. 1279 (*Ch. Bury*, p. 70). Permission to make testament 18 Oct. 1290 (*CPR 1281–92*, p. 389). D. 27 Oct. 1301 and bur. 12 Nov. (PRO, C84/14/19; cf. *CFR 1272–1307*, p. 445). D., lic. to el. 30 Nov. 1301 (*CPR 1301–07*, p. 4).

Thomas of Tottington (Totyngton, Tytyngton) **1302–1312** Sub-pr. of Bury, eln pres. to king for royal ass. 7 Jan. 1302, temps. 10 Aug. 1302 (*CPR 1301–07*, pp. 10, 52). Papal conf. of eln 1 June 1302 (*CPL*, I, 601; Sayers, no. 1039). D. 8 Jan. 1313 (PRO, C84/17/13). D., lic. to el. 18 Jan. 1313 (*CPR 1307–13*, p. 520). Fragment of ledger stone at Hedgerley, Bucks (*Earliest English Brasses*, p. 43).

Richard of Draughton (Draghton, Drangton, Drauhton) **1312–1335** M. of Bury, royal ass. 4 Mar. 1313, writ *de intendendo* 17 May 1313 (*CPR 1307–13*, pp. 556, 593–4). Third pr. of Bury, papal conf. of eln 7 Apr. 1313; having been bl. by Berengar, bp of Tusculum, mand. to return to his monastery 22 Apr. 1313 (*CPL*, II, 111; *Orig. Papal Letters*, p. 36, no. 73). 31 Oct. 1328 letter concerning his abduction (*Reg. Martival*, II, i, 579–81). D. by 6 May 1335 (*CCR 1333–37*, p. 394). D., lic. to el. 15 May 1335 (*CPR 1334–38*, p. 100). Possible fragment of monument at Ingham, Norfolk (*Earliest English Brasses*, p. 43).

William de Bernham 1335–1361 Sub-pr. of Bury, royal ass. 31 May 1335, temps. 22 Jan. 1336 (*CPR 1334–38*, pp. 110, 195). Papal conf. of eln 11 Oct. 1335 (*CPL*, II, 523; *Orig. Papal Letters* p. 86, no. 172). Bl. by Anibaldo, bp of Tusculum; mand. to William to return to Bury 29 Oct. 1335 (*CPL*, II, 529). Papal faculty to dispose of his personal property by will 13 Feb. 1345 (ibid., III, 166). D. 28 Feb. 1361 (*Cal. Misc. Inq.*, III, 221). D., lic. to el. 3 Mar. 1361 (*CPR 1358–61*, p. 556).

Henry of Hunstanton (Huntstanton) **1361** M. of Bury, royal ass. 18 Mar. 1361 (ibid., p. 572).

John of Brinkley (Brinkele, Brynkele) **1361–1378** M. of Bury, temps. 12 Nov. 1361 (*CPR 1361–64*, p. 104). Fealty 12 Nov. 1361 (*CCR 1369–74*, p. 60). D. 31 Dec. 1378 (*Mem. Bury*, III, 113; cf. PRO, C84/32/17). Lic. to el. 6 Jan. 1379 (*CPR 1377–81*, p. 296).

CANTERBURY (Kent), CHRIST CHURCH CATHEDRAL PRIORY (Holy Trinity) f. 997

Lists based on *Le Neve 1066–1300*, II, 8–12; *Le Neve 1300–1541*, IV, 5–6; Greatrex, *Biog. Reg.*, pp. 66–335 (Canterbury monks); also lists in *Heads*, I, 33–4; *VCH Kent*, II, 119–20.

Walter 1213–1222 El. *c.* June 1213 (*Gervase*, II, 108). Temps. 1 June 1213 (*Rot. Lit. Pat.*, p. 99b). D. 1222 (*Gervase*, II, 112), 6 Feb (or 7 Jan.: BL, Cotton ms. Nero C IX, ff. 3r (7 Jan.), 5r (6 Feb.); BL, Arundel ms. 68, ff. 12v (7 Jan.), 15v (6 Feb.)).

Mag. John of Sittingbourne 1222– M. of Christ Church, succ. 1222 (*Gervase*, II, 112). Archbp-el. of Canterbury Mar.–June 1232 (*Le Neve 1066–1300*, II, 6). Poss. the pr. John who occ. Sept. 1234 (Canterbury, Reg. E, f. 376v). Certainly d. by 1238 (*Gervase*, II, 133) and poss. by 1236 (see below). Obit 18 July (BL, Arundel ms. 68, f. 35r; Lambeth, ms. 20, fl. 203r).

John de Chetham –1238 Occ. Dec. 1237 (*Gervase*, II, 131), but presumably the unnamed pr. who was apparently apptd by the archbp and approved by the convent before 11 Aug. 1236 (*Reg. Greg. IX*, no. 3277). Forced by archbp to res. and became a Carthusian early Nov. 1238 and d. shortly afterwards (*Gervase*, II, 133; *Ann Waverley*, p. 320). Obit as *quondam* pr. 8 July (BL, Arundel ms. 68, f. 33v; Lambeth, ms. 20, f. 199v).

Roger de la Lee 1239–1244 M. of Christ Church, el. 7 Jan. 1239 (*Gervase* II, 146–7). Archbp's conf. withheld and monks excommunicated 14 Jan. (ibid., 150–1, cf. *MPCM*, II, 493). Appeals to pope and dispute continued until d. of archbp 1240 (*Gervase*, II, 151–80). Occ. 9 Oct. 1244 (Canterbury, Reg. A, f. 63r). Res. 1244 (*Gervase*, II, 202). D. 1258 (ibid., 206). Obit as Roger *quondam* pr. 24 Aug. (BL, Arundel ms. 68, f. 39r; Lambeth, ms. 20, f. 213r). Seal (*BM Seals*, no. 2832).

Nicholas of Sandwich 1244–1258 M. of Christ Church, succ. 1 Nov. 1244 (*Gervase*, II, 202, n. 1). Apptd and installed by archbp-el. 25–27 Oct. 1244 (*Ang. Sac.*, I, 174–5). Occ. 16 July 1258 (CUL, ms. Ee. V.31, f. 9r–v). Res. 1258 (*Gervase*, II, 207). Obit as *quondam* pr. 11 Feb. (BL, Arundel ms. 68, f. 16r; Lambeth, ms. 20, f. 163r). Seals (*BM Seals*, no. 2833).

Roger of St Alphege (de Sancto Elphego) **1258–1263** Sub-pr. of Christ Church, eln conf. by archbp 12 Nov. 1258 (BL, Add. ms. 6159, f. 5r; *Gervase*, II, 207). D. 29 Sept. 1263 (*Gervase*, II, 226). Obit as *quondam* pr. 29 Sept. (BL, Arundel ms. 68, f. 43v). Seal (*Mon. Seals*, p. 19).

Adam of Chillenden (Chillendenne) **1263/4–1274** Chamberlain of Christ Church, archbp's lic. to el. sought Sept./Oct. 1263 (*Gervase*, II, 226–7). El. and conf. by archbp 1263/4 (ibid., 228); installed 16 Apr. 1264 (ibid., 229). Archbp-el. of Canterbury 1270–2 (*Le Neve 1066–1300*, II, 7). D. 13 Sept. 1274 (*Gervase*, II, 278). Obit 13 Sept. (BL, Arundel ms. 678, f. 41v; Lambeth, ms. 20, f. 217v).

Thomas of Ringmer (Ringmere, Ryngemere, Ryngmere) **1274–1285** M. of Christ Church and archbp's chaplain, succ. and installed 19 Sept. 1274 (*Gervase*, II, 278). Res. to become a Cistercian at Beaulieu 17 Mar. 1285 (BL, Cotton ms. Galba E IV, f. 109v; *Ch. Bury*, p. 84, cf. *Reg. Pontissara*, I, 318; *Reg. Peckham*, III, 918). Archbp Pecham gtd absolution to Thomas for joining the Cistercians 16 July 1291 (*Reg. Peckham*, III, 980). Letter of Pope Celestine V to the archbp of Canterbury enabling him to gt a dispensation to Thomas who had res. as pr. and entered the Cistercian order and then left to become a hermit, 6 Oct. 1294 (*Reg. Winchelsey*, I, 496). Letter of archbp to pr. of Christ Church, remonstrating with him for ungenerous treatment of ex-pr. Thomas and non-payment of his pension 16 Apr. 1300 (ibid., II, 1321–2, cf. Smith, *Canterbury Cathedral Priory*, p. 61). Obit 11 May (BL, Arundel ms. 68, f. 27r; Lambeth, ms. 20, f. 186r).

Henry of Eastry 1285–1331 Treasurer of Christ Church, el. 8 Apr. 1285 (BL, Cotton ms. Galba E IV, f. 109v); conf. by archbp 9 Apr. (BL, Cotton ms. Julius D V, f. 62r). Installed 10 Apr. 1285 (*Gervase*, II, 292). D. 8 Apr. 1331, in the 92nd year of his age (BL, Arundel ms. 68, f. 23v). Seal (*BM Seals*, no. 2834; *Northumberland and Durham Seals*, p. 104, suppl. no. 46). See Sharpe, *Latin Writers*, pp. 167–8; N. Ramsay in P. Collinson et al. eds., *A History of Canterbury Cathedral*, pp. 353–62.

Richard de Oxenden 1331–1338 M. of Christ Church. el. 25 Apr and appt announced by the archbp 26 Apr. 1331 (Canterbury, Reg. G, f. 22v). D. 4 Aug. 1338 (BL, Add. ms. 6160, f. 252v; Canterbury, Lit. ms. D.12, f. 16v). Obit 4 Aug. (BL, Arundel ms. 68, f. 37r).

Robert Hathbrande 1338–1370 M. of Christ Church, el. 11 Sept. 1338 (BL, Add. ms. 6160, f. 252v). D. 16 July 1370 (Lambeth, Reg. Whittlesey, f. 31v). Seal (*BM Seals*, no. 2835).

Richard Gillyngham 1370–1376 M. of Christ Church, el. 2 Aug. and appt announced by archbp 3 Aug. 1370 (Lambeth, Reg. Whittlesey, f. 31v). Notification of pr.'s d. brought to archbp 31 Aug. 1376 (Lambeth, Reg. Sudbury, f. 27v; cf. Lambeth, ms. 20, f. 214v; BL, Arundel ms. 68, f. 40r – obit, 31 Aug.).

Stephen Mongeham (Mongham, Monyngham) **1376–1377** M. of Christ Church, el. 9 Sept. 1376, apptd 10 Sept. 1376 (Lambeth, Reg. Sudbury, ff. 27v, 30r, 33v). D. 14 June 1377 (Lambeth, ms. 20, f. 194r).

John Fynch (Fynche) **1377–1391** M. of Christ Church, apptd 25 July 1377 (Lambeth, Reg. Sudbury, ff. 30v, 39r–v, cf. Greatrex, p. 163 for the confusion over the eln date). D. 25 Jan. 1391 (Lambeth, Reg. Courtenay, ff. 333v–334v). Obit 25 Jan. – he was pr. for 13 years, 6 months, 2 weeks (BL, Arundel ms. 68, f. 14r).

CANTERBURY, ST AUGUSTINE St Peter and St Paul (Kent) f. 598 x 605
List in *VCH Kent*, II, 132; *Heads*, I, 34–7.

Master Alexander 1213/14–1220 M. of St Augustine's, bl. by pope (Thorne, pp. 170–1, with date 1212; Elmham, p. 41. *Ann. Dunstable*, p. 41 gives eln of unnamed abb. 1213, desc. as previously chamberlain of St Augustine's). Certainly the abbey was vacant on 4 Mar. 1213 (*Rot. Lit. Pat.*, p. 97). Bl. by Innocent III 18 May 1214 (Cheney, *Innocent III and England*, p. 206, n. 108). D. 4 Oct. 1220 (Thorne, pp. 180–1; Elmham, p. 41; Feltoe, *Three Canterbury Kalendars*, p. 26). Sharpe, *Latin Writers*, p. 47.

Hugh 1220–1225 Chamberlain of St Augustine's, el. Aug. 1220 (Thorne, p. 183, gives 24 Aug.; Elmham, p. 41, gives 26 Aug.); eln conf. by papal legate (Thorne, pp. 183–5). (H.) royal ass. 17 Nov. 1220 (*CPR 1216–25*, pp. 270–1). Occ. as abb.-el. when given royal protection on setting out for the Roman Curia 22 Jan. 1221 (ibid., p. 280). Bl. 1 Apr. 1221 at the Roman Curia (Elmham, p. 41) or 4 Apr. 1221 by S(tephen) de Nova Fossa (cardinal dcn of S. Angelo, later cardinal pr. of the Twelve Apostles) (Thorne, p. 188). D. 3 Nov. (ibid., p. 193) or 5 Nov. (Elmham, p. 42) 1224 (*sic*). D. (H.), lic. to el. 7 Nov. 1225 (*CPR 1225–32*, p. 2; cf. *Ann. Dunstable*, p. 100 – unnamed abb. d. 1226).

Robert of Battle (Bello) **1225/6–1253** Sacrist of St Augustine's, el. 23 Nov. 1224 (*sic*) (Thorne, p. 193) or 24 Nov. (Elmham, p. 42); royal ass. 22 Jan. 1226 (*CPR 1225–32*, p. 12). Bl. 8 May 1225 (*sic*, presumably for 1226) (Elmham, p. 42). Occ. from 21 Sept. 1227 to Nov. 1251 (*Kent F.*, p. 85; *Black Book*, p. 174). D. 14 Jan. 1253 (Thorne, p. 223) or 16 Jan. 1253 (Elmham, p. 48) or 17 Jan. 1253 (PRO, C84/1/24). Lic. to el. 29 Jan. 1253 (*CPR 1247–58*, p. 174). Seal (*BM Seals*, no. 2847).

Roger of Chichester (Cicestre, Cicestria, Cycestre) **1253–1272** Chamberlain of St Augustine's, el. 3 Feb. 1253 (Thorne, p. 223; Elmham, p. 48); royal ass. 22 Feb. 1253, writ *de intendendo* 30 June 1253 (*CPR 1247–58*, pp. 179, 203). Papal conf. 5 May 1253 (*CPL*, I, 286). Bl. by bp of London 20 Aug. 1253 (Thorne, p. 223; Elmham, p. 48). Apptd a papal chaplain 1258 (*CPL*, I, 360). D. 13 Dec. 1272 (*Ch. Bury*, p. 53). Lost ledger stone (*Earliest English Brasses*, p. 193, cf. Thorne, p. 257, n. 1). Seal (*BM Seals*, no. 2848; *Northumberland and Durham Seals*, p. 104, suppl. no. 47).

Nicholas Thorne (Thorn, de Spina) **1273–1283** 3rd pr. of St Augustine's, el. 3 Jan. 1273 (Thorne, p. 257; Elmham, p. 53); notification to pope of royal ass. 17 Jan. 1273 (*CPR 1272–81*, p. 3); temps. 15 June 1273 (ibid., p. 10). Eln conf. 4 Apr. 1273; bl. by [John of Toledo] cardinal bp of Porto 9 Apr. 1273 (Thorne, p. 257; Elmham, p. 53). Mand. for temps. by archbp of York and R. Burnell, archdn of York, acting on behalf of the king 18 May 1273 (PRO, C84/4/43). Res. acc. by pope 12 May 1283 (*CPL*, I, 468; Thorne, pp. 283–4; Elmham, p. 54); became a Carthusian (*Ch. Bury*, p. 79 – according to this source he went to the Curia on the pretext of a pilgrimage to St Nicholas at Bari). Order to take the abbey into the king's hands 21 June 1283 (*CFR 1272–1307*, p. 186, cf. Thorne, pp. 285–6). 6 Oct. 1283 pardon to abb. Thomas for trespass of Nicholas late abb., who having obtained the king's lic. to go on pilgrimage to Monte Cassino went to the Roman Curia and in the pope's presence, without consulting the king, ceded the monastery in favour of Thomas de Fyndon, m. of St Augustine's, wherefore the monastery was seized into the king's hands (*CPR 1281–92*, p. 79); 12 Oct. 1283 similar pardon to the abbey for the trespass, for a fine of 400 marks (*CFR 1272–1307*, p. 192). Pension gtd to ex-abb. 1294 (Thorne, pp. 324–5).

Thomas de Fyndon (Fyndona) **1283–1310** 3rd pr. of St Augustine's, apptd by pope 14 May 1283 and commn to archbp of Dublin or bp of London to bl. him (*CPL*, I, 468; Sayers no. 855), Thomas was in England at the time of the provision (*CFR 1272–1307*, p. 192) Papal bull of provision delivered to king 29 June 1283 (Thorne, p. 284). Bl. at London 4 Apr. [?1284] by archbp of Dublin (Thorne, p. 284; Elmham, p. 54). D. 16 Feb. 1310 (Elmham, p. 60; Thorne, p. 394). D., lic. to el. 23 Feb. 1310 (*CPR 1307–13*, p. 210). Lost ledger stone (*Earliest English Brasses*, p. 193). Seal (*BM Seals*, no. 2849).

Ralph de Borne (Bourne, Burne, Burun) **1310–1334** M. of St Augustine's, el. 7 Mar. 1310; eln conf. 15 June 1310 (Thorne, p. 395). Royal ass. 13 Mar. 1310, temps. 15 Oct. 1310 (*CPR 1307–13*, pp. 214, 283). Lic. to go overseas to prosecute the business of his eln 13 Mar. 1310 (*CCR 1307–13*, p. 200). Papal conf. of his eln 22 June 1310 (*CPL*, II, 69–70). Bl. 21 June 1310 at Avignon (Elmham, p. 60) or 22 June 1310 by bp of Ostia (Thorne, p. 395). D. 2 Feb. 1334 (Elmham, p. 63) or 3 Feb. 1334 (Thorne, p. 482). D. (R.), lic. to el. 9 Feb. 1334 (*CPR 1330–34*, p. 511).

Thomas Poucyn (Poucin, Poucy, Pousyn) **1334–1343** M. of St Augustine's, el. 1 Mar. 1334 (Thorne, p. 482; Elmham, p. 63); royal ass. 12 Mar. 1334, temps. 13 Sept. 1334 (*CPR 1330–34*, p. 524; *CPR 1334–38*, p. 7). Papal conf. of eln 3 June 1334 (*CPL*, II, 405); bl. at Avignon 12 June 1334 (Thorne, p. 482; Elmham, p. 63). D. 13 Sept. 1343 (Thorne, p. 503; Elmham, p. 64). D., lic. to el. 16 Sept. 1343 (*CPR 1343–45*, p. 120, cf. *CCR 1343–46*, p. 177). Lost ledger stone (*Earliest English Brasses*, p. 193). Sharpe, *Latin Writers*, p. 676.

William of Throwley (Thrulegh, Drulege, Thruley, Thrulleye, Thurlegh) **1343–1346** M. of St Augustine's, el. 2 Oct. 1343 (Thorne, p. 503; Elmham, p. 64); royal ass. 14 Oct. 1343, temps. 24 Feb. 1344 (*CPR 1343–45*, pp. 128, 211). Papal conf. of eln 19 Dec. 1343 (*CPL*, III, 125). Bl. at Avignon by bp of Sabina n.d. (Thorne, p. 503, but 11 Oct. according to Elmham, p. 64). D. 22 Sept. 1346 (Thorne, p. 504; Elmham, p. 64). D., lic. to el. 24 Sept. 1346 (*CPR 1345–48*, p. 190, cf. *CCR 1346–49*, p. 103).

[William de Kenyngton (Kemyngton, Keningtone, Kenynton) M. of St Augustine's, el. 5 Oct. 1346 (Thorne, p. 504; Elmham, p. 65); royal ass. 11 Oct. 1346 (*CPR 1345–48*, p. 192). Occ. as abb.-el. 15 Oct. 1346 when he was ordered not to leave the realm without the king's special order (*CCR 1346–49*, p. 157). Eln made in ignorance of papal provision and annulled 23 May 1347 (*CPL*, III, 240, 251). Occ. 17 June 1347 (ibid., 221). In a report of 25 July 1348 it is recorded that William was el. and the king forbade his proceeding to the Curia for conf. William petitioned the pope to issue a commn to examine the eln. The pope quashed the eln and provided John Devenys by apostolic authority (*CPR 1348–50*, p. 142; see *Nottingham Medieval Studies*, XXXV (1991), 79).]

John (de) Devenys (Devenesthe, Devenish, Devenissh, Devenysse) **1347–1348** M. of Winchester cath. and previously el. as bp of Winchester (ineffective), apptd by pope 23 May 1347 (*CPL*, III, 240, also 34–5, 38–9); mand. for induction 4 Oct. 1347 (ibid., 251). Admission refused by king and council until the king is informed further on the matter 3 July 1347 (*CPR 1345–48*, p. 345). Occ. 14 July, 22 July 1347 (*CPL*, III, 250, 246; *CPP*, p. 335). John went to the Curia 3 Apr. 1348 (Thorne, p. 556). D. 23 June 1348 and bur. in the Franciscan friary at Avignon (ibid., p. 557; Elmham, p. 65). D., lic. to el. 25 July 1348 (*CPR 1348–50*, p. 142). D. at the Apostolic See (*Orig. Papal Letters*, pp. 112–13, no. 222).

Thomas de Colwell (Colewell, Colewelle, Colwelle) **1348–1375** Sacrist of St Augustine's, el. 5 Aug. 1348 (Thorne, p. 557, but cf. Elmham, p. 65 – 5 Apr. (*sic*)); royal ass. 12 Aug. 1348, temps. 19 Dec. 1348 (*CPR 1348–50*, pp. 143, 220). Papal notification to king of his appt of Thomas 3 Oct. 1348 (*CPL*, III, 278; *Orig. Papal Letters*, pp. 112–13, no. 222); bl. at Avignon 4 Oct. 1348 (Elmham, p. 65); received insignia from cardinal bp of Sabina 12 Oct. 1348 (Thorne, pp. 557–8); lic. to return to abbey 15 Oct. 1348, Thomas having been bl. by Anibaldo [Frascati], cardinal bp of Tusculum (*CPL*, III, 302). D. 28 May 1375 (Elmham, p. 67). D., lic. to el. 4 June 1375 (*CPR 1374–77*, p. 111).

Michael de Pecham (Petham) **1375–1387** Chamberlain of St Augustine's, eln pres. to king for royal ass. 27 June 1375 (PRO, C84/31/29); royal ass. 2 July 1375, temps. 8 Oct. 1375 (*CPR 1374–77*, pp. 122, 172). Papal provision 17 Sept. 1375; bl. and prof. obed. to Holy See 7 Oct. 1375 (*Reg. Wykeham*, I, 66–9; cf. Thorne, p. 606 who says 6 Oct.). D. 11 Feb. 1387 (Thorne, p. 654; Elmham, p. 68). D., lic. to el. 19 Feb. 1387 (*CPR 1385–89*, p. 283).

CANWELL (Staffs), St Mary, St Giles and All Saints (Binns, p. 66). f. –1148 (priory) Lists in *VCH Staffs*, III, 216; Heads, I, 37.

H. Last recorded occ. 1209+ (*Mon. Angl.*, IV, 112, cf. Cheney, *Inn. III*, no. 846 for date. Possibly the same as Hugh (*Shenstone Chts.*, p. 249, no. 10; mentd *SHC*, XV, 37). Hugh occ. *temp.* Henry III (*Reg. Repingdon*, III, p. 79, no. 122).

Thomas Occ. 14 Sept. 1289 (*Mon. Angl.*, IV, 104, citing Shaw, *Hist. of Staffs*, II, 3); 1291 (PRO,

C85/55/27); 8 Dec. 1294 (Bodl., Staffs Cht. 17); Hil. 1295 (PRO, CP40/107, m. 34d); n.d. (late 13th/early 14th cents.) (Staffs RO, 3764/1).

Walter Occ. 5 Sept. 1315 (*Magnum Reg. Album Lichfield*, p. 42).

Henry of Rowley (Roulegh) **–1355** D. by 11 May 1355 (Lichfield, B/A/1/2, f. 197r).

John of Kingston (Kengeston, Kyngeston) **1355–** M. and *mansionarius* of Bermondsey, eln conf. 11 May 1355 (ibid.). Occ. Hilary term 1365 (*Staffs Plea Rolls 1360–87*, p. 40); 24 June 1368 (Bodl., Staffs Cht. 18).

The next recorded pr., **John**, occ. 7 Richard II (June 1383 x June 1384) (Bodl., Staffs Cht. 19). Prob. to be identified with **John Molton**, who occ. *temp.* Richard II (*Reg. Repingdon*, III, p. 78, no. 122).

CERNE (Dorset), St Peter and St Ethelwold f. –987

Lists in *VCH Dorset*, II, 57; *Heads*, I, 37.

Denis **–1219/20** Occ. 1204 x 5 (*Ped. Fin.*, II, 94); 1206 (*Rot. Lit. Pat.*, p. 64b); 1216 x 1220 (*Ctl. Loders*, pp. 62–4; see Axmouth); 1 Dec. 1218 (*Dorset F.*, p. 23). Res. shortly before 12 Feb. 1220 (*CPR 1216–25*, p. 228). See note in *HMC Middleton*, p. 52.

Richard **1220–?1232** (R.) pr. of Cerne, royal ass. 12 Feb. 1220 (*CPR 1216–25*, p. 228). Occ. n.d. *c.* 1225 (*HMC Middleton*, p. 59); 1231 (ibid., p. 61). Lic. to el. (no reason given for vacancy) 30 Mar. 1232 (*CPR 1225–32*, p. 468).

William of Hungerford **1232–?1244** M. of Cerne, royal ass. 30 Mar. 1232 (ibid.). Occ. Mich. Term 1228, East. Term 1229 (*CRR*, XIII, nos. 1146, 1907); 13 Apr. 1237 (*Ctl. Cerne*, p. 202); (W.) 16 Aug. 1242 (*Sarum Chts.*, p. 280, no. ccxxxix). Lic. to el. (no reason given for vacancy) 2 Mar. 1244 (*CPR 1232–47*, p. 420).

Richard de Suwell (Siwel) **1244–1260** M. of Cerne, royal ass. 20 Mar. 1244, writ *de intendendo* 24 Mar. 1244 (ibid., pp. 421–2). Bl. by bp of Salisbury at Potterne 15 May 1243 (*Sarum Chts.*, p. 283, no. ccxliii). D., lic. to el. 2 Apr. 1260 (*CPR 1258–66*, p. 119).

Philip of Bloxworth (Blokeswurth) **1260–1274** Pr. of Cerne, royal ass. 27 Apr. 1260, temps. 1 May 1260 (ibid., pp. 121, 67). D. by 4 Nov. 1274 (PRO, C84/5/8). D., lic. to el. 7 Nov. 1274 (*CPR 1272–81*, p. 63).

Thomas de Ebblosbury (Ebbelesborne, Ebleburn) **1274–1295/6** M. of Cerne, eln pres. to king for royal ass. 15 Nov. 1274 (PRO, C84/5/9); writ *de intendendo* 5 Dec. 1274 (*CPR 1272–81*, p. 74). Cert. conf. eln by bp of Salisbury 10 Dec. 1274 (PRO, C84/4/48). D., lic. to el. 2 Jan. 1296 (*CPR 1292–1301*, p. 180).

Gilbert of Minterne (Mynterna, Mynterne) **1296–1312** M. of Cerne, royal ass. 16 Jan. 1296 temps. 1 Feb. 1296 (ibid., pp. 182, 184). Cert. conf. eln by bp of Salisbury 26 Jan. 1296 (PRO, C84/12/27). D. by 30 Mar. 1312 (PRO, C84/17/2). D., lic. to el. 10 Apr. 1312 (*CPR 1307–13*, p. 452).

Ralph of Cerne (Cernelio) **1312–1324** Pr. of Cerne, royal ass. 17 May 1312, temps. 4 July 1312 (ibid., pp. 457, 467). Eln pres. to bp 5 June, commn to examine eln 20 June, eln conf. 26 June 1312 (*Reg. Gandavo*, II, 795–9; PRO, C84/17/4). D., lic. to el. 7 Apr. 1324 (*CPR 1321–24*, p. 402; cf. BL, Add. ms. 6165, f. 29r).

Richard of Osmington (Osmyn(g)ton) **1324–1356** M. of Cerne, royal ass. 17 Apr. 1324, temps. 11 May 1324 (*CPR 1321–24*, pp. 406, 410). Eln pres. to bp 19 Apr. 1324, eln conf. 8 May 1324, bl. 13 May 1324 (*Reg. Martival*, I, 419; PRO, C84/20/31). D. 16 Oct. 1356 (*Dorset IPM* no. 238; BL, Add. ms. 6165, f. 33r). D., lic. to el. 25 Oct. 1356 (*CPR 1354–58*, p. 464).

Stephen Sherrard (Sherard) **1356–1361** M. of Cerne, royal ass. 8 Nov. 1356, temps. 29 Nov. 1356 (ibid., pp. 468, 481). D., lic. to el. 7 Sept. 1361 (*CPR 1361–64*, p. 57).

Thomas Sewale **1361–1382** M. of Cerne, royal ass. 17 Sept. 1361, temps. 23 Sept. 1361 (ibid., pp. 61, 77). Eln conf. 20 Sept 1361 (Salisbury, Reg. Wyvil II, f. 294r). D. 29 June 1382 (PRO, C84/32/45; *Dorset IPM* no. 240). D., lic. to el. 4 July 1382 (*CPR 1381–85*, p. 150).

CHERTSEY (Surrey), St Peter ref. –964

Lists in V*CH Surrey*, II, 63; *Ctl. Chertsey*, II, pp. ix ff.; obits in Bodl., ms. Lat. Liturg. e. 6, ff. 4r–8v; *Heads*, I, 39.

Adam 1210–1223 El. *c.* 25 Apr. 1210 (*PR 10 John*, pp. 94–5). Abb. in post by Mich. 1210 (*PR 12 John*, pp. 79, 101, 162). Obit 4 Apr. (f. 5v). House vacant 4 Apr. 1223 (*CPR 1216–25*, pp. 369–70). Lic. to el. (no reason given for vacancy) 5 Apr. 1223 (ibid., p. 370). Unnamed abb. d. 1223 (*Ann. Waverley*, p. 298).[4]

Alan 1223–1261 M. of Chertsey, royal ass. 9 Apr. 1223 (*CPR 1216–25*, p. 371). Occ. from Oct. 1232 x Oct. 1223 to Oct. 1260 x Oct. 1261 (*Surrey F.*, pp. 18, 40). Obit 26 May (f. 6r). Lic. to el. (no reason given for vacancy) 12 July 1261 (*CPR 1258–61*, p. 165).

John of Medmenham (Medmeham) **1261–1272** M. of Chertsey, royal ass. 18 July 1261; temps. 29 July 1261, the eln having been conf. by B., archbp of Canterbury (ibid., pp. 168, 170). Prof. obed. 7 Aug. 1261 (*Arch. Cant.*, XXXVII (1925), 63; Canterbury D. & C., Ch. Ant. A41/25). Obit 22 Sept. (f.8r). D., lic. to el. 22 Sept. 1272 (*CPR 1266–72*, p. 678). Seal (*BM Seals*, nos. 2902–3).

Bartholomew of Winchester (Wintonia) **1272–1307** M. of Chertsey, eln pres. to king for royal ass. 4 Oct. 1272 (PRO, C84/4/16); royal ass. (Robert) 10 Oct. 1272; temps. (Bartholomew) 21 Oct. 1272 (*CPR 1266–72*, pp. 680, 684). Obit 15 July (f. 7r). D. by 2 Sept. 1307 (*Reg. Woodlock*, I, 200–1, 218, cf. *CPR 1307–13*, p. 1). Seal (*BM Seals*, no. 2904).

John of Rotherwick (Rotherwyk, Rothurwike, Rutherwike, Rutherwyk) **1307–1347** M. of Chertsey, royal ass. 2 Sept. 1307, temps. 27 Sept. 1307 (*CPR 1307–13*, pp. 1, 7). Proclamation of eln 13 Sept. 1307 – citation of opposers to be issued; letters testimonial of conf. and mand. to induct 29 Oct. 1307 (*Reg Woodlock*, I, 200–1, 218, 225). Cert. conf. eln by bp of Winchester 23 Sept. 1307 (PRO, C84/15/46). D. by 14 Jan. 1347 (*CCR 1346–49*, p. 134). D., lic. to el. 19 Jan. 1347 (*CPR 1345–48*, p. 223).

John of Benham 1347–1361 M. of Chertsey, royal ass. 28 Jan. 1347, temps. 15 Feb. 1347 (ibid., pp. 243, 250; PRO, SC1/56/86; SC1/40/47). Commn to enquire into eln 9 Feb. 1347; eln conf., bl. and prof. obed. 11 Feb. 1347 (*Reg. Edington*, I, nos. 157–61). D. by 9 Nov. 1361 (PRO, C84/28/17). D., lic. to el. 12 Nov. 1361 (*CPR 1361–64*, p. 104).

William (de) Clyve 1361–1370 Eln pres. to king for royal ass. 19 Nov. 1361 (PRO, C84/28/20). Eln conf. and bl. 4 Dec. 1361 (*Reg. Edington*, I, nos. 1476–79). M. of Chertsey, temps. 5 Dec. 1361 (*CPR 1361–64*, p. 124). D. by 4 Aug. 1370 (PRO, C84/30/26). D., lic. to el. 5 Aug. 1370 (*CPR 1367–70*, p. 457).

John (of) Usk (Uske) **1370–1400** M. of Chertsey, eln pres. to king for royal ass. 24 Aug. 1370 (PRO, C84/30/27); royal ass. 25 Aug. 1370; temps. 21 Sept. 1370 (*CPR 1367–70*, p. 465). Eln presented to bp 19 Sept., eln conf. 20 Sept.; bl. and prof. obed. 22 Sept. 1370; mand. to install s.d. (*Reg. Wykeham*, I, 32–5). D. 7 Sept 1400 (ibid., 229). D., lic. to el. 21 Sept. 1400 (*CPR 1399–1401*, p. 336).

CHESTER St Werburgh f. 907; 1092 x 3

Lists in *VCH Cheshire*, III, 144–5; *Ctl. Chester*, I, pp. 1ff.; basis in *Ann. Chester* and obits (ed. M. V. Taylor in *Liber Luciani*, pp. 85–102, with notes on abbots from other mss. of Ann.); *Heads*, I, 39.

---

[4] Maurice is mentd as former abb. in a case at Easter term 1236 (*CRR*, XV, no. 1694). This prob. refers to Martin 1197–1206 (*Heads*, I, 39).

Hugh Grylle 1208–1226 M. of Spalding (BL, Harley ms. 2071, f.16(2)r). El. 1208 (*Ann. Chester*, p. 48; cf. p. xx: installed 30 Mar. 1214 after Interdict). Occ. (H.) 1209, 1215 x 1216 (*Ctl. Chester*, I, nos. 60, 307); (H.) 2 Sept. 1216 (*Ctl. Burscough*, no. 166). D. 22 July 1226 (Ann. Chester, pp. xx, 54, 127). Cf. Obits, p. 96 which gives other d. dates too, 21 June, 21 Apr.

William Marmion (Marmiun) **1226–1228** El. 26 July 1226, bl. 28 July 1226 (*Ann. Chester*, pp. xx, 54 and n. 1, cf. 127). Occ. 6 Oct. 1226 (*Derbys F. (1886)*, p. 19). D. 1228 (*Ann. Chester*, pp. xx, 54, 127, cf. *Ctl. Chester*, p. ii, n. 15 (? 26 Sept.).

Walter of Pinchbeck (Pincebec(k), Pincebech) **1228–1240** El. 1228 and bl. 29 Sept. 1228 (ibid.). Occ. 7 Mar. 1230 (*Reg. Wells*, III, 183); 10 Jan. 1231 (*CPR 1225–32*, p. 444); 1238 (PRO, CP25/1/73/12, no. 223). D. 16 July 1240 (*Ann. Chester*, pp. xx, 60, 128). Obit 16 July (Obits, p. 97).

Roger Frend 1240–1249 Pr. of Chester, mand. for seisin 19 Aug. 1240 (*CR 1237–42*, p. 215). Bl. 21 Sept. 1240 (*Ann. Chester*, pp. xx, 60, 128). D. 1249 (ibid., pp. xx, 66, 128). Obit 23 Sept. (Obits, p. 100). Lic. to el. (no reason given for vacancy) 1 Oct. 1249 (*CPR 1247–58*, p. 48).

Thomas of Capenhurst (Capenthurst) **1249–1265** Pr. of Chester, royal ass. 15 Oct. 1249 (ibid., p. 51); mand. for seisin 2 Nov. 1249 (*CR 1247–51*, p. 234). D. 17 Apr. 1265 (*Ann. Chester*, p. 92), but later in *Ann.* it is stated that he d. 28 Apr. 1265 (ibid., p. 131). Obit 29 Mar. (Obits, pp. 92–3). Possibly 4 kal. May (28 Apr.) is a mistake for 4 kal. Apr. (29 Mar.), or vice versa.

Simon of Whitchurch (de Albo Monasterio) **1265–1291** El. 28 Apr. 1265 in the 45th year of his age and the 22nd after becoming a monk (*Ann. Chester*, p. 92), but cf. succ. 17 Apr. 1265 (ibid., p. 131). Eln conf. 25 May, bl. 31 May (ibid., p. 92). D. 22 Feb. 1291 (ibid., p. 116, cf. p. 134 – 22 Feb. 1294). Obit 22 Feb. (Obits, p. 91). D., lic. to el. 1 Mar. 1291 (*CPR 1281–92*, p. 423).

Thomas de Burchelles 1291–?1323 M. of Chester, el. 12 Mar. 1291 (*Ann. Chester*, p. 118); royal ass. 21 May 1291 temps. 24 May 1291 (*CPR 1281–92*, pp. 425, 429); mand. to deliver all issues received during the voidance 24 Jan. 1292 (*CCR 1288–96*, p. 216). Obit 23 Dec. (Obits, p. 102), so presumably 1323 from the date of his successor. Ledger stone (now lost) (*Earliest English Brasses*, p. 184).

William of Bebington (Bybynton, also Bynynton) **1324–1351/2?** M. of Chester, eln conf. 5 Feb. 1324 (Lichfield, B/A/1/2, ff. 100v–101r). House vacant by 21 July 1352 on d. of William (*CPL*, III, 468). Obit 20 Nov. [?1351] (Obits, p. 101).

Richard of Seynesbury (Seynesburi) **1352–1362** M. of Chester, papal order to enquire about eln and receive his fealty 21 July 1352 as Richard had been prevented from going to the Curia to obtain conf., having been bl. by order of the Court of Canterbury when at London (*CPL*, III, 468). 2 May 1362 Constable of Denbigh Castle ordered to receive the body of Richard of Seynesbury, last abb. of Chester, and to keep him safely in the castle until further notice (*Reg. Black Prince*, III, 442). 22 May 1362 testimony of Edward, prince of Wales, that Richard had voluntarily res. office to the abb. of St Albans, and now proposes to go into foreign parts to prosecute many processes to the destruction of the abbey. He is to be followed, arrested and held securely so that he may not be able to do anything prejudicial to the king or the abbey (*CPR 1361–64*, p. 214). House void by his res. at the Curia by 6 Mar. 1363 (*Reg. Stretton*, I, 162–3). Indictment of two monks and others accused of assaulting ex-abb. Richard n.d. (?1362–3) (Chester RO, Pentice ctl., CHB/2, f. 77r–v). 4 Feb. 1364 the Constable of Conway castle, in whose keeping he is on account of notorious faults, destructions and damage done to the abbey, is ordered to deliver him to the abb. of Chester, to sojourn in the abbey as a monk (*Reg. Black Prince*, III, 463–4). He refused obed. to his successor, Thomas, and left the abbey without permission in 1368. Papal mand. to compel his return 10 May 1368 (*CPL*, IV, 70; Logan, *Runaway Religious*, p. 192). 31 Oct. 1374 safe conduct for 6 months for Richard, 'abb.' of Chester in going to England and other parts and in returning hence to the Papal Curia (*CPL*, IV, 196). Obit 22 July (Obits, p. 97–8).

Thomas of Newport (Neuport) **1363–1386** M. of Chester, priest, papal provision 6 Mar. 1363, mand. to install by bp 27 Sept. 1363 (*Reg. Stretton*, II, 162–3). Obit 26 May (prob.) (Obits, p. 95). D. 26 May 1386 (PRO, C84/33/45). D., lic. to el. 1 June 1386 (*CPR 1385–89*, p. 152).

COLCHESTER (Essex), St John f. 1096 x 1097
   Lists in *VCH Essex*, II, 40; basis in BL, Cotton ms. Nero D VIII, ff. 345–6; *Ctl. Colchester*, pp. xix–xxi; *Heads*, I, 40.

Adam de Campes *c.*1194/5–1238 ruled 44 years. Occ. 23 Jan. 1197 (*FF. 7–8 Richard I*, no. 74); 14 Dec. 1237 (*ECSP*, no. 99). D. 20 Feb. 1238 (Bodl., ms. Gough Essex 1. f. 24v). Lic. to el. (no reason given for vacancy) 27 Feb. 1238 (*CPR 1232–47*, p. 211). Said in 1302 inquisition to have died 68 years previously (*Cal. Misc. Inq.*, I, 523).

William de Wande (Wanda, Waude) **1238–1245** M. of Colchester, royal ass. 6 Mar. 1238 (*CPR 1232–47*, p. 211); mand. for seisin 8 Mar. 1238 (*CR 1237–42*, pp. 32–3). Cess. in his 8th year (Bodl., ms. Gough Essex 1. f. 24v). Res., lic. to el. 17 Apr. 1245 (*CPR 1232–47*, p. 450).

William of Spaldwick (Spaldewic, Spaldewik) **1245–1272** Royal ass. 21 Apr. 1245, writ *de intendendo* 22 Apr. 1245 (ibid., p. 451). Occ. 8 Apr. 1272 (*CPR 1266–72*, p. 641). D. 29 June 1271 (*recte* 1272) in his 27th year as abb. (Bodl., ms. Gough Essex 1. f. 25r). D., lic to el. 8 July 1272 (*CPR 1266–72*, p. 665).

Robert of Greensted (Grenstede, Grinsede) **1272–1306** Temps. 6 Aug. 1272, eln having been conf. by Fulk Lovel, guardian of the spirituality of London (ibid., pp. 668, 672). D. 13 Oct. 1306 in his 36th (*sic*) year as abb. (Bodl., ms. Gough Essex 1. f. 25r). D., lic. to el. 27 Oct. 1306 (*CPR 1301–07*, p. 466).

John de Bruges 1306–1311 M. of Colchester, royal ass. 8 Dec. 1306 (ibid., p. 485). Notification of conf of eln by bp of London and mand. to restore temps. 27 Jan. 1306 (*Cal. Chanc. Warr.*, pp. 258–9). D. 31 Oct. 1306 in his 6th year as abb. (Bodl., ms. Gough Essex 1. f. 25r) *or* 1 Nov. 1311 (PRO, C84/16/46). D. (J.), lic. to el. 6 Nov. 1311 (*CPR 1307–13*, p. 397).

Walter of Huntingfield (Huntingfeld, Huntyngfelde) **1311–1326** Pr. of Colchester, eln pres. for royal ass. 12 Nov. 1311 (PRO, C84/16/47); royal ass. 13 Nov. 1311, temps. 30 Nov. 1311 (*CPR 1307–13*, pp. 399, 404). Cert. conf. eln by bp of London 27 Nov. 1311 (PRO, C84/16/50). Lic. for annual absences 20 Oct. 1312 (*Reg. Baldock*, p. 149). D. 15 Nov. 1326 in his 16th year as abb. (Bodl., ms. Gough Essex 1. f. 25r; cf. PRO, C84/10/29).

William of Glemham 1326–1327 M. of Colchester, royal ass. 10 Dec. 1326, temps. 19 Dec. 1326 (*CPR 1324–27*, pp. 338, 339). D. 30 Aug. 1327 in his 1st year as abb. (Bodl., ms. Gough Essex 1. f. 25r; PRO, C84/21/38). D., lic. to el. 2 Sept. 1327 (*CPR 1327–30*, p. 147).

John of Wymondham (Wymund(e)ham) **1327–1349** M. of Colchester, eln pres. to king for royal ass. 9 Sept. 1327 (PRO, C84/21/39); royal ass. 12 Sept. 1327, temps. 3 Sept. 1327 (*CPR 1327–30*, pp. 164, 167). Cert. conf. eln by bp of London [ ] Oct. 1327 (PRO, C84/21/41). D. 24 Aug. 1349 in his 23rd year as abb. (Bodl., ms. Gough Essex 1. f. 25r) *or* D. 25 Aug. 1349 (PRO, C84/26/15). D., lic., to el. (John) 25 Aug. 1349, cf. 24 Aug. (Robert) (*CPR 1348–1350*, pp. 362, 363). Seal (*BM Seals*, no. 2984; *Mon. Seals*, p. 25).

Simon of Blyton 1349–1353 Letter to the king announcing Simon's eln 4 Sept. 1349 (PRO, C241/126/154). Royal ass. 6 Sept. 1349, temps. 23 Sept. 1349 (*CPR 1348–50*, pp. 373, 378). Cert. of conf. eln by bp of London 19 Sept. 1349 (PRO, C84/24/23). Cess. by 3 July 1353

(PRO, C84/27/13). Res., lic. to el. 4 July 1353 (*CPR 1350–54*, p. 476). Seal (M.R. Hull, 'Fourteenth-century seal of Simon de Blyton, abbot of Colchester', *TEAS*, n.s. XXIV (1951), 69–96).

Thomas Moveron (Moveroun) **1353–** Eln pres. to king for royal ass. 7 July 1353 (PRO, C84/27/14); royal ass. 10 July 1353, temps. 12 July 1353 (*CPR 1350–54*, pp. 478–9). Cert. of conf. eln by bp of London 11 July 1353 (PRO, C84/27/16). Occ. 28 Sept. 1353 (*CCR 1349–54*, p. 619).

Simon of Blyton (again) **–1368** Occ. 25 June 1358 (*CCR 1354–60*, p. 513); 1360 (*Colchester Leger Book*, p. 108); 1361 (ibid., pp. 110, 118; *Reg. Sudbury*, I, 227–8); 1363 (*CPL*, IV, 35); 1364 (*Ctl. Colchester*, II, 498; *Reg. Sudbury*, II, 142). D. 29 Nov. 1368 (Bodl., ms. Gough Essex 1. f. 25v) *or* D. 3 Dec. 1368 (*Reg. Sudbury*, I, 144). D., lic. to el. 4 Dec. 1368 (*CPR 1367–70*, p. 184).

Thomas Stukele(e) (Stucle) **1368–1369** M. of Colchester, doctor of canon law, eln pres. to king for royal ass. 13 Dec. 1368 (PRO, C84/29/45); royal ass. 16 Dec. 1368, temps. 21 Dec. 1368 (*CPR 1367–70*, pp. 181, 185). Commn to examine eln 15 Dec. 1368; cert. 19 Dec.; eln conf. 20 Dec. 1368 (*Reg. Sudbury*, II, 142–50). D. 8 Oct. 1369 and bur. 9 Oct. (ibid., 112; PRO, C84/30/13; Bodl., ms. Gough Essex 1. f. 25v). D., lic. to el. 9 Oct. 1369 (*CPR 1367–70*, p. 309).

Richard of Colne 1369–1375 Pr. of Snape, m. of Colchester, el. 15 Oct. 1369 (*Reg. Sudbury*, I, 112–18); eln pres. to king for royal ass. 16 Oct. 1369 (PRO, C84/30/14); royal ass. 17 Oct. 1369, temps. 26 Oct. 1369 (*CPR 1367–70*, pp. 310, 311; *Reg. Sudbury*, I, 109–10). Commn to examine eln 21 Oct.; cert. 23 Oct. 1369 (*Reg. Sudbury*, I, 110–12). D. 26 July 1375 (*Colchester Leger Book*, p. 97; PRO, C84/31/33; Bodl., ms. Gough Essex 1. f. 25v). D., lic. to el. 29 July 1375 (*CPR 1374–77*, p. 129).

John (of) Dedham 1375–1377 M. of Colchester, eln pres. to king for royal ass. 3 Aug. 1375 (PRO, C84/25/28); royal ass. 5 Aug. 1375, temps. 12 Aug. 1375 (*CPR 1374–77*, pp. 130–1). D. 25 Oct. 1377 (PRO, C84/32/4; Bodl., ms. Gough Essex 1. f. 25v). D., lic. to el. 28 Oct. 1377 (*CPR 1377–81*, p. 33).

William de Gritton (Grettone, Grittone) **1377–1380** M. of Colchester, eln pres. to king for royal ass. 5 Nov. 1377 (PRO, C84/32/5); royal ass. 11 Nov. 1377, temps. 14 Nov. 1377 (*CPR 1377–81*, pp. 58–9). Cert. of conf. eln by bp of London 13 Nov. 1377 (PRO, C84/32/6). D. 24 Nov. 1380 in his 3rd year as abb. (Bodl., ms. Gough Essex 1. f. 25v) *or* D. 25 Oct. 1380 (PRO, C84/32/26). D., lic to el. 27 Nov 1380 (*CPR 1377–81*, p. 560).

COVENTRY (Warws), St Mary, St Peter, St Osburga, and All Saints f. 1043; 1102 (Cath. Priory) Lists in *VCH Warws*, II, 58; *Heads*, I, 40–1; *Le Neve 1300–1541*, X, 4–5 (from 1294). Greatrex, *Biog. Reg.*, 336–76 for biographical details of the monks of Coventry.

Geoffrey 1216–1235 Royal ass. 8 July 1216 (*Rot. Lit. Pat.*, p. 190). Occ. from Mich. 1221 (*Warws F.*, I, no. 245); 27 May 1233 (*CPL*, I, 134). Unnamed pr. d. 1235 (*Ann. Tewkesbury*, p. 102). Lic. to el. (no reason given for vacancy) 16 Sept. 1235 (*CPR 1232–47*, p. 118). See Sharpe, *Latin Writers*, p. 123; *EEA*, 17, 120–3.

Master Roger of Watton (Wotton) **1235–1249** M. of Coventry, royal ass. 19 Sept. 1235; writ *de intendendo* 28 Apr. 1236 (*CPR 1232–47*, pp. 118, 143). Eln quashed, but bp apptd him (*Magnum Reg. Album Lichfield*, p. 340, no. 712). Occ. 3 Nov. 1236 (*Staffs F.* 2, p. 234); 8 July 1248, 6 Feb. 1249 (*Magnum Reg. Album Lichfield*, p. 169, no. 345; p. 287, no. 596). Cess., lic. to el. 26 May 1249 (*CPR 1247–58*, p. 42).

William of Brightwalton (Brithwauton, Brichtwalton, Brythwalton) **1249–1280** M. of Coventry, occ. 21 Sept. 1249 (ibid., p. 48). Cess. by 2 May 1280 (PRO, C84/6/38). Cess., lic. to el. 9 May 1280 (*CPR 1272–81*, p. 369).

Thomas (de) Pavy 1280–1294 M. of Coventry, eln pres. to king for royal ass. 15 May 1280 (PRO, C84/7/3); royal ass. 19 May 1280, temps. 3 June 1280 (*CPR 1272–81*, pp. 370, 376). D. 11 Jan. 1294 (PRO, C84/11/36–7). D., lic. to el. 16 Jan. 1294 (*CPR 1292–1301*, p. 60). Seal (*Mon. Seals*, p. 27).

Henry of Leicester (Leycestre) 1294– M. of Coventry, petition to king for royal ass. 27 Jan. 1294 (PRO, C84/11/38); royal ass. 2 Feb. 1294, temps. 11 Feb. 1294 (*CPR 1292–1301*, pp. 61, 62). Cert. of conf. of eln by bp of Lichfield 8 Feb. 1294 (PRO, C84/11/41–2). Occ. (Henry) 1299 (*HMC R. R. Hastings*, I, 21); 7 Nov. 1305 (*CPR 1301–07*, p. 395); 26 Mar. 1313 (*CPR 1307–13*, p. 600); 2 May 1313 (*CCR 1307–13*, p. 530); 1318 (BL, Add. Cht. 21237); Mich. 1320 (PRO, KB27/242, m. 21); 19 Feb. 1324 and [ ] 1325 (*Parliamentary Writs*, II, div. 3, p. 732).

Henry *dictus* Houwhel Papal mand. 25 Apr. 1324 to enquire touching charges of simony, perjury and sortilege against him (*CPL*, II, 237). (see below).

Henry Irreys 12 Sept. 1328 arrangements completed for the chantry, at the altar of the Holy Trinity and St Mary, for Henry Irreys *nuper* prior and for the family, Robert and William of Leicester, canons of Lichfield, etc. (Lichfield, B/A/1/3, f. 27r). See Greatrex, p. 359. Initially this would suggest that Henry Irreys and Henry of Leicester were one and the same person, but the evidence is difficult. Henry of Leicester was named at his admission in 1294; likewise a Henry of Leicester vacated the priory by death in 1342 (see below), but in 1328 there is a reference to Henry [Irreys] former pr., thereby indicating at least two pr. Henrys. Add to this the reference of Houwhel in 1324 (see above). Occ. (Henry of Leicester) 31 Oct. 1326, 24 Feb. 1329, 14 Aug. 1333 (Bodl., Ashmole ms. 794, ff. 16v, 29v, 47r; Greatrex, p. 362); (Henry) 20 Apr. 1326 (*CChR 1300–26*, p. 488); 21 July 1329 (PRO, E326/3925); 1336 (*Select Cases of Trespass*, pp. 182–3); Mich. 1337 (PRO, CP40/213, attorneys m. 9); 25 Jan. 1339 (*Ctl. Boarstall*, p. 8). D. (Henry), lic. to el. 6 Feb. 1342 (*CPR 1340–43*, p. 375). Conf. of eln of his successor notes that priory was vacant by the d. of Henry of Leicester (Lichfield, B/A/1/2, ff. 38v–39r).

William Irreys 1342–1349 Sacrist of Coventry, royal ass. 7 Mar. 1342, temps. 4 May 1342 (*CPR 1340–43*, pp. 390, 431). Eln conf. 19 Apr. 1342 on the d. of Henry de Leyc' (Lichfield, B/A/1/2, ff. 38v–39r). D. by 29 July 1349 (PRO, C84/26/8). D., lic. to el. 1 Aug. 1349 (*CPR 1348–50*, p. 353).

William of Dunstable (Dunstaple) 1349–1361 Sacrist of Coventry, royal ass. 10 Aug. 1349, temps. 1 Sept. 1349 (ibid., pp. 357, 373). Cert. of conf. of eln by bp of Lichfield 26 Aug. 1349 (PRO, C84/26/16). D. by 30 June 1361 (PRO, C84/28/49). D., lic. to el. 2 July 1361 (*CPR 1361–64*, p. 35).

William de Greneburgh (Grenburgh) 1361–1390 M. of Coventry, royal ass. 13 July 1361, temps. 27 July 1361 (ibid., pp. 42, 47). Eln conf. 23 July (*Reg. Stretton*, I, 20). D. by 12 Sept. 1390 (PRO, C84/34/42). D., lic. to el. 16 Sept. 1390 (*CPR 1388–92*, p. 301).

CROWLAND (Lincs), St Bartholomew and St Guthlac (cf. Binns, p. 69 St Mary, St Bartholomew and St Guthlac) ref. +971.

Lists in *VCH Lincs*, II, 117; basis in Orderic, II, 281ff.; 15th cent. list from BL, Cotton ms. Vespasian B. XI, (Vita abbatum Croylandie) ff. 80r–82r; F. M. Page, *Estates of Crowland Abbey*, p. 159; *Heads*, I, 41–2.

Henry de Longo Campo (Longchamp) 1190–1236 Brother of William de Longchamp, bp of Ely, m. of Evesham, el. 1190 (Fulman, I, 457; date confirmed by *Walt. Cov.*, I, p. xli; *Ch. Peterborough*, p. 3). Abb. 46 years (list; Vita Abb., f. 81r). D. 1236 (unnamed abb.) (*Ann. Dunstable*, p. 144). House void, lic. to el. (no reason given for vacancy) 20 Sept. 1236 (*CPR 1232–47*, p. 158). Notif. to king of d. of abb. n.d. (1236) (BL, Add. Cht. 5863). Seal (*BM Seals*, no. 3017).

[**Walter of Weston** M. of Crowland, royal ass. 28 Sept. 1236 (*CPR 1232–47*, p. 159; cf. p. 161). El. by conv. against the form of the [Lateran] Council *c.* Sept. 1236 (*Reg. Grosseteste*, p. 11) and see above.]

Richard 1236–1248 Cellarer of Bardney, apptd by bp of Lincoln by authority of the Council Sept. 1236 x June 1237, *c.* Sept.–Oct. 1236 (ibid.). Writ *de intendendo* 18 Oct. 1236 (*CPR 1232–47*, p. 161). Occ. 12 Nov. 1247 (*Lincs F.*, II, 45). Ruled 11 years D. 17 June (1248) (Vita Abb., f. 81v; list – Fulman, I, 479, gives 10 years). Lic. to el. (no reason given for vacancy) 22 June 1248 (*CPR 1247–58*, p. 20).

Thomas de Welle (Well') **1248–1254** M. of Crowland, eln conf. & bl. on death of Richard, June 1248 x June 1249 (*Reg. Grosseteste*, p. 105). Called sub-pr. of Crowland (Fulman, I, 479). Mand. for seisin 19 July 1248 (*CPR 1247–51*, pp. 66–7). Lic. to el. (no reason given for vacancy) 12 Oct. 1254 (*CPR 1247–58*, p. 33). Rules 6 years '*letali morbo decoctus*' 8 Oct. (Vita Abb., f. 81v), but cf. d. 15 Oct. 1254 (*Mon. Angl.*, II, 102).

Ralph Merk (de Merch(e)) **1254–1280** M. of Crowland, royal ass. 26 Oct. 1254, writ *de intendendo* 9 Nov. 1254 (*CPR 1247–58*, pp. 373, 391). Ruled 26 years; d. 29 Sept. 1281 (*sic*) (Vita Abb., ff. 81v–82r). D., lic. to el. 7 Oct. 1280 (*CPR 1272–81*, p. 398). D. Mich. 1280 (*Mon. Angl.*, II, 102).

Richard of Crowland (Crouland, Croyland, Croylaund) **1280–1303** M. of Crowland, el. 27 Oct. 1280, eln quashed and apptd by bp of Lincoln 6 Nov. 1280, bl. 10 Nov. 1280 (*Reg. Sutton*, I, 8–9). Writ *de intendendo* 5 Nov. 1280 (*CPR 1272–81*, p. 402). In 1290 described as papal chaplain (*CPL*, I, 515). Cess. 10 Nov., lic. to el. 26 Nov. 1303 (*CPR 1301–07*, pp. 167, 200; PRO, C84/15/3).

Simon of Luffenham (Suthluffenham) **1303–1324** M. of Crowland, eln pres. to king for royal ass. 20 Dec. 1303 (PRO, C84/15/5); royal ass. 25 Dec. 1303 to Simon, 'secretary' of the cell of Freiston to be abb., temps. 28 Jan. 1303 (*CPR 1301–07*, pp. 204, 207). Eln conf. 16 Jan. 1304. bl. 19 Jan. 1304 (Lincoln, Ep. Reg., II, f. 9v). Attended Council of Vienne 1311 (*CPR 1307–13*, pp. 388–9). Cess. 16 Sept. 1324 (PRO, C84/20/34). Cess. of Simon de Luffenham deceased (*sic*), lic. to el. 22 Sept. 1324 (*CPR 1324–27*, p. 24). House vacant by cess. of Simon (*Reg. Burghersh*, I, no. 120). '*Pro demeritis depositus est*' (Vita Abb., f. 82r).

Henry of Casewick (Casewik, Casewyk) **1324–1359** Pr. of Crowland, el. pres. to king for royal ass. 3 Oct. 1324 (PRO, C84/20/39); royal ass. 9 Oct. 1324, temps. 30 Nov. 1324 (*CPR 1324–27*, pp. 33, 55). Eln conf. 29 Nov. 1324, bl. 23 Dec. 1324 (*Reg. Burghersh*, I, no. 120). 18 Aug. 1344 royal protection and custody on acct of its poverty, gtd to archbp of Canterbury and the earl of Northampton (*CPR 1343–45*, p. 339). D., lic. to el. 1 Feb. 1359 (*CPR 1355–61*, p. 168). Ruled 35 years (Vita Abb., f. 82r).

Thomas (of) Barnack (Bernak) **1359–1378** M. of Crowland, eln pres. to king for royal ass. 10 Feb. 1359 (PRO, C84/27/44); royal ass. 19 Feb. 1359, temps. 11 Mar 1359 (*CPR 1358–61*, pp. 178, 181). Eln pres. to bp of Lincoln 20 Feb. 1359, eln examined 7 Mar. 1359, conf. 7 Mar. 1359 (Lincoln, Ep. Reg., IX, f. 137r). Occ. 14 Feb. 1378 (*CPR 1377–83*, p. 76). Ruled 14 years and died 12 March (1378) (Vita Abb., f. 82r). D., lic. to el. 15 Mar. 1378 (*CPR 1377–81*, p. 146).

DURHAM CATHEDRAL PRIORY, St Cuthbert f. 28 May 1083

List based on *Le Neve 1066–1300: II, Monastic Cathedrals*, pp. 32–36; *Le Neve 1300–1541: VI, Northern Province*, pp. 109–10; other lists in *VCH Durham*, II, 102–3; *Heads*, I, 43–4. Medieval lists from DCD, Cart. II, pd *Simeon of Durham*, I, pp. xlviii–l (list 1 – unreliable); DCD, Reg. II, f. 350v (list 2); BL, Cotton ms. Vespasian A VI, f. 62v (list 3). I am grateful to Mr A. J. Piper for help with this list.

William (of Durham) 1212/13–1218 El. 1212/13 (*Scriptores Tres*, p. 27 (states he was a native of Durham); list 1 gives –1208, list 2 1212–14); occ. *c.* 1213 (*Rot. Chart.*, p. 208a–b); 20 Feb. 1214 (ibid., p. 207b); 22 Jan. 1217 (*Feodarium Prioratus Dun.*, p. 158n); late Jan. 1218 (*Ch. Melrose*, p. 70). D. 14 May 1218 (ibid.; cf. obit (*LV Durham*, p. 150; BL, Harl. ms. 1804, f. 14r); '1214' in list 1).

Ralph Kerneth 1218–1234 Called Gernet (*Cal. Misc. Inq.*, II, 219). Said to have been el. 1214 (DCD, Reg. II, f. 350v), but this is impossible if predecessor d. in office 1218. Occ. 11 Nov. 1218 (DCD, 4.13.Spec.34, m. 1); 10 Dec. 1218 (*Misc. D. M. Stenton*, p. 213 = *Lincs F.*, I, p. 143). 17 May 1231 papal dispensation for illegitimacy (*CPL*, I, 128). D. 4 Mar. 1234 (*Obit roll of W. Ebchester and J. Burnby*, pp. 45–8). Commem. 8 Mar. (*LV Durham*, p. 149; BL, Harl. ms. 1804, f. 13v); 9 Mar. (BL, Harl. ms. 4664, f. 127r).

Thomas of Melsonby 1234–1244 Pr. of Coldingham (*Feodarium Prioratus Dun.*, p. 217). Bp's lic. to el. 4 Mar. 1234 (DCD, Loc. XIII: 2). Occ. 11 June 1234 (DCD, 3.2.Spec.10). El. Bp. of Durham 1 June 1237 (*Ann. Durham*, p. 6); royal objections (ibid., p. 7; *Scriptores Tres*. p. 38). After suit before archbp of York and pope (cf. *CPR 1232–47*, pp. 198, 206, 223, 231). Last occ. 22 May 1244 (DCD, 3.2.Spec.12b). Said to have res. 1244 (*Scriptores Tres*, p. 41; DCD, Cart. II, f. lv). D. by 18 Sept. 1244 (DCD, 1.6. Pont. 15). Commem. 15 Sept. (*LV Durham*, p. 151; BL, Harl. ms. 1804, f. 15r; BL, Harl. ms. 4664, f. 130r).

Bertram of Middleton (Medilton) **1244–1258** Bp's lic. to el. 18 Sept. 1244 on d. of pr. Thomas (DCD, 1.6.Pont. 15). El. 22 Sept. 1244 (*Ann. Durham*, p. 9; *Scriptores Tres*, p. 41). Res. acc. by bp 15 Aug. 1258 (*Ann. Durham*, pp. 12–14; *Scriptores Tres*, pp. 43–4). Case brought against ex-pr. 15 May 1266 (*Ann. Durham*, p. 16). Commem. 8 Feb. (*LV Durham*, p. 149; BL, Harl. ms. 1804, f. 13r). Seal (*Durham Seals*, p. 552, no. 3431).

Hugh of Darlington (Derlington) **1258–1273** Sub-pr. of Durham, bp's lic. to el. 15 Aug. 1258 (*Ann. Durham*, p. 14). El. 16 Aug. 1258 (ibid., pp. 14–15; *Scriptores Tres*, p. 44). Res. 26 Dec. 1272 (*Ann. Durham*, pp. 19–20: *Scriptores Tres*, pp. 48–9). Res. accepted 8 Jan. 1273 (*Ann. Durham*, pp. 26–30; *Scriptores Tres*, p. 53). Seal (*Durham Seals*, p. 552, no. 3432). For second term see below. Occ. as former pr. Easter 1275 acting as an executor of the testament of Bp Robert of Durham (PRO, CP40/9, mm. 11d, 31d).

Richard of Claxton 1273–1285 Pr. of Holy Island. Bp's lic. to el. 11 Jan 1273 (*Ann. Durham*, pp. 32–6). El. 26 Jan. 1273 (DCD, Loc. I: 60 m. 2; *Ann. Durham*, pp. 36–41; *Scriptores Tres*, p. 55). Installed 2 Feb. 1273 (*Ann. Durham*, pp. 44–5; *Scriptores Tres*, p. 55). Res. 27 Dec. 1285 (*Ann. Durham*, p. 65). Commem. 27 Mar. (*LV Durham*, p . 150; BL, Harl. ms. 1804, f. 13v; BL, Harl. ms. 4664, f. 127r). Seal (*BM Seals*, no. 3094; *Durham Seals*, pp. 552–3, nos. 3433–4).

Hugh of Darlington (Derlington, Derlyngton) **1286–1290** Bp's lic. to el. 28 Dec. 1285, el. for second term 11 Jan. 1286 (*Ann. Durham*, pp. 67, 75, 82); eln conf. 22 Jan. 1286 (ibid., p. 84; cf; DCD, Misc. Cht. 7209). Installed 7 Feb. 1286 (*Scriptores Tres*, p. 72); 7 Feb. (*Ann. Durham*, p. 84). Res. 11 Mar. 1290 (*Scriptores Tres*, p. 72). Still alive 16 Mar. 1290 (DCD, 1.6.Pont. 11; *Recs. A. Bek*, pp. 20–1, refer to provision made for him). Commem. ?25 June (*LV Durham*, p. 150; BL, Harl. ms. 1804, f. 14r; BL, Harl. ms. 4664, f. 128v). Bp's lic. to el. 16 Mar. 1290 (DCD, 1.6.Pont. 11; *Recs. A. Bek*, pp. 20–1, no. 17).

Richard de Hoton
Henry of Lusby (Luceby)

Hoton, pr. of Lytham, el. 24 Mar. 1290, eln conf. 28 Mar. 1290 (*Scriptores Tres*, p. 73). Installed 9 Apr. (ibid.). For the great struggle between Bp Bek and Pr. Hoton see C. M. Fraser, *A history of Antony Bek, bishop of Durham 1283–1311* (Oxford, 1957), chap. 7 'The signifi-cance of the visitation by Bishop Bek of the convent of Durham in 1300' (pp. 123–52) and chap. 8 'An ecclesiastical *cause célèbre*' (pp. 153–75); also *Gesta Dunelmensia A.D. MCCC*, ed. R. K. Richardson in *Camden Miscellany XIII* (Camden, 3rd ser., 34, 1924), pp. i–xiv,

1–58. Hoton excommunicated by bp 20 May 1300 for contumacy at visitation (*Recs. A. Bek*, pp. 62–67, no. 67); depr. 21 May 1300 (ibid., pp. 68–72, nos. 69–70). Award made by king between bp and pr. and convent 20 June 1300 (ibid., pp. 72–4. no. 71), but not put into effect (*Gesta Dunelmensia*, pp. 17–22).

Lusby, pr. of Holy Island, apptd by bp 10 Aug. 1300 (*Recs. A. Bek*, pp. 74–6; *Scriptores Tres*, p. 76). Eln of Lusby conf. 16 Aug. 1300 (*Gesta*, p. 30). Lusby made forcible entry into priory 20 Aug. 1300 (*Gesta*, p. 31; *Scriptores Tres*, p. 76). Hoton removed from stall and imprisoned and Lusby formally installed 24 Aug. 1300 (*Gesta*, pp. 36–9). Hoton res. 29 Sept. 1300, exemplification by bp 2 Oct. (*Recs. A. Bek*, pp. 76–8, no. 73). Hoton in the priory prison 29 Sept.–16 Dec. 1300 (*Gesta*, p. 52). Hoton had royal leave to go to papal court for two years 1, 26 Mar. 1301 (*CPR 1292–1301*, pp. 578, 582). Eln of Lusby declared uncanonical and the restoration of Hoton ordered by the pope 29 Nov. 1301 (*CPL*, I, 597; *Scriptores Tres*, p. 79). Lusby excommunicated by archbp of York 14 Feb. 1302 for his part in the deprivation of Hoton (*Recs. A. Bek*, p. 84). Lusby left Durham 19(?) Apr. 1302 (*Scriptores Tres*, p. 79). Hoton's proctor put in possession 21 Apr. 1302 (DCD, Loc. VII: 80; Misc. Cht. 5523(49)). Hoton returned from Rome 1 Aug. 1303 (*Scriptores Tres*, p. 81). Hoton suspended by pope and Bp Bek made administrator of the convent 5 Mar. 1306 (*Recs. A. Bek*, pp. 118–19, no. 112; *CPL*, II, 6). Lusby apptd as bp's proctor to administer the convent but resisted by monks 31 Mar. 1306 (*Recs. A. Bek*, pp. 119–21, no. 113; *Scriptores Tres*, p. 83). Royal letters forbidding execution of papal mand. 29 Apr. 1306, 16 June 1306 (*CCR 1302–07*, pp. 444, 452). Lusby d. *c.* 1306 (*Ch. Walt. of Guisborough*, p. 365).

Hoton had king's protection to go to papal court for one year 7 Aug. 1306 (*CPR 1301–07*, p. 459). Hoton's suspension lifted by pope and restored to office 1 Dec. 1307 (*CPL*, II, 32). Hoton d. at papal court 9 Jan. 1308 (*Scriptores Tres*, p. 84). Commem. 9 Jan. (*LV Durham*, p. 149; BL, Harl. ms. 1804, f. 13r). News of d. reached Durham 2 Feb. 1308 (DCD, Cellarer's Ac. 1307–8; Fraser, *Hist. A. Bek*, p. 169). Seal (*Durham Seals*, p. 553, no. 3435).

William of Tanfield (Tainfelde, Tanfeld) **1308–1313** Pr. of Wetheral. Papal prov. 22 Feb. 1308 (*CPL*, II, 40); apptd 24 Feb. 1308 at suggestion of king and bp. (*Scriptores Tres*, p. 85). Installed 4 Sept. 1308 (ibid.). Res. 13 June 1313 (DCD, Reg. II, f. 21r; *Reg. Pal, Dun.*, I, 361–2). Provision made for the former pr. 13 June 1313 (*Reg. Pal. Dun.* I, 362–5). D. 7 Feb. 1314 (*Ch. York*, p. 65). Seal (*Durham Seals*, p. 553, no. 3436).

Geoffrey of Burdon 1313–1321 Petition for lic. to el. 14 June 1313; lic. gtd 15 June 1313 (*Reg. Pal. Dun.*, I, 355–6). El. 2 July 1313 (DCD, Reg., II, ff. 16r–17v); eln conf. and prof. obed. n.d.; mand. to obey 14 July 1313 (*Reg. Pal. Dun.*, I, 392–4); installed 14 July 1313 (DCD, Reg. II, f. 22v). Res. 22 Jan. 1321 (DCD, Loc. XIII: 3a). Seal (*Durham Seals*, p. 553, no. 3437). See Emden, *BRUO*, I, 307. Master of Monkwearmouth 1321 (q.v.). Still living 1333 (*Scriptores Tres*, p. 120). Commem. 27 Oct. (*LV Durham*, p. 152; BL, Harl. ms. 1804, f. 15r). Previously pr. of Finchale; pr. of Lytham (q.v.).

William of Guisborough 1321 Date fixed for eln 24 Jan. 1321 (DCD, Loc. XIII: 3A); el. 6 Feb. 1321; renounced eln 8 Feb. 1321 (*Scriptores Tres*, p. 102; cf. DCD, Loc. XIII: 3b).

William of Cowton (Couton, Cotony) **1321–1341** El. 2 Mar. 1321 (DCD, Loc. XIII: 3c). Lic. to bp of Durham to conf. eln in York diocese 19 Mar. 1321 (*Reg. Melton*, I, no. 218). Conf. 11 Apr. 1321 (DCD, 2.6.Pont. 10). Installed 3 May 1321 (DCD, Reg. II, f. 74r; *Scriptores Tres*, p. 102). D. 26 Jan. x 23 Feb. 1341 (*Durham Acct Rolls*, II, 538); in the week before Lent (*Scriptores Tres*, p. 130). Commem. 18 Feb. (*LV Durham*, p. 149; BL, Harl. ms. 1804, f. 13r). Seal (*Durham Seals*, p. 554, no. 3438).

John Fossor 1341–1374 Master of Wearmouth, lic. to el. 4 Mar. 1341 (*Reg. Bury*, p. 139). El. 16 Mar. 1341 (*Scriptores Tres*, p. 130). Eln conf. 31 Mar. 1341 (*Reg. Bury*, p. 143). Installed 31 Mar. 1341 (*Scriptores Tres*, p. 131). D. 11 Nov. 1374 (DCD, Loc. XIII: 8a). Commem. 12

Nov. (*LV Durham*, p. 149; BL, Harl. ms. 1804, f. 15v). Seal (*BM Seals*, no. 3095; *Durham Seals*, p. 554, no. 3439). Previously pr. of St Leonard's, Stamford (q.v.).

Robert Berrington of Walworth (Walleworth, Wallworht) **1374–1391** Bp's lic. to el 20 Nov. 1374; commn to examine future eln s.d. (Durham, Reg. Hatfield, ff. 78v–79r). El. 11 Dec. 1374 (*Scriptores Tres*, p. 136); eln conf. 20 Dec. 1374 (DCD, Loc. XIII: 8a); installed 24 Dec. 1374 (DCD, Magnum Repertorium, 2.6.Pont.2). Res. 21 July 1391 (*Scriptores Tres*, app. no. cxliv). Formal res. before bp 14 Aug. 1391 (DCD, Loc. XIII: 10a). Commem. 27 July (*LV Durham*, p. 151). Seal (*Durham Seals*, p. 555, no. 3441). D. 1399 (DCD, Bursar's Ac. 1399–1400 Pensions). Also commem. 31 July (BL, Harl. ms. 1804, f. 14v).

ELY (Cambs), St Peter and St Etheldreda ref. 970; cathedral priory from 1109.

Lists in *VCH Cambs*, II, 209–10; *Le Neve* 1066–1300, II, 47–50; 1300–1541, IV, 16–17; *Heads*, I, 44–6. For monks of Ely see Greatrex, *Biog. Reg.*, pp. 377–465.

Roger de Bergham **–?1229** M. of Ely (*CRR*, II, 140). Occ. before Feb. 1215 (BL, Cotton ms. Tiberius C IX, f. 152r). Last occ. June 1225 x Dec. 1228 (CUL, Add. ms. 3020, f. 172r; CUL, ms. G. 3. 28, p. 407). Bentham, *Ely*, I, 27 gives date of death as early 1229, citing the lost ff. 39–40 of BL, Add. ms. 9822. House vacant 6 Mar. 1229 (*CR 1227–31*, p. 235). See Greatrex, *Biog. Reg.*, p. 391.

Ralph ?1229– Said to have been confirmed as pr. *c.* 25 Mar. 1229 (Bentham, *Ely*, I, 218). First occ. Aug. 1233 (BL, Cotton ms. Tiberius B II, f. 252r). Occ. 17 June 1235 (PRO, Cambs F. CP25/24/17, no. 45); Oct. 1237 x Oct. 1238 (*Suffolk F. (Rye)*, p. 39). Last known occ. Apr–May 1238 (CUL, ms. G. 3.28, pp. 599–600). See Greatrex, *Biog. Reg.*, p. 432.

Walter First known occ. (W.) 3 Apr. 1241 (*CPR 1348–50*, p. 28). Occ. Oct. 1244 x Oct. 1245 (*Suffolk F. (Rye)*, p. 47); 26 Mar. 1258 (Hailstone, *History of Bottisham*, p. 207). Last known occ. 16 Mar. 1259 (Madox, *Form.*, p. 310). Obit 13 May (BL, Cotton ms. Vespasian A VI, f. 133v; BL, Add. ms. 9822, f. 105r; BL, Add. ms. 33381, f. 12r; CUL, Add. ms. 2950, f. 13r). See Greatrex, *Biog. Reg.*, pp. 455–6.

Robert of Leverington **–1271** Said to occ. 6 Mar. 1260 (Bentham, *Ely*, I, 218); Jan. 1261 (CUL, ms. G. 3. 28, p. 599). Last recorded occ. 1 Jan. 1271 (ibid., pp. 316–17). D. shortly before 23 Sept. 1271 (ibid., p. 195). Obit 12 Sept. (BL, Cotton ms. Vespasian A VI, f. 130v). See Greatrex, *Biog. Reg.*, p. 421.

Henry de Bancs **1271–1273** Bp's lic. to el. gtd 23 Sept. 1271 (CUL, ms. G. 3. 28, p. 195). El. between 20 Oct. 1271, when priory still vacant (*CPR 1266–72*, p. 581), and 12 Nov. 1271, when first occ. as pr. (Bodl., Ashmole ms. 801, f. 102v). Last occ. 28 Nov. 1273 (BL, Add. ms. 41612, f. 5r). D. 25 Dec. 1273 (*Ch. Bury*, p. 56). See Greatrex, *Biog. Reg.*, p. 389.

John of Hemingstone **1273–1288** M. of Ely, bp's lic. to el. gtd 27 Dec. 1273 (CUL, ms. G. 3. 28, p. 196). El. 1273/4 (*Ch. Bury*, p. 56). Last occ. 24 Feb. 1288 (BL, Add. ms. 41612, ff. 14v–15r). D. shortly before 16 Nov. 1288 (CUL, ms. G. 3. 18, p. 208). Obit 9 Nov. (BL, Cotton ms. Vespasian A VI, f. 130v; BL, Add. ms. 33381, f. 12r). See Greatrex, *Biog. Reg.*, p. 416.

John of Shepreth **1288–1292** M. of Ely, bp's lic. to el. gtd 16 Nov. 1288 (CUL, ms. G. 3. 28, p. 208, cf. *Ch. Bury*, p. 91). D. 22 Apr. 1292 (*Ch. Bury*, p. 113). See Greatrex, *Biog. Reg.*, p. 438.

John Salmon *alias* **of Ely** **1292–1299** Sub-pr. of Ely, el. pr. 1292 (*Ch. Bury*, p. 113). El. bp of Ely in disputed eln 19 May 1298 (*Ch. Bury*, p. 148), but royal ass. given to other candidate (*CPR 1292–1301*, p. 357). Last recorded occ. as pr. 26 Oct. 1299 (*CPR 1292–1301*, pp. 457, 520). El. bp of Norwich 1299, papal prov. by 18 June (*Le Neve 1066–1300*, II, 58). Said to have been el. 15 June 1299 (*Bart. Cotton*, p. 170). See Greatrex, *Biog. Reg.*, p. 436.

Robert of Orford **1299–1302** El. after 26 Oct. 1299 (see Salmon entry above). Presum. the unnamed pr. who occ. 10 June 1300 (*CPR 1292–1301*, p. 522). El. bp of Ely 14 Apr. 1302, consecr. 28 Oct. 1302 (*Le Neve 1300–1541*, IV, 13). Priory void by res. 4 Dec. 1302 (*CPL*, I, 604). See Greatrex, *Biog. Reg.*, p. 428.

William de Clare 1303 El. and d. 1303 (*Sacrist rolls of Ely*, II, 18). See Greatrex, *Biog. Reg.*, p. 398.

John of Fressingfield (Fresingfield) **1303–1321** First recorded occ. 24 Dec. 1303 (BL, Egerton ms. 3047, f. 177v). Res. 16 Feb. 1321 (BL, Cotton ms. Titus A I, f. 115v). See Greatrex, *Biog. Reg.*, pp. 412–13.

John de Crauden (Crouden, Crowden) **1321–1341** El. after 30 Mar. 1321 (BL, Cotton ms. Titus A I, f. 125v). Succ. 20 May 1321 (CUL, Add. ms. 2957, f. 65r). D. 25 Sept. 1341 (Ely, G/1/1, part 1, f. 25r–v). Lic. to el. 14 Oct. 1341 (ibid.). See Greatrex, *Biog. Reg.*, p. 401.

Alan of Walsingham 1341– Sacrist of Ely, el. 25 Oct. 1341; eln conf. 19 Nov. 1341 (Ely, G/1/1, part 1, f. 25r–v). Latest recorded occ. 12 July 1363 (BL, Egerton ms. 3047, f. 224r). Obit 15 May (BL, Add. ms. 33381, f. 12r). ? d. 1364. See Greatrex, *Biog. Reg.*, pp. 453–4.

William [de] Hathfield Mentd as predecessor of John de Bukton (BL, Egerton ms. 3047, f. 218v). See Greatrex, *Biog. Reg.*, p. 415.

John [de] Bukton (Bucton) **–1396** Occ. 24 Sept. 1364 (CUL, EDC. 7/7/2); 14 Oct. 1376 (Ely, G/1/2, f. 18r). D. about 21 Oct. 1396 (CUL, EDC.5/4/19; cf. obit 21 Oct. BL, Add. ms. 33381, f. 12r). Seal (*Mon. Seals*, p. 33). See Greatrex, *Biog. Reg.*, pp. 393–4.

EVESHAM (Worcs), St Mary and St Ecgwin f. *c.* 970; community expelled *c.* 975; ref. 995 x 997. Lists in *VCH Worcs*, II, 126; *Heads*, I, 46–8.

Randulf (Ralph, Ranulf, Rannulf) 1214–1229 M. of Evesham, pr. of Worcester, [bp-el. of Worcester 2 Dec. 1213 to Jan. 1214 (*Le Neve 1066–1300*, II, 100–1)], el. 22 Jan. 1214 (*Ch. Evesham*, p. 255, cf. p. 266 – 1215 in 2nd year). Royal ass. 24 Jan. 1214 (*Rot. Lit. Claus.*, I, 162; cf. *Ann. Worcs*, p. 403). Bl. by papal legate at St Mary's abbey, York 10 March 1214 (*Ch. Evesham*, p. 256, cf. *Ann. Worcs*, p. 403 – 23 Feb.: for the legate's movements see H. Tillmann, *Die päpstlichen Legaten in England* (Bonn, 1926), p. 106). D., lic. to el. 15 Dec. 1229 (*CPR 1225–32*, p. 320), but cf. D. 17 Dec. 1229 (*Ch. Evesham*, p. 263 and n. 2; *Ann. Tewkesbury*, p. 73; *Penwortham Docts*, p. 89). Seal (Randulf) (*Mon. Seals*, pp. 33–4).

Thomas of Marlborough (Marlebarwe) **1230–1236** Pr. of Evesham, royal ass. 7 Jan. 1230 (*CPR 1225–32*, p. 321). El. 1229 but not adm. except by provision of the pope; bl. *c.* 11 July 1230; enthroned 29 Sept. 1230 (*Ann. Tewkesbury*, pp. 73–5); bl. 1230 by bp of Coventry at Chester (*Ann. Worcs*, p. 421). Papal mandate to bp of Coventry to receive res. of abbot who has asked to be relieved of his charge, on account of age and infirmity 13 July 1236 (*CPL*, I, 154); provision is to be made if he is too infirm to share the refectory and dormitory 29 July (ibid., 156). D. 12 Sept. 1236 (*Ch. Evesham*, p. 278; *Penwortham Docts*, p. 89); bur. 13 Sept. (*Ann. Tewkesbury*, p. 101). Lic. to el. (no reason given for vacancy) 20 Sept. 1236 (*CPR 1232–47*, p. 158). See Sharpe, *Latin Writers*, p. 667.

Richard le Gras (Crassus) **1236–1242** Pr. of Hurley, el. 25 Sept. 1236, bl. by bp of Coventry 30 Nov.; installed 6 Dec. 1236 (*Flor. Hist.*, II, 217; *Ch. Evesham*, p. 278; *MPCM*, III, 379). Cf. el 23 Sept. 1236 (*Ann. Tewkesbury*, pp. 101–2). Royal ass. 4 Oct. 1236 (erroneously called pr. of Carlisle); temps. 19 Oct. 1236 (*CPR 1232–47*, pp. 159, 166). Apr. 1240 appointed Chancellor and Keeper of the Great Seal (*Chronology*, p. 85). El. Bp of Coventry 1241, but declined office (*Ann. Tewkesbury*, p. 121), or died before disputed eln settled (*CPL*, I, 203). Ment. of the abb. falling sick at La Réole (*CPR 1232–47*, p. 348). D. 8 Dec. 1242 (*Ann. Tewkesbury*, p. 128). D. in Gascony 9 Dec. 1242 (*Ch. Evesham*, p. 279, cf. *CPL*, I, 203; *Penwortham Docts*, p. 89). Lic. to el. (no reason given for vacancy) 26 Mar. 1243 (*CPR 1232–47*, p. 370).

Thomas of Gloucester (Gloucestria, Glovernia) **1243–1255** M. of Evesham, pr. of Penwortham, el. 1243 (*Ann. Tewkesbury*, p. 133; *Ann. Worcs.*, p. 435). Royal ass. 8 July 1243 (*CPR 1232–47*, p. 385). Papal conf. 17 Dec. 1243 (*CPL*, I, 203); mand. to bp of Ely to bl. abb.-el. 1 Jan. 1244 (ibid., p. 204). Attended Papal Council 1245 (*CPR 1232–47*, p. 454). D. 15 Dec. 1255 (*Ch. Evesham*, p. 280; *Penwortham Docts*, p. 89). Lic. to el. (no reason given for vacancy) 22 Dec. 1255 (*CPR 1247–58*, p. 454).

Henry of Worcester (Wigornia) **1256–1263** Pr. of Evesham, papal conf. 27 Apr. 1256 and request to king to gt temps. (*CPL*, I, 330); writ *de intendendo* 8 June 1256 (*CPR 1247–58*, p. 479). Grant to the pr. and conv. for a fine of next custody of the abbey when vacant by the cess. or d. of Henry 24 May 1263 (*CPR 1258–66*, p. 276). D. 13 Nov. 1263 (*Ch. Evesham*, p. 282; *Penwortham Docts*, p. 89). D., lic. to el. (no name) 12 Nov. 1263 (*CPR 1258–66*, p. 299). According to *Ch. Evesham*, the abbey was vacant after Henry's death for almost 3 yrs (p. 282).

William of Marlborough (Marleberg, Maleberge) **1263–1266** M. of Evesham, royal ass. 13 Dec. 1263 (*CPR 1258–66*, p. 304). Papal mand. to legate to examine eln and bl., if the elect is found to be a fit person 9 Apr. 1264 (*CPL*, I, 392). Mand. to the legate, Cardinal Ottobuono, to bl. abb.-el. 18 June 1265 (ibid., p. 420). House void by 23 July 1266 (*CPR 1258–66*, p. 619).

William of Whitchurch (Whitechurch, Wytchurche, Wytechurche) **1266–1282** M. of Pershore, abb. of Alcester, apptd by the legate Ottobuono *c.* 14 Sept. 1266 (*Ch. Evesham*, p. 282); writ *de intendendo* 15 Sept. 1266 (*CPR 1258–66*, p. 638). Cess. by 1 Aug. 1282 (*CFR 1272–1307*, p. 166; *CPR 1281–92*, p. 31). D. 1 Aug. 1282 (*Ann. Worcs.*, p. 484). But cf. D. 3 Aug. 1282 (*Ch. Evesham*, p. 283; *Penwortham Docts*, p. 90). D. (*sic* not cess.), lic. to el. 10 Aug. 1282 (*CPR 1281–92*, p. 32).

John of Brockhampton (Brochampton, Brockhamptone) **1282–1316** Cellarer of Evesham, eln pres. to king for royal ass. 17 Aug. 1282 (PRO, C84/7/33); Royal ass. 23 Aug. 1282, temps. 11 Apr. 1283 (*CPR 1281–92*, pp. 34, 61). Papal conf. of eln 15 Feb. 1283 (*CPL*, I, 467; Sayers, no. 852). D. 18 Aug. 1316 and bur. beside font in the nave of the church (*Ch. Evesham*, p. 289, cf. n. 2, citing 16 Aug. date; *Penwortham Docts*, p. 90). D. (J.), lic. to el. 29 Aug. 1316 (*CPR 1313–17*, p. 543).

William de Chiriton (Cheryton, Chiryngton, Chenaitone, Chyrinton) **1316–1344** M. of Evesham, el. 30 Aug. 1316, papal conf. at Avignon 6 Feb. 1317 (*Ch. Evesham*, p. 289, cf. *CPL*, I, 136 which gives 13 Feb. as date of papal conf.). Safe conduct for abb.-el. 25 Sept. 1316, royal ass. 15 Oct. 1316, 31 Mar. 1317 (*CPR 1313–17*, pp. 549, 555, 633). Mand. for letters recommending him to pope and cardinals 21 Oct. 1316 (*Cal. Chanc. Warr.*, p. 446). D. 13 Dec. 1344 and bur. beside font in the nave of the church (*Ch. Evesham*, p. 293; *Penwortham Docts*, p. 90). Cf. house void by death by 10 Dec. 1344 (*CCR 1343–46*, p. 434). D., lic. to el. 22 Dec. 1344 (*CPR 1343–45*, p. 374).

William (du/de) Boys 1345–1367 El. 1 Jan. 1345 (*Ch. Evesham*, p. 293; PRO, E135/2/26). Papal conf. at Avignon 20 March 1345 (*CPR 1343–45*, p. 293, but cf. 21 March, *CPL*, III, 148). Papal safe-conduct for William, promoted at the Holy See and returning to Evesham 27 March 1345 (ibid., 17). Temps. 28 Apr. 1345 (*CPR 1343–5*, pp. 458–9). Installed 15 May 1345 (*Ch. Evesham*, p. 293). 1366 lic. to go on pilgrimage to Amiens, Cologne, Assisi and Santiago (*CPR 1364–7*, p. 217). D. 6 June 1367 and bur. 20 June in the nave before the image of the Virgin Mary (*Ch. Evesham*, p. 299; *Penwortham Docts*, p. 90). D., lic. to el. 8 June 1367 (*CPR 1364–67*, p. 405).

John of Ombersley (Ambresley(e), Ombresley) **1367–1379** Cellarer of Evesham, el. 4 July 1367, bl. by bp of Lincoln at Banbury 18 July, installed 1 Aug. (*Ch. Evesham*, p. 299). Royal ass. 10 July 1367 (*CPR 1364–67*, p. 420). D. 30 Oct. 1379 and bur. in the nave of the church in front of the screen (*Ch. Evesham*, p. 303; *Penwortham Docts*, p. 90). D., lic. to el. 8 Nov. 1379 (*CPR 1377–81*, p. 395).

EYNSHAM (Oxon), St Mary (etc., see Binns, p. 72) f. 1005; ref. –1086 and again in 1091 (at Stow, Lincs); 1094 x 5 (returned to Eynsham).

Lists in *VCH Oxon*, II, 67; *Ctl. Eynsham*, I, pp. xiii–xxxii; *Heads*, I, 48–9.

Adam 1213/14–1228 Sub-pr. and possibly pr. of Eynsham (see *Mag. Vit.*, I, pp. viii ff). Occ. 1 July 1214 (*Ctl. Eynsham*, I, n. 230; *Bucks F.*, II, 105); 1219 (*Oxford F.*, p. 57); 1225 (ibid., p. 74). Dep. 1 June 1228 by Hugh, bp of Lincoln (*Ann. Tewkesbury*, p. 70; *Ann. Dunstable*, p. 109; *Walt. Cov.*, I, p. xli), but cf. occ. 10 June 1228 (*Reg. Wells*, II, 145). Author of *Magna Vita* of St Hugh. See Sharpe, *Latin Writers*, pp. 16–17. Protection for Adam, former abb. 8 Apr. 1233 and exemption for life from doing suit in person 20 May 1233 (*CPR 1232–47*, pp. 14, 16).

Nicholas 1228–1238/9 Pr. of Freiston, succ. 1228 (*Ann. Dunstable*, p. 109). Occ. *ante* Dec. 1228 (*Reg. Wells*, II, 30); from 29 Oct. 1229 to 15 Sept. 1238 (*Oxford F.*, pp. 86, 104). Res. June 1238 x June 1239 (*Reg. Grosseteste*, p. 457). D. as former abb. 9 Feb. 1243 (*Ann. Tewkesbury*, p. 126).

John of Dover (Dovor') **1238/9–1241** Pr. of Eynsham, eln conf. and bl. by Walter, bp of Ossory June 1238 x June 1239 (*Reg. Grosseteste*, p. 459). Occ. (J.) 13 Mar. 1241 (*Luffield Chts.*, I, no. 22; *Ctl. Eynsham*, I, no. 231).

Gilbert of Gloucester (Glovern') **1241–1264** M. and cellarer of Eynsham, eln quashed but apptd by bp June 1240 x June 1241, [Mar. x Apr. 1241], no reason given for vacancy (*Reg. Grosseteste*, p. 468). Occ. 14 Apr. 1241 (*Oxford F.*, p. 118). D. by 23 May 1264 (*Reg. R. Gravesend*, p. 217). See Sharpe, *Latin Writers*, p. 145.

Alexander of Brackley (Brackele) **1264–1268** M. of Eynsham, apptd by bp 23 May 1264 (*Reg. R. Gravesend*, p. 217). D. 15 Mar. 1268 (*Ann. Osney*, p. 213).

John of Oxford (Oxon') **1268–1281** Cellarer of Eynsham, apptd by bp who had been empowered by convent to choose 7 Apr. 1268 (*Reg. R. Gravesend*, p. 220). Occ. 29 Sept. 1281 (*Ctl. Eynsham*, I, no. 468). Cess. mentd as former abb. gtd pension and the buildings where the former abb. Nicholas used to live 23 Oct. 1281 (*Ctl. Eynsham*, II, no. 452). Modification by Archbp Pecham of Bp Sutton's provision for him 10 Nov. 1298 (*Reg. Peckham* III, 843–5).

Thomas de Well(e) 1281–1307 Occ. frequently in *Ctl. Eynsham* from 30 Nov. 1281 to 18 June 1306 (I, no. 311; II, no. 731). D. by 19 May 1307; lic. to el. (Lincoln, Ep. Reg., II, ff. 152r–153r). Indulgence offered for soul 4 Dec. 1308 (Lincoln, Ep. Reg., III, f. 144v). Poss. grave slab at Hardwick, Oxon. (*Earliest English Brasses*, p. 205 and fig. 56; *Trans. of the Monumental Brass Society*, XI, 308–11).

Adam (of) Lambourn (Laumbourn) **1307–1316/17** M. of Eynsham, eln conf. 21 June 1307, bl. 24 June 1307 (Lincoln, Ep. Reg., II, ff. 152r–153r). Occ. 17 Nov. 1316 (*Ctl. Eynsham*, II, no. 723). D. by 7 Jan. 1317 (Lincoln, Ep. Reg., II, f. 168r). Indulgence of 20 days for his soul gtd 17 May 1323 (Lincoln, Ep. Reg., V, f. 339v).

John of Cheltenham (Chiltenham) **1317–1330** Pr. of Eynsham, eln quashed but apptd by bp 7 Jan. 1317 (Lincoln, Ep. Reg., II, f. 168r). Bl. by ex-archbp of Armagh and prof. obed. 9 Jan. 1317 (Lincoln, Ep. Reg., III, f. 361r). Res. deed 27 Mar. 1330 (Lincoln, Ep. Reg., IV, f. 262r–v). Mutilated grave slab of John as *quondam abbas* survives in the church of Elsfield, Oxon. (*Earliest English Brasses*, p. 205; *Trans. of the Monumental Brass Society*, X, 384–6).

John of Broughton 1330–1338 M. of Eynsham, apptd by bp 13 Apr. 1330 (Lincoln, Ep. Reg., IV, f. 262r–v). Cess. by 17 Oct. 1338 (ibid., f. 280v).

Nicholas of Upton (Upptone) **1338–1344** M. of Eynsham, eln conf. 17 Oct. 1338 (ibid.). Lic. to receive bl. from any catholic bp 17 Oct. 1338 (Lincoln, Ep. Reg., V, f. 565r). Depr. by 20 May 1344 (Lincoln, Ep. Reg., VI, f. 86r). A report of 10 Jan. 1345 states that he had been depr. by the bp of Lincoln at his visitation but subsequently returned with 1500 armed men and turned out William of Stamford and other monks (5 of whom came to the Curia, and another 9 were dispersed throughout England) (*CPL*, III, 174).

William of Stamford (Staunford) **1344–1344/5** M. of Eynsham apptd by bp 20 May 1344 (Lincoln, Ep. Reg., VI, f. 86r). Driven out by Nicholas of Upton and his armed supporters by 10 Jan. 1345 (*CPL*, III, 174). Signified for arrest 18 Oct. 1345 (Logan, *Runaway Religious*, p. 189).

Nicholas of Upton ?**1345–** Re-occ. from 25 Feb. 1345 to 15 July 1345 (*CCR 1343–46*, pp. 555, 638). In prison in Oxford Castle for trespass of vert 6 Apr. 1345 (ibid., p. 518). Ment. of dispute between the two claimants in papal mand. of 18 July 1345 (*CPL*, III, 189). Occ. 8 May 1346 (*CCR 1346–49*, p. 65). 2 monks apptd as custodians and administrators of the abbey 14 May 1349 (Lincoln, Ep. Reg., IX, f. 18r); Nicholas re-adm. to administration of abbey 17 May 1349, following his recent suspension and the d. of the above custodians (ibid., f. 22v). Occ. 13 June 1350 (*Ctl. Eynsham*, I, no. 573). Presumably res. by 1352 (see below). Occ. as former abb. 16 June 1360 (*CCR 1360–64*, p. 59); Oct. 1366 (*Ctl. Eynsham*, II, p. 118, no. 673).

Geoffrey of Lambourn (Lamburn) **–1388** Occ. from 26 Jan. 1352 to 6 June 1353 (*CCR 1349–54*, pp. 464, 604). In Oct. 1366 it was stated that it was abb. Geoffrey's 15th year (*Ctl. Eynsham*, II, p. 118, no. 673). 21 Nov. 1358 ment. of Nicholas of Upton, m. of Eynsham, in dispute with the abb. and convent and accused of stealing chalices, books and vestments (*CPR 1358–61*, p. 123). Attorneys apptd 8 Aug. 1386 on account of abb.'s blindness and old age (*CPR 1385–89*, p. 193). D. by 13 Aug. 1388, lic. to el. (Lincoln, Ep. Reg., XI, f. 314v).

FAVERSHAM (Kent), St Saviour f. 1148

Lists in *VCH Kent*, II, 141; *Heads*, I, 49–50.

Nicholas 1215–1234 Cellarer of Faversham, el. 1215 (*Gervase*, II, 109; *Rot. Lit. Pat.*, p. 127b). Res. on account of old age and sickness, lic. to el. 9 Dec. 1234 (*CPR 1232–47*, p. 85). Seal (*BM Seals*, no. 3150).

Peter 1234–1267 Cellarer of Faversham, royal ass. 20 Dec. 1234, writ *de intendendo* 23 Dec. 1234 (*CPR 1232–47*, p. 85). Prof. obed. n.d. (Canterbury D. & C., Ch. Ant. A41/21, 26). Occ. 22 Oct. 1267 (*CPR 1266–72*, p. 120). Petition to king wishing to retire as abb. after 32 years *c.* Dec. 1267 (PRO, SCI/3/103). Res. 21 Nov. 1267 (PRO, C84/3/34). Cess., lic. to el. 1 Dec. 1267 (*CPR 1266–72*, p. 170). Seal (*BM Seals*, no. 3151).

John de Horapeldre 1268–1271 Cellarer of Faversham writ *de intendendo* 25 Jan. 1268 (*CPR 1266–72*, p. 184). Cert. conf. eln by archbp of Canterbury 24 Jan. 1268 (PRO, C84/3/39). Prof. obed. n.d. (Canterbury D. & C., SVSB.I/71/2). House void by 12 Jan. 1271 (*CPR 1266–72*, p. 505). D., lic. to el. 18 Jan. 1271 (ibid., p. 508).

Peter de Erdeslose (Herdeslo) **1271–1272** M. of Faversham, royal ass. 13 Feb. 1271, writ *de intendendo* 20 Feb. 1271, eln having been conf. by mag. Hugh de Mortimer, archdn of Canterbury *sede vacante* (ibid., pp. 517, 519). Prof. obed. 4 Mar. 1271 (Canterbury D. & C., SVSB.I/69/2). Occ. 4 Dec. 1272 (*CPR 1272–81*, p. 1). D. by 8 Dec. 1272 (PRO, C84/4/32). D., lic. to el. 10 Dec. 1272 (*CPR 1272–81*, p. 2).

Peter of Rodmersham (Redmersham) **1272–1275** M. of Faversham, royal ass. 26 Dec. 1272, temps. 20 Jan. 1273 (ibid., pp. 2–3). Cert. conf. eln by archbp-el. of Canterbury 30 Dec. 1272 (PRO, C84/4/34). Letters of protection, going overseas 1273 (*CPR 1272–81*, pp. 9,

28). 17 Aug. 1275 Fulk Peyforer and mag. Hamo Doges apptd during pleasure to the custody of the abbey fallen into debt (ibid., p. 102). Unnamed abb. dep. 12 Sept. 1275 (*Gervase*, II, 280). Lic. to el. (no reason given for vacancy) 22 Sept. 1275 (*CPR 1272–81*, p. 106). Case still going on in 1283 (*CPL*, I, 470–1).

[**John de Romenhale** M. of Faversham, eln quashed by archbp 6 Nov. 1275 (*CPR 1272–81*, p. 109)]

Oswald (Osward) of Eastry (Eastria, Estry) *alias* **Heye 1275–1292** M. of Christ Church, Canterbury, request from archbp of Canterbury (who has conf. his eln) to king to gt temps. 6 Nov. 1275 (*CCR 1272–79*, p. 253); writ *de intendendo* 6 Nov. 1275 (*CPR 1272–81*, p. 109). Prof. obed. n.d. (Canterbury D. & C., Ch. Ant. A41/27). Bl. 10 Nov. by Archbp Kilwardby (*Gervase*, II, 282). D., lic. to el. 15 May 1292 (*CPR 1282–91*, p. 490). Obit 10 May (Greatrex, *Biog. Reg.*, p. 146).

Geoffrey de Bocton(e) 1292–1308 Sub-pr. of Faversham, royal ass. 20 June 1292, temps. 30 Sept. 1292 (*CPR 1282–91*, pp. 496, 508). Cert. conf. eln by archbp of Canterbury 12 July 1292 (PRO, C84/10/46; cf. *Reg. Peckham*, III, 984). D., lic. to el. 25 Sept. 1308 (*CPR 1307–13*, p. 138).

Clement de Lodenne (Leden) **1308–1318** Pr. of Faversham, eln pres. to king for royal ass. 9 Oct. 1308 (PRO, C84/16/11); royal ass. 12 Oct. 1308, temps. 29 Oct. 1308 (*CPR 1307–13*, pp. 139–40). Cert. conf. eln by archbp of Canterbury 29 Oct. 1308 (PRO, C84/16/13). Prof. obed. n.d. (Canterbury D. & C., Reg. A, f. 253r). D., lic. to el. 26 Oct. 1318 (*CPR 1317–21*, p. 219).

Thomas of Wingham (Wengeham, Wyngeham) **1318** Pr. of Faversham, eln pres. to king for royal ass. 8 Nov. 1318 (PRO, C84/19/44); royal ass. 19 Nov. 1318 (*CPR 1317–21*, pp. 223, 239). Cess. by 28 Dec. 1318 (ibid., p. 257; cf. PRO, C84/19/44).

John (le) Orfreiser (Lorfreyser, Orfre(y)ser) **1318–1325** Sub-pr. of Faversham, royal ass. 28 Dec. 1318, temps. 21 Jan. 1319 (*CPR 1317–21*, pp. 257, 268). Commn to proceed against abb. for certain offences arising out of recent visitation 23 Apr., 21 May 1325 (Lambeth, Reg. Reynolds, ff. 136v–137r). 28 Aug. 1325 appt of Stephen de la Dane to custody of the abbey, fallen into debt (*CPR 1324–27*, p. 163). Res. on 15 Sept. 1325 and provision made for ex-abb. (Lambeth, Reg. Reynolds, ff. 140v–141r). Res., lic. to el. 17 Sept. 1325 (*CPR 1324–27*, p. 178). Alleged to be guilty of dilapidation and simony, having been deprived it was claimed he was kept in custody by the king's officers 1328 (*CPL*, II, 279).

John *dictus* **Ive 1325–1356** Sub-pr. of Faversham, eln reported to king 26 Sept. 1325, mand. to issue royal letters 1 Oct. 1325 (*Cal. Chanc. Warr.*, p. 568); royal ass. 1 Oct. 1325, temps. 11 Nov. 1325 (*CPR 1324–27*, pp. 176, 188). Eln conf. by archbp 8 Nov. 1325 (Lambeth, Reg. Reynolds, f. 144v, cf. f. 151r). Later dispute between Orfreiser and Ive, papal mand. to archbp of Canterbury to settle the matter 30 Aug. 1328 (*CPL*, II, 279). D., lic. to el. 24 June 1356 (*CPR 1354–58*, p. 326).

William of Maidstone (Maidenstan, Maidenston, Maydenstan, Maydestan) **1356–1370** Pr. of Faversham, royal ass. 8 Feb. 1356, temps. 9 Mar. 1356 (ibid., pp. 343, 352–3). On 23 Feb. 1356 abb.'s proctor appeared with William's eln decree. On 5 Mar. witnesses were examined and on 6 Mar archbp apptd commissaries to proceed in the matter. Eln conf. 9 Mar.; mand. to install 14 Mar. (Lambeth, Reg. Islip, f. 113r–v). D. by 6 Sept. 1370 (PRO, C84/30/28). D., lic. to el. 10 Sept (*CPR 1367–70*, p. 461).

Robert of Faversham (Faverisham, Feversham) **1370–1409** M. of Faversham, eln pres. to king for royal ass. 17 Sept. 1370 (PRO, C84/30/29); royal ass. 20 Sept. 1370, temps. 8 Oct. 1370 (*CPR 1367–70*, pp. 465–6). Commn to examine eln 25 Sept. 1370, eln conf. 2 Oct. 1370; mand. for induction 13 Oct. 1370 (Lambeth, Reg. Whittlesey, ff. 33r–34r). D. by 10 Dec. 1409 (Lambeth, Reg. Arundel II, ff. 122v–123r).

GLASTONBURY (Soms), St Mary ref. 940

Lists in *VCH Soms*, II, 98; *Heads*, I, 50–2.

Jocelin of Wells 1213–1219 Bp of Bath 1206–1242, took the title of Bath and Glastonbury in 1213 and abandoned it in 1219; the royal chancery conceded it to him in Nov. 1214; the papacy never (*ex inf.* C. R. Cheney; see *Le Neve 1066–1300*, VII, forthcoming); but in 1218–19 a compromise was reached (*Ctl. Glastonbury*, I, pp. xlff., 73ff.), and William of St Vigor was el. abb. (*Ad. Dom.*, II, 466–76).

William of St Vigor 1219–1223 El. 8 July 1219 (*Ad. Dom.*, II, 466–76; *John of Glastonbury*, II, 253–4). Occ. 12 Nov. 1220 (*Ctl. Glastonbury*, I, p. 102, no. 149); 1222 x 1223 (PRO, DL.36/1/211). D. 18 Sept. 1223 (*John of Glastonbury*, II, 256; *Ann. Waverley*, p. 299; *Ann. Tewkesbury*, p. 63; *Ctl. Glastonbury*, III, p. 706, no. 1310).

Robert of Bath (Bathonia) **1223–1235** Pr. of Bath, el. 1223 (*Ad. Dom.*, II, 478; *Ann. Tewkesbury*, pp. 66–7; *Ann. Waverley*, p. 299). Bl. 23 Oct. 1223 (*John of Glastonbury*, II, 257). Dep. 29 Mar. 1235 and returned to Bath (ibid., 259; Greatrex, *Biog. Reg.*, p. 13).

Michael of Amesbury (Ambresburi) **1235–1252/3** Chamberlain of Glastonbury, el. 3 Apr. 1235 and bl. 25 Apr. 1235 (*John of Glastonbury*, II, 260); cf. bl. at London 11 Nov. 1235 (*Ann. Tewkesbury*, p. 96). Occ. many times in *Ctl. Glastonbury* from 20 Jan. 1236 to 29 Sept. 1252 (I, p. 209, no. 340; III, p. 710, no. 1316). Cess. [?1252] after almost 18 years; d. 24 June 1253 in the year after his cess. (*John of Glastonbury*, II, 272–3). Register (Longleat mun. 10590, 10592).

Roger of Forde 1253–1261 Chamberlain of Glastonbury, el. 4 Mar. 1253, but **Robert of Petherton**, sacrist, was also el. They renounced their eln and Roger was re-el. and bl. 9 Mar. 1253 (ibid., 273–5). Robert continued to cause problems. Commn of oyer and ter-miner touching trespasses lately committed against the king and abb. Roger in respect of the abbey 13 Mar. 1256 (*CPR 1247–58*, p. 511); on 28 Mar. 1256 royal prohibition to mer-chants from lending anything to the bp of Bath and Wells and Robert the m. of Glastonbury falsely bearing themselves as abb. of Glastonbury by the common seal of Glastonbury, which Robert and the monks fraudulently detain from Roger the true abb. (ibid., p. 467). Occ. from 9 Feb. 1255 to 30 June 1260 (*Ctl. Glastonbury*, I, p. 235, no. 388; II, p. 466, no. 848) and in many undated chts.; occ. as royal envoy 1257 (*CPR 1247–58*, p. 568). D. at Bromley 2 Oct. 1261 and bur. at Westminster (*John of Glastonbury*, II, 285, cf. *CPR 1258–66*, p. 177). See Sharpe, *Latin Writers*, p. 589.

Robert of Petherton (Pederton) **1261–1274** Bl. Nov. 1261 (*John of Glastonbury*, II, 286). Occ. many times in *Ctl. Glastonbury* from 19 Feb. 1262 to 18 Nov. 1273 (II, p. 424, no. 761; I, p. 215, no. 356). D. 31 Mar. 1274 (*John of Glastonbury*, II, 294, cf. *CFR 1272–1307*, p. 20).

John of Taunton (Tanton(ia)) **1274–1291** M. of Glastonbury, el. 14 June 1274 (*John of Glastonbury*, II, 297); archbp of Canterbury quashed eln and provided John as abb. 15 Feb. 1275 (ibid., 299). Royal ass. (to bp of Bath and Wells) 27 Aug. 1274, (to archbp of Canterbury) 26 Dec. 1274; temps. 9 May. 1275 (*CPR 1272–81*, pp. 55, 74, 85, 88). Bl. 18 Feb. 1275 (*Arch. Cant.*, XXXVII, 64). D. by 7 Oct. 1291 (PRO, C84/10/22). D., lic to el. 8 Oct. 1291 (*CPR 1281–92*, p. 447, cf. BL, Cotton ms. Cleopatra D III, f. 49r).

John of Kent (Cancia, Kancia) **1291–1303** M. of Glastonbury, eln pres. to king for royal ass. 18 Oct. 1291 (PRO, C84/10/24); royal ass. 22 Oct. 1291, temps. 26 Oct. 1291 (*CPR 1281–92*, p. 448). Occ. 13 Nov. 1303 (*Ctl. Glastonbury*, III, p. 720, no. 1328). D. by 24 Nov. 1303, prob. d. 14 Nov. since vacancy calculated from that date (*CFR 1272–1307*, p. 485; cf. PRO, C84/15/2, d. by 18 Nov.). D (J.), lic. to el. 6 Dec. 1303 (*CPR 1301–07*, p. 203).

Geoffrey Fromond (Fromound, Fromund) **1303/4–1322** M. of Glastonbury, el. 29 Dec. 1303 (*John of Glastonbury*, II, 314). Royal ass. 18 Jan. 1304, temps. 10 Feb. 1304 (*CPR 1301–07*, pp. 205, 209). Cert. conf. eln by bp of Bath and Wells 3 Feb. 1304 (PRO, C84/15/8). D. 14

or 15 (St Brice's day) Nov. 1322 (*John of Glastonbury*, II, 321). House void from 21 Nov. 1322 (*Reg. R. Shrewsbury*, I, nos. 802, 860). D., lic. to el. 26 Nov. 1322 (*CPR 1321–24*, p. 220). Register (Longleat mun. 10591, 10593). See I. Keil, 'The abbots of Glastonbury in the early fourteenth century', *Downside Review*, 82 (1964), 327–48, at 331–7.

Walter of Taunton (Tanton(ia)) **1322–1323** Pr. of Glastonbury, el. 7 Dec. 1322 (*John of Glastonbury*, II, 322). Royal ass. 20 Dec. 1322, d., lic. to el. 30 Jan. 1323 before temps. restored (*CPR 1321–24*, pp. 229, 239). Bl. *c.* 13 Jan. 1323; D. 23 Jan. 1323 (*John of Glastonbury*, II, 324, 322). See I. Keil, 'The abbots of Glastonbury in the early fourteenth century', *Downside Review*, 82 (1964), 327–48, at 337.

Adam of Sodbury (Sobbury) **1323–1334** Sacrist of Glastonbury, el. 5 Feb. 1323, bl. 6 Mar. 1323 (*John of Glastonbury*, II, 325). Royal ass. 16 Feb. 1323, temps. 12 Mar. 1323 (*CPR 1321–24*, pp. 241, 265). Cert. conf. eln by bp of Bath and Wells 6 Mar. 1323 (PRO, C84/20/18). Occ. 4 Oct. 1334 (*Ctl. Glastonbury*, III, p. 709, no. 1314). D. by 30 Oct. 1334 (PRO, C84/23/29). D., lic to el. 6 Nov. 1334 (*CPR 1334–38*, p. 43). See I. Keil, 'The abbots of Glastonbury in the early fourteenth century', *Downside Review*, 82 (1964), 327–48, at 337–40.

John de Breynton(e) (Brenketon, Breyketon) **1334–1342** Pr. of Glastonbury, el. 23 Dec. 1334 (*John of Glastonbury*, II, 334), but cf. eln pres. to king for royal ass. 16 Nov. 1334 (PRO, C84/23/19). Royal ass. 20 Nov. 1334, temps. 24 Dec. 1334 (*CPR 1334–38*, pp. 47, 53). Royal commn to take fealty 3 Dec. 1334 (PRO, C84/23/21). Cert. conf. eln by bp of Bath and Wells 23 Dec. 1334 (PRO, C84/23/25). D., lic. to el. 29 Sept. 1342 (*CPR 1340–43*, p. 517). See I. Keil, 'The abbots of Glastonbury in the early fourteenth century', *Downside Review*, 82 (1964), 327–48, at 341–2.

Walter de Monyton(e) (Monyngton, Monynton) **1342–1375** M. of Glastonbury, royal ass. 13 Oct. 1342, temps. 11 Nov. 1342 (*CPR 1340–43*, pp. 530, 568). El. 25 Oct. 1342 (*sic*) (*John of Glastonbury*, p. xxiv – error). Commn to examine eln 25 Oct. 1342, conf. and mand. to install 7 Nov. 1342 (*Reg. R. Shrewsbury*, nos. 1682, 1685). D. by 14 July 1375 (PRO, C84/31/31). D., lic. to el. 18 July 1375 (*CPR 1374–77*, p. 128). See I. Keil, 'The abbots of Glastonbury in the early fourteenth century', *Downside Review*, 82 (1964), 327–48, at 342–47; epitaph ibid., 347. Abb. Walter's register 1352–66 is BL, Arundel ms. 2; his feodary is Longleat mun. 10588). See also A. Watkin, 'The correspondence of Walter de Monyton, abbot of Glastonbury', *Proc. Dorset NHAS*, 85 (1964), 135–40; Sharpe, *Latin Writers*, p. 738.

John Chynnok *(alias* **Wynchestre)** **1375–1420** M. of Glastonbury, eln pres. to king for royal ass. 25 July 1375 (PRO, C84/31/32); royal ass. 1 Aug. 1375, temps. 17 Aug. 1375 (*CPR 1374–77*, pp. 130, 132). Prof. obed. 12 Aug. 1375 (*HMC Wells*, I, 275); cert. conf. eln by bp of Bath and Wells 13 Aug. 1375 (PRO, C84/31/34). D., lic to el. 10 Aug 1420 (*CPR 1416–22*, p. 297). See I. Keil, 'Profiles of some abbots of Glastonbury', *Downside Review*, 81 (1963), 355–70, at 356–62, which details the struggle with Thomas Coffyn, m. of Glastonbury, who went to the Papal Curia on behalf of those monks wishing to have Chinnock's eln annulled (see also Logan, *Runaway Religious*, p. 192; Emden, *BRUO*, I, 455).

GLOUCESTER St Peter ref. ? 1022

Lists in *VCH Glos.*, II, 61; *Heads*, I, 52–3.

Henry Blont 1205–1224 Prev. pr. of Gloucester, bl. 29 Sept. 1205; installed 1 or 2 Oct. 1205 (*Ctl. Gloucester*, I, 23; *Heads*, I, 53). Occ. 30 Apr. 1214 (Cheney, *Inn. III*, no. 964); 1222 (PRO, Glos F., CP25/1/73/5, no. 54). D. 23 Aug. 1224 (*Ctl. Gloucester*, I, 26; *Ann. Tewkesbury*, p. 67). Seal (*Hereford Seals*, p. 8).

Thomas of Bredon (Bredone) **1224–1227/8** Prev. pr. of Gloucester, el. 1224 (*Ann. Tewkesbury*, p. 67; *Ann. Worcs.*, p. 416). Succ. 31 Aug. 1224 (*Ctl. Gloucester*, I, 26). Royal ass. 6 Sept. 1224 (*CPR 1216–25*, p. 468). Bl. by bp of Worcester 22 Sept. 1224 and installed

29 Sept. (*Ctl. Gloucester*, I, 26–7), but cf. bl. at Worcester 15 Jan. 1225 (*Ann. Worcs.*, p. 416). Occ. 3 Feb., 7 Feb. 1227 (PRO, Glos. F., CP25/1/73/7, no. 100; 73/8, no. 116). D. 1227 (*Ann. Worcs.*, p. 420) or 1228 (*Ann. Tewkesbury*, p. 70). D. after 3½ years (*Ctl. Gloucester*, I, 27).

Henry Foliot (Folet, Foliet) **1228–1243** El. 1228 (*Ann. Tewkesbury*, p. 70); bl. by bp of Worcester and installed by archdn of Gloucester 1228 (*Ctl. Gloucester*, I, 27–8). M. of Gloucester, pr. of Bromfield, royal ass. 26 May 1228 (*CPR 1225–32*, p. 189); mand. for seisin 27 May 1228 (*CCR 1227–31*, p. 52). D. 15 July 1243 (*Ann. Tewkesbury*, p. 130); 1243 (*Ann. Worcs.*, p. 435). Lic. to el. (no reason given for vacancy) 12 Aug. 1243 (*CPR 1232–47*, p. 390).

Walter of St John (de Sancto Iohanne) **1243** Pr. of Gloucester, el. abb., royal ass. 28 Sept. 1243; writ *de intendendo* 1 Oct. 1243 (ibid., pp. 396–7), bl. 4 Oct. 1243, but d. on day he should have been installed (*Ann. Worcs.*, p. 435, *Ctl. Gloucester*, I, 29; *Ann. Tewkesbury*, p. 131). D., lic. to el. 29 Oct. 1243 (*CPR 1232–47*, p. 407).

John de Felda (Feld, de la Feld) **1243–1263** Precentor of Gloucester, bl. 6 Dec. 1243; installed 13 Dec. 1243 (*Ann. Tewkesbury*, p. 132). Royal ass. 26 Nov. 1243; writ *de intendendo* 27 Nov. 1243 (*CPR 1232–47*, p. 408). D. 27 Mar. 1263 (*Ctl. Gloucester*, I, 30, cf. PRO, C84/3/3).

Reginald de Homme 1263–1284 M. of Gloucester, eln pres. to king for royal ass. 6 Apr. 1263 (PRO, C84/3/2); royal ass. 2 Apr. 1263, temps. 29 Apr. 1263, eln having been conf. by the bp of Worcester (*CPR 1258–66*, pp. 254, 256); installed 1 July 1263 (*Ctl. Gloucester*, I, 31). Abb. Felda's chaplain (ibid.). D. 1283 (*Ann. Worcs.*, p. 489), but D. 13 Sept. 1284 (*Ctl. Gloucester*, I, 34). Seal (*Hereford Seals*, p. 8).

John de Gamages 1284–1306 Prev. pr. of St Guthlac's, Hereford, el. 1 Oct. 1284 (*Ctl. Gloucester*, III, 26–7). Installed 30 Nov. 1284 (ibid., I, 34). M. of Gloucester, royal ass. 4 Oct. 1284 (*CPR 1281–92*, p. 135). Succ. 1283, *nobilissimus vir morum elegantia et parentum nobilitate* (*Ann. Worcs.*, p. 489). Request to king for confirmation 10 Oct. 1285 (*Reg. G. Giffard*, p. 252). Mand. to obey 18 Nov. 1284 (ibid., p. 250). D. 17 Apr. 1306 (*Ann. Worcs.*, p. 559; *Ctl. Gloucester*, I, 39; BL, Cotton ms. Cleopatra D III, f. 57r). Bur. 19 Apr. 1306 (*Worcs Liber Albus*, p. 62; *Ann. Worcs.*, p. 559). D., lic. to el. 21 Apr. 1306 (*CPR 1301–07*, p. 429).

John Thoky (Toky) **1306–1328** Sub-pr. of Gloucester, succ. 1306 and bl. at Hartlebury 25 June (*Ann. Worcs.*, p. 559). El. 1 May 1306 (*Ctl. Gloucester*, I, 41). Eln pres. to king for royal ass. 1 May 1306 (PRO, C84/15/41); royal ass. 3 May 1306; temps. 16 May 1306 (*CPR 1301–07*, pp. 430, 432). Cert. conf. eln by bp of Worcester 13 May 1306 (PRO, C84/15/42). Bl. and prof. obed. 24 June 1306 (*Reg. Gainsborough*, pp. 151–2). Installed 29 June 1306 (*Ctl. Gloucester*, I, 41; *Worcester Liber Albus*, I, no. 363). 1322 abb. 'stricken with old age' (*CPR 1321–24*, p. 78). Cess. by 25 Oct. 1328 (PRO, C84/16/12). Cess., lic. to el. 27 Oct. 1328 (*CPR 1327–30*, p. 325). D. Jan. 1329 x Jan 1330 (*Ctl. Gloucester*, I, 45).

John of Wigmore (Wygemor(e), Wyggemor, Wygmor) **1328–1337** Pr. of Gloucester, royal ass. 11 Nov. 1328, temps. 10 Dec. 1328 (*CPR 1327–30*, pp. 332, 342). Eln conf. 1 Dec. 1328 (*Reg. Orleton (Worc.)*, nos. 258–9). 1328 too infirm to attend to business in the courts personally (*CPR 1327–30*, p. 345); 1330 believed to be suffering from incurable disease (ibid., p. 343). D. 28 Feb. 1337 (*Ctl. Gloucester*, I, 47). D., lic. to el. 3 Mar. 1337 (*CPR 1334–38*, p. 384).

Adam of Staunton (Stauntone) **1337–1351** M. of Gloucester, royal ass. 18 Mar. 1337, temps. 11 Apr. 1337 (ibid., pp. 397, 420). Cert. conf. eln by bp of Worcester 9 Apr. 1337 (PRO, C84/24/1). D. after 14½ years' rule and bur. at altar of St Thomas Martyr (*Ctl. Gloucester*, I, 48). D. by 26 Oct. 1351 (PRO, C84/26/45). D., lic. to el. 28 Oct. 1351 (*CPR 1350–54*, p. 172). Seal (*Mon. Seals*, p. 37).

Thomas de Horton 1351–1377 M. of Gloucester, eln pres. to king for royal ass. 15 Nov. 1355 (PRO, C84/26/46); royal ass. 19 Nov. 1351, temps. 12 Dec. 1351 (*CPR 1350–54*, pp. 185,

191). Sacrist of Gloucester (*Ctl. Gloucester*, I, 48). Commn to bp of Hereford to conf. eln 19 Nov. 1351; cert. conf. eln 4 Dec. 1351; notif. to king 9 Dec.; mand. to install 10 Dec. (Worcester, Reg. Thoresby, pp. 78–9; PRO, C84/26/47). Occ. 10 Sept. 1377 (*Gloucester Reg.*, p. 31, no. 74). Cess., lic. to el. 8 Nov. 1377 (*CPR 1377–81*, p. 59). D. 30 Mar. 1378 (*Ctl. Gloucester*, I, 50–1).

John (de) Boyfeld 1377–1380 Precentor of Gloucester, el. 26 Nov. 1377 (*Ctl. Gloucester*, I, 51–2). Royal ass. 2 Nov. 1377, temps. 31 Dec. 1377 (*CPR 1377–81*, pp. 73, 82). Bl. by bp of Hereford 20 Dec. 1377, installed 24 Dec. (*Ctl. Gloucester*, I, 52). D. by 31 Dec. 1380 (PRO, C84/32/31). D., lic. to el. 7 Jan. 1381 (*CPR 1377–81*, p. 564).

HULME, *see* ST BENET OF HULME

HUMBERSTON (Lincs), St Mary and St Peter f. *c.* 1160

Lists in *VCH Lincs.* II, 134; Heads, I, 53. See A. E. Kirkby and A. R. Taithby, *The Abbey of St Mary and St Peter, Humberston, Lincolnshire* (Waltham, 1974).

Simon Occ. 20 Apr. 1203 (*Lincs F. 1199–1216*, p. 80, no. 170); 19 Oct. 1224 (*Lincs. F.*, I, p. 168).

William of Coxwold (Kukewald) **1225/6–1261/2** Pr. of Humberston, el. & conf. Dec. 1225 x Dec. 1226, no reason given for vacancy (*Reg. Wells*, III, 151). D. Nov. 1261 x Nov. 1262 (*Reg. R. Gravesend*, p. 9).

Geoffrey 1261/2– Cellarer of Humberston el. Nov. 1261 x Nov. 1262 (ibid.).

Thomas of Sutterby 1274–1289 Pr. of Humberston, eln conf. 9 May 1274 on d. of prev. unnamed abb.; bl. & prof. obed. 10 May 1274 (*Reg. R. Gravesend*, p. 58). D. by 8 June 1289 (*Reg. Sutton*, I, 120).

John of Bratoft (Braytoft) **1289–1311** Pr. of Humberston, eln quashed but apptd by bp 8 June 1289 (ibid., 120–1). D. by 11 Sept. 1311 (Lincoln, Ep. Reg., II, f. 37r).

William of Sutterby 1311–1339 M. of Humberston, eln quashed but apptd by bp 11 Sept. 1311 (ibid.). D. by 1 Dec. 1339 (*Reg. Burghersh*, I, no. 619).

John of Horkstow (Horkestowe) **1339–** M. of Humberston, eln quashed but apptd by vicar-general of bp of Lincoln 1 Dec. 1339 (ibid.). Lic. to be bl. by any Catholic bp 1 Dec. 1339: bl. by bp of Carlisle, cert. 5 Dec. 1339 (*Reg. Kirkby*, I, nos. 517–18). Presumably vacated abbey 1355 (see below). 2 Oct. 1359 a corrody granted to him as former abb. (Lincoln, Ep. Reg., VIII, f. 137v).

Henry of Binbrook (Binbrok, Bynbrok) **1355–1364** Commn to exam. eln dated 19 Nov. 1355, no reason given for vacancy (ibid., f. 77v). M. of Humberston, eln conf. 19 Nov. 1355, bl. 25 Dec. 1355 (Lincoln, Ep. Reg., IX, ff. 117v–118r). Cess. by 13 Feb. 1364 (Lincoln, Ep. Reg., X, f. 6v).

Ranulph of Haltham (Holtham) **1364–1381** M. of Humberston, apptd by bp of Lincoln, to whom the right of appt had been transferred, 13 Feb. 1364 (ibid.). Occ. 1377, 1381 (*Clerical Poll-Taxes*, pp. 31, 169, nos. 420, 2091; also (as Ralph) 1381, p. 121, no. 1490). Pardoned for the death of Robert Neuland of Humberston 15 June 1380 (*CPR 1377–1381*, p. 501). Cess. by 18 May 1381 (Lincoln, Ep. Reg., X, f. 114r). Mandate to make provision for ex-abb. 26 May 1381 (ibid.).

LUFFIELD (Bucks and Northants), St Mary f. 1116 x 1118. diss. 1494 (priory)

Lists in *VCH Bucks*, I, 349–50; *VCH Northants.*, II, 97; *Luffield Chts.*, II, p. lxxix; Heads, I, 53–4.

Roger –1231 Occ. 1 July 1214 (*Bucks F.*, II, 105); 1214 (*CRR*, VII, 52); Oct. 1220 x Oct. 1221 (*Luffield Chts.*, I, no. 196). D., lic. to el. 30 Apr. 1231 (*CPR 1225–32*, p. 432).

William of Brackley (Brackele) **1231–1263** (W.) M. of Luffield, royal ass. 3 June 1231 (ibid.).

El. and adm. Dec. 1230 x Dec. 1231 (bp's pontifical year), no reason given for vacancy (*Reg. Wells*, II, 163). D., lic. to el. 16 Jan. 1263 (*CPR 1258–66*, p. 239). D. Nov. 1262 x Jan. 1263 (*Reg. R. Gravesend*, p. 294 – Nov. 1262 being the start of the bp's pontifical year). D. by 10 Jan. 1263 when lic. to el. sought (PRO, C84/2/44).

Ralph of Silverstone *alias* **of Luffield** (Selveston, Silverston, Luffeld) **1263–1275** M. of Luffield, eln pres. to king for royal ass. 18 Jan. 1263 (PRO, C84/2/46); royal ass. 20 Jan. 1263, temps. (Robert) 18 Jan. 1263 (*CPR 1258–66*, pp. 240, 242). Eln quashed but apptd by bp Nov. 1262 x Nov. 1263 (*Reg. R. Gravesend*, pp. 102, 292); bp's cert. to king 29 Jan. 1263 (PRO, C84/2/48). Occ. (R.) 14 Apr. 1275 (*Luffield Chts.*, II, p. 436, app. A1). Res. ? *c.* June 1275 (*Reg. R. Gravesend*, p. 127). Res. by 11 June 1275 (PRO, C84/5/31). Cess., lic. to el. 13 June 1275 (*CPR 1272–81*, p. 94).

William of Easton Neston (Esteneston, Esteston, Estniston, Estinton) **1275–1280** M. of Luffield, eln pres. to king for royal ass. 17 June 1275 (PRO, C84/5/33); royal ass. and writ *de intendendo* 20 June 1275 (*CPR 1272–81*, p. 96). Eln conf. *c.* June 1275 (*Reg. R. Gravesend*, pp. 127, 303); bp's cert. to king 23 June 1275 (PRO, C84/9/35). Res. by 7 Mar. 1280 (*Reg. Sutton*, II, 2). Res., lic. to el. 26 Feb. 1280 (*CPR 1272–81*, p. 364). Mand. of archbp of Canterbury to bp-el. of Lincoln forbidding him to assign to former prior William a portion outside the monastery (*Reg. Peckham*, I, 101–2). Revocation of privileges gtd to former pr. by Bp Sutton of Lincoln 15 Nov. 1284 (ibid., III, 854–5).

Adam of Hendred (Handred, Henred) **1280–1284** M. of Luffield, royal ass. 2 Mar. 1280; writ *de intendendo* 8 Mar. 1280 (*CPR 1272–81*, pp. 364, 366). Eln conf. 7 Mar. on res. of William of Easton Neston (*Reg. Sutton*, II, 2). Cess., lic. to el. 21 Dec. 1284 (*CPR 1281–92*, p. 146).

William of Brackley (Brackele, Brakk') **1285** M. of Luffield, el. on res. of Adam, royal ass. 2 Jan. 1285 (ibid., p. 150). Eln quashed by bp 18 Jan. 1285 (*Reg. Sutton*, II, 44).

Adam of Hendred 1285–1287 M. of Luffield, re-apptd 26 Jan. 1285 (ibid., II, 44). Bp Sutton had preferred Adam to be pr. without renewed lic. to el. having been sued or royal ass. obtained. Order to deliver Adam late prior the temps. of the priory until the next Parliament after Easter, 2 Feb. 1285 (*CFR 1272–1307*, p. 210). Temps. 1 May 1285 (*CPR 1281–92*, p. 160). Cess. by 24 May 1287 (PRO, C84/9/4). Cess., lic. to el. 26 May 1287 (*CPR 1281–92*, p. 270, cf. *Reg. Sutton*, II, 59).

Richard of Silverstone (Selveston, Silveston, Milveston) **1287** Sub-pr. of Luffield, eln pres. to king for royal ass. 18 June 1287 (PRO, C84/10/1); royal ass. 18 June 1287 (*CPR 1281–92*, p. 271). El. but refused to accept eln (*Reg. Sutton*, II, 59). Res., lic. to el. 18 June 1287 (*CPR 1281–92*, p. 271).

John de Houton 1287–1289 Eln pres. to king for royal ass. 4 July 1287 (PRO, C84/9/8); royal ass. 6 July 1287, temps. 16 July 1287 (*CPR 1281–92*, pp. 271, 276 – says M. of Luffield). El. on 3 July, conf. 11 July 1287 (*Reg. Sutton*, II, 59–60 – says M. of Daventry; PRO, C84/9/10). Res. to join Franciscans (*Reg. Sutton*, II, 74); house void 24 Apr. 1289 by cess. of John de Houton (*CFR 1272–1307*, p. 259). Cess., lic. to el. 28 Apr. 1289 (*CPR 1281–92*, p. 314).

Gilbert de Merse (Mersch') **1289** M. of Luffield, royal ass. 3 May 1289 (ibid., p. 315). El. but renounced eln (*Reg. Sutton*, II, 74). Res. of pr.-el., lic. to el. 8 May 1289 (*CPR 1281–92*, p. 315; PRO, C84/9/2).

Peter of Shalstone (Saldeston, Schaldeston, Shaldeston, Scaldeford) **1289–1294** M. of Luffield, eln pres. to king for royal ass. 14 May 1289 (PRO, C84/9/33); royal ass. 15 May 1289, temps. 22 May 1289 (*CPR 1281–92*, p. 316). El. on 14 May and conf. 21 May 1289 (*Reg. Sutton*, II, 74; PRO, C84/9/34). Dismissed from office for failure to obey the bp's injunctions 21 Oct. 1294 (*Reg. Sutton*, II, 119; V, 37–8). Dep., lic. to el. 4 Nov. 1294 (*CPR 1292–1301*, p. 101).

William of Brackley (Brackele) **1294–1316** M. of Luffield, eln pres. to king for royal ass. 31

Oct. 1294 (PRO, C84/12/22); royal ass. 20 Nov. 1294, temps. 28 Dec. 1294 (*CPR 1292–1301*, pp. 125, 128). Eln conf. 19 Dec. 1294 (*Reg. Sutton*, II, 119; PRO, C84/12/24). D. by 23 May 1316 (PRO, C84/18/28). D. (W.), lic. to el. 28 May 1316 (*CPR 1313–17*, p. 462).

John of Westbury 1316–1344 M. of Luffield, royal ass. 13 June 1316, temps. 13 July 1316 (ibid., pp. 470, 511). Eln quashed but apptd by bp 9 July 1316 (Lincoln, Ep. Reg., II, f. 130r; PRO, C84/18/40). D., lic. to el. 14 Oct. 1344 (*CPR 1343–45*, p. 343).

William of Skelton (Skilton, Skylton) **1344–1349** M. of Luffield, royal ass. 22 Oct. 1344, temps. 1 Nov. 1344 (ibid., pp. 350, 361). Eln quashed but apptd by bp 3 Nov. 1344 (Lincoln, Ep. Reg., VI, f. 59r). D. by 28 May 1349 (PRO, C84/25/47). D., lic. to el. 29 May 1349 (*CPR 1348–50*, p. 293).

William (of) Horwood (Horwode) **1349–1383** M. of Luffield, royal ass. 8 June 1349, temps. 30 June 1349 (ibid., pp. 302, 334). Eln quashed but apptd by bp 25 June 1349 (Lincoln, Ep. Reg., IX, f. 287v). Res., lic. to el. 23 Apr. 1383 (*CPR 1381–85*, p. 242; cf. Lincoln, Ep. Reg., X, f. 230r–v).

MALMESBURY (Wilts), St Mary and St Aldhelm f. *c.* 965

Lists in *VCH Wilts*, III, 230–1; *Heads*, I, 54–6.

Walter Loring 1208–1222 M. of Malmesbury el. 1208 (*PR 10 John*, p. 195). M. 30 years, abb. '19' years (*Ctl. Malmesbury*, I, 251). D. 1222 (not named) (*Ann. Dunstable*, p. 77). D., lic. to el. 30 Oct. 1222 (*CPR 1216–25*, p. 349).

John Walensis 1222–?1246 M. of Malmesbury, royal ass. 10 Nov. 1222 (ibid., p. 351). Occ. from 20 Jan. 1224 to 8 July 1241 (*Wilts F.*, I, 13, 35); 17 Oct. 1230, (J.) 25 July 1231 (*Ctl. Malmesbury*, II, 29, 52–3); 25 July 1231 (PRO, E40/4850); 8 Feb. 1236 (*Ctl. Glastonbury*, I, p. 209, no. 342). Lic. to el. (no name or reason given) 10 Mar. 1246 (*CPR 1232–47*, p. 475).

Geoffrey 1246–1260 Abb. 15 years (*Ctl. Malmesbury*, I, 251). Sacrist of Malmesbury, royal ass. 25 Mar. 1246, writ *de intendendo* 30 Mar. 1246 (*CPR 1232–47*, pp. 476–7). Bl. (G.) by bp of Salisbury 20 Apr. 1246 (*Sarum Chts.*, p. 301, no. cclvi). D., lic. to el. 7 Apr. 1260 (*CPR 1258–66*, p. 120).

William of Colerne (Colern) **1260–1296** Abb. 25 years (*Ctl. Malmesbury*, I, 251, cf. II, 380). M. of Malmesbury, royal ass. 20 Apr. 1260; temps. 29 Apr. 1260 (*CPR 1258–66*, pp. 121, 67). D. 21 Sept. 1296 (BL, Cotton ms. Cleopatra D. III, f. 51r). D., lic. to el. 3 Oct. 1296 (*CPR 1292–1301*, p. 205).

William of Badminton (Badmynton, Bamynton) **1296–1324** M. of Malmesbury, royal ass. 25 Oct. 1296, temps. 6 Nov. 1296 (ibid., pp. 208–9). Cert. conf. eln by bp of Salisbury 1 Nov. 1296 (PRO, C84/12/36). Said to be sick and infirm 23 Feb. 1324 (*Parliamentary Writs*, II, div. 3, p. 1135). D. by 23 May 1324 (PRO, C84/20/33). D., lic. to el. 26 May 1324 (*CPR 1321–24*, p. 416).

Adam de la Hok(e) 1324–1340 Sacrist of Malmesbury, eln pres. to king for royal ass. 8 June 1324 (PRO, C84/20/35); eln pres. to bp 14 June 1324, eln conf. 21 June 1324, bl. 29 July 1324 (*Reg. Martival*, I, 419–27; PRO, C84/20/36). Royal ass. 12 June 1324, temps. 29 June 1324 (*CPR 1321–24*, pp. 423, 426). D., lic. to el. 29 Mar. 1340 (*CPR 1338–40*, p. 441).

John of Tintern (Tinterne, Tynterne) **1340–1349** M. of Malmesbury, royal ass. 10 Apr. 1340, temps. 25 Apr. 1340 (ibid., pp. 452, 467). Cert. conf. eln by bp of Salisbury 26 Apr. 1340 (PRO, C84/24/15). D. 8 Aug. 1349 (*Eulog. Hist.*, II, 214). D., lic. to el. 9 Aug. 1349 (*CPR 1348–50*, p. 357).

Simon de Aumeney (Ammeneye, *alias* Segre) **1349–1361** M. of Malmesbury, eln conf. 5 Sept. 1349 Sept. (Salisbury, Reg. Wyvil, II, ff. 217v–218r; PRO, C84/26/19). Eln pres. to king for royal ass. 17 Aug. 1349 (PRO, C84/26/11); royal ass. 19 Aug. 1349, temps. 11 Sept. 1349

(*CPR 1348-50*, pp. 366, 377). D. by 10 Oct. 1361 (PRO, C84/28/12). D., lic. to el. 13 Oct. 1361 (*CPR 1361-64*, p. 85).

Walter (de) Camme 1361-1396 M. of Malmesbury, made abb. 31 Oct. (*Eulog. Hist.*, III, 313), royal ass. 4 Nov. 1361, temps. 25 Nov. 1361 (*CPR 1361-64*, pp. 93, 115). Eln conf. 9 Nov. 1361 (Salisbury, Reg. Wyvil, II, f. 287r). D. 23 Feb. 1396 (BL, Add. ms. 6165, f. 59r). D., lic. to el. 27 Feb. 1396 (*CPR 1391-96*, p. 661). Seal (*BM Seals*, no. 3599; *Hereford Seals*, p. 8).

MILTON (Dorset), St Mary, St Michael, St Samson and St Branwalader f. 964

Lists in *VCH Dorset*, II, 62; J. P. Traskey, *Milton Abbey: a Dorset monastery in the middle ages* (Tisbury, 1978), pp. 201-2; *Heads*, I, 56.

Eustace 1198- Sacrist of Milton el. 1198 (*Ann. Winchester*, p. 69). Occ. Oct. 1206 (*Rot. Ch.*, p. 163); 16 June 1219 (*Dorset F.*, p. 21); 1216 x 1220 (*Ctl. Loders*, pp. 62-4). House void by 8 Nov. 1222 (*CPR 1216-25*, p. 351).

William de Stoke(s) 1222-1256 Royal ass. and writ *de intendendo* 10 Nov. 1222 (*Rot. Lit. Claus.*, I, 520, cf. *CPR 1216-25*, p. 351). Gt of future custody of abbey to the pr. and convent when it shall fall vacant by the cess. or d. of William de Stokes 12 Nov. 1256 (*CPR 1247-58*, p. 530). An unnamed abb. d. 1256 (*Ann. Winchester*, p. 96). D. by 17 Nov. 1256 (PRO, C84/1/44). Lic. to el. (no reason given for vacancy) 18 Nov. 1256 (*CPR 1247-58*, p. 531).

William of Taunton (Tantone) **1256-1273** Formerly pr. of Winchester, St Swithun, succ. 1256 (*Ann. Winchester*, p. 96). Eln pres. to king for royal ass. 26 Nov. 1256 (PRO, C84/1/45); royal ass. 6 Dec. 1256, temps. 7 Dec. 1256, the eln having been conf. by 3 vicegerents of Giles, bp of Salisbury (*CPR 1247-58*, pp. 532, 533). El. Bp of Winchester by majority of Chapter 3 Feb. 1261 (*Le Neve 1066-1300*, II, 86). Eln quashed by Pope before 22 June 1262; given further dispensation to continue as abb. of Milton and to be a bp if el., 6 July 1262 (ibid.; *CPL*, I, 377-8). Gt of future custody of abbey to the pr. and convent when it shall fall vacant by the d. or cess. of abb. William, 12 Apr. 1273 (*CPR 1272-81*, p. 7; *CFR 1272-1307*, p. 3). D. by 13 Apr. 1273 (PRO, C84/4/41). D., lic. to el. 15 Apr. 1273 (*CPR 1272-81*, p. 8).

Walter of Corfe (Corf, Corffe) **1273-1291** Pr. of Milton, el. 1 May 1273 (PRO, C84/4/42); royal ass. (Robert) 19 May 1273, temps. (Walter) 17 June 1273 (*CPR 1272-81*, pp. 9, 10). Cert. conf. eln by bp of Salisbury 10 June 1273 (PRO, C84/4/44). D., mand. to issue lic. to el. 22 Feb. 1291 (*Cal. Chanc. Warr.*, p. 30).

Walter de Sideling (Sidelingge, Sydelungg') **1291-1314** M. of Milton, eln pres. to king for royal ass. 5 Mar. 1291 (PRO, C84/10/11); royal ass. 10 Mar. 1291, temps. 18 Mar. 1291 (*CPR 1281-92*, pp. 425, 426). Cert. conf. eln by bp of Salisbury 15 Mar. 1291 (PRO, C84/10/14). D. 25 Nov. 1314 (PRO, C84/17/45). D. (W.), lic. to el. 11 Dec. 1314 (*CPR 1313-17*, p. 201). Ledger stone (*Earliest English Brasses*, p. 186 and fig. 82).

Robert le Fauconer (Faukener) **1314-1331** M. of Milton, eln pres. to king for royal ass. 22 Dec. 1314 (PRO, C81/90/3221); royal ass. 26 Dec. 1314, temps. 21 Jan. 1315 (*CPR 1313-17*, pp. 206, 210). Cert. conf. eln by bp of Salisbury 18 Jan. 1315 (PRO, C84/18/7). Occ. 10 May 1331 (*CFR 1327-37*, p. 261). D. by 21 May 1331 (PRO, C84/22/44). D., lic. to el. 28 May 1331 (*CPR 1330-34*, p. 121).

Richard Maury (Mauri) **1331-1352** M. of Milton, royal ass. 8 June 1331, temps. 2 July 1331 (ibid., pp. 123, 150). Cert. conf. eln by archbp of Canterbury *ratione visitationis* 26 June 1331 (PRO, C84/22/47). Ratification of the conf. by archbp of Canterbury, Bp Wyvil being *in remotis* 14 Nov. 1336; prof. obed. 15 Nov. 1336 (Salisbury, Reg. Wyvil I, f. 34v;). Commn to take the abbey into the king's hands, now in a state of great depression and indebtedness by reason of the dissensions between the abb. and some of his monks 24 Apr. 1344 (*CPR 1343-45*, p. 264). Res. 13 Nov. 1352 (Salisbury, Reg. Wyvil I, f. 141r). Res., lic. to el. 18 Nov. 1352 (*CPR 1350-54*, p. 357). Seal (*Mon. Seals*, p. 61).

Robert (de) Burbach(e) 1352–1382 M. of Milton, royal ass. 30 Nov. 1352, temps. 12 Dec. 1352 (*CPR 1350–54*, pp. 367, 376). D. by 3 Oct. 1382 (PRO, C84/33/1). D., lic. to el 7 Oct. 1382 (*CPR 1381–85*, p. 165).

MONK BRETTON (Yorks W.), St Mary Magdalen f. *c.* 1153 x 1155 (dependent on Pontefract); *c.* 1279 (independent Benedictine priory).

Lists in *VCH Yorks*, III, 94; J. W. Walker, *Monk Bretton Priory*, p. 60; *Heads*, I, 120. For earlier priors see under Cluniac Houses.

William de Rihale (Riall, Ryhal(1), Rykale, Rykall) **–1291** First Benedictine pr. Occ. 4 Jan. 1281 (*Ctl. Monk Bretton*, p. 216; *Reg. Wickwane*, p. 139; BL, Lansdowne ms. 402, ff. 115v–116r); 17 Apr. 1283 (*CPR 1281–92*, p. 61); 1287 (*Yorks F.*, 1272–1300, p. 81); testimonial to good behaviour 10 May 1290; letter to king asking him to recall a writ against the pr. since he was not an apostate 29 May 1290 (*Reg. Romeyn*, II, 98–9, 100, cf. Logan, *Runaway Religious*, pp. 199–200). Res. 21 Sept. 1291 (*Reg. Romeyn*, II, 114).

William of York 1291– M. of Monk Bretton, recognition as new pr. 21 Sept. 1291 (ibid.). Occ. 21 Apr. 1297 (*Ctl. Monk Bretton*, p . 180); Easter 1299 (PRO, CP40/127, m. 178d).

Richard de Halgton (Haulghton) **1305–1323** M. of Monk Bretton, eln quashed, but apptd by Dean and Chapter of York *sede vacante*, mand. to install 16 Nov. 1305 (*Reg. Corbridge*, II, 168). 2 July 1323 mand. to him to give up the keys to the goods of the house to the sub-pr. and cellarer (York, Reg. 9A, f. 194v). Dep. 22 Aug. 1323 (ibid., f. 196r). Provision made for him 3 Jan. 1324 (ibid., f. 196v). Seal (*BM Seals* no. 3659; Clay, *Seals*, p. 26).

Disputed election between William de Went' and William de Staynton (York, Reg. 9A, f. 196r). Elns quashed by archbp 27 Aug. 1323 (ibid.).

William of Wentbridge (Went, Wentebrigg) **1323–1338** Apptd by archbp 26 Sept. 1323 (ibid.). Occ. 3 Oct. 1324, purgation from visitation charges (ibid., f. 205r). Papal commn to investigate charges made against pr. of dilapidation and other crimes 8 Nov. 1326 (*CPL*, II, 254). Res. 10 July 1338 (ibid., f. 261v). Provision made for him 17 July 1338 (ibid.).

William of Appleby (Appelby) **1338–** M. of Monk Bretton, el. immediately on res. of William of Went[bridge]. Conf. by archbp is undated, but order to convent to obey him dated 17 July 1338 (ibid.).

William of Stainton (Staynton) **–1349** Occ. 1347 (Baildon, I, 141). D. by 17 Oct. 1349 (York, Reg. 10, f. 39v).

Hugh of Brierley (Brereleye) **1349–** M. of Monk Bretton, eln conf. 17 Oct. 1349 (ibid.); prof. obed. s.d. (ibid., f. 40r). Mentd as former pr. 1361 (PRO, CP40/406, m. 33).

John of Birthwaite (Birkethwayt, Birthwait, Birthwat, Birthwayt, Byresthwayt, Byrthwayt) Occ. 2 Dec. 1350 (*Ctl. Monk Bretton*, p. 182); 28 Mar. 1353 (ibid., pp. 220–1); 3 Feb. 1357 (*Yorks Deeds*, I, 144); 10 July 1361, 15 Feb. 1363 (*CPR 1361–64*, pp. 40, 310); 8 Sept. 1363 (*Ctl. Monk Bretton*, p. 31); going to Rome, lic. to cross sea 12 Jan. 1368 (*CPR 1367–70*, p. 74); 1369, Hilary 1370 (Baildon, I, 142).

The next recorded pr., **William**, occ. 7 July 1385 (*Ctl. Monk Bretton*, p. 47).

MUCHELNEY (Soms), St Peter Ref. *c.* 959

Lists in *VCH Soms*, II, 107; *Ctl. Muchelney*, pp. 18–19; *Le Neve 1300–1541*, VIII, 52–3; *Heads*, I, 56–7.

Richard I –1235 Occ. Lent 1195 x 1 May 1204 (*EEA*, 10, no. 234); 17 Oct. 1198 (*Ctl. Bath*, II, no. 18); from 1 Dec. 1201 to 14 Feb. 1231 (*EEA*, 10, no. 240; *Ctl. Muchelney*, p. 76, no. 58). D. 1235 (*Ann. Tewkesbury*, p. 97). D. (R.), lic. to el. 14 May 1235 (*CPR 1232–47*, p. 105).

Richard II 1235–1237 Sacrist of Muchelney, royal ass. 21 May 1235, writ *de intendendo* 19 June 1235 (ibid., pp. 105, 109). Succ. 1235, called Glestonie (? of Glastonbury) (*Ann. Tewkesbury*,

p. 97). D. 30 Sept. 1237 (ibid., p. 105). Lic. to el. (no reason given for vacancy) 8 Oct. 1237 (*CPR 1232–47*, p. 198).

Walter of Cerne 1237–1252 Pr. of Muchelney, royal ass. (no name) 22 Oct. 1237 (ibid., p. 199); mand. for seisin 23 Nov. 1237 (*CR 1237–42*, p. 6). Surname (*Ctl. Muchekney*, p. 71, no. 47). Occ. from 1 July 1238 to 12 Mar. 1243 (*Ctl. Muchelney*, pp. 81, 108). Lic. to el. (no reason given for vacancy) 22 June 1252 (*CPR 1247–58*, p. 143).

John de Barnevill 1252– M. of Muchelney, royal ass. 29 June 1252 (ibid., p. 144); mand. for seisin and writ *de intendendo* 3 July 1252 (*CR 1251–53*, p. 117). Cert. conf. eln by bp of Bath and Wells 3 July 1252 (PRO, C84/1/28). Occ. frequently in *Ctl. Muchelney* from 6 Apr. 1254 to 16 Feb. 1268 (pp. 60–1, 65); 21 May 1269, 15 July 1269 (*Soms Pleas*, II, 86, 96).

William de Gyvele 1274–1294 Pr. of Muchelney, royal ass. 27 Sept. 1274, writ *de intendendo* 8 Oct. 1274 (*CPR 1272–81*, pp. 58–9). Cert. conf. eln by bp of Bath and Wells 6 Oct. 1274 (PRO, C84/5/5). D. by 15 June 1294 when lic. to el. sought (PRO, C84/12/8). D., lic. to el. 19 June 1294 (*CPR 1292–1301*, p. 74).

Ralph of Muchelney (Michelnya) **1294–1305** M. of Muchelney, petition for royal ass. 25 June 1294 (PRO, C84/12/12). Royal ass. 3 July 1294, temps. 5 Aug. 1294 (*CPR 1292–1301*, pp. 78, 83). Cert. conf. eln by bp of Bath and Wells 25 July 1294 (PRO, C84/13/16). D (R.), lic. to el. 19 Jan. 1305 (*CPR 1301–7*, p. 310).

John de Henton (Hentone, Neuton) **1305–1334** Petition for royal ass. 3 Feb. 1305 (PRO, C84/15/26). Sacrist of Muchelney, royal ass. 1 Mar. 1305, temps. 10 Apr. 1305 (*CPR 1301–7*, pp. 315, 328). Cert. conf. eln by bp of Bath and Wells 6 Apr. 1305 (PRO, C84/15/29). Recently created (Neuton) 26 May 1305 (*C. Chanc. Warr.*, p. 249). D. 9 June 1334 (*Ctl. Muchelney*, p. 21). Lic. to el. sought 14 June 1334 (PRO, C84/23/10). D., lic. to el. 21 June 1334 (*CPR 1330–34*, p. 551).

John of Somerton (Somertone) **1334–1347** Pr. of Muchelney, eln notified to king 2 July 1334 (PRO, C84/23/11). Royal ass. 8 July 1334, temps. 24 July 1334 (*CPR 1330–34*, pp. 559, 567). Eln conf. 19 July 1334 (*Reg. R. Shrewsbury*, I, no. 690; PRO, C84/23/12). D., lic. to el. 9 Sept. 1347 (*CPR 1345–48*, p. 375). Chantry in Wells cathedral to celebrate for his soul by 15 Apr. 1350 (*Reg. R. Shrewsbury*, II, no. 2325).

John of Cudworth (Codeworth, Cudeworth) **1347–1349** Pr. of Muchelney, royal ass. 17 Sept. 1347, temps. 1 Nov. 1347 (*CPR 1345–48*, pp. 403, 424). D., lic. to el. 22 May 1349 (*CPR 1348–50*, p. 293).

Thomas of Overton 1349–1370 Pr. of Muchelney, royal ass. 29 May 1349, temps. 16 June 1349 (ibid., pp. 295, 306; *Reg. R. Shrewsbury*, II, no. 2359). D. 17 Nov. 1370 (PRO, C84/30/35). Lic. to el. sought 18 Nov. 1370 (ibid.). D., lic. to el. 21 Nov. 1370 (*CPR 1370–74*, p. 13).

William (of) Shepton (Schepton(e)) **1370–1398** M. of Muchelney, eln pres. to king for royal ass. 27 Nov. 1370 (PRO, C84/30/31); royal ass. 1 Dec. 1370, temps. 19 Dec. 1370 (*CPR 1370–74*, pp. 23, 28). Cert. conf. eln by bp of Bath and Wells 16 Dec. 1370 (PRO, C84/30/32). D. before 20 Feb. 1398 when lic. to el. sought (PRO, C84/37/13). D., lic. to el. 23 Feb. 1398 (*CPR 1396–99*, p. 276).

MULLICOURT (Norfolk), St Mary (de Bello Loco) f. ?–1086 (priory)
  List in *VCH Norfolk*, II, 350.

Simon Occ. Oct. 1247 x Oct. 1248 (Blomefield, *Norfolk*, VII, 477, without source). Occ. as former pr. 1250 (PRO, Just. 1/560, m. 36d).

Edward Occ. 1276 (Blomefield, *Norfolk*, VII, 477, without source).

Robert Occ. Hil. 1295 (PRO, CP40/107, mm. 44d, 156d); Nov. 1296 x Nov. 1297 (*Norfolk F (Rye)*, p. 149).

Andrew Occ. 1306 (Blomefield, *Norfolk*, VII, 477, citing a fine without precise reference).

William de Merstone 1316– M. of Mullicourt, eln quashed, but apptd by bp, no reason given for vacancy 6 Oct. 1316 (Norwich, Reg/1/1, f. 66r).

John de Malteby 1320–1333 M. of Mullicourt, custody and admin. of house committed to him 3 Mar. 1320, no reason given for vacancy (ibid., f. 82v). Apptd pr. by bp 1 May 1320 (ibid., f. 83v). D. by 2 Nov. 1333 (Norwich, Reg/1/2, ff. 61v–62r).

David of West Dereham (Westderham, Derham) 1333–1369 M. of Mullicourt, eln conf. 2 Nov. 1333 (ibid.). D. by 11 Apr. 1369 (Norwich, Reg/2/5, f. 85r).

John of Dereham (Derham) 1369–1390 M. of Mullicourt, apptd by bp 1 Apr. 1369, there being no eln on account of lack of monks (ibid.). D. by 9 July 1390 (Norwich, Reg/3/6, f. 147r).

NORWICH Holy Trinity Cathedral priory f. 1096 x 1101 (B. Dodwell in *TRHS*, 5th ser., VII (1957), 11).

Lists in *VCH Norfolk*, II, 327; *Le Neve 1066–1300*, II, 58–61, *1300–1541*, IV, 25–26; *Heads*, I, 57–8. Biographical details in Greatrex, *Biog. Reg.*, pp. 466–576 (Norwich monks).

William of Walsham –?1217 Said to have been apptd 1201 (*Bart. Cotton*, p. 92) – presumably wrong since predecessor occ. 1202 (*Heads*, I, 58). First occ. 10 Feb. 1205 (*Norfolk F. 1201–15*, no. 68). Last occ. 3 Feb. 1212 (*CRR*, VI, 221). Said to have d. 1217 (*Bart. Cotton*, p. 109). Prob. d. 23 Feb. (obit).

Master Ranulph of Wareham 1217 Said to have been el. 1217 (*Bart. Cotton*, p. 109), but el. bp of Chichester before 17 Dec. 1217 (*Le Neve 1066–1300*, VI, 4).

William son of Odo of Norwich 1219–1235 Said to have been installed 1219 and d. 1235 (*Bart. Cotton*, pp. 110, 118). Occ. 8 Feb. 1220 (Coxe, *Cal. Bodl. Chts.*, p. 244) and prob. earlier c. 11 Apr. 1219 (*Le Neve 1066–1300*, II, 60, citing *Reg. Greg.* IX, no. 3835). D. (W.) 12 Apr. 1235 (*Ann. Tewkesbury*, p. 99).). Obit of pr. William II 12 Apr. (BL, Harl. ms. 3950, f. 40v).

Simon of Elmham 1235–1257 Said to have succ. 1235, d. 8 June 1257 (*Bart. Cotton*, pp. 118, 137; cf. *CR 1256–59*, p. 137). Occ. from 1 July 1235 (*Norwich Cath. Chts.*, no. 331). He had been el. bp of Norwich before 9 Nov. 1236, but eln quashed by pope 17 Jan. 1239 (*Le Neve 1066–1300*, II, 57). Priory vacant by 13 June 1257 (*CCR 1256–59*, p. 137). Obit 8 June (BL, Harl. ms. 3950, f. 5v).

Roger de Skerning 1257–1266 M. of Norwich, el. 1257 (*Bart. Cotton*, p. 137). El. bp of Norwich 23 Jan. 1266, royal ass. 9 Feb. 1266 (*First Reg. Norwich*, p. 142; *CPR 1258–66*, p. 548; *Le Neve 1066–1300*, II, 57–8). Conf. by legate, followed by return of temps. 17 Mar. 1266, cons. 4 Apr. 1266 (ibid.).

Nicholas de Bramertone 1266–1269 El. 1266, eln conf. 18 Apr. 1266 (*Bart. Cotton*, p. 141). D. 19 Feb. 1269 (ibid., p. 143). Obit 19 Feb. (*Norwich Customary*, p. 2; BL, Harl. ms. 3950, f. 3v; Norfolk RO, DCN. Reg. XI, p. 2).

William of Burnham 1269–1272 Succ. before 25 Mar. 1269 (*Bart. Cotton*, p. 143). Res. 27 Sept. 1272 (ibid., p. 149, cf. *CPR 1266–72*, pp. 324, 682; *CCR 1268–72*, p. 526 – Binham, *recte* Norwich). Cf. res. 26 Sept. 1272 and gtd ch. of Worstead (*Flor. Hist.*, III, 26). D. 12 Feb. 1273 (ibid., III, 27).

William of Kirkby (Kirkeby) 1272–1289 El. and conf. 1 Oct. 1272; installed 2 Oct. 1272 (*Bart. Cotton*, p. 149; *Flor. Hist.*, III, 26). Sub-pr. of Norwich, temps. 20 Oct. 1272 (*CPR 1266–72*, p. 682). D. 25 Feb. 1289 (*Ch. Bury*, p. 92) but 9 Mar. 1289 (*Bart. Cotton*, p. 170). Obit 9 Mar. (BL, Harl. ms. 3950, f. 4r; Norfolk RO, DCN. Reg. XI, p. 3; BL, Arundel ms. 68, f. 19v; Lambeth ms. 20, f. 171r).

Henry of Lakenham 1289–1310 Sacrist of Norwich (*Ch. Bury*, p. 92). First occ. 27 June 1289

(*Le Neve 1066–1300*, II, 61, citing Norfolk RO, DCN., Norwich Cht. no. 1068). Res. shortly before 5 Feb. 1310 (Norwich, Reg/1/1, f. 35r). Obit 21 Oct. (*Norwich Customary*, p. 10; BL, Harl. ms. 3950, f. 7v); 22 Oct. (Norfolk RO, DCN, Reg. XI, f. 6v). Prob. d. 1310 (Norfolk RO, DCN.1/1/22).

Robert of Langley (Langele) **1310–1326** Sub-pr. of Norwich, el. 29 Jan. 1310 (Lambeth ms. 368, f. 4r); eln conf. 5 Feb. 1310 (Norwich, Reg/1/1, f. 35r). Occ. 16 Aug. 1325 (ibid., Reg/1/2, f. 1r). Res. by 4 Sept. 1326 (ibid., f. 9r–v). Obit 25 Aug. (BL, Harl. ms. 3950, f. 6v).

William of Claxton (Claxtone) **1326–1344** M. of Norwich, pr. of Yarmouth (q.v.), eln conf. 4 Sept. 1326 (Norwich, Reg/1/2, f. 9r–v); cert. of install. 5 Sept. 1326 (ibid., f. 9v). Occ. 26 July 1344 (*Reg. Bateman*, I, no. 98). D. by 25 Aug. 1344 (ibid., no. 102).

Simon Bozoun 1344–1352 M. of Norwich, eln conf. 25 Aug. 1344, installed 27 Aug. 1344 (ibid.). Res. by 24 Apr. 1352 (Norwich, Reg/2/4, f. 138v). Pr. of St Leonard's, Norwich 1352 (q.v.).

Laurence de Leek(e) (Leck) **1352–1357** M. of Norwich, eln quashed, but apptd by bp 24 Apr. 1352 (Norwich, Reg/2/4, f. 138v). See Sharpe, *Latin Writers*, p. 361. D. by 12 Dec. 1357 (Norwich, Reg/2/5, f. 23r–v).

Nicholas de Hoo 1357–1381 M. of Norwich, eln conf. 12 Dec. 1357, installed 14 Dec. (ibid.). Occ. 2 May 1381 (*CPR 1377–81*, p. 593). Res. by 24 June 1381 (Norfolk RO, DCN. 1/6/20).

PERSHORE (Worcs), St Mary f. c. 870

Lists in *VCH Worcs*, II, 136; *Heads*, I, 58–9.

Gervase 1204–1234 El. and bl. 1204 (*Ann. Worcs*, p. 392; *Ann. Tewkesbury*, p. 57). D. 1234 (*Ann. Worcs*, p. 425; *Ann. Tewkesbury*, p. 93). Lic. to el. 25 Apr. 1234 (*CPR 1232–47*, p. 44).

Roger de Rudeby (Rudby) **1234–1251** Chamberlain of Pershore, succ. 1234 (*Ann. Worcs*, p. 425; *Ann. Tewkesbury*, p. 93). Royal ass. 1 May 1234, writ *de intendendo* 9 May 1234 (*CPR 1232–47*, pp. 44, 45); mand. for seisin 9 May 1234 (*CR 1231–34*, p. 421). Cert. conf. eln by bp of Worcester n.d. (PRO, C84/1/7). D. (R.) 1251 (*Ann. Worcs*, p. 440). D., lic. to el. 4 Mar. 1251 (*CPR 1247–58*, p. 89).

Elerius 1251–1264 Succ. 1251 (*Ann. Worcs*, p. 440). Pr. of Cogges, royal ass. 19 Mar. 1251, writ *de intendendo* 15 Apr. 1251 (*CPR 1247–58*, pp. 90, 92). Cert. conf. eln by commissaries of bp 11 Apr. 1251 (PRO, C84/1/23). Apptd escheator this side Trent 4 Aug. 1251 (*CPR 1247–58*, p. 104); sent as royal envoy to Wales 1255 (ibid., p. 449); on pilgrimage to Pontigny 1257 (ibid., p. 514). 1253 royal letter to the earl of Cornwall and master W. of Kilkenny, archdeacon of Coventry, ordering that as soon as a Benedictine abbey 'fit for so great a man as abb. Elerius falls void in England, they are to endeavour by such means as seems most efficacious to promote him thereto' (ibid., p. 211). Gt to pr. and convent of custody of the abbey on its next voidance by the d. or cess. of abb. Elerius 30 June 1264 (*CPR 1258–66*, p. 351). Cess. by 19 Oct. 1264 (PRO, C84/3/13). Cess. (no name). lic. to el. 24 Oct. 1264 (*CPR 1258–66*, p. 355).

Henry of Bidford (Bideford) **1264–** M. of Pershore, writ *de intendendo* 12 Nov. 1264, the eln having been conf. by W., bp of Worcester (ibid., p. 387). Occ. 1269 (*Reg. G. Giffard*, p. 31); 25 Mar. 1271 (PRO, E210/241); Mich. 1272 x Mich. 1273 (PRO, E159/47, m. 14).

Henry de Caldewelle 1274–1290 M. of Pershore, writ *de intendendo* 3 Dec. 1274 (*CPR 1272–81*, p. 73). D. 2 Mar. 1290 (*Ann. Worcs*, p. 500). D., lic. to el. 6 Mar. 1290 (*CPR 1281–92*, p. 348).

William de Leghe (Leg(a)) **1290–1307** Cellarer of Pershore, royal ass. 10 Mar. 1290, writ *de intendendo* 12 Mar. 1290 (ibid., p. 348). Eln conf. 11 Mar. 1290 (*Reg. G. Giffard*, p. 368, cf. *Ann. Worcs*, p. 500; PRO, C84/9/27). D. (W.), lic. to el. 22 Apr. 1307 (*CPR 1301–07*, p. 520).

William of Harvington (Herwynton, Herewinton) **1307–1340** Royal ass. 16 May 1307, temps. 4 June 1307 (ibid., pp. 525, 529). M. of Pershore, commn to bp of Hereford to bl. abb.-el. 5 July 1307 (*Reg. Gainsborough*, p. 30). Asked permission to res. on account of old age and bodily infirmity 24 Sept. 1340, formal res. 26 Sept. 1340, acc. by bp 27 Sept. (*Reg. Bransford*, nos. 351, 352). Cess., lic. to el. 2 Oct. 1340 (*CPR 1340–43*, p. 34). As former abb., apptd by bp to administer spiritualities and temporalities 21 Oct. 1340 (*Reg. Bransford*, no. 141, see below).

Two candidates for el., **Thomas of Pirton** (Pyriton), Cellarer of Pershore, who gained 15 votes and **Robert de Lutlynton** who gained 13 votes. Both elns were quashed by bp (ibid., nos. 361–2, 366).

Thomas of Pirton (Pyriton, Piriton) **1340–1349** Cellarer of Pershore, royal ass. 25 Oct. 1340, temps Nov. 1340 (*CPR 1340–43*, pp. 48, 60). Apptd by bp 14 Nov. 1340 and request to king for restitution of temps. 14 Nov. 1340; mand. to install and to convent to obey 26 Nov. 1340 (*Reg. Bransford*, nos. 367–8, 374–6; cf. PRO, C84/24/17). D. by 16 July 1349 (*CCR 1349–54*, p. 40). D., lic. to el. 21 July 1349 (*CPR 1348–50*, p. 344).

Peter of Pendock (Pendok) **1349–1363** M. of Pershore, royal ass. 5 Aug. 1349, temps. 30 Aug. 1349 (ibid., pp. 357, 380). Res. acc. 8 Aug. 1363 (Worcester, Reg. Barnet, pp. 56–9). Cess., lic. to el. 18 Aug. 1363 (*CPR 1361–64*, p. 387).

Peter (de) Bradewey(e) **1363–1379** M. of Pershore, eln pres. to king for royal ass. 7 Sept. 1363 (PRO, C84/29/8–9); royal ass. 9 Sept. 1363, temps. 23 Sept. 1363 (*CPR 1361–64*, pp. 388, 389). Commn to conf. eln 15 Sept. 1363; eln conf. 20 Sept.; bl. 24 Sept. 1363 (Worcester, Reg. Barnet, pp. 56–9). D., lic. to el. 18 Sept. 1379 (*CPR 1377–81*, p. 390).

PETERBOROUGH (Northants), St Peter ref. c. 966

Lists in *VCH Northants*, II, 93; Ctl. *Peterborough*, pp. 224–5; *Heads*, I, 59–61.

Robert of Lindsey (Lindesei(a), Lindesey) **1214–1222** M. and sacrist Peterborough, el. 11 June 1214, pres. to king 15 Aug. 1214 (Sparke, II, 108; CUL, Peterborough ms. 1, f. 37v; *Ch.* p. 7 cf. *Rot. Lit. Pat.*, p. 109). El. 1213 (*Ann. Dunstable*, p. 40). Abb. 9 years and 10 weeks; d. 25 Oct. 1222 (Sparke, II, 115; CUL, Peterborough ms. 1, f. 40r). D. 1222 (*Ann. Dunstable*, p. 76; *Ann. Tewkesbury*, p. 66). D., lic. to el. 30 Oct. 1222 (*CPR 1216–25*, p. 349). Seal (*Mon. Seals*, p. 71).

Alexander of Holderness **1222–1226** Pr. of Peterborough, royal ass. 10 Nov. 1222 (*CPR 1216–25*, p. 351). D. 15 or 17 Nov. (lists – 17 Nov. *Archaeologia*, 51, p. 39); 1226 (*Ann. Dunstable*, p. 100); 19 Nov. 1226 (*Ch. Peterborough*, p. 9). House vacant by 16 Nov. 1226 (*CPR 1225–32*, p. 92). D., lic. to el. 28 Nov. 1226 (no name given) (*CPR 1225–32*, p. 93).

Martin of Ramsey (Rameseia, Rammese) **1226–1233** El. 2 Dec. 1226; received by king 7 Dec., conf. by bp of Lincoln in the chapel of St Katherine, Westminster, and bl. at Fingest 27 Dec. 1226 (*Ch. Peterborough*, p. 9; Sparke, II, 116; CUL, Peterborough ms. 1, f. 40r). M. and almoner of Peterborough, royal ass. 7 Dec. 1226 (*CPR 1225–32*, p. 95). D. 23 June 1233 (*Ch. Peterborough*, p. 13); or 26 June (*Archaeologia*, 51, p. 34). Lic. to el. (no reason given for vacancy) 30 June 1233 (*CPR 1232–47*, p. 19).

Walter of St Edmund (de Sancto Edmundo) **1233–1245** Sacrist of Peterborough, el. 1233 (Sparke, II, 117); royal ass. 8 July 1233 (*CPR 1232–47*, p. 20). (W.) mand. for seisin 29 July 1233 (*CR 1231–34*, p. 242). D. 22 Dec. 1245 (*MPCM*, IV, 502); or 23 Dec. 1245 (*Ch. Peterborough*, p. 15); or 26 Dec. 1245 (*Archaeologia*, 51, p. 40). Lic. to el. (no reason given for vacancy) 6 Jan. 1246 (*CPR 1232–47*, p. 469).

William de Hotot (Hoccot(e), Hocthone) **1246–1249** El. 6 Feb. 1246 (Sparke, II, 125) Eln conf. & bl. Jan. x June 1246 on death of Walter of St Edmund (*Reg. Grosseteste*, p. 225). Royal as. 17 Jan. 1246, writ *de intendendo* 11 Feb. 1246 (*CPR 1232–47*, pp. 470, 473). Entered (*ingressus*) 29 June 1246 (*Ch. Peterborough*, p. 15). Cess. 6 Dec. 1249 (*Ch. Peterborough*, p. 15)., but cf. res. June 1250 x June 1251 (*sic*) (*Reg. Grosseteste*, p. 244). Cess., lic. to el. 27 Dec. 1249 (*CPR 1247–58*, p. 56). Obit 6 Jan. (*Archaeologia*, 51, p. 29). For William (de) Hotot and the Hotot family see E. King, *Estate Records of the Hotot Family*, p. 8 and n. 46.

John de Caux (Caleto, Cauez, Cauz, Kaleto) **1250–1263** Pr. of St Swithun's, Winchester, postulated, el. 1249 (i.e. early 1250) (Sparke, II, 128); eln conf. and bl. June 1250 x June 1251 (*sic*) (*Reg. Grosseteste*, p. 244), but cf. cert. of conf. of postulation by bp of Lincoln 6 Feb. 1250 (PRO, C84/1/20). Royal ass. 15 Jan. 1250 (*CPR 1247–58*, p. 58). Mand. for seisin 8 Feb. 1250 (*CR 1247–50*, p. 263); transl. 1250 (*Ann. Tewkesbury*, p. 140). Entered (*ingressus*) into abbey St Peter's day (?29 June) 1250 (*Ch. Peterborough*, p. 15). Occ. as abb.–el. 9 Feb. 1250 (*CPR 1247–58*, p. 59). King's envoy to Scotland 1257 (*CPR 1247–58*, p. 574). Apptd. a papal chaplain 23 July 1260 (*CPL*, I, 374); Treasurer of England 1260–1263 (*Chronology*, p. 104; *CChR 1257–1300*, p. 119). Occ. 28 Sept. 1262 (*CPR 1266–72*, p. 732). D. 3 Mar. 1263 (*Ch. Peterborough*, pp. 16–17; Sparke, II, 132). D. Nov. 1262 x Nov. 1263 (*Reg. R. Gravesend*, p. 102). Obit 1 Mar. (*Archaeologia*, 51, p. 31). D. (J.), lic. to el. 8 Mar. 1263 (*CPR 1258–66*, p. 251).

Robert of Sutton (Sottone) **1263–1274** M. of Peterborough, el. 16 Mar. 1263 (Sparke, II, 132); eln conf. Nov. 1262 x Nov. 1263 (*Reg. R. Gravesend*, pp. 102, 294), cf. cert. conf. eln by bp of Lincoln 28 Mar. 1260 (PRO, C84/3/1). D. 11 Mar. 1274 (*Ch. Peterborough*, p. 20); cf. d. 17 Mar. in his 11th year en route for Council of Lyons (Sparke, II, 143); obit 21 Mar. (*Archaeologia*, 51, p. 31). D., lic. to el. 28 Mar. 1274 (*CPR 1272–81*, p. 45). Seal (*BM Seals*, no. 3835).

Richard of London (de Londiniis) **1274–1295** M. of Peterborough, el. 9 Apr. 1274 and eln conf. 17 Apr. 1274 (*Ch. Peterborough*, p. 20; *Reg. R. Gravesend*, p. 122; Sparke, II, 145 says he was sub-chamberlain, 3rd pr., and sacrist of Peterborough), but cf. eln pres. to king for royal ass. 28 Mar. 1274 (PRO, C84/5/2). Royal ass. 9 Apr. 1274, temps 20 Apr. 1274 (*CPR 1272–81*, pp. 46–7). D. 16 Aug. 1295 (Sparke, II, 150); cf. of obit 1 Aug. (*Archaeologia*, 51, p. 36). D., lic. to el. 24 Aug. 1295 (*CPR 1292–1301*, p. 143).

William of Woodford (Wodeford) **1295–1299** Sacrist of Peterborough, el. 29 Aug. 1295 (Sparke, II, 150); royal ass. 6 Sept. 1295, temps. 19 Sept. 1295 (*CPR 1292–1301*, pp. 146–7). Eln conf. 11 Sept. 1295, bl. 25 Sept. 1295 (*Reg. Sutton*, II, 131–2). D. 25 Sept. 1299 (Sparke, II, 153); cf. obit 2 Sept. (*Archaeologia*, 51, p. 37). D., lic. to el. 30 Sept. 1299 (*CPR 1292–1301*, p. 440). See Sharpe, *Latin Writers*, p. 819.

Godfrey of Crowland (Croyland) **1299–1321** M. of Peterborough, el. St Sergius and St Bacchus ? 7 Oct. 1299 (Sparke, II, 153). Royal ass. 10 Oct. 1299, temps 5 Nov. 1299 (*CPR 1292–1301*, pp. 441, 451). Eln conf. 19 Oct. 1299, bl. 25 Oct. 1299 (*Reg. Sutton*, II, 165). Entered monastery (*ingressus*) 29 Dec. 1299 (Sparke, II, 153). Cert. of purgation dated 26 May 1313 of abb. Godfrey who had been charged with adultery, procuring the death of his chamberlain, disclosing confessions of his monks and other offences. The abb. denied the charges and purged himself by 12 of his monks before the bp at his visitation 14 May 1313 (Lincoln, Ep. Reg., III, f. 274v); similar cert. of purgation 14 Oct. 1313 (ibid., f. 285r). D. in his 22nd year as abb. 21 Aug. 1321, bur. 29 Aug. (Sparke, II, 166, cf. 217). D., lic. to el. 3 Sept. 1321 (*CPR 1321–24*, p. 22). Indulgence of 40 days for his soul 11 Nov. 1322 (Lincoln, Ep. Reg., V, f. 324r). Mon. brass (*Earliest English Brasses*, p. 203). Seal (*BM Seals*, no. 3836).

Adam of Boothby (Botheby) **1321–1338** M. Peterborough, sub-cellarer, el. 7 Sept. 1321 (Sparke, II, 218). Royal ass. 25 Sept. 1321, temps 7 Oct. 1321 (*CPR 1321–24*, p. 26). Eln conf. 2 Oct. 1321; bp's letter to convent 18 Oct. (Lincoln, Ep. Reg., IV, f. 163r–v). D. 25 Nov. 1338, bur. 5 Dec. (*Ch. Angl. Petr.*, p. 167; Sparke, II, 232); cf. obit 23 Nov. (*Archaeologia*, 51, p. 39). D., lic. to el. 26 Nov. 1338 (*CPR 1338–40*, p. 169; PRO

SC1/42/97). Indulgence of 40 days for his soul 22 May 1340 (Lincoln, Ep. Reg., V, f. 580v). Mon. brass (*Earliest English Brasses*, p. 203). Seal (*Mon. Seals*, p. 71).

Henry of Morcott (Morcote) **1338–1353** M. of Peterborough, el. 8 Dec. 1338 (Sparke, II, 234); royal ass. 12 Dec. 1338, temps. 16 Jan. 1339 (*CPR 1338–40*, pp. 164, 175–6). Eln quashed 11 Jan. 1339 but apptd by vicar-general of bp of Lincoln 12 Jan. 1339 (Lincoln, Ep. Reg., IV, f. 224v). Bl. 13 Jan. 1339 (Sparke, II, 234). D. by 31 May 1353 (PRO, C84/27/11). D., lic. to el. 3 June 1353 (*CPR 1350–54*, p. 469).

Robert of Ramsey (Rameseye, Rammesaye) **1353–1360/1** Eln pres. to king for royal ass. 18 June 1353 (PRO, C84/24/29); royal ass. 20 June 1353, temps. 15 July 1353 (*CPR 1350–54*, pp. 470, 482). Cert. conf. eln by bp of Lincoln 10 July 1353 (PRO, C84/27/15). King's order to bp of Lincoln to appt suitable guardians at Peterborough 'as it is presumed that the abb. is dead, since no news of him has reached England since he lately departed for the Court of Rome' 3 June 1361 (*CFR 1356–68*, p. 162); gt of custody of vacant abbey to pr., sub-pr. and 2 monks 14 June 1361 (Lincoln, Ep. Reg., VIII, f 162v); gt to pr. and convent of the guardianship of the abbey 27 June 1361 (*CFR 1356–68*, p. 162). D., lic. to el. 22 Aug. 1361 (*CPR 1361–64*, p. 54). Obit 6 Oct. (*Archaeologia*, 51, p. 38).

Henry of Overton 1361–1391 M. of Peterborough. Pr. and convent el. Henry 'on receiving a sure report that the late abb. had died in parts beyond seas immediately after his departure from England and that the abbey had thus been void for a year or more' 20 Nov. 1361 (*CFR 1356–68*, p. 175). Eln pres. to king for royal ass. 28 Sept. 1361 (PRO, C84/28/9). Eln conf. 5 Nov. 1361 (Lincoln, Ep. Reg., IX, f. 238r). Royal ass. 2 Oct. 1361, temps. 10 Nov. 1361 (*CPR 1361–64*, pp. 79, 103). mand. for fealty 10 Nov. 1361 (*CCR 1360–64*, p. 305). D. by 4 Apr. 1391 (PRO, C84/35/8). D., lic. to el. 5 Apr. 1391 (*CPR 1388–92*, p. 387).

RAMSEY (Hunts), St Benedict f. 969

Lists in *VCH Hunts*, I, 384; basis in *Ch. Ramsey*; dates in 14th cent. Ann. ed. in *Ch.*, pp. 339–46; *Heads*, I, 61–3.

Richard 1214–1216 Prev. abb. of Selby res., apptd to Ramsey 1214 (*Walt. Cov.*, II, 216; *Ad. Dom.*, II, 449; *Ann. Worcs.*, p. 403 (no name); cf. 1213 (*Ann. Dunstable*, p. 40). Given seisin May x June 1214 (*Rot. Lit. Claus.*, I, 207). Occ. 9 Jan. 1215 (*Ctl. Glastonbury*, I, no. 141). D. 1216 (after 2 years, Ann., p. 342). Seal (*BM Seals*, no 3870; *Mon. Seals*, p. 74).

Hugh Foliot 1216–1231 Pr. of Ramsey, apptd 1216, bl. by bp of Bath (Ann., p. 342). Royal ass. 14 June 1216 (*CPR 1216–25*, p. 177). Occ. Trin. term 1230 (*CRR*, XIV, no. 1934); (H.) 8 Apr. 1230 (*CPR 1225–32*, p. 355). D. 1231 (*Ann. Dunstable*, p. 126). Abbey vacant 11 July 1231 (*CR 1227–31*, p. 526). D., lic. to el. 12 July 1231 (*CPR 1225–32*, p. 440). Seal (*Mon. Seals*, p. 74).

Ran(n)ulf Brito 1231–1253 Pr. of Ramsey, royal ass. 22 July 1231 (*CPR 1225–32*, p. 441). D. 14 Aug. 1253 (Lambeth, ms. 1106, f. 120v, cf. *CPR 1247–58*, p. 221). D. (Randulf), lic. to el. 8 Sept. 1253 (*CPR 1247–58*, p. 241). Seal (*BM Seals*, no. 3871; *Mon. Seals*, p. 74).

William de Acholt (Akolt) **1253–1254** Power given to Queen and the earl of Cornwall to give royal ass. to William de Acholt to be abb. – if the pr. and convent choose another they are to send him to the king to request royal ass. 8 Sept. 1253 (*CPR 1247–58*, p. 241). M. of Ramsey, el. 6 Oct. 1253 (Lambeth, ms. 1106, f. 120v); royal ass. 10 Oct. 1253 (*CPR 1247–58*, p. 223); cert. conf. eln by archbp of Canterbury 18 Oct. 1253 (PRO, C84/1/36); mand. for seisin 21 Oct. 1253 (*CR 1251–53*, p. 423). D. 16 Oct. 1254 and bur. 21 Oct. before altar of St John the Evangelist in the abbey church (Lambeth, ms. 1106, f. 120v).

Hugh of Sulgrave 1254–1268 M. of Ramsey, previously pr. of St Ives, el. 1254, ruled 13½ years (Ann., pp. 343–4). Royal ass. 20 Dec. 1254, writ *de intendendo* 1 Jan. 1255 (*CPR*

1247–58, pp. 386, 392). D. 14 Feb. 1268 (Lambeth, ms. 1106, f. 120v, cf. *Reg. R. Gravesend*, p. 172; PRO, C84/3/40). Seal (*BM Seals*, no. 3872; *Mon. Seals*, pp. 74–5).

William of Godmanchester (Gomcestre, Gommecestr', Gumecestre, Gumescestr' Gurmecestr') **1268–1285** Sacrist of Ramsey, el. 22 Feb. 1268 (Lambeth, ms. 1106, f. 120v); royal ass. 26 Feb. 1268 (*CPR 1266–71*, p. 197). Eln conf. by legate Ottobuono (Ann., p. 344; cf. PRO, E135/19/44); bl. by bp of Lincoln 3 Mar. 1268 (*Reg. R. Gravesend*, p. 172). Installed by archdn of Huntingdon 22 Mar. 1268 (Lambeth, ms. 1106, f. 120v). Ruled 18 years and in his 19th year was stricken with paralysis and res. Lived for one year afterwards and d. in his second year after res. (Ann., p. 344). Res., lic. to el. 8 June 1286 (*CChR 1427–1516*, App., p. 288). Seal (*BM Seals*, no. 3873; *Mon. Seals*, p. 75).

John of Sawtry (Sautre, Sawtrey) **1286–1316** El. year 7 of Bp Sutton (19 May 1286 x 18 May 1287) (Bodl., Dodsworth ms. 107, f. 147v). Temps. 26 July 1286 (*CPR 1281–92*, p. 250). Ruled 30 years and d. in his 31st year. He had been blind for 6 years before his d. (Ann., pp. 344–5). Commn to appt a co-adjutor for abb. John, who was blind, 20 May 1313 (Lincoln, Ep. Reg., III, f. 274v); br. Simon of Eye, m. of Ramsey, attpd coadjutor 11 June 1313 (ibid., f. 276r–v). D. prob. 4 Nov. 1316, date vacancy calculated to have begun (*CFR 1307–19*, p. 310). Petition for lic. to el. n.d. (Hill, *Eccles. Letter-Books*, pp. 208–9). D., lic. to el. 18 Nov. 1316 (*CPR 1313–17*, p. 566). Indulgence of 40 days for his soul issued 24 Nov. 1318 (Lincoln, Ep. Reg., III, f. 401v). Seal (*BM Seals*, no. 3874; *Mon. Seals*, p. 75).

Simon of Eye (Eya) **1316–1342** *juris canonici professor*, el. 1316 and ruled 26 years; bur. before the high altar (Ann., p. 345). M. of Ramsey, royal ass. 9 Dec. 1316; temps. 29 Dec. 1316 (*CPR 1313–17*, pp. 569, 603). Eln conf. 23 Dec. 1316 (Lincoln, Ep. Reg., II, f. 240v). Bl. by ex-archbp of Armagh and prof. obed. 25 Dec. 1316 (Lincoln, Ep. Reg., III, f. 360r). Lic. to appt deputy 5 May 1342 (*CPR 1340–43*, p. 424). D., lic to el. 23 Nov. 1342 (ibid., p. 559). Seal (*BM Seals*, no 3875; *Mon. Seals*, p. 75).

Robert of Nassington (Nassinton, Nassyngton) **1342–1349** El. abb. 1342 and was abb. 6½ years (Ann., p. 345; cf. PRO, E135/22/66). M. of Ramsey, royal ass. 13 Dec. 1342, temps. 22 Jan. 1343 (*CPR 1340–43*, pp. 574, 579). Eln conf. 11 Jan. 1343, bl. 12 Jan. 1343 (Lincoln, Ep. Reg., X, f. 105r–v). Occ. 15 Apr. 1349 (PRO, E40/5085). D., lic. to el. 6 June 1349 (*CPR 1348–50*, p. 301). Seal (*BM Seals*, no. 3876; *Mon. Seals*, p. 75).

Richard of Shenington (Sheningdon, Schenyngdon, Scheryngden, Shenengdon, Shenyngdon, Shenyngton) **1349–1378** M. of Ramsey, royal ass. 28 July 1349, temps. 21 Aug. 1349 (*CPR 1348–50*, pp. 360, 367). Eln conf. 19 Aug. 1349; bl. 23 Aug. 1349 (Lincoln, Ep. Reg., IX, f. 385v; cf. PRO, C84/26/12). D. 27 Oct. 1378 (*Cal. Misc. Inq.*, IV, 57; cf. *CFR 1377–83*, p. 115). but d. 28 Oct. 1378 (PRO, C84/32/15). D., lic. to el. 11 Nov. 1378 (*CPR 1377–81*, p. 289). Seal (*BM Seals*, no. 3877; *Mon. Seals*, p. 75).

READING St Mary and St John the Evangelist f. 1121 but not fully established under an abbot until 1123.

List based on *Ctl. Reading*, I, 25–31; other lists *VCH Berks*, II, 72–3; *Heads*, I, 63.

Simon the Chamberlain 1213–1226 El. 1213 (*Ann. Dunstable*, p. 40) . D. 13 Feb. 1226 (*Ann. Rad.*, p. 402; cf. *Ann. Dunstable*, p. 100; *Ann. Worcester*, p. 419). 12 Feb. (obit) (BL, Cotton ms. Claudius D III, f. 143r); 14 Feb. in Trokelowe, ed. Hearne, p. 385; 11 Feb. (*Mon. Angl.*, IV, p. 30). Lic. to el. 16 Feb. 1226 (*CPR 1225–32*, p. 18).

Adam of Lathbury 1226–1238 Pr. of Leominster, royal ass. 7 Mar. 1226 (ibid., p. 21; cf. *Ann. Rad.*, p. 402). Bl. by bp of Salisbury 15 Mar. 1226 (*Reg. St Osmund*, II, 48–9, cf. bl. 30 Nov. 1226 *Ann Tewkesbury*, p. 69). D. 1238 (*Ann. Waverley*, p. 318). Abbey vacant by 7 Apr. 1238 (*CR 1237–42*, p. 40). D., lic. to el. 8 Apr. 1238 (*CPR 1232–47*, p. 215). Obit 15 Apr. (BL, Cotton ms. Claudius D III, f. 147r).

Richard of Chichester (Cycestre) **1238–1262** Sub-pr. of Reading, succ. 1238 (*Ann. Waverley*, p. 218). El. 12 Mar. 1238 (*Ann. Tewkesbury*, pp. 106–7). Royal ass. 18 Apr. 1238 (*CPR 1232–47*, p. 216). D. 22 Mar. 1262 (*Ann. Rad.*, p. 403). D., lic. to el. 26 Mar. 1262 (*CPR 1258–66*, p. 207). Obit 24 Mar. (BL, Cotton ms. Claudius D III, f. 145v).

Richard of Reading (Radinges) *alias* **Banastre 1262–1269** Sub-pr. of Reading, royal ass. 26 Mar. 1262, temps. 1 Apr. 1262, the eln having been conf. by E., bp of Salisbury (*CPR 1258–66*, pp. 207–8). Res. on grounds of ill health 11 July 1269 (PRO, C84/3/49).

Robert of Burgate 1269–1290 M. of Reading, royal ass. 15 July 1269, writ *de intendendo* 20 July 1269 (*CPR 1266–72*, pp. 354, 357). Eln conf. by bp of Salisbury 19 July 1269 (PRO, C84/3/50). Res. 26 Oct. 1290 (PRO, C84/10/33). Cess., lic. to el. 2 Nov. 1290 (*CPR 1281–92*, p. 393). Seal (*BM Seals*, no. 3885).

William of Sutton 1290–1305 Chamberlain of Reading. El. 20 Nov. 1290; cert. conf. eln by bp of Salisbury 9 Dec. 1290 (PRO, C84/10/5–6). Bl. 14 Jan. 1291 (Salisbury Cath. Muniment room, I Bil 1/7). Royal ass. 27 Nov. 1290, commn to take fealty and gt temps. if eln is conf. 28 Nov. 1290 (*CPR 1281–92*, p. 409; *CCR 1288–96*, pp. 154–5). Abbey void by 24 June 1305 (*CCR 1302–07*, p. 274). D. (W.), lic. to el. 27 June 1305 (*CPR 1301–07*, p. 367). Obit 17 June (BL, Cotton ms. Claudius D III, f. 151v).

Nicholas of Whaplode (Quappelode) **1305–1328** [From Whaplode, Lincs: cf. indulgence for the parents of abb. Nicholas, whose bodies are buried in Whaplode church 27 Sept. 1317 (Lincoln, Ep. Reg., III, f. 372v)]. Commn to absolve monks of Reading in view of the forthcoming eln of an abb. 5 July 1305 (*Reg. Gandavo*, I, p. 165). Precentor of Reading. El. pres. to king for royal ass. 23 July 1305 (PRO, C84/15/32). Mand. for royal ass. 27 July 1305 (*Cal. Chanc. Warr.* p. 251). Eln pres. to bp 4 Aug. and quashed but Nicholas provided by bp 10 Sept. 1305 (*Reg. Gandavo*, II, 655–9; PRO, C84/15/33). D. 11 Jan. 1328 (PRO, C84/22/2). D., lic. to el. 16 Jan. 1328 (*CPR 1327–30*, p. 202).

John of Appleford (Appleford) **1328–1342** M. of Reading, royal ass. 12 Feb. 1328, temps. 8 Mar. 1328 (ibid., pp. 233, 250). D. 22 Jan. 1342 (PRO, C84/24/21). D., lic. to el. 30 Jan. 1342 (*CPR 1340–43*, p. 368).

Henry of Appleford (Appelford, Appilford) **1342–1361** M. of Reading, royal ass. 10 Feb. 1342, temps. 21 Mar. 1342 (ibid., pp. 372, 393). House void by his d. by 29 July 1361 (*CCR 1360–64*, p. 197; *Ctl. Reading*, I, no. 496). Seal (*Mon. Seals*, p. 75).

William of Dumbleton 1361–1369 M. of Reading, previously pr. of Leominster, royal ass. 15 Aug. 1361, temps. 7 Sept. 1361 (*CPR 1361–64*, pp. 52, 58). Eln of unnamed abb. conf. 1361 (Salisbury, Reg. Wyvil II, f. 294r). Had licence to leave abbey for a year and go to the cell of Leominster with a few household servants 31 May 1364 (*CPR 1361–64*, p. 504). D. 29 June 1369 (PRO, C84/29/50). D., lic. to el. 2 July 1369 (*CPR 1367–70*, p. 275).

John of Sutton (Sotton) **1369–1378** Pr. of Reading eln pres. to king for royal ass. 11 July 1369 (PRO, C84/30/1).; royal ass. 12 July 1369; temps. 15 Aug. 1369 (*CPR 1367–70*, pp. 276, 295–6). Cert. conf. eln by bp of Salisbury 12 Aug. 1369 (PRO, C84/30/11). D. 6 Apr. 1378 (PRO, C84/32/8). D., lic. to el. 9 Apr. 1378 (*CPR 1377–81*, p. 175).

ROCHESTER CATHEDRAL PRIORY (Kent), St Andrew ref. 1080

Lists based on *Le Neve 1066–1300*, II, 78–80; *Le Neve 1300–1541*, IV, 40–1; Greatrex, *Biog. Reg.*; also lists in *Heads*, I, 63–4; Flight, *The Bishops and Monks of Rochester 1076–1214*, pp. 241–2; *VCH Kent*, II, 125.

Elias Previously sacrist of Rochester (Flight, p. 242). Occ. 1 Nov. 1214 (Rochester D. & C., T. 193/1; Flight, app. 3, no. 821); (H.) after 1215 (Bodl., Rawlinson ms. B461, f. 57r).

William Occ. 6 Oct. 1218, 1 May 1222 (*Kent F.*, pp. 57, 75 and corrigenda, vii; *Reg. Roff.*, p. 368); n.d. (1217 x 1218 (*Ctl. Colchester*, II, 557); (W.) 29 May 1223 (*HMC De L'Isle and Dudley*, I, 82).

Richard of Darenth (Darente) **1225–** Pr. of Darenth, el. as pr. of Rochester (*Flor. Hist.*, II, 183). El. *c.* 26 May 1225 (Ann. Roff. in BL Cotton ms. Vespasian A XXII, f. 33v). Occ. Oct. 1228 x Oct. 1229 (*Surrey F.*, p. 15); 30 Nov. 1238 (Ann. Roff. in *Flor. Hist.*, II, 226, 230, cf. 103).

William de Hoo 1239–1242 Sacrist of Rochester, el. 25 June 1239 (ibid., 235). Last occ. as pr. 1 June 1242 (*Reg. Roff.*, pp. 344–5; *Reg. Hethe*, I, 38). Res. 1242 went to Woburn to be a Cistercian, prob. June x Nov. (*Reg. Roff.*, p. 125).

Alexander de Glanvill (Glanville) **1242–1252** M. of Rochester, el. 5 Nov. 1242 (Ann. Roff. in *Flor. Hist.*, II, 256). D. 5 Mar. 1252 (ibid., II, 376).

Simon de Clyve 1252–1262 Sacrist of Rochester, succ. after 5 Mar. 1252 (ibid., 377). Res. through illness 1262 (ibid., II, 477–8). Seal (*BM Seals*, no. 3919).

John of Rainham (Renham, Reynham) **1262–1283** Succ. 1262 (*Flor. Hist.*, II, 477–8); occ. 10 Feb. 1263 (*Kent F.*, pp. 343–4). Commn to remove Pr. John following archbp's visitation 3 Dec. 1283 (*Reg. Peckham*, II, 641–2). Res. by 24 Dec. 1283 on account of illegitimacy (Ann. Roff. in *Flor. Hist.*, III, 59; BL, Cotton ms. Vespasian A XXII, f. 34r; *Les Registres d'Honorius IV*, no. 537).

Thomas of Wouldham *alias* **Southfleet** (Wuldham) **1283–1291** Succ. 24 Dec. 1283 (Ann. Roff. in *Flor. Hist.*, III, 59; BL Cotton ms. Vespasian A XXII, f. 34r). El. Bp of Rochester 6 June 1291 (*Le Neve 1066–1300*, II, 78); D. as bp 28 Feb. 1317 (ibid.).

John of Rainham (Renham) **1292–1294** Re-el. 7 Jan. 1292 (Ann. Roff. in *Flor. Hist.*, III, 74) having been dispensed for illegitimacy being the son of a priest 13 June 1286 (*Les Registres d'Honorius IV*, no. 537; *CPL*, I, 487). D. 1294 (Ann. Roff. in *Flor Hist.*, III, 92; BL, Cotton ms. Vespasian A XXII, f. 34r). Sharpe, *Latin Writers*, p. 299.

Thomas de Shelford (Seleforde) **1294–1301** Succ. 1294 (Ann. Roff. in *Flor. Hist.*, III, 92; BL, Cotton ms. Vespasian A XXII, f. 34r). Dispensed for illegitimacy and permitted to retain office 19 June 1295 (*Les Registres de Boniface VIII*, no. 249; *CPL*, I, 559). Res. on account of illness *c.* 2 Feb. 1301 (Ann. Roff. in *Flor. Hist.*, III, 110; BL, Cotton ms. Vespasian A XXII, f. 34r).

John de Greenstreet 1301–1314 El. Feb. 1301 (*Ang. Sac.*, I, 355); after 2 Feb. 1301 (Ann. Roff. in *Flor. Hist.*, III, 110). Res. by 8 May 1314 (*Ang. Sac.*, I, 355).

Hamo de Hethe 1314–1317 El. 8 May 1314 (ibid., 356). El. Bp of Rochester 18 Mar. 1317, consecr. 26 Aug. 1319. Res. 1352. D. 4 May 1352 (*Le Neve 1300–1541*, IV, 37; *Chronology*, p. 267).

John of Westerham 1320–1321 El. 14 Jan. 1320 (*Ang. Sac.*, I, 361). D. by 31 Jan. 1321 (ibid., 362).

John of Speldhurst (Spelderhurst, Speldherst, Speldhurst) **1321–1333** El. 31 Jan. 1321 (ibid.). Res. 12 Aug. 1333, res. acc. 19 Aug. 1333 (ibid., 371; *Reg. Hethe*, I, 531–2).

Master John de Sheppey (Scapeya, Shepeye) **1333–1350** STP, sub-sacrist of Rochester, el. 19 Aug. 1333 (*Reg. Hethe*, I, 531–4). 1 Feb. 1350 petition gtd and lic. given to res. – pr. for 16 years, claims to have freed house from the debts incurred by his predecessors; built refectory, hospice and vestibule of church, repaired other buildings at great expense; added land and rents of churches and obtained confirmation of same; enclosed the whole with a strong wall. Now feeling that he can do no more prays lic. to res. the priory and have apportioned to him a yearly pension of £40 (*CPP*, p. 192; *CPL*, III, 400). 21 Feb. 1350 king gave his assent for pension gtd by pope to the former pr. (*CPR 1350–4*, p. 41). M. of Rochester, lately pr., occ. 14 July 1351 (*CPP*, p. 217). Provided to bishopric of Rochester 22 Oct. 1352, consecr. 10 Mar. 1353, d. 19 Oct. 1360 (*Le Neve 1300–1541*, IV, 37). For further details see *Greatrex, Biog. Reg.*, pp. 634–5; Sharpe, *Latin Writers*, p. 317.

Robert of Southfleet (Southflete) **?1351–1361** Pr. of Felixstowe. El. before 18 Aug. 1351 (*CCR 1349–54*, p. 379). D. by 6 Aug. 1361 (*Angl. Sac.*, I, 394).

John of Hartlip (Hertlepe, Hertelep) **1361–1380** Pr. of Felixstowe, el. 6 Aug. 1361 (ibid.). Ment. 18 June 1376 as former chief master of the king's works at Rochester castle and the manor of Gravesend (*CCR 1374–77*, p. 321). Res. 6 Nov. 1380 (BL, Cotton ms. Faustina C V, f. 19r). Seal (*BM Seals*, no. 3920).

ST ALBANS (Herts), St Alban ref. *c.* 970

Lists in *VCH Herts*, IV, 414–15; *Heads*, I, 64–7. See also R. Vaughan, 'The election of abbots at St Albans in the thirteenth and fourteenth centuries', *Proc. Cambs. AS*, XLVII (1954), 1–12.

William of Trumpington (Trumpinton) **1214–1235** 22nd abb. M. of St Albans, el. 20 Nov. 1214, bl. by bp of Ely 30 Nov. 1214 (*GASA*, I, 253). D. 24 Feb. 1235, bur. 27 Feb. (ibid., 300, 306; cf. *MPCM* VI, 274); 1234 (? for 1234/5) (*Ann. Tewkesbury*, p. 93); 1235 (*Ann. Dunstable*, p. 141; *Ann. Worcs.*, p. 427). D. 24 Feb. also Belvoir obit., Nichols, *Leics*, II, i, app. II, p. 27; 23 Feb. obit. D., lic. to el. 28 Feb. 1235 (*CPR 1232–47*, p. 95).

John of Hertford 1235–1263 23rd abb. (cf. *GASA*, I, 312). El. 27 Mar. 1235 (Bodl., Digby ms. 20, ff. 105r–109r, collection of letters re eln; cf. PRO, C84/1/10). Pr. of Hertford (J.), royal ass. 1 Apr. 1235, writ *de intendendo* 17 Aug. 1235 (*CPR 1232–47*, pp. 98, 116). Succ. 1235 (*Ann. Dunstable*, p. 141). Eln conf. by bp of London on behalf of pope; bl. by bp of London 9 Sept. 1235 (*GASA*, I, 310). D. 19 Apr. 1260 sic, for 1263 (ibid., 396). Seal (*BM Seals*, no 3947). Pr. and convent apptd to custody of the abbey, vacant by his d. 23 Apr. 1263 (*CPR 1258–66*, p. 257).

Roger of Norton(e) 1263–1290 24th abb. El. 7 May 1263 (Vaughan, 'Election', citing Bute ms. 3, p. 278). Papal conf. 9 Sept. 1263 (*CPL*, I, 393; Sayers, no. 692). Temps. 21 Dec. 1263 (*CPR 1258–66*, p. 304). Bl. by bps of London and Ely 23 Dec. 1263 (*GASA*, I, 400). Said 1 Aug. 1290 to be too infirm to ride (*CPR 1281–92*, p. 379). D. 3 Nov. 1290, bur. 6 Nov. (*GASA*, I, 485; *Ch. Bury*, pp. 95–6); D. 1 Nov. 1290 (*Ann. Dunstable*, p. 363). D., lic. to el. 11 Nov. 1290 (*CPR 1281–92*, p. 394).

John of Berkhamsted (Berkhamstede, Berkamsted(e)) **1290–1301** 25th abb. (*GASA*, II, 3). Sacrist of St Albans, el. 9 Dec. 1290 (ibid., 6–7); royal ass. 14 Dec. 1290, writ *de intendendo* 2 June 1291 (*CPR 1281–92*, pp. 409, 430). Papal conf. 13 Mar. 1291 & bl. by bp of Ostia (*CPL*, I, 531–2; Sayers, no. 948, cf. *GASA*, II, 8–14). D. 19 Oct. 1301, bur. 6 Nov. (*GASA*, II, 50, 52, cf. *CCR 1302–7*, p. 43). D., lic. to el. 15 Nov. 1301 (*CPR 1292–1301*, p. 617). Mon. brass (*Earliest English Brasses*, p. 191).

John de Maryns (Marines, Marinis, Marynes) **1302–1309** 26th abb. Pr. of St Albans, el. 2 Jan. 1302 (*GASA*, II, 53, cf. Bodl., Digby ms. 20, ff. 160v–163v). Royal ass. 30 Jan. 1302, temps. 12 Aug. 1302 (*CPR 1301–07*, pp. 11, 53); fealty taken 12 Aug. (*CCR 1302–7*, p. 43, cf. *GASA*, II, 56). Papal conf. of eln 25 May 1302, bl. 27 May 1302 (*GASA*, II, 55; cf. [cert. of] papal conf. and subsequent bl. by bp of Albano, 1 June 1303 (*CPL*, I, 601; Sayers, no. 1040)). Feast expenses on eln 1302 (*Reg. Whethamstede*, II, 330–3). D. 23 Feb. 1309 (*GASA*, II, 108; PRO, C84/16/17). D. (J.), lic.. to el. 28 Feb. 1309 (*CPR 1307–13*, p. 101).

Hugh of Eversden (Everesden, Everisdene) **1309–1327** 27th abb., Cellarer of St Albans (cf. *GASA*, II, 114). Occ. as abb.-el. 27 Apr., 6 May 1309 (*CPR 1307–13*, p. 112). Royal authority to bp of Worcester to accept the fealty of the abb.-el. if, during the king's absence in the north, the eln is conf. by the pope, and to restore temps. 7 Oct. 1309 (*CPR 1307–13*, p. 194). Papal conf. of eln 11 Feb. 1310 (*CPL*, II, 66); lic. to receive bl. from Nicholas, cardinal bp of Ostia (ibid.). Temps. 1 Apr. 1310 (*CPR 1307–13*, p. 221). Indulgence of 30 days for those praying for the health of abb. Hugh and for the souls of William and Margery de Eversden his parents 14 Sept. 1312 (Lincoln, Ep. Reg., III, f. 261r). D. the night of 7–8 Sept. 1327 (*GASA*, II, 178). Ledger stone attributed to abb. Hugh (*Earliest English Brasses*, p. 191). D., lic. to el. 20 Sept. 1327 (*CPR 1327–30*, p. 167). See D. Preest and M. Still, *Hugh of Eversden, Abbot of St Albans* (Fraternity of the Friends of St Albans Abbey, occasional paper 2, 1998).

Richard of Wallingford (Walyngford) **1327–1336** 28th abb. M.of St Albans, el. 29 Oct. 1327 (*GASA*, II, 183–5). Royal ass. 8 Nov. 1327, temps. 19 May 1328 (*CPR 1327–30*, pp. 184, 272). Royal order to permit the abb.-el. to cross the sea from Dover. He is going to the Curia in respect of his eln 22 Nov. 1327 (*CCR 1327–30*, p. 235). Apptd by pope, having res. his earlier eln 1 Feb. 1328 (*CPL*, II, 269, cf. *GASA*, II, 189–90). 6 Feb. 1329 given permission to live elsewhere to save expense (*CPR 1327–30*, p. 362). Papal enquiry about alleged leprosy of abb. 1332 (*CPL*, II, 509, cf. *GASA*, II, 199). D. 23 May 1336, bur. 27 May (*GASA*, II, 293–4). Mon. brass (*Earliest English Brasses*, p. 191). See Sharpe, *Latin Writers*, p. 518; H. H. Turner, W. A. Wigram, H. W. Garrod & R. T. Gunther, 'Richard of Wallingford, abbot of St Albans', *Trans. St Albans & Herts AAS*, 1926, 221–39; J. D. North, *Richard of Wallingford* (Oxford, 1976); G. Henwood, *Abbot Richard of Wallingford, a fourteenth-century astronomer and instrument maker* (Wallingford, 1988). House void by 24 May 1336 (*CCR 1333–37*, p. 583). D., lic. to el. 29 May 1336 (*CPR 1334–38*, p. 270).

Michael of Mentmore (Mentemor) **1336–1349** 29th abb. M. of St Albans, el. 1 June 1336 (*GASA*, II, 300). Royal ass. 16 July 1336, temps. 11 Mar 1337 (*CPR 1334–38*, pp. 304, 380). Papal conf. of eln 18 Nov. 1336, bl. by bp of Albano (*CPL*, II, 531); papal safe conduct 30 Nov. (ibid.). D. of plague 12 Apr. 1349, bur. 16 Apr. (*GASA*, II, 369–70). D., lic. to el. (no name given) 18 Apr. 1349 (*CPR 1348–50*, p. 277).

[**Hugh of Stukeley** (Stukele) Pr. of Wymondham, el. 1349 but refused the office (*GASA*, II, 382).]

Thomas de la Mare 1349–1396 30th abb. Pr. of Tynemouth, el. n.d. (1349) (ibid.). Eln conf. by pope 8 July 1349 (*CPL*, III, 339; *Orig. Papal Letters*, pp. 114–15, no. 226). Lic. to return to his abbey, 14 July 1349, having been bl. by Bertrand, cardinal bp of Sabina (ibid., 336). Temps. 22 Nov. 1349 (*CPR 1348–50*, p. 430). D. 15 Sept. 1396 in his 88th year (*GASA*, III, 422). See also E. Woolley, 'A study of the character of Abbot Thomas de la Mare', *Trans. St Albans & Herts AAS*, 1928, 163–71, cf. Knowles, *Religious Orders*, II, 39–48. Mon. brass (photo in Knowles, *Religious Orders*, II, frontis., & E. Woolley, 'The brass of Thomas de la Mare, St Albans abbey church', *Trans. St. Albans & Herts AAS*, 1928, 172–5); see also H. K. Cameron, '14th-century Flemish brasses to ecclesiastics in English churches', *TMBS*, XIII(1) (1980), 3–23, Thomas de la Mare at 3–13; N. Rogers, 'The earliest known description of the de la Mare brass at St Albans Abbey', *TMBS*, XIV(2) (1987), 154–7. D., lic. to el. 18 Sept. 1396 (*CPR 1396–99*, p. 25). Seal (*BM Seals*, no. 3948).

ST BENET OF HULME (Norfolk), St Benedict (Home, Hulme) ref. 1019

Lists in *VCH Norfolk*, II, 336; *Ctl. Hulme*, II, 191–8; *Ch. Oxenedes*; 15th cent. list and extracts from calendar etc. in *Worcestre* (ed. Harvey), pp. 203ff.; *Heads*, I, 67–9.

Lic. to el. 25 July 1213 (*Rot. Lit. Claus.*, I, 150).

Reginald c. **1215–1229** M. of Hulme (*Ch. Oxenedes*, p. 296). Occ. c. 1217 x 1218, as j.d. acting on papal commn of 23 Nov. 1216 (CUL, ms. Mm. 2. 20, f. 30r); 6 Feb. 1219 (BL, Cotton ms. Galba E.II, f. 87r); Oct. 1220 x Oct. 1221, Oct. 1228 x Oct. 1229 (*Norfolk F. (Rye)*, pp. 36, 48); 10 July 1227 (*CPR 1225–32*, p. 159); 3 May 1229 (BL, Cotton ms. Galba E II, f. 88r; Lambeth, Ch. Ant. X/32). D. 24 May 1229 (*Worcestre*, pp. 230, 232; *Ch. Oxenedes*, pp. 297, 435). D. (R.), lic. to el. 29 May 1229 (*CPR 1225–32*, p. 251).

Sampson 1229–1237 Pr. of Hulme, royal ass. 11 July 1229 (ibid., p. 252). Occ. from Oct. 1228 x Oct. 1229 to Oct. 1234 x Oct. 1235 (*Norfolk F. (Rye)*, pp. 48, 49, 57); 1231 (Lambeth, Ch. Ant. X/32). D. 27 May 1237 (*Worcestre*, p. 230; *Ch. Oxenedes*, p. 297). Custodian apptd for vacant abbey 30 May 1237 (*CPR 1232–47*, p. 183).

Robert of Torksey (Thorkeseye) **1237–1251** Pr. of Ramsey, royal ass. 15 June 1237, writ *de intendendo* 14 (*sic*) June 1237 (ibid., pp. 185, 186). D. 12 Aug. 1251 (*Worcestre*, p. 230; *Ch. Oxenedes*, p. 298). Lic. to el. (no reason given for vacancy) 20 Aug. 1251 (*CPR 1247–58*, p. 106).

William de Ringefeude (Ringefeld, Ringgefelde) **1251–1256** Precentor of Hulme, royal ass. 15 Oct. 1251 (ibid., p. 112); mand. for seisin 16 Oct. 1251 (*CR 1247–51*, p. 514). D. 18 Apr. 1256 (*Worcestre*, p. 230). cf. D. 21 Apr. 1256 (*Ch. Oxenedes*, p. 298). Appt of custodians of vacant abbey 24 Apr. 1256 (*CPR 1247–58*, p. 470). Lic. to el. (no reason given for vacancy) 19 Apr. 1256 (ibid.).

Adam of Neatishead (Neteshyrd, Neteshirde, Neteshurde, Nottishurd) **1256–1268** M. of Hulme, royal ass. 8 May 1256, writ *de intendendo* 10 May 1258 (ibid., p. 472). D. 19 Aug. 1268 (*Worcestre*, p. 230; *Ch. Oxenedes*, p. 299). House void by 26 Aug. 1268 (*CPR 1266–72*, p. 253).

Richard of Buckenham (Bukenham) **1268–1275** Pr. of Hulme, royal ass. 3 Oct. 1268, temps. 24 Oct. 1268, the eln having been conf. by R., bp of Norwich (ibid., pp. 261, 266–7). D. 8 June 1275 (*Worcestre*, p. 230; *Ch. Oxenedes*, p. 300; cf. *Flor. Hist.*, III, 46). D. (no name given), lic. to el. 13 June 1275 (*CPR 1272–81*, p. 94; cf. PRO, C84/5/30).

Nicholas of Walsham (Walesham) **1275–1302** Pr. of Hulme, royal ass. 15 June 1275, writ *de intendendo* 4 July 1275 (*CPR 1272–81*, pp. 96, 98). Cert. conf. eln by bp of Norwich 3 July 1275 (PRO, C84/5/37; cf. *Earliest English Law Reports*, I, 95). D. 15 Nov. [1302] (*Worcestre*, p. 230). D. (N.), lic. to el. 23 Nov. 1302 (*CPR 1301–07*, p. 96). Seal (*BM Seals*, no. 3300).

Henry de Brok 1302–1325 M. of Hulme, royal ass. 15 Dec. 1302, temps. 8 Jan. 1303 (*CPR 1301–07*, pp. 100, 104). Eln quashed but apptd by bp of Norwich 2 Jan. 1303 (Norwich, Reg/1/1, f. 111r; PRO, C84/14/27). D. 14 Dec. [1325] (*Worcestre*, p. 232); d. notified to king 28 Dec. 1325 (*Cal. Chanc. Warr.*, p. 572, cf. *CFR 1319–27*, p. 372). Mand. to issue lic. to elect 2 Jan. 1326 (*Cal. Chanc. Warr.*, p. 572). D., lic. to el. 2 Jan. 1326 (*CPR 1324–27*, p. 201).

John of Aylsham (Aylesham) **1326–1347** Pr. of Hulme, royal ass. 11 Jan. 1326, temps. 21 Jan. 1326 (ibid., pp. 203, 214). Eln conf. 16 Jan. 1326 (Norwich, Reg/1/2, f. 5v). D. 7 Feb. [1347] (*Worcestre*, p. 230). D. by 15 Feb. 1347 (*CCR 1346–49*, p. 181).

Robert of Aylsham (Aylesham) **1347–1349** M. of Hulme, royal ass. 24 Feb. 1347, temps. 18 Mar. 1347 (*CPR 1345–48*, pp. 256, 268; PRO, SC1/40/49). Eln conf. 12 Mar. 1347 (*Reg. Bateman*, I, no. 276). D. 4 July [1349] (*Worcestre*, p. 230). D., lic. to el. 12 July 1349 (*CPR 1348–50*, p. 339).

William of Haddiscoe (Hadesco, Haddisco, Hadischo) **1349–1365** M. of Hulme, royal ass. 20 Aug. 1349, temps. 25 Sept. 1349 (ibid., pp. 363, 403). Eln quashed but apptd by bp 15 Sept. 1349 (Norwich, Reg/2/4, f. 108v). D. 18 Mar. 1365 (*Cal. Misc. Inq.*, III, 221–2; *Worcestre*, p. 230). D., lic. to el. 23 Mar. 1365 (*CPR 1364–67*, p. 100; cf. *CCR 1364–68*, p. 110).

William (of) Methwold (Medwold, Methelwold(e), Methewold) **1365–1296** M. of Hulme, eln pres. to king for royal ass. 30 Mar. 1365 (PRO, C84/29/18); royal ass. 3 Apr. 1365; temps. 14 May 1365 (*CPR 1364–67*, pp. 101, 118). Eln conf. 9 May 1365 (Norwich, Reg/2/5, f. 64v). D. 18 Feb. [1396] (*Worcestre*, p. 230). D., lic. to el. 2 Mar. 1396 (*CPR 1391–96*, p. 670).

SANDWELL (Staffs), St Mary Magdalen f. *c.* 1180 (priory)
Lists in *VCH Staffs*, III, 219; *Heads*, I, 69.

John Occ. 1195 x 1222 (*Mon. Angl.*, IV, 107, no. vi); 15 July 1218 (*Bucks F.*, I, 37).

William Occ. (W.) n.d. (*ante* 1228) (*Ctl. Rydeware*, p. 271); 2 Nov. 1227 (*Staffs Pleas, SHC*, IV, p. 52); Hil. term 1230 (*CRR*, XIII, no. 2324); Jan. 1230 (*Ctl. Trentham*, p. 77; *Staffs F.* 2, p. 222).

Eudo Occ. 20 Jan. 1245 (*Bucks F.*, I, 85).

John Occ. 7 Apr. 1269 (*Staffs Pleas*, *SHC*, IV, p. 170).

Richard de la Barre In a case of 1293 pr. Richard was mentd as a predecessor of the present pr. (*SHC*, VI, i, 220). Presumably this Richard is the same as Richard de la Barre, pr. of Sandwell *temp.* Henry III (*SHC*, VII, 18).

Thomas –1316 Occ. 7 Jan. 1293 (*SHC*, VI, i, 224 – initially the pr. had been named as Roger but the other parties took exception to the writ because the pr. was named Thomas not Roger, and the suit was dismissed (ibid., p. 220). Occ. 1294 (*SHC*, VII, 17); Trin. 1297 (PRO, CP40/119, m. 81d). D. by Oct. 1316 (Lichfield, B/A/1/1, f. 55v).

John de Buckebroc (Buckebrok) 1316–1323 M. of Much Wenlock, his eln by monks of Sandwell earlier in the year had been quashed, but he was apptd by the bp Oct. 1316 (ibid.). Res. by 31 Mar. 1323 (Lichfield, B/A/1/2, f. 137r–v). Provision made for pr. 'R. de H.' (*sic*) made n.d. (*c.* Aug. 1323) (Lichfield B/A/1/3, f. 39r).

Richard de Eselberg (Eselbourgh) 1323–1330 M. of Sandwell, right of appt transferred to bp and he apptd Richard 31 Mar. 1323 (Lichfield, B/A/1/2, f. 137r–v). Res. by 25 May 1330 (ibid., f. 147r).

William de la Lee 1330– M. of Sandwell, eln quashed, but apptd by bp 25 May 1330 (ibid.).

William Harell 1333– M. of Thorney, apptd by bp 13 Feb. 1333, no reason given for vacancy (Lichfield, B/A/1/3, f. 153r). Occ. 21 Apr. 1333 (Lincoln, Ep. Reg., IV, f. 342v).

Richard le Warde –1349 Occ. Mich. 1341 (*SHC*, XI, 122); 10 Oct. 1341 (*CPR 1340–43*, p. 320). D. by 20 June 1349 (Lichfield, B/A/1/2, f. 181r).

Nicholas of Compton (Cumpton) 1349– M. of Sandwell, apptd by bp since he alone remained of the professed monks 20 June 1349 (ibid.).

John Occ. 20 Dec. 1360 (PRO, C81/1786/42).

William del Ree –1361 D. by 18 Sept. 1361 (*Reg. Stretton*, I, 108).

Henry of Kidderminster (Kydermynstre) 1361– Priest and the sole m. of Sandwell, apptd by bp 18 Sept. 1361 (ibid.).

John of Kingston (Kyngeston) –1380 Occ. Easter term 1371, Trin. term 1372 (*SHC*, XIV, 130, 132) – in this case pr. John claimed he had been shot in the arm with an arrow by the defendant on 29 June 1370. The defendant claimed **Richard de Tudenham**[5] was pr., not John, but the latter denied this and appealed on this issue to the jury (ibid., 132). A pr. Richard is found in a signification of 1372 (PRO, C88/197/14). Richard (Budenham) had papal prov. 21 Jan. 1374 (*Accts of Papal Collectors*, p. 509). John occ. 16 Dec. 1379 (*CCR 1377–81*, p. 343) and cess. by 24 Mar. 1380 (*Reg. Stretton*, I, 147–8).

SELBY (Yorks W.), St Mary and St Germanus f. 1069 x 1070

Lists in *VCH Yorks*, III, 99–100; *Ctl. Selby*, I, 1 ff.; *Heads*, I, 69–70.

Alexander 1214–1221 Pr. of Selby, royal ass. 14 Dec. 1214 (*Rot. Lit. Pat.*, p. 125). Occ. 1219 (*Ctl. Selby*, II, 59). Res. 1221 (no name) (*Walt.Cov.* II, 250). Lic. to el. (no name or reason given) 21 June 1221 (*CPR 1216–25*, p. 293).

Richard 1221–1223 Pr. of St Ives, royal ass. 15 Aug. 1221 (ibid., p. 300). Res., lic. to el. 17 Jan. 1223 (ibid., p. 363). Seal of this abb. Richard or poss. his successor (*BM Seals*, no. 3984; Clay, *Seals*, p. 32).

Richard 1223–1237 Sub-pr. of Selby, royal ass. 7 Feb. 1223, writ *de intendendo* 5 Apr. 1223 (*CPR 1216–25*, 364, 370). Occ. 1 Aug. 1237 (*Ctl. Selby*, I, 270 – but cf. below). D. or res. 1237 (*Ctl. Guisborough*, I, 216n.).

---

[5] A Richard de Tudenham, monk, is found gtd the keeping of Stratfield Saye priory in 1378–9 (*CFR 1377–83*, pp. 95, 161; *CPR 1377–81*, p. 305).

Alexander 1237–1245 Succ. 1237 (Baildon, I, 196, no source given). Occ. June 1236 x June 1237 (*Reg. Grosseteste*, p. 10). Lic. to el. (no reason given for vacancy) 14 Sept. 1245 (*CPR 1232–47*, p. 460).

Hugh of Drayton 1245–1254 M. of Selby, royal ass. 1 Oct. 1245 (ibid., p. 461). Mand. for seisin 30 Oct. 1245 (*CR 1242–47*, p. 368). House void by 14 Sept. 1254 (*CR 1252–54*, pp. 96–7). D., lic. to el. 27 Sept. 1254 (*CPR 1247–58*, p. 358).

Thomas of Whalley (Qualley, Whalleye) **1254–1264** Pr. of Selby, royal ass. 25 Dec. 1254 (ibid., p. 390). Occ. to 1 Apr. 1263 (*Ctl. Selby*, II, 92, 328); 15 Apr. 1263 (*Yorks F. 1246–72*, p. 127). Dep. 1263 (*VCH* without source). Ref. to his cess. (*CPR 1258–66*, p. 408). Occ. as former abb. 1267 (*CR 1264–8*, p. 371). Cess. notified to king 1 Apr. 1264 (PRO, C84/3/8). Seal (*Durham Seals*, II, p. 580, no. 3540; Clay, *Seals*, p. 32).

David of Cawood (Cawod) **1264–1270** M. of Selby, eln pres. to king for royal ass. 30 Apr. 1264 (PRO, C84/3/10); royal ass. 28 May 1264 (*CPR 1258–66*, p. 319). Cess., lic. to el. 1 Apr. 1270 (*CPR 1266–72*, p. 420; cf. PRO, C84/3/46).

Thomas of Whalley (Qualle(y), Qwalle, Wallaye) **1270–1280** M. of Selby, eln quashed by archbp but Thomas apptd 24 June 1270; mand. to convent to obey 3 July; notif. to king 4 July (*Reg. W. Giffard*, pp. 217–20). Dep. in visitation 9 Jan. 1280 (*Reg. Wickwane*, pp. 22–4, no. 75; PRO, C84/6/31). Cess., lic. to el. 20 Jan. 1280 (*CPR 1272–81*, p. 361). Excommunicated as a fugitive M. of Selby *c*. Mar. 1280 (*Reg. Wickwane*, pp. 211–12, 271, nos. 507, 682); still apostate 29 Mar. 1281 (Logan, *Runaway Religious*, p. 185).

William of Aslackby (Aslakby, Aselakeby, Aslakeby) **1280–1294** Pr. of Selby, royal ass. 4 Mar. 1280, writ *de intendendo* 23 Apr. 1280 (*CPR 1272–81*, pp. 365, 368). King notified of eln & adm. 11 Apr. 1280 (*Reg. Wickwane*, p. 27, no. 84). Cert. conf. eln by archbp of York 11 Apr. 1280 (PRO, C84/6/36). D. by 4 Mar. 1294 (PRO, C84/11/46). D., lic. to el. 12 Mar. 1294 (*CPR 1292–1301*, p. 66). For his seal matrix found on Dogger Bank 1914 see BI, PR. Sel. 322.

John of Wistow (Wistowe, Wykestou, Wykestowe, Wystowe, Wyxstouwe) **1294–1300** Sub-pr. of Selby, eln pres. to king for royal ass. 1 Apr. 1294 (PRO, C84/11/47); royal ass. 12 Apr. 1294, temps. 17 May 1294 (*CPR 1292–1301*, pp. 67, 70). Cert. conf. eln by archbp of York 8 May 1294 (PRO, C84/11/51; C84/12/1). Mand. to obey & to install 8 May 1294 (*Reg. Romeyn*, I, p. 139, no. 383). Cess. by 15 Nov. 1300 (PRO, C84/13/47). Res., lic. to el. 19 Nov. 1300 (*CPR 1292–1301*, p. 542; cf. *Reg. Corbridge*, I, 39–41).

The archbp was requested by the abbey, unable to agree on a new abb., to choose one. He had apptd William of Aslackby; notification to king 29 Nov. 1300. Inquiry ordered 3 Dec. 1300 to examine report that John had not resigned willingly but through menace and fear (*Cal. Chanc. Warr.*, p. 124).

William of Aslackby II (Aslakby, As(e)lagby) **1300–1313** Sacrist of Selby, royal ass. 27 Nov. 1300, temps. 13 Dec. 1300 (*CPR 1292–1301*, pp. 558, 559 – royal ass. 2 Dec. acc. to *Reg. Corbridge*, I 40). Abb.-el. 3 Dec. 1300 (*Cal. Chanc. Warr.*, p. 124). Eln conf. 9 Dec. 1300; mand. to install 18 Dec. (*Reg. Corbridge*, I, 40–1). House void by 5 Nov. 1313 by death of William of Aslakby (*CFR 1307–19*, p. 182). D., lic. to el. 7 Nov. 1313 (*CPR 1313–17*, p. 35).

Simon of Scarborough (Scardeburgh, Scarth(e)burgh) **1313–1321** Occ. as pr. of Selby 1309 (*Reg. Greenfield*, V, no. 2759). Pr. of Selby, eln pres. to king for royal ass. 21 Nov. 1313 (PRO, C84/17/28–9); royal ass. 7 Dec. 1313, temps. 13 Jan. 1314 (*CPR 1313–17*, pp. 48, 77). Citation of opposers to eln 17 Dec. 1313 – to appear 7 Jan. 1314; eln conf. 7 Jan. 1314 (*Reg. Greenfield*, II, nos. 1035, 1039); bl. & prof. obed. 27 Jan. 1314 (ibid., p. 175, n. 1). D. by 27 Dec. 1321 (PRO, C84/20/9). D., lic. to el. 3 Jan. 1322 (*CPR 1321–24*, p. 42).

John of Wistow II (Wistowe, Wystouwe, Wystowe) **1322–1335** M. of Selby, eln pres. to king for royal ass. 15 Jan. 1322 (PRO, C84/21/11); royal ass. 20 Jan. 1322, temps. 23 Feb. 1322

(*CPR 1321–24*, pp. 50, 71; York, Reg. 9A, f. 184r). Eln conf. 9 Feb. 1322 (ibid., f. 183r; PRO, C84/20/12); prof. obed. 15 Mar. 1322 (York, Reg. 9A, f. 185v); mand. to install 16 Mar. 1322 (ibid., f. 184v). House void by his death by 6 July 1335 (*CFR 1327–37*, p. 450). D., lic. to el. 10 July 1335 (*CPR 1334–38*, p. 151). Indulgence of 40 days for those praying for the soul of John of Wistow II, buried in the new choir of the conventual church, issued 28 July 1336 (Lincoln, Ep. Reg., V, f. 535v). Seal (*Durham Seals*, II, p. 580, no. 3541).

John of Heslington (Heslyngton, Heselyngton) **1335–1342** M. of Selby, eln pres. to king for royal ass. 16 July 1335 (PRO, C84/23/34); royal ass. 18 July 1335, temps. 2 Aug. 1335 (*CPR 1334–38*, pp. 154, 159). Proclamation *si quis* 19 July 1335 (York, Reg. 9A, ff. 247v–248r); eln conf. 31 July 1335 (ibid., f. 247v); mandate to install & prof. obed. 15 Aug. 1335 (ibid., f. 248r). D. 25 Sept. 1342 (PRO, DL. 42/8, f. 1r). D., lic. to el. 3 Sept. 1342 (*CPR 1340–43*, p. 519). Fragment of register (Bodl., ms. Top. Yorks d. 2).

Geoffrey de Gaddesby (Gatesby) **1342–1368** M. of Selby, royal ass. 24 Oct. 1342, temps. 14 Dec. 1342 (*CPR 1340–43*, pp. 533, 574). Cert. conf. eln by archbp of York 14 Dec. 1342 (PRO, C84/29/47). Mand. to obey & to install 30 Dec. 1342 (York, Reg. 10, f. 1r). D. 30 Nov. 1368 (*YAJ*, XLII (1967), 25). D., lic. to el. 9 Dec. 1368 (*CPR 1367–70*, p. 184). Seal (*Mon. Seals*, p. 80; Clay, *Seals*, p. 32). Register (PRO, DL.42/8).

John of Sherburn (Shirburn, Shyrburn) **1369–1408** M. of Selby. Eln pres. to king for royal ass. 14 Feb. 1369 (PRO, C84/29/47); eln said to be simoniacal, king asks archbp to examine eln before he gives royal assent 26 Feb. 1369, temps. 20 Apr. 1369 (*CPR 1367–70*, pp. 220, 231). Eln conf. and prof. obed. 27 Mar. 1369 (York, Reg. 11, f. 151r–v). In 1386 the abb. said to be aged 50 and more (*Scrope-Grosvenor*, I, 91). D. by 12 Feb. 1408 (PRO, C84/39/43). D., lic. to el. 18 Feb. 1408 (*CPR 1405–08*, p. 394). Grave slab, Selby abbey (see J. Mountain, *The History of Selby* (York, 1800), p. 92 for inscription). See G. S. Haslop, 'The creation of brother John Sherburn as abbot of Selby', *YAJ*, XLII (1967), 25–30. Seal (*Mon. Seals*, p. 80). Registers (BL, Cotton mss. Vitellius E XVI, ff. 97–162; Cleopatra D. III, ff. 184–202).

SHERBORNE (Dorset), St Mary f. *c.* 933 (cath. Pr.); 1075 x 8 (Priory); 1122 (abbey).

Lists in *VCH Dorset*, II, 68–9; *Heads*, I, 70; *Le Neve 1066–1300: IV Salisbury*, pp. 95–7.

Philip Abbey vacant on 3 June 1213 (*Rot. Litt. Pat.*, I, 99b). Occ. 1211 x 1214, presumably 1213 x 1214 (*EEA*, 19, no. 239; *Reg. St Osmund*, I, 265; cf. *Le Neve 1066–1300*, IV, p. 96, n. 1); 1215 x 1222 (*Ctl. Bruton*, no. 252, with Pandolf bp.-el. of Norwich); *c.* 13 Oct. 1217 (*Dorset F.*, p. 19); 15 Aug. 1222 (*Reg. St Osmund*, II, 18); 18 Aug. 1222 (ibid., I, 339); 3 Feb. 1225 (*Dorset F.*, p. 27).

Henry 1227–1242 Pr. of Sherborne, royal ass. 7 July 1227 (*CPR 1225–32*, p. 132). Protection overseas 7 May 1241 until he returns from pilgrimage (*CPR 1232–47*, p. 250). Cess., lic. to el. 7 Oct. 1242 (ibid., p. 304).

John de (la) Hele 1242–1246 M. of Sherborne, royal ass. 15 Oct. 1242 (ibid.). Bl. by bp of Salisbury at Ramsbury 6 Dec. 1242: Salisbury cathedral had been assigned but the bp was ill - the right of the cathedral is safeguarded in a letter of 21 Dec. (*Sarum Chts.*, pp. 281–2, no. ccxli). Occ. j. i. 1244 (*Devon F.*, I, 187–440 *passim*). Lic. to el. (no reason for name given) 29 Oct. 1246 (*CPR 1232–47*, p. 492).

Laurence of Bradford (Bradeford) **1246–1260** M. of Sherborne, royal ass. 7 Nov. 1246 (ibid.). Occ. 11 Nov. 1246 (*CR 1242–47*, p. 485). D. (L.), lic. to el. 18 Oct. 1260 (*CPR 1258–66*, p. 97). Seal (*BM Seals*, no. 4011).

John de Saunde (Sonde) **1260–1286** M. of Sherborne, royal ass. 28 Oct. 1260, temps. 2 Nov. 1260 (*CPR 1258–66*, pp. 124, 125). Cess. by 19 Apr. 1286 (PRO, C84/8/42). Cess., lic. to el. 25 Apr. 1286 (*CPR 1281–92*, p. 232). Seal (*Mon. Seals*, p. 81).

Hugh of Stalbridge (Stapelbrigg(e)) **1286–1310** M. of Sherborne, royal ass. 30 Apr. 1286, temps 10 May 1286 (*CPR 1281–92*, pp. 242, 247). D. 23 Apr. 1310 (*Reg. Gandavo*, II, 736). D., lic. to el. 1 May 1310 (*CPR 1307–13*, p. 225).

John of Thornford (Thorneford(e)) **1310–1316** Precentor of Sherborne, eln pres. to king for royal ass. 13 May 1310 (PRO, C84/16/39); royal ass. 19 May 1310, temps. 15 June 1310 (*CPR 1307–13*, pp. 227, 231). El. 13 May 1310, eln conf. 20 May, bl. and prof. obed. 21 June 1310 (*Reg. Gandavo*, II, 734–45). Occ. *c.* Mar. x Apr. 1316 (*Reg. Martival*, II, 98). D. by 16 Sept. 1316 (PRO, C84/18/51). D. (J.), lic. to el. 24 Sept. 1316 (*CPR 1313–17*, p. 547).

Robert of Ramsbury (Remmesbir', Remmesbury) **1316–1329** M. of Sherborne, eln pres. to king for royal ass. 18 Oct. 1329 (PRO, C84/19/1); royal ass. 20 Oct. 1316 (*CPR 1313–17*, p. 555). Eln pres. to bp 29 Oct. 1316, eln conf. 16 Nov. 1316, bl. 21 Nov. 1316 and mand. to install s.d. (*Reg. Martival*, I, 413–14). Occ. 24 Jan. 1329 (ibid., II, ii, 597). D., lic. to el. 23 Sept. 1329 (*CPR 1327–30*, p. 447).

John of Compton 1329–1342 Pr. of Sherborne, eln pres. to king for royal ass. 18 Oct. 1329 (PRO, C84/22/31); royal ass. 25 Oct. 1329, temps. 2 Feb. 1330 (*CPR 1327–30*, pp. 453, 485). Inhibition by the Official of Canterbury of prejudicial action against John of Compton, m. of Sherborne, or the monks who have el. him during the hearing of an appeal against them. Mand. for their citation to answer Thomas le Gilden, who objects to Compton because he has incurred excommunication for violence to clerks 17 Dec. 1329 (*Reg. Martival*, IV, pp. 130–1, no. 180). Cert. conf. eln by bp of Salisbury 30 Jan. 1330 (PRO, C84/22/33). Petition to Black Prince for lic. to el. 30 Nov. (1342) (PRO, SC1/42/113). D., lic. to el. 7 Dec. 1342 (*CPR 1340–43*, p. 573). Compton may possibly be the same as the pr. of Horton (dependency of Sherborne) who occ. in 1310 (q.v.).

John of Henton 1342–1348 M. of Sherborne, royal ass. 26 Dec. 1342 (ibid., p. 574); temps. 12 Feb. 1343 (*CPR 1343–45*, p. 7). Cert. conf. eln by bp of Salisbury 9 Feb. 1343 (PRO, C84/24/26). Occ. 6 Feb. 1348 (*CPR 1348–50*, p. 60). D., lic. to el. 27 Dec. 1348 (ibid., p. 220). Seal (*BM Seals*, no. 4013).

John (de) Frith (Fryth) **1349–1373** M. of Sherborne, royal ass. 18 Jan. 1349, temps. 16 Feb. 1349 (*CPR 1348–50*, pp. 227, 259). Eln conf. 7 Feb. 1349 (Salisbury, Reg. Wyvill, II, f. 199r). D. 18 Sept. 1373 (PRO, C84/30/53). D., lic. to el. 24 Sept. 1373 (*CPR 1370–74*, p. 337). Seal (*BM Seals*, no. 4014).

Edward Goude (Gode) **1373–1385** (Pr.) M. of Sherborne, eln pres. to king for royal ass. 5 Oct. 1373 (PRO, C84/30/53); royal ass. 8 Oct. 1373, temps. 24 Oct. 1373 (*CPR 1370–74*, pp. 341, 345). Cert. conf. eln by bp of Salisbury 23 Oct. 1373 (PRO, C84/30/54). D. by 28 July 1385 (PRO, C84/33/40). D., lic. to el. 2) Aug. 1385 (*CPR 1385–89*, p. 10).

SHREWSBURY (Shrops), St Peter and St Paul f. *c.* 1083 x 87, (? 1087)
Lists in *VCH Shrops*, II, 37; *Ctl. Shrewsbury*, I, pp. xxvii–xxv (to 1333); M. Webb, *The Abbots of Shrewsbury 1087–1540* (Shrewsbury, 1985); *Heads*, I, 71.

Hugh de Lacy **–1221** Occ. 23 Oct. 1190 (*Ctl. Shrewsbury*, II, 354); 22 Nov. 1192 (Eyton, *Salop*, VI, 329); 6 Feb. 1196 (*Lancs F.*, p. 2 = PRS, XVII, no. 113); 7 May 1197 (PRS, XX, no. 151); 12 Nov. 1219 (Salop. F., *Trans. Salop. Arch. Soc.* VI (1906), 168). Unnamed abb. dep. by July 1221 (*Rolls of Justices in Eyre 1221–2*, pp. 462, 503–4). Abbey vacant 6 July 1221 (*CPR 1216–25*, p. 296). Seal (*Durham Seals*, II, pp. 580–1, no. 3543).

Walter **1221–?1223** (W.) pr. of Leominster, royal ass. 23 July 1221 (*CPR 1216–25*, p. 297). El. abb. 1221 (W.) (*Ann. Tewkesbury*, p. 65). Unnamed abb. d. 1223 (ibid., p. 67). Lic. to el. (no reason given for vacancy) 13 Aug. 1223 (*CPR 1216–25*, p. 381).

Henry **1223–?1244** Pr. of Shrewsbury, royal ass. 24 Aug. 1223 (ibid., pp. 382–3). (H.) el. 1223 (*Ann. Tewkesbury*, p. 67). Occ. 1227, 1236, 18 Nov. 1240 (Salop F., *Trans. Salop, Arch. Soc.*, 4th series, I, 385; IV, 161, 173; VI, 176). Abbey void 4 Aug. 1244 (*CPR 1232–47*, p. 433).

Adam II 1244–1250 Pr. of Shrewsbury, royal ass. 7 Aug. 1244 (ibid., p. 433); mand. for seisin 14 Apr. 1244 (*CR 1242–47*, pp. 220–1). Cess., lic. to el. 2 May 1250 (*CPR 1247–58*, p. 64).

[**Adam [III]** Sacrist of Shrewsbury, royal ass. 21 May 1250 (ibid., p. 65). Bp of Coventry refused to conf. eln (*CPL*, I, 269).]

William 1250–1251 M. of Coventry, apptd by bp of Coventry (ibid). Royal ass. 19 Aug. 1250, writ *de intendendo* 28 Aug. 1250 (*CPR 1247–58*, pp. 72–3). Occ. 22 Oct. 1250 (ibid., p. 76). Adam appealed to the Pope, who quashed both his eln and that of William, and apptd Henry (*CPL*, I, 269).

Henry⁶ 1251–1258 M. of Evesham and chaplain to Cardinal J. of St Lawrence in Lucina (ibid.). Apptd 6 Mar. 1251 and William ordered to res. (ibid). Writ *de intendendo* 5 May 1251 (*CPR 1247–58*, p. 94). Mand. for seisin 5 May 1251 (*CR 1247–51*, pp. 437–8). Reproved by king for appealing to Rome against W[illiam], sub-pr. of Coventry 15 Oct. 1251 (ibid., p. 565). 1257 the king's envoy to Castile (*CPR 1247–58*, pp. 572, 575). Returned from Castile June 1258 (*CR 1256–59*, p. 314). Res. at bp's visitation; notif. of res. 12 Dec. 1258 (PRO, C84/2/5). Cess., lic. to el. 25 Dec. 1258 (*CPR 1258–66*, p. 7). Mentioned 1277 as apostate fugitive from the order (*Chapters of English Black Monks*, I, 83; Logan, *Runaway Religious*, p. 185).

Thomas 1258–1266 Precentor of Shrewsbury, royal ass. 26 Dec. 1258, writ *de intendendo* 10 Jan. 1259 (*CPR 1258–66*, pp. 7–8, 9; cf. PRO, C84/2/4). D., lic. to el. 21 May 1266 (*CPR 1258–66*, p. 600).

William of Upton 1266–1271 M. of Shrewsbury, writ *de intendendo*, eln having been conf. by R., bp of Coventry and Lichfield 11 Aug. 1266 (ibid., p. 625). Cess., lic. to el. 27 Dec. 1271 (*CPR 1266–72*, p. 612).

Luke of Wenlock (Wenlok) **1272–1278** M. of Shrewsbury, royal ass. 24 Jan. 1272, writ *de intendendo*, eln having been conf. by bp of Coventry and Lichfield (ibid., pp. 617–18). Cess., lic. to el. 3 Jan. 1279 (*CPR 1272–81*, p. 296). Bp Anian II of St Asaph informs the king that he was present at the res. of the abb. *c.* 4 Dec. 1278 (PRO, SC1/20/140).

John of Drayton (Dreyton) **1279–1292** M. of Shrewsbury, eln pres. to king for royal ass. 19 Jan. 1279 (PRO, C84/6/13); royal ass. 24 Jan. 1279, writ *de intendendo* 11 Feb. 1279 (*CPR 1272–81*, pp. 299, 301). Cert. conf. eln by bp of Coventry and Lichfield 5 Feb. 1279 (PRO, C84/6/15). D. by 14 May 1292 (PRO, C84/10/41). D., lic. to el. 28 May 1292 (*CPR 1281–92*, p. 492).

William of Muckley (Mockeleye, Mokeleg, Mokeley(e), Mokileg) **1292–1333** M. of Shrewsbury, eln pres. to king for royal ass. 13 June 1292 (PRO, C84/10/43); royal ass. 20 June 1292, temps. 2 July 1292 (*CPR 1281–92*, pp. 496–7). Cert. conf. eln by bp of Coventry and Lichfield 26 June 1292 (PRO, C84/10/45). House void by his death 22 Apr. 1333 (*CFR 1327–37*, p. 358). D., lic. to el. 26 Apr. 1333 (*CPR 1330–34*, p. 424).

Adam of Cleobury (Cleburi, Clebury, Clubury) **1333–1355** Pr. of Shrewsbury, royal ass. 20 May 1333, temps. 8 June 1333 (ibid., pp. 430, 437). Eln conf. 5 May 1333 (Lichfield, B/A/1/2, f. 211r–v). D. by 16 July 1355 when extent taken (BL, Add. ms. 6165, f. 43r). D., lic. to el. 22 July 1355 (*CPR 1354–58*, p. 274).

Henry of Alston 1355–1361 M. of Shrewsbury, eln pres. to king for royal ass. 29 July 1355 (PRO, C84/27/27); royal ass. 3 Aug. 1355, temps. 11 Aug. 1355 (*CPR 1354–58*, pp. 272, 276). Eln conf. 8 Aug. 1355 (Lichfield, B/A/1/2, f. 230r). D., lic. to el. 12 Oct. 1361 (*CPR 1361–64*, p. 85).

Nicholas Stevens (Stevenes) **1361–1399** M. of Shrewsbury, royal ass. 17 Nov. 1361, temps. 11 Dec. 1361 (ibid., pp. 104, 135). Commn to examine eln 22 Nov. 1361, eln conf. by commis-

---

⁶ For a note on the disputed eln of 1250–1, and the career of Abb. Henry see *Ctl. Shrewsbury*, I, p. xxvi.

sary 1 Dec. 1361 (*Reg. Stretton*, II, 194). D. after 24 June 1399 (*Ctl. Shrewsbury*, II, p. 436n). D. by 21 July 1399 (PRO, C84/38/2). D., lic. to el. 25 July 1399 (*CPR 1396–99*, p. 591).

SNELSHALL (Bucks), St Leonard f. –1166 (as cell of Prémontré); 1203 x 1219 (Ben. priory). Lists in *VCH Bucks*, I, 353.

William Occ. Apr. 1219 (*Ctl. Dunstable*, no. 273; *Mon. Angl.*, IV, 235, no. ii).

Hugh Occ. n.d. (1219 x 1231) (*Ctl. Snelshall*, p. 11, no. 25); n.d. (PRO, E326/5263). *Mon. Angl.*, IV, 233, gives occ. 1226, but without source.

John Occ. (J.) 15 June 1231 (*Ctl. Snelshall*, p. 66, no. 213 = *Bucks F.*, I, 60)[7]; (J.) 18 Nov. 1237 (*Ctl. Snelshall*, p. 64, no. 208 = *Beds F.*, I, p. 107, no. 400); 1237 (PRO, F. Divers Cos. CP25/1/283/10, no. 139); 8 Nov. 1242 (*Luffield Chts.*, I, no. 42); 12 Nov. 1247 (*Bucks F.*, I, 91).

Hugh of Dunstable (Dunstapl') **1251/2–1273** Sub-pr. of Snelshall, eln conf. June 1251 x June 1252, no reason given for vacancy (*Reg. Grosseteste*, p. 381). Res. by 28 Sept. 1273 (*Reg. R. Gravesend*, p. 249).

Warin 1273– Eln conf. 28 Sept. 1273 (ibid., pp. 249, 344).

Nicholas of Hanslope (Hameslape, Hamslap) **1280/1–1300** El. pr. year 1 of bp Sutton (19 May 1280 x 18 May 1281), lic. to el. from Richard FitzJohn, knight, patron (Bodl., Dodsworth ms. 107, f. 140v). Occ. *c.* 1280 (*Ctl. Snelshall*, p. 16, no. 40). Res. 16 July 1300 (Lincoln, Ep. Reg., III, f. 12r).

Richard of Eye (Eya) **1300–1302** M. of Snelshall, pres. 30 Oct. 1300, eln quashed but apptd by bp of Lincoln 19 Nov. 1300 (Lincoln, Ep. Reg., II, f. 174r–v). D. by 20 May 1302 (ibid., f. 175r).

Nicholas of Hanslope (Hameslap, Hamslap) **1302–1319** M. of Snelshall, eln quashed but apptd by bp 20 May 1302 (ibid.). D. by 5 Mar. 1319 (ibid., f. 191v).

John of Cosgrove (Conesgrave or Covesgrave) **1319–** M. of Snelshall, eln quashed but apptd by bp 5 Mar. 1319 (ibid.). Occ. 29 Nov. 1329, 30 Nov. 1329 (*Luffield Chts.*, II, p. 442, no. A. 11; p. 31, no. 18a).

Hugh of Leckhampstead (Lekhamsted) **1334–1358** M. of Snelshall, commn to examine eln 21 Nov. 1334 (Lincoln, Ep. Reg., V, f. 487r). D. by 12 May 1358 (Lincoln, Ep. Reg., IX, ff. 310v–311r).

Ralph (Richard) of Nibley (Nibbeley, Nuble) **1358–1367** M. of Snelshall, right of appt transferred by bp of Lincoln and he apptd Ralph 12 May 1358 (ibid.). D. (Richard) by 25 Nov. 1367 (Lincoln, Ep. Reg., X, f. 414v).

Roger (of) Oving (Ovyng) **1367–1392** M. of Snelshall, eln quashed but apptd by bp 25 Nov. 1367 (ibid.). D., lic. to el. 21 Nov. 1392 (*CPR 1391–96*, p. 199; cf. Lincoln, Ep. Reg., XI, f. 408r).

TAVISTOCK (Devon), St Mary and St Rumon f. 975 x 80; destroyed 997, but reestablished. See Finberg (1951), pp. 1 ff.

Lists in H. P. R. Finberg in *Devon and Cornwall Notes and Queries*, XXII (1943), 159–62, 174–5, 186–8, 194–7, partly based on Ann. Tavistock in *Newburgh* ed. Hearne, III, 709–10, checked by Finberg with Oxford, Bodl. ms. Digby, 81, ff. 67 ff.; brief list in H. P. R. Finberg, *Tavistock Abbey: a study in the social and economic history of Devon* (Newton Abbot, 1969), p. 277; *Heads*, I, 71–3.

Jordan *c.* **1203–1219/20** See *DCNQ*, p. 186. D. late 1219 or early 1220 (cf. *CRR*, VIII, 327; 1220, Ann.).

---

[7] *Mon. Angl.*, IV, 233 gives a pr. Nicholas occ. 1232, but no source is given and prob. this is an error.

William de Kernet (Kermet) **1220–1224** Pr. of Otterton, royal ass. 20 Feb. 1220 (*CPR 1216–25*, p. 229). D. by 27 Mar. 1224 (ibid., p. 432). See *DCNQ*, pp. 186–7.

John of Rochester (Rofa) **1224–1233** Chaplain of Archbp Stephen Langton of Canterbury, royal ass. 3 June 1224 (*CPR 1216–25*, p. 443, cf. *DKR* 4, app. ii, p. 143, no. 55). El. 1224 (*Ann. Tewkesbury*, p. 67). Occ. 15 June 1232 (*CChR 1226–57*, p. 157). D. 13 Apr. 1233 (Ann.). Lic. to el. (no reason given for vacancy) 27 Apr. 1233 (*CPR 1232–47*, p. 15). See *DCNQ*, p. 187.

Alan of Cornwall (Cornubiensis) **1233–1248** Pr. of Scilly, royal ass. 8 June 1233 (*CPR 1232–47*, p. 18, cf. Ann. give 11 Aug. as his accession date). Mand. for seisin 24 July 1233 (*CR 1231–34*, p. 241). D. 1248 (Ann., – Willis, I, 173 version 28 Feb., but Hearne's date of 31 May may refer to Robert's eln not Alan's d.). Lic. to el. (no reason given for vacancy) 4 May 1248 (*CPR 1247–58*, p. 14). See *DCNQ*, p. 187.

Robert of Kidknowle (Kitenoll) **1248–1257** M. of Tavistock, royal ass. 2 June 1248 (*CPR 1247–58*, p. 18). Mand. for seisin 12 June 1248 (*CR 1247–51*, p. 60). Cess., lic. to el. 16 June 1257 (*CPR 1247–58*, p. 560). See *DCNQ*, p. 187.

Henry of Northampton 1257–1259 Cellarer of Bermondsey, royal ass. 7 Aug. 1257, writ *de intendendo* 12 Sept. 1257 (*CPR 1247–58*, pp. 573, 577). Cert. conf. eln by bp of Exeter 3 Sept. 1257 (PRO, C84/1/46). D., lic. to el. 18 May 1259 (*CPR 1258–66*, p. 22). After d. of John (*sic*) of Northampton two men refused office and patronage lapsed to bp of Exeter (*Reg. Bronescombe*, p. 265; *Reg. W. Bronescombe*, I, no. 109). See *DCNQ*, p. 187.

Philip Trenchfoil (Trenchefoyl(e), Trencheful) **1259–1260** M. of St Swithun's, Winchester, provided by bp 10 Aug. 1259, bl. 12 Oct. 1259 (*Reg. Bronescombe*, p. 265; *Reg. W. Bronescombe*, I, nos. 109, 153). Royal ass. 22 July 1259, temps. 14 Aug. 1259 (*CPR 1258–66*, pp. 35, 39). D. by 27 July 1260 (*CPR 1258–66*, p. 84). D., lic. to el. 9 Aug. 1260 (ibid., p. 87). See *DCNQ*, pp. 187–8.

Alfred 1260–1262 Pr. of Tavistock, eln quashed but apptd by bp, no reason given for vacancy, 7 Sept. 1260; bl. and prof. obed. 29 Sept. 1260 (*Reg. Bronescombe*, p. 266; *Reg. W. Bronescombe*, I, nos. 258, 273; PRO, C84/2/17). Eln pres. to king for royal ass. 24 Aug. 1260 (PRO, C84/2/16); royal ass. 30 Aug. 1260, writ *de intendendo* 15 Sept. 1260 (*CPR 1258–66*, pp. 91, 92). D. (A.) by 23 June 1262 (PRO, C84/2/32). Lic. to el. (no reason given for vacancy) 1 July 1262 (*CPR 1258–66*, p. 219). See *DCNQ*, p. 194.

John Chubb(e) 1262–1269 M. of Tavistock and pr. of Scilly, el. as abb. and pres. to king n.d. [?June 1262] (*CR 1261–64*, p. 132). Eln quashed but apptd by bp 8 Sept. 1262, bl. 2 Feb. 1263 (*Reg. Bronescombe*, pp. 183, 266; *Reg. W. Bronescombe*, I, nos. 451, 471). Royal ass. (Robert) 7 Aug. 1262, temps. 30 Sept. 1262 (*CPR 1258–66*, p. 227). He was suspended for 3 years for extravagance and finally dep. 19 Mar. 1269 (*Reg. Bronescombe*, pp. 183, 266–8; *Reg. W. Bronescombe*, II, no. 733, and see *DCNQ*, p. 194, n. 12). House void 12 Dec. 1269 (*CPR 1266–72*, p. 398). Dep., lic. to el. 14 Jan. 1270 (ibid., p. 402). See *DCNQ*, p. 194.

Robert Colbern 1270–1285 Precentor of Tavistock, royal ass. 14 Mar. 1270, temps. 28 Mar. 1270 (*CPR 1266–72*, pp. 415, 417). Bl. 6 Apr. 1270 (*Reg. Bronescombe*, p. 299; *Reg. W. Bronescombe*, II, no. 803). D., lic. to el. 29 Mar. 1285 (*CPR 1281–92*, p. 155). See *DCNQ*, pp. 194–5.

Robert Champeaux (de Campellis, Campell, Champiaus, Champyaux) **1285–1324** M. of Tavistock, royal ass. 21 Apr. 1285, temps. 2 May 1285 (*CPR 1281–92*, pp. 157, 159). D. by 13 Dec. 1324 (PRO, C84/20/42). D., lic. to el. 23 Dec. 1324 (*CPR 1324–27*, p. 62). See *DCNQ*, p. 195.

Robert Bosse (Busse) and **John (de) Courtenay 1325** Commns to bp of Exeter to examine double eln 15 Feb., 3 Mar. 1325 (*CPR 1324–27*, pp. 89, 109). Royal protection for Robert Bosse, abb.-el. 6 Mar. 1325 (ibid., p. 106). Appt of John Everard to custody of the abbey until the eln dispute is resolved. Robert and John have refused to accept decision of the bp of Exeter and have appealed to the Curia 5 Apr. 1325 (*CPR 1324–27*, p. 113). 23 Sept. 1325 royal protection for 1 year: temps. granted to pr. and convent as abbey vacant (ibid., p. 179). Robert res. his eln and John's eln quashed (*CPL*, II, 265). Letter of recommendation from king to pope about John de Courtenay, m. of Tavistock and son of Hugh de Courtenay, el. in discord, 20 Aug. 1327 (*Reg. Berkeley*, p. 33). See *DCNQ*, p. 195. Robert said to be illegitimate etc. (PRO, C84/20/49A).

Bonus 1327–1333 Abb. of Larreule-en-Bigorre, dioc. of Tarbes, apptd by pope 30 Oct. 1327 (*CPL*, II, 265). Temps. 5 May 1328 (*CFR 1327–37*, pp. 89–90). Commn to induct 12 June 1328 (*Reg. Grandisson*, I, 346). Occ. 10 May 1328 (*CCR 1327–30*, p. 385). Abbey under interdict: commn for admin. of its goods 8 July 1333 (*Reg. Grandisson*, II, 702–6). Monition 8 Dec. 1332 (ibid., 675–8); sentence of deprivation 24 Oct. 1333 (ibid., 716–18). Dep. by bp, royal lic. to el. 22 Nov. 1333 (*CPR 1330–34*, p. 483). Marginal comment by Bp Grandisson in *Reg.* I, 395 'Iste abbas qui dicebatur bonus erat pessimus quasi hereticus'. See *DCNQ*, p. 195, and also H. P. R. Finberg, 'The tragi-comedy of Abbot Bonus' in W. G. Hoskins and H. P. R. Finberg, *Devonshire Studies* (1952), pp. 198–211, repd in H. P. R. Finberg, *West-Country Historical Studies* (Newton Abbot, 1969), pp. 169–81.

John de Courtenay (Courteneye, Curtenay) **1334–1349** See above and under Lewes. Son of Hugh de Courtenay. M. of Tavistock, had been installed at Lewes, but had to res. 17 Sept. 1329 and return to Tavistock (*Reg. Grandisson*, I, p. 231). Eln proclaimed 13 Jan. 1334, eln conf. 24 Apr. 1334, bl. and prof. obed. s.d. (ibid., II, 725–6, 740–1). Temps. 13 Mar. 1334 (*CPR 1330–34*, p. 524). Suspension of abb. 1338 and again 27 June 1348 *qui per multos annos bona mobilia ipsius monasterii dilapidavit notorie et consumpsit* (*Reg. Grandisson*, II, 887, 1050–1); mand. to publish suspension 5 July 1348 (ibid., 1052). D., lic. to el. 11 July 1349 (*CPR 1348–50*, p. 342). See *DCNQ*, pp. 195–6.

Richard de Esse (Asshe) **1349–1362** Pr. of Tavistock, royal ass. 3 Sept. 1349, temps. 1 Nov. 1349 (*CPR 1348–50*, pp. 377, 418). Commn to receive fealty of abb.-el. 17 Oct. 1349 (*Reg. Grandisson*, I, p. 71). D., lic. to el. 13 Feb. 1362 (*CPR 1361–64*, p. 165). See *DCNQ*, p. 196.

Stephen (of) Langdon (Langedon, Langedone, Langhedon(e)) **1362–1380** M. of Tavistock, eln pres. to king for royal ass. 14 Mar. 1362 (PRO, C84/28/39); royal ass. 29 Mar. 1362 (*CPR 1361–64*, p. 178). Letter of bp of Exeter stating he had quashed the eln and that Stephen had appealed to the Court of Canterbury. The bp, on the Black Prince's instructions to conf. or reject, commns the bp of Bath and Wells to examine eln and to conf. if canonical and bl. 10 Oct. 1362 (*Reg. Grandisson*, III, 1239–40). The bp commns several to examine the eln: certif. 14 Oct. 1362 by commissaries that they had conf. eln and given him lic. to be bl. by any bp in the province of Canterbury. The bp of Bath and Wells bl. him 20 Oct. 1362 (*Reg. R. Shrewsbury*, II, app. no. 95). Adm. as abb. 20 Oct. 1362 and renunciation of his appeal to the Court of Canterbury s.d. (*Reg. Grandisson*, III, 1240–1). D. 28 Nov. 1380 (*DCNQ*, p. 196). D., lic. to el. 8 Dec. 1380 (*CPR 1377–81*, p. 563).

TEWKESBURY (Glos), St Mary ref. *c.* 980 (dep. on Cranborne); 1102 (independent).
Lists in *VCH Glos.* II, 65; basis in *Ann. Tewkesbury* and *Mon. Angl.*, II, 59, obit 1 in calendar in BL, Royal ms. 8 C VII, ff. 6r–8v; obit 2 in calendar in CUL, ms. Gg. 3. 21, ff. 5r–9v; *Heads*, I, 73.

Peter of Worcester 1216–1232 Cellarer, proposed by king 9 Apr. 1216 (*Rot. Lit. Claus.*, I, 270). M. of Tewkesbury, royal ass. 26 May 1216 (*Rot. Lit. Pat.*, p. 194). Seisin gtd 27 May 1216 (*Rot. Lit. Claus.*, I, 271). Bl. 8 Sept. 1216 (*Ann. Worcs*, p. 405; cf. *Ann. Tewkesbury*, p. 62). (P.) Set out for Rome 13 Mar. 1225 and was absolved by Honorius III from accusations made by the bp of Worcester (*Ann. Tewkesbury*, p. 68). D. 30 Mar. 1232 (*Ann. Tewkesbury*, p. 83; *Ann. Worcs*, p. 424; and in Tewkesbury obits 1, 2, cf. *Heads*, I, 73).

Robert III 1232–1254 4 Apr. 1232 appeal in chapter of Tewkesbury for a free eln (*Ann. Tewkesbury*, p. 83); 28 Apr. 1232 bp of Worcester absolved convent from excommunication (ibid.). Pr. of Tewkesbury, el. 9 May 1232, bl. 30 May 1232 (ibid., p. 84; *Ann. Worcs*, p. 424; see *Mon. Angl.*, II, 80–1, no. lxxxv). D. 20 Nov. 1254 (*Ann. Tewkesbury*, p. 155).

Thomas de Stoke (Stokes) **1255–1276** Pr. of St James, Bristol, el. 7 Jan. 1255; bl. 7 May 1255; installed 14 Mar. 1255 (ibid.). D. by 20 Aug. 1276 (*Reg. G. Giffard*, p. 89).

Richard of Norton 1276–1282 Eln conf. 20 Aug. 1276 (ibid.). D. 14 Apr. 1282 (*Ann. Worcs.*, p. 483).

Thomas of Kempsey (Kemeseye, Kemes) **1282–** Adm. of el 24 May 1282, no reason given for vacancy (*Reg. G. Giffard*, 151; cf. succ. 21 May 1282 (*Mon. Angl.*, II, 55)). Bl. 24 May 1282 (*Ann. Worcs*, pp. 484–5). Occ. Easter 1328 (*Index to Placita de Banco*, pp. 174, 717); 8 May 1328 (*Reg. Orleton (Worcester)*, no. 273).

John de Cotes –1347 Occ. as pr. of Tewkesbury 1317 (*Worcs. Liber Albus*, II, no. 765). Occ. as abb. 19 Jan. 1330, 25 June 1330 (*Reg. R. Shrewsbury*, I, pp. 51, 66, nos. 261, 205). D. 22 July 1347, bur. 31 July 1347 (*Reg. Bransford*, nos. 933, 940). Ledger stone (*Earliest English Brasses*, p. 189).

Thomas de Leghe (Leighe) **1347–1361** Lic. of patron for eln 4 Aug. 1347 (*Reg. Bransford*, no 932); pr. of Tewkesbury, el. by compromise 20 Aug. 1347 (ibid., nos. 927, 933, 940–1); consent of patron 30 Aug. (ibid., no. 928); eln conf. 10 Sept. 1347 (ibid., no. 926). See also 'The election of an abbot of Tewkesbury in 1347' in R. M. Haines, *Ecclesia Anglicana: studies in the English Church of the later middle ages* (Toronto, 1989), pp. 15–25. D. 7 Oct. 1361 (*Worcs Reg. Sede Vacante*, pp. 214–15; 16 Oct. acc. to *Mon. Angl.*, II, 55).

Thomas of Chesterton 1361–1389 Cellarer of Tewkesbury, el. 24 Nov. 1361; appt of abbey proctors s.d.; patron pres. eln to bp 29 Nov. 1361; appt of proctors to seek bp's conf. 10 Dec. 1361; commn to examine eln 14 Dec. 1361 (*Worcs Reg. Sede Vacante*, pp. 213–15). Occ. 1384 (PRO, C115/78, f. 94v). D. 1389 (*Mon. Angl.*, II, 55). Presumably the unnamed abb. who d. 17 Nov. 1389 (*Cal. Misc. Inq.*, V, no. 253).

THORNEY (Cambs), St Mary, Holy Trinity, St Botolph f. 973 (possibly 972)
Lists in *VCH Cambs*, II, 217; *Heads*, I, 73–5.

Ralph Simplex 1198–1216 El. 1198. D. after 18 years in 1215 18 John (i.e. 1216 in CUL, Add. ms. 3021, ff. 424r, 427v; 1216 in *Ann. Thorney*, p. 21). D. by 5 June 1216 (*Rot. Lit. Claus.*, I, 274).

[**Robert of Elm** Pr. of Deeping, mks attempted to el. him abb. but the legate Guala forced him to res. (*Guala Letters*, no. 158, cf. no. 119n.).]

Robert of Graveley 1217–1237 Sacrist of Bury, newly-el. occ. 6 Dec. 1217 (*Guala Letters*, no. 119 and n.). Royal ass. 17 Dec. 1217 (*CPR 1216–25*, p. 132; *Guala Letters*, no. 158). El. 1216 (*sic*), bl. at Northampton by William, bp of Chester, 2 Henry III (Oct. 1217 x Oct. 1218), ruled 21 years (CUL, Add. ms. 3021, f. 427v). Sacrist of Bury St Edmunds, succ. 3 Nov. 1217 (*Ann. Thorney*, p. 21). Mand. to attend legate 6 Dec. 1217 (*Guala Letters*, no. 119). Eln conf. by Guala and by the king at Northampton 17 Dec. 1217 and entered into possession 21 Dec. (ibid., no. 158). D. 16 Aug. 1237 and bur. in the chapel of the BVM (CUL, Add. ms. 3021, f. 437v). Lic. to el. (no reason given for vacancy) 18 Aug. 1237 (*CPR 1232–47*, p. 193).

Richard of Stamford (Stanford) **1237–1238** M. of Thorney, pr. of Deeping, royal ass. 28 Aug. 1237, writ *de intendendo* 9 Nov. 1237 (ibid., pp. 194, 204). Eln conf. at London 22 Aug. 1237 by Cardinal Otto, the legate; bl. 13/14 Nov. (St Brice's day) 1237 at Balsham by Hugh, bp of Ely (CUL, Add. ms. 3021, f. 437v). D. 13 July 1238 (ibid.). D., lic. to el. 17 July 1238 (*CPR 1232–47*, p. 226).

David 1238–1254 Pr. of Thorney, royal ass. 25 July 1238 (ibid., p. 228). Eln conf. in London by the legate Otto, 2 Feb. 1239, bl. by bp of Ely 6 Feb. 1239 (CUL, Add. ms. 3021, f. 437v). D. by 1 Oct. 1254 (PRO, C84/1/39). D., lic. to el. 9 Oct. 1254 (*CPR 1246–58*, p. 373). D. *c.* Michaelmas 1255 (*sic*) in 17th year of office (CUL, Add. ms. 3021, f. 441r). Seal (*BM Seals*, no. 4167).

Thomas of Castor (Castre) **1254–1261** Pr. of Thorney, royal ass. 26 Oct. 1254, writ *de intendendo* 7 Nov. 1254 (*CPR 1247–58*, pp. 373, 391). Eln conf. by Hugh de Mortimer, official of Archbp Boniface at Canterbury on 31 Oct. bl. by Walter, bp of Norwich on 25 Nov., installed 13 Dec. by Richard de Wotton, administering the Officiality of Ely, *sede vacante* (CUL, Add. ms. 3021, f. 441r). D. 21 Mar. 1261 (ibid., f. 441v). Lic. to el. (no reason given for vacancy) 25 Mar. 1261 (*CPR 1258–66*, p. 147).

William of Yaxley (Jakele, Jakesle) **1261–1293** Pr. of Deeping, el. 1261 (CUL, Add. ms. 3021, f. 441v); royal ass. 18 Apr. 1261, temps. 3 June 1261, the eln having been conf. by mag. R. de Leycestre, Official of H., bp of Ely (*CPR 1258–66*, pp. 149, 156). D. 17 June 1293 in his 32nd year of office (CUL, Add. ms. 3021, f. 449r). D., lic. to el. 25 June 1293 (*CPR 1292–1301*, p. 28).

Odo of Whittlesey (Witleseye, Wittelseye, Wytlesheya) **1293–1305** M. and almoner of Thorney, royal ass. 7 July 1293, temps. 17 July 1293 (ibid., pp. 30, 32). El. 4 July 1293, received by king at Canterbury 7 July 1293, ruled 12 years, eln conf. and bl. by William of Louth, bp of Ely, installed 8 Sept. 1293 (CUL, Add. ms. 3021, f. 449r; cf. PRO, C84/11/22, el. 3 July 1293); cert. conf. eln by bp of Ely 12 July 1293 (PRO, C84/11/23 A–B). D. 28 Sept. 1305 (CUL, Add. ms. 3021, f. 453r). D., lic. to el. 7 Oct. 1305 (*CPR 1301–07*, p. 380).

William of Clopton (Claptona, Cloptone) **1305–1323** M. of Thorney, royal ass. 24 Oct. 1305, writ *de intendendo* 6 Nov. 1305 (*CPR 1301–07*, pp. 387, 397). El. 20 Oct. 1305, eln conf. and bl. by Robert Orford, bp of Ely (CUL, Add. ms. 3021, f. 453r). Cert. conf. eln by bp of Ely 3 Nov. 1305 (PRO, C84/15/37). Installed 9 Jan. 1306 (ibid.) D. 8 Mar 1323 and bur. 12 Mar. 1323 (ibid., f. 464v). D., lic. to el. 12 Mar. 1323 (*CPR 1321–24*, p. 263). Indulgence of 40 days for his soul, bur. before the high altar, 14 Mar. 1323 (Lincoln, Ep. Reg., V, f. 334r).

Reginald of Waternewton (Waterneuton, Neuton) **1323–1347** M. of Thorney, royal ass. 23 Mar. 1323, temps. 13 Apr. 1323 (*CPR 1321–24*, pp. 266, 273). Eln conf. by the vicar-general of the bp of Ely 7 Apr. 1323. temps. 13 Apr. 1323, bl. 17 Apr. by Stephen, bp of London, installed 25 May 1323 (CUL, Add. ms. 3021, ff. 464v–465r). D. 16 Apr. 1347 (Ely, G/1/2, f. 49r; BL, Harl. ms. 3658, f. 3v; *Ann. Thorney*, p. 24). D., lic. to el. 17 Apr. 1347 (*CPR 1345–48*, p. 268; cf. PRO, C84/25/11).

Consent of Edw. III to an el. 30 Apr. 1347 (PRO, SC1/40/53). Thomas Gosberkirk, pr. of Deeping went to king as abbey's proctor after death of Reginald (CUL, Add. ms. 3021, f. 471v). Lic. to el. 17 Apr. 1347 (ibid.).

William of Haddon and **Robert Corby** Disputed eln, both el. by scrutiny. The supporters of William of Haddon guarded the cloister doors; formal protestation by Robert Corby dated 27 Apr. 1347 (ibid., ff. 471v–472v).

William of Haddon (Haddone) **1347–1365** M. of Thorney (M. of Crowland – *Ann. Thorney*, p. 24), royal ass. 30 Apr. 1347, temps. 22 May 1347 (*CPR 1345–48*, pp. 280, 294). El. 27 Apr. 1347; eln conf. 29 Apr. 1347; lic. to bl. abb. 9 May; bl. 20 May 1347 (Ely, G/1/1 part 2, ff, 49r–50v). Cert. conf. eln by bp of Ely 20 May 1347 (PRO, C84/25/13). Order to release temps. 22 May 1347 (PRO, SC1/40/53). Lic. to bp of Ely to bl. William, abb.-el. 8 May

1347 (Lincoln, Ep. Reg., VII, f. 91r). Mand. to install 22 May 1347 (Ely, G/1/1 part 2, f. 51r). D. 6 Nov. 1365 (*Ann. Thorney*, p. 24; cf. PRO, C84/29/28). D., lic. to el. 15 Nov. 1365 (*CPR 1364-67*, p. 181).

Provision for two monks' portions, a fitting room in the monastery and a yearly pension of 8 marks for Robert Corby, the elder, who was lately abb., but res. for the sake of peace, dated 1 Sept. 1351 (*CPP*, p. 219).

John (of) Deeping (Depyng) **1365-1397** M. of Thorney, succ. 25 Nov. 1365 (*Ann. Thorney*, p. 24). Eln pres. to king for royal ass. 28 Nov. 1365 (PRO, C84/29/29); royal ass. 1 Dec. 1365, temps. 17 Dec. 1365 (*CPR 1364-67*, pp. 188, 191). Cert. conf. eln by bp of Ely 17 Dec. 1365 (PRO, C84/29/30). Rules 31 years, 8 weeks and 1 day. D. 21 Jan. 1397 (*Ann. Thorney*, p. 25; cf. PRO, C84/36/50). D., lic. to el. 26 Jan. 1397 (*CPR 1396-99*, p. 60).

UPHOLLAND (Lancs), St Thomas the Martyr (Holande in Wigan) f. 1310 (secular coll.); 1319 (priory).

List in *VCH Lancs*, II, 112.

Thomas of Doncaster (Doncastre) **1319–** First pr. M. of Pontefract, absolved by pr. of Pontefract from his obedience, so that he can become pr. 31 Mar. 1319, and similarly by pr. of Lewes 2 Apr. (*Magnum Reg. Album Lichfield*, pp. 183-4, nos. 371-2); patron pres. him to bp of Coventry as pr. 12 Apr. 1319 (ibid., p. 183, no. 370); adm. 11 May 1319 (ibid., p. 185, no. 375). Letter of Walter Langton, bp of Coventry, transferring the collegiate ch. of St Thomas, the college having been dispersed, to the monks of the Benedictine Order, and constituting Thomas of Doncaster as pr. 10 June 1319; conf. by king 20 June 1319 (*CPR 1317-21*, p. 383). Presumably the 'William' of Doncaster former pr., who occ. 17 July 1334 (Lichfield, B/A/1/3, f. 71v) and who, in 1334, was living at the manor of Greston at the time of the bp's visitation (ibid., f. 60v).

John of Barnby (Barneby) Occ. 18 Nov. 1334 (*CPR 1334-38*, p. 45); 23 July 1340 (PRO, C81/1786/20); 23 May 1343 (*CCR 1343-46*, p. 115); 18 Oct. 1344 (Lincoln, Ep. Reg., VI, f. 41r); 14 Feb. 1348 (*CFR 1347-56*, p. 80); 16 Mar. 1349 pardon, having been indicted for abduction and other felonies (*CPR 1348-50*, p. 269); 19 Sept. 1356 (Lichfield, B/A/1/3, f. 139r).

William –1389 Occ. 1379 (Bennett, 'Lancs and Cheshire Clergy', p. 22). Res. by 18 Nov. 1389 (Lichfield, B/A/1/6, f. 54r).

WALDEN (Essex), St Mary and St James (Saffron Walden) f. ?1136 (priory); 1 Aug. 1190 (abbey)

Lists in *VCH Essex*, II, 114-15; Ann. Walden (15th cent.) in BL, Cotton ms. Titus D XX, ff. 68r-91v (sometimes erratic, cf. *Ch. Walden*, pp. lviii-lix, 167-8); *Heads*, I, 75-6.

Master Reginald 1st abb. D. 3 x 5 Feb. 1200 or 1203 (see *Heads*, I, 76; *Ch. Walden*, pp. xxxvi-vii).

Robert I 2nd abb. Occ. +24 Apr. 1206 as j.d. (BL, Add. ms. 46353, f. 294v; *Heads*, I, 76). D. 1210, ? for 1213, according to BL, Cotton ms. Titus D XX, f. 81r; *Heads*, I, 76).

Roger 3rd abb. Said to have d. 1222 (BL, Cotton ms. Titus D. XX, f. 83v), but see below under Robert II. Occ. Trin. 1215 (*Essex F.*, I, p. 47).

Robert II 4th abb. Said to have d. 1231 (BL, Cotton ms. Titus D. XX, f. 84v, but cf. later entries). Occ. as Robert in 1220 but also as Roger later in the same cht. (BL, Harl. ms. 3697, f. 211r-v). Occ. 1221 (*Ctl. Colchester*, II, 534-5); 1221 x 1227 (*temp.* Bp Eustace of London and pr. R. of Anglesey) (BL, Harl. ms. 3697, f. 44v); 1222 x 22 May 1224 (*Waltham Chts.*, no. 306); (R.) [*c.* 1 Aug.] 1234 (WAM 3761); (R.) 30 Sept. 1234 (*CChR 1226-57*, pp. 196-7).

An unnamed abb. d. 1236 (*Ann. Dunstable*, p. 144). It could be Thomas (below) but in view of the evident dating discrepancies could refer to Robert.

Thomas Occ. Mich. 1236 (*Essex F.*, I, 115); 25 Nov. 1236 (BL, Harl. ms. 3697, f. 24r).

Richard **–1241** 5th abb. Said to have d. 1241 (BL, Cotton ms. Tiberius D XX, f. 86r).

Roger Called 6th abb., said to have d. 1251 (ibid.), but succ. by 1244 (see below). Occ. n.d. (1229 x 1237), *temp.* Abb. Sampson of St Benet's, Hulme (BL, Harl. ms. 3697, f. 43r); n.d. (1234/5 x 1241), *temp.* Bp Roger of London and Peter de Neuport, archdn of London (ibid., f. 201v; *HMC 9th Rept*, app., p. 39); 18 July 1236 (BL, Harl. ms. 3697, f. 45r). Seal (*BM Seals*, no. 4242).

Absolom (Absalon, Aspolon) **–1263** Occ. 29 Mar. 1244, 6 Oct. 1247 (BL, Harl. ms. 3697, ff. 208v, 159r); 24 & 26 Nov. 1248 (*CChR 1226–57*, p. 337); 17 June 1263 (*Staffs F.*, p. 250); from 26 Apr. 1248 to Easter 1251 (*Essex F.*, I, 159, 187); (A.) 1254 (BL, Harl. ms. 3697, f. 175v); Hil. term 1256 (ibid., f. 64v); 22 Sept. 1263 (ibid., f. 82v). 7th abb. D 1263 (BL, Cotton ms. Titus D XX, f. 86v).

Thomas **–1270** 8th abb. Res. 1270 to join Dominican friars at Cambridge (ibid., f. 87r).

John (of) Feering (Feryng, Fering) **–1285** Name (BL, Harl. ms. 3697, f. 214r). Occ. Mich. 1272 (*Essex F.*, I, 282); 13 Oct. 1272 (PRO, F. Divers Cos. CP25/1/283/17, no. 502); (J.) 1281 (PRO, DL25/181); 25 Oct. 1285 (BL, Harl. ms. 3697, f. 188r). Called 9th abb. D. 1285 (BL, Cotton ms. Titus D XX, f. 87v).

William de Polhey (Palhey, Poley, Polley) **–1304/5** Occ. 15 Mar. 1286, 19 July 1296, 5 Mar. 1298 (BL, Harl. ms. 3697, ff. 192r, 110v, 255r–v); 16 Nov. 1299 when absolved from excommunication for infringing *Clericis Laicos* (*Reg. Winchelsey*, I, 372); Whitsun 1303 (BL, Harl. ms. 3697, f. 54r). 10th abb. D. 1304 (? 1304/5) (BL, Cotton ms. Titus D XX, f. 88r). Convent wrote to Humphrey, earl of Hereford and Essex asking as patron lic. to el. on d. of abb. William 6 Feb. 1305 (PRO, DL34/1/9).

John de Plesseto (Plesset) **1305–** Name (BL, Harl. ms. 3697, ff. 83r, 94r, 105v). Occ. 29 Apr. 1305, 1306, 1308 (ibid., ff. 255v, 106r, 54r); 7 Aug. 1311 (*Worcs. Liber Albus*, I, no. 530); 29 Oct. 1311 (*CPR 1307–13*, p. 397); 1321 (BL, Harl. ms. 3697, f. 83r); 20 July 1322 (PRO, E40/14864; *HMC 9th Rept*, app., p. 633); 8 Feb. 1327 (Norwich, Reg/1/2, f. 13r).

Andrew Occ. 8 Nov. 1329 (BL, Harl. ms. 3697, f. 244r); 1332 (*Reg. S. Gravesend*, p. 299); 8 Oct. 1335 (Lincoln, Ep. Reg., IV, f. 211v); Jan. 1344 (PRO, DL27/17; BL, Harl. ms. 3697, ff. 258r, 261r–v).

William Coleman of Hatfield (Hatfeld) Occ. 29 Apr. 1345 (ibid., ff. 181r); 8 Dec. 1350 (CPL, III, 404); Mich. 1351 (PRO, KB27/365, rex roll m. 31d); 1361 (*Reg. Sudbury*, I, 227); 26 Nov. 1361 (*CPR 1361–64*, p. 133); 19 Nov. 1361, 24 Oct. 1362, 12 Feb. 1362, 6 May 1362 (*CCR 1360–64*, pp. 297, 360, 398, 399); 1365 (BL, Harl. ms. 3697, f. 151v); 1365 (Lambeth, Reg. Islip, f. 211v). D. 30 Sept. 1366 (*Reg. Sudbury*, I, 127).

John of Finningham (Fynyngham) **1366–1374** M. of Walden, el. 9 Oct. 1366; commn to examine eln 15 Oct.; cert. 20 Oct.; bp conf. eln 22 Oct. 1366 (ibid., 124–34). Occ. 4 Feb. 1368 (*CPL*, IV, 67). Res. 2 May 1374 (*Reg. Sudbury*, I, 170).

Peter of Hatfield (Hatefeld) **1374–** M. of Walden, el. 31 May 1374 (ibid., 169–75). Occ. 1375, 1377 (BL, Harl. ms. 3697, ff. 259r, 107r); 1381 (London, Reg. Braybrooke, f. 280v); 17 Jan. 1382 (BL, Harl. ms. 3697, f. 107v).

The next recorded abb., **John Pentelowe**, was apptd by bp of London *pro hac vice* 17 June 1385, no reason given for the vacancy (London, Reg. Braybrooke, ff. 318v–319r).

WESTMINSTER St Peter ref. *c.* 959
    Lists in *VCH London*, I, 454–5; *Heads*, I, 76–7.

William du Hommet (Humez) **1214–1222** A Norman, m. of Caen, pr. of Frampton (q. v.). El. 4 May 1214, bl. by Bp William of London 25 May 1214 (*Flete*, p. 101, from *Flor. Hist.*, II, 147f.). D. 20 Apr. 1222 and bur. in south part of the cloister (*Flete*, p. 102, cf. *Ann. Dunstable*, p. 76).

Richard of Barking (Berchinhes, Berking, Berkinges) **1222–1246** Pr. of Westminster. El. 1222 (*Ann. Dunstable*, p. 76). Mand. to examine eln and to conf. it if canonical 5 July 1222 (*CPL*, I, 88). Bl. by bp of Winchester 18 Sept. 1222 (*Flete*, p. 103). D. 23 Nov. 1246 and bur. in Lady Chapel (*Flete*, p. 106). D., lic. to el. (no name given) 10 Dec. 1246 (*CPR 1232–47*, p. 495).

Richard de Crokesle(y) (Crockelee, Crokele) **1246–1258** El. 16 Dec. 1246 (*Flete*, p. 108; *Flor. Hist.*, II, 320). Royal ass. 25 Mar. 1247 (*CPR 1232–47*, p. 499). 1256 described as papal chaplain (*CPL*, I, p. 338). D. 17 July 1258 at Winchester at the parliament held there, and bur. in the chapel of St Edmund of Canterbury (*Flete*, p. 110). D. by poison 1258 (*Ann. Burton*, p. 460). D., lic. to el. 23 July 1258 (*CPR 1247–58*, p. 642).

Philip (de) Levesham 1258 Pr. of Westminster, el. Aug. 1258 (*Flete*, p. 113; *CPL*, I, 376). Occ. as pr. of Westminster and abb.-el. n.d. (PRO, E159/55, m. 14d). El. 1258 but had died same year. Lic. to el. 1 Dec. 1258 (*CPR 1258–66*, p. 7). Cf. *Flete*, p. 113 – D. 17 July 1259 (*sic*).

Richard of Ware (Wara) **1258–1283** M. of Westminster, royal ass. 15 Dec. 1258, temps. 17 Aug. 1259, the eln having been conf. by pope (*CPR 1258–66*, pp. 7, 39). 11 March 1259 apptd papal chaplain (*CPL*, I, 364). Apptd Treasurer of England 18 June 1280 (*Chronology*, p. 104). D. on the king's service. £50 to be delivered to the abb.'s clerk for his burial etc. ment. 9 Dec. 1283 (*CCR 1279–88*, p. 247). D. 8 Dec. 1283 and bur. before high altar (*Flete*, p. 115). D. 1 Dec. 1283 (*Ch. Bury*, p. 80); d. c. 30 Nov. 1283 (*Ann. Worcs.* p. 479). D., lic. to el. 11 Dec. 1283 (*CPR 1281–92*, p. 107). Seal (*Mon. Seals*, p. 96; *BM Seals*, no. 4306).

Walter of Wenlock (Wenlac, Wenlok) **1283–1307** El. 31 Dec. 1283 (*Flete*, p. 116; *Ann. Worcs*, p. 489). Royal ass. 22 Jan. 1284, temps. 20 June 1284 (*CPR 1281–92*, pp. 110, 124). Papal conf. of eln and mand. to bp of Ostia to bl. 8 May 1284 (*CPL*, I, 472). D. 25 Dec. 1307 (*Flete*, p. 119). D., lic. to el. 10 Jan. 1308 (*CPR 1307–13*, p. 34). See E. H. Pearce, *Walter de Wenlok, Abbot of Westminster* (London, 1920); B. F. Harvey ed., *Documents illustrating the rule of Walter de Wenlok, abbot of Westminster, 1283–1307* (Camden 4th ser., 2, 1965).

Richard de Kedyngton (Kedyngton(e), Kidington, Kidinton, Kidyngton, Kydyngton, *alias* **de Sudburia** (*CPL*, II, 132; PRO, C84/14/9) **1308–1315** M. of Westminster, el. 26 Jan. 1308 (*Flete*, p. 121). Royal ass. 23 Feb. 1308, temps. (John) 25 Apr. 1310 (*CPR 1307–13*, pp. 45, 225). Commn to hold an enquiry into the dissensions between the mks of Westminster during the voidance of the abbey 14 July 1308 (*CPR 1307–13*, p. 124). Papal mand. to enquire into Richard's merits and if he is worthy to be apptd 28 Jan. 1310, the pr. of Sudbury having appealed against his el. (*CPL*, II, 65). Notif. by papal judges of pope's conf. of eln 15 Apr. 1310 (PRO, C84/16/38). Mand. to bp of Worcester to bl. abb. 23 July 1310 (*CPL*, II, 71); same day further mand. to bp of Winchester to bl. abb., the latter's el. having been conf. by the bp of Worcester and mag. William Testa (ibid., 75). D. 9 Apr. 1315 (*Flete*, p. 122). D., lic. to el. 21 Apr. 1315 (*CPR 1313–17*, p. 272). Ledger stone (now lost) (*Earliest English Brasses*, p. 200).

William de Curtlyngton (Curtlinton, Curlyngton, Kertlyngton, Kirtlington, Kurtlyngton) **1315–1333** M. of Westminster, el. 24 Apr. 1315 (*Flete*, p. 122); royal ass. 11 June 1315, temps. 27 Jan. 1317 (*CPR 1313–17*, pp. 298, 613; cf. *Cal. Chanc. Warr.*, p. 416). Papal conf. of eln 30 Oct. 1316 (*CPL*, II, 132). Commn to absolve from excommunication 1320 (ibid.,

209). D. 11 Sept. 1333, and bur. before St Benedict's altar (*Flete*, p. 123; cf. *CFR 1327–37*, pp. 373, 381). D., lic. to el. 13 Sept. 1333 (*CPR 1330–34*, p. 467). Ledger stone (now lost) (*Earliest English Brasses*, p. 200). Seal (*Mon. Seals*, p. 96).

Thomas de Henle(e) (Henelee) **1333–1344** M. of Westminster, el. Sept. 1333 (*Flete*, p. 125); royal ass. 30 Sept. 1333, temps. 29 June 1334 (*CPR 1330–34*, pp. 465, 556). Abb.-el. 6 Oct. 1333 going to Roman Curia (*CCR 1333–37*, p. 175). Occ. 14 July 1344 (*CPR 1343–45*, p. 391). D. 29 Oct. 1344 (*Flete*, p. 126; cf. *CFR 1337–47*, p. 402). D., lic. to el. 4 Nov. 1344 (*CPR 1343–45*, p. 365).

Simon de Bercheston (Bircheston) **1344–1349** M. of Westminster, el. 10 Nov. 1344 (*Flete*, p. 128); royal ass. 15 Nov. 1344, temps. 23 Mar. 1345 (*CPR 1343–45*, pp. 369, 445). Papal conf. of eln 7 Feb. 1345 (*CPL*, III, 176, 182). D. 7 May 1349 (PRO, C84/25/37), cf. d. of plague 15 May 1349 (*Flete*, p. 128); bur. in cloister (ibid., p. 129).

Simon de Langham 1349–1362 El. 18 May 1349, eln pres. to king 20 May 1349 (PRO, C84/25/40), cf. el. 27 May 1349 (*Flete*, p. 130). Papal conf. of eln 20 July 1349 (*CPL*, III, 339). Pr. of Westminster, temps. 16 Sept. 1349 (*CPR 1348–50*, p. 404). Apptd Treasurer of England 23 Nov. 1360 (*Chronology*, p. 105). Consecrated Bp. of Ely 20 Mar. 1362 (ibid., p. 244); made Chancellor by the king 21 Feb. 1363 (ibid., p. 86). Translated to Canterbury 24 July 1366 (*Reg. Langham*, pp. 119–20). Res. 28 Nov. 1368 and made Cardinal priest of S. Sixtus (*Eubel*, I, 21). Lic. to el. to Westminster 7 Apr. 1362 (*CPR 1361–64*, p. 182). D. 21 July 1376 (*Flete*, p. 132). Seal (*Durham Seals*, II, p. 585, no. 3558).

Nicholas de Litlington (Lytlyngton, Lyttlyngton) **1362–1386** Pr. of Westminster, el. Apr. 1362 (*Flete*, p. 134); eln pres. to king for royal ass. 12 Apr. 1362 (PRO, C84/28/41); royal ass. 14 Apr. 1362, temps. 12 Dec. 1362 (*CPR 1361–64*, pp. 182, 277). 1 Apr. 1375 gtd lic. to dispose of property by will (*CPL*, IV, 204). D. 29 Nov. 1386 (*Flete*, p. 137; PRO, C84/34/11). D., lic. to el. 12 Dec. 1386 (*CPR 1385–89*, p. 245).

WHITBY (Yorks N.), St Peter and St Hilda ref. 1097 (as priory); 1109 (as abbey)
Lists in *VCH Yorks*, III, 104–5; *Ctl. Whitby*, I, 1–7 and XXXVIII ff.; *Heads*, I, 77–8.
Abbey vacant 18 Aug. 1212 and 16 Jan. 1214 (*Rot. Lit. Pat.*, pp. 94, 108).

John (? of Evesham) ?1214–1223 Said to have been apptd 1214 by papal legate and to have d. 1222 (prob. rightly 1223) by L. Charlton in *History of Whitby and of Whitby Abbey* (York, 1779), pp. 158, 169, but he gives no sources. Occ. 1219 x 1223 (*Ctl. Whitby*, I, no. 39, cf. nos. 42, 94). D. 1222 (Baildon, I, 222) but cf. lic. to el. (no reason given for vacancy) 31 May 1223 (*CPR 1216–25*, p. 374).

Roger of Scarborough (Scardeburgh) **1223–?1245** Pr. of Whitby, royal ass. 18 June 1223 (ibid., p. 375; ment. Charlton, *History of Whitby*, p. 169). Occ. (R.) 26 May 1224 (*Ctl. Brinkburn*, p. 61); 11 Aug. 1240 (*Yorks F., 1232–46*, p. 9). Lic. to el. (no reason for vacancy) 15 June 1245 (*CPR 1232–47*, p. 454).

John of Stonegrave (Staingreve, Staingreve, Stayngreve, Stayngrive) **1245–1258** Sub-pr. of Whitby, royal ass. 27 June 1245 (ibid., p. 455); mand. for seisin 12 July 1245 (*CR 1242–47*, p. 327). Gt to pr. and convent of next keeping of abbey on the cess. or d. of John of Stonegrave 7 Feb. 1258 (*CPR 1247–58*, p. 615). Had become a Cistercian on 20 Nov. 1258 (PRO, C84/2/1). Cess., lic. to Dec. 1258 (*CPR 1258–66*, p. 7).

William de Brineston (Briniston) **1259–?1265** M. of Whitby, royal ass. 6 Jan. 1259, writ *de intendendo* 23 Jan. 1259, the eln having been conf. by G[odfrey], archbp of York (ibid., pp. 8, 10). Occ. 8 July 1260 (*Yorks F., 1246–72*, p. 119); (W.) 1 Aug. 1264 (*Ctl. Bridlington*, p. 98). D. 19 Dec. 1265 (PRO, C84/3/21).

Robert of Langtoft (Langetoft) **1266–1278** M. of Whitby, temps. 4 Feb. 1266, the eln having been conf. by the dean and chapter of York Minster *sede vacante* (*CPR 1258–66*, p. 545). D., lic. to el. 28 Sept. 1278 (*CPR 1272–81*, p. 278).

William of Kirkham (Kirkeham) **1278–1304** Pr. of Whitby, royal ass. 27 Oct. 1278, writ *de intendendo* 7 Nov. 1278 (ibid., pp. 280–1). D. 11 Oct. 1304 (PRO, C84/15/18). D. (W.), lic. to el. 17 Oct. 1304 (*CPR 1301–07*, p. 263).

Thomas of Malton 1304–1322 Sub-pr. of Whitby, royal ass. 24 Oct. 1304, temps. 31 Oct. 1304 (ibid., pp. 265–6). Mand. 26 Oct. 1304 to proceed to abbey and cite all those opposing the eln of a new abb. to appear in York on 29 Oct. (*Reg. Corbridge*, II, 176). Ordinance recording the appearance of Thomas's proctors seeking the abb.'s res. on account of bodily infirmity and accepting the archbp's award for the ex-abb. Res. 13 July 1322 (*Reg. Melton*, II, no. 187). Cess., lic. to el. 16 July 1322 (*CPR 1321–24*, p. 179; PRO, C84/27/30).

Thomas de Haukesgarth 1322–1356 M. of Whitby, royal ass. 26 July 1322, temps. 1 Aug. 1322 (*CPR 1321–24*, pp. 184, 195, cf. *Reg. Melton*, II, no. 196 – royal ass. 25 July). Mand. to cite objectors to eln to appear before the archbp on 31 July, dated 28 July 1322 (*Reg. Melton*, II, no. 195). Eln conf. 31 July 1322 (ibid., nos. 199–202). Cess. of unnamed abb. 21 Mar. 1356 (York, Reg. 11, f. 173v). Cess., lic. to el. 21 Mar. 1356 (*CPR 1354–58*, p. 350). Letter to abb. of convent of Whitby to pay the expenses of Thomas, ordered to stay at Selby abbey for 2 years 24 Mar. 1365 (York, Reg. 11, f. 182v). Thomas became the leader of the opposition to the next abb. in 1366, signified for excommunication 1371 (Logan, *Runaway Religious*, p. 192).

William (of) Burton 1356–1374 M. of Whitby, commn to examine eln (*BIB*, 3, p. 54, no. 166); eln conf. and prof. obed. n.d.; mand. to install 12 Apr. 1356 (York, Reg. 11, f. 173v). Eln pres. to king for royal ass. 2 Apr. 1356 (PRO, C84/27/30). Temps. 13 Apr. 1356 (*CPR 1354–58*, p. 365). D., lic to el. 10 May 1374 (*CPR 1370–74*, p. 439).

John of Richmond (Richemond, Richemund, Richmund) **1374–1393** M. (Sacrist) of Whitby, eln pres. to king for royal ass. 26 May 1374 (PRO, C84/31/10); royal ass. 6 June 1374, temps. 26 June 1374 (*CPR 1370–74*, pp. 446, 451). Eln conf. by archbp's vicar-general 17 June 1374 (York, Reg. 12, f. 36r–v); commn to suffragan to bl. abb. 24 June 1374; bl. and prof. obed. 1 July 1374 (York, Reg. 11, ff. 393v–394r; Reg. 12, f. 36r–v). D. by 30 Aug. 1393 (PRO, C84/35/46). D., lic. to el. 31 Aug. 1393 (*CPR 1391–96*, p. 308).

WINCHCOMBE (Glos.) St Mary and St Kenelm ref. 970, dedicated 972.
Lists in *VCH Glos*, II, 72; *Ctl. Winchcombe*, II, pp. xvi, ff.; *Heads*, I, 78–9.

Master Robert of Hasleton 1196–1221 Dates as Greg. Caerwent, f. 200r–v. D. 8 June (cf. *Ctl. Winchcombe*, I, 44). Lic. to el. (no reason given for vacancy) 23 June 1221 (*CPR 1216–25*, p. 294). D. 1221 (*Ann. Worcs*, p. 414).

Thomas 1221–1232 Pr. of Winchcombe, royal ass. 8 July 1221 (*CPR 1216–25*, p. 296). Bl. 11 July 1220 (*Ann. Worcs*, p. 413; *Ann. Tewkesbury*, p. 65). D. 1232 (*Ann. Worcs*, p. 424); 3 Oct. 1232 (*Ann. Tewkesbury*, p. 89).

Henry of Tuddington (Tudington, Tudintone) **1232–1247** (H.) sacrist of Winchcombe, royal ass. 12 Oct. 1232 (*CPR 1225–32*, p. 505). El. 1232 and bl. at Worcester 13 Mar. 1233 (*Ann. Worcs.*, p. 424); mand. for seisin 18 Oct. 1232 (*CCR 1231–34*, p. 118); installed 28 Oct. 1232 (*Ann. Tewkesbury*, p. 87). Cess. (H.) 1247 (*Ann. Worcs.*, p. 438). Lic. to el. (no reason given for vacancy) 10 July 1247 (*CPR 1232–47*, p. 504).

John of Yanworth (Yaneworth, Yaneworthe, Yanewinch) **1247–1282** Cellarer of Winchcombe, writ *de intendendo* 26 July 1247 (ibid., p. 505). Succ. 1247 and bl. at Worcester by bp of Hereford acting on commn (*Ann. Worcs.*, p. 438). Cess. 1282 (ibid., p. 485; *Reg. G.*

Giffard, p. 165). Bp of Worcester writes to king about the vacancy 8 Oct. [1232] (PRO, SC1/23/103); letters of sheriff of Glos. to king re cess. of abb. *c.* 10 Oct. 1282 (PRO, SC1/20/185). Cess. by 8 Oct. 1282 (PRO, C84/8/6). Cess., lic. to el 13 Oct. 1282 (*CPR 1281–92*, p. 37).

Walter de Wickwane (Wyckewane, Wykewane) **1282–1314** Cellarer of Winchcombe, succ. 1282 and bl. by bp of Worcester (*Ann. Worcs.*, p. 485). Commn to conf. eln 20 Oct. 1282; eln conf. 29 Oct. 1282 (*Reg. G. Giffard*, pp. 180, 165; PRO, C84/8/9). Writ *de intendendo* 5 Nov. 1282 (*CPR 1281–92*, p. 39). Occ. 28 Mar. 1314 (*CFR 1307–19*, p. 192). D., lic. to el. 31 May 1314 (*CPR 1313–17*, p. 119).

Thomas of Sherborne (Shirebourn(e), Shireburne) **1314–1316** Pr. of Winchcombe, eln pres. to king for royal ass. 21 June 1314 (PRO, C84/17/35); royal ass. 25 June 1314, temps. 10 July 1314 (*CPR 1313–17*, pp. 126, 155). Eln pres. to bp for examination 10 July 1314, eln conf. 12 July 1314 (Worcester, Reg. Maidstone, p. 29). D. by 24 May 1316 (*CFR 1307–19*, p. 279). D. (T.), lic. to el. 28 May 1316 (*CPR 1313–17*, p. 462).

Richard of Idbury (Id(d)ebury) **1316–1340** Sacrist of Winchcombe, eln pres. to king for royal ass. 5 June 1316 (PRO, C84/18/30); royal ass. 14 June 1316, temps. 1 July 1316 (*CPR 1313–17*, pp. 471, 481). Cert. conf. eln by bp of Worcester 26 June 1316 (PRO, C84/18/36). Petition to be relieved of office 7 Jan. 1340, subsequent petition 22 Mar. 1340, agreed by bp 23 Mar. 1340 (*Reg. Bransford*, nos. 109, 284). Cess., lic. to el. 27 Mar. 1340 (*CPR 1338–40*, p. 441). Provision made for former abb. 19 May 1340 (*Reg. Bransford*, no. 318).

William of Sherborne (Shiburn, Shireb(o)urn, Shirburn) **1340–1352** M. of Winchcombe, apptd by bp 26 Apr. 1340, after eln had been quashed; mand. to convent to obey s.d. (ibid., nos. 289, 195–9, 301). Royal ass. 10 Apr. 1340, temps. 28 Apr. 1340 (*CPR 1338–40*, pp. 452, 477). Prof. obed. 14 May 1340 (Worcester Cath. Lib., mun. B.832). Mand. to install 14 May 1340 (*Reg. Bransford*, no. 300). Res. 18 Sept. 1352 (Worcester, Reg. Thoresby, pp. 110, 113). Res., lic. to el. 18 Sept. 1352 (*CPR 1350–54*, p. 328).

Robert of Ipwell (Ippewell, Ypwell) **1352–1360** M. of Winchcombe, royal ass. 22 Sept. 1352, temps. 26 Sept. 1352 (ibid.). Notif. to king of Robert's appt 24 Sept. 1352 (Worcester, Reg. Thoresby, p. 110). Permission from bp of London to bp of Worcester to bl. Robert in the chapel in the bp's manor in the suburbs of London 25 Sept. 1352; letter of appt and mand. to install 27 Sept. 1352 (ibid., pp. 110, 113). Cess., lic. to el. 16 Oct. 1360 (*CPR 1358–61*, p. 467).

Walter of Winferton (Wynferton, Wynforton) **1360–1395** M. of Worcester, apptd by bp of Worcester after eln dispute, petition for royal ass. 14 Nov. 1360 (PRO, C84/28/3); royal ass. 20 Nov. 1360, temps. 1 Dec. 1360 (*CPR 1358–61*, pp. 493, 497; cf. Worcester, Reg. Brian I, p. 67). D. 22 June 1395 (*Worcs. Sede Vacante Reg.*, p. 366). D. 22 June 1395 (PRO, C84/36/13). D., lic. to el. 28 June 1395 (*CPR 1391–96*, p. 593).

WINCHESTER, Hyde Abbey, formerly New Minster, St Peter and St Grimbald. ref. 964; 1110 (to Hyde).
  Lists in *VCH Hants*, II, 121; *Heads*, I, 80–2.

John Suthil *c.* **1180–1222** Succeeded 1181 according to Ann. (2) BL Harl. ms. 1761, ff. 14ff. Occ. *temp.* Richard I (*CPR 1343–5*, p. 364); 1219 (PRO, Hants F., CP25/1/202/4 no. 58). D. 1222 (*Ann. Winchester*, p. 84; *Ann. Waverley*, p. 296). House vacant 1 June 1222 (*CPR 1216–25*, p. 333). Seal (*BM Seals*, no. 3311).

Walter de Aystun 1222–1248 M. of Hyde, royal assent 7 July 1222 (*CPR 1216–25*, p. 335). D. 1248 (*Ann. Winchester*, p. 91). Obit 2 Apr. (*Hyde Breviary*, G.5v).

Roger of St Valery (de Sancto Valerico, Walerico) **1248–1263** Sub-pr. of Hyde, royal assent

27 Apr. 1248, writ *de intendendo* 10 May 1248 (*CPR 1247–58*, pp. 12, 15). (R.) letter of res. 21 Sept. 1263 (PRO, SC1/3/179). Lic. to el. (no reason given) 29 Sept. 1263 (*CPR 1258–66*, p. 282). D. 1263 (*Ann. Winchester*, p. 100). Obit 23 Sept. (*Hyde Breviary*, G. 8r).

William of Worcester (Wigornia) **1263–1282** M. of Hyde, writ *de intendendo* 12 Nov. 1263 on cess. of Roger (*CPR 1258–66*, p. 298). Cert. conf. eln by bp of Winchester 18 Oct. 1263 (PRO, C84/3/4). D., lic. to el. 2 May 1282 (*CPR 1281–92*, p. 18). Obit 21 Apr. (*Hyde Breviary*, G. 5v).

Robert of Popham (Sopham) **1282–1292** M. of Hyde, eln pres. to king for royal ass. 13 May 1282 (PRO, C84/7/25); royal assent 17 May 1282, writ *de intendendo* 2 June 1282 (*CPR 1281–92*, pp. 19, 24). Bl. 11 June 1282 (*Reg. Pecham*, I, 186). Mentd 1289, going overseas (*CPR 1281–92*, p. 312). D. by 25 June 1292 (PRO, C84/10/44) D., lic. to el. 6 July 1292 (ibid., p. 499). ? Obit 19 June (*Hyde Breviary*, G. 6v).

Simon de Caningges (Kaning(g)es, Kanynges, Keninges) **1292–1304** Sacrist of Hyde, royal assent 26 July 1292, temps. 12 Aug. 1292 (*CPR 1281–92*, pp. 503–4). Cert. conf. eln by bp of Winchester 5 Aug. 1292 (*Reg. Pontissara*, I, 346; PRO, C84/10/48). Mentd 1293, going to Ireland, attorneys apptd for 2 years (*CPR 1292–1301*, pp. 36–7). D., lic. to el. 23 Sept. 1304 (*CPR 1301–7*, p. 259).

Geoffrey de Feringges (Fer(r)ynges) **1304–1317** M. of Hyde, royal assent 15 Oct. 1304 (*CPR 1313–17*, p. 263). Eln conf. 23 Oct. 1304 (*Reg. Pontissara*, I, 181); temps. 30 Oct. 1304 (*CPR 1301–7*, p. 265). Cert. conf. eln by bp of Winchester 23 Oct. 1304 (PRO, C84/15/19). Commn to bl. 12 Nov., bl. by bp of Salisbury 15 Nov. 1304 (*Reg. Gandavo*, II, 642–3); mand. to induct 21 Nov. 1304 (*Reg. Pontissara*, I, 181). Cess. by 26 Feb. 1317 (*CFR 1307–19*, p. 319). Res., lic. to el. 13 Mar. 1317 (*CPR 1313–17*, p. 626). Ob. 28 Feb. (*Hyde Breviary*, G. 4v).

William of Odiham (Odyham) **1317–1319** M. of Hyde, royal assent 25 Mar. 1317 (*CPR 1313–17*, p. 631). Proclamation of eln: commn to cite objectors 29 Mar. 1317 (*Reg. Sandale*, p. 34); petition for restitution of temps. 26 Apr.; temps. 26 Apr. 1317 (ibid., p. 38; *CPR 1313–17*, p. 643; PRO C84/19/12); mand. to install 1 May 1317 (*Reg. Sandale*, pp. 38–9). Occ. 21 May 1319 when abb. and conv. petition for custody of the abbey in a future vacancy (PRO, SC1/34/102). D. 5 June 1319 (*Reg. Sandale*, p. 108, n. 1, cf. *CFR 1307–19*, p. 404). Lic. to el. (no reason given) 8 June 1319 (*CPR 1317–21*, p. 345).

Walter (of) Fifehead (Fifide, Fyfyde) **1319–1362** M. of Hyde, royal assent 26 June 1319 (*CPR 1317–21*, p. 356). Eln pres. to bp 12 July 1319, adjourned to 28 July (*Reg. Sandale*, pp. 108–10). Cert. conf. eln by bp of Winchester 30 July 1319 (PRO, C84/19/49). Temps. 1 Aug. 1319 (*CPR 1317–21*, p. 385). D., lic. to el. 11 Sept. 1362 (*CPR 1361–64*, p. 244; cf. PRO, C84/28/46).

Thomas (de) Pethy (Pechi, Pechy, Peythy) **1362–1380** M. of Hyde, eln pres. to king for royal ass. 16 Sept. 1362 (PRO, C84/28/47); royal assent 17 Sept. 1362 (*CPR 1361–64*, p. 246); examination of eln 24 Sept.; eln conf. 24 Sept.; bl. 25 Sept. 1362 (*Reg. Edington*, I, nos. 1526–8; PRO, C84/28/48). Temps. 26 Sept. 1362 (*CPR 1361–64*, p. 245). D. 27 Dec. 1380 (*Reg. Wykeham*, I, 110; PRO, C84/32/39). D., lic. to el. 28 Dec. 1380 (*CPR 1377–81*, p. 583).

WINCHESTER CATHEDRAL PRIORY (Hants), St Swithun ref. 964

Lists in *VCH Hants*, II, 114–15; *Le Neve*, 1066–1300, II, 88–91; 1300–1541, 47–48; *Heads*, I, 79–80. Biographical details in Greatrex, *Biog. Reg.*, pp. 651–753 (Winchester monks).

Stephen [de Lucy] **–1214** For name see *Le Neve, Fasti 1066–1300*, p. 89, n. 2 Last recorded occ. 23 Jan. 1214 when royal ass. given to his eln as abb. of Burton (*Rot. Lit. Pat.*, pp. 108b–109; cf. *Rot. Lit. Claus.*, I, 161b).

Walter II **–1239** Occ. *c.* 1216 (Cheney, *Inn. III*, no. 1174); from 1227 to 1236 (*Wilts F.*, I, 17,

25); 7 Apr. 1236 (*Soms. F.*, I, 82). Last occ. after 9 June 1238 (*Ctl. Winchester*, no. 310). D. 1239 (*Ann. Waverley*, p. 323). Presum. d. 10 Nov. 1239, as obit kept 10 Nov. (Lambeth, ms. 20, f. 237v; BL, Arundel ms. 68, f. 47v).

Andrew 1239–1243 Third-pr. of Winchester. Apptd by king, *sede vacante*, 23 Nov. 1239 (*CR 1237–42*, p. 138); against the will of the convent (*Ann. Waverley*, pp. 323–4). Excommunicated by archbp of Canterbury before Nov. 1240, papal mand. for investigation and possible fresh eln 26 Sept. 1243 (*CPL*, I, 200); Occ. 16 Dec. 1243 (*CPR 1232–47*, p. 412). D. 1243 (*Ann. Tewkesbury*, p. 132; *MPCM*, IV, 265). D. by 26 Dec. 1243 (*CPR 1232–47*, p. 413). Commem. 27 Dec. (Winchester obit: BL, Add. ms. 29436, f. 44r).

John de Caux (Calceto, Cauz) **1243–1244** Apptd (no name) by king, *sede vacante*, 26 Dec. 1243 (*CPR 1232–47*, pp. 413–14). Writ *de intendendo* 8 Jan. 1244 (ibid., p. 415). Dep. by bp *c.* 29 Aug. 1244 (*MPCM*, IV, 390). Re-apptd later (see below).

Walter III 1244–1247 Perhaps apptd by bp as result of papal mandate of 22 Dec. 1244 (*CPL*, I, 210). Occ. 18 Apr. 1245 (*Reg. Roff.*, p. 13); 19 Apr. 1245 (Windsor, Arundel White Book, ff. 143v–144r). Res. 3 Apr. 1247 (*Ann. Winchester*, p. 90).

John de Caux 1247–1250 Succ. Walter, presum. soon after 3 Apr. 1247 (ibid.). Occ. 1246 x 1249 (*Ctl. Winchester*, no. 472). Royal ass. to eln as abb. of Peterborough 15 Jan. 1250 (*CPR 1247–58*, p. 58).

William of Taunton (Tanton(e)) **1250–1255** M. of Winchester, succ. 1250 (*Ann. Tewkesbury*, p. 140). Succ. 10 Feb. 1250 (*Ann. Winchester*, p. 91). Expelled before 5 Feb. 1255, but still calling himself prior (*CPR 1247–58*, p. 397). Royal ass. to his eln as abb. of Milton 6 Dec. 1256 (*CPR 1247–58*, p. 532). El. bp of Winchester by a majority 3 Feb. 1261 but elns quashed by pope before 22 June 1262 (*Le Neve 1066–1300*, II, 86–7). Seal (*BM Seals*, no. 4342). Papal chaplain (*CPL*, I, 326); son of a clerk in minor orders, disp. for illegitimacy (ibid., 377–8).

Andrew of London *alias* **of St Martin** (de Sancto Martino) **1255–1261** First occ. as pr. 20 July 1255 (*CPR 1247–58*, p. 439). Said to have been intruded and conf. by bp-el. of Winchester 1256 (*MPCM*, V, 568, 591). Occ. 21 Oct. 1255, 28 July 1256 (*CR 1254–5*, pp. 147, 337); 18 Nov. 1256 (*CR 1255–6*, pp. 9–10). Res. 12 July 1258, but re-el. same day (*Ctl. Winchester*, no. 22; *Ann. Winchester*, p. 97). Eln conf. 21 Aug. 1258 (*Ctl. Winchester*, no. 24). 11 Dec. 1258 papal disp. for illegitimacy (*CPL*, I, 361); apptd papal chaplain 20 Aug. 1259 (ibid., 366). El. bp of Winchester and royal ass. to eln 29 July 1259 (*CPR 1258–66*, p. 35) – invalidated by subsequent consecration of Aymer de Valence (*Le Neve 1066–1300*, II, 86, n. 4). El. Bp. of Winchester by a minority 3 Feb. 1261 but elns quashed by pope before 22 June 1262 (ibid., 86–7, see also William of Taunton above). Dep. of priorate by bp of Winchester and then by archbp of Canterbury in 1261 for disobedience, and made appeal to Rome (*Ann. Winchester*, p. 99, cf. p. 100). Priory treated by king as vacant from 15 Feb. 1262 (*CR 1261–64*, p. 105). Occ. styled as pr. 1264 (*CPL*, I, 418). 13 Jan. 1268 the bp, on his deathbed, absolved Andrew from excommunication and restored him – ineffective (*Ctl. Winchester*, no. 23). Continued calling himself prior as late as 26 Mar. 1276 (*Reg. Pontissara*, II, 645) and 8 Apr. 1278 (*Les Registres de Nicolas III*, no. 100).

Walter Ruffus M. and hordarius of Winchester. Apptd by bp. shortly after 25 Dec. 1262 (*Gervase Cant.*, II, 218).

Ralph Russell –1265 Occ. 28 May 1263 (PRO, Hants F., CP25/204/10, no. 73); 1265 (BL, Cotton ms. Tiberius D. VI, part 1, f. 6r–v). D. 8 July 1265 (*Ann. Winchester*, p. 102).

Valentine 1265–1267; 1268–1276 Hordarius of Winchester (*Ctl. Winchester*, no. 547a). Succ. 21 July 1265 (*Ann. Winchester*, p. 102). Res. 7 Aug. 1267 (ibid., p. 105). House void from cess. 5 Nov. 1267 (*CPR 1266–72*, p. 164). Restored 3 July 1268 (*Ann. Winchester*, p. 107).

Res. again *c.* 19 May 1276 (ibid., pp. 122–3). Restored again 1 Aug. 1276 (ibid., p. 123). Deprived by bp before 3 Dec. 1276 (ibid.). Still living 8 Oct. 1289, desc. as former pr. (*CPL*, I, 504).

John de Durevill(e) (Urevilla) **1276–1278/9** Almoner of Winchester (*CPR 1232–47*, pp. 413–14). Apptd by bp, inst. and installed 3 Dec. 1276 (*Ann. Winchester*, p. 123). Last occ. 22 June 1278 (*Reg. Pontissara*, II, 649). Presumably d. or res. before 14 Jan. 1279 when priorate vacant (*CCR 1272–79*, p. 519).

House void 1 Mar. 1279 (*CPR 1272–81*, p. 304).

Adam of Farnham 1279–1283 M. of Winchester, apptd 1279 (*Ann. Worcs*, p. 476). Presumably apptd before 4 Apr. 1279 (*CCR 1272–79*, p. 525). Excommunicated for disobedience July 1282 but absolved (*Ann. Winchester*, p. 476; *Reg. Pecham*, I, 188). Occ. 14 Dec. 1282 (*Reg. Pontissara*, I, 240). Summoned to meet with the king about reform of the house 12 Jan. 1283 (PRO, E135/3/39B). Commn to receive his res. 13 Feb. 1283 (*Reg. Pontissara*, I, 246, cf. 245–6).

William de Basing (Basinges, Basingstoke) **?1283–1284; 1284–1295** M. of Winchester. Perhaps apptd by bp's Official before 9 Apr. 1283 (*Reg. Pontissara*, I, 246). Occ. Trin. 1283 (PRO, CP40/50, m. 25); 4 June 1284 (*Reg. Pontissara*, I, 281–2). Res. before 13 July 1284 (ibid., I, 284–6). Bp.'s lic. to el. sought 18 July 1284 on William's cess., granted 20 July (ibid., 285–7). Mand. to convent to obey newly conf. pr. 25 Aug. 1284 (ibid., 294–5). Occ. 4 Nov. 1294 (*Ctl. Winchester*, no. 442). D. shortly before 30 May 1295; petition for lic. to el. (*Reg. Pontissara*, I, 71–2).

Henry Woodlock de Merewell (Merewelle) **1295–1305** M. of Winchester. El. 6 June 1295, bp's ass. and conf. 7 June 1295 (*Reg. Pontissara*, I, 72–8). Royal ass. to el. as bp of Winchester 29 Jan. 1305 (*CPR 1301–07*, p. 312; cf. *Reg. Winchelsey*, II, 797).

Nicholas de Tarente 1305–1309 M. of Winchester, bp's lic. to el. gtd 13 June 1305 (*Reg. Woodlock*, I, 32). Eln pres. to bp 29 July and eln conf. 7 Aug. 1305; mand. to install s.d. (ibid., 33–4, 36–7). D. by 18 June 1309 (ibid., 369).

Richard of Enford (Eneford) **1309–1328** M. of Winchester, bp's lic. to el. gtd 18 June 1309 (*Reg. Woodlock*, I, 369). Eln conf. 25 Aug. 1309 (ibid., 384–5). Papal faculty to bp of Winchester to appt a pr. in place of Richard, who 'seeing he is unfit to govern the monks' is ready to res. 10 May 1328 (*CPL*, III, 274). Res. on 25 June 1328 (Winchester, Reg. Stratford, f. 107r).

Alexander Herierd (Heriard, Herierde) **1328–1349** M. of Winchester, bp's lic. to el. sought 27 June 1328, gtd 29 June 1328 (Winchester, Reg. Stratford, f. 107r). Eln pres. to bp 7 July and conf. 13 July 1328 (ibid., ff. 107r–108r). D. by 5 Mar. 1349 (*Reg. Edington*, I, no. 556).

John de Merlawe 1349–1361 M. of Winchester, bp's lic. to el. gtd 7 Mar 1349 (*Reg. Edington*, I, no. 557); proclamation of eln 21 Mar. 1349; commn to examine 31 Mar. 1349; conf. s.d. (ibid., nos. 558–67). D. by 9 Dec. 1361 (ibid., I, no. 1490).

[**William de Thudden 1361–1362** El. 9 Dec. 1361 (*Reg. Edington*, I, no. 1490). Bp's commissary quashed eln since he discovered irregularity and the monks were deprived of their right to el. 11/14 Feb. 1362 (ibid., nos. 1490–3).]

Hugh (de) Basyng (Basynge) **1362–1384** M. of Winchester, apptd 11 Feb. 1362 (William *in error*) (*Reg. Edington*, I, nos. 1493–6). D. 26 Sept. 1384 (*Reg. Wykeham*, I, 149).

WORCESTER CATHEDRAL PRIORY, St Mary ref. 964 or 969 (see *Heads*, I, 82).

Lists based on *Le Neve 1066–1300*, II, 102–4; *1300–1541*, IV, 59–60; and see lists in *VCH Worcs*, II, 112; *Heads*, I, 82–4; Greatrex, *Biog. Reg.*, pp. 908–9. Biographical details in Greatrex, Biog. Reg., pp. 754–901 (Worcester monks).

Silvester of Evesham 1214/15–1216 M. of Worcester, el. pr. 21 Jan. 1214 or 1215 (*Ann. Worcs*, p. 403 and see *Ctl. Worcester*, p. lix). El. Bp of Worcester 3 Apr. 1216 (*Ann. Worcs.* p. 405; *Ann. Tewkesbury*, p. 62).

Simon Pimme 1216–1222 For name see *Le Neve 1066–1300*, II, 103, n. 2. Chamberlain of Worcester, el. Oct. 1216 (*Ann. Worcs*, p. 407; *Ann. Tewkesbury*, p. 66). Bp tried unsuccessfully to remove him 1220 (*Ann. Worcs*, p. 411). Summoned to Rome before 22 Mar 1222 (*CPL*, I, 86), and on return dep. by bp (*Ann. Worcs*, pp. 414–15; cf. *CPR 1216–25*, p. 320, *Ann. Tewkesbury*, p. 66, *CPL*, I, 92–3). Absolved by archbp of Canterbury, appealed against bp, re-excommunicated and returned to Rome 1222 (*Ann. Worcs*, p. 415). Suspended by the pope for using falsified letters 1223 (*CPL*, I, 92–3). D. 1223 (*Ann. Worcs*, p. 415; *Ann. Tewkesbury*, p. 67).

William Norman 1222–1224 Pr. of Malvern, apptd by bp against will of monks 1222 (*Ann. Worcs*, pp. 417, 415). Controversy between bp and convent and pr. William and convent 1223 (ibid.). Res. 3 Oct. 1224 (ibid., pp. 416–17, cf. *Liber Pensionum Prioratus Wigorn.*, no. 142).

A composition was made between Bp William de Blois of Worcester and the priory in 1224 about the choice of a pr. In future the priory were to nominate seven candidates from amongst their own number, from whom the bp would choose one as pr. (*Acta Langton*, app. 3, pp. 160–3; *EEA*, 13, p. xxvi; *CPL*, I, 103).

Master William of Bedford (Bedeforde) **1224–1242** Pr. of Tynemouth, presumably one of monks' nominees, 3 Oct. 1224 (*Ann. Worcs*, p. 417). Apptd by bp 21 Nov. 1224 (ibid., *Ann. Tewkesbury*, p. 67). D. 29 Oct. 1242 (*Ann. Worcs*, p. 434; *Ann. Tewkesbury*, p. 127; *MPCM*, VI, 276). See C. H. Talbot and E. A. Hammond, *The Medical Practitioners of Medieval England: a biographical register*, pp. 384–5, cf. 131.

Richard de Gundicote 1242–1252 Probably Condicote, see *Le Neve 1066–1300*, p. 103, n. 3. Sacrist of Worcester, apptd by bp and installed 19 Nov. 1242 (*Ann. Worcs*, p. 434; *Ann. Tewkesbury*, p. 127). D. 29 Sept. 1252 (*Ann. Worcs*, p. 441).

Thomas 1252–1260 Sub-pr. of Worcester, for 32 years, installed 1 Nov. 1252 (*Ann. Worcs*, p. 441; cf. *Ctl. Worcester*, no. 324). Occ. Mar. 1260 (*Burton Chts.*, no. 164). D. by 24 Dec. 1260 (*Ann. Worcs*, p. 446).

Richard of Dumbleton (Dunbleton) **1260–1272** Cellarer of Worcester, installed 24 Dec. 1260 (ibid.). D. by 21 Dec. 1272 (ibid., p. 462; *Reg. G. Giffard*, pp. 50–1).

William of Cirencester 1272–1274 Sacrist of Worcester, succeeded 21 Dec. 1272 (*Reg. G. Giffard*, pp. 50–1; cf. *Ann. Worcs*, p. 462). D. by 20 Sept. 1274 (*Reg. G. Giffard*, pp. 61–2; cf. *Ann. Worcs*, p. 466). See also Sharpe, *Latin Writers*, p. 759.

Richard of Feckenham 1274–1286 Chamberlain of Worcester. one of the monks' seven nominees 21 Sept. 1274 (ibid., p. 467). Apptd by bp 25 Sept. 1274, with mand. to install (*Reg. G. Giffard*, pp. 61–2). D. 29 Dec. 1286 (*Ann. Worcs*, pp. 492–3). Bur. 1 Jan. 1287 in Worcester cathedral between the high altar and the chapel of St Mary (*Reg. G. Giffard*, p. 325). See also Sharpe, *Latin Writers*, p. 435.

Philip de Aubyn (Obyn) *alias* **of Worcester 1287–1296** Sub-pr. of Worcester, one of the monks' seven nominees 2 Jan. 1287 (*Reg. G. Giffard*, p. 304). Apptd by bp 6 Jan. 1287 (ibid., pp. 304, 325; *Ann. Worcs*, p. 493 gives 7 Jan.). Installed 19 Jan. 1287 (*Ann. Worcs*, p. 493). D. 7 July 1296 (ibid., p. 527; Bl, Cotton ms. Cleopatra D III, f. 51r). D. 7 July the third hour and buried the following Tuesday in Worcester cathedral before the altar of the Holy Cross by the abb. of Evesham (*Reg. G. Giffard*, p. 480).

Simon de Wyre *alias* **de Wirecestre 1296–1301** Sub-pr. of Worcester, among nominees pres. to bp 11 July 1296 (ibid.). Apptd by bp 13 July 1296 (ibid., p. 481; *Ann Worcs*, p. 527);

installed 23 Sept. 1296 (*Ann. Worcs*, p. 528). 24 June 1299 pr. Simon and convent absolved from excommunication imposed for offence against *Clericis Laicos* (*Reg. Winchelsey*, I, 343–4). Res. 13 July 1301 (*Ann. Worcs*, p. 550; cf. *Reg. G. Giffard*, p. 547 – res. on account of bodily infirmity and old age).

John de Wyke (Wyk) **1301–1317** Sub-pr. of Worcester, apptd 18 July 1301 by archbp (*Ann. Worcs*, p. 550; *Reg. G. Giffard*, p. 547). Installed 20 July 1301 (*Ang. Sac.*, I, 549). D. 5 Oct. 1317 (Worcester Liber Albus, f. 83r). Seal (*Hereford Seals*, p. 9).

Wulstan of Bransford (Branesford) **1317–1339** El. of seven candidates by convent 20 Oct. 1317, pres. to bp 18 Nov. 1317; mand. to install 23 Nov. 1317, installed 2 Dec. 1317 (Worcester, Liber Albus, ff. 83v–84v). bp commns vicar-general to appt one of seven nominees as pr. 21 Nov. 1317 (*Reg. Cobham*, pp. 1–2). Unsuccessful eln as bp of Worcester 1327, set aside (*Le Neve 1300–1541*, IV, 56; *CPL*, II, 487). Lic. to el. bp 28 Dec. 1338; el. as bp 5 Jan. 1339; royal ass. to eln as bp of Worcester 16 Jan. 1339 (*CPR 1338–40*, pp. 172, 175; Worcester Cath. ms. F.41, cited in Greatrex, *Biog. Reg.*, p, 780).

Simon le Botiller 1339 Hosteler of Worcester, eln of seven candidates by convent 12 Apr. 1339; apptd by bp 13 Apr.; mand. to convent to obey new pr. s.d. (*Reg. Bransford*, nos. 38–40, 92). D. 28 Oct. 1339 (ibid., no. 29; Worcester Cath. Lib., mun. C.298).

Simon Crompe (Cromp) **1339–1340** M. of Worcester, apptd 6 Nov. 1339 (*Reg. Bransford*, nos. 229–30); installed 7 Nov. 1339 (Worcester Cath. Lib., mun. C.298). D. 10 Apr. 1340 (*Reg. Bransford*, no. 290).

Master John of Evesham 1340–1370 B. Th., eln of seven candidates by convent 21 Apr. 1340, apptd by bp and mands. to install and obey 22 Apr. 1340 (ibid., nos. 290–4). Unsuccessful eln as bp of Worcester 1349, set aside (*Le Neve 1300–1541*, IV, 56; *CPL*, III, 311). D. 27 Mar. 1370 (*Ang. Sac.*, I, 549). See J. Greatrex, 'Prior John de Evesham of Worcester: One of St Benedict's worthy stewards?' in V. King and A. Horton eds., *From Buckfast to Borneo: essays presented to Father Robert Nicholl on the 85th anniversary of his birth, 27 March 1995* (Hull, 1995), pp. 64–76.

Walter de Legh (Lye) **1370–1388** Almoner of Worcester, eln of seven candidates by convent 2/3 Apr. 1370 (Worcester, Liber Albus, f. 246r–v; Reg. Lenn, p. 46); apptd by bp 4 Apr. 1370 (ibid.). Unsuccessful eln as bp of Worcester 1373–5, set aside (*Le Neve 1300–1541*, IV, 57). D. *c.* 15 Aug. 1388 (Worcester Cath. Lib. mun. C. 179). Bur. 22 Aug. 1388 (*Reg. Wakefield*, no. 788).

YORK, St Mary Offshoot of the same community as Whitby. f. *c.* 1078 (at Lastingham); moved to York before 1086 (A. H. Thompson in *YAJ*, XXVII (1924), 388–95); *Domesday Book* I, 305, ref. to 'abbas Eboracensis'.

List (1) of names and dates to 1258 in *Ch. York* (hereafter *Ch.*) pp. 1–2 = (*Mon. Angl.*, III, 569) some demonstrably false, list (2) in *Anonimalle Chronicle* (hereafter *Anon.*), pp. xlvii–xlviii. Also lists in *VCH Yorks*, III, 111; *Heads*, I, 84; A. Stacpoole ed., *The Noble City of York* (York, 1972), pp. 676–8.

Robert II de Longo Campo (Longchamp) **1197–1239** 7th abb. [Brother of William de Longchamp]; Pr. of Ely, el. 17 Mar. 1197, bl. 23 Mar. 1197 (by Archbp Hubert Walter), installed 2 Apr. 1197 (Diceto, II, 151–2; for the year see also Howden, IV, 17; Florence, II, 162; cf. *Ctl. Guisborough*, II, no. 673; *Le Neve 1066–1300*, I, 48). D. 11 Jan. 1239 (*Ch.*, p. 2, obit, p. 111). Tenure 43 years (*Ch.*, p. 2; *Anon.*, p. xlvii). Seal (*Mon. Seals*, p. 104; *BM Seals*, no. 4390).

William Roundell (*dictus* Rondele) **1239–1244** 8th abb. M. of York, el. 1239 (*Ch.*, p. 2). Occ. as elect (W.) June 1239 x June 1240 (*Reg. Grosseteste*, p. 48). D. 30 Aug. 1244 (obit, *Ch.* p.

114, see below). Lic. to el. (no reason given) 3 Sept. 1244 (*CPR 1232–47*, p. 435). D. 29 Nov. 1244 (*Ch.*, p. 2–3 cal. Dec. probably an error for 3 cal. Sept.).

Thomas of Warthill (Wardhull, Warthille, Warthyll) **1244–1258** 9th abb. el. 1244 (*Ch.*, p. 2). Papal chaplain 4 Feb. 1244 (*CPP*, p. 40). *c.* 15 Sept. 1244 the keeper of the abbey reports to the steward of the king's household that the royal request to the prior and convent to elect one of his nominees has been ignored (PRO, SC1/11/76). Royal ass. 15 Oct. 1244, writ *de intendendo* 28 Oct. 1244 (*CPR 1232–47*, pp. 436, 445). Future grant to convent of custody of next vacancy by the cess. or d. of abb. Thomas of Warthill 5 May 1258 (*CPR 1247–58*, p. 627). D. 17 May 1258 (*Ch.* p. 2, obit p. 112). Lic. to el. 29 May 1258 (*CPR 1247–58*, p. 631).

Simon of Warwick (Warwik, Warrewik) **1258–1296** 10th abb. M. of York, royal ass. 4 July 1258, temps. 25 July 1258 (ibid., pp. 640, 642). El. 24 June 1258 in the 14th year of his conversion; eln conf. 12 July 1258 (by D. & C. York *sede vacante*); bl. by bp of Durham 14 Sept. 1258 (*Ch.*, pp. 2–3). 1264 went to live at his own house for over a year on account of the quarrel with the citizens of York (*Ch.*, p. 6); D. 4 July 1296 (*Ch.* p. 26; obit p. 113). Tenure 39 Years (*Ch.* p. 26). D., lic. to el. 15 July 1296 (*CPR 1292–1301*, p. 191). Seal (*BM Seals*, no. 4391, *Durham Seals*, II, p. 586, no. 3563).

Benedict of Malton (Meuton) **1296–1303** 11th abb. Pr. of York, el. 25 July 1296 (*Ch.*, pp. 27, 34). Royal ass. 7 Aug. 1296, temps. 23 Aug. 1296 (*CPR 1292–1301*, pp. 191, 193). Cert. conf. eln by D. & C. of York *sede vacante* 17 Aug. 1296 (PRO, C84/12/29). Commn to bp of Carlisle from D. & C. of York to bl. abb. 17 Aug. 1296; lic. from the bp of Durham for the ceremony to take place in his diocese 23 Aug.; bl. by bp of Carlisle at Linstock near Carlisle 26 Aug. 1296 (*Reg. Halton*, I, 76–7; *Ch.*, p. 28). Commn to receive cess. and to make provision for him 17 July 1303 (*Reg. Corbridge*, I, 90–1). Res. 26/27 July 1303 (*Ch.*, p. 34; *Anon.*, p. xlvii); 27 July 1303 (PRO, C84/14/60). Cess., lic. to el. 31 July 1303 (*CPR 1301–07*, p. 151). Lic. from archbp to el. an abb. without intrigues and unanimously 6 Aug. 1303 (*Reg. Corbridge*, I, 91–2). Abb. 7 years, d. 22 Oct. 1307 at Deighton, bur. at abbey in front of altar of St Benedict (*Ch.*, p. 42).

John of Gilling (Gillyng, Gyllyng(e)) **1303–1313** 12th abb. M. of York, pr. of Wetheral, el. 8 Aug. 1303 in the 18th year of his conversion (*Ch.*, pp. 34–5; *Anon.*, p. xlviii). Royal ass. 9 Aug. 1303, temps. 19 Aug. 1303 (*CPR 1301–07*, p. 151). Citation of opposers 12 Aug. to appear on 16 Aug.; eln conf. 17 Aug.; prof. obed. & bl. 18 Aug. 1303 (*Reg. Corbridge*, I, 93–4). Installed 29 Sept. 1303 (*Anon.*, p. xlviii). D. 24 May 1313 (obit. *Ch.*, p. 112; *Anon.*, p. xlviii) ruled 10 years less 11 weeks, bur. before high altar beside abb. Simon on the south side (*Ch.*, p. 55). D. (J.) lic. to el. 13 June 1313 (*CPR 1307–13*, p. 594). Seal (*Durham Seals*, II, pp. 586–7, no. 3565).

Alan of Ness (Nesse) **1313–1331** 13th abb. Pr. of St Bees, pr. of York, el. 14 July 1313 in the 26th year of his conversion (*Ch.* pp. 61–2; *Anon.*, p. xlviii). Eln pres. to king for royal ass. 5 July 1313 (PRO, C84/17/190); royal ass. 20 July 1313, temps. 2 Sept. 1313 (*CPR 1313–17*, pp. 2, 13). Citation 22 July for opposers to eln to appear on 20 Aug. (*Reg. Greenfield*, II, p. 152, no. 1001); eln conf. 25 Aug. & bl. 26 Aug. 1313 (*Reg. Greenfield*, II, no. 1007 – bl. 25 Aug. *Anon.*, p. xlviii); installed 30 Sept. 1313 (*Ch.*, pp. 62–3; *Anon.*, p. xlviii). D. 16 Apr. 1331 (obit, *Ch.*, p. 112; *Anon.*, p. xlviii). D. lic. to el. 20 Apr. 1331 (*CPR 1330–34*, p. 102). Seal (*Durham Seals*, II, p. 587, II, p. 587, no. 3566).

Thomas of Moulton (Multon) **1331–1359** 14th abb. El. 15 May 1331 (*Anon.*, p. xlviii; PRO, C84/22/42). Royal ass. 25 May 1331 (*CPR 1330–34*, p. 121). Proclamation *si quis* 31 May 1331; opposers to appear 14 June (York, Reg. 9A, f. 226r); el. conf. 15 June (ibid., f. 228r–v); prof. obed. & bl. 16 June 1331 (ibid., f. 227r); installed 15 Aug. 1331 (*Anon.*, p. xlviii). D. 9

Apr. 1359 (obit, *Ch.*, p. 112; *Anon.*, p. xlviii – abb. 27 years, 11 months, 3 weeks and 1 day from his el. to his death). Lic. to el. when the abb. (broken by age and bodily weakness) shall *cede* [*sic*] 11 Apr. 1359 (*CPR 1358–61*, p. 192). Seal (*Durham Seals*, II, p. 587, no. 3567).

William (de) Marreys 1359–1382 15th abb. El. 2 May 1359 (*Anon.*, p. xlviii). Royal ass. 9 May 1359 (*CPR 1358–61*, p. 196); temps. 1 June 1359 (*ibid.*, p. 204); conf. of ein & bl., prof. obed. 26 May 1359 (York, Reg. 11, ff. 104r–v, 103Ar; *Anon.*, p. xlviii; PRO, C84/27/46); installed 20 June 1359 (*Anon.*, p. xlviii). D. 9 July 1382 (obit, *Ch.*, p. 113). Lic. to el. 15 July 1382 (*CPR 1381–85*, p. 152). Seal (*BM Seals*, no. 4392).

THE BENEDICTINE HOUSES:
DEPENDENCIES

Some small cells yield no names and have not been included.

ALDEBY (Norfolk), St Mary (Norwich) f. *c.*1166 x 1135
List in *VCH Norfolk*, II, 328; cf. Greatrex, *Biog. Reg.*, pp. 466–576 (Norwich monks).
John of Bedingfield (Bedingfeld) Occ. 27 May 1355 (*Mon. Angl.*, IV, 461); occ. 1352 x 1357
(DCN, Reg. IX, f. 20r).
John of Kirkby (Kirkeby, Kyrkeby) Occ. Mich. 1380–Mich. 1381 (DCN.2/2/1); infirmarer of
Norwich cath. priory occ. from 1387–8 (DCN.1/12/33).

ALKBOROUGH (Lincs)
No further priors found after Hugh (see *Heads*, I).

ALVECOTE (Warws), St Blaise (Great Malvern) f. 1159
Lists in *VCH Warws*, II, 62; *Heads*, I, 85.
Thomas Occ. 1161 x 77 (*HMC Middleton*, p. 8)
William de la Were Ment. 1327 as pr. long before the statute of mortmain (1279) (*Cal. Misc.
Inq.*, II, 248).
Walter of Worcester −1279 M. of Great Malvern, occ. 30 Sept. 1269 (PRO, Leics F.,
CP25/1/122/27, no. 523). El. as abb. of Alcester 1279 (q.v.).
William of Wickwane −1282 Res. 1282 to be pr. of Great Malvern (*Reg. Peckham*, II, 751).
William de Beulu (Beulow) 1305− M. of Great Malvern, adm. 29 Oct. 1305, no reason given
for vacancy, on pres. of pr. of Great Malvern (Lichfield, B/A/1/1, f. 16r).[1] Occ. 1327 (*Cal.
Misc. Inq.*, II, 248); Mich. 1334 (*Select Cases of Trespass*, I, 146).
Richard *dictus* **of Malvern** Occ. 19 July 1341 (Lichfield, B/A/1/2 ,f. 37v).
John of Painswick −1349 Res. to become pr. of Great Malvern 27 June 1349 (WAM, no.
32656).
The next recorded pr., **William Newton**, occ. 17 May 1397 (WAM, no. 22943).

BEADLOW (Beds), St Mary Magdalen (St Albans) (Beaulieu, Bello Loco) f. 1140 x 1146
(at Millbrook); abandoned 1435
List in *VCH Beds*, I, 352–3.
Walter of Standon (Standone) 1234− Adm. 15 Mar. 1234, no reason given for vacancy (*Reg.
Wells*, III, 32).
Roger 1237/8− Adm. June 1237 x June 1238, no reason given for vacancy (*Reg. Grosseteste*, p.
309). Occ. 3 Feb. 1254 (*Beds F.*, I, no. 548).
Reyner Occ. 20 Apr., 29 June, 11 July 1275 (WAM, nos. 5862, 5868, 5863); (R.) 23 Oct. 1275 as
collector of the tenth for the Holy Land (*Luffield Chts.*, II, p. 446, no. A17); ? *c.* Apr. 1279
(*Reg. R. Gravesend*, p. 207).
Roger de Thebregg' 1281− M. of St Albans, letter of pres. 15 Mar. 1280 – delayed; 2nd letter
of pres. 16 Oct. 1281; inst. 30 Oct. 1281, no reason given for vacancy (*Reg. Sutton*, VIII, 95).

---

[1] The date of 1315 given in the *VCH* is incorrect.

John of Stopsley (Stoppesle) **1285–** M. of St Albans, letter of pres. 4 Apr. 1285. After having borrowed a knife and cut out certain words from the letter of pres., the bp of Lincoln inst. him 9 Apr. 1285, no reason given for vacancy (ibid., 100–1).

John de Stakedorn **–1297** Transf. to Belvoir 1297 (ibid., 120).

William de Parys 1297– M. of St Albans, letter of pres. 24 June 1297; adm. 20 Aug.1297 (ibid.).

Peter of Maidford (Maydenford) **1299–** M. of St Albans, pr. of Belvoir 1295–97, letter of pres. 6 May 1299, adm. 25 May 1299 (ibid., 124–5). Oath of obedience 30 June 1301 (Lincoln, Ep. Reg., III, f. 33r). Occ.1 June 1303 (*CPL*, I, 601).

Gregory of St Albans (de Sancto Albano) **1303–** M. of St Albans, letter of pres. 22 Feb.1303, adm. 17 July 1303, no reason given for vacancy (Lincoln, Ep. Reg., II, f. 257v).

Richard of Northampton 1305– M. of St Albans, letter of pres. 12 Nov. 1305, adm. 15 Nov. 1305, no reason given for vacancy (ibid., ff. 258v–259r).

William of Kirkeby 1310–1312 M. of St Albans, letter of pres. 19 Aug. 1310, adm. 6 Sept. 1310, no reason given for vacancy (ibid., f. 263v). Transf. to be pr. of Hertford 14 Apr. 1312 (ibid., f. 244r).

Richard of Hertford 1312– M. of St Albans, pr. of Hertford, letter of pres. 9 Apr. 1312, adm. 8 (*sic*) Apr. 1312, no reason given for vacancy (ibid., f. 267r).

Henry of St Neots (de Sancto Neoto) **1317–** M. of St Albans, letter of pres. 29 Dec. 1316, adm. 2 Jan. 1317 (ibid., ff. 271v–272r).

Adam of Newark (Neuwerk) **1340–** M. of St Albans, letter of pres. 30 Nov. 1340, adm. 12 Dec. 1340, no reason given for vacancy (Lincoln, Ep. Reg., IV, f. 321r). Occ. 8 July 1349 (*CPL*, III, 339).[2]

John of Caldwell (Caldewell(e)) **1351–** M. of St Albans, letter of pres 25 Aug. 1351, adm. 29 Aug. 1351, no reason given for vacancy (Lincoln, Ep. Reg., IX, f. 427v).

Thomas Occ. 14 Nov.1369 (Lincoln, Ep. Reg., X, f. 384r).

William (of) Winslow (Wynslowe, Wynslawe) Occ. 1 July 1374 (ibid., f. 390r); 1379 (*Clerical Poll-Taxes*, p. 83, no. 1018).

The next recorded pr., **John Warram**, occ. 9 Oct. 1396 (*GASA*, III, 425).

BEDEMANS BERG (Essex) (Barrow) **-1135.** diss. *c*.1536 (dependent on Colchester abbey)

Walter Occ. as pr., signification of excommunication 19 Oct. 1381 (McHardy, *Church in London*, no. 652).

BELVOIR (Lincs), St Mary (St Albans) f. 1076 x 1088

Lists in *VCH Lincs*, II, 126. Obits in Cambs. Trinity Coll. ms. O.9.25, pd in Nichols, *Leics.*, II, i, pp. 25ff.; *Heads*, I, 85.

Master Ralph Simplex Preceded Roger of Wendover (*GASA*, I, 270). Possibly d. as a monastic archdn 13 Oct.1217 (*MPCM*, VI, 270).

Roger of Wendover (Wendoure) **–1226** The historian, occ. 6 Oct.1224 (*HMC Rutland*, IV, 143; PRO, Leics F., CP25/1/121/10, no. 92). Dep. by Abb. William (*GASA*, I, 270, 274,cf. 273), but cf. *Reg. Wells*, III, 150 entry for 1226 below stating that Roger *propter ipsius debilitatem ad quietem et pacem claustri revocato*. D. 6 May 1226 (*MPCM*, VI, 274; commemorated on 6 May in obits, f. 158v).

Martin de Bodekesham 1226–1249 Brother of Winemer, late archdn of Northampton, adm.

---

[2] *CPL*, III, 326 mentions Raymond Capelli, claustral pr. of Beaulieu, Lincoln dioc. occ. 18 June 1349, but the diocesan ascription must be wrong.

27 May 1226 (*Reg. Wells*, III, 150, cf. *GASA*, I, 274). Occ. *c.* 1220 x 1234, before 1235 (*Ctl. Bushmead*, no. 290, cf. no. 297); 2 Feb. 1240 (*HMC Rutland*, IV, 131). D. 3 Jan. 1249 (*MPCM*, VI, 278).

Ralph of Watlington Occ. 12 June 1250 (*Lincs F.*, II, 67); Mar. 1263 (*HMC Rutland*, IV, 164); 1264,1269 (Nichols, *Leics*, II, i, 81, citing Willis); 9 Feb. 1265 (BL, Add. ms. 4936, f. 84r). Pr. of Wallingford (q.v.).

William of Huntingdon (Huntedon) Occ. Aug. 1270, Christmas 1271 (*HMC Rutland*, IV, 153, 124); 1277 (BL, Add. ms. 4936, f. 87r).

Reyner (Rayner) 1278– M. of St Albans, inst.17 Mar. 1278, no reason given for vacancy (*Reg. R. Gravesend*, p. 80). Occ. (R.) 23 May 1284 (BL, Add. ms. 4936, f. 89r); 9 Feb. 1285 (*HMC Rutland*, IV, 125; PRO, Leics F., CP25/1/123/36, no. 142).

Roger of Hendred (Hanred(e), Henred', Henreye) 1287–1295 M. of St Albans, on 7 July 1287 Roger appeared before the bp with a letter of pres. dated 1 May 1287 (no reason given for vacancy). The bp took no action because it was irregular. A second letter of pres. dated 14 July 1287; adm. 18 July 1287 (*Reg. Sutton*, I, 97–8). D. by 11 Dec. 1295 (ibid., II, 203–5).

Peter of Maidford (Maydenford) 1295–1297 M. of St Albans., Letter of pres. dated 11 Dec. 1295 on d. of Roger; adm. 19 Dec. 1295 (ibid.). Recalled to St Albans before 23 June 1297 (ibid., 218–19). Made pr. of Beadlow 1299 (q.v.).

John de Stakedern 1297– M. and pr. St Albans, letter of pres. 23 June 1297; adm. 25 June 1297 (ibid.). Occ. 6 Jan. 1299 (BL, Add. ms. 4936, f. 97r); 1 June 1303 (*CPL*, I, 601); Aug. 1303, Apr. 1305, Apr. 1307, Apr. 1310 (*HMC Rutland*, IV, 149, 104, 162, 169); 1312 (PRO, E326/8638).

William of Kirkeby 1315– M. of St Albans, letter of pres. 22 July 1315; adm. 15 Aug. 1315, no reason given for vacancy (Lincoln, Ep. Reg., II, f. 56v).[3]

John de Stakedern (Stakethorn) 1316– M. of St Albans, letter of pres. 12 Oct. 1316; adm.19 Oct. 1316, no reason given for vacancy (ibid., f. 62v). Occ. 22 Sept. 1317 (*HMC Rutland*, IV, 104).

William de Beauver 1319– M. of St Albans, letter of pres.14 July 1319; adm. 6 Aug. 1319, no reason given for vacancy (Lincoln, Ep. Reg., II, f. 80r).

John of Kendal (Kendale) 1320– M. of St Albans, letter of pres. dated 11 Apr. 1320, adm.by Official *sede vacante*, 28 Apr. 1320, no reason given for vacancy (ibid., f. 352r). Occ. 16 Dec. 1322 (*Hatton's Book of Seals*, no. 16); 1324, 1325, 1329 (*HMC Rutland*, IV, 150, 143, 120); 14 June 1331 (Lincoln, Ep. Reg., IV, f. 132r). Obit 19 Oct. (Nichols, *Leics*, II, i, app. ii, p. 36).

William of Belvoir (Belvero) 1333– M. of St Albans, letter of pres. 26 Oct. 1333, no reason given for vacancy; inst. 24 Nov. 1333 (*Reg. Burghersh*, I, no. 400). Occ. 23 Sept. 1334 (*CCR 1333-7*, p. 336); 12 Nov. 1334, 9 Mar. 1335 (*Reg. Burghersh*, I, nos. 435, 457); 4 Apr. 1340 (PRO, E315/31/167); Jan. 1344 x Jan. 1345 (PRO, E326/9804); 1345, July 1346 (*HMC Rutland*, IV, 155, 146); 8 July 1349 (*CPL*, III, 339); 1349 (*GASA*, II, 382). Obit 17 Aug. *De domino Willelmo de Belvero secundo priore egregio et actis suis bonis* (Nichols, *Leics*, II, i, app., p. 21, no. 80; p. 34). Nichols says he d. 17 Aug. 1361, and bur. in old church; *Mon. Angl.* states he res. priory 2 yrs earlier (ibid., II, i, 81, also giving him the surname Heron and linking him with the pr. of Wallingford of the same name; *Mon. Angl.*, III, 287). I have found no evidence for these dates. A pr. William occ. 8 Sept. 1364 (*HMC Rutland*, IV, 144). Whether it is William of Belvoir, William de Stevington, or another William is unclear.

[**William de Stevington** Nichols, *Leics*, II, i, 81 says he succ. 1361 and d.1367 and bur. in the

---

[3] On 7 Mar. 1316 mention is made of John de Kirkby, then pr. ? a scribal error for William (*HMC Rutland*, IV, 125).

old church (repeated in *Mon.*, III, 287). William de Stevington was pr. of Wallingford *c.* 1360–1370 (q.v.).]

Richard of Belvoir (Belvero) **1369–** M. of St Albans, letter of pres. dated 29 Apr. 1369, no reason given for vacancy; letter presented 14 May 1369 and Richard subsequently adm. (Lincoln, Ep. Reg., XII, f. 70v).[4] Occ. 1374 (*HMC Rutland*, IV, 122, 172); 1381 (Lincoln, Ep. Reg., X, f. 277r; *Clerical Poll-Taxes*, nos. 1249, 2055); 1384 (*HMC Rutland*, IV, 173); 13 Apr. 1385 (Lincoln, Ep. Reg., XI, f. 13r).
The next recorded pr., **Stephen de Suthrey**, adm. 25 July 1386, no reason given for vacancy (ibid., f. 24v).[5]

BINHAM (Norfolk), St Mary (St Albans) f. –1093
  Lists in *VCH Norfolk*, II, 345–6; *Heads*, I, 85–6.
Richard Occ. 3 May 1215 (*Norfolk F. 1201–1215*, no. 279); 18 Nov. 1219 (PRO, Cambs F., CP25/1/23/10, no. 7); 18 Nov. 1220 (BL, Cotton ms. Claudius D XIII, f. 140r).
Milo (Miles) Occ. n.d. (ibid., ff. 37r, 55r, 94r). His precise place in the sequence of priors is uncertain.
Richard of Kent (Kantia) and **Miles** were referred to as former priors in 1250 (PRO, Just.1/560, m. 53).
William of Gedding **–1227** D. at Wymondham 17 Apr. 1227 (*MPCM*, VI, 272).
Richard de Parco *alias* **Rufus de Winchelcumbe** (le Rus) **–1244** Occ. Oct. 1233 x Oct. 1234, Oct. 1234 x Oct. 1235 (*Norfolk F. (Rye)*, pp. 53, 57); Mich. term 1230, Easter term 1231, Trin. term 1231 (*CRR*, XIV, nos. 660, 1246, 1827). Transferred to Tynemouth in 1244, el. before 20 Feb. (*MPCM*, VI, 89, cf. 279). As Richard le Rus mentd as former pr. in 1250 (PRO, Just.1/560, m. 53).
Richard de Selford (Schalford, Seldefort) **1244–** Succ. 1244 (ibid., 89–90). Occ. *c.* Mich. 1244 (BL, Cotton ms. Claudius D XIII, f. 92v); from Oct. 1246 x Oct. 1247 to Oct. 1261 x Oct. 1262 (*Norfolk F.(Rye)*, pp. 71, 98); 25 June 1262 (BL, Cotton ms. Claudius D XIII, f. 179v. cf. f. 153v for full name).
Adam de Mota Occ. May 1264, Sept. 1267 (ibid., ff. 152v, 171r).
Robert of Waltham (Wautham) Occ. 23 Sept. 1272, 20 Oct. 1272 (*CPR 1266–72*, pp. 679, 682); Nov. 1273 x Nov. 1274 (*Cal. Misc. Inq.*, II, 308); Mich. 1275 x Mich. 1276, desc. as former keeper of Norwich priory (PRO, E159/50, mm. 13, 14d); 7 Nov. 1277 (BL, Cotton ms. Claudius D XIII, f. 150v); 2 Feb. 1279 (ibid., f. 133r); 3 Apr. 1289 (ibid., f. 152r); 13 Mar. 1291 (*CPL*, I, 531). Obit 17 Oct. (Nichols, *Leics* II, i, app. II, p. 36).
Walter of Somerton (Somartone) Occ. 23 Nov. 1295 (BL, Cotton ms. Claudius D XIII, ff. 82r, 83v); 1 June 1303 (*CPL*, I, 601); Mich. 1305 (PRO, CP40/153, m. 132); 7 Aug. 1315 (Norwich, Reg/1/1, f. 62r); 20 Nov. 1316 (ibid., f. 67r). Priory impoverished through ill-keeping – taken into king's hands 5 May 1320 (*CFR 1319–27*, p. 22). King's protection during pleasure to William of Leicester (Leycestre) and br. Nicholas of Flamstead (Flamstede) to whom he had gtd custody of the priory of Binham 4 June 1320 (*CPR 1317–21* p. 455). Order for his arrest 28 Oct.1320, William of Somerton, calling himself pr. of Binham and 13 named monks – disobedient to St Albans (*CCR 1318–23*, p. 271). Case between pr. William and abb. of St Albans. Pr. appealed to pope. Subsequently commn to archbp of Canterbury to investigate 17 July 1321 (*CPL*, I, 213–14). See also E.B. Burstall, 'Three priors of Binham: William de Somerton, Henry Halstede, William Dixwell', (ts. account, Norfolk RO, NRS. 24077).

---

[4] *HMC Rutland*, IV, 170 notes a pr. William occ. 1 Jan. 1370. Whether this is a scribal error or whether pr. Richard had two terms of office is unclear.
[5] *Mon. Angl.*, III, 287 gives a pr. Geoffrey occ. 1251, citing Willis, and a pr. Minion of Barton between Reyner and Roger de Hendred. I have not found the sources for these statements.

Nicholas of Flamstead (Flamstede) **1323–** Order to William of Leicester and Nicholas of Flamstead, m. of St Albans not to meddle further with custody of the priory previously gtd to them 10 Aug. 1323 (*CCR 1323–27*, p. 14). M. of St Albans, 3 Oct. 1323 exhibited letters of pres. from abb. and convent of St Albans, and was adm. 4 Oct. 1323 (Norwich, Reg/1/1, f. 102v). Later pr. of Hertford (q.v.), and pr. of St Albans.

William Occ. 4 Sept. [1332] (PRO, C270/7/20).

John of Caldwell (Caldewell(e)) **1337–** M. of St Albans, letter of pres. dated 12 Aug. 1337, adm. 1 Oct. 1337, no reason given for vacancy (Norwich, Reg/1/3, ff. 8v–9r). Occ. 8 May 1338 (ibid., f. 12v); 2 Feb. 1340 (PRO, C81/1786/ 35); 1349 (*GASA*, II, 382).

Adam Occ. 29 June 1353 (BL, Cotton ms. Claudius D XIII, f. 53v). Presumably the **Adam of Newark** (Neuwerchia), dep. by abb. Thomas de la Mare of St Albans (1349–96) (*GASA*, II, 394).

William Occ. *temp.* Richard II (1377 x 1381) (PRO, E179/45/7C).

Richard Occ. in clerical subsidy n.d. (*c.* 1378 x 1381) (PRO, E179/45/114). The sequence of these two priors is uncertain.

The next recorded pr., **Thomas of Walsingham** (Walsyngham), m. of St Albans, pres. 4 Sept. 1394, adm. 15 Sept. 1394, no reason given for vacancy (Norwich, Reg/3/6, f. 195r).

BRECON, St John the Baptist (Battle) f. ?*c.*1110
List in *Heads*, I, 86.

John Occ. 1203 (*Gir.Camb.*, II, 308, cf. IV, 36); 1203 x 1214 (*Reg. Gloucester*, nos. 45, 62; *St Davids Acta*, nos. 58–9); 1219 x 1229 (ibid., nos. 75–6); 1221 (Eyton, *Salop*, III, 26; *Salop F.*, 3rd series,VI, p. 177, no. 31); 1222 (*St Davids Acta*, no. 107); 10 May 1226 (PRO, Worcs F., CF25/1/258/3, no. 9).

Ralph Occ. 19 May 1235 (*CR 1234–37*, p. 181).

Reginald **–1260** Occ. 8 Sept. 1248 (*Welsh Episcopal Acts*, I, no. 579; *Ctl. Brecon*, p.288); Royal ass to el. as abb. of Battle, 27 Nov. 1260 (*CPR 1258–66*, p.130).

Stephen de Oteringeber Mentd 12 Nov. 1265 as former pr., now a vagabond, signified for arrest (PRO, C81/1786/4; Logan, *Runaway Religious*, pp. 184–5).

Sampson Mentd in 1336 as pr. *temp.* Henry III (*CCR 1332–37*, p. 551). Occ. n.d. (late 13th cent.) (*HMC Var. Coll.*, IV, 103).

Nicholas Sampson's next successor, occ. *temp.* Henry III, mentd in 1336 (ibid.); also mentd as having been pr. long before the statute of mortmain (1279) (*Cal. Misc. Inq.*, II, 372).

Michael Occ. 2 or 16 July 1277 (*CCR 1288–96*, p. 393).

William Occ. Easter 1282 (PRO, CP40/45, m. 11d).

Visitation of Battle abbey 1283 – '*memorandum de priore de Brekynok qui amotus fuerit pro incontinentia et nunc remissus est per abbatem ut sit prior*' (*Reg. Pecham*, I, 198).

Nicholas Occ. Trin. 1309 (PRO, CP40/178, m. 107).

Goderinggus Occ. Mich. 1310 (PRO, CP40/183, m. 166d).

John de Cherring Occ. 20 Oct. 1312 (PRO, C85/7/57); 23 July 1315 (*Reg. Gloucester*, no. 56); 29 May 1326 (*Reg. Orleton (Hereford)*, p. 295).

R. de Horwod res. n.d. (1328 x 1347); A. abb. of Battle (1324–51) pres. to H., bp of St Davids (1328–47) **W. of Exeter** (Exon'), conventual pr. of Battle as the new pr. of Brecon (BL, Harl. ms. 3586, f. 21v). Is he to be identified with pr. **Walter** who occ. Mich. 1337 (PRO, CP40/312, m. 366)?

Nicholas Wardeden Mentd as predecessor of John Lose (*Accts of Papal Collectors*, p. 245).

John (de) Lose (Lese, Losa, Loze) Occ. 4 July 1355 (Longleat mun. 523). Bps. of Hereford, St Davids and Worcester informed that he had been absolved from excommunication arising out of archbp's visitation of Battle abbey, and had been restored to admin. of Brecon, 22

Dec. 1355 (Lambeth, Reg. Islip, f.108v). Occ. 4 July 1363, 30 Oct. 1368 (*CPL*, IV, 31,75); prov. by Urban V 9 July 1363 (*Accts of Papal Collectors*, p. 263); 10 May 1365 (*CCR 1364–68*, p. 173); 27 Nov. 1367 (BL, Harl. ms. 3586, f. 28v).

John ?the same Occ. 29 Sept. 1375 (Longleat mun. 524); 1380 x 1381 (PRO, E179/21/8, m. 1). The next recorded pr., **John Echyndenn**, order to arrest him 28 Mar. 1411 (*CPR 1405–13*, p. 315).

BRISTOL (Glos.), St James (Tewkesbury) f. *c.*1137
Lists in *VCH Glos.*, II, 74–5; *Heads*, I, 86.

Walter Occ. (W.) 1186 x 1202 (*Glam.Chts.*, II, p. 256, no. 256); (W.) 2 Apr. 1207 (*Magnum Reg. Album Lichfield*, pp. 140–1, no. 291); 22 Apr. 1224 (*Ctl. Bradenstoke*, no. 340).

Jordan −1231 D. 19 Sept. 1231 (*Ann. Tewkesbury*, p. 80).

Henry of Washbourne (Wasseburne) −1234 Res. *c.* 29 Sept. 1234 (ibid., p. 94).

Thomas of Keynsham (Keynesham) 1234− Apptd *c.* 29 Sept. 1234 (ibid.).

Thomas de Stokes −1254 Occ. 1 Aug. 1253 (*BGAS*, 58, p. 229, n. 9). El. abb. of Tewkesbury 1254 (*Ann. Tewkesbury*, p. 155).

Richard of Devizes (Devises) 1255− Cellarer of Tewkesbury, apptd 27 Mar. 1255 (ibid., p. 157).

William Isaac 1262− Apptd 22 June 1262 (ibid., p. 160).
King's order to deliver to G., bp of Worcester, custody of the priory, a cell of Tewkesbury abbey, since the earl Gilbert de Clare of Gloucester and Hereford asserts he has the right of custody in the voidance of Tewkesbury and the king has taken it into his own hands 19 May 1282 (*CCR 1279–88*, p. 157); appt of Bp G(odfrey) to the custody until 3 weeks after Michaelmas when the claim between the king and the earl is to be decided (*CPR 1281–92*, pp. 21–2).

Henry Occ. 20 June 1304 (*Reg. Gainsborough*, p. 207); 29 July 1310 (*CPR 1307–13*, p. 309); 1 Sept. 1310 (ibid., p. 310); July 1310 x July 1311 (Birch, *Bristol Original Docts*, 295).

William Foliot(h) Occ. as pr. 7 July 1328 and as lately pr. 28 Mar. 1329 (*Reg. Orleton (Worcs)*, nos. 532, 571).

Robert de Seddyngton Occ. 18 Feb. 1335 (*Reg. Montacute*, no. 218).

William of Campden (Campeden) M. of Tewkesbury, occ. 20 Aug. 1347 (*Reg. Bransford*, p. 164, no. 941).

Thomas of Norton Occ. 30 Nov. 1374 (Bristol RO, P/StJ/D/1/4; Nicholls and Taylor, *Bristol Past and Present*, II, 30, cf. 36).

John Occ. 1379 (PRO, E179/58/5, m. 4).

Richard Wircestre (Worcetr') Occ. 30 Aug. 1393 (*BGAS*, 56, 166); 25 Mar. 394 (Bristol RO, 5139 (77); Nicholls and Taylor, *Bristol Past and Present*, II, 36); 8 June 1400 (*CPR 1399–1401*, p. 306); 20 June 1400 (*Great Red Book of Bristol* (Bristol Record Soc. IV), p. 243).

BROMFIELD (Salop), St Mary (Gloucester) f. 1155
Lists in *VCH Salop*, II, 29; *Heads*, I, 86. See A.L. Moir, *Bromfield Priory and Church in Shropshire* (Chester, 1947); list at p. 45.

Elias Last recorded occ. Nov. 1208 (Eyton, *Salop*, V, 213, 218, citing Shropshire eyre roll). Mentd as former pr. 1243 (*CRR*, XVII, no. 1631).

Henry Foliot (Foliet) −1228 Occ. (H.) n.d. (early 13th cent.) (SRRC, 20/6/2); M. of Gloucester, el. abb. of Gloucester 1228 (*Ctl. Gloucester*, I, 27).

Alexander Occ. n.d. (1228 x 1243) (SRRC, 20/6/1; 356/MT/1024).

Sampson Occ. 1243 (Moir, *Bromfield Priory*, p. 45, no source).

Reginald of Radnor (Radenouer) Occ. n.d. (1263 x 1284, *temp.*, Robert de Ledebur', pr. of St Guthlac, Hereford) (Hereford Cath. mun. 1500).

John de Worme Occ. 28 Sept. 1284, 1 Oct. 1284 (*Ctl. Gloucester*, III, 22, 24).

Thomas de Hourgulhulle Occ. 15 Sept. 1312 (*CPR 1307–13*, pp. 535–6); 3 Dec. 1313 (*CPR 1313–17*, p. 72). For name see Moir, *Bromfield Priory*, p. 45.

John Toky Occ. Nov. 1346 (SRRC, 20/1/2, m. 1d).

John de Eldesfelde Occ. 24 Feb., 25 Apr. 1355 (ibid., 20/1/3, mm. 2, 3).

In 1378 x 1379 clerical subsidy the priory is noted as being in the king's hands (PRO, E179/58/5, m. 2).

The next recorded pr., **Thomas Penyord**, occ. 28 Apr. 1385 (SRRC, 20/1/7).

CARDIFF (Glamorgan), St Mary (Tewkesbury) f. -1106
  Lists in *South Wales and Mon. Rec. Soc.* II (1960), p. 151; *Heads*, I, 86–7.

Eustace Occ. 1193 x 1218 (*Glam. Chts.*, VI, no. 1612; *Welsh Episcopal Acts*, II, 697).

Elias of Radnor –1230 Cons. as bp of Llandaff 1 Dec. 1230 (*Chronology*, p. 293).

Richard of Derby –1248 Occ. 1243 (*Ann. Tewkesbury*, p. 131(unnamed pr. absolved by bp of Llandaff (ibid., p. 136). Cess. 1248 (ibid., p. 137; *Welsh Episcopal Acts*, II, 729 says d.).

Alan of Cornwall (Cornubie) **1248**– Succ. Richard (*Ann. Tewkesbury*, p. 137).

Philip de Leche (Lecche) –**1261** Succ. on d. of Alan (ibid.). D. 15 Dec. 1261 (though not named as pr. of Cardiff) (ibid., p. 169).

Roger de Boyfeld M. of Tewkesbury, mentd as former pr. 1258. No indication of date. He could precede Richard of Derby. (*Ann. Tewkesbury*, p. 166).

William of Deerhurst (Derherst) **1262**– Apptd 27 June 1262 (ibid., p. 170; *Welsh Episcopal Acts*, II, 744).

Simon mentd as former pr. 15 Aug. 1295 (*CPR 1292–1301*, p. 140); must occ. late 13th cent. since *temp.* Nicholas, abb. of Keynsham and Gilbert de Clare, earl of Gloucester and Hereford.

CARDIGAN, St Mary (Chertsey) f. 1110 x 1115 (dependent on Gloucester); 1165+ (dependent on Chertsey)
  Lists in *Heads*, I, 87; E.M. Pritchard, *Cardigan Priory in the olden days* (London, 1904), p. 48.

Robert of Henley (Enley) Occ. 1277–78 (*West Wales Ministers' Accounts*, pp. 6, 9–11, accounts 2 Feb. 1277–22 Feb. 1280, although it is not certain whether he was still pr. at the end of the period); 23 Oct. 1278, 30 May 1279 (*Litt. Wallie*, nos. 231–2; Cowley, *Monastic Order in South Wales*, p. 219).

John Occ. 3 Aug. 1294 (*CPR 1317–21*, p. 77).

[Appt during pleasure of Robert de Malleye to the custody of the priory which has fallen into debt, 29 Oct. 1322 (*CPR 1321–24*, p. 211).]

John de Whitele Occ. 1 July 1349 (*CPR 1422–29*, p. 521).

Thomas Cymy (Chymy) **of Wales** (de Wallia) M. of Battle, prov. 2 *or* 5 Sept. 1368, ineffective as priory not vacant (*Accts of Papal Collectors*, pp. 355–6, 397).

No further heads recorded until the fifteenth century.

COLNE, *see* EARL'S COLNE

CRANBORNE (Dorset), St Mary and St Bartholomew (Tewkesbury) f. *c.* 980 (abbey); 1102 (cell of Tewkesbury).
  Lists in *VCH Dorset*, II, 71; *Heads*, I, 87.

Adam of Preston (Prestune) –**1262** Occ. 22 Dec. 1246 (*Sarum Chts.*, p. 309, no. cclxi). D. 18 Oct. 1262 (*Ann. Tewkesbury*, p. 169).

Walter de Appeleigh Occ. 3 Mar. 1314 (*Ctl. Glastonbury*, III, p. 636, no. 1187)

Peter of Broadway (Bradeway, Bradewey) Occ. 21 Apr. 1329 (*CPR 1327–30*, p. 384); 10 Dec. 1332 (*CPR 1330–34*, p. 382).

John de Stradull (Stradhull) M. of Tewkesbury, occ. 26 Aug. 1347 (*Reg. Bransford*, no. 940).

William of Putley (Putteleye) Occ. 24 Nov. 1361 (*Worcs Reg. Sede Vacante*, pp. 214–15).

The next recorded pr., **Henry Bromall**, occ. 1535 (*Valor*, II, 485).

DARENTH (Kent) f. 1195+ (Rochester cath. priory)

Biographical details in Greatrex, *Biog. Reg.*, pp. 577–650 (Rochester monks).

Richard of Darenth (Darente) Pr. of Darenth (Ann. Roff. in *Flor. Hist.* II, 183), el. pr. of Rochester May 1225 (*Le Neve 1066–1300*, II, 80).

Ralph occ. n.d. (? late 13th/early 14th cent. (before 1311) *temp.* Henry de Cobham justice (*Kentish Ctl.*, pp. 124–5, cf. also p. 14 and p. 25n).

But cf. conf. to pr. and conv. of Rochester of the order made by them 10 years since, that the church and chapel in their manor of Darenth should be served by chaplains instead of by 2 monks 9 Dec. 1255 (*CPL*, I, 325).

DEEPING (Lincs), St James (Thorney) f. 1139

Lists in *VCH Lincs*, II, 129; *Heads*, I, 87.

Robert of Elm Occ. as pr. ? 1216 x 1217 when the monks of Thorney tried to el. him as abb. but the legate Guala forced him to res. (*Guala Letters*, no. 158).

Richard [of Stamford] –1237 Occ. 3 Apr. 1231 (BL, Harl. ms. 3658, f. 64v); n.d. (1217 x 1237) (CUL, Add. ms. 3021, f. 462v). Royal ass. to el. as abb. of Thorney 28 Aug. 1237 (*CPR 1232–47*, p. 194).

William of Yaxley (Jakesle) –1261 Occ. 25 Mar. 1261 (*CPR 1258–66*, p. 147). Royal ass. to el. as abb. of Thorney 18 Apr. 1261 (ibid., p. 149).

Robert of Nassington (Nassyngton) Occ. 5 July 1299 (BL, Harl. ms. 3658, f. 20r).[6]

Thomas of Gosberton (Gosberkirk) M. of Thorney, occ. *c.* Jan. 1330 (ibid., f. 52v); 17 Apr. 1347 (*CPR 1345–48*, p. 268); 27 Apr. 1347 (Ely, G/1/1, part 2, f. 49r). Went to king as proctor of Thorney after death of abb. (1347) (CUL Add. ms. 3021, f. 471v).

John of Chatteris (Chateriz) Occ. 30 Dec. 1364 (BL, Harl. ms. 3658, f. 21v).[7]

Richard Occ. 1381 (*Clerical Poll-Taxes*, p. 107, no. 1290).

DOVER (Kent), St Martin (Canterbury, Christ Church) f. 1131 (Aug. priory); 1136 (Ben. priory).

List based on information kindly provided by Miss Melanie Barber; other lists in *VCH Kent*, II, 136; Haines, *Dover Priory*, pp. 183–322; *Heads*, I, 87–8; Ann. (not altogether reliable) in BL, Cotton ms. Julius D V, ff. 14ff, partly pd (to 1270) in *Mon. Angl.*, IV, 536–7; 14th cent. list in *Lit. Cant.*, III, 376; another incomplete list in Canterbury Cath., ms. Litt. D.4, f. 17r. See Greatrex, *Biog. Reg.*, pp. 66–335 (for Canterbury monks who were priors of Dover).

Reginald of Sheppey 1212–1228/9 M. of Christ Church, Canterbury (*Lit. Cant.*, III, 376 also giving his name); 11th pr. (Ann. ff. 25v, 28v but d. under end of Ann. for 1228, as he d. 1 Feb. (BL, Arundel ms. 68, f. 15r, this may mean 1229). Occ. 12 Nov. 1223 (*Kent F.*, p. 80).

William of Dover (*alias* Staunford) 1229–1235 M. of Christ Church, Canterbury; 12th pr., apptd by Archbp Grant 26 June 1229, installed at Dover 1 July 1229 (Ann., f. 29r); d. 1235,

---

[6] *VCH* gives his name, erroneously, as James.

[7] *VCH* gives occurrences in 1358 and 1365, but only cites the above Harl. ms. reference.

possibly one of the prs. William who d. in July (5 or 10) (Lambeth ms. 20, ff. 198r, 200r; BL, Arundel ms. 68, ff. 32v–33r). It is not clear from the Ann. (f. 30r) whether he died in 1234 or 1235. *Lit. Cant.*, III, 376 calls him de Staunford. Greatrex, *Biog. Reg.*, p. 277 (under Sandford).

Robert of Ulcumbe (Olecombe) **1235–1248** M. of Christ Church, Canterbury; 13th pr., apptd by Archbp Edmund July 1235, installed 22 July 1235 (Ann., f. 30v; Lambeth ms. 241, f. 30v). D. 1248 (ibid.; *Gervase*, II, 202). Obit 14 May (Lambeth ms. 20, f. 187r; BL, Arundel ms. 68, f. 27v) or 30 June (Lambeth ms. 20, f. 197r; BL, Arundel ms. 68, f. 32r). Greatrex, *Biog. Reg.*, p. 201 (under Holekumbe).

[Eustace of Faversham apptd as pr. of Dover by Archbp Edmund on the d. of pr. R. 7 Mar. 1240 (Canterbury, Ch. Ant. D.76; Greatrex, *Biog. Reg.*, p. 158 – not effective since Robert not dead, see Haines, *Dover Priory*, p. 214; Lawrence, *St Edmund of Abingdon*, pp. 318–19, cf. p. 149; *Lit. Cant.*, III, 377). See Sharpe, *Latin Writers*, p. 114.]

John of Northfleet 1248–1251 M. of Christ Church, Canterbury, 14th pr., apptd by Archbp Boniface *post* 30 June 1248; suspended by archbp 1250; restored 21 Mar. 1250; res. 1251 – could possibly be early 1252 (Ann., f. 30v; *Gervase*, II, 203). Occ. 1 July 1249 (*Kent F.*, p. 229). Greatrex, *Biog. Reg.*, p. 245.

House vacant 1251–1253

Guy de Walda 1253?–1260 M. of Christ Church, Canterbury, prev. sub-pr. of Dover, 15th pr., apptd by Archbp Boniface 1253; prof. 16 Feb. 1253 or 1254? (Ann., f. 31r; cf. *Gervase*, II, 203–4); res. 7 Apr. 1260 (ibid., f. 33v). Greatrex, *Biog. Reg.*, p. 312. See also Sharpe, *Latin Writers*, p. 157.

William of Buckwell (Buckwelle) **1260–1268** M. of Christ Church, Canterbury, 16th pr., apptd by Archbp Boniface Apr. 1260, installed 2 May 1260 (Ann., f. 33v; *Gervase*, II, 211). D. 12 Oct. 1268 (Ann., f. 49v; Lambeth ms. 20, f. 231v; BL, Arundel ms. 68, f. 45r). Greatrex, *Biog. Reg.*, p. 104.

Richard de Wencheape (Wincheap) **1268–1273** M. of Christ Church, Canterbury, 17th pr., apptd by Archbp Boniface 28 Oct. 1268, installed 8 Nov. 1268 (Ann., f. 49v; *Gervase*, II, 247). 1270–3 Retired to Tournai and then Canterbury (see *Gervase*, II, 253–74; Greatrex, *Biog. Reg.*, p. 331). Restored as pr. but then deposed 9 Mar. 1273 and returned to Canterbury (Ann., f. 53r; *Gervase*, II, 274–7, 282–3). Mention of the contention between the pr., and the sub-pr. and convent of Dover July 1272 (*CPR 1266–72*, p. 694). See Greatrex, p. 331; Haines, *Dover Priory*, pp. 221–34.

[Robert de Arcubus M. of Reading, writ *de intendendo* 4 Nov. 1272, to whom the king has gtd the priory by reason of the voidance of the archbishopric (*CPR 1266–72*, p. 712).]

House vacant 9 Mar. 1273–19 Dec. 1275.

Anselm of Eastry 1275–1283 M. of Christ Church, Canterbury, 18th pr., apptd by Archbp Kilwardby 21 Dec. 1275, installed 22 Dec. 1275 (Ann., f. 54v; *Gervase*, II, 282). Occ. 8 July 1278 (PRO, Kent F., CP25/1/98158, no. 71); Oct. 1281 x Oct. 1282 (PRO, E159/55, mm. 9, 11d); (A.) *c.* 11 Apr. 1273 (PRO, SC1/20/6). Dep. by Archbp Pecham 24 Sept. 1283 (Ann., f. 59r–v). Called Ascelinus in *Lit. Cant.*, III, 377. Greatrex, *Biog. Reg.*, pp. 143–4. Said to be brother of Henry of Eastry, prior of Christ Church, Canterbury (Haines, p. 235n, cited Greatrex, *Biog. Reg.*, p. 143).

Vacancy Sept. 1283 – Dec. 1289 (cf. *CFR 1272–1307*, p. 106; Ann., ff. 59r–60r)

Excommunication of those who have assumed custody of the priory which belongs to the archbp 3 Feb. 1284 (*Reg. Pecham*, II, 222–3).

Robert de Wetacre (Wetakere, Whiteacre) **1289–1318** M. of Dover, 19th pr., apptd by Archbp Pecham 30 Dec. 1289 (*Reg. Peckham*, I, 89; Lambeth ms. 241, f. 26r). Occ. 3 Nov. 1317 (*CPR 1317–21*, p. 42). D. 1318, gt of custody by Archbp Winchelsey 13 Dec. 1318 (Lambeth ms. 241, f. 25v, cf. *CPR 1317–21*, p. 339).

House vacant 1318–29 May 1321. The king sends enclosed writings to his chancery clerks to discuss what he should do. The sub-pr. and convent complain to him of hardships and oppressions committed by the pr. and convent of Christ Church, Canterbury, who claim the right to appt a pr. of Dover in the present vacancy 2 Apr. 1319 (*Cal. Chanc. Warr.*, p. 495). Sub-pr. and convent of Dover give detailed statement of their claim to the right of electing their pr. *c.* Mich. 1320 (PRO, SC1/36/129). Order to sub-pr. of Dover to adm. a person deputed by the archbp of Canterbury to supervise, along with him, the custody of the priory vacant by the d. of pr. Robert, on account of the dissension which arose over the appt of a successor 5 June 1320 (*CCR 1318–23*, p. 195). Restitution of the advowson of Dover priory to the archbp of Canterbury 24 Nov. 1320 (*CPR 1317–21*, p. 531).

John of Sholden (Scholdon) **(senior) 1321–*c.* 1328/9** Cellarer of Dover, 20th pr., apptd by archbp 29 May 1321 (Lambeth, Reg. Reynolds, f. 28r; Lambeth ms. 241, f. 26v). Occ. 23 Sept. 1325 (*CCR 1323–27*, p. 511); 8 Oct. (1325) (Lambeth, Reg. Reynolds, f. 142r–v); 3 Apr 1325 (ibid, f. 166v).; 1327–8 (*Index to Placita de Banco*, p. 247). Dep. by Archbp Meopham 1328/9 (*Lit. Cant.*, III, 377).

Robert de Hathbrand of Ringwould (Rydelyngeweald) **1328/9–1350** M. of Dover, 21st pr., apptd by Archbp Meopham 1328/9, occ. as pr. 11 Nov. 1329 (Lambeth ms. 241, f. 214r). Occ. from 5 Mar. 1331 (*CCR 1330–33*, p. 287) to 28 Mar. 1349 (Lambeth ms. 241, f. 102r). Vacated priory by 11 Mar. 1350 (Lambeth, Reg. Islip, f. 252r). Seal (*BM Seals*, no. 3068).

Richard of Hougham (Hugham) **1350–1351** M. of Dover, 22nd pr., apptd by archbp 29 Apr 1350, no reason given for vacancy (Lambeth, Reg. Islip, f. 253v). Occ. 20 May 1350 (ibid., f. 25r). Res. by 17 Sept. 1351 (ibid., f. 50v). Former pr. apptd sub-pr. 17 Sept. 1351 (ibid., f. 51r). Seal (*BM Seals*, no. 3067).

William de Puryton 1351 M. of Battle, 23rd pr., apptd by archbp 17 Sept. 1351 (Lambeth, Reg. Islip, f. 50v). Mand. to obey him 10 Oct. 1351 (ibid. ff. 50v, 51r). Res. 23 Nov. 1351 (ibid., f. 51r).

Thomas Beauveys (Beaneys) **1351–1356** M. of Battle, 24th pr., apptd by archbp 25 Nov. 1351 (ibid.). Mand. to install 28 Nov. 1351, installed by commissary 3 Dec. 1351 (ibid.). Occ. 1354 (BL, Add. Cht. 16430). Occ. 11 Mar. 1356 (Lambeth ms. 241, f. 220v). Vacated priory by 7 July 1356 (Lambeth, Reg. Islip, f. 272v). Royal lic. for annexation of Dover priory to Christ Church, Canterbury, for default of good government 20 May 1356 (*CPR 1354–58*, pp. 379, 382–3; *Reg. Langham*, pp. 274–5). However, an appt was made (see below).

William of Chartham (Chertham) **1356–1366** M. of Christ Church, Canterbury, 25th pr., apptd by archbp 7 July 1356 (Lambeth, Reg. Islip, f. 272v, cf. f. 136v). Occ. 1357, 1358, 1359 (ibid. ff. 136v, 144r–v, 282r); 10 Mar. 1360 (*CPR 1358–61*, p. 343); 1362 (BL, Add. Cht. 16425); 20 Nov. 1365 (Lambeth ms. 241, f. 220v). D. 1366 (possibly between June and Nov., cf. *CCR 1364–68*, p. 317, priory taken into custody of the Crown on account of the vacancy of the see of Canterbury). Greatrex, *Biog. Reg.*, p. 114.

James de Ston(e) of Oxney (Oxneye) **1367–1371** M. of Christ Church, Canterbury, 26th pr., apptd 19 Jan. 1367 (*Reg. Langham*, pp. 276–7, cf. appt for life 19 Sept. 1369, Lambeth, Reg. Whittlesey, f. 16r). Prof. obed. (Ann., f. 68r; Lambeth ms. 241, f. 26r–v). D. by 24 May 1371 (Lambeth, Reg. Whittlesey, ff. 85v–86r). Greatrex, *Biog. Reg.*, p. 292.

John Newenham 1371– M. of Dover, apptd by archbp 24 May 1371 (Lambeth, Reg. Whittlesey, ff. 85v–86r, cf. ibid., f. 93r).

The next recorded pr., **William (of) Dover**, was apptd by the archbp 16 Aug. 1393, on the d. of the last (unnamed) pr. (Lambeth, Reg. Courtenay II, f. 212r–v).

DUNSTER (Soms), St George (see Binns, p. 70) (Bath) f. 1090+
    Lists in *VCH Soms*, II, 82; *Ctl. Bath*, p. lxxix; Maxwell-Lyte, *History of Dunster*, II, 552–3; Hancock, *Dunster Church and Priory*, pp. 65–6; *Heads*, I, 88. Biographical details in

Greatrex, *Biog. Reg.*, pp. 1–49 (Bath monks).

? Martin Occ. ? late 12th cent. (*Heads*, I, 88; *Ctl. Buckland*, no. 338). See Greatrex, *Biog. Reg.*, p. 34, where it is suggested that the 13th-cent date ascribed to him by Maxwell-Lyte, *History of Dunster*, II, 552, perhaps confuses another m. of Bath, Martin of Dunster.

R. Occ. 11 Apr. 1301 (*Ctl. Bath*, II, no. 580; see Greatrex, *Biog. Reg.*, p. 37 note).

Walter Occ. 23 Sept. 1308 (*Ctl. Bath*, II, no. 560).

Roger de Grutelyngthon Apptd before 11 June [1323] (Somerset RO, Reg. Drokensford, f. 203v – not in pd reg., cited Greatrex, *Biog. Reg.*, p. 26).

Robert of Sutton 1332–1337 Pr. of Bath (q.v.), apptd to Dunster 30 Sept. 1332 when papal nominee promoted to Bath; financial provision 24 Oct. 1332 (*Reg. R. Shrewsbury*, I, nos. 697, 486). Occ. 10 Nov. 1335 (*Reg. Montacute*, p. 209). Vacated priory in 1337 (see next entry). See Greatrex, *Biog. Reg.*, pp. 42–3.

Adam of Cheddar 1337– Apptd 5 July 1337 in succession to Robert of Sutton (*Ctl. Bath*, II, no. 780). Occ. 25 June 1340 and 1344 but had ceased to be pr. by 6 Oct. 1345 (ibid., nos. 812, 878, 876). See Greatrex, *Biog. Reg.*, p. 18.

William Tondre (Tover) Occ. 1354/55 (PRO, Just.1/772/1, m. 27, cited by Greatrex, *Biog. Reg.*, p. 44, and Maxwell-Lyte, *History of Dunster*, II, 552).

Richard de Childeston Occ. Jan. [?1357]. Date 1357 according to Maxwell-Lyte, *History of Dunster*, II, 393, but it could be 1303 and relate perhaps to pr. R. above (see Greatrex, *Biog. Reg.*, p. 19).

John Hervey Occ. 1376 (Maxwell-Lyte, *History of Dunster*, II, 552, citing Somerset RO, DD/L/P1/4).

The next recorded pr., **William Bristow**, occ. 1411 (Maxwell-Lyte, *History of Dunster*, II, 552, citing Somerset RO, DD/L/P11/1).

EARLS COLNE (Essex), St Mary, St Andrew and St John the Evangelist (Abingdon) f. 1107

Lists in *VCH Essex*, II, 104–5; *Heads*, I, 88–9.

William Occ. 1204 x 1221 (*Ch. Abingdon*, II, 294–5); Hil. term 1209, *c.* Easter 1221 (*Essex F.*, I, 43, 67).

Richard Occ. from 2 Nov. 1227 to 14 Jan 1248 (ibid., 77, 170); Trin. term 1231 (*CRR*, XIV, no. 1802); (R.) 8 Sept. 1248 (Hill, *Eccles. Letter-books*, p. 71).

Henry Occ. 18 Nov. 1255 (*Essex F.*, I, 204); 22 July 1262 (ibid., 243); n.d. (*c.* 1260) (Hill, *Eccles. Letter-books*, p. 74). Possibly the **H. de Essintun**, pres. by Hugh de Vere, earl of Oxford (1233–63) to be pr. (Hill, *Eccles. Letter-books*, p. 72).

John de Campeden Occ. 22 Sept. 1316 (Norwich, Reg/1/1, f. 65v); 31 Mar. 1321 (*CPR 1321–24*, p. 25).

Roger Occ. 9 Sept. 1352 (Longleat, mun. 99); 13 May 1355 (London, Reg. Gilbert, f. 208v); 30 Apr. 1365 (London, Reg. Braybrooke, f. 24v).

Richard of Sudbury –1371 D. 23 Mar 1371 (*Reg. Sudbury*, I, 163).

Elias de Beauchamp (de Bello Campo) 1371– M. of Earls Colne, el. 1 May 1371 (ibid., 163–9). Ass. of abb. of Abingdon given 14 May 1371 (ibid., 161–2). Commn to examine eln 10 May and report 15 June 1371 (ibid., 162–3).

Thomas of Maldon –1390 Occ. 18 Jan. 1384 (*CCR 1381–85*, p. 427); 22 May 1386 (London, Reg. Braybrooke, f. 23v). D. by 23 July 1390 (ibid. f. 331v).

EWENNY (Ogmore) (Glamorgan), St Michael (Gloucester) f. 1141

Lists in Birch, *History of Margam*, p. 338; Birch, *History of Neath Abbey*, p. 210; *Heads*, I, 89.[8]

Peter Occ. n.d. (1207 x 1214) (*Glam. Chts.*, VI, 2306; cf. *JHSCW*, XXIV, 55).

---

[8] Adam is given by Birch as pr. without dates or source.

David Occ. 1205 x 1224; *ante* 1243 (*Glam. Chts.*, II, 440, 523).

John de Gamages Occ 12 Mar. 1261 (Hereford Cath. mun. 2300). Pr. of Hereford, St Guthlac, after being pr. of Ewenny. El. abb. of Gloucester 1284 (q.v.). See Cowley, *Monastic Order in South Wales*, pp. 161, 234.

Henry of Wigmore (Wig(g)emore) Occ. 28 Sept.–1 Oct. 1284 (*Ctl. Gloucester*, III, 22–4).

John de Helyon (Heliun) Occ. 14 Feb. 1303 (Hereford Cath. mun. 2298); 3 Oct. 1303 (*Glam. Chts.*, VI, 2359).

Reginald of Standish (Stanedish) 1333– Letter from John, abb. of Gloucester, to Henry, earl of Lancaster as patron, requesting ass. to their eln of Reginald as pr. of Ewenny 22 Sept. 1333 (PRO, DL25/255). ? Unsuccessful, or held office for a short while, see below.

Reginald of Standish 1338– Letter from Adam, abb. of Gloucester, as above 17 Apr. (?) 1338 (PRO, DL27/107).

John of Tewkesbury (Teukesbury) 1339– Similar letter from Adam, abb. of Gloucester, as above 26 July 1339 (PRO, DL25/256).

The next recorded. pr., **John Stowell**, occ. 5 Aug. 1382 (*CPR 1381–85*, p. 196).

EWYAS HAROLD (Hereford), St. James and St Bartholomew (Binns, p. 71) (Gloucester) f. 1100+; diss. ? 1359 (monks recalled to Gloucester)
   List (without sources) Bannister, *History of Ewyas Harold*, p. 134.

Adam Occ. 1205 x 1224 (Bannister, p. 50, no. 16, with H. abb. of Gloucester).

Thomas Occ. 29 Oct. 1243 (*CPR 1232–47*, p. 407).

William of London (Londiniis) Occ. 1266 x 1300 (Walker, *Eccles. Miscellany*, p. 50, no. 150; Bannister, p. 56, no. 53).

William son of Alan Prob. same as above, occ. 1265 x 1300 (list, p. 134).

Richard le Norman (Noreman) Occ. 1265 x 1300 (Walker, *Eccles. Miscellany*, p. 44, no. 123); 1283 (Bannister, p. 51, nos. 26–7).

Richard of Bibury (Beyburia, Beybury) Poss. same as above. Occ. 27 Sept. 1284 – 1 Oct. 1284 (*Ctl. Glos.*, III, 22–3, 26).

William of Potterne (Potern, Poterne) Occ. 27 Feb. 1311 (Bannister, p. 60, no. 76), 8 Mar. 1318 (PRO, E315/49/295).

Walter of Monmouth Last pr. Occ. 1352–58 (list, p. 134); 28 Aug. 1357, 14 Oct. 1359 (Walker, *Eccles. Miscellany*, pp. 47, 55, nos. 134, 171). Notarial instrument recording case 6 Oct. 1360: Roger la Warr of Ewyas to the abb. of Gloucester – consents to the recall of the monks at Ewyas to Gloucester on account of financial difficulties of the priory, on condition that a secular vicar is apptd 7 May 1358 (Bannister, p. 60, no. 78, cf. nos. 79–80). On 22 July 1361 a tithe case between the abb. and convent of Gloucester and W., still described as pr. of Ewyas, on the one part, and Thomas de Bergham, rector of All Cannings, dioc. Salisbury, on the other (Worcester Cath. Lib. mun. B.1A).

EXETER, St. Nicholas (Battle) f. 1087
   Lists in Oliver, pp. 114–15; 15th-cent list in BL, Cotton ms. Vitellius D IX, f. 23r (which does not entirely accord with the evidence set out below); *Heads*, I, 89.

Peter Occ. 1212 (*Ctl. Exeter*, p. 184, nos. 77–8); 23 Mar. 1219 (*Devon F.*, I, p. 44, no. 75); ?1219 x 1220 (Devon RO, ED/SN/23, dated by reeves of Exeter); 1221 x 1222 (*Ctl. Exeter*, p. 63, no. 39).

Roger Occ. 1224/5 x 1229/30 or 1234/5 (ibid., p. 381, no. 333; Devon RO, ED/SN/27, dated by mayoralty of Exeter).

John Occ. 1227 (*Ctl. Exeter*, I, p. 188, no. 158).

Hugh Occ. 15 July 1238, 17 July 1238 (*Devon F.*, I, pp. 136, 158, nos. 273, 317).

A. (?Alan) Occ. (A.) 1244 (*Ctl. Exeter*, p. 387, no. 393; Devon RO, ED/SN/34); (Alan) 11 July 1246 (Devon RO, ED/SN/36–7); n.d. (1246/7 x 1248/9 or 1253/4) (ibid., ED/SN/38, dated by mayoralty of Exeter); 25 Oct. 1249 (BL, Cotton ms. Vitellius D IX, f. 99v).

Robert de Cumbwelle –1262 Occ. 1255/6 x 1262/3 (ibid., ED/SN/45, dated by mayoralty of Exeter); 1260 (*Ctl. Exeter*, p. 383, no. 351); 29 Aug. 1261 (Devon RO, ED/SN/46). Res. by 29 June 1262 (*Reg. Bronescombe*, pp. 80, 140; *Reg. W. Bronescombe*, I, no. 445).

Robert de Rya 1262– Adm. 29 June 1262 (ibid.). Occ. Nov. 1272 x Nov. 1273 (*Ctl. Exeter*, p. 375, no. 228).

Alan Occ. Nov. 1274 x Nov. 1275 (ibid., p. 375, no. 224); Easter 1276 (PRO, CP40/14, m. 22d).

Roger Occ. Nov. 1294 x Nov. 1295 (*Ctl. Exeter*, p. 380, no. 324); 24 June 1295 (Devon RO, ED/SN/52; *TDA*, 44 (1912), 199); 23 Oct. 1296 (Devon RO, ED/SN/53); 6 Mar. 1297 (*CPR 1292–1301*, p. 269); 26 May 1302, 8 Feb. 1306 (*CPR 1301–07*, pp. 38, 414); 4 Oct. 1306 (PRO, C241/50/246).

Richard Occ. 1 June 1308 (*CPR 1307–13*, p. 75).

Roger of Pevensey (Pevenese) –1318 Occ. 31 Aug. 1310 (*Reg. Stapeldon*, p. 388); 2 Feb. 1311, 2 May 1313 (*CPR 1307–13*, pp. 306, 569); 1 June 1316 (*CPR 1313–17*, p. 468); 1 Oct. 1317 (BL, Cotton ms. Vitellius D IX, f. 120v). Royal ass. (John (*sic*) de Pevenese) to eln as abb. of Battle, 19 Mar. 1318 (*CPR 1317–21*, p. 120). Abb.-el. had left Exeter dioc. by 18 Mar. 1318 (*Reg. Stapeldon*, p. 438, cf. ibid., pp. 214–15).

William de Burum 1318–1320 M. of Battle, adm. 28 Aug. 1318 (ibid., p. 215). Res. by 14 Jan. 1320 (ibid.).

Robert *dictus* Laurencz de Guyngis 1320– M. of Battle, inst. 14 Jan. 1320 (ibid.).

Richard Horwode Occ. 1326 (*Ctl. Exeter*, p. 389, no. 344). Presumably also pr. of Brecon (q.v.).

John de Bordene (Bordenne) –1334 Occ. Jan. 1327 x Jan. 1328, 1333, 1338 (ibid., pp. 377, 386, 184, nos. 269, 384, 80). Occ. 15 June 1327 (*CPR 1327–30*, p. 126); 7 Aug. 1328; commn for purgation of John, charged with various crimes 2 Aug. 1329 (*Reg. Grandisson*, I, 519–21). Res. by 9 Sept. 1334 *propter impotenciam* (ibid., III, 1303, cf. BL, Harl. ms. 3586, f. 21v).

John of Brecon (Brechon(e)) 1334–1349 M. of Battle, pres. by abb. of Battle to bp n.d. (BL, Harl. ms. 3586, f. 21v); adm. 9 Sept. 1334 (*Reg. Grandisson*, III, 1303). Collector for the archdeaconry of Exeter, 1340 (ibid., I, 63). D. by 26 Mar. 1349 (ibid., III, 1380).

John of Wye (Wy) 1349 M. of Battle, adm. 26 Mar. 1349 (ibid.; cf. II, 1081). D. by 6 June 1349 (ibid., III, 1390).

Thomas Ovyngge 1349–1353 M. of Battle, inst. 6 June 1349 (ibid.). Went to Battle, but failed to return, commn to receive res. 26 Feb. 1353. Cert. 14 Mar. 1353 that he had appeared in the bp of Hereford's house in London and had res. 12 Mar. 1353 (ibid., 1426).

Matthew of Exeter (Exonia) 1353–1359 Pres. 18 Mar. 1353, commn for instn 17 Apr. 1353 (ibid.). Occ. 22 Sept. 1359 (Devon RO, ED/SN57). Res. by 3 Dec 1359 (*Reg. Grandisson*, III, 1454).

Gilbert (of) Lindsey (Lyndeseye) 1359– M. of Battle, inst. 3 Dec. 1359 (ibid.). Occ. 1373, 1384 (*Reg. Brantingham*, I, 145, 88); 20 Apr. 1377 (*CPR 1374–77*, p. 450); 1385 (Devon RO, ED/SN/58); 1387 (ibid., ED/SN/59; *Reg. Brantingham*, II, 647). William Cantelbyry, m. of St Nicholas, apptd coadjutor for pr. who is old and in ill health 16 July 1388 (*Reg. Brantingham*, II, 658). Occ. 10 Aug. 1390 (ibid., 704).[9]

FARNE (Northumberland), St Cuthbert f. *c.* 676; by 1208 (cell of Durham) (AJP)
List kindly provided by Mr A.J. Piper from his biographical register of Durham monks (forthcoming). Also list (without sources) in Raine, *North Durham*, p. 34.

---

[9] A pr. William occ. 28 Jan. 1374 (*CPR 1370–74*, p. 403), but this is prob. a scribal error.

MASTERS

Robert of Kilvington Occ. 13 Jan. 1292 (DCD, Misc. Cht. 4655).

Thomas of Bamburgh Occ. 31 Mar. 1311 (DCD, Loc.VI: 9a).

William of Ripon Occ. 6 Nov. 1316 (DCD, Misc. Cht. 2630); 2 Mar. 1321 (DCD, Loc.XIII: 3d).

John Lutterell 1325– Apptd 11 Apr. 1325 (DCD, Reg., II, f. 88r).

William of Hexham 1326– Apptd 28 Mar. 1326 (ibid.).

John Lutterell In office 2 Oct. 1328 x 1 Oct. 1329 (DCD, Westoe Ac. 1328–9); 11 Nov. 1329 x 11 Nov. 1330 (DCD, Norham Ac. 1329–30).

William of Hexham In office 11 Nov. 1330 x 11 Nov. 1331 (DCD, Norham Ac. 1330–1).

Robert of Birtley Relieved of office 1332 x 1333, to be replaced by Simon of R[othbury] (BL, Cotton ms. Faustina A. VI, ff. 12v–13v).

Simon of Rothbury Allegedly too young for office *c.* 1332 (DCD, Loc.XXVII: 12; 2.9.Pont.6). In office *c.* 11 Nov. 1332 x *c.* 11 Nov. 1333 (DCD, Bursar's Ac. 1332–3).

William of Hexham In office *c.* 11 Nov. 1332 x *c.* 11 Nov. 1333 (ibid.). Relieved of office 1 May [?1333] (BL Cotton ms. Faustina A VI, f. 53v).

William of Holy Island In office *c.* 7 Nov. 1333 x *c.* 6 Nov. 1334 (DCD, Bursar's Ac. 1333–4).

Robert of Middleham Occ. 29 Sept. 1335 (BL Cotton ms. Faustina A VI, f. 36v).

Simon of Rothbury In office 11 Nov. 1335 x 11 Nov. 1336, 11 Nov. 1338 x 11 Nov. 1339 (DCD, Norham Ac. 1335–6, 1338–9). Occ. 28 Oct. 1339 (DCD, Misc. Cht. 3796).

William of Holy Island In office *c.* 11 Nov. 1341 x *c.* 12/19 May 1342 (DCD, Bursar's Ac. 1341–2).

John of Shaftoe In office [1344 x 1345] (DCD, Norham Ac. 1344–5). Master of Monkwearmouth *c.* 1354–60 (q.v.).

William of Holy Island Occ. 15 Aug., 30 Nov. 1348 (DCD, Misc. Chts. 4811, 4097).

[**Simon of Alwinton** Accounted for Farne (? master) before 22 May 1357 (DCD, Farne Ac. 1357–8).]

John Abell –1358 Accounts 22 May 1357 – 24 June 1358 (ibid.). Master of Jarrow 1358–63 (q.v.).

Richard of Sedgebrook Accounts 24 June 1358 – 15 May 1363 (DCD, Farne Ac. 1358–63). Master of Jarrow to 1367 (q.v.).

John of Herrington Accounts 6 May 1364 – 26 May 1365, [?26 May 1365 x ?31 May 1366] (DCD, Farne Ac. 1364–6).

Robert of Faceby Accounts 6 Oct. 1366 – 4 Sept. 1368 (DCD, Farne Ac. 1366–8).

Richard of Sedgebrook Accounts 31 Aug. 1368 – [31 May 1378] (DCD, Farne Ac. 1368–78). Occ. 11 Dec. 1374 (DCD, Loc.XIII: 8a).

The next recorded master, **Adam of Knaresborough**, accounted up to 7 May 1380 (DCD, Farne Ac. 1380–1).

FELIXSTOWE (Suffolk), St Felix (Rochester) (Walton, St Felix), f. *c.* 1090 x 1100
List in *VCH Suffolk*, II, 81; cf. Greatrex, *Biog. Reg.*, pp. 577–650 (Rochester monks).

Alan Occ. 31 March 1217, 1223 (Maidstone, Centre for Kentish Studies, DRc/BZ1; *Reg. Roff.* p. 381).

John Occ. June 1291 (Bodl., Suffolk Cht. 1384).

John of Meopham (Mepham) Occ. Easter 1328 (*Index to Placita de Banco*, p. 614).

Robert of Southfleet –1351 *custos* of Felixstowe until el. pr. of Rochester, before 18 Aug. 1351 (*CCR 1349–54*, p. 379).

John of Hartlip –1361 *custos* of Felixstowe until el. pr. of Rochester 6 Aug. 1361 (*Ang. Sac.*, I, 394).

John Morel –1382 Occ. (John) June 1380 x June 1381 (PRO, E179/45/5B, m. 2); 17 May [1382] (BL, Cotton ms. Faustina C V, f. 10v); removed 30 Nov. 1382. Morel apptd as sub-pr. of Rochester (ibid., f. 15r).

FINCHALE (Durham), St John the Baptist and St Godric (see Binns, p. 73). f. (cell of Durham by 1174, following Godric's death in 1170), 1196 (AJP).
   List kindly provided by Mr A.J. Piper from his biographical register of Durham monks (forthcoming). Other lists in *VCH Durham*, II, 105, from *Finchale Priory*, p. xxv; *Antiquities of Sunderland*, VII (1908 for 1906), 30–34; *Heads*, I, 89.
P. Occ. ? *c.* 1215 (Raine, *North Durham*, p. 101, no. dlxxxi). ? same as below.
Peter Occ. *c.* 1225 (*Feodarium Prioratus Dun.*, p. 266). Seal (*Durham Seals*, II, p. 563, no. 3473).
Ralph Occ. 29 May 1230 (*Reg. Gray*, p. 49n); 23 Aug. 1235 (DCD, Misc. Cht. 6430); *c.* 1234 x 1237 (DCD, Misc. Cht. 2362); 25 May x 28 Oct. 1242 (*Finchale Priory*, pp. 108–9). ? same as below. Seal (*Durham Seals*, II, p. 563, no. 3474).
Ralph of Elvet Occ. [4 Mar. 1234 x 15 Sept. 1244] (DCD, 4.16.Spec.162).
M. Occ. 1242 x 1260, after Ralph and before Robert of Stichill (DCD, 1.5.Finc.10, 12; 3.7.Spec.5*; *Finchale Priory*, pp. 88–9).
Gilbert Occ. 22 Sept. 1244 x 15 Aug. 1258 (DCD, 3.3.Finc.7 and 7*).
Clement Occ. 22 Sept. 1244 x 15 Aug. 1258 (DCD, 3.1.Finc.7).
Robert Occ. 1 Aug. 1255 (or ? 1256) (DCD, Cart., IV, f. 106v). ? same as below.
Robert of Stichill –1260 Occ. n.d. (*Finchale Priory*, pp. 87–8). El. bp of Durham 30 Sept. 1260 (DCD, Misc. Cht. 5519; *Le Neve 1066–1300*, II, 32).
Geoffrey Occ. 22 July 1265 (*Finchale Priory*, pp. 143–4).
Robert of Holy Island –1274 Occ. 26 Jan. 1273 (*Ann. Durham*, pp. 40–1). El. bp of Durham 24 Sept. 1274 (ibid., p. 50; *Le Neve 1066–1300*, II, 32).
Richard Occ. 26 Mar. 1280 (DCD, 4.1.Finc.11*); *c.* 11 Nov. 1282 (DCD, 4.5.Spec.35); 9 July 1283 (DCD, Misc. Cht. 5709a). Possibly Richard of Escrick below.
Richard of Escrick Occ. 29 Apr. 1284 (*Reg. Wickwane*, no. 129); 11 Jan. 1286 (*Ann. Durham*, p. 76); 30 Sept. 1289 (DCD, 2.3.Finc.9).
Richard Occ. 11 Nov. 1289 (DCD, 4.1.Finc.19). ? the same as above.
Henry of Teesdale Occ. 21 Apr. 1295 (*Reg. Romeyn*, I, p. 150, no. 416); 1297 (DCD, Finchale Cat. f. 17v, no. 12); 14 June 1300 (DCD, Misc. Cht. 5526); 19 Apr. 1301 (DCD, 4.1.Finc.30*).
Geoffrey of Burdon Occ. 28 Apr., 12 May 1303 (*Finchale Priory*, p. i; DCD, Misc. Cht. 5700); 14 June 1307 (*Reg. Greenfield*, II, 32). Left office 9 Jan. x 24 Feb. 1308 (*Recs. A. Bek*, pp. 143–4). Pr. of Oxford cell 1302–3; pr. of Lytham 1311; pr. of Durham 1313–21; master of Monkwearmouth *c.* 1321–33 (q.v.). See also Emden, *BRUO*, I, 307.
Henry of Stamford Sub-pr. of Durham 12 Jan. 1311, occ. as pr. 31 Mar. 1311 (DCD, Lib. ms. B.II.1, f. 270r); 11 Nov. 1312 (DCD, 4.1.Finc.51); 2 July 1313 (DCD, Reg., II, f. 16v); 30 Mar. 1316 (DCD, Loc.XXVII: 16). El. bp of Durham 6 Nov. 1316 – set aside (DCD, Misc. Cht. 2630; *Le Neve 1300–1541*, VI, 107). Left office 11 Nov. 1316 (*Finchale Priory*, p. ix). Seal matrix (*Trans. AAS Durham and Northumberland*, VII (1937), 106–9).
John of Layton took delivery of status [?took office] 6 Nov. 1317 (ibid., p. xi). Pr. of Holy Island *c.* 1321–28 (q.v.).
Henry of Newcastle ?1317– Apptd after 27 Nov. 1317 (*Scriptores Tres*, pp. cxvi–cxvii). Occ. 2 Feb. 1319 (DCD, 1.5.Finc.28); 2 Mar. 1321 (DCD, Loc.XIII: 3c).
Richard of Aslackby Occ. 12 Dec. 1324, 12 Jan. 1325 (York, Reg. 9A, ff. 201v, 203r); 11 Nov. 1326 (DCD, 1.5.Finc.22). Drew up status 7 Apr. 1331 (*Finchale Priory*, p. xiv).
Thomas (of) Lund Occ. 15 Oct. 1333 (*Scriptores Tres*, p. 120); Drew up status 11 Nov. 1333,

12 Oct. 1336, 21 Sept. 1338 (*Finchale Priory*, pp. xv, xvii, xviii). See Emden, *BRUO*, II, 1178.

Emery of Lumley Occ. 15 Apr. 1339 (DCD, Misc. Cht. 4390); 11 Nov. 1341 (DCD, 1.5.Finc.24a); 8 Apr. 1342 (DCD, 4.1.Finc.17*). Ledger stone, Durham, styled pr. of Finchale (*Earliest English Brasses*, p. 186). Pr. of Lytham 1333; master of Jarrow to 1344 (q.v.).

William of Dalton Occ. *c.* 19 Jan. 1343 (*RDB*, p. 155).

[**John of Beverley senior** Accounted shortly before 7 June 1344 (DCD, Finchale Ac. 1344–5). Pr. of Oxford cell 1333; Master of Jarrow *c.* 1339–41 (q.v.). See also Emden, *BRUO*, I, 183.]

John of Barnby Accounts 7 June 1344 – 4 June [1346] (DCD, Ac. ?; 4.1.Finc.22). Pr. of Lytham *c.* 1331–2 (q.v.).

Nicholas of Lusby Accounts 3 June 1346 – 25 May 1349 (*Finchale Priory*, pp. xxii, xxvii, xxxi). Pr. of St Leonard's, Stamford 1338–46 (q.v.).

John of Norton Held office before *c.* 1352 (DCD, Finchale Ac. *c.* 1352). Master of Monkwearmouth 1349–50; master of Jarrow to 1355 (q.v.).

Thomas of Graystanes –1355 Accounts 26 May 1354 – 1 Mar. 1355 (*Finchale Priory*, p. xxxiv). Master of Jarrow 1344–48 (q.v.).

William of Goldsborough 1355–1360 Accounts 1 Mar. 1355 – 3 June 1359 (ibid., pp. xli–ii, xlv, xlvii, xlix). Delivered status [? left office] 24 May 1360 (ibid., p. li). Pr. of Holy Island 1367–74 (q.v.).

John of Newton 1360–1363 Accounts 18 May 1360 – 15 May 1363 (ibid., pp. liv, lvi, lix). Master of Monkwearmouth 1367–69 (q.v.).

John of Tickhill 1363–1367 Accounts 15 May 1363 – 16 Aug. 1367 (ibid., pp. lxii, lxv, lxviii, lxxi, lxxiii). Drew up status [? left office] 15 Aug. 1367 (ibid., p. lxxviii). Master of Jarrow 1367–69 (q.v.).

Uthred of Boldon 1367–1369 Accounts 7 Aug. 1367 – 14 May 1369 (ibid., pp. lxxix, lxxxii). See below.

Richard of Birtley 1369–1373 Took office 14 May 1369 (ibid., p. lxxxiv). Accounts 10 May 1372 – 30 May 1373 (ibid., p. lxxxiv). Accounted up to 15 Oct. 1373 (ibid., pp. lxxxviii, lxxxix). Pr. of Lytham from 1373 (q.v.); master of Farne 1380.

John of Normanby 1373–1375 Accounts 15 Oct. 1373 – 4 June 1375 (ibid., pp. lxxxviii, xc). Occ. 11 Dec. 1374 (DCD, Loc.XIII: 8a). Pr. of Lytham 1362–73; pr. of Holy Island 1379 (q.v.).

Uthred of Boldon 1375– Accounts 4 June 1375 – 7 May 1380 (*Finchale Priory*, pp. xciii, xcvi, xcviii). Occ. 1379 (PRO, E179/62/4, m. 2); 1 Mar., 16 and 24 May 1381; Sub-pr. of Durham 30 May 1381 (DCD, Reg., II, f. 199r). Uthred again accounts as pr. 19 May 1382 – 5 Oct. 1383 (DCD, Finchale Ac. 1382–3 and 1383). He also occ. as pr. of Finchale 1386–1396; see also Oxford cell 1349 x 1368. See also Emden, *BRUO*, I, 212–13; D. Knowles, *The Historian and Character and other essays* (Cambridge, 1963), pp. 129–70, bibliography on p. 129, n. 2; Sharpe, *Latin Writers*, pp. 699–702.

The next recorded pr., **John of Berrington**, occ. 14 Oct. 1383 (DCD, Misc. Cht. 2653).

FREISTON (Lincs), St James (Crowland) f. 1114+
Lists in *VCH Lincs*, II, 129; *Heads*, I, 90.

Nicholas –1228 M. of Crowland, occ. 18 Nov. 1208 (*Lincs F.*, *1199–1216*, no. 286). Res. 1228 to be abb. of Eynsham (*Ann. Dunstable*, p. 109; Ch. Barnwell in *Walt. Cov.*, I, p. xlin.).

Brice ? (Briciaius) Occ. 7 June 1232 (PRO, Notts F., CP25/1/182/5, no. 131).

John of Northampton (Northamton) Occ. 23 Apr. 1246 (BL, Cotton ms. Vespasian E XX, f. 31v).

Alexander Mentd 30 May 1293 as former pr. (*Reg. Sutton*, IV, 85).

William de Marcheford Mentd 12 Dec. 1312 as former pr., when indulgence issued for his soul (Lincoln, Ep. Reg., III, f. 266r).

John of Oundle (Oundell) Occ. 1377 (*Clerical Poll-Taxes*, p. 14, no. 169).

Simon of Langtoft Occ. 1381 (ibid., p. 115, no. 1402).

GREAT MALVERN (Worcs), St Mary and St Michael (Westminster) f. 1085; dependent on Westminster soon after.

Lists in *VCH Worcs*, II, 142; *Heads*, I, 90; M.G. Cheney, *Roger, Bishop of Worcester 1164–1179* (Oxford, 1980), app. III, pp. 374–6 'The priors of Great Malvern, 1177–1191'.

Walter *c.* 1190–*c.* 1216 For *c.* 1190 see Cheney, *Roger, Bishop of Worcester*, pp. 374–6. Latest recorded occ. 1204 (Westminster, Domesday, ff. 574v–576r; WAM, no. 22492). Prob. the W. who was dep. before 1224 (*Acta Langton*, pp. 160 ff.; cf. *GFL*, no. 239n.; cf. *Reg. G. Giffard*, p. 61 – provided with the manor of Cleeve Prior for his maintenance).

Thomas de Wichio *c.* 1216/1218–1242 Apptd by Bp Silvester (1216–18) (*Reg. G. Giffard*, p.18). Occ. n.d. (3 July 1216 x 16 July 1218) (WAM, no. 22493); n.d. (WAM, no. 32658; Hereford Cath. mun. 732). D. 1242 (*Reg. G. Giffard*, p. 198; *Ann. Worcs*, p. 434). Seal (*BM Seals*, no. 3603).[10]

John of Claines (Claynes) *alias* **Worcester** 1242–1259 (J.) succ. 17 June 1242 (Westminster Domesday, f. 307r; *Ann. Worcs*, p. 434). Eln conf. by Bp Cantilupe (*Reg. G. Giffard*, p.178, cf. 189). Occ. 3 Feb. 1249, 5 July 1251 (PRO, Worcs F., CP25/1/258/6, no. 48; /258/7, no. 6). Res. 20 Oct. 1259 (*Mon.*, III, 442, citing Nash, II, 124).

Thomas of Bredon (Brudone) –1267 Succ. on d. (*sic*) of John de Claynes 1259 x 1266 (*Reg. G. Giffard*, p. 178). Res. on account of bodily infirmity 25 Jan. 1267 (WAM, no. 32631).

William of Wickwane (Wykewane) 1267– On Thomas's d. Bp Cantilupe conferred priory on William (*Reg. G. Giffard*, p. 178, cf. 198). Cellarer of Great Malvern, eln pres. to abb. and convent of Westminster for approval 29 Jan. 1267 (WAM, no. 32632). William occ. 7 Jan. 1269 (*Reg. G. Giffard*, p. 9).

William of Ledbury (Ledbiry, Ledebure, Ledeburi, Ledebyre) –1282 Eln conf. by Bp Giffard n.d. (ibid., p. 178). Occ. 2 June 1275 (WAM, no. 22458); Mich. 1277 x Mich 1278 (PRO, E159/51, m. 15d). 4 Mar. 1279 sub-pr. and convent declare that William was canonically el. (*Reg. G. Giffard*, p. 188). Occ. 12 May 1280 (PRO, Worcs F., CP25/1/258/10, no. 17). Convicted of excesses and dep. 28 Sept. 1282, following archbp's visitation (*Reg. G. Giffard*, p. 164; *Ann. Worcs*, p. 484; *Reg. Peckham*, II, 423–4). Excommunication of pr. 23 Mar. 1283; repeated 11 May 1283; archbp refuses to repeal it 13 May 1283 (*Reg. Peckham*, II, 527–8. 543–4, 547–8). Absolution of those excommunicated by associating with William of Ledbury acting as pr. 18 June 1283 (ibid., 571). Papal judges delegate conf. excommunication of pr. 23 July 1283; absolution 7 Nov. 1283 (*Reg. G. Giffard*, pp. 210, 219).

William of Wickwane (Wyckewan, Wykewane) 1282 Pr. of Alvecote, el. 1282 in succ. to William of Ledbury (*Reg. Peckham*, II, 751). Letter of G., bp of Worcester, dated 17 Oct. [1282] to Edward I re. disputed eln; his jurisdiction has been challenged by the abb. of Westminster (PRO, SC1/23/104). Letter of bp of Worcester to the bp of Bath and Wells asking him to inform the king of what was happening at Great Malvern 17 Oct. 1282. Bp Giffard had removed William of Ledbury who was defamed of crimes of fornication with 22 women. William of Wickwane was el. pr. by the sub-pr. and convent. When Wickwane went to obtain the consent of the abb. of Westminster, he was imprisoned by the abb. who

---

[10] Pr. William occ. [*c.* Aug.] 1228 (*CR 1227–31*, p. 114). He is not mentd in the succ. of priors given in *Reg. G. Giffard*, p. 178.

claimed that the bp of Worcester had no jurisdiction in the priory (*Reg. G. Giffard*, p. 178). Bp writes to abb. of Westminster to release the pr.-el. of Great Malvern 16 Oct. 1282 – abb. replies that allegations are untrue (ibid., p. 179). King orders Bp Giffard to cease violating the rights of Westminster abbey 18 Oct. 1282 (ibid., pp. 182–3). Royal writ to take possession of vacant priory of Great Malvern 3 Nov. 1282 (ibid., p. 181): bp appts Henry de Wynton, his clerk, to be keeper of the spiritualities of the vacant priory 7 Nov. 1282 (ibid., p. 182). Bp Giffard writes to archbp of Canterbury complaining that the abb. of Westminster is imprisoning the el. of Great Malvern 10 Nov. 1282 (ibid., p. 183). Sentence of interdict on the priory 16 Nov. 1282 (ibid., p. 184). King orders sheriff of Worcestershire to restore priory to William of Ledbury the pr. 23 Nov. 1282 (ibid.). Bp Giffard excommunicates William of Ledbury, 'former' pr. 12 Dec. 1282 (ibid., p. 185). Letter of bp of Worcester, dated 8 Feb. [1283] to Edward I on release of pr.-el from the prison of the abb. of Westminster (PRO, SC1/18/5). Letter from archbp of Canterbury to king, dated 9 Feb. [l283], on dispute between the monks of Malvern and the abb. of Westminster (PRO, SC1/19/201). Letter of the Queen Mother on imprisonment of pr.-el. by abb. of Westminster dated 26 Feb. 1283 (PRO, SC1/16/166; *Reg. Peckham*, II, 749). Letter to archbp of Canterbury about imprisoned pr. 23 Mar 1283 (*Reg. G. Giffard*, p. 193). Letter to Cardinal Hugh of Evesham asking him to try to obtain the release of William de Wickwane, alleged to be the cardinal's nephew, imprisoned by the abb. of Westminster 9 Feb. 1283; further letter 8 June 1283 (*Reg. G. Giffard*, pp. 189, 195, 201). Ledger stone (*Earliest English Brasses*, p. 213).

William of Ledbury 1282–1287 King ordered his restoration 23 Nov. 1282 as he had been defamed (*Reg. G. Giffard*, p. 182). Request from pr. William to the abb. and convent of Westminster to retain in their monastery William of Wickwane and his accomplices who have lately sown great discord and dissension in the priory 24 Feb. 1283 (WAM, no. 22940). Occ. 9–10 Oct. 1283 (*CPR 1281–92*, p. 91; WAM, nos. 32643, 32635). Ratification by pr. William of the peace made between the king and the abb. of Westminster 18 Oct. 1283 (*Reg. G. Giffard*, p. 219; *CCR 1279–88*, p. 242). Occ. 1 Nov. 1283 (*CPR 1281–92*, p. 85); 15 May 1285 (ibid., p. 205). Dep. 5 Nov. 1287 by abb. of Westminster (*Ann. Worcs.*, p. 494).

Richard de Estone 1287–1301 Succ. 1287, *qui erga Willelmum de Wykewane aliquando extiterit ingratus* (ibid.). Occ. 15 July 1292 (PRO, Hereford F. CP25/1/81/22, no. 131); 27 Oct. 1299 (Worcester Cath. Lib., B.838). D. 5 Mar. 1301 (*Ann. Worcs.*, p.548).[11]

Hugh de Wyke (Wykes) –1341 Occ. 2 Feb. 1305 (*CPR 1301–07*, p. 312); 6 Nov. 1314 (Worcester, Reg. Maidstone, p. 34); 1316 (*SHC*, IX, p. 69); 8 Mar. 1318 (WAM, no. 32646); 30 Aug. 1333 (Worcs. Cath. Lib., B.392B); Mich. 1337 (PRO, CP40/312, attorneys m. 17); 24 Jan. 1341 (WAM, no. 32648). Res. by 7 Feb. 1341 on account of old age and infirmity (WAM, nos. 32649, 32651*).

Thomas de Legh(e) (Lega) 1341–1349 El. 7 Feb. 1341 and eln pres. to abb. and convent of Westminster for approval 10 Feb. 1341 (WAM, nos. 32649–51*). Commn to punish pr. Thomas for his repeated acts of insubordination and contumacy 13 Dec. 1346 (WAM, no. 32653, cf. 32655). Occ. 1 May 1349 (Staffs RO, D593/A/1/32/12). D. 17 June 1349 (WAM, no. 32656).

---

[11] WAM no. 32645 is an undated (early 14th cent.) letter from (? abb. of) Westminster addressed to the subpr. and convent of Great Malvern, thanking them for the honour they have done him in asking him to choose them a new pr. out of the names submitted to him, viz. brs. John de Wantynge, John de Wygornia, Ranulph de Westburi, John de Buttierleye, Gilbert de Cotes, and Simon de Henle, but he declines to make a selection, as he finds their merits to be equal. He warns them not to proceed to an eln without lic. of Westminster abbey. On the dorse is a note that if their choice falls upon W. de Wyrbertone he will never agree to it.

John of Painswick (Payneswykes) **1349–1361** Pr. of Alvecote, el. 27 June 1349 (ibid.). D. 24 Sept. 1361 (WAM, no. 32657).

Simon of Bisley (Byscheley, Bysscheleye) **1361–1397** Notarial instrument of eln 11 Oct. 1361 (ibid.; cf. no. 32659). D. 3 May 1397 (WAM, no. 22943, cf. 32661).

HATFIELD PEVEREL (Essex) St Mary (St Albans) f. 1100+

Lists in *VCH Essex*, II 106–7; *Heads*, I, 90. Also in T.M. Hope, *The Township of Hatfield Peverel: its history, natural history and inhabitants* (Chelmsford, 1930), p. 110.

Matthew Last recorded Occ. 13 Oct. 1206 (*CRR*, IV, 225).[12]

Alexander de Burgo Dep. ?–1226 by abb. of St Albans (*GASA*, I, 274, see below).

Richard of Bramfield (Brantefeld) **–1239** Succ. Alexander (ibid., 275). Occ. 30 Oct. 1226 (*EEA London 1189–1228* (forthcoming), no. 216, citing Southampton Univ. Lib., ms. 28/9). D. 14 July 1239 (*MPCM*, VI, 275).

William of Huntingdon (Huntendune) Occ. 16 Aug. 1254 (*MPCM*, V, 461)? the same as (W.) 20 Apr. 1269 (*CPR 1266–72*, p. 332);

Adam Occ. 1285 (PRO, Just.1/242, mm. 23d, 26).

Luke of Bovingdon (Bovindon) Occ. as cellarer of St Albans, 1290–5 (*Mon. Angl.*, II, 212n). Occ. as pr. n.d. (BL, Lansdowne ms. 860A, f. 248r–v); 11 Feb. 1310 (*CPL*, II, 66).

Peter de Maydenford Occ. 28 Nov. 1311, 25 Apr. 1317 (Norwich, Reg/1/1, ff. 44r, 70r); 7 Oct. 1317 (*CCR 1409–13*, p. 219). ? pr. of Beadlow.

William of Norton Occ. 20 Nov. 1351 (*CPL*, III, 452).

John Occ. 23 Jan. 1369 (*Reg. Sudbury*, I, 264); Easter 1370 (PRO, KB27/437, m. 7d).

William Eversdon D. in Flanders 1383 (*GASA*, II, 416).

Ralph Whichchirche Mentd as former pr. of Hatfield Peverel and pr. of Wallingford. Papal chaplain 1386/7, but on account of great age allowed to live in cell of Belvoir (ibid., 418). No indication when he was pr. of these cells.

HENES and **SANDTOFT** (Lincs) (York, St Mary) f. Henes, date unknown; Sandtoft 1147 x 1186, diss. +1291 (*KH*) but see below.

Lists in *Ch. York, St Mary*, p. 80; *Heads*, I, 96.

Ralph Rachel Professed by Abb. Robert Longchamp (1197–1239) (*Ch.*, p. 14). Occ. as pr. 24 June 1258 (ibid., p. 4). D. 11 Feb. 1271 '*homo magne etatis ac idem susceptus atque in eodem monasterio lvi annos et amplius vivens, quinto languoris sui anno migravit ab hoc seculo*' (ibid., pp. 14–15).

Thomas Plunket (Plunketh) **–1264** Said by Leland to have been the first pr. (Leland, *Coll.*, (2nd edn.), I, 25). *Socius* of the pr. of Wetheral 1258 when Ralph was pr. Henes (*Ch.*, p. 4). D. at Henes 3 Oct. 1264 (ibjd., p .7).

William of Thornton (Thorneton) **1264–** Succ. 1264 (ibid., p. 80). Succ. after 3 Oct. 1264 (ibid., p. 7). D. at Richmond 22 Oct. 1278, prob. not still pr. (ibid., pp. 19, 130).

Robert of Grimston (Grimeston) **–1281** Next in list (ibid., p. 80). D. 9 Feb. 1281 (ibid., p. 131).

Robert de Mideforth Received 1259 (ibid., p. 48). Occ. n.d. next in Henes list (ibid., p. 80) Became sub-pr. of York by 1286 (ibid., p. 23). D. 28 Nov. 1310, '*homo magne etatis et bone conversationis*' and bur. at York (ibid., pp. 48, 131).

William de Bracton (Brayton, Braxton) Professed 2 Dec. 1266 (ibid., p. 8). Occ. n.d. next in Henes list (ibid., p. 80). Also n.d. on Lincoln list (ibid., p. 79). Pr. of Lincoln, St Mary

---

[12] BL, Lansdowne ms. 860A, f. 248v notes a pr. Henry but there is no clue to the dating of the document. Hope, p. 195 also cites a pr. Geoffrey occ. in a cht. without ref. which he dates palaeographically to the 13th cent.

Magdalen 1286, 1293 (ibid., pp. 24, 132); chamberlain of York 1295, sub-pr. 1296 (ibid., pp. 79, 132); occ. 1296 at eln of Abb. Benedict, but office not mentioned (ibid., p. 27); *c.* 1296 succ. Osbert of Ripon at Richmond (ibid., p. 25). D. 20 Apr. 1312 at Rumburgh and bur. there (ibid., p. 53).

William de Sexdecim Vallibus Received 1260 (ibid., p. 5). Occ. n.d. next in Henes list (ibid., p. 80). Pr. of Henes 1286 (ibid., pp. 24, 131). D. at Richmond 8 June 1309 (ibid., p. 45).

John de Birne (Byrune) Received and tonsured 4 Feb. 1262, professed 1262/3 (ibid., p. 5). Occ. n.d. on lists of Rumburgh, Lincoln and Henes, (ibid., pp. 78–80). Travelled to Rome 25 Oct. 1300 (ibid., p. 31). Occ. 1313 (ibid., p. 62).

Richard de Craveton Brother of the hospital of St Leonard, York, received at York 14 Apr. 1281 (ibid., pp. 21, 135). M. of York 1293 (ibid., p. 24). Occ. n.d. next in Henes list (ibid., p. 80).

Thomas of Garton M. at St Bees 1293 (ibid., p. 135); occ. n.d. next in Henes list (ibid., p. 80). Proctor of convent 1313 at eln of Alan of Nesse as abb. of St Mary's, York (*Reg. Greenfield*, II, 154).

Robert de Gisburne (*dictus* Twentiman, Twentyman) Occ. n.d. next in Henes list (*Ch.*, p. 80). M. and priest of Durham, had obtained Wetheral 13 June 1310 by papal provision (ibid., p. 47). Renounced Wetheral 1313 to Abb. Alan (ibid., p. 64). Apparently came to Henes after 1313. A pr. of Henes is mentd on 1 May 1322 (*CPR 1321–24*, p. 105).

HEREFORD, St Guthlac and St Peter (Gloucester) f. *c.* 1100 x 1101 in St Peter's, Hereford, amalgamated with St Guthlac's and moved outside the city 1143.
List in *Heads*, I, 91.

Henry Last occ. (H.) 30 Apr. 1214 (Cheney, *Inn. III*, no. 964). Mentd before 18 Nov. 1215 as former pr. (Oxford, Balliol ms. 271, f. 50r). BL, Add. ms. 5827, f. 201v (Cole ms.) states he occ. 1226, but no source.

S. Occ. ?1220, dated 1228 in error (*Ctl. Shrewsbury*, II, no.368b n.; *EEA*, 7, no. 365; *Heads*, I, 91).

Jocelin Occ. 1220 x Aug.1224, 1231 x 1234 (*EEA*, 7, no. 371; Oxford, Balliol ms. 271, ff. 49v, 55r); 26 Sept. 1227 (PRO, Hereford F., CP25/1/80/6, no. 97). (J.) 13 Aug. 1232 (*CPR 1225–32*, p. 523).

Robert of Ledbury (Ledebur') Occ. 20 Jan. 1249 (PRO, Hereford F., CP25/1/80/12, no. 228); 3 June 1272 (ibid., 81/15, no. 316); 1263 x 1284 (Hereford Cath. mun. 1500).; 1276 (*HMC Rye and Hereford*, p. 292).

John de Gamages –1284 Occ. *ante* 1284 (Hereford Cath. mun. 319); 27–28 Sept. 1284 (*Ctl. Gloucester*, III, 22). El. abb. of Gloucester 1 Oct. 1284 (ibid., 26).

Hugh of Radnor (Radenor(e)) Occ. n.d. (Oxford, Balliol ms. 271, f. 26r). Mentd as previous pr. in case of Trin. 1297 (PRO, CP40/119, m. 78).

Ralph Forest Occ. 1293 (*Mon. Angl.*, III, 621, citing BL, Add. ms. 5827, f. 201v (Cole ms.), no source); Trin. 1297 (PRO, CP40/119, m. 78); Trin. 1298 (PRO, KB27/155, m. 37).

Laurence Occ. 12 Mar. 1304 (*Reg. Swinfield*, p. 395); 25 Sept. 1304 (Lincoln, Ep. Reg., III, f. 73r); [1305] (*Reg. Swinfield*, p. 407).

William (de) Ireby (Irby) (W.) citation for bp's visitation 26 Sept. 1321 (*Reg. Orleton (Hereford)*, p. 199). King orders sheriff of Hereford to take house into custody Jan. 1322 because of dispute between pr. and Thomas de Burghill who had intruded therein. Protection and safe conduct for William (*CPR 1321–24*, p. 49; *CCR 1318–23*, p. 416). Appeal against excommunication 11 July 1323 (*Reg. Orleton (Hereford)*, p. 258); 1324 bp orders dean of Ross to publish further excommunication (ibid., p.285; *Reg. Cobham*, p. 171). 19 Feb. 1324 bp of Hereford's commn to adm. a new pr. should one be presented (*Reg.*

Orleton (Hereford), p. 277). William appealed to the Court of Canterbury against the excommunication; the bp of Hereford acknowledges summons from the Court 26 May 1324 (ibid., pp. 297–8); Dean of Arches dismisses appeal 31 July 1324 and bp orders excommunication against pr. 2 Aug. 1324; bp commns several clergy to act for him in the matter of William de Ireby who has come asking for absolution 17 Aug.; further appeal by William to the Court of Canterbury 12 Nov. 1324 (ibid., pp. 305–9). Occ. 9 Nov. 1324 (*CFR 1319–27*, p. 314); 20 Feb. 1325 (*Reg. Martival*, III, no. 537); 3 July 1325 (*CCR 1323–27*, p. 382); 14 Mar. 1326 (PRO, C241/103/48); 10 May 1328 (PRO, C241/95/50). See A.T. Bannister, 'A note on an obscure episode in the history of St Guthlac's priory, Hereford', *Trans. Woolhope Soc.* (1908–11), pp. 20–24.[13]

John of Longney (Longoneye) Occ. 14 Oct. 1335 (PRO, E315/35/30).

John de la Forde Occ. 16 Apr. 1336 (*CPR 1334–38*, p. 286; PRO, C270/9/7).

John Mangeaunt (Maungeaunt) 14 Oct. 1341 (*Reg. R. Shrewsbury*, II, no. 1636); 3 Apr. 1342 (PRO, C241/115/346); 10 Nov. 1346 (Hereford Cath. mun. 2699); 19 May 1348 (Reg. Trillek, p. 129).

Richard Toky Occ. 29 June 1370 (PRO, C115/82, ff. 35v, 57r).

The next recorded pr., **Roger**, occ. 5 Nov. 1380 (PRO, E315/37/39); presumably the same as **Roger Appelby**, who occ. 1394 (Hereford Cath. mun. 3206).

HERTFORD, St Mary (St Albans) f. –1093

Lists in *VCH Herts*, IV, 421; *Heads*, I, 91.

William de Sandruge (Sandridge?) ?1213–1222 ? Inst. 1213 in place of the pr. who died that year (*Ann. Dunstable*, p. 41). D. 6 July 1222 (*MPCM*, VI, 270).

John 1223–1235 M. of St Albans, adm. 10 Jan. 1223 on d. of pr. William (*Reg. Wells*, III, 44–5). Royal ass. to his eln as abb. of St Albans 1 Apr. 1235 (*CPR 1232–47*, p. 98; cf. Hill, *Eccles. Letter-books* pp. 83–4). Occ. 13 Oct. 1225 (PRO, Herts F., CP25/1/84/11, no. 76); 30 Nov. 1227 (ibid., /84/13, nos. 129–30).

Richard 1237/8– Inst. June 1237 x June 1238, no reason given for vacancy (*Reg. Grosseteste*, p. 255). Occ. 25 Apr. 1238 (PRO, Herts F., CP25/1/85/17, no. 237); 1240 (ibid., 85/18, no. 267); 4 May 1242 (*Warws F.*, I, no. 602).

[?**Simon** Simon *dictus* prior d. at Hertford 10 Sept. 1247 (*MPCM*, VI, 277) – is he actually pr. of Hertford?].

Richard [de Wendene] –1253 Occ. 9 June 1252 (PRO, Herts F., CP25/1/88/24, no. 413). D. 4 Mar. 1253 (*MPCM*, VI, 279). Plea of June 1254 adjourned *sine die* because pr. Richard is dead (*SHC*, IV(1), p. 132).

Thomas Martel 1254/5– M. of St Albans, adm. May 1254 x May 1255, no reason given for vacancy (*Reg. Lexington*, pp. 509–10). Occ. May 1255 x May 1256 (ibid., p. 510); 30 Aug. 1269 (PRO, C85/117/35).

William of Hertford 1271– M. of St Albans, adm. 3 Jan. 1271, no reason given for vacancy (*Reg. R. Gravesend*, pp. 174, 317). Occ. 2 May 1272 (*Staffs F.* 2, p. 262; *Warws F.*, I, no. 906).

Martin of St Edmund (de Sancto Edmundo) 1277– M. of St Albans, adm. 6 Sept. 1277, no reason given for vacancy (*Reg. R. Gravesend*, p. 185).

William of Romsey 1299– Letter of pres. 10 Feb. 1299; adm. 14 Feb. 1299, no reason given for vacancy (*Reg. Sutton*, VIII, 91).

Richard of Hertford 1303–1312 M. of St Albans, on 13 July 1303 Richard appeared but the bp did not acc. his letters of pres. because they were letters close not patent; Richard reappeared with letters patent of pres. dated 11 June 1303 and was adm. 15 July 1303, no reason

---

[13] BL, Add. ms. 5827, f. 201v (Cole ms.) gives pr. Thomas Burghill 'about 1330', but no source.

given for vacancy (Lincoln, Ep. Reg., II, f. 234r). Occ. 3 May 1309 (*CPR 1307–13*, p. 112). El. pr. of Beadlow, Beds, 1312 (q.v.).

William de Kirkeby 1313– M. of St Albans, formerly pr. of Beadlow (q.v.), appeared 8 Apr. 1313 and letters of pres. rejected; he appeared with other letters of pres. dated 9 Apr. and was adm. 14 Apr. 1312, no reason given for vacancy (Lincoln, Ep. Reg., II, f. 244r).

John of Walsingham (Walsyngham) **1315–** M. of St Albans, letters of pres. 29 Sept. 1315, adm. 9 Oct. 1315, no reason given for vacancy (ibid., f. 248r).

William de Kirkeby 1316– M. of St Albans, letters of pres. 15 Oct. 1316, adm. 24 Oct. 1316, no reason given for vacancy (ibid., f. 249v).

Stephen de Withenham (Wythenham) **1317–** M. of St Albans, letters of pres. 28 Nov. 1317, adm. 7 Dec. 1317, no reason given for vacancy (ibid., f. 251v).

Richard of Wheathampstead (Wathamstede) **1319–** M. of St Albans, letters of pres. 10 Mar. 1319, adm. 17 Mar. 1319 (ibid., ff. 253v–254r).

Geoffrey of St Albans (de Sancto Albano) **1323–** M. of St Albans, formerly pr. of Redbourn 1290, pr. of Beadlow, 1302 (q.v.). Letters of pres. 20 July 1323, previous letters rejected 11 July, no reason given for vacancy; bp apptd him 11 Aug. 1323 (Lincoln, Ep. Reg., IV, f. 365r).

Nicholas of Flamstead (Flamstede) Occ. *c.* Nov. 1327 (*GASA*, II, 184, 187). Previously pr. of Binham (q.v.), and subsequently pr. of St Albans, coadjutor of abb. of St Albans 1332, d. 1349 (ibid., 209–10, 289–91, 381).[14]

Adam of Doncaster (Dancastr') **1349–** Prob. vacant 24 July 1349 when pres. made to a vicarage (Lincoln, Ep. Reg., IX, f. 384r). M. of St Albans, letters of pres. 10 Dec. 1349, adm. 22 Dec. 1349, no reason given for vacancy (ibid., f. 388v).

Robert Nony 1352– M. of St Albans, letters of pres. 20 Aug. 1352, adm. 21 Aug. 1352, no reason given for vacancy (ibid., f. 395r–v).

John Occ. June 1378 x June 1379 (*YB 8–10 Richard II*, p. 3). Perhaps the same as the next recorded pr., **John de Colby**, occ. 30 Apr. 1389 (Lincoln, Ep. Reg., XII, f. 359r).

HOLY ISLAND (Northumberland), St Peter (Lindisfarne) f. 635, refounded by 1172 (cell of Durham) (AJP)

List kindly provided by Mr A.J. Piper from his biographical register of Durham monks (in preparation); other lists in *Heads*, I, 94; Raine, *North Durham*, pp. 81–2.

Simon Occ. (S.) 17 July 1202 (*Ctl. Lanercost*, no. 300); 1203 x 1212 (DCD, Misc. Cht. 1040; *North Durham*, no. cclxix); n.d. (early 13th cent.) (*Northumberland and Durham Deeds*, p. 94).

Ralph Occ. n.d. (1220s) (DCD, 2.1.Spec.33; *North Durham*, no. dclxii); before 1242–3 (DCD, 1.1.Spec.28).

W. Occ. 14 Feb. 1235 (DCD, 1.2.Spec.14; *North Durham*, no. dcclxxxviii); ?1234 x 15 Sept. 1244 (DCD, Misc. Cht. 1104, cf. *North Durham*, no. cccxliv). ? same as William below.

William Occ. ? 1230 x 1242–3 (DCD, 3.1.Spec.47, 51, 52); 1234? x 15 Sept. 1244 (DCD, 3.1.Spec.69).

Thomas Occ. 12 Jan. 1242 (DCD, 1.2.Spec.10; *North Durham*, no. dcclxxxiv); 23 Apr. 1256 (*Northumberland and Durham F.*, I, p. 89, no. 210).

A. of Neasham Apptd [after 8 Sept. 1259] (DCD, Misc. Cht. 6151*).

Andrew compromissary 30 Sept. 1260 (DCD, Misc. Cht. 5519c).

Richard of Claxton –1273 El. pr. of Durham 26 Jan. 1273 (*Ann. Durham*, p. 37).

Nicholas Occ. 24 Sept. 1274 (*Hist. Ch. York*, III, 191); n.d. (1270s) (*North Durham*, nos. dclxix, dcciii). ? same as below.

---

[14] Browne Willis in his app. to Tanner, *Notitia Monastica* lists John de Longeney as pr. 1338, but this is an error for Hereford, St Guthlac.

Nicholas of Walworth Occ. before 4 Apr. 1281 (DCD, Misc. Cht. 5234); res. acc. *senio et corporis debilitate confractus* 26 Jan. 1273 x 27 Dec. 1285 (DCD, 2.9.Pont.13).

[**Gilbert of Sherburn** commn to restore finances after Nicholas of Walworth 26 Jan. 1273 x 27 Dec. 1285 (ibid.). Pr. of St Leonard's, Stamford 1286–7 (q.v.).]

Richard of Barnby Occ. 9 July 1283 (*Recs. A. Bek*, p. 182); 1 Mar. 1284 (DCD, Misc. Cht. 5820/14).

Roger Occ. 20 Dec. 1284 (DCD, Cart.II, ff. 11v–12r). ? same as below.

Roger of Methley Occ. 27 Dec. 1285 (*Ann. Durham*, p. 65); 11 Jan. 1286 (ibid., p. 76).

William of Middleton Occ. late 13th cent. (after 20 Dec. 1284) (DCD, Cart. II, ff. 11v–12r; 2.1.Spec.25; *North Durham*, no. dclxxvi).

Henry of Lusby –1300 Occ. 14–15 June 1300 (DCD, Misc. Cht. 5526); apptd pr. of Durham 10 Aug. 1300. (*Recs. A. Bek*, pp. 74–6).

[**Hugh de Monte Alto** keeper, apptd and removed before 23 Dec. [1302] (DCD, Loc.VII:79).]

Richard Kellawe Occ. 26 Apr. 1305 (DCD, Loc.VII:6); delivered status (? left office) 25 Feb. 1308 (DCD, Holy Island status 1308).

Stephen of Howden junior Occ. 31 Mar. 1311 (DCD, Loc.VI: 9a); 30 Oct. 1316 (DCD, Loc.VI: 10p).

John of Layton Occ. 6 Feb., 2 Mar. 1321 (DCD, Loc.XIII: 3b–c); 21 Feb. 1325 (DCD, Reg., II, f. 87r); 11 Oct. 1326, 14 Mar. 1327, 25 Sept. 1328 (DCD, Holy Island status 1326–8). Pr. of Finchale 1317 (q.v.).

Gilbert of Elwick 1328– Apptd 18 Nov. 1328 (DCD, Reg., II, f. 98v). Occ. 6 Dec. 1330, 18 Nov. 1332, 19 July 1333 (DCD, Holy Island status 1330, 1332–3); 15 Oct. 1333 (*Scriptores Tres*, p. 120). Accounts 16 May 1339 – [25 Apr. 1343], 25 Apr. 1344 – [14 May 1346] (DCD, Holy Island Ac.). Occ. 19 June 1343 (*Reg. Bury*, pp. 154–5). See Emden, *BRUO*, I, 637. Pr. of Oxford cell 1316 (q.v.).

[**John of Beverley** drew up status 16 Aug. 1348, but not desc. as pr. (DCD, Holy Island status 1348). Master of Jarrow *c.* 1339–41; pr. of Finchale *c.* 1344 (q.v.).]

Michael of Gunnerton *alias* **Chilton** –1352 In office 29 Sept. 1348 – 19 Apr. 1349 (DCD, Norham Ac. 1348–9). Accounts 16 May 1350 – 5 June 1351 (DCD, Holy Island Ac.). Left office shortly before 6 Oct. 1352 (ibid., 1352–3).

William of Bamburgh Accounts 6 Oct. 1352 – 26 May 1354 (ibid.). Occ. 29 Jan. 1353 (Durham, Reg. Hatfield, f. 10v). Pr. of Coldingham 1355–62 (*Priory of Coldingham*, pp. 34, 37).

Robert of Hexham In office 11 Nov. 1357 x 11 Nov. 1358 (DCD, Bursar's accts 1357–8). Pr. of St Leonard's, Stamford 1348–52 (q.v.).

John of Goldsborough Accounts 13 Dec. 1358 – 2 June 1359, 18 May 1360 – 10 May 1361 (DCD, Holy Island Ac.). Master of Jarrow 1357–8; master of Monkwearmouth *c.* 1367 (q.v.).

[**John of Elwick** accounted for the cell [?up to] 7 Oct. 1362 (ibid.). Master of Jarrow 1363–66 (q.v.).]

Richard of Beckingham Accounts for the cell 7 Oct. 1362 (styled keeper) – 19 Feb. 1363 (in 1363 desc. as pr.) (ibid.). Master of Monkwearmouth 1360–62 (q.v.).

John of Billesfield Accounts [15 May 1363] – 12 Sept. 1367 (ibid.). Also pr. of Holy Island again 1384–88; pr. of St Leonard's, Stamford 1373–75 (q.v.).

William of Goldsborough Accounts 12 Sept. 1367 – 15 May 1374 (ibid.). Pr. of Finchale 1355–60 (q.v.).

Thomas of Hardwick Occ. 11 Dec. 1374 (DCD, Loc.XIII: 8a). Accounts [15 May] 1374 – 4 June 1375; [25 May] 1376 – 23 May 1379 (DCD, Holy Island Ac.). Occ. 10 Jan. 1379 (Durham, Reg. Hatfield, f. 153v)

The next recorded pr., **William Fayrfax**, occ. 1379 (PRO, E179/62/4, m. 1d). It is possibly a fake name, like others connected with certain Ricardian clerical subsidies. See F.P. Mackie, 'The Clerical Population of the Province of York: an edition of the clerical poll tax enrolments 1377–81' (University of York, unpublished D. Phil. thesis, 1998), pp. 50–55. Mr Alan Piper tells me that he has not found this monk at Durham (preparatory to his forthcoming register of Durham monks).

HORTON (Dorset), St Wolfrida (? formerly St Mary) (Binns, p. 75) (Sherborne) f. ?10th cent. (as abbey of nuns); ref. c. 1050 (1033 x 1061) (as abbey of monks); 1122 x 1139 (as subject to Sherborne).

Lists in *VCH Dorset*, II, 73[15]; *Heads*, I, 53.

John of Compton Occ. (J.) 13–14 May 1310 (*Reg. Gandavo*, II, 737, 741, 744); 14 May 1310 (ibid., 737, 744); ? Is he the same as John of Compton el. abb. of Sherborne 1329 (q.v.).

William Occ. 22 Mar 1336 (*CCR 1333–37*, p. 654); 25 Mar. 1337 (*CCR 1337–39*, p. 109).

John of Bradford (Bradeford) Occ. 6 Feb. 1348 (*CPR 1348–50*, p. 60).

Peter de Whitsand Occ. 16 Jan. 1370 (Lambeth, Reg. Whittlesey, f. 161r); 1 Dec. 1376 (Lambeth, Reg. Sudbury, f. 96r); 28 Nov. 1384 (*CPR 1381–85*, p. 483).

HOXNE (Suffolk), St Edmund (cell of Norwich) f. 1130

Lists in *VCH Suffolk*, ii, 77 from Blomefield, *Norfolk*, III, 609–10; *Heads*, I, 91–2. Blomefield evidently took the names from the cartulary, then in the possession of T. Martin of Palgrave, but now only surviving as a fragment (Suffolk RO, Ipswich, ms. HD.1538/265; see Blomefield, p.607; Davis, *Medieval Cartularies*, no. 496). He was unable to determine the order of the dates of the first five priors given. Biographical details in Greatrex, *Biog. Reg.*, pp. 456–576 (Norwich monks).

Hervey
Richard of Hoxne
Roger
William of Acle
John de Shamelisford

Richard of Hoxne and William of Acle are known from other sources (see below) and Roger may poss. be Roger de Thurston, unless Blomefield's list actually reflects a precise chronological sequence.

Richard of Hoxne Occ. as pr. of Hoxne *temp.* pr. William of Norwich (presumably one of the four pr. Williams between 1205 and 1289: Greatrex, p. 526, citing from a fragment of the Hoxne ctl.)

William of Acle (Akel, Hocle) Occ. second half of 13th cent., but no document yet found referring to him as pr. of Hoxne. He was almoner of Norwich 1260 (*Cal. Misc. Inq.* II, no. 2001) and occ. as m. of Norwich 1282/3 (Norfolk RO, DCN.1/6/5).

H. of Elmham prob. pr. of Hoxne, occ. ? 1317 (Norfolk RO, DCN, Reg. IX, f. 9v). D. Mich. 1317 x Mich. 1318 (ibid., DCN.1/5/5).

Robert of Ormesby Occ. ? before 1336, for at least 2 years (Windsor DC, I.C. 1).

William of Lynn (Lenn) Prob. pr. of Hoxne 1343 x 1351 about whose dismissal the pr. of Norwich wrote to the bp (ibid.; DCN. Reg. X, f. 38r).

John of Worstead (Wirstede, Worsted(e)) *or of* **Norwich** (Norwico) Removed as pr. 1343 x 1351 at pr. of Norwich's request (Norfolk RO, DCN., Reg. X, f. 2v).

Roger of Thurston (Thurstone, Thurton, Turston, Turton) In a letter 1343 x 1351 the pr. of

---

[15] Pr. Hugh listed in *VCH* occ. 1286 actually relates to the priory of Monks Horton.

Norwich asks Bp Bateman to adm. him in place of John de Worstede (ibid.). Occ. Mich. 1351 – Mich. 1352 (Windsor DC, I.C.3).

Alexander of Caistor (Castre) Occ. Mich. 1375 – Mich. 1376 (ibid., I.C.4).

Richard of Bilney (Bilneye, Bulneye, Bylneye) Occ. Mich. 1376 – Mich. 1378 (ibid.). He occ. as precentor of Norwich 1382–85 (Norfolk RO, DCN.1/9/20–22).

The next recorded pr., **John**, occ. June 1380 x June 1381 (PRO, E179/45/5B, m. 2).

HURLEY (Berks), St Mary (Westminster) f. –1087
  Lists in *VCH Berks*, II, 76; F.T. Wethered, *St Mary's Hurley in the Middle Ages*, (London, 1898), pp. 84–5, revised in F.T. Wethered, *Corrections and amendments to St Mary's Hurley in the Middle Ages* (London, 1903), pp. 6–7, and F.T. Wethered, *Hurley Church and Priory* (Reading, 1917), p. 9, also Wethered, 'Hurley Church and Priory', p. 102; *Heads*, I, 92.

William de Stanford Occ. (W.) –1205 (Canterbury D. & C., Eastry Correspondence, Group III, no. 25); (W.) 1199 x 1213 (*Ctl. Missenden*, III, no. 725); 1213 x 1214, Oct. 1221 x Oct. 1222 (WAM, nos. 3379, 2185); n.d. (*c.* 1221) (ibid., 474, 2083).

Richard le Gras –1236 For name see WAM, no. 3744. Occ. Hilary term 1226 (*CRR*, XII, no. 2018); 1231 (WAM, nos. 2971, 20619–20); 1235 (PRO, Berks F., CP25/1/7/11, no. 17); 27 Feb. 1236 (*CChR 1226–57*, p. 218; WAM, no. 2028). El. abb. of Evesham 1236 (q.v.).

Samson de Eswelle Succ. 1236 (*Ann Dunstable*, p. 145).

Theobald Occ. Easter term 1237 (*Essex F.*, I, 116); *c.* Trin. 1239 (*CRR*, XVI, no. 556); 3 Nov. 1243 (*Kent F.*, p. 179); 1247, 2 Nov. 1248 (PRO, Berks F., CP25/1/7/15, no. 27; /15, no. 29); 1248 (*Berks Eyre*, no. 219); *c.* 1250 x 1258 (*Basset Chts.*, no. 77); (Th.) 15 Feb. 1253 (*CR 1251–53*, p. 321); 24 June 1254, 1 May 1255 (WAM, nos. 2029, 7605). In the Wethered list he is given the surname of 'de Ayswelle'.

Thomas Occ. 30 Jan. 1256 (*CR 1254–56*, p. 391), ? error for Theobald.

Geoffrey Occ. (Godfrey) 1258 (BL, Harl. ms. 3697, f. 68r); 29 June 1259 (*Oxford F.*, p. 177); 23 Feb. 1261 (PRO, Berks F., CP25/1/8/24, no. 19); n.d. (1258 x 1274) (WAM, nos. 2125, 2193, 2264, 2303). In the Wethered list he is given the surname of 'de Suttone'.

John de Lyra (Lyre) Occ. 3 June 1274 (WAM, no. 2180; PRO, Berks F., CP25/1/9/29, no. 4); Nov. 1274 (WAM, nos. 2298, 2310, 2316); Nov. 1275 x Nov. 1276 (*London and Middlesex F.*, p. 219); 15 May 1276 (PRO, F. Divers Cos.CP25/1/284/20, no. 43).

Walter of London Occ. 3 Sept. 1279, (W.) 25 Apr. 1283; 4 June 1285 (WAM, nos. 2124, 2320, 2327).

Adam Occ. Nov. 1292 x Nov. 1293, 17 June 1295 (ibid., nos. 2081, 2204); n.d. (1292 x 1295, 1285 x 1299) (ibid., nos. 3631, 3554).

William Seger Said to be pr. *c.* 1299 (*VCH*), ref. to as late pr. in cht of 10 Apr. 1352 (WAM, no. 3714). Also occ. n.d. (late 13th cent.: pal.) (ibid., no. 3707). His precise place in the sequence of priors is uncertain.

Richard de Waleden(e) –1304 Occ. from 21 June 1299 to 24 Mar. 1304 (ibid., nos. 2179, 3634). D. by 3 Sept. 1304 (PRO, DL34/1/7).

Alexander de Neuport 1304– Sub-pr. and convent petition Humphrey, earl of Hereford, asking his ass. to eln of Alexander 3 Sept. 1304 (ibid.). Occ. 1 Aug. 1305, 2 July 1306 (WAM, nos. 2318, 2263); 9 Aug. 1306 (PRO, DL27/138); 4 Apr. 1309 (*Goring Chts.*, no. 129); 15 May 1309 (WAM, no. 3772); 23 July 1310 (*Reg. Gandavo*, II, 746); but cf. 16 July 1310 a pres. deed issued by sub-pr. and convent (?vacancy) (ibid.).

Henry Occ. 17 Apr. 1311 (*Reg. Gandavo*, I, 403); 17 June 1311, 16 Dec. 1313 (WAM, nos. 3792, 3595).

Richard de Coleworth(e) (Colewrth, Culeworth) Occ. from 1 Oct. 1320 to 13 Sept. 1336 (ibid., nos. 2165, 3758); 8 Dec. 1325 (*CCR 1323–27*, p. 530).

John de Tothale (Tuttehale) Occ. from 1338 to 25 July 1348 (WAM, nos. 19620, 7608); 18 Sept. 1340, 8 May 1342 (*CPR 1340–43*, pp. 95, 455); 22 Oct. 1342 (*CCR 1343–46*, p. 91). As former pr. gtd a corrody at Westminster 28 Feb. 1352 (*CPR 1350–54*, p. 225).

Thomas de Cumbrok (Combrok) Occ. 14 Apr. 1352 (*CCR 1349–54*, p. 466); from 7 July 1352 to 10 July 1363 (WAM, nos. 3711, 2159).

William (de) Bromley (Bromle, Bromleyge) Occ. from 10 Oct. 1365 to 5 Dec. 1375 (ibid., nos. 2314, 3598).

William of Ipswich (Geppeswych, Yepiswich, Ypeswiche, Ypeswyche, Zepeswich, Zepiswych), occ. from 8 Oct. 1377 to 15 Sept. 1400 (ibid., nos. 3600, 3590).

JARROW (Durham), St Paul (Durham) f. 681; 1073/4 (as priory); cell by 1235 (AJP)

List based on A.J. Piper, *The Durham Monks at Jarrow* (Jarrow Lecture, 1986), app. I, pp. 23–30, repd *Bede and his World*, II *The Jarrow Lectures 1979–1993* (1994), 711–18; also lists in *VCH Durham*, II, 85 from *Jarrow and Wearmouth*, ed. J. Raine, xiv–xv; *Heads*, I, 92.

MASTERS

Ralph of Middleham Occ. 15 June 1300 (DCD, Misc. Cht. 5526); ? left office before 21 Aug. 1303 (Piper list).

Adam de Boyville delivered subsidy from cell 11 Nov. 1309 x 3 Oct. 1310 (DCD, Bursar's acct); occ. 31 March 1311 (Durham Cath. Lib. ms. B.II.1, f. 270r).

[**Geoffrey of Haxby** delivered status 14 June 1313 (*Jarrow and Wearmouth*, no. XIII).]

[**William of Tanfield** assigned cell on res. as pr. of Durham 13 June 1313. D. 7 Feb. 1314 (*Ch. St Mary's, York*, p. 65)].

[**Thomas of Newcastle** accounts 14 June 1313 – 18 Apr. 1314 (*Jarrow and Wearmouth*, nos. III–VI).]

Geoffrey of Haxby Occ. 3 Nov. 1316 to 7 Sept. 1319 (DCD, Misc. Chts. 5231, 5083; 2.2.Arch.Dun.19). See Emden, *BRUO*, II, 893.

Robert of Durham 1321– Master of Monkwearmouth 1321 (q.v.). Took delivery of status 17 May 1321 (XIV); occ. 4 Dec. 1323 (DCD, Misc. Cht. 4562).

Emery of Lumley Occ. from 1 Oct. 1326 to 9 May 1333 (*Jarrow and Wearmouth*, nos. XV–XIX). Pr. of Lytham 1333 (q.v.).

Alexander of Lamesley Occ. 15 Oct., 11 Nov., 29 Dec. 1333 (*Scriptores Tres*, p. 120)

[**Walter of Scarisbrick** produced status 7 Nov. 1334, 9 Nov. ?1335 (DCD, originals)]

[**Emery of Lumley** produced status 6 Oct. 1338 (*Jarrow and Wearmouth*, no. XXII)]

John of Beverley senior In office *c.* 12 May 1339 x *c.* 12 May 1340 (DCD, Bursar's Ac.). Accounts 16 Apr. 1340 – [?25 Apr.] 1341 (*Jarrow and Wearmouth*, no. XXIII); occ. 20 July 1341 (DCD, Misc. Cht. 5383). Seal (*Durham Seals*, II, p. 570, no. 3500). Pr. of Oxford cell 1333; accounted at Finchale 1344 (q.v.). See Emden, *BRUO*, I, 183.

Emery of Lumley –1344 Occ. *c.* 19 Jan., 11 Nov. 1343 (*Reg. Bury*, p. 155; DCD, Misc. Cht. 5239); accounted up to 1 Aug. 1344 (*Jarrow and Wearmouth*, no. XXV). Pr. of Lytham 1333; pr. of Finchale *c.* 1339–42 (q.v.). Ledger stone, styled pr. of Finchale, at Durham (*Earliest English Brasses*, p. 186).

Thomas of Graystanes 1344–1348 Accounts from 1 Aug. 1344 to 16 Aug. 1348 (*Jarrow and Wearmouth*, nos. XXV–XXIX). Prior of Finchale 1354–5.

[**Adam of Wearmouth** Accounts up to 17 Sept. 1350 (DCD, Jarrow Ac. 1350–1).]

John of Goldsborough 1350–1351 Accounts 17 Sept. 1350 to 30 May 1351 (*Jarrow and Wearmouth*, no. XXXI). Pr. of Holy Island 1358–61; master of Monkwearmouth *c.* 1367 (q.v.).

John of Norton –1355 Occ. 29 Jan. 1353, 5, 25 Aug. 1354 (Durham, Reg. Hatfield, ff. 10r, 17v; DCD, 2.8.Pont.9); drew up status 23 March 1355 ? when he left office (DCD, Jarrow status 1355). Pr. of Finchale *c.* 1352; accounted at Monkwearmouth 1349–50 (q.v.).

Richard of Bickerton 1355–1357 Accounts 30 March 1355 to 21 Sept. 1357 (*Jarrow and Wearmouth*, nos. XXXIII–VI).

John of Goldsborough 1357–1358 Accounts 2 Oct. 1357 to 13 Dec. 1358 (ibid., nos. XXXVII–XXXVIII). Prior of Holy Island 1358–61. Master of Monkwearmouth *c*.1367 (q.v.).

John Abell 1358–1363 Accounts 13 Dec. 1358 to 18 Feb. 1363 (ibid., nos. XXXIX–XLII, XLIV). Master of Farne to 1358 (q.v.).

John of Elwick 1363–1366 Accounts 10 March 1363 – 18 May 1366 (ibid., nos. XLV–XLVIII).

Richard of Sedgebrook –1367 Left office 15 Aug. 1367 (ibid., no. XLIX). Master of Farne 1358–63 (q.v.).

John of Tickhill 1367–1369 Pr. of Finchale 1363–67. Accounts 15 Aug. 1367 – 14 May 1369 (ibid., nos. XLIX–L).

John of Bolton 1369–1370 Accounts 19 Aug. 1369 – 8 Nov. 1370 (ibid., nos. LI, LIII).

John of Lumley 1370–1373 Accounts 4 Nov. 1370 – 20 July 1373 (ibid., nos. LIV–LIX).

William Vavasour 1373–1375 Accounts 20 July 1373 – 4 June 1375 (ibid., nos. LX–LXI).

John of Lumley Accounts [16 Sept.] 1376 to 11 May 1377 (ibid., no. LXII); occ. 20 March 1378 (DCD, Misc. Ch. 5098); accounts 31 May 1378 to 3 Oct. 1379 (*Jarrow and Wearmouth*, nos. LXIII–IV).

The next recorded master, **Thomas Legat**, accounts from 27 Sept. 1381 (ibid., no. LXV).

KIDWELLY (Carmarthen), St Mary (Sherborne) f. 1114

List in D. Daven Jones, *A History of Kidwelly* (Carmarthen, 1908), pp. 54–5.

Abraham Occ. 1231 x 1247 (*St Davids Acta*, no. 99; *Welsh Episcopal Acts*, I, p. 375, no. 546).

Gervase 1286– Letter of J., abb. of Sherborne, to Pain de Chaworth, requesting his ass. as patron of Kidwelly to the eln of Gervase, m. of Sherborne, as pr., vacant by d. of unnamed pr. 9 Apr. 1268 (PRO, DL34/1/3).

Ralph of Beaminster (Bemenster) **–1284** Dep. by Archbp Pecham, ordered to be recalled to Sherborne 22 Aug. 1284 (*Reg. Peckham*, III, 810–11; Cowley, *Monastic Order in South Wales*, p. 107).

Geoffrey of Coker Occ. 15 Oct. 1301 (*Mon.*, IV, 64, no. i); 15 Oct. 1301 (PRO, E328/144 (1); *Hist. Kidwelly*, app. I, p. 111); n.d. late 13th or early 14th cent. (PRO, E315/44/212); 29 Sept. year illeg. (PRO, E315/49/270).

Richard de Coker Occ. 13 May 1310 (*Reg. Gandavo*, II, 742).

The next recorded pr., **Philip Morevyle**, m. of Sherborne, received the ratification of his estate as pr. of Kidwelly 10 May 1399 (*CPR 1396–99*, p. 521).[16]

KILPECK (Hereford) (Gloucester) f. 1134

List in *Heads*, I, 92.

Richard Occ. 27 Oct. 1219 x 7 Aug. 1234 (*EEA*, 7, no. 327; *Ctl. Gloucester*, II, 224).

John Occ. 25 Mar. 1262 (Hereford Cath. mun., no. 725).

William of Shrivenham (Schrivenham) Occ. 4 Sept. 1276 *or* 16 Jan. 1277 (St Marcellus feast-day) (*Ctl. Gloucester*, I, 347); 27 Sept. – 1 Oct. 1284 (ibid., III, 22–4, 26).

Thomas Occ. 16 Apr. 1336 (*CPR 1334–38*, p. 287).

John de Longen' Occ. 7 Dec. 1353 (Hereford Cath. mun., no. 2734).

[**John Hancok**, vicar of Dewchurch and **John le Waren'** occ. as guardians of the priory 4 Nov. 1388 (ibid., no. 726).]

The next recorded pr., **William Coveley**, occ. 1403 (ibid., no. 2628).

---

[16] *Hist. Kidwelly* lists Robert Dunsterr as pr. in 1346 and John Flode in 1361, but no sources.

KINGS LYNN (Norfolk), St Margaret (Lynn) (Norwich Cathedral) f. *c.*1100
  Lists in *VCH Norfolk*, II, 329; *Heads*, I, 93; H.J. Hillen, *History of the Borough of King's Lynn*, II, 868–70; biographical details in Greatrex, *Biog. Reg.*, pp. 466–576 (Norwich monks)
Adam Mentd as late pr. in cht. *temp.* pr. John de Hoxnedis, n.d. (early 13th cent.: pal.) (Norfolk RO, DCN.44/76/165).
Nicholas Occ. *c.* 1200 (Owen, *King's Lynn*, p. 77, no. 12).
John of Oxnead (Hoxnedis) Occ. n.d. (early 13th cent.: pal.) (Norfolk RO, DCN.44/76/165).
John Grym Occ. *c.* Mich. 1239 (Norfolk RO, DCN.44/81/2).
Alexander Occ. as 'pr. of St Margaret's' 12 June 1245 (*Lincs F.*, II, p. 18).
Nicholas of Rattlesden Occ. n.d. (mid/late-13th cent.: pal.) (Norfolk RO, DCN.44/76/140).
Adam of Shipdham (Schipdam) Called late pr. in 1285 (*Mon.*, IV, 463) but source not found (cf. Greatrex, pp. 554–5).
Guy Occ. 1291–2 (*Communar Rolls*, p. 61), possibly to be identified with Guy de Sancto Edmundo who occ. as a m. of Norwich in 1288 (*Norwich Cath. Chts.*, I, no. 155; Greatrex, p. 552).
John Occ. Trin. 1298 (PRO, KB27/155, m. 9), possibly the same as the next pr.
John of Bromholm (Brompholm) Occ. 5 Feb. 1310 (Norwich, Reg/1/1, f. 35r); 24 July 1313 (*CPR 1313–17*, p. 57); 26 Dec. 1313 (PRO, Just.1/612, m. 2). D. 1321–2, possibly still as pr. of Lynn (DCN, 1/5/6).
J. de Stocton Addressed as pr. of Lynn by pr. Robert of Norwich in a letter on behalf of a nephew of John of Bromholm after the latter's death *c.* 1321 x 1326 (DCN, Reg. IX, f. 32r).
John of Stratton (Strattone) Occ. 19 Feb. 1326 (Norwich, Reg/1/2, f. 79v).
Ralph of Mundesley (Monesele) Occ. 7 Sept. 1332 (ibid., f. 53r).
John de Mari D.Th. Occ. 27 Sept. 1342 (Norwich, Reg/1/3, f. 61v). D. 1343–4, but not necessarily as pr. of Lynn (DCN, 1/5/12). See Emden, *BRUO*, II, 1221–2.
Laurence of Tunstall Occ. 7 Dec. 1361 (Owen, *King's Lynn*, p. 106, no. 87); pr. of Yarmouth by 1366 (q.v.).
Nicholas Occ. 23 Apr. 1372 (Norfolk RO, DCN.44/76/102); 25 Mar. 1374 (Owen, *King's Lynn*, p. 87, no. 53).
Ralph of Martham Occ. Mich. 1372–Mich. 1373, 1379–Jan. 1393 (DCN, 2/1/2–20); 1375–6 (Owen, *King's Lynn*, p. 122, no. 106) and 1377 (ibid., p. 149, no. 162). By 25 Jan. 1393 had d. at Lynn (DCN, 2/1/20).

LAMANNA (Cornwall), St Michael (Glastonbury) f. -1114; in 1239 Glastonbury had lic. to dispose of it (see Oliver, p. 70; *KH*, p. 69).
  List in *Heads* I, 93.
Elias Occ. prob. early 13th cent., dated by O.J. Padel to 1199 x 1220 (see Oliver, p. 70; from *Ad. Dom.*, II, Auct., pp. 599–600; *Heads*, I, 93; O.J. Padel in L. Abrams and J.P. Carley, eds., *The Archaeology and History of Glastonbury Abbey*, pp. 253–4).

LEOMINSTER (Hereford), St Peter and St Paul (Reading) f. *c.* 666; 1139 (deans/priors)
  List in *Heads*, I, 93, cf. B.R. Kemp, 'The monastic deans of Leominster', *EHR*, 83 (1968), 505–15.
Walter −1221 Occ. (W.) 1216 x 1219 (*EEA*, 7, nos. 301–2); 1216 x 1221 (ibid., no. 315); 1220 (PRO, E329/186). El as abb. of Shrewsbury 1221 (q.v.).
Adam of Lathbury (Latebiry) −1226 El. as abb. of Reading 1226 (q.v.).
Thomas Occ. as dean 1226 x 1234 (*Ctl. Reading*, I, no. 364; *EEA*, 7, no. 353); 1239, after 8 Apr. (BL, Cotton ms. Domitian A. III, f. 96v).

Hubert Occ. n.d. (ibid., f. 169r, with Walter de la Lee who also occ. in a cht. of 1251, ibid.). Occ. as former pr. with pr. Roger de Lilford (ibid., ff. 134v, 135r).

Roger de Lilford Occ. n.d. (late 13th cent. entries) (ibid., ff. 134v, 135r, 167v), on two occasions with former pr. Hubert.

[Appt of Roland de Herlegh, knight, to custody of the priory which had fallen into debt, 26 Dec. 1275 (*CPR 1272–81*, p. 128, cf. *Reg. Cantilupe*, pp. 37–8).]

Stephen de Wattone (Waketon) –1281 Occ. 11 Jan. 1277, 6 Sept. 1279 (*Reg. Cantilupe*, pp. 116, 218); occ. as dean 1 May 1277 (BL, Cotton ms. Domitian A III, f. 140v); n.d. (ibid., ff. 140r, 162v, 165r). Unnamed pr. seems to have been removed by by abb. of Reading 7 May 1281 (ibid., pp. 269–70, 296). Stephen mentd as recalled and William de Kyntone apptd, in letter of 5 July 1281 (*Reg. Swinfield*, pp. 38–41).

William of Kinton (Kyntone) 1281– Succ. Stephen 1281 (ibid.).

John Gerard (Gerand, Geraud, Geroud) Occ. 4 Apr. 1282 (*CPR 1281–92*, p. 14); 6 Apr. 1283 (*Reg. Swinfield*, p.15); 28 Mar. 1284 (*CCR 1279–88*, p. 294). Mentd as former pr. 19 June 1287 – request to the abb. of Reading to discipline him on account of his incontinence with many women (*Reg. Swinfield*, p. 149).

[Appt of John de Bruges, king's clerk, to custody of the cell for 4 years, the monastery being in debt and under the king's protection, 18 Oct. 1285 (*CPR 1281–92*, p. 197).]

Stephen de Wabeton Occ. 21 Apr. 1292 (PRO, E315/47/153; *Records of Wroxall*, p. 13, n. 30). Prob. same as above –1281.

Walter de Meders Occ. as dean 1290 x 1305, *temp.* abb. William of Reading (*EHR*, 83, 509, citing BL, Cotton ms. Domitian A III, ff. 161v–162r).

William of Finchampstead (Fynchampstede) Occ. 17 June 1332 *qui se gerit pro priore de L.* (*Reg. T. Charlton*, p. 16).

John of Gloucester (Gloucestre, Gloucestria) Occ. n.d. (between entries Nov. 1346 x Feb. 1347) (*Reg. Trillek*, p. 107); 20 July 1347 – shortly to be recalled to Reading (ibid., p. 304; BL, Cotton ms. Domitian A III, f. 52r–v).

William of Dumbleton –1361 Occ. as 'monastic dean' 2 Oct. 1359 (*JSA*, 7, no. 8 (1985), p. 518). El. as abb. of Reading 1361 (q.v.).

Robert Han . . . rd Mentd as dean in inqn of 1386, from the context prob. *c.* 1380 (*Cal. Misc. Inq.*, IV, no. 368).

Note

Robert de Arcubus occ. without date (BL, Cotton ms. Domitian A III, f. 171r) and cannot be placed in the sequence with any accuracy. The entry in the ctl. is in a mid-late 13th cent. hand.

LEONARD STANLEY (Glos), St Leonard (Gloucester) f. 1121 x 30 (Aug.); 1146 (Ben.) Lists in *VCH Glos.*, II, 73; *Heads*, I, 93.

William of Cirencester Occ. ?Jan. x Aug. 1203 (Cheney, *Inn. III*, no. 505).

Peter Occ. *c.* 1230 (Gloucester Cath. Lib., Seals and Documents, V, 1; cf. *Archaeologia*, 71 (1921), pp. 210–11 (1230 x 1238)).

Thomas de Lakinton Occ. 1263 x 1284, *temp.* Abb. R(eginald) of Gloucester (Hereford Cath. mun. 742). Seal (*Hereford Seals*, p. 9).

Thomas de Tyringham Occ. 27 Sept. – 1 Oct. 1284 (*Ctl. Gloucester*, III, 22–4); 23 Apr. 1295 (Worcester Cath. mun. B.563).

Maurice of Minsterworth –1362 Occ. 21 Aug. 1361 (Walker, *Eccles. Miscellany*, p. 38, no. 96). Abb. of Alcester 1362 (q.v.).

Richard Occ. 1378 x 1379 (PRO, E179/58/5, m. 2).

The next recorded pr., **John Crosse**, occ. 1449 (*Mon. Angl.*, IV, 469).

LINCOLN, St Mary Magdalen (York, St Mary) f. *c.* 1135 (?)
> List in *Heads*, I, 93. The following list is taken from the *Ch. of St Mary's York* (pp. 79–80 and *passim*) and except for a few added items is unsupported by any other authority. The order may be correct but where dates of death are given it must be remembered that the priors of the York dependencies were moved around and the man at that date may no longer have been in office at Lincoln.

Hugh Occ. prob. 1210 (*Reg. Ant. Lincoln*, VIII, no. 2304, cf. editor's note).

William of Rothwell (Rothwelle) **–1262** Occ. 1258 (*Ch. York*, p. 4). M. and priest of St Mary's, York. D. at Lincoln 8 Feb. 1262 (ibid., pp. 5–6, 79). Called Robert p. 79. *See also* St Bees.

Robert of Cawood (Kawode, Kauode) **1262–1268** Succ. William of Rothwell (ibid., p. 7). M. and priest of St Mary's, York. D. 28 Sept. 1268 (ibid., p. 13).

Gilbert of Leverton After Robert of Cawood in list. Occ. n.d. (ibid., p. 79); Easter x Trin. terms 1275 (*Select Cases in the Exchequer of Pleas*, pp. 72–3); Mich. 1278 (PRO, KB27/41, m. 52).

Henry of Fangfoss (Fangfosse) Occ. 1283 (*Ch. York*, p. 79). *Plumbarius* of York 1286 (ibid., p. 23).

Walter of Leicester (Leycestria) Occ. 1285 (ibid., p. 79). D. at York 24 Oct. 1299, '*predicator optimus*' (ibid., p. 30). Received 1260, '*bonus scolaris in arte dialectica*' (ibid., p. 5); attended the Council of Lyons 1274 (ibid., p. 16).

Henry of Fangfoss *dictus* Scot Occ. second time on list, n.d. (ibid., p. 79). D. 5 Feb. 1304 at Richmond and bur. there (ibid., p. 38).

William de Bracton (Braxton) After Hugh of Fangfoss (2nd time) in the list, ? an error. Occ. n.d. (ibid., p. 79). Pr. of Lincoln 1290 x ?1293 (ibid., p. 24). Chamberlain at York 1295 (ibid., p. 25). D. 20 Apr. 1312 at Rumburgh (ibid., p. 53). *See also* Henes.

John de Birne (Byrne) Occ. n.d. (ibid., p. 79). Occ. Mar. 1297 (*CPR 1292–1301*, p. 268; *CCR 1296–1302*, p. 96). *See also* Henes, Rumburgh.

Lambert of Moulton (Multona) Occ. n.d. (*Ch. York*, p. 79). *See also* Rumburgh.

Hugh de Competon Occ. n.d. (ibid., p. 79). D. 21 May 1314 at York after being five years in the infirmary, and having been professed for 47 years (ibid., p. 65). *See also* St Bees.

Stephen of Austwick (Austewik, Oustewyk) Occ. n.d. (ibid., p. 79). *See also* Rumburgh, St Bees. Assaulted at 'La Maudelyne' cell, Lincoln, 1311, 1312 (*CPR 1307–13*, pp. 419–20, 471). Afterwards sacrist of St Mary's.

Adam of Thwing (Tweng) Occ. as pr. of Lincoln 4 July 1313 (*Ch. York*, p. 62). Ruled 4 years (ibid., p. 79). D. 21 Mar. 1318 (obit, ibid., p. 135).

William of Towthorpe (Thouthorpe) Pr. 2 years (ibid., p. 79). M. at York 1293 (ibid., p. 136). *See also* Rumburgh.

Thomas of Dalton Made pr. 5 July [no year given] (ibid., p. 80).

LINDISFARNE, *see* **HOLY ISLAND**

LITTLE MALVERN (Worcs), St Giles (Worcester) (Malvern) f. 1171
> Lists in *VCH Worcs*, II, 147; *Heads*, I, 94.

William Norman **–1222** Occ. (W.) 1200 x 1212 (*CDF*, no. 281). El. pr. of Worcester 1222 (*Ann. Worcs*, pp. 415–17; see under Worcester).

Roger Occ. 6 Oct. 1227 (PRO, Hereford F., CP25/1/80/7, no. 107).

Richard **–1269** Occ. 6 Oct. 1233 (PRO, Worcs F., CP25/1/258/4, no. 15); 1236 (PRO, Hereford F., CP25/1/80/8, no. 126); 1238 (PRO, Worcs F. CP25/1/258/5, no. 14); 1253 (*Ctl. Eynsham*, I, no. 205); 1255 (PRO, Worcs F., CP25/1/258/7, no. 48; Hereford F.,

CP25/1/80/13, no. 269); 1262 (Worcester RO, BA3814.ref.821, f. 59v); 1264 (Hereford Cath. mun. 394); 1265 (WAM, no. 22939). D. by 18 Apr. 1269 (*Reg. G. Giffard*, p. 7). ? Seal (*Hereford Seals*, p. 8).

William of Broadway (Bradeweie) **1269–** Inst. 18 Apr. 1269 (*Reg. G. Giffard*, p. 7). Occ. 18 Nov. 1272 (PRO, C115/58/4084).

John de Shockeleg' **–1280** Occ. 5 Feb. 1274 (ibid., pp. 65, 114); 20 Dec. 1275 (BL, Sloane Cht. XXXIII. 14); Easter 1278 (PRO, CP40/26, m. 46). D. by 1 July 1280 (*Reg. G. Giffard*, p. 122).

John de Colewell (Colevylle) **1280–1286** M. of Little Malvern, apptd and ind. 1 July 1280 (ibid.). Res. 4 Dec. 1286 (ibid., p. 300, cf. p. 330).

John of Worcester (Wigorn', Wygorn(ia)) **1287–1299** Letter to convent to obey new pr. 23 May 1287 in place of John of Colewell (ibid., p. 330). D. by 4 Nov. 1299 (ibid., p. 513, but cf. *Reg. Winchelsey*, II, 865, when he occ. as former pr., provision having been made for him by the archbp in his visitation injunctions 28 July 1301).

John of Dumbleton (Dombleton, Dumbletone) **1299–1300** M. of Worcester, apptd 4 Nov. 1299; mand. to install 17 Nov. 1299 (ibid.; *Ann. Worcs*, p. 542). Res. Christmas 1300, but not acc. by chapter of Worcester (ibid., p. 548). 25 Mar. 1302 Dumbleton still claiming to be pr. and staying at Oxford until a decision was arrived at by the Benedictine General Chapter (*Worcs Reg. Sede Vacante*, pp. 2–3). See Greatrex, p. 800.

William de Molendinis 1301–1303 Apptd ('imposed') by bp 17 Jan. 1301 (*Ann. Worcs*, p. 548). Occ. 11 Mar. 1301 (*Worcs Reg. Sede Vacante*, p. 73). Res. 4 Oct. 1303 in visitation, res. acc. 17 Oct. 1303 (*Reg. Gainsborough*, p. 77).

Roger de Pyribroke (Piriebrok, Pyrie) **1303–1326** M. of Little Malvern, apptd 19 Oct. 1303 (ibid.). Res. deed dated 9 Apr. 1326 (*Reg. Cobham*, pp. 198–9).

Hugh de Pyribroke (Piribrok) **1326–1360** Adm. 10 Apr. 1326 (ibid., p. 246). Occ. 9 Jan. 1360 (Worcester, Reg. Brian, I, p. 61). D. by 25 June 1360 (ibid., p. 63).

Henry of Staunton (Stanton) **1360–1369** M. of Little Malvern, apptd 25 June 1360 (ibid., pp. 63–4). D. by 29 Nov. 1369 (Worcester, Reg. Lenn, pp. 45–6).

John of Worcester (Wygornia) **1369–** M. of Little Malvern, apptd 29 Nov. 1369 (ibid.). Occ. 18 Sept. 1373 (WAM no. 32665).

Richard of Wenlock (Wenlak) **1379–1392** Given lic. to go to Little Malvern as pr. 16 Feb. 1379 (Worcester, Liber Albus, f. 271v). Res. by 24 Oct. 1392 (*Reg. Wakefield*, no. 708). Greatrex, p. 890.

LYNN, *see* KING'S LYNN

LYTHAM (Lancs), St Cuthbert (Durham) f. 1189 x 1199 (AJP)

List kindly provided by Mr A.J. Piper from his biographical register of Durham monks (forthcoming); other lists in *VCH Lancs*, II, 110; *Heads*, I, 94; H. Fishwick, *The history of the parish of Lytham in the county of Lancaster* (Chetham Soc., new ser. 60, 1907), pp. 70–2.

Clement Occ. before 13 Dec. 1234 (*Ann. Durham*, pp. 119–20).

Thomas Occ. 22 July 1250 (PRO, E315/40/6).

William Mentd in 1287 x 1288 as former pr. *temp.* Henry III, before 50 Henry III (Oct. 1265 x Oct. 1266) (*SHC*, IX, p. 108). See *Heads*, I, 94 for dating of ref. to pr. William in doct of 1325 (DCD, 2.4.Ebor.41).

Stephen Occ. 5 Jan. 1259 (DCD, 2.2.4.Ebor.36); poss. the pr. S. who occ. 23 June 1262 (*Ann. Durham*, p. 120). Prob. the same as below.

Stephen of Dalton Occ. before 14 Apr. 1268 (*Ann. Durham*, p. 120; *Reg. R. Gravesend*, p. 148).

Stephen Occ. 9 Feb. 1272 (DCD, 2.4.Ebor.14a).

Stephen of Durham Occ. late 13th cent. (DCD, 1.2.4.Ebor.12).

Walter of Norton Occ. before 7 Dec. 1283 (DCD, Loc.XIV: 2e); 1 Mar. 1284 (DCD, Misc. Cht. 5820/14).

Richard de Hoton –1290 apptd and removed 11 Jan. 1286 x 11 Mar. 1290 (*Scriptores Tres*, p. 72). El. pr. of Durham 24 Mar. 1290 (ibid., p. 73).

Ambrose of Bamburgh Apptd [11 Jan. 1286 x 11 Mar. 1290] (*Ann. Durham*, p. 122). Occ. Nov. 1287 x Nov. 1288 (*SHC*, IX, p. 109); 23 May 1288 (DCD, 4.4.Ebor.3d). Mentd Sept. 1296 as former pr. (DCD, Misc. Chts. 3668).

Henry of Faceby Occ. 30 July 1291 (PRO, Just.1/407, m.3); n.d. (DCD, 1.2.4.Ebor.13).

Walter of Craven *alias* **of Giggleswick** Occ. 14 June 1300 (DCD, Misc. Cht. 5526).

Robert of Ditchburn Occ. 4 May 1307 (DCD, Misc. Chts. 5456).

Geoffrey of Burdon Occ. 31 Mar. 1311 (DCD, Loc.VI: 9a). See Emden, *BRUO*, I, 307. Pr. of Finchale *c.* 1303–8; pr. of Durham 1313–21; master of Monkwearmouth *c.* 1321–33 (q.v.).

Roger of Stanhope Held office before Roger of Tynemouth below (DCD, Lytham status 1338); occ. (Roger) 1 Nov. 1316 (DCD, Loc.XVI: 1). Perhaps pr. R. who occ. 2 July 1313 x 25 Jan. 1321 (DCD, Misc. Cht. 5560).

Roger of Tynemouth 1320– Pres. 22 Apr. 1320 (DCD, Misc. Cht. 5622). Occ. 6 Feb., 2 Mar. 1321 (DCD, Loc.XIII: 3b–c); 11 Nov. 1325 (DCD, 2.2.4.Ebor.25). Pr. of St Leonard's, Stamford from 1308 (q.v.).

John of Barnby Occ. (John) 28 July 1331 (*Reg. Burghersh*, I, no. 1012); 20 Mar. 1332 (DCD, 3.4.Ebor.33). Pr. of Finchale *c.* 1344–46 (q.v.).

Emery of Lumley Occ. 15 Oct. 1333 (*Scriptores Tres*, p. 120). Pr. of Finchale *c.* 1339–42; master of Jarrow to 1344 (q.v.).

Hugh of Woodburn Drew up status 9 Oct. 1338; 30 Apr. 1341, 21 Apr., 9 Oct. 1342 (DCD, Lytham status 1338, 1341, 1342A–B). Master of Monkwearmouth *c.* 1343–45 (q.v.).

Robert of Cambois 1342–1349 Adm. 31 Oct. 1342 (DCD, Lytham Ac. 1342–3). Drew up status 11 June 1343, 7 June 1344, 29 May 1346, 14 May 1347, 2 June 1348 (DCD, Lytham status 1343–4, 1346–8). House void 1349 (*EHR*, V (1890), 526). Pr. of St Leonard's, Stamford 1333–38 (q.v.).

Simon of Darlington 1349–1351 Pres. 28 Oct. 1349 (DCD, Reg., II, f. 138r). Left office 6 July 1351 (DCD, Lytham Ac. 1351–2).

Robert of Kelloe 1351–1362 Adm., inst. and inducted 9 July 1351 (DCD, 2.4.Ebor.35, 39). Accounts [6 July 1351]–22 May 1357, 14 May 1358–30 May 1362 (DCD, Lytham Ac.). Occ. 5 Aug. 1354, 20 Oct. 1354, 10 Jan. 1355, 17 Mar. 1355, 14 Apr. 1355 (Durham, Reg. Hatfield, ff. 17r, 18v, 19r, 20v, 23v). In 1361 Robert obtained a bull from Innocent VI granting that during his lifetime he was not to be moved from Lytham by his superior without good reason. The pr. of Durham demanded he give up the bull and renounce any rights it gave him (*Arch. Aeliana*, 4th ser., XXXVI, 96). Left office by 5 June 1362 (DCD, Lytham status 1362).

John of Normanby 1362–1373 Pres. 4 June 1362, adm. 28 June 1362, inducted 3 July 1362 (DCD, Misc. Cht. 5622; 2.4.Ebor.34). Occ. 29 Dec. 1356 (DCD, 3.4.Ebor.14a). Seal (*Durham Seals*, II, p. 573, no. 3510). Pr. of Finchale 1373–75; Holy Island 1379–82 (q.v.).

Richard of Birtley 1373– [Apptd] 29 Sept. 1373, adm. 24 Oct. 1373, inducted 29 Oct. 1373 (DCD, Misc. Cht. 5622; 2.4.Ebor.38; 3.4.Ebor.31). Accounts 7 Oct. 1373–24 Sept. 1379 (DCD, Lytham Ac. and Ac. B.). Occ. 11 Dec. 1374 (DCD, Loc.XIII: 8a). Said to have striven to be relieved as pr. (DCD, Loc.IX: 14). Pr. of Finchale 1369–73 (q.v.); master of Farne 1380.

The next recorded pr., **William of Aslackby**, adm. 25 Oct. 1379 (*Reg. Archdny Richmond*, p. 186, no. 135).

MALVERN, *see* **GREAT MALVERN, LITTLE MALVERN**

MIDDLESBOROUGH (Yorks N.), St Hilda (cell of Whitby) f. *c.* 1120 x 30
   List in *VCH Yorks*, III, 106.
Thomas de Haukesgarth (Hakisgarth) The abb. of Whitby 1322–56 had the same name, but
   ? another person. Occ. as pr. Mich. 1386 (*Ctl. Whitby*, II, p. 504, no. 562); 4 Sept. 1393 (ibid.,
   p. 316, no. 377, cf.Young, *History of Whitby*, I, 391n.).
The next recorded pr., **Stephen of Ormesby**, occ. 25 Jan. 1398 (*YAJ*, XVIII, 68, n.1, citing
   York, Reg. 5A, f. 234v).

MONKWEARMOUTH (Durham), St Peter (Durham) f. 674; *c.* 1075 (as priory); Cell of
Durham by 1235 (AJP)
   List kindly provided by Mr A.J. Piper from his biographical register of Durham monks (in
   preparation); other lists in *VCH Durham*, II, 85 from *Jarrow and Wearmouth*, ed. J. Raine;
   Heads, I, 92.

MASTERS
Richard of School Aycliffe Occ. 7 Nov. 1310 (DCD, 2.2.Archd.Dun.19); 31 Mar., 2 Apr. 1311
   (DCD Lib. ms. B.II.1, f. 270r); 3 June, autumn 1315 (DCD, Loc.IV: 59; Loc.IV: 50).
Robert of Durham Said [*c.* Dec. 1320] to have been apptd improperly (DCD, Loc.XXVII:
   30–1). Occ. 18 Jan. 1321 (DCD, Misc. Cht. 4554). Drew up status 11 May 1321 [?left office]
   (*Jarrow and Wearmouth*, p. 139). Master of Jarrow 1321 (q.v.).
[**Geoffrey of Burdon** Assigned cell on res. as pr. of Durham 25 Jan. 1321; in possession 15 Oct.
   1333 (*Scriptores Tres*, pp. 102, 120). See Emden, *BRUO*, I, 307. Also pr. of Oxford cell
   1302–3; pr. of Finchale *c.* 1303–8; pr. of Lytham 1311 (q.v.).]
John of Howden In office 6, 13 Nov. 1334 x 30 Apr. 1335 (DCD, Bursar's acct 1334–5).
Alan of Marton Occ. '1335' (DCD, Loc.II: 6). Delivered status 24 Jan. 1338 [?left office]
   (*Jarrow and Wearmouth*, p. 141).
John Fossour ?1338–1340 [?took office] took delivery of status 24 Jan. 1338 (ibid.). Occ.
   1338–1340 (DCD, Loc.II: 6). Pres. as pr. of Coldingham 8 Jan. 1340 (BL, Cotton ms.
   Faustina A VI, f. 55r; *Priory of Coldingham*, p. xvi). El. prior of Durham 16 Mar. 1341 (q.v.).
   Previously pr. of St Leonard's, Stamford to 1333 (q.v.).
Hugh of Woodburn Occ. *c.* 19 Jan. 1343 (*Reg. Bury*, p. 155). Accounts 9 June 1343 – 1 June
   1348 (*Jarrow and Wearmouth*, pp. 143, 145–6, 148, 150). Occ. 29 Apr. 1345 (DCD, Misc.
   Cht. 2636). Pr. of Lytham *c.* 1338–42 (q.v.).
[**John of Norton** Accounts 18 Oct. 1349 – 10 May 1350 (*Jarrow and Wearmouth*, p. 151 –
   Neuton' *recte* Norton). Occ. as pr. of Finchale *c.* 1352; master of Jarrow to 1355 (q.v.).]
John of Shaftoe Occ. [23 July], 5, 25 Aug. 1354 (DCD, 1.8.Pont.1; Durham, Reg. Hatfield, f.
   17r; DCD, 2.8.Pont.5, 9); [11 Nov. 1357 x 26 May 1358] (DCD, 1.9.Pont.16); 11 Nov. 1359
   x 11 Nov. 1360 (DCD, Bursar's Ac. 1359–60). Drew up *status* [?left office] 6 Aug. 1360
   (*Jarrow and Wearmouth*, p. 152). Master of Farne *c.* 1344–5 (q.v.). Noted as having medical
   knowledge (DCD, 2.8.Pont.12).
Richard of Beckingham Accounts 10 Aug. 1360 – 30 May 1362 (ibid., pp. 154–5). Drew up
   status [?left office] 11 Sept. 1362 (ibid., p. 158). Pr. of Holy Island 1362–3 (q.v.).
[**John of Goldsborough** accounted shortly before 31 May 1367 (ibid., p. 161). Occ. as master
   of Jarrow 1357–8; pr. of Holy Island 1358–61 (q.v.)]
John of Newton Accounts 31 May 1367 – 14 May 1369 (ibid.). Pr. of Finchale 1360–63
   (q.v.).
John of Bishopton Accounts 10 Aug. 1369 – 23 May 1384 (ibid., pp. 162, 166–71, 174–7); 15
   May 1385 – 22 Feb. 1386 (DCD, Wearmouth Ac. 1385–6B). Occ. 11 Dec. 1374 (DCD,
   Loc.XIII: 8a); 1379 (PRO, E179/62/4 m. 2); 30 May 1381 (DCD, Reg., II, f. 199r). See also
   Emden, *BRUO*, I, 194.

The next recorded master, **John of Aycliffe**, accounts from [4 June 1386] to 11 May 1388 (*Jarrow and Wearmouth*, p. 178).

MORVILLE (Salop), St George f. *c.* 1138 (as cell of Shrewsbury)
  List in *VCH Salop*, II, 30.
John Occ. Mich. 1220 (*CRR*, IX, 313).
John Wallensis Occ. 28 May 1253 (Eyton, *Salop*, I, 38 & n. 26).
John Perle Occ. 15 June 1353 (*Reg. Trillek*, pp. 176, 177).
Walter Occ. 11 Sept. 1364 (PRO, E32/308).
The next recorded pr., **Ralph de Wybunbury**, m. of Shrewsbury, occ. 4 Feb. 1398 (PRO, C67/30 m. 33).

NORWICH, St Leonard (Norwich cathedral priory) f. *c.* 1095; dep. on cathedral after *c.* 1101.
  List in *VCH Norfolk*, II, 329; biographical details in Greatrex, *Biog. Reg.*, pp. 466–576 (Norwich monks).
William of Yaxham (Jakisham, Jaxham) Occ. 1345–6 and poss. before. D. at St Leonard's (Norfolk RO, DCN, 1/12/25).
John of Hingham (Hengham) Occ. 1348 (ibid., DCN.2/3/7).
Walter of Stockton (Stokton(e)) Occ. Mich. 1349 – Mich. 1350 (ibid., DCN.2/3/1).
Simon Bozoun (Bosonii) **1352–** Pr. of Norwich cathedral 1342–52; apptd pr. of St Leonard's 30 Aug. 1352 (ibid., DCN, Reg. X, f. 40r).
John of Hethersett (Haterset, Hedersett, Hedirset(e), Hetersete, Hoderset) Papal lic. to choose a confessor 18 Jan. 1353 (*CPL*, III, 492). Occ. Mich. 1353 – Mich. 1357 (Norfolk RO, DCN.2/3/2–5).
William of Rickinghall (Rykinghale) Occ. Mich. 1358 – Mich. 1366, 1369 (ibid., DCN.2/3/6–7).
John of Happisburgh (Hapisburgh, Hasbrough) Occ. Mich. 1368 – Mich. 1376 (Norfolk RO, DCN.2/3/6–8).
Richard of Blakeney (Blakene(e), Blakeneye) Occ. Mich. 1386 – 5 Feb. 1405, except for several months between Sept. 1390 and Feb. 1391 (ibid., DCN.2/3/9–22). D. by 1 Sept. 1405 (ibid., DCN.1/5/35) and obit celebrated 4 Aug. (ibid., DCN, Reg. XI, f. 5v).

OXFORD, Cell of Durham Cathedral Priory (later **DURHAM COLLEGE**) f. 1286 x 1291 (cell); *c.* 1380–1 (Durham College)
  List kindly provided by Mr A.J. Piper from his biographical register of Durham monks (forthcoming). List also in *Collectanea III* (Oxford Historical Society 32, 1896), pp. 23–25. See also M.R. Foster, 'Durham monks at Oxford *c.* 1286–1381: a house of studies and its inmates', *Oxoniensia*, LV (1990), 99–114; *VCH Oxon*, II, 69.
Geoffrey of Burdon Delivered allowance 11 Nov. 1302 x 11 Nov. 1303 (DCD, Bursar's Ac. 1302–3); held office before becoming pr. of Finchale 1303 (DCD, Loc. XXVII: 31). See Emden, *BRUO*, I, 307. Pr. of Durham 1313–21; master of Monkwearmouth *c.* 1321–33 (q.v.).
Gilbert of Elwick Occ. as pr. 6 Nov. 1316 (DCD, Misc. Cht. 2630). See Emden, *BRUO*, I, 637. Pr. of Holy Island from 1328 (q.v.).
John of Beverley senior Occ. as pr. 15 Oct. 1333 (*Scriptores Tres*, p. 120). See Emden, *BRUO*, I, 183. Master of Jarrow *c.* 1339–41; pr. of Finchale *c.* 1344 (q.v.).
Robert of Hallington **1343–** Apptd 24 Sept. 1343 (DCD, Reg. II, f. 117v). Occ. 29 Apr. 1345 (DCD, Misc. Cht. 2636). Pr. of St Leonard's, Stamford 1346 (q.v.).

[**Uthred of Boldon** Received money from the bursar on behalf of monks in Oxford 11 Nov. 1349 x 11 Nov. 1352, 11 Nov. 1358 x 11 Nov. 1360; 5 June 1362 x 5 Mar. 1363; 12 May 1365 x 12 May 1368 (DCD, Bursar's Ac. 1349–52, 1358–60, 1362–3, 1365–8). See Emden, *BRUO*, I, 212–13; D. Knowles, *The Historian and Character and other essays* (Cambridge, 1963), pp. 129–70, bibliography on p. 129, n. 2; Sharpe, *Latin Writers*, pp. 699–702. Pr. of Finchale 1367–9, 1375–83, 1386–96 (q.v.).]

John of Aycliffe Received money from the bursar on behalf of the monks in Oxford 15 Dec. 1371 x 29 Sept. 1379 (DCD, Bursar's Ac. 1371–79). Sub-pr. of Durham 29 Sept. 1378 x 29 Sept. 1379 (ibid., Ac. 1378–9); occ. 20 May 1381 (DCD, Reg. II, f. 200v). See Emden, *BRUO*, I, 10–11. Master of Monkwearmouth from 1386.

The next pr., **Robert of Blacklaw**, was apptd 14 Sept. 1381 (BL, Cotton ms. Faustina A VI, f. 81r).

OXFORD, Cell of Gloucester Abbey (later **GLOUCESTER COLLEGE**), St John the Evangelist and St Benedict (St Benedict) f. 1283 (cell of Gloucester). From 1291 general house of studies under the abbots-president of the English Benedictine province, known as Gloucester College (*KH*, pp. 56, 72). See also *VCH Oxon*, II, 70–1; *Snappe's Formulary*, p. 342).

Henry de Helyon(e) M. of Gloucester. Occ. (H.) as pr. of Oxford 1 Oct. 1284 (*Ctl. Gloucester*, III, 26); pr. of St Benedict, Oxford, Mich. 1286 x Mich. 1287 (PRO, E159/60, m. 14); 11 Sept. 1291 (*Ctl. Winchester*, no. 66). In 1291 it was decided that an independent house of studies should be established under Henry as pr., and Gloucester abbey released him from all subjection and renounced any special claims upon their cell. Henry was apptd pr. of Gloucester College (ibid., no. 62, cf. no. 65; Emden, *BRUO*, II, 905; *Chapters of English Black Monks*, I, 130; *Snappe's Formulary*, p. 345). It appears that this arrangement was not immediately effective since the pr. and monks of Gloucester abbey dwelling at Oxford are mentd in 1295 (*CFR 1272–1307*, p. 366). Further documents about the process of foundation are found in 1298–9 (*Snappe's Formulary*, pp. 342, 345–8, 361–7).

PENWORTHAM (Lancs), St Mary (Evesham) f. -1122(?)

Lists in *VCH Lancs*, II, 106; *Penwortham Docts*, pp. xl–xli; *Heads*, I, 94.

Roger Norreis 1213–1214; 1218 x 19–1224 x 25 Prev. abb. of Evesham, apptd to Penwortham 27 Nov. 1213, held office 5 months then dep.; restored about 5 years later by legate Pandulph (i.e. after 3 Dec. 1218, the effective start of Pandulph's second legation (*CS*, II, I, 52)); held office for 6 years, d. 16 July (*Ch. Evesham*, pp. 251, 253 and n.; *Penwortham Docts*, p. 89).

John Occ. early 13th cent. (*Ctl. Burscough*, p. 140 no. 141).

Thomas of Gloucester −1243 M. of Evesham, pr. of Penwortham, royal ass. to his el. as abb. of Evesham 8 July 1243 (*CPR 1232–47*, p. 385). See Evesham.

Philip de Neldesle Occ. as former *custos* n.d. in cht of abb. John of Evesham (1282–1316) (*Penwortham Docts*, p. 53, no. xliv, ascribed there to *c.* 1290).

Walter de Walecote Occ. as pr. n.d. in cht. of abb. John of Evesham (1282–1316) (ibid., p. 28, no. xxvi, ascribed there to *c.* 1300, but no real evidence for the sequence of these two priors.

Ralph de Wilecote (Wylicote) Occ. as *custos* 1320, 6 Apr. 1320 (ibid., p. 105, cf. p. 97; p. 21, no. xx).

Thomas of Blockley Occ. 'the translation of St Andrew' 1321 (ibid., p. 22, no. xxi).

Ralph de Wylecote Re-apptd. Occ. 1 Feb. 1332 (*CPR 1330–34*, p. 244); 2 July 1341 (*Penwortham Docts*, pp. 54–5, no. xlv).

Ralph de Whateley Occ. 10 Jan. 1350 (ibid., p. 55, no. xlvi).

Roger Occ. 1371 (PRO, KB27/442, m. 244).

The next recorded pr., **William de Mersehton**, occ. 26 May 1383 (*Penwortham Docts*, p. 56, no. xlvii).

PILTON (Devon), St Mary (Malmesbury) f. 12th cent.
List in *Heads*, I, 95.
J. Occ. n.d. (1199 x 1208, ?1206 x 1208 (*Ctl. Buckland*, no. 206; ex inf. Professor B.R. Kemp).
John Occ. 30 June 1228 (*Devon F.*, I, p. 116, no. 240).
Adam de Beteslegh(e) 1261–1282 Letter of pres. of abb. of Malmesbury (A. de B., *in margin* Adam) 5 Dec. 1260, inspected by bp 16 Dec. (*Ctl. Malmesbury*, II, 79); adm. 4 May 1261 (*Reg. Bronescombe*, p. 162; *Reg. W. Bronescombe*, I, no. 330). D. by 29 Aug. 1282 (*Reg. Quivil*, p. 351).
Richard de Iweleghe (Ouppelegh) 1282– Inst. 29 Aug. 1282 (ibid.). Occ. 7 May 1283 (Oliver, *Supplement*, p. 21).
John de Stanleghe 1283– Adm. 2 Dec. 1283 (*Reg. Quivil*, p. 351).
William de Wrockeshale –1316 Occ. 13 Nov. 1311 (*Reg. Stapeldon*, p. 35). Warned about behaviour 27 Dec. 1311 (ibid., p. 314). D. by 29 Apr. 1316 (ibid., p. 242; *Reg. Bytton*, p. 421).
Henry de Pekynghulle 1316–1336 M. of Malmesbury, inst. 29 Apr. 1316 (ibid.). Absolution for marrying a couple without lic. or banns 24 Mar. 1332; letter from papal penitentiary 23 Feb. (*Reg. Grandisson*, II, 642). Res. by 19 May 1336 (ibid., III, 1312).
John de Lokyngham (Lakenham) 1336–1349 M. of Malmesbury, priest, inst. 19 May 1336 (ibid.). Collector for archdeaconry of Cornwall 18 June 1340 (ibid., I, 63). D. by 7 May 1349 (ibid., III, 1386).
Simon de Aveneye 1349 M. of Malmesbury, inst. 7 May 1349 (ibid.).
John of Rodbourne (Rodebourne) 1349–?1361 M. of Malmesbury, inst. 12 Oct. 1349, no reason given for vacancy (ibid., III, 1400). Occ. Mich. 1351 (PRO, KB27/365, rex roll m. 23). Priory vacant 16 Dec. 1361 by death of last (unnamed) pr., and sequestrators apptd (ibid., 1235).
Thomas Brokeneborwe 1362– M. of Malmesbury, inst. 25 Jan. 1362, no reason given for vacancy (ibid., 1473).
Richard Totton Occ. 22 Nov. 1373 (*Reg. Brantingham*, I, 319); n.d. (?1377) (PRO, E179/24/10b); n.d. (?1379 x 1381) (PRO, E179/24/10a, m. 3).
The next recorded pr., **William**, occ. 22 Feb. 1391 (*Reg. Brantingham*, II, 721).

REDBOURN (Herts), St Amphibalus (St Albans) f. *c.* 1198 +
Lists in *VCH Herts*, IV, 418; *Heads*, I, 95.
Martin Occ. 17 Dec. 1215 (*Ctl. Dunstable*, no. 391).
Gilbert of Sisserfens (Sisseverne) Occ. 1218 x 1235 (*GASA*, I, 289).
Vincent –1249 D. 27 Jan. 1249 (*MPCM*, VI, 277).
Geoffrey of St Albans (de Sancto Albano) Occ. 7 Nov. 1290 (*GASA*, II, 7).
Richard de Hatford Occ. Jan. 1302 but dep. soon after (ibid., 53–4).
J. Woderove Mentd in connection with agreement of 1383 as *bone memorie* pr. of Redbourn, *temp.* Thomas de la Mare, abb. of St Albans (1349–96) (*GASA*, III, 258). It is not known exactly where he should be placed in the sequence of priors.
John of Rickmansworth (Rykemersworth) Occ. 6 May 1376 (*CCR 1385–89*, p. 631).
William of Flamstead (Flamstede) Occ. 1380 (BL, Cotton ms. Nero D. VII, f. 81v).

RICHMOND (Yorks N.), St Martin (York, St Mary) f. 1100 x 1137
Lists in *VCH Yorks*, III, 112; *Ch. York*, pp. 78–9; *Heads*, I, 95.
John of Poppleton (Popilton) Occ. Mich. 1258 – Hil. 1259 (Baildon, I, 174); 24 June 1258 (*Ch. York*, p. 3).

Michael *dictus* **Roundel** (Rondele) Former pr., d. 7 Sept. 1281 as pr. York (ibid., p. 21). Follows John of Poppleton in list (ibid., p. 79).

Geoffrey of Monkton (Monketon) –1295 Occ. 1290 x ?1293 (ibid., p. 24). D. as pr. of Richmond 8 June 1295 and bur. there (ibid., p. 25).

Osbert of Ripon (Ripona, Rypon) Chamberlain of York, then succ. Geoffrey of Monkton (ibid.). Occ. 25 July 1296 (ibid., p. 27). Dep. and sent to St Bees, where he d. 21 Apr. 1301 (ibid., pp. 79, 32).[17]

Roger of Ulrome (Wlerham) Occ. Easter 1300 (Baildon, I, 174). Deposed and made infirmarian at York (*Ch. York*, p. 79); he died at Hornsea 12 Mar. 1303 (ibid., p. 34).

Thomas of York (Eboraco) Succ. Roger (ibid., p. 79).

Adam of Dalton senior Son of Richard of Newby (ibid., p. 49). Occ. 26 May 1313 (ibid., p. 59). Succ. Thomas of York (ibid., p. 79). Installed as pr. York 5 Oct. 1313 (ibid., pp. 63, 75).

John of Pickering (Pikeryng) **senior** Next in list to Adam of Dalton (ibid., p. 79). Pr. Wetheral for one year in 1309–10 (ibid., p. 76). Sacrist of York by 1313 (ibid., p. 62).

William of Tanfield (Tanefeld) **junior** 1318– Succ. John Pickering 24 July 1318 (ibid., p. 79).

Thomas of Stonegrave (Stayngreve) Occ. 22 Oct. 1387 (*Ctl. St Bees*, p. 126).

RUMBURGH (Suffolk), St Michael f. 1047 x 1064 (dep. on Hulme, St Benet); 1135 (dep. on York, St Mary)

Lists in *VCH Suffolk*, II, 78; *Ch. York*, (hereafter *Ch.*), pp. 77–8; *Heads*, I, 95.

Henry Called **de Paumiflet** in list (*Ch.*, p. 77). Occ. 1199 x 1206 (BL, Harl. Cht. 44 I 24, cf. Cheney, *Inn. III*, no. 593).

The list (*Ch.*, pp. 77–8) follows Henry de Paumiflet with the names **Clement of Poppleton, Lambert de Multon, Herbert** (who d. at Rumburgh),

H. Occ. 5 Sept. 1221 or 1222 (*Ctl. Eye*, I, no. 62). If the list is correct, prob. to be identified with Herbert.

There then follows **Daniel** (who was pr. at York), **Walter of Harpham, John of Belton** (who was pr. at York), and then:

Odo Occ. 1228 (*CRR*, XIII, no. 844). D. at Rumburgh (*Ch.*, p. 77).

The list (*Ch.*, pp. 77–8) then continues with **William of Myton** and **Godfrey**, and **Peter of Easingwold** who was pr. for a long time, and then:

Ralph of Forsett (Forset) Prob. the pr. Ralph who occ. n.d. with Stephen, pr. of Thetford i.e. after 1237, cited 12 Nov. 1339 (*CPR 1338–40*, p. 332).

John Birne Occ. Oct. 1254 x Oct. 1255 (*Suffolk F. (Rye)*, p. 57). Mentd 20 Feb. 1287 as former pr., to be delivered from gaol where he had been since the last eyre for the death of a chaplain (*CPR 1281–92*, p. 285). A pr. John occ. 1259 (Bodl., Dodsworth ms. 95, f. 45Ar), but it is unclear which pr. John he is.

John of Acaster (Acastre) Occ. in list after Ralph de Forset (ibid., p. 78). D. 9 May 1266 (but not desc. as pr.) (*Ch.*, pp. 9, 128).

John de Camera Occ. 1258 (ibid., pp. 3–4); in list (ibid., p. 78).

Henry of Tutbury (Totesbiry, Tuttesbyri) In list (p. 78). D. at Richmond 2 Mar. 1274, but desc. as m. of St Mary's and former pr. of Wetheral (ibid., p. 16). And see Wetheral.

Stephen of Gilling (Gillyng) **senior** D. at Rumburgh 2 Apr. 1273 (*Ch.*, p. 16). In list after Henry (ibid., p. 78).

---

[17] Peter de Fissheburn is found as 'tunc priore castri Richmond' on 9 Nov. 1299 (Ctl. Scrope of Bolton, f. 39v). It is doubtful whether he should be included in this list.

John de Birne follows Stephen in list (ibid.).

Robert de Brune Follows John de Birne in list (ibid.).

Peter of Newton (Neuton) Occ. [12]85 (ibid.); 1290 x ?1293, 1296 (ibid., pp. 24, 27).

Peter of Burton Ruled the cell for 9 weeks (ibid., p. 78).

Peter of Newton –1300 Occ. after res. of Peter of Burton and remained until he died [1300] (ibid.).

Geoffrey Occ. 1302 (PRO, E40/14290).

Stephen of Austwick (Austewik) Occ. 1305, 1307 (PRO, E40/14291; /14292). In office 7 years, occ. 1300 (*Ch.*, p. 78). And see St Bees.

William de Tolberton (Toleton, Tolktona) 1308–1311 Adm. 4 July 1308, no reason given for vacancy (Norwich, Reg/1/1, 28r). D. 20 Nov. 1311 (*Ch.*, p. 51).

Matthew of York *alias* **Northstreet** (Northstreth) 1311– Succ. William 1311 (ibid.). Adm. 19 Dec. 1311 (Norwich, Reg/1/1, f. 44v). Occ. 4 July 1313 (*Ch.*, p. 62).

James de Morlande (Morlound) 1316–1319 Adm. 30 Oct. 1316, no reason given for vacancy (Norwich, Reg/1/1, f. 66v). Ruled 3 years less 12 weeks (*Ch.*, p. 78).

William of Towthorpe (Touthorp(e)) 1319– Adm. 27 Dec. 1319, no reason given for vacancy (Norwich, Reg/1/1, f. 82r). Ruled 2 full years (*Ch.*, p. 78).

Geoffrey of Rudston (Rodestan, Rudstan) 1322– Adm. 1 Apr. 1322, no reason given for vacancy (Norwich, Reg/1/1, f. 94v). Royal protection for 2 years 1 July 1325 (*CPR 1324–27*, p. 131).

Adam de Sancto Botolpho 1331– Letter of pres. dated 23 Feb. 1331; adm. 29 Apr. 1331, no reason given for vacancy (Norwich, Reg/1/2, f. 41r).

William of Newton (Neuton) 1332 M. of St Mary's, York, adm. 12 Feb. 1332, no reason given for vacancy (ibid., f. 46r).

John of Maunby (Maghenby) 1332 M. of St Mary's, York, adm. 12 July 1332, no reason given for vacancy (ibid., f. 49v).

William of Tanfield 1332– M. of St Mary's, York, adm. 26 Oct. 1332, no reason given for vacancy (ibid., f. 53v).

Roger of Aslackby (Aslakby) –1343 Occ. 1 Aug. 1337 (PRO, E40/7669). Recalled to York by 8 Oct. 1343 (Norwich, Reg/1/3, f. 72v).

John of Maunby (Mauneby) 1343– M. of St Mary's, York, adm. 9 Nov. 1343 (ibid., f. 72v).

Alexander of Wath –1347 Certificate of recall by 28 Dec. 1347 (*Reg. Bateman*, I, no. 355).

Richard of Burton 1348– M. of St Mary's, York, letter of pres. dated 28 Dec. 1347, adm. 14 Jan. 1348 (ibid.).

John de Gayterigg –1357 Occ. 1350 (PRO, E40/14293). Recalled to York by 24 Sept. 1357 (Norwich, Reg/2/5, f. 22r).

John of Marton (Martone) 1357–1360 M. of St Mary's, York, letter of pres. dated 24 Sept. 1357, adm. 22 Nov. 1357 (ibid.). Recalled by 12 June 1360 (ibid., f. 38v).

Alexander of Wath 1360–1361 M. of St Mary's, York, letter of pres. dated 12 June 1360, adm. 25 June 1360 (ibid.). D. by 27 Aug. 1361 (ibid., f. 49v).

Richard of Appleton (Apilton, Appilton) 1361–1370 M. of St Mary's, York, letter of pres. dated 27 Aug. 1361, adm. 9 Sept. 1361 (ibid.). Recalled by 1 Apr. 1370 (Norwich, Reg/3/6, f. 2r).

Thomas (de) Lascels 1370–1373 M. of St Mary's, York, letter of pres. dated 1 Apr. 1370, adm. 29 July 1370 (ibid.). Recalled by 18 June 1373 (ibid., f. 21v).

John of Garton 1373– M. of St Mary's, York, letter of pres. dated 18 June 1373, adm. 29 June 1373 (ibid.).

Nicholas of Kelfield (Kelfeld) –1392 Occ. 1377 x 1381 (PRO, E179/45/18); June 1380 x June 1381 (PRO, E179/45/5b, m. 2); recalled by 16 July 1392 (Norwich, Reg/3/6, f. 168r).

ST BEES (Cumberland) (York, St Mary) f. 1120

Lists in *VCH Cumberland*, II, 183; *Ctl. St Bees*, pp. 602–7 (long list); pp. 608–9 (short list); *Ch. York*, pp. 76–7; *Heads*, I, 95.

Daniel Occ. 2 Feb. 1211 (*Ctl. St Bees*, p. 435).

Ralph Occ. early 13th cent. (*c.* 1200?) (ibid., pp. 303–4).

Guy (Wydo) Occ. 1231/2 x 1239, *temp.* Ralph, pr. of Carlisle and before William Roundel became abb. of St Mary's, York (*Ctl. Wetheral*, p. 345). Pr. 10 years then made m. at Furness (*Ch. York*, p. 76).

John of Lastingham (Lestingham) Said to have followed Guy and ruled 11 years and then made pr. York, St Mary (ibid., p. 74). D. 13 Sept. 1266 (ibid., p. 8).

William of Rothwell (Rothewel, Rothwelle) –1262 Occ. 26 May 1256 (*Ctl. St Bees*, pp. 257–8, no. 231). Ruled 2½ years and d. in office at St Bees 8 Feb. 1262 (*Ch. York*, pp. 76, 130).

Nicholas of Langton (Langeton) Pr. of St Bees 1258 (ibid., p. 4). Occ. from 25 Apr. 1258 (N.) to 14 Sept. 1282 (*Ctl. St Bees*, pp. 180–1, 410). Pr. 29 years until removed from office by Abb. Simon (ibid., p. 76). D. as former pr. 5 Sept. 1298 at York (ibid., p. 29).

Benedict of Malton –1286 Occ. 11 Nov. 1282, 10 May 1286 (ibid., pp. 409, 145–6). Succ. Nicholas ruled 7 years, made pr. of St Mary's, York 1286 (*Ch. York*, p. 76); abb. 1296 and d. 22 Oct. 1307 4 years after retirement (ibid., p. 42).

William of Derby (Dereby) Pr. of St Bees for 7 years (ibid., p. 77). Occ. 11 Nov. 1288, 1288 x 1294, 10 Mar. 1295 (*Ctl. St Bees*, pp. 436–7, 405, 101–2); 1290 x ?1293 (*Ch. York*, p. 24). Chosen pr. of St Mary's, York 1296 (ibid., p. 28). Went to Rome 1300, broke his leg and 'left this vale of misery' 7 Jan. 1301, bur. at Rome 1301 (ibid., p. 31).

Hugh of Compton (Cumpton) –1303 Succ. William and ruled 7½ years, deposed 29 Jan. 1303 in visitation of Archbp Corbridge (ibid., p. 56). Occ. 21 Nov. 1301 (*Ctl. St Bees*, pp. 260–1). D. 21 May 1314 at York after 5 years in the infirmary and 47 years in orders (*Ch. York*, pp. 65, 136).

Alan of Ness (Nesse) 1303–1308 Succ. Hugh and ruled 4½ years (ibid., p. 76). Occ. 1307 (ibid., p. 42). Made pr. of St Mary's, York 1308 (ibid., p. 43). El. abb. of St Mary's, York 4 July 1313 and d. 16 Apr. 1331 (ibid., pp. 59, 112).

Stephen of Gilling 1308–1316 Succ. Alan. Received by brethren at St Bees 5 June 1308 (ibid., p. 43). Occ. 1309 (ibid., pp. 44, 46); 1312 (ibid., p. 53); 1315 (ibid., p. 68). D. 22 Oct. 1316 (ibid., p. 70).

Stephen of Austwick (Austewik, Oustewyke) 1316–1323 Succ. Stephen of Gilling 1316 (ibid.). Ruled 7 years and 4 weeks up to 21 Dec. [1323] (ibid., p. 77). Res. and returned to York (ibid., p. 23). And see Lincoln, St Mary Magdalen and Rumburgh.

Thomas of Sutton 1323–1324 Made pr. 21 Dec. 1323 (ibid., p. 77) and ruled 35 weeks (ibid.). D. as pr. 29 Aug. 1324 and bur. before the high altar of St Bees 2 Sept. (ibid., p. 73).

John Occ. 10 Dec. 1330 (*Ctl. St Bees*, p. 563).

William de Seynesbury (Seynesburi, Sluynesbur', Swynesburi, Swynesbury, Weynesbury) Papal conf. of coll. 27 June 1360 (*CPP*, pp. 315, 357); further papal conf. 24 Aug. 1360 (ibid., pp. 316, 358; *Accts of Papal Collectors*, pp. 157, 205, 239, 302, the last-mentd with additional note: 'Iste prioratus non est in diocesi Dunelmensi sed est in diocesi Eboracensi, et non habuit effectum ut patet per bullam factam super revocatione dicte gratie, cuius copia remanet penes registrum collectorie'). Poss. from Saintbury, Glos.

John of Harome (Harom) Mentd in 1368 as late pr. of St Bees, ref. to acquisition of land 7 years previously [1361] (*Cal. Misc. Inq.*, III, 261).

Thomas of Brignall (Brignal) Occ. 21 Sept. 1370, 3 Feb. 1371 (*Ctl. St Bees*, pp. 264–6).

Thomas of Cottingham (Cotingham) Occ. 24 May 1379, 8 June 1379, 30 June 1379 (ibid., pp. 268–9, 276–7).

ST IVES (Hunts) (Ramsey) f. -1066
  Lists in *VCH Hunts*, I, 389; *Heads*, I, 95-6.
Richard Scot -1221 Possibly the same as (R.) 1198 x 1200 (Cheney, *Inn. III*, no. 248). Named
  in full as former pr. 1251 (*Ctl. Ramsey*, I, 296, cf. 285). Royal ass. to el. as abb. of Selby 21
  June 1221 (*CPR 1216-25*, p. 300).
Benedict Occ. n.d. (*temp*. Abb. Rannulf 1231 x 1253) (*Ctl. Ramsey*, II, 225); n.d. (ibid., I, 285).
Hugh of Sulgrave (Sulegrave) Occ. n.d. (*c.* 1250) (PRO, E40/1246); n.d. (*temp*. Abb. Rannulf
  of Ramsey 1231 x 1253) (PRO, E326/8436). Mentd as former pr. in doct of 16 Jan. 1264
  (PRO, E40/1203). Abb. of Ramsey 1255, but prob. was not pr. of St Ives at time of his eln
  (q.v.).
Martin Occ. Oct. 1252 x Oct. 1253 (*Hunts F.*, p. 27).
Simon Occ. n.d. (PRO, E326/1550, 1551 pal.: mid-late 13th cent.).
Walter of Lilford (Lilleford) Mentd in Ramsey library catalogue s. xiv ex. (*Ch. Ramsey*, p.
  366). Sharpe, *Latin Writers*, p. 736, 'libri fratris Walteri de Lilleford quondam prioris sancti
  Ivonis'.
Robert of Nassington -1343 Occ. 19 May 1333 (*Ctl. Bushmead*, p. 66, no. 54). El. abb. of
  Ramsey 1343 (q.v.).
Richard of Raveley (Rauele) Occ. 24 Oct. 1348 (*CPL*, III, 287).
The next recorded pr., **John Alkmundbury**, occ. 1432 (*Lincoln Visitations*, I, 105).

SCILLY (Cornwall), St Nicholas (Tavistock) f. *c.* -1114
  Lists in Oliver, pp. 73-4; *Heads*, I, 96; cf. *JRIC*, n.s. 3(4) (1960), 490-1.
Alan of Cornwall -1233 El. as abb. of Tavistock 1233 (*CPR 1232-47*, p. 18).
John Chubb(e) -1262 M. of Tavistock and pr. of Scilly, el. as abb. of Tavistock 1262 (*CR
  1261-64*, p. 132).
John Occ. 31 Mar. 1305 (*CPR 1301-7*, p. 351).
Robert Deneys Occ. 4 Jan. 1331 (*Reg. Grandisson*, I, 594).
John Duraunte -1373 Res. at visitation 1373 on account of old age and sickness, returned to
  Tavistock (*Reg. Brantingham*, I, 29-30).
Richard Auncel(le) 1373-?1385 M. of Tavistock, apptd by bp of Exeter 28 Sept. 1373 (ibid.).
  Occ. 11 Oct. 1375 (ibid., 363). As m. of Tavistock, inst. as pr. of St Michael's Mount 7 Dec.
  1385 (ibid., 94).

SNAITH (Yorks W.), cell of Selby abbey St Laurence f. 1101+, 1310 (ordination *Reg.
Greenfield*, II, no. 875) (*KH*, p. 76; C.B. Robinson, *History of the Priory and Peculiar of Snaith
in the county of York* (London, 1861).
No named pr. found before **Thomas (de) Warneford**, who occ. 28 Mar. 1398 (York, Reg. 5A,
  f. 241v). He also occ. as *custos* of the spirituality of Snaith (? pr.) 28 Apr. 1393 (YMA,
  M2/1g, f. 83v).

SNAPE (Suffolk), St John the Evangelist (Colchester) f. 1155
  Lists in *VCH Suffolk*, II, 80 (from 1307); *Heads*, I, 96.
John Occ. 15 Oct. 1255 (*Ctl. Eye*, I, no. 83); (J.) 17 Dec. 1257 (ibid., no. 98); n.d. (mid-13th cent.:
  pal.) (PRO, E40/3559; /3786).
Nicholas Occ. n.d. (13th cent., possibly before John – sequence uncertain (PRO, E42/381;
  E40/3344).
Thomas Occ. 7 June 1300 (*CPR 1292-1301*, p. 551); Feb. 1301 (*Ctl. Colchester*, II, 599); Mich.
  1305 (PRO, CP40/153, m. 118); (T.) 28 Jan. 1306 (Norwich, Reg/1/1, f. 19r).
Gilbert of Polstead (Polstede) 1308– M. of St John, Colchester, apptd on pres. of abb. and

convent 15 Feb. 1308, no reason given for vacancy (ibid., f. 26v). Occ. 27 Apr. 1311, 9 Oct. 1311, 16 Mar. 1323 (ibid., ff. 41r, 42v, 99v).

Thomas of Neyland (Neylonde) **1328–** M. of St John, Colchester, apptd on pres. of abb. and convent 21 Jan. 1328, no reason given for vacancy (Norwich, Reg/1/2, f. 18v). Occ. 1328 (PRO, E42/237); 29 Sept. 1311 (PRO, E40/3340).

Simon de Blyton 1349 M. of St John, Colchester, apptd 10 July 1349, on d. of last (unnamed) pr. (*Reg. Bateman*, I, no. 768). Royal ass. to el as abb. of Colchester, 6 Sep. 1349 (*CPR 1348–50*, p. 373).

John of Colne 1349– M of St John, Colchester, adm. 27 Oct. 1349, no reason given for vacancy (Norwich, Reg/2/4, f. 113r–v).

Richard of Colne (Calne) **1361–1369** M. of St John, Colchester, apptd 19 Jan. 1361, no reason given for vacancy (Norwich, Reg/2/5, ff. 42v–43r). El. abb. of Colchester 1369 (*Reg. Sudbury*, I, 112).

William de Grytton 1369– M. of St John, Colchester, apptd by archbp of Canterbury 11 Dec. 1369 (Lambeth, Reg. Whittlesey, f. 146r).

Thomas Monyron (Morn') **1377–** M. of St John, Colchester, apptd 14 Dec. 1377 (Norwich, Reg/3/6, f. 54v). Occ. 29 Sept. 1378 (BL, Add. Cht. 26263); June 1380 x June 1381 (PRO, E179/45/5b, m. 2).

Richard of Bury 1381– M. of St John, Colchester, adm. 13 Feb. 1381, no reason given for vacancy (Norwich, Reg/3/6, ff. 72v–73r).

STAMFORD (Lincs), St Leonard (Durham) f. *c.* 1082

List based on Alan Piper's list in *Stamford Historian*, VI (1982), pp. 15–20; also lists in *VCH Lincs*, II, 128; *Heads*, I, 96.

Matthew Occ. j.d. after 26 Oct. 1218 (CUL, Add. ms. 3021, f. 299r–v).

Walter 1222– Inst. 14 June 1222 (*Reg. Wells*, III, 121).

W. Occ. *c.* 11 Nov. 1235 (DCD, 2.3 Ebor.5).

A(?dam) of Norham 1242/3– Inst. June 1242 x June 1243, on res. of unnamed pr. (*Reg. Grosseteste*, p. 66).

William of Elvet 1260–1261 M. of Durham, inst. 18 Mar. 1260 (*Reg. R. Gravesend*, p. 4 as 'Richard'). Occ. 30 Sept. 1260 (DCD, Misc. Cht. 5519C); 1 May 1261 (*Ann. Durham*, p. 122 no. 55). Res. *c.* Easter 1261, ment. in letter to bp 24 Apr. 1261 x 25 Oct. 1261 (ibid.).

Geoffrey of Newcastle (Castro) **1262** M. of Durham, adm. 3 Sept. 1262 on cess. of William of Elvet (*Reg. R. Gravesend*, p. 11, said in *Ann. Durham*, p. 220n to be prob. error as regards year). Letter of pres. n.d. (*Ann. Durham*, p. 126, no. 56). D. 27 Dec. 1262 (ibid., p. 124, no. 58).

William of Wearmouth (Wermuth) **1263–?1264** M. of Durham, adm. 30 Aug. 1263 (*Reg. R. Gravesend*, p. 13; *Ann. Durham*, pp. 124–6, nos. 58–61). D., successor apptd after lapse (? of 6 months at least) 30 Nov. 1264 (*Reg. R. Gravesend*, p. 17).

John of Burford (Bureford) **1264–1272** M. of Durham, apptd by bp *per lapsum* 30 Nov. 1264 on d. of William (ibid.). Res. by 18 Dec. 1272 (ibid., p. 53).

William of Masham (Massam) **1272–1274** M. of Durham, inst. 18 Dec. 1272 (ibid., pp. 53, 278). Sent to General Council 4 May 1274 (*Ann. Durham*, p. 46). Res. by 7 Oct. 1274 (*Reg. R. Gravesend*, p. 60).

Nicholas of Ireland (Ybernia) **1274–1278** M. of Stamford, inst. 7 Oct. 1274 (ibid.). Res. by 4 Mar. 1278 (ibid., p. 79).

William de Rybus 1278–1281 M. of Durham, inst 4 Mar. 1278 (ibid., pp. 79, 286). Res. by 14 Apr. 1281 (*Reg. Sutton*, I, 12).

William Lutterell (Luterel) **1281–1284** Eln conf. 14 Apr. 1281 (ibid). Res. on account of ill health; letter of res. 21 Dec. 1284; successor pres. 5 Jan. 1285 (ibid., 61–3).

Robert of Wackerfield (Wakerfeld, Wakerfeud) **1285–1286** M. of Durham, pres. 5 Jan. 1285, adm. 31 Jan., mand. to induct 1 Feb. 1285 (ibid.). Letter of res. on account of ill-health 7 July 1286 (ibid., 86).

Gilbert of Sherburn (Schireburn, Schyreburn) **1286–1287** M. of Durham, letter of pres. 18 July 1286, adm. 5 Aug. 1286 (ibid.). Letter of res. on account of ill-health 10 Apr. 1287 (ibid., 96–7).

Peter of Sedgefield (Seggefeud) **1287–1290** M. of Durham, letter of pres. 20 Apr. 1287, adm. 10 July 1287 (ibid.). Letter of res. on account of ill-health 31 Oct. 1290 (ibid., 145–6).

Geoffrey of Boston (de Sancto Botulpho) **1290–1292** M. of Durham, letter of pres. 2 Nov. 1290, adm.13 Nov. 1290 (ibid.). Letter of res. 8 Jan. 1292 (ibid., 162–3).

Ingram of Chatton (Chaton) **1292–1293** M. of Durham, letter of pres. 9 Jan. 1292, adm. 2 Feb. 1292 (ibid.). Letter of res. 31 Mar. 1293 (ibid., 175–6).

Geoffrey of Boston 1293–1302 M. of Durham, letter of pres. 21 Apr. 1293, adm. 30 Apr. 1293 (ibid.). D. by 1 May 1302 (Lincoln, Ep. Reg., II, f. 16v).

Robert of Killingworth (Kyvelingworth) **1302–1308** M. of Durham, letter of pres. 30 Apr. 1302, nothing done immediately since pr. Richard of Durham was deprived. On the pr.'s restoration the bp of Lincoln adm. Richard of Killingworth n.d. (27 Dec. 1305 x 19 Jan. 1306) (ibid). D. by 20 Sept. 1308 (ibid., f. 23v).

Roger of Tynemouth 1308– M. of Durham, letter of pres. 20 Sept. 1308, adm. 7 Oct. 1308 (ibid.). Occ. *c.* 1 Nov. 1312 (DCD, Reg., II, f. 5r); 24 June 1313 (ibid., f. 14v); 17 May 1314 (DCD, Misc. Cht. 6836). Pr. of Lytham from 1320 (q.v.).

Adam of Pontefract 1314– M. of Durham, letter of pres. 28 Sept. 1314 (DCD, Reg., II, f. 258r; DCD, Misc. Cht. 6835). Occ. 6 Nov. 1316 (DCD, Misc. Cht. 2630); 2 Mar. 1321 (DCD, Loc. XIII: 3c). Adam became pr. of Coldingham 1325 (*Priory of Coldingham*, p. 13).

John Fossour −1333 Occ. 15 Oct. 1333 (*Scriptores Tres*, p. 120). Res. by 29 Dec. 1333 (*Reg. Burghersh*, I, no. 411). Master of Monkwearmouth ?1338–40 (q.v.); pr. of Coldingham 1340; pr. of Durham 1341–74 (q.v.).

Robert de Cambois (Cambehow, Cambok, Cambou) **1333–1338** M. of Durham, letter of pres. 29 Dec. 1333, adm. 24 Feb. 133[4] (*Reg. Burghersh*, I, no. 411). Lic. to preach 13 Dec. 1334; lic. to hear confessions in the Lincoln archdeaconry 3 Oct. 1336 (Lincoln, Ep. Reg., V, ff. 488r, 539v). Res. by 13 Oct. 1338 (*Reg. Burghersh*, I, no. 591). Pr. of Lytham 1342–49 (q.v.).

Nicholas of Lusby (Lusceby) **1338–1346** M. of Durham, letter of pres. 13 Oct. 1338, adm. 28 Oct. 1338 (*Reg. Burghersh*, I, no. 591). Res. by 12 July 1346 (Lincoln, Ep. Reg., VI, ff. 23v–24r). Pr. of Finchale *c.* 1346–49 (q.v.). See Emden, *BRUO*, II, 1171.

Robert of Hallington 1346– M. of Durham, letter of pres. 12 July 1346, adm. 21 July 1346 (ibid.). Proctor for Benedictine General Chapter app. 29 Aug. 1346 (BL, Cotton ms. Faustina A. VI, f. 28r). Pr. of Oxford cell from 1343 (q.v.).

Robert of Hexham 1348–1352 Pres. 12 July 1348 (DCD, Reg., II, f. 132v). Commissioned to act in divorce case 29 June 1352 (Lincoln, Ep. Reg., VIII, ff. 6v–7v). Res. by 21 Nov. 1352 (Lincoln, Ep. Reg., IX, f. 103r–v). Pr. of Holy Island 1357–8 (q.v.).

John of Langton (Langeton) **1352–1355** priest, pres. 21 Nov. 1352, adm. 28 Nov. 1352 (ibid.). Res. by 30 Jan. 1355 (ibid., f. 115r–v). At the 1354 visitation of Durham it was claimed that pr. Fossour of Durham had apptd Langton as pr. of Stamford in spite of the latter's imprudence and lack of judgment (DCD, 1. 8. Pont. 1).

John of Barnard Castle (de Castro Bernardi) **1355–1366** priest, pres. 20 Jan. 1355, adm. 16 May 1355 (Lincoln, Ep. Reg., IX, f. 115r–v). Res. by 4 Nov. 1366 (Lincoln, Ep. Reg., X, f. 15v).

Robert of Claxton 1366–1372 M. of Durham, pres. 4 Nov. 1366, adm. 3 Dec. 1366 (ibid.). Res. by 21 June 1373 (ibid., f. 57v).

John of Billesfield 1373–1375 M. of Durham, pres. 21 Jan. 1373, adm. 14 July 1373 (ibid.). Allegedly improvident; withdrawn (DCD, Misc. Cht. 421, f. 15r). Res. by 16 June 1375 (Lincoln, Ep. Reg., X, f. 73r–v). Pr. of Holy Island 1363–67, 1384–88 (q.v.).

John of Hemingbrough (Hemyngburgh) **1375–1391** M. of Durham, pres. 16 June 1375, adm. 1 Nov. 1375 (ibid.). Accounts, Summer 1375 – 11 May 1377, 31 May [1378] – 16 May 1390 (DCD, Stamford Accs). El. pr. of Durham 1391 (*Le Neve 1300–1541*, VI, 110).

STANLEY, *see* LEONARD STANLEY

SUDBURY (Suffolk), St Bartholomew (Westminster) f. *c.* 1115
   List in *Sudbury Chts.* p. xv.

Brian Occ. 28 Oct. 1222 (*Essex F.*, I, 62).

Gilbert Occ. mid-13th cent. (*Sudbury Chts.*, nos. 7, 9–10, 26; cf. no. 20).

John of Rickmansworth (Rikemaresworze) Occ. mid-13th cent. (*Sudbury Chts.*, nos. 8, 11, 97 cf. no. 22).

[**Richard de Dol** occ. as proctor etc. but not desc. as prior, between 21 Oct. 1279 and 5 May 1285 (ibid., nos. 106, 31, 112, 115–16). It is thought that he was perhaps in charge of Sudbury's interests at this time).]

Gregory Occ. late-13th cent. (ibid., nos. 60, 104).

Henry of London Occ. late-13th cent. (ibid., nos. 27, 34).

Nicholas of Ware Occ. *ante* 1286 (ibid., no. 38); cf. endorsements to ibid. nos. 89–90, of prob. ? 1303.

Simon Occ. 29 June 1299 (ibid., no. 37); 12 March 1300 (ibid., no. 35).

Roger de Buiyns Occ. *ante* 28 Jan. 1310, having appealed to the pope against the eln of Richard de Kidinton as abb. of Westminster (*CPL*, II, 65).

Simon de Henlegh Occ. 9 Sept. 1323 (*Sudbury Chts.*, nos. 44–5).

The next recorded prior, **Thomas Flete**, was appointed in 1499 (ibid., no. 131).

TICKHILL (Yorks W.), ? St Thomas (ref. to unnamed pr. of the chapel of St Thomas 1251 *CPR 1247–58*, p. 87); cell of Humberston abbey, Lincs., otherwise a hospital 'in the marsh', acquired by Humberston (*KH*, p. 398, cf. *Mon. Angl.*, IV, 430; J. Hunter, *South Yorkshire: the history and topography of the deanery of Doncaster* (2 vols., London, 1828–31), I, 244). *VCH Yorks*, III, 332 suggests that the leper hospital of St Leonard, Tickhill, and the hospital in the marsh may be identical.

Robert Acra Occ. as pr. of the cell (*prior celle vestre de Tykhull*) 3 May 1360 (Lincoln, Ep. Reg., VIII, f. 145v).

Robert of Humberston (Humberstayn) Occ. as pr. of chapel of St Thomas the Martyr in the Marsh at Tickhill 14 Aug. 1368 (Nottingham Univ., Clifton of Clifton Hall, Cl. D.576).

TYNEMOUTH (Northumberland), St Mary, St Oswin (St Albans) f. *c.* 1083–85 (dep. on Durham); -1089 (dep. on St Albans).
   Lists in *Hist. Northumberland*, VIII, 122–3; *Heads*, I, 96–7.

Ralph Gubion -*c.*1216 For name see *GASA*, I, 271–3. Occ. 20 Nov. 1208, 3 Feb. 1212 (*Northumberland and Durham F.*, I, nos. 40, 50). Asks to res. but is dissuaded by abb. of St Albans (*GASA*, I, 271–2). Res. *c.* 1216 (ibid., 272–3; *Heads*, I, 97, n. 1).

Master William of Bedford –1224 Apptd pr. of Worcester 21 Nov. 1224 (q.v.).

C. Occ. *post* 28 Jan. 1224, date of papal mand. (*Ctl. Newminster*, p. 214). ? error for G(erman).

German Occ. Mich. term 1225, Hil. term 1226, Easter term 1227 (*CRR*, XII, nos. 1400, 2043;

XIII, no. 85); 16 May 1227 (*Northumberland and Durham F.*, I, p. 40, no. 95). Seal (*Durham Seals*, II, p. 583, no. 3553).

?**Henry** Possibly 13th or 14th cent. D. 17 Apr. (Belvoir obit, Nichols, *Leics*, II, i, app. ii, p. 28). His position in the sequence of priors is unclear.

Walter de Bulun **–1244** Occ. 8 Feb. 1235, 18 Nov. 1236, 13 Oct. 1241 (*Northumberland and Durham F.*, I, pp. 49, 58, 67, nos 117, 134, 162); Easter term 1236 (*CRR*, XV, no. 1758). D. 10 Jan. 1244 (*MPCM*, VI, 276).

Richard de Parco *alias* **Rufus de Winchelcombe** **1244–1252** Pr. of Binham 1226–44 (q.v.). El. to Tynemouth before 20 Feb. 1244 (ibid., 89). D. 25 Apr. 1252 (ibid., 279). Presumably the same as **Richard of Binham** (Bynham) mentd as pr. *temp.* abb. John of St Albans 1235–60 (*GASA*, I, 348).

Ralph de Dunham **1252–?1266/7** Name (Ctl. Tynemouth, f. 73r). El. on or before 1 May 1252 (*Hist. Northumberland*, list, no source). Occ. 23 Apr. 1256, 7 May 1256 (*Northumberland and Durham F.*, I, pp. 88, 94, nos. 207, 231); 1257 (Gibson, *Tynemouth*, app., p. lvii, no. lxxxiv); 11 Dec. 1264 (*Reg. Whethamstede*, II, 319). D. 13 Aug. (Belvoir obit, Nichols, *Leics*, II, i, app. ii, p. 33). Seal (*Northumberland and Durham Seals*, no. 244). Appt of custodians on d. of pr. Ralph n.d. (? *c.* 1266–7) (Hill, *Eccles. Letter-books*, pp. 87–8, cf. pp. 90, 93).

William of Horton (Hortune) Prev. pr. of Wymondham (q.v.); also cellarer of Tynemouth 1244 (*MPCM*, VI, 90). Mentd as former pr. of Tynemouth in inquisition of 16 Aug. 1291 (Gibson, *Tynemouth*, app., p. lxix, no. lxxxix). Also mentd as pr. *temp.* Henry III, *cito post bellum Evesham* [i.e. 1265] (ibid., p. lxviii).

Adam of Meppershall (Meperdeshall) Occ. 20 Oct. 1273 (*Northumberland and Durham F.*, II, p. 1, no. 2). Mentd in 1291 inquisition as predecessor of William (Gibson, *Tynemouth*, app., p. lxix, no. lxxxix).

William Bernard Mentd in 1291 inquisition as immediate predecessor of the then pr. (Gibson, *Tynemouth*, app., p. lxix, no. lxxxix). *Hist. Northumberland*, VIII, 123 gives his death as 1280, but the two refs. given, *CPR* and PRO, Just.1/1254, have both been searched without success. In an assize plea of Nov. 1282 x Nov. 1283 it is stated that pr William had d. 3 years previously (Ctl. Tynemouth, f. 179r).

Simon of Walden **–1294/5** Occ. 1280 (*Hist. Northumberland*, list, no source); Apr. & Sept. 1282 (Ctl. Tynemouth, ff. 177r, 178r); Easter 1291 (*King's Bench Edward I*, II, 39, 41; Ctl. Tynemouth, f. 183r); 1293 (Brand, *Hist. Newcastle*, II, 86, n. 6; Ctl. Tynemouth, ff. 192r, 203v–204r); 25 Sept. 1294 (*Hist. Northumberland*, VIII, 82, n. 2, citing BL, Cotton ms. Vespasian E VI, f. 154v).

Adam of Tewing Occ. Christmas 1295 (*Hist. Northumberland*, XII, 220, citing BL, Cotton ms. Tiberius E. VI, f. 120r; cf. ibid., VIII 123); 14 Oct. 1300 (*Northumberland Assize Roll*, p. 263). Rebellious, pr. made prisoner and banished to St Albans n.d. by Abb. John of Berkhampstead (1290–1301) (*GASA*, II, 21–2, but cf. *Hist. Northumberland*, VIII, 82, who thinks this relates to Simon of Walden).

Simon of Walden Occ. 11 June 1301 (Ctl. Tynemouth, f. 168r); 30 June 1307 (ibid., f. 190r). D. 17 Apr. (Belvoir obit, Nichols, *Leics*, II, i, app. ii, p. 28).

Simon of Taunton (Thwangton) **1311–** Pres. to bp by abb. of St Albans 1 July 1311, adm. 21 July 1311 (*Reg. Pal. Dun.*, I, 79–81). Mentd. 1314 (*Northumberland De Banco Rolls*, p. 44; cf. next entry).

Roger of Norton Occ. 25 Nov. 1313 (*CPR 1313–17*, p. 42).

Richard of Tewing (Tewyng, Tewyngge, Tywinge) **1315–1340** Pres. to bp 20 Mar. 1315 by abb. of St Albans (*Reg. Pal. Dun.*, II, 699); adm. 31 Mar. 1315 (ibid., p. 696). Occ. from 1328 to 1338 (Ctl. Tynemouth, ff. 159r, 162r, 175r). D. 29 Sept. (Belvoir obit, Nichols, *Leics*, II, i, app. ii, p. 36). D. 1340 (*GASA*, II, 375). Seal (*Mon. Seals*, p. 91; *Durham Seals*, II, p. 583, no. 3554).

Thomas de la Mare 1340–1349 Promoted to be pr. on d. of Richard of Tewing (*GASA*, II, 375). Pres. 6 Oct. 1340 (*Reg. Bury*, p. 75; *Reg. Pal. Dun.* III, 378). Occ. 1344 to 1347 (PRO, Just.1/1435, mm. 4, 49, 49d, 54); 30 Jan. 1345 (*CPR 1343–45*, p. 492). El. abb. of St Albans 1349 (q.v.). Cf. *GASA*, II, 375 for his rule at Tynemouth.

Clement of Wheathampstead (Wathmastede) **1350–** Abb. Thomas obtains papal leave to pres. one of his monks to the priory (ibid., 390–1). Adm. 1350 (Durham, Reg. Hatfield, f. 1r -faded, date unclear, followed by entries of Sept. & Nov. 1350). Occ. 5 Apr. 1352 (*CPL*, III, 444); 1376 (*CPR 1374–77*, p. 317); 4 Apr. 1380 (*Hist. Northumberland*, XII, 214); 22 Oct. 1386 (*Northumberland and Durham Deeds*, p. 234). Supposed to be alive 1389 (Hodgson, *Northumberland*, II, ii, 252).

Robert de Wyk Occ. June 1378 x June 1379 (PRO, E179/62/4, m. 3). Is this the case of a 'bogus' pr. as Lanercost?

The next recorded pr., **John Macrell**, occ. 11 Apr. 1394 (*CPL*, IV, 487).

WALLINGFORD (Berks) Holy Trinity (St Albans) f. *c.* 1087 x 1089
  Lists in *VCH Berks*, II, 79, *Heads*, I, 97.

Rualend Occ. 13th cent., but in a cht. conf. in 1284 (Bodl., Berks Cht. 117*). His precise place in the sequence of priors is uncertain.

Richard Occ. May 1210 (*Oxford F.*, p. 43).

Thomas Occ. (T.) 1216 x 1227 (*Ctl. Reading*, II, no. 785); May 1224 (*Oxford F.*, p. 68); Hilary 1229, Easter term 1229 (*CRR*, XIII, nos. 1567, 2074).

John Occ. 20 May 1229 (*Oxford F.*, p. 85).

German Occ. 30 June 1235, 1 July 1235 (ibid., pp. 97, 98).

Geoffrey Occ. 10 June 1247, 17 June 1247 (ibid., pp. 143, 146); *c.* 1250 (*Muniments of Wallingford*, p. 64, no. 14); Oct. 1250 x Oct. 1251 (Bodl., Berks Cht. 33); n.d. (mid 13th cent.) (*HMC R. R. Hastings*, I, 277).

John occ. 8 July 1268 (*Oxford F.*, p. 196).

Ralph Occ. 22 Sept. 1275 (Bodl., Berks Cht. 46). Prob. the same as **Ralph of Watlington** who occ. n.d. (late 13th cent.) (ibid., Berks Chts. 15, 41). The pd catalogue ascribes to them dates of *c.* 1255, 1260, but this is clearly too early since abb. R. of St Albans is mentd, who must be Roger (1263–90). Ralph of Watlington occ. n.d., *temp.*, Bp Oliver Sutton of Lincoln and abb. Roger of St Albans (i.e. 1280 x 1290) (*GASA*, I, 456).

Gregory Occ. 9 Dec. 1284 (Bodl., Berks Chts. 117*, 51); 3 Feb. 1285 (*Goring Chts.*, II, no. 337); 3 Feb. 1285, 26 Apr. 1289 (*Medieval Archives of Christ Church*, pp. 145, 146).

William de Kirkeby Occ. n. d. (*Mon. Angl.*, II, 196), ? *temp.* Edward I, when Richard of Wallingford (abb. of St Albans 1326–34) was about 10 years old (BL, Cotton ms. Claudius E IV, f. 201r). Occ. n.d. (late 13th cent.) (Bodl., Berks Cht. 45).

John Occ. 1300 (PRO, Just.1/1318, m. 7).

Simon de Thanington Occ. 18 Sept. 1311 (PRO, C241/74/322).

Stephen of Wittenham (Wytte(n)ham) Occ. 10 Sept. 1315 (Bodl., Berks Cht. 57); 16 Apr. 1317 (*Muniments of Wallingford*, p. 65, no. 16); 3 Aug. 1317 (*YB*, XXIII, 9–10); still alive Mich. 1318 but no longer pr. (ibid.).

William Occ. 30 Nov. 1321, 6 June 1322 (*Reg. Martival*, II, ii, pp. 375, 398). *VCH*, following Willis, calls him 'of Huntingdon', but is this a confusion with the St Albans m., William of Huntingdon who occ. as pr. of Belvoir in the late 13th cent. (q.v.)?

William Heron (Heyron) Occ. 24 June 1328 (Bodl., Berks Cht. 70); 25 Apr. 1329 (*Muniments of Wallingford*, p. 67, no. 18); 12 Mar. 1334, 19 Apr. 1336 (*Medieval Archives of Christ*

Church, pp. 140, 141); 18 Aug. 1334 (Lincoln, Ep. Reg., IV, f. 270r); 20 Dec. 1337 (*CCR 1337–39*, p. 284); 3 July 1339 (*CCR 1339–41*, p. 228); 10 Dec. 1346 (Bodl., Berks Cht. 91); 6 May 1358 (ibid., Berks Cht. 97).

William of Steventon (Stevington, Stevyngton) Occ. from 30 Sept. 1360 to 12 Sept. 1369 (Bodl., Berks Chts. 99, 109); 13 Aug. 1370 (*HMC Rutland*, IV, 151). Possibly pr. of Belvoir (q.v.).

Robert Occ. 1372 (PRO, C85/107/14).

The next recorded pr. **William (de) Bynham** (Binham) occ. 1 Oct. 1378 (*Ctl. Boarstall*, p. 260); 10 Mar. 1381 (Dynham – *Muniments of Wallingford*, p. 69, no. 19); 10 May 1383 (Bodl., Berks Cht. 125); Oct. 1396 (*GASA*, III, 426). See Sharpe, *Latin Writers*, p. 754.

Ralph Whichchirche is mentd as former pr. of Hatfield Peverel and pr. of Wallingford. Papal chaplain 1386/7, but on account of great age allowed to live in cell of Belvoir (*GASA*, II, 418). No indication when he was pr. of these cells.

WEARMOUTH, *see* MONKWEARMOUTH

WETHERAL (Cumberland), Holy Trinity, St Mary, and St Constantine (York, St Mary) f. *c.* 1106

Lists in *VCH Cumberland*, II, 188; *Ctl. Wetheral*, pp. 504–11; *Ch. St Mary's, York*, pp. 75–6; *Heads*, I, 97.

Thomas Occ. 1203 x 1214 (*Ctl. Holm Cultram*, no. 16).

Suffred (Sophred) Occ. (S.) 1219 x 1223 (*Ctl. Lanercost*, nos. 178–9; *Ctl. Whitby*, I, no. 39; Bodl., ms. Top. Yorks e 8, ff. 70v–71r).

William Roundell −1241 Occ. (W.) 2 Oct. 1225 (*Ctl. Wetheral*, no. 225); Hil. 1229 (*CRR*, XIII, no. 1508). El. as abb. of St Mary's, York 1241 (q.v.).

Thomas Occ. Whitsun 1241 (*Ctl. Wetheral*, no. 171).

Richard of Rouen (Rothomago) Occ. n.d. (mid 13th cent.) (ibid., no. 87); 25 Jan. 1252 (ibid., p. 405, no. x, cf. p. 504). Prob. the Richard de Reme noted in the list before Henry of Tutbury (*Ch. York*, p. 75).

Henry of Tutbury (Tutesbyrie, Tuttesbyri) −1265 Occ. 11 Nov. 1257 (*Ctl. Wetheral*, no. 66); (H.) n. d. (*ante* 1266) (*Yorks Deeds*, VII, 50). Res. 5. 13 July 1265 and entered Dominicans at Carlisle but left 14 Nov. 1265 and received back at St Mary's (*Ch. York*, pp. 7–8, 130, cf. list p. 75). D. (as former pr.) 2 Mar 1274 at Richmond (ibid., p. 16). See also Rumburgh.

Thomas of St Bees (de Sancta Bega) 1265− Succ. Henry. Pr. of Wetheral 1265 for one year, then pr. of York (ibid., pp. 74, 75, cf. p. 9).

Thomas of Wymondham (Wymundham) −?1292 Pr. 1266 (ibid., p. 129). Occ. 16 Feb. 1271 (*Ctl. Wetheral*, no. 96). D. prob. shortly before 1292 (ibid., p. 427). Bur. in choir of Wetherhal ch. (*Ch.*, p. 75). Ment. of Robert de Wymondham, brother of the pr. of Wetheral Mich. 1280 (PRO, E159/54, m. 12d).

William of Tanfield I (Tainfelde, Tan(e)feld, Tanefeud) −1299 Occ. n.d. (1290 x ?1293) (*Ch. York*, p. 24); Nov. 1292 (*Ctl. Wetheral*, no. 230, and p. 427); 1293 (PRO, Just.1/650, m. 33d); (W.) 18 Dec. 1294 (*Reg. Halton*, I, 25). Made pr. of York 1299, but dep. by Archbp Corbridge 29 Jan 1303 (*Ch. York*, p. 37). later restored (ibid., p. 34).

John of Gilling (Gillyng(e)) 1299–1303 Apptd to Wetheral 1299 and ruled 4½ years (ibid., p. 75). El. abb. of St Mary's, York 1303 (q.v.).

John of Thorpe (Thorp) 1303–1304; 1309 *Homo parve stature sed magnus in astutia* (ibid., pp. 46, 135). Pres. 10 Nov. 1303 by Abb. John of Gilling to fill his place and he ruled Wetheral from 22 Nov. 1303 to 25 June 1304 when he was made pr. of St Mary's, York (*Ch. York*, p. 75; *Ctl. Wetheral*, p. 508). Res. from York 1309 and returned to Wetheral (ibid., p. 43). Occ.

6 May 1309 (*CPR 1307–13*, p. 112); 10 May 1309 (*Reg. Halton*, I, 326); 14 Sept. 1309 (*Ch.*, p. 46). D. 27 Sept. 1309 (ibid.).

William of Tanfield I (restored) **1304–1309** Adm. 18 Mar. 1304, no reason given for vacancy (*Reg. Halton*, I, 216). Occ. 20 Feb. 1306 (ibid., 247). Papal prov. to Durham priory 21 Feb. 1308 by Clement V (*CPL*, II, 40); installed 4 Sept. 1309 (*Ch. York*, p. 43). D. 7 Feb. 1314 (ibid., p. 65).

[**John of Pickering** (Pikeryng) After John of Thorpe's d. he was sent by abb. of St Mary's as *custos*. He stayed there for a year (ibid., p. 76).]

Robert de Gisburn (Giseburn, Gyseburgh) *alias* **Twentyman 1309–1314** Twentyman claimed priory (ibid., p. 75). Occ. 26 Apr. 1309 when papal lic. to contract a loan of 2,000 gold florins (*CPL*, II, 53). Apptd by pope. Prohibition of Robert's induction to the priory until the king and his council should have examined the papal letters of collation, in regard to any encroachment upon royal prerogative 18 Sept. 1309 (*CPR 1307–13*, p. 190; *Reg. Halton*, II, 11–12). Occ. 1 Mar. 1311 (*CPL*, II, 94). Excommunicated 2 Jan. 1314 and convent placed under interdict; Robert res. (*Reg. Halton*, II, 87; *Ctl. Wetheral*, p. 403).

Gilbert de Botile (Botil(l)) **1314–1319** Sub-pr. of York 1313 (*Ch. York*, p. 62). Apptd to Wetheral 25 Jan. 1314 (ibid., p. 64). Inst. 27 Mar 1314 on res. of Robert (*Reg. Halton*, II, 87–8). Made pr. York by 8 Mar. 1319 and removed from Wetheral (ibid., 183), but cf. pr. **John** (*sic*) occ. 14 Mar. 1316 and 28 May 1316 (*Reg. Halton*, II, 119, 121).

Adam of Dalton 1319–1341 M. of York, Letters of pres. by abb. of St Mary's, York, since Gilbert de Botile had been apptd pr. of St Mary's 8 Mar. 1319 (*Reg. Halton*, II, 183). Occ. 1331 (*Reg. Kirkby*, I, no. 57); 7 Feb., 27 Mar. 1341 in dispute with dean and chapter of York *sede vacante* over tuitorial appeal to Canterbury (ibid., nos. 577, 579, 593).

William of Tanfield II (Tanfeld) **1341–** M. of York, adm. 19 Nov. 1341, no reason given for vacancy (ibid., no. 623). Occ. 5 Aug 1342 (*Ctl. Wetheral*, no. 244). Re-inst. 21 June 1354 but no reason given (*Reg. Welton* no. 35). Occ. 6 Feb. 1360 (ibid., no. 297).

William de Bridford (Brudford) **1374–1382** M. of York, adm. [ ] Aug. 1374, no reason given for vacancy (Carlisle, DRC/1/2, p. 258). El. abb. of St Mary's, York 1382, royal ass. 16 Aug. 1382 (*CPR 1381–85*, p. 159).

WYMONDHAM (Norfolk) St Mary (St Albans) f. 1107

Lists in *VCH Norfolk*, II, 342–3; early 14th cent. list in Oxford, Magdalen Coll. ms. 53 (deposited in the Bodl.), p. 4 – the list for this period goes from Alexander 9th pr.; then Ralph of Whitby; Thomas *medicus*; William of St Albans, William of Horton, William of Waltham, Roger of Acre, Adam Puleyn, and the list ends with his successor the 17th pr., John de Stevenache; Bodl., Wood ms. D.18, f. 117; *Heads*, I, 97–8. See *Heads*, I, corrigenda for a discussion of the succession of priors to Thomas *medicus*.

Alexander of Langley (Langleya) Made pr. *temp.* William abb. of St Albans (1214–35) but soon recalled to St Albans (*GASA*, I, 260).

Ralph de Stanham *alias* **of Whitby** (Witeby, Wyteby) Former m. and pr. of Whitby, replaced Alexander (ibid.). Complaints made against him (ibid., 272). Dep. and returned to his cell at Whitby (ibid., 274). Is he to be identified with pr. **R.** who occ. 15 May 1220 (*Norwich Cath. Chts.*, II, no. 75)?

William of Fécamp Replaced Ralph as pr. but held office only a short time. Eln quashed on complaint of the earl of Arundel who secured the promotion of Thomas *medicus*, his son (ibid., 274–5).

Thomas *Medicus* –1248 Succ. William (ibid.). Occ. from Oct. 1224 x Oct. 1225 to Oct. 1236 x Oct. 1237 (*Norfolk F. (Rye)*, pp. 39, 59); 10 Aug. 1229 (*CPR 1225–32*, p. 301). D. 6 Apr. 1248 (*MPCM*, VI, 278). See Talbot and Hammond, p. 330. *GASA*, I, 275 notes that

Thomas accompanied the earl of Arundel on crusade 1218 and brought back the earl's body for burial at Wymondham. The earl died before 30 Mar. 1221 (*Complete Peerage*, I, 236–8; cf. *Reg. Whethamstede*, II, 343). What is not clear is whether Thomas was pr. when he went on crusade or was apptd later. I suspect the latter. A pr. **John** occ. Hil. term 1229 (*CRR*, XIII, no. 1503). Whether this is just a scribal error for Thomas is uncertain.

William of St Albans –**1262** Occ. Oct. 1256 x Oct. 1257 (*Norfolk F. (Rye)*, p. 92). D. 12 Mar. 1262, after which there followed a dispute between St Albans and Isabel, countess of Arundel, the patron (*GASA*, I, 408).

William of Horton (Hortone) Occ. 14 Sept. 1264 (ibid., 407–8); royal escheator 1268 (*Ch. Barnwell*, p. 80 & n. 2).

Prob. **William of Waltham** should be inserted as 14th pr., if the Magdalen list can be accepted.

Roger Occ. n.d. (*c.* 1274) (Ctl. Marham, f. 31r). Presumably the **Roger of Acre** of the Magdalen list.

Adam Pulleyn (Poleyn, Puleyn) –**1303** Apptd by abb. Roger of St Albans (1263–90) (*GASA*, II, 82). Occ. (A.) 12 Apr. 1301 (*HMC Var. Coll.*, II, 341); 22 Aug. 1303 (*GASA*, II, 145–7). D. 25 Dec. 1303 (ibid., 83; Bodl., Magd. Coll. ms. 53, p. 2).

John of Stevenage (Stevenache, Stethenache, Stithenache) **1304**– M. of St Albans, pres. to priory 13 Jan. 1304 (*GASA*, II, 86; Bodl., Magd. Coll. ms. 53, p. 3); entered possession of priory 10 Feb. 1304 (*GASA*, II, 88, cf. 148). Occ. 26 Jan. 1304 (ibid., 89); May–June 1306 (PRO, Just.1/591, mm. 10, 13); 20 Nov. 1306 (PRO, E40/6201); 13 Dec. 1307 (PRO, C241/58/5); 1 June 1308 (PRO, C241/57/188).

John de Hurle(e) **1318**– Pres. by Abb. Hugh of St Albans, adm. 11 Feb. 1318, no reason given for vacancy (Norwich, Reg/1/1, f. 72v). Occ. 20 Dec. 1318 (ibid., f. 78r); 29 Oct. 1326 (*GASA*, II, 184).

Richard of Hethersett (Hedersete) **1334**– M. of Wymondham, adm. 23 Sept. 1334 (Norwich, Reg/1/2, f. 67v). Occ. 16 Dec. 1346 (*CCR 1346–49*, p. 174). Recent d. of unnamed pr. mentd 14 Sept. 1347 (*CPR 1345–48*, p. 404).

Henry of Stukeley (Steukle, Stukle) **1347**– M. of St Albans, pres. by Abb. Michael, dated 11 Sept. 1347, adm. 14 Oct. 1347, no reason given for vacancy (Norwich, Reg/2/4, f. 64v). El. abb. of St Albans 1349 but refused to acc. office (*GASA*, II, 382). Occ. 8 July 1349 (*CPL*, III, 339); 4 Feb. 1350, 8 Feb. 1350, 17 July 1350 (*CCR 1349–54*, pp. 202, 203, 239); 10 Oct. 1361 (PRO, C241/141/176).

Nicholas de Radclif (Radeclyf) **1369**– M. of St. Albans, *sacre pagine professor*, pres. by letter of Abb. Thomas, dated 5 Feb. 1369, adm. 7 Mar. 1369, no reason given for vacancy (Norwich, Reg/2/5, f. 84v). Occ. 20 Mar. 1376, 8 July 1376 (*CPR 1374–77*, pp. 318, 328). Ordered by bp of Norwich to collect subsidy *c.* 1380; a dispute led to his recall and appt as archdn of St Albans (*GASA*, III, 122–3, 281–2, 396; cf. *Ch. Amundesham*, I, 436). See Emden, *BRUO*, III, 1539.

John occ. *c.* 1378 x 1381 (PRO, E179/45/14), presumably 1381, unless this is another instance of a 'suspect' or bogus name being found in these Ricardian clerical subsidy rolls (see Lanercost; Tynemouth).

The next recorded pr., **William de Kylyngworthe**, occ. *c.* 1381 (*GASA*, III, 343; *Walsingham*, II, 28).

YARMOUTH, (Great Yarmouth) (Norfolk) (Ben. Cell of Norwich) f. –1101
List in *VCH Norfolk*, II, 329; biographical details in Greatrex, *Biog. Reg.*, pp. 466–576 (Norwich monks).

Ralph of Ellingham (Elingham, Elyngham) Occ. as *custos* 1291–2 (*Communar Rolls*, p. 61).

Ralph Occ. Mich. 1305 (PRO, CP40/153, m. 132) ? same as Ralph of Ellingham.

William of Claxton (Clackiston, Clasthun, Claston, Claxisthon) –1326 Occ. 6 Apr. 1325 (NRO, DCN.44/57/1); 1 Jan. 1326 (Norwich, Reg/1/2, f. 79r); pr. of Norwich 1326–44 (q.v.)

Roger de Wolterton (Wlterton, Waltyrton) Occ. Mich. 1350–56 (DCN.2/4/1).

Laurence of Tunstall (Tunstale) On 20 June 1366 the pr. of Norwich wrote to 'Lawrence de T.', pr. of Yarmouth requesting his return to a Black Monk Chapter visitation (*Chapter of English Black Monks*, III, 55–6) – likely to be identified with Laurence de Tunstall (Greatrex). Previously pr. of Lynn 1361.

The next recorded pr., **John of Hoo**, D.Th., occ. Mich. 1386–88, 1400–1, 1404–6 (DCN.2/4/2–4; -1/12/33); 10 July 1393, 29 Sept. 1394 (NRO, DCN.44/31/57; 44/119/3).

THE BENEDICTINE
HOUSES:ALIEN PRIORIES

No names have been found in this period for Monkland, Spettisbury, and Tooting Bec. For the status of the last named see A. Hughes, 'The manor of Tooting Bec and its reputed priory', *Surrey Arch. Coll.*, 59 (1962), 1–14.

ABERGAVENNY (Monmouth), St Mary (S. Vincent, Le Mans) f. 1087 x 1100
  List in *Heads*, I, 99.
Richard Occ. May 1291 (*Wilts F.*, II, 36);
Giles de Lummier' (Limenei) **1291–1293** M. of Le Mans, inst. 27 Feb.1292 by archbp of Canterbury *sede vacante*, no reason given for vacancy (*Reg. Pecham*, I, 96); res. 21 June 1293 on account of infirmity (*Canterbury Sede Vacante Institutions*, p. 1).
William de Lonboul 1293– M. of Le Mans, adm. 9 Aug.1293 (ibid.).
Fulk Gastard Bp Orleton of Hereford commnd by pope to investigate state of priory – Fulk removed from office by 27 Sept. 1320 (*Reg. Orleton (Hereford)*, pp. 151–3, 190–4; Cowley, *Monastic Order in South Wales*, pp. 111–12). Ment. in mand. of 29 Mar. 1321 as having been removed by bp without consulting the abb. and convent of St Vincent (*CPL*, II, 211).
Richard of Bromwich (Bromwico) **1320–** M. and precentor of Worcester (*Reg. Bransford*, p. vii). Bp Orleton asks pr. of Worcester to sanction appt of Richard of Bromwich, m. of Worcester, as pr. of Abergavenny 27 Sept. 1320 (*Reg. Orleton*, pp. 154–5); apptd by bp on removal of Fulk (ibid., pp. 151–3, 155, 190–4). Permission to be pr. given 4 Oct.1320 (*Worcester Liber Albus*, II, no. 887). 1325 appeal from the pr. of Worcester for Richard of Bromwich, formerly their lecturer, now pr. of Abergavenny, to return (ibid., nos. 1083–4). For Richard see Greatrex, *Biog. Reg.*, pp. 782–3.
1325 ment. of the French pr. and monks of Abergavenny having been replaced *temp*. John, bp of Llandaff (1294/7–1323) (*CCR 1323–27*, pp. 270–1).
John le Peleter Occ. 17 Feb.1344 (*CCR 1343–46*, p. 353).
William Pelliparius Occ. 1 June 1348 (*CCR 1346–49*, p. 522); 15 Mar. 1351 (*CFR 1347–56*, p. 283); 17 Mar. 1351 (*CCR 1349–54*, p. 352). Mentd in respect of arrears before 1354 (PRO, E372/200, rot. 9).
John Hegan Occ. 24 Mar. 1354 (*CFR 1347–56*, p. 392); Mich. 1354 x Mich. 1355 (PRO, E372/200, rot. 9).
Void 4 Oct.1369 (*CPR 1367–70*, p. 307) – safe-conduct to John de la Ferte, m. of Abergavenny, who is going to St Vincent for the eln and creation of a new pr. of Abergavenny on the d. of the last (unnamed) pr.
William Petrowe (Peydrowe, Peytrau) Occ. 28 Oct. 1371 (*CFR 1368–77*, p.117); 15 Feb. 1378 (*CFR 1377–83*, p. 84); 10 July 1387 (PRO, C85/11/33).

ALLERTON MAULEVERER (Yorks W.), St Martin (Marmoutier) f. 1100+
(dependent on York, Holy Trinity); *c*. 1110 (dependent on Marmoutier)
  List in *VCH Yorks*, III, 387;
Waleran Occ. *c*.1235 (BL Cotton ms. Claudius D. XI, f. 62r).
Gilbert Occ. *c*.1245 (ibid., f. 62v); 1247 x 1252 *temp*. Stephen, abb. of Fountains (*Ctl. Fountains*, II, 855).

Richard Occ. late Henry III or Edward I (BL, Add. Chts. 1293, 1297). Mentd as former pr. in 1279 (PRO, Just.1/1056, m. 55d).

Geoffrey Occ. 7 Sept.1272 (*CPR 1266–72*, p. 676); 1300 (Baildon, I, 1).

John Dugas Occ. 1344 (*VCH* citing Baildon's ms. notes, no precise source mentioned).

John de Passu –1362 M. of Marmoutier, occ. 1 Mar. 1345 (*CFR 1337–47*, p. 410). Occ. Mich. 1348 x Mich. 1349 (PRO, E372/194, rot. 8d); Mich. 1354 x Mich. 1355 (PRO, E372/200, rot. 6, 6d); Mich. 1358 x Mich. 1359 (PRO, E372/204, rot. 7d). D. *ante* 30 June 1362 (*YAJ*, XXV, p. 168, no. 7).[1]

Denis Rabarus 1362– M. of Marmoutier, adm.30 June 1362 on presentation of John Fresney, pr. of Tickford, vicar-general of abb. of Marmoutier, on d. of John de Passu (ibid.).

Francis Quatresout 1363– Adm. 24 Jan. 1363 on presentation of John de Fresneya, pr. of Tickford, no reason given for vacancy (ibid., p. 170, no. 22).

William de Virgulto 1364–1365 Adm. 2 Apr.1364, no reason given for vacancy (ibid., p.171, no.30). Res. by 9 Feb. 1365 (ibid., no. 32).

John Pratt(e) *alias* de Newport (Neuport) 1365–1400 M. of Marmoutier, adm. 9 Feb.1365 on res. of William de Virgulto, on presentation of abb. of Marmoutier (ibid., no. 32 & p. 200, no. 236a). D. by 29 Apr. 1400 (ibid., p. 200, no. 236).

ANDOVER (Hants), St Mary (S. Florent, Saumur) f. -1087
Lists in *VCH Hants*, II, 221; *Heads*, I, 99.

John Occ. early 13th cent., perhaps *temp*. Henry III (pal.: WCM, no. 2126)

Nicholas Hermita Occ. first half 13th cent. (pal.: WCM, nos. 2125, 2131); 19 Dec. 1234 (*CChR 1226–57*, p. 189).

Mag. Berard of Naples 1250– subdeacon and papal chaplain – apptd by Pope Innocent IV 23 July 1250; papal letter of commendation to Henry III 26 Sept. 1250 (*Reg. Woodlock*, II, 1026–26; Sayers, nos. 371–2, 378). Occ. 31 May 1264 (*CPL*, I, 418).

John of St John (de Sancto Johanne) ?1289/90–1305 Said, on 23 June 1293, to have been pr. for 4 years (*Select Canterbury Cases*, p. 416). Occ. Nov. 1295 x Nov. 1296 (PRO, E106/3/19, m. 6); Nov. 1296 x Nov. 1297 (PRO, E106/4/2, m. 4); 23 Mar. 1297 (*CPR 1292–1301*, p. 270); Nov. 1297 x Nov. 1298 (PRO, E106/4/8, m. 3); Nov. 1298 x Nov. 1299 (PRO, E106/4/9, m. 3d; E106/4/10, m. 5); 1300 (PRO, E106/4/14, m. 7); Nov. 1302 x Nov. 1303 (PRO, E106/4/18, m. 9d); 14 Mar. 1305 (*Reg. Woodlock*, I, 2).

Robert de Combo(u)r 1305– Occ. 28 Mar. 1305 – prohibition of a suit in Court Christian by John de Sancto Johanne against pr. Robert (ibid., II, 880). Mand. to the dean of Andover to cite Robert de Combour, monk, and to sequester the revenues of Andover priory. By a campaign of slander against John de Sancto Johanne, pr. of Andover, Robert persuaded the abb. of S. Florent to pres. him to Bp Pontissara of Winchester in John's stead, and although never canonically adm. as pr., Robert acted as pr. When the truth was put to him, the abb. ordered John to be reinstated but Robert still retains the post he usurped, 17 Mar. 1305 (ibid., I, 3–4). Robert submits to the bp's ruling in the matter of the priory 22 Aug. 1305; mand. to relax sequestration same day (ibid., 34–5). Bp Woodlock writes to the abb. of S. Florent and commends John de Sancto Johanne. He did good work: now elderly and worn out he deserves peace and some compensation for his past hardship n.d. (*c*. Sept. 1305) (ibid., 44–5). Robert adm. 22 Oct. 1305 (ibid., II, 715; *Reg. Wykeham*, II, 613).

Helias de Combor 1307– M. of S. Florent, mand. to induct 17 Sept. 1307 (*Reg. Woodlock*, II, 726; *Reg. Wykeham*, II, 614). Occ. 16 May 1313 (*Reg. Woodlock*, II, 738).

---

[1] *VCH* has John Passu occ. 1366, citing Pipe Roll 40 Edward III.

Ralph de Combor(e) 1316– Adm. 26 Sept. 1316, no reason given for vacancy (*Reg. Sandale*, pp. 119–20; *Reg. Wykeham*, II, 614).

Helias de Combor 1320– M. of S. Florent, inst. Nov. 1320 (*Reg. Wykeham*, II, 614).

John de Pomariis (Pomeries, Pomeriis) **–1341** Born in Aquitaine (*CPR 1324–27*, p. 181). Proceedings in a case between Andrew de Caprasia, m. of S. Florent, pres. by the abb. of S. Florent to the priory, and John de Pomer', m. of S. Florent and pr. of Andover by virtue of a papal provision 1324. Andrew did not appear and the case against John was dismissed (Winchester, Reg. Stratford, f. 161r–v). Occ. 4 Aug. 1324, 10 Nov. 1324, 17 Oct. 1325, safe-conduct to the Court of Rome 20 Aug. 1326 (*CPR 1324–27*, pp. 16, 46, 181, 311); lic. to be absent for 3 years 20 July 1326 (Winchester, Reg. Stratford, f. 16r); further lic. 20 Nov. 1331 (ibid., f. 63v); monition to reside 9 Dec. 1332 (ibid., f. 76r); gtd keeping of Sele priory now void, 10 Mar. 1338 (*CFR 1337–47*, p. 71). Occ. Mich. 1338 x Mich. 1339 (PRO, E372/184, rot. 13d). Priory vacant by 7 Sept. 1341 by John's appt as pr. of Sele (Winchester, Reg. Orleton, II, f. 89r–v, cf. *CFR 1337–47*, p. 248).

Philip Matheu (Maghe) **1341–** M. of S. Florent, adm. 7 Sept. 1341 (Winchester, Reg. Orleton, II, f. 89r–v; *Reg. Wykeham*, II, 614). Occ. 5 Feb. 1342 (*CFR 1337–47*, p. 265); 11 July 1345 (*CCR 1343–46*, p. 636); 30 Aug. 1361 (*Reg. Edington*, I, no. 1303).

Denis Canoun (Cano(n), Chanon) **1363–1399** Adm. 16 Jan. 1363 (ibid., no. 1556; *Reg. Wykeham*, II, 615). D. by 20 Oct. 1399 (*CPR 1399–1401*, p. 23). Successor adm. 23 Oct. 1399 on d. of Denis Canoun (*Reg. Wykeham*, I, 221).

ANDWELL (Hants), St Mary (Tiron) (Mapledurwell) f. *temp.* Henry II; diss. 1391 and granted to Winchester College.

Lists in *VCH Hants*, II, 225; *Heads*, I, 99.

Gervase Occ. *c.* Sept. 1210 (*Basset Chts.*, no. 210); n.d. (*c.*1213 x 1232) (ibid., no. 239); 1213+ (*HMC 4th Rept.* App., p.455); 14 June 1219 (PRO, Hants. F. CP25/1/203/4, no. 22).

Nicholas Occ. 2 Feb. 1267, 14 Mar. 1277 and frequently *temp.* Henry III and Edward I (WCM, nos. 2818, 2835, etc.).

William Occ. 2 Feb. 1282 (WCM, no. 2868).

Robert Occ. 27 Jan. 1290 (WCM, no. 2871); 1292 (ibid., no. 2898); Nov. 1295 x Nov. 1296 (PRO, E106/3/19, m. 9d); 1 Nov. 1297 (WCM, no. 2873); Nov. 1298 x Nov. 1299 (PRO, E106/4/9, m. 5); 2 May 1303 (WCM, no. 2854); 25 Nov. 1306 (ibid., no. 2916).

Richard Occ. 30 Apr.1309 (ibid., no. 2840).

Ralph Hermite Occ. 22 Nov. 1314 (*Reg. Gandavo*, I, 828); 31 May 1315 (WCM, no. 2874); 6 Nov. 1317 (ibid., no. 2915); 23 June 1319 (ibid., no. 2890); 25 Apr. 1320 (ibid., no. 10666); July 1325 x July 1326 (PRO, E106/5/4, m. [8]); 8 Oct. 1326 (*Memo. Roll 1326–7*, p. 272); 25 July 1327 (*Reg. Martival*, I, 376), 8 May 1333 (WCM, no. 2895).

Geoffrey Burgeys of Isle of Wight *alias* **de Lille** (del Ile, de Insula Vectis) Occ. 17 Mar 1331 (ibid., no. 2842); 11 Nov. 1332 (ibid., no. 2897); 3 Dec. 1332 (ibid., no. 10667); 8 May 1335 (ibid., no. 2897); (Burgeys) 1 June 1338 (ibid., no. 2891); 1 Aug. 1340 (ibid., no. 2875). Possibly the unnamed pr. too aged and infirm to administer priory and the abb. of Tiron appts br. **Robert Renard**, m. of Tiron, to administer 6 Mar. 1341 (*CFR 1337–47*, p. 214).

Robert Renard (Reynard) Occ. 9 Mar.1342 (*CFR 1337–47*, p. 273). Mentd 28 Apr. 1344 as former pr. (ibid., p. 370); mentd 1354 x 1355 as occ. before 16 Edward III (Jan. 1342 x Jan. 1343) (PRO, E372/200, rot. 28d).

Richard de Beaumont (Beaumond, Beumond) Occ. 31 Dec. 1343 (WCM, no. 2876); gtd keeping of priory 28 Apr. 1344 (*CFR 1337–47*, p. 370); occ. 10 Dec. 1344 (WCM, no. 2892). And see Hamble.

Robert Renard (Reynard) Occ. 11 July 1345 (*CCR 1343–46*, p. 636).

James Pasquerii 1346– M. of Tiron, proctor-general in England of abb. of Tiron, gtd keeping of priory on account of French war 15 Aug. 1346 (*CFR 1337–47*, p. 476).
1 Feb. 1385 memorandum that the priory is in the hands of Thomas Driffelde and Eleanor his wife (*Reg. Wykeham*, II, 354). On 18 Nov. 1381 Thomas Driffeld is desc. as *tenens et occupans prioratum de Endewelle* (PRO, C85/155/38).

APPULDURCOMBE (Isle of Wight), St Mary (Montebourg) f. *c.* 1100
Lists in *VCH Hants*, II, 232; *Heads*, I, 99. See also J.L. Whitehead, 'The Priory and Manor of Appuldurcombe, Isle of Wight', *Hants Field Club* 5 (1904–6), pp. 185–95.
Richard Occ. 1228 x 1238 (*Chts Quarr*, p. 75, nos. 306–7); *c.* 1241 (ibid., p. 79, no. 322). cf. St Cross.
Stephen Occ. Nov. 1295 x Nov. 1296 (PRO, E106/3/19, m. 10); Nov. 1297 x Nov. 1298 (PRO, E106/4/8, m. 3); Nov. 1298 x Nov. 1299 (PRO, E106/4/9, m. 5; E106/4/10, m. 5); Nov. 1302 x Nov. 1303 (PRO, E106/4/18, m. 10). Prob. **Stephen de Collevilla** who occ. in n.d. cht. (PRO, PRO31/8/140B, part 2, p. 189).
Laurence Occ. 1324 (PRO, SC6/1127/1); *c.* Mich. 1324 (PRO, E106/5/2, m. 4d); July 1325 x July 1326 (PRO, E106/5/4, m. [3]); 8 Oct. 1326 (*Memo. Roll 1326–7*, p. 272); 1331 (Laurence Bertram) (*Hants. Field Club* 5, p. 191, n. 4 – no source given); Mich. 1338 x Mich. 1339 (PRO, E372/184, rot. 14d).
Roger Haryel (Hariel) Occ. 12 July 1342 (*CFR 1337–47*, p. 275); 24 Feb. 1343 (*CCR 1343–46*, p. 92).
John (de) Osanne (Osanna, Ozanna) **1345–** M. of Montebourg, adm. 8 July 1345 (*CFR 1337–47*, p. 428). Papal conf. of colln by abb. of Montebourg 25 Feb.1350 on d. of last pr. (*CPL*, III, 354; *CPP*, p. 194; cf. *Accts of Papal Collectors*, pp. 94, 145, 175, 189, 270, 326, 366, 488). Occ. Mich. 1354 x Mich. 1355 (PRO, E372/200, rots. 28d, 29d); 16 June 1355 (as pr.), 8 Nov. 1355 (as m. of Montebourg, see Loders) (*CFR 1347–56*, pp. 431, 436).
Simon de la Launde M. of Montebourg, royal gt of keeping of priory during the French war 24 July 1359 (*CFR 1356–68*, p. 105).
Sampson Trygal (Trigall) Occ. 11 June 1369, 6 Oct. 1369 (*CFR 1368–77*, pp. 15, 23); 18 Mar. 1370 (*CPR 1367–70*, p. 380).
Peter de Mouster Occ. 8 Mar. 1377 (*CFR 1368–77*, p. 393); 16 Feb. 1378 (*CFR 1377–83*, p. 75); m. of Montebourg, 1 Feb. 1385 (*Reg. Wykeham*, II, 354); 25 Feb. 1389, 4 May 1390, but described as late pr. by 15 Nov. 1390 when the above docts were inspected and conf. (*CPR 1385–92*, p. 507).

ARUNDEL (Sussex), St Nicholas (Sées) f. -1094. Dissolved 1380 (when secular college
founded – M.T. Elvins, *Arundel Priory 1380–1980: The College of the Holy Trinity* (Chichester, 1981), pp. 8–12.
Lists in *VCH Sussex*, II, 120; *Heads*, I, 100.
William Occ. *c.* 1210 x 35 (PRO, E326/3905). Possibly the same as the William who occ. 20 June 1199 (*Rot.Cur.Reg.*, I, 405). The Walter who occ. 18 Nov. 1200 (*Sussex F.*, I, no. 48) is possibly a slip for William.
Nicholas Occ. (N.) 28 Sept. 1222, 1 Apr.1233 (*Ctl. Chichester*, nos. 1120, 246).
Warner Occ. 15 July 1241 (ibid., no. 379); 26 Aug. 1241 (*Ctl. Sele*, no. 30; *St Richard of Chichester*, p. 46, no. 70).
Gervase de Mota Occ. 1254 x 1259 (*Ctl. Chichester*, no. 820); 9 Jan. 1262 (PRO, E326/9305). Desc. as former pr. in 1271–2 (PRO, Just.1/913, m. 2).
Denis Occ. 24 June 1269 (BL, Lansdowne Cht. 92). Apptd attorney for the abb. of Sées 'shortly before Henry III's death', conf. 6 Feb. 1276 (*CPR 1272–81*, p. 135). Occ. 18 May 1272 (*CPR*

1266–72, p. 651). Occ.in *Sussex F.* from 25 Nov. 1275 to 25 June 1288 (nos. 859, 1000); Mich. 1276, Mich. 1280 (PRO, E326/12829–30); Nov. 1295 x Nov. 1296 (PRO, E106/3/19, m. 8d); 7 Feb. 1296 (*CPR 1292–1301*, p. 176); Nov. 1296 x Nov. 1297 (PRO, E106/4/2, m. 1); Nov. 1297 x Nov. 1298 (PRO, E106/4/8, m. 1); Nov. 1298 x Nov. 1299 (PRO, E106/4/9, m. 1; E106/4/10, m. 1d); Easter 1300 (PRO, E106/4/14, m. 1d); Nov. 1302 x Nov. 1303 (PRO, E106/4/18, m. 1d).

William de Mesnillo Occ. 29 Jan. 1318 (BL, Lansdowne cht. 105); midsummer 1322 (*CFR 1319–27*, p. 318); *c.* Mich. 1324 (PRO, E106/5/2, m. 3d); July 1325 x July 1326 (PRO, E106/5/4, m. [2]); 8 Oct. 1326 (*Memo. Roll 1326–7*, p. 271); 30 May 1328 (BL, Lansdowne Cht. 105); Easter-Mich. 1328 (*Index to Placita de Banco*, p. 658).

Gervase Occ. Mich. 1337 (PRO, CP40/312, m. 32).

Michael de Nanchal (Nonchal) **1349–1354** [occ. as proctor in England of abb. of Sées 1342, 1345 and Mich. 1346 (*CFR 1337–47*, p. 276; *CPR 1340–43*, pp. 388, 423; *CPR 1343–45*, p. 469; PRO, E106/9/21; E401/383)]. Petition to Queen Isabel to receive Michael, el. by Sées abbey to be pr. 1349, no reason given for vacancy (PRO, E40/15644). Occ. 10 Mar. 1350 (*CFR 1347–56*, p. 219); 13 Oct. 1353, 20 Jan. 1354 (*CCR 1349–54*, pp. 623, 624); 12 May 1354 to 20 June 1354 (*CCR 1354–60*, pp. 15, 80). D. by 20 Oct. 1354 (*CFR 1347–56*, p. 404).

Nicholas (le) Corner (Cromer) **1354–** Occ. 20 Oct. 1354 (*CFR 1347–56*, p. 418); 26 Apr. 1357 (*CCR 1354–60*, p. 404); Mich. 1358 x Mich. 1359 (PRO, E372/204, rot. 21d). Ref. in 1360 to him as late pr., deceased (*CFR 1356–68*, p. 117).

John Mercer ((le) Merser, Messer, Messier) M. of Sées, occ. 7 Feb. 1360 (ibid.); [occ. as proctor in England of abb. of Sées 1354, 1356, 1361 – not desc. as pr. (*CFR 1347–56*, p. 404; *CFR 1356–68*, p. 13; *CPR 1361–64*, p. 12)]; 30 Sept. 1364 (*CPL*, IV, 46); going overseas 1368 (*CPR 1367–70*, p. 96); 1370 (PRO, E106/10/11); 1374 (*Cal. Misc. Inq.*, III, 351); 1377 (PRO, E179/11/1A); 8 Feb. 1378 (*CFR 1377–83*, p. 79); 19 May 1378 (*CCR 1377–81*, p. 134). ? the same as the bailiff of Atherington (q.v.).

ASTLEY (Worcs), St Peter (S.Taurin, Evreux) f. *c.* 1085
  Lists in *VCH Worcs*, II, 182; *Heads*, I, 100.

W. Occ. 1193 x 1205 (*HMC Var. Coll.*, I, 239).[2]

Robert de Sanarvill 1289– Inducted 22 Nov. 1289, no reason given for vacancy (*Reg. G. Giffard*, p. 365).

Guy de Villaribus 1294– Inst. 16 Aug. 1294, no reason given for vacancy (ibid., p. 444). Occ. Nov. 1295 x Nov. 1296 (PRO, E106/3/19, m. 7d); 5 Mar. 1296 (ibid., p. 466); Nov. 1296 x Nov. 1297 (PRO, E106/4/2, m. 6); Nov. 1298 x Nov. 1299 (PRO, E106/4/9, m. 9; E106/4/10, m. 7); Easter 1300 (PRO, E106/4/14, m. 11). He also occ. in the return of aliens Nov. 1302 x Nov. 1303 (PRO, E106/4/18, m. 13) – is this an error? (see next entry).

Ralph de Portes (Porters, le Porter) **–1304** Occ. 15 June 1300 (*Reg. G. Giffard*, p. 526). July–Aug.1303 (*Reg. Worcs. Reg. Sede Vacante*, pp. 57, 59). Res. by 31 July 1304 (*Reg. Gainsborough*, p. 85).

Stephen de Meisiaco (Mesiaco, Meysiaco) **1305–1313** Custody gtd to Stephen de Meisiaco, m. of S. Taurin, in the absence of Ralph le Porter until Assumption next, on condition that the bp is satisfied of the res. of Ralph and that a suitable person is presented, 9 May 1304 (ibid., p. 135). Inst. to Astley, vacant by the res. of Ralph de Portes, 31 July 1304 (ibid., p. 85). Letter to king for arrest 30 March 1313 (*Reg. Reynolds*, p. 63); res. 11 Oct. 1313 (ibid., p. 74).

---

[2] Simon occ. in *VCH* list for 1280, but the source (*Reg. G. Giffard*, p. 122) describes him as monk of Astley, not pr.

Robert de Louers (Lavers) 1313–1329/30 M. of S. Taurin, pres. 11 Oct.1313 (ibid.); adm. same day (ibid., p. 157). Adm. 29 Nov. 1313 (*Worcs. Reg. Sede Vacante*, p. 139). D. by 13/23 June 1329/1330 (*Reg. Orleton (Worcester)*, nos. 88, 727).

John Heribel 1329/30–1334 M. of S. Taurin, adm. 13 or 23 June 1329/1330 (ibid., no. 88). Res. by 8 July 1334 (*Reg. Montacute*, nos. 179, 199).

William Busquet (Busqet) 1334– M. of S. Taurin, letter of pres. 8 July 1334; adm. 27 Oct. 1334 (ibid.).

Ralph de Valle (Walle) 1341– M. of S. Taurin, inst. 18 Apr. 1341, no reason given for vacancy (*Reg. Bransford*, no. 400). Occ. 10 Feb. 1342 (*CFR 1337–47*, p. 273); 11 July 1345 (*CCR 1343–46*, p. 636), but see next entry.

William Prevot (Provot) 1343–1349 M. of S. Taurin, inst. 5 June 1343, no reason given for vacancy (*Reg. Bransford*, no. 506). Recalled 1349 (ibid., p. 427).

Hugh de Valle 1349– Inst. 18 June 1349 when William Prevot recalled on account of his infirmity (ibid.).

John Ogerii 1361 Adm. pr. 9 Mar. 1361, no reason given for vacancy (Worcester, Reg. Brian, I, p. 68); res. by 4 June 1361 (ibid., p. 70).

John Bonnet 1361– Adm. 4 June 1361 (Worcester, Reg. Brian, I, p. 70).

William de Atrio (Attrio) 1362– [br. John Ogerii & br. William de Attrio, monks of S. Taurin, gtd keeping of the priory during French war 20 Jan. 1361 (*CFR 1356–68*, p. 147)]. M. of S. Taurin, adm. 3 Feb. 1362, no reason given for vacancy (*Worcs. Reg. Sede Vacante*, p. 208).

Commn to enquire into charges of committing damages, waste etc., against Percival le Walssh, to whom the king has committed the custody of the priory, 15 June 1374 (*CPR 1370–74*, p. 483).

John M. of Conches, occ. 1374 (*Worcs. Reg. Sed. Vac.*, p. 307); 14 Mar. 1376 (*CFR 1368–77*, p. 345); 8 Feb. 1378 (*CFR 1377–83*, p. 80).

[**Richard of Hampton** was apptd by letters patent of 5 Aug. 1380 to custody of the priory during the French war and he was to have the priory for life at a yearly rent of £20, 24 Feb. 1381 (*CPR 1377–81*, p. 602).]

ASTON PRIORS (Aston Tirrold) (Berks). The church of Aston Tirrold, along with land at Watlington and the church of Newbury formed an estate grouping, one of four priories or 'estate offices' administering the English possessions of the abbey of St Peter, Préaux (Matthew, *Norman Monasteries*, p. 53). Only the following reference has been found to it as a 'priory' and it was probably not so in a technical sense.

Amfrid Meret Occ. as *dictus* pr. of Aston (Priors) and proctor-general in England of Préaux 19 Apr. 1322 (*Reg. Martival*, I, 249).

ATHERINGTON (Sussex) (Sées) (Bailiwick, prob. administering all the Sées estates in England not specifically allotted to the abbey's English cells, Matthew, *Norman Monasteries*, pp. 54–5). f. -1102? diss. *c.*1414 (granted to Syon Abbey)

List in *VCH Sussex*, II, 120.

[**?John of Alençon** (Alenchon) occ. as pr. of 'Aurinton', witn. to a cht. of H., abb. of Sées (Madox, *Form.*, p. 115, no. 196). Abb. H. ? Henry/Hugh, late 12th, early 13th cents. (*Gallia Christiana*, XI, 721). Is this to be identified with Atherington? It seems likely that John was based in Atherington before he moved to be pr. of Lancaster (q.v.)]

William Occ. as bailiff 9 Sept. 1295 (*Reg. Sutton*, I, 201).

William Oliver (Olyver) Occ. as bailiff n.d. (PRO, E326/3485); Nov. 1302 x Nov. 1303 (PRO, E106/4/18, m. 1); occ. as proctor of abb. of Sées midsummer 1304 (PRO, E326/3315).

Peter de Orgericiis (Orgeriz) Occ. 1324 (PRO, E326/9282); as bailiff and proctor-general of abb. of Sées in England: protection for 1 year, 6 Dec. 1325 (*CPR 1324–27*, p. 194).

Gervase A(r)miger/Le Squyer Occ. as bailiff 9 July 1330, 20 May 1331, 6 June 1331 (*Reg. Burghersh* I, nos. 267, 296, 299); occ. as proctor of Sées 15 Apr. 1334 (ibid., no. 412).

Emeric Occ. as bailiff 28 July 1337 (*CPR 1334–38*, p. 483).

Michael bro. of Richard, earl of Arundel, a monk of St Martin's, secretary, now bailiff of Atherington [*c.* July– Aug.] 1345 (*CPP*, p. 102); occ. as bailiff 29 Jan. 1349 (*CPR 1348–50*, p. 311).

Michael Nanchal Occ. as bailiff 11 June 1353 (PRO, E326/3753). ? same as above. Pr. of Arundel 1349–54 (q.v.).

John (le) Merser/Messer bailiff of Atherington, pardon for his outlawry in connection with a plea of debt, he having now surrendered to Fleet prison 22 Apr. 1371 (*CPR 1370–4*, p. 69). Occ. as bailiff 25 Aug. 1356, 24 Nov. 1356 (*CFR 1356–68*, pp. 12, 24)? same as pr. of Arundel. (q.v.).

Richard Occ. as bailiff 29 Sept. 1376 (PRO, E326/173).

AVEBURY (Wilts) (S. Georges, Boscherville) f. 1114+ Diss. 1378
List in *VCH Wilts*, III, 393.

John de Wymonville Occ. n.d. (1209 x 1232) (*Ctl. Bradenstoke*, no. 112).

William Occ. 1249 (*Wilts Crown Pleas*, p. 223, no. 374).

William Occ. Nov. 1295 x Nov. 1296 (PRO, E106/3/19, m. 9); Nov. 1296 x Nov. 1297 (ibid., E106/4/2, m. 4); Nov. 1297 x Nov. 1298 (ibid., E106/4/8, m. 3); Nov. 1298 x Nov. 1299 (ibid., E106/4/9, m. 3d); Easter 1300 (ibid., E106/4/14, m. 6d); Nov. 1302 x Nov. 1303 (ibid., E106/4/18, m. 9).

Robert Maynard Occ. *c.* Mich. 1324 (ibid., E106/5/2, m. 6d); July 1325 x July 1326 (ibid., E106/5/4, m. [5d]). See also below, 1336.

Richard Botayl −1336 Recalled to Boscherville 1336 (*Ctl. Cirencester*, III, no. 736).

Robert Maynard (Menart, Taynard) **1336–** Apptd 1336 (ibid.). Occ. (Taynard) 8 Feb. 1342 (*CFR 1337–47*, p. 261); 11 July 1345 (*CCR 1343–46*, p. 636), but see next entry.

Walter Barre Occ. 8 May 1343 (*CFR 1337–47*, p. 330); Mich. 1348 x Mich. 1349 (PRO, E372/194, rot. 36). Mentd 15 Mar. 1350 as having been removed from office by his superior (*CFR 1347–56*, pp. 220–1).

Hugh de Abifago Occ. 15 Mar. 1350 (ibid.). Infirm and cannot attend to the rule of the priory, replaced by 8 Aug. 1350 (ibid., p. 251).

John de la Haye (Haia, Haya, de la Heye) **1350–** M. of S. Georges, gt of keeping of priory 8 Aug. 1350 (ibid.). Occ. 18 Oct. 1353 (*CPR 1354–58*, p. 4).

Robert de Verretot M. of S. Georges, gt of keeping of priory 10 Mar. 1354 (*CFR 1347–56*, p. 390; mentd PRO, E372/200, rot. 34). Occ. 1369 (PRO, C47/18/2/35, old ref., not yet reclassified to C270).

Stephen Fosse Occ. 20 Sept. 1370, 18 June 1377 (*CFR 1368–77*, pp. 83, 405).
House dissolved 1378.

AXMOUTH (Devon) (Montebourg) f. *temp.* Henry II; diss. 1414
List in *Heads*, I, 100.

Baldwin Occ. 1195 x 1205 (*HMC Wells*, I, 50; II, 551); presumably also pr. of Loders.

R. Occ. 1216 x 1220 (*Ctl. Loders*, pp. 62–4, for date see *Heads*, I, 100).

Ralph de Witeville Occ. as pr. 1 Nov. 1275 (PRO, PRO31/8/140B, part 2, pp. 195–6).
Sometimes reckoned as a priory, sometimes a parcel of Loders priory (*KH*, p. 86).

BLYTH (Notts), St Mary (S. Trinité du Mont, Rouen) f. 1088; *c.*1409 (independent)
Lists in *VCH Notts*, II, 88; *Ctl. Blyth*, pp. xlvii–li (to 1344); Raine, *Hist. Blyth*, pp. 50–1; *Heads*, I, 100 and *Heads*, I, corrigenda, to p. 100.

Richard Occ. n.d. (ascribed by ed. to late 12th cent./early Henry III, i.e., before 1224 (*Ctl. Blyth*, nos. 22, 408) but there is no precise evidence to confirm this dating. The ctl. is late 13th cent. so Richard must be pr. before that time but precisely when is unclear.

Ascelin Occ. n.d. (possibly early 13th cent.) (*Ctl. Blyth*, no. 284 – revised dating).

William Occ. n.d. (*c.* 1213 x 1223, *temp.* Reginald, abb. of Roche and Richard, abb. of Welbeck) (*HMC Duke of Leeds etc.* p. 91). This could possibly be the pr. William referred to as William de Welles in 1279 (PRO, Just.1/1056, m. 48d) and in several chts. in the ctl. (see below under William).

Gilbert Occ. 1224 (*Ctl. Blyth*, nos. 317, 318); 30 Sept. 1226 (PRO, Notts F., CP25/1/182/3, no. 47); Mich. 1227 (Ctl. Beauchief, f. 70v); n.d. (prob. 1228 or shortly after) (*Ctl. Blyth*, no. B.107, cf. p. l).

William Occ. as William 30 July 1231 (*Ctl. Blyth*, no. 207); identified with pr. **William de Well(es)** who occurs in n.d. 13th-cent. charters (ibid., nos. 130, 141, 143, 406), but Welles may be the earlier William desc. above, and this William is prob. to be identified with **William Wastel**, whose prof. obed. to Archbp Walter de Gray (1215–55) is in BL, Lansdowne ms. 402, f. 77v. A witness (without title) is Laurence of Lincoln, who occ. as a can. of York from Oct. 1237 and archdn of York from before Feb. 1241 till his d. in 1245 (*Le Neve 1066–1300*, VI, 34, 107).

? Ralph See *Heads*, I, corrigenda to p. 100.

Nicholas Occ. n.d. (BL, Lansdowne ms. 415, f. 7r) (? *c.* 1231 x 1248, *temp.* abb. William I of Holy Trinity, Rouen: *Gallia Christiana*, XI, 128, cf. 126–7).

Theobald Said to have been inst. by Archbp Gray (1215–1255) (*Reg. Greenfield*, IV, no. 1754). Occ. 28 Apr. 1252 (PRO, Notts F., CP25/1/182/10, no. 391); 30 Apr. 1252, 22 Oct. 1255, 13 Oct. 1258 (*Ctl. Blyth*, nos. 315, 223, 372); inhibition, forbidding him to go beyond the seas 2 Mar. 1261 (*Reg. Greenfield*, IV, no. 1754); in this same decree of Archbp Godfrey Ludham the pr. is also referred to as Thomas.

William Occ. n.d. *temp.* the Queen and her firstborn, the Lord Edward (from 1272 Edward I) (*Ctl. Blyth*, no. B.36). Either pr. William Burdon became pr. before the unsubstantiated 1273 date (see below) or there is another pr. William.

William Burdon (Burdon) **-1303** Stated to have been installed 1273 but no source (Raine, *Hist. Blyth*, p. 50). Occ. in *Ctl. Blyth* from Dec. 1275 to 26 Mar. 1302 (nos. 50, A.528); in 1291 Archbp Romeyn asked the abb. Holy Trinity not to recall (unnamed) prior, as he was very useful (*Reg. Romeyn*, I, pp. 302–3, no. 853). Occ. 16 Feb. 1281 (*Yorks F., 1272–1300*, p. 61); 1287 (W.) (*Reg. Romeyn*, I, p. 368n.); Nov. 1295 x Nov. 1296, Nov. 1302 x Nov. 1303 (PRO, E106/3/19, m. 6d; E106/4/18, m. 10d). Archbp Corbridge wrote to the abb. of Holy Trinity that on 6 Sept. 1303 he visited the priory and found the (unnamed) prior unfit for office by reason of illness and old age. He had not removed him at present but the abb. was to appt a new pr. by 1 Nov., as the archbp will not allow the pr. to remain in office. If the abb. should choose a monk from Blyth, the archbp recommends Nicholas de Brettevill (*Reg. Corbridge*, I, pp. 261–2). Pr. res. 30 Oct. 1303 (ibid., pp. 268–9). Mentioned 31 Mar. 1309 as late pr. (Nottingham Univ., Clifton of Clifton Hall, Cl. D. no. 57).

Nicholas de Bret(t)eville **1303–1310** M. of Blyth, (said in 1291 to be useful to the priory (*Reg. Romeyn*, I, no. 844, cf. no. 843)), nominated 10 Oct., adm. 30 Oct. 1303, mandate to install 1 Nov. (*Reg.Corbridge*, I, pp. 268–9). 20 June 1310 archbp reports to abb. of Holy Trinity that Nicholas was worn out with age and paralysed; the archbp had apptd John de Passewyke, rector of Carlton in Lindrick as coadjutor; the abb. was to nominate another pr. by 29 Sept. (*Reg. Greenfield*, IV, nos. 1828, 1825). Cess. 26 Aug.1310 (ibid., no. 1850).

Robert de Clivilla **1310–1328** Presented 20 July 1310 (ibid.). M. of Rouen, adm. 26 Aug. 1310 and an ordinance made for the support of Nicholas (ibid.). Occ. in *Ctl. Blyth* from 24 May

1311 to 7 Mar. 1326 (nos. A.114, A.100); Hil..–Trin. 1328 (*Index to Placita de Banco*, p. 512). D. by 30 Sept. 1328 (York, Reg. 9B, ff. 442v–443r).

Ralph de Toto 1328–1335 M. of Rouen, pres. by abb. in letter dated 10 Sept. 1328, adm. 30 Sept. 1328 on death of Robert de Clivilla (ibid.). Res. by 5 Apr. 1335 (ibid., f. 464r).

Peter Meslier 1335–1344 M. of Rouen, apptd by archbp 5 Apr. 1335 (ibid.). Letter of presentation dated 13 Mar. 1335 (ibid., f. 464v). Res. 17 June 1344 (York, Reg. 10, f. 109r). Mentioned 18 Sept. 1349, after res., as proctor of S. Wandrille (ibid., f. 38v).

Peter Textor (Textoris) *alias* **de Aneslevilla 1344–** M. of Rouen, apptd 17 June 1344 (ibid., f. 109r). Occ. 28 June 1344 (*CFR 1337–47*, p. 371); Mich. 1348 x Mich. 1349 (PRO, E372/194, rot. 21); Mich. 1358 x Mich. 1359 (PRO, E372/204, rot. 18); 30 Sept. 1361 (*Ctl. Blyth*, no. A.128).

Gilbert Occ. 1365, citing information in inquisition of 8 Sept. 1379 (Raine, *Hist. Blyth*, pp. 42–3, 51).

Thomas Wymond -1377 Occ. [*c.* Jan.] 1370 (PRO, E179/63/5); 13 July 1373 (*CPR 1370–74*, p. 390). Res. by 26 Jan. 1377 (York, Reg. 12, f. 73v).

Nicholas Anglicus (Anglia, Anglice, English) **1377–1409** M. of Rouen, pres. by abb., adm. 26 Jan. 1377 (York, Reg. 12, f. 73v). Occ. from 25 Feb. 1377 (YMA, M2/1h, f. 7v) to 4 Aug. 1402 (*Reg. Scrope*, I, no. 600); Jan. 1403 (*Privy Council* I, 195). House void by his death 17 July 1409 (*CFR 1405–13*, p. 97).

The next pr., **William Ouston**, was inst. 11 Aug. 1409, vacant by Nicholas's death (York, Reg. 18, f. 211v).

BOXGROVE (Sussex), St Mary and St Blaise (Lessay) f. 1105+ (dependent on Lessay); 1339 (independent).

Lists in *VCH Sussex*, II, 59; *Ctl. Boxgrove*, pp. xliii–xliv (to 1350); *Heads*, I, 100.

Robert Occ. 1215, 1216 (*Ctl. Boxgrove*, nos. 350, 98).

Ansketil Occ. ?*c.* 1216 x 1222 (ibid., no. 99); (A.) 1225 (ibid., no. 352). Occ. 8 May 1233 (*Bucks F.*, I, 63); 1 July 1235 (*Lincs F.*, I, 290); 3 Nov. 1235 (*Sussex F.*, I, no. 288); 26 Aug. 1241 (*St Richard of Chichester*, p. 46, no. 70); 30 Sept. 1249 (*Sussex F.*, I, no. 451); (A.) 1252 (*Ctl. Boxgrove*, no. 277).

Walter of Shoreham Occ. 1253 (ibid., app., p. 182); 30 Sept. 1256 (*Sussex F.*, II, no. 566); (W.) 28 Sept. 1260 (ibid., no. 369); (W.) Mich. 1261 (ibid., no. 370); (W.) Mich. 1266 (ibid., no. 339); 1271 (ibid., no. 410); n.d. (1268 x 1272) (*Ctl. Bruton*, no. 354);1271–72 (PRO, Just.1/913, mm. 1d, 10d).

Ralph de Dumo M. of Lessay, chosen by abbey as pr. of Boxgrove, occ. *c.* 1276 when bp of Chichester refused to admit him (*CPL*, I, 483).

Robert M. of Boxgrove, el. by monks. Appeal over eln in times of Popes John XXI, Nicholas III and Martin IV (1276) (ibid.). Occ. Mich. 1278 (PRO, KB27/41, m. 55); 1279 (PRO, Just.1/914, m. 8); 25 Nov. 1279 (*Sussex F.*, II, no. 916; Farrer, *Honors and Knights' Fees*, I, 86); 1280 (BL, Add. Cht. 20067); 8 July 1281 (*Ctl. Boxgrove*, no. 3a). Renounced right n.d. (*CPL*, I, 483).

William El. after Robert's renunciation but res. his right (ibid.).

John of Winchester (Wynton') **–1283** El. after William and res. his right (ibid.). Removed 1283 (*Reg. Peckham*, II, 683). Ordered to go to Battle abbey – mand. to enforce order 25 June 1283 (ibid., 574–5). Archbp permits ex-pr. to return to Boxgrove from Battle 2 Mar. 1284 (ibid., 682–3).

Thomas El. after John's renunciation. Occ. 1286 (*CPL*, I, 483); 1288 (PRO, Just.1/929, m. 38d); 13 Jan. 1289 (*Ctl. Boxgrove*, no. 298); Easter 1298, July 1303 (PRO, Just.1/1312, m. 4d; Just.1/1329, m. 29).

Laurence of Gloucester (Gloucestre) King's protection for pr. 13 June 1313 (*CPR 1307–13*, p. 594). Occ. July 1313 x July 1314 (*Ctl. Boxgrove*, no. 301); 27 Sept. 1314, 14 Mar. 1316, 18 Jan. 1317 (*CPR 1313–17*, pp. 182, 439, 610); 28 July 1318 (*CPL*, II, 178); 7 Jan. 1319 (*Ctl. Boxgrove*, no. 300); protection for 1 yr, staying overseas 1 Jan. 1318, and for a further 2 yrs 12 Feb. 1319 (*CPR 1317–21*, pp. 67, 310). On 30 Apr. 1319 Cardinal Colonna proposed that Laurence should be given the see of Rochester but the pope refused (*Reg. Hethe*, p. xii).

John de Wareng(e) –1348 Occ. July 1322 x July 1323 (*Ctl. Boxgrove*, p. xliv, citing De Banco Roll 224, m. 155d); 21 Sept. 1322 (PRO, Just.1/938A, mm. 29, 30d); c. Mich. 1324 (PRO, E106/5/2, m. 3d); July 1325 x July 1326 (PRO, E106/5/4, m. [2]); 8 Oct. 1326 (*Memo. Roll 1326–7*, p. 271); 7 Oct. 1328 (*Ctl. Boxgrove*, no. 302; *CPR 1354–58*, p. 599); Mich. 1338 x Mich. 1339 (PRO, E372/184, rot. 13). D. by 24 Oct. 1348 (PRO, C84/25/20). D., lic. to el. 25 Oct. 1348 (*CPR 1348–50*, p. 197).

[It is not absolutely certain whether John de Wareng was in office continuously or was pr. for two separate periods. The doubt arises from a document of 1351 in which John atte Stroude testifies that John son of John de Seintcler was born on 27 Mar. 1328. John atte Stroude was at Boxgrove where his brother, **Robert**, had been el. pr. when news of John son of John de Seintcler's birth arrived and he caused his brother to enrol it in the missal of Boxgrove (*Sussex Arch. Coll.*, XII, 27). If the dating of this record is correct it would suggest John de Wareng was pr. for two periods of office, punctuated by the tenure of a pr. Robert.]

Nicholas de Stanle (Stanlygh(e)) **1348–1349** M. of Boxgrove, eln pres. to king for royal ass. 16 Nov. 1348 (PRO, C84/25/22); royal ass. 18 Nov. 1348 (*CPR 1348–50*, p. 210). Eln pres. to king but elect d. before conf. and lic. to el. asked for again 18 Apr. 1349 (PRO, C84/25/30). D., lic. to el. 20 Apr. 1349 (*CPR 1348–50*, p. 280), but says on d. of John de Wareng.

John Occ. 28 Aug. 1357 (*CPR 1354–58*, p. 599), but see below.

Richard Bonehomme Excommunicated 8 Oct. 1355; mand. to denounce him – he had been excommunicate for over 3 yrs, 12 June 1359 (Lambeth, Reg. Islip, f. 148v).

Robert [Dutot] **1363–** M. of Lessay, coll. by lapse by bp of Chichester 31 May 1363, no reason given for vacancy (PRO, PRO31/8/140B, part 2, pp. 74–5).

John de Lunda (Landa, Lande, Louda) **1369–** Papal prov. 5 Sept. 1369 (*Accts of Papal Collectors*, pp. 360, 402, 412). Occ. 10 Apr. 1370 (PRO, E106/10/11); 6 Apr. 1374 (*Cal. Misc. Inq.*, III, 351); 27 July 1376 (*Reg. Wykeham*, II, 258); 1377 (PRO, E170/11/1A); Jan. 1381 (PRO, E179/11/9); 12 Feb.1383 (*CPR 1381–85*, p. 228).

BRIMPSFIELD (Glos) (S. Wandrille) f. -1100. Diss. -1441

List in *VCH Glos*, II, 103; R.F. Butler, 'Brimpsfield church history, part IV: the priory', *BGAS*, 82 (1963), 127–42, at 141.

Hugh de Blevill' Occ. Mich. Term 1232 (*CRR*, XIV, no. 2283).

Gilbert **1289–** M. of St Stephen, Fontenay, mand. to induct as pr. 16 Oct. 1289, no reason given for vacancy (*Reg. G. Giffard*, II, 357). Prob. the Gilbert de Dremis apptd by the abb. and convent of Fontenay as their proctor in England (ibid., 365).

Robert le Masiner (*dictus* le Masuer) **1290–1311** M. of Fontenay, custody gtd 4 Apr 1291, inst. 4 June 1291 (ibid., 368–9). D. by 23 Sept. 1311 (*Reg. Reynolds*, p. 152).

Thomas de Brykebek (Brikebec, Briqubect) **1311–** M. of Fontenay, custody gtd 23 Sept. 1311 (ibid.). Adm. and inst. 10 Nov. 1311 (ibid., pp. 152–3). Occ. 29 Apr. 1317 (*Worcs. Reg. Sede Vacante*, p. 183).

Roger de Argenciis **1327–** Inst. 30 July 1327, no reason given for vacancy (*Reg. Cobham*, p. 249).

Richard Hette (Hente) **1328–** M. of Fontenay, adm. 12 Apr. 1328, no reason given for vacancy (*Reg. Orleton (Worcs)*, nos. 42, 662).

Roger de Haketo (Hegnet, Hequeto) **1331–** Letter of pres. 17 July 1331, no reason given for vacancy; adm. 14 Sept. 1331 (ibid., nos. 141, 847). Occ. 13 Nov. 1343, 27 Nov. 1343 (*Reg. Bransford*, no. 524). Notification by official of Bayeux of renunciation of pr. Roger de Hegnet 10 June 1361 (Worcester, Reg. Brian I, p. 226).

John Fabri 1361– M. of Fontenay, adm. 2 March 1361, no reason given for vacancy (ibid., p. 68).

Peter le Tubonour/Cerboneur (?) **–1363** Res. by 30 July 1363 (Worcester, Reg. Barnet, p. 54).

Simon Halley 1363– M. of Fontenay, adm. 30 July 1363 (ibid.).

Stephen Prev. abb. St Mary, Calais, gtd keeping of priory during pleasure on account of the French war 22 Jan. 1371 (*CPR 1370–74*, p. 30).

BURSTALL (Yorks E.), St Helen (S. Martin, Aumale) f. 1115
  Lists in *VCH Yorks*, III, 388.

[John de Belsted Occ. as proctor of the abbey of Aumale in England (not styled pr.) 12 Feb. 1267 (*CPR 1266–72*, p. 35).]

Gilbert Occ. n.d. (Oct. x Nov. 1274) (*Reg. W. Giffard*, p. 254). Occ. as proctor of Aumale abbey in England 17 Dec. 1279, not styled as pr. (*Reg. Wickwane*, p. 31, no. 100 and p. 97, no. 322).

[Hugh Occ. as proctor of the abbey in England (not styled pr.) 20 Sept. 1281 (ibid., p. 113, no. 362).]

[Reynold M. of Aumale living at Burstall, proctor of the abbey in England (not styled pr.) 18 Oct. 1289 (*Reg. Romeyn*, I, p. 209, no. 587).]

Ralph (de) Moussores (Monsures, Monsuris, Mussures) Occ. 16 June 1291 (*Reg. Romeyn*, I, p. 219, no. 623); (R.) 24 Sept. 1295 (ibid., p. 239, no. 691); 16 Nov. 1300, 16 Dec. 1301 (*Reg. Corbridge*, I, 158, 170); 1306 (*Reg. Greenfield*, III, p. 121, no. 1390); 1312 (Norwich, Reg/1/1, f. 47v); 1313 (ibid., pp. 211–13, nos. 1582, 1585, 1589); 1314 (ibid., p. 214, no. 1594); 1 Mar. 1318 (York, Reg. 9A, f. 322r). Occ. as proctor of Aumale (and not desc. as pr.) 1314, 1316 and 4 Oct. 1319 (*Reg. Greenfield*, III, p. 228, no. 1621 & p. 230, no. 1627; ibid., IV, pp. 268, 270, nos. 2857, 2867; Norwich, Reg/1/1, f. 81v).

Richard de Borrenco (Barenco, Boreco) **1322–** M. of S. Martin, Aumale, occ. 27 Jan. 1323, 12 Aug. 1323 (York, Reg. 9A, f. 350r); 1324 (PRO, E106/5/2, m. 10d); July 1325 x July 1326 (PRO, E106/5/4, m. [10]). Lic. for one year's absence 6 Sept. 1328 (ibid., f. 370r). Occ. 7 Feb. 1328 (*CCR 1327–30*, p. 359). Occ. as proctor (not desc. as pr.) 1324 (York, Reg. 9A, f. 353r).

[Gt of alien priory to Isabel, the king's eldest daughter 8 Mar. 1355 (*CPR 1354–58*, p. 189).]

Thomas of Sées Occ. 26 Aug. 1369, 6 Oct. 1369 (*CFR 1368–77*, pp. 13, 25); 6 Oct. 1377 (*CFR 1377–83*, p. 16); 1 Nov. 1377 (*CPR 1377–81*, p. 618). Permission to remain in England 1378 (D. Matthew, *The Norman Monasteries and their English possessions*, app. III, p. 156). Priory of Durham gtd priory of Burstall 6 Mar. 1381 (*CPR 1377–81*, pp. 606–7); Thomas Sées, former proctor of the abbey of Sées demits all right in the priory or cell of Burstall to Durham cath. priory 8 May 1381 (Bodl., Dodsworth ms. 7, f. 234r–v), but cf. below, presumably ineffective. Occ. 26 June 1385, 28 June 1385 (*CCR 1385–89*, pp. 4, 1).[3] Durham presumably farmed it for a while cf. DCD, Misc. Cht. 7036 of 1382 and 3.6.Ebor.3, Exchequer plea, Hilary term 1388, mentioning inquisition at Hull March 1387 over claim, that the pr. of Durham and a fellow-monk, John Beryngton, 'fecerunt vastum in una bercaria in prioratu de Brustell' . . . tempore quo ipsi eundem prioratum de Rege ad firmam tenuerunt'.

---

[3] A cht. issued by an unnamed pr. of Burstall on 22 Feb. 1371 bears a seal (damaged) with the remaining legend: *S' Ioh'is Gomers . . . de Brustall* (*HMC R.R. Hastings*, I, 199; Clay, *Seals*, p. 36). Did Thomas of Sées have two terms of office, with a pr. John intervening?

Aumale abbey sold its dependent priory of Burstall to Kirkstall abbey for 10,000 pounds tours in 1395 (D. Matthew, *The Norman Monasteries and their English possessions*, p. 118 and n.; G.D. Barnes, *Kirkstall Abbey 1147–1539: an historical study*, p. 68).

BURWELL (Lincs), St Michael (La Grande-Sauve, Bordeaux) f. -1110
  Lists in *VCH Lincs*, II, 239; J.F. Trabut-Cussac, *Les possessions Anglaises de l'abbaye de la Sauve-Majeure. Le prieuré de Burwell, Lincolnshire*, app. I, pp. 173–4; *Heads*, I, 101.
Adam Occ. early 13th cent., *c.*1200 x 1230 (BL, Harl. Cht. 47 I 22, *temp.* abb. Robert of Barlings; BL, Cotton Cht. XXIX 15); 13th cent. (BL, Harl. Cht. 51 D 24, *temp.* abb. Clement of Barlings, *c.* 1236 x 1242).
Raymond −1266 D. by 7 Apr. 1266 (*Reg. R. Gravesend*, p. 21).
Amfred (Anfredus) 1266–1293 Adm. 7 Apr.1266 (ibid.). D. by 15 Apr. 1293 (*Reg. Sutton*, I, 174).
Peter Pelata 1293–1315 Adm. 15 Apr. 1293 (ibid.). D. by 8 Mar. 1315 (Lincoln, Ep. Reg., II, f. 55r).
John of Louth (Luda) 1315–1317 M. of La Grande-Sauve, letter of pres.8 Mar. 1315, adm. 28 Apr. 1315 (ibid.). Res. by 6 Nov. 1317 (ibid., f. 69r).
Hugh de Valibus 1318– M. of La Grande-Sauve, letter of pres. 6 Nov. 1317, adm. 9 Jan. 1318 (ibid.; Trabut-Cussac, p. 174, n. 1).
John de Ponte 1324–1345 M. of La Grande-Sauve, apptd by bp by lapse 2 June 1324 (*Reg. Burghersh*, I, no. 102). D. by 20 Feb. 1345 (Lincoln, Ep. Reg., VI, f. 12v).
William Arnald de Calhauet (Arnaldi, Chalhavek) 1345–1349 M. of La Grande-Sauve, adm. 20 Feb. 1345 (ibid.). D. by 23 Aug. 1349 (Trabut-Cussac, p. 153 and n.1).
23 Aug. 1349 the King gtd the priory to John Kirkby, bp of Carlisle for the duration of the war at an annual rent of 10 pounds (PRO, E371/108, m. 2, cited in Trabut-Cussac, p. 153).
Arnulph Farsey 1352– M. of Le Grande Sauve, gtd keeping of the priory 24 May 1352, previously preferred as pr. (*CFR 1347–56*, p. 352; Trabut-Cussac, p. 153 and n. 4). Mentioned in the sheriff's accounts 1352–1362 (Trabut-Cussac, p. 154, nn. 1–2, citing PRO, E372). Letter from Gilbert de Umfraville, earl of Angus. to abb. of La Grande-Sauve, asking for a new pr. in place of Arnulph, 20 Dec. [no year] (*Mon. Angl.*, VII, 1015; BL, Harl. Cht. 43 B 19).
John Occ. 3 July 1369 (Lincoln, Ep. Reg., X, f. 291r).
Peter de Monte Ardito of Aquitaine 1375–1416 Prov. by Pope Gregory XI n.d. (*Accts of Papal Collectors*, p. 507). Gt of keeping of priory 26 Feb. 1375 (*CFR 1368–77*, p. 284). Occ. 1381 (*Clerical Poll-Taxes*, p. 133, no. 1686; p. 159, no. 1969), 1389 (PRO, C85/109/3–4; C202/C/92/103–4); 1403 (*Privy Council*, I, 193). D. 25 Dec. 1416 (BL, Add. ms. 6165, f. 75r).

CALDY (Pembr.) (Tiron) (St Dogmells) f. +1113–15 diss. 1536
No list.
Philip Fadir Occ. as pr. 1381 (PRO, E179/21/9, m. 3)

CARISBROOKE (Isle of Wight), St Mary (Lire) f. 1070; *c.* 1156. Diss. 1414
  Lists in *VCH Hants*, II, 231; *Ctl. Carisbrooke*, App. B., pp. 187–8; *Heads*, I, 101.
William de Gloz (Glos) Occ. 1205 (*Ctl.*, nos. 174–5); n.d. (ibid. nos. 102–3, dated *c.* 1240 in ctl. edn but prob. earlier).
J. Occ. *after* 24 Jan. 1226, judge delegate (Oxford, Queen's Coll. Archives, catalogue I, no. 227B).
Hugh Occ. 1228 x 1238 (*Quarr Chts.*, p. 75, nos. 306–7; cf. *Ctl.*, no. 158 later than edn date of *c.* 1202).

Lambert Occ. n.d. (*c.* 1240, according to ctl. list, but date not at all certain) (BL, Add. ms. 70511, f. 40v).

William of Jumièges (Gemitico, Gymeges) Occ. n.d. (1230 x 1240) (*Ctl.*, no. 181); 1241 (ibid., no. 170); n. d. (*c.* 1241) (*Quarr Chts.*, p. 79, no. 322).

Ralph de Romily (Romilego) junior Occ. in 1260 library catalogue, by then ex-pr. (*Annales de Normandie* (1953) p. 87, n. 2, cf. p. 88). Became abb. of Lire (*Ctl.*, p. 187). Cf. Randulf de Romuleyo, proctor-general in England of the abbey of Lire 1275 (*Reg. Cantilupe*, p. 7).

Robert of S. Pierre sur Dives (de Sancto Petro super Divam) Occ. 14 Nov. 1257 (*Ctl.*, no. 251). Occ. in library catalogue of 1260 (*Annales de Normandie* (1953) p. 87, n. 2).

Andrew Occ. 1264 (*Ctl.*, no. 219); 1271 (PRO, E329/166); 16 Feb. 1272 (PRO, Hants F. CP25/1/204/11, no. 73); Nov. 1277 (*Ctl.*, no. 220). Seal (*Mon. Seals*, pp. 19–20). Called 'le Cornu' in list (*Ctl.*, p. 187); *Cornutis* in *Annales de Normandie* (1953) p. 87, n. 3.

Richard de Preaus Occ. 24 Oct. 1279 (*Ctl.*, no. 222).

John de Insula Occ. mid-13th cent. (*Ctl.*, nos. 115, 166, *temp.* Isabel de Fortibus, mar. William III de Fortibus 1248, d. 1293).

John de Caleto Occ. 18 Nov. 1283 (*King's Bench, Edward I*, I, p. 120); 26 Mar. 1283, 31 Mar. 1285 (*Reg. Pontissara*, I, 312, 310–11); 26 Mar. 1284, 30 May 1286 (*Ctl.*, nos. 223, 225); Nov. 1295 x Nov. 1296 (PRO, E106/3/19, m. 10). Removed from priory *c.* 1298, mentd in letter of 3 May 1298 (*Ctl.*, no. 235).

Warin (*dictus*) **Piel** (Pyel) Occ. 3 May 1298 (ibid.); *c.* 1298 (*Quarr Chts.*, p. 78, no. 318); 28 May 1309 (*Reg. Gandavo*, I, 711); occ. styled proctor of Lire 11 Mar. 1310, 28 July 1312 (*Reg. Woodlock*, II, 733, 736).

John Poucyn (Pontyng, Pouncyn) 1313–1336 M. of Lire, adm. 28 July 1313 (*Reg. Woodlock*, II, 740; *Reg. Wykeham*, II, 614). Res. by 14 May 1336 when he, as proctor of Lire, pres. Blaise Doublel (Winchester, Reg. Orleton II, f. 53v).

Blaise *dictus* **Doublel** (Dublel) 1336–1348 M. of Lire, adm. 14 May 1336 (ibid.; *Reg. Wykeham*, II, 614). Occ. 5 Jan. 1348 (*Reg. Edington*, I, no. 223). Res. acc. 4 May 1348 (ibid., no. 262). Occ. in Sheen inventory of chts. as Blaise Blomblell (*sic*) (BL, Cotton ms. Otho B XIV, f. 51v).

John Pepyn 1348–1350 Entered Lire as a m. 1321(Guery, *Hist. Lyre*, p. 380). Pr. of Hinckley to 1348, adm. to Carisbrooke 5 May 1348 (ibid., no. 263). As pr. of Carisbrooke, apptd keeper of Wareham 4 Nov. 1348 (*CFR 1347–56*, p. 101). D. by 20 Feb. 1350 (*CFR 1347–56*, p. 207).

Almaric (Emery) de Pugnenay (Pugneia, Pugneya, Pugueya) M. of Lire, occ. 29–30 Sept. 1353 (ibid., pp. 432, 378); 1354 (Salisbury, Reg. Wyvil II, f. 264r); 1355 (ibid., p. 432); 1356 (*CPR 1354–58*, p. 460); 18 Oct 1359, 8 Feb. 1360 (*CFR 1356–68*, pp. 110, 118).

Nicholas Gaugire (Gavaire) 1361– M. of Lire, adm. 27 Jan. 1361, no reason given for vacancy (*Reg. Edington*, I, no. 1240; *Reg. Wykeham*, II. 615).

Robert de Gasturia 1362– M. of Lire, adm. 19 Mar. 1362, no reason given for vacancy (*Reg. Edington*, I, no. 1456).

Peter de Ultra Aquam 1364–1369 M. of Lire, inst. 15 Mar. 1364, no reason given for vacancy (ibid., no. 1619). Occ. 11 June 1369 (*CFR 1369–77*, p. 14). D. by 19 Aug. 1369 (ibid., p. 18).

Thomas de Val Oseul (de Valle Osoul, De Val Osoul, Vallosoul, Ozoul(es)) 1371–1400/1 Previously proctor of the abb. and convent of Lire 1360, 1361, 1364 (*CFR 1356–68*, p. 135; *Reg. L. Charlton*, pp. 63–4; *Reg. Stretton*, I, 21, 33). M. of Lire, coll. on d. of Peter, 20 June 1371 (*Reg. Wykeham*, I, 39; II, 615). Occ. 28 Jan. 1400 (ibid., I, 225). D. by 12 Jan. 1401 (ibid., II, 230).

CHEPSTOW (Monmouth), St Mary (Striguil) (Cormeilles) f. -1071
List in *Heads*, I, 101.
Nicholas Occ. 6 Oct. 1213 (BL, Add. ms. 15668, f. 3v).
S. Occ. 19 May 1239 (*Llandaff Episcopal Acta*, no. 78; *Glam. Chts.*, II, no. 505; *Welsh Episcopal Acts*, II, 714).
Nicholas Occ. July 1254 (BL, Add. Cht. 17653).
Ralph Occ. *c.* 1334 (PRO, C269/15/12).
Robert Occ. Mich. 1364 (PRO, KB27/416, m. 47d).
[**John Fabri**, pr. of Newent, apptd by the abb. of Cormeilles to rule the priory of Chepstow during its voidance 1368 (PRO, E42/409).]
In 1384 the unnamed pr. was described as 'an alien of France' (*Glos IPM 1359–1413*, p. 136).
The next recorded pr., **William Auger** (Anger), occ. 14 May 1389 (*CPR 1383–91*, p. 286).

CLATFORD (Wilts) (Hullavington) (S.Victor-en-Caux) f. 1104+
List in *VCH Wilts*, III, 394.
[**Michael de la Lunde** Occ. 28 Sept. 1294, proctor general of the abbey in England, not desc. as pr. (*CPR 1292–1301*, p. 95).]
Matthew Occ. from Nov. 1295 x Nov. 1296 to Nov. 1298 x Nov. 1299 (PRO, E106/3/19, m. 9d; E106/4/9, m. 3d); 6 Oct. 1297 (*Reg. Gandavo*, II, 559); Easter 1300 (PRO, E106/4/14, m. 7).
Thomas Occ. 6 Feb. 1308 (*Reg. Gandavo*, II, 696).
Thomas de Valle Perhaps the same. Occ. 1321 (ECR, 18/97; *HMC, 9th Rep.* p. 356); *c.* Mich. 1324 (PRO, E106/5/2, m. 6d); July 1325 x July 1326 (PRO, E106/5/4, m. [5d]). On 19 Aug. 1320 he is desc. as proctor of the abbey, not as pr. (*Reg. Martival*, II, 286).
Michael Clarel −1357 Occ. 12 Mar. 1342 (*CFR 1337–47*, p. 274); 11 July 1345 (*CCR 1343–46*, p. 636). D. by 15 Mar. 1357 (*CFR 1356–68*, p. 30).
Nicholas Laloyer (Lalomer, Lalouier, Lalouyer, Lassimer, Loloyer) 1357– M. of S. Victor, gt of keeping of priory 15 Mar. 1357 (*CFR 1356–68*, p. 30); custody of priory committed to him by the king during the French war 15 July 1357 (*CPR 1354–58*, p. 578). Occ. Mich. 1358 x Mich. 1359 (PRO, E372/204, rot. 26); 1365 (ECR, 18/98); 1369, 1377 (*CFR 1368–77*, pp. 15, 405); 1378 (*CFR 1377–83*, p. 71); 1384 (ECR, 18/103). Unnamed pr. had d. by 29 Jan. 1391 (poss. Nicholas) (*CPR 1388–92*, p. 437).

COGGES (Oxon), St Mary (Fécamp) f. 1103
Lists in *VCH Oxon*, II, 162; *Heads*, I, 101. See also J. Blair and J.N. Steane, 'Investigations at Cogges, Oxfordshire 1978–81: the priory and the parish church' *Oxoniensia*, XLVIII (1982), 37–125, esp. 47–53.
Michael Last recorded occ. 1205 (*Rot. de Finibus*, pp. 319–20).
Roger −1225/6 M. of Fécamp. Occ. *c.* 1221 (*Ctl. Oseney*, IV, no.144). Res. Dec. 1225 x Dec. 1226 (*Reg. Wells*, II, 23).
Hugh 1225/6–1226/7 Adm. Dec. 1225 x Dec. 1226 (ibid.). Res. Dec. 1226 x Dec. 1227 (ibid., 27).
John of London 1226/7– Adm. Dec. 1226 x Dec. 1227 (ibid.).
Elerius 1238– Installed 18 May 1238, no reason given for vacancy (*Reg. Grosseteste*, p. 454). Occ. (E.) 24 Oct. 1250; 8 Mar. 1251 (*CPR 1247–58*, pp. 77, 90). Royal ass. to el. as abb. of Pershore 19 Mar. 1251 (ibid., p. 90).[4]

---

[4] From the documentary evidence it must be presumed that pr. Elerius made way in 1248/9 for pr. Gervase and then at some point resumed office as pr. of Cogges before his elevation to Pershore in 1251. Interestingly Elerius occ. as proctor in England of the abbey of Fécamp in 1248, without the Cogges title (*CPR 1247–58*, p. 7).

Gervase 1248– Inst. June 1248 x June 1249, no reason given for vacancy (*Reg. Grosseteste*, p. 494).

William de Esmerville 1251/2– M. of Fécamp, inst. June 1251 x June 1252, no reason given for vacancy (ibid., p. 501).

Hugh –1262 Res. by 12 July 1262 (*Reg. R. Gravesend*, p. 215)

William *dictus* Barbeyn 1262–1277 M. of Fécamp, adm. 12 July 1262 (ibid.). Res. by 29 Dec. 1277 (ibid., p. 233).

Hugh 1277– M. of Fécamp, inst. 29 Dec. 1277 (ibid., pp. 233, 337).

Stephen de Alba Malla –1291 Res. by 28 Aug. 1291 (*Reg. Sutton*, VIII, 176).

Matthew Dupont 1291–1299 Adm. 28 Aug. 1291 (ibid.). Letter of res. 24 May 1299 (ibid., 201). Matthew also mentd Nov. 1302 x Nov. 1303 (PRO, E106/4/18, m. 2d). ? scribal error.

Roger *dictus* Hardy 1299–1302 M. of Fécamp, letter of pres. 30 Apr. 1299, adm. 29 May 1299 (ibid.). Res. by 11 Nov. 1302 (Lincoln, Ep. Reg., II, f. 144v). Mentd s.d. as former pr. in commn about dilapidated state of priory (Lincoln, Ep. Reg., III, f. 50v).

Vigor 1302–1303 M. of Fécamp, adm. 11 Nov. 1302 (Lincoln, Ep,. Reg., II, f. 144v). Res. 18 Mar. 1303 (ibid., f. 145v). [Poss. to be identified with the br. Vigor of Fécamp, who occ. as proctor-general in England of the abbey of Fécamp 1297 (*CPR 1292–1301*, pp. 241–2), cf. occ. as bailiff in England in 1293, 1294 and 1296, 1298–1300 (ibid., pp. 10, 75, 92, 176; PRO, E106/1/1, m. 3; E106/1/2, m. 2; also *CCR 1288–96*, p. 501).]

William de Limpevilla (Limpvill) 1303–1333 M. of Fécamp, letter of pres. dated 17 Sept. 1303, custody not granted 21 Oct. 1303, pending receipt of a more suitable letter (Lincoln, Ep. Reg., II, f. 145v). New letter of pres. 21 Feb. 1304, adm. 10 Mar. 1304 (ibid., f. 147r). D. by 6 Apr. 1333 (Lincoln, Ep. Reg., IV, f. 267v).

Ralph le Frison (Frisoun) 1333–1341 M. of Fécamp, letter of pres. 6 Apr. 1333, adm. 29 Apr. 1333 (ibid.). Res. by 30 July 1341 (ibid., f. 289r).

William Hamonis *alias* Hamon (Hamond) 1341– M. of Fleury, inst. 30 July 1341 (Lincoln, Ep. Reg., X, f. 289r). Priory conf. to him for life by pope 28 Oct. 1344, when said to have been in office three years (*CPP*, p. 80). Occ. 17 Oct. 1349 as the king's surgeon who, although a Norman, was not to be treated as an alien (*CPR 1348–50*, p. 407); in Ireland on the king's service 1362 (*CPR 1361–64*, p. 244). Protection for 1 year gtd 3 Oct. 1364 while he was in Ireland on the king's business (*CPR 1364–67*, p. 39). Occ. 4 Oct. 1366 (Bodl., Oxon. Cht. 77). See also C.H. Talbot and E.A. Hammond, *The Medical Practitioners of Medieval England: a biographical register* (1965), p. 397.[5]

Thomas Tymy Occ. 16 Nov. 1377 (*CFR 1377–83*, p. 41).

Nicholas Goyn 1380– M. of Holy Trinity, Fécamp, adm. 12 Feb. 1380, no reason given for vacancy (Lincoln, Ep. Reg., X, f. 370r). Induction 1 Apr. 1380 (WCM, no. 872).

CORSHAM (Wilts), St. Bartholomew (Marmoutier) f. *temp.* Henry I. Diss. 1294 and administered from Tickford.

Gilbert Occ. n.d., *temp.* Richard, earl of Cornwall (cr. 1227, d. 1272) (*CPR 1330–34*, p. 311; *Wilts AM*, XLIII, 513 and plate ii; *CTG*, II, 318).

[**William de la Menere** Occ. as proctor of abb. of Marmoutier Nov. 1299 x Nov. 1300 (PRO, E210/2889) – writ of Edward I to enquire whether the manor of Corsham is held for the abb. of Marmoutier by br. William de la Menere, his proctor, or by another.]

COVENHAM (Lincs), St Mary and St John (S. Calais) f. *c.*1082; diss. 1306
Lists in *VCH Lincs*, II, 238 (from 1238); *Heads*, I, 101.

Reginald Occ. late 12th cent. (*Reg. Ant. Lincoln*, V, no. 1621).

---

[5] Br. Philip Ranulphy occ. on 6 Apr. 1374 as proctor in England of the abbey of Fécamp, but there is no ref. to his being pr. of Cogges (*Cal. Misc. Inq.*, III, 351).

Geoffrey −1237 Res. 28 June 1237 (*Reg. Grosseteste*, p. 16).

William 1237− M. of S. Calais, adm. 28 June 1237 (ibid.).

Matthew de Pinneaus 1262–1282 M. of S. Calais, pres. 26 Aug. 1262, adm. and inst. 11 Sept. 1262, vacant by the res. of unnamed pr. (*Reg. R. Gravesend*, pp. 11, 266). Occ. 9 Feb 1282 (PRO, Lincs F., CP25/1/133/54, no. 9). D. by 16 Sept. 1282 (*Reg. Sutton*, I, 35–6). Name n.d. (PRO, DL25/321).

James 1283–1285 M. of S. Calais, letter of pres. 16 Sept. 1282, inst. 19 Jan. 1283 (ibid.). Res. by 15 Oct. 1285 (ibid., 82).

Peter le Beschu 1286− M. of S. Calais, letter of pres. 15 Oct. 1285, adm. 12 Apr. 1286 in place of James who had res. (ibid., 82–3). Occ. from Nov. 1295 x Nov. 1296 to Nov. 1298 x Nov. 1299 (PRO, E106/3/19, m. 10d; E106/4/9, m. 1d; E106/4/10, m. 2d).

Sold by S. Calais to Kirkstead Abbey. Conf. of Bp Bek of Durham of a gt by abb. Philip and convent of S. Calais to Kirkstead abbey of their manor of Covenham etc. 1303 (DCD, Misc. Cht. 7125d). Letter of Bp Dalderby to the official of the archdn of Lincoln, dated 18 May 1306, about the transfer of Covenham priory from S. Calais to Kirkstead (Lincoln, Ep. Reg., III, f. 96r–v).

COWICK (Devon), St Andrew (Bec) f. 1144, but cf. −1137 (G. Yeo, *The Monks of Cowick*, p. 2).

Lists in Oliver, pp.153–4; *Heads*, I, 101–2.

Hugh of St Edmund (de Sancto Edmundo) Occ. 20 May 1219 (*Devon F.*, I, p. 45, no. 78; corrected ibid., II, p. vii).

William App. 1218 x 1221 by the legate Pandulph, prob. 1220 x 1221 by mayoralty of Exeter (Devon RO, ED/M/28). Occ. 7 July 1228, 13 June 1233 (*Devon F.*, I, pp. 119, 127, nos. 246, 258). Mentd 1313 as pr. *temp.* John (? mistake or another William) (*YB*, XIV, part 2, p. 97).

Maurice Occ. 27 Jan. 1245, 6 June 1249 (*Devon F.*, I, pp. 223, 251, nos. 448, 497).

Thomas −1263 Res. by 4 Feb. 1263 (*Reg. Bronescombe*, pp. 59, 127–8; *Reg. W. Bronescombe* I, no. 472).

[*blank*] **de Columbers** 1263− Adm. 4 Feb. 1263 (ibid.).

Adam de Buris (Bures) 1275− M. of Cowick, adm. 16 Aug. 1275, no reason given for vacancy (*Reg. Bronescombe*, p. 128; *Reg. W. Bronescombe*, II, no. 1107). Occ. Easter 1276 (PRO, CP40/14, m. 78); July 1286 (PRO, Just.1/1273, m. 40). See below.

William de Ponte Episcopi (Pont l'Evêque) 1291− writ *de intendendo* in favour of William, m. of Bec, apptd by the abb. of Bec to the custody thereof, the priory being in the king's hands, 4 Sept. 1291 (*CPR 1282–91*, p. 507).

Adam de Buris Either the above writ was ineffective, or Adam de Buris came back for a second term as pr., since William de Porta was coll. in succession to Adam *temp.* Bp Bitton (1292–1307) (*Reg. Stapeldon*, p. 204; cf. *Reg. Bytton*, p. 407). Adam also occ. in returns of aliens Nov. 1295 x 1296 (PRO, E106/3/19, m. 11d); Nov. 1296 x Nov. 1297 (PRO, E106/4/2, m. 2); Nov. 1297 x Nov. 1298 (PRO, E106/4/8, m. 2); Nov. 1298 x Nov. 1299 (PRO, E106/4/9, m. 1d; E106/4/10, m. 2d); Easter 1300 (PRO, E106/4/14, m. 4); Nov. 1302 x Nov. 1303 (PRO, E106/4/18, m. 5).

William de Porta Occ. 25 Jan. 1306 (Devon RO, Tavistock archives, W1258M/D82(3)). Coll. by authority of the Lateran Council by Bp Bitton (1292–1307) in succession to Adam de Buris – William had now deserted priory, mentd in commn of 23 Dec. 1315. Bp Stapeldon gts custody to mr Walter de Buris, rector of Whimple (*Reg. Stapeldon*, p. 204; cf. *Reg. Bytton*, p. 407).

Eustace Occ. 24 Feb. 1317 (*Reg. Stapeldon*, p. 261); lic. to visit mother-house 5 June 1317, to return by 1 Aug. (ibid., p. 125); 2 Jan. 1327 (*HMC Var. Coll.* I, 274). Called de Ponte Episcopi (Yeo, p. 2).

Thomas de Leonibus –1334 Occ. 22 Jan. 1329 (*Reg. Grandisson*, I, 453). Letter of abb. of Bec to bp of Exeter. He has absolved Thomas de Leonibus from admin. of the priory and pres. Alexander de Rothis 30 May 1334 (Devon RO, Tavistock archives, W1258M/D82(6)). Res. by 22 Aug. 1334 (*Reg. Grandisson*, III, 1303).

Alexander de Rothis (Rotis) 1334–1352 M. of Bec, inst. 22 Aug. 1334 (ibid.). Occ. 7 Oct. 1351 (PRO, C69/15/31). Asked permission to res. and return to Bec, 10 Feb. 1352 (*Reg. Grandisson*, III, 1421).

Durand of St Stephen (de Sancto Stephano) 1352–1361 Previously pr. of Wilsford (q.v.). Adm. 8 Mar. 1352 (ibid.; Devon RO, Tavistock archives, W1258M/D82(9)). Res. by 2 Apr. 1361 (*Reg. Grandisson*, III, 1461).

John de Ponte Episcopi (Pont l'Evêque) 1361– M. of Bec, pres. 2 Apr. 1361, commn to inst. 14 May 1361; prof. obed. 20 May 1361 (ibid.).

John de Petra Ficta (Pierrefitte) Occ. 1370 (PRO, E106/10/2). Yeo, p. 2, gives *c.* 1370–1374.

Robert de Glanvilla –1382 Royal gt of keeping of priory during French war 5 Oct. 1377 (*CFR 1377–83*, p. 14). D. by 2 Aug. 1382 (*Reg. Brantingham*, I, 80).

CREETING (Suffolk), St Mary (Bernay) f. –1156. During this period this house and Everdon, Northants, were often supervised by a single prior. See also Everdon list. There was also a small cell, Creeting, St Olave, belonging to Grestein abbey (sold 1360) (VCH Suffolk, II, 153–4). It is just possible that some of the earlier references below relate to Creeting St Olave.

Robert Occ. as pr. of Creeting Oct. 1218 x Oct. 1219 (*Suffolk F. (Rye)*, p. 17).

Richard Occ. as pr. of Creeting *c.* 1225 (widest limits 1220 x 1230) (*Ctl. Daventry*, p. 197, no. 604).

William Occ. as pr. of Creeting and Everdon from Nov. 1295 x Nov. 1296 to Nov. 1298 x Nov. 1299 (PRO, E106/3/19, m. 8; E106/4/9, m. 9; E106/4/10, m. 8); Easter 1300 (PRO, E106/4/14, m. 12d).

Nicholas Occ. as pr. of Creeting *c.* Mich. 1324 (PRO, E106/5/2, m. 10); July 1325 x July 1326 (PRO, E106/5/4, m. [9d]); (Creeting and Everdon) 8 Oct. 1326 (*Memo. Roll 1326–7*, p. 272).

Jerome de Cormellis (Carletens) Occ. as pr. of Creeting and Everdon 23 Nov. 1335 (Lincoln, Ep. Reg., IV, f. 212v); 10 Feb. 1342 (*CFR 1337–47*, p. 272); 11 July 1345 (*CCR 1343–46*, p. 636).

Robert de Ponte (Pount) Occ. 6 Oct. 1349 (*CFR 1347–56*, p. 165). Removed by abb. of Bernay by 6 May 1352 (ibid., p. 332).

Robert de Fraccinis (Fraccynis) 1352– M. of Bernay, apptd to custody of priory of Creeting and Everdon 6 May 1352 (*CPR 1358–61*, p. 356; *CFR 1347–56*, p. 332). Occ. Mich. 1354 x Mich. 1355 (PRO, E372/200, rot. 19); 1 May 1360 (*CPR 1358–61*, p. 356).

Roger Faber Occ. 11 Oct. 1367, 21 Oct. 1367, (Lincoln, Ep. Reg., X, f. 170v); Easter 1375 (*Accts of Papal Collectors*, p. 498). Occ. as proctor-general of Bernay 22 Oct. 1367 (*Reg. Wykeham*, I, 10).

Nicholas Avenis Occ. as pr. of Creeting and Everdon 8 Nov. 1376, 18 June 1377 (*CFR 1368–77*, pp. 372, 404).

DEBDEN (Essex) The Norman abbey of Hambye held property here but it was not technically a cell of the abbey (Matthew, *Norman Monasteries*, p. 13, n. 2). However, in the returns of aliens in the late 13th century a 'prior' of Debden is described.

Ralph Occ. as pr. Nov. 1295 x Nov. 1296 (PRO, E106/3/19, m. 9); Nov. 1296 x Nov. 1297 (PRO, E106/4/2, m. 6d); Nov. 1297 x Nov. 1298 (PRO, E106/4/8, m. 4); Nov. 1298 x Nov. 1299 (PRO, E106/4/9, m. 5d); Easter 1300 (PRO, E106/4/14, m. 8d).

DEERHURST (Glos), St Mary and St Denis (S. Denis) ref. -1059
Lists in *VCH Glos*, II, 105; *Heads*, I, 102.
Andrew Occ. Oct. 1209 (*Oxford F.*, p. 43); 25 June 1221 (PRO, Glos F., CP25/1/73/5, no. 33);
1227 (PRO, Glos F., CP 25/1/73/8, no. 118).
William 1233– Mand. for seisin 6 June 1233 (*CR 1231–34*, p. 225). Occ. 1 July 1235 (*Oxford F.*,
p. 97); (W.) June 1236 x June 1237 (*Reg. Grosseteste*, p. 448).
Nicholas 1237– Mand. for seisin; pres. to king by abb. Odo of S. Denis 5 Sept. 1237 (*CR
1234–37*, p. 492); Trin. 1237 (*CRR*, XVI, no. 149 J); June 1237 x June 1238 (*Reg. Grosseteste*,
p. 453).
Henry 1242– M. of S. Denis, apptd by abb. Odo of S. Denis, mand. for seisin 3 June 1242 (*CR
1237–42*, p. 44); writ *de intendendo* 4 June 1242 (*CPR 1232–47*, p. 299). Occ. 27 May 1248
(PRO, Glos F., CP25/1/74/17 no. 335; and 74/18, no. 362).
Robert de Trembliaco 1251– Royal ass. 6 Nov. 1251 (*CPR 1247–58*, p. 118). Occ. 8 July 1252
(*Oxford F.*, p. 162); 1255 (PRO, Glos F., CP25/1/74/20, no. 421; 74/21, nos. 466–7); 28
June 1258, royal protection, going to France (*CPR 1247–58*, p. 639).
Benedict 1258– M. of S. Denis, mand. to sheriffs to give full admin. of priory; adm. by king to
cure and temps. of house on pres. of abb. and convent of S. Denis 17 Oct. 1258 (*CPR
1247–58*, p. 653)
John de Strenes 1260– M. of S. Denis, temps. 14 July 1260 (*CPR 1258–66*, p. 81). Occ. 1260
(P. Chaplais, *Diplomatic Documents*, I, no. 319); 27 Jan. 1261 (*Oxford F.*, p. 185).
Priory void by 10 Feb. 1265 when William de Wenling, king's clerk, gtd custody of the priory
during pleasure (*CPR 1258–66*, p. 405).
Stephen of Paris (Parys) **1269–** Writ *de intendendo* 23 Sept. 1269, mand. to restore temps. 6
Oct. 1269, having been apptd by the abb. of S. Denis (*CPR 1266–72*, pp. 367–8). Adm. 4
Apr 1270 (*Reg. G. Giffard*, pp. 37–8; *Reg. Reynolds*, p. 40). Royal protection 30 Mar. 1270
(*CPR 1266–72*, p. 418); 9 July 1270 (*Reg. R. Gravesend*, p. 222). House void by 30 July 1272
(*CPR 1266–72*, p. 669).
William of Bermondsey (Bermundeseye) **1272** M. of La Charité, adm. and temps. 1 Aug.
1272 (ibid.).
Robert de Elleboef 1272– M. of S. Denis, Mand. to bp's Official to gt custody to Robert 20
Aug. 1272; inst. 17 Oct. 1272, no reason given for vacancy (*Reg. G. Giffard*, p. 49). Occ.
Easter 1275 (PRO, CP40/9, m. 62); 1277 (*HMC Var. Coll.*, II, 9); Easter 1278 (PRO,
E326/12891); 8 May 1278 (*Oxford F.*, p. 209).
Stephen de Moysiaco *alias* **de Sorfrato** (Soysiac) **1278–1301** Inst. 5 Aug. 1278, no reason
given for vacancy (*Reg. G. Giffard*, p. 98, cf. *Reg. Reynolds*, p. 40 which gives the date as 5
Aug. 1279). Occ. 1294 (*Reg. Sutton*, VIII, 185); 1296 (*Reg. G. Giffard*, p. 483); 1297
(Sorfrato) (PRO, C146/618); 6 Apr. 1301 (*CPR 1292–1301*, p.586). Res. on grounds of age
by 9 Nov. 1301 (*Worcs Liber Albus*, I, no. 76). Mentd as former pr. 3 Jan. 1302 (*CPR 1301–07*,
p. 8).
Peter de Torniaco (Thorigniaco, Thorny, Toreignyaco, Torigniac(o), Torrigniac) **1302–1315**
Pres. by abb. of S. Denis 9 Nov. 1301 (*Worcs Liber Albus*, I, no. 76); temps. 3 Jan. 1302 (*CPR
1301–07*, pp. 7–8). Occ. 1308, 2 Aug. 1312 (Lincoln, Ep. Reg., II, ff. 154v, 162r). In dispute
over priorship, signified for arrest 1310 (Logan, *Runaway Religious*, p. 187). Mentd 1312 as
having been deprived and excommunicated by the abb. of S. Denis (*CPL*, II, 103). Lic. to
go to S. Denis 8 Nov. 1312 (*Reg. Reynolds*, p. 90). Appt of royal keepers of the priory, now
in the king's hands, 24 Sept. 1313 (*CPR 1313–17*, p. 17). Mentd 12 Nov. 1313, as claiming
to be pr. (ibid., p. 38). Res. 31 May 1315 (Worcester, Reg. Maidstone, pp. 67–70).
Philip de Sarnay (Cernaie, Cerniaco, Sarnaye, Sarneio, Sarney(a), Sarneye, Sarneyo,
Sarnyaco, Sernayco, Sernayo, Serneye) **1315–1329** M. of S. Denis, letter committing to

Philip, desc. as king's chaplain, the custody of the priory during pleasure 26 Oct. 1313 (*CFR 1307–19*, p. 181; *CPR 1364–67*, p. 184); styled keeper of the priory 20 Mar. 1314 (*CPR 1313–17*, p. 94). Purgation and absolution, having been accused of the crime of intrusion into the priory, 8 Jan. 1314 (*Worcs Sede Vacante Reg.*, p. 146). Abb. of S. Denis requests king to restore temps. to new pr., who is replacing a rebel and excommunicate 18 Jan. (1315) (PRO, SC1/38/135). Temps. 7 Mar. 1315 (ibid., p. 259). Cert. of appt by abb. of S. Denis 4 Apr. 1315, on recall of Peter de Torniaco (PRO, C84/18/14). Letter of pres. 10 June 1315, commn to enquire 21 Aug.; adm. and inst. 21 Aug. 1315 (Worcester, Reg. Maidstone, pp. 67–70); occ. 1328 (*Index to Placita de Banco*, p. 170); 26 Apr. 1328 (*Reg. Orleton (Worcester)*, no. 659). Going overseas 3 Oct. 1328 (*CPR 1327–30*, p. 322). Dep. by 18 Aug. 1329 (ibid., p. 419).

John de Vetolio 1329–1339 M. of S Denis, preferred by abb. of S. Denis, temps. 18 Aug. 1329 (ibid.). Occ. 1 Oct. 1329 (ibid., p. 441); 1335 (J.) (*Reg. Montacute*, no. 210); 1338, 11 May 1339 (*CPR 1338–40*, pp. 87, 226). Lic. 1 July 1339 to overstay leave until next Whitsun, owing to bodily weakness, the badness of the way and the peril of the sea (ibid., p. 388). Dep. by abb. of S. Denis? Mich. 1339, mentd 8 Mar. 1340, certainly had returned to S. Denis by 9 Dec. 1339 (*CFR 1337–47*, p. 163; *Reg. Bransford*, no. 256).

Ralph de Ermenovill(a) (Ermenevilla) **1340–?1344/45** M. of S. Denis, pres. by abb. of S. Denis on the recall of John de Vetolio through infirmity 9 Dec. 1339; inst. 8 Feb. 1340 (ibid., nos. 256–7). Gt, during pleasure, of the keeping of the priory, having been deputed by the abb. of S. Denis, the previous pr. having returned to S. Denis to stay there permanently 12 Jan. 1340 (*CFR 1337–47*, p. 155). Further gt of priory with issues from Mich. 1339, the abb. of S. Denis having deposed John de Vetolio and apptd Ralph in his place, 8 Mar. 1340 (ibid., p. 163). Occ. Mich. 1342 (*YB 16 Edward III, part 2*, p. 301); 29 Apr. 1343, 17 Jan. 1345, 8 Mar. 1345 (*CPR 1343–45*, pp. 86, 378, 501). Removed before 10 Mar. 1345 (*CPL*, III, 16), but prob. disputed, since he occ. 10 Oct. 1345 (*CPR 1343–45*, p. 589, see also next entry).

Thomas Graculi (Garculi, Gratuli) **?1344–1345** M. of S. Denis, royal protection who claims he has been pres. to the priory by the abb. of S. Denis 15 Aug. 1344 (*CPR 1343–45*, p. 338; BL, Add. Cht. 11306); apptd before 10 Mar. 1345 on removal of Ralph (*CPL*, III, 16). Res. 26 Nov. 1345 and apptd to 'a more acceptable position' (*Reg. Bransford*, nos. 759–60).

John Godelli 1346–1349 M. of S. Denis, pres. 26 Nov. 1345 (*Reg. Bransford*, no. 759; PRO, C84/24/51). Gt of keeping of priory during French war 28 Jan. 1346 (*CFR 1337–47*, p. 51). Inst. and mand. to induct 17 Feb. 1346 (*Reg. Bransford*, nos. 761–2). Royal protection 20 Dec. 1347 (*CPR 1345–48*, p. 436). Occ. 23 Apr. 1348, going overseas on the king's service (*CPR 1348–50*, p. 58). Association of br. Geoffrey Julyen, m. of S. Denis, with John Godelli in the keeping of Deerhurst 20 May 1349 (*CFR 1347–56*, p. 110). D. by 20 Sept. 1349 (ibid., p. 164).

John Coci (Cocus) **1349–** Abb. of S. Denis requests king for temps. to be restored to new pr. 4 Aug. 1349 (PRO, SC1/38/134). M. of S. Denis, adm. by king *sede vacante* 20 Sept. 1349 (*CPR 1348–50*, p. 375); adm. and inst. by pr. of Worcester 29 Sept. 1349 (*Worcs Reg. Sede Vacante*, p. 237).

Peter Cudoe (*dictus* Cudoue, Cudone) **1351–1361** M. of S. Denis, inst. 25 Oct. 1351, no reason given for vacancy (Worcester, Reg. Brian, I, p. 4). D. by 18 Oct. 1361 (PRO, C84/28/13).

John de Medunta (Medinka) **1361–1368** M. of S. Denis, letters of pres. from abb. of S. Denis 18 Oct. 1361 (ibid.); temps. 16 Feb. 1361; fealty to king 10 Nov. 1361 (*CPR 1361–64*, p. 112). Adm. 26 Nov. 1361 (Worcester, Reg. Brian, I, p. 84). D. by 8 Mar. 1368 (*CFR 1356–68*, p. 378; *CPR 1367–70*, p. 91).

Peter (de) Ponfichet (Pounchefichet) **1368–1375** M. of S. Denis, letters of pres. 12 Feb. 1368; adm. 22 Mar. 1368 (Worcester, Reg. Whittlesey, p. 48); temps. 8 Mar. 1368 (*CPR 1367–70*,

p. 91, cf. *CFR 1356–68*, p. 378). House said to be void 26 Oct. 1375 (*CFR 1368–77*, p. 306). D. by 18 Dec. 1375 (*Reg. Wakefield*, no. 11).

[**John Walkelyn** (Wallcelyn) M. of SS. Serge and Bacchus, Angers – prov. by pope Urban V 17 June 1369 on d. of John de Medunta (*Accts of Papal Collectors*, pp. 359, 400) – ineffective.]

Drogo Carnarii (Carnerii, Garyner, Grayner) **1375–1393** Inst. 18 Dec. 1375 (*Reg. Wakefield*, no. 11). Occ. 24 Jan. 1378, 28 June 1379, 13 Feb. 1383 (*CPR 1377–83*, pp. 67, 160, 351); 4 June 1388 (*CFR 1383–91*, p. 237). At an inquisition held in July 1397 it was stated that pr. Drogo had been killed (*interfectus*) on Christmas eve 3 years previously (i.e. 1393) and that the priory had been vacant since then (Worcester, Reg. Winchcombe, pp. 32–3). Mentd as late pr. 8 Feb. 1394 (*CPR 1391–96*, p. 366).

DUNWICH (Suffolk), ? St Felix (cf. Binns, pp. 96–7) (Eye) f. 1080+; swallowed by the sea *temp.* Edward I.

The pr. **Thomas** who supposedly occ. Oct. 1227 x Oct. 1228 (*Suffolk F. (Rye)*, p. 25) is in fact a mistranscription for 'parson' (cf. *Suffolk F. 1199–1214*, no. 303).

ECCLESFIELD (Yorks W.), St Mary (S. Wandrille) f. *temp.* Henry I; 1386 gtd to Carthusian priory of Coventry.

Lists in *VCH Yorks*, III, 389; *Fasti Parochiales*, I, 95–104 (14th cent.).

Peter de Sancto Romano Occ. 28 June 1287 (*Reg. Romeyn*, I, p. 69, no. 167); Nov. 1295 x Nov. 1296 (PRO, E106/3/19, m. 11d). A Ralph (*sic*) de Sancto Romano occ. as a M. of S. Wandrille at Ecclesfield 1279 (*Yorks F., 1272–1300*, p. 42).

Alan Mentioned as former pr., deceased, 7–8 Aug. 1349 (*CPR 1347–56*, pp. 146,149).

Robert de Bosco **–1328** M. of S. Wandrille, claiming to be pr. 21 June 1308, occ. 23 June 1309 (*Reg. Greenfield*, V, no. 2688). Custody of the sequestration of Ecclesfield church gtd to him 12 July 1308 (ibid., II, no. 795). Ment. as M. of S. Wandrille, then staying at Ecclesfield 20 July 1310 (ibid., IV, no. 1850). Inst. as vicar of Ecclesfield 16 Apr. 1311 (ibid., II, no. 927). Occ. 28 Jan. 1315, 24 Apr. 1315 (*CPR 1313–17*, pp. 212, 321); 10 Oct. 1323 (York, Reg. 9A, f. 195v); 1324 (PRO, E106/5/2, m. 14); July 1325 x July 1326 (PRO, E106/5/4, m. [10d]). Commn to adm res. 19 Nov. 1328 (ibid., f. 217v). Letter of res. 30 Nov. 1328 (ibid., f. 218r).

John dictus Fauvel (Fauvell, Favell) **1329–1349** M. of S. Wandrille, letter of pres. 30 Nov. 1328, adm. 6 Feb. 1329 (ibid., f. 218r–v). Occ. 11 July 1345 (*CCR 1343–46*, p. 636). D. by 7 Aug. 1349 (*CFR 1347–56*, p. 152; cf. York, Reg. 10, f. 38r, and see also letter of proxy below, 16 Feb. 1348 where John is described as the present pr.).

Robert Guilliam (Guillelmi) **1349–** M. of S. Wandrille, letter of Robert, abb. of S. Wandrille. appointing proctors (including Peter Textoris, pr. of Blyth) to pres. Robert to priory of Ecclesfield, 16 Feb. 1348 (York, Reg. 10, ff. 37v–38r); inst. on d. of John Fauvel 18 Sept. 1349 (ibid., f. 38v). Gt of keeping of priory on d. of John Favell 7 Aug. 1349 (*CFR 1347–56*, p. 152). 1357 summoned to S. Wandrille to answer charges of evil life and embezzlement (J. Eastwood, *History of the parish of Ecclesfield in the county of York* (London 1862), p. 512). Occ. 28 Aug. 1356 (*CFR 1356–69*, p.12, in room of Peter Volet, see below); Mich. 1358 x Mich. 1359 (PRO, E372/204, rot. 7–7d). Prob. pr. until 1369 (see below). See also Emden, *BRUO*, II, 836–7.

[**Peter Volet** M. of S. Wandrille, styled proctor of the abbey in England, gtd keeping of Ecclesfield priory in the room of Robert Guillelmi 14 Mar. 1356 (*CFR 1356–68*, pp. 2–3). However, Robert Guilliam seems to have remained styled as pr., see above and below.]

Robert Occ. 3 Nov. 1360 (York, Reg. 11, f. 106v) ? Robert Guilliam. Robert Guillelmi is said to have died by 29 Oct. 1369, leaving the *vicarage* of Ecclesfield vacant (ibid., f. 156r). At this time the pr. seems also to have been styled vicar (see *Fasti Parochiales*, I, 102–4).

John Burdet Occ. 6 Oct. 1369 (*CFR 1368–77*, p. 24). Pres. by king to vicarage of Ecclesfield 26 June 1370 (*CPR 1367–70*, p. 441, see *Fasti Parochiales*, I, 103–4 for subsequent litigation). Occ. 1372 (Baildon, I, 50); 14 Sept. 1372, 30 Oct. 1373 (*CCR 1369–74*, pp. 457, 594).

EDITH WESTON (Rutland) (S. Georges, Boscherville) f. *c.*1114; diss. 1394 (sold to Carthusian priory of Coventry)
  No list in *VCH*.

John Occ. from Nov. 1295 x Nov. 1296 to Nov. 1297 x Nov. 1298 (PRO, E106/3/19, m. 6d; E106/4/8, m. 4d); Easter 1300 (PRO, E106/4/14, m. 12d); Nov. 1302 x Nov. 1303 (PRO, E106/4/18, m. 14).

Hugh Occ. *c.* Mich. 1324 (PRO, E106/5/2, m. 10); July 1325 x July 1326 (PRO, E106/5/4, m. [9d]); 8 Oct. 1326 (*Memo. Roll 1326–7*, p. 272). Prob. the same as Hugh de Altifago, M. of S. Georges, who was alleged to have been assaulted by Robert Bernard, rector of Edith Weston, ment. 14 Nov. 1321 (*CPR 1321–24*, pp. 59–60).

Robert Cunebaud (Dounebaut) Prob. the Robert de Unebato, M. of S. Georges, who was gtd keeping of the priory 15 Dec. 1339 (*CFR 1337–47*, p. 154). Desc. as late pr. in inquisition of 11 Oct. 1355 – he had behaved in a scandalous manner, did not use monastic habit or tonsure, lived luxuriously, alleged to have fathered children and had concubines, dissipated priory's revenues etc. (*Cal. Misc. Inq.*, III, 74–5; cf. PRO, SC8/227/11337).

William de Beauvey M. of S. Georges. Proctor of S. George, keeper of Edith Weston. Occ 1 May 1355 as recently apptd (*CPR 1354–58*, p. 205).

William Silvestr(e) Occ. 29 Jan. 1366 (Lincoln, Ep. Reg., X, f. 164r); ment. as previous pr. in 1375 (*Cal. Misc. Inq.*, III, 366).

Robert Occ. 27 Apr. 1367 (Lincoln, Ep. Reg., X, f. 168v).

John Occ. 22 Nov. 1375 (*CFR 1368–77*, p. 311); 10 Oct. 1377 (*CFR 1377–83*, p. 19); 1377 (*Clerical Poll-Taxes*, p. 66, no. 878).

ELLINGHAM (Hants) St Mary (S. Sauve le Vicomte) f. 1160
  List in *VCH Hants*, II, 230.

Richard de Wauville Occ. 1240 (Cht. in Archives of St Lô, destroyed 1944, cited in *VCH*); 1243, 6 Dec. 1244 (Winchester Cath. Lib., Ellingham priory transcripts no. 9).
6 Mar. 1284 custody of the priory gtd to the vicar of Ellingham in the absence abroad of unnamed pr., without leave (*Reg. Pontissara*, I, 11).

Michael –1292 D. by 13 July 1292 (ibid., 52).

Thomas *dictus* le Petit 1292– Mand. for induction 13 July 1292 (ibid., 52–3; *Reg. Wykeham*, II, 613).

William Cancelot (Canchelot, Cauchelot) Occ. 1298 (*HMC, 9th Rept.*, p. 350); 9 May 1298 (PRO, E106/4/8, m. 3d); Nov. 1298 x Nov. 1299 (PRO, E106/4/9, m. 5; E106/4/10, m. 5); Easter 1300 (PRO, E106/4/14, m. 7d); Nov. 1302 x Nov. 1303 (PRO, E106/4/18, m. 10).

Denis 1301– Adm. 19 June 1301, lic. being given to him to stay in the abbey of S. Sauve for one year (*Reg. Pontissara*, I, 109; *Reg. Wykeham*, II, 613).

Geoffrey Occ. Sept. 1305 (*HMC, 9th Rept.*, p. 350); lic. to visit mother house 10 Apr. 1311 (*Reg. Woodlock*, I, 562).

John le Vyoun (Vion) 1311–1328 Adm. 11 July 1311 (ibid., II, 735);lic. to visit mother house 5 Sept. 1318 (*Reg. Sandale*, p. 101); lic. to be absent for 1 year 19 Oct. 1327 (Winchester, Reg. Stratford, f. 32v). D. by 19 Jan. 1328 (ibid., f. 34v).

Michael Pellene (Poillevey) 1328– M. of S. Sauve, adm. 23 Mar. 1328 (ibid., f. 104r, cf. *Reg. Wykeham*, II, 614, called Richard Pelleue). Occ. 1331, 1335 (Winchester Cath. Lib., Ellingham priory transcripts nos. 16*, 12*); 1337 (*CPR 1334–38*, p. 484; Winchester, Reg. Orleton II, f. 61r).

Michael Belny −1347 Occ. 5 Mar. 1342 (*CFR 1337–47*, p. 274); 1345 (*CCR 1343–46*, p. 636); 1346 (*Reg. Edington*, II, no. 609). D. by 6 Nov. 1347 (*CFR 1347–56*, p. 54).

Galvan de Hambeya 1348– M of S. Sauve, inst. 22 Feb. 1348, no reason given for vacancy (*Reg. Edington*, I, no. 242). Occ. 5 Mar. 1348 (*CFR 1347–56*, p. 74). Revocation of letters patent giving custody 10 Apr. 1348 (*CPR 1348–50*, p. 50).

William de Albigneye (Aubegneio, Aubegneyo, Daubeney(e)) 1361– M. of S. Sauve, gt of keeping of the priory during the French war 30 Dec. 1356 (*CFR 1356–68*, p. 25); mentd 4 Mar. 1359 as having lately been gtd custody of Ellingham by the king (*CPR 1358–61*, p. 178); adm. by bp 1 Sept. 1361, no reason given for vacancy (*Reg. Edington*, I, no. 1304; *Reg. Wykeham*, II, p. 615). Occ. 1370 (PRO, E106/10/2); 1 Apr. 1366 (*Reg. Edington*, I, no. 1734); 10 July 1371(*CPR 1368–77*, p. 117); Nov. 1373 (*HMC, 9th Rept.*, p. 350).

EVERDON (Northants) (Bernay) f. -1100. Diss. *c.* 1399. Granted to Eton College 1440.
Run together with Creeting, St Mary, Suffolk from 1327 (*KH*, p. 88), but see below.
Details in *VCH Northants*, II, 182 (no list). See also Creeting list.

William Occ. as pr. of Creeting and Everdon Nov. 1298 x Nov. 1299 (PRO, E106/4/9, m. 9; E106/4/10, m. 8).

Nicholas Sauvalle Occ. 28 Feb. 1330 (Lincoln, Ep. Reg., IV, f. 183v). Occ. as pr. of Creeting and Everdon July 1325 x July 1326 (PRO, E106/5/4, m. [9d]); 8 Oct. 1326 (*Memo. Roll 1326–7*, p. 272).

Jerome de Cormelis (Carletens') Occ. as pr. of Creeting and Everdon 23 Nov. 1335 (ibid., f. 212v); 10 Feb. 1342 (*CFR 1337–47*, p. 222); 11 July 1345 (*CCR 1343–46*, p. 636).

Robert de Ponte Occ. as pr. of Creeting and Everdon 6 Oct. 1349 (*CFR 1347–56*, p. 165). Removed by abb. of Bernay by 6 May 1352 (ibid., p. 332).

Robert de Fraccinis (Fraccynis) M. of Bernay, apptd to custody of priory of Creeting and Everdon 6 May 1352 (*CPR 1358–61*, p. 356; *CFR 1347–56*, p. 332). Occ. 1 May 1360 (*CPR 1358–61*, p. 356).

Roger Faber Occ. 11 Oct. 1367, 21 Oct. 1367 (Lincoln, Ep. Reg., X, f. 170v). Occ. as pr. of Creeting and proctor-general of the abb. of Bernay at presentation to Everdon parish church 22 Oct. 1367 (*Reg. Wykeham*, I, 10).

Nicholas Avenis Occ. as pr. of Creeting and Everdon 8 Nov. 1376, 18 June 1377 (*CFR 1368–77*, pp. 372, 404).

EYE (Suffolk), St Peter (Bernay) f. *c.* 1080
Lists in *VCH Suffolk*, II, 75–6; *Ctl. Eye*, II, pp. vii–x; *Heads*, I, 102–3; obits in BL, Egerton ms. 3140.

Roger de Mungumbray Occ. 1203 (*Reg. Pinchbeck*, pp. 421–2 = *Ctl. Eye*, II, no. 366); 30 Sept. 1228 (*Ctl. Eye*, I, no. 93). He was paralysed by June 1230 when another pr. was substituted (*CRR*, XIV, no. 228). Obit 6 Sept. (BL, Egerton ms. 3140, f. 68r; *Ctl. Eye*, II, p. vii).

Roger de la Bruer' name (*Ctl. Eye*, I, no. 270); prob. the unnamed pr. who had succeeded by June 1230 (*CRR*, XIV, no. 228). Occ. Oct. 1231 x Oct. 1232, Oct. 1234 x Oct. 1235 (*Suffolk F. (Rye)* pp. 32,34); 25 Apr. 1232 (*Ctl. Eye*, I, no. 92); 18 Nov. 1234 (ibid., no. 96). Obit 11 Apr. [?1237] (ibid., II, p. viii & n.).

William Puleyn (Poleyn) Occ. as pr. William 9 Mar. 1243 (ibid., I, no. 47); 19 June 1244 (ibid., no. 95). Obit 1 July (BL, Egerton ms. 3140, f. 67r; *Ctl. Eye*, II, p. viii & n.).

William of St Peter Had become pr. before *c.* 1260 (ibid., p. viii, n. 12), poss. occ. as pr. William 12 Sept. 1255 (ibid., no. 379); Nov. 1259 (*CPR 1258–66*, p. 61); 1268 (*Ctl. Eye*, II, no. 392); 1270 (ibid., no. 381); 1276 (pro, Lincs F., CP25/1/132/51, no. 49); full name 1 Dec. 1278 (*Ctl. Eye* II, no. 395). Obit 12 Dec. (BL, Egerton ms. 3140, f. 69v), prob. 1282 (*Ctl. Eye*, II, p. viiii & n. 10).

Richard Jacob –**1294** Occ. as pr. Richard 8 July 1288 (*Suffolk F. (Rye)*, p. 91). Obit given as 14 June 1237 (*sic*) (BL, Egerton ms. 3140, f.66v; *Ctl. Eye*, II, p. viii & n. 10; cf. *Heads*, I, 103 for poss. identification with pr. Richard, dep. 1202 x 1203), but was d. by 8 Apr. 1294 when the earl of Cornwall took custody of the priory on his d. (*CCR 1288–96*, p. 479; *Cal. Misc. Inq.*, I, 480–1; cf. *HMC Westmorland etc.*, p. 518). ?Vacancy until 1300; presumably the **Richard de I**(*rest illegible*) who had d. as pr. by 30 Nov. 1300 (PRO, C84/13/49).

Nicholas Ivelyn (Yvelyn, Evelyn) **1300–1313** M. of Bernay, adm. 8 July 1300, no reason given for vacancy (Norwich, Reg/1/1, f. 6r), but cf. occ. as pr.-el. 1298 (*Ctl. Eye*, II, p. viii & n.19). Eln pres. to king for royal ass. 30 Nov. 1300 (PRO, C84/13/49); royal ass. 26 Dec. 1300, temps. 4 Jan 1301 (*CPR 1292–1301*, pp. 560–1). D. 18 June 1313 (BL, Egerton ms. 3140, f. 66v; *Ctl. Eye*, II, p. viii; cf. *CPR 1313–17*, pp. 53–4).

Durand Frowe (Froue, Froe) **1313–1323** M. of Bernay, pres. to king by abb. of Bernay 10 July 1313 (PRO, C84/17/20); temps. 10 Aug. 1313 (*CPR 1313–17*, p. 11). Cess. by 15 Nov. 1323 (*CCR 1323–27*, pp. 46–7), but see below.

Robert Morpayn 1323–1348 M. of Bernay, eln quashed, but apptd by bp 19 Oct. 1323 (Norwich, Reg/1/1, ff.102v–103r). Preferment by abb. of Bernay mentd 15 Nov. 1323 (*CCR 1323–27*, p. 47). Pres. to king by abb. of Bernay 27 Feb. 1324 (PRO, C84/20/23); temps. 10 Mar. 1324 (*CPR 1321–24*, p. 392). D. 10 Jan. 1348 (BL, Egerton ms. 3140, f. 64r; *Ctl. Eye*, II, p. ix).

Michael Reynard (Renard) –**1380** Occ. 3 July 1348 (*CCR 1346–49*, p. 474); 10 Sept. 1348 (*CFR 1347–56*, p. 94); 16 May 1351 (Norwich, Reg/2/4, f.129Ar); Mich. 1354 x Mich. 1355 (PRO, E372/200, rots. 16–16d, 17); Mich. 1358 x Mich. 1359 (PRO, E372/204, rot. 16–16d). An unnamed alien pr. reported to be blind and so weak in body and broken with age that he is no wise able to labour about the rule of the priory 20 Feb. 1379 (*CFR 1377–83*, p. 129). D. by 4 Oct. 1380 (Norwich, Reg/3/6, f. 71r).

FOLKESTONE (Kent), St Mary and St Eanswith (Lonlay) f. 1095
List in *VCH Kent*, II, 237.

Peter Occ. 7 Feb. 1296 (royal protection) (*CPR 1292–1301*, p. 177); Nov. 1295 x Nov. 1296 (PRO, E106/3/19, m. 5d); Nov. 1296 x Nov. 1297 (PRO, E106/4/2, m. 2d); Nov. 1298 x Nov. 1299 (PRO, E106/4/10, m. 3d); Easter 1300 (PRO, E106/4/14, m. 5); Nov. 1302 x Nov. 1303 (PRO, E106/4/18, m. 6).

John Occ. Trin. 1309 (PRO, CP40/178, m. 208).

Robert de Stokeys (Stokeyo) Occ. *c.* Mich. 1324 (PRO, E106/5/2, m. 12d); July 1325 x July 1326 (PRO, E106/5/4, m. [12d]); 8 Oct. 1326 (*Memo. Roll 1326–7*, p. 273); Mich. 1338 x Mich. 1339 (PRO, E372/184, rots. 9, 10d).

William Waterham Occ. 18 Feb. 1342 (*CFR 1337–47*, p. 273); 11 July 1345 (*CCR 1343–46*, p. 636), but see next entry.

William Medici 1344– M. of Lonlay, papal conf. of 3 Nov. 1345 of prov. by abb. of Lonlay dated 10 Oct. 1344 (*CPL*, III, 214). Gt of keeping of priory to br. William Medici whom the abb. and convent have preferred to be pr. – same gt as that to William Waterham late pr. 22 Jan. 1345 (*CFR 1337–47*, p. 406). Occ. *c.* 1349 (*Accts of Papal Collectors*, pp. 78, 92, 120, 142, 173).

Thomas le Provost (Prepositus) –**1361** Occ. 26 Sept. 1349 (*CFR 1347–56* p. 166); Mich. 1354 x Mich. 1355 (PRO, E372/200, rot. 10–10d); 15 July 1356 (*CPR 1354–58*, p. 428); 20 July 1356, 24 May 1357 (*CFR 1356–68*, pp. 10, 37); Mich. 1358 x Mich. 1359 (PRO, E372/204, rot. 10). D. by 11 Sept. 1361 (Lambeth, Reg. Islip, f. 292r).

James de Suessione 1361– M. of Lonlay, letter of pres. dated 11 Sept. 1361; adm. 25 Oct. 1361 (*ibid.*).

John (de) Huscen (Husten') Occ. 16 Jan. 1370 (Lambeth, Reg. Whittlesey, f. 161r); 1370 (PRO, E106/10/10).

Sampson Senex (Veilard, Senioris, Senys) **1372–1376** M. of Lonlay, adm. 3 June 1372, no reason given for vacancy (Lambeth, Reg. Whittlesey, ff. 90v–91r), but occ. 27 May 1372 (*CFR 1368–77*, p. 159). Res. 5 July 1376 (Lambeth, Reg. Sudbury, f. 118v).

Nicholas Barbarot(e) 1376– M. of Folkestone, adm. 5 July 1376 (ibid.). Occ. 3 July 1376, 10 May 1377 (*CFR 1368–77*, pp. 352, 400); 10 Oct. 1377 (*CFR 1377–83*, p. 17); 22 July 1386 'so holden with sickness of leprosy that he cannot uphold governance and rule of priory' (*CPR 1383–91*, p. 148); 2 Mar. 1388 (ibid., p. 212).

The next recorded pr., **Nicholas Cheryton** (Chiriton), m. of Westminster, pres. to priory in the king's gift by reason of the war with France 10 Jan. 1393 (*CPR 1391–96*, p. 213). Occ. 22 Oct. 1398 (PRO, C67/31, mm. 9, 10).

FRAMPTON (Dorset) (S. Etienne, Caen) f. *temp.* William I

Lists in *VCH Dorset*, II, 116; *Heads*, I, 103.

Roger Occ. 1193+ or 1214+ (*Ctl. Montacute*, p. 173, no. 49).

William du Hommet –1214 M. of Caen, el. abb. of Westminster 4 May 1214 (*Flor. Hist.*, II, 147f.; *Flete*, p. 101; *Walt. Cov.*, II, 216).

Michael Occ. 3 Aug. 1238 (PRO, PRO31/8/140B, part 2, p. 144).

Guymond Occ. 17 July 1251 (ibid., p. 172) Said to occ. 1261 (*Mon. Angl.*, VII, 1000, from Hutchins, no other source), but this is prob. an error for the 1251 ref. Mentd as prev. pr. in an inquisition of 1376 (*Cal. Misc. Inq.*, III, 383).

Richard de Mondrevilla Occ. 1 May 1255 (PRO, PRO31/8/140B, part 2, p. 164).

Robert Occ. 16 Apr. 1275 (PRO, SC1/17/125).

Richard Occ. n.d. (*Mon. Angl.*, VII, 1000, no source); 13th cent. (*JBAA*, VI (1852), 162). Seal matrix (13th cent.) (G. Dru Drury, 'Catalogue of seal casts in the Dorset County Museum, 1944', *Proc. Dorset NHAS*, 66 (1944), p. 101, no. 74).

Martin Occ. Easter 1287 (PRO, CP40/67, m. 32d); 1296 ?; 9 Sept. 1302, 7 Oct. 1302 (*Reg. Gandavo*, II, 615–16).

James de Troarn (Troarn, Trowarno) **1302–** M. of Caen, adm. 10 Nov. 1302 (ibid., 620). Occ. 29 Apr. 1307, 9 July 1308, 7 May 1311, 12 July 1311 (ibid., 689, 703, 764–5, 768); 28 July 1317, 9 Aug. 1317 (*Reg. Martival*, I, 89).

Nicholas (Richard) de Montigneyo 1317–1329 (Nicholas) inst. 24 Nov. 1317, no reason given for vacancy (ibid., 94). Occ. (Nicholas) 1324 (PRO, E106/5/2, m. 5d). Res. (Richard) by 28 May 1329 (*Reg. Martival*, I, 394).

William de Ruscavilla 1329–1335 M. of Caen, pres. 28 May 1329, adm. and inst. 29 May 1329 (ibid.). Res. 24 Oct. 1335 (Salisbury, Reg. Wyvill II, f. 40v).

Laurence de Brioto (Breoto, Brioco, Briout) **1335–1370** M. of Caen, adm. 30 Nov. 1335 (ibid.). Previously inst. to priory and has ruled it well, mentd in petition of bp of Salisbury, appt conf. by pope 24 Oct. 1343 (*CPP*, p. 26). Occ. 11 June 1369 (*CFR 1368–77*, p. 16). D. by 6 Apr. 1370 (ibid., p. 72).

[**William de Tour** Occ. re keeping of priory, not styled pr. 6 Oct. 1369 (ibid., p. 25).]

William Nag(u)et 1370– Gtd keeping of priory 6 Apr. 1370 on d. of Laurence de Briout (ibid., p. 72). Mentd 15 Oct. 1375 as former pr., along with Laurence de Brioto his predecessor (*CPR 1374–77*, p. 219).

John Letour 1377– Gt. of keeping of priory 6 Mar. 1372 (*CFR 1368–77*, p. 158). M. of Caen, coll. by bp 5 Oct. 1377, no reason given for vacancy (Salisbury, Reg. Erghum, f. 28r).

The next recorded pr., **Ralph de Nubibus,** m. of Caen, coll. by bp *per lapsum temporis* 1 Jan. 1400, no reason given for vacancy (Salisbury, Reg. Mitford, f. 67v).

GOLDCLIFF (Monmouth), St Mary Magdalen (cf. Binns, p. 98) (Bec) f. 1113
List in *Heads*, I, 103.

Vincent Occ. 11 x 18 Aug. ? 1203 x 1204 (*EEA*, 3, no. 476 and n.; cf. Adams and Donahue, *Select Canterbury Cases*, p. 107, no. 26). Evidently there were two Williams.

William –1219 Royal ass. to his eln as bp of Llandaff 16 July 1219 (*CPR 1216–25*, p. 196). Res. from Goldcliff Oct. 1219 (*Ann. Margam*, p. 64; cf. *Lib. Landav.*, pp. 303, 312; Ann. Dore, BL, Egerton ms. 3088, f. 133r). ?Seal (*BM Seals* no. 3213).

Maurice Occ. 1233 (Evreux, Arch. dép. Eure, H1453). Mentd 15 Sept. 1341 as former pr. (*CCR 1341–43*, p. 264). A pr. Maurice is said to occ. 47 Henry III (Oct. 1262 x Oct. 1263) in a later inquisition (*Cal. Misc. Inq.*, II, 431). Either there was a second pr. Maurice or the act was misdated.

Henry Occ. 25 Apr. 1249 (*Soms F.*, I, 148; *HMC Wells*, I, 2); n.d. (mid-13th cent.) (D. Crouch & G. Thomas, 'Three Goldcliff Charters', *Nat. Lib. Wales Jnl*, 24 (1985), p. 157).

Walter desc. as 'long since' pr. in inquisition of 28 Mar. 1357 (*Cal. Misc. Inq.*, III, 92). His precise place in the sequence of priors is uncertain.

Osbert Occ. Nov. 1295 x Nov. 1296 (PRO, E106/3/19, m. 7d); Nov. 1296 x Nov. 1297 (PRO, E106/4/2, m. 6); 19 Apr. 1297 (*CPR 1292–1301*, p. 270); Nov. 1297 x Nov. 1298 (PRO, E106/4/8, m. 4); Nov. 1298 x Nov. 1299 (PRO, E106/4/9, m. 5d; E106/4/10, m. 7); 1300 (PRO, E106/4/14, m. 11); Nov. 1302 x Nov. 1303 (PRO, E106/4/18, m. 12); 21 Nov. 1311 (*Reg. Droxford*, p. 46); 16 May 1313 (*CPR 1307–13*, p. 585).

Ralph de Roncevill(e) (Ronchevilla, Runcevill(a)) 1313–1318 Abb. of Bec writes to king requesting the adm. of a new pr. 2 Aug. 1313 (PRO, SC1//33/25). M. of Bec, fealty to king made 7 Aug. 1313 (*CCR 1318–23*, p. 10); temps. 24 Aug. 1313 (*CPR 1313–17*, p. 12). Occ. 1 May 1318 (*CFR 1319–27*, p. 325). In dispute over priorship – writ for arrest 15 Jan. 1319 (Logan, *Runaway Religious*, p. 187). Order to pr. of Ogbourne for his arrest – the pr., having rejected the habit of religion, was wandering about in secular dress 10 Apr. 1319 (*CCR 1318–23*, p. 133). 1319 x 1322 had remained for 6 months in disobedience to abb. of Bec, who had removed him (*Cal. Anc. Pet. Wales*, p. 118). Absolution gtd by cardinal bp of Tusculum (Frascati) 12 Apr. 1320 to Roger de Wilyntone who had seized and imprisoned pr. Ralph (*Reg. Orleton (Hereford)*, p. 132). Ralph had held the priory for half a year against William de Sancto Albino and has not permitted him to enter 6 Nov. 1320 (*CPR 1317–21*, pp. 544–5).

William de Sancto Albino 1318–1328 Abb. of Bec writes to king requesting adm. of a new pr. 5 June 1318 (PRO, SC1/33/29). M. of Bec, temps. 10 June 1318 (*CPR 1317–21*, p. 158); 19 July 1319, temps. previously restored to him but order subsequently (9 Sept.) revoked when Ralph de Roncevill, calling himself pr., claimed he had done fealty and had been canonically el. Letters of institution of J., bp of Llandaff, admitting Ralph as pr. were exhibited. Ralph claims that he is perpetual pr. and has not been canonically removed (*CCR 1318–23*, p. 15; cf. ibid., pp. 10–11). Occ. 23 Oct. 1320 (ibid., p. 332); 30 Dec. 1327 (*CPR 1327–30*, p. 197). House void by cession by 2 Apr. 1328, order made to take over the temps. (*CFR 1327–37*, p. 86). 2 seals (*Arch. Camb.*, 137 (1988), p. 127, nos. 282–3; *Mon. Seals*, p. 38; *BM Seals*, nos. 3214–15; D.H. Williams, *Catalogue of Seals in the National Museum of Wales*, I, (Cardiff, 1993). p. 45, nos. W165–6).

Philip de Goupillariis (Gepillar', Gopillariis) 1328–1332 Temps. 5/6 Apr. 1328 (*CPR 1327–30*, p. 255; *CFR 1327–37*, p. 86). Protection gtd 22 Dec. 1331 (*CPR 1330–34*, p. 225). Supposedly removed by 1 Feb. 1332 (*CPR 1330–34*, p. 244), but occ. 26 Mar. 1332 (*CCR 1330–33*, p. 553). 6 Sept. 1332 absolved from excommunication for non-payment of tenth (*Reg. R. Shrewsbury*, no. 438). Seal (*Mon. Seals*, p. 38; *Arch. Camb.*, 137 (1988), pp. 126–7, no. 281).

William Martel 1332 M. of Tintern, claiming to have been apptd by apostolic authority, temps. 1 Feb. 1332 on. removal of former pr. (*CPR 1330–34*, p. 244; cf. *CCR 1330–33*, p. 433). Occ. 24 Mar. 1332 (PRO, E40/3215); 6 Apr. 1332 (*CCR 1330–33*, p. 554). Temps. revoked 11 June 1332 since the king has learned that the papal bull by which William pretended to be apptd to the priory is a forgery; gt of custody of temps. to Peter le Counte, sub-pr. of Goldcliff (*CFR 1327–37*, p. 316). Occ. 1332 x 1333 (*Cal. Anc. Pet. Wales*, pp. 65–6). Mentd 20 Aug. 1337 as former pr., who had made himself pr. by false and forged bulls (*CCR 1337–39*, p. 175). Seal (*Mon. Seals*, p. 38; *BM Seals*, no. 3213).

Philip de Goupillariis (restored) **1333–1334** Occ. 10 Jan., 24 Jan. 1333 (PRO, CP40/293, m. 1). Mand. 6 Feb. 1333 to restore temps. to Philip. The king had lately taken fealty of Philip as pr., on the pres. of the abb. of Bec, and had restored temps., but these had been revoked at the suit of William Martel, claiming to be presented by the pope, and Philip was removed. The papal bull was found to be forged and Philip unjustly removed (*CPR 1330–34*, p. 406). 28 Aug. 1334 escheator ordered to recall temps. as Philip been absolved by abb. of Bec from the administration of the house (*CFR 1327–37*, p. 415).

Thomas de Leonibus (de Leone) **1334–1336** M. of Bec, temps. 28 Aug. 1334 (*CPR 1334–38*, p. 12). Apptd by abb. of Bec. but relieved of his charge by the abb. before 10 July 1336 (ibid., p. 279).

William de Sancto Albino (Seint Aubyn) (restored) **1336–1349** Apptd by abb. of Bec. in place of Thomas de Leonibus. Temps. 10 July 1336 (ibid., p. 279). Occ. 12 Apr. 1347 (*CPR 1345–48*, p. 332). Retired infirm before 13 May 1349 (*CFR 1347–56*, p. 136).

Betrand Maheil (Maahiel) **1349–1351/2** Pr. of Steventon, apptd by abb. of Bec and pres. to king 30 Apr. 1349 (PRO, C84/25/33). Keeping of priory gtd to him 12 May 1349 in place of William de Sancto Albino who was relieved of office by abb. of Bec on account of his weakness (*CPR 1347–56*, p. 136). Relieved of keeping of priory by abb. of Bec by 28 Mar. 1352, prob. much earlier, 1351 (*CFR 1347–56*, p. 326; see below).

William de Sancto Vedasto 1351/2– Occ. Mich. 1351 (PRO, KB27/365, rex roll, m. 7). Care and rule gtd by abb. of Bec to William de Sancto Vedasto, m. of Bec – gt of keeping of priory by king 28 Mar. 1352 (*CFR 1347–56*, p. 326).

German de Sancto Vedasto Occ. 1 Oct. 1367 (*CPR 1377–81*, p. 341); 11 June 1369 (*CFR 1368–77*, p. 13); 26 Oct. 1377 (*CFR 1377–83*, p. 26); restoration of priory 31 Mar. 1400 (*CPR 1399–1401*, p. 72); 13 Feb. 1406 (*CPR 1405–08*, p. 142); 28 Apr. 1410 (*CPR 1408–13*, p. 193).

GROVEBURY (La Grove, Leighton Buzzard). (Beds) (Fontevrault) f. 1164+; diss. *c*.1414
Lists in *VCH Beds*, I, 404 (from 1258); *Heads*, I, 103.

Vitalis Latest recorded occ. 26 May 1196 (*Beds F.*, I, no. 8). Possibly pr. of Nuneaton (*DC*, no. 329).

William Occ. 1227 (*Bucks Eyre*, p. 25, no. 287); Mich. term 1230 (*CRR*, XIV, no. 645); Oct. 1234 x Oct. 1235 (*Surrey F.*, p. 19). He is poss. to be identified with William, proctor of the abbs. and convent of Fontevrault in England *c.* 1220 (*Reg. Ant. Lincoln*, III, no. 646).

Nicholas de Ambr' Occ. 1244 x 1253 (*Ctl. Missenden*, III, no. 908); 12 Nov. 1256 (*Bucks F.*, I, 105); 1257 (*Beds F.*, I, no. 85); Oct. 1257 x Oct. 1258 (PRO, E210/222); pardon for the death of Philip de Leshawe and his subsequent outlawry 1260 (*CPR 1258–66*, p.95); 18 Nov. 1262 (PRO, Glos. F., CP25/1/74/27, no. 606); June 1263 (PRO, E210/331).

William de Verney (Verny) priest. Previously pr. of Nuneaton *c.* 1256–60. Occ. 30 Oct. 1268 as attorney of abbs. of Fontevrault (*CPR 1266–72*, p. 296); as proctor of abbey 21 Oct. 1276 (*Reg. W. Bronescombe*, II, no. 1194). Occ. 5 Oct. 1282 (*CFR 1272–1307*, p. 191); 7 Oct. 1283 (*CPR 1281–92*, p. 78); (W.) 1284 x 6 (PRO, SC1/23/123); 12 Oct. 1287 (*CPR 1281–92*, p. 278); 10 Nov. 1289 (*CCR 1288–96*, p. 27); in Dec. 1291 referred to as '*quondam procurator*' of Grovebury (BL, Add. Cht. 48,003); former pr., but still alive 7 May 1300 (BL, Add. Cht. 48,521). Mentioned *c*.1297 x 1302 as former pr. (PRO, SC1/27/14).

William de Lyencourt Occ. 22 Feb. 1297 (*CPR 1292–1301*, p. 263).

Richard de Greneburgh Previously pr. of Nuneaton 1329–30. Occ. 19 June 1333 (*CPR 1330–33*, p. 438). Pr. of Westwood occ. 1342 (q.v.).

No further prs known.

HAMBLE (Hants), St Andrew (Tiron) f. -1128; Diss. 1391 and granted to Winchester College.

Lists in *VCH Hants*, II, 223; *Heads*, I, 103; WCM, no. 10704 (1393 certificate of admissions to priory 1318–91).

Walter Occ. 24 June 1194 (WCM, no. 10631).

Ambrose Occ. 6 May 1219 (PRO, Hants F., CP25/1/203/4, no. 66).

William mentd 1263 as former pr. (*CR 1261–64*, pp. 301–2).

William Occ. Nov. 1295 x Nov. 1296 (PRO, E106/3/19, m. 7d); Nov. 1296 x Nov. 1297 (PRO, E106/4/2, m. 4); Nov. 1297 x Nov. 1298 (PRO, E106/4/8, m. 3).

John Occ. Nov. 1298 x Nov. 1299 (PRO, E106/4/9, m. 5; E106/4/10, m. 5).

William Occ. Easter 1300 (PRO, E106/4/14, m. 7).

William Goyer Occ., n. d. (*temp.* Edw. II) (WCM, nos. 10763, 12494, the latter *temp.* Simon, abb. of Tiron, i.e. 1297–*c*. 1313, *Gallia Christiana*, VIII, 1265).

Alan Occ. 24 Sept. 1313, 28 Oct. 1313, 26 Nov. 1313 (*CPR 1313–17*, pp. 60, 64, 69).

Richard de Florie −1318 Res. by 4 Jan. 1318 (*Reg. Sandale*, p. 139).

John de Estrepanacho (Estrepamacho, Estrepaniacho) 1318– M. of Tiron, adm. 4 Jan. 1318 (ibid.; WCM, no. 10704). Mentd, but not desc. as pr. 1320 (*Reg. Asserio*, p. 438).

Richard de Beaumont (de Bello Monte) M. of Tiron, gt *in commendam* of house 21 Sept. 1320 (ibid., pp. 437–8; WCM, no. 10704), but occ. as pr. 25 Apr. 1320 (WCM, no. 10666).

John de Estrepanacho −1322 House vacant by his cess. by 14 July 1322 (*Reg. Asserio*, p. 492).

Richard de Beaumont (de Bello Monte, Beaumond) 1322–1345 Inst. 14 July 1322 (ibid., pp. 492–3; *Reg. Wykeham*, II, 614; WCM, no. 10704). Occ. 15 Oct. 1325, 30 Aug. 1326, 3 Dec. 1332; 8 Dec. 1332, 6 Apr. 1337 (WCM nos. 10637, 10668, 10667, 10638, 10669). Order to arrest Richard (not desc. as pr.), who is of the king's enmity of France 29 July 1342 (*CCR 1341–43*, p. 638). Res. by 10 Mar. 1345 (Winchester, Reg. Orleton, II, f. 106r). See Andwell.

James Pasquier (Pasquerii) 1345–1362 M. of Tiron, adm. 10 Mar. 1345 (ibid.; *Reg. Wykeham*, II, 614; WCM, no. 10704). Priory in king's hand 4 Apr. 1349, 22 Mar. 1350 on account of the war with France (*Reg. Edington*, I, nos. 436, 741). Occ. as pr. of Hamble and proctor-general in England of Tiron 1 Apr. 1359 (*CPR 1358–61*, p. 189). Occ. as pr. of Hamble and Andwell, 24 May 1350, 6 June 1359 (WCM, nos. 10676, 10678). D. by 28 Feb. 1362 (*Reg. Edington*, I, no. 1487; WCM, no. 10704).

William de Monasteriis 1362–1371 Occ. as proctor of abbey of Lire 1361–2 (*Reg. Edington*, I, nos. 1266, 1302, 1312, 1338, 1389, 1437). M. of Tiron, inst. 28 Feb. 1362 (ibid., I, no. 1487; WCM, no. 10704). 6 Mar. 1364 Richard Wynnegod occ. as custodian of Hamble, Andwell and St Cross by comm. of John abb. St Mary de Arcisses, vicar-general of abb. Tiron in England (WCM, no. 17216). Admonished to come into residence within 6 mths 14 Jan. 1368; the monition had no effect, the pr. apparently being in foreign parts; commn to sequester temps. 28 Jan. 1369 (*Reg. Wykeham*, II, 15–16). Res. acc. 13 Nov. 1371 (ibid., 17).

Custody of the spiritualities gtd by bp of Winchester to three named men 15 Nov. 1371 (cf. ibid., 17–18; WCM, no. 10683).

William of Foxley (Foxele, Foxle) 1375–1386 M. of Chertsey, coll. by lapse 10 Aug. 1375 (*Reg. Wykeham*, I, 62; II, 615). Certificate of inst. 1 (*sic*) Aug. 1375 (WCM, no. 10704). Occ. 1

Mar. 1380 (WCM, no. 2921a); 3 Oct. 1383 (WCM, no. 13163). On 8 Aug. 1386 Richard II, for the benefit of Sir Bernard Brocas and Tideman, the monk, gtd them the priory of Hamble, after the death of William Foxley, last prior, which took place on 31 May last past, for the term of their lives during the war with France (WCM, no. 2921a; *CPR 1385–89*, p. 19). See T.F. Kirby, 'The alien priory of St Andrew, Hamble, and its transfer to Winchester College in 1391', *Archaeologia*, L (1887), 251–62.

HARMONDSWORTH (Middlesex) (S. Catherine du Mont, Rouen) f. *temp.* William I
List in *VCH Middlesex*, I, 202.
William Occ. 6 July 1260 (*CR 1259–61*, p. 12).
John mentd in 1279 as predecessor of pr. Richard (*CPR 1272–81*, p. 346).
Richard Occ. 17 July 1279 (ibid.; PRO, Just.1/1248, m. 8).
William de Bosco *alias* **de Yvelont** Occ. Nov. 1295 x Nov. 1296 (PRO, E106/3/19, m. 7); 21 Mar. 1296 (WCM, no. 11460); 23 Mar. 1297 (*CPR 1292–1301*, p. 270); Nov. 1298 x Nov. 1299 (PRO, E106/4/9, m. 9; E106/4/10, m. 8); Easter 1300 (PRO, E106/4/14, m. 13).
John de Ibelound Occ. 12 June 1305 as proctor of S. Catherine (Lincoln, Ep. Reg., II, f. 178v).
Humphrey *dictus* **le Contepoyntour** Occ. as general proctor in England of the abbey of S. Catherine 15 May 1317 (Norwich, Reg/1/1, f. 70r).
John de Fraunkevyle (Frankavilla, Frankevill) Occ. as pr. 2 July 1314 (Lincoln, Ep. Reg., II, f. 186v);. proctor of S Catherine 11 Nov. 1318 (ibid., f. 191r); as general proctor in England of the abbey of S. Catherine 1 May 1321 (Norwich, Reg/1/1, f. 89r).
William de Pestlamore Occ. as pr. *c.* Mich. 1324 (PRO, E106/5/2, m. 10d); July 1325 x July 1326 (PRO, E106/5/4, m. [2d]); 8 Oct. 1326 (*Memo. Roll 1326–7*, p. 272); as general proctor in England of the abbey of S. Catherine 29 July 1329 (Norwich, Reg/1/2, f. 30r).
John Busot(is) Proctor of S. Catherine at Harmondsworth 29 Aug. (1332) (PRO, C270/9/4).
Roger Sorel −1351 Occ. 12 Feb. 1342 (*CFR 1337–47*, p. 262); 11 July 1345 (*CPR 1343–46*, p. 636). D. by 21 Nov. 1351 (*CFR 1347–56*, p. 314).
John Cibe 1351–1352 M. of S. Catherine, gtd keeping of priory 21 Nov. 1351 (ibid.); ceased to hold priory by 27 Mar. 1352 (ibid., pp. 325–6).
Robert de Bello Campo 1352 -1391 M. of S. Catherine, gt of keeping of priory 27 Mar. 1352 (ibid.); appt conf. by pope 28 Dec. 1358 (*CPP*, p. 310). Occ. 20 Sept. 1361 (Norwich, Reg/2/5, f. 51r); 6. Oct. 1369 (*CFR 1368–77*, p. 22); 24 Oct. 1372 (WCM, no. 11337); 20 Oct. 1377 (*CFR 1377–83*, p. 4); 18 Sept. 1378 (*CCR 1377–81*, p. 212); 1381 (Richard) (McHardy, *Church in London*, no. 337); 16 June 1388 (*CCR 1385–89*, p. 500); 8 Feb. 1391, 30 May 1391 (*CCR 1389–92*, pp. 248, 265). Described as lately pr. 9 June 1392 (WCM, no. 11379).

Priory given to Bp Wykeham by the abb. and convent of Rouen 15 Oct. 1391(WCM, no. 11380). Dissolved 1391 and granted to Winchester Coll. (*KH*, pp. 83, 88).

HATFIELD REGIS (Broad Oak) (Essex), St Mary and St Melaine (S.Melaine, Rennes) f. *c.* 1135; ref. 1254 (independent)
Lists in *VCH Essex*, II, 110; *Heads*, I, 103.
Eudo Occ. early 13th cent. (pal: BL, Add. Cht. 28396).
Hervey Occ. -1214 (*temp.* Aubrey de Vere, earl of Oxford) (BL, Add. Cht. 28354, cf. ibid., 28360, 28362, 28364); 1222 x 22 May 1224, prob. *c.* 22 May 1224 (*Waltham Chts.*, no. 306, cf. no. 307).
R. Occ. 1229 (*CPR 1225–32*, p. 268).
Stephen −1235 Occ. 22 July 1232 (PRO, Cambs F., CP25/1/24/14, no. 11); 13 Oct. 1233 (*Basset Chts.*, no. 142); 9 Feb. 1235 (*Essex F.*, I, 108). D. by 21 Feb. 1235 (*CR 1234–37*, p. 51).

William 1235– Occ. 25 Nov. 1235 (*CPR 1232–47*, p.131); (W.) 1246 (PRO, E40/13875); 1246 x 1252 (PRO, E40/514, *temp.* Robert, precentor of St Paul's and John de Neville, can. of Chichester). 1236 papal judge delegate case between the abb. of S. Melaine and the bp of London over the right of appt of a pr. The bp and the earl of Oxford had put in W. a monk of St John's, Colchester (? William) (*CPL*, I, 152). Prob. to be identified with **William of Hereford** who occ. *temp.* Hugh de Vere, earl of Oxford (1233–63) (Bodl., Dodsworth ms. 90, f. 117v).

Thomas Occ. 11 Nov. 1254 (*HMC 8th Rept.*, app. I, p. 632); 28 Oct. 1255, May 1259, 25 Mar. 1271 (*TEAS*, new ser., II, 130); 10 Feb. 1261 (PRO, Cambs F., CP25/1/25/30, no. 6); 1272 (PRO, Just.1/84, m. 18); Mich. 1274 x Mich. 1275 (PRO, E159/49, m. 26d).

Michael Occ. 3 Nov. 1278 (PRO, Cambs. F., CP25/1/25/37, no. 6/8); Mich. 1274 x Mich. 1275 (PRO, E159/49, m. 26d).

Roger de Cristeshale (Christehall, Cristehall) Occ. 26 Mar. 1288, 5 July 1292 (BL, Add. Chts. 28534, 28530) and in 8 n.d. chts (late 13th/early 14th cents.) (*TEAS*, new ser., II, 132–3).

John of Colchester (Colcestria) Occ. 18 Sept. 1327 (ibid., 137); 24 Mar. 1338 (ibid., 138); 26 Mar. 1338 (BL, Add. Chts. 28590–1); 15 Aug. 1338 (*HMC 7th Rept.*, p. 582).

Alexander de Berd(e)feld 1344–1369 Sub-pr. of Hatfield Regis, appt of proctors to pres. eln to Ralph, bp of London, 20 Nov. 1344 (BL. Add. Cht. 28596). Occ. 1361 (*Reg. Sudbury*, I, 227); 24 July 1368 (*TEAS*, new ser., II, 142). Res. acc. 15 May 1369 (*Reg. Sudbury*, I, 93).

Thomas of Bradeleye 1369–1380 M. of Hatfield Regis, eln held 25 May 1369 (*Reg. Sudbury*, I, 93–100); commn to examine eln 28 May, certif. 4 June (ibid., 91–3); ass. of earl of Oxford to eln 29 May (ibid., 89–90). D. by 16 July 1380 (PRO, C84/32/24). D., lic. to el. 21 July 1380 (*CPR 1377–81*, p. 526).

HAUGHAM (Lincs) (St Sever) f. 1080; granted 1394 to Carthusian priory, Coventry (Lincoln, Ep. Reg., XII, f. 456r–v).

List in *VCH Lincs*, II, 241.

Nicholas –1226/7 Res. Dec. 1226 x Dec. 1227 (*Reg. Wells*, III, 158).

J. 1226/7–1229/30 Adm. Dec. 1226 x Dec. 1227 (ibid.). D. Dec. 1229 x Dec. 1230 (ibid., 186).

John 1229/30– Adm. Dec. 1229 x Dec. 1230 (ibid.)

Adam 1235– Adm. by archdn of Lincoln *sede vacante* Feb. x June 1235, no reason given for vacancy (*Reg. Wells*, III, 186 – later entry; cf. *AASRP*, XXXIX, 181). Occ. 12 May 1240 (*Lincs F.*, I, 314).

William of Beaulieu (de Bello Loco) **1277–** M. of St Sever, inst. 3 Oct. 1277, no reason given for vacancy (*Reg. R. Gravesend*, pp. 71, 284).

Thomas Hugolini Mentioned 22 Dec. 1290 as predecessor of pr. William Lovel (*Reg. Sutton*, I, 133). Said on 23 Dec. 1290 to have sold spiritualities for two years to Simon Bek, a merchant of Flanders, and gone off with the money (*Reg. Sutton*, I, 131).

William Lovel (Luvel, Lovill) **1291–1298** Appeared before bp 22 Oct. 1289 to answer for having acted as pr. before inst. (ibid.). He pleaded ignorance. The priory's spiritualities were sequestered and he was sent to get letters of recommendation from the earl of Lincoln. 17 Feb. 1290 bp allowed his custody until 1 month after Easter. Nothing was done since the earl of Lincoln was abroad. On 23 Dec. 1290 William was forbidden to act as custodian; 24 Apr. 1291 William appeared before the bp with letters from the earl of Lincoln dated 19 Feb. 1291, stating the abb. St Sever had designated William to Haugham; William was inst. without delay 24 Apr. 1291 (ibid., 131–4); D. by 18 Mar. 1298 (ibid., 227–8).

[**Henry** Occ. as pr. in the returns of aliens from Nov. 1295 x Nov. 1296 to Nov. 1298 x Nov. 1299 (PRO, E106/3/19, m. 10d; E106/4/9, m. 1d; E106/4/10, m. 2). ? a scribal error]

William le Vavasur 1298– M. of St Sever, letter of pres. 18 March 1298, adm. 3 Apr. 1298 (*Reg. Sutton*, I, 227–8).

John de Baunevilla (Bannevilla, Barnevilla) **–1319** Occ. 20 July 1313 (Lincoln, Ep. Reg., II, f. 47v), but as M. of St Sever, adm. 29 Feb. 1317, no reason given for vacancy (ibid. f. 64r). Res. by 11 Dec. 1319 (ibid., f. 350v).

Henry de Sancto Landulo 1319– Letter of pres. by abb. St Sever dated 11 Dec. 1319, adm. by Official *sede vacante* 11 Feb. 1319 (ibid.).

Nicholas de Hamars 1329– M. of St Sever, inst. by bp's vicar-general 7 July 1329, no reason given for vacancy (*Reg. Burghersh* I, no. 230). Commn to inquire into those holding property of the priory of which Nicholas de Hamars, pr., has been wickedly despoiled 4 Sept. 1335 (Lincoln, Ep. Reg., V, f. 509r). Signification to king for the capture of the excommunicate (unnamed) pr. of Haugham 30 Oct. 1339 (ibid., f. 574r). Occ. 1337 (PRO, CP40/312, m. 118); 1340 (PRO, C241/115/380); 1343 (PRO, C85/106/11); 1347, 21 Oct. 1352 (*CFR, 1347–56*, pp. 47, 341); Mich. 1354 x Mich. 1355 (PRO, E372/200, rot. 14); Mich. 1358 x Mich. 1359 (PRO, E372/204, rot. 12).

HAYLING (Hants) (Jumièges) f. *c.* 1067. Diss. 1413 and subsequently gtd to Sheen
No list in *VCH*.

Simon Occ. as pr. *temp.* Bp Jocelin of Bath (1206–42) (BL, Cotton ms. Otho B XIV, f. 65v).

Robert Occ. 20 Oct. 1238 (*Soms F.*, I, 104). Mentd as former pr. 23 Feb. 1245 (*CPL*, I, 214).

Hugh Occ. Nov. 1295 x Nov. 1296 (PRO, E106/3/19, m. 9d); Nov. 1297 x Nov. 1298 (PRO, E106/4/8, m. 5).

Henry Renard (Renart, Reynard) Occ. *c.* Mich. 1324 (PRO, E106/5/2, m. 4); 10 Nov. 1324 (*CFR 1319–27*, p. 314); June 1325 (PRO, E106/8/26); July 1325 x July 1326 (PRO, E106/5/4, m. [3]); 8 Oct. 1326 (*Memo. Roll 1326–7*, p. 272); n.d. in Sheen inventory (BL, Cotton ms. Otho B XIV, f. 63r).

William de Blossevill (Blossevile, Blossevylle) Occ. 23 Mar. 1330 (*CCR 1330–33*, p. 128); 7 Oct. 1337 (*CCR 1337–39*, p. 264); 18 Oct. 1343 (*CCR 1343–46*, p. 244). House void 23 Feb. 1349 (*CPR 1348–50*, p. 261). Occ. as attorney of the abbey of Jumièges 8 Nov. 1341 (not styled pr.) (*CPR 1340–43*, p. 339) and nominated as attorney for 3 years 25 July 1344 (*CPR 1343–45*, p. 319).

Peter de Veulys Occ. 20 Jan. 1360 (*CFR 1356–68*, p. 116).

John Buket (de Busqueto, Bewcot, Boket, Dusqueto, Ousqueto) Letter of collation n.d. mentd in Sheen inventory of chts. (BL, Cotton ms. Otho B XIV, f. 60r). Occ. 6 Oct. 1370, 14 Apr. 1374 (*CFR 1368–77*, pp. 84, 242, 346); 4 Oct. 1377 (not styled pr.), 5 July 1379, 1382 (late farmer of the priory) (*CFR 1377–83*, pp. 16, 161, 284). Gtd custody of the priory 30 Mar. 1382 (ibid., p. 295). Occ. (Ousqueto) 1 Feb. 1385 (*Reg. Wykeham*, II, 354); 1385 (Dusqueto) (PRO, C269/15/56). Gt of keeping of priory 26 Oct. 1399 (*CFR 1399–1405*, p. 13). Occ. Jan. 1403 (*Privy Council*, I, 193).

Note
The Sheen inventory of chts. also notes **Stephen**, pr. of Hayling (BL, Cotton ms. Otho B XIV, ff. 61r, 62v, 63r) and **John**, *custos* of the priory (ibid., f. 62v). There is no clear indication of dates.

HEADLEY (Yorks W.), St Mary (Holy Trinity, York, and Marmoutier) f. –1125; diss. 1414.
No list in *VCH Yorks*.

William described as 'monk at Headley' 25 Jan. 1291 (*Mon. Angl.*, IV, 687, no. iii).

HINCKLEY (Leics), St Mary (Lire) f. -1173; diss. 1409
Lists in *VCH Leics*, II, 52–3; *Heads*, I, 104.

Richard de Capella (Cappella) **1224/5–1230/1** M. of Lire, adm. as administrator Dec. 1224 x Dec. 1225, no reason given for vacancy (*Reg. Wells*, II, 300). Occ. as pr. 1226 (*Ctl. Tutbury*, nos. 266–7); Mich. 1230, Trin. 1231 (*CRR*, XIV, nos. 589, 1633). Res. by 11 Oct. 1231 (*Reg. Wells*, II, 315–16).

John de Capella 1230/1–1233/4 adm. 11 Oct. 1231 (ibid.). Res. Dec. 1233 x Dec. 1234 (ibid., 324).

Richard de Paceio 1233/4–1236/7 M. of Lire, pres. by abb. and conv. of Lire Dec. 1233 x Dec. 1234 (ibid.). Res. (Ralph) June 1236 x June 1237 (*Reg. Grosseteste*, p. 392).

Peter Lombard (Lombardus) **1236/7–1244/5** Adm. June 1236 x June 1237 (ibid.). Res. June 1244 x June 1245 (ibid., p. 423).

William de Aquila 1244/4–1246/7 M. of Lire, pres. June 1244 x June 1245 (ibid.). Res. June 1246 x June 1247 (ibid., p. 427).

Hugh of Winchester (Winton) **1246/7–** M. of Lire, adm. June 1246 x June 1247 (ibid.).

Gilbert –1265 D. by 16 Apr. 1265 (*Reg. R. Gravesend*, p. 145).

Adam de Trungey (Trungeio) **1265–1268** M. of Lire, adm. 16 Apr. 1265 (ibid.). Res. by 23 Apr. 1268 (ibid., p. 148).

Richard de Audreia (Aldereya) **1268–1271** Adm. 23 Apr. 1268 (ibid.). Res. by 9 Aug. 1271 to join the Dominican friars (ibid., p. 152).

Nicholas *dictus* **Bynet** (Binet) **1271–** Adm. 9 Aug. 1271 (ibid.). Occ. as proctor in England of the abbey of Lire (not desc. as pr.) 17 July 1280 (*Reg. Pontissara*, II, 393); appt as proctor in England by abb. of Lire 21 July 1282 (ibid., I, 263).

William de Arena –1289 D. by 20 Nov. 1289 (*Reg. Sutton*, VIII, 43).

Henry (Hervey) de Alneto (d'Aunay) **1289–1300** M. of Lire, adm. (Henry) 20 Nov. 1289 (ibid.). Occ. (Hervey) Nov. 1295 x Nov. 1296, Nov. 1296 x Nov. 1297 (PRO, E106/3/19, m. 11; E106/4/2, m. 4d); (Henry) 1300 (E106/4/14, m. 8d). Letter of res. (Hervey) dated 24 Sept. 1300 and res. adm. same day (Lincoln, Ep. Reg., II, f. 195v).

Reyner de Jarieta 1300–1310 M. of Lire, letter of pres. 24 Sept. 1300, adm. 25 Sept. 1300 (ibid.) Occ. 18 Feb. 1302, 15 Mar. 1305 as proctor of Lire. (ibid., ff. 198r, 199r) D. by 14 Dec. 1310 (ibid., f. 205r).

Matthew de Puteo (Gote) **1310–1319** M. of Lire, letter of pres. dated 14 Dec. 1310; adm. 27 Feb. 1311 (ibid.). D. by 2 Apr. 1319 (referred to as Matthew Gote) (ibid., f. 217v).

Henry de Rie 1319–1333 M. of Lire, letter of pres. dated 2 Apr. 1319, adm. 23 May 1319 (ibid.). Res. by 16 Mar. 1333 (*Reg. Burghersh* I, no. 1032).

Michael de Gayniaco (Ganiaco, Gaynaco) **1333–1334** M. of Lire, letter of pres. by Abb. Robert and convent dated 16 Mar. 1333 (ibid.); adm. and inst. 29 Apr. 1333 (ibid.). Res. by 28 Oct. 1334 (ibid., no. 1066). Occ. later as proctor-general of Lire in 1355 (*CFR 1347–56*, p. 428). D. by 1360 (*CFR 1356–68*, p. 135).

Nicholas de Gaynaire (Ganaire) **1334–** M. of Lire, letter of pres. by Abb. William and convent dated 28 Oct. 1334, adm. and inst. 1 Dec. 1334 (*Reg. Burghersh*, I, no. 1066). Lic. for one year's study 27 July 1340 (Lincoln, Ep. Reg., V, f. 201r).

John Pepyn –1348 Occ. 24 Mar. 1342 (*CFR 1337–47*, p. 262); 4 Dec. 1347 (*CFR 1347–56*, p. 61). Letter from Abb. to proctor to pres. on res. or dimission of John, dated 5 Mar. 1348 (Lincoln, Ep. Reg., IX, f. 340r). A Br. John Pepyn, m. of Lire, was adm. to Carisbrooke priory 5 May 1348 (*Reg. Edington*, I, no. 263).

John Morelli (Morell, Morelly) **1348–1367** M. of Lire, letter from Abb. to proctor to pres. on res. or dimission of John Pepyn, dated 5 Mar. 1348; John Morelli adm. 23 May 1348 (Lincoln, Ep. Reg., IX, f. 340r). Vacant by d. or dimission by 16 June 1367 (Lincoln, Ep. Reg., X, f. 240v). Seal (*Mon. Seals*, p. 40; *BM Seals*, no. 3282).

John de Fonte 1367–1368 M. of Lire, letter of pres. dated 16 June 1367, inst. by bp 5 Aug. 1367 (Lincoln, Ep. Reg., X, f. 240v). Res. by 18 June 1368 (ibid., f. 241v).

Ralph le Cornu (Cornuti, Cornuz, Corane) 1368–1376 M. of Lire, letter of pres. dated 18 June 1368, inst. by bp 28 July 1368 (ibid.). D. by 1 Mar. 1376 (ibid., f. 264r).

Michael Aufri (Aufreye, Aufrie, Aufry, Aufrye, Ausfrie) 1376– M. of Lire, adm. 1 Mar. 1376 (ibid.). He had previously been gtd keeping of the priory, with Ralph Maylok, 24 May 1375 (*CFR 1368–77*, p. 286). Occ. 1377 (*Clerical Poll-Taxes*, p. 28, no. 377); gt of keeping of priory 14 Feb. 1397 (*CFR 1391–99*, p. 204); restoration of priory 26 Jan. 1400 (*CFR 1399–1401*, p. 71). Occ. 11 Aug. 1400 (Worcester, Reg. Winchcombe, pp. 100–1); 20 Feb. 1404 (*CFR 1399–1405*, p. 241). Prob. the last pr.; Hinckley dissolved 1409; gtd to Mountgrace priory (*KH*, pp.83, 88).

HOLBECK (Yorks W.) (Cell of Holy Trinity, York) See D.J.H. Michelmore, 'A monastic cell at Holbeck' in M.L. Faull and S.A. Moorhouse, *West Yorkshire Archaeological Survey to A.D. 1500* (3 vols., Wakefield, 1981), 3, p. 798, app. 2; ment. in 13th cent. chts. See also ref. to the master of Holbeck in a taxation list in *Ctl. Sallay*, II, 177.
No names found.

HORSHAM ST FAITH (Norfolk), St Mary and St Faith (Conques) f. 1105
Lists in *VCH Norfolk*, II, 348; *Heads*, I, 104.

Eustorgius (Austorgius) Occ. early 13th cent. (pal.: BL, Add. Cht. 15185), Oct. 1227 x Oct. 1228 (*Norfolk F., (Rye)*, p. 42); doubtless the same as Austorgius (*HMC Lothian*, p. 10, there dated *c.* 1120 x 30?).

Peter Desc. as former pr. at Easter 1243 (*CRR*, XVII, no. 2363). His position in the sequence of priors is uncertain).

Berengar Carbunel Occ. 18 Jan. 1245 (PRO, Just.1/560, m. 48); from Oct. 1246 x Oct. 1247 to Oct. 1271 x Oct. 1272 (*Norfolk F (Rye)*, pp. 71, 111); *c.* 1256 (Norfolk RO, NRS.27204); 14 May 1269 (*HMC Lothian*, p. 7); n.d. (mid-13th cent.) (Norfolk RO, Blickling, Lothian ms. MC/3/1 XII).

Reymund de Cotrodes Occ. 1281 and 1293 (Blomefield, *Norfolk*, X, 440, with no source). (R.) 20 May 1292 (BL, Add. Cht. 19294); n.d. (late 13th cent) (Norfolk RO, Phi/216/1.577 x 3); n.d. (PRO, LR14/415). Seal (*BM Seals*, nos. 3294–6).

William Occ. (W.) 29 Dec. 1300 (*Norwich Cath. Chts.*, I, no. 383); 15 Apr. 1303 (*CPR 1301–07*, p. 131); 8 Dec. 1307, going to Gascony 24 Apr. 1311 (*CPR 1307–13*, pp. 25, 339).

Hugh Targe 1313– M. of Conques, adm. 21 Dec. 1313, no reason given for vacancy (Norwich, Reg/1/1, f. 54v). Occ. 1320 (BL, Add. Chts. 15189–90); 15 Apr. 1322 (PRO, C241/102/150); *c.* Mich. 1324 (PRO, E106/5/2); 1326 (*Memo. Roll 1326–7*, p. 272); 6 Aug. 1331 (PRO, C241/102/126).

An unnamed pr. d. by 10 Jan. 1338 (*CFR 1337–47*, p. 71).

Pontius de Serveria (Cerveria, Cirveria, Servera, Severia) 1338–1349 M. of Conques, adm. 8 May 1338, no reason given for vacancy (Norwich, Reg/1/3, f. 12v). Gt of keeping of priory during pleasure 10 May 1338 (*CFR 1337–47*, p. 82). Occ. 21 July 1340, 16 Feb. 1342 (ibid., pp. 186, 265); 12 Aug. 1344 (*CPR 1343–45*, p. 334); 11 July 1345 (*CCR 1343–46*, p. 636). D. by 24 Sept. 1349 (*Accts of Papal Collectors*, p. 98).

Hugh de Pardines (Pertinis) 1349–1351 M. of Conques, adm. 19 Nov. 1349, no reason given for vacancy (Norwich, Reg/2/4, f. 115v). Occ. 15 June 1351 (*CPR 1354–58*, p. 28). D. by 19 Nov. 1351 (*CPL*, III, 429, cf. *CFR 1347–56*, p. 331).

[**Bernard Jori** (Joly) M. of Souillac, dioc. Cahors, apptd, but res. before 19 Nov. 1351 (*CPL*, III, 429); cf. prov. 24 Sept. 1349 on d. of Pontius de Serveria (*Accts of Papal Collectors*, pp. 98, 126, 218, 232–3, 260, 272, 312).]

Ber(n)ard de Seintoill (Centolli, Sentoll) **1351–1356** Papal prov. 19 Nov. 1351 (ibid.). Occ. 1 May 1352 (*CFR 1347–56*, p. 331); 3 June 1355 (*CPR 1358–61*, p. 429). Res. by 14 Oct. 1356 (Norwich, Reg/2/5, f. 171r–v).

Berengar Natas (Nathas) **1357–** M. of Conques, letter of pres. 14 Oct. 1356, adm. 21 Jan. 1357 (ibid.; cf. entry of 17 July 1357 (*CFR 1356–68*, p. 43)). Occ. Mich. 1358 x Mich. 1359 (PRO, E372/204, rot. 16d); 26 Oct. 1370, 12 May 1377 (*CFR 1368–77*, pp. 83, 401); 30 Jan. 1378 (*CFR 1377–83*, p. 67); 24 June 1381 (ibid., p. 261).

Thomas Bertholt 1389– M. of Horsham, apptd by bp to whom the collation has devolved this turn 18 Sept. 1389, no reason given for vacancy (Norwich, Reg/3/6, f. 139v).

HORSLEY (Glos) (Troarn; Bruton) f. *temp.* William I (alien priory); diss. 1260 and given to Bruton. 1262 (Aug. cell); 1380 (diss.).

Lists in *VCH Glos.*, II, 93; *Heads*, I, 104.

Gilbert Occ. 1214 (*CRR*, VII, 161).

Stephen Prob. first Aug. pr. adm. *c.* 12 July 1262 (*Ctl. Bruton*, p. 79, no. 316; *EEA*, 13, no. 114); 11 Apr. 1269 (*Reg. G. Giffard*, p. 21).

Walter of Horwood (Horwode) Can. of Bruton, having previously been pres. to priory by the pr. and convent of Bruton and adm. as pr., the bp gives permission for him to live at Bruton for 4 years and to use the fruits of Horsley for the payment of Bruton priory's debts 15 May 1271 (ibid., p. 46).

Richard de la Grave 1292– Inst. n.d. [between entries July – Sept. 1292] (ibid., p. 425). Occ. 8 Apr. 1297 (*CPR 1292–1301*, p. 276).

William 1298– Inst. 11 Nov. 1298 (*Reg. G. Giffard*, p. 507).

William de Wasoun (Wason) ?the same. Occ. 9 Mar. 1307 (Worcester Cath. Lib., mun. B.477); 19 Jan. 1313 (*CCR 1307–13*, p. 564).

William of Milverton –1329 D. by 5 Oct. 1329 (*Reg. Orleton (Worc.)*, no. 98).

Laurence de Haustede 1329– Can. of Bruton, adm. 5 Oct. 1329 (ibid., nos. 98, 746).

Henry de Lisle (de Insula, Lile, Lyle) **1335–1357** Can. of Bruton, adm. 21 Sept. 1335, no reason given for vacancy (*Reg. Montacute*, no. 276 and p. 305). Lic. to make a pilgrimage 31 Dec. 1349 (*Worcs Reg. Sede Vacante*, p. 245). Occ. 3 May 1355 (*CPR 1354–58*, p. 244); June 1355 (*Ctl. Bruton*, nos. 358, 363); 10 July 1355 (*CPR 1354–58*, p. 266 = Lambeth, Reg. Islip, f. 100r). Mentd that he had been to Rome and Venice without the pr. of Bruton's leave, and had dissipated the revenues of Horsley (*Cal. Misc. Inq.*, III, 73). In dispute over priorship, signified for arrest 20 Mar. 1357 (Logan, *Runaway Religious*, p. 222). Res. by 19 Oct. 1357 (Worcester, Reg. Brian I, p. 50). Mentioned 5 Nov. 1358 as deposed pr. (*CCR 1354–60*, p. 469).

Richard de Holte 1357–1363 Can. of Bruton, pres. to Horsley by pr. and convent of Bruton 21 Sept. 1357 (*Ctl. Bruton*, no. 362); adm. 19 Oct. 1357 (Worcester, Reg. Brian I, p. 50). Res. by 10 Dec. 1363 (Worcester, Reg. Barnet, p. 10).

Henry Cary 1363– Can. of Bruton, adm. by vicar-general 10 Dec. 1363 (ibid.).

Replacement of a can. of Bruton called pr. of Hurley by another mentd 15 July 1371 (*CPR 1370–74*, p. 126).

William Cary (Gary) Occ. Jan. 1368 x Jan. 1369 (PRO, E42/421; E326/11644). Dispute at the Curia – William styling himself pr., occ. 19 Jan. 1372, 14 Nov. 1373 – William committed to Bruton for safe custody (*King's Bench Edward III*, VI, 168–70).

Richard Cary (most prob. an error for William, see above and below). Priory sequestered on account of pr.'s absence 30 July 1375 (*Worcs Reg. Sede Vacante*, p. 347).

William Cary (Cari, Gary) William's (*sic*) sequestration released 17 Aug. 1375 (ibid., p. 348). Sequestration of fruits of priory owing to bad governance and long absence of pr.

William, who is excommunicate 26 Mar. 1376 (*Reg. Wakefield*, no. 42). Pr. absent and long excommunicate – signification for arrest 16 Apr. 1376 (Logan, *Runaway Religious*, p. 224). Ordinance governing the future relationship of Bruton priory and the dependent priory of Horsley 5 July 1376 (*Reg. Wakefield*, no. 43). Occ. 13 June 1377 (PRO, C67/283, m. 1).

ISLEHAM, *see* LINTON

William Occ. as pr. 12 Sept. 1219 (Maidstone, Centre for Kentish Studies, DRb/Ar.2).
Roland Occ. as pr. Isleham (i.e. Linton) 31 Aug. 1332 (PRO, C270/9/18).

KIRBY, *see* MONKS KIRBY

LANCASTER, St Mary (Sées) f. 1094

Lists in *VCH Lancs.*, II, 172–3; *Lancaster Hist.*, IV, 771; *Heads*, I, 104.

In 1208–9 the priory was vacant (*PR 11 John*, p. 105).

John de Alench' (?Alençon) Occ. *c.*1210 x 1235 (PRO, E326/3905). (John Redufo) early 13th cent. (*Ctl. Cockersand*, III, i. 922).

Geoffrey 1230– The house was taken in the sheriff's hands when mand. to release to br. Geoffrey, assigned to the priory by the abb. of Sées, issued 2 Nov. 1230 (*CR 1227–31*, p. 460; cf. *Lancaster Hist.*, I, 150–1). Occ. 12 Nov. 1241 (*Lancs. F.*, I, 82; *Lancaster Hist.*, I, 32–3).

Garner Occ. n.d. but stated to be the successor of Geoffrey (*Ctl. Whalley*, II, 428). Occ. July 1250 (*Lancaster Hist.*, I, 47–8, cf. 44–5, where the original composition is dated 1259(/60) – a likely error); n.d. (ibid., 155–6).

William de Reyo (Reo, Reio) **1251–** Mand. for seisin 15 Feb. 1251 (*CR 1247–51*, p. 414). Occ. 4 July 1251 (*Ctl. Whalley*, II, 428); 10 July 1251 (*CPR 1247–58*, p. 101); 13 Jan. 1253 (PRO, E315/33/201); 13 Jan. 1253 (*Lancaster Hist.*, I, 34); 1256 (ibid., II, 288); Oct. 1256 x Oct. 1257 (ibid., 410–11); ? Oct. 1258 x Oct. 1259 (ibid., 418–19).

Ralph de Truno 1266– M. of Sées, temps. 9 Mar. 1266 (*CPR 1258–66*, p. 566; *Lancaster Hist.*, II, 474–5). Occ. 31 Dec. 1271 (*Lancaster Hist.*, I, 59–60); Nov. 1283 x Nov. 1284 (ibid., II, 332–3); 25 Feb. 1287 (ibid., I, 35–6); n.d. (late 13th cent.) (PRO, E315/42/111).

John *dictus* Rex ((de) le Ray) **1290–** M. of Sées, adm. by Edmund, son of Henry III n.d. (*Lancaster Hist.*, II, 475–6); mand. to install 25 Oct. 1290 (ibid., 476–7). Occ. from 8 July 1292 (ibid. I, 41–3) to 17 June 1306 (*Ctl. Furness*, II, i, 181).

Fulcher Occ. 8 Aug. 1305 (PRO, E315/33/202); 25 Feb. 1306 (BL, Harl. Cht. 83 A 31). Mentd 1322–3 as predecessor of Nigel and had d. (*Lancaster Hist.*, II, 508–11).

Nigel Occ. 29 Sept. 1315 (*Ctl. Furness*, II, i, 217); 9 Aug. 1316 (*Reg. Greenfield*, V, app., p. 279, no. 2886); 1318 (*Lancaster Hist.*, II, 495–8); 14 July 1323 (ibid., 510–11); 22 Aug. 1323 (ibid., 477–9); *c.* Mich. 1324 (PRO, E106/5/2, m. 5d); July 1325 x July 1326 (PRO, E106/5/4, m. [2d]); 8 Oct. 1326 (*Memo. Roll 1326–7*, p. 272).

Ralph Courait (Courrat) **1328–1337** Letter of pres. 7 July 1328, inst. 5 Aug. 1328 (*Reg. Melton*, I, p. 41, nos. 127–9). Called Adam Courrat 1331 (*Lancaster Hist.*, II, 471–2). D. by 27 July 1337 (*CFR 1337–47*, p. 35, cf. *CPR 1334–38*, p. 489).

Emery de Argenteles (Argentels) **1337–** M. of Lancaster, pres. by king 11 Aug. 1337 (*CPR 1334–38*, p. 489, cf. *CFR 1337–47*, p. 35; *CCR 1337–39*, p. 162). Occ. 7 Mar. 1338 (*CCR 1337–39*, p. 335); 13 Apr. 1340 (*CFR 1337–47*, p. 176).

John de Condreto -?1349 Occ. 24 Feb. 1342, 14 Dec. 1344 (ibid., pp. 265, 404); 25 May 1344 (PRO, E315/32/75); 9 Jan. 1345, 14 Jan. 1345, 11 July 1345 (*CCR 1343–46*, pp. 483, 435, 636); Mich. 1348 x Mich. 1349 (PRO, E372/194, rot. 18). Probably d. 1349, ref. to him as dead by 18 Nov. 1349 (*CFR 1347–56*, p. 183).

Peter Martini (Martyn) **–1366** Occ. 18 Nov. 1349 (ibid.); 24 Nov. 1356, 14 Nov. 1358 (*CFR 1356–68*, pp. 25, 76); Mich. 1358 x Mich. 1359 (PRO, E372/204, rot. 24d). Res. 1366 to be abb.of Sées (*Mon. Angl.*, VII, 998, no. ii; *Gallia Christiana*, XI, 722–3).

William Raymbaut (Raynbote, Raynbo(u)t, Reynboud) **1366–1369** Apptd by Pope Urban V 25 Nov. 1366 (ibid.; cf. *Accts of Papal Collectors*, pp. 297, 348). Occ. 7 Feb. 1368 (*CPR 1367–70*, p. 128); 11 June 1369 (*CFR 1368–77*, p. 16); 2 July 1369 (*CCR 1369–74*, p. 97). D. by 24 July 1369 (*CFR 1368–77*, pp. 18–19).

John Innocent 1369–1396 M. of Sées, adm. 23 Sept. 1369 (*Reg. Archdny Richmond*, p. 174, no. 60). D. by 6 Sept. 1396 (*CFR 1391–99*, p. 187).

LAPLEY (Staffs), (S. Rémi, Rheims) f. 1061
  Lists in *VCH Staffs*, III, 343; *Heads*, I, 105.
Inganus Latest recorded occ. 1206 x 1207 (*PR 9 John*, p. 9).
John 1233– M. of S. Rémi, apptd by abb. of S. Rémi; mand. for seisin 10 Nov. 1233 (*CR 1231–34*, p. 337).
Walcher Occ. 19 Mar. 1266 (*Lichfield Mag. Reg. Album*, no. 318).
Order to take priory into the king's hands 2 June 1288: unnamed pr. had gone overseas without royal lic. (*CFR 1272–1307*, p. 248).
Reginald Occ. 1293 (PRO, Just.1/805, m. 39d); Nov. 1295 x Nov. 1296 to Nov. 1297 x Nov. 1298 (PRO, E106/3/19, m. 7d; E106/4/8, m.5).
Roger Occ. Nov. 1298 x Nov. 1299 (PRO, E106/4/9, m. 9); Easter 1300 (PRO, E106/4/14, m. 13).
Peter de Passiaco –1305 Res. by 16 Aug. 1305 (Lichfield, B/A/1/1, f. 16r).
John de Tannione (Tanyen – *Staffs Plea Rolls 1360–87*, p. 62) **1305–1320** M. of S. Rémi, adm. 16 Aug. 1305 (Lichfield, B/A/1/1, f. 16r). Occ. 14 June 1314 (ibid., f. 46v). Res. on 5 Nov. 1320 (ibid., f. 90v).
Gobert de Brabantia (Barbantia) **1320–1322** Adm. 5 Nov. 1320 (ibid.; PRO, LR14/350). Res. by 24 July 1322 (Lichfield, B/A/1/2, f. 136r).
John de Acey(o) 1322–1328 M. of S. Rémi, adm. 24 July 1322 (ibid.; PRO, LR14/350). Res. by 30 Apr. 1328 (ibid., ff. 143v–144r).
Baldwin de Spinallo (Spinalo, Spynale, Spynal(l)o, Spynarle) **1328–?1361** Custody gtd to Baldwin, m. of S. Rémi, 28 Feb. 1328 (ibid. f. 143v). pres. 30 Apr. 1328, adm. 27 May 1328 (ibid., ff. 143v–144r; PRO, LR14/350). Occ. 11 Dec. 1332 (Lichfield, B/A/1/2, f. 152r); 27 Nov. 1349 (ibid., f. 186v). Process against Gobert (Gobertus) de Lapione, m. of S. Rémi, intruded as pr., excommunicated, and Baldwin declared the regularly instd pr. 11 Mar. 1335 (ibid., B/A/1/3, ff. 72v–73r). Gobert had appeared, styled as pr. 17 Feb. 1335 (*CPR 1334–38*, p. 75). Occ. 14 Feb. 1335, 1 Apr. 1335, 5 June 1335 (*CPR 1334–38*, pp. 136, 91, 145); 1 May 1338, 6 July 1338, 8 Mar. 1341, 17 June 1345 (*CFR 1337–47*, pp. 75, 87, 212, 473); 16 May 1347 (*CPR 1345–48*, p. 540). Pardoned 6 Sept. 1352 for homicides, felonies, trespasses and robberies (*CPR 1350–54*, p. 320). Occ. 28 Feb. 1354 (*CPR 1354–58*, p. 11); 28 June 1354, 16 Feb. 1356, 20 May 1357 (*CCR 1354–60*, pp. 26, 301, 356, 358; *CFR 1356–68*, p. 2).
Priory vacant on 23 Nov. 1361 (*Reg. Stretton*, I, 110).
Peter de Geninero (Gennerey(o), Gennerye) **1361–** M. of S. Rémi, inst. 26 Jan. 1362 (*Reg. Stretton*, I, 110; PRO, LR14/350). Peter occ. Mich. term 1367 (*Staffs Plea Rolls 1360–87*, p. 62); 1370 (PRO, E106/10/2).
Peter de Romelot –1399 Occ. in return of aliens in response to a writ of 6 Mar. 1374 (PRO, C269/15/36); 21 Apr. 1377 (*CFR 1368–77*, p. 395); 8 Oct. 1377 (*CFR 1377–81*, p. 18); 1382 (*SHC*, XIV, 160); 1385 (PRO, C269/15/55); 1388 (*CPR 1383–91*, p. 273); gtd keeping of

priory 22 July 1397, 23 Oct. 1397 (*CPR 1391–99*, pp. 221, 237). D. by 4 Nov. 1399 (*CPR 1399–1401*, p. 42).

LEWISHAM (Kent) (St Peter, Ghent) f. 918; ref. 1044. Diss. 1414.
Lists in *VCH Kent*, II, 238; *Heads*, I, 105.

Arnold Occ. 14 Feb. 1229 (*CChR 1226–57*, p. 91). A pr. **Arnulph** occ. n.d. (PRO, E42/524), ? the same.

Sigor Occ. morrow of St Augustine (prob. 27 May) 1257 (PRO, E40/4760).

John de Ostborth Occ. as proctor of Lewisham and Greenwich *c*. Mar. 1288 (PRO, E40/3389).

[4 Oct. 1295 David le Graunt, king's clerk, apptd to custody of the priory as the number of foreigners staying there constitutes a danger (*CPR 1292–1301*, p. 151; *CFR 1272–1307*, p. 366).]

John Occ. from Nov. 1295 x Nov. 1296 to Nov. 1298 x Nov. 1299 (PRO, E106/3/19, m. 6d; E106/4/9. m. 3); Trin. 1297 (*Coram Rege Roll*, p. 87); 24 Sept. 1298 (*CPR 1292–1301*, p. 362).

James de Dovra Occ. 25 Nov. or 7 Dec. 1317 (Lambeth, Reg. Reynolds, f. 22r – 7 [calends/ides] Dec.); 10 Sept. 1321, 15 Dec. 1321, 25 Sept. 1322 (*Reg. Hethe*, I, 99, 101, 116). Letter of the convent of St Peter's, Ghent, to the king explaining the reasons why they cannot grant Lewisham priory to the king's nominee 18 Feb. 1319 (PRO, SC1/34/56). Possibly the James de Dousa (*sic*), m. of Lewisham, mentd in the Sheen inventory of chts. (BL, Cotton ms. Otho B XIV, f. 76r).

William (de) Sergotz (Segrotis, Sergods, Sergortz) **1330–1332** Inst. to 'stewardship' (*yconomatus*) of Lewisham, no reason given for vacancy 7 Feb. 1330 (*Reg. Hethe*, I, 434). Occ. as pr. 6 Nov. 1330 (ibid., 435). Suspended for contumacy and cited to appear 27 Apr. 1332 (ibid., 472).

James (John) Brounyng 1332– M. of St Peter, Ghent, cited to make his oath of obedience as *yconomus* 28 Sept. 1332 [James in heading/John in text] (ibid., 478). Adm. (James) 11 Oct. 1332, no reason given for vacancy (ibid., 523).

Livinus Piscarius 1334– M. of St Peter, Ghent, adm. 20 Nov. 1334, no reason given for vacancy (ibid., 548).

William (de) Sergotz (Segrotis) Occ. as pr. or *iconomus* 3 Feb. 1339 (ibid., 586); 8 Feb. 1342 (*CFR 1337–47*, p. 261); as proctor of the abbey of Ghent at Lewisham July 1343 (*Reg. Hethe*, II, 713); 11 July 1345 as pr. of Lewisham and Greenwich (*CCR 1343–46*, p. 636); 13 Sept. 1343 (*CPR 1345–48*, p. 68; *CCR 1343–46*, p. 81). Mentd in the Sheen inventory of chts. (BL, Cotton ms. Otho B XIV, ff. 74v, 76r).

Gossewin (Gossuin) Riym (Riim, Rym) M. of St Peter, Ghent, occ. 20 Oct. 1357 (*CFR 1356–68*, p. 50); 25 June 1360, 20 Nov. 1360 (*CPR 1361–64*, pp. 432, 502); 22 Jan. 1360 (*CFR 1356–68*, p. 115); 18 Oct. 1362 (PRO, C241/143/67); going overseas 12 Dec. 1362 (*CPR 1361–64*, p. 277); going overseas 18 July 1364 (*CPR 1364–67*, p. 8). Ment. as attorney in England of the abbey of Ghent, not desc. as pr. 15 Oct. 1366, 25 Nov. 1366 (ibid., pp. 321, 340). Mentd several; times in the Sheen inventory of chts. (BL, Cotton ms. Otho B XIV, ff. 73v, 75r, 78r, 83r).

Note
The Sheen inventory also mentions **Theodoric**, *procurator* of Lewisham (BL, Cotton ms. Otho B XIV, ff. 78r, 80r), and **Giles**, pr. of Lewisham (ibid., f. 80r). There is no indication of dates.

LINTON and ISLEHAM, St Margaret (Cambs) (S. Jacut de Mer) f. Isleham -1100;
Linton -1163. Monks of Isleham moved to Linton 1254. It was parcel of Linton 1291 when a prior of Linton and Isleham recorded, and this double title is used regularly, although in 1332

the pr. of Isleham alone is recorded (see under Roland below). Diss. 1414 (*VCH Cambs*, II, 314–5 (article but no list)).

William Occ. as pr. of Isleham 12 Sept. 1219 (Maidstone, Centre for Kentish Studies, Drb/Ar.2).

Alan Mentd 1312 as a previous pr. *temp.* Edward I (*YB XIII*, p. 70).

Roland Occ. Nov. 1295 x Nov. 1296 (PRO, E106/3/19, m. 9); Nov. 1296 x Nov. 1297 (PRO, E106/4/2, m. 6); Nov. 1297 x Nov. 1298 (PRO, E106/4/2, m. 6); Nov. 1298 x Nov. 1299 (PRO, E106/4/9, m. 5d; E106/4/10, m. 6d); Mich. 1312 (*YB XIII*, pp. 68–70); *c.* Mich. 1324 (PRO, E106/5/2, m. 9d); July 1325 x July 1326 (PRO, E106/5/4, m. [8d]); (pr. of Isleham) 31 Aug. 1332 (PRO, C270/9/18). Mentd in royal writ and cert. of 10 Feb. 1344 notes that pr. Roland d. 6 years ago (Ely, G/1/1, part 1, ff. 90r, 93r).

John Occ. 24 Dec. 1339 (ibid., f. 83r).

R./John Porty (Porci) Occ. (R.) lic. for absence 6 Jan. 1341 (ibid., f. 9v); (John) res. acc. 14 May 1341 (ibid., f. 20r).

William Bourdet 1341– M. of S. Jacut, letter of pres. 20 Feb. 1341; adm. 21 May 1341 in place of John Porci, deceased (ibid., f. 20r–v). Occ. 15 Dec. 1344 (*CPR 1343–45*, p. 456; *CFR 1337–47*, p. 402); 4 Mar. & 14 Oct. 1346 (Ely, G/1/1, part 2, ff. 67v, 69v); 6 Oct. 1351 (PRO, C269/15/30). D. by 11 Mar. 1357, prob. *c.* 1355 (*CPP*, p. 294, and see below).

John of Whittlesey (Withelsey, Witlesey(e), Wytleseye) 1355– M. of Thorney, coll. by bp by lapse 22 June 1355, no reason given for vacancy (Ely, G/1/3, f. 131v; ibid., G/1/1, part 2, f. 46v). Mentd 11 Mar. 1357 as having intruded on d. of William Bourdet (*CPP*, p. 294, see below).

Robert Renaut (Renant, Reynaudii) M. of S. Jacut, appealed to Pope (case committed to papal auditor 11 Mar. 1357) stating that his abbot had presented him on the d. of William Bourdet (?1355), but John had intruded (*CPP*, p. 294). On 25 May 1358 sentence of the papal commissary in an appeal of the convent and Robert el. their pr. against John Wittlesey, m. of Thorney, pretending to the same (*HMC 1st Rept*, p. 70). John appealed against the papal decision in favour of Robert; Pope Innocent VI commns the bp of Rochester to sequester the priory until the final result 13 June 1358 (*Orig. Papal Letters*, p. 127, no. 249). Royal protection for Robert 24 Sept. 1359 (*CPR 1358–61*, p. 273).[6]

Nicholas Menfrey (Manfray, Menfray) 1370– M. of S. Jacut, adm. 28 Mar.1370 (Ely, G/1/3, f. 131v). Occ. 1377 (*CFR 1368–77*, p. 401; *CFR 1377–83*, p. 24); 1378 (*CPR 1377–81*, p. 203); 1382 (*CFR 1377–83*, p. 285); 16 June 1385 (*CCR 1381–85*, p. 557); 8 Feb. 1385, 20 Feb. 1387 (*CPR 1383–91*, pp. 86, 172); Jan. 1403 (*Privy Council*, I, 196). Gt of keeping of priory 30 Jan. 1403 (*CFR 1399–1405*, p. 191).

LIVERS OCLE (Hereford) (Lire) f. 1100. Diss. *c.* 1414

William Occ. 26 July 1221 (PRO, Glos.F., CP25/1/73/4, no. 16).

W. de Insula Possibly the same as above. Occ. *c.* 1225 (BL, Cotton ms. Domitian A III, f. 87v, cht. n.d. but conf. of abb. of Lire on same folio dated 1225).

Peter Occ. 29 Apr. 1246 (PRO, Hereford F., CP25/1/80/11, no. 202); n.d. (1247 x 1262 with John, abb. of Wigmore) (*Reg. Trillek*, p. 49).

The next recorded pr., **Ralph Maylock** (Mayloc, Maylot), occ. Mich. 1389, 18 Nov. 1399 and 1 March 1400 (*YB 13 Richard II*, p. 74; *CPR 1399–1401*, pp. 71, 408). However, Maylock occ. frequently as M. of Lire and proctor in England of the abbot and convent of Lire, but without the Livers Ocle title between 18 Nov. 1367 and 20 Feb. 1387 (*CPR 1367–70*, p. 58; *Buckingham Writ Reg.*, p. 108, no. 326).

---

[6] *Mon. Angl.*, VII, 1045 lists John Walkelyn as pr. 1362 but without source.

Note
Albricus Occ. n.d. as pr. of 'Acle' (?Ocle) in the Sheen inv. of chts. (BL, Cotton ms. Otho B XIV, f. 16v). There is no indication of when he might have held office.

LLANGENNITH (Glamorgan) (S. Taurin, Evreux) f. -1119
List in *Heads*, I, 105.
William Gabriel(e) Occ. early 13th cent. (pal. *Glam. Chts.*, II, p. 105, no. 497 = BL, Harl. Cht. 75 C 28); 1231 x 1247 (*St Davids Acta*, nos. 96 (William), 99 (W. Gabriele); *Ctl. Brecon*, p. 14; *Welsh Episcopal Acts*, I, nos. D546, D593).
Thomas Occ. 31 May 1300 (*Glam. Chts.*, III, p. 966, no. 838); n.d. (late 13th/early 14th cents.: pal.) (PRO, E210/8500).
John Pelagay Occ. Jan. 1337 x Jan. 1338 (PRO, C146/9339).
[**William de Pire** M. of S. Taurin, gtd keeping of priory during the French war 8 Mar. 1350 (*CFR 1347-56*, pp. 218-19).]
Richard de Fonte (de la Fountaigne) Occ. 16 Oct. 1371 (*CFR 1368-77*, p. 117); 18 Feb. 1379 (*CFR 1377-83*, p. 129); as m. of S. Taurin, gtd custody of priory 8 May 1381 (ibid., p. 248).
The next recorded pr., **Richard de Augo**, m. of S. Taurin, was adm. and the priory restored to him 22 Feb. 1401 (*CFR 1399-1401*, p. 442).

LLANGUA (Monmouth) (Llangwyfan) (Lire) f. -1183
Lists in *Mon. Angl.*, V, 735; *Heads*, I, 105. See F. Hockey, 'Llangua, alien priory of Lyre', *JHSCW*, vol. XXVII, no. 32 (1990), 8-13.
Hilary de Llangiwen (?Llangwyfan) Occ. 26 Aug. 1196 (*FF.*, PRS XVII, no. 220).
Peter Maunsell Occ. 29 May 1268 (*CChR 1257-1300*, p. 150).

LODERS (Dorset), St Mary Magdalen (Montebourg) f. *c.* 1107
Lists in *VCH Dorset*, II, 118; *Heads*, I, 105.
R. ? also pr. of Axmouth, q.v. Occ. prob. 1205+ (*Sarum Chts.*, p. 80).
Peter de Criencis (Crienciis, Criensis, Crient) Occ. from 14 Oct. 1246 to 2 Feb. 1263 (PRO, PRO31/8/140B, part 2, pp. 134-5).
Robert Osmondi Occ. 5 May 1297 (PRO, PRO31/8/140B, part 2, p. 157); 1305 (ibid., p. 197); 9 July 1308 (*Reg. Gandavo*, II, 703).
William de Carentonio (Karenton) *alias dictus* le Condu 1313-1321 M. of Montebourg, adm. 1 June 1313 (ibid., 807-8). Occ. 12 Dec. 1319 (*Reg. Martival*, I, 141). Gt of adm. revoked by abb. of Montebourg 1 Feb. 1321 and bp. asked to accept Roger *dictus* Hariel (ibid., I, 225).
Roger (Oger) *dictus* **Hariel** (Hariol, Haryel) 1321-1355 Exhibited letters of pres. dated 17 Dec. 1320, adm. 16 Feb. 1321; mand. to induct 17 Feb. 1321 (*Reg. Stapeldon*, p. 187); commn to adm. 2 Feb. 1321 (*Reg. Martival*, I, 225-6). Papal indult that he shall not be removed from the priory without reasonable cause 27 Apr. 1344 (*CPL*, III, 116). D. by 8 Nov. 1355 (*CFR 1347-56*, p. 437; cf. *CPR 1354-58*, p. 305).
[**John (de) Osanne** M. of Montebourg, pr. of Appledurcombe. Gt of keeping of priory on d. of Roger Hariel 8 Nov. 1355 (*CFR 1347-56*, pp. 436-7); ceased to have keeping by 1 Feb. 1356 (*CFR 1356-68*, pp. 1-2)].
Simon de Londa (de la Lounde, Clouda) 1355/6- M. of Montebourg, priest, letter of pres. from abb. of Montebourg, no reason given for vacancy, dated 17 Nov. 1355; adm. to rectory and manor of Axmouth 31 Dec. 1355 (*Reg. Grandisson*, III, 1437-8; cf. PRO, PRO31/8/140B, part 2, p. 194; prov. conf. 31 Jan. 1355 *or* 1356, prob. the latter (*Accts of Papal Collectors*, pp. 96, 146, 176). Gt of keeping of priory in place of John Osanne 1 Feb. 1356 (*CFR 1356-68*, pp. 1-2).

Robert Dore (Doree) **1361–1364** Adm. 15 Oct. 1361, no reason given for vacancy (Salisbury, Reg. Wyvill II, f. 285r); adm. to rectory and manor of Axmouth 5 Nov. 1361 (*Reg. Grandisson*, III, 1466). Res. by (?19) March 1364 (Salisbury, Reg. Wyvill II, f. 305r).

Samson Trygal (Trigal, Trygel) **1364–** M. of Montebourg, adm. (?19) March 1364 (ibid., cf. *Reg. Grandisson*, III, 1495). Conf. of inst. 10 Jan. 1372 (*Accts of Papal Collectors*, pp. 474, 491). Occ. 11 June 1369 as pr. of Appledurcombe and pr. of Loders (*CFR 1368–77*, pp. 15, 17); 1370 (PRO, E106/10/2); 26 July 1376 (*CFR 1368–77*, p. 360); 8 Oct. 1377 (*CFR 1377–83*, p. 151); n.d. (*c.* 1377–78) (Salisbury, Reg. Erghum, f. 131v); priory restored to him 13 Nov. 1399 (*CPR 1399–1401*, p. 60).

The next recorded pr., **William Burnell**, occ. 20 Jan. 1401 (*CPR 1399–1401*, p. 364); Jan. 1403 (*Privy Council*, I, 192).

MERSEA, *see* WEST MERSEA

MINSTER (Cornwall), St Marteriana (Talcarn) (S. Serge, Angers) f. -1190

Lists in Oliver, p. 63; Watkin, *Totnes Priory*, II, 1042–3; priors mentd in L. Guilloreau, *Prieurés Anglais de la dépendance de Saint-Serge d'Angers: Totnes, Tywardreath, Minster* (Ligugé 1909).

Geoffrey de Swavesey (Swanesey) **1263–** Adm. 26 Aug. 1263, pres. by Geoffrey, pr. of Tywardreath. (*Reg. Bronescombe*, p. 156; *Reg. W. Bronescombe*, II, no. 491).

Nicholas Occ. Mich. 1279 x Mich. 1280 (PRO, E159/53, m. 11d).

Robert Occ. Easter 1276 (PRO, CP40/14, m. 75).

[**Robert Sturmy** Occ. 12 Mar. 1289 (Guilloreau, pp. 47–8); cf. *Reg. Bronescombe*, pp. 152–3 for the confusion between this Minster and (Minster) Manaccan. Robert de Stormy was inst. to the latter church in 1265.]

Ralph Occ. Nov. 1296 x Nov. 1297 (PRO, E106/4/2, m. 1d); Easter 1300 (PRO, E106/4/14, m. 2).

Philip Occ. 2 Apr. 1311 (*Reg. Stapeldon*, p. 235). Lic. to Philip to make pilgrimage abroad s.d. – to return before Whitsun (ibid., p. 290).

Richard Portel 1314– M. of Minster, inst. 26 Feb. 1314, pres. by Philip, pr. of Tywardreath and Jocelin pr. of Totnes (ibid., p. 235; *Reg. Brantingham*, I, 568).

William (de) Bouges (Bages, Boges) **1323–1333** M. of S. Serge, coll. by lapse 20 July 1323 (*Reg. Stapeldon*, p.235, cf. *Reg. Brantingham*, I, 568). Occ. 17 Sept. 1331 when co-adjutor to Philip, pr. of Tywardreath (*Reg. Grandisson*, II, 631); 18 Sept. 1331 disp. for non-residence until Christmas (ibid., 633). Coll. by lapse as pr. of Tywardreath 17 Nov. 1333 (ibid., III, 1296)

House vacant 12 Sept. 1334 (ibid., II, 764).

Gehelius (Joel) le Fertrer (Ferorer) **1335–** Commendation during pleasure 10 Dec. 1334, no reason given for vacancy (ibid., III, 1304). M. of Tywardreath, coll. by lapse 7 Oct. 1335 (ibid., III, 1310). Occ. 3 Jan. 1340, 31 Jan. 1340 (ibid., I, 59; II, 924).

William de la Hune 1341–1349 M. OSB, priest, coll. by lapse 20 Sept. 1341, no reason given for vacancy (ibid., III, 1332; *Reg. Brantingham*, I, 569). D. 26 Apr. 1349 (Oliver, p. 63, no source; Guilloreau, p. 50).

William Decimarii (Dimier, Dyme, Willelmi) **1349–1375** Inst. 8 July 1349, no reason given for vacancy (*Reg. Grandisson*, III, 1394; *Reg. Brantingham*, I, 569). Occ. 6 Mar. 1375 (*Reg. Brantingham*, I, 195). D. by 12 Mar. 1375 (ibid., 36, 569).

Miletus Andreas (Andrew, Andree) **1375–** M. of S. Serge, coll. by lapse 12 Mar. 1375 (ibid.), but occ. 10 Oct. 1374, he does not know the English or the Cornish tongue and the king appts a secular chaplain to serve the parish church (*CPR 1374–77*, p. 7). Appt as custodian of priory 30 Jan. 1378 (*CPR 1377–81*, p. 102); 1380 x 1381 (PRO, E179/24/5, m. 4).

The next recorded pr., **John de Stratton**, was coll. by lapse 26 Jan. 1386, no reason given for vacancy (*Reg. Brantingham*, I, 94).

MINSTER LOVELL (Oxon), St Kenelm (Ivry) f. 1200 x 6. Diss. 1415
List in *VCH Oxford*, II, 163. See also A.J. Taylor, 'The Alien Priory of Minster Lovell', *Oxoniensia* 2 (1937), 103–17.

Robert 1225/6– Adm. Dec. 1225 x Dec. 1226, no reason given for the vacancy (*Reg. Wells*, II, 23).

Geoffrey 1246/7– Inst. June 1246 x June 1247, no reason given for vacancy (*Reg. Grosseteste*, p. 489).

Simon de Paris –1260 Res. Nov. 1259 x Nov. 1260 (*Reg. R. Gravesend*, p. 213).

Gracius 1260–1264 M. of Ivry, adm. Nov. 1259 x Nov. 1260 (ibid., pp. 213, 329). Res. by 12 Feb. 1264 (ibid., p. 217).

James 1264–1265 M. of Ivry, adm. 12 Feb. 1264 (ibid., pp. 217, 330). Res. by 30 June 1265 (ibid., p. 219).

Gacius [*sic, for* Gracius] 1265–1269 M. of Ivry, adm. 30 June 1265 (ibid., pp. 219, 331). Res. by 7 Nov. 1269 (ibid., p. 221).

John 1269–1291 M. of Ivry, adm. 7 Nov. 1269 (ibid., pp. 221, 332). D. by 22 Feb. 1291 (*Reg. Sutton*, VIII, 173).

Stephen de Habitu of Ivry 1291–1293 Letter of pres. 22 Feb. 1291, adm. 4 Apr. 1291 (ibid., 173). Letter of res. dated 4 Oct. 1293 (ibid., 183).

Ralph de Montfort of Ivry (de Ibrayo) 1293–1299 Adm. 7 Oct. 1293 (ibid.). Attack on him mentd 1294 (ibid., IV, 165, 172–3). Letter of res. dated 18 Sept. 1299 (ibid., VIII, 203).

John de Monte Calvet (Calveti) 1299–1305 M. of Ivry, letter of pres. 25 July 1299, adm. 10 Nov. 1299 (ibid.). D. by 18 Jan. 1305 (Lincoln, Ep. Reg., II, f. 148r–v).

Robert de Hodenco 1305–1307 M. of Ivry, 28 Feb. 1305 exhibited letter of pres. dated 18 Jan. 1305, adm. 1 Mar. 1305 (ibid., f. 148r–v). Letter of res. dated 29 June 1307 (ibid., f. 153r).

Geoffrey de Ruffeto (Rufeto) 1307–1309 M. of Ivry, letter of pres. dated 7 July 1307, adm. 31 Aug. 1307 (ibid., f. 153r). Letter of res. dated 4 Sept. 1309 (ibid., f. 156v).

Bertaud (Berthold) de Mondrevilla 1309– M. of Ivry, letters of pres. dated 7 July (*sic*) 1309, adm. 7 Dec. 1309 (ibid., f. 156v). Occ. 1324 (PRO, E106/5/2, m. 8d); 14 June 1332 (*CPR 1330–34*, p. 350).

William (de) Rouge (Ronge) 1341– M. of Ivry, coll. by lapse 10 May 1341, no reason given for vacancy (Lincoln, Ep. Reg., IV, f. 288r). Occ. 28 May 1341, 4 May 1344 (*CFR 1337–47*, pp. 226, 377; *CPR 1343–45*, pp. 258, 263).

Peter de Curry (Cury, Urry) 1352–1361 M. of Ivry, letters of pres. dated 5 Oct. 1351, no reason given for vacancy; adm. 22 Jan. 1352 (Lincoln, Ep. Reg., IX, f. 254r). Res. by 29 June 1361 (ibid., f. 276r). Cf. br. Peter (not described as prior) named as patron of Minster Lovell vicarage in institution of 17 Nov. 1361 (ibid., f. 278r), but of course the presentation could have taken place much earlier.

Matthew de Villa Nova 1361–1368 M. of Ivry, priest. pres. by Ivry, adm. 29 June 1361 (ibid., f. 276r). D. by 27 Nov. 1368 (Lincoln, Ep. Reg., X, f. 344v). Cf. royal appt as custodian of the priory 22 Oct. 1360 (*CPR 1358–61*, p. 474).

Vincent le Courour (le Tournour) 1368– M. of Ivry, adm. 27 Nov. 1368 (Lincoln, Ep. Reg., X, f. 344v). Occ. (Tournour) 12 Mar. 1363 (Norwich, Reg, 2/5, f. 59v); 6 Oct. 1369 (*CFR 1368–77*, p. 26). cf. Taylor, 'Alien Priory of Minster Lovell', p. 113.

Peter Corp Last recorded pr. Royal grant of keeping of priory during French War committed to him 12 May 1370 (*CFR 1368–77*, p. 87).

MINTING (Lincs), St Andrew (S. Benoît-sur-Loire, Fleury) f. c. 1129. Diss. 1414.
Lists in *VCH Lincs*, II, 239–40; *Heads*, I, 105.

Raymond Occ. c. 29 June 1213 (BL, Cotton ms. Vespasian E, XVIII, f. 164r–v).

John 1238/9–1248 M. of Fleury, adm. June 1238 x June 1239, no reason given for the vacancy
(*Reg. Grosseteste*, p. 27). D. by c. 29 Sept. 1248 (ibid., p. 111).

Stephen 1248–1251/2 Inst. c. 29 Sept. 1248 on d. of John (ibid.). Occ. Nov. 1251 (BL, Cotton
ms. Vespasian E XX, f. 106r). Res June 1251 [Nov. 1251] x June 1252 (ibid., p. 129).

Robert 1251/2–1281 M. of Fleury, inst. June 1251 x June 1252 on res. of Stephen (ibid.). Res.
by 25 Nov. 1281 (*Reg. Sutton*, I, 17).

Iterus (Iterius) *dictus* **de Turre 1281–1289** M. of Minting, eln conf. 25 Nov. 1281 (ibid.). Res.
by 31 Oct. 1289 (ibid., 135–6).

Theobald de Thoriaco 1291–1308 M. of Fleury. On 4 Dec. 1289 Bp Sutton received a letter
from the abb. of Fleury, dated 31 Oct. 1289, presenting Theobald in place of Iterus de Turre
who had res. (ibid., 134–5). Letters were also necessary from the earl of Lincoln and Theobald
was sent to get them. On 3 Jan. 1290 Theobald's proctor appeared with the earl's letter of
pres. dated 27 Dec. 1289. They were found to be irregular. Custody was given to Theobald
until 24 June 1290 (ibid., 134–6); custody extended to 16 Aug. 1290 (ibid., 136–7). On 23 Dec.
1290 noted as acting as *custos* without authority (ibid., 133). Letters of pres. dated 6 Aug. 1290,
adm. 29 Jan. 1291 (ibid., 147–9). D. by 18 Dec. 1308 (Lincoln, Ep. Reg., II, f. 28v).

Hugh *dictus* **Folon (Fullonis) de Lorriaco 1309–1310** M. of Fleury, letter of pres. 18 Dec.
1308; adm. 3 Jan. 1309 (ibid.). Res. letter dated 13 Sept. 1310, on account of his promotion
to be sub-pr. of Fleury (ibid., ff. 34v–35r).

John Cheuen (Cheveu, Chenen, Chauvell, Chauvelli) 1310–1320 M. of Fleury, adm. 3 Nov.
1310 (ibid.). Res. dated 7 Nov. 1320 (*Reg. Burghersh*, I, no. 70.

William de Jargolio 1320–1331 M. of Fleury, letter of pres. 7 Nov. 1320 on res. of John de
Chauvelli, adm. 4 Jan. 1321 (ibid.). Commn to visit the priory to grant William absolution
from excommunication imposed by the bp 20 Dec. 1322 (Lincoln, Ep. Reg., V, f. 327v). Res.
by 18 Jan. 1331 (*Reg. Burghersh*, I, no. 285).

William Lespicer (Aposticarii) 1331–1334 M. of Fleury, inst. 18 Jan. 1331 (ibid.). occ. 16 Jan.
1331 (*CCR 1330–33*, p. 180). Res. by 23 Feb. 1334 (*Reg. Burghersh*, I, no. 414).

John Chaperon (Caperon) 1334– Pres. by Abb. Peter, letter dated 23 Feb. 1334, adm. 4 Apr.
1334 (ibid.). Occ. 1342 (*CFR 1337–47*, p. 272); 11 July 1345 (*CCR 1343–46*, p. 63).

Peter de Soliaco (Suliaco) 1353–1357 As M. of Minting granted keeping of the priory 12 Oct.
1349 (*CFR 1347–56*, p. 1670). M. of Fleury, adm. on d. of lst pr. 28 Jan. 1353 (Lincoln, Ep.
Reg., IX, f. 104r–v). Letter of pres. dated 9 Nov. 1349 (*sic*) (ibid.). Letter of res. dated 31
Aug. 1357 (ibid., ff. 131r–134r).

Simon de Naudaria 1358– M. of Fleury, letter of pres. dated 3 Nov. 1357, adm. by bp. 5 Sept.
1358 (ibid.). Occ. 1357 (*CFR 1356–68*, p. 49); Mich. 1358 x Mich. 1369 (PRO, E372/204,
rots. 12, 13d); 1361 (Lincoln, Ep. Reg., IX, f. 148v); security for good behaviour 1369 (PRO,
C47/18/3/33, under rearrangement but no new number yet allocated); 24 Oct. 1377 (*CFR
1377–83*, p. 26); permission to remain in England Feb. 1378 (Matthew, *Norman Monasteries*,
p. 160).

MODBURY (Devon), St George (S. Pierre-sur-Dives) f. c. 1140
Lists in Oliver, p. 298; J. M. James, 'The Norman Benedictine alien priory of St George,
Modbury, AD c. 1135–1450', *TDA*, 131 (1999), 81–103, at 103; *Heads*, I, 105.

Ralph Pres. to patron by abb. of S. Pierre, no reason given for vacancy, n.d. (1213 x 1225) (ECR,
Modbury ctl., p. 44). Occ. 1207 x 1227 (ECR, 32/30).

Gervase and **Durand** Occ. in ECR, 32/1 and 17, without dates, but the latter was perhaps late
12th cent.

Geoffrey –1240 predecessor of Richard – had been removed from office [i.e. 1240] (*EEA*, 12, no. 288).

Richard 1240– Inst. by bp of Exeter 19 Aug. 1240 (ibid.)

William de Curcy (Cocy, Curceyo, Curly) Occ. 1259 (ECR, Modbury ctl., pp. 26–7); 30 Sept. 1260 (BL, Add. Cht. 72399); 1269 (ECR, 1/13); n.d. (ECR, 1/12, 16).

William de Sagio Occ. 7 Feb. 1274 (ECR, 1/18).

Vincent de Fulchis 1275– Adm. 21 July 1275 (*Reg. Bronescombe*, p. 207; *Reg. Bronescombe*, II, no. 1095); 1285 (ECR, I/18, 19); 4 Jan. 1286 (ECR, I/22). Priory mentd as void 12 Feb. 1289 (*CCR 1288–96*, p. 5).

Stephen Occ. 7 June 1290 (ECR, I/24). Priory mentd as void 4 May 1292 (*CCR 1288–96*, p. 230).

Robert Occ. 10 May 1294 (ECR, Modbury ctl., p. 29); Nov. 1295 x Nov. 1296 (PRO, E106/3/19, m. 9); Nov. 1296 x Nov. 1297 (PRO, E106/4/2. m. 2); 29 Sept. 1297 (ECR, Modbury ctl., pp. 8–9); Nov. 1297 x Nov. 1298 (PRO, E106/4/8, m. 1d; E106/4/9, m. 1d).

Robert Truwerd Prob. the same as above, occ. 16 Sept. 1302 (ECR, 1/25), Occ. (Robert) Nov. 1302 x Nov. 1303 (PRO, E106/4/18, m. 4d).

William de Nova Mansione (de Nova Domo) **1305–1321** Inst. by bp of Exeter 19 Aug. 1305, no reason given for vacancy (ECR, 1/26). D. 27 May 1321 (*Reg. Stapeldon*, p. 235).

Nicholas la Barbe *alias* **de Seint Piere** (Seynt Piere) **1321–1345** M. of S. Pierre, inst. 21 Sept. 1321 (ibid.). Occ. 11 July 1345 (*CCR 1343–46*, p. 636). Res. by 12 Feb. 1346 (*CFR 1337–47*, p. 453).

John de Fovea 1346– M. of S. Pierre, priest, nomination to be pres. to priory 26 Mar. 1345 (*CPR 1343–45*, p. 471). Gt of keeping of priory to John who has been adm. pr. on res. of Nicholas de Seint Piere 12 Feb. 1346 (*CFR 1337–47*, p. 453). Inst. 14 June 1346 (*Reg. Grandisson*, III, 1347).

John Walteri (Galteri) **1349–1351** M. of S. Pierre, inst. 9 June 1349 (ibid., 1390). D. by 3 Apr. 1351 (ibid., 1416).

Robert de Cury (Cureio, Curie, Cureyo) **1351–1361** M. of S. Pierre, inst. 3 Apr. 1351 (ibid.). Inquisition held on 28 July 1363 found that pr. Robert had d. on Tuesday the feast of St Andrew, no year [would be 30 Nov. 1361] (ECR, 1/38). Certainly he was d. by 5 Apr. 1362 (*Reg. Grandisson*, III, 1480–1).

Philip Furnarii (Fornerii) **1362–1369** M. of S. Pierre, nomination by abb. of S. Pierre to Thomas de Campo Arnulphi, lord of Modbury 3 Mar. 1362; pres. to bp by Thomas 4 Apr.; adm. 5 Apr. 1362 on d. of Robert de Cureyo (ibid.). D. by 6 Oct. 1369 (*CPR 1367–70*, p. 310).

Gilbert de Billeyo (Beliow, Bellayo, Belywo) **1369–1375** M. of S. Pierre, nomination to Thomas de Campo Arnulphi for him to pres. to bp 6 Oct. 1369 (ibid.). Gt of keeping of priory 6 Oct. 1369 (*CFR 1368–77*, p. 23). D. by 20 Apr. 1375 (*CPR 1374–77*, p. 93; cf. *Reg. Brantingham*, I, 37).

John Michel 1375–1399 Nomination to Thomas de Campo Arnulphi for him to pres. to bp 20 Apr. 1375 (*CPR 1374–77*, p. 93). M. of S. Pierre, inst. 5 May 1375 (*Reg. Brantingham*, I, 37). Gt of keeping of priory 1 May 1375 (*CFR 1368–77*, p. 284). Res. by 7 Feb. 1399 (*CPR 1396–99*, p. 480; cf. *Reg. Stafford*, p. 188; ECR, 1/44).

MONK SHERBOURNE (Hants), St Mary and St Fromund (Cerisy-la-Forêt) f. *c.* 1120 x 1130

Lists in *VCH Hants*, II, 228–9; *Heads*, I, 106.

William Occ. early 13th cent. (*HMC 4th Rept.*, pp. 453–4); n.d. (1204 x 1226) (WCM, no. 2804, cf. ibid., nos. 2879, 2889); 1225 (*CRR*, XII, no. 1428); 10 Oct. 1235 (*Ctl. Sandford*, II, no. 333); June 1238 x June 1239 (*Reg. Grosseteste*, p. 34); 6 Oct. 1240 (*CRR*, XVI, no. 1198); 29 Nov. 1242 (BL, Add. Cht. 20372 – pr. not named in cht. but seal bears name William, cf. *BM Seals*, no. 4015, wrongly placed under Sherborne abbey); 16 Dec. 1249 (*CPR 1247–58*,

p. 56). Prob. to be identified with **William of St Fromund**, pr., occ. n.d. (1st half of 13th cent.) (Oxford, Queen's Coll. mun. catalogue, I, no. 74).

Roger Occ. *?temp.* Henry III (WCM, no. 2878). His precise place in the sequence of priors is uncertain, unless he is to be identified with the late 12th/early 13th cent. pr. of that name (*Heads*, I, 106).

Michael Occ. 7 Apr. 1254 (*Selborne Chts.*, II, 18, with seal); 30 Apr. 1256 (PRO, Hants F., CP25/1/204/9, no. 56); Oct. 1257 x Oct. 1258 (Oxford, Queen's Coll. mun. catalogue, I, no. 191).

James Occ. n.d. (13th cent.) (Oxford, Queen's Coll. muns. catalogue, I, no. 22). Is he to be identified with pr. J. who occ. 30 June 1262 (ibid., no. 78)?

Michael Occ. Oct. 1270 x Oct. 1271 (Oxford, Queen's Coll. mun. catalogue, I, no. 275); Feb. 1272 (ibid., no. 42).

Richard de Bourdigny Occ. n.d. (1272 x 1274) (Oxford, Queen's Coll. mun. catalogue, I, nos. 103, 194; cf. F. A.G. Davidson in *Hants Field Club*, m. 7 (1914–16), p. 103).

Nicholas Occ. 25 July 1277 (Oxford, Queen's Coll. mun. catalogue, I, no. 64); n.d. (1274 x 1283) (Oxford, Queen's Coll. mun. catalogue, I, nos. 199, 201).

Reginald de Caen (Cadomo) **1293–1308** M. of Cerisy, prov. by bp 2 Oct. 1293, no reason given for vacancy (*Reg. Pontissara*, I, 57). Res. acc. 16 June 1308 (*Reg. Woodlock*, I, 278).

Thomas Galouber (de la Bere, le Galoberr, Galobirii, de Galobre, Galobre) **1308–1345** Eln conf. and mand. to induct 5 Nov. 1308 (ibid., 313, cf. 325). D. 9 May 1345 (*Reg. Edington*, I, no. 229).[7]

Robert Corbel (Corbett) **1345/7–1349** Public instrument concerning the eln. of Robert, cantor of Cerisy on d. of Thomas 9 Aug. 1345 and when lic. is obtained from Sir William Trussell, the patron by reason of wardship (Oxford, Queen's Coll. mun. catalogue, I, no. 136). Royal protection for, 20 May 1346, who being chosen to be pr. of Monk Sherborne, is coming to England (*CPR 1345–48*, p. 119). M. of Cerisy el. on 23 June 1347 – a delay in presenting him for conf.; citation for opposers 6 Dec. 1347; eln conf. 22 Dec. 1347 (*Reg. Edington*, I, no. 229). D. by 22 Oct. 1349 (ibid., no. 695).

Denis de Vanceye (Vauceye, Vauxeio, Wange) **1349–1361/2** M. of Cerisy, eln, conf. by commissary 22 Oct. 1349 (ibid.). D. by 28 Feb. 1362 (ibid., no. 1485), but cf. ibid., no. 1374 instn to parochial benefice on Crown's pres. by reason of the vacancy of the priory 22 Oct. 1361.

William Benart (Benard, Bernandi) **1362–1375** Claustral pr. Cerisy, adm. 28 Feb. 1362 (ibid., nos. 1485–6). Lic. to choose a confessor 20 Mar. 1369 (*Reg. Wykeham*, II, 79). D. by 24 Aug. 1375 (ibid., I, 63).

Inguerand (Ingelram, Ingerald) **de Dinno** (Dumo) *alias* **de Roppia 1375–1397** M. of Cerisy, letters of pres. exhibited 24 Aug. 1375, proclamation of eln 24 Aug. 1375, and common to cite opposers 1 Sept. 1375 (ibid., II, 239); eln quashed by commissary, but apptd 26 Sept. 1375 (ibid., I, 63–6). Gtd custody of the priory by king 28 Apr. 1380 (*CPR 1377–81*, p. 489). Thought to be dying n.d. [1396/7] (*Reg. Wykeham*, II, 469). D. by 2 Feb. 1397 (ibid., I, 205). (Roppia) (Oxford, Queen's Coll. mun. catalogue, I, no. 146).

MONKS KIRBY (Warws), St Mary, St Nicholas, and St Denis (S. Nicholas, Angers) f. 1077
Lists in *VCH Warws*, II, 131; *Heads*, I, 106.

Ralph Last recorded occ. 30 Sept. x 6 Oct. 1200 (*Bucks F.*, I, 19).

Nicholas –**1221** Vacated pr. in 1221 (R. A. B. Mynors, *Catalogue of the Manuscripts of Balliol College*, p. 263).

---

[7] The mention of Ellis de Galumberd in 1340 (*Cal. Misc. Inq.*, II, 425) is most prob. a scribal error for pr. Thomas (de Galumberd).

John of Angers 1221–1237 Succ. 1221, res. 1237 (ibid.). Occ. Oct. 1220 x Oct. 1221 (PRO, E210/7744); 1 July 1221 (PRO, Leics F., CP25/1/121/9, no. 63); 30 Sept. 1221 (PRO, Leics F., CP25/1/121/9, no. 62); 1226 (*Ctl. Tutbury*, nos. 266–7); Feb.–Mar. 1230 apptd pr. of Spalding but not accepted (*Reg. Wells*, III, 182–6): Mich. 1230, Trin. 1231 (*CRR*, XIV, nos. 589, 1633).

M. 1237– Occ. 1237 (PRO, E326/8787). Prob. to be identified with **Mathew**, occ. n.d. (13th cent.) (Oxford, BNC, Burrow deed 1) and also n.d. (*Ctl. Burton Lazars*, p. 43).

Defensor Occ. 20 Jan. 1247 (PRO, Leics F., CP25/1/122/19, no. 315); Oct. 1250 x Oct. 1251 (PRO, E210/3542); 1256 (Madox, *Form.*, p. 85, no. 158): 8 July 1255, 22 May 1272, 3 Nov. 1278 (*Warms F.*, I, nos. 747, 905, 941); 28 Jan. 1285 (*Warms F.*, II, p. 3 no. 994); 1285 (PRO, Just. 1/956, m. 33, 33d). In 1347 mention is made of **Defensor de Neubold**, former pr. (*Cal. Misc. Inq.*, II, 509).

Geoffrey Occ. 12 Oct. 1289 (*CPR 1281–92*, p. 324).

John –1315 Occ. 17 Feb. 1296, royal protection, alien (*CPR 1292–1301*, p. 177); from Nov. 1295 x Nov. 1296 (PRO, E106/3/19, m. 8) to Nov. 1302 x Nov. 1303 (PRO, E106/4/18, m. 10d); 1304 (*CPR 1301–07*, p. 237); 21 Aug. 1310 (*CPR 1307–13*, p. 242). D. by 18 Jan. 1315 (Lichfield, B/A/1/1, f. 39r).

Peter Franciscus (Fraunceys) **1314–1326** Name (*YB 19 Edward III*, p. 205). M. of Angers, letter of pres. 18 Jan. 1315; adm. 6 Feb.; mand. to induct 7 Feb. 1315 (Lichfield, B/A/1/1, f. 39r; PRO, LR14/350). Occ. July 1317 x July 1318 (PRO, E210/9000); 1320 (*CPR 1321–24*, p. 412). Dep. by 8 June 1326 (Lichfield, B/A/1/2, f. 20r), but occ. 8 Oct. 1326 (*Memo. Roll 1326–7*, p. 272).

William Eisneille (Esnelli, le Esneile) **1326–1335** M. of Angers, adm. 8 June 1326 (Lichfield, B/A/1/2, f. 20r). Pres. 1325 (PRO, E210/1349). D. 13 Apr. 1335 (Lichfield, B/A/1/2, f. 28v).

William of St Clement (de Sancto Clemente) **1335–1349/50** Previously at Wing (q.v.). M. of Angers, adm. 22 June 1335 (Lichfield, B/A/1/2, f. 28v; PRO, LR14/350). Occ. 1342 (*CFR 1337–47*, p. 267); 1345 (*CCR 1343–46*, p. 636); 1346 (PRO, E326/8824); 20 Oct. 1348 (*CPR 1348–50*, p. 194); 30 Nov. 1348 (PRO, E326/4367); Jan. 1349 x Jan. 1350 (PRO, E210/6499). Mentd 12 Oct. 1349 As late pr., deceased (*CFR 1347–56*, p. 167). D. by 16 Oct. 1350 (Lichfield, B/A/1/2, ff. 53v–54r).

Maurice Aubery (Auberi, Aubiry) **1350–1353** M. of Angers, letter of pres. 16 Oct. 1350, adm. 13 Nov. 1350 (ibid.; PRO, LR14/350). Occ. 1 Mar. 1353 (*CPR 1350–54*, p. 530; BL, Add. Cht. 21388). D. by 20 Aug. 1353 (*CFR 1347–56*, p. 380).

Oliver de Desertis (Sertis) **1353–1359** M. of Angers, letter of pres. 13 Sept. 1353; adm. 1 Dec. 1353 (Lichfield, B/A/1/2, f. 57v; PRO, LR14/350). 29 July 1356 John de Fess, m. of Monks Kirby, apptd to custody of priory by reason of the dilapidations of pr. Oliver (Lichfield, B/A/1/3, f. 137v). res. by 16 Feb. 1359 (*CPP*, p. 311). Provided by Pope to be pr. of Vieux Belesme (ibid.).

William Camon 1359– M. of Kenilworth, inst. 4 Jan. 1359 (*Reg. Stretton*, I, 5; PRO, LR14/350).

William de Grauleriis (Crauleriis, Gralerio, Granlerio, Granleriis, Gravelereio, Grablerio) **1359–** Petition presented on behalf of William de Grauleriis, m. of S. Theodore in Vienne, for the priory of Monks Kirby, void by the papal provision of Oliver de Desertis to Vieux Belesme, about which William was litigating in the palace, notwithstanding that he holds the priory of Gilion in dioc. Vienne, which he is ready to res. Papal prov. 16 Feb. 1359 (*CPP*, p. 338; cf. *Accts of Papal Collectors*, pp. 152–3, 200, 236, 262, 274, 370, 507). M. of Angers, gt of keeping of priory during French war 20 Aug. 1360 (*CPR 1356–68*, p. 136). Occ. 1364 (Oxford, BNC, Burrow deed 50); 1365 (*CCR 1364–68*, p. 172; *CPR 1364–67*, p. 112); 1370

(*CPR 1377–81*, p. 376); 14 July 1375 (*CFR 1368–77*, p. 291); 1376 (PRO, E326/9816). Mentd 12 July 1382 as former pr. (*CPR 1381–85*, p. 195). Seal (*Mon. Seals*, p. 61).

MONMOUTH St Mary and St Florent (S. Florent, Sauumur) f. -1086
  List in *Heads*, I, 106; K.E. Kissack, *Medieval Monmouth* (Monmouth, 1974), p. 75.
Gilbert Occ. 1 Aug. 1221 (PRO, Hereford F., CP25/1/80/4, no. 29).
Walter de Coleville Transferred to Sele, as pr. before 1232 (*Ctl. Sele*, no. 39, and see intro., pp. xiv–xv).
Florence Occ. 1230 x 1240, *temp.* Bp Elias of Llandaff (*Mon. Angl.*, IV, 595–8; *Welsh Episcopal Acts*, II, 718); n.d. (PRO, E210/3415, E210/5784; E315/21/5). Seal (*Mon. Seals*, p. 62; *Arch. Camb.* 137 (1988), p. 129, no. 287).
John Occ. 15 July 1245 (PRO, Hereford F., CP25/1/80/10, no. 200).
Geoffrey Moreteau –1270 Occ. 9 June 1264 (P. Marchegay, 'Les prieurés anglais de Saint-Florent près Saumur: notice et documents inédits', p. 190, no. 29). El. abb. of S. Florent 1270 (P. Marchegay, *Les prieurés anglais de S. Florent*, p. 41 n. 2; Cowley, pp. 229, 234).
Matthew Occ. 16 Oct. 1270 (PRO, E210/328). Mentd 1311 as former pr. (*YB IX*, 93).
Peter de Bosco Occ. Nov. 1295 x Nov. 1296 (PRO, E106/3/9, m. 11); Nov. 1296 x Nov. 1297 (PRO, E106/4/2, m. 6); Nov. 1297 x Nov. 1298 (PRO, E106/4/8, m. 4d); Nov. 1298 x Nov. 1299 PRO, E106/4/9, m. 9); Easter 1300 (PRO, E106/4/14, m. 12); 1302 x 1306 (*Ctl. Cirencester*, III, no. 342); Nov. 1302 x Nov. 1303 (PRO, E106/4/18, m. 14).
David de Coleville (Colevyle) **1300**– M. of S. Florent, appt. conf. 29 Sept. 1300, no reason given for vacancy (*Reg. Swinfield*, p. 376). Occ. 1303, July 1313 x July 1314 (PRO, E210/6999; /9052; /9062).
Helias 1315– M. of S. Florent, letter of pres. dated 1 Mar. 1315, no reaason given for vacancy (*Reg. Swinfield*, p. 500); adm. 16 July 1315 (ibid., pp. 500–1); letter to monks to obey 28 July 1315 (ibid., p. 501).
Ralph de Combornio 1320– Adm. 18 Nov. 1320 (*Reg. Orleton (Hereford)*, p. 168). Occ. July 1325 x July 1326 (PRO, E106/5/4, m. [7]); 1 Nov. 1330 (*Reg. T. Charlton*, p. 4); 26 June 1344 (Hereford Cath. mun. 2614); 20 Oct. 1346 (*Reg. Trillek*, p. 288o; 16 June 1347 (PRO, E210/7798).
William Pepyn (Pipun) **1349**– M. of S. Florent, inst. 13 Sept. 1349, no reason given for vacancy (*Reg. Trillek*, p. 44). Occ. 1351 (PRO, C269/15/32); 1357 (Hereford Cath. mun. 2620); Jan. 1359 x Jan. 1360 (PRO, E210/1662).
John Blewyn (Blew, Blewen, Blowyn) Occ. 27 June 1362 (BL, Add. ms. 15668, f. 103v); Jan. 1375 x Jan. 1376 (PRO, E210/6537; /8191); 8 Oct. 1377, 12 Feb. 1378 (*CFR 1377–83*, pp. 19, 72–3).
The next recorded pr., **Thomas Tymy** (Tynny), adm. 11 July 1379, no reason given for vacancy (*Reg. J. Gilbert*, p. 7). Gt of keeping of priory 10 Dec. 1379 (*CFR 1377–83*, p. 174).

NEWENT (Glos.), St Mary (Cormeilles) f. -1086. Diss. 1399
  List in *VCH Glos*, II, 106.
Andrew Occ. as pr. late 12th cent. (*temp.* Harduin, abb. of Cormeilles) (BL, Add. ms. 15668, f. 17r; BL, Add. ms. 18461, f. 55v).
John de Calvicuria (Calvericia, Cauinco(u)rt) Occ. as proctor of abbey 19 Feb. 1238 (BL, Add. ms. 15668, f. 53v); as bailiff n.d. (BL, Add. ms. 18461, f. 119r).
Simon Moyaz (Moaz, Mohauz, Moiaz, Moraus) Occ. as bailiff with Reginald de Acle (BL, Add. ms. 15668, f. 57r; BL, Add. ms. 18461, f. 58v). [Reginald known 1258 (BL, Add. ms. 15668, f. 69r) and see below]; 10 Apr. 1241 (BL, Add. ms. 18461, f. 130v); Aug. 1253 (BL, Add. ms. 15668, f. 61r); 15, 18 Aug. 1253 (ibid., f. 63r).

John (de) Moyaz (Moaz, Moiauz, Moiaz, Moraus, Moyas) Possibly before Simon, occ. several times with Reginald de Acle (ibid., ff. 58v, 59r, 63r, 68r). With Sir William de Ebroicis, knight (ibid., f. 33v).

John ?Moyaz or Havage, occ. as bailiff 12 Mar. 1259 (BL, Add. ms. 18461, f. 32r); pr. early to mid 13th century (BL, Add. ms. 15668, f. 52r, cf. f. 117r).

John Havage Occ. *temp.* Abb. Simon of Cormeilles *c.* 1260 (ibid., f. 70v); with Reginald de Acle when sheriff of Glos., i.e. 1265–67, 1273 (ibid., f. 34v; *List of Sheriffs*, p. 49). Mentd as deceased pr. in cht. of 1275 (BL, Add. ms. 15668, f. 48v, cf. ff. 13v, 30r).

Simon de Goupilleriis (Genpilliariis, Gopileres, Gopil(l)er(s), Gorpilers, Goupill, Goupill(i)eres) Occ. many times in both ctls. between 25 Nov. 1275 (ibid., f. 10r) and Nov. 1302 x Nov. 1303 (ibid., f. 18v); 30 July 1290 (*Reg. Swinfield*, p. 239); from Nov. 1295 x Nov. 1296 to Nov. 1298 x Nov. 1299 (PRO, E106/3/19, m. 8; E106/4/9. m. 5d; E106/4/10, m. 7); 10 June 1296 (PRO, E326/1570); 19 Apr. 1297 (*CPR 1292-1301*, p. 270); 12 Mar. 1298 (*Reg. Swinfield*, p. 358); Nov. 1302 x Nov. 1303 (PRO, E106/4/18, m. 13).

William de Hakeville (Hakevill, Hakevilla, Hakkeville) Occ. 8 June 1301 (BL, Add. ms. 15668, f. 85r); 27 Apr. 1303 (BL, Add. ms. 18461, f. 30v); 20 Mar. 1304 (ibid., f. 30v); 8 Feb. 1311 (PRO, C241/76/64); 13 June 1311 (ibid., f. 95v); 14 June 1311 (BL, Add. ms. 15668, f. 78r).

Thomas de Bosco Occ. *c.* Mich. 1324 (PRO, E106/5/2, m. 6); 26 Nov. 1324 (BL, Add. ms. 15668, f. 83v); July 1324 x July 1325 (ibid., f. 82r); 8 Oct. 1326 (*Memo. Roll 1326-7*, p. 272).

Baldwin Occ. 4, 14 Apr. 1331 (ibid., f. 86v); 17 Jan. 1332 (ibid., f. 87v); 7 Dec. 1333 (ibid., f. 88r); 24 Oct. 1335 (ibid., f. 89v); 8 Nov. 1335 (ibid., f. 88r).

Robert Crohadas (Brohadas) Occ. 24 June 1336, 2 Feb. 1337 (ibid., f. 93r, in both these cases not actually styled pr.); 24 Apr., 6 May 1339 (*CFR 1337-47*, p. 128).

Richard de Corneville (Cornevilla) Occ. Sept. 1337–Sept. 1338 (BL, Add. ms. 15668, f. 94v); 24 July 1341, 12 Sept. 1342 (*CFR 1337-47*, pp. 235, 298); gtd keeping of priory during French war 5 Feb. 1342 (ibid., p. 265); 20 Oct. 1346 (*Reg. Trillek*, p. 289); 20 Sept. 1348 (BL, Add. ms. 15668, f. 102v).

Jakes de Beauver Occ. 10 Sept. 1350, 19 Dec. 1350 (ibid., f. 103r); in return of aliens in response to a writ of 1 Sept. 1351 (PRO, C269/15/32).

Peter de Duro Sensu Occ. 18 Oct. 1346 (BL, Add. ms. 15668, f. 102v); 18 Apr., 12 June, 29 Oct. 1349 (ibid., f. 102v); 20 July 1350 (ibid., f. 103r); 20 June 1358 (ibid., f. 101r). Gt of keeping of priory during French war 20 June 1358 (*CFR 1356-68*, p. 72). Occ. Mich. 1358 x Mich. 1359 (PRO, E372/204, rot. 8); Jan. 1360 x Jan. 1361 (BL, Add. ms. 15668, f. 96r).

John Fabri (Faber, Fabry, Le Fever, Lefevre) Occ. 1 Sept. 1361 (ibid., f. 98r); 5 Nov. 1361 (Worcester, Reg. Brian, I, p. 82); 27 June 1362 (BL, Add. ms. 15668, f. 103v).

Peter du Duro Sensu Occ. Jan. 1363 x Jan. 1364 (ibid., f. 96r) to Jan. 1368 x Jan. 1369 (ibid., f. 96v).

John Fabri Apptd as pr. by Robert, abb. of Cormeilles, to rule the priory with the church of Beckford and to rule the priory of Striguil (Chepstow) in Wales during its voidance 1368 (PRO, E42/409). Occ. 1368 (*Reg. L. Charlton*, p. 72); going overseas 9 June 1368 (*CPR 1367-70*, p. 1440); occ. 11 June 1369, 6 Oct. 1369 (*CFR 1368-77*, pp. 13, 24); appt by abb. of Cormeilles as his attorney for 1 year 3 Nov. 1370 (*CPR 1370-74*, p. 10).

Peter de Duro Sensu Occ. Jan. 1370 x Jan. 1371 (BL, Add. ms. 15668, f. 96r); Jan 1371 x Jan. 1372 (ibid., f. 104r).

John Fabri Occ. 1374 (*Worcs Reg. Sede Vacante*, p. 308); June 1377 x June 1378 (BL, Add. ms. 15668, f. 97r); 8 Feb. 1378, 1 July 1379 (*CFR 1377-83*, pp. 68, 160).

OGBOURNE ST GEORGE (Wilts), St George (Bec) f. -1147

Lists in *VCH Wilts*, III, 396; *Heads*, I, 107.

Ogbourne became the administrative centre of the English lands of the abbey of Bec and the 'pivot of administration' was the pr. of Ogbourne, sometimes referred to as the proctor or proctor-general in England of the abbey of Bec, rather than the title of pr. (M. Morgan, *English Lands of Bec*, pp. 38–40). The use of both titles makes for some confusion.

Ranulf Occ. 1206 (*PR 8 John*, p. 40).

William Occ. 23 Mar. 1219 (PRO, Berks F., CP25/1/7/6, no. 10). Possibly the same as William of Wantage who is desc. as proctor of the monks of Bec in 1218 (M. Morgan, *English Lands of Bec*, p. 43).

Ralph Occ. 1227 (*Bucks Eyre*, nos. 102, 353); Hil. term 1228 (*CRR*, XIII, no. 424).

William de Guineville (Genvyll, Ginevill', Gynevill') Occ. Mich. term 1228 (*CRR*, XIII, no. 779). Occ. (G.) Trin. term 1237 (*CRR*, XVI, no. 149E); desc. not as pr. but as proctor-general of Bec in England 16 Feb. 1242 (*CPR 1232–47*, p. 272); and 1245 x 1246 (PRO, DL36/1/152) and 8 Sept. 1246 (*HMC Var. Coll.*, VII, 30); as pr. 16 May 1248 (*CChR 1226–57*, p. 331). D. by 25 Nov. 1258 (*CR 1256–59*, p. 345). See M. Morgan, *English Lands of Bec*, pp. 43–5.

[**John de Plessac** (Plessetis) M. of Bec, apptd by abb. of Bec as his bailiff and proctor for the keeping of the abbey's goods and lands in England 9 Dec. 1254 (Ogbourne not mentd) (*CPR 1247–58*, p. 390); occ. as proctor recently apptd on d. of William de Guineville 25 Nov. 1258 (*CR 1256–59*, p. 345).]

Richard de Flammaville (Flammavill, Flamma Villa, Flamavil, Flaumville, Frenanvill) Occ. as pr. Easter 1260 (BL, Cotton ms. Faustina A IV, f. 139v); as proctor-general in England 9 Jan. 1261, 17 Nov. 1265 (*CPR 1258–66*, pp. 135, 507); 12 Feb. 1270 (*CPR 1266–72*, p. 408); 6 Jan. 1275 (*CPR 1272–81*, p. 75). Occ. as pr. 12 Dec. 1263 (*CR 1261–64*, p. 325); 9 Nov. 1268 (*Reg. R. Gravesend*, p. 221); 30 July 1273 (*CCR 1272–79*, p. 57); 8 July 1276 (Cambridge, King's Coll. OGB.179); 1288 x 1289 (*Bec Documents*, pp. 127, 140–1).

[**Robert de Leone** (Merial) Occ. as attorney-general of abb. of Bec in England 20 May 1282 (*CFR 1272–1307*, p. 163); as proctor-general in England 25 Apr. (*CPR 1281–92*, p. 158); 1285 (PRO, Just.1/956, m. 9d); 1286 (*Bucks F.*, II, 60); 11 Apr. 1288 (*Reg. Pecham*, I, 73); 28 Sept. 1289 (*CPR 1281–92*, p. 323.]

[**William de Sancto Paterno** Occ. as proctor-general in England 25 Jan. 1286 (ibid., p. 219).]

Theobald de Cambremer (Cambermer, Cambrem', Caunbermer, Combremer) Occ. Nov. 1295 x Nov. 1296 (PRO, E106/3/19, mm. 6, 12d); Nov. 1297 x Nov. 1298 (PRO, E106/4/8, mm. 3, 5); Trin. 1298 (PRO, KB27/155, m. 45d); Nov. 1298 x Nov. 1299 (PRO, E106/4/9, m. 11d; E106/4/10, m. 4d); 1299 (*CPR 1292–1301*, pp. 462, 466, 474); 1300 (PRO, E106/4/14, m. 6d); 1 Aug. 1303, 26 Aug. 1304, 26 Apr. 1305, 25 Jan. 1306, 20 Feb. 1306 (*CPR 1301–07*, pp. 193, 285, 356, 472, 473).

[**Raymond de Got** Cardinal of Sta Maria Nova. In Feb. 1312 the pope absolved from excommunication the abb. and convent of Bec for having oposed the late Cardinal Raymond's provision to the priory 'four years ago' (*CPL*, II, 94).]

William de Ponte Episcopi (Pont L'Evêque) Occ. as proctor(-general) in England of abbey 1306–7 (*Bec Documents*, p. 151); 10 June 1307 (*CPR 1301–07*, p. 529); 16 Apr. 1308 (Lincoln, Ep. Reg., II, f. 154r); (pr.) Trin. 1309 (PRO, CP40/178, m. 36); 21 June 1317 (Lincoln, Ep. Reg., II, f. 168v); adm. as proctor for 4 yrs 8 Jan. 1318 (*CPR 1317–21*, p. 70); 28 Mar. 1319, 10 Apr. 1319 (*CCR 1318–23*, pp. 132–3); 8 Jan. 1322 (*CPR 1321–24*, p. 52). Occ. as pr. 25 Nov. 1310 (Lincoln, Ep. Reg., II, f. 159v); 15 Jan 1319 (*CPR 1317–21*, p. 268); 8 May 1319 (Lincoln, Ep. Reg., II, f. 172v); 9 May 1322 (*Reg. Asserio*, p. 485).

Richard de Beausevall (Beusevall) Occ. as pr. 29 Sept. 1323 (*HMC Var. Coll.*, VII, 31,); 26 July 1324 (Lambeth, Reg. Reynolds, f. 252v); July 1325 x July 1326 (PRO, E106/5/4, m. [5d]); 1327, 1335 (*CFR 1326–37*, pp. 64, 72, 443); 24 May 1340, 31 Jan. 1342, 27 Sept. 1343

(Salisbury, Reg. Wyvil II, ff. 77r, 125r–v); 1 Feb. 1341 (Norwich, Reg./1/3, f. 43r); 11 Mar. 1345 (Winchester, Reg. Orleton, II, f. 106r): mentd as ill 27 Aug. 1345 (*CFR 1337–47*, p. 437); 21 Sept. 1347, 15 Dec. 1347 (Lincoln, Ep. Reg., IX, f. 174r); 8 July 1346, 10 Feb. 1349, 24 Mar. 1349, 24 Apr. 1349, 3 July 1349 (*Reg. Edlington*, I, nos. 112, 352, 403, 476, 615). Also occ. as proctor-general in England 1322 and later (*CPR 1321–24*, p. 197; *CPR 1324–27*, p. 157).

Peter de Falk (Fulconis) *alias* **of St Stephen** (de Sancto Stephano, Peris de Seynt Stevene) **1349–1364** Gt of keeping of priory 18 July 1349 (*CPR 1358–61*, p. 447). Occ. 18 July 1349 (*CFR 1347–56*, p. 14); Nov. 1351 (Salisbury, Reg. Wyvil, II, f. 264r); 17 Aug. 1354 (*CPL*, III, 534); Aug. 1360 (Lambeth, Reg. Islip, f. 285r): 1361 (*Reg. Sudbury*, I, 7; Lambeth, Reg. Islip, f. 294v): 30 Mar. 1363 (Norwich, Reg/2/5. f. 60r); 28 Jan. 1364 (*Reg. Edlington*, I, no. 1614). Previously pr. of St Neots (q.v.).

William de Sancto Vedasto M. of Bec, occ. as proctor in England 7–8 Mar. 1364 (*CPR 1361–64*, p. 471); as pr. from 12 March 1365 (Cambridge, King's Coll., OGB.9) to 3 Sept. 1405 (*CPR 1408–13*, p. 267); gt for 5 yrs of office as proctor-general in England of Bec 10 Sept. 1368 (*CPR 1367–70*, p. 149). Gt of keeping of St Neots priory 8 July 1370 (*CFR 1368–77*, p. 26, cf. *CPR 1377–81*, p. 446); gt of keeping of Stoke by Clare priory 28 July 1374 (ibid., p. 257). Occ. 14 Sept. 1391 (Norwich, Reg/3/6, f. 162r); 3 Dec. 1391 (London, Reg. Braybrooke, f. 365r); 12 June 1398 when also pr. of St Neots (PRO, C67/30, m. 14); 2 Aug. 1398, 3 Dec. 1404 (*CPR 1401–05*, pp. 5, 466). D. by 28 Nov. 1410 (*CPR 1408–13*, p. 267).

After the death of the last pr., Ogbourne was in the custody of the Duke of Bedford. The spiritualities were transferred in 1421 to St George's, Windsor, and from 1440 other possessions were divided between King's College, Cambridge, Eton College, the London Charterhouse and other establishments (*KH*, p. 90).

OTTERTON (Devon), St Michael (Mont S. Michel) f. *temp.* William I
Lists in Oliver, pp. 248–9; Heads, I, 107.

Nicholas Last recorded occ. 1212 (BL, Cotton ms. Vitellius D. IX, ff. 48v–49v).

William de Kernet **–1220** Occ. n.d. (*c.* 1215 x 1218 *temp.* Robert Courtenay, sheriff of Devon (Devon RO, Petre 123M/TB429; TD42, Ctl. Otterton, p. 55). El. abb. of Tavistock 1220; royal ass. 20 Feb. 1220 (*CPR 1216–25*, p. 229).

Henry Occ. 30 June 1228 (*Devon F.*, I, p. 83, no. 162); n.d. (early 13th cent.) (PRO, E326/4202; Devon RO, TD42, Ctl. Otterton, p. 86).

William de Tordousta (?) Name in Ctl. Otterton but not very legible. Occ. n.d. and Aug. 1231 (Devon RO, TD42, Ctl. Otterton, pp. 47–8); 13 Jan. 1235 (Madox, *Form.*, p. 307, no. 538).

Ralph Uddewin occ. as pr. of Otterton in Devon RO, TD42, Ctl. Otterton, p. 52 in n.d. cht. His position in the sequence of priors is uncertain, but the bulk of the Otterton Ctl. was compiled in the mid-13th cent., *temp.* pr. Geoffrey Legat.

John de Medunta (Medonta, Meonta, Medmita) Occ. May 1251 (Devon RO, TD42, Ctl. Otterton, p. 59); 17 July 1251 (PRO, PRO31/8/140B, part 2, p. 172); Sept. 1252 (Devon RO, Petre 123M/TB434); 1 May 1255 (PRO, PRO31/8/140B, part 2, p. 164); Oct. 1256 x Oct. 1257 (Devon RO, TD42, Ctl. Otterton, p. 57).

Geoffrey *dictus* **Legat** Occ. 17 July 1259, 15 Nov. 1265 (*CPR 1258–66*, pp. 31, 506); Feb. 1260 (Devon RO, TD42, Ctl. Otterton, p. 56); 1260 (ibid., p. 92); 26 Mar. 1264 (ibid., p. 89).

William de Pratellis **1266–** Custody of priory gtd to William (*scribal error rectified*) 23 Sept. 1266; inst. 21 Dec. 1266 (*Reg. Bronescombe*, p. 160; *Reg. W. Bronescombe*, II, nos. 636, 650).

Richard *dictus* **Jordan** (Jurdan) **1276–1310** M. of Mont S. Michel, coll. by lapse 11 Apr. 1276 (*Reg. Bronescombe*, p. 161; *Reg. W. Bronescombe*, II, no. 1157). Occ. 14 June 1284 (*Reg.*

Quivil, p. 332).Commn to appt coadjutor, blind and old, 16 Nov. 1309 (*Reg. Stapeldon*, p. 303). Res. 28 Mar. 1310 (*Reg. Bytton*, p. 421), but res. 29 Mar. 1310 (*Reg. Stapeldon*, p. 239).

Robert Lovel (Lowel) **1310–1316** M. of Mont S. Michel, letter of pres. 20 Apr. 1310, adm. 27 Apr. [1310] (*Reg. Stapeldon*, p. 239: correct version in Devon RO, Exeter, Reg. Stapeldon, f. 49v; cf. PRO, PRO31/8/140B, part 2, p. 353). Lic. to visit mother-house of Mont S. Michel 31 Mar. 1312. Lic. was for 2 months, but he had not returned after a year and six months and on 23 July 1316 was found to be ill to travel (*Reg. Stapeldon*, p. 303). Res. 13 Aug. 1316 in the presence of Richard de Albo Dyoto, m. of Mont S. Michel, who had been nominated his successor (ibid., pp. 239, 303).

Richard de Albo Dyoto (Albo Ducto, Alboryvo, Blandoyt, Doyto) **1316–1319** M. of S. Michel, letter of pres. 27 Aug. 1316 (PRO, PRO31/8/140B, part 2, p. 355); inst. 12 Sept. 1316 (*Reg. Stapeldon*, p. 240). Lic. to visit mother-house, two months' leave gtd 26 May 1319 (ibid., p.303). Res. by 30 July 1319 (ibid., p. 240). Seal (*Mon. Seals*, p. 70).

Oger de Bueys *alias* **Cordon** *alias* **de Monte** (Mone) **1319–1352** Letter of pres. 30 July 1319 (*Reg. Stapeldon*, p. 240). Occ. 12 Sept. 1334 (Roger *alias* Oger) (*Reg. Grandisson*, II, 763–4). D. (de Monte) by 26 Feb. 1352 (*Reg. R. Shrewsbury*, II, no. 2645; *CFR 1347–56*, pp. 322–3), cf. d. (Bueys) by 30 May 1352 (*Reg. Grandisson*, III, 1423)).

Thomas Sedile (Sedille) **1352–1373** M. of S. Michel, inst. 30 May 1352 on death of Oger Bueys (ibid.). Royal gt of keeping of priory during French war 28 Apr. 1352 (*CFR 1347–56*, p. 326). Instn conf. by Pope Innocent VI 31 Jan. 1357 (*Orig. Papal Letters*, p. 124, no. 244; cf. *Accts of Papal Collectors*, pp. 97, 124, 147, 177). D. by 13 Sept. 1373 when goods of priory sequestered (*Reg. Brantingham*, I, 309).

Gt to br. Thomas Payen, m. of Otterton, of keeping of priory void by d. of last pr. 27 Jan. 1374 (*CFR 1368–77*, p. 240).

Simon Garyn (Garren, Guarin) **1374–** Inst. *c.* June 1374 (*Reg. Brantingham*, I, 32). Occ. 9 June 1374, 28 Nov. 1376 (*CFR 1368–77*, pp. 248, 370); 26 Jan. 1378 (*CFR 1377–83*, p. 66). Commn to denounce pr., excommunicate, charged with fornication with Isabel Bourne 14 Aug. 1374 (*Reg. Brantingham*, I, 340). Occ. 15 May 1387 (*CFR 1383–91*, p. 177).

The next recorded pr., **Thomas Pagam**, inst. 19 Aug. 1393 (*Reg. Brantingham*, I, 130)

PANFIELD (Essex), and **WELL** (Norfolk) (S. Etienne, Caen) f. 1070 x 1077. Diss. 1413
List in *VCH Essex*, II, 199.

Peter Occ. from Nov. 1295 x Nov. 1296 to Nov. 1298 x Nov. 1299 (PRO, E106/3/19, m. 9; E106/4/9, mm. 3d, 5; E106/4/10, m. 4); Easter 1300 (PRO, E106/4/14, m. 6); Nov. 1302 x Nov. 1303 (PRO, E106/4/18, m. 8).

John Occ. (pr. of 'Welles') 21 Jan. 1319 (Norwich, Reg/1/1, f. 78r); 29 Mar. 1321 (*Reg. S. Gravesend*, p. 227); as pr. of 'Welle' Mich. 1327 (*Index to Placita de Banco*, p. 470).

Laurence de Brycoo Occ. 11 Apr. 1335 (*Reg. S. Gravesend*, p. 306).

William Pogier (Piogier, Poeges) Occ. 14 May 1341 (*CFR 1337–47*, p. 225); 28 Oct. 1341 (*CPR 1340–43*, p. 330). Mentioned 29 Aug. 1342 as former pr. (ibid., p. 297).

William Naget (Naguet) Occ. 29 July 1342 in order to sheriff to arrest William Naget m. of St Stephen, Caen, whom the abb. app. to Panfield and Well and sent to England to remove William Poeges the present pr. and farmer (*CCR 1341–43*, p. 638). Occ. 29 Aug. 1342, 2 Dec. 1345 (*CFR 1337–47*, pp. 297, 347); 1343 (*Cal. Misc. Inq.*, II, 466); 18 Oct. 1350 (going abroad) (*CPR 1348–50*, p. 578). Replaced as pr. 6 Aug. 1351 because he stayed in France without the king's licence and left no deputy (*CFR 1347–56*, p. 303).

William Pougier 1351– (? same as pr. of similar name above) M. of St Stephen, Caen, gtd keeping of priory 6 Aug. 1351 (ibid.).

William Naget (Naguet) M. of St Stephen, Caen, gt of keeping of priory in place of William

Pougier, m. of Caen, late farmer of priory, 24 Aug. 1352 (ibid., p. 338). Occ. Mich. 1354 x Mich. 1355 (PRO, E372/200, rot. 4); Mich. 1358 x Mich. 1359 (PRO, E372/204, rot. 16); 1363 (BL, Harl. ms. 3697, f. 44r–v); 11 June 1369, 16 Jan. 1370 (*CFR 1368–77*, pp. 16, 38). Mentioned 22 Oct. 1371 as late pr. (ibid., p. 135).

Gt of keeping of priory to Thomas Howlet from 1 Oct. past 'until a prior shall come from parts beyond seas' 22 Oct. 1371 (ibid.).

The next recorded pr., **John Moryn**, m. of St Stephen, Caen, gtd keeping of priory 4 Feb. 1403 (*CFR 1399–1405*, p. 195).

PEMBROKE, St Nicholas (Sées) f. *c.* 1098
List in *Heads*, I, 107.

John de Quisse M. of Sées, occ. 1231 x 1247 (*Ctl. Brecon*, p. 141; *St Davids Acta*, nos. 95–6; *Welsh Episcopal Acts*, I, no. D540); mand. to receive fealty and mand. for seisin 28 May 1246 – the abb. of Sées had apptd him to custody of the priory (*CCR 1242–47*, p. 426). (J.) n.d. (?mid 13th cent. – *c.* 1236 in catalogue) (Hereford Cath. mun. 801).

John Occ. 1256 x 1272 (*Welsh Episcopal Acts*, I, no. D696); 3 Aug. 1260 (PRO, E210/112; *Arch. Camb.*, 6th ser., IX, 173). ? the same as above.

Ralph –1284 Dep. by Archbp Peckham July 1284. Letter to abb. of Sées notifying him that the archbp has ordered pr. Ralph to return to Sées on account of his crimes, discovered at the visitation (*Reg. Peckham*, III, 786–8; *Arch. Camb.*, 6th ser., IX, 173; Cowley, *Monastic Order in South Wales*, p. 107).

John *dictus* Oysel Occ. 11 May 1290, 29 June 1299 (*CPR 1330–34*, p. 67). Is he to be identified with John III Loisel, abb. of Sées (*Gallia Christiana*, XI, 722)?

John *dictus* Sauvage Occ. 15 May 1308 (*CPR 1330–34*, p. 67).

John de Alneyo Occ. *c.* Mich. 1324 (PRO, E106/5/2, m. 13d).

William Menillo Occ. Easter 1330 (*Welsh Memoranda*, no. 642); 4 Mar. 1331 (*CPR 1330–34*, p. 80).

John de Vivacio (Vyviaco) **1357–** M. of Sées, royal gt of keeping of priory 2 June 1357 (*CFR 1356–68*, p. 40). Occ. 30 Nov. 1359 (ibid., p. 115); 22 Apr. 1364 (Lambeth, Reg. Islip, f. 202v); 6 Oct. 1369 (*CCR 1369–77*, pp. 22, 27); protection gtd 9 Dec. 1370 – he was going to Rome to have his eln as abb. of Sées conf. (*CPR 1370–74*, p. 27, presumably the abb. John IV mentd in *Gallia Christiana*, XI, 723).

[**Richard le Verrer** M. of Sées, gtd keeping of priory 24 July 1371, 7 Oct. 1371 (*CFR 1368–77*, pp. 129, 133).]

John de Rougecok(e) (Rugecok) Occ. 13 Dec. 1371 (ibid., p. 133); 8 Oct. 1377, 10 July 1379 (*CFR 1377–83*, pp. 14, 155–6); 1380 x 1381 (PRO, E179/21/9, m. 3).

The next recorded pr., **Gervase le Brek** (Breek), occ. 22 Dec. 1399 (*CPR 1399–1401*, p. 71); 12 Feb. 1404 (*CFR 1399–1405*, p. 241).

PILL (Pembroke), St Mary and St Budoc (Tiron) f. +1113 x 1115 (St Dogmells)
List in E.M. Pritchard, *The history of St Dogmaels Abbey, together with her cells, Pill, Caldy and Glascareg, and the mother abbey of Tiron*, (London 1907), p. 217.

Robert Occ. 1248 x 1255 (*St Davids Acta*, no. 124; *Welsh Episcopal Acts*, I, 390).[8]

Henry Robert and Henry desc. as former prs. in 1294 (Longleat mun. 10543).

Philip Occ. 26 Oct. 1280 (Longleat mun. 11297.6); 16 Sept. 1294 (Longleat mun. 10543); 18 July 1319 (Longleat mun. 248); 8 Mar. 1320 (Longleat mun. 249).

Philip Rey(n)bod Occ. 1380 x 1381 (PRO, E179/21/9, m. 2).

---

[8] *Welsh Episcopal Acts*, I, 412 gives pr. J. 1256 x 1272, but a more recent edn of this cht does not give any initial for the pr. of Pill (*St Davids Episcopal Acta*, no. 151).

RUISLIP (Middlesex) (Bec) f. *c.* 1090. ? Conventual until ? *c.* 1250 (*KH*).
  Lists in *VCH Middlesex*, I, 204; *Heads*, I, 107.
William Occ. July 1224 (*Oxford F.*, p. 72). A pr. of Ruislip d. 1225 (*Ann. Dunstable*, p. 94). cf.
  Ogbourne.
Ralph Occ. 27 Jan. 1226 (*Oxford F.*, p. 76); 17 May 1226 (PRO, Hants F., CP25/1/203/5, no.
  12); 1227 (*Bucks Eyre*, pp. 13, no. 164); 22 Oct. 1227 (*CPR 1225–32*, p. 167); Hil. term 1228,
  Easter term 1228, Hil. term 1230 (*CRR*, XIII, nos. 418, 508, 2769). cf. Ogbourne.
Michael Occ. Hil. term 1230 (ibid., no. 2432); Oct. 1229 x Oct. 1230 (*London and Middlesex F.*,
  p. 17). Possibly the Michael de Turnebu, who occ. as proctor of Bec in 1232 (Morgan,
  English Lands of Bec, p. 43).

RUNCTON (Sussex) (Troarn) f. -1086; 1100+?; diss. 1260 when it passed to Bruton.
  No list in *VCH*
William Occ. n.d. (13th cent.) (*Ctl. Bruton*, no. 351; ment. *CPR 1388–92*, p. 149). A related
  charter (*Ctl. Bruton*, no. 352, with 2 witnesses the same as in no. 351, also includes W[illiam]
  IV, earl of Arundel (i.e. William IV d'Aubigny, earl of Arundel 1221–1224)).

ST CROSS (Isle of Wight) (Tiron) f. 1132+; diss. 1391 and granted to Winchester College.
  List in *Heads*, I, 107.
Walter Occ. 1202 x 1203 (*Hants F.*, PRO transcripts); 1228 x 1238 (*Quarr Chts.*, no. 306).
Gir' Occ. ?1250 (BL, Harl. Cht. 55 D 22), but cf. *Quarr Chts.*, no. 489 which dates this cht. 1191
  x 1194.
Geoffrey Occ. Nov. 1296 x Nov. 1297 (PRO, E106/4/2, m. 4); 1 Nov. 1297 (WCM, no. 2873);
  Nov. 1297 x Nov. 1298 (PRO, E106/4/8, m. 3); Nov. 1298 x Nov. 1299 (PRO, E106/4/9,
  m. 5; E106/4/10, m. 5); 1300 (PRO, E106/4/14, m. 7); 14 Apr. 1301 (*Reg. Swinfield*, p. 379);
  3 Apr. 1306 (*Reg. Gandavo*, II, 676).
Ralph Occ. 24 Sept. 1313, 28 Oct. 1313, 26 Nov. 1313 (*CPR 1313–17*, pp. 60, 64, 69); 22 Nov.
  1314 (*Reg. Gandavo*, II, 828).
Theodore Occ. 1324 (PRO, SC6/1127/1; PRO, E106/5/2, m. 4d); July 1325 x July 1326 (PRO,
  E106/5/4, m. [3d]); 8 Oct. 1326 (*Memo. Roll 1326–7*, p. 272). Mentd (as former pr.) 1338
  x 1339 in PRO, E372/184, rots. 14d, 15d).
Peter Pulein Occ. 8 Dec. 1332 (WCM, no. 10638).
Robert Reynard Occ. 27 Dec. 1337 (WCM, no. 17215); 1341 (PRO, SC6/1127/2); 15 Feb. 1343
  (*CPR 1337–47*, p. 316).
John Bernerii (Bernyer) Gt of keeping of priory during French war 15 June 1345 (*CFR
  1337–47*, p. 422). Occ. from 1348 until his d. on 18 Apr. 1350 (*Cal. Misc. Inq.*, III, 21).
Peter le Gros Occ. 1350 (PRO, SC6/1127/2); 5 May 1361 (WCM, no. 17214).
Richard Wynnegod Occ. as custodian of priories of Hamble, Andwell and St Cross 6 Mar.
  1364 (WCM, no. 17216).
[Inquisition of 1381 reported that **Thomas Dryffeld** held priory by title unknown for 12 years
  preceding Edward III's death (1377), but ? as farmer or pr. (*Cal. Misc. Inq.*, IV, 31).]
Peter, abb. of Tiron, gtd the priories of Andwell, St Cross and Titley to Winchester College 1
  Sept. 1391 (WCM, nos. 2970–2, cf. 2969a).

ST DOGMELLS (Pembroke), St Mary and St Dogmell (Cammeis) (Tiron) f. *c.* 1115
(priory); 1120 (abbey).
  Lists in *Heads*, I, 107; E. M. Pritchard, *The History of St Dogmells Abbey* (1907), p. 217,
  without sources.
Walter Last occ. 15 Apr. 1203, when his eln as bp of St Davids was quashed (Cheney, *Inn. III*,
  no. 468).

Andrew Occ. ? early 13th cent. (*Mon. Angl.*, IV, 503, no. i – foundation cht. of Pill priory, cf. *Heads*, I, 107, n.5).

J. Occ. 9 May 1292 (WCM, no. 10664). Possibly the same as below.

John Occ. 13 Dec. 1302 (Longleat mun. nos. 241, 3442).

John le Rede –1330 D. by 1 Mar. 1330 (*CCR 1327–30*, p. 455).

David Occ. 15 Feb. 1354 (*Reg. Grandisson*, III, 1431).

John Paid homage at Newport 4 June 1364 (*Baronia de Kemeys*, p. 88). Occ. 20 June 1364 (ibid., pp. 86–7); 18 Aug. 1376 (*Reg. Brantingham*, I, 44).

No further recorded abbots until the fifteenth century.

ST MICHAEL'S MOUNT (Cornwall) (Mont. S. Michel) f. -1050 (cell); *c.* 1087 x 91 (priory)

Lists in *Ctl. St Michael's Mount*, p. 63 (to 1262); *Heads*, I, 108.

Ralph de Kankale Occ. *c.* 1209 x 1214 (*Ctl. St Michael's Mount*, nos. 12, 13).

John Mentioned 1226 as former pr. (ibid., no. 16).

R. Occ. 11 Oct. 1240 (ibid., no. 65).

Aluinus Mentioned 16 Aug. 1261 (ibid., p. 63 & n.).

Ralph *dictus* Vyel Occ. 1 May 1262 (ibid., no. 35).

Ralph de Cartaret 1266– Inst. 21 Dec. 1266 (*Reg. Bronescombe*, p. 175, cf. ibid., p. 160; *Reg. W. Bronescombe*, II, nos. 636, 650: custody committed to William de Cartaret, m. of St Michael's, 23 Sept. 1266 ? scribal error). Occ. 31 Mar. 1267 (*Ctl. St Michael's Mount*, no. 39).

Richard Perer 1276– M. of St Michael's, coll. by lapse 11 Apr. 1276 (*Reg. Bronescombe*, p. 179; *Reg. W. Bronescombe*, II, no. 1158).

John Occ. 18 June 1282 (*Ctl. St Michael's Mount*, no. 3).

Geoffrey de Jernon (Gernon, Seroion, Sernon) 1283–1316 Adm. 9 July 1283, no reason being given for the vacancy (*Reg. Quivil*, p. 354). Occ. 26 June 1295, 22 Nov. 1295, 18 Sept. 1299 (*Ctl. St Michael's Mount*, nos. 90, 36, 34). Res. dated and acc. 13 Aug. 1316 (*Reg. Stapeldon*, p. 256; *Reg. Bytton*, p. 423).

Peter de Carville (Caraville, Carvilla, Craville, Karaville, Karville) 1316–1342 M. of St Michael's Mount, inst. 12 Sept. 1316 (*Reg. Stapeldon*, p. 256). Res. by 24 Sept. 1342 (*Reg. Grandisson*, III, 1336).

Nicholas Isabella (Isabel) 1342–1348 Inst. 24 Sept. 1342 (ibid.). Occ. *c.* 12 June 1348 (*CPR 1348–50*, p. 107). 28 Oct. 1348 king had given it to Nicholas Isabella, pr., and it has been taken from him because he sold corrodies, made alienations and demises of land without the licence of the king and has converted the money to uses not only unprofitable but dishonest (*CFR 1348–56*, p. 97).

John Hardy (Harde) 1349–1362 M. of S. Michel, priest, inst. 3 Oct. 1349, no reason being given for the vacancy (*Reg. Grandisson*, III, 1399). 1356 acquitted after being indicted of having, in 1354, sent his brother across the sea to Normandy as a messenger to the king's enemies with secret letters and money (*CPR 1354–58*, p. 460). D. by 24 Apr. 1362 (*Reg. Grandisson*, III, 1481–2).

John (le) Volant (Voland) 1362– Priest, inst. 24 Apr. 1362 (ibid.). Occ. from 13 July 1362 to 19 Apr. 1372 (*Ctl. St Michael's Mount*, nos. 11, 50); 1370 (PRO, E106/10/2); 1373–74 (*Reg. Brantingham*, I, 303, 194); 21 Jan. 1380 (ibid., 415); 1380 x 1381 (PRO, E179/24/5, m. 4).

The next recorded pr. of St Michael's Mount occ. in a royal mand. of 15 June 1383 mentioning **Richard Harepathe** who had obtained the priory by false letters and was now occupying it (*Reg. Brantingham*, I, 497). Richard became pr. of St Germans in 1385 (ibid., I, 93; II, 586–7).

ST NEOTS (Hunts) (Bec) (Eynesbury) f. *c.* 974 (dependent on Ely); *c.* 1081 x 2 (cell of Bec).

Lists in *VCH Hunts*, I, 388; *Heads*, I, 108.

William Last recorded occ. 11 Jan. [1210] (CUL Add. ms. 3021, f. 376v).

Roger -?1225 Occ. *c.* 15 July 1219 (ibid., f. 50r; Soc. of Ant. ms. 38, f. 121v); Oct. 1223 x Oct. 1224 (*Hunts F.*, p. 9); n.d. (PRO, E210/3789); 15 July 1219 (PRO, Northants F. CP25/1/172/16, no. 7; BL, Cotton ms. Faustina A IV, f. 50r); 27 Jan. 1224 (ibid., f. 51v). Prob. the unnamed pr. who d. 1225 (*Ann. Dunstable*, p. 94).[9]

Reginald 1225–1230 M. of St Neots, adm. 9 Feb. 1225, no reason given for vacancy *(Reg. Wells*, III, 54), erroneously said to have been inst. 15 Feb. 1226, citing above ref. (*Mon.*, III, 464). Occ. 1227 (*Beds Eyre*, no. 95); Oct. 1227 x Oct. 1228 (*Hunts F.*, p. 11); Apr. 1230 (*Sarum Chts.*, p. 202, no. clxxviii).

Hugh de Fagerlon 1230–1248/9 Occ. 13 Sept. 1230 (BL, Cotton ms. Faustina A IV, f. 105r); Jan. 1231 (*Records of Turvey*, p. 91); 24 June x 1 July 1235 (*Warws F.*, I, no. 505); 6 Oct. 1236 (*Beds F.*, I, p. 103, no. 384); 20 Jan. 1244 (BL, Cotton ms. Faustina A IV, f. 52v); Oct. 1247 x Oct. 1248 (*Hunts F.*, p. 25). Res. June 1248 x June 1249 (*Reg. Grosseteste*, p. 295).

Henry de Mesnill 1248/9–1258/9 M. of Bec, inst. June 1248 x June 1249 (ibid.). Res. Nov. 1258 x Nov. 1259 (*Reg. R. Gravesend*, p. 167).

William de Bonesboz (Boneboz) 1258/9–1262 Adm. Nov. 1258 x Nov. 1259 (ibid., pp. 167, 315). Occ. July 1260 (BL, Cotton ms. Faustina A IV, f. 135r). D. Nov. 1262 x Nov. 1263, clearly 1262 by reference to the following entry (*Reg. R. Gravesend*, p. 168).

Elias de Ponte Episcopi 1262–1265 M. of Bec, adm. Nov. 1262 x Nov. 1263 (ibid.). Fealty had been taken by 17 Oct. 1262 (*CR 1261–64*, pp. 159–60); temps. 15 Nov. 1262, the priory being in the king's hands by virtue of his wardship of the land and heirs of Richard de Clare, earl of Gloucester (*CPR 1256–66*, p. 237). Occ. 11 Jan. 1265 (BL, Cotton ms. Faustina A IV, f. 139v). Res. by 30 Sept. 1265 (*Reg. R. Gravesend*, p. 170).

Henry of St Neots (de Sancto Neoto) 1265–1272 Inst. 30 Sept. 1265 (ibid., pp. 170, 316). Bp's letter to patron of house 3 Oct. 1265 (ibid.). Res. by 11 June 1272 (ibid., pp. 176, 317).

Walter de Bernaio 1272–1275 Letter of pres. 11 June 1272, inst. 17 July 1272 (ibid.). Res. by 10 Dec. 1275 (ibid., p. 182).

Thomas de Benseval 1275– M. of Bec, adm. 10 Dec. 1275 (ibid., pp. 182, 319).

William de Bougevilla Occ. as m. of Bec and pr. of St Neots late 13th cent. (Sharpe, *Latin Writers*, p. 756). Prob. fits into this gap, and may coincide with the missing Huntingdon archdeaconry roll of Bp Sutton. According to information kindly provided by Dr Richard Sharpe he had ceased to be pr. by 1281: 'Tempore bone memorie domini Petri quondam abbatis Becci frater Willelmus de Bugevilla tunc prior sancti Neoti recessit a dicto prioratu at apud Beccum venit non mandatus nec licenciatus et expositus domino abbati causis adventus sui absolutus fuit a dicto prioratu' (BL, Cotton ms. Domitian A XI, f. 114r). Peter de la Chambrie, abb. of Bec died on 2 Nov. 1281 (*Gallia Christiana*, XI, 232).

John de Bosco Reynaldi –1292 Occ. 30 Sept. 1286 (BL, Cotton ms. Faustina A IV, f. 27v); (J.) 24 Dec. 1290 (ibid., f. 22v). Letter of res. dated 31 Aug. 1292 (*Reg. Sutton*, VIII, 80–2).

John de Siccavalle (Suta Valle) 1293–1302 M. of Bec, letter of pres. 30 June 1292, adm. 23 Apr. 1293 (ibid.). D. by 30 May 1302 (Lincoln, Ep. Reg., II, f. 233r–v).

William of Bec (Becco) *alias dictus* Lecaron 1302–1317 M. of Bec, letter of pres. 30 May 1302, assent of patron the earl of Gloucester and Hertford dated 20 June 1302; adm. by bp 1 July 1302 (ibid.). Letter of res. dated 3 July 1317 (ibid., f. 250v).

---

[9] William who is said to occur 1224 (*Mon. Angl.*, III, 464, citing BL, Cotton ms. Faustina A IV, f. 51r) is an error, the document in question being dated 8 John, not 8 Henry III.

Geoffrey _dictus_ Fae 1317–1321 M. of Bec, letter of pres. by abb. of Bec dated 10 July 1317; consent of patron, Maud de Clare, countess of Gloucester and Hertford, dated 19 July 1317; adm. by bp 23 July 1317 (ibid., ff. 250v–251r). D. or res. by 15 Nov. 1321 (PRO, SC1/33/30). Request by Abb. of Bec to Edward II for admission of a new pr. 15 Nov. 1321 (ibid).

Clement of St Stephen (de Sancto Stephano) **1322–** M. of St Neots, writ _de intendendo_ 19 Apr. 1322, having been preferred by abb. of Bec (_CPR 1321–24_, p. 104). Occ. 24 Jan. 1325 (_CPR 1324–27_, p. 83); 8 Oct. 1326 (_Memo. Roll 1326–7_, p. 272); 30 May 1331 (_CCR 1330–33_, p. 319); Mich. 1338 x Mich. 1339 (PRO, E372/184, rot. 3). Poss. the unnamed pr. who was so infirm that he could not adm. the goods of the house and br. Peter de Sancto Stephano, m. of Bec, was associated with him 18 Feb. 1340 (_CFR 1337–47_, p. 161).

Peter de Falco (Falk) _alias_ **of St Stephen** (de Sancto Stephano) **1341–?1349** M. of Bec, coll. by lapse, the abb. of Bec having neglected to pres., no reason given for vacancy 5 Apr. 1341 (Lincoln, Ep. Reg., IV, f. 393v). Occ. 12 Feb. 1342 (_CFR 1337–47_, p. 272). Referred to as former pr. of St Neots 11 July 1349 (_CFR 1347–56_, p. 146). Pr. of Ogbourne 1349 (q.v.).

William de Beaumont (Bello Monte, Beaumond) **1349–1351** M. of Bec, letter of pres. dated 11 June 1349, no reason given for vacancy; adm. 10 Aug. 1349 (Lincoln, Ep. Reg., IX, f. 385r). Royal gt of keeping of priory during the French War 11 July 1349 (_CFR 347–56_, p. 146). Res. by 17 Mar. 1352 (Lincoln, Ep. Reg., IX, f. 395v).

Geoffrey de Branvilla 1352– M. of Bec, letter of pres. dated 17 Mar. 1352, adm. by bp 30 Apr. 1352 (ibid.). Cess. by [_blank_] Nov. 1353 (ibid., f. 397v).

Peter de Villaribus 1353– M. of Bec, letter of pres. dated [-] Nov. 1353; adm. by bp 29 Nov. 1353 (ibid.).

Peter of Bec (Becke, Becko, Beco, Bek) Occ. as pr. in return of aliens 16 Jan. 1370 (_Buckingham Writ Reg._, p. 39, no. 116; PRO, E179/35/4): ? same as above, but see below for apparent incompatibility of date. In Feb. 1378, as a m. of St Neots, he received permission to leave England (D. Matthew, _The Norman Monasteries and their English possessions_, app. III, p. 153).

Christian of Troarn (de Troarno) **1364–1372** Adm. 20 May 1364, no reason given for vacancy (Lincoln, Ep. Reg., X, f. 284v). D. by 20 July 1372 (ibid., ff. 301v–302r).

Robert de Glanvilla 1372–1378 M. of Bec. Letter of William de Sancto Vedasto, pr. of Ogbourne, proctor of Bec, presenting him dated 20 July 1372; inst. 10 Aug. 1372 (ibid.). Commn to proceed against Robert de Glanvilla, calling himself pr. of St Neots 16 June 1375 (Lincoln, Ep. Reg., XII, f. 128v). Pr. of Ogbourne given custody 18 Oct. 1377 (_CFR 1377–83_, p. 19; _CPR 1377–81_, p. 446). Res. of Robert de Glanvilla, claiming to be pr. of St Neots 31 Jan. 1378 (Lincoln, Ep. Reg., XII, f. 177r).

The next pr., **William de Sancto Vedasto**, was apptd by bp 29 Dec. 1378 (Lincoln, Ep. Reg., X, f. 321v).

SELE (Sussex), St Peter (S. Florent, Saumur) f. -1126; letters of denization 9 June 1396 (Oxford, Magdalen Coll., Sele Cht. 62).

Lists in _VCH Sussex_, II, 62, from W.D. Macray, _Notes from the Muniments of Magdalen College, Oxford_ (Oxford and London, 1882), pp. 8–9; _Heads_, I, 108.

Robert Occ. n.d. (early 13th cent. pal: ?_c_. 1220 x 1230) (Oxford, Magdalen Coll., Bidlington and Bramber Cht. 13).[10]

Walter de Coleville Formerly pr. of Monmouth (_Ctl. Sele_, pp. xiv–xv). Occ. in _Ctl. Sele_ from 1232 (no. 39) to 21 Nov. 1272 (no. 48), many times his full name given. Occ. 24 Aug. 1273 (Oxford, Magdalen Coll., Thakeham Cht. 12).

---

[10] _VCH_, citing Macray, gives William Malherbe _c_. 1224, but I have not located this cht. at Magdalen College, Oxford.

David Occ. 26 Jan. 1282, 6 July 1286 (*Ctl. Sele*, nos. 177, 78); 22 Nov. 1284 (Oxford, Magdalen Coll., Binelands and Grinstead Cht. 16); 1288 (PRO, Just.1/929, m. 47d).

Peter de Nabynaux Occ. 20 Jan. 1292, going overseas (*CPR 1281–92*, p. 468); (P.) 9 Oct. 1294 (*Ctl. Sele*, no. 60); 30 Nov. 1294, 27 Jan. 1298, 1300, 12 Dec. 1304 (ibid., nos. 76, 61, 182, 188); presumably the unnamed pr. , an alien, permitted to remain in his priory 4 Oct. 1295 (*CCR 1288–96*, p. 460); 30 Dec. 1295 (*CPR 1292–1301*, p. 176); Nov. 1295 x Nov. 1296, Nov. 1297 x Nov. 1298, Nov. 1298 x Nov. 1299 (PRO, E106/3/9, m. 8; E106/4/8, m. 1; E106/4/9, m. 1; E106/4/10, m. 1); 1 Apr. 1304, 21 May 1306 (*CPR 1301–7*, pp. 222, 437); 1306 (PRO, Just.1/934, m. 27).

Robert of Beeding (Bedinge, Bedyng) Occ. 29 Sept. 1307, *c.* 1312, 15 Mar. 1331 (*Ctl. Sele*, nos. 165, 67, 183); July 1308 x July 1309 (BL, Add. ms. 4535, f. 191r); 29 Nov. 1308 (*CPR 1307–13*, p. 147); 1324 (PRO, E106/5/2, m. 3d); July 1325 x July 1326 (PRO, E106/5/4, m. [2]); 8 Oct. 1326 (*Memo. Roll 1326–7*, p. 271);19 Mar. 1330 (*CCR 1330–33*, p. 127).

An unnamed pr. was dead by 10 Feb. 1338 (*CFR 1337–47*, p. 65). Matthew de Duno, sub-pr. of Sele, renders account for his custody 1338 (PRO, E372/184, rot. 13d).

Gilbert of Wimborne (Wymbourn) Occ. 10 Feb. 1339 (ibid., p. 115); Feb. x Mich. 1339 (PRO, E372/184, rot. 13); 8 June 1343 (*CPR 1343–45*, p. 39).

John de Pomeriis (Pomariis, Pomeries) 1341– Pr. of Andover, apptd to Sele 6 Nov. 1341, noted in royal mand. (*CPR 1340–43*, p. 338; *CFR 1337–47*, p. 248), cf. Winchester, Reg. Orleton II, f. 89r–v, Andover priory vacant by 7 Sept. 1341 by the appt of John de Pomeries to Sele; 1342 (*Cal. Misc. Inq.*, II, 448); 1343 (*CCR 1343–46*, p. 111); 1344 (PRO, C47/109/4); 1353 (*CPR 1350–54*, p. 436); 26 June 1358 (*CCR 1354–60*, p. 522).

Gerard de Parell (Parellis) Occ. 1 Oct. 1368 (Gerald) (*CPR 1370–74*, p. 415; *CPR 1377–81*, p. 269); 1370 (PRO, E106/10/11); 28 June 1374 (*CFR 1369–77*, p. 252); Jan. 1374 x Jan. 1375 (PRO, LR14/1103); 6 Apr. 1374 (*Cal. Misc. Inq.*, III, 351).

Nicholas Comyn (Goyn, Gouyn) M. of S. Florent, gtd keeping of priory 19 Feb. 1378 (*CFR 1377–83*, p. 76); received permission to leave England Feb. 1378 (Matthew, p. 155). Occ. as m. of Sele, gtd custody of priory 20 July 1379 (*CFR 1377–83*, p. 157).

Stephen de Sens (Saus/Sans) 1378–1429 Apptd by the abb. of S. Florent 1 Oct. 1378 (Oxford, Magdalen Coll., Sele Cht. 6). M. of Monmouth, pres. by king to bp of Chichester for instn 5 Mar. 1379 on d. of previous pr. (*CPR 1377–81*, p. 332). Occ. 4 May 1380, 9 June 1380 (*CFR 1377–83*, pp. 198, 201); 1396 (Oxford, Magdalen Coll., Sele Cht. 62); Jan. 1403 (*Privy Council*, I, 195). Res. by 27 Oct. 1429 (*Reg. Chichele*, III, 486).

SHERBORNE, *see* MONK SHERBORNE

SPALDING (Lincs), St Mary (S. Nicholas, Angers) f. 1052 (dependent on Crowland); 1074 (dependent on St. Nicholas, Angers).

Lists in *VCH Lincs*, II, 123–4; *Heads*, I, 109.

J. Occ. as pr. *c.* 8 Jan. 1215, in letter of pres. for instn made by bp of Lincoln on that day (Lincoln, Ep. Reg. II, ff. 27v–28r).

Ralph le Mansel –1230 Occ. 3 Nov. 1224 (*Lincs F.*, I, 173); Dec. 1224 x Dec. 1225 (*Reg. Wells*, III, 135); Easter term 1226 (*CRR*, XII, no. 2173); Easter term 1229 (*CRR*, XIII, no. 1806). D. by 10 Feb. 1230 (*Reg. Wells*, III, 182).

[**John** Pr. of Monks Kirby, given custody of Spalding priory 10 Feb. 1230 (ibid., 182–6). On 7 Mar. objections were made and he subsequently renounced his claim (ibid.).]

Simon de Hauton' (Hautone, Haut') 1230–1253 M. of Spalding, eln conf. 7 Mar. 1230 (ibid.). Occ. 16 June 1252 (*Lincs F.*, II, 95). D. 14 Mar. 1253 (*Ch. Angl. Petr.*, pp. 139–41; cf. *Mon. Angl.*, III, 209n.; *Ch. Peterborough*, p. 16). Seal (*BM Seals*, no. 4067; *Mon. Seals*, p. 83; *Northumberland and Durham Seals*, p. 110, suppl. no. 81).

John the Almoner 1253–1274 Succ. Simon 1253 and ruled for 22 years (BL, Add. ms. 35296, f. 422r); conf. by Bp Grosseteste, hence before Oct. 1253 (*Ch. Angl. Petr.*, p. 141). Occ. 3 June 1274 (PRO, Lincs F., CP25/1/132/51 no. 5). D. at St-Denis in France 24 Sept. 1274, while on a pilgrimage to Pontigny (*Ch. Angl. Petr.*, pp. 149–51; cf. *Mon. Angl.*, III, 209; BL Add. ms. 35296, f. 422r; cf. *Reg. R. Gravesend*, p. 61).

William of Littleport (Litleport, Littelport) **1274–1294** Succ. 1274 (*Ch. Angl. Petr.*, p. 151). Eln conf. Nov. 1274 x Nov. 1275, ? *c.* Jan. 1275 (*Reg. R. Gravesend*, pp. 61, 282). D. 25 Jan. 1294 (*Ch. Angl. Petr.*, pp.156–7; cf. *Mon. Angl.*, III, 209–10 & n.; *Reg. Sutton*, I, 186). Indulgences offered to all who go to Spalding to pray for his soul. 6 Oct. 1298, 3 May 1301 (ibid., VI, 113; Lincoln, Ep. Reg., III, f. 29v).

Clement of Hatfield (Hatfeld, Hattefeud) **1294–1318** Sub-pr. of Spalding, eln conf. 11 Apr. 1294 (*Reg. Sutton*, I, 186; II, 113). D. [22 Oct.]1318 (*Mon. Angl.*, III, 210, but the note cited, i.e. *Ch. Angl. Petr.*, p. 161, only mentions the year; cf. Lincoln, Ep. Reg., II, f. 76r–v).

Walter of Halton 1319–1333 M. of Spalding, el. appeared before bp 23 Jan. 1319 and eln conf. 25 Jan. 1319 (ibid.). Br. Hugh de Lenn' occ. as coadjutor of unnamed pr. 4 Apr. 1333 (Lincoln, Ep. Reg., IV, f. 47r). D. 1332 *recte* 1333 (*Ch. Angl. Petr.*, pp. 166–7). Commn to Hugh de Lenn, sub-pr. of Spalding, of the admin. of priory during the vacancy 16 May 1333 (Lincoln, Ep. Reg., V, f. 464v).

[James of Haugh (Hagh) *or* **Haugham]**

Thomas of Nassington *alias* **of Spalding** (Nassyngton, Spaldyng) **1333–1353** Commn to act in the disputed eln of Thomas of Nassington and James of Haugh, mm. of Spalding, 16 Aug. 1333 (Lincoln, Ep. Reg., V, f. 473v). Disp. went to Roman Curia; eln quashed and Thomas apptd. (*Ch. Angl. Petr.*, p. 170, which refers to James as 'of Haugham' (Haghem); cf. *Accts of Papal Collectors*, p. 91). Thomas occ. as pr. 28 Oct. 1333 (*Reg. Burghersh*, I, no. 399). Commn to appt a suitable m. of Spalding to the admin. of the priory, Hugh de Lenn, sub-pr., having died, and the pr. being *in remotis* 3 Nov. 1334 (Lincoln, Ep. Reg., V, f. 485r–v). D. by 4 Dec. 1353 (Lincoln, Ep. Reg., IX, ff. 108v–109r; cf. *Ch. Angl. Petr.*, p. 170).

John (of) Eastfield (Estfeld(e), Estrefeld) **1353–1384** El. appeared before bp 4 Dec. 1353; eln examined 2 Jan. 1354; eln conf. 4 Jan. 1354 (Lincoln, Ep. Reg., IX, ff. 108v–109r). D. by 3 July 1384 (Lincoln, Ep. Reg., XI, ff. 9v–12r).

SPORLE (Norfolk), St Mary (S. Florent, Saumur) f. -1123
Lists in *VCH Norfolk*, II, 464; *Heads*, I, 109.

Stephen Occ. n.d. (Norfolk RO, NRS. 18199, mid-14th cent. Sporle ctl., f. [26r]). His position in the sequence of priors is unclear.

John de Montimato Occ. n.d. *temp.* Bp Roger Skerning of Norwich (1266–78) (*HMC 9th Rept.*, app., p. 351).

Guy Occ. 1270 (ibid., p. 350).

John Occ. Trin. 1309 (PRO, CP40/178, m. 310d).

John de Cernoun Occ. Mich. 1324 (PRO, E106/5/2, m. 15d).

[?John of Sporle A vicar pres. to Sporle vicarage by Br. John of Sporle, monk, (?pr.) and the brothers of the place, 20 Dec. 1328 (Norwich, Reg/1/2, f. 26r).]

Alan Mahe (Maher, Mathe, Mathei) **1335–** M. of S. Florent, adm. 7 Mar. 1335, no reason given for vacancy (ibid., f. 70v). Occ. 13 Oct. 1335 (Norfolk RO, NRS. 18199, Sporle ctl., f. [21v]); 5 Feb. 1342 (*CFR 1337–47*, p. 274); Mich. 1342 (*HMC 9th Rept.*, p. 351); 11 July 1345 (*CCR 1342–46*, p. 636); 9 June 1352 (*CFR 1347–56*, p. 330).[11]

[11] *VCH* gives the appt of William de Leke in 1349, citing Norwich, Reg/2/4, f. 97r, but there is no such entry there, cf. *Reg. Bateman*, I. *VCH* also gives Thomas Eliot res. 1345 and John de Braidesdale apptd 1345, but these are vicars of Sporle, not priors (*Reg. Bateman*, I, nos. 170–1).

John Godes (Goddes) 1361–1379 M. of S. Florent, adm. 20 Nov. 1361, no reason given for vacancy (Norwich, Reg/2/5, f. 56r). D. by 17 Feb. 1379 (*CPR 1377–81*, p. 332, cf. Norwich, Reg/3/6, f. 62v).

STANDON (Herts), St Michael (dependent on Stoke by Clare) f. 1173 x 1178
List in *VCH Herts*, IV, 422.

John of Salburn (Salebourne) 1269– Apptd warden of the house of Salburn by Gilbert de Clare, earl of Gloucester, 27 May 1269 (BL, Add. ms. 6041, f. 73r, no. xix).

[**Roger de Castone** Apptd 'a brother in the chapel of Salburn' 11 June 1306, ? error for warden (ibid., no. xx).]

Letter of Elizabeth de Burgh, lady of Clare, appting a warden (*gardeyn*) of the chapel of Salburn (no name) 16 May 1334 (ibid., f. 73v, no. xxii).

STEVENTON (Berks), St Michael (S. Mary du Pré, Rouen and Bec-Hellouin) f. *temp.* Henry I.
No list in *VCH*.

Clarus First known pr., occ. Hil. term 1228, Hil. term 1230 (*CRR*, XIII, nos. 418, 2769).

William Occ. from Nov. 1295 x Nov. 1296 to Nov. 1298 x Nov. 1299 (PRO, E106/4/2, m.1d; E106/4/9, m. 1; E106/4/10, m. 2); Trin. 1309 (PRO, CP40/178, attorneys m. 20).

Bertrand of Pont-Audemer (de Ponte Odomeri, Maheil) Occ. 5 Feb. 1342 (*CPR 1337–47*, p. 262); 11 July 1345 (*CCR 1343–46*, p. 637); 18 Apr. 1348 (*CCR 1346–49*, p. 445); former pr. (Maheil) by 12 May 1349, when gtd keeping of Goldcliff priory (*CFR 1347–56*, p. 136). Mentioned as former pr. (Maheil), relieved of the keeping of Goldcliff 25 Mar. 1352 (ibid., p. 326).

John de Anglica Villa 1349 M. of Bec, keeper of Steventon, gtd keeping of priory during French war 12 May 1349 (ibid., p. 136). Had been removed by abb. of Bec by 16 Oct. 1349 (ibid., p. 167).

William de Calida 1349–1356 M. of Bec, preferred as pr. in place of John de Anglica Villa 16 Oct. 1349 (ibid.). D. by 18 Nov. 1356 (*CFR 1356–68*, p. 23).

[br. **Stephen of St Stephen** (de Sancto Stephano) and br. **Thomas de Lineya**, MM. of Bec, gtd keeping of the priory in place of William de Calida, deceased, 18 Nov. 1356 (ibid.).]

John Hudicot Occ. 6 Oct. 1369 (*CFR 1368–77*, p. 24).

William de Estrepany Occ. 2 Dec. 1376 (ibid., p. 373); 26 Oct. 1377 (*CFR 1377–83*, p. 27).

STOGURSEY (Soms), St Andrew (Lonlay) f. 1100 x 1107
Lists in *VCH Soms*, II, 171; *Stogursey Chts.*, p. xxviii; *Heads*, I, 109–10.

G. Occ. *c.* 1220 x 1242 (*HMC Wells*, I, 367; cf. *Gallia Christiana*, XIV, 484: this doct is dated to *c.* 1219 in *Stogursey Chts* list).

Vincent Occ. 11 Nov. 1251, 1258 x 1259, 1259 x 1260 (*Stogursey Chts.*, nos. 43, 38, 46); *c.* 1260 (*Hylle Ctl.*, nos. 106, 107).

Robert Occ. before 10 Sept. 1270, by which time he had become abb. of Lonlay (*Stogursey Chts.*, no. 49).

James de Malitote (Malecote, Maletote) Occ. 1282 x 1283 (*Ctl. Bath*, II, p. 169, no. 842); n.d. (1274 x 1284) (*Stogursey Chts.*, nos. 39, 40).

Giles Occ. 30 Apr. 1284 (*Stogursey Chts.*, no. 50).

Nicholas Occ. Nov. 1295 x Nov. 1296 (PRO, E106/3/19, m. 9d); Nov. 1296 x Nov. 1297 (PRO, E106/4/2, m. 6); Nov. 1297 x Nov. 1298 (PRO, E106/4/8, m. 4d); Nov. 1298 x Nov. 1299 (PRO, E106/4/9, m. 9; E106/4/10, m. 7d); Easter 1300 (PRO, E106/4/14, m. 11d).

Vincent Tybout –1309/10 Recalled to Lonlay 1309/10 (*Reg. Droxford*, p. 27).

Peter de Grana 1310–1316 M of Lonlay, pres. by abb. of Lonlay, inst. 11 Jan. 1310 (ibid., pp. 27–8). D. by 30 July 1316 (ibid., p. 8).

Giles Rosee (Rosey) 1316–1328 Said to be a priest aged 40, inquisition's findings 31 July 1316, inst. 14 Aug. 1316 (ibid., pp. 8–9). Occ. 7 Dec. 1316 (*Stogursey Chts.*, no. 53). Recalled Apr. 1328 (*Reg. Droxford*, p. 287).

Godfrey de Bu (Bew, de Duc) 1328– M. of Lonlay, pres. Apr. 1328, inst. 18 June 1328 (ibid.). Occ. 7 Oct. 1332 (*Reg. R. Shrewsbury*, I, no. 461); 1332, 1337 (*Stogursey Chts.*, nos. 57–9); 1 July 1340 (*CPR 1340–43*, p. 3). Pr. appealed to the Court of Canterbury against the bp of Bath and Wells and his commissaries who had cited him for dilapidations; Canterbury inhibition 7 Aug. 1334 (*Reg. R. Shrewsbury*, I, nos. 696, 734). Mentd 20 Mar. 1342 as former pr. (*CFR 1337–47*, p. 278). Ref. in 1374 to his being pr. about 30 years before (*Cal. Misc. Inq.*, III, 353).

Thomas (le) Provost (Provest) –1349 Occ. 20 Mar. 1342, 15 June 1342 (*CFR 1337–47*, pp. 278, 292); 1343 forged common seal of Lonlay abbey (*Stogursey Chts.*, no. 260); 1346, 1347, 1348, 26 July 1349 (ibid., nos. 60, 62–5). Res. by 11 Sept. 1349 (*Reg. R. Shrewsbury*, II, no. 2401).

William (de) Hodierne (Oderne) *alias* **Fraunces** 1349–1350/1 Mentd as William Fraunces (*Stogursey Chts.*, no. 76). M. of Lonlay, adm. 11 Sept. 1349 (*Reg. R. Shrewsbury*, II, no. 2401). Res. by 7 Jan. 1351 (ibid., no. 2509, and see below).

John Gallard(i) (Galard(us), Gal(l)art, Gayl(l)ard) 1351–1374 Gt of keeping of priory 5 Sept. 1350, styled pr. (*CFR 1347–56*, pp. 253–4). M. of Lonlay, adm. 7 Jan. 1351 on res. of William (*Reg. R. Shrewsbury*, II, no. 2509). Occ. 20 Apr. 1360 (*CPR 1358–61*, p. 360); 26 Oct. 1371 (*CFR 1368–77*, p. 117). D. by 10 Oct. 1374 (*Stogursey Chts.*, no. 70).

Richard Amys (Armys) 1374– M. of Lonlay, pres. to king by vicar-general of the abb. of Lonlay 10 Oct. 1374 (PRO, C84/31/15); commn to administer goods of the priory, together with the care and rule of the monks 10 Oct. 1374 (*Stogursey Chts.*, no. 70). Pres. to bp of Bath and Wells for adm. on d. of last pr. 14 Oct. 1374 (*CPR 1374–77*, p. 9); adm. 1 (*sic, ? recte* 21) Oct. 1374 (*Stogursey Chts.*, no. 69). Occ. 1377 (*CFR 1368–77*, p. 405); 1384 (PRO, C269/15/43); 1386 'of the age of 40 years and more' (*Stogursey Chts.*, no. 76); 1389 (BL, Add. Cht. 76149); 1397 (*CPR 1399–1401*, p. 444); restoration of priory 13 Nov. 1399 (ibid., p. 71); 1 July 1400 (*Stogursey Chts.*, no. 82); 19 Apr. 1402 (*Reg. Bowet*, p. 30); 1403 (*Privy Council*, I, 192); 29 Sept. 1406 (*Stogursey Chts.*, no. 223).

STOKE BY CLARE (Suffolk), St John the Baptist (Bec) f. 1090 (at Clare); 1124 (at Stoke).

Lists in *VCH Suffolk*, II, 155; *Ctl. Stoke by Clare*, III, xi–xii; *Heads*, I, 110.

Richard Occ. 25 Apr. 1205 (*Ctl. Stoke*, I, no. 14; *Essex F.*, I, 34); Nov. 1219 x Jan. 1229 (ibid., p. 82 no. 104); 10 July 1225 (ibid., no. 103; *Llandaff Episcopal Acta*, no. 65); Easter term 1229 (*CRR*, XIII, no. 2110); 31 May 1229 as pr. of Stoke, parson of Crimplesham (*CPR 1225–32*, p. 290).

John de Havelers For name see *Ctl. Stoke*, II, no. 373. John de Havelers preceded John de Gineville in office (ibid., nos. 373n, 375) but it is impossible to distinguish the pr. Johns who occ. Oct. 1233 x Oct. 1234 to Oct. 1246 x Oct. 1247 (*Norfolk F. (Rye)*, pp. 50, 72). Occ. 27 Oct. 1234, 14 Apr. 1247, 23 Nov. 1247, 27 Apr. 1250 (*Ctl. Stoke*, I, nos. 13, 11, 12, 42). Occ. Easter 1250 to Mich. 1259 (*Essex F.*, I, 183, 231). Seal (E. Farrer. 'The seal of a prior of Stoke-by-Clare', *Proc. Suffolk Inst.*, XX (1930), 265–9).

John de Gineville (Guineville) –1265 Occ. mid-13th cent. (*Ctl. Stoke*, I, no. 375). Became abb. of Bec in Dec. 1265 (ibid., list, p. xi; *Gallia Christiana*, XI, 232–3; *Reg. Eudes of Rouen*, p. 607).

William Occ. Hil. 1278 (*Essex F.*, II, 17); Mich. 1278 (PRO, KB27/41, m. 39d); (W.) 1278 x 9

(*Chapters of Black Monks*, III, 266–8); Nov. 1279 x Nov. 1280, Nov. 1280 x Nov. 1281 (*Norfolk F. (Rye)*, p. 121).

Henry de Leone 1287– Pres. 18 Jan. 1287 (*Ctl. Stoke*, list, citing Bibliothèque Nationale, ms. Lat. 13905, f. 46r). Occ. Nov. 1295 x Nov. 1296 (PRO, E106/3/19, m. 11); Nov. 1296 x Nov. 1297 (PRO, E106/4/2, m. 4); Nov. 1298 x Nov. 1299 (PRO, E106/4/9, m. 3d); Easter 1300 (PRO, E106/4/14, m. 6); Nov. 1302 x Nov. 1303 (PRO, E106/4/18, m. 8d); 6 Nov. 1303 (*Ctl. Stoke*, II, no. 429b).

Henry de Dyva (Dyve) 1326– Adm. 6 Mar. 1326, no reason given for vacancy (Norwich, Reg/1/2, f. 6v). Occ. 8 Oct. 1326 (*Memo. Roll 1326–7*, p. 272); 30 May 1331 (*CCR 1330–33*, p. 319); 18 Feb. 1342 (*CFR 1337–47*, p. 273); 1343 (PRO, C269/15/18); 11 July 1345 (*CCR 1343–46*, p. 636). Ceased to be pr. by 12 Nov. 1349 (*CFR 1347–56*, p. 181).

John de Aqua Partita 1349–1352 M. of Bec, gt of keeping of priory during French war 12 Nov. 1349 (ibid., pp. 180–1). Cess. 17 Mar. 1352 (Norwich, Reg/2/4, f. 140v; cf. *CFR 1347–56*, pp. 328–9).

William de Bellomonte 1352– M. of Bec. letter of pres. 17 Mar. 1352; adm. 20 Apr. 1352 (Norwich, Reg/2/4, f. 140v). Royal gt of keeping of priory 20 May 1352 (*CFR 1347–56*, pp. 328–9).

Geoffrey de Braunvill 1354– Royal gt of keeping of priory 24 Apr. 1354 (ibid., p. 393). Occ. Mich. 1354 x Mich. 1355 (PRO, E372/200, rots. 16, 17d); Mich. 1358 x Mich. 1359 (PRO, E372/204, rots. 16–16d, 17d); 13 Oct. 1361 (*Reg. Sudbury*, I, 226).

Peter de Valle 1368– M. of Bec, pres. 28 Feb. 1368, adm. 22 Mar. 1368 (Norwich, Reg/2/5, f. 80r–v).

Priory void by d. of the last (unnamed) pr. 28 July 1374 when William de Sancto Vedasto, pr. of Ogbourne gtd keeping of the priory (*CFR 1368–77*, p. 257).

John (de) Henditot (Henditoft, Heuditot, Hudito) **1374/6–1391** M. of Bec, letter of pres. by abb. of Bec 4 Apr. 1374 (*sic*), adm. 6 Mar. 1376 (Norwich, Reg/3/6, ff. 42v–43r). Letter of pres. of abb. of Bec to Edmund Mortimer, earl of March 2 Nov. 1374 (BL, Add. ms. 6041, f. 63r, no. lviii); letter of pres. of same to same by pr. of Ogbourne, proctor of Bec, 2 Feb. 1376 (ibid., f. 63v, no. lix); letter of pr. of Ogbourne excusing certain faults found in the abb. of Bec's letter n.d. (ibid., f. 63v, no. lx); letter of Edmund Mortimer, earl of March, to bp of Norwich asking for John's instn Feb. 1376 (ibid., f. 63v, no. lxv). D. by 14 Sept. 1391 (Norwich, Reg/3/6, ff. 161v–162r; cf. *CPR 1388–92*, p. 514).

STRATFIELD SAYE (Berks), St Leonard (Valmont) f. c. 1170. Diss. 1399
No list in *VCH*.
John Occ. n.d. (mid-13th cent.) (Oxford, Queen's Coll. archives catalogue I, no. 249).
Roger Mentd as former pr. in 1265 (ECR., 18/26).
W. Occ. 1265 (ibid.).
Richard Temvile Occ. 8 June 1310, 25 Jan. 1316 (ibid., 18/29–30).
William Valeran (Waleran) Occ. 24 Mar. 1332 (*CPR 1330–34*, p. 262); 30 Nov. 1332, (?26) May 1334 (ECR., 18/32–3).
William Parmenter Occ. 9 Jan. 1340 (ibid., 18/34).
[**John le Fevre de Cormellan** OSB of the hermitage of Stratfield Saye. Occ. 25 Apr. 1341 (*CPR 1340–43*, p. 166) – does not say whether he is pr.]
Ralph (le) Provost of Valmont (de Valido Monte, Vaumont) M. of Valmont, attorney in England of the abb. of Valmont 8 May 1342 (*CPR 1340–43*, p. 418). Occ. as *custos* 12 June 1342 (ibid., p. 467); 3 Mar. 1345 (*CCR 1343–46*, p. 547); 11 July 1345 (Noion and Neufmarché) (ibid., p. 636); 1 Nov. 1345 (ECR., 18/35); 20 Nov. 1346 (*CFR 1337–47*, p. 488); 25 Nov. 1346 (*CCR 1346–49*, p. 123).

Peter Guyser (Guysyer) Gtd keeping of priory, not styled pr. 13 Oct. 1349 (*CFR 1347–56*, p. 165); as *custos* 7 Apr. 1353, 24 Aug. 1353 (ECR., 18/38, 40). Mentd as d. by 1 July 1359 (*CPR 1358–61*, p. 247).

Richard Anketil Occ. 1 July 1359, when gtd keeping of priory (ibid.).

William Helyes (Elya) Occ. 3 July 1363, 6 Jan. 1364, 13 Apr. 1365 (ECR., 18/41–3).

Richard Tud(d)enham, monk, gtd keeping of priory during French war, not styled pr. 22 May 1378 (*CFR 1377–83*, p. 95); desc. as farmer of the priory 23 Aug. 1378 (*CPR 1377–81*, p. 95). As m., gtd custody of the priory again 8 July 1379 (*CFR 1377–83*, p. 161).

SWAVESEY (Cambs), St Andrew (S. Serge, Angers) f. -1086

Lists in *VCH Cambs*, II, 318; Palmer, *Swavesey Priory*, pp. 34–40; *Heads*, I, 110.

John Occ. 1213+ (*Berkeley Chts.*, no. 91); 1228 (*CR 1227–31*, p. 91); Trin. term 1231, Easter term 1232 (*CRR*, XIV, nos. 1936, 2471); n.d. (*temp.* Henry III) (Tyson, *Rylands Chts.*, no. 49).

W. Occ. 1247 (PRO, C85/66/1).

Roger –1272 Occ. 31 Aug. 1257 (Tyson, *Rylands Chts.*, no. 50). Res. by 22 Nov. 1272 (Ely, G/1/3, f. 131v).

Geoffrey de Brynkeleye 1272– M. of S. Serge, adm. 22 Nov. 1272 (ibid.). Occ. Apr. 1288 (*Select Cases, Law Merchant*, I, 34–5). D. by 18 Apr. 1291 (ibid., 68–9).

John de Ponteseye (Punteseie) -1312 Occ. 6 May 1295 (ibid., 68); Nov. 1295 x Nov. 1296 (PRO, E106/3/19, m. 7); Nov. 1297 x Nov. 1298 (PRO, E106/4/8, m. 4); Nov. 1298 x Nov. 1299 (PRO, E106/4/9, m. 5d; E106/4/10, m. 6d); 1300 (PRO, E106/4/14, m. 9); Nov. 1302 x Nov. 1303 (PRO, E106/4/18, m. 12). Res. by 16 Feb. 1312 (Ely, G/1/3, f. 131v).

Oliver Britenis de Faugeriis (Filgeriis, Frangeriis, Fulgeriis) 1312–1314 M. of S. Serge. adm. 16 Feb. 1312 (ibid.). D. by 31 July 1314 (ibid.). D. at Carpentras mentd 1343 (*CPL*, III, 124).

Richard Burgensis 1314– M. of S. Serge, adm. 31 July 1314 (Ely, G/1/3, f. 131v). Occ. 30 Oct. 1339 (*CPR 1338–40*, p. 338). Lic. for absence 22 Oct. 1340 (Ely, G/1/1, part 1, f. 9v).

Stephen Guyntran(d) (de Gurtery, Bertrand, Brand) 1345– Petition to pope for prov. to priory gtd 20 Nov. 1343 (*CPP*, p. 30). M. of S. Serge, adm. 15 Jan. 1345, no reason given for vacancy (Ely, G/1/3, f. 131v). Pr. Oliver had d. within 2 days of the Curia and the priory was reserved by John XXII, Benedict XII and then by Clement VI. On 15 Jan. 1345 letters of Clement VI were exhibited reserving the priory to Stephen Guyntrand, m. of S. Serge. Previously, the abb. of S. Serge, not knowing of the reservation, had pres. Richard Burionus to William la Zouche, knt, by virtue of a composition, and he, in turn, had pres. him to the bp, who had adm. him. The pr. of Horsham, one of the executors of the papal letters of grace, had removed Richard Burionus and had invested Stephen with the priory. The abb. of S. Serge and Alan Zouche in due course pres. Stephen to the bp, who adm. him 15 Jan. 1345 (Ely, G/1/1, part 1, ff. 33v–34r, cf. *CPL*, III, 124; *Accts of Papal Collectors*, pp. 98, 126, 149). Occ. 20 Jan. 1345 (*CFR 1337–47*, p. 405); 17 Feb. 1347 (Ely, G/1/1, part 2, f. 9v); 2 Dec. 1347 (*CPR 1345–1348*, p. 437); 28 Apr. 1350 (*CCR 1349–54*, p. 216); 16 Mar. 1351 (*CFR 1347–56*, p. 284); Mich. 1354 x Mich. 1355 (PRO, E372/200 rot. 2).

John Witlesey 1355– M. of Thorney, coll. by bp 22 June 1355, no reason given for vacancy (Ely, G/1/3, f. 131v).

John Walk(e)lyn (Walkelin) 1362– M. of Westminster, coll. 31 Aug. 1362 *per lapsum temporis* (Ely, G/1/3, f.131v). Papal conf. of coll. 17 May 1363 (*CPP*, p. 422; cf. *Accts of Papal Collectors*, pp. 243, 281–2, 335, 375). Occ. 9 Feb. 1369 (*CCR 1369–74*, p. 70); going to Roman Curia 16 Feb. 1369 (*CPR 1367–70*, p. 215).

John Goldale 1370 M. of Selby, adm. 22 Jan. 1370, no reason given for vacancy (Ely, G/1/3, f. 131v).

Laurence Russell 1370–1388 M. of S. George de Hulso, adm. 6 Dec. 1370, no reason given for vacancy (Ely, G/1/3, f. 131v). Royal nomination to Hugh la Zouche, knt, 20 Nov. 1370 (*CPR 1370–74*, p. 14). Desc. as Englishman (PRO, C269/15/46). Res. by 7 Dec. 1388 (*CPR 1388–92*, p. 1).

TAKELEY (Essex), (S. Valéry) f. 1066 x 1086. Diss. *c.* 1391 and gtd to New College, Oxford
List in *VCH Essex*, III, 200.

Hugh Occ. early 13th cent. (pal: BL, Add. Cht. 28384).

[John de Mareskallo M. of S. Valéry. Removed as the abbey's proctor in England by 24 Feb. 1272 (*CPR 1266–72*, p. 630).]

[Bartholomew M. of S. Valéry. Royal protection for, apptd as proctor in England of abb. and convent of S. Valery, 24 Feb. 1272 (ibid.).]

John Occ. as 'pr. of S. Valéry in England' 13 June 1283 (Oxford, New College, Takeley 160/13023); 31 Mar. 1294 (*Cal. Chanc. Warr.*, p. 40); as pr. of Takeley 2 Nov. 1283 (Oxford, New College, Takeley 217/13071); 12 Mar. 1294 (Oxford, New College, Takeley 165/13029); Easter 1300 (PRO, E106/4/14, m. 9). Inq. held 20 May 1313 following John's d. (Oxford, New College, Takeley 218/13072);

Andrew de (la) Goue (Gova, Gova, Gave, Gora) M. of S. Valéry, occ. 25 Oct 1320 (*CPR 1317–21*, p. 512); 1324 (PRO, E106/5/2, m. 9); 6 Dec. 1325 (*CPR 1324–27*, p. 194); 1330 (*CCR 1330–33*, p. 2); 1336, 1337 (*CPR 1334–38*, pp. 356, 365, 443); 1338 (*CCR 1337–39*, pp. 523, 504); Mich. 1338 x Mich. 1339 (PRO, E372/184, rot. 5); 26 Feb. 1339, 2 July 1340, 2 Nov. 1340 (*CCR 1339–41*, pp. 103, 489, 647); 3 Feb. 1340 (*CPR 1338–40*, p. 416).

John de Maisiulio (Maisnilio, Maisuyl, Marsoilia, Masnilio, Meizinl) **–1357** Occ. 10 Mar. 1342, 26 Sept. 1344 (*CFR 1337–47*, pp. 267, 399); 11 July 1345 (*CCR 1343–46*, p. 636); 12 June 1348 surrendered custody (*CPR 1348–50*, p. 160), but gtd keeping of priory 16 June 1348 (*CFR 1347–56*, p. 867). Occ. 10 Dec. 1348 (*CPR 1348–50*, p. 216); Mich. 1348 x Mich. 1349 (PRO, E372/194, rot. 7); 20 June 1354 (Oxford, New College, Takeley 63/12938); Mich. 1354 x Mich. 1355 (ibid., E372/200, rot. 4); 20 July 1357 (Oxford, New College, Takeley 138/13002).

Firmin de Founteynes (Fontanis, Founteneys) M. of S. Valéry, proctor in England of the abbey of S. Valéry, gtd keeping of priory during the French war 24 Nov. 1357 on d. of John de Maisiulio (*CFR 1356–68*, p. 52; Oxford, New College, Takeley 233/13086). Occ. Jan. 1358 x Jan. 1359 (PRO, E210/6425); 1 May 1360 (*CPR 1377–81*, p. 181; *CPR 1370–74*, p. 265); 1362, 1367, 1368 (*Reg. Sudbury*, I, pp. 231, 254, 261); 11 June 1369, 20 May 1370 (*CFR 1368–77*, pp. 16, 82); 1370 (PRO, E179/42/31); 1374 (PRO, Coram Rege roll 48 Edward III, cited *TEAS*, XVII, 48).

Gerard de Oissencourt (Doissencourt, Oessencourt, Ossencourt) **1375–** Gtd custody of Takeley by Firmin, abb. of S. Valéry 30 Sept. 1375 (Oxford, New College, Takeley 16/12896). Occ. *c.* 1373 x 1376 in a petition to the king (A. K. McHardy, 'Effects of war on Church . . . in fourteenth century', p. 292, no. 6); 19 July 1376 (*CPR 1368–77*, p. 358); 5 Nov. 1377, 8 May 1378, 15 May 1381 (*CFR 1377–83*, pp. 32, 88, 251); 24 Feb. 1384, 8 Sept. 1386 (*CFR 1383–91*, p. 39; *CPR 1383–91*, pp. 39, 149).

3 June 1391 Abb. of S. Valéry gts all English properties to New College, Oxford (Oxford, New College, Takeley 14/12894; 15/12895).

THROWLEY (Kent) (S. Bertin, S. Omer) f. *c.* 1150. Diss. *c.* 1414
List in *VCH Kent*, II, 240.

Folcard M. of St Bertin, occ. as proctor (?in England) in case concerning Throwley June 1218 (*Chartes de S. Bertin*, I, no. 562).

Hugh Occ. as proctor in England of abbey from 1 May 1221 to 16 March 1233 (ibid., I, nos. 605, 632, 679–81, 759, 808); n.d. proctor of Throwley (ibid., no. 843); 1225 (S. Omer, ms. 746, part II, ff. 223v, 225r).

[br. **Richard** *dictus* **Digun/?im** occ. as *custos* of the churches of Throwley and Chilham 10 Aug. 1269 (S. Omer, ms. 746, part II, f. 236r).]

Walter Occ. as proctor of Throwley Oct. x Nov. 1272 (*Chartes de S. Bertin*, II, no. 1153; S. Omer, ms. 746, part II, f. 195r).

Peter de Insula M. and proctor of Throwley. Occ. Nov. 1295 x Nov. 1296 (PRO, E106/3/19, m. 5d); 10 July 1296 (S. Omer, ms. 746, part II, f. 242v); Nov. 1296 x Nov. 1297 (PRO, E106/4/2, m. 2d); 9 July 1297 (*Chartes de S. Bertin*, II, no. 1380); Nov. 1297 x Nov. 1298 (PRO, E106/4/8, m. 2); Nov. 1298 x Nov. 1299 (PRO, E106/4/9, m. 3; E106/4/10, m. 3d). Mentd as dead on 5 Feb. 1309 (*Chartes de S. Bertin*, no. 1433; S. Omer, ms. 746, part II, ff. 244v–246r).

William de Poperinghes (Poperinge, Poperinghe) Occ. proctor 1 May 1305 (*Chartes de S. Bertin*, II, no. 1424; S. Omer, ms. 746, part II, f. 238v); 5 Feb. 1309 (*Chartes de S. Bertin*, no. 1433; S. Omer, ms. 746, part II, f. 245v); proctor 11 Feb. 1310 (*Chartes de S. Bertin*, no. 1436); 15 July 1315 (S. Omer, ms. 746, part II, ff. 242r, 246v).

Walter *dictus* **Bloc** (le Blok) Occ. July 1325 x July 1326 (PRO, E106/5/4, m. [13]); 6 July 1326 (S. Omer, ms. 746, part II, f. 257r); 8 Oct. 1326 (*Memo. Roll 1326–7*, p. 273); 25 Feb. 1327 (S. Omer, ms. 746, part II, f. 244r).

Giles de Ardembourgh (Ardenburgh, Audenburgh) M. of S. Bertin, occ. as proctor 8 July 1344 (*Chartes de S. Bertin*, II, no. 1611; S. Omer, ms. 746, part II, f. 250v); proctor 1345 (*Chartes de S. Bertin*, no. 1613; S. Omer, ms. 746, part II, f. 203r); proctor 1356 (*Chartes de S. Bertin*, no. 1678; S. Omer, ms. 746, part II, f. 255r); 1356 (*CCR 1354–60*, p. 321); proctor 1361 (Lambeth, Reg. Islip, ff. 289r, 291v); pr. 1367 (*Chartes de S. Bertin*, II, nos. 1740, 1748; S. Omer, ms. 746, part II, ff. 256r, 261r); 11 June 1369, 6 Oct. 1369 (*CFR 1368–77*, pp. 16, 26).

Bartholomew Occ. 16 Jan. 1370 (Lambeth, Reg. Whittlesey, f. 161r).

James Scotelare (Scoteler, Stotelare) Occ. 18 July 1376, 20 Feb. 1377 (*CFR 1368–77*, pp. 358, 383; *Chartes de S. Bertin*, II, nos. 1876, 1885); 17 July 1377 (ibid., no. 1893).

TICKFORD (Newport Pagnell) (Bucks), St Mary (Marmoutier) f. 1110
   Lists in *VCH Bucks*, I, 364; *Heads*, I, 110.

Hugh −1220 Occ. 1214 (*CRR*, VII, 51). Res. by 23 June 1220 (*Reg. Wells*, II, 51–2).

William 1220–1231 Adm. 23 June 1220 (ibid.). 1228 disturbance at Tickford and pr. William and all but three of the monks exiled (*Ann. Dunstable*, p. 109). Res. 28 July 1231 (*Reg. Wells*, II, 87–8).

John of Colne (Colna, Kolna) **1232–1233** M. of Spalding, coll. by bp *per lapsum temporis* 24 Jan. 1232 (ibid., 87–9). Res. 26 Sept. 1233 (ibid., 93–5). Chapel of Eastwood assigned to him for his maintenance (ibid., 94–5).

Robert Hamelin 1233− M. of Tickford, adm. 11 Oct. 1233 (ibid., 93–6).

Oliver Occ. 18 Feb. 1236 (BL, Cotton ms. Vespasian E XIX, f. 42v); 29 Oct. 1254 (PRO, Bucks F., CP25/1/16/33, no. 14). *Mon. Angl.*, V, 201 gives occ. 1259, but no source. Erroneously (?) occ. 1 Apr. 1271 (*YB 7 Richard II*, p. 91).

Gilbert −1268 Occ. *c.* 1262 (*Mon. Angl.*, V, 201, from Willis). Res. by 7 May 1268 (*Reg. R. Gravesend*, p. 242).

Bartholomew 1268–1270 Adm. 7 May 1268 (ibid.). D. by 22 Oct. 1270 (ibid., p. 246).

Reginald de Cossam *alias* **Bernevalle 1270–** M. of Tickford, apptd 22 Oct. 1270. inst. 25 Oct. 1270 (ibid., pp. 246, 343). On 4 Feb. (1275) countess Alice of Blois writes to Edward I asking for priors to be established by force at Holy Trinity, York, and Tickford (PRO, SC1/15/71); abb. of Marmoutier writes to the king about disputes at the two priories 11 Feb. 1275 (PRO, SC1/19/99). Reginald (de Bernevalle) signified for arrest; excommunicated now for more than 2 years (Logan, *Runaway Religious*, p. 185; PRO, C81/1786/26).

Simon de Reda (Redd', Rede, Beda) **–1291** Occ. 13 Oct. 1275 (*Bucks F.*, II, 33); royal protection for 2 years 21 Apr. 1278 (*CPR 1272–81*, p. 262). Pr. Simon reported as imprisoned by renegade monks led by Reginald de Donynton. Reginald de Grey apptd to custody of priory and pr. Simon taken into the king's protection. Grey is to reinstate the pr. 25 June 1278 (ibid., p. 272). Commn of oyer and terminer regarding the enormities committed against pr. Simon 17 Sept. 1278 (ibid., p. 293). Occ. Mich. 1278 x Mich. 1279; Mich. 1280 x Mich. 1281 (E159/52, m. 11; E159/54, m. 23d); 1282 (PRO, C85/100/36). Occ. 7 Oct. 1290 in connection with visitation dispute between the bp of Lincoln and the abb. of Marmoutier (*CPL*, I, 521). Dep. 27 Sept. 1291 in bp's visitation for dilapidations, incontinence and homicide (*Reg. Sutton*, VIII, 128). Visitation dispute settled Feb. 1292 (ibid.).

Geoffrey Villicus (Vig') **1292–1302** M. of Marmoutier, adm. 20 Feb. 1292, prof. obed. 1 Nov. 1292 (ibid., 128–37, 138–43). Occ. 14 Apr. 1301 (PRO, C85/6/25). Res. by 5 June 1302 (Lincoln, Ep. Reg., II, f. 175r–v).

William Occ. as *custos* from Nov. 1295 x Nov. 1296 to Nov. 1298 x Nov. 1299 (PRO, E106/3/19, m. 7; E106/4/9, m. 12); (as pr.) E106/4/10, m. 2d).

William de Meneria (Manureria, Manuteria) **1302–1332** M. of Marmoutier, pres. 5 June 1302, adm. 4 July 1302 (Lincoln, Ep. Reg., II, f. 175r–v). Occ. going overseas 22 Apr. 1309 (*CPR 1307–13*, p. 110). Res. by 17 May 1332 (Lincoln, Ep. Reg., IV, f. 341r).

Fulk of Champagne (Caumpaynettes, Champynettes, Chaumpaignetes, Chaumpaynettes) **1332–1349** M. of Marmoutier, letter of pres. 17 May 1332, adm. 15 June 1332 (ibid.). Occ. (Hugh) 6 Mar. 1349 (*CFR 1347–56*, p. 105). D. by 2 July 1349 (ibid., p. 143), presumably by 26 May (see next entry).

William Conqueterre (Caiketre, Canqueterre, Cauketere, Cauketre, Coketarre) **1349–1351** M. of Marmoutier, apptd by abb. of Marmoutier on the d. of pr. Fulk 2 July 1349 (ibid.); letter of pres. 26 May 1349, adm. 13 Aug. 1349 (Lincoln, Ep. Reg., IX, f. 287r). Occ. 1 Mar. 1351, 14 June 1351 (*CCR 1349–54*, pp. 349, 369); exchanged priory with John de Garriz 2 Mar. 1351 (*CPL*, III, 362). Had ceased to be pr. by 16 Sept. 1351 (*CFR 1347–56*, p. 307).

John de Garriz (Gariz, Garroz, Garrys, Garryz, Guryz) **1351–** Papal prov. 2 Mar. 1351, by way of exchange with William Conqueterre, prev. pr. (*CPL*, III, 362). Royal gt of keeping of priory 16 Sept. 1351 (*CPR 1347–56*, p. 307). Occ. Mich. 1358 x Mich. 1359 (PRO, E372/204, rots. 1, 31d); 22 Oct. 1359 (*CPR 1358–61*, p. 289); 2 Aug. 1360 (ibid., p. 448). On 17 Sept. 1361 an instn was made to Bradwell vicarage on the pres. of 2 named monks of Tickford, neither designated as pr., ? a vacancy (Lincoln, Ep. Reg., IX, f. 320r).

[**John de Fresnay** Occ. 1362 (*Mon. Angl.*, V, 201, no source).]

Francis Quatersoule 1364– M. of Marmoutier, adm. 20 Jan. 1364, no reason given for vacancy (Lincoln, Ep. Reg., X, f. 409r).

William de Alneto (Dathy, Lateneus) **1365–** M. of Marmoutier, adm. 13 Feb. 1365, no reason given for vacancy (ibid., f. 410v). Occ. 6 Oct. 1369 (*CFR 1368–77*, p. 23); in return of aliens 1370 (*Buckingham Writ Reg.*, p. 40, no. 116). Priory desc. as being without a pr. 28 Oct. 1375 (*CFR 1368–77*, p. 305), although John is desc. as pr. in return of aliens in response to writ of 6 Mar. 1374 (PRO, C269/15/36).

John Drieu (Drewe, Drien) Occ. 1374 (see previous entry); 20 July 1376 (*CFR 1368–77*, p. 359). Mentd as farmer of the priory 26 Oct. 1389 (*CPR 1388–92*, p. 143). Occ. Hil. 1393 (*Bucks*

Inquests and Indictments, no. 570). Priory restored to him 6 Dec. 1399 (*CPR 1399–1401*, p. 71).
John Colle occ. Jan. 1403 (*Privy Council*, I, 194). Revocation of letters patent gting priory to John Colle, m. of Shrewsbury, as by letters patent it was gtd to John Drieu. He was expelled by John Colle but is now returned to possession 13 July 1403 (*CPR 1401–05*, pp. 246–7).

TITLEY (Hereford), St Peter (Tiron) f. 1120 x 1. Diss. 1391.
Geoffrey Occ. from Nov. 1295 x Nov. 1296 to Nov. 1297 x Nov. 1298 (PRO, E106/3/19, m. 10d; PRO, E106/4/8, m. 4d); Easter 1300 (PRO, E106/4/14, m. 12).
William de Silesiis 1301– M. of Tiron, adm. 14 Apr. 1301 in the pres. of Geoffrey, pr. of St Cross, proctor of the abb. and convent of Tiron, no reason given for vacancy (*Reg. Swinfield*, pp. 378–9).
Thomas de Marigneio 1313– M. of Tiron, inst. 5 June 1313, no reason given for vacancy (ibid., p. 488).
Richard of Beaumont-le-Roger (de Beaumont Rogeri) Put in charge by abb. of Tiron, in the pres. of the abbey's proctors 8 July 1314 (ibid., p. 493).
William de Yllesiis –1325 Res. by 12 Apr. 1325 (*Reg. Orleton (Hereford)*, p. 323).
Ralph le Heremite 1325– M. of Tiron, adm. 12 Apr. 1325 (ibid.).
Geoffrey de Insula Occ. 25 July 1327 (*Reg. Martival*, I, 376; WCM, no. 4280a).
Richard Baderum (Baderoun) **1332–** M. of Tiron, mand. to induct after instn 20 May 1332, cert. of induction 25 May 1332 (*Reg. T. Charlton*, pp. 19–20, 77).
Arnold Occ. 20 Oct. 1346 (*Reg. Trillek*, p. 288).
Arnulph de Scopulo 1347–1348 M. of Tiron, adm. (Arnuld) 31 Dec. 1347 (ibid., p. 374). Res. (Arnulph) by 3 Oct. 1348 (ibid., pp. 39–40).
William Sallerii 1348– M. of Tiron, inst. 3 Oct. 1348 (ibid.), in return of aliens in response to writ of 1 Sept. 1351 (PRO, C269/15/32).
Gt to William Bastard, chaplain, of the keeping of the alien priory of Titley, void, to hold from Easter last 'until a pr. come there from parts beyond seas', 20 June 1372 (*CFR 1368–77*, p. 174).
No further prs. known, but the house was void 4 July 1374 (ibid., p. 252). Dissolved 1391 and granted to Winchester College.

TOFT MONKS (Norfolk), St Margaret (S. Pierre, Préaux). f. *temp*. William II. Diss. *c*. 1414 granted to Witham Charterhouse.
Nicholas Occ. from Nov. 1295 x Nov. 1296 to Nov. 1298 x Nov. 1299 (PRO, E106/3/19, m. 11; E106/4/9. m. 3d; E106/4/10, m. 4); 7 Feb. 1296, 23 Mar. 1297 (*CPR 1292–1301*, pp. 177, 270).
[**Ralph Morel** occ. 10 Oct. 1318 as proctor-general in England of abbey of Préaux (*Reg. Martival*, I, 115) ? pr. of Toft Monks.]
Roger de Gresteno Occ. 17 Feb. 1327 as pr. of Toft Monks and proctor of Préaux (*Reg. Martival*, I, 369, cf. ibid., 370, 372 where he is just described as proctor of Préaux).
Unnamed pr. occ. 26 July 1338 but had ceased to be pr. by 1 Sept. 1338 (*CFR 1337–47*, p. 93).
Thomas Heynfre (Heinfre, Hemfr', Hynefrend) Occ. as proctor in England of Préaux abbey 15 May 1341, 20 May 1341 (*CFR 1337–47*, p. 224; *CPR 1340–43*, p. 199). Occ. as pr. 6 Feb. 1342 (*CFR 1337–47*, p. 273); 20 June 1344 (*CCR 1343–46*, p. 391); 11 July 1345 (ibid., p. 637).
Robert de Magnavilla Occ. 25 June 1349 (*CFR 1347–56*, p. 143); Mich. 1354 x Mich. 1355 (PRO, E372/200, rot. 16–16d); Mich. 1358 x Mich. 1359 (PRO, E372/204, rots. 16, 17, 25).
Richard Vateman (Vatemon) Also pr. of Warmington occ. 1366 (q.v.), proctor-general of Préaux, occ. 13 Feb., 17 June 1360, 17 Aug. 1361 (*CFR 1356–68*, pp. 118, 127; *Reg. Stretton*,

I, 22); as pr. of Toft Monks 4 Jan. 1362 (ibid., 27); also as pr. of Toft Monks and Warmington 31 Jan. 1366 (ibid., 37–8); 11 June 1369, 11 June 1370 (*CFR 1368–77*, pp. 13, 81).

Clement Hulyn (Hugelyn) **–1385** Occ. 22 July 1376, 28 May 1377 (ibid., pp. 358, 403); 5 Nov. 1377, 8 May 1378 (*CFR 1377–83*, pp. 32, 93). Mich. 1379 – Feb. 1383 (*Cal. Misc. Inq.*, IV, 134). Desc. as former pr. by 10 Feb. 1385 (*CCR 1381–85*, p. 611). Desc. as m. not pr. when gtd keeping of the priory 13 Mar. 1388, also occ. 28 Nov. 1388 (*CFR 1383–91*, pp. 225, 263).

TOTNES (Devon), St Mary (S. Serge, Angers) f. *c.* 1088
   Lists in Oliver, pp. 239–40; Watkin, *Totnes Priory*, II, pp. 998–9; *Heads*, I, 110–11.
John Occ. n.d. (early 13th cent. ? *c.* 1216) (Devon RO, Hole of Park, 312M/TY53; TY62; Watkin, I, 113–14, 122–3, 125).
[**G. de Molesia** Occ. as pr. n.d. (? early-mid 13th cent.) (Oliver, p. 239, no source).]
Peter Occ. n.d. (13th cent., *temp.* William Cantilupe junior, lord of Totnes – poss. William II succ. 1239, d. 1251) (Devon RO, Hole of Park 312M/TY67).
Nicholas Occ. 30 Jan. 1260 (*Reg. Bronescombe*, p. 272; *Reg. W. Bronescombe*, I, no. 212); 3 May 1262, 10 Feb. 1263 (Devon RO, Hole of Park, 312M/TY69–70); 10 Feb. 1263 (*Devon F.*, I, p. 321, no. 629; Watkin, *Totnes*, I, p. 162); 15 Apr. 1269 (Devon RO, Hole of Park, 312M/TY77); 7 Mar. 1276, 4 Jan. 1277, 5 June 1280, 29 Sept. 1281 (ibid., TY90–93). Oliver, p. 239, gives occ. 3 Mar. 1283 (no source).
John de Vendagio 1284– Adm. 12 Mar. 1284, no reason given for vacancy (*Reg. Quivil*, p. 357).
Robert Occ. 29 Dec. 1288, 11 Mar. 1289, 23 Apr. 1289 (Devon RO, Hole of Park, 312M/TY94–5, 97).
Geoffrey Occ. 6 Apr. 1294, 15 Apr. 1306 (Devon RO, Hole of Park, 312M/TY98–9); Nov. 1295 x Nov. 1296 (PRO, E106/3/19, m. 10d); Nov. 1296 x Nov. 1297 (PRO, E106/4/2, m. 2); Trin. term 1297 (*Coram Rege Roll*, pp. 189, 207); Nov. 1298 x Nov. 1299 (PRO, E106/4/9, m. 1d; E106/4/10, m. 2d); Easter 1300 (PRO, E106/4/14, m. 4); Nov. 1302 x Nov. 1303 (PRO, E106/4/18, m. 4d).
Jocelin (Josselin) –1322 Occ. 27 Nov. 1307, 22 Dec. 1307 (Devon RO, Hole of Park, 312M/TY100–1); 26 Feb. 1314 (*Reg. Bytton*, p. 424); monition to reside in priory 23 Mar. 1317 (*Reg. Stapeldon*, pp. 390–1); 26 Feb. 1314 (ibid., pp. 235, 265); 7 May 1318 (ibid., p. 86). D. 22 July 1322 (ibid., p. 265).
Robert de Conka 1323– M. of S. Serge, inst. 13 Jan. 1323 (ibid.). Occ. Mich. 1328 (*Index to Placita de Banco*, p. 92); 12 Sept. 1334 (*Reg. Grandisson*, II, 764); 31 Jan 1340 (ibid., II, 924). Suspended from admin. of temps. during bp's visitation 23 Dec. 1348, and Br. Peter Burgoil, m. of Totnes and Andrew de Cheverestone, priest, apptd administrators of priory 24 Dec. 1348 (ibid., II, 1075). D. 3 Mar. (Watkin, I, p. 273, 'according to the obituary calendar of Tywardraith (*sic*) priory').
Roger Occ. 7 Oct. 1351 (PRO, C269/15/31).
Michael (de) Bouges (Boges) **1353–1372** M. of S. Serge, proxy for William Bouges, pr. of Tywardreath to nominate 7 Oct. 1353; letter of pres. 16 Dec. 1353; inst. 27 Dec. 1353 (*Reg. Grandisson*, III, 1429–30). Occ. 1 Apr. 1354 (*CPR 1347–56*, p. 392); 28 Oct. 1361 (*CPR 1381–85*, p. 205). D. by 27 Oct. 1372 (*Reg. Brantingham*, I, 23).
[**Thomas de la Ryvere 1373–** Gt of keeping of priory 8 Mar. 1373 (*CFR 1368–77*, p. 205). (Note below, 'Vacat' because priory gtd to J. le Bouers as appears below).]
John (de/le) Bouers (Boners, Bouer', Boures, Rouers) **1372–1382** M. of S. Serge, nominated by king for pres. by William la Zouche, lord of Harringworth 14 Oct. 1372 (*CPR 1370–74*, p. 204). Adm. 29 Oct. 1372 on death of Michael de Bouges (*Reg. Brantingham*, I, 23). Gt of keeping of priory 12 May 1373 (*CFR 1368–77*, p. 212). Occ. 1379 x 1380 (PRO, E179/24/9,

m. 1). D. by 10 July 1382 (*CFR 1377–83*, p. 322). Commn to sequestrate goods of the priory on d. of pr. John 11 July 1382 (*Reg. Brantingham*, I, 471).

TUTBURY (Staffs), St Mary (S. Pierre-sur-Dives) f. 1080
  Lists in *VCH Staffs*, III. 339; *Ctl. Tutbury*, p. 21; *Heads*, I, 111.
Bartholomew Occ. (B.) j. d. +28 July 1210 (*HMC Rutland*, IV, 33–4; cf. Cheney, *Inn. III*, no. 873); (B.) 1215 x 1216 (*Cheshire Chts.*, p. 23); 1216 x 1222 (*Burton Chts.*, nos. 72–3); 7 Apr. 1218 (*Ctl. Tutbury*, no. 356). For his name see also *Derbys Chts.*, nos. 1159, 2125.
Nicholas Occ. 17 May 1226 (*Derbys F. (1886)*, p. 17= *Ctl. Tutbury*, no. 290); 11 Aug. 1227 (*CPR 1225–32*, p. 137); Nov. 1227 (*Staffs F.*, 2, pp. 224, 226; *Staffs Plea Rolls, Henry III*, p. 59); 24 June 1230, 4 Sept. 1230 (*Ctl. Tutbury*, nos. 296, 291); 6 Oct. 1230 (*Staffs Plea Rolls, Henry III*, p. 80); 4 Sept. 1230 (*Derbys F. (1886)*, p. 28); Mich. term 1230 (*CRR*, XIV, no. 563).,
Fulk Occ. *c.* 1235, *c.* 1240 (*Ctl. Tutbury*, nos. 287, 141); 8 Oct. 1234 (*CPR 1232–47*, p. 73).
William de Sentelleys Mentd as pr. *temp.* Henry III (*Staffs Plea Rolls 1360–87*, p. 192). His position in the sequence of priors is unclear.
William de Truard Occ. *c.* 1245 (*Ctl. Tutbury*, no. 260).
William Occ. 29 May 1248 (*Warws F.*, I, no. 681; *Ctl. Tutbury*, no. 292); 1256, *c.* 1260 (ibid., nos. 201, 212); 5 Apr. 1252 (*Derbys F. (1886)*, p. 56).
William de Favers (Faveriis) **–1262** Occ. 28 Apr. 1262 (*Ctl. Tutbury*, no. 94). D. 1262 (*Ann. Burton*, p. 500).
Geoffrey de Beumes (Beumys) **1262–1266** Succ. 1262 (ibid.). Occ. 5 Feb. 1263 (*CR 1261–64*, p. 283); 28 Sept. 1263, 1266 (*Ctl. Tutbury*, nos. 95, 289).
William Occ. 18 Nov. 1285 (*Derbys F. (1891)*, p. 16).
Robert Mentd as former pr. 1316, ? before 1286 (*Ctl. Tutbury*, p. 96, no. 100, n.4). His place in the sequence of priors is uncertain.
Walter (?**le Mouner**) Prob. the Walter le Mouner, m. of Tutbury, el. *temp.* Edward I (*YB 11–12 Edward III*, pp. 17–22, see below). Occ. Nov. 1296 x Nov. 1297 (PRO, E106/4/2, m. 6d); 22 Apr. 1301 (Lichfield, B/A/1/1, f. 23v); 27 Oct. 1303 (*Ctl. Tutbury*, p. 159, no. 17, citing PRO, DL27/96). Seal (*Mon. Seals*, pp. 90–1).
Robert de Longden (Langedon, Longedon) **1308–1329** The right of appt had devolved to the bp of Lichfield and he commns the archdn of Chester to choose a pr. in his name 17 July 1308 (Lichfield, B/A/1/1, f. 71r). Coll. (Walter) by lapse [ ] Aug. 1308 (PRO, LR14/350). Bp conf. commissary's appt 12 Mar. 1309 (Lichfield, B/A/1/1, f. 71r). Occ. Mich. 1327 – Trinity 1329 (*Index to Placita de Banco*, p. 89). Abb. of Burton 1329 (q.v.).
John de Sancto Albino (Albyno) **1329–1336** M. of S. Pierre, pr. of Wolston in 1324 x 6; letter of pres. 21 Sept. 1329, adm. 30 Sept. 1329 (Lichfield, B/A/1/1, f. 145v; PRO, LR14/350). Occ. [1332 x 1333] (PRO, C270/12/18). Res. by 24 Jan. 1336 (Lichfield, B/A/1/2, f. 159r). Previously occ. as proctor in England of abb. of S. Pierre 10 Oct. 1327 (*CCR 1327–30*, p. 229).
Hilary term 1337 sub-pr. and convent of Tutbury summoned to answer Henry, earl of Lancaster, in a plea that they should permit him to pres. a fit person to the priory which was vacant. The earl said he had pres. John de Sancto Albino, by whose res. the priory was now vacant. The convent said that in the reign of Edward I they had el. one Walter le Mouner, m. of Tutbury, and had pres. him to earl Thomas, who had pres. him to the bp. As for John de Sancto Albino they say that the vacancy they el. **Giles of Longford** (Longeford), m. of Tutbury, and had pres. him to the earl who had refused to adm. him. John de Sancto Albino had been pres. by the earl. The convent had moved a plea in the Court Christian against John and had appealed to the Papal Curia, and the said plea was now pending. John had res.

the priory 'perceiving that the judgment would be against him'. Judgment in favour of the earl. (*Staffs Plea Rolls 1–15 Edward III*, pp. 72–3; *YB 11–12 Edward III*, pp. 17–22).

Alexander de Portu 1336–1347 Kidnapped on way back from visiting the bp (*SHC*, I, 267). M. of S. Pierre, letter of pres. 14 Jan. 1336, adm. 25 Jan. 1336 (Lichfield, B/A/1/2, f. 159r; PRO, LR14/350). See mand. of Pope Clement VI of 27 June 1342 to revoke Alexander's possession of the priory. He had been intruded by the abbey of S. Pierre, of which he was a monk (*Orig. Papal Letters*, pp. 89–90, no. 178). Res. on 14 Dec. 1347 (Lichfield, B/A/1/2, ff. 179v–180r).

Peter Vasseur (Vasseour, Wasseur) **1347–** M. of S. Pierre, letter of pres. 9 Dec. 1347, adm. 16 Dec. 1347 (ibid.; PRO, LR14/350). Occ. 10 Feb. 1348 (*CFR 1347–56*, p. 73); 1354 (*CCR 1354–60*, p. 55); 1356 (*CPR 1354–58*, p. 465); Mich. 1358 x Mich. 1359 (PRO, E372/204, rot. 24–24d); Easter 1361 (PRO, CP40/406, attorneys m. 4); 12 May 1361 (*CCR 1360–64*, p. 261).

William Beloc 1362– M. of S. Pierre, inst. 10 June 1362, no reason given for vacancy (*Reg. Stretton*, I, 111). Occ. 1 May 1364, 25 Apr. 1371 (*Ctl. Tutbury*, nos. 101–2); 1364 (*Staffs Plea Rolls 1360–87*, p. 47); 1366 (Lincoln, Ep. Reg., X, f. 166r); 1370 (PRO, E106/10/2); also in return of aliens in response to a writ of 6 Mar. 1374 (PRO, C269/15/36).

John Bellocier 1377–1404 M. of S. Pierre, m. of Tutbury, (Philip) apptd 26 Nov. 1377, no reason given for vacancy (*Reg. Stretton*, I, 144). Occ. as John 8 Feb. 1378 (*CFR 1377–83*, p. 82); 31 May 1392 (*Ctl. Tutbury*, no. 298); 13 Feb. 1404 (*CPR 1401–5*, p. 366). Res. 18 June 1404 (Lichfield, B/A/1/7, f. 58v).

TYWARDREATH (Cornwall), St Andrew (S. Serge, Angers) f. *c.* 1088
Lists in Oliver, pp. 34–5; *Heads*, I, 111.

Andrew Occ. late 12th or early 13th cent. (Oliver, p. 42; *Heads*, I, 111 and n. 8).

Simon Occ. n.d. (1220 x 1244) (Cornwall RO, AR.1/815).

Theobald Occ. n.d. ? *c.* 1225 (ibid., AR.1/60–1); (T.) *c.* 1225 (*Ctl. Launceston*, no. 533; cf. *EEA*, 11, no. 110B).

Michael –1263 Occ. 11 June 1251 (Cornwall RO, AR.1/841); 8 July 1251 (*Cornwall F.*, I, p. 71, no. 139). D. 4 Mar. 1263 (*Reg. Bronescombe*, p. 277; *Reg. W. Bronescombe*, I, no. 473). [A pr. Odo occ. 13 Oct. 1251 (*Cornwall F.*, I, p. 69, no. 138), but since the other party in this final concord is also called Odo there is the possibility of a scribal error.].

Geoffrey 1263– Adm. 22 May 1263 (*Reg. Bronescombe*, pp. 277–8; *Reg. W. Bronescombe*, II, no. 478). Occ. 26 Aug. 1263 (*Reg. Bronescombe*, p. 156; *Reg. W. Bronescombe*, II, no. 491).

Roger de Fontibus 1270– Adm. 13 June 1270 (*Reg. Bronescombe*, p. 188; *Reg. W. Bronescombe*, II, no. 808). Obit 12 Oct. (Oliver, p. 34).

John Occ. 14 May 1284 (*Cornwall F.*, I, p. 175, no. 303). If he is to be identified with pr. John Leonter, his obit was kept on 6 Apr. (Oliver, p. 34).

James Occ. Easter 1288 (PRO, CP40/72, m. 35d). Obit 22 Mar. (Oliver, p. 34).

Philip –1333 Occ. Nov. 1296 x Nov. 1297 (PRO, E106/4/2, m. 6); Nov. 1297 x Nov. 1298 (PRO, E106/4/8, m. 4d); Nov. 1298 x Nov. 1299 (PRO, E106/4/9, m. 9); Easter 1300 (PRO, E106/4/14, m. 11d). Lic. to visit mother house 13 Aug. 1310, 27 Apr. 1318, 23 June 1319 (*Reg. Stapeldon*, p. 395). Occ. July 1325 x July 1326 (PRO, E106/5/4, m. [7d]). Priory restored to him 22 Jan. 1329 following his suspension during visitation (*Reg. Grandisson*, I, 454–5). Commn to hear accts of William, pr. of Minster, apptd co-adjutor, 17 Sept. 1331 (ibid., II, 631). D. 25 May 1333 after long rule (*CTG*, III, 107; cf. *Reg. Grandisson*, II, 695–6).

William Bouges (Boges, Bouge) **1333–1370** Pr. of Minster, coll. by lapse 17 Nov. 1333 (*Reg. Grandisson*, III, 1296). Occ. 1370 (PRO, E106/10/2). D. by 1 Nov. 1370 (*Reg. Brantingham*, I, 12).

William de la Hay(e) (Lahaie) 1370–?1396 M. of Tywardreath, previously gtd keeping of the priory 2 May 1370 (*CFR 1368–77*, p. 76). Royal pres. to priory on acct of the war 25 Oct. 1370; nomination to Edward, prince of Wales 30 Oct. (*CPR 1370–74*, pp. 5, 7). Inst. 1 Nov. 1370 (*Reg. Brantingham*, I, 12). Papal mand. to conf. eln if found fit after the usual examination in Latin 25 Apr. 1372 (*CPL*, IV, 174; cf. *Accts of Papal Collectors*, pp. 463–4). Excommunication of pr. 1386 (*Reg. Brantingham*, II, 625). Said to d. 18 June 1399 (*CTG*, III, 107). D. by 3 Nov. 1399 when his succ., John Maslyn, pres. (*CPR 1399–1401*, p. 138; cf. *Reg. Stafford*, p. 216), but cf. *CFR 1391–99*, p. 173, gt to William Arundell and John Pygot of keeping of the priory, to hold the same from the time of the death of William de la Hay, late pr. and last farmer of priory, for as long as the French war shall last, 20 June 1396.

UPAVON (Wilts), (S. Wandrille) f. -1086. Cell 12th cent. Granted to Ivychurch in 1423
  List in *VCH Wilts*, III, 397.
Robert de Bella Aqua Occ. 10 Apr. 1262 (*CR 1261–64*, p. 106).
Gilbert of Carcutt Occ. 20 Jan. 1289 (*HMC Var. Coll.*, I, 346).
John Occ. from Nov. 1295 x Nov. 1296 (PRO, E106/3/19, m. 9) to Nov. 1298 x Nov. 1299 (PRO, E106/4/9, m. 3d; E106/4/10, m. 4d). Poss. the same as below.
John de Millevill Occ. 12 Nov. 1306 (*Reg. Gandavo*, II, 682).
William de Sancta Genoveva (Genovefa, Genovesa, Genovisa) Occ. 27 June 1308 (ibid., I, 322); 12 Aug. 1308, styled m. at Upavon and proctor-general of the abbey (ibid., II, 704); 31 July 1319 (proctor-general) (*Reg. Martival*, I, 137); occ. as pr. 1320, 1321 (ibid., IV, 61, 68) and 31 Jan. 1325 (ibid., I, 334–5).
Richard le Provost Occ. as proctor of S. Wandrille, not styled pr. 27 June 1337 (*CCR 1337–39*, p. 163); gt of keeping of priory 10 Aug. 1337 (*CFR 1337–47*, p. 35); as proctor in England of S. Wandrille order to release to him the sequestration of Upavon 29 July 1339 (*CCR 1339–41*, pp. 243–4).
Unnamed pr. d. by 14 Oct. 1341 (*CFR 1337–47*, p. 245).
Protection for br. **William de Freauvyll** and br. **Robert William** who render 30 marks a year for the custody of Upavon priory 10 May 1342 (*CPR 1340–43*, p. 389). [Robert William is later found as pr. of Ecclesfield]
William de Freauvill Occ. as pr. 22 Oct. 1346 (PRO, E401/383); Mich. 1348 x Mich. 1349 (PRO, E372/194, rot. 36, mentd with Robert William, both desc. as monks); both also mentd Mich. 1358 x Mich. 1359 as acting up to 1350 (PRO, E372/204, rot. 26).
William Ponhier Occ. 27 July 1352 (*CFR 1347–56*, p. 326); Mich. 1354 x Mich. 1355 (PRO, E372/200, rot. 34); Mich. 1358 x Mich. 1359 (PRO, E372/204, rot. 26).
Robert Abbot (Labbe) Gt of keeping of priory during French war 17 Jan. 1361 (*CFR 1356–68*, p. 147). Mentioned as late pr. 8 Sept. 1368 (ibid., p. 388). D. by 24 Nov. 1368 (ibid., p.390).

WARE (Herts), St Mary (S. Evroul) f. -1081. Diss. 1414
  Lists in *VCH Herts*, IV, 457; H.P. Pollard, 'The alien Benedictine priory at Ware', *East Herts Arch. Soc. Trans.*, 3 (1905–7), 119–32, at 132; *Heads*, I, 111–12.
Herbert Last occ. *c.*1214 x 1215 (erroneously described as pr. of Warwick (*Reg. Wells*, I, 6; for dating see *BIHR*, XLV (1972), 57–70)). Seal (Demay, no. 3117).
A. occ. *c.* 1217 (*Reg. Wells*, I, 49).
William Occ. *c.* 1220 (*Ctl. Daventry*, no. 502); 22 Sept. 1221 (PRO, Leics F. CP25/1/121/7, no. 18); 8 Nov. 1221 (*Warws F.*, I, no. 326); identified as **William de Sancta Eugenia** 1222 (Alençon, Archives dép. de l'Orne, H.930); occ. (William) 1224 (PRO, Worcs F., CP25/1/258/3, no. 7); Mich. term 1225 (*CRR*, XII, no. 956); 1226 (PRO, F. Divers Cos. CP25/1/282/8, no. 45); Dec. 1233 x Dec. 1234 (*Reg. Wells*, II, 323).

Nicholas Occ. Oct. 1235 x Oct. 1236 (PRO, E40/2447); from 1237 to 1240 (PRO, PRO31/8/140B, part 1, pp. 222–4); June 1239 x June 1241 (*Reg. Grosseteste*, pp. 409, 411–12); 1242 (*Wilts F.*, I, p. 35); June 1242 x June 1243 (ibid., p. 477).

Peter Occ. Feb. 1244 (PRO, PRO31/8/140B, part 1, pp. 226–7); 17 Jan. 1247, 24 Jan. 1247 (*Reg. Grosseteste*, pp. 428, 229). Seal (Demay, no. 3066).

John Occ. (J.) June 1249 x June 1250 (*Reg. Grosseteste*, p. 434); (J.) Nov. 1258 x Nov. 1259, Nov. 1259 x Nov. 1260 (*Reg. R. Gravesend*, pp. 138–9); (J.) May 1259 (Alençon, Archives dép. de l'Orne, H.928, *ex inf.* N. Vincent); 9 Jan. 1260 (BL, Harl. Cht. 84 D 56). Seal (*BM Seals*, no. 4261; Pollard, p. 131).[12]

William de Parnys Occ. 1262 x 1263 (*Ctl. Holy Trinity, Aldgate*, no. 124; PRO, E42/386); 1268 (PRO, PRO31/8/140B, part 1, pp. 232–3); 1272 (Parnys) (ibid., p. 333); (W.) 1275 (*Reg. R. Gravesend*, pp. 157, 227). Absolved from excommunication 4 Sept. 1279 (*Reg. Pecham*, I, 140; cf. *Reg. Peckham*, III, 1020); 29 Sept. 1279 (PRO, PRO31/8/140B, part 1, pp. 245, 290–1); Trin. 1280 (PRO, CP40/34, m. 56d). Seal (*Mon. Seals*, p. 93).

Fulk Occ. 11 Nov. 1282 (*Reg. Peckham*, II, 432), possibly the unnamed pr. occ. 22 July 1281 who was being sued in the same case mentd in 1282 (ibid., I, 209–10); 21 Dec. 1286 (*Reg. Sutton*, VIII, 36).

Richard Occ. 26 Feb. 1288. 25 Mar. 1288, 10 Nov. 1288 (ibid., 39–40); 24 Mar 1288 (ibid., II, 65); 26 Apr. 1290, 12 May 1290 (ibid., 44–5).

Ralph le Graunt 1292– Prof. obed. 23 May 1292 (ibid., IV, 3). Occ. 19 Oct. 1292 (ibid., VIII, 52); 1295, 1298 (ibid., 55, 68–9); 1301, 1304 (Lincoln, Ep. Reg., II, ff. 196v, 200v); 1306 (PRO, E315/31/67c; E326/8506); 1308 (PRO, C241/70/15); 1310 (Lincoln, Ep. Reg., II, f. 204v); 4 May 1312 (PRO, KB27/211, m. 60); 4 Oct. 1315, 13 Oct. 1315 (Lincoln, Ep. Reg., II, f. 209v). Seal (*BM Seals*, no. 4263; *Mon. Seals*, p. 93; Pollard, p. 131).

William de Botteville Occ. 23 Mar. 1317, 6 Dec. 1317 (Lincoln, Ep. Reg., II, ff. 213v, 214v); prof. obed. 31 July 1319 (Lincoln, Ep. Reg., III, f. 422r). Occ. Oct.-Nov. 1319, June 1320 (Lincoln, Ep. Reg., II, ff. 140v, 218v, 219r, 357v); 19 Aug. 1321, 22 June 1322 (*Reg. Burghersh*, I, no. 838; Lincoln, Ep. Reg., IV, f. 164v); 1324 (PRO, E106/5/2, m. 9d); 8 Oct. 1326 (*Memo. Roll 1326–7*, p. 272); 5 Apr. 1327 (Lincoln, Ep. Reg., IV, f. 177v).[13]

Richard le Gregi Occ. 2 July 1329, 15 July 1329, 21 June 1330 (*Reg. Burghersh*, I, no. 234; Lincoln, Ep. Reg., IV, ff. 182v, 262v).

John Gerond (Gerald, Gerant, Geraud, Guerand, Guerard, Guerond, Gueront, de Keneyo) Occ. 18 June 1331 (*Reg. Burghersh*, I, no. 1010); 1332 (ibid., nos. 1020, 1024); Easter 1334 (*Select Cases of Trespass*, II, 380–1); 1336 (*Reg. Burghersh*, I, nos. 1082–3); 1342 (*CFR 1337–47*, p. 266); 1345 (*CCR 1343–46*, p. 636); 1349 (*CFR 1347–56*, p. 165 – Keneyo); 1352 (PRO, DL25/315); 1354 (ibid., p. 393); Mich. 1354 x Mich. 1355 (PRO, E372/200, rot. 32 – Keneyo); 1356 (*CPR 1354–58*, pp. 351, 373); 1362 (*Reg. L. Charlton*, p. 64); 1364 (Lincoln, Ep. Reg., X, f. 233r); 11 June 1369, 6 Oct. 1369 (*CFR 1368–77*, pp. 14, 24); 28 Oct. 1370 (*CCR 1369–74*, p. 165); 1374 (PRO, C241/5/36); 16 May 1375 (*CFR 1368–77*, p. 286). Seal (*Mon. Seals*, p. 93; Pollard, p. 131).

William Herberd(e) (Heberd, Herbert) Occ. 7 Nov. 1376 (ibid., p. 368); 4 Nov. 1377 (*CPR 1377–81*, p. 32). Occ.1380 (*CCR 1385–89*, p., 291); 1381 (*CPR 1381–85*, p. 139); 1385 (PRO, C269/15/55); 1387 (*CPR 1385–89*, p. 336); 22 Nov. 1399 (*CFR 1399–1405*, p. 24); 20 May 1405 (*CCR 1402–05*, p. 449).

---

[12] The transcript of a cht. in PRO, PRO31/8/140B, part 1, pp. 231–2 has pr. T. occ. in May 1259, but it is likely that this is a transcription error for J.

[13] The pr. Hugh listed in the *VCH* for Trin. 1327–Mich. 1328 is described in a plea of debt as 'Hugh of the Priourye of Ware', not pr. of Ware (*Index to Placita de Banco*, p. 209), and I do not think he is to be included in the list of priors.

The next recorded pr., **Nicholas Champene** (Chanpyn), occ. 8 Feb. 1410, lic. to bring a monk from his chief house of S. Evroul with a servant in his company into the realm to dwell with him in the priory for life, for the maintenance of divine service (*CPR 1408–13*, p. 157). Prob. the same as the monk gtd keeping of the priories of Noyon and Neufmarché in the counties of Oxford and Berkshire 1403 (*CFR 1399–1405*, p. 193).

WAREHAM (Dorset) St Mary (Lire) f. *temp*. Henry I.
   Lists in *VCH Dorset*, II, p. 122; *Heads* I, 112.
W. Occ. 15 Oct. 1216 (*Rot. Lit. Pat.*, p. 199).
Geoffrey Mentioned in earlier undated cht. inspected on 30 Nov. 1280 (*CChR 1257–1300*, p. 245). Occ. in Sheen inv. of chts. (BL, Cotton ms. Otho B XIV, f. 34r).
Nicholas Bynet Occ. 6 Mar. 1297 (*CFR 1292–1301*, p. 267).
Peter de Deserto Occ. as 'rector' 23 Sept. 1302 (*Reg. Gandavo*, II, 857).
John Mabere (Mabyre) **1309–1311** Adm. 28 May 1309, no reason given for vacancy (ibid., 711). D. by 26 Oct. 1311 (ibid., 772).
Hilderic de Paceyo 1311–1323 Pres. 26 Oct. 1311 on the d. of John Mabere – enquiry ordered if priory vacant (ibid.). Res. by 8 Apr. 1323 (*Reg. Martival*, I, 280).
Ralph *dictus* Coudray (Coudraio) **1323–** M. of Lire, pres. to bp by Lire 8 Apr. 1323 (ibid.). Occ. *c*. Mich. 1324 (PRO, E106/5/2, m. 5d); July 1325 x July 1326 (PRO, E106/5/4, m. [4d]); 8 Oct. 1326 (*Memo. Roll 1326–7*, p. 272).
William (de) Bally 1330–1332 Pres. to bp by Lire 13 Jan. 1330, no reason given for vacancy (*Reg. Martival*, I, 405). Inst. 9 Feb. 1330 (ibid.). Res. by 17 Oct. 1332 (Salisbury, Reg. Wyvil II, f. 18r).
John de Bodiers (Bediers) **1332–1334** Adm. 17 Oct. 1332 (ibid.). Res. by 8 Sept. 1334 (ibid., f. 31v).
Michael de Molis (Molys) **1334–1344** Adm. 8 Sept. 1334 (ibid.). Occ. 20 Mar. 1342 (*CFR 1337–47*, p. 274). Res. by 4 Feb. 1344 (Salisbury, Reg. Wyvil II, f. 131v).
William de Barly (Barli) **1344–** M. of Lire, pres. by Blaise Doublel, pr. of Carisbrooke, adm. 4 Feb. 1344 (ibid.).
Michael de Molis Occ. 11 July 1345 (*CCR 1343–46*, p. 636). D. by 4 Nov. 1348 and custody of priory committed to John Pepyn, pr. of Carisbrooke (*CFR 1347–56*, p. 101).
William de Noys 1349–1354 M. of Lire, adm. 29 May 1349, no reason given for vacancy (Salisbury, Reg. Wyvil II, f. 208r). Occ. 13 Aug. 1352 (*CFR 1347–56*, p. 339). Res. by 16/17 May 1354 (Salisbury, Reg. Wyvil II, f. 264r).
[**Richard de Frigideo Monte** M. of Lire, gtd keeping of the priory during the French war 20 Feb. 1350 (*CFR 1347–56*, p. 207).]
Robert de Gascur 1354– M. of Lire, pres. by Almeric de (Pugn)eya, pr. of Carisbrooke, adm. 16/17 May 1354 (Salisbury, Reg. Wyvil II, f. 264r).
Peter de Elemosina M. of Lire, gtd keeping of the priory during the French war 20 Sept. 1359 (*CFR 1356–68*, p. 106). Occ. as pr. Easter 1361 (PRO, CP40/406, m. 175d).
Lewis Goulaffre 1362 M. of Lire, pres. by Robert de Gascur, proctor of Lire, adm. 13 Apr. 1362 (Salisbury, Reg. Wyvil II, f. 295v). Res by [ ] Oct. 1362 (ibid., f. 298r).
Peter de Ultra Aqua 1362–1364 Adm. [ ] Oct. 1362 (ibid.). Res. by 31 Mar. 1364 (ibid., f. 305v).
William Minguet (Mignot) **1364–** M. of Lire, adm. 31 Mar. 1364 (ibid.). Previously occ. as proctor of Lire abbey 6 May 1363 (*Reg. Edington*, I, no. 1574).
Stephen de Barra −1414 Occ. 8 Oct. 1371 (*CFR 1368–77* p. 132); 8 Oct. 1377 (*CFR 1377–83*, p. 17); 3 times in Sheen inv. of chts. (BL, Cotton ms. Otho B XIV, ff. 41r, 42r, 43v); 1403 (*Privy Council*, I, 192). Gt of keeping of priory 28 Jan. 1403 (*CFR 1399–1405*, p. 193). D. 4 Nov. 1414 (*Reg. Hallum*, no. 376).

WARMINGHURST (Sussex) (Fécamp) f. *c.* 1085. Diss. 1414. See *VCH Sussex*, II, 124 – this was in the nature of a grange with a bailiff (sometimes called pr.); cf. Matthew, *Norman Monasteries*, p. 95.

John Palmer (Palmarii, Paumier, Paumer(e)) Occ. as bailiff of the abb. of Fécamp 10 Feb. 1340 (*CCR 1339–41*, p. 351); as bailiff of Warminghurst 19 Apr. 1341 – arrested for sending bows and arrows to Normandy, to be sent to Westminster (*CCR 1341–43*, p. 128). Occ. as proctor of abbey 1 Nov. 1335, 28 July 1341, 15 May 1342 (*CFR 1327–37*, p. 459; *CFR 1337–47*, p. 236; *CPR 1340–43*, p. 430).

Philip Arnulphi (Arnulphy) Occ. as bailiff of Warminghurst 1367–8 (Matthew, *Norman Monasteries*, p. 68). Philip occ. as proctor in England of the abbey of Fécamp (but with no Warminghurst title) 1374 (*Cal. Misc. Inq.*, III, 351).

Hugh Veretot Occ. as bailiff 1378 (Matthew, *Norman Monasteries*, p. 157; *CFR 1383–91*, p. 57). Occ. as m. of Fécamp 2 June 1409 (Matthew, *Norman Monasteries*, p. 164).

WARMINGTON (Warws.) (S. Pierre, Préaux) f. -1123
List in *Heads*, I, 112.
Ralph Occ. 29 Sept. 1206 (*Warws. F.*, I, no.157).
Robert Occ. 8 July 1252 (PRO, Leics F., CP25/1/122/21, no. 358).
Nicholas de Campeney (Canpyngnio) Occ. 8 July 1274 (*Warws. F.*, I, no. 910); 1285 (BL, Cotton Cht. IV. 14 (4)); 11 Nov. 1307, 12 Sept. 1309 (Lichfield, B/A/1/1, ff. 27v, 35v). Occ. as general proctor of abbey (not styled pr. of Warmington) 17 Sept. 1311 (ibid., f. 37r).
Peter Burdon (Burdone) absolution from excommunication 1328 [between entries of 24–25 Oct.] (*Reg. Grandisson*, I, 417–18). Occ. as proctor of the abbey of Préaux 13 Oct. 1331 (not styled pr. of Warmington) (Lincoln, Ep. Reg., IV, f. 102v).
Richard Vateman (Vatemon) Occ. as pr. Toft Monks and Warmington 31 Jan. 1366, 28 Nov. 1366 (*Reg. Stretton*, II, 37–8). See also Toft Monks.

WATH (Yorks N.) (Mont S. Michel) f. *ante* 1196 (see also *EYC*, V, p. 46 & n.).
List in *Heads*, I, 112.
Richard Occ. *c.* 1200 (*EYC*, V, no. 141); n.d. (early 13th cent.) (*Ctl. Fountains*, II, 500).
Mand. to make enquiry about dispute over the manor of Wath between the abb. of Mont S. Michel and Sir Robert Marmion, knight, following a duel at which the abb.'s predecessor renounced his right. The present abb. petitions the pope to annul the renunciation which was not made with the consent of the convent, 1239: the Marmions were apparently successful in their claim (*CPL*, I, 179–80; *VCH North Riding Yorks*, I, 391).

WEEDON BECK (Northants) (Bec; S. Lambert de Mallassis) f. -1086; +1126; under Ogbourne but in 1329 a pr. (unnamed) of Weedon mentd (M. Morgan, *English Lands of Bec*, pp. 23–4; *VCH Northants*, II, 183).
No named priors recorded for this period, but at Trin. 1298, a Henry le Baillif of Weedon is found in company with pr. Theobald of Ogbourne (PRO, KB27/155, m. 45d).

WEEDON LOIS (Northants), St Mary (S. Lucien, Beauvais) (Weedon Pinkney) f.-1123; diss. 1392 and granted to Biddlesden abbey.
Lists in *VCH Northants*, II, 185; *Heads*, I, 112.
Philip Occ. prob. early 13th cent. (BL, Harl. ms. 4714, f. 247r).
Nicholas -1238/9 Occ. (N.) Dec. 1227 x Dec. 1228 (*Reg. Wells*, II, 143); 30 Dec. 1228, 25 Feb. 1232 (ibid., 230, 247). Res. June 1238 x June 1239 (*Reg. Grosseteste*, p. 175).
Roger 1238/9- Adm. June 1238 x June 1239 (ibid., 175–6).

Baldwin 1240/1– M. of S. Lucien, Beauvais, inst. June 1240 x June 1241, no reason given for vacancy (ibid., p. 202). Occ. 18 June 1256 (PRO, Northants F. CP25/1/174/42, no. 701).

William Occ. *temp.* Henry III, mentd in case of 1297 (*Coram Rege Roll*, p. 174). Unfortunately the institution to Plumpton church mentd in the case is not recorded in the extant Lincoln episcopal registers. Pr. William is said to have given the advowson to William le Mareschal, grandfather of one of the 1297 parties. As pr. Nicholas is found presenting to Plumpton (*Reg. Wells*, II, 143) it must be after 1238/9, and prob. William fits in the sequence either between Roger and Baldwin, or Baldwin and Matthew Charite.

Matthew Charite –1265 Occ. 8 July 1261 (PRO, Northants F. CP25/1/174/44, no. 774). Res. by 7 Jan. 1265 (*Reg. R. Gravesend*, p. 104).

Matthew *dictus* Pressour 1265–1266 M. of S. Lucien, Beauvais, adm. 7 Jan. 1265 (ibid.). Res. by 15 July 1266 (ibid., p. 107).

Matthew 1266–1276 M. of S. Lucien, Beauvais, adm.15 July 1266 (ibid., pp. 107, 296). Res. by 23 June 1276 (ibid., p. 129).

John 1276–1277 M. of S. Lucien, Beauvais, adm. 23 June 1276 (ibid., pp. 129, 304). Res. by 3 July 1277 (ibid., p. 132).

Matthew 1277–1282 Adm. 3 July 1277 (ibid.). D. by 21 July 1282 (*Reg. Sutton*, II, 19).

Walter *dictus* Gleyne 1282–1285 M. of S. Lucien, Beauvais, adm. 21 July 1282 (ibid., 19–20). Letter of res.15 Dec. 1285 on account of ill-health (ibid., 53–4).

Thomas de Compendio 1286–1287 M. of S. Lucien, Beauvais, letter of pres. 15 Dec. 1285 – bp refused to acc. letter and gave him custody 26 Jan. 1286; second letter of pres. 19 Apr. 1286; adm. 28 May 1286 (ibid., 53–5). Letter of res. 16 Nov. 1287 on account of ill-health; produced before bp 21 Dec. 1287 (ibid., 60–2).

Thomas de Sancto Marcello (*alias* de Villa Nova) 1287–1290/1 M. of S. Lucien, Beauvais, letter of pres. Oct. 1287 – given custody 10 Nov. 1287 pending receipt of pr. Thomas's letter of res.; adm. 21 Dec. 1287 (ibid.). Letter of res. dated 29 May 1290 – declared invalid as was not in correct form; second letter of res. 21 Nov. 1290 (ibid., 92–3).

Hugh de Patay 1290/1–1294 M. of S. Lucien, Beauvais, given custody 19 Aug. 1290 until problem with letter of res. resolved; adm. 1 July 1291 (ibid.). Letter of res. dated 6 Feb. 1294; res. by 15 May 1294 (ibid., 110–11).

Hugh de Tyenloy (Tilloy, Tyculoy, Tyenloi) **1294–1302** M. of S. Lucien, Beauvais. 1 Oct. 1293 Hugh exhibited letters of pres. dated 31 Jan. 1293 – bp refused to acc. letters. On 14 May 1294 he appeared again with new letters of pres. dated 7 Feb. 1294; adm. 15 May 1294 (ibid.). Absent without leave, but spiritualities restored 17 Dec 1298 after submission to bp (ibid., VI, 128). Res. by 6 Apr. 1302 (Lincoln, Ep. Reg., II, f. 105v), but Hugh occ. in return of aliens Nov. 1302 x Nov. 1303 (PRO, E106/4/18, m. 14d, and see also next entry).

Peter de Dyion (Dyon, Dyoun) **1302–1315** M. of S. Lucien, Beauvais, appeared on 6 Apr. 1302 with letters of pres., including the res. of Hugh. Bp had not been informed but gave custody; he appeared again with letter of pres. dated 7 Aug. 1302 and Hugh's letter of res. dated 6 Aug. 1302; adm.10 Nov. 1302 (Lincoln, Ep. Reg., II, f. 105v). Occ. 16 Nov. 1310 (ibid. f. 120v). Letter of res. dated 20 July 1315 (ibid., f. 129v).[14]

Thomas de Nova Villa 1316– M. of S. Lucian, Beauvais, letter of pres. dated 10/17 Feb. 1316 (ibid., ff. 129v–130r); adm. 21 Apr. 1316 (ibid.). Occ. 11 Aug. 1319 (*CPR 1317–21*, p. 385).

Peter de Dygon –1322 ? same as pr. from 1302. Letter of res. dated 9 Sept. 1322 (Lincoln, Ep. Reg., IV, f. 167r–v).

Thomas de Villa Nova *alias* de Sancto Marcello 1322– M. of S. Lucien, Beauvais, letter

---

[14] Robert occ. as pr. 30 Jan. 1304 (*CCR 1302–07*, p. 197). Whether this is a scribal error or whether Peter de Dyion had two terms of office punctuated by the tenure of a pr. Robert is uncertain.

of pres. 20 Aug. 1322, adm. 23 Dec. 1322 (ibid.). Occ. July 1325 x July 1326 (PRO, E106/5/4, m.[9d]);(de Sancto Marcello), 23 Mar. 1329, 15 July 1329, 21 July 1329, 20 Oct. 1329, 8 Dec. 1329 (*CRR 1327–30*, pp. 533, 560, 561, 575, 587).

Robert de Calceya Augi 1330– M. of S. Lucien, Beauvais, letter of pres. dated 13 Nov. 1330; adm. 13 Dec. 1330, no reason given for vacancy (Lincoln, Ep. Reg., IV, f. 187v).

William de Meiaco (Moiaco) **1342–** M. of S. Lucien, Beauvais, adm. 12 Jan. 1342, no reason given for vacancy (ibid., f. 244r). Occ. 8 Mar. 1342 (*CFR 1337–47*, p. 273); 11 July 1345 (*CCR 1343–46*, p. 636).

Robert de Novavilla 1360– M. of S. Lucien, Beauvais, letter of pres. dated 20 Sept. 1360; adm. 11 Dec. 1360 (Lincoln, Ep. Reg., IX, f. 232r).

John de Malengiene (Mailgneure) **1366–1368** M. of S. Lucien, Beauvais, adm. 19 Mar. 1366 (Lincoln, Ep. Reg., X, f. 164r). Res. by 16 Mar. 1368 (ibid., f. 172v).

Ralph de Ponte 1368– M. of S. Lucien, Beauvais, letter of pres. dated 16 Jan. 1368; adm. 4 Apr. 1368 (ibid., f. 172v). Occ. 6 Oct. 1369 (*CFR 1368–77*, p. 24); 1370 (*Buckingham Writ Register*, no. 116); 23 Oct. 1377 (*CFR 1377–83*, p. 27).

The next recorded pr., **John of Ludlow** (Lodelowe), occ. 3 May 1392 (ibid., f. 253v). It is prob. that John was pr. of Weedon Lois, but the document is actually ambiguous. It is a notarial instrument made in the chapter house of Biddlesden abbey concerning the grant of Weedon Lois priory from Beauvais to Biddlesden and the witnesses to this instrument include John of Ludlow (. . . *priore dicti monasterii*. . .). Whether the monastery is Weedon or Biddlesden is not entirely clear.

In 1392 the priory was conveyed by Beauvais abbey to Biddlesden abbey (BL, Harl. ms. 4714, ff. 248r–253v).

WELL, *see* PANFIELD

WEST MERSEA (Essex), St Peter and St Paul (S. Ouen, Rouen) f. (?)1046. Diss. 1400
List in *VCH Essex*, II, 197.

Ralph Occ. Trin. term 1233 (*Essex F.*, I, 94).

James Occ. 25 Oct. 1236 (Guildhall, St Paul's D & C. ms. 25121/510); 23 Nov. 1248, mand. to let pr. James have custody of his priory, which had been taken into the king's hands, up to the octaves of Easter, provided that before then the abb. of S. Ouen shall come to the king to make fealty regarding the priory and that James shall have letters of pres. (*CR 1247–51*, p. 218); Occ. n.d. when allowed by Abb. Hugh of S. Ouen (1235–51) to dispose of property in London (*HMC 9th Rept.*, p. 10).

Gilbert Occ. Nov. 1295 x Nov. 1296 (PRO, E106/3/19, m. 8); Nov. 1296 x Nov. 1297 (PRO, E106/4/2, m. 6d); Nov. 1297 x Nov. 1298 (PRO, E106/4/8, m. 4; E106/4/9, m. 5d); Nov. 1298 x Nov. 1299 (PRO, E106/4/10, m. 6); Easter 1300 (PRO, E106/4/14, m. 8d).

John Occ. 1312 (Colchester court rolls, cited in *TEAS*, 17, p. 48).

Walter Occ. *c.* Mich. 1324 (PRO, E106/5/2, m. 9d); July 1325 x July 1326 (PRO, E106/5/4, m. [8d]); 8 Oct. 1326 (*Memo. Roll 1326–7*, p. 272); 4 Feb. 1328, 22 Mar. 1328 (*CPR 1327–30*, pp. 276, 292).

John Morel Occ. 17 May 1329 (*Reg. S. Gravesend*, p. 288).

William de Reel Occ. 4 May 1330 (*CCR 1330–33*, p. 25); 12 Feb. 1342 (*CFR 1337–47*, p. 272); 23 July 1343 (PRO, C269/15/18); 11 July 1345 (*CCR 1343–46*, p. 636).

Stephen de Caus M. of S. Ouen, occ. 16 Jan. 1370 (PRO, E179/42/3B).

Stephen Foukes Occ. 4 May 1377 (*CFR 1368–77*, p. 396); 26 Oct. 1377 (*CPR 1377–83*, p. 29).

Gt of the keeping of the priory to **John Ramseye**, monk, 18 Feb. 1378 (*CFR 1377–83*, p. 75); gt repeated 26 Aug. 1382 (ibid., p. 316).

WILMINGTON (Sussex), St Mary (Grestain) f. -1086 (as cell); -1243 (as priory).

Lists in *VCH Sussex*, II, 122–3 (from 1243); *Heads*, I, 112).

Robert de Avalon (Avalin) Occ. 14 June 1238 (*Ctl. Chichester*, no. 4); June 1238 x June 1239 (*Reg. Grosseteste*, p. 264).

John Occ. 6 Oct. 1243 (*Sussex F.*, I, no. 416); 8 Jan. 1250 (PRO, C85/1/8).

Robert de Pickard (Pykard) Occ. 12 Sept. 1261 (*CR 1259–61*, p. 492); 15 Sept. 1261 (*CPR 1258–66*, p. 175).

William de Gymeges Occ. (W.) 27 Dec. 1256 (*Ctl. Chichester*, no. 218); 26 July 1267 (*Reg. R. Gravesend*, p. 108); 13 July 1268 (*CPR 1266–72*, p. 244).

Reginald Occ. 13 July 1268 (PRO, Just.1/913, m. 4); 10 July 1270, (R.) 3 May 1271, 19 Apr. 1277 (*Reg. R. Gravesend*, pp. 115, 174, 255); 1 May 1283 (*Reg. Sutton*, II, 27).

William Occ. 16 Mar 1299 (*CPR 1292–1301*, p. 398). Could be the same as below.

William de Banville (Bamvill(a), Bannvilla, Banvyll, Baumvill(a), Baunvilla, Beauvill) –1343/4 Occ. 23 Feb. 1306 (Norwich, Reg/1/1, f. 19v); 12 May 1307, 15 July 1307, 28 Sept. 1309 (Lincoln, Ep. Reg., II, ff. 236r, 180r, 116v); (W.) 1312 (*Reg. Droxford*, p. 52); 1315 (Lincoln, Ep. Reg., III, f. 317r); 1317 (Lincoln, Ep. Reg., II, f. 189r); 1317, 1318 (*Reg. Sandale*, pp. 136,151); 1320 (*CFR 1317–21*, pp. 542, 549); July 1325 x July 1326 (PRO, E106/5/4, m. [2]); 1342 (*CFR 1337–47*, p. 272); 3 Dec. 1343 (*CPR 1343–45*, p. 151). D. by 17 Mar 1344 (*CFR 1337–47*, p. 364).

[br. **John Maigre** M. of Wilmington, gtd keeping of the priory following the d. of William de Banville 17 Mar. 1344 (ibid.). Prob. the John Maigre who became abb. of Grestain in 1362 (*Sussex Arch. Coll.*, LXIX, p. 39, n. 49).]

Peter Crispyn (Crispin, Crispy, Cryspyn) 1344–?1349 Previously proctor of the abb. of Lire occ. 1331–1335 (*Reg. Burghersh* I, nos. 998, 1001, 1017, 1040, 1073; *Reg. T. Charlton*, p. 20). M. of Grestain, gt of keeping of priory 16 May 1344, having been apptd pr. by the abb. of Grestain (*CFR 1337–47*, p. 374). Occ. 2 Oct. 1344 (*CCR 1343–46*, p. 413). D. by 18 May 1349 (*CFR 1347–56*, p. 139), but did he hold office twice (see next entry)?

William de Beauvill Occ. 11 July 1345 (*CCR 1343–46*, p. 636).

John Picot (Pyket) 1349– M. of Grestain, apptd pr. by the abb. of Grestain, gtd keeping of the priory 18 May 1349 (*CFR 1347–56*, p. 139). Occ. 13 July 1351 (*CCR 1349–54*, p. 375); Lent 1353 (PRO, Just.1/941A, m. 56d). ? the John Picot who was abb. of Grestain in 1377 (*Sussex Arch. Coll.*, LXIX, p. 44).

John Putt Occ. 23 Apr. 1363 (*Reg. Sudbury*, I, 24).

William Occ. 16 Jan. 1370 (PRO, E179/42/3B).

John de Vaux (Vaal, Vale, Valle, Walle) Occ. 10 Apr. 1370 (PRO, E106/10/11); 31 July 1371 (*Ctl. Chichester*, no. 775); 18 Oct. 1371 (*CFR 1368–77*, p. 132); 6 Apr. 1374 (*Cal. Misc. Inq.*, III, 351).

Thomas Auncel(l) Occ. 14 Nov. 1375 (*CFR 1368–77*, p. 308); fit sustenance to be found for him by the pr. of Michelham 3 Feb. 1378 (*CFR 1377–83*, p. 68); 13 May 1388 (*CPR 1388–91*, p. 230).

WILSFORD (Lincs) (Bec) f. 1135 x 1154; granted to Bourne Abbey 1401.

Lists in *VCH Lincs*, II, 240; *Heads*, I, 112.

Roger Occ. 6 July 1202 (*Lincs F., 1199–1216*, no. 79).

Adam de Subiria (Subyr') 1225/6–1228/9 Adm. Dec. 1225 x Dec. 1226, no reason given for the vacancy (*Reg. Wells*, III, 151). Occ. 14 Jan. 1228 (*CPR 1225–32*, p. 209). Res. '*maxime propter ipsius recentem incontinentiam*' Dec. 1228 x Dec.1229 (*Reg. Wells*, III, 172–3).

Peter de Kambreis 1228/9– Adm. Dec. 1228 x Dec. 1229 (ibid.). Occ. 1231 (BL, Harl. ms. 3658, f. 64v); 22 Feb. 1235 as attorney for Bec (*CR 1234–37*, p. 615); (P.) June 1238 x June 1239 (*Reg. Grosseteste*, p. 33).

Richard Perpelun(?) 1239/40– Inst. June 1239 x June 1240, no reason given for vacancy (ibid., p. 46). Occ. (Perpelun?) 15 May 1246 (ibid., pp. 85–6).

Richard de Maunvill –1247/8 Res. June 1247 x June 1248 (ibid., p. 96)

Roger de Guilemore 1247/8–1250/1 M. of St Neots, inst. June 1247 x June 1248 (ibid.). Res. June 1250 x June 1251 (ibid., p. 118).

Jordan de Hotot 1250/1– Inst. June 1250 x June 1251 (ibid., pp. 118–19).

Robert de Gomervill –1258/9 Res. Nov. 1258 x Nov. 1259 (*Reg. R. Gravesend*, p. 2).

Henry of St Neots (de Sancto Neoto) 1258/9–1265 M. of Bec., inst. Nov. 1258 x Nov. 1259 (ibid.). Res. by 30 Sept. 1265 (ibid., p. 19).

John de Lilebon 1265– Adm. 30 Sept. 1265 (ibid.). Prob. the same as John de Insula Bona below.

Gilbert Occ. *temp.* Edward I, an alien (*Cal. Misc. Inq.*, IV, 163). Poss. occ. at this point in the sequence.

William de Tribus Montibus –1275 Res. by 11 July 1275 (*Reg. R. Gravesend*, p. 65).

John de Insula Bona (Lillebonne) 1275–1282 M. of Bec., inst. 11 July 1275 (ibid.). Relieved of office by abb. of Bec by 23 Mar. 1282 (*Reg. Sutton*, I, 22–3).

Stephen de Stok(e) 1282–1290 M. of Bec., letter of pres. 23 Mar. 1282, inst. 8 Apr. 1282 (ibid.). D. by 27 July 1290 (ibid., III, 28–9).

Walter of Pont-Audemer (de Ponte Audomari, Audem') 1290–1299 M. of Bec, Walter appeared before bp 27 July 1290 saying he had been apptd pr. in succession to Stephen who had died: the bp deferred consideration of the case until the following Mich. (ibid.). Letter of pres. 18 Aug. 1290, deemed irregular and Walter given custody until next Candlemas on 26 Sept. 1290, no reason given for vacancy (ibid., I, 142–4); second letter of pres. 4 Dec. 1290 and adm. 24 Jan. 1291 (ibid., 149–50). Letter of res. dated 9 Jan. 1299 on account of ill-health (ibid., 239–40).

John de Sauvarvilla 1299–1300 M of Bec, letter of pres. 10 Dec. 1298, adm. 11 Jan. 1299 (ibid.). Res. by 16 July 1300 (Lincoln, Ep. Reg., II, f. 2r).

Richard de Boneboz 1300–1302 M. of Bec, letter of pres. 16 July 1300; adm. 29 Aug. 1300 (ibid.). Res. by 10 Sept. 1302 (ibid., f. 6v).

Michael de Ponte Antonis 1302– M. of Bec, letter of pres. 10 Sept. 1302, adm. 11 Oct. 1302 (ibid.). Occ. 26 June 1309 (ibid., f. 240r); 9 Mar 1311 (ibid., f. 242r).

John de Burneville –1312 D. 7 Oct. 1312 (*Cal. Misc. Inq.*, II, 40).

Richard de Fangnellon (Fanguellon) 1313–1314 M. of Bec, letter of pres. 2 Nov. 1312 on d. of Richard Flagellon (*sic*); adm 27 Oct. 1313 (Lincoln, Ep. Reg., II, f. 49v; cf. PRO, C84/17/12). D. by 2 Dec. 1314 (Lincoln, Ep. Reg., II, f. 54r).

William de Sancto Albino 1315– M. of Bec, letter of pres. 2 Dec. 1314; adm. 13 Jan. 1315 (ibid.; PRO, C84/17/46). Occ. 6 Sept. 1315 (Lincoln, Ep. Reg., II, f. 56v); 27 Oct. 1316 (ibid., f. 249v).

William de Nassaundres 1320– M. of Bec, letter of pres. 29 Oct. 1319, no reason given for vacancy; inst. by Official of Lincoln *sede vacante* 15 Feb. 1320 (ibid., f. 356v). Occ. 1324 (PRO, E106/5/2, m. 12); 1326 (*Memo. Roll 1326–7*, p. 273); 23 Apr. 1327 (Lincoln, Ep. Reg., IV, f. 368v); Mich. 1338 x Mich. 1339 (PRO, E372/184, rots. 31, 32d).

Durand of St Stephen (de Sancto Stephano) 1341– M. of Bec, adm. 8 Apr. 1341, no reason given for vacancy (*Reg. Burghersh* I, no. 677). Occ. 4 Mar 1342 (*CFR 1337–47*, p. 275); (de Sancto Botulpho) 9 Feb. 1343 (Lincoln, Ep. Reg., VII, f. 23r); 11 July 1345 (*CCR 1343–46*, p. 636). Pr. of Cowick 1352–61 (q.v.).

John de Efreno –1366 House vacant by dimission of John de Efreno by 20 Apr. 1367 (Lincoln, Ep. Reg., X, f. 17r)

John de Lacmers 1367– Pres. by abb. of Bec, adm. 20 Apr. 1367 (ibid.).

John de Aquila Occ. 14 Oct. 1372 (*CFR 1368–77*, p. 159)

[William de la Bark Pr. of S. Pierre du Château, gtd keeping of priory, having been despoiled of his former priory forcibly by the king's enemies 6 Aug. 1378 (*CFR 1377–83*, p. 106). Remission for 2 years to William de la Bark, late pr. of St Peter de Castro in Aquitaine, to whom the custody of Wilsford priory was gtd, of the farm of 12 marks due to the sheriff of Northampton and the clerical subsidy of 12 marks (*CPR 1377–81*, p. 506).]

WING (Bucks) (St Nicholas, Angers) f. -1086; 1416 granted to St Mary de Pré.
List in *VCH Bucks*, I, 396.

Geoffrey Occ. Nov. 1270 x Nov. 1271, 5 July 1271 (*Reg. R. Gravesend*, pp. 222, 247).

Robert de Bures Occ. 30 Nov. 1312 (Lincoln, Ep. Reg., II, f. 185r).

William of St Clement (de Sancto Clemente) Proctor of abb. of St Nicholas at Wing, 17 Aug. 1332 (PRO, C270/12/28). Pr. of Monks Kirby 1335–1349/50 (q.v.).

John de Fessinis (Feffynis, Felyng, Fesyniis, Fessunis) Occ. 7 Feb. 1366 (*CPR 1367–70*, p. 234); 6 Feb. 1367 (*CCR 1364–68*, p. 365); 16 Jan. 1370 (*Buckingham Writ Register*, p. 40, no. 116); 15 May 1370 (*CPR 1367–70*, p. 400).

Peter de Monte Ardito 1377– Bp. apptd him *per lapsum temporis* 27 Nov. 1377 (Lincoln, Ep. Reg., X, ff. 442v–443r).

WINGHALE (Lincs). (Sées) f. -1115. Diss. 1400
List in *VCH Lincs*, II, 242.

Philip 1228– M. of Sées, adm. 17 June 1228, no reason given for vacancy (*Reg. Wells*, III, 132–3).

William de Rupe 1241/2– Adm. June 1241 x June 1242 on d. of unnamed pr. (*Reg. Grosseteste*, pp. 62–3)

Galganus –1276 Res. by 20 Nov. 1276 (*Reg. R. Gravesend*, p. 71).

Geoffrey de Oumayo 1276– M. of Sées, inst. 20 Nov. 1276 (ibid., pp. 71, 284). Occ. from Nov. 1295 x Nov. 1296 (PRO, E106/3/19, m. 9d; E106/4/9, m. 1d; E106/4/10, m. 2); Easter 1300 (PRO, E106/4/14, m. 3).

William Occ. *c*. Mich. 1324 (PRO, E106/5/2, m. 12).

John de Croquet Occ. 5 Feb. 1342 (*CFR 1337–47*, p. 261); 11 July 1345 (*CCR 1343–46*, p. 636).

Gerard le Cordwayner M. of Sées, occ. 22 May 1345, the previous (unnamed) pr. now being dead (*CPR 1337–47*, p. 421). See next entry.

Simon Pynart Gtd keeping of the priory at the suit of br. Gerard le Cordowaner, m. of Sées 1 Aug. 1345 (*CPR 1343–45*, p. 539; *CFR 1337–47*, p. 433). He had been removed for waste by the abb. of Sées before 8 Feb. 1348 (*CPR 1347–56*, p. 67).

John de Radouno M. of Sées, apptd by abb. of Sées, occ. 8 Feb. 1348 (*CPR 1348–50*, p. 7; *CFR 1347–56*, p. 67). Removed by abb. before 26 Jan. 1352 (ibid., p. 319).

Robert Romny Occ. 26 Jan. 1352 (ibid.); 1 Oct. 1358 (*CFR 1356–68*, p. 81); Mich. 1358 x Mich. 1359 (PRO, E372/204, rot. 13d).

William Occ. 6 Oct. 1369 (*CFR 1368–77*, p. 23).

Richard le Verrer Occ. 1 May 1372 (ibid., p. 159); 12 Nov. 1377 (*CFR 1377–83*, p. 49); 7 Feb. 1378 (ibid., p. 71); 14 May 1382 (*CCR 1381–85*, p. 132); gtd keeping of priory 13 June 1384 (*CFR 1383–91*, p. 38). Described as previous farmer of the priory 25 July 1388 (ibid., p. 245).

WOLSTON (Warws) St Aubyn (S. Pierre-sur-Dives) f. 1086 x 94
(No list in *VCH Warws*.)

John de Sancto Albino Occ. as pr. *c*. Mich. 1324 (PRO, E106/5/2, m. 9); July 1325 x July 1326

(PRO, E106/5/4, m. [8]). Previously occ. 12 July 1309 as m. of S. Pierre and attorney for the abbey (*CPR 1307–13*, p. 176).

Alexander Occ. as proctor and *custos* of the abbey of S. Pierre-sur-Dives at Wolston 1332 x 1333 (PRO, C270/12/40).

Sampson Occ. 7 Mar. 1344 (*CFR 1337–47*, p. 362); mentioned as former pr. 4 Aug. 1346 (ibid., p. 476).

Ralph of Coventry (Coventre) 1346– M. of S. Pierre, gtd keeping of the priory during the French war, deputed by his abb. to be his proctor-general in England 4 Aug. 1346 (ibid.). Pr. and proctor of S. Pierre in England, occ. 20 Oct. 1346 (*CPR 1345–48*, p. 194); 26 Mar. 1347 (*CCR 1346–49*, p. 249).

26 Oct. 1353 keeping of priory committed to William Belet, proctor-general of S. Pierre in England (*CFR 1347–56*, p. 381).

Stephen Boutyn M. of S. Pierre, occ. as proctor of the abbey at Wolston 29 June 1366 (Lincoln, Ep. Reg., X, f. 166r).

John Chatet (Chatel) Permission to stay in England 1378 (D. Matthew, *The Norman Monasteries and their English possessions*, app. III, p. 159). Occ. 10 Feb. 1378 (*CPR 1377–83*, p. 79); 16 Jan. 1385 (PRO, C269/15/55); 28 Oct. 1384, 12 June 1387 (*CFR 1383–91*, pp. 89, 183).

WOOTTON WAWEN (Warws), St Peter (Conches) f. 1066

Lists in *VCH Warws*, II, 135, citing Dugdale, *Warwickshire*, II, 815 from the cartulary at Evreux, Dép. Eure, II, f. 148; W. Cooper, *Wootton, its history and records* (Leeds, 1936), p. 50; *Heads*, I, 113. I am grateful for information on the priors and proctors kindly provided by Mr A.E.B. Owen from the archives of King's College, Cambridge.

Reginald Occ. 22 Sept. 1221 (Cambridge, King's Coll., WOW 231, ff. 9v–10r; *Warws F.*, I, no. 294); Oct. 1225 x Oct. 1226 (*Rot. Lit. Claus.*, II, 150); 25 Sept. 1227 (PRO, Hereford F. CP25/1/80/7, no. 115).

Ralph Occ. *c.* 1225 x 1230 (*Ctl. Reading*, I, no. 592); 3 Nov. 1240 (Cambridge, King's Coll., WOW 231, f. 25v; King's, WOW 586, f. 7v; *Warws F.*, I, no. 588); 1240 (Evreux ctl., f. 28r; *EEA* 13, no. 50); called *quondam prior* in undated cht of pr. Gerard (see below) *c.* 1251 (Cambridge, King's Coll., WOW 231, f. 21v; WOW 586, f. 10r). Seal (*Mon. Seals*, p. 101).

Taurin Occ. ? *temp.* Henry III (Cambridge, King's Coll., WOW 89).

Richard of St John (de Sancto Johanne) Occ. 13th cent., but date uncertain, prob. mid-13th cent, since one of the witnesses is found in cht. of 1243 (PRO, E315/38/41; Cambridge, King's Coll., WOW231, f. 10r; ibid., 586, f. 8v; cf. Evreux ctl., ff. 6r, 9r–v).

Gerard Occ. 3 May 1251 (Cambridge, King's Coll., WOW 94) and n.d. (ibid., 231, ff. 21v, 27r, 33v; 586, ff. 10r, 12r, 15v; Evreux ctl., ff. 12v–13v).

[**William Godin** occ, as proctor-general of Conches, not styled pr., from 30 May 1250 to 1261 (Cambridge, King's Coll., WOW 311, 273).]

[**John de Ebolo** Occ. as proctor 1 July 1250 (ibid., 305).]

Roger de Conchis Occ. 1 July 1260 (ibid., 305) and n.d. (ibid., 95; 231, ff. 30r, 37v; 586, ff. 13r, 17v).

[**John de Cleydon** Occ. as proctor 24 Aug. 1262 (Cambridge, King's Coll., WOW 484).]

Philip Occ. ? late 13th cent. (pal.: ibid., WOW 470). His position in the sequence of priors is unclear.

W. Bonndaye Occ. 5 Edward I (Nov. 1276 x Nov. 1277) (ibid., WOW 586, f. 16v) but this date seems unlikely, see Roger de Pavely below.

Peter de Altaribus Accused of attacking a monk and drunkenness – inquisition on 8 Apr. 1281; Peter to retire to Conches for penance 23 Apr. 1281 (*Reg. G. Giffard*, I, 129–33). Occ. 11 Feb. 1283 (ibid., 172).

[**Robert de Quercii** Occ. as proctor ? late 13th cent. (Cambridge, King's Coll., WOW 306).]

John de Barqueto (Barquarto) **–1285** Proctor-general of Conches, occ. 12 Mar. 1285 (*Reg. G. Giffard*, p. 255). Letter from bp of Worcester to the abbey of Conches touching the appt of a pr. 15 July 1285 (ibid., p. 262). Letter from bp to abb. that he is unwilling to proceed with the business of the pres. of Roger de Palliaco to Wootton, as J. de Barqueto has made no res. to the bp 30 Aug. 1285; notif. of recall of former pr. J. and vacancy of priory 26 Sept. 1285 (ibid., pp. 265–6).

Roger de Pavilliaco (Palliaco, Paveliaco, Pavely) **1285–1288** Inst. 21 Dec. 1285 on res. of John de Barquarto (ibid., p. 275, cf. 265 Roger's indemnity to bp for adm. by him without former pr.'s res. n.d. (ibid., p. 276). Occ. 10 Nov. 1287 (Cambridge, King's Coll., WOW 80). Res. by 25 May 1288 (*Reg. G. Giffard*, p. 341). Mentioned as *quondam prior* in memorandum of W. Bonndaye (see above), whose purported date is questionable (Cambridge, King's Coll., WOW 586, f. 16v).

John de Brocia (Broyca, Brocher, Brokschawe) **1288–** M. of Conches, inst. 25 May 1288 (ibid.). Occ. 8 Sept. 1295 (PRO, KB27, roll 146, m. 6d); Nov. 1295 x Nov. 1296 (PRO, E106/3/19, m. 11); Nov. 1296 x Nov. 1297 (PRO, E106/4/2, m. 4d); Nov. 1297 x Nov. 1298 (PRO, E106/4/8, m. 4); 3 June 1298 (Cambridge, King's Coll., WOW 5140); Nov. 1298 x Nov. 1299 (PRO, E106/4/9, m. 5d; E106/4/10, m. 6d); also occ. 18 Sept. 1300 (ibid., 231, f. 34r; 586, f. 15v) and Nov. 1302 x Nov. 1303 (PRO, E106/4/18, m. 11), but see below next entry. Brocia occ. as proctor 27 May 1304 (ibid., 168)

John de Avyroun (Avrion, Avyron) **1300–1305** Inst. 3 Aug. 1300, no reason being given for vacancy (*Reg. G. Giffard*, p. 527). Res. by 14 Oct. 1305 (*Reg. Gainsborough*, p. 116).

John de Brocia 1305– M. of Conches, inst. 14 Oct. 1305 (ibid.). Occ. 2 May 1308 (Norwich, Reg/1/1, f. 27v) and as proctor of the abbey 5 Apr. 1307 (*Reg. Gainsborough*, p. 178); 17 July, 26 Nov. 1308 (Cambridge, King's Coll., WOW 231, f. 35r; 555); as proctor 7 May 1308 (ibid., 437).

William de Lavercoyo 1309– M. of Conches, adm. 6 Nov. 1309 (*Reg. Reynolds*, p. 150). Occ. c. Mich. 1324 (PRO, E106/5/2, m. 9); July 1325 x July 1326 (PRO, E106/5/4, m. [8]); 8 Oct. 1326 (*Memo. Roll 1326–7*, p. 272).

Robert de Souef' –1328 Res. by 26 July 1328 (*Reg. Orleton (Worcs)*, no. 51).

John le Tonnelier 1328– Adm. 26 July 1328 (ibid., nos. 51, 675).

John de Lovers (Lotoveris) **–?1341** Occ. 29 Sept. 1338 (Cambridge, King's Coll., WOW 54); 12 Apr. 1340 (*CCR 1339–41*, p. 465); 22 July 1340 (Cambridge, King's Coll., WOW 114). Res. by 2 Jan. 1341 (*Reg. Bransford*, no. 384).

John de Silvaneto (Silvanetto) **1341–** Inst. 2 Jan. 1341 (ibid., no. 384). Previously occ. as proctor of Conches 1333 (Cambridge, King's Coll., WOW 585); 1336 (*Reg. Montacute*, no. 387).

John de Seyntliz (Senctlys) Occ. from 1 Aug. 1341 to 15 July 1343 (Cambridge, King's Coll., WOW 115, 590).

Michael de la Bouch –1349 Occ. 22 Feb. 1349 (ibid., WOW 352). D. by 13 Oct. 1349 (*Worcs. Reg. Sede Vacante*, p. 238).

William (Guillermus) (*sic*) *dictus* **Pinchart** (Pinchard, Pynchard) **1349–** Pres. 13 Oct. 1349, adm. 24 Oct. 1349 (ibid.). Occ. 18 Jan. 1352, 27 Mar. 1353 (Cambridge, King's Coll., WOW 119–20); Mich. 1354 x Mich. 1355 (PRO, E372/200, rot. 32).

[**Nicholas Malet** Occ. as proctor 22 Feb. 1349 to 23 Dec. 1359 (Cambridge, King's Coll., WOW 352, 465); as proctor-general of the abbey of Conches when gtd keeping of the priory during the French war 24 July 1358 (*CFR 1356–68*, p. 73).]

[**Michael Cheyne** (Chayne, Cheine, Scheneye) Occ. as proctor 1 Dec. 1364, 16 May 1373 (Cambridge, King's Coll., WOW 122–3); 23 Mar. 1364, 1367 (*Reg. T. Charlton*, pp. 66, 72).]

Occ. also as proctor-general of the abbey 14 Dec. 1373, 20 Nov. 1374, 24 Oct. 1377 (*CFR 1368–77*, pp. 227, 265; *CFR 1377–83*, p. 29).]

William de Chesnayo –1372 Occ. 11 June 1369, 6 Oct. 1369 (*CFR 1368–77*, pp. 15, 22). D. by 7 Mar. 1372 (Worcester, Reg. Lenn, p. 11).

John Maubert (Mambard, Mauberd, Mauberti, Mawebrede) **1372–1400** M. of Conches, adm. as pr. 7 Mar. 1372 (ibid.). occ. 20 Nov. 1374 (*CFR 1368–77*, p. 265); 24 Oct. 1377, 6 Feb. 1378, 14 July 1379 (*CFR 1377–83*, pp. 29, 78, 158); permission to remain in England 1378 (Mawebrede) (Matthew, *Norman Monasteries*, p. 157). D. by 11 Aug. 1400 (Worcester, Reg. Winchcombe, p. 101).

YORK, Holy Trinity (Marmoutier) f. 1089
Lists in *VCH Yorks*, III, 390; J. Solloway, *The Alien Benedictines of York*, p. 324; *Heads*, I, 113.
T. ? Occ. early 13th cent. (*EYC*, I, no. 208n).

Robert Latest known occ. 2 Nov. 1208 (*Yorks F., John*, p. 134). Presumably the pr. R. removed by abb. H. of Marmoutier *c.* 1208 x 1214 (addressed to S. dean of York, mentd in letter of 22 Nov. 1309 (*Reg. Greenfield*, II, pp. 76–7, no. 860 ?=Ralph, occ. n. d. (*CChR 1300–26*, p. 150).

William Presumably the pr. W. apptd in place of R. by abb. H. of Marmoutier *c.* 1207 x 1214, mentd 22 Nov. 1309 (*Reg. Greenfield*, II, pp. 76–7, no. 860). Occ. (W.) 9 Sept. 1216 (*Rot. Lit. Pat.*, p. 196b); 9 Oct. 1220 (*Ctl. St Bees*, no. 104); 1223, 1226 (*Yorks F. 1218–31*, pp. 54, 88); 1226 (*Lincs F.*, I, 216); Dec. 1228 x Dec. 1229 (*Reg. Wells*, III, 170).

Stephen 1231– Letter from the abb. of Marmoutier seeking admission for Stephen, m. of Marmoutier, as pr. 1231 (*Reg. Wickwane*, p. 249, no. 608). Occ. 1233 (*Reg. Wells*, II, 93–96); 1236 (BL, Cotton ms. Vespasian E XIX, f. 42v); 1237 (*Yorks F. 1232–46*, p. 48); Easter term 1241 (*CRR*, XVI, no. 1807).

Isembert 1242 Adm. 1242 (Martène, *Marmoutier*, II, 213, no source given).

Ranulf 1242– Adm. late 1242 (ibid., no source given).

William 1248– Adm. 1248 (ibid., no source given); W., m. of Marmoutier, gtd custody by Archbp Gray from 5 Nov. [1248] to the following Easter, on condition that he brought a letter of presn to the priory from the abb. of Marmoutier and sought instn. Otherwise his custody should be revoked (*Reg. Gray*, pp. 258–9). Occ. n.d. [1248 x 9] (*Ctl. Sallay*, II, 89–91).

Geoffrey Norman 1249– Adm. 1249 (Martène, *Marmoutier*, II, 213, no source given). Occ. 20 Oct. 1251, 27 Oct. 1252 (*Yorks F. 1246–72*, pp. 28, 89); Oct. 1251 x Oct. 1252 (*CCR 1327–30*, p. 33); Mich. 1252 x Trin. 1253 (Baildon, I, 238–9); 24 Nov. 1254 (*CPR 1247–58*, p. 383). Surname mentd in plea of Mich. 1289 (Baildon, I, 240).

Master Roger Pepyn Occ. Mich. 1260 (Baildon, I, 239). Solloway, *Alien Benedictines*, pp. 138–40, thinks Pepyn was pr. in 1258 and 1263, based on court case evidence.

William Wenge Mentioned as former pr. in plea of Hil. 1292 (Baildon, I, 240). His precise place in the sequence of priors is uncertain. Is he the pr. William allegedly ousted by pr. Hamo (see below)?

Hamo (Aymo) Occ. 12 Nov. 1265 (*CPR 1258–66*, p. 502); 1 Oct. 1267 (*Reg. W. Giffard*, p. 105); 17 Mar. 1272 (*CPR 1266–72*, p. 694); 31 Oct. 1272 (Baildon, I, 104); 8 July 1274 (PRO, Lincs F. CP25/1/132/51, no. 7). It was claimed in 1291 that Hamo by lay force in time of war occupied the priory over one William, then prior. Hamo was later removed by sentence of the court of Rome at the suit of Theobald, who had been apptd by the abb. Marmoutier. Hamo claimed to have been canonically apptd by the abb. (Baildon, I, p. 104). Removed by papal judges delegate before the death of Clement IV (29 Nov. 1268) (*CPL*, I, 447–8).

Theobald Apptd pr. by the abb. of Marmoutier in opposition to Hamo, who was in possession, mentd in case of 1291 (Baildon, I, 104).

Bartholomew Solloway states he was first nominated by abb. Stephen of Marmoutier in 1265 and gives him the surname Panem (Solloway, *Alien Benedictines*, p. 146). M. of Marmoutier, apptd on removal of Hamo, before d. of Clement IV (29 Nov. 1268), case – sentence against Hamo 5 Oct. 1274 (*CPL*, I, 447–8). Is this the same as Baldwin who occ. 10 May 1268 (*CPR 1266–72*, p. 226).

[4 Feb. (1275) countess Alice of Blois wrote to Edward I for priors to be established by force at Holy Trinity and Tickford priories (PRO, SC1/15/71); abb. of Marmoutier also wrote to Edward I about disputes at the two priories 11 Feb. 1275 (PRO, SC1/19/99). Similar letter from the duke of Brittany 26 Feb. 1275 (Solloway, *Alien Benedictines*, pp. 147–9).]

Geoffrey de Beaumont (Bellomonte) –?1281 Occ. 12 Apr. 1276 (*CCR 1272–79*, p. 417); Mich. 1280 x Mich. 1281 (PRO, E159/54, m. 23d); Easter 1288, Hil. 1292 ref. to as former prior (Baildon, I, 121, 240). In 1288 it was stated that Geoffrey had d. seven years earlier (ibid., 121).

[**Simon de Reda** Occ. *post* 1278 (Solloway, pp. 153, 324, citing ms. 'Histoire de Marmoutier' by Anselme Le Michel, ff. 122–3), but he occ. as pr. of Tickford from 1275 till he was dep. in 1291 (q.v.).]

John de Insula 1283–1305 Philip III of France writes to Edward I on behalf of the new pr. 22 June [1283] (PRO, SC1/17/156, cf. Solloway, *Alien Benedictines*, p. 156 who gives his appt as 1282). Occ. Trin. 1283 (PRO, CP40/50, m. 12); Mich. 1283, 1289 (Baildon, I, 239–40). Memorandum that unnamed pr. is to present letters of presentation of his abb. and to make obed. to archbp before 11 June 1284 (*Reg. Wickwane*, p. 331, no. 902); occ. several time from 15 Sept. 1284 to 6 Feb. 1292 (*CPR 1281–92*, pp. 134, 475); assault on unnamed pr. in Leeds parish church mentd in letter of 5 Jan. 1291 (*Reg. Romeyn*, I, p. 108, no. 285); excommunication of unnamed pr. 28 Jan. 1294, notification to king 9 May 1294 (ibid., pp. 138, 233, nos. 375, 670); signification 1294, 1298–9, 1301 (PRO, C85/173/95; C85/176/32 & 40; C85/177/162, 24 & 48); from Nov. 1295 x Nov. 1296 to Nov. 1298 x Nov. 1299 (PRO, E106/3/119, m. 6; E106/4/9, m. 3; E106/4/10, m. 3). Excommunicated 11 Oct. 1300 (*Reg. Corbridge*, I, 31); occ. 24 Feb. 1302 (*CPR 1301–07*, p. 20). D. by 23 July 1305 (*Yorks Inq.*, IV, 106–7), but Trin. 1306 the sheriff was ordered to distrain pr. John (Baildon, II, 88) – is this evidence for another pr. John, or merely a scribal error?

[br. **John de Bello Ramo** Occ. as *custos* of priory 19 July 1300 (*Reg. Corbridge*, I, 26); unnamed *custos* mentd 26 Nov. 1302 (ibid., 77)]

Oliver de Bages Notification of excommunication for contumacy 3 Feb. 1308 (*Reg. Greenfield*, II, p. 48, no. 776; cf. PRO, C85/178/16). Occ. 26 Mar. 1308 (*CPR 1307–13*, p. 57); Mich. 1310 (PRO, CP40/183, m. 138d). Unnamed pr. alleged to be absent at Marmoutier 20 Nov. 1309 (*Reg. Greenfield*, II, p. 76, no. 860).

Geoffrey de Chiveny (?) Occ. Mich. 1317 (Baildon, II, 88); 8 Dec. 1318 (*Ctl. Fountains*, I, 282); 1322 (*CCR 1318–23*, p. 674); 16 May 1323 (*CCR 1318–23*, p. 127) mentd as former pr. 13 Feb. 1327 (*CCR 1327–30*, p. 33).

Hugh Aubyn Occ. *c.* Mich. 1324 (PRO, E106/5/2, m. 10d); 8 Oct. 1326 (*Memo. Roll 1326–7*, p. 272); Easter 1327, Mich. 1328 (*Index to Placita de Banco*, pp. 823, 751, 766); Mich. 1327, 1330 (Baildon, I, 240–1); 25 Apr. 1331 (*CCR 1330–33*, p. 303); going overseas 28 Apr. 1331 (*CPR 1330–34*, p. 110).

John de Boys Brimol –1340/1 Occ. 20 July 1335 (*CCR 1333–37*, p. 508); 1336, 1337 (Baildon, II, 89); Hil. 1338 (ibid., I, 41); 2 June 1340 (*CCR 1339–41*, p. 482). Ceased to be pr. by 1 Feb. 1341 (*CFR 1337–47*, pp. 206–7).

Odo (Eudo) Fryket (Friquet) M. of Marmoutier, royal gt of keeping of priory 1 Feb. 1341 – the abbot of Marmoutier had made him pr. in place of John de Boys Brimol (ibid.). Occ. Trin. 1341 (*YB 15 Edward III*, pp. 172–6). Solloway states he was dep. by the abb. of Marmoutier (*Alien Benedictines*, pp. 209, 211).

Richard de Chichele (Chicole) Occ. 8 Oct. 1341, 8 Feb. 1342 (*CFR 1337–47*, pp. 243, 261); 1344 (*Cal. Misc. Inq.* II, 488); 11 July 1345 (*CCR 1343–46*, p. 636).

John de Chosiaco (Choziaco) Occ. 20 Mar. 1350 (*CFR 1347–56*, p. 221); 25 Nov. 1356 (*CPR 1354–58*, p.476); 13 Apr. 1361, 31 May 1363 (DCD, Loc. XXVI. 26). Seal (*Durham Seals*, II, p. 592, no. 3592).

Peter Carpenter Occ. 11 June 1369, 6 Oct. 1369 (*CFR 1369–77*, pp. 14, 25); 1369 (Baildon, I, 241); 1370 (PRO, E179/63/5); 5 May 1377 (*CFR 1369–77*, p. 396); 14 Mar. 1378, 18 Oct. 1381 (*CPR 1377–83*, pp. 81, 269); 8 Apr. 1381 (*Cal. Misc. Inq.*, IV, 84).

The next recorded pr., **John Castell** (*alias* **Eschall**), m. of Marmoutier, was pres. to priory, in king's gift on account of the French war 7 Nov. 1383 (*CPR 1381–85*, p. 325).

THE CLUNIAC HOUSES

No names have been found in this period for Aldermanshaw and Nottingham (Basford).

ACRE, see **CASTLE ACRE**

BARNSTAPLE (Devon), St Mary Magdalen (S.Martin des Champs) f. *c.* 1107
  Lists in Oliver, pp. 196–7; *Heads*, I, 114.
Richard Occ. early 1227 (Prynne, *Records*, III, 74).
Baldwin Occ. 4 July 1238 (*Devon F.*, I, p. 174, no. 353).
Peter Occ. 6 June 1249 (*Devon F.*, I, p. 249, no. 492).
Unnamed pr. prof. obed. 22 July 1261 (*Reg. Bronescombe*, p. 24; *Reg. W. Bronescombe*, I, no. 349).
Simon de Gorney (Gurneye) **1265–** Adm. 20 Aug. 1265, no reason given for vacancy (*Reg. Bronescombe*, p. 112; *Reg. W. Bronescombe*, II, no. 596). Occ. 8 Dec. 1270 (*CPR 1266–72*, p. 497). Excommunicated 20 Apr. 1272 (*Reg. Bronescombe*, p. 24; *Reg. W. Bronescombe*, II, no. 901).
Monition, dated 25 Feb. 1275, to the pr. and convent of S. Martin des Champs to present a suitable person to be pr. of Barnstaple, *diutius vacantis*, by 1 May (ibid., pp. 24–5; *Reg. W. Bronescombe*, II, no. 1053).
Theobald de Curtipalacio 1275– M. of Barnstaple, adm. and prof. obed. 29 June 1275 (ibid., p. 25; *Reg. W. Bronescombe*, II, no. 1087). Letter of caption 1279 (*Reg. Pecham*, I, 24). Previously pr. of St James, Exeter. mentd 1279 (*Cluniac Visitations*, p. 25). Occ. 10 June 1278, 31 May 1279 (PRO, C85/3/5–6).
Pascasius (Paschasius) Occ. going overseas 19 Mar. 1291 (*CPR 1281–92*, p. 425); Nov. 1295 x Nov. 1296 (PRO, E106/3/19, m. 10d); Nov. 1296 x Nov. 1297 (PRO, E106/4/2, m. 2); Nov. 1297 x Nov. 1298 (PRO, E106/4/8, m. 1d; E106/4/9. m. 1d); Nov. 1298 x Nov. 1299 (PRO, E106/4/10, m. 2d); Easter 1300 (PRO, E106/4/14, m. 4); Nov. 1302 x Nov. 1303 (PRO, E106/4/18, m. 5); n.d. (PRO, C146/3642; /3881; /5469).
John Occ. 18 Mar. 1308 (PRO, C146/4562). ? the same as John de Nantolio below.
John de Nantolio 1314– As pr. of Barnstaple, given custody of St James' priory, Exeter 17 Mar. 1314 and coll. by lapse 1 Aug. 1314, mand. for induction 2 Aug.1314 (*Reg. Stapeldon*, p. 214, cf. p. 188; *Reg. Bytton*, p. 412).
John Notarial instrument regarding prof. obed. to archdn of Barnstaple 1 Dec. 1319 (PRO, C270/30/12). Commn apptd 25 Sept. 1323 to investigate charges against pr. John and to suspend him if reports were true (*Reg. Stapeldon*, p.41; PRO, C270/30/13). Occ. 1324 (PRO, E106/5/2, m. 7d); 1326 (*Memo. Roll 1326–7*, p. 272); Trin. 1327 (*Index to Placita de Banco*, p. 92). Prob. to be identified with John de Sancta Gemma (see next entry).
John de Sancta Gemma Occ. 3 Nov. 1332 (*Reg. Grandisson*, I, 263). House under interdict following desertion by John de Sancta Gemma 21 Nov. 1332 (ibid., I, 670). Res. by 18 Mar. 1333 (ibid., III, 1292).
[**John** *dictus* **de Parys** Commn to remove John *dictus* de Parys from the rule and administration of the priory 29 Sept. 1332. He had intruded himself, while pr. John de Sancta Gemma was still alive (ibid., II, 658–9).]
John Sayer (Soier, Soyer) **1333–1334** M. of Cluny, priest, inst. 18 Mar. 1333 on res. of John de Sancta Gemma (ibid., III, 1292). Pres. to priory but bp reluctant to adm. him as he was publicly defamed – dissolute, having children, dilapidations, etc. – while he was in Wales (ibid.,

I, 263). He was previously pr. of St Clears (q.v.). Occ. 8 May 1333 (ibid., I, 265–6). Appt of custodians of priory 5 Aug. 1334 vacant by d. of John Soyer (ibid., II, 760–1). Referred to in 1335 as *maledictus predecessor suus immediatus* (ibid., I, 289).

Imbert de Dannanchiis (Dauneschies) **1334–1349** M. of Cluny, inst. 10 Nov. 1334 on d. of John Soyer (ibid., III, 1304). Lic. to visit mother-house 22 June 1335 (ibid., II, 787). Occ. (Tibert) 9 Aug. 1347 (*CPR 1345–48*, p. 397); Mich. 1348 x Mich. 1349 (PRO, E372/194, rot. 5). D. by 11 Apr. 1350 (*CFR 1347–56*, p. 230), but cf. next inst. below.

Reginald Pizdoe (Pyzdone) **1349–1351** M. of Barnstaple, inst. 9 Dec. 1349, no reason given for vacancy (*Reg. Grandisson*, III, 1402). Occ. 11 Apr. 1350 (*CPR 1347–56*, p. 230). Res. by 7 Nov. 1351 (*Reg. Grandisson*, III, 1420), cf. gt of keeping of priory during French war to br. Roger Capy, m. of S. Martin des Champs 16 Oct. 1351 (*CFR 1347–56*, p. 309, see next entry).

Roger Hayn *dictus* **de Capiago** (Capi, Capiaco, Cappe, Capy) **1351–1376** Notif. to the monks of Barnstaple that Roger had been apptd pr. by the vicar-general of the pr. and convent of S. Martin des Champs 26 Aug. 1351 (PRO, C270/30/15). Adm. 7 Nov. 1351 on res. of Reginald (*Reg. Grandisson*, III, 1420). 23 June 1376 'has been so infirm for the last 5 years, and still is, that he cannot help himself and govern the priory': Ralph Chelpham, m. of Barnstaple, born in England, gtd keeping of priory (*CFR 1368–77*, p. 353, and see next entry). Pr. Roger d. by 17 Dec. 1376 (*Reg. Brantingham*, I, 48).

Ralph Chelpham (Chalfham, Chalveham, Chelfham, Chelsham) **1376–1392** M. of Cluny, nominated by king 17 Dec. 1376 (*CPR 1374–77*, p. 393; *Reg. Brantingham*, I, 48). Inst. 29 Dec. 1376 (*Reg. Brantingham*, I, 48; PRO, SC1/41/190). D. by 28 May 1392 (*Reg. Brantingham*, I, 120).

BERMONDSEY (Surrey), St Saviour (La Charité) f. 1089

Lists in *VCH Surrey*, II, 75–7 (from unreliable *Ann. Bermondsey*; but on the annals see revised version by M. Brett, 'The annals of Bermondsey, Southwark and Merton' in D. Abulafia, M. Franklin and M. Rubin eds., *Church and City 1000–1500: essays in honour of Christopher Brooke* (Cambridge, 1992), pp. 279–310); *Heads*, I, 114–16; R. Graham, *English Ecclesiastical Studies*, pp.121ff.; Graham, 'Bermondsey', pp. 188–91.

Hugh **–1235** Occ. 4 Dec. 1202 (PRO, CP25/1/225/2, no. 37); 16 Oct. 1219, 25 Feb. 1227 (*Soms F.*, I, 39, 57); from 27 Jan. 1222 to 20 Jan. 1230 (*Kent F.*, pp. 73, 107); Oct. 1221 x Oct. 1222, Oct. 1225 x Oct. 1226, Oct. 1232 x Oct. 1233 (*Surrey F.*, pp.12, 13, 18); 1227 (*Bucks Eyre*, no. 112; *Bucks F.*, I, 55); 9 Feb. 1235 (*Essex F.*, I, 100); 16 Apr. 1235 (PRO, Herts F., CP25/1/84/15, no. 192). D. 1235 (Bodl., Rawlinson ms. B.177, f. 222v).

Peter **1235–** Mand. for seisin 16 Nov. 1235, sent to England by Landric, pr. of La Charité (*CR 1234–37*, p. 209). Occ. 1 July 1236, 12 Nov. 1236 (*Soms F.*, I, 84, 101).

Guichard (Wyschard) **1238–** Writ *de intendendo* 10 June 1238. apptd by Theobald, pr. and convent of La Charité (*CPR 1242–47*, p. 223); Occ. 27 Oct. 1238 (PRO, Surrey F., CP25/1/225/10, no. 14; *Surrey F.*, p. 21); (G.) n.d. (*c.* 1240) (*Chartes de Cluny*, VI, no. 4782).

Imbert (Humbert, Hymbert) Prob. also pr. of Much Wenlock. Occ. from Oct. 1241 x Oct. 1242 to 12 June 1250 (*Surrey F.*, pp. 26, 33; PRO, Surrey F., CP25/1/226/14, no. 13); Oct. 1246 x Oct. 1247 (*London & Middlesex F.*, p. 31); 1248 (PRO, Just.1/231, m. 24d); 1249 x 1253 (*Ctl. Holy Trinity Aldgate*, no. 462).

Aymo (Aymon, Eymo) **de Montibus** **1252–1261** Fealty to king and mand. for seisin 22 Aug. 1252 (*CR 1251–53*, p. 148). Apptd to Much Wenlock 9 Apr. 1261 (*CPR 1258–66*, p. 148; *EHR*, 44, p. 101).

Gilbert de Bussa **1261–** M. of Bermondsey, writ *de intendendo* 5 Aug. 1261, apptd by pr. of La Charité (*CPR 1258–66*, p.171).

John de Chartres (Tickford) **1266–1272** Temps. 5 Feb. 1266, apptd by Miles, pr. of La Charité (*CPR 1258–66*, p. 544). Occ. Oct. 1268 x Oct. 1269 (*Surrey F.*, p.45); 20 July 1270 he was committed the rule of Northampton, St Andrew by the pr. of La Charité, as well as Bermondsey (*CPR 1266–72*, p. 445). Occ. 26 Apr. 1271 (*CR 1268–72*, pp. 409–10); 9 June 1272 (PRO, E315/37/224). Apptd to Much Wenlock 1272 and then pr. of Lewes 1285 (q.v.). Seal (*Mon. Seals*, p. 8; R. Graham, 'The seals of the Cluniac monastery of Bermondsey', *Surrey Arch. Coll.*, XXXIX (1931), 78–9).

Henry de Montemauri 1272– Writ *de intendendo* 12 Nov. 1272, apptd by pr. of La Charité (*CPR 1266–72*, p. 714). Occ. 15 Nov. 1274 (PRO, E40/767); 18 Feb. 1275 (PRO, C85/2/25). Seal (Graham, 'Bermondsey', p. 185).

11 Dec. 1275 pr. of La Charité informs king that he has apptd the pr. of Much Wenlock as keeper of Bermondsey (PRO, SC1/16/26, cf. *CPR 1272–81*, p. 131); another letter 16 Aug. 1279; his agreement with Adam de Stratton over Bermondsey. The cellarer of Bermondsey has been apptd pr. (? Peter below) (PRO, SC1/16/27).

John (de Chartres) For name see *Cluniac Visitations*, p. 21. Occ. 8 July 1276 (PRO, Herts F., CP25/1/86/35, no. 49); 15 July 1279 (PRO, F. Divers Cos. CP25/1/284/21, no. 84; *Essex F.*, II, 24). In 1279 it was stated that the unnamed pr. had been in office 4 years (*Cluniac Visitations*, p. 21).

Peter of Mont St Vincent (de Monte Sancti Vincentii) Occ. Nov. 1278 x Nov. 1279, Nov. 1281 x Nov. 1282 (*Surrey F.*, pp. 53, 56); 20 Sept. 1279 (*CFR 1272–1307*, p. 117); 21 Sept. 1279 (*CPR 1272–81*, p. 325); Mich. 1280 x Mich. 1281 (PRO, E159/54, m. 22d); 20 Jan. 1281 (PRO, F. Divers Cos., CP25/1/284/21, no. 92).

Robert 1285– Styled sub-cellarer of La Charité, apptd to Bermondsey by pr. of La Charité, petition for temps. 1 Oct. 1285 (PRO, C84/8/38). Royal gt of keeping of priory, now void, to Robert, pr. of Coulonges 5, 7 Oct. 1285 (*CPR 1281–92*, p. 194; *CFR 1272–1307*, p. 221). Occ. as pr. Mich. 1285 x Mich. 1286 (PRO, E159/59, mm. 1(2), 6). A dispute arose, since a letter of the mayor of London to the king's treasurer refers to the ejection of a pr. of Bermondsey by the pr. of Much Wenlock and his replacement by a foreigner n.d. (*c.* 1284 x 1286) (PRO, SC1/48/73).

Henry de Bonville (de Bono Villar') *alias* **Normanus 1285/6–1293** Petition for temps. by pr. of La Charité on behalf of Henry *quondam* of Payern 21 Sept. 1284 (PRO, C84/8/31). Late dean of Payern (Patriniaco), apptd by pr. of La Charité, temps. 5 May 1285 (*CPR 1281–92*, p. 159). Also received temps. of Much Wenlock 10 Sept. 1285 (ibid., p. 192). A Norman, almoner of St Andrew, Northampton, apptd by the pr. of La Charité 1286, after Mich. (*EHR*, 44, p. 98; Cambridge, Corpus Christi ms. 281, f. 33v); 8 Feb. 1287, 14 Feb. 1288, 20 July 1290, 24 Oct. 1292 (*CPR 1281–92*, pp. 263, 290, 376, 508); 8 July 1293 (*CPR 1292–1301*, p. 27). D. 28 Aug. 1293 (*Cal. Misc. Inq.*, I, 458; cf. PRO, C84/11/29).

William of La Charité *alias* **Kant 1293–1297** Sub-cellarer of La Charité, cert. to king of his appt by the pr. of La Charité 9 Sept. 1293 (PRO, C84/11/29); temps. 5 Oct. 1293 (*CPR 1292–1301*, p. 39). Res. by 1 June 1297 (PRO, C84/13/2).

Peter de Sancto Simphoriano 1297–1298 Pres. by pr. of La Charité 1 June 1297 (ibid.); writ *de intendendo* 4 July 1297, mand. to keeper of priory to restore temps. 13 Dec. 1297, pr. Peter is staying overseas in the king's service (*CPR 1292–1301*, pp. 289, 325). D. by 27 Nov. 1298 (ibid., p. 386).

Henry 1298–1312 Mentd as a former pr. of St Helen's, temps. 27 Nov. 1298 (ibid.). Occ. 1303–1305 (*CPR 1301–07*, pp. 188, 273–4, 277, 368); 1308 (*CPR 1307–13*, pp.138–9); 9 Oct. 1311 (*CCR 1307–1313*, p. 441). D. (H.) by 23 Aug. 1312 (ibid., p. 548).

Peter of St Laurence (de Sancto Laurentio) **1312–** Letter to pr. of La Charité recommending eln in succession to pr. H. 23 Aug. 1312 (ibid.). Cert. by pr. of La Charité of his appt of Peter 9 Oct. 1312 (PRO, C84/17/10). M. of Bermondsey, temps. 28 Oct. 1312 (*CPR 1307–13*, p.505). Occ. 20 Apr. 1316 (*CPR 1313–17*, p. 448); 3 Nov. 1317, 26 Feb. 1320 (*CPR 1317–21*, pp. 9l, 422); 11 Mar. 1321, 13 June 1322 (*CPR 1321–24*, p.441). Appt during pleasure of 2 keepers of the priory which is in debt 17 June 1320; king restores priory to pr. 26 Oct. 1320; further appt of keepers 20 Nov. 1320 (*CPR 1317–21*, pp. 457, 513, 529); order to restore to Peter all the goods of the priory 1 Oct. 1321 (*CCR 1318–23*, p. 403). Request to the pr. of La Charité to recall the present pr. of Bermondsey and to abstain from sending another pr. until the king shall inform him of some circumspect and industrious religious man 21 Nov. 1320 (*CCR 1318–23*, pp. 344–5). Letter from Edward II to the pr. of La Charité thanking him for nominating John de Cusancia, m. of Lewes, 'a wise and circumspect man supported by the protection of powerful friends' as pr. of Bermondsey. The king urges his pres. to the priory with all speed 8 Feb. 1321 (ibid., p. 358 – for John see below). Letter of pr. of La Charité to Edward II about the deposition of the pr. of Bermondsey – a man not in orders cannot be apptd 4 Jan. (no year, ?1321) (PRO, SC1/16/28). Occ. 18 Sept. 1321 (PRO, C81/1787/1). Protection for 1 yr for Peter de Sancto Laurentio, late pr. of Bermondsey, prosecuting business in the king's courts 12 Jan. 1327 (*CPR 1324–27*, p. 347).

Walter de Diluiz (Deluiz, Duluyd, Duluydz, de Lutz) **1322–1324** Temps. 6 July 1322, apptd by pr. Peter of La Charité (*CPR 1321–24*, pp. 143–4). Order for his arrest and committal to the Tower 6 Jan. 1324, for harbouring the king's rebellious knights (*Reg. Asserio*, p. 618; *CPR 1321–24*, p. 358). 9 Jan. 1324 house in custody as pr. in gaol (*CPR 1321–24*, p. 361; *Reg. Asserio*, pp. 618–19). Safeconduct for former pr. returning home to his native country 13 May 1324 (ibid., p. 397). The king takes the priory into his protection because of a dispute between Walter and pr. John de Cusancia and custody gtd to Nicholas de Gildeburgh and Nicholas de Acton, king's clerks 8 July 1327 (*CPR 1327–30*, p. 136). Walter de Duluydz, late pr. of Bermondsey, came to the king and has shown that he held the priory until Robert de Baldock, Edward II's chancellor, falsely charged him with being of the party of Thomas, earl of Lancaster, and caused him to be detained in the Tower of London until he res. his priory for fear of perpetual imprisonment. The king requests the pr. of La Charité to restore Walter to Bermondsey 12 Aug. 1327 (*CCR 1327–30*, pp. 215–16). Order to Roger de Gildesburgh and Nicholas de Acton not to meddle further with the custody of the priory, which the king committed to them by reason of the dispute between Walter and John de Cusancia, pr. of Bermondsey. Concord has been established between Walter and pr. John 4 May 1328 (ibid., p. 278).

John de Cusancia (Cusance) **1324–1360** Brother of James de Cusancia, pr. of Prittlewell (*CCR 1323–27*, pp. 310–11) and of William de Cusancia, king's clerk (*CFR 1337–47*, p. 277). Cert. of appt by pr. Peter of La Charité 1 Apr. 1324 (PRO, C84/20/19). M. of Lewes, temps. 18 Apr. 1324 (*CPR 1321–24*, p. 407). Protection gtd 30 Sept. 1324 (born in Burgundy) (ibid., p. 30). Res. by 15 Oct. 1360 (*CFR 1356–68*, p. 140).

John de Caro Loco (Cariloco) **1360–1364** Occ. 15 Oct. 1360 (ibid.); 1363 (Bodl., ms. Gough Norfolk 18, f. 12r); 5 Feb. 1364 (ibid.). Abb. of Cluny transfers him to be pr. of Lewes 22 May 1364 (PRO, SC1/42/17).

Peter de Telonio (Tenolio, Tevolio, Tolonio) **1364–1372** Late pr. of Pontefract, king conf. gt of custody of Bermondsey, made by the pr. of Much Wenlock, vicar-general of the pr. of La Charité in England 14 June 1364 (*CPR 1361–64*, p. 505). Occ. (Peter de Cendio) 29 Nov. 1372 (*Reg. John of Gaunt 1371–5*, I, no. 62). D. 29 Dec. 1372 (*Ann. Bermondsey*, p. 478).

Richard de Dounton (Dunton) **1373/4–1390** Pres. by pr. of La Charité 28 Mar. 1373, no reason given for vacancy (PRO, C84/30/46). Temps. 30 Apr. 1374 (*CPR 1370–74*, p. 433). First English pr. (*Ann. Bermondsey*, p. 478). Occ. 18 Jan. 1374, 14 June 1374, 5 July 1374

(*CFR 1368–77*, pp. 237, 250, 252, cf. 232). Denization of priory at request of pr. Richard 29 May 1381 (*CPR 1381–85*, p. 18). Cess. by 1 Dec. 1390 (PRO, C84/34/51; cf. *CPR 1385–92*, pp. 332–3).

BRETTON, *see* MONK BRETTON

BROMHOLM (Norfolk), St Andrew (Cluny) f. Apr. 1113 (dependent on Castleacre). 1195 (dependent on Cluny).

Lists in *VCH Norfolk*, II, 363; *Heads*, I, 116.

Wlricus Occ.12th or 13th cent. (CUL, ms. Mm 2.20, ff. 43v–44).

W. Possibly the same. Occ. 28 Jan. 1226 (ibid., f. 10r–v).

Vincent –1248 Occ. +12 Apr. 1229 (BL, Harl. ms. 2110, f. 141r–v); Oct. 1236 x Oct. 1237 (*Suffolk F. (Rye)*, p. 39); Mar. 1239 (*Cluny Chts.*, II, 262); 20 Apr. 1245 (*CChR 1226–57*, p. 283; CUL, ms. Mm 2.20, ff. 2v–3). D. by 17 July 1248 (*CR 1247–51*, p. 65).

Clement 1248– Mand. for seisin 17 July 1248 (ibid.). Occ. 1250 (Oxford, Merton Coll. mun. 1726); from Oct. 1252 x Oct. 1253 to Oct. 1267 x Oct. 1268 (*Norfolk F. (Rye)*, pp. 85, 94); Oct. 1257 x Oct. 1258 (*Suffolk F. (Rye)*, p. 59); 2 monks nominated as attorneys on account of his debility 28 Mar. 1256 (*CPR 1247–58*, p. 512). Coadjutor apptd at General Chapter 4 May 1259 – '*Item diffiniunt quod priori de Brimoh. propter eius debilitatem et impotentiam detur unus monachus eiusdem ecclesie utilis coadjutor*' (Charvin, I, no. 50).

John Occ. 1 July 1268 (CUL, ms. Mm 2.20, f. 52r); from Oct. 1267 x Oct. 1268 to Oct. 1273 x Oct. 1274 (*Norfolk F. (Rye)*, pp. 105, 113); Oct. 1269 x Oct. 1270, Oct. 1270 x Oct. 1271 (*Suffolk F. (Rye)*, pp. 71, 73).

Roger Occ. 11 Feb. 1286 (Charvin, I, no. 119); 24 Dec 1290, 21 Dec. 1292 (CUL, ms. Mm 2.20, ff. 37r, 50r); 22 Mar. 1293 (Charvin, II, no. 140). In 1294 it was reported: '*Prior est impotens sui, set habet bonam memoriam*' (Charvin, II, no. 144).

William of Tuttington (Tutingdon, Tutington) –1313 Occ. 13 May 1304, 18 June 1307 (CUL, ms. Mm 2.20, ff. 21r, 46r). D., lic. to el. 18 Feb. 1313 (*CPR 1307–13*, p. 552, cf. *CCR 1307–13*, p. 526; *CFR 1307–19*, p. 163). Mentd as late pr. by 23 May 1313 (*CPR 1307–13*, p. 526).

William of Witton (Wittone, Wytton) 1313–1335 M. of Bromholm, eln pres. to king for royal ass. 2 Mar. 1313 (PRO, C84/17/14); royal ass. 30 Mar. 1313, temps. 3 Apr. 1313 (*CPR 1307–13*, pp. 562, 560). Occ. as pr.-el. 2 Apr. 1313 (*CCR 1307–13*, p. 526). Occ. 1314, 1318, 1319 (CUL, ms. Mm 2.20, ff. 25r, 50r, 89v); 23 Nov. 1321 (Norwich, Reg/1/1, f. 93r). D., lic. to el. for John, earl of Cornwall 26 Feb. 1335 (Norwich, Reg/1/2, f. 71r–v).

John of Hardingham 1335– M. of Bromholm, bp's bl. requested; bl. and prof. obed. 22 Mar. 1335 (ibid.). Occ. 6, 13 Sept. 1337, 22 July 1340 (CUL, ms. Mm 2.20, ff. 29r, 28v, 25r).

The next recorded pr., **Thomas Herlyngg**, occ. in clerical subsidy 1378 x 1381 (PRO, E179/15/14).

CASTLE ACRE (Norfolk), St Mary (Lewes) f. 1089; denizen 1351 x 1374

Lists in *VCH Norfolk*, II, 358; a 15th cent. list (names only) in BL, Harl. ms. 2110, f. 143v; *Heads*, I, 117.

Philip de Mortimer (Mortemer) Latest recorded occ. 18 Jan. 1209 (*Norfolk F. 1201–15*, no. 134).

Robert (de Bozoun so list, ?d'Alencon). Occ. 6 Oct. 1220 (BL, Harl. ms. 2110, f. 115r); Oct. 1219 x Oct. 1220 (*Norfolk F. (Rye)*, p. 36); Easter 1224 (*Essex F.*, I, 67); Mich. term 1228, Hil. term 1230 (*CRR*, XIII, nos. 834, 2642).

Henry named inserted in BL, Harl. ms. 2110 list. Occ. n.d. (13th cent.) (BL, Add. Cht. 15508).

Ralph of Weasenham (Wesenham) Occ. Oct. 1234 x Oct. 1235 (*Norfolk F. (Rye)*, p. 56); (R.) 1235 (*Ctl. Lewes, Norfolk*, no. 146); (*c.* June–July) 1235 (*CR 1234–37*, p. 184).[1]

William of Kent Pr. of Prittlewell, fealty to king and mand. for seisin 16 May 1241 (*CR 1237–42*, p. 301). Occ. 23 Nov. 1243 (*Ctl. Lewes, Norfolk*, no. 143).

Adam Occ. Oct. 1250 x Oct. 1251 (*Norfolk F. (Rye)*, pp. 81, 83).

John de Grangiis Occ. from Oct. 1252 x Oct. 1253 to Oct.1259 x Oct. 1260 (*Norfolk F. (Rye)*, pp. 85, 88, 97).

Walter de Stanmer Occ. Oct. 1268 x Oct. 1269 (*Norfolk F. (Rye)*, p. 106); (William) 19 Oct. 1269 (*Ctl. Lewes, Norfolk*, no. 142 & n.).

Robert de Hakebeach (Hakebeche) Occ. n.d. (*c.* 1270) (Norfolk RO, ms. 3794/8A.2); Easter 1278 (PRO, CP40/24, m. 81d); Mich. 1279 x Mich. 1280 (PRO, E159/53, m.13d).

William de Schorham (Soram) Occ. Mich. 1280 x Mich. 1281, Mich. 1281 x Mich. 1282 (PRO, E159/54, m. 22d; E159/55, m. 9). Noted at General Chapter 9 May 1283 that he had been removed by the pr. of Lewes but was *contumax, rebellis et inobediens* (Charvin, I, p. 422, no. 111).

Benedict of Cluny (Cluniaco) Apptd by pr. of Lewes on removal of William de Soram but could not gain possession, mentd at General Chapter 9 May 1283 (ibid.). Occ. Mich. 1284 x Mich. 1285 (PRO, E159/58, m. 17); 12 May 1285 (PRO, C85/4/15); Jan. 1286 (PRO, E159/59, m. 6d); July 1286 (PRO, C241/6/71); Mich. 1286 (PRO, E159/60, m. 14); June 1287 – Aug. 1288 (PRO, C241/2/21; /8/90, 330).

Robert Porter Full name in BL, Harl. ms. 2110 list. Occ. 22 Oct. 1292 (*CPR 1281–92*, p. 510).

John Hamelyn Occ. 1296 (PRO, E210/8461); 23 July 1304 (BL, Harl. ms. 2110, f. 130v; BL, Add. ms. 46353, f. 262r). Mentd in 1314 as a former pr. (*YB XVIII*, 199), and prob. the former pr. John referred to in 1305 (PRO, CP40/153, m. 31).

The king has heard that the pr. of Lewes had conferred Castle Acre (vacant by the d. of the last pr.) upon the pr. of Clifford. The King requests the pr. of Lewes not to omit to make Arnald de Pinoliis, m. of Lewes and the king's chaplain, pr. of Castle Acre if it is still vacant, or at least pr. of Clifford, 20 Jan. 1302 (*CCR 1302–07*, p. 6). No record of this name is known for either house.

John of Acre Occ. 6 June 1307 (PRO, C241/53/65). Indulgence of 40 days issued by Bp Gilbert of Annaghdown for those hearing masses of pr. John and praying for his health and state while he lives and for his soul when he shall die, 30 Jan. 1308 (PRO, E135/6/40).

Walter le Frounceys Full name in BL, Harl. ms. 2110 list. Occ. 14 Dec 1311 (Norwich, Reg/1/1, f. 44r); 12 Jan. 1314 (ibid., f. 55r); 14 Feb. 1314 (ibid., f. 56v); 25 Nov. 1314 (ibid., f. 59r).

Peter de Jocellis Occ. 9 Jan. 1317 (Norwich, Reg/1/1, f. 67v); 26 Apr. 1317 (ibid., f. 70r); 1320 (*CCR 1318–23*, p. 225); 1321 (PRO, CP40/238, m. 1); 1322 (Norwich, Reg/1/1, f. 94v); 20 May 1327 (*CPR 1327–30*, p. 105); Easter 1327 – Trin. 1328 (*Index to Placita de Banco*, p. 424). Pr. of Lewes (q.v.)

Guy de Charrins (Charyns) Occ. 28 Feb. 1330 (Norwich, Reg/1/2, f. 34v); 29 Nov. 1330 (*CCR 1330–33*, p. 166); 4 Feb. 1331 (ibid., p. 274); 5 May 1334 (*Reg. Burghersh*, I, no. 417); 1336 (*CCR 1333–37*, p. 651); 2 Dec. 1337 (Norwich, Reg/1/3, f. 4v); 21 Aug. 1338 (ibid., f. 16r); 10 Feb. 1340 (*CPR 1338–40*, p. 487).[2]

William de Warenne (Varena, Varenne, Warrenna) illegitimate son of Earl John de Warenne (of Surrey). Pr. of Monks Horton (q.v.). Said to have been prov. by Pope Clement VI May

---

[1] Blomefield, *Norfolk*, VIII, 375 also gives Ralph occ. 1239 and Walter de Stanmer in 1258, 1267, but no sources are provided and their reliability is in doubt.

[2] Pr. John occ. 20 Mar. 1333 (*Newington Longville Chts.*, no. 129), but this is prob. a scribal error. He does not feature in the BL, Harl. ms. 2110 list.

1342 x May 1343 (*Accts of Papal Collectors*, pp. 195, 232, 328, 368, 497). Dispensation (John) for a conventual priory, previously having had a disp. for illegitimacy for a non-conventual priory 17 Jan. 1344 (*CPP*, p. 38; *CPL*, III, 139, cf. 12, 124); made papal chaplain 3 Feb. 1348 (*CPL*, III, 264). Fled after his father's death and was signified for arrest 1 Nov. 1348; writs of 25 Oct. 1348 and 8 Feb. 1351 (Logan, *Runaway Religious*, pp. 200–1). Occ. 21 Dec. 1361 (*Reg. Sudbury*, I, 230); 27 Jan. 1364, had been apptd by Pope Clement VI (1342–52) (*CPL*, IV, 6; cf. *Accts of Papal Collectors*, pp. 98, 125–6, 148). Mentd as late pretender to the priory 1385 (PRO, SC8/88/4388).

Walter Picot (Pykot) Occ. 25 Oct. 1348 (*CPR 1348–50*, p. 244); 1 Nov. 1348 (PRO, C81/1787/5); 1350 (*Cal. Misc. Inq.*, III, 17); 8 Feb. 1351 (*CPR 1350–54*, p. 78); 26 June 1352 (*CCR 1349–54*, p. 488); occ. in clerical subsidy *c.* 1378 x 1381 (PRO, E179/45/14).

The next recorded pr., **Thomas**, occ. 26 June 1394 (*CPL*, IV, 489), identified in the BL, Harl. ms. 2110 list as **Thomas of Wiggenhall** (Wygenhall).

CHURCH PREEN (Salop). St John the Baptist f. 1150+. Diss. 1539.
List in *VCH Salop*, II, 38.

Richard of Wistanstow (Welstaunestowe) –1301 Occ. Nov. 1291 x Nov. 1292 (SRRO, 1514/254). Res. by 6 Apr. 1301 (Eyton, *Salop*, VI, 222, cf. *Cal. Inq. Misc.*, I, no. 1863).[3]

Roger of Little Hereford (Parva Hereford) 1301– Temps restored to Roger, apptd as keeper of cell by pr. of Much Wenlock 8 May 1301 (*CPR 1292–1301*, p. 594; cf. PRO, C84/21/24).

The next recorded pr. was called **Cambridge** and was pr. 'for the space of about 7 years and after him John Castle for the space of and above 20 years . . . that the said John Castle continued prior of the said priory, which was about 3 years before the dissolution of Wenlock' (Sparrow, *History of Church Preen*, p. 80, citing Exchequer depositions Hil. 1590). John Castle/Castell occ. in 1521 (Graham, *English Ecclesiastical Studies*, p. 126), so that Cambridge's tenure was likely to have been in the 1510s.

CLIFFORD (Hereford), St Mary (Lewes) f. 1129 x 30 (dependent on Lewes); 1351 x 1374 (independent)

Adam Occ. n.d. 1st half of 13th cent. (PRO, E315/40/177)

William Occ. n.d. (1st half to mid-13th cent.: pal.) (PRO, E326/207).

John Occ. from Nov. 1295 x Nov. 1296 to Nov. 1298 x Nov. 1299 (PRO, E106/3/19, m. 6d; E106/4/9, m.9; E106/4/10, m. 7d). Mentd in 1347 as former pr. Nov. 1300 x Nov. 1301 (*CCR 1346–49*, p. 217).

[**Arnold de Pinoliis** (Pujols) Letter from the pr. of Lewes *c.* 1301–2 to Edward I, concerning the appt. of Arnold as pr. of Clifford (PRO, SC1/19/10). 20 Jan. 1302 the king has heard that the pr. of Lewes has conferred the priory of Castleacre void by the d. of the last pr. on the pr. of Clifford. He asks the pr. of Lewes to appt Arnold de Pinoliis, king's chaplain, as pr. of Castleacre or at least pr. of Clifford (*CCR 1302–07*, p. 6). Not found at either house.]

Peter de Ripariis Occ. n.d. (1309 x 1324, *temp.* John de Monte Martini, pr. of Lewes) (BL, Campbell Cht., XVI, 16).

Roger of Lewes Occ. 1326 (PRO, E210/9055).

Richard Kenting 1330– Adm. by bp by lapse 7 May 1330 (*Reg. T. Charlton*, p. 76).

In the Cluniac General Chapter of 7 May 1335 the unnamed pr. of Clifford was said to be *leprosus* (Charvin, III, no. 258, p. 186).

Peter de Caro Loco Occ. 3 July 1344 (*CFR 1337–47*, p. 371).

---

[3] Sparrow, *History of Church Preen*, p. 21, suggests that Henry of Preen who occ. in a case in 1244 (*recte* Mich. 1224, cf. Eyton, *Salop*, III, 288 and n. 264) may have been pr. of Church Preen, but there is no corroboration of this.

Thomas of Ludlow (Lodelove, Lodelowe) Occ. 12 Dec. 1344 (ibid., p. 402); 20 Oct. 1346 (*Reg. Trillek*, p. 288); 6 May 1347 (*CCR 1346–49*, p. 217).

William Occ. 2 Sept. 1349 (*CCR 1349–54*, p. 137); in return of aliens in response to writ of 1 Sept. 1351 (PRO, C269/15/32).

The next recorded pr., **Nicholas of Malling**, occ. 1394 (PRO, E210/2539).

DAVENTRY (Northants), St Augustine (La Charité) f. *c.* 1090 (at Preston Capes); 1107 x 1108 (at Daventry)

Lists in *VCH Northants*, II, 113; *Ctl. Daventry*, p. xlviii; *Heads*, I, 117–18.

Alelm Occ. 1206 (*CRR*, IV, 255); 1 Apr. 1208 (*Ctl. Daventry*, no. 670; PRO, Northants F., CP25/1/171/12, no.216); 1 Jan. x 2 July 1215 (BL Stowe ms. 937, f. 147r; Cheney, *Inn. III*, no. 1008n).

James Occ. 1215 x 17 (*Ctl. Daventry*, nos. 270, 652).

Reyner Occ. 1217 x *c.* 1220 (*Ctl. Daventry*, no. 897); *c.* 1220 (Reginald) (ibid., no. 923).

Peter Occ. ? *c.*1220 (ibid., no. 898).

Walter of Sawbridge (Saleberg') –1230 Occ. Dec. 1224 x Dec. 1225 (*Reg. Wells*, II, 123); 24 May 1225 (*Ctl. Daventry*, no. 556); 1227 (*Bucks Eyre*, nos. 61, 401; PRO, Northants F., C125/1/179/22, no. 224); 27 Oct. 1228 (*Ctl. Daventry*, no. 392); Easter term 1229 (*CRR*, XIII, no. 1659); late Sept. 1229 (*Ctl. Daventry*, no. 542). D. 7 Sept. 1230 (*Reg. Wells*, II, 163).

Nicholas of Ely 1231–1264/5 M. of Daventry, coll. by bp by authority of the (Lateran) Council 28 Jan. 1231 (ibid.). D. by 5 Jan. 1265 (*Reg. R. Gravesend*, p. 104). Seal (*BM Seals*, no. 3041).

Robert of Hellidon (Heliden(e)) 1264–1270 Cellarer of Daventry, eln conf. 9 Jan. 1265 (ibid.). D. by 17 May 1270 (*Reg. R. Gravesend*, p. 114).

John of Staverton (Stampton) 1270–1281 Eln conf. 17 May 1270 (ibid.). Res. by 16 May 1281 (*Reg. Sutton*, II, 10–11). Bp conf. provision for ex-pr. 9 June 1281 (ibid., 12–13).

[**Robert of Winwick** (Wynewike) El by monks 16 May 1281, but eln quashed on account of irregularity and bastardy (ibid., 10–11)]

William of Leamington (Lemington, Lemyngton) 1281–1289 Sub-pr. of Daventry, eln quashed but apptd by bp prob. late May/June 1281 (ibid., 10–12). Occ. 9 June 1281 (ibid., 12). Res. by 1 June 1289 (ibid., 75).

Peter of Ashby (Esseby) 1289– M. of Daventry, eln pres. to bp 1 June and conf. 2 June 1289 (ibid.). Occ. in *Ctl. Daventry* from 22 July 1289 to 26 June 1322 (nos. 911, 100). Seal (*BM Seals*, no. 3038).

Peter of Harpole (Horpol) –1352 Occ. in *Ctl. Daventry* from 28 Oct. 1328 to 12 Feb. 1349 (nos. 45, 848). Still a pr. in office on 6 Aug. 1352 when an instn made to West Haddon church (Lincoln, Ep. Reg., IX, f. 198r). D. by 20 Sept 1352 (ibid, f. 198r–v), but cf. ment. 18 Aug. 1350 (*CPL*, III, 401).

John of Fawsley (Fawesl', Falwesle) 1352–1360 M. of Daventry, eln quashed but apptd by bp 20 Sept. 1352 (Lincoln, Ep. Reg., IX, f. 198r–v). D. by 30 Mar. 1360 (ibid., f. 228r–v).

Thomas of Stockingford (Stokkyngford) 1360–1361 M. of Daventry, eln quashed but apptd by bp 30 Mar. 1360 (ibid.). D. by 23 Aug. 1361 (ibid., f. 235r–v).

William (of) Grendon 1361–1396 M. of Daventry, eln quashed but apptd by bp 23 Aug. 1361 (ibid.). D. 20 Aug. 1396 (Lincoln, Ep. Reg., XI, f. 182r).

DERBY, St James (Bermondsey) f. -1140

Lists in *VCH Derbys*, II, 46; *Heads*, I, 118.

Arnold Occ. *temp.* Henry III (PRO, Just.1/167, m. 29d).

Frumund Occ. *temp.* Henry III (ibid.).

Stephen Occ. Feb. 1222 (*Derbys. F.* (1885) p. 214). The sequence of these three priors is unclear. On 28 Aug. 1279 it was reported that the unnamed pr. was new, having come at the Purification (Feb. 1279): 'bone et laudabilis vite et fame . . . novus est, venit ibi in ista Purificacione' (Charvin, I, p. 387, no. 99).

Peter Occ. as *custos* Nov. 1287 x Nov. 1288 (Farnham, *Charnwood Forest*, p. 192); from Nov. 1295 x Nov. 1296 to Nov. 1298 x Nov. 1299 (PRO, E106/3/19, m. 9; E106/4/9, m.5; E106/4/10, m. 5d); 1300 (PRO, Just.1/156, m. 1d); Easter 1300 (PRO, E106/5/2, m. 8); 1299, 1303, 1 July 1306 (Lugard, *Trailbaston*, I, 47, 49).

Nicholas of Clifford Occ. 1325 (PRO, SC6/1127/18).

John of Kingston (Kyngeston) Royal protection for 2 years 1 Jan. 1347 (*CPR 1345–48*, p. 217); Occ. 1349 (WAM no. 9511); 11 Sept. 1350 (*CPR 1348–50*, p. 568). The next recorded pr., **Henry**, occ. 22 Dec. 1393 (PRO, C85/60/16); 28 May 1393 (*CPL*, IV, 454); 11 Mar. 1394 (PRO, C202/C/98/2).

DUDLEY (Worcs), St James (Much Wenlock) f. 1149 x 1160
Lists in *VCH Worcs*, II, 161–2; *Heads*, I, 118.

William Frond Occ. 1190 x 1203 (*Ctl. Staffs 2*, p. 217). Poss. the pr. William occ. n.d. (?early 13th cent.) (Lyttelton, Hagley Hall Chts. 351065).

Walter Occ. n.d. (? *c.* 1220s, early 13th cent.) (*Ctl. Rydeware*, p. 262).

Robert Occ. 6 Oct. 1262 (PRO, Berks F., CP25/1/8/26, no. 6); mentd in 1291–2 as pr. *temp.* Henry III (*YB 21–2 Edward I*, pp. 156–7).

In Nov. 1272 an unnamed pr. of Dudley was present regarding a forest plea involving the receiving of malefactors of venison. In 14 Edward I (Nov. 1285 x Nov. 1286) the then pr. stated he was the third pr. of Dudley since the one in 1272 and that the latter was now dead (*Staffs Forest Pleas*, p. 160).

Walter Occ. 20 Jan. 1276 (PRO, Leics F., CP25/1/123/32, no. 31). Prob. the pr. W. who occ. 5 Jan. 1276 and Nov. 1275 x Nov. 1276 (*Ctl. Rydeware*, pp. 270–1).

Roger Occ. 27 Jan. 1278 (PRO, Worcs. F., CP25/1/258/10, no. 13).

John de C. Mentd in 1292 as predecessor of the present pr. (*YB 20–1 Edward I*, pp. 204–5).

Robert de Malleya (Malleye) Conf. by archbp of Canterbury of pr.'s excommunication for manifest offences 25 Sept. 1292 (*Reg. G. Giffard*, p. 426; *Reg. Pecham*, II, 247; cf. PRO, C85/162/51, 53 of 22 Apr., 27 Aug. 1292). Occ. 6 May 1297 (Lyttelton, Hagley Hall Chts. 351093); 20 May 1298 (*Reg. G. Giffard*, p. 496).

Geoffrey Mentd in Nov. 1301 x Nov. 1302 as a predecessor of the present pr., but with no indication of when he precisely held the office of pr. (*YB 30–1 Edward I*, pp. 268–9).

William Occ. Nov. 1301 x Nov. 1302 (ibid.).

John Occ. 19 Oct. 1329 (*Reg. Martival*, III, no. 846).

Thomas of London (Londoniis) Occ. Mich. 1337 (PRO, CP40/312, m. 306); 23 Mar. 1338 (Dugdale, *Baronage*, II, 214–15); Easter 1339 (*Staffs Plea Rolls 1–15 Edward III*, p. 90); 3 Jan. 1346 (*Reg. Bransford*, nos. 763–4); Mich. 1346 (*Staffs Plea Rolls 16–33 Edward III*, p. 62).

William Occ. Hil. term 1352 (ibid., p. 111); Mich. 1354 (ibid., 129); detained in Stourton prison for a trespass of venison and vert 20 Oct. 1360 (*CCR 1360–64*, p. 74); 26 July 1361 (Worcester, Reg. Brian I, p. 72). Prob. the same as:

William of Pontefract (de Ponte Fracto, Ponfreit) –1376 Occ. 1370 (PRO, E106/10/2); gtd keeping of Much Wenlock priory 1 Apr. 1376 (*CFR 1368–77*, p. 344). Apptd to Much Wenlock, temps. restored 14 Oct. 1376 (*CPR 1374–77*, p. 54).

The next recorded pr., **Roger**, occ. 12 June 1380 (*Reg. Wakefield*, no. 862), presumably the same as **Roger Wynel** or **Wyvel**, who occ. Easter term 1383 (*Staffs Plea Rolls 1360–87*, p. 181).

EXETER, St James (S. Martin des Champs) f. 1141

Lists in Oliver, p. 192; *Heads*, I, 118. I am grateful for information on the priors kindly provided by Mr A.E.B. Owen from the archives of King's College, Cambridge.

John Occ. 26 Nov. 1232 (*Devon F.*, I, p. 126, no. 257).

Gilbert (Guybert, Gwibert) Occ. n.d. (*c.*1249 by mayoralty of Exeter) (Watkin, *Totnes*, I, p. 98, no. 987; Oliver, p. 195, no. x); n.d. (mid-13th cent.) (Cambridge, King's Coll., SJP.56, 60, 67).

John de Gery Occ. *c.* 1253 x 1254, dated by Exeter mayoralty (Devon RO, ED/M/81).

Ivo Occ. 3 Feb. 1263 (Cambridge, King's Coll., SJP.64); 1264 (ibid., 65).

Auger Attests doct with Simon de Gurney, pr. of Barnstaple (1265 x 1272) (Oliver, p. 192).

Tuyn Occ. n.d. (1264/5 x 1268/9 *or* 1270/1 x 1271/2, dated by mayoralty of Exeter (Cambridge, King's Coll., SJP.66).

Theobald 1272– M. of S. Martin, adm. 11 Feb. 1272 (*Reg. Bronescombe*, p. 140; *Reg. W. Bronescombe*, II, no. 879). Occ. n.d. (late 13th cent.) (Cambridge, King's Coll., SJP.70); *c.* 22 Jan. 1274 (ibid., SJP.59). Pr. of Barnstaple 1275 (q.v.).

John Myrel 1276/7– M. of St James, pres. 20 Sept. 1276; inst. 6 Jan. 1277 (*Reg. Bronescombe*, p. 140; *Reg. W. Bronescombe*, II, no. 1210). Occ. 1284 (Cambridge, King's Coll., SJP.93); Hil. 1286 (PRO, Just.1/1273, mm. 5d, 10).

William de Arenis Occ. 1290 (Oliver, *Supplement*, p. 18); 21 Mar. 1290 (Cambridge, King's Coll., SJP.74).

Peter de Seynt Moys –1304 Occ. 25 Dec. 1294 (Cambridge, King's Coll., SJP.94–5); Nov. 1296 x Nov. 1297 (PRO, E106/4/2, m. 2); Nov. 1298 x Nov. 1299 (PRO, E106/4/9, m. 1d); Easter 1300 (PRO, E106/4/14, m. 4); Nov. 1302 x Nov. 1303 (PRO, E106/4/18, m. 4d). D. by 4 Nov. 1304 (*Reg. Stapeldon*, p. 214).

Stephen 1304– M. of S. Martin, mand. to ind. 4 Nov. 1304, cert. of ind. 17 Nov. 1304 (ibid.; *Reg. Bytton*, p. 417). Lic. gtd 20 Oct. 1308 to visit mother house; to return by Dec. (*Reg. Stapeldon*, p. 155).

John de Nantolio 1314– Pr. of Barnstaple (q.v.), given custody 17 Mar. 1314; coll. by lapse; mand. to ind. 2 Aug. 1314 (*Reg. Stapeldon*, p. 214; cf. p. 293).

William de Bitteden(e) (Byttedene, Bytynden) Letters test. re excommunication 8 May 1334; mand. to denounce 15 May – pr. did not appear before bp's commissary undertaking visitation (*Reg. Grandisson*, II, 745–6). Occ. 31 July 1334, 30 Sept. 1334, 24 Apr. 1335 (ibid., 759, 765, 781); 1336 (Devon RO, ED/M/327–8); 12 Nov. 1336 (*CPR 1334–38*, p. 332). Desc. in 1338 as *per fatuum et incautum regimen . . . ab administratione eiusdem in forma suspensi, qui vitam ducens enormiter dissolutam* – he had dilapidated priory and bp appts administrators (*Reg. Grandisson*, II, 883); 3 Jan. 1340 *vagabundus et nullibi residens* (ibid., I, 58–9). Occ. 5 Sept. 1341 (*CCR 1341–43*, p. 272). Commn of oyer and terminer 24 Mar. 1344: whereas the king had lately gtd to William custody of his priory by reason of the French war, the priors of Barnstaple, Bermondsey and Montacute and others in order to expel him from his custody had imprisoned him at Bermondsey etc. (*CPR 1343–45*, pp. 288–9). Gt of keeping of priory 4 Nov. 1344 (*CFR 1337–47*, p. 399). 17 Mar. 1345 desc. as now a fugitive, intending to carry the goods of the priory overseas to the king's enemies (ibid., p. 413).

John de Puteolis (Peutolis) 1341– Inst. 7 Nov. 1341 on presentation of Imbert, pr. of Barnstaple, no reason given for vacancy (*Reg. Grandisson*, III, 1332). Ref. to as former pr. in return to royal writ of 27 Oct. 1349; he had violated the bp's sequestration and carried off the priory's goods (*Reg. Grandisson*, I, 72).

John Lespard (Lespert) 1348/9– Letter of pres. from the pr. of S. Martin des Champs to Hugh Courtenay, patron, on d. of last (unnamed) pr. 20 Oct. 1349 (BL, Add. Cht. 13915). Inst. 9 Dec. 1348 (*sic*) (*Reg. Grandisson*, I, 72). Inst. 9 Nov. 1349 (ibid., III, 1401, cf. 1402 which gives 9 Dec.). Occ. 7 Oct. 1351 (PRO, C269/15/31); 28 Feb. 1362 (*CPR 1377–81*, p. 257).

John Vignorosi 1363– M. of S. Martin, inst. 3 June 1363, patron: Gerald, pr. of Lewes (*Reg. Grandisson*, III, 1492–3). Adm. (John de Worcester)10 June 1363 (*Mon. Angl.*, V, 105. presumably an error). At the General Chapter 30 Apr. 1368 the priory said *in spiritualibus et temporalibus male regitur* (Charvin, IV, no. 340).

Ralph (de) Chelfham 1369– Royal nomination to Hugh Courtenay, earl of Devon 6 Oct. 1369, no reason given for vacancy (*CPR 1367–70*, p. 310; *CFR 1368–77*, p. 23 – styled keeper of the priory). Occ. 1370 (PRO, E106/10/2). Also Pr. of Kerswell; Barnstaple (q.v.).

John Bevyle (Beofvylle) **1370–** M. of Montacute, coll. by lapse 12 Oct. 1370, no reason given for vacancy (*Reg. Brantingham*, I, 12). Royal nomination to Hugh Courtenay, earl of Devon, for adm. 20 Apr. 1371, in king's hands (*CPR 1370–74*, p. 67).

Ralph (de) Leghe (Leye) Occ. 2 Sept. 1371 (Cambridge, King's Coll., SJP. 77). For some time in possession of priory, res. into bp's hands and then bp adm him 20 Feb. 1374 (*Reg. Brantingham*, I, 31; Cambridge, King's Coll., SJP.89). Occ. 29 Oct. 1374 (*CFR 1368–77*, p. 262); 1 Nov. 1377, 7 Feb. 1380 (*CFR 1377–83*, pp. 31, 177); 28 Jan. 1381 (Cambridge, King's Coll., SJP. 79).

The next recorded pr., **Walter Marschall**, occ. 2 Feb. 1397 in inspeximus conf. 6 Apr. 1397 (*CPR 1396–99*, p. 108).

FARLEIGH, *see* MONKTON FARLEIGH

HOLM, *see* SLEVES HOLM

HOLME EAST (Dorset), St Mary (Montacute) f. *c.* 1107 (alien priory); 1407 (denizen) Lists in *VCH Dorset*, II, 82; *Heads*, I, 118.

Adam Last recorded occ. 13 Oct. 1218 (*Dorset F.*, I, 19).

Geoffrey Occ. 1262 (*Cluniac Visitations*, p. 12; *Cluny Chts.*, II, 123).

On 1279 it was stated that the unnamed pr. had been in office for 3 years (Charvin, I, p. 385, no. 99).

Walter M. of Montacute and pr. of Holme, occ. 18 June 1281 (*Cal. Misc. Inq.*, I, 361).

William Occ. as pr. 'Holne' (? Holme East) 21 Apr. 1302 (*CPR 1301–07*, p. 32).

Walter de Welham Occ. 24 Apr. 1317 (Charvin, III, p. 415, no. 212); 25 May 1330 (*CPR 1327–30*, p. 520); 23 Jan. 1331, 16 Feb. 1331 (*CPR 1330–34*, pp. 63, 131); ?5 May 1331 and the king's 9th year (i.e. Jan. 1335 x Jan. 1336) (*sic*) in inspeximus (*CPR 1348–50*, p. 91).

Gerard de Noiale (Noial) Occ. Mich. 1338 x Mich. 1339 (PRO, E372/184, rot. 25); 10 July 1339 (ref. to the previous pr. being dead), 6 Aug. 1344 (Gerard having returned from overseas and replacing a similar gt of custody made 23 June 1344 to Peter de Bosco, m. of Montacute, on the grounds that Gerard had gone overseas without lic.) (*CFR 1337–47*, pp. 135, 385, cf. 370); 28 Apr. 1344 (*CCR 1343–46*, p. 369); Mich. 1354 x Mich. 1355 (PRO, E372/200, rot. 26).

William Occ. Easter 1361 (PRO, CP40/406, m. 163).

Denis Gt of keeping of priory during the French war 6 July 1377, to hold from 22 June (*CFR 1377–83*, p. 4).

The next recorded pr., **Thomas Tyntenhull**, occ. 16 May 1381 (ibid., p. 251).

HORKESLEY (Essex), St Peter (Thetford, St Mary) f. -1127 (*KH*, pp. 97, 100; cf. Binns, p. 112); 1376 (denizen).

List in *VCH Essex*, II, 138–9.

Nicholas Occ. *c.* 1200, *c.* 1196 x *c.* 1207 (*Ctl. Hospitallers*, II, no. 545, citing PRO, E40/13896).

Philip Occ. ? *c.* 1200 x 1210 (Bodl., Essex Cht. 70 – dating in annotated Bodl. catalogue, altered from *c.* 1230).

Robert Occ. *temp.* Henry III, ? 1229 (ibid., Essex Cht. 42).

Roger Occ. Oct. 1234 x Oct. 1235 (PRO, E40/14039); *temp.* Henry III, after 1251 (pr. of Leighs) (BL, Harl. Cht. 50 G 23).

Reginald Occ. *c.* 1244 x 1259 (*temp.* Fulk Basset, bp of London) (*HMC 9th Rept.*, p. 31).

Robert Occ. Mich. 1261 (*Essex F.*, I, 240).

Simon Occ. 23 July 1260, 10 July 1263 (Bodl., Essex Roll 17).

In 1279 the unnamed pr. was stated to have not long entered his duties – '*prior novus est*' (Charvin, I, p. 389, no. 99; *Cluniac Visitations*, p. 35).

Henry Occ. 22 Feb. 1295 (Bodl., Essex Roll 17).

Stephen de Larriens (Larryens, Laryans) Occ. 10 Sept. 1309 going overseas in the service of Queen Isabella, 18 Aug. 1310 (*CPR 1307–13*, pp. 188, 277); 1 Feb. 1310 (PRO, E40/3836); 26 Aug.1312 (*CPR 1307–13*, p. 488).

Peter Occ. 1314 (PRO, C85/119/20; *TEAS*, II, 367).

William de Boys Occ. 23 July 1343 (PRO, C269/15/18).

In 1368 the priory was said to be '*in temporalibus male regitur*' (Charvin, IV, p. 51, no. 340).

Roger (de) Ware Occ. 16 Jan. 1370 (PRO, E179/42/3B). Signified for arrest by the pr. of Thetford 15 June 1374 but Roger secured supersedence by appealing tuitorially to the Pope on grounds that Horkesley was not subject to jurisdiction of Thetford (Logan, *Runaway Religious*, p. 201; PRO, C81/1787/20). Mand. to stay the taking of Roger de Ware, m. of Thetford, whom the king, on the representation of pr. John of Thetford that he was a vagabond in secular attire, lately ordered to be arrested and delivered to the pr., as the said Roger pretending he is and has long been pr. of Horkesley, and that the pr. of Thetford has no power or jurisdiction over him, has appealed to the Apostolic See and tuition of the Court of Canterbury (*CPR 1374–77*, p. 56). Occ. 23 Mar. 1375 (*Reg. Sudbury*, II, 141); 1386 (Bodl., Essex Chts. 63, 64a); 12 Mar. 1388 (ibid., Essex Cht. 64b).

John Occ. 12 Apr. 1374 (*Reg. Sudbury*, II, 140).

HORTON, *see* MONK'S HORTON

KERSAL (Lancs.) St Leonard (Lenton) f. 1145 x 1153 (alien cell); 1392 (denizen).

List in *VCH Lancs*, II, 114.

John of Ingleby (Ingilby) Occ. 1332, accused of wounding (PRO, Just.1/428, m. 5).

KERSWELL (Devon) (Montacute) f. 1119 x 1129

Lists in Oliver, p. 312; *Heads*, I, 118; some priors mentd in R. Graham, 'The Cluniac Priory of St Mary, Carswell', *TDA*, 84 (1952), 115–17.

Nicholas Occ. 1 July 1201 x 2 (*Devon F.*, I, 25).

Richard Occ. 1 Aug. 1228 (ibid., 87); Mich. term 1228 (*CRR*, XIII, no. 1172).

Unnamed pr. in 1278 reported by the Cluniac visitors to be 'good, wise, modest and discreet, although he is an Englishman' (*TDA*, 84, p. 116, citing *Cluny Chts.*, II, 136).

12 Oct. 1295 cert. that unnamed pr. is not an alien born in the power of the king of France (*CCR 1288–96*, p. 461).

Bartholomew Occ. from Nov. 1295 x Nov. 1296 (PRO, E106/3/19, m. 9d) to Nov. 1298 x Nov. 1299 (PRO, E106/4/9, m. 1d; E106/4/10, m. 2d); 1297 (*Reg. Bytton*, p. 414); Easter 1300 (PRO, E106/4/14, m. 4).

Guichard 1299– M. of Montacute, cert. of appt notified to king 18 Mar. 1299 (PRO,

C84/13/38); apptd to Kerswell by Stephen, pr. of Montacute; mand. to escheator to restore the cell to him 28 Mar. 1299 (*CPR 1292–1301*, p. 400). Prob. to be identified with Guichard de Jou, apptd pr. of Montacute 1326 (q.v.)., but, if so, had given up Kerswell before his elevation to Montacute (see below).

Philip de Chintriaco (Chintry) –?1339 Occ. *c*. Mich. 1324 (PRO, E106/5/2, m. 7d); July 1325 x July 1326 (PRO, E106/5/4, m. [6d]); 12 Sept. 1334 (*Reg. Grandisson*, II, 763); 1337 (Chintry) (*TDA*, 84, p. 116); Mich. 1338 x Mich. 1339 (PRO, E372/184, rot. 26); mentd 12 Mar. 1339 as deceased pr. (*CFR 1337–47*, p. 124).

John Gyot Occ. 19 Aug. 1339, 3 Jan. 1340 (*Reg. Grandisson*, II, 916; I, 58).

Peter de Bosco Gt of keeping of priory (*not* adm.) 22 May 1348 (*CFR 1347–56*, p. 87). Occ. as pr. Mich. 1348 x Mich. 1349 (PRO, E372/194, rot. 5d).

Ralph (de) Chelfham (Chalfham, Shalfham, Shalsam) Pr. of St James, Exeter 1369 (q.v.). Occ. 1370 (English) (PRO, E106/10/2); *c*. Mar. 1374 (*Reg. Brantingham*, I, 194); n.d. (*Reg. Grandisson*, II, 763n). Is he to be identified with the pr. of Barnstaple of the same name 1376?

William Criche (Cryche) Occ. 16 Nov. 1377 (*CFR 1377–83*, p. 40); n.d. (?1377) (PRO, E179/24/10B).

Thomas Crich (Cryche) Occ. 8 May 1381 (*CFR 1377–83*, p. 253); Jan. 1403 (*Privy Council*, I, 192).

LENTON (Notts), Holy Trinity (Cluny) f. 1102 x 1108

Lists in *VCH Notts*, II, 100; *Heads*, I, 118–19; J.T. Godfrey, *The History of the Parish and Priory of Lenton in the County of Nottingham* (London and Derby, 1884), pp. 179–90.

R. Occ. 1214 (*HMC Middleton*, pp. 55–6), ? same as below.

Roger Occ. 17 Nov. 1225 (BL, Stowe Cht. 58); 1226 (R.) (*Nottingham Borough Records*, I, 20–1, no. 10; *Derbys Chts.*, no. 1696); 6 Oct. 1226 (PRO, Notts F., CP25/1/182/4, no. 69); 25 Oct. 1227 (PRO, Northants F., CP25/1/172/22, no. 232); Hil. term 1230 (*CRR*, XIII, no. 2324); 15 Nov. 1230 (*CPR 1225–32*, p. 443); 1231 (*Reg. Gray*, p. 43); 1232 (PRO, Notts F., CP25/1/182/5, no. 142); 1239 (*Reg. Gray*, p. 73n); 23 Feb. 1240 (PRO, Notts F., CP25/1/182/8, no. 276); 16 Aug. 1240 (ibid., 182/8, no. 279).

Hugh Burgundiensis –1243 Royal ass. to his appt as abb. of Cluny and mand. for seisin 18 Dec. 1243 (*CR 1242–47*, p. 147).

Hugh Bluet Occ. (H.) 21 Jan. 1244 (Bruel, *Cluny Chts.*, VI, no. 4805); 6 July 1245 (PRO, Notts F., CP25/1/182/9, no. 325); 2 July 1247 (*Staffs F. 2*, p. 238; *Magnum Reg. Album Lichfield*, p. 253); (H.) 1251 (BL, Harl. Cht. 84 F 35); 1252 (PRO, Notts F., CP25/1/182/10, no. 399); 29 Jan. 1258 (*Derbys F., (1889)*, p. 151). At the visitation 4 May 1259 it was noted that the unnamed pr. '*non redeat ad monasterium Lentonie propter inimicitias capitales quas ibi habet*' (Charvin, I, p. 50, no. 232).

Dalmatius 1259–1260 In the last General Chapter the abb. of Cluny had removed Hugh and had apptd Dalmatius, m. of Cluny; mand. for seisin 24 June 1259 (*CR 1256–59*, p. 400). Occ. 6 Dec. 1259 (*CPR 1258–66*, p. 107); (D.) 1 Apr. 1260 (*Magnum Reg. Album Lichfield*, no. 523). D. 1260 (*EHR*, 44, p. 101). House mentd as void 6 Sept. 1260 (*CPR 1258–66*, p. 92). D. by 16 Sept. 1260 (ibid., p. 93).

Roger de Clepenville (Cliponvill) 1260– Name (PRO, C146/3925). Pr. of Montacute, coll. by abb. of Cluny, writ *de intendendo* 16 Sept. 1260 (*CPR 1258–66*, p. 93). Occ. 1263 (PRO, Leics F., CP25/1/122/7, no. 596); 24 Sept. 1267 (R.), 23 June 1268 (R.), 24 Aug. 1268 (*Reg. W. Giffard*, pp. 75, 85, 86); 3 Nov. 1268 (PRO, Northants F., CP25/1/174/48, no. 867); 27 Apr. 1269 (*Derbys F., (1889)*, p. 101). At the General Chapter 14 Apr. 1269 the unnamed pr. '*dicatur esse diffamatus apud bonos et graves super incontinentia, dilapidatione et mala*

administratione; ordinant diffinitores quod per visitatores anni sequentis super premissis fiat inqui-
sitio et ad sequens Generale Capitulum deferatur, nisi dominus abbas interim, ex causa, aliud
duxerit ordinandum' (Charvin, I, p. 70, no. 310). Presumably this is the same pr. as **Roger of**
Normanton (or ? Norman) cited in Nichols, *Leics.* II(i), 110 from Croxton register *temp.*
abb. Geoffrey, supposedly *c.* Mich. 1241 (very doubtful) with mention of Roger's predecessor Damascenus (*sic*, for Dalmatius?).

Matthew 1270– Late almoner of Lewes, apptd pr. by abb. Ivo of Cluny, temps. 14 Mar. 1270
(*CPR 1266–72*, p. 415). Occ. 22 May 1280 (*CCR 1279–88*, p. 13).

Peter de Siriniaco –1289 Occ. 1 Dec. 1281, protection for 3 yrs, going overseas (*CPR
1281–92*, p. 4); 1283 (*CPR 1334–38*, p. 185; *CChR 1257–1300*, p. 270); 1285 (*CPR 1281–92*,
p. 195; *Reg. Romeyn*, I, 252); 7 July 1287 (*CPR 1281–92*, p. 275). Dep. by abb. of Cluny
(*CCR 1288–96*, p. 313). Letter to Edward I asking him to restore Peter de Siriniaco to full
possession of the priory, since he had been wrongfully dep. 5 Nov. 1289 (*CPL*, I, 505);
similar letter 11 Dec. 1289 (ibid., 507; Sayers, no. 931).

Reginald de Jora 1289–1290 Apptd pr. on dep. of Peter. By 5 Nov. 1289 Reginald had been
ind. by the king (*CPL*, I, 505). Going overseas 12 Feb. 1290 (*CPR 1281–92*, pp. 342, 344);
4 Mar. 1290 (*CCR 1288–96*, p. 150). Res. by 22 Sept. 1290 (*CFR 1272–1307*, p. 283).

William de Dolyna Occ. 30 Aug. 1291, going overseas (*CPR 1281–92*, p. 441); 20 Mar. 1292
(ibid., p. 480); 1300, 1302 (*Reg. Corbridge*, I, 208, 243); 1302 (Lincoln, Ep. Reg., II, f. 256v);
10 Apr. 1305, 11 Apr. 1306 (*CPR 1301–07*, pp. 332, 426). 1295 cert. that unnamed pr. is not
an alien born in the power of the king of France (*CCR 1288–96*, p. 461).

Stephen de Moerges 1309–1313 Occ. as a farmer of the priory 1302 x 1303 (PRO, E106/4/18,
m. 15d). Notif. by the abb. of Cluny to the king of his appt of Stephen as pr. 13 Nov. 1309
(PRO, C84/16/30); temps. 19 Dec. 1309 (*CPR 1301–07*, p. 203). Occ. 2 May 1313 (*Reg.
Greenfield*, IV, no. 1954).

Reginald de Crespy 1313–1316 M. of Cluny, apptd by abb. of Cluny, temps. 3 Aug. 1313 (*CPR
1313–17*, p. 14). Occ. 15 Oct. 1315, 22 Nov. 1314 (ibid., pp. 30, 203). Res. by 7 Mar. 1316
(ibid., p. 439).

Geoffrey de Chintriaco (Chantry, Cintriaco) **1316–1332** Pr. of Froville, apptd by abb. of Cluny
on res. of Reginald, temps. 7 Mar. 1316 (ibid.). Occ. 29 Sept. 1321, 2 Apr. 1324 (*CPR
1321–24*, pp. 31, 400); 19 Nov. 1324, 1 Aug. 1324 (*CPR 1324–27*, pp. 56, 63); 25 Apr. 1327
(Lincoln D. & C. Dij/53/1/3); 7 Feb., 13 Oct. 1327 (*CPR 1327–30*, pp. 91, 181). In mand.
of 7 Nov. 1323 mentd as having been excommunicate for 3 yrs for having disobeyed a papal
mand. to carry out the provision of benefice (*CPL*, II, 234–5). mand. to absolve him from
excommunication 9 Dec. 1328 (ibid., 284). Promoted to be pr. of Montacute 1330 (ibid., 346)
– ?ineffective, *see* Montacute. D. as pr. of Lenton by 13 Oct. 1332 (*CCR 1330–33*, p. 499).[4]

[**Guichard de Jou** M. of Cluny, papal reservation of priory, about to be void by the appt of
Geoffrey de Chintriaco to be pr. of Montacute 4 Dec. 1330 (*CPL*, II, 346, *but see*
Montacute). Ineffective.]

Guy de Arlato 1332–1333 Mand. to restore issues to Guy, preferred as pr. by the abb. of Cluny
13 Oct. 1332 on the d. of pr. Geoffrey (*CCR 1330–33*, p. 499). Occ. 15 Feb. 1333, 8 Oct. 1333
(*CPR 1330–34*, pp. 408, 471). D. by 22 Dec. 1333 (*CCR 1333–37*, p. 167).

Astorgius de Corciis (Gorciis) **1333–1349** Fealty 22 Dec. 1333 (ibid.). Note that he had
returned from overseas and now lives continually in his priory 2 Oct. 1341 (*CFR 1337–47*,
p. 242). D. by 18 Aug. 1349 (*CFR 1347–56*, p. 147).

[Gt to br. Vincent de Fiscampo, sub-pr. of Lenton and two others, of the keeping of the priory
4 June 1349, ? vacant (*CFR 1347–56*, p. 137).]

---

[4] *Mon. Angl.*, V, 109 cites in list of priors William de Pinnebury occ. 1324, citing plea roll 17 Edward II.

Peter de Abbeville (de Abbatis Villa, Dabbevill) **1349–?1376** M. of Cluny, gt of keeping of priory 18 Aug. 1349, having been preferred as pr. of Lenton by the abb. of Cluny (ibid.). Occ. 1350 (*CCR 1349–54*, p. 223; *CPR 1350–54*, p. 150); 1354 (*CPR 1354–58*, pp. 107, 136); 1357 (*Lenton Chts.*, pp. 23–4, no. 12); 1360 (*CPR 1358–61*, p. 342); 1366 (Nottingham Univ., Middleton Mi.D.778); 1367 (*CPR 1374–77*, p. 286); 11 June 1369 (*CFR 1368–77*, p. 11); 1370 (PRO, E106/10/2); 18 Oct. 1371 (*CFR 1368–77*, p. 117). At General Chapter 30 Apr. 1369 Lenton was said '*in temporalibus . . . pessime regitur*' (Charvin, IV, p. 52, no. 340). Possibly the unnamed pr. who had d. by 28 Sept. 1376 (PRO, C84/31/42), and see next entry.

[Gt to br. Robert Castelacre and br. Nicholas de Ilkeston, monks of Lenton, of the keeping of the priory 27 Aug. 1376 (*CFR 1368–77*, p. 360).]

Geoffrey de Rocherio (Rocharia, Rochero, Rothario) *alias* **of Guernsey** (Gernesey) **1376–1412** Pres. by abb. of Cluny on d. of last unnamed pr. 25 Sept. 1376 (PRO, C84/31/42). Gt of keeping of priory to hold from Mich. last as long as the French war lasts 1 Dec. 1376 (*CFR 1368–77*, p. 371); 1377 (*CFR 1377–83*, p. 18); 1389 (*CPR 1388–92*, pp. 57, 36); 1392 (*CPR 1391–96*, p. 195; *CCR 1392–96*, p. 98); 1403 (*Privy Council*, I, 195); 27 Nov. 1408 (*CPR 1408–13*, p. 11). Res. by 6 Feb. 1412 (ibid., p. 367).

LEWES (Sussex), St Pancras (Cluny) f. 1077

Lists in *VCH Sussex*, II, 69–70; *Heads*, I, 119.

Humbert Last recorded occ. May 1209 (*Norfolk F. 1201–15*, no. 225).

Stephen Occ. 25 May 1218 (*Sussex F.* I, no. 140; *Ctl. Lewes*, II, p. 75n.); 1218 (PRO, DL25/9); 18 Apr. 1219, 19 May 1219 (PRO, F. Unknown cos. CP25/1/282/6, no. 20 and no. 23). Presumably the pr. who res. 1220 (*CRR*, IX, 69; *Bracton's Note Book*, III, 355), but a pr. Stephen occ. 1222 (PRO, E40/14216); 1220 x 1224 (PRO, E40/14196). Seal (*BM Seals*, no. 3464; *Mon. Seals*, p. 51 – counterseal reads Stephen de Hzi (? Hussey), but amended to ?G[ ]vzi in ts. seal catalogue at PRO; cf. *Sussex Arch. Coll*, II, 19).

Hugh Occ. 20 Jan. 1225, 23 Feb. 1226 (*Sussex F.*, I, nos. 189, 198; PRO, F. Unknown cos. CP25/1/282/6, no. 37); Hil. term 1226 (*CRR*, XII, no. 1777); 1230 (*Yorks F., 1218–31*, p. 129; *EYC*, VIII, no. 129); Easter term 1231 (*CRR*, XIV, no. 1199); 27 Nov. 1234 (PRO, E40/5555).

Albert **–1244** Occ. Nov. 1239, 1243 (PRO, E40/8010; E40/10698); 1240 (Charvin, I, no. 25); 1241 (*St Richard of Chichester*, p. 46, no. 70; *Ctl. Sele*, no. 30); 1243 (*Sussex F.*, I, no. 414); Feb. 1244 (PRO, E40/1416). D. 1244 (*Ch. Lewes*, p. 24).

Guichard de Osays **1244–1248** M. of Cluny, succ. 1244; entered Lewes 11 May 1244 (*Ch. Lewes*, pp. 24–5). Adm. 7 May 1245, the king having custody of the priory by reason of his custody of the land and heir of W., earl Warenne (*CPR 1232–47*, p. 453). D. 7 Dec. 1248 (*Ch. Lewes*, p. 25).

William (de) Russelun (Russelons, Russinoll) **1249–?1256** Came to Lewes 1249 (ibid.). Occ. 1251 (PRO, E40/14973–4); travelled to the Papal Curia and returned to England 25 Mar. 1255 (*Ch. Lewes*, p. 26); signification for arrest 20 May 1255 (PRO, C85/43/7); 25 Nov. 1255 (*Sussex F.*, II, no. 588); Mar. 1256, 1 May 1256 (*Lincoln Reg. Ant.*, II, nos. 388–90). Left England ?1256 and did not return (*Ch. Lewes*, p. 27).

William de Fouville (Fouvill, Fovile, Fovill, Fovyll) **1257–1268** Pr. of St Andrew's, Northampton, arrived at Lewes 1257 (ibid.). 18 Oct. 1257 the king understands, having inspected letters of the abb. of Cluny, that although the abb. of Cluny preferred William to Lewes, he enjoined him to retain the priory of St Andrew's, Northampton, until further provision was made concerning it, and since the pr. of La Charité has not preferred anyone to Northampton, the king has restored the free administration of St Andrew's to William

(*CPR 1247-58*, p. 582). Noted on 14 Dec. 1257 that William had shown to the itinerant justices that Lewes was vacant by the cess. of his predecessor. (*CR 1256-59*, p. 173). Occ. from 1258 (*Ctl. Lewes*, I, 83-4; PRO, E40/14047); 10 Jan. 1267, 25 Sept. 1268 (*Reg. W. Giffard*, pp. 20, 27). D. 28 Sept. 1268 (*Ch. Lewes*, p. 29).

Miles de Columbers 1268-1274 Came to Lewes 30 Jan. 1269 (ibid., p. 30), but clearly received appt earlier since he occ. 29 Sept. 1268 (PRO, E40/2974). Occ. 11 July 1273 (*Ctl. Lewes*, I, 50). Left house 1274 on becoming abb. of Vézelay (*Ch. Lewes*, p. 31).

Peter de Villiaco 1275 Pr. of Souvigny, entered Lewes 1 May 1275, but res. 5 Nov. that year on appt as pr. of St Martin des Champs, Paris (*Ch. Lewes*, p. 31). Occ. 1275 (PRO, E40/15457-8; cf. *Ctl. Lewes*, I, 81).

John de Teyngiis (Dwyanges, Teng(es), Tengys, Teynges, Tyanges) **1276-1285** Pr. of 'Gayfes', entered Lewes 29 May 1276 (*Ch. Lewes*, p. 31). Occ. Nov. 1277 x Nov. 1278 (*Norfolk F. (Rye)*, p. 117); 8 June 1278, 26 May 1281 (*CPR 1277-81*, pp. 268, 437); 1283 (*Reg. Peckham*, II, 610). Crossed overseas to attend the General Chapter and about 2 Feb. 1285 was made pr. of St Mary la Woute, Auvergne, and did not return to Lewes (*Ch. Lewes*, p. 35). Seal (*BM Seals*, no. 3465; *Mon. Seals*, p. 51). Archbp Pecham sends advice to abb. of Cluny about the management of the priory and the appt of a new pr. 1 June 1285 (*Reg. Peckham*, III, 902-4).

John of Avignon (Avinona, Avynon, Davynium, Davyun) **1285-1298** Previously called Chartres/Tickford (see Bermondsey/Much Wenlock). Pr. of Much Wenlock, entered Lewes 15 Aug. 1285 (ibid.). Occ. 3 Nov. 1285 (PRO, Leics F., CP25/1/123/36, no. 146); going overseas 23 Nov. 1288, 24 Oct. 1290, 20 Jan. 1291, 18 Oct. 1292 (*CPR 1281-92*, pp. 310, 391, 419, 508-9). Certif. that pr. of Lewes should not be molested *c*. Oct. 1295 (PRO, SC1/27/5). D. 28 Mar. 1298 (*Ch. Lewes*, p. 36).

John of Newcastle (de Castro Novo) **1298-1302** Entered the priory 24 May 1298 (ibid., pp. 36-7), but pres. to priory 13 June 1298 (*Record Evidences of Cluny*, p. 17, no. 26). D. 10 Jan. 1302 (*Ch. Lewes*, p. 37).

Stephen de Sancto Romano 1302-1307 Entered priory 12 May 1302 (ibid.). Occ. 1303 (*Ctl. Lewes, Norfolk*, p. 12; PRO, E40/2295, E40/3143); 1304 (*CPR 1301-7*, pp. 205, 215; PRO, E40/1415); 1305 (*CPR 1301-7*, pp. 328, 331); 28 Apr. 1306 (*Reg. Greenfield*, II, p. 1, no. 658). 1307 became pr. of Beaulieu in Argonne (PRO, E41/468).

John de Monte Martini 1307-1324 Pr. of Prittlewell, apptd pr of Lewes by the abb. of Cluny in succession to Stephen de Sancto Romano promoted to the priory of Beaulieu in Argonne 29 Mar. 1307 (ibid.). Occ. 29 Aug. 1308 (*Ctl. Lewes*, I, 164). D. by 15 Sept. 1324 (*CCR 1323-27*, p. 310, cf. *CFR 1319-27*, p. 313). **James de Cusancia**, pr. of Prittlewell, and his brother, **John de Cusancia**, pr. of Bermondsey, commn to administer Lewes in the vacancy after John de Monte Martini's death (*CPR 1323-27*, pp. 310-11). Seal (*Mon. Seals*, p. 51).

Adam of Winchester (Wintonia, Wyncestr', Wynton') **1324-** M. of St Swithin's, Winchester, occ. late 1324 (PRO, E106/5/2, m. 4); July 1325 (*CPR 1324-27*, pp. 149, 158-9; *CCR 1323-27*, pp. 495, 497); 12 Dec. 1325 order to be released by the constable of Dover, having been arrested for attempting to cross sea to visit Cluny (*CCR 1323-27*, p. 532); protection for 1 year 28 June 1327 (*CPR 1327-30*, p. 133). Occ. 4 Jan. 1328 (PRO, C84/21/47).

[**John de Courtenay** (Courthenay, Curtenay) eldest son of Hugh, 5th Baron Courtenay, letter re papal provision 13 Sept. 1329, ment. of obstacles by earl Warenne (*Reg. Grandisson*, I, 230-1). M. of Tavistock, papal mand. at king's request, to assign the priory of Lewes to John, void by the d. of the last pr. 27 Dec. 1328. Adam of Winchester, m. of Winchester, had obtained the priory and held it for 2 years and was turned out by Peter de Jocellis, pr. of Castleacre, who in his turn was deprived for having acted while the appeal against Adam's appt was pending. Adam's appt was made under papal reservation which did not apply to Cluniac houses and is therefore void (*CPL*, II, 293–4). Occ. as pr. 1 Oct. 1330 (ibid., 346). Unsuccessful abbatial candidate for Tavistock 1325 and abb. of Tavistock 1334–49 (q.v.).]

Peter de Jocellis (Joceaux, Jocelles, Insshewes) –**1344** Pr. of Castleacre (see previous entry); cf. letter of John, earl Warenne, on installation of pr. 22 Apr. 1327 (*Record Evidences of Cluny*, p. 17, no. 29). Occ. 14 Mar. 1329 (*Reg. Martival*, I, 391); 15 Apr. 1329 (Norwich, Reg/1/2, f. 28r); (Peter Insshewes) 10 Oct. 1331 (*CCR 1331–33*, p. 343); 12 Mar. 1344 (*CPR 1343–45*, p. 220). House void 15 Nov. 1344 (*CPL*, III, 12, and see next entry).

John de Janicuria (Jacourt) **1344**– Papal letter of recommendation addressed to John, earl Warenne 15 Nov. 1344 (ibid.), but occ. 23 Aug. (*sic*) 1344 (ibid., 179). However, John occ. as m. of Cluny (not styled pr.) 21 Oct. 1344 (*CPR 1343–45*, p. 360). Occ. 21 Jan. 1349 (PRO, E41/467). Instn to rectory of Whaddon 25 July 1349, pres. by John fourth pr. of Lewes, the pr., the sub-pr., and the third pr. all being dead (Ely,G/1/1 pt 2, f. 24r), but he occ. 28 Jan. 1350 (BL, Campbell Cht. IV. 7).

Hugh de Chintriaco (Chyntriaco) –**1362** Occ. 21 Sept. 1350 (PRO, E40/15524); from 25 Feb. 1351 to 17 Apr. 1353 (*CPR 1350–54*, pp. 47, 530); 1355 (PRO, E40/15637; Bodl., Gough ms. Norfolk 18, f. 45v); 1357 (PRO, E40/1417); 1360 (*Ctl. Lewes, Norfolk*, p. 116); 16 Apr. 1361, 2 Oct. 1361, 23 Nov. 1362 going overseas (*CPR 1361–64*, pp. 5, 79, 270). Seal (*Mon. Seals*, p. 52). Became pr. of Tournus by 16 Aug. 1362 (*Accts of Papal Collectors*, pp. 171, 229).

Gerald Rothonis (Rocho, Rotho, Bothonis) **1362**– Prov. 16 Aug. 1362 (ibid., p. 171). B. Decr. (ibid., p. 229). Pr. of Montacute, occ. 7 Jan. 1363 (*CPL*, IV, 2); 3 June 1363 (*Reg. Grandisson*, III, 1492–3); 28 July 1363, 10 Oct. 1363 (*CPR 1361–64*, pp. 386, 448).

John de Cariloco (Carlioco, Caroloco, Cherles, Cherlu) **1364–1396** Pr. of Bermondsey, transfered to Lewes by abb. of Cluny 22 May 1364 (PRO, SC1/42/17). Occ. 25 Oct. 1366 subcollector of apostolic camera in England (*CPP*, p. 536). D. by 8 Nov. 1396 (London, Reg. Braybrooke, f. 207r). Seal (*Mon. Seals*, pp. 51–2).

MALPAS (Monmouth), St Mary (Montacute) f. -1122; (denizen) 1407
Robert de Beck' Occ. 30 July 1303 (Walker, *Eccles. Misc.*, p. 33, no. 82 = Hereford Cath. mun. 2222).
William Occ. *c.* 1334 (PRO, C269/15/12).

MENDHAM (Suffolk), St Mary (Castle Acre) f. -1155 (alien priory); 1351 x 1374 (denizen).
Lists in *VCH Suffolk*, II, 87; *Heads*, I, 120.
John of Lindsey Occ. *c.* 1200 x 1202 (*Mon. Angl.*, V, 59; for date cf. *Ctl. Eye*, I, no. 87n.); (J.) 5 Sept. 1221 (*Ctl. Eye*, I, no. 62).
John Occ. Oct. 1239 x Oct. 1240 (*Norfolk F. (Rye)*, p. 61).
Simon Occ. 1250 (PRO, Just.1/560, m. 29d); Oct. 1250 x Oct. 1251 (*Norfolk F. (Rye)*, p. 84); 20 Oct. 1251 (*Cal. Misc. Inq.*, I, 34); n. d. (mid 13th cent.) (PRO, E42/216). Seal (*Mon. Seals*, p. 60).
John Occ. Nov. 1295 x Nov. 1296 (PRO, E106/3/19, m. 10d); Nov. 1296 x Nov. 1297 (PRO, E106/4/2, m. 4); 28 June 1308 (PRO, E327/638); Easter 1328 (*Index to Placita de Banco*, p. 601). Seal (*BM Seals*, no. 3626; *Mon. Seals*, p. 60).
Nicholas Cressi –**1338** Occ. 1336 (Blomefield, *Norfolk*, V, 376, citing court roll). Priory void by his d. by 18 Apr. 1338 (*Cal. Misc. Inq.*, II, 397).
John of Walton Occ. 1340 (Blomefield, *Norfolk*, V, 376, citing court roll).
Henry de Berlegh M. of Castle Acre, apptd by pr. of Castle Acre; pres. to king 25 Apr. 1343 (PRO, C84/24/27); fealty to king 3 May 1343 (*CCR 1343–46*, p. 47).

William Occ. 1353 (Blomefield, *Norfolk*, V, 376, citing court roll).
The next recorded pr., **John of Thompson** (Tomston), occ. 1382 (ibid., citing court roll).

MONK BRETTON (Yorks W.), St Mary Magdalen f. *c.* 1153 x 1155 (dep. on Pontefract); *c.* 1279 (independent Benedictine priory).
  Lists in *VCH Yorks*, III, 94; J.W. Walker, *Monk Bretton Priory*, p. 60; *Heads*, I, 120.
William Occ. *c.* 1185 x 1211 (*EYC*, III, no. 1819; cf. *Heads*, I, 120, n. 1).
Adam Occ. 6 Oct. 1226 (*Lincs F.*, I, 213); 12 Nov. 1226 (*Yorks F., 1218–31*, p. 77); 1227 (Baildon, I, 140); Trin. term 1230 (*CRR*, XIV, no. 88).
Roger Occ. Mich. term 1232 (ibid., no. 2431); 23 Feb. 1240 (*Derbys F. (1886)*, p. 44); 4 Oct. 1240 (PRO, Notts F., CP25/1/182/8, no. 281).
Isaak le Moyne of Pontefract Intruded himself as pr. of Monk Bretton after d. of pr. Roger, mentd 1279 (PRO, Just.1/1055, m. 15).
Adam of Northampton (Norhampton) M. of Pontefract, intruded by the pr. of Pontefract *temp.* Innocent IV (1243–54); dispute continued through the pontificates of Alexander IV (1254–61) and Urban IV (1261–64); Pope Clement IV pronounced eln of Adam void – mentd in bull of 30 Mar. 1265 (*Ctl. Monk Bretton*, pp. 214–15). Occ. 1259 (BL, Harl. Cht. 112 F 28); 1268 in case against sub-pr. and convent of Pontefract (PRO, Just.1/1050, m. 13); 1265 (PRO, C85/198/4).
R. Occ. 16 May 1267 (*Reg. W. Giffard*, p. 155).
William de Rihale (Riall, Ryhal(l), Rykale, Rykall) –**1291** First Ben. pr. Occ. 4 Jan. 1281 (*Ctl. Monk Bretton*, p. 216; *Reg. Wickwane*, p. 139; BL, Lansdowne ms. 402, ff. 115v–116r); 17 Apr. 1283 (*CPR 1281–92*, p. 61); 1287 (*Yorks F., 1272–1300*, p. 81); testimonial to good behaviour 10 May 1290; letter to king asking him to recall a writ against the pr. since he was not an apostate 29 May 1290 (*Reg. Romeyn*, II, 98–9, 100, cf. Logan, *Runaway Religious*, pp. 199–200). Res. 21 Sept. 1291 (*Reg. Romeyn*, II, 114).
For later priors see under Benedictines: Independent Houses.

MONKS HORTON (Kent), St Mary and St John the Evangelist (Lewes) f. 1142
  Lists in *VCH Kent*, II, 152; *Heads*, I, 120.
Adam Occ. Oct. 1218 x Oct. 1219 (*Suffolk F. (Rye)*, p. 18); 13 Oct. 1227 (*Kent F.*, pp. 97–8).
Peter de Aldinge Occ. *c.* 1246 x 1248 (BL, Stowe ms. 935, f. 26v); Oct. 1257 x Oct. 1258, Oct. 1263 x Oct. 1264 (Hasted, *Kent*, (1790), III, 319, citing (now missing fos.) from BL, Stowe ms. 935, chts. nos. 76 and 92, dated 42 and 48 Henry III); 2 Dec. 1262 (*Kent F.*, pp. 328–9).
Geoffrey Occ. 1263 (Charvin, I, no. 55); n.d. (BL, Stowe ms. 935, f. 44v).
William Occ. 8 Mar. 1278 (BL, Stowe ms. 935, f. 12v – date conf. by *List of Sheriffs*, p. 67); 24 Oct. 1279 (*Reg. G. Giffard*, p. 117). In 1279 unnamed pr. *est optima persona, vite honeste et redolentis fame, anglicus* (Charvin, I, no. 99).
Hugh Occ. 26 June 1282 (BL, Stowe ms. 935, f. 45r); 1284 (PRO, C241/1/63; C241/1/139); 4 Apr. 1286, 5 Apr. 1286 (*CPR 1281–92*, pp. 230, 229); Mich. 1286 x Mich. 1287 (PRO, E159/60, mm. 12d, 15d).
James Occ. Nov. 1295 x Nov. 1296 (PRO, E106/3/19, m. 6d); 26 June 1297, 4 July 1297, 30 Jan. 1298 (*CPR 1292–1301*, pp. 270, 289, 328); Nov. 1296 x Nov. 1297 (PRO, E106/4/2, m. 2d); 5 Nov. 1297 (BL, Stowe ms. 935, f. 46r); Nov. 1297 x Nov. 1298 (PRO, E106/4/8, m. 2d); Nov. 1298 x Nov. 1299 (PRO, E106/4/9, m. 3; E106/4/10, m. 3d); 1300 (PRO, E106/4/14, m. 5); 18 July 1302 (*CPR 1301–07*, p. 44); 29 Mar. 1310 (BL, Stowe ms. 935, f. 30r).
Conon (Cono) –**1320** Occ. 15 May 1318 (BL, Stowe ms. 935, f. 10v); July 1319 x July 1320 (*CPR 1324–27*, p. 52). Transferred to Northampton, St Andrew, before 27 Feb. 1320 (*CPR 1317–21*, p. 426).

John Occ. *c.* Mich. 1324 (PRO, E106/5/2, m. 14); 15 Nov. 1324 (*CPR 1324–27*, p. 52); 29 Oct. 1325 (*CCR 1323–27*, p. 519); July 1325 x July 1326 (PRO, E106/5/4, m. [13]); 8 Oct. 1326 (*Memo. Roll 1326–7*, p. 273).

James Occ. 23 Mar. 1327 (*CCR 1327–30*, p. 111).

John de Cabulone Occ. 5 July 1328 (*CCR 1327–30*, p. 401); 17 Apr. 1331, 20 Apr. 1331 (*CCR 1330–33*, pp. 301, 304).

William de Warenne M. of Lewes, illegitimate s. of John, Earl Warenne, born at Conisbrough Castle (*Cal. Misc. Inq.*, II, 397). Occ. 1 June 1335 (BL, Stowe ms. 935, f. 45r); Mar. 1337 (*CCR 1337–39*, pp. 106, 109); 22 Feb. 1339, 8 May 1339 (*CCR 1339–41*, pp. 18, 82). Transferred to Castleacre (q.v.) from Monks Horton (*CPL*, III, 124).

Hugh de Faloniis (Falcouns, Falouns) –1356 Occ. 8 Feb. 1342 (*CFR 1337–47*, p. 261); 11 July 1345 (*CCR 1343–46*, p. 636); 26 Nov. 1346 (*CPR 1345–48*, p. 215); 21 Dec. 1347, 15 Feb. 1348 (*CCR 1346–49*, pp. 418, 491). D. by 4 June 1356 (*CFR 1356–68*, p. 20).

Peter de Tenolio (Tevolio, Tonelio) **1356–** Apptd by abb. of Cluny *ante* 4 June 1356 on d. of Hugh (ibid.). Occ. Mich. 1358 x Mich. 1359 (PRO, E372/204, rot. 10); 3 Feb. 1363 petition gtd to be given Prittlewell priory when Francis de Baugiaco got the priory of Montacute (*CPP*, p. 401). In fact he was apptd to Bermondsey in 1364 and d. there in 1372 (q.v.).

[**Denis de Hopton** (Opton) Subpr. and almoner of Prittlewell, petition for priory gtd when Peter obtains that of Prittlewell 3 Feb. 1363 (ibid.). Papal prov. 7 Feb. 1363 – ineffective (*Accts of Papal Collectors*, p. 299).]

John Occ. 11 June 1369 (*CPR 1368–77*, p. 18).

Peter (de) Witsand (Whitsand, Whytsond) Occ. 1370 (PRO, E106/1–/10); 11 Nov. 1371 (*CFR 1368–77*, p. 117); 1384 (PRO, C269/15/35; *CPR 1381–85*, p. 483); 20 Jan. 1397 (BL, Stowe ms. 935, f. 22r); Mar. 1401 (ibid., f. 22r); 14 Mar. 1404 (ibid., f. 30r).

MONKTON, *see* WINTERBORN MONKTON

MONKTON FARLEIGH (Wilts), St Mary Magdalen (Lewes) f. 1120 x 1123

Lists in *VCH Wilts*, III, 268; *Heads*, I, 120.

Mainer (Mayno) 1191– M. and Chamberlain of Lewes, el. 21 Apr. 1191 (PRO, DL27/3). Occ. 6 Oct. 1204 (*Wilts F.*, I, 9); 1213 (PRO, E326/11639); Oct. 1218 (*Ctl. Lewes, Wilts etc.*, p. 13, no. 32).

Henry de Flegly (Fleg') –1247 Occ. 16 Feb. 1227 (*Soms F.*, I, 56); 1227 (*Wilts F.*, I, 18); (H.) 3 Sept. 1227 (*Sarum Chts.*, p. 185); 1236 (*Wilts F.*, I, 23); 24 July 1247 (BL, Harl. ms. 61, f. 92v; Wilts RO, Acc.192/54); 10 Sept. 1247 (*Ctl. Lewes, Wilts etc.*, p. 6 no. 12). Res. by 14 Sept. 1247 (ibid., p. 9, no. 18). Mentd as former pr. in 1249 (*Wilts Civil Pleas*, p. 96, no. 284).

Thomas Occ. [*c.* Sept.] 1248 (PRO, E326/469).

Simon Occ. 25 Apr. 1249 (*Wilts F.*, I, 37); 9 May 1249 (PRO, Hants F., CP25/1/203/8, no. 45); 1251 (*CR 1247–51*, p. 550; PRO, F., Various Cos, CP25/1/284/19, no. 97); 1256 (*Wilts F.*, I, 49); 27 Apr. 1259 (*Cornwall F.*, I, no. 253); 6 July 1265 (PRO, E210/320).

William of Chichester (Cicestr', Cystr') –1281 Occ. 13 Feb. 1267 (*Ctl. St Nicholas, Salisbury*, p. 20); 7 Feb. 1271 (*Ctl. Tropenell*, I, 300 but date given as 1261); Mich. 1277 x Mich. 1278 (PRO, E159/51, m. 18/2); 21 Mar. 1278 (*CCR 1272–75*, p. 494); Easter 1278 (PRO, CP40/24, m. 19). In 1279 the pr. '*est incorrigibilis, rebellis, publice diffamatus de incontinentia, de usuria, de inobedientia, et est excommunicatus, et fuit bene per x annos, prout ipsemet recognovit et dicit*' (Charvin, I, no. 99). D. by 4 Apr. 1281 (*Ctl. Lewes, Wilts etc.*, pp. 9–10, no. 19).

Stephen –1292 Occ. 13 Jan. 1282 (*Ctl. Tropenell*, I, 67); 16 Nov. 1282, 2 Dec. 1282, 23 Dec. 1282 (*Highworth Hundred Rolls*, II, 223, 225, 227); 1285 (PRO, E326/2273); 1289 (*CPR*

1281–92, p. 313). Letter of res. dated 15 Mar. 1292; notification of his res. in Lent 1292 and the breaking of his seal certified by letters dated 7 Apr. 1292 (*Ctl. Lewes, Wilts etc.*, p. 6, no. 11, p. 8, no. 16; and pp. 16–17, no. 26).

Thomas de Montargis (Muntagis, Muntargy) –**1300** Occ. 1292 x 1296 with William of Colerne, abb. of Malmesbury (*Ctl. Malmesbury*, II, 351, 353); Hil. 1295 (PRO, CP40/107, m. 129). Petition from sub-pr. and convent to the earl of Hereford and Essex reporting the dep. of Thomas and requesting the pres. of a new pr. under an agreement with Lewes priory, 1300 (PRO, DL36/1/205). 27 Nov. 1300 it was reported that Thomas de Montargis had been deposed at the pr. of Lewes's visitation (*Ctl. Lewes, Wilts etc.*, pp. 14–15, no. 23). Occ. as m. and *mansionarius* of Lewes and former pr. of Monkton Farleigh 9 May 1309 (Charvin, II, no. 179).

John de Castro Novo 1300/1– Gardener of Lewes, succ. as pr. and entered Monkton Farleigh 2 Jan. 1301 (*Ch. Lewes*, p. 37). Occ. 12 May 1305 (*CCR 1302–07*, p. 332); (John Leuwes) 9 July 1305 (*Wilts Gaol Deliveries*, no. 797); 3 May 1313 (*Ctl. Lewes, Wilts etc.*, p. 21, no. 31); 11 Apr. 1314 (PRO, E40/9366).

Thomas Occ. 13 Sept. 1318 (*CCR 1318–23*, p. 98).

John of Fécamp (Fiscampo) **1323–1326** Occ. in letter of pr. of Lewes dated 12 Mar. 1323 'at your creation as pr.' (*Ctl. Lewes, Wilts etc.*, p. 21, no. 32). Cess. by 13 Apr. 1326 (PRO, C84/21/3; cf. *CPR 1324–27*, pp. 260–1), and mentd 28 Apr. 1326 as former pr. (*CCR 1323–27*, p. 477).

Robert de Strete 1326– M. of Lewes, mentd 28 Apr. 1326 as having been adm. (*CCR 1323–27*, p. 478); cert. to king of his appt 30 Apr. 1336 (PRO, E135/2/29). Occ. 18 July 1326 (ibid., p. 634); 17 Mar. 1327 (*CCR 1327–30*, p. 108); Jan. 1328 x Jan. 1329 (PRO, DL36/1/233).

William de Balsham (Balcham, Barsham) Occ. 9 July 1330, 2 Feb. 1331 (*Reg. Burghersh*, I, nos. 268, 288); 3 Dec. 1330 (*CCR 1330–33*, p. 165); 1334 (Salisbury, Reg. Wyvil II, f. 30r; PRO, E210/2591); 16 Mar. 1336, 22–3 Mar. 1336 (*CCR 1333–37*, pp. 649, 654); 25 Oct. 1336 (*CPR 1374–77*, p. 205). Inhibition from the Court of Canterbury n.d. (*Ctl. Lewes, Wilts etc.*, p. 13, no. 21). Mentd 28 Mar. 1343 as former pr., when his arrest is ordered (*CPR 1343–45*, p. 78).

Laurence Archebaud (Archenbaud) –**1350** Occ. 11 Apr. 1337 (PRO, E315/35/195); 20 Mar. 1342 (*CFR 1337–47*, p. 274); 11 July 1345 (*CCR 1343–46*, p. 636); 26 Aug. 1346 (*Ctl. Lewes, Wilts etc.*, p. 19, no. 30). D. by 1 July 1350 (*CFR 1347–56*, p. 245).

John de Chalons (Chalouns) **1350–1354** Occ. 1 July 1350 (ibid.); Mich. 1351 (PRO, KB27/365, m. 87). Ceased to hold office by 31 Jan. 1354 (*CFR 1347–56*, p. 392).

Geoffrey of Walton 1354– Occ. 31 Jan. 1354 (ibid., pp. 391–2). Occ. 7 May 1356 (*Med. Deeds of Bath*, I, no. 143); 16 July 1358 (*CPR 1358–61*, p. 82); 6 Oct. 1358 (*CCR 1354–60*, p. 464); 22 Nov. 1364 (Lincoln, Ep. Reg., X, f. 9v).

The next recorded pr., **William Preston**, occ. 1380 x 1381 (Kirby, 'Clerical poll-taxes', p. 166).

MONTACUTE (Soms), St Peter (and St Paul) (Cluny) f. ?1078 (Ann., f. 162v).

Lists in *VCH Soms*, II, 114–15; *Ctl. Montacute*, pp. lxviii–lxxv; *Heads*, I, 121–2; 14th cent. Ann. in BL, Cotton ms. Tiberius A X, ff. 145–76, 181 (list pd in *Mon. Angl.*, V, 164).

Durand –1220 Occ. 1197 x 1205 (*HMC Wells*, I, 57); ejected 21 Dec. 1207 (*Rot. Lit. Pat.*, p. 78); restored 1217, but again ejected in 1220 (BL, Cotton ms. Tiberius A X, f. 167, partly quoted in *Mon. Angl.*, V, 163 and n.).

Mark 1221–1251 Succ. 1221 (ibid.). Occ. 14 Oct. 1231 (*Soms F.*, I, 74); 1236 (*Reg. Bronescombe*, p. 5); 1237 (*Ctl. Montacute*, no. 187); 1238 (*Cornwall F.*, I, no. 74); 1246 (*CChR 1226–57*, p. 304; *Ctl. Montacute*, no. 22); 1 July 1250 (*Devon F.*, I, 268, no. 532). Ejected 1251 by the abb. of Cluny (Ctl. list citing Ann.); house void by cess. by 13 July 1251 (*CPR 1247–58*, p. 102).

Roger de Cliponvill 1251–1260 Mand. for seisin 20 July 1251 (*CCR 1247–51*, p. 477). Occ. 6 Dec. 1259 (*CPR 1258–66*, p. 107). Transf. to Lenton 1260 (q.v.). House vacant by his cess. and promotion by 16 Sept. 1260 (*CPR 1258–66*, p. 93).

Hugh de Noyers 1260– Royal ass. 17 Sept. 1260, writ *de intendendo* 16 Sept. 1260, having been coll. by abb. of Cluny (ibid.). Occ. 1 July 1261 (*Ctl. Montacute*, no. 112).

John de Wylton Occ. as *custos* 6 Oct. 1265 (*Reg. W. Giffard (Bath)*, p. 3).

Gilbert de Broxolio 1266– M. of Cluny, temps. 30 Jan. 1266 (*CPR 1258–66*, p. 541). Occ. 2 May 1267, 18 Oct. 1267 (*CPR 1266–72*, pp. 58, 118).

Guy de Marchant 1270–1283 M. of Cluny, apptd by abb. of Cluny [July x Aug.] 1270 (*CCR 1268–72*, p. 290); temps. 15 Aug. 1270 (*CPR 1266–72*, p. 454). 3 July 1279 pardoned for coin-clipping (*CPR 1272–81*, p. 318; *CFR 1272–1307*, p. 113). Ref. to recent voidance of house 16 Dec. 1283 (*CFR 1272–1307*, p. 196). Order to the keeper of the Tower 15 Sept. 1284 to cause Guy, former pr. of Montacute, now in the Tower for certain trespasses, to be replevied from prison if he finds sufficient mainpernors who undertake to have him before the king 15 days from Michaelmas (*CCR 1279–88*, p. 277). Pardon to Guy, former pr., of trespasses concerning the clipping of money and for receiving the chattels of certain Jews 27 Dec. 1284 (*CPR 1281–92*, p. 147; *CFR 1272–1307*, p. 209).

Peter Gaydenzar 1283– Pr. of Reyny, mand. to make letters for Peter to be adm. pr. of Montacute 29 Nov. 1283 (*Cal. Chanc. Warr.*, p.17). Temps. 12 Dec. 1283, now appptd as pr. by abb. Ivo of Cluny (*CPR 1281–92*, p. 108). Occ. 7 May 1284 (*Cornwall F.*, I, no. 314); 27 Mar. 1290 (*CPR 1281–92*, p. 348).

John de Bello Ramo 1292–1293 M. of Cluny, notif. to king by abb. William of Cluny of his appt of John as pr. 26 Apr. 1292 (PRO, C84/10/38; cf. C84/10/47); temps. 8 June 1292 (*CPR 1281–92*, p. 493). 9 June 1292 promised he would let the king's chancellor have a letter of protection (*?recte* pres.) under seal of the abb. (*CCR 1288–96*, p. 266). D. at Kerswell 9 Apr. 1293; his heart bur. there in front of the high altar; his body bur. in front of the high altar at Montacute (*TDA* 84, p. 116, citing BL, Cotton ms. Tiberius A X, f. 174r).

Geoffrey de Dosa 1293–?1297 M. of Cluny, notif. to king by abb. William of Cluny of his appt of Geoffrey as pr. 13 July 1293 (PRO, C84/11/24); temps. 26 July 1293 (*CPR 1292–1301*, p. 33). Occ. Nov. 1295 x Nov. 1296 (PRO, E106/3/19, m. 7). Unnamed pr. had d. by 18 Mar. 1297 (PRO, SC1/63/61, prob. by 6 Mar., cf. *CPR 1292–1301*, p. 267, ref. to sub-pr. and convent).

Stephen Raulun 1297–1316 Abb. of Cluny asks king to receive new (unnamed) pr. 27 May 1297 (PRO, SC1/63/61). M. of Cluny, notif. to king by abb. of Cluny of his appt of Stephen as pr. 10 June 1297 (PRO, C84/21/30); writ *de intendendo* 4 July 1297 (*CPR 1292–1301*, p. 288). Res. 7 Aug. 1316 (*CFR 1307–19*, p. 300).

John Cheverer (Caprarii, Caprario) *alias* **de Gigny** (Giniaco) **1316–1326** Pr. of Breuil, notif. to king by abb. Henry of Cluny of his appt of John as pr. 12 July 1316 (PRO, C84/18/41); temps. 12 Oct. 1316 (*CPR 1313–17*, p. 553). 16 Feb. 1317 order to sheriff to stay the execution of the order to arrest pr. John and the former pr. Stephen (*CCR 1313–18*, p. 395). 1322 papal reservation to John of the priory of Montacute (*CPL*, II, 223, cf. 216). 15 Feb. 1326 granted leave of absence for a year, resident in France (ibid., 248–9). Res.by 29 Apr. 1326 (PRO, C84/21/5, cf. *CPR 1324–27*, p. 274).

Guichard de Iou (Jou) **1326–1340** M. of Cluny, notif. to king by abb. Peter of Cluny of his appt of Guichard as pr. 22 Apr. 1326 (PRO, C84/21/5); writ *de intendendo* 6 June 1326 (*CPR 1324–27*, p. 274; cf. *CPR 1334–38*, p. 48). Pope claimed the right to present and app. Robert Bosse, m. of Tavistock, who was refused by the Abb. of Cluny and the convent, and died during the litigation. Guichard cited before the pope 8 Sept. 1327 (*CPL*, II, 278). Permission to Guichard to leave Dover to go to the Roman Curia 14 Oct. 1328, mand. to restore issued 22 Oct. 1328 (*CCR 1327–30*, pp. 415, 330). Papal reservation to Guichard of Lenton priory about to become vacant by the appt of Geoffrey de Cintriaco to Montacute 4 Dec. 1330 (*CPL*, II, 346) – ineffective (see petitions, PRO, SC8/210/10488–9; *Ctl. Montacute*, pp. lxxi–lxxii). Guichard going overseas, appts attorneys 10 Feb. 1331 (*CPR 1330–34*, p. 75). Occ. 31 Jan. 1340 (*Reg. Grandisson*, I, 58). House void by d. of last (unnamed) pr. by 6 Mar. 1340 (*CPR 1338–40*, p. 435); house void (no reason given) by 12 Feb. 1340 (*Reg. R. Shrewsbury*, I, no. 1596).

[**Robert Busse** M. of Tavistock – unsuccessful candidate for Tavistock abbey (q.v.). Papal commn to cite Guichard de Jou touching his title to the priory. On the transfer of John Cheverer the pope had put Robert in his place at Montacute, but the abb. of Cluny had apptd Guichard and the papal order to remove him was resisted (*CPL*, II, 257). Robert d. during litigation before 22 Aug. 1328 (ibid., 277).]

[**Peter de Mortmart** Cardinal of St Stephen's on the Caelian. Papal appt to the priory on the d. of Robert Busse 22 Aug. 1328 (ibid.).]

[**Geoffrey de C(h)intriaco** Papal appt to the priory 4 Dec. 1330 (ibid., 347). Prev. pr. of Lenton (q.v.) – appt ineffective.]

[**Humbert de Banhaco** prov. from Montacute to the priory of Parois le Monail by 2 Nov. 1332 (ibid., 370).]

[**Philip de Cheyntriaco** Pr. of Kerswell. Papal prov. 2 Nov. 1332 on transfer of Humbert de Banhaco. He is to res. Kerswell (ibid.) – appt ineffective]

John de Henton 1340–1342 [as m. of O. Clun., gtd keeping of priory 3 Oct. 1338 (*CFR 1337–47*, p. 96); further gt of custody to him 20 Dec. 1338 the pr. being too ill to labour thereon – petition and information proved to be false (*CFR 1337–47*, pp. 112, 124). On 18 Feb. 1340 gt of keeping of priory to John Gyot, m. of Montacute (ibid., p. 160).] Pres. by attorneys of William de Montacute, earl of Salisbury 28 Apr. 1340 on d. of Guichard; commn to examine matter of pres. 26 May 1340 (*Reg. R. Shrewsbury*, I, nos. 1391–2). Priory vacant and the abb. of Cluny had failed to pres. and the power of colln had devolved on the bp: citation 15 Feb. 1341 (ibid., no. 1596). Royal ass. as abb. of Sherborne 26 Dec. 1342 (*CPR 1340–43*, p. 574).

John (de) la Porta I (La Porte) –1345 Of Uzerches, dioc. Limoges, B.Cn.L., chaplain of G., cardinal of St Sabina (*CPP*, p. 25). Occ. from 22 Apr. 1343 to 6 Aug. 1345 (*CPR 1343–45*, pp. 44, 540); 24 Oct. 1343, 7 Dec. 1345 (*CPP*, pp. 25, 89). 16 Jan. 1345 Pope ordered abb. of Cluny to receive the res. of John and give priory to a suitable person (*CPL*, III, 15, 172). D. by 17 Dec. 1345 (*CPP*, p. 90).

John (de) la Porta II 1345– 17 Dec. 1345 Papal prov. of priory to John la Porta, on the d. of his brother John at the Curia. He was chamberlain of Montacute and must give up that office (*CPL*, III, 186; *CPP*, p. 90; cf. *Accts of Papal Collectors*, pp. 87, 98, 124). Occ. 19 Jan. 1346, 14 Oct. 1347 (ibid., pp. 24, 249); 28 Mar. 1346 (*CCR 1346–49*, p. 55). At the General Chapter of 3 May 1349 it was reported that the unnamed pr. *percussus est morbo paralitico et incurabili* (Charvin, III, p. 437, no. 505).

Gerald (William) Roche (Rothonis) –1362/3 Occ. (William) 15 Aug. 1356 (*CPL*, III, 621); Easter 1361 (PRO, CP40/406, m. 217); 21 Oct. 1362 (*Reg. R. Shrewsbury*, II, app., no. 98); 6 Dec. 1362, 2 Jan. 1363 (*Ctl. Montacute*, nos. 200, 202). Occ. as pr. of Lewes 1363 (q.v.).

Francis de Baugiaco (Barchiato, Barghiato) 1362/3–1404 Pr. of Prittlewell, petition for priory of Montacute void by the promotion of the last pr. to Lewes 30 Dec. 1362 (*CPP*, p. 393). Prov. 30 Dec. 1362 *or* 3 *or* 11 Jan. 1363 (3 [ ] Jan.) (*Accts of Papal Collectors*, pp. 194, 218). Occ. 10 Nov. 1371 (*CFR 1368–77*, p. 136); 15 July 1380 (*CPR 1377–81*, p. 569); 1371, 1382 (*Ctl. Montacute*, no. 217); 6 Feb. 1382 (PRO, C67/29, m. 17); in return of aliens 20 Sept. 1384 (PRO, C269/15/43). Commn to enter priory and expel those attempting to arrest pr. Francis 6 Dec. 1385 (*CPR 1385–89*, pp. 88–9). Order to arrest Francis de Baugiaco, pr. of Montacute and to bring him before the king and his council 16 Jan. 1386 (ibid., p. 164). Revocation of letters gtd to Francis, former pr., giving him custody of the priory 21 Jan. 1386 (ibid., p. 111). Revocation of the commn to arrest the evildoers who had entered the priory and expelled Francis, late pr. 21 Jan. 1386 (ibid., pp. 166–7); 10 Feb. 1386 commn to induct **Nicholas Hornyk**, confessor of Queen Anne, to whom the king has gtd custody of priory 4 June last into possession thereof (ibid., p. 167); similar commn, with power to arrest and imprison contrariants 28 Feb. 1386 (ibid., p. 174). [1386] the new pr., Nicholas Hornyk, petitioned the king asking for commn to arrest Francis, former pr., who is disobedient to the king and the crown, indicted of felonies and treasons (PRO, SC8/250/12495). 2 petitions from Francis (PRO, SC8/125/6219; SC8/199/9917). Revocation of gt of priory's custody to Nicholas Hornyk and to restore the priory to pr. Francis 12 July 1387 (*CPR 1385–89*, p. 331, cf. pp. 385–6). Francis occ. again 23 May 1389 (PRO, C85/39/1); Hil. 1390, and July 1393, 12 May 1395 (*YB 13 Richard II*, pp. 115, 118, 120–1); apptd papal chaplain 28 Apr. 1398 (*CPL*, IV, 302). Restoration of priory to him by crown 14 Nov. 1399 (*CPR 1399–1401*, p. 70). D. by 18 Jan. 1404 (Lambeth, Reg. Arundel I, f. 292v).

MUCH WENLOCK (Shrops), St Milburga (La Charité sur Loire) f. 1080 x 1081
Lists in *VCH Shrops*, II, 46–7; R. Graham, *The history of the alien priory of Wenlock* (HMSO 1965, from *JBAA*, 3rd ser., 4 (1939)) pp. 24–6; *Heads*, I, 122–3. See also W.F. Mumford, 'Monks of Wenlock priory', *Trans. Shrops ANHS*, LX (1975–6), 97–111.
Master Josbert (Joybert) –1216 Pr. of Coventry; pr. of Bermondsey. He was pr. of Much Wenlock by 1198 (*MPCM*, II, 445–6). D. 14 June 1216 (Dugdale, *Warwickshire*, I, 164, citing lost Ch. of Geoffrey, pr. of Coventry). Mumford, p. 104; Greatrex, *Biog. Reg.*, p. 360.
Humbert (Imbert, Inbert, Hymbert) –1261 Prob. also pr. of Bermondsey (q.v.). Occ. in *Shrops F.* from 8 Nov. 1221 to 30 Apr. 1245 (*Trans. Shrops ANHS*, 3rd ser., VI, 173); 4th ser., VI, 184); 1222 (Stenton, *Eyre 1221–2*, no. 1463); royal envoy 1236 (*CPR 1232–47*, p. 154); (H.) 1245 (*Cluny Chts*, VI, no. 4833); 1249 (PRO, E368/23, m. 3); 13 Feb. 1254 (*Reg. Pontissara*, II, 726); Jan 1256 (PRO, Shrops F., CP25/1/193/4, no. 76; 173/4, no. 82). D. 1261 (*EHR*, 44, p. 102). Mumford, pp. 103–4.
Aymo de Montibus 1261–1272 Pr. of Bermondsey, succ. 1261 (*EHR*, 44, p. 102). Occ. Feb. 1262 (*CChR 1257–1300*, p. 419); 7 Mar. 1262, 22 Aug. 1263, 5 Dec. 1265 (*CPR 1258–66*, pp. 207, 276, 518); 7 Feb. 1265 gt to pr. Aymo of the priory of St Andrew, Northampton, until further notice – the priory is so deteriorated by occasion of the late conflict in the town of Northampton and the pr. cannot stay there, later revoked (ibid., pp. 403, 441). Occ. as pr. of Wenlock 1267 (*CPR 1266–72*, pp. 1, 112, 118); 11 Sept. 1271 (Hereford Cath. mun 731). Payment for custody of vacant priory 26 Oct. 1272 (*CR 1268–72*, p. 535). Mumford, p. 105.
John de Thifford (Tickford, Tycford, Tyeford) 1272–1285 Previously pr. of St Andrew, Northampton (*Cluniac Visitations*, p. 22). Apptd by pr. of La Charité, writ *de intendendo* 12 Nov. 1272 (*CPR 1266–72*, p. 714). Occ. 11 Nov. 1276 (PRO, SC1/21/63); 11 May 1276, 15 July 1279 (*CPR 1272–81*, pp. 140, 322); 15 Oct. 1281 (*CCR 1279–88*, p. 134); in 1279 claimed by the visitors to be manoeuvring for the see of Rochester (*Cluniac Visitations*, p. 30). 22 Sept. 1284 apptd to custody of Bermondsey priory, taken under king's protection (*CPR 1281–92*, p. 134). Res. 1285 to go to be pr. of Lewes (q.v.). Mumford, p. 108.
Henry de Bonvillars (Bono Villar', Bonville, Benilar', Beuelard) 1285–1320 Pr. of Bermondsey, apted by pr. of La Charité, petition for temps. 10 Sept. 1285 (PRO, C84/8/36); temps. 10 Sept. 1285 (*CPR 1281–92*, p. 192). Occ. from 10 June 1290 to 26 Mar.

1292 (ibid., pp. 362, 481); from 6 Feb. 1294 to 1 Feb. 1301 (*CPR 1292–1301*, pp. 61, 568); 1302, 1305 (*CPR 1301–7*, pp. 94–5, 351, 375); 1308 (*CPR 1313–17*, p. 273); D. by 20 Jan. 1320 (*Cal. Chanc. Warr.*, p. 504). Mumford, p. 100.[5]

Hearing the pr. of Much Wenlock is dead, the king desires that **Adam of Cleobury**, m. of Shrewsbury and brother of Richard of Cleobury, the king's servant, be made pr. of Wenlock 20 Jan. 1320. The pr. of La Charité responds that before the royal letter had arrived he had given the priory to another; mand. 10 Mar. 1320 (*Cal. Chanc. Warr.*, pp. 504, 506).

Guichard de Charlieu (de Caro Loco) **1320–** Pr. of St Andrew, Northampton, temps. 26 Feb. 1320 (*CPR 1317–21*, p. 425). Occ. 5 Feb. 1342, 16 Mar. 1342, 16 May 1345 (*CFR 1337–47*, pp. 258, 276, 421); 2 Dec. 1344 (*CPL*, III, 160; *CPP*, p. 81); 20 Oct. 1346 (*Reg. Trillek*, p. 288); 16 Apr. 1350 (*CFR 1347–56*, p. 232); *c.* Sept. 1351 (PRO, C269/15/32). Mumford, p. 101. Also pr. of Pontefract (q.v.).

Henry de Miouns (Meones, Mionus) *alias* de Chay **–1370** Occ. 12 Jan. 1354 (*CFR 1347–56*, p. 383); 10 May 1355 (*CPR 1354–58*, p. 212); 10 May 1358 (*CPR 1358–61*, p. 50); 1 Dec. 1361 (*Reg. Stretton*, II, 194); 2 Feb. 1363 (*Ctl. Holy Trinity, Aldgate*, no. 796). D. by 3 Jan. 1370 when *extenta temporalium* taken (BL Add. ms. 6165, f. 51r). Seal (*Mon. Seals*, p. 62). Mumford, p. 105.

Otto de Fleury (Floriaco) **1370–** Apptd by the pr. of Bermondsey, vicar-general of the pr. of La Charité in England; temps. 6 Feb. 1370 (*CPR 1367–70*, pp. 362, 377). Occ. 16 Feb. 1372 (*CFR 1368–77*, p. 156). Mumford, p. 102.

John Bally –1376 Res. by 14 Oct. 1376 (PRO, C84/31/43).

William of Pontefract (de Ponte Fracto) **1376–** Pr. of Dudley. The pr. of Bermondsey, vicar-general of the pr. of La Charité in England, pres. William 14 Oct. 1376 (ibid.); temps. 14 Oct. 1376 (*CPR 1374–77*, p. 354). Occ. 24 Oct. 1377 (*CFR 1377–83*, p. 25); 6 Sept. 1379 (*Mon. Angl.*, V, p. 77, no. viii). Mumford, p. 106.

Roger Wyvel (Wevell, Wynelle) **–1397** Gt of keeping of priory 8 June 1388 (*CFR 1383–91*, p. 237). Priory vacant by 13 Jan. 1397 (PRO, C84/34/38). D. by 18 Jan. 1397 (*CPR 1396–99*, p. 61). Mumford, p. 109.

NEWTON LONGVILLE (Bucks), St Faith (Longueville, Ste Foi) f. –1102. Diss. 1414. Lists in *VCH Bucks*, I, 396; *Heads*, I, 123; *Newington Longeville Chts.*, pp. xlvi–xlvii. The pr. of Newton Longville and the proctor in England of the priory of Longueville were usually the same man and in the earlier period the title proctor was more common (ibid., p. xlvi).

William Occ. 1199 x 1216 (proctor) (*Newington Longeville Chts.*, no. 47).

Richard of Whaddon (Waddon) Occ. 1225 (proctor) (ibid., no. 80).

Ralph Occ. 1227 (proctor) (ibid., no. 86); Hil. term 1229 (*CRR*, XIII, no. 1577).

William of Lincoln Occ. 1232 x 1234 (proctor) (*Newington Longeville Chts.*, no. 27).

Richard of Whaddon (Waddon) Occ. *c.* 1235 (proctor) (ibid., no. 49).

William Ginneux Occ. 26 Mar. 1238 (proctor) (ibid., no. 54).

Walter de Enerardemeville Occ. 14 Aug. 1251 (proctor-general) (ibid., no. 40); 18 Dec. 1258 (proctor), 1258 x 1263 (pr.), 14 Aug. 1262 (proctor-general) (ibid., nos. 34, 79, 84).

John de Pennavilla (Panneuil, Paynel) Apptd as proctor in England 17 May 1265, 1266 (proctor) (ibid., nos. 82, 83); pr. 19 Mar. 1274 (ibid., no. 42); 18 July 1279 (*Reg. R. Gravesend*, p. 256, cf. ibid., p. 257, where he occ. as proctor 25 Feb. 1279).

Odo (Eudo) Occ. 14 Nov. 1281 (pr.) (*Newington Longeville Chts.*, no. 108). Desc. as former pr. of Newton Longville when apptd to St Andrew, Northampton 1285 (*CPR 1281–92*, p. 169). Occ. as pr. of Newton Longville (Eudo) 15 July 1290, 20 July 1290 (ibid., pp. 375–6).

---

[5] Adam (*sic*), pr. of Wenlock, is recorded 28 Jan. 1291 (*Reg. Swinfield*, p. 253).

Richard Occ. Nov. 1295 x Nov. 1296 (PRO, E106/3/19, m. 8d); Nov. 1296 x Nov. 1297 (PRO, E106/4/2, m. 2); Nov. 1297 x Nov. 1298 (PRO, E106/4/8, m. 1d); Nov. 1298 x Nov. 1299 (PRO, E106/4/9; m. 1d; E106/4/10, m. 2d); Easter 1300 (PRO, E106/4/14, m. 3d); Nov. 1302 x Nov. 1303 (PRO, E106/4/18, m. 4).

William de Tronolio Occ. 31 Mar. 1306 (Oxford, New Coll., Liber Niger, f. 7v).

William de Talaya (Tallia) Occ. as proctor-general 13 Mar. 1308, 3 Mar. 1314, 1 Dec. 1314 (Lincoln, Ep. Reg., II, ff. 180r, 185v, 186r); 16 Mar. 1311 (*Newington Longeville Chts.*, no. 14).

William de Tonolio Occ. *c.* Mich. 1324 (PRO, E106/5/2, m. 10d); July 1325 x July 1326 (PRO, E106/5/4, m.[10]); 8 Oct. 1326 (*Memo. Roll 1326–7*, p. 272); 27 Jan. 1330 (*Reg. Martival*, I, 406); 5 Nov. 1330 (Lincoln, Ep. Reg., IV, f. 337v); n.d. [1332] as *custos* (PRO, C270/10/21). See also below.

Richard Occ. 20 Mar. 1333 (*Newington Longeville Chts.*, no. 129).

William de Tonolio (Tholonio, Thonolio, Thonoile, Touolio, Tevolio, Thernolio) –1358 Occ. proctor 5 Nov. 1330, 2 Sept. 1334 (Lincoln, Ep. Reg., IV, ff. 337v, 346r); 6 May 1342 (ibid., no. 132); 28 July 1339 (*CPR 1338–40*, p. 309); 12 Feb. 1342 (*CFR 1337–47*, p. 272); 16 Aug. 1344 (*Newington Longeville Chts.*, no. 133); 11 July 1345 (*CCR 1343–46*, p. 636). Mentd as late proctor 5 Aug. 1358 (*Newington Longeville Chts.*, no. 134). William mentd 13 Mar. 1359 as now broken with age and so weak as to be unable to admin. the priory (*CFR 1356–68*, p. 90).

Peter de Sales (Salis) Occ. proctor 5 Aug. 1358 (*Newington Longeville Chts.*, no. 134); 27 Oct., 16 Nov. 1358 (ibid., nos. 50, 43); pr. 3 July 1359 (ibid., no. 135).

Arnald Lanuci (Lamici) Occ. proctor 29 Sept. 1365 (ibid., no. 51). On 20 Oct. 1367 desc. as pr. of St Mary de Bellomonte Petroso, proctor in England of the pr. and convent of Longueville (ibid., no. 137).

John Fabri (Fever) Appt with two others to be proctor in England of the pr. and convent of Longueville 'to govern our house of Newton and all other possessions of the priory' 2 July 1368; appt as sole proctor in England 4 Oct. 1369 (ibid., nos. 138–9); occ. as proctor 1 May 1375 (ibid., no. 104).

NORMAN'S BURROW (Norfolk), St Mary and St John the Evangelist (Castleacre) f. *c.* 1160 (Aug.); *c.* 1200 (Cluniac cell, dependent on Castleacre); 1351 x 1374 (denizen)

List in *VCH Norfolk*, II, 359; *Heads*, I, 123.

Simon Occ. Oct. 1227 x Oct. 1228 (*Norfolk F. (Rye)*, p. 45); Easter term 1228 (*CRR*, XIII, no. 611); 26 July 1228 (BL, Harl ms. 2110, f. 115r); n.d. (BL, Egerton ms. 3137, f. 184v).

Gervase Occ. n.d. (BL, Egerton ms. 3137, ff. 184r–v, 214v). No clear idea as to date or place in the sequence of priors.

NORTHAMPTON, St Andrew (La Charité) f. 1093 x 1100

Lists in *VCH Northants*, II, 108–9; *Heads*, I, 123; R.M. Serjeantson, 'The Priory of St Andrew, Northampton', *Northants. Nat. Hist. Society and Field Club*, XIII (1905), 143–4.

Walter Latest recorded occ. 1207 x 1208 (Northants F. PRO transcripts).

Ralph –1228 Occ. 24 May 1220 (*Reg. Wells*, II, 185); 1224 (*CPR 1216–25*, p. 477; PRO, Northants F., CP25/1/172/18 no. 112); 19 Oct. 1226 (PRO, Leics F., CP25/1/121/10, no. 98). Vacated priory by 19 May 1228 (*Reg. Wells*, II, 145).

Thomas de Longavilla 1228– Letter of pres. sealed 19 May 1228, adm. in place of pr. Ralph 10 June 1228 (ibid., 144–7). Occ. 1228 x 1233 (*Berkeley Chts.*, no. 446); 31 July 1232 (PRO, Northants F., CP25/1/172/25, no. 298); n.d. (*Basset Chts.*, no. 58).

Thomas de Theovill 1234–1240 M. of Longville, mand. for seisin 4 Nov. 1234 (*CR 1234–37*,

p. 6, cf. *CPR 1232–47*, p. 80). Occ. 1 Oct. 1236 (PRO, Northants F., CP25/1/173/28, no. 351); 1238 (*Cluny Chts.*, II, 110–11). D. by Sept. 1240 (*Reg. Grosseteste*, p. 201).

Arnulf (Ernulph) 1240–1245/6 Letter of pres. on d. of pr. Thomas Sept. 1240; adm. 7 Oct. 1240 (ibid., pp. 200–1). Pr. of St Stephen, Nevers, mand. for seisin 16 Sept. 1240, having been apptd by the pr. of La Charité (*CR 1237–42*, p. 222). Adm. 7 Oct. 1240 (*Reg. Grosseteste*, pp. 200–1). Occ. 26 Apr. 1243 (PRO, Northants F., CP25/1/173/32, no. 468). Had become pr. of Longpont by 25 Aug. 1246 (*Reg. Grosseteste*, p. 223) but see below.

William de Fouville (Fovill) 1245/6–1258/9 Apptd Aug. 1245 (*EHR*, 44, 97) but adm. 26 Aug. 1246 (*Reg. Grosseteste*, p. 223). Occ. Aug. 1246 x June 1247 (ibid., pp. 226–7); 1 May 1250 (*Lincs F.*, II, 69). 18 Oct. 1257 the king understands, having inspected letters of the abb. of Cluny, that although the abb. preferred William, pr. of St Andrew's, Northampton, to be pr. of Lewes, he enjoined him to retain the priory of St Andrew's until another ordinance was made concerning it. Whereas the pr. of La Charité has not preferred anyone to St Andrew's, the king has restored to William free administration of Northampton priory (*CPR 1247–58*, p. 582). Seal (*BM Seals*, no. 3739). Res. by Jan. 1259 to go to Lewes (*Reg. R. Gravesend*, p. 98), but occ. as pr. of Lewes 14 Dec. 1257, 31 Oct. 1258 (*CR 1256–59*, pp. 173, 335).

Guy (Wido) de Busseria 1258/9–1270 Apptd pr. s.a. 1258 (*EHR*, 44, 100); letter of pres. from pr. of La Charité to king, pr. William having gone to Lewes May 1258 (PRO, C84/1/49); pres. to bp Jan. 1259, adm. 24 Jan. 1259 (*Reg. R. Gravesend*, p. 98). Mand. for seisin (Ivo) 31 Oct. 1258 (*CR 1256–59*, p. 335). Gt to Aymo, pr. of Much Wenlock, of the priory of St Andrew's, until further order, 7 Feb. 1265 – the priory of Northampton is so deteriorated by occasion of the late conflict in the town of Northampton and the pr. cannot stay there (*CPR 1258–66*, p. 403). House void by 10 July 1270 (*CPR 1266–72*, p. 439). Conf. of the gt by the pr. of La Charité to John, pr. of Bermondsey, of custody of the priory of St Andrew's 20 July 1270 (*CPR 1266–72*, p. 445). Res. by 19 Dec. 1270 (*Reg. R. Gravesend*, p. 117).

John de Thifford (Tickford) 1270–1272 Pr. of La Charité notifies king that he had chosen John, pr. of Bermondsey as the new pr. 13 Nov. 1270 (PRO, C84/4/5). Letters of pres. dated 19 Dec. 1270, adm. 21 Mar. 1271 (*Reg. R. Gravesend*, pp. 117, 299). Res. by 11 July 1272 (ibid., pp. 119, 300). Pr. of Much Wenlock 1272–85 (q.v.).

Bernard de Caroloco (Carilaco, Kariloco) 1272–1285 M. of La Charité, letters of pres. 11 July 1272; adm. 25 Aug. 1272 (ibid.). Writ *de intendendo* 30 July 1272 and temps. 1 Aug. 1272 (*CPR 1266–72*, pp. 669, 670). Occ. Mich. 1284 x Mich. 1285 (PRO, E159/58, m. 14). Departed secretly on account of uneasy conscience (*Reg. Sutton*, II, 68–9). Pr. Bernard departed from St Andrew's about the first Sunday of Lent 1285 and the monks reported to the king 'about Easter' that they were *velud oves sine pastore* (Cambridge, Corpus Christi Coll. ms. 281, part II, f. 33r). Mand. to deliver priory to the proctor of the pr. of La Charité, apptd keeper until the coming Parliament, 8 Apr. 1285 (*CPR 1281–92*, p. 156).

Odo (Eudo) 1285/8–1293 Former pr. of Newton Longville, preferred by pr. of La Charité, temps. 2 June 1285 (*CPR 1281–92*, p. 169). Occ. 12 Nov., 2 Dec. 1285 (PRO, Northants F., CP25/1/174/54, no. 182; 175/55, no. 203); 3 Jan. 1286, 20 July 1287 (ibid., pp. 214, 275). M. of La Charité, had been given custody by the Cluniac visitors after Bernard's departure; letter of pres. 23 Oct. 1287 – adm. deferred, finally adm. by bp 21 Oct. 1288 (*Reg. Sutton*, II, 68–70). Occ. 29 Sept. 1292 (PRO, C241/18/115; C241/22/66). D. by 12 June 1293, prob. by 19 May (*CPR 1292–1301*, p. 23, and see below).

Robert d'Arcy (Arceio, Arcey, Arceyo) 1293–1298 Pr. of La Charité notifies king of his pres. of Robert 19 May 1293 (PRO, C84/10/18). Sometime pr. of Moiremont, dioc. Chalons, temps. 12 June 1293 (*CPR 1292–1301*, p. 23). M. of La Charité, no letters of pres. and given custody 16 June 1293 until 8 Sept.; he again appeared on 24 Oct. 1293 with letters of pres.

dated 19 May 1293; inst 25 Oct. 1293 (*Reg. Sutton*, II, 104–7). Occ. (going overseas) 8 July 1293, 8 Apr. 1298 (*CPR 1292–1301*, pp. 30, 339). Res. by 21 Sept. 1298 (ibid., p. 360). Recalled to take up a position overseas (*Reg. Sutton*, II, 154–5).

Bartholomew de Bosco 1298/9–1316 Intruded himself on the res. of Robert d'Arcy. He appeared before the bp on 8 Jan. 1299 saying he did not realise a letter of pres. was necessary; he was given custody until 25 Mar. next (ibid., 154–6). Sometime pr. of Cassouel, preferred by pr. of La Charité, temps. 21 Sept. 1298 (*CPR 1292–1301*, p. 360). On 18 Mar. 1299 letters of pres. dated 11 Feb. 1299 were brought to the bp and rejected, and new letters provided; adm. 24 Apr. 1299 (*Reg. Sutton*, II, 159–62). Occ. (going overseas) 4 Apr. 1300 (*CPR 1292–1301*, p. 502); 7 Apr. 1313 (*CPR 1307–13*, p. 569); 18 May 1316 (*CPR 1313–17*, p. 464). Res. by 17 Aug. 1316 (PRO, C84/18/46; cf. *CPR 1313–17*, p. 546).

Guichard de Caroloco (Baraloco *sic*) **1316/19–1320** Pr. of La Charité notifies king of his pres. of Guichard 17 Aug. 1316 (PRO, C84/18/46). M. of La Charité, whom the pr. of La Charité had preferred, temps. 20 Sept. 1316 (ibid.). Letters of pres. 2 Apr. 1317, adm. 26 Jan. 1319 (Lincoln, Ep. Reg., II, ff. 137v–138r). Res. by 26 Feb. 1320 to be pr. of Much Wenlock (*CPR 1317–21*, p. 425).

Conan (Cono) 1320–?1338 Pr. of Monks Horton, temps. 27 Feb. 1320 (*CPR 1317–21*, p. 426). Occ. 16 Mar. 1330, 6 July 1331, 16 July 1331 – protection for him during his visitation of the English houses of the order (*CPR 1330–34*, pp. 95, 153, 157); 24 Apr. 1331, 7 May 1331, 16 Nov. 1331 (*CCR 1330–33*, pp. 302, 311, 402); 21 June 1334, 8 Apr. 1336 (*CCR 1333–37*, pp. 320, 666); 28 June 1336 (Lincoln, Ep. Reg., IV, f. 386v); Mich. 1337 (PRO, CP40/312, m. 322).

Possibly the unnamed pr. who had d. by 10 Jan. 1338 (*CFR 1337–47*, p. 61).

[br. **William de Thonoile** gtd keeping of the priory 10 June 1339 (ibid., p. 137).]

[br. **Stephen of Bridgnorth** (Briggenorth) gtd keeping of the priory 9 Mar. 1341 (ibid., p. 220). On 26 Mar. 1341 the priory was noted as being void, the previous unnamed pr. having d. (*CPR 1340–43*, p. 168); similar gt of custody 15 Mar. 1342 (*CFR 1337–47*, p. 276).]

Francis de Bruges (Brugiis, Brugis) **1342–1345** Letter of pres. by pr. of Much Wenlock, commissary of pr. of La Charité 2 May 1345 (PRO, C84/24/39). M. of La Charité, temps. 23 May 1342 (*CPR 1340–43*, p. 438, cf. *CFR 1337–47*, pp. 290–1). Res. by 2 May 1345 (PRO, C84/24/39) but mentd in papal mand. 12 June 1345 (*CPL*, III, 19).

Thomas de Synartcleus (Sinarcleus, Sinartcleus) **1345–** M. of La Charité (PRO, C84/24/39). Adm. and gtd keeping of priory on res. of pr. Francis 16 May 1345 at request of Guichard, pr. of Montacute (*CFR 1337–47*, p. 421). Occ. Mich. 1348 x Mich. 1349 (PRO, E372/194, rot. 23d); Mich. 1354 x Mich. 1355 (PRO, E372/200, rot. 18); Mich. 1358 x Mich. 1359 (PRO, E372/204, rots. 14, 15).

[br. **William de T(h)onoile** gtd custody of the priory by the king before 14 May 1347 at the request of the earl of Suffolk and subsequently discharged of his custody (*CPR 1345–48*, p. 288).][6]

In 1368 the priory visitors noted that *in temporalibus male et turpissime regitur* (Charvin, IV, 53).

Thomas –?1387 Uncertain whether he is to be identified with Thomas de Synartcleus above. Occ. 11 June 1369, 4 July 1370 (*CFR 1368–77*, pp. 15, 83); 1370 (*Buckingham's Writ Register*, p. 39, no. 116); 18 Nov. 1377 (*CFR 1377–83*, p. 35); 18 June 1386 (*CPR 1383–91*, p. 138). Possibly the unnamed pr. who d. in 1387 (see below).

John Dokesworth, can. of St Andrew's, was gtd the priory, void by the d. of the last pr. and in the king's gift by reason of the French wars, 13 May 1387 (*CPR 1385–89*, p. 303).

---

[6] The transfer of a pr. William of St Andrew's to the priory of Lewes in 1358 (*Mon.*, V, 5) must surely be an error for the events of 1258 above.

PONTEFRACT (Yorks W.), St John the Evangelist (La Charité sur Loire) f. *c.* 1090
(dependent on la Charité); 1393 (denizen)
  Lists in *VCH Yorks*, III, 186; C.T. Clay, 'The early priors of Pontefract', *YAJ*, XXXVIII
  (1955), 456–64; *Heads*, I, 124; *Ctl. Pontefract*, II, 681.
Fulk Last recorded occ. -1211 (Clay, p. 461); *c.* 1212 (*Ctl. Pontefract*, II, 545).[7]
Walter Occ. 21 Jan. 1219 (*Yorks F., 1218–31*, p. 11). See Clay, p. 462 for dismissal of the notion
  of a pr. Walter *c.* 1230.
Hugh Occ. 8 June 1225, 8 Nov. 1226 (*Yorks F., 1218–31*, pp. 60 and n., 74; *Ctl. Pontefract.* II,
  327–8); 1226 (Baildon, I, 166).
Stephen Occ. 20 Jan. 1235 (*Yorks F., 1232–46*, p. 37); 1235 (*Ctl. Pontefract*, I, 75–6, 199); n.d.
  (1233 x 1235) (*Reg. Gray*, p. 182).
Peter Occ. (P.) 13 Feb. 1238 (*Ctl. Pontefract*, I, 77); 1238 (ibid., 41); (P.) 24 June 1239 (ibid.,
  233).
Dalmatius –1260 Occ. 1 Aug. 1240 (ibid., II, 660); 20 Jan. 1241 (*Yorks F., 1232–46*, p. 104);
  1248 (*Ctl. Pontefract*, II, 574); 1250 (BL, Harley ms. 2101, f. 73v); 1251–2 (*Yorks F.,
  1246–72*, pp. 28, 68); 1253 (Baildon, I, 166); Cess. by 17 May 1260 (*CR 1259–61*, p. 42).
Peter 1260– Pr. of Prittlewell, moved to Pontefract, mand. for seisin 17 May 1260, pres. by the
  pr. of La Charité and the priory being in the king's hands by reason of the land and heirs
  of Edmund de Lacy (*CR 1259–61*, pp. 42–3). Occ. 22 Nov. 1265 (*CPR 1258–66*, p. 508).
S. Occ. 16 May 1267 (*Reg. W. Giffard*, p. 21).
Godfrey/Geoffrey All entries note Godfrey unless otherwise stated. Occ. 20 May 1268 (*Yorks
  F.,1246–72*, p. 144); 29 June 1268 (*Reg. W. Giffard*, p. 20); 1268, 1276, 1282 (PRO,
  C85/170/5, 65; 173/23); Mich. 1273 x Mich. 1274 (PRO, E159/48 m. 15); 1277 (*CPR
  1272–81*, p. 243); Mich. 1279 x Mich. 1280 (PRO, E159/53, m. 12d, where the last part of
  the surname is evident: *Geoffrey . . . side*). In 1279 the pr. was said to have been pr. for 12
  years (*Cluniac Visitations* p. 33). Occ. 1 Dec. 1281 (*CPR 1282–91*, p. 5); 25 Aug. 1283 (PRO,
  DL25/65–6). Seal (Godfrey) (*BM Seals*, no. 3854; Clay, *Seals*, p. 29).
John 1285–1286 M. of Pontefract, el. pr. by command of the earl of Lincoln 1285, dep. 1286
  by the visitor from La Charité and another pres. by the prior of La Charité and received by
  the earl (*EHR*, 44 (1929), 98; Cambridge, Corpus Christi ms. 281, part II, f. 33v).
William Occ. Easter 1286 (PRO, E159/59, m. 9d); 1300 (Baildon, I, 168). Presumably to be
  identified with **William de Brigges**, former pr., mentd in a case of 1317 (BI, CP. E. 9).
Robert Occ. 3 Oct. 1308, Mich. 1309 (*YB II*, 95; *Select Cases of Trespass*, II, 192–3).
Guichard (Wichard) de Caro Loco (Cherleu) **1311–1316** Occ. 1 Apr. 1310 (*CPR 1307–13*, p.
  223). Desc. as newly-created pr. 3 Feb. 1311, occ. 14 May 1311 (*Reg. Greenfield*, II, nos. 919,
  930); 24 July 1313 (*CPR 1313–17*, p. 2). Pr. of Northampton, St Andrew 1316; later to Much
  Wenlock.
Simon of Castleford (Castelford) Occ. 24 July 1316 (*Reg. Greenfield*, V, no. 2801); 31 Mar.
  1319 (*Magnum Reg. Album Lichfield*, p. 183, no. 371). Priory void by 7 Aug. 1322, no reason
  given for vacancy (*CCR 1318–23*, p. 585). Ment. as predecessor of present pr. 1348 (Baildon,
  I, 170).
Stephen de Cherobles (Chirobols) **1322–** Temps. 22 Aug. 1322, having been preferred by
  Peter, pr. of La Charité (*CPR 1321–24*, p. 197 – or 23 Aug., *CCR 1318–23*, p. 594). Prof.
  obed. 17 Dec. 1322 (York, Reg. 9A, f. 193r). Occ. 1324 (PRO, E106/5/2, m. 13); 1326
  (*Memo. Roll 1326–7*, p. 272); 1333 (Charvin, III, no. 251); 1341 (PRO, DL25/75); 15 July

---

[7] The occurrence of a pr. Reiner in the early 13th cent. (Clay, pp. 461–2; *Ctl. Pontefract* (list); Baildon, I, 166;
  VCH etc.) is an error; Reiner was the proctor of the pr. and convent, not the pr. (*Letters of Innocent III*,
  no. 403). The mention of a pr. Robert in 1225 (*VCH*, *Ctl. Pontefract* list) is also an error. The pr. in question was Hugh.

1343 (*CPR 1343–45*, p. 163); 1348 (Baildon, I, 170); 1348 – 26 May 1349 (*Wakefield Court Rolls 1348–50*, pp. 7, 126). Sharpe, *Latin Writers*, p. 621. Seal (*Mon. Seals*, p. 73).

Simon of Balderstone (Baldreston) Occ. 20 Feb. 1351 (*CCR 1349–54*, p. 346); 14 Oct. 1353 (*CFR 1347–56*, p. 379); 5 July 1359 (*CFR 1356–68*, p. 97); 11 July 1360 (PRO, SC1/50/188).

Peter de Tevolio ment. as late pr. of Pontefract 14 June 1364 when king conf. gt of custody of Bermondsey priory (*CPR 1361–64*, p. 505). But also pr. of Monks Horton from 1356 (q.v.).

[**John of Methley** (Metheley, Mateleye, Melcheley) Papal prov. conf. 10 Sept. 1365 – ineffective (*Accts of Papal Collectors*, pp. 292, 343, 383–4).]

Richard of Eston Occ. 5 Oct. 1367 – going overseas (*CPR 1367–70*, p. 8); 6 Oct. 1369 (*CFR 1368–77*, p. 38); 1370 (PRO, E179/63/5).

Walter Occ. 1 June 1372 (PRO, C81/1787/14).

Geoffrey of Walton –1372 D. by 29 Nov. 1372 (*Reg. John of Gaunt 1371–5*, I, no. 61).

Richard of Hetton (Hethton) 1372– M. of Pontefract, notif. to John of Gaunt by pr. of Bermondsey, the vicar-general of the pr. of La Charité, of appt 29 Nov. 1372 (ibid., nos. 61–2); gt of keeping of priory 26 Oct. 1377 (*CFR 1377–83*, p. 28). Occ. 1379 (PRO, E179/63/5).

The next recorded pr., **John Tunstall**, occ. 12 May 1380 (*CFR 1377–83*, p. 184).

PREEN, *see* CHURCH PREEN

PRITTLEWELL (Essex), St Mary (Lewes) f. -1121

Lists in *VCH Essex*, II, 140–1; *Heads*, I, 124.

William –(?)1241 Occ. 1190 x 1200 (*ECSP*, no. 172); *c.* Easter 1203, 22 Apr. 1235 (*Essex F.*, I, nos. 80, 400); n.d. (*c.* 1233) (PRO, E40/13828(b)). ? same as pr. William who res. 1241 to be pr. of Castleacre (*CR 1237–42*, p. 301). There may have been more than one pr. William.

Simon de Waltham (Walthon) 1241– M. of Lewes, apptd by the king, the right of patronage being in his hands by reason of the honour of Essex 12 May 1241 (*CPR 1232–47*, p. 251). Occ. 1242 (Guildhall, Dean & Chapter of St Paul's, 25121/240, dated by shrievalty); 17 Feb. 1248 (*Essex F.*, I, 160); Oct. 1248 x Oct. 1249 (*Suffolk F. (Rye)*, p. 49).

Peter 1249–1260 M. of Cluny, mand. for seisin 29 Aug. 1249 (*CR 1247–51*, p. 197). Occ. 12 Nov. 1259 (*Kent F.*, p. 306). Transferred to be pr. of Pontefract by 17 May 1260 (*CR 1259–61*, p. 42).

John of Northampton (Norhampt') 1260– M. of Lewes, pres. by W., pr. of Lewes, in place of Peter who had moved to Pontefract; mand. for seisin 18 May 1260 (ibid., p. 43).

William de Verge (Vergeris) 1261–1281 Pres. By Miles, pr. of Lewes 3 Aug. 1261 (PRO, C84/2/24).Occ. 4 Nov. 1275 (*CCR 1272–79*, p. 252); Mich. 1278 (*Essex F.*, II, 17); 15 Nov. 1279 (*Cal. Misc. Inq.*, I, 347). Priory vac. by promotion of William to priory of Mergey by 21 May 1281 (PRO, C84/7/27).

Nicholas de Cukefeld (Cok(e)feld) 1281–1290 Pr. of Clifford, pres. by pr. of Thetford and sub-pr. of Lewes, vicegerents of John, pr. of Lewes, 21 May 1281 (ibid.); writ *de intendendo* 26 May 1281 (*CPR 1272–81*, p. 437). D. by 24 Oct. 1290 (*CPR 1281–92*, p. 391). Seal (*BM Seals*, no. 3860; *Mon. Seals*, p. 73).

Peter de Montellier 1290– M. of Lewes, apptd by pr. of Lewes, writ *de intendendo* 24 Oct. 1290 (*CPR 1281–92*, p. 391). Lic. to unnamed pr., though an alien, to remain in priory 4 Oct. 1295 (*CCR 1288–96*, p. 460, cf. PRO, SC1/27/4, certif. that Peter is a Savoyard and should not be molested *c*. Oct. 1295). Occ. 26 June 1297 (*CPR 1292–1301*, p. 270); Easter 1300 (PRO, E106/4/14, m. 8d.); Nov. 1302 x Nov. 1303 (PRO, E106/4/18, m. 11d.). Mentioned as former pr. 7 Mar. 1303 (*CPR 1301–07*, p. 119).

John de Monte Martini 1303–1307 Apptd by pr. of Lewes, temps. 10 Mar. 1303 (*CCR*

1302–07, p. 18), but cf. cert. of appt *ad rogatum* of Queen Margaret 22 Oct. 1301(?) (PRO, C84/14/18). Occ. 15 Oct. 1303 (*CCR 1302–07*, p. 58); 23 Aug. 1304, 22 Mar. 1305, 7 Nov. 1305 (*CPR 1301–07*, pp. 256, 321, 395). Pr. of Lewes 1307 (q.v.).

Henry de Fautrariis (Fautrerus) **1308–** Cert. of appt by pr. of Lewes 25 Apr. 1308, no reason given for vacancy (PRO, C84/16/8); temps. 4 May 1308 (*CPR 1307–13*, p. 69). Occ. (going overseas) 14 May 1308 (ibid., p. 72).

Giles de Seduno 1309– M. of Lewes, cert. of appt by pr. of Lewes 21 June 1309 (PRO, C84/16/25); temps 1 July 1309 (*CPR 1307–13*, p. 123). Occ. 22 Feb. 1310, 7 Mar. 1310, 10 Oct. 1310 (ibid., pp. 210, 212, 244).

Thomas de Shelevestrode (Shelenestrode) **1310–** Apptd by pr. of Lewes, no reason given for vacancy, temps 4 July 1310 (ibid., p. 234).

William de (le) Avernaz (Advernaz, Aumuniaco, Auvergnat, Auvernay, Auvernaz, Avernas, Avernatz, Lavernas) **1311–** M. of Lewes, temps. 20 Apr. 1311 (ibid., p. 333). Apptd by pr. of Lewes, mand. to escheator not to molest him: he has done fealty 28 Apr. 1311 (*CCR 1307–13*, p. 309). Attempt to dep. him in 1315 (see below under Guichard de Caro Loco). At General Chapter noted William had been deprived by pr. of Lewes *suis demeritis exigentibus privatus* – order for him to be taken 24 Apr. 1317 (Charvin, II, p. 414, no. 212). Order made to redress his grievances 31 May 1318 (*Cal. Chanc. Warr.*, p. 487); protection for 1 year 5 June 1318 (*CPR 1317–21*, p. 155). Occ. 16 Aug. 1318, 18 Nov. 1318 (*CCR 1318–23*, pp. 8, 29). Order for his removal and to take priory into the king's hands 28 Dec. 1318 (*CPR 1317–21*, p. 262). He had again entered priory – royal order to remove malefactors 28 Dec. 1318 (*CCR 1318–23*, pp. 51–2). See below under James de Cusancia.

[**Guichard de Caro Loco** Cert. to king by John, pr. of Lewes, of the appt of Guichard as pr. of Prittlewell on the dep. of William Avernatz 27 Sept. 1315 (PRO, CP84/18/23) – presumably ineffective.]

James de Cusancia 1316–1334 M. of Lewes, brother of John de Cusancia, pr. of Bermondsey (*CPR 1324–27*, p. 30; *CCR 1323–27*, pp. 310–11), born in Burgundy (*CPR 1324–27*, pp. 30, 41). Temps. 1 Dec. 1316 (*CPR 1313–17*, p. 570; cf. *Reg. Sandale*, p. 357). Petition from pr. James 8 Jan. 1318 (*Cal. Chanc. Warr.*, p. 481). Mand. to escheator to deliver the priory to James, because the king had learned from the complaint of James, that William de Avernaz, who asserted he had been inst. pr., had entered the priory by force and had held the priory by armed force. The king had previously accepted the promotion of James to the priory, made by the pr. of Lewes. William then entered the priory before the morrow of St James last past, on which day the king ordered the escheator to summon James to appear in Chancery to show cause why the temps. should not be delivered to William. William came in person on the morrow of the Assumption and expressly renounced any right in the priory, 16 Aug. 1318 (*CCR 1318–23*, pp. 8–9). Case cited as above. The king has learned that William has drawn James into a plea before the archbp of Canterbury in Court Christian. The king signifies to the archbp what was done in the royal presence 18 Nov. 1318 (ibid., p. 29). Appt during pleasure of two custodians of the priory 2 Jan. 1319. At the suit of William le Avernaz, alleging he had been deprived of possession of the priory at the procurement of James de Cusancia, whom the pr. of Lewes had preferred to be pr. William had entered the priory with an armed mob. (*CPR 1317–21*, pp. 261–2). In papal commn to the archbp of Canterbury of 25 Mar. 1321 it is recited that James de Cusancia expelled William de Avernaz. The latter appealed to the archbp of Canterbury, and the pr. of Dunmow to whom the case was committed, restored William. James then appealed to the archbp and ejected William and the convent. The archbp's judges replaced William and James again appealed to the archbp and the pope. Two monks of Lewes came to Prittlewell, wounded William in the head while he was celebrating mass and putting the pr. and three monks, bound hand and foot, into a cart, imprisoned them at Lewes (*CPL*, II, 211–12); William, mentd in commn of 1 July 1321 as having died (ibid., 214). James obviously resumed possession – he occ. 1324, 1325, 1327 (*CCR 1323–27*, pp. 310–11, 500; *CFR 1327–37*, p. 246).

Robert *dictus* le Palmere Cert. to king from Adam de Wynton', pr. of Lewes, of his appt of Robert as pr. of Prittlewell, no reason given for vacancy 4 Jan. 1328 (PRO, C84/21/47). Either ineffective – or else Robert was pr. for a while and then James de Cusancia returned (see below).

James de Cusancia **–1334** Res. by 5 Aug. 1334 (*CCR 1333–37*, p. 246). Pr. of Thetford St Mary 1334–55 (q.v.).

John Chaluns Occ. 23 May 1341 (PRO, C81/1787/8); 5 Mar. 1342 (*CFR 1337–47*, p. 262); 11 July 1345 (*CCR 1343–46*, p. 636).

Ralph de Myouns Occ. 4 Sept. 1351 (*CFR 1347–56*, p. 318); Mich. 1354 x Mich. 1355 (PRO, E372/200, rot. 4).

Guichard de Chentriaco **1361–** Apptd by pr. of Lewes, temps. 24 Mar. 1361 (*CPR 1361–64*, p. 3).

Francis de Baugiaco (Bargiaco) **1361–1362** Apptd by pr. of Lewes, petition for temps. 16 Sept. 1361 (PRO, C84/28/8); temps. 2 Oct. 1361 (*CPR 1361–64*, p. 79). Going overseas 3 Oct. 1362 (ibid., p. 253). Petition to transfer to Montacute, void by the transfer of its pr. to Lewes gtd 30 Dec. 1362 (*CPP*, p. 393).

[**Peter de Tenoleo** (Tenolio) Pr. of Monk's Horton, petition for priory of Prittlewell on its voidance by transfer of Francis de Baugiaco to Montacute gtd 3 Feb. 1363 (ibid., p. 400) – Papal prov. 26 June 1363 – ineffective (*Accts of Papal Collectors*, p. 299).]

John Saver (Sauer(e)) **1363–** Apptd by pr. of Lewes, petition for temps. 25 July 1363 (PRO, C84/29/7); temps. 28 July 1363 (*CPR 1361–64*, p. 386). Occ. 18 Apr. 1364 (ibid., p. 484); 11 June 1369, 28 Nov. 1371 (*CFR 1368–77*, pp. 14, 132).

Richard Ysewode **1377–** Apptd by pr. of Lewes, petition for temps., no reason given for vacancy 3 Mar. 1377 (PRO, C84/31/46); temps. 5 Mar. 1377 (*CPR 1374–77*, p. 434).

The next recorded pr., **James Wygepole**, was pres. to king by pr. of Lewes 8 Jan. 1386, no reason given for vacancy (PRO, C84/33/43); temps. 12 Jan. 1386 (*CPR 1385–89*, p. 93).

ST CARROK (Cornwall) (Cell of Montacute) f. 1100 x 1140; (denizen) 1407

Robert Occ. 30 May 1339 (*Reg. Grandisson*, II, 908).

John Occ. 1381 (PRO, E179/24/5, m. 3).

The next recorded pr., **William Smethe**, occ. 29 July 1385 (*Reg. Brantingham*, II, 582), prob. the same as occ. as pr. William 5 May 1396 (Cornwall RO, Art.1/55).

ST CLEARS (Carmarthen) (S. Martin des Champs, Paris) f. 1147 x 84. Diss. *c.* 1414.

List in R. Graham, 'The Cluniac Priory of St Martin des Champs, Paris, and its dependent priories in England', *JBAA*, 3rd ser., XI (1948), 36–59, at p. 48.

William de Airaines **–1288** Absconded 1288 leaving debt unpaid to Bp of St David's (Paris, Bibl. Nat. L875, no. 38, cited by R. Graham in list above; F.G. Cowley, *Monastic Order in South Wales*, p. 230).

John Seyer (Soier, Soyer) **–1333** Res. by 13 Sept. 1333 (*CPR 1330–34*, p. 467); transferred to Barnstaple 1333, although Bp Grandisson reluctant to adm. him as he was publicly defamed (for being dissolute, having children, dilapidation and simony) while in Wales; later referred to as 'maledictus predecessor suus immediatus' (*Reg. Grandisson*, I, 263, 265–6, 289).

Peter Seyer **1333–** M. of S. Martin des Champs, pr. and convent of St Martin report to king that new (unnamed) pr. of St Clears has been apptd 14 July 1333 (PRO, SC1/38/120). Temps. 13 Sept. 1333 (*CPR 1330–34*, p. 467).

Poncius M. of St Clears, gtd keeping of the priory during the French War 16 July 1339 (*CFR 1337–47*, p. 136); as pr., preferred by the pr. of St Martin des Champs, gtd keeping of priory 30 Apr. 1341 (ibid., p. 222; Cowley, *Monastic Order in South Wales*, p. 222). Unnamed pr. (? Poncius) dead by 12 Feb. 1346 (*CFR 1337–47*, p. 452).

William Troies –1370 D. by 1 Sept. 1370, when custody gtd to John Barlus, m. of St Clears (*CFR 1368–77*, p. 85).

Thomas of Thetford (Tetford) Mentd as newly preferred to priory by the pr. of St Martin des Champs 22 Sept. 1372; occ. 14 Mar. 1376 (ibid., pp. 186, 345); 8 Oct. 1377, 20 Feb. 1381 (*CFR 1377–83*, pp. 19, 240); June 1377 x June 1378 (PRO LR14/282); 9 Feb. 1393 (*CPR 1391–96*, p. 243).

The next recorded pr., **Richard Lodelowe**, m. of Bermondsey, apptd by the archbp of Canterbury and abb. of Bermondsey, on the d. of the last (unnamed) pr. 18 Feb. 1403 (Lambeth, Reg. Arundel I, f. 286v); occ. 24 Sept. 1403 (*CPR 1401–05*, p. 298).

ST HELEN'S (I. of Wight) (Much Wenlock) f. *c.* 1090 x 1155. Diss. 1414.
List in *VCH Hants*, II, 216.

Robert Occ. 20 Jan. 1249 (PRO, Hants F. CP25/1/203/8, no. 54); n.d. (early-mid. 13th cent. pal.) (IOW, STH/P/27).

Henry Occ. Nov. 1295 x Nov. 1296 (PRO, E106/3/19, m. 10); 17 Apr. 1296 (BL, Stowe ms. 935, f. 43r); Nov. 1296 x Nov. 1297 (PRO, E106/4/2, m. 4); Nov. 1297 x Nov. 1298 (PRO, E106/4/8, m. 3); Nov. 1298 x Nov. 1299 (PRO, E106/4/9, m. 5; E106/4/10, m. 5). Made pr. of Bermondsey 1298, temps. restored 27 Nov. 1298 (*CPR 1292–1301*, p. 386) and d. 1312 (q.v.), but still desc. as pr. of St Helen's (or another Henry?) Easter 1300 (PRO, E106/4/14, m. 7); Nov. 1302 x Nov. 1303 (E106/4/18, m. 9d).

Aymo Occ. 10 Feb. 1307 (*Reg. Woodlock*, II, 722); absolved from sentence of excommunication 20 Nov. 1316 (*Reg. Sandale*, p. 17). Occ. 30 Mar. 1318 (ibid., p. 87; PRO, C85/155/2 – Emeric).

Guy de Bosco Occ. *c.* Mich. 1324 (PRO, E106/5/2, m. 5); 3 Sept. 1325 (IOW, STH/P/15); July 1325 x July 1326 (PRO, E106/5/4, m. [3d]); 15 June 1326 (IOW, STH/P/23); 8 Oct. 1326 (*Memo. Roll 1326–7*, p. 272); 5 Feb. 1330 (IOW, STH/P/37); Mich. 1338 x Mich. 1339 (PRO, E372/184, rots. 14d, 15d).

John de Wythyford Occ. 24 Apr. 1344 (*CFR 1337–47*, p. 369); his unnamed predecessor, mentd on 12 July 1342 as having been removed by his superior (ibid., p. 275).

Peter de Chyerbitz (Chirlu) Occ. 13 Nov. 1347 (PRO, E326/539, 677); n.d. (PRO, E326/533, 535).

William Occ. 21 Sept. 1346 in return of aliens (*Reg. Edington*, II, no. 609), but see below.

Otto de Floriaco Occ. 20 June 1346 (IOW, STH/P/18); 8 Mar. 1349 (*CFR 1347–56*, p. 105); Mich. 1348 x Mich. 1349 (PRO, E372/194, m. 18d).

Richard of Billingsley (Billyngesleye) Occ. 30 Sept. 1353 (*CFR 1347–56*, p. 378). Mentd Mich. 1354 x Mich. 1355 (PRO, E372/200, m. 28d).

John of Fécamp (Fescamp, Fiscampo) Occ. 20 June 1354 (*CFR 1347–56*, p. 398); 13 May 1355 (*Reg. Edington*, I, no. 1031); Mich. 1354 x Mich. 1355 (PRO, E372/200, rots. 28, 29d).

William of York (Ebor') Occ. 4 May 1373 (PRO, C85/155/32); 18 Nov. 1381 (PRO, C85/155/38), but see next entry.

Richard Newebury (Neubury, Nubury) M. of Much Wenlock, gtd custody of priory 12 Sept. 1381 (*CFR 1377–83*, p. 267). Occ. as pr. 24 Oct. 1383 (PRO, C85/155/40); 8 May 1388 (CPR, 1385–89, p. 459).

SLEVES HOLM (Norfolk), St Mary and All Saints (Castleacre) f. 1222–6
Lists in *VCH Norfolk*, II, 359, citing Blomfield, *Norfolk*, II, 210.

Paul Occ. 1222 x 1226 (*Mon. Angl.*, V, 72, no. iii cites Blomfield, *temp.* Stephen (*sic*); *EYC*, VIII, pp. 135–6, no. 98).

The two other priors mentd in the list occ. in the 15th cent. A br. John, monk in the hermitage of Sleves Holm is found *temp.* Bp Walter Suffield of Norwich (1245–57) (BL, Harl. ms. 2110, f. 7r) but it is unclear whether he was pr.

STANSGATE (Essex), St Mary Magdalen (Lewes) f. 1112 x 1121; 1351 x 1374 (denizen)
Lists in *VCH Essex*, II, 142; *Heads*, I, 124.

Gilbert Occ. *c.* 1195 x 1238 (*Ctl. Colchester*, II, 555).

Nicholas Occ. Easter term 1228 (*CRR*, XIII, no. 679). The order of these two priors is uncertain.

Alan Occ. 2 Nov. 1254 (*Essex F.*, I, 211).

William of Petersfield (Petresfeld) Occ. *c.* 1260 (Bodl., Essex Cht. 73).

Theobald Occ. n.d. (PRO, E40/828).

Alexander Occ. from Nov. 1296 x Nov. 1297 to Nov. 1298 x Nov. 1299 (PRO, E106/4/2, m. 6d; E106/4/9, m. 5; E106/4/10, m. 6); 1300 (PRO, E106/4/14, m. 8d); Nov. 1302 x Nov. 1303 (PRO, E106/4/18, m. 11).

John Darcy Occ. 11 Sept. 1332 (*CPR 1330–34*, p. 332).

Peter Occ. 26 Nov. 1356 (*CFR 1356–68*, p. 24).

William of Canterbury (Caunterbury) Occ. 11 June 1369 (*CFR 1368–77*, p. 14); 20 Nov. 1371 (ibid., p. 132); 8 Mar. 1374 (Bodl., Essex Cht. 76).

The next recorded pr., **John**, occ. Nov. 1400 (Bodl., Essex Cht. 77).

THETFORD (Norfolk), St. Mary (Cluny) f. 1103 x 1104 (dependent on Lewes); 1114 (dependent on Cluny); 1376 (denizen).
Lists in *VCH Norfolk*, II, 368; *Heads*, I, 125.

?W. Occ. -1216 (*Ctl. Cockersand*, II, i, pp. 466–7; *Mon. Angl.*, V, 150; but possibly pr. of Holy Sepulchre, Thetford, or just possibly Vincent (*Heads*, I, 125).

Richard Occ. (R.) 15 May 1220 (*Norwich Cath. Chts.*, II, no. 75); Oct. 1223 x Oct. 1224, Oct. 1234 x Oct. 1235 (*Suffolk F. (Rye)*, pp. 23, 27, 34, 36); Oct. 1227 x Oct. 1228 (*Norfolk F. (Rye)*, p. 40); 9 Feb. 1235 (*Essex F.*, I, 110). D. by Trin. 1237 (*CRR*, XVI, no. 91).

Stephen Occ. Oct. 1237 x Oct. 1238, Oct. 1238 x Oct. 1239, Oct. 1242 x Oct. 1243 (*Suffolk F. (Rye)*, pp. 40, 46); Oct. 1242 x Oct. 1243, Oct. 1243 x Oct. 1244 (*Norfolk F. (Rye)*, pp. 69, 70); n.d. (*ante* 1245) (Charvin, I, no. 32); 13 Oct., 27 Oct. 1247 (PRO, Cambs F., CP25/1/24/22, nos. 13–14). *MPCM*, V, 31–2 gives a portrait of the bad character of the pr. and his subsequent murder by a Welsh monk *sub anno* 1248.

Aymo (Hamo) Occ. Easter 1259 (*Essex F.*, I, 231); Oct. 1257 x Oct. 1258 (*Norfolk F. (Rye)*, p. 95); 13 Apr. 1260 (*Ctl. Blythburgh*, II, no. 404); 1262 (*CR 1261–64*, p. 267). At the 1263 visitation the unnamed pr. did not appear, *proprii corporis infirmitate detentus* (Charvin, I, no. 55).

William Occ. Oct. 1270 x Oct. 1271 (*Suffolk F. (Rye)*, p. 73); 15 May 1272 (PRO, Cambs F., CP25/1/25/34, no. 25); Easter 1273 (PRO, CP40/3, m. 3).

Thomas Occ. 8 Apr. 1276, excusing his absence from the General Chapter (Charvin, I, no. 87).

Vincent Occ. 12 Sept. 1279 (ibid., I, no. 99); 4 Apr. 1281 (*Ctl. Lewes, Wilts etc.*, p. 9); (W., ? for V.) 26 May 1281 (*CPR 1272–81*, p. 437); 26 May 1281 (*CPR 1272–81*, p. 437); Easter 1282 (PRO, CP40/45, mm. 59, 75); 16 Mar. 1287, 22 Jan. 1291 (*CPR 1281–92*, pp. 266, 419);

Nov. 1289 x Nov. 1290 (*Norwich Cath. Chts.*, II, no. 235); Nov. 1293 x Nov. 1294 (*HMC Var. Coll.*, II, 228); Nov. 1295 x Nov. 1296 (PRO, E106/3/19, m. 5d); Nov. 1296 x Nov. 1297 (PRO, E106/4/2, m. 2d); Nov. 1297 x Nov. 1298 (PRO, E106/4/8, m. 2d); Nov. 1298 x Nov. 1299 (PRO, E106/4/9, mm. 7, 8); Easter 1300 (PRO, E106/4/14, m. 5d).

Aymo de Chaumes (Chaves) Archbp of Canterbury writes to bp of Norwich asking him to publish excommunication which the sub-pr. and monks have incurred by their refusal to receive Aymo as pr., nominated by abb. of Cluny, and by their presumption in electing a pr. and intruding him with the support of laymen 14 Apr. 1300 (*Reg. Winchelsey*, II, 703–4). Aymo (Haymo) occ. 12 Oct. 1305 (*CCR 1302–07*, p. 349); 24 Apr. 1306 *qui se dicebat priorem* (Charvin, II, no. 181).

Reginald of Eye (*alias* **de Montargi**) On the d. of pr. Vincent, Roger, earl of Norfolk, during the war between Edward I and the king of France, caused Reginald to be el. pr. and delivered temps. to him, mentd 1308 (*CCR 1307–13*, p. 78). El. by convent and conf. by bp before 5 Apr. 1301. He resisted the abb. of Cluny and the pope ordered the dep. of Reginald if the charges proved true (*CPL*, I, 594–5). Archbp of Canterbury writes to the bp of Norwich informing him that the archbp had discovered during his visitation that Reginald, then acting as pr., had never been professed as a monk and therefore his nomination was void. The Archbp wrote to the patron, the earl of Norfolk, to ask him to lic. sub-pr. and convent to el. and they informed the archbp that their choice was Thomas Bigod, m. of Walden. The archbp refers the matter to the bp of Norwich 14 Oct. 1304 (*Reg. Winchelsey*, II, 792).

Thomas (le) Bigod 1304–1308 For eln see above. Adm. 11 Dec. 1304, no reason given for vacancy (Norwich, Reg/1/1, f. 14v). Occ. 14 Oct. 1305 (*CPR 1301–07*, p. 384). D. by 3 Oct. 1308 (*CFR 1307–19*, p. 30).

William of Ventadour (Ventodoro, Vent(h)adoro, Venthodoro, Wentodoro) **1309–1311** Dean of priory of St Peter of Caremac, dioc. Cahors. Gtd custody of temps. 7 Oct. 1308, renewed 26 Jan. 1309, 7 Oct. 1309 as *custos* (*CPR 1307–13*, pp. 140, 99, 193; *Cluny Chts.*, I, 115–17). Cert. by abb. Henry of Cluny of his appt as pr. 22 June 1309 (PRO, C84/16/26); temps. 1 Dec. 1309 (*CPR 1307–13*, p. 200). Occ. 25 Feb. 1310, 1 Apr. 1310, 14 May 1311 (ibid., pp. 211, 223, 343). Res. (W.) by 20 July 1311 (*CFR 1307–19*, p. 98), prob. by May (see below).

Martin de Ruihiaco (Rinhiaco) **1311–** M. of Cluny, cert. by abb. Henry of Cluny of his appt as pr. 25 May 1311 (PRO, C84/16/43); temps. 18 Dec. 1311 (*CPR 1307–13*, p. 409). Occ. 6 May 1313 (Charvin, II, no. 200); 16 Aug. 1313, 17 Aug. 1313, assaulted by rioters (*CPR 1313–17*, pp. 12, 55); Easter 1313–July 1314 (PRO, Just.1/593, m. 21d); 4 May, 21 May 1314 (PRO, C85/119/19, 21). On 24 Apr. 1314 at the General Chapter the unnamed pr. of Thetford was instructed to become a priest, or vacate his office *quia prior dicti loci non est professus, nec sacerdos, diffiniunt diffinitores quod prior dictus infra annum profiteretur et ad sacerdotium ordinetur* . . . (Charvin, II, no. 203).

Peter de Bosco Occ. 25 Apr. 1316 (Norwich, Reg/1/1, f. 64r); 26 May 1318 (*CCR 1313–18*, p. 613); 4 June 1318, (ibid., p. 618); 9 Oct. 1318 (PRO, CP40/225, m. 1); 23 Jan. 1324 (*CCR 1323–27*, p. 153); July 1325 x July 1326 (PRO, E106/5/4, m. [11]); 8 Oct. 1326 (*Memo. Roll 1326–7*, p. 272); could also be the pr. Peter of Thetford who occ. Easter 1327 – Trin. 1328 (*Index to Placita de Banco*, pp. 386, 633), but it could equally be pr. Peter of Holy Sepulchre, Thetford (q.v.).

John Occ. 15 Aug. 1331 (*CCR 1330–33*, p. 333); 17 Sept. (1332) (PRO, C270/12/4).

James de Cusancia Prev. pr. of Prittlewell, q. v. Prittlewell void by 5 Aug. 1334 (*CCR 1333–37*, p. 246); 14 Sept. 1335 (Bodl., ms. Gough Norfolk 18, f. 15v); 7 May 1336 (*CCR 1333–37*, p. 673); 1338 (*CPR 1338–40*, p. 91); 1339 (PRO, CP40/320, m. 1d); 1341 (*CFR 1337–47*, pp. 226, 246); 1343 (PRO, C269/15/18); 11 Sept. 1350 (*CPR 1348–50*, p. 568); 1 June 1352 (*CCR 1349–54*, p. 448); 6 May 1354 (*CCR 1354–60*, p. 68); 10 May 1355 (*CPR 1354–58*, p.

340); 24 Oct. 1355 (Bodl., ms. Gough Norfolk 18, f. 45v). According to *Mon. Angl.*, V, 146, citing Blomefield, *Norfolk*, he was dep. in 1355, source not located.

Geoffrey de Rochario (Rocherio) **1369–** Had custody from 11 June 1369 (Bodl., ms. Gough Norfolk 18, f. 38r). Occ. 20 Oct. 1370 (*CFR 1368–77*, p. 83). See Sharpe, *Latin Writers*, p. 127. The fragment of the history of Thetford priory attributed to Geoffrey is pd, Martin, *Hist. Thetford*, app. vi, pp. 29–34.[8]

James Occ. 20 June 1371 (Bodl., ms. Gough Norfolk 18, f. 17r).

John of Fordham Occ. 10 July 1371, 8 July 1372, 7 May 1373 (*CFR 1368–77*, pp. 129, 157, 212). ? had custody from 7 May 1373 (Bodl., ms. Gough Norfolk 18, f. 38r). Occ. several times ibid. from Dec. 1372 to 20 July 1397 (ff. 10r, 27v); 28 Oct. 1374 (*CPR 1374–77*, p. 56); 1378 (CUL, EDC.1A/3, no. 22); 24 Feb. 1388 (*CPR 1385–89*, p. 467); Mich. 1389 (*YB 13 Richard II*, p. 94); 1404 (Lambeth, Reg. Arundel I, f. 292v); 13 July 1411 (*CPR 1408–13*, p. 259). Prob. the pr. John who occ. *c.* 6 Apr. (1416) (PRO, SC1/43/190).

WANGFORD (Suffolk), St Mary (*alias* St Peter and St Paul) (Thetford, St Mary) f. -1159 (as alien priory); 1376 x 1393 (denizen)

List in *VCH Suffolk*, II, 89.

John Occ. 7 Nov. 1218. ? *recte* 1217 (*Ctl. Eye*, I, no. 75).

William Occ. Oct. 1248 x Oct. 1249, Oct. 1249 x Oct. 1250, Oct. 1251 x Oct. 1252 (*Suffolk F. (Rye)*, pp. 49, 50, 55); 13 Apr. 1260 (*Ctl. Blythburgh*, II, no. 404).

Reginald Occ. 1275 (*Hundred Rolls*, II, 149).

James Occ. Nov. 1295 x Nov. 1296 (PRO, E106/3/19, m. 8); Nov. 1296 x Nov. 1297 (PRO, E106/4/2, m. 4); Nov. 1297 x Nov. 1298 (PRO, E106/4/8, m. 2d); Nov. 1298 x Nov. 1299 (PRO, E106/4/9, m. 3d; E106/4/10, m. 4); Easter 1300 (PRO, E106/4/14, m. 6); Nov. 1302 x Nov. 1303 (PRO, E106/4/18, m. 8).

Henry Occ. Mich. 1305 (PRO, CP40/153, m. 301).

Master Martin de Rinhaco, monk of Cimorra, dioc. Auch Occ. going overseas in king's service 9 Dec. 1308 (*CPR 1307–13*, p. 96); papal disp. to retain priory with other benefices 23 June 1309 (*CPL*, II, 57); staying overseas on king's service 30 May 1310 (*CPR 1307–13*, p. 229).

At General Chapter 13 Apr. 1315 unnamed pr. 'non est professus' (Charvin, II, p. 380, no. 205).

John Occ. *c.* Mich. 1324 (PRO, E106/5/2, m. 13).

Roger of Shropham Occ. 16 Mar. 1376 (Bodl. ms. Gough Norfolk 18, f. 44r; *CFR 1368–77*, p. 345); 28 Oct. 1377 (*CFR 1377–83*, p. 29); occ. subsidy 1377 x 1381 (PRO, E179/45/18); June 1380 x June 1381 (PRO, E179/45/5b, m. 2).

The next recorded pr., **Walter**, mentd 18 June 1402 as having lately obtained papal appropriation of Northales church, i.e. gt of 11 July 1398, revoked 1 Mar. 1399 (*CPR 1401–5*, p. 105; *CPL*, V, 156, 240–1).

WENLOCK, *see* **MUCH WENLOCK**

WINTERBORN MONKTON (Dorset), St Michael (Cluny) (De Vasto, Wast) f. -1214 (Cluniac grange) *KH*, p. 103 says it was not a cell or priory and was leased to a layman, but there are named priors of 'Winterburn Wast' found.

John Occ. n.d. (early-mid 13th cent.: pal.) (PRO, E40/11002)

---

[8] *VCH* gives pr. Roger de Berton occ. 1370, citing as the source Norwich Ep. Reg. Huyden, 10, 5–167. Dr John Alban, the County Archivist of Norfolk, kindly suggests that this is likely to be a ref. to Norwich Consistory Court Will Register Heydon 1370–83, and indeed on f. 16r Roger de Berton occ. as pr. of the Dominican friary of Thetford, occ. 13 Sept. 1371.

Hugh Occ. 31 Oct. 1269 (PRO, E40/4833; PRO, E40/356); 15 Feb. 1270 (*CPR 1266–72*, p. 476).

Walter Occ. Nov. 1276 x Nov. 1277 (PRO, E42/240); 1277 (PRO, E40/480); 29 June 1280 (PRO, E40/239); 30 Sept. 1281 (PRO, E40/6358); 5 June 1286 (PRO, E40/4601, /4747); 30 June 1288 (PRO, E40/4867).

Peter Occ. 10 Feb. 1291 (*CPR 1281–92*, p. 419).

Thomas predecessor of pr. Bertrand de Vallibus; removed as pr. but still alive 1367 (see next entry).

Bertrand de Vallibus Mentd as late pr. in writ of 24 Apr. 1367. Note from P., abb. of Cluny, that the priory is donative not elective and that the abb. of Cluny had removed pr. Thomas, Bertrand's predecessor, who is still alive (*CPR 1367–70*, p. 165).

THE GRANDMONTINE
HOUSES

ALBERBURY (Salop), St Mary (New Abbey) f. 1221 x 1226 (dependent on Lilleshall), subsequently Lilleshall renounced claims (R. Graham, 'Alberbury Priory', app. III, pp. 291–2); ref. before 1232 (Grandmontine) (cf. *EEA*, 7, no. 316A).

Lists in *VCH Salop*, II, 50; R. Graham, *English Ecclesiastical Studies*, pp. 209–46, at 243, also in *Archaeologia* 75 (1926), 159–210; R. Graham, 'Alberbury Priory', *Trans. Shropshire ANHS*, 44 (1928), 257–303, at 288.

Lambert Occ. as former *custos* 1245 (All Souls, Oxford, Whadborough Cht. 19: C218/19). Prob. the same as *generalis custos domorum ordinis Grandimontis in Anglia*, who occ. Easter–Trin. 1245 (*CRR*, XVIII, no. 1743).

Geoffrey Occ. as *custos* 1245 (ibid.); n.d. (All Souls, Whadborough Cht. 18: C218/18).

Peter London Occ. Hockday 1247 (ibid., Whadborough Cht. 23: C218/23); as corrector 1248 (ibid., Alberbury Cht. 71: C1/71); prob. the Peter who occ. as pr. (of the order of Grandmont in England) Oct. 1256 x Oct. 1257 (ibid., Whadborough Cht. 26: C218/26) and n.d. (1241 x 1264) (PRO, E211/477).

John Occ. as corrector Oct. 1256 x Oct. 1257 (All Souls, Oxford, Whadborough Cht. 26:C218/26); n.d. (1241 x 1264) (PRO, E211/477).

Randolph (Ranulph) 12 Feb. 1259 prior. of pr. Ranulph and others held in prison at Shrewsbury for the death of Kennthreth le forester (*CCR 1256–59*, p. 360). Occ. as corrector 7 Oct. 1259 (All Souls, Alberbury Cht. 117: C1/117); corrector 1267 (ibid., Alberbury Cht. 47: C1/117). Occ. as former corrector 1287 (Arch. dép. Haute Vienne, 5HH25/16).

Laurence Occ. as pr. Trin. 1280 (PRO, CP40/34, m. 73).

Peter de Corcellis priest, occ. as corrector 27 Mar. 1286 when apptd as the order's proctor in England; as corrector 1287 (Arch. dép. Haute Vienne, 5HH25/16); 9 May 1289; pr. or corrector 26 July 1289; pr. 27 July 1289 (*Reg. Swinfield*, pp. 216, 217, 220, 223).

Gerard Occ. 11 Mar., 31 Mar. 1298 (All Souls, Oxford, Whadborough Chts. 27–8: C218/27–8, cf. ibid., Alberbury Cht. 90: C1/90).

Roger Occ. 26 Mar. 1299 (ibid., Whadborough Cht. 29: C218/29).

Arnold Rissa Occ. as corrector 7 Mar. 1316 (ibid., Alberbury Cht. 120: C1/120); pr. 1 Feb. 1338 (ibid., Alberbury Cht. 121: C1/121; Graham, *English Ecclesiastical Studies*, p. 243 also cites Arch. dép. Haute Vienne, 5HH25/16). Seal (Graham, *English Ecclesiastical Studies*, p. 245; 'Alberbury Priory' p. 290).

Stephen Occ. 1343 (PRO, C85/90/15); 20 Oct. 1346 (*Reg. Trillek*, p. 288).

Richard of Stretton Apptd as pr. by abb. Jean Chabrit of Grandmont (1347–55). He ruled there for some years but owing to an accident he had absented himself for many years. He occ. in return of aliens in response to writ of 1 Sept. 1351 (PRO, C269/15/32). In 1364 he requested restoration from the abb. of Grandmont (All Souls, Oxford, Alberbury Cht. 123: C1/123). As former pr., he had received royal pardon for the death of Alice of Chirbury 12 June 1363 (*CPR 1361–64*, p. 347; Logan, *Runaway Religious*, p. 203; 'Alberbury Priory', pp. 274–5).

John of Cublington –**1359** Apptd by abb. Adémar Crespi of Grandmont (1355–78). Presumably the unnamed pr. accused of alienating property, killing Agnes Peckenhale and wounding a fellow monk 26 Jan. 1357 (*CPR 1354–58*, pp. 547–8). 8 May 1359 charges laid by 2 monks of Alberbury against their pr.: he was illegitimate and had entered the order by simony; after many misdeeds he had left Alberbury, and was an apostate; priory laid under interdict by the bp of Hereford ('Alberbury Priory' pp. 272–4, citing Arch. dép. Haute Vienne, 5HH25/16). 16 Sept. 1359 abb. Adémar issued a special commn to Robert of Newton, pr. of Grosmont, appointing him pr. of Alberbury. He was to institute new priors at Craswell and at Grosmont, vacant either *de jure* or *de facto* (All Souls, Oxford, Alberbury Cht. 122: C1/122).

Robert of Newton 1359– Apptd 16 Sept. 1359 (ibid.).

Richard of Hatton Apptd by abb. Adémar Crespi of Grandmont (1355–78). In 1364 the former pr. Richard of Streeton asked to be reinstated and both he and pr. Richard were summoned to Grandmont (see above). Richard of Hatton remained pr. He occ. 3 Oct.1365 (*CPR 1364–67*, p. 202); 5 May 1373 (*CCR 1369–74*, p. 547); 21 May 1373 (All Souls, Oxford, Alberbury Cht. 24 C1/24); 16 Nov. 1381 (*CPR 1381–85*, p. 40); 12 Feb. 1388, 14 Mar. 1388 (*CFR 1383–91*, pp. 206, 214). 9 May 1388 restitution to Geoffrey of Stafford, can. of Ronton, of the custody of the priory, to which he had been apptd by letters patent of 20 May 1386 as from the following 1 June, so long as the war with France should last at a yearly rent of 20 marks. Upon the false suggestion of Richard of Hatton and Richard Westbury, pr. of Sandwell, who 12 Feb. 1388 obtained letters patent appointing them to the custody, Geoffrey was removed. The king now revokes the letters to Richard of Hatton and Richard Westbury, as well as others of 14 Mar. 1388 granting custody to Richard of Hatton and Fulk FitzWarin (*CPR 1385–89*, pp. 438–9).

John Colle 1391– M. of Shrewsbury, pres. by Crown to priory, which was in the king's hands on account of the French war and because the son and heir of the patron, Fulk FitzWarin, was a minor, 1 Dec. 1391, no reason given for vacancy (*CPR 1391–96*, p. 1).

CRASWELL (Hereford), St Mary (Grandmont) f. *c.* 1225

List in R. Graham, *English Ecclesiastical Studies*, pp. 209–46, at 242; also in *Archaeologia*, 75 (1926), 159–210.

Simon of Clifford Occ. n.d. early 13th cent., dated by R. Graham *ante* 1231 (*Mon. Angl.*, IV, 490, no. iii; Graham, *English Ecclesiastical Studies*, p. 242).

Geoffrey Occ. *c.* 25 Mar. 1233 (BL, Harl. ms. 6203, f. 23v).

Reginald (R.) apptd by the abb. of Grandmont as corrector 1252 (ibid., f. 26r–v); occ. 1253 'rector omnium domorum Grandimontensis ordinis in Anglia et specialiter rector et prior domus de Cresswelle Hereford' diocesis' (ibid., ff. 26v–27r; PRO, C115/58/4015); n.d. (*temp.* Bp Peter d'Aigueblanche of Hereford 1240–68) (BL, Harl. ms. 6203, ff. 41v–42r).

Hugh Occ. as corrector 7 Oct. 1259 (All Souls, Oxford, Alberbury Cht. 117: C1/117).

Roger Occ. 1287 (Graham, *English Ecclesiastical Studies*, pp. 233, 242, citing Arch. Dép. Haute Vienne, 5HH25/16); 26 July 1289 (*Reg. Swinfield*, p. 223).

In 1315 the pr. of Grandmont claimed that the lord who claimed a founder's right at Craswell had turned out the unnamed corrector and all except one of the monks (All Souls, Oxford, Alberbury Cht. 120).

Peter Grimoaldi Occ. as pr. of Craswell n.d. [*c.* 1317] in dispute with Arnold Rissa, pr. of Alberbury (Graham, *English Ecclesiastical Studies*, p. 236, citing Arch. Dép. de la Haute Vienne, liasse 1672, but cf. Graham, 'Alberbury Priory', pp. 269–70 ment. him as pr. (i.e. vicar-general) of the order of Grandmont in England, and cf. Graham, *English Ecclesiastical Studies*, p. 231; *Archaeologia* 75, 180).

John of Cublington −1359 Pr. of Alberbury, also apptd pr. of Craswell by abb. Adémar Crespi of Grandmont (1355–78). Removed 1359 (All Souls, Oxford, Alberbury Cht. 122: C1/122, see Alberbury entry for further details).

GROSMONT (Yorks N.), St Mary (Grosmont in Eskdale) f. *c.* 1204 (Grandmont); 1394 (denizen)

List in *VCH Yorks*, III, 194; R. Graham, *English Ecclesiastical Studies*, pp. 209–46, at 242; see also N. Vickers, 'Grosmont Priory', *YAJ*, 56 (1984), 45–49.

James Occ. 15 Nov. 1273 (PRO, C85/170/34).

Roger of Craswell (Cressewell) Occ. 22 Apr. 1287 (*Ctl. Guisborough*, II, 154); as corrector at Eskdale 24 Aug. 1294 (J.C. Atkinson, *Cleveland Ancient and Modern*, I, 202n).

Reginald Occ. 11 Nov. 1318 (*CCR 1318–23*, p. 106).

Stephen Occ. 18 Aug. 1333 (*CCR 1333–37*, p. 130).

Robert of Newton –1359 Apptd by abb. Adémar Crespi of Grandmont as pr. of Alberbury 16 Sept. 1359 (Oxford, All Souls, Alberbury Cht. 122).

THE CISTERCIAN HOUSES

All dedications were to St Mary except where stated.

ABBEY CWMHIR (Radnor) (Cwmhir) (Whitland) f. 22 July 1143 (at Tyfaenor); 1 Aug. 1176 (at Cwmhir)

Lists in *Fasti Cistercienses Cambrenses*, p. 188; *Heads*, I, 126.

G(wrgeneu) Occ. 1215 x 1229 (*Welsh Episcopal Acts*, I, p. 352, no. 453). Possibly the Gwrgenau who occ. as pr. of Abbey Cwmhir 1206 (*Ystrad Marcell Chts.*, no. 42).

A. Occ. 15 July 1227 (ibid., no. 70).

Philip Occ. n.d., ? *c.* 1241 (*Arch. Camb.*, 4 (1849), 240; Williams, *Hist. of Radnor*, p. 341).

Griffin −1261 D. 15 Sept. 1261 (*Ann. Camb.*, p. 99).

Cadwgan Occ. 13 May 1276 (*Litt. Wallie*, no.44), ? same as below.

Cadwgan Ap Yeva (Caducus, Caducanus) unnamed abb. ment. in case of Dec. 1279 as 'newly created abb.' (*Welsh Assize Roll 1277–84*, p. 288). Abb. from at least 1278, another Cadwgan may have been abb. 1276–78 (*Fasti Cistercienses Cambrenses*, p. 188n). Occ. 1281 (*Welsh Assize Roll 1277–84*, p. 312); 10 June 1297 (*CPR 1292–1301*, pp. 290–1).

David Las Abb. of Abbey Cwmhir when intruded into the abbey of Strata Marcella, mentd in letter of archbp of Canterbury to bp of St Asaph 6 Nov. 1352 (Lambeth, Reg. Islip, ff. 60v–61r).

The next recorded abb., **John**, occ. 1381 (PRO, E179/21/8, m. 1).

ABBEY DORE (Hereford) (Dore) (Morimond) f. 26 Apr. 1147

Lists in *Monmouthshire Antiquary* II, part 2 (1966), 83–6; *Fasti Cistercienses Cambrenses*, p. 189; *Dore Abbey*, p. ix; *Heads*, I, 126. Cf. Annals of Dore (BL, Egerton ms. 3088, ff. 133v–134v) which appears to be confused about the numbering of abbots (see below) and produces other chronological difficulties.

Adam II Occ. (A.) 2 Oct. 1213 (*St Davids Acta*, no. 67n; PRO, C115/A1/6683, ff. 151v–152v, sec. viii, nos. 77–81, esp. f. 152r, no. 80); 28 July 1216 (*Rot. Lit. Pat.*, p. 191); 1217 (*Gir. Camb.*, iv, 206); 1221, 1226, 6 Oct. 1227 (PRO, Hereford F., CP25/1/80/3, no. 10; 80/5, no. 64; 80/6, no. 78); Oct. 1226 x Oct. 1227 (PRO, E210/9456); 15 July 1227 (*Ystrad Marchell Chts.*, no. 70). See Sharpe, *Latin Writers*, pp. 9–10.

Godfrey Occ. 1230 (*Monmouthshire Antiquary* II, part 2 (1966), p. 83 & n. 124, citing M. Gibson, *Churches of Door, Home Lacy and Hempsted* (1727), p. 15; n.d. (PRO, C115/A1/6683, f. 31v, sec. i, no. 92); 1240 (*Mon. Angl.*, V, 553, from Tanner, no source given, but the date is most prob. erroneous, see below).

Stephen of Worcester (Wygornia) Occ. 1236 (PRO, E326/11,297); 1238 (PRO, Hereford F., CP25/1/80/9, no. 161); 1241 (*CChR, 1226–57*, pp. 126, 260); 1243 (PRO, Hereford F., CP25/1/80/10, no. 196); (S.) 1247 (*Welsh Episcopal Acts*, I, p. 372, no. D.535); (S.) 1248 (ibid., II, p. 730, no. L.443); 1250 (PRO, F. Divers Cos. CP25/1/283/12, no. 208); (S.) 1252 (PRO, E329/210; PRO, F. Divers Cos. CP/25/1/ 283/13, no. 272); 1253 (BL, Harl. Cht. 75 D 11; *An. Sac. Ord. Cist.*, XX, 100; Williams, *Strata Florida*, pp. xxx–xxxi; *Glam. Chts*, II, p. 609, no. 581); 12 Nov. 1255 (PRO, Hereford F., CP25/1/80/13, no. 267b).

Reginald −1257 6th abb., d. 1 Apr. 1257 (BL, Egerton ms. 3088, f. 133v).

Henry (?King) (King) n.d. (PRO, E40/8575). Occ. 1263 (BL, Harl. Cht. 48 C 30–31; PRO, E326/12, 634); 1265 (*CR 1264–68*, p. 126); 1266 (*Reg. Gloucester*, p. 50, no. 149); 1267 (*CChR*

1257–1300, p. 304; *Welsh Episcopal Acts*, II, p. 752, no. L.544); 1268 (PRO, Hereford F., CP25/1/80/14, no. 295); Mich. 1272 x Mich. 1273 (PRO, E159/47, m. 14d). 7th abb., d. 20 Nov. 1273 (BL, Egerton ms. 3088, f.133v). Seal (*BM Seals*, no. 3062; *Hereford Seals*, p. 7).

William Wrohz 9th abb., d. 1281 and bur. at L'Arrivour (BL, Egerton ms. 3088, f. 134r)

William of Hereford (Heref', Herford) **1274–** El. 1 Jan. 1274 (BL, Egerton ms. 3088, f. 133v). Occ. 1279 (*Welsh Assize Roll 1277–84*, p. 283). As *quondam* abb. 10th abb., d. 12 March 1297 (BL, Egerton ms. 3088, f.134r). An abb. William occ. n.d. (1267 x 1276) (PRO, DL25/326 – it could be William of Hereford 1274 x 1276 or it could be another.

Hugh Cromus (Crone) **1294–** Prof. obed. & bl. 8 Aug. 1294 (*Reg. Swinfield*, p. 302). Occ. 1297 (*Cal. Chancery Rolls*, pp. 26, 53). D. 1312, 13th abb. as *quondam* abb. (BL, Egerton ms. 3088. f. 134r). ? presumably res. earlier on.

John de Grosmont (Grossemont, Grossomont) **1298–** Bl. 11 June 1298 (*Reg. Swinfield*, p. 346). Occ. 5 Mar. 1301 (PRO, E315/50/155). Presuambly res. D. as *quondam* abb. 1310, 11th abb. (BL, Egerton ms. 3088, f. 134r).

Richard of Madeley (Madely) *alias* **Straddel** (Straddull) **1305–1346** Prof. obed. 7 July 1305 (*Reg. Swinfield*, p. 419). Incepted at Oxford 1312 (BL, Egerton ms. 3088, f. 134r). D. 29 July 1346, 12th abb. (BL, Egerton ms. 3088, f. 134v). See C.H. Talbot, 'Richard Straddell, abbot of Dore 1305–46', *Downside Review*, 61 (1943), pp. 11–20; Sharpe, *Latin Writers*, p. 512; Emden, *BRUO*, III, 1795.

Roger ?1346– An unnamed abb. was bl. 12 Nov. 1346 (*Reg. Trillek*, p. 38). Roger occ. 13 June 1347 (*CPL*, III, 246). ? the abb. Roger who occ. n.d. (mid-14th cent.: pal.) (PRO, E315/41/23).

Robert Wroth ?1347–1362 Lic. to bp of Hereford from bp of Salisbury to confer bl. on unnamed abb. when he is in the Salisbury diocese 29 Nov. 1347 (*Reg. Trillek*, p. 122) – possibly Robert Wroth. Occ. (R.) 1351 (*Reg. Grandisson*, I, 147); 1354 (PRO, E326/4100); (?)1355 (PRO, E315/48/24). D. 22 June 1362, 13th abb. (BL, Egerton ms. 3088, f. 134v).[1]

John 1363– Bl. & prof. obed. 24 Dec. 1363 (*Reg. L. Charlton*, pp. 10–11). Occ. 1 June 1384 (PRO, C85/90/38).

The next recorded abb., **Richard**, was bl. 6 Jan. 1385 (*Reg. J. Gilbert*, p. 68).

BASINGWERK (Flint) (Savigny) f. 11 July 1231

Lists in *Fasti Cistercienses Cambrenses* p. 188; *Heads*, I, 126. See also D. Williams, 'Basingwerk abbey', *Cîteaux*, 32 (1981), 87–113.

W. Occ. June x July 1198 (*Epp. Cant.*, pp. 423–5).

Geoffrey Occ. early 13th cent., mentd as former abb. *temp.* Ranulph, earl of Chester (*Chester City Courts*, p. 59, note: the chronology in the accounts is somewhat confused).

A. Occ. *temp.* Philip Orreby, justice and Hugh, abb. of Chester (1208–26) (L. Owen, *MSS. in BM relating to Wales* (1930), II, p. 124, no. 329, citing BL, Harl. ms. 280, f. 77v (list by D'Ewes), said to be *c.* 1390 but clearly much earlier).

Simon Occ. 22 Sept. 1226 (*Derbys F.* (1886), p. 17).

John Occ. 10 Nov. 1245 (*CChR 1226–57*, p. 289).

Hugh Occ. 27 Jan. 1282 (*Chester City Courts*, p. 41; *Ctl. Chester*, II, pp. 294–5, nos. 513–14); Nov. 1285 x Nov. 1286 (Cheshire RO, DLT/B17, f. 4v); 1286 x 1287 (A. Jones, 'Basingwerk Abbey', *Historical Essays in honour of James Tait*, ed. J.G. Edwards and others, 1933, pp. 169–78, at p. 175).

Robert Occ. 25 Aug. 1292 (BL, Harl. ms. 2162, f. 28r).

William Occ. 27 Apr. 1316 (*Ctl. Whalley*, II, 548); 10 Mar. 1317 (*DKR 36*, app. II, no. 1, p. 24).

---

[1] Robert Wroth, m. of Dore, was ordained acolyte 1350, subdeacon 1351, deacon 1351, and priest 1352 (*Reg. Trillek*, pp. 533, 562, 567, 575), but since he was not described as abb. he is prob. a namesake.

German Mentd in 1330 as previous abb. – it is unclear how much earlier he was abb. (*Derbys Arch. and Nat. Hist. Soc.*, 47 (new ser. 1), 1924–5, p. 225).

Richard de Kokenfeld *alias* **Dokynfeld** Occ. *c.* June 1330 (PRO, Just. 1/167, m. 54); Mich. 1344 (BL, Add. Ch. 72289); 25 Jan. 1345 (*CPL*, III, 159). Mentd as late abb. 29 May 1357 (*Reg. Black Prince*, III, 245).

Ralph Occ. 4 July 1351 (*DKR 36*, app. II, no. 1, p. 25); 23 Aug. 1359 (*Reg. Black Prince*, III, 359).

Richard Occ. 22 Apr., 6 May 1362 (*DKR 36*, app. II, no. 1, p. 25); 1378 x 79 (PRO, E179/1/4, m. 2).

The next recorded abb., **Henry**, occ. 15 Sept. 1394 (L. Owen, *MSS. in BM relating to Wales* (1930), III, p. 705, no. 1296); 2 Oct. 1395 (*DKR 36*, app. II, no. 1, p. 25); 11 Oct. 1405 (*Signet Letters*, no. 447).

BEAULIEU (Hants), St Mary Magdalen (Cîteaux) f. 2 Nov. 1203 (at Faringdon); 15 June 1204 (at Beaulieu).

Lists in *VCH Hants*, II, 146; *Heads*, I, 126; lists in BL, Arundel ms. 17, ff. 45r, 53r.

Hugh of Cardeville (of Beaulieu) 1203– Occ. (H.) 25 Aug. 1206, 2 Jan. 1214, 8 Jan. 1215 (*Rot. Lit. Pat.*, pp. 67, 107, 126b); 9 Jan. 1215 (*Ctl. Glastonbury*, I, p. 90, no. 141). In 1218–19 he became bp of Carlisle: el. .–1 Aug. 1218, temps. 25 Aug. 1218, consec. 24 Feb. 1219 (*CPR 1216–25*, p. 164; cf. *Ann. Waverley*, p. 291; *Ann. Worcs.*, p. 410). According to *Ann. Waverley*, p. 291, he had previously been dep. as abbot, and this seems to be confirmed by an entry in *Reg. Wells*, I, 58, referring to William de Grisneto, *nepos domini abbatis quondam de Bello Loco*. This entry is undated but can be ascribed with some confidence to *c.* 1217 (cf. *BIHR*, XLV (1972), 157–70; cf. also Knowles, *Mon. Order*, pp. 658–9; Canivez, I, 445, 460).

Hugh (II) Occ. 3 Nov. 1220 (*Oxford F.*, p. 64). Is this a scribal error or a second abb. Hugh?[2]

Acius (Aceus, Aso) de Gisors (Gisortio) Occ. 1227 x 1243 (*Ctl. St Michael's Mount*, p. 5, no. 4); (A.) 24 Jan. 1226 (*Ctl. Fountains*, I, 216); (A.) 1233 x 1235; *c.* 1235 (*Ctl. Beaulieu*, nos. 233, 254, 60); 1 June 1236 (ibid., no. 273; *Cornwall F.*, I, p. 29, no. 60); (A.) 1 Apr. 1245 (*Ctl. Winchester*, no. 453; *CPR 1313–17*, p. 676).

Denis –1280 Occ. 1261 (BL, Royal ms. 12 E XIV, f. 73r); 3 Feb. 1262 (PRO, Beds F., CP25/1/2/21, no. 1); 22 Apr. 1263 (*Ctl. Beaulieu*, no. 275; *Cornwall F.*, p. 100, no. 189); 10 Jan. 1269 (*CChR 1257–1300*, p. 115); 1272 (*Ctl. Beaulieu*, App., p. 258); 1272 (PRO, Hants. F., CP25/1/204/11, no. 74; 204/11, no. 38); D. 1280 (*Ann. Waverley*, p. 395, *Ann. Worcs.*, p. 479).[3]

William de Gisors (Gisortio, Gizors, Gysors) **1281–** Cellarer of Beaulieu, el. 23 Apr. 1281 (*Ann. Waverley*, p. 397; *Ann. Worcs.*, p. 479).

Robert of Buckland (Boclande, Boclonde) **–1302** D. *ante* 26 Dec. 1302 (*CPR 1301–07*, p. 100).

Peter of Chichester (Chicestria) Occ. 1308 (C.H. Talbot, 'Cîteaux and Scarborough', p. 141, no. xxvii); Mich. 1310 (PRO, CP40/123, m. 149); 1311 (PRO, DL27/123); (P.) 20 Sept. 1316, 21 Sept. 1316, 1 Aug. 1316 (*Ctl. Beaulieu*, nos. 94, 95, 281); 1319 (PRO, SC1/31/15); 29 Mar. 1326 (*CPR 1324–27*, p. 288); (P.) 1331 (BL, Cotton ms. Nero A. XII, f. 32r, cf. f. 58v full name). n.d. (1332 x 1333) (PRO, C270/7/15); Mich. 1337 (PRO, CP40/312, m. 240). Seal (*Mon. Seals*, p. 7)

William of Hameldon 1340– S.T.P. Lic. to receive bl. from any Catholic bp 7 Sept. 1340 (Winchester, Reg. Orleton I, f. 96r). Occ. 11 Aug. 1343 to 2 Nov. 1345 (*CPR 1343–46*, pp.

---

[2] The first list in BL, Arundel ms. 17 (f. 45r) names only one abb. Hugh, but the second list (f. 53r) begins with: Hugh, first abb.; Hugh afterwards bp of Carlisle; Acius etc. While this order of the two abbots Hugh does not seem to equate with the extant evidence, the presence of two abbots named Hugh as first and second abbots is perhaps significant (2 abbots Hugh would also confirm John Petrus as 9th abb.).

[3] The reference to abb. H. in Oct. 1275 (*Reg. Ant. Lincoln*, III, no. 946) is prob. a scribal error.

229, 655); 6 Feb. 1346 to 19 Dec. 1346 (*CPL*, III, 212, 224); 3 May 1346 to 14 Oct. 1348 (*CCR 1346–49*, pp. 68, 589); 1 Jan. 1347 (*CPP*, p. 123); 27 Mar. 1349 (*CCR 1349–54*, p. 64).

John Petrus (Peres, Piers) **–1372** Called the 9th abb., although only the eighth named in the first list (BL, Arundel ms. 17, f. 45r). Occ. 28 Sept. 1350, 28 May 1351 (*CCR 1349–54*, pp. 264, 362); Mich. 1351 (PRO, KB27/365, m. 62); c. 19 June 1355 (*Ctl. Winchester*, nos. 345–6); 1370 (*Reg. Wykeham*, II, 102); 14 Mar. 1372 (ibid., I, 41). D. by 18 Aug. 1372 (ibid., 44).

Walter Heryng(e) 1372–1392 M. of Beaulieu, eln pres. to bp 18 Aug. 1372, bl. and prof. obed. 22 Aug. 1372 (ibid. 44–5). D. by 6 Jan. 1392 (*CPR 1391–96*, p. 12). Seal (*Mon. Seals*, p. 7).

BEGARE (Yorks N.) (?cell/grange dependent on abbey of Bégard). f. *temp.* Henry III; diss. 1414. Sometimes called Richmond mills. See *VCH Yorks*, III, 391 (no list); and survey of the property of the abb. of Bégard in Richmond and area (NYCRO, ZRL.3/77).

br. **Hugh** Occ. as *custos molendinorum Richem'* Nov. 1295 x Nov. 1296 (PRO, E106/3/19, m. 5d); Nov. 1297 x Nov. 1298 (PRO, E106/4/8, m. 2); Nov. 1298 x Nov. 1299 (PRO, E106/4/9, m. 3; E106/4/10, m. 3); as proctor of the abb. of Bégard Nov. 1302 x Nov. 1303 (PRO, E106/4/18, m. 5).

BENNINGTON, *see* LONG BENNINGTON

BIDDLESDEN (Bucks) (Garendon) f. 10 July 1147

Lists in *VCH Bucks*, I, 367–8; *Heads*, I, 126–7.

Adam of Bath 1198– For his name see BL, Harl. ms. 4714, f. 33r. Cellarer of Bruern, el. 1198 (*Ann. Waverley*, p. 251). Occ. 24 Apr. 1202, 1209 (BL, Harl. ms. 4714, ff. 59v, 154v); c. 1210 (*Ctl. Oseney*, II, 443); 1210 x 1213 (*Luffield Chts*, II, no. 413).

Simon n.d. (late 14th cent. transcript of charter) (*Medieval Archives of Christ Church*, p. 157) *temp.* William Foliot senior of Evenley? 12th cent./13th cent. His precise place in the sequence of abbots is uncertain.

Maurice (Maricius, Ahamric(us)) Occ. 12 Apr. 1220 (PRO, Northants F., CP25/1/172/16, no. 69); 1222 (ibid., /172/17, no. 89); 1 June 1225 (BL, Cotton ms. Vespasian E XIX, f. 9v); 9 Sept. 1226 (*Lincs F.*, I, 214); 29 Oct. 1226 (PRO, Northants F., CP25/1/172/22, no. 219; BL, Harl. ms. 4714, f. 44v). An unnamed abb. d. 1228 (*Ann. Dunstable*, p. 109).[4]

Thomas Occ. 21 July 1232 (PRO, Northants F. CP25/1/172/25, no. 278); 12 Oct. 1232 (*Bucks F.*, I, 62). Seal (*BM Seals*, no. 2660).

Giffard (Giffardus) –1236 El. abb. of Waverley 1236 (*Ann. Waverley*, p. 316). Seal (*BM Seals*, nos. 2658–9). Occ. n.d. (BL, Harl. ms. 4714, ff. 26r, 135v).

Walter Occ. c. 1236 x 1240 (*Ctl. Cirencester*, II, no. 649); (W.) 29 Sept. 1237 (*Luffield Chts.*, II, no. 475); n.d. (1238 x 1240) (*Ctl. Daventry*, no. 691).

William Occ. 1239, ? 2 Nov. ('de animarum' *sic, for* die animarum) (BL, Harl. ms. 4714, f. 20v).

Henry Mallore 1241– Bl. 24 Mar. 1241, no reason given for vacancy (*Reg. Grosseteste*, p. 205).

Philip Occ. 29 June 1244 (BL, Harl. ms. 4714, f. 20r; *CChR 1226–57*, p. 279); 1245, 1247 (BL, Harl. ms. 4714, ff. 123v, 316r, 132r); 1250 (PRO, Northants F., CP25/1/173/37, no. 584); 9 July 1251 (PRO, Northants F. CP25/1/283/13, no. 259); 20 Oct. 1251 (*Bucks. F.*, I, 96). Seal (*BM Seals*, nos. 2661–4).

William Occ. 29 Oct. 1254 (*Bucks F.*, I, 103); 1 Feb. 1255 (BL, Harl. ms. 4714, f. 196r).

Roger Occ. 9 Jan. 1260 (BL, Harl. Cht. 84 D 56); 17, 19 Jan. 1260 (BL, Harl. ms. 4714, ff. 6r, 96r); 7 May 1262 (*Beds F.*, I, p. 177, no. 627); 14 June 1262 (BL, Harl. ms. 4714, f. 11v).

---

[4] It is prob. that the abb. Henry who is said to occ. in 1226 (Willis, *Hist. Buckingham*, p. 357) is a scribal error for Maurice (Maricius, Ahamricus).

William de Byham *alias* **Wiham** Occ. (W.) Easter 1266 (BL, Harl. ms. 4714, f. 338r); 1268, 1272, 1275, 1278, 1285 (ibid., ff. 130v, 96v, 97r, 6r, 105r); Mich. 1284 x Mich. 1285 (PRO, E159/68, m. 13); 8 Aug. 1286 (*CPR 1281–92*, p. 250).

John de Thornber Occ. (J.) 30 July 1290 (*Luffield Chts.*, II, no. 715); Mich. 1291 (BL, Harl. ms. 4714, f. 126r); 14 Mar. 1292, 1293, 1295 (BL, Harl. Chts. 84 E 20, 24, 25); 1 May 1294 (PRO, C81/1788/4).

Walter of Thornborough (Tornberge) **1296–** Bl. 21 Sept. 1296 (*Reg. Sutton*, V, 186). Occ. 28 Oct. 1300 (BL, Harl. Cht. 84 E 29). Vacated office before 9 Apr. 1302 – he had left house taking the common seal and leaving debts (*Cal. Chanc. Warr.*, I, 163), presumably before 24 June 1301 (see below). Abbey taken into the king's protection for debt 12 Apr. 1302 (*CPR 1301–07*, p. 28).

John of Salisbury (Salesbir', Sarum) Occ. 24 June 1301, 17 Sept. 1307 (BL, Harl. Chts. 84 E 28, 38); 15 Sept. 1301 (PRO, C81/1788/5); 9 Apr. 1302 (*Cal. Chanc. Warr.*, p. 163). Seal (*BM Seals*, no. 2672).

Thomas of Buckingham (Bokyngham) **1309–** Bl. 6 Jan. 1309 (Lincoln, Ep. Reg., III, f. 147v). Occ. 20 Nov. 1315, 6 Dec. 1315 (BL, Harl. Chts. 84 E 43, 29).

John 1317– Bl. by ex-archbp of Armagh and prof. obed. 7 May 1317 (Lincoln, Ep. Reg., III, f. 368r); Occ. Mich. 1320 (PRO, KB27/242, m. 2d); 21 Dec. 1320 (BL, Harl. Cht. 84 E 47).

Roger of Gotham Occ. 3 May 1325 (BL, Harl. ms. 4714, f. 303v); 28 Oct. 1325 (*CCR 1323–27*, p. 518); 18 Jan. 1327 (ibid., p. 659); 24 Mar. 1328 (BL, Harl. ms. 4714, f. 127r); 13 Aug. 1334 (*CCR 1333–37*, p. 329); 13 May 1339, 9 Feb. 1340 (*CCR 1339–41*, pp. 120, 440). Seal (*BM Seals*, no. 2673).

Griffin 1340– Lic. to Benedict, bp *Cardicensis*, to bl. him 3 Aug. 1340 (Lincoln, Ep. Reg., V, f. 585v). Occ. 26 Mar. 1341 (BL, Harl. Cht. 84 F 1).

William of Loughborough (Loughteburgh) Occ. Jan. 1346 x Jan. 1347, Jan. 1357 x Jan. 1358 (Willis, *Hist. Buckingham*, p. 158, with no sources); apptd papal chaplain 28 Nov. 1353 (*CPL*, III, 490); 29 Sept. 1354, 10 Aug. 1356 (BL, Harl. Chts. 86 B 8, 84 F 2).

John Occ. 1360 (PRO, E210/9045).

Peter Devias of Charwelton For name see BL, Harl. ms. 4714, f. 254r. Occ. from 25 Jan. 1380 to 5 July 1394 (BL, Harl. ms. 4714, ff. 268v, 239v).

The next recorded abb., **John**, commn to suffragan to bl. him 16 Apr. 1397 (Lincoln, Ep. Reg., XII, f. 444v.).

BINDON (Dorset) (Forde) f. 22 or 27 Sept. 1172

Lists in *VCH Dorset*, II, 86; *Heads*, I, 127; G. Dru Drury, 'The Abbots of Bindon', *Proc. Dorset NHAS* 55 (1934), 1–19.

Henry –1212 Res. 1212 to be bp of Emly, Ireland (*Ann. Waverley*, p. 267). The abbey was possibly vacant 27 July 1213 when King John visited Bindon and made a gift to the monks, not the abb. and monks (*Rot. Lit. Claus.*, I, 148).

Ralph Occ. (R.) 1213 x 1214 (*temp.* Nicholas of Tusculum, papal legate) (BL, Cotton roll XIII 26); 20 Mar. 1227 (*Dorset F.*, p. 30).

John Occ. 8 Mar. 1232 (*CPR 1225–32*, p. 513).

Robert Occ. from 18 Nov. 1235 to 6 June 1249 (*Dorset F.*, pp. 66, 85); 1236 (*Wilts. F.*, I, 23); 6 June 1249 (*Ctl. Malmesbury*, II, 319). Prob. the **Robert of St Edward** referred to as former abb. in 1276 case (PRO, CP40/17, m. 41d).

Reginald Occ. 1275 (Hutchins, III, 355).

Roger Occ. *c.* 1274 x 1291 with John, abb. of Glastonbury (*CChR 1257–1300*, p. 215); 25 Nov. 1278 (*Dorset F.*, p. 184).

William de Haliburn Occ. 8 June 1290 (*CPR 1281–92*, p. 357); 22 Feb. 1296, appeal against abb. William and 2 other monks for the d. of br. Nicholas Wyther of Bexinton, sometime m. of Bindon (*CPR 1292–1301*, p. 216). Abbey taken into the king's hands on account of a felony charged to abb. 1296 (*CFR 1272–1307*, pp. 368–9). Occ. 22 Feb. 1296 (*CPR 1292–1301*, p. 216); 20 Apr. 1299 (PRO, C81/1788/3); 12 July 1300 (PRO, C241/34/397); 8 Sept. 1300 (PRO, C241/20/24; C241/34/396).

Letters for unnamed abb. of Bindon, by reason of his feebleness, nominating 2 monks as his attorneys 18 Apr. 1303 (*CPR 1301–07*, p. 133).

Henry Occ. 19 Sept. 1303 (PRO, Just.1/1329, m. 16d).

Richard de Maners Occ. Mich. 1305 (PRO, CP40/153, m. 470d); Trin. 1309 (PRO, CP40/178, mm. 9, 105d, 357); grave slab at Bindon (R. Graham, 'Richard de Maners, abbot of Bindon', *JBAA*, new ser., 39 (1934), 186; *Earliest English Brasses*, p. 186 and fig. 83).

Walter 1309– Prof. obed. 9 Nov. 1309 (*Reg. Gandavo*, II, 716). Occ. 17 Apr. 1311 (ibid., I, 403).

Richard of Hailes (Hayles) Occ. 1315 to 1318 (R. Graham, *art. cit.*, 186); 1316 (*Reg. Martival*, II, 98); 27 Mar. 1318 (*HMC Var. Coll.*, I, 358); 1319 (PRO, Just.1/1430, m. 105).

William of Keynsham Occ. 30 Nov. 1321, 6 June 1322 (*Reg. Martival*, II, ii, 375, 397); recently abb. 12 Jan. 1329 (*Reg. Grandisson*, I, 196–7).

John de Monte Acuto (Mountagu) Occ. 29 Oct. 1327 (*Reg. Martival*, II, ii, 544); 12 Jan 1329, excommunicated (*Reg. Grandisson*, pp. 197, 206). Commn of oyer and terminer, on complaint of the abb. of Bindon (presumably William), that John de Monte Acuto, feigning himself to be abb., and others took away property, goods etc. 16 Feb. 1331 (*CPR 1330–34*, p. 131). Claimed to be abb. – allegedly broke into the monastery at night with his supporters and stole 100 oxen, 7000 sheep, chalices, books, vestments and ornaments, as well as the common seal. Writ for arrest 22 Mar. 1331 (Logan, *Runaway Religious*, p. 206). John, an apostate monk, under arrest – writ of aid for taking him back to Bindon 29 Apr. 1331 (ibid., p. 142). Appt of persons to retake and conduct to Bindon abbey to be chastised according to the rule of his order John de Monte Acuto, sometime abb., who had escaped from the custody of William Trussel, to whom he had been delivered by the sheriffs of London when arrested by the king's mand. as an apostate 1 Aug. 1331 (ibid., p. 201). Removed by order of the General Chapter on account of excesses whereby he had harmed the abbey by 'indiscreet government and detestable presumption'. John had entered into possession of the abbey by armed force, mentd Nov. 1332 (*CCR 1330–33*, p. 619).

William Occ. 12 Oct. 1331 (*CPR 1330–34*, p. 203). Presumably the unnamed abb. mentd 16 Feb. 1331 (see above).

Roger Harnhull of Faringdon (Faryndon) 1332– Bl. 30 Sept. 1332 (Salisbury, Reg. Wyvil II, f. 17r). Occ. 26(?) Nov. 1332 (*CCR 1330–33*, p. 619); 1 May 1333 commn of oyer and terminer touching trespasses of named parties for imprisoning abb. Roger and others etc. (*CPR 1330–34*, p. 449); 15 June, 13 Aug. 1334, 29 Oct. 1335 (*CCR 1333–37*, pp. 320, 329, 530); Mich. 1337 (PRO, CP40/312, m. 458).

William of Cumnor (Comenore) 1338– Bl. 5 April 1338 (Salisbury, Reg. Wyvil II, f. 57v). Occ. 2 Dec. 1338 (*CCR 1337–39*, p. 624); 25 Mar. 1339 (*CCR 1339–41*, p. 111); 27 Apr. 1344 (*CCR 1343–46*, p. 365); 21 Dec. 1348 (Salisbury, Reg. Wyvil II, f. 194r). Seal (*Mon. Seals*, p. 9). Abb. of Forde, occ. 1350–51 (q.v.).

Philip Occ. 1349, 1353 (Dru Drury list, p. 17, citing Fordington court rolls, now in the Duchy of Cornwall Office); 8 Nov. 1350, 4 Feb. 1351 (*CPL*, III, 404, 399); 9 Sept. 1352 (*CCR 1349–54*, p. 497). Pardon to former abb. of king's suit against him 20 May 1362 (*CPR 1361–64*, p. 199).

John Occ. 1359 (Dru Drury list, p. 17, citing Fordington court rolls, now in the Duchy of Cornwall Office).

William 1361– Bl. 14 Nov. 1361 (Salisbury, Reg. Wyvil II, f. 286v). *VCH* gives his surname as Cletus, but this is a misreading of *electus* in the Salisbury register.

John de Hales original seal matrix [1383] (G. Dru Drury, 'Catalogue of Seal Casts in the Dorset County Museum, 1944', *Proc. Dorset NHAS*, 66 (1944), p. 100, no. 70).

William Occ. 1386 (PRO, CP40/503, m. 418d).

BORDESLEY (Worcs) (Garendon) f. 22 Nov. 1138
 Lists in *VCH Worcs*, II, 154; *Heads*, I, 127.

Richard Occ. 7 June 1221 (PRO, Worcs F., CP25/1/258/2, no. 28); 20 Oct. 1222 (*Warws F.*, I, no. 325). Presum. the unnamed abb. who d. 1223 (*Ann. Waverley*, p. 298).

Philip Occ. 3 Nov. 1237 (*Warws F.*, I, no. 553); 27 Jan. 1237 (ibid., no. 562); 1243 (PRO, Worcs F. CP25/1/258/6, no. 8); 1244 (ibid., 258/6, no. 6); 6 Oct. 1248 (*Soms F.*, I, p. 130). Seal (Demay, no. 2999).

William Occ. 3 Feb. 1250 (PRO, E326/3335); 7 June 1250 (BL, Add. Roll 51525(21)).

Walter Seal on cht. of Apr. 1253, not named in cht. (*Mon. Seals*, pp.10–11; PRO, E327/268).

Ralph of Biddlesden (Bitlesden, Butlesden) Occ. 8 July 1251 (*Warws. F.*, I, no. 695); 20 Oct. 1255 (PRO, Worcs F., CP25/1/258/7, no. 44); 16 Apr. 1257, mand. to overseas merchants in London not to lend money on seal taken by late abb. (*CPR 1247–58*, p. 591); 30 June 1257, king orders arrest of Ralph of Biddlesden sometime abb. of Bordesley who has secretly left his house and furtively taken with him the conventual seal (ibid., p. 565).

William −1270/1 Occ. *c.* 25 Mar. 1258 (BL, Cotton Cht. XXIX. 56); 5 Oct. 1258 (PRO, Worcs F., CP25/1/258/8, no. 7); 27 Jan. 1260, 8 July 1261, 17 July 1262 (*Warws F.*, I, nos. 783, 786, 817); Oct. 1266 x Oct. 1267 (PRO, C146/8168); n.d. (1260s) (Worcester Cathedral mun. B.789).

1270 deposition or cession of unnamed abb. made by abbots of Garendon, Neath and Abbey Dore (Canivez, III, 89; cf. 97 – cess. of William acc. 1271).

Henry −1277 Occ. 1 July 1275 (PRO, Worcs F. CP25/1/258/9, no. 59). D. 1277 (*Ctl. Stoneleigh*, p. 253).

Thomas de Orlescote 1277– Abb. of Stoneleigh, but res. 1277 to be abb. of Bordesley (ibid.). Occ. Nov. 1281 x Nov. 1282 (PRO, E315/39/67); 20 Jan. 1285 (*Warws F.*, II, no. 1009); 1285 (PRO, Just.1/956, m. 19). In 1278 **John** is mentd as former abb. – *abbas . . . loci eiusdem tertius ante ipsum qui nunc est* (*Rot. Parl.*, I, 1).

William de Heyford(e) 1292– Abb. of Stoneleigh, apptd to Bordesley 1292 (*Ctl. Stoneleigh*, p. 253). Occ. n. d. (late 13th cent.) (PRO, E329/148); Nov. 1292 x Nov. 1293 (PRO, E159/39/209); *c.* 30 Nov. 1294 (PRO, E315/46/64). ? Seal (*Mon. Seals*, p. 10).

John of Twyford (Twiford) Occ. Nov. 1295 x Nov. 1296 (PRO, E326/6132); 14 June 1296 (BL, Add. ms. 18641, f. 93v); *c.* 2 Feb. 1297 (PRO, E326/4144); 1301 (*HMC Abergavenny*, p. 103); 1302 (PRO, E326/8971); 1 July 1303 (PRO, Glos F. CP25/1/75/39, no. 229); Nov. 1306 x July 1307 (PRO, E326/6295).

John de Edoreston (Edereston) **1309–** Lic. to receive bl. from bp of Llandaff 2 May 1309, bl. by bp of Llandaff & prof. obed. 30 May 1309 (*Reg. Reynolds*, pp.7–8, 10, 149). Occ. *c.* July 1312 x July 1313 (PRO, E326/9308).

Lic. to unnamed abb. of Bordesley to receive bl. from any bp 5 Feb. 1314 (*Worcs Reg. Sede Vacante*, p. 152).

William Occ. 29 June 1316 (PRO, E315/38/232); 1319 (*CPR 1317–21*, p. 369); 3 May 1322 (PRO, E326/73); 1323 (PRO, LR14/997).

Thomas of Witherley (Wythirdeleye) Occ. 10 July 1325 (PRO, E315/39/172); 1326 (PRO, E326/8974–5); 1328 (*Worcester Liber Albus* (1920), p. 222); 1329 (*CPR 1327–30*, p. 456); 6 Dec. 1329 (PRO, E315/39/173); 16 Dec. 1330 (*CCR 1330–33*, p. 171); Jan. 1329 x Jan. 1330

(PRO, E326/6262); Jan. 1334 x Jan. 1335 (PRO, E326/5467); 1341 (PRO, E315/31/122); 1345 (PRO, E315/38/8); 6 Nov. 1346 (PRO, E326/1491). ? the same as the abb. of Merevale in 1348 (q.v.).

Robert Occ. 6 July 1349 (PRO, E326/8970) .

Thomas Occ. 18 Oct. 1349 (PRO, E315/42/8); 1350 (PRO, E326/5176); but occ. 30 June 1351 (PRO, E315/44/205, cf. below).

William de Edoreston (Edreston, Eldrestone) 1350– Commn from bp of Worcester to bp of Hereford to bl. & take prof. obed. 7 Dec. 1350 (Worcester, Reg. Thoresby, p. 50). Bl. by bp of Hereford 6 Jan. 1351 (*Reg. Trillek*, pp. 164–5). Occ. 1352 (*Ctl. Stoneleigh*, p. 254); 7 Feb. 1355 (PRO, E315/43/221).

John (de) Acton 1361– Prof. obed. 8 Sept. 1361 (Worcester, Reg. Brian, I, p. 76). Occ. 22 Feb. 1362 (PRO, E315/41/155); 1363 (PRO, E326/1921); 12 Feb. 1366 commn to arrest John de Acton, monk of Bordesley, who went to foreign parts and purposes to usurp possession of the abbey (*CPR 1364–67*, p.280); 14 May 1366 custody of abbey granted to Ralph, earl of Stafford (ibid., p.245); occ. 14 Aug. 1366 (PRO, E315/33/51); Jan. 1367 x Jan. 1368 (PRO, E326/5260); 22 Dec. 1368 (*CPL*, IV, 80); 8 June 1369 (*CCR 1369–74*, p. 92); Jan. 1370 x Jan. 1371 (PRO, E326/5109, 5115); June 1379 x June 1380 (PRO, E326/5453); June 1381 x June 1382 (PRO, E326/5430).

The next recorded abb., **John Braderugge**, was bl. and prof. obed. 25 Sept. 1384 (*Reg. Wakefield*, no. 294).

BOXLEY (Kent) (Clairvaux) f. 23 Oct. 1143 or 1146
Lists in *VCH Kent*, II, 155; *Heads*, I, 128.

John ?1216– Said to have been pr. of Robertsbridge, el. 1216 (*VCH*, but incorrect reference). Occ. 20 Jan. 1219 (*Kent F.*, p. 61).

W. Occ. *c.* 8 Aug. 1224 (PRO, SC1/1/63; P. Chaplais, *Diplomatic Docts I: 1101–1272*, p. 98, no. 144).

John –1236 Occ. 1229 (*CR 1227–31*, p. 250); visitor of English Benedictines 1233 (*Ann. Dunstable*, p. 133). Res. 1236 to be 20th abb. of Cîteaux (*Ann. Waverley*, p. 316).

Richard Occ. 1238 (PRO, E326/5422).

Simon Prof. obed. to Archbp Edmund Rich (1234–40) n.d. (*Arch. Cant.*, 37 (1925), p. 57; Canterbury D. & C., Register A, f. 261r). Occ. 12 July 1243 (*Kent F.*, p. 177).

Alexander Occ. 20 Oct. 1248, 2 June 1258 (ibid., pp. 214, 293).

Robert Prof. obed. to Archbp Boniface (1245–70) n.d. (*Arch. Cant.*, 37, p. 58; Canterbury D. & C., Ch. Ant. A41/24).

Henry Occ. 30 April 1279 (PRO, Kent F. CP25/1/98/60, no.123), Mich. 1281 x Mich. 1282 (PRO, E159/55, m.7). See Canivez, III, 185, *super promotione abbatis de Buxeria que fuit conspirator . . .*, 1279.

Gilbert 1289– Bl. and prof. obed. 5 Apr. 1289 (Gervase, II, 294; *Arch. Cant.*, 37, p. 58; Canterbury D. & C., Ch. Ant. A41/28).

Robert Occ. 4 June 1303 (*Reg. Hethe*, I, 55).

John de Burstallis 1312/13– Lic. to bp of Rochester to bl. him n.d. (Dec. 1312 x Feb. 1313) (*Reg. Woodlock*, I, 601). Occ. 30 Mar. 1318 (*Reg. Sandale*, p. 87; PRO, C85/155/1); 28 Oct. 1318 (PRO, E315/50/258); 2 Mar. 1321 (PRO, E210/4030).

Alan Occ. Easter 1327 – Trin. 1328 (*Index to Placita de Banco*, p. 644).

William of Romney (Romenee) Occ. 8 Nov. 1336 (PRO, E315/51/242); 19 June 1346, 4 June 1348 (*CPL*, III, 192, 308).

John of Harrietsham (Heriettisham) Occ. 4 June 1357 (Worcester, Reg. Brian I, p. 161); Sept. 1360 (Lambeth, Reg. Islip, f. 163r; PRO, E40/11500); *c.* Mich. 1364 (PRO, E210/9216);

1 Sept. 1368 (PRO, E315/31/155); Jan. 1371 x Jan. 1372 (PRO, E210/4739); 1379 (PRO, E210/923); 20 May 1397 (*CPR 1396–99*, p. 140).
The next recorded abb., **Richard Shepey** was bl. as abb. 9 Feb. 1416 (*Reg. Chichele*, I, 25–6).

BRUERN (Oxon) (Waverley) f. 10 July 1147
  Lists in *VCH Oxon*, II, 81; *Heads*, I, 128.
W. Occ. 15 Mar. 1216 *or* 13 Mar. 1217 (*Ctl. Oseney*, IV, 207).
Richard 1218–1228 Pr. of Waverley, apptd 1218 (*Ann. Waverley*, p. 291). Occ. (R.) 7 Feb. 1221 (*Ctl. Oseney*, III, 78); (Ranulf) 6 July 1221 (PRO, Glos. F., CP25/1/73/6, no. 2); 1222 (*Oxford F.*, p. 67; BL, Cotton ms. Nero A XII, f. 41v); 12 Nov. 1223 (PRO, Glos. F. CP25/1/73/7, no. 77). D. 1228 (*Ann. Waverley*, p. 304).
Thomas Occ. Easter term 1229 (*CRR*, XIII, no. 2013); from 9 June 1230 to 3 May 1243 (*Oxford F.*, pp. 86, 126). Excommunicated by the bp of Lincoln *c.* 1240 (Canivez, II, 223).
John Occ. 20 Jan. 1246 (*CPR 1232–47*, p. 472); *c.* 25 Mar. 1249 (Oxford, BNC, Dunthorp deed 10); 6 Oct. 1249 (PRO, F. Var. Cos., CP25/1/284/19, no. 88); 13 Oct. 1249 (*Oxford F.*, p. 238); 6 June 1255 (PRO, Glos. F., CP25/1/74/22, no. 495). Seal (*BM Seals*, no. 2740).
Roger –1279 Occ. n.d. (1274 x 1283) (PRO, E40/4864); 27 Jan. 1274 (PRO, Glos F., CP25/1/75/30, no. 9). Dep. 2 May 1279 (*Ann. Worcester*, p. 479; see also Canivez, III, 199 (Auger)).
Robert de Estal 1279– M. of Bruern, succ. Roger 1279 (ibid.). Occ. *c.* Mich. 1280 (PRO, E315/52/111).
Robert The abb. in office 1285 had been there 3 years (*Placita de Quo Warranto*, p. 663). Occ. *c.* Mich. 1284 (PRO, E315/52/111); 8 Oct. 1286 (*CPR 1281–92*, p. 251).
Hugh Occ. Easter 1286 (*sic*) (PRO, E159/59, m. 8d). He is most likely to be identified with abb. **Hugh de Schulstone**, predecessor of the present (unnamed) abb. in a case of Jan. 1286 (PRO, Just.1/1273, m. 21).
Robert Occ. 19 May 1290 (*CCR 1288–96*, p. 130).
Roger de Lecebourne Occ. 25 Mar. 1294 (ibid., p. 383); 1282 x 1314 (*Ctl. Winchcombe*, I, 292–3); 1296 (Oxford, BNC, Dunthorp deed 13).
John Occ. *c.* 11 June 1303 (Oxford, BNC, Dunthorp deed 15); 1311 (*CPR 1307–13*, p. 372); 3 Apr. 1315 (Oxford, BNC, Stoke Bruern deed 1); 3 May 1315 (PRO, E315/32/157).
Thomas Occ. 25 June 1320, 4 May 1321, 26 Aug. 1321, 5 Oct. 1321 (*CCR 1318–23*, pp. 241, 371, 490–1, 502); 13, 25 Feb. 1325 (*CCR 1323–27*, pp. 347, 351); 3 May 1325 (PRO, E315/46/218); 20 Feb., 23, 27 Mar. 1327 (*CCR 1327–30*, pp. 96, 111); Easter 1327 – Mich. 1328 (*Index to Placita de Banco*, p. 531). Letter for the arrest of Thomas, former abb. 18 Jan. 1331 (Lincoln, Ep. Reg., V, f. 443v).
Robert Lic. to receive bl. from bp of Winchester, 29 Apr. 1330 (ibid., f. 430v). Lic. to unnamed abb. to receive bl. from Peter, bp *Corbaviensis* 1 Dec. 1330 (ibid., f. 440v). Occ. 16 July, 8 Dec. 1330 (*CCR 1330–33*, pp. 147, 167); 2, 10 Feb. 1333 (PRO, E315/48/41; 48/157); 25 Sept. 1334 (*CCR 1333–37*, p. 335); 18 July 1338 (*CCR 1337–39*, p. 520); 4 Apr. 1340 (*CCR 1339–41*, p. 464); 14 Apr. 1341 (PRO, C241/114/15).
[**Roger** Occ. 1350 (*VCH* cites Kennett, *Parochial Antiquities*, p. 298, but this ref. cannot be found).]
Geoffrey Occ. 24 Jan. 1352 (*CCR 1349–54*, p. 404).
William Lynham Occ. 24 July 1356 (Oxford, BNC, Dunthorp deed 16).
John of Dunster (Donsterre, Dounstarre, Dunsterre) Deposed in a cause of spoliation but restored by 27 Nov. 1343 by the Cardinal of Boulogne, auditor of the cause (*CPP*, pp. 470–1) – on 12 Aug. 1343 it was stated that the case had been in the papal curia for 2 years (ibid., p. 446). Mentd as imprisoned at Hailes abbey 8 Jan. 1364, 17 Apr. 1364 (*CPR 1361–64*, pp.

454, 483); Occ. 4 June 1364 (PRO, E315/44/256); 3 June 1364 (*CCR 1364–67*, p. 61); 20 July 1364 mentd as having been imprisoned by abb. of Garendon, when noted that the abbey had been occupied by an intruded person for 5 years (*CPR 1364–67*, p. 9). King apptd custodians for the abbey, very greatly in debt and placed it under royal protection 9 Feb. 1365 (ibid., p. 86); further royal gt of custody 14 May 1366 (ibid., pp. 244–5). Occ. 3 Jan. 1366 (*CPP*, p. 511). 6 Oct. 1366 desc. as m. of Bruern, pardoned for having gone abroad to attempt matters against the abb. of Bruern (*CPR 1364–67*, p. 310).

William Occ. Jan. 1369 x Jan. 1370 (PRO, E326/9416); 5 Apr. 1375 (PRO, E326/1319); 1375 (PRO, E326/1319); June 1388 x June 1389 (PRO, E210/2529); 8 June 1396 (PRO, E315/35/25).

The next recorded abb., **Walter**, bl. 8 May 1405 (*Reg. Repingdon*, I, 28–9).

BUCKFAST (Devon) (Savigny) f. 1018, suppressed ?-1100 (Benedictine); 27 Apr. 1136 (Cistercian).

Lists in Oliver, pp. 371–2; Dom John Stephan, *Buckfast Abbey* (revised edn 1962), p. 33; *Heads*, I, 128.

Nicholas 1205– Abb. of Stanley, el. 1205 (*Wm. Newb.*, II, 508). Occ. n.d. (*Cist. Devon*, pp. 61–2; *TDA*, 8 (1876), 817).

Michael Occ. 3 May 1223 (*Ctl. Buckfast*, pp. 1579, 1598); 3 June 1228 (*Devon F.*, I, p. 89, no. 176); n.d. (1217 x 1226) (*Hatton's Book of Seals*, no. 469).

Peter Occ. 29 Sept. 1242 (*Ctl. Buckfast*, p. 1568).

Howell Occ. 1242 x 1243 (Devon RO, ED/M/51); (H.) Oct. 1243 x Oct. 1244 (BL, Harl. ms. 6974, f. 30r); n.d. (BL, Add. ms. 37640, f. 13r).

William Occ. n.d. (mid-13th cent.) (Seymour, *Torre Abbey*, p. 32, no. 6, citing Devon RO, 312M/TY65); 17 Sept. 1246 (*Cist. Devon*, p. 67; *TDA*, 8 (1876), 823). Is he the same as W., occ. 29 Sept. 1257 (*Ctl. Buckfast*, p. 1591)?

Durand Occ. n.d. (BL, Harl. ms. 6974, f. 30r; Bodl., Tanner ms. 342, f. 178r). His place in the sequence of abbots is unclear.

Henry Occ. (H.) 25 Dec. 1264 (Devon RO, Petre 123M/TB6); 15 Apr. 1268 (*Reg. Bronescombe*, p. 120n.); 1 Nov. 1269 (Devon RO, Petre/123M/TB60); 2 Feb. 1270 (*Ctl. Buckfast*, p. 1592). Presumably the unnamed abb. disciplined in 1270 (Canivez, III, 89).

Simon 1272– Bl. 24 June 1272 (*Reg. Bronescombe*, pp. 39, 120; *Reg. W. Bronescombe*, II, no. 889). Occ. from 9 Apr. 1273 (*Ctl. Buckfast*, p. 1577) to 14 Apr., 3 May 1280 (*TDA*, 45 (1913), 157).

Robert 1280– Bl. 3 July 1280 (*Reg. Bronescombe*, p. 120; *Reg. W. Bronescombe*, II, no. 1421). Occ. from 1282 (PRO E40/9370) to 21 Sept. 1284 (BL, Add. ms. 37640, f. 3r); July 1286 (PRO, Just.1/1273, m. 39).

Peter de Colepitte Occ. 2 Feb. 1290 (BL, Add. ms. 37640, f. 30v); from 2 Feb. 1291 to 17 Aug. 1307 (Devon RO, Petre/123M/TB12, 23); 4 Oct. 1311 (PRO, E40/8702). Name in Devon RO, Petre/123M/TB22.

Robert 1316– Bl. 1 Aug. 1316 (*Reg. Stapeldon*, p. 198).

William atte Slade Occ. Trin. 1327 (*Index to Placita de Banco*, pp. 95, 106).

Stephen 1328–1332 Bl. and prof. obed. 24 June 1328 (*Reg. Grandisson*, I, 350). Occ. 2 July 1328 (ibid., p. 356). Ref. to those detaining the goods of Stephen, late abb. 4 Nov. 1332 (ibid., II, 662–3).

John of Churchstow (Churstowe) **1332–** Bl. and prof. obed. 1 Nov. 1332 (ibid., 662). Occ. 4 Nov. 1332 (ibid., 662–3); 16 Nov. 1335 (*CPR 1334–38*, p. 214), but see below.

William Giffard 1333– Bl. and prof. obed. 6 June 1333 (*Reg. Grandisson*, II, 693). Occ. 8 Feb. 1336 (*CPR 1334–38*, p. 281); Mich. 1337 (PRO, CP40/312, m. 241); 1341 (*Reg. Grandisson*, II, 971); 13 Feb. 1342 (*CPR 1340–43*, p. 439); Easter 1346 (*YB 20 Edward III, part 1*, pp. 237, 295).

Stephen of Cornwall (Cornubia) 1348– Bl. and prof. obed. 8 June 1348 (*Reg. Grandisson*, II, 1046–7).

Philip 1349– Bl. and prof. obed. 21 May 1349 (*Reg. Grandisson*, III, 1082).

Robert Simon Occ. 9 Jan. 1356 (Devon RO, Petre/123M/TB62); 11 Aug. 1356 (PRO, C146/542); 8 July 1360 (*CPR 1358–61*, p. 423); 1365 (*Devon Gaol Delivery*, p. 14); 1371 (*Select Cases of Trespass*, II, 384–6); 1373 (*Reg. Brantingham*, I, 303, 319); 1379 (*CPR 1377–81*, p. 418); June 1379 x June 1380 (PRO, E179/24/9, m. 1); 22 Sept. 1382 (Devon RO, Petre/123M/TB97); 17 Apr. 1390 (ibid., /TB98); Hil. 1391, Trin. 1394, Mich. 1394 (*TDA*, 8 (1876), pp. 839, 841–3, 845).

The next recorded abb., **William Paderstow**, occ. 22 June 1395 (Devon RO, Petre/123M/TB91); Sept. 1395 (*Reg. Stafford*, p. 151).

BUCKLAND (Devon) (Quarr) (Locus Sancti Benedicti) f. 1278
List in Oliver, pp. 380–1.

Robert 1st abb. mentd in foundation cht. of Amice, countess of Devon (*TDA*, 7 (1875), 353–4). Occ. 1281 (ibid., 8 (1876), 799); 1282 (Bodl., Tanner ms. 342, f. 178r; BL, Harl. ms. 6974, f. 30r).

William Occ. 1288 (*Cist. Devon*, p. 36, citing Redvers cht.); 27 Jan. 1289 (*Arch. J.*, V, 34, 58); 19 June 1289 (Oliver, p. 385); (W.) 26 June 1289 (BL, Add. Cht. 13971).

Geoffrey Occ. 1304 (*Mon. Angl.*, V, 712; *Cist. Devon*, p. 36; Oliver, p. 380, no source).

Thomas of Dunstone (Dunstane) Occ. Mich. 1310 (PRO, CP40/183, attorneys m. 7); 13 Nov. 1311 (*Reg. Stapeldon*, p. 198); 27 Mar. 1316 (Tyson, *Rylands Chts.*, p. 4, no. 48); 27 July 1317 (*CPR 1317–21*, p. 19); 5 Oct. 1327 (*CCR 1327–30*, p. 173); Trin.–Mich. 1328 (*Index to Placita de Banco*, p. 108); 3 May 1329 (*Reg. Grandisson*, I, 491); 8 June 1330 (*CPR 1327–30*, p. 563); 13 May 1331 (*CPR 1330–34*, p. 143).

William Occ. n.d. (before 1333) (*HMC Var. Coll.*, IV, 77); 16 Nov. 1335 (*CPR 1334–38*, p. 214).

John Occ. 8 Feb. 1336 (ibid., p. 282).

Thomas Occ. 13 Feb. 1342 (*CPR 1340–43*, p. 440).

John Brytone Occ. 12 May 1358 (*CPL*, III, 597), but prof. obed. 1 Aug. 1358 (*Reg. Brantingham*, I, 583).

Thomas de Wappesleghe Occ. Easter 1361 (PRO, CP40/406, mm. 177d, 235d); Easter 1364 (*TDA*, 8 (1876), p. 799; *Cist. Devon*, pp. 43–4); 20 Oct. 1369 (*Cal. Misc. Inq.*, III, 272); 24 May 1373, 22 Nov. 1373 (*Reg. Brantingham*, I, 303, 319); June 1379 x June 1380 (PRO, E179/24/9, m. 2).

The next recorded abb., **Walter**, occ. Oct. 1392 (Oliver, p. 387, no. xiii).

BUILDWAS (Shrops), St Mary and St Chad (Savigny) f. 8 Aug. 1135
Lists in *VCH Shropshire*, II, 58–9; *Heads*, I, 129.

Huctred Occ. *c.* 1210 (Eyton, *Salop*, VII, 244); (H., ? for Huctred) 1216 x 1222 (*Ctl. Shrewsbury*, II, no. 357).

William Occ. prob. 1215 x 1223, although it could be 1206 x 1208 (*EEA*, 17, no. 137 & n.; see *Heads*, I, corrigenda).

Stephen Occ. 28 Oct. 1227 (Eyton, *Salop*, II, 39); 28 Oct. 1226 (*Salop F.*, 3rd ser, VII, p. 383, no. 42).

S. Simon or Stephen? Occ. 1228 (*Glam. Chts.*, II, no. 465; *Margam Abbey*, no. 133; *An. Sac. Ord. Cist.*, II, 65–6).

Simon Occ. July 1233 (Eyton, *Salop*, VI, 76, ref. to essoins).

Nicholas Occ. 18 Nov. 1236, 23 Nov. 1236, 7 Dec. 1240, 14 June, 1243, 1 July 1247, 26 Nov. 1247 (*Salop F.*, 4th ser., I, p. 397; 4th ser., IV, p. 162; 4th ser., VI, pp. 176, 180, 188, 190);

Oct. 1247 x Oct. 1248 (*CChR 1257–1300*, p. 419); 1249 (PRO, Shrops F., CP25/1/193/4, no. 1); 1251 (SRRC, 972/220/1/7); 20 Jan. 1256 (PRO, Shrops. F. CP25/1/193/4 no. 70).

William Occ. 14 Apr. 1258 (*Staffs F. 2*, p. 248); *c.* 1263 (Eyton, *Salop*, VI, 333, without source). Prob. the **William Bungy**, former abb., mentd in 1278 case (PRO, CP40/24, m. 6d).

Adam Occ. (A.) Easter 1271 (SRO, 6000/6302); 8 July 1272 (*Staffs F. 2*, p. 258). 14 Nov. 1272 (PRO, Shrops. F. CP25/1/193/4, no. 132).

William Tyrry *alias* **Bruges** (Brugges) Occ. 1277 (Oxford, Balliol Coll. ms. 35a, f. 3r; Sheppard, *The Buildwas Books*, p. 165 and fig. 11); Easter 1278 (PRO, CP40/24, mm. 6d, 12d, 69d); (W.) ?autumn 1282 (PRO, SC1/22/139); 8 Aug. 1286 (*CPR 1281–92*, p. 250); 1289 (PRO, C81/1788/15); 1292 (*YB 20–21 Edward I*, pp. 244–5); 12 Nov. 1292 (PRO, Shrops F. CP25/1/193/6, no. 58).

Henry Said to occ. Nov. 1298 x Nov. 1299, surnamed Burnell (Eyton, *Salop*, VI, 334, citing Blakeway note). Occ. 1303 (PRO, Shrops F., CP25/1/193/7, no. 56); 1304 (SRRC, 6000/3998); Mich. 1315 (*Staffs Plea Rolls 1307–27*, p. 56).

John Occ. 10 Aug. 1318 (*CPR 1317–21*, p. 276).

Henry Letter to Edward III n.d. (? latter half of 1332) (PRO, SC1/33/81, pd *Cal. Anc. Corr. Wales*, p. 177, although the king addressed could poss. be Edward II and hence be the earlier abb. Henry). Occ. Mich. 1337 (PRO, CP40/312, m. 442).

An unnamed abb. was murdered in 1342. His accused murderer, br. Thomas de Tonge, m. of Buildwas, placed in monastic prison, from which he broke out. Writ for arrest 12 Sept. 1342; papal mand. to reconcile 20 Nov. 1343; yet another writ for arrest 18 Aug. 1344 (*CPR 1345–48*, p. 110; Logan, *Runaway Religious*, p. 207).

Roger Occ. 18 Aug. 1344 (*CCR 1343–46*, p. 460).

1 Apr. 1346 mention of electoral dissension and 2 rival abbots. King takes abbey into his special protection and appts overseers of the revenues (*CPR 1345–48*, p. 110).

Nicholas Occ. 13 Apr. 1347 (ibid., p. 312); 3 Feb. 1348 (*CPR 1348–50*, p. 17).

Hugh Possibly same as below. Occ. 18 Apr. 1355 making visitation of St Mary's, Dublin (*CPR 1354–58*, p. 206); 1352 (SRRC, 6000/6145, 17th-cent ref. to lost doct); 22 Dec. 1354 (*CPP*, p. 269).

Hugh Fikeys Occ. 1377 (PRO, E179/15/3, no. 1). Occ. (Hugh) 13 May 1381, 4 Apr. 1391, 29 Sept. 1397 (SRRC, 972/220/8/2, 8, 10).

BYLAND (Yorks N.) (Savigny) (Bella Landa) f. 10 Jan. 1135 (at Calder); 1138 (at Hood); Sept. 1142 (at Old Byland); 1247 (at Stocking); 30 Oct. 1177 (at Byland).

Lists in *VCH Yorks*, III, 133; *Heads*, I, 129; Clay, *Early Abbots*, pp. 9–13 (to 1268).

Walter Last recorded occ. Whitsun 1212 (*Ctl. Fountains*, II, 626); n.d. (1210 x 1213 (*Yorks Deeds*, III, no. 144)); (W.) n.d. (1211 x 1217) (Bodl., Fairfax ms. 7, f. 99r, with R. Marsh, archdn of Northumberland). Presumably deposed, since Walter former abb. was to be sent to Clairvaux in 1218 to be punished '*ad arbitrium Claraevallensis et tam ille quam monachi qui cum eo exierunt, sententie conspiratorum subiacebunt*' (Canivez, I, 490, see also 519). Seal (*BM Seals*, no. 2821).

Robert Occ. (R.) *c.* 1219 (*Ctl. Sallay*, I, nos. 61–62); *c.* 1220 (*Ctl. Furness*, II, ii, 475; *Yorks Deeds*, VI, no. 164, cf. no. 163); 1223 (Baildon, I, 27); 1224, 1226 (Yorks F., 1218–31, pp. 55, 95); (R.) 1226 (*Ctl. Fountains*, I, 216–17); 3 Feb. 1230 (*Yorks. F., 1218–31*, p. 125). Seal (wrongly ascribed to Richard) (*Durham Seals*, II, p. 548, no. 3421). Mentd as former abb. 1243 (*CRR*, XVII, no. 2163).

Henry of Battersby (Bathersby, Bathirsby) 1230 (DCD, Misc. Cht. 4940). Occ. 6 Apr. 1231 (*Yorks. F., 1218–31*, p. 132); from 1235 to 1246 (*Yorks F., 1232–46*, pp. 32, 157); from 3 May 1247 to 24 June 1262 (*Yorks F., 1246–72*, pp. 6, 125); 1267 (*Reg. W. Giffard*, p. 49); *c.*

Whitsun 1268 (BL., Egerton ms. 2823, f. 55v); (H.) *c.* Sept. 1268 (*Reg. W. Giffard*, p. 190). Desc. as former abb. in late 1268 case (PRO, Just.1/1050, m. 26). Surname provided from reference in 1292 assize roll (PRO, Just.1/1100, m. 84, cited *VCH* p. 133, n. 19) and in BL, Egerton ms. 2823, f. 97r.

Adam of Husthwaite (Hustwayt) Occ. 3 June 1272 (*Yorks F., 1246–72*, p. 183); 1279 (*Ctl. Sallay*, II, no. 412; *Ctl. Fountains*, I, 322); 1280 (*Yorks F., 1272–1300*, p. 43); 1282 (*HMC Westmorland etc.*, pp. 323–4); (A.) 2 Apr. 1283 (*Ctl. Fountains*, I, 142; Baildon, I, 31).

Thomas Occ. 1285 (Baildon, I, 27), possibly the unnamed abb. going overseas 1 Aug. 1286 (*CPR 1281–92*, p. 250).

John 1287– Prof. obed. 30 Mar. 1287 (*Reg. Romeyn*, I, p. 163, no. 454). Occ. 1287 (Baildon, I, 27); (J.) 1292 (BL, Add. ms. 38816, f. 11v.); 21 Aug. 1293 (*CPR 1292–1301*, p. 37).

Henry 1300– Prof. obed. 4 Sept. 1300 (*Reg. Corbridge*, I, 119). Occ. 1301 (Baildon, II, 8); abb. of 'Benyngdon' occ. 6 Mar. 1302, 19 Mar. 1302 (*Ctl. Fountains*, I, 62) but is this to be identified with Byland?

William Occ. 22 Apr. 1302 (*Reg. Corbridge*, I, 72); 1304 (YAS, Grantley mss, no. 124).

Adam [of Husthwaite] Occ. July 1309 x July 1310 (BL, Egerton ms. 2823, f. 80v); 21 Sept. 1314 (*CPR 1313–17*, p. 177); 1315 (Baildon, I, p.27 – which gives the surname, but without source).

John of Winkburn (Winkeburn) Occ. 22 Apr. 1316 (*Reg. Greenfield*, V, p. 260, no. 2837); 7 Sept. 1317 (Bodl., Dodsworth ms. 7, f. 110r).

John 1318– Bl. & prof. obed. 25 June 1318 (*Reg. Melton*, II, pp. 19–20, no. 40).

John of Myton (Miton) **1322–** Bl. & prof. obed. 11 July 1322 (ibid., p. 80, no. 191). Occ. 1325 (*CCR 1323–27*, p. 518); 1327 (*CCR 1327–30*, p. 214); 1332 (*Reg. Melton*, II, p. 157, no. 418); 29 Nov. 1333 (*CCR 1333–37*, p. 185); 1333 (Baildon, I, p.31).

Walter [of Dishforth (Disceford) *alias* **of Yarm** (Jarum)] **1334–**[5] Prof. obed. to Roland Jorz, ex-archbp of Armagh (acting for Archbp Melton of York) 3 July 1334 (*Reg. Melton*, II, p. 167, no. 430). Occ. 7 Dec. 1334 (*CCR 1333–37*, p. 355); Mich. term 1342 (Baildon, I, 31). Seal (Clay, *Seals*, p. 14).

John 1349– Bl. & prof. obed. 1 Nov. 1349 (York, Reg. 10, f. 166v). Occ. 1351 (*CPR 1350–54*, p.158); 5 Feb. 1355 (*CPL*, III, 577).

William of Helmsley (Helmeslay, Helmesleye) **1357–** Bl. & prof. obed. 17 Sept. 1357 (York, Reg. 11, f. 174Ar). Occ. 22 Nov. 1357 (Ctl. Scrope of Bolton, f. 48r). Intruded into the abbey, by the power of magnates and bribery, it is claimed in letter of 16 Dec. 1360 (*CPR 1358–61*, p. 507). Occ. June 1361–Mar. 1362, when indicted for extortion (*Yorks Sessions of the Peace 1361–64*, p. 101–2, 108, 115, 122, 124).

John de Difford styled true abb., in dispute with William of Helmsley – dead by 16 Dec. 1360 but case to continue (ibid., pp. 507–8). Claimant 16 Dec. 1360 (*CCR 1354–60*, p. 50).

An unnamed abb. about 1364 was still in office in early 1367 (*Cal. Misc. Inq.*, III, 243).

Robert of Helmsley (Helmeslay) **1370–** Bl. & prof. obed. 9 June 1370 (York, Reg. 11, f. 190r). Occ. 1381 (Baildon, I, p.27); 8 Nov. 1389 (*CPR 1385–92*, p. 86). In 1386 the unnamed abb. was said to be 50 years old (*Scrope-Grosvenor*, I, 96).

The next recorded abb., **Geoffrey of Pickering** (Pikeryng) occ. 12 June 1397 (*Reg. Waldby*, p. 16), cf. Sharpe, *Latin Writers*, p. 127.

CALDER II (Cumberland) (Furness) f. 1142 x 1143
Lists in *VCH Cumberland*, II, 177–8; *Heads*, I, 129–30.

G. Occ. 1214+ (*Ctl. St Bees*, pp. 300–1, no. 288).

---

[5] The surnames are given in *VCH* but the reference to Archbishop Melton's register is incorrect and I have not been able to find the correct source.

[**Ralph** and **Nicholas** prof. obed. to Archbp Walter of York (Gray 1215–55 or Giffard 1266–79) (*Mon. Angl.*, V, 340, citing BL, Harl. ms. 6972, f. 49r). Nicholas is presumably to be identified with the abb. Nicholas in 1251, but Ralph's place in the sequence is uncertain.]

Jol(l)an Occ. from Oct. 1241 x Oct. 1242 to Oct. 1246 x Oct. 1247 (*Cumbd F.*, pp. 222–4); 10 May 1243 (*Ctl. Furness*, I, iii, 654).

Nicholas Occ. Jan. 1251 (*Ctl. Furness*, II, ii, p. 326).

Walter Occ. Oct. 1255 x Oct. 1256 (*Cumbd F.*, pp. 224, 225).

William Occ. Nov. 1262 (*Mon. Angl.*, V, 341, no. ii).

Warin Occ. 1286 (*Trans. CWAAS*, IX, 232, citing Senhouse collection deed).

Elias 1289– Prof. obed. 11 Dec. 1289 (*Reg. Romeyn*, I, 340). Occ. 1293 (PRO, Just.1/650, m. 37d).

Richard 1322– Bl. and prof. obed. 12 Dec. 1322 (*Reg. Melton*, I, nos. 67, 69). Occ. n.d. (? *c.* Jan. 1328 (ibid., no. 108); 10 Dec. 1330 (*Ctl. St Bees*, p. 563); n.d. (1332 x 1333) (PRO, C270/8/1); 17 Jan. 1334 (CCR 1333–37, p. 169).

[**William de Lobenham** Occ. 1347 (*Trans. CWAAS*, new ser., LIII (1953), p. 95, no source).]

Robert 1351– Commn to bl. 8 Jan. 1351 (York, Reg. 10, f. 79r.). Possibly the same abb. as **Robert de Willoughby** whose tomb slab survives at Calder (*Trans. CWAAS*, new ser., LIII (1953), p. 89).

Nicholas of Bretby [1369–] Prof. obed. n.d. [between entries of 22 Jan. 1369 and 25 Nov. 1369] (York, Reg. 11, f. 293v); Mentd (Nicholas de Byrby) (*Obit of W. Ebchester and J. Burnby*, p. 58).

The next recorded abb., **Richard**, occ. 7 Apr. 1432 (*Test. Ebor.*, III, 327).

CLEEVE (Soms) (Revesby) f. 25 June 1198

Lists in *VCH Soms*, II, 118; *Heads*, I, 130

Hugh 1198– First abb., occ. 1199 (*Bec Documents*, pp. 4–5, 12–13, cf. *Mon. Angl.*, V, 734).

William Occ. 30 Apr. 1219 (*Soms F.*, I, 35).

J. Occ. Sept. 1228 (*Ctl. Launceston*, no. 406); 14 May 1230 (*CPR 1225–32*, p. 376). Mentd 3 Jan. 1237 as still alive but former abb. (*CR 1234–37*, p. 518).

Simon Occ. 14 May 1234 (*Cornwall F.*, I, p. 25, no. 52); 23 June 1238 (*Devon F.*, I, 140); Jan. 1243 (*Somerset Pleas*, no. 1151); 13 Oct. 1254 (*Devon F.*, I, 274).

John Goddard 1248– Abb. of Newenham, el. to Cleeve 4 Apr. 1248 and ruled many years (Oliver, pp. 363–4). Occ. 1255 (*CPR 1317–21*, p. 581); 8 July 1256 (*Soms. F.*, I, 178).

Henry Occ. (H.) *c.* Apr. 1275 (PRO, SC1/16/45); 18 May 1284 (*Cornwall F.*, I, p. 167, no. 286); 4 Nov. 1297 (*Reg. R. Shrewsbury*, I, no. 1346).

Richard le Bret 1315– Occ. as abb.-el. 15 May 1315 (*Reg. Droxford*, p. 85). Bl. and prof. obed. 21 Sept. 1315 (ibid., pp. 97–8).

Henry Occ. July 1318 x July 1319 (PRO, SC8/124/6200).

Robert of Cleeve (Clyve) 1321– Bl. and prof. obed. 29 Sept. 1321 (*Reg. Droxford*, p. 193). Trin. 1327 – Mich. 1328 (*Index to Placita de Banco*, pp. 92, 100).

Michael de Caldun Occ. Mich. 1337 (PRO, CP40/312, m. 197); 12 Mar. 1338 (*Reg. Grandisson*, II, 869); 13 Feb. 1342 (*CCR 1341–43*, p. 469); 8 Apr. 1343 (*CCR 1343–46*, p. 107); Trin. 1343 (*YB 17 Edward III*, p. 595). Former abb. by 1344 when his successor refused to pay his annual pension and was ordered by the General Chapter to pay (Canivez, III, 478).

James Occ. 14 Oct. 1344, 24 Oct. 1344 (*CCR 1343–46*, pp. 458, 473); 28 Nov. 1346 (*CCR 1346–49*, p. 178); 20 Jan. 1364 (*CCR 1360–64*, p. 561); 28 Mar. 1367 (*Cleeve Chts.*, p. 49); 1 Aug. 1367 (BL, Add. Cht. 11164).

Gilbert Occ. 30 Sept. 1374 (PRO, C85/38/27).

The next recorded abb., **John**, occ. 3 Oct. 1381 (PRO, C85/38/40) and 29 Mar. 1383 (*CPR 1396–99*, p. 484), perhaps the same as **John Mason** who occ. 23 May 1389 (PRO, C85/39/1;

SDNQ, XIII, 356) and 30 Nov. 1394 (*Cal. Misc. Inq.* VII, no. 525). John also occ. 8 Nov. 1400 (*CPR 1399–1401*, p. 413); 22 June 1406 (Hugo, *Nunneries*, p. 69).

COGGESHALL (Essex) (Savigny) f. 3 Aug. 1140
Lists in *VCH Essex*, II, 128–9; *Heads*, I, 130.

Ralph 1207–1218 Sixth abb., m. of Coggeshall, el. 1207 and res. 1218 after eleven years and two months, on account of ill-health (*Ralph Coggeshall*, pp. 162, 187).

Benedict of Stratford 1218–1223 Seventh abb., prev. abb. of Stratford Langthorne, el. 1218 and d. 1223 (ibid., pp. 187, 192, cf. *Ann. Waverley*, p. 297).

Geoffrey 1223– Eighth abb., prev. pr. of Coggeshall, el. 1223 (*Ralph Coggeshall*, p. 192).

William Occ. Trin. term 1227 (*CRR*, XIII, no. 349); Mich. term 1230 (*CRR*, XIV, no. 655).

[**Stephen** M. of Rievaulx 1230 'Frater Stephanus, monachus Rievallis, curam domus de Coqueshale, ad quam electus est, suscipere compellatur' (Canivez, II, 90).]

Richard Occ. Mich. term 1230, Trin. term 1231 (ibid., nos. 961, 1585); 25 Nov. 1230 (PRO, Herts F., CP25/1/84/14, no. 157); 1235 (ibid., /85/15, no. 178); 1236 (*Essex F.*, I, 113); 27 Jan. 1248 (ibid., 162).

Robert Occ. n.d. (mid-late 13th cent.) (PRO, LR14/543). His precise place in the sequence of abbots is uncertain.

Thomas Quintyn Occ. from Easter 1251 to Trin. 1258 (ibid., 186, 223); 1255 (PRO, Herts F., CP25/1/85/26, no. 466); 1255 x 1256 (*CChR 1341–1417*, p. 1); 1257 (*C. Misc. Inq.*, III, 290).

William of Tolleshunt Succ. on d. of Thomas and was in possession of a certain manor for 26 years or more until in 20 Edward I (Nov. 1291 x Nov. 1292) the king's bailiff intervened (PRO, SC8/98/4871, 4873; *CChR 1341–1417*, p. 1). Occ. 29 July 1262, 11 Apr. 1266 (*Essex F.*, I, 246, 263); 1270 (PRO, LR14/46); 1285 (PRO, Just.1/242, m. 59d).

John Occ. *c.* May 1299 (PRO, SC1/16/51).

William Occ. 2 Jan. 1310 (*HMC Var. Coll.*, I, 358).

John Occ. 30 Nov. 1318 (PRO, CP40/225, m. 2d).

Richard of Panfield (Pantfeld) Occ. 30 May 1327 (PRO, SC8/98/4870–75); cf. 'Tolleshunt Major and Coggeshall abbey', *TEAS*, IX (1903), 181.

William Joldayn Occ. 12 Feb. 1341 (*CChR 1341–1417*, p. 1); said to occ. 1348 (*sic*) (*TEAS*, new ser., XI, 49), but see next entry.

Roger Port(e) Occ. 25 June 1346 (PRO, KB27/356, rex roll m. 32d); 13 Nov. 1350 (*CCR 1349–54*, p. 276); 18 June 1352 (*CPL*, III, 467); 29 May 1354 (*CCR 1354–60*, p. 77).

Thomas Occ. Easter 1361 (PRO, CP40/406, m. 58d).

Robert Occ. Mich. 1364 (PRO, KB27/416, m. 57d); 7 Aug. 1380 (PRO, C81/1788/16).

The next recorded abb., **John**, bl. 23 June 1387 (London, Reg. Braybrooke, f. 376v).

COMBE (Warws) (Waverley) f. 10 July 1150
Lists in *VCH Warw.*, II, 75; *Heads*, I, 130.

William II Occ. 20 Jan. 1200 (BL, Cotton ms. Vitellius A I, f. 58v); 1201, 1206 (*Basset Chts.*, nos. 85, 102); 1208 x 1209 (*Warws. F.*, I, no. 188). Presumably the **W. de Suham**, former abb, alive 1226 (*Magnum Reg. Album Lichfield*, no. 414, for date see no. 410).

Michael –1234 Occ. (M.) 1217+ (*Ctl. Tutbury*, no. 264); Easter 1224 (*Warws. F.*, I, no. 342); 11 Nov. 1226 (ibid., no. 374); 29 Sept. 1227 (*CPR 1225–32*, p. 165); 12 May 1230 (*Warws. F.*, I, no. 437). Res. 1234 (*Ann. Waverley*, p. 315).

Robert 1234 M. of Swineshead, succ. 1234 *quo celeriter de medio sublato subrogatur* (ibid.).

William 1234– Sub-pr. of Garendon, el. 1234 (ibid.). Occ. 25 June 1236 (*Warws. F.*, I, no. 512).

Roger 1237–1238 M. of Waverley, succ. 1237 (*Ann. Waverley*, p. 317). D. 1238 (ibid., p. 319).

Roger II 1238– Precentor of Combe, succ. 1238 (ibid.). Occ. 27 Oct. 1240 (*Warws. F.*, I, no. 596).

William of Chester (Chestre) **1241–1262** M. of Waverley, succ. 1241 (*Ann. Waverley*, p. 328). Occ. 25 June 1248 (PRO, Berks. F., CP25/1/8/17, no. 41); 24 May 1255 (PRO, Glos. F. CP25/1/74/21 no. 462). D. 1262 (*Ann. Waverley*, p. 353).

Philip Occ. 9 Feb. 1259 (*sic*, see above) (*YB, XIV (ii)*, p. 148); 3 July 1272 (*Staffs F. 2*, p. 254; *Staffs Plea Rolls, Henry III*, p. 206); Oct. 1271 x Oct. 1272 (*Pedigrees from the Plea Rolls*, p. 501).

Warin –1279 Occ. 20 Jan. 1279 (*Warws. F.*, I, no. 946). Cess. 1279 (*Ann. Waverley*, p. 392; *Ann. Worcester*, p. 476).

Jordan of Twangham 1279– Pr. of Waverley, succ. 1279 (*Ann. Waverley*, p. 392; *Ann. Worcester*, p. 476). Occ. 27 Jan. 1285 (*Warws F.*, II, no. 1018); 1285 (PRO, Just.1/956, m. 4).

William Occ. 20 Jan. 1288 (*Warws. F.*, II, no. 1061); 14 Aug. 1289 going overseas (*CPR 1281–92*, p. 319); (W.) 4 June 1291 (PRO, E326/105; E315/46/85); 7 Apr. 1298 (BL, Add. Cht. 48519A–B).

Henry Occ. *c.* Mar. 1305 (PRO, SC1/16/59); Mich. 1305 (PRO, CP40/153, m. 351); Trin. 1309 (PRO, CP40/178, attorneys m. 2d).

Simon Mentd 1313 as a former abb. (*YB, XIV (ii)*, p. 147). His position in the sequence of abbots is unclear.

Richard Occ. 30 Dec. 1329, 31 Jan. 1332 (*CCR 1327–30*, p. 591; *CCR 1330–33*, p. 531).

Geoffrey Occ. 20 Aug. 1332 (*CCR 1330–33*, p. 594).

John Brid –1333/5 Occ. n.d. as abb. of Combe (*Hatton's Book of Seals*, p. 344, no. 499). Res. 1333; provided as bp of Cloyne, 10 Aug. 1333 (*Orig. Papal Letters*, p. 83, no. 165), but did not gain full possession until 1335 (*Chronology*, p. 342).

Geoffrey –1345 Occ. 1 Feb. 1337 (Cheshire RO, DCR.26/1B/19); Mich. 1337 (PRO, CP40/312, attorneys m. 5d). Killed at Combe 6 July 1345, commn of oyer and terminer about his death 29 July 1345 (*CPR 1343–45*, pp. 573, 580).

John Occ. 28 Oct. 1351 (*CCR 1349–54*, p. 396).

Robert of Atherstone (Atherestone) **1352–** Abb. of Stoneleigh, made abb. of Combe 23 May 1352 (*Ctl. Stoneleigh*, p. 254). Mentioned 6 Feb. 1364 as former abb. (*CPR 1351–64*, p. 526).

John Occ. 22 June 1361 (PRO, C81/1788/18).

The next recorded abb., **William of Bretford**, occ. 20 Jan. 1397 (*CPR 1396–99*, p. 55).

COMBERMERE (Ches.), St Mary and St Michael (Savigny) f. 3 Nov. 1135

Lists in *VCH Ches.*, III, 155–6; *Heads*, I, 130–1. See also J. Hall, *Book of the Abbey of Combermere*.

Thomas Was apparently dep. *c.* Apr. 1201 (*CRR*, I, 454; II, 9) but he, or another of the same name, occ. 1203 x 1204 (Cheney, *Inn. III*, no. 542). Occ. (T.) 1215 x 1223 (*Ctl. Dieulacres*, p. 311); 1216 x 1219 (BL, Harl. ms. 3868, f. 7r); 29 Aug. 1228 (*CPR 1225–32*, p. 223).

Robert Occ. 1228+ ?1230 x 1232 (*Ctl. Staffs 3*, p. 423; Staffs RO, D(W). 1721/1/1, f. 29r); 15 July 1236 (*Staffs F. 2*, p. 230).

Richard Occ. 1237 (Staffs RO, D(W). 1721/1/1, f. 33r); (R.) *c.* 1237 x 1240 (SRRC, 972/222/4/6).

Simon Occ. (S.) *c.* 1237 x 1240 (*Ctl. Staffs. 3*, p. 425); (S.) 4 Apr. 1241 (*Ctl. Dieulacres*, p. 362; *Ches. Sheaf*, XXXV, 57); 1 Aug. 1242 (*Ctl. Trentham*, pp. 314–15); 6 Oct. 1242 (*Salop F.*, 4th Ser. VI, 179); 8 Nov. 1245 (*CChR 1327–41*, p. 203); 3 Feb. 1248, 18 Nov. 1249 (*Staffs F. 2*, p. 242).

William de Waresley (Warley) Occ. 23 Feb. 1255 (Staffs RO, B/1/20/1/5); Jan. 1256

(*Shropshire Eyre*, nos. 741–2). Desc. as former abb. by Easter 1263 (Eyton, *Salop*, VIII, 13, citing PRO, KB26/172, m. 19d); as former abb. in 1272 (*Earliest English Law Reports*, I, p. 12).

A case at Easter term 1271 involved the pr. and cans. of Combermere, the abbey presumably being vacant (Eyton, *Salop*, VIII, 13, citing PRO, KB26/203, mm. 2, 48d).

Richard –?1281 Occ. Easter 1279 (*Staffs Plea Rolls 1272–94*, p. 93); 31 Oct. 1280, 23 Jan., 27 July 1281 (PRO, C85/3/20; 3/26; 3/54).

Sequestration and citation of unnamed abb. 26 July 1281; letter of caption 27 July 1281 (*Reg. Pecham*, I, 147, 175–6). In 1281 an unnamed abb. of Combermere was dep. by authority of the General Chapter of Cîteaux (Canivez, III, 216).

Adam Occ. Easter 1282 (PRO, CP40/45, m. 74); 10 Aug 1289 (*CPR 1281–92*, p. 318); Easter 1289 (Hall, *Combermere*, p. 16); 25 Feb. 1293 (*Staffs F. 3*, p. 52); 1296 (Hall, *Combermere*, p. 15); 1296 x 1297 (Hill, *Eccles. Letter-books*, p. 171); 21 July 1300 (*CPR 1292–1301*, p. 529); Dec. 1300 (Duke of Hamilton's Archive, Lennoxlove, bundle 3020).

William de Lee Occ. (W.) possibly 1302 (Whitaker, *Whalley*, I, 178); 4 Apr. 1305 (*Staffs Plea Rolls 1294–1307*, 126–7); 28 Apr. 1306 (*Mon. Angl.*, V, 321; Whitaker, Whalley, I, 90, n,2).

Robert Occ. 1 Mar. 1310 (*CPR 1307–13*, p. 213). Is this the same as abb. R. (*Mon. Seals*, p. 26), who occ. in PRO, C146/5852, n.d. but dated *c.* 1304?

Richard (de) Rodeyerd (Rodierd, Rodiherde) –1316 Name (*Staffs Plea Rolls 1307–27*, p. 117). Occ. 21 Sept. 1314 (PRO, C81/1788/19). M. of Whalley before he became abb. of Combermere, d. 1316 (BL, Cotton ms. Titus F. III, f. 261v).

Adam of Burton Occ. 1320 (Whitaker, *Whalley*, I, 93); 1322 (PRO, Wales 29/190); Easter 1326 (*Staffs Plea Rolls 1307–27*, p. 115), but cf. n.1 where it is argued that this is a scribal error for Nicholas (see below), who also occ. in pleas of this term..

Nicholas de Thokeby [Kesteven] M. of Croxden, received *temp.* abb. William de Overa (1297–1308); afterwards abb. of Hulton (q.v.). Occ. 20 Oct. 1324, Nov. 1328 (*DKR 36*, app. II, no. 1, p. 119); Mich. 1326 (*Staffs Plea Rolls 1307–27*, p. 117); Hil. 1327 – Mich. 1328 (*Index to Placita de Banco*, pp. 80, 588); 1330 (PRO, Just.1/167, m. 59d); 1336 (SRRC, 327/12/43); 1338 (*HMC Westmorland etc.*, p. 360).

Roger Lyndley Noted in list of monks of Whalley, afterwards abb. of Combermere (Whitaker, *Whalley*, I, 112). Occ. 16 Feb. 1339 (BL, Harl. ms. 2072, f. 69r). Roger briefly removed from office in or just before 1344 (Canivez, III, 481). Said to be d. by 1348 (*VCH* citing PRO, SC8/244/15406). This is an incorrect reference and as yet the correct document cannot be located. Ancient petition 15406 (SC8/309/15406) has been checked without success.

John of Chester Occ. 19 Apr. 1350 (SRRC, 327/12/46); 6 Dec. 1352 (SRRC, 327/12/21); 24 & 26 Feb. 1355 (*DKR 36*, app. II, no. 1, p. 119; Ormerod, *Cheshire*, III, 403).

Richard of Chester Occ. 6 June 1360 (*CPR 1358–61*, p. 419); 1362 (Ormerod, *Cheshire*, III, 403); Jan. 1362 x Jan. 1363 (*DKR 28*, app. 6, p. 61); 20 July 1377 (BL, Add. Cht. 50876), presumably the unnamed abb. reported to be 'so feeble in body' that he could not act as a collector of the subsidy 8 June 1377 (*CFR 1368–77*, p. 400). *VCH Lancs*, II, 136 mentions his attempts in 1365 to oust abb. Lindley of Whalley and replace him with William Banaster. The next recorded abb., **John**, occ. 1379 (Bennett, 'Lancs and Cheshire Clergy', p. 23).

CONWAY (Caernarvon) (Strata Florida) (Aberconway, Maenan) f. 24 July 1186 (at Rhedynog-felen); ref. 1283 by Edward I (at Maenan).

Lists in Rhys Hays, *History of Aberconway* (in index); *Fasti Cistercienses Cambrenses*, p. 188.

Unnamed abb. excused from attendance at the General Chapter on account of infirmity 1216 (Canivez, I, 454).

Anian Occ. 17–28 June 1258 (*CPR 1247–58*, pp. 639, 664; *Litt. Wallie*, nos. 7, 33).

Maredwt Occ. 21 July 1278 (*Litt. Wallie*, no. 203); (M.) 5 Sept. 1281 (ibid., no. 30).

David Occ. 15 Oct. 1284 (ibid., no. 71; *CCR 1279–88*, p. 407); (D.) 27 Oct. 1284 (*Litt. Wallie* no. 187). Fealty taken 28 Apr. 1301 (*CPR 1343–45*, p. 231).

Tudor Occ. 1303 (Hays, pp. 86, 117, citing A. Hadley, *Register of Conway* (London, 1900), p. x).

Ieuan ap Rhys occ. uncertain date (prob. 14th cent.) (Hays, p. 155 and n.). Possibly a misreading for John ap Rhys a century later (*Fasti Cistercienses Cambrenses*, p. 198). See also 1385 below.

Clement Occ. 4, 19 Feb. 1344 (*CCR 1343–46*, pp. 338, 351).

Cynfrig Occ. in relation to debts dating from before 12 May 1343 (Hays, p. 122, citing PRO, SC6/1171/5, m. 2); 12 Mar. 1353 a prisoner in Denbigh castle (Hays, p. 94); (Cynric) 1356–7 (ibid., p. 97).

The next recorded abb., **John**, occ. 1378 x 1379 (PRO, E179/1/4, m. 1; Hays, p. 128). Perhaps the same as **John ap Rees** who occ. 1385 (PRO, SC8/139/6928).[6]

CROXDEN (Staffs) (Aunay-sur-Odon) f. 1176 (at Cotton); 19 May 1178 (at Croxden). Lists in *VCH Staffs*, III, 230; Ann. and list in BL, Cotton ms. Faustina B. VI, ff. 68v–94v; *Heads*, I, 131.

Thomas of Woodstock 1178–1229 1st abb. el. 28 May 1178, abb. 51½ years, d. 4(?) Dec. 1229 (Ann., ff. 72r–73v; list, f. 93r). Occ. Hil. term 1229 (*CRR*, XIII, no. 1557). Bur. in Chapter House (Ann., f. 73v).

Walter of Chacombe (Chacumbe, Chakumbe) **1230–1234** 2nd abb., el. 1230 (Ann., f. 73v; list, f. 93r). Occ. 21 May 1234 (*Staffs F. 2*, p. 228).

William of Ashbourne (Esseburn) **1234–1237** 3rd abb., el. 1 July 1234 (Ann., f. 74r; list, f. 93r). Occ. (W.) 1236 (Staffs RO, D593/A/2/23/22). D. 22 Sept. 1237, returning, it is believed, from Cîteaux; bur. overseas (Ann., f. 74r).

John of Tilton 1237–1242 4th abb., el. 1237, res. 1242 (Ann., f. 74r; list, f. 93r). Occ. 23 Feb. 1240 (*Staffs F. 2*, p. 234); 4 Apr. 1241 (*Ctl. Dieulacres*, p. 362; *Cheshire Sheaf*, XXXV (1940), 57).

Walter of London 1242–1268 5th abb., pr. of Stratford Langthorne, el. and took up office 25 May 1242 (Ann., f.74r; list, f. 93r). Occ. 1256 (PRO, Shrops F., CP25/1/103/4, no. 54). D. 29 Oct. 1268 *relinquens posteris memoriam sui in benedictione* (Ann., f. 75v). Abbey vacant 4 months 3 days (ibid.).

William of Howton (Houton) **1269–1274** 6th abb., succ. 22 Feb. 1269 (Ann., f. 75v; list, f. 93r). D. 16 Sept. 1274 at Dijon, bur. at Cîteaux and more than 400 abbs. present (Ann., f. 76r).

Henry of Measham (Meisam, Meysam, Moysam) **1274–1284** 7th abb., succ. 13 Dec. 1274 and ruled well for 10 years, res. 11 June 1284 on account of infirmity (Ann., f. 76r; list, f. 93r). D. 1286 (Ann., f. 77r). Abbey vacant 3 months less 3 days (Ann., f. 76r).

John of Billesdon (Billisdone, Billysdon(e)) **1284–1293** 8th abb., el. 11 June 1284, d. 8 July 1293, bur. in Chapter House beside Thomas, the 1st abb. (Ann., ff. 76v, 77v; list, f. 93r). Abbey vacant one year less three weeks three days (Ann., f. 77v).

Richard of Twyford (Twiford, Twyforde) **1294–1297** 9th abb., el. 13 June 1294, d. 9 June 1297 (Ann., ff. 77v–78r; list, f. 93r). Bur. in Chapter House (Ann., f. 78r). Abbey vacant 7 months 6 days (ibid.).

William of Over (Oure, Overa, Overe) **1297–1308** 10th abb. el. 30 Dec. 1297, dep. 1308 by General Chapter for failure to attend meeting (Ann., ff. 78r, 79r; list, f. 93r).

---

[6] *Arch. Camb.* 136 (1987), p. 145, no. 233 desc. a seal of Henry, abb. of Conway late 14th or 15th cents. It is just possible that the legend transcript is mistaken and it refers to Henry, abb. of Abbotsbury 1354–76.

Richard of Ashby (Esseby) **1309–1313** 11th abb., el. 12 Mar. 1309, res. 23 May 1313 (Ann., f. 79v; list, f. 93r).

Thomas of Casterton (Castreton(e)) **1313–** 12th abb., pr. of Croxden, el. 24 May 1313 (Ann., f. 79v; list, f. 93r).

Richard of Ashby 1319–1329 Re-el. 11 June 1319 (Ann., f. 80v; list, f. 93r – called 13th abb.). Res. 23 May 1329 on account of infirmity (Ann., f. 81v – called 11th abb.). D. 10 Nov. 1333 in the 52nd year of his conversion and, it is believed, aged 70 (ibid., f. 83v – called 11th abb.).

Richard of Shepshed (Schepisheved) **1329–** 13th abb., el. 24 May 1329 (Ann., ff. 81v, 86v; list, f. 93r – called 14th abb.). Occ. 1329, 1331 (*Staffs Plea Rolls 1–15 Edward III*, pp. 11, 35); 7 Jan. 1335 (Ann., f. 83v, cf. f. 86v); Mich. 1337 (PRO, CP40/312, m. 391).

Alexander of Cubley (Colbeley, Cubbeley) **–1368** Dep. 13 Jan. 1368 by Visitors (Ann., f. 89v; list, f. 93r *sub anno* 1367– called 15th abb.).

William (of) Gunston (Gunstone) **1368–** El. 13 Jan. 1368 (Ann., ff. 89v–90r; list, f. 93r – called 16th abb.). Occ. 1375, 1380 (*Staffs Plea Rolls 1360–87*, pp. 124, 167). Mentd as late abb. 6 May 1382 (PRO, C67/29, no. 7). Occ. as *monachus de Oken'* 22 Nov. 1398 – Oaken belonged to Croxden (*SHC*, new ser. VI, pt 2, p. 183).

CWMHIR, *see* ABBEY CWMHIR

CYMMER (Merioneth) (Abbey Cwmhir) f. 1198 x 9

Lists in *Fasti Cistercienses Cambrenses*, p. 188; *Heads*, I, 131.
Esau Occ. 1209 (*Mon. Angl.*, V, 459).
Llywelyn Occ. 9 July 1274, 7 Nov. 1281 (*Lit. Wallie*, nos. 45, 69).
Cadwgan (Caducanus) Occ. 27 Oct. 1284 (ibid., no. 189).
Philip Occ. 19 Oct. 1343 (*CCR 1343–46*, p. 244).
The next recorded abb., **John Loncastell**, occ. 20 Sept. 1398 (*CPL*, IV, 304).

DARNHALL (Ches.) (Abbey Dore, Vale, Royal) f. 1266 x 1272 (foundation cht. 14 Jan. 1274); moved to Vale Royal 1281.

See under **VALE ROYAL**

DIEULACRES (Staffs), St Mary and St Benedict (Combermere) f. 12 May 1153 (at Poulton); 1 May 1214 (at Dieulacres).

Lists in *VCH Staffs*, III, 234; *Heads*, I, 131.
Richard Occ. 1214 and later (*CCR 1339–41*, pp. 204–5; *SHC*, 1913, p. 73).
Robert Occ. 1216 x 1219 (?) (BL, Harl. ms. 3868, f. 7r); Mich. term 1228 (*CRR*, XIII, no. 825); 3 Nov. 1228 (*Lancs F.*, pp. 54–5, no. 30).
Adam Occ. n.d. (1230 x 1232) (*Ctl. Staffs 3*, p. 423; BL, Cotton Cht. XI. 38); n.d. (*Arley Chts.*, p. 45).
William Occ. n.d. (1237 x1240) (*Ctl. Staffs 3*, p. 425).
Joseph Mentd as former abb. in case of 1282, *temp.*, grandfather of the then plaintiff (*Chester City Courts*, p. 40). His precise place in the sequence is uncertain.
Stephen Occ. 17 Apr. 1244, 3 Nov. 1244 (BL, Harl. ms. 2101, f. 43r: *Ctl. Dieulacres*, p. 360); 3 Nov. 1244 (*Staffs F. 2*, p. 236)
William Occ. 3 Feb. 1251 (*Staffs F. 2*, p. 244); n.d. (mid-13th cent.) (Eaton estate cht. 37); n.d. (1250 x 1259) (*Ctl. Staffs 3*, p. 428).[7]

---

[7] In 1272 Ralph is mentd as former abb. (*Staffs Plea Rolls, Henry III*, p. 200) but this prob. refers to abb. Ralph *c.* 1191 x 1211 (*Heads*, I, 131).

Hamo Occ. n.d. (mid-late 13th cent., ascribed to 1266 or 1267 acc. to mayor of Chester, a witness) (Eaton estate cht. 53; Sleigh, *Leek*, p. 63).

Walter of Morton M. of Croxden (ann., f. 93r); occ. 1272 (*Staffs Plea Rolls, Henry III*, p. 200).

Ranulph Occ. 6 Oct. 1279 (*Staffs F. 3*, p. 34); Easter 1282 (PRO, CP40/45, m. 74).

Elias Occ. n.d. (late 13th cent, ascribed to 1274 x 1279) (*Ctl. Staffs 3*, p. 430); 8 June 1287 (*CPR 1281–92*, p. 269).

Richard Occ. Hilary 1292 (*Staffs Plea Rolls 1272–94*, p. 205). ? Vacated abbey by Nov. 1292 since his unnamed successor stated in assize roll that he had only been abb. 3 months (ibid., p. 267).

Richard Occ. 25 July 1293 (PRO, C241/22/41, 44).

Robert le Burgiloun (Burgulun, Burgyloun) **1294–** Bl. 30 May 1294 (*Reg. Sutton*, V, 3). Occ. 29 Sept. 1294, *c.* 29 Sept. 1299 (Eaton estate chts. 97, 107); 1 Mar. 1302 (*Ctl. Staffs 3*, p. 433).

Nicholas of Banbury (Bannebur') Occ. 1 Dec. 1308 (ibid.); 22 Aug. 1312 (PRO, E40/8239; *Reg. Greenfield*, IV, no. 1745n); July 1315 x July 1316 (BL, Harl. ms. 2063, f. 50r); Easter 1317 (PRO, CP40/218, m. 215).

Peter Occ. 1 Nov. 1330 (Sleigh, *Leek*, pp. 63–4); (P.) *post* 14 Aug. (1332) (PRO, C270/8/31).

Ralph Occ. Trin. term 1345 (*SHC*, XIV, p. 65); (Randolf) Trin. term 1345 (*CPR 1345–48*, p. 83); 12 July 1345 (BL, Add. Cht. 72165).

Robert of Brigge (Brugge) Occ. 12 Aug. 1352 (*CPP*, p. 233); 12 Nov. 1353 (*Reg. Black Prince*, III, 130).

William of Lichfield (Lichfeld, Lichefeld, Lychefeld) Occ. 23 May 1377 (PRO, C67/28B, m. 6); 1379, 1380 (*CPR 1377–81*, pp. 362, 516); Jan. 1381 or 1382 committed to Marshalsea (*SHC*, XIV, p. 154); 29 Apr. 1382 (PRO, C67/29, m. 9).

DORE, *see* ABBEY DORE

DUNKESWELL (Devon), St Mary and St Nicholas (Forde) f. 16 Nov. 1201
Lists in Oliver, p. 394; *Heads*, I, 131; *TDA*, 9 (1877), 391.

William Occ. 1202 x 1219 (*Ctl. Canonsleigh*, no. 62).

John Occ. 19 Mar. 1219 (*Dorset F.*, I, 24). An unnamed abb., prob. John, d. 1223 (*Ann. Waverley*, p. 298).

Richard Occ. 25 July 1228 (*Devon F.*, I, p. 79, no. 152); 18 Feb. 1233 (*CR 1231–34*, p. 295); n.d. (early Henry III?) (Devon RO, Magee catalogue no. 416).

John Occ. 28 June 1238 (*Devon F.*, I, p. 142, no. 283).

Ralph 1245–1252 M. of Waverley, abb. of Tintern, el. 1245 (*Ann. Waverley*, p. 336). Occ. 1 July 1249 (*Devon F.*, I, p. 232, no. 462). El. abb. of Waverley 1252 (*Ann. Waverley*, p. 345).

Thomas Occ. 13 Oct. 1253, 18 Nov. 1255, 25 Nov. 1256 (*Devon F.*, I, pp. 273–4, 284, 295–6, nos. 541, 559, 578).

John Occ. 12 Mar. 1260 (Hants RO, Wriothesley deeds 5M53/153); n.d. (1274 x 1283) (PRO, E40/4864); 12 May 1275 (*Devon F.*, II, pp. 9–10, no. 779); n.d. (1257 x 1278) (PRO, DL25/214). Desc. as predecessor of the then abb. in Hil. 1286 (PRO, Just.1/1273, m. 6).

William of Combe (Comba) Occ. 6 Dec. 1307 (Seymour, *Torre Abbey*, p. 194, nos. 189, 190); Mich. 1310 (PRO, CP40/183, attorneys m. 13).

John 1311– Bl. and prof. obed. 17 Oct. 1311 (*Reg. Stapeldon*, p. 207).

William 1318– Bl. 16 Apr. 1318 (ibid., p. 208).

William of Stanlake 1321– Bl. 8 Sept. 1321 (ibid.). Occ. Mich. 1325 (*TDA*, 9 (1877), 386).

William of Combe (Coumbe) Occ. Trin. 1327 (*Index to Placita de Banco*, p. 112).

William (? the same as above) Occ. Easter–Mich. 1328 (ibid., p. 100); 6 July 1329 (*CCR 1327–30*, p. 558).

John Occ. 31 Jan. 1340 (*Reg. Gandavo*, II, 924); 8 Oct. 1341 (ibid., 971).

Simon 1341– Bl. and prof. obed. 22 Feb. 1341 (*Reg. Grandisson*, II, 943).

John de Wellis 1346– Cellarer of Newenham, el. 22 Apr. 1346 (Bodl., ms. Top. Devon d. 5, f. 6r). Occ. 6 Oct. 1347, 11 Oct. 1347, 28 May 1348 (*CCR 1346–49*, pp. 396, 394, 518); 1 Oct. 1346 (PRO, C81/1788/22).

William of Wedmore (Wedmour) 1353– Bl. and prof. obed. 7 Apr. 1353 (*Reg. Grandisson*, II, 1123). Occ. 24 May 1373, 22 Nov. 1373 (*Reg. Brantingham*, I, 304, 319).

Richard Occ. n.d. (?1377) (PRO, E179/24/10B); 29 Aug. 1378 (*CPR Supplement*, no. 70); 22 Sept. 1378 (ibid., no. 74; *CCR 1377–81*, p. 211).

The next recorded abb., **Robert Orcharde**, was professed 20 Apr. 1382 (*Reg. Brantingham*, I, 459–60).

FLAXLEY (Dene) (Glos) (Bordesley) f. 30 Sept. 1151
   Lists in *VCH Glos*, II, 96; *Ctl. Flaxley*, pp. v–vi, 85–6; *Heads*, I, 131–2.

Roger Last recorded (R.) 2 Oct. 1213 (*St Davids Acta*, no. 67n.).

William Occ. 15 July 1221 (PRO, Glos F. CP25/1/73/5, no. 40).

Osmund Occ. as pr. of Flaxley under abb. William 1221 (ibid.). Occ. as abb. Easter 1229 (*CRR*, XIII, no. 1707). 6 Oct. 1231 (PRO, Glos F. CP25/1/73/9, no. 135). Occ. (O.) n.d. (PRO, E315/43/171).

William Aug. 1253 (BL Add. ms. 15668, f. 61n; BL Add. ms. 18461, f. 86v). Occ. 30 May 1255, 6 June 1255, 13 June 1255, 6 May 1257 (PRO, Glos F., CP25/1/74/23, no. 504; 74/23, no. 503; 74/22, no. 494; 74/24, no. 526). Presumably the unnamed abb. who was sent to Wales on the king's business in 1255 (*CPR 1247–58*, p. 452).

Hugh Occ. 5 Sept. 1276 (PRO, C106/53). Seal (*Mon. Seals*, p. 35).

William 1277– Prof. obed. n.d. (between entries of 11 Feb. 1278 and 31 Dec. 1277 (*Reg. Cantilupe*, p. 157). Occ. Mich. 1277 x Mich. 1278 (PRO, E159/51, m. 20d); Trin. 1280 (PRO, CP40/34, m. 7d); (W.) Mich. 1281 x Mich. 1282 (PRO, E159/55, m. 6).

Nicholas 1288– Prof. obed. 1 Aug. 1288 (*Reg. Swinfield*, p. 185).

William Occ. 8 July 1307 (PRO, Glos F. CP25/1/75/41, no. 310).

William de Rya 1314– Bl. 15 Sept. 1314 (*Reg. Swinfield*, p. 495); 14 Sept. 1316 (PRO, E42/412). Seal (*Mon. Seals*, p. 35).

J. Occ. 20 Nov. 1321 (*Reg. Orleton (Hereford)*, pp. 204–5).

Robert Occ. 23 Aug. 1332 (PRO, C270/8/46).

Hugh Occ. 2 May 1338 (*CCR 1337–39*, p. 362).

William Occ. 20 June 1361 (*HMC Var. Coll.*, IV, 178).

Richard Peyt 1372– Bl. 6 June 1372 (*Reg. Courtenay*, pp. 9–10).

FORDE (Dorset, formerly Devon) (Waverley) f. 3 May 1136 (at Brightley); 1141 (at Forde)
   List in *Ctl. Forde*, pp. i–ii; *Heads*, I, 132.

Roger 1214–1236 Sub-pr. of Forde, app. 1214 (after 21 Apr.) (*Ann. Waverley*, p. 282). Occ. 1227 and 1228 (*Devon F.*, I, nos. 151, 728, 730); 1235 (*Soms F.*, I, 97); 27 Mar. 1236 (Oliver, p. 339). Cess. 1236 (*Ann. Waverley*, p. 316).

John of Warwick 1236–1240 M. of Forde, el. 1236 (ibid.). Occ. from 9 Feb. 1237 to 9 July 1238 (*Devon F.*, I, nos. 264, 287); 1239 x 1240 (Exeter D. & C., vicars choral doct no. 3076). D. abroad in 1240 on his return from the Cistercian General Chapter (*Ann. Waverley*, p. 328).

Adam 1240– M. of Waverley, succ. 1240 (ibid.). Occ. from 3 Feb. 1243 to 22 July 1256 (*Soms F.*, I, 118, 162); 12 June 1244, 6 June 1249 (*Devon F.*, I, nos. 396, 503).

Thomas Occ. 11 June 1258 (*Ctl. Forde*, no. 605).

William –1262 D. at Waverley 1262, bur. in the chapter-house (*Ann. Waverley*, p. 353).

William (le Fria *alias* **Fry) of Crewkerne** (Crook, Crukerne) **–1284** Occ. ?1267, Hil. term 1268 to 1273 (*Ctl. Forde*, nos. 627, 374, 423); 20 Jan. 1268 (*Devon F.*, I, no. 671); 1272 (Cornwall RO, AR.1/1076); 1275 (*Reg. W. Bronescombe*, II, no. 1089). Excommunicated May 1276; signification to king 24 May (*Reg. Bronescombe*, pp. 86–7, 89–91; *Reg. W. Bronescombe*, II, nos. 1176–7, 1215). Occ. Mich. 1278 x Mich 1279 (PRO, E159/52, m. 4d); 6 Mar. 1282 (*Reg. Quivil*, p. 357).

Nicholas 1284– Bl. 1 Jan. 1284 (ibid., p. 345). Occ. (N.) 26 June 1289 (BL, Add. Cht. 13971); Mich. 1284 x Mich. 1285 (PRO, E159/58, m. 13). Occ. Nov. 1285 x Nov. 1286 to 14 July 1289, ?1290 (*Ctl. Forde*, nos. 407, 360, 624); 19 June 1289 (Oliver, p. 385).

William (le Fria) **–1297** Occ. *c.* 1290 x 1297, 1291 to 1297 (*Ctl. Forde*, nos. 1, 11, 59, 65, 477). Abb. of Newenham 1297 (q.v.). Subsequently returned from Newenham *ubi prius per plurimos annos abbatizavit*; bur. at Forde 1303 (Bodl., ms. Top. Devon D. 5, f. 5r).

Thomas Occ. 26 May 1301 (*Ctl. Forde*, no. 641).

Robert Occ. 1302 x 1305, *temp.* Henry, dean of Wells (ibid., no. 325).

Henry Occ. 16 Jan. 1313 (*Reg. Stapeldon*, p. 218). Mentd as former abb. in case of 1342 (*YB 16 Edward III, part 2*, p. 216).

William 1319– Bl. 22 Sept. 1319 (ibid.). Occ. 12 Mar. 1320, 7 Feb. 1321, 16 Oct. 1327 (*Ctl. Forde*, nos. 245, 244, 438); n.d. (Devon RO, Exeter deeds ED/M/300).

John de Worton *alias* **Worterlegh** (Worteleigh) **1328–** Bl. and prof. obed. 24 June 1328 (*Reg. Grandisson*, I, 350, cf. 368). Occ. 10 Apr. 1329 (ibid., 222); 11 June 1337 (*Beauchamp Reg.*, p. 87); 27 July 1337 (*Ctl. Forde*, no. 30).

Nicholas Occ. n.d. (after 1336 x 1337, ?1338 x 1340 (ibid., no. 133).

John (of) Childhay (Childehegh, Childehey(e)) Occ. 17 Sept. 1340 (*Beauchamp Reg.*, p. 91); 10 Apr. 1341, 11 Oct. 1341 (*Ctl. Forde*, nos. 361, 658); 1341 (*Reg. Grandisson*, II, 971); 1342 (PRO, C241/129/199); Easter 1343 (*Cist. Devon*, p. 180); excommunicated 18 July 1343 (Salisbury, Reg. Wyvil I, f. 127v); 17 Nov. 1345 (*CPR 1345–48*, p. 9).

William of Cumnor (Comenore) Previously abb. of Bindon (q.v.). Occ. 15 Oct. 1350 (PRO, C241/129/199); 9 Nov. 1350, 4 Feb. 1351 (*CPL*, III, 404, 399).

Adam 1354– Bl. and prof. obed. 29 Sept. 1354 (*Reg. Grandisson*, II, 1134). Occ. 5 Aug. 1359 (*Ctl. Forde*, no. 490).

John of Faringdon Occ. 15 Aug. 1365 (ibid., no. 495).

John Chylheglys Occ. 29 May 1373, 22 Nov. 1373 (*Reg. Brantingham*, II, 304, 319); n.d. (? 1377) (PRO, E179/24/10B).

The next recorded abb., **Walter Burstoke**, prof. obed. 11 Apr. 1378 (*Reg. Brantingham*, I, 387). Seal (*Hatton Wood MSS.*, p. 12).

FOUNTAINS (Yorks W.) (Clairvaux) f. 27 Dec. 1132

Lists in *VCH Yorks*, III, 137–8; *Heads*, I, 132–3. See Clay, *Early Abbots*, for ch. of the abbots in *Mem. Fountains* I, 130ff. – note particularly that usually no details of vacancy periods are given, that some abbots are omitted from the numbering scheme adopted by the ch., and that the calculations of an abbot's rule are based on the lunar month of 28 days not the calendar month.

John II 1211–1220 Described as 9th abb. (*Mem. Fountains*, I, 134). Abb. (not named) bl. at Melrose 13 Dec. 1211 (*Ch. Melrose*, p. 55). Occ. Whitsun 1212 (*Ctl. Fountains*, II, 626); 7 Dec. 1218, 27 Jan. 1219 (*Yorks. F., 1218–31*, pp. 7, 15). Pandulf, bp of Norwich, provides him to the see of Ely 16 Jan. [1220] (PRO, SC1/4/131). Royal ass. to eln as Bp of Ely 24 Jan. 1220 (*CPR 1216–25*, p. 224). Consecrated 8 Mar. 1220 (*Mem. Fountains*, I, 171). D. 6 May 1225 (*Mem. Fountains*, I, 134).

John of Kent (Cancia) **1220–1247** Described as 10th abb., formerly cellarer of Fountains

(*Mem. Fountains*, I, 135). Succ. 1220 (Baildon, I, 61). Occ. (J.) 20 Oct. 1220 (*Ctl. Wetheral*, p. 52). D. 25 Nov. 1247. Ruled 28 years, 7 months, 7 days (*Mem. Fountains*, I, 134–5); m.i. (10th abb. D. 25 Nov.) in chapter house (Gilyard-Beer, p. 47).

Stephen of Eston 1247–1252 Described as 11th abb. (*Mem. Fountains*, I, 137). Cellarer of Fountains, abb. of Sallay, abb. of Newminster. Occ. 16 Nov. 1248 (*Ctl. Fountains*, II, 532). D. at Vaudey 6 Sept. 1252 (*Ctl. Fountains*, II, p. 765); d. 6 Sept. 1252, ruled 5 years, 10 months, 5 days, bur. in chapter house at Vaudey '*ubi miraculis choruscat*' (*Mem. Fountains*, I, 137–8). See Sharpe, *Latin Writers*, p. 622; B.K. Lackner ed., *Stephen of Sawley: Treatises* (Cistercian Fathers 36, Kalamazoo 1984).

William of Allerton 1252–1258 Described as 12th abb., formerly pr. of Fountains, cr. abb. 22 Sept. 1252 (*Mem. Fountains*, I, 138) or 23 Sept. (*Ctl. Fountains*, II, 766). D. 1 Dec. 1258, ruled 5 years, 3 months, 2 days (*Mem. Fountains*, I, 138); m.i. (d. 1 Dec., 12th abb.), chapter house (Gilyard-Beer, p. 47).

Adam 1258–1259 Described as 13th abb., succ. William (*Mem. Fountains*, I, 138). Occ. *c.*1 May 1259 (*Ctl. Fountains*, II, 713) but acc. to Ch. Fountains, D. 30 April 1259 (*Mem. Fountains*, I, 138); m.i. (damaged: 13th abb.) chapter house (Gilyard-Beer, p. 47).

Alexander 1259–1265 Described as 14th abb. (*Mem. Fountains*, I, 139). Occ. in *Ctl. Fountains* from 15 June 1259 to 1265 (II, 565; I, 156). D. 11 Oct. 1265, ruled 5 years, 7 months, 9 days, bur. in chapter house (*Mem. Fountains*, I, 139).

Reginald –1274 Described as 15th abb. (*Mem. Fountains*, I, 139). Occ. from 5 Nov. 1267 to 23 June 1273 (*Ctl. Fountains*, I, 433, 590). D. 25 Oct. 1274, ruled 9 yrs, 7 months (*Mem. Fountains*, I, 139) but d. 24 Oct. and bur. in chapter house (m.i.) (Gilyard-Beer, p. 47).

Peter Aling (Alyng) **1275–1279** El. 1275 (Baildon, I, 61). Occ. 4 July 1275 (*Ctl. Fountains*, II, p. 545). Cess. 8 July 1279, ruled 4 years, 3 months, 23 days (*Mem. Fountains*, I, 139 – not given a number in the sequence of abbots) but occ. 18 July 1279 (*Ctl. Fountains*, I, 322). D. 11 Aug. 1282 (*Mem. Fountains*, I, 139).

Nicholas 1279 Described as 16th abb., cr. 8 July 1279 and d. 26 Dec. 1279, ruled 6 months, 9 days, bur. in chapter house (*Mem. Fountains*, I, 139). Occ. before Mich. 1279 (PRO, E159/52 m. 13).

Adam Raveneswath 1280–1284 Described as 17th abb., cr. 1 July 1280 (*Mem. Fountains*, I, 139). D. 16 May 1284, ruled 3 years, 11 months, 11 days, bur. in chapter house (*Mem. Fountains*, I, 139–40).

Henry Otley (Ottelay) **1284–?1290** Abbey vacant for 26 days after Adam's d. (*Mem. Fountains*, I, 140). El. 1284 (Baildon, I, 61). D. 23 Dec. 1290, ruled 6 years, 6 months, 27 days, bur. at entrance to chapter house – '*hic non habetur in cathalogo abbatum*' (*Mem. Fountains*, I, 140). See below. Did abb. res. or cede, cf. date of earliest occs. of his successor?

Robert Thornton *c.* **1289/90** Occ. (going to General Chapter) 24 Aug. 1289 (*CPR 1281–92*, p. 319); 21 Dec. 1289 (*Mem. Fountains*, I, 140). D. as *quondam* abb. 1306, bur. in chapter house (*Mem. Fountains*, I, 140).

Robert Bishopton (Byssihopton) *c.* **1290/1–1311** Described as 18th abb. (*Mem. Fountains*, I, 141). 1291 '*petitio abbatis de Fontanis in Anglia qui petit dispersionem conventus sui, de patris abbatis consilio, exauditur*' (Canivez, III, 258). Ruled 20 years, 2 months, 28 days from the d. of Henry (*sic*), viz. *temp.* Edward I 16 years, 7 months, 6 days, and *temp.* Edward II 3 years, 8 months, 22 days (*Mem. Fountains*, I, 141). Occ. Mich. 1305 (PRO, CP40/153, mm. 371, 522); Epiphany 1307 (PRO, Just./1107, m. 32); 4 Apr. 1307 (*CPR 1301–7*, p. 547); 14 Nov. 1307 (*CPR 1307–13*, p. 39); 10 June 1310 (*Ctl. Fountains*, II, 565). D. 16 March 1311, bur. in chapter house; abbey vacant for 21 days (*Mem. Fountains*, I, 141).

William Rygton 1311–1316 Described as 19th abb., cr. 6 Apr. 1311 (*Mem. Fountains*, I, 141).

Prof. obed. and bl. 20 May 1311 (*Reg. Greenfield*, II, no. 930a). D. 31 May 1316, ruled 5 years, 1 month, 27 days, bur. in chapter house in front of lectern (*Mem. Fountains*, I, 141).

Walter (of) Coxwold (Cokewold) **1316–1336** Described as 20th abb. (*Mem. Fountains*, I, 142); commn to bp of Durham to bl. 7 June 1316 (*Reg. Greenfield*, V, no. 2796; *Reg. Pal. Dun.*, II, 806). Cess. 1336, ruled 19 years, 12 months, 25 days; d. 8 May 1338, bur. in chapter house (*Mem. Fountains*, I, 142).

Robert Copgrave (Coppegrayve) **1336–1346** Described as 21st abb, cr. 27 May 1336 (*Mem. Fountains*, I, 143–4). Occ. 9 Sept. 1336 (*Ctl. Fountains*, I, 111). Full name (in *Ctl. Fountains*, II, 807). D. 14 March 1346, ruled 9 years, 10 months, 11 days, bur. in chapter house (*Mem. Fountains*, I, 144).

Robert (of) Monkton (Munketon) **1346–1369** Described as 22nd abb., cr. 19 Apr. 1346 (*Mem. Fountains*, I, 144). Bl. and prof. obed. 30 Apr. 1346 (York, Reg. 10, f. 70r). Fully named (*Ctl. Fountains*, I, 367). D. 27 Nov. 1369, ruled 23 years, 8 months, 4 days, bur. in church before the altar of St Peter (*Mem. Fountains*, I, 144).[8]

William Gower 1369–1384 B. Sac. Th. Described as 23rd abb., cr. 11 Nov. [1369, but see previous entry] (*Mem. Fountains*, I, 145). Bl. and prof. obed. 25 Nov. 1369 (York, Reg. 11, f. 293v.). Res. 3 Feb. 1384, ruled 14 years, 3 months, 14 days; in old age he became blind, d. 1390 and bur. before the 9 altars (*Mem. Fountains*, I, 145). Seal (*BM Seals*, no. 3171).

FURNESS (Lancs) (Savigny) f. 4 July 1124 (at Tulketh); 1127 (at Furness)

Lists in *VCH Lancs*, II, 130; *Ctl. Furness*, I, iii, pp. xxvff.; cf. II, iii, pp. xi, 836; based on medieval lists in *Ctl.*, I, i, pp. 8–10; *Heads*, I, 133–4.

Nicholas 1211–*c.* 1217 x 1219 Previously Can. of Warter, m. of Meaux (cf. *Ch. Meaux*, I, 380). Occ. 1211 (*Ctl. Furness*, II, ii, 576–7; *Ctl. Fountains*, I, 61–2) and so the unnamed abb., who was bl. 13 Dec. 1211 (*Ch. Melrose*, f. 29, p. 55); (N.) 1211 x 1214 (*Ctl. Guisborough*, II, 319). Bp. of the Isles 1217 x 9 Nov. 1219 – 1224 x 1225 (res.) (cf. *Fasti Ecclesiae Scoticanae*, p. 200; cf. *Ctl. Furness*, II, iii, 712). N. abb. of Furness occ. with N., bp. of the Isles in PRO, DL 27/111. Presumably to be identified with Nicholas of Meaux, 17th abb. in the medieval list (*Ctl.*, I, i, 9).

[**William** ?William Niger, prev. abb. of Swineshead, then 10th abb. of Furness, acc. to medieval list *Ctl.* I, i, 9; and a William, abb. of Swineshead occ. 1200–1209+; also a William *quondam* abb. of Furness ?1200–1216 (*Ctl. Furness*, II, ii, 477). But this may be the later William of Middleton, who occ. mid-13th cent. (see below).]

Gerard Occ. *c.* 1219 x 1225 (*Ctl. Sallay*, II, no. 417; cf. *Heads*, I, 134, n. 3); n.d. (PRO, DL 25/449); ? = G. occ. n.d. (*Ctl. Furness*, I, i, 246; *Ctl. Sallay*, I, no. 372). Presumably to be identified with the Gerard Bristaldun who occ. as 11th abb. in the medieval list (*Ctl.*, I, i, 9).

Robert –?1236/7 Occ. (R.) 24 Jan. 1225 (?1226) (BL, Egerton ms. 2823, f. 78r–v = *Ctl. Fountains*, I, 216); 1228 (*Reg. Gray*, pp. 23, 161n); 15 June 1231 (*Yorks F., 1218–31*, p. 138); 1232 (*Reg. Gray*, p. 191n); (R.) 14 May 1235 (*Ctl. Furness*, I, i, 253–4; II, i, 270). D. by 8 Apr. 1237 (*CR 1234–37*, p. 430), and presumably the unnamed abb. who was d. by 4 Dec. 1236 (ibid., p. 400). Acc. to medieval list (*Ctl.*, I, i, 9) he was Robert of Denton, prev. abb. of Swineshead, and then 18th abb. of Furness. See *Heads*, I, corrigenda to p. 133.

[**Laurence de Acclome** Occ. in medieval list as 19th abb. between Robert of Denton and William of Middleton (*Ctl.*, I, i, 9) but nothing is known of him, and he does not seem to fit into the sequence.]

---

[8] The charter dated the Wednesday the feast of St Luke 1370 with abb. Robert is clearly a scribal error since St Luke's day fell on a Friday in 1370; it was on a Wednesday in 1368 (*Ctl. Fountains*, I, 68).

William of Middleton (Mideltona) –1267 Occ. in medieval list as 20th abb. (*Ctl.*, I, i, 9). Occ. 8 Apr. 1237 (*CR 1234–37*, p. 430); Mich. 1246 (*Yorks Deeds*, IV, no. 506); 18 Nov. 1246 (*Yorks F., 1246–72*, p. 1; *Ctl. Furness*, II, ii, 425); 3 Feb. 1252 (*Ctl. Furness*, II, ii, 442; *Yorks F., 1246–72*, p. 78). Visited Cîteaux 1252 (*Chron. SHR*, II, 536). Occ. 11 Nov. 1253 (*Ctl. Furness*, II, i, 328); 28 Oct. 1260 (ibid., I, iii, 655). D. after over 30 years rule on 27 Mar. 1267 (*Chron. SHR*, II, 552).

Hugh le Brun (Bron) 1267– Occ. in medieval list as 21st abb. (*Ctl.*, I, i, 9). Sub-pr. of Furness, el. 25 May 1267 (*Chron. SHR*, II, 552); bl. by archbp of York 1 Nov. 1267 (ibid., 553–4). Occ. 1 July 1268 (*Yorks F., 1246–72*, p. 152); 11 Apr. 1271 (*Ctl. Furness*, I, ii, 262); Feb. 1273 (ibid., I, ii, 448–9); (H.) 5 Dec. 1272 (ibid., I, ii, 472); Easter 1282 (PRO, CP40/45, m. 25d).

William of Cockerham (Cokerham, Kokerham, Kokirham) Occ. in medieval list as 22nd abb. (*Ctl.*, I, i, 9–10). Occ. 28 July 1289 (*CPR 1281–92*, p. 317); 8 Feb. 1290 (*CCR 1288–96*, p. 124); May 1292 (*Ctl. Furness*, II, i, 181; BL, Harl. Cht. 83 A 31); 1294 (*Ctl. Furness*, II, ii, 320); 28 Jan. 1294 (ibid., 449).

Hugh Skilhare (Skyllar) Occ. in medieval list as 23rd abb., who was later dep. (ibid., I, i, 10). Occ. 29 Sept. 1297 (ibid., I, ii, 477); 13 Apr. 1299 (ibid., II, iii, 693; BL, Woolley Cht. IX 10); 14 June 1301 (*Ctl. Furness*, II, i, 87). Thomas, earl of Lancaster, requests letters for the abb. of Cîteaux for the release of the former (unnamed) abb. accused of forging seals 6 Nov. [1308] (PRO, SC1/37/49). Alive 24 Nov. 1308 but not abb. (*Cal. Chanc. Warr.*, p. 280).

John of Cockerham (Cokerham, Kokerham) 1303–1347 Occ. in medieval list as 24th abb. (*Ctl.*, I, i, 10). Prof. obed. 1 Nov. 1303 (*Reg. Corbridge*, I, 300). Occ. frequently in *Ctl. Furness* from (J.) Mich. term 1303 (II, ii, 324) to 27 Jan. 1337 (I, ii, 482); 12 Feb. 1338, 6 Feb. 1340 (*CPR 1338–40*, pp. 7, 412); 28 Jan. 1343 (*CPR 1343–45*, p. 10). D. by 9 Dec. 1347 (*CCR 1346–49*, p. 459, cf. York, Reg. 10, f. 70r for date).

Alexander of Walton 1347–?1367 Occ. in medieval list as 25th abb. (*Ctl.*, I, i, 10). Bl. and prof. obed. 9 Dec. 1347 (York, Reg. 10, f. 70r). Occ. 14 June 1349 (*CPP*, p. 169); 14 Feb. 1355 (*CPR 1354–58*, p. 177); 18 June, 26 July 1357 (ibid., pp. 567, 589). Abbey vacant from *c.* 10 Aug. 1367 (*Ctl. Furness*, II, ii, 357 & n).

John de Cokayn (Cokan) 1367– Occ. in medieval list as 26th abb. (*Ctl.*, I, i, 10). Bl. and prof. obed. 19 Sept. 1367 (York, Reg. 11, f. 293r). Name (*Cal. Misc. Inq.*, III, 397). Occ. 18 Apr. 1370, going to Ireland (*CPR 1367–70*, p. 389); 16 May 1373 (*CPR 1370–74*, p. 285). A John occ. 12 Nov. 1383 (*Yorks Deeds*, IV, no. 506), who may be this man, or his successor, the 27th abb., **John Bolton** who occ. 1388 x 1389, 1393 (PRO, DL36/2/98; *York Memo. Bk*, II, 30).

GARENDON (Leics) (Waverley) f. 28 Oct. 1133
Lists in *VCH Leics*, II, 7; *Heads*, I, 134–5.

Adam –1219 (A.) Occ. n.d. (early 13th cent.) (PRO, E315/42/262; *Berkeley Chts.*, no. 212). Res. 1219 to be abb. of Waverley (*Ann. Waverley*, p. 292).

William –1226 Cess. 1226 (ibid., p. 302).

Reginald 1226–1234 Pr. of Garendon, succ. 1226 (ibid.). Said to be the 10th abb. but only eight known (ibid.). Occ. 3 Nov. 1226 (PRO, Leics. F. CP25/1/121/11, no. 11). Cess. 1234 (*Ann. Waverley*, p. 315).

Andrew 1234– Pr. of Garendon, succ. 1234 (ibid.). Occ. 1 Oct. 1235 (PRO, Notts. F. CP25/1/182/6, no. 182); n.d., *temp.* John de Wynton, archdn of Leicester 1235 x 1252 (PRO, E329/180).

Henry Occ. Oct. 1246 x Oct. 1247 (PRO, E210/5860); 13 Oct. 1247 (PRO, Notts F., CP25/1/182/9, no. 347).

Simon Occ. (S.) 27 May 1251 (BL, Harl. Cht. 44 D 47); 16 June 1252 (PRO, Leics F., CP25/1/122/2, no. 375); 15 July 1252 (PRO, Leics F., 122/20, no. 349); 20 Oct. 1255 (PRO, Notts F., CP25/1/183/11, no. 420). Seal (*BM Seals*, no. 3180).

Robert of Thorp Occ. 6 Oct. 1266 PRO, Leics F. CP25/1/122/27, no. 508); 1274 (*Ctl. Sandford*, I, nos. 98–100); 20 Jan. 1275 (PRO, Leics F. CP25/1/123/31, no. 14; Farnham, *Leics Notes*, II, 27); 9 Mar. 1275 (*Reg. R. Gravesend*, p. 157).

Roger Occ. 18 Nov. 1280 (PRO, Notts F. CP25/1/183/15, no. 60).

Eustace 1290– Bl. 24 Sept. 1290 (*Reg. Sutton*, III, 46). Occ. 1290 (BL, Lansdowne ms. 415, f. 39r); 8 Mar. 1293 (ibid., f. 36r); Hil. 1294 (Farnham, *Leics Notes*, VI, 356, citing De Banco roll).

John 1295– Bl. 22 June 1295 (*Reg. Sutton*, V, 92). Occ. (J.) 1295 x 6 (BL, Lansdowne ms. 415, f. 31v.); 10 Aug. 1299 (*CPR 1292–1301*, p. 431).

Henry 1303– Bl. & prof. obed. 16 June 1303 (Lincoln, Ep. Reg., III, f. 57v.).

John Occ. Mich. 1310 (PRO, CP40/183, attorneys m. 21); 3 Aug. 1317, 12 Aug. 1318, 12 Jan. 1319 (*CPR 1317–21*, pp. 84, 279, 307); 13 Dec. 1330 (*CChR 1327–41*, p. 196).

Walter of Holy Cross (de Sancta Cruce) **1334–1350** Lic. to receive bl. from any Catholic bp 16 Aug. 1334 (Lincoln, Ep. Reg., V, f. 480r). Occ. 8 Mar. 1340 (*HMC R.R. Hastings*, I, 7); 12 July 1340 (*CChR 1327–41*, p. 472). Res. (William) by 24 Mar. 1350 to be president and 1st abb. of the new abbey of St Mary Graces, London (*CPR 1348–50*, p. 560).

John Occ. 6 May 1360 (*CPR 1358–61*, pp. 358, 412; PRO, C81/1788/27).

Thomas of Loughborough (Loghteburgh, Lughtburgh) **1361–** Bl. and prof. obed. 11 Apr. 1361 (Lincoln, Ep. Reg., VIII, f. 155r). Occ. 20 July 1364 (*CPR 1364–67*, p. 9); 1377 (*Clerical Poll-Taxes*, p. 27, no. 370); 26 Mar. 1382 (*CPR 1381–85*, p. 101).

The next recorded abb., **John**, occ. 15 Feb. 1406 (*CPL*, VI, 79).

GRACE DIEU (Monmouth) (Abbey Dore) f. 24 Apr. 1226

Lists in *Monmouthshire Antiquary*, I, part 4 (1964), 96; *Fasti Cistercienses Cambrenses*, p. 189. See also J. Harrison, 'The troubled foundation of Grace Dieu abbey', *Monmouthshire Antiquary*, 14 (1998), 25–9.

John Occ. 26 Mar. 1236 (*CCR 1234–37*, p. 343). No longer abb. but alive and engaged on king's business in Gascony 19 Nov. 1236, 27 Nov. 1236, 6 Aug. 1237 (*CPR 1232–47*, pp. 169, 201, 192).

Walter Occ. 3 July 1236 (PRO, Herefords F., CP25/1/80/8 no. 150); ?1240 (*Monmouthshire Antiquary*, I, part 4 (1964), p. 96, citing Bodl., Jesus Coll. ms. 131 – possibly a forgery). Prob. the abb. Walter who occ. n.d. in an earlier cht. confirmed on 10 Mar. 1337 (*CChR 1327–41*, p. 390).

Roger Occ. 22 Aug. 1246 (Gloucester D. & C., register B, p. 474, no. 1091).[9]

William Occ. 1267 (*CPR 1334–38*, p. 334; *CChR 1257–1300*, p. 304; *Welsh Episcopal Acts*, II, p. 752, no. L.544).

Warin Occ. 15 Aug. 1281, 25 Aug. 1281 (*Ctl. Oseney*, II, 453, 456–7); 3 Sept. 1281 (*Ctl. Thame*, I, no. 39).

A. ? Occ. *ante* 1304 (*Monmouthshire Antiquary*, I, part 4 (1964), p. 96, citing *YB 33–35 Edward I*, p. 330. It is not exactly certain whether A. is the actual initial of the abb. or a year-book convention).

Robert Occ. 1350 and 4 May 1351 (*CPL*, III, 385).

---

[9] *Monmouthshire Antiquary* list (p. 96 and n. 150) cites ? Gilbert de Lacy as abb. *ante* 1256, citing BL, Add. Cht. 40796(2), but the note does suggest that Gilbert and the abb. mentd in the charter recited in 1256 may have been different people.

Roger of Chepstow -1351 Res. 1351 and provision made for him (*Monmouthshire Antiquary*, I, part 4 (1964), p. 95, citing BL, Royal ms. 12 E XIV, f. 23r).

John Wysbeche Occ. *ante* 1387, later abb. of Tintern 1387–1407 (G. Williams, *The Welsh Church from Conquest to Reformation* (Cardiff, 1962), p. 208, citing PRO, C85/167/32; *Monmouthshire Antiquary*, I, part 4 (1964), pp. 96, 107).

HAILES (Glos.) (Beaulieu) f. 17 July 1246
List in *VCH Glos.*, II, 99.

Jordan Occ. 1246 (BL, Harl. ms. 3725, f. 33v).

Walter Occ. 1270 (BL, Cotton ms. Cleopatra D III, f. 46v).

An eln took place in 1272 (Canivez, III, 108–9).

Martin de Billeslye Occ. 8 July 1275 (PRO, C85/2/16).

Prof. obed. of unnamed abb. 27 Apr. 1276 (*Reg. Bronescombe*, p. 99).

Adam Occ. 11 June 1280 (*Ctl. Winchcombe*, II, 294).

Hugh of Dumbleton (Dombelton) Name from BL, Cotton ms. Cleopatra D III, f. 54v. Occ. 18 Mar. 1287 (PRO, E210/653); 3 Dec. 1299 (*Berkeley Chts.*, no. 463); absolved 6 Feb. 1300 from excommunication imposed for infringing *Clericis laicos* (*Reg. Winchelsey*, I, 375–6); occ.1300, 1302 (BL, Cotton ms. Cleopatra D III, ff. 53v, 54v) from 12 Feb. 1301 to 10 Nov. 1302 (*CCR 1296–1302*, pp. 478, 609); 2 Aug. 1301 (*CPR 1292–1301*, p. 603); 26 Apr. 1302, 26 Nov. 1302 (*CPR 1301–07*, pp. 30, 98); 13 Oct. 1302 (*Cornwall F.*, I, no. 381); 6 Feb. 1303 (*CCR 1302–07*, p. 67); 9 Nov. 1304 (*Reg. Gainsborough*, p. 210); 19 Apr. 1305 (*CPR 1301–07*, p. 339).

John of Gloucester 1305– Bl. and prof. obed. 18 Aug. 1305 (*Reg. Gainsborough*, p. 114). Occ. 15 June 1309 (*Ctl. Winchcombe*, II, 295); (J.) 1312 (PRO, E210/6841); 1325 (*Reg. Cobham*, p. 198); 13 Feb. 1327 (*CCR 1327–30*, p. 94); 19 June 1328, 29 July 1330, 7 Sept. 1330, 8 Sept. 1330 (*Reg. Orleton (Worc.)*, nos. 529, 773, 634, 635); 8 Jan. 1333 appt of attorneys on testimony that he is too old to work (*CPR 1330–34*, p. 385).

Thomas Occ. 26 Dec. 1345, 3 Feb. 1346 (*CPR 1345–48*, pp. 35, 101). Mentd 25 Sept. 1352 as recipient of earlier gt (*CPR 1350–54*, p. 325).

House void 1354 (*CPR 1361–64*, p. 10).

Thomas 1354– Bl. 15 June 1354 (Worcester, Reg. Brian, I, p. 23). Occ. Easter 1361 (PRO, CP40/406, m. 185d); 3 Nov. 1367 (PRO, C241/147/52).

John of Gloucester (Gloucestre, Gloucestria) **1368–1397/1399** Bl. by bp of Hereford and prof. obed. to bp of Worcester 8 Apr. 1368 (*Reg. L. Charlton*, p. 52). Occ. 19 June 1377 (PRO, C67/28B, m. 11). Occ. 10 Jan. 1397, abb. of Hailes but claiming to be abb. of Beaulieu (*Cal. Misc. Inq.*, VI, no. 155). On 20 May 1397 the king accepts him as abb. of Beaulieu, to which abbey Richard Middelton had also laid claim (*CPR 1396–99*, pp. 139–40). Writ *de intendendo* in favour of John as abb. of Beaulieu 15 Sept. 1399 (ibid., p. 515).

The next recorded abb., **Robert**, occ. 1380 (*Mon. Angl.*, V, 687).

HOLM CULTRAM (Cumbria, formerly Cumberland) (Melrose) (Abbey Town) f. 30 Dec. 1150
Lists in *VCH Cumberland*, II, 172–3; *Ctl. Holm Cultram*, pp. 133–5, 146–7; *Heads*, I, 135.

Adam of Kendal -1223 Occ. (A.) 1215 x 1223 (*Ctl. Holm Cultram*, p. 7, no. 23a). Presumably the unnamed abb. who in 1222 had not been to the Cistercian General Chapter in 8 years (Canivez, II, 16). According to *Scotichronicon* tried by bribery to get the see of Carlisle and went out of his mind when he failed (*Ctl. Holm Cultram*, pp. 133–4). Res. 1223 (*Ch. Melrose*, p. 76). D. 23 May 1224 (*Ctl. Holm Cultram*, p. 134).

Ralph 1223– Prev. abb. of Gray Abbey, Ireland, succ. 1223 (*Ch. Melrose*, p. 76). Occ. (R.) 1224 x 1226 (PRO, SC1/6/61).

William −1233 Res. 1233 (*Ch. Melrose*, p. 82).

Gilbert 1233–1237 Master of *conversi* of Holm Cultram, succ. 1233 (ibid.). Occ. Oct. 1234 x Oct. 1235 (*Cumbd F.*, p. 222). D. 1237 at Canterbury on way home from Cistercian General Chapter (*Ch. Melrose*, p. 86; *Ctl. Holm Cultram*, pp. 76, 134).

John 1237–1255 Prev. abb. of Gray Abbey, Ireland, succ. 1237 (*Ch. Melrose*, p. 86). D. 1255 (ibid., p. 113).

Henry 1255– M. of Holm Cultram, succ. 1255 (ibid.). Occ. (H.) *c.* 1255, 1262, (H.) 4 Apr. 1270 (*Ctl. Holm Cultram*, pp. 38, 70, 43, nos. 99, 202, 108a). Dep. 1267 by Adam, abb. of Melrose, but reinstated by the Cistercian General Chapter (*Ch. Melrose*, p. 129; cf. Canivez, III, 45, where the year is given as 1266). In 1304 (*temp.* abb. Robert) it was stated that Henry was the third predecessor of the present abb. (*Ctl. Holm Cultram*, p. 88, no. 254b).

Gervase Occ. (G.) 15 May 1274 (*Ctl. Newminster*, p. 238); 25 Nov. 1278 (*Cumbd F.*, p. 228; *Ctl. Holm Cultram*, p. 26, no. 60); (G.) n.d. (1279) ('Ctl. Meaux', pp. 214–17, no. 126).

Robert of Kelsick (Keldesik) −1318 Occ. *c.* 1288, 21 Feb. 1289 (?1290), 1292, 1294 (*Ctl. Holm Cultram*, pp. 58, 88, 60, 12, nos. 152, 255, 156e, 36a). Paid homage to the King of Scots 28 Aug. 1296 (ibid., p. 132). Occ. (R.) Mar. 1284 (PRO, SC1 23/137); Easter 1292, Nov. 1295 x Nov. 1296 (*Arch. Aeliana*, XXXIX (1961), p. 339); Trin. 1297 (PRO, CP40/119, m. 77d); (R.) Mar. 1303 (*Ctl. Fountains*, I, 62–3); (R.) 1312 (*Reg. Halton*, II, 56); (R.) 14 Mar. 1316 and 28 May 1316 (ibid., pp. 119, 121). D. by 12 Aug. 1318 (*CPR 1317–21*, p. 196).

12 Aug. 1318 King issued letter of safe conduct to the abb. of Melrose to journey to Holm Cultram, daughter-house of Melrose, to el. a successor to the late abb. R., which could not be done without the presence of the abb. of Melrose (ibid.).

Lic. to bp of Carlisle to bl. unnamed abb. of Holm Cultram within the diocese of York 31 Oct. 1318 (*Reg. Melton*, I, p. 71, no. 199). Unnamed abb. going to the Cistercian General Chapter 1321 (*CCR 1318–23*, p. 492).

Thomas de Talkan (Talkane) M. of Holm Cultram, ordained dcn 1319, pr. 1320 (*Reg. Halton*, II, 191, 202). Still a m. on 2 Feb. 1327 (ibid., 142). Occ. as abb. 1330 (*Ctl. Holm Cultram*, p. 105, no. 294b); 1331 (PRO, DL25/244); 1 May 1332, 6 Sept. 1332, 13 Mar. 1334, 19 June 1336 (*Reg. Kirkby*, I, nos. 114–15, 167, 306); 25 June 1336 (PRO, CP40/210, m. 1); 1336 (*Ctl. Holm Cultram*, p. 146). Seal (*BM Seals*, no. 3290; *Mon. Seals*, p. 41).

Robert de Sothayk (Sitthayk, Southaik) Occ. 5 July 1351, 29 Feb. 1352 (*CPL*, III, 461, 453; *CPP*, p. 215); 8 Aug. 1359, 6 Feb. 1360, 17 Oct. 1362 (*Reg. Welton*, nos. 265, 297, 509).

Robert de Rawbankes (Rabankes, Raubank, Rawebankes, Raybankes) 1365– As m. of Holm Cultram ordained dcn 1344 (*Reg. Kirkby*, I, 165). Prof. obed. as abb. 24 Aug. 1365 (Carlisle, Reg. Appleby, DRC/1/2, p. 144). Occ. 1366, 1368 (*Cal. Misc. Inq.*, III, 261); *c.* 1379 (Carlisle, Reg. Appleby, DRC/1/2, p. 314); 1379 (PRO, E179/60/1, m. 1); 20 May 1382 (PRO, C67/29 m. 7).

HULTON (Staffs) (Combermere) f. 26 July 1219, but cf. J. T. Tomkinson, 'The documentation of Hulton abbey: two cases of forgery', *Staffs Studies*, 6 (1994), 73–99.
List in *VCH Staffs*, III, 237.

A. Occ. 1224 x 1238 (*temp.* Bp Alexander Stainsby) (*Ctl. Stone*, p. 19).

Robert Occ. 1237 x 1240 (*Ctl. Staffs 3*, p. 425); Aug. 1240 (*Ctl. Dieulacres*, p. 319); 4 Apr. 1241 (*Ctl. Dieulacres*, p. 362; *Cheshire Sheaf*, XXXV (1940), 57).

William Occ. 1 Aug. 1242 (*Ctl. Trentham*, pp. 314–15); (W.) 1242 (*Ctl. Shrewsbury*, II, p. 357, no. 391); 17 Apr. 1244 (*Ctl. Dieulacres*, p. 360);

Simon Occ. 1246 (Staffs RO, D593/B/1/23/2/6); Oct. 1245 x Oct. 1246 (*Ctl. Trentham*, p. 306); Oct. 1254 x Oct. 1255 (ibid., p. 315)

William de Wersleg Occ. from *c.* 1265 to *c.* 1280 x 1286 (*Ctl. Staffs 3*, p. 443); 1284 (*Ctl.*

Trentham, p. 333); n.d. (BL, Add. Chts. 46634–37); surname from n.d. (late 13th cent.) (Staffs RO, D1790/A/12/14).

Richard Occ. *c.* 1286 (*Ctl. Staffs 3*, p. 443).

Henry Occ. *c.* 1288, 1302 (ibid., p. 443).

Stephen Occ. 1306 (*Ctl. Staffs 2*, p. 439; *Salt MSS.*, p. 26, no. 4).

Henry Occ. 3 Aug. 1317 (BL, Add. Cht. 46640; *Ctl. Staffs 2*, p. 433).

Nicholas of Kesteven M. of Croxden (BL, Cotton ms. Faustina B VI, f. 93r). El. abb. of Combermere by 1324 (q.v.).

William 1332 (Hutchinson, *Archdeaconry of Stoke*, 35, without source); Easter term 1336 (*SHC*, XIV, 46).

Robert Occ. 1340 (PRO, E210/11247).

Simon of Barton 1341– Bl. 25 Mar. 1341 by bp of Worcester (*Reg. Bransford*, no. 397).

See Canivez, III, 480–1 about the disturbances at Hulton in 1344 and the forcing of the cess. of the unnamed abb. etc.

Henry Occ. 1369 (BL, Add. Cht. 46641); 1373 (*Staffs Plea Rolls 1360–87*, p. 100); Mich. term 1374 (ibid., 115).

The next recorded abb., **Denis**, occ. 20 May 1389 (*CCR 1385–89*, p. 675).

JERVAULX (Wensleydale) (Yorks N.) (Byland) f. 1143 (at Fors); 10 Mar. 1150 (as abb.); 1156 (Jervaulx).

Lists in *VCH Yorks*, III, 142; Clay, *Early Abbots*, pp. 21–3 (to 1258); *Heads*, I, 135.

William 3rd abb. (grave slab: *YAJ*, XXI, 319); n.d. (early 13th cent.) (Ctl. Scrope of Bolton, f. 138v); last recorded occ. 1209 x 11 (*Ctl. Furness*, II, ii, 343).[10]

Thomas Occ. 1 July 1218 (*Yorks. F., 1218–31*, p. 2); (T.) 1219 x 1221 (*Ctl. Fountains*, I, 200); n.d. (early 13th cent) (NYCRO, ZDX, Bellerby Chts.).

Eustace 1221– 5th abb. (grave slab: *YAJ*, XXI, 319). El. 1221 (TCD, ms. 516, f. 214r, *ex inf.* Julian Harrison). Occ. 12 May 1224 (*Yorks. F., 1218–31* p. 56); (E.) 24 Jan. 1225 (*Ctl. Fountains*, I, 217); 1234 to 1246 (*Yorks. F., 1232–46*, pp. 11, 99, 159); 20 Jan. 1252, 27 Jan. 1254 (*Yorks F., 1246–72*, pp. 62, 94).

Thomas Occ. 1258 (Baildon, I, 93); Whitsun 1259 (NYCRO, ZQH, Clervaux ctl., f. 25v); 12 Nov. 1266 (*Yorks. F., 1246–72*, p. 130).[11] Possibly the **Thomas de Alverton**, former abb., mentd in 1279 (PRO, Just.1/1055, m. 27).

Philip –1279 Occ. n.d. (NYCRO, ZQH, Clervaux ctl., f. 25v); murdered 1279 (*VCH*, citing Just.1/1064, m.31d; see also Canivez, III, 187). His murderer, br. William de Modlether, M. of Jervaulx, fled and was declared an outlaw (Logan, *Runaway Religious*, p. 204).

Thomas Occ. 1279 (PRO, Just.1/1055, m. 27); 8 & 15 July 1280 (*Yorks. F., 1272–1300*, pp. 53–4, 48). Possibly the **Thomas de Wandesleye** former abb., mentd in 1309 (PRO, CP40/178, m. 143d).

Ralph de Aldeburg (?Aldburgh/Aldborough) Occ. 18 Sept. 1288 (PRO, C85/174/56); 16 Aug. 1289, 7 Feb. 1290 (*CPR 1281–92*, pp. 319, 340); 1289, 1300, 1301 (Baildon, I, 95–6; II, 17); (R.) 4 Aug. 1302 (*Ctl. Fountains*, I, 62).

Simon de Miggele (?Midgley) 1304– Lic. to bp of Coventry and Lichfield for bl. 17 Oct. 1304 (*Reg. Corbridge*, II, no. 1016).

John –1312 D. 24 June 1312 (*Reg. Greenfield*, IV, no. 2115). Possible grave slab, where he is described as 8th abb. (*YAJ*, XXI, 319).

[10] In an annotated copy of Baildon at the Borthwick Institute the name of Peter de Tolvero is given as abb. in 1209. No source has been found for this statement and indeed William was abb. at this time.

[11] 11 Jan. 1275 appt during pleasure of Guichard de Charron to the custody of the abbey, which was in debt (*CPR 1272–81*, p. 76).

Thomas of Gristhwaite (Gristhwayt, Grysethweyt) 1313– Prof. obed. & bl. 21 Jan. 1313 (*Reg. Greenfield*, IV, pp. 217–18, no. 2115); occ. Jan. 1336 x Jan. 1337 (PRO, E210/9385); 16 Oct. 1338 (*CPR 1338–40*, p. 178). [occ. as m. of Jervaulx 1308 (*Reg. Greenfield*, V, no. 2696)].

Hugh of Ferrybridge (Feribrig) 1342– Prof. obed. & bl. 8 Dec. 1342 (York, Reg. 10, f. 65r). Occ. 1344 (Burghley mss. 204/96); *c.* Sept. 1347 (PRO, SC1/40/6).

John of Newby (Neuby) 1349– Prof. obed. and bl. 25 Oct. 1349 (York, Reg. 10, f. 77v); 1351 (PRO, Just.1/1129, m. 17); 1355 (PRO, E326/7997); 1367/8 (Baildon, II, 18); 1376 (*Yorks F. 1347–77*, 200); 8 July 1376 (Ctl. Scrope of Bolton, f. 88r). Mentioned Easter 1378 as former abb. (Baildon, I, 96).

The next recorded abb., **John of Rookwith** (Rukewyk), occ. June 1396 x June 1397 (PRO, E326/6021); 16 June 1398 (PRO, C67/30, m. 5).

KINGSWOOD (Glos) (Tintern) f. 7 Sept. 1139 (at Kingswood); *c.* 1149/50 (at Hazelton); *c.* 1150 x 1154 (at Tetbury); *c.* 1164 or 1166 x 1170 (at Kingswood, see *GFL*, pp. 510ff.)

Lists in *VCH Glos*, II, 101; *Heads*, I, 135–6; E.S. Lindley, in *BGAS*, 73 (1954), pp. 128–9.

William 1188– Previously pr. of Kingswood, el. abb. 1188 (*Ann. Waverley*, p. 245). Occ. several times late 12th cent. and early 13th cent. (see *Heads*, I, 135–6); 19 Oct. 1210 (Gloucester Cath., Reg. A, f. 97v).

Thomas Occ. 1215 x 1241 (*BGAS*, 22, p. 190); 5 May 1224 (PRO, Glos F., CP25/1/73/7, no. 78); n.d. (*BGAS*, 73, p. 167, n. 8).

John Occ. 30 May 1236 (PRO, Glos F., CP25/1/73/10, no. 171); 1238 (*Glam. Chts.*, II, p. 509, no. 504); 1 July 1241 (PRO, Glos F., CP25/1/73/13, no. 240); 22 July 1241 (*Berkeley Chts.*, no. 273); (J.) 1 Aug. 1244 (PRO, C115/L1/6689, f. 16r).

Andrew Occ. 3 May 1248 (PRO, Glos F., CP25/1/74/19, no. 385); 29 May 1248 (ibid., 74/18, no. 352); 12 June 1248 (ibid. 74/18, no. 360).

Sampson Occ. 20 Jan. 1263 (PRO, Glos F. CP25/1/74/27, no. 607); Hil. term 1263 (*Berkeley Chts.*, p. 137, no. 433); 16 Dec. 1263 (BL, Harl. Chts. 48 C 81); n.d. (*Ctl. Bruton*, no. 333). Seal (*BM Seals*, no. 3357).

Henry of Horton Succ. ?1272 (see end of entry). Occ. 8 June 1287 (PRO, Glos F., CP25/1/75/35, no. 126); stone at Haselden barn (now lost) inscribed 1290 and with abb. Henry's name (*BGAS*, 73, p. 148); 20 Mar. 1297 (PRO, SC1/48/55). Another stone in a barn at Calcot built in 1300 in abb. Henry's 29th year (hence succ. ?1272) (*BGAS*, 73, p. 142 and plate XIX).

Robert of Tetbury Occ. 10 Feb. 1303 (*Berkeley Chts.*, no. 468); 30 Dec. 1305 (*Reg. Gainsborough*, p. 145).

Commn to unnamed abb. to receive bl. from any bp in the province of Canterbury 25 Feb. 1308 (*Worcester sede vacante reg.*, p. 88). Is this John below?

John Occ. 1 May [1309] ('Ctl. Meaux', no. 189); Mich. 1310 (PRO, CP40/183, attorneys m. 16d); 8 Dec. 1316, 17 June 1317 (*CCR 1313–18*, pp. 442, 483).

On 7 June 1318 an undated lease of abb. **Richard** was conf. (*CPR 1317–21*, p. 157). The date of the original lease is not absolutely certain but it would appear to be close in date to the conf.

Richard 1319– Bl. and prof. obed. 22 Feb. 1319 (*Reg. Cobham*, p. 15). Occ. 6 Oct. 1319 (Perkins, *BGAS*, 22, p. 247; *BGAS*, 73, p. 169, no. 43); 16 Nov. 1321 (*CCR 1318–23*, p. 507).

John Occ. Hil.–Mich. 1328 (*Index to Placita de Banco*, p. 170).

Richard Occ. 2 Mar. 1335 (*CCR 1333–37*, p. 468).

Nicholas Hayl 1351– M. of Kingswood, commn to bp of Hereford to bl. him as abb. and to take his prof. obed. 24 Oct. 1351 (Worcester, Reg. Thoresby, p. 75).[12]

---

[12] Richard Hampton is said to occ. as abb. 1369 (Bigland,*Glos.*, II, 129, but no source).

Nicholas Occ. 12 Apr. 1376 (*BGAS*, 73, p. 171); 1378 x 1379 (PRO, E179/58/5, no. 3). Is he the same as Nicholas Hayl?

KIRKSTALL (Yorks W.) (Fountains) f. 19 May 1147 (at Barnoldswick); 19 May 1152 (at Kirkstall).

Lists in *VCH Yorks*, III, 145; Clay, *Early Abbots*, pp. 23–7 (to 1249); *Heads*, I, 136; G.D.Barnes, *Kirkstall Abbey 1147–1539* (Thoresby Soc. 58, 1984), pp. 95–7.

Ralph of Newcastle *c.* 1204–1231/3 M. of Fountains (*Mem. Fountains*, I, 123). Occ. (R.) *post* 9 Dec. 1204 (*EYC*, III, no. 1560); from 20 Oct. 1209 to 1 Dec. 1226 (*Ctl. Kirkstall*, pp. 10, 15, nos. 14, 18); from 9 Feb. 1219 to 1 Dec. 1226 (*Yorks F., 1218–31*, pp. 20, 84); (R.) 22 Sept. 1230 (*Reg. Greenfield*, II, p. 209, no. 1106). D. 6 Apr. 1231/3 (*Fundacio*, p. 187; cf. Clay, *Early Abbots*, p. 27).[13]

Walter Succ. abb. Ralph *temp.* Henry III (*Fundacio*, p. 188; Clay, *Early Abbots*, p. 27). D. 14 oct. (no year given, but ? 1231 x 1233, possibly 1232) (ibid.).

Maurice –1249 *Fundacio* says he succ. abb. Walter in 1222 (p. 188) but this is clearly an error; possibly 1232 is intended (Clay, *Early Abbots*, p. 27). Occ. from 16 May 1234 to 6 May 1246 (*Ctl. Kirkstall*, pp. 46, 24, nos. 62, 30); 1235 (*Yorks Deeds*, I, 107); from 28 June 1237 to 6 May 1246 (*Yorks F., 1232–46*, pp. 48–9, 128); (Martin) 6 Oct. 1237 (ibid., p. 49); 20 Jan. 1247 (*Yorks. F., 1246–72*, p. 3); 21 Apr. 1247 (ibid.); Oct. 1248 x Oct. 1249 (PRO, DL36/3/14). D. 26 Mar. 1249 (*Fundacio*, p. 188).

Adam 1249– Succ. 23 Apr. 1249 (ibid.). Occ. from 1 May 1250 to 29 June 1253 (*Yorks. F., 1246–72*, pp. 14, 91); 25 Jan. 1252 (*Yorks Deeds*, VII, no. 12); 30 Sept. 1256 (*Lincs. F.*, II, 114); 10 June 1257 (*Ctl. Kirkstall*, p. 30, no. 39).

Hugh Mikelay (Mykelay) 1260–1262 Created abb. 16 Mar. 1260 (i.e. 1259 in ms.) (*Fundacio*, p. 188). D. 1 June 1262 (ibid.). Seal (Thoresby Soc. 2, p. 18 and pl. I).

Simon 1262–1270 Created abb. 17 June 1262 (*Fundacio*, p. 188). Occ. (S.) 27 Apr. 1267, 29 July 1268 (*Ctl. Kirkstall*, pp. 43, 49, nos. 58, 66); 8 July 1268 (*Yorks Deeds*, X, no. 163); 26 July 1269 (*Yorks F., 1246–72*, pp. 173–4). D. 17 Feb. 1270 (*Fundacio*, p. 188).

William (of) Leeds (Ledes, Ledys) 1270–1275 Succ. 6 Mar. 1270 and was abb. up to the Assumption of the BVM (15 Aug.) 1275 (ibid.).

Gilbert of Cotes (Cothes, Cotles) 1275–1280 Created abb. 23 Aug. 1275, ruled 3 years, 1 month, 4 days. (ibid.). Occ. 11 Apr. 1277 (*Lancs F.*, I, 153). He presumably res., for he was again created abb. 12 Dec. [1278] and ruled to 1 Aug. 1280 (*Fundacio*, p. 188). Occ. 22 July 1280 (*Yorks F., 1272–1300*, p. 49). Prob. the unnamed abb. deposed by the General Chapter (Canivez, III, 203).

Henry Carr (Kar) 1280– Created abb. 29 Nov. 1280 (*Fundacio*, p. 188). Occ. 1282 x 1283 (PRO, C85/173/31); Mich. 1282 x Mich. 1283 (PRO, E159/56); Mich. 1283 (PRO, KB27/80, m. 12d); 10 July 1284, 20 Jan. 1285 (*Ctl. Kirkstall*, pp. 26, 27, nos. 31, 32).

William [of Darlington (or Parlington)] Occ. 8 June 1285 (*Ctl. Kirkstall*, p. 32, no. 41); Nov. 1285 x Nov. 1286 (ibid., p. 33, no. 42); 28 June 1287, 9 Oct. 1288 (ibid., p. 343, no. 415 & p. 344, no. 417).

Hugh of Grimston (Grimeston, Grymeston, Grymston) 1289–1304 *Fundacio*, p. 188 states that Henry Carr was succeeded by Hugh of Grimston, created abb. 17 Sept. 1284, but this totally ignores abb. William and is clearly an error, and the 1284 date is prob. that of William's accession. Hugh prof. obed. 27 Feb. 1289 (*Reg. Romeyn*, I, 85). Occ. Easter

---

[13] Baildon, I, p. 112, no. 25 refers to a court document of Easter term 1368 which records an abb. Robert in the time of Henry III and Edward I. However the preceding document (no.24) shows clearly that the abb. in question was actually Ralph (and that the 14th-century scribe was also erratic in his chronology).

1291–Mich. 1292, Easter/Trin. 1300 (Baildon, I, 110–11); Nov. 1295 x Nov. 1296 (Bodl., Dodsworth ms. 144, f. 49r). D. 1 May 1304 (*Fundacio*, p. 188). Seal (Thoresby Soc. 2, p. 18 and pl. I).

John of Birdsall (Briddesale) **1304–** Succ. Hugh of Grimston (ibid.). Prof. obed. 16 May 1304 (*Reg. Corbridge*, I, 112). Occ. 3 Feb. 1310 (*Ctl. Kirkstall*, p. 235, no. 332); 15 Jan. 1311 (*Reg. Greenfield*, IV, p. 111, no. 1909); 25 Mar. 1311 (*Calverley Chts.*, p. 153); 4 Apr. 1312 (*Yorks Deeds*, III, no. 211). Seal (*BM Seals*, no. 3367; Clay, *Seals*, p. 24).

Walter 1314– Prof. obed. and bl. 2 June 1314 (*Reg. Greenfield*, II, pp. 183–4, no. 1063).

William of Driffield (Driffeld) **1318–1349** Prof. obed. 17 Dec. 1318 (York, Reg. 9A, f. 160r). Occ. 1322 (Bodl., ms. Top. Yorks e 7, f. 99r); 1324 (PRO, C81/1788/32); 1327 (*CPR 1327–30*, p. 132); from 24 Sept. 1332 to Mich. 1337 (*Ctl. Kirkstall*, pp. 268, 309, nos. 369, 398); 1343 (*Yorks Deeds*, III, no. 427; *CPR 1343–45*, p. 163); 1348 *(Ctl. Kirkstall*, p. 275, no. 375). Last occ. 17 Mar., 7 Apr. 1349 (*Wakefield Court Rolls 1348–50*, pp. 90, 97). Seal (*BM Seals*, no. 3368; Clay, *Seals*, p. 24; Thoresby Soc. 2, p. 18 and pl. I).

Roger of Leeds (Ledes) **1349–** Prof. obed. and bl. 15 Dec. 1349 (York, Reg. 10, f. 43r). Occ. 17 Feb. 1351 (*CPL*, III, 375). Ref. in 1374 to his being abb. within last 25 years (*Cal. Misc. Inq.*, III, 350).

John Topcliff of Thirkleby (Thurkelby) Occ. 1 July 1354 (*Ctl. Kirkstall*, p. 294, no. 387); 1 Oct. 1355 (*CCR 1354–60*, p. 225); 10 July 1356 (*CPR 1354–58*, p. 498); 17 July 1364 (York, Reg. 11, f. 131r.); 26 Oct. 1366 (*CPR 1364–67*, p. 362); 6 Mar. 1368, Easter term 1368 (*Ctl. Kirkstall*, pp. 299–300, no. 391; Baildon, I, 112).

John de Thornbergh Occ. Easter term 1369 (Baildon, I, 113); 30 Nov. 1377 (*CPR 1377–81*, p. 95); 16 Feb. 1379 (ibid., p. 357). In Hilary term 1399 John was described as former abb., predecessor of present abb. (Baildon, I, 114).

The next recorded abb., **John of Bardsey**, is said to occ. 1392 (*VCH* citing Baildon's ms. notes, without further source). Possibly the abb. John who occ. 1394 ('Ctl. Meaux', p. 387, no. 210), although with a succession of abb. Johns it is not always possible to distinguish them.

KIRKSTEAD (Lincs) (Fountains) f. 2 Feb. 1139 (at Kirkstead I); 1187 (to Kirkstead II). Lists in *VCH Lincs*, II, 137–8; *Heads*, I, 136.

William Last recorded occ. 26 Nov. 1210 (*Lincs F. 1199–1216*, p. 160, no. 316; BL, Cotton ms. Vespasian E XVIII, f. 207v).

Henry Occ. (H.) 1215 (BL, Harl. Cht. 43 B 47; *An. Sac. Ord. Cist.*, XX (1964), 98); 1219 (BL, Cotton ms. Vespasian E XVIII, f. 106v); occ. in *Lincs F.*, I, from 12 June 1222 to 19 Oct. 1234 (pp. 162, 253); and in BL, Cotton ms. Vespasian E XVIII from 1 Aug. 1221 to 7 May 1234 (ff. 28v, 67v).

Hugh Occ. 17 Apr. 1239 (*Lincs F.*, I, 301; BL, Cotton ms. Vespasian E XVIII, f. 192r); 1240, 1242, 1243 (ibid., ff. 6r, 65r, 29r, 137r); 4 Apr. 1245 (ibid., f. 29v).

Simon Occ. 20 Oct. 1249, 12 June 1250 (*Lincs F.*, II, 49, 316–17; BL, Cotton ms. Vespasian E XVIII, ff. 190v, 189r); May 1251 (ibid., f. 66v).

William Occ. 13 Oct. 1253, 30 May 1255, 18 May 1259, 8 July 1260 (ibid., ff. 192v, 190v, 7v, 6v, 191v; *Lincs F.*, II, 100, 110, 171, 174); 6 May 1257 (ibid., 129); 4 May 1259 (BL, Cotton ms. Vespasian E XVIII, f. 7v).

John Occ. 15 Apr. 1263, 22 Sept. 1263 (*Lincs F.*, II, 191, 195); 30 Dec. 1266 (BL, Harl. Cht. 44 F 1).

William Occ. 13 Oct. 1271 (*Lincs. F.*, II, 233).

Simon Occ. 6 June 1277 (PRO, Lincs F., CP25/1/132/52, no. 4); 1 Sept. 1281 (*CPR 1272–81*, p. 454). Seal (*BM Seals*, no. 3371).

Robert of Withcall (Widkal, Withcale, Whital) Occ. 1286 (Lancs RO, DDTO (Lord

O'Hagan), Towneley mss. K/24/24); 29 Aug. 1297 (BL, Harl. Cht. 45 H 15); 16 Aug. 1300 (*CPR 1292–1301*, p. 532); 13 Oct. 1303 (PRO, Lincs F., CP25/1/132/69, no. 50). Indulgence of 40 days gtd 26 Jan. 1313 for the soul of the late abb., whose body is bur. at Cîteaux (Lincoln, Ep. Reg., III, f. 268v.); further indulgence 13 Sept. 1322 (Lincoln, Ep. Reg., V, f. 317v).

Thomas 1313– Bl. by bp of Down and prof. obed. 11 Mar. 1313 (Lincoln, Ep. Reg., III, f. 271r). Occ. 12 Aug. 1313 (*CPR 1313–17*, p. 59).

John of Louth (Luda) **1315–** Bl. by ex-archbp of Armagh and prof. obed. 21 Dec. 1315 (Lincoln, Ep. Reg., III, ff. 335v–336r). Occ. 1323 (*CPR 1321–24*, pp. 372, 379); 21 Sept. 1331 (BL, Harl. Cht. 44 F 7); 1332 (BL, Cotton ms. Vespasian E XVIII, f. 156v); 1333 (PRO, Just.1/535, m. 5).

John 1336– Prof. obed. 28 June 1336 (Lincoln, Ep. Reg., V, f. 532r); bl. 29 June 1336 (ibid., f. 536r). Occ. 19 Nov. 1339 (*CCR 1339–41*, p. 327).[14]

William Occ. 19 Feb. 1348 (*CPL*, III, 246).

Thomas Occ. Hil. 1354 (*King's Bench Edward III*, VI, 91).

Robert de Alverton Occ. Mich. 1364 (PRO, KB27/416, m. 48).

Thomas of Nafferton (Naffirton) Occ. 20 July 1372 (BL, Harl. Cht. 44 F 9);[15] 1377 (*Clerical Poll-Taxes*, p. 55, no. 767); 1381 (occ. as Nassryngton) (ibid., p. 131, no. 1644).

Richard of Upton mentd as the predecessor of **Thomas** who occ. 26 July 1404 (*CPL*, V, 610), where it is stated that Thomas was el. on res. of Richard of Upton made to Robert, abb. of Fountains, father-abb. (1383–1410). William of Louth, m. of Kirkstead, had opposed Thomas's eln and had intruded himself. Papal judges delegate adjudged the abbey to Thomas and William appealed. He lost and the pope conf. the proceedings.

LLANTARNAM (Monmouth) (Caerleon) (Strata Florida) f. 22 July 1179

Lists in *Heads*, I, 136; *Monmouthshire Antiquary*, I, part 4 (1964), pp. 108–9; *Monmouthshire Antiquary*, II, part 3 (1967), p. 143; *Fasti Cistercienses Cambrenses*, p. 189.

Walter Occ. 1193 x 1218 (*Welsh Episcopal Acts*, II, p. 697, no. L.306; *Glam. Chts.*, VI, 2335; Price, *Valle Crucis Abbey*, pp. 239–41).

Kenweryc (Cynwrig) Occ. 15 July 1227 (*Ystrad Marchell Chts.*, no. 70).

Anian Occ. 7 Jan. 1280 (*Welsh Assize Roll 1277–84*, p. 301).

Griffin Occ. 15 Oct. 1313 (WAM, no. 5982).

David Occ. mid-fourteenth cent., mentd in 16th-century case as occurring about 200 years previously (Lewis and Davies, *Records of Court of Augmentations*, pp. 134–5; Cowley, *Monastic Order in South Wales*, p. 243).

John Occ. 25 Jan. 1377 (*Reg. Wykeham*, II, 267); 2 Dec. 1383 (*CCR 1381–85*, p. 343).

LONDON, St Mary Graces (Beaulieu) f. 20 Mar. 1350

List in *VCH London*, I, 464.

William of Holy Cross (de Sancta Cruce) **1350–** 24 Mar. 1350 William (?Walter) de Sancta Cruce, late abb. of Garendon, at the king's request came to the free chapel of St Mary Graces in the Tower, founded by the king to stay as president of a convent of monks to be constituted there at £20 yearly from the Exchequer to keep him and monks while arrangements made (*CPR 1348–50*, p. 560).

John of Gloucester (Gloucestre) Occ. 1 May 1354 (*CCR 1354–60*, p. 22).

William (of) Wardon (Wardone) Said to have been made abb. 27 Aug. 1360 (*Mon. Angl.*, V, 717, without source). Described as 3rd abb., 3 June 1368 (*Reg. Sudbury*, II, 58). Occ. 27 Aug.

---

[14] *VCH* calls him John of Lincoln, but source of information not found.

[15] *VCH* gives occ. of abb. Thomas in 1367, citing BL, Lansdowne ms. 207B, f. 143. This is an incorrect ref.

1369 (*CPR 1358–61*, p. 457); and many references to abb. William among PRO, E210 and E326 deeds series until 4 Feb. 1405 (PRO, E326/843).

LONG BENNINGTON (Lincs) with FIELD DALLING (Norfolk) (granges of Savigny) f. (Long Bennington) ?1200; (Field Dalling) *c.* 1138

List in *VCH Lincs*, II, 242.

[**William** Occ. as m. of (Long) Bennington and proctor of the abbey of Savigny Dec. 1230 x Dec. 1231 (*Reg. Wells*, III, 188).]

[**William de Brettevill** M., occ. as proctor of the abbey of Savigny in a final concord about land in Long Bennington 10 May 1242 (*Lincs F.*, I, 339).]

Robert M. of Savigny, occ. as keeper 12 July 1319 (*CPR 1317–21*, p. 378).

Richard M. of Savigny, occ. as keeper – protection for 1 year 7 Oct. 1321 (*CPR 1321–24*, p. 27). Occ. as warden of Long Bennington and Field Dalling 24 Jan. 1323 (ibid., p. 238).

Grant of keeping of Long Bennington and Field Dalling to br. **John de Lupynyaco** and br. **John de Escayo**, monks of Savigny, 10 Dec. 1343; regrant in similar terms 20 Sept. 1344 (*CFR 1337–47*, pp. 348, 385). Ment. 2 Mar. 1346 of br. John de Lupiniaco *et aliis firmariis prioratus* (PRO, E401/383).

Michael Roger(s) Occ. 26 Apr. 1368 (*CPR 1367–70*, p. 132); 11 June 1369, 10 Feb. 1372, 6 June 1377 (*CFR 1368–77*, pp. 15, 156, 404); 8 June 1375 (*CCR 1374–77*, p. 139); 23 Oct. 1377, 16 May 1381 (*CFR 1377–83*, pp. 27, 256); 8 Nov. 1399, 28 Jan. 1403 (*CFR 1399–1405*, pp. 24, 194); 30 May 1401 (*CPR 1399–1401*, p. 503); Jan. 1403 (*Privy Council*, I, 193).

LOUTH PARK (Lincs) (Fountains) (De Parco Lude) f. 1137 (at Haverholme); 2 Feb. 1139 (at Louth Park).

Lists in *VCH Lincs*, II, 140–1; *Heads*, I, 136–7.

Warin Occ. (W.) 1203 x 5 (*HMC Var. Coll.*, I, 236ff.); 1203 x 11 (*Reg. Ant. Lincoln*, V, no. 1614); 3 Nov. 1205 (*Lincs. F. 1199–1216*, no. 203); 2 Aug. 1207 (ibid., no. 228); 1213 (Bodl., ms. Laud misc. 625, f. 130v); 1217 (Soc. of Ant. ms. 38, f. 125v); 6 Oct. 1226 (*Lincs F.*, I, 215). Seal (*BM Seals*, no. 3578).

Richard de Dunham 1227–1246 M. of Kirkstead, el. 1227 (*Ch. Louth Park*, p. 12); Occ. 13 Jan. 1228 (*CPR 1225–32*, p. 209); 8 July 1236 (*Lincs F.*, I, p. 294). D. 18 Apr. 1246 (*Ch. Louth Park*, p. 13). Obit 18 Apr. (Newhouse obit, *HMC Ancaster*, p. 483). Seal (*BM Seals*, no. 3581).

John of Louth –1261 D. 1261 (*Ch. Louth Park*, p. 17).

Walter Pylath (Pilat) of Welton 1261–1273 El. 1261 (ibid.). Res. 1273 (ibid., p. 18).

Alan de Ake 1273–1291 El. 1273 (ibid.). Occ. 8 May 1278 (PRO, Lincs F., CP25/1/132/52, no. 15); 14 June 1278 (Bodl., ms. Laud misc. 642, f. 38r); going overseas 1281 (*CPR 1272–81*, p. 454). Presumably res. ?1291; as former abb. d. 25 Feb. 1305 (*Ch. Louth Park*, p. 20, cf. *Cîteaux*, 30 (1979), p. 275).

Ralph 1291– Bl. 15 Aug. 1291 (*Reg. Sutton*, III, 138). On 9 Sept. 1293 the unnamed abb. of Louth Park said he was newly-appointed and his predecessor was still alive (ibid., IV, 113–14).

Gilbert Pacok 1294–1308 Bl. 21 Sept. 1294 (ibid., V, 31). Excommunicated 12 Feb. 1299 (ibid., VI, p. 144). Cess. 24 July 1308 (*Ch. Louth Park*, p. 20).

Robert of Algarkirk 1308–1312 El. 25 July 1308 (ibid.). Bl. & prof. obed. 2 Mar. 1309 (Lincoln, Ep. Reg., III, f. 149v). Occ. 13 Jan. 1312 (ibid., f. 239v). Cess. 1312 (*Ch. Louth Park*, p. 21).

Adam of Louth 1312–1320 El. 28 Oct. 1312 (ibid.). Bl. by bp of Down and prof. obed. 11 Mar. 1313 (Lincoln, Ep. Reg., III, f. 271r). Cess. 1320 (*Ch. Louth Park*, p. 26). ? d. 1333 (*Cîteaux*, 30 (1979), p. 273).

Gilbert Pacok (Peacok) **1320–1332** Re-el. 28 June 1320 (*Ch. Louth Park*, p. 26). D. 18 Sept. 1332 (ibid., p. 33).

Walter of Louth 1332–1349 El. 5 Oct. 1332 (ibid.). Royal protection for abbey in its impoverished state and appt of custodians 15 July 1344 (*CPR 1343–5*, pp. 334, 336; *CFR 1337–47*, p.382). D. 13 July 1349 (*Ch. Louth Park*, p. 35).

Richard of Lincoln Occ. 1353 (*Ch. Meaux*, III, 85).

[In 1375 the brother of the then abb. of Louth Park was called Alan Pulter (*Lincs. Sessions of Peace 1360–75*, p. 90, no. 403)]

Robert de Downham Occ. 1377, 1381 (*Clerical Poll-Taxes*, p. 56, no. 771; p. 134, no. 1693, cf. p. 159, no. 1972 (Cowham)); 1379 x 1380 (*Cal. Misc. Inq.*, V, no. 307).

MARGAM (Glam.) (Clairvaux) f. 21 Nov. 1147

  Lists in Birch, *Margam Abbey*, p. 375; *Arch. Camb.*, 3rd ser., XIII, 313–14; *Heads*, I, 137.

John of Goldcliff (Golcliva) **1213–1236/7** El. 17 June 1213 (*Ann. Margam*, p. 32). Occ. 1213 x 1216 (*Ctl. Bristol, St Mark*, no. 89); (J.) 1228 (*Glam. Chts.*, II, p. 459, no. 465). D. Nov. 1236 *or* 24 Aug. 1237 (*Ann. Tewkesbury*, p. 101; PRO, E164/1, p. 33; *Welsh Episcopal Acts*, II, p. 714, no. 374; *Glam. Chts.*, III, p. 859, no. 758; BL, Harl. ms. 838, f. 116r).

John de la War(r)e 1237–1250 Succ. after Nov. 1236 (*Ann. Tewkesbury*, p. 101); succ. 1237 (BL, Harl. ms. 838, f. 116r; *Glam. Chts.*, III, p. 859, no. 758). Occ. Oct. 1247 x Oct. 1248 (*Bristol F.*, p. 185); 12 June 1248 (PRO, Glos. F. CP25/1/74/18, no. 358). Res. 29 June 1250 (*Margam Abbey*, p. 264, n. 1; *Glam. Chts.*, III, p. 860, no. 758; BL, Harl. ms. 838, f. 116v; *Welsh Episcopal Acts*, II, p. 730). Royal ass. to eln as bp of Llandaff 26 July 1253 (*CPR 1247–58*, p. 217)

Thomas of [Portskewit] (Pertchiwet, Perithiwet) **1250–** Succ. 22 Sept. 1250 (BL, Harl. ms. 838, f. 116v; *Welsh Episcopal Acts*, II, p. 730, no. 444; *Margam Abbey*, p. 264, n. 1; *Glam. Chts.*, III, p. 860, no. 758). Occ. Mich. 1252 (*Glam. Chts.*, III, p. 599, no. 574); 11 Nov. 1267 (ibid., p. 687, no. 634; BL, Harl. Cht. 75 A 41).

Roger Occ. 1267 x 1268 (*Ctl. Bristol, St Mark*, p. 72, no. 92).

Gilbert Occ. *c.* 1270 x 1295, certainly before the d. of Gilbert, earl of Gloucester and Hereford, 1295 (BL, Harl. Chts., 75 A 36, 75 C 38).

Roger Occ. *c.* 1305 (*Glam. Chts.*, III, p. 988, no. 850).

Thomas Occ. 25 July 1307, 25 July 1308 (ibid., pp. 1005, 1008, nos. 853, 855); 25 July 1308 (BL, Harl. Cht. 75 A 43).

John de Cantelo Occ. 22 Feb. 1326 (*Margam Abbey*, p. 299); 5 Nov. 1326 (*CPR 1324–27*, p. 336); Jan. 1330 x Jan. 1331 (*Select Bills in Eyre*, p. 84).

Henry Occ. 31 Dec. 1338 (*Glam. Chts.*, IV, pp. 1227–8, no. 871), 19 Apr. 1340 (ibid., p. 1244, no. 982); 8 Nov. 1359 (Birch, *Neath Abbey*, p. 249). Poss. grave slab marked 'Henricus IX', but if this indicates the 9th abb. of Margam, presumably not the above, unless they followed the strange rule at Furness of only counting abbots who ruled for more than ten years (C.A.R. Radford, *Margam Museum, Glamorgan* (1949), p. 29, no. 20; for Furness rule see *Heads*, I, 133, n. 3, and corrigenda).

John Occ. 22 June 1366 (*Glam. Chts.*, IV, p. 1318, no. 1029).

David ap Rice Occ. 7 Aug. 1371 (*Ctl. Bristol, St Mark*, pp. 72–3, no. 93).

The next recorded abb. **John**, occ. 5 June 1385 (BL, Harl Cht. 75 A 33).

MEAUX (Yorks E.) (Fountains) f. 1 Jan. 1151

  Lists in *VCH Yorks*, III, 149, based on *Ch. Meaux* and abbatial list, printed ibid., I, 47–9; Clay, *Early Abbots*, 27–31 (to 1249); *Heads*, I, 137–8.

Hugh 1210–1220 Pr. of Meaux (over 5 years), el. 5th abb. 6 Dec. 1210 (*Ch. Meaux*, I, 353). Occ.

1212 x 1214 (*Hatton's Book of Seals*, no. 444); 16 June 1219 (*Yorks F.,1218–31*, p. 33). Res. 1220 (in 10th year) and d. 1222 (*Ch. Meaux*, I, 353, 380).

Geoffrey 1220–1221 6th abb. Came from Sawtry, apptd 1220 on res. of Hugh, but d. within a year on way to General Chapter (ibid., I, 405). Abb. by Whitsun 1220 (ibid., 406).

Richard of Ottringham (Otringham) **1221–1235** Cellarer of Meaux, 7th abb., el. 1221 on d. of Geoffrey (ibid., 407). Occ. from 24 Apr. 1222 to 5 July 1231 (*Yorks F.,1218–31*, pp. 45, 154); (R.) 22 Mar. 1228 (*Reg. Gray*, p. 158); 4 Dec. 1234 (*Yorks F.,1232–46*, p. 24). D. 1235 in the 14th year of his abbacy and the 35th of his profession (*Ch. Meaux*, I, 433).

Michael de Bruno (Buron') **1235–1249** El. 8th abb. in succession to Richard (ibid., II, 3). Occ. from 22 July 1240 to 25 June 1246 (*Yorks F.,1232–46*, pp. 78, 155); 1246 (PRO, Just.1/1045, m. 34). Seal (*Durham Seals*, II, p. 575, no. 3517). D. 1249 in the 14th yr of his abbacy and 35th of his profession (*Ch. Meaux*, II, 65). For Buron' see *EYC*, VII, no. 40.

William of Driffield (Dryffeld) **1249–1269** 9th abb., succ. 1249 on d. of Michael (*Ch. Meaux*, II, 75). Occ. 1249 x 1254 (*Reg. Gray*, p. 59n); from 20 Jan. 1252 to 24 June 1268 (*Yorks F.,1246–72*, pp. 64, 151). D. 1269 after ruling nearly 20 years, and miracles were performed at his tomb (*Ch. Meaux*, II, 119).

Richard of Thornton (Thorntona) **1269–** 10th abb, el. 1269 on d. of William of Driffield (ibid., II, 141). Said to have d. in 1270 after only one and a half years in office (ibid., 147), but this is evidently wrong since abb. Richard occ. 7 Feb. 1275 (Bodl., ms. Top. Yorks e 7, f. 94v); 1276 (PRO, C85/170/66); 25 Nov. 1276 (*Yorks F., 1272–1300*, p.12).

Robert of Skerne (Skyren, Skyrena) **–1280** 11th abb., succ. Richard of Thornton (*Ch. Meaux*, II, 147). Occ. 1278 (*Select Cases in Exchequer of Pleas*, p. 93); 4 June 1278, 3 Oct. 1279 (*CPR 1340–43*, p. 459); Mich. 1279 x Mich. 1280 (PRO, E159/53, m. 12d(2)); 12 Dec. 1279, 9 Feb. 1280, 22 July 1280 (*Yorks F.,1272–1300*, pp. 41, 39, 50). Cess. 1280 and d. 6 years later (*Ch. Meaux*, II, 157).

Richard of Barton (Bartona) **1280–1287** 12th abb., succ. Robert of Skerne (ibid., 169); prof. obed. 19 Aug. 1280 (*Reg. Wickwane*, p. 98, no. 327). Occ. 1282, 1284 (Baildon, I, 132–3). Cess. 1 Feb. 1287 in sixth year of office, but lived another 14 years and was buried next to Richard of Thornton, his predecessor, in the chapter house (*Ch. Meaux*, II, 175–6).

Roger of Driffield (Driffeld, Dryffeld) **1287–1310** 13th abb., succ. Richard of Barton (ibid., 183); prof. obed. 2 Feb. 1287 (*Reg. Romeyn*, I, p. 198, no. 556). Occ. 2 May 1309 (*CPR 1307–13*, p. 111). Cess. 1310 and lived 8 years after (*Ch. Meaux*, II, 238, 287). Res. but still living 14 Sept. 1310 (*Reg. Greenfield*, III, no. 1525).

Adam of Skerne (Skirne, Skyren, Skyrne) **1310–1339** 14th abb., succ. 15 May 1310 (*Ch. Meaux*, II, 238, 287); prof. obed. 28 May 1310 (*Reg. Greenfield*, III, no. 1507). D. 1339 having ruled the abbey for 30 years (*Ch. Meaux*, II, 313).

Hugh of Leven (Levena) **1339–1349** Sub-cellarer of Meaux, made 15th abb. *c.* 21 Dec. 1339 on d. of Adam of Skerne (ibid., III, 3). Occ. 25 Sept. 1343 (PRO, CP40/336, m. 1); 1347 (York, Reg. 10, f. 185v); 30 June 1349 (Lincoln, Ep. Reg., IX, f. 86r). Plague abating 1349 but Hugh d. (*Ch. Meaux*, III, 77).

William of Dringhoe (Drynghowe) **1349–1353** Sub-cellarer of Meaux, one of the ten survivors of the Black Death el. 1349 (ibid.). Occ. 1353 (PRO, Just. 1/1129, m. 1). Dep. 18 Apr. 1353 (*Ch. Meaux*, III, 86, cf. 83–6) – not placed in the numbered sequence of abbots (ibid., 87).

John de Ryslay (Ryselay) **1353–1356** Cellarer of Meaux, born in Wales and apptd by Visitor 1353 as convent unable to agree on eln (ibid., 93). Prof. obed. 29 Aug. 1353 (York, Reg. 11, f. 22r). Occ. 1355 (Baildon, I, 131). Called to Rome to reply to William of Dringhoe, recently abb. about spoliation and intrusion (*Ch. Meaux*, III, 113). John res. voluntarily 4 July 1356 (ibid.). See A.D.M. Barrell, *The Papacy, Scotland and Northern England 1342–78*, pp. 222–3.

Robert of Beverley 1356–1367 Styled 16th abb. Cellarer of Meaux, el. *c.* July 1356 on res of John Ryslay, and William of Dringhoe asked to drop his suit (ibid., 113–16). Commn to suffragan to bl. abb.-el. 2 Aug. 1356 (York, Reg. 11, f. 194v). Prof. obed. 27 Sept. 1356 (*BIB*, 3, p. 61, no. 216). D. 27 Nov. 1367, having ruled 11 years 8 months and 11 days (*Ch. Meaux*, III, 151–2).

After Robert's d. there was a disputed eln between **John of Hull** and **John of Newton**, then pr. of Meaux. John, abb. of Kirkstall attempted to be transferred to Meaux but the convent did not consent and restored William of Dringhoe, former abb. (ibid., 163).

William of Dringhoe 1367–1372 Styled 17th abb., el. 6 Dec. 1367. (ibid.). Occ. Mich. 1368 (Baildon, I, 135); 25 Sept. 1371 ('Ctl. Meaux', no. 201). D. 6 May 1372 (*Ch. Meaux*, III, 167).

After William's death there was a repeat of the 1367 disputed eln between **John of Hull**, then pr. of Meaux, and **John of Newton**, m. of Meaux, before William of Scarborough was chosen by compromise (ibid., 171).

William of Scarborough (Scardburgh) **1372–1396** Cellarer of Meaux for 16 years, el. 18th abb. 23 May 1372 (ibid., 171). Notif. to archbp by pr. and convent of Meaux of eln 23 May 1372 (York, Reg. 11, f. 228v); prof. obed. n.d. (ibid.). Occ. 1377 (Baildon, I, 136); 1386, 1394 ('Ctl. Meaux', nos. 186, 205, 210). Res. 6 July 1396, after 24 years, 7 months and 16 days in office (*Ch. Meaux*, III, 233).

MEDMENHAM (Bucks) (Woburn) f. 3 Jan. 1201; ref. 18 June 1212
  List in *VCH Bucks*, I, 376–7.
Adam Occ. 21 Apr. 1241 with Richard, abb. of Woburn (*Bucks F.*, I, 80). Has been identified with Adam of Luton who d. as abb. of Woburn *c.* Mar.1248 (*Ann. Dunstable*, p. 175).
Nicholas −1248 Occ. 29 May 1248 (*Bucks F.*, I, 92). Later el. to Woburn to replace Adam of Luton 1248 (*Ann. Dunstable*, p. 175).
Roger Occ. 25 June 1257 (*Bucks F.*, I, 106); 25 Nov. 1259 (*Bucks F.*, II, 1).
Abbey recorded as vacant Oct. 1272 (*Reg. R.. Gravesend*, p. 249).
Peter 1295– Bl. 24 Aug. 1295 (*Reg. Sutton*, V, 116). Occ. 25 June 1303 (*Bucks F.*, II, 86).
John of Medmenham Occ. 23 Nov. 1333 (Lincoln, Ep. Reg., IV, f. 343r).[16]
Geoffrey Occ. [?8} Oct. 1318 (BL, Campbell Cht. X. 8; Bodl., Rawlinson ms. B.461, f. 8r); 2 Oct. 1321 (*CCR 1318–21*, p. 501).
Stephen of Thame 1375– M. of Medmenham, lic. to receive bl. from any Catholic bp 20 May 1375 (Lincoln, Ep. Reg., XII, f. 128r).
The next recorded abb., **Henry**, occ. 1416 (Langley, *Hist. of Desborough Hundred*, I, 340, with no source given).

MEREVALE (Warws) (Bordesley) f. 10 Oct. 1148
  Lists in *VCH Warws*, II, 78; *Heads*, I, 138.
Henry 1195– Succ. as abb. 1195 (*Ann. Waverley*, p. 250). Last recorded occ. May 1210 x May 1211 (*Warws F.*, I, no. 202).
John Occ. 1216 x 1222 (*temp.* abb. Nicholas of Burton) (*Burton Chts.*, nos. 72, 73).
William Occ. *c.* 1226 in response to papal mand. of 31 Oct. 1225 (*Ctl. Darley*, I, 179).
Robert Occ. 1230 (*Gresley Chts.*, no. 44); 20 Jan. 1232 (PRO, Leics F., CP25/1/21/13, no. 158); 22 June 1236 (PRO, Leics F. 121/14, no. 199); n.d. (*temp.* Henry III) (*Gresley Chts.*, no. 81).
Ralph Occ. *c.* Oct. 1241 x Oct. 1242 (PRO, E210/79); *c.* 1242 (PRO, E210/95); 12 July 1243 to

---

[16] The reference to abb. John in 1308 (Langley, *Hist. of Desborough Hundred*, II, 340) is actually an error for Mendham priory.

3 Feb. 1248 (PRO, Leics F., CP25/1/121/17, no. 271; 122/204, no. 333); 21 Apr. 1247 (*Warws F.*, I, no. 628).

Richard Occ. 30 Apr. 1251 (*Lancs F.*, I, p. 133 no. 132); 2 June, 16 June 1252 (PRO, Leics F., CP25/1/122/22, nos. 398, 380).

Robert Occ. 13 Oct. 1254 (PRO, Leics F., CP25/1/122/23, no. 408); 1254 (PRO, LR14/1001); 30 Apr. 1256 (PRO, Leics F., CP25/1/122/23, no. 424); 25 Apr. 1260 (*Lancs F.*, I, 132); 11 June 1262 (*Warws F.*, I, no. 821). Prob. the same as the next abb.

Robert de Hocthorp (Okthorpe) Occ. June 1273 (*Ctl. Rydeware*, p. 271). Mentd as former abb. in case of 1346 (*YB 20 Edward III, part 2*, p. 367).

Robert Occ. 16 Feb. 1276, 25 Nov. 1276, 8 May 1278 (PRO, Leics F., CP25/1/123/32, nos. 30, 40, 45). Prob. the same as above.

William de Wavere Occ. *temp.* Edward I (*Derby Chts.*, no. 2033; *Gresley Chts.*, no. 159); 9 Nov. 1284 (*Gresley Chts.*, no. 129); Jan. 1285 (PRO, Just.1/956, mm. 30, 32); 18 Sept. 1290, 15 May 1292 (*CPR 1281–92*, pp. 406, 516).

John 1294– Bl. 21 Sept. 1294 (*Reg. Sutton*, V, 31).

Ralph Occ. July 1302 x July 1303 (*Ctl. Rydeware*, p. 262); 22 Feb. 1317 (Staffs RO, D1790/A/13/18).

Thomas 1321– Bl. by bp of Worcester on commn from bp of Coventry and Lichfield 21 Sept. 1321 (*Reg. Cobham*, p. 31).

William of Leicester (Leycestre, Leycestria) Occ. 9 Oct. 1342 (*Gresley Chts.*, no. 257); 6 Oct. 1343 (*CCR 1343–46*, p. 243); 28 Feb. 1345 (*CPR 1343–45*, p. 443); Mich. 1346 (*YB 20 Edward III, part 2*, p. 367).

Thomas of Witherley (Wytherle) Occ. 15 Feb. 1348 (*CCR 1346–49*, p. 490); 29 Sept. 1348 (PRO, E315/45/232). ? the same as the abb. of Bordesley (q.v.).

Robert Occ. 26 June 1351 (*CPL*, III, 448).

Thomas de Scheynton Occ. 9 Oct. 1370 (*Reg. Stretton*, II, 139); 12 Mar. 1378 (PRO, C146/6593).

NEATH (Glam.), St Mary and Holy Trinity (Savigny) f. 25 Oct. 1130
Lists in Birch, *Neath Abbey*, pp. 167–9; Birch, *Margam Abbey*, pp. 333–4; *Heads*, I, 138.

Abraham Occ. (A.) 1201 (*Glam. Chts.*, II, 263); n.d. (*Gir. Camb.*, IV, 131).

Clement –1218 Prob. prev. pr. 1201 (*Glam. Chts.*, II, 263). D. 1218 (*Ann. Margam*, p. 33).

Gervase 1218– Pr. of Neath, succ. 1218 (ibid.).

Robert Excommunicated and the secular arm instructed to jail him 1245 x 1253 (*Llandaff Episcopal Acta*, no. 86).

Adam of Carmarthen (Kaermerdyn) Occ. (A.) 25 June 1266 (PRO, DL25/254); 1283 (*Glam. Chts.*, III, 860); 13 Apr. 1289 (*CChR 1327–41*, p. 357; *Glam. Chts.*, V, 1677–9). Seal (*Mon. Seals*, p. 63).

David Occ. 14 Oct. 1322 (PRO, E40/3213); 1322 (Cowley, *Monastic Order in South Wales*, p. 247).

William Occ. 11 Apr. 1336, 19 Apr. 1340, 20 Oct. 1341 (*Glam. Chts.*, IV, nos. 962, 982, 989).

Thomas Occ. 18 June 1358 (*Glam. Chts.*, IV, no. 1018). Mentd 8 Nov. 1359 (Birch, *Neath Abbey*, p. 84).

John Occ. 17 Dec. 1401, ordained priest (*Regs. St Davids*, I, 228).

NETLEY (Hants), St Mary and St Edward the Confessor (Beaulieu) (De Sancto Edwardo, Edwardstowe, Letley, Lettele) f. 27 July 1239
List in *VCH Hants*, II, 149.

Robert de Clare –1260 Occ. 30 June 1240 (BL, Add Cht. 20234); 14 Jan. 1241, 1 July 1243

(PRO, Hants F., CP25/1/203/7, nos. 57, 68); Oct. 1243 x Oct. 1244 (*Surrey F.*, p. 27); 1244 (WAM no. 7122); (R.) 1 Apr. 1245 (*Ctl. Winchester*, no. 453; *CPR 1313–17*, p. 676; *Reg. Sandale*, p. 271); 1251 (PRO, E210/230); 1258 (PRO, Hants F., CP25/1/203/7, no. 83; 204/10, no. 10). D. by 11 Jan. 1260 (*CR 1259–61*, p. 24). Full name (*Winchester Common Seal Reg.*, no. 306). Desc. as former abb. 1277 (*Earliest English Law Reports*, I, p. 79).

Richard 1260– Mand. for seisin 11 Jan. 1260 (*CR 1259–61*, p. 24); n.d. (Surrey RO, Loseley ms. 334/26).

Simon Occ. n.d. (late 13th cent.) (PRO, E210/1703). The sequence of abbots at this period is uncertain.

Stephen Occ. n.d. [1275 x 1290] (WCM no. 3518); Easter 1278 (PRO, CP40/24, m. 29).

Walter de Chesledene Going to General Chapter 10 June 1290 (*CPR 1281–92*, p. 362). Occ. 17 Apr. 1303 (PRO, E210/323).

William Deverel Occ. 5 Nov. 1311 (PRO, E210/630); (W.) 1312 (PRO, E210/6841); Jan. 1329 x Jan. 1330 (BL, Harl. Cht. 44 F 22); 1 Jan. 1331 (*CPR 1330–34*, p. 34); 3 Feb. 1341 (*Ctl. St Denys*, I, no. 169); Jan. 1341 x Jan. 1342 (PRO, E326/9332); 24 Jan. 1348 (*CCR 1346–49*, p. 425).[17]

John 1348– Bl. 21 Dec. 1348, no reason given for vacancy (*Reg. Edington*, II, no. 196). Occ. 29 Nov. 1351 (*CCR 1349–54*, p. 399).

William 1355– Bl. 30 Aug. 1355, no reason given for vacancy (*Reg. Edington*, II, no. 534). Occ. Jan. 1356 x Jan. 1357 (PRO, E210/1901); 29 Jan. 1356 (*Reg. Edington*, I, no. 1059).

John –1372 Occ. Jan. 1370 x Jan. 1371 (PRO, E210/7828). Cess. by 2 Mar. 1372 (*Reg. Wykeham*, I, 41).

Henry (of) Inglesham 1372–1374 Eln proceedings 2 Mar. 1372; bl. and prof. obed. 14 Mar. 1372 (ibid., 40–2; II 164). D. by 4 Sept. 1374 (ibid., I, 52–3).

John Stelharde (Stillard) 1374–1387 Abb.-el., pres. to bp 4 Sept.; bl. and prof. obed. 8 Sept. 1374 (ibid.). Cess. by 3 June 1387 (ibid., 163).

NEWENHAM (Devon) (Beaulieu) f. 6 Jan. 1247

Lists in Oliver, pp. 358–9 from *Mon. Angl.*, V, 690, 693–4; Davidson, *History of Newenham Abbey*, pp. 11–88, based upon the accounts in Bodl., ms. Top. Devon d. 5 and BL, ms. Arundel 17. Also lists in *TDA*, 9 (1877), p. 379; *Cist. Devon*, p. 157.

John Godard 1246–1248 First abb., native of Canterbury, adm. 6 Jan. 1247 (Bodl., ms. Top. Devon d. 5, f. 3v). Res. Newenham, 18 Aug. 1248 (Bodl., ms Top. Devon d.5, f. 3v, cf. BL, ms. Arundel 17, f. 53v which gives 4 Apr. 1247). Abb. of Cleeve 1248 (q.v.). See Sharpe, *Latin Writers*, p. 258.

Henry of Sparsholt (Sparsholte, Spersolte) **1248–1250** Native of Berkshire, cellarer of Newenham, succ. 6 Sept. 1248 (Bodl., ms. Top. Devon d. 5, f. 3v; cf. BL, ms. Arundel 17, f. 53v which gives 6 Apr. 1247). Occ. 14 May 1249 (*Devon F.*, I, p. 259, no. 514). Res. owing to illness 3 May 1250 (Bodl., ms. Top. Devon d. 5. f. 4r; BL, ms. Arundel 17, f. 53v).

John of Robertsbridge (de Ponte Roberti) **1250–1252/3** Pr. of Beaulieu, succ. Henry. Cess. 25 Feb. 1252/3 (Bodl., ms. Top. Devon d. 5, f. 4r; BL, ms. Arundel 17, ff. 53v–54r).

Geoffrey de Blanchevile 1252/3–1262 *Placitator* of Beaulieu, succ. 29 Mar. 1252 (Bodl., ms. Top. Devon d. 5, f. 4r) but more likely 9 Mar. 1253 (BL, ms. Arundel 17, f. 53v). D. early June 1262 while absent from Newenham (Bodl., ms. Top. Devon d. 5, f. 4r).

Hugh de Cokiswell (Cokeswille) **1262–1265** Porter of Beaulieu, succ. 14 June 1262 but never received episcopal bl. (Bodl., ms. Top. Devon d. 5, f. 4r; BL, ms. Arundel 17, f. 54r). Went

---

[17] B., abb. of Netley, occ. 1319 (S.O. Addy, *XVI Charters of Roche Abbey, now first published* (Sheffield 1878), p. 20, no. viii; id., 'Roche abbey charters', *Trans. Hunter AS*, 4 (1929–37), pp. 227–48, at 239). Is this an error or were there two abb. Williams?

to Beaulieu and secretly res. 5 July 1265 (Bodl., ms. Top. Devon d. 5, f. 4r; BL, ms. Arundel 17, f. 54r).

John of Northampton (Norhamton) **1265–1272** M. of Beaulieu, *custos* of the manor of Faringdon, el. 8 July 1265, received abbey 9 July 1265 (Bodl., ms. Top. Devon d. 5, f. 4r–v; BL, ms. Arundel 17, f. 54r–v). Cess. 11 Sept. 1272 (Bodl., ms. Top. Devon d. 5, f. 4v; BL, ms. Arundel 17, f. 54r–v). Said in error to occ. Oct. 1275 (*Ctl. Glastonbury*, III, p. 580, no. 1065).[18]

William of Cornwall (Cornubia) **1272–1288** Pr. of Beaulieu, apptd 12 Sept. 1272 (Bodl., ms. Top. Devon d. 5, f. 4v; BL, ms. Arundel 17, ff. 54v–55r). Occ. 1281 x 1282 (*London and Middlesex F.*, pp. 57–8); 26 Apr. 1284 (*Ctl. Glastonbury*, I, p. 54, no. 77); Mich. 1286 x Mich. 1287 (PRO, E159/60, m. 16d). William went blind, returned to Beaulieu and cess. 1288 (Bodl., ms. Top. Devon d. 5, f. 5r).[19]

Richard of Chichester (Chichestre, Chykestr') **1288–1293** M. of Beaulieu, succ. 13 Sept 1288. Removed from office 15 Oct. 1293 (Bodl., ms. Top. Devon d. 5, f. 5r). But cf. occ. 20 Oct. 1287 (*Cornwall F.*, p. 184, no. 320); Easter 1288 (PRO, CP40/72, m. 91); 14 Apr. 1288 (*CPR 1281–92*, p. 292).

Richard of Petherton (Pederton, Pedirton) **1293–1297** Sub-cellarer of Beaulieu, succ. 11 Nov. 1293; cess. 13 Apr. 1297 (Bodl., ms. Top. Devon d. 5, f. 5r; BL, ms. Arundel 17, f. 55r).

William le Fria (Frie, Frye) **1297–1304** Previously abb. of Forde, succ. 14 Apr. 1297; cess. 3 Feb. 1304 and bur. at Forde (Bodl., ms. Top. Devon d. 5, f. 5r).

Richard of Petherton (Pedirtone) **1304** Recalled to office 4 Feb. 1304; d. returning from the General Chapter 5 Nov. 1304 and bur. at Waverley (Bodl., ms. Top. Devon d. 5, f. 5r; BL, ms. Arundel 17, f. 55r).

Ralph of Shapwick (Sapewyk, Shapewyk) **1304–1314** Pr. of Newenham, a native of Somerset, succ. 6 Dec. 1304; cess. at Beaulieu 13 Aug. 1314 but returned to Newenham and bur. there (Bodl., ms. Top. Devon d. 5, f. 5r–v; BL, ms. Arundel 17, f. 55r–v). Occ. Mich. 1310 (PRO, CP40/183, attorneys m. 21).

Robert of Pupplisbury (Publesburi) **1314–1321** Cellarer of Beaulieu, a native of Somerset, succ. 30 Sept. 1314 (Bodl., ms. Top. Devon d. 5, f. 5v). Bl. 15 Jan. 1315 (*Reg. Stapeldon*, p. 237). Cess. 12 May 1321 and returned to Beaulieu where he d. (Bodl., ms. Top. Devon d. 5, f. 5v).

John de Cokiswell (Cokeswelle, Cokiswille, Kokiswille) **1321–1324** Pr. of Beaulieu, succ. 13 May 1321 (Bodl., ms. Top. Devon d. 5, f. 5v). Bl. 2 Feb. 1322 (*Reg. Stapeldon*, p. 237). D. 26 Dec. 1324 after long illness and buried at Newenham (ibid.; Bodl., ms. Top. Devon d. 5, f. 5v; BL, ms. Arundel 17, f. 45v).

John de Geytyngton 1325–1338 Native of Northants, archdeacon of Lewes, canon of Chichester cathedral, *portarius* of Beaulieu. Succ. 22 Feb. 1325 (Bodl., ms. Top. Devon d. 5, ff. 5v–6r; BL, ms. Arundel 17, f. 45v). Bl. 17 Mar. 1325 (*Reg. Stapeldon*, p. 237). Occ. 1328 (*Index to Placita de Banco*, p. 107); 23 Sept. 1332 (*Reg. Grandisson*, II, 658). Went blind, cess. 11 May 1338 and d. 22 Feb. 1339 (Bodl., ms. Top. Devon d. 5, ff. 5v–6r).

Walter de la Houe (atte Houe) **1338–** Native of Devon, *portarius* of Newenham, succ. 13 May 1338 (Bodl., ms. Top. Devon d. 5, f. 6r; BL, ms. Arundel 17, f. 45v). Bl. and prof. obed. 31 May 1338 (*Reg. Grandisson*, II, 878). Occ. 1341 (ibid., 971); Easter 1343, Easter 1344, 1353 x 1354 (*TDA*, 9 (1877), pp. 368–70; *Cist. Devon*, pp. 146–8); 30 June 1349 (WAM no. 3532)

---

[18] This is a cht. dated Oct. 1275 between John (Taunton) abb. of Glastonbury (1274–91) and John (of Northampton) abb. of Newenham (who d. 1272) (*TDA*, 10 (1878), 375). The abb. of Newenham at that date (1275) was William of Cornwall (1272–88). At no date could the two Johns have met.

[19] In BL, ms. Arundel 17, ff. 54v–55r William is said to have been dep. 15 Oct. 1293 (*sic*) and Richard of Chichester is omitted from the list.

Richard of Branscombe *alias* **Exeter** (Exceter) 1361– Born in Devon (BL, ms. Arundel 17, f. 45v). Bl. 7 Mar. 1361 (*Reg. Grandisson*, III, 1220). Occ. Easter 1361 (PRO, CP40/406, mm. 14, 53); 24 May, 22 Nov. 1373 (*Reg. Brantingham*, I, 304, 319); n.d. (?1377) (PRO, E179/24/10B); 24 June 1380 (Devon RO, Petre 123M/TB.224); 26 June 1380 (ibid., TB.225).

The next recorded abb., **John Legga**, prof. obed. 24 Sept. 1391 (*Reg. Brantingham*, II, 737).

NEWMINSTER (Northumberland) (Fountains) f. 5 Jan. 1138 (? for 1139)
   Lists in *Ctl. Newminster*, pp. xii ff.; A.M. Oliver, 'A list of the abbots of Newminster', *Arch. Aeliana*, 3rd ser., XII (1915), 206–15; *Heads*, I, 138–9.

Walter –1217 D. at Cîteaux General Chapter *c.* 14 Sept. 1217 (*Ch. Melrose*, f. 35v (34v); cf. Canivez, I, 484).

Henry 1217–1219 Pr. of Roche, succ. Walter 1217. D. 1219 (*Ch. Melrose*, f. 35v (34v), 38r–v (37r–v)). Occ. (H.) 1 June 1218 (*Ctl. Rievaulx*, p. 223, wrongly dated 1317; cf. *Arch. Aeliana*, list, p. 206).

Robert Occ. 20 Apr. 1220 (*Northumberland and Durham F.*, I, 28); 2 May 1221 (*Ctl. Newminster*, p. 180); n.d. (1218 x 1224) (ibid., p. 215; *EEA Durham*, no. 277 forthcoming).

Stephen of Eston –1247 Cellarer of Fountains, abb. of Sallay to *c.* 1233 x 1234 (q.v.). Occ. 6 Oct. 1241, 13 Oct. 1241 (*Northumberland and Durham F.*, I, 66, 69, nos. 157, 172); (Simon – scribal error) (*Ctl. Newminster*, p. 68); (S.) 15 Mar. 1245 (*CPL*, I, 278). El. abb. of Fountains 1247 (*Mem. Fountains*, p. 137). D. 6 Sept. 1252 (*Ctl. Fountains*, II, 765). Seal (*Durham Seals*, II, p. 577, no. 3527). See Sharpe, *Latin Writers*, p. 622.

Adam Occ. *temp.* Archbp Walter de Gray (d. 1255) (*Ctl. Newminster*, p. 65); n.d. (1251 x 1255) with William, archdn of Richmond (*Reg. Gray*, pp. 290–1); 1256 x 1265 (*Ctl. Sallay*, II, 101); (A.) 1258 x 1273 (*Ann. Durham*, p. 199 no. 178); *c.* 1260 x 1275 (*Northumberland and Durham Deeds*, p. 9); 1269 (*Northumberland Assize Roll*, p. 154); Whitsun 1272, 1274 (*Ctl. Newminster*, pp. 141, 238); (A.) *c.* 12 Apr. [1275] (PRO, SC1/17/153). Said to be called Pennington (Willis).[20]

Roger de Akeden (Akden) Occ. 1279 (*Northumberland Assize Roll.*, p. 241). Mentd as former abb. in a deed of 1 Nov. 1302 (Hodgson, *Northumberland*, vol. II, pt. ii, 344, 417).

John of York El. before 1289 (*Arch. Aeliana*, list, p. 220, citing BL, Harl. ms. 112, f. 154, *temp.* Henry, abb. of Fountains). Occ. 1291 and 1295 (*Arch. Aeliana*, list, citing PRO, CP40/91, m. 216 and CP40/110, m. 280d). Possibly John of York rather than John of Whelpington who occ. 11 June 1296 (*Ctl. Newminster*, p. 143); Trin. 1297 (PRO, CP40/119, m. 71), but it is of course unclear exactly when John of York vacated office and John of Whelpington succ.

John of Whelpington For name see BL, Lansdowne ms. 436, f. 120v; Oliver list. Prob. occ. from 1303 to 1311 (DCD, Misc. Chts. 4152, 4175, 4208, 4214, 4263, 4329, 4345, 4349); 24 Nov. 1305 (*Northumberland Ass. Roll*, pp. 386–7, 391); 10 Apr. 1308 (*Ctl. Newminster*, p. 49); Trin. 1309 (PRO, CP40/178, mm. 275, 301d); 20 Mar. 1314 (*Ctl. Newminster*, p. 51); 1315 (*Reg. Pal. Dun.*, II, 731); 20 Sept. 1315 (*CPR 1313–17*, p. 566; *Ctl. Newminster*, p. 49). Could be Whelpington/Thornton Seal (*Durham Seals*, II, p. 577, nos. 3528–9).

J. of Thornton Occ. 16 Mar. 1310 (*Ctl. Fountains*, I, 352–3).

Walter Occ. Mich. 1328 (*Index to Placita de Banco*, p. 510).

William Occ. 7 Mar. 1334 (*CCR 1333–37*, p. 300).

Walter Occ. 30 Sept. 1335 (Oxford, Merton Coll. mun. 546); 22 June 1337 (*CCR 1337–39*, p. 138).

---

[20] Tanner, *Notitia Monastica*, app. is the only source for abb. William of Edmundsbury, said to occ. 1276 but no supporting documentary evidence has been located.

John Occ. 1 Nov. 1356 (*Ridley Chts.*, p. 68).

Walter Occ. 7 July 1358 (*Northumberland and Durham Deeds*, p. 96). Willis says Walter de Hink occ. 1368, but his source has not been located.

The next recorded abb., **John Pape**, occ. June 1378 x June 1379 (PRO, E179/62/4, m. 3d).

PIPEWELL (Northants) (Newminster) f. 13 Sept. 1143
  Lists in *VCH Northants*, II, 121; early 14th cent. list in BL, Cotton ms. Otho B. XIV, f. 197r; *Mon. Angl.*, V, 433n; *Heads*, I, 139.

Robert (?of Pattishall) Occ. 1209 x 1210 (BL, Cotton ms. Caligula A. XIII, f. 145v); *c.* 13 Oct. 1211 (BL, Stowe ms. 937, ff. 23r, 120v); ?1214 x 1215 (Cheney, *Inn. III*, no. 1008); 1230 (*CPR 1225–32*, p. 354; *CR 1227–33*, p. 396); 17 Sept. 1235 (BL, Stowe ms. 937, f. 26r; BL, Cotton ms. Caligula A. XII, ff. 26v–27r). For prob. surname see *Heads*, I, 139, n.1.

William (?de Kynton) For prob. surname see ibid. William de Kynton occ. as cellarer 1235 (BL, Cotton ms. Caligula A XII, f. 27r). Occ. as abb. 12 July 1243 (PRO, Northants F., CP25/1/173/32, no. 473); 1244 (ibid., CP25/1/173/33, no. 478); 1245 (PRO, Rutland F., CP25/1/192/3, no. 25); 27 May 1247 (*Warws F.*, I, no. 643); 20 Oct. 1247 (PRO, Northants F., CP25/1/173/38, no. 561). Referred to 1275 as former abb. Kynton (PRO, CP40/9, m. 27); similarly in 1285 (PRO, Just.1/956, m. 22d).

Robert of Newbold (Neubold) For surname see BL, Cotton ms. Otho B XIV, f. 197r. Occ. 18 Nov. 1251 (*Warws F.*, I, no. 699); 10 May 1254 (PRO, Northants F., CP25/1/173/41, no. 690); 20 Oct. 1256 (ibid., CP25/1/174/42, no. 704).

Gerard de Lega In office for 10 years (BL, Cotton ms. Otho B XIV, f. 197r). Occ. 16 June 1269 (PRO, Northants F., CP25/1/174/48, no. 873); n.d. (PRO E326/3134).

Reginald In office for 1 year (BL, Cotton ms. Otho B XIV, f. 197r).

Thomas of Grafton (Graftone) Abb. for 8 years (ibid.). Occ. 3 Nov. 1278 (*Warws F.*, I, no. 941); Mich. 1278 x Mich. 1279 (PRO, E159/52, m. 11d).

John de Hillum (Hillom) 1280–?1295 Abb. for 15 years (BL, Cotton ms. Otho B XIV, f. 197r). Bl. 10 June 1280 (*Reg. Sutton*, II, 4). Occ. Nov. 1280 x Nov. 1281 (PRO, E326/11658); 1284 x 1289 (*Ctl. Sallay*, II, no. 572); 28 Jan. 1285 (*Warws F.*, II, no. 994); 1285 (PRO, Northants F. CP25/1/174/54, no. 192); 24 Apr. 1287 (PRO, C81/1788/38); 14 Aug. 1289 (*CPR 1281–92*, p. 319).

Richard de Heyham ?1295–1298 Abb. for 4 years (BL, Cotton ms. Otho B XIV, f. 197r). Occ. Nov. 1296 x Nov. 1297 (PRO, E210/8474); 29 Sept. 1297 (BL, Add. Cht. 22547).

Andrew de Royewelle (?Rothwell) ?1298–1308 Abb. for 10 years '*optime officium occupavit*' (BL, Cotton ms. Otho B XIV, f. 197r). Bl. of unnamed abb. 21 Sept. 1298 (*Reg. Sutton*, VI, 110). Occ. Mich. 1305 (PRO, CP40/153, m. 145).

Thomas of Thockrington (Thokerington) 1309–1320 Former pr. of Newminster. Abb. for 12 years and 21 weeks (BL, Cotton ms. Otho B XIV, f. 197r). Bl. and prof. obed. 6 Jan. 1309 (Lincoln, Ep. Reg., III, f. 147r). Occ. 27 Sept. 1311 (*CPR 1307–13*, pp. 421–2); 1312 (BL, Cotton ms. Otho B XIV, f. 197r); Easter 1317 (PRO, CP40/218, m. 11); 22 July 1318 (*CCR 1318–23*, p. 94); 28 Feb. 1320 (ibid., p. 223); Mich. 1320 (PRO, KB27/242, attorneys m. 11d).

William de Lalleford ?1320–1322 Abb. '*qui non bene se habuit in regimine domus*' for 2 years and 16 weeks (BL, Cotton ms. Otho B XIV, f. 197r).

Nicholas Occ. 22 Jan. 1324 (PRO, E315/52/157); 14 Dec. 1327 (*CCR 1327–30*, p. 238); 25 July 1331, 13 Oct. 1331 (*CCR 1330–33*, pp. 256, 347); 12 Aug. 1334, 26 Aug. 1334 (*CCR 1333–37*, pp. 329, 332); 3 June 1337 (*CCR 1337–39*, p. 131); 11 Apr. 1340 (*CCR 1339–41*, p. 456); 1340 (BL, Sloane Cht. XXXII. 3); 10 Aug. 1344 (*CPL*, III, 158); 18 Aug. 1344, 23 Aug. 1344

(*CCR 1343–46*, pp. 453, 454); 18 Aug. 1344 (*CPR 1343–45*, p. 335); 29 May 1346 (Lincoln D. & C., Dij/52/3/18); 14 Aug. 1350 (*Reg. Bateman*, I, no. 25).[21]

John Occ. 7 Oct. 1354 (PRO, E315/44/274); 6 Feb. 1358 (Lincoln, Ep. Reg., X, f. 171r).

Thomas Occ. 11 Jan. 1376 (PRO, E326/8636, /8444). Mentd 21 Sept. 1383 as former abb. (PRO, E315/46/348).

Roger Occ. 21 Sept. 1383 (ibid.).

QUARR (Isle of Wight) (Savigny) f. 27 Apr. 1132

Lists in *VCH Hants*, II, 139; S.F. Hockey, *Quarr Abbey and its Lands 1132 – 1631*, pp.259–60; *Quarr Chts.*, p. 138; *Heads*, I, 139.

H. Occ. 1206 (*Ctl. Canonsleigh*, no. 181; *Quarr Chts.*, no. 458).

Hugh Occ. n.d. (*ante* Sept. 1217) (*Quarr Chts.*, no. 340, dated *c.* 1215 – dated by the d. of William de Redvers, earl of Devon). ? the same as abb. H. above. The *Quarr Chts.* list identifies the above as Henry but I have found no evidence for the full name.

John Occ. 24 Apr. 1219 (PRO, Hants F., CP25/1/203/4, no.30; *Quarr Chts.*, no. 141, incorrectly dated).

Henry Occ. n.d. (*c.* 1227) (*Quarr Chts.*, no. 436); 7 Apr. 1228 (ibid., no. 287); 29 Apr. 1228 (ibid., no. 441); 22 June 1228 (*Devon F.*, I, no. 228; *Quarr Chts.*, no. 461).

Philip –1238 Occ. n.d. (early 13th cent.) (PRO, E326/8887; *Quarr Chts.*, nos. 119, 307, dated *c.* 1228 x 1238); 1235 (*An. Sac. Ord. Cist.*, VIII, pp. 303–5, no. 91); 1235 x 1238 (*Quarr Chts.*, nos. 127, 474). D. 1238 (*Ann. Waverley*, p. 319).

Augustine 1238– Pr. of Quarr succ. 1238 (ibid.). Occ. 6 Apr. 1239 (*Quarr Chts.*, no. 465); 1247 (ibid., no. 425); 1248 (ibid., no. 185); Jan. 1249 (ibid., nos. 432, 517); Feb. 1249 (ibid., nos. 120, 128).

Andrew Occ. 13 Oct. 1253 (PRO, F. Var. Cos. CP25/1/284/19, no. 108); 1254 (*Quarr Chts.*, nos. 314, 422); 1254 x 1258 (ibid., no. 536); Feb. 1256 (ibid., nos. 158–9); 1258 (ibid., nos. 447–8).

Philip Occ. 19 May 1262 (PRO, Hants F., CP25/1/204/10, no. 37);. n.d. (mid-13th cent.) (*Quarr Chts.*, no. 160, where it is dated *c.* 1260); *c.* 1268 (ibid., no. 160). Prob. the abb. dep. in 1269 (Canivez, III, 74).[22]

Elias Occ. Advent 1270 (*Quarr Chts.*, no. 505); 1279 (E326/2642; /2946).

Adam of Arundel Occ. 21 Mar. 1274 (*Quarr Chts.*, no. 40); (A.) 5 Mar. 1277 (*Ctl. Kirkstall*, p. 45, no. 60); 1282 (PRO, E326/5185; E315/33/108); 1283 (BL, Cotton ms. Tiberius D VI, part 1, f. 32v); 1284 (*Quarr Chts.*, nos. 116, 365); 1286, 1287 (PRO, C241/6/35; /7/27; /7/250); 1292 (ibid., no. 156); 1295 (PRO, C241/32/129); 1303 (ibid., no. 418; BL, Add Cht. 20219); Christmas 1304 (*Quarr Chts.*, no. 162). For full name see Madox, *Form.*, p. 305, no. 535.

Walter Occ. several times from 24 June 1308 (*Quarr Chts.*, no. 138) to July 1323 (ibid., nos. 368–70); 18 July 1323 (BL, Cotton ms. Tiberius D VI, part 1, f. 53r–v).[23]

Geoffrey 1325– Bl. and prof. of obed. 29 Jan. 1325 (Winchester, Reg. Stratford, f. 11v). Occ. 25 June 1330 (*Quarr Chts.*, no.205); from 1331 to 1342 (ibid., nos. 144, 245, 388); 31 Mar. 1346 (ibid., no. 194).

Robert 1349– Bl. 24 May 1349 (*Reg. Edington*, II, no. 215). Occ. from 28 June 1349 to 19 July 1352 (*Quarr Chts.*, nos. 412, 263 – the latter is dated incorrectly in the edition).

William Occ. 5 Feb. 1357 (*Quarr Chts.*, no. 218); many times between 1358 and 1365 (ibid., nos. 221, 18); 12 June 1366 (*CPR 1364–67*, p. 253).

The next abb., **John Wynchestre**, was bl. and prof. obed. 25 Jan. 1381 (*Reg. Wykeham*, I, 112).

---

[21] *Mon. Angl.*, V, 433 has abb. Nicholas, then abb. Thomas, abb. William de Lalleford re-el., and then Nicholas (without sources). It is more prob. that Nicholas occ. as abb. 1324–50 – no ref. to Thomas or a second term for William de Lalleford has been found so far.
[22] The ref. to an abb. Peter *c.* 1264 in the *Quarr Chts.* list relates to the mid-12th century abb. of the same name.   [23] The ref. to an abb. Geoffrey occ. 1314 in the *Quarr Chts.* list has not been found.

REVESBY (Lincs), (St Laurence) St Mary and St Laurence (Rievaulx) f. 9 Aug. 1143
Lists in *VCH Lincs*, II, 142; *Heads*, I, 140.

Ralph Latest recorded occ. 20 Oct. 1208 (*Lincs F.*, *1199–1216*, p. 126, no. 250).

Elias 1217– Abb. of Rievaulx 1211–1215, el. abb. of Revesby Dec. 1217 (*Ch. Melrose*, pp. 59, 68). Occ. 1230 (*CR 1227–31*, p. 390); *c.* 1230 (*HMC Var. Coll.*, IV, 326); July 1231 (*Lincs F.*, I, 229); n.d. (1231 x 43) (PRO, DL36/3/185). Stated 1335 to have occ. 100 years earlier (*CCR 1333–37*, p. 461).

William Occ. mid-13th cent., stated in 1335 to have occ. 80 years earlier (ibid).[24]

Walter Occ. from 9 Dec. 1256 to 6 May 1273 (*Lincs F.*, II, pp. 139, 222); 26 May 1257 (BL, Cotton ms. Vespasian E XVIII, f. 207r); Oct. 1262 x Oct. 1263 (*CCR 1333–37*, p. 461).

William Occ. 12 Nov. 1271 (*Lincs F.*, II, 249).

Robert Occ. late 13th cent., stated in 1335 to have occ. 60 years earlier (*CCR 1333–37*, p. 461).

Walter Occ. 19 May 1284 (PRO, Lincs. F., CP25/1/133/58, no. 54).

Henry Occ. 13 Oct. 1286 (PRO, Lincs F., CP25/1/133/59, no. 36); 25 Nov. 1291 (ibid., 133/63 no. 4).

William 1294– Bl. 29 Sept. 1294 (*Reg. Sutton*, V, 32). Occ. n.d. (*temp.* Edward I) (BL, Add. Cht. 5305).

Walter of Keal (Kele) Occ. 26 Aug. 1295 (*Reg. Halton*, I, 54).

Henry 1302– Prof. obed. 14 Jan. 1302 (Lincoln, Ep. Reg., III, f. 411r). Occ. (E.) 4 Aug. 1302 (*Ctl. Fountains*, I, 62); 9 Aug. 1308 (*Reg. Greenfield*, III, no. 1194); 26 Mar. 1335, 29 May 1337 (*Reg. Burghersh*, I, nos. 461, 537); 29 June 1346 (*HMC Delisle & Dudley*, I, 17).

Robert of Raithby (Ratheby) Occ. Jan. 1358 x Jan. 1359 (*Cal. Misc. Inq.*, IV, 163).

William Occ. 2 Jan. 1362 (Lincoln, Ep. Reg., VIII, f. 165r).

Simon of Spilsby (Spillesby) Occ. 1377 (*Clerical Poll-Taxes*, p. 55, no. 766).

Henry Occ. 1381 (ibid., p. 117, no. 1424, and p. 163, no. 2034); 26 Nov. 1385 (*CPR 1385–89*, p. 64).

REWLEY (Oxon) (Thame) (Bello Loco Regis; Locus Regalis) f. 11 Dec. 1281
List in *VCH Oxford*, II, 83.

Richard Previously abb. of Thame, occ. 1284 x 1285 (PRO, Just.1/710, mm. 9, 42).

Warin Occ. Mich. 1284 x Mich. 1285 (PRO, E159/58, m. 19); going overseas 4 June 1286 (*CPR 1281–92*, p. 249).

Robert Occ. 6 Dec. 1287 (*CChR 1257–1300*, p. 339); 28 June 1289 (*CPR 1281–92*, p. 316).

Richard Occ. (R.) 4 June 1291 (PRO, E326/105; E315/46/85); 21 June 1294 (*Ctl. Eynsham*, I, no. 501); 14 July 1297 (*Ctl. Thame*, I, no. 40; *Ctl. Oseney*, II, no. 1059).

Richard 1302– Bl. and prof. obed. 27 Dec. 1302 (Lincoln, Ep. Reg., III, f. 51v).

Thomas 1310– Bl. and prof. obed. 10 May 1310 (ibid., f. 180v).

Peter de Duvone 1317– Bl. by ex-archbp of Armagh and prof. obed. 7 May 1317 (ibid., f. 368r). Occ. 1320 (C.H. Talbot, 'Cîteaux and Scarborough', p. 144, no. xxx). Born in France, occ. 21 Aug. 1324, 4 Nov. 1324 (*CPR 1324–27*, pp. 20, 42).

Simon Occ. 1 Aug. 1330 (*CPR 1327–30*, p. 541); 28 Sept. 1332 (*CPR 1330–34*, p. 341); 17 Jan. 1337 (Lincoln, Ep. Reg., V, f. 544v); Jan. 1337 x Jan. 1338 (Wood, *City of Oxford*, II, 302).

Adam de Stanlegh(e) Occ. 24 May 1352 (*Ctl. Stoneleigh*, p. 254); 20 Aug. 1352 (PRO, C241/130/97); 14 June 1353 (*CPR 1350–54*, p. 466); 27 Aug. 1354 (*Reg. Grandisson*, II, 1132); 1368 (*Mon. Angl.*, V, 699); 15 Feb. 1370 (*Assize of Nuisance*, no. 570); 28 Oct. 1370 (PRO, E315/37/137). See Sharpe, *Latin Writers*, p. 21.

William Hacleston Occ. 14 June 1384 (PRO, C85/108/5); 18 Nov. 1386 (*CCR 1385–89*, p. 266); 5 Nov. 1391 (PRO, C202/C/95/5); 19 Oct. 1391, 15 Dec. 1392 (PRO, C85/11/68, 82).

---

[24] Poss. the abb. mentioned in 1246: '*abbas de Reueshi, qui episcopum suum processionaliter iterato recepit contra Ordinis instituta, viginti diebus sit extra stallum, et tribus diebus sit in levi culpa, uno eorum in pane et aqua*' (Canivez, II, 308).

RIEVAULX (Yorks N.) (Clairvaux) f. 5 Mar. 1132
  Lists in *VCH Yorks*, III, 152–3; *Ctl. Rievaulx*, pp. lxxxviii–cix; Clay, *Early Abbots*, pp. 31–37 (to 1260); *Heads*, I, 140.
Henry 1215–1216 Abb. of Wardon, succ. Elias 8 Apr. 1215 (*Ch. Melrose*, p. 59). D. at Rufford 1216 and bur. there (ibid., p. 63).
William III 1216–1223/4 Abb. of Holm Cultram, abb. of Melrose; el. abb. of Rievaulx 31 Aug. 1216 (ibid., pp. 61, 63). D. 1 Feb. 1223 or 1224 (ibid., p. 76 under 1223; *Ann. Waverley*, p. 299 under 1224).
Roger 1223/4–1239 Abb. of Wardon, el. 1223 or 1224 (ibid.). Occ. (R.) 24 Jan. 1225 (*Ctl. Fountains*, I, 216); 5 Feb. 1238 (*Glam. Chts.*, II, no. 504); Easter 1239 (*Ctl. Rievaulx*, p. 390). Res. 1239 (*Ch. Melrose*, pp. 76, 86).
Leonius 1239–1240 M. of Melrose, Abb. of Dundrennan, el. 1239; d. 8 Jan. 1240 (*Ch. Melrose*, pp. 86–7). Presumably the same as the abb. Leo, predecessor of abb. Adam, mentd in a plea of 1252 (*Yorks F., 1246–72*, p. 53n.).
Adam de Tilletai 1240– Succ. after Easter 1240 (*Ch. Melrose*, p. 87). Occ. from 25 June 1240 to 13 Oct. 1246 (*Yorks F., 1232–46*, pp. 63, 165); 1257 (*Ctl. Rievaulx*, p. 227); 19 Aug. 1260 (ibid., p. 226; Bodl., Dodsworth ms. 7, f. 140r); (A.) [Aug. 1265 x Sept. 1266] (PRO, SC1/60/77).[25]
William Occ. 8 July 1268 (*Yorks F., 1246–72*, p. 155).
William [?(of) Ellerbeck (Ellerbec, Ellerbek)] **1275–** Prof. obed. 21 July 1275 (*Reg. W. Giffard*, p. 270). Occ. 18 July 1279 (*Ctl. Fountains*, I, 322); 1 July 1280 (*Yorks F., 1272–1300*, p. 55); Easter term 1282 (PRO, CP40/45, m. 60); Mich. 1284 – Mich. 1285 (Baildon, I, 178); presumably the unnamed abb. going overseas 1282, 1285 (*CPR 1281–92*, pp. 18, 157); Easter 1286 (PRO, E159/59, m. 9d). Surname from *Ctl. Rievaulx*, p. c, citing Bodl., Dodsworth ms. 63, f. 68r, and by refs. to him as late abb. in 1304–5 case (Baildon, I, 179). It is just possible if there were two abbs. William in succession at this period and that the 1268 abb. could be Ellerbeck. *VCH* calls the later abb. Daneby but no source given.
Thomas 1286/7– Prof. obed. 2 Feb. 1287 (*Reg. Romeyn*, I, p. 162, no. 449). Occ. 24 May 1286 (*Yorks F., 1272–1300*, p. 77) ? the same abb. or another Thomas; Mich. 1286 x Mich. 1287 (PRO, E159/59, m. 9d); Sept. 1291 (*Ctl. Rievaulx*, p. 377). Canivez, III, 258 records that in 1291 *petitio abbatis de Rievalle, qui petit dispergi conventum suum per generationem suam, et quod suscipientes absoluti sint a susceptione aliorum hospitum per triennium, exauditur.*
Henry –1302 Occ. Mich. 1300, Hil. 1302 (Baildon, I, 179); 27 Mar. 1301 (NYCRO, ZQH, Clervaux ctl., f. 2v).
Robert 1302–1307/8 Prof. obed. 2 Feb. 1302 (*Reg. Corbridge*, I, 130). Occ. Mich. 1304, Hil. 1305 (Baildon, I, 179); Mich. 1305 (PRO, CP40/153, m. 310). D. *c.* 1307/8, possibly at Margam (? on visitation) – grave-slab at Margam (C.A.R. Radford, *Margam Museum, Glamorgan*, p. 28, no. 18).
Peter 1308 Prof. obed. 28 Jan. 1308 (*Reg. Greenfield*, III, p. 20, no. 1171 and p. 128, no. 1417).
Henry Occ. 23 Aug. 1308 (PRO, C241/61/19); 20 Apr. 1311 (*CCR 1307–13*, p. 306).
Thomas Occ. 7 Apr. 1314, 2 May 1315 (Cheshire RO, Ctl. Scrope of Bolton, ff. 7r, 7v).
Richard Occ. 3 June 1317 (*CPR 1313–17*, p. 697).
William 1318– Prof. obed. and bl. 25 June 1318 (*Reg. Melton*, II, pp. 19–20, no. 40). Possibly the same as below.
William of Ingleby (Ingelbi, Inggelby) Occ. 4 Jan. 1322 (*CPR 1321–24*, p. 61); Jan. 1332 x Jan. 1333 (PRO, E43/108); 27 June 1332 (*CPR 1330–34*, p. 316); 13 Nov. 1332 (PRO, C81/1788/40).[26]

[25] *VCH*, citing Baildon's ms. notes, gives abb. Thomas Stangrief occ. 1268, but no source has been found.
[26] The occ. of abb. John in 1327 (*Ctl. Rievaulx*, p. c, citing ibid., p. 421, and repeated in *VCH* and Baildon)

William of Langton (Langeton) **1335–** Commn to bp of Lincoln to bl. him 5 Jan. 1335 (*Reg. Melton*, II, p. 168, no. 435). Occ. 11 Oct. 1338 (*CCR 1337–39*, p. 270).

Richard 1349– Prof. obed. and bl. 1 Nov. 1349 (York, Reg. 10, f. 166v).

Ref. to an unnamed newly-el. abb. 22 Oct. 1359 (*Cal. Misc. Inq.*, III, 127).

William ?1361– Prof. obed. and bl. n.d. (between entries Jan 1361 x Oct. 1361) (York, Reg. 11, f. 178Ar). Occ. 17/18 Oct. 1363 (PRO, E41/457); 14 Feb. 1369 (*CPR 1377–81*, p. 529); 20 Aug. 1369 (Lincoln, Ep. Reg., XII, f. 77r); 22 Oct. 1369 (*Reg. Sudbury*, I, 269); 20 Feb. 1380 (*CPR 1377–81*, p. 441). Seal (*Mon. Seals*, p. 77; Clay, *Seals*, pp. 30–1).

The next recorded abb., **John**, occ. 10 July 1380 (*CPR 1377–81*, p. 529).

ROBERTSBRIDGE (Sussex) (Boxley) (Salehurst) f. 29 Mar. 1176 (at Salehurst); ? *c.* 1250 (at Robertsbridge).

Lists in *VCH Sussex*, II, 73–4; fragment of Ann. (BL, Add. ms. 28550, summarised in *Archaeologia* XLV, 432–40); *Heads*, I, 141.

William Occ. (W.) 1194 (*HMC De L'Isle and Dudley*, I, 43–4); 1203+ (*Ctl. Lewes, Norfolk*, p. 33; cf. Cheney, *Inn. III*, no. 500); occ.in *Sussex F.* I from 16 May 1204 to 1 July 1219 (I, nos. 93, 162); 1215 x 17 (*Ctl. Chichester*, p. 92 no. 346); 23 June 1219 (*HMC De L'Isle and Dudley*, I, 71); 1222 (*Robertsbridge Chts.*, no. 285).

Nicholas Occ. 19 June 1222 (*Kent F.*, p. 76).

William of St Neots (de Sancto Neoto) Occ. Oct. 1222 x Oct. 1223 (*HMC De L'Isle and Dudley*, I, 128). Ment. in 1299 as former abb. (*Cal. Misc. Inq.*, I, 497).

John Occ. 20 Oct. 1223, 22 Nov. 1229 (*Sussex F.*, I, nos. 183, 218); (J.) *c.* 1224 (PRO, SC1/1/63); 4 Sept. 1229 (*CR 1227–31*, p. 252); 1229 (*HMC De L'Isle and Dudley*, I, 83); 8 June 1231 (*Kent F.*, p. 109).[27]

William Occ. in *Sussex F.* from 11 Nov. 1235 to 2 Dec. 1248 (I, nos. 299, 498); 5 Jan. 1243 (PRO, E326/2974); 8 Feb. 1244 (BL, Egerton Cht. 375; *Archaeologia* XLV, 459);15 July 1248 (*Kent F.*, p. 202); Apr. 1252 (*HMC De L'Isle and Dudley*, p. 105). Seal (*BM Seals*, no. 3913).

Roger Occ. Apr. 1258, 1265, 24 July 1276, 15 July 1279 (*HMC De L'Isle and Dudley*, pp. 107, 120, 121, 123); 1 July 1258 to 25 Nov. 1275 (*Sussex F.*, II, nos. 626, 855); (Robert) 6 Oct. 1259, 13 Apr. 1271 (*Kent F.*, pp. 305, 363); 20 Jan. 1275 (PRO, F. Divers Cos, CP25/1/284/20, no. 22); 10 Aug. 1277 (San Marino, Huntington Lib., HEH/BA/1528); Easter 1278 (PRO, CP40/24, m. 7d).

Mainard Occ. 25 Nov. 1279 (*Sussex F.*, II, no. 925); ? 1279 (*HMC De L'Isle and Dudley*, I, 121).

Walter Occ. 25 Nov. 1286 (ibid., 123); 1288 (PRO, Just.1/929, m. 46d).

Thomas Occ. 10 June 1293 (*HMC De L'Isle and Dudley*, I, 128; *CPR 1292–1301*, p. 21).

Giles Occ. 11 June 1303 (*HMC De L'Isle and Dudley*, I, 129).

Laurence −1311 Occ. 26 Apr. 1304 (*Sussex F.*, II, no. 1156); 10 June 1304, 11 Oct. 1304 (*Ctl. Chichester*, nos. 289, 290); 30 July 1308, Nov. 1310 (*HMC De L'Isle and Dudley*, I, 129, 132); Mich. 1310 (*YB IV*, 218). Res. 8 Sept. 1311 (*Archaeologia* XLV, 432).

John de Wallyngfeld 1311– El. 10 Sept. 1311 (ibid., 432–3). Occ. 27 Apr. 1313 (*Ctl. Chichester*, no. 907; *HMC De L'Isle and Dudley*, I, 132); 1313–14 (*YB VIII*, 167, 213);

Alan Occ. 1 Aug. 1315, going overseas (*CPR 1313–17*, p.338); n.d. (*c.* 1315) (*HMC De L'Isle and Dudley*, I, 185).

Nicholas Occ. 20 Jan. 1320, 20 June 1320 (*HMC De L'Isle and Dudley*, I, 137).

John of Lamberhurst −1333 Occ. 5, 8 July 1323, 1 Nov. 1323, 23 June 1324, 20 Nov. 1329

is the result of a misreading of an exemplification of chts. in 1380. John was the abb. in 1380, not earlier (see list). *VCH*, citing Baildon's ms. notes, also gives an abb. John in 1363. No source has been found.

[27] Abb. Robert occ. 1231, day set for 8 June (*CRR*, XIV, no. 1140), but see above – abb. John occ. 8 June 1231. Is Robert an error?

(*HMC De L'Isle and Dudley*, I, 137–8); 19 May 1332, 2 Mar. 1333 (ibid., 140). D. 24 June
and bur. 3 July 1333 (*Archaeologia* XLV, 439–40).

John de Wormedale 1333– M. of Robertsbridge, el. 23 July 1333 (ibid.); bl. and prof. obed.
by bp of Rochester at request of bp of Chichester 29 Dec. 1333 (*Reg. Hethe*, I, 536). Occ.
from 28 Feb. 1334 to 25 Apr. 1340 (*HMC De L'Isle and Dudley*, I, 142, 145); 19 June 1346
(*CPL*, III, 192; *CPP*, p. 93).

Simon Occ. 1 July 1349 (*CPL*, III, 326).

John Wysdon (Wysdoun) Occ. Nov. 1352, Jan. 1353 (PRO, Just.1/941A, mm. 6, 9, 19d, 37, 38).

Adam Occ. 2 Oct. 1357 (*HMC De L'Isle and Dudley*, I, 146).

John Occ. 9 Dec. 1369, 24 Apr. 1373 (ibid., 148).

The next recorded abb., **William Lewes**, occ. 20 May 1399 (*CPL*, IV, 307).

ROCHE (Yorks W.) (Newminster) f. 30 July 1147

Lists in *VCH Yorks*, III, 155–6; based on medieval list (*successio abbatum*) in St Mary's Tower,
York in *Mon. Angl.*, V, 505, no. xiv; Clay, *Early Abbots*, 37ff.; *Heads*, I, 141.

Reginald *c.* 1213–*c.* 1228 M. of Roche, ruled 15 years (*Mon. Angl.*, V, 505, cf. Clay (1952), p.
38n). Occ. 25 June 1219 (*Lincs F.*, I, 138); 1223 (ibid., 165); 1225 (BL, Egerton ms. 2827, f.
181v); Mich. 1227 (Ctl. Beauchief, ff. 68r, 70v).[28]

Richard Ruled 16 years (*Mon. Angl.*, V, 505). Occ. 8 Sept. 1229, 1 Jan. 1230 (*CPR 1225–32*, pp.
305, 352); (R.) 22 Sept. 1230 (*Reg. Greenfield*, II, no. 1106); 23 Aug. 1230, 10 July 1231
(*Yorks F., 1218–31*, pp. 128, 156); 29 Apr. 1240 (PRO, Notts F., CP25/1/182/8 no. 278); 17
June 1240, 8 July 1240, 14 Jan. 1241 (*Yorks F., 1232–46*, pp. 60, 70, 97).

Walter of Wadworth (Waddeworth) Ruled 14 years (*Mon. Angl.*, V, 505). Occ. 18 May 1246
(*Yorks F., 1232–46*, p. 139); 18 Nov. 1246 (*Yorks F., 1246–72*, p. 2); 1 July 1249 (*Lincs F.*, II,
49); (W.) 23 Sept. 1252 (Leeds, Newby Hall mss. NH.273)

Jordan Occ. 6 May 1263 (*Lincs F.*, II, 216); ment. 1282 as former abb. (Baildon, I, 184).

Alan 1268– Succ. 1268 (Baildon, I, 183, no source given). In *Mon. Angl.*, V 505, Alan precedes
Jordan who is followed by Philip.

Philip Occ. in list (*Mon. Angl.*, V 505).[29]

Robert Occ. Mich. 1279 x Mich. 1280 (PRO, E159/53 m. 16); 27 Jan. 1280 (*Yorks F. 1272–1300*,
p. 32); 3 Feb. 1281 (ibid., p. 60); 9 Feb. 1281 (ibid., p. 62); Trin. – Mich. 1282 (Baildon, I,
184).

Walter Occ. July 1285 (*State Trials*, p. 1).

Stephen of Stainton (Steynton) 1286– Prof. obed. 3 Nov. 1286 (*Reg. Romeyn*, I, 66–7, 253,
nos. 157, 728).[30] Occ. 13 Feb. 1287 (Hull University Archives, Constable of Everingham
Collection, DDEV 41/1); 1287 (*Yorks F., 1272–1300*, p. 81; Bodl., ms. Top. Yorks e 9, f.
69r); 1293 (*CPR 1292–1301*, p. 28; *CCR 1288–96*, p. 323); 1293 (PRO, Lincs F.,
CP25/1/134/64 no. 19); Easter 1296 – Trin. 1297 (Baildon, I, 185); Trin. 1297 (PRO,
CP40/119, m. 101).

John 1300 Prof. obed. 30 May 1300 (*Reg. Corbridge*, I, 23); Easter term 1300 (Baildon, I, 185).

Robert 1300– Prof. obed. and bl. 18 Dec. 1300 (ibid., 41). Occ. Mich. 1305 (PRO, CP40/153,
m. 238).

---

[28] Roger, abb. of Roche, occ. as a witness *post* 13 Oct. 1224 (*Ctl. Sallay*, I, no. 219) but this may be a scribal
error for Reginald.

[29] *VCH* gives occ. 1276 x 1277 and cites Patent Roll 5 Edward I, m. 18d, but the entry cannot be located in
CPR 1272–1281. Philip may poss. be the abb. who, in 1278, having not attended the General Chapter of
Cîteaux for many years, was deposed by the General Chapter (Canivez, III, 178–9).

[30] Baildon, I, 183 gives, copying *Mon. Angl.* V, 501, Thomas, as abb. of Roche, eln conf. 7 Nov. 1286, but this
date is clearly at variance with the evidence in *Reg. Romeyn*.

William 1324– Prof. obed. 9 Dec. 1324 (York, Reg. 9A, f. 200v). Occ. Mich. 1328 (*Index to Placita de Banco*, p. 795).

Adam of Giggleswick (Gykeleswyk) **1330–** Prof. obed. and bl. 4 Nov. 1330 (York, Reg. 9A, f. 231r).

John Occ. Trin. 1341 (Baildon, I, 186); 8 Dec. 1344 (*Yorks Deeds*, III, no. 190).

Adam 1347–1349 Prof. obed. and bl. 20 May 1347 (York, Reg. 10, f. 118Ar). Occ. 1348 – 26 May 1349 (*Wakefield Court Rolls 1348–50*, pp. 7, 127).

Simon of Bakewell (Baukewell *or* Bankewell) **1349–** Prof. obed. and bl. 25 Oct. 1349 (York, Reg. 10, f. 41r).

John of Aston 1358– Prof. obed. and bl. 23 Nov. 1358 (York, Reg. 11, f. 102r).

John of Durham (Dunelmia) j.d. case 17 July 1364: John of Durham, claiming to be abb. of Roche against br. John of Retford, m. of Roche '*super spoliacione dicti monasterii et administracione bonorum et dignitatis abbatis monasterii eiusdem*' (ibid., f. 131v); 20 Nov. 1369 (Nottingham Univ., Clifton of Clifton Hall ms. 580); Easter 1372 (Baildon, I, 186).

The next recorded abb., **Robert de Kesburgh**, occ. 3 July 1392 (*CPR 1391–96*, p. 166).

RUFFORD (Notts) (Rievaulx) f. 13 July 1146

Lists in *VCH Notts*, II, 104; *Rufford Chts.* I, pp. lxxx–lxxxiii; *Heads*, I, 141.

Walter Occ. *c.* 13 Oct. 1211 (*EYC*, XII, no. 115; *Rufford Chts.*, II, no. 307); 25 July 1215 (*Rot. Lit. Pat.*, p. 150b). May have d. 1217 as in that year an abb. of Rufford was excused attendance at the General Chapter on account of illness (Canivez, I, 469).

Robert Apptd p.j.d. 13 Nov. 1219 (*Reg. Ant. Lincoln*, VIII, 113n). Occ. (R.) 24 Jan. 1226 (*Ctl. Fountains*, I, 217); 27 Oct. 1226 (PRO, Notts F., CP25/1/182/4, no. 93); 20 Jan. 1228 (*Rufford Chts.*, I, no. 110; *Derbys F. (1886)*, p. 26).

Simon de Rise 1231– El. 25 Jan. 1231 in chapter house at Melrose (*Ch. Melrose*, p. 80). Occ. 25 June 1232 (*Rufford Chts.*, II, no. 424); 7 Aug. 1233 (ibid., I, no. 128); 1235 x 7 (ibid., II, 629); 16 Jan. 1235 (PRO, Notts F., CP25/1/182/6, no. 178); 24 Sept. 1236 (*Rufford Chts.*, III, no. 857; PRO, Notts F., CP25/1/182/6, no. 185).

Geoffrey Occ. in *Rufford Chts.* from (G.) 25 Aug. 1239 to 11 June 1257 (II, no. 409; III, no. 985). Occ. 23 Feb. 1240 (PRO, Notts F., CP25/1/182/8, no. 271); 19 Apr. 1244 (ibid., 182/9 no. 301); 1 May 1250, 19 June 1250, 18 May 1253 (*Lincs F.*, II, 69, 83, 104).

William Occ. 15 June 1259 (PRO, Notts F., CP25/1/183/12, no. 168); 19 June 1259, 29 Sept. 1260 (*Rufford Chts.*, III, no. 863; I, no. 262).

John Occ. 1261 x 1276 (ibid., III, no. 812).

Henry An eln dispute took place in 1276–77 and firstly the abbs. of Neath and Coggeshall, and then the abbs. of Coggeshall and Jervaulx investigated on behalf of the General Chapter. Henry, m. of Rufford had been el. and then ejected – '*frater Henricus monachus dicti loci ius in ipsa electione habeat et repulsus fuerit minus iniuste*' (Canivez, III, 156–7, 165). It is just possible that Henry is the same as the later abb., Henry of Fring.

Thomas of Stonegrave (Stangreve, Steyngreve) Occ. 22 July 1278 (*CPR 1413–16*, p. 367); 23 Apr. 1284 (*Yorks F., 1272–1300*, pp. 69–70); *c.* 1278 x 1288 (*Rufford Chts.*, II, no. 331); 12 Apr. 1282 (PRO, Lincs F. CP25/1/138/55 no. 53); n.d. (*ante* 1283) (*CChR 1257–1300*, p. 264).

Henry of Fring Occ. 14 Jan. 1287 (*CChR 1341–1417*, p. 67); Easter 1288 (PRO, CP40/72, m. 44d); going overseas 5 Aug. 1288 (*CPR 1281–92*, pp. 297–8); in *Rufford Chts.* from 8 Sept. 1290 to 9 May 1305 (II, no. 321; III, no. 1001); 9 Feb. 1310 (*Yorks F., 1300–1314*, p. 77); 1314–1315 (PRO, C85/179, 42, 56); 1315 (*Reg. Greenfield*, IV, p. 186, no. 2058A); 25 May 1315 (*YB 6 Richard II*, pp. 134–5).

Robert 1318– Prof. by Archbp Melton *c.* June 1318 (York, Reg. 9B, f. 402r).

Elias Lyvet Occ. 3 Dec. 1320 (*CCR 1318–23*, p. 346); Apr. 1331 (*Rufford Chts.*, III, no 871); Easter 1341 (*Select Cases of Trespass*, II, 241); Trin. 1342 (*YB 16 Edward III, part 2*, p. 231). D. by 28 Oct. 1347 (*CChR 1341–1417*, p. 68).

Thomas Occ. 10 May 1350 (*Rufford Chts.*, III, no. 993; York, Reg. 10, f. 150v; Southwell minster ms. 1, f. 131r).

Robert of Maplebeck (Mapelbeck) **1352–** Commn to receive prof. obed. 2 Aug. 1352 (*York Sede Vacante Reg. 1352–3*, p. 77, no. 12).

Richard Occ. 29 Aug. 1363 (*Rufford Chts.*, III, no. 1003).

Thomas 1366– Bl. and prof. obed. 6 Sept. 1366 (York, Reg. 11, f. 264r).

John of Harlsey (Harlesay) **1372–** Bl. and prof. obed. 28 Nov. 1372 (ibid., f. 277r).

The next recorded abb., **Thomas de Sewoldby**, occ. 14 June 1383 (*Rufford Chts.*, III, no. 881).

SALLAY (Yorks W.) (Newminster) (Sawley) f. 6 Jan. 1147
  Lists in *VCH Yorks*, III, 157–8; *Ctl. Sallay*, II, 197–9; Clay, 39–41 (to 1246); *Heads*, I, 141–2.
William Occ. 1209 x 1211 (*Ctl. Furness*, II, ii, 343); j.d. +18 Dec. 1218 (*Ctl. Kirkstall*, pp. 252–3).
Richard Occ. 1220 x 1224 (*Ctl. Sallay*, II, no. 534n.).
Stephen of Eston *c.* 1233/4 Cellarer of Fountains; abb. of Sallay for ten years, abb. of Newminster *c.* 1234–47; 11th abb. of Fountains 1247 till his d. 6 Sept. 1252. Buried in chapter-house at Vaudey (*Mem. Fountains*, I, 137–8); see J. McNulty 'Stephen of Eston, abbot of Sallay' in *YAJ*, XXXI (1934), 49–64; Sharpe, *Latin Writers*, p. 622; B.K. Lackner ed., *Stephen of Sawley: Treatises* (Cistercian Fathers 36, Kalamazoo, 1984). Occ. as abb. of Sallay *c.* 1225 (*Ctl. Healaugh Park*, p. 171); 8 May 1225 (BL, Egerton ms. 2827, f. 181v); 1226 (*Ctl. Fountains*, I, 217; *Reg. Gray*, p. 328; *Ctl. Sallay*, I, no. 301; *Yorks F. 1218–31*, p. 85); (S.) 1230 (*Reg. Greenfield*, II, pp. 208–9, no. 1106); 1231 (*Yorks F. 1218–31*, p. 159); *c.* 1231 (*Pudsay Deeds*, p. 113). Last occ. as abb. of Sallay 19 Oct. 1233 (*Ctl. Newminster*, pp. 81–2)).[31] In 1322 and 1325 Stephen is described as abb. 'a hundred years ago' (*CCR 1318–23*, p. 595; *CCR 1323–27*, p. 290).
Walter Occ. n.d. (Bodl. Dodsworth ms. 91, f. 59r; *Ctl. Sallay*, II, no. 558); 1233 x 1240 (*EYC*, VIII, no. 171); 1234 x 1240 (*Ctl. Sallay*, I, no. 208); 1234 x 1245 (PRO, E40/317); *c.* 1241 x 2 (*Percy Ctl.*, p. 27, cf. ibid., p. 90, *ante* 1244, where abb. is called William (? error for Walter)); 1242 x 1245 (*Ctl. Sallay*, I, no. 34). Seal (*Mon. Seals*, p. 80).
Warin Occ. 4 June 1246 (*Ctl. Sallay*, I, no. 38n; *Yorks F., 1232–46*, p. 142); *c.* 1246 x 51 (*Ctl. Whalley*, I, 134); Whitsun 1255 (*Percy Ctl.*, p. 52). Seal (*Durham Seals*, II, pp. 579–80, no. 3539).
Hugh de Wighale (Wyghale) Occ. (H.) n.d. (*c.* 1260) (*Pudsay Deeds*, p. 122); 12 Aug. 1265 (*Ctl. Sallay*, II, no. 621); (H.) *c.* 1265 x 70 (ibid., I no. 146); (H.) 1268 x 72 (ibid., no. 249); *c.* 1269 (ibid., no. 38); 9 June 1269 (*Yorks F., 1246–72*, p. 169). Mentd as former abb. 1279–80 (PRO, Just.1/1055; Just.1/1056, m. 63d).[32]
Thomas of Driffield Occ. 27 May 1278 (*Yorks F., 1272–1300*, p. 14; *Ctl. Sallay*, I, no. 50); 1279 (*Ctl. Fountains*, I, 322; *Ctl. Sallay*, II, no. 412; *Pudsay Deeds*, pp. 7, 71, 94); 1280 (Baildon, II, p. 35, no. 1; *Yorks F., 1272–1300*, pp. 49, 52; *Pudsay Deeds*, p. 150); Nov. 1279 x Nov. 1280 (*Ctl. Healaugh Park*, p. 173); 1282, 1285, 1287 (Baildon, I, 191); 1284 (*Ctl. Sallay*, I, no. 199); 1290 (ibid. II, no. 620; *Reg. Romeyn*, I, 107); last occ. 15 July 1292 (Whitaker, *Whalley*, II, 401).
Roger Occ. Mich. 1299 (Baildon, I, 191); 1300 (ibid. p. 192, nos. 9–10, cf. also no. 11 where the

---

[31] For a mistaken 1210 date ascribed to abb. Stephen, see *Ctl. Sallay*, II, 193, n.5.
[32] An abb. B. is mentd by Baildon (I, 190) as occ. 1277 but no source is given.

abb. is named Robert; *Pudsay Deeds*, p. 71); 1301 (Baildon, I, 192); *c.* 1299 x 1302 (*Ctl. Sallay*, I, no. 364). He is tentatively identified with Roger de Neuby, monk of Sallay 1275 (ibid., II, 194).

John of Howden (Houden, Houedene, Hoveden) 1303– M. of Sallay, prof. obed. 25 Mar. 1303 (*Reg. Corbridge*, I, 81). Order to deliver him from bp's prison 15 Sept. 1306 (*CCR 1302–7*, p. 458). Excommunicated for contumacy 1306 (*Reg. Greenfield*, II, pp. 7–8, no. 686); absolved 1314 (ibid., p. 180, no. 1055, where the abb. is called Thomas of Howden). Occ. 10 Dec. 1306 (*CCR 1302–7*, p. 521); 1310 (*Ctl. Sallay*, I, nos. 67, 154); 1311 (*Cal. Chanc. Warr.*, p. 340); 1314 (*Ctl. Sallay*, I, no. 75); last occ. 11 Nov. 1318 (*CCR 1318–23*, p. 106).

John de Heton 1321– Pr. of Sallay, bl. & prof. obed. 2 May 1322 (York, Reg. 9A, ff. 186v, 187v). Occ. 12 Mar. 1322 (*Ctl. Whalley*, III, 709); last occ. Mich. 1332 (Baildon, I, 192).

Adam Occ. 1335 (*Trans. Lancs. & Ches. Hist. Soc.*, new ser., 32 (1916), p. 128n.); Hil. 1344 (Baildon, II, 37).

John of Gisburn Commn to suffragan bp. to bl. abb-el. 8 Jan. 1350 (York, Reg. 10, f. 286v). Occ. 1351 (*CPL*, III, 407); 1354 (ibid., 534; *Ctl. Sallay*, II, 182–3); last occ. 24 Dec. 1362 (*Ctl. Sallay*, II, no. 476n.).

Geoffrey Occ. 1366 as sponsor to Thomas Mowbray, earl of Nottingham (Harland, *Hist. Acct. of Sallay Abbey*, p. 42; Whitaker, *Craven* (London, 1805), p. 52).

John Occ. 6 Aug. 1371 (*Ctl. Sallay*, I, no. 191); 1376 (Lancs RO, DDTO/K/9); 1377 (*Ctl. Sallay*, II, 189; *Mon.*, V, 516, no. xxiv; *Percy Ctl.*, pp. 373–4); 1380 (*Ctl. Sallay*, II, 195); 1392 (ibid., I, no. 221); last occ. 30 Nov. 1394 (ibid., II, no. 391).

The next recorded abb., **Richard of Clitheroe** (Cliderowe, Clyderou), prof. obed. [Apr.] 1398 (York, Reg. 5A, f. 246v).

SAWTRY (Hunts) (Wardon) f. 3 July 1147
Lists in *VCH Hunts*, I, 392; *Heads*, I, 142.

Ralph Occ. (R.) j. d. 30 Dec. 1210 (CUL, Add. ms. 3021, f. 322r); Oct. 1217 x Oct. 1218 (*Hunts F.*, p. 5); (R.) *c.* 1220 (PRO, SC1/11/95).

Alard (Athelard) Occ. 27 May 1228 (*Waltham Chts.*, no. 135); Oct. 1231 x Oct. 1232 (*Hunts F.*, p. 14).

Adam Occ. Oct. 1236 x Oct. 1237, Oct. 1247 x Oct. 1248 (*Norfolk F. (Rye)*, pp. 59, 72); from Oct. 1240 x Oct. 1241 to Oct. 1252 x Oct. 1253 (*Hunts F.*, pp. 20–3, 25–6); 4 June 1278 (*CPR 1272–81*, p. 266); Mich. 1280 x Mich. 1281 (PRO, E159/54, m. 19). Presumably the abb. dep. in 1282 (Canivez, III, 226, cf. 211).

William Occ. Nov. 1285 x Nov. 1286 (*Norfolk F. (Rye)*, p. 132); 25 Mar. 1289 (BL, Add. Cht. 33468); 1293 (PRO, C146/9470).

Laurence Occ. 28 Mar. 1299 (*CPR 1292–1301*, p. 402). Said to occ. *temp.* Henry III (*sic*) in case of 1343–4 (*YB 17–18 Edward III*, p. 271).

Richard Said to occ. *temp.* Edward I in case of 1343–4 (ibid.).

John 1303– Bl. & prof. obed. 7 July 1303 (Lincoln, Ep. Reg., III, f. 58v); occ. (J.) 23 Nov. 1311 (Norwich, Reg/1/1, f. 43v).

John 1314– Bl. from ex-archbp of Armagh & prof. obed. 2 June 1314 (Lincoln, Ep. Reg., III, f. 299v).

William 1316– Lic. to receive bl. from ex-archbp of Armagh 6 Mar. 1316 (ibid., f. 343r).

Roger de Herford Occ. 12 Aug. 1320 (*CCR 1318–23*, p. 324); 1323 (*CPR 1321–4*, p. 288); 1324 (PRO, E106/5/2, m. 9d); July 1325 x July 1326 (PRO, E106/5/4, m. [9]); Hil. 1327–Trin. 1328 (*Index to Placita de Banco*, p. 225); 1332 (*CCR 1330–33*, p. 583); 14 Feb. 1338 (*CCR 1337–39*, p. 382).

Ralph de Beville 1347– Lic. to receive bl. from any Catholic bp 24 Apr. 1347; bl. by bp of Ely 20 May 1347 (Ely, G/1/1 part 2, f. 50v). Occ. 1348 (BL, Harl. Cht. 83 C 9).

William Occ. 25 Dec. 1351 (BL, Add. Cht. 34229); 24 Oct. 1358, 11 July 1359 (*CCR 1354–60*, pp. 530, 628).

William of Ramsey (Rameseye) Occ. Easter 1361 (PRO, CP40/406, m. 129). ? the same as above.

Thomas of Spalding (Spaldyng) Occ. 6 May 1362 (PRO, C241/143/23); 2 Dec. 1365 (*CPR 1364–67*, p. 207); 5 Nov. 1373 (*CCR 1369–74*, p. 590); 24 June 1388, Hil. 1390 (*YB 13 Richard II* p. 84); 11 June 1391 (BL, Harl. Cht. 83 B 30).

SCARBOROUGH (Yorks N.), St Mary (cell of Cîteaux) f. -1203 (royal grant 1189); diss. *c.* 1407 (see C.H. Talbot, 'Cîteaux and Scarborough' in *Studia Monastica*, II (1960), 95–158; A. Rowntree, *The History of Scarborough* (London, 1931), pp. 54–72).[33]

Maurice Occ. as M. of Cîteaux and *custos* 28 Sept. 1268 (*Reg. W. Giffard*, p. 52).

[Robert Occ. as M. and proctor of Cîteaux abbey 23 Sept. 1290, 15 July 1291 (*Reg. Romeyn*, I, pp. 212, 220) ? *custos.*]

James de Portu Occ. as warden 5 Nov. 1295 (*CFR 1272–1307*, p. 366); 25 July 1298 (Talbot, 'Cîteaux and Scarborough', p. 139, no. xxvia; *Ctl. Bridlington*, pp. 428–9); 13 May, 10 June 1300 (*Reg. Corbridge*, I, 150, 119); 1305 (*Rot. Parl.*, I, 178); 16 Dec. 1306 (*Reg. Greenfield*, III, p. 12, no. 1157); 12 May 1311 (ibid., pp. 195–6, no. 1542, cf. pp. 195–6, n. 2).

Bartholomew Occ. as warden 17 Nov. 1313 (ibid., p. 213, no. 1589).

Hugh de Sancto Lupo Occ. as proctor of abbey of Cîteaux 10 Sept. 1320 (York, Reg. 9A, f. 279v); as *custos c.* Mich. 1324 (PRO, E106/5/2, m. 10d); 8 Oct. 1326 (*Memo. Roll 1326–7*, p. 272); 28 Apr. (1333) (PRO, C270/11/24); 27 Jan. 1336 (York, Reg. 9A, f. 394r); 5 Feb. 1342 (*CFR 1337–47*, p. 267); 11 July 1345 (*CCR 1343–46*, p. 636); Feb. 1346 (PRO, E401/383); 15 Oct. 1348 (*CFR 1347–56*, p. 98); Mich. 1348 x Mich. 1349 (PRO, E372/194, rot. 8).

Peter de Castro Novo (Novo Castro) Occ. as *custos* 6 Nov. 1369 (*CFR 1368–77*, p. 41); 15 July 1376 (ibid., p. 354); 6 Oct. 1377 (*CFR 1377–83*, p. 14); 8 Feb. 1378 (ibid., p. 78); gtd keeping of the cell 28 Feb. 1380 (ibid., p. 184); 17 Apr. 1380, 13 May 1381 (ibid., pp. 191, 197, 253); 11 May 1392 (YMA, M2/1g, f. 66r); 19 May 1397 (*Reg. Waldby*, p. 19).

SIBTON (Suffolk) (Warden) f. 22 Feb. 1150
Lists in *VCH Suffolk*, II, 90–1; *Ctl. Sibton*, I, 4–6; *Heads*, I, 142.

Alexander Occ. before 1212 (*Ctl. Blythburgh*, II, no. 474); Easter term 1212 (*CRR*, VI, 241).

S. Occ. *c.* 1210 x June 1230 (*Ctl. Leiston*, no. 68; dated by Robert, archdn of Suffolk and Roger, pr. of Eye, *Heads*, I, *corrigenda*); early 13th cent., after 1205–6 (*Ctl. Sibton*, III, no. 771).

G. Occ. before 1233 (d. of Robert de Meisi) and therefore must be a predecessor of Constantine (*Ctl. Sibton*, III, no. 784). May be identified with Geoffrey (see below).

Constantine Occ. in *Ctl. Sibton* from 3 May 1229 to 20 Jan. 1243 (IV, nos. 1140, 957). Occ. Oct. 1228 x Oct. 1229, Oct. 1229 x Oct. 1230, Oct. 1234 x Oct. 1235 (*Suffolk F. (Rye)*, pp. 30, 31, 35); Hil. term 1230 (*CRR*, XIII, no. 2387); Oct. 1242 x Oct. 1243 (*Norfolk F. (Rye)*, p. 69).

Henry Occ. Oct. 1244 x Oct. 1245 (*Ctl. Sibton*, II, no. 253); 15 July 1245 (ibid., III, no. 707). D. by 6 Oct. no year (*Ctl. Sibton* list, p. 5 citing Elveden Hall, Iveagh collection 345(1), no. 46 – the 1246 charter mentd on p. 5 is actually dated 1251, see below).

---

[33] There is a monumental brass from Scarborough, St Mary's (now in a local museum) to br. William de Thornton, early 14th cent. (*Earliest English Brasses*, p. 214). William need not of course have been monk-*custos*.

Alexander of Walpole Succ. on d. of Henry before 6 Oct. no year (ibid.). Occ. 27 Jan. 1251 (*Ctl. Sibton*, III, no. 698); Oct. 1250 x Oct. 1251 (*Suffolk F. (Rye)*, p. 51). For name, see *Ctl. Sibton*, IV, no. 984.

John Occ. n.d. (mid 13th cent.) (*Ctl. Sibton*, III, no. 495). Prob. the abb. J. who occ. 31 Mar. 1259 (list, citing Suffolk RO, Ipswich, HA3/50/9/16.5 (15), f. 1r).

Geoffrey Possibly same as G. above. A contemporary of Norman father of Robert Henry (*Sibton Abbey Estates*, p. 72), mentd in rent roll of 1328. Robert Henry occ. 1287 (*Ctl. Sibton*, III, no. 587), so a mid 13th cent. date is a probability (see *Ctl. Sibton*, list, p. 5 for further discussion).

Henry Occ. 11 June 1267 (SRO, Ipswich, HA3/50/9/16.5 (15), f. 2r).

Richard of Ely For name see *Ctl. Sibton* list, citing BL, Add. ms. 34560, f. 26r. Occ. in *Ctl. Sibton* from 8 July 1268 to 13 Oct. 1278 (IV, nos. 1003, 1144). Occ. Oct. 1267 x Oct. 1268, Oct. 1268 x Oct. 1269 (*Norfolk F. (Rye)*, pp. 105, 107); Oct. 1268 x Oct. 1269, Oct. 1276 x Oct. 1277, Oct. 1277 x Oct. 1278 (*Suffolk F. (Rye)*, pp. 70, 78, 79); 1 July 1271 (PRO, F. Divers Cos. CP25/1/283/17, no. 484); (R.) 20 Jan. 1279 (Suffolk RO, Ipswich, HA3/50/9/16.5 (15), f. 4v).

Walter Occ. in *Ctl. Sibton* from 7 July 1280 to 3 May 1288 (III, nos. 884, 585); Nov. 1280 x Nov. 1281, Nov. 1281 x Nov. 1282 (*Norfolk F. (Rye)*, p. 123).

John of Aldeby For name see *Ctl. Sibton*, III, no. 774. Occ. 1 July 1290 (ibid., IV, no. 990); Oct. 1289 x Oct. 1290 (*Suffolk F. (Rye)*, p. 93); (J.) 31 May 1293 (PRO, SC1/31/13); 1296 (PRO, E210/8475); Easter 1298 (PRO, CP40/123, m. 180); 1310 (Suffolk RO, Ipswich, HA3/50/9/15.2 (5), f. 1r).

Eustace Occ. in *Ctl. Sibton* from 25 Mar. 1313 to 14 May 1318 (III, nos. 617, 774); 27 Oct. 1316 (Norwich Reg/1/1, f. 66v).

Ralph Occ. 22 Jan. 1320 (*Ctl. Sibton*, IV, no. 981).

Edmund of Beccles Occ. 6 July 1320 (*Ctl. Sibton*, IV, no. 967); 1323 (Suffolk RO, Ipswich, HD533/345/1/6); Jan. 1328 x Jan. 1329 (SRO, Ipswich, HA3/50/9/15.2 (5), f. 2v, for name see ibid., ff. 1–2).

Ralph of Bradenham Occ. in *Ctl. Sibton* c. Jan. 1331, 1342 (IV, no. 1147; II, no. 5); 12 Aug. 1334 (*CCR 1333–37*, p. 329).

Roger de Helghton (Helgeton) **1343–** M. of Sibton, lic. from bp of London to receive bl. 16 May 1343, bl. and prof. obed. 1 June 1343 (Norwich, Reg/1/3, f. 70v).

Roger of Loddon (Lodne) Occ. before Oct. 1345 (*Ctl. Sibton*, II, no. 5); 25 Nov. 1346 (ibid., III, no. 579).

John of Cratfield (Cratefeld) Former Cellarer of Sibton (*Ctl. Sibton*, II, no. 5). Occ. as abb. 26 June 1351 (ibid., III, no. 630); 1354 (Suffolk RO, Ipswich, HD1538/345/1/68); 12 Mar. 1364 (PRO, E329/2449); 6 Aug. 1367 (Suffolk RO, Ipswich, HA 3/50/9/15.3 (2), f. 23v); 25 Oct. 1367 (PRO, E326/2875).

Walter 1375– Bl. and prof. obed. 30 Nov. 1375 (Norwich, Reg/3/6, f. 43r). Occ. 1377 x 1381 (PRO, E179/45/18); June 1380 x June 1381 (PRO, E179/45/5b, m. 2).

The next recorded abb., **John of Sibton**, held his first court 9 Sept. 1391 (*Ctl. Sibton* list, using BL, Add. ms. 19082, f. 176r, BL, Add. ms. 8172, f. 169r, and court rolls in Suffolk RO, Ipswich).

STANLEY (Wilts) (Quarr) f. 1151 (at Loxwell); 1154 (at Stanley)
  Lists in *VCH Wilts*, III, 274–5; *Heads*, I, 142.

Thomas of Calstone 1205– Pr. of Stanley, el. 1205 (*Ch. SHR*, II, 508). Occ. c. 13 Oct. 1212 (*Wilts F.*, I, 11); ?1214 (*Ch SHR*, II, 517); 1217+ (*Ctl. Chertsey*, I, no. 74).

Ralph –1221 Occ. (R.) 7 Oct. 1221 (*Sarum Chts.*, p. 114, no. ccxxxii). Became Cistercian m. at

Quarr 1221, *vir nobilis genere sed scientia et moribus nobilior* (*Ann. Dunstable*, p. 67). Mentioned 28 Mar. 1224 as former abb. – still alive (*Rot. Lit. Claus.*, I, 590).

Stephen of Lexington (Lexintona) –**1229** Occ. (S.) Mich. term 1223 (*CRR*, XI, no. 1248); 1224 (PRO, Glos. F., CP25/1/73/7, no. 76); 1225 (BL, Cotton ms. Domitian A XIV, f. 154v); from 1225 to 1227 (*Wilts F.*, I, 13, 19); 1228 (*Glam. Chts.*, II, 457). Easter term 1229 (*CRR*, XIII, no. 2032); 1229 made visitor of Irish monasteries (*Ann. Dunstable*, p. 116). El. abb. of Savigny 1229 (*Ann. Waverley*, p. 307; *Ann. Dunstable*, p. 116). Later abb. of Clairvaux from 1243. D. 1260 (*DNB*; Emden, *BRUO*, III, 1140–1; Sharpe, *Latin Writers*, pp. 632–3).

William Occ. 4 Apr. 1229, going to Wales (*CPR 1225–32*, p. 243); 4 Sept. 1229 (*CCR 1227–31*, p. 252).

Walter of Pucklechurch –?**1235** Occ. 17 Oct. 1230 (*Ctl. Malmesbury*, II, 29); 1229 x 1232 (*Ctl. Bradenstoke*, no. 26); Mentd 1337 as occ. *temp.* Henry III (*CCR 1337–39*, p. 193). Abb. Stephen of Lexington wrote to Philip, abb. of Quarr, re poor state of Stanley: the cess. of the abb. is necessary and to be received with maximum haste n.d. [27 May x 13 June 1235] (*An. Sac. Ord. Cist.*, VIII, pp. 303–5, no. 91). The electors had decided upon the pr. of Quarr as the new abb. of Stanley *sed infirma eius valetudo impedimentum videbatur*; Abb. of Quarr is to judge and decide 23 June 1235 (ibid., p. 305, no. 92).

Peter Occ. 1236 (*Wilts F.*, I, 25).

Robert –**1248** Called 9th abb. Occ. 2 June 1241, 16 June 1241, 3 Nov. 1246, 28 Apr. 1247 (*Wilts F.*, I, 32, 34, 37); 1239 x 1248 (*Lacock Chts.*, no. 339); 3 Feb. 1245 (PRO, Glos F., CP25/1/74/17, no. 237). D. 10 Apr. 1248 (*Ch. SHR* II, 535).

William Chinnoc(k) **1248–1268** Called 10th abb., succ. presumably 1248 (ibid., 551). Occ. 13 Oct. 1253 (*Soms F.*, I, 155); 27 Apr. 1259, 23 Apr. 1262 (*Wilts F.*, I, 52, 54). D. 27 Mar. 1268 (*Ch. SHR*, II, 551).

William Occ. 25 Jan. 1272 (*Ctl. Hungerford*, no. 249).

Richard Occ. 9 May 1280 (PRO, E212/46); n.d. (late 13th cent.) (PRO, E326/1954; E329/19). Seal (*Mon. Seals*, p. 84).

William de Tynghurst Occ. 8 Aug. 1286 (*CPR 1281–92*, p. 250); (W.) 9 Apr. 1287 (*Ctl. Glastonbury*, III, p. 667, no. 1231).

Nicholas **1298–** Prof. obed. 25 May 1298 (*Reg. Gandavo*, II, 575). Occ. 17 June 1301 (PRO, E40/4611; E40/7488); 9 Feb. 1303 (PRO, Glos F., CP25/1/75/39, no. 232); 15 Sept. 1303 (PRO, Just.1/1329, m. 13).

John de Southber Occ. 10 June 1304 (*CPR 1301–07*, p. 229); 24 Feb. 1310 (PRO, E40/9280); 17 Apr. 1311 (*Reg. Gandavo*, I, 403); 11 Jan. 1312 (*HMC Var. Coll.*, I, 358); *c.* Mar. x Apr. 1316 (*Reg. Martival*, II, 98). Mentd as late abb. 5 Feb. 1330 (*CPR 1327–30*, p. 484).

Robert Occ. 4 Aug. 1320 (*CCR 1318–23*, p. 318). Mentd as late abb. 5 Feb. 1330, 8 Feb. 1330 (*CPR 1327–30*, pp. 484, 486).

William Occ. 30 Nov. 1321, *c.* 6 June 1322 (*Reg. Martival*, II, ii, 375, 397); 8 May 1323 (*CPR 1321–24*, p. 284).

John Occ. 6 Mar. 1324, 17 Nov. 1324 (*CCR 1323–27*, pp. 158, 326); 29 Oct. 1327 (*Reg. Martival*, II, ii, 544). Mentd as late abb. 5 Feb. 1330 (*CPR 1327–30*, p. 484).

John de la Stone Occ. n.d. (1332 x 1333) (PRO, C270/11/40); Mich. 1337 (PRO, CP40/213, m. 34 and attorneys m. 15); 27 Mar. 1342 (*CCR 1341–43*, p. 496; PRO, E42/215); 13 Oct. 1342 (Salisbury, Reg. Wyvil, I, f. 83v).

William of Combe Name from seal (*BM Seals*, no. 4082; *Mon. Seals*, p. 84). Occ. 4 Oct. 1351, 20 Oct. 1351, 18 Apr. 1352, 2 Apr. 1353 (*CCR 1349–54*, pp. 388, 395, 482, 589); 3 Mar. 1355 (*CCR 1354–60*, p. 183); Jan. 1354 x Jan. 1355 (PRO, E326/11781). Said to occ. 1357 (*VCH* citing Soms RO, Ctl. Hungerford, f. 362, but as yet this reference cannot be located. The Soms RO, Ctl. Hungerford does not run to 362 folios).

John Occ. 23 and 24 Jan. 1363 (PRO, E40/5869, /6974); 28 Apr. 1363 (*CPR 1361–64*, pp. 327–9); 1 June 1363 (ibid., p. 347; PRO, E40/170); 28 Apr. 1363 (BL, Harl. Cht. 111 C 13); Jan. 1363 x Jan. 1364 (PRO, E42/382; /513). Said to be called Serrige by Sir Thomas Phillipps, citing Wyvil's Salisbury register, but the entry has not been found (*VCH Wilts*, III, 275, n. 52).

Robert Occ. 13 June 1377 (PRO, C81/1788/47).

The next recorded abb., **William**, bl. 14 Sept. 1393 (*Reg. Waltham*, no. 824).

STANLOW *or* STANLAW (Ches).
see WHALLEY

STONELEIGH (Warws) (Bordesley) f. 1141 (at Radmore); *c.* 1156 x 9 (at Stoneleigh).
Lists in *VCH Warws*, II, 81; 'Acta abbatum' in *Ctl. Stoneleigh*, pp. 249–54; *Heads*, I, 143.

William of Tysoe (Tyso, Tysto) *c.* 1204–1217 7th abb. (Acta, *Ctl.*, p. 251). Occ. 12 May 1204 (?1205), Mich. 1208 (*Ctl. Stoneleigh*, p. 21; *Heads*, I, 143, n.4; *Warws F.*, I, no. 187); + 1209 (*Mon. Angl.*, IV, 112; for date cf. Cheney, *Inn. III*, no. 846). D. 23 July 1217 after 12 years as abb. (Acta, *Ctl.*, p. 251).

Ralph (Ranulph) *c.* 1217–1221 8th abb., succ. William and abb. for 3 years (ibid., p. 252). Occ. (R.) 1217 or a little later (*Ctl. Tutbury*, no. 264). Cess. 1221 (Acta, *Ctl.*, p. 252).

William de Gyleforde 1221–1231 9th abb. (ibid.). Occ. 11 Nov. 1226 (*Warws F.*, I, no. 381). Dep. 1231, abb. for 10 years (acta, *Ctl.*, p. 252).

Osbert de Westwelle 1231–1258 10th abb., succ. William (ibid.). Occ. 13 Oct. 1245, 21 Apr. 1247 (*Warws F.*, I, nos. 618, 666). Res. 5 Sept. 1258 after 26 years as abb. (Acta, *Ctl.*, p. 252).

Peter Wyche 1258–1262 11th abb., prev. cellarer of Bordesley, succ. Osbert 11 Nov. 1258 (ibid.). D. 21 Feb. 1262 after 3½ years as abb. (ibid).

Richard of Alkrington (Alcryntone) 1262–1272 12th abb., succ. Peter 5 June 1262 (ibid., pp. 252–3). Removed 1272 after d. of Henry III (16 Nov.) after 10 years as abb. (ibid., p. 253). Called Merynton (*VCH*).

Thomas de Orlescote 1273–1277 13th abb., succ. Richard 10 Jan. 1273 (Acta, *Ctl.*, p. 253). Occ. 29 Sept. 1273 (PRO, E315/48/214). Res. 1277 to be abb. of Bordesley after 5 years (Acta, *Ctl.*, p. 253).

William de Heyford 1277–1292 14th abb. succ. Thomas 1 Dec. 1277 (ibid). Occ. 1280 (PRO, E210/4602); 1287 (BL, Add. Chts. 49059–61). Res. before 10 Aug. 1292 after 14 years, to be abb. of Bordesley (Acta, *Ctl.*, p. 253).

John de la Sale 1292–1308 15th abb., succ. William 10 Aug. 1292 (ibid.). Occ. 7 July 1307 (*Ctl. Stoneleigh*, p. 127). Dep. before 15 Dec. 1308 after 16 years 2 months (Acta, *Ctl.*, p. 253).

Robert de Horkeleye (Hockele) 1308–1349 16th abb., succ. John 15 Dec. 1308 (ibid.). D. 1349 (St Desiderius the Bishop's Day – *impossible to identify definitely which of the several Bishops Desiderius it might be*) after 40 years 4 months as abb. (ibid., p. 254).

Robert of Atherstone 1349–1352 17th abb., succ. Robert 26 May 1349 (ibid.). Bl. 19 July 1349 by lic. from bp of Coventry and Lichfield (*Reg. Bransford*, no. 1537). Res. 23 May 1352 after 3 years as abb. to be abb. of Combe (Acta, *Ctl.*, p. 254).

Thomas (de) Pype (Pipe) *alias* **Weston(e)** 1352– 18th abb., succ. Robert 24 May 1352 (ibid.). Lic. to receive bl. from any bp 16 June 1352 (Lichfield, B/A/1/3, f. 127v). Occ. 10 Oct. 1363, 5 Feb. 1364 (*CPR 1361–64*, pp. 447, 460); 6 May 1364 (Oxford, BNC, Yatford deed 1); 21 June 1364 (Stratford, SBT, DR.18/1/713–14). Apostate, signified for arrest (PRO, C81/1788/48; Logan, *Runaway Religious*, p. 209). 26 Oct. 1364 king takes abbey, heavily in debt, into his royal protection and appts Richard de Stafford and Richard de Piryton as custodians (*CPR 1364–67*, p. 29).

Alexander of Evesham M. of Bordesley, said to have been imposed on monastery after depriv. of abb. Thomas (*CPL*, IV, 80). Subsequently res., fearing depriv. (ibid.). Ordered 6 May 1365 to arrest Thomas Pipe, now a vagabond (*CPR 1364–67*, p. 145). Occ. 1 May 1365 (PRO, C81/1788/48); 24 Sept. 1365 (*CPR 1364–67*, p. 178). The present (unnamed) abb., for fear of the previous abb. and his accomplices, dares not labour about his business. The king takes the abbey into his special protection and gts custody of the house to John of Gaunt, duke of Lancaster, and Richard de Stafford 30 June 1365 (*CPR 1364–67*, pp. 133–4).

William (of) Aston M. of Stoneleigh, succ. Alexander (*CPL*, IV, 80). Occ. 20 Mar. 1367, 28 Jan. 1369 (*CPR 1367–70*, pp. 1, 259); 12 Feb. 1369 (PRO, C81/1788/49).

Thomas (de) Pype (Pipe) *alias* **Weston** Apparently restored. Occ. 19 May 1370, 12 Mar. 1372 (Stratford, SBT, DR.18/1/715; DR.18/3/1148); 1371 (PRO, C85/59/15); Jan. 1373 x Jan. 1374 (PRO, E326/6687); Jan. 1375 x Jan. 1376 (PRO, E210/7863); June 1379 x June 1380 (PRO, E210/2285); 24 Mar. 1380 (*CPR 1377–81*, p. 618); June 1380 x June 1381 (PRO, E42/469). Occ. as former abb. 11 Sept. 1383, when gtd certain lands for his use and maintenance for life (*CPR 1381–85*, p. 312).

The next recorded abb., **Thomas Haltone** (Haloughton), occ. 12 Mar. 1391 (Stratford, SBT, DR.18/1/716); 5 June 1392 (ibid., DR.18/1/56); 24 Oct. 1392 (PRO, E315/41/7); 30 Jan. 1393 (Stratford, SBT, DR.18/3/957).

STRATA FLORIDA (Cardigan) (Whitland) f. 1 June 1164; rebuilt 1184+ after fire.

Lists in *Fasti Cistercienses Cambrenses*, p. 190; S.W. Williams, *The Cistercian Abbey of Strata Florida* (1889), app., p. cxii; *Heads*, I, 143.

An unnamed abb. was dep. Sept. 1217 (*Ch. Melrose*, f. 35v (34v); cf. Canivez, I, 484).

Cedifor –**1225** D. 1225 (*Brut Red Book*, p. 227; *Brut Peniarth*, p. 100).

P. Occ. 1226, 15 July 1227 (*Ystrad Marchell Chts.*, nos. 69–70).

Gruffud Occ. 1248 (*Brut Red Book*, p. 241).

Joab –**1268** D. 1268 (ibid., p. 269; *Brut Peniarth*, p. 115).

Philip Coch (Goch) –**1280** Occ. 6 Nov. 1278 (PRO, SC1/20/189). 13th abb. D. 1280 (*Brut Red Book*, p. 269; *Brut Peniarth*, p. 120).

Anian Sais **1280**– Occ. 1280 (*Brut Red Book*, p. 269; *Brut Peniarth*, p. 120); (A.) *c.* Nov. 1284 (*Lit. Wallie*, no. 149); 3 Aug. 1294 (*CPR 1317–21*, p. 77); n.d. (Williams, *Strata Florida*, app., pp. xvi–xvii). ? to be identified with later archdn of Anglesey and bp of Bangor 1309–28 (*Fasti Cistercienses Cambrenses*, p. 192; *Le Neve 1300–1541*, XI, 3, 9).

John Occ. 10 Feb. 1299 (*Cal. Anc. Pet. Wales*, p. 368).

Meredith (Maredudd) **Bool** Occ. 2 Oct. 1336 (*CChR 1327–41*, p. 382; *CPR 1377–81*, p. 551); excommunicated 1 Oct. 1338 (PRO, C85/167/22; G. Williams, *Welsh Church*, p. 141).

Llewelyn Vaughan (Vichan) **1344**– 1344 the abbs. of Beaulieu and Thame commissioned by General Chapter to investigate, and subsequently conf. the eln of Llewelyn (Canivez, III, 494). M. of Strata Florida, eln disputed with Clement ap Richart (see below). Llewelyn complains that Clement and other monks have carried off goods etc. of the abbey – order to the justice of South Wales not to adm. the said monks to sustenance at the abbey 18 July 1346 (*Reg. Black Prince*, I, 2); dispute continues in Court Christian 8 Feb. 1347 (ibid., 44). Llewelyn appealed to the Court of Arches and the Official of Canterbury asks the bp of Hereford and other judges delegate to send a record of the suit now in progress 27 Apr. 1347 (*Reg. Trillek*, pp. 112–13). Order to aid abb. Llewelyn in obtaining restitution and possession of property etc. occupied by Clement and others 25 Oct. 1347 (ibid., 132). Abb. Llewelyn occ. 2 Aug. 1377 (*CPR 1377–81*, p. 14); 20 Oct. 1380 (ibid., p. 551).

[**Clement ap Richart** (Richard, Rycard) had been ejected by Llewelyn Vaughan, m. of Strata
Florida. Papal commn to bp of Hereford to adjudicate 1 Mar. 1345; bp appts deputy to hear
case 1 June 1345; another deputy apptd to hear case 25 Apr. 1346 (*Reg. Trillek*, pp. 52, 62).]
The next recorded abb., **John**, occ. 1385 (PRO, SC8/139/6928).

STRATA MARCELLA (Montgomery) (Whitland) (Ystrad Marchell) f. 22 June 1170;
1172(?) (second site)
   Lists in *Fasti Cistercienses Cambrenses*, p. 190; *Montgomeryshire Coll.*, VI, 366; *Heads*, I, 144.
David (Dafydd) Occ. 1215 (*Ystrad Marchell Chts.*, nos. 59, 61; *Montgomeryshire Coll.*, 51, p.
   185, no. 31).
Ieuaf (Joab) Occ. as *quondam* abb. 1234 (*Ystrad Marchell Chts.*, no. 82). His position in the
   sequence of abbs. is uncertain.
Goronwy Occ. 1225 x 1230, (G.) 15 July 1227 (*Ystrad Marchell Chts.*, nos. 67, 70; *Ctl.
   Shrewsbury*, I, no. 188); (Grennou) Sept. 1233 x Apr. 1234 (*Ctl. Shrewsbury*, II, no. 368d).
Gregory Occ. 1248 (*Welsh Assize Roll*, p. 27, citing PRO, KB26/135, m. 10).
James Occ. ?1 Mar. 1271, 10 June 1278 (*Cal. Chancery Rolls*, pp. 172–3; *Litt. Wallie*, no. 233).
Edeneweyn Occ. 25 Apr. 1281 (*Welsh Assize Roll 1277–84*, p. 323).
C. Occ. 3 Nov. 1284 (*Litt. Wallie*, no. 301).
H. Occ. 27 Feb. 1286 (*CCR 1279–88*, p. 413).
Unnamed abb. removed by abbs. of Abbey Dore, Hailes and Thame, commissaries lately
   deputed by the abb. of Cîteaux and *diffinitores* of General Chapter mentd 16 Aug. 1328
   (*CCR 1327–30*, p. 410).
Gruffudd (Griffin) 'Lately dead' 28 Feb. 1333 (*CCR 1333–37*, pp. 93–4); also mentd as late
   abb. 12 Apr. 1367 (*Ystrad Marchell Chts.*, no. 88).
Matthew On d. of abb. Griffin, Matthew was el. by the pr. and convent of Strata Marcella at
   the abbey of Valle Crucis, as they did not dare to proceed with an eln at Strata Marcella
   because of diverse threats of death and other damages made to them by John de Cherleton,
   lord of la Pole in Wales. John, upon Matthew's eln being conf., entered the abbey of Strata
   Marcella by armed force whilst the pr. and convent were at Valle Crucis. The king orders
   John to withdraw from the abbey and restore it to Matthew 28 Feb. 1333 (*CCR 1333–37*,
   pp. 93–4; *Cal. Anc. Pet. Wales*, p. 400; PRO, SC8/239/11937).
John Wade Letter to bp of St Asaph, stating that the abb. of Clairvaux and other abbatial col-
   leagues had removed John Wade from office, subsequently imprisoned him and had intruded
   David Las, abb. of Abbey Cwmhir. Subsequently other Cistercian abbs. had restored John
   and their action been ratified by the General Chapter. The bp is to take action against John's
   opponents – letter dated 6 Nov. 1352 (Lambeth, Reg. Islip, ff. 60v–61r; cf. Canivez, III, 525).
William Occ. 12 Apr. 1367 (*Ystrad Marchell Chts.*, no. 88).
David Occ. Jan. x June 1377 (PRO, E179/1/3); 6 Aug. 1396 (*Reg. Trefnant*, p. 128).
The next recorded abb., **John**, occ. 29 June 1406 (*Montgomeryshire Coll.*, I, 307, 312).

STRATFORD LANGTHORNE (Essex), St Mary and All Saints (Savigny) (Ham) f.
25 July 1135
   Lists in *VCH Essex*, II, 1333; *Heads*, I, 144.
Benedict *c.* 1197–1218 El. *c.* 1197. Res. 1218 after 19 years to be abb. of Coggeshall (*Ralph
   Coggeshall*, p. 187).
Richard 1218– Occ. from Trin. 1218 to 8 Feb. 1235 (*Essex F.*, I, 49, 113); 1227 (PRO,
   Just.1/229, m. 12); Mich. term 1228, Trin. term 1229 (*CRR*, XIII, nos. 772, 2210); 1229
   (*CR 1227–31*, p. 238); Trin. term 1230, Trin. term 1231 (*CRR*, XIV, nos. 409, 1686); Hil.
   term 1233 (*CRR*, XV, no. 123); 1233 (PRO, E40/14033).

Hugh Occ. from Hil. 1237 to Hil. 1259 (*Essex F.*, I, 115, 232); 20 Oct. 1237 (*Kent F.*, p. 148); 26 Feb. 1248 (*CPR 1247–58*, p. 9); 20 Oct. 1248 (PRO, F. Divers Cos. CP25/1/283/12, no. 230).

John Occ. from 29 July 1262 to 20 Oct. 1272 (*Essex F.*, I, 247, 277).

Robert Occ. Trin. 1280 (PRO, CP40/34, mm. 2d, 5); 1285 (PRO, Just.1/242, m. 26); Trin. 1286 (PRO, E159/59, m. 11d); Mich. 1286 (*Essex F.*, II, 55); 6 Aug. 1288 (*CPR 1281–92*, p. 297); 25 Nov. 1288 (*Beds F.*, II, no. 146).

Henry Occ. 24 Jan. 1292 (*CPR 1281–92*, p. 513); 1296 (*TEAS*, 11, 368).

Richard de Wyght (Wight) Occ. 9 May 1311 (*HMC Var. Coll.*, I, 358); 21 Feb. 1315, enrolled 1316 (*CCR 1313–18*, p. 337); (Feb. x July) 1316 (PRO, CP40/213, m. 1d); 1319 (WAM no. 29412); 1320 (C.H. Talbot, 'Cîteaux and Scarborough', p. 144, no. xxx); Trin. 1327 – Mich. 1328 (*Index to Placita de Banco*, p. 156); 1329 x 1330 (*Cal. Misc. Inq.*, III, 307); n.d. (1332 x 1333) (PRO, C270/11/44); 28 Dec. 1336 (Longleat mun. 808).

William of Coggeshall (Coggeshale) –1349 Name (*YB 19 Edward III*, p. 487). Occ. 20 Feb. 1340 (*CCR 1339–41*, p. 448); 16 Oct. 1342 (*CPR 1340–43*, p. 558); 10 Dec. 1343 (*CFR 1337–47*, p. 348); 20 Sept. 1344 (ibid., p. 385); Mich. 1348 x Mich. 1349 (PRO, E372/194, rot. 16). D. by 23 Mar. 1349 (*CCR 1349–54*, p. 22).

William Occ. 7 Aug. 1350 (ibid., p. 242).

John Normand Occ. 17 Dec. 1351 (ibid., p. 406; *Ctl. Pyel*, p. 97); Mich. 1351 (PRO, KB27/365, m. 65); Jan. 1351 x Jan. 1352 (PRO, E326/6661); 26 Apr. 1353 (Longleat mun. 769). Name, see *TEAS*, 10, 109.

William Occ. 6 July 1358, 26 Mar. 1359 (*CCR 1354–60*, pp. 512, 618); 16 Nov. 1358 (*CPR 1358–61*, p. 120).

Nicholas Occ. 14 Dec. 1363 (*CCR 1360–64*, p. 560).

The next recorded abb., **Herman Hunnyfeld**, occ. 5 May 1380 (*Hornchurch Priory*, p. 53, no. 236); 6 Mar. 1383, 2 Jan. & 6 Feb. 1385 (*CCR 1381–85*, pp. 267, 508, 608); 1388 (Longleat mun. 1160); 22 Feb. 1393 (London, Reg. Braybrooke, f. 292v); 1395 (Longleat mun. 10974 (full name)).

SWINESHEAD (Holland) (Lincs) (Furness) f. 1 Feb. 1135
  Lists in *VCH Lincs*, II, 146; *Heads*, I, 144.

?Robert of Denton (Dentona) If it is correct that he was abb. of Swineshead before he was abb. Furness he must have been in office before 1225 (?1226) (*Ctl. Furness*, I, i. 9; BL, Egerton ms. 2823, f. 78r–v).

Jordan Occ. n.d. (*temp.* Henry III) (BL, Add. Cht. 26205); 1235 (*Ctl. Furness*, II, ii, 509). Seal (*BM Seals*, no. 4137).

Geoffrey Occ. 5 May 1240 (*Lincs F.*, I, 306); 1 May 1250 (*Lincs F.*, II, 80).

Henry Occ. from 20 Jan. 1253 to 3 June 1263 (ibid., 104, 218).

Elias Occ. *c.* Apr. 1270 (*Reg. R. Gravesend*, p. 41); 1277 (PRO, C85/171/9). Mentd. as being abb. before the statute of mortmain (1279) (*Cal. Misc. Inq.*, II, 54).

Thomas Occ. 22 Oct. 1286 (*Reg. Romeyn*, I, p. 253, no. 727).

Lambert –1298 Occ. 9 Apr. 1290 (PRO, C81/1788/51); 16 Feb. 1298 (*CPR 1292–1301*, p. 331).

Thomas of Wensley 1298– Apptd 7 Sept. 1278 (TCD, ms. 516, f. 217v).

John 1309– Bl. and prof. obed. 6 Jan. 1309 (Lincoln, Ep. Reg., III, f. 147r). Occ. n.d. (Jan. 1332 x Jan. 1333 (PRO, C270/11/45); 23 Apr. 1338 (*CPR 1338–40*, p. 77).

John Occ. Mich. 1351 (PRO, KB27/55, m. 18d).

John de Rale (Ryale) Occ. 28 Apr. 1368 (Lincoln, Ep. Reg., XII, f. 97v; Lambeth, Reg. Whittlesey, f. 116v).

William of Swineshead (Swynesheved) Occ. 1377, 1381 (*Clerical Poll-Taxes*, p. 52, no. 758; p. 115, no. 1403).
The next recorded abb., **John**, occ. 27 Aug. 1411 (PRO, SC1/57/23).

THAME (Oxon), St Mary (Waverley) f. 22 July 1137 (at Otley); *c.* 1140 (at Thame)
   Lists in *VCH Oxon*, II, 85; medieval list in *Ctl. Thame*, II, 201; *Heads*, I, 145.
Simon 1205–1224 4th abb., prev. pr. of Bruern, el. 1205 (*Ctl. Thame*, II, 201). Occ. 1210 x 1211 (*Ctl. St Frideswide*, II, 246; cf. Cheney, *Inn. III*, no. 871); 26 Aug. 1211 (*Ctl. Thame*, II, 125); from 7 Dec. 1218 to 2 Feb. 1224 (*Oxford F.*, pp. 59, 72). D. 1224 (?for 1225, see below, *Ann. Waverley*, p. 300).
Laurence 1224 (?1225)– 5th abb., m. of Thame, apptd 1224 on d. of Simon (ibid.). Apptd 1225 (*Ctl. Thame*, II, 201). Occ. 13 Apr. 1225 (PRO, Berks F., CP25/1/7/7, no. 25); 25 Oct. 1232 (*Bucks F.*, I, 62); 1232 (*Ctl. Sandford*, II, no. 244). Commn to abb. of L'Aumône to investigate charges against unnamed abb. *qui arma pugili dicitur ministrasse* 1232 (Canivez, II, 109).
Robert of Tetsworth (Tettesworth) **1232–** Apptd 1232 (*Ctl. Thame*, II, 201, where name given as 'de Tett'). Occ. 20 Oct. 1235 (*Oxford F.*, p. 93); Oct. 1236 x Oct. 1237, Oct. 1238 x Oct. 1239 (*London and Middlesex F.*, pp. 23, 25).
Hilary 1243– Apptd 1243 (*Ctl. Thame*, II, 201). Occ. from 18 Nov. 1244 to 22 July 1248 (*Oxford F.*, pp. 131, 154); 25 Oct. 1246 (*Ctl. Thame*, I, no. 35); Oct. 1248 x Oct. 1249 (*London and Middlesex F.*, p. 33).
Roger (of) Marcham 1252– Apptd 1252 (*Ctl. Thame*, II, 201). Occ. 6 Oct. 1252 (*Oxford F.*, p. 160); 18 Mar. 1257, 1252 x 1259 (*Ctl. Thame*, I, nos. 33, 34, 58).
Richard Barton(e) 1259– Apptd 1259 (ibid., II, 201). Occ. 3 Feb. 1261 to 8 July 1276 (*Oxford F.*, pp. 179, 207); 1262 (PRO, Bucks F., CF25/1/16/37, no. 8); 1266 (*Cal. Misc. Inq.*, I, 108); 1274, 25 Aug. 1281 (*Ctl. Thame*, I, nos. 77–8, 39); Mich. 1280 x Mich. 1281 (PRO, E159/54, m. 22); 15 Aug. 1281, 25 Aug. 1281 (*Ctl. Oseney*, II, 452, 455). Abb. of Rewley (q.v.).
Roger Hoveton (Houttone) **1283–** Poss. the Roger, pr. of Thame, who occ. 1281 (*Ctl. Thame*, I, no. 39); apptd 1283 (ibid., II, 201). Occ. Trin. 1283 (PRO, CP40/50, mm. 57, 61, 63); 3 Feb. 1285, 25 Nov. 1285 (*Oxford F.*, pp. 218, 223); 12 May 1286 (*Bucks F.*, II, 59); 14 May 1287 (*Ctl. Thame*, II, no. 190); 10 Oct. 1294 (*CPR 1292–1301*, p. 97); Hil. 1295 (PRO, CP40/107, m. 47d); Easter 1298 (PRO, Just.1/1312, m. 2d).
William Stratton 1302/4– Apptd 1302 (*Ctl. Thame*, II, 201); bl. and prof. obed. 1 Jan. 1304 (Lincoln, Ep. Reg., III., f. 62r).
John of Thame (Thama) **1316–** Apptd 1316 (*Ctl. Thame*, II, 201). Lic. to receive bl. from bp of Salisbury 11 Dec. 1316 (Lincoln, Ep. Reg., III, f. 359r; *Reg. Martival*, II, 165). Engaged on the king's affairs 1321 (*CCR 1318–23*, p. 476); occ. Mich. 1328 (*Index to Placita de Banco*, p. 531); 25 July 1337, 3 Nov. 1337 (*CCR 1337–39*, pp. 144, 273).
William de Steynton (Styventon) **1349–** Apptd 1349 (*Ctl. Thame*, II, 201). Occ. 27 Jan. 1352, 4 July 1353 (*CCR 1349–54*, pp. 463, 606); 26 Jan. 1355 (*CCR 1354–60*, p. 178).
John de Esingdon 1355– Apptd 1355 (*Ctl. Thame*, II, 201).
Richard de Wath[ ] (? for Watlyngton) **1356–** Apptd 1356 (*Ctl. Thame*, II, 201). Occ. 1 Feb. 1358, 21 Feb. 1359 (*CCR 1354–60*, pp. 487, 612). Abb. Richard occ. 6 June 1372 (PRO, C146/5769). Possibly to be identified with abb. Richard Watlyngton below.
Richard Watlyngton Occ. 1 May 1379 (PRO, C67/28B, m. 13). Possibly the same as the above.
The next recorded abb., **Henry Toursey**, occ. 14 Nov. 1393 (*CPL*, IV, 482).

TILTY (Essex) (Wardon) f. 22 Sept. 1153
   Lists in *VCH Essex*, II, 126; *Heads*, I, 145.

Simon –**1214** Last occ. *ante* 14 Oct. 1213 (*Cartae Antiquae 11–20*, p. 49, no. 363). D. 1214 (*Ralph Coggeshall*, p. 169).

Walter Occ. Mich. 1219, 2 Nov. 1227, Hil. 1230 (*Essex F.*, I, 56, 79, 86); 23 Apr. 1228 (PRO, Cambs F., CP25/1/23/12, no. 41); Hil. term 1230 (*CRR*, XIII, no. 2283); Mich. term 1230, Trin. term 1231 (*CRR*, XIV, nos. 717,1580).

Robert Occ. from Trin. 1247 to Hil. 1264 (*Essex F.*, I, 154, 261); 1249, 7 Jan. 1253, 17 May 1253, Mich. 1257 (Essex RO, T/B3, p. 153, no. 121; p. 265, no. 180; p. 29, no. 25 and p. 13, no. 10); 13 Oct. 1254 (PRO, Cambs F., CP25/1/25/28, no. 6); Oct. 1266 x Oct. 1267 (*Suffolk F. (Rye)*, p. 65).

Nicholas Occ. 22 May 1272 (PRO, Cambs F., CP25/1/25/33, no. 17); from Hil. 1276 to Mich. 1285 (*Essex F.*, II, 12, 49); 20 Jan. 1276 (PRO, F. Divers Cos. CP25/1/284/20. no. 39); 6 Feb. 1277 (Essex RO, T/B3, p. 17, no. 14); n.d. (ibid., p. 19, no. 15 and p. 95, no. 71; (1268 x 1285) (PRO, E40/14346). Seal (*Mon. Seals*, p. 89).

Adam Occ. 11 Nov. 1293 (PRO, C241/18/1; C241/24/45); 1 July 1295 (PRO, Cambs F., CF25/1/26/45, no. 23); n.d. (BL, Harl. ms. 662, f. 107r).

Edmund Occ. 1307 (PRO, Assize roll 254, m. 2d, cited in *TEAS*, XVII, 48); mentioned 20 Feb. 1318 in a conf. (*CPR 1317–21*, p. 123).

Simon Occ. 14 Jan. 1328 (PRO, C146/10,064). Seal (*Mon. Seals*, p. 89; see also R.C. Fowler, 'An abbot and seal of Tiltey', *TEAS*, n.s., XVI (1921), 57).

John of Wardon Occ. 8 Aug. 1347 (*CPR 1345–48*, p. 393).

Richard Chishull Occ. 7 July 1350 (*CCR 1349–54*, p. 239); n. d. (Essex RO, T/B3. p. 95, no. 72).

The next recorded abb., **William**, occ. 1381 (McHardy, *Church in London*, p. 33, no. 296).

TINTERN (Monmouth) (L'Aumone) f. 9 May 1131

Lists in *Heads* I, 145; *Monmouthshire Antiquary*, I, part 4 (1964), pp. 107–9; *Fasti Cistercienses Cambrenses*, pp. 190–1.

Ralph –**1245** Said to be abb. 1232–45 (*Monmouthshire Antiquary*, I, part 4 (1964), pp. 107–8). Occ. 16 June 1234 (*CPR 1232–47*, p. 56). Abb. of Dunkeswell 1245–1252 (q.v.); abb. of Waverley 1252–1266 (q.v.).

J. Occ. 22 Oct. 1253 (*Glam. Chts.*, II, no. 581; BL, Harl. Cht. 75 D 11; Williams, *Strata Florida*, pp. xxx–xxxi; *An. Sac. Ord. Cist.*, XX, 100).

There was a vacancy and an eln at Tintern in 1259 (cf. *'Abbas de Brueria in Anglia qui abbatiam de Tinterna de mandato patris abbatis providere debebat, secundum formam Ordinis, de pastore, et in generali capitulo confessus est se ibidem clandestinam electionem fecisse, ut similis motu poene ab huiusmodi abusivo processu ceteri terreantur, sex diebus sit in levi culpa, duobus eorum in pane et aqua, et quadraginta diebus extra stallum abbatis. Predictam vero electionem que facta fuit nulla forma iuris vel ordinis observata, generale capitulum denuntiat esse nullam; verum quoniam ipsa electio non persone sed fame vitio reprobatur, concedit capitulum generale ut ille idem in eadem abbatia possit eligi, si ei aliquid canonicum non obsistat'* Canivez, II, 453).

John –**1277** Occ. 1267 (*CChR 1257–1300*, p. 304; *Welsh Episcopal Acts*, II, p. 752, no. L.544); 1270 (*CCR 1268–72*, p. 285); 3 Nov. 1271 (*Sussex F.*, II, no. 780); 1276 (*Ann. Waverley*, p. 387). On account of ill-health the unnamed abb. of Tintern (presumably John) had not been to the Cistercian General Chapter for a long time; if he did not come to the following General Chapter the father-abb. was to receive his cession; note of his deposition 1277 (Canivez, III, 171, 169).

Ralph Occ. Oct. 128[ ] (PRO, C81/1788/53); 13 May 1294 (*Berkeley Chts.*, no. 459); Nov. 1302 x Nov. 1303, Nov. 1303 x Nov. 1304 (*Norfolk F. (Rye)*, p. 159).

Hugh de Wyke (le Wyke) **1305–1320** Made abb. 1305 (*Flor. Hist.*, III, 328). Occ. 25 May 1306

(*CPR 1301–07*, p. 434). D. midnight 10 Nov. 1320 in London and bur. at Stratford (London) (*Flor. Hist.*, III, 343).

Walter of Hereford 1321– Cellarer of Tintern el. 9 Feb. 1321 (ibid., 343–4). Occ. 26 Mar. 1327 (*CPR 1327–30*, p. 64).

Roger de Camme (Kamme) Occ. 3 Dec. 1330, 10 Oct. 1331 (*CPR 1330–34*, pp. 19, 201); 27 Mar. 1331 (*Cal. Misc. Inq.*, II, 339); 9 Nov. 1331 (*CCR 1330–33*, p. 370).

Walter Occ. 29 Jan. 1333 (*CPR 1330–34*, p. 397).

Gilbert Occ. 21 July 1340 (*CCR 1339–41*, p. 492); (G.) 17 May 1340 – 22 Oct. 1341 (NLW, Badminton manorial records 1645).

John Occ. 31 July 1349 – 29 June 1375. Possibly more than one man (NLW, Badminton manorial records 1646–53). Occ. *c.* 16 Jan. 1370 (*CCR 1381–85*, p. 638).

John Wysbech(e) (Westbych, Wisbech) **1387–1407** Previously abb. of Grace Dieu (q.v.). Occ. 6 Apr. 1387 (PRO, C81/1788/55b); 1390 (G. Williams, *The Welsh Church from Conquest to Reformation* (Cardiff, 1962), p. 208, citing PRO, C85/167/32); 1395 (BL, Add. Cht. 7488); abb. 1387–1407 (NLW, Badminton manorial records 1571, 1654–6). Styled 23 Apr. 1390 as former abb., *intrusor fuit* (PRO, C85/167/32).

VALE ROYAL (Cheshire), St Mary, St Nicholas, and St Nicasius (Abbey Dore) f. 1266 x 1272 (foundation cht. 14 Jan. 1274) (at Darnhall), monks from Abbey Dore poss. resident from as early as 1268; 29 Apr. 1281 (at Vale Royal, old abbey); 15 Aug. 1333 (Vale Royal, new abbey). See T. Bostock & S. Hogg, *Vale Royal Abbey and the Cistercians 1277–1538* (Northwich, 1998).

Lists in *VCH Cheshire*, III, p. 164; *Vale Royal Ledger*, pp. 20–1.

At DARNHALL

Walter Occ. *temp.* Henry III (d. 1272) (*Vale Royal Ledger*, pp. viii, 20).

Henry Mentd as former abb. in assize record of 1294 (BL, Harl. ms. 2072, f. 50r). The assize mentions two former abbots, John (to be identified with John Champneys below) and Henry. While the *VCH* gives Henry the dates 1270 x 1275 it is uncertain when Henry was actually abb. *Vale Royal Ledger*, p. 20 suggests Henry might be a scribal error for abb. Walter.

John Champneys See *Vale Royal Ledger*, pp. 13–14. Occ. Mich. 1273 x Mich. 1274 (PRO, E159/48, m. 18); 8 Nov. 1275 (*CCR 1272–79*, pp. 254–5); 25 July 1277 (PRO, E315/51/133); 1278 (*CChR 1257–1300*, p. 207; *Derbys AJ*, 13 (1891), 100–1); Mich. 1280 x Mich. 1281 (PRO, E159/54, m. 23). Moved to Vale Royal 29 Apr. 1281 (*Vale Royal Ledger*, p. 5). Occ. 2 June 1282 (*Chester City Courts*, p. 45); 1283 (BL, Harl. ms. 2162, f. 17r); 1286 (Hill, *Ecclesiastical Letter Books*, p. 182); 28 June 1289 (*Chester City Courts*, p. 141). Seal (*BM Seals*, no. 4235).

At VALE ROYAL (Moved to Vale Royal 29 Apr. 1281: *Vale Royal Ledger*, p. 5).

Walter of Hereford See *Vale Royal Ledger*, pp. 14–15. Occ. 27 Apr. 1294 (BL, Harl. ms. 2072, f. 50r); Trin. term 1297 (*Coram Rege roll*, pp. 65, 258); 1301 x 1307 (Ormerod, *Cheshire*, II, 147). Mentd 20 Nov. 1311 as former abb. *temp.* Edward I (*CFR 1307–13*, p. 402).

John of Hoo (Oo) See *Vale Royal Ledger*, pp. 15–17. Occ. 20 Mar. 1305 (*Vale Royal Ledger*, p. 149); 4 Oct. 1308 (BL, Harl. ms. 2162, ff. 16v, 17r); 1311 (*Vale Royal Ledger*, p. 91); 16 Nov. 1311 (BL, Harl. ms. 2072, f. 53v); 1314 x 1315 (*DKR 36*, app. II, no. 1, p. 482).

Richard of Evesham See *Vale Royal Ledger*, pp. 17–19. Occ. 1316 (*DKR 36*, app. II, no. 1, p. 482); 24 May 1320 (*Vale Royal Ledger*, p. 84); 2 Jan. 1326 (BL, Harl. ms. 2162, f. 23r).

Peter El. *c.* 1322 (*Vale Royal Ledger*, pp. 74 & 75n.). In 1336 it was the abb.'s 13th year (ibid., p.

37). Occ. from 1325 x 6 to 12 Mar. 1330 (ibid., pp. 122, 28); 21 July 1330 (*DKR 36*, app. II, no. 1, p. 482). Moved to Vale Royal New Abbey, 15 Aug. 1330 (ibid., p. 6). Occ. 15 Aug. 1330 to 21 Feb. 1338 (ibid., pp. 179, 116). Still abb. Aug. 1339 (BL, Harl. ms. 2272, ff. 76v, 77r). Pardon to Roppert ap Griff', saving the king's suit, for the death of abb. Peter 9 Nov., 20 Dec. 1341 (*DKR 36*, app. II, no. 1, p. 205; cf. *Vale Royal Ledger*, p. 164).

Robert (de) Cheyneston *c.* 1340– Occ. 1337 as m. of Vale Royal (*Vale Royal Ledger*, p. 27). Succ. *c.* 1340 (ibid., pp. 29, 163). Occ. 14 July 1341, 24 Feb. 1343 (ibid., pp. 177, 59); 18 June 1344 (*CCR 1343–46*, p. 380); 1349 (*Vale Royal Ledger*, p. 159).

Thomas Ragon Occ. 26 Mar. 1351, 8 May 1356, 13 Dec. 1364, 1 Aug. 1366 (ibid., pp. 60, 62). Supposed to have d. in 1369 in third great pestilence (Ormerod, *Cheshire*, III, 897, but no source). Mentd 1383–4 as former abb. *temp.* the Black Prince (*Rot. Parl.*, III, 182).

Stephen Occ. 27 Jan. 1373 (*Vale Royal Ledger*, p. 62); 1375 (ibid., p. 86); 1379 (Bennett, 'Lancs. and Cheshire Clergy', p. 22); 20 July 1395 (*CPR 1391–96*, p. 606); 1400 (*DKR 36*, app. II, no. 1, p. 483); Aug. 1401 (*Vale Royal Ledger*, p. 37n.). In 1386 he was stated to be aged 40 and more (*Scrope-Grosvenor*, I, 253).

VALLE CRUCIS (Denbigh) (Strata Marcella) f. 28 Jan. 1201

Lists in G. Vernon Price, *Valle Crucis Abbey*, pp. 41–50; *Fasti Cistercienses Cambrenses*, p. 191; *Heads*, I, 145–6; and *ex inf.* Dr Michael Rogers.

John Occ. July 1213 x Jan. 1214 *or* Nov. 1214 x Oct. 1215 (*Acta Langton*, no. 35; *Ctl. Haughmond*, no. 838; *Montgomeryshire Coll.*, IV, 315; Eyton, *Salop*, X, 347–8).

M. Occ. 1226 (*Ystrad Marchell Chts.*, no. 69).

Tenhaer Occ. 15 July 1227 (ibid., no. 70); Abb. of Thelanegwistel[34], occ. Sept. 1233 x Apr. 1234 (*Ctl. Shrewsbury*, II, p. 333, no. 368d); (T.) July 1225 x Feb. 1333 (*Ctl. Haughmond*, no. 3)[35]; (T.) 1234 (*CChR 1257–1300*, p. 458).[36]

Madoc Poss. M., pr. of Valle Crucis in 1234 (*CChR 1257–1300*, p. 458). Occ. 1254 as former abb. (*Arch. Camb.*, I (1846), 152; K. Maund ed., *Handlist of Acts of Native Welsh Rulers 1132–1283*, no. 237).

Anian ap Meredith Abb. 1251, ?1265 (Price, p. 43). Occ. 8 Sept. 1254 (*Arch. Camb.* I (1846), 152; K. Maund ed., *Handlist of Acts of Native Welsh Rulers 1132–1283*, no. 237).

Gervase (Iorwerth) Occ. 30 Dec. 1270 (K. Maund ed., *Handlist of Acts of Native Welsh Rulers 1132–1283*, no. 238, cf. nos. 235–6; *Powys Fadog*, I, 173–4).

Madoc Occ. 1 Sept. 1275 (PRO, C85/167/12); 17 May 1276 (*Litt. Wallie*, no. 58); (M.) 1 Aug. 1280 (ibid., no. 53); 2 Nov. 1284 (ibid., nos. 90, 94).

Hywel Occ. Feb. 1294 (Denbighshire RO, Ruthin, DD/WY/1591); *c.* July 1295 (PRO, SC1/27/174).

Adam (Ad(d)af, Atha) Occ. May 1330 (BL, Add. ms. 10013, f. 174r); Jan. 1331 x Jan. 1332, Jan. 1343 x Jan. 1344 (Price, p. 44; *Arch. Camb.* V (1888), p. 370); Aug. 1343 (BL, Add. ms. 10013, f. 172r).[37]

Thomas Occ. 1380 x 1381 (PRO, E179/1/6).

---

[34] Tenhaer, abb. Thelanegwistel = Llyn Egwistel, better known as Valle Crucis (*Brut y Twysogyon (Peniarth)*, pp. 195, 104).

[35] In one ms. the initial of the abb. is given as G., but T. seems likely given the other evidence of this period.

[36] There is an inscription *Adam abbas fecit hoc opus in pace quiescat Amen* in a gable end at the abbey site (*Arch. Camb.* (1846), 21, 25–6, cf. Price, p. 42 – date queried *Fasti Cistercienses Cambrenses*, p. 191). The identification (1846) with Adam (Adda) Vras, a poet *c.* 1240 is not likely (cf. *Dict. Welsh Biography*, p. 4). More recent investigations have placed this inscription to the 14th cent. which fits in with the abb. Adam of the 1330s and 1340s (see D.H. Evans, *Valle Crucis Abbey* (CADW, revised edn, 1995), p. 24).

[37] Price, pp. 44–5 has abb. Ieuan (John Trevor) but no source.

VAUDEY (Lincs) (Fountains) f. 23 May 1147 (at Bayham); 1149 (at Vaudey)
  Lists in *VCH Lincs*, II, 144–5; *Heads*, I, 146.
William Occ. (W.) ?1214 x 15 (Cheney, *Inn. III*, no. 1008); July 1214 x July 1216 (*Ctl. Daventry* no. 924); 1219+ (*Mon. Angl.*, VI, 693); 23 Apr. 1219 (BL, Cotton ms. Vespasian E XVIII, f. 106v); occ. as former abb. *temp.* Nicholas below (LAO, 2 Anc.1/1/10).
John Occ. 26 Apr. 1225 (*Lincs. F.,* I, 174); occ. as former abb. *temp.* Nicholas below (LAO, 2 Anc.1/1/10).
Nicholas Occ. 16 Feb. 1227 (*Ctl. Glastonbury*, I, p. 188, no. 303); 29 Sept. 1227 (*CPR 1225–32*, p. 165); 1228, 1229 (ibid., pp. 209, 289); 1228 (*Lincs F.*, I, 221); Hil. term 1229, Hil. Term 1230 (*CRR*, XIII, nos. 1362, 2569); (N.) *c.* 18 May 1230 (PRO, SC1/6/155); 11 July 1231, 8 May 1232 (*Lincs F.*, I, 232, 248); 5 Feb. 1238 (*Glam. Chts.*, II, no. 504).
Godfrey Occ. 18 June 1245, 5 June 1250, 12 June 1250 (*Lincs. F*, II, 24, 55, 63). 14 Apr. 1247 (PRO, Leics F., CP25/1/122/19, no. 303).
Henry Occ. 3 Feb. 1251, 2 June 1252, 25 June 1252, 8 July 1258 (*Lincs. F.*, II, 91, 96, 94, 163). 1254 (*Ctl. Burton Lazars*, p. 37); 1264 (ibid.).
William Occ. 26 Nov. 1271 (LAO, 3 Anc 2/1, f. 24r, no. 103).
James Occ. 1 July 1281 to 7 May 1284 (PRO, Lincs F., CP25/1/132/53, no. 16; CP25/1/133/58, no. 87); Easter 1282 (PRO, CP40/45, m. 24). [On 7 May 1292 the king takes abbey under his protection and gtd custody during pleasure to William de Hamelton, king's clerk (*CPR 1281–92*, p. 491).]
Roger Occ. Hil. 1295 (PRO, CP40/107, m. 13); n.d. and 1 Nov. 24 Edward (? I, i.e. 1296) (PRO, C81/1788/58–60).
Richard Occ. Trin. term 1297 (*Coram Rege Roll*, p. 257); n.d. (*Ctl. Burton Lazars*, p. 37)
William Occ. Mich. 1305 (PRO, CP40/153, m. 284); Mich. 1310 (*YB IV*, 209; PRO, CP40/183, m. 111d). Poss. the deceased abb. William mentd in case of 1346 (*YB 20 Edward III, part 1*, p. 55).
Simon 1314– Bl. 3 Mar. 1314 by ex-archbp of Armagh and prof. obed. (Lincoln, Ep. Reg., III, f. 292v).
Walter Occ. 1 Sept. 1323, 8 Feb. 1325, 11 May 1325 (*CCR 1323–27*, pp. 136, 343, 372); 25 Oct. 1325 (*CPR 1324–27*, p. 232); Easter 1327, Mich.1327 (*Index to Placita de Banco*, pp. 348, 282).
John Occ. 20 Apr. 1331 (*CCR 1330–33*, p. 304); 17 July 1332 (ibid., p. 579); 31 Mar. 1335, 28 Sept. 1336 (*CCR 1333–37*, pp. 475, 705). 2 May 1338, 8 Oct. 1338, 16 Dec. 1338 (*CCR 1337–39*, pp. 407, 538, 627); 14 Aug. 1349 (*CPR 1348–50*, p. 414).
It is possible that some or all the above entries concern John of Howden below.
John of Howden (Howdeyn) Occ. from 13 Oct. 1349 to 31 Oct. 1350 as abb. in the manor court rolls (LAO, 2 Anc. 2/19/7).
John de Berham Occ. as abb. in the manor court rolls from 25 Nov. 1354 to 25 July 1360 (ibid., 2 Anc 2/19/10).
John Occ. 1377 (*Clerical Poll-Taxes*, p. 54, no. 764). Could be the same as above.
Thomas Occ. 1381 (ibid., p. 106, no.1272 and p.166, no.2078).

WARDON (Beds), St Mary de Sartis (Rievaulx) f. 8 Dec. 1136
  Lists in *VCH Beds*, I, 365; *Ctl. Wardon*, pp. 357–8 (to 1346); *Heads*, I, 146–7.
Roger II 1215–1223/4 M. of Wardon, master of *conversi*, el 29 Apr. 1215 (*Ch. Melrose*, p. 59). Occ. Oct. 1217 x Oct. 1218 (BL, Cotton ms. Faustina C. I, f. 20v); 25 June 1219 (*Beds F.*, I, p. 53, no. 227); 1221 (Robert) (*Ctl. Colchester*, II, 534); 19 Oct. 1223 (*Ctl. Wardon*, no. 109); 20 Oct. 1223 (PRO, Northants F., CP25/1/12/17, no. 98). El abb. of Rievaulx 1223/4, res. 1239 (Clay, 'Early abbots', p. 36, citing *Ch. Melrose*, pp. 76, 86).

William 1223/4– Pr. of Wardon 1223/4 (*Ch. Melrose*, p. 76). Occ. Oct. 1224 x Oct. 1225 (*Hunts F.*, p. 10); from 8 June 1225 to 30 Sept. 1232 (*Beds F.*, I, pp. 70, 90, nos. 270, 335); (W.). 28 June 1225 (*Ctl. Newnham*, no. 129); Hil. term 1229 (*CRR*, XIII, no. 1244); 10 Dec. 1229 (*CR 1227–31*, p. 386); 22 July 1232 (PRO, Cambs F, CP25/1/24/14, no. 12).

Adam –1242 Occ. from 3 Feb. 1234 to 2 Dec. 1240 (*Beds F.*, I, pp. 96, 120, nos. 359, 443); (A.) Feb. 1235 (*Ctl. Newnham*, nos. 128, 130); 26 July 1240 (PRO, Herts F., CP25/1/85/18, no. 254). El. Bp. of Connor *ante* 27 Jan 1242, d. 7 Nov, 1244 (*Chronology*, p. 343).

[**Alexander** M. of Wardon, el. abb. but not yet professed for a year, so eln set aside – mentd in General Chapter in 1244 (Canivez, II, 278).]

Geoffrey Occ. 29 June 1244 (*CChR 1226–57*, p. 279; *Ctl. Wardon*, no. 348); 10 Feb. 1246 (Beds RO, Russell (Duke of Bedford) R.O. 5/6); from 12 Nov. 1246 to 3 Feb. 1258 (*Beds F.*, I, pp. 133, 166, nos. 475, 590); 17 Apr. 1253 (PRO, Cambs.,F, CP25/1/24/26, no. 24); 7 Dec. 1254 (*Ctl. Wardon*, no. 342k); 6 June 1255 (PRO, Glos. F.,CP25/1/74/20, no. 424); 26 May 1256 (PRO, F. Unknown Cos., CF25/1/282/7, nos. 125–6).

Alexander de Reynes Occ. 1259 (*Ctl. Wardon*, nos. 255, 262); 8 July 1269 (PRO, Herts F. CP25/1/86/32, no. 615); 8 July 1271 (*Beds F.*, I, p. 188, no. 672).

Elias (Helias) Occ. (H.) Aug. 1272 (*Ctl. Newnham*, no. 135); 6 Oct. 1276 (*Beds F.*, II, no, 20); 1276 (PRO, C115/Li/6689, f. 73v).

Robert Occ. Trin. 1285 (*King's Bench, Edward I*, I, p. 153).

John of Dalling Occ. July 1288 (PRO, Just.1/1276, m. 20); 12 July 1290 (*CPR 1281–92*, p. 371).

Laurence Occ. 19 Oct. 1302 (*Ctl. Wardon*, no. 139); 1 May 1304 (PRO, C85/6/74).

Ralph of Harrold (Harewold) 1304– Bl. and prof. obed. 11 Apr. 1305 (Lincoln, Ep. Reg. III, f. 81r). Occ. 25 Nov. 1306 (*Ctl. Wardon*, no. 268). Desc. as former abb. 1312 (*YB XII*, 139). D. by 7 Oct. 1313 when indulgence offered for prayers for his soul (Lincoln, Ep. Reg., III, f. 284v).

Geoffrey of Stamford (Staneford) 1313/14– Lic. to receive bl. 7 Oct. 1313 (ibid.). Bl. by ex-archbp of Armagh and prof. obed. 3 Mar. 1314 (ibid., f. 292v). Occ. Aug. 1316 (*Ctl. Wardon*, no. 266).

Thomas 1318– Bl. by ex-archbp of Armagh and prof. obed. 1 Nov. 1318 (Lincoln, Ep. Reg., III, f. 399v). Occ. 29 July 1318 (*CPR 1317–21*, p. 275); 6 July 1320 (*Ctl. Sibton*, IV, no. 967).

Robert Wodhulle Mentd as previous abb. in 1345/46 homage (*Ctl. Wardon*, no. 204g).

William of Helmsley (Helmeslee) Occ. 21 Dec. 1327 (Lincoln, Ep. Reg., IV, f. 316r); Easter 1327 – Mich. 1328 (*Index to Placita de Banco*, p. 1); 18 July 1330, Jan. 1345 x Jan. 1346 (*Ctl. Wardon*, nos. 199, 204f); Mich. 1337 (PRO, CP40/213, m. 351); 18 Apr. 1338, 30 Oct. 1338 (*CCR 1337–39*, pp. 465, 610); 6 Oct. 1340 (*CCR 1339–1341*, p. 638); 11 June 1346 (*CPL*, III, 222).

Walter of Clifton (Clyfton) Occ. 7 Feb. 1377, 12 Feb. 1377 (*CCR 1374–77*, pp. 513, 531); 1379 (*Clerical Poll-Taxes*, p. 79, no. 995).

The next recorded abb., **John**, occ. 20 May 1397 (*CPR 1396–99*, p. 139).

WAVERLEY (Surrey) (L'Aumône) f. 24 Nov. 1128
Lists in *VCH Surrey*, II, 88 from *Ann. Waverley*; *Heads*, I, 147.

John III 1201–1216 Seventh abb. Cellarer of Waverley, el. 1201 (*Ann. Waverley*, p. 253). D. 3 Aug. 1216 (ibid., p. 286).

Adam 1216–1219 Sub-pr. of Waverley, succ. 1216 (ibid.). Occ. 1216 x 1217 (*Ctl. Chichester*, no. 756. Seventh abb. (*sic*, should be eighth), cess. 1219 (*Ann. Waverley*, p. 292 & n. 2). D. 1229 (ibid., p. 305). Obit (could be Adam I or II) 1 May (BL, Cotton ms. Claudius D III, f. 148v).

Adam II 1219–1236 Eighth abb. (*sic*, should be ninth), former abb. of Garendon, succ. 1219

(*Ann. Waverley*, p. 292). Occ. 27 Jan., 1 Feb. 1236 (PRO, Hants F., CP25/1/203/6, nos. 39, 37). Cess. 1236 (*Ann. Waverley*, p. 316).

Walter Giffard 1236–1252 Tenth abb. Abb. of Biddlesden succ. 1236 (ibid.). Occ. 1241 (PRO, Hants F., CP25/1/203/7, no. 22); Oct.1246 x Oct. 1247, Oct. 1247 x Oct. 1248 (*Surrey F.*, p. 28). D. 1252 (*Ann. Waverley*, p. 345).

Ralph 1252–1266 Eleventh abb. M. of Waverley, abb. of Dunkeswell, abb. of Tintern, succ. 1252 (ibid.). Res. 1266 on account of infirmity *vir quidem morum honestate et scientie probitate non mediocriter adornatus* (ibid., p. 373).

William of London (Londonia) **1266–** M. of Waverley, succ. 1266 (ibid.). Occ. 29 May 1269 – had no friendship with Simon de Montfort and is not to be molested (*CPR 1266–72*, p. 346). Abb. William occ. 21 Mar. 1274 (*Quarr Chts.*, no. 40); 24 May 1275 (PRO, Hants F., CP25/1/204/12, no. 10), but whether to be identified with William of London or William of Hungerford is uncertain (if indeed they are two persons).

William of Hungerford –1276 Cess. on account of infirmity (*Ann. Waverley*, p. 387).

Hugh of Lewknor (Leuckenor, Leukenor) **1276–1286** M. of Waverley, el. 16 Nov. 1276 (ibid.). Occ. (H.) 5 Mar. 1277 (*Ctl. Kirkstall*, no. 60); 1282 (BL, Add. Cht. 5548). D. 18 Mar. 1286 (*Ann. Waverley*, p. 403).

Philip of Bedwyn (Bedewinde, Bedwindo) **1286–** Succ. and bl. in Winchester cath. 14 Apr. 1286 (ibid.). Occ. 22 Oct. 1286, 1295 (*Reg. Pontissara*, I, pp. 332. 536); 1289 (*Wilts F.*, II, 30); 1308 (Talbot, 'Cîteaux and Scarborough', p. 141, no. xxvii); 25 July 1310 (*Ctl. Winchester*, no. 409); Mich. 1310 (PRO, CP40/183, attorneys m. 41d).

Bl. to unnamed abb. 24 Apr. 1312 by bp of Bath and Wells, acting under commn from vicargeneral of bp of Winchester (*Reg. Droxford*, p. 50). Presumably William below.

William Occ. 17 June 1313 (Spencer muns. II/1/1421–NRA list); Hil. and Mich. 1314 (*YB XVI*, 63–4); 1321 (*CCR 1318–23*, p. 482); 9 July 1324, 17 Jan. 1325 (*CCR 1323–27*, pp. 306, 336); Trin. 1328 (*Index to Placita de Banco*, p. 655).

Robert Occ. n.d. (after May 1334) (PRO, SC1/39/132); 26 Aug. 1334 (*CCR 1333–37*, p. 330); 4 Aug. 1340 (*CCR 1339–41*, p. 494); 29 Sept. 1340 (*CPR 1340–43*, p. 293); 12 May 1341 (ibid. p. 186); 5 Feb. 1342 (*CFR 1337–47*, p. 267); 2 Feb. 1344 (*HMC R. R. Hastings*, I, 8).[38]

John of Collingham (Colyngham) Occ. 14 May 1344 (Winchester, Reg. Orleton, f. 125v). Mentd 15 May 1352 as late abb. (*CPR 1350–54*, p. 286).

John 1349– Bl. 24 May 1349 (*Reg. Edington*, II, no. 215). Broken by age and infirmity 20 Apr. 1357 (*CPR 1354–58*, p. 524). Occ. 10 Dec. 1360 (Spencer muns. II/1/1398–9–NRA list); 1 Aug. 1362 (Spencer muns. II/1/1400); 28 Oct. 1370 (PRO, E315/37/137); 24 Mar. 1379 (*CPR 1377–81*, p. 635). It is impossible to tell how many different abb. Johns are included here. *VCH* says one abb. John d. 1361 but gives no source. On 10 Feb. 1386 the abb. was **John Enford** (*VCH* citing Winchester, Reg. Wykeham II, ff. 224v–225r; his name is not noted in the calendar *Reg. Wykeham*, II, 386–7). When he came into office is impossible to determine.

The next recorded abb., **William**, occ. 26 Jan. 1397 (*CPR 1396–99*, p. 40); 20 May 1397 (*CPR 1396–99*, p. 139), presumably the same as **William Hakeleston** occ. 5 Oct. 1398 (PRO, C67/31, m. 13).

WHALLEY (Lancs) (Combermere) f. 11 Nov. 1172 (at Stanlow, Ches.); 4 Apr. 1296 (moved to Whalley).

Lists in *VCH Lancs*, II, 139; transcript of medieval list (to 1355) in BL, Cotton ms. Titus F III, f. 261r–v; *Heads*, I, 142–3 (under Stanlow).

---

[38] Abb. William occ. 22 Jan. 1341 (*CCR 1339–41*, p. 662) – ? scribal error.

Abbots of Stanlow

W. Occ. 1209 x 11 (*Ctl. Furness*, II, ii, p. 343: not in list).

Charles Called 3rd abb.; d. 3 Jan. (BL, Cotton ms. Titus F III, f. 261r). Occ. (K.) 1224 x 1231 (PRO, DL25/273; see Norton (Ches.); 3 Jan. 1226 (*CPR 1225–32*, p. 71; cf. *Ctl. Whalley*, I, 89); (K.) June 1232 (*Ctl. Burscough*, no. 155); 1232 x 1240 (*Ctl. Kirkstall*, no. 271; *Ctl. Sallay*, I, 157); *c.* 1231 (BL, Cotton Cht. XI 38),; 1238 (*Magnum Reg. Album Lichfield*, no. 529); 3 Aug. 1241 (*Ctl. Chester*, I, no. 306a; *Ctl. Whalley*, II, 545); Whitsun 1244 (BL, Harl. ms. 2063, f. 80v; *Ctl. Whalley*, III, 882–3).

Peter Called 4th abb.; d. 6 Mar. (BL, Cotton ms. Titus F III, f. 261r).

Simon –1268 Called 5th abb.; occ. 29 Oct. 1259; d. 7 Dec. 1268 (ibid.).

Richard Thornton –1269 Called 6th abb.; d. 7 Dec. 1269 (ibid.).

Richard Northburn –1273 Called 7th abb.; d. 1 Jan. 1273 (ibid.).

Robert (of) Haworth (Haword) Called 8th abb.; d. as former abb. 22 Apr. 1304 (ibid., f. 261r–v). Occ. (R.) 1268 x 1272 (*Ctl. Sallay*, I, p. 153, no. 249); n.d., 5 June 1276 (*Ctl. Whalley*, III, 882–3); 8 Sept. 1280 (Cheshire RO, DLT/B17, f. 3v). Remained behind at Stanlow and d. there 22 Apr. 1304 (BL, Cotton ms. Titus F III, f. 261v).

Gregory of Norbury (Northbur') –1296 Called 9th abb. of Stanlow and 1st abb. of Whalley (BL, Cotton ms. Titus F. III, f. 261v). Occ. 8 June 1292 (*Ctl. Whalley*, III, 810); 1294 (*Cal. Misc. Inq.*, II, 489); 10 Feb. 1295 (*CCR 1288–96*, p. 440); 5 June 1295 (*Lancs F.*, I, 179).

Papal lic. had been given for the transfer to Whalley 23 July 1289 (*CPL*, I, 499). Move made 4 Apr. 1296 and Gregory, abb. of Stanlow, became first abb. of Whalley (BL, Cotton ms. Titus F III, f. 261r; cf. BL, Cotton ms. Cleopatra C III, f. 321v, see also ff. 318v, 321r).

Abbots of Whalley

Gregory of Norbury 1296–1310 Became first abb. of Whalley 1296 (ibid.). Occ. 27 May 1297 (BL, Harl. ms. 2162, f. 51r); 1298 (*Ctl. Whalley*, I, 205). D. St Vincent's day 1309 [22 Jan. 1310] (BL, Cotton ms. Titus F III, f. 261v).

Elias de Workesle 1310–1318 Prof. obed. 12 Apr. 1310 (Lichfield, B/A/1/1, f. 57v). D. 28 Sept. 1318 and bur. at Boxley abbey (BL, Cotton ms. Titus F III, f. 261v).

John Belfeld –1323 Occ. 23 Dec. 1321 (*Ctl. Whalley*, III, p. 710); 2 Jan. 1322, 16 Jan. 1322, 27 Nov. 1322 (ibid., III, pp. 711, 713, 410); 12 Mar. 1323 (ibid., III, 709). D. 25 July 1323 – styled 11th abb. (i.e. incl. the Stanlow sequence) (BL, Cotton ms. Titus F III, f. 261v).

Robert of Topcliffe (Topcliff, Toppecliff, Toppeclyf) Occ. 10 Apr. 1328 (*CPR 1327–30*, p. 294); 12 Mar. 1331 (BL, Cotton ms. Titus F III, f. 261v); 29 Sept. 1333, 13 Jan. 1334, 25 Apr. 1335 (*Ctl. Whalley*, IV, 1025; I, 312, 314); 30 Mar. 1334, 7 May 1335, 4 May 1336 (*CCR 1333–37*, pp. 305, 482, 671); 7 May 1335, 4 May 1336 (*CPR 1334–38*, pp. 99, 258); Jan. 1339 x Jan. 1340 (*Cal. Misc. Inq.*, III, 333). Pension as former abb. 1344 (Canivez, III, 479). As former abb. d. 20 Feb. 1351 – styled 12th abb. (BL, Cotton ms. Titus F III, f. 261v).

John of Lindley (Lindelay, Lindeley, Lyndelay, Lyndeley(e), Lynneley) ? Occ. 1342 (Whitaker, *Whalley*, I, 95, n.2: John del Clough gtd to Adam de Gristhwaite and John de Topcliffe in trust for the abbey the tenth part of the manor of Revel 1342. In the *Status de Blackburnshire* it is stated that *tempore Johannis Lyndlay abbatis 10ᵐᵃ pars manerii de Revard adquisita fuit*). Occ. 29 Aug. 1344 (*CPR 1343–45*, p. 338); 19 Dec. 1346, 2 Nov. 1354, 25 Aug. 1359 (*CPL*, III, 224, 532, 609); 1 Jan. 1347 occ. as M. Theol. (*CPP*, p. 123); 1349 (*CPR 1348–50*, p. 469); 1353 (*CPR 1350–54*, p. 466); 1354 (*CPR 1354–58*, p. 97); 1356 (*CFR 1356–68*, p. 12); 1357 (*CPR 1354–58*, p. 601); 1359 (Lambeth, Reg. Islip, f. 161v); 1362, 1363 (*CCR 1360–64*, pp. 429, 531); 1364, 1365, 1366 (*CCR 1364–68*, pp. 84, 167, 187, 296). 1365–6 ref. to abb. John against William Banastre and others who have tried to replace him (PRO, C81/1788/62–3).

Occ. 1370, 1371 (PRO, C241/148/17; /152/29); 7 Oct. 1373 (*Ctl. Whalley*, IV, 1139); 28 Jan. 1375 (*CFR 1368–77*, p. 280); 13 June 1377 (PRO, C67/28B, m. 12). See also Emden, *BRUO*, II, 1150.

The next recorded abb., **William Selby**, occ. 1379 (Bennett, 'Lancs and Cheshire Clergy', p. 22).

WHITLAND (Carmarthen) (Alba Landa, Alba Terra, Ty Gwynn) (Clairvaux) f. 16 Sept. 1140 (at Trefgarn); *c.* 1151 (at Whitland).

Lists in *Fasti Cistercienses Cambrenses*, p. 191; *Heads*, I, 147.

Cadwgan of Llandyfai –1215 Abb. of Whitland until his res. in 1215 to become bp of Bangor; consecrated Bp. Bangor 21 June 1215, res. 1235 x 1236 (*Brut, Red Book*, p. 205; *Brut, Peniarth*, p. 91; *Ann. Worc.*, p. 404; *Chronology*, p. 291; *Dict. of Welsh Biography*, p. 65). Retired to Abbey Dore, where he died 11 Apr. 1241. A noted bishop, writer and preacher (Cowley, *Monastic Order in South Wales*, pp. 150, 153–4, 192; Sharpe, *Latin Writers*, p. 82; C.H. Talbot, 'Cadogan of Bangor' in *Cîteaux*, 9 (1958), 18–40).

An unnamed abb. was dep. Sept. 1217 (*Ch. Melrose*, f. 35v (34v); for date see Canivez, I, 484).

Hoedlew Occ. (H.) 1226; 15 July 1227 (*Ystrad Marchell Chts.*, nos. 69–70).

James Occ. 15 July 1275 (Longleat mun. 622).

Llewelyn Occ. 7 Jan. 1280 (*Welsh Assize Roll 1277–84*, p. 301); 10 Feb. 1299 (*Cal. Anc. Pet. Wales*, p. 368).

Howel Seys Occ. 13 Aug. 1352 (*CPR 1350–54*, p. 316).

The next recorded abb., **Lewis Dew**, occ. 6 Oct. 1399 (*Regs. St Davids*, I, 128–9).

WOBURN (Beds) (Fountains) f. 28 May 1145

Lists in *VCH Beds*, I, 370; *Heads*, I, 147–8.

Richard –1234 Occ. j. d. +19 Dec. 1208 (BL, Lansdowne ms. 375, ff. 131v–132r, cf. Cheney, *Inn. III*, no. 808); Oct. 1214 (WAM no. 15684); from 2 July 1218 to 29 Oct. 1227 (*Bucks F.*, I, 37, 58); 23 June 1219 to 14 Jan. 1228 (*Beds. F.*, I, nos. 230, 248, 269, 288); May 1224 (*Oxford F.*, p. 70); 1227 (*Beds Eyre*, no. 47; *Bucks Eyre*, nos. 293, 463); 9 May 1227 (*Ctl. Fountains*, I, 60); 1228 (*Ann. Dunstable*, p. 108). Dep. 1234 (ibid., p. 140). House then so poor that most of the monks dispersed temporarily to other houses (*KH*, p. 128).[39]

Roger 1234– M. of Fountains, succ. 1234 (*Ann. Dunstable*, p. 140). Occ. from 16 Apr. 1235 to 26 July 1236 (*Bucks. F.*, I, 65, 67); from 27 Sept. 1236 to 27 Jan. 1241 (*Beds F.*, I, nos. 371, 417; *Ctl. Dunstable*, no. 920).

Richard Occ. 21 Apr. 1241 (*Bucks F.*, I, 80).

Adam of Luton –1248 ? Prev. abb. of Medmendham (q. v.). D. *c.* 12 Mar. 1248 (*Ann. Dunstable*, p. 175).

Nicholas 1248– Abb. of Medmendham, succ. *c.* 12 Mar. 1248 (ibid.). Occ. 3 Nov. 1251 (*Bucks F.*, I, 99); 25 June 1252 (*Beds. F.*, I, no. 529; PRO, F. Unknown Cos. CP25/1/282/7, no. 112).

Roger –1281 Occ. 23 Apr. 1262 (*Bucks F.*, II, 10); 7 Apr. 1269 (ibid., 20). D. 1281 (*Ann. Dunstable*, p. 287).

Hugh of Soulbury (Suleburi) **1281–** Succ. 1281 (ibid.).

William Occ. 16 Aug. 1286, going overseas (*CPR 1281–92*, p. 250).

Robert de Stok' 1297– Lic. to receive bl. from any bp of the Canterbury province 5 Dec. 1297 (*Reg. Sutton*, VI, 48). Occ. 18 Apr. 1301 (*CPR 1292–1301*, p. 627); July 1308 x July 1309 (*YB*

---

[39] The L., abb. of Woburn, in *Cart. de la Couture*, p. 191, no. cclx, along with F. (*recte* R.), pr. of Dunstable in a document of 1218 is presumably an error.

I, 104); Trin. 1309 (PRO, CP40/178, mm. 10d, 316); Mich. 1310 (PRO, CP40/183, attorneys m. 41).

Henry 1313– Bl. by bp of Down and prof. obed. 11 Mar. 1313 (Lincoln, Ep. Reg., III, f. 271r).

Robert Occ. 8 July 1324, protection for 2 years (*CPR 1324–27*, p. 6); 21 Dec. 1327, 28 Oct. 1332 (Lincoln, Ep. Reg., IV, ff. 316r, 342r)

Thomas of Thornton 1336– Bl. 17 Nov. 1336 (Lincoln, Ep. Reg., V, f. 543r).

William (of) Wheldrake (Queldrik, Queldryk) **1346–** Lic. to receive bl. from any Catholic bp 1 Oct. 1346 (Lincoln, Ep. Reg., VII, f. 86v). Occ. 5 Sept. 1348 (PRO, C81/1788/ 24 Jan 1358, 6 May 1358, 27 Nov. 1359 (Lincoln, Ep. Reg., VIII, ff. 97v, 73v, 145r); (W.) Jan. 1357 x Jan. 1358 (PRO, E43/111). Seal (*Mon. Seals*, p. 101).

John of Upton Occ. 29 July 1363, 30 July 1363, 6 May 1366 (Lincoln, Ep. Reg., XII, ff. 42r, 5r, 31r); 17/18 Oct. 1363 (PRO, E41/457, using seal with legend: 'Sigillum fratris Willelmi de Wardone', *Mon. Seals*, p. 101, cf. London, St Mary, Graces); 1379 (*Clerical Poll-Taxes*, p. 83, no. 1019)

The next recorded abb., **William Manepeny**, had lic. to receive bl. 20 Nov. 1396 (Lincoln, Ep. Reg., XII, f. 440r).

THE CARTHUSIAN MONKS

BEAUVALE (Notts), Holy Trinity, St Mary and All Saints f. 1343

List in *VCH Notts*, II, 109.

Walter Occ. 4 May 1367 (Herts RO, Panshanger papers, Potternewton deeds 32b).

William Occ. 14 Feb. 1st regnal year , [1378 or 1400, Richard II or Henry IV, uncertain which] (PRO, E315/41/203). A pr. William occ. 19 Sept. 1398 (PRO, E315/33/213).

John Occ. 20 Oct. 1394 (BL, Add. ms. 6060, f. 38r, named f. 35v).

HINTON (Soms), St Mary, St John the Baptist and All Saints f. 1222 (at Hatherop); 1227 x 1232 (at Hinton).

Lists in *VCH Soms*, II, 123; Thompson, *Somerset Carthusians*, p. 305; Hogg, *Priors*, pp. 26–7.

Ralph Occ. (as pr. of Locus Dei) 1240 (PRO, E326/11312).

Robert Occ. 1 Dec. 1246 (*Ctl. Bath*, II, p. 34, no. 156); 6 Oct. 1248, 8 July 1249 (*Soms F.*, I, 130, 133).

Thomas Occ. n.d. (1243 x 1260 *or c.* 1282 x 1287) (*Ctl. Bradenstoke*, no. 622).

Peter Occ. 30 Apr. 1273 (Watkin, *Totnes Priory*, II, 1049); 11 June 1273, 8 July 1275 (*Soms F.*, I, 234, 237).

Edbert According to A. Gray, *List of Obiits of Carthusians of the English Houses from the earliest times to the present day* (typescript at Parkminster, cited by Hogg, *Priors*), he occ. 1304.

Thomas Occ. 26 Oct. 1343, 20 Nov. 1343 (*CCR 1343–46*, pp. 245, 241).

John Luscote Occ. 9 Mar. 1368, 26 Mar. 1368 (*CPR 1367–70*, pp. 93, 130; cf. Thompson, *Carthusian Order*, p. 253). Rector of the new foundation in London 1370 and subsequently pr. of the London Charterhouse, 1371–98 (q.v.).

Adam Occ. 4 Sept. 1377 (*CCR 1377–81*, p. 93); 14 Apr. 1391 (PRO, C81/1787/24); 9 May 1391 (*CPR 1388–92*, p. 441). According to A. Gray, *List of Obiits of Carthusians of the English Houses from the earliest times to the present day* (typescript at Parkminster, cited by Hogg, *Priors*), he d. 1401.

KINGSTON-UPON-HULL (Yorks E.), St Mary, St Michael and All Angels, and St Thomas the martyr. f. 1377

List in *VCH Yorks*, III, 191–2; Hogg, *Priors*, p. 28.

Walter de Kele 1377– First pr., occ. 13 June 1377 (*CCR 1374–77*, p. 552). Apptd pr. in Michael de la Pole's 'foundation charter' of 18 Feb. 1379 (*Mon. Angl.*, VI, 20–1, no. ii, cf. Thompson, *Carthusian Order*, p. 200).

John, described as sometime pr. d. 1404 (according to A. Gray, *List of Obiits of Carthusians of the English Houses from the earliest times to the present day* (typescript at Parkminster, cited by Hogg, *Priors*).[1]

LONDON, Charterhouse, The Salutation f. 1371

Lists in *VCH Middlesex*, I, 169 from PRO, LR2/61, f. 15v, pd Hope, *History of London Charterhouse*, p. 147, who also edits and trans. foundation history pp. 1–36; Hogg, *Priors*, pp. 27–8.

---

[1] The *VCH* reference to a pr. John Craven in 1410 is incorrect. John Craven was pr. of the Carmelite friary in Hull, not the Charterhouse (York, Reg. 18, f. 303v).

John Luscote 1371–1398 First pr., formerly pr of Hinton, transferred to London as rector 1370; arrived in London *c.* 8 Sept.; apptd pr. in foundation charter 28 Mar. 1371 (Hope, *London Charterhouse*, p. 13; PRO, LR2/61, f. 21r; Thompson, *Carthusian Order*, pp. 171–2). Pr. for 27½ years (list; Hope, *London Charterhouse*, pp. 41, 49, 147). Hope suggests he may have res. office shortly before his death (ibid., p. 148). D. 15 June 1398 (ibid., p. 59; Hogg, *Priors*, p. 43, n. 55; *Analecta Cartusiana*, 100: 7, p. 19).

WITHAM (Soms) St Mary, St John the Baptist and All Saints (Binns, p. 176) f. 1178 x 1179

Lists in *VCH Soms*, II,128; Hogg, *Priors*, p. 26; Thompson, *Somerset Carthusians*, p. 110; *Heads*, I, 149.

Robert II of Keyford (Caveford) occ. Palm Sunday 1210 x 13 (*Ch. Witham*, p. 504 (229); *Heads*, I, 149, n. 6); (R.) *c.* 1212 (*Mag. Vit.*, I, p. 1 and n. 1). For his name see *Ch. Witham*, p. 504 (229) and n.

Philip occ. 1209 x 1218 as 'pr. of the Charterhouse', presumably Witham (*Med. Deeds of Bath*, pt. i, no. 163 – *temp.* Hugh II, bp of Lincoln and before William de Hammes became precentor of Wells). A. Gray, *List of Obiits of Carthusians of the English Houses from the earliest times to the present day* (typescript at Parkminster, cited by Hogg, *Priors*), notes a pr. Philip d. *c.* 1233, prob. at the Grande Chartreuse. See also Thompson, *Carthusian Order*, pp. 133–4.

Giles Occ. Sept. x Oct. 1223 (*John of Glastonbury*, II, 256); 15 Aug. 1226, 30 Oct. 1226, 10 June 1229 (*CPR 1225–32*, pp. 79, 85, 292).

R. Occ. 1233 (Thompson, *Carthusian Order*, p. 135; *Proc. Soms ANS*, LXIV, 24–5; also A. Gray, *List of Obiits of Carthusians of the English Houses from the earliest times to the present day* (typescript at Parkminster, cited by Hogg, *Priors*).

J. Occ. 22 Sept. 1242, going to the king in Bordeaux (*CPR 1232–47*, p. 326).

John Occ. 26 Mar. 1260 (Thompson, *Carthusian Order*, p. 138).

John of Canterbury Mentd as former pr. in 1280 (*Soms Pleas*, I, 367–70). Possibly to be identified with J. and John above.

William Mentd as former pr. in 1280 (*Soms Pleas*, I, 198); no clear indication of his precise place in the sequence of priors.

John of Pevensey (Pevenseye) Occ. 29 July 1280 (*Soms Pleas*, I, 367, cf. 17).

Walter Occ. 14 June 1318 (Madox, *Form.*, pp. 316–17, no. 557).

Luke Occ. 1320 (PRO, E135/3/42); 23 Dec. 1321 (PRO, E315/34/200).

Richard Occ. Jan. 1329 x Jan. 1330 (PRO, E43/113); 1331 (PRO, E326/6982).

William de Cokkyng Occ. 1356 (Bodl., Rawlinson ms. D.318, f. 78r; Thompson, *Carthusian Order*, pp. 252–3).

William Occ. 1363 (A. Gray, *List of Obiits of Carthusians of the English Houses from the earliest times to the present day* (typescript at Parkminster, cited by Hogg, *Priors*). Possibly to be identified with the above.

Thomas Occ. 3 Feb. 1366 (Longleat mun. 5844); 4 Sept. 1377 (*CCR 1377–81*, pp. 92–3).

The next recorded pr., **John Langryche**, occ. 20 June 1382 (PRO, C241/170/69).

THE AUGUSTINIAN
CANONS

No names have been found in this period for the cells of Halywell (Rocester), Hood (Newburgh), and Marsh Barton (Plympton).

ALNESBOURN (Suffolk), St Mary f. c. 1200
List in *VCH Suffolk*, II, 91.
Roger Occ. n.d. (pal.: mid-13th cent.) (Suffolk RO, Ipswich, HD1538/113/1/(15)).
Robert Occ. 25 June 1286 (*Norwich Cath. Chts.*, II, nos. 237–8, 246; Suffolk RO, Ipswich, HD1538/113/1/(17)).
Walter of Creeting (Cretyngge) 1312– Can. of Alnesbourn, eln quashed but apptd by bp 4 Jan. 1312, no reason given for vacancy (Norwich, Reg/1/1, f. 45r).
John of Stoke (Stok) 1316–1345 Can. of Alnesbourn, apptd by bp 9 July 1316, no reason given for vacancy (ibid., f. 64v). D. by 9 Nov. 1345 (*Reg. Bateman* I, no. 187).
John of Finningham (Fynyngham) 1345– Can. of Alnesbourn, eln quashed but apptd by bp 9 Nov.1345 (ibid.).
Henry of Haughley (Hawele) 1349–1350 Can. of Alnesbourn, eln quashed but apptd by bp 16 May 1349, no reason given for vacancy (ibid., no. 518). House vacant by d. of Henry of Fynyngham (*sic*) by 17 July 1350 (Norwich, Reg/2/4, f. 123r–v).
Robert Dwyt (Duyt) 1350 Can. of Alnesbourn, apptd 17 July 1350 (ibid.). Res. on 30 July 1350 (ibid., f. 124r).
John of Lynn (Lenn(e)) 1350– Can. of Alnesbourn, apptd by bp, no eln having taken place as so few canons survived 7 Aug. 1350 (ibid., f. 124v). Occ. Mich. 1364 (PRO, KB27/416, rex roll, mm. 12d, 34 – the latter desc. him as former pr. and lists his offences 1358–63 and mentions Robert, *custos* of priory).
John (? another) Occ. 13 Oct. 1365 (Suffolk RO, Ipswich, HD1538/113/1/(19)); Hilary 1378 (*Select Cases of Trespass*, II, 291–2); June 1380 x June 1381 (PRO, E179/45/5B, m. 2)
Robert Brethenham Occ. 1391 (Blomefield, *Norfolk*, V, 107, no source).
Richard Susanne 1392– Can. of St Sepulchre, Thetford, coll. 28 Nov. 1392, no reason given for vacancy (Norwich, Reg/3/6, f. 170v). Occ. 10 Oct. 1401 (Suffolk RO, Ipswich, HD1538/113/1/(16)).

ANGLESEY (Cambs), St Mary and St. Nicholas f. (hosp.) ? 12th cent.; c. 1212 (priory)
Lists in *VCH Cambs*, II, 234; Hailstone, *History of Bottisham*, pp. 174–5.
Richard Occ. (R.) c. 1220 (PRO, SC1/11/95); Easter 1221 (*CRR*, X, 34); Oct. 1221 x Oct. 1222 (PRO, E326/10518); 27 Oct. 1222 (PRO, Cambs. F., CP25/1/23/10, no. 12). Prob. identical with the rector of the Hospital of Blessed Mary of Anglesey n.d., (PRO, E40/7671).
William of Fordham Occ. June 1227 (*Newington Longeville Chts.*, no. 85); 1 Aug. 1232 (PRO, Cambs F., CP25/1/24/14, no. 26; F. Unknown Cos. CP25/1/282/6, no. 56); 22 Sept. 1232 (ibid., CP25/1/24/14, no. 2); 10 June 1235 (ibid., CP25/1/24/16, no. 14); 17 June 1235 (ibid., CP25/1/24/16, no. 9; F. Unknown Cos. CP25/1/282/6, no. 61); 1236 (W.) (E40/14492–3, 14496–7; Hailstone, pp. 196–7); 14 June 1254 (PRO, Cambs F., CP25/1/25/28, no. 4). Full name (PRO, E40/14475, 14477).

Hugh Occ. 17 June 1263 (PRO, Cambs F. CP25/1/25/31, no. 18); 29 Sept. 1264 (PRO, E315/39/123).

John of Terrington (Teringtone) Occ. 13 Oct. 1272 (PRO, Cambs F., CP25/1/25/36, no. 1); 1272 (PRO, Just.1/84, m. 24); 18 June 1273 (ibid., 25/36, no. 4; PRO, E315/41/254); 20 Oct. 1275 (PRO, Herts F., CP25/1/86/35, no. 40); n.d. (late 13th cent.) (BL, Add. Cht. 8415; PRO, E210/5356).

William Occ. n.d. (after 1276), mentions pr. John his predecessor (*Casus Placitorum*, p. 111).

Henry Occ. 1278 (Hailstone, p. 225); n.d. (late 13th cent.) (PRO, E315/45/112; E315/48/68); n.d. (after 1275) (*Casus Placitorum*, p. 129).

John of Bottisham (Bodekesham) –1299 Occ. Nov. 1290 x Nov. 1291 (PRO, E326/6123); Trin. 1298 (PRO, KB27/155, m. 23d). Found guilty of misdeeds and res. before 7 Jan. 1299, when lic. to el. given (*Reg. Winchelsey*, I, 299–300). Mentd as alive 1314 (Hailstone, p. 247).

Roger of Weston 1299– Can. of Anglesey, notif. to sub-pr. and convent that their eln of Roger de Weston was invalid and therefore the archbp of Canterbury has the right to nominate a pr., the see of Ely being vacant. Yet, if their choice of another pr. is unanimous he will nominate him, 16 Mar. 1299 (*Reg. Winchelsey*, I, 324). Notif. to Roger de Weston that as the recent el. was invalid, the archbp has apptd him n.d.; mandate to install n.d. (entries Apr. x May 1299) (ibid., 330–1). Occ. 1299–1300 (Hailstone, pp. 155, 248); 1300 (PRO, E40/14502); Nov. 1305 x Nov. 1306 (PRO, E40/14504).

Walter of Withersfield (Wetherisfeld, Withersfeld, Wytheresfeld) 1316–1338 Installed 1316 (E40/14505, cf. Hailstone, p. 174). Occ. 1325 (PRO, E315/36/151); Jan. 1337 x Jan. 1338 (PRO, E326/5478). D. by 10 Sept.1338 (Ely, G/1/1, pt. 1, ff. 4v–5r).

Walter de Yelveden(e) (Zweldene, Yhevelden) 1338–1352 Eln pres. to bp of Ely 10 Sept. 1338. commn to Official to examine eln 24 Sept. 1338, eln conf. 19 Sept. 1338 (ibid.). Congé d'élire from Elizabeth de Burgh, patroness of the priory, on the d. of William de Yelveden, 20 June 1352 (BL, Add. Cht. 20580).

Richard de Wrottinge (Wrottyng(e), Wrattynge) 1352– Can. of Anglesey, comm. to examine eln dated 15 July 1352, eln conf. by commissary 16 July, bp approved conf. 17 July 1352 (Ely, G/1/1 part 2, ff. 52v–53r). Occ. 30 Sept 1352 (PRO, E315/42/234); 1358 (PRO, E315/31/180); 1360 (BL, Harl. Cht. 47 E 41); Jan. 1368 x Jan. 1369 (PRO, E329/343).

William (of) Quy (Queye, Quye) –1393 Occ 3 Aug. 1373 (Lambeth, Reg. Whittlesey, f. 153v); 1379 (PRO, E179/23/1.m.2); 1385 (PRO, E315/32/57); 4 July 1391 (PRO, E315/34/163; Hailstone, p. 290). D. by 10 Oct. 1393 (PRO, C84/36/4).

Note
A pr. **Robert** is found mentd in a seal cast, supposedly 14th cent., but if this is so he cannot be placed in the sequence of priors with any certainty (*BM Seals*, no. 2558).

ARBURY (Warws), St Mary f. 1154+
Lists in *VCH Warws*, II, 91; *Heads*, I, 150.

Adam Latest recorded occ. 13 Aug.1202 (*Warws F.*, I, no. 139); (A.) n.d. (early 13th cent.) (BL, Add. Cht. 48491) – could be Adam or Alexander (see below)

Alexander Occ. n.d. (early 13th cent. pal.) (PRO, E326/3964). His precise place in the sequence of priors is unclear.

Roger Occ. Easter term 1226 (*CRR*, XII, no. 2376).

Albin Occ. 1227 x 1228 (PRO, E40/5785).

Hugh Occ. 8 June 1236 (*Warws F.*, I, no. 534).

Nicholas Occ. n.d. (mid-late 13th cent. pal.) (PRO, E326/3354). His precise place in the sequence of priors is unclear.

Simon Corbet Occ. 1277 (PRO, E210/4632); 15 May 1282 (BL, Add. Cht. 47564A); n.d. (*c.* 1290 x 1300) (BL, Add. Cht. 48066).

Thomas Occ. 1 Dec. 1308 (Lichfield, B/A/1/1, f. 34v); Mich. 1310 (PRO, CP40/183, attorneys m. 3).

William of Bloxham 1315–1322 Conf. 27 Mar. 1315 of appt by vicar-general as right of eln had devolved to the bp of Lichfield this time (ibid., f. 39v). Occ. 27 Apr.1320 (PRO, E315/45/1). Commn dated 22 Aug.1322 to inquire into William's wish to res. (Lichfield, B/A/1/1/3, ff. 4v–5r). Res. by 12 Oct. 1322 (Lichfield, B/A/1/2, f. 18r–v). Provision made for him n.d. (Lichfield, B/A/1/3, ff. 68v–69r).

John of Burbage (Borebach, Burbach(e)) **1322–** Commn to examine eln 4 Oct. 1322 (ibid., f. 7r). Can. of Arbury, eln conf. 12 Oct. 1322 (Lichfield, B/A/1/2, f. 18r–v). John de Borebach who claimed to be pr. of Arbury cited by archbp of York (papal judge delegate) to appear in York Minster to answer a case brought against him by John de Sutton, pr. of Arbury, 30 May 1329 (*Reg. Melton*, III, p. 94, no. 172). Case between John de Borebach and the commissary of Lichfield – papal letter of appt 28 June 1329; archbp of York's letters as papal judge delegate dated 15 Nov. 1330; appeal to Rome (ibid., pp. 108–9, no. 187). Depr. n.d. (*c.* 1329), John de Sutham, can. of Arbury, previously having been apptd coadjutor (Lichfield, B/A/1/3, f. 20v).

John de Southam (Sutton) **1329–** Occ. 20 May 1329 – see above entry (*Reg. Melton*, III, p. 94, no. 172). Prof. obed. 4 July 1329 (Lichfield, B/A/1/2, f. 22v). Occ. 10 Jan. 1347 (ibid., f. 45r).

Robert de Merston –1379 Occ. 29 July 1373 (PRO, C81/1789/10). Res. by 16 Oct. 1379 (*Reg. Stretton*, I, 60–1; PRO, E326/8439).

ARUNDEL, *see* PYNHAM BY ARUNDEL

ASHBY, *see* CANONS ASHBY

BAMBURGH (Northumberland) (Aug. cell of Nostell) f. -1221 (see below); diss. *c.* 1537 List in *Hist. Northumberland vol. 1: Parish of Bamburgh with the chapelry of Belford* (Newcastle, 1893), p. 95; for details of the cell, ibid., pp. 73–94.

N. Occ. as *procurator* of Bamburgh 20 Jan. 1221 (BL, Cotton ms. Vespasian E XIX, f. 121r).

William of Breedon (Bredona) Occ. as *procurator* of Bamburgh 16 Sept. 1240 (ibid., f. 120v).

William of Clifford Occ. as master n.d. (mid-13th cent.) (DCD, 1.1.Spec.25; Raine, *North Durham*, app., p. 124, no. dccvii, dating the cht. to *c.* 1248). Prob. the William of Clifford who became pr. of Nostell 1255–77 (q.v.).

John of Braham Occ. as master Nov. 1285 x Nov. 1286 (*Arch. Aeliana*, 4th ser., XXXIV (1956), 186).

Henry de Dermor master or *custos* of ch. of Bamburgh, cited to appear before the archbp of York following his visitation of Nostell 28 Oct. 1313, to appear on 26 Nov. (*Reg. Greenfield*, II, p.165, no.1022). Occ. 6 Oct. 1315 (*Reg. Pal. Dun.* II, 734).

Richard of Dewsbery Occ. as master Apr. [1337] (Leeds Archives, NP/C1/1/1, p. 103)

Adam of Allerton Occ. 1376 (*Hist. Northumberland*, I, 95, with no source given).

The next recorded master, **Roger Radcliff**, occ. 1381 (PRO, E179/62/6, m. 1).

BARDSEY (Caernarvon), St Mary f. -1240 (abbey)

Ralph Occ. as abb. 'Ynes' (?Bardsey) 6 July 1221 (*Ctl. Furness*, II, ii, 321).

A. Occ. 11 July 1252 (*Mon. Angl.*, IV, 659).

Adam Occ. 5 May 1301 (*CPR 1343–45*, p. 233).

Kenric –1346 Res., lic. to el. 23 Dec. 1346 (*Reg. Black Prince*, I, 41).

Gregory de Eglewyskadell 1347– Can. of Bardsey, prince's ass. 1 Feb. 1347; temps. 27 Feb. 1347, the eln having been conf. by Matthew, bp of Bangor (ibid., 42, 46).

John Occ. 8 Nov. 1362, 28 Aug. 1372 (*Caernarvon Court Rolls 1361–1402*, pp. 20, 76).

Unnamed abb. d. by 10 Sept. 1377 (PRO, C84/32/2). Lic. to el. on d. of unnamed abb. 26 Sept. 1377 (*CPR 1377–81*, p. 27).

Gervase ap David 1377–1381 Can. of Bardsey, eln pres. to king for royal ass. 8 Oct. 1377 (PRO, C84/32/3); royal asst 26 Oct. 1377 (*CPR 1377–81*, p. 35); temps. 10 Nov. 1377 (ibid., p. 60). Res. by 30 Apr. 1381 (PRO, C84/32/40). Res., lic. to el. 22 May 1381 (*CPR 1381–85*, p. 9).

BARLINCH (Soms), St Nicholas f. 1174 x 91 (?*c.* 1180)
   Lists in *VCH Soms*, II, 134; *Heads*, I, 150.
Elias Occ. 1191 x 1225, prob. *c.* 1200 (*Ctl. Canonsleigh*, no. 151).
John Occ. Oct. 1225 x Oct. 1226 (*Rot. Lit. Claus.*, II, 112); 3 Feb. 1243 (*Soms F.*, I, 120).
Robert Occ. 4 Aug.1267 (Oliver, *Supplement*, p. 7); 8 Nov. 1268 (*HMC Wells*, I, 106); Mich. 1273 x Mich. 1274 (PRO, E159/48, m. 17); 5 Dec.1272, 18 Mar. 1278 (*HMC Wells*, I, 110, 148).
Hugh Occ. Mich. 1283 x Mich. 1284 (PRO, E159/57, m. 11d).
[**Humphrey** Occ. 1288 (Collinson, *Hist. Soms*, III, 503, in list, but no source). Might possibly be a dating error for Humphrey de Lymbiri below.]
Hugh –1321[1] Sought permission to res. on account of age and infirmity 13 Jan. 1321; bp acc. res. 20 Jan. and lic. to el. (*Reg. Droxford*, p. 177).
Humphrey de Lymbiri –1347 Occ. 20 Sept. 1321 (*Reg. Stapeldon*, p. 45); 1329 (*Reg. Grandisson*, III, 1270); 1332 (ibid., II, 651); 30 July 1334 (*HMC Var. Coll.*, IV, 77); Mich. 1337 (PRO, CP40/312, attorneys m. 18). Res. accepted 6 (*sic, see next entry*) Mar. 1347 (*Reg. R. Shrewsbury*, II, no. 1984).
Simon Pile 1347– Eln conf. 5 Mar 1347 (ibid., no. 1982).
The next recorded pr., **William**,[2] occ. 8 July 1386, 22 July 1386 (*HMC Wells*, I, 397). In a 1390 inq. **John Taunton** was mentd as late pr. and **William Wrokkeshale** as his succ. (*Caal. Misc. Inq.*, V, no. 283). They prob. followed Simon, but their precise place in the sequence is uncertain, although the 1386 William could well be William Wrokkeshale.

BARNWELL (Cambs), St Giles f. 1092 (at Cambridge); 1112 (at Barnwell)
   Lists in *VCH Cambs*, II, 248–9; *Ch. Barnwell*, pp. xv–xviii; *Heads*, I, 150–1.
Laurence of Stansfield (Stanesfeld) Can. of Barnwell and pr.'s chaplain (*Ch. Barnwell*, p. 69). Occ. from 12 Apr. 1220 to 25 May 1253 (PRO, Cambs F., CP25/1/23/10, no. 2; /24/26, no. 18). D. in 38th year of office [*c.* 1254] (*Ch. Barnwell*, p. 69).
Henry of Eye (Eya) ?1254/5–1256/7 Chamberlain and sub-pr. of Barnwell, succ. Laurence (ibid., p. 70). Occ. 2 May 1255, 6 Oct. 1256 (PRO, Cambs F., CP25/1/25/28, no. 7; 25/28, no. 11). Res. in his 3rd year as pr. in the hands of the Official of Canterbury, and provision made for him. This was when the see of Ely was vacant, i.e. 21 Sept. 1256 x 14 Oct. 1257 (after the d. of Bp William of Kilkenny and Bp Hugh Balsham's eventual consec. 14 Oct. 1257) (*Ch. Barnwell*, p. 70). D. 14 years after res. (ibid.).
Jolan of Thorley (Thorleye) ?1257–1267/8 Succ. Henry (ibid., p. 71). Occ. 15 Aug. 1257, 1258, Oct. 1267 x Oct. 1268 (ibid., pp. 94, 218, 120; cf. pp. 127–8). Res. in his 11th year of office, but lived another 18 years in the priory, and bur. before the altar of St Thomas the martyr (ibid., p. 72)
Master Simon de Ascellis (Asceles, Aschele, Hasseles) ?1267/8–1297 El. 6 Sept., installed 18 Oct., no year given (ibid., p. 73). Occ. 29 May 1272 (PRO, Cambs F., CP25/1/25/33,

---

[1] *VCH* gives his surname as Price (no source).
[2] *VCH* gives his surname as Wroxhale but no other source except those cited.

no. 4). Res., lic. to el. 20 June 1297 (*CPR 1292–1301*, p. 253). Occ. Trin. 1297 (PRO, CP40/119, m. 152). Res. about 24 June 1297 after 30 years of office and d. 8 Sept.1297 and bur. before the altar of St Katherine (*Ch. Barnwell*, pp. 73–4). See Emden, *BRUC*, p. 17.

Benedict of Welton(e) 1297–1315 Can. of Barnwell, eln pres. to king for royal ass. 24 June 1297 (PRO, C84/13/4); royal ass. 26 June 1297, temps. 3 July 1297 (*CPR 1292–1301*, pp. 255, 289–90). Cert. conf. eln by bp of Ely 28 June 1297 (PRO, C84/13/5). Res., lic. to el. 3 Dec. 1315 (*CPR 1313–17*, p. 371).

Fulk de Stanton 1316–1330 Pardon for his transgression in procuring conf. of his eln by bp. J. of Ely before getting royal ass. 23 Jan. 1316, temps. 24 Jan. 1316 (ibid., p. 79; cf. PRO, C47/15/2/4). D., lic. to el. 23 Jan. 1330 (*CPR 1327–30*, p. 469). For surname see PRO, C84/22/34.

John of Quy (Queye, Quye) 1330–1340 Can. of Barnwell, eln pres. to king for royal ass. 7 Feb. 1330 (PRO, C84/22/34); royal ass. 9 Feb. 1330, temps. 22 Mar. 1330 (ibid., pp. 485, 502). D., lic. to el. 10 Nov. 1340 (*CPR 1340–43*, p. 61).

John de Brunne 1340–1349 Can. of Barnwell, el. 22 Nov. 1340; eln conf. 15 Dec. 1340 (Ely, G/1/1, pt 1, f. 23r–v). Royal ass. 27 Nov. 1340, temps. 23 Dec. 1340 (*CPR 1340–43*, pp. 65, 74). Occ. 10, 12 Apr. 1349 (Ely, G/1/1, pt 2, ff. 18v, 19r). D. by 25 May 1349 (PRO, C84/25/46). D., lic. to el. 28 May 1349 (*CPR 1348–50*, p. 293).

Ralph of Norton 1349–1392 Can. of Barnwell, cert. of appt by vicar-general of bp of Ely *iure devoluto* 27 June 1349 (PRO, C84/26/6). Temps. 1 July 1349 (*CPR 1348–50*, p. 334). D. by 2 Mar. 1392 (PRO, C84/35/21). D., lic. to el. 6 Mar.1392 (*CPR 1391–96*, p. 36).

[**Simon of Sées** came to England in 1349 with papal bull of provision to the priory. The king ordered his arrest and a writ of prohibition forbade giving effect to the provision. *Accts of Papal Collectors*, p. 111 states his prov. was 10 Oct. 1351. Subsequently, in 1356, he tried to claim the abbey of Bourne (q.v.) and was committed to the Tower (*Nottingham Medieval Studies*, XXXV (1991), 79–80; *CPR 1348–50*, pp. 334, 519; *CPR 1350–54*, pp. 272, 244; *CPR 1354–58*, p. 335; *King's Bench Edward III*, VI, 111–12). See also J.M. Gray, 'The Barnwell canons and the Papal Court at Avignon', *Proc. Cambs. Ant. Soc.*, XXXIII (1933), 98–107.]

BARTON (Isle of Wight), Holy Trinity f. 1275; gtd to Winchester Coll. 1439 (see R.G. Davis, 'The Oratory at Barton', *Hants Field Club*, 2 (1890–3), 295–307).

List in *VCH Hants*, II, p. 181 (without sources).

ARCHPRIEST OR PRIOR

Jordan de Marisco Occ. n.d. (1275 x 1285) (WCM no. 3452); also occ. n.d. (ibid., nos. 3519–21).

William Occ. 2 May 1285 (*CPR 1281–92*, p. 159); n.d. (*temp.* Edward I) (WCM no. 3462). Bp of Winchester, being dissatisfied with the administration of the archpriest W., orders the dean of the Isle of Wight to take charge of the house 17 July 1286 (*Reg. Pontissara*, I, 327–8).

Simon Occ. 10 June 1290 (WCM no. 3456); 25 Mar. 1298 (*Lacock Chts.*, no. 458).

Nicholas of Alresford 1307–1343 priest, coll. by bp *pro hac vice* 20 May 1307 (*Reg. Woodlock*, II, 723–4). Occ. from 17 July 1307 to 4 Feb. 1340 (WCM nos. 3512, 2528). D. by 21 Apr. 1343 (Winchester, Reg. Orleton, I, f. 120r).

Richard de Dene 1343– Priest, eln quashed, but apptd by bp 21 Apr. 1343 (ibid.). Occ. 21 Mar. 1347 (WCM no. 3643).

Roger of Exeter *alias* **Pope** (de Exon') **1349–1352** Commn to examine eln 22 May 1349, no reason given for vacancy (*Reg. Edington*, I, no. 531). Occ. 25 July 1352 (WCM no. 7850). Res. by 26 Nov. 1352 (*Reg. Edington*, I, no. 923).

Robert of Somborne 1352–1387 Bp conf. 26 Nov. 1352 (ibid., nos. 923–5). Occ. from 10 Feb. 1358 to 16 Nov. 1385 (WCM nos. 17830, 17832). D. by 3 June 1387 (*Reg. Wykeham*, II, 401).

BECKFORD (Glos) & **COLSTERWORTH** (Lincs) (Ste Barbe-en-Auge) f. 1128 x 1135.

Lists in *VCH Glos.*, II, 102; *Heads*, I, 151.

Sampson Occ. 2 June 1225 (*Lincs F.*, I, 175).

Peter de Haya −1298 D. by 15 Oct. 1298 (*Reg. G. Giffard*, p. 505).

William de Bonyn (*dictus* Bony, Boyn) **1298–** (Previously apptd proctor in England of Ste Barbe 25 July 1293 (ibid., pp. 504–5)). Prof. obed. 15 Oct. 1298 (ibid., p. 505). Occ. Christmas 1298, 31 Mar. 1303 (ECR, 8/14,15); 1300 (PRO, E106/4/14, m. 11); 4 Apr. 1305 (Lincoln, Ep. Reg., III, f .13r).

Giles Boyn(e) Occ. *c.* Mich. 1324 (PRO, E106/5/2, m. 6); July 1325 x July 1326 (PRO, E106/5/4, m. [5]); 8 Oct. 1326 (*Memo. Roll 1326–7*, p. 272); Mich. 1338 x Mich. 1339 (PRO, E372/184, rot. 22).

John de Haseyo Occ. 11 July 1341 (ECR, 8/19).

Laurence Gerard Occ. 10 Mar. 1342 (*CFR 1337–47*, p. 273). Mentd as former pr. 26 Jan. 1343 (ibid., p. 315), but occ. as pr. 11 July 1345 (*CCR 1343–46*, p. 636, and see below).

Giles Boyn −1352 Occ. 26 Jan. 1343 (*CFR 1337–47*, p. 315); 1 Oct. 1344 (ECR, 8/20). Removed by pr. of Ste Barbe before 28 Mar. 1352 (*CFR 1347–56*, p. 320).

Nicholas Malet Occ. 28 Mar. 1352 (ibid.); Mich. 1354 x Mich. 1355 (PRO, E372/200, rot. 8); 28 Apr. 1358 (*CFR 1356–68*, p. 61); proctor-general of abbey of Conches, 24 July 1358, and gtd keeping of priory of Wootton Wawen (ibid., p. 73). Royal gt of keeping of priory during the French war to br. **Alberic Vassal**, can. of Ste Barbe, and one *chivaler* 5 June 1358 (ibid., pp. 66, 83).

[**John Fabri**, apptd pr. of Newent with the church of Beckford (PRO, E42/409).]

Robert de Rotes Can. of Ste Barbe, occ. 11 June 1369 (*CFR 1368–77*, p. 15); 1374 (*Worcs Reg. Sede Vacante*, p. 308); 5 Oct. 1377, 26 Jan. 1378 (*CFR 1377–83*, pp. 14, 17). Obtained permission to remain in England 1378 (Matthew, *Norman Monasteries*, p. 158).

The next recorded pr., **Geoffrey le Gascoing**, priest, can. of Ste Barbe, was apptd 18 May 1401 (PRO, PRO31/8/1140B, part 1, pp. 40–1).

BEDDGELERT (Caernarvon.), St Mary f. 6th cent.; *c.*1200

Madoc Occ. 10 May 1286 (*Mon. Angl.*, VI, 200–1, no. ii).

Philip −1293 Occ. 12 June 1289 (*Cal. Misc. Inq.*, I, 416). Cess. by 1 Nov. 1293; power gtd to Robert de Staundon, justice of North Wales to gt lic. to el., give royal ass. to eln and to restore temps. in due course s.d. (*CPR 1292–1301*, pp. 40–1).

Philip II −1322 D., lic. to el. 25 Apr. 1322 (*CPR 1321–24*, p. 101).

Llewelyn 1322–1337 Can. of Beddgelert, temps. 20 May 1322 (ibid., p. 126). Cert. conf. eln by bp of Bangor 20 May 1322 (PRO, C84/20/15). Res. by 3 Mar. 1337, prob. 1 Mar. (PRO, C84/23/46–7). Res., lic. to el. 12 Mar. 1337 (*CPR 1334–38*, p. 392).

John de Leyn 1337– Can. of Beddgelert, eln pres. to king for royal ass. 2 Apr. 1337 (PRO, C84/23/50); temps. 10 Apr. 1337 (*CPR 1334–38*, p. 419).

Cuhelyn (Keelin) −1376 Occ. 7 Mar. 1375 (*Caernarvon Court Rolls 1361–1402*, p. 89). Commn to archdn of Bangor to proceed to eln of a new pr. on the d. of Keelin, 7 May 1376 (Lambeth, Reg. Sudbury, f. 117r).

John Occ. 1379 (PRO, E179/3/3).

The next recorded pr., **Jevan ap Bled**, d. 13 Aug. 1390; lic. to el. issued 7 Sept. 1390 (PRO, C84/34/41, 43; *CPR 1388–92*, p. 300).

BEESTON (Norfolk), St Mary f. *c*. 1216
    List in *VCH Norfolk*, II, 374.
Roger −1283 Occ. from Oct. 1261 x Oct. 1262 to Oct. 1271 x Oct. 1272 (*Norfolk F. (Rye)*, pp. 99, 111); n.d. (PRO, E40/4918). D. by 26 Feb. 1283 (PRO, C84/8/12).
William of Gateley (Gatele, Gaterele) 1283– Can. of Beeston, eln pres. to king for royal ass. 26 Feb. 1283 (PRO, C84/8/12); mand. to bp of Norwich to deliver seisin if his eln as pr., which the king has accepted, is conf. by the diocesan 6 Mar. 1283. The priory was in the king's hands by reason of the minority of William le Mareschal, patron of the priory (*CCR 1279–88*, p. 203). Occ. 9 Mar. 1290 (Norfolk RO, DCN.44/21/1).
Thomas Occ. 24 June 1297 (PRO, E40/5577).
Walter (William) of Beeston 1314–1326 Can. of Beeston, eln conf. 16 Aug. 1314, no reason given for vacancy (Norwich, Reg/1/1, ff. 57v–58r). In Dec. 1316 the pope ordered the bp of Norwich to enjoin penance on John de Walsam, can. of Beeston, who 'had inflicted wounds on his prelate with a sword', from which he having now recovered, the pope has gtd canonical absolution (*CPL*, II, 136). D. (William) by 12 Feb. 1326 (Norwich, Reg/1/2, f. 5v).
Geoffrey de Botone 1326– Can. of Beeston, apptd by bp on d. of William of Beeston 12 Feb. 1326 (ibid.).
The next recorded pr., **Simon de Calthorp**, can. of Beeston, apptd by bp 20 Dec. 1390, no reason given for vacancy (Norwich, Reg/3/6, f. 151r).

BENTLEY (Middlesex). St Mary Magdalen f. ? 1171 (but cf. Binns, p. 120)
    List in *VCH Middlesex*, I, 170. By the 14th cent. the priory seems to have been annexed to St Gregory's priory, Canterbury (*KH*, p. 147).
Martin Occ. Hil. Term 1229 (*CRR*, XIII, no. 1576).
A pr., unnamed, was suffocated under a mow of corn in 1248 (*MPCM*, V, 33–4).
John de Bere predecessor of William of Carlton, mentd 1301 (*Reg. Winchelsey*, II, 748).
William of Carlton Occ. 1301 [between entries of June and July] (ibid.).
John Taleboth Occ. 10 Nov. 1315 (London Metropolitan Archives, court rolls of manor of Harrow *alias* Sudbury, Acc. 76/2410).
Robert Occ. 10 Jan. 1321 (ibid., 76/2411).
John de Merston Occ. as can. of St Gregory at Bentley 13 Dec. 1330; br. John de Hagh apptd coadjutor due to his old age 1 Feb. 1331 (*Lit. Cant.*, I, 337–9, 345).
Adam Occ. 30 June 1334 (London Metropolitan Archives, Acc. 76/2412).
Walter de Hancrisham Occ. 29 July 1337 (ibid.)
No later prs. known.

BERDEN (Essex), St. John the Evangelist f. 12th cent. ?; –1214
    List in *VCH Essex*, II, 143–4.
Stephen Occ. n.d. (Bodl., Dodsworth ms. 74, f. 26r).
S. (?Stephen) Occ. −1221 (*Ctl. Colchester*, II, 534).
Gilbert −1241 Occ. 20 Jan. 1235 (*Essex F.*, I, 104). Mentd as former pr. 1248 (PRO, Just.1/231, m. 27); n.d. (BL, Harl. ms. 3697, f. 148r).
John Occ. n.d. (*?temp.* Henry III) (BL, Add. ms. 5827, f. 196v, citing deed, now untraced).
Nicholas Occ. 1285 (PRO, Just.1/242, m. 21).
William Occ. (W.) 29–30 Sept. 1317 (BL, Add. Cht. 28556; *HMC 7th Rept.*, p. 581); 2 Dec. 1318 (*Reg. Hethe*, p. 57); 4 Feb. 1337 (PRO, C146/2948).

The next recorded pr., **John de Marchia**, res. by 23 Dec. 1393 (London, Reg. Braybrooke, f. 340r).

BICESTER (Oxon), St Edburga and St Mary f. 1182 x 1185
  Lists in *VCH Oxon*, II, 95; *Heads*, I, 151.
Robert Occ. late 12th to early 13th cent. (PRO, E315/49/277); early 13th cent.(BL, Add. Cht.
  10594); j.d. +25 Apr. 1212; +3 Mar. 1217 (*Ctl. St Frideswide*, II, 50–1, 267; cf. Cheney, *Inn.
  III*, no. 899; *Ctl. Oseney*, IV, 433); (R.) 28 July 1216, 7 Aug. 1217 (*Ctl. Oseney*, V, 57; IV,
  450); 26 Nov. 1224 (*Bucks F.*, I, 51).
[**Henry** Henry occ. twice in the *Ctl. Bradenstoke*, 1226 x 1250 (no. 568) and ostensibly 1239 x
  1242 (no. 360) but the latter could actually be dated before earl William Longespée of
  Salisbury's death in 1226. Therefore there is the possibility of a pr. Henry *c.* 1224 x 1227,
  or of course it could be a scribal error for Hervey (see below).]
William Occ. 7 Mar. 1227 (*Oxford F.*, p. 78); 8 Apr. 1236 (PRO, E210/1104).
Robert –1239/40 Occ. n.d. (PRO, E210/3053). D. June 1239 x June 1240 (*Reg. Grosseteste*, pp.
  462–3).
Hervey 1239/40– Can. of Bicester, el. and adm. June 1239 x June 1240 (ibid.). Occ. 13 Oct.
  1252 (*Oxford F.*, p. 160); (Henry) 1239 x 1242, 1226 x 1250 (*Ctl. Bradenstoke*, nos. 360, 568);
  n.d. (mid-13th cent.) (dated to 1254, apparently without authority, Kennett, *Parochial
  Antiquities*, I, 350–1, followed by Dunkin, *History of Bicester*, p. 65).
Reginald –1269 Occ. Oct. 1261 x Oct. 1262 (PRO, E210/7728); 27 Jan. 1262 (*Bucks F.*, II, 6);
  20 Oct. 1267 (*Oxford F.*, p. 243). Res. by 17 Dec. 1269 (*Reg. R. Gravesend*, p. 221).
Walter de Quenton (Quenthone) 1269– Eln quashed, but apptd by bp 17 Dec. 1269 (ibid., pp.
  221, 333). Occ. 1275 (PRO, F. Divers Cos. CP25/1/284/20, no. 23); 1277 (BL, Add. Cht.
  10620); 1278 (*CCR 1272–79*, p. 498); Trin. 1280 (PRO, CP40/34, m. 9d); 20 Jan. 1285, 13
  Oct. 1288 (*Oxford F.*, pp. 221, 225). Presumably res. 1289/90 (see below) but provision
  made for him by convent 14 Aug. 1298 and conf. by bp 17 Aug. 1300 (Lincoln, Ep. Reg., III,
  f. 16r–v).
William de Thornberg(e) 1289/90–1300 El. during 10th year of Bp Sutton (i.e. 19 May 1289
  x 18 May 1290, lic. to el. having been given by Henry de Lacy, earl of Lincoln (Bodl.,
  Dodsworth ms. 107, f. 146v). Occ. Nov. 1298 x Nov. 1299 (PRO, E210/8526); 14 Aug. 1300
  (Lincoln, Ep. Reg., III, f. 16r–v). Bp adm. cess. 5 Oct. 1300 (ibid., f. 18r).
Roger of Cottisford (Cotesford) 1300–1331 Can. of Bicester, el. and appeared before bp 28
  Oct. 1300, any opposers to eln cited for 15 Nov. 1300, on which day bp conf. eln (Lincoln,
  Ep. Reg., II, f. 142v). D. by 26 Nov. 1331 (Lincoln, Ep. Reg., IV, f. 264v).
Robert of Kirtlington (Curtlington, Curtlyngton, Kyrtlyngton) 1331–1348 Can. of Bicester,
  eln quashed, but apptd by bp 26 Nov. 1331 (ibid.). Res. by 30 May 1348 (Lincoln, Ep. Reg.,
  IX, f. 244v).
Roger Warde 1348–1349 Can. of Bicester, right of appt transferred to bp and he apptd Roger
  30 May 1348 (ibid.). D. by 22 June 1349 (ibid.).
Nicholas de Shobindon 1349–1350 Can. of Bicester, eln quashed, but apptd by bp 22 June
  1349 (ibid.). D. by 8 Jan. 1350 (ibid., ff. 244v–245r).
Peter de Grete 1350–1354 Can. of Bicester, eln quashed, but apptd by bp 8 Jan. 1350 (ibid.).
  Occ. 1 May 1354 (PRO, C241/133/160). Res. by 9 Dec. 1354 (Lincoln, Ep. Reg., IX, f. 261v).
Robert Blaket 1354–1383 Can. of Bicester, eln quashed, but apptd by bp 9 Dec. 1354 (ibid.).
  D. by 5 Mar. 1383 (Lincoln, Ep. Reg., XI, f. 296r).

BICKNACRE (Essex), St John the Baptist (Woodham Ferrers) f. 1175
  Lists in *VCH Essex*, II, 145–6; *Heads*, I, 151.
Fulk Mentioned 1232 as former pr. (*CRR*, XIV, no. 2066).

Ralph of Ely −1237 Occ. 13 Jan. 1230, 9 Feb. 1235 (*Essex F.*, I, 87, 100); *c.*1195 x 1238 (*Ctl. Colchester*, II, 555). D., lic. to el. 17 Mar. 1237 (*CPR 1232–47*, p. 177). For surname see BL, Lansdowne ms. 860A, f. 116r (*ex inf.* Professor N. Vincent); and see *Heads*, I, 151.

Andrew 1237–1255 Sub-pr. of Bicknacre, royal ass. 5 Apr. 1237, writ *de intendendo* 15 Apr. 1237 (*CPR 1232–47*, pp. 178, 179). Cess. by 17 Apr. 1255 (PRO, C84/1/40). Cess., lic. to el. 21 Apr. 1255 (*CPR 1247–58*, p. 407).

Ralph de Dunham 1255–1268 Can. of Bicknacre, eln pres. to king for royal ass. 25 Apr. 1255 (PRO, C84/1/41); royal ass. 26 Apr. 1255 (*CPR 1247–58*, p. 407); mand. for seisin 9 May 1255, having been conf. by F., bp of London (*CR 1254–56*, p. 80). Cess. by 3 Nov. 1268 (PRO, C84/3/44).

John of St Edmund (de Sancto Edmundo) **1268–1272** Prev. pr. of Lessness, eln pres. to king for royal ass. 3 Nov. 1268 (ibid.); temps. 12 Nov. 1268, eln having been conf. by master G. de Sancto Dunstano, Official of the bishopric of London in the bp's absence abroad (*CPR 1266–72*, p. 302). Res., lic. to el. 18 May 1272 (ibid., p. 653).

Ralph de Dunham 1272–1273 Can. of Bicknacre, royal ass. 3 June 1272 (ibid., p. 658; PRO, C84/4/14). D., lic. to el. 24 Mar. 1273 (*CPR 1272–81*, p. 7).

William of Wilbraham (Wilburg(e)ham, Wylburham) **1273–1281** Can. of Bicknacre, royal ass. 5 Apr. 1273 (ibid.; cf. PRO, C84/4/39). Cert. conf. eln by bp of London 8 Apr. 1273 (PRO, C84/4/40). D. by 24 Dec. 1281 (PRO, C84/7/42). D., lic. to el. 28 Dec. 1281 (*CPR 1281–92*, p. 7).

Alan of Barking (Bercking, Berkinges) **1282–1288** Can. of Bicknacre, eln pres. to king for royal ass. 23 Jan. 1282 (PRO, C84/7/47); temps. 18 Feb. 1282 (*CPR 1281–92*, p. 12). Cert. conf. eln by bp of London 5 Feb. 1282 (PRO, C84/7/49). D. by 12 Oct. 1288 (PRO, C84/9/29). D., lic. to el. 14 Oct. 1288 (*CPR 1281–92*, p. 301).

Benedict of Rochester (Roff') *alias* **Woldham 1288–1300** Can. of Bicknacre, royal ass. 8 Nov. 1288, temps. 25 Nov. 1288 (ibid., pp. 303, 310). Cert. conf. eln by bp of London 16 Nov. 1288 (PRO, C84/9/20). D., lic. to el. 13 Dec. 1300 (*CPR 1292–1301*, p. 559; cf. PRO, C84/13/52).

Robert of Blakenham 1300–1315 Eln pres. to king for royal ass. 18 Dec. 1300 (PRO, C84/13/52); royal ass. 22 Dec. 1300, temps. 10 Jan. 1301 (*CPR 1292–1301*, pp. 559, 562; *CCR 1296–1302*, p. 475). Cert. conf. eln by bp of London 3 Jan. 1301 (PRO, C84/14/3). Res. by 29 Jan. 1315 (PRO, C84/18/10). Res., lic. to el. 8 Feb. 1315 (*CPR 1313–17*, p. 217).

Robert de Ramesden(e) (Rammesden) *alias* **Burre 1315–1320** Can. of Bicknacre, royal ass. 10 Feb. 1315, temps. 4 Mar. 1315 (ibid., pp. 220, 256). Cert. conf. eln by bp of London 3 Mar. 1315 (PRO, C84/18/13). Occ. (Burre) Feb. 1318 (*CPR 1317–21*, p. 79). Res. by 21 Dec. 1320 (PRO, C84/20/2). Res. (Ramesdene), lic. to el. 20 Jan. 1321 (*CPR 1317–21*, p. 554).

Matthew of Grafton (Graftone) *alias* **Langeton 1321–1324** Can. of Bicknacre, royal ass. 27 Jan. 1321, temps. 4 Mar. 1321 (ibid., pp. 555, 579). Cert. conf. eln by bp of London 25 Feb. 1321 (PRO, C84/20/5). D. by 1 Mar. 1324 (PRO, C84/20/24). D. (Langeton), lic. to el. 6 Mar. 1324 (*CPR 1321–24*, p. 396).

Reginald of Theyden 1325–1341 Can. of Thremhall, pres. to be pr. of Bicknacre by S., bp of London, patron *pro hac vice*, temps. 28 June 1325 (*CPR 1324–27*, p. 133). Res., lic. to el. 7 Mar. 1341 (*CPR 1340–43*, p. 143).

Ralph of Chishall (Chishull) **1341–1361** Can. of Bicknacre, royal ass. 14 Mar. 1341, temps. 28 Mar. 1341 (ibid., pp. 150, 160–1). Cert. from bp of London of quashing of eln and his appt of Ralph 20 Mar. 1341 (PRO, C84/24/19). D. 9 Nov. 1361 (PRO, C84/28/19). D., lic. to el. 29 Nov. 1361 (*CPR 1361–64*, p. 120).

William de Purle(e) 1361–1375 Can. of Bicknacre, eln pres. to king for royal ass. 30 Nov. 1361 (PRO, C84/28/26); royal ass. 2 Dec. 1361, temps. 18 Dec. 1361 (*CPR 1361–64*, pp. 128,

144). Cert. conf. eln by bp of London 15 Dec. 1361 (PRO, C84/28/31). D., lic. to el. 6 Nov. 1375 (*CPR 1374–77*, p. 191).

John (of) Thaxted (Thaxstede) **1375–1386** Can. of Bicknacre, eln pres. to king for royal ass. 9 Nov. 1375 (PRO, C84/31/38); royal ass. 11 Nov. 1375, temps. 14 Nov. 1375 (*CPR 1374–77*, pp. 189, 196). D. 31 May 1386 (PRO, C84/33/46). D., lic. to el. 4 June 1386 (*CPR 1385–89*, p. 154).

BILSINGTON (Kent), St Mary f. 1253

Lists in *VCH Kent*, II, 156; 15th-cent. list in *Ctl. Bilsington*, pp. 57–8 (incl. some errors over calculation of regnal years), 139–40.

William de Campesete [1253–1255/6] 1st pr. 1253; d. Oct. 1255 x Oct. 1256 (*Ctl. Bilsington*, p. 139).

Walter of Rye (Rya) **[1255/6–1261/2]** 2nd pr., succ. Oct. 1255 x Oct. 1256; d. Oct. 1261 x Oct. 1262 (ibid.). But said to occ. Oct. 1254 x Oct. 1255 (*CCR 1330–33*, p. 73), possibly an error.

Ralph of South Malling (Suthmallynges) **[1261/2–1272/3]** 3rd pr., made pr. Oct. 1261 x Oct. 1262. Res. 29 May 1263 and after 6 mths was restored by Simon de Montfort. D. Nov. 1272 x Nov. 1273 (*Ctl. Bilsington*, p. 139). Cf. priory vacant by 9 Mar. 1266 (*CPR 1258–66*, p. 566).

Adam of Micheldever (Micheldevere) **[1272/3–1273/4] –1276** 4th pr., succ. Nov. 1272 x Nov. 1273. Pr. for 1 yr (*Ctl. Bilsington*, p. 139). But d. by 3 Oct. 1276 (PRO, C84/6/1) but see the following: (*cancelled entry*) pardon to the sub-pr. and conv. for trespass committed in admitting on two occasions a pr. apptd by R. archbp of Canterbury, the king's ass. not having been asked for (*CPR 1272–81*, p. 145); lic. to el. 5 June 1276; further gt to sub-pr. and convent on matter of eln and royal ass. 8 June 1276 (ibid., p. 146).

John of Romney (Romene, Romenal) **1276–1279** Can. of Leeds, 5th pr., succ. Adam and lived for 2 yrs (*Ctl. Bilsington*, p. 139). Postulation pres. to king for royal ass. 3 Oct. 1276 (PRO, C84/6/1); royal ass. 29 Oct. 1276 (*CPR 1272–81*, p. 164); cert. of adm. by archbp of Canterbury 31 Oct. 1276 (PRO, C84/6/2). Occ. 12 May 1279 (PRO, Kent F., CP25/1/98/60, no. 108). D. by 17 Oct. 1279 (PRO, C84/6/28).

Hamo of Warwickshire (Warewykschire) *alias* **Clopton 1279–1293** 6th pr., succ. John and d. Nov. 1291 x Nov. 1292 (*sic*) (*Ctl. Bilsington*, p. 139). Can. of Bilsington, eln pres. to king for royal ass. 17 Oct. 1279 (PRO, C84/6/28); royal ass. 20 Oct. 1279 (*CPR 1272–81*, p. 328). D. by 28 Apr. 1293 (PRO, C84/10/15). In a later source he is said to have occ. Nov. 1275 x Nov. 1276 (*CCR 1330–33*, p. 73) but this is prob. an error.

John of Sandwich (Sandwico, Sandwyco) **1293–1317** 7th pr., apptd Nov. 1292 x Nov. 1293, ruled 24 yrs and d. July 1316 x July 1317 (*Ctl. Bilsington*, p. 139). Can. of Bilsington, eln pres. to king for royal ass. 28 Apr. 1293 (PRO, C84/10/15); royal ass. 7 May 1293, temps. 20 June 1293 (*CPR 1292–1301*, pp. 13, 26). Eln conf. by pr. and convent of Canterbury *sede vacante* 6 June 1293; mand. to install 27 June 1293 (*Canterbury Sede Vacante Institutions*, p. 11; PRO, C84/10/19). D. by 7 Feb. 1317 (*CPR 1313–17*, p. 614).

Simon of Hawkeswell (Hauekeshell, Hauekeswelle, Haukeshulle) **1317–1320** 8th pr., apptd July 1316 x July 1317; res. July 1320 x July 1321 (*Ctl. Bilsington*, p. 139). Can. of Bilsington, royal ass. 7 Feb. 1317, temps. 24 Feb. 1318 (*CPR 1313–17*, p. 614, *CPR 1317–21*, p. 108). Cess. by 16 Sept. 1320 (*CCR 1318–23*, p. 261).

John of Wye (Wy) **1320–1342** 9th pr., made pr. July 1320 x July 1321, ruled 22 yrs (*Ctl. Bilsington*, pp. 139–40). Can. of Bilsington, royal ass. 22 Oct. 1320, temps. 13 July 1321, the eln having been conf. by W. archbp of Canterbury (*CPR 1317–21*, p. 512; *CPR 1321–24*, p. 4). Occ. 7 Oct. 1328 (*CPR 1354–58*, p. 599; *Ctl. Boxgrove*, no. 302).

John of Romney (Romene, Romenal, Romeneye) **1342–1349** 10th pr., succ. John of Wye Jan.

1342 x Jan. 1343 and ruled almost 6 yrs (*Ctl. Bilsington*, p. 140). Sacrist of Bilsington, royal ass. 30 July 1342 (*CPR 1340–43*, p. 492). D. by 21 Sept. 1349 (*Canterbury Sede Vacante Institutions*, p. 11; cf. *CPR 1348–50*, p. 412).

Edmund of Canterbury (Cant', Cantuaria) *alias* **Roper 1349–1361–1390** 11th pr., succ. John Mich. 1349 and ruled 40 yrs (*Ctl. Bilsington*, p. 140). Royal ass. 9 Oct. 1349 (*CPR 1348–50*, p. 412). Can. of Bilsington, provided by pr. and convent of Canterbury on d. of John of Romenal, 21 Sept. 1349, installed 12 Oct. 1349 (*Canterbury Sede Vacante Institutions*, p. 11). Res. by 19 Sept. (1361) (Lambeth, Reg. Islip, f. 278v). Res., lic. to el. 16 Apr. 1361 (*CPR 1361–64*, p. 6). Ex-pr. transferred to St Gregory's priory, Canterbury 28 Dec. 1363 (Lambeth, Reg. Islip, f. 200r). There prob. must have been some dispute which eventually resulted in Edmund's restoration (see below). *Ctl. Bilsington* ignores John de Aldeham and John of Romney in the sequence of priors at this date.

John of Aldham (Aldeham) **1361–1363** Request by the archbp of Canterbury for the release of temps. 10 May 1361 (ibid., f. 172v); archbp chooses John and conf. him as pr. 20 May 1361 (ibid., ff. 173r–174r). Can. of Leeds, royal ass. 14 May 1361, the convent having transferred the right of appt to the archbp of Canterbury (*CPR 1361–64*, p. 19). Cess. by 13 Mar.1363 (ibid., p. 320), but presumably by 3 Mar. (see below). Notif. to king of vacancy by res. of John 12 Mar. 1363 (Lambeth, Reg. Islip, f. 191r–v).

John of Romney (Romene) **1363–** 3 Mar. 1363 convent transfer right of appt to archbp of Canterbury; he chooses and conf. John of Romney (ibid., f. 192r–v). Can. of Bilsington, royal ass. 13 Mar. 1363 (*CPR 1361–64*, p. 320).

Edmund of Canterbury (Canterberi) *alias* **of Westgate** (Westgat') **–1390** Pr., became a monk of Christ Church, Canterbury, by 3 Mar. 1390 (Lambeth, Reg. Courtenay, f. 333r).

The next recorded pr., **Thomas Brenchesle(s)**, styled 12th pr., succ. Edmund *c.* 15 Jan. 1390 (*Ctl. Bilsington*, p. 140; cf. *CPR 1388–92*, p. 193).

BISHAM (Berks), Jesus Christ and St Mary, *alias* Holy Trinity (Bisham Montagu) f. 22 Apr. 1337 (cf. dedication plate 1333, *Earliest English Brasses*, pp. 181–2).
  List in *VCH Berks*, II, 84.
Thomas (de) Wiltshire (Wiltesschire, Wilteshire, Wyltshire, Wyltshyr) **1337–** Can. of Christchurch, had permission from bp to transfer to the new priory of Bisham (Winchester, Reg. Orleton, I, f. 51v). Eln pres. to bp 27 Mar. 1337; commn to examine eln 1 Apr. 1337, cert. of commissary 3 Apr. 1337 (Salisbury, Reg. Wyvil, I, f. 38v). Compotus of pr. Thomas 1337–38 (Longleat mun. 510). Occ. 1339 (Winchester, Reg. Orleton, I, f. 73r); 1341 (PRO, C241/160/46); 1343 (PRO, C241/118/88); 1344 (*CCR 1343–46*, pp. 347, 395, 452, 454); 1345 (BL, Harl. Cht. 44 B 40; *CPR 1345–48*, p. 22; PRO, E40/9451); 12 July 1347 (*CCR 1346–49*, p. 364); occ. between 22 Aug. 1344 and 8 July 1348 (*Reg. Edington*, II, nos. 645–6, 655, 657, 660–1). Mentioned 1355 as former pr. (*CCR 1354–60*, p. 222). Seal (*BM Seals*, nos. 2643–4).
Robert Occ. 26 July 1355 (*CCR 1354–60*, p. 222).
Richard of Marlborough (Marlebergh) **–1378** D. by 13 Feb.1378 (Salisbury, Reg. Erghum, f. 131r).

BLACKMORE (Essex), St Laurence f. 1152 x 1162
  Lists in *VCH Essex*, II, 147; *Heads*, I, 151.
Richard Occ. *c.* June 1203 (*Essex F.*, I, 33); 1199 x 1209 (*EEA London II* forthcoming, from London, Reg. Stokesley, f. 54r–v).
Roger Mentd in 1248 as having been pr. *temp.* King John (PRO, Just.1/231, m. 5).
William Occ. n.d. (*c.* 1226 x 1239 *temp.* Fulk Basset, provost of Beverley) (PRO, E40/501;

Basset Chts., no. 248); Trin. term 1231, Mich. term 1232 (*CRR*, XIV, nos. 1800, 2343A); Oct. 1232 x Oct. 1233 (*London and Middlesex F.*, p. 20); 1242 (PRO, DL27/65); Easter term 1234, 1 July 1240, Trin. term 1244 (*Essex F.*, I, 95, 128, 147). Seal (*Mon. Seals*, p. 10).

John Occ. 3 Feb. 1248 to Mich. 1261 (*Essex F.*, I, 169, 241); 3 May 1248 (PRO, Herts F., CP25/1/85/22, no. 359); 27 Oct. 1257 (PRO, F. Var. Cos. CP25/1/284/19, no.132).

Roger Occ. 17 May 1270 (Oxford, New Coll., Writtle 403/13887).

Thomas Occ. Mich. 1285 (*Essex F.*, II, 47); 10 Aug. 1290 (PRO, C241/15/104). ? ledger stone (Thomas de ?Veer) (*Earliest English Brasses*, p. 187).

Nicholas Occ. 6 Apr. 1310 (*Reg. Baldock*, p. 126); 1321 (*YB XXVI*, 117, 121).

William Occ. 22 Oct. 1327 (*Reg. Martival*, I, 380).

James Occ. Mich. 1351 (PRO, KB27/365, m. 98); 12 June 1360 (*CCR 1360–64*, p. 117).

Walter Bumsted –1385 D. by 2 Dec. 1385 (London, Reg. Braybrooke, f. 322v).

BLYTHBURGH (Suffolk), St Mary (St Osyth) f. -1135

Lists in *VCH Suffolk*, II, 94; *Ctl. Blythburgh*, I, 5; *Heads*, I, 152.

William [of Hingham] Occ. very early 13th cent. (*Ctl. Blythburgh*, II, no. 441); -1212 (ibid., no. 319); (W.) 1198 x 1216 (Cheney, *BIHR*, XLIV (1971), p. 101, no. 1204). Prob. William of Hingham who occ. prob. *ante* 1218 (*Ctl. Blythburgh*, I, no. 183).

Guy Occ. 7 Nov. 1218, ? 1217 (*Ctl. Eye*, I, no. 75); (G.) early 13th cent. (*Ctl. Blythburgh*, I, nos. 56, 95, 237, 234); prob. same as pr. Wyth (ibid., II, no. 480).

Osbert Occ. after 1240, mid-late 13th cent. (ibid., nos. 369, 240, 315).

William ?de Suberi (Sudbury) Occ. after 1237 (ibid., I, no. 178); *c.* 1242 x 1252, 13 Apr. 1260 (ibid., II, nos. 440, 404); *c.*1264–5 (ibid., no. 313); *c.*1240 x 1264 (ibid., I, nos. 17, 49, 97, 108, 185–7); mid-late 13th cent. (ibid., nos. 59a, 54, 153, 178–9, 238, 186–7). Prob. William de Suberi (ibid., no. 185).

Geoffrey Occ. after 1237, probably after William (list, p. 5); mid-late 13th cent (ibid., I, no. 180).

Thomas Occ. n.d. (1264 x 1287) (ibid., I, nos. 52, 53; II, no. 286).

Adam Occ. Nov. 1286 x Nov. 1287 (*Suffolk F.(Rye)*, p. 89); from *ante* 1290 to Nov. 1293–Nov. 1294 (*Ctl. Blythburgh*, I, nos. 57, 2).

Nicholas Occ. 10 Apr. 1304 (ibid., II, no. 325).

Alexander of Dunwich (Donewyco) 1311– Can. of St Osyth, adm. 24 Mar 1311 (Norwich, Reg/1/1, f. 40v). Occ. 26 Dec. 1319, 14 Sept. 1324 (*Ctl. Blythburgh*, I, nos. 55, 96); 24 Oct. 1322 (Norwich, Reg/1/1, f. 98v).

Nicholas of Dagworth (Daggeworth) 1332– Can. of St Osyth, adm. 27 Nov. 1332, no reason given for vacancy (Norwich, Reg/1/2, f. 54r). Occ. 25 June 1340, 6 May 1343 (*Ctl. Blythburgh*, II, nos. 453, 454); Jan. 1346 x Jan. 1347 (ibid., I, no. 154).

Robert de Parco Occ. 12 Nov. 1349, 16 Aug. 1361 (ibid., II, nos. 310, 311).

John (of) Norton 1361–1371 Can. of St Osyth, adm. 2 Oct. 1361, no reason given for vacancy (Norwich, Reg/2/5, f. 52r–v). Occ. Jan. 1362 x Jan. 1363 (*Ctl. Blythburgh*, I, no .115). D. by 8 Oct. 1371 (Norwich, Reg/3/6, f. 10r).

Walter of Stansted (Stanstede) 1371–1374 Can. of St Osyth, adm. 8 Oct. 1371 (ibid.). D. by 9 Nov. 1374 (ibid., f. 28v).

John Alnele (?Alvele) 1374– Can. of St Osyth, adm. 9 Nov. 1374 (ibid.).

John of Colchester (Colcestria) Possibly same as above – occ. 18 Feb. 1376 (*Ctl. Blythburgh*, II, no. 340). Prob. the pr. John who occ. in clerical subsidy 1379 x 1381 (PRO, E179/45/18); June 1380 x June 1381 (PRO, E179/45/5B, m. 2).

The next recorded pr., **William Wykham**, can. of St Osyth, adm. 22 Dec. 1382, no reason given for vacancy (Norwich, Reg/3/6, f. 85v).

BODMIN (Cornwall), St Petroc f. *c.* 1124
Lists in Oliver, p.16; *Heads*, I, 152.

Hugh Occ. n.d. (1200 x 1220) (Cornwall RO, AR.1/793–5). Prob. the Hugh, pr. of St Petroc, d. 30 Dec. (BL, Add. ms. 29436, f. 44r).

John Occ. n.d. (first half of 13th cent., ? 1220 x 1230) (Cornwall RO, AR.1/801); (J.) n.d. (ibid., 800); (J.) n.d. (*c.* 1225) (*Ctl. Launceston*, no. 533; *EEA*, 11, no. 110B).

Baldwin Occ. n.d. (*temp.* Richard, count of Poitou and earl of Cornwall, i.e. after 1227) (*CPR 1374–77*, p. 26); (B.) 1236 (?30 Mar.) (Cornwall RO, AR.1/802).

Richard Occ. 13 Oct. 1256 (*Cornwall F.*, p. 80, no. 157); 2 Oct. 1277 (*Reg. Bronescombe*, p. 32; *Reg. W. Bronescombe*, II, no. 1237); excommunicated 12 Nov. 1284 and signification for capture (*Reg. Quivil*, p. 315); 25 Aug. 1286 (*Reg. G. Giffard*, II, 293).

Edmund Occ. 22 Feb. 1296 (*CCR 1286–96*, p. 474); Trin. 1297 (PRO, CP40/119, m. 41d).

German **–1310** Occ. 27 Oct. 1302 (*Cornwall F.*, I, p. 208, no. 368); said to be old and ill; coadjutor apptd 7 Mar. 1309, provision made for retirement 22 May 1310 (*Reg. Stapeldon*, pp. 48–50). Res. May 1310 (*Reg. Bytton*, p. 413); res. 10 May 1310 (*Reg. Stapeldon*, p. 49).

John of Kilkhampton (Kilkhamptone, Kylkhamptone) **1310–1349** Petition for lic. to el. 11 May 1310; on 13 May convent gtd bp the right to provide a new pr. (ibid., p. 49). Can. of Bodmin, apptd by bp 20 May 1310 (ibid., pp. 49, 191–2). Order to escheator to restore priory to pr. John upon his finding two sureties to answer to the king for his journey overseas without royal lic. 2 Nov. 1313 (*CCR 1313–18*, p. 21). Occ. 1314 (*Reg. Stapeldon*, pp. 50–1; *CCR 1313–18*, p.103); 1316 (*CPR 1313–17*, p. 580). Bp associates br. William Bagge with pr. John in admin. of temps. and spiritualities 12 Aug. 1328 (*Reg. Grandisson*, I, 371–2, cf. ibid., 423–4). Clearly the unnamed pr. described on 22 June 1340 as too feeble of body to act (*CPR 1338–40*, p. 503). 30 Nov. 1343 appt of Ralph,, rector of Withiel and William Bagge, can. of Bodmin, as custodians of the priory (*Reg. Grandisson*, II, 979–81). D. 27 Feb. 1349 (ibid., 1077).

Auger Bant (Eger, Ouger) **1349–** 17 Mar. 1349 all but two cans. dead on account of the plague. Power of appt transferred to bp who apptd Ouger Bant, can. of Launceston, 22 Mar. 1349 (ibid., 1076–8). Bp writes to pr. of Launceston to allow Bant to become pr. of Bodmin; pr. of Launceston consents 21 Mar. (ibid., 1077–8). Occ. Easter 1361 (PRO, CP40/406, m. 276). Restitution of pr., previously suspended 20 Mar. 1362 (*Reg. Grandisson*, II, 1238). Occ. Mich. 1364 (PRO, KB27/416, rex roll m. 10).

Restitution to unnamed pr. of the priory, which had been taken into the king's hands because the present pr. was el. without the king's lic. 5 May 1366 (*CPR 1364–67*, p. 241).

William Carnellow (Camehelowe, Carnhellowe) **–1403** Occ. 22 July 1372 (PRO, E40/10365); 24 May 1373, 22 Nov. 1373 (*Reg. Brantingham*, I, 303, 319); 1375 (Lambeth, Reg. Sudbury, f. 83v); 1377 (PRO, C67/28B, m.12); 1380 (*CPR 1377–81*, p. 517); 1380 x 1381 (PRO, E179/24/5); 1386 (*Reg. Brantingham*, II, 612, 625). D. 10 Nov. 1403 (*Reg. Stafford*, p. 107).

BOLTON (Yorks W.), St Mary (Bolton in Wharfedale, Bolton in Craven) f. 1120 x 21 (Embsay, St Mary and St Cuthbert); 1154 x 5 (Bolton)
Lists in *VCH Yorks*, III, 199; *Heads*, I, 152; *EYC*, VII, app. E, pp. 293–6 'The early priors of Bolton'.

John Occ. -1203, *c.*1218 x 1220 (*EYC*, VII, nos. 65, 102); 24 Jan. 1206 (*Yorks F., John*, p. 97); 1219 (*Ctl. Kirkstall*, p. 252, no. 350); 27 Jan. 1219, 19 Feb. 1219 (*Yorks F., 1218–31*, pp. 15, 27).

Robert Occ. from 17 Apr. 1222 to 14 Dec. 1226 (ibid., pp. 44, 96); 2 Feb. 1223 (*Ctl. Fountains*, II, 464), cf. also 1200 x 1220 (*Ctl. Furness*, II, ii, 420–1).

Thomas Occ. 1232 (Bodl., Dodsworth ms. 144, f. 13v, cal. *EYC*, VII, no. 89n.); 8 July 1233 (*Yorks F., 1232–46*, p. 6; *Bolton Priory*, p. 61); n.d. (*post* 1226 x 1240) (*Yorks Deeds*, V, no. 464).

Richard Occ. (R.) 15 Aug. 1243 (*EYC*, VII, no. 134A); n.d. (before 1246) (*Yorks Deeds*, V, no. 469); 19 May 1247 (*EYC*, VII, no. 78).

Adam Occ. 20 June 1255 (*Yorks F.*, *1246–72*, p. 102; *Bolton Priory*, p. 61); (A.) 27 May 1257 (*EYC*, VII, no. 43); Oct. 1257 x Oct. 1258 (Bodl., Dodsworth ms. 144, f.12r).

Henry Occ. 29 Apr.1263 (*Yorks F.*, *1246–72*, p. 128; *Bolton Priory*, p. 62); (H.) n.d. (mid-13th cent. (*Yorks Deeds*, V, no. 333).

William of Tanfield (Tanefeud, Danfeld) **1267–** Can. of Bolton, eln conf. 28 Apr.1267, mandate to install 1 May 1267 (*Reg. W. Giffard*, p. 153). Occ. 2 Dec. 1267 (ibid., p. 145); 1271(?) (BL, Add. Cht. 20927). D. or res. in 1270 according to *Bolton Priory*, p. 64, but no precise source given (see next entry), but occ. as former pr. in 1268 case (PRO, Just.1/1050, m. 63d).

Richard of Beachampton (Bachampton, Bakhamton, Bakhampton) **1270–1275** Eln conf. 3 Nov. 1270, no reason given for vacancy (*Reg. W. Giffard*, p. 32). Letter of res. 14 Jan. 1275, acc. by archbp 15 Jan. 1275 and provision made for him (ibid., pp. 264–5, 305–7; see I. Kershaw, *Bolton Priory 1286–1325*, p. 8).

William Hog 1275 Can. of Bolton, eln pres. to king for royal ass. 21 Jan. 1275 (PRO, C84/5/19); royal ass. 18 Mar. 1275 (*CPR 1272–81*, p. 83). Order to receive fealty if he is conf. by archbp 19 Mar. 1275 (*CCR 1272–79*, p. 158). Deposed by archbp of York 7 Oct. 1275 (*Reg. W. Giffard*, p. 307, cf. *Bolton Priory*, pp. 66–69). Letter of archbp to king informing him he had deposed the pr. 20 Oct. 1275 (PRO, SC1/18/28).

John of Lund (Lond, Lound, Lunda, Lunde) **1275–?1286** Can. of Bolton, el. 19 Oct. 1275 (*Reg. W. Giffard*, pp. 307–12; cf. PRO, C84/5/49). Royal ass. 2 Nov. 1275 (*CPR 1272–81*, p. 103). Occ. 6 Feb. 1276 (ibid., p. 260); 9 Feb. 1276 (York, Reg. 9A, f. 186v); Nov. 1279 x Nov. 1280 (Bodl., Dodsworth ms. 144, f. 35v); 1281 (Yorke records, Halton Place, Hellifield, Skipton 5). Res. by 16 July 1286, when at the archbp of York's visitation it was stated that John of Lund, former pr., was to be specially honoured and to have 20s. a year (*Reg. Romeyn*, I, p. 56, no. 133). He was apptd pr. of Marton 1287 (ibid., I, 164–5, nos. 458, 460).

John of Laund (Landa) **–1331** Occ. 1290 (Baildon, I, 13); 28 Nov. 1291 (*CPR 1281–92*, p. 461); 1292 (*CCR 1288–96*, p. 331); 25 May 1298, 25 Aug. 1300 (*Yorks F.*, *1272–1300*, pp. 137, 143); 25 Oct. 1300 went to Rome, accompanied by John of Lund, pr. of Marton (*Ch. York*, p. 31); 26 Apr. 1304 pardoned for trespass (*CPR 1300–07*, p. 222); occ. 1323 (Chatsworth box XVII, Fountains abbey no. 40); 1327 (*Calverley Chts.*, p. 105; Baildon, I, 13). Letter of res. 3 Jan. 1331; acc. 25 Jan 1331; lic. to el. 26 Jan. 1331 (York, Reg. 9B, f. 722r). Seal (*Mon. Seals*, p. 10).

Thomas of Copley (Coppelay) **1331–1340** Unnamed pr. of Bolton had done fealty to the king 4 May 1331 (*CCR 1330–33*, p. 229). D. by 17 Oct. 1340 (York, Reg. 5A, f. 86r-v).

Robert of Harton 1340–1369 Can. of Bolton, eln conf. 17 Oct. 1340 (ibid.). D. by 2 Oct. 1369 (York, Reg.11, f. 155r-v); 'worn out by great year of pestilence' (Baildon, I, 12).

Robert of Otley (Otteley, Ottelay) **1369–** Sub-pr. of Bolton, eln conf. 2 Oct. 1369 (York, Reg. 11, f. 155r-v). Occ. 1373 (*Yorks Deeds*, IV, p. 25; York, Reg.11, f. 192v); 1377 (PRO, E179/63/100); 1385 (Baildon, I, 15).

The next recorded pr., **Robert Greene**, occ. 26 May 1397 (*CPL*, V, 59).

BOURNE (Lincs), St Peter Arrouaisian Abbey f. 1138
  Lists in *VCH Lincs*, II, 178; *Heads*, I, 152–3.

Baldwin Occ. 15 Apr. 1212 (*Lincs F.*, *1199–1216*, p. 106, no. 328); 7 Jan. 1219, 3 Nov. 1222 (*Lincs F.*, I, 126, 166).

Everard Cut –1236/7 Occ. (E.) after 28 Nov. 1224, date of papal mand. (CUL, Add. ms. 3021, f. 257v). For surname see *CCR 1323–27*, p. 62. Occ. from 3 Feb. 1225 to 21 Oct. 1234 (*Lincs*

F., I, 173, 275). Res. June 1236 x June 1237 (*Reg. Grosseteste*, p. 11). D. 14 Sept. (BL, Cotton ms. Caligula A. VIII, f. 20v)

Walter of Ripton 1236/7– Cellarer of Huntingdon, el. and inst. June 1236 x June 1237 (*Reg. Grosseteste*, p.11). (Erroneously called William in *Mon. Angl.*, VI, 370).

[**Robert of Haceby** (Hasceby), can. of Bourne **William Swinstead** (Swinehamstede), Can. of Bourne Both el. on d. unnamed abb. but subsequently res. into the bp of Lincoln's hands June 1247 x June 1248 (*Reg. Grosseteste*, p. 101). For Haceby see below 1259/60–1275.]

Robert de Hamme 1247/8–1259/60 Can. of Waltham, postulated and adm. June 1247 x June 1248 on d. of unnamed abb. (*Reg. Grosseteste*, p. 101). D. Nov. 1259 x Nov. 1260 (*Reg. R. Gravesend*, p. 4).

Robert of Haceby (Hasceby) **1259/60–1275** Can. of Bourne, eln quashed but apptd by bp who bl. him Nov. 1259 x Nov. 1260 (ibid.). Res. by 29 Nov. 1275 (ibid., p. 67).

William of Spalding 1275–1277 Pr. of Bourne, el. 29 Nov. 1275 on res of Robert, el. conf. 3 Dec. 1275 (ibid., pp. 67, 283). D. by 16 Oct. 1277 (ibid., p.78).

Alan de Wauz 1277–1291 Pr. of Bourne, eln conf. 16 Oct. 1277 (ibid., pp. 78, 286). D. by 3 Nov. 1291 (*Reg. Sutton*, I, 160).

Thomas of Colsterworth (Colstwrth') **1291–1313** Can. of Bourne, eln pres. to bp 3 Nov. 1291, eln quashed but apptd by bp 4 Nov. 1291 (ibid., 160–1). Lic. to Thomas Wake, a minor in the king's custody, that he may grant lic. to el. on d. of abb. Thomas 3 Apr. 1313 (*CPR 1307–13*, p. 563).

William of St Albans (de Sancto Albano) **1313–1314** Can. of Bourne, eln examined by commissaries 23 Apr. 1313, but eln quashed but William apptd by bp 24 Apr. 1313 (Lincoln, Ep. Reg., II, f. 46v). Lic. granted 6 May for bl. by bp of Down (suffragan) on 13 May 1313 (Lincoln, Ep. Reg., III, f. 274r). Res. before bp 29 Oct. 1314. who issued lic. to el. (ibid., f. 307v), but cf. house void by his cess. 28 Sept. 1314, royal lic. to el. (*CPR 1313–17*, pp. 184, 181).

William of Abbotsley (Abbotesle(e)) **1314–1324** Pr. of Bourne, eln conf. 2 Dec. 1314 (Lincoln, Ep. Reg., II, ff. 53v–54r). Bl. 22 Dec. 1314 (Lincoln, Ep. Reg., III, f. 310v). Mentioned 12 Feb. 1324 as former abb., now deceased (*CCR 1323–27*, p. 62).

John de Wycheton (Wytheton) **1324–1334** Can. of Bourne, commn to examine eln 25 Feb. 1324 (Lincoln, Ep. Reg., V, f. 358r). D. by 20 Apr. 1334 (*CCR 1333–37*, p. 217).

House vacant 13 Oct., 26 Dec. 1334 (*Reg. Burghersh* I, nos. 433, 468). 12 Dec. 1334 commn to grant administration of vacant abbey to suitable canon (Lincoln, Ep. Reg.,V, f. 488r).

Simon of Walton 1334–1354 Papal conf. of eln 22 Nov. 1334 – the eln was opposed by Thomas Wake, Lord Liddel, the patron, but Simon's appeal to the pope was successful (*CPL*, II, 523). D. by 24 June 1354 (Lincoln, Ep. Reg., IX, f. 112r–v).

[21 Mar. 1355 pope asked to provide a suitable candidate to vacant abbey (*CPL*, III, 574) – not actually vacant. Simon de Sagio (Sées), claimant for papal provision to abbey, which was not vacant – ment. in royal letters of prohibition 21 Jan. 1356 – see under Barnwell (*CPR 1354–58*, p. 335; *Nottingham Medieval Studies*, XXXV (1991), 90)]

Thomas of Grantham (Graaham, Graham) **1354–1369** Can. of Bourne, eln quashed but apptd by bp 24 June 1354 (Lincoln, Ep. Reg., IX, f. 112r–v). D. by 19 Sept. 1369 (Lincoln, Ep. Reg., X, f. 34v).

Geoffrey of Deeping (Depyng) **1369–** Can. of Bourne, eln pres. to bp of Lincoln 19 Sept. 1369, el. quashed but apptd by bp 14 Oct. 1369 (ibid.). Occ. Easter 1381 (*Select Cases of Trespass*, I, 53–4); 1381 (*Clerical Poll-Taxes*, p. 111, no. 1343 and p. 156, no. 1932); mentd 1406 (unsure whether alive or not) as having executed papal mand. *c.* 1392 (*CPL*, VI, 75).

BRADENSTOKE (Wilts), St Mary (Clack) f. 1139
  Lists in *VCH Wilts*, III, 288; *Ctl. Bradenstoke*, p. 199; *Heads*, I, 153.
The house was prob. vacant when committed to the keeping of William Longespée, earl of
  Salisbury, in 1208 (*Rot. Lit. Claus*, I, 109b).
Simon (Simeon) Occ. (S.) 9 July 1215 (*Rot. Chart.* p. 212b); over thirty times in the *Ctl.* from
  20 Oct. 1221 to 22 May 1243 (nos. 531, 445).
William Occ. 25 Nov. 1246 (*Wilts F.*, I, 36 = *Ctl.* no. 540); 27 May 1247 (*Ctl.* no. 542); 3 June
  1247 (wrongly dated 1237) (*Oxford F.*, p. 133); 1249 (*Wilts F.*, I, 40 = *Ctl.* no. 543); 13 Oct.
  1260 (*Ctl.* no. 545).
Geoffrey Occ. 21 May 1263 (*Ctl.* no. 246); 30 Apr. 1266 (*Ctl. Glastonbury*, II, p. 539, no. 1005);
  n.d. (1260 x 1270) (*HMC Var. Coll.*, IV, 99); (G.) 6 Jan. 1271, Nov. 1282 x Nov. 1283, 25
  Feb. 1285 (*Ctl.* nos. 343, 64, 334); Easter 1288 (PRO, CP40/72, m. 7d).
W. Occ. 9 Apr. 1287 (*Ctl. Glastonbury*, III, p. 667, no. 1231).
Hugh Called ninth pr. (*Ctl.* no. 415). Occ. 29 June 1295, 25 Apr. 1306, 7 Jan. 1307 (ibid., nos.
  594, 405, 250); 1300 (PRO, Just.1/1318, m. 16); Mich. 1310 (PRO, CP40/183, m. 101); 17
  Apr. 1311 (*Reg. Gandavo*, I, 403).
John of Botwell (Botewell) 1312– Called tenth pr. (*Ctl.* no. 415). Can. of Bradenstoke, eln
  pres. to bp 6 Mar. 1312; eln conf. 15 Apr. 1312, no reason given for vacancy (*Reg. Gandavo*,
  II, 779–81). Occ. 1316 (*Reg. Martival*, II, 98); 1321 (ibid., II, ii, 375); 15 Jan. 1327, 29 Oct.
  1327 (ibid., 530, 544); 1328 (*Index to Placita de Banco*, pp. 475, 702); 23 Sept. 1332 (Lincoln,
  Ep. Reg., IV, f. 377r).[3]
Richard de Cernecote 1339– Can. of Bradenstoke, eln conf. 12 Jan. 1339, no reason given for
  vacancy (Salisbury, Reg. Wyvil II, f. 63r). Occ. 25 Dec. 1344, 1346 (*Ctl.* nos. 448, 349); 20
  May 1347 (*Lacock Chts.*, no. 291 = *Ctl.* no. 305).
Presentations to benefices by reason of house's vacancy 1 July 1349, 16 Aug. 1350 (*CPR 1348–50*,
  pp. 332, 565).
Thomas Spicer –1354 Occ. 14 June 1352 (*CPL*, III, 473); 7 Feb. 1354 (Salisbury, Reg. Wyvil
  I, f. 149r). Res. 9 Mar. 1354 (ibid., f. 150v) and gt of custody of priory to Geoffrey Besils,
  can. of Bradenstoke same day (ibid., f. 150r–v). Res., lic. to el. 16 Mar. 1354 (*Reg. Black
  Prince*, IV, 113).
Geoffrey de Besiles (Besilis, Besils) 1354– Can. of Bradenstoke, royal ass. 6 Apr. 1354 (ibid.).
  Eln conf. 18 Apr. 1354 (Salisbury, Reg. Wyvil II, f. 263v). Occ. 24 Apr. 1362 (*HMC Var.
  Coll.*, IV, 112); 25 May 1365 (*CCR 1364–68*, p. 176). Case touching G. Besiles, former pr.,
  19 June [1367] (Salisbury, Reg. Wyvil I, ff. 210v–211r).
Richard Redborn Occ. 23 Jan. 1371, 25 Mar. 1372 (*Ctl.*, nos. 251, 252).
Geoffrey de Besiles Pardon 8 Jan. 1377 (*CPR 1374–77*, p. 404).
The next recorded pr., **Richard Boterwell**, occ. 29 Jan. 1380 (*Ctl.*, no. 253); 6 Nov. 1389
  (Botuell) (Wilts RO, Brudenell-Bruce mss., no. 30); 17 Feb. 1397 (Salisbury, Reg. Mitford,
  f. 117v), and had ceased to be pr. by Easter term 1402 (*Ctl.*, no. 571).

BRADLEY (Leics), f. 1220+
  List in *VCH Leics*, I, 25.
Robert de [blank] 1233/4– Can. of Bradley, el. and adm. Dec. 1233 x Dec. 1234 (*Reg. Wells*,
  II, 324–5).
Henry 1263–1290 Can. of Caldwell, apptd by bp by authority of the Council, on the d. of the

---

[3] *Abbrev. Rot. Orig.*, II, 16 has Richard le Best, pr. of Bradenstoke occ. 1327, but his does not seem to fit with
  the occs. of pr. John. It could possibly be that this 1327 reference is to two individuals: Richard le Best and
  an unnamed pr. of Bradenstoke.

last (unnamed) pr. 9 Nov. 1263 (*Reg. R. Gravesend*, pp. 143, 309). D. by 10 July 1290 (*Reg. Sutton*, VIII, 46).[4]

Walter of Drayton 1290–1295 Adm. 10 July 1290 on the d. of pr. Henry, with the consent of Hugh, the only other can. (ibid., 46–7). Res. by 28 Feb.1295 (ibid., 55).

John of Kirkeby (Kyrkeby) **1295–1300** Can. of Launde, eln quashed but apptd by bp 28 Feb. 1295 (ibid.). Cess. by 18 Aug. 1300 (Lincoln, Ep. Reg., II, f. 195r).

Walter of Drayton 1300–1302 Can. of Bradley, eln conf. 18 Aug. 1300 (ibid.). Removed from office *propter ipsius demerita* and lic. to el. 26 Jan. 1302 (Lincoln, Ep. Reg., III, f. 41v).

John of Quorndon (Queringdon) **1302–** Can. of Bradley, eln quashed but apptd by bp 21 Feb. 1302 (Lincoln, Ep. Reg., II, f. 198r). Occ. 22 Sept. 1314 (Ctl. Scrope of Bolton, f. 160v).

Robert of Horninghold (Hornyngwald) **1336–** Can. of Bradley, commn to examine eln 29 May 1336 (Lincoln, Ep. Reg., V, f. 534r).

Vacant 1349 by d. of unnamed pr. Right of appt transferred to bp (Lincoln, Ep. Reg., IX, f. 191r).

(John) of Quorndon (Queryngton) **1349–** Can. of Bradley, apptd by bp 7 Aug. 1349 (ibid.). Occ. Jan. 1374 x Jan. 1375 (Nichols, *Leics*, II, ii, 510); 1377 (*Clerical Poll-Taxes*, p. 28, no. 375).

Richard Brownknave *alias* **Chanon 1381–** Can. of Bradley, apptd by bp 2 July 1381, no reason given for vacancy (Lincoln, Ep. Reg., X, f. 275v). Occ. (Chanon) 23 Dec. 1389 (*CPR 1388–92*, p. 170).

Richard Stokes –1394 Res. by 16 Feb. 1394 (Lincoln, Ep. Reg., XI, f. 226v). Poss. the same as the above.

BRADLEY *see* MAIDEN BRADLEY

BREADSALL (Derbys), Holy Trinity f. 1200+
List in *VCH Derbys*, II, 56.

Hugh of Mackworth (Macworth) **1306–** Adm. 7 June 1306, no reason given for vacancy (Lichfield, B/A/1/1, f. 14v).

Hamund de Merston 1309– Can. of Breadsall, adm. pr. 15 Nov. 1309, on the pres. of Richard de Corzon of Breadsall, no reason given for the vacancy (ibid., f. 71v). Presumably at some point Hamund res. and was replaced, and then was apptd for a second time in 1323 (see below).

Hamund de Merston 1323–1329 Can. of Breadsall, adm. on pres. of Henry Curzon of Breadsall 8 Feb. 1323, no reason given for vacancy (Lichfield, B/A/1/2, f. 64r). Res. by 31 May 1329 (ibid., f. 68r).

William of Repton (Repingdon, Repyngdon) **1329–1347** Can. of Breadsall, adm. on same presentation 31 May 1329 (ibid.). Res. by 4 Oct. 1347 (ibid., f. 180r).

Thomas de Castello (Castel, **Kyver** (Kyner) of Newcastle) **1347–1350** Can. of Breadsall. Commn to adm. him 4 Oct. 1347, adm. 6 Oct. 1347 (ibid.). Killed by a can. of Breadsall, Roger de Cothale, who was later pardoned 25 Aug. 1350 (*CPR 1348–50*, p. 563; cf. *CCR 1349–54*, p. 245, *CPR 1350–54*, p. 126).

Thomas of London 1365–1370 M. of Burton, coll. by bp *pro hac vice* 7 Aug. 1365, no reason given for vacancy (*Reg. Stretton*, I, 79). Res. by Sept. 1370 (ibid., 88).

[**Gregory of Stafford 1370** Occupied priory, vacant by Sept. 1370 by the res. of Thomas of London (ibid.). Res. 15 Dec.1370 (ibid). Had never held priory canonically.]

---

[4] There is a slightly puzzling entry in the Ctl. Scrope of Bolton, f. 160v: a request by the canons of Bradley to Sir William de Kyrkeby, knight, who has the advowson of the priory, for permission to el. a new pr., on the cession of the last pr., John de Kyrkeby, made into the hands of the bp of Lincoln 8 Sept. 1290. There was a vacancy in 1290 but John de Kyrkeby, previously can. of Launde, was pr. of Bradley 1295–1300. It is prob. a copyist's error.

Thomas (of) Lewes 1371– Inst. 8 Jan. 1371 (ibid., br. Thomas having res. as vicar of Bradbourne). Occ. 8 Jan. 1371 when apptd penitentiary in the archdeaconry of Derby for 2 years (ibid., I, 53).

The next recorded pr., **Roger of Upton**, was adm. 22 Mar. 1385, no reason given for vacancy (ibid., II, 105).

BREAMORE (Hants), St Michael f. 1128 x 1133
 Lists in *VCH Hants*, II, 172; *Heads*, I, 153.
Ralph Occ. 22 July 1202 (*Wilts.F.*, I, 8).
Walter Occ. *c.* 1225 (*Ctl. Beaulieu*, no. 155); (W.) 7 Mar. 1226 (*Sarum Chts.*, p. 166, no. cxlvi). Mentioned *c.* 1230 as former pr. (*Ctl. Beaulieu*, no. 187).[5]
Simon Occ. 9 June 1241, 14 May 1249 (*Wilts F.*, I, 32, 38); (S.) 1244, 1249 (Madox, *Form.*, pp. 84, 136, nos. 155, 229); 29 Sept. 1249 (PRO, E315/50/217); *c.* 1254, (S.) 1250 x 1260 (*Ctl. Beaulieu*, nos. 154, 294); n.d. (1259 x 1264) (*Sarum Chts.*, p. 333. no. cclxxx); 26 Apr. 1263 (PRO, Hants F.,CP25/1/204/10, no. 82); 27 Oct. 1268 (PRO, E315/48/232).
Thomas of Pimperne (Pymperne) Occ. 1273 (PRO, E326/11,817); 25 Nov. 1275 (PRO, Hants F., CP25/1/204/12, no. 20); 1276 x 1277 (PRO, E42/403); 1283 x 1284 (PRO, E159/37, rn. 15d); 1285 (PRO, E315/41/192); 1288 (PRO, E315/38/248); 1289 (PRO, E315/42/177; E315/46/280); 1291 (*CPR 1313–17*, p. 125; *TDA*, 7 (1895), p. 359); 1292 (PRO, E315/37/32); 1295 (PRO, E315/53/225); 1298 x 1299 (PRO, E326/11,277); 1301 (*CPR 1292–1301*, p. 585); (T.) 1302 (*Reg. Pontissara*, I, 123); 8 May 1307 (*Reg. Woodlock*, II, 723). Seal (*Mon. Seals*, p. 12).
Thomas de Dountone 1308– Citation for objectors to eln 2 July 1308 (ibid., I, 282–3). Occ. 22 May 1309 (PRO, E326/1594); 7 May 1311 (PRO, E326/3603).
William le Eyr –1327 Res. by 19 Oct. 1327 (Winchester, Reg. Stratford, f. 105r).
James de Wyttenham (Wittenham) **1327–1342** Apptd 19 Oct. 1327, no reason given for vacancy (ibid.). Mandates to obey and induct the same day (ibid.). D. by 26 Aug. 1342 (Winchester, Reg. Orleton, I, ff. 112r–113r).
John of Wallop (Wollop) **1342–** Can. of Breamore, commn to examine eln 26 Aug. 1342; eln conf. 28 Aug. 1342 (ibid.; cf. *Dorset IPM*, no. 195). Occ. 6 Oct. 1342 (PRO, E326/3494); 6 Jan. 1344 (PRO, E315/32/66); 24 Dec. 1348 (PRO, E326/611); 15 Mar. 1349 (PRO, E315/31/140). An unnamed pr. mentioned as recently dead 19 June 1349 (*Reg. Edington*, I, no. 601).
Thomas Occ. Jan. 1350 x Jan. 1351 (PRO, E326/9179); 24 Dec. 1352 (PRO, E326/611); 8 Jan. 1356 (PRO, E315/48/75); 29 Dec. 1356 (PRO, E326/675).
John de Tyssebury *alias* **Sussebury 1361–1395** Commn to examine eln 16 Oct. 1361 to inquire into eln of John de Tyssebury, can. of Breamore, with power to conf. or annul (*Reg. Edington*, I, no. 1358); occ. Aug. 1366 (PRO, E326/3584); 23 Apr. 1368 (PRO, E326/676); 20 July 1370 (PRO, E315/31/105); 7 Mar. 1374 (PRO, E326/1318); 14 June 1389 (PRO, E315/52/93); 7 July 1390 (PRO, E315/37/174); 2 Oct. 1390 (PRO, E326/78); but cf. 4 Mar. 1371 pardon for trespass to John *late* pr. of Breamore (*CPR 1370–74*, p. 53). D. on 20 July 1395 (*Reg. Wykeham*, I, 198).

BREEDON (Leics), St Mary and St Herdulf (Nostell) f. -1122
 Lists in *VCH Leics*, II, 9; *Heads*, I, 154.
Gervase 1223–1244/5 Sub-pr. of Nostell, adm. 30 July 1223, no reason given for vacancy (*Reg.*

---

[5] Nicholas de Meoles apparently occ. as pr. in an undated cht (*c.* 1240), inspected *CPR 1313–17*, p. 19. However, the identification of 'Nicholas de Meoles, the pr. of Breamore' as two people is confirmed by *Ctl. Beaulieu*, no. 175, and p. xlviii.

Wells, II, 290); 5 Mar. 1229 ('Ctl. Breedon', no. 75); *c*.1230 (*HMC Var. Coll.*, IV, 326). Res. June 1244 x June 1245 (*Reg. Grosseteste*, p. 424).

Walter de Stokes 1245– Can. of Nostell, inst. June 1244 x June 1245 (ibid.). Letter of pres. to bp of Lincoln on cess. of Gervase, 30 Sept. 1245 (BL, Cotton ms. Vespasian E XIX, f. 126r).

T. Described as former pr., witness to a cht. of 1253 ('Ctl. Breedon', no. 80).

G. Occ. June 1252 x June 1253 (*Reg. Grosseteste*, p. 440).

Thomas de Acum (Oake(n)) **–1293** Occ. 14 Mar. 1288 ('Ctl. Breedon', no. 73); 5 July 1289 (ibid., no. 154). D. by 23 Mar 1293 (*Reg. Sutton*, VIII, 53).

William (de) Willeys (Wyles, Wylleys) **1293–1313** Can. of Nostell, pres. by Nostell priory on d. of Thomas Oaken, inst. 23 Mar. 1293 (ibid.). Cited to appear before archbp of York following his visitation of Nostell 28 Oct. 1313, to appear 26 Nov. (*Reg. Greenfield*, II, p. 165, no. 1022). Cess. by 4 Dec. 1314 (Lincoln, Ep. Reg., II, f. 208v). Provision made for him as former pr. 13 Dec. 1314 (Lincoln, Ep. Reg., III, ff. 309v–310r).

Robert of Pontefract (Pontefracto) **1314–1324** Adm. 4 Dec. 1314 (Lincoln, Ep. Reg., II, f. 208v; cf. 'Ctl. Breedon', no. 16). D. by 7 May 1324 (PRO, C84/20/28; cf. *CPR 1321–24*, p. 415).

John de Insula 1324–1328 Can. of Nostell, letter of pres. from pr. of Nostell 7 May 1324 (PRO, C84/20/28); royal ass. to pres. dated 18 May 1324, given by Edward II, the lands of Thomas, earl of Lancaster, being then in his hands (*CPR 1321–24*, p. 415; 'Ctl. Breedon', no. 17). Inst. and adm. 30 May 1324 (*Reg. Burghersh* I, no. 890). El. pr. of Nostell 1328 (q.v.).

William Buttrebuske (Boterbusk, Botrebusk, Butterbosk) **1328–1342** John de Insula, then pr. of Nostell, asked the earl of Lancaster to approve the presn of William Buttrebuske, sub-pr. of Nostell, to Breedon, 3 Sept. 1328 ('Ctl. Breedon', no. 20). Adm. and inst. 8 Sept. 1328 (*Reg. Burghersh*, I, no. 955). Occ. 1341 ('Ctl. Breedon', no. 156). Commn dated 19 Nov. 1342 to examine him about res., and to accept it if offered (Lincoln, Ep. Reg., VII, f. 180r). Res. by 26 Nov. 1342 (Lincoln, Ep. Reg., VI, f. 311r–v).

Richard de Farbourn 1342– Can. of Nostell, pres. 26 Nov. 1342, consent of Henry, earl of Lancaster, patron, given 23 Nov. 1342, adm. 29 Nov. 1342 (ibid.). Occ. 30 Aug. 1348 (*CPR 1348–50*, p. 177).

Geoffrey of Leeds (Ledes) **1358–?1367** Can. of Nostell, adm. 23 Jan. 1358, no reason given for vacancy (Lincoln, Ep. Reg., IX, f. 369r–v). Vacant by his res. n.d. (? *c*. 1367) (Lincoln, Ep. Reg., XII, f. 40v).

John de Culchief ?1367– Pres. by pr. and convent of Nostell on res. of Geoffrey n.d (?*c*. 1367) (ibid.). Adam of Bilton, can. of Nostell, apptd co-adjutor to John, then infirm, 15 Mar. 1374 (ibid., f. 123v).

Adam of Bilton –1385 Occ. 1377 (Hilton) (*Clerical Poll-Taxes*, p. 28, no. 373); 17 Mar. 1378 (Lincoln, Ep. Reg., X, f. 268v). Occ. June 1384 x May 1385 (PRO, E326/8108). Vacant by his cess. on eln as pr. of Nostell, 9 May 1385 (Lincoln, Ep. Reg., XI, f. 200r). Seal (*BM Seals*, no. 2706).

BRICETT *see* **GREAT BRICETT**

BRIDLINGTON (Yorks E.) St Mary f. –1114
   Lists in *VCH Yorks*, III, 204; *Heads*, I, 154.

Elias (Helias) Last recorded occ. 1210 (*Ch. Meaux*, I, 354).

H. Occ. *c*. 1213 x 14 (BL Cotton ms. Nero D. III, f. 55r). ? (H.)elias or Hubert.

Hubert Occ. 4 Apr . 1226, 2 Jan. 1227 (*Ctl. Bridlington*, pp. 28, 246); 22 Dec. 1226 (*Yorks F, 1218–31*, p. 99 = *Ctl.* p. 141); Mich. term 1228, Hil. term 1229 (*CRR*, XIII, nos. 759, 1365). Still alive 1243 when mentd as former pr. (*Reg. Gray*, p. 254).

Thomas Occ. many times in *Ctl. Bridlington*, from 10 June 1231 to (T.) 20 Oct. 1249 (pp. 191, 324); in *Yorks F., 1218–32*, from 10 June 1231 to 17 June 1231 (pp. 133, 142); in *Yorks F., 1232–46* from 7 June 1232 to 10 June 1246 (pp. 3, 151); in *Yorks F., 1246–72* on 20 Oct.1249 (pp. 10–11).

John Occ. 27 Oct. 1251 (*Lincs F.*, II, 91); 5 Feb. 1252 (*Ctl. Bridlington*, pp. 167–8). Papal mand. to archbp of York to receive res. of pr. John, who is incurably sick, and to make him a fitting provision 13 Jan. 1255 (*CPL*, I, 310).

Geoffrey of Nafferton (Nafreton) Occ. very many times in *Ctl. Bridlington* from 1 July 1259 to (G.) 25 Nov. 1286 (pp. 424, 290);[6] 29 July 1268, 26 May 1269 (*Yorks F., 1246–72*, pp. 162, 166); (G.) 7 Dec. 1268 (*Reg. W. Giffard*, p. 53); 7 Feb. 1273 (*Reg. Romeyn*, I, p. 353, no. 1012); 1277, 1280, 1286 (*Yorks F., 1272–1300*, pp. 10, 35, 77); 27 Jan. 1287 (*Reg. Romeyn*, II, p. 50). Res. by 23 July 1289 (*Reg. Romeyn*, I, p. 208, no. 584). Eln. conf. (presumably Geoffrey was re-el.) 4 Aug. 1289 (ibid., pp. 208–9, no. 586). Occ. (G.) 6 Aug. 1290 (*Ctl. Bridlington*, p. 65); (Geoffrey of Nafferton) 23 Sep. 1291 (ibid., p. 56).

Gerard of Burton (Burtona) –1315 Occ. in *Ctl. Bridlington* from 25 Nov. 1293 to 20 Jan. 1310 (pp. 228, 454); Mich. 1310 (PRO, CP40/183, m. 30d); 3 Feb. 1311 (*CPR 1307–13*, pp. 363–4); 25 Sept. 1313, 27 Apr.1314, 20 Nov. 1314 (*CPR 1313–17*, pp. 60, 148, 245); 11 May 1314 (*Reg. Greenfield*, III, p. 218, no. 1605); provision made for his retirement 11 Jan. 1315 (ibid., pp. 240–2, no. 1636).

Peter of Weaverthorpe (Wyrthorp, Wyverthorp) 1315–1321 Archbp's exhortation to sub-pr. and convent to lay aside all prejudice in electing a new pr. 10 Mar. 1315 (*Reg. Greenfield*, III, p. 245, no. 1639, cf. no. 1641). Can. of Bridlington, eln pres. to archbp 27 Mar 1315 on death of Gerard; eln conf. 11 Apr. 1315 (*Reg. Greenfield*, III, no.1646). Res. and cess. 25 Aug. 1321 (York, Reg. 9A, f. 346r); house vacant by cess.; pr.'s seal to be broken 3 Sept. 1321 (ibid.,ff. 342v–343r). Provision made for ex-pr. 6 Aug. 1321 and conf. by archbp 11 Sept. 1321 (ibid., f. 346r). After res. had lic. to travel and study for 3 years from 13 Jan. 1322 (ibid., f. 346v); lic. for absence for 1 year 12 Sept. 1324 (ibid., f. 356v); further lic. to study for 2 years 25 Apr. 1326 (York, Reg. 9B, f. 710r); similar lic. for 1 year 28 Aug. 1325 (York, Reg. 9A, f. 346v). Lic. for absence gtd to ex-pr. and *custos* of the manor of Little Kelk (ibid., f. 370r). Ordered to reside on the manor of Little Kelk 4 Apr. 1330 (ibid., f. 377v).

Henry of Melkinthorpe (Melkanthorp) and **William of Driffield** (Driffeld) both el. on 9 Sept. 1321 in a dispute but neither apptd. Sub-pr. and convent asked archbp to appt a pr. (ibid., ff. 343r, 351v).

Robert of Scarborough (Scardborogh, Scardeburgh) 1321–1343 Cellarer of Bridlington, apptd by archbp 18 Sept. 1321 (ibid.). D. by 15 Feb.1343 (York, Reg.10, f. 175v).

Peter of Appleby (Appelby, Appilby) 1343–1357 Can. of Bridlington, eln conf. 15 Feb. 1343 (ibid.). Cess. admitted, lic. to el. 23 Jan. 1357 (York, Reg. 11, f. 195r).

Peter de(l) Cotes 1357–1362/3 Can. of Bridlington, commn to examine eln 29 Jan 1357; opposers cited to appear 6 Feb. (ibid.). D. by 3 Jan. 1363 (ibid., f. 207v).

John of Thwing (Thweng, Twenge) (*afterwards* St John of Bridlington) 1363–1379 Can. of Bridlington, eln conf. and prof. obed. 3 Jan. 1363 (ibid.; see also J.S. Purvis, *St John of Bridlington*, app. C: 'The date of St John's election to the priorate', pp. 42–3). D. 10 Oct. 1379 (Purvis, *St John of Bridlington*, p. 24, citing the *Life* by Hugh the canon; cf. York, Reg. 12, f. 60r). Commn to investigate his miracles 26 June 1386 (ibid., f.97v). Papal bull of canonisation 24 Sept. 1401 (Purvis, *St John of Bridlington*, pp. 31–42); translation 11 Mar. 1404 (*Walsingham*, II, 262). See Sharpe, *Latin Writers*, p. 220; P. Grosjean, 'De S. Iohanne Bridlingtoniensi collectanea', *Analecta Bollandiana*, 53 (1935), 101–29.

---

[6] William, pr. of Bridlington, occ. 15 May 1271 (*Yorks F., 1246–72*, p. 178). Either this is a scribal error, or Geoffrey res. and was replaced by William for a short while, before resuming office.

BRINKBURN (Northumberland), St Peter and St Paul (Pentney) f. *c.* -1135, (dependent on Pentney); *c.* 1188 (independent).

Lists in *Ctl. Brinkburn*, pp. xiii–xiv; *Hist. Northumberland*, VII, 465; *Heads*, I, 154.

Ralph Occ. 18 Mar. 1186 x 7 (*PUE*, I, no. 241); (R.) 1185 x 1195 (*Ctl. Brinkburn*, p. 181).

Alan Occ. 20 June 1231 (*CPR 1225–32*, p. 447); 9 Feb. 1235 (*Northumberland and Durham F.*, I, p. 51, no. 121); 1239 (DCD, 4.2.Spec.14); 1240, Feb. 1242 (*Ctl. Brinkburn*, pp. 126, 163). Seal (*Durham Seals*, II, p. 546, no. 3411).

William Occ. *post* 23 Dec. 1243 (papal commn) (DCD, 2.4.Ebor.26); 29 Oct. 1248 (DCD, 4.2.Spec.40); 25 Nov. 1248, 24 June 1249, 6 May 1252 (*Ctl. Brinkburn*, pp. 91, 113, 121); 1254 (PRO, E42/400); 25 Dec. 1253, 31 Jan. 1255, Feb. 1257 (*Ctl. Brinkburn*, pp. 183, 42, 160). Seal (*Mon. Seals*, p. 13; *Durham Seals*, II, pp. 546–7, nos. 3412–13).

Nicholas of Cramlington (Cramelington) Occ. 1260 x 75 (*Northumberland and Durham Deeds*, p. 9); n.d. (before 1271) (*CChR 1257–1300*, p. 170); (N.) Feb. 1273 (*Ctl. Brinkburn*, p. 119); n.d. (1267 x 1273) (ibid., p. 151, Wilchard de Charron, sheriff of Northumberland witn.); n.d. (1267 x 1272) (*Hatton's Book of Seals*, p. 169, no. 234); Mich. term 1275 (*Northumberland Pleas*, I, p. 90, no. 298). Seal (*Durham Seals*, II, p. 507, no. 3414).

William Occ. 1279 (*Northumberland Assize Rolls*, pp. 264–5, 283).[7]

Ralph Occ. Mich. 1305 (PRO, CP40/153, mm. 48, 522). ? same as next entry.

Ralph of Preston −1343 Occ. 22 May 1334 (*Ctl. Brinkburn*, p. 145). Res. 13 Jan. 1343 (*Reg. Pal. Dun.*, III, 519; cf. *Reg. Bury*, pp. 10–16).

Robert de Throunclon 1343– Commn to cite opposers to eln 23 Jan. 1343; commn to pres. eln to bp 3 Feb. 1343; eln quashed but apptd by bp 6 Feb. 1343 (*Reg. Bury*, pp. 10–16).

Peter of Durham (Dunolm') −1352 Res. 15 Sept. 1352 (Durham, Reg. Hatfield, f. 7r–v).

Robert de Aldewod(e) 1352– Sub-pr. of Brinkburn, el. 19 Sept.1352, eln conf. 20 Sept. 1352 (ibid., ff. 7v–8v).

Peter Occ. 4 May 1367 (*CPR 1364–67*, p. 437).

Robert de Aldewod(e) Occ. 25 Jan. 1372 (*Ctl. Brinkburn*, p. 170).

The next recorded pr., **William Lassy**, occ. June 1378 x June 1379 (PRO, E179/62/4, m. 1d).

BRISTOL (Glos), St Augustine f ?1148 (Victorine) (abbey)

Lists in *VCH Glos*, II, 79 from Abb. Newland's roll (*BGAS*, XIV (1889–90),117–30); *Heads*, I, 155.

The abbey was vacant on 18 Feb. 1216 (*Rot. Lit. Pat.*, p. 166).

Joseph 1216 Pr. of St Augustine's; royal ass. 6 Apr. 1216 (ibid., p. 174b). D. 17 Sept. 1216, after 31 wks, before he had been installed (Newland's roll, p. 127) – i.e. from the d. of the previous abb. John (*Heads*, I, 155).

David Hundered 1216–1234 Succ. and ruled 19 years, d. 3 July 1253 (Newland's roll, p. 127). Dep. 1234 by bp of Worcester (*Ann. Tewkesbury*, p. 93). Cess., lic. to el. 24 May 1234 (*CPR 1232–47*, p. 47). Seal (*Hereford Seals*, p. 7).

William of Bradstone *alias* **of Berkeley** (Berkele) **1234–1242** El. 21 May 1234, ruled 8 years, d. 20 May 1252 (Newland's roll, p. 127). Pr. of St. Augustine's, succ. 1234 (*Ann. Tewkesbury*, p. 93). (W.) royal ass. 28 May 1234; writ *de intendendo* 4 June 1234 (*CPR 1232–47*, pp. 50, 54). Mand. for seisin 4 June 1234 (*CR 1231–34*, p. 444). Res. (W.), lic. to el. 21 Apr. 1242 (*CPR 1232–47*, p. 281). Seal (either Bradstone or Longe) (*BM Seals*, no. 2721).

---

[7] The pr. Geoffrey, said to occ. *c.* 1280 (Ctl. list) or 1288 x 1292 (*Durham Seals*, II, p. 547, no. 3415), is wrongly placed in the sequence. As *BM Seals*, no. 2717 correctly indicates the pr. belongs to the 12th cent. The original cht. involved, DCD, Misc. Cht. 1226, also includes Bernard, pr. of Newburgh 1186–99, and thus is to be identified with pr. Geoffrey also found 1185 x 1187 (*Heads*, I, 154).

[**Walter** pr. of St Augustine's; royal ass. 6 May 1242; s.d. power to archbp of York and W. de Cantilupo to give royal ass. to eln of Walter, or to the eln of any other person if the said el. is not sufficient (*CPR 1232–47*, p. 288). Eln must have been quashed because lic. to el. issued 20 June 1242 *on cess. of abb. William* (ibid., 299).]

William Longe 1242–1264 El. 10 Aug. 1242, ruled 22 years, d. 17 May 1264 (Newland's roll, p. 127). Chamberlain of Keynsham, royal ass. 16 July 1242; writ *de intendendo* 5 Aug. 1242 (*CPR 1232–47*, pp. 299, 300).

Richard of Malmesbury 1264–1275 Succ. and ruled 12 years, d. 13 Sept. 1276 *recte* 1275 (see below) (Newland's Roll, p. 127). Can. of St Augustine, royal ass. 5 June 1264 (*CPR 1258–66*, p. 321); cert. of conf. of eln by bp of Worcester 13 June 1264 (PRO, C84/3/11). D., lic.to el. 17 Sept. 1275 (*CPR 1272–81*, p. 105).

John de Marina 1275–1280 Succ. and ruled 10 years, d. 21 Feb. 1286 (Newland's Roll, p. 127). Chamberlain of St Augustine's, el. 28 Sept. 1275 (PRO, C84/5/47); royal ass. 4 Oct. 1275; writ *de intendendo* 10 Oct. 1275 (*CPR 1272–81*, p. 106); cert of conf. of eln by bp of Worcester 7 Oct. 1275 (PRO, C84/5/48). 25 Aug. 1280 bp of Worcester's commn to visit abbey since abb. John is unable to attend to business on account of illness (*Reg. G. Giffard*, pp. 123–4). Cess. by 28 Oct. 1280 (PRO, C84/7/6). Cess., lic. to el. 3 Nov. 1280 (*CPR 1272–81*, p. 401).

Hugh de Dadyngtone (Dadinton) 1280–1293 Succ. and ruled 8 years, d. 26 Nov. 1294 (*recte* 1293 (see below) (Newland's Roll, p. 127). Can. of St Augustine's, temps. 22 Nov. 1280 (*CPR 1272–81*, p. 415). Detained in prison in Cardiff by Gilbert de Clare, earl of Gloucester and Hereford (*Reg. G. Giffard*, p. 271). D., lic. to el. 1 Dec.1293 (*CPR 1292–1301*, p. 53).

James Barry (Barri) 1293–1306 Succ. and ruled 12 years, d. 12 Nov. 1306 (Newland's Roll, p. 128). Sacrist of St Augustine, el. 9 Dec. 1293 (PRO, C84/11/34); royal ass. 17 Dec. 1293, temps.2 Jan. 1294 (*CPR 1292–1301*, pp. 58, 59); cert. of conf. of eln by bp of Worcester 22 Dec. 1293 (PRO, C84/11/35). D., lic. to el. 30 Nov. 1306 (*CPR 1301–07*, p. 485).

Edmund of Knulle 1306–1332 El. 21 Dec. 1306, ruled 26 years, d. 9 June 1332 (Newland's Roll, p. 128). Can. of St Augustine, royal ass. 7 Jan. 1307, temps. 22 Feb. 1307 (*CPR 1301–07*, pp. 487, 499). See R.H. Warren, 'St Augustine's abbey, Bristol: the work of Abbot Knowle' (*Procs. Clifton Antiquarian Club* 5 (1904), 162–9).

John Snow(e) 1332–1341 El. 17 June, ruled 9 years, d. 3 July [no years given] (Newland's Roll, p. 128). Pr. of St Augustine's, eln pres. to bp 2 July 1332, eln conf. 17 July 1332 (*Reg. Orleton (Worcester)*, no. 427). D. by 2 Aug. 1341 (*Reg. Bransford*, no. 421).

Ralph de Asshe (Assch(e)) 1341–1353 Succ. and ruled 12 years, el. 18 July, d. 1 Mar. 1353 (Newland's Roll, p. 128). Bp's mand. to cite opposers to eln 21 July 1341; eln conf. 31 July 1341; letter to Queen Philippa 2 Aug. 1341; mand. for induction 30 Aug. 1341 (*Reg. Bransford*, nos. 417, 419–22). D. 1 Mar. 1353 (*Worcs Reg. Sede Vacante*, p. 193).

William Cok(e) 1353–1365 Succ. and ruled 13 years, res. 1 Oct. 1365, d. 8 Apr. 1366 (Newland's Roll, p. 128). Sub-pr. of St Augustine's, el. 15 Mar 1353; commn to examine eln 25 Mar.; eln conf. 8 Apr. 1353; mand. to induct 8 Apr. 1353 (*Worcs Reg. Sede Vacante.*, p. 195). Letter of Queen Philippa to the king asking for the release of temps. to new abb. 20 Mar. 1353 (PRO, SC1/40/1137).

Henry de Shalyngforde *alias* Blebury 1365–1388 Succ. and ruled 23 years, d. 2 Dec. 1388 (Newland's Roll, pp.128–9). Occ. 14 Sept. 1371 (*CPR 1370–74*, p. 178 – accused of misrule); 26 Oct. 1371 accused of neglecting abbey, bp of Worcester ordered to visit abbey (*CCR 1369–74*, p. 259; Worcester, Reg. Lynn, p. 105, cf. *Cal. Misc. Inq.*, III, 304–5; *Glos IPM 1359–1413*, pp. 66–7). D. 9 Dec. 1388 (*Dorset IPM*, no. 159) but prob. 2 Dec. as Newland's roll, cf. informal letter from archbp of Canterbury 2 Dec. 1388 recommending William Lane, can. of St Augustine's, for the vacant abbey; lic. to el. 16 Dec. 1388 (*Reg. Wakefield*, nos. 796–7).

BROMEHILL (Norfolk), St Mary and St Thomas the Martyr f. -1224
  Lists in *VCH Norfolk*, II, 37.
Geoffrey Occ. Oct. 1239 x Oct. 1240 (*Norfolk F. (Rye)*, p. 64).
Henry Occ. Oct. 1267 x Oct. 1268 (ibid., p. 103).
William Occ. July 1308 x July 1309 (Blomefield, *Norfolk*, II, 164, no source, but prob. a cht. of
  John de Brampton, see p. 165).
Ralph of Threxton (Threkestone) **1311–1342** Can. of Bromehill, eln quashed, but apptd by
  bp 14 Dec. 1311 (Norwich, Reg/1/1, f. 44v). Res. by 4 May 1342 (Norwich, Reg/1/3, ff.
  54v–55r).
John de Welle 1342–1344 Can. of Bromehill, eln conf. 4 May 1342 (ibid.). D. by 26 July 1344
  (*Reg. Bateman*, I, nos. 96, 98).
Thomas of Saham 1344– Can. of Bromehill, eln conf. 8 Aug. 1344 (ibid.).
Peter de Bernham –1394 [El. 1349, according to *VCH* (Norwich, Reg/2/4, f. 103 but the
  entry has not been located in the original register nor in *Reg. Bateman*, I, nor is it in the later
  ms. index to this register Norfolk RO, ms. 21509/60).] D. by 27 Apr. 1394 (Norwich,
  Reg/3/6, f. 190r–v).

BROOKE (Rutland), St Mary (Kenilworth) f. -1153
  Lists in *VCH Rutland*, I, 160–1; *Heads*, I, 155.
Ralph Occ. 1180 (*Mon. Angl.*, VI, 234). R. occ. ?1199 (1198 x 1200; Cheney, *Inn. III*, no. 814).
Richard of Luddington (Ludintone) **1222–** Can. of Kenilworth, adm. 20 May 1222, no
  reason given for vacancy (*Reg. Wells*, II, 110). Occ. 3 Nov. 1226 (PRO, Leics. F.,
  CP25/1/121/12 no. 141).
Richard of Lichfield (Lichefeude, Luchefeude) **1230–1242/3** Can. of Brooke, adm. 16 Nov.
  1230, no reason given for vacancy (*Reg. Wells*, II, 158–9). D. June 1242 x June 1243 (*Reg.
  Grosseteste*, p. 214).
John of Wootton (Wotton, Wutton) **1242/3–** Can. of Kenilworth, inst. June 1242 x June 1243
  (ibid.). Occ. June 1248 x June 1249 (ibid., p. 240).
Robert of Ledbury (Ledebir', Ledebur', Ledbyr') **1250/1–1285** Can. of Kenilworth, inst.
  June 1250 x June 1251 (ibid., p. 246). Occ. 1259, 1276 (*CPR 1258–66*, p. 21; PRO, Rutland
  F., CP25/1/192/3 no. 50). Res. dated 11 Sept. 1285 (*Reg. Sutton*, II, 45–6).
Nicholas of Breedon (Bredon') **1285–1294** Can. of Kenilworth, letter of pres. 27 Sept., adm.
  17 Oct. 1285 (ibid.). Res. dated 7 Nov. 1294 on account of ill-health (ibid., 117–18).
Richard of Bromsgrove (Bremesgrave) **1294–1299** Can. of Kenilworth, letter of pres. 11
  Nov. 1294, adm. 29 Nov. 1294 (ibid., 117–19). On 7 May 1298 Bp Sutton wrote to the pr.
  of Kenilworth about Brooke following the episcopal visitation; interview with pr.'s proctors
  on 11 May. A respite was requested until Michaelmas before a new pr. of Brooke was presented (ibid., 145–7). On 26 Oct. 1298 Geoffrey of Whitwell (Whitewell), can. of
  Kenilworth, presented letters from Kenilworth dated 28 Sept. 1298 appointing to Brooke.
  Archdn of Northampton, upon enquiry, found that previous pr. had neither died, nor res.,
  but he was said by Geoffrey to have been recalled to Kenilworth. Bp. Sutton ordered
  Richard to return to Brooke or to explain his absence. Richard did neither and was removed
  from office 10 Apr. 1299 (ibid., 157–8).
Richard of Ketton (Ketene) **1299–1300** Can. of Kenilworth, letter of pres. 6 Apr., adm. 11
  Apr. 1299 (ibid., 157–9). Res. dated 25 (*sic*) Oct. 1300 (Lincoln, Ep. Reg., II, f. 103r).
John of Flore (Flora) **1300–1302** Can. of Kenilworth, presented 28 Oct. 1300, letter of pres.
  dated 24 Oct. 1300 and letter of res. of Richard de Keten dated 25 (*sic*) Oct. 1300. Adm. 8
  Nov. 1300 (ibid.). Res. dated 23 June 1302 (ibid., f. 105r).
Stephen of Ketton (Keten(e)) **1302–1305** Can. of Kenilworth, presented 27 June 1302, letter

of pres. dated 26 June 1302; adm. 11 July 1302 (ibid.) Res. dated 20 July 1305 (ibid., f. 109v). On 1 July 1310 papal mand. to bp of Ely to enquire about Stephen, pr. of Brooke and 2 other cans. of Kenilworth. After the bp of Lincoln's visitation of the priory, pr. Stephen had appealed to the archbp of Canterbury and in order to hinder his appeal was dragged from before the high altar of Torksey priory, where he had been placed by the bp of Lincoln, and was imprisoned by the pr. of Torksey. The 2 canons escaped and came to the pope. If their tale is true, the bp of Ely is to liberate Stephen, if he is still alive (*CPL*, II, 77).

Richard of Ketton 1305–1310 Can. of Kenilworth, presented 13 Aug. 1305, letter of pres. dated 22 July 1305 on res. of Stephen of Ketton; adm. 20 Sept. 1305 (Lincoln, Ep. Reg., II, f. 109v). Res. dated 10 Oct. 1310 (ibid., f. 120v). Pr. of Calwich 1312.

Robert of Pershore (Persora) **1310–** Can. of Kenilworth, presented 8 Oct. 1310, letter of pres. dated 10 *(sic)* Oct. 1310 on res. of Richard of Ketton; adm. 15 Nov. 1310 (ibid.).[8]

Robert of Shackerstone (Shakereston, Schakeston) **1328–1331** Can. of Kenilworth, presented 19 June 1328, letter of pres. dated 13 June 1328; adm. 3 Sept. 1328, no reason being given for vacancy (Lincoln, Ep. Reg., IV, f. 179v). Res. by 27 June 1331 (ibid., f. 191r–v).

Stephen of Wormleighton (Wirmeleghton, Wylmeleston) **1331–1346** Can. of Kenilworth, pres. exhibited to bp 17 July 1331, letter of pres. dated 27 June 1331; adm. 4 Aug. 1331(ibid.). Res. dated 27 *(sic)* March 1346 (Lincoln, Ep. Reg., VI, f. 70v).

Henry Waleys 1346– Can. of Kenilworth, presented 24 Mar. 1346, letter of pres. dated 24 Mar. 1346 on res. of Stephen of Wormleighton; adm. 27 Mar. 1346 (ibid.).

Richard of Oxendon (Oxenden) **1362–1366** Can. of Kenilworth, adm. 17 Jan. 1362, no reason given for vacancy (Lincoln, Ep. Reg. IX, f. 238v). Res. by 9 Feb. 1366 (Lincoln, Ep. Reg., X, f. 164r).

Ralph of Towcester (Toucestr', Toycestr') **1366–1375** Priest, adm. 9 Feb. 1366 on res. of Richard of Oxendon (ibid.). Res. acc. 6 Nov. 1375 (ibid., f. 202r–v).

Thomas de Farnecote 1375– Can. of Kenilworth, adm.6 Nov. 1375 by abb. of Owston, commissary of bp (commn dated 16 Oct. 1375 and the commissary's certificate 14 Nov. 1375). The commissary had received the res. of Ralph of Towcester, and also the purgation of Thomas of Farnecote, defamed of the murder of Richard Palfraymen, late servant of pr. Ralph at Brooke (ibid., f. 202r–v; Lincoln, Ep. Reg., XII, f. 140r–v). Occ. 1377 (*Clerical Poll-Taxes* p. 67, no. 889); 10 June 1377 (PRO, C67/28B, m. 3).

The next recorded pr., **Robert of Leicester** (Leicestr'), can. of Kenilworth, adm. 21 July 1379, no reason given for the vacancy (Lincoln, Ep. Reg., X, f. 214r).

BRUTON (Soms.), St Mary f. 1127 x 1135
Lists in *VCH Soms*, II,138; *Ctl. Bruton*, pp. xxxi–xxxiii; *Heads*, I, 155–6.

Ralph Occ. ? early 13th cent. (*Ctl. Bruton*, no.81).

William Occ. n.d. *temp.* Bp Jocelin of Bath (1206–42) (ibid., no. 165). The sequence of priors is unclear.

Richard Occ. 1222 (PRO, PRO31/8/140B, part 1, pp. 125–7); 25 Mar. 1222, May 1231 x May 1232 (*Ctl. Bruton*, nos. 425, 131); 21 May 1222 (*Soms. F.*, I, 45); 1206 x 1235 (*HMC Wells*, I, 42); 1234 x May 1238 (*Ctl. Bruton*, no. 205, cf. no. 206).

Stephen de Kari –1255 Occ. 7 Apr. 1236 (*Soms F.*, I, 85); 1236 (*Ctl. Bruton*, no. 113); (S.) Apr. 1251 (ibid., no.271); 1251 (ibid., no.303). Removed 5 July 1255 (*Cal. Misc. Inq.*, I, 73).

William of St Edward (de Sancto Edwardo) *dictus* of **Shaftesbury** (Sheftysbery) **1255–** Provided 10 Aug. 1255 (ibid.). Occ. 1256, 1260, 29 Sept. 1262 (*Ctl. Bruton*, nos. 35, 438,

---

[8] On 26 Jan. 1319 a safe conduct was issued for William, pr. of 'Brok', who had come to the king as a nuncio from the pope and was returning beyond the seas (*CPR 1317–21*, p. 268). I have not been able to identify the priory.

288, 194); 9 Sept. 1258 (Devon RO, Petre 123M/TB.116); 21 Jan. 1266 (*Reg. W. Giffard (Bath)*, p. 9); 1 Nov. 1267 (*Ctl. Bruton*, no. 175). Pr. for 12 years (Soms RO, DD/L.P.37/5[6]).

Thomas de Deverell Pr. for 3 years (ibid.). Occ. n.d. (1268 x 1272) (*Ctl. Bruton*, no. 354); 14 Apr. 1269 (*Soms F.*, I, 225; *Ctl. Bruton*, no. 37).

William Occ. 1 July 1271 (*Ctl. Bruton*, no. 448).

Stephen de Carevyle −1275 Pr. for 4 years (Soms RO, DD/L.P.37/5[6]). Occ. 1274 (ibid., no. 39). D. by 26 Jan. 1275 (Soms RO, DD/L.P.37/3).

John de Grindham (Gryndenham, Gundham) 1275–1297 Chosen as pr. in succ. to Stephen de Carevyle 26 Jan. 1275 (ibid.). Occ. 18 Nov. 1276 (*Ctl. Bruton*, no. 211); Nov. 1279 x Nov. 1280 (Devon RO, Petre 123M/TB.124; *Ctl. Bruton*, no. 161); 1285 (ibid., no. 163); 1295 (ibid., no. 211). D. (J.) 3 July 1297 (ibid., no. 370; cf. *Glos IPM 1236–1300*, p. 200).

Richard de la Grave 1298–1309 Cert. of appt by bp of Bath and Wells, eln having been quashed 18 July 1298 (PRO, C84/13/15). Can. of Bruton, temps. 26 Aug. 1298 (*Ctl. Bruton*, no. 370). Recently promoted as pr. by W., bp of Bath and Wells: king's mand. to escheator to gt him certain manors 26 Aug. 1298 (*CCR 1296–1302*, p. 178). D. 2 Jan. 1309 (*Ctl. Bruton*, no. 371). Pr. for 10 years (Soms RO, DD/L.P.37/5[6]).

Walter de Legh(e) 1309–1334 Pr. for 26 years (ibid.). Can. of Bruton, mand. to cite any opposers to eln 5 Mar. 1309 (*Reg. Winchelsey*,II, 1107–8); temps. 14 Apr. 1309 (*Ctl. Bruton*, no. 371; Soms RO, DD/L.P.37/5[5]). D. 23 Dec. 1334 (*Cal. Misc. Inq.*, II, 356).

Robert Coker 1335–1361 Occ. 22 May 1335 (*Ctl. Bruton*, no. 356); 26 May 1335 (*CCR 1333–37*, p. 400; Soms RO, DD/L.P.37/5[4]); 1340 (PRO, E329/298); Jan. 1340 x Jan. 1341 (PRO, E326/8472); 1344 (*Reg. R. Shrewsbury*, I, no. 1510); 1347 (*CPR 1345–48*, p. 273); 1348 (*Ctl. Bruton*, no. 220); 1349, 1353 (*Reg. R. Shrewsbury*, II, nos. 2214, 2244, 2723); 21 Sept. 1357 (*Ctl. Bruton*, no. 362). D. 3 Oct. 1361 (ibid., no. 365), but cf. D. 17 Sept. 1361 (*Cal. Misc. Inq.*, III, 311). Pr. for 27 years (Soms RO, DD/L.P.37/5[6]).

Richard Cockyng (Cokkyng(e)) 1361–1396 Eln conf. 26 Oct. 1361 (*Ctl. Bruton*, no. 364, cf. *CCR 1360–64*, p. 213; Soms RO, DD/L.P.37/5[3]); temps. 30 Oct. 1361 (*Ctl. Bruton*, no. 365; *Cal. Misc. Inq.*, III, 311). D. by 2 May 1396 (*CFR 1391–99*, p. 173). Pr. for 35 years (Soms RO, DD/L.P.37/5[6]).

BUCKENHAM (Norfolk), St James (perhaps also St Mary and All Saints, cf. Binns, p. 124) f. *c.* 1146

    Lists in *VCH Norfolk*, II, 378; *Heads*, I, 156

W. Occ. (W.) 15 May 1220 (*Norwich Cath. Chts.*, II, no. 75). Blomefield states a pr. William occ. 1216, but gives no source (*Norfolk*, I, 387).

Walter Said to occ. 1221 (Blomefield, *Norfolk*, I, 387, no source). Occ. Oct. 1242 x Oct. 1243 (*Norfolk F. (Rye)*, p. 70).

Hugh Occ. 1269 (Blomefield, *Norfolk*, I, 387, no source).

Richard of Otley (Otteley) Occ. 1286 (ibid.).

Richard Betts Succ. Richard (ibid.).

John de Malton (Multon) 1308–1327 Can. of Buckenham, eln conf. 9 Feb. 1308, no reason given for vacancy (Norwich, Reg/1/1, f. 26r). D. by 4 Mar. 1327 (PRO, C84/21/34). D., lic. to el. 8 Mar. 1327 (*CPR 1327–30*, p. 33).

Nicholas of Colton 1327– Sub-pr. of Buckenham, royal ass. 17 Mar. 1327 (ibid., p. 37).

Hugh de Brom 1329–1354 Can. of Buckenham, eln quashed, but apptd by bp 15 June 1329 (Norwich, Reg/1/2, f. 29v). D. by 11 Oct. 1354 (Norwich, Reg/2/4, f. 154r).

William of Spixworth (Spykesworth) 1354–1381 Can. of Buckenham, eln conf. 11 Oct. 1354 (ibid.). Res. by 26 Sept. 1381 (Norwich, Reg/3/6, f. 75v).

BURSCOUGH (Lancs), St Nicholas f. *c.* 1190
  Lists in *VCH Lancs*, II,151; *Ctl. Burscough*, p. 17; *Heads*, I, 156.
Geoffrey Occ. before Benedict (*Ctl. Burscough*, no. 19).
Benedict Occ. 1229, 14 May 1235 (*Ctl.* nos. 16, 14); 14 May 1236 (*Lancs F.*, p. 60, no. 39); (B.)
  n.d. (? 1228 x 1240) (PRO, DL36/2/158).
William Occ. Whitsun 1245 (*Ctl.* no. 115, cf. nos. 71–2).
Nicholas Occ. *c.*1260 x *c.*1275 (*Ctl.* nos. 53, 113); n.d. (*c.* 1260) (*Scarisbrick Chts.*, nos. 15–17, p.
  264).
Warin Occ. *c.*1275 x 1303, 1280 x 1290 (*Ctl.* nos. 112, 40, app. I, nos. 28–9).
Richard Occ. 25 Mar. 1303, 29 May 1303, 1 Sept. 1303, 5 Feb.1304 (*Ctl.* nos. 75, 54, 63, app. I,
  no. 30; *Scarisbrick Chts.*, nos. 44, 47, pp. 273, 275).
John de Donyngton –1348 Occ. several times in the *Ctl.* from 8 Sept.1322 to 11 Nov. 1338 (*Ctl.*
  no. 32, app. I, no. 23); Mich. 1328 (*Index to Placito de Banco*, p. 259); 1344 (PRO,
  Just.1/1435, m. 38d). D. by 28 Feb. 1347[9] (Lichfield, B/A/1/2, f. 120v).
Thomas of Litherlond (Lytherland, Lytherlond) 1347–1385 Can. of Burscough, commn to
  examine eln 28 Feb. 1347; cert. of conf. by commissaries 7 Mar. 1347 (ibid.). Royal mand.
  to stay process against pr. Thomas, who with others was indicted of the rape of Margery
  late wife of Nicholas de la Beche 28 Nov. 1347 (*CPR 1345–48*, p. 436). Occ. 1348 (*CFR
  1347–56*, p. 80); 1349 (*CPR 1348–50*, p. 269); 1379 (Bennett, 'Lancs and Cheshire Clergy',
  p. 22); 1381 (*Ctl.* no. 180); 1383 (*Reg. Stretton*, I, 145). Res. by 25 May 1385 when John
  Wrightynton's eln conf. by bp (*Ctl.* no. 201).

BURTLE (Soms), Holy Trinity, St Mary, and St Stephen (Sprawlesmede) f. –1270 (subject
to Glastonbury).; diss. 1439
  List in *VCH Soms*, II, 139.
[**Walter** the hermit of Sprawlesmede, mentd in cht. of William son of Geoffrey n.d., inspected
  by William Bitton I, bp of Bath and Wells (1248–64), itself inspected by Archbp Boniface
  of Canterbury 14 July 1261 (*Ctl. Glastonbury*, I, p. 117, no. 162).]
Stephen Occ. 21 Jan.1271 as *custos* or pr. (ibid., p. 120, no. 165). Presumably the **Stephen of
  Burtle**, former pr. of 'Sproulesmede' mentd in 1309 (PRO, CP40/178, m. 358).
William of Foulbrook (Foulbrok) –1312 D. by 10 May 1312 (ibid., I, p. 121, no. 166).
Nicholas Drake 1312– Can. of Burtle, eln pres. to Glastonbury by cans. of Burtle 10 May 1312
  (ibid., p. 122, no. 167); eln quashed but apptd by bp by lapse 23 Sept. 1312, no reason given
  for vacancy – among the irregularities found was that the eln dated in May did not actually
  occ. until Sept. (*Reg. Droxford*, p. 54).
Robert de Cadecote 1345– Can. of Burtle, apptd by bp, to whom the power had devolved, 25
  Nov. 1343, no reason given for vacancy (*Reg. R. Shrewsbury*, II, pp. 479–80, no. 1764).
Robert of Baltonsborough (Baltisborw) –1350 D. by 27 Feb.1350 (ibid., p. 603, no. 2325).
William of Foulbrook (Fulbroke, Fulbrok) 1350–1362 Can. of Burtle, priest, mand. to induct
  27 Feb. 1350 (ibid.). D. by 31 Dec. 1362 (ibid., II, app., no. 110).
William Tannere 1362–1409 Can. of Burtle, priest, adm. 31 Dec. 1362 (ibid.). D. reported to
  Glastonbury and lic. to el. sought 10 Nov. 1409 (*Hylle Ctl.*, p. 57, no. 143).

BUSHMEAD (Beds), St Mary f. *c.* 1195; became regular –1215 (*Ctl. Bushmead*, pp. xv–xvi)
  Lists in *VCH Beds*, I, 386–7; *Ctl. Bushmead*, pp. xv–xvii, late 14th-cent. (and sometimes unreliable) list (ibid., p.1); *Heads*, I, 156.

---

[9] The year given in the bp's register is 1347 [i.e. 1347/8] and 25th pontifical year. The position of the entry
at the beginning of the 1347 section and the pontifical year confirms this is a scribal error for 1346/7.

Joseph of Coppingford (Copmanford) –1232/3 Occ. 30 Aug. 1215 (*Ctl.*, no. 13); (John) 1227 (*Beds Eyre*, no. 98); 3 Nov. 1231 (*Beds F.*, I, p. 89, no. 330; *Ctl.*, no. 193); possibly earlier chaplain of Coppingford hermitage (*Ctl.* no. 238; cf. ibid., p. xvi). D. by Dec. 1232 x Dec. 1233 (*Reg. Wells*, III, 31).

John de Wildbof (Oyldebouf) 1232/3– Can. of Bushmead, el. and adm. Dec. 1232 x Dec. 1233 (ibid.). Occ. Oct. 1234 x Oct. 1235 (*Hunts F.*, p. 16); 1236 (*Beds.F.*, I, p. 104, no. 386); 25 Nov. 1240 (ibid., p. 123, no. 455; *Ctl.*, no. 190); (J.) 1247 (BL, Cotton ms. Faustina A IV, f. 130v); 30 May 1255 (*Beds F.*, II, p. 81, no. 277; *Ctl.*, no. 39; PRO, Glos F. CP25/1/74/21, no. 470). According to *Ctl.* list he d. a monk of Wardon 1251 (*sic*) – obviously a wrong date, unless the 1255 ref. is to another pr. John.

Simon de Colesden(e) –1265 Occ. Oct. 1260 x Oct. 1261 (*Hunts F.*, p. 32); 1261 (*Ctl.*, no. 262). D. by 25 Aug. 1265 (*Reg. R. Gravesend*, p. 192, cf. p. 91).

Unnamed pr. (presumably Peter below) ment. in a commn to examine recent eln 25 Aug. 1265 (*Reg. R. Gravesend*, p. 91).

[**Peter Ratlesden** El. on death of Simon, but eln quashed 13 Sept. 1265 (ibid., pp. 192, 323).]

Richard Foliot (Folyot(h)) 1265–1298/9 Can. of Bushmead, apptd (Peter) by bp 13 Sept. 1265 (ibid.). Occ. as Richard: 1268 (*CR 1264–68*, p. 521); 1270 (*Reg. R. Gravesend*, p. 41); 1283 (*CPR 1281–92*, p. 97); 1292 (*Ctl.*, no. 278); 1295 (*Select Cases, Law Merchant*, I, 70). D. (Richard), n.d. (? Nov. 1298 x Feb. 1299) (*Reg. Sutton*, VIII, 124).

[**Jocelin of Stockton** El. by cans. but eln quashed n.d (? Nov. 1298 x Feb. 1299) (ibid.).]

Simon de Redbourn(e) (Redebourn) 1298/9–1321 Cellarer of Bushmead, apptd by bp n.d.(? Nov. 1298 x Feb. 1299) to succeed Richard Foliot (ibid.). Cess. by 5 Jan. 1321 (Lincoln, Ep. Reg., IV, f. 291r). *Ctl.* list (p. 1) says he res. after priorate of 50 years (*sic*).

Robert of Lubbenham (Lobbenham, Lubenham, Lubbynham) 1321–1348 Can. of Bushmead, eln pres. to bp 5 Jan. 1321, quashed but apptd by bp 7 Jan. 1321 (Lincoln, Ep. Reg., IV, f. 291r). Res. by 12 Apr. 1348 (Lincoln, Ep. Reg., IX, f. 417v). *Ctl.* list (p. 1) says res. after priorate of 34 years (*sic*).

Richard of Stockton (Stoketon, Stokton) 1348–1349 Can. of Bushmead, right of appt transferred to bp and he apptd 12 Apr. 1348 (Lincoln, Ep. Reg., IX, ff. 417v, 421v). D. by 2 Dec. 1349 (ibid., f. 422v). *Ctl.* list (p. 1) says he d. after priorate of 2 years.

Simon de Grantesdon (Grantesdene) 1349– Can. of Bushmead, eln quashed but apptd by bp 2 Dec. 1349 (Lincoln, Ep. Reg., IX, f. 422v). *Ctl.* list (p. 1) says he res. after priorate of 1½ years.

Adam de Leverington (Leveryngton) –1355 Res. by 3 Feb. 1355 (Lincoln, Ep. Reg., IX, f. 432r). *Ctl.* list (p. 1) says he res. after priorate of 2½ years.

John de Rysle (Rysele, Ryslee) 1355–1386 Can. of Bushmead, apptd by bp to whom the right of appt had been transferred 3 Feb. 1355 (Lincoln, Ep. Reg., IX, f. 432r). Commn to receive res. and proceed to el. 6 Jan. 1386 (Lincoln, Ep. Reg., XI, f. 344r; Lincoln, Ep. Reg., XII, f. 319r). Res. conf. 15 Jan. 1386 (Lincoln, Ep. Reg., XI, f. 344r).

BUTLEY (Suffolk), St Mary f. 22 Feb. 1171

Lists in *VCH Suffolk*, II, 98–9; *Butley Chts.*, p. 51; *Heads*, I, 156–7; J.N.L. Myres, 'Butley priory, Suffolk', *Arch. J.*, XC (1933), 177–281, list at 222.

Robert Occ. 20 Jan. 1213 (*Suffolk F. 1199–1214*, no. 556).

Adam Occ. 6 Oct. 1219 (*Lincs F.*, I, 119); (A.) 1227 x 1230 (Norfolk RO, DCN no. 4194); Oct. 1233 x Oct. 1234, Oct. 1236 x Oct. 1237 (*Suffolk F. (Rye)*, pp. 33, 39); 3 Feb. 1235 (*Essex F.*, I, 103). 17 May 1237 (PRO, F. Divers Cos., CP25/1/283/10, no. 134).

William Occ.18 Nov. 1235 (*Ctl. Leiston*, nos. 89–90); n.d. (13th cent.) (Suffolk RO, Ipswich, HD1538/172/2).

During the vacancy of the see of Norwich (1236–39), Archbp Edmund of Canterbury dep. an unnamed pr. of Butley (Lincoln D. & C., Dij/62/4, f. 19r).

Peter Occ. Oct. 1249 x Oct. 1250 (*Suffolk F. (Rye)*, p. 50); said to occ. 1251 (Myres, 'Butley priory', p. 182).

Hugh Occ. 1255 (ibid.; BL, Harl. ms. 639, f. 62r).

Walter Occ. Oct. 1260 x Oct. 1261, Oct. 1267 x Oct. 1268 (*Norfolk F. (Rye)*, pp. 98, 102); 18 June 1262 (*Essex F.*, I, 246); Oct. 1262 x Oct. 1263 (*Suffolk F. (Rye)*, p. 64).

Robert Occ. Oct. 1268 x Oct. 1269 (ibid., p. 66); 18 Nov. 1271 (*Lincs F.*, II, 273).

Thomas Occ. Nov. 1276 x Nov. 1277, Nov. 1285 x Nov. 1286 (*Norfolk F. (Rye)*, pp.117,129); 1290 (*State Trials*, p. 62); 27 Oct. 1290 (*King's Bench, Edward I*, II, 87).

John Myres, 'Butley priory', pp. 184, n. 2, 196, notes there is some evidence for a pr. John at some point between 1290 x 1293 and Richard of Yaxley's eln in 1303, citing *CPR 1446–52*, p. 234; *CPR 1452–61*, p. 16.

Richard of Yaxley (Jakesle) **1303–** Apptd by bp, the right having lawfully devolved upon him 16 Sept. 1303, no reason given for the vacancy (Norwich, Reg/1/1, f. 12v).

Nicholas de Witteleyham 1307– Can. of Butley, adm. 7 Dec. 1307, no reason given for the vacancy (ibid., f. 25v).

Richard of Hoxne 1309– Can. of Butley, eln conf. 27 July 1309 (ibid., f. 33r).

William de Geyton(e) 1312–1332 Cellarer of Butley, eln conf. 21 Feb. 1312, no reason given for the vacancy (ibid., f. 46r). D. by 22 Aug. 1332 (Norwich, Reg/1/2, ff. 51v–52r). Ledger stone at Hollesley, Suffolk (*Earliest English Brasses*, p. 209 & fig. 85; Salter, *Essays*, p. 201 & n. 1).

Alexander of Stratford 1332–1333 Can. of Butley, commn to examine eln 22 Aug. 1332; eln conf. 5 Sept. 1332 (Norwich, Reg/1/2, ff. 51v–52r). D. by 21 July 1333 (ibid., f. 58r)

Matthew of Pakenham 1333–1353 Can. of Butley, eln conf. 21 July 1333 (ibid.). Occ. 12 Jan. 1353 (*CPL*, III, 504). Res. by [ ] Sept. 1353 (Norwich, Reg/2/4, f.148r–v).

Alexander of Drinkstone (Drenkeston) **1353–** Can. of.Butley, eln conf. [ ] Sept. 1353 (ibid.). Occ. autumn 1362 (Putnam, *Justices*, p. 360).

Roger of Bungay Suggested without ref. Myres list. A 14th-cent. seal of his survives (*BM Seals*, no. 2817). His precise place in the sequence of priors is uncertain.

John Baxter –1375 Res. by 30 Jan. 1375 (Norwich, Reg/3/6, f. 30r–v).

William of Halesworth 1375– Can. of Butley, commn to examine eln 30 Jan. 1375; eln con.31 Jan. 1375 (ibid.).

The next recorded pr., **William Bandeworth**, was apptd by the bp of Norwich 31 May 1410, no reason being given for the vacancy (Norwich, Reg/3/7, f. 27r).

CALDWELL (Beds), St John the Baptist and St John the Evangelist (see Binns, pp. 125–6). f. *c.* 1154

Lists in *VCH Beds*, I, 384–5; *Heads*, I, 157.

Alexander 1212–1229 Sub-pr. of Dunstable, postulated autumn 1212, installed 28 Oct. 1212 (*Ann. Dunstable*, p.39). Occ. 24 Nov. 1228 (*Beds F.*, I, no. 295). D. 1229 (*Ann. Dunstable*, p. 115).

William 1229–1244 Succ. Alexander 1229 (ibid.). El. and adm. Dec. 1228 x Dec. 1229 (*Reg. Wells*, III, 22). D. after Christmas 1244 (*Ann. Dunstable*, p. 166).

[**Thomas of Cardington** (Kerdinton) Eln quashed by bp's official June 1244 x June 1245 '*tam pro debilitate visus quam propter morbum paraliticum*' (*Reg. Grosseteste*, p. 325).]

Eudo 1244/5–1249 Can. of Caldwell, apptd June 1244 x June 1245 (ibid.). Occ. 9 July 1249 (*Bucks F.*, I, 93). Res. 2 Aug.1249 in visitation after being accused by brethren, and on 6 Aug. joined the Cistercians at Merevale (*Ann. Dunstable*, p. 179).

Walter of Caddington (Cadendone) **1249–1272** Sub-pr. of Dunstable, el. 2 Aug.1249, eln conf. 3 Aug., installed 15 Aug. 1249 (ibid., p. 179). El. and adm. June 1249 x June 1250 (*Reg. Grosseteste*, p. 336). Res. (W.) by 25 Sept. 1272 on account of old age and ill-health (*Reg. R. Gravesend*, p. 196). D. within 8 days of res. (*Ann. Dunstable*, p.254).

Matthew of Bedford (Bedeford) **1272–1287/8** Can. of Caldwell, el. 1272 on day that Walter res. (ibid.); eln conf. 25 Sept. 1272 (*Reg. R. Gravesend*, p. 196). Res. 1287 during visitation (*Ann. Dunstable*, p. 340). Res. by 21 Feb. 1288 (*Reg. Sutton*, VIII, 104).

John de Ypre (Ipre, Le Dypre) **1287/8–1303** Can. of Caldwell, el. and installed on day Matthew res. (*Ann. Dunstable*, p. 340). Eln conf. 21 Feb. 1288 (*Reg. Sutton*, VIII, 104). Res. by 12 Aug.1303 (Lincoln, Ep. Reg., II, f. 257v).

John de Lacu 1303–1318 Can. of Caldwell, eln quashed but apptd by bp 12 Aug. 1303 (ibid.). D. by 21 Nov. 1318 (ibid., f. 273r–v).

Hugh de Beauchamp (Bello Campo) **1318–1326** Can. of Caldwell, eln quashed but apptd by bp 21 Nov. 1318 (ibid.). Res. by 15 Jan. 1326 (Lincoln, Ep. Reg., IV, f. 298v).

Roger of Wennington (Wenyngton) **1326–** Can. of Huntingdon, Subpr. and convent gtd power of appt to bp, who apptd Roger 15 Jan.1326 (ibid.). Occ. 19 Oct. 1328 (Lincoln, Ep. Reg., VI, f. 124r); 22 Aug. 1332 (*CCR 1330–33*, p. 582). Administration of vacant priory gtd to subpr. and convent 12 Oct. 1337 (Lincoln, Ep. Reg., V, f. 550r); commn to examine an eln of a future pr., no reason given for vacancy 31 Oct. 1337 (ibid., f. 551r).

Robert de Lufwyk –1338 Occ. 1 May 1338 (*CCR 1337–39*, p. 408). Cess. by 22 Aug. 1338 (Lincoln, Ep. Reg., IV, f. 319r).

William of Souldrop (Suldrop) **1338–1348** Can. of Caldwell, eln conf. 22 Aug.1338 (ibid.). Cess. by 11 June 1348 (Lincoln, Ep. Reg., IX, f. 418r).

Richard of Hardwick (Herdewyk) **1348–1349** Can. of Oxford, St Frideswide, right of appt transferred to bp who apptd him 11 June 1348 (ibid.). House vacant by 1 Sept. 1349 (Lincoln, Ep. Reg., IX, f. 420v). D. by 9 Nov. 1349 (ibid., f. 422r).

Ralph of Derby 1349–1375 Can. of Caldwell, eln quashed but apptd by bp 9 Nov. 1349 (ibid.). D. by 10 Oct. 1375 (Lincoln, Ep. Reg., X, f. 392v).

Thomas (of) Stratford 1375–1396 Can. of Caldwell, eln conf. 10 Oct. 1375 (ibid.). D. 12 June 1396 (Lincoln, Ep. Reg., XI, f. 369r).

CALWICH (Staffs), St Margaret (Kenilworth) f. -1148; -1169 (cell of Kenilworth).
Lists in *VCH Staffs*, III, 239–40; *Heads*, I, 157.

KEEPERS

Henry Occ. *c*. 1197 x 1210 (F.Taylor in *BJRL*, XXXIII (1950–1), 155).

Nicholas –1259 Can. of Kenilworth. Occ. 10 May 1259 (*CPR 1258–66*, p. 21). Royal ass. to his el. as pr. of Kenilworth 1 June 1259 (ibid., p. 27).

Hugh Occ. 20 Jan. 1274 (*Staffs F. 3*, p. 28).

Thomas de Boweles 1305– Adm. 14 Oct. 1305, no reason given for vacancy (Lichfield, B/A/1/1, f. 16r).

William of Sheldon (Scheldon) Letter from pr. of Kenilworth to Joan de Langeford, asking her approval of William's nomination to Calwich 20 July 1309 (*Anglesey Chts.*, pp. 125–6, no. 1801).

John of Leicester (Leicestr') **1311–** Can. of Kenilworth, adm. 30 June 1311, no reason given for vacancy (Lichfield, B/A/1/1, f. 44v).

Richard of Ketton (Keten) **1312** Can. of Kenilworth, adm. 30 Mar.1312, no reason given for vacancy (ibid., f. 45v). Previously pr. of Brooke 1299–1300, 1305–1310.

John of Leicester 1312– Presumably the same as in 1311. Can. of Kenilworth, adm. 17 May 1312, no reason given for vacancy (ibid., f. 32v).

Geoffrey of Whitwell (Whitewell) 1318– Can. of Kenilworth, adm. 23 Feb. 1318, no reason given for vacancy (ibid., f. 89r).

Nicholas of Blagrave (Blacgreve) 1323– Can. of Kenilworth, adm. 2 Aug. 1323, no reason given for vacancy (Lichfield, B/A/1/2, f. 138r).

William Boydyn 1333–1334 Can. of Kenilworth, adm. 14 Oct. 1333, no reason given for vacancy (ibid., f. 154v). Recalled 1334 (see below).

Geoffrey Irreys 1334– Pr. and conv. of Kenilworth had pres. William Boydyn, can. of Kenilworth and he had been inst. pr. Later he had been recalled to Kenilworth and Geoffrey Irreys, can. of Kenilworth, pres. in his place. The bp of Lichfield suspended the admission of Geoffrey while considering whether the recall of William was prejudicial to the episcopal jurisdiction. After witnesses were examined, the bp pronounced in favour of the right of the priory and Geoffrey was adm. 29 Nov. 1334 (Lichfield, B/A/1/3, f. 72v).

Thomas of Hellidon (Helyden) 1337– Can. of Kenilworth, letter of pres. from pr. and conv. of Kenilworth 2 Jan. 1337, no reason given for vacancy; ass. of Nicholas de Longeford, knight, 28 Mar. 1337, adm. 5 Apr. 1337 (Lichfield, B/A/1/2, f. 160r).

Robert of Shackerstone (Sakerston) 1340– Can. of Kenilworth, letter of pres. from pr. and conv. of Kenilworth 27 Mar. 1340, no reason given for vacancy; ass. of Nicholas de Langeford, knight, 31 Mar. 1340, adm. 26 July 1340 (ibid., f. 166r–v). Previously pr. of Brooke 1328–31.

Geoffrey of Hampton 1346– Can. of Kenilworth, letter of pres. from pr. and conv. of Kenilworth 2 May 1346, no reason given for vacancy; ass. of Nicholas de Langeford 3 May 1346, adm. 4 May 1346 (ibid., f. 178r–v).

Roger of Birmingham (Bermyng(e)ham) 1349 Can. of Kenilworth, letter of pres. from pr. and conv. of Kenilworth ?21 Aug. 1349, no reason given for vacancy; ass. of Nicholas de Longford 23 Aug. 1349 [*sic*, Friday after Assumption]; adm. 20 Aug. 1349 (ibid., f. 184r).

Henry de Bradewey 1349 Can. of Kenilworth, letter of pres. from pr. and conv. pof Kenilworth 4 Sept. 1349, no reason given for vacancy; ass. of Nicholas de Longford 6 Sept. 1349; adm. 7 Sept. 1349 (ibid., ff. 184v–185r).

PRIORS

Memorandum that the cell of Calwich is made into an independent priory under the patronage of the Longford family, its founders, paying a pension of 60s. a year to Kenilworth priory, the mother church 4 Nov. 1349 (Lichfield, B/A/1/3, ff. 125v–126r; cf. BL Add. ms. 47677, ff. 116r–117v).

Richard Mayel (Mayell) 1349– Can. of Calwich, apptd 4 Nov. 1349, no reason given for vacancy (ibid., f. 186r–v); n.d. (BL Add. ms. 47677, f. 123v).

On 10 Mar. 1384 it was reported that the unnamed pr. was too feeble through age to labour and too poor to hire others to labour for him (*Reg. Stretton*, I, 152).

Hugh de Beley –1385 D. by ? Apr. 1385 (Lambeth, Reg. Courtenay, f. 347r [between entries of 11 and 29 Apr. 1385]).

CANONS ASHBY (Northants), St Mary f. 1147 × 1151

Lists in *VCH Northants*, II, 132; *Heads*, I, 157.

Peter Occ. n.d. (late 12th/early 13th cent.: pal.) (PRO, E326/10312), definitely before 1219 × 1220 when a witness, Philip, ceased to be rector of Eydon (*Reg. Wells*, II, 98) and prob. much earlier.

Hugh Occ. 1213 × 1214, 20 Jan. 1215 (PRO, E326/5129; BL, Egerton ms. 3033, ff. 117v, 98v).

A. Occ. 1215 × 1225 (*Luffield Chts.*, II, no. 348).

Osbert –1226 Occ. n.d. (early Henry III) (BL, Add. Cht. 7534; BL, Egerton ms. 3033, f. 80v); 14 Feb. 1226 (*Reg. Wells*, II, 217). Res. by 6 Nov. 1226 (ibid., 134).

Geoffrey de Eketone 1226– Precentor of Dunstable, eln conf. 6 Nov. 1226 (ibid.); succ. 1226 (*Ann. Dunstable*, p. 100). Occ. (G.) Dec. 1226 x Dec. 1227 (*Reg. Wells*, III, 15); 1228 (*CPR 1225–32*, p. 222); 1236 (PRO, Northants F., CP25/1/172/27, no. 350; BL, Egerton ms. 3033, f. 99v); 1240 (BL, Harl. Cht. 84 D 33); Trin. 1242 (*CRR*, XVIII, no. 218); 12 July 1243 (*Warws F.*, I, no. 609); *c.* June 1244 (PRO, E326/11383). Seal (*Mon. Seals*, p. 18).

Adam Occ. 23 Oct. 1253 (BL, Egerton ms. 3033, f.5v); 1255 (ibid., f. 99r; PRO, E326/8492; PRO, Northants F., CP25/1/173/41, nos. 695, 698); 1259 (BL, Egerton ms. 3033, f. 109r); 1260 (PRO, E326/11458); 1261 (BL, Egerton ms. 3033, f. 41v); 3 Mar. 1267 (PRO, E326/11479).

Elias of Chacombe 1272/3–1294 Can. of Canons Ashby, eln conf. n.d. (?Dec. 1272 x Jan. 1273), no reason given for vacancy (*Reg. R. Gravesend*, pp. 120, 300). Occ. 28 Dec. 1275 (PRO, E326/2958). D. by 18 Aug. 1294 (*Reg. Sutton*, II, 116).

Robert of Wardington 1294–1311 Can. of Canons Ashby, eln pres. to bp 18 Aug. 1294; eln quashed but apptd by bp 19 Aug. (ibid., 116–17). Res. by 9 June 1311 (Lincoln, Ep. Reg., II, f. 121v). Provision made for him 13 Jan. 1312, conf. by bp 25 Nov. 1312 (Lincoln, Ep. Reg., III, ff. 256v–257r).

Robert Lovel (Luvel) **1311–1319** Can. of Canons Ashby, eln quashed but apptd by bp 9 June 1311 (Lincoln, Ep. Reg., II, f. 121v). Occ. 24 Jan. 1319 (ibid., f. 273v). D. by 30 Jan. 1319 (ibid., f. 138v).

John of Dodford (Dodeford) **1319–1320** Can. of Canons Ashby, eln quashed but apptd by bp 30 Jan. 1319 (ibid.). Cess. by 4 June 1320 (ibid., f. 354r).

Robert of Gawcott (Gauecot(e), Gavecote) **1320–1323** Can. of Canons Ashby, eln quashed 4 June 1320 but apptd by Official *sede vacante* 18 June 1320 (ibid.). Res. by 22 Feb. 1323 (Lincoln, Ep. Reg., IV, f. 167v).

Adam of Buckingham 1323– Can. of Canons Ashby, eln pres. to bp 22 Feb. 1323; eln quashed but apptd by bp 24 Feb. 1323 (ibid.). Occ. 1 May 1323 (PRO, E326/4065); 1325 (PRO, E326/1153; *CCR 1323–27*, p. 530); 5 Feb. 1328 (BL, Egerton ms. 3033, f. 25r); Trin. 1327 – Mich. 1328 (*Index to Placita de Banco*, pp. 473, 487).

Walter Neyrnuyt (Neyrenuyt) **–1344** Occ. 14 Nov. 1333 (Lincoln, Ep. Reg., IV, f.306v); 1334 (ibid., f. 307v); 1341 (PRO, E326/1937). D. by 28 Feb. 1344 (Lincoln, Ep. Reg., VI, f. 55v).

Thomas of Heigham (Hegham, Heyham) **1344–1359** Can. of Canons Ashby, eln quashed but apptd by bp 28 Feb. 1344 (ibid.). D. by 10 Dec. 1359 (Lincoln, Ep. Reg., IX, f. 228r).

Robert of Ashby (Asscheby, Assheby) **1359–** Can. of Canons Ashby, eln conf. 10 Dec. 1359 (ibid.). Occ. 1362 (PRO, E315/34/168); Jan. 1371 x Jan. 1372 (PRO, E329/1182); 1 Sept. 1392 (BL, Add. Cht. 22016); 1 Aug. 1397 (*CPL*, V, 44).

CANONSLEIGH (Devon), St Mary and St John the Evangelist f. *c.* 1161; 1284 refounded as abbey for canonesses.

Lists in *Ctl. Canonsleigh*, p. 116; *Heads*, I, 157–8.

R. Occ. 1206 (*Ctl. Canonsleigh*, no. 181); poss. identical with Richard 1200 x 1219 (ibid., no. 153).

Roger Occ. 26 Sept. 1238 (ibid., no. 142); *c.* 1240 (Devon RO, ED/M/48).

Henry Occ. 6 June 1249 (*Devon F.*, I, p. 258, no. 513; *Ctl. Canonsleigh*, no. 26); (H.) 11 Aug. 1253 (*Ctl. Canonsleigh*, no. 185); n.d. (1256 x 1259) (ibid., no. 201).

[**William of Chagford** (Chaggeforde) Eln quashed by bp's commissaries 1260 (*Reg. Bronescombe*, pp. 41, 120; *Reg. W. Bronescombe*, I, no. 282).]

Henry de Trewvineke 1260– Can. of Launceston, apptd by bp's commissaries 17 Dec. 1260 (*Reg. Bronescombe*, pp. 41, 122; *Reg. W. Bronescombe*, I, no. 282). Occ. from 1262 x 1263 to 28 Oct. 1282 (*Ctl. Canonsleigh*, app. I, no. xv; no. 29).

William de Ronetone 1283–1284 Inst. 26 Feb. 1283 by bp to whom the right of appt had been transferred (*Reg. Quivil*, p. 339). Evicted and gaoled 14 Aug. 1284 (PRO, KB27/106, m. 16).

On 12 Nov. 1299 a commn was issued to the pr. of Barlinch to act for the archbp of Canterbury who had received a papal mandate to judge the case of William de Burlescumbe and other cans. of Canonsleigh, who pleaded that they had been unjustly expelled from their monastery (*Reg. Winchelsey*, I, 364–5).

CANTERBURY (Kent), ST GREGORY f. 1086 (hospital); c. 1123 (priory)

Lists in *VCH Kent*, II, 159; *Ctl. St Gregory, Canterbury*, pp. 172–3 (to 1271); *Heads*, I, 158.

Robert of Osney (Oseneye) 1213–c. 1215 El. 1213 (*Ann. Dunstable*, p. 41). Res. 'post aliquot annos' to become a m. at Clairvaux (ibid., p. 41; cf. *Ctl. St Gregory*, p. 172).

Peter Occ. (P.) -1216 (*Ctl. St Gregory*, no. 45); c. 1222 (ibid., no. 170); 14 May 1223 (*Kent F.*, p. 78 = *Ctl. St Gregory*, no. 88).[10]

Thomas –?1241 Occ. July 1227 (*Ctl. St Gregory*, app. I, no. 5); 20 Oct. 1227 (*Kent F.*, p. 102 = *Ctl. St Gregory*, no. 83); 1230 (*Chartes de Saint-Bertin*, I, no. 759); 1234 (*Ctl. St Gregory*, no. 188); July 1240 (ibid., no. 219); 18 Oct. 1240 (ibid., app. I, no. 7). Lic. to el. (no reason given for vacancy), 1 July 1241 (*CPR 1232–47*, p. 254).

Nicholas of Shottenden (Shotindon) 1241– Can. of St Gregory's, royal ass. 22 July 1241, writ *de intendendo* 8 Aug. 1241 (ibid., pp. 255–6). Occ. 1243 (Canterbury D. & C., Ch. Ant. C.37); 15 July 1248 (*Kent F.*, p. 204).

Robert Occ. 2 June 1252, 13 Oct. 1253 (ibid., pp. 241, 251); May 1260 (*Ctl. St Gregory*, no. 209). ? Seal (*BM Seals*, no. 2856, could possibly be earlier Robert).

Hugh Occ. 1263 (Hasted, *Hist. of Kent* (2nd edn, 1801), XII, 142). Seal (*BM Seals*, nos. 2857–8).

William Pig Occ. 1 June 1271, 7 June 1271 (*Kent F.*, pp. 376–7; Canterbury D. & C., SVSB.III/87).

Henry Occ. 1279 x 1292, *temp.* Archbp Pecham (BL, Harl. Cht. 75 F 50); 25 Nov. 1276 (PRO, Kent F., CP25/1/98/58, no. 55). Seal (*BM Seals*, no. 2859).

Custody of temps. of the priory during vacancy gtd to Adam de Rouceby, priest, until the appt of a new pr., 19 Sept. 1279 (*Reg. Pecham*, I, 14–15).

Guy –1294 Occ. 4 July 1293 (BL, Harl. Cht. 80 D 5). D. 2 June 1294 (PRO, C84/12/6). D., lic. to el. 6 June 1294 (*CPR 1292–1301*, p. 71).

Elias of Sandwich (Sandwyco) 1294– Royal ass. 30 June 1294, temps. 14 July 1294 (ibid., pp. 77, 80). Eln conf. by pr. and convent of Christ Church, Canterbury *sede vacante* 10 July 1294 (*Canterbury Sede Vacante Institutions*, p. 28); mand. to install 25 July 1294 (ibid.).

[Mand. to archbp's commissary to order William de Heth', administrator of the temps. of the priory, to continue in office 7 Jan. 1299 (*Reg. Winchelsey*, I, 299).]

William de Lyndestede 1301– Eln conf. and commn to install 9 Dec. 1301 (ibid., I, 426).

John Occ. 25 Jan. 1325 (*CCR 1323–27*, p. 337). Possibly the unnamed pr. suspended following archbp's visitation, when 2 cans., Thomas Nichol and Robert de Wenchepe, were apptd to administer temps. n.d. (c. Mar. 1326) (Lambeth, Reg. Reynolds, ff. 148v–149r).

Thomas Occ. 28 Oct. 1340 (*CCR 1339–41*, p. 639).

Robert de Wenchepe –1349 D. by 10 June 1349 (*Canterbury Sede Vacante Institutions*, p. 28).

William atte Thorne 1349–1378 Can. of St Gregory's, eln conf. 10 June 1349 (ibid.). D. 5 Jan. 1378 (Lambeth, Reg. Sudbury, ff. 45r, 47r).

CARHAM (Northumberland), St Cuthbert (Kirkham) f. 1131+

Robert Chanbard Occ. 1293 (*Hist. Northumberland*, XI, 13, citing assize roll 21 Edward I).

---

[10] See *Ctl. St Gregory*, p. 172, n. 1 amending the *VCH* inclusion of Elias of Derham as pr. in 1225.

William of Thoralby (Thoraldby) Can. of Kirkham, papal prov. to vicarage of Newark 20 Jan. 1359; he is to res. the priory of Carham, about which he is litigating at the Curia (*CPL*, III, 604; *CPP*, p. 337).

The next recorded 'master' of Carham is **Richard Colyn**, can. of Kirkham, occ. 23 Apr. 1432 (*Reg. Langley*, IV, no. 996).

CARLISLE (Cumberland), St Mary (Arrouaisian) f. 1122 or ?1102 (priory); 1133 (Cath. priory).

List based mainly on *Le Neve 1066–1300*, pp. 22–3; *1300–1541*, pp. 99–100; lists also in *VCH Cumberland*, II, 150–1; *Heads*, I, 158.

Henry de Mareis 1214–?1217 Can. of Merton, el. 26 June x 25 Aug. 1214 (*Rot. Lit. Claus.*, I, 211b). Occ. Nov. 1214 (*Ch. Lanercost*, p. 14); (H.) *c.* 1203 x 14 (*HMC 10th Rep.*, IV, 322). House prob. vacant by 26 Apr. 1217 (Rymer, *Foedera*, I, 147; *Le Neve 1066–1300*, p. 22).

Bartholomew –1231/2 Prob. appointed by legate Guala 1218 (*CChR 1257–1300*, pp. 363–5; *Guala Letters*, no. 13n.; Sayers, *Honorius III*, p. 175). Prob. the unnamed pr. who occ. 20 July, 21 Aug. 1219 (*Reg. Hon. III*, nos. 2156, 2181). Occ. (B.) 1219 x 23 (*Ctl. Wetheral*, no.20 – as Bartholomew prob. 1219 x 1223, no. 29; *Ctl. Lanercost*, nos. 178–9; Bodl., ms. Top. Yorks e. 8, ff. 70v–71r; *Ctl. Newminster*, p. 216); Hil. term 1229 (*CRR*, XIII, no. 1508). Last occ. 1230 or 1231(*Ctl. Wetheral*, nos. 59, 129). D. 1231(x 1232) (*Ch. Lanercost*, p. 41).

Ralph Barri 1231/2–1248 Succ. 1231(x 1232) (ibid., p. 41). Nephew of Walter Mauclerc, bp of Carlisle (ibid). Occ. (R.) 12 May 1232 (*Ctl. Holm Cultram*, no. 223). D. 9 Feb. 1248 (*Ch. Lanercost*, p. 53).

Robert 1248–?1258 First occ. 22 Oct. 1248 (Hodgson, *Northumberland*, III, ii, 144). Occ. 1251 (*Ctl. Fountains*, I , 202). Last certain ref. 31 Dec. 1252 (*Ctl. Lanercost*, no. 185); 1248 x 1256 (ibid., no. 56). Res. by 14 Jan. 1258 (*Northumberland Pleas*, p. 192, nos. 570–1), cf. 17 Dec. 1258 at time of bp's visitation when ordered by the Pope to return from the church of Corbridge (to which he had been sent by the bp of Carlisle) to the cloister of Carlisle (*Les Registres d'Alexandre IV*, no. 1734; *CPL*, I, 361–2).

John Occ. 14 Jan. 1258 (*Northumberland Pleas*, p. 192, nos. 570–1); 15 May 1263 (Hull Univ., DDCA(1)/20/86).

Robert II Occ. (R.) 27 Aug. 1267 (*Ctl. Lanercost*, no. 314); 1276 (*Northumberland & Durham Deeds*, p. 40n.); 2 Nov 1278, 19 Nov 1278 (*Cumbd. F.*, p. 228; PRO, Cumb. F., CP25/1/35/5 no. 6; 35/5 no. 8); 27 Dec. 1278 (PRO, C84/6/12); Easter 1282 (PRO, CP40/45, m. 66); 11 July 1282 (*Letters from Northern Regs.*, p. 251). 24 Apr. 1283 (*Reg. Halton*, I, 32).

Adam of Warwick (Warthwyk) **–1304** Said to have succ. 1284, but no source (*Reg. Halton*, I, p. xxxii). Occ. 3 Nov. 1285 (*CPR 1330–34*, p. 111); 1287, 1288, (A.) 1296, 1301, 1302 (*Ctl. Lanercost*, nos. 239, 241; *Reg. Halton*, I, 39, 89, 119, 177). Res. 18 Sept. 1304 (ibid., 223–4); provision made for him 19 Sept. 1304 (ibid., 224–6).

William of Haltwhistle (Hautewysil) **1304–1308** Lic. sought to el. new pr. 18 Sept. 1304 (ibid., 223–4). Occ. 17 May 1306 (ibid., 251). Res. and lic.to el. new pr. sought 28 Sept. 1308 (ibid., 297–8).[11]

Robert de Helpeston 1308–1314 Ass. of bp 1 Oct. 1308 (ibid, 301). Occ. (R.) 3 Aug. 1309 (ibid., 323); 9 Nov. 1309 (*Ctl. Lanercost*, no. 251); 14 Jan. 1310, 21 Dec. 1312 (*Reg. Halton*, I, 13, 66). Commn to vicar-general with authority to adm. the cess. of pr. Robert 4 July 1314 (ibid., 99). But cf. mentioned 6 Nov. 1333 as having demised property 14 Edward II (July 1320 x July 1321 (*CCR 1330–33*, p. 357).

Gilbert of Crosby (Crosseby) **1314–** Prof. obed. for the priory's churches in the Durham

---

[11] In a case of Trin. 1309 William is still described as pr. (PRO, CP40/178, m. 203).

diocese 10 Sept. 1314 (*Reg. Pal. Dun.*, I, 605–6). Occ. 13 Jan. 1316, (G.) *c.* 14 Mar. 1316, (G.) 28 May 1316 (*Reg. Halton*, II, 233, 119, 121); 21 Oct. 1318 (ibid., 233).

Alan Occ. 28 Jan. 1319 (*CPR 1317–21*, p. 270); 18 June 1321(*CPR 1321–1325*, p. 3).

Simon of Haltwhistle (Hautwysell) –**1325** Occ. (S.) 1 Feb. 1324 (*Reg. Halton*, II, 233; *Parlty Writs*, II, div. 3, p. 646); 11 Feb. 1325 (York, Reg. 9B, f. 589r). D., lic. to el. sought by conv. 13 July 1325 (*Reg. Kirkby*, I, no. 78).

William Occ. Mich. 1327 (*Index to Placita de Banco*, p. 75).

John of Kirkby (Kirkeby) –**1332** Occ. 6 Oct. 1330 when excommunicated for not paying tenths; excommunicated 3 Jan. 1331 (*Reg. Kirkby*, I, nos. 11, 57); commn to proceed against pr. John and remove him from office 1 Feb. 1331 (ibid., no. 18). Occ. 4 May 1331 (*CCR 1330–33*, p. 310). Bp. of Carlisle 1332.

Geoffrey Occ. 8 Mar. 1334 (*CCR 1333–37*, p. 302); 9 Mar. 1334 (York, Reg. 9A, f. 64r); (G.) n.d. (late 1337) (*Reg. Kirkby*, I, no. 421).

John of Horncastle (Horncastell, Horncastre) ?**1352–1376** Lic. of archbp of York to eln of a new pr. 2 July 1352 (PRO, C84/23/51). Occ. as. pr. 10 Jan. 1353, when royal ass. given to his eln as bp of Carlisle (*CPR 1350–54*, p. 384), temps. 22 Feb. 1353 (ibid., pp. 408–9). Eln set aside by provision of Gilbert of Welton as bp 13 Feb. 1353 (*Le Neve 1300–1541*, p. 97); temps gtd to Bp Gilbert 26 June 1353 (*CPR 1350–54*, p. 470). Occ. as pr. 1359 (*Reg. Welton*, no. 261); 1360, 1362 (ibid., nos. 297, 509); 1363 (*CPP*, p. 437). Commn to receive res. 10 Nov. 1376 (Carlisle, DRC/1/2, p. 289).

John (of) Penrith (Penreth) **1376–1381** Lic. to el. sought 13 Nov. 1376 and gt n.d. (ibid.). Occ. 17 Feb. 1378 (ibid., p. 306); 1379 (PRO, E179/60/1, m. 1). Res. by 9 Aug 1381 (ibid., p. 337).

CARMARTHEN, St John the Evangelist and St Theulac f. -1127 (Aug.)

List in *Heads*, I, 158; also list by G.E. Evans in *Trans. Carmarthenshire Antiq. Soc. & Field Club*, V (1909–10), 69–70.

Robert of Carmarthen (Kaermerdin) **1246–1253** Royal ass. 9 Nov. 1246 (*CPR 1232–47*, p. 492). Cess., lic. to el. 23 Mar. 1253 (*CPR 1247–58*, p. 185).

Walter of Haverford 1253–1266 Mand. for seisin 15 June 1253 (*CR 1251–53*, pp. 369–70). Cess. by 15 Feb. 1266 (PRO, C84/3/23). Lic. to el. 27 Feb. 1266 (*CPR 1258–66*, p. 561).

Walter's successor (name illegible, ? Thomas) postulated and pres. to king for royal ass. 15 Feb. 1266 (PRO, C84/3/23).

Thomas Occ. 20 Apr. 1272 (*CPR 1266–72*, p. 709).

Request from convent to Edmund son of King Henry III for permission to el. a fit person as pr. 15 June 1277 (PRO, DL25/974).

William of Wycumbe (Wycomb) –**1281** Letter from Queen Eleanor to Robert Burnell, bp of Bath and Wells requesting him to expedite the business of her chaplain, pr. William 16 Feb. [no year] (1276 x 1281) (*Cal. Anc. Corr. Wales*, p. 116). Transferred to abbey of Hartland (PRO, C84/7/23). Lic. to el. 1 May 1281 (*CPR 1272–81*, p. 430).

John Edrich (Edrych, Istrigge) **1281–** Can. of Carmarthen, eln pres. to king for royal ass. 11 May 1281 (PRO, C84/7/23); royal ass. 24 May 1281, temps. 26 May 1281 (*CPR 1272–81*, pp. 437, 440). Occ. late 13th cent. (*Ctl. Carmarthen*, nos. 2–4, 10, 23–4); 22–3 Jan. 1289 (*Litt. Wallie*, nos. 313, 315); 10 Feb. 1299 (*Cal. Anc. Pet. Wales*, p. 368). Is he the unnamed pr. apptd treasurer of West and South Wales 2 Apr. 1299 (*CFR 1272–1307*, p. 411)?

Robert de Daviston –**1324** Occ. Sept. 1314 x May 1315 (*Welsh Memoranda*, no. 418); 1 Nov. 1315 (*Cal. Anc. Pet. Wales*, p. 195); 23 Nov. 1318 (*CChR 1300–26*, p. 397); (unnamed) apptd chamberlain of South Wales 1318 (*CFR 1307–19*, p. 375). Res. by 27 Sept. 1324 'senex et decrepitus' (PRO, C84/20/38). Res., lic. to el. 5 Oct. 1324 (*CPR 1324–27*, p. 33)

John Chaundos (Chaundoys) **1324–1332** Can. of Carmarthen, eln pres. to king for royal ass. 15 Oct. 1324 (PRO, C84/20/40); royal ass. 30 Oct 1324, temps. 10 Nov. 1324 (*CPR 1324–27*, pp. 37, 45); cert. of conf. of eln by bp of St Davids 4 Nov. 1324 (PRO, C84/20/41). Res., lic. to el. 13 Jan. 1332 (*CPR 1330–34*, p. 381).

John Wynter Occ. 21 Mar. 1333 (*CCR 1333–37*, p. 21); Hilary 1338 (*CPR 1338–40*, p. 553); 1354, 27 Mar. 1355, 12 Oct. 1355, chamberlain of South Wales (*Ctl. Carmarthen*, nos. 121, 119). The 1355 case lists the succession of priors from the late 13th cent., viz. John Istrygge (Edrich); Robert; John Chaundos; and John Wynter (ibid., no. 119).

William Symunds (Symond, Symonis) Occ. many times in *Ctl. Carmarthen* from 27 Aug. 1359 to 15 Aug. 1369 (nos. 109, 96).

John Jussell Occ. 1369 (*Mon. Angl.*, VI, 431); 1 Mar. 1371, 28 Jan. 1384 (*Ctl. Carmarthen*, nos. 117–18).

The next recorded pr., **Walter Taymer**, occ. 1391 (*Ctl. Carmarthen*, no. 77); 15 Nov. 1393 (*CFR 1391–96*, p. 100).

CARTMEL (Lancs), St Mary f. 1189 x 1194
Lists in *VCH Lancs*, II, 148; *Heads*, I, 158; see also J. Stockdale, *Annales Caermoelenses* (1872), p. 23; J.C. Dickinson, *The Priory of Cartmel* (1991), app. 3, p. 117.

William Latest recorded occ. 14 Aug. 1214 (*Ctl. Furness*, II, ii, 312; PRO, DL.27/133). Seal (*Mon. Seals*, p. 20).

Absolon Occ. 1219, 6 July 1221 (*Ctl. Furness*, I, iii, 806; II, ii, 321); (A.) Christmas 1230 (*Reg. Gray*, p.161n.); (A.) 1 Jan. 1231 (*Ctl. Furness*, I, ii, 442). Seal (*Mon. Seals*, p. 20 – from PRO, DL25/282, n.d., early 13th cent., but erroneously dated 1285 x 1288 in calendar).

Election custom annulled 1233, whereby on the d. of a pr. two persons are pres. to their patron that he may choose one of them, with the approval of the diocesan bp (*CPL*, I, 135).

John Occ. 5 Mar. 1236 (*Ctl. Furness*, II, i, 90).

Richard Occ. 25 June 1250 (*Lancs F.*, I, 111).

William of Walton Occ. 3 Nov. 1279 (ibid.,156); 1292 (PRO, Just.1/410, m. 53d); presumably the unnamed pr. going to Ireland and given the king's protection for 2 years Nov. 1292 (*CPR 1281–92*, p. 510); 1300 (Stockdale list, with no source). Ledger stone in Cartmel church (R.H. Kirby ed., *The Rural Deanery of Cartmel*, p. 22; *Earliest English Brasses*, p. 196 & fig. 206; J.C. Dickinson, *The Priory of Cartmel*, p. 56).

Simon Occ. n.d. (1332 x 1333) (PRO, C270/8/6); 1334 (PRO, KB27/298, m. 27).

A lic. to el. (no reason for vacancy) was issued 20 Sept. 1349 (*CPR 1348–50*, p. 411).

William of Kendal (Kendale) **–1356** Occ. 21 Jan. 1353 (*CPR 1350–54*, p. 383); July 1354 (PRO, DL35/3, m. 1). Cess. by 5 Mar. 1356 (PRO, C84/27/50). Cess., lic. to el. 18 Mar. 1356 (*CPR 1354–58*, p. 350).

Richard of Kellet (Kellech') **1356–1381** Can. of Cartmel, eln pres. to king for royal ass. 26 Sept. 1356 (PRO, C84/27/50); royal ass. 8 Oct. 1356, temps. 24 Oct. 1356 (*CPR 1354–58*, pp. 439, 458). Cert. of conf. of eln by archdn of Richmond 18 Oct. 1356 (PRO, C84/27/33). Conf. by Pope Urban V 7 Mar. 1369 (*Accts of Papal Collectors*, pp. 320, 358, 399, 512). D., lic. to el. 22 Jan. 1381 (*CPR 1377–81*, p. 584; PRO, C84/32/32).

CATHALE (Herts), f. -1189?; -1240 (granted to Cheshunt)
See *VCH Herts*, IV, 426 (no list).

Hugh Occ. 1216 x 1226 (BL, Stowe Cht. 157); Oct. 1221 x Oct. 1222 (WAM, no. 2185, pd Wethered, *St Mary's Hurley in the middle ages*, p. 107, no. 50); occ. 1220 (BL, Harl. ms. 3697, f. 211r, cited in H.C. Andrews, 'Cathale priory, Herts.: its history and site' in *Trans. East Herts. Arch. Soc.*, VI (1915), 90–7, at 92–3).

CHACOMBE (Northants), St Peter and St Paul f. *temp.* Henry II
Lists in *VCH Northants*, II, 134–5 (from 1241); *Heads*, I, 159.

Thomas Occ. 3 Nov. 1222 (PRO, Leics F. CP25/1/121/10 no. 82); 3 Nov. 1226 (ibid., 121/12, no. 137); 19 Nov. 1226 (*Warws F.*, I, no. 384); Oct. 1226 x Oct. 1227 (PRO, E210/7745).

An unnamed pr., prob. Thomas, d. 1230 and a pr. of Osney succeeded (*Ann. Dunstable*, p. 125).

William of Collingham (Colingham) **1240/1–1279** Can. of Chacombe, inst. June 1240 x June 1241, no reason given for vacancy (*Reg. Grosseteste*, p. 204). Occ. 1251 (PRO, Northants F. CP25/1/173/37 no. 585); 3 Feb. 1262, 13 June 1266 (*Oxford F.*, pp. 190, 194); Nov. 1278 x Nov. 1279 (PRO, E315/45/298). D. by *c.* Nov. 1279 (*Reg. R. Gravesend*, p. 307).

Adam of Appleby (Appelby) **1279–1299** El. and adm. *c.* Nov. 1279 (ibid.). D. by 1 May 1299 (*Reg. Sutton*, II, 162).

Robert of Wardon 1299–1302 Can. of Chacombe, eln conf. 1 May 1299 (ibid.). D. by 18 Nov. 1302 (Lincoln, Ep. Reg., II, f. 105v).

Alexander de Kaysthorp (Kaystorp) **1302–1326** Can. of Chacombe, eln quashed but apptd by bp 18 Nov. 1302 (ibid.). D. by 14 Apr. 1326 (PRO, C84/21/4; cf. *CCR 1323–27*, p. 469).

Roger of Sileby (Silby, Syleby) **1326–1333** Can. of Chacombe, royal. ass. 19 Apr. 1326 (*CPR 1324–27*, p. 258). Eln quashed but apptd by bp 5 May 1326 (Lincoln, Ep. Reg., IV, f. 174v). D. by 16 (22) Mar. 1333 (*CCR 1337–39*, p. 24; cf. *CPR 1330–34*, p. 416). Prob. the pr. Roger mentd in 1387 as a predecessor of the then pr. (*Staffs Plea Rolls 1387–1405*, p. 5).

Thomas of Saxton 1333–1340 Can. of Chacombe, royal ass. 16 Mar. 1333 (*CPR 1330–34*, p. 416). Eln pres. to bp 13 Apr. 1333; eln quashed but apptd by bp 17 Apr. 1333 (Lincoln, Ep. Reg., IV, f. 195v). Res. by Jan x Mar. 1340 (ibid., f. 230r).

Henry of Kegworth 1340–1371 Sub-pr. and conv. asked bp's vicar-general to appt; Henry, can. of Chacombe, apptd by vicar-general n.d. [between entries 28 Jan. x 3 Mar. 1340] (ibid.). D. by 20 Mar. 1371 (PRO, C84/30/34, cf. *CCR 1369–74*, p. 219). Seal (*Mon. Seals*, p. 21; *BM Seals*, no. 2897).

Edmund (of) Thorpe (Throp) **1371–** Can. of Chacombe, royal. ass. 20 Mar. 1371 (*CPR 1370–74*, p. 56; cf. PRO, C84/30/34). Occ. 1372 (PRO, E40/6182); (Esmond) 1376 (BL Harl. Cht. 85 G 32); June 1380 x June 1381 (PRO, E42/469); 1386 (PRO, E326/8662); 6 Dec. 1405, 6 Apr. 1406 (*Reg. Repingdon*, I, 59, 105).

CHARLEY (Leics), St Mary f. -1190
Lists in *VCH Leics*, II, 24; *Heads*, I, 159.

William Occ. 1207 x 1219 (Nichols, *Leics*, III, i, 120); *temp.* Henry III (pal.) (*HMC Hastings*, I, 12).

Simon –1264 Res. by 29 Jan. 1264 (*Reg. R. Gravesend*, p. 143).

Robert of Grimsby (Grimesby) **1264–1272** Can. of Charley, apptd and inst. by bp 29 Jan. 1264 (ibid., pp. 143, 309). Res. by 19 June 1272 (ibid, p. 153).

John of Bawtry (Bautr(e)) **1272–1285** Can. of Charley, eln conf. 19 June 1272 (ibid., pp. 153, 312). Commn of oyer and terminer, pr. and others accused of robbery 18 Oct. 1283 (*CPR 1281–92*, p. 102). Res. by 9 Apr. 1285 (*Reg. Sutton*, III, 94). Pr. of Charley was instructed 20 June 1296 to report on the visit to Ireland of John of Bawtry their late pr. and on the circumstances of his return (ibid., V, 161).

Stephen of Keyham (Cainham, Cayham) **1285–1291** Can. of Charley, apptd *per lapsum* by bp 9 Apr 1285, 3 months having elapsed without an eln (ibid., III, 93–4). Commn to receive res. 4 May 1291 (ibid., III, 95). Res. by 9 May 1291 (ibid.,VIII, 48).

Thomas of Evesham 1291–1298 Can. of Ulverscroft, eln quashed but apptd by bp 9 May 1291 (ibid.). Res. by 19 Mar. 1298 to join Cistercians and entered Garendon (ibid, 68).

[**Robert de Radeclive** Can. of Charley, eln quashed on ground of unsuitability 19 Mar. 1298 (ibid.).]

John of Bawtry 1298–1309 El. on res. of Thomas of Evesham and the rejection of Robert of Radeclive; eln quashed but apptd by bp 3 Aug. 1298 as the best of three candidates in the depressed state of the house (ibid.). Res. by 9 Aug. 1309 (Lincoln, Ep. Reg., II, f. 203v).

William of Seagrave (Segrave) **1309–1319** Can. of Charley, eln quashed but apptd by bp 9 Aug. 1309 (ibid.). D. by 16 May 1319 (ibid., f. 217r–v).

William of Leicester (Leicestr') **1319–** Can. of Ulverscroft, eln quashed but apptd by bp's official 16 May 1319 (ibid.). Occ. 26 Jan. 1328 (*CPR 1327–30*, p. 275).

Henry de Stretford –1335 Commn to receive cess. and supervise eln 1 June 1335 (Lincoln, Ep. Reg., V, ff. 498v–499r).

Roger of Glen Occ. Hil. 1368 (Farnham, *Charnwood Forest*, p. 193). Pardon for receiving an apostate Franciscan friar and others who had committed felonies 21 Oct. 1371 (*CPR 1370–74*, p. 140).

John Attewell Occ. 1377 (*Clerical Poll-Taxes*, p. 28, no. 376).

Ralph of Bingham (Byngham) **1382–** Can. of Ulverscroft, apptd by bp, the right of appt having devolved to bp *hac vice*, no reason given for vacancy 19 May 1382 (Lincoln, Ep. Reg., X, f. 277v). Occ. Hil. term 1390 (Farnham, *Charnwood Forest*, p. 193).

Richard de Haitlee 1382 Can. of Rocester, pres. 26 July 1382, in the king's gift by reason of the custody of the land and heir of Henry de Beaumont, knight (*CPR 1381–1385*, p. 157). Presumably ineffective.

CHETWODE (Bucks), St Mary and St Nicholas f. 1245 (1460–1 annexed to Notley as a cell)

   List in *VCH Bucks*, I, 381.

[**Robert de Keinton** Chaplain of hermitage inst. to hermitage June 1242 x June 1243 (*Reg. Grosseteste*, p. 361).] **Thomas of Hanworth** (Haneworth) **1245–1262** Can. of Thurgarton, adm. June 1244 x June 1245, presumably 1245 (foundation) (*Reg. Grosseteste*, p. 369). Res. 13 Jan. 1262 (PRO, C84/2/26). Cess., lic to el. 18 Jan. 1262 (*CPR 1258–66*, p. 197).

John of Woodstock (Wodestok) **1262–** Sub-pr. of Bicester, eln pres. to king for royal ass. 7 Feb. 1262 (PRO, C84/2/27); royal ass. 10 Feb. 1262 (*CPR 1258–66*, p. 200). Postulated and inst. Nov. 1261 x Nov. 1262 on res. of unnamed pr. (*Reg. R. Gravesend*, p. 237). Occ. 7 Feb. 1262 (ibid., p. 8); 11 Apr. 1266 (*Ctl. Oseney*, V, 480). Mentioned 12 Aug. 1267, as former pr. (*CPR 1266–72*, p. 98)

William de Dadington (Dadigton) **1270–** Can. of Chetwode, royal ass 8 Nov. 1270 (ibid., p. 490). First eln irregular, but chosen at the second eln and provided and preferred by the bp's commissary 13 Nov. 1270, no reason given for vacancy (*Reg. R. Gravesend*, pp. 246–7, 343). Occ. 5 Dec. 1286 (*CPR 1281–92*, p. 261).

William of Brixworth (Brickelesworth, Brikelesworth, Brikhill) **–1304** The house had been taken by the escheator on grounds of William's infirmity but bp's mand. to recover dated 7 Mar. 1304 (Lincoln, Ep. Reg., III, f. 64v). Res. on 3 Nov. 1304 (ibid., f.. 75r; PRO, C84/15/20). Res., lic. to el. 11 Nov. 1304 (*CPR 1301–07*, p. 267).

Roger of Lyneham (Lenham, Linham, Lynham) **1304–1317** Can. of Chetwode, eln pres. to king for royal ass. 20 Nov. 1304 (PRO, C84/15/23); royal ass. 26 Nov. 1304, temps. 12 Dec. 1304 (*CPR 1301–07*, pp. 291, 303). Eln conf. 8 Dec. 1304 (Lincoln, Ep. Reg., II, f. 176v; PRO, C84/15/24). Res., lic. to el. 18 Mar. 1317 (*CPR 1313–17*, p. 60).

John of Warmington (Warmyn(g)ton) **1317–1337** Can. of Chetwode, royal ass. 31 Mar. 1317, temps. 4 May 1317 (ibid., pp. 633, 647). Eln quashed but apptd by bp 28 Apr. 1317 (Lincoln, Ep. Reg., II, f. 189v). D., lic. to el. 28 June 1328 (*CPR 1327–30*, p. 304).

Robert of Brackley (Brackele) 1328–1337 Can. of Chetwode, royal ass. 15 July 1328, temps.
11 Aug. 1328 (ibid., pp. 305, 313). D. by 8 Aug. 1337 (PRO, C84/24/2). D., lic. to el. 10 Aug.
1337 (*CPR 1334–38*, p. 485).

William of Halton 1337–1349 Can. of Chetwode, royal ass. 16 Aug. 1337, temps. 26 Aug. 1337
(ibid., pp. 488, 500). Sub-pr. and convent asked bp to appt; he apptd 26 Aug. 1337 (Lincoln,
Ep. Reg., IV,f. 350r). D. by 14 May 1349 (PRO, C84/25/38). D., lic. to el. 15 May 1349 (*CPR
1348–50*, p. 292).

Henry de Wykham 1349–1361 Can. of Chetwode, royal ass. 28 May 1349, temps. 20 June 1349
(ibid., pp. 295, 325). Eln quashed but apptd by bp 9 June 1349 (Lincoln, Ep. Reg., IX, ff.
287v–288r; PRO, C84/26/3). D. by 7 Oct. 1361 (PRO, C84/28/11). D., lic. to el. 11 Oct.
1361 (*CPR 1361–64*, p. 81).

John of Westbury 1361–1387 Can. of Chetwode, eln pres. to king for royal ass. 23 Oct. 1361
(PRO, C84/23/38); royal ass. 26 Oct. 1361, temps. 22 Nov. 1361 (*CPR 1361–64*, pp. 99,
116–17). Commn to examine eln dated 4 Nov. 1361; eln conf. 13 Nov. 1361 (Lincoln, Ep.
Reg., IX, f. 321v). D., lic. to el. 29 Jan. 1387 (*CPR 1385–89*, p. 266; cf. Lincoln, Ep. Reg.,
XI, f. 385r).

CHIPLEY (Suffolk), St Mary f. -1235
List in *VCH Suffolk*, II, 99.

Adam Occ. Oct. 1234 x Oct. 1235, Oct. 1239 x Oct. 1240 (*Suffolk F. (Rye)*, pp. 34, 45).

John of Cavendish (Cavenedisch, Cavendissh) 1308–1333 Can. of Chipley, eln conf. 1 Feb.
1308, no reason given for vacancy (Norwich, Reg/1/1, f. 26r). D. by 8 Dec. 1333 (Norwich,
Reg/1/2, f. 62r).

Richard of Norwich (Norwico) 1333–1350 Can. of Chipley, eln conf. 8 Dec. 1333 (ibid.). D.
by 15 Mar. 1350 (Norwich, Reg/2/4, f. 120r).

David de Fornham/Thornham 1350 Can. of Chipley, apptd 15 Mar. 1350 (ibid.). Res. by 17
Dec. 1350 (ibid., f. 129r).

Reginald of Rushford (Russheworth) 1350– Can. of Chipley, apptd by bp 17 Dec. 1350, no
eln having taken place on account of the lack of canons (ibid.).

Thomas of Hepworth (Heppeworth) –1370 Res. by 2 Dec. 1370 (Norwich, Reg/3/6, f. 3v).
Thomas became pr. again in 1396 (ibid., f. 210r).

Richard Man 1370–1396 Can. of Chipley, apptd by bp 2 Dec. 1370 (ibid., f. 3v). Res. by 5 May
1396 (ibid., f. 210r).

CHIRBURY (Salop), St Michael f. c. 1190 (at Snead); c. 1195 (at Chirbury)[12]
Lists in *VCH Salop*, II, 61–2; *Heads*, I, 159.

Richard –1217 Res. to be abb. of Wellow, royal ass. 10 Aug. 1217 (*CPR 1216–25*, p. 83).

Philip Occ. n.d. (1219 x 1227) (*EEA*, 7, no. 319; *CChR 1226–57*, p. 53); ante 23 July 1227, when
cht. inspected (*CChR 1300–26*, p. 225); 20 Nov. 1256 (PRO, E326/2640); n.d. (PRO,
E315/38/194; 315/42/272; E326/926; E326/3960).

?Wa(lter) Pr.'s seal (bearing the name Wa . . . (? Walter), is attached to 13th-cent. cht. (PRO,
E326/8687; *Mon. Seals*, p. 22).

Osbert –1280 Occ. n.d. (13th cent.) (PRO, E326/3168; E326/8027). Unnamed pr. of
Wormsley apptd as coadjutor for unnamed pr. of Chirbury 9 Jan. 1280 (*Reg. Cantilupe*, p.
228). Bp of Hereford received res. 6 June 1280 (PRO, SC1/30/10). Res., lic. to. el. 23 June
1280 (*CPR 1272–81*, p. 383).

---

[12] The canons remained at Chirbury until the Dissolution although a lic. to return to Snead was issued 21
May 1281 (*CPR 1272–81*, p. 436).

Geoffrey de Menedep 1280–1287 Can. of Wormsley, eln pres. to king for royal ass. 1 July 1280 (PRO, C84/6/44); royal ass. 6 July 1280, writ *de intendendo* 2 Aug. 1280, having been postulated and conf. by vicegerent of bp of Hereford (*CPR 1272–81*, pp. 385, 392). D., lic. to el. 18 June 1287 (*CPR 1281–92*, p. 271).[13]

Adam de Hopton 1287–1299 Can. of Chirbury, eln pres. to king for royal ass. 4 July 1287 (PRO, C84/9/7); royal ass. 16 July 1287, temps. 21 July 1287 (*CPR 1281–92*, p. 276). Cert. conf. eln by bp of Hereford 18 July 1287 (PRO, C84/9/11). Letter of res. 26 Oct. 1299 on account of age and ill-health (*Reg. Swinfield*, p. 365), but cf. Res. by 16 Sept. 1299 (PRO, C84/13/35). Res., lic. to el. 26 Sept. 1299 (*CPR 1292–1301*, p. 440).

Roger of Rorrington (Rorinton, Romertone) *alias* **Rufin** (Ruffyn) **1299–1314** Can. of Chirbury, eln pres. to king for royal ass. 7 Nov. 1299 (PRO, C84/9/42); royal ass. 16 Nov. 1299, temps. 14 Dec. 1299 (*CPR 1292–1301*, pp. 454, 483). Eln conf. 25 Nov. 1299 (*Reg. Swinfield*, p. 365; PRO, C84/13/41). Occ. (Rufin) Nov. 1299 x Nov. 1300 (PRO, E326/11640). D. by 4 Aug. 1314 (PRO, C84/17/36; cf. (Ruffyn) *Reg. Swinfield*, p. 494). D. (R.), lic. to el. 11 Aug. 1314 (*CPR 1313–17*, p. 163).

Philip de Montgomeri 1314–1322 Sub-pr. of Chirbury, el. 16 Aug. 1314 (*Reg. Swinfield*, p. 494); royal ass. 27 Aug. 1314, temps. 13 Sept. 1314 (*CPR 1313–17*, pp. 167, 173; *Reg. Swinfield*, p. 494). Mand. to convent to obey him 7 Sept. 1314 (ibid., pp. 494–5; cf. PRO, C84/17/39). Cited to appear before bp 6 Mar. 1321 (*Reg. Orleton (Hereford)*, p. 212). Removed from office by bp 16 Mar. 1322 (ibid., pp. 215–16). Request for lic. to el. on Philip's cess. 14 Apr. 1322, mand. to issue letters 23 Apr. 1322 (*Cal. Chanc. Warr.*, p. 528). Res., lic. to el. 24 Apr. 1322 (*CPR 1321–24*, p. 102).

Hugh of Hereford (Herefordia) (Henry *VCH*) **1322–** Can. of Chirbury, eln pres. to king for royal ass. 30 Apr. 1322 (PRO, C84/20/14); royal ass. 14 May 1322, temps. 20 June 1322 (*CPR 1321–24*, pp. 112, 135). Any opposers to eln cited 16 May 1322 (*Reg. Orleton (Hereford)*, pp. 226–7). Commn to examine eln 8 June 1322 (ibid., p. 229). King informed 10 June 1322 that eln of Hugh had been conf. (ibid., p. 228; PRO, C84/20/16). Mentd 14 Mar. 1345 relating to events *temp.* Bp Orleton – it is not clear whether he is still alive in 1345 (*Reg. Trillek*, p. 68).

Thomas of Chirbury (Chirebury) **1369–1374** Adm. 27 Feb. 1369 by *sede vacante* custodians (*Reg. L. Charlton*, p. 57). Vacated by 16 Jan. 1374 when convent asked patron, Edmund Mortimer, earl of March, to adm. a pr. and write to bp of Hereford to conf. him (BL, Add. ms. 6041, f. 32r. no. xii).

The next recorded pr. **Walter**, occ. 1406 (SRRC, 3365/816).

CHRISTCHURCH (Hants), Holy Trinity (Twynham) f. -1066 (secular canons); *c.* 1150 (Augustinian).

Lists in *VCH Hants*, II, 10; *Heads*, I, 159. List in ctl., BL, Cotton ms. Tiberius D VI, part 2, f. 134v.

Roger 4th pr., *temp.* Henry III, anno 9 (ctl. list, i.e. Oct. 1224 x Oct. 1225). Occ *temp.* John – ? early thirteenth cent (? pal.: *Berkeley Chts.*, no. 96); 20 Jan. 1225, 20 Mar. 1227 (*Dorset F.*, pp. 27, 30; BL, Cotton ms. Tiberius D VI, part 1, f. 100v; part 2, ff. 4r, 9r); 23 Mar. 1228 (PRO, Hants F., CP25/1/203/5, no. 24).

Richard 1229– 5th pr. (ctl. list). (R.) sub-pr. of Christchurch, royal ass. 22 Sept. 1229 (*CPR 1225–32*, p. 267). Occ. 15 Jan. 1231 (*CCR 1227–31*, p. 578); 10 Feb. 1232 (BL, Cotton ms. Tiberius D VI, part 1, f. 47v).

Nicholas de Warham and **Nicholas of Sturminster** (Sturmynstr') 6th pr. and 7th pr. (ctl. list). It is impossible to distinguish between the two priors Nicholas. In the ctl. list the date

---

[13] Pr. Geoffrey, said to occ. 14th cent. (*HMC Westmorland etc.*, p. 399), is actually late 13th cent. (pal.) (now NLW, Powis Castle records, box 14 (uncatalogued)), and fits in with Geoffrey de Menedep.

1272 is placed midway between the names of Nicholas of Sturminster and John of Abingdon. From the other evidence it would seem that it refers to John. Nicholas occ. Trin. term 1236 (*CRR*, XV, no. 2000); 1244 (*Sarum Chts.*, p. 291, no. ccxlix); 1245 (ibid. p. 294, no. cclii); 1249 (*Devon F.*, I, p. 243, no. 478); 25 June 1256 (BL, Cotton ms. Tiberius D VI, part 2, f. 3r); 11 May 1258 (ibid., part 1, f. 161v); 25 Dec. 1261 (ibid., f. 84r).

John of Abingdon (Abyngdon) 8th pr. (ctl. list). Occ. 15 Apr. 1263 (PRO, Hants F., CP 25/1/203/10, no. 45); from 1263 to 30 May 1277 (BL, Cotton ms. Tiberius D VI, part 1, ff. 98r, 99r, 101r; part 2, f. 20r); 23 Feb. 1272 (PRO, Hants F., CP25/1/204/11, no. 49); (J.) 24 Feb. 1278 (BL, Cotton ms. Tiberius D VI, part 1, f. 68v), but see next entry.

William of Netheravon (Nitheravene, Nytherhavene) 9th pr., conf. Nov. 1276 x Nov. 1277 (according to ctl. list, but see previous entry). Occ. 18 Mar. 1279, 9 Feb. 1280, 12 Mar. 1283, 24 Feb. 1284, 29 Aug. 1285 (BL, Cotton ms. Tiberius D VI, part 1, ff. 131r–v, 32v, 143v; part 2, f. 10r).

Richard Maury (Mauri) 1287–1302 10th pr. (ctl. list). Sub-pr. of Christchurch, adm. and mand. to induct 15 May 1286 (*Reg. Pontissara*, I, 23, 322–3). D., lic. to el. 7 Mar. 1302 (*CPR 1301–07*, p. 24; *Reg. Pontissara*, I, 134).

William Quintin (Quentyn, Quintyn, Quyntin, Quynton, Quyntyn) 1302–1317 11th pr. (ctl. list). Sub-pr. of Christchurch, eln pres. to king for royal ass. 23 Mar. 1302 (PRO, C84/14/13); royal ass. 3 Apr. 1302, writ *de intendendo* 16 Apr. 1302 (*CPR 1301–07*, pp. 26, 31); fealty 16 Apr. 1302 (*CCR 1296–1302*, p. 524). Can. of Christchurch, eln conf. and mand. to induct 11 Apr. 1302 (*Reg. Pontisssara*, I, 134). Occ. Trin. 1309 (PRO, CP40/178, m. 339); 29 Oct. 1313 (BL, Cotton ms. Tiberius D VI, part 2, f. 65v).

William de Tydolveshyde (Tidelneshyde) 1317– 12th pr. (ctl. list). Letter of proclamation of eln and citation of opposers 5 May 1317 (*Reg. Sandale*, p. 36).

Edmund of Ramsbury (Remmysbury) –1337 13th pr. (ctl. list). Occ. 6 May 1321, 18 July 1323, 24 June 1325, 22, 25 Aug. 1336 (BL, Cotton ms. Tiberius D VI, part 2, f. 33r; part 1, ff. 53r–v, 143v, 66v). D. by 28 Mar. 1337 (Winchester, Reg. Orleton, I, ff. 53r–54r). Seal (*BM Seals*, no. 4224; *Mon. Seals*, p. 22).

Richard de Bustethorn (Busthorne) 1337– 14th pr. (ctl. list). Can. of Christchurch, eln conf. 28 Mar. 1337 (Winchester, Reg. Orleton, I, ff. 53r–54r). Commn to sub-pr. of Christchurch giving him full admin. of temps. and spiritualities during the vacancy 2 May 1338 (ibid., f. 58v). Institution to a vicarage 3 June 1339 on pres. of sub-pr. and convent, priory being vacant (ibid., II, f. 73r).

Robert de Legh(e) 1340–1349 15th pr. (ctl. list). Can. of Christchurch, apptd by the archbp of Canterbury to whom the power of appt had been transferred by the convent 19 July 1340, no reason given for vacancy; inhibition of Bp Orleton against anyone attempting to install him 28 July (Winchester, Reg. Orleton, I, f. 93r–v); installed 23 Aug. 1340 (ctl. list). Case and appeal, archbp of Canterbury v. bp of Winchester July–Aug. 1340 (BL, Cotton ms. Tiberius D VI, part 1, ff. 44v–45r). Commn from bp to archbp to provide a pr. 8 Aug. 1340, re-appt of Robert by archbp 19 Aug.; mand. to install 21 Aug.; prof. obed. 21 Aug. 1340 (Winchester, Reg. Orleton, I, ff. 93v–95v). Occ. 28 Nov. 1348 (BL, Cotton ms. Tiberius D VI, part 1, f. 68r). D. by 7 Mar. 1349 (*Reg. Edington*, I, no. 426).

William (de) Tyrewache (Tyrenache, Trynach) 1349– 16th pr. (ctl. list). Can. of Christchurch, eln conf. 7 Mar. 1349 (ibid., nos. 425–9); installed 18 Mar. 1349 (ctl. list). Occ. 6 Feb. 1356 (Bl, Cotton ms. Tiberius D VI, part 1, f. 88v); Mich. 1356 (*King's Bench, Edward III*, VI, 113).

Henry Eyr 1357–1377 17th pr., installed [ ] Mar. 1357 (ctl. list). Occ. Trin. term 1359 (BL, Cotton ms. Tiberius D. VI, part 2, ff. 65v, 66v). 'So weak and broken with age that he cannot in person labour about the business of the house' 1368 (*CPR 1367–70*, pp. 98, 99). Enjoined to appt a co-adjutor, on account of failing sight. Peter Travers, can. of Christchurch, apptd coadjutor 20 June 1368 (*Reg. Wykeham*, II, 18–19). Lic. for attorney, being so weak and broken with age 22 Nov. 1370, 27 Nov. 1370 (*CPR 1370–74*, pp. 18, 21). Occ. 1 Apr. 1377 (BL, Cotton ms. Tiberius D VI, part 1, f. 102v). D. by 20 July 1377 (*Reg. Wykeham*, I, 87).

John Wodenham 1377–1397 18th pr., installed [ ] July 1377 (ctl. list). Can. of Christchurch, commissary ordered to proclaim eln 13 July 1377, cert. of no opposers 16 July (ibid., II, 271); eln pres. to bp 20 July 1377, eln conf. 21 July 1377 (ibid., 87–90). D. by 5 Oct. 1397 (PRO, C84/37/2). D., lic. to el. 12 Oct. 1397 (*CPR 1396–99*, p. 224).

CHURCH GRESLEY (Derbys), (St Mary and) St George (see Binns, p. 129) f. *temp.* Stephen

Lists in *VCH Derbys*, II, 57–8; *SHC*, new ser., I (1898), pp. 175ff.; *Heads*, I, 159.

An unnamed pr. res. 1228 (*Ann. Dunstable*, p. 112).

Walter Occ. prob. *c.* 1210 x 1240 (BL, Add. ms. 6671, f. 15v; *Heads*, I, 159 & n.6).

Richard Occ. 6 July 1245 (PRO, Notts F., CP25/1/182/9, no. 337; *Derbys F. (1886)*, p. 52); n.d. *c.* 1250, mid 13th cent. (*Burton Chts.*, no. 116; *Gresley Chts.*, nos. 76, 152).

Henry Occ. 15 Apr. 1252 (*Derbys F. (1886)*, p. 57).

Richard –1281 Occ. 28 Jan. 1281(*Derbys F. (1890)*, p. 31); n.d. (*temp.* Edward I) (*Gresley Chts.*, no. 152). D. by 26 May 1281, when petition to el. (*SHC*, new ser., I, p. 176, citing BL, Add. ms. 8157, f. 52r).

Robert [Bakewell] –1286 Res. by 16 Feb. 1286 to be abb. of Rocester (*CPR 1281–92*, p. 221).

William Occ. n.d. (late 13th cent.) (*Ctl. Rydeware*, p. 269). The *SHC* list calls him Seile.

Robert Occ. 25 Feb. 1309 (Lichfield, B/A/1/1, f. 70v).

Roger of Aston [1311–] Commn to examine eln n. d. (between items 5 July and 25 Sept. 1311) (Lichfield, B/A/1/1, f. 45r). Occ. 11 x 12 Mar. 1340 (Lichfield, B/A/1/3, f. 80r); 4 Apr. 1341 (ibid., f. 87v).

John Walrant 1349– Can. of Church Gresley, apptd by bp, the right having been transferred to him by the convent 26 Aug. 1349, no reason given for vacancy (Lichfield, B/A/1/2. f. 87r).

John Hethcote –1400 D. by 6 Sept. 1400 (Lichfield, B/A/1/7, f. 78r).

CIRENCESTER (Glos), St Mary f. 1131 (as abbey).

Lists in *VCH Glos*, II, 834; *Ctl Cirencester*, I, p. xliii; *Heads*, I, 159–60.

Master Alexander Nequam 1213–1217 Lic. to el. 24 July 1213 (*Rot. Lit. Claus.*, I, 146b); temps. 1 Aug. 1213 (*Ctl. Cirencester*, I, no. 86). D. 31 Mar. 1217, bur. at Worcester (*Ann. Worcs*, p. 409; for the day see Floyer and Hamilton, *Worcester MSS.*, p. 92, cf. *Ann. Worcs*, p. 409). See Sharpe, *Latin Writers*, pp. 51–3; R.W. Hunt, *The Schools and the Cloister: the Life and Writings of Alexander Nequam (1157–1217)*, ed. M.T. Gibson (Oxford, 1984).

Walter of Gloucester 1217–1230 Cellarer of Cirencester, royal ass. 27 Apr. 1217 (*Rot. Lit. Claus.* I, 37). Occ. from 9 May 1219 to 18 Nov. 1230 (*Ctl. Cirencester*, I, nos. 193, 199). Occ. 20 Oct. 1219, 12 Nov. 1230 (*Soms F.*, I, pp. 36, 74); 20 June 1227 (*Wilts. F.*, I, p. 16); 19 June 1229 (*CR 1222–31*, p. 244). Occ. 18 Nov. 1230 (*Ctl. Cirencester*, I, no. 199). D. 1230 (*Ann. Worcs*, p. 422). D., lic. to el. 5 Dec. 1230 (*CPR 1225–32*, p. 418).

Hugh of Bampton (Bampt', Bamptone, Bamton) **1230–?1250** Cellarer of Cirencester, royal ass. 8 Dec. 1230 (*Ctl. Cirencester*, I, no. 90). Bl. 25 Dec. 1230 at Worcester (*Ann. Tewkesbury*, p. 77; (Henry) *Ann. Worcs*, p. 421). Occ. 17 May 1249 (*Ctl. Cirencester*, I, no. 214). Lic. to el. (no reason given for vacancy) 7 Dec. 1250 (*CPR 1247–58*, p. 82).

Roger of Rodmarton (Rodmerton) **1250–?1267** Can. of Cirencester, royal ass. 12 Dec. 1250, writ *de intendendo* 18 Dec. 1250 (ibid.). Latest occ. found 26 May 1265 (*Ctl. Cirencester*, II, no. 624). Fine paid for the pr. and conv. to have keeping of the abbey in the impending vacancy 24 Jan. 1267 (*CPR 1261–72*, p. 29).

Henry de Mundene 1267–1281[14] Can. of Cirencester, royal ass. 10 Oct. 1267, writ *de intendendo* 4 Nov. 1267, eln having been conf. by N., bp of Worcester (ibid., pp. 115, 163; cf. PRO, C84/3/27). Occ. 23 Mar. 1281 (*Ctl. Cirencester*, II, no. 656). Res. (H.) by 28 Dec. 1281 (PRO, C84/7/43).

Henry of Hampnett (Hampton, Hamptonet, Hamtonet) **1281–1307** Can. of Cirencester, royal ass. 28 Dec. 1281, writ *de intendendo* 2 Jan. 1282 (*CPR 1281–92*, pp. 7–8; cf. PRO, C84/7/44). D. 1 Nov. 1307 (*Ctl. Cirencester*, I, no. 94), but D. 2 Nov. 1307 and bur. following Monday (6 Nov.) (*Worcs Sede Vacante Reg.*, pp. 99, 101; cf. PRO, C84/15/49). D. (H.), lic. to el. 6 Nov. 1307 (*CPR 1307–13*, p. 12; cf. PRO, C81/58/50B).

Adam of Brokenborough (Brokenbarewe, Brokenberwe, Brokeneberg, Brokeneborwe) **1307–1320** Chamberlain of Cirencester, royal ass. 23 Nov. 1307, temps. 14 Dec. 1307 (*CPR 1307–13*, pp. 20, 26, cf. royal ass. 24 Nov (*Worcs Sede Vacante Reg.*, p. 99)). On 5 Nov. 1307 it was agreed to hold eln on St Brice's day (13 or 14 Nov.); witnesses examined 29 Nov.; eln quashed but apptd by pr. of Worcester *sede vacante* 3 Dec. 1307; prof. obed. same day; mand. to install 9 Dec. 1307 (*Worcs Sede Vacante Reg.*, pp. 98–103; cf. PRO, C84/16/1). Succ. 14 Dec. 1309 (*Ctl.*, I, 94). D. by 9 Oct. 1320 (*CFR 1319–27*, p. 34). D., lic. to el. 31 Oct. 1320 (*CPR 1317–21*, p. 508).

Richard of Charlton (Cherleton, Cherlton) **1320–1335** Chamberlain of Cirencester, royal ass. 25 (*sic*) Oct. 1320, temps. 13 Nov. 1320 (ibid., pp. 511, 519). Res. by 18 June 1335 (*CCR 1333–37*, p. 405). Cess., lic. to el. 19 June 1335 (*CPR 1334–38*, p. 126).

William Hereward 1335–1352 Can. of Cirencester, royal ass. 7 July 1335, temps. 6 Aug. 1335 (ibid., pp. 151, 161). Cert. conf. eln by bp of Worcester 29 July 1335 (PRO, C84/23/35). Excused attendance at Parliament on account of age and infirmity 17 Feb. 1350 (*CPR 1348–50*, p. 476). D. 25 Apr. 1352, bur. 28 Apr. (Worcester, Reg. Thoresby, p. 90; cf. PRO, C84/26/51). D., lic. to el. 28 Apr. 1352 (*CPR 1350–54*, p. 253).

Ralph of ?Eastcott (Escote, Estcote) **1352–1358** Pr. of Cirencester, royal ass. 14 May 1352, temps. 19 May 1352 (ibid., p. 263). El. 11 May 1352, eln conf. 20 May 1352 (Worcester, Reg. Thoresby, pp. 90–99). D. by 25 Nov. 1358 (PRO, C84/27/37). D., lic. to el. 28 Nov. 1358 (*CPR 1358–61*, p. 124).

William of Martley (Marteleye) **1358–1361** Can. of Cirencester, eln pres. to king for royal ass. 14 Dec. 1358 (PRO, C84/27/41); royal ass. 16 Dec. 1358, temps. 12 Jan. 1359 (*CPR 1358–61*, pp. 137, 144). Eln conf. 5 Jan. 1359, bl. 6 Jan. 1359 (Worcester, Reg. Brian I, p. 55; PRO, C84/27/43). D., lic. to el. 21 Oct. 1361 (*CPR 1361–64*, p. 98).

William of Lyneham (Lynham, *also* Lynton) **1361–1363** Pr. of Cirencester, royal ass. 10 Nov. 1361 (there called Lynton), temps. 8 Dec. 1361 (ibid., pp. 104, 127). Eln conf. 27 Nov. 1361 (Worcester, Reg. Brian I, p. 85). D., lic. to el. 8 June 1363 (*CPR 1361–64*, p. 350).

Nicholas (of) Ampney (Ameneye, Aumeneye) **1363–1393** Can. of Cirencester, formerly parson of Holwell, Dorset (*Ctl. Cirencester*, II, nos. 573n., 574). Royal ass. 3 July 1363, temps. 13 Aug. 1363 (*CPR 1361–64*, pp. 379, 386). Commn to enquire about eln 23 July 1363, eln conf. 29 July, bl. 30 July 1363 (Worcester, Reg. Barnet, pp. 52–3). D. 15 Aug. 1393 (*Dorset IPM*, no. 271). D., lic. to el. 23 Aug. 1393 (*CPR 1391–96*, p. 308).

---

[14] One of these abb. Henrys (Mundene/Hampnett) was also known as Clerbaud (Clerebaud) from references in later 14th-cent. documents. Unfortunately the evidence is contradictory, since Clerbaud is mentioned in a writ as occ. 8 Edward I (Nov. 1279 x Nov. 1280), hence Mundene (*Ctl. Cirencester*, I, no. 129 (p. 109)), but in another inquisition as having occ. 20 Edward I (Nov. 1291 x 1292), hence Hampnett (ibid., no. 126 (p. 107)).

COCKERHAM (Lancs), St Michael f. 1207 x 1208
Lists in *VCH Lancs*, II, 153; *Heads*, I, 160.

A. Occ. 1208 (*Lancs PR*, p. 365).

Henry Occ. n.d. (? mid-13th cent.) (*Lancaster Hist.*, II, 431–2).

William of Hexham (Hext', Hextildesham) Can. of Leicester and pr. or guardian (*gardianus*) of Cockerham, occ. 30 Nov. 1335 (*Reg. Melton*, I, no. 178); 18 June 1335, 20 Nov. 1337 (York, Reg. 9A, ff. 71v, 78v).

COLCHESTER (Essex), St Botolph and St Julian (St Botolph) f. *c.* 1093 (secular); 1100 x 1106 (Aug.)
Lists in *VCH Essex*, II, 150; *Heads*, I, 160.

Henry Last occ. 1206 (*Ctl. Colchester*, II, 541–2); 1215 x 1218 (ibid., 557–8, *temp.* pr. William of Rochester and abb. Ralph of Coggeshall).

Robert Occ. 11 Jan. 1221 (ibid., 534).

Hasculf Occ. Trinity 1224, Hil. 1228, 9 Feb. 1235, 25 June 1240, 3 Nov. 1240 (*Essex F.*, I, 66,73, 111, 123, 139); 1227 (*Ctl. Colchester*, II, 545).

John −1279/80 Occ. 8 July 1246 (PRO, Cambs F., CP25/1/24/21, no. 2); 1259 (*Ctl. Colchester*, II, 511); Easter 1260 (*Essex F.*, I, 236). El. abb. of St Osyth 1279 x 1280 (*Reg. Pecham*, II, 95–6; *Reg. Peckham*, III, 1063).

Simon Occ. Hil. 1280 (*Essex F.*, II, 26); 23 May 1281 (*Ctl. Colchester*, II, 570); *temp.* ? Edw. I (BL, Add. Cht. 14990).

Richard Occ. 3 Aug. 1290, 17 Sept. 1296 (*Ctl. Colchester*, II, 493, 577); Nov. 1295 x Nov. 1296 (*Rot. Parl.*, I, 228).

John Occ. as 'pr. of Colchester' 28 Feb. 1312 (*Court Rolls Colchester*, I, 67) – could possibly be the conventual pr. of St John's abbey.

Richard le Brun Occ. 1323 (PRO, KB27/253, m. 77).

John Occ. 1326 (*VCH*, citing *CPR 1324–27*, but not located in pd calendar); 27 Jan. 1338 (*Ctl. Colchester*, II, 502–3).

Richard de Westbrom 1348 (BL, Campbell Cht. XXIII. 14).

John de Colum Occ. n. d., *temp.* abb. Simon of Colchester (1349–53, 1368) (*Ctl. Colchester*, II, 552).

Thomas Sakkot −1361 Occ. 15 July 1360 (*Court Rolls Colchester*, II, 117). D. 1361 (Morant, *Essex*, I, 148, but with no source).

Mention of priory vacant *c.* Sept. 1361 and at 14 Oct. 1361 (*Reg. Sudbury*, I, 12, 227).

John Pruet Mand. for excommunication 1 July 1363 (*CPL*, IV, 35); occ. 24 June 1364 (*Ctl. Colchester*, II, 498).

John of Nayland (Neilond, Neyland(e)) −1391 Occ. 14 Nov. 1371, 23 Mar. 1375 (*Reg. Sudbury*, I, 214; II,141); 12 Oct. 1383 (BL, Add. Cht. 15601); 24 Nov. 1388 (*Colchester Leger Book*, p. 108). Letter of res. dated 2 July 1391; acc. 19 July (London, Reg. Braybrooke, f. 334v). Seal (*BM Seals*, no. 2986).

COLD NORTON (Oxon), St John the Evangelist and St Giles (cf. Binns, p. 130: St John the Evangelist) f. 1148 x 1158
Lists in *VCH Oxon*, II, 97; *Heads*, I, 160.

Master Samuel Last recorded occ. (S.) +25 Apr. 1212 (*Ctl. St Frideswide*, II, 50); (S.) 1200 x 1218 (*Ctl. Oseney*, V, pp. 96–8 = Cheney, *Inn. III*, no. 1158).

Roger Occ. Easter term 1229 (*CRR*, XIII, no. 1717).

Ralph −1236 Occ. n.d. (1212 x 1236) (*Hatton's Book of Seals*, no. 478); 2 July 1235 (*Oxford F.*, p. 98). Dep. at visitation by Bp Grosseteste 1236 (not named) (*Ann. Dunstable*, p. 143).

[**William de Berton** Can. of Osney, eln quashed by bp June 1235 x June 1236 (*Reg. Grosseteste*, p. 447).]

Walter of Wilton (Willtone) **1236–** Can. of Dunstable, succ. 1236 (*Ann. Dunstable*, p. 144). Apptd by bp June 1235 x June 1236 (*Reg. Grosseteste*, p. 447). Occ. 21 Apr. 1241, 13 Oct. 1249 (*Oxford F.*, pp. 116, 238); 27 Oct. 1248 (BNC, Rollright deed 14); 25 Mar. 1249 (BNC, Dunsthorp deed 10); 6 Oct 1249 (PRO, F. Var. Cos. CP25/1/284/17 no. 88).[15]

Adam Occ. n .d. (1254 x 1268) (*Ctl. Oseney*, VI, no. 1065).

Roger Occ. 27 Jan. 1261 (*Oxford F.*, p. 184); 3 Nov 1262 (PRO, Notts F., CP25/1/183/12 no. 488). Could be Norton, Ches. (q.v.).

Simon de Frollesham (Rolesham) **1264–1283/4** Can. of Cold Norton, adm. 13 Dec. 1264, no reason given for vacancy (*Reg. R. Gravesend*, p. 218). Occ. 1277 (BNC, Wideford deed 2). D. by 19 May 1283 x 18 May 1284, 4th year of Bp Sutton (Bodl., Dodsworth ms. 107, f. 145r).

Adam of Woodford (Wodford) **1283/4–** El. 19 May 1283 x 18 May 1284 (ibid.). Occ. c. 1283 x 1293 (BNC, Cold Norton deed 16*).

Peter de Wadington 1284/5– El. 19 May 1284 x 18 May 1285, lic. to el. having been sought from Lady Isabel de Mortimer, patron (Bodl., Dodsworth ms. 107, f. 145v)

Hugh Occ. Mich. 1285 (PRO, CP40, roll 60, m. 28). Obit 15 Jan. (*Ctl. Oseney*, I, p. xviii).

Walter [**de Stratton**] **1288/9–1292** El. 19 May 1288 x 18 May 1289, lic. to el. having been sought from Robert Hastang, patron (Bodl., Dodsworth ms. 107, f. 146v). Cess. by c. Nov. 1292 (*Reg. Sutton*, IV, 51–2; VIII, 178).

Robert of Ravensden (Ravenesden, Ravesden) **1292–1297** Can. of Canons Ashby, apptd to succ. Walter n.d. [between entries of 26 and 30 Nov. 1292] (ibid.,VIII, 178). As late pr., ordered on 7 Oct. 1297 to return to Canons Ashby and stay there (ibid., VI, 32; VIII, 195).

William de Twye 1297–1322 Can. of Cold Norton, eln quashed but apptd by bp 7 Oct. 1297 (ibid.,VIII, 195). Cess. by 25 Feb. 1322 (Lincoln, Ep. Reg., IV, f. 247v).

John of Wootton (Wotton) **1322–1330** Can. of Cold Norton, eln pres. to bp 25 Feb. 1322, eln quashed but apptd by bp 26 Feb. 1322 (ibid.). D. by 24 Apr. 1330 (ibid., f. 262v).

John of Thenford 1330–1334 Can. of Cold Norton, eln conf. 24 Apr. 1330 (ibid.). Res. adm. and lic. issued 26 Nov. 1334 for him to transfer to the Benedictines of Eynsham (Lincoln, Ep. Reg., V, f. 488r; *Ctl. Eynsham*, I, p. xxiv).

William of Hook Norton (Hogenorton, Hokenorton) **1335–1343** Commn to examine eln 14 Apr. 1335 (Lincoln, Ep. Reg., V, f. 496r). Commn following visitation to enquire into excesses of pr. William, to correct them and if necessary to remove him from office 26 June 1343 (Lincoln, Ep. Reg., VII, ff. 37v, 184v). Deprived by 16 Sept. 1343 (Lincoln, Ep. Reg., VI, f. 82v).

William of Tewkesbury (Teukesbur') **1343–** Can. of Cold Norton, apptd by bp 16 Sept. 1343 (ibid.). Occ. 27 Apr. 1346 (BNC, Chipping Norton deed 13); 24 July 1356 (BNC, Dunthorp deed 16).

Robert (of) Enstone (Enstan, Enestan) **1357–1396** Can. of Cold Norton, commn to examine eln 19 Dec. 1357 (Lincoln, Ep. Reg., VIII, f. 99r). Conf. of provision made for Robert Enstone, recently res., 28 Apr. 1396 (Lincoln, Ep. Reg., XII, f .435r).

COLSTERWORTH, *see* BECKFORD

COMBWELL (Kent), St Mary Magdalen f. *temp.* Henry II (abbey); *c.* 1216 x 1220 (priory). Lists in *VCH Kent*, II, 161; *Heads*, I, 161.

---

[15] Pr. Andrew who occ. 10 May 1247 (*Oxford F.*, p. 148) is prob. to be identified with the pr. of Norton, Ches., rather than Cold Norton.

ABBOTS

William Last recorded occ. Mich. term 1210 (*CRR*, VI, 94). Res. *temp.* Stephen Langton, prob.
1216 x 1219 (Combwell Chts. – *Arch. Cant.*, V, 214 cf. *Acta Langton* no. 44 and n.; Coll. of
Arms, mss. 5–6).

Henry Succ. William *c.* 1216 x 19 (*Arch. Cant.*, V, 212–13, cf. *Acta, ut supra*).

PRIORS

Henry (cont.) Occ. 21 Sept. 1227 (*Kent F.*, p. 85; BL, Harl. Cht. 79 B. 44); Hil. 1230 (*CRR*,
XIII, no. 2546); (H.) 1234 (Coll. of Arms, ms. 15); 20 Apr. 1236 (*Kent F.*, p. 126).

Robert Occ. 9 Feb. 1249, 9 May 1249 (*Kent F.*, pp. 227–8).

W. Occ. 1250, 1251 (*HMC De L'Isle and Dudley*, I, 105). Prob. to be identified with the abb.
William (seal) who occ. in n.d. cht., mid-13th cent. (*BM Seals*, no. 3082, from BL, Egerton
Cht. 382).

Godfrey Occ. 14 June 1254 (*Sussex F.*, II, no. 542); (Geoffrey) 24 Jan. 1257 (Coll. of Arms, ms.
65).

Walter Occ. 21 June 1271 (*Kent F.*, p. 384); 5 Mar. 1279 (Coll. of Arms, ms. 113/3).

John of Marden (Meredonn') Occ. *c.* Nov. 1275 (BL, Harl. Cht. 78 A 19).

Lic. to el. a new pr. on the res. of last unnamed pr., during archbp's visitation 1 Sept. 1278 (*Reg.
Winchelsey*, I, 282).

John de Lose 1315– Can. of Combwell, commn to examine eln 13 Mar. 1315 (Lambeth, Reg.
Reynolds, f. 52r). Eln conf. 16 Apr. 1315 (ibid., f. 62v).

John Talbot 1318– Can. of St Gregory, Canterbury, apptd by archbp 30 Jan. 1318, no reason
given for vacancy (ibid., f. 22v).

Comm. to proceed to eln of a new pr., no reason given for vacancy 25 June 1323 (ibid., f. 131v).
Prob. Stephen below.

Stephen –1324 D. by 28 July 1324 (ibid., f. 252v).

[**Guy de Natyngton** El. by convent, on d. of Stephen, but he renounced eln and as convent
failed to el. a pr. within statutory time they asked archbp to provide one 28 July 1324 (ibid.).]

John de Hawe (Hagh) **?1324–1363** Can. of Combwell, apptd by archbp, n. d. [*c.* 1324] (ibid.,
ff. 252v–253r). Occ. 29 June 1336, 27 May 1338 (Lincoln, Ep. Reg., IV, ff. 349r, 351r); 17
Dec. 1339 (Lincoln, Ep. Reg., V, f. 247v). D. by 3 Feb. 1363 (Lambeth, Reg. Islip, ff.
190v–191r).

William of Chart (Chert) **1363–** Can. of Combwell, eln conf. 3 Feb. 1363 (ibid.).

Roger of Tycehurst (Tychesherst, Tyshirst, Tyshurst) Left with goods of house 6 Aug. 1387
(Logan, *Runaway Religious*, p. 224); removed in visitation 16 Sept. 1387 (Lambeth, Reg.
Courtenay, ff. 168v–169r). Subsequently restored. 7 May 1395 mand. to the pr. of St
Gregory, Canterbury, to absolve from excommunication and to gt dispensation to Simon
dictus Mudiston, can. of Combwell, between whom and Roger Tyshurst (who asserted he
had obtained the priory by authority of the ordinary and that Simon had despoiled him of
it) a suit arose and was heard in the apostolic palace. Roger obtained a definitive sentence
before the papal auditor. Simon was removed and Roger restored (*CPL*, IV, 522–3). Occ.
14 June 1398 (PRO, C67/30, m. 16); 20 May 1399 (*CPL*, IV, 307); 29 Sept. 1409 (BL, Harl.
Cht. 75 G 1).

CONISHEAD (Lancs), St Mary f. -1181

Lists in *VCH Lancs*, II, 143; *Heads*, I, 161.

T. Last recorded occ. 14 Aug. 1214 (*Ctl. Furness*, II, ii, 312–13).

Augustine Occ. 6 July 1221 (ibid., 321); n.d. (*Ctl. St Bees*, pp.300–1; PRO, DL25/439).

John Occ. 21 Dec. 1230 (*Ctl. Furness*, II, ii, 555); 13 May 1235 (*Lancs F.*, I, 63); 1239 (PRO,
Westmorland F. CP25/1/249/3, no. 32); (J.) 1243 (*Ctl. Furness*, I, iii, 654); 1246 (*Cumbd F.*,

p. 224); 8 July 1255 (ibid.); 26 May 1256 (PRO, Westmorland F. CP25/1/249/4, no. 27); 20 Oct. 1261 (*Cumbd F.*, p. 226).

Thomas de Morthyng Full name n.d. (*temp.* abb. Hugh le Brun of Furness) (PRO, DL25/383). Occ. 4 May 1270 (PRO, F. Divers Cos. CP25/1/283/17, no. 466); Oct. 1270 x Oct. 1271 (*Cumbd F.*, p. 227).

John Occ. Nov. 1280 x Nov. 1281 (ibid., p. 229).

Robert Occ. 1292 (PRO, Just.1/480, m. 40d).

Simon Occ. 17 May 1294 (*Reg. Halton*, I, 8). Former pr. d. 7 June 1309 (*Ch. York*, p. 45).

Thomas Trawers −1309 D. 6 June 1309 and bur. in south part of choir (ibid.).

William Flemyng Occ. 21 Feb. 1310 (*CPR 1307–13*, p. 255); 21 Dec. 1310 (*Ctl. Furness*, II, iii, 779; PRO, DL25/380).

Thomas Morthyng Occ. 29 Dec. 1339 (*Ctl. Furness*, I, ii, 426).

John Occ. *c.* 1340 (PRO, DL36/2/106); 26 Mar. 1343 (PRO, Just.1/1435, m. 41); 22 Oct 1354 (*Reg. Welton*, no. 60).

Richard of Bolton Occ. 1373 (PRO, DL.25/1191); 1376 (PRO, DL.25/1127); 18 Feb. 1400 (*Reg. Archdny Richmond*, p. 200, no. 235); 1401 (PRO, PL15/1, m. 26d).

COTTINGHAM, *see* HALTEMPRICE

COXFORD (Norfolk), St Mary f. *c.* 1140 (at Rudham); *c.* 1216 (at Coxford)
Lists in *VCH Norfolk*, II, 380; *Ctl. Coxford*, pp.284 ff.; *Heads*, I, 161.

Herbert (Hubert) Latest recorded occ. 15 Apr. 1212 (*Norfolk F., 1201–15*, no. 265; Norfolk RO, DN/SUN.8, f. 15v; BL, Add. ms. 47784, f. 25r); 1212 (Norfolk RO, DN/SUN.8, f. 16r).

?Robert Occ. 1212 x 1223 (*Ctl. Coxford*, p. 346; BL, Add. ms. 47784, f. 16v), *temp.* Robert, pr. of Castle Acre, but his existence is not definitely established, cf. Norfolk RO, DN/SUN.8, f. 17v – Robert, pr. of Castle Acre and *William*, pr. of Coxford.

William −?1233/4 Occ. 6 Oct. 1223, June 1230 (Norfolk RO, DN/SUN.8, f.52r); Oct. 1222 x Oct. 1223 to Oct. 1232 x Oct. 1233 (*Norfolk F. (Rye)*, pp. 38, 50); 27 Jan. 1233 (BL, Add. ms. 47784, f. 30r; Norfolk RO, DN/SUN.8, f. 17v). Presumably the unnamed pr. who d. 1233 (*Ann. Dunstable*, p. 135, cf. p. 139 – 1234).

Adam of Dalling Name mentd 1244 x 1245 (no source) according to Blomefield, *Norfolk*, VII, 155–6. Occ. Oct. 1234 x Oct. 1235 (*Norfolk F. (Rye)*, p. 56); 14 Jan. 1235 (BL, Add. ms. 47784, f. 30r); 17 Nov. 1242 (*Ctl. Coxford*, p. 347; Norfolk RO, DN/SUN.8, f. 52v); Easter 1244 (*CRR* XVIII, no. 1404); 7 May 1245 (BL, Add. ms. 47784, f. 74r).

John Occ. from Oct. 1249 x Oct. 1250 to Oct. 1257 x Oct. 1258 (*Norfolk F.(Rye)*, pp. 75, 95); 26 May 1251, 21 June 1254, 13 Oct. 1258 (Norfolk RO, DN/SUN.8, ff. 47r, 46r, 12r), but see below ?date of last entry an error.

William Occ. 21 Dec. 1255, 21 Apr. 1257, 3 Feb. 1258 (ibid., ff. 38r, 8r, 6v; BL, Add. ms. 47784, ff. 61v, 12v, 11r); Oct. 1257 x Oct. 1258 (*Norfolk F. (Rye)*, p. 95).

Thomas Occ. n.d. (BL, Add. ms. 47784, ff. 35v, 51r, 61v) – f. 35v ment. of Roger son of Ralph Colomb of West Rudham: Ralph Colomb occ. *temp.* priors Adam and John (ibid., ff. 37r, 36v). Thomas's precise place in the sequence of priors is uncertain.

Hugh of Elmham Occ. *c.* 29 Sept. 1272 (ibid., f. 90v); 20 Feb. 1274 (ibid., f. 26v); (H.) 1275 x 1288 (PRO, SC1/22/168); July 1277 (BL, Add. ms. 47784, f. 35v; Norfolk RO, DN/SUN.8, f. 21r); Trin. 1280 (PRO, CP40/34, m. 59); Nov. 1285 x Nov. 1286 (Blomefield, *Norfolk*, VII, 156, no source).

Reyner −1289 Occ. Sept. 1288 (PRO, Just.1/1282, m.19d); n.d. (BL, Add. ms. 47784, ff. 17v, 19r, 68v; Norfolk RO, DN/SUN.8, ff. 11v, 12v, 45r). Ceased to be pr. by 7 Dec. 1289 (*CCR 1288–96*, p. 59).

Robert 1289– Occ. 7 Dec. 1289 (ibid.); 5 Feb. 1299, 26 May 1299 (*CPR 1292–1301*, pp. 460, 469); 1 Nov. 1301 (BL, Add. ms. 47784, f. 63v); July 1314 (PRO, Just.1/593, m.32d).

William of Hempton 1315– Sub-pr. of Coxford, eln conf. 12 June 1315, no reason given for vacancy (Norwich, Reg/1/1, f. 61v). Occ. 8 Jan. 1319, Jan. 1320 (BL, Add. ms. 47784, f. 19v; Norfolk RO, DN/SUN.8, ff. 12v, 13v).

John of Thorpe –1342 Occ. 28 Apr. 1326 (Norwich, Reg/1/2, f. 80v); 1327 (*Index to Placita de Banco*, p. 43); 1 Apr. 1331 (BL, Add. ms. 47784, f. 70r); 27 Aug. 1332 (PRO, C270/8/23). D. by 18 Dec. 1342 (Norwich, Reg/1/3, f. 64r–v).

John of Thornham 1342–1346 Can. of Coxford, commn to examine eln 18 Dec. 1342; eln conf. 19 Dec. 1342 (ibid.). Cess. by 31 July 1346 (*Reg. Bateman*, I, no. 228).

Peter of Flecknoe (Flekenhowe) **1346–** Can. of Coxford, eln conf. 31 July 1346 (ibid.). Occ. 7, 14 June 1349 (BL, Add. ms. 47784, f. 1v).

Henry of Elmham –1405 Occ. 1369 (ibid., f. 80v). D. by 15 Jan. 1405 (Norwich, Reg/3/6, f. 314r).

CREAKE, see NORTH CREAKE

DARLEY (Derbys), St Mary (formerly St Helen) (Derby; St Mary of the Derwent) f. 1137 (at Derby); *c.* 1146 (at Darley) (abbey)

Lists in *VCH Derbys*, II, 53; *Ctl. Darley*, I, p. lxxx; *Heads*, I, 161–2.

Henry of Repton 1214–1233 Occ. as abb.-el. in j. d. decision +28 July 1210 (*Ctl. Darley*, II, 414; cf. Cheney, *Inn. III*, no. 873). Put in possession 21 Dec. 1214 (*Rot. Lit. Pat.*, p. 125). Occ. (H.) 1222 (*Ctl. Tutbury*, no. 14); 28 Oct. 1225 (*Ctl. Darley*, I, 341–2); 22 Sept. 1226 (*Derbys F. (1886)*, p. 18); 1227 (*Glapwell Chts.*, nos. 19–20). D. 1233 (*Ann. Dunstable*, p. 135, but cf. ibid., p. 139, d. 1234). D., lic. to el. 20 Aug. 1233 (*CPR 1232–47*, p. 24).

Ralph of Leicester (Leicestre) **1233–** Sub-pr. of Darley, royal ass. 29 Aug. 1233 (ibid., p. 24); mand. for seisin 28 Aug. 1233 (*sic*) (*CR 1231–34*, p. 255). Succ. 1233 (*Ann. Dunstable*, p. 135). Occ. 18 Oct. 1239 (*Ctl. Darley*, II, 345); 17 Feb. 1240 (*Derbys F. (1886)*, p. 44).

Walter of Walton 1248–?1261 Royal ass. 4 May 1248 (*CPR 1247–58*, p. 14). Occ. in *Ctl. Darley* from 18 Aug. 1249 to 23 May 1259 (I, 192; II, 385–6); 20 Oct. 1252, 20 Jan. 1256, 13 Oct. 1257 (*Derbys F., (1887)*, pp. 85, 89, 90). Cess. 20 June [1261] (PRO, C84/2/10). Presumably the abb. who vacated the abbey in 1261.[16] Lic. to el. (no reason given for vacancy) 22 June 1261 (*CPR 1258–66*, p. 160).

William of Wymondham (Wymundeham) **1261–1275** Canon of Darley, eln pres. to king for royal ass. 15 July 1261 (PRO, C84/2/23); royal ass. 18 July 1261, temps. 26 July 1261 (*CPR 1258–66*, pp. 168, 170). Occ. from 1264 to 1271 (*Glapwell Chts.*, nos. 144, 44, 50). Cess. by 10 Jan. 1275 (PRO, C84/5/17).

Henry of Kedleston (Keccheleston, Ketteleston, Kettlestone) **1275–1287** Royal ass. 3 Feb. 1275, writ *de intendendo* 9 Feb. 1275 (*CPR 1272–81*, pp. 78, 79). Formerly pr. of Darley, occurs in *Ctl. Darley* from Jan. 1276 to 24 June 1286 (II, 453, 364). D. by 31 Mar. 1287 (PRO, C84/8/48). D., lic. to el. 7 Apr. 1287 (*CPR 1281–92*, p. 267).

William de Alsop (Alssopp, Aslop, Dalsop) **1287–1330** Can. of Darley, (cellarer of Darley) eln pres. to king for royal ass. 11 Apr. 1287 (PRO, C84/8/13); royal ass. 6 May 1287, writ *de intendendo* 11 May 1287 (*CPR 1281–92*, p. 268). Cert. conf. eln by bp of Coventry and Lichfield 11 May 1287 (PRO, C84/9/3). Occ. in *Ctl. Darley* from 29 Sept. 1288 to 18 Nov.

---

[16] *VCH* gives an abb. Andrew in 1259, but this is most prob. incorrect and confuses Andrew of Spondon, can. of Darley, one of those to seek lic. to el. in 1261 (see *Ctl. Darley*, I, p. lxxx).

1330 (I, 139; II, 365). D. by 6 Dec. 1330 (PRO, C84/22/39). D., lic. to el. 12 Dec. 1330 (*CPR 1330–34*, p. 24).

William of Clifton (Clyfton, Clyston) **1331–1352** Can. of Darley, eln pres. to king for royal ass. 21 Jan. 1331 (PRO, C84/22/40); royal ass. 3 Feb. 1331 (Clyston), temps. 3 Mar. 1331 (*CPR 1330–34*, pp. 70, 83). Occ. 6 May 1352 (*Ctl. Darley*, I, 216–17). D., lic. to el. 30 Oct. 1352 (*CPR 1350–54*, p. 348).

Laurence of Burton 1352–1383 Can. of Darley, royal ass. 23 Nov. 1352, temps. 12 Dec. 1352 (ibid., pp. 359, 378). Eln conf. 3 Dec. 1352 (Lichfield, B/A/1/2, ff. 92v–93r). D. by 29 May 1383 (PRO, C84/33/15). D., lic. to el. 31 May 1381 (*CPR 1381–85*, p. 276).

DODFORD (Worcs), St Mary f. 1184 x 1186; absorbed by Halesowen in 1464.

Simon Occ. 9 Dec. 1226 (PRO, Worcs F., CP25/1/258/3, no. 36).

Guy de Hersinton (*also* Herforton) **1291–1332** Eln conf. 19 June 1291 (*Reg. G. Giffard*, p. 385). Occ. n.d. (Worcester Cath. mun. B.734). Apptd pr. of Warwick, St Sepulchre 23 Oct. 1332 (*Reg. Orleton (Worc)*, no. 395).

William of Aston **–1362** D. 9 Feb. 1362, bur. 10 Feb. 1362 (*Worcs. Reg. Sede Vacante*, p. 209).

Thomas Doul 1362–1376 Apptd by bp 15 Feb. 1362, there being no way or form of eln in the same priory (ibid.). Res. by 16 Apr. 1376 (*Reg. Wakefield*, no. 23).

William at Pole 1376– Can. of Dodford, apptd by bp at the request of the convent 16 Apr. 1376 (ibid.). Occ. 1379 (PRO, E179/58/11, m. 3).

The next recorded pr., **John**, occ. 18 Oct. 1402 (*Reg. Clifford*, no. 148).

DODLINCH, *see* WOODSPRING

DODNASH (Suffolk), St Mary f. *c.* 1188

Lists in *VCH Suffolk* II, 100 (from 1346); *Dodnash Chts.*, p. xix; *Heads,* I, 162.

Jordan Occ. 13 Oct. 1228, 12 Nov. 1234 (*Dodnash Chts.*, nos. 62, 38, cf. *Suffolk F. (Rye)*, pp. 24, 34); Mich. term 1228 (*CRR*, XIII, no. 1201). Prob. the pr. J. mentd early-mid 13th cent. (*Dodnash Chts.*, no. 18).

Richard Occ. mid-13th cent. (ibid., nos. 160, 194) (prob. but not certainly before Robert).

Robert Occ. mid-13th cent. (ibid., nos. 21, 24A, 161); Oct. 1252 x Mich. 1257 (ibid., no. 42).

John Occ. Dec. 1279 (ibid., no. 209).

Ralph Occ. (R.) Mich. 1284 (ibid., no. 206); from 12 Mar. 1285 to 29 Sept. 1301 (ibid., nos. 27, 127); 1 Dec. 1286 (ibid., no. 64, cf. *Suffolk F. (Rye)*, p. 89).

[**Edmund de Stowe** el. 1304 and disqualified (Norwich, Reg/1/1, f. 5v).]

Henry of Framlingham 1304– Can. of Dodnash, apptd by bp of Norwich 13 Apr. 1304, the right having devolved upon him on account of the canonically irregular election of Edmund de Stowe and his subsequent disqualification (ibid.).

John Occ. from 25 Oct. 1304 to 2 Feb. 1316 (*Dodnash Chts.* nos. 195, 163).

John of Gusford (Godelesford, Gudlesford) **1317–1346** Can. of Dodnash, eln conf., no reason given for vacancy 26 Mar. 1317 (Norwich, Reg/1/1, f. 69v). Res. by 10 May 1346 (*Reg. Bateman*, I, no. 216).

Adam (le) Neuman 1346– Can. of Dodnash, eln quashed but apptd by bp of Norwich 10 May 1346 (ibid.). Occ. 25 Nov. 1348 (*Dodnash Chts.*, no. 156).

Henry of Benacre 1349– Can. of Dodnash, eln quashed but apptd by bp of Norwich, no reason given for vacancy 19 June 1349 (*Reg. Bateman*, I, no. 640). Occ. from 20 June 1350 to 11 June 1362 (*Dodnash Chts.*, nos. 180, 168).

Roger Occ. from 24 Sept. 1363 to 15 Dec. 1382 (ibid., nos. 169, 215).

Thomas of Thornham **–1383** Res. by 10 July 1383 to be pr. of Holy Trinity, Ipswich (Norwich, Reg/3/6, f. 98v). The next appt to Dodnash, vacant by his cession, was on 12 Apr. 1384 (ibid., f. 98v).

DORCHESTER (Oxon), St Peter, St Paul and St Birinus (Arrouaisian) f. *c.* 1140 (abbey)
  Lists in *VCH Oxon*, II, 89; *Heads*, I, 162.
Roger Occ. 1215 x 1222 (*Reg. Ant. Lincoln*, III, no. 955): 1216 x 1217 (*Ctl. Oseney*, IV, 228); (R.)
  7 Feb. 1221 (ibid., III, 78); (R.) 1220 (BL, Cotton ms. Domitian A III, f. 109r). Prob. the
  unnamed abb. who retired to St Frideswide's priory, Oxford, shortly before 1225 (*Bracton's
  Note Book*, I, 551).[17]
An unnamed abb. dep. 1236 at Bp Grosseteste's visitation (*Ann. Dunstable*, p. 143).
Richard de Wrthe **1236–1258/9** Can. of Osney, made abb. 1236 (*Ann. Osney*, p. 83). Occ. from
  21 Apr. 1241 to 8 July 1248 (*Oxford F.*, pp. 110, 152). D. (R.), Nov. 1258 x Nov. 1259 (*Reg.
  R. Gravesend*, pp. 213, 329).
John of Warwick (Warewik) **1258/9–1270** Can. of Dorchester, eln conf. Nov. 1258 x Nov.
  1259 (ibid.). Res by 23 Mar. 1270 to join the Dominican Order (ibid., p. 222).
Walter of Peterborough (de Burgo) **1270–** Eln conf. and bl. 23 Mar. 1270 (ibid. pp. 222, 333).
  Occ. 26 July 1272 (*Oxford F.*, p. 202); (W.) 24 May 1278 (PRO, C81/1789/8); 1 Oct. 1282
  (Oxford, Merton Coll. muns. 810).
Thomas Occ. 9 Feb. 1285 (*Oxford F.*, pp. 218–19); 1285 (PRO, Just. 1/710, m. 7d); Mich. 1286
  x Mich. 1287 (PRO, E159/60, m. 14d).
Ralph of Didcot **–1294** D. by 28 Jan. 1294 (*Reg. Sutton*, VIII, 184).
William of Rufford (Rofford, Ropford) **1294–1298** Can. of Dorchester, eln conf. 28 Jan. 1294
  (ibid.). D. by 17 Jan. 1298; lic. to el. (ibid., VI, 54).
Alexander of Waltham **1298–1304** Can. of Dorchester, eln conf. 7 Feb. 1298, bl. 9 Feb. 1298
  (ibid., VIII, 198–9). Mand. to install 24 Feb. 1298 (ibid., VI, 66). Lic. to el. requested on his
  removal from office 25 Nov. 1304, issued 27 Nov. 1304 (Lincoln, Ep. Reg., III, f. 77r; cf.
  Lincoln, Ep. Reg., II, f. 148r).
John of Caversham (Kaversham) **1304–1333** Can. of Dorchester, el. on dep. of Alexander, eln
  pres. to bp 5 Dec. 1304, eln quashed but apptd by bp 7 Dec. 1304, bl. 13 Dec. 1304 (Lincoln,
  Ep. Reg., II, f. 148r). D. by 27 Sept. 1333 (Lincoln, Ep. Reg., IV, f. 268r).
John of Sutton **1333–?1349** Can of Dorchester, eln pres. to bp 27 Sept. 1333, pr. and conv.
  renounced eln and bp apptd 8 Oct. 1333, bl. 28 Oct 1333 (ibid.). Occ. Mich. 1337 (PRO,
  CP40/312, m. 173); 5 Mar. 1347 (Lincoln, Ep. Reg., VII, f. 99v); 30 Sept. 1347 (Lincoln,
  Ep. Reg. IXC, p. 14). Lic. to el. (no reason given for vacancy) 19 Apr. 1349 (Lincoln, Ep.
  Reg., IX, f. 21r). Ledger stone (*Earliest English Brasses*, p. 205 and fig. 158).
Robert of Winchendon (Wynchedon, Wynchendon, Wynchyndon) **1349–1380** Can. of
  Dorchester, eln quashed but apptd by bp 11 May 1349 (Lincoln, Ep. Reg., IX, f. 245v). D
  by 2 Oct. 1380 when lic. to el. requested, lic. gtd 6 Oct. 1380 (Lincoln, Ep. Reg., X, f. 372r).

DRAX (Yorks, WR.) St Nicholas f. 1130 x 1139
  Lists in *VCH Yorks*, III, 208; *Heads*, I, 162.
Alan Occ 13 Jan. x 3 Feb. 1205 (*Yorks F., John*, p. 93); *c.* 1213 (Bodl., ms. Top. Yorks c. 72, f.
  69v); n.d. (1205 x 1223) (*EYC*, VI, no. 107).

---

[17] Abb. Richard occ. in n.d. cht (*Ctl. Sandford*, I, no. 246), which the editor has dated to 1219. The final
  concord that deals with the rent mentd in this cht. is indeed dated 1219 (*Oxford F.*, p. 58), but this particular cht. could date from much later. Richard could be either the unnamed abb. deposed in 1236 or
  Richard de Wrthe 1236–58/9.

Adam Occ. 3 Sept. 1226, mentd in case of Hil. 1346 (Bodl., ms. Top. Yorks c. 72, f. 87r).[18]

Robert Occ. 7 Jan. 1227 (*Yorks F., 1218–31*, p. 105; Bodl., ms. Top. Yorks c. 72, ff. 81r–v, 95v); Hil. 1234 (Baildon, I, 38); 2 Aug. 1243 (*Lincs F.*, I, 341).

Gervaganus Occ. as pr. *temp.* Henry III, mentd in case Trin. 1335 (Baildon, I, 38); also occ. n.d. (Bodl., ms. Top. Yorks c. 72, f. 85v), desc. as pr. *temp.* Henry III and having been unjustly disseised by Hugh Paynel. Paynel died before 6 June 1244 (*EYC*, VI, 11). The correct sequence of this pr. and John of Rasen is not entirely certain.

John of Rasen Occ. n.d. (Bodl., ms. Top. Yorks c. 72, f. 94v) – a record of a plea, ment. of John de Rasen appearing before Roger of Thirkleby and fellow-justices at York. Roger of Thirkleby was a justice from *c.* 1239 till his death in 1260 (*EYC*, VI, 196).

Robert Occ. 8 Sept. 1250 (*CCR 1247–51*, p. 369); 5 May 1252 (*Yorks F., 1246–72*, p. 83).

Thomas of Campsall (Camsal) –1286 Occ. Trin. 1280 (PRO, CP40/34, m. 15); 3 Feb. 1282 (PRO, Lincs F., CP25/1/133/55, no. 74); (T.) 23 Nov. 1285 (*Ctl. Fountains*, I, 294). Cess. 13 Dec. 1286 on account of ill-health (*Reg. Romeyn*, I, p. 63, no. 149).

Elias de Byrton 1287– Can. of Drax, eln conf. 22 Jan. 1287 (ibid., pp. 64–5, no. 151). Occ. 1289 (Baildon, I, 38, without source).

John of Lincoln 1291– Can. of Drax, eln conf. 14 Aug. 1291, no reason given for vacancy (*Reg. Romeyn*, I, pp. 110–11, no. 298). Occ. Mich. 1291–Mich. 1292, Mich. 1295 (Baildon, I, 39); Hil. 1295 (PRO, CP40/107, m. 132d).

Henry of Sherwood (Shirewode) –1332 Occ. 20 July 1301 (*Cal. Inq. PM*, VI, 264; Baildon, II, 10); 16 Aug. 1310 (*CPR 1307–13*, p. 310); 1313 (Bodl., ms. Top. Yorks e. 9, f. 88v). D., lic. to el. 9 Dec. 1332 (*CPR 1330–34*, p. 374). Surname mentd *Cal. Inq. PM*, VI, 264.

Gilbert de Ounesby (?*alias* of York) 1332–?1349 Can. of Drax, eln conf. 23 Dec. 1332 (York, Reg. 9A, ff. 235v–236r). D. (York) by 14 Aug. 1349 (York, Reg. 10, f. 35v).

John of Saxton 1349–1354 Can. of Drax, el. on d. of Gilbert of York (Ebor'). Eln conf. 14 Aug. 1349, mand. to obey him 15 Aug. 1349 (ibid.). Commn to adm. cess. 3 Oct. 1354 (York, Reg. 11, f. 29v). Cess., lic. to el. 26 Nov. 1354 (*BIB*, 3, pp. 44–5, nos. 100, 105).

John of Wigton (Wiggeton) 1354– El. conf. 1 Dec. 1354 (ibid.).

Thomas of Sherburn (Shirburn) –1391 Leave of absence granted for one year 28 Aug. 1360, 1 Aug 1364 (*studium generale*), 2 Oct. 1366, 1 Oct. 1367 (for 2 years) (York, Reg. 11, ff. 106v, 138v, 140v, 143v). Occ. Mich. 1387, Hil. 1388 (Baildon, I, 43); 1389 (PRO, C85/184/26). D. by 30 Sept. 1391 (York, Reg. 14, f. 24r).

DUNMOW, *see* **LITTLE DUNMOW**

DUNSTABLE (Beds), St Peter f. -1125

Lists in *VCH Beds*, I, 377; *Ctl. Dunstable*, p. 16; *Heads*, I, 162–3; *Ann. Dunstable* is basis on which see C. R. Cheney in *Essays in Medieval History presented to B. Wilkinson*, pp. 79–98.

Richard de Mores 1202–1242 Can. of Merton, el. 1202 (*Ann. Dunstable*, p. 28). Occ. in *Beds F.*, I from 5 Nov. 1202 to 3 July 1237 (nos. 110, 399); Trin. term 1240 (*CRR*, XVI, no. 1867). D. 9 Apr. 1242 (*Ann. Dunstable*, p. 18). On him see S. Kuttner and E. Rathbone in *Traditio*, VII (1949–51), pp. 327 ff.; Sharpe, *Latin Writers*, pp. 494–6. Lic. to el. (no reason for vacancy) 14 Apr. 1242 (*CPR 1232–47*, p. 280).

Geoffrey of Barton (Barthon) 1242–1262 Can. of Dunstable, el. 17 Apr., conf. by bp 5 June, installed 19 June 1242 (*Ann. Dunstable*, p. 158). Royal ass. 20 Apr. 1242, writ *de intendendo* 8 June 1242 (*CPR 1232–47*, pp. 282, 299). El. and adm. June 1241 x June 1242 (*Reg. Grosseteste*, p. 319). Mand. for seisin 8 June 1242 (*CR 1237–42*, p. 444). Res. 2 Dec. 1262

---

[18] *VCH* and Baildon, I, 38 following Burton, *Mon. Ebor.*, p. 114, give the date as 1272.

(*Ann. Dunstable*, pp. 219–20, cf. *Reg. R. Gravesend*, p. 191, res. Nov. 1262 x Nov. 1263). Cess., lic to el. 1 Jan. 1263 (*CPR 1258–66*, p. 238).

Simon of Eaton (Eton, Etone) **1263–1274** 6th pr., el. 19 Jan. 1263, conf. 26 Jan. 1263, installed 21 (*sic*) Jan. 1263 (*Ann. Dunstable*, p. 220). Cert. conf. eln by bp of Lincoln 16 Jan. 1263 (PRO, C84/2/45; cf. *Reg. R. Gravesend*, pp.191, 323). Temps. 15 Jan. 1263 (*CPR 1258–66*, p. 240). Pr. 11 years, 9 months (*Ann. Dunstable*, p. 263). D. 23 Oct. 1274 (ibid.; PRO, C84/5/6; cf. d. 29 Oct. (*Mon. Angl.*, VI, 238, no source).

William le Bretun (Bretun, Brothan) **1274–1280** Can. of Dunstable, eln [? conf.] 7 Nov. 1274 (*Reg. R. Gravesend*, p. 200); but cf. Sub-pr. of Dunstable, el. 29 Oct. 1274, conf. by bp 6 Nov., and 11 Nov. adm. by king at Northampton; installed 25 Nov. 1274 (*Ann. Dunstable*, p. 264). Eln pres. to king for royal ass. 29 Oct. 1274 (PRO, C84/5/7); royal ass. 1 Nov. 1274, writ *de intendendo* 11 Nov. 1274 (*CPR 1272–81*, pp. 62, 64). Removed following visitation and provision made for him 1280 (*Ann. Dunstable*, p. 284, cf. *Reg. Sutton*, VIII, 94). Cess., lic to el. 9 Dec. 1280 (*CPR 1272–81*, p. 418). Went to Ruxox and lived there for 7 years dying in 1288 and bur. in the priory chapter house (*Ann. Dunstable*, p. 340).

William de Wederhore (Wederover, Wederowe) **1280–1302** Can. of Dunstable, el. 7 Jan 1281, conf. by bp 26 Jan. (but see below); adm. by king 2 Feb. and installed 9 Feb. 1281 (*Ann. Dunstable*, p. 284). Eln quashed and apptd by bp 25 Jan. 1280 (*Reg. Sutton*, VIII, 94; PRO, C84/7/16). Writ *de intendendo* 2 Feb. 1281 (*CPR 1272–81*, p. 423). Cess., lic. to el. 16 Nov. 1302 (*CPR 1301–07*, p. 74). Seal (*BM Seals*, nos. 3083–4).

John of Cheddington (Chedindon, Chedingdon(e), Chetingdon, Chetindon) **1302–1342** Can. of Dunstable, royal ass. 1 Dec. 1302, temps. 8 Dec. 1302 (*CPR 1301–07*, p. 98). Appeared before bp 5 Dec. 1302, eln conf. 6 Dec. 1302 (Lincoln, Ep. Reg., II, f. 256v); installed within the octaves of Christmas 1302, eln expenses given (*Ann. Dunstable*, p. 409). 3 Aug. 1330 order for release from prison where he was held on an indictment of felony (*CCR 1330–33*, p. 51). 1 Oct. 1330 the pr. was so ill that his life was despaired of and he could not come before the justices (ibid., pp. 62–3). D. by 3 Feb. 1342 (PRO, C84/24/23). D. (unnamed), lic. to el. 12 Feb. 1342 (*CPR 1340–43*, p. 374).

John of London 1342–1348 Eln conf. n. d. (between entries of 17 Jan. 1342 and 22 Mar. 1342) (Lincoln, Ep. Reg., IV, f. 323r). Can. of Dunstable, eln pres. to king for royal ass. 3 Feb. 1342 (PRO, C84/24/23); royal ass. 24 Feb. 1342, temps. 27 Mar 1342 (*CPR 1340–43*, pp. 379, 393). Res. by 9 Apr. 1348 (PRO, C84/25/10). Res., lic. to el. 10 Apr. 1348 (*CPR 1348–50*, p. 52). House void 12 Apr. 1348 by deposition of pr. (*CFR 1347–56*, p. 77).

Roger of Gravenhurst 1348–1351 Can. of Dunstable, royal ass. 15 Apr. 1348, temps. 23 Apr. 1348 (*CPR 1348–50*, pp. 50, 58). Eln conf. on cess. of John of London 12 Apr. 1348 (Lincoln, Ep. Reg., IX, f. 421v) (given as 17 Apr. on f. 416v). D. 8 Sept. 1351 (PRO, C84/26/42, cf. *CFR 1347–56*, p. 305). D., lic. to el. 10 Sept. 1351 (*CPR 1350–54*, p. 135).

Thomas (le) Marescall (Mareschal(l)) **1351–1413** Can. of Dunstable, eln held 15 Sept. 1351 (PRO, C84/26/43); royal ass. 17 Sept. 1351, temps. 13 Oct. 1351 (*CPR 1350–54*, pp. 136, 148–9). Eln quashed but apptd by bp 9 Oct. 1351 (Lincoln, Ep. Reg., IX, f. 428r; cf. PRO, C84/26/44). He had prev. served as vicar of Flitwick (a church in the patronage of Dunstable) (ibid.). Occ. 1406 (BL, Add. Ch. 19953). D. 12 Oct. 1413 (*Mon. Angl.*, VII, 239, no source). D., lic. to el. 13 Oct. 1413 (*CPR 1413–16*, p. 112).

ELSHAM (Lincs), St Mary and St Edmund f. -1166

Lists in *VCH Lincs.*, II, 172; *Heads*, I, 163.

Henry Occ. (H.) 2 Sept. 1201 (BL Harl. Cht. 53 D 10). Last recorded occ. 25 Nov. 1218 (*Lincs. F.*, I, p. 124).

William Escrop 1228/9– Can. of Elsham, el. & adm. Dec. 1228 x Dec. 1229, no reason given for vacancy (*Reg. Wells*, III, 173). Occ. 1229 (*CR 1227–31*, p. 386);1229 x 1234 (BL, Harl. Cht. 44 G 30); Oct. 1245 (LAO, Lincoln D. & C., Dij/78/3/86).

Robert of Clifton **–1271** Occ. 6 Oct. 1256 (*Lincs F.*, II, 121); 1260 (*CR 1259–61*, p. 97); 1260 x 2 (*Reg. Ant. Lincoln*, X, no. 2812); Res. by 29 Sept. 1271 (*Reg. R. Gravesend*, p. 49). Seal (*BM Seals*, no. 2550).

William of Coates (Cotes) **1271–1285** Can. of Elsham, eln conf. 29 Sept. 1271 (*Reg. R. Gravesend*, p. 49). Res. acc. 3 Sept. 1285 (*Reg. Sutton*, I, 65).

William of Barton **1285–1304** Sub-pr. of Elsham, eln quashed but apptd by bp 6 Sept. 1285 (ibid., 65–6). Occ. 3 Feb. 1304 (Lincoln, Ep. Reg., II, f. 5v; PRO, Lincs F. CP/25/1/134/70 no. 9). D. by 27 Feb. 1304 (Lincoln, Ep. Reg., II, ff. 9v–10r). Seal (*BM Seals*, no. 2548).

Robert of Newsham (Neusum) **1304–1323** Cellarer of Elsham, eln quashed but apptd by bp 27 Feb. 1304 (Lincoln, Ep. Reg., II, ff. 9v–10r). D. by 10 April 1323 (*Reg. Burghersh*, I, no. 76). Seal (*Durham Seals*, II, p. 560, no. 3463).

Stephen of Keelby (Keleby) **1323–1332** Can. of Elsham, eln pres. to bp 10 Apr. 1323, eln quashed but apptd by bp 12 Apr. 1323 (*Reg. Burghersh*, I, no. 76). D. by 5 Sept. 1332 (ibid., no. 349).

Richard of Thornton **1332–1339** Can. of Elsham, eln quashed but apptd by bp 5 Sept. 1332 (ibid.). D. by 3 Nov. 1339 (ibid., no. 618).

John of Torksey (Torkeseye) **1339–1341** Can. of Elsham, eln quashed but apptd by vicar-general 3 Nov. 1339 (ibid.). D. by 27 Nov. 1341 (ibid., no. 692).

Ralph de Crossholm (Crosholm) **1341–1343** Can. of Elsham, renounced his eln but submitted to the disposition of the Official *sede vacante* who apptd him 27 Nov. 1341 (ibid.). Cess. by 16 Apr. 1343 (Lincoln, Ep. Reg., VI, ff. 3v–4r), but house noted as vacant 21 Feb. 1343, when Richard de Amcotes, rector of Scawby, was given custody and administration of the goods of the priory (Lincoln, Ep. Reg., VII, f. 24r).

William of Grimsby (Grymesby) **1343–** Can. of Thornholm, apptd by bp 16 Apr. 1343 (Lincoln, Ep. Reg., VI, ff. 3v–4r). William de Ardern, can. of Elsham, apptd co-adjutor 2 Oct. 1346 on account of age and infirmity of pr. (Lincoln, Ep. Reg., VII, f. 86r).

Alexander Disny (de Isny) **1347–1352** Can. of Elsham, commn to examine eln 28 Feb. 1347, no reason given for vacancy; eln conf. 6 May 1347 (Lincoln, Ep. Reg., VI, f. 27v; commn repeated Lincoln, Ep. Reg., VII, f. 205v). Res. by 6 Dec. 1352 (Lincoln, Ep. Reg., IX, f. 103v). Provision made for him 10 Mar. 1353 (Lincoln, Ep. Reg., VIII, f. 41v).

Simon of Driffield (Driffeld) **1352–1378** Can. of Elsham, apptd by bp to whom the power of appt had been unanimously transferred 6 Dec. 1352 (Lincoln, Ep. Reg., IX, f. 103v). Occ. 1377 (*Clerical Poll-Taxes*, p. 45, no. 633). D. by 23 June 1378 (Lincoln, Ep. Reg., X, f. 90r).

FELLEY (Notts), St Mary (?and St Helen, but cf. Binns, p. 133) f. 1152
Lists in *VCH Notts*, II, 112; *Heads*, I, 163.

William de Lovetot Occ. as pr. n.d. re cht. of Ivo de Heriz (BL, Add. ms. 36872, f. 90r). He is prob. 12th cent. or early 13th cent. (depending on whether Ivo I or II, cf. the Heriz details in *Ctl. Thurgarton*, pp. cxlvii–cli).

Walter Occ. Easter 1231 (BL, Add. ms. 36872, f. 74v); n.d. (before 1232 x 1233) (ibid., f. 62v); n.d. (1234 x 1241) (ibid., ff. 75v–76r); 9 Feb. 1240 (PRO, Notts F., CP25/1/182/8 no. 254); c. 1240 (*Nottingham Borough Records*, I, pp. 38–9, no. 19); c. 1250 (*HMC Var. Coll.* IV, 327).

Adam of Nocton (Nok(e)ton) Occ. 29 Sept. 1252 (BL, Add. ms. 36872, ff. 32v–33r); n.d. (*temp*. Henry III) (*Ctl. Crich*, p. 67, no. 30); n.d. (BL, Add. ms. 36872, ff. 26r, 29r).

Henry Occ. c. March 1261 (ibid., f. 132r); n.d. (*temp*. Henry III ?) (ibid., ff. 84r–v, 106r); (H.) n.d. (*temp*. Henry III) (*Ctl. Crich*, p. 66, no. 29).

Ralph of Pleasley (Plesleye) **–1276** Occ. n.d. (BL, Add. ms. 36872, ff. 91r, 92r–93r, not 1268 as in *VCH*). Articles against pr. 9 July 1276 at archbp's visitation (*Reg. W. Giffard*, p. 319). Dep. on 10 July 1276 (ibid., p. 312); In 1303 an agreement involving pr. Ralph was said to have been made 'about 35 years previously' (*Reg. Corbridge*, I, 265).

Thomas of Watnall (Wathenowe) **1276–** Can. of Felley, el. 11 July 1276, eln conf. 13 July 1276 (*Reg. W. Giffard*, pp. 312–13). Occ. 1279 (BL, Add. ms. 36872, ff. 79v, 126r–128r); 9 Dec. 1280 (PRO, Notts F., CP25/1/183/15 no. 51).

Alan de Elkeley 1281– Apptd 2 Sept. 1281, no reason given for vacancy (*Reg. Wickwane*, p. 76, no. 247); n.d. (BL, Add. ms. 36872, f. 105r).

William of Toton (Toveton) **–1315** Occ. 28 Jan. 1295 (ibid., f. 116v). Gave up office (?d./res.) by 5 Apr. 1315 (*Reg. Greenfield*, IV, p. 173, no. 2038).

Elias of Linby (Lyndeby) **1315–1328** Can. of Felley, notice to subpr. and convent that his eln was quashed but he had been apptd by the archbp 5 Apr. 1315 (ibid.). D. by 25 Nov. 1328 (York, Reg. 9B, f. 446v).

John of Kirkby (Kyrkeby) **1328–** Can. of Felley, commn to examine eln 25 Nov. 1328; any opposers to appear 14 Dec.; eln conf. by commissary 18 Dec. 1328 (ibid.). Occ. 25 Sept. 1339 (ibid., f. 475v); 7 July 1344 (York, Reg. 10, f. 110v).

John of Holbrook (Holbrok) **–1349** D. by 11 Sept. 1349 (ibid., f. 133v).

Richard of Shirebrook (Shyrebrok) **1349–** Can. of Felley, eln conf. 11 Sept. 1349 (ibid.).

Richard Ewys –1378 D. by 11 Oct. 1378 (York, Reg. 12, f. 76r–v).

FERRIBY, *see* NORTH FERRIBY

FINESHADE (Northants), St Mary (Castle Hymel) f. -1208

List in *VCH Northants*, II, 136.

William Engaine 1226– Eln conf. 28 May 1226, no reason given for vacancy (*Reg. Wells*, II, 133–4).

Philip of Bedford (Bedeforde) **1232/3–** Can. of Newnham, adm. Dec. 1232 x Dec. 1233, no reason given for vacancy (ibid., 176). Occ. 18 Nov. 1247 (CUL, Peterborough ms. 1, f. 171v; PRO, Northants F., CP25/1/173/36, no. 565); 25 Mar. 1248 (*Basset Chts.*, no. 274).[19]

Constantine Occ. 4 Apr. 1250 (*Lincs F.*, II, 84).

John of Billing 1250/1– Pr. of St James, Northampton, el. and apptd June 1250 x June 1251, no reason given for vacancy (*Reg. Grosseteste*, p. 246). Occ. Oct. 1252 x Oct. 1253 (PRO, E315/48/194); 19 Aug. 1258 (CUL, Peterborough ms. 1, f. 290r).

William of St Neots (de Sancto Neoto) *alias* **Dolerti 1266–1275** Can. of Fineshade, eln conf. 1 Apr. 1266, no reason given for vacancy (*Reg. R. Gravesend*, pp. 106, 296). D. by 20 July 1275 (ibid., p. 128).

Arnold of Slawston (Slauston') **1275–1289** Cellarer of Owston. Eln by compromise agreed 22 July 1275; on 25 July the compromissors go to Owston abbey and choose Arnold and postulate him on 26 July. Eln conf. 15 Aug. 1275 (ibid., pp. 128, 303–4). Res. by 15 Apr. 1289 (*Reg. Sutton*, II, 73). Abb. of Owston 1289 (q.v.).

Thomas of Tachbrook (Tachbrok') **1289–1305** Can. of Fineshade, eln conf. 15 Apr. 1289 (*Reg. Sutton*, II, 73–4). D. by 18 Nov. 1305 (Lincoln, Ep. Reg., II, f. 110r).

Stephen de Stanford (Staunford) **1305–1310** Can. of Fineshade, eln conf. 18 Nov. 1305 (ibid.). Cess. by 20 Mar. 1310 (ibid., f. 119r). Provision made for him as former pr. 17 Oct. 1310 (Lincoln, Ep. Reg., III, f. 201r).

---

[19] The ref. in *VCH* to Ralph le Messag as pr. in 1248 is an error. In Soc. of Ant. ms. 38, f. 94r, Ralph le Messag appears as the proctor of the abb. of Peterborough, not the pr. of Fineshade.

Richard de Holt 1310–1341 Can. of Fineshade, eln quashed, but apptd by bp 20 Mar. 1310 (Lincoln, Ep. Reg., II, f. 119r). D. by 30 May 1341 (Lincoln, Ep. Reg., IV, f. 240r–v).

John Bacon (Bacoun) 1341–1343 Can. of Fineshade, eln quashed, but apptd by Official *sede vacante* 30 May 1341 (ibid.). D. by 24 Oct. 1343 (Lincoln, Ep. Reg., VI, f. 53v).

William of Spalding (Spaldyng) 1343– Can. of Fineshade, eln quashed, but apptd by bp 24 Oct. 1343 (ibid.).

Robert –1356 D. by 10 Aug. 1356 (Lincoln, Ep. Reg., IX, f. 215r).

John de Piry 1356– Aug. can. and priest, right of appt transferred to bp and he apptd John 10 Aug. 1356 (ibid.). Occ. 29 Sept. 1358 (PRO, E315/44/187); 14 Feb. 1362 (PRO, E315/45/186); Jan. 1363 x Jan. 1364 (PRO, E326/3633); 25–26 Mar. 1366 (PRO, E326/428–9); Jan. 1374 x Jan. 1375 (PRO, E210/11189).

The next recorded pr., **Henry Sutton**, cess. by 9 Sept. 1421 (*Reg. Fleming*, I, no. 506).

FLANESFORD (Hereford), St Mary and St John the Baptist. f. 1346 – first stone laid 1346 (*Reg. Trillek*, pp. 88–9).

John Cosyn 1346– Can. of Wormsley, commn to install him as first pr. 12 Oct. 1346 (*Reg. Trillek*, p. 89).

The next recorded pr., **John Walker** (Waller), can. of Wormsley, was pres. 28 June 1400, no reason being given for vacancy (*CPR 1399–1401*, p. 340; *Reg. Trefnant*, p. 184). Another pr., **Nicholas Stormy**, occ. n.d. in a copy cht. in Bodl., Dodsworth ms. 90, f. 121v.

FLITCHAM (Norfolk), St Mary ad Fontes f. 1216+
List in *VCH Norfolk*, II, 381.

Philip Occ. n.d. (13th cent.) (Norfolk RO, Flitcham estate records no. 724); 1244 x c. 1250 (*Ctl. Reading*, I, p. 328, no. 408); 1256 (PRO, Just.1/567, m. 58).

Fulk Bretoun (Briton) –1332 Said to have been pres. in 1300 by William Anemer but patron's right set aside (Blomefield, *Norfolk*, VIII, 418, with no source). Occ. 23 Mar. 1332 (*CCR 1330–33*, p. 543). D. by 7 Sept. 1332 (Norwich, Reg/1/2, f. 53r).

Vincent of Flitcham (Flicham) 1332– Can. of Flitcham, eln conf. 7 Sept. 1332 (ibid.).

John of Flitcham (Flycham) 1349– Can. of Flitcham, eln quashed but apptd by bp 5 Aug. 1349, no reason given for vacancy (*Reg. Bateman*, I, no. 949).

William de Caterford Occ. 1351 x 1352 (Norfolk RO, Flitcham estate records, bundle 1/58).

John Occ. 20 Dec. 1365, 31 Dec. 1365 (ibid., nos. 795–6).

Laurence of Weston 1374– Can. of Flitcham, eln quashed but apptd by bp 26 Sept. 1374, no reason given for vacancy (Norwich, Reg/3/6, f. 28r).

John of Hillington (Hillyngton, Hyllington, Hyllyngton) 1376– Can. of Flitcham, eln quashed but apptd by bp, no reason given for vacancy 5 Mar. 1376 (ibid., f. 42v). Occ. c. 1378 x 1381 (PRO, E179/45/14); 30 Nov. 1380 (Norfolk RO, Holkham, misc. deeds no. 802).

The next recorded pr., **John of Flitcham** (Flycham), can. of Flitcham, eln quashed but apptd by bp 4 Aug. 1404, no reason given for vacancy (Norwich, Reg/3/6, f. 308v).

FRITHELSTOCK (Devon), St Mary and St Gregory f. c. 1220
Lists in Oliver, p. 219; cf. R. Pearse Chope, 'Frithelstock priory', *TDA*, 61 (1929), 167–91.

John Occ. 28 May 1224, 9 Apr. 1228 (*Devon F.*, I, pp. 72, 76, nos. 139, 146); Easter term 1228 (*CRR*, XIII, no. 516).

William Occ. 31 May 1249, 6 June 1249 (*Devon F.*, I, pp. 250, 241–2, nos. 493, 476).

Henry Kaynnes 1262– Adm. and installed 16 Aug. 1262, no reason given for vacancy (*Reg. Bronescombe*, pp. 92, 141; *Reg. W. Bronescombe* I, no. 448). Occ. 8 July 1270 (*Devon F.*, I, p. 345, no. 674).

Johel 1276– Eln conf. 27 Jan. 1276 (*Reg. Bronescombe*, p. 141; *Reg. W. Bronescombe*, II, no. 1148).

Thomas Leaute 1284–1287 Letter of bp of Exeter re admission of a new pr. 15 July 1284 (PRO, SC1/20/21). Order for temps to be restored 1 Aug. 1284 (ibid., SC1/20/21A). Can. of Mottisfont, apptd by bp of Exeter, temps. 2 Aug. 1284 (*CPR 1281–92*, p. 127). Permission gtd to leave Mottisfont 22 July 1284 (*Reg. Pontissara*, I, 283). D., lic. to el. 8 Sept. 1287 (*CPR 1281–92*, p. 277).

Robert of Oxford (Oxonia) **1287–** Can. of Frithelstock, eln pres. to king for royal ass. 19 Sept. 1287 (PRO, C84/9/12); royal ass. 25 Oct. 1287 (*CPR 1281–92*, p. 278).

Oliver –1323 Pr, noted as being old and infirm; Humphrey vicar of Monkleigh apptd as coadjutor 10 Nov. 1311 (*Reg. Stapeldon*, p. 162). Commn to receive res. and make provision for him, and to examine subsequent eln 28 Feb. 1323 (ibid., pp. 162–3); res. 28 Feb. 1323 (*Reg. Bytton*, p. 418). Request to Sir John Beauchamp for lic. to el. a new pr. 31 Mar. 1323 and lic. s.d. (*DKR 8*, p. 148).

Richard de Bittedene Occ. 17 Jan. 1334, 8 Oct. 1341, 18 Mar. 1349 (*Reg. Grandisson*, II, 730, 971, 1079).

John Oc. 8 Jan. 1365 (Lambeth, Reg. Islip, f. 346r). He is prob. to be identified with **John Henycie** who occ. as can. of Frithelstock in 1391 in a case about his unpaid pension but 'formerly for seventeen years its faithful, diligent and laborious prior' who had res. on account of his infirmities and provision had been made for him (*CPL*, IV, 374–5).

William Occ. 22 Nov. 1373 (*Reg. Brantingham*, I, 319), but cf. below.

Thomas Rede (Red) Occ. 24 May 1373 (ibid., 304); n.d. (?1377) (PRO, E179/24/10B). ? Same as below.

The next recorded pr., **John Pynnok(e)**, commn to examine eln 4 July 1379, no reason given for vacancy (*Reg. Brantingham*, I, 402–3, cf. I, 155). Occ. n.d. (?1379 x 1381) (PRO, E179/24/10A, m. 2). At the 1400 episcopal visitation John Pynnok was suspended from the administration of the temps. and Thomas Rede, can. of Frithelstock, was entrusted therewith (*Reg. Stafford*, p. 107). Rede was eventually el. pr. on Pynnok's death in 1417 (ibid., p. 108).

GLOUCESTER, St Oswald f. *c*. 909 (as college); –1153 (as priory)

Lists in *VCH Glouc.*, II, 87; *Heads*, I, 163–4; *BGAS*, XIII (1888–89), pp. 128–9 (without sources); A.H. Thompson, *BGAS*, XLIII (1922), pp. 177–8.

A. Occ. 1223 x *c*. 1227 (*Ctl. Brecon*, XIV, 274, j.d. to Honorius III (in the pd ctl. A. pr. of Gloucester acts with A. pr. of Worksop, the latter evidently being a mistake for R(obert) – so A. could also be a mistake for Gloucester).

William Occ. 1218 (*Ctl. Gloucester*, I, 83; see *Heads*, I, corrigenda); 19 Mar. 1230 (*HMC 5th Rept*, App, p. 335); (W.) 13 Feb. 1231 (*Reg. Gray*, p. 43, no. cc); n.d. (1225 x 1241) (PRO, E164/20, f. 61r); 19 Mar. 1231 (*BGAS*, 22 (1899), p. 182).

E. Occ. 4 Aug. 1235 (*Newington Longueville Chts.*, no. 62).

Nicholas Occ. July 1241 (PRO, Glos. F., CP25/1/73/14 no. 265; CP25/1/73/15, nos. 284, 296).

An unnamed pr. was dep. by the bp of Worcester and replaced by the sub-pr. 1251 (*Ann. Tewkesbury*, p. 146).

Walter Occ. 6 Oct. 1256 (PRO, Glos. F., CP25/1/74/23, no. 514).

William Occ. 1260 (*BGAS*, XIII, 128, no source; *Ann. Tewkesbury*, p. 78, n. 1).

Alfred (Alured) Occ. 15 May 1261 (PRO, Glos. F., CP25/1/74/26, no. 592).

Richard –1281 D. by 10 June 1281 (*Reg. Wickwane*, p. 234, no. 574).

Richard of Bathampton (Bathamptone) **1281–** Chaplain to Archbp. Wickwane, provided 10 June 1281 (ibid., pp. 233–5, no. 574). Presumably the unnamed pr. excommunicated by the archbp of Canterbury 23 Mar. 1283 (*Reg. Peckham*, II, 527–8). Occ. 24 Oct. 1283 (*Reg. Pontissara*, I, 277).

Guy –1289 D. 24 Apr. 1289; petition to appt a new pr. 25 Apr. Archbp of York defers appt until his arrival (*Reg. Romeyn*, II, p. 60, no. 1266).

Peter de Melbourn *alias* **Le Norreis 1289–1301** Apptd 24 May 1289 (ibid., p. 61n). Occ. 10 Sept. 1300 (*Reg. Corbridge*, II, 35). Removed by 5 July 1301 on account of age and ill-health (ibid., II, 63). Ment. as former pr. 25 Feb. 1302 – he had first been sent to Drax priory and now was being transferred to Bridlington priory (ibid., I, 170–1).

Walter of Bingham (Byngham) **1301–1310** Can. of Thurgarton, apptd after removal of Peter (ibid., 170n). Mandate to obey him 5 July 1301 (ibid., II, 63). Mand. 1 June 1310 to return to Thurgarton, handing over St Oswald's to Humphrey of Lavington – ineffective, see below (*Reg. Greenfield*, I, pp. 220–2, no. 513). Deposed by archbp 25 Sept. 1312 (ibid., I, pp. 250–1, no. 579). Mentd 18 Oct. 1312 (*CPR 1307–13*, pp. 536–7).

[**Humphrey of Lavington** Can. of St Oswald's, Gloucester, apptd. 1 June 1310 (*Reg. Greenfield*, I, pp. 220–2, no. 513).]

John of Ashwell (Ashwelle, Asshewelle) **1312–1313** Can. of St Oswald's, Gloucester, apptd 25 Sept. 1312 (ibid., pp. 250–1, no. 579). Occ. 3 Dec. 1312 (ibid., p. 251). Res. by 21 Mar. 1313 (ibid., p. 253, no. 586). As can. of St Oswald's apptd archbp's receiver in the jurisdiction of Churchdown 4 May 1313 (ibid., p. 255, no. 593).

Robert of Kidderminster (Kyddermynster) **1313–1314** Can. of St Oswald's, Gloucester, apptd 21 Mar. 1313 (ibid., p. 253, no. 586). Removed from office 6 Oct. 1314 (ibid., pp. 264–5, no. 623).

John of Ashwell 1314– Re-apptd 6 Oct. 1314 (ibid.).

Robert of Kidderminster –1321 Occ. 19 Aug. 1318 (York, Reg. 9B, f. 482r). Cess. by 5 Apr. 1321 (ibid., f. 492r–v). 14 Apr. 1322 pr. of Thurgarton asked to adm. the former pr. (ibid., f. 417r); 20 Oct. 1322 Robert to be sent back from Thurgarton to St Oswald's (ibid., f. 421v). Sent 16 Jan. 1327 to Healaugh Park priory (ibid., f. 715v).

John of Walton 1321– Can. of St Oswald's, Gloucester, apptd 5 Apr. 1321 (ibid., f. 492r–v).

Thomas Occ. 25 Jan. 1331 (ibid., f. 722r).

John de Harescombe (Harscombe) **–1349** Occ. 31 May 1339 (York, Reg. 9A, f. 81v); 9 Mar. 1347 (York, Reg. 10, f. 293r). D. by 1 June 1349 (ibid., f. 296r).

John of Compton (Cumpton) **1349** Can. of St Oswald's, Gloucester, apptd 1 June 1349 (ibid.). D. by 7 Aug. 1349 (ibid.).

William Heved 1349–1367 Apptd 7 Aug. 1349 (ibid.). Res. by 1 Feb. 1367 (York, Reg. 11, f. 304v).

John Wyneyerde 1367– Can. of St Oswald's, Gloucester, apptd 1 Feb. 1367 (ibid.). Occ. 2 Feb. 1367 (ibid., f. 305r).

Thomas Duk Occ. 4 Mar. 1371 (ibid., f.306r–v); 9 Aug. 1398 (*Reg. Scrope*, I, no. 648).

John of Shipton –1405 Res. by 17 Mar. 1405 (ibid., no. 684).

GRAFTON REGIS (Northants) St Mary and St Michael (occasionally St Michael, cf. Binns, p. 133) f. 1180 x 1205; diss. late 14th/early 15th cents. and granted to Northampton, St James.

List in *VCH Northants*, II, 137.

Richard of Harlestone (Herleston) **1267–1284** chaplain, adm. to custody of hermitage 17 May 1268 (*Reg. R. Gravesend*, p. 110). D. by 30 June 1284 (*Reg. Sutton*, II, 41).

Walter Frusselu 1284–1313 chaplain, pres. 1284; the hermits opposed the presn at first but later withdrew their candidate. Inst. 30 June 1284 (ibid.). D. by 21 July 1313 (Lincoln, Ep. Reg., II, f. 125v).

Adam of Caversfield (Caveresfeld, Karisfeld) **1313–1340** priest, adm. 21 July 1313 (ibid.). D. by 26 July 1340 (Lincoln, Ep. Reg. IV, f. 235r).

William of Radford (Radeford) **1340–1349** priest, inst. 26 July 1340 (ibid.). D. by 28 June 1349 (Lincoln, Ep. Reg., IX, f. 179r).

Simon of Olney (Olneye) **1349–** priest, adm. 28 June 1349 (ibid.)

Walter Child 1370– priest, coll. by bp *per lapsum temporis*, no reason being given for vacancy 28 Apr. 1370 (Lincoln, Ep. Reg., X, f. 180r).

No more admissions have been found in the Lincoln episcopal registers after 1370. Thomas Widevill, esquire, conveyed the hermitage by will dated 12 Oct. 1434 to St James's abbey, Northampton (Baker, *Northants*, II, 162–3, cf. *VCH Northants*, II, 137 for the history of the property later in the 15th century).

GREAT BRICETT (Suffolk), St Leonard (Nobiliac) f. 1114 x 1119

Lists in *VCH Suffolk*, II, 95 (from 1312); *Heads*, I, 164.

Bernard Occ. (B.) 4 May 1218 (*Ctl. Eye*, I, 64–5); 15 July 1224 (PRO, F. Unknown Cos. CP25/1/ /6. no. 35); pr. 'Breseley' occ. Oct. 1227 x Oct. 1228 (*Suffolk F. (Rye)*, p. 24); occ. from *c.* 29 Sept. 1241 to 1 Nov. 1252 (Cambridge, King's Coll., GBR 64–5, 103).

John composition 28 May 1259 between Nobiliac and Great Bricett re his eln (Cambridge, King's Coll., GBR 287); occ. 29 Sept. 1266 (ibid., GBR 73).

Geoffrey Occ. Oct. 1268 x Oct. 1269 (*Suffolk F. (Rye)*, p. 68); 16 June 1269 (Cambridge, King's Coll., GBR 484).

Bartholomew Occ. from Feb. 1272 to 28 Oct. 1276 (ibid., GBR 485, 72).

Stephen Occ. 10 Aug. 1283 (ibid., GBR 96).

Augustine Occ. from 19 Dec. 1292 to 18 Mar. 1300 (ibid., GBR 72, 66).

Robert Occ. from 12 Nov. 1305 to 5 June 1311 (ibid., GBR 72, 281).

William Randulf 1312–1337 Can. of Great Bricett, eln conf. 5 Apr. 1312, no reason given for vacancy (Norwich, Reg/1/1, f. 46v). D. by 21 May 1337 (Norwich, Reg/1/3, f. 5r).

John of Essex (Essexia) **1337–1352** Can. of Great Bricett, eln conf. 21 May 1337 (ibid.). D. by 4 Mar. 1351/2 (Norwich, Reg/2/4, f. 137r).

John of Loddon (Lodene, Lodne) **1352–1365** Can. of Great Bricett, eln quashed but apptd by bp 4 Mar. 1351/2 (ibid.). Cess. by 23 May 1365 (Norwich, Reg/2/5, f. 64v).

Adam of Darsham (Dersham) **1365–** Can. of Great Bricett, eln quashed but apptd by bp 23 May 1365 (ibid.).

Alan of Coddenham (Codenham) **1372–** Can. of Great Bricett, eln conf. 16 Apr. 1372 (Norwich, Reg/3/6, f. 14r), but cf. occ. 30 Jan. 1371 (Thurs. after Conversion of St Paul 45 Edward III) (Cambridge, King's Coll., GBR 274); June 1380 x June 1381 (PRO, E179/45/5B, m. 2).

Alan Borel –1400 D. by 18 Mar. 1400 (ibid., f. 256r–v).

GREAT MASSINGHAM (Norfolk), St Mary, St Nicholas f. –1260

List in *VCH Norfolk*, II, 387.

William Occ. Oct. 1260 x Oct. 1261 (*Norfolk F. (Rye)*, p. 98).

Robert Occ. Oct. 1271 x Oct. 1272 (ibid., p. 110).

Richard –1299 Cess. by 4 Feb. 1299 (PRO, C84/13/26).

Geoffrey of Fakenham 1299– Cellarer of Gt. Massingham, eln pres. to king for royal ass. 4 Feb. 1299 (ibid.); royal ass. to eln 18 Feb. 1299, the lands of Richard son of John, tenant in chief, deceased, being in the king's hands (*CPR 1292–1301*, p. 395). Occ. July 1310 x July 1311 (*Norfolk F. (Rye)*, p. 227); July 1311 x July 1312 (ibid., p. 232).

John of Lynn (Lenn(e), Len) **1325–1355** Cellarer of Gt. Massingham, royal ass. 20 Mar. 1325 (*CPR 1324–27*, p. 112). Eln conf. 3 Apr. 1325, no reason given for vacancy (Norwich, Reg/1/1, f. 115r). D., lic. to el. 4 Jan. 1355 (*CPR 1354–58*, p. 152).

John Brandon of Weasenham (Wesenham) (*also* **of Brandon**) 1355–1372 Can. of Gt.
Massingham, eln conf. 20 Jan. 1355 (Norwich, Reg/2/4, f. 156r). Temps. 22 Jan. 1355 (*CPR
1354–58*, p. 155). Cess. by 26 Oct. 1372 (PRO, C84/30/42). Res., lic. to el. 9 Nov. 1372 (*CPR
1370–74*, p. 215).

John of Raynham (Reynham, Roynham) 1372– Can. of Gt. Massingham, el. 11 Nov. 1372
(PRO, C84/30/44); royal ass. 18 Nov. 1372, temps. 27 Nov. 1372 (*CPR 1370–74*, pp. 216,
220). Eln quashed but apptd by bp 26 Nov. 1372, no reason given for vacancy (Norwich,
Reg/3/6, f. 17v).

Roger of Brisley (Brisele) 1378– Can. of Flitcham, eln quashed but apptd by bp 23 Aug. 1378,
no reason given for vacancy (ibid., f. 59r–v). Occ. in clerical subsidy n.d. (*c.* 1379 x 1381)
(PRO, E179/45/14).[20]

GRESLEY, *see* CHURCH GRESLEY

GUISBOROUGH (Yorks N.), St Mary (Gisburn) f. 1119

Lists in *VCH Yorks*, III, 212; *Ctl. Guisborough*, II, pp. xxxix ff.; *Heads*, I, 164.

Laurence Occ. 1204 x 1210 (*Hatton's Book of Seals*, no. 460; *EYC*, X, no. 122); 2 Feb. 1212 (*Ctl.
Guisborough*, II, no. 1133; *Lincs F.*, II, 304); 17 July 1217 (*Northumberland and Durham
Deeds*, p. 255). Res. 1216 x 1218, presumably 1217 x 1218 into hand of legate, Guala, according to a doct of 1238 (*Ctl. Guisborough*, II, 358; *Reg. Gray*, pp. 80–1, cf. *Guala Letters*, no.
34). Occ. as former pr. 1219 x 1223, 1222 x 1223 (*Ctl. Whitby*, I, nos. 39, 42).

Michael Occ. many times in *Ctl. Guisborough* from Nov. 1218 to 7 Dec. 1234 (II, nos. 921,
687A); 25 Nov. 1218 to 6 July 1231 (*Yorks F., 1218–31*, pp. 5, 155); 8 Nov. 1234 to 7 Dec.
1234 (*Yorks F., 1232–46*, pp. 10, 26); 14 Jan. 1236 (*Durham Assize Rolls*, p. 98).

John of Overton Occ. Apr. 1239 (Bodl., ms. Top. Yorks e. 9, f. 44r); occ. in *Ctl. Guisborough*
from 13 Oct. 1239 to 3 Nov. 1257 (I, no. 232; II, no. 703B); 20 Oct. 1239 to 6 May 1246
(*Yorks F., 1232–46*, pp. 55, 129); 3 and 8 Nov. 1251 (*Yorks F., 1246–72*, p. 37). 11 Jan. 1255
papal mand. to archbp of York to receive the res. of the (unnamed) pr. of Guisborough
who is uncurably sick, and to assign him a fitting provision (*CPL*, I, 309; *Reg. Gray*, p.
215), but John occ. 20 Oct. 1256 (*Lincs F.*, II, 120). Seal (*Durham Seals*, II, p. 566, nos.
3482–3).

Ralph of Irton (Ireton) –1278 Occ. (R.) 16 July 1261 (*Reg. Giffard*, p. 213); also occ. in *Ctl.
Guisborough* from 18 Oct. 1262 to 12 Nov. 1278 (II, nos. 943, 886); 19 Jan. 1276, 12 Nov.
1278 (*Yorks F., 1272–1300*, pp. 7, 16). El. Bp of Carlisle 14 Dec. 1278; d. 1 Mar. 1292 (*Le
Neve 1066–1300*, II, 21).

Adam of Newland –1281 Occ. 1279–80 (PRO, Just.1/1056, m. 42d); 8 July 1280 (*Ctl.
Guisborough*, II, no. 668B; *Yorks F., 1272–1300*, p. 58). Cess. (A.) by 9 July 1281, when provision made for his retirement (*Ctl. Guisborough*, II, pp. 362–4, no. v; *Reg. Wickwane*, no.
399).

William of Middlesbrough (Middelesburgh, Midelesburg, Mydlesburg) –1320 Occ. in *Ctl.
Guisborough* from 9 July 1281 to 7 June 1293 (II, p. 362, no. v; no. 891A); 29 Mar. 1308 (*Recs
A. Bek*, p. 14, no. 9); (W.) 31 Dec. 1312 (*Reg. Pal. Dun.*, I, 105). Res. on account of bodily
infirmity, lic. to el. 19 Jan. 1321 (*Reg. Melton*, II, pp. 66–7, no. 141).

Robert of Wilton (Wylton) 1321–1346 Can. of Guisborough, proclamation *si quis* 28 Jan.
1321; commn to hear objections 14 Feb. 1321 (ibid., p. 67, nos. 142–3). Conf. of eln n.d. and
mand. to obey 18 Feb. 1321 (ibid., nos. 144–6). Occ. 12 Apr. 1346 (Bodl., ms. Top. Yorks e.
8, f. 20v). D. by 28 Nov. 1346 (York, Reg. 10, ff. 159v–160r).

---

[20] Stephen de Helgeye ment. in *VCH* was gtd the wardenship of the *hospital* of Great Massingham (dependent on the priory), not the priory itself, 16 May 1395 (*CPR 1391–96*, p. 569).

John of Darlington (Derlington, Derlyngton) **1346–1364** Proclamation *si quis* 28 Nov. 1346 (ibid., f. 159v); eln conf. 5 Dec. 1346 (ibid., f. 160r). D. by 18 May 1364 (York, Reg. 11, f. 182v). Seal (Clay, *Seals*, pp. 19–20; *Durham Seals*, II, p. 566, no. 3484).

John of Hurworth (Horeworth, Hurreworth) **1364–1393** Can of Guisborough, Commn to examine eln 18 May 1364 (ibid.). In 1386 the pr. was said to be aged 66 (*Scrope-Grosvenor* I, 98). Cess. by 19 Oct. 1393 (York, Reg. 14, ff. 43v–44r).

HALTEMPRICE (Yorks W.), St Mary and Holy Cross f. 1322 (at Cottingham); 1325 x 6 (at Haltemprice – BL, Add. Ch. 20554).
   List in *VCH Yorks*, III, 215.

Thomas of Overton 1327–1329 Can. of Bourne, nominated by founder 9 May 1327, apptd 11 May 1327 (York, Reg. 9A, f. 366r). D. by 28 Jan. 1329 (ibid., f. 375v).

Robert Engayne (Engayn) **1329–1331** Can. of Haltemprice, commn to examine eln 28 Jan. 1329 (ibid.); eln conf. and Robert installed 22 Feb. 1329; certif. of conf. dated 28 Feb. 1329 (ibid. f. 376r). Lic. to el. as house vacant by cess. of Robert 30 Aug. 1331 (ibid., ff. 379v–380r).

John of Hickling (Hickelyng, Hikeling) **1331–1333** Eln quashed but apptd by archbp of York 13 Sept. 1331 (ibid., f. 380r). D. by 3 Feb. 1333 (ibid. f. 383r).

Thomas of Ella (Elvelee, Elveley) **1333–1338** Commn to examine eln 3 Feb. 1333 (ibid.); eln conf. 6 Feb. 1333 (ibid. f. 383r–v). Res. by 4 Apr. 1338 (ibid. f. 396v).

William de Wolfreton 1338–1349 Can. of Haltemprice, eln conf. 4 Apr. 1338 (ibid.). D. by 29 Aug. 1349 (York, Reg. 10, f. 196v).

Robert of Hickling (Hikling, Hiklyng, Hyklyng) **1349–1357** Can. of Haltemprice, eln conf. 29 Aug. 1349 (ibid.). Res. by 30 Nov. 1357 (York, Reg. 11, f. 197v).

Peter of Harpham 1357–1362 Can. of Haltemprice, eln conf. 30 Nov. 1357 (ibid.). Res. by 14 Dec. 1362 (ibid., f. 207r–v).

Robert of Hickling (Hikelyng) **1362–** Can. of Haltemprice, eln conf. 14 Dec. 1362 (ibid.). A co-adjutor, Robert de Burton, can. of Haltemprice, apptd for pr. Robert 2 June 1366 (ibid., f. 217v).

Peter Occ. Easter and Trinity 1370 (Baildon, I, 82).

Robert of Clayworth (Claworth) **–1392** D. by 25 Jan. 1392 (York, Reg. 14, f. 31v).

HARDHAM (Sussex) St Cross f. 1248
   List in *VCH Sussex*, II, 75

Robert Occ. n.d. *ante* 1253 (*Ctl. Chichester*, no. 828).

Richard Occ. as former pr., mentd 1279 (PRO, Just.1/914, m. 25).

Robert Occ. 1279 (ibid.).

Robert de Glottyng' *alias* **de Bodeketon –1299/1300** Dep. by Archbp. Winchelsey for misconduct in visitation and notification to bp of Chichester 31 Jan. 1300 in visitation (*Reg. Winchelsey*, II, 699–700). Mentd (Bodeketon) 27 Apr. 1300 in letter to pr. and convent forbidding them to permit the late pr. Robert de Bodeketon, who was dep. by the archbp and sent to Tortington, to return to Hardham (ibid., I, 383–4). Letter to the bp of Chichester questioning the suitability of Robert, late pr. of Hardham who had been dep., to become pr. of Shulbrede 3 Sept. 1300 (ibid., II, 718–19).

Henry Occ. 1306 (PRO, Just.1/934, m. 18).

John Occ. Hil. – Mich.1328 (*Index to Placita de Banco Rolls* p. 673).

John Occ. 1336 (PRO, Just.1/1423, m. 66), possibly same as above or below.

John of Kent Occ. 1350. In a proof of age case, a witness deposed that William son of Walter del Isle was 21 years old on 1 Aug. 1371 and that at his baptism (1350) John of Kent, then pr. of Hardham, was one of his sponsors (*Sussex Arch. Coll.*, XII, 35).

John Baron Occ. Jan. 1381 (PRO, E179/11/9).

HARTLAND (Devon), St. Nectan (Arrouaisian) f. -1066 (college); 1161 x 1169 (abbey).
   Lists in Oliver, p. 205; *Heads*, I, 164–5.
T. Occ. 5 Oct. 1214 x 16 July 1216 (*Ctl. Launceston*, no. 30).
Wl'icus (?Wulfric) Occ. n.d. (1224 x 1226) (*EEA*, 12, no. 227n).
Thomas Occ. *c.* 1224 x 1242 (*Ctl. Launceston*, no. 184); n.d. (?1248 by mayoralty of Exeter)
   (Oliver, *Supplement*, p. 19).
Hugh Occ. 31 May 1249, 6 June 1249 (*Devon F.*, I, pp. 249, 239–40, nos. 491, 473).[21]
Walrand Occ. 18 Nov. 1256 (*Devon F.*, I, p. 296, no. 579).
Oger de Kernic 1261– Eln conf. 3 Apr. 1261, bl. 10 Apr. 1261 (*Reg. Bronescombe*, p. 100; *Reg.
   W. Bronescombe*, I, nos. 299, 306). Occ. 3 Nov. 1269 (*Cornwall F.*, I, pp. 125–6, no. 231); n.d.
   (1272/3 – 1274/5 or 1277/8, dated by mayoralty of Exeter) (Devon RO, ED/SJ/8).
William [of Wycombe] 1281 Pr. of Carmarthen, transl. to be abb. by 1 May 1281 (*CPR
   1272–81*, p. 430).
Thomas de Wybbebire 1281– Eln conf. 4 Oct. 1281, bl. 5 Oct. 1281 (*Reg. Quivil*, p. 346). Occ.
   Trin. 1283 (PRO, CP40/50, m. 11).
John Occ. 28 Dec. 1300 (PRO, Just.1/1318, m. 22). Prob. the same as John of Exeter below.
John of Exeter –1330 Occ. 15 Nov. 1307 (PRO, C241/65/146); 17 Apr. 1308 (*Reg. Bytton*, p.
   418); 29 May 1308 (PRO, C241/57/105); Mich. 1310 (PRO, CP40/183, mm. 143, 149); 6
   July 1312 (*Reg. Stapeldon*, pp. 170–1); 1314 (ibid., p. 104); 1316 (ibid., p. 279); 23 July 1329
   appt of coadjutors for abb. John (pr. of Hartland, Nicholas (de) Galby, and Henry Bokerel);
   appt revoked 31 July 1329 (*Reg. Grandisson*, I, 516–18). Res. 18 Sept. 1329 and soon died
   (*Mon. Angl.*, VI, 435; Oliver, p. 205, no source). D. *ante* 4 Feb. 1330 when gt of custody of
   spiritualities (*Reg. Grandisson*, I, 554).
John/Roger de Raleghe (Raleye) 1330– There seems to be a recurring problem over the fore-
   names of this abb. (Roger) el. 18 Feb. 1330 and bl. 11 Mar. 1330 (Oliver, p. 210). Occ. (John)
   as abb.-el. 8 Mar. 1330 (*Reg. Grandisson*, I, 560); (Roger) 24 Sept. 1330 (ibid., 582); (Roger)
   1336 (*HMC Var. Coll.*, IV, 78); (Roger) 41 (*Reg. Grandisson*, I, 56; II, 971); (Roger) 1348
   (ibid., II, 1054). D. (John, altered by editor to Roger) by 13 Mar. 1349 (ibid., 1079).
David de Wynscote 1349–1354 Can. of Hartland, eln pres. to bp 13 Mar. 1349; commn to
   examine eln 18 Mar. 1340; bl. 20 (*sic* for 29) Mar. 1349 (ibid., 1079–81). Occ. as abb.-el.
   26 Mar. 1349 (ibid., III, 1380). Death notified to patron 7 May 1354 (Oliver, p. 211, no.
   xii).
William Beaumond (Beamound(e), Beawmond) 1355– Prof. obed. 2 Feb. 1355; mand. to ind.
   3 Feb. (*Reg. Grandisson*, II, 1144). Occ. 24 Apr. 1362 (PRO, C241/143/86); 24 May 1373,
   22 Nov. 1373 (*Reg. Brantingham*, I, 304, 319); n.d. (?1379 x 1381) (PRO, E179/24/10A).
The next recorded abb., **Philip**, occ. 1 Mar. 1398 (*CPR 1408–13*, p. 29).

HASTINGS (Sussex), Holy Trinity f. -1176 (cf. *Heads*, I, 165).
   Lists in *VCH Sussex*, II, 77; *Heads*, I, 165.
John Occ. 1215 x 1217, called abbot (*Ctl. Chichester*, p. 92).
Roger Occ. n.d. (*c.* 1224 x 1229) (ibid., no. 276).
Nicholas Occ. *c.* 1232 (mentd as occ. 'about 30 yrs ago' in case of 1262) (PRO, Just.1/912A, m.
   16).
Thomas Occ. 1266 (*Mon. Angl.*, VI, 168, citing BL, Add. ms. 6343, f. 59r).
Adam Occ. 27 Apr. 1278 (ESRO, T466/43).

---

[21] Oliver, p. 205, gives John Westcott as prob. successor of Hugh, but with no source.

Alexander Occ. 25 Nov. 1279 (*Sussex F.*, II, no. 914); Mich. 1280 x Mich. 1281 (PRO, E159/54, m. 5); complaint about conduct of unnamed pr. 1283 (*Reg. Peckham*, II, 608–9); 20 Nov. 1290 (*HMC De L'Isle and Dudley*, I, 125; *Robertsbridge Chts.*, no. 280).

John −1300 Res. by 8 June 1300 after being accused of negligence and crimes. Bp of Chichester ordered him to be sent to Michelham, so that the cans. can el. a new pr. (*Reg. Winchelsey*, II, 712). He is prob. to be identified with **John Longe**, who is mentd as a former pr. in the time of the grandfather of a party in a case of Trin. 1344 (*YB 18 Edward III*, pp. 317, 319).

Henry Occ. 15 Sept. 1326 (Lambeth, Reg. Reynolds, f. 158r); 4 Feb. 1331 (ESRO, T466/38).

Philip Mentd as former pr. in a case of Trin. 1344 (*YB 18 Edward III*, p. 317).

William de Dene Occ. 21 Jan. 1350 (ESRO, T466/54); 1352 when he had been pr. *c.* 3 years (PRO, Just.1/941A, m. 31); Mich. 1352 (ESRO, T466/58); 28 Oct. 1353 (ESRO, T466/59); Hil. 1359 (*Select Cases of Trespass*, II, 223–4).

John Occ. 12 Jan. 1382 (ESRO, T466/23); 30 Nov. 1385 (ESRO, T466/89); perhaps the same as **John Hassok**, who res. 16 Aug. 1402 (*Reg. Rede*, II, 215).

HAUGHMOND (Shropshire), St John the Evangelist f. 1110 or *c.* 1120 (abbey)
Lists in *VCH Shropshire*, II, 69–70; *Ctl. Haughmond*, p.16; *Heads*, I, 165.

Ralph Occ. 1204 x 1211 (*Ctl. Shrewsbury*, II, no. 358); 1206 (Eyton, *Salop*, VII, 300); 1204 x 1210 (*Ctl. Haughmond*, no. 691); 1204 x *c.* 1218 (ibid., no. 1325); 1203 x 1221 (Oxford, Balliol Coll., ms. 271, f. 102r).

Nicholas Occ. 1217 x 1221 (*Ctl. Haughmond*, no. 861).

Osbert Occ. 1216 x 1222 (*Ctl. Shrewsbury*, II, no. 357); 1219 x 1229, prob. 1217 x 1223 (*EEA*, 7, no. 334; *Ctl. Haughmond*, no. 271; cf. *EEA*, 17, no. 137n.); (O.) 1221 x 1223 (*Ctl. Shrewsbury*, II, no. 363).

William Occ. 1226 x 1227 (*Ctl. Haughmond*, no. 274n; *Ctl. Lilleshall*, no. 143); *c.* 1227 (*Ctl. Haughmond*, no. 1318n.); 28 Oct. 1227 (*Salop F.*, 4th ser., I (1911), p.387).

Ralph Occ. *c.* 1227 x 1236 (*Ctl. Haughmond*, no. 729). For the sequence of abbots at this period see ibid., no. 499.

Hervey (Henry) Occ. (H.) Nov. 1234 x Dec. 1239 (*Ctl. Shrewsbury*, II, no. 339); 27 June 1236 (*Ctl. Haughmond*, no. 917; PRO, Hereford F., CP25/1/80/8, no. 144).

Engelard 1241 Can. of Haughmond, royal ass. 1 Apr. 1241 (*CPR 1232–47*, p. 248). Cess., lic. to el. 30 Apr. 1241 (ibid., p. 250).

Gilbert 1241–1252/3 (G.) pr. of Stone, royal ass. 10 Aug. 1241 (ibid., p. 256). Writ *de intendendo* 24 Aug. 1241 (ibid, p. 257). Occ. 9 Feb. 1245, 17 May 1248 (*Salop F.*, 4th ser., VI, pp. 185, 191); 19 Aug. 1252 (*Ctl. Haughmond*, no. 451). Prob. vacated abbey by 1253 (ibid., no. 412, and see below). Seal (*BM Seals*, no. 3239).

Alexander 1253– ?is he to be identified with Alexander de Ercalwe, pr. of Haughmond, in 1240 (*Ctl. Haughmond*, no. 625). Mand. for seisin and *intendendo* (unnamed abb.) 28 Jan. 1253 (*CR 1251–3*, p. 310). Occ. 1256, 2 Apr. 1258 (*Ctl. Haughmond*, nos. 586, 1357); 29 Dec. 1259 (Staffs RO, D593/A/1/2/15).

John of Morton Occ. 2 Feb. 1264 (*Ctl. Haughmond*, no. 579).

Alan of Shrewsbury (Salop) −1280 Occ. (A.) Oct. 1272, 11 Dec. 1273, 20 Oct. 1277 (ibid., nos. 725, 688, 332); Mich. 1277 x Mich. 1278 (PRO, E159/51, m. 15). Res. by 23 Oct. 1280 (PRO, C84/7/4).

Henry of Astley (Astlegh) 1280–1284 Can. of Haughmond, eln pres. to king for royal ass. 12 Nov. 1280 (PRO, C84/7/9); royal ass. 22 Nov. 1280, temps. 4 Dec. 1280 (*CPR 1272–81*, pp. 415, 417). Cert. of conf. of eln by bp of Lichfield 1 Dec. 1280 (PRO, C84/7/10). D., lic. to el. 18 July 1284 (*CPR 1281–92*, p. 125).

Gilbert of Campden (Caumpeden(e)) 1284–1304 Can. of Haughmond, royal ass. 27 July

1284 (ibid., p. 127; cf. PRO, C84/8/29). Cert. of conf. of eln by bp of Lichfield 5 Aug. 1284 (PRO, C84/8/30). Cess. by 19 Dec. 1304 (PRO, C84/15/25). Provision made for him, after his res had been acc. by the bp during his recent visitation, n.d. (Lichfield, B/A/1/1, f. 65Av). Cess., lic. to el. 25 Dec. 1304 (*CPR 1301–07*, p. 305; *Ctl. Haughmond*, no. 416).

Richard of Brooke (Brock, Broke) **1305–1325** Can. of Kenilworth, royal ass. 15 Jan. 1305, temps. 1 Feb. 1305 (*CPR 1301–07*, pp. 309–10, 312). Occ. in *Ctl. Haughmond* from 1 Feb. 1305 to 15 May 1324 (nos. 450, 1324). D. by 10 June 1325 (Lichfield, B/A/1/2, f. 205r–v; cf. *Ctl. Haughmond*, no. 722).

Nicholas of Longnor (Longenor(l)e, Longenolre) **1325–1346** Can. of Haughmond, eln conf. 10 June 1325 (Lichfield, B/A/1/2, f. 205r–v). Desc. in 1340 as too weak to work (*CPR 1338–40*, p. 503). D. by 7 Feb. 1346 (Lichfield, B/A/1/2, f. 220r).

Richard de Brugge (Brigge) **1346–1362** Can. of Haughmond, eln conf. 7 Feb. 1346 (ibid.). D. by 28 May 1362 (*Reg. Stretton*, I, 195–6).

John of Smethcote (Smethecote) **1362–** Can. of Haughmond, commn to examine eln 28 May 1362; eln conf. 10 June 1362 (ibid.). Occ. 5 Oct. 1373 (*Ctl. Haughmond*, no. 173); 1377 (PRO, E179/15/3, m. 1).

The next recorded abb., **Nicholas of Berrington** (Biriton), occ. June 1377 (Eyton, *Salop*, VII, 302, no source); 24 June 1379 or 1380, 6 Oct. 1381 (*Ctl. Haughmond*, nos. 1309, 407).

HAVERFORD WEST (Pembroke), St Thomas the Martyr f. -1200

Geoffrey Occ. 1231 x 1247 (*Ctl. Brecon*, p. 141; *St Davids Acta*, nos. 95–6; *Welsh Episcopal Acts*, I, p. 373, nos. D539–40); n.d. (first half of 13th cent.) (PRO, E315/53/237).

John Occ. 23 Aug. 1272 (*St Davids Acta*, no. 142; *Welsh Episcopal Acts*, I, p. 411, no. D694).

Richard de Honyburgh (Houyngburgh) **–1331** D. 28 Aug. 1331 (PRO, C84/22/48). D., lic. to el. 8 Sept. 1331 (*CPR 1330–34*, p. 168).

John de Honyngburgh (Hovyngborgh) **1331–** Letter of inst. 11 Dec. 1331 (PRO, SC1/42/44; *Cal. Anc. Corr. Wales*, pp. 191–2, no. xlii). Can. of Haverford, temps. 20 Jan. 1332, eln having been conf. by H., bp of St David's (*CPR 1330–34*, p. 231).

Philip Harold **–1379** Occ. 3 July 1363 (*CPR 1361–64*, p. 378). D. 30 Mar. 1379 (PRO, C84/32/19). D., lic. to el. 20 Apr. 1379 (*CPR 1377–81*, p. 340).

HEALAUGH PARK (Yorks W.), St John the Evangelist. f. -1184 (hermitage); 1218 (Aug. priory).

Lists in *VCH Yorks*, III, 218–19; *Ctl. Healaugh Park*, pp. 3–6.

William de Hamelech (Hameleco) **1218–1233** 1st pr., installed 13 Dec. 1218, d. 21 July 1233, ruled 18 years (*Ctl. Healaugh Park*, list, pp. 3–4). Occ. 1218 (Baildon, I, 89); 22 Feb. 1219, 23 June 1230 (*Yorks F.*, *1218–31*, pp. 31, 128).

Elias **1233–1256** 2nd pr., installed 29 July 1233, res. 21 Sept. 1256, ruled 23 years 1 month (*Ctl.*, list, p. 4). Occ. c. 1233 (*Yorks Deeds*, I, no. 424); 20 Jan. 1252 (*Yorks F.*, *1246–72*, p. 58).[22] Seal (Clay, *Seals*, p. 21).

John Nocus **1257–1261** 3rd pr., installed 9 Oct. 1257, res. 10 Jan. 1261, ruled 4 years 3 months (*Ctl.*, list, p. 4).

Hamo of York (Eboraco) **1261–1264** 4th pr., installed Mar. [/] kal. April] 1261 (*Ctl.*, list, p. 4; *Ctl. Guisborough*, I, 204n.). Occ. n.d. (Bodl., ms. Top. Yorks e 8, f. 153r). Res. 20 May 1264, ruled 3 years, 1 month (*Ctl.*, list, p. 4).

Henry of Wheatley (Quetelay) **1264–1281** 5th pr., el. 4 July 1264, conf. 6 July 1264, installed 8 July 1264. D. June 1281, ruled 15 days short of 17 years (*Ctl.*, list, p. 4). Occ. 2 June 1269

---

[22] Cf. pr. John, occ. 20 Jan. 1249 (*Yorks F.*, *1246–72*, p. 8) – presumably an error.

(*Yorks F., 1246–72*, p. 168); 29 July 1280 (*Yorks F., 1272–1300*, p. 52). Commn to conf. or quash the eln of a future pr. 26 June 1281 (*Reg. Wickwane*, p. 216, no. 520).

Adam of Blyth (Blide, Blithe, Blythe) **1281–1300** 6th pr., el. 27 June 1281, eln conf. 3 July 1281, installed 6 July 1281 (*Ctl.*, list, p. 4). Occ. 1281–1293 (*Ctl.*, pp. 187–8); 1284 (Baildon, I, 89). Res. 20 Oct. 1300. Ruled 19 years 15 weeks, i.e. from the day of the octaves of St Peter and St Paul up to the morrow of St Luke (*Ctl.*, list, p. 4).

William of Grimston (Gremeston, Grymeston) **1300–1320** 7th pr., cellarer of Healaugh Park, el. 20 Oct. 1300 and conf. s.d. Installed 21 Oct. 1300 (*Ctl.*, list, p. 5) but commn to install 8 Dec. 1300 (*Reg. Corbridge*, I, 35). Res. 10 Apr. 1320 (York, Reg. 9A, f. 167v – *Ctl.*, list, p. 5 gives 9 Apr.). Ruled 19 years 6 months 10 days (*Ctl.*, list, p. 5).

Robert of Spofforth (Spofford) **1320–1333** 8th pr., cellarer of Healaugh Park, eln conf. 10 Apr. 1320 (York, Reg. 9A, f. 167v – *Ctl.*, list, p. 5 says el. 9 Apr 1320 and conf. s.d.). D. by 12 Aug. 1333 (York, Reg. 9A, f. 240v). Ruled 13 years (*Ctl.*, list, p. 5). See also York, Reg. 9A, ff. 388v–389r – transfer of Richard of Bilton, can. of Healaugh Park, on account of his attack on Richard of Spofforth, former pr., 19 Jan. 1334.

Stephen of Leavington (Levington) **1333–1352** 9th pr., can. of Healaugh Park, el. on d. of Robert, eln conf. 12 Aug. 1333 (York, Reg. 9A, ff. 240v–241r). Installed 19 Kal. (*sic*) Aug. 1333 (*Ctl.*, list, p. 5). Occ. Lent 1352 (PRO, Just.1/1129, m. 14d). Res. by 4 Oct. 1352 (*BIB*, 1, p. 83, nos. 65–6).

Richard of Leavington (Levyngton, Benington) **1352–1357** 10th pr., installed 14 Aug. 1357 (*sic*) (*Ctl.*, list, p. 5), but cf. petition for conf. of eln 4 Oct. 1352 (*BIB*, 1, p. 83, no. 65). Eln conf. 20 Oct. 1352 on cess. of Stephen of Leavington (ibid., p. 83, no. 66). Richard was prob. vicar of Wighill before his eln, cf. ibid., p. 85, no. 77). Res. 10 Nov. 1357; lic. to el. 11 Nov. (York, Reg. 11, f. 97r).

Thomas of Yarm (Yarum) **1357–1377** 11th pr., can. of Healaugh Park, installed 16 Mar. 1358/9 (*Ctl.*, list, p. 5), but cf. eln conf. 29 Nov. 1357 on res. of Richard of Leavington (York, Reg. 11, f. 97r). Commn to admit cess. 6 Apr. 1377 (York, Reg. 12, f. 23r).

Stephen Clarell 1377–1424 Commn to conf. eln of unnamed pr. 11 Apr. 1377 (ibid.). 12th pr., installed 30 Apr. 1378 (*sic*) and was pr. 45 years 9 months and 3 days (*Ctl.*, list, p. 5). D. 31 Jan. 1424 (York, Reg. 5A, f. 348r).

HEMPTON (Norfolk), St Stephen f. -1135

Lists in *VCH Norfolk*, II, 383; *Heads*, I, 165

Henry Occ. n.d. (?1240) (*Norwich Cath. Chts.*, II, no. 140).

Richard Occ. Oct. 1269 x Oct. 1270, Oct. 1271 x Oct. 1272 (*Norfolk F. (Rye)*, pp. 108, 110).

Giles Occ. 4 Feb. 1298 (*CPR 1292–1301*, p. 376).

Guy Ferret Occ. Nov. 1298 x Nov. 1299 (*Mon. Angl.*, VI, 571).

Richard of Westacre (Westacr') **1302–** Can. of Hempton, apptd by bp 22 Jan 1302 (Norwich, Reg/1/1, f. 7v). Occ. 1305–Jan. 1307 (PRO, Just.1/591, mm. 17, 19d); Easter 1317 (PRO, CP40/218, attorneys m. 8).

Alexander of Lynn (Lenn) **1325–1339** Sub-pr. of Hempton, eln conf. 8 Mar. 1325, no reason given for vacancy (Norwich, Reg/1/1, f. 114v). D. by 10 Apr. 1339 (Norwich, Reg/1/3, f. 24r).

Nicholas of Kettlestone (Ketleston) **1339–** Can. of Hempton, eln conf. 10 Apr. 1339 (ibid.).

Nicholas Curle Occ. 17 June 1352 (*CPL*, III, 465). Probably the same as Kettlestone.

Nicholas Occ. in clerical subsidy n.d. (*c.* 1378 x 1381) (PRO, E179/45/14); 15 Apr. 1381 (Holkham, Coke mun. 2364).

Nicholas of Kettlestone (Kettleston) **–1386** D. by 29 Oct. 1386 (Norwich, Reg/3/6, f. 119v).

HERRINGFLEET (Suffolk), St Olave f. *c.* 1216
  Lists in *VCH Suffolk*, II, 101.[23]
Henry Occ. 22 Apr. 1259 (*Norwich Cath. Chts.*, II, no. 454).
William Occ. Oct. 1268 x Oct. 1269 (*Suffolk F., (Rye)*, p. 69); 3 Oct. 1273 (PRO, E326/8918;
  Suckling, *Suffolk*, II, 15; *JBAA*, new ser. 31 (1925), p. 111).
Benedict Occ. in agreement of Nov. 1300 x Nov. 1301 (Blomefield, *Norfolk*, IX, 417, no source;
  repeated *JBAA*, new ser. 31 (1925), p. 111).
Thomas of Norwich (Norwyco) **1308–** Can. of St Olave, eln conf. 22 Nov. 1308, no reason
  given for vacancy (Norwich, Reg/1/1, f. 31r). Occ. 27 Jan. 1314 (ibid., f. 55r).
[**John of Norwich** (Norwico) Can. of St Olave, eln quashed by bp by 16 June 1329 (Norwich,
  Reg/1/2, f. 29v).]
John of Tibenham (Tybenham) **1329–1341** Apptd by bp 16 June 1329 (ibid.). D. by 24 Apr.
  1341 (Norwich, Reg/1/3, f. 45r).
Philip of Poringland Magna (Porynglond Magna) **1341–1354** Can. of St Olave, eln conf. 24
  Apr. 1341 (ibid.). D. by 17 Nov. 1354 (Norwich, Reg/2/4, f. 155r).
John of Surlingham (Surlyngham) **1354–** Can. of St Olave, eln quashed, but apptd by bp 17
  Nov. 1354 (ibid.).
Roger de Haddiscoe Occ. 1370 (BL, Add. ms. 19098, f. 158r, no source).
John Occ. June 1380 x June 1381 (PRO, E179/45/5b, m. 2).
The next recorded pr., **John de Hanewell** eln conf. 3 Feb. 1392, no reason given for vacancy
  (Norwich, Reg/3/6, f. 164r).

HEXHAM (Northumberland), St Andrew f. ?1113
  Lists in *Heads*, I, 165–6; *Hist. Northumberland*, III, 164–5 from Raine, *Hexham Priory*, pp. cxl–
  cxlxxxii; *Fasti 1066–1300*, VI, 96–7; *Fasti 1300–1541*, VI, 76–8.
William Occ. 26 May 1209 (*Yorks F., John*, p.156); 1215+ (Raine, p. clviii from BL, Cotton
  ms. Claudius B. III, f. 31r (29r)); *c.* 1215 x 1226 (*Reg. Gray*, pp. 275–6); Jan. 1221 x Feb.
  1223 (*Arch. Aeliana*, 3rd ser., XXI (1924), 189–90); Mar. 1222 (Bodl. ms. Top. Yorks e 9,
  f. 82v).
Bernard Occ. 5 Aug. 1226 (Raine, p. clviii from BL, Cotton ms. Claudius B. III, ff. 45v–46r
  (43v–44r)); (B.) 1226 x 1242 (*Northumberland and Durham Deeds*, p. 110); (B.) 1243 (*Ctl.
  Newminster* p. 68); from 11 Feb. 1227 to 15 July 1246 (*Northumberland and Durham F.*, I, pp.
  38, 73, nos. 84, 179).
John of Lazenby (Lasenby, Lasyngby, Laysingby) Occ. n.d. (1250 x 1255) (BL, Lansdowne
  ms. 402, ff. 15v–16r; *Reg. Gray*, pp. 290–1); 1251 (*CTG*, 6, p. 42); 23 Apr. 1256, 20 Oct.
  1266 (*Northumberland and Durham F.*, I, pp. 87, 102, nos. 204, 249); ? *c.*1270, prob. earlier
  (*Northumberland and Durham Deeds*, p. 216). Raine, p. clix has pr. John occ. in a cht. of 19
  July 1271, citing BL, Lansdowne ms. 326, f. 138r and Hodgson, *Northumberland*, III, ii, 13,
  but this is clearly wrong. Hodgson prints an undated cht. mentioning John de Lasenby
  which was conf. by Henry III on 29 March 1269 (13–14). Is he the same as **John de Biwelle**,
  mentd as former pr. in case of 1343 (*YB 17 Edward III*, p. 399, n. 5)?
[**Richard of York** (Ebor') [? **1269**] Eln quashed by archbp on account of canonical irregular-
  ity and illegitimacy of elect, no reason given for vacancy n.d. [?1269, see below] (*Reg. W.
  Giffard*, p. 156; *Hist. Northumberland*, III, 136; Raine, app., p. xxii, no. xiv).]
Henry de Merdene 1269–1281 Pr. of Osney, el. 11 Nov. 1269 (*Ann. Oseney*, p. 229). D. by 29
  Jan. 1281; lic. to el. 2 Feb. 1281 (*Reg. Wickwane*, pp. 226–7, no. 550).
William del Clay (de le Cley) **1281–** Can. of Hexham, eln conf. 28 Feb. 1281 (ibid.); mandate

---

[23] Two prs. of Woodbridge have been interpolated in 1371 in the *VCH* list.

to install as canon of York (Preb. Salton) s.d. (ibid., p. 5, no. 22). Prob. the pr. W. who occ. ? autumn 1291 (YMA, M2/4, f. 4r, *ex inf.* Professor D. Greenway).

[**John de le Cley** Occ. 25 July 1284 (*Northumberland and Durham Deeds*, p. 244). ? an error for William de le Cley above.]

Thomas of Fenwick (Fennewyke) **1292–1311** Eln conf. 5 Mar. [1292] (YMA, M2/4, f. 5r, among 1292 entries). Occ. 9 Feb. 1294 (*Yorks F., 1272–1300*, p. 105); 28 Apr. 1310 *recte* 1311 (*Reg. Greenfield*, I, p. 233, no. 556). Provision made for retirement 29 Apr. 1311 (ibid., p. 233n; Raine, I, p. xlix.)

Gilbert of Boroughbridge (de Ponteburgi) **1311–1312** Can. of Nostell, pr. of Thurgarton (1284–90), apptd by archbp 4 July 1311 (*Reg. Greenfield*, I, pp. 235–6, no. 561). Mandate to subpr. & conv. to receive him as pr. within 3 days under pain of excommunication (ibid., pp. 236–7); letter of archbp's vicar-general to conv. stating that Gilbert's appt should not prejudice their right in future elns 22 July 1311 (ibid., pp. 237–8, no. 564); several canons excommunicated 2 Aug. 1311; commn to relax interdict on priory 20 Nov. 1311; petition for lic. to el. 5 Dec., lic. to el. 19 Dec. 1311 (ibid., pp. 238–44, nos. 564–5). Res. all claims to be pr. 26 Jan. 1312 (ibid., pp. 240–2, no. 565). The pr. of Nostell to receive £10 per annum from Hexham for Gilbert (ibid., p. 243, no. 565).

Robert of Whelpington (Qwelpington, Qwelpyngton) **1312–1328** Can. of Hexham, eln examined 8 Jan., adjourned and eln conf. 26 Jan. 1312 (ibid., pp. 239–44, no. 565). Res. deed (R.) dated 12 Sept. 1328 (York, Reg. 9B, f. 535v); petition for lic. to el. a new pr. 12 Sept. (ibid., f. 536r); lic. to el. 19 Sept. 1328 (ibid.). 27 Dec. 1328 Archbp confirms provision made for ex-pr. Whelpington on 9 Nov. 1328 (ibid., f. 537r).

Thomas of Appleton (Appelton) **1328–1345** Can. of Hexham, proclamation *si quis* 10 Oct. 1328; opposers to appear 21 Oct. (York, Reg. 9B, f. 536v); eln conf. 21 Oct. 1328 (ibid.). D. by 10 Oct. 1345 (YMA, H1/2, f. 19v).

John of Bridekirk (Bridkirk) **1345–1349** Can. of Hexham, eln conf. 22 Oct. 1345, no reason given for vacancy (York, Reg. 10, f. 292r–v). Occ. 7 Feb. 1348 (ibid., f. 295v). D. by 10 Oct. 1349 (YMA, H1/1, f. 66v).

John of Walworth 1349–1358 Adm. sought as preb. Salton (York Minster), attached to priory 10 Oct. 1349 (ibid.). Prof. obed. n.d. (York, Reg. 10, f. 294Br). Occ. 19 Aug. 1350 (*Hist. Northumberland*, IV, 11); 1352 (*BIB*, 1, p. 78, no. 18); 1356 (*Reg. Welton*, no. 119); 12 Jan. 1358 (York, Reg. 11, f. 302r); vacated priory and preb. Salton by 16 Aug. 1358 (YMA, H1/3, f. 28v). Mentioned as former pr. 26 Oct. 1360 (York, Reg. 11, f. 316r).

William of Kendal (Kendall, Kendale) **1358–1366/7** Adm. as preb. of Salton (York Minster) 16 Aug. 1358 (YMA, H1/3, f. 28v). Occ. 5 Apr. 1359 (*Reg. Welton*, no. 251). D. by 21 July 1367 (York, Reg. 11, f. 305r, cf. YMA, AC.1352–1426, f.84v which says d. by 26 June 1366, ?*recte* 1367).

Alexander of Marton 1367–1398 Can. of Hexham, commn to examine eln 21 July, eln conf. 28 July 1367 on d. of William Kendall (York, Reg. 11, f. 305r). Mand. to adm. him as can. of York (preb. Salton), 3 July [*recte* Aug.] 1367 (ibid., f. 305v). Occ. 11 Apr. 1397 (*Reg. Waldby*, pp. 4–5). Res. by 5 Nov. 1398 (*Reg. Scrope*, I, no. 653). Seal (*Durham Seals*, II, p. 569, no. 3494).

HICKLING (Norfolk), St Mary, St Augustine and All Saints. f. 1185
Lists in *VCH Norfolk*, II, 1385–6; list of prs. in *Ch. Oxenedes*, pp. 433–8 (not entirely reliable); *Heads*, I, 166.

Roger –1232 2nd pr., succ. 1209 (*Ch. Oxenedes*, p. 434), but cf. occ. *c.* 25 Apr. 1204 (Bodl., Tanner ms. 425, f. 46v). Occ. 1212 (*CRR*, VI, 293); 1217 x 18 (CUL, ms. Mm 2. 20, ff. 30v–31r); Oct. 1219 x Oct. 1220, Oct. 1227 x Oct. 1228 (*Norfolk F. (Rye)*, pp. 36,41). Cess. 1232 (*Ch. Oxenedes*, p. 435).

Nicholas 1232–1248 3rd pr., succ. 1232. D. 1248 (ibid.). Occ. n.d. (Bodl., Tanner ms. 425, ff. 9r, 48r).

Alan 1248–1270? 4th pr., succ. 1248 (*Ch. Oxenedes*, p. 435). Occ. (A.) at general chapter at Dunstable, prob. 1249 (Bodl., Tanner ms. 425, f. 54r; *Chap. Aug. Cans.*, p. xii); Oct. 1256 x Oct. 1257 (*Norfolk F. (Rye)*, p. 91). D. 1270 (*Ch. Oxenedes*, p. 436).

Hubert ?1270–1286 5th pr., succ. 1270. D. 1286 (ibid.). But he occ. 8 May 1264, (H.) 6 June 1264 and 25 Apr. 1265 (Bodl., Tanner ms. 425, ff. 11v–12r, 47r); (H.) 21 Aug. 1275 (ibid., f. 48v); 28 Jan. 1276 (ibid.).

Geoffrey 1286–1288? 6th pr., succ. 1286. D. 1288 (*Ch. Oxenedes*, p. 436). But occ. n.d., with R., bp of Norwich, therefore after 20 Mar. 1289 (Bodl., Tanner ms. 425, f. 53v).

Ranulf ?1288–1293 7th pr. Can. of Butley, coll. by bp of Norwich 1288. D. 1293 (*Ch. Oxenedes*, p. 436). But occ. 2 Oct. 1286 (Bodl., Tanner ms. 425, f. 48r).

John 1293–1319 8th pr., succ. 1293 (*Ch. Oxenedes*, p. 436). D. 1319 (ibid., p. 437). Occ. (J.) 1295 (Bodl., Tanner ms. 425, f. 53v).

Richard of Hemsby (Hemesby, Hemmesby) 1319–1349 9th pr. succ. 1319 (*Ch. Oxenedes*, p. 437). Can. of Hickling, eln quashed but apptd by bp 14 Apr. 1319, no reason given for vacancy (Norwich, Reg/1/1, f. 79v). D. by 17 July 1349 (*Reg. Bateman*, I, no. 828; *Ch. Oxenedes*, p. 437).

[**Simon Wodewale** El. 1349 while in infirmary, but d. (*Ch. Oxenedes*, pp. 437–8).]

John Netisherde (Hetisherde, Grys de Netesherde) 1349–1358 10th pr., succ. 1349 (ibid., p. 437). Can. of Hickling, apptd by bp 17 July 1349, there being no eln on account of lack of canons (*Reg. Bateman*, I, no. 828). Only 2 cans. left in 1349 and John, an unprofessed novice became pr. (*Ch. Oxenedes*, pp. 437–8). Occ. 4 May 1351 (*CPL*, III, 411). Res. by 18 Nov. 1358 (Norwich, Reg/2/5, ff. 27v–28r; *Ch. Oxenedes*, p. 438).

Richard of Hemsby (Hemmesby) 1358–1366/7 Succ. 1358, styled 11th pr. (*Ch. Oxenedes*, p. 438). Can. of Hickling, eln conf. 18 Nov. 1358 (Norwich, Reg/2/5, ff. 27v–28r). Occ. 27 Feb. 1364 (*CPL*, IV, 41). Cess. 1366 (*Ch. Oxenedes*, p. 438). Res. by 22 Jan. 1367 (Norwich, Reg/2/5, f. 73r).

William (of) Wroxham (Wrexham) 1367–1390/1 12th pr., succ. 1366 (*Ch. Oxenedes*, p. 438). Can. of Hickling, eln conf. 22 Jan. 1367 (Norwich, Reg/2/5, f. 73r). Occ. 1369 (Lambeth, Reg. Whittlesey, f. 76r); 5 Nov. 1383 (Norwich, Reg/3/6, f. 342r); Mar. 1386 (Lambeth, Reg. Courtenay, f. 223r). D. 1390 (*Ch. Oxenedes*, p. 438, but could be 1390/1, see below).

The next recorded pr., **John de Tudyngton**, 13th pr., eln conf. 20 Mar. 1391, no reason given for vacancy (Norwich, Reg/3/6, f. 153v; *Ch. Oxenedes*, p. 438).

HIRST (Lincs), St Mary (Cell of Nostell) f. -1135

Benedict of Dudley (Dodeley) Can. of Nostell, occ. as master or *custos* of Hirst 1 July 1314 (*Reg. Greenfield*, II, p. 184, no. 1065).

John of Leeds (Ledes) Can. of Nostell, dwelling at 'Le Hirst',? as master or *custos*, occ. 17 June 1374 (*Cal. Misc. Inq.*, III, 404).

HOLME, see STEEP HOLME

HORSLEY (Glos) (Troarn; Bruton) f. *temp.* William I (alien priory); diss. 1260 and given to Bruton. 1262 (Aug. cell); 1380 (diss.).

Lists in *VCH Glos.*, II, 93; *Heads*, I, 104.

Gilbert Occ. 1214 (*CRR*, VII, 161).

Stephen Prob. first Aug. pr. adm. *c.* 12 July 1262 (*Ctl. Bruton*, p. 79, no. 316; *EEA*, 13, no. 114); 11 Apr. 1269 (*Reg. G. Giffard*, p. 21).

Walter de Horwode Can. of Bruton, having previously been pres. to priory by the pr. and convent of Bruton and adm. as pr., the bp gives permission for him to live at Bruton for 4 years and to use the fruits of Horsley for the payment of Bruton priory's debts 15 May 1271 (ibid., p. 46).

Richard de la Grave 1292– Inst. n.d. [between entries July – Sept. 1292] (ibid., p. 425). Occ. 8 Apr. 1297 (*CPR 1292–1301*, p. 276).

William 1298– Inst. 11 Nov. 1298 (*Reg. G. Giffard*, p. 507).

William de Wasoun (Wason)? the same. Occ. 9 Mar. 1307 (Worcester Cath. Lib., mun. B.477); 19 Jan. 1313 (*CCR 1307–13*, p. 564).

William of Milverton –1329 D. by 5 Oct. 1329 (*Reg. Orleton (Worc.)*, no. 98).

Laurence de Haustede 1329– Can. of Bruton, adm. 5 Oct. 1329 (ibid., nos. 98, 746).

Henry de Lisle (de Insula, Lile, Lyle) **1335–1357** Can. of Bruton, adm. 21 Sept. 1335, no reason given for vacancy (*Reg. Montacute*, no. 276 and p. 305). Lic. to make a pilgrimage 31 Dec. 1349 (*Worcs Reg. Sede Vacante*, p. 245). Occ. 3 May 1355 (*CPR 1354–58*, p. 244); June 1355 (*Ctl. Bruton*, nos. 358, 363); 10 July 1355 (*CPR 1354–58*, p. 266 = Lambeth, Reg. Islip, f. 100r). Mentd that he had been to Rome and Venice without the pr. of Bruton's leave, and had dissipated the revenues of Horsley (*Cal. Misc. Inq.*, III, 73). In dispute over priorship, signified for arrest 20 Mar. 1357 (Logan, *Runaway Religious*, p. 222). Res. by 19 Oct. 1357 (Worcester, Reg. Brian I, p. 50). Mentioned 5 Nov. 1358 as deposed pr. (*CCR 1354–60*, p. 469).

Richard de Holte 1357–1363 Can. of Bruton, pres. to Horsley by pr. and convent of Bruton 21 Sept. 1357 (*Ctl. Bruton*, no. 362); adm. 19 Oct. 1357 (Worcester, Reg. Brian I, p. 50). Res. by 10 Dec. 1363 (Worcester, Reg. Barnet, p. 10).

Henry Cary 1363– Can. of Bruton, adm. by vicar-general 10 Dec. 1363 (ibid.).

Replacement of a can. of Bruton called pr. of Hurley by another mentd 15 July 1371 (*CPR 1370–74*, p. 126).

William Cary (Gary) Occ. Jan. 1368 x Jan. 1369 (PRO, E42/421; E326/11644). Dispute at the Curia – William styling himself pr., occ. 19 Jan. 1372, 14 Nov. 1373 – William committed to Bruton for safe custody (*King's Bench Edward III*, VI, 168–70).

Richard Cary (most prob. an error for William, see above and below). Priory sequestered on account of pr.'s absence 30 July 1375 (*Worcs Reg. Sede Vacante*, p. 347).

William Cary (Cari, Gary) William's (*sic*) sequestration released 17 Aug. 1375 (ibid., p. 348). Sequestration of fruits of priory owing to bad governance and long absence of pr. William, who is excommunicate 26 Mar. 1376 (*Reg. Wakefield*, no. 42). Pr. absent and long excommunicate – signification for arrest 16 Apr. 1376 (Logan, *Runaway Religious*, p. 224). Ordinance governing the future relationship of Bruton priory and the dependent priory of Horsley 5 July 1376 (*Reg. Wakefield*, no. 43). Occ. 13 June 1377 (PRO, C67/283, m. 1).

HOUGH (Lincs) (Notre Dame de Voeu, Cherbourg) f. *c.* 1164.

Lists in *VCH Lincs.*, II, 243, *Heads*, I, 166.

William –1227/8 Occ. 27 Oct. 1208 (*Lincs. F. 1199–1216*, no.260). Res. Dec. 1227 x Dec. 1228 to be abb. of Cherbourg (*Reg. Wells*, III, 166; *Gallia Christiana*, XI, 942).

Nicholas 1227/8– Adm. Dec. 1227 x Dec. 1228 (ibid.); (N.) occ. June 1238 x June 1239 (*Reg. Grosseteste*, p. 34).

Robert Painpare (Paynpare) **1273–1286** Inst. 3 July 1273 on d. of unnamed pr. (*Reg. R. Gravesend*, p. 55). Letter of res. dated 25 June 1286, acc. 2 Sept. (*Reg. Sutton*, I, 88).

John de Insulis (Insula) **1286–1329** Can. of Cherbourg, letter of pres. 13 Aug. 1286; inst. 2 Sept. 1286 (ibid.). Occ. Trinity 1328 (*Index to Placita de Banco*, p. 282). D. by 1 Apr. 1329 (*Reg. Burghersh*, I, no. 252).

Nicholas Warin (Varun, *dictus* Wary) **1329–1346** Can. of Cherbourg, letter of pres. 1 Apr. 1329, inst. 21 Apr. 1329 (ibid.). D. 1 May 1346 (*CFR 1337–47*, p. 469).

William de Gardino **–1359** Can. of Hough, gtd keeping of priory 1 May 1346 (ibid.). Occ. 8 Apr. 1348 (*CFR 1347–56*, p. 88); Mich. 1348 x Mich. 1349 (PRO, E372/194, rot. 17d). Res. by 22 Feb. 1359 (Lincoln, Ep. Reg., IX, f. 137v).

Richard de Londa (Louda) **1359–** Can. of Cherbourg, letter of pres. 22 Feb. 1359, adm. 22 Mar. 1359 (ibid.). Gtd keeping of the priory during the French war 13 Mar. 1359 (*CFR 1356–68*, p. 91; cf. PRO, E372/204, rot. 13d).

John Feverer *alias* **Smyth** (Faber) Occ. 11 June 1369 (*CFR 1368–77*, p. 15); (Faber) 9 June 1371 (ibid., p. 132); 9 Oct. 1371 (ibid.); (Faber) 17 July 1376 (ibid., p. 357); gt of keeping of priory (Smyth) 17 Apr. 1377 (ibid., p. 395); (Smyth) 24 Oct. 1377 (*CFR 1377–83*, p. 21); (Smyth) 1377 (*Clerical Poll-Taxes*, p. 51, no. 739).

Giles **–1387** D. by 10 June 1387 (Lincoln, Ep. Reg., XI, f. 302r–v).

HUNTINGDON, St Mary f. -1091; *c.* 1108? (finally Augustinian).
Lists in *VCH Hunts*, I, 395; *Heads*, I, 166.

John **–1225** Occ. 1211 x 12 (*Hunts F.*, p. 4); (J.) 1219 (PRO, E40/14067); (J.) 30 Oct. 1219 (*Ctl. Lewes, Norfolk*, pp. 32–3); (J.) 1221 (*HMC Rutland*, IV, 158); Oct. 1222 x Oct. 1223 (*Hunts F.*, p. 8). Res. Dec. 1224 x Dec. 1225 (*Reg. Wells*, III, 54); res. 1225 (Lambeth ms. 1106, f. 120r). D. 1234 (ibid.).

Roger de Frasebii (Eusebii) **1225–1237** El. & adm. Dec. 1224 x Dec. 1225 (*Reg. Wells*, III, 54). Sacrist of Huntingdon, succeeded 1225 (Lambeth ms. 1106, f. 120r). D. June 1237 x June 1238 (*Reg. Grosseteste*, p. 256); D. 1237 (Lambeth ms. 1106, f. 120v).

Richard **1237–1256** Sub-pr. of Huntingdon, adm. June 1237 x June 1238 (*Reg. Grosseteste*, p. 256). Occ. 28 Dec. 1250 (*CChR*, I, 350); Oct. 1254 x Oct. 1255 (*Hunts F.*, p. 29). D. 8 Nov. 1256 (Lambeth ms. 1106, f. 120v).

John of Cambridge (Cantebrig', Cauntebrig') **1256–1302** Succeeded 1256 (ibid.). Occ. 20 Jan. 1258 (PRO, Northants F., CP25/1/174/42, no. 711); Nov. 1280 x Nov. 1281 (PRO, LR14/668); 1294 (PRO, Lincs F., CP25/1/134/64, no. 14). Res. acc. and lic. to el. issued 4 May 1302 (Lincoln, Ep. Reg., III, f. 45r). Order to let John, former pr., to have 4 oaks in the forest of Wauberge fit for timber 30 March 1305 (*CCR 1302–7*, p. 248). Ratification of indulgences granted by other bps for the soul of John of Cambridge 18 Feb. 1311 (Lincoln, Ep. Reg., III, f. 207r).

Walter of Evenley (Evenle(e)) Can. of Huntingdon, eln annulled by bp of Lincoln; Pope apptd bps of Ely and Norwich to investigate Walter's appeal 10 Jan. 1303 (*CPL*, I, 605). House vacant 7 Dec. 1303, 25 June 1305, 15 Aug. 1305, 4 Apr. 1305 (Lincoln, Ep. Reg., II, ff. 234v, 235r–v). Void by his death 29 Jan. 1308 at the apostolic see (*CPL*, II, 37; *Orig. Papal Letters*, p. 26, no. 50). Notification of proceedings against Walter de Evenley, former pr., who had removed the seal 2 July 1307 (Lincoln, Ep. Reg., III, f. 117r). Unnamed pr. excommunicate and absent from England 20 Aug. 1307 (Lincoln, Ep. Reg., II, f. 237v).

Robert of Stamford (Stanfordia, Staunford) **1308–1322** Late pr. of Newstead by Stamford, exhibited papal letters of Clement V, providing him to Huntingdon on death of Walter of Evenley, who called himself pr. Letters dated 29 Jan. 1308, prof. obed. 28 May 1308 (ibid., f. 238v; *CPL*, II, 37; *Orig. Papal Letters*, p. 26, no. 50). Cess., lic. to el. 26 Feb. 1322 (*CPR 1321–24*, p. 75).

Reginald (Robert) of Bluntisham (Blundesham, Blontesham, Bluntysdon) **1322–1349** Can. of Huntingdon, eln pres. to king for royal ass. 28 Mar. 1322 (PRO, C84/20/13); royal ass. 3 Apr. 1322, mandate to escheator to restore issues of priory (Reginald) 6 June 1322 (*CPR 1321–24*, p. 88; *CCR 1318–23*, p. 456). Eln of Robert (*sic*) de Blundesham, can. of

Huntingdon, pres. to bp of Lincoln 20 Apr. 1322, eln quashed but apptd by bp 28 Apr. 1322 (Lincoln, Ep. Reg., IV, f. 363r–v). Occ. 28 June 1322 (BL, Cotton ms. Faustina C. I, f. 28r). D. (Reginald) by 13 Aug. 1349 (Lincoln, Ep. Reg., IX, f. 386r).

John of Weston 1349– Can. of Huntingdon, eln quashed but apptd by bp of Lincoln 13 Aug. 1349 (ibid.). Occ. 6 July 1351 (*CPL*, III, 447); 28 Sept. 1354, 26 July 1357 (*CCR 1354–60*, pp. 90, 417); 10 Aug. 1357 (John de West') (BL, Cotton ms. Faustina C. I, f. 23r); 24 Jan. 1358 (Lincoln, Ep. Reg., VIII, f. 97r).

Thomas of Nassington Occ. 16 Sept. 1363 (Lincoln, Ep. Reg., XII, f. 8r).

Thomas of Shenington (Schenyngton) **–1375** Occ. 18 Apr. 1371 (*CPL*, IV, 162). D. by 1 Aug. 1375 (Lincoln, Ep. Reg., X, f. 310r).

Henry of Roxton (Rokesden, Rokeston) **1375–1404** Can. of Huntingdon, eln pres. to bp of Lincoln 1 Aug. 1375, eln conf. 7 Sept. 1375 (ibid.). D. by 14 June 1404 (Lincoln, Ep. Reg., XIII, f. 281v).

IPPLEPEN (Devon) S. Pierre-de-Rillé (near Fougères) f. *c.* 1145?; diss. *c.* 1414 List in Oliver, p. 300.

Thomas –1274 Res. by 14 Sept. 1274 (*Reg. Bronescombe*, p.146).

Luke 1274– Can. of S. Pierre Fougères, inst. 14 Sept. 1274 (ibid.).[24]

Geoffrey Lic. to visit relatives and friends abroad for 10 weeks 11 Sept. 1315 (*Reg. Bytton*, p. 419; *Reg. Stapeldon*, pp. 224, 272). Lic. to visit mother house and return within 2 months 12 Apr. 1317 (*Reg. Stapeldon*, p.272); occ. 12 Sept. 1334 (*Reg. Grandisson*, II, 764); *c.* 1334 (PRO, C269/15/9). Is he the same as the Geoffrey, can. of S. Pierre, Fougères, resident at Ipplepen 3 Jan. 1340 (ibid., I, 58)?

1355 transfer of priory patronage to the college of St Mary, Ottery (*CPL*, III, 564).

IPSWICH (Suffolk), Holy Trinity f. c. 1133; before 1139 (*Heads*, I, 166).

Lists in *VCH Suffolk*, II, 104 (which erroneously incl. priors of Ipswich, St Peter and St Paul 1253–1304); *Heads*, I, 166–7.

John Occ. 27 Jan. 1203 (*Suffolk F. 1199–1214*, no. 400); 13 Oct. 1211 (ibid., no. 548); 1217 (PRO, E40/14067); 18 Nov. 1223 (*CRR*, XI, no.1208).

William Occ. (W.) 2 Sept. 1226 (*Ctl. Eye*, I, no. 59); (W.) 12 Nov. 1226 (*Ctl. Stoke by Clare*, II, no. 505). Occ. Trin. term 1231 (*CRR*, XIV, no. 1531); and from Oct. 1227 x Oct. 1228 to Oct. 1239 x Oct. 1240 (*Norfolk F. (Rye)*, pp. 47, 63); from Oct. 1230 x Oct. 1231 to Oct. 1250 x Oct. 1251 (*Suffolk F. (Rye)*, pp. 31, 51).

William Occ. 1269 (PRO, C85/130/71). ? The same as above or below.

William Aubry Occ. Nov. 1273 x Nov. 1274 (*Cal. Misc. Inq.*, II, 77).

Hugh Occ. *c.* 1280 (PRO, E42/425).

William Occ. *c.* Nov. 1286 (PRO, E40/3288); Nov. 1286 x Nov. 1287 (*Suffolk F. (Rye)*, p. 90); 27 June 1289 (PRO, CP40/178, m. 295).

William de Brecles Described as former pr. in 1310, not too long before (*YB III*, 66). ? same as above.

Hugh Occ. Trin. 1309 (PRO, CP40/178, m. 157); Easter 1310 (ibid.); Mich. 1310 (PRO, CP40/183, m. 118d).

John of Kentford (Kenteford, Kentforde) **1324–1353** Can. of Holy Trinity, apptd 15 Feb. 1324, no reason given for vacancy (Norwich, Reg/1/1, f. 105v). Occ. 21 Nov. 1328 (Norwich, Reg/1/2, f. 85v); 1337 (Norwich, Reg/1/3, f. 2r); 21 Apr. 1347 (*CPL*, III, 234; *CPP*, p. 109). D. by 31 Jan. 1353 (Norwich, Reg/2/4, f. 145v).

[24] Oliver, p. 300 has pr. Roland occ. first week of Lent 1310, but this must surely be Roland, *can.* of Ipplepen, ordained priest (in the first week of Lent) 6 Mar. 1311 (*Reg. Stapeldon*, p. 481).

William de Braunforde 1353– Can of Holy Trinity, eln quashed, but apptd by bp 31 Jan. 1353 (ibid.). Accounts 1359 (Suffolk RO, Ipswich, HD1538/271/5).

Thomas Accounts as pr. Mich. 1360 – Mich. 1361, Mich. 1361 – Mich. 1362 (ibid., /271/6, 5).

John Baxstere –1383 Occ. ?1379 x 1381 (PRO, E179/45/17). D. by 10 July 1383 (Norwich, Reg/3/6, ff. 90v–91r).

IPSWICH (Suffolk), St Peter and St Paul f. -1189
Lists in *VCH Suffolk*, II, 103; *Heads*, I, 167.

Michael Latest recorded occ. 16 Apr. 1208 (*Suffolk F., 1199–1214*, no. 484).

Gilbert 1225–?1248 Sub-pr. of Ipswich, royal ass. 13 Apr. 1225 (*CPR 1216–25*, p. 519). Occ. (G.) 22 Sept. 1226 (*Ctl. Stoke by Clare*, II, pp. 328–9, no. 505); Oct. 1229 x Oct. 1230 (*Suffolk F., (Rye)*, p. 31); 5 May 1230 (Suffolk RO, Ipswich, HD226, f. 94r). Lic. to el. (no reason given for vacancy) 23 May 1248 (*CPR 1247–58*, p. 16).

William de Colneys 1248–?1252 Can. of Ipswich, royal ass. 2 June 1248 (ibid., p. 18). Occ. Oct. 1250 x Oct. 1251 (*Suffolk F., (Rye)*, p. 54); 21 May 1251 (Suffolk RO, Ipswich, HD226, f. 94v). Lic. to el. (no reason given for vacancy) 29 Dec. 1252 (*CPR 1247–58*, p. 169).

Nicholas of Ipswich (Gippewyz, Gypeswic) **1253–1267** Can. of Ipswich, royal ass. 8 Jan. 1253; temps. 15 Jan. 1253 (ibid., pp. 170, 172). Cert. conf. eln by bp of Norwich 15 Jan. 1253 (PRO, C84/1/33). Occ. Jan. 1267 (PRO, E40/3377). D., lic. to el. 20 Sept. 1267 (*CPR 1266–72*, p. 111).

William of Sedgeford (Secheford, Seggeford) **1267–1289** Can. of Ipswich, royal ass. 14 Oct. 1267, temps. 4 Nov. 1267, eln having been conf by R., bp of Norwich (ibid., pp. 116, 163). Cess., lic. to el. 7 Feb. 1289 (*CPR 1281–92*, p. 313; cf. PRO, C84/9/23 of 5 Feb. 1289).

John of St Nicholas (de Sancto Nicholao) **1289–1304** Sub-pr. of Ipswich, eln pres. to king for royal ass. 30 Apr. 1289 (PRO, C84/9/32); royal ass. 3 May 1289, temps. 5 May 1289 (*CPR 1281–92*, p. 315). Res. 2 July 1304 (PRO, C84/15/13, 15). Cess., lic. to el. 7 July 1304 (*CPR 1301–07*, p. 234). Seal (*Mon. Seals*, p. 43).

Henry of Burstall (Brusstalle, Burstalle) **1304–1311** Can. of Ipswich, eln conf. 3 Aug. 1304 (Norwich, Reg/1/1, f. 13v). Eln pres. to king for royal ass. 5 Aug. 1304 (PRO, C84/15/16); royal ass. 15 Aug. 1304, writ *de intendendo* 25 Aug. 1304 (*CPR 1301–07*, pp. 247, 258). 23 Aug. 1304 Henry of Burstall, pr.-el. of Ipswich St Peter and St Paul to answer the king for having obtained confirmation from John, bp of Norwich, before the king had given his assent to the election (*CCR 1302–7*, p. 218). D., lic. to el. 20 Oct. 1311 (*CPR 1307–13*, p. 395).

Henry of Kersey (Kerseya, Kerseye) **1311–1343** Can. of Ipswich, eln pres. to king for royal ass. 24 Oct. 1311 (PRO, C84/16/45); royal ass. 31 Oct. 1311, temps. 23 Nov. 1311 (*CPR 1307–13*, pp. 397, 400). Eln conf. 18 Nov. 1311 (Norwich, Reg/1/1, f. 43v; PRO, C84/16/48). Unnamed pr. too weak to work 10 June 1340 (*CPR 1338–40*, p. 503). D., lic. to el. 16 Sept. 1343 (*CPR 1343–45*, p. 120).

Clement of Ipswich (Gippewico) **1343–1349** Can. of Ipswich, royal ass. 22 Sept. 1343, temps. 14 Oct. 1343 (ibid., pp. 121, 128). Occ. 16 Feb. 1349 (PRO, E40/3406).

William of Ipswich (Gippewico, Gyppewico) **1349–1381** Cellarer of Ipswich, royal ass. 8 May 1349, temps. 18 May 1349 (*CPR 1348–50*, pp. 286, 296). Bp's provision of pr. 16 (*sic*, see below) May 1349 (PRO, SC1/56/59). Eln quashed but apptd by bp 17 May 1349 (*Reg. Bateman*, I, no. 521). D., lic. to el. 25 June 1381 (*CPR 1381–85*, p. 26).

IVYCHURCH (Wilts), St Mary (Ederoso) f. -1154
Lists in *VCH Wilts*, III, 295; *Heads*, I, 167.

Nicholas Occ. 10 July 1214 (*Sarum Chts.*, p. 78; *Reg. St Osmund*, I, 236–7).

Thomas Occ. 7 Oct. 1221 (*Sarum Chts.*, p. 114). An unnamed pr. occ. as papal judge delegate 5 July 1227 (ibid., p. 183).

David Occ. 9 Oct. 1235 (*Selborne Chts.*, I, 20).[25]

Thomas Griffin 1247–1250 Can. of Osney, royal ass. 26 Apr. 1247 (*CPR 1232–47*, p. 500). Occ. 14 May 1249 (*Wilts F.*, I, 40). Cess., lic. to el. 26 Dec. 1250 (*CPR 1247–58*, p. 83; PRO, C84/1/21).

Henry de Boteham (Bocham) **1250–1281** Can. of Ivychurch, royal ass. 29 Dec. 1250 (*CPR 1247–58*, p. 83). D., lic. to el. 2 Sept. 1281 (*CPR 1272–81*, p. 454).

Richard of Catherington (Katerington) **1281–1303** Can. of Ivychurch, royal ass. 22 Sept. 1281 (ibid., p. 457). Mand. for lic. to el. in place of Richard of Catherington 25 Oct. 1303 (*Cal. Chanc. Warr.*, p. 194). D. by 14 Sept. 1303 (PRO, C84/14/52). D. (R.), lic. to el. 1 Nov. 1303 (*CPR 1301–07*, p. 162).

Mag. William of Calne (Calna) *alias* **Braybrok 1303–1347** Sub-pr. of Ivychurch, eln pres. to king for royal ass. 18 Nov. 1303 (PRO, C84/14/53; C84/15/1); royal ass. 23 Nov. 1303, temps. 17 Dec. 1303 (*CPR 1301–07*, pp. 200, 203). Eln quashed but apptd by bp 6 Dec. 1303 (*Reg. Gandavo*, II, 650–1; PRO, C84/15/4). Res. lic. to el. 18 May 1347 (*CPR 1345–48*, p. 293), but cf. lic. to el. 16 May 1347 (PRO, SC1/40/55).

Stephen of Moredon (Mordon, Morton) **1347–1349** Can. of Ivychurch, royal ass. 30 May 1347, temps 27 June 1347 (*CPR 1345–48*, pp. 295, 346; PRO, SC1/40/57). Apptd by bp's commissaries 12 June 1347; bp's notification to king 14 June 1347 (Salisbury, Reg. Wyvil II, ff. 159v–160r). D. (unnamed pr.) by 25 Feb. 1349 (*CPR 1348–50*, p. 260; CFR 1347–56, p. 106).

James de Groundewell (Grundewell(e)) **1349–1350** Can. of Ivychurch, royal ass. 25 Feb. 1349, as if he had been el., all the other cans. having died; temps. 16 Mar. 1349 (*CPR 1348–50*, pp. 260, 268). Apptd by bp, there being only 1 can. left 6 Mar. 1349 (Salisbury, Reg. Wyvil II, f. 201v; PRO, C84/25/26). Res. by 20 Mar. 1350 (PRO, C84/26/34). Cess., lic. to el. 1 Apr. 1350 (*CPR 1348–50*, p. 484).

John of Langford (Langeford) **1350–1357** Temps. 3 May 1350 (ibid., p. 502). Cess., lic. to el. 29 Sept. 1357 (*CPR 1354–58*, p. 600). Apostate, signified for arrest 8 July 1358 (Logan, *Runaway Religious*, p. 222).

Roger of Chiseldon (Chesuldene, Chuselden(e)) **1357–1361** Cert. conf. eln by bp of Salisbury 10 Oct. 1357 (PRO, C84/27/36). Temps. 25 Oct. 1357 (*CPR 1354–58*, p. 629). D. ? Oct. 1361 (Salisbury, Reg. Wyvil II, f. 282r). House void 14 Oct. 1361 (*CPR 1361–64*, p. 88).

John (of) Bromleye (Bremle, Brymlee) **1361–1374** Can. of Ivychurch, apptd by bp of Salisbury, no reason given for vacancy ? Oct. 1361 (Salisbury, Reg. Wyvil II, f. 282r); cert. of appt by bp 2 Oct. 1361 (PRO, C84/28/10)); temps. 20 Oct. 1361 (*CPR 1361–64*, p. 90). D. by 8 May 1374 (PRO, C84/31/8). D., lic. to el. 17 May 1374 (*CPR 1370–74*, p. 446).

Roger Virgo (Viro) **1374–1404** Sub-pr. of Ivychurch, eln pres. to king for royal ass. 25 May 1374 (PRO, C84/31/9); royal ass. 29 May 1374; temps. 6 June 1374 (*CPR 1370–74*, pp. 446, 443). D. by 1 Dec. 1404 (PRO, C84/38/49). Warrant for lic. to priory to elect a new pr. in place of Roger Virgo whose death is reported by the sub-pr., 9 Dec. 1404 (*Signet Letters*, no. 215). D., lic. to el. 10 Dec. 1404 (*CPR 1401–05*, p. 475).

IXWORTH (Suffolk), St Mary f. 1170

Lists in *VCH Suffolk*, II, 106–7 (from 1338); *Heads*, I, 167.

Adam Occ. (A.) Nov. 1206 (CUL, Add. ms. 4220, f. 103r–v); 1207 (*CRR*, V, 82); 1218 (*Guala Letters*, no. 120); (A.) 1 July 1221 (*Ctl. Eye*, I, no. 64, cf. no. 69).

---

[25] *Ctl. Glastonbury*, II, pp. 157–8, no. 231 (and I, p. lxiii) identifies an unnamed pr. of Ivychurch in a papal delegation case of 1 May 1245 as William of Calne. No source has been found for this identification and it may be an error for the pr. of the same name who occ. a century later.

Gilbert Occ. 18 June 1228 (Cambridge, Emmanuel Coll. box 20, A1, no. 2; *Norfolk F. (Rye)*, p. 41); Oct. 1234 x Oct. 1235 (*Suffolk F. (Rye)*, pp. 33, 36, 38).

Philip Occ. Oct. 1250 x Oct. 1251, Oct. 1255 x Oct. 1256 (ibid., pp. 54, 57).

William Occ. Nov. 1274 x Nov. 1275 (ibid., p. 76); Jan. 1276 (Suffolk RO, Ipswich, HD1538/278/1/13); 4 Oct. 1283 (*CPR 1281–92*, p. 89).

J. Occ. May 1293 (BL, Harl. Roll L. 42).

Reginald Occ. 1293 and 22 Edward I (Nov. 1293 x Nov. 1294) (*Letter-book of William of Hoo*, p. 149, app. no. 15); Nov. 1297 x Nov. 1298 (Suffolk RO, Ipswich, HD1538/278/1/19).

William of Ixworth (Ixeworth) **1307–1338** Can. of Ixworth, adm. 17 Oct. 1307, no reason given for vacancy (Norwich, Reg/1/1, f. 25r). D. by 7 May 1338 (Norwich, Reg/1/3, ff. 11v–12v).

Roger of Kirkstead (Kirkestede, Kyrkested) **1338–1352** Can. of Ixworth, eln conf. 7 May 1338, installed 10 May 1338 (ibid.). Res. by 20 Apr. 1352 (Norwich, Reg/2/4, f. 140v).

John of Swaffham (Swafham) **1352–** Can. of Ixworth, eln quashed, but apptd by bp 20 Apr. 1352 (ibid.). Occ. 27 May 1353 (*CPL*, III, 493).

Nicholas de Monesle 1383– Can. of Ixworth, eln conf. 8 Feb. 1383, no reason given for vacancy (Norwich, Reg/3/6, f. 86v).

KENILWORTH (Warws), St Mary f. *c.* 1125

Lists in *VCH Warws*, II, 89; *Heads*, I, 167–8.

W. 1214– sub-pr. of Osney, el. May–July 1214, the lic. to el. having been given 25 July 1213 (*Rot. Lit. Claus.*, I, 207, 148, cf. *Ann. Dunstable*, p. 41, see appendix I). Prob. the same as William below.

William –1221 Occ. 20 May 1218 (*Staffs F. 2*, p. 218); 12 May 1219 (BL, Add. ms. 47677, f. 19r); 1221 (*Magnum Reg. Album Lichfield*, p. 146, no. 299; Stenton, *Eyre*, no. 652). d. 2 Sept. 1221 (BL, Add. ms. 35295, f. 251v).

William of Burton (Borton) Occ. 8 Nov. 1221 (*Warws F.*, I, nos. 323–4); 12 Nov. 1223 (*Staffs F. 2*, p. 222); (W.) 1226 (PRO, C146/1871); 7 Mar. 1227 (*Warws F.*, I, no. 354). Lic. to el. (no reason given for vacancy) 4 Sept. 1227 (*CPR 1225–32*, p. 141).

Henry 1227–1236 Sub-pr. of Kenilworth, royal ass. 11 Sept. 1227 (ibid., p. 142). Occ. 3 Nov. 1227 (*Staffs Plea Rolls, Henry III*, p. 53); 15 June 1236 (PRO, Leics F., CP25/1/121/15, no. 205). Res. (no name given), lic. to el. 8 July 1236 (*CPR 1232–47*, p. 153).

David 1236–1259 Can. of Kenilworth, royal ass. and writ *de intendendo* 16 July 1236 (ibid., p. 154). House void by his cess. by 4 May 1259 (*CPR 1258–66*, p. 20); lic. to el. 10 May 1259 (ibid., p. 21).

Nicholas 1259–?1265 Can. of Kenilworth, pr. of Calwich, royal ass. 1 June 1259 (ibid., p. 27). Cert. conf. eln by bp of Coventry and Lichfield 2 June [1259] (PRO, C84/4/25). Occ. 7 July 1260 (*Reg. G. Giffard*, p. 105); 9 Feb. 1262 (*Warws F.*, I, no. 831). Prob. the pr. (name lost) who had res. by 12 Jan. 1265 (PRO, C84/3/16).

Humphrey 1265–1266 Cellarer of Kenilworth, royal ass. 10 Feb. 1265, temps. 11 Feb. 1265 (*CPR 1258–66*, pp. 404–5). Cert. conf. eln by bp of Coventry and Lichfield 11 Feb. 1265 (PRO, C84/3/17). Occ. 10 Nov. 1266 (*CPR 1266–72*, p. 8). Lic. to el. (no reason or name given) 2 Nov. [*sic, recte* Dec.] 1266 (ibid., p. 13).

Robert of Astley (Esteley, Estleg) **1266–1276** Writ *de intendendo* 22 Dec. 1266, his eln having been conf. by the legate O[ttobono], cardinal deacon of St Adrian (ibid., p. 19). Res. by 6 Mar. 1276 (PRO, C84/5/51). Res., lic. to el. 14 Mar.1276 (*CPR 1272–81*, p. 137).

William of Evesham 1276–1279 Can. of Kenilworth, eln pres. to king for royal ass. 17 Mar. 1276 (PRO, C84/5/54); royal ass. 23 Mar. 1276, writ *de intendendo* 31 Mar. 1276 (*CPR 1272–81*, p. 137). Occ. 29 Dec. 1278 (*CPR 1281–92*, p. 190; PRO, DL25/149). D. by 25 Jan. 1279 (PRO, C84/6/14).

Richard of Thelsford (Tyvelesford) **1279–1292** Can. of Kenilworth, almoner of the queen mother, eln pres. to king for royal ass. 16 Feb. 1279 (PRO, C84/6/17); royal ass. 18 Feb. 1279, writ *de intendendo* 3 Mar. 1279 (*CPR 1272–81*, pp. 302–3). Cert. conf. eln by bp of Coventry and Lichfield 28 Feb. 1279 (PRO, C84/6/16). D. by 6 Aug. 1292 (PRO, C84/10/49). D., lic. to el. 12 Aug. 1292 (*CPR 1281–92*, p. 504).

Robert de Salle (Salve) **1292–1312** Can. of Kenilworth, eln pres. to king for royal ass. 22 Aug. 1292 (PRO, C84/10/50); royal ass. 27 Aug. 1292, temps. 8 Sept. 1292 (*CPR 1281–92*, pp. 505, 507). Cert. conf. eln by bp of Coventry and Lichfield 2 Sept. 1292 (PRO, C84/11/1). D. by 26 July 1312 (PRO, C84/17/6). Death of unnamed pr. announced 26 July 1312, to be bur. on 30 July (*Worcs Liber Albus*, I, no. 550). D., lic. to el. 30 July 1312 (*CPR 1307–13*, p. 483, cf. *CFR 1307–19*, p. 141).

Thomas of Warmington (Warminton, Warmyngton(e), Warmynton, Worminton) **1312–1345** Can. of Kenilworth, eln pres. to king for royal ass. 9 Aug. 1312 (PRO, C84/17/7); royal ass. 18 Aug. 1312, temps. 5 Sept. 1312 (*CPR 1307–13*, pp. 486, 490). Cert. conf. eln by vicar-general of the bp of Coventry and Lichfield 30 Aug. 1312 (PRO, C84/17/8). D. by 28 Feb. 1345 (PRO, C84/24/35). D., lic. to el. 6 Mar. 1345 (*CPR 1343–45*, p. 440; cf. *CCR 1343–46*, pp. 506–7). Seal (*Mon. Seals*, p. 45).

John de Peyto (Peito) **1345–1361** Can. of Kenilworth, eln pres. to king for royal ass. 15 Mar. 1345 (PRO, C84/24/36); royal ass. 20 Mar. 1345, temps. 18 Apr. 1345 (*CPR 1343–45*, pp. 444, 451–2). Eln conf. 12 Apr. 1345 (Lichfield, B/A/1/2, f. 42v; PRO, C84/24/37). D., lic. to el. 28 July 1361 (*CPR 1361–64*, p. 45).

Henry de Bradewey (Bradeway) **1361–1375** Can. of Kenilworth, royal ass. 8 Aug. 1361, temps. 23 Aug. 1361 (ibid., pp. 45, 54). Commn to examine eln 16 Aug. 1361 on death of John de Peyto, but commissaries conf. eln 28 Aug. (*Reg. Stretton*, I, 23; cf. PRO, C84/28/7 cert. conf. eln 22 Aug. 1361). D. by 18 Mar. 1375 (PRO, C84/31/20). D., lic. to el. 20 Mar. 1375 (*CPR 1374–77*, p. 82).

Walter of Charlton (Cherleton, Cherlton) **1375–1385** Sub-pr. of Kenilworth, eln pres. to king for royal ass. 30 Mar. 1375 (PRO, C84/31/21); royal ass. 3 Apr. 1375, temps. 14 Apr. 1375 (*CPR 1374–77*, pp. 90, 87). Cert. conf. eln by bp of Coventry and Lichfield 12 Apr. 1375 (PRO, C84/31/23–4). D. by 28 Feb. 1385 (PRO, C84/33/27). D., lic. to el. 4 Mar. 1385 (*CPR 1381–85*, p. 535).

KERSEY (Suffolk), St Mary and St Anthony f. *c.* 1218 (as hospital) but soon converted to priory. Diss. 1443.

    List in *VCH Suffolk*, II, 108 (from 1331). I am grateful for information on the priors kindly provided by Mr A.E.B. Owen from the archives of King's College, Cambridge.

Henry Occ. Oct. 1218 x Oct. 1219, Oct. 1234 x Oct. 1235 (*Suffolk F. (Rye)*, pp. 18, 38); *c.* 1240 x 1250 (PRO, E24/427); 1245 (Cambridge, King's Coll, KER 787). Seal (*Mon. Seals*, p. 45; *BM Seals*, no. 3344).

William Occ. 22 July 1245 (Cambridge, King's Coll, KER 641); Oct. 1246 x Oct. 1247 (*Suffolk F. (Rye)*, p. 48); 13 Oct. 1247 (Cambridge, King's Coll, KER 635–6, 639).

Reginald Occ. Oct. 1257 x Oct. 1258, Oct. 1258 x Oct. 1259, Oct. 1260 x Oct. 1261 (*Suffolk F. (Rye)*, pp. 59, 62, 63); Easter 1261 (*Essex F.*, I, 241); 2 Dec. 1257, 13 Jan. 1260 (Cambridge, King's Coll, KER 636, 641).

William Occ. Oct. 1268 x Oct 1269 (*Suffolk F. (Rye)*, p. 69). ? the same as **William de Len'** who occ. n.d. (mid- 13th cent.) (Cambridge, King's Coll, KER 579).

Roger Occ. 1285 (PRO, Just.1/242, m. 4); n.d. (Cambridge, King's Coll, KER 583, 632).

Henry Occ. 5 June 1301, 15 Apr. 1302 (Cambridge, King's Coll, KER 643, 70).

Richard *dictus* **le Waleis** (Waleys) **of Kersey** (Kerseye) **1303–1331** Apptd by bp 6 Feb. 1303, no reason given for vacancy (Norwich, Reg/1/1, f. 11r). Occ. 8 Mar. 1331 (Cambridge, King's Coll, KER 240). D. by 12 Dec. 1331 (Norwich, Reg/1/2, f. 45r–v).

Robert of Akenham 1331–1339 Can. of Kersey, commn to examine eln 12 Dec. 1331, eln conf. 9 Jan. 1332 (ibid.). D. by 26 June 1339 (Norwich, Reg/1/3, f. 27v).

John Parker de Illegh 1339– Can. of Kersey, eln conf. 26 June 1339 (ibid.). Occ. Easter 1346 (*YB 20 Edward III, part 1*, p. 215); from 26 Nov. 1340 to 27 Mar. 1349 (Cambridge, King's Coll, KER 630, 248).

Baldwin de Sauston 1350– Can. of Kersey, apptd 21 Jan. 1350 on d. of unnamed pr. (Norwich, Reg/2/4, f. 119r). Occ. 15 Feb. 1350 (Cambridge, King's Coll, KER 596).

John Call(e) –1388 Occ. from Jan. 1360 x Jan. 1361 to 9 Oct. 1381 (Cambridge, King's Coll, KER 781, 638); June 1380 x June 1381 (PRO, E179/45/56, m. 2). Res. by 15 Jan. 1388 (Norwich, Reg/3/6, f. 126v). Prov. made for ex-pr. 28 Jan. 1387 (Cambridge, King's Coll, KER 627).

KEYNSHAM (Soms), St Mary, St Peter and St Paul f. 1172 x 1173 (see N. Vincent, 'The early years of Keynsham abbey', *BGAS*, CXI (1994 for 1993), 95–113).
  Lists in *VCH Soms*, II, 131–2; *Heads*, I, 168.

Richard 1214/15–1233 Pr. of Keynsham, el. 1214 (*CRR*, VII, 82, cf. Lambeth ms. 1212, f. 110v); but, chamberlain of Keynsham, royal ass. and temps. 15 Jan. 1215 (*Rot. Lit. Claus.*, I, 187). D. 17 Aug. 1233 (*Ann. Tewkesbury*, p. 92). Lic. to el. 20 Aug. 1233 (*CPR 1232–47*, p. 24).

John of Swineshead (Swinesheved) **1233–1243** Pr. of Keynsham, royal ass. 20 Aug. 1233 (ibid., p. 24). Bl. 21 Sept. 1233 (*Ann. Tewkesbury*, p. 92). Occ. 6 Oct. 1243 (*Sarum Chts.*, p. 228). El. abb. of Wigmore 1243 (*Ann. Tewkesbury*, p. 134).

Peter de Pratis 1243– Succ. John (ibid.). Occ. 1 July 1249 (PRO, Herts F., CP25/1/55/23, no. 393B); 31 June 1255 (PRO, Glos F., CP25/1/74/21, no. 469); 15 July 1249, 22 July 1256, 29 July 1256, 9 Feb. 1259 (*Soms F.*, I, 145, 160, 168, 182).

Robert Occ. May 1266 (*Reg. W. Giffard (Bath)*, p. 11); 1268 (*Wilts F.*, I, 56); 30 Apr. 1273 (*Soms F.*, I, 234); 1271 (*CR 1268–72*, p. 412); 24–25 Oct. 1277 (*CPR 1272–81*, p. 245).

Adam Occ. 1 Apr. 1288 (PRO, C241/3/8; C241/9/182; C241/21/16); 4 June 1291 (PRO, C241/21/7; C241/52/12); 14 Oct. 1292 (PRO, C241/21/4); 21 Oct. 1292 (PRO. C241/21/15); n.d. (*temp.* Simon Adrian and Richard *orparius* junior, bailiffs of Bristol, early Edward I) (BL, Add. Cht. 15205).

Nicholas –1349 Occ. 20 Oct. 1294, 4 Apr. 1297 (*CPR 1292–1301*, pp. 98, 273); 1297 (*Cal. Chancery Rolls*, p. 44); Easter 1299 (PRO, CP40/127, m. 179d); 1308, 1313 (*CPR 1307–13*, pp. 140, 555); 1316 (*CPR 1313–17*, p. 451); 1318 (*CPR 1317–21*, p. 134); 1325 (*HMC Wells*, I, 210); 1328 (*CPR 1327–30*, p. 322); 1336, 1337 (*CPR 1334–38*, pp. 279, 497); 1337 (*HMC Wells*, I, 397); 9 May 1343, 8 Sept. 1344 (*CPR 1343–45*, pp. 26, 341); 30 Mar. 1346 (*CPR 1345–48*, p. 66); 10 Jan. 1349 (*Reg. R. Shrewsbury*, II, no. 2139). *VCH* gives him the surname Taunton.

John of Bradford (Bradeford) **1349–** Can. of Keynsham, eln conf. 23 Feb. 1349 (ibid., no. 2207). Occ. 30 Mar. 1350 (*CPR 1348–50*, p. 484); 13 June 1357 (*CPR 1354–58*, p. 562).

William Peschon Occ. Easter 1361 (PRO, CP40/406, m. 85); 28 Oct. 1367 going overseas (*CPR 1367–70*, p. 55); 18 Nov. 1373 (*CCR 1369–74*, p. 590); 1377 (PRO, E179/4/2, m. 1); 1389 (*Cal. Misc. Inq.*, V, no. 214).
The next recorded abb., **Thomas**, occ. 30 Apr. 1393 (*Cal. Misc. Inq.*, VI, no. 17).

KIRKBY BELLARS (Leics) St Peter f. 1316 (as college); 1359 (as priory)
  List in *VCH Leics*, II, 26.

Roger of Cotes 1360–1369 Can. of Owston, apptd to the new Aug. priory 21 Mar. 1360

(Lincoln, Ep. Reg., IX, ff. 372v–373v; *Trans. Leics AHS*, XVI (1929–31), 207–12). D. by 5 Apr. 1369 (Lincoln, Ep. Reg., X, f. 244v; Lincoln, Ep. Reg., XII, f. 69r).

Roger of Sewstern (Seusterne, Sewesterne) **1369–1379** Pres. to bp by convent on d. of Roger of Cotes 5 Apr. 1369; can. of Kirkby, commn to adm. his eln 7 Apr., adm. by commissary 12 Apr. 1369. Mand. to install 10 Apr., installed 12 Apr. 1369 (Lincoln, Ep. Reg., X, ff. 244v, 247v–248r; Lincoln, Ep. Reg., XII, f. 69r). Res. adm. 6 June 1379 (Lincoln, Ep. Reg., XII, f. 181v).

KIRKHAM (Yorks E.), Holy Trinity f. *c.* 1122

Lists in *VCH Yorks*, III, 222; *Heads*, I, 168–9.

Andrew Last recorded (A.) *c.* 1213 x 14 (BL, Cotton ms. Nero D. III, f. 57v).

William de Muschamp Occ. 22 Feb. 1219 to 22 May 1228 (*Yorks F., 1218–31*, pp. 30–1, 116); 1225 (*Ctl. Kirkstall*, p. 266, no. 368); 11 Feb. 1227 (*Northumberland and Durham F.*, I, p. 33, no. 69). For his name see *Ctl. Rievaulx*, no. 47. Possibly the pr. G. (? for Guillelmus) mentd in 1314 as occ. *temp.* Henry III (*YB XVIII*, 150).

Richard Occ. 3 Dec. 1234 to 18 May 1246 (*Yorks F., 1232–46*, pp. 23, 139); 1235, 1241 (*Northumberland and Durham F.*, I, pp. 41, 67, nos. 98, 163); Easter 1244 (Baildon, I, 18); Easter 1245 (Bodl., Dodsworth ms. 7, f. 194v). Prob. **Richard Poterel** former pr., mentd in 1279 *temp.* father of one of the parties in the case (PRO, Just.1/1055, m. 56).

Roger Occ. 20 Oct. 1251, 21 Apr. 1252 (*Yorks F., 1246–72*, pp. 29, 82; Bodl., Fairfax ms. 7, f. 2v); 6 Apr. 1252 (PRO, E135/37/146).[26] Presumably the former pr., **Roger de Kyrkholm**, mentd in case of 1268 (PRO, Just.1/1050, m. 23).

Hugh of Beverley Occ. 1 Oct. 1255 (Bodl., Fairfax ms. 7, f. 101r); 1257 (ibid., f. 3r); 1261 (BL, Cotton ms. Nero D. III, f. 30v); 15 Apr. 1263 to 8 July 1268 (*Yorks F., 1246–72*, pp. 199, 154); (H.) 8 Sept. 1267 (*Reg. W. Giffard*, p. 23); 1268 (PRO, Just.1/1050, m. 69). Possibly the unnamed pr. mentd when commn issued to receive his res. 19 May 1269 (*Reg. W. Gifford*, p. 131).

William of Wetwang (Wetewang) **–1304** Occ. Easter 1276 (PRO, CP40/14, m. 77); 1279 (PRO, Just.1/1056, mm. 65, 66d); 2 Dec. 1279 to 14 June 1294 (*Yorks F., 1272–1300*, pp. 42, 110); 1289 (PRO, C81/1789/18); Trin. 1301 (Baildon, II, 20). Attornies apptd 24 Apr. 1303 on account of debility (*CPR 1301–07*, p. 139). Mand. to pr. William and his convent to obey the archbp's commissary, sent to correct the *comperta* at the recent visitation 30 Apr. 1304 (*Reg. Corbridge*, I, 199–200).

John of Kirkella (Elvelee, Elveley(e)) **1304–1311** Can. of Kirkham, eln quashed but apptd by archbp 3 May 1304 (ibid., 198). Purgation of (unnamed) pr. for several articles discovered at archbp's visitation 1309 (*Reg. Greenfield*, III, pp. 150–1, no. 1471). Provision made for retirement 22 May 1310 (ibid., pp. 170–2, no. 1508). Res. acc. 14 Feb. 1311 (ibid., pp. 190–2, no. 1533A). Commn of oyer and terminer against ex-pr. John for robbery and breach of the peace 1 June 1312 (*CPR 1307–13*, p. 476). Monition to pr. and convent to support ex-pr. John *c.* Sept. 1312 (*Reg. Greenfield*, III, p. 204, no. 1563). Occ. Mich. 1313 (*YB XV*, p. 176). Pension altered 14 July 1314 (*Reg. Greenfield*, III, p. 80, no. 1324).

Robert of Aldborough (de Veteri Burgo) **1311–1321** Can. of Kirkham, eln conf. 14 Feb. 1311 (ibid., pp. 190–2, no. 1533A). D. 25 Oct. 1321 (York, Reg. 9A, f. 348r).

He had previously been an obedientiary of Kirkham (*YB XV*, p. 180).

John of Yarm (Jarum, Yarum) **1321–1333** Cellarer of Kirkham, citation for any opposers to eln 10 Nov. 1321; eln conf. 18 Nov. 1321 (York, Reg. 9A, f. 346r–v). Purgation for adultery acc. by archbp 17 June 1331 (ibid., f. 379v). Occ. 4 June 1333 (*CCR 1333–1337*, p. 116). D. (J.) by 17 Nov. 1333 (York, Reg. 9A, f. 388r).

---

[26] Pr. Roger occ. 20 Jan. 6 Henry III (1222), but since Silvester, bp. of Carlisle (1247–54) also occ., it clearly must be an error for 36 Henry III (1252) (*YB XVIII*, 154).

Adam of Warter (Wartria) **1333–1350** Can. of Kirkham, any opposers to eln cited 20 Nov. 1333; eln conf. 27 Nov. 1333 (ibid.). D. by 6 Mar. 1350 (York, Reg. 10, f. 202v).

John of Hartlepool (Hertenpole, Hertilpole) **1350–1363** Can. of Kirkham, eln conf. 6 Mar. 1350 (ibid., ff. 202v–203r). Mand. to obey him 11 Mar. 1352 (ibid., f. 210v). Cess. by 27 Feb. 1363 (York, Reg. 11, f. 208r).

William of Driffield (Driffeld) **1363–1366** Can. of Kirkham, eln conf. 27 Feb. 1363 (ibid.). D. by 13 July 1361 (ibid., f. 218r).

John of Bridlington (Bridlyngton, Brydlington) **1366–1398** Sub-pr. of Kirkham, eln conf. 13 July 1366 (ibid.). Occ. 14 Jan. 1398 (*Cal. Misc. Inq.*, VI, no. 212). D. by 11 May 1398 (York, Reg. 5A, f. 250r–v).

KYME (Lincs), St Mary (South Kyme) f. -1156
  Lists in *VCH Lincs*, II, 173–4; *Heads*, I, 169.
Roger Last recorded occ. 1 July 1202 (*Lincs F., 1199–1216*, no. 57; *Basset Chts.*, nos. 87–8).
Jordan –**1236/7** Occ. n.d. (1227 x 1230) (BL, Add. ms. 6118, f. 381r). Res. June 1236 x June 1237 (*Reg. Grosseteste*, p. 11).
Roger of Toft 1236/7– Sub-pr. of Thornholm, apptd by authority of the (Lateran) Council & inst. June 1236 x June 1237 (ibid.).
Henry –**1250/1** Occ. 12 June 1245 (*Lincs F.*, II, 5). Res. June 1250 x June 1251 (*Reg. Grosseteste*, p. 119).
John of Bampton 1250/1– Can. of Osney, eln conf. June 1250 x June 1251 (ibid.). Occ. from 20 Oct. 1256 to 7 Feb. 1257 (*Lincs F.*, II, 124, 157).
Peter of Lincoln –**1268** Res. by 27 May 1268 (*Reg. R. Gravesend*, p. 27).
John of Timberland (Timberlund) **1268–1275** Can. of Kyme, eln quashed but apptd by bp 27 May 1268 (ibid., pp. 27–8). Res. by 29 Apr. 1275 (ibid., pp. 63–4).
Thomas of Spalding 1275–1291 Sub-pr. of Kyme, el. 1 May & conf. 9 May 1275 (ibid.). Res. by 20 Jan. 1291 (*Reg. Sutton*, I, 151).
[**Nicholas of Swarby** (Swarreby) **1291** Can. of Kyme, eln quashed on grounds of irregularity by bp who accused the house of conspiracy and deprived them of the right to el. on this occasion 20 Jan. 1291 (ibid., I, 151–2, III, 67–8).]
Arnold 1291–1293 Cellarer of Thornton, apptd by Bp Sutton in the place of Nicholas and inst. 11 Feb. 1291 (ibid., I, 151–2; III, 71). (Arnold had refused Nocton Park in May 1286 (ibid., II, 83–4)). Res. by 23 Sept. 1293 (ibid., I, 179).
Walter of Harby (Herdeby) **1293–1300** Can. of Kyme, appeared before bp of Lincoln 23 Sept. 1293; eln quashed & apptd by bp 24 Sept. 1293 (ibid., 179–80). Res. by 5 Apr. 1300 (Lincoln, Ep. Reg., II, f. 1r).
Thomas of Spalding (Spaldyng) **1300–1309** Can. of Kyme, eln conf. 5 Apr. 1300 (ibid.). Co-adjutors app. to pr. (no name) 2 Aug. 1308 (Lincoln, Ep. Reg., III, f. 139v). Res. by 15 June 1309 (Lincoln, Ep. Reg., II, ff. 28v–29r). Provision made 25 Sept. by successor, conf. by bp 1 Apr. 1310 (Lincoln, Ep. Reg., III, f. 178r–v).
William of Spalding 1309–1317 Can. of Kyme, eln quashed but apptd by bp 15 June 1309 (Lincoln, Ep. Reg., II, ff. 28v–29r). Res. by 26 Apr. 1317 (ibid., ff. 66v–67r).
Drogo Breton (Bretoun) **1317–1326** Can. of Kyme, eln quashed but apptd by bp 26 Apr. 1317 (ibid.). Letter to king for the capture of Drogo, pr. of Kyme, and of the sub-pr., sacrist and cellarer at the instance of Gilbert, vicar of Croft, in a tithe cause 26 Nov. 1320 (Lambeth, Reg. Reynolds, f. 291r). Res. by 26 Apr. 1326 (*Reg. Burghersh*, I, no. 144).
Robert of Lincoln 1326– Can. of Kyme, eln conf. 26 Apr. 1326 (ibid.).
Henry of Whaplode (Quappelade, Quaplod(e), Wapelode) **1376**– Can. of Kyme, commn. to examine eln, dated 3 Dec. 1376, no reason given for vacancy. Eln conf. by commissary 10

Dec. 1376 (Lincoln, Ep. Reg., X, f. 87r). Occ. 1381 (*Clerical Poll-Taxes*, p. 109, no. 1320 & p. 155, no. 1909).

John of Gosberton (Gosberkirke) –**1385** D. by 19 Apr. 1385 (Lincoln, Ep. Reg., XI, ff. 16v–17r).

LANERCOST (Cumberland), St Mary Magdalen f. *c.* 1166

Lists in *VCH Cumberland*, II, 160–1; J.R.H. Moorman, *Lanercost Priory* (1945), p. 31; *Heads*, I, 169.

John Occ. n.d. (1185 x 1210) (*Ctl. Lanercost*, pp. 152, 155, nos. 112, 115); 1205 x 1225 (ibid., pp. 105, 392, nos. 52, 356); 1219 x 1223, ? 1220 (*Ctl. Holm Cultram*, no. 17; *Ctl. Lanercost*, p. 401, no. A3); 1223 x 1229 (*Ctl. Wetheral*, no. 79; Bodl., ms. Top. Yorks e 8, ff. 70v–71r).

S. Occ. 1223 x 1229 (*Ctl. Wetheral*, no. 131).

W. Occ. 26 Dec. 1224 *or* 1225 (*Ctl. Lanercost*, p. 275, no. 226). The sequence is unclear at this point.

Thomas Occ. 1231 x 1240 (ibid., p. 388, no. 352); 1231 x 1246 (ibid., p. 389, no. 353).

Walter Occ. n.d. (1238 x 1256) (ibid., p. 194, no. 166); Oct. 1255 x Oct. 1256 (*Cumbd F.*, p. 226); June 1256 (*Ctl. Lanercost*, p. 237, no. 201).

John of Galloway (Galwythia) –**1283** Prob. the pr. John II mentd in ctl. heading (ibid., p. 241). Occ. Whitsun 1271 (ibid., pp. 309–12, no. 259); 26 Apr. 1272 (ibid., p. 253, no. 211); 2 Feb. 1278 (ibid., pp. 330–2, no. 283). Cess. by 16 Aug. 1283, with provision conf. by Ralph, bp of Carlisle (*Ch. Lanercost*, p. 113). As former pr., d. 1289 (ibid., p. 133).

Simon of Driffield (Driffeld) **1283**– El. 16 Aug. 1283 (ibid., p. 113). Occ. 23 Oct. 1304 (*Ctl. Lanercost*, pp. 387–8, no. 351); 6 Nov. 1306 (*Reg. Halton*, I, 270).

Henry de Burgh –**1315** Occ. 20 Sept. 1310 (*Ctl. Lanercost*, pp. 407–8, no. A7); 22 Nov. 1310 (ibid., pp. 408–9, no. A8). D. 9 Dec. 1315 (*Ch. Lanercost*, p. 232; cf. *Reg. Halton*, II, 112).

Robert of Meaburn (Meburne) **1315**– Commn to examine eln of an unnamed pr. 30 Dec. 1315 (*Reg. Halton*, II, 112). Occ. (R.) *c.* 14 Mar. 1316, 28 May 1316 (ibid., 119, 121).

William de Suthayk (Suthaik) –**1337** Occ. 18 Jan. 1325 (*Ctl. Lanercost*, pp. 383–4, no. 343). D. by 18 June 1337 (*Reg. Kirkby*, I, no. 373).

John of Boothby (Bowethby) **1337**–**1338** Sacrist of Lanercost, eln announced to bp 18 June 1337 (ibid.); eln conf. n.d. (ibid., no. 376). Occ. 8 Nov. x 3 Dec. 1337 (ibid., no. 404). D. by 14 Oct. 1338 (ibid., no. 459).

John of Bewcastle (Bothecastre) **1338**–**1354** Can. of Lanercost, original eln date set for 17 Oct. but postponed to Oct. 21; priory apptd proctors Oct. 23; eln quashed but apptd by bp n.d. (ibid., no. 461). Occ. 6 Apr. 1340 (ibid., no. 535); 1343 (*Ctl. Lanercost*, pp. 371–2, no. 331). Cess. by 2 Dec. 1354 (*Reg. Welton*, no. 69). Provision made 2 Dec. 1354, conf. 10 Dec. 1354 (ibid., nos. 71–2).

Thomas of Hexham (Hextildesham) **1354**–**1355** Can. of Lanercost, el. 2 Dec. 1354 and bp conf. n.d. (ibid., nos. 69–70). D. by 15 July 1355 (ibid., no. 100, cf. no. 102).

Richard of Ridale **1355**– Can. of Carlisle, post. 15 July 1355, conf. by bp 27 July (ibid., no. 102). Some cans. had el. John de Nonyngton (ibid., no. 101). Occ. 6 Feb. 1360 (ibid., no. 297). Absent without leave 30 Nov. 1360 and custody of priory gtd to br. Martin of Brampton, can. of Lanercost, by bp (ibid., no. 355).

The next recorded pr., **Peter Froste**, occ. 1379 (PRO, E179/60/1, m. 1, probably a fake name, see *Trans. CWAAS*, n.s. 52 (1952), 75, and pp. 71–2 for a discussion of the forgery. See also F.P. Mackie, 'The Clerical Population of the Province of York: an edition of the clerical poll tax enrolments 1377–81' (University of York, unpublished D. Phil. thesis, 1998), pp. 50–55. The next mention of a pr. is **John** in 1380 (*Trans. CWAAS*, n.s. 52, 81).

LANTHONY, *see* LLANTHONY

LATTON (Essex), St John the Baptist f. -1200 [re-dated 1177 x 1230, ? *c.* 1196, *Waltham Chts.*, no. 256 & n. – but *Heads*, I, cites V. pr. in 1207]

Lists in *VCH Essex*, II, 154–5 (from 1426); *Heads*, I, 169.

Geoffrey Occ. *c.* 1240 (Oxford, Merton Coll. mun., XII, 3175); 3 Apr. 1276 (Cambridge, King's Coll., LAT.1, no. 7); n.d. (ibid., no. 6, preceding item dated 17 June 1280); mentd as former pr. in 1292 (PRO, Just.1/252, m. 7d). Could be earlier in date (cf. *Waltham Chts.*, no. 256, 1177 x 1230, ? 1196).

John Occ. 8 Oct. 1357 (*CCR 1354–60*, p. 422).

Peter Occ. 27 Oct. 1361 (*Reg. Sudbury*, I, 227).

John Occ. 23 Mar. 1375 (ibid., II, 141); 1374 x 1375 (PRO, C85/121/63).

Peter Occ. 1381 (McHardy, *Church in London*, no. 328); 20 Feb. 1393 (London, Reg. Braybrooke, f.292v)

LAUNCESTON (Cornwall), St Stephen f. 1127

Lists in *Ctl. Launceston*, pp. 219–20; *Heads*, I, 169.

Godfrey Occ. 29 Apr. 1202 (*Cornwall F.*, I, p. 6, no. 11); (G.) n.d. (?*c.* 1220) (*Ctl. Launceston*, no. 482).

Richard Occ. n.d. (*c.* 1220–1244); (R.) n.d. (*c.*1228–1238) (ibid., nos. 310, 297).

William Occ. n.d. (28 Oct. 1232 x 27 Oct. 1233) (ibid., no. 217); 1 July 1235, 2 June 1238 (*Cornwall F.*, I, pp. 29, 33, nos. 59, 69; *Ctl. Launceston*, nos. 530, 345).

Henry Occ. 1 May 1244 (*Cornwall F.*, I, p. 43, no. 87; *Ctl. Launceston*, no. 564).

Robert de Fissacre −1261 Occ. *ante* 1256 (ibid., no. 461). Excommunicated 17 Sept. 1259 on account of disobedience and '*manifestam offensam*', sentence published 18 Sept. 1259, Robert absolved as penitent 20 Sept. 1259; appeared before bp 30 Sept. (*Reg. Bronescombe*, pp. 200–2; *Reg. W. Bronescombe*, I, no. 135). Desc. as former pr. 2 Nov. 1259 (*Reg. W. Bronescombe*, I, no. 168) but see below. Res. 4 Sept. 1261 and lic. to el. and provision made for him 12 Sept. 1261 (*Reg. Bronescombe*, pp. 200–2; *Reg. W. Bronescombe*, I, no. 378).

On 17 Oct. after res. of Robert de Fissacre, both **Laurence** and **Richard of Upton** were el. and both elns quashed and bp decided to provide Richard (ibid., p. 198n; *Reg. Quivil*, p. 361; *Reg. W. Bronescombe*, I, no. 405). Laurence res. his eln 24 Jan. 1262 (*Reg. Bronescombe*, p. 202; *Reg. W. Bronescombe*, I, no. 418).

Richard of Upton (Uppetone) **1261–1273** Occ. 7 July 1261 (*Ctl. Launceston*, no. 298); 20 Oct. 1262 (*Cornwall F.*, I, p. 97, no. 185); 3 Nov. 1262 (ibid., p. 108, no. 203); 31 May 1271 (*Ctl. Launceston*, no. 22). D., lic. to el. 13 Jan. 1273 (ibid., no. 18).

Henry Occ. 28 Feb. 1277 (ibid., no. 350); 15 Feb. 1279 (ibid., no. 424).

Roger Occ. 22 Sept. 1281 (ibid., no. 371).

Henry Occ. 21 Feb. 1285 (ibid., no. 575).

William Teingterer 1285– Can. of Launceston, eln quashed, but apptd by bp 27 Aug 1285, no reason given for vacancy (*Reg. Quivil*, p. 361)

Richard de Brykevile −1307 Occ. many times in the cartulary from Easter Sunday (10 Apr.) 1289 to 14 Nov. 1302 (*Ctl. Launceston*, nos. 258, 391). Pr. until early 1308 (*Reg. Bytton*, p. 419). D. by 26 Dec. 1307 (PRO, C84/16/3). D. (R.), lic. to el. 14 Jan. 1308 (*CPR 1307–13*, p. 43).

Roger of Horton(e) 1308– Can. of Launceston. Eln proclaimed 5 Apr. 1308 on d. of Richard, eln conf. 3 May 1308, commn for installation 4 May 1308 (*Reg. Stapeldon*, pp. 180, 229–30; PRO, C84/16/9). Temps. restored 6 May 1308 (*CPR 1307–13*, p. 69). Bp admonished pr. to exhibit within 2 years his disp. for illegitimacy 20 Feb. 1309 (*Reg. Stapeldon*, p. 180); papal conf. of a former lic. to hold the priory, he already being disp. for illegitimacy 1 Aug. 1309 (*CPL*, II, 63). Occ. Mich. 1310 (PRO, CP40/183, m. 12d; attorneys m. 8d); 1312 (*YB XIII, 1312–13*, p. 139). Roger being blind and infirm, br. Ralph de Huggeworthi, can. of Launceston, is apptd coadjutor 29 Sept. 1316 (*Reg. Stapeldon*, p. 279). Occ. 31 July 1318, 29 Oct. 1320 (*Ctl. Launceston*, nos. 379, 518).

Adam (de) Knoll(e) –1346 Occ. 20 June 1327 (ibid., no. 268). Occ. in *Reg. Grandisson* from 1328 to 1339 (I, 367, 432, 453, 581, 601; II, 907). Occ. in *Ctl. Launceston* from 20 Jan. 1332 to 16 Aug. 1344 (nos. 351, 231). Commn to enquire into state of priory and the excesses of pr. Adam 10 Feb. 1337 (*Reg. Grandisson*, II, 837). Brs. Richard de Trelouny and William de Mershe, cans. of Launceston, apptd co-adjutors 22 Dec. 1344, and William Mershe, Ouger Bant and David atte Hole, cans. of Launceston, apptd administrators of the priory 13 Jan. 1345 (ibid., 989–90). Lic. to el. a new pr. 19 June 1346 (ibid., 1002–3). Bp ordered pr. Adam to res. 21 June 1346; certified he had done so in a letter of 27 June (ibid., 1003–4). Letter of res. 26 June 1346 (ibid., 1004).

Thomas de Burdon(e) (Bourdone) 1346– Can. of Launceston, eln pres. to bp 3 July 1346 (ibid.). 13 July 1346 bp quashed eln, but apptd him and issued mand. to install (ibid., 1004–7; III, 1355). Occ. from 21 May 1348 to 3 July 1361 (*Ctl. Launceston*, nos. 93–4); 1349, 1357, 1362 (*Reg. Grandisson*, II, 1078; III, 1444, 1485); 7 May 1367 (*CPR 1364–67*, p. 388).

Roger Leye Occ. 20 July 1370 (*Ctl. Launceston*, no. 467); 24 May 1373, 22 Nov. 1373 (*Reg. Brantingham*, I, 303, 319).

Stephen Trediddan (Tredydan) –1403 Occ. between 2 Sept. 1377 and 24 Nov. 1384 (*Cal. Misc. Inq.*, VII, no. 454); 1 June 1379 (*Ctl. Launceston*, no. 354); 27 Oct. 1379 (*Reg. Brantingham*, I, 408); 1380 x 1381 (PRO, E179/24/5); 1399 (*Cal. Misc. Inq.*, VI, no. 376). D. 8 Dec. 1403 (*Reg. Stafford*, p. 237).

LAUNDE (Leics.), St John the Baptist f. 1219 x 1225
Lists in *VCH Leics*, II, 12; *Heads*, I, 169–70.

William of Brompton Occ. 1208 x 1209 (PRO, Leics. F., Transcripts, vol. III); n.d. (W.) (late 12th/early 13th cent., with pr. W. of Chacombe) (PRO, E326/8776).

Hugh Occ. 7 May 1223 (PRO, Leics. F., CP25/1/121/10, no. 84).

Osbert Occ. 6 Oct. 1230 (PRO, Northants F., CP25/1/172/23, no. 247); n.d. (early Henry III) (*Berkeley Chts.*, no. 263).

Unnamed pr. deposed at Bp Grosseteste's visitation 1236 (*Ann. Dunstable*, p. 143).

Robert (de) Martival (Martivals, Martivaus, Martiwast) –1252 Occ. from 15 June 1236 to 2 July 1251 (PRO, Leics. F. CP25/1/121/15, no. 204; 122/20, no. 345); 1240 (*HMC Rutland*, IV, 131); 25 July 1248 (*CChR 1226–57*, p. 333); 3 Feb. 1248 (PRO, Notts. F., CP25/1/182/9, no. 350); cancelled entry 25 Jan. 1252 (*CR 1251–53*, p. 190). D. 1252 (*Ann. Dunstable*, p. 185).

Reginald of Kirkby (Kirkeby) –1273 Occ. 6 July 1259 (PRO, Notts. F., CP25/1/183/12, no. 469); 7 Mar. 1268 (*Reg. W. Giffard*, p. 78); 14 Apr. 1269 (PRO, Notts. F. CP25/1/183/13, no. 528); 22 Sept. 1272 (*Staffs. F. 2*, p. 258). D. by 11 July 1273 (*Reg. R. Gravesend*, p. 154). Indulgence for his soul (pr. bur. in priory ch.) 8 June 1318 (Lincoln, Ep. Reg., III, f. 389r).

Richard (de) Martival (Martivallis, Martivaus) 1273–?1289 Eln conf. 11 July 1273 (*Reg. R. Gravesend*, pp. 154, 312). Occ. 13 Oct. 1284 (PRO, Leic. F., CP25/1/123/35, no. 116; 123/36, no. 130); 27 Jan. 1285 (PRO, C85/54/48). D. (William Martival) by ? summer 1289 (*Reg. Sutton*, VIII, 42). Indulgences for his soul (pr. bur. in priory ch.) 9 Oct. 1300 and 8 June 1318 (Lincoln, Ep. Reg., III, ff. 18r, 389r).

William of Somerby (Someredby, Someredeby) ?1289–1300 Ralph Basset, patron of priory, given lic. to el. year 10 of Bp Sutton (May 1289 x May 1290) (Bodl., Dodsworth ms. 107, f.

140r). Apptd by bp n.d. (? summer 1289) after disputed eln with Hugh of Dingley (Dingele) (*Reg. Sutton*, VIII, 42). Res. by 8 Oct. 1300 (Lincoln, Ep. Reg., II, f.195v). Provision made for him 21 Dec. 1301 (Lincoln, Ep. Reg., III, ff. 39v–40r). Indulgence for his soul (pr. bur. in priory ch.) 8 June 1318 (ibid., f. 389r).

John of Kirkby (Kirkeby, Kyrkeby) **1300–1309** Can. of Launde, appeared before bp 8 Oct. 1300, eln conf. 30 Oct. 1300 (Lincoln, Ep. Reg., II, f. 195v). Absolved from excommunication 5 Jan. 1309 (Lincoln, Ep. Reg., III, f. 146v). D. by 29 Mar. 1309 (Lincoln, Ep. Reg., II, f. 203r). Indulgence for his soul (pr. bur. in priory ch.) 8 June 1318 (Lincoln, Ep. Reg., III, f. 389r).

John de Burgo 1309–1319 Can. of Launde, eln quashed, but apptd by bp 29 Mar. 1309 (Lincoln, Ep. Reg., II, f. 203r). Occ. 15 Sept. 1319 (Lincoln, Ep. Reg., III, f. 424r). D. (J.), lic. to el. 13 Nov. 1319 (*CPR 1317–21*, p. 400, cf. *CFR 1319–27* p. 9). Indulgence for soul 20 Dec. 1319 (Lincoln, Ep. Reg., III, f. 430r).

Henry of Braunston (Barnedeston, Braundeston(e), Braunseton) **1319–1344** Can. of Launde, royal ass. 3 Dec. 1319 (*CPR 1317–21*, p. 405). Eln quashed , but apptd by bp 20 Dec. 1319 (Lincoln, Ep. Reg., II, f. 219r–v). Res. by 28 June 1344 (Lincoln, Ep. Reg., VI, ff. 37v–38r).

John of Peatling (Petlyng) **1344–1354** Can. of Launde, apptd by bp 28 June 1344 (ibid.). Occ. n.d. (*c.* Aug. 1353) (York, Reg. 11, f. 20v). D. by 25 Mar. 1354 (Lincoln, Ep. Reg., IX, f. 359r–v).

John de Wytherington (Wetheryngton) **1354–1366** Can. of Launde, bp nominated him 25 Mar. 1354, formal eln 26 Mar; eln conf. 5 June 1354 (ibid.). Res. 6 Dec.1366 (Lincoln, Ep. Reg., X, ff. 237v, 238r).

Disputed eln 1366 between **John de Bolewyk**, sub-pr. of Launde, and **Peter of Leicester** (Leycestr'), can. of Launde. The sub-pr. and convent subsequently transfer right of appt to bp of Lincoln 20 Dec. 1366 and he chose **John of Leicester**, can. of Launde (ibid., f. 238r–v).

John of Leicester (Leicestr(ia)) **1366–1369** The convent el. him on the bp's nomination and eln conf. [ ] Dec. 1366 (ibid.). D. by 6 Aug. 1369 (ibid., f. 246r–v).

John of Rearsby (Rerisby, Rerysby) **1369–1376** Can. of Launde, el. 6 Aug. 1369; eln conf. by commissary 7 Aug. 1369 (ibid.). Res. by 8 Mar. 1376 (Lincoln, Ep. Reg., XII, f. 143v).

[**Walter de Staunford** Can. of Launde, el. but res. his right 1376 (Lincoln, Ep. Reg., X, f. 266r); commn to examine eln 8 Mar. 1376 (Lincoln, Ep. Reg., XII, f. 143v).]

Thomas Colman of Lichfield (Lichefeld) **1376–1388** Eln pres. to bp 28 Aug. 1376; eln conf. 5 Sept. 1376 (Lincoln, Ep. Reg., X, f. 266r). Complaints by the sub-pr and *sanior pars* of the convent against him n.d. (? Apr. 1377) (Lincoln, Ep. Reg., XII, f. 146r–v). Occ. 1377 (John of Lichfield) (*Clerical Poll-Taxes*, p. 28, no. 379). 3 Aug. 1388 ordered under pain of forfeiture to cease expelling, beating and imprisoning cans., dispersing books, ornaments, jewels, property and goods of the priory (*CCR 1385–89*, p. 519). Res. by 20 Nov. 1388 (PRO, C84/34/25). Res., lic. to el. 23 Nov. 1388 (*CPR 1385–89*, p. 527). Occ. as can. of Launde 11 Feb. 1392 – previously pr. and deprived of his priory earlier by papal judges delegate (*CPL*, IV, 435).

LEEDS (Kent), St Mary and St Nicholas f. 1119
  Lists in *VCH Kent*, II, 164; *Heads*, I, 170.
Fulk Occ. 27 Oct. 1205, 1214 (*Kent F.*, pp. 37, 52); (F.) 1212 (*Essex F.*, I, 48); 1217 x 1218 (*Ctl. Colchester*, II, 557); 9 Feb. 1222 (*Kent F.*, p. 74); Hil. term 1225 (*CRR*, XII, no. 217); Trin. term 1227 (ibid., XIII, no. 378); 1227 (PRO, Just.1/229, m. 11d); 9 Apr. 1228 (*Kent F.*, p. 106); n.d. (after 1229, ? *c.* 1230 x 1231) (College of Arms ms. 8).

Roger Occ. 25 Nov. 1231 (*Kent F.*, p. 109).

William Occ. 29 May 1237 (ibid., p. 147).

F. Occ. 1250 (*HMC De L'Isle and Dudley*, I, 105); n.d. (mid-13th cent.) (BL, Egerton Cht. 382). Seal (*BM Seals*, no. 3426).

Richard Occ. Apr. 1258 (*HMC De L'Isle and Dudley*, I, 107); 1 July 1260, 10 Feb. 1263 (*Kent F.*, pp. 311, 343).

Stephen Occ. 3 Feb. 1267, 14 June 1271 (ibid., pp. 348, 381); 1279 (Canterbury D. & C., Ch. Ant. B.320); 27 Apr. 1282 (*CChR 1341–1417*, p. 199); n.d. (*CChR 1257–1300*, p. 29).

Adam of Maidstone (Maydenstan) Occ. 1288–89 (Lambeth, Ch. Ant. V 84); 1289–90 (ibid., V 109); 20 July 1296 (PRO, E40/10238). Res. by 1 Mar. 1299 (PRO, C84/13/29; cf. *CPR 1292–1301*, p. 401, cf. 400; see also *CCR 1337–39*, p. 295).

William of Borden (Bordenn(e)) *alias* **Verduno** 1299– Can. of Leeds, eln pres. to king for royal ass. 1 Mar. 1299 (PRO, C84/13/29); royal ass. 28 Mar. 1299 (*CPR 1292–1301*, p. 400). Gt to canons that the intrusion lately made by the escheator on the voidance of the priory shall not be a precedent 30 Mar. 1299 (ibid., p. 401). Occ. (W.) 23 Dec. 1301 (PRO, SC1/27/84); 21 Oct. 1302 (Sayers, no. 1046); 29 Sept. 1307 (PRO, C241/55/175).

R. Occ. 1316 (*Reg. Hethe*, I, 15). Prob. Robert below.

Robert of Maidstone (Maidenstan) –1338 Occ. 8 Aug. 1326 (Lambeth, Reg. Reynolds, f. 262v). D. by 9 Feb. 1338 (*CCR 1337–39*, p. 294).[27]

Thomas Perci Occ. 23 Mar. 1346 (Lambeth, Ch. Ant. XI 23; *Reg. Edington*, II, no. 37).

Thomas of Rochester (Roffa) –1380 Occ. 16 July 1347 (*CCR 1346–49*, p. 366); 20 Apr. 1351 (*CPL*, III, 377); 18 Mar. 1359 (*CPR 1358–61*, p. 187); Easter 1361 (PRO, CP40/406, m. 73d); 21 Feb. 1362 (*CCR 1360–64*, p. 393); 1367 (*CPR 1367–70*, p. 46); visitation charges against him 25 Apr. 1368 (*Reg. Langham*, pp. 235–6); 31 Oct. 1377 (Lambeth, Reg. Sudbury, f. 43v). D. by 31 May 1380 (PRO, C84/32/22; cf. Lambeth, Reg. Sudbury, f. 62v; *CPR 1377–81*, p. 496).

LEICESTER, St Mary de Prato, Pratis f. 1143 (abbey)

Lists in *VCH Leics*, II, 18–19; *Heads*, I, 170–1. Abbs. also treated in A.H. Thompson, *The Abbey of St Mary of the Meadows* (1949), *passim*. List (damaged) in BL, Cotton ms. Vitellius F XVII, f. 46r, with Wharton transcript in Lambeth ms. 585, f. 215r, the latter pd in *AASRP*, XIV (1876), 277.

William Pepyn 1204/5–1221/2 5th abb., in list abb. 19 years from 1205 = 15 John (*sic*). Occ. 26 Feb. 1206 (*Lancs F.*, p. 24); 1212 x 13 (*Bucks F.*, I, 35); (W.) 14 Jan. 1215 (*Reg. Ant. Lincoln*, III, no. 878); Feb. 1218 (ibid., no. 875); 29 Sept. 1221 (*Warws F.*, I, no. 246); 13 Oct. 1221 (ibid., no. 229).

Osbert of Dunton 1222–1229 6th abb., in list abb. 5 years from 1224 (*sic*). Royal ass. 22 Aug. 1222 (*Rot. Lit. Claus.*, I, 508; *CPR 1216–25*, p. 338). D. 1229 (*Ann. Dunstable*, p. 115). D., lic to el. 22 Jan. 1229 (*CPR 1225–32*, p. 235).

Matthew de Bray 1229–1235 7th abb., in list abb. 6 years. Pr. of Leicester, royal ass. 29 Jan. 1229, writ *de intendendo* 2 Apr. 1229 (*CPR 1225–32*, pp. 237, 243); mand. for seisin 29 Jan. 1229 (*CR 1227–31*, p. 147). Removed by Bp Grosseteste at his visitation 1236 (*sic*) (*Ann. Dunstable*, p. 143). Res. June x Sept. 1235 during visitation (*Reg. Grosseteste*, p. 385; PRO, C84/1/11). Lic. to el. 4 Sept. 1235 (*CPR 1232–47*, p. 117).

Alan of Chesham (Cestreham) 1235–?1244 8th abb., in list el. 1 Nov. (*sic*), abb. 9 years. Can. and sacrist of Leicester, el. and adm. *c.* Sept. 1235 (*Reg. Grosseteste*, p. 385). Royal ass. 16

---

[27] The mention in 1339 of a Nicholas being pr. of Leeds 30 years before the publication of the Statute of Mortmain (1279) (*Cal. Misc. Inq.*, II, 408) may provide a reference to a new pr., or could merely be an unreliable calculation and actually refer to the 12th-century pr. Nicholas (*Heads*, I, 170).

Sept. 1235, writ *de intendendo* 29 Sept. 1235 (*CPR 1232–47*, p. 118); mand. for seisin 29 Sept. 1235 (*CR 1234–37*, p. 144). Occ. 15 July 1236 (PRO, Leics F., CP25/1/121/14, no. 187); Oct. 1241 x Oct. 1242 (*Casus Placitorum*, p. 119); 25 June 1242 (PRO, Leics F., CP25/1/121/17, no. 266). Lic. to el. (no reason given for vacancy) 13 Nov. 1244 (*CPR 1232–47*, p. 445).

Robert Furmentin (Furmenteyn) **1244–1247** 9th abb., in list el. 2 Nov., abb. 3 years. Can. and sacrist of Leicester, royal ass. 26 Nov. 1244, writ *de intendendo* 18 Dec. 1244 (*CPR 1232–47*, pp. 446–7). Occ. 6 May 1246 (*York F., 1232–46*, p. 131); 20 Jan. 1247 (PRO, Leics F., CP25/1/122/19, no. 316); 27 Jan. 1247 (ibid., /122/18, no. 295).

Henry of Rothley (Rothelegh, Rotheley, Rottele) **1247–1270** 10th abb., in list el. 1 Aug. (?), abb. 24 years. Can. of Leicester, royal ass. (Richard) 23 Sept. 1247 (*CPR 1232–47*, p. 510). El. and adm. June 1247 x June 1248 and bl. by W(alter Mauclerc), former bp of Carlisle, no reason given for vacancy (*Reg. Grosseteste*, p. 429). Occ. 13 Sept. 1270 (*CPR 1266–72*, p. 460). Cess., lic. to el. 25 Sept. 1270 (ibid., p. 463). Seal (*BM Seals*, no. 3442).

William of Shepshed (Schepished, Sepehevid, Shepheved) **1270–1291** 11th abb., in list el. 6 Oct., abb. 21 years. Pr. of Leicester, royal ass. 9 Oct. 1270 (*CPR 1266–72*, p. 464). Eln conf. 15/16 Oct. 1270 (18 cal. Nov. *sic*); bl. 19 Oct. 1270 (*Reg. R. Gravesend*, pp. 151, 311). Going to Scotland 2 Sept. 1286 (*CPR 1281–92*, p. 251). D. 1291 (*Reg. Sutton*, VIII, 49). D. by 7 Sept. 1291 (PRO, C84/10/18). D. (W.). lic. to el. 11 Sept. 1291 (*CPR 1281–92*, p. 444). Seal (*BM Seals*, no. 3443). Prob. the William whose obit was kept on 17 Aug. at Lire (*HF*, XXIII, 473).

William of Malvern (Malverne, Malvernia) **1291–1317** 12th abb., in list el. 9 Sept., abb. 26 years. Can. of Leicester, eln pres. to king for royal ass. 17 Sept. 1291 (PRO, C84/10/19); royal ass. 21 Sept. 1291, temps. 6 Oct. 1291 (*CPR 1281–92*, pp. 446–7). Eln pres. to bp 27 Sept. and eln quashed and apptd by bp 29 Sept. 1291; bl. 30 Sept. 1291 (*Reg. Sutton*, VIII, 49). Occ. 7 Dec. 1317 (*CFR 1307–19*, p. 348). D. by 30 Dec. 1317 (PRO, C84/19/19). D., lic. to el. 4 Jan. 1318 (*CPR 1317–21*, p. 68).

Richard (de) Tours (Toures) **1318–1345** 13th abb., in list el. 20 Dec., abb. 28 years. Can. of Leicester, eln pres. to king for royal ass. 20 Jan. 1318 (PRO, C84/19/21); royal ass. 25 Jan. 1318, temps. 15 Feb. 1318 (*CPR 1317–21*, pp. 73, 80). Eln conf. 3 Feb. 1318 (Lincoln, Ep. Reg., II, f. 214v; PRO, C84/19/25). Bl. by ex-archbp of Armagh and prof. obed. 5 Feb. 1318 (Lincoln, Ep. Reg., III, f. 380v). D. by 9 Oct. 1345 (*CCR 1343–46*, p. 615). D., lic. to el. 11 Oct. 1345 (*CPR 1343–45*, p. 560).

William Cloune (Clone) **1345–1378** 14th abb., in list el. 21 Oct., abb. 33 years. Can. of Leicester, eln pres. to king for royal ass. 22 Oct. 1345 (PRO, C84/24/50); royal ass. 25 Oct. 1345 (*CPR 1343–45*, p. 558); temps. 28 Nov. 1345 (*CPR 1345–48*, p. 25). Eln conf. 26 Nov. 1345 (Lincoln, Ep. Reg., VI, f. 44r–v). Temps. taken into the king's hands 18 Sept. 1352 since the abb. had left the court without licence when asked to answer certain complaints (*CFR 1347–56*, pp. 339–40). D. 22 Jan. 1378 (*Ch. Knighton*, pp. 198–9, but cf. pp. 200–1 and n., stating that he died on a Sunday, which would have been 24 Jan.). Lic. to el. 28 Jan. 1378 (*CPR 1377–81*, p. 104).

LEIGHS (Essex), St Mary and St John the Evangelist (cf. Binns, p. 140). (Little Leighs) f. - 1200

Lists in *VCH Essex*, II, 165; *Heads*, I, 171.

William Occ. early 13th. cent. (*HMC Rutland*, IV, 40); 1209 x 1217, 1227 x 1228, 1207 x 1230 (*Caen Chts.*, nos. 14, 18, 20); Easter 1228 (*Essex F.*, I, 74); Oct. 1228 x Oct. 1229, Oct. 1234 x Oct. 1235 (*Suffolk F. (Rye)*, pp. 29, 38); Easter term 1229 (*CRR*, XIII, no. 1736); Trin. term 1230, Easter term 1231, Trin. term 1231 (*CRR*, XIV, nos. 413, 1331, 1585).

Hugh Occ. from Mich. 1246 to Mich. 1251 (*Essex F.*, I, 156, 188). 3 Nov. 1246 (PRO, F. Divers Counties CP25/1/283/2, no. 210); 1248 (PRO, Just.1/231, m. 2).

Walter Occ. Oct. 1257 x Oct. 1258 (*Suffolk F. (Rye)*, p. 58); 8 July 1262 (*Essex F.*, I, 251); n.d. (*temp.* Henry III) (BL, Harl. Ch. 50 G 23; Essex RO, T/B.3, p. 267, no. 182).

Simon of Saling (Salynge) Occ. *temp.* Henry III (*YB 19 Edward III*, p. 85, n. 3); 30 Sept. 1272 (*Essex F.*, I, 278); from Easter 1276 to Trin. 1279 (*Essex F.*, II, 9, 22); Easter 1282 (PRO, CP40/45, m. 75d).

Thomas de Beauchamp (de Bello Campo) –1308 Succeeded Simon (*YB 19 Edward III*, p. 85, n. 3). Occ. Nov. 1286 x Nov. 1287 (*Suffolk F. (Rye)*, p. 87). D. by 7 Feb. 1308 (*Reg. Baldock*, p. 65).

Thomas de Chelmesho 1308– Can. of Leighs, commn to examine eln n.d., opposers cited to appear on 7 Feb. 1308 (ibid., pp. 65–6). Occ. 29 May 1319 (*Reg. S. Gravesend*, p. 212).

Henry de Hegsete –1345 On Thomas de Chelmesho's d., Henry de Hegsete succ. and the priory is now (1345) vacant by his d. (*YB 19 Edward III*, p. 85, n. 3). Henry occ. Trin. 1327–Mich. 1328 (*Index to Placita de Banco*, p. 157).

Hugh Occ. Mich. 1351 (PRO, KB27/365, mm. 83d, 99d); 1355 (PRO, CP40/376, m.254).

Henry Occ. Mich. 1364 (PRO, KB27/416, m. 4d).

William Curteys Occ. 5 July 1370 (*Reg. Sudbury*, I, 157).

The next recorded pr., **Henry of London** (*alias* **Brompton**), commn to examine eln 18 Aug. 1385; eln conf. 19 Aug. 1385 (London, Reg. Braybrooke, f.322v)

LESSNESS (Kent), St Thomas Becket (Westwood) (Arrouaisian) f. 1178 (abbey)

Lists in *VCH Kent*, II, 166; *Heads*, I, 171; H.C. Westlake, *Hornchurch Priory* (1923).

ABBOTS

Fulk An unnamed abb., prob. Fulk, d. 1208 (*CRR*, V, 157, cf. 145–6).

Mark Prob. prev. pr. (ibid., III, 322). Occ. Mich. term 1219 (*Essex F.*, I, 55); (M.) 29 May 1223 (*HMC De L'Isle and Dudley*, I, 89); n.d. (early 13th cent.) (*Ctl. Missenden*, III, no. 782) Seal (*BM Seals*, no. 3461).

W. Occ. 15 Feb. 1228 (*Ctl. Chertsey*, I, 89).

Hugh Occ. 16 July 1234 (*Kent F.*, p. 122); 9 Feb. 1237 (ibid., p. 146).

Alan Occ. July 1245 (*Hornchurch Priory*, no. 529); 27 Apr. 1248 (*Essex F.*, I, 174); n.d. (PRO, E40/15765).

Richard Occ. 25 Nov. 1265 (*Kent F.*, p. 347); *c.* 1270 (*Hornchurch Priory*, no. 420).

Robert Occ. 29 May 1279 (PRO, Kent F., CP25/1/98/59, no. 87).

Elias Occ. Trin. 1286 (PRO, E159/59, m. 11d); Nov. 1286 x Nov. 1287 (*Suffolk F. (Rye)*, p. 89); Mich. 1286 x Mich. 1287 (PRO, E159/60, m. 18); Easter 1287 (PRO, CP40/67, m. 19); 26 June 1291 (*Select Canterbury Cases*, p. 506).

Thomas of Sandwich (Sandwico) Occ. 11 Feb. 1315 (BL, Cotton ms. Nero E VI, f. 202v); July 1314 x July 1315 (PRO, E40/15716); Trin. 1317 (*Select Cases of Trespass*, II, 348).

Adam de Hanifeld (Halifeld) 1319–1321 Mand. of archbp of Canterbury to install, having conf. and bl. him, dioc. Rochester *sede vacante* 9 Oct. 1319 (*Reg. Hethe*, I, 103–4). D. by 9 Dec. 1321 (ibid., 187).

Roger of Dartford (Derteford) 1321–1327 Can. of Lessness, eln pres. to bp 26 Nov.; eln conf. 26 Nov. 1321, mand. to install 27 Dec. 1321 (ibid., 184–8, 102). D. before 8 Nov. 1327 (ibid., 234).

John of Hoddesdon (Hodesdon(e), Hodeston, Hodisdon) 1327– Can. of Lessness, eln reported 8 Nov. 1327 (ibid., 234–6); eln conf. 25 Nov. and mand. to install s.d.; bl. 23 (*sic*) Nov. 1327 (ibid., 181–2, 506–9). Occ. 9 Nov. 1330 (ibid., 439). 19 Nov. 1336 certificate that he had appeared before the bp on 27 July 1336 and confessed to fornication (ibid., II,

646–9). 6 May 1340 charged with repeated adultery with Agnes Saltere of Bromley who has borne him two children, and also with the wife of John Farmer of Tonge. Archbp of Canterbury requests bp's sanction to deal with the offences (ibid.). Apostate, signified for arrest 11 July 1341 (Logan, *Runaway Religious*, p. 220). Mentd as former abb. in case of 1342 (*YB 16 Edward III, part 2*, p. 481).

Robert de Clyve –1347 Occ. 20 Dec. 1344 (*CPR 1343–45*, p. 425). Buried 10 Feb. 1347 (*Reg. Hethe*, II, 811).

Richard de Gayton 1347–1362 Lic. to el. from patron 18 Feb. 1347 (ibid., 810); el. 24 Feb. (ibid., 811–18); appt of proctor to pres. eln of Richard of Gayton, pr. of Lessness, to bp 9 Mar.; eln pres. to bp 10 Mar. (ibid., 802–4, 806–7); commn to conf. eln 14 Mar.; eln conf. by commissaries 15 Mar. 1347 (ibid., 807–8). D., lic. to el. 4 Oct. 1362 (*CPR 1361–64*, p 247).

William de Hethe 1362–1366 Can. of Lessness, el. 2 Nov. 1362 (Rochester, Reg. Whittlesey, ff. 9v–10v). D., lic. to el. 1 May. 1366 (*CPR 1364–67*, p. 232); similar lic. 16 May 1366 (ibid., p. 239).

John Haunsard –1386 Occ. 25 Sept. 1368 (Rochester, Reg. Trillek, f. 13r); 18 Oct. 1378 (PRO, E40/7372). D. by 11 Sept. 1386 (PRO, C84/34/4). D., lic. to el. 12 Sept. 1386 (*CPR 1385–89*, p. 208).

LETHERINGHAM (Suffolk), St Mary (St Peter and St Paul, Ipswich) f. -1200
List in *VCH Suffolk*, II, 108.

Brice (Bricus) Occ. Oct. 1234 x Oct. 1235 (*Suffolk F. (Rye)*, p. 38).

Richard de Hetham (Hecham) 1308– Can. of St Peter, Ipswich, apptd by bp, no reason given for vacancy, 15 Feb. 1308 (Norwich, Reg/1/1, f. 26v). Occ. as former pr. at visitation of Ipswich *c.* 1327 x 1336 (C.R. Cheney, 'A visitation of St Peter's priory, Ipswich', *EHR*, 47 (1932), pp. 268–72, at 272).

Luke of St Edmund (de Sancto Edmundo) 1316– Can. of St Peter, Ipswich, granted admin. and custody of priory 10 July 1316; apptd pr., no reason given for vacancy, 24 Sept. 1316 (Norwich, Reg/1/1, ff. 64v–65v).

Ralph of Framlingham (Framelyngham) –1349 Res. by 16 Aug. 1349 (Norwich, Reg/2/4, f. 104v). Pr. of Pentney 1349.

Roger of Huntingfield (Huntyngfeld) 1349– Can. of St Peter, Ipswich, eln conf. 16 Aug. 1349 (ibid.).

William of Thornham 1357–1361 Can. of Butley, pres. by St Peter, Ipswich and apptd by bp, no reason given for vacancy, 27 Apr. 1357 (Norwich, Reg/2/5, f. 19r). D. by 19 Sept. 1361 (ibid., f. 50v).

William of Creeting (Cretyng(g)) 1361–1378 Can. of St Peter, Ipswich, eln quashed but apptd by bp 19 Sept. 1361 (ibid., f. 50v). Res. by 1 May 1378 (Norwich, Reg/3/6, f. 57r).

LILLESHALL (Shrops), St Mary (Arrouaisian) f. *c.* 1143 (at Lizard); *c.* 1144 (at Donnington Wood); *c.* 1148 (at Lilleshall) (abbey).
Lists in *VCH Shrops*, II, 79; *Ctl. Lilleshall*, pp. xx–xxi; *Heads*, I, 171.

Ralph Occ. 6 Oct. 1203 (*Ctl. Lilleshall*, no. 203); 5 Nov. 1208 (SRRC, 972/223/1/1; Eyton, *Salop*, VI, 369); (R.) 6 July 1216 (ibid., X, 139; *Ctl. Shrewsbury*, I, p. 72, no. 74); *c.* 1211 x 1216 (*Brewood Chts.*, p. 194; *Ctl. Staffs.* 2, p. 193).

Alan –1226 Occ. *c.* 1220 (*Ctl. Lilleshall*, no. 248); 20 Oct. 1221 (PRO, Leics F., CP25/1/121/9, no. 64; *Ctl. Lilleshall*, no. 213). Res., lic. to el. 12 Apr. 1226 (*CPR 1225–32*, p. 26).

William de Dorleg 1226–1235 Royal ass. 6 May 1226 (ibid., p. 29). D., lic. to el. 27 July 1235 (*CPR 1232–47*, p. 114). Seal (R. Graham, *English Ecclesiastical Studies*, p. 245).

Simon of Fotheringay (Fodringheye) **1235–1240** Pr. of Lilleshall, royal ass. 9 Aug. 1235, temps. 2 Sept. 1235 (*CPR 1232–47*, pp. 115, 117). Res., lic. to el. 3 Dec. 1240 (ibid., p. 239).

Richard of Shrewsbury (Salopia) **1240–1253** Can. of Lilleshall, royal ass. 14 Dec. 1240 (ibid., p. 240); mand. for seisin 11 Jan. 1241 (*CR 1237–42*, p. 265); occ. 25 July 1252 (*Derbys F.* (1887), p. 85). Lic. to el. (no reason given for vacancy) 3 June 1253 (*CPR 1247–58*, p. 194).

Robert of Ercall (Arkalaw, Ercaluue) **1253–1270** Can. of Lilleshall, royal ass. 15 June 1253, writ *de intendendo* 28 June 1253 (ibid., pp. 198, 203). Fine paid for custody 'during the instant voidance' 12 Nov. 1270 (*CPR 1266–72*, p. 492). House vacant by 16 Nov. 1270 (*CR 1266–72*, p. 307).

William de Hales 1270–?1275 Pr. of Lilleshall, royal ass. 30 Nov. 1270, writ *de intendendo* 12 Dec. 1270 (ibid., pp. 495, 499). Occ. Easter 1272 (*King's Bench, Edward I*, II, 97, 100, 104); 3 Nov. 1273 (PRO, Shrops F., CP25/1/193/5, no. 2; *Ctl. Lilleshall*, no. 249); 1275 (Eyton, VIII, 226, but no source cited). Res. n.d. (prob. 1275) (PRO, C84/6/8).

Luke of Shrewsbury (Sallopia) **1275–1284** Can. of Lilleshall, writ *de intendendo* 4 Sept. 1275 (*CPR 1272–81*, p. 103). Cert. conf. eln by bp of Coventry and Lichfield 4 Sept. 1275 (PRO, C84/5/44). D., lic. to el. 25 May 1284 (*CPR 1281–92*, p. 121).

Ralph of Shrewsbury (Salopia) **1284–1291** Can. of Lilleshall, note of appt 13 June 1284 (PRO, C84/8/26); temps. 22 June 1284 (*CPR 1281–92*, p. 123). Cess., lic. to el. 4 Apr. 1291 (ibid., p. 427). Seeking pension 11 Oct. 1297. Letter to the Official of Coventry and Lichfield requiring him to do speedy justice to Ralph who asks that he may have from the abbot and convent the provision made for him on his res. by the late bp of Lichfield (*Reg. Winchelsey*, I, 196–7). Occ. as former abb. 29 Sept. 1304 (PRO, C241/19/67).

William of Bridgnorth (Bruges, Brugg', Brugges) **1291–1308** Can. of Lilleshall, royal ass. 22 Apr. 1291, temps. 9 May 1291 (*CPR 1281–92*, p. 428). Cert. conf. eln by bp of Coventry and Lichfield 29 Apr. 1291 (PRO, C84/10/15). Res. by 18 Jan. 1308 (PRO, C84/4/35). Res., lic. to el. 26 Jan. 1308 (*CPR 1307–13*, p. 44).

John of Chetwynd (Chetewynde, Chetwud) **1308–1330** Can. of Lilleshall, eln pres. to king for royal ass. 29 Feb. 1308 (PRO, C84/16/4); royal ass. 10 Mar. 1308, temps. 13 Mar. 1308 (*CPR 1307–13*, pp. 50, 58). Cert. eln having been conf. by the bp of Coventry and Lichfield 12 Mar. 1308 (PRO, C84/16/5). Provision for John who is retiring, 30 May 1330 (Lichfield, B/A/1/3, f. 24r–v). Conf. by bp. of the provision and also by present abb. Henry 19 kal. June (*sic*) 1331 (ibid., ff. 31r–32r). Vacant by 28 June 1330 when extent taken (BL, Add. ms. 6165, f. 37r). Cess., lic. to el. 1 July 1330 (*CPR 1327–30*, p. 538).

Henry de Stoke (Stok) **1330–1350** Temps. 2 Aug. 1330 (ibid., p.545). Occ. 30 July 1331 (SRO, Acc.938/723). Provision *c.* 1350 for Henry who is resigning (Lichfield, B/A/1/3, f. 115v). Occ. 4 July 1350 (SRRC, 972/219/1/11). House void by 6 July 1350 (*CFR 1347–56*, p. 246). Res., lic. to el. 8 July 1350 (*CPR 1348–50*, p. 544).

Robert of Ashby (Asscheby, Assheby) **1350–1353** Pr. of Lilleshall, royal ass. 31 July 1350, temps. 10 Aug. 1350 (ibid., pp. 555, 560). Eln conf. by bp of Lichfield 6 Aug. 1350 (Lichfield, B/A/1/3, ff. 226v–227r). Occ. 12, 25 Mar. 1353 (SRRC, 972/219/2/5; 972/220/2/8). D., lic. to el. 30 Apr. 1353 (*CPR 1350–54*, p. 429).

William of Peplow (Peppelowe, Pippelowe, Pottelowe) **1353–1369** Pr. of Lilleshall, royal ass. 17 May 1353, temps. 3 June 1353 (ibid., pp. 437, 465). Eln conf. by bp of Lichfield 29 May 1353 (Lichfield, B/A/1/3, f. 228r; PRO, C84/27/10). D. 30 June 1369 (PRO, C84/29/51). D., lic. to el. 5 July 1369 (*CPR 1367–70*, p. 276).

Roger Norreys 1369–1375 Can. of Lilleshall, eln pres. to king for royal ass. 19 July 1369 (PRO, C84/30/3); royal ass. 26 July 1369, temps. 14 Aug. 1369 (*CPR 1367–70*, pp. 286, 299). D. 2 Apr. 1375 (BL, Add. ms. 6165, f. 49v). Bede-roll of abb. Norreys (Bodl., Shropshire roll 2). D., lic. to el. 19 Apr. 1375 (*CPR 1374–77*, p. 91; cf. PRO, C84/31/25).

William (de) Peynton (Penynton) 1375–1398 Can. of Lilleshall, eln pres. to king for royal ass. 26 Apr. 1375 (PRO, C84/31/26); royal ass. 30 Apr. 1375, temps. 7 May 1375 (*CPR 1374–77*, pp. 92, 93). Cert. conf. eln by bp of Coventry and Lichfield 5 May 1375 (PRO, C84/31/27). D. by 18 Mar. 1398 (PRO, C84/36/53). D., lic. to el. 22 Mar. 1398 (*CPR 1396–99*, p. 318).

LITTLE DUNMOW (Essex), St Mary f. 1104

Lists in *VCH Essex*, II, 153–4; basis in Ann. Dunmow in *Mon. Angl.*, VI, 147–8; *Heads*, I, 171 (which gives details of ms. versions of Ann. Dunmow).

Durand –1217 Occ. 1209 x 1217 (*Caen Chts.*, no. 14). D. or Res. 1217 (*Mon. Angl.*, VI, 147 – d. in BL, ms. Cotton Cleopatra C III, f. 282r; res. in BL, ms. Cotton Vespasian A IX).

William 1217–1221 Succ. 1217. D. 1221 (*Mon. Angl.*, VI, 147; BL, ms. Cotton Cleopatra C III, f. 282r).

Thomas of Taunton (Tanton) 1221–1238 Succ. 1221. D. 1238 (ibid.). Occ. Oct. 1225 x Oct. 1227 (PRO, E212/97); 8 Nov. 1227 (*Essex F.*, I, 77; BL, Harl. ms. 662, f. 15r); 1 Dec. 1227 (PRO, Hants F. CP25/1/84/12 no. 112); Trin. term 1230 (*CRR*, XIV, no. 236); Oct. 1234 x Oct. 1235 (*Norfolk F (Rye)*, p. 56); 9 Feb. 1235 (*Essex F.*, I, 111).

John de Sateforde 1238–1245 Succ. 1238. D. 1245 (*Mon. Angl.*, VI, 147; BL, ms. Cotton Cleopatra C III, f. 282r).

Hugh de Steveinheth 1245–1246 Succ. 1245. D. 1246 (*Mon. Angl.*, VI, 147–8; BL, ms. Cotton Cleopatra C III, f. 282r).

Edmund 1246–1247 Succ. 1246. D. 1247 (*Mon. Angl.*, VI, 148; BL, ms. Cotton Cleopatra C III, f. 282r).

Geoffrey 1247–1248 Succ. 1247. D. 1248 (*Mon. Angl.*, VI, 148; BL, ms. Cotton Cleopatra C III, f. 282r). Occ. 3 May 1248 (*Essex F.*, I, 176).

John de Cobham (Codham) 1248–1270 Succ. 1248. Suspended 1268 for not paying tenth D. 1270 (*Mon. Angl.*, VI, 148; BL, ms. Cotton Cleopatra C III, f. 282r).

Hugh de Poflington 1270–1279 Succ. 1270. Cess. 1279 (*Mon. Angl.*, VI, 148; BL, ms. Cotton Cleopatra C III, f. 282v). Occ. Trin. 1273 and Mich. 1274 (*Essex F.*, II, 1, 5).

Richard de Wicham (Witham) 1279– Succ. 1279 (*Mon. Angl.*, VI, 148; BL, ms. Cotton Cleopatra C III, f. 282v). Occ. Hil. term 1281 (*Essex F.*, II, 29); Mich. 1286 x Mich. 1287 (PRO, E159/60, m. 11); from 1283 to 21 Sept. 1294 (BL, Harl. ms. 662, ff. 5r, 116v). Letter of Stephen, sub-pr. addressed to R. bp of London, making provision for Richard de Witham, late pr., who had res. on account of bodily weakness and ill-health n.d. (ibid., f. 114v).

Stephen de Noble (Notele) Occ. 16 Apr. 1301, 1303, 1305 (ibid., ff. 114v, 115r, 116r); Mich. 1305 (PRO, CP40/153, mm. 16, 212). D. 1312 (*Mon. Angl.*, VI, 148; BL, ms. Cotton Cleopatra C III, f. 282v).

Robert (of) Feering (Feryng) 1312–1329 Succ. 1312 (ibid.). D., lic. to el. 22 Apr. 1329 (*CPR 1327–30*, p. 383; cf. PRO, C84/21/31).

John de Gelham 1329– Can. of Little Dunmow, royal ass. 5 May 1329 (*CPR 1327–30*, p. 385), temps. 15 June 1329 (ibid., p. 400). Cert. conf. eln by bp of London 17 May 1329 (PRO, C84/22/22). Occ. 17 Jan. 1345 (*HMC Var. Coll.*, VII, 315).

Robert de Wodehouse Occ. n.d. (Newcourt, *Repertorium*, II, 228). His precise place in the sequence of priors is uncertain.

Richard de Plescy (Plescyo, Plesye) –1365 Occ. Mich. 1351 (PRO, KB27/365, m. 94d); 6 Apr. & 5 May 1365 (*CCR 1364–68*, p. 171). Res., lic. to el. 8 May 1365 (*CPR 1364–67*, p. 113; cf. PRO, C84/29/20).

Nicholas de Helmenden (Emeldon) 1365–1370 Can. of Little Dunmow, eln pres. to king for royal ass. 17 May 1365 (PRO, C84/29/22); royal ass. 18 May 1365, temps. 16 July 1365

(*CPR 1364–67*, pp. 125, 163). Notice of conf. of eln 15 July 1365 (*Reg. Sudbury*, II, 142; PRO, C84/29/29). Commn to receive res. 17 June; res. acc. 20 June 1370 (*Reg. Sudbury*, I, 150–1, 153).

John Swaffham (Swafham) **1370–1391** Can. of Little Dunmow, patron's ass. to eln 29 June 1370; commn to examine eln 30 June; eln conf. 5 July 1370 (ibid., I, 151–61). D. by 7 Jan. 1391 (London, Reg. Braybrooke, f. 332r–v).

LLANTHONY PRIMA (Monmouth), St John the Baptist f. 1103

Lists in *Heads*, I, 172–3; list in *Ch. Llanthony* in BL, Cotton ms. Julius D X, f. 32r–v.

Walter 10th pr. (*Ch.*, f. 32r). Occ. (W.) 1217 x 1224 (*Ctl. Llanthony (Irish)*, pp.141–2); 29 Oct. 1224 (PRO, Hereford F., CP25/1/80/5, no. 60); 26 Sept. 1227 (ibid., /80/7, no. 112).

Stephen 11th pr. (*Ch.*, f. 32r).

Philip 12th pr. (ibid.). Occ. 6 July 1236 (PRO, Hereford F., CP25/1/80/7, no. 125).

David 13th pr. (*Ch.*, f. 32r). Occ. 15 July 1241 (PRO, Hereford F., CP25/1/80/10, no. 191); Aug. 1242 (*Ctl. Llanthony (Irish)*, p. 23).

Thomas 14th pr. (*Ch.*, f. 32v). Occ. 13 Oct. 1251 (PRO, F.,Var. Cos. CP25/1/284/19, no. 100).

Simon Occ. 30 June 1253 (*Ctl. Llanthony (Irish)*, p. 133, cf. p. 55).

Bartholomew Occ. Oct. 1258 x Oct. 1259 (*Norfolk F., (Rye)*, p. 96).

Walter Occ. 19 June 1266 (*Reg. Gloucester*, p. 50, no. 149; Bannister, *Ewyas*, p. 56, no. 52); 8 Sept. 1267 (*CCR 1264–68*, p. 382); (W.) *c.* 1281, but prob. earlier, see below (*Ctl. Llanthony (Irish)*, p. 237).

Nicholas Occ. 2 July 1279 (*Welsh Assize Roll 1277–84*, p. 293); 12 Nov. 1279 (*CPR 1272–81*, p. 350); 1280, 1281 (*Welsh Assize Roll*, pp. 309, 326, 329, 337); pardoned of outlawry 10 Sept. 1284 (*CPR 1281–92*, p. 132); 1286 (PRO, C85/87/3); (N.) ?Sept. 1288 (PRO, SC1/23/188); 6 Nov. 1287, 28 Sept. 1288 (*CPR 1281–92*, pp. 280, 300); 1289 (*Ctl. Carmarthen*, no. 40); 23 Oct. 1293 (*Reg. Sutton*, IV, 130); 22 Sept. 1295 (*CPR 1292–1301*, p. 141).

Thomas of Gloucester (Glocestria, Glovernia) Occ. 5 & 8 Oct. 1296 (ibid., pp. 205, 206); 1297 (*Select Cases in Exchequer of Pleas*, p. 156). Mentd 9 Mar. 1301 in report to bp of St Davids to recall the former pr., *vagabundus*, after his res. back to his priory; similar letter 8 June 1301 (*Reg. Winchelsey*, II, 732–3, 744).

Walter Occ. 4 Oct. 1305 (*CPR 1301–07*, p. 391); 4 Dec. 1314 (*CPR 1313–17*, p. 200).

John of Kingston (Kyngeston) Occ. 16 July 1316 (Hereford Cath. mun. 1169). Seal (*Hereford Seals*, p. 8 and plate II(6)).

John de Rufford Occ. 4 Apr. 1321 (*CPR 1317–21*, p. 574); 29 Oct. 1325 (*CCR 1323–27*, p. 518); 12 July 1327 (*CPR 1327–30*, p. 140); Apr. 1331, 22 Jan. 1332, 4 May 1334, 29 Nov. 1332 (*CPR 1330–34*, pp. 108, 232, 542, 373); 16 Apr. 1336, 20 Mar. 1337 (*CPR 1334–38*, pp. 242, 394). Mentd 27 Jan. 1348 as late pr. (*CPR 1348–50*, p. 1). He prob. d. 1338 – on 27 Feb. 1338 note that the previous pr. John had d. (*CCR 1337–39*, p. 316), more likely to be Rufford than Kyngeston in the circumstances.

John of Gloucester (Gloucestr(e)) Occ. 27 Feb. 1338 (ibid.); 20 Feb. 1340 (*CPR 1338–40*, p. 428); 20 Jan. 1342 (*CPR 1340–43*, p. 356); 28 Oct. 1352 (*CPR 1350–54*, p. 351); 18 Jan. 1353 (*CPL*, III, 493); 24 Oct. 1357 (*CPR 1354–58*, p. 621).

Adam Occ. 1 July 1362 (*CPR 1361–64*, p. 283).

Nicholas Trilley (Trillek, de Trinleye, Trinbeye) **–1373/76** Occ. 12 Feb. 1363, going to Ireland (ibid., p. 307); 12 Mar. 1367 (*CPR 1364–67*, p. 385); 2 Oct. 1368 (PRO, C241/149/120); 11 Nov. 1373 (PRO, C81/1789/19). Dep. *propter suum proprium delictum* 4 Aug. 1373, *prout in libro scripto de eius vita detestabili et actu proproso ad exemplum aliorum tanquam memorie commendandum plene continetur* (*Ch. Wigmore*, p. 92). Mand. to receive res. 8 Feb. 1376; after ruling well for eleven years when saying the Office for the Dead he was thrown to the ground and his eyes torn out by three cans. The pr. now dare not dwell within 40 miles of the priory and is ready to res. (*CPL*, IV, 223). Still alive, as former pr., 1380 (PRO, C115/78, f. 55r).

John (de) Yatton 1376– Occ. 6 Apr. 1376 (ibid., f. 54v); 5 May 1376 (*CPR 1374–77*, p. 261); 1377 x 1378 (*HMC Rye and Hereford*, p. 298); 6 Feb. 1379, 15 Nov. 1379 (*CPR 1377–81*, pp. 318, 403); 1380 x 1381 (PRO, E179/21/3, m. 1); 27 Nov. 1391 (*CPR 1399–1401*, p. 283); 14 Nov. 1391 (*CPR 1388–92*, p. 501).

The next recorded pr., **John Welynton**, occ. 15 July 1395, 8 Nov. 1397 (PRO, C81/1789/20).

LLANTHONY SECUNDA (Glos), St Mary (Llanthony by Gloucester) f. 25 May 1136 (dependent on Llanthony Prima); 1205 (independent).

Lists in *VCH Glos.*, II, 91; J.N. Langston, 'Priors of Lanthony in Gloucester', *BGAS*, 63 (1942), pp. 1–144; *Heads*, I, 173.

Gilbert 8th pr. of Llanthony Secunda. Last recorded occ. 3 July 1216 (*Ctl. Oseney*, IV, 226). Seal (*BM Seals*, no. 3417).

John of Hempstead I-II? **–?1240** 9th pr. of Llanthony Secunda. Occ. (J.) 1217 x 1224 with W., pr. of Llanthony Prima (*Ctl. Llanthony (Irish)*, pp. 141–2); 6 July 1221 (PRO, Glos. F., CP25/1/73/5, no. 49); (J.) Oct. 1224 (*Ctl. Gloucester*, II, 171); 1227 (PRO, F. Var. Cos. CP25/1/284/18, no. 28); 1228 (*Cal. Docs. Ireland*, I, no. 1618; *CR 1227–31*, p. 113); 8 Sept. 1234 (*Cal. Docs. Ireland*, I, no. 2164); 1236 (PRO, Glos. F., CP25/1/73/10, no. 160); 1237 (ibid., 73/11, no. 190). Two priors called John of Hempstead are thought to have been in office successively in this period (Langston, p. 40) but their terms of office are not known. D. 29 Dec. 1240 (*Ann. Tewkesbury*, p. 116), but pr. John occ. 29 July, 2 Aug. 1241 (PRO, CP25/1/73/14, no. 269; 73/13, no. 236); (J.) 1 Aug. 1244 (PRO, C115/L1/6689, f. 16r); 9 Nov. 1245 (PRO, C115/L1/6687, ff. 38v, 72v).

Godfrey of Banbury –1251 Thought to have succ. *c.* 1241 (Langston, p. 46). Occ. *c.* 1250 (*Ctl. Cirencester*, III, no. 375n). Prob. the unnamed pr. whose cess. is recorded 1251 (*Ann. Tewkesbury*, p. 146).

Everard 1251– Can. of Llanthony Secunda, succ. 1251 (ibid.).

Godfrey Apparently re-instated occ. *c.* 1261, 1264 (Langston, p. 49, citing *BGAS*, 7, 153–4, 154–6). Occ. n.d. with abb. Roger of Cirencester 1250 x 1267 (PRO, C115/LI/6689, f. 130r).

William of Ashwell (Assewell, Asshewell, Axewell, Esshewell) Occ. n.d. (*either* Oct. 1260 x June 1261 *or* July 1263 x Aug. 1265, *temp.* Hugh le Despenser, justiciar of England (PRO, C146/3024); (W.) 27 Jan. 1267 (*Reg. G. Giffard*, II, 361); 1266 (PRO, Glos. F., CP25/1/74/27, nos. 609–10); 1265 x 1268 (*Reg. Gloucester*, p. 51, no. 152); 1275, 1276 (PRO, C115/LI/6689, ff. 26v, 73v); Nov. 1278 x Nov. 1279 (PRO, C115/82, f. 33v); 1279 (PRO, Glos F., CP25/1/75/31, nos. 38, 41).

Walter of Martley (Martleg', Martleya, Martleye) **1283–** Eln conf. 18 Mar. 1283, no reason given for vacancy; mand. to install. 1 Apr. 1283 (*Reg. G. Giffard*, pp. 174–5). Occ. 1287 (PRO, Glos. F., CP25/1/75/35, no. 128; *CPR 1281–92*, p. 268); 1293 (*CPR 1292–1301*, p. 9); 12 May 1297 (PRO, F. Unknown & Var. Cos. CP25/1/285/27, no. 36); 1300 (Bodl., ms. Top. Glos. c 5, p. 646).

John (de) Chaundos 1300– El. 1300 (Langston, p. 68, citing Bodl., ms. Top. Glos. c 5, p. 646). n.d. [1300] 'what ought to be done about the elect of Llanthony against whom it is objected that he is excommunicated' (*Reg. G. Giffard*, p. 515). Occ. 13 June 1300 (*CPR 1292–1301*, p. 514); 15 Mar. 1302, 8 Jan. 1304 (*CPR 1301–07*, pp. 25, 205); 18 Oct. 1302 (*Wilts. IPM 1242–1316*, p. 292); (J.) 14 Feb. 1306 (*Reg. Gainsborough*, p. 147); 6 Sept. 1307 (*CPR 1307–13*, p. 2); 1309 (PRO, C115/L1/6689, f. 59r); 20 Mar. 1314, 21 May 1316 (*CPR*

1313–17, pp. 94, 442); 14 Oct. 1318 (Worcester Cath. Lib. B.541); 16 Mar. 1318, 22 Feb. 1320 (*CPR 1317–21*, pp. 119, 423).

William of Penbury (Pendebury, Pondebury, Pyndebury) –**1324** Prob. succ. *c.* 1322 but not mentd by name until he res. in 1324 (Langston, p. 76). Res. by 8 Mar. 1324 (PRO, C84/20/26). Res., lic. to el. 12 Mar. 1324 (*CPR 1321–24*, p. 393). 6 Apr. 1324 letter from Bp Cobham to William de Pendebury, late pr., stating that following William's res. on account of dissensions he orders him to transfer to Studley until a new eln is held at Llanthony (*Reg. Cobham*, p. 170).

Custody of house gtd during pleasure to Adam de Helnak 28 May 1324 owing to discord among the cans. and disputed eln of **Robert of Gloucester** and **Walter of Longeney** (Longeneye, Langeneie, Langeneye) (*CPR 1321–24*, pp. 419–20; cf. *Reg. Cobham*, p. 208).

Robert of Gloucester (Gloucestre) **1324** Eln pres. to king for royal ass. 30 Apr. 1324 (PRO, C84/20/27); royal ass. 13 July 1324 (*CPR 1324–27*, p. 3), but never installed. Went to St Thomas's abbey, Dublin, and gtd 40 marks a year for life (Langston, pp. 79–80).

William of Penbury (Pendebury) **1326–1362** William de Pendebury opposed the above elns, stating his res. was not valid. Bp of Winchester to arbitrate: his ordinance of 8 July 1325 annulled the elns and declared initial res. invalid. Bp Cobham ratifies the bp of Winchester's ordinance and reinstates William de Pendebury 24 Sept. 1326 (*Reg. Cobham*, pp. 208–12). Occ. 5 Mar. 1326 (*Ctl. Winchester*, no. 323). Ref. 9 Nov. 1330 to the madness which recently had afflicted pr. William (*Reg. Orleton (Worcs)*, no. 129). D. 14 Nov. 1362 (Bodl., ms. Top. Glos. c 5, p. 648; Langston, p. 81). House void by 21 Nov. 1362 by d. of William (*CCR 1360–64*, p. 373; PRO, C115/82, f. 5r–v).

Simon of Brockworth (Brocworth, Brokworth) **1362–1377** Petition for royal ass. 25 Nov. 1362 (PRO, C115/82, f. 5v); royal ass. 2 Dec. 1362 (*CPR 1361–64*, p. 276). D. 10 Feb. 1377 (PRO, C84/31/44, cf. *CCR 1374–77*, p. 479; Bodl., ms. Top. Glos. C 5, p. 659). Register of pr. (PRO, C115/82).

William de Chiriton 1377–1401 Can. of Llanthony Secunda, eln pres. to king for royal ass. 28 Feb. 1377 (PRO, C84/31/45); royal ass. 5 Mar. 1377 (*CPR 1374–77*, p. 438; PRO, C115/78, f. 17r). Debts relating to William's installation n.d. (PRO, C115/78, f. 13r). Occ. 1380 (*CPR 1377–81*, p. 541); 1391 (*CPR 1388–92*, p. 444); 5 Jan. 1400 (*CPR 1399–1401*, p. 2); June–July 1401 (PRO, C115/78, f. 218r). D. 1401 (Bodl., ms. Top. Glos c 5, p. 648). Register of pr. (PRO, C115/78).

LONDON, Holy Trinity, Aldgate f. 1107 x 1108

Lists in *VCH London*, I, 474 the basis in Ann. (unreliable) in *Newburgh* ed. Hearne, III, 690–707, checked by the ms. (Glasgow Univ. Lib. Hunterian 2.6, ff. 1 ff), and by the edn. of the cartulary ed. G. Hodgett (1971), *Ctl.*, pp. 2–5; *Heads* I, 173–4.

Peter of Cornwall 1197–1221 4th pr. El. 9 May 1197, D. 7 July 1221 (Ann., p. 707; *Ctl.*, p. 3). Occ. 1 May 1198, (P.) 3 May 1221 (PRO, E40/1888, E40/2226). Theologian, see R.W. Hunt in *TRHS*, 4th ser., XIX (1936), 33–4, 38–42; idem Powicke, *Studies*, pp. 143–56; Sharpe, *Latin Writers*, pp. 425–6. Seal (*Mon. Seals*, p. 55).

Richard de Templo 1222–1250 5th pr. Prob. el. 16 July 1222 (1223 in Ann., p. 708; *Ctl.*, p. 3), but before 25 Oct. 1222 when royal ass. given (*CPR 1216–25*, p. 342). Occ. many times in *Ctl.* from Mon. 21 Aug. (*sic*) 1222 to 11 Mar. 1250 (nos. 629, 218); 30 Sept. 1248 (*Kent F.*, p. 206); 25 Dec. 1249 (PRO, E40/7315); 16 May 1250 (PRO, E40/2294). D. 14 Aug. 1248 (*sic*) (*Ctl.*, p. 3), but clearly 1250 is correct. D., lic. to el. 26 Aug. 1250 (*CPR 1247–58*, p. 73).

John of Tooting (Totinges, Totynge) **1250–?1261** 6th pr. Sacrist of Holy Trinity, el. 24 Aug. 1250 (*Ctl.*, p. 4). Royal ass. 5 Oct. 1250 (*CPR 1247–58*, p. 75). Occ. in the *Ctl.* from Oct. 1250 x Oct. 1251 to 1259 (nos. 88, 1016); Oct. 1250 x Oct. 1251 to Oct. 1260 x Oct. 1261

(*London and Middlesex F.*, pp. 34, 41). D. 15 June 1258 (*sic*) (*Ctl.*, p. 4). Lic. to el. (no reason given for vacancy) 16 June 1261 (*CPR 1258–66*, p. 160).

Gilbert de Wrotting 1261–?1268 7th pr. Can. of Holy Trinity, el. 1260 (*sic*) (*Ctl.*, p. 4). Royal ass. 21 June 1261, writ *de intendendo* 2 July 1261 (*CPR 1258–1266*, pp. 160, 161). Occ. in *Ctl.* from 1262 x 1263 to 1268 (nos. 24, 68); 18 June 1262 (PRO, E40/5514); 25 Nov. 1267 (PRO, Herts F., CP25/1/85/31, no. 600). Apptd a papal chaplain 31 Jan. 1264 (*CPL*, I, 408). D. 30 Dec. 1264 (*sic*) (*Ctl.*, p. 4), but clearly 1268 is more likely (see next entry).

Eustace 1269–1284 8th pr. Can. of Holy Trinity, el. 7 Jan. 1265 (*sic, recte* 1269) (*Ctl.*, p. 4). Writ *de intendendo* 12 Jan. 1269, eln having been conf. by master G., Official of London (*CPR 1266–72*, p. 312). Occ. in *Ctl.* from 17 Mar. 1269 to 25 Dec. 1278 (nos. 97, 534); (E.) Nov. 1280 x Nov. 1281 (PRO, E40/2487). D. 20 Dec. 1280 (*sic*) (*Ctl.*, p. 4). D., lic. to el. 27 Dec. 1284 (*CPR 1281–92*, p. 147).

William Aiguel (Aignel, Aygnel) 1285–1294 9th pr. Can. of Holy Trinity, el. 31 Dec. 1280 (*sic*) (*Ctl.*, p. 4). Royal ass. 10 Jan. 1285, temps. 19 Jan. 1285 (*CPR 1281–92*, pp. 151, 152). Occ. 24 June 1285 to 21 Sept. 1292 (*Ctl.*, nos. 45, 646); Nov. 1292 (PRO, E40/2077); 1293 (PRO, E40/11674). D. 21 May 1289 (*sic*) (*Ctl.*, p. 4). D. by 23 May 1294 (PRO, C84/12/2). D., lic. to el. 24 May 1294 (*CPR 1292–1301*, p. 70).

Stephen de Watton 1294–1303 10th pr. Can. of Holy Trinity, el. 1289 (*sic*) (*Ctl.*, p. 4). Eln pres. to king for royal ass. 28 May 1294 (PRO, C84/12/3–4); royal ass. 29 May 1294 (*CPR 1292–1301*, p. 70). Cert. conf. eln by bp of London 3 June 1294 (PRO, C84/12/5). Occ. 23 Aug. 1294 to 1 Nov. 1302 (*Ctl.*, nos. 920, 73). Res. 11 Mar. 1302 (*sic*), d. 5 Oct. [?1302] (*Ctl.*, p. 4). Res. by 7 Mar. 1303 (PRO, C84/14/43). Dep., lic. to el. 8 Mar. 1303 (*CPR 1301–07*, p. 120).

Ralph of Canterbury (Cantuaria) 1303–1316 11th pr. Can. of Holy Trinity, el. 12 Mar. 1302 (*sic*) (*Ctl.*, p. 4). El. 12 Mar. 1303 (PRO, C84/18/35). Royal ass. 13 Mar. 1303, temps. 19 Mar. 1303 (*CPR 1301–07*, pp. 123, 125). D. 18 June 1314 (*sic*) (*Ctl.*, p. 4). D. by 20 June 1316 (*CFR 1307–19*, p. 283; PRO, C84/18/35). Lic. to el. 27 June 1316 (*CPR 1313–17*, p. 480).

Richard (de) Wymbyssh(e) (Wymbissh(e)) 1316–1325 12th pr. Can. of Holy Trinity. el. 25 June 1314 (*sic*) (*Ctl.*, p. 4). Royal ass. 27 June 1316, temps. 12 July 1316 (*CPR 1313–17*, pp. 478, 508). Res. 2 June 1325, d. 17 Mar. [?1326] (*Ctl.*, p. 4). Cess., lic. to el. 29 May 1325 (*CPR 1324–27*, p. 124).

Roger (de) Poly (Poleye) 1325–1331 13th pr. Can. of Holy Trinity, el. 3 June 1325 (*Ctl.*, p. 4). Sub-pr. and convent ask king for royal ass. 5 June 1325 (PRO, SC1/36/55A); royal ass. 7 June 1325 (*CPR 1324–27*, p. 125, cf. PRO, SC1/36/55); temps. 21 June 1325 (*CPR 1324–27*, p. 126). Res. 26 May 1331 (*Ctl.*, p. 4). Cess. by 18 May 1331 (PRO, C84/22/43). Cess., lic. to el. 20 May 1331 (*CPR 1330–34*, p. 120). D. 7 Jan. [?1332] (*Ctl.*, p. 4).

Thomas Heyron (Heron, Heroun) 1331–1340 14th pr. Can. of Holy Trinity, el. 27 May 1331 (ibid.). cf. Eln pres. to king for royal ass. 24 May 1331 (PRO, C84/22/45); royal ass. 26 May 1331, temps. 11 June 1331 (*CPR 1330–34*, pp. 121, 123). Cert. conf. eln by bp of London 9 June 1331 (PRO, C84/22/46). D. 20 Feb. 1340 (*Ctl.*, p. 4, cf. PRO, C84/24/14), but d. by 19 Feb. 1340 (*CFR 1337–47*, p. 160). D., lic. to el. 20 Feb. 1340 (*CPR 1338–40*, p. 429).

Nicholas of Aldgate *alias* **of London** (Algate) 1340–1377 15th pr. Can. of Holy Trinity, el. 26 Feb. 1340 (*Ctl.*, p. 4). Royal ass. 29 Feb. 1340, temps. 20 Mar. 1340 (*CPR 1338–40*, pp. 430, 443). D. 6 July 1377 (*Ctl.*, p. 4). D. by 17 July 1377 (PRO, C84/32/1; *CPR 1377–81*, p. 10). D., lic. to el. 18 July 1377 (*CPR 1377–1381*, p. 5).

William (de) Risyng(g) (Rysyng) 1377–1391 16th pr. Can. of Holy Trinity. el. 27 July 1377 (*Ctl.*, p. 5). Royal ass. 29 July 1377 (*CPR 1377–1381*, p. 12). D. 5 Aug. 1391 (*Ctl.*, p. 5). D., lic. to el. 8 Aug. 1391 (London, Reg. Braybrooke, f. 336r).

LONDON, St Bartholomew f. *c.* Mar. 1123

Lists in *VCH London*, I, 479–480; *Heads*, I, 174.

G. 1213 Can. of Oseney, el. 1213 and res. within a few days (*Ann. Dunstable*, p. 41); became m. at Abingdon.

John –1232 Occ. Easter 1226 (*Essex F.*, I, 71); Easter term 1229, Hil. term 1230 (*CRR*, XIII, nos. 1666, 2344). Gave up office in 1232 (*Ann. Dunstable*, p. 130).

Gerard 1232– Succ. John 1232 (ibid.); Mich. term 1232 (*CRR*, XIV, no. 2244); Easter 1234, Mich. 1237, Hil. 1239 (*Essex F.*, I, 97, 119, 122); 17 July 1236 (*Bucks F.*, I, 67); Oct. 1237 x Oct. 1238 (*London and Middlesex F.*, p. 24).

Peter –1255 Occ. 25 Nov. 1246 (PRO, Herts F., CP25/1/85/21, no. 329); 3 Feb. 1248 (*Essex F.*, I, 172); n.d. (*c.* 1240 x 1255) (PRO, DL36/1/34). House void by cess. of Peter; lic. to el. 4 Nov. 1255 (*CPR 1247–58*, p. 447). *VCH* gives him the surname Le Duc.

Robert 1255–1261 Sub-pr. of St Bartholomew's, royal ass. 23 Nov. 1255 (*CPR 1247–58*, p. 451). Occ. Oct. 1259 x Oct. 1260 (PRO, E42/353). D. by 26 (24) Nov. 1261 (PRO, C84/2/25).

Gilbert of Walden (Waleden, Waledon) 1261–1263 Can. of St Bartholomew's, temps. 24 Nov. 1261 (*CPR 1258–66*, p. 192). Cert. of conf. eln by bp of London 26 Nov. 1261 (PRO, C84/2/25). D. by 28 Dec. 1263 (PRO, C84/3/5).

John Bacun 1264– Letter of Richard, king of the Romans, to the chancellor about the new pr. 10 Jan. 1264 (PRO, SC1/8/5). Can. of St Bartholomew's, royal ass. 11 Jan. 1264 (*CPR 1258–66*, p. 305); temps. 20 Jan. 1264. eln having been conf. by B., archbp of Canterbury (ibid.). Occ. 1264 x 1265 (*Ctl. Holy Trinity, Aldgate*, no. 785).

Hugh –1295 Occ. 11 June 1273 (PRO, Herts F., CP25/1/86/34, no. 17); 1274 (*CCR 1272–79*, p. 117); 1279 (PRO, Herts F., CP25/1/86/37, no. 79); Nov. 1286 x Nov. 1287 (*Suffolk F. (Rye)*, p. 89). D., lic. to el. 11 Mar. 1295 (*CPR 1292–1301*, p. 131).

John of Kensington (Kensingthon) –1316 Occ. 22 July 1306 (*Assize of Nuisance*, no. 93); July 1315 x July 1316 (PRO, E210/9086). D., lic. to el. 4 Nov. 1316 (*CPR 1313–17*, p. 560).

John of Pegsdon (Pekesden(e)) –1350 Occ. 28 Jan. 1321 (*CCR 1318–23*, p. 288); 26 July 1321 (WAM no. 29439); 13 Dec. 1323 (*CCR 1323–27*, p. 149); 1327 (PRO, E326/9954); 1331, 1334, 1338 (Lincoln, Ep. Reg., IV, ff. 339r, 342v, 351r); Jan. 1338 x Jan. 1339 (PRO, LR14/561); 1 Dec. 1339 (*CCR 1339–41*, p. 330); 6 June 1349 (*CCR 1349–54*, p. 84). D., lic. to el. 25 May 1350 (*CPR 1348–50*, p. 505; *CCR 1349–54*, pp. 182–3).

Edmund of Braughing (Braghyng(g), Braughyng(g), Brauhyngg) 1350–1355 Can. of St Bartholomew's, eln pres. to king for royal ass. 3 June 1350 (PRO, C84/26/35); royal ass. 3 June 1350, temps. 23 June 1350 (*CPR 1348–50*, pp. 535, 538). Cert. of conf. eln by bp of London 22 June 1350 (PRO, C84/26/36). Res. by 13 Apr. 1355 (PRO, C84/27/24). Cess., lic. to el. 18 Apr. 1355 (*CPR 1354–58*, p. 206; *CCR 1354–60*, p. 128).

John of Carlton (Carelton, Carleton) 1355–1361 Eln pres. to king for royal ass. 20 Apr. 1355 (PRO, C84/27/25); royal ass. 20 Apr. 1355, temps. 22 Apr. 1355 (*CPR 1354–1358*, pp. 202, 204). Cert. of conf. eln by bp of London 22 Apr. 1355 (PRO, C84/27/26). D. by 15 May 1361 (*CFR 1356–68*, p. 158). D., lic. to el. 16 May 1361 (*CPR 1361–1364*, p. 21).

Thomas of Watford 1361–1382 Can. of St Bartholomew's, royal ass. 21 May 1361, temps. 29 May 1361, eln having been conf. by M., bp of London (*CPR 1361–64*, pp. 19, 22). D. 4 Jan. 1382 (London, Reg. Braybrooke, f. 306r).

LONGLEAT (Wilts), St Radegund f. –1235

List in *VCH Wilts*, III, 302–3.

[**John de Mora** who occ. *c.* 1225 x 1233 as pr. of Langley, Soms (*Ctl. Cirencester*, II, no. 599) may actually be pr. of Longleat. For the connection between the two houses see *KH*, p. 165; *Ctl. Cirencester*, I, p. xix.]

Richard Occ. 25 Nov. 1271, 15 July 1281 (*Soms F.*, I, pp. 233, 256); n.d. (late 13th cent.) (Longleat mun. nos. 8022, 8032).

Everard Occ. n.d. – ctl. dates from *temp.* Edward I, so ref. before that date (*Ctl. Bruton*, no. 44). The precise place in the sequence of priors is uncertain.

William Occ. 22 Sept. 1322 (Longleat mun. no. 8018); 1326 (*Mon. Angl.*, VI, 583, no source, ? error).

Peter Occ. 13 Apr. 1324 (*Reg. Martival*, II, i, p. 441).

Henry Occ. 29 Sept. 1334 (Longleat mun., no. 8016).

Richard Axebrugge Occ. 1380 x 1381 (Kirby, 'Clerical poll-taxes', p. 166).

MAIDEN BRADLEY (Wilts), St Mary f. -1164 (hospital); -1201 (priory)
  Lists in *VCH Wilts*, III, 301; *Heads*, I, 174.

Andrew Latest recorded occ. 8 July 1212 (BL, Add. ms. 37503, f. 29r).

Hugh Occ. 1225 (*Wilts F.*, I, 13); 15 Aug. 1226 (*CPR 1225–32*, p. 79); (H.) 20 Oct. 1226 (ibid., p. 85); Hil. term 1230 (*CRR*, XIII, no. 2604); 1225 x 1233 (*Ctl. Cirencester*, II, no. 599); n.d. (Wilts RO, 1332/7–8, 11, 20).

William Occ. 1235 (BL, Add ms. 37503, f. 26r).

Ralph Occ. 27 Jan. 1249 (ibid., f. 14r); n.d. (Wilts RO, 1332/27).

Geoffrey Occ. n.d. (mid-late 13th cent.) (PRO, E329/137). His precise place in the sequence of priors is uncertain.

John of Heytesbury/John le Frye It is impossible to separate the two pr. Johns. *VCH* gives John of Heytesbury 1260–1286 and John Le Frye 1298–1306 but the dates are not certain. The 1286 date is prob. a misreading of PRO, E135/21/69, an indulgence issued by Bp Godfrey Giffard of Worcester for pr. John while he lives and for his soul when he shall die 1 Sept. 1286. There is no indication he died shortly after this indulgence was gtd. In almost all cases the refs. below only mention the forename of the pr. Pr. John occ. 13 Oct. 1260 (*Soms F.*, I, 186); 20 Apr 1267 (PRO, E210/291); 1267 PRO, E315/37/194); 1268 (*Wilts F.*, I, 57); 1270 (PRO, E210/308); 1272 (PRO, E210/202); 1273 (PRO, F. Divers Cos. CP25/1/284/20, no. 4; *Wilts F.*, II, 2, 61); 1278 (PRO, E210/4630); Nov. 1278 x Nov. 1279 (PRO, E329/85); (J.) 21 Feb. 1280 (BL, Add. ms. 37503, f. 34v); 1283 (PRO, E210/7077); Nov. 1284 x Nov. 1285 (PRO, E326/10705); 1286 (PRO, E326/8417); 1287 (PRO, E210/7098); Nov. 1289 x Nov. 1290 (PRO, E210/7103); Nov. 1293 x Nov. 1294 (PRO, E210/6459); Nov. 1296 x Nov. 1297 (PRO, E210/8456); 1298 (PRO, E210/727); 1301 (PRO, Just.1/1318, m. 15d); 1 May 1303 (BL, Add. ms. 37503, f. 27v); 23 Jan 1306 (ibid., f. 35v).

John le Frye −1306 Name (Longleat ms. 38A, f. 15r). Cess. by 12 Sept. 1306 (*Reg. Gandavo*, II, 680).

John of Tilshead (Tydolves(s)yde) 1306− Request for ass. to eln 9 Sept. 1306 (PRO, SC1/48/76). Can. of Maiden Bradley, eln pres. to bp 12 Sept. 1306 (*Reg. Gandavo*, II, 679). Eln conf. 8 Oct. 1306 (ibid., 680–1). Occ. July 1309 x July 1310 (PRO, E210/8975); July 1310 x July 1311 (PRO, E210/8329); 1312 (PRO, SC1/49/127); 1319 (Wilts RO, 1332/37); 10 Mar. 1323 (BL, Harl. Cht. 43 A 9); July 1323 x July 1324 (PRO, E210/8328).

William de Welewe 1325− Eln pres. to bp 23 Mar. 1325, no reason given for vacancy; eln conf. 1 Apr. 1325 (*Reg. Martival*, I, 428). Occ. Jan. 1327 x Jan. 1328 (PRO, E210/1808); Jan. 1331 x Jan. 1332 (PRO, E210/2323); 4 Apr. 1333 (PRO, E315/45/154); 3 June 1334 (BL, Harl. Cht. 44 G 8); Jan. 1334 x Jan. 1335 (PRO, E210/2176).

Henry of Frome Occ. 1 Apr. & 5 Apr. 1335 (BL, Add. ms. 37503, ff. 37v, 38v); Nov. 1335 (*Reg. Montacute*, no. 292); Jan. 1336 x Jan. 1337 (PRO, E210/1811); 11 Dec. 1340 (*Reg. Bransford*, no. 153); 7 Feb. 1341 (BL, Add. ms. 37503, f. 54r); 7 Apr. 1343 (PRO, E315/50/280).

John de Welles Previous land acquisition mentd in cht. of 22 Feb. 1348 (BL, Harl. Cht. 57 E 41).

Thomas of Tidcombe (Tidecombe) **1349–** Can. of Maiden Bradley, eln conf. 8 Feb. 1349, no reason given for vacancy (Salisbury, Reg. Wyvil, II, f. 199r). Occ. 20 Mar. 1350 (BL, Add. ms. 37503, f. 60r); Jan.1351 x Jan. 1352 (PRO, E210/9295; /9394); Jan. 1352 x Jan. 1353 (PRO, E210/7758); 25 Apr. 1355 (PRO, E315/43/269); 26 June 1355 (PRO, E210/921); Jan. 1357 x Jan. 1358 (PRO, E210/1962).

William of Frome 1361– Eln quashed, but apptd by bp 10 Nov. 1361 (Salisbury, Reg. Wyvil, II, f. 287v). Occ. 28 Aug. 1362 (PRO, E210/338); Jan. 1366 x Jan. 1367 (PRO, E210/6829); Jan. 1369 x Jan. 1370 (PRO, E210/9305); 8 Nov. 1370 (PRO, E315/49/143); Jan. 1373 x Jan. 1374 (PRO, E210/6494).

Edward (of) Frome 1376–1389 Can. of Maiden Bradley, eln conf. by commissaries 4 Aug. 1376, no reason given for vacancy (Salisbury, Reg. Erghum, f. 21r). Res. by 8 Nov. 1389; provision made for him 8 Dec. 1389 (*Reg. Waltham*, nos. 58, 60).

MARKBY (Lincs), St Peter f. ? *temp.* Henry II
  Lists in *VCH Lincs*, II, 175; *Heads*, I, 174–5.
Simon –1225 Occ. 1202 (*Lincs Assize Roll*, no. 1079); occ. 1203 x 5 (*HMC Var. Coll.*, I, 238). D. 1225 (*Medieval Lindsey Marsh*, pp. 65, 69).
Eudo –1227/8 Res. Dec. 1227 x Dec. 1228 (*Reg. Wells*, III, 166).
Geoffrey de Holm' 1227/8–1231/2 El. and adm. Dec. 1227 x Dec. 1228 (ibid., 166–7). Postulated as abb. of Thornton Curtis Dec. 1231 x Dec. 1232 (ibid., 202).
Alan 1231/2– Chamberlain of Thornton, postulated Dec. 1231 x Dec. 1232 (ibid.). Occ. (A.) June 1237 x June 1238 (*Reg. Grosseteste*, pp. 17–18).
John of Hedon 1246/7–1259/60 Can. of Osney, el. and inst. June 1246 x June 1247, no reason given for vacancy (ibid., p. 87). Res. Nov. 1259 x Nov. 60 (*Reg. R. Gravesend*, p. 4).
Roger of Walmsgate (Walmesgar(e)) **1259/60–1273** Can. of Markby, el. and inst. Nov. 1259 x Nov. 1260 (ibid.). Res. by 12 July 1273 (ibid., p. 55).
Simon of Ottringham (Oteringham, Otringham) **1273–1291** Can. of Markby, eln conf. 12 July 1273 (ibid.). D. by 4 Feb. 1291 (*Reg. Sutton*, I, 150).
Roger of Bratoft (Braytoft) **1291–1306** Can. of Markby, eln quashed but apptd by bp 4 Feb. 1291 (ibid., 150–1). D. by 23 Dec. 1306 (Lincoln, Ep. Reg., II, f. 19r). Indulgence of 30 days for the soul of Roger granted 5 Mar. 1309 (Lincoln, Ep. Reg., III, f. 150r).
William of Laughton (Laghton) **1306–** Cellarer of Markby, eln conf. 23 Dec. 1306 (Lincoln, Ep. Reg., II, f. 19r). Occ. 23 Feb. 1319 (ibid., f. 76r).
Thomas of Hagworthingham –1346 Occ. 25 June 1332 (Lincoln, Ep. Reg., IV, f. 39r); Jan. 1332 x Jan. 1333 (PRO C279/10 no. 6); 1342 (*CPR 1340–43*, p. 453). D. by 19 Mar. 1346 (Lincoln, Ep. Reg., VI, f. 21r–v).
John of Edlington (Edelington, Edlyngton) **1346–1349** Can. of Markby, commn to examine eln 19 Mar. 1346, eln conf. by commissaries 29 Mar. 1346 (ibid.). (commn repeated Lincoln, Ep. Reg., VII, f. 201r). Occ. 22 June 1349 (*CPL*, III, 336). D. by 9 July 1349 (Lincoln, Ep. Reg., IX, f. 67r–v)
Richard de Leek (Lek) **1349–1373** Can. of Markby, eln conf. 9 July 1349 (Lincoln, Ep. Reg., IX, f. 67r–v). D. by 30 Mar. 1373 (Lincoln, Ep. Reg., XII, f. 117v).
Peter of Scotton 1373–1395 Can. of Markby, commn to examine eln 30 Mar. 1373, eln conf. by commissary 13 Apr. 1373 (Lincoln, Ep. Reg., X, f. 68r–v) (commn repeated Lincoln, Ep. Reg., XII, f. 117v). D. by 24 Mar. 1395 (Lincoln, Ep. Reg., XI, f. 75v).

MARTON (Yorks N.), St Mary (Marton in Galtres) f. 1135 x 54
  Lists in *VCH Yorks*, III, 225; *Heads*, I, 175.
Henry Occ. 1199 x 1203 (Raine, *North Durham*, app. p. 140); (H.) 1203 (*Ctl. Healaugh Park*, p.

11); c. Whitsun 1212 (*Ctl. Fountains*, II, 626); c. 1213 x 14 (BL, Cotton ms. Nero D. III, f. 57v); 14 Dec. 1226 (*Yorks F., 1218–31*, p. 99); Easter term 1227 (*CRR*, XIII, no. 134). Seal (*BM Seals*, no. 3621; Clay, *Seals*, p. 25).

Richard Occ. 20 Jan. 1235 (*Yorks F., 1232–46*, p. 36).

Simon Occ. 6 Mar. 1239 (BL, Egerton ms. 2823, f. 43r).

John Occ. 9 Sept. 1252 (*Yorks F., 1246–72*, p. 86); n.d. (mid-13th century) (*York Vicars Choral Chts.*, no. 465). Prob. the John of Askham (Askam) described as former pr. in 1280 (*Yorks F., 1272–1300*, p. 56).

William Occ. c. 1262 x 1263, shortly after 11 Nov. 1262 (*York Vicars Choral Chts.*, no. 533); 1279 (PRO, Just.1/1055, mm. 56d, 61 – in the first entry the pr. is called Walter, in the later one William).

Walter –1280 Occ. 16 Feb. 1280, 15 July 1280 (*Yorks F., 1272–1300*, pp. 36, 53). Res. acc. 2 Aug. 1280 (*Reg. Wickwane*, pp. 58–9, no. 193).

Gregory of Lissett (Lesset) 1280–?1286 Can. of Newburgh, apptd 4 Aug. 1280; mand. to convent to obey 5 Aug. (ibid., pp. 59–60. no. 193). At the archiepiscopal visitation of Newburgh priory on 26 Nov. 1286 he was described as former pr. of Marton and was instructed to return to Newburgh. The manor he had in Craven by provision is to revert to Marton and the letter of provision is to be restored (*Reg. Romeyn*, I, p. 161, no. 447).

John of Wilton (Wylton) –1287 Occ. 24 June 1287 (*CChR 1300–26*, p. 137). Cess. by 27 Oct. 1287, lic. to el. (*Reg. Romeyn*, I, 164, no. 458).

[**William of Bulmer** Sub-pr. of Marton, eln quashed and power to provide a new pr. reserved to the archbp (ibid.)]

John of Lund (Lound) 1287– Can. of Bolton (former pr. of Bolton), provided ?13 Nov. 1287, mandate to install 16 Nov. 1287 (ibid., pp. 164–5, nos. 458, 460). Occ. 30 Sept. 1300 (*Ch. York*, p. 31); 30 Apr. 1301 (*Reg. Corbridge*, I, 124).

Alan of Morton 1305– Can. of Marton, eln conf. 22 Dec. 1305, no reason given for the vacancy (*Reg. Corbridge*, II, 173).

Simon of Brawby (Brauby, Branby) 1308–1318 Can. of Marton, apptd by the vicar-general 29 Feb. 1308, no reason given for the vacancy (*Reg. Greenfield*, V, no. 2658). Cess. accepted and lic. to el. issued 15 June 1318 (*Reg. Melton*, II, no. 37).

[**Alan of Sherburn** (Shirburn) Cellarer of Marton, eln quashed 17 July 1318 (ibid., nos. 42–4). 21 Dec. 1318 absolution to Alan and a fellow-canon from sentences of excommunication for attempting to poison a fellow-canon, Robert of Tickhill (prior 1321–40) (*Reg. Melton*, II, no. 64); permission for him to visit the Roman Curia 4 Aug. 1319 (ibid., no. 98).]

Henry of Melkinthorpe (Melkanthorp, Melkingthorp) 1318–1321 Can. of Bridlington, apptd by archbp 17 July 1318 (*Reg. Melton*, II, nos. 42–4). Cess. by 22 May 1321, when provision made for him by the priory (ibid., no. 156). Seal (*Durham Seals*, II, p. 574, no. 3515). Unsuccessful candidate at Bridlington 1321 (q.v.)

Roger of Tickhill (Tikhil(l)) 1321–1340 Can. of Marton, eln quashed but apptd by archbp 21 July 1321 (*Reg. Melton*, II, nos. 154–5).[28] Pardoned 19 Apr. 1322 for selling garb tithes and not attending synods in person (ibid., no. 178). D. by 28 Nov. 1340 (York, Reg. 5A, f. 105v).

William of Craven (Cravene) 1340–1345 Can. of Marton, eln quashed but apptd by Chapter of York *sede vacante* 28 Nov. 1340 (ibid.). D. by 3 Feb. 1345 (York, Reg. 10, f. 156v).

Hugh of Riccall (Rikal, Rikhale) 1345–1349 Can. of Marton, eln conf. 3 Feb. 1345 (ibid.). D. by 18 Sept. 1349 (ibid., f. 165v).

John of Thirsk (Thresk) 1349–1357 Can. of Marton, eln conf. 18 Sept. 1349 (ibid.). Res. 1357 (Baildon, I, 128, without source). Seal (*BM Seals*, no. 3622; Clay, *Seals*, p. 25).

---

[28] In 1318 an attempt was made by two fellow-canons to poison him (*Reg. Melton*, II, no. 64). See above under Alan of Sherburn.

Robert Occ. 1369 (Baildon, I, 129).

William Occ. Mich. 1370, Hil. 1371 (Baildon, I, 128–9).

Robert of Hutton (Hoton) Occ. Trin. 1371, Hil. 1372, 1378, Hil. 1388 (Baildon, I, 130); 23 Feb. 1398 (BI, Prob. Reg. 2, f. 13r).

The next recorded pr., **Robert of Stillington** (Stillyngton), occ. 1403 (*VCH* citing Baildon ms. notes).

MASSINGHAM, GREAT, *see* GREAT MASSINGHAM

MAXSTOKE (Warws), St Michael (Holy Trinity, St Mary, St Michael and All Saints – *KH*) f. 1331 (college); 1336 x 7 (priory)
List in *VCH Warws*, II, 94

John Deyville (Deyvill) **1336–1339/40?** Letter of pres. by William de Clynton, knight, for br. John Deyvill, can. OSA, to be pr. of the newly-founded house of Maxstoke dated 14 July 1336; John adm. 15 July 1336 (Lichfield, B/A/1/2, f. 29v). Occ. Midsummer 1337 (PRO, E326/2259). Res. n.d. [between entries of May x Sept. 1339] (Lichfield, B/A/1/2, ff. 34v–35r) but cf. ment. 30 May 1340 (*CPR 1338–40*, p. 525).

Robert of Watford 1339/40?- Sub-pr. of Maxstoke, eln conf. by bp n.d. [between entries of May x Sept. 1339] (Lichfield, B/A/1/2, ff. 34v–35r). Occ. 2 Jan. 1340 (Worcester Cath. Lib. B809); 1344 (*Warws F.*, II, 197, nos. 1949, 1952); 1345 (Worcester Cath. Lib. B66a); 1346 (PRO, E315/35/68); from 1346 to 1347 (*CCR 1346–49*, pp. 74, 488); Jan. 1347 x Jan. 1348 (PRO, E210/1584 I); 18 Oct. 1355 (PRO, C241/134/49); mentd in inspeximus of 29 Jan. 1365 but could be much earlier (*CCR 1364–68*, p. 161).

Reginald of Bromwich (Bromwych) Occ. 4 May 1383 (PRO, E326/1086); 15 Aug. 1383 (PRO, E326/3730); 25 June ?1386 (PRO, E210/729).

MERTON (Surrey), St Mary f. 25 Mar. 1117
Lists in *VCH Surrey*, II, 102; *Heads*, I, 175; Heales, *passim*; Annals in Eton ms. of *Flor. Hist.* ed. Luard I, p. liii (Ann. 1, quoted from Luard); BL, Cotton ms. Faustina A. VIII, ff. 137–42 (Ann. 2); Cambridge, Corpus Christi College ms. 59, ff. 158 ff. (Ann. 3); 17th cent. copy in Lambeth ms. 585, pp. 105 ff.; Ann. to 1218 ed. M. Brett, *Annals*; list in BL, Cotton ms. Cleopatra C. VII, f. 196r.

Walter 1197/8–1218 Entered office 17 May 1198 = Whit Sunday (Ann 3, f. 168v; Brett, *Annals*, p.304). 7th pr., res. to became Carthusian in 1218 (Ann. 3, f. 173v; year confirmed by list Ann. 1, 2, but list and Ann. 2 also give date of accession as 1198; Bodl., Rawlinson ms. B.177, f. 219r–v). List gives 1218 as 20th year. Occ. 20 Sept. 1197 (*Beds. F.*, no. 19 – which suggests he was apptd 13 Aug. x 20 Sept. 1197, unless there is an error or anachronism in the fine). Also occ. 1202 (ibid., no. 172); 10 Mar. 1218 (Heales, p. 74); Trin. term 1218 (*Essex F.*, I, 49). Became a Carthusian 1218 (*Ann. Waverley*, p. 290; *Ann. Southwark*, pp. 53–4; Brett, *Annals*, p. 310); Nov. 1217 (*Ann. Dunstable*, p. 52). Lic. to el. 2 Oct. 1218 (*CPR 1216–25*, p. 169).

Thomas de Wllst 1218–1222 For name see *Mon. Angl.*, VI, 604, no. ii. 8th pr. Cellarer of Merton, royal ass. 6 Nov. 1218 (*CPR 1216–25*, p. 178). Succ. 10 Nov. 1218 (Bodl., Rawlinson ms. B.177, f. 219r–v) *or* 11 Nov. 1218 (Ann. 3); 1218 (*Ann. Dunstable*, p. 53). Occ. 8 July 1219 (PRO, Cambs F., CP25/1/23/9. no. 17)); 1222 (WAM, no. 12753); 26 June 1222 (PRO, Hants F., CP25/1/203/5, no. 4). D. 1222 (*Ann. Waverley*, p. 297; BL, Cotton ms. Cleopatra C VII, f. 196r; Bodl., Rawlinson ms. B.177, f. 219v). D., lic. to el. 12 Sept. 1222 (*CPR 1216–25*, p. 339).

Giles de Burn(e) 1222–1231 9th pr. Can. of Merton, succ. 1222 (Bodl., Rawlinson ms. B.177,

f. 219v); royal ass. 28 Sept. 1222 (*CPR 1216–25*, p. 341). Succ. 1222 (*Ann. Dunstable*, p. 76; *Ann. Waverley*, p. 297). ?Installed (*impositus*) by P., bp of Winchester 25 Oct. 1222 (BL, Cotton ms. Cleopatra C VII, f. 196r). Occ. 12 Nov. 1223 (*Bucks F.*, p. 50). Became Cistercian at Beaulieu 1231 (*Ann. Dunstable*, p. 128; *Ann. Waverley*, p. 310; *Ann. Southwark*, p. 56; BL, Cotton ms. Cleopatra C VII, f. 196r; Bodl., Rawlinson ms. B.177, f. 221v). Lic. to el. (no reason given for vacancy) 30 Oct. 1231 (*CPR 1225–32*, p. 451).

Henry de Basinges (Basing') **1231–1238** 10th pr. Sub-cellarer of Merton, succ. 1231 (*Ann. Dunstable*, p. 128, cf. *Ann. Waverley*, p. 310). Can. of Merton, royal ass. 10 Nov. 1231 (*CPR 1225–32*, p. 451); mand. for seisin 13 Nov. 1231 (*CR 1231–34*, p. 3). Succ. (?installed) 17 Nov. 1231 (BL, Cotton ms. Cleopatra C VII, f. 196r; Bodl., Rawlinson ms. B.177, f. 221v). D. 22 Dec. 1238 (ibid.; cf. *Mon. Angl.*, VI, 245 (27 Dec.); *Ann. Waverley*, p. 319).

Robert de Heyham (Helyham) **1238–1249** 11th pr. Can. of Merton, succ. 1238 (*Ann. Waverley*, p. 319). Installed 6 Jan. 1239 (BL, Cotton ms. Cleopatra C VII, f. 196r; Bodl., Rawlinson ms. B.177, f. 223v). Res. 10 Oct. 1249 (ibid.). Res., lic. to el. 12 Oct. 1249 (*CPR 1247–58*, p. 50).

Eustace 1249–1263 12th pr. Can. of Merton, writ *de intendendo* 13 Oct. 1249 (ibid.).; mand. for seisin 14 Oct. 1249 (*CR 1247–51*, p. 208). Succ. (?installed) 25 Oct. 1249 (BL, Cotton ms. Cleopatra C VII, f. 196r). D. 31 Jan. 1263 (ibid.; cf. PRO, C84/1/29).

Gilbert de Aette (Eytte) **1263–1292** 13th pr. Sub-pr. of Merton, temps. (G.), whose eln had been conf. by the bp of Winchester (*CPR 1258–66*, p. 244). Installed 22 Feb. 1263 (BL, Cotton ms. Cleopatra C VII, f. 196r, cf. f. 197r for surname and prev. office of cellarer). D. 21 Mar. 1292 (ibid., f. 196r). D., lic. to el. 24 Apr. 1292 (*CPR 1281–92*, p. 486).

Nicholas (of) Tregony 1292–1296 14th pr. Sub-pr. of Merton, el. 28 Apr. 1292 (PRO, C84/10/39); royal ass. 4 May 1292; temps. 15 May 1292 (*CPR 1281–92*, pp. 488, 490). Cert. of conf. eln by bp of Winchester 7 May 1292 (PRO, C84/10/40). Installed 1 June 1292 (BL, Cotton ms. Cleopatra C VII, f. 196r). D. 26 Sept. 1296 (ibid.). D. (Philip *sic*), lic. to el. 8 Oct. 1296 (*CPR 1292–1301*, p. 207).

Edmund of Herriard (Herierd, Her(e)yerd) **1296–1305** 15th pr. Can. of Merton, eln pres. to king for royal ass. 29 Oct. 1296 (PRO, C84/12/35); royal ass. 6 Nov. 1296, temps. 28 Nov. 1296 (*CPR 1292–1301*, pp. 209, 223). Cert. of conf. eln by vicegerent of bp of Winchester 23 Nov. 1296 (PRO, C84/12/37). Released from excommunication 4 May 1301 (*Reg. Pontissara*, I, 106).

Acts of the bp's commissaries at Merton – inquiry into the pr.'s alleged contravention of the archbp of Canterbury's inhibition met with a flat denial from the pr. (*Reg. Woodlock*, I, 102–4). Pr. Edmund, on the ground of dissensions, offered his res. to bp, subject to a declaration of his innocence of the charges laid against him at the archbp's visitation. The bp acc. the res. but disallowed the condition and made provision for the ex-pr. 25 Sept. 1305 (ibid., 104–6, cf. BL, Cotton ms. Cleopatra C VII, f. 196r; PRO, C84/15/35). Cess. (E.), lic. to el. 20 Oct. 1305 (*CPR 1301–7*, p. 385).

An election dispute followed: on 1 Dec. 1305 proctors of the 2 el. candidates, **Edmund of Herriard** (re-el.) and **William of Broxbourne** (Brokesbourne), cans. of Merton, produced royal letters dated 12 Nov. 1305 asking the bp to deal with the matter (*Reg. Woodlock*, I, 76–8). On 3 Dec. bp found it impossible to intervene since one of the proctors maintained right to proceed to a new eln. Letter from the sub-pr. and convent to bp asking him to provide one of their cans. as pr. 30 Dec. 1305; royal letter in similar vein 27 Dec. (ibid., 91–4). In a letter from the archbp of Canterbury to the bp of Winchester, the former had found at his visitation of the priory that Edmund had caused serious trouble and he reduced him to living in the cloister as an ordinary canon. The bp is to provide a new pr. 28 Feb. 1306 (*Reg. Woodlock*, I, 99–101).

Geoffrey of Alconbury (Alkemondbury, Alkemundburia) **1306–1307** 16th pr. Can. of Merton, provision as pr. 5 Mar. 1306; letters to convent and king 6 Mar. (*Reg. Woodlock*, I, 94–7); notif. of appt to king 7 Mar. 1306 (ibid., 101–2). Temps. 6 Mar. 1306 (*CPR 1301–07*, p. 419). Installed 25 Mar. 1306 (BL, Cotton ms. Cleopatra C VII, f. 196r). D. 15 Mar. 1307 (ibid.). D. (G.), lic. to el. 26 Mar. 1307 (*CPR 1301–07*, p. 511).

William of Broxbourne (Brokesborn, Brokesbourne, Brokesburn) **1307–1335** Can. of Merton, royal ass. 3 May 1307, writ *de intendendo* 4 June 1307 (ibid., pp. 524, 529). Eln conf. 10 June 1307, no reason given for vacancy (*Reg. Woodlock*, I, 184–5, cf. ibid., II, 725). Installed 25 June 1307 (BL, Cotton ms. Cleopatra C VII, f. 196r). Occ. 20 Jan. 1335 (Lincoln, Ep. Reg., IV, f. 312r). D., lic. to el. 18 Mar. 1335 (*CPR 1334–38*, p. 87).

Thomas of Kent (Kantia) **1335–1339** Can. of Merton, royal ass. 24 Mar. 1335, temps. 30 Apr. 1335 (ibid., pp. 87, 102). El. 20 Mar. 1335, proclamation of eln 1 Apr., eln conf. 26 Apr. 1335 (Winchester, Reg. Orleton I, ff. 16v–18v). Inhibition of the Court of Canterbury re tuitorial appeal by the archdn of Surrey in a dispute over the installation of pr. Thomas (ibid., f. 23v); complaint by pr. Thomas about the installation dispute 29 Nov. 1335 (ibid., f. 29*r–v); commn to install 17 Mar. 1336 (ibid., f. 34r). D. by 20 Sept. 1339 (PRO, C84/24/12). D., lic. to el. 24 Sept. 1339 (*CPR 1338–40*, p. 316).

John de Lytlynton (Lutelynton, Lutlynton) **1339–1345** Can. of Merton, royal ass. 13 Oct. 1339, temps. 10 Nov. 1339 (ibid., pp. 322, 330). Eln conf. 6 Nov. 1339 (Winchester, Reg. Orleton I, f. 81r–v). Dep. by 12 Aug. 1345 (PRO, C84/24/45). Dep., lic. to el. 14 Aug. 1345 (*CPR 1343–45*, p. 537).

William de Friston (Freston) **1345–1361** Can. of Merton, royal ass. 24 Aug. 1345 (ibid., p. 536); cert. conf. of eln by archbp of Canterbury *sede vacante* 30 Aug. 1345 (PRO, C84/24/47). D., lic. to el. 22 Aug. 1361 (*CPR 1361–64*, p. 53).

Geoffrey de Chaddesley (Chaddesle, Chaddeslegh, Chaddesleye) **1361–1368** Can. of Merton, royal ass. 31 Aug. 1361, temps. 10 Sept. 1361 (ibid., pp. 56, 58). Eln conf. 4 Sept. 1361 (*Reg. Edington*, I, nos. 1458–63). D. 6 Oct. 1368 (PRO, C84/29/39). D., lic. to el. 7 Oct. 1368 (*CPR 1367–70*, p. 151).

Robert of Windsor (Windsore, Wyndesore) **1368–1403** Can. of Merton, royal ass. 18 Oct. 1368, writ *de intendendo* 27 Oct. 1368 (ibid., pp. 150, 158). Eln conf. 27 Oct. 1368 and mand. to install s.d. (*Reg. Wykeham*, I, 18–22). D. 6 May 1403 (*Mon. Angl.*, VI, 246). D., lic. to el. 11 May 1403 (*CPR 1401–05*, p. 226; cf. PRO, C84/38/41).

MICHELHAM (Sussex), Holy Trinity f. 1229

List in *VCH Sussex*, II, 79; Salzmann, *Hailsham*, ch. xv, pp. 214–38.

Roger I Occ. 19 Nov. 1235 (*Sussex F.*, I, no. 313).

Peter Occ. from 18 Nov. 1248 to 8 July 1249 (ibid., I, nos. 465, 506); from 19 Oct. 1254 to 8 July 1256 (ibid., II, nos. 547, 606). From *CCR 1333–37*, p. 369 it is prob. that Peter was pr. when John de Warenne became earl (1240).

Roger II Occ. from 8 May 1261 to 2 Dec. 1262 (ibid., II, nos. 646, 648); 3 June 1261 (*Kent F.*, p. 317); n.d. (before 1268) (PRO, E40/15533).

William Occ. 5 July 1273 (*CChR 1257–1300*, p. 410).

Roger III Occ. from 1 July 1277 to 25 June 1288 (*Sussex F.*, II, nos. 863, 1014); (R.) 7 Apr. 1279 (*Ctl. Chichester*, no. 655); 1286 (PRO, Just.1/86, m. 17); 1287 (PRO, E326/12632); 1288 (PRO, Just.1/929, m. 36d); 20 Nov. 1290 (*HMC De L'Isle & Dudley*, I, 125; *Robertsbridge Chts.*, no. 280); 26 Nov. 1300 (PRO, Just.1/1318, m. 6); 1304 (Cambridge, King's Coll., MIC.1); Mich. 1310 (PRO, CP40/183, attorneys m. 8d).

William de Shelvestrode (Scalvestrod) Occ. n.d. (*c.* 1322) (Bodl., Kent roll 6, dated by Salzmann, p. 219); Trin. 1328 (*Index to Placita de Banco*, p. 668); (W.) [1332 x 3] (PRO, C270/10/11). Mentd as former pr. 4 Feb. 1335 (*CCR 1333–35*, p. 369).

John of Worth Mentd as former pr. in proceedings of 1346 x 1347 (PRO, Just.1/941A, m. 5d).

John Occ. Dec. 1352 (ibid., m. 24).

John Leme (Leem) Occ. 1377 (PRO, E42/456); 10 Feb. 1381 (*CPR 1377–81*, p. 576); 1377–1382 as receiver of the honour of Aquila (Salzmann, *Hailsham*, pp. 222–3); 27 Sept. 1392 (PRO, E40/4085); 1402 (*Reg. Rede*, II, 216, 218); 1405 (ibid., I, 60); 20 Jan. 1414 (ibid., 97); 29 May 1415 (*CPR 1413–16*, p. 408).

MISSENDEN (Bucks), St Mary f. 1133 (abbey)

Lists in *VCH Bucks*, I, 375; *Ctl. Missenden*, III, xxiv–xxvi; *Heads*, I, 176.

Adam Last recorded occ. 1212 (*CRR*, VI, 220).

Martin –1236 Occ. *c.* 20 Oct. 1219 (*Bucks F.*, I, 42; *Basset Chts.*, no. 114; *Devon F.*, I, p. 53, no. 94); 1219, 25 Apr. 1220 (*Ctl. Colchester*, II, 562, 564); 20 Oct. 1219 (Devon F., I, no. 94); from 1219 to 2 June 1234 (*Ctl. Missenden*, III, nos. 857, 886); from Easter 1227 to Trin. 1231 (*CRR*, XIII, no. 146; XIV, no. 1543). Res. June 1236 x June 1237 (*Reg. Grosseteste*, p. 343). Unnamed abb. dep. at Bp Grosseteste's visitation 1236 (*Ann. Dunstable*, p. 143).

Robert 1236/7–1240/1 Can. of Missenden, el. and inst. June 1236 x June 1237 (*Reg. Grosseteste*, p. 343). Occ. 30 Mar. 1239 (*Ctl. Missenden*, I, no. 191). Res. June 1240 x June 1241 (*Reg. Grosseteste*, p. 355).

Roger of Aylesbury (Eylesbir') 1240/1–1258/9 Can. of Missenden, el., adm. and bl. June 1240 x June 1241 (ibid.). Res. Nov. 1258 x Nov. 1259 (*Reg. R. Gravesend*, p. 236). Seal (*BM Seals*, nos. 3652–3).

Simon of London (Lond') 1258/9–1262 Apptd by bp after eln quashed, Nov. 1258 x Nov. 1259 (*Reg. R. Gravesend*, p. 236). Occ. (S.) 20 Sept. 1259 (*Ctl. Missenden*, II, no. 321); 10 Feb. 1262 (*Bucks F.*, II, 8). Res. Nov. 1261 x Nov. 1262 (*Reg. R. Gravesend*, p. 237). Simon, former abb., writes to Edward I about the failure of the abb. and convent to support him n.d. (PRO, SC1/19/117); a further letter about his plight n.d. (PRO, SC1/55/20–20A).

Geoffrey of Whelpley (Welpele, Welepeleye, Welpesle, Whelpelegh) 1262–1268 Inst. Nov. 1261 x Nov. 1262, after Feb. 1262 (*Reg. R. Gravesend*, pp. 237, 339, and see above). Res. by 27 May 1268 (ibid., p. 242, but see next entry). Protection for 3 years for Geoffrey, sometime abb., 5 May 1268, 18 Oct. 1271 (*CPR 1266–72*, pp. 224, 580). Occ. as former abb. 5 Oct. 1268 (PRO, C85/98/55).

William of London 1268– Can. of Missenden, eln [?conf.] 27 May 1268 (*Reg. R. Gravesend*, p. 242). Occ. 15 Sept. 1268, 1273, June 1279 (*Ctl. Missenden*, I, no. 101; III, nos. 728, 889); 30 Oct. 1278 (*CCR 1272–79*, p. 563); 7 Nov. 1278 (ibid., p. 512); 11 June 1279 (*Bucks F.*, II, 41); 1280 (PRO, CP40/34, m. 75; C85/3/19); Mich. 1281 x Mich. 1282 (PRO, E159/55 mm. 15, 16(2)); unnamed abb. going overseas, attorneys apptd for 3 years 23 Apr. 1282 (*CPR 1281–92*, p. 18).

Matthew of Tring (Treng) –1307 Occ. in *Ctl. Missenden* from 26 Nov. 1293 to 12 July 1304 (III, nos. 775, 575); 19 July 1304 (BCL, Hampton 492825). D. by 20 Feb. 1307 (Lincoln, Ep. Reg., II, ff. 179v–180r).

Richard le Mareschal 1307–1323 Can. of Missenden, eln conf. 20 Feb. 1307, prof. obed. and bl. 26 Feb. 1307 (ibid.; repeated Lincoln, Ep. Reg., IV, f. 356r). D. by 10 June 1323 (Lincoln, Ep. Reg., IV, f. 328v).

Robert of Kimble (Kinebell, Kynebell) 1323–1340 Can. of Missenden, eln pres. to bp 10 June 1323, but renounced by convent who asked bp to appt. He apptd Robert 12 June 1323 (ibid.). Cess. by 22 Feb. 1340 (ibid., f. 335r–v). Provision made for him 29 Mar. 1340 (Lincoln, Ep. Reg., VIIB, ff. 76v–77r).

William de la Mare 1340 Pr. and convent asked vicar-general to appt in a letter of 22 Feb. 1340. Can. of Missenden, apptd 2 Mar. 1340 (Lincoln, Ep. Reg., IV, f. 355r–v). D. by 8 Oct. 1340 (ibid., f. 359v).

Henry of Buckingham (Bokyngham) **1340–1347** Can. of Missenden, eln renounced but apptd by bp's Official 8 Oct. 1340 (ibid.). Commn to receive res. 28 Apr. 1347 (Lincoln, Ep. Reg., VII, 91r). Occ. 6 May 1347 (*CCR 1346–49*, p. 274). Res. acc. 8 May 1347 (Lincoln, Ep. Reg., VII, f. 91r).

John of Abingdon (Abyndon) **1347–1348** Can. of Missenden, commn to examine eln 11 May 1347 (ibid., f. 207v). Similar commn with different named commissaries 19 May 1347 (ibid., f. 208r). Lic. to receive bl. from any Catholic bp 11 May 1347 (ibid., f. 91r). D. by 4 Oct. 1348 (Lincoln, Ep. Reg., IX, f. 288v).

William of Bradley (Bradele) **1348–1356** Can. of St Mary de Pratis, Leicester, apptd by bp *per lapsum temporis* 4 Oct. 1348 (ibid.). Occ. 8 Mar. 1351 (*Ctl. Missenden*, III, no. 856). Res. by 3 June 1356 (Lincoln, Ep. Reg., IX, ff. 306v–307r). Alteration of the provision made for him 12 July 1356 (Lincoln, Ep. Reg., VIII, f. 102r).

Ralph Mareschall 1356–1374 Can. of Missenden, commn to examine eln dated 3 June 1356 (ibid.). Lic. to receive blessing from any Catholic bp 3 June 1356 (Lincoln, Ep. Reg., VIII, f. 64r). Accused of forging and clipping money – sentenced to be drawn and hanged Mich. 1357 (*King's Bench, Edward III*, VI, 118). Admin. of the abbey given to the pr. while abb. Ralph is absent in prison, dated 21 Apr. 1358 (Lincoln, Ep. Reg., VIII, ff. 98v–99r). Letter from the king to Bp Gynwell, dated 18 July 1359, concerning the abbot now in custody in Nottingham Castle, but to be transferred to a monastic prison. Bp's letter to the abbot and convent of Bourne dated 29 July 1359 to take charge of him (ibid., f. 115v). Pardon gtd to abb. who had received the death sentence for feloniously clipping the king's money in the 30th and 31st years of the king's reign (1356–58), 3 Sept. 1361 (*CPR 1361–64*, p. 59). D. by 21 Nov. 1374 (Lincoln, Ep. Reg., X, ff. 435v–436r).

William (de) Thenford 1374–1383 Pr. of Missenden, pres. as abb.-el. to bp 21 Nov. 1374, eln conf. 12 Dec. 1374 (ibid.). D. by 4 Oct. 1383 (ibid., ff. 461v–462r).

MOBBERLEY (Ches.), St Mary and St Wilfrid f. 1198 x 1204; annexed to Rocester 1228 x 1240. See F. I. Dunn, 'The priory of Mobberley and its charters', *Cheshire History*, 8 (1981), 73–88.

List in *Heads*, I, 176.

No names found after **Walter,** first pr. (*Heads*, I, 176).

MOTTISFONT (Hants), Holy Trinity f. 1201

List in *VCH Hants*, II, 175.

Gregory Occ. 15 July 1218 (*Wilts F.*, I, 11); 21 May 1223 (PRO, Hants F., CP25/1/203/5, no. 13).

Stephen Occ. 2 May 1227 (PRO, Hants F., CP25/1/203/5, no. 13); Easter term 1229 (*CRR*, XIII, no. 1682); 1230, 1234 (*Ctl. Winchester*, nos. 300, 398; *EEA*, 9, nos. 48–50); 1230 (PRO, Hants F., 203/6 no. 5); Easter term 1231 (*CRR*, XIV, no. 1273); 1234, 1235 (*Selborne Chts.*, I, 9, 16, 20); 1241, 1244 (PRO, Hants F., 203/7, nos. 28, 74); 1246 (*CChR 1226–57*, p. 310); 1252 (*Wilts F.*, I, 45); 5 July 1253 (*Ctl. St Denys*, II, no. 342).

Letter of A., bp-el. of Winchester to sub-pr. and convent 10 Aug. 1256; lic. to el. another pr., the (unnamed) person el. to be pr. having excused himself on acct of bodily weakness (*per debilitatem corporis*) (Hants RO, 13M63/2, f. 1v).

Joseph Occ. 25 Mar. 1259, 15 Nov. 1262 (ibid., ff. 163r, 124r); 29 Apr. 1263 (PRO, Hants F., 204/10, no. 59); 1268, 9 Feb. 1272 (ibid., 204/11, nos. 11, 72); Sept. 1272 (*Ctl. Winchester*, no. 312); 4 June 1273 (BL, Campbell Cht. V. 3); Nov. 1274 x Nov. 1275 (Hants RO, 13M63/2, f. 60v).

Henry of Winchester (Wynton) –**1294** Occ. Nov. 1276 x Nov. 1277 (ibid., f. 79r); 1277 (PRO, DL27/232); 1280 (PRO, E210/6856); 1281 (PRO, Hants F., 204/13, no. 23); (H.) 22 July 1284 (*Reg. Pontissara*, I, 283–4); Mich. 1284 x Mich. 1285 (PRO, E159/58, m. 15); 30 Nov. 1289 (BL, Harl. Cht. 44 G 13). 26 Jan. 1284 archbp of Canterbury send visitation injunctions to unnamed pr. about whom there had been serious complaints (*Reg. Peckham*, II, 645–9). House void by his cess. and lic. issued 4 Feb. 1294 (*CPR 1292–1301*, pp. 61–2). Seal (*BM Seals*, no. 3662; *Mon. Seals*, p. 62).

Thomas de Berton(e) (Berthon) **1294–** Can. of Mottisfont, el. 15 Feb. 1294 and request to bp for conf. 26 Feb. (*Reg. Pontissara*, I, 60, 367–70; PRO, C84/11/44); royal ass. 22 Feb. 1294, temps. 4 Mar. 1294 (*CPR 1292–1301*, pp. 62–3; *Reg. Pontissara*, I, 366–7). Cert. conf. eln by bp of Winchester 28 Feb. 1294 (PRO, C84/11/45). Occ. 11 June 1296 (*HMC De L'Isle and Dudley*, I, 9); 25 Dec. 1296, 19 Jan. 1298 (Hants RO, 13M63/2, ff. 60v, 119v).

William Kay 1300– Can. of Mottisfont, apptd by the bp, mand. for induction 11 Mar. 1300 (*Reg. Pontissara*, I, 94). Occ. 1308 (Hants RO, 13M63/2, f. 84r); 16 June 1310 (*Reg. Woodlock*, I, 466); 29 Sept. 1310, 2 Apr. 1315 (Hants RO, 13M63/2, ff. 59v, 83v, 85r).

John of Durnford (Durneford) **1317–** Can. of Mottisfont, commn to cite any objectors to eln 13 Mar. 1317 (*Reg. Sandale*, pp. 31–2). Mand. to install 29 Mar. 1317 (ibid., pp. 33–4). Occ. 10 Aug. 1317, 25 Nov. 1319 (Hants RO, 13M63/2, ff. 60r, 175r).

Walter of Wallop (Walhup) **1323–** Commn to examine eln 30 Aug. 1323 (*Reg. Asserio*, pp. 609–10).

Benedict of Wallop (Wollop) –**1331** Occ. 12 June 1330 (*Ctl. Winchester*, no. 131). Court gave bp of Winchester right to provide a new pr. 6 Jan. 1331 (Winchester, Reg. Stratford, f. 121v). Res. acc. 8 Feb. 1331 (ibid., ff. 121v–122r). Mand. to pr. John about provision for former pr. n.d. (*c*. June 1331) (ibid., f. 56v).

John of Durnford (Derneford, Durneford) **1331–1344** Can. of Mottisfont, apptd by bp 8 Feb. 1331 (ibid., ff. 121v–122r). D. by 9 Feb. 1344 (Winchester, Reg. Orleton II, f. 101v).

Walter (le) Blount 1344– Can. of Mottisfont, commn to examine eln 9 Feb. 1344 (ibid., ff. 101v–102r).

Robert of Breamore (Brommore) **1349–1351** Sub-pr. of Mottisfont, commn to examine eln 17 Apr. 1349 (*Reg. Edington*, I, nos. 459–60). Cert. of commissary 13 May 1349 (ibid., no. 543). D. by 14 Dec. 1351 (ibid., no. 866).

Richard de Can(e)ford 1351–1352 Coll. by lapse 14 Dec. 1351 (ibid.). Res. by 9 Aug. 1352 (ibid., no. 909).

Ralph of Thurlaston (Thorleston) **1352–1366** Can. of Leicester, apptd by bp, having been asked by the convent to appt on this occasion 6 Oct. 1352 (ibid., nos. 909–12). D. by 25 Mar. 1366 (ibid., no. 1726).

John Netheravene (Netherhaven) **1366–** Can. of Mottisfont, commn to examine eln 25 Mar. 1366; eln conf. 1 Apr. 1366 (ibid., nos. 1726–32). Mentd n.d. (*Cal. Misc. Inq.*, VII, no. 387).

John Occ. 1382, 29 July, 1 Sept. 1383, 11 Jan. 1392, 4 Apr. 1395 (Hants RO, 13M63/2, ff. 46v, 169v, 171r, 156v, 64v). ? the same as John Netheravene.

The next recorded pr., **John Brykenyle**, commn to examine eln 27 Dec. 1398, no reason given for vacancy (*Reg. Wykeham*, I, 218–19).

MOUNTJOY (Haveringland) (Norfolk), St Laurence f. 1189 x 99 (cell of Wymondham); + 1199 (Aug. priory)
Lists in *VCH Norfolk*, II, 388; *Heads*, I, 176.

Hur' Occ. 1265 x 80 (*Ctl. Holy Trinity Aldgate*, p. 7, no. 43).

Thomas Occ. 29 Sept. 1294 (PRO, E40/2782). Possibly the same as below.

Thomas de Carlemle (?Carlevile *see below*) **de Swenington** −1304 Notification to the bp of Norwich that the archbp of Canterbury has dep. Thomas. The patron has presented John de Weeting and the archbp asks the bp to adm. him, 11 May 1304 (*Reg. Winchelsey*, II, 791–2).

John of Weeting (Weting, Wetyng) 1304– Can. of Bromehill, apptd 19 May 1304, no reason given for vacancy (Norwich, Reg/1/1, f. 13r). Notification of his appt at archbp's visitation, following deposition of previous pr. 16 Oct. 1304 (*Reg. Winchelsey*, I, 484).

Thomas Carleville 1306– Can. of Mountjoy, apptd by bp 11 Feb. 1306, no reason given for vacancy (Norwich, Reg/1/1, f. 19r). Occ. 26 Mar. 1306 (PRO, E40/2788).

Peter of Cley (Cleye) 1308– Eln quashed but apptd by bp 7 July 1308, no reason given for vacancy (Norwich, Reg/1/1, f. 28r). Occ. 1315 (PRO, E40/3045); 1319 (PRO, E40/3043); 1322 (PRO, E40/3051); 23 Dec. 1324 (PRO, E40/2807).

John Occ. 1341 (PRO, E40/14059); 31 Oct. 1344 (PRO, E40/2733); 29 Sept. 1347 (PRO, E40/2844).

An unnamed pr. d. by 16 July 1349, along with all the canons (*Reg. Bateman*, I, no. 825).

Simon de Fleg' 1349– Can. of Wormegay, apptd by bp 16 July 1349 (ibid.).

John of Elveden −1370 Occ. 7 Oct. 1357 (PRO, E40/2884); 21 May 1362 (PRO, E40/2742). D. by 7 Feb. 1370 (Lambeth, Reg. Whittlesey, f. 147v).

John of Catton 1370– Can. of Mountjoy, eln conf. 7 Feb. 1370 (ibid.). Occ. 27 May 1375 (PRO, E40/2793).

Philip de Tadeshale 1379– Can. of Pentney, eln quashed but apptd by bp 12 June 1379, no reason given for vacancy (Norwich, Reg/3/6, f. 64r). Occ. 1387 (PRO, E40/2839); 1389 (PRO, E40/3078); 8 May 1395 (PRO, E40/2756).

NEWARK (Surrey), St Mary and St Thomas Becket (Aldbury; de Novo Loco, etc.) f. *temp.* Henry II; ?*c.* 1169 or later.

Lists in *VCH Surrey*, II, 105; *Heads*, I, 176.

John −1226 First pr. D. 1226 after 'sacerdotio functus est' for 57 years (*Ann. Waverley*, p. 302). Known to occ. *c.* 1191 x *c.* 1192 (*EEA*, 8, no. 226); (L.) 1200 x 1202 (*Ctl. Chertsey*, I, no. 87 – Aldbury); 1205 (*CRR*, III, 262); Mich. term 1225 (ibid., XII, no. 1508). Prob. the pr. John whose obit celebrated 8 Dec. (BL, Cotton ms. Claudius D III, f. 162v).

Thomas Occ. Mich. term 1231 (*Essex F.*, I, 93); Mich. term 1232 (*CRR*, XIV, nos. 1995, 2277); from Oct. 1234 x Oct. 1235 to Oct. 1247 x Oct. 1248 (*Surrey F.*, pp. 19, 29); 16 Apr. 1235 (*Essex F.*, I, 104); Oct. 1237 x Oct. 1238 (*London and Middlesex F.*, p. 24); Oct. 1242 x Oct. 1243 (ibid., p. 27); n.d. (1249 x 1252) (BL, Cotton Cht. XXI 25).

Richard Occ. Oct. 1252 x Oct. 1253 (*London and Middlesex F.*, p. 35); from Oct. 1258 x Oct. 1259 to Oct. 1260 x Oct. 1261 (*Surrey F.*, pp. 38, 40); Mich. 1260 (*Essex F.*, I, 240); 8 July 1262 (*Ctl. Chertsey*, II, no. 873).

Geoffrey of London −1280 Occ. from Oct. 1265 x Oct. 1266 to Nov. 1278 x Nov. 1279 (*Surrey F.*, pp. 44, 52); Oct. 1265 x Oct. 1266, Nov. 1272 x Nov. 1273 (*London and Middlesex F.*, pp. 44, 50). Cess., lic. to el. 29 May 1280 (*CPR 1272–81*, p. 373; cf. PRO, SC1/19/194, archbp of Canterbury notifying the king that he has removed the pr. and asks for lic. to el. 29 May [no year]). Seal (*Surrey Arch. Coll.*, 40 (1932), p. 39).

Walter de Chapmannesford (Chepmannesforde) 1280– Can. of Newark, archbp writes to king asking for restitution of temps. 19 July 1280 (*Reg. Peckham*, I, 392g–h); writ *de intendendo* 24 July 1280 (*CPR 1272–81*, p. 392). Occ. 8 Oct. 1281 (BL, Harl Cht. 50 F 47); 27 Nov. 1281 (*CPR 1281–92*, p. 42); Nov. 1301 (*Cal. Chanc. Warr.*, p. 147); Mich. 1310 (PRO, CP40/183, m. 12). cf. visitation injunctions for priory – unnamed pr. is old and feeble, 2 cans. apptd as administrator and receiver 1 Apr. 1309 (*Reg. Woodlock*, I, 523–4).

Roger de Eynham (Enham) 1312–1344 Eln proclaimed 26 Sept. 1312, opposers to appear on 11 Oct. (ibid., 586–7). Eln quashed, but apptd by bp 11 Oct. 1312; mand. to induct 12 Oct. 1312 (ibid.). Commn to acc. cess. 29 June 1344; res. adm. 1 July 1344 (Winchester, Reg. Orleton, I, ff. 126r–127v).

John of Barton 1344– Power of appt a new pr. transferred by convent to bp of Winchester 1 July 1344 and he apptd John de Barton, can. of Newark, 1 July (ibid.). Occ. 22 Mar. 1348 (BL, Harl. Cht. 58 D 7); 12 Jan. 1351 (*CPL*, III, 372). Mentd as late pr. 15 May 1352 (*CPR 1350–54*, p. 286).

The next recorded pr., **Alexander Culmeston**, res. acc. 25 Oct. 1387 on account of infirmity (*Reg. Wykeham*, I, 165).

NEWBURGH (Yorks N.), St Mary (Coxwold) f. 1142/3 (at Hood); 1145 (at Newburgh)
  Lists in *VCH Yorks*, III, 229; *Heads*, I, 176–7; *EYC*, IX, app. C, pp. 248–50 'The early priors of Newburgh' (to 1228).

Walter Latest occ. *c.* 13 May 1212 (*Ctl. Fountains*, II, 626); –1214 (*EYC*, VI, no. 136).

Philip Occ. (as unnamed pr.) in p.j.d. commn of 20 Dec. 1224 (BL, Egerton ms. 2823, f. 93r) – the award in the case issued by pr. Philip and other p.j.d. 1 July 1225 (*Ctl. Kirkstall*, no. 368); 7 Jan. 1227, 27 Jan. 1228 (*Yorks F., 1218–31*, pp. 104, 115).

John Occ. Whitsun 1231 (Bodl., Fairfax ms. 9, f. 27r; *HMC R.R. Hastings*, I, 188); 10 Mar. 1234 (BL, Egerton ms. 2823, f. 81v).

Simon Occ. Mich. 1241 (Bodl., Dodsworth ms. 7, f. 151v).

Ingram (Ingelram) Occ. 1 July 1246, 4 Sept. 1246 (*Yorks F., 1232–46*, pp. 161, 164); 27 Jan. 1249 (*Yorks F., 1246–72*, p. 9).

William of Lowthorpe (Louthorpe) Mentioned 1284 as former pr. and placed by Baildon before John of Skipton (Baildon, I, 145–6), but there is no clear evidence for his position in the sequence of priors.

John of Skipton (Schipton) King's chaplain, occ. 12 Jan. 1251, 21 Jan. 1251 (going overseas as envoy of the king), 20 June 1251 (*CPR 1247–58*, pp. 84,85, 99; as king's chaplain *CPR 1247–58*, pp. 270, 273). King issues letters patent to earl of Cornwall and mag. William of Kilkenny to give royal ass. to eln of pr. John as bp of Carlisle. If the pr. and convent of Carlisle do not el. him, they are to send the person el. to the king, 25 May 1254 (ibid., p. 292 – the cath. priory el. Thomas de Vipont as bp). Occ. as pr. 8 June 1256, 12 June 1256 (*CPR 1350–54*, p. 217); 12 June 1256 (*HMC Var. Coll.*, IV, 256); 28 June 1256 (PRO, E315/49/200). See Sharpe, *Latin Writers*, p. 318.

Richard 1256– Occ. as pr.-el. 15 Oct. 1256 (*CR 1254–56*, p. 366). Occ. as pr. 20 Jan. 1258 (BL, Egerton ms. 2823, f. 94r).

William of Staplet[on] Occ. 10 Aug. 1262 (*Yorks Deeds*, II, 37); (W.) Easter 1267 (Bodl., Dodsworth ms. 91, f. 49v).

Robert of Hovingham Occ. (R.) 10 Aug 1269 (*Reg. W. Giffard*, p. 45); 5 June 1278 (Bodl., Dodsworth ms. 91, f. 54r); 1279 (ibid., ff. 37v, 48v); 22 July 1279, 29 July 1280, 6 Oct. 1280 (*Yorks F., 1272–1300*, pp. 19, 43, 49). Surname provided from mention of previous priors in 1329 (Baildon, I, 147–8).

William of Empingham 1281–1304 Can. of Newburgh, eln conf. 28 Jan. 1281, no reason given for vacancy (*Reg. Wickwane*, p. 125, no. 396). Cess. by 3 May 1304 (PRO, C84/15/10). Surname given as Implyngham in mention of previous priors in 1329 (Baildon, I, 148).

John of Foxholes 1304–1318 Can. of Newburgh, royal ass. 4 May 1304, writ *de intendendo* 10 May 1304 (*CPR 1301–07*, pp. 221, 222). Mand. to adm. pr., having now been conf. by archbp 6 May 1304; request to king to restore temps. 10 May (*Reg. Corbridge*, I, 145; PRO, C84/15/11). Dispensation to allow him to continue in office although convicted of immorality 2 Aug. 1314 (*Reg. Greenfield*, III, pp. 80–1, no. 1325). Mand. 14 Apr. 1318 to hold eln after his res. (*Reg. Melton*, II, no. 19). Conf. of provision made for him after his res. 14 Apr. 1318 (ibid., nos. 20–1); new provision made 8 June 1318 (ibid., no. 36); letter from archbp ordering him to amend his life and restore alienated property of the priory 3 Aug. 1318 (ibid., no. 50); summary of evidence against ex-pr. 9 Sept. 1326 (ibid., no. 86); conditional conf. of new provision made for him 16 Mar. 1319 (ibid., no. 87). Letters to the pr. of Shelford to adm. John of Foxholes, late pr. of Newburgh 19 July 1327 (York, Reg. 9B, f. 433v). Mand. 11 July 1328 to the pr. of Shelford concerning the offences and penance of John of Foxholes late pr. of Newburgh (ibid., f. 439v). Mand. for the payment of a pension to the ex-pr. 8 Nov. 1332 (*Reg. Melton*, II, no. 412). Mand. to John to obey the present pr. 17 Mar. 1334 (ibid., no. 428).

John of Hutton (Hoton) **1318–1322** Can. of Newburgh, commn to cite any opposers to eln 16 Apr. 1318 (ibid., no. 24). Eln quashed but apptd by archbp; mand. to install 4 May 1318 (ibid., nos. 26–7). D. by 12 Feb. 1322 (ibid., no. 174).

John of Catterick (Caterigge, Caterik, Cateryk) **1322–1332** Cellarer of Newburgh, mand. to cite any opposers to eln 12 Feb. 1322 – they are to appear on 18 Mar. (ibid.). Eln conf. 20 Mar. 1322 (ibid., nos. 175–6). D. by 15 Feb. 1332 (ibid., no. 385).

John of Thirsk (Thresch, Thresk) **1332–1351** Mand. to cite any opposers to the eln 15 Feb. 1332 (ibid.); eln conf. 29 Feb. 1332 (ibid., nos. 387–9). Occ. Sept. 1332 (Bodl., Dodsworth ms. 91, f. 14r); 1341 (Lincoln, Ep. Reg., IX, f. 72v); 20, 26 July 1350 (*CPL*, III, 369). Commn to adm. cess. of John and to supervise the eln of a successor 8 May 1351 (York, Reg. 10, f. 170v); conf. of a corrody made to John of Thirsk, ex-pr. by the pr. and convent 11 May 1351, conf. by archbp 4 June 1351 (ibid., f. 171v); 2 letters over the provision made for the former pr. John of Thirsk 15 May, 17 May 1358 (York, Reg. 11, f. 175v).

Thomas of Husthwaite 1351– Obtained priory by authority of Archbp Zouche (1342–52) on res. of John of Thirsk, 1351, mentd in papal indult 30 May 1359 (*CPL*, III, 607). **John de Kylington**, can. of Newburgh, said to be in unlawful occupation, since he had obtained it simoniacally. Thomas had appealed to the Curia and the bp of Lincoln was to make enquiries and to correct and punish crimes and excesses 30 May 1359 (ibid.). For this dispute see A.D.M. Barrell, *The Papacy, Scotland and Northern England, 1342–1378*, p. 223.

John of Thirsk (Tresk) **1359–1369** Ex-pr. John of Thirsk conf. by bp of Lincoln acting on papal commn [1359] (*Accts of Papal Collectors*, p. 514). Occ. Mich. 1368, Hil. 1369 (Baildon, I, 148). D. as pr. by 13 Sept. 1369 (York, Reg. 11, f. 189r).

Thomas of Husthwaite (Hustewaite, Hustewayt) **1369–** Can. of Newburgh, letters testimonial of conf. of eln on d. of John of Thirsk 13 Sept. 1369 (ibid., ff. 188v–189r). Occ. 13 Oct. 1369 (ibid., f. 190r); Mich. 1385 (Baildon, I, 148).
The next recorded pr., **William**, occ. 6 May 1387 (York, Reg. 12, f. 44r).

NEWNHAM (Beds), St Paul f. –1086 (secular college at Bedford); *c.* 1165 (regular cans. at Bedford); *c.* 1180 (1178 x 81) (at Newnham).
Lists in *VCH Beds*, I, 381; *Heads*, I, 177.

Eustace –1225 Occ. 20 Jan. 1214 (*Ctl. Newnham*, no. 841; *Beds F.*, I, p. 43, no. 179); D. 1225 (*Ann. Dunstable*, p. 93).[29]

Hervey 1225– Pr. of Osney, apptd 1225 (ibid.). Occ. (H.) 28 June 1225 (*Ctl. Newnham*, no. 129; (Henry) 1228 (*CR 1227–31*, p. 91); (Henry) Easter term 1229 (*CRR*, XIII, no. 2190); 1230

---

[29] On 26 Mar. 1292 an order was issued to supersede the demand made upon the pr. of Newnham for a debt due to Sampson son of Sampson, sometime a Jew of Cambridge, from Hugh, pr. of Newnham. An inquisition had subsequently found that there never was any pr. of Newnham of the name of Hugh (*CCR 1288–96*, p. 224).

(*Ctl. Newnham*, no. 24); 1232 (*Beds F.*, I, p. 89, no. 329; *YB XVIII*, 193, 195–6); 1232, 1235, Aug. 1236 (*Ctl. Newnham*, nos. 128, 147, 435, 928); (H.) 6 July 1238 (*Reg. Grosseteste*, p. 314); 1240 (*Ctl. Wardon*, p. 187, no. 240).

Walter –1247 Occ. 5 June 1244, 6 Oct. 1247 (*Beds F.*, I, pp. 131, 138, nos. 468, 497); 1244 (*Ctl. Newnham*, nos. 746, 877); 1247 (*Beds Eyre Roll 1247*, p. 97, no. 283). D. about Trinity Sunday 1247 (*Ann. Dunstable*, p. 172). Prob. to be identified with the pr. Walter de Galner who occ. n.d. (*Ctl. Harrold*, no. 105).

Walter de Chauvertune 1247–1254 Can. of Newnham, installed 18 June 1247 (*Ann. Dunstable*, p. 172). Occ. 1247 (*Ctl. Newnham*, no. 858). D. suddenly 1254 (*Ann. Dunstable*, p. 191).

Stephen 1254–1264 Can. of Dunstable, succ. 1254 (ibid.). Occ. 18 Nov. 1254 (*Beds F.*, I, p. 156, nos. 554, 558; *Ctl. Newnham*, nos. 615, 780). Memorandum that at the bp's visitation on 21 Jan. 1255 William de Beauchamp acknowledged that he had exceeded his rights in taking upon himself to install pr. Stephen after his eln (ibid., no. 103). D. by 7 July 1264 (*Reg. R. Gravesend*, p. 191).

William le Franceys 1264–1271 Can. of Newnham, eln quashed and apptd by bp 7 July 1264 (ibid., pp. 191, 323). In Apr. 1270 the unnamed pr. was too infirm to act as a collector (*CPR 1266–72*, p. 421). D. (W.) by 4 Nov. 1271 (*Reg. R. Gravesend*, p. 324).

William le Rus 1271–1272/3 Can. of Newnham, eln conf. 4 Nov. 1271 (ibid., pp. 195, 324). Occ. (W.) Aug. 1272 (*Ctl. Newnham*, no. 135). D. 1272 (*Ann. Dunstable*, p. 255). D. by 10 Jan. 1273 (*Reg. R. Gravesend*, p. 196).

Michael of Goldington 1272/3–1283 Can. of Newnham, eln conf. 10 Jan. 1273 (ibid.). Succ. 1272 (*Ann. Dunstable*, p. 255). D. 1283 (ibid., p. 297). D. by 1 July 1283 (*Reg. Sutton*, VIII, 98).

John of Bedford (Bedeford(e)) 1283–1300 Can. of Newnham, succ. July 1283 (*Ann. Dunstable*, p. 297). Eln quashed and apptd by bp 1 July 1283 (*Reg. Sutton*, VIII, 98). Cess. by 8 July 1300 (Lincoln, Ep. Reg., II, f. 255r–v). Provision made by convent in charter dated 29 Apr. 1300, and conf. by bp-el. 1 May 1300 (Lincoln, Ep. Reg., III, f. 5r). Priory still vacant 22 May 1300 (ibid., f. 8r).

[**Adam de Schireborn** 1300 Sub-pr. of Newnham, bp's commn to archdn of Bedford to cite opposers dated 14 June 1300 (ibid., f. 9r); renounced eln 8 July 1300 (Lincoln, Ep. Reg., II, f. 255r–v). Convent gave bp power to provide but he instructed them to nominate another person. (ibid.).]

William of Biddenham (Bidenham, Bydenham) 1300–1308 Cellarer of Newnham, chosen by convent and apptd by bp 4 Aug. 1300 (ibid.). D. by 11 Jan. 1308 (ibid., f. 260r).

William of Thorpe (Thorp) 1308–1315 Can. of Newnham, eln conf. 11 Jan.1308 (ibid.). Letter of res. dated 7 May 1315 (Lincoln, Ep. Reg., III, f. 319v). Provision made 7 Apr. 1315 and conf. by bp 7 May 1315 (ibid., ff. 319v–320r). Additional provision made 15 Dec. 1318 (ibid., f. 404r). Signified for arrest as an apostate 23 May 1317 (Logan, *Runaway Religious*, p. 218).

John of Astwick (Astwyk, Estwik, Estwyk) 1315–1347 Can. of Newnham, eln conf. 23 July 1315 (Lincoln, Ep. Reg., II, f. 270v). Mand. to sub-pr. and convent to obey John, who during the recent visitation had tendered his res. which the bp had refused to accept, 18 May 1322 (Lincoln, Ep. Reg., V, f. 318r). D. by 26 Jan. 1347 (Lincoln, Ep. Reg., VI, f. 95v; cf. *CCR 1346–49*, pp. 212–13; *Ctl. Newnham*, no. 53), but see also notification that priory was vacant by his cess. 1348 (*Ctl. Wardon*, no. 3420). Ref. to him as former pr. 17 July 1348, when it was alleged he had been assaulted by a can. of Newnham (Lincoln, Ep., Reg., IX, f. 17r).

John of Amersham (Agmundesham) 1347–1348 Can. of Newnham, commn to examine eln 26 Jan. 1347; eln quashed but apptd by bp's commissaries 29 Jan. 1347 (Lincoln, Ep. Reg.,

VI, f. 95v). House void by 17 July 1348 when Henry of Woodford, can. of Newnham, apptd to administer the spiritualities and temporalities of the vacant priory (Lincoln, Ep. Reg., IX, f. 17v – John had res., cf. ibid., f. 421r).

Henry of Woodford (Wodeford) **1349** Commn to examine elns of Henry of Woodford and John of Hornby (Horneby), cans. of Newnham, 22 Oct. 1348, 31 Oct. 1348 (ibid., ff. 18v, 35v). Commn to examine eln of Henry 8 Jan. 1349 (ibid., f. 20r). Eln quashed but apptd by bp 19 Jan. 1349 (ibid., f. 421r). Occ. 29 Jan. 1349 (*CPL*, III, 275); 3 May 1349 (Lincoln, Ep. Reg., XII, f. 184r). D. by 18 Sept. 1349 (Lincoln, Ep. Reg., IX, f. 421r–v).

William of Woodford (Wodeford) **1349–** Can. of Newnham, eln quashed but apptd by bp 18 Sept. 1349 (ibid.). Occ. 24 Feb. 1359 (*Ctl. Newnham*, no. 234).

Nicholas of Baldock (Baldoc, Baldok) **–1369** Occ. 4 July 1361 (*Ctl. Newnham*, no. 235); 7 Apr. 1364 (*CPL*, IV, 39). D. 17 Aug. 1369 (PRO, C84/30/15). D., lic. to el. 26 Oct. 1369 (*CPR 1367–70*, p. 314; *Ctl. Newnham*, no. 59).

John of Biddenham (Byd(d)enham) **1369–1392** Can. of Newnham, eln pres. to king for royal ass. 4 Nov. 1369 (PRO, C84/30/18); royal ass. 8 Nov. 1369 (*CPR 1367–70*, p. 325). Eln pres. to bp 14 Nov. 1369, eln conf. 28 Nov. 1369 (Lincoln, Ep. Reg., X, f. 348r–v). D. 13 Dec. 1392 (Lincoln, Ep. Reg., XI, f. 365v).

NEWSTEAD (Notts), St Mary in Sherwood f. *c.* 1163
Lists in *VCH Notts*, II, 117; *Heads*, I, 177.

Eustace Occ. 8 July 1215 (*Rot. Lit. Pat.*, p. 148); 25 Nov. 1225 (PRO, Notts F., CP25/1/182/3, no. 30); 30 Sept. 1226 (PRO, Notts F., CP25/1/182/3, no. 45); 6 Oct. 1226 (PRO, Notts F., CP25/1/182/4, no. 73); 13 Nov. 1226 (*Ctl. Tutbury*, no. 270); n.d. (Dec. 1231 x 1233) ('Ctl. Breedon', no. 115); n.d. *post* 1231 (*Reg. Wickwane*, p. 252, no. 615 – occ. with pr. Walter of Worksop).[30]

Robert **1234–?1241** Can. of Newstead, royal ass. 9 Dec. 1234 (*CPR 1232–47*, p. 85). Occ. 9 Feb. 1240 (PRO, Notts F., CP25/1/182/8 no. 268). Lic. to el. (no reason given for vacancy) 27 Apr. 1241 (*CPR 1232–47*, p. 250).

William of Mottisfont (Motesfunt) **1241–1267** Cellarer of Newstead, mand. for seisin 7 May 1241 (*CR 1237–42*, p. 298). Occ. 1255 (BL, Harl. Cht. 112 F 34); 23 May 1259 (*Ctl. Darley*, II, 385); 9 July 1262 (PRO, Notts F., CP25/1/183/12, nos. 482, 485). Letter of res. (W.) to archbp of York 24 Oct. 1267 (*Reg. W. Giffard*, p. 211; PRO, C84/3/33) but occ. 30 Oct. 1267 (*CPR 1266–72*, p. 163).

[**Augustine** sub-pr. of Newstead, eln pres. to king for royal ass. 28 Dec. 1267 (PRO, C84/3/36). ? ineffective.]

14 July 1270 sub-pr. and convent paid a fine for the custody of the priory in its present vacancy (*CR 1268–72*, p. 209); priory mentd as void 15 July 1270 (*CPR 1266–72*, p. 442).

John de Lexington (Laxton, Lessingtone, Lexinton) **–1288** Occ. 26 Apr. 1271 (PRO, Notts F., CP25/1/183/13, no. 542); July 1279 (BL, Add. ms. 36872, ff. 126r–128r); 12 Nov. 1280 (PRO, Notts F., CP25/1/183/14, no. 31). Cess., lic. to el. 8 July 1288 (*CPR 1281–92*, p. 297; cf. PRO, C84/9/16). Sub-pr. and conv. submitted to archbp because they had el. a new pr. before he had acc. cess. of old one 1 Aug. 1288; adm. of cess. by archbp's vicar-general 1 Aug. 1288 (*Reg. Romeyn*, I, pp. 275–6, no. 767). At the archbp's visitation 19 Aug. 1293 it was enjoined that the former pr. John was to be honoured and his counsel followed, for his services and generosity to the house about his pension – detailed provision made for him (ibid., p. 318, no. 903).

---

[30] The Pr. Thomas, occ. 1232 x 33 (*Heads*, I, 177) has been identified with pr. Thomas of Newark priory (Surrey).

Richard of Hallam (Halum) **1288–1292** Sub-cellarer of Newstead, eln quashed but apptd by archbp's vicar- general 2 Sept. 1288 (ibid., p. 276, no. 767; PRO, C84/9/18). Royal ass. 23 Aug. 1288, temps. 5 Sept. 1288 (*CPR 1281–92*, p. 300). Res. 29 Nov. 1292 (PRO, SC1/19/154; PRO, C84/11/4). Res., lic. to el. 10 Dec. 1292 (*CPR 1292–1301*, p. 1). Ex-pr. to be punished 19 Aug. 1293 (*Reg. Romeyn*, I, p. 319, no. 903).

Richard de Grangia (de la Grainge) **1293–1324** Can. of Newstead, eln pres. to king for royal ass. 26 Dec. 1292 (PRO, C84/11/7); royal ass. 4 Jan. 1293, temps. 12 Jan. 1293 (*CPR 1292–1301*, p. 3). Eln conf. 9 Jan. 1293 (*Reg. Romeyn*, I, p. 308, no. 872; PRO, C84/11/8). Commn to receive purgation of pr. charged with incontinency with 2 women 27 Jan. 1308 (*Reg. Greenfield*, IV, pp. 25–6, no. 1727). Lic. to el. on res. of Richard 9 Dec. 1324 (*Reg. Melton*, IV, p. 82, no. 385). Res., lic. to el. 13 Dec. 1324 (*CPR 1324–27*, p. 61).

William of Thurgarton (Thurgerton) **1324–1349** Can. of Newstead, royal ass. 18 Dec. 1324, temps. 10 Jan. 1325 (ibid., pp. 62, 85). Proclamation *si quis* 22 Dec. 1324 (*Reg. Melton*, IV, p. 82, no. 387). Eln quashed but apptd by archbp 5 Jan. 1325 (ibid., nos. 384, 386; PRO, C84/20/44). D., lic. to el. 19 Aug. 1349 (*CPR 1348–50*, p. 368).

Hugh of Collingham (Colyngham) **1349–1356** Can. of Newstead, eln pres. to king for royal ass. 20 Sept. 1349 (PRO, C84/26/24); royal ass. 24 Sept. 1349, temps. 26 Oct. 1349 (*CPR 1348–50*, pp. 376, 408). Notif. to king for temps. 4 Oct. 1349 (York, Reg. 10, f. 135r). Eln conf. 3 Oct. 1349 (ibid.). Res. 21 Sept. 1356 (PRO, C84/27/31). Res., lic. to el. 17 Oct. 1356 (*CPR 1354–56*, p. 440). Pension granted by priory 3 Dec. 1356 and conf. by king 10 Mar. 1359 (*CPR 1358–61*, p. 183). Mentioned as former pr. 15 Feb. 1357 (York, Reg. 11, f. 238v).

John of Wilsthorpe (Willesthorp, Wilsthorp, Wylesthorp) **1356–1366** Can. of Newstead, eln pres. to king for royal ass. 29 Oct. 1356 (PRO, C84/27/34); royal ass. 6 Nov. 1356, temps. 7 Nov. 1356 (*CPR 1354–58*, pp. 467, 472). Eln quashed but apptd by archbp 7 Nov. 1356; mand. to induct 8 Nov. (York, Reg. 11, f. 237r). Res. by 22 Apr. 1366 (PRO, C84/29/33). Res., lic. to el. 6 May 1366 (*CPR 1364–67*, p. 234). Commn to examine reasons for proposed cess. n.d. (*c.* Mar. x May 1366) (York, Reg. 11, f. 263r).

William of Allerton 1366–1406 Can. of Newstead, eln pres. to king for royal ass. 9 May 1366 (PRO, C84/29/34); royal ass. 12 May 1366 (*CPR 1364–67*, p. 242). Eln conf. 28 May 1366 (York, Reg. 11, f. 263r). D. 23 Aug. 1406 (PRO, C84/39/31). D., lic. to el. 29 Aug. 1406 (*CPR 1405–08*, p. 226).

NEWSTEAD BY STAMFORD (Lincs), St Mary f. -1200 (hospital at Uffington); -1247 (priory)

List in *VCH Lincs*, II, 177.

Walter 1224/5– chaplain, adm. to the hospital as master Dec. 1224 x Dec. 1225 (*Reg. Wells*, III, 135).

Adam de Herefeld 1225/6– Can. of Missenden, adm. to hospital of Uffington Dec. 1225 x Dec. 1226 (ibid., 150).

Walter 1231/2– Can. of 'Wilemerdel' (?Wymondley). adm. to hospital of Uffington Dec. 1231 x Dec. 1232 (ibid., 202).

PRIORS

Walter de Crek 1246– Can. of Newstead (Uffington), royal ass. 8 Sept. 1246, in the king's hands by virtue of the custody of the land late of William de Albiniaco, patron of the priory (*CPR 1232–47*, p. 488). Eln quashed but apptd by bp June 1246 x June 1247 (*Reg. Grosseteste*, p. 88). Occ. 5 Oct. 1258, 25 Nov. 1260 (*Lincs F.*, II, 161, 181).

Hamo of Greatford (Gretford) **1263–1285** Eln quashed but apptd by bp on the d. of the last (unnamed) pr. Nov. 1262 x Nov. 1263 (*Reg. R. Gravesend*, p. 12). Occ. 1276 (PRO, Lincs. F., CP25/1/132/5, no. 44); 1278 (PRO, Rutland F., CP25/1/192/4 no. 4); 9 Dec. 1281 (PRO,

Lincs F., CP25/1/133/54, no. 5). Joined the Dominicans by 16 Sept. 1285 (*Reg. Sutton*, I, 70–1).

[**Robert of Stamford** (Staumford) Can. of Newstead, eln pres. to bp 16 Sept. 1285 in place of Hamo, but eln quashed 17 Sept. (ibid.).]

Peter de Berham 1285–1287 Can. of Bourne, apptd by bp 30 Sept. 1285 (ibid., 71). D. by 21 July 1287 (ibid., 99).

Thomas of Deeping (Deping) **1287–1292** Can. of Newstead, eln conf. 21 July 1287 (ibid.). Res. by 13 Sept. 1292 (ibid., 169).

Robert of Stamford (Staumford, Staunford) **1292–1308** Can. of Newstead, eln quashed but apptd by bp 13 Sept. 1292 (ibid). Absolved from excommunication 23 Mar. 1306 (Lincoln, Ep. Reg., III, f. 93v). Translated to be pr. of Huntingdon before 29 Jan. 1308 (Lincoln, Ep. Reg., II, f. 22v). Papal provision to priory of Huntingdon on d. of pr. Walter 29 Jan. 1308 (*CPL*, II, 37).

Henry of Overton 1308– Can. of Newstead, exhibited letter of provision of Clement V, dated 29 Jan. 1308 appointing him in place of Robert of Stamford; appt accepted by bp and Henry made prof. obed. 28 May 1308 (ibid., 38; Lincoln, Ep. Reg., II, f. 22v). Occ. Mich. 1310 (PRO, CP40/183, m. 45). An unnamed pr. of Newstead ill and the pr. of Fineshade apptd coadjutor 11 May 1323 (Lincoln, Ep. Reg., V, f. 339r). Pr. of Fineshade and mag. John de Beby, rector of Folkingham, apptd coadjutors; the pr and convent of Newstead inhibited from interference in the admin. of the house; the prev. commn to pr. of Fineshade now revoked, 23 May 1323 (ibid., f. 340r). To mag. (John) de Beby, rector of Folkingham his appt as coadjutor reaffirmed, the pr. of Fineshade being unable to act 1 Aug. 1323 (ibid., f. 348v). Henry occ. Hil. x Mich. 1328 (*Index to Placita de Banco*, p. 347).

Geoffrey Occ. 1377 (*Clerical Poll-Taxes*, p. 12, no. 151); 1381 (ibid., p. 106, no. 1276).

The next recorded pr., **William of Prestwold**, occ. 14 June 1391 (*CCR 1389–1392*, p. 354).

NOCTON PARK (Lincs), St Mary Magdalen f. *temp.* Stephen

Lists in *VCH Lincs*, II, 169–70; *Heads*, I, 177–8.

Alan Occ. 25 Sept. 1205 x 10 May 1206 (*EEA*, 4, no. 268, cf. *YB XVI*, 120, 124–5).

William Occ. ante 1218 (Bodl., Dodsworth ms. 143, f. 28r, cited *Ctl. Thurgarton*, no. 394n.); *c.* 1212 x 1224 (ibid., citing Lancs RO, DDTO/K24/2); *c.* 1220 x 1224 (*Reg. Ant. Lincoln*, IV, no. 1388); 1 May 1230 (Leeds Archives, Vyner ms. 5163).

Ivo of Scarle (Scarla) **1230/1–** Cellarer of Nocton Park, el. and adm. Dec. 1230 x Dec. 1231, no reason given for vacancy (*Reg. Wells*, III, 195).

Thomas of London (Londiniis) Can. of Nocton Park, eln conf. June 1240 x June 1241, no reason given for vacancy (*Reg. Grosseteste*, p. 53). Occ. 3 Aug. 1243 (*Lincs F.*, I, 344); 1243 (Lancs RO, DDTO/ K/1/9).

Philip Occ. 6 May 1250, 26 June 1250 (*Lincs F.*, II, 85, 60).

William Occ. 30 Sept. 1256 (ibid., 120).

Philip of Gunness (Gunesse) **–1258/9** Res. Nov. 1258 x Nov. 1259 (*Reg. R. Gravesend*, p. 1).

Thomas of Navenby (Navenebi, Navenesb') **1258/9–1268** Can. of Nocton Park, eln conf. Nov. 1258 x Nov. 1259 (ibid.). Res. by 16 June 1268 (ibid., p. 28).

Peter of Thurlby (Thorlebi, Thurlebi) **1268–1277** Can. of Nocton Park, apptd by bp at the request of the convent 16 June 1268 (ibid.). Dep. 1277 (ibid., p. 77). Mentd as former pr. Mich. 1277 x Mich. 1278 (PRO, E159/51, m. 19d).

Richard of Yarwell (Jarewell) **1277–1286** Eln conf. [1277, poss. July x Sept.] on dep. of Peter (*Reg. R. Gravesend*, p. 77). Occ. Mich. 1277 x Mich. 1278 (PRO, E159/51, m. 19d). Res. by 10 May 1286 to join the Franciscans (*Reg. Sutton*, I, 83–4).

[**Philip of Hanworth** (Hanewrth) Sub-pr. of Nocton Park, eln quashed by bp 10 May 1286 (ibid.).]

[**Arnold** Cellarer of Thornton, next el. but refused office 1286 (ibid.). Pr. of Markby 1291.]

John of Grimsby (Grimesby) **1286–1292** Can. of Thornton, apptd by bp 19 June 1286 (ibid., 84–5). Res. by 26 July 1292 to join Franciscans (ibid., 168).

John de Gevelston (Geveleston) **1292–1296** Cellarer of Nocton Park, eln conf. 26 July 1292 (ibid., 168–9). Eln conf. (*sic*) 7 Aug. 1292 (ibid., IV, 14–15). Res. by 14 Aug. 1296 (ibid., I, 209).

[**Philip of Hanworth** (Hanewurth) Sub-pr. of Nocton Park, eln pres. to bp 14 Aug. 1296 but again rejected by Bp Sutton 9 Sept. 1286 and new eln ordered (ibid., 209–10).]

Thomas of Louth (Luda) **1296–1301** Can. of Nocton Park, el. 14 Sept. 1296 (ibid., 209). Eln conf. 20 Sept. 1296 (ibid., 209–11). Cess. by 26 Sept. 1301 (Lincoln, Ep. Reg., II, f. 5r).

John of Hough (Hagh) **1301–1303** Eln quashed but apptd by bp 26 Sept. 1301 (ibid.). D. by 11 May 1303 (ibid., f. 7v).

William of Grimsby (Grimesby, Grimmesby) **1303–1320** Can. of Nocton Park, appeared before bp 11 May 1303; eln conf. 20 May 1303 (ibid.). Cess. by 28 Jan. 1320 (ibid., f. 352r).

Thomas of Louth (Luda) **1320–1323** Can. of Nocton Park, el. 28 Jan. 1320, but due to his negligence in not appearing within 3 months, the power of appt devolved upon the Official *sede vacante* who adm. him 9 May 1320 (ibid.; see also Lincoln D. & C., Dij/53/2/11–13). Res. by 13 Aug. 1323 (*Reg. Burghersh* I, no. 81).

Walter of Navenby 1323–1349 Can. of Nocton Park, pres. to bp 13 Aug. 1323, eln quashed but apptd by bp 17 Aug. 1323 (ibid.). Cess. by (?early) 1349 (Lincoln, Ep. Reg. IX, f. 70r).

William de Mere 1349 Can. of Nocton Park, apptd by bp n.d. [early 1349 *from surrounding dated entries*], to whom the power of appt had been transferred by the convent, on the cess. of William of Navenby (ibid., – entry A). ·

Hugh of Dunston 1349– Can. of Nocton Park, apptd by bp to whom the power of appt had been transferred by the convent 5 Aug. 1349 (ibid., f. 70r – entry B). Occ. 1377 (*Clerical Poll-Taxes*, p. 38, no. 532).

The next recorded pr., **Hugh Triffour**, occ. 1381 (ibid., p. 111, no. 1347), ? same as Hugh of Dunston. The next pr., **Robert Frysby**, res. 1400 (no day or month given) (Lincoln, Ep. Reg., XIII, f. 141r).

NORTH CREAKE (Norfolk), St Mary de Pratis f. -1189 (as hospital) (*KH*; suggested redating shortly after 1217, *Ctl. Creake*, p. xiv); 1206 (priory) (*KH*; suggested redating *c.* 1227, *Ctl. Creake*, p. xiv); 1231 (abbey)
   Lists in *VCH Norfolk*, II, 372; *Ctl. Creake*, p. xxv.

PRIORS

William of Guist (de Geyste) Master of hospital, apptd as pr. *c.* 1227, *temp.* Bp Thomas de Blundeville of Norwich (1226–36) (*Ctl. Creake*, p. 1, no. 1, cf. p. xiv – this is dated 1226 x 1231 in *EEA* 21, app. II, no. 21); 1225 x 1228 (*Ctl. Creake*, p. 9, no. 16).

Robert Occ. 1228 (Blomefield, *Norfolk*, VII, 75–6), ref. to untraced agreement.

ABBOTS

[**Robert** Occ. 1231 (ibid., 78), acc. to *Ctl. Creake* list. but ref. not located.].

Auger (Ogier) Occ. 1237 (Blomefield, *Norfolk*, VII, 78, no source).

Richard Ref. in a deed of 1255 x 1265 to Richard, former abb. (*Ctl. Creake*, p. 63, no. 116). No other ref. has been found.

William –1262 Occ. from Oct. 1246 x Oct. 1247 to Oct. 1255 x Oct. 1256 (*Norfolk F. (Rye)*, pp. 71, 89); 20 Apr. 1248 (*Ctl. Creake*, p. 77, no. 145); 12 July 1259 (Cambridge, Christ's

Coll., drawer 7, no. 10). D., lic. to el. 11 July 1262 (*CPR 1258–66*, p. 223). ? de Geyste (Guist), ref. to John son of William de Geyste, brother of abb. William (*Ctl. Creake*, p. 59, no. 108), but cf. above.

Geoffrey 1262–1281 Bp of Norwich informs king of his conf. of eln of a new abb. *c.* July–Aug. 1262 (PRO, SC1/63/6). Pr. of Creake, royal ass. 4 Aug. 1262; temps 13 Aug. 1262 (*CPR 1258–66*, p. 26). Res. acc. 13 Jan. 1281 on account of his age (*Reg. Peckham*, I, 392j–k). Res., lic. to el. 22 Jan. 1281 (*CPR 1272–81*, p. 423). Bp conf. an el. *c.* July – Aug. 1362 (SC1/63/6).

John (le) Chevre (Chevere) *alias* of Creake (Creyk') **1281–1303** Can. of North Creake; eln pres. to king for royal ass. 10 Feb. 1281 (PRO, C84/7/18); writ *de intendendo* 11 May 1281 (*CPR 1272–81*, p. 432). Cert. conf. eln by bp of Norwich 12 May 1281 (PRO, C84/7/24). D. by 9 May 1303 (PRO, C84/11/17). D. (J.), lic. to el. 21 May 1303 (*CPR 1301–07*, p. 140; *Cal. Chanc. Warr.*, p. 176).[31]

Thomas of South Creake (Suth Craik, Suthcrek) **1303–1334** Can. of North Creake, royal ass. 4 June 1303, temps. 3 July 1303 (*CPR 1301–07*, pp. 143, 146). Eln conf. 1 July 1303 (Norwich, Reg/1/1, f. 12r). D. 25 Aug. 1334 (PRO, C84/23/14). D., lic. to el. 7 Sept. 1334 (*CPR 1334–38*, p. 5).

John of Harpley (Harple, Harpele) **1334–1352** Can. of North Creake, eln pres. to king for royal ass. 18 Sept. 1334 (PRO, C84/23/16); royal ass. 23 Sept. 1334, temps 23 Oct. 1334 (*CPR 1334–38*, pp. 13, 33). Eln conf. 6 Oct. 1334 (Norwich, Reg/1/2, f. 67v; PRO, C84/23/18). Res. by 17 Jan. 1352 (PRO, C84/26/48). Res., lic. to el. 20 Jan. 1352 (*CPR 1350–54*, p. 196).

Robert of Docking (Dockyng(g), Dokkyng) **1352–1353** Can. of North Creake, eln pres. to king for royal ass. 2 Feb. 1352 (PRO, C84/26/49); royal ass. 9 Feb. 1352, temps. 11 Feb. 1352 (*CPR 1350–54*, p. 226). Eln conf. 10 Feb. 1352 (Norwich, Reg/2/4, f. 136r; PRO, C84/26/50). Res. by 30 Apr. 1353 (PRO, C84/27/7). Res., lic. to el. 3 May 1353 (*CPR 1350–54*, p. 429).

Thomas of Redham 1353–1356 Can. of North Creake, eln pres. to king for royal ass. 9 May 1353 (PRO, C84/27/8); royal ass. 15 May 1353, temps 17 May 1353 (*CPR 1350–54*, pp. 441, 439). Eln conf. 17 May 1353 (Norwich, Reg/2/4, f. 146v; PRO, C84/27/9). Res. by 12 Dec. 1356 (PRO, C84/27/35). Cess., lic. to el. 12 Jan. 1357 (*CPR 1354–58*, p. 488).

Thomas of Brandon (Brandone) **1357–1360** Can. of North Creake, temps. 16 Apr. 1357 (ibid., p. 524). Eln conf. [-] Feb. 1357 (Norwich, Reg/2/5, f. 18r). D., lic. to el. 30 Sept. 1360 (*CPR 1358–61*, p. 461).

John de Assh 1360–1393 Temps. 21 Nov. 1360 (ibid., p. 491). Can. of North Creake, eln quashed, but apptd by bp 24 Oct. 1360 (Norwich, Reg/2/5, f. 41v). D. by 26 Apr. 1393 (PRO, C84/35/35). D., lic. to el. 30 Apr. 1393 (*CPR 1391–96*, p. 264).

NORTH FERRIBY (Yorks E.), St Mary f. *c.* 1140 (?)

List in *VCH Yorks*, III, 242–3.

Robert Occ. early Henry III (*EYC*, XII, no. 95); 12 Nov. 1234 (*Yorks F., 1232–46*, p. 12).

Simon Occ. 29 July 1240 (ibid., p. 86).

Ralph Occ. 27 Jan. 1258 (PRO, Notts F., CP25/1/183/12, no. 459).

Walter of St Edmund (de Sancto Eadmundo) Claims to be pr. 17 Mar. 1272 (*Reg. W. Giffard*, p. 66); Occ. 1272 (Baildon, I, 59, without source, cf. *Mon. Angl.*, VI, 590).

Robert Occ. 1284 (Baildon, I, 59); ment. as former pr. summer 1286 (*CPR 1340–43*, p. 460).

---

[31] Blomefield, *Norfolk*, VII, 76 gives Bartholomew de Burgate as abb. 1285–1303, ths sole ref. being to a plea roll which cannot now be traced. The Patent Roll and Chancery Warrant entries of 1303 (see above) appear to contradict this and make abb. Bartholomew's existence questionable. (*Ctl. Creake*, p. xxiii).

William Occ. n.d. [Sept. x Oct. 1300] (*Reg. Corbridge*, I, 156); 1303 x 1307 (Bodl., ms. Top. Yorks e 9, f. 68r).

Walter of Hessle (Hesill) –1349 Occ. 1315, 1329 (Baildon, I, 59–60); 1328 (*Index to Placita de Banco*, p. 756). D. by 23 July 1349 (York, Reg. 10, f. 197v).

John of Beverley (Beverlac(o)) 1349 Can. of North Ferriby, commn to examine eln 23 July 1349; eln conf. by commissaries 24 July 1349 (ibid.). D. by 3 Aug. 1349 (ibid.).

John of Preston 1349– Can. of North Ferriby, eln quashed but apptd by archbp 3 Aug. 1349 (ibid.).

John of Hedon –1372 Occ. Hilary 1369 (Baildon, I, 60). Former pr., provision made for him by successor 12 Mar. 1372 and conf. by archbp 27 Aug. 1372 (York, Reg. 11, f. 229r–v).

John of Kilham (Killom, Killum) 1372–1389 Occ. 12 Mar. 1372 (ibid.); 5 May 1373 (YMA, M2/1c, f. 13r). D. by 1 Dec. 1389 (York, Reg. 14, f. 18r).

NORTHAMPTON, St James f. *c.* 1145 x 1150 (abbey)

Lists in *VCH Northants*, I, 129–30; 15th-cent. list in BL, Cotton ms. Tiberius E V, f. 234r, damaged – copy made before damage in Bodl., ms. Top. Northants c. 5, pp. 479–80, cf. Bridges, *Hist. Northants*, I, 503; *Heads*, I, 178.

Thomas *c.* 1205 x 6–1220 4th abb. (list). Occ. 1206 x 1207 (*Ctl. Cirencester*, II, no. 669 = Cheney, *Inn. III*, no. 1160); 1215 (*Ctl. Cockersand*, II, i, 392–5). D. 13 Oct. 1220 (BL, Cotton ms. Tiberius E V, f. 234r; Bodl., ms. Top. Northants c. 5, p. 479). D. 1220 (not named) (*Ann. Dunstable*, p. 50).

Adam of Duston 1220–1231 5th abb. (list). Can. of St James, royal ass. 30 Oct. 1220 (*CPR 1216–25*, p. 269). Occ. 1 July 1228 (*Oxford F.*, p. 105). D. 25 Sept. 1231 (Bodl., ms. Top. Northants c. 5, p. 479; BL, Cotton ms. Tiberius E V, f. 234r).

Walter of Melton (Meltone) 1230/1–1237 6th abb. (list). El. and adm. Dec. 1230 x Dec. 1231, no reason given for vacancy; bp of Coventry to bl. him (*Reg. Wells*, II, 164). D. 26 May 1237 (Bodl., ms. Top. Northants c. 5, p. 479; BL, Cotton ms. Tiberius E V, f. 234r). D., lic. to el. 27 May 1237 (*CPR 1232–47*, p. 183).

Adam Gylly (? for Grylly, see below) 1237 Can. of St James, royal ass. 7 June 1237 (ibid., p. 184). Lic. to el. (no reason given for vacancy) 30 July 1237 (ibid., p. 190).

Osbert of Luffenham (Lufenham) 1237–1242 Pr. of St James, royal ass. 15 Aug. 1237 (ibid., p. 193); mand. for seisin 22 Aug. 1237 (*CCR 1234–37*, p. 489). El., adm. and bl. June 1237 x June 1238 (*Reg. Grosseteste*, p. 171). Res. 1241/2 (BL, Cotton ms. Tiberius E V, f. 234r; Bodl., ms. Top. Northants c. 5, p. 479). Res., lic. to el. 16 Feb. 1242 (*CPR 1232–47*, p. 272).

Adam Grilli (Grilly, Grylly, Gilly) 1242–1266 7th abb. (list). Can. of St James, royal ass. 25 Feb. 1242; writ *de intendendo* 8 Mar. 1242 (ibid., pp. 273, 275). Eln quashed but apptd by bp June 1240 x June 1241 (*sic*) (*Reg. Grosseteste*, p. 205). D. 6 July 1266 (Bodl., ms. Top. Northants c. 5, p. 479; BL, Cotton ms. Tiberius E V, f. 234r). D. (no name given), lic. to el. 8 July 1266 (*CPR 1258–66*, p. 613; *Reg. R. Gravesend*, p. 107).

John *dictus* **(Le) Lu** (Lupus) 1266–1270 8th abb. (list). Eln pres. to king for royal ass. 17 July 1266 (PRO, C84/3/25). Eln conf. 21 July 1266 (*Reg. R. Gravesend*, p. 107); writ *de intendendo* 23 July 1266 (*CPR 1258–66*, p. 618). D. 6 Mar. 1270 (Bodl., ms. Top. Northants c. 5, p. 479; BL, Cotton ms. Tiberius E V, f. 234r). D., lic. to el. 8 Mar. 1270 (*CPR 1266–72*, p. 415). Seal (*BM Seals*, no. 3745).

Adam of Kelmarsh (Keylmer, Keylemers, Keylmarsch, Keylmersch, Keylmersh) 1270–1274 9th abb. (list). Can. of St James, eln conf. 27 Mar. 1270; bl. and prof. obed. 30 Mar. 1270 (*Reg. R. Gravesend*, p. 114). Writ *de intendendo* 4 Apr. 1270 (*CPR 1266–72*, p. 420). D. 28 Nov. 1274 (Bodl., ms. Top. Northants c. 5, p. 479; BL, Cotton ms. Tiberius E V, f. 234r; PRO, C84/5/10). D. by 13 Dec. 1274 (*Reg. R. Gravesend*, pp. 124, 302).

Ralph of Higham (Hecham, Hegham, Hehgham, Heyham) **1274–1300** 10th abb. (list). Can. of St James, eln pres. to king for royal ass. 3 Dec. 1274 (PRO, C84/5/11); royal ass. 7 Dec. 1274, writ *de intendendo* 15 Dec. 1274 (*CPR 1272–81*, p. 73). Eln conf. 13 Dec. 1274; bl. 16 Dec. 1274 (*Reg. R. Gravesend*, pp. 124, 302; PRO, C84/5/15). D. 27 Dec. 1298 (*sic*) (Bodl., ms. Top. Northants c. 5, p. 479; BL, Cotton ms. Tiberius E V, f. 234r). D., lic. to el. 7 Jan. 1300 (*CPR 1292–1301*, p. 484). Seal (*BM Seals*, no. 3746).

Nicholas of Flore (Flora) **1300–1334** 11th abb. (list). Can. of St James, royal ass. 24 Jan. 1300, temps. 18 Mar. 1300 (*CPR 1292–1301*, pp. 486, 493). Eln examined 27 Mar. 1300 (*sic*, presumably for 25 Feb., ?6 kal. April written in error for 6 kal. Mar.); eln conf. 19 Mar.; bl. 20 Mar. 1300 (Lincoln, Ep. Reg., II, f. 102r). Lic. to receive bl. 19 Mar. 1300 (Lincoln, Ep. Reg., III, f. 1r). D. 19 Aug. 1334 (Bodl., ms. Top. Northants c. 5, p. 479). D., lic. to el. 22 Aug. 1334 (*CPR 1334–38*, p. 5).

Gerard de Combes 1334–1354 12th abb. (list). Can. of St James, temps. 19 Sept. 1334 (ibid., p. 8). Cert. conf. eln by bp of Lincoln 18 Sept. 1334 (PRO, C84/23/17). D. 8 Mar. 1354 (Bodl., ms. Top. Northants c. 5, p. 479; BL, Cotton ms. Tiberius E V, f. 234r). D., lic. to el. 14 Mar. 1354 (*CPR 1354–58*, p. 19).

William of Thorpe (Thorp) **1354–1378** 13th abb. (list). Can. of St James, royal ass. 24 Mar. 1354; temps. 2 Apr. 1354 (ibid., pp. 23, 26). Eln pres. to bp 22 Mar. 1354; eln conf. 29 Mar. 1354 (Lincoln, Ep. Reg., IX, f. 203r–v). D. 3 June 1378 (Bodl., ms. Top. Northants c. 5, p. 480; BL, Cotton ms. Tiberius E V, f. 234r). D., lic. to el. 6 June 1378 (*CPR 1377–81*, p. 228).

NORTON (Ches), St Mary and St Bertelinus f. *c.* 1115 (at Runcorn); 1134 (at Norton); 1391 (abbey)

Lists in *VCH Ches.*, III, 170; *Cheshire Charters*, p. 26 (to late 13th cent.); *Heads*, I, 178.

PRIORS

Ranulf Last recorded occ. 1215 x 1223, prob. 1220+ (*Ctl. Whalley*, I, 139).

Andrew Occ. (A.) *c.* 1223 x 1227 (*Ctl. Whalley*, II, 398 & n.); 1224 x 1231 (PRO, DL25/273); (A.) *c.* 1232 (*Ctl. Burscough*, no. 155 – extended in ms. to Adam); n.d. (Cheshire RO, DLT/B3, f. 136v); 1232 x 1240 (Lichfield, B/A/1/1, f. 63r); 3 Aug. 1238 (*Magnum Reg. Album Lichfield*, no. 529); 10 May 1247 (*Oxford F.*, p. 48).

Hugh of Donington (Doninton) Prob. succ. Andrew (*Cheshire Chts.*, p. 26, citing Cheshire RO, DLT/B3, f. 149v). Occ. n.d. (mid-13th cent.; pal.) (Cheshire RO, DLT/A14/3, 6).

Roger of Budworth (Buddeworthe) and **Roger of Lincoln** (Lincolne) They were the next two priors according to *Cheshire Chts.*, p. 26, citing Cheshire RO, DLT/B3, ff. 190r (Budworth), 155v (Lincoln)). It is difficult to distinguish them. Pr. Roger occ. n.d. (1249 x 1261) (JRL, Arley Chts, Box 1, no. 87); 27 Jan. 1261 (*Oxford F.*, p. 148); 3 Nov. 1262 (PRO, Notts F., CP25/1/183/12, no. 488); Whitsun 1278 (PRO, E40/8920); 27 Oct. 1283 (PRO, Notts F., CP25/1/183/15, no. 69); 15 Aug. 1285 (Budworth) (PRO, E40/8971); 29 Sept. 1285 (Budworth) (Cheshire RO, DCH/F/800); 1286 (*Ctl. Whalley*, II, 403).[32] It looks as if Roger of Lincoln preceded Roger of Budworth.

Acharius Occ. 25 Oct. 1288 (*Chester City Courts*, p. 155).

Richard Occ. 31 Dec. 1293 (*Reg. Romeyn*, I, 330).

Roger of Mamecestre Occ. Nov. 1297 x Nov. 1298 (Cheshire RO, DCH/E/255); n.d. (after 1295) (*Arley Chts.*, p. 14).

---

[32] In *Cheshire Chts.*, p. 26, n. 10 Barraclough notes that he had found no evidence for pr. Roger of Manchester, but *VCH* list still includes this pr. 1249 x 1261 and equates Roger of Budworth with Roger of Lincoln. From the Cholmondeley charter evidence it is clear that Roger de Mamecestre was pr. at the close of the 13th cent. (see list for 1297 x 1298).

Roger de Cuddeworth –1308 D. by 29 June 1308 (Lichfield, B/A/1/1, f. 29r).

Gilbert *dictus* Puttok 1308– Can. of Norton, eln conf. 29 June 1308 (ibid.). Occ. July 1308 x July 1309 (BL, Harl. ms. 2162, f. 15r); 12 Sept. 1310 when br. William de Wyco and br. Adam de Dysewortham cans. of Norton, apptd coadjutors because pr. squandering goods of the house (Lichfield, B/A/1/1, f. 58v); Mich. 1310 (PRO, CP40/183, attorneys, m. 41).

John de Colton 1314– Can. of Trentham, commn to examine eln 15 Jan. 1314, no reason given for vacancy (Lichfield, B/A/1/1, f. 60v). Occ. 18 May 1318 (*DKR 36*, app. II, no. 1, p. 366); 27 Oct. 1322 (*Ctl. Whalley*, II, 410).

Robert Bernard 1329– Can. of Norton, eln quashed, but apptd by bp 4 Jan. 1329, no reason given for vacancy (Lichfield, B/A/1/2, f. 104r). Occ. 1 Nov. 1331 (Cheshire RO, DLT/A16/5); 24 June 1336 (*CCR 1333–37*, p. 592); 1339 (BL, Harl. ms. 2072, f. 78v); 24 Oct. 1344 (Lichfield, B/A/1/3, f. 113r); 9 June 1346, 10 Aug. 1346 (Lichfield, B/A/1/2, f. 119r–v); 22 Oct. 1346 (*CPL*, III, 233).

Thomas de Fraunkevylle 1349– Commn to examine eln dated 9 Aug. 1349, no reason given for vacancy. Can. of Norton certificate of eln conf. dated 23 Aug. 1349 (Lichfield, B/A/1/2, f. 125r).

Walter of Weaverham (Weeverham, Wevirham) Occ. 2 June 1355 (*DKR 36*, app. II, no. 1, p. 366); 30 Aug. 1356 (Lichfield, B/A/1/3, f. 138v); 18 Jan. 1357 (*DKR 36*, app. II, no. 1, p. 366); 8 Feb. 1358 (Lichfield, B/A/1/3, f. 144v); 14 Apr. 1358 (PRO, E40/9847); 1 Aug, 5 Aug. 1358 (*Ctl. Burscough*, nos. 170–1).

Richard (del) Wyche –1391 (as prior) Occ. 1366 (*VCH Lancs*, III, 413, citing plea roll); 1379 (Bennett, 'Lancs & Ches. Clergy', p. 22); 12 Mar. 1379 (Cheshire RO, DCH/E/96); 1 July 1380, 2 Nov. 1388 (Cheshire RO, DLT/A11/71–2).

ABBOT

Richard (del) Wyche 1391–1400 Priory elevated to abbey 10 May 1391 with Richard Wyche as abb. (*CPL*, IV, 405). Lic. to receive bl. from any Catholic bp 7 June 1391; indult for use of mitre, ring, pastoral staff and other pontifical insignia 18 June 1391 (ibid., 408, 410). D. 12 Dec. 1400 (Lambeth, Reg. Arundel, I, f. 484v). See J.P. Greene, 'The elevation of Norton priory, Cheshire, to the status of mitred abbey', *Trans. Lancs and Ches. Hist. Soc.*, 128 (1979), 97–112.

NORTON, *see* **COLD NORTON**

NOSTELL (Yorks W.), St Oswald (St Oswald by Pontefract) f. *c.* 1114
Lists in *VCH Yorks*, III, 234; *Fasti 1066–1300*, VI, 60–62; *Fasti 1300–1541*, VI, 38–9; *Heads*, I, 178–9; account of priors in Leeds, NP/C1/1/1, pp. 88ff ('De gestis et actibus priorum monasterii sancti Oswaldi de Nostell' ' (Ch.)).

John 1208–1237 Occ. 1209 and frequently to 13 Oct. 1236 (BL, Cotton ms. Vespasian E XIX, f. 166v; *Yorks F., 1232–46*, p. 44). Pr. for 29 years, 2 months and 3 days, and d. 27 Sept. 1237, so suggests he was el. *c.* 24 July 1208 (Ch., p. 92).

Ambrose 1237–1240 Pr. for 3 years, 7 weeks and 3 days, and d. 18 Nov. 1240 (Ch., p. 92).

Stephen 1240–1244 Pr. for 4 years and ceded office in 1244 (Ch., p. 92). Occ. (S.) 29 Sept. 1240 (*sic*) (BL, Harl. Cht. 84 D 33); 1241 (*Ctl. Tockwith*, p. 206).

Ralph [junior] 1244–1246 Succ. and was pr. for 2 years. D. 18 May 1246 (Ch., p. 92).

Robert de Behall 1246–1255 Pr. for 8 years and 5 months. D. 4 Jan. 1255 (Ch., p. 93). Occ. 13 Dec. 1247 (*Reg. Gray*, p. 205; (R.) 1248 (*Magnum Reg. Album Lichfield*, p. 228; *Reg. Gray*, p. 206). 9 June 1252 (*Yorks F., 1246–72*, p. 84). Surname identified as Beal, pa. Kellington (*Fasti 1066–1300*, VI, 62, n. 146).

William of Clifford (Clifforth, Clyfford) **1255–1277** Pr. for 22½ years and d. 16 Aug. 1277 (Ch., p. 93). Occ. Hil. 1255 (Baildon, I, 153); 1256 (*Northumberland and Durham F.*, I, p. 96, no. 336); 1263 (*Lincs F.*, II, 202); (W.) 1267 (*Reg. W. Giffard*, p. 23); 1 July 1269 (*Yorks F., 1246–72*, p. 172).

Richard of Warter (Wartria) **1277–1291** Pr. for 15 years and d. 26 Aug. 1291 (Ch., pp. 93–4). Occ. 9 Feb. 1279 (*Northumberland and Durham F.*, II, 12, no. 28); 1280 (PRO, E42/484); 24 May 1286 (*Yorks F., 1272–1300*, p. 76).[33]

William of Birstall (Bristall) **1291–1312** Pr. for 21½ years and ceded office on account of old age and infirmity about the feast of St Alphege (19 Apr.) 1312 (Ch., pp. 94–5, but see below). Can. of Nostell, eln conf. 2 Oct. 1291 (*Reg. Romeyn*, I, p. 114. no. 312). Res. on account of ill-health and old age 10 Apr. 1312 (*Reg. Greenfield*, II, p. 117, no. 950). Lic. to el. 12 Apr. 1312 (ibid.). Provision made for ex-pr. 15 June 1312, conf. by archbp 18 June 1312 (ibid., pp. 118–21, no. 952).

Henry of Aberford (Abirforth, Aburford) **1312–1328** El. 9 May 1312 by compromise. 9 compromissaries chosen, 4 choosing Henry and the rest between other candidates, Gilbert de Petirburgh and Robert of Pontefract; subsequently Henry was conf. After almost 15 years in office Henry res. 20 June [1328] and subsequently retired to the cell of Woodkirk and lived there 8 months and 2 days, dying on 3 June 1329 (Ch., pp. 95–9). Can. of Nostell, eln quashed and apptd by archbp 5 June 1312 (*Reg. Greenfield*, II, p. 118, no. 952). Purgation at archbp's visitation 12 Dec. 1313 (ibid., p. 171, no. 1033). Letter of res. dated 20 June 1328 (York, Reg.9A, f. 214r). Lic to el. 22 June 1328 (ibid., f. 213v). Provision made for Henry 7 Aug. 1328 (ibid., f. 214v).

John de Insula 1328–1331 El. 9 July 1328 – 13 chose John and 15 chose William de Butturbuske, sub-pr. of Nostell. On 10 July William renounced his right and after a few days John's eln was conf. by Archbp. John was pr. for 2 years and 8 months and 1 day and d. 8 Mar. 1331 (Ch., pp. 99–102). Can. of Nostell, pr. of Breedon (q.v.). Eln quashed but apptd by archbp n.d., proclamation *si quis* 14 July 1328, opposers to appear on 3rd law day after St James (28 July 1328) (York, Reg. 9A, ff. 214v–215r). Accepted by the steward of the Honour of Pontefract 13 July 1328 (ibid., f. 214v). Mand. to install 29 July 1328 (ibid., f. 215v). Occ. 1330 (PRO, Just.1/167, mm. 7, 85); Hil. term 1331 (Baildon, I, 155).

John of Dewsbury (Dewsbery) *alias* **Wodehous 1331–1337** El. 27 Mar. 1331 and after a few days conf. by the vicar-general of the archbp and was installed 'feria quinta in die sinodi in capitulo et choro Ebor''. He d. 31 Mar. 1336, presumably error for 1337 – see below (Ch., pp. 102–3). (Wodehous) adm. to prebend of Bramham (York Minster) annexed to the pr.'s office 28 Apr. 1331 (YMA, L1/7 (Torre's ms.), p. 1213). Occ. 13 June 1331, 12 May 1336 (Lincoln, Ep. Reg., IV, ff. 190r, 348v).

Thomas of Darfield (Derfeld(e), once Driffeld) **1337–1372** El. 14 Apr. [1337] and d. about the feast of St Ambrose (4 Apr.) 1372 (Ch., pp. 103–5) Can. of Nostell, eln conf. 30 Apr. 1337 (York, Reg. 9A, f. 258r). D. by 10 May 1372 (York, Reg. 11, f. 165v).

Richard of Wombwell (Wombewell) **1372–1385** Cellarer of Nostell, el. n.d., ruled priory for 13 years and d. 1385 (Ch., p. 105). Can. of Nostell, eln conf. 10 May 1372 (York, Reg. 11, f. 165v). Occ. 1377 (*CPR 1374–77*, p. 494; *CPR 1377–81*, p. 43); Easter 1378 (Baildon, I, 157).

His successor, **Adam of Bilton**, previously pr. of Breedon, had vacated the latter by 9 May 1385 (Lincoln, Ep. Reg., XI, f. 200r).

---

[33] Baildon, I, 152 cites a pr. Thomas in an unidentified fine of 1286. This has not been located, only a fine of 1286 with pr. Richard (*Yorks F., 1272–1300*, p. 76).

NOTLEY (Bucks), St Mary (Crendon Park, De Parco-super-Thamam) f. -1162 (abbey)
Lists in *VCH Bucks*, I, 379–80; list of abbots from lost ctl. (17th cent. extract) in Jenkins, 'Lost cartulary', p. 382; *Heads*, I, 179.

Edward *c.* 1201–*c.* 1218 Abb. for 17 years ('Lost cartulary', p. 382). Occ. 1200 x 1205 (*Newington Longeville Chts.*, no. 38); 21 Jan. 1204 (*Bucks F.*, I, 28; Jenkins, 'Lost cartulary', p. 390, no. 30); *c.* 1206 (*Ctl. Sandford*, II, 188–9, no. 261).

John de Essesden *c.* 1218–1236 Abb. for 17 years ('Lost cartulary', p. 382). Occ. Oct. 1221 x Oct. 1222 (*Cambs F.*, p. 11; PRO, E326/ 10518); *c.* 1225 (*Ctl. Boarstall*, p. 79); Hil. term 1233 (*CRR*, XV, no. 19); 21 May 1234 (*Bucks F.*, I, 65). Res. June 1236 x June 1237 (*Reg. Grosseteste*, p. 343). Presumably the unnamed abb. deposed by Bp Grosseteste at his 1236 visitation (*Ann. Dunstable*, p. 143).

[Walter de Augens El. by convent but quashed by bp (*Reg. Grosseteste*, p. 343).]

Henry de Sancta Fide 1236/7–1251/2 Abb. for 16 years ('Lost cartulary', p. 382). Pr. of Notley, apptd by bp June 1236 x June 1237 (*Reg. Grosseteste* p. 343). Cf. abb. H. occ. 1235 (*sic*) (*Newington Longeville Chts.*, no. 63).

John of Grendon (Crendon) 1251/2–1269 Abb. for 17 years ('Lost cartulary', p. 382). Can. of Notley, eln conf. June 1251 x June 1252, no reason given for vacancy (*Reg. Grosseteste*, p. 381). Occ. 30 Nov. 1264 (*Reg. R. Gravesend*, p. 17). D. (J.) by 5 Jan. 1269 (ibid., pp. 243, 342).

John of Gloucester (Gloucestr') 1269 Abb. for 1½ years ('Lost cartulary', p. 382, but clearly not correct, see next entry). Can. of Notley, eln quashed but apptd by bp 5 Jan. 1269 (*Reg. R. Gravesend*, pp. 243, 342).

Richard of Dorchester (Dorckcestr') 1269–1273 Abb. for 3½ years; entered Cistercian abbey at Thame ('Lost cartulary', p. 382). Pr. of Notley, el. 17 Sept. 1269; eln conf. 18 Sept.; bl. 22 Sept. 1269 (*Reg. R. Gravesend*, pp. 243, 342). Had joined Cistercians by 6 July 1273 (ibid., p. 249).

Henry *dictus* **Medicus** (Le Mysere?) 1273–1289/90 Abb. for 17 years ('Lost cartulary', p. 382). Can. of Notley, eln quashed, but apptd by bp 6 July 1273 (*Reg. R. Gravesend*, pp. 249, 344). Occ. Mich. 1272 x Mich. 1273 (PRO, E159/47, m. 13d).

William of Sheringham (Scheringham, Sciringham) 1290–1308 Abb. for 20 years; el. 18 Feb. [1290], d. 14 Aug. [1308] ('Lost cartulary', p. 382). El. in Bp Sutton's tenth year (May 1289 x May 1290); lic. to el. obtained from Matilda de Mortimer, claiming to be patron, but the earl of Gloucester said he should be patron (Bodl., Dodsworth ms. 107, f. 142v). Occ. 24 June 1292 (Oxford, Oriel College mun., Shadwell III. 16). D. 14 Aug. 1308 (Lincoln, Ep. Reg., II, f. 181r–v).

John of Thame 1309–1329 Abb. for 20 years ('Lost cartulary', p. 382). Can. of Notley, el. 9 Feb. 1309 (?*rectius* 9 Jan.). Opposition heard 20 Jan. 1309, ?27 Feb., third lawday after St Matthias eln quashed, but apptd by bp; bl. 2 Mar. 1309 (Lincoln, Ep. Reg., II, f. 181r–v). Occ. 1323 (*CPR 1321–24*, pp. 258, 369). D. by 28 May 1329 (*CCR 1327–30*, pp. 464–5).

Richard of Crendon (Crondon) 1329–*c.* 1361 Abb. for nearly 32 years ('Lost cartulary', p. 382). Commn to examine eln 2 May 1329 (Lincoln, Ep. Reg., V, f. 416v). Commn to bp of Worcester to bl. 11 June 1329; bl. 12 June 1329 (*Reg. Orleton (Worcester)*, no. 726). Occ. 1331 (BL, Add. Cht. 14519); 12 Sept. (1332) (PRO, C270/ 10 no. 30); 1333 (*CPR 1330–34*, p.444); 1340 (*HMC 1st Rept*, app., p. 70); 1343 (Lincoln, Ep. Reg., VI, f. 82r–v; Oxford, Oriel College mun. Shadwell III. 22); 21 Jan. 1350 (*CCR 1349–54*, p. 156); 26 June 1351 (*CPL*, III, 448).

John Wychenden *c.* 1361–*c.* 1374 Abb. for 12 years and 9 months ('Lost cartulary', p. 382). Occ. 6 Apr. 1368 (Lambeth, Reg. Whittlesey, p. 49).

John de Cherdesle(y) (Scherdesle) *c.* 1374–1384 Abb. for 10 years, after which he res. office for the benefice of [*blank*] ('Lost cartulary', p. 382). Occ. 13 June 1379 (Lincoln, Ep. Reg.,

XII, f. 183v). Pardon for the death of William Dunstone, can. of Notley, 17 June 1381 (*CPR 1381–85*, p. 14). 13 June 1381 suspended *propter dilapidacionem suam notoriam* following visitation (Lincoln, Ep. Reg., XII, f. 226v); appeal to Rome 8 Dec. 1383, apostles refused 28 Dec. 1383 (ibid., f. 269r–v).

The next abb., **Nicholas Amcotes**, commn to examine eln 3 Oct. 1384 (Lincoln, Ep. Reg., XII, f. 285v). Abb. for 11 years ('Lost cartulary', p. 382).

OSNEY (Oxon), St Mary f. 1129 (priory); *c.* 1154 (abbey).

Lists in *VCH Oxon*, II, 93; *Ctl. Oseney*, I, xii–xiv (list); *Heads*, I, 179–80.

Clement 1205–1221 Pr. of Osney, el. 22 Apr. 1205 (*Ann. Osney*, p. 62). D. 17 Sept. 1221 (list; ibid.); D., lic. to el. 23 Sept. 1221 (*CPR 1216–25*, p. 301).

Richard de Gray (Crey, Grai) **1221–1229** Pr. of Osney, succ. Sept. 1221 (*Ann. Osney*, p. 62). Royal ass. 26 Sept. 1221 (*CPR 1216–25*, pp. 301–2). D., lic. to el. 10 July 1229 (*CPR 1225–32*, p. 56); but cf. D. 11 July 1229 (*Ann. Osney*, p. 70; list, p. xiii); obit 11 July (*Ctl. Oseney*, I, p. xxiii).

John of Reading (Redinges) **1229–1235** Sub-pr. of Osney, royal ass. 13 July 1229; writ *de intendendo* 22 July 1229 (*CPR 1225–32*, pp. 256, 258); succ. 1229 (*Ann. Osney*, p. 70). Res. 2 July [1235] (PRO, C84/1/9). Joined Franciscans at Northampton 3 Oct. 1235 (ibid., p. 82; A.G. Little ed., *Fratris Thomae vulgo dicti de Eccleston: De Adventu Fratrum Minorum in Angliam*, p. 18 & note p – 'qui nobis omnis perfectionis exempla reliquit'). Lic. to el. 4 Oct. 1235, abb. having become a Franciscan (*CPR 1232–47*, p. 119).

John de Leche (Lecche) **1235–1249** 7th abb., el. 4 Oct. 1235 (list, p. xiii). Can. of Osney, royal ass. 7 Oct., writ *de intendendo* 19 Oct. 1235 (*CPR 1232–47*, pp. 119, 121). Bl. 4 Nov. 1235 (*Ann. Osney*, p. 83). Eln conf. n.d. [Oct. 1235 x June 1236] (*Reg. Grosseteste*, p. 447). Res. before 11 June 1249 on account of illness (list, p. xiii; *Ann. Osney*, p. 101). Cess., lic. to el. 6 June 1249 (*CPR 1247–58*, p. 43). D. 1 Nov. 1250, ruled 14 years; obit 3 Nov. (*Ann. Osney*, p. 100; *Ctl. Oseney*, I, p. xxvi).

Adam de Berners 1249–1254 8th abb., ruled 5 years. Can. of Osney, el. 11 June 1249; bl. 24 June, installed 29 June 1249 (list, p. xiii; *Ann. Osney*, pp. 101–2). El. June 1249 x June 1250 (*Reg. Grosseteste*, p. 496). Royal ass. 14 June 1249 (*CPR 1247–58*, p. 43); mand. for seisin 17 June 1249 (*CR 1247–51*, p. 174). Cert. conf. eln by bp of Lincoln 18 June 1249 (PRO, C84/1/18). D. 2 Aug. 1254 (*Ann. Osney*, p. 106; list, p. xiii). Lic. to el. (no reason given for vacancy) 9 Sept. 1254, earl of Cornwall empowered to give royal asst (*CPR 1247–58*, p. 328).

Richard II of Appletree (Appeltre) **1254–1268** 9th abb., ruled 13½ years, el. 5 Oct. 1254, bl. 1 Nov. 1254, installed 11 Nov. 1254 (list, pp. xiii–xiv; *Ann. Osney*, p. 107). Pr. of Osney, royal ass. 9 Oct. 1254, temps. 26 Oct. 1254 (*CPR 1247–58*, pp. 373–4). Occ. 25 Nov. 1267 (PRO, Bucks F., CP25/1/16/40, no. 12). Res. after 1 Jan. 1268 on account of infirmity (*Ann. Osney*, p. 208). Res. 4 Jan. 1268 (PRO, C84/3/37). Richard de Appeltre, former abb. d. 28 Dec. 1269 (*Ann. Osney*, pp. 229–230; list, p. xiv). Obit 28 Dec. (*Ctl. Oseney*, I, p. xxvii).

William of Sutton (Suttone) **1268–1285** 10th abb., ruled 17 years 1 month (list, p. xiv). Can. of Osney, royal ass. 17 Jan. 1268, writ *de intendendo* 26 Jan. 1268 (*CPR 1266–72*, pp. 181, 183). El. 14 Jan. 1268, installed 22 Jan. 1268 (list, p. xiv); eln conf. and bl. 22 Jan. 1268 (*Reg. R. Gravesend*, pp. 220, 331–2; *Ann. Osney*, pp. 210–11). He attended Council of Lyons 1274 (*Ann. Osney*, pp. 257–8). D. 9 Feb. 1285 (list, p. xiv; *Ann. Osney*, p. 302). D., lic. to el. 12 Feb. 1285 (*CPR 1281–92*, p. 154).

Roger of Coventry (Coventre) **1285–1297** 11th abb. Can. of Osney, royal ass. 23 Feb. 1285, temps. 7 Mar. 1285 (ibid., pp. 154–5). El. 19 Feb. 1285, eln conf. and bl. 3 Mar. 1285, installed 22 Mar. 1285, 10th abb. ruled 17 years 1 month (list, p. xiv; *Ann. Osney*, pp. 302–3).

Obit. 28 Mar. (*Ctl. Oseney*, I, p. xxi). D., lic. to el. 4 Apr. 1297 (*CPR 1292–1301*, p. 246).

John of Bibury (Bebur', Beybury, Bibir') **1297–1317** Can. of Osney, royal ass. 25 Apr. 1297, temps. 8 May 1297 (ibid., pp. 247–8). Eln conf. 2 May 1297, bl. 3 May 1297 (*Reg. Sutton*, VIII, 194; PRO, C84/12/44). Prof. obed. to Bp Dalderby 29 July 1300 (Lincoln, Ep. Reg., III, f. 14r). Cess., lic to el. 4 Feb. 1317 (*CPR 1313–17*, p. 615). Indulgence issued for his soul 13 Sept. 1319 (Lincoln, Ep, Reg., III, f. 424r).

John of Osney (Oseney(e), Osneye) **1317–1330** Can. of Osney, eln pres. to king by pr. and convent 24 Feb. 1317, mand. for letters 27 Feb. (*Cal. Chanc. Warr.*, p. 464). Royal ass. 27 Feb. 1317, temps. 7 Apr. 1317 (*CPR 1313–17*, pp. 623, 637). Eln conf. 30 Mar. 1317 (Lincoln, Ep. Reg., II, f. 168v). D., lic to el. 16 July 1330 (*CPR 1327–30*, p. 537).

Thomas of Kidlington (Chudlyngton, Cudelyngton, Cudyngton, Kydlyngton) **1330–1373** Can. of Osney, royal ass. 20 July 1330 (ibid., p. 542). Eln pres. to bp 8 Aug. 1330; eln quashed but apptd by bp 9 Aug. 1330 (Lincoln, Ep. Reg., IV, ff. 262v–263r). Occ. 2 May 1373 (Lincoln, Ep. Reg., X, f. 366r). D. by 12 May 1373 (PRO, C84/30/47). D., lic. to el. 13 May 1373 (*CPR 1370–74*, p. 279).

John (of) Buckland (Bokelond, Buckelond) **1373–1404** Can of Osney, eln pres. to king for royal ass. 19 May 1373 (PRO, C84/38/43); royal ass. 21 May 1373, temps. 1 June 1373 (*CPR 1370–74*, pp. 285, 290). Eln pres. to bp 25 May 1373, eln conf. 5 June 1373, but mand. to install and letter of benediction 1 June (*sic*) 1373 (Lincoln, Ep. Reg., X, ff. 358r–359r; cf. cert. conf. eln 30 May 1373 (PRO, C84/30/49)). D. by 1 Feb. 1404 (PRO, C84/38/43). D., lic. to el. 14 Feb. 1404 (*CPR 1401–05*, p. 366).

OWSTON (Leics), St Andrew f. – 1161 (abbey)

Lists in *VCH Leics*, II, 22–3; *Heads*, I, 180.

Peter of Buckland (Bocland) **–1236** Occ. 1208 x 9 (Leics F., PRO transcripts, III); 3 Nov. 1226 (PRO, Leics F., CP25/1/121/12, no. 128); (P.) 1227 (CUL, ms. Dd. III. 87 (20), f. 21v); (P.) 24 Feb. 1231 (*Ctl. Cockersand*, II, I, 379–80). Unnamed abb. deposed by Bp Grosseteste at his visitation 1236 (*Ann. Dunstable*, p. 143). Res. June 1235 x June 1236 (*Reg. Grosseteste*, p. 388).

Richard of Watlington 1236–?1241 Precentor of Osney, apptd by bp by authority of the Council on res. of Peter of Bocland (ibid.). El. 1236 (*Ann. Osney*, p. 83). Writ *de intendendo* 27 June 1236 (*CPR 1232–47*, p. 151 – desc. as can. of Osney). Occ. June 1237 x June 1238 (*Reg. Grosseteste*, p. 397). Lic. to el. (no reason given) 10 July 1241 (*CPR 1232–47*, p. 254).

Peter of Leicester (Leirc', Leycestre) **1241–1264** Can. of Owston, el. and adm. June 1241 x June 1242, no reason given for vacancy (*Reg. Grosseteste*, p. 415). Royal ass. 10 Aug. 1241, writ *de intendendo* 28 Sept. 1241 (*CPR 1232–47*, pp. 256, 259). D. (P.) on the day of St Edward the Confessor 1264 – prob. the translation 13 Oct. (PRO, C84/3/6). D. by 19 Nov. 1264 (*Reg. R. Gravesend*, p. 144).

William of Flamstead (Flamested, Flamsted) **1264–1268** Pr. of Owston, eln conf. 17 Nov. 1264 (ibid.). Eln pres. to king for royal ass. 7 Nov. 1264 (PRO, C84/3/14); royal ass. 13 Nov. 1264 (*CPR 1258–66*, p. 387). (W.) D. by 6 Apr. 1268 (*CPR 1266–72*, p. 217; *Reg. R. Gravesend*, p. 148; cf. PRO, C84/4/20).

Ivo of Cosby (Cosseby) **1268–1280** Can. of Owston, eln conf. 29 Apr. 1268 (*Reg. R. Gravesend*, pp. 148, 310). Royal ass. 17 Apr. 1268 (*CPR 1266–72*, p. 219). Bp of Lincoln writes to the king about the cess. of the abb. 27 May 1280 (PRO, SC1/20/193). Cess. by 29 May 1280 (*CFR 1272–1307*, p. 127). Cess., lic. to el. 1 June 1280 (*CPR 1272–81*, p. 374).

John (le) Chaumberleyn 1280–1284 Can. of Owston, royal ass. 10 June 1280, writ *de intendendo* 23 June 1280 (ibid., pp. 378, 383). El. abb. year 1 of Bp Sutton (19 May 1280 x 18 May 1281) (Bodl., Dodsworth ms. 107, f. 138r). Cess., lic. to el. 11 Dec. 1284 (*CPR 1281–92*, p. 146).

Ivo of Cosby (Cosseby) **1284–1286** Can. of Owston, eln pres. to king for royal ass. 21 Dec. 1284 (PRO, C84/8/32); royal ass. to re-election 23 Dec. 1284, temps. 9 Jan. 1285 (*CPR 1281–92*, pp. 147, 150). Cess., lic. to el. 30 Mar. 1286 (ibid., p. 229). Had entered Cistercian order by 26 Mar. 1286 (PRO, C84/8/41).

Robert of Lincoln 1286–1289 Can. of Owston, royal ass. 10 Apr. 1286, temps. 26 Apr. 1286 (*CPR 1281–92*, pp. 230, 234). D. by 19 Feb. 1289 (PRO, C84/9/25). D., lic. to el. 24 Feb. 1289 (*CPR 1281–92*, p. 312).

Arnold (Ernald) of Slawston 1289–1298 Pr. of Fineshade (q.v.) and late can. of Owston, ref. to eln n.d. (*Reg. Sutton*, II, 73). Eln pres. to king for royal ass. 15 Mar. 1289 (PRO, C84/9/28); royal ass. and temps. 20 Mar. 1289 (*CPR 1281–92*, p. 314). D. by 4 Oct. 1298 (PRO, C84/13/17). D., lic. to el. 6 Oct. 1298 (*CPR 1292–1301*, p. 364).

Richard of Boxworth (Bokesworth, Bokeswrth') **1298–1316** Can. of Owston, eln pres. to king for royal ass. 6 Nov. 1298 (PRO, C84/13/19–20); royal ass. 16 Nov. 1298, temps. 5 Dec. 1298 (*CPR 1292–1301*, pp. 372, 387). Eln pres. to bp 28 Nov. 1298, eln conf. 29 Nov. 1298, bl. 28 Dec. 1298 (*Reg. Sutton*, VIII, 69; PRO, C84/13/21). Occ. 1 Aug. 1313 (CUL, ms. Dd. III, 87(20), f. 3v). D. by 4 June 1316 (PRO, C84/18/31). D. (R.), lic. to el. 13 June 1316 (*CPR 1313–17*, p. 470).

Robert of Stamford (Staunford) **1316–1322** Can. of Owston, eln pres. to king for royal ass. 18 June 1316 (PRO, C84/18/34); royal ass. 20 June 1316, temps. 31 July 1316 (*CPR 1313–17*, pp. 480, 522). Eln quashed but apptd by bp 23 July 1316 (Lincoln, Ep. Reg., II, f. 210v; PRO, C84/18/42). Lic. for blessing from ex-archbp of Armagh, same day (Lincoln, Ep. Reg., III, f. 349v). Cess., lic. to el. 21 Jan. 1322 (*CPR 1321–24*, p. 51).

William of Braunstone (Braundeston) **1322–1328** Can. of Owston, eln pres. to king for royal ass. 15 Mar. 1322 (PRO, C84/20/6); royal ass. 18 Mar. 1322, temps. 2 Apr. 1322 (*CPR 1321–24*, pp. 83, 93). El. 24 Mar. 1322, eln quashed but apptd by bp 25 Mar. 1322 (Lincoln, Ep. Reg., IV, ff. 114v–115r; PRO, C84/20/7). D., lic. to el. 22 Mar. 1328 (*CPR 1327–30*, p. 253).

Roger of Barkby (Barkeby) **1328–1349** Can. of Owston, royal ass. 8 Apr. 1328, temps. 30 Apr. 1328 (ibid., pp. 255, 258). Cert. conf. eln by bp of Lincoln 27 Apr. 1328 (PRO, C84/22/8). Occ. 19 Jan. 1349 (Lincoln, Ep. Reg., XII, f. 139r). D., lic. to el. 25 Apr. 1349 (*CPR 1348–50*, p. 278).

John of Kibworth (Kybbeworth) **1349–1355** Can. of Owston, (pittancer of Owston), eln pres. to king for royal ass. 1 May 1349 (PRO, C84/25/35); royal ass. 6 May 1349, temps. 19 May 1349 (*CPR 1348–50*, pp. 280, 293).[34] Eln quashed but apptd by bp, cert. 19 May 1349 (PRO, C84/25/39). D. by 6 Mar. [1355] (PRO, C84/26/41). D., lic. to el. 11 Mar. 1355 (*CPR 1354–58*, p. 193).

William of Cottesmore (Cotesmor(e)) **1355–1401** Can. of Owston, eln pres. to king for royal ass. 14 Mar. 1355 (PRO, C84/27/21); eln quashed but apptd by bp 28 Mar. 1355 (Lincoln, Ep. Reg., IX, f. 361r–v). Temps. 30 Mar. 1355 (*CPR 1354–58*, p. 201). Letter from pr. and convent 12 Sept. 1401 announcing res. of abb. and seeking lic. to el. (PRO, C241/192/99). Res., lic. to el. 23 Nov. 1401 (*CPR 1401–05*, p. 18).

OXFORD, St Frideswide f. 1002 (secular canons); 1122 (Augustinian).

Lists in *VCH Oxon*, II, 100; *Ctl. St Frideswide*, I, pp. xiii–xiv; *Heads*, I, 180.

Simon –1228 Occ. 27 Nov. 1195 (*Oxford F.*, p. 1); (S.) 1197 (*CDF*, no. 145); Oct. 1219, 27 Jan. 1226, 7 Mar. 1227 (*Oxford F.*, pp. 53, 76, 79). Res., lic. to el. (no name given) 6 June 1228 (*CPR 1225–32*, p. 194).

---

[34] The *VCH* ref. to an abb. John in 1344 is an error; it is a document referring to abb. John Chaumberleyn dated Feb. 1283, being mentd in 1344 (*CPR 1343–45*, p. 214).

Elias Scotus 1228–1235 Can. of St Frideswide, royal ass. 20 July 1228 (ibid., p. 195). Succ. 1228 (*Ann. Dunstable*, p. 112); adm. July x Dec. 1228 (*Reg. Wells*, II, 30). Occ. 2 July 1235 (*Oxford F.*, p. 94). Dep. June 1235 x Sept. 1235 (*Reg. Grosseteste*, p. 446, cf. *CPL*, I, 163; PRO, C84/1/12). Dep. (E.), lic. to el. 2 Sept. 1235 (*CPR 1232–47*, p. 117).

[**Walter de Crokesby** Can. of St Frideswide, royal ass. 19 Sept. 1235 (ibid. p. 118). Lic. to el. (no reason given) 8 Oct. 1235 (ibid., p. 119). Presumably ineffective, see below.]

[**Gilbert** Sub.-pr. of St Frideswide, royal ass. 17 Oct. 1235 (ibid., p. 120). Presumably ineffective, see below.]

An unnamed pr. dep. at Bp Grosseteste's visitation 1236, but presumably an error of year and referring to Elias Scotus (*Ann. Dunstable*, p. 143, and see below).

William of Gloucester (Glouc', Gloucestre, Glovernia) **1236–1249** Cellarer of Dunstable, put into St Frideswide 1236 (*Ann. Dunstable*, pp. 143–4). Apptd by bp by authority of the [Lateran] Council June 1235 x June 1236 to house vacant by deposition of E. Scotus (*Reg. Grosseteste*, p. 446). Writ *de intendendo* 2 Feb. 1236 (*CPR 1232–47*, p. 135). D., lic. to el. 26 May 1249 (*CPR 1247–58*, p. 42).

Robert (of) Weston (Westone) **1249–1260** Sub.-pr. of St Frideswide, royal ass. 3 June 1249, temps. 6 June 1249 (ibid., p. 43). Eln conf. June 1248 x June 1249, presumably June 1249 (*Reg. Grosseteste*, p. 494). D. 23 July 1260 (*Ann. Oseney*, p. 127; cf. PRO, C84/2/14). D. (R.), lic. to el. 25 July 1260 (*CPR 1258–66*, p. 83).

Robert of Olney (Olneia, Olneya, Olneye, *alias* **Mundam**) **1260–1278** For the surname Mundam see *Ctl. St Frideswide*, I, 493. Sub.-pr. of St Frideswide, eln pres. to king for royal ass. 27 July 1260 (PRO, C84/2/12); royal ass. 28 July 1260, writ *de intendendo* 29 July 1260 (*CPR 1258–66*, p. 84). Eln conf. (called John) Nov. 1259 x Nov. 1260 (*Reg. R. Gravesend*, pp. 214, 329). D., lic. to el. 17 Sept. 1278 (*CPR 1278–81*, p. 278, cf. *Reg. R. Gravesend*, p. 234).

John of Lewknor (Leukenhouer(e), Leukenor(e)) **1278–1283** Letter about newly-el. pr. 28 Sept. 1278 (PRO, SC1/9/3). Sub.-pr. of St Frideswide, royal ass. 1 Oct. 1278 (*CPR 1272–81*, p. 279). Eln quashed but apptd by bp 8 Oct. 1278 on d. of Robert of Olney (*Reg. R. Gravesend*, pp. 234, 338). House vacant by his cess. 21 Nov. 1283 (*CPR 1281–92*, p.107). Cess., lic. to el. 5 Dec. 1283 (ibid., p. 107).

[**John of Sandon 1283–** Can. of St Frideswide, eln pres. to king for royal ass. 15 Dec. 1283 (PRO, C84/8/17); royal ass. 24 Dec. 1283 (*CPR 1281–92*, p. 108). Prob. ineffective.]

Robert of Ewelme ((del) Euwelme, Ewelm(e), Lewelm, Lewelin) **1284–1294** Sub.-pr. of St Frideswide, bp notifies king of his eln 29 Jan. 1284 (PRO, SC1/21/155); temps. 3 Feb. 1284 (*CPR 1281–92*, p. 111). Res. 30 Mar. 1294 on account of ill-health (*Reg. Sutton*, IV, 182). By 6 Apr. 1294 had been removed by authority of the bp of Lincoln (*Cal. Chanc. Warr.*, p. 41). Cess., lic. to el. 12 Apr. 1294 (*CPR 1292–1301*, p.67, cf. *Reg. Sutton*, VIII, 184–5).

Alexander of Sutton 1294–1316 Sub.-pr. of St Frideswide, eln pres. to king for royal ass. 17 Apr. 1294 (PRO, C84/11/49); royal ass. 20 Apr. 1294, temps. 29 Apr. 1294 (*CPR 1292–1301*, p.69). Eln conf. 24 Apr. 1294 (*Reg. Sutton*, VIII, 184–5; PRO, C84/11/50). Occ. 19 May 1316 (Oxford, Merton Coll. mun, I, 317). D. by 8 July 1316 (PRO, C84/18/39). D., lic. to el. 20 July 1316 (*CPR 1313–17*, p. 515). Indulgence for his soul issued 9 July 1319 (Lincoln, Ep. Reg., III, f. 420v).

Robert de Thorveston (Torveston) **1316–1337** Can. of St Frideswide, eln pres. to king for royal ass. 27 July 1316 (PRO, C84/18/44); royal ass. 4 Aug. 1316, temps. 27 Aug. 1316 (*CPR 1313–17*, pp. 521, 539). Eln conf. 25 Aug. 1316 (Lincoln, Ep. Reg., II, f. 166v; PRO, C84/18/48). Cess. by 10 Jan. 1337 (PRO, C84/23/44). Cess. (Tornestone *sic*), lic. to el. 11 Jan. 1337 (*CPR 1334–38*, p. 344), but cf. commn to make provision for his cess. 24 Jan. 1337 (Lincoln, Ep. Reg., V, f. 545r–v; commn to adm. cess. and supervise the eln of a successor 24 Jan. 1337 (ibid., f. 545v).

John of Littlemore (Litlemore, Littelmor(e), Lutelmore, Luttlemore, Lyttelmore) **1337–1349** Can. of St Frideswide, temps. 2 Feb. 1337 (*CPR 1334–38*, p. 379). Occ. 22 Jan., 25 Jan. 1349 (Lincoln, Ep. Reg., IX, f. 28v). D. by 19 Apr. 1349 (PRO, C84/25/31). D., lic. to el. 25 Apr. 1349 (*CPR 1348–50*, p. 278).

Nicholas of Hungerford (Hougford) **1349–1369/70** Can. of St Frideswide, eln quashed but appointed by bp 11 May 1349 (Lincoln, Ep. Reg., IX, f. 245r–v); royal ass. 15 May 1349, temps. 1 June 1349 (*CPR 1348–50*, pp. 292, 300). On 20 May 1354 the priory was taken into the king's special protection out of compassion for the depression of the priory by misrule, adversities and debts (*CPR 1354–58*, p. 51). Mand. to cite sub-pr. and convent in their case against Nicholas of Hungerford, pretended pr., 15 Dec. 1362 and certif. 22 Dec. (Lambeth, Reg. Islip, f. 189v); further citation 3 Jan. 1363; commn to visit priory 10 Jan. 1363 (ibid., ff. 189v–190r). Formerly chaplain of Edward, prince of Wales, Nicholas of Hungerford, former pr., had ruled 16 years, then exchanged the priory for a certain vicarage with **John of Dodford**, can. of Carlisle.[35] Papal prov. of Dodford on d. of pr. Nicholas 20 Nov. 1369, 19 *or* 20 Jan. 1370 (*Accts of Papal Collectors*, pp. 361–2, 403–4, 502). John's trickery and Nicholas's own simplicity caused him to be guilty of simony and pr. Nicholas was subsequently deprived of both offices. The pope is petitioned to absolve Nicholas and restore him as pr. – 10 Dec. 1365 case recommitted to the Cardinal of Nîmes (*CPP*, p. 509). 20 Mar. 1370, John of Dodford, chaplain, order for him to be arrested for trying to intrude. He had intended to deprive the king of patronage and had done other things prejudicial to the king (*CPR 1367–70*, p. 423); warrant for arrest 1374 (*CPR 1370–74*, pp. 480–1). For Dodford's activities, see *Nottingham Medieval Studies*, XXXV (1991), 81–2. Presumably he was reinstated. D. by 20 Jan. 1370 (PRO, C84/30/21; cf. *Accts of Papal Collectors*, p. 361). D., lic. to el. 23 Jan. 1370 (*CPR 1367–70*, p. 337).

John (of) Wallingford (Wal(l)yngford) **1370–1374** Can. of St Frideswide, commn to examine eln 28 Feb. 1370 (Lincoln, Ep. Reg., XII, f. 88r). Eln pres. to king for royal ass. 28 Jan. 1370 (PRO, C84/30/22); royal ass. 1 Feb. 1370, temps. 18 Mar. 1370 (*CPR 1367–70*, pp. 342, 379). Cert. conf. eln by bp of Lincoln 15 Mar. 1370 and cert. by bp's commissary 16 Mar. (PRO, C84/30/24–5). Commn to abb. of Osney to act in the name of the bp of Lincoln (as a p.j.d.) to execute the definitive sentence in the Papal Curia for John of Dodford against John of Wallingford and to adm. the former into possession of the priory 28 Dec. 1372 (Lincoln, Ep. Reg., XII, f. 113r). Petition of convent to king for lic. to el. on res. of John of Wallingford 23 July 1373 (*sic*) (*Ctl. St Frideswide*, I, 476; but cf. PRO, C84/30/52). Provision made for res. 24 Aug. 1374, 1 Dec. 1374 (*CPR 1374–77*, pp. 48, 55). Res., lic. to el. 14 Nov. 1374 (ibid., p. 27; *Ctl. St Frideswide*, I, 477 has 20 Nov.). Subsequently in dispute over priorship – signified for arrest 16 Oct. 1377, 14 July 1378 (Logan, *Runaway Religious*, p. 224).

John (of) Dodford (Dedeford, Dodefford, Dodeford(e), Doderford) **1374–1391** Petition of conv. for royal ass. 6 Dec. 1374 (*Ctl. St Frideswide*, I, 478). Royal ass. 15 Jan. 1375, temps. 8 Feb. 1375 (*CPR 1374–77*, pp. 44, 74). Cert. conf. eln by bp of Lincoln 6 Feb. 1375 (PRO, C84/31/19). 22 July 1377 gt of protection for priory for 3 years and appt of John, duke of Lancaster, to custody of the house (*CPR 1377–81*, p. 8). 26 Feb. 1378 indicted of offences; to be brought from the Marshalsea to answer the king (ibid., p. 122); commn to investigate 27 July 1378 (ibid., p. 302). D. by 26 Mar. 1391 (PRO, C84/35/6). D., lic. to el. 27 Mar. 1391 (*CPR 1388–92*, p. 378).

---

[35] If this John of Dodford is the man who became pr. 1374–91, he is found in 1357 described as a can. of St Frideswide, when a papal provision apptd him vicar of Whittingham, dioc. Durham (*CPL*, III, 583).

PATRIXBOURNE (Kent) (Beaulieu, Normandy) f. *c.* 1200; sold to Merton priory 1409
List in *VCH Kent*, II, 239.

Walter Occ. from Nov. 1295 x Nov. 1296 to Nov. 1298 x Nov. 1299 (PRO, E106/3/19, m. 5d; E106/4/9, m. 3; E106/4/10, m. 3d; Easter 1300 (PRO, E106/4/14, m. 5).

Ralph de Valle Occ. *c.* Mich. 1324 (PRO, E106/5/2, m. 12d); July 1325 x July 1326 (PRO, E106/5/4, m. [12d]); 8 Oct. 1326 (*Memo. Roll 1326–7*, p. 273). Mentd (? former pr.) in pipe roll of Mich. 1338 x Mich. 1339 (PRO, E372/184, rot. 9).

John de Pychervill proctor in England of the pr. of Beaulieu, gtd keeping of the manor of Patrixbourne 27 July 1337 (*CFR 1337–47*, p. 35).

Richard Septennent (Septennant) proctor of the pr. of Beaulieu and keeper of the manor of Patrixbourne: occ. 6 Oct. 1369 (*CFR 1368–77*, p. 43); 18 Nov. 1377 (*CFR 1377–83*, p. 35).

PENMON (Anglesey), St Seiriol f. 1237+

J. –1294 Cess. (J.) by 14 Feb. 1294 (PRO, C84/11/43). Res., lic. to el. 17 Apr. 1294 (*CPR 1292–1301*, p. 68). Power to Robert de Staundon, justice of North Wales, to give royal ass. and restore temps. in due course 16 Apr. 1294 (ibid.).

John –1310 Cess., lic. to el. 3 Aug. 1310 (*CPR 1307–13*, p. 273).

Gervase of Bristol (Bristoll) 1310–1316 Can. of Penmon, royal ass. 27 Sept. 1310, temps. 20 Jan. 1311 (ibid., pp. 279, 303). Res. by 8 July 1316 (PRO, C84/18/38). Res., lic. to el. 21 July 1316 (*CPR 1313–17*, p. 514).

John Seys 1316–1317 Can. of Bardsey, eln pres. to king for royal ass. 16 Aug. 1316 (PRO, C84/18/45); royal ass. 25 Aug. 1316, temps. 21 Sept. 1316 (*CPR 1313–17*, pp. 537, 546). Cert. conf. eln by bp of Bangor 6 Sept. 1316 (PRO, C84/18/49). Res. by 12 June 1317 (PRO, C84/19/13). Res., lic. to el. 17 June 1317 (*CPR 1313–17*, p. 669).

Matthew (Martin) Goch (Cogh') 1317–1335 Can. of Penmon, eln pres. to king for royal ass. 15 July 1317 (PRO, C84/19/14); royal ass. 22 July 1317, temps. 17 Aug. 1317, eln having been conf. by Bp Anian of Bangor (*CPR 1317–21*, pp. 4, 17). Res. by 17 May 1335 (PRO, C84/23/39–40). Cess., lic. to el. 7 June 1335 (*CPR 1334–38*, p. 116).

Anais son of Goroun (Goronw, Gorouw) 1335– Can. of Penmon, royal ass. 2 July 1335, temps. 26 July 1335 (ibid., pp. 129, 157).

PENTNEY (Norfolk), Holy Trinity, St Mary, and St Mary Magdalen f. *c.* 1130
Lists in *VCH Norfolk*, II, 390; *Heads*, I, 180–1.

Simon Occ. 27 Jan. 1200 (*CRR*, I, 352).

Simon ? the same. Occ. from Oct. 1227 x Oct. 1228 to Oct. 1254 x Oct. 1255 (*Norfolk F. (Rye)*, pp. 40, 88); (S.) 6 July 1241 (BL, Add. ms. 47784, f. 79v; Norfolk RO, DN/SUN.8, f. 59r).[36]

William Occ. n.d. in BL, Cotton ms. Titus C VIII, f. 51r (13th cent. ctl.). His precise place in the sequence of priors is unknown (see n. 36 below).

Hugh of Narborough (Narburch, Narburg) Occ. Nov. 1294 x Nov. 1295, Nov. 1295 x Nov. 1296 (PRO, LR14/317, 449); n.d. (ibid., /155, 411).

Richard of Marham 1302– Eln conf. 20 Sept. 1302, no reason given for vacancy (Norwich, Reg/1/1, f. 10r). Occ. 1306 (PRO, Just.1/591, m. 3d); 1307 (PRO, LR14/56); 1310 (PRO, Just.1/593, m. 13d); July 1311 x July 1312 (*Norfolk F. (Rye)*, p. 232); 3 Feb. 1312 (Norfolk RO, ms. Fel. 30, f. 7r); ?pr. 8 Aug. 1322 (Norfolk RO, Hare 1256).

Giles of Whitwell (Whitewelle) –1342 Occ. 21 Aug. 1338 (Norwich, Reg/1/3, f. 16r). D. by 19 Oct. 1342 (ibid., f. 62r).

---

[36] Pr. Ralph, said by the *VCH* to occ. 1225 is an error; the entry refers to Ralph, abb. of Fontenay ('Funtenay') not Pentney (*Norfolk F., (Rye)*, p. 39; cf. *Gallia Christiana*, XI, 414). Blomefield, *Norfolk*, IX, 41 lists after Simon a pr. Geoffrey *temp*. Henry III, followed in the sequence by a pr. William (possibly the same as occ. in BL, Cotton ms. Titus C VIII above), but without any sources for either. *VCH*, citing only Blomefield, gives Geoffrey a date *c.* 1260 and William *temp.* Edward I.

Thomas de Helgeye 1342–1349 Can. of Pentney, eln conf. 19 Oct. 1342 (ibid.). Occ. 20 Apr. 1349 (PRO, LR14/576).

Ralph of Framlingham (Framelyngham) 1349–1351 Can. of St Peter, Ipswich, former pr. of Letheringham, apptd by bp 16 Aug. 1349, no reason given for vacancy (Norwich, Reg/2/4, f. 104v). Res. by 27 Sept. 1351 (ibid., f. 133v).

Vincent of Caldecote 1351–1353 Can. of Pentney, eln conf. 27 Sept. 1351 (ibid., f. 133v). Res. by 16 July 1353 (ibid., f. 147v).

Peter Bysshop *alias* **of Buckenham** (Bokenham) 1353–1381 Can. of Pentney, eln conf. 16 July 1353 (ibid.). Res. by 26 Oct. 1381 (Norwich, Reg/3/6, f. 76v).

PETERSTONE (Norfolk), St Peter f. -1200

List in *VCH Norfolk*, II, 391.

Thomas Occ. *temp.* Henry III (Blomefield, *Norfolk*, VII, 24).

Philip Mentioned 1250 as predecessor of Simon (PRO, Just.1/560, m. 11).

Simon Occ. 1250 (ibid.); Oct. 1250 x Oct. 1251 (*Norfolk F. (Rye)*, p. 83).

Geoffrey Occ. Oct. 1258 x Oct. 1259, Oct. 1269 x Oct. 1270 (ibid., pp. 96, 108).

Roger Occ. 1271 x Oct. 1272, Oct. 1275 x Oct. 1276 (ibid., pp. 111, 115); 1262 x 1281 (*Ctl. Creake*, p. 77); 15 Aug. 1277 (BL, Harl. ms. 2110, f. 101r).

Eustace of Barsham 1308–1314 Eln conf. 3 July 1308, no reason for vacancy (Norwich, Reg/1/1, f. 28r). Res. by 8 Oct. 1324 (ibid., f. 58r).

Warin of Repps (Reppes) 1314– Can. of Peterstone, apptd and installed during bp's visitation 8 Oct. 1314 (ibid.). Occ. 1318 (*Lordship and Landscape*, pp. 213–14); 22 July 1321 (Norwich, Reg/1/1, f. 91r).

Thomas (of) Warham 1324–1339 Sub-pr. of Peterstone, eln quashed, but apptd by bp 27 Oct. 1324, no reason given for vacancy (ibid., f. 112r). Cess. by 22 Nov. 1339 (Norwich, Reg/1/3, f. 31v).

Thomas of Warham 1339– Thomas de Warham (*sic*), eln quashed, but apptd by bp 22 Nov. 1339 (ibid.).

John de Howham 1349– Can. of Peterstone, apptd by bp 20 Nov. 1349, no reason given for vacancy (Norwich, Reg/2/4, f. 115v).

Roger de Drynyngham –1366 Cess. by 28 Jan. 1366 (Norwich, Reg/2/5, f. 67v).

John of Massingham (Massyngham) 1366–1376 Can. of Flitcham, postulation quashed, but apptd by bp 28 Jan. 1366 (ibid.). D. by 12 Apr. 1376 (Norwich, Reg/3/6, f. 44r).

John of Dunton 1376– Can. of Peterstone, eln quashed, but apptd by bp 12 Apr. 1376 (ibid.).

The next recorded pr., **William Bryght de Wyghton**, received the priory on the bp's collation 18 Nov. 1393, no reason given for vacancy (ibid., f. 183v).

PLYMPTON (Devon), St Peter and St Paul f. -909 (College); 24 Aug. 1121 (Aug.).

Lists in Oliver, pp.131–3; transcript of med. list from lost ctl. in BL, Harl. ms. 6974, f. 28r–v; Bodl., Tanner ms. 342, f. 177r; *Heads*, I, 181. It is possible that the regnal figures in the list included vacancies. If this is so, the dates of d. etc. may not be reliable.

Anthony 1214–1225 8th pr., el. 1214, ruled 10 yrs, 10 mths, 15 days (med. list). Occ. n.d. *temp.* Bp Simon of Exeter 1214–23 (Devon RO, Hole of Parke 312M/TY64); 3 May 1223 (*Reg. Grandisson*, pp. 1579, 1598). 1224 is possible for his d. but 1225 is more likely (cf. *Heads*, I, 181, n. 2).

Richard de Brugis 1225–1236 9th pr., el. 1225, ruled 10 yrs 11 mths (med. list). Occ. Easter 1228 (*CRR*, XIII, no. 519); 30 June 1228 (*Devon F.*, I, nos. 200, 232); 13 May 1233 (PRO, F. Divers Cos. CP25/1/284/18, no. 47).

Robert de Molton (Moltona) 1236–1252 10th pr., el. 1236, ruled 15½ yrs (med. list). Occ. 25

June 1238 (*Devon F.*, I, no. 274); 25 Mar. 1242 (*CChR 1257–1300*, p. 303; *CPR 1385–89*, p. 104); 20 Oct. 1245 (*Devon F.*, I, no. 447).

Baldwin 1252–1263 11th pr., el. 1252, ruled 11 yrs (med. list). D. 26 Mar. 1263 (*Reg. Bronescombe*, p. 223n; *Reg. W. Bronescombe*, I, no. 474).

Robert *dictus* Blund 1263–1272/3 12th pr., el. 1263, ruled 9 yrs (med. list). Dispute between bp and convent over eln of Robert and advowson and custody of the temps. of the priory 19–31 Aug. 1263 (*Reg. Bronescombe*, pp. 225–7; *Reg. W. Bronescombe*, II, no. 488); eln conf. 1 Nov. 1263 (*Reg. Bronescombe*, pp. 227–8; *Reg. W. Bronescombe*, II, no. 508). Occ. 13 Dec. 1267 (BL, Add. Cht. 27552); 17 June 1268 (*Devon F.*, I, no. 670).

Peter de Sancto Antonio (Antonino) **1273–1280** 13th pr., el. 1273, ruled 8 yrs (med. list). Adm. 2 Apr. 1273 (*Reg. Bronescombe*, p. 162; *Reg. W. Bronescombe*, II, no. 950, cf. Peter el. on d. of pr. Robert *temp.* John (*sic*), record of later inquisition *Cal. Misc. Inq.*, IV, 40–1). Occ. 20 May 1277 (Seymour, *Torre Abbey*, p. 261, no. 297).

Richard of Tregony 1280–1302 14th pr., el. 1280, ruled 22 yrs (med. list). Cf. record of later inquisition: On d. of pr. Peter, Richard el. *temp.* Henry III (*sic*) (*Cal. Misc. Inq.*, IV, 40–1). Attorneys apptd for 3 yrs, debility mentd 16 Apr. 1297; apptd for a further 3 yrs 22 Apr. 1301 (*CPR 1292–1301*, pp. 247, 590). On his d. *temp.* Edward I, pr. John el. (*Cal. Misc. Inq.*, IV, 40–1). Seal (*BM Seals*, no. 3847).

John de la Sturte (Sterte) **1302–1305** 15th pr., el. 1302, ruled 3 yrs (med. list).

Mathias (Matthew) de Mymmelonde (Memminglound, Mimminglond) **1305–1332** 16th pr., el. 1305, ruled 26 yrs (med. list). Occ. Mich. 1310 (PRO, CP40/183, m. 58); 19 Aug. 1312 (*CCR 1307–13*, p. 582); 1316, 1318 (*Reg. Stapeldon*, pp. 279, 242); cited to appear before pope, letter dated 22 June 1326 (*CPL*, II, 252); 7 Jan. 1329, 6 Aug. 1329, 4 June 1330 (*Reg. Grandisson*, I, 441, 522, 566). D. in office (*Cal. Misc. Inq.*, IV, no. 60).

John of Englebourne (Engleborn(e), Englebourn(e), Engleburne) **1332–1347** 17th pr., el. 23 Jan. 1332 (med. list).Can. of Plympton, pres. for conf. on d. of Mathias 28 Mar. 1332 (*Reg. Grandisson*, III, 1287). Lic. to examine eln 22 Mar. 1332, eln quashed but apptd by bp 28 Mar. 1332, mand. for induction 9 Apr. 1332 (ibid., I, 640–1, 643–4, cf. *Reg. Brantingham*, I, 183). D. on 14 Sept. 1347; lic. to el. 16 Sept. 1347; gt of custody of vacant priory 17 Sept. (*Reg. Grandisson*, II, 1031–2).

Robert (of) Forde (Ford) **1347–1364** Succ. Engleburne 'nescio quot annis' (med. list). Can. of Plympton, mand. to cite opposers to his eln 22 Oct. 1347, eln quashed, but apptd by bp 3 Nov. 1347, mand. for induction 4 Nov. 1347 (*Reg. Grandisson*, II, 1033–6; cf. *Reg. Brantingham*, I, 183). D. by 4 Dec. 1364: Robert d. while a plea was pending between the king and the priory over the advowson of the priory – the sub-pr. and convent are to hold the priory until the question should be settled in the king's court (*CFR 1356–68*, p. 299). Lic. to el. 12 May 1365, provided that Thomas Doulyssh, can. of Plympton, selected by the convent to be pr. without the king's lic., be not present or have any voice in the eln (*CPR 1364–67*, pp. 120–1).

[Thomas Doulyssh (Doulissh(e), Deulysh) El. without consent of king 12 May 1365, dep. and forbidden to take part in el. of successor (ibid.; cf. PRO, C84/29/52; *CPR 1377–81*, pp. 250–1). Bp of Exeter acc. res. of Thomas 28 May 1365 (PRO, C84/29/23).]

Ralph Person (Persona, Persone, Persoun) **1365–1378** Sub-pr. of Plympton, eln pres. to king for ass. 8 June 1365 (PRO, C84/29/24); royal ass. 15 June 1365 (*CPR 1364–67*, p. 126). Cert. of conf. of eln by bp of Bath and Wells acting on commn from the bp of Exeter 26 Oct. 1365 (PRO, C84/29/27). Temps. 4 Feb. 1366 (*CPR 1364–67*, pp. 214–15). D., lic. to el. 2 Mar. 1378 (*CPR 1377–81*, p. 121).

POUGHLEY (Berks), St Margaret f. *c.* 1160 x 1178

Lists in *VCH Berks*, II, 86; *Heads*, I, 181.

Robert Occ. *c.* 20 Apr. 1214 (*Ped. Fin.*, I, 149–50); *ante* 23 July 1222 (WAM, no. 7138).

William Occ. from [1234] (WAM no. 3865); 20 Oct. 1235 to 22 July 1248 (PRO, Berks F., CP25/1/7/11, no. 26; CP25/1/8/18, no. 62); 17 Apr. 1236 (Madox, *Form.*, p. 374); 1 Aug. 1242 (Salter, 'Priory', pp. 107–9); 29 Nov. 1242 (BL, Add. Cht. 20372, pr. unnamed in cht, but name given on seal legend); (W.) 12 May 1244 (BL, Add. Cht. 10604); (W.) 24 June 1246 (WAM nos. 8528–9). Seal (*BM Seals*, nos. 3856–7).

Robert Occ. 3 Nov. 1252 (PRO, Berks F., CP25/1/8/21, no. 4); 1253 (WAM nos. 3889, 7163); 1259 (WAM no. 7154); 23 Feb. 1261 (PRO, Berks F., CP25/1/9/25, no. 29); 25 Jan. 1267 (WAM no. 3908); 1268 (*Wilts F.*, I, 58; WAM no. 696).

James Occ. 29 Nov. 1281 (WAM no. 876); Nov. 1288 x Nov. 1289 (WAM no. 854); 28 Apr. 1292 (WAM no. 755).

Thomas Occ. n.d. (1293 x 1299) (WAM no. 7159); 1 Nov. 1297 (*Reg. Gandavo*, I, 560); 25 May 1298 (WAM no. 7204); 21 Dec. 1299 (WAM nos. 7198, 7217); 28 Jan. 1300 (WAM no. 7541).

Ivo (Yvo) –1314 Occ. 20 Dec. 1306 (WAM no. 8539); 23 Dec. 1309, 17 Apr. 1311 (*Reg. Gandavo*, I, 470, 403). Res. by 15 Feb.1314 (ibid., II, 819).

John of Lambourn 1314– Can. of Poughley, eln pres. to bp 13 Feb. 1314; eln quashed, but apptd by bp 25 Feb. 1314 (ibid., II, 818–21). Occ. Jan. 1315 (WAM nos. 805, 807); 28 Dec. 1316 (WAM no. 3894).

Thomas Ferthyng (Ferthing, Forthyng) Occ. 28 Feb. 1330 (WAM no. 1930); 1334 (WAM no. 1923); 1335 (WAM no. 7181); 25 Dec. 1341 (WAM no. 7123); n.d. (?1329 x 1341) (WAM no. 7136).

William Appleford (Apelford, Appelford) Occ. 23 July 1346 (WAM no. 761); 25 Dec. 1347 (WAM no. 7080); 12 Jan. 1348 – order not to restrain the pr. as the prince has received his fealty (*Reg. Black Prince*, I, 162).

Ralph de Pesmere 1348– Can. of Poughley, eln conf. 24 June 1348, no reason given for vacancy (Salisbury, Reg. Wyvil, II, f. 185v).

Geoffrey Foy Occ. 11 Apr. 1350 (PRO, E40/4720); fealty to Prince of Wales 15 June 1352 (*Reg. Black Prince*, IV, 53); 1355, 1365 (WAM nos. 781–2, 902); 25 Mar. 1375 (*Hearne's Coll.*, VII, 157); 11 Mar. 1381 (*Goring Chts.*, p. 258, no. 350).

The next recorded pr., **John**, occ. 12 May 1402 (WAM no. 7205).

PUFFIN ISLAND (Gwynedd, Anglesey) (Cell of Penmon) (Priestholme, Ynys Lannog, Ynys Seiriol) f. 1237 x 1414 (Augustinian)

Gervase de Perrouse Occ. 1303 [Feb. x Apr.] mandate to bp of Bangor to enquire into charges made against him by 2 of his canons. (*Reg. Winchelsey*, II, 776).

The next recorded pr., **John**, occ. 1 July 1379 (PRO, E179/3/2). He may possibly be the same as **John de Castell** who had res. by 21 May 1414 (PRO, C84/40/39).

PYNHAM BY ARUNDEL (Sussex), St Bartholomew (Cauce, Chauces, de Calceto, La Chauce) f. -1151

List in *VCH Sussex*, II, 80–1.

Ivo Occ. 30 Nov. 1229, 6 Dec. 1229, 20 Jan. 1230 (*Sussex F.*, I, nos. 232, 242, 251); n.d. (*Ctl. Chichester*, no. 669).

Stephen Occ. 6 Oct. 1253 (*Sussex F.*, II, no. 531).

Thomas Occ. *c.* 1270 x 1280 (*Cal. Bodl. Chts.*, p. 579, Sussex Cht. 49); 1285 (ibid., p. 579, Sussex Cht. 60).

William Occ. Hil. 1324–Easter 1325 (PRO, Just.1/938/1, mm. 19, 21, 22).

Henry Occ. 1346, 14 Sept. 1356 (*Cal. Bodl. Chts.*, p. 578, Sussex Chts. 67, 64).[37]

---

[37] *VCH*, following *Hist. Shulbrede*, pp. 78–9, states that in or before 1355 Robert Coytar was dep. as pr. of Pynham and sent to Shulbrede to do penance, citing Lambeth, Reg. Islip, ff. 101v–102r. The original entry in Islip's register does not in fact describe Robert as former pr., merely can. of Pynham.

John Occ. 8 Sept. 1376 (ibid., Sussex Cht. 69); 1381 (PRO, E179/11/9).

RANTON (Staffs), St Mary (de Essarz, de Sartis, Ronton) f. -1166 (dependent on Haughmond); 1246 x 7 (independent).
  Lists in *VCH Staffs*, III, 254; *Heads*, I, 181.
Alfred Occ. (A.) *c.* 1220 or + (*Ctl. Staffs 2*, pp. 210–11); 22 Sept. 1221 (*Warws F.*, I, no. 235); 1221 (*Ctl. Ranton*, p. 295); 1240 (ibid., p. 281); 1 Dec. 1240 (*Staffs F. 2*, p. 236); 13 Feb. 1247 (*Magnum Reg. Album Lichfield*, no. 106; *Ctl. Haughmond*, no. 946).
Philip of Chester (Cestria) Can. of Ranton, letter from R. de Narecurt, patron, to Roger, bp of Coventry and Lichfield (1245–56 *or* 1258–95) requesting him to conf. appt of Philip as pr. n.d. (BL, Cotton Cht. V 65).
Gilbert Occ. 1253, 1255 (*Ctl. Ranton*, pp. 293, 271); (G.) 1267 (BL, Cotton ms. Vespasian C XV, f. 39r); n.d. (mid 13th cent.) (Staffs RO, D798/1/1/6).
Thomas Occ. 13 Feb. 1272 (*Magnum Reg. Album Lichfield*, no. 503); 1 Aug. 1274, 1275, 24 Aug. 1279 (*Ctl. Ranton*, pp. 270, 284, 280).
John Occ. 9 Nov. 1284 (*Staffs Plea Rolls 1360–87*, p. 185).
Thomas of Evesham Occ. 1293 (*Staffs Plea Rolls 1272–94*, pp. 217, 231, 233); 2 Apr. 1293, 13 Mar. 1298, 26 Sept. 1298 (*Ctl. Ranton*, pp. 276, 278); 7 Sept. 1299 (*Staffs Plea Rolls 1294–1307*, p. 60).
Henry de Tywe Occ. 24 Aug. 1301 (*Ctl. Ranton*, p. 285); 5 Apr. 1313 (*Magnum Reg. Album Lichfield*, no. 484); n.d. (*Ctl. Ranton*, p. 270).
Robert of Bradley (Bradel(e)) **1326–** Can. of Ranton, eln quashed, but apptd by bp 21 June 1326, no reason given for vacancy (Lichfield, B/A/1/2, ff. 141v–142r).
Richard de Mul(e)wych (Mulewyk) **1349–1359** Can. of Ranton, commn to examine eln 9 Apr. 1349, no reason given for vacancy; eln conf. 13 Aug. 1349 (ibid., f. 187r). Occ. 28 Jan. 1351; 20 Sept. 1351 (*Ctl. Ranton*, p. 273); 1356 (Staffs RO, D3764/12). D. by 13 Nov. 1359 (*Reg. Stretton*, I, 13).
John Harecourt **1359–** Can. of Ranton, eln conf. 13 Nov. 1359 (ibid.). Occ. 21 Nov. 1360 (ibid., 105).
John of Eccleshall (Eccleshale, Ecclissale) **–1380** Occ. Mich. term 1372 (*Staffs Plea Rolls 1360–87*, p. 95); 1373 (ibid., 101); 1376 (*SHC*, XIV, 141). D. by 20 June 1380 (*Reg. Stretton*, II, 149).

RATLINGHOPE (Salop), St Margaret Victorine f. -1200; -1209 (cell of Wigmore)
  List in *VCH Salop*, II, 80.
Roger Occ. 1256, 1262 (Eyton, *Salop*, VI, 162, citing Forest Assize of 1262 – pr. Roger had taken one of the king's deer 7 Dec. 1256).

RAVENSTONE (Bucks), St Mary f. 1254 x 1255
  List in *VCH Bucks*, I, 381–2.
William de Divisis **1255–1271** request to bp of Lincoln to adm. William to the priory, newly founded by the king, 16 June 1255 (*CPR 1247–58*, p. 413). Notification to bp H(enry) of Lincoln of the appt of John de Chishull as the king's proctor in all that concerns the priory, recently founded – his presn thereto of William de Divisis 9 Sept. 1255 (ibid., p. 441). His recent cess. mentd 15 Aug. 1271 (*CR 1268–72*, p. 370). Res., lic. to el. 11 Aug. 1271 (*CPR 1266–72*, p. 568, cf. *Reg. R. Gravesend*, p. 247).
Adam of Wymondley (Wilemundele, Wymundele) **1271–1275** Can. of Dunstable, royal ass. 28 Aug. 1271 (*CPR 1266–72*, p. 572). Eln quashed but apptd by bp's vicegerent 2 Sept. 1271 on res. of W. (*Reg. R. Gravesend*, p. 247). Res. by 27 Jan. 1275 (PRO, C84/5/23). Res., lic. to el. 5 Feb. 1275 (*CPR 1272–81*, p. 78).

Ralph of Ravenstone (Raviniston) **1275–1285** Can. of Ravenstone, el. 1 Mar. 1275 (PRO, C84/6/25); royal ass. 9 Mar. 1275, writ *de intendendo* 16 Mar. 1275 (*CPR 1272–81*, p. 83). Eln conf. 9 Mar. 1275 on res. of unnamed pr. (*Reg. R. Gravesend*, pp. 253, 345). Cess., lic. to el. 8 Feb. 1285 (*CPR 1281–92*, p. 154). Seal (*BM Seals*, no. 3879).

John de Beneton 1285–1309 Can. of Caldwell, royal ass. 26 Mar. 1285 (*CPR 1281–92*, p. 155). D. by 24 Feb. 1309 (PRO, C84/16/16). D. (J.), lic. to el. 27 Feb. 1309 (*CPR 1307–13*, p. 100, cf. Lincoln, Ep. Reg., II, f. 182r).

Roger de Clere 1309–1324 Can. of Ravenstone, el. 23 Apr. 1309 (PRO, C84/16/20); royal ass. 27 Apr. 1309, writ *de intendendo* 27 May 1309 (*CPR 1307–13*, pp. 111, 116). Commn to examine eln (no name) 1 Apr. 1309 (Lincoln, Ep. Reg., III, f. 151v). Eln conf. 15 May 1309 (Lincoln, Ep. Reg., II, f. 182r; PRO, C84/16/22). D. by 4 Mar. 1324 (PRO, C84/20/25). D., lic. to el. 10 Mar. 1324 (*CPR 1321–24*, pp. 392, 394). Mentioned 16 Mar. 1324 as recently dead (*Cal. Chanc. Warr.*, p. 552).

William Aubel 1324–1328 Eln pres. to king 16 Mar. 1324, mand. for letters of ass. 21 Mar. (*Cal. Chanc. Warr.*, p. 552). Cellarer of Ravenstone, royal ass. 21 Mar. 1324, temps. 27 Apr. 1324 (*CPR 1321–24*, pp. 398, 408). Eln pres. to bp 23 Apr. 1324 on d. of Roger; eln renounced by priory and William apptd by bp 23 Apr. (Lincoln, Ep. Reg., IV, ff. 330v–331r). Bp of Lincoln reports appt of William; 24 Apr.; mand. for royal letters (*Cal. Chanc. Warr.*, p. 554). House void by 25 Oct. 1328 (*CCR 1327–30*, p. 345). D., lic. to el. 27 Oct. 1328 (*CPR 1327–30*, p. 325).

Robert of Yardley (Yerdele) *alias* **Maunsel** (Mauncel) **1328–1349** Sub-cellarer of Ravenstone, eln pres. to king for royal ass. 9 Nov. 1328 (PRO, C84/22/12). Eln conf. 7 Dec. 1328 (Lincoln, Ep. Reg., IV, ff. 335v–336r). Royal ass. 8 Dec. 1328, temps. 10 Dec. 1328 (*CPR 1327–30*, pp. 341, 339). Pr. mentd as pres. an incumbent at an instn of 1 July 1349 (Lincoln, Ep. Reg., IX, f. 283v). D., lic. to el. 16 Aug. 1349 (*CPR 1348–50*, p. 355).

Gilbert of Molesworth (Mollesworth, Molseworth) **1349–1363** Can. of Ravenstone, royal ass. 25 Aug. 1349, temps. 9 Oct. 1349 (ibid., pp. 362, 395). Res. 14 Feb. 1363 (PRO, C84/29/6). Res., lic. to el. 8 May 1363 (*CPR 1361–64*, p. 332).

John Jerdele –1397 D. by 8 Dec. 1397 (PRO, C84/37/5). D., lic. to el. 10 Dec. 1397 (*CPR 1396–99*, p. 266).

REIGATE (Surrey) St Mary and Holy Cross f. +1217

List in *VCH Surrey*, II, 107.

Adam Occ. *c.* 1298 (Cox, *Mag. Brit.*, V, 448, no source given).

Richard of Froyle (Froille) **–1309** Occ. as *custos* Mich. 1305 (PRO, CP40/153, m. 473d). Res. (R.) 15 Mar. 1309 and lic. to el. (*Reg. Woodlock*, II, 348). Order to the new pr. to seal a maintenance provision 22 Nov. 1309 (ibid., 396–7); provision to be made for him 11 Dec. 1310 (ibid., 505).

Walter de Timberdene (Tymberden(e)) **1309–1337** Can. of Reigate, eln conf. 11 May 1309 (ibid., II, 731, cf. I, 373). D. by 20 Sept. 1337 (Winchester, Reg. Orleton I, ff. 65v–66r).

John atte Breth(e) 1337–1341 Can. of Reigate, eln quashed but apptd by bp of Winchester 20 Sept. 1337 (ibid). Cess. by 3 Mar. 1341 (ibid., ff. 101v–102r).

John de (la) Pyrie (Pirie) **1341–** Can. of Reigate, eln quashed and apptd by bp of Winchester 3 Mar. 1341 (ibid.). Occ. 13 Oct. and 25 Oct. 1344 (*Reg. Edington*, II, no. 84).

Robert of Scotney (Scoteney(e)) **1349–1367** Can. of Tandridge, apptd by bp of Winchester *per lapsum* 2 Aug. 1349, no reason given for vacancy (ibid., I, no. 644). Res. by 9 Dec. 1367 (*Reg. Wykeham*, I, 11–12).

John Kente 1367–1374 Can. of 'Heryngham', commissary to conduct proceedings 20 Dec. (*recte* Nov.) 1367; convent ask bp of Winchester to choose a successor, coll. 9 Dec. 1367 (ibid). D. by 18 Nov. 1374 (ibid., 55).

Richard Warnham 1374–1395 Can. of Reigate, el. 18 Nov., commissary quashed eln and apptd him 20 Nov. 1374 (ibid., 54–8). D. 31 May 1395 (ibid., 198).

REPTON (Derbys), Holy Trinity and St Wistan (formerly St Giles and St Wistan, Calke) f. 1130 x 1136 (at Calke); c. 1153 x 1160 (at Repton, but the main transfer took place in 1272). Lists in *VCH Derbys*, II, 62–3; *Heads*, I, 182.

Richard Occ. 15 Nov. 1208 (*Derbys F.* (1885), p. 205); (R.) 23 Jan. 1215 x 14 June 1216 (*Cheshire Chts.*, p. 23).

N. Occ. 1215 x 1223 (*Derbys Chts.*, no. 1681).

John Occ. 1218 x 21 (ibid., no. 2572); 1218 x 1223 (*Burton Chts.*, p. 33); 31 May 1220 (*Derbys F. (1885)*, p. 214); 17 May 1226 (ibid. *(1886)*, p. 16); 6 Oct. 1226 (PRO, Notts F., CP25/1/182/4, no. 85; *HMC R.R. Hastings*, I, 128).

Reginald Occ. n.d. (*c.* 1230) (BL, Woolley Cht. X 34; *Derbys Chts.*, nos. 1755–6); 29 Sept. 1236 (PRO, Notts F. CP25/1/182/6, no. 197); 10 Aug. 1243 (*Ctl. Burton*, no. 99); Oct. 1244 x Oct. 1245 (*Hunts F.*, p. 21).

Peter Occ. 20 Jan. 1247 (PRO, Notts F. CP25/1/182/9, no. 344; *HMC R.R. Hastings*, I, 130); 1252 (*Derbys F. (1886)*, p. 62); 1252 (BL, Stowe Cht. no. 145; *Derbys Chts.*, no. 2582); 8 July 1260 (*Derbys F. (1889)*, p. 93). Seal (*Mon. Seals*, p. 76).

Richard de Smytherby Occ. 26 July 1268 (*HMC R.R. Hastings*, I, 105); n.d. (mid-late 13th cent.) (ibid., 131). Mentd in 1335 as pr. of Repton who d. *temp.* Devorguilla de Balliol (*Cal. Misc. Inq.*, II, 372). Devorguilla succ. her sister in 1246, married John de Balliol (d. 1268) and d. 1290 (*English Baronies*, p. 119). The precise sequence of priors is unclear.

Robert of Staunton Occ. 26 Oct. 1289 (*Derbys Chts.*, no. 1964; BL, Stowe Cht. no. 162). Priory vac. by his d. *temp.* Edward I, before John de Balliol's forfeiture (1296) (*CCR 1333–37*, p. 624). Mentd 25 Oct. 1336 as former pr. (*CPR 1340–43*, p. 391).

Ralph of Ticknall (Tykenhale, Tykenhall) –1336[38] El. on d. of Robert de Staunton *ante* 1296 (*CCR 1333–37*, p. 624). Occ. 1327, 1328 (*Index to Placita de Banco*, pp. 79, 87). 1330 accused of receiving a stolen horse (PRO, Just.1/169, m. 42d). D. 1 Oct. 1336 (*CFR 1327–37*, p.. 497). D., lic. to el. 5 Oct. 1336 (*CPR 1334–38*, p. 324).

John of Lichfield (Lich(e), Lichefeld, Lych', Lychfeld) **1336–1346** Can. of Repton, royal ass. 16 Oct. 1336 (ibid., p. 325). Eln quashed, but apptd by bp 25 Oct. 1336 (Lichfield, B/A/1/2, f. 74r–v). D. by 22 June 1346 (*CFR 1337–47*, p. 473). D., lic. to el. 1 July 1346 (*CPR 1345–48*, p. 132).

Simon of Sutton 1346–1356 Can. of Repton, eln pres. to king for royal ass. 27 July 1346 (PRO, C84/25/4); royal ass. 1 Aug. 1346, temps. 4 Sept. 1346 (*CPR 1345–48*, pp. 155, 164–5, 409). Eln conf. 25 Aug. 1346 (Lichfield, B/A/1/2, f. 82r–v). D., lic. to el. 10 Feb. 1356 (*CPR 1354–58*, p. 344).

Ralph of Derby 1356–1399 Sub-pr. of Repton, eln pres. to king for royal ass. 9 Mar. 1356 (PRO, C84/27/29). Commn to examine eln 11 Mar. 1356; eln conf. 28 Mar. 1356 and king notified 30 Mar. 1356 (Lichfield, B/A/1/2, f. 95r–v). Sub-pr. of Repton, royal ass. 14 Mar. 1356, temps. 9 Apr. 1356 (*CPR 1354–58*, pp. 346, 362). D. by 16 June 1399 (PRO, C84/37/44). D., lic. to el. 26 June 1399 (*CPR 1396–99*, p. 589). Seal (*Mon. Seals*, p. 76).

ROCESTER (Staffs), St Mary f. *c.* 1146 (abbey)
Lists in *VCH Staffs*, III, 251; *Heads*, I, 182.

W. Occ. 1215 x 1223 (*Ctl. Dieulacres*, p. 311); 1216 (*Ctl. Staffs 3*, p. 425).

---

[38] BL., Harl. ms. 6959, f. 101, refers to Ralph's appt in 1316, citing rolls in the Tower of London, but no ment. has been found in *CPR* etc.

House vacant by 24 May 1233 (*CR 1231–34*, p. 220). An unnamed abb. d. 1234 (*Ann. Dunstable*, p. 139).

Philip –**1256** Occ. ?early Henry III (*Ctl. Stone*, pp. 1, 17); 8 Jan. 1235 (*CR 1234–37*, p. 160); 1233 x 1238 (*Ctl. Stafford*, p. 156); 1240 (*Ctl. Staffs 3*, p. 425); 18 Oct. 1251 (PRO, F. Various Counties, CP25/1/284/19, no. 99). D. 1256 (*Ann. Burton*, p. 376). Lic. to el. (no reason given for vacancy) 29 June 1256 (*CPR 1247–58*, p. 485).

Richard 1256–1257/8 Can. of Rocester, eln pres. to king for royal ass. 6 July 1256 (PRO, C84/1/42); royal ass. 16 July 1256, writ *de intendendo* 31 July 1256 (*CPR 1247–58*, pp. 488, 490). Succ. 1256 (*Ann. Burton*, p. 376). D. 1257 (ibid., p. 409). Lic. to el. (no reason given for vacancy) 18 Jan. 1258 (*CPR 1247–58*, p. 613).

Walter 1258–1269 Pr. of Rocester, royal ass. 4 Feb. 1258, writ *de intendendo* 4 Mar. 1258 (ibid., pp. 614, 618). Occ. 2 Mar. 1269 (*CPR 1266–72*, p. 323). Res. by 28 July 1269 (ibid., pp. 360–1).

Walter de Dodlegh (Dodele) **1269–1285** Can. of Rocester, royal ass. 3 Oct. 1269, writ *de intendendo* 8 Oct. 1269, the eln having been conf. by R., bp of Coventry and Lichfield (ibid., pp. 367, 368). Cess., lic. to el. 15 Dec. 1285 (*CPR 1281–92*, p. 214).

Robert 1286–1289 Pr. of Church Gresley, preferred by R., bp of Coventry and Lichfield, temps. 16 Feb. 1286 (ibid., p. 221). D. by 29 Jan. 1289 (PRO, C84/9/21). D., lic. to el. 12 Feb. 1289 (*CPR 1281–92*, p. 312).

Roger of Loughborough (Lughteburgh) **1289–1316** Can. of Rocester, eln pres. to king for royal ass.19 Mar. 1289 (PRO, C84/9/30); writ *de intendendo* 20 Mar. 1289 (ibid., p. 314). Res., lic. to el. 7 Dec. 1316 (*CPR 1313–17*, p. 569).

Walter of Aston 1316–1324 Can. of Rocester, eln pres. to king for royal ass. 21 Dec. 1316 (PRO, C84/19/5); royal ass. 29 Dec. 1316, temps. 1 Feb. 1317 (*CPR 1313–17*, pp. 603, 616). D., lic. to el. 17 Apr. 1324 (*CPR 1321–24*, p. 406; cf. Lichfield, B/A/1/2, ff. 139v–140r).

Gilbert de Bosco 1324–1334 Can. of Rocester, royal ass. 6 May 1324 temps. 23 May 1324 (*CPR 1321–24*, pp. 410, 416). Eln conf. 18 May 1324 (Lichfield, B/A/1/2, ff. 139v–140r). Res/ by 16 Dec. 1334 (PRO, C84/23/23). Cess., lic. to el. 27 Jan. 1335 (*CPR 1334–38*, pp. 54–5), but cf. house void by d. of Gilbert de Bosco by 20 May 1335 (ibid., p. 86; Lichfield, B/A/1/2, f. 158r).

Henry of Hopton 1335–1349 Can. of Rocester, eln pres. to king for royal ass. 27 Dec. 1334 (PRO, C84/23/26); royal ass. 19 [*sic*] Jan. 1335, temps. 25 May 1335 (*CPR 1334–38*, pp. 56, 103). Right of appt transferred to bp and he apptd Henry 20 May 1335 (Lichfield, B/A/1/2, f. 158r; PRO, C84/23/33). D. by 14 Aug. 1349 (PRO, C84/26/9). D., lic. to el. 21 Aug. 1349 (*CPR 1348–50*, p. 368; cf. Lichfield, B/A/1/2, f. 186r).

William of Cheadle (Chedle) **1349–1364** Can. of Rocester, temps. 21 Oct. 1349 (*CPR 1348–50*, p. 413). Right of appt transferred to bp and he apptd William 16 Oct. 1349 (Lichfield, B/A/1/2, f. 186r). D. 13 Nov. 1364 (BL, Add. ms. 6165, f. 55r). D., lic. to el. 18 Nov. 1364 (*CPR 1364–67*, p. 38).

Thomas of Rocester (Roucestre) **1364–1375** Can. of Rocester, temps 21 Dec. 1364 (*CPR 1364–67*, pp. 53–4). D., lic. to el. 8 Mar. 1375 (*CPR 1374–77*, p. 80).

John of Cheswardine (Chesewardyn, Ches(e)worthyn) **1375–1386** Can. of Ranton, now vicar of Seighford, eln pres. to king for royal ass. 11 Apr. 1375 (PRO, C84/31/22); royal ass. 1 June 1375, temps. 28 June 1375 (*CPR 1374–77*, pp. 113, 120). Eln conf. 22 June 1375 (*Reg. Stretton*, I, 141; PRO, C84/31/30). Pardon 12 Dec. 1385 to John Chesewardyn of the felonies whereof he is indicted and of outlawry, in consideration of his having been driven from the abbey and the county by evil-doers, who got him indicted so as to make him res. and el. another in his place, and are also lying in wait night and day to kill him because he has complained to the king (*CPR 1385–89*, pp. 71–2). Res. by 30 July 1386 (PRO, C84/34/2). Res., lic. to el. 8 Aug. 1386 (*CPR 1385–89*, p. 193).

ROSELAND, *see* ST ANTHONY IN ROSELAND

ROYSTON (Herts), St John the Baptist and St Thomas Becket (de Cruce Roisia) f. 1173 x 1179

Lists in *VCH Herts*, IV, 440; *Heads*, I, 182.

William Occ. (W.) Oct. 1229 (*CR 1227–31*, p. 225); 20 Jan. 1230 (PRO, Herts F. CP25/1/84/13, no. 150). Seal (*Hereford Seals*, p. 7).

Osbert Occ. Oct. 1247 x Oct. 1248 (*Hunts F.*, p. 25); (O.) June 1248 x June 1249 (*Reg. Grosseteste*, p. 105); 25 May 1253 (PRO, Cambs F., CP25/1/24/29, no. 9); 28 Oct. 1254 (*CPR 1247–58*, p. 378); 1262 (PRO, E40/14415); Trin. 1263 (*Essex F.*, I, 259).

Laurence Occ. 13 Oct. 1278 (PRO, Lincs F., CP25/1/132/52, no. 25).

Richard de Leccinton Occ. (R.) n.d. (?1279) (PRO, SC1/8/96); 1290 (PRO, E368/62, m. 6d); Nov. 1293 x Nov. 1294 (*Suffolk F. (Rye)*, p. 98). Mentd 8 Apr. 1298 as former pr. (*CPR 1292–1301*, p. 377).

Thomas Occ. 9 Apr. 1302, 29 Dec. 1302 (*Cal. Chanc. Warr.*, pp. 163, 168); 11 May 1302 (*CCR 1296–1302*, p. 553); 5 May 1303 (PRO, Herts F., CP25/1/87/48, no. 373); Mich. 1305 (PRO, CP40/153, m. 85).

Geoffrey Hakoun –1314 Occ. 10 Apr. 1313 (*Reg. Baldock*, p. 175). Res. by 24 Oct. 1314 (PRO, C84/17/43). Res., lic. to el. 5 Nov. 1314 (*CPR 1313–17*, p. 195).

John de Broome (Brome) 1314– Can. of Colchester, St Botolph, eln pres. to king for royal ass. 27 Nov. 1314 (PRO, C84/17/44); royal ass. 6 Dec. 1314, temps 4 Jan. 1315 (*CPR 1313–17*, pp. 202, 209). Cert. conf. eln by bp of London 23 Dec. 1314 (PRO, C84/18/1). Occ. Easter 1317 (PRO, CP40/218, attorneys m. 6).

John de Beauchamp Occ. 11 Dec. 1339 (BL, Add. Cht. 44502).

Thomas Occ. 1346 (*FA*, V, 53).

John (de) Arniburgh (Arneburgh) –1369 Occ. 3 July 1351 (*Cal. Misc. Inq.*, III, 39); 20 July 1351 (*CFR 1347–56*, p. 331); 1354 (BL, Add. ms. 5843, f. 120r); 1361 (*CPR 1361–64*, p. 40); 1362 (*CCR 1360–64*, p. 408). D. 25 July 1369 and bur. 30 July (*Reg. Sudbury*, I, 103–4). D., lic. to el. 6 Aug. 1369 (*CPR 1367–70*, p. 298).

John West 1369–?1378 Sub-pr. of Royston, eln pres. to king for royal ass. 11 Aug. 1369 (PRO, C84/30/10); royal ass. 13 Aug. 1369 (*CPR 1367–70*, p. 298; *Reg. Sudbury*, I, 101). El. 9 Aug. 1369 (ibid., I, 103–9); commn to examine eln 14 Aug., cert. 17 Aug. (ibid., 102–3); eln conf. 18 Aug. 1369 (ibid., 109). Letter of sub-pr. and convent to Edmund Mortimer, earl of March, asking for lic. to el. 12 Apr. 1378 (BL, Add. ms. 6041, f. 94v, no. lxviii); letter to the same asking him to adm. the eln of a new unnamed pr. 25 Apr. 1378 (ibid., f. 94v, no. lxix).

ST ANTHONY IN ROSELAND (Cornwall) (cell of Plympton) f. -1288; diss. 1538

No priors found named until **James Davy** in 1443 (*JRIC*, new ser., 2(3) (1955), 23).

ST DENYS (Hants) f. 1127

Lists in *VCH Hants*, II, 163–4; *Ctl. St Denys*, p. xix; *Heads*, I, 182–3.

Alard Occ. n.d. (1202 x 1215) (*Ctl. God's House*, p. 81); 21 Feb. 1211 (*Ctl. St Denys*, I, p. xx, n. 5). House void by 28 Nov. 1215 (*Rot. Lit. Claus.*, p. 239; *Ctl. St Denys*, I, p. xx, n. 6).

Walkelin 1220–?1233 Can. of S. Denys, royal ass. 10 Mar. 1220 (*CPR 1216–25*, p. 230). Occ. 7 Oct. 1228 (*Ctl. St Denys*, II, no. 329). Lic. to el. (no reason given for vacancy) 20 Aug. 1233 (*CPR 1232–47*, p. 24).

Rowland (Ruel, Rueland, Rothuland) 1233–1252 Can. of St Denys, royal ass. 12 Sept. 1233 (ibid., p. 25). Res. (R.) by 24 Sept. 1252 (*CPR 1247–58*, p. 151). Lic. to el. (no reason given for vacancy) 26 Sept. 1252 (ibid.).

William le Angele 1252 Can. of St Denys, royal ass. 9 Oct. 1252 (ibid., p. 152). D., lic. to el. (no reason given for vacancy) 27 Oct. 1252 (ibid., p. 155).

Nicholas of Hampton 1252–1280 Can. of St Denys, royal ass. 19 Nov. 1252 (ibid., p. 165). Cert. of conf. of eln by bp-el. of Winchester [ ] Nov. 1252 (before 25 Nov.) (PRO, C84/1/32). Occ. 19 Feb. 1280 (*Ctl. St Denys*, I, no. 114). Res. by 4 July 1280 (PRO, C84/6/45). Res., lic. to el. 14 July 1280 (*CPR 1272–81*, p. 388).

Henry de Hamelton (Hameledon) **1280–1294** Can. of St Denys, el. 17 July 1280 (PRO, C84/6/46); royal ass. 20 July 1280, writ *de intendendo* 8 Aug. 1280 (*CPR 1272–81*, pp. 390, 394). Cert. of conf. of eln by archbp of Canterbury *sede vacante* 6 Aug. 1280 (PRO, C84/6/49). Cess., lic. to el. 16 Aug. (*CPR 1292–1301*, p. 84). Res. acc. 18 Aug. 1294 (*Reg. Pontissara*, I, 64; PRO, C84/12/114, 16).

Richard of Chacombe (Chacumbe, Chaucombe) **1294–1314** Eln pres. to king for royal ass. 20 Aug. 1294 (PRO, C84/12/17); royal ass. (Robert) 21 Aug. 1294, temps. (Richard) 23 Aug. 1294 (*CPR 1292–1301*, p. 84; *Reg. Pontissara*, I, 65). Notif. of bp's conf. and mand. to induct 22 Aug. 1294 (ibid., 64–5; PRO, C84/12/18). Attorney apptd by reason of pr.'s weakness 28 Jan. 1298 (*CPR 1292–1301*, p. 328); similar appt 26 Sept. 1300 (ibid., p. 537). Res. by 5 Jan. 1314 (PRO, C84/17/30). Cess., lic. to el. 8 Jan. 1314 (*CPR 1313–17*, p. 78).

Robert of Stoneham (Stonham) **1314–1328** Cellarer of St Denys, eln pres. to king for royal ass. 18 Jan. 1314 (PRO, C84/17/31); royal ass. 23 Jan. 1314, temps. 22 Feb. 1314 (*CPR 1313–17*, pp. 79, 88). Cert. conf. eln by bp of Winchester 5 Feb. 1314 (PRO, C84/17/32). House void by 8 Mar. 1328 (*CFR 1327–37*, p. 85). Res., lic. to el. 9 Mar. 1328 (*CPR 1327–30*, p. 251).

Thomas of Newton 1328 Can. of St Denys, eln pres. to king for royal ass. 5 Apr. 1328 (PRO, C84/22/5); royal ass. 12 Apr. 1328 (*CPR 1327–30*, p. 256). 13 May 1328 custody of priory gtd to the sub-pr. and convent (ibid., p. 269). Commn to examine eln 14 May 1328; further commn 11 June; Thomas renounced eln and sub-pr. and convent transferred the right of appt to the bp 28 June 1328 (Winchester, Reg. Stratford, ff. 108v–110r).

William de Warham 1328–1349 Can. of St Denys, apptd by bp 13 July 1328, letter to convent to obey 26 July (Winchester, Reg. Stratford, ff. 109v–110r; PRO, C84/22/10). Temps. 20 July 1328 (*CPR 1327–30*, p. 307). Papal disp. for illegitimacy 11 Sept. 1328 (but desc. as can. of St Denys) (*CPL*, II, 282). D. by 12 Feb. 1349 (PRO, C84/25/23). D., lic. to el. 13 Feb. 1349 (*CPR 1348–50*, p. 255).

Richard (de) Staunford (Standforde, Staunfeld, Staunton) **1349–1391** Can. of St Denys, commn to examine eln 28 Feb. 1349 (*Reg. Edington*, I, no. 431). Temps. 10 Mar. 1349 (*CPR 1348–50*, p. 265). John Staunforde, can. of St Denys, apptd coadjutor 14 Mar. 1382 (*Reg. Wykeham*, II, 335). D. by 7 Mar. 1391 (PRO, C84/35/2). D., lic. to el. 8 Mar. 1391 (*CPR 1388–92*, p. 382). Seal (*Mon. Seals*, p. 82).

ST FRIDESWIDE, *see* OXFORD, ST FRIDESWIDE

ST GERMANS (Cornwall) f. -1184

List in *Heads*, I, 183.

Auger Last recorded occ. 8 July 1202 (*EEA*, 12, no. 208).

Alvred Occ. as Auger's successor Trin. term 1224 (*CRR*, XI, no. 1680); (A.) 1225 (*Ctl. Launceston*, no. 533).

Godfrey Occ. 17 June 1230 (*Cornwall F.*, I, p. 23, no. 49).

Henry Occ. 18 Apr. 1244 (ibid., p. 43, no. 88).

Godfrey Occ. 25 June 1245 (ibid., p. 54 no. 110).

Richard –1279 Recently dead 11 Aug. 1279; excommunication of those disturbing the bp's officers in the vacancy (*Reg. Bronescombe*, pp. 247–8; *Reg. W. Bronescombe*, II, no. 1342).

Geoffrey 1280– Can. of St Germans, eln conf. 16 Mar. 1280 (*Reg. Bronescombe*, p. 248; *Reg. W. Bronescombe*, II, no. 1406).

Henry Occ. 16 July 1293 (*Ctl. Launceston*, no. 36); Trin. 1297 (PRO, CP40/119, m. 153d); Mich. 1305 (PRO, CP40/153, m. 109); 31 Aug. 1315 (*Reg. Stapeldon*, p. 331). Mentd in 1357 as former pr. *temp.* Edward II (*CPR 1354–58*, p. 637; *Reg. Black Prince*, II, 114).

Richard Occ. n.d. [1332 x 1333] (PRO, C270/11/17).

Bp appts custodians of vacant priory 14 Sept. 1341 (no reason given for vacancy); lic. to el. 20 Sept. (*Reg. Grandisson*, II, 950).

Richard Michael Occ. 8 Oct. 1341 (*Reg. Grandisson*, II, 971). Mentd in 1357 as former pr. (*Reg. Black Prince*, II, 114).

Richard (de) Polgover **–1355** Occ. 17 Mar. 1342 (*Reg. Grandisson*, II, 954); 21 July 1343 (*CPR 1343–45*, p. 110). Said to have d. 14 Aug. 1355, but *recte* 7 Aug. (Friday before rather than after St Laurence – scribal error); bur. 12 Aug. 1355 (*Reg. Grandisson*, II, 1168–9). Lic. to el. 8 Aug. 1355 and appt of custodians of vacant priory (ibid., 1162–3). Mentd in 1357 as former pr. (*Reg. Black Prince*, II, 114).

John Prechour 1355–1367 Sub-pr. of St Germans, el. 14 Aug. 1355; bp conf. eln and mand. to induct 27 Aug.; ind. 3 Sept. (*Reg. Grandisson*, II, 1166–73). D. by 22 Jan. 1367 (PRO, C84/29/38). D., lic. to el. 8 Feb. 1367 (*CPR 1364–67*, p. 376).

William (de) Treskelly 1367–1385 Can. of St Germans, royal ass. 16 Mar. 1367, temps. 7 May 1367, having been conf. by bp of Exeter (ibid., pp. 385, 388). 28 Aug. 1377 Commn to appt co-adjutor because William was blind and old (*Reg. Brantingham*, I, 382–3). Commn to remove John Avery, can. of St Germans, whom pr. William had chosen as co-adjutor and to appt another can. in his place 16 Nov. 1379; mand. to take oath from br. Richard Harepathe, chosen as co-adjutor 26 Dec. 1379 (ibid., 410, 414). Bp writes to Harepathe the co-adjutor. During his visitation the bp has forbidden pr. William admin. of the temps.; provision of £10 a year made for pr. to be paid by co-adjutor, 9 June 1381 (ibid., 447). Res., lic. to el. 20 Aug. 1385 (ibid., II, 586–7).

ST OLAVE'S, *see* HERRINGFLEET

ST OSYTH (Essex), St Peter and St Paul and St Osyth f. 1121 (priory); –1161 (abbey).

Lists in *VCH Essex*, II, 162; *Heads*, I, 183; Walcott's list in *TEAS*, V, 13–14.

David Occ. 1207 x 1221 (*Ctl. Lewes*, II, 119); 11 Jan. 1221 (*Ctl. Colchester*, II, 532 ff.); 26 Oct. 1221 (*Waltham Chts.*, no. 262); 1227 (PRO, Just.1/229, m. 7); Hil. term 1229 (*CRR*, XIII, no. 1311); from 4 May 1229 to Easter 1244 (*Essex F.*, I, 83, 147); Oct. 1242 x Oct. 1243 (*Suffolk F. (Rye)*, p. 46); 28 Jan. 1247 (*Ctl. Blythburgh*, I, no. 1).

Henry **–?1272/3** Occ. Trin 1256, Hil. 1261 (*Essex F.*, I, 214, 239); Oct. 1257 x Oct. 1258, Oct. 1262 x Oct. 1263 (*Suffolk F. (Rye)*, pp. 58, 64); Easter 1265 (*Essex F.*, I, 262); 15 July 1272 (PRO, Cambs F. CP25/1/25/35, no. 57). Mentd 10 May 1273 as having been dep. and replaced by Adam (*CPR 1272–81*, p. 33).

Adam de Wyham ?1272/3–1280 Mentd 10 May 1273 as present abb. (ibid.). Occ. Mich. 1272 x Mich. 1273 (PRO, E159/47, m. 17d); (William) 6 Aug. 1273 (*CPR 1272–81*, p. 12);[39] 10 Oct. 1279 (*YB, XX*, 78). Res. by 7 Jan. 1280 (*Reg. Pecham*, II, 95–6; *Reg. Peckham*, III, 1063). Reduction of pension of former (unnamed) abb. 20 Feb. 1281 (*Reg. Pecham*, II, 119).

John 1280– Pr. of Colchester, St Botolph. Eln conf. 7 Jan. 1280 (ibid., II, 95–6; *Reg. Peckham*, III, 1063). Occ. Jan. x Mich. 1280 (PRO, E159/53, m. 13d); 17 Mar. 1281 (*HMC 9th Rept.*,

---

[39] This may be the source for Walcott's (? erroneous) statement, without source, (*TEAS*, V, 14), that Adam was *elected* 6 Aug. 1272.

app. 56); 1284 (BL, Harl. ms. 3697, f. 260v); 9 Sept. 1285 (BL, Harl. Cht. 83 A 11); 4 Feb. 1286 (BL, Harl. Cht. 44 C 17); 26 July 1289 (PRO, Just.1/1282, mm. 29, 31).[40]

David Occ. (D.) n.d., after Mar. 1303 (PRO, SC1/28/93); Mich. 1305 (PRO, CP40/153, mm. 23, 335); Trin. 1309 (PRO, CP40/178, m. 13d); Mich. 1310 (PRO, CP40/183, m. 11); 19 Aug. 1311 (*Reg. Baldock*, p. 148); 29 Apr. 1311, 2 Dec. 1311, 15 Dec. 1316 (Norwich, Reg/1/1, ff. 41r, 44r, 67r).

William Occ. 31 July [1332] (PRO, C270/11/21).

Thomas Occ. 12 Aug. 1345 (*CCR 1343–46*, p. 600); 31 Mar. 1351 (*CPL*, III, 410); 1 Nov. 1354 (ibid., 535); 13 Dec. 1361 (*Reg. Sudbury*, I, 229); 1363 and Mich. 1364 (PRO, KB27/416, rex roll, m. 28d, cited *TEAS*, XVII, 48).

John Storey −1375 Occ. 1 June 1370 (*Reg. Sudbury*, I, 135–6). D. 27 Sept. 1375 (ibid., 179).

Eln of new abb. (no name of elect) 4 Oct. 1375 on d. of John Storey (ibid., 179–81).

John Occ. June 1385 x June 1386 (*Pedigrees from the Plea Rolls*, p. 166).

SANDALEFORD (Berks), St John the Baptist f. 1193 x 1202
 List in *VCH Berks*, II, 88.

Walter Occ. -23 July 1222 (WAM no. 7138). Mentd 1248 as previous pr., *temp.* grandmother of party in case (*Berks Eyre*, no. 80).

John Occ. n.d. (1230 x 40) (Oxford, Queens Coll. Chts. of Monk Sherborne, I, no. 6); 7 Oct. 1235 (PRO, Berks F., CP25/1/7/11, no. 33); 27 Jan. 1236 (*Wilts F.*, I, 22); 14 Jan. 1241 (PRO, Hants F., CP25/1/203/7, no. 47); Oct. 1243 x Oct. 1244 (*Surrey F.*, p. 27); 1248 (*Basset Chts.*, no. 170); 12 Nov. 1252 (PRO, Berks F., CP25/1/8/21, no. 14).

Gervase Occ. 6 June 1255 (PRO, Berks F., CP25/1/8/21, no. 26).

Stephen Occ. 1256 x 1262, *temp.* Bp Giles of Salisbury (Money, *Newbury*, p. 131).

Robert of Winchester (Wynton) 1301− Sub-pr. of Sandaleford, eln conf. 18 Dec. 1301, no reason given for vacancy (*Reg. Gandavo*, II, 608). Occ. 17 Apr. 1311 (ibid., I, 403).

Thomas Occ. 12 June 1330 (*CCR 1330–33*, p. 142).[41]

Robert [Gilbert] 1334− Occ. 27 Jan. 1336 (PRO, E315/31/116); 28 Sept. 1348 (Madox, *Form.*, p. 62, no. 122; PRO, E327/122). Seal (*Mon. Seals*, p. 80).

John Occ. 2 Feb. 1354 (WCM, no. 12291).

John Occ. 11 Feb. 1384 (Salisbury, Reg. Erghum, f. 178r).

SELBORNE (Hants), St Mary f. 1234 (see *EEA* 9 no. 48n.)
 Lists in *VCH Hants*, II, 179–80; *Selborne Chts.*, I, xiii; Deirdre Le Faye, 'Selborne priory, 1233–1486', *Proc. Hants. Field Club* 30 (1973), pp. 47–71 (list at p. 69).

John de Wich 1234− First pr. occ. 1234 (*Selborne Chts.*, I, 14–15); Oct. 1235 (ibid., 19); 1236 (PRO, Hants F., CP25/1/203/6, no. 47); 1241 (ibid., 203/7, no. 25); (J.) 12 Jan. 1237 (*Selborne Chts.*, I, 20); Oct. 1250 x Oct. 1251 (*Surrey F.*, p. 33); 20 Jan. 1256 (*Selborne Chts.*, I, 48); 3 May 1258 (ibid., p. 49 = PRO, Hants F. CP25/1/204/10, no. 16); 9 Feb. 1260 (*Selborne Chts.*, II, 8), but cf. the same doct is also dated 9 Feb. 1261 (*YB*, XXII, 2: the correct dating of the former is conf. by PRO, Hants F., CP25/1/204/10, no. 30). Wich was possibly related to Richard Wich, bp of Chichester: see *EEA*, 9, no. 49n.; *St Richard of Chichester*, pp. 203–4, 241.

---

[40] Walcott's list (*TEAS*, V, 13–14) gives Robert de Bokelow occ. 1299, and Robert de Glotinges as having been removed for various crimes 1299 (the latter repeated *VCH*). The former entry has not been found and the latter, in Archbp Winchelsey's register, actually refers to the removal of Robert de Glotinges, pr. of Hardham (q.v.).

[41] The *VCH* ref. to a pr. Thomas occ. 1311 (citing Money, *Newbury*, p. 161) is to a Thomas of Sandaleford, not a pr. Thomas.

Richard of Kent *or* **Canterbury** (Cant', Cantuaria) **1261–** Sub-pr. of Selborne, royal ass. 8 Oct. 1261, temps. 24 Dec. 1261, the eln having been conf. by B[oniface], archbp of Canterbury (*CPR 1258–66*, pp. 177, 195). Occ. 2 Feb. 1262 (*Selborne Chts.*, II, 57; WCM, no. 6656); (R.) 24 June 1262 (*Selborne Chts.*, I, 56).

Peter de Disenhurste Occ. 1266 (*Hatton's Book of Seals*, p. 99, no. 142); 9 Sept. 1267 (*Selborne Chts.*, I, 60); 1268 (ibid., 61); 1271 (ibid., 64); 1273 (ibid., II, 82). Seal (*BM Seals*, no. 3976; *Northumberland and Durham Seals*, p. 109, suppl. no. 78).

Richard Occ. 1 Sept. 1277 (*Selborne Chts.*, I, 66); 1278, 1279 (ibid., II, 40); 15 July 1280 (ibid., I, 67); 25 July 1280 (ibid., 68); 1281 (ibid., II, 67); 1289 (ibid., 60); 1291 (PRO, Hants F., CP25/1/204/14, no. 38; *Selborne Chts.*, I, 76); Trin. 1298 (PRO, KB27/155, m. 54d).

William de Basyng(e) 1300–1323 Mand. for induction, no reason being given for vacancy 11 Mar. 1300 (*Reg. Pontissara*, p. 94). D., lic. to el. 25 Aug. 1323, and power to bp of Exeter to grant royal ass. to eln (*CPR 1321–24*, p. 341; *Reg. Asserio*, p. 608).

Walter de Insula 1324–1339 Can. of Selborne, pres. 18 July 1324, no reason being given for vacancy; eln quashed but apptd by bp 20 July 1324 (Winchester, Reg. Stratford, f. 6r). Occ. 21 Jan. 1339 (*Selborne Chts.*, I, 90). Cess. by 4 Nov. 1339 (Winchester, Reg. Orleton I, f. 82r–v).

Thomas of Winchester (Wynton', Wynt') **1339–1349** Sub-pr. of Selborne, apptd by bp of Winchester 6 Nov. 1339 (to whom the right had been transferred on 4 Nov.) (ibid.). D. by 29 June 1349 (*Reg. Edington*, I, no. 618). Seal (ascribed to *John* of Winchester) (*BM Seals*, no. 3979).

Edmund of Popham 1349– Can. of Selborne, commn to examine eln 29 June 1349 (*Reg. Edington*, I, no. 618). Occ. 1352, 1357 (*Selborne Chts.*, I, 91, 93). Accusations brought against him of wasting the priory's goods and incontinency and other faults 19 June 1359 (*Reg. Edington*, II, no. 372). Deprived of all right to alienate the priory's goods 16 Aug. 1359 (ibid., no. 375).

Nicholas of Winchester (Wynton') **1361–1378** Sacrist of Selborne, commn to examine eln, no reason being given for vacancy 31 Dec. 1361 (ibid., I, no. 1484). Suspended for dilapidation of goods 9 Aug. 1376 (*Reg. Wykeham*, II, 258–9). Res. on account of age and infirmity dated 10 Feb. 1378 and accepted 14 Feb. (ibid., I, 94–5).

SHELFORD (Notts), St Mary f. *temp.* Henry II

Lists in *VCH Notts*, II, 120; *Heads*, I, 183.

Laurence 1215– El. 1215 (*Rot. Lit. Pat.*, p. 131). Occ. 7 June 1220 (*Lincs F.*, I, 153); n.d. (*c.* 1220 (*HMC Middleton*, p. 57). On his d. he was succeeded by Thomas of Lexington, mentd in pleas of 1258 and 1320 (PRO, KB27/242, m. 153).

Thomas of Lexington (Lexinton) Occ. 1219 x 1223 (*Reg. Ant. Lincoln*, VII, no. 2077); from 21 May 1221 to 6 Oct. 1226 (PRO, Notts F., CP25/1/182/3, no. 16; 182/4, no. 82); Mich. term 1225 (*CRR*, XII, no. 1360); 13 Nov. 1226 (*Ctl. Tutbury*, no. 270); Easter, Trin. term 1227, Trin. term 1229 (*CRR*, XIII, nos. 228, 252, 2233); Dec. 1228 x Dec. 1229 (*Reg. Wells*, III, 171).

Robert Occ. 25 June 1232 (PRO, Notts F. CP25/1/182/6, no. 157); 25 Sept. 1236 (ibid. /186/6, no. 190); Mich. 1236 (ibid., /182/6, nos. 202, 205); 11 Nov. 1236 (ibid. /182/7, no. 243).

Walter Occ. 1244. In a case of 1308 it was stated that pr. Walter had pres. John de Ludham to Burton Joyce church *temp.* Henry III (*Reg. Greenfield*, IV, p. 48, n.1). Ludham was inst. 19 June 1244 (*Reg. Gray*, p. 94).

William Occ. n.d. (Thoroton, *Notts.*, I, 288); cf. *Ctl. Thurgarton*, nos. 423, 477, dated *c.* 1250, mid-13th cent. His precise place in the sequence of priors is uncertain.

John of Nottingham (Notingham) **–1289** Occ. 27 Jan. 1263 (*Lincs F.*, II, 289); 1269 (PRO,

Notts F., CP25/1/183/13, no. 529); 3 Feb. 1272 (*Lincs F.*, II, 248); 1271 (*Nottingham Borough Records*, I, 48); (J.) 15 Apr. 1275 (PRO, SC1/20/177). Res., lic. to el. 30 Mar. 1289 (*Reg. Romeyn*, I, pp. 281–2, no. 782).

Richard of Tythby (Tytheby) **1289–** Sacrist of Shelford, eln conf. 21 Apr. 1289 (ibid., I, p. 284, no. 787). D. by 20 Apr. 1315, lic. to el. (*Reg. Greenfield*, IV, p. 179, no. 2047).

Robert of Mansfield (Mamesfeld, Mammesfeld) **1315–1320** Citation for opposers to eln 7 May 1315, to appear 23 May (ibid., p. 179, n. 2). Can. of Shelford, eln quashed, but apptd by archbp 29 May 1315 (ibid., p. 198, no. 2076). D. by 17 Sept. 1320, lic. to el. (*Reg. Melton*, IV, no. 180).

William (le) Breton 1320–1340 Sub-pr. of Shelford, citation for opposers to eln 23 Oct. 1320 (ibid., no. 188). Eln quashed but appt. 26 Nov. 1320 (ibid., no. 196). Cess. by 27 Apr. 1340 (York, Reg. 5A, f. 109v).

William of Leicester (Leycestr(ia)) **1340–1349** Can. of Shelford, eln conf. 27 Apr. 1340 (ibid.). Occ. 5 May 1349 (York, Reg. 10, f. 128v). D. by 29 Oct. 1349 (ibid., f. 135v).

Stephen of Bassingbourne (Bassingborn, Bassyngbourne) **1349–1350** Can. of Shelford, eln conf. 29 Oct. 1349 (ibid.). Cess. by 10 Feb. 1350 (ibid., f. 139r).

Thomas of Chilwell (Chilewell) **1350–** Can. of Shelford, eln conf. 10 Feb. 1350 (ibid.). Occ. 17 May 1350 (*CPR 1348–50*, p. 509).

[**Alexander de Insula** El. 1358, but quashed by archbp (York, Reg. 11, f. 244r).]

Roger of Greystoke (Craystok, Graystok) **1358–1365** Can. of Shelford, apptd by archbp 20 Dec. 1358, the prev. eln of Alexander having been quashed; letter to install 20 Dec. 1358 (ibid.). Cess. by 6 Nov. 1365 (ibid., f. 262r).

William of Kinoulton (Kynalton) **1365–1404** Can. of Shelford, eln quashed, but apptd by archbp 6 Nov. 1365 (ibid.). Occ. 18 May 1394 (*CPR 1391–96*, p. 403). D. by 20 Nov. 1404 (*Reg. Scrope*, I, no. 613).

SHULBRED (Sussex), St Mary, St Eustace, Holy Cross (Lynchmere, Wolinchmere) f. c. 1200

Lists in *VCH Sussex*, II, 82; *Hist. Shulbrede*, p. 100.

John Occ. 1242 (*Hist. Shulbrede*, p. 69); n.d. (*c.* 1247 x 1252) with Valentine, abb. of Durford (BL, Cotton ms. Vespasian E XXIII, f. 58r). Mentd as former pr. in case of 1262 x 1263 (PRO, Just.1/912A, m. 13d).

Henry Occ. 40 Henry III (Oct. 1255 x Oct. 1256) (*CCR 1330–33*, p. 17); 1263 (*Hist. Shulbrede*, pp. 69–70). In 1329 stated to have been pr. long before the publication of the Statute of Mortmain (1279) (*Cal. Misc. Inq.*, II, 266).

John Occ. 20 Apr. 1265 (*Ctl. Chichester*, no. 699).

Thomas de Henton Occ. 19 Jan. 1300 (ibid., II, 852; *Hist. Shulbrede*, p.70).

Robert de Glottyng Occ. 30 Sept. 1300 when Archbp Winchelsey wrote to bp of Chichester questioning the suitability of Robert, deposed from Hardham for various causes, to be pr. of Shulbred (*Reg. Winchelsey*, II, 718–19).

Roger Occ. 1320 (*Hist. Shulbrede*, list, p. 100, no source); 1334 (ibid., p. 74, no source).

John Occ. 1354 (*Hist. Shulbrede*, list, p. 100, no source); 10 Sept. 1358 (Lambeth, Reg. Islip, f. 102r); 6 Mar. 1358 (PRO, E40/14223); before 12 Feb. 1373 (*CPL*, IV, p. 186).

William Harethorn –1404 Occ. Jan. 1381 (PRO, E179/11/9); 1385 (*Hist. Shulbrede*, p. 80). Res. by 6 Dec. 1404 (*Reg. Rede*, II, p. 212).

SKEWKIRK (Yorks W.), All Saints (Nostell) (Scokirk, Tockwith) f. *temp.* Henry I
No list in *VCH*.

Nicholas Wlfe Occ. 11 Nov. 1229 (*Yorks Deeds*, VI, no. 544; *Ctl. Tockwith*, p. 154, n.4).

SOUTHWARK (Surrey), St Mary Overy f. 1106

Lists in *VCH Surrey*, II, 111; *VCH London*, I, 484; basis in BL, Cotton ms. Faustina A. VIII, ff. 119v, 131v; BL, Harl. ms. 544, f. 100r, and see on the annals M. Brett, 'The annals of Bermondsey, Southwark and Merton' in D. Abulafia, M. Franklin and M. Rubin eds., *Church and City 1000–1500; essays in honour of Christopher Brooke* (Cambridge, 1992), pp. 279–310); *Heads*, I, 183–4.

Martin *c.* 1205–1218 Can. of Merton (Bodl., Rawlinson ms. B.177, f. 219r). Occ. 1212 x 1215 (*EEA*, 9, no. 57 & n.); 1215 (*CPR 1301–07*, p. 339). D. 11 June 1218 (*Ann. Southwark*, p. 53; Bodl., Rawlinson ms. B.177, f. 219r); pr. 15 years (*sic*) (BL, Harl. ms. 544, f. 100r).

Robert of Osney (Osneya) 1218–1223 pr. of Osney, el. 1 Sept. 1218 (*Ann. Southwark*, p. 53; cf. *Ann. Dunstable*, p. 41 *sub anno* 1213; see Brett, p. 310). D. 18 Apr. 1223 (*Ann. Southwark*, p. 53), but d. 19 Apr. 1223 (Bodl., Rawlinson ms. B.177, f. 220r). Ruled 5 years (BL, Harl. ms. 544, f. 100r).

Alexander Occ. Mich. 1225 (*CRR*, XII, no. 1137). Not in BL, Harl. ms. list. An unnamed pr. d. 1225 (*Ann. Dunstable*, p. 94). Possibly an error.

Humphrey 1223–?1240 Succ. 1 May 1223 (Bodl., Rawlinson ms. B.177, f. 220r). Occ. Mich. term 1225, Trin. term 1227 (*CRR*, XII, no. 1113; XIII, no. 373); (H.) *c.* 1226 x 1227 (PRO, E40/14070, 14197); 30 Sept. 1227 (*Kent F.*, p. 89); (Hugh) Oct. 1236 x Oct. 1237 (*Surrey F.*, p. 21). Ruled 17 years (BL, Harl. ms. 544, f. 100r).

[**Eustace** Ruled 13 years (bracketed with Stephen below, so presumably 13 years is the joint total) (BL, Harl. ms. 544, f. 100r). Not in Rawlinson ann. (see next entry).]

Stephen 1240–1252 Succ. 27 June 1240 (Bodl., Rawlinson ms. B.177, f. 223v). D. 1252 (ibid., f. 229v). Occ. Trin. term 1243, Mich. term 1244 (*Essex F.*, I, 144, 147); Oct. 1247 x Oct. 1248, Oct. 1248 x Oct. 1249 (*Surrey F.*, pp. 29, 32); 30 Sept. 1248, 13 Oct. 1251 (*Kent F.*, pp. 206, 237). Ruled 13 years (linked with Eustace, see above).

Alan 1252–1283 Succ. 1252 (Bodl., Rawlinson ms. B.177, f. 229v). Occ. 14 May 1253 (PRO, Cambs F., CP25/1/24/27, no. 5); 1 May 1260 (PRO, Berks F., CP25/1/8/23, no. 12); 23 Apr. 1262, 6 Oct. 1263 (*Bucks F.*, II, 10, 14); Oct. 1259 x Oct. 1260, Oct. 1264 x Oct. 1265 (*Surrey F.*, pp. 39, 42); 13 Oct. 1275 (*Sussex F.*, II, no. 837). Res., lic. to el. n.d. [Sept./Oct.] 1283 (*Reg. Pontissara*, I, 275). Ruled 33 years (*sic*) (BL, Harl. ms. 544, f. 100r).

William le Waleys (Walys) 1283–1305 Ruled 23 years (ibid.). Occ. Mich 1285 (*Essex F.*, II, 48, 51). Occ. 20 Jan. 1300 (*Cal. Early Mayors' Court Rolls, 1298–1307*, p. 56); 5 Nov. 1302 (*CCR 1296–1302*, p. 554). Dep. by bp's commissaries following archbp's visitation of priory *sede vacante* 12 Aug. 1305 (*Reg. Woodlock*, I, 108–12). Petition for lic. to el. 9 Sept. 1305; lic. gtd 10 Sept. (ibid., 40–1). D. 1305 (Bodl., Rawlinson B.177, f. 286v).

Peter of Cheam (Cheyham) 1305–1327 Can. of Southwark, eln pres. to bp 13 Oct. 1305, eln quashed 30 Oct. 1305; bp appts him 10 Nov. 1305 (*Reg. Woodlock*, I, 49–51, 62–4). D. by 5 Sept. 1327; lic. to el. 7 Sept. 1327 (Winchester, Reg. Stratford, ff. 104r–105r). Ruled 20 years (*sic*) (BL, Harl. ms. 544, f. 100r).

Thomas of Southwark (Southwerke, Suthewerk) 1327–1331 Eln pres. to bp 22 Sept.; commn to examine eln 13 Oct. 1327; eln conf. 16 Oct. 1327 (Winchester, Reg. Stratford, ff. 104r–105r). Res. by 23 Oct. 1331, when sub-pr. and convent gave bp the right to provide a new pr. (ibid., f. 124v). Ruled 4 years and res. (BL, Harl. ms. 544, f. 100r).

Robert (de) Welles (Willys) 1331–1349 Can. of Southwark, apptd by bp 25 Oct. 1331 (Winchester, Reg. Stratford, ff. 124v–125r). D. by 24 May 1349; lic. to el. (*Reg. Edington*, I, no. 545). Ruled 17 years (BL, Harl. ms. 544, f. 100r).

John (de) Pecham (Peccham, Pekham) 1349 Can. of Southwark, eln conf. 10 June 1349; mand. to induct s.d. (*Reg. Edington*, I, nos. 545, 583–6). Commn to visit priory after the bp has heard that certain reforms are needed to avoid scandals 23 Aug. 1349 (ibid., II, no. 256). Res. 24–25 Aug. 1349 (ibid., I, no. 661).

Richard de Stakes 1349– Provided 24–25 Aug. 1349. At the visitation the bp received John's res. and apptd Richard (ibid.). Occ. 30 Apr. 1351 (*CCR 1343–54*, p. 359). Not in BL, Harl. ms. list.

John de Pecham (restored) **–1361** Sub-pr. mentd as locumtenens of absent pr. John 25 June 1355 (*Reg. Edington*, I, no. 1036). Pr. John occ. 18 Sept. 1357 (ibid., no. 1120); 1358 (BL, Harl Cht. 44 I 54). Res. 16 Mar. 1361 (*Reg. Edington*, I, no. 1245). Ruled 11 years and res. (BL, Harl. ms. 544, f. 100r).

Henry (of) Collingbourne (Colyngborne, Colyngbourne, Colingham) **1361–1395** Petition for lic. to el. 24 Mar. 1361; nomination by bp at request of community s.d.; eln conf. 27 Mar. 1361 (*Reg. Edington*, I, nos. 1246–51). D. 15 June 1395 (*Reg. Wykeham*, I, 196). Ruled 34 years, 9 weeks, 3 days (BL, Harl. ms. 544, f. 100r). Seal (*BM Seals*, no. 4051).

SOUTHWICK (Hants), St Mary f. 1133 (at Porchester); *c.* 1145 x 1155 (at Southwick). Lists in *VCH Hants*, II, 168; *Heads*, I, 184; *Ctl. Southwick*, I, lxiv–lxvii.

Guy Latest recorded occ. 5 Feb. 1206 (*Ctl. Chichester*, pp. 48–9). Obit. 2 Nov. (BL, Cotton ms. Claudius D III, f. 160v); 3 Nov. (Trokelowe, ed. Hearne, p. 392). See Sharpe, *Latin Writers*, p. 157.

Luke –1227 Occ. n.d. (PRO, E210/100); (L.) *after* 24 Jan. 1226, judges delegate (Oxford, Queen's Coll., archives catalogue I, no. 227B). D., lic. to el. 24 May 1227 (*CPR 1225–32*, p. 125).

Walkelin 1227–1235 Sacrist of Southwick, royal ass. 3 June 1227 (ibid., p. 127). Occ. Mich. term 1228 (*CRR*, XIII, no. 777); 1234 (PRO, Hants F., CP25/1/203/6, no. 11). D., lic. to el. 29 Sept. 1235 (*CPR 1232–47*, p. 118). Obit 11 Sept. (BL, Cotton ms. Claudius D III, f. 157r).

Matthew 1235–1266 Can. of Southwick, royal ass. 17 Oct. 1235, writ *de intendendo* 25 Nov. 1235 (*CPR 1232–47*, pp. 120, 131). Occ. 12 Nov. 1236 to 16 Feb. 1256 (PRO, Hants F. CP25/1/203/7, no. 3; 204/9, no. 103). D., lic. to el. 4 Mar. 1266 (*CPR 1258–66*, p. 565).

Peter (de) Maupol (Maupudre) **1266–1273** Can. of Southwick, royal ass. 3 Apr. 1266, temps. 7 Apr. 1266 (ibid., pp. 576, 579). At bp of Winchester's visitation removed from office 15 Nov. 1273 (PRO, C84/4/47). Petition for lic. to el. 20 Nov. 1273 (ibid.). Cess. 30 Nov. 1273 (*CPR 1272–81*, p. 40)

Andrew of Winchester 1273–1281 Can. of Southwick, eln pres. to king for royal ass. 30 Nov. 1273 (PRO, C84/11/33); royal ass. and writ *de intendendo* 4 Dec. 1273 (*CPR 1272–81*, pp. 40, 41). Cert. conf. eln by bp of Winchester 20 Dec. 1273 (PRO, C84/4/49). D. (*sic*), lic. to el. 23 Nov. 1281 (*CPR 1281–92*, p. 2). Provision made for Andrew, who had res. office as pr. at the archbp of Canterbury's visitation, 12 Feb. 1282 (*Reg. Peckham*, I, 292–3). On 10 Jan. 1282 the archbp wrote to the unnamed pr. of Southwick to send him the decision of the chapter regarding the deposed (unnamed) pr. (ibid., III, 1065); letter regarding his excommunication 3 Nov. 1284 (ibid., 837–8).

John de Clere 1281–1291 Can. of Southwick, eln pres. to king for royal ass. 26 Nov. 1281 (PRO, C84/7/39); royal ass. 28 Nov. 1281, temps. 9 Dec. 1281 (*CPR 1281–92*, pp. 4, 6). Cert. conf. eln by archbp of Canterbury (PRO, C84/7/40). D. by 13 Dec. 1291 (PRO, C84/10/31). D., lic. to el. 14 Dec. 1291 (*CPR 1281–92*, p. 464).

Robert of Hempton (Houton, Henton(e)) **1291–1315** Can. of Southwick, eln pres. to king for royal ass. 21 Dec. 1291 (PRO, C84/18/20); royal ass. 28 Dec. 1291, writ *de intendendo* 5 Jan. 1292 (*CPR 1281–92*, pp. 463, 466). Mand. to convent to obey their newly-adm. pr. 17 Jan. 1292 (*Reg. Pontissara*, I, 50). D., lic. to el. 13 May 1315 (*CPR 1313–17*, p. 287).

William of Winchester (Wynton(ia)) **1315–1316** Can. of Southwick, eln pres. to king for royal ass. 23 May 1315 (PRO, C84/18/20); royal ass. 28 May 1315, temps. 11 June 1315

(*CPR 1313–17*, pp. 289, 298). Notif. by bp of Winchester of his conf. 9 June 1315; royal mand. for letters 11 June 1315 (*Cal. Chanc. Warr.*, p. 416). D., lic. to el. 6 Mar. 1316 (*CPR 1313–17*, p. 435).

Nicholas of Cheriton (Cherynton, Chiriton) **1316–1334** Can. of Southwick, royal ass. 20 Mar. 1316, temps. 4 Apr. 1316 (ibid., pp. 439, 446). Commn to examine eln 22 Mar. 1316; any objectors to appear 31 Mar., petition to king for restitution of temps. 2 Apr. 1316 (*Reg. Woodlock*, I, 664–5, 667–8). D. by 8 Jan. 1334 (PRO, C84/23/3). D., lic. to el. 20 Jan. 1334 (*CPR 1330–34*, p. 492).

John of Gloucester (Gloucestria, Gloucestre) **1334–1349** Can. of Southwick, eln pres. to king for royal ass. 7 Feb. 1334 (PRO, C84/23/7); royal ass. 13 Feb. 1334, temps. 24 Sept. 1334 (*CPR 1330–34*, p. 507; *CPR 1334–38*, p. 13). Eln conf. 12 Apr. 1334 (Winchester, Reg. Orleton I, ff. 1v–2v). D. by 12 Dec. 1349 (PRO, C84/26/33). D., lic. to el. 15 Dec. 1349 (*CPR 1348–50*, p. 437).

Richard (of) Bromden (Bramden) **1349–1381** Royal ass. 28 Dec. 1349 (ibid., p. 440). Commn to examine eln 1 Jan. 1350 (*Reg. Edington*, I, no. 726). Temps. 4 Jan. 1350 (*CPR 1348–50*, p. 433). D. 28 Apr. 1381 (*Ctl. Southwick*, I, p. 183, no. II 32). D., lic. to el. 30 Apr. 1381 (*CPR 1377–81*, p. 619).

SPINNEY (Cambs), St Mary and Holy Cross f. -1227/8

List in *VCH Cambs*, II, 253–4.

Hervey Occ. 13 Apr. 1228, 15 July 1232 (PRO, Cambs F., CP25/1/23/12, no. 40; 24/14, no. 28).

Henry Malebisse (Malebysse) Occ. 1265 (PRO, C85/130/28); 12 Mar. 1272 (CUL, EDR, G3/28, p. 451; *Mon. Angl.*, VI, 479).

Simon de Lydgate Occ. before 1286, when mentd as former pr. (PRO, Just.1/86, mm. 7, 19d).

Nicholas Occ. 1286 (ibid.); 3 Feb. 1302 (PRO, Cambs F., CP25/1/26/48, no. 18).

John of Burwell (Borewell) **1305–1333** Eln conf. 7 Aug. 1305, no reason given for vacancy (Norwich, Reg/1/1, f. 17v). D. by 25 Aug. 1333 (Norwich, Reg/1/2, f. 58v).

Thomas of Comberton (Cumberton) **1333–1339** Can. of Spinney, eln conf. 25 Aug. 1333 (ibid.). D. by 8 May 1339 (Norwich, Reg/1/3, f. 25r).

Robert of Isleham (Iselham) **1339–** Can. of Spinney, eln conf. by 8 May 1339 (ibid.).

Henry Wylmyn 1366– Can. of Spinney, eln conf. 27 Feb. 1366, no reason given for vacancy (Norwich, Reg/2/5, f. 68v).

Henry of Cambridge (Cantebrig') **–1390** Res. by 15 Feb. 1390 (Norwich, Reg/3/6, ff. 143v–144r).

STAFFORD, St Thomas the Martyr (Baswich) f. 1173 x 1175

Lists in *VCH Staffs*, III, 266–7; *Ctl. Stafford*, pp. 129–30; *Heads*, I, 184.

Philip Occ. ?1215 x 1225 (*Ctl. Stafford*, pp. 161–2); n.d. (*c.* 1220) (*Ctl. Chetwynd*, p. 275); 20 Oct. 1221 (*Staffs F. 2*, p. 220); 3 Nov. 1227 (ibid., pp. 224–5).

Richard Occ. 3 Feb. 1248 (ibid., pp. 238, 240).

Nicholas of Aspley (Aspeleghe, Aspeley) Occ. 29 Jan., 24 Feb. 1256 (Staffs RO, Acc. 938/528–30); 1257, 1271 (*Ctl. Stafford*, pp. 144, 171); 1261 (ibid., pp. 178–9); (N.) 24 June 1259, 1 May 1271 (ibid., pp. 173, 189; Staffs RO, Acc. 938/166, 465–6); 25 June 1257 (*Staffs F. 2*, p. 248); 4 Feb. 1263 (*Kniveton Leiger*, nos. 209–10); 1271 (Staffs RO, Acc. 938/409, 534); 1272 (ibid., /541); 2 Feb. 1273 (ibid., /587); 25 June 1273 (*Ctl. Stafford*, p. 151). See below.

John of Ercall (Erkelawe) Occ. 22 Apr. 1274 (*CPR 1272–81*, p. 67).

Nicholas (?of Aspley) Occ. 1276 (Staffs RO, Acc. 938/546); 29 June 1276 (ibid., /547); 21 June 1277 (*Magnum Reg. Album Lichfield*, no. 323). See below.

Richard Occ. 1 July 1277 (*Staffs F. 3*, p. 30).

Nicholas of Aspley Occ. 6 July 1278 (*Magnum Reg. Album Lichfield*, no. 322); 1278 (ibid., no. 320); 1280 (ibid., no. 26); 1281 (*CCR 1279–88*, p. 134); 1282 (*Ctl. Stafford*, pp. 138–9); 1284 (ibid., p. 154); 1286 (*Staffs F. 3*, p. 42); 3 Dec. 1292 (Staffs RO, Acc.938/16); 9 Mar. 1293 (ibid., /119); 16 Nov. 1294 (ibid., /276).

Richard of Hilderstone ((Hildreston, Hylderston, Ildreston) –1343 Occ. 24 Aug. 1295 (Staffs RO, Acc. 938/121); 2 Oct. 1295 (*Ctl. Stafford*, pp. 188–9). 10 Jan. 1296 letter of archbp of Canterbury to justices of gaol delivery to hand over pr. Richard and six cans. to the pr. of Stone and pr. of Ranton (*Reg. Winchelsey*, I, 70). Occ. 1297, 1298, 1302 (*Ctl. Stafford*, pp. 138, 181, 197); 5 June 1308 (ibid., p. 138); 30 Dec. 1312 (Staffs RO, Acc. 938/474–5); July 1312 x July 1313 (*Ctl. Stafford*, p. 171); 25 Aug., 26 Nov. 1314 (Staffs RO, Acc. 938/128; /110); 1321 (ibid., /558); 13 Feb. 1322 (ibid., /561); 1323 (ibid., /420); 1324 (ibid., /477–8); Christmas 1325 (*Ctl. Stafford*, p. 150); 1333 (ibid., pp. 178–9). D. 25 Jan. 1343 (Lichfield, B/A/1/2, ff. 171v–172v).

Thomas de Tydnesouere 1343–1347 Sub-pr. of Stafford, el. 3 Feb. 1343; eln conf. 18 Feb. 1343 (ibid.). Res. by 6 Aug. 1347 (ibid., f. 179r).

Robert of Cheadle (Chedele, Chedle) 1347– Can. of Stafford, eln conf. 6 Aug. 1347 (ibid., ff. 178v–179r). Occ. from 1348 (Staffs RO, Acc. 938/421) to 14 June 1361 (ibid., /363).

Richard de Mere Bp examines eln and conf. eln n.d. [prob. 1365] (*Reg. Stretton*, I, 119). **Robert of Hilderstone** (Hylderston) also el. but bp declares his eln void. Occ. Mich. term 1367 (*Staffs Plea Rolls 1360–87*, p. 62); 27 Oct. 1367 (Staffs RO, Acc. 938/643).

Nicholas de Huxton Occ. 1 Aug. 1373 (ibid., /138); 1374 (ibid., /592); 1376 (ibid., /202, 369); 1377, 1383 (*Ctl. Stafford*, pp. 186, 193); 1388 (ibid., pp. 146–7); 1389 (ibid., pp. 196–7); 4 Nov. 1390 (*CPR 1388–92*, p. 349); 1397 (Staffs RO, Acc. 938/373); 1402 (*Ctl. Stafford*, p. 138); 1404 (ibid., p. 183). The surname *atte Stretehende* is found for pr. Nicholas in 1395 and 1396 (*Cheshire Plea Rolls*, p. 31), prob. a variant rather than two priors called Nicholas in succession.

The next recorded pr., **Thomas**, occ. Mich. 1406 and Mich. 1409 (ibid., pp. 49, 67).

STAVORDALE (Soms), St James f. –1243 (Victorine)

List in *VCH Soms*, II, 141.

William Occ. n.d. (*c.* 1233 x 1242, after d. of Eva Sanzaver (alive 1233) and before d. of Bp Jocelin of Wells) and n.d. (1243 x 1249) (E.H. Bates Harbin, 'Two deeds relating to Stavordale priory and the family of Sanzaver', *Proc. Soms ANHS*, 61 (1916 for 1915), 105–14, at 105 and 107).

Walter Occ. 15 July 1249 (*Soms F.*, I, 134).

Robert Occ. 14 June 1254 (ibid., 158); 19 July 1263 (*HMC Wells*, I, 152).

Robert of Charlton (Charleton) –1310 Occ. Mich. 1305 (PRO, CP40/153, m. 100); Trin. 1309 (PRO, CP40/178, m. 67). House vacant by his d. by 8 Mar. 1310 (*Reg. Droxford*, p. 30).

Walter de Eton 1310–1322 Commission to examine eln 8 Mar. 1310 (ibid., pp. 30–1). 2 Aug. 1322 inquiry to be made into his wastefulness (ibid., p. 204). Res., lic. to el by bp 13 Aug. 1322 (ibid., p. 205).

Walter of Nympsfield (Nymfield, Nymesfeld) 1322–1333 Can. of Evesham, commn to examine eln 1 Sept. 1322 (ibid.). D. by 19 July 1333 (*Reg. R. Shrewsbury*, I, no. 577).

Henry of Nympsfield (Nymesfeld) 1333– Can. of Stavordale, eln pres. to bp 19 July 1333, eln quashed, but apptd by bp 24 July 1333 (ibid.).

John Bodman –1361 D., lic. to el. 12 Oct. 1361 (*CPR 1361–64*, p. 87).

John (of) Wincanton (Wyncanton, Wyncaulton) 1361– Can. of Stavordale, apptd 3 Nov. 1361,

the convent have transferred right of appt to the bp (*Reg. R. Shrewsbury*, II, app., no. 49). Occ. 1377 (PRO, E179/4/1, m. 4).
The next recorded pr., **Robert**, occ. 5 Nov. 1382 (PRO, C146/3694).

STEEP HOLME (Soms), St Michael (dependent on Studley) f. -1260; diss. *c.* 1300
No list in *VCH*. See E.H. Bates Harbin, 'The priory of St Michael on the Steep Holme', *Proc. Soms ANHS*, 62 (1917 for 1916), 26–45.
William Occ. 2 Nov. 1235 (*Soms F.*, I, 95).

STONE (Staffs), St Wulfardus and St Mary (Kenilworth) f. c. 1135
   Lists in *VCH Staffs*, III, 246–7; *Heads*, I, 184; Bowers and Clough, *Hist. of Parish and Parish Church of Stone*, p. 17 (without sources).
Richard Last occ. n.d. (early 13th cent.) (*Ctl. Stone*, p. 9). Desc. as former pr. 1221 (*Eyre Roll 1221–2*, no. 714) and in 1242 (*CRR*, XVII, no. 373).
Reginald Occ. 3 Nov. 1227 (*Staffs Plea Rolls, Henry III*, p. 53).
Gilbert –1241 Res. 1241, royal ass. to his el. as abb. of Haughmond 10 Aug. 1241 (*CPR 1232–47*, pp. 256–7). Presumably the abb. G. who occ. n.d. (*Salt MSS.*, p. 8, no. 21) and Gill' who occ. n.d. (*Ctl. Stone*, p. 13).
Humphrey Said to occ. Oct. 1245 x Oct. 1246 (*SHC*, new ser., XII, 101, but no source). Occ. n.d. (*Ctl. Stone*, p. 14). Ref. to as former abb. 1319 (*YB XXIV*, 64).
Roger of Worcester Occ. 7 July 1260 (*Reg. G. Giffard*, p. 105); 1265 (*Ctl. Stone*, p. 25); 1266, 1267 (Oxford, Merton Coll. muns. 698–9, 690); 22 Dec. 1272 (*Staffs F.*, 2 p. 256); 1279 (*Staffs Plea Rolls 1272–94*, p. 101; *Reg. G. Giffard*, p. 106); 3 Oct. 1288 (ibid., p. 323). See also BL, Harl. ms. 3868, f. 5r. Mentd as former pr. Nov. 1292 x Nov. 1293 (*Staffs Plea Rolls 1272–94*, p. 278). Possibly the Roger of Worcester, pr. of *Graves* who was apptd a papal chaplain 4 Mar. 1261 (*CPL*, I, 375).
John Tiney Occ. 18 Jan. 1292 (*CPR 1334–38*, p. 308); 23 Dec. 1292 (*Staffs Plea Rolls 1294–1307*, p. 33); 25 Feb. 1293 (*Staffs F.*, 3, p. 50); 1 Aug. 1294 (*Staffs Plea Rolls 1272–94*, p. 293); 9 Dec. 1294 (PRO, C241/21/62).
Thomas de Mulwych –1309 Occ. Trin. 1298 (PRO, KB27/155, m. 45). D. by 23 Feb. 1309 (Lichfield, B/A/1/1, ff. 41v–42r). Said to occ. from 1296 (Bowers and Clough, p. 17, no source).
John de Atteberge (Atleberge) 1309–1327 Sub-pr. of Stone, eln quashed, but apptd by bp. Bp ordered Kenilworth to deliver temps. to John 23 Feb. 1309; mand. to install same day (Lichfield, B/A/1/1, ff. 41v–42r). D. by 23 Apr. 1327 (ibid., B/A/1/2, f. 142v).
John of Stallington (Stalinton, Stalyngton) 1327– Sub-pr. of Stone, eln conf. 23 Apr. 1327 (ibid.). Occ. 1339 (*Staffs Plea Rolls 16–33 Edward III*, p. 93); Jan. 1344 x Jan. 1345 (PRO, E210/11246); 17 Aug. 1345 (Lichfield, B/A/1/2, f. 176v); Mich. term 1348 (*Staffs Plea Rolls 16–33 Edward III*, p. 87).
Walter (of) Podmore (Podemor(e)) 1349–1391 Can. of Stone, comm. to examine eln dated 28 July 1349, no reason given for vacancy; eln conf. by commissaries 3 Aug. 1349 (Lichfield, B/A/1/2, f. 186v). Occ. 13 Aug. 1349 (ibid., f. 187r). Apptd honorary papal chaplain 1366 (*CPP*, p. 534). D. by 10 Sept. 1391 (Lichfield, B/A/1/6, f. 39v).

STONELY (Hunts), St Mary f. *c.* 1180
   List in *VCH Hunts*, I, 396.
Alexander 1263– Can. of Stonely, adm. 31 Oct. 1263, no reason given for vacancy (*Reg. R. Gravesend*, p. 169). Occ. n.d. (PRO, E210/3299; E210/6727).
Seman (Semannus) 1273– Can. of Stonely, eln conf. as 'master' 7 Oct. 1275, no reason given

for vacancy (*Reg. R. Gravesend*, pp. 183, 320). Occ. 8 July 1274 (*Beds F.*, II, no. 8). Occ. n.d. (PRO, E210/180; E210/8654; E326/5146; E326/5159).

Simon –1290 Same as above? D. by 19 July 1290 (*Reg. Sutton*, VIII, 72–3). An unsuccessful attempt made to elect Walter of Gidding and Simon of Woolley, cans. of Stonely (ibid).

John of Ripton 1290–1309 Can. of Huntingdon, apptd by bp 19 July 1290, with lic. from Humphrey de Bohun, patron 18 July (ibid.). D. by 27 May 1309 (Lincoln, Ep. Reg., II, f. 239v).

Simon of Woolley (Wolle, Wulle) 1309–1310 Can. of Stonely (see above), eln quashed but apptd by bp 27 May 1309 (ibid.). D. by 26 Mar. 1310 (ibid., ff. 240v–241r).

William of Brampton 1310– Can. of Stonely, (once called Richard), eln quashed but apptd by bp 26 Mar. 1310 (ibid.). Occ. 22 June 1329 (PRO, E315/40/52); Jan. 1330 x Jan. 1331 (PRO, E210/9069); 12 Mar. 1346 (PRO, E326/1928); 3 May 1346 (PRO, E326/1955); Jan. 1346 x Jan. 1347 (PRO, E210/5454). An unnamed pr., prob. William, was d. by 5 Aug. 1349 (Lincoln, Ep. Reg., IX, f. 385v).

John de Stowe (Stoue, Stone) 1349–1369 Can. of Stonely, apptd by bp to whom the right of appt had been transferred 5 Aug. 1349 (ibid.). D. by 28 Feb. 1369 (Lincoln, Ep. Reg., X, f. 295v).

John (of) Ellington (Elyngton) 1369–1387 Can. of Stonely, apptd by bp 1 Mar. 1369, to whom right of appt had been transferred on 28 Feb. 1369 (ibid.). Res. by 29 July 1387 (Lincoln, Ep. Reg., XI, f. 253v).

STUDLEY (Warws), St Mary f. *c.* 1135 (at Witton); *c.* 1151 (at Studley).
Lists in *VCH Warws*, II, 97; *Heads*, I, 185.

Ralph Occ. Mich. 1209 (*Warws F.*, I, nos. 197, 193–4).

Nicholas Occ. 6 July 1221, 1226, 11 July 1236 (ibid., nos. 291, 375, 397, 551); Trin. term 1227 (*CRR*, XIII, no. 276); 14 Apr. 1241 (PRO, Worcs. F., CP25/1/258/5, no. 26).

Richard Occ. 20 Jan. 1246 (ibid., 258/6, no. 13); 1 July 1250 (*Soms F.*, I, 149).

Adam Occ. from 8 July 1252 to 3 June 1272 (*Warws F.*, I, nos. 706, 879); 1255, 1263 (PRO, Worcs. F. CP25/1/258/7, no. 35; /258/8, no. 19); (A.) 17 Apr. 1257 (*HMC Middleton*, p. 67).

William Occ. n.d. (1275 x 1287) (PRO, SC1/24/125); Trin. 1280 (PRO, CP40/34, m. 12).

John de Wytenhull 1293– Adm. 18 July 1293, no reason given for vacancy (*Reg. G. Giffard*, p. 394). Occ. (J.) 7 Jan. 1306 when absolved from excommunication imposed for paying taxes to the king against the pope's orders (*Reg. Gainsborough*, p. 145).

Adam de Honnburne Ment. of papal disp. for illegitimacy gtd 7 July 1310 – the pr. was the child of a deacon and an unmarried woman. (*Worcs Reg. Sede Vacante*, p. 92); n.d. (early 14th cent.) (Worcester Cath. mun. B.735).[42]

Robert de Hoyland (Holand(e)) 1316– Can. of Fineshade, given permission to go to Studley 11 Jan. 1316 (Lincoln, Ep. Reg., III, f. 336v). Ref. to unnamed pr. who had been expelled by some of the brethren (mentd 12 Mar. 1319) (*Reg. Cobham*, pp. 15–16). 27 Aug. 1319 the Bp wrote to the pr. of Horsley instructing him to take in Robert Holande until peace been made between him and brethren (ibid., p. 38). Appt of William de Stoke, rector of Welford, as *custos* of priory reduced to depths of poverty n.d. (Aug. x Sept. 1319) (ibid., pp. 33–4). Bp recalled Robert to rule over his monastery 8 Mar. 1320 (ibid., pp. 23–4). Pr. Robert sent to another house to do penance for certain defaults found by the bp of Worcester in his visitation and has now done penance and returned 4 May 1320 (*CCR 1318–23*, p. 190).

---

[42] *Mon. Angl.*, VI, 185 gives occ. of pr. Adam Tessull in 1319, but no source.

Adam de Hambury 1321– Prof. obed. 2 Jan. 1321 (*Reg. Cobham*, p. 28).

Robert of Langdon (Langedon) –1349 D. by 6 July 1349 (*Reg. Bransford*, no. 1504).

John la Suche (Southe) 1349– Cert. of citation delivered 6 July; eln examined and quashed 8 July, but apptd by bp 9 July 1349 (ibid.).

John de Gorecote –1372 Occ. 26 Apr. 1353 (*CPR 1350–54*, p. 459); 27 Jan. 1360 (Worcester, Reg. Brian I, p. 198). D. by 9 Jan. 1372 (Worcester, Reg. Lenn, p. 47).

John of Evesham 1372– Can. of Studley, apptd 9 Jan. 1372 (ibid.). Occ. 1379 (PRO, E179/58/11, m. 1d); 29 Oct. 1383 (*CPR 1381–85*, p. 323); 5 Oct. 1402, but desc. as 'lately prior' 14 May 1404 (*CPR 1401–05*, pp. 399–400).

TANDRIDGE (Surrey), St James f. *temp.* Richard I (hospital); +1218 (priory).

Lists in *VCH Surrey*, II, 113; Heales, *Tandridge Priory*, pp. 80–95.

Thomas Occ. 9 Feb. 1226 (*Surrey F.*, p. 13).

Adam Occ. Oct. 1234 x Oct. 1235, ?13 Oct. 1235 (ibid., p. 19).

Humphrey Occ. 25 Nov. 1248 (*Sussex F.*, I, no. 478); Oct. 1262 x Oct. 1263, ?27 Jan. 1263 (*Surrey F.*, p. 41).

Nicholas Occ. Nov. 1277 x Nov. 1278 (ibid., p. 51); Easter 1278 (PRO, CP40/24, m. 9).

John de Codham Occ. 3 Aug. 1296 when archbp of Canterbury ordered his suspension if found guilty of dilapidations (*Reg. Winchelsey*, I, 125–6).

Walter de Pedeleshurst *alias* Hatfeld 1306–1309 Can. of Tandridge, eln pres. to bp 1 June; eln quashed but bp apptd him 13 June 1306 (*Reg. Woodlock*, I, 127–9). Thomas of Waltham when sacrist of Tandridge mistook the (unnamed) pr. one night in the dark for a robber and attacked him but without serious consequences. Peter, cardinal bp of Sabina, the nuncio, has absolved Thomas and the bp enjoins a salutary penance 26 Sept. 1307 (ibid., 210). Res. (W.) acc. 12 Mar. 1309 and lic. to el. (ibid., 347). Cess. of Walter de Hatfeld mentd (ibid., 368).

Thomas of St Albans (de Sancto Albano) 1309–1322 Convent submitted to bp's ordination to appt a pr.; the pr-el. summoned to bp on 17 June 1309; mand. to obey and install 17 June 1309 (*Reg. Woodlock*, I, 367–9). Can. of Newark, letter to pr. of Newark requesting release to be pr. of Tandridge (ibid., 362). Coadjutor to be apptd 22 Nov. 1312 (ibid., 598–9). Mand. to inquire into his acts and administration 3 Aug. 1321 (*Reg. Asserio*, pp. 409–10). Res. by 10 Feb. 1322 (ibid., p. 481).

Henry (de) Pecham (Pekham) 1322–1324 Can. of Tandridge, eln pres. to vicar-general 10 Feb. 1322; eln conf. 31 Mar. 1322 (*Reg. Asserio*, pp. 481–2). D. by 17 Mar. 1324 (Winchester, Reg. Stratford, f. 3r–v).

John Hansard 1324–1335 Can. of Tandridge, eln pres. to bp 17 Mar. 1324; on 31 Mar. he quashed eln and on 2 Apr. 1324 he was apptd by bp (ibid.). Coadjutor apptd 1330 (ibid., f. 51r). Commn 22 May 1334 to enquire into the state of the pr., suspended by bp from all administration, temporal and spiritual (Winchester, Reg. Orleton I, f. 4r). Res. 4 Sept. 1335 during bp's visitation '*propter sui corporis debilitatem et sue insufficientiam persone*' (ibid., f. 28v).

Philip of Wokingham (Wokyngham) 1335–1341 Can. of Newark, apptd 4 Sept. 1335 (ibid.). Mand. to reside 17 June 1341, similar mand. 28 July, commn to deprive 22 Sept. 1341, deprived 26 Sept. 1341 (ibid., ff. 108r–109r).

John of Merstham (Mertsham) 1341–1380 Can. of Tandridge, el. 11 Nov. 1341; conf. 13 Nov. 1341 (ibid., ff. 109r–v). Res. by 8 May 1380 (*Reg. Wykeham*, II, 317–18).

TAUNTON (Soms), St Peter and St Paul f. *c.* 1120

Lists in *VCH Soms*, II, 144; *Heads*, I, 185.

John Occ. 1197 x 1205 (*HMC Wells*, I. 57), (J.) 5 Oct. 1204 (*Devon F.*, I, p. 31, no. 51); 31 July 1228 (*Soms F.*, I, 71).

Robert Occ. 3 Nov. 1235 (ibid., 86).

Richard Occ. n.d. as predecessor of John (*Soms Pleas*, III, 49).

John Occ. 28 July 1276 when it is stated that John was the successor of Richard, who had died, and the latter had succeeded Robert, who had died (ibid.); Mich. 1278 (PRO, KB27/41, mm. 21, 54); Nov. 1279 x Nov. 1280 (ibid., IV, 217). Coadjutors apptd 1 Sept. 1313 on account of his age (*Reg. Droxford*, p. 158).

Stephen de Pykouteston (Pycoteston) –1325 Occ. 1315 (*Mon. Angl.*, VI, 166; Collinson, *Hist. Soms*, III, 235, no source). Petition by Ralph of Culmstock, sub-pr. and convent for lic. to el. a new pr. on d. of Stephen 26 Dec. 1325; lic. issued 29 Dec. 1325 (Winchester, Reg. Stratford, f. 13r).

Ralph of Culmstock (Colmestock, Col(u)mpstoke, Culmpstock) 1326–1339 Sub-pr. of Taunton, eln pres. to bp of Winchester as patron 7 Jan. 1326; bp's assent and acceptance of the el. 11 Jan. 1326 (ibid., f. 13r–v). Cert. to bp of Winchester that bp of Bath and Wells had conf. and installed him, 29 Jan. 1326 (*Reg. Droxford*, p. 276). Res. made 22 Mar. 1339 and acc. 24 Mar. (*Reg. R. Shrewsbury*, I, no. 1332). Intimation by bp of Bath and Wells of the res. of Ralph 24 Mar 1339 (Winchester, Reg. Orleton II, ff. 71v–72r). Lic. to el. 28 Mar. 1339 (ibid., f. 72r; *Reg. R. Shrewsbury*, I, no. 1332). Letter from the sub-pr. seeking lic. to el. from Bp Orleton, patron, 5 Apr. 1339 (Winchester, Reg. Orleton II, f. 71v).

Robert de Messyngham 1339–1346 Can. of Taunton, eln pres. to bp 20 Apr. 1339; ass. of patron 24 Apr 1339 (ibid., f. 72r–v). Eln held 10 Apr. 1339 (*Reg. R. Shrewsbury*, I, no. 1332). D., lic. to el. by bp of Winchester 2/21 Mar. 1346, eln date fixed for 29 Mar. (ibid., II, no. 1963; *Reg. Edington*, I, no. 52).

Thomas Cook (Le Couk, Coke) 1346– Can. of Taunton, eln announced to bp 30 Mar. 1346 (ibid., no. 72). Bp's ass. and request to bp of Bath and Wells to proceed 4 Apr. 1346 (ibid., no. 73). Opposers to eln cited 6 Apr. 1346, to appear 2 May (*Reg. R. Shrewsbury*, II, no. 1942). Homage paid to bp n.d. [June 1347] (*Reg. Edington*, II, no. 77). Occ. 21 July 1353 (*Reg. R. Shrewsbury*, II, app., no. 2).

Thomas of Petherton (Pedirton, Pedyrton) –1361 D., lic. to el. 23 Nov. 1361 (*Reg. Edington*, I, no. 1475; *Reg. R. Shrewsbury*, II, app., no. 2).

Walter Gratel(e)y (Grategh) 1362–1377 Can. of Taunton, commn to cite opposers to eln 12 Jan. 1362; ass. of bp of Winchester 17 Jan. (ibid.). Ass. of bp of Winchester 17 Jan. 1362 (*Reg. Edington*, I, no. 1488). Pr. alleged to be incompetent; after examination of witnesses he res. 29 Nov. 1377 (*Reg. Wykeham*, II, 291).

John of Kingsbury (Kyngesbury) 1378–1391 Can. of Taunton, nom. to bp of Bath and Wells for appt 18 Apr. 1378 (ibid., 291–2). D.6 Nov. 1391 (ibid., 430).

THELSFORD (Warws), St John the Baptist and St Radegund f. +1170 (Aug.); ?1224 x 1240 (passed to Trinitarians, see p. 534).

> List in *VCH Warws*, II, 106. See L. Watts and P. Rahtz eds., M. Gray, *The Trinitarian Order in England: excavations at Thelsford priory* (BAR, British ser., 226, 1993, pp. 15–20).

Geoffrey Occ. 6 Oct. 1221, Mich. 1221 (*Warws F.*, I, nos. 243, 267); Oct. 1231 x Oct. 1232 (PRO, E326/767).

THETFORD (Norfolk), Holy Sepulchre f. +1139

> Lists in *VCH Norfolk*, II, 393; *VCH Suffolk*, II, 110; *Heads*, I, 185.

Richard Occ. 3 Nov. 1202 (*Norfolk F. 1201–15*, no. 10).

William Occ. 1218 'Thetford Canonicorum' (*Guala Letters*, no. 120); Oct. 1227 x Oct. 1228 (*Norfolk F. (Rye)*, p. 45); Oct. 1234 x Oct. 1235, pr. of St Cross (*Suffolk F. (Rye)*, p. 37).

Richard Occ. Oct. 1242 x Oct. 1243 (*Norfolk F. (Rye)*, p. 69).

Baldwin 1246– Cellarer of Thetford, royal ass. 6 Apr. 1246; patronage belongs to the king by virtue of his custody of the land and heir of W., earl Warenne (*CPR 1232–47*, p. 477).

[**Roger of Kersey** El. 1247, D. 1273 (Martin, *Thetford*, p. 189, citing Blomefield's mss., but see below, William first occ. 1272).]

William Occ. 15 May 1272 (PRO, Cambs F., CP25/1/25/34, no. 25); 16 June 1275 (PRO, F. Divers Cos. CP25/1/284/20, no. 28).

Nicholas Occ. as former pr. Trin. 1283, in case regarding corrody gtd by him (PRO, CP40/50, m. 10).

Peter [de Horsage] El. 1315 (*VCH* citing Norwich, Reg/1/1, f. 63, but cannot be located on this folio). Occ. 21 Sept 1318 (*CCR 1318–23*, p. 99). Possibly the pr. Peter of Thetford who occ. Easter 1327 – Trin. 1328 (*Index to Placita de Banco*, pp. 386, 633), but it could equally be pr. Peter of St Mary's, Thetford (q.v.).

Richard of Wintringham (Wyntringham, Wyntryngham) 1329–1338 Can. of Thetford, eln quashed, but apptd by bp 11 May 1329, no reason given for vacancy (Norwich, Reg/1/2, f. 28v). Res. by 20 Dec. 1338 (Norwich, Reg/1/3, f. 19v).

John of Thetford (Thefford) 1338– Can. of Thetford, eln conf. 20 Dec. 1338 (ibid.).

Robert of Thetford (Thefford) 1349– Can. of Thetford, eln quashed, but apptd by bp 15 July 1349, no reason given for vacancy (*Reg. Bateman*, I, no. 811).

Robert Edwyne –1351 ? same as above. Res. by 14 Nov. 1351 (Norwich, Reg/2/4, f. 134v).

Adam of Hockwold (Hokewold(e)) 1351–1359 Can. of Ixworth, eln quashed, but apptd by bp 14 Nov. 1351 (ibid.). D. by 25 Jan 1359 (Norwich, Reg/2/5, f. 29r–v).

William of Hanworth (Haneworth) 1359– Can. of Thetford, eln quashed, but apptd by bp 25 Jan. 1359 (ibid.).

Adam of Worstead (Worstede) 1378– Can. of Pentney, eln quashed, but apptd by bp 9 June 1378, no reason given for vacancy (Norwich, Reg/3/6, f. 58r). Former pr., apostate signified for arrest 20 Jan. 1395 by present pr. Robert (PRO, C81/1789/60; Logan, *Runaway Religious*, p. 225).

THOBY (Essex) St Leonard, St Mary (Ginges) f. 1141 x 1150
Lists in *VCH Essex*, II, 163; *Heads*, I, 185.

Ralph and H. Occ. in two documents of *c.* 1200 or early 13th cent. the former with Henry, pr. Colchester, St Botolph (*Ctl. Colchester*, II, 304–5).

William Occ. 1227 (PRO, Just.1/229, m. 13).

Henry Occ. 1240 (PRO, E42/384); Hil. 1242, Easter 1245, Trin. 1252 (*Essex F.*, I, 142, 149, 189). Seal (*Mon. Seals*, p. 88).

Thomas Occ. 17 May 1270 (Oxford, New College, Writtle 403/13887).

Roger Occ. Whitsun 1292 (PRO, Just.1/252, m. 2).

John de Pleyces (Plessych) 1306– Can. of Blackmore, postulation of pr. conf., mand. to obey and install 25 Aug. 1306; formal episcopal letter of appt 27 Aug. (*Reg. Baldock*, pp. 21–2). Prob. occ. 12 Mar 1313 (*CCR 1307–13*, p. 569 – calendared as John Prior (surname) of Thoby, but prob. pr. John).

Nicholas Occ. July 1317 x July 1318 (PRO, E326/9040).

William Occ. 2 May 1324 (*CCR 1323–27*, p.177).

Thomas de Parco –1393 Occ. 22 Feb. 1393; res. acc. 29 Apr. 1393 (London, Reg. Braybrooke ff. 292v, 337v).

THORNHOLME (Lincs), St Mary f. *temp.* Stephen
Lists in *VCH Lincs.* II, 168; *Heads*, I, 185.

Andrew Occ. 1205 x 1223 (*EYC*, VI, no. 107); 1216 x 1218 (BL, Cotton ms. Claudius D. XI, f. 217r–v); 1218 (*Ctl. Peterborough*, no. 522); 6 Oct. 1226 (*Lincs. F.*, I, 194).

R. Occ. Dec. 1222 x Dec. 1223 (*sic*) (*Reg. Wells*, I, 219).

Geoffrey Occ. 9 Feb. 1230 (*Lincs. F.*, I, 225).

Roger Occ. 26 Apr. 1254 (*Lincs F.*, II, 108); 7 May 1262 (*Lincs F.*, II, 184; BL, Harl. Cht. 54 E 13).

John of Sixhills (Sixel, Sixil) **1262–1270** Eln conf. May x Nov. 1262, no reason given for vacancy (*Reg. R. Gravesend*, p. 89, cf. p.10). Res. by 14 June 1270 (ibid., p. 92).

Laurence of Goxhill (Gousel) **1271–1280** Eln conf. 14 June 1270 (ibid., pp. 92, 291). Res. by 15 July 1280 (*Reg. Sutton*, VIII, p. 1).

[**Simon** Pr. of Markby postulated on res. of pr. Laurence 15 July 1280 but eln quashed by bp 23 July 1280 (ibid.).]

Thomas of Hedon 1280–1307 Can. of Thornholme, apptd by bp on res. of Laurence 25 July 1280 (ibid.). D. by 24 Aug. 1307 (Lincoln, Ep. Reg., II, f. 91r–v). Seal (*Mon. Seals*, p.88; *BM Seals*, no. 4168).

Walter of Roxby (Roxeby) **1307–** Sub-pr. of Thornholme, el. and appeared. before bp 24 Aug. 1307 (Lincoln, Ep. Reg., II, f. 91r–v). Eln quashed by bp's commissary who apptd Walter 16 Sept. 1307 (ibid.). Occ. 1310 (ibid., f. 94v); 1320, 1321 (*CPR 1317–21*, pp. 545, 603). Lic. to choose a confessor 6 Feb. 1323 (Lincoln, Ep. Reg., V, f. 331v).

Richard of Gainsborough (Geynesburgh) Occ. 12 Oct. 1333 (Lincoln, Ep. Reg., IV, f. 48v); 12 Mar. 1346 (*CPR 1345–48*, p. 107). Unnamed pr. d. by 7 (11) Aug. 1349 (Lincoln, Ep. Reg., IX, f. 157r).

William of Seagrave (Segrave) **1349** Can. of Thornholme. Canons transferred right of appt. to bp of Lincoln 7 Aug. 1349; he apptd William 11 Aug. 1349, no reason given for vacancy (ibid., ff. 156r, 157r). D. on 2 Oct. 1349 (ibid., f. 159r–v).

Roger of Belton 1349– Can. of Thornholme, eln quashed but apptd by bp. 22 Oct. 1349 (ibid.). Occ. 2 July 1351 (*CPR 1350–54*, p. 120).

John de Wa(s)celyn –1383 Occ. 1365 (BL, Harl. Cht. 45 A 7); 1377 (*Clerical Poll-Taxes*, p. 66, no. 874). D. by 19 Dec. 1383 (Lincoln, Ep. Reg., X, f. 149r). Seal (*BM Seals*, no. 4172).

THORNTON CURTIS (Lincs), St Mary f. 1139 (abbey)

Lists in *VCH Lincs*, II, 166; *Heads*, I, 186. List in Bodl., Tanner ms. 166, ff. 4r–13v; BL, Add. ms. 6118, ff. 335–6 (Holles transcript), pd *Mon. Angl.*, VI, 326, partly corrected (to the end of the 12th century) in *PUE*, III, 24 (and see comments in *Heads*, I, 186). The dates given in this list are not always reconcilable, cf. the early 13th-cent. abbots below. In addition the tenure of abbots ignores vacancies (i.e. runs from one abb.'s death to the next).

Jordan de Villa 5th abb., occ. 22 Feb. 1193 (K.J. Stringer in *Essays on the Nobility of Medieval England* (Edinburgh, 1985), pp. 64–5); el. 1203 (Bodl., Tanner ms. 166, f. 7v); said to have d. 7 Nov. 1223 after rule of 20 years and 4 days (list). Seal (*BM Seals*, no. 4183).

Richard de Villa 6th abb., el. 1223 (list, f. 8r), but occ. 1221 x 1223, *temp.* Richard, abb. of Selby (Bodl., Dodsworth ms. 90, f. 118r); 20 Jan. 1222 (*Lincs F.*, I, 162). Occ. 1226 (R.) (*Ctl. Guisborough*, II, 281); Mich. Term 1228, Hil. Term 1229 (*CRR*, XII, nos. 39, 1326); 30 Aug. 1231 (*Lincs F.*, I, 239). D. 6 Feb. 1234 (list, f. 8v – abb. for 10 years), cf. an unnamed abb. d. 1233 (*Ann. Dunstable*, p. 135). Seals (*BM Seals*, no. 4176).

Geoffrey Holme 1231/2– 7th abb., el. 1233/4 (list) but cf. Pr. of Markby, postulated Dec. 1231 x Dec. 1232; letter to bp of Coventry to bl. him, no reason given for vacancy (*Reg. Wells*, III, p. 202). Occ. 30 June 1233 (*Lincs. F.*, I, 252). D. 24 July 1245 (list, f. 8v – abb. for 12 years and 24 weeks), but see below. Cf. also *Ann. Dunstable*, p. 143 – an unnamed abb. deposed by Bp Grosseteste in his visitation of 1236.

Robert –1258/9 8th abb., el. 1245 (list, f. 9r), but occ. 14 Jan. 1235, 9 July 1240 (*Yorks F., 1232–46*, pp. 31, 84–5); Hil. 1243 (*CRR*, XVII, no. 1573; 18 May 1257, 20 Oct. 1258 (*Lincs F.*, II, 129, 161). D. by Nov. 1258 x Nov. 1259 (*Reg. R. Gravesend*, p. 2), cf. D. 15 Mar. 1257/8 (list, f. 9r – abb. for 12 years, 33 weeks, and 2 days).

William of Lincoln (Lincolnia, Lyncolne) **1258/9–1273** 9th abb. el. 1257/8 (list). Cellarer of Thornton, eln conf. & bl. Nov. 1258 x Nov. 1259 (*Reg. R. Gravesend*, p. 2). D. 4 Apr. 1273 (list, f. 10r – abb. for 16 years 4 days, cf. *Reg. R. Gravesend*, p. 54, d. by 3 May 1273). Seal (*BM Seals*, no. 4186).

Walter of Huttoft (Hotoft, Hotot) **1273–1290** 10th abb., el. 1273 (list). Can. of Thornton, eln conf. 3 May 1273 (ibid.). Excused attendance at synod 20 Sept. 1287 (*Reg. Romeyn*, I, p. 204, no. 568). Notice of res. on account of illness 24 Aug. 1290, res. acc. 25 Aug. (*Reg. Sutton*, III, 38–9). Bp of Lincoln tells pr. and convent to proceed to eln of a new abb. 26 Aug. 1290 (PRO, SC1/31/21). Cess., lic. to el. 31 Aug. 1290 (*CPR 1281–92*, p. 383). Seal (*BM Seals*, no. 4179). List, f. 10v has abb. d. 26 June 1291.

Thomas of Glanford Brigg (Bryge, de Ponte/Glauntefordbrig) **1290–1322** 11th abb. Pr. of Thornton, eln pres. to bp of Lincoln 17 Sept. 1290, eln conf. 18 Sept., bl. 24 Sept. 1290 (*Reg. Sutton*, I, 141–2); temps. 19 Sept. 1290 (*CPR 1281–92*, p. 387). Prof. obed. [for churches in the York dioc.] 2 Nov. 1290 (*Reg. Romeyn*, I, p. 215, no. 607). Pardon for trespasses 1319 (*CPR 1317–21*, p. 330). Cess. by 6 Nov. 1322 (*CCR 1318–23*, p. 607). Cess., lic. to el. 21 Nov. 1322 (*CPR 1321–24*, p. 218). Seal (*Mon. Seals*, p. 88). D. 9 Oct. 1323 – abb. 23 years and 15 weeks (list, f. 11v).

William of Grasby (Grasseby, Gresseby, Gryssby) **1322–1348** 12th abb. Can. of Thornton, royal ass. 3 Dec. 1322 (*CPR 1321–24*, p. 221). Eln pres. to bp of Lincoln at York 1 Dec. 1322 (*Reg. Burghersh*, I, no. 60). Commn to examine eln 4 Dec. 1322 (Lincoln, Ep. Reg., V, f. 326r). Eln conf. by bp's commissaries 20 Dec. 1322 (*Reg. Burghersh*, I, no. 60). Prof. obed. 4 June 1324 (York, Reg. 9A, f. 353v). Cess., lic. to el. 7 July 1348 (*CPR 1348–50*, p. 114). D. 10 Feb. 1349 (list, f. 12v – abb. 24 years, 16 (*sic*) months and 6 days).

Robert of Darlington (Derlington, Derlyngton, Derlyncton, Dernyngton) **1348–1364** 13th abb. Can. of Thornton, royal ass. 13 Aug. 1348, temps. 3 Sept. 1348 (*CPR 1348–50*, pp. 142, 150). Commn to examine eln 24 Aug. 1348 (Lincoln, Ep. Reg., IX, f. 12v). Cert. conf. eln by bp of Lincoln 28 Aug. 1348 (PRO, C84/25/18). D. by 2 Nov. 1364 (PRO, C84/29/13), but d. 11 Nov. 1364 – abb. 16 years (list, f. 13v). D., lic. to el. 16 Nov. 1364 (*CPR 1364–67*, p. 37).

Thomas (of) Greetham (Gretham) **1364–1393** Can. of Thornton, eln pres. to king for royal ass. [ ] Nov. 1364 (PRO, C84/29/14); royal ass. 5 Dec. 1364, temps. 21 Dec. 1364 (*CPR 1364–67*, pp. 51, 54). Eln pres. to bp of Lincoln 10 Dec. 1364; eln conf. 20 Dec. 1364 (Lincoln, Ep. Reg., X, f. 21r–v; PRO, C84/29/15). D. by 30 Aug. 1393 (PRO, C84/35/45). D., lic. to el. 31 Aug. 1393 (*CPR 1393–96*, p. 308). After his death a local cult developed against which action was taken by Pope Alexander V in 1410 (L. E. Boyle, *A Survey of the Vatican Archives and of its medieval holdings* (Toronto, 1972), pp. 143–4).[43]

THREMHALL (Essex), St James f. c. 1150

List in *VCH Essex*, II, 164; *Heads*, I, 186.

William Occ. late 1202 (*Essex F.*, I, 27); early 13th cent. (before 1208) (*Hatton's Book of Seals*, p. 113, no. 157).

Robert Occ. as witness to a cht. n. d. (Essex RO, T/B.3, p. 303, from destroyed Reg. Tilty, II, f. 41). The cht. is one of a series of undated (and connected) chts. *VCH*, places Robert between William and John but in fact his precise sequence is uncertain. The chts. would appear to date from the 12th or 13th cents.

---

[43] Cf. Bodl., Tanner ms. 166, f. 13v, note made by Tanner in the Thornton chronicle: 'This fourteenth abbot was Thomas Gretham . . . His time (with the leafe) was torne out by a freind of mine that had the booke, to prevent, as he sayd, the scandall of the church. The truth is the account given of him was that he was a very wicked man, a Sodomite, and what not. . .'.

John Occ. 18 Mar. 1231, Hilary 1259, Easter 1261 (*Essex F.*, I, 88, 231, 241); 1250 (*HMC 9th Rep.*, p. 33).

John of Stortford Occ. 14 Aug. 1299 (PRO, C241/172/50).

John Occ. Trin. 1306 (*Essex F.*, II, 108); 25 Sept. 1306 (*HMC 9th Rep.*, p. 39).

William of Shereford (Sherford) –1368 D. on 15 June 1368 (*Reg. Sudbury*, I, 86).[44]

John of Takeley (Takeleye) 1368– Can. of Thremhall, eln pres. to bp of London 1 July; commn to examine el. 9 July; el. conf. 15 July 1368 (ibid., 86–9).

Archbp of Canterbury writes to the royal chancellor requesting secular assistance in reinstating the rightful pr. 21 July 1375 (PRO, SC1/56/46).

The next recorded pr., **Richard of Braintree** (Brangtre), res., lic. to el. 3 July 1403 (*CPR 1401–05*, p. 239).

THURGARTON (Notts), St Peter f. 1119 x 1139

Lists in *VCH Notts.*, II, 125; Foulds, *Trans. Thoroton Soc.*, 84 (1980) 31–2; *Ctl. Thurgarton*, pp. cci–ccvi; *Heads*, I, 187.

Priory vacant summer 1208 (*CRR*, V, 276).

Henry Occ. 19 Nov. 1208, 22 Nov. 1208 (*Ctl. Thurgarton*, nos. 1037, 1036); 6 Oct. 1218 (*Lincs F.*, I, 117).

Elias Occ. 25 June 1219 (ibid., I, 122–3; *Ctl. Thurgarton*, no. 1023); Hil. term 1221 (*CRR*, X, 21; cf. Southwell ms. 1, p. 42); 25 Apr. 1221 (PRO, Notts F. CP25/1/182/3, no. 6).

John Occ. Trin. term 1227 (*CRR*, XIII, no. 252); c. 1227 (*Ctl. Thurgarton*, no. 1103).

William (?Lucian) Occ. with William de Lisurs who was d. by 10 July 1231 (*Excerpta e Rot. Fin.*, I, 222; *Ctl. Thurgarton*, p. cciii); 20 Jan. 1234 (*Ctl. Thurgarton*, no. 1042); 13 Oct. 1236, 26 Aug. 1240 (*Lincs F.*, I, 292, 335); (W.) 2 Apr. 1240 (*Reg. Gray*, p. 90); 12 Nov. 1244 (*Lincs F.*, II, 3); 6 July 1245 (PRO, Notts F., CP25/1/182/9, no. 316; *Ctl. Thurgarton*, no. 1038). Possibly the pr. William Lucian mentd in a deed c. 1200 x 1232 (*Ctl. Thurgarton*, no. 60).

Richard Occ. from 19 June 1250 to 2 Dec. 1257 (ibid., no. 1046; *Lincs. F.*, II, 88, 97, 114, 152, 284); 2 Dec. 1257 (PRO, Notts, F. CP25/1/183/12, no. 451; F. Divers, CP25/1/283/14, no. 335; *Ctl. Thurgarton*, no. 1029).

Robert of Basford (Baseford) Occ. 20 May 1262 (*CPR 1338–40*, p. 522; *Ctl. Thurgarton*, no. 41 & n. – the editor of the *Ctl.* considers the date, and hence the document, possibly suspect). See below.

Adam of Sutton *alias* **Winton** Occ. 27 Jan. 1263, 3 June 1263, 12 Feb. 1272 (*Lincs. F.*, II, 187, 199, 267; *Ctl. Thurgarton*, no. 1044); 6 May 1263 (PRO, Notts. F., CP2511/183/12, no. 495); 1276, 1277 (PRO, Lincs F. CP25/1/132/51, no. 49; ibid., Notts F., CP25/1/183/14, no. 9; /183/14, no. 14; *Ctl. Thurgarton*, no. 1035); 15 June 1278 (*Ctl. Thurgarton*, no. 958). For name see *Rufford Chts.*, II, no. 622; brother of Gerard of Sutton in Ashfield (*Ctl. Thurgarton*, no. 516n.).

Robert of Basford –1284 Occ. 22 May 1280 (*CCR 1279–88*, p. 14); 25 Nov. 1280 (PRO, Notts F. CP235/1/183/14, no. 38; *Ctl. Thurgarton*, no. 1022); Mich. 1283 x July 1284 (PRO, E159/57, m. 11d). Res. by 9 July 1284 (*Reg. Wickwane*, p. 300, no. 733). Conf. of provision made for ex-pr. 22 Aug. 1284 (ibid., p. 147, no. 438).

Following the. res. of Robert of Basford in 1284 two elns were held. In the first **Alexander of Gedling** and **Nicholas de Gamelay**, cans. of Thurgarton, were el. but both were quashed (ibid., pp. 300–2, no. 733). In the second eln **Roger de Batelay**, can. of Thurgarton, and

---

[44] A document dated 25 July 1330 between the pr. and convent of Thremhall and John Bataille of Manuden has had the name 'William de Sterteforde' written in above the word 'Priorem' in a very much later hand (H.T. Jantzen, East Grinstead, catalogue no. 120, Sept. 1973).

Gilbert of Boroughbridge, can. of Nostell, were el. Again both elns were quashed but Gilbert was provided by the archbp (ibid.).

Gilbert of Boroughbridge (de Ponte Burgi) **1284–1290** Letter to the patron asking for his ass. 9 July 1284; can. of Nostell, mand. to obey him and to install, dated 9 July 1284 (ibid., pp. 300–2, no. 733). Occ. July x Mich. 1284 (PRO, E159/57, m. 11d). Purgation of pr. Gilbert accused of incontinence with Margery wife of Reginald Canun of Lowdham 19 May 1286 (*Reg. Romeyn*, I, p. 245, no. 711). Lic. to el. on res. 17 Oct. 1290 (ibid., I, p. 294, no. 827). Sent back to Nostell 25 Oct. 1290 (ibid., p. 104, no. 278). He was apptd to Hexham 1311 (q. v.).

Alexander of Gedling (Gedeling) **1290–1304** Can. of Thurgarton, provided 20 Nov. 1290 after eln been quashed by archbp (ibid., I, p. 296, no. 831). Dep. by archbp 13 Mar. 1304 (*Reg. Corbridge*, I, 272–3). Plea by sub-pr. and convent to restore Alexander n.d., and archbp's reply 25 Mar. 1304 (ibid., 274–7); archbp's mand. to choose a new pr. 31 Mar. 1304 (ibid., 278).

[J(ohn) of Hickling (Hikeling) Can. of Thurgarton, eln quashed and new eln ordered 18 Apr. 1304 (ibid., 278–9). See below.]

John of Rudston (Rodeston, Ruddestan, Ruddestayn, Rudestan, Rudstan) **1304–1319** Can. of Thurgarton, eln quashed but apptd by archbp 3 May 1304 (ibid., 279); Occ. 11 Dec. 1319 (York, Reg. 9B, f. 409v). Res. by 12 Dec. 1319 when lic. to el. gtd (ibid.). Provision made for him 11 Feb. 1324 (ibid. f. 425v). Pr. again 1337–8.[45]

John of Hickling (Hicling, Hikleling, Kykeling) **1320–1331** Sub-pr. of Thurgarton, eln proclaimed 4 Jan 1320; eln quashed but apptd by archbp 1 Feb. 1320 (ibid., ff. 409v, 410r). Lic. to visit Rome 24 May 1322 (ibid., f. 420r). Res. by 23 Sept. 1331 (ibid., f. 454r).

Robert of Hathern 1331–1337 Can. of Thurgarton, eln quashed but apptd by archbp 23 Sept.1331 (ibid.). D. by 28 Aug. 1337 (ibid., f. 472r).

John of Rudston 1337–1338 Can. of Thurgarton, commn to examine eln 28 Aug. 1337; eln conf. 6 Sept. 1337 (ibid., f. 472r–v). Res. 5 June 1338 (ibid., f. 473r).

Richard of Thurgarton 1338–1346 Can. of Thurgarton, commn to examine eln 20 June 1338; eln conf. 27 June 1338 (ibid., f. 473r–v). D. by 12 Jan. 1346 (York, Reg.10, f. 92v).

Robert of Hickling (Hikelyng, Hiklyng) **1346–1349** Can. of Thurgarton, eln conf. 12 Jan 1346 (ibid.). D. by 28 Aug.1349 when presn to Timberland vicarage made by sub-pr. and convent (Lincoln, Ep. Reg. IX, f. 64v; cf. York, Reg. 10, f. 135v).

Robert of Claxton 1349–1379 Can. of Thurgarton, eln conf. 5 Oct. 1349 (York, Reg.10, f. 135v). D. by 23 Aug. 1379 (York, Reg. 12, f. 78v).[46]

TIPTREE (Essex), St. Mary and St. Nicholas f. -1200
List in *VCH Essex*, II,165.

Benedict Occ. *c*. 1221 x 1228 (BL, Harl. Cht. 50 C 3, *temp.* Bp Eustace of London, cited from *TEAS*, XVII, 48); 1240 (PRO, E42/384); Mich. 1243 (*Essex F.*, I, 148).

John Occ. n.d. (first half of 13th cent.: pal.) (PRO, E40/14525).

Walter Occ. n.d. (*c*. 1260) (Bodl., Essex Cht. 16).

Robert Occ. July 1309 (ibid., Essex Cht. 24).[47]

---

[45] R. White, *Dukery Records*, 390, refers to Alexander of Thurgarton succeeding John of Rudston in 1316 (cf. Foulds, *Trans. Thoroton Soc.*, 31). John actually res. in 1319 but this earlier event seems to be the appt of an attorney or proctor in a particular lawcase (*CCR 1313–18*, p. 438).

[46] John of Caunton occ. as pr. 9 Jan. 1379 (*CPR 1377–81*, p. 425), in an inspeximus of 23 Jan. 1380. This is actually an error for 9 Jan. 1380 new style (cf. *Mon. Angl.*, VIII, 1315–16): the archbp's commn is dated 18 July 1379. Caunton (Calveton)'s eln was not conf. until 23 Aug. 1379 (York, Reg. 12, f. 78v).

[47] *VCH* has reference to pr. John in 1355 and pr. [*blank*] de Wyndesore in 1358, citing Bodl. Chts. These chts. have not been located.

Thomas (de) Multon (Malton) **–1391** Occ. 1374 x 1375 (PRO, C85/121/63); 23 Mar. 1375 (*Reg. Sudbury*, II,141); 4 Aug. 1376 (*CCR 1374–77*, p. 439); 19 Sept.1386 (*CCR 1385–89*, p. 279); 2 Sept.1389 protection for 2 years as he holds of the king by the service of carrying on the day of the coronation the irons wherein the king's wafers are made and assaying them before the king; upon his petition that John de Boys, patron of the priory, had despoiled him thereof (*CPR 1388–92*, p. 109; see also R.F[owler], 'Tiptree Priory and the Coronation', *TEAS*, n.s. VIII (1901), 334–5). Occ. 12 Nov. 1389 (PRO, C85/122/37). Res. by 6 Feb. 1391 when eln process began (London, Reg. Braybrooke, f. 333r).

TOCKWITH, *see* SKEWKIRK

TONBRIDGE (Kent) St Mary Magdalen f. -1192
Lists in *VCH Kent*, II. 168; Hailstone, *History of Bottisham*, p. 153; *Heads*, I, 187.

John last recorded occ. 5 Jan. 1202 (Cheney, *Inn. III*, no. 368, cf. nos. 369–71).

John Occ. Oct. 1242 x Oct. 1243 (*Surrey F.*, p. 26); 20 Oct. 1248, 25 Nov. 1248 (*Kent F.*, pp. 220, 224).

Peter Occ. (P.) 23 Jan. 1268 (*Reg. Hethe*, I, 45); 29 May 1272 (PRO, Cambs F., CP25/1/25/33, no. 8). Mentd as previous pr. 1308 x 1309 (*YB I*, 65, 67).

David –1279 Occ. *c.* Nov. 1273, 25 Feb. 1274 (*Cal. Bodl. Chts.*, pp. 117, 133, 136). D. (D.) by 13 June 1279 (*Reg. G. Giffard*, p. 107).

John 1279– Sub-pr. of Tonbridge. The earl of Gloucester and Hereford asks the bp of Worcester to inst. John 13 June 1279. The bp commns the pr. of Combwell to proceed to conf. eln 14 June 1279 (ibid.). Occ. Nov. 1285 x Nov. 1286, 7 Feb. 1305 (Bodl., Kent Cht. 72*; Kent Cht. 79); Easter 1298 (PRO, CP40/123, m. 181d); 3 Apr. 1303 (PRO, E40/3139).

Roger Occ. 25 Nov. 1307, called de Snotbrame (PRO, C85/143/36); *c.* Mich. 1311 (Bodl., Kent Chts. 83–88 (roll)).

John Osprengge Occ. 25 Mar. 1320 (Hill, *Eccles. Letter-books*, p. 216);11 Sept. 1320, July 1323 x July 1324, 1 Aug. 1336 (ibid., Kent Chts. 82, 88*, Kent Roll 7). Unnamed pr. on 26 Apr. 1326 was also pr. on 8 Sept. 1317 (*CCR 1323–27*, p. 470).

William Frendesbury Occ. 17 June 1337, 5 Jan. 1349 (Bodl., Kent Roll 7, Kent Cht. 101).

William of Malling (Mallyng) Occ. 27 Nov. 1352 (ibid., Kent Roll 8); 2 Oct. 1358 (PRO, E40/7971).

John Pecham 1361– Can. of Tonbridge, eln conf. 5 Nov. 1361, no reason given for vacancy (Lambeth, Reg. Islip, f. 226r–v). Occ. Jan. 1372 x Jan. 1373 (Bodl., Kent Cht. 115).

Robert Mallyng –1379 Occ. 29 Sept. 1376 (Bodl., Kent Cht. 116). Res. by 19 Sept. 1379 (Lambeth, Reg. Sudbury, f. 57v).

TORKSEY (Lincs), St Leonard f. *temp.* Henry II
Lists in *VCH Lincs*, II, 171; *Heads*, I, 187.

Absalom Occ. 21 Jan. 1186 (B. Dodwell, 'A papal bull for Torksey priory', *BIHR*, 52 (1979), 87–90); 1201 (BL, Lansdowne ms. 402, ff. 33v–34r). Mentioned as former pr. 16 Aug. 1268 in inspected charter n.d. (1186 x 1200) (*CChR 1257–1300*, p. 106).

John –1236/7 Occ. 5 Oct. 1234, 16 Oct. 1234 (*Lincs F.*, I, 280, 261). Res. June 1236 x June 1237 (*Reg. Grosseteste*, p. 138).

Ivo (Yvo) 1236/7–1247/8 Cellarer of Torksey, el. and adm. June 1236 x June 1237 (ibid.). Res. June 1247 x June 1248 (ibid., p. 153).

Henry 1247/8– Can. of Thornton, postulated and inst. June 1247 x June 1248 (ibid.).

John –1262/3 Res. Nov. 1262 x Nov. 1263 (*Reg. R. Gravesend*, p. 90).

John of Lincoln 1262/3– El. and inst. Nov. 1262 x Nov. 1263 (ibid., pp. 90, 290).

John of Owmby (Ouneby) –1282 D. by 25 July 1282 (*Reg. Sutton*, VIII, 3).

William of Rasen 1282–1286 Can. of Torksey, el. 25 July 1282 but quashed by bp who apptd him n.d. (? late July) (ibid.). Res. by 14 July 1286 (ibid., 8).

[**William of Keelby** (Kellby) Can. of Thornton, el. before 14 July 1286, but refused office (ibid.).]

Joel of Lincoln 1286–1292 Sub-pr. of Torksey, el. on res. of William of Rasen and the refusal of William of Keelby to assume office; eln conf. 14 July 1286 (ibid.). Res. by 26 July 1292 (ibid., 22).

William of Rasen 1292–1295 Sub-pr. of Torksey, eln submitted for confirmation 26 July 1292 el. conf. 27 July 1292 (ibid.). Res. by 13 Apr. 1295 (ibid., 25).

Geoffrey of Beckering (Bekering) 1295–1296 Can. of Kyme, postulated to Torksey on res. of William of Rasen; eln conf. 13 Apr. 1295 (ibid.). Res. priory and permitted to return to Kyme 13 May 1296 (ibid., V, 152).

William of Rasen 1296–1316 Can. of Torksey, eln conf. 13 May 1296. Letter to Kyme about re-admittance of Geoffrey who had res. (ibid., VIII, 27). Res. by 18 Nov. 1316, when provision made for him as former pr. (Lincoln, Ep. Reg., III, f. 358r–v, cf. Lincoln, Ep. Reg. II, f.98r–v).

Robert de Sandale 1316– Can. of Torksey, eln quashed but apptd by bp 19 Nov. 1316 (Lincoln, Ep. Reg., II, f. 98r–v). Occ. 1 July 1323 (*CPR 1321–24*, p. 16).

Henry of Thornhaugh (Thornhagh) –1333 Res. by 20 Mar. 1333 (Lincoln, Ep. Reg., IV, f. 103v).

[**Robert of Kelfield** Can. of Torksey, eln quashed 20 Mar. 1333 (ibid.). Previously as can. of Torksey (Kekfeld) collector in the diocese of York for the fabric of the priory (*Reg. Melton*, III, no. 70).]

Henry of Buckingham (Buckyngham) 1333– Can. of Missenden, apptd by bp 4 Apr. 1333 (*Reg. Burghersh*, I, no. 779).

Robert of Willingham (Wylyngham) –1347 Cess. by 24 May 1347 (Lincoln, Ep. Reg., VI, f. 30v). House vacant by 12 May 1347 when Robert Pie, can. of Torksey, was apptd administrator of the priory during the vacancy (Lincoln, Ep. Reg., VII, f. 91v).

Henry of Crowland (Crouland, Croyland) 1347–1348 Can. of Torksey, eln quashed by Official *sede vacante* 24 May 1347 (entry unfinished) (Lincoln, Ep. Reg.,VI, f. 30v). Cess. by 20 Mar. 1348 (Lincoln, Ep. Reg., IX, f. 154r.)

John Poignant (Poynnaunt, Poynyant, Pugniant) 1347–1352 Can. of Osney, right of appt transferred by convent to the bp, who apptd John 20 Mar. 1348 (ibid.). Occ. 5 Apr. 1351 (*CCR 1349–54*, p. 360). House vacant by 11 Dec. 1351 when an appt. made to a vicarage in the priory's patronage (Lincoln, Ep. Reg., IX, f. 162v). D. by 24 Sept. 1352 (*CFR 1347–56*, p. 340).

Robert of Willingham (Wyulyngham) 1353– Can. of Torksey, apptd by archbp of Canterbury 1 June 1353, no reason given for the vacancy, the right having devolved by the negligence of the canons and the bp of Lincoln (Lambeth Palace, Reg. Islip, f. 68v). Occ. 9 May 1354 (*CCR 1354–60*, p. 68); Easter 1361 (*CPR 1361–64*, p. 166; PRO, CP40/406, m. 162).

Thomas of Saxilby 1366–1374 Since house vacant over three months the right to appt devolved to bp and he comm. William Hunte to adm. Thomas of Saxilby, can. of Torksey, and install him n.d. (Lincoln, Ep. Reg., XII, f. 34v). Similar commn 26 Apr. 1366 (ibid., f. 30v). Res. by 2 June 1374 (Lincoln, Ep. Reg., X, f. 140r).

John (of) Boston (de Sancto Botulpho) 1374–1392 Can. of Torksey, eln conf. 2 June 1374 (ibid.). Cess. by 4 Feb. 1392 (Lincoln, Ep. Reg., XI, f. 107v)

TORTINGTON (Sussex), St. Mary Magdalen f. *c.* 1180
  Lists in *VCH Sussex*, II, 83; *Heads*, I, 187.
Nicholas Occ. 1180 x 1197 (*Ctl. Chichester*, no. 182).
Henry Occ. 1218 (*Ctl. Lewes*, II, p. 75, n. 1); 1220 x 1224 (PRO, E40/14196).
R. Occ. 28 Sept. 1222 (*Ctl. Chichester*, no. 1120). Prob. Reyner below.
Reyner (Reiner) Occ. from 23 Nov. 1229 to 18 Nov. 1248 (*Sussex F.*, I, nos. 219, 464); 1232,
  1235, Dec. 1247 (*Ctl. Chichester*, nos. 542, 543, 37); Oct. 1253 x Oct. 1254 (*Surrey F.*, p. 35);
  14 June 1254 (Merton Coll. mun., IV, 572); n.d. (PRO, E326/3196).
Robert Occ. 1254 x 72 (*Ctl. Chichester*, no. 30); 26 Aug. 1262 (Merton Coll. mun., IV, 573).
Matthew Occ. 18 Nov. 1255 (*Sussex F.*, II, no. 577); *temp.* Henry III (PRO, Just.1/912A, m. 4d).
William (de) Launcel Occ. 2 Mar. 1274 (PRO, SC1/7/28); 1278 (PRO, KB27/38, m. 16);
  Mich. 1278 (PRO, KB27/41, m. 21d).
Roger Occ. Nov. 1296 x Nov. 1297 (PRO, E210/6943).
Walter Occ. *c.* Sept. 1320 (PRO, Just.1/938/1, m. 36d); 8 Oct. 1329 (*CCR 1327–30*, p. 572); Jan.
  1331 x Jan. 1332 (PRO, E40/14670); 5 Feb. 1331, 27 Apr. 1331 (*CPR 1330–34*, pp. 128, 142).
William Bradewell Occ. Jan. 1356 x Jan. 1357 (PRO, E212/136).
William Occ. 5 May 1361 (*CPP*, pp. 317, 367). Possibly the same as above.
John Palmer(e) John Palmer, calling himself pr. in sanctuary at Westminster abbey 10 Oct.
  1366 (*CPR 1364–67*, pp. 312–13). Occ. 2 July 1376 (Lambeth, Reg. Sudbury, f. 26v).
John Occ. 1381 (PRO, E179/11/9). Possibly the same as John above.

TREGONEY (Cornwall) St James (Le Val) f. -1125 (?). Diss. 1267 and granted to Merton
priory.
  List in Oliver, p. 65; cf. *JRIC*, n.s. 3(4) (1960), 450–2.
Nicholas de Sancto Remigio 1260– Can. of Le Val, inst. 30 Mar. 1260, no reason given for
  vacancy (*Reg. Bronescombe*, pp. 187–8; *Reg. W. Bronescombe*, I, no. 229).
Geoffrey de Algia 1264– Can. of Le Val and proctor of the abbot and convent in England,
  custody gtd to him until 20 Apr. next on 27 Jan. 1264 (*Reg. Bronescombe*, pp. 274–5; *Reg. W.
  Bronescombe*, II, no. 528).
Deed of exchange of priory – Br Richard de Ponte, proctor of the abb. and convent of Le Val to
  Bp Walter of Exeter, 4 Aug. 1267 (Oliver, *Supplement*, p. 7). Priory of Tregoney exchanged
  between Le Val and Merton for the priory of Cahagnes, dioc. Bayeux – bp of Exeter's letter
  dated 29 May 1278 (*Reg. Bronescombe*, II, no. 1277; cf. *Reg. Quivil*, p. 379; Matthew, *Norman
  Monasteries*, p. 102, n. 5; cf.).

TRENTHAM (Staffs), St Mary and All Saints f. 1155
  Lists in *VCH Staffs*, III, 259–60; *Ctl. Trentham*, p. 299; *Heads*, I, 187.
Alan Occ. n.d. (late 12th/early 13th cent.: pal.) (Cheshire RO, DCR.26/6A/1).
William Mentd, along with Richard and Roger, in a plea of Mich. 1305, as pr. *temp.* Henry
  III (BL, Lansdowne ms. 207B, ff. 282v–283r). His place in the sequence of priors is uncer-
  tain.
Richard ? early Henry III (*Ctl. Stone*, p. 11; cf. p. 17); 1224 x 1238 (ibid., p. 19); 25 June 1234
  (*Lincs F.*, I, 288).
Roger Occ. 1 Aug. 1242 (*Ctl. Trentham*, pp. 314, 315); 1246 (ibid., p. 306); 9 July 1251 (*Derbys
  F. (1886)*, p. 56); 12 July 1255 (PRO, E326/3823); 1255 (*Ctl. Trentham*, p. 315).
Geoffrey Occ. *c.* Mich. 1261 (*Reg. R. Gravesend*, p. 322).
Roger Occ. 25 Nov. 1267 (*Lincs F.*, II, 226).
Richard Occ. *c.* 1272, early Edward I (*Ctl. Trentham*, p. 318).
Robert de Seintpere Can. of Trentham, el. pr. *temp.* Henry III, pres. to king and was adm. and

install. by bp of Coventry and Lichfield. Died *temp.* Edmund, earl of Lancaster (1267–96) and was succeeded by John de Conyngston (*YB 18 Edward III*, p. 49).

John de Conyngston (Conynston) **–1297** Can. of Trentham, el. *temp.* Edward I and pres. to Edmund, earl of Lancaster, and by him to the bp of Coventry and Lichfield who adm. and install. him (ibid.). Occ. from 25 Mar. 1280 to 1296 (*Ctl. Trentham*, pp. 319, 325, 327); 1282 (PRO, E326/11833); 1293 (*Staffs Plea Rolls 1272–94*, p. 225); 1297 (PRO, E210/10580). Res. by 9 May 1297 (PRO, C84/12/45). Cess., lic. to el. 11 May 1297 (*CPR 1292–1301*, p. 248).

Richard de Lavinden (Lavendene, Lavynden, Layndon) **1297–** Sub-pr. of Trentham, eln pres. to king for royal ass. 24 May 1297 (PRO, C84/12/47); royal ass. 5 June 1297, temps. 20 June 1297, having been conf. by the vicegerent of bp of Coventry and Lichfield, the latter being overseas (*CPR 1292–1301*, pp. 252–3). Occ. 1299 to 1 June 1302 (*Ctl. Trentham*, pp. 325, 307, 310–12).

Richard de Dulverne (also Bulmere) **–1343** Can. of Trentham, el. on d. of pr. Richard de Lavinden (*YB 18 Edward III*, p. 51). Occ. 18 Mar. 1305 (*CPR 1301–07*, p. 347); Trin. 1307 (*Staffs Plea Rolls 1294–1307*, p. 187); 1313 to 1338 (*Ctl. Trentham*, p. 334). Pardon to Richard de Dulverne. Upon the past voidance of the house by the d. of pr. Richard de Lavinden, Thomas, earl of Lancaster, asserting the advowson of the priory belonged to him, although it belonged to the king, compelled the sub-pr. and convent to obey him; and Richard on his eln did fealty to him. The king pardons him and takes fealty from pr. Richard 25 Mar. 1322 (*CPR 1321–24*, p. 92). D., lic. to el. 10 Oct. 1343 (Bulmere) (*CPR 1343–45*, p. 125; cf. Lichfield, B/A/1/2, f. 174v (Dulverne)).

Richard de Whatton (Watton) **1343–1352** Can. of Trentham, royal ass. 25 Oct. 1343, temps. 1 Dec. 1343 (*CPR 1343–45*, pp. 135, 140). Henry, earl of Lancaster, brought a case of *quare impedit* against the sub-pr. and convent 1343 (*YB 18 Edward III*, pp. 49–51). Eln conf. 21 Nov. 1343 (Lichfield, B/A/1/2, f. 174v). D. 14 June 1352 (PRO, C84/27/1). D., lic. to el. 20 June 1352 (*CPR 1350–54*, p. 294).

Nicholas of Mucklestone (Mokeleston, Mokeliston, Mokelyston, Moleston, Muc(k)leston) **1352–1402** Can. of Trentham, eln pres. to king for royal ass. 24 July 1352 (PRO, C84/27/3); royal ass. 3 Aug. 1352, temps. 26 Aug. 1352 (*CPR 1350–54*, pp. 308, 319). Commn to examine eln 29 July 1352; eln conf. by commissary 11 Aug. 1352. Prof. of obed. 23 Aug. 1352 (Lichfield, B/A/1/2, ff. 192v–193r). Notarial instrument of res. 23 July 1402 (PRO, C270/24/10, cf. PRO, C84/38/29). Res., lic. to el. 28 July 1402 (*CPR 1401–05*, p. 110). Seal (*BM Seals*, no. 4206).

TWYNHAM, *see* CHRISTCHURCH

ULVERSCROFT (Leics), St Mary f. 1134

Lists in *VCH Leics.*, II, 20–1; *Heads*, I, 187.

Walter Occ. 1219 x 1234, prob. soon after 1219 (Nichols, *Leics*, III, 1085); 30 Sept. 1221 (PRO, Leics. F., CP25/1/121/8, no. 34); 1222 (Alençon, Archives Dép. de l'Orne, H.930; PRO, PRO31/8/140B, part 1, p. 216); c. 1230 (BL, Harl. Cht. 112 C 27).

Thomas –1269 Occ. n.d. (mid-13th cent.: pal.) (PRO, E40/12096); Aug. 1243 (PRO, PRO31/8/140B, part 1, p. 226). Res. by 16 Jan. 1269 (*Reg. R. Gravesend*, p. 148). Poss. the pr. T. who occ. *temp.* Henry III (pal. *HMC R.R. Hastings*, I, 12).

William of Spondon 1269–1276 Can. of Ulverscroft, adm. 16 Jan. 1269 (*Reg. R. Gravesend*, p. 148). Occ. (W.) 10 June 1276 (*Reg. W. Giffard*, p. 262). Res. by 27 Oct. 1276 to join Franciscans (*Reg. R. Gravesend*, p. 159).

Robert of Gaddesby (Gaddisby, Gadesby) **1276–1304** Can. of Ulverscroft, adm. 27 Oct. 1276 (ibid.). Occ. 1288 (Farnham, *Charnwood Forest*, p. 120); 1297 (*Cal. Chancery Rolls*, p. 55). House vacant by his death 3 Aug. 1304 (Lincoln, Ep. Reg., II, f. 200r). Seal (*BM Seals*, no. 4229).

John of Normanton 1304–1305 Can. of Ulverscroft, eln quashed but apptd by bp 13 Aug. 1304 (Lincoln, Ep. Reg., II, f. 200r). House vacant by his cess. by 15 June 1305 (ibid., f. 201r). Presumably res. on 29 May 1305 – Lincoln, Ep. Reg., III, f. 83r has the res. of Robert Gaddesby acc. on 29 May 1305, *recte* John of Normanton.

Walter of Evesham 1305–1315 Can. of Ulverscroft, eln quashed but apptd by bp 15 June 1305 (Lincoln, Ep. Reg., II, f. 201r). Res. on 22 Apr. 1315 (ibid., f. 209r).

Roger of Glen 1315–?1338/9 Can. of Ulverscroft, commn to examine eln 22 Apr. 1315 (ibid.). Eln quashed but apptd by bp's commissary 10 May. 1315 (ibid.). Occ. 25 Nov. 1330 (*Reg. Burghersh*, I, no. 993). House vacant by d. of unnamed pr. by 30 Jan. 1339 (ibid., no. 1155). Convent to proceed to eln 22 Jan. 1339 (Lincoln, Ep. Reg., V, f. 566v).

Roger of Shepshed (Schepesheved, Shepesheved) **1339–1368** Vicar-general's commn to official of archdn of Leicester giving leave to make appt 30 Jan 1339 (*Reg. Burghersh*, I, no. 1155). Commn to enquire into vacancy of priory 30 Jan. 1339 (Lincoln, Ep. Reg., V, f. 244r). Can. of Ulverscroft, apptd by lapse, the convent having failed to make an eln within the permitted time 10 Apr. 1339 (*Reg. Burghersh*, I, no. 1155). Occ. 1352 (PRO, DL25/313); 20 July 1363 (*CPR 1361–64*, pp. 445–6); 20 Sept. 1365 (York, Reg. 11, f. 262v). Mentioned in will dated 1 June 1368; his successor Thomas ment. in undated codicil (Lambeth, Reg. Whittlesey, f. 124v). Seal (*Mon. Seals*, p. 91).

Thomas of Lockington (Lokyngton) **1368–1387** Can. of Ulverscroft, commn to examine eln 28 Dec. 1368 (Lincoln, Ep. Reg., XII, f. 62r–v). D. by 24 Nov. 1387 (Lincoln, Ep. Reg., XI, f. 207v).

WALSINGHAM (Norfolk), St Mary f. c. 1153

Lists in *VCH Norfolk*, II, 401; *Heads*, I, 188; 15th cent. list in BL, Cotton ms. Nero E VII, f. 157v, printed in J.C. Dickinson, *The Shrine of Our Lady of Walsingham*, (Cambridge, 1956), pp. 133–4, on occasion (see below, Thomas de Clare) in error and prob. to be used with caution.

William *c.* **1207–c. 1254** 4th pr., ruled 47 years (list, p. 133). Occ. morrow St Edward 1235, 6 Jan. or 19 Mar. (BL, Cotton roll, IV 57, no. 48); Occ. from Oct. 1238 x Oct. 1239 to Oct. 1250 x Oct. 1251 (*Norfolk F. (Rye)*, pp. 60, 84); Oct. 1249 x Oct 1250 (*Suffolk F. (Rye)*, p. 50); 26 Apr. 1250 (Bodl., Norfolk cht. 554); 25 Nov. 1250 (*Lordship and Landscape*, p. 65).

Peter 5th pr. (coupled with Alan 6th pr., in 16 years' rule (list, p. 133). In the margin of the list (BL, Cotton ms. Nero E VI, f. 157v) is a note *Memorandum quod anno vj. Petri prioris factum [?] fuit statutum Quia Emptores terrarum*. This is presumably an error: *Quia Emptores* dates from 1290!

Alan 6th pr. Occ. Oct. 1267 x Oct. 1268, Oct. 1268 x Oct. 1269 (*Norfolk F. (Rye)*, pp., 104, 106); 1273 (Blomefield, *Norfolk*, IX, 277).

William 7th pr. ruled 9 years (list, p. 133). Occ. Nov. 1275 x Nov. 1276 (*Norfolk F. (Rye)*, p. 115); Mich. 1278 (PRO, KB27/41, m. 25d).

John 8th pr., ruled 20 years (list, p. 133). Occ. Mich. 1279 x Mich. 1280 (PRO, E159/53, m. 9d); Easter 1282 (PRO, CP40/45, m. 80); Trin. 1283 (PRO, CP40/50, m. 63); 21 May 1291 (*Norwich Cath. Chts.*, II, no. 223); Easter 1298 (PRO, CP40/123, mm. 175d, 180d).

Philip 9th pr., ruled 14 years (list, p. 133). Occ. 16 May 1306 (*Lordship and Landscape*, p. 111).

Walter de Wyghtone 1314–1335 10th pr., ruled 22 years (list, p. 133). Eln conf. 12 Jan. 1314, no reason given for vacancy (Norwich, Reg/1/1, f. 55r). Occ. 6 Oct. 1327 (*CPR 1327–30*, p. 214). D. by. 9 Sept. 1335 (Norwich, Reg/1/2, f. 75r).

Simon de Wyneton *alias* **Storm 1335–1349** 11th pr., ruled 14 years (list, p. 133). Sub-pr. of Walsingham, eln conf. 9 Sept. 1335 (Norwich, Reg/1/2, f. 75r). D. by 31 July 1349 (*Reg. Bateman*, I, no. 912 & n. 87).

Thomas de Clare 1349–1374 12th pr., ruled 10 years – evidently wrong (List, p. 133). Can. of Walsingham, eln quashed but apptd by bp 31 July 1349 (Norwich Reg/2/4, f. 100r–v). Occ. 10 Sept. 1350, 3 Jan. 1355 (*CPL*, III, 402, 550); 27 Feb. 1364 (*CPL*, IV, 41). 12 June 1374 letter of sub-pr. and convent to earl of March for lic. to el. (BL, Add. ms. 6041, f. 70r, no. xix); earl's lic. to el. 3 Feb. 1376 (*sic*) (ibid., f. 70r, no. xx – *error*). Res. by 9 July 1374 (Norwich, Reg/3/6, ff. 26v–27r).

John of Snoring (Naryng, Norryngge, Snoryng(e), Snoryngg) **1374–** 13th pr., ruled 27 years (list, p. 133). Letter of sub-pr. and convent asking earl of March to write to bp of Norwich asking for John's conf., 4 July 1374 (BL, Add. ms. 6041, f. 70r, no. xxi). Can. of Walsingham, commn to examine eln 9 July 1374, eln conf. 15 July 1374 (Norwich, Reg/3/6, ff. 26v–27r). Occ. 1378 x 1381 (PRO, E179/45/14); 9 Mar. 1384 (*CPR 1381–85* p. 389; *CCR 1381–85*, p. 434). In dispute with the bp of Norwich over conversion of the priory into an abbey etc. from 1382, leading to his removal by the bp in 1389, but later restored (Dickinson, pp. 28–31, cf. ibid., p. 134 quoting from BL, Cotton ms. Nero E VII, f. 157r (marginal note to list of priors): *Memorandum quod Johannes Herford' gessit officium et nomen prioris predicto Johanne Snoryng existente Rome in placito pro abbathia de prioratu fienda; sed dominus Henricus Spenser episcopus Norwicensis cum maiori parte conventus huic officium [?] restituit et sic totus labor predicti domini Johannis, licet multum sumptuosus est, erat cassatus*). Removed by Archbp Arundel of Canterbury after his visitation 1400 (ibid., p. 32).

WALTHAM (Essex), Holy Cross f. –1060 (secular); 1177 (priory); 1184 (abbey).

Lists in *VCH Essex* II, 170–1; *Heads*, I, 188; *Waltham Chts.*, pp. xi–xii.

Richard *c.* **1201/2–1230** Bl. 29 Dec. 1201 x 10 June 1202 (*Waltham Chts.*, p. xi and no. 413 and n. 23). Occ. 1203 (*Essex F.*, I, 31); (R.) 1218 (*CPR 1216–25*, p. 177); 1219 (*Lincoln Reg. Ant.*, III, no. 653); Trin. 1220, 8 Nov. 1227 (*Essex F.*, I, 56, 75); 14 July 1220, 1 May 1221, 20 May 1223 (*Lincs F.*, I, 155, 157, 166); 16 June 1224 (*Beds F.*, I, p. 67, no. 262); 1225 (*CPR 1225–32*, p. 2); 27 May 1228 (BL, Cotton ms. Tiberius C IX, f. 153r–v). D., lic. to el. 22 Mar. 1230 (*CPR 1225–32*, p. 330).

Henry of Amwell 1230–1248 Pr. of Waltham, royal ass. 1 Apr. 1230 (ibid., pp. 330–1). Occ. from 6 Oct. 1240 to 16 Feb. 1248 (*Essex F.*, I, 127, 177). 3rd abb., d. 25 Mar. 1248 (Bodl., Rawlinson ms. B.177, f. 228v). D. by 30 Mar. 1248 (*CPR 1247–58*, p. 11). For his origin see *Waltham Chts.*, p. xii, n. 7, citing BL, Harl. ms. 3776, f. 38r.

Simon of Saham 1248–1264 Can. of Waltham, royal ass. 11 Apr. 1248 (*CPR 1247–58*, p. 12). Formerly cellarer, lic. to bps of Ely and Rochester to bl. 21 May 1251 (*CPL*, I, 272). D., lic. to el. 15 Apr. 1264 (*CPR 1258–66*, p. 312).

Adam de Wiz (Wich) **1264–1270** Can. of Waltham, writ *de intendendo* 20 Aug. 1264, the eln having been conf. by Guy, bp of Sabina, papal legate (ibid., p. 342). D. 17 Sept. 1270 and bur. next day (*Ch. Bury*, p. 48). Lic. to el. 18 Sept. 1270 (*CPR 1266–72*, p. 461). Seal (*BM Seals*, no. 4255).

Richard de Harewes (Heregens, Herghes) **1270–1273** Can. of Waltham, royal ass. 5 Oct. 1270 (*CPR 1266–72*, p. 464). D., lic. to el. 2 Nov. 1273 (*CPR 1272–81*, p. 31). Seal (*Mon. Seals*, p. 93). Waltham been in debt since Richard de Heregens, el. three years ago, had d. at Bologna on his way to Rome for blessing. House now void, 3 Dec. 1273, and papal commissaries to conf. or arrange an eln (*CPL*, I, 445). 21 Dec. 1273, Reginald de Maydenethe the cellarer, got more votes than Richard the sub-pr. Legate to choose between them (ibid., 446).

Reginald de Maydenethe (Maidenheth) **1273–1289** Cellarer of Waltham, writ *de intendendo*

29 Jan. 1274, having been conf. by R. archbp of Canterbury and Raymond de Nogeriis, papal nuncio (*CPR 1272–81*, p. 42; cf. PRO, C84/5/1). D. (no name)1288 (*Ann. Dunstable*, p. 341). D. *c.* St Peter ad Vincula (22) Feb. 1289, bur. 25 Feb. 1289 (*Ch. Bury*, p. 92; cf. *Ann. Dunstable*, p. 341 – *vir bene religiosus*). Seal (*BM Seals*, no. 4256; *Durham Seals*, II, p. 584, no. 3555).

Robert of Ellington (Elenton) **1289–1302** Eln conf. by pope 29 Sept. 1289 (*CPL*, I, 504; Sayers, no. 922). Writ *de intendendo* 25 Dec. 1289 (*CPR 1281–92*, p. 335). D. 13 Jan. 1302 (PRO, C84/14/21). D., lic. to el. 2 Feb. 1302 (*CPR 1301–07*, p. 12). Indulgence for the soul of Robert, late abb. 16 July 1305 (Lincoln, Ep. Reg., III, f. 85v). Ledger stone (*Earliest English Brasses*, p. 189 and figs. 25, 53).

John of Babraham (Badburgham) **1302–1307** Cellarer of Waltham. Eln pres. to king for royal ass. 11 Mar. 1302 (PRO, C84/14/22); royal ass. 30 Mar. 1302; temps. 6 Feb. 1303 (*CPR 1301–07*, pp. 25, 113, cf. 111). Papal conf. of eln 2 July 1302 (*CPL*, I, 602; Sayers, no. 1041). D. [1 Nov.] 1307 (PRO, C84/15/50). D. (J.), lic. to el. 6 Nov. 1307 (*CPR 1307–13*, p. 12). Indulgence for the soul of the late abb. John 25 Sept. 1310 (Lincoln, Ep. Reg., III, f. 195v).

Richard of Hertford 1308–1345 Writ *de intendendo* 5 June 1308 (*CPR 1307–13*, p. 76). Papal conf. of eln 25 Feb. 1308 (*CPL*, II, 37). Occ. 28 Oct. 1344 (*CCR 1343–46*, p. 474). House void by 18 July 1345 (*CCR 1343–46*, p. 596). Warrant for lic. to el. 19 July 1345 (PRO, SC1/39/177). D., lic. to el. 20 July 1345 (*CPR 1343–45*, p. 525).

Thomas of Wolmersty (Wolmersey, Wolmerty) **1345–1371** Can. of Waltham, eln pres. to king for royal ass. 30 July 1345 (PRO, C84/24/44); royal ass. 2 Aug. 1345 (*CPR 1343–45*, p. 536). Eln conf. by pope 19 Oct. 1345 on death of abb. 'Ricoldus' (*CPL*, III, 198); mand. to return to Waltham, having been bl. by Geoffrey, bp of Lausanne 12 Nov. 1345 (ibid., 189). Writ *de intendendo* 27 Dec. 1345 (*CPR 1345–48*, p. 23). D. 25 Aug. 1371 (PRO, C84/30/37). Letter of pr. and convent to king announcing d. of the abb. and asking for admin. of temps. during the vacancy 27 Aug. 1371 (PRO, SC1/40/189). D., lic. to el. 6 Sept. 1371 (*CPR 1370–74*, p. 133).

Nicholas Morice (Morys) **1371–1389** Eln pres. to king for royal ass. 27 Sept. 1371 (PRO, C84/30/38). Cellarer of Waltham, royal ass. 1 Oct. 1371, temps. 6 Aug. 1372 following provn by the pope (*CPR 1370–74*, pp. 137, 191). Notification from Pope Gregory XI to the king that he had apptd Nicholas as abb. 17 Nov. 1371 (*Orig. Papal Letters*, p. 163, no. 320). Order to escheator to take abbey into king's hands since Nicholas, can. of Waltham, elected abb. thereof and to whose eln royal ass. was given, has spurned such eln and has received temps. from the pope, by virtue of a reservation lately made by the pope and not from the king 8 Feb. 1372 (*CFR 1368–77*, p. 158). D. 14 Dec. 1389 (PRO, C84/34/35). D., lic. to el. 18 Dec. 1389 (*CPR 1388–92*, p. 167).

WARTER (Yorks N.) St James f. *c.* 1132 (priory); 1140 x 1 (Arrouaisian abbey); 1181 x 1192 (priory again)

    Lists in *VCH Yorks*, III, 238; *Heads*,I, 188–9; C.T. Clay, 'The early priors and abbots of Warter', *EYC*, X, 140–2 (using 15th-cent. list in Bodl., ms. Fairfax 9, ff. 57r–v, 93r – most of the details of lengths of tenure appear reliable).

Richard Last recorded occ. 21 May 1212 (Bodl., ms. Fairfax 9, f. 34r).

Thomas *c.* **1223–c. 1229** 5th pr., el. *c.* 1223 (list in Ctl. Warter in *Mon. Angl.*, VI, 298–9 and Clay, pp. 140 n. 4, 142). Ruled 6 years and cess. (ibid.) Occ. n.d. (1220 x 1247) (*Ctl. Fountains*, II, 814); n.d. (Bodl., ms. Top. Yorks e 7, f. 161r).

Ranulf *c.* **1229–c. 1235** 6th pr., ruled 6 years (Clay, p. 140). Occ. 4 July 1231 (*Yorks F., 1218–31*, p. 152; Bodl., ms. Fairfax 9, f. 49r).

John (of) Lastingham (Lestyngham) *c.* **1235–c. 1236** 7th pr. Succ. 1235 (Baildon, I, 210, no source, prob. following Burton, *Mon. Ebor.*, p. 384). Ruled *dimidio anno et sex mensibus* (*sic*) (list, f. 57r–v, cf. *dimidio anno et iij mensibus* list, f. 93r; Clay, p. 140).

John of Durham (Dunelm(ia)) *c.* 1236–*c.* 1249 8th pr. Occ. 1236 (Baildon, I, 210, no source). Ruled 13 years and cess. (list; Clay, p. 140). Occ. 6 May 1246 (*Yorks F., 1232–46*, p. 134).

Robert of Lund (Lunde) *c.* 1249–*c.*1264 9th pr. Ruled 15 years and cess. (list; Clay, p. 140). Occ. 1249, 1253 (Bodl., ms. Fairfax 9, ff. 36v, 78r); 3 Nov. 1253 (*Yorks F., 1246–72*, p. 93). Asked permission to res. as old and infirm; papal mand. to archdn of the East Riding to receive res. 29 Jan. 1256 (*CPL*, I, 328) – presumably ineffective. Occ. 25 Mar. 1256, 1259, 1261 (Bodl., ms. Fairfax 9, ff. 28v, 84v, 35r, 36v).

John of Wheldrake (Queldreke, Queldri(c)ke, Qweldreke) *c.* 1264–1280 10th pr., ruled 16 years (list; *Mon. Angl.*, VI, 299). Occ. 20 Oct. 1271 (*Yorks F., 1246–72*, p. 179); 25 Nov. 1273 (*Yorks F., 1272–1300*, p. 2); 11 June 1279, 23 Feb. 1280 (ibid.. pp. 18, 37). Res. acc. *imbecillitatem tuam et impotenciam considerans* and conf. of provision made for him 14 Dec. 1280 (*Reg. Wickwane*, pp. 106–8, no. 342).

John of Thorpe (Thorp) 1280–1314 11th pr., ruled 33 years, res. 1309 (*sic*) (list; *Mon. Angl.*, VI, 299; 34 years, list, f. 93r). Can. of Warter, eln quashed, but apptd by archbp 19 Dec. 1280 (*Reg. Wickwane*, p. 107). Provision for when he gives up office conf. 13 Oct. 1291 (*Reg. Romeyn*, I, p. 221, no. 631); dispensation from eating in frater, sleeping in dorter, or rising for mattins 23 Feb. 1293 (ibid., p. 226, no. 649). Conf. of provision made 28 Mar. 1309 in recognition of his good service (*Reg. Greenfield*, III, pp. 1164–6, no. 1499). Occ. 20 Apr. 1310 (*Yorks F. 1300–14*, p. 413). Cess. by 28 Oct. 1314 (*Reg. Greenfield*, III, p. 228, no. 1623). Conf. by archbp of provision made by the convent for their late pr., John of Thorpe, *causa imbecillitatis sue ac impotencie a regimine prioratus eiusdem nuper per nos absoluto* n.d. [1314] (*Reg. Greenfield*, III, p. 228, n. 3).

Richard of Welwick (Welewyk, Wellewyk) 1314–1359 12th pr., ruled 44 years (list; *Mon. Angl.*, VI, 299). Can. of Warter, eln pres. to archbp 28 Oct. 1314; eln quashed, but apptd by archbp 29 Oct. 1314; mand. to convent to obey 30 Oct. (*Reg. Greenfield*, III, pp. 228–9, no. 1623). Cess. by 6 June 1359 (York, Reg. 11, f. 200r).

Robert (of) Balne 1359–1364 13th pr., ruled 4 years and res. (list; *Mon. Angl.*, VI, 299). Can. of Warter, eln conf. 6 June 1359 (York, Reg. 11, f. 200r). Bl. and prof. obed. 20 Nov. 1359 (ibid., f. 201r). Occ. 1 Oct. 1359 (*Reg. Welton*, no. 281). Cess. by 19 Aug. 1364 (York, Reg. 11, f. 211r).

William of Ferriby (Feriby, Feryby) 1364–1380 14th pr., ruled 16 years and d. (list; *Mon. Angl.*, VI, 299). Can. of Warter, eln conf. 19 Aug. 1364 (York, Reg. 11, f. 211r). Occ. 24 July 1372 (ibid., f. 327r); 25 May 1377 (Bodl., ms. Fairfax 9, f. 102r).

WARWICK, St Sepulchre (Canons of the Holy Sepulchre) f. *c.* 1119 x 1123
Lists in *VCH Warws*, II, 98–9; *Heads*, I, 189.

Master Thomas Last recorded occ. 1203 x 1208 (BL, Egerton ms. 3033, f. 2v; cf. *Heads*, I, 189, n.1).

Richard Occ. in *Warws F.*, I, from 27 Jan. 1245 to 20 June 1260 (nos. 617, 785); 2 May 1252 (PRO, E315/54/62); 20 June 1260 (PRO, Fines, Divers Cos. CP25/1/283/15, no. 382); 25 Sept. 1264 (PRO, E315/43/65).

Robert de Breyles Occ. 2 June 1270 (*Reg. W. Giffard*, p. 167). Possibly the pr. R. removed by the Official of the bp of Worcester 1280 (*Reg. G. Giffard*, p. 126).

William Letter n.d. to the earl of Warwick informing him of the departure of pr. William (between entries of 1284) (ibid., p. 247) – presumably the unnamed predecessor of William de Bereford (see below) and prob. the **William** *dictus* **de Sancto Johanne**, desc. as former pr. in a signification of 1286 (PRO, C85/162/5).

William of Barford (Bereford) Occ. as can. of St Sepulchre, mand. to excommunicate those who attacked and imprisoned him when he exhibited to the canons letters of the bp's Official about the removal of pr. R. 5 Dec. 1280 (*Reg. G. Giffard*, p. 247). Bp commands William de Bereford, can. of St Sepulchre, to take charge of the priory until the return of the unnamed pr. who has retired from it without reasonable cause 22 Aug. 1284 (ibid., pp. 246–7). Mand. to the sub-pr. and convent to obey William de Bereford their new pr. 22 Oct. 1284 (ibid., p. 250). Hugh Tankard apptd co-adjutor for pr. William 5 Sept. 1288 (ibid., p. 335).

Hugh de Brok (Brekes) **1289–1292** Can. of Kenilworth, el. by convent of St Sepulchre, inst. 22 Mar. 1289; letter to the earl of Warwick, the patron of the priory about this eln 25 Mar. (ibid., p. 349). 8 July 1292 bp visited priory to absolve him from cure committed to him (ibid., p. 432).

R. de Coucham Occ. n.d. (between entries of May 1287) (ibid., p. 330).

Paul de Stanleye (Stonle, Stolton) **1292/3–1316** Adm. 5 Sept. 1292 *or possibly* 1293, no reason given for vacancy (ibid., p. 394). Occ. 16 Aug. 1309, 8 Nov. 1309 (*CPR 1307–13*, pp. 164, 166). Res. by 1 Oct. 1316 (PRO, C84/18/53). Res., lic. to el. 6 Oct. 1316 (*CPR 1313–17*, p. 552).

William of Cotheridge (Coderigge, Coderugge, Coterigge, Coterugge) **1316–1332** Can. of St Sepulchre, royal ass. 25 Oct. 1316, temps. 20 Jan. 1317 (ibid., pp. 556–7, 608). Cert. conf. of eln by bp of Worcester 23 Nov. 1316 (PRO, C84/19/4). Bp of Worcester to bp of Exeter: 'The pr. of St Sepulchre going from bad to worse, has troubled us in many ways in the Court of Arches and elsewhere, about which more when we meet' (c. June 1325) (*Reg. Cobham*, p. 187). Res. by 23 Oct. 1332 (*Reg. Orleton (Worc.)*, nos. 394–5). Seal (*BM Seals*, no. 4267).

Guy de Herforton (Hereforton) **1332–1338** Pr. of Dodford, apptd by bp (to whom the sub-pr. and convent had devolved the appt) 23 Oct. 1332 (*Reg. Orleton (Worc.)*, nos. 394–5). Occ. 1 Dec. 1335 (*Reg. Montacute*, no. 1087). Res. by 9 Oct. 1338 when notification by sub-pr. and convent of a day chosen for the eln of a pr. (Worcester Cath. mun. B. 821).

William de Wilton (Wylton, Witton) **1339–1349** Eln conf. 9 Jan. 1339 (*Worcs Reg. Sede Vacante*, p. 292); mand. to install s.d. (ibid., p. 268). Removed before 16 June 1349 (*Reg. Bransford*, no. 1452). Mentd as former pr. 1354 (*CPR 1354–58*, p. 106).

Peter of Warwick (Warrewic) *alias* le Skynnere **1349–1402** El. appeared 16 June and witnesses examined; eln conf. 17 June 1349 (*Reg. Bransford*, no. 1452). Occ. (le Skynnere) 1368 (Worcester, Reg. Whittlesey, p. 61). D. by [?13] Sept. 1402 (PRO, C84/338/34). D., lic. to el. 27 Sept. 1402 (*CPR 1401–05*, p. 123).

WELLOW (Grimsby) (Lincs) St Augustine and St Olaf f. ? 1132. (abbey)
Lists in *VCH Lincs*, II, 162–3; *Heads*, I, 189.

Richard I Last recorded occ. 19 June 1202 (*Lincs. F., 1199–1216*, p. 15, no. 27).

Roger Occ. *temp.* abb. Simon of Humberston (*c.* 1203 x 1217) (BL, Cotton ms. Vespasian E XVIII, f. 91r).
Lic. to el. 24 July 1213, repeated 30 Jan. 1214 x 1215 (*Rot. Lit. Claus.*, 147, 181).

Richard II 1217–?1234 Pr. of Snead (Chirbury), royal ass. 10 Aug. 1217 (*CPR 1216–25*, p. 83); Occ. between 9 Feb. 1219 and 30 Sept. 1226 (*Lincs. F.*, I, 125, 182, 213). Lic. to el. (no reason for vacancy given) 21 Aug. 1234 (*CPR 1232–47*, p. 65). Seal (*BM Seals*, no. 3232).

Reginald 1234–?1250/1 or 1252 Pr. of Wellow, royal ass. 8 Sept. 1234, writ *de intendendo* 30 Sept. 1234 (*CPR 1232–47*, pp. 68, 72). Occ. 12 June 1250 (*Lincs F.*, II, 70). D. June 1250 x June 1251 (*Reg. Grosseteste*, p. 123), but cf. D. (R.) 27 Feb. 1252 (PRO, C84/1/26). Lic. to el. (no reason given for vacancy) 9 Mar. 1252 (*CPR 1247–58*, p. 131).

[**Philip de Gummes** Royal ass. 23 Mar. 1252 (ibid., p. 132). Eln renounced before bp of

Lincoln, and lic. to el. sought 29 Apr. 1252 (PRO, C84/1/27). Lic. to el. (no reason for vacancy given) 6 May 1252 (*CPR 1247–58*, p. 137)]

William of Cabourne (Kaburn) ?1250/1 or 1252–1271 Can. of Wellow, eln conf. on death of Reginald June 1250 x June 1251 (*Reg. Grosseteste*, p. 123) but cf. royal ass. 14 May 1252, writ *de intendendo* 26 May 1252 (*CPR 1247–58*, pp. 138, 140). Occ. 7 May 1271 (*CPR 1266–72*, p. 534). House vacant by 27 Sept. 1271 (ibid., p. 575). D. by 3 Dec. 1271 (*Reg. R. Gravesend*, p. 50).

John 1271 Pr. of Wellow, royal ass. 27 Sept. 1271 (*CPR 1266–72*, p. 575). D. on journey to the bp's vicegerent, the archdn of Buckingham, and his companions afterwards went to the king at Merton and asked for lic. to el., n.d. (ibid., p. 576).

Simon of Wainfleet (Waynflet, Weynflete) 1271–1293 Can. of Wellow, royal ass. 4 Nov. 1271 (*CPR 1266–72*, p. 603). Eln on d. of William conf. 3 Dec. 1271 (*Reg. R. Gravesend*, p. 50). D. by 5 Aug. 1293 (PRO, C84/11/26). D., lic. to el. 16 Aug. 1293 (*CPR 1292–1301*, p. 36).

William of Croxby (Croxeby) 1293–1317 Can. of Wellow, eln pres. to king for royal ass. 1 Sept. 1293 (PRO, C84/11/28); royal ass. 13 Sept. 1293, temps. 28 Sept. 1293 (*CPR 1292–1301*, p. 38). Eln pres. to bp 20 Sept., conf. 21 Sept. 1293, bl. 4 Oct. 1293 (*Reg. Sutton*, I, 178–9; PRO, C84/11/30). D by 24 Dec. 1317 (PRO, C84/19/18). D., lic. to el. 4 Jan. 1318 (*CPR 1317–21*, p. 67).

Thomas of Wellingore (Welinghour(e), Welynghoure) 1318–1341 Can. of Wellow, eln pres. to king for royal ass. 18 Jan. 1318 (PRO, C84/19/22); royal ass. 25 Jan. 1318, temps. 18 Feb. 1318 (*CPR 1317–21*, pp. 73, 106). Eln quashed but apptd by bp 11 Feb. 1318 (Lincoln, Ep. Reg., II, f. 71r; PRO, C84/19/26–7). Bl. by former archbp of Armagh & prof. obed. 12 Feb. 1318 (Lincoln, Ep. Reg., III, f. 381r). D., lic. to el. 20 Mar. 1341 (*CPR 1340–43*, p. 163).

John de Houton 1341–1348 Can. of Wellow, royal ass. 10 Apr. 1341, temps. 3 May 1341 (ibid., pp. 165, 180). Eln conf. (14–30) Apr. 1341 (*Reg. Burghersh*, I, no. 682). Dep. by bp (*CPR 1348–50*, p.150). Res, lic. to el. 28 Aug. 1348 (ibid., p. 142).

Henry of Allington (Alyngton, Aylyngton) 1348–1349 Can. of Huntingdon, royal ass. 17 Sept. 1348, temps. 18 Sept. 1348 (ibid., pp. 147, 150). Commn to examine eln 21 Sept. 1348 (Lincoln, Ep. Reg., IX, f. 14v), but convent agreed to leave eln to bp (*CPR 1348–50*, p. 150), but bp cert. to king that convent had transferred right to him and he had apptd Henry 13 Sept. 1348 (PRO, C84/25/19). House void by his death by 25 July 1349 (*CFR 1347–56*, p. 146). Lic. to el. 30 July 1349 (*CPR 1348–50*, p. 352).

Richard of Utterby 1349–1369 Can. of Wellow, royal ass. 20 Sept. 1349, temps. 28 Sept. 1349 (ibid., p. 399). Cert. conf. eln by bp of St David's, as commissary of bp of Lincoln, 28 Sept. 1349 (PRO, C84/26/26). King took house into his hand for debt 6 July 1350 (*CPR 1348–50*, pp. 549–50) and again on 15 Oct. 1359 (*CPR 1358–61*, p. 292). Mandate 31 July 1359 to cite abb. to appear before bp to answer charges of excesses arising out of recent visitation (Lincoln, Ep. Reg., VIII, ff. 116v–117r). On 30 Sept. 1367 the King apptd 5 individuals and the abb. to have the custody of the abbey, depressed and impoverished by the dissensions of the canons (*CPR 1367–70*, p. 7). D. by 14 July 1369 (PRO, C84/30/2). D., lic. to el. 24 July 1369 (*CPR 1367–70*, p. 290).

[**William of Utterby** Can. of Wellow, el. by convent, pres. to bp 6 Sept. 1369; subsequent examn found him ineligible on acount of illegitimacy and eln quashed (Lincoln, Ep. Reg., X . ff. 35v–36r; *CPR 1367–70*, pp. 319–20). William renounced eln 10 Oct. 1369 (Lincoln, Ep. Reg., XII, f. 80v).]

John of Utterby 1369–1373 Can. of Wellow, he appeared before the bp on 10 Oct. 1369, apptd by bp 18 Oct. 1369 (Lincoln, Ep. Reg., X, f. 35v). Appt. annulled by king, 4 Nov. 1369, and fresh lic. to el. ordered (*CPR 1367–70*, p. 320; PRO, E135/3/19). Because John publicly renounced right and to spare the convent a long vacancy the king gave his ass. 1 Dec. 1369 and restored temps. 18 Dec. 1369 (*CPR 1367–70*, pp. 332, 336). Eln conf. 15 Dec. 1369, mand. to induct same day, bl. 23 Dec. 1369 (Lincoln, Ep. Reg., X, f. 38r). Dep. by 20 Nov. 1373 when petition for lic. to el. (PRO, C84/31/3). Bp suspended John 4 Dec. 1372 on complaints by the convent and sent administrators for the house until he could make visitation (Lincoln, Ep. Reg., XII, f. 111v). Commn to impose penances on John for crimes and excesses 30 Dec. 1372 (ibid., f. 113r). Commn to adm. cess. 2 Jan 1373 (ibid., f. 114r). Dep., lic. to el. 26 Nov. 1373 (*CPR 1370–74*, p. 369).

John de Thorpe (Thorp) **1374–1410** Can. of St Mary, Leicester, apptd by bp *per lapsum temporis* 19 Apr. 1374 (Lincoln, Ep. Reg., X, f. 61r). King notified 20 Apr. 1374 (ibid., f. 61r–v). Royal ass. 29 Apr. 1374, temps. 5 May 1374 (*CPR 1370–74*, pp. 433–4). Occ. 1381 (*Clerical Poll-Taxes*, p. 121, no. 1489 and p. 168, no. 2090); 1388 (*CPR 1385–89*, p. 506); 24 Oct. 1395 (Lincoln, Ep. Reg., XII, f. 458r). D. 28 Aug. 1410 (BL, Add. ms. 6165, f. 69v; cf. PRO, C84/40/14).

WESTACRE (Norfolk), St Mary and All Saints f. *temp.* Henry I (*c.* 1135); 1102 x 1126 (cf. N. Vincent, 'The foundation of Westacre priory 1102 x 1126', *Norfolk Archaeology*, 41(4) (1993), 490–94)

Lists in *VCH Norfolk*, II, 404; J.H. Fairweather and H.I. Bradfer-Lawrence, 'The priory of St Mary and All Saints, Westacre, and excavations upon its site', *Norfolk Archaeology*, 23 (1929), 359–94, at 370; *Heads*, I, 189.

William Latest occ. 1200 (*CRR*, I, 352).

William ? the same, occ. Oct. 1227 x Oct. 1228 (*Norfolk F. (Rye)*, p. 43).

Richard Occ. (R.) Mar. 1229 (PRO, E40/2915); n. d. (PRO, E40/2907).

Robert de Alenzun Occ. from Oct. 1231 x Oct. 1232 to Oct. 1256 to Oct. 1257 (*Norfolk F. (Rye)*, pp. 49, 94); n. d. (PRO E40/2871;/2954).[48]

John Occ. n.d. (with Mary, prs of Blackborough 1258/9 x 1261) (BL, Egerton ms. 3137, f. 95v); Oct. 1267 x Oct. 1268 (*Norfolk F. (Rye)*, p. 103); 11 July 1273 (Ctl. Marham, f. 2r).

Hubert/Herbert Occ. Nov. 1285 x Nov. 1286 (*Norfolk F. (Rye)*, p. 130).

Richard Occ. Sept. 1288 (PRO, Just.1/1282, m. 21); Trin. term 1297 (*Coram Rege Roll*, p. 93).

Henry of Acre (Acra) **1301–** Can. of Westacre, adm. 14 Jan. 1301, no reason given for vacancy (Norwich, Reg/1/1, f. 6r). Occ. 1308 (PRO, Just.1/593, m. 3d); Easter 1313 (ibid., m. 23); (H.) 26 Jan. 1317 (Norwich, Reg/1/1, f. 69r); 27 Sept. 1321, 7 Jan. 1322 (ibid., ff. 91v, 93v)

William of Weasenham (Wesenham) **1323–1328** Cellarer of Westacre, eln conf. 17 Aug. 1323 (ibid., f. 102r). D. by 16 Mar. 1328 (Norwich, Reg/1/2, ff. 20v–21r).

Gilbert of Whaplode (Qwaplode, Wappelod) **1328–1349** Can. of Westacre, eln conf. 16 Mar. 1327/8 (ibid.). D. by 24 July 1349 (*Reg. Bateman* I, no. 862).

John of Swaffham (Swafham) **1349–** Can. of Westacre, eln conf. 24 July 1349 (ibid.).

Walter Occ. 29 Sept. 1352, 29 Sept. 1357, 1 Oct. 1358 (Holkham, Coke muns. Tittleshall deeds 62, 64, 66).

John de Stowe **–1367** D. 1 Apr. 1367 (Norwich, Reg/2/5, f. 74r).

Geoffrey de Warham **1367–1373** Can. of Westacre, eln conf. 1 Apr. 1367 (ibid.). D. by 12 May 1373 (Norwich, Reg/3/6, ff. 19v–20r).

Nicholas (of) Butley (Butle, Buttele) **1373–** Commn to examine eln 12 May 1373, eln conf. 24 May 1373 (ibid.). Occ. n.d. (*c.* 1378 x 1381) (PRO, E179/45/14).

The next recorded pr., **John of Acre**, eln conf. 7 Dec. 1390, no reason given for vacancy (Norwich, Reg/3/6, f. 151r).

---

[48] Blomefield, *Norfolk*, IX, 160, gives Simon occ. 1249, but without source.

WEYBOURNE (Norfolk), St Mary and All Saints f. +1199 (dependent on Westacre); 1314 (independent).

List in *VCH Norfolk*, II, 406; F.H. Fairweather, 'The Augustinian priory of Weybourne', *Norfolk Arch.*, 24 (1932), 201–228, at 203–6.

Roger of Hoxne –1314 Occ. 1309 (Blomefield, *Norfolk*, IX, 450, no source); 3 Aug. 1312 (PRO, C241/76/289). Blomefield notes (IX, 450, citing 'inter Archiv. Dec. et Capit. Norw.') that at Roger's d. a struggle ensued between the sub-pr. and cans. of Weybourne and the pr. of Westacre. The former claimed free eln, the latter as the ruling house that the cans. of Weybourne should el. but that their choice should be a can. of Westacre. The matter being put to arbitration, it was ruled that Weybourne should have free eln for ever on payment of an annual pension to Westacre of 7s. 6d. The bp of Norwich conf. this agreement in 1315 and the pope in 1319 (mentd Fairweather, p. 203).

John of Frenze (Frenes) **1315–1344** Can. of Weybourne, eln quashed, but apptd by bp 7 Jan. 1315, no reason being given for vacancy (Norwich, Reg/1/1, f. 59v). D. by 1 Dec. 1344 (*Reg. Bateman* I, no. 129).

Roger de Geystwayth 1344– Can. of Weybourne, eln conf. 1 Dec. 1344 (ibid.).

Thomas Occ. 1377 x 1381 (PRO, E179/45/7c).

The next recorded pr., **John of Ellingham** (Elyngham), can. of Buckenham, coll. 14 Oct. 1391, no reason given for vacancy (Norwich, Reg/3/6, f. 161r).

WEYBRIDGE (Norfolk), St Mary f. –1225

Lists in *VCH Norfolk*, II, 407.

Robert Occ. *temp.* Edward I (Blomefield, *Norfolk*, XI, 92, citing a n.d. cht. of Roger Bigod, earl of Norfolk (1270–1306) not traced).

Hugh Said to occ. Nov. 1285 x Nov. 1286 (ibid., no source).

Humphrey –1308 D. by 10 Nov. 1308 (*CPR 1307–13*, p. 142).

Custody of vacant priory gtd to John de Kayly, rector of Rollesby, 17 June 1308 (Norwich, Reg/1/1, f. 28r).

Matthew of Horsey (Horseye) **1308–** Can. of Weybridge. Adm. to custody of house 14 Nov 1308, no reason given for vacancy, on pres. of Edward II, the lands of Roger Bigod, late earl of Norfolk being in his hands (ibid., f. 29v). Notif. to bp of his pres. to be keeper of the house 10–12 Nov. 1308 (*CPR 1307–13*, pp. 142–3); temps. 15 Nov. 1308 (ibid., p. 143). Occ. Mich. 1310 (PRO, CP40/183, attorneys m. 20).

Nicholas Occ. 3 Oct. 1321 (Norwich, Reg/1/1, f. 92r)

Matthew of Horsey (Horseye) **1323–** Can. of Weybridge, apptd by bp, the right having devolved to him 3 Aug. 1323, no reason given for vacancy (ibid., f. 101v).

Laurence of Billockby (Billokby) Sub.-pr. of Weybridge, commn to examine eln 17 Feb. 1328 (Norwich, Reg/1/2, f. 84v); eln conf. 21 June 1328, no reason given for vacancy (ibid., f. 23r).

Adam of Hickling (Hikelyng) –1334 D. by Jan. 1334 (ibid., f. 64r).

Robert of Martham 1334–1340 Can. of Weybridge, eln conf. 3 Jan. 1334 (ibid.). Res. by 3 Nov. 1340 (Norwich, Reg/1/3, f. 41v).

William of Acle 1340– Can. of Weybridge, eln conf. 3 Nov. 1340 (ibid.).

John of Tofts (Toftes) –1370 D. by 1 Mar. 1370 (Lambeth, Reg. Whittlesey, f. 148v).

John de Berton 1370–1397 Can. of Weybridge, eln conf. 1 Mar. 1370 (ibid.). D. by 30 Sept. 1397 (Norwich, Reg/3/6, f. 227v).

WIGMORE (Hereford), St James f. 1131 x 35 (at Shobdon); 1172 (at Wigmore) (abbey)

Lists in *Arch. J.*, XC (1933), app. 1, pp. 41–5; *Heads*, I, 190: Ann. to 1306 in Manchester, John Rylands Lib., Latin ms. 215, ff. 1r–8v.

Ralph 1194–1216 Succ. 1194. D. 1216 (Ann., ff. 3v, 4v). Occ. (R.) n.d. (early 13th cent.) (*HMC Westmorland etc.*, p. 416).

Walter –1243/4 Occ. 25 Apr. 1232 (PRO, Worcs F., CP25/1/258/4, no. 13); 1234 (ibid., 258/4, no. 16); Easter term 1236 (*CRR*, XV, no. 1538); 6 July 1236 (PRO, Hereford F., CP25/1/80/8, no. 149). D. 1244 (Ann., f. 5r, but see below). Seal (*BM Seals*, no. 4333).

John of Swineshead 1243/4–1274 Prev. abb. of Keynsham (q. v.) el. 1243 (*Ann. Tewkesbury*, p. 134), but poss. 1244 (see above; John last occ. as abb. of Keynsham 6 Oct. 1243 (q.v.)). Occ. 14 Jan. 1249 (Hereford Cath. Mun., no. 2090); 1256 (PRO, Shrops. F., CP25/1/193/4, no. 63); 3 May 1258 (PRO, Hereford F., CP25/1/80/13, no. 274). D. 29 Nov. 1274 (Ann., f. 6r).

Adam –1293 Occ. 23 Apr. 1281 (BL, Cotton Cht. XXI. 43); (A.) 6 Apr. 1283 (*Reg. Swinfield*, p. 15); 5 Sept. 1284 (*CPR 1281–92*, p. 130); 12 July 1292 (Hereford Cath. Mun., no. 2532). Commn to enquire into physical condition of abb. and to assign him adequate provision if he is to res. 5 July 1293 (*Reg. Swinfield*, p. 301); letter of res. on account of age and ill-health 14 July 1293 (ibid., pp. 301–2). Res. *c.* 22 July 1293 (Ann., f. 7r). Seal (*Hereford Seals*, p. 9).

John of Arleston (Erleston, Eorleslon) 1293–1295 Succ. 1293 (Ann., f. 7r). Res. 13 Apr. 1295 and lic. to el. (*Reg. Swinfield*, pp. 335–6); provision made for him 13 Apr. 1295 (ibid., pp. 336–7).

John de Whittone (Eytone, Wyttone) 1296– Eln conf. 24 Apr. 1296 (ibid., pp. 338–9). Occ. Nov. 1296 x Nov. 1297 (PRO, E210/8330); 10 June 1297 (*CPR 1292–1301*, pp. 290–1); 13 Oct. 1299 (*Reg. Swinfield*, p. 363); 7 June 1300 (ibid., p. 372).

[**Walter of Ludlow** (Lodelawe) El. but res. all claim and new eln ordered 12 May 1302 (ibid., p. 382).]

Philip le Galeys (*dictus* le Waleys) 1302–1318 Can. of Wigmore, commn to examine eln 27 May 1302; eln conf. 1 June 1302; inducted 3 June 1302 (ibid., pp. 382–3). Res. 28 Dec. 1318 (*Reg. Orleton (Hereford)*, p. 92).

John of Clehonger (Clehangre, Clehongre) 1318–1332 Pr. of Wormsley, pres. to Roger de Mortimer, patron, and apptd by bp 28 Dec. 1318 (ibid., pp. 90–1). D., lic. to el. 10 July 1332 (*CPR 1330–34*, p. 320).

Richard de Turpitone (Turpletone, Turpyntone, Turpyton) 1332–1351 Can. of Wigmore, notif. to king of conf. of eln 14 Aug. 1332, bl. 5 Sept. 1332 (*Reg. T. Charlton*, pp. 19, 21). Temps. 20 Aug. 1332 (*CPR 1330–34*, p. 327). D. by 14 Mar 1351 (*Reg. Trillek*, p. 165). Seal (*Mon. Seals*, p. 98). From the description it would appear that seal casts ascribed to an unknown abb. Richard in the 13th cent. actually relate to this abb. Richard (*BM Seals*, no. 4334; *Hereford Seals*, p. 9).

John of Stapleton (Stapeltone, Stepeltone, Steppulton) 1351–1359 Eln conf. and mand. to induct 14 Apr. 1351 (*Reg. Trillek*, p. 165). Ruled 8 years and 9 months and d. 22 Nov. 1359 (*Ch. Wigmore*, p. 87). D. by 24 Dec. 1359 (*Reg. Trillek*, p. 254).

Richard of Brompton (Bromptone) 1359–1390 Eln conf. 24 Dec. 1359 and bl. 25 Dec. (ibid., pp. 253–4). D., lic. to el. 7 July 1390 (*CPR 1388–92*, p. 279; cf. PRO, C84/34/40).

WOMBRIDGE (Shropshire) St Mary and St Leonard f. 1130 x 1135
    Lists in *VCH Shrops.*, II, 82–3; Eyton, *Salop*, VII, 370; *Heads*, I, 190.

Roger Last recorded occ. 1207 (*CRR*, V, 80),

Henry Occ. *c.* 1220, *ante* 1225, when Baldwin de Hodnet d. (Eyton, *Salop*, II, 133n.; *Ctl. Wombridge*, nos. 308, 322); *c.* 1226 (*Ctl. Wombridge*, no. 485); 21 Nov. 1236 (*Salop F.*, 4th ser., *Trans. Shrops. ANHS*, IV, 171).

Baldwin Occ. 18 June 1245 (*Salop. F.*, 4th ser., *Trans. Shrops. ANHS*, VI, p. 184, no. 151); 15, 22 Nov. 1248 (PRO, Shrops F., CP25/1/193/4, nos. 28, 34).

Walter Occ. n.d. (*Ctl. Wombridge*, no. 1, dated *c.* 1240 x 60); Oct. 1270 (Eyton, *Salop*, VII, 361, but no source); n. d.(*Ctl. Wombridge*, no. 319). Mentd as former pr. *c.* 1284 when request to king for some provision for his upkeep (PRO, SC1/24/198).

S. Occ. n.d. (*Ctl. Wombridge*, no. 89, dated *c.* 1290, but this seems unlikely with pr. Philip (below) occ. from 1284 and his precise position in the sequence of priors is uncertain).

Philip –1321 Occ. in *Ctl. Wombridge* from 16 Nov. 1284 (no. 282) to 18 Oct. 1318 (no. 233). D. by 19 Apr. 1321 (Lichfield, B/A/1/1, f. 81r).[49]

Richard of Melton 1321– Eln quashed, but apptd by bp 19 Apr. 1321 (ibid.). Occ. 1332 x 1333 (PRO, C270/12/41); 3 May 1344 (*Ctl. Wombridge*, no. 44); 19 Mar. 1346 (ibid., no. 98); 17 Oct. 1346 (ibid., no. 70).

John of Lawley (Lauelay, Lauley) 1349–1373 Can. of Wombridge, el. 14 July 1349, conf. by commissaries – cert. dated 27 July 1349 (Lichfield, B/A/1/2, f. 225v). D. by 11 Nov. 1373 (*Reg. Stretton*, I, 204–5).

John (de) Watford (Watteford) 1373– Can. of Wombridge, eln conf. 11 Nov. 1373 (ibid.). Occ. 21 May 1377 (*Ctl. Wombridge*, no. 487); Jan. x June 1377 (PRO, E179/15/3, m. 1).

The next recorded pr., **John**, occ. July 1425 (Eyton, *Salop*, VII, 372; *Ctl. Wombridge*, app., no. v).

WOODBRIDGE (Suffolk) St Mary f. 1146 x 1166 (see *Heads*, I, corrigenda)
  Lists in *VCH Suffolk* II, 112; *Heads*, I, 190.

During the vacancy of the see of Norwich (1236–1239), Archbp Edmund of Canterbury deposed an unnamed pr. of Woodbridge (LAO, Lincoln D/C, Dij/62/4, f. 19r).

Amisus occ. Oct. 1266 x Oct. 1267 (*Suffolk F. (Rye)*, p. 65, cf. Ambrose 1267 (*Proc. Suffolk Inst.*, IV, 224)).

Henry of Oakley (Oclee) 1305– Can. of Woodbridge, eln quashed, but apptd by bp 23 June 1305, no reason being given for the vacancy (Norwich, Reg/1/1, f. 17r).

John de Athelyngton(e) 1326–1343 Can. of Woodbridge, eln conf. 28 Nov. 1326, no reason being given for the vacancy (Norwich, Reg/1/2, f. 11v). D. by 25 Jan. 1343 (Norwich, Reg/1/3, f. 68r).

John de Burnedissh (Brundissh) 1343– Commn to examine eln 25 Jan. 1343; eln conf. 31 Jan. 1343 (ibid.).[50]

John of Hadleigh (Hadeley) 1349– Can. of Woodbridge, eln quashed, but apptd by bp 4 July 1349, no reason being given for the vacancy (*Reg. Bateman*, I, no. 735).

William of Holton –1371 Res. by 9 Aug. 1371 (Norwich, Reg/3/6, f. 9r).

Henry Brom 1371– Can. of Herringfleet, eln conf. 9 Aug. 1371 (ibid.).

Thomas of Troston 1372–1395 Can. of Ixworth, eln conf. 25 Aug. 1372, no reason being given for the vacancy (ibid., f. 16r). D. by 2 Mar. 1395 (ibid., f. 197v).

WOODKIRK (Yorks W.), St Mary (Nostell) f. -1135 Cell of Nostell
  List in *Heads*, I, 190.

Richard of Selby (Selebi) Occ. as *custos* n.d. (*EYC*, III, no. 1617, dated 1180 x 1200 but could be later).

Nicholas Occ. prior n.d. (early 13th cent.) (*EYC*, XII, no. 80).

Richard Tonge occ. as master 1424 (Baildon, II, 53).

---

[49] *Ctl. Wombridge*, no. 372 notes a pr. John occ. 20 Edward. The date given does not seem to fit the 20th year of Edward I, II, or III, and may be a scribal error.

[50] *VCH* gives Thomas as occ. 1286 and William Bast as occ. 1345, following the list in *Proc. Suffolk Inst.*, IV (1864), p. 224, but without source.

WOODSPRING (Soms), St Thomas the Martyr (see Binns, p. 158) (Worspring)
(Victorine) f. -1210 (at Dodlinch); -1226 (at Woodspring).

List in *VCH Soms*, II, 146.

John Occ. Mich. 1223 (*Essex F.*, I, 64).

Reginald (Reynold) -1243 Occ. *temp.* Henry III (*Cal. Misc. Inq.*, II, 84); n.d. (PRO, E326/11006, 11008). D. in vacancy of see of Bath and Wells (Nov. 1242 – Sept. 1244), but prob. 1243, see below (*HMC Wells*, I, 98).

Richard 1243– Can. of Keynsham, formerly parson of Stoke, eln pres. to chapter of Wells 16 Aug. 1243; conf. by chapter 18 Aug. 1243 (ibid.).

John Occ. Oct. 1255 x Oct. 1256 (*Cal. Misc. Inq.*, II, 84; mentd *Abbrev. Rot. Orig.*, I, 240b); 22 July 1266, 16 Aug. 1266 (*HMC Wells*, I, 396–7, 153); 6 Oct. 1276 (*Soms F.*, I, 240); 4 July 1277 (*HMC Wells*, I, 70–1).

Reginald Occ. 16 Aug. 1318 (*CFR 1307–19*, p. 373).

Henry Occ. 7 Feb. 1325 (*CPR 1324–27*, p. 86); Mich. 1337 (PRO, CP40/312, m. 21).

Nicholas Chill' Occ. 1377 (PRO, E179/4/1, m. 6)

The next recorded pr., **Thomas**, occ. 1 July 1382 (*HMC Wells*, I, 413).

WORKSOP (Notts), St Mary and St Cuthbert f. *c.* 1120

Lists in *VCH Notts*, II, 129; *Heads*, I, 190–1.

Robert (? of Pickburn (Pykeburn): R.White, *Dukery Records*, p. 417). Occ. (R.) *c.* 1213 x 14 (BL, Cotton ms. Nero D III, f. 57v)., -1216 (Cheney, *Inn. III*, no. 1148); 1216 x 1223 (*Rufford Chts.*, no. 847); -1218 (*EYC*, III, no. 1288); 6 Oct 1226 (PRO, Notts F. CP25/1/182/4, no. 81); 18 Nov. 1230 (*Yorks F., 1218–31*, pp. 130–1); Easter term 1231 (*CRR*, XIV, no. 1358). [A., pr. of Worksop occ. 1223 x *c.* 1227 with A. pr. of St Oswald's, Gloucester, as j.d.; evidently A., pr. of Worksop is an error for R(obert) (*Ctl. Brecon*, p. 274).]

Walter of Lenton (also Leirtone) Occ. *c.* 1231 x 1233 (*Reg. Wickwane*, p. 252, no. 615; BL, Harl. Cht. 112 I 55); from 12 June 1233 to 6 July 1245 (PRO, Notts F. CP25/1/182/6, no. 175; 182/9, no. 326); 1240 (*Yorks F., 1232–46*, p. 67); *c.* 1244 (*EYC*, VI, p. 210); 5 May 1252 (*Yorks F., 1246–72*, p. 83); n.d. *temp.* A(ymer), bp-el. of Winchester 1250 x 1260 (BL, Add. Cht. 46918). Possibly the pr. Walter mentd in 1331 as having been pr. *temp.* Edward I (*CCR 1330–33*, p. 197).

John Occ. *temp.* Archbishop Ludham 1258–65, and before Mar. 1261 (BL, Add. ms. 36872, f. 130v); 18 Nov. 1262 (PRO, Notts F., CP25/1/183/12, no. 490); 3 June 1263 (*Lincs F.*, II, p. 188); (J.) 12 Sept. 1267 (*Reg. W. Giffard*, p. 75).

Ralph Mentd in 1367 inquisition as having been pr. of Worksop 'long before' the publication of the Statute of Mortmain (1279) (*Cal. Misc. Inq.*, III, 254). His precise place in the sequence of priors is uncertain.

Alan of London –1303 Occ. 6 Oct. 1279 (*Yorks F., 1272–1300*, p. 17); 18 Nov. 1280 (PRO, Notts F. 25/1/183/14, no. 33); 14 Mar. 1301 (*Reg. Corbridge*, I, 215). Res., broken by old age, by 11 Oct. 1303, when lic. to el. gtd – vacancy to be filled by 1 Nov. (ibid., 266).

John of Tickhill (Tykehille, Tykhill) 1303–1314 Can. of Worksop, eln quashed but apptd by archbp 4 Nov. 1303 (ibid., 269–70). 3 cans. of Worksop (incl. Robert of Carlton, see below) apptd as coadjutors of pr. John 1 Aug. 1311 (*Reg. Greenfield*, IV, p. 119, no. 1922 & n.1). Dep. 6 Mar. 1314 and lic. to el. (ibid., pp. 149–50, no. 2000). Provision made for him 14 Apr. 1315 (ibid., pp. 179–80, no. 2048).

Robert of Carlton (Carleton) 1314– Can. of Worksop, citation 14 Mar. 1314 for opposers to his eln to appear on 22 Mar. (ibid., p. 150, n. 1); eln conf. 22 Mar. 1314 (ibid.). Occ. Mich.

1325 (*Ctl. Kirkstall*, p. 353, no. 424); Trin. term 1328 (*Index to Placita de Banco*, pp. 529, 819); 1330 (PRO, Just.1/167, m. 78); 25 Sept. 1337 (Lincoln, Ep. Reg., IV f.. 221r).

Commn to receive the res. of unnamed pr., and proceed to eln 20 Mar. 1375 (York, Reg. 12, f. 69v).

The next recorded, pr., **John**, occ. 1396 (R. White, *Dukery Records*, p. 305, citing YMA, Torre ms. – precise source not found in York, Reg. 14). **Roger of Upton** (Uptone), former vicar of Sheffield, elevated to be pr. of Worksop by 18 Dec. 1397 (*Reg. Waldby*, p. 37).

WORMEGAY (Norfolk). St Mary, Holy Cross and St John the Evangelist (Binns, p. 158) f. -1175 (Vincent)

> List in *VCH Norfolk*, II, 407. See also N. Vincent, 'The foundation of Wormegay priory', *Norfolk Archaeology*, 43(2) (1999), 307–12.

Ralph Occ. Mich.1228 (*CRR*, XIII, no. 834); Oct. 1233 x Oct. 1234, Oct. 1234 x Oct. 1235 (*Norfolk F. (Rye)*, pp. 55–6); 1238 (BL, Egerton ms. 3137, f. 62r).

Nicholas Occ. Nov. 1285 x Nov. 1286 (Blomefield, *Norfolk*, VII, 500; *Mon. Angl.*, VI, 591, no source).

John of Boyland (Boylound) **1300–** Can. of Wormegay, apptd [2] Nov. 1300, no reason given for vacancy (Norwich, Reg/1/1, f. 3v).

Nicholas of Elm 1303– Can. of Wormegay, apptd by bp 19 Mar. 1303, no reason given for vacancy (ibid., f. 11r).

Robert of Cranworth (Craneworthe) **1315–1330** Can. of Wormegay, eln quashed but apptd by bp 13 May 1315, no reason given for vacancy (ibid., f. 61r). D. 4 May 1330 (PRO, C84/22/36). D., lic. to el. 11 May 1330 (*CPR 1327–30*, p. 521, cf. Norwich, Reg/1/2, f. 36v).

John of Cantley (Cauntele, Cantele, Cauntelle) **1330–1349** Can. of Wormegay, royal ass. 15 May 1330, temps. 7 Dec. 1330 (*CPR 1327–30*, p. 525; *CPR 1330–34*, p. 24). Eln conf. 25 May 1330 (Norwich, Reg/1/2, f. 36v; PRO, C84/22/37). D. by 16 July 1349 (*Reg. Bateman*, I, no. 826).

Simon of Leverington 1349– Can. of Wormegay, eln quashed but apptd by bp 16 July 1349 (ibid.).

Michael of Thornham –1370 House vacant by his res. by 31 July 1370 (Norwich, Reg/3/6, f, 2r).

Robert of Fordham 1370–1387 Can. of Wormegay, eln conf. 31 July 1370 (ibid.). D. 18 Dec. 1387 (PRO, C84/34/16). D., lic. to el. 23 Jan. 1388 (*CPR 1385–89*, p. 380; cf. Norwich, Reg/3/6, f. 128r).

WORMSLEY (Hereford), St Leonard and St Mary (Victorine) (Pyon) f. *c.* 1216 (+1200)
> List in *Heads* I, 191.

Hugh Occ. prob. *temp.* Henry III (Bodl., Rawlinson ms. B. 329, f. 129r). His precise place in the sequence of priors is uncertain.

Ralph Occ. 15 Feb. 1222 (BL, Harl. ms. 3586, f. 84v).

William Occ. 1225 x 1231 (Hereford Cath. muns. 2001, 2011); Hil. term 1229 (*CRR*, XIII, no. 1622); n. d. (*Ctl. Brecon*, pp. 31–2).

John (?of Pembridge (Panbregg)) Occ. 19 May 1235 (*CR 1234–37*, p. 181); 28 Apr. 1241 (PRO, Hereford F., C25/1/80/10, no. 176). Prob. to be identified with John de Panbregg mentd 1280 as former pr. (*Soms Pleas*, IV, 367).

Robert Occ. 3 Nov. 1248 (PRO, Hereford F., CP25/1/80/11, no. 220); 9 Nov. 1248 (PRO, Hereford F., CP25/1/80/12, no. 233); chaplain to Bp Peter of Hereford, 30 May 1252 (*CPR 1247–58*, p. 231); 8 July 1275 (PRO, Hereford F., CP25/1/81/17, no. 8); 29 July 1280 (*Soms Pleas*, IV, 367–8); 1280, Nov. 1282 x Nov. 1283 (BL, Harl. ms. 3586, f. 90r).

John (de) Ros Occ. Hil. 1295 (PRO, CP40/107, m. 99); 14 Sept. 1304 (BL, Harl. ms. 3586, f. 143r). Res. 7 July 1307 and acc. by bp 8 July (*Reg. Swinfield*, p. 438).

John de Bruges 1307–1310 Can. of Wormsley, el. 10 July 1307, eln conf. 15 July 1307 (ibid., pp. 438–9). Res. 3 May 1310 owing to bad health (ibid., p. 453).

John of Clehonger (Clehangre) **1310–1318** El. 5 May 1310, eln conf. 7 May 1310 (ibid.). El. abb. of Wigmore 28 Dec. 1318 (*Reg. Orleton (Hereford)*, p. 90).

John de Kyneford 1319–1331 Convent of Wormsley assigned to bp the choice of a new pr. from three cans. nominated by the convent, viz.: John de Kyneford, Alexander de Kyngestone and William de Berdetone, priests. The bp chose John and apptd him 5 Jan. 1319 (ibid., pp. 93–4). Res. 1331 (*Reg. T. Charlton*, p. 65).

William (de) Berton(e) 1331–1354 Can. of Wormsley, el. in succession to John, but renounces right. Convent appt a proctor to cede their right to choose a pr. into the bp's hands 18 Jan. 1331; bp appts William 20 Jan. 1331 (ibid., pp. 65–7). Commn to receive his res. 20 Mar. 1354 (*Reg. Trillek*, pp. 214–15). Seal (*Hereford Seals*, p. 9).

Richard of Brockhampton (Brochamptone) **1354–** Eln conf. by commissaries 22 Mar 1354 (*Reg. Trillek*, p. 215).

Thomas of Wormsley Occ. 7 May 1370 (PRO, C241/151/50).

Richard Occ. 11 July 1375 (BL, Harl. ms. 3586, f. 108v).

The next recorded pr., **William**, occ. 11 May 1395 (PRO, C241/187/19), 26 Oct. 1402 (*CPR 1401–05*, p. 142) and 18 June 1407 (Hereford Cath. mun. 2847).

WROXTON (Oxon) St Mary f. *c.* 1217

Lists in *VCH Oxon*, II, 102; *Heads*, I, 191.

Roger Called first prior (*Placita de Quo Warranto*, p. 533).

Geoffrey Occ. first half of 13th cent. (pal. Oxford, New College Archives, Swalcliffe Cht. no. 127), possibly later than Richard.

Richard 1231/2– Pr. of St James, Northampton, el. and adm. Dec.1231 x Dec.1232, no reason given for vacancy (*Reg. Wells* II, 40–1).

Walter Occ. 10 Jan. 1236, 8 July 1241 (*Oxford F.*, pp. 101, 117).

Hugh 1242/3–1263 Can. of Wroxton, eln conf. June 1242 x June 1243, no reason given for vacancy (*Reg. Grosseteste*, p. 477). (H.) Res. or d. by 20 June 1263 (*Reg. R. Gravesend*, p. 216).

William of Caldwell (Caudewell) **1263–1271** Can. of Wroxton, eln quashed but apptd by bp 20 June 1263 on res. or d. of pr. H. (ibid., pp. 216–17). Occ. 26 Nov. 1263 (*Oxford F.*, p. 193). Dep. by 12 Dec. 1271 (*Reg. R. Gravesend*, p. 223).

Nicholas de Cerney 1271–1272 Eln conf. 12 Dec. 1271 (ibid., pp. 223, 333). (N.) D. by 9 Jan. 1272 (ibid., p. 224).

William de Dayleford 1272– el. [? conf.] 9 Jan. 1272 (ibid., pp. 224, 334); occ. Mich. 1272 x Mich. 1273 (PRO, E159/47, mm. 15d(2), 16, 17).

Richard de Deen (Den) **–1305** occ. 18 Nov. 1285 (PRO, Northants F. CP25/1/175/55 no. 217); Mich. 1286 x Mich. 1287 (PRO, E159/60, m. 13d). D. by 7 Apr. 1305 (Lincoln, Ep. Reg., II, f. 148v). Indulgence of 30 days for his soul 13 Oct. 1305 (Lincoln, Ep. Reg., III, f. 88r).

Robert de Faningho 1305–1340 Can. of Wroxton, eln conf. 7 Apr. 1305 (Lincoln, Ep. Reg., II, f. 148v). D. by 14 May 1340 (Lincoln, Ep. Reg., V, f. 579r, cf. Lincoln, Ep. Reg., IV, f. 284r).

William of Adderbury (Abburbur(y), Eadburbury) **1340–1349** Can. of Wroxton, commn to examine eln 14 May 1340 (Lincoln, Ep. Reg., V, f. 579r); eln quashed but apptd by bp 15 May 1340 (Lincoln, Ep. Reg., IV, f. 284r). D. by 2 July 1349 (Lincoln, Ep. Reg., IX, f. 245r).

Thomas de la Grove 1349– Can. of Wroxton, eln quashed but apptd by bp 2 July 1349 (ibid.).

Occ. Jan. 1352 x Jan. 1353 (PRO, E210/9239); 10 May 1371 (Lincoln, Ep. Reg., X, f. 184r); 18 June 1377 (Lincoln, Ep. Reg., XII, f. 175v).
The next recorded pr., **Richard**, Occ. 10 Oct. 1410 (*CChR 1341–1417*, p. 443).

WYMONDLEY (Herts), St Mary f. -1218

Lists in *VCH Herts*, IV, 442–3; *Heads*, I, 191.

William Occ. early 13th cent. (BL, Cotton ms. Nero E VI, f. 128r–v; BL, Cotton ms. Tiberius C IX, ff. 95v–96r); 1223 x 1226 (*temp.* Philip de Fauconberg archdn of Huntingdon and John, pr. of Newark) (BL, Add. ms. 43972, f. 18r). Seal (*Hatton Wood MSS.*, pp. 6–7).

Hugh –1246/7 Occ. 2 July 1234 (PRO, Herts F. CP25/1/84/14, no. 183; BL, Add. ms. 43972, f. 19r). D. (H.) by June 1246 x June 1247 (*Reg. Grosseteste*, p. 291).

Martin 1246/7–1247/8 Can. of Wymondley, eln quashed but apptd by bp June 1246 x June 1247 (ibid.). D. June 1247 x June 1248 (ibid., p. 292).

[[*blank*] **of Wymondley** (Wilemundel) and **John of Eynsham** (Eynisham), cans. of Wymondley, both el. and subsequently res. June 1247 x June 1248 (ibid.).]

Richard de Waldia 1247/8– Can. of Dunstable, postulat. and adm. June 1247 x June 1248 on d. of Martin (ibid.). Installed 16 Mar. 1248 (*Ann. Dunstable*, p. 175). Occ. 17 Apr. 1250 (PRO, Herts F. CP25/1/85/24, no. 403); 28 Oct. 1252 (PRO, E210/506; BL, Add. ms. 43972, ff. 52v, 53v).

John de Mordon (Moredon, Morton) 1273–1290 Can. of Wymondley, eln conf. 13 Oct. 1273, no reason given for vacancy (*Reg. R. Gravesend*, p. 178). Res. by 17 June 1290 (*Reg. Sutton*, III, 12). D. by 27 Nov. 1290 (ibid., VIII, 74).

John of Wymondley 1290– Can of Wymondley, el. to succ. John de Mordon, who is dead; eln conf. 27 Nov. 1290 (ibid.). House vacant by deposition of unnamed pr. made by the late Bp Sutton (i. e. before 13 Nov. 1299, cf. Lincoln, Ep. Reg., II, f. 230r). Lic. 11 July 1300 for long overdue election (Lincoln, Ep. Reg., III, f. 11r).

John de Mordon 1300– Can. of Wymondley, eln conf by bp's commissary 3 Nov. 1300 (Lincoln, Ep. Reg., II, f. 230r–v). Occ. 13 Mar. 1302 (Lincoln, Ep. Reg., III, f. 43r).

House vacant 18 Jan. 1304 by deposition of unnamed pr. (Lincoln, Ep. Reg., II, f. 234v).

[**Elias of Wheathampstead** (Wethamstede) Eln quashed 1304 (ibid., f. 234v).]

John of Wymondley (Wilemundele, Wylemundele) 1304–1310 Apptd by bp 18 Jan. 1304 (ibid.). Res. by 6 Aug. 1310 (ibid., f. 241r–v).

Elias of Wheathampstead (Whethamsted) 1310–1340 Can. of Wymondley, eln again quashed but apptd by bp 6 Aug. 1310 (ibid.). D. by 5 May 1340; lic. to el. (Lincoln, Ep. Reg., V., f. 579r).

John of Buckden (Buckeden, Bukeden) 1340–1347 Can. of Wymondley, commn to examine eln 16 May 1340 (ibid., f. 579r–v). Bur. 17 Feb. 1347 (PRO, C84/25/9). D., lic. to el. 28 Mar. 1347 (*CPR 1345–48*, p. 262; PRO, SC1/40/51).

William Legat of Preston 1347–1349 Can. of Wymondley, comm. to examine eln 14 Apr. 1347 (Lincoln, Ep. Reg., VII, f. 206v). D. by 11 July 1349 (Lincoln, Ep. Reg., IX, f. 386r).

Roger de Beston 1349–1374 Can. of Wymondley, right of appt transferred to bp who apptd Roger 11 July 1349 (ibid.). Res. 1 May 1374 (Lincoln, Ep. Reg., XII, f. 136v).

Roger Occ. 1379 (*Clerical Poll-Taxes*, p. 88, no. 1064).

The next recorded pr., **William Bydenham**, occ. 19 Feb. 1403 (PRO, C85/110/37).

THE PREMONSTRATENSIAN
CANONS

ALNWICK (Northumberland), St Mary (Newhouse) f. 1147 x 1148
Lists in Colvin, pp. 392–3; A.M Oliver in *Proc. of Soc. of Antiquaries of Newcastle upon Tyne*,
3rd ser., IX (1919–20), 42–4; *Heads*, I, 192.

Benedict Occ. 1212 (*Heads*, I, 192).

Bartholomew Occ. 13 Jan. 1219, 25 Oct. 1224 (*Northumberland and Durham F.*, I, pp. 26, 30,
nos. 54, 64); (B.) 20 Jan. 1222 (BL, Cotton ms. Vespasian E XIX, f. 121r).

Peter Occ. 1224 (Oliver, p. 42, source not found); 7 Dec. 1235 (DCD, Misc. Cht. 491); n.d. (1228
x 1241 (BL, Egerton ms. 2827, f. 166v); n.d. (1237 x 1241) (Ctl. Scrope of Bolton, f. 67r);
7 Oct. 1239 (DCD, 4.2.Spec.14). Seal (*Durham Seals*, II, p. 544, no. 3402).

Walter Occ. Oct. 1245 x Oct. 1246 (*Hist. Northumberland*, II, p. 16, n. 1); n.d. (mid 13th cent.)
(ibid., II, p. 84, n. 1).

Reginald Occ. 20 Aug. 1249 -St Oswin's day (*Percy Ctl.*, p. 347). Obit 14 Apr. (*HMC Ancaster*,
p. 483).[1]

William of Alnmouth (Alnemuth) Occ. *c*. June 1269 (BL, Harl. Cht. 44 A.4); 5 June 1269
(*Northumberland and Durham Deeds*, p. 231); 8 Sept. 1270 (*CChR 1257–1300*, p. 166); 12
Sept. 1275 (*Percy Ctl.*, p. 253). Seal (*BM Seals*, no. 2555; *Durham Seals*, II, p. 544, no.
3403).

Thomas of Kirkby (Kirkeby) Occ. 12 Jan. 1283 (*Hist. Northumberland*, II, 340, n. 3); 13 Feb.
1284 (*Percy Ctl.*, pp. 233–4).

Alan de Staunforde Occ. 10 Feb. 1288 (prob. 1289) (*Ch. Alnwick*, p. 38); 4 July 1304 (*Priory of
Coldingham*, p. 3).

Thomas Occ. 11 May 1310 (BL, Harl. ms. 3897, f. 17r).

John of Otley (Otteley) Occ. 23 July 1310 (*CAP*, I, p. 3, no. 3); 1 Sept. 1334 (*Percy Ctl.*, p. 320);
1334 (BL, Harl. ms. 3897, ff. 18v, 30v); 15 Aug. 1339 (ibid., ff. 21r, 31v); 11 June 1340
(Norwich, Reg/1/3, f. 39r).

John of Alnwick (Alnewyk) **1340–1350** Pres. to bp for bl. 30 Nov. 1340 (*Reg. Pal. Dun.*, III,
324–5). Lic. from Dean and Chapter of York *sede vacante* to bp of Durham to bl. new abb.
within the York diocese 12 Jan. 1341 (ibid., 327–8). Occ. 30 Apr. 1343 (DCD, Misc. Cht.
4891); 29 June 1347 (BL, Harl. ms. 3897, f. 26r). D. 1350 (*Ch. Alnwick*, p. 40).

Henry of Bamburgh (Baumburgh) Occ. 8 Feb. 1354 (*Percy Ctl.*, p. 344).

Walter −1362 Res. 1362 (*Ch. Alnwick*, pp. 41–2).

Robert of Rothbury 1362− El. 1362 (ibid., p. 41). Occ. 25 Mar. 1364 (BL, Harl. ms. 3897, f.
33r). Retired to Oxford and there for 4 years and at length died in raging pestilence (*Ch.
Alnwick*, pp. 41–2).

Walter of Hepscott (Hepescotes) Occ. 15 Aug. 1376 (ibid., p. 43).

John Frechevyl Occ. 1379 (PRO, E179/62/4, m. 1d).

---

[1] Tate, *Hist. of Alnwick*, II, 18 gives abb. Richard *c*. 1250 but this ref. has not been located.

BARLINGS (Lincs), St Mary (Oxeney) f. 1154 x 1155; cf. Colvin, p. 73.
Lists in *VCH Lincs*, II, 204; Colvin, p. 394; *Heads*, I, 192.

Robert of Rampton (Rampthon) Surname recorded in act of 1216 (BL, Cotton ms. Faustina
B I, f. 112r, cf. f. 108r–v). Occ. 1203 x 1206 (*Lincoln Reg. Ant.*, I, nos. 216–18); 1209 (*Lincs
F. 1199–1216*, p. 156, no. 309); 1221 x 1222 (CUL, Peterborough D. and C. ms. 5, f. 82r =
ms. l, f. 173r); *c.* 1227 x 1230 (BL, Add. ms. 6118, f. 381r, *temp.* abbs. Helias of Revesby and
Adam of Bardney). Obit 6 July (BL, Cotton ms. Caligula A VIII, f. 16r).

Clement Occ. 6 May 1236 (BL, Harl. Cht. 43 A 61a); n.d. (BL, Harl. Cht. 51 D 24); 14 Jan.
1242 (PRO, Notts F., CP25/1/182/8, no. 287). Obit 23 Dec. (BL, Cotton ms. Caligula A
VIII, f. 27r).

Robert Occ. *c.* 1245 x 1247 (*Lincoln Reg. Ant.*, V, no. 1625).

Ing(e)ram (Ingelram) Occ. 20 Jan. 1257, 6 May 1263, 13 Oct. 1267 (*Lincs F.*, II, 134, 203, 224);
1261, 1263 (BL, Cotton ms. Faustina B I, ff. 90v, 39v, 169v); 5 Mar.1267 (*CChR 1257–1300*,
p. 109); Nov. 1266 x Nov. 1267 (*Reg. R. Gravesend*, p. 24); 23 Aug. 1268 (BL, Cotton Cht.
XXVII 60); 16 Sept. 1268 (BL, Harl. Cht. 54 F 59); n.d. (1263 x 1271) (Bodl., ms. Top.
Yorks e 8, f. 49v). Obit 15 Sept. (BL, Cotton ms. Caligula A VIII, f. 20v).

William Occ. 3 Nov. 1271 (*Lincs F.*, II, 247; BL, Cotton ms. Faustina B I, f. 80v). Possibly the
William Galle former abb. referred to in a n.d. cht (ibid., f. 94v).

Ralph Occ. *c.* 6 July 1277 (BL, Cotton ms. Vespasian E XX, f. 95r).

Richard of Hanworth (Haneworth) Surname (BL, Cotton ms. Faustina B I, f. 104r). Occ.
Mich. 1278 x Mich. 1279 (PRO, E159/52, m. 15d); 17 Oct. 1281 (BL, Cotton ms. Faustina
B I, f. 108v); 8 July 1281, 20 Jan. 1282 (PRO, Lincs F., CP25/1/132/53, no. 32; 133/54, no.
11). Res., and subsequently joined Franciscans at York 8 Sept. 1285 (*Medieval Lindsey
Marsh*, p. 68; BL, Cotton ms. Faustina B I, f. 110r).

Richard of Sutton (Suthon) **1282–** El. 1282 (PRO, E36/71, p. 24). Occ. 17 Mar. 1286 (BL,
Cotton ms. Faustina B I, f. 104r); 1287, 1288, 1289 (PRO, C241/7/219; C241/8/42;
C241/10/19); 1288, 1291 (BL, Cotton ms. Faustina B I, ff. 110r–v, 112r, 113r); parliamen-
tary proxies to 1321 (PRO, SC10/244, 268, 323); 1294 (PRO, C241/25/17); 1310 (BL, Harl.
Cht. 44 H 16; *CAP*, I, p. 3, no. 3); 5 Feb. 1312 (Norwich, Reg/1/1, f. 45v); 29 Dec. 1316
(PRO, E36/71, p. 24); Trin. 1317 (*YB XXI*, 180).

Thomas of Edenham Letters of protection issued 10 July 1322 (*CPR 1321–24*, p. 175); 1324
(*Parlty Writs*, II, div. 3, p. 485); 14 May 1327 (*CPR 1327–30*, p. 104); 9 Aug. [1332] (PRO,
C270/7/8); from to 9 Jan. 1336 (*Reg. Burghersh* I, nos. 292, 345, 376); 1333 (PRO, E36/71,
p. 28); 19 Nov. 1340 (BL, Cotton ms. Faustina B I, f. 170r). Seal (*BM Seals*, no. 2597).

Alexander of Ramsey (Ramesey(e), Ramusey) Occ. 29 Apr. 1341 (*CPR 1340–43*, p. 179); 1342
(BL, Cotton ms. Faustina B I, f. 96v); 10 June 1344 (*CPR 1343–45*, p. 261); 7 Mar.1345
(*CPL*, III, 161; *CPP*, p. 76); desc. as king's chaplain 20 Aug. 1349, 4 Feb. 1353 (*CCR
1349–54*, pp. 104, 529); 28 Apr. 1350 (BL, Cotton ms. Faustina B I, f. 97r); from 30 Sept.
1342 to 14 May 1368 (PRO, E36/71, pp. 24, 28).

John of Kirton (Kirkketon, Kyrketon) Occ. from 3 Feb. 1370 to 3 Oct. 1395 (ibid., pp. 29, 31);
1374 (*CPR 1370–74*, p. 484); 29 Oct. 1377 (*CPR 1377–83*, p. 30); 28 June 1382, 28 Apr.1383
(*CPR 1381–85*, pp. 150, 242); 21 Feb. 1387 (PRO, C81/17890/4); 5 Mar. 1387 (*CPR
1385–89*, p. 321). The mention of abb. **George**, occ. 7 July 1393 (*CPL*, IV, 463) is prob. an
error, since John of Kirton occ. 24 June 1393 and 29 Apr. 1394 (PRO, E36/71, p. 31).

BAYHAM (Sussex), St Mary and St Laurence f. 1199 x 1208 by amalgamation of Brockley,
f. -1182 and Otham, f. 1180 x 1187.
Lists in *VCH Sussex*, II, 88; Colvin, p.395; *Heads*, I, 193.

Jordan of St Quintin Last recorded occ. 1215 (Lambeth ms. 1212, f. 106r, cf. *Heads*, I, 193, n.

1). For name see *Ctl. Bradenstoke*, no. 523. See Colvin, p. 116, n. 7 for the possibility that he res. to become archdn of St. Davids, but cf. *St Davids Acta*, p. 28 for his identification as Jordan of Three Mountains (Trismontium).

Reginald Occ. in *Sussex F.*, I, from 5 June 1222 to 13 Apr. 1236 (nos. 175, 333); Mich. term 1228, 1239 (*CRR*, XIII, no. 963; XVI, no. 866, but cf. ibid., XII, no. 1354 (Osmund, Mich. term 1225); 1228 (*CR 1227–31*, p. 92); 13 July 1231 (*Yorks F., 1218–32*, p. 160); 25 June 1242 (*Kent F.*, p. 174); 8 Feb. 1244 (BL, Egerton Cht. 375).

Benedict Occ. 14 May 1245 (*Sussex F.*, I, no. 424).

Reginald Occ. 1 July 1246, 2 Dec. 1248 (ibid., nos. 429, 492); 29 Apr. 1247 (*Ctl. Chichester*, no. 286; *St Richard of Chichester*, pp. 39–40, no. 51); 22 July 1248, 2 May 1249 (*Kent F.*, pp. 204, 228). He may have been one of Archbp Edmund's estate stewards (*St Richard of Chichester*, p. 41, no. 55; Lawrence, *St Edmund*, pp. 98–9, 166–7).

John Occ. 8 July 1251, 1 July 1255 (*Kent F.*, pp. 236–7, 264); 18 Oct. 1253 (*CR 1251–53*, p. 511); from 3 Nov. 1255 to 17 June 1257 (*Sussex F.*, II, nos. 557, 617).

Thomas Occ. 25 May 1262, 2 Dec. 1262 (*Sussex F.*, II, nos. 657, 691). Prob. the former abb. Thomas referred to in 1279 (PRO, Just.1/914, m. 42).[2]

Richard Occ. Mich. 1275 x Mich. 1276 (PRO, E159/50, m. 17d); 1279 (PRO, Just.1/914, mm. 40, 42); 1280–81 (PRO, C85/43/41; C85/44/1, 3; C85/3/13, 17, 56–7); 1287 (PRO, E326/12632); 1288 (*Sussex F.*, II, no. 1014); 1290 (*HMC De L'Isle and Dudley*, I, 125; *Robertsbridge Chts.*, no. 280); 1292 (BL, Cotton ms. Otho A II, ff. 57v, 58r); 8 June 1296 (*HMC De L'Isle and Dudley*, I, 128); 20 July 1296 (PRO, E40/10238).

Laurence −1315 Occ. n.d. (early 14th cent.) (PRO, C81/1790/2); -1304 (Belvoir Castle ms. 71, f. 136r); 7 Nov. 1305 (*CPR 1301–07*, p. 394); 13 June 1308 (*CCR 1307–13*, p. 68); 1311 (*CAP*, I, no. 16). Res. 1315 (Cambridge, Corpus Christi College ms. 59, ff. 231v–235r).

Luke of Sholdon 1315– El. 1315 (ibid.). Occ. 1320 (PRO, Just.1/938A, m. 36); Mich. 1337 (PRO, CP40/312, mm. 161, 213); 18 June 1344 (*CPL*, III, 179).[3]

Simon Occ. 5 Oct. 1345 (*CAP*, III, no. 543).

William Occ. 1352 (PRO, Just.1/941A, mm. 3, 23d, 31, 54); 9 Apr. 1355 (*HMC 5th Rept.*, app. p. 509; R. Dell, *The records of Rye Corporation: a catalogue* (Lewes, 1962), p. 214).

Richard Worth Occ. 6 May 1363 (PRO, C241/144/98).

Robert Occ. from 1 Aug. 1366 to 19 Feb. 1367. By 4 May 1367 he was no longer abb. (*Cal. Misc. Inq.*, III, 257).

The next recorded abb., **Robert**, occ. 27 Nov. 1395 (BL, Add. Cht. 29536).

BEAUCHIEF (Derbys), St Mary and St Thomas of Canterbury f. 1173 x 1176

Lists in *VCH Derbys*, II, 69; Colvin, pp. 396–7; obits in BL, Cotton ms. Caligula A.VIII, ff. 4–27 (translated in Addy, *Beauchief Abbey*, pp. 22–60, with list of abbots p. 72); *Heads*, I, 193.

Gilbert Latest recorded occ. 1209 x 1219 (Colvin, pp. 347–8). cf. BL, Cotton ms. Caligula A VIII, f. 27r (his mother's obit).

Stephen Prob. earlier than William. Occ. early Henry III (*Derbys. Chts.*, no. 1032); ?1217 x 1218 (*Ctl. Darley*, II, 372); c.1217 x 1218 (*Glapwell Chts.*, no. 147); n.d. (Ctl. Beauchief, f. 10v). Obit 5 July (BL, Cotton ms. Caligula A VIII, f. 16r); obits of his father and sister (ibid., ff. 25v, 18r).

William Occ. early Henry III (*Derbys. Chts.*, no. 1862; BL, Woolley Chts. IV. 46).

Jordan Occ. 25 June 1232 (PRO, Notts F., CP25/1/182/5, no. 150). Obit 9 Sept. (Addy, p. 48).

---

[2] Abb. John is said to occ. 1272 (Cooper, 'The Premonstratensian Abbey of Bayham', *Sussex Arch. Coll.*, IX, (1857), 179, without source).   [3] Not surnamed Coldone as in *VCH*.

Gilbert of Salmonby (Salmanby) Occ. 6 May 1236 (BL, Harl. Cht. 43 A 61a); 22 Apr. 1237 (*Reg. Ant. Lincoln*, III, no. 700); July 1243 (Bodl., ms. Top Yorks e 7, f. 119v). 8 Apr. 1247 (PRO, Leics F., CP25/1/122/19, no. 305). Obit 16 May (BL, Cotton ms. Caligula A VIII, f. 12v; Addy, p. 37; also Newhouse obit *HMC Ancaster*, p. 485, former can. of Newhouse).[4]

Roger Occ. n.d. (*temp.* Edward I) (BL, Harl. Cht. 83 E 15); n.d. (Ctl. Beauchief, f. 40v); n.d. *temp.* late Henry III/Edward I (*Derbys. Chts.*, no. 131). Obit. 13 Aug. (BL, Cotton ms. Caligula A VIII, f. 18v; Addy, p. 46).

Ivo –1278 Res. acc. by visitors 1278 (BL, Lansdowne ms. 207C, f. 359r–v).

R. of Fulstow (Foulstowe, Fulstowe) 1278– El. Apr. 1278 (BL, Lansdowne ms. 207C, f. 359r–v; Addy, p. 73, extending R. to Roger). Is he the same as Ralph below?

Ralph Occ. Nov. 1282 x Nov. 1283 (BL, Lansdowne ms. 207C, f. 357v); n.d. (Ctl. Beauchief, f. 85r).[5] Obit 24 Oct. (BL, Cotton ms. Caligula A VIII, f. 23r; Addy, p. 53).

William of Folkingham (Folkyngham) –1324 Occ. 10 Apr. 1296 (Ctl. Beauchief, f. 56v); 28 Aug. 1318 (*CPR 1317–21*, p. 281); n.d. (*temp.* Edward II) (*Derbys. Chts.*, no. 1775; *DAJ*, II (1880), p. 7). Obit 14 Feb. 1324 (BL, Cotton ms. Caligula A VIII, f. 6v).[6]

Robert Occ. Mich. 1328 (*Index to Placita de Banco*, p. 734).

Robert of Radcliffe (Radclive, Radclyf(e), Raddecliffe, Radeclif, Ratcliffe) Occ. 6 Nov. 1347 (York, Reg. 10, f. 325r); 7 Apr. 1350 (Ctl. Beauchief, f. 50v); Jan. 1355 x Jan. 1356, Jan. 1364 x Jan. 1365 (BL, Lansdowne ms. 207C, f. 357v); 19 May 1366 (*Glapwell Chts.*, no. 152); 18 Oct. 1367, 22 Oct. 1367 (Ctl. Beauchief, ff. 46r, 50r). Obit 3 July (BL, Cotton ms. Caligula A VIII, f. 16r; Addy, p. 42).

John of Darley (Derleye) Occ. June 1392 x June 1393 (BL, Lansdowne ms. 207C, f. 358r).

Robert of Rotherham (Roderham) and **Thomas of Doncaster** (Donecastre) are both named as abbots in the Beauchief obituary but their place in the sequence of abbots is unknown. Obits 14 Mar., 8 Nov. (BL, Cotton ms. Caligula A VIII, ff. 8v, 24r; Addy, pp. 30, 55). Robert Roderham is noted as a can. of Beauchief in 1310 (Pegge, *Beauchief*, p. 65), so he may possibly be identified with abb. Robert who occ. above in 1328.

BEELEIGH (Essex), St Mary and St Nicholas (Maldon, Parndon) f. -1172 (at Great Parndon); 1180 (at Beeleigh, near Maldon)

    Lists in *VCH Essex*, II, 176; Colvin, pp. 397–8; R.C. Fowler and A.W. Clapham, *Beeleigh Abbey*, pp. 5, 51; *Heads*, I, 193.

Henry Occ. 1183 x 1189 (BL, Woolley Cht. I 43); Sept. x Oct. 1189 (Colvin, p. 350, cf. p. 136); (H.) 1208 (*CRR*, V, 302); (H.) Trin. 1209 (*Essex F.*, I, 101); Trin. 1234 (*CRR*, XV, no. 1378); 3 Feb. 1235 (*Essex F.*, I, 108). Prob. refer to more than one man (see *TEAS*, X (1908), 350–1).

John Occ. 8 July 1247 (PRO, Cambs F., CP25/1/24/22, no. 2); Mich. 1249 (*Essex F.*, I, 181).

Walter Occ. Easter 1253 (ibid., 194); (W.) 5 Aug. 1253 (BL, Campbell Cht. VIII 22 – William according to seal, *BM Seals*, no. 3595). obit. 13 Apr. (Newhouse obit, *HMC Ancaster*, p. 483).

Roger Occ. from 27 Oct. 1254 to 15 July 1262 (*Essex F.*, I, 196, 249); (R.) 1257 (PRO, DL27/70); (R.) 1262 (Newcourt, *Repertorium*, II, 399).

Andrew Occ. Easter 1265 (*HMC 9th Rept.*, p. 37).

Reginald Occ. 13 Mar. 1268 (BL, Stowe ms. 935, f. 27r); 6 Nov. 1269 (*CPR 1266–72*, p. 390),

---

[4] *VCH* calls him 'of Malmesbury' in error.

[5] *VCH*, following Pegge, *Beauchief*, gives the date 1285 for this entry, but that is the date of the next cht. on f. 85r of the Beauchief ctl.

[6] An abb. John occ. in 1310 (*CAP* I, p. 3, no. 3), but this may be a scribal error, or else William of Folkingham had two terms of office.

where it is mentd that discords and contentions had arisen between the abb. and convent. Cf. 10 Nov. 1269 gt of keeping of abbey to Fulk Lovel, archdn of Colchester and John de Wytham, chaplain (ibid., p. 392).

Andrew Occ. 30 July 1272 (ibid., p. 669); Trin. 1280 (*Essex F.*, II, 27).

Richard of Purleigh (Purle) Occ. 22 May 1298 (Longleat mun. 750); n.d. (PRO, E40/14543).

William of Rockland (Rokelaunde) –1323 Cess. by 26 July 1323 (*Reg. S. Gravesend*, p. 233).

William of Compton 1323– Eln notified to bp 26 July 1323 and pres. for bl. (ibid., pp. 233–4). Bl. 10 Aug. 1323 (ibid., p. 234, cf. *Beeleigh Abbey*, pp. 8–9). Occ. 14 Sept. 1331 (BL, Cotton Cht. XXI 8).

Alexander Occ. 29 Sept. 1341 (Longleat mun. 751).

William –1379 Occ. 21 May 1373 (*Reg. Sudbury*, I, 42). D. by 30 Sept. 1379 when Pope Urban VI deputed the hearing a case about the abbey to the archbp of Canterbury. On the d. of abb. William 5 cans. had excluded Giles the cellarer and 6 others and el. John de Ecclesia, one of the five, as abb. (*Orig. Papal Letters*, p. 81, no. 354).

BLANCHLAND (Northumberland), St Mary (Croxton) f. 1165

Lists in Colvin, p. 398; *Heads*, I, 193.

Adam D. 7 Oct. (BL, Cotton ms. Caligula A VIII, f. 22r).

William D. 17 Nov. (ibid., f. 25r). Both these entries in the Beauchief obit are in 13th-cent. hands.

Ingram Occ. 26 July 1274 (BL, Cotton Cht. V 30).

William of Norton 1315– Can. of Blanchland, el. pres. to bp for bl. 8 June 1315, prof. obed. n.d. (*Reg. Pal. Dun.*, II, 722, 725). Occ. 7 Oct. 1320 (DCD, 1. 17. Spec. 14). Seal (*Durham Seals*, p. 546, no. 3409).

John of Stainton (Staynton) 1322– Request from bp of Durham for permission to bl. to abb. in the York diocese 12 May 1322 (*Reg. Melton*, I, p. 76, no. 222); lic. for bl. 14 May 1322 (ibid., p. 77, no. 223).

In 1327 the unnamed abb. of Blanchland was said to be the cousin of the Scottish lord, Lord Lindsay (*Hist. Northumberland*, VI, 319, n. 2).

John de Stanton 1342– (? the same as above) Appt conf. by bp of Durham 7 Sept. 1342 (*Reg. Pal. Dun.*, III, 501).

William of Brampton Occ. 1379 (PRO, E179/62/4, m. 3).

BRADSOLE, *see* ST RADEGUND

CAMMERINGHAM (Lincs), St Michael (Blanchelande, Normandy) f. *c.* 1192; sold to Hulton 1396

Robert Occ. Dec. 1218 x Dec. 1219 (*Reg. Wells*, I, 133).

[**Julian** Occ. 1 June 1282 as proctor-general of the abbey of Blanchelande at the instn of a vicar of Cammeringham, ? pr. (*Reg. Sutton*, VIII, 3).]

William Occ. as keeper of the manor of Cammeringham 13 Apr. 1293 (ibid., 23). Occ. as pr. from Nov. 1295 x Nov. 1296 to Nov. 1298 x Nov. 1299 (PRO, E106/3/19, m. 7; E106/4/9, m. 1d; E106/4/10, m. 2). Perhaps the same as William Sampson, proctor-general of the abbey of Blanchelande, who occ. at instn of a vicar of Cammeringham 9 May 1298 (*Reg. Sutton*, VIII, 29).

Ralph Occ. 1303 (PRO, E101/568/15, no. 4, quoted *Mon. Seals*, p. 17).

[**Michael Tierry** Occ. 4 Dec. 1326 as proctor of the abbey of Blanchelande at instn of a vicar of Cammeringham (Lincoln, Ep. Reg., IV, f. 99v).]

Nicholas Fovet/Fouet Occ. 1 Apr. 1318 as proctor-general in England of the abbey of Blanchelande at instn of a vicar of Cammeringham (Lincoln, Ep. Reg., II, f. 99v). Occ. as pr. *c.* Mich. 1324 (PRO, E106/5/2, m. 12); July 1325 x July 1326 (PRO, E106/5/4, m. [12]); 8 Oct. 1326 (*Memo. Roll 1326–7*, p. 273).

John Occ. 16 Sept. 1327 (*CPR 1334–38*, p. 484). ? the same as below.

John Lutehale (Lutehare) Occ. 5 Feb. 1342 (*CFR 1337–47*, p. 274); 11 July 1345 (*CCR 1343–46*, p. 636).

Peter Richere (Richer, Rycher, Ryther) Occ. 11 June 1369 (*CFR 1368–77*, p. 16); 1370 (*Buckingham Writ Reg.*, p. 40, no. 106); 23 June 1374 (*Lincs Sessions of the Peace 1360–75*, p. 57, no. 241); 13 Nov. 1387 (*CPR 1383–91*, p. 209).

[On 28 Jan. 1381 John Bilneye, king's chaplain, can. of Torre, was apptd for life to the custody of the priory of Cammeringham (*CPR 1377–81*, p. 589).]

CHARLTON (Wilts) (L'Isle-Dieu, Normandy) f. c.. 1187. Alienated to hospital of St Katherine by the Tower, London, 1380. In the 14th century the abbey of L'Isle-Dieu often apptd one of its cans. to be 'rector' of Upchurch and keeper of Charlton manor (*VCH Wilts*, III, 393); see also Upchurch.

William Occ. as *custos* of manor of Charlton 19 May 1324 (PRO, E106/8/26).

COCKERSAND (Lancs), St Mary (de Marisco) f. -1190

Lists in *VCH Lancs*, II, 158–9; Colvin, pp. 398–9; *Ctl. Cockersand*, I, pp. xxi–xxiii; *Heads*, I, 193–4.

Roger Occ. 1205 x 1206 (*Lancaster Hist.*, II, 385–6); (R.) 1209 x 1212 (DCD, 4.2.4. Ebor. 4); early 13th cent. (*Ctl. Cockersand*, III, ii, 1013–14, cf. II, ii, 738–9).

Hereward Occ. prob. 1216 (*Lancaster Hist.*, I, 48–9, cf. 51–2); Occ. 27 Jan. 1227 (*Ctl. Cockersand*, III, ii, 1021; PRO, Westmorland F., CP25/1/249/13, no.12).); 1234 x Oct. 1235 (*Ctl. Dieulacres*, p. 346); 13 May 1235 (*Ctl. Cockersand*, I, ii, 169; *Lancs F.*, I, 63). Obit 28 Dec. (BL, Cotton ms. Caligula A VIII, f. 27v).

Richard Occ. 15 July 1240 (*Ctl. Cockersand*, II, i, 520–1; *Yorks F.,1232–46*, p. 76).

Henry Occ. 20 Oct. 1246, 27 Oct. 1246, 26 Apr. 1254, Easter 1261 (*Ctl. Cockersand*, I, ii, 225; II, i, 443; III, i, 764; I, i, 147). Occ. in *Lancs F.*, I, from 20 Oct. 1246 to 26 Apr. 1254 (pp. 103, 115); 8 Apr. 1261 (Cheshire RO, DLT/A63/1). Described as former abb. in case of 1268 (PRO, Just.1/1050, m. 84).

Adam le Blak Occ. 26 July 1269 (*Yorks F.,1246–72*, p. 174; *Ctl. Cockersand*, II, i, 529); 26 Mar. 1271 (*Ctl. Cockersand*, I, i, 150); 13 Dec. 1271, 2 Nov. 1277 (ibid., II, ii, 739–40; *Arley Chts.*, no. 34; *Ctl. Cockersand*, III, ii, 1095); Mich. 1278 (PRO, KB27/41, m. 30).

Thomas Occ. 2 Sept. 1286 (*CPR 1281–92*, p. 251; *Ctl. Cockersand*, III, iii, 1106); 1288 (PRO, CP40/73, m. 7).

Robert of Formby 1289– Can. of Cockersand, abb.-el., pres. for bl. 27 Sept. 1289 (*Reg. Romeyn*, I, pp. 338–9, no. 974). Occ. 10 Sept 1290 (*CPR 1281–92*, p. 384; *Ctl. Cockersand*, III, iii, 1107).[7]

Lic. to bp of Carlisle to bl. unnamed abb. 18 Nov. 1302 (*Reg. Corbridge*, II, 153).

Thomas Occ. Aug. 1305 (PRO, KB27/183, m. 26); Mich. term 1306 (*Ctl. Cockersand*, III, ii, 1096); 22 Mar. 1307 (ibid., III, i, 784)

Roger 1311– Prof. obed. and bl. 23 Mar. 1311 (*Reg. Greenfield*, V, p. 214, no. 2108). Occ. 1 June 1326, 21 May 1329 (*Ctl. Cockersand*, III, ii,1097); 5 Aug. 1331 (ibid., III, ii, 1098).

---

[7] *CAP*, II, 105 has Roger occ. 1300, without source.

William of Bosden (Bosdon(a), Boston) Occ. n.d. (1332 x 1333) (PRO, C270/8/13); 28 May, 11 Aug. 1338 (*Chetham Misc.*, new ser. VII, pp. 44, 87, 97); 28 Mar. 1340 (*Ctl. Cockersand*, II, ii, 750); 10 Oct. 1340 (ibid., II, i, 385).[8]

Robert of Carlton (Carleton) –1354 Occ. Hil. term 1347, 24 Nov. 1348 (ibid., III, ii, 1102; III, ii, 1103); 8 July 1347 (ibid., III, iii, 1110; *CPR 1348–50*, p. 387); 1 Oct. 1352 (*Ctl. Cockersand*, III, ii, 1100). D. 20 Mar. 1354 (*CCR 1360–1364*, p. 235; cf. York, Reg.11, f. 31r).

Jordan of Bosden (Bosdon, Bosdoun) 1354– Can. of Cockersand, pres. for bl. 8 Apr. 1354; commn to bps of Carlisle and Sodor to bl. 4 May 1354 (York, Reg. 11, f. 31r). Lic. to seek bl. from any suffragan of York 28 July 1354; bl. and prof. obed. by bp of Carlisle 3 Aug. 1354 (*Reg. Welton* no. 540). Occ. 10 Dec. 1355, 24 July 1357, 25 Sept. 1357 (*Ctl. Cockersand*, III, ii, 1100–1); 1 Aug. 1360, 30 Nov. 1364 (ibid., III, ii, 1101; II, i, 386); 30 Sept. 1369 (*Chetham Misc.*, new ser. VII, p. 20).

Thomas de Burgh Can. of Cockersand, commn to suffragan to bl. Thomas 8 July 1377, no reason given for vacancy (York, Reg. 12, f. 87v). Occ. 1387 (Lancs RO, DDTO.H/3/1–17); June 1388 x June 1389 (*Ctl. Cockersand*, II, ii, 750).

COVERHAM (Yorks N.), St Mary (?Durford) f. *c.* 1187 (at Swainby); 1197 x 1202 (at Coverham).

Lists in *VCH Yorks*, III, 245; Colvin, pp. 399–400; *Heads*, I 194; *YAJ*, XXV, 287; *CAP*, II, 128.

Laurence Occ. *c.* 1209 and *c.* 1213 x 14 (BL, Cotton ms. Nero D. III, f. 51r–v).

Conan Occ. 17 Apr. 1222; 12 June 1231 (*Yorks F., 1218–31*, pp. 44, 136); 1221 x 2 (Bodl., Dodsworth ms. 144, f. 17v); 1226 (BL, Egerton ms. 2827, f. 301r); n.d. (1228 x 1241) (ibid., f. 166v).

John of Knaresborough (Knaresburg) Occ. 25 Nov. 1251 (*Yorks F., 1246–72*, p. 52); 12 Dec. 1261 (*Yorks Deeds*, VII, no. 144); 2 Feb. 1262 (Ctl. Scrope of Bolton, f. 23r).

William Occ. 21 July 1262 (*Yorks F., 1246–72*, p. 126).

Nicholas Occ. 1287 (Baildon, I, 35); 18 Mar. 1300 (Ctl. Scrope of Bolton, f. 27v).

John 1300– Prof. obed. 5 June 1300 (*Reg. Corbridge*, I, 284). Occ. 28 Aug. 1306 (BL Harl. Cht. 44 H 54); Trin. 1309 (PRO, CP40/178, m. 169d).

Thomas Occ. 27 Mar. 1312 (Madox, *Form.*, p. 385, no. 698).

Bernard Occ. 25 Aug. 1320 (*Reg. Melton*, I, p. 10, no. 25).

William of Aldborough (Aldeburg) 1331– Prof. obed. 16 June 1331 (ibid., p. 46, no.142). Occ. Mich. 1337 (PRO, CP40/312, attorneys m. 5); 15 Jan. 1340, 2 Nov. 1341 (*Reg. Pal. Dun.*, III, 241, 408); 10 Feb. 1348 (*CPR 1348–50*, p. 65).

Robert Occ. [*c.* July] 1351 (PRO, Just.1/1129, m. 17).

Elias Occ. Hil. – Mich. 1371 (Baildon, I, 35); grave-slab (*YAJ*, XXV, 294) – the inscription refers to him as *quondam* abb., so poss. he res. before he d.

The next recorded abb., **John**, occ. 1 May 1387 (*York Memo. Bk*, III, 26); Sept. 1404 x Sept. 1405, 6 Henry IV (PRO, E326/9422).

It has proved impossible to fit the following two abbots in their correct sequence.

Robert There is an obit of an abb. Robert on 8 Feb. written in a 13th-century hand in BL, Cotton ms. Caligula A VIII, f. 6r.

Gilbert A cht. of abb. Gilbert is noted as having been taken away from Ellerton priory in Swaledale by the Scots in 1342. There is no indication of the date of the missing document. (*CPR 1345–48*, p. 453, cf. *EYC*, V, p. 33, no. 132n.).

---

[8] *CAP*, II, 106 has William of Brackley occ. 1340, without source. Presumably this is an error for William of Bosden; cf. Croxton Kerrial, p. 498.

CROXTON KERRIAL (Leics), St John the Evangelist f. 1162

Lists in *VCH Leics.*, II, 31; Colvin, pp. 400–1; *Heads*, I, 194.

Adam Occ. 1202 (*Lincs. Assize Roll*, p. 52). 27 Jan. 1212 (*Lincs F. 1199–1216*, no. 326; *Lincs F.*,II, 304); 1219 (BL, Cotton ms. Vespasian E XVIII, f. 106v); 28 Sept. 1221 (PRO, Leics F. CP25/1/121/8, no. 28); 12 June 1222 (PRO, Northants F. CP25/1/172/17, no. 9). D. 12 Nov. (BL, Cotton ms. Caligula A VIII, f. 24v).

Elias Occ. 22 June 1228 (BL, Add. ms. 4936, f. 76r); 20 Dec. 1228 (Nichols, *Leics.*, II, i, p. 93); 20 Jan. 1231 (PRO, Leics F. CP25/1/121/13, no. 157).

Ralph of Lincoln 1231– Can. of Croxton, adm. Dec. 1230 x Dec. 1231, clearly after 20 Jan. 1231 (see previous entry) (*Reg. Wells*, II, 318). Occ. 7 June 1232 (PRO, Notts F., CP25/1/182/5, no. 128); 19 May 1235 (*Lancs F.*, p. 67); 3 May 1236 (*Berkeley Chts.*, no. 239); 3 May 1237 (PRO, Leics F. CP25/1/121/16, nos. 226, 229); 20 Jan. 1240 (ibid.,121/16, no. 244); 1240 (Farnham, *Leics Notes*, II, 193).[9]

Geoffrey 1241/2– Can. of Croxton, bl. June 1241 x June 1242, no reason given for vacancy (*Reg. Grosseteste*, p. 416). Occ. 10 June 1246 (*Lancs F.*, p. 94); 25 June 1246 (*Derbys F. (1886)*, p. 54); 1247 (PRO, Leics F., CP25/1/122/18, no. 271); 1249 (*HMC Rutland*, IV,141); 1252 (PRO, Leics F., CP25/1/122/21, no. 364); 1261 (PRO, Northants F., CP25/1/174144, no. 752; PRO, Leics F. CP25/1/122/24, no. 40); 1263 (ibid., 122/27, no. 5); 18 Nov. 1271 (*Lincs F.*, II, 269). Obit Geoffrey *quondam* abb. 12 Aug. (BL, Cotton ms. Caligula A VIII, f. 18v).[10]

William of Grantham (Graham) 1274– Pr. of Croxton, bl. and prof. obed. 16 Dec. 1274, no reason given for vacancy (*Reg. R. Gravesend*, p. 156). Occ. 30 Oct. 1280, 5 Dec. 1281 (*CPR 1272–81*, pp. 413, 467).[11]

William of Huntingdon (Huntyngdon, Hunt') Occ. 3 Feb. 1285 (PRO, Leics F., CP25/1/123/36, no. 143); (W.) 27 Sept. 1289 (*Reg. Romeyn*, I, p. 339, no. 974); n.d. (Soc. of Ant., ms. 38, f. 37r).

William 1294– El. by 4 Oct. 1294 and bl. 31 Oct. 1294 (*Reg. Sutton*, V, 39–40); (W.) 30 Mar. 1297 (PRO, SC1/47/199); Trin. 1297 (PRO, CP40/119, m. 89); (W.) Aug. 1303 (*HMC Rutland*, IV, 150). ? the same as below.

William of Brackley (Brackeleye, Brakley) Occ. 23 July 1310 (*CAP*, I, no. 3); 24 May 1315 (PRO, C241/77/10); 1316 (PRO, C241/82/177); 14 Aug. 1319, 2 Sept. 1319 (Lincoln, Ep. Reg., II, f. 344r–v).[12]

H. Occ. n.d. (*ante* 1343) (*CAP*, II, no. 271; Colvin, p. 401 dates this document 1304 x 1333).

William Occ. 8 Nov. 1338 (*Reg. Burghersh*, I, no. 1141); 8 Jan., 23 Jan. 1347 (*CPL*, III, 246, 249); 5 Feb. 1348 (Nichols, *Leics*, II, ii, app.1, p. 100); 30 Oct. 1348 (*CCR 1346–49*, p. 595).

Thomas of Loughborough (Loughteburgh) Occ. 8 Apr. 1354 (York, Reg. 11, f. 31r); 13 June 1357 (BL, Harl. Cht. 43 G 30); 21 Mar. 1360 (Lincoln, Ep. Reg., IX, f. 373v), 30 Aug. 1360 (Lincoln, Ep. Reg., VIII, f. 18r); 1363 (*CPL*, IV, 32; *Ctl. Cockersand*, III, iii, 1119); 1364 (*CPR 1361–64*, p. 508); 1371 (Lincoln, Ep. Reg., X, f. 252r); 1374 (*HMC Rutland*, IV, 122); 19 May 1380 (Lincoln, Ep. Reg., XII, f. 209r).

The next recorded abb., **John of Grantham**, can. of Croxton, petition for bl. 17 Nov. 1394, bl. 8 Dec. 1394 (ibid., f. 420r).

---

[9] Nichols, *Leics*, II, i, 157 and *Mon. Angl.*, VII, 876 both give an abb. John in 1241 but without reference.

[10] Nichols, *Leics*, II, i, 157 lists an abb. Thomas in 1250 and an abb. William de Houghton, d. 1274 (the latter repeated in *Mon. Angl.*, VII, 876), both without any source.

[11] The abb. Thomas who occ. *c.* 1279 (*CAP*, II, no. 329) is actually *recte* 1379.

[12] Abb. John occ. 1310, according to *Mon. Angl.*, VII, 876, without source.

DALE (Derbys), St. Mary (Newsham) (De Parco iuxta Dereleyam; de Parco Stanley). f.
temp. Stephen (as hermitage); 1153 x 58 (Aug. priory); ? *c.* 1185 x *c.* 1192 (Prémont. priory);
and again *c.* 1196 (as abbey); *c.* 1200 (*Ctl. Dale*, pp. 2ff; cf. Colvin, pp. 170–6).
    Lists in *VCH Derbys*, II, 75; *Ctl. Dale*, p. 45 (13th-cent. list); Colvin, p. 402, based on *Ch. Dale*,
ed. W. H. St John Hope, *DAJ*, 5 (1883), l ff. and medieval list (ibid., 81–100; *Heads*, I, 194–5.
See also A. Saltman, 'The history of the foundation of Dale abbey or the so-called
Chronicle of Dale', *DAJ*, 87 (1967), 18–38.

Walter de Senteney *alias* **de Todeni** *c.*1200–1231 1st abb. Can. of Easby; cf. *Heads*, I, 195;
and Newhouse. Abb. 31½ years (list). Occ. (W.) 24 Jan. 1226 (*Ctl. Fountains*, I, 217); 4 May
1229 (*Ctl. Dale*, no. 539). Possibly Walter, canon of Newbo, formerly abb. of 'Stanley Park',
obit. 3 Jan. (BL, Cotton ms. Caligula A VIII, f. 4r).

William 1231–1233 El. abb. of Prémontré in 1233 after rule of 2½ years (*Ann. Dunstable*, p.
135; list, p. 82 gives eln date as 10 Oct.).

John Grauncourt (Grauncorth) 1233–1253 Abb. 19 years 39 weeks (list). Occ. Trin. 1234 x
Easter 1235 (*CRR*, XV, no. 1185); 1237 (J.) (*Magnum Reg. Album Lichfield*, p. 357, no. 750);
8 July 1237, 27 Oct. 1241 (*Ctl. Dale*, nos. 541, 540); 2 Feb.1239 (BL, Lansdowne Cht. 584);
Oct. 1241 x Oct. 1242 (*Derbys Chts.*, no. 1504); 6 Jan. 1243 (BL, Harl. Cht. 44 A 9); 8 July
1247 (*Lincs F.*, II, 280).

Hugh of Lincoln (Lincon) 1253–1268 Abb. 14½ years (list). Occ. n.d. (1259 x 1261) (*Hatton's
Book of Seals*, p. 241, no. 353); 1251 x 1268 (*Kniveton Leiger*, p. 134, no. 264); 28 June 1260
(*Ctl. Dale*, no. 181); 1266 (*Ctl. Tutbury*, no. 289).

Simon 1268–1273 Abb. 5 years 11 days (list). Occ. 21 Mar. 1271, *c.* 1269 (*Ctl. Dale*, nos. 19,
46). Obit 27 Sept. (BL, Cotton ms. Caligula A VIII, f. 21v; Addy, p. 51).

Laurence Teuren 1273–1289/90 Abb. 16½ years (list). Occ. in *Ctl. Dale* from 23 Apr. 1275
to 5 Mar. 1286 (nos. 273, 558); 1278 (PRO, F. Divers Cos. CP25/1/284/21, no. 68); 3 May
1286 (*Derbys Chts.*, no. 387). (L.) desc. as former abb. *ante* 1287 (*CAP*, I, no. 350; II, p. 165).

Richard of Normanton ?1290–1297 Abb. 8 years all except 10 days (list). Commn to bp of
Lincoln from bp of Coventry to bl. abb. dated 16 Sept. 1290; bl. before 21 Sept. 1290 (*Reg.
Sutton*, II, 44–5).

John of Lincoln (Lync') 1297–?1303 Abb. 6 years (list). Occ. 9 Dec. 1298 (Lichfield,
B/A/1/1, f. 1v); 22 Aug. 1300 (*Ctl. Dale*, no. 153); 1303 (Colvin, p. 402).

Richard of Normanton 1303–1304 Restored, abb. 1 year 38 weeks (list).

John of Horsley (Horseley(e)) ?1306–1332/3 Abb. 26 years, 45 weeks and a few days (list). Bl.
by bp of Worcester; prof. obed. 5 Aug. 1306 (*Reg. Gainsborough*, p. 165). Presumably res.
1332 (see below). D. 1333, obit. 9 Nov. (BL, Cotton ms. Caligula A VIII, f. 24v). Ledger
stone (*Earliest English Brasses*, p. 185; *DAJ*, 1 (1879), p. 112).[13]

John (de) Wodhous(e) 1332 Abb. 15 weeks (list). Cess. by 14 Aug. 1332 (*CAP*, II, p. 168, no.
353).

William of Horsley (Horseleye, Horslaye) 1332–1354 Abb. 21 years 41 weeks (list). Can. of
Dale, el. 14 Aug. 1332 (*CAP*, II, pp. 168–70, no. 353; *DAJ*, 5, 88–90); (W.) *post* 26 June 1332
(PRO, C270/8/26); 1336 (*CAP*, I, p. 59, no. 33); 1337 (BL, Add. Cht. 21,181); 5 Feb. 1337
(*Ctl. Dale*, no. 563); 28 Feb. 1351 (*CPL*, III, 411); 15 Dec. 1351 (*Ctl. Crich*, p. 85, no. 57).

Roger de Kyrketon 1354–1358 Abb. 3 years 20 weeks (list).

William de Bonay 1358–1400 Abb. 42 years 13 weeks (list). Occ. 28 Nov. 1381 (*CPR 1381–85*,
p. 82); 13 Feb. 1386 (Jeayes, *Derbys. Chts.*, no. 942).

DEREHAM, WEST *see* WEST DEREHAM

---

[13] An abb. William of Dale occ. 23 July 1310 in a list of 14 named English abbs. (*CAP*, I, p. 3, no. 3), but this
is prob. a scribal error.

DURFORD (Sussex), St Mary and St John the Baptist (Welbeck) f. -1161
  Lists in *VCH Sussex*, II, 91; Colvin, pp. 402–3; *Heads*, I, 195.
William Last recorded occ. 1209 x 1219 (Colvin, pp. 346, 348, cf. *Heads*, I, 193, n. 2).
Jordan Occ. July 1218 x Sept. 1220 (when William de Waude was promoted from precentor to
  dean of Salisbury) (*Sarum Chts*, pp. 88, 91, 93; *Ctl. Malmesbury*, I, 401); n.d. (1218 x 1220)
  (*Ctl. Malmesbury*, I, 395–8); 1209 (prob. 1217) x 1228 (*Ctl. Sele*, no. 59; *Heads*, I, 195, n. 3).
Robert Occ. 7 Apr. 1222 (BL, Cotton ms. Vespasian E XXIII, ff. 21v–22r). His occurrence 1229
  (Colvin, citing above) is an error.
William Occ. 15 June 1231, 2 July 1244 (*Sussex F.*, I, nos. 267, 419); 17 Nov. 1239–12 Nov. 1244
  (*Wilts F.*, I, 29, 65); 14 Jan. 1241 (PRO, Hants F., CP/25/1/203/7, no. 52); 12 Nov. 1243,
  12 June 1244 (PRO, F. Divers Cos. CP25/1/283/11, no. 189; 283/11, no. 196; *Kent F.*, p.
  405).
Valentine Occ. 8 July 1247 (PRO, Hants F. CP/25/1/203/8, no. 10); 3 Nov. 1248, 1 July 1252
  (*Sussex F.*, I, nos. 447, 526); 25 Apr. 1249 (*Kent F.*, p. 228). Obit 27 Sept. (BL, Cotton ms.
  Caligula A VIII, f. 21v).
Nicholas Occ. *temp.* Henry III, mentd as former abb. in case of 1288 (PRO, Just.1/929, m. 12d).
  His precise place in the sequence of abbots is uncertain.
John Occ. 25 Nov. 1257 (*Sussex F.*, II, no. 622); 16 Sept. 1266 (*Ctl. Chichester*, no. 700); 1268 to
  1281 (PRO, Hants F.,CP/25/1/204/11, no. 8; 204/13, no. 5); 1293 (*Ctl. Hungerford*, nos.
  678–9; *HMC R.R. Hastings*, I, 244); Nov. 1296 x Nov. 1297 (PRO, E210/8479).
Osbert Occ. 4 Jan., 17 Oct. 1310 (PRO, C241/81/184, 189); 23 July 1310 (*CAP*, I, no. 3); 1311
  (PRO, C241/81/196); 28 Apr. 1315 (*CCR 1313–18*, p. 225); Easter 1317 (PRO, CP40/218,
  attorneys m. 8d).
Walter Occ. 16 Aug. 1318 (*Ctl. Chichester*, no. 394).
John Occ. 13 July 1321 (BL, Cotton ms. Vespasian E XXIII, f. 103v).
Thomas Occ. 26 July 1323 (*Reg. S. Gravesend*, p. 233); 20 Jan. 1328 (*Sussex Arch. Coll.*,VIII, 77,
  citing BL, Harl. ms. 1761, f. 162r); 7 Oct. 1329 (*CCR 1327–30*, p. 571).
Henry Occ. 19 Jan. 1334, 23 Sept. 1334 (*CCR 1333–37*, pp. 191, 336).
John Occ. Easter 1361 (PRO, CP40/406, m. 84d). Prob. the same as below.
John atte Re Occ. 23 June 1364 (BL, Cotton ms. Vespasian E XXIII, f. 76r).
The next recorded abb., **John Heuerwyk**, occ. Jan. 1381 (PRO, E179/11/9); 16 Sept. 1384
  (London, Reg. Braybrooke, f. 369v).

EASBY (Yorks N.) St. Agatha (Richmond: St Agatha) f. 1151
  Lists in *VCH Yorks*, III, 248–9; Colvin, p. 404; *Heads*, I, 195.
Geoffrey Occ. July 1204 (*Yorks F., John*, p. 91; BL, Egerton ms. 2827, f. 282v); 1209 (*EYC*, V,
  no. 313n.); (G.) *c.* 1213 x 1214 (BL, Cotton ms. Nero D III, f. 58r); (G.) 1219 x 1223 (*Ctl.
  Fountains*, I, 200).
Elias –1228 Occ. 12 May 1224 (*Yorks F.,1218–31*, p. 56). Mentd as former abb. in Aug. 1228
  (*Reg. Gray*, p. 25, no. cxix).[14]
Roger Occ. Hil. term 1230 (*CRR*, XIII, no. 2373); 1230 (BL, Egerton ms. 2827, f. 283r); 1231
  (Baildon, I, 45); 13 June 1231 (*Yorks F.,1218–31*, p. 138); 20 June, 30 Sept. 1231 (BL, Egerton
  ms. 2827, ff. 283r, 284r); (R.) 11 Nov. 1238 (ibid., f. 304r); (R.) 8 Dec. 1239 (ibid., f. 296r).[15]
Henry Occ. 6 Oct. 1241 (*Northumberland and Durham F.*, I, p. 62, no. 139; BL, Egerton ms. 2827,
  f. 284v); 1242 (BL, Egerton ms. 2827, f. 10r); 25 June 1246 (Roger is mentioned as predecessor) (*Yorks F.,1232–46*, p. 158; BL, Egerton ms. 2827, f. 285r).

---

[14] Baildon, I, 45 says Elias was dep. 1228 but gives no source.
[15] Clarkson, *Hist. of Richmond*, p. 375 lists Robert 1230 and Roger [of St Agatha] apptd 17 Oct. 1237, but
  this appears to be an error.

William Occ. 30 May 1249 (ibid., ff. 173v–174r); from 1251 to 1255 (*Yorks F.,1246–72*, pp. 26, 100); 1256 (PRO, Westmorland F., CP25/1/249/4, no. 26); 20 Oct. 1257 (BL, Egerton ms. 2827, f. 260r). Obit (late 13th cent. hand) 20 June (BL, Cotton ms. Caligula A VIII, f. 15r).

John of Newcastle (de Novo Castro, de Castro) Occ. 29 Sept. 1260 to 1291 (BL, Egerton ms. 2827, ff. 160v, 161r, 220v); 12 Dec. 1261 (*Yorks Deeds*,VII, no. 144); 24 Apr. 1299 (Ctl. Scrope of Bolton, f. 42v); 1300 (Baildon, I, 48).[16]

Richard of Barningham (Bernyngham) **1302–1307** Prof. obed. 1 Nov. 1302 (*Reg. Corbridge*, I, 299); Res. by 15 June 1307 (*Reg. Greenfield*, IV, p. 205, no. 2090).

William of Eryholme (Ergum, Eriom) **1307–1308** Can. of Easby, prof. obed. 15 June 1307 (ibid.). Res. 1308, still living 1311 (Colvin, p. 404, n.11).

Roger de Walda 1308– Bl. 29 June 1308, no reason given for vacancy (*Reg. Greenfield*, IV, p. 208, no. 2095). Occ. 11 Jan. 1310 (BL, Add. ms. 38816, f. 15r); 23 July 1310 (*CAP*, I, p. 3, no. 3); 6 Nov. 1310 (*CPR 1307–13*, p. 245).

William of Burrill (Burel, Burelle) **1311–** Prof. obed. 22 Feb. 1311 (*Reg. Greenfield*, IV, p. 214, no. 2108). Occ. 15 Apr. 1311 (BL, Egerton ms. 2827, f. 240v).

[BL, Egerton ms. 2827, f. 239r–v – charter of Robert de Eglisclive dated 17 Apr. 1311 refers to John de Castro, Richard de Bernyngham, William de Ergum, Roger de Walda and William de Burelle as *successive abbates*. There is no mention of Thomas (1302) in this list: see n.16.]

Philip of Sigston (Siggeston, Syggeston) **1315–1320** Can. of Easby, eln announced 15 June 1315, commn to bp of Durham to bl. abb.-el. 16 June 1315 (*Reg. Greenfield*, V, p. 144, no. 2589, cf. *Reg. Pal. Dun.*, II, 709–10); similar commn to bp of Durham 17 June 1315 (ibid., IV, p. 231, no. 2133); bl. 22 June 1315 (*Reg. Pal. Dun.*, II, 709–11). Res. by 25 Aug. 1320 (*Reg. Melton*, I, p. 10, no. 25).

Nigel of Irby (Ireby) **1320–** Can. of Easby, eln reported to archbp 25 Aug. 1320 (ibid.).

John of Piercebridge (Percebrigg, Percebrugg) **1328–** Abb.-el. pres. for bl. 22 July 1328 (ibid., I, p. 36, no. 121); prof. obed. n.d. (? July x Aug. 1328) (ibid., no. 122). Occ. 1 June 1334 (*Yorks Deeds*, II, no. 525; Ctl. Scrope of Bolton, f. 68r); 1343 (Baildon, I, 49).

Thomas de Haxley 1345– Prof. obed. & bl. 16 Oct. 1345 (York, Reg. 10, f. 70r). Occ. [*c.* July] 1351 (PRO, Just.1/1129, m. 17).

Thomas ? same a the above. Occ. 19 Sept. 1364 (York, Reg. 11, f. 357r); 2 Jan. 1367 (Ctl. Scrope of Bolton, f. 43r); 7 Sept. 1371 (*Reg. Archdnry Richmond*, p. 177, no. 82).

[**William Isaac** Occ. 1375 (Clarkson, p. 375, without source, and then repeated in *VCH*, Colvin).]

The next recorded abb., **John**, occ. 24 June 1382 (*Yorks Deeds*, III, no. 335); 16 Feb. 1399 (ibid., I, no. 576); 29 Aug. 1403 (*Ridley Chts.*, p. 75, no. 102). In 1386 he was said to be aged 40 and more (*Scrope-Grosvenor*, I, 95).

EGGLESTONE (Yorks N.), St John the Baptist f. -1198

Lists in *VCH Yorks*, III, 251; Colvin, p. 405; *YAJ*, XVIII (1905), 175–8; *Heads*, I, 195.

H. Occ. *c.* 1214 (BL, Cotton ms. Nero D III, f. 52v).[17]

In a case of 1218–19 which Maud widow of Robert of Applegarth brought against an unnamed abb. over land in Skeeby, it is recorded that a certain (unnamed) can. came and said that he was abb. until he was deposed by the General Chapter (Stenton, *Yorkshire Eyre*, no. 406).

William Occ. 18 Nov. 1226 (*Yorks F., 1218–31*, p. 80).

Roger Occ. Oct. 1228 x Oct. 1229 (Plantagenet-Harrison, *Gilling West*, p. 61, citing advowson

---

[16] 28 Jan. 1301 attorney nominated by unnamed abb. for 3 yrs on account of his debility (*CPR 1292–1301*, p.563). Baildon, I, 45 names Thomas as abb. in 1302 (repeated in *VCH*, Colvin), but no source given.

[17] Baildon and *YAJ*, XVIII, list Robert, said to occ. 1216, but without source.

case). The *YAJ* also gives abb. Roger n.d. regarding a chantry in Romaldkirk, citing *Yorks Chantry Surveys*, I, 143. It is prob. that he is to be identified with this abb. Roger, although Colvin tentatively places him after abb. Robert occ. 1251–54.

Hamo Occ. 26 Nov. 1238, 8 July 1240 (*Yorks F., 1232–46*, pp. 52, 73); n.d. (1228 x 1241) (Cheshire RO, Ctl. Scrope of Bolton, f. 67r; BL, Egerton ms. 2827, f. 166v)

Robert Occ. 18 Nov. 1251, 3 May 1254 (*Yorks F., 1246–72*, pp. 42, 95).

John of Easby (Eseby) –1307 Occ. Easter–Trin.1296 (Baildon, I, 51); 1299, 1303 (Cheshire RO, Ctl. Scrope of Bolton, ff. 50r–v); 1303 (*Yorks F., 1300–1314*, p. 174). D. by 4 Nov. 1307 (*Reg. Greenfield*, IV, p. 207, no. 2092).

Thomas of Durham (Dunolmo) 1307– Can. of Egglestone, eln pres. 4 Nov. 1307 in succession to John, deceased, and prof. obed. 24 Dec. 1307 (ibid.).

William 1309– Commn to bps of Carlisle and Whithorn to bl. 30 June 1309 (*Reg. Greenfield*, V, p. 71, no. 2506). He was prob. the W. de C., former abb., whose restoration as abb. was ordered by the abb. of Prémontré *c.* 1309 (*CAP*, II, p. 204, no. 391; Colvin, p. 405, n. 7). Prob. res. 1313, if he is to be identified with W. former abb. of Egglestone, whom the abb. of Torre was ordered to receive *c.* 1313 (*CAP*, II, pp. 208–9, no. 396, cf. no. 395).

Bernard of Langton (Langeton) 1313– Prof. obed. & bl. 23 Dec. 1313 (*Reg. Greenfield*, IV, p. 220, no. 2121). Dispersed – went to Langdon abbey, mentd 20 Sept. 1323, not described as abb. (*CCR 1323–27*, p.139). Occ. 25 Dec. 1328, Mich. 1329 (*YAJ*, XVIII, 176; Baildon, II, 64).

Thomas Occ. 25 Aug. 1320 (*Reg. Melton*, I, p. 10, no. 25). At dispersal in 1323 3 canons called Thomas mentd (Thomas de Dunolm', Thomas de Thexton, Thomas de Oteryngton) (*CCR 1323–27*, p. 139).

John of Theakston (Thexton) 1330– Occ. as can. 1323 – dispersed to Barlings abbey (*CCR 1323–27*, p. 139); as abb.-el. pres. for bl. 28 Mar. 1330, prof. obed. 1 Apr. 1330 (*Reg. Melton*, I, p. 46, nos. 140, 141, 145).

Alexander of Easby (Easeby, Eseby) 1349– Occ. as can. 1323 – dispersed to Newhouse abbey (*CCR 1323–27*, p.139). Prof. obed. and bl. 25 Oct. 1349 (York, Reg.10, f. 77v). Occ. [*c.* July] 1351 (PRO, Just.1/1129, m. 17, ascribed in error to the year Jan. 1353 x Jan. 1354 (Plantagenet-Harrison, *Gilling West*, p. 53)).

William de Stratford (Stretteford) (? Startforth) 1351– Commn to bl. 18 Oct. 1351 (York, Reg. 10, f.8or).

John Occ. Jan. 1354 x Jan. 1355 (plea roll 28 Edward III, cited by Plantagenet-Harrison, *Gilling West*, p. 47).

Peter of Easby (Eseby) 1377– Prof. obed. 5 Oct. 1377 (York, Reg.12, f. 88r).
The next recorded abb., **John Inglys**, occ. 5 Sept. 1401 (*CPL*, V, 414).

HAGNABY (Lincs), St Thomas of Canterbury (Welbeck) f. 1175 x 1176 (priory); *c.* 1250 (as abbey)
  Lists in *VCH Lincs.*, II, 206; Colvin, p. 406; *Heads*, I, 196.

PRIORS

Thomas Occ. *c.* 1200 (pal. *DC*, no. 68).

W. Occ. n.d. (BL, Harl Cht. 45 C 36), but before 1225, d. of S(imon), pr. of Markby who also occ. in cht.

William de Fultorp Can. of Hagnaby, adm. *provisor* and *custos* of house Dec. 1227 x Dec. 1228 (*Reg. Wells*, III, 166). Called prior in BL, Cotton Cht. XXIX 72, prob. to be dated before Dec. 1229 when new instn to vicarage of Alford). Perhaps W. '*rector domus de Hagneby*' who occ. Dec. 1227 x Dec. 1228 (*Reg. Wells*, III, 158).

Peter Occ. 1228 x 32 (BL, Cotton Cht. XXVII 65), *temp.* Geoffrey, pr. of Markby.

ABBOTS

Roger of Retford (Rethford) **1250–1270** El. as first abbot, 1 Jan. 1250 (*Medieval Lindsey Marsh*, no. 31, pp. 65, 70). Res. '*propter impotenciam*' before 4 June 1270 and went to end his days at Welbeck (ibid., pp. 66, 70, cf. pp. 63–4). D. 22 Feb. 1276, bur. at Welbeck (ibid., pp. 66, 70).

John of Barrow (Barwe) **1270–** 2nd abb. El. 4 June 1270 (ibid., pp. 66, 70). Occ. 1278 (BL, Cotton Cht. XXVII 120); 1281 (PRO, Lincs F., CP25/1/132/53 no. 26); (J.) 4 April 1287 (PRO, SC1/47/124). Presumably res. 1290 (see below). D. as former abb. 17 Feb. 1291 (*Medieval Lindsey Marsh*, p. 69). Obit 17 Feb. (*Mon. Angl.*, VII, 891).

John 1290– Bl. 27 Aug. 1290 (*Reg. Sutton*, III, 39). Occ. (J.) 4 Apr. 1297 (PRO, SC1/47/124).

Alan 1300– 4th abb. El. 15 July 1300 (*Medieval Lindsey Marsh*, pp. 69, 73).

William Occ. 23 July 1310 (*CAP*, I, p. 3).

Walter 1313– Bl. by bp of Down & prof. obed. 11 Mar. 1313 (Lincoln, Ep. Reg. III, f. 271r). Occ. 8 Aug. 1316 (*CCR 1313–18*, p. 427).

William Occ. *c*. 1336 (*CAP*, I, p. 57, no. 32); 29 June 1338 (Bodl., Dodsworth ms. 95, f. 65r); 1343 (BL, Harl. Cht. 44 E 15); 21 July 1346 (*CPL*, III, 233). Seal (*BM Seals*, no. 3242).

John Occ. 1377 (*Clerical Poll-Taxes*, p. 42, no. 594).

John of Fordington (Forthyngton) Occ. 1381 (ibid., p. 119, no. 1460). Possibly the same as the above.

HALESOWEN (Worcs), St Mary and St John the Evangelist (Welbeck) f. 1215 x 1218
  Lists in *VCH Worcs*, I, 166; Colvin, p. 407.

Roger First abb., obit 2 Dec. (BL, Cotton ms. Caligula A VIII, f. 26r); 20 Jan. 1222 (*Salop F.*, 3rd Series, VII, p. 379); n.d. (*Cat. Lyttelton Papers*, p. 14, no. 7).

Richard –1232 Occ. Hil. term 1226, Easter term 1227 (*CRR*, XII, no. 2017; XIII, no. 206); 12 Nov. 1227 (*Staffs F.* 2, p. 226); 1229 (*Staffs Plea Rolls, Henry III*, p. 75); 15 Aug. 1232 (*CPR 1225–32*, p. 524 – could be Richard II below). Presumably the unnamed abb. translated to Welbeck 1232 (*Ann. Worcs.*, p. 424, but cf. Colvin, p. 407, n. 3 on the difficulties of placing him in the sequence of abbots of Welbeck).

Richard II 1232– Can. of Halesowen, el. 1232 (*Ann. Worcs.*, p. 424). Occ. 13 Oct. 1238 (*Staffs F.* 2, p. 234); (R.) 27 July 1240 (*Magnum Reg. Album Lichfield*, p. 344); 15 July 1245 (*CChR 1226–57*, p. 287; *Ctl. Walsall*, p. 24); 18 Oct. 1247 (*Cat. Lyttelton Papers*, p. 16, no. 9); 1 June 1251 (*CChR 1226–57*, p. 362); 15 May 1261 (*Staffs F.* 2, p. 250).

Henry de Branewyk Transferred from Titchfield, *c*. 1262? (*CTG*, I, 14; *JBAA*, XXXIV (1878), 346, said to be 'after 1250').

William Occ. 3 Nov. 1273 (PRO, Worcs F., CP25/1/258/9, no. 1).

Martin Occ. n.d. (13th century), his precise place in the sequence of abbots is uncertain (Bodl., Shropshire roll 1).

Nicholas Occ. 7 Dec. 1277 (*Magnum Reg. Album Lichfield*, p. 81); May 1278 (ibid., p. 171; *Staffs F.* 3, p. 32); 1280 (PRO, Worcs F., CP25/1/258/10, no. 18); 1284–1292 (*Select Bills in Eyre*, pp. 24–5); 1289 (*CCR 1288–96*, p. 54). Occ. n.d. three times in Bodl., Shropshire roll 1. D. 'first day of the new year' ?25 Dec. 1298 (Benedictine source) rather than 25 Mar. 1299, see next entry (*Ann. Worcs.*, p. 539).

John of Coventry 1299– Bl. by bp of Hereford 25 Jan. 1299 (ibid., p. 540). Occ. Easter 1301 (PRO, KB27/164, m. 51); 27 Oct. 1303 (PRO, Worcs F. CP25/1/259/13, no. 6).

Walter de la Flagge 1305/6– Lic. to receive bl. from bp of Whithorn 8 Dec. 1305 (*Reg. Gainsborough*, p. 143); prof. obed. and bl. by bp of Whithorn 25 June 1306 (ibid., p. 162). Occ. Trin. 1309 (PRO, CP40/178, m. 37d); 23 July 1310 (*CAP*, I, p. 3).

Bartholomew 1314– Can. of Halesowen, bl. and prof. obed. 11 May 1314 (Worcester, Reg.

Maidstone, p. 14). Possibly the unnamed abb. who had res. by 17 June 1322 (*CAP*, II, pp. 238–40, no. 429).

Thomas de Lech 1322–1331 Apptd by abb. of Welbeck 17 June 1322 (ibid.). Occ. Easter 1330 (*Select Cases of Trespass*, II, 235–6). Res. by 15 May 1331 (*Reg. Orleton (Worcs)*, no. 822).

Thomas of Birmingham (Burmeigham) 1331– Can. of Halesowen, letters requesting bl. 15 May 1331, bl. 16 May 1331 (ibid.). Occ. 1335 (*SHC*, XIV, p. 44); 1343 (BL, Harl. Cht. 44 E 15). Seal (*BM Seals*, no. 3245).

William of Bromsgrove (Brumsgreve) 1366– Can. of Halesowen, former vicar of Walsall, had vacated vicarage on his creation as abb. by 28 Apr. 1366, no reason given for vacancy (*Reg. Stretton*, I, 120).

Richard of Hampton 1369– Bl. 23 Sept. 1369, no reason given for vacancy (Worcester, Reg. Lenn, p. 45). Occ. 1370 (*Reg. Wykeham*, I, 30–1); 24 June 1383 (Lambeth, Reg. Courtenay, f. 216v); 28 May 1391 (*CPR 1388–96*, p. 420).

The next recorded abb., **John Hampton**, can. of Halesowen, eln pres. to bp 13 June 1391, no reason given for vacancy; bl. 16 July 1391 (*Reg. Wakefield*, no. 604).

HORNBY (Lancs), St Wilfrid (Croxton Kerrial) f. *c.* 1172+
List in *VCH Lancs*, II, 161.

Richard of Croxton Occ. as master of Hornby 20 Jan. 1227 (*Lancs F.*, I, 51; *Ctl. Cockersand*, III, i, 901–2).

H. Occ. n.d. (*temp.* J., bp of the Isles 1217 x 1226) (*Lancaster Hist.* I, 154–5).

Robert –?1246 D. *c.* 1246. It was presented at assizes at Lancaster Mich. term 1246 that pr. Robert had been killed by his own horse, which carried him against a certain cross, which he struck with such violence that he died (*Lancs Assize Rolls*, I, 104; *Lancs F.*, I, 95n.).

The next recorded pr., **Robert of Gaddesby**, was apptd 1379 (*CAP*, II, no. 329) but wrongly dated *c.* 1279).

LANGDON (Kent), St Mary and St Thomas of Canterbury (West Langdon) f. 1189
Lists in *VCH Kent*, II, 171; Colvin, pp. 407–8; *Heads*, I, 196.

Richard Last recorded occ. 20 Jan. 1206 (*Kent F.*, p. 38; PRO, E164/29, f. 96v).

Peter Occ. 30 Sept. 1227 (*Kent F.*, p. 89; PRO, E164/29, f. 132v); Easter term 1229, Hil. term 1230 (*CRR*, XIII, nos. 1951, 2546); n.d. (with ref. to Richard, former abb.) (PRO, E164/29, f. 73v).

Robert Prof. obed. n.d. (*Arch. Cant.*, 37, p. 71; Canterbury D. & C., Ch.Ant. A41/4). Occ. 20 Apr. 1236 (*Kent F.*, p. 125); 10 May 1236 (ibid., p. 141).

John Prof. obed. n.d. (*Arch. Cant.*, 37, p. 71; Canterbury D. & C., Ch.Ant. A41/18). Occ. 15 July 1248 (*Kent F.*, p. 201).

William Prof. obed. to Archbp Boniface (1245–70) (*Arch. Cant.* 37, p. 71; Canterbury D. & C., SVSB.I/70/2). Occ. 1 Feb. 1258 (PRO, E164/29, f. 122r–v)

Nicholas Occ. 25 Dec. 1276 (PRO, E164/29, f. 40v).

William Occ. 25 Mar. 1284 (ibid., f. 124v).

Roger de Ore 1289– Bl. and prof. obed. 28 Aug. 1289 (*Gervase*, II, 295; *Arch. Cant.*, 37, p. 72; Canterbury D. & C., Register A, f. 265r; SVSB.I/70/4). Occ. 1291 (PRO, C241/2/122); Nov. 1291 x Nov. 1292 (PRO, E164/29, f. 40r).

William de Digepet There is prob. more than one abb. William here. Digepet is the surname given in the 1305 entry. Occ. 9 Sept. 1302 (PRO, E164/29, f. 147v); 1305 (PRO, E135/6/18); 18 Oct. 1310 (*CAP*, I, nos. 7, 73); 14, 30 Apr. 1312 (ibid., nos. 25–6); from 1312 to Mar. 1341 (PRO, E164/29, ff. 171v, 169r); 8 June 1315 (*Reg. Pal. Dun.*, II, 722–3); 16 June 1315 (*Reg. Greenfield*, V, no. 2589); 5 Aug. 1324 (PRO, C81/1790/7); 4 Apr. 1325, 23 Sept. 1325 (*CCR*

1323–27, pp. 489, 511); 28 Aug. 1325 (*CPR 1324–27*, p. 164); revocation by Adam, abb. of Prémontré, of the sentence of suspension and excommunication against abb. William July 1327 (Lambeth, Reg. Reynolds, f. 155v); 14 Feb. 1331 (*CCR 1330–33*, p. 286); (W.) Aug. 1345 (*CAP*, III, no. 645); (W.) 6 Nov. 1345 (ibid., no. 463).

A new abb. was summoned to receive bl. from the pr. and convent of Canterbury *sede vacante* 1348 (*HMC 8th Rept.*, app., p. 336).

Stephen Occ. 1358 (PRO, E101/462/19).

John of Hackington (Hakynton) 1369– Prof. obed. 31 May 1369 (Lambeth, Reg. Whittlesey, ff. 70v–71r).

The next recorded abb., **Robert of Eastry (Estry)**, lic. to receive bl. from any Catholic bp 31 Jan. 1382 (Lambeth, Reg. Courtenay, f. 5r).

LANGLEY (Norfolk), St Mary f. 1195

Lists in *VCH Norfolk*, II, 421; Colvin, pp. 408–9; *Heads*, I, 196.

Gilbert Latest recorded occ. 18 Jan. 1209 (*Norfolk F. 1201–15*, no. 133).

Hugh Said to be the third abb. (BL, Add. ms. 5948, ff.3r–5r). Occ. from Oct. 1218 x Oct. 1219 to Oct. 1246 x Oct. 1247 (*Norfolk F. (Rye)*, pp. 34, 71); 15 May 1220 (*Norwich Cath. Chts.*, II, no. 75); 1248, 1249 (BL, Add. ms. 5948, f. 4r–v). Possibly Hugh *quondam* abb. of Langley whose obit was on 27 Apr. (BL, Cotton ms. Caligula A VIII, f. 11v).

Simon de Milham −1269 Occ. from Oct. 1249 x Oct. 50 to Oct. 1267 x Oct. 1268 (*Norfolk F. (Rye)*, pp. 76, 100); from Oct. 1250 x Oct. 1251 to Oct. 1257 x Oct. 1258 (*Suffolk F. (Rye)*, pp. 52, 59); 25 Nov. 1260 (*CPR 1258–66*, p. 129); 1267 (BL, Add. Cht. 19291). D. 1269 (Leland, *Iter.*, IV, 95). Seal (*BM Seals*, no. 3402).

Richard (Richer) of Massingham 1269– Fifth abb. succ. 1269 (Leland, *Iter*, IV, 95). Occ. 1269 x 1280 (PRO, E42/430); Oct. 1270 x Oct. 1271, Oct. 1271 x Oct. 1272 (*Norfolk F. (Rye)*, pp. 109, 111); 1271–2, 1275 (PRO, C85/130/77, 80; 131/35); 29 Jan. 1276 (Bodl., Norfolk Cht. 229–30).

William Sixth abb. (BL, Add. ms. 5948, f. 14r). Occ. Nov. 1277 x Nov. 1278 (*Norfolk F. (Rye)*, p. 118).

Thomas Occ. 5 July 1280 (*CCR 1279–88*, p. 60).

Adam de Phileby Occ. 1288–9 (*HMC Lothian*, p. 60); 1289 (Bodl., ms. 242, f. 39r); 12 Feb. 1293 (BL, Add. Cht. 75880); (A.) Nov. 1296 x Nov. 1297 (PRO, E210/7918).

Ralph Occ. 12 July 1300 (*HMC Lothian*, p. 60); 13 June 1302 (Norfolk RO, Phillipps mss. Phi/141.577xl); 8 Apr. 1304 (PRO, C241/43/15); Mich. 1305 (PRO, CP40/153, mm. 32, 494); Mich. 1309 (*YB II*, 151); Trin. 1309 (PRO, CP40/178, m. 261); Mich. 1310 (PRO, CP40/183, attorneys, m. 13); (R.) 20 Feb. 1311 (Norwich, Reg/1/1, f. 39v).

Geoffrey −1340 Occ. 8 Aug. 1316 (*CCR 1313–18*, p. 427); 27 Apr. x 25 Aug. 1327 (Lambeth, Reg. Reynolds, f. 198r); 7 May 1329 (Norwich, Reg/1/2, f. 28v); Mich. 1337 (PRO, CP40/312, m. 7); 4 July 1339 (Norwich, Reg/1/3, f. 27v). Cess. by 11 June 1340 (ibid., f. 39r).

John de Strumpeshagh 1340– Can. of Langley, pres. by John, abb. of Alnwick, on cess. of Geoffrey; bl. and prof. obed. 11 June 1340 (ibid.). Occ. 24 May 1345 (*CAP*, III, p. 197, no. 644).

William Occ. 23 Sept. 1350 (BL, Add. ms. 6275, f. 52v).

Geoffrey 1368– Bl. 19 Mar. 1368 (Norwich, Reg/2/5, ff. 80v–81r). Occ. 22 May 1369 (Bodl., Norfolk Cht. 232).

Peter 1375– Bl. and prof. obed. 30 Nov. 1375 (Norwich, Reg/3/6, f. 43r). Occ. n.d. (*c.* 1378 x 1381) (PRO, E179/45/14); 3 July 1382 (*Reg. Archdnry Richmond*, p. 189, no. 154).

The next recorded abb., **John of Norwich (Norwyco)**, bl. and prof. obed. 3 Nov. 1392, no reason given for vacancy (Norwich, Reg/3/6, f. 170r).

LAVENDON (Bucks), St John the Baptist (Sulby) f. 1155 x 8
  Lists in *VCH Bucks*, I, 386; Colvin, pp. 409–10; *Heads*, I, 196.
Ralph Occ. (R.) 1209 x 1220 (Colvin, p. 339; Bodl., Rawlinson ms. B.336, p. 42); 13 May 1218
  (*Beds. F.*, I, p. 45, no. 185).
Augustine Occ. 1227 (*Beds Eyre*, no. 85); Easter term 1231 (*CRR*, XIV, no. 1242); 24 Sept. 1232
  (*Beds F.*, I, p. 94, no. 354); 13 Oct. 1233 (PRO, C146/2280); 1233 (PRO, E42/279); 26 July
  1236, 15 June 1237 (*Bucks F.*, I, 66,72); Oct. 1237 x Oct. 1238 (*Norfolk F. (Rye)*, p. 59); 24
  Dec. 1250 (*HMC, 7th Rept.*, app. p. 56). Obit 16 Apr. (BL, Cotton ms. Caligula A VIII, f.
  11r; *HMC Ancaster*, p. 483). Seal (*Mon. Seals*, p. 49).
Jordan Occ. 9 Aug. 1267 (*CPR 1266–72*, p. 97); 3 June 1272 (*Bucks F.*, II, 27).[18]
Philip Occ. 3 Feb. 1279 (*CCR 1272–79*, p. 556); 3 May 1286 (*Derbys Chts.*, no. 387); 5 May 1286
  (*Ctl. Dale*, no. 558; BL, Woolley Chts. X 33); Sept. 1287, July 1288 (PRO, Just.1/1276, mm.
  17, 20).
William Occ. 23 July 1310 (*CAP*, III, p. 3).
John de Lathbury 1313– Bl. by bp of Down; prof. obed. 1 Jan. 1313 (Lincoln, Ep. Reg., III, f.
  266v). Occ. Easter 1317 (PRO, CP40/218, m. 179).
Order to permit an unnamed abb. to go to Prémontré to make his obed. to the abb., due to his
  new creation 24 Sept. 1331 (*CCR 1330–33*, p. 335).
Richard de Emerton (Emburton) –1380 Occ. 14 Apr. 1339 (*CPR 1338–40*, pp. 281, 283); 13
  June 1350 (*CPL*, III, 369). D. by 19 May 1380 (Lincoln, Ep. Reg., XII, f. 209r).

NOTE
A **William**, abb. of Lavendon, is commemorated in the Beauchief Obituary on 17 Oct. (BL,
  Cotton ms. Caligula A VIII, f. 23r): the hand of this entry is 13th cent. and the entry is
  linked in the list with abb. William of Welbeck (d. 1229). He is prob. to be identified with
  abb. W. who occ. ? May–Aug. 1207 (*Heads*, I, addenda).

LEISTON (Suffolk), St Mary f. 1183
  Lists in *VCH Suffolk*, II, 119; Colvin, p. 410; *Ctl. Leiston*, p. 50; *Heads*, I, 196.
Philip Formerly pr., successor to Robert (Colvin, p. 347). Occ. several times in *Ctl. Leiston* and
  Butley Chts. after 1193 x 1205 (*Butley Chts.*, no. 130); 7 Nov. 1218, ?recte 1217 (*Ctl. Eye*, I,
  no. 75); 15 May 1220 (*Norwich Cath. Chts.*, II, no. 75). D. 8 Feb. (BL, Cotton ms. Caligula
  A.VIII, f. 6r). Seal (*BM Seals*, no. 3429; Suckling, *Suffolk*, II, 442).
Gilbert Recorded 29 Jan. in 13th-cent. obit (BL, Cotton ms. Caligula A.VIII, f. 5v). His exact
  position in the sequence is uncertain.
Hugh Occ. Oct. 1228 x Oct. 1229, Oct. 1229 x Oct. 1230 (*Suffolk F. (Rye)*, pp. 29, 30).
Peter Occ. Oct. 1234 x Oct. 1235 (ibid., p. 34); Mich. 1242 (*CRR*, XVII, no. 698); (P.) 10 Feb.
  1243 (*Ctl. Leiston*, no. 22).
Matthew Occ. 1243 x *c*. 1250 (*Ctl. Eye*, I, no. 91); Oct. 1246 x Oct. 1247, Oct. 1250 x Oct. 1251
  (*Suffolk F. (Rye)*, pp. 48, 51).
Geoffrey Occ Oct. 1256 x Oct. 1257 (ibid., p. 58).
Gregory Occ. 1260 x 1275 (*Ctl. Leiston*, no. 116). *VCH* suggests 1285 for this cht.
Robert Occ. Nov. 1274 x Nov. 1275 (*Suffolk F. (Rye)*, p. 76).
Nicholas Occ. 20 Sept. 1278 (*CChR 1341–1417*, p. 321); Nov. 1291 x Nov. 1292 (*Suffolk F.
  (Rye)*, p. 95); 1293, *c*. 1294 (*Ctl. Leiston*, nos. 112–13); Trin. 1297 (PRO, CP40/110, m.
  152d); Easter 1299 (PRO, CP40/127, m. 51). Mentd 1302 as late abb. (*Cal. Misc. Inq.*, I,
  518).
John of Glemham 1301– Bl. 21 Dec. 1301 (Norwich, Reg/1/1, f. 7v). Occ. 1302 (*Cal. Misc.*

---

[18] Lipscombe, *Bucks*, IV, 215, gives an occ. in 1254 but with no source.

Inq., I, 518, 641); Mich. 1305 (PRO, CP40/153, m. 470); 12 June 1308 (*CPR 1307–13*, p. 88).

Alan Occ. 23 July 1310 (*CAP*, I, no. 3).

Simon Occ. 8 Aug. 1316 (*CCR 1313–18*, p. 427).

William Occ. n.d. (first half of 14th century) (Bodl., Suffolk Cht. 221).

John Occ. 24 Nov. 1344 (*CCR 1343–46*, p. 478); 10 July 1367 (*Ctl. Leiston*, no. 117); n.d. clerical subsidy (*c.* 1378 x 1381) (PRO, E179/45/18); June 1380 x June 1381 (PRO, E179/45/5b, m. 2); 20 Feb. 1399 (*CPL*, V, 233). It is impossible to say how many abb. Johns are actually included here.

NEWBO (Lincs), St Mary (Newhouse) f. 1198
  Lists in *VCH Lincs*, II, 209; Colvin, p. 411.

Ralph Occ. 1227 (*Bracton's Note Book*, III, p. 632, case 1831). Obit of Ralph *quondam* abb. 7 July (BL, Cotton ms. Caligula A VIII, f. 16r).

Matthew Occ. 6 Jan. 1243 (BL, Harl Cht. 44 A 9).

Luke Occ. 1249 (*HMC Rutland*, IV, 141); n.d. (ibid., 164).

William Occ. 22 Apr. 1257 (PRO, Leics F., CP25/1/122/24, no. 426).

Wiliam (?another) Occ. *temp.* Edward I, referred to as predecessor of abb. William (below) in 1308 (*Reg. Greenfield*, IV, p. 24n.).

William 1277– Prof. obed. and bl. 1 Jan. 1277 (*Reg. R. Gravesend*, pp. 71, 130). Occ. 17 Jan. 1308 (*Reg. Greenfield*, IV, p. 23, no. 1723); 23 July 1310 (*CAP*, I, p. 3, no. 3); Nov. 1310 (ibid., p. 8, no. 7 and p. 126, no. 74).

J. Occ. 28 Apr. 1314 (PRO, C81/1790/8).

Ralph Occ. 4, 10 Mar. 1318 (*YB XXIV*, 59); Hil. 1319 (ibid., 58).

Geoffrey Occ. 18 July 1347 (York, Reg. 10, f. 120v); Mich. term 1348 (*CPR 1348–50*, p. 233).

Roger de Thurverton Occ. 10 June 1356 (*BIB*, 3, p. 56, no. 176); 16–17 Feb. 1358 (*CCR 1354–60*, pp. 491, 489); Easter 1361 (PRO, CP40/406, m. 174); 20 Apr. 1369 (*CPR 1367–70*, p. 232); mentd 28 Apr. 1382 as former abb. (*CCR 1381–85*, p. 125).

Robert of Bennington (Benyngton) Occ. 20 Oct. 1386 (Lincoln, Ep. Reg., XII, f. 219v); before Easter 1396 (*Lincs Sessions of Peace 1381–96*, I, pp. 32–3, no. 125).

NEWHOUSE (Lincs), St Mary and St Martial (Licques) (Newsham) f. 1143
  Lists in *VCH Lincs*, II, 201; Colvin, pp. 412–13; *Heads*, I, 197.

Geoffrey –1226 Occ. 1211 (LAO, Yarb/3/3/1/1, f. 30r, no. 287, where he is called Geoffrey II); (G.) Apr. 1212 (ibid., f. 12r, no. 107); 16 Feb. 1219, 25 June 1219 (*Lincs F.*, I, 120, 123); 13 June 1226 (*Ctl. Dryburgh*, pp. 168–9). The next abb. occ. 28 Sept. 1226 (see below) and so Geoffrey sems to have d. June x Sept. 1226 and not to have been the pr. Geoffrey who d. 3 May (BL, Cotton ms. Caligula A. VIII, f. 12r).

Osbert Occ. 22 Jan. 1226 (BL, Harl. Cht. 49 G 1); 28 Sept. 1226 (*Lincs F.*, I, 183–4); 1229 x 1234 (BL, Harl. Cht. 44 G 30); 5 Dec. 1234 (*Yorks F.*, *1232–46*, p. 25); (O.) June 1237 x June 1238 (*Reg. Grosseteste*, p. 32); 1237 x 1241 (Ctl. Scrope of Bolton, f. 67r). Osbert *quondam* abb., obit 2 Oct. (BL, Cotton ms. Caligula A VIII, f. 22r). Seal (*BM Seals*, nos. 3713–21).

Thomas Occ. 6 Jan. 1242 (BL, Harl. Cht. 44 A 9).

Robert Occ. 12 Nov. 1256, 15 Apr. 1263 (*Lincs F.*, II, 147, 207); 15 Apr. 1263 (BL, Harl. Cht. 44 G. 45).

Thomas Occ. 1267 (BL, Harl. Cht. 44 F 31); 13 Oct. 1271, 20 Oct. 1271, 2 Dec. 1271 (*Lincs F.*, II, 235–6, 275); 5 May 1275 (PRO, Lincs F., CP25/1/132/51, no. 31). 28 Dec. 1275 (*CCR 1272–79*, p. 233; BL, Harl. Cht. 44 H 10);

John of Cave (Kave) –?1296 Occ. (J.) 1278 (BL, Lansdowne ms. 207C, f. 359r–v); presumably

the unnamed abb. going to Scotland for visitation of his order 1284 (*CPR 1282–91*, p. 119);
occ. 9 Feb. 1286 (PRO, Lincs F., CP25/1/133/59, no. 19); 23 Nov. 1293 (LAO,
Yarb/3/3/1/1, f. 48v, no. 492); 8 Sept. 1294 (BL, Harl. Cht. 52 D 20); (J.) 4 Oct. 1294 (*Reg.
Sutton*, V, 39–40); 23 July 1295 (PRO, C241/27/181). Abbey recently vacant June 1296
(*Reg. Sutton*, V, 159). Surname from BL, Harl. Cht. 44 H 13, dated 24 Sept. 1296 and men-
tioning him as lately deceased abb. Seal (*BM Seals*, no. 3709).

Thomas of Hedon 1296– Bl. 21 Sept. 1296 (*Reg. Sutton*, V, 186). Occ. Trin. 1297 (PRO,
CP40/119, m. 48); 2 May 1305 (PRO, Lincs F., CP25/1/134/71, no. 17); 15 June 1307 (*Reg.
Greenfield*, IV, p. 205, no. 2090); 23 July 1310 (*CAP*, I, p. 3, no. 3); 1310 (BL, Harl. Cht. 44
H 16).

John Occ. 25 Aug. 1320 (*Reg. Melton*, I, p. 10, no. 25); 13 May 1322 (York, Reg. 9B, f. 420r).

Ralph Occ. 18 Apr. 1324 (BL, Harl. Cht. 44 H 20); 29 Mar. 1330 (*Reg. Burghersh*, I, no. 257).

Alan 1335– Bl. 12 Mar. 1335 (Lincoln, Ep. Reg., V, ff. 491v–492r). Occ. 8 Aug. 1335 (*CPR
1334–38*, p. 161); 1335 (York, Reg. 9B, f. 467r); 1338 (BL, Harl. Cht. 44 H 26); 1339 (*Reg.
Burghersh*, I, no. 807); 1340 (*Reg. Pal. Dun.*, III, 324); 1341 (*CPR 1340–43*, p. 281; *Reg.
Kirkby*, I, no. 609); 26 Sept. 1344 (*CPR 1343–45*, p. 346); 13 Mar. 1354 (*CPL*, VI, 159).

Robert of Thornton 1355– Can. of Newhouse, lic. to receive bl. from any Catholic bp 21 Feb.
1356 (Lincoln, Ep. Reg., VIII, f. 76v). Occ. 13 June 1357 (BL, Harl. Cht. 43 G 30).

William of Tealby (Teleby, Tevelby) Occ. 15 Aug. 1373 (*CPR 1370–74*, p. 394); 1377
(*Clerical Poll-Taxes*, p. 56, no. 770; p. 134, no. 1697; p. 154, no. 1906); 6 Oct. 1381 (*CPR
1381–85*, p. 80); 22 Apr. 1383 (Lincoln, Ep. Reg., X, f. 125r).

The next recorded abb., **Henry**, occ. 17 Nov. 1394 (Lincoln, Ep. Reg., XII, f. 420r); 20 Sept. 1396
(*CCR 1396–99*, p. 78).

RAVENDALE, WEST, *see* WEST RAVENDALE

ST RADEGUND (Kent) (Bradsole) f. 1193

Lists in *VCH Kent*, II, 174; Colvin, p. 413; *Heads*, I, 197.

Hugh Bl. by Archbp Hubert Walter 1193 x 1205 (*Gervase*, II, 410). Occ. (H.) 1201 x 1203
(Colvin, p. 339); d. before 1219 (ibid., pp. 339–40).

Simon Occ. 15 Sept. 1221 (BL, Add ms. 4934, f. 160r).

Richard 1221– Prof. obed. 29 Dec. [1221] to Archbp Stephen Langton in presence of Bp
Benedict of Rochester (*Arch. Cant.*, XXXVII, 59; Canterbury D. & C., Ch. Ant. A41/19).
Occ. 20 Jan. 1222 (*Kent F.*, p. 73); 1225 (*HMC De L'Isle and Dudley*, p. 83); Easter term 1227
(*CRR*, XIII, no. 79).

Henry Said to be third abb. (Colvin, p. 413, citing Obituary of Prémontré, p. 154). Prof. obed.
n.d. (Canterbury D. & C., SVSB.I/70/3; Ch. Ant. A41/15). Occ. 12 July 1235 (Oxford,
Merton Coll. mun. 1006); 1236 (Bodl., Rawlinson ms. B.461, f. 3r); 1242 (Bodl., Rawlinson
ms. B.336, p. 6); Oct. 1241, 6, 13 Oct. 1258, 20 Jan. 1265 (*Kent F.*, pp. 171, 295–6, 346); (H.)
c. Apr. 1265 (PRO, SC1/3/93); 1269 (Bodl., ms. Gough Kent 18, p. 22, no. 223); 1 Aug.
1276 (*sic*) (Bodl., Rawlinson ms. B.461, f. 16r; Bodl., ms. Gough Kent 18, p. 66, no. 570).
Obit 24 July (BL, Cotton ms. Caligula A VIII, f. 17r). Seal (*BM Seals*, no. 2703).[19]

Roger Came between the two abbots Henry (see note 19).

John 1271– Prof. obed. and bl. by Anian, bp of St Asaph 1271 (*Arch. Cant.*, XXXVII, 59;

---

[19] A case in Trin. 1297 (PRO, CP40/119, m. 115) indicates that there are two abbots Henry. The case details
the previous succession of abbots, viz: Henry, Roger, Henry and John, the immediate predecessor of the
1297 abb. Nothing else had been found relating to abb. Roger or to indicate the likely dates of the first and
second Henrys.

Canterbury D. & C., Ch. Ant. A41/29). Occ. 1273 (Oxford, Merton Coll. muns. 965, 968, 971); 17 June 1273 (PRO, Kent F., CP25/1/98/56, no. 15); 1 July 1274 (ibid., Kent F., 98/56, no. 25); 1274, 1275 (Bodl., Rawlinson ms. B.336, pp. 136–7, 121); *c.*11 Apr. 1278 (PRO, SC1/20/96); (J.) 14 June 1279 (*Reg. Pecham*, I, 4); 1280 (Bodl., Rawlinson ms. B.336, p. 195); 1293 (Oxford, Merton Coll. mun. 1857). Obit 16 May, Newhouse obit (*HMC Ancaster*, p. 485).

William Prof. obed. to Archbp Robert n.d. (1294+) (Canterbury D. & C., Register A, f. 262r). Occ. Nov. 1296 x Nov. 1297 (PRO, E210/8573); Nov. 1301 x Nov. 1302, Nov. 1302 x Nov. 1303 (Bodl., Rawlinson ms. B.336, pp. 91, 123); 6 May 1305 (PRO, C81/1790/12); 14 Apr. 1312 (*CAP*, II, pp. 42–3, no. 25); Mich. 1320 (PRO, KB27/242, m. 31; attorneys m. [7d]). He is most prob. to be identified with **William de Preston** abb. ? first half of 14th cent., mentd in the will of Thomas de Askham, rector of Southfleet, dated 29 May 1357 ('Item conventui monasterii sancte Radegund(is) iuxta Dovor' viginti solidos et volo quod restituantur eidem monasterio decretales ... quod frater Willelmus de Preston quondam abbas loci dedit mihi scolas exercendi') (Rochester, Reg. Sheppey, DRb/Ar.1/2, f. 211r).

Robert de Monyngeham (Monegham) 1325–1327 Letter to archbp of Canterbury from the pr. and convent asking for R. to be bl. 29 Mar. 1325; cert. from the abbs. of Newbo and Titchfield of conf. of R.'s eln 15 Mar. 1325; prof. obed. n.d.; bl. 31 Mar. 1325 (Lambeth, Reg. Reynolds, f. 254v; Canterbury D. & C., Register A, f. 262r). Occ. 23 Sept. 1325 (*CCR 1323–27*, p. 511). Res. [1327] (Lambeth, Reg. Reynolds, f. 198r).

Richard de Offynton 1327– Can. of St Radegund, prof. obed. n.d. [Apr. – Aug. 1327] (ibid.). Occ. 29 Sept. 1328 (*Index to Placita de Banco*, p. 248); 1329 (Bodl., Rawlinson ms. B.336, p. 96A); 19 Oct. 1338 (PRO, E164/29, f. 18v).[20]

Henry de S. –1345 Cess. by 4 Oct. 1345 (*CAP*, III, p. 89, no. 542); provision made for former abb. 5 Oct. 1345 (ibid., pp. 92–5, no. 543).

John R. 1345– El. 4 Oct. 1345 (ibid., pp. 89–92, no. 542). Occ. 1354 (PRO, E101/462/17).

Warisius de Cant' 1362– Prof. obed. 31 July 1362 (Lambeth, Reg. Islip, f. 298r–v).

John Strete –1384 Occ. 26 Oct. 1371, 20 Nov. 1371 (Bodl., Rawlinson ms. B.461, f. 16r); 18 Oct. 1384 (Lambeth, Reg. Courtenay, ff. 302v–303r); lic. to el. new abb. following his res. 2 Nov. 1384 (ibid., f. 58r). Can. of St Radegund, intruded by John, abb. of Welbeck, mentd 1393 (*CPL*, IV, 463). He presumably became abb. again later, for he died as abb. by 1 Jan. 1397 (PRO, C84/36/49). However, **Richard Brygge** was dep. by 19 June 1397 and **Clement**, can. of St Radegund's, el. in his place (PRO, E164/29, f. 173r).

SHAP (Cumbria, formerly Westmorland), St Mary Magdalen (Cockersand) (Valle Magdalene de Heppe) f. 1192(?) (at Preston Patrick); –1201 (at Shap)
Lists in Colvin, p. 414; *Heads*, I, 197.

Walter Last recorded occ. 22 Feb. 1209 (?1210) (BL, Cotton ms. Nero D. III, f. 52v).

Richard Occ. Easter term 1229 (*CRR*, XIII, no. 1850); Hil. term 1231 (*CRR*, XIV, no. 1088); 2 May 1235 (PRO, Westmorland F., CP25/1/249/3 no. 27).

Peter Occ. 6 Oct. 1246 (PRO, Cumberland F., CP25/1/35/3 no. 46); 20 Jan. 1257 (PRO, Westmorland F. CP25/1/249/4, no. 31); 14 Sept. 1265 (*CR 1264–68*, p. 131).

Robert Occ. 27 Jan. 1279 (*Northumberland Assize Rolls*, p. 307); 12 May 1279 (PRO, Westmorland F. CP25/1/249/5 no. 7).

Roger Occ. 28 May 1311 (*Reg. Halton*, II, 33).

John Occ. *c.* 14 Mar. 1316, 28 May 1316 (ibid., 119, 121); n. d. (1332 x 3) (PRO, C270/11/27).

William Occ. 28 Oct. 1343 (*Reg. Kirkby*, I, no. 748).

---

[20] *Mon. Angl.*, VII, 940 gives abb. Gilbert, Jan. 1328 x Jan. 1329, following Hasted.

Lambert of Morland Occ. 4 Sept. 1354 (*Reg. Welton*, no. 544); 1359, 1360 (ibid., nos. 265, 297); *c.* 1379 (ibid., p. 314); 1379 (PRO, E179/60/1). [As a can. of Shap ordained subdcn 26 Mar. 1345 and dcn 21 May 1345 (*Reg. Kirkby*, I, pp. 163–4)].

Robert Mareschall 1380– Prof. obed. Feb. x Apr. 1380 (Carlisle, DRC 1/2, p. 321; Nicholson and Burn, *History of Westmorland*, I, pp. 475–6). Occ. 13 June 1398 (PRO, C67/30 m. 6).

SULBY (Northants), St Mary (Welford) f. 1155

Lists in *VCH Northants*, II, 142; Colvin, pp. 414–15; *Heads*, I, 197–8.

John Occ. 1206 x 1207 (Northants F., PRO transcripts); 1 July 1221 (PRO, Leics F., CP25/1/121/8, no. 29; *Basset Chts.*, no. 116); n.d. (BL, Add. Cht. 20850 – early 13th cent., not late as *CAP*, III, 106).

William Occ. 19 June 1222 (PRO, Northants F., CP25/1/172/17, no. 91). The obit of this abb. William or the one adm. in 1231/2 was celebrated on 12 Oct. (BL, Cotton ms. Caligula A VIII, f. 22v).

Walter –1231/2 Occ. 29 Dec. 1225 (*HMC R.R. Hastings*, I, 134); 29 Oct. 1226., 3 Nov. 1226 (PRO, Leics F., CP25/1/121/11, nos. 102, 113); 9 Jan. 1227 (*CPR 1225–32*, p. 152); 25 Sept. 1227 (PRO, Northants F., CP25/1/172/19, no. 139). Dep. by the General Chapter of Prémontré Dec. 1231 x Dec. 1232 (*Reg. Wells*, II, 171). Seal (*BM Seals*, no. 4130).

William 1231/2– Can. of Sulby, adm. Dec. 1231 x Dec. 1232; bp of Coventry to bl. him (*Reg. Wells*, II, 171). Occ. 9 July 1234, 1236, 18 Nov. 1239 (PRO, Northants F., CP25/1/172/27, no. 340; 172/27, no. 346; 173/29, no. 386); 1236, 1237, 20 Jan. 1247 (PRO, Leics F., CP25/1/121/15, no. 202; 121/16, no. 288; 122/19, no. 324). Seal (*BM Seals*, nos. 4125, 4131).

Robert Occ. 9 June 1252 (PRO, Leics F., CP25/1/122/21, no. 368); 25 Dec. 1257 (Westminster Domesday, f. 499v); 22 Jan. 1258 (BL, Add. Cht. 22423). Obit 14 May (Newhouse obit, *HMC Ancaster*, p. 485).

Hugh Occ. 7 May 1262 (PRO, Leics F., CP25/1/122/24, no. 446).

Henry Occ. 28 June 1273 (PRO, C81/1790/16).

Hugh 1276– Pr. of Barlings, bl. and prof. obed. 17 Nov. 1276, no reason given for vacancy (*Reg. R. Gravesend*, p. 130). Occ. n.d. (*temp.* Edward I) (BL, Add. Cht. 20617, 22464; PRO, E315/40/169); n.d. (*c.* 1276 x 1300) (BL, Add. Cht. 22430). Seal (*BM Seals*, no. 4132).

Henry Occ. 29 May 1286 (Westminster Domesday, f. 500r); (H.) 12 Mar. 1293 (*Reg. Romeyn*, I, p. 228, no. 650); 7 Sept. 1297 (BL, Add. Cht. 21583); Easter 1301 (BL, Add. Cht. 20854); 18 Oct. 1310 (*CAP*, I, p. 6, no. 7; p. 125, no. 73)

Simon Occ. n.d. (said to be *temp.* Edward I) (BL, Add. Cht. 21389).

John of Welford 1314– Lic. 3 May 1314 to receive bl. from the ex-archbp of Armagh (Lincoln, Ep. Reg., III, f. 297v). Occ. 1317 (PRO, DL36/2/251).

Walter Occ. 20 Apr. 1323 (PRO, E315/54/161); 10 Mar. 1326 (*CCR 1323–27*, p. 550); 1328 (*Index to Placita de Banco*, p. 308).

Walter of Belgrave (Belegrave) 1329– 5 Dec. 1329 lic. for bl. by a Catholic bp (Lincoln, Ep. Reg., V, f. 398v); bl. by archbp of York 10 Dec. 1329, by virtue of lic. from bp of Lincoln (*Reg. Melton*, I, no. 284). Occ. 26 Oct. 1335 (Lincoln, Ep. Reg., IV, f. 211v); 24 Aug. 1339 (*CPR 1338–40*, p. 359); 20 July 1341 (*CAP*, III, p. 168, no. 620); Oct. 1342 (BL, Add. Cht. 21090); 7 Nov. 1342 (BL, Add. Cht. 20611). Mentd 22 July 1346 as former abb. (BL, Add. Cht. 20858).

Walter Occ. 1 Nov. 1348 (Lincoln, Ep. Reg., IX, f. 72r); 6 Nov. 1348 (ibid., f. 186v); 1349 (*CPL*, III, 359); 1353 (*Ctl. Pyel*, nos. 29, 34–6); 24 Apr. 1353, 28 Nov. 1353 (*CCR 1349–54*, pp. 590, 617); Jan. 1355 x Jan. 1356 (PRO, E329/313).

Richard of Burton 1356– Can. of Sulby, bl. 2 June 1356 (Lincoln, Ep. Reg., VIII, ff. 63v–64r). Occ. 1356, 24 Aug. 1360 (BL, Add. Chts. 21365, 22444).

John Occ. 13 June 1377 (*CCR 1374–77*, p. 551); 19 May 1380 (Lincoln, Ep. Reg., XII, f. 209r). The next recorded abb., **William de Gysburgh**, occ. 28 Oct. 1414 (BL, Add. ms. 25288, f. 15v).

TALLEY (Carmarthen), St Mary and St John the Baptist (see Binns, p. 168). f. 1184 x 1189
List in *Heads*, I, 198.

Iorwerth (Gervase) –1215 Res. 1215 to be bp of St David's, royal ass. to eln 18 June 1215 (*Rot. Lit. Pat.*, p. 143; *Gir. Camb.*, III, 361ff.; IV, 150f.; *Brut (Peniarth)*, p. 91; *Brut Red Book*, p. 205). D. *ante* 27 Jan. 1229 (*HBC*, p. 297).

G. Occ. 1215 x 1229 (*Welsh Episcopal Acts*, I, p. 357, no. D473).

Gruffudd (Griffin,Gruffin) Possibly the same. Occ. 1 Apr. 1239 (ibid., p. 368, no. D517; *St Davids Acta*, p. 178; *Mon.*, IV, 164; *Arch. Camb.* X (1893), pp. 227–8).

E. Occ. 1 May 1281 (*Litt. Wallie*, no. 200).

Simon Occ. 6 Dec. 1284 (*CPR 1282–91*, p. 146 – indexed under Ireland).

Thomas of Pagham Occ. 8 July 1347 (*Reg. Black Prince*, I, 118).

Rees ap David Occ. *temp.* Black Prince (Cowley, *Monastic Order in South Wales*, p. 210, n. 76, cf. *Arch. Camb.*, 1893, p. 236, dated 1343 x 1344).

The next recorded abb., **Rees ap Jevan**, occ. 20 Sept. 1381 (*CPR 1381–85*, p. 41).

TITCHFIELD (Hants), St Mary (Halesowen) f. 1232 x 1233 (cf. 1231 x 1232, *EEA*, 9, no. 67).
Lists in *VCH Hants*, II, 186; Colvin, p. 416, based on *CTG*, I, 14–16 and *CAP*, III, 123–4; BL, Add. ms. 70506, ff. 214r–215v; Hants RO, 46M48/109, p. 80.

Richard 1232/3– First abb., came with the brethren from Halesowen 1222 (*recte* 1232) (*CTG*, I, 14; BL, Add. ms. 70506, f. 214r). Occ. (R.) n.d. (BL, Harl. ms. 3640, f. 129r); 2 Mar. 1238 (*EEA*, 9, no. 52); Feb. 1237, 11 Mar. 1238 (*Selborne Chts.*, pp. 21, 23). D. 16 June (*CTG*, I. 14; BL, Add. ms. 70506, f. 214r).

Isaac 2nd abb., succ. Richard (ibid.). Occ. in PRO, Hants F. from 3 Feb. 1239 to 20 Jan. 1249 (CP25/1/203/7, no. 16; ibid., /203/8, no. 47); 1246 (Hants RO, 46M48/109, 3, p. 113; Winchester Cath. Lib., Allchin Scrapbook, II/Hen.III/9). D. 19 June (*CTG*, I, 14; BL, Add. ms. 70506, f. 214r).

Henry de Branewyk Succ. on Isaac's d. Later became abb. of Halesowen (*CTG* I, 14). Colvin gives succ. date at Titchfield 1249.

Henry of Sparsholt (Spersholte) Succ. Henry. Cess. D. 22 Sept. (*CTG*, I, 14; BL, Add. ms. 70506, f. 214r–v). Occ. 1 Mar. 1272 (PRO, Hants F., CP25/1/204/11, no. 65).

Ivo Succ. Henry. Cess. D. 3 Mar. (obit) (*CTG*, I, 14; BL, Add. ms. 70506, f. 214v).

Adam Called 3rd abb. D. 14 Sept. (*CTG*, I, 14; BL, Add. ms. 70506, f. 214v). Occ. 9 Feb. & 22 Sept. 1281 (PRO, Hants F. CP23/1/204/13, nos. 25, 39).

William of Bickton (Byketon) Called 4th abb. D. 8 Nov. (*CTG*, I, 14; BL, Add. ms. 70506, f. 214v). Said to occ. 20 and 22 Edward I (Nov. 1290 x Nov. 1291, Nov. 1293 x Nov. 1294 (*CTG*, I, 14, n. c, no sources)). D. 8 Nov. (obit) (ibid., 124; Hants RO, 46M48/109, p. 80). Indulgence of 40 days for late abb. 5 Oct. 1314 (*Reg. Pal. Dun.*, I, 616).

John Sydemanton Called 5th abb. D. 3 Dec. (*CTG*, I, 14–15; BL, Add. ms. 70506, f. 214v). Said to occ. 34 Edward I (Nov. 1305 x Nov. 1306) (*CTG*, I, 14, n. d, no source).

Roger of Candover (Candevere) *c.* 1309–*c.* 1328 Called 6th abb. Ruled abbey about 18 years. D. 5 Aug. (*CTG*, I, 15; BL, Add. ms. 70506, f. 214v). Abb.'s first year (*recognitio novi abbatis*) given as 2 Edward II, *c.* 1309 (*CTG*, I, 15, n. a; Colvin, p. 416, n. 3).

John of Combe *c.* 1329–*c.* 1348 Called 7th abb. Ruled abbey about 20 years. D. 5 May (*CTG*,

I, 15; BL, Add. ms. 70506, f. 214v). *Recognitio novi abbatis* given as 3 Edward III Jan. 1329 x Jan. 1330 (*CTG*, I, 15, n. b). Occ. 8 July 1331 (*Ctl. Winchester*, no. 70a); 24 Aug. 1332 (Winchester, Reg. Stratford, f. 71v). D. 5 May (obit) (*CAP*, III, 124).

Peter of Winchester (Wynton(e)) **1348–1349** Called 8th abb. Ruled for one year and 6 months. (*CTG*, I, 15; BL, Add. ms. 70506, f. 214v). Bl. 8 June 1348 (*Reg. Edington*, I, no. 272, cf. no. 271). D. ?14 Aug. (*CTG*, I, 15; BL, Add. ms. 70506, f. 214v).

William of Wallop (Wallope) **–1370** Called 9th abb. Ruled 20 years 9 months 3 days (*CTG*, I, 15; BL, Add. ms. 70506, f. 215r). Occ. 13 Mar. 1356 (BL, Add. ms. 70506, ff. 47r, 48v); 1 Feb. 1362 (Hants RO, Wriothesley deeds 5M53/12); 13 Feb. 1368 (BL, Add. ms. 70506, f. 108v). D. 23 May 1370 (obit) (*CAP*, III, 124).

John (de) Thorney (Thony, Thorneye, Thorni, Thorny) **1370–?1390** Called 10th abb. Ruled 19 years 13 weeks 5 days (*CTG*, I, 15; BL, Add. ms. 70506, f. 215r). Can. of Titchfield, bl. and prof. obed. 8 Sept. 1370 (*Reg. Wykeham*, I, 30–1). Occ. 1371 (Putnam, *Justices*, p. 207); Jan. 1375 x Jan. 1376 (BL, Add. ms. 70506, f. 110v); 2 June 1380 (ibid., f. 107r). D. 30 Sept (?1390) (*CTG*, I, 15; BL, Add. ms. 70506, f. 215r).

The next recorded abb., **John (of) Romsey**, was bl. 20 Nov. 1390 (*Reg. Wykeham*, I, pp. 176–7).

TORRE (Devon), Holy Trinity, St Saviour (Welbeck) f. 1196

Lists in Colvin, p. 416; Seymour, *Torre Abbey*, 26–45; *Heads*, I, 198. All references from Seymour, *Torre Abbey*, are citing the cartularies: PRO, E164/19; TCD ms. 524.

W. Occ. n.d. (1207 x 1208) (Seymour, *Torre Abbey*, pp. 30–1, 187, nos. 3, 174; TCD ms. 524, f. 114v; PRO, E164/19, f. 57v).

Robert Occ. 2 June 1223, 22 June 1228, 7 Aug. 1228 (ibid., pp. 31, 164, 243, 194, nos. 146, 253, 187); other copies 2 June 1223 (*Lincs F.*, I, 164); 22 June 1228, 7 Aug. 1228 (*Devon F.*, I, nos. 201, 731).

Laurence Occ. from 1231 to 29 June 1246 (Seymour, *Torre Abbey*, pp. 31–2, 261, nos. 5, 295); from 19 Apr. 1238 to 18 Nov. 1239 (*Devon F.*, I, nos, 279, 366).

Simon Occ. 1246, 8 Apr. 1253, 19 May 1254, 24 June 1254, 4 Apr. 1260 (Seymour, *Torre Abbey*, pp. 32–3, 85, 261, 164–5, 220, nos. 6, 13, 293, 147, 230); 8 July 1253 (*Lincs. F.*, II, 103); 11 May 1259, 10 Feb. 1263 (*Devon F.*, I, nos. 615, 629).

Brian **1264–** Bl. 8 June 1264 (*Reg. Bronescombe*, p. 271; *Reg. W. Bronescombe*, II, no. 553). Occ. 15 Mar. 1265 (*Reg. Bronescombe*, p. 167; Seymour, *Torre Abbey*, pp. 33–4; *Reg. W. Bronescombe*, II, no. 586); 1264 x 1270 (Seymour, *Torre Abbey*, p. 205, no. 205).

Richard **1270–** Bl. 22 May 1270 (*Reg. Bronescombe*, p. 271; *Reg. W. Bronescombe*, II, no. 805). Occ. from 1275 to 19 Oct. 1301 (Seymour, *Torre Abbey*, pp. 34–5, 243, 110, nos. 254, 32); July 1286 (PRO, Just.1/1273, m. 11); Easter 1287 (PRO, CP40/67, m. 65).

John le Rous Occ. 16 Feb. 1305, 6 Dec. 1307, 1309 (Seymour, *Torre Abbey*, pp. 35–7, 194, 261, nos. 189, 299); 23 June 1316 (*CPR 1313–17*, p. 503). Occ. in parliamentary writs from 1305 to 1323 (Seymour, *Torre Abbey*, pp. 36–7); Trin. 1327, Mich. 1328 (*Index to Placita de Banco*, pp. 95, 101).

Simon of Plympton **1330–1345** Bl. and prof. obed. 15 Aug. 1330 (*Reg. Grandisson*, I, 568–9; Seymour, *Torre Abbey*, pp. 37–8). D. by 13 Dec. 1345 (*Reg. Grandisson*, II, 1109–10).

Richard de Cotelford (Cotelleford) **1345–**

John dictus Gras (Cras) **1345–**

See Seymour, *Torre Abbey*, pp. 53–6. Cotelford, can. of Torre, el. as abb. after the d. of abb. Simon but Robert, abb. of Welbeck, the father-abbot of Torre, refused to conf. eln. and apptd John *dictus* Gras, can. of Torre. Abb. Richard appealed to the apostolic see and afterwards on John's d. (*sic*) while the appeal was pending at the Curia, of his own accord ceded to the pope all right in his eln. and was subsequently apptd abb. of Torre by the pope. King

Edward III takes abb. under his special protection 26 Aug. 1351 (*CPR 1350–54*, pp. 130–1; *Reg. Black Prince*, IV, 24; *CPL*, III, 340). John *dictus* Gras appeared before bp of Exeter 13 Dec. 1345; bl. by bp of Exeter and prof. obed. 21 Dec. 1345 (*Reg. Grandisson*, II, 1002, 1109–10; III, 1349). John bl. (again, or is he another abb. as Seymour thinks?) by bp of Exeter 21 May 1349 (ibid., II, 1082). John d. in the course of the appeal (*sic*) and the pope apptd Richard abb. 13 Nov. 1349; bl. by Bernard, bp of Porto (*CPL*, III, 340). John occ. 6 Nov. 1348 (*CPR 1348–50*, p. 206). A mob stormed the abbey and John (*sic*) complained to the king of the loss of goods and the ill-treatment of his men and on 20 Nov. 1351 a royal commn to inquire into the riots (*CPR 1350–54*, p. 204). 6 Dec. 1351 John was restored by letters of Bp Grandisson referring to his bl. in 1345 and Cotelford renounced his claim before the bp (*Reg. Grandisson*, II, 1309–10). Royal pardon to Geoffrey Cras of Teignbrewer of the king's suit for the imprisonment of Richard de Cotelford, can. of Torre, for the d. of the same Richard, and for the d. of Roger de Queryngdon and other offences 18 June 1352 (*CPR 1350–54*, p. 292).

John (de) Berkadone (Berkedene, Berkaden) Occ. 27 May 1352 (*CPL*, III, 472); Easter 1361 (PRO, CP40/406, mm. 109d, 209); 1363 (*CPR 1361–64*, p. 369; *Reg. Grandisson*, III, 1489); 1369 (*CCR 1369–74*, p. 89); 1373 (*Reg. Brantingham*, I, 288, 319); 1374 (ibid., 33); June 1379 x June 1380 (PRO, E179/24/9, m. 1).

The next recorded abb., **William Nortone**, was bl. and prof. obed. 27 July 1382 (*Reg. Brantingham*, I, 476). He was previously vicar of Bradworthy which he had vacated on his eln and conf. as abb. by 14 July 1382 (ibid., 78–9).

TUPHOLME (Lincs.), St Mary (Newhouse) f. 1155 x 1166

Lists in *VCH Lincs*, II, 207; Colvin, pp. 417–18; *Heads*, I, 198.

Geoffrey Occ. 19 June 1202 (*Lincs. F. 1199–1216*, p. 16, no. 28); 1203 x 6 (*Reg. Ant. Lincoln*, I, no. 216); 25 Nov. 1218 (*Lincs F.* I, 124); 1230 (*CR 1227–31*, p. 404); early 13th cent. (BL, Cotton Cht. V 63); n.d. [*c.*1227 x 1230] (BL, Add. ms. 6118, f. 381r)

William Occ. 12 Nov. 1247 (*Lincs. F.* II, 45; *Lincs. N. & Q.*, VII (1912–13), 116); 29 May 1250, 29 Apr. 1263 (*Lincs F.*, II, 70, 223); 22 Sept. 1263 (ibid., 193); 1267 x 1271, *temp.* Walter, rector of Halton (BL, Harl. Cht. 56 E 33; cf. *Reg. R. Gravesend*, pp. 26, 45); Whitsun 1273 (*Reg. Ant. Lincoln*, V, no. 1745).

Thomas Occ. 1276 (BL, Harl. Cht. 45 A 14); 2 Dec. 1281 (PRO, Lincs F., CP.25/1/133/55, no. 104); 12 Apr. 1282 (PRO, Lincs F. CP25/1/133/54, no. 48); 3 Feb. 1289 (*CCR 1288–96*, p. 33).

Ralph 1292– Bl. 1 June 1292 (*Reg. Sutton*, IV, 4); (R.) occ. 15 July 1300 (*Medieval Lindsey Marsh*, no. 31, p. 73).

William 1310– Bl. and prof. obed. 10 May 1310 (Lincoln, Ep. Reg., III, f. 181r). Occ. 22 Feb. 1317 (BL, Harl. Cht. 45 A 19).

Philip Occ. 15 Sept. 1330 (*Reg. Burghersh*, I, no. 276).

William of Thorpe (Thorp) **1336–** Lic. to receive bl. from any Catholic bp 21 Mar. 1336 (Lincoln, Ep. Reg., V, f. 525v). Occ. 3 July 1336 (*Reg. Burghersh*, I, no. 500).

Roger of Blankney (Blaunkenay) **1341–** Lic. to receive bl. from any Catholic bp 7 Aug. 1341 (*Reg. Kirkby* I, no. 609); occ. 15 June 1348 (BL, Harl. Cht. 45 A 20, 45 A 21); 29 July 1348 (Lincoln, Ep. Reg., X, f. 20v); n.d. (BL, Harl. Chts. 45 A 17, 45 A 18).

Simon of Lincoln 1349– Can. of Tupholme, bl. and prof. obed. 13 July 1349, no reason given for vacancy (Lincoln, Ep. Reg., IX, f. 60r).

Thomas Occ. 4 Apr. 1354 (*CCR 1354–60*, p. 66).

John of Beelsby (Belesby) **1373–** Bl. and prof. obed. 9 Oct. 1373 (Lincoln, Ep. Reg., XII, f. 121v). Occ. 1377, 1381 (*Clerical Poll-Taxes* p. 56, no. 769 & p. 127, no. 1579).

The next recorded abb., **William de Tynton** (Tyneton), can. of Tupholme, was pres. for bl. by William abb. of Newhouse, 22 Apr. 1383 (Lincoln, Ep. Reg., X, f. 125r). Occ. 3 May 1385 (*CPR 1381–85*, p. 522).

UPCHURCH (Kent) Rectory of church given to Prem. abbey of L'Île-Dieu in Normandy (cf. *Reg. Langham*, p. 395, n.2). The can. in charge seems to have been called *custos*, rector, or prior. In 1361 Upchurch was described as an alien priory (*CPR 1358–61*, p. 560, cf. p. 558).

Hugh *custos* of Upchurch, alien, royal protection gtd 7 Feb. 1296 (*CPR 1292–1301*, p. 177). Occ. from Nov. 1295 x Nov. 1296 to Nov. 1298 x Nov. 1299 (PRO, E106/3/19, mm. 5d, 16; E106/4/10, m. 3d); Nov. 1302 x Nov. 1303 (PRO, E106/4/18, m. 6).

William Bense Occ. as proctor-general in England of the abbey when pres. clerk to the vicarage of Upchurch, 14 Sept. 1311 (*Reg. Winchelsey*, II, 1225).

William Occ. as *custos* of Upchurch *c*. Mich. 1324 (PRO, E106/5/2, m. 12d); July 1325 x July 1326 (PRO, E106/5/4, m. [12d]).

br. Peter Hugonis Occ. as 'rector' of Upchurch 27 July 1337 (*CFR 1337–47*, p. 27); *custos*, Mich. 1338 x Mich. 1339 (PRO, E372/184, rot. 9).

Richard of L'Île-Dieu (del Ilde Dieu, del Ild Dieu) Occ. as 'prior' of Upchurch in return of aliens 16 Jan. 1370 (Lambeth, Reg. Whittlesey, f. 161r; cf. PRO, E106/10/10).

br. Richard Beton (Becon) Occ. as proctor of the abbey when instn made to Upchurch vicarage 21 Oct. 1367 (*Reg. Langham*, p. 294). Gt of keeping of priory 20 Oct. 1371 (*CFR 1368–77*, p. 135); canon of L'Île-Dieu and keeper of Upchurch occ. 18 July 1376 (ibid., p. 358); 3 May 1377 (ibid., pp. 396–7); 20 Oct. 1377 (*CFR 1377–83*, p. 27); 11 July 1379 (ibid., p. 156).

WELBECK (Notts), St James (Newhouse) f. 1153 x 1154

Lists in *VCH Notts.*, II, 138; Colvin, p. 418; A.H. Thompson, *The Premonstratensian Abbey of Welbeck*, pp. 58ff., 113; *Heads*, I, 198.

Richard of Southwell ?1197– El. prob. 1197 (9 Richard I, Ch. Hagnaby, BL, Cotton ms. Vespasian B XI, f. 11r). For his name see *Ch. Dale*, p. 12. His predecessor, Adam, may have left Welbeck in 1196 to become the first abb. of Torre (*EEA*, 12, no. 209n.). Occ. 1203 (*CRR*, II, 258); 1198 x 1216 (*Ctl. Tutbury*, no. 268; Cheney, *Inn. III*, no. 1148); 8 July 1215 (*Rot. Lit. Pat.*, p. 148b); 1217 x 1224 (*Ctl. Healaugh Park*, pp. 7–8); 20 Jan. 1222 (*Derbys F. (1885)*, p. 214; BL, Harl. ms. 3640, f. 117r). D. 24 Oct. (Beauchief obit, BL, Cotton ms. Caligula A. VIII, f. 23r). ?Seal (*BM Seals*, no. 4288).

William –?1229 Occ. 27 Jan. 1223 (PRO, Notts F., CP25/1/182/3, no. 21); 18 Nov. 1223 (ibid., /182/3, no. 25; BL, Harl. ms. 3640, ff. 119r, 117v); 30 Sept. 1226 (*Derbys F. (1886)*, p. 24; BL, Harl. ms. 3640, f. 117r); Mich. 1227 (Ctl. Beauchief, ff. 68r, 70v); D. 17 Oct. (possibly this William) (Beauchief obit, BL, Cotton ms. Caligula A VIII, f. 23r). Possibly the abb. William who occ. 1 Apr. 1229 (*CPR 1225–32*, p. 285). An unnamed abb. of Welbeck d. 1229 (*Ann. Dunstable*, p. 115).

William of Croxton (Croxeton) –1247[21] Occ. 18 Jan. 1232 (PRO, Notts F., CP25/1/182/5, no. 116); 25 June 1232 (ibid., 182/6, no. 155); 1236 (ibid., 182/6, nos. 186, 189–90); 12 May 1240 (*Lincs F.*, I, 316); 6 Jan. 1243 (BL, Harl Cht. 44 A 9); 25 Mar. 1243, (W.) 24 Mar. 1244 (BL, Harl. ms. 3640, f. 70r; *Derbys Chts.*, nos. 1086, 1087); 1245 (PRO, Notts F., CP25/1/182/9, no. 317); 1246 (BL, Harl. ms. 3640, f. 101r); 3 Dec. 1247 (*Reg. Ant. Lincoln*, III, no. 699; BL, Harl. ms. 3640, f. 140r).[22]

[21] [Richard], abb. of Halesowen was stated to have been translated to Welbeck in 1232 (*Ann. Worcs*, p. 424), but cf. Colvin, p. 407, n. 3 on the difficulties of placing him in the sequence of abbots of Welbeck.

[22] *VCH Notts* gives a second abb. Richard occ. 1250, 1252, 1256 x 1257 and an abb. Adam occ. 1263, 1272 and 1276, referring to the cartulary (BL, Harl. ms. 3640) but these are all mistaken and their names should be deleted from the sequence of abbs.

Hugh Occ. from 28 Apr. 1252 to 6 Oct. 1257 (PRO, Notts F., CP25/1/182/10, no. 375; /183/11, no. 429; *Derbys F. (1886)*, p. 59); Oct. 1261 x Oct. 1262 (BL, Harl. ms. 3640, f. 23v); 1263 (Thompson, p. 69). Obit 3 May (BL, Cotton ms. Caligula A VIII, f. 12r).

N. Occ. 16 Nov. 1273 (BL, Harl. ms. 3640, ff. 38v–39r; cf. Thompson, p. 69). He is prob. to be identified with abb. **Nicholas** who occ. in several n.d. chts. (BL, Harl. ms. 3640, ff. 70r, 81r, 101v, 105r, 123r).

Thomas of Sutton Occ. Mich. 1278 x Mich. 1279 (PRO, E159/52, m. 11); 3 & 25 Nov. 1280 (PRO, Notts F., CP25/1/183/14, nos. 29, 37); 1281 (ibid., /183/15, nos. 55, 64); 9 June 1287 (BL, Harl. ms. 3640, f. 25r); 11 June 1292 (BL, Woolley Cht., I, 52; *Derbys Chts.*, no. 1093); (T.) 1300 (*Medieval Lindsey Marsh*, no. 31, p. 73). Presumably the unnamed abb. who went to Norway on the king's service in 1290 (*CPR 1281–92*, pp. 349–50). Occ. 20 Jan. 1307 (BL, Harl. ms. 3640, f. 21v).[23]

John of Duckmanton (Dugmanton) **1309–1310** Prev. pr. of Welbeck (Thompson, p. 70). Prof. obed. 13 Apr. 1309 (*Reg. Greenfield*, IV, pp. 54–5, no. 1783). Occ. 23 July 1310 (*CAP*, I, p. 3, no. 3).

John of Chesterfield (Cesterfeld) **1310–** Prof. obed. and bl. 6 Dec. 1316 (*Reg. Greenfield*, IV, p. 111, no. 1908A). Occ. (J.) 5 Jan. 1311 (*Derbys Chts.*, no. 1094; BL, Woolley Cht. I 51).

William of Kendal (Kendale) **1316–1322** Commn to Bp *Recreensis* to bl. 24 July 1316 (*Reg. Greenfield*, V, p. 274, no. 2877). Res. by 13 May 1322 (York, Reg. 9B, f. 420r).

John of Nottingham (Notingham) **1322–** Can. of Welbeck, el. and pres. to archbp for bl. 13 May 1322 (ibid.); prof. obed. 23 May 1322 (ibid., f. 419r). Occ. 29 Dec. 1324 (*CCR 1323–27*, p. 334); 15 May 1325 (*CAP*, III, p. 210, no. 661); 10 Sept. 1327 (*CCR 1327–30*, p. 222); 1329 (BL, Harl. Cht. 45 A 31; BL, Harl. ms. 3640, ff. 131v, 147r); 1330 (PRO, Just.1/167, mm. 16, 29); 21 Sept. 1334 (*CPR 1334–38*, p. 63).

William of Aslockton (Aslaghton, Aslaketon) **1335–** Can. of Welbeck, prof. obed. and bl. 14 Dec. 1335 (York, Reg. 9B, f. 466r), cf. eln pres. to archbp for bl. 30 Dec. (*sic, recte* Nov.) 1335 (ibid., f. 467r).

Robert of Spalding (Spaldyng) **1341–** Abb. of Langdon to abb. of Sulby, who is to cite Robert of Spalding, can. of Welbeck, recently el. as abb., lately convicted of certain crimes at Welbeck. He is to cite him to answer 20–21 July 1341 (*CAP*, III, pp. 167–9, no. 620). Occ. 13 Dec. 1345 (*Reg. Grandisson*, II, 1109–10); 13 Nov. 1349 (*CPL*, III, 340).

John de Wirsop 1349– Prof. obed. and bl. [*c.* late Oct.] 1349 (York, Reg. 10, f. 136r). Occ. 22 Dec. 1351 (*CPL*, III, 440).

Hugh of Langley (Langeley) **1360–** Prof. obed. 25 Mar. 1360 (York, Reg. 11, f. 246r). Occ. 19 Sept. 1360 (ibid., f. 247r); 13 Mar. 1368 (Norwich, Reg/2/5, f. 80v).

George of Gamston (Gamelston) **1369–** Prof. obed. 25 Jul 1369 (York, Reg.11, f. 270r). Occ. 28 Apr. 1383 (*CPR 1381–85*, p. 242); 20 Oct. 1386 (*CCR 1385–89*, p. 309); 21 Feb. 1387 (PRO, C81/1790/4).

The next recorded abb., **John (de) Baukwell**, occ. Apr. 1388 (*CPL*, V, 334; Thompson, pp. 79, 82–3 re appropriation of Flintham church during his tenure of office).

WENDLING (Norfolk), St Mary (Langley) f. -1267
Lists *VCH Norfolk* II, 423: Colvin, pp. 419–20.

Nicholas Said to be first abb. and occ. 1267 (Blomefield, *Norfolk*, X, 89–90; Colvin, p. 192); Oct. 1268 x Oct. 1269 (*Norfolk F. (Rye)*, p. 106); 22 July 1268 (PRO, F. Divers Cos., CP25/1/283/16, no. 446) n. d. (2nd half of 13th cent.) (PRO, E40/10572).

Robert Occ. 1 June 1282 (Holkham Hall, Longham deeds no. 23); Oct. 1292 (PRO, E40/10919);

---

[23] Nash, *Worcs*, I, 514 notes an abb. E. of Welbeck, whose cht. (n.d.) was inspected by Nicholas, abb. of Halesowen (*c.* 1278 x 1299). Thompson (p. 69) thinks his existence is doubtful.

June 1303 (PRO, E40/10610); 1307 (PRO, E42/209); 1 Feb. 1315 (Norwich, Reg/1/1, f. 59v); 6 Feb. 1317 (ibid., f. 70r).[24]

John –1329 Occ. 10 Dec. 1325 (Norwich, Reg/1/2, f. 5r); 30 Dec. 1325 (Holkham Hall, Longham deeds no. 30); 1327 (Lambeth, Reg. Reynolds, f. 198r). Res. by 7 May 1329 (Norwich, Reg/1/2, f. 28v).

William of Saxlingham (Saxlyngham) **1329**– Can. of Wendling, eln conf. by Geoffrey, abb. of Langley and John, abb. of West Dereham, and bl. 7 May 1329 (ibid.).[25]

John of Norwich (Norwic', Norwyce) –1339 D. by 4 July 1339 (Norwich, Reg/1/3, f. 27v)

Thomas of Tittleshall (Tytleshale) **1339**– Can. of Wendling, pres. by Geoffrey, abb. of Langley and Nicholas, abb. of West Dereham, bl. 4 July 1339 (ibid.). Assaulted and stoned on 29 May 1356 (*Cal. Misc. Inq.*, III, 84). The unnamed abb. to show cause why his eln should not be declared null Aug. 1345. His predecessor, John of Norwich, now dead, was not properly el. (*CAP*, III, pp. 198–9, no. 645). Occ. 12 Aug. 1356 (*CPR 1354–58*, p. 452).

John de Snytton Occ. in n.d. clerical subsidy (1377/8 x 1381) (PRO, E179/45/14; E179/45/7c).

The next recorded abb., **John (de) Brissele** (Brysele) occ. 14 Dec. 1400 (PRO, E40/10,081); 6 Nov. 1406 (Norfolk RO, ms. 3812/8.A.3).

WEST DEREHAM (Norfolk), St Mary (Welbeck) f. 1188
Lists in *VCH Norfolk*, II, 418; Colvin, pp. 420–1; *Heads*, I, 199

Ralph (II) Can. of Welbeck, pr. and novice-master of Durford, occ. 1209 x 1219 (Colvin, pp. 345ff.); Oct. 1217 x Oct. 1218, Oct. 1221 x Oct. 1222, Oct. 1227 x Oct. 1228 (*Norfolk F. (Rye)*, pp. 32, 38, 43); *c.* 24 June 1218 (BL, Add. ms. 46353, f. 12v); 26 Apr. 1225 (*Lincs F.*, I, 174). This abb. or Ralph I d. 17 May (BL, Cotton ms. Caligula A VIII, f. 13r; *Heads*, I, 199).

Angerus (Anger, Aunger) Occ. *Norfolk F. (Rye)* from Oct. 1230 x Oct. 1231 to Oct. 1252 x Oct. 1253 (pp. 48, 86); 1236 (PRO, E40/14021); 1237 (*CPL*, I, 171; PRO, Notts F., CP25/1/182/7, no. 247); 4 Apr. 1250 (*Lincs. F.*, II, 73); 30 Sept. 1251 (*Yorks F., 1246–72*, p. 17). Seal (*BM Seals*, no. 3053; *Mon. Seals*, p. 95).

Roger Occ. Oct. 1267 x Oct. 1268 (*Norfolk F. (Rye)*, p. 104); 9 June 1269 (*Yorks F., 1246–72*, p. 169).

Walter Occ. 8 July 1279 (*Yorks F.,1272–1300*, p. 22); 1280 (*Ctl. Sallay*, I, 23); Nov. 1285 x Nov. 1286 (*Norfolk F. (Rye)*, p. 129); Nov. 1287 (PRO, E40/15045). Called Denis Walter in Blomefield, *Norfolk*, VII, 325.

Simon Occ. 23 July 1304 (*Lordship and Landscape*, p. 68).

Walter of Dunton (Dontone, Duntona) **1306**– Commn to receive bl. from bp of Ely 1 Mar. 1306 (Norwich, Reg/1/1, f. 19v). Occ. 18 May 1307 (BL, Add. ms. 46353, f. 269v); Mich. 1309 (PRO, Just.1/593, mm. 12d, 15d).

Paul of Tilney (Tilneye) **1313–1325** Prof. obed. 21 Dec. 1313 (Norwich, Reg/1/1, f.54v). Occ. Easter 1317 (PRO, CP40/218, attorneys m. 1d). D. by 6 May 1325 (*CCR 1323–27*, p. 287; Norwich, Reg/1/1, f. 117r; *CAP*, III, pp. 210–11, no. 661).[26]

John de Rutham 1325– Can. of West Dereham, abb.-el., pres. to bp for bl. 15 May 1325

---

[24] *VCH* gives Robert occ. 1281 citing Tanner's Norwich ms. In fact, Norfolk RO, Tanner, Norwich ms. I, p. 136 gives occ. 14 Edward I (1285 x 1286) not 1281, and cites 'Iter Norf. Ass. 93'. PRO, Just.1/93 is actually the assize roll for Cambridgeshire and Huntingdonshire for 1288 x 1289 and I cannot locate any ment. of abb. Robert.

[25] Blomefield, *Norfolk*, X, 90 has occ. 1352, which is presumably an error.

[26] Abb. Bartholomew occ. 8 Aug. 1316 (*CCR 1313–18*, p. 427) but this is most prob. a scribal error for Halesowen (q.v.).

(Norwich, Reg/1/1, f. 117r); lic. from vicar-general to receive bl. from any Catholic bp 21 May 1325 (ibid., f. 117r–v; cf. *CAP*, III, pp. 210–11, no. 661). Occ. 1 Feb. 1328 (PRO, C81/1790/3); 7 May 1329 (Norwich, Reg/1/2, f. 28v); 8 Aug. 1329 (BL, Add. Cht. 17737). Seal (*BM Seals*, no. 3054).

Richard Occ. 6 Mar. 1330 (*CPL*, II, 497).

Nicholas Occ. 4 July 1339 (Norwich, Reg/1/3, f. 27v); 15 Oct. 1348 (*CPL*, III, 271).

John of Weeting (Wetyng) Occ. 24 Oct. 1351 (*CPR 1350–54*, p. 169); 10 June 1363 (*CPR 1361–64*, p. 377).

William (of) Holt 1368– Can. of West Dereham, petition for bl. 13 Mar. 1368, no reason given for vacancy; bl. 6 Apr. 1368 (Norwich, Reg/2/5, f. 80v). Occ. 8 May 1378, 15 May 1378 (*CPR 1377–81*, pp. 196, 211); 16 Aug. 1384 (*Cal. Misc. Inq.*, IV, no. 322). Desc. as former abb., apostate, signified for arrest 21 Feb. 1387 (Logan, *Runaway Religious*, p. 233).

The next recorded abb., **Constantine**, occ. 5, 20 Oct. 1387 (Ely, G/1/2, f. 60r); 1 Feb. 1389 (*CPR 1385–89*, p. 489).

WEST RAVENDALE (Lincs) (Beauport, Brittany) f. *c.* 1202. Diss. -1413 (priory)
List in *VCH Lincs*, II, 244.

Roger Occ. 1197 x 1219, ? Dec. 1219 (*Waltham Chts.*, no. 415).

Roald Occ. 7 Feb. x 17 June 1235, during vacancy of the see of Lincoln (*AASRP*, XXXIX, 183).

Nicholas Occ. June 1245 x June 1246 (*Reg. Grosseteste*, p. 84); June 1246 x June 1247 (ibid., p. 86); June 1248 x June 1249 (ibid., p. 106).

Paul Occ. as proctor of Beauport abbey at West Ravendale (? pr.) Nov.1261 x Nov. 1262 (*Reg. R. Gravesend*, pp. 10, 266).

John de Sola Occ. 8 March 1270 (ibid., p. 38).

Martin Occ. as proctor of Beauport abbey at West Ravendale 21 Sept. 1273 (ibid., p. 279); as pr. 23 Oct. 1275 (*CPR 1272–81*, p. 107).

Richard Occ. as proctor of Beauport abbey at West Ravendale 31 July 1280 (*Reg. Sutton*, I, 5).

Robert Occ. as proctor of Beauport abbey (in West Ravendale vicarage institution entry) 31 Mar. 1282 (ibid., 22).

Ralph *dictus* **Galeard** Occ. as proctor of Beauport 26 June 1282, 19 Dec. 1282, 4 Mar. 1284 (ibid., 26, 34, 51); occ. as pr. of West Ravendale 23 Jan. 1284 (ibid., 51).

[**William** *dictus* **Rucof** Occ. as proctor of Beauport (no mention of being at West Ravendale) 6 June 1286 (ibid., 91).]

William de Houteville (Houtevile) Pr. of West Ravendale, proctor of Beauport 18 Jan. 1288 (pr.), 18 Dec. 1289 (proctor), 27 May 1290 (pr.) (ibid., 115, 130, 140).

Ralph *dictus* **Maleherbe** Occ. as proctor of Beauport abbey at West Ravendale 16 June 1291 (ibid., 155).

Nicholas Occ. as pr. from Nov. 1295 x Nov. 1296 to Nov. 1298 x Nov. 1299 (PRO, E106/3/19, m. 9d; E106/4/9, m. 1d; E106/4/10, m. 2); as proctor-general of abbey in England 3 March 1298 (no mention of West Ravendale) (ibid., 224); as pr. Easter 1300 (PRO, E106/4/14, m. 2d).

Sampson Occ. 24 July 1301 (Lincoln, Ep. Reg., II, f. 4v).

Michael (*dictus*) **Moryn** Occ. as proctor of abbey at West Ravendale 7 Oct. 1303, 14 Jan. 1314 (PRO, C146/1865; Lincoln, Ep. Reg., II, f. 335v); proctor (no mention of West Ravendale) 1323–24 (*Reg. Burghersh*, I, nos. 75, 93); pr. *c.* Mich. 1324 (PRO, E106/5/2, m. 12); July 1325 x July 1326 (PRO, E106/5/4, m. [11d]); proctor at West Ravendale 1327, 9 Sept. 1328 (*Reg. Burghersh*, I, nos. 162, 206).

Nicholas de Dinanno (Divanno, Dynanno) Occ. as proctor of abbey at West Ravendale 7 Jan. 1330, 27 Feb. 1330 (ibid., nos. 249, 253).

William Occ. 2 Mar. 1334 (*CPR 1330–34*, p. 519); 5 Mar. 1334 (*CCR 1333–37*, p. 305). Is pr. William to be identified with br. **William Cillardy**, who occ. 11 June 1332 as proctor in England of Beauport abbey (no mention of West Ravendale) (*Reg. Burghersh*, I, no. 339)?

[**Thomas Tryquet** (Triquet) occ. as proctor of Beauport abbey (no mention of West Ravendale) 23 Nov. 1334 (ibid., no. 437); 29 Mar., 3 May 1335 (ibid., nos. 580, 594, 641, 644).]

Nicholas de Dinanno (Dynanno, Dynauno, Dyvanno) Occ. as prior 27 Jan. 1344 (*CFR 1337–47*, p. 355); previously occ. as proctor of Beauport (no mention of West Ravendale) 6 July, 4 Dec. 1338, 9, 27, June 1340 (*Reg. Burghersh*, I, nos. 580, 594, 641, 644).

Oliver Gelyn (Gelin, Gleyne) Occ. 12 Aug. 1349 (*CFR 1347–56*, p. 147); 28 Feb. 1361 (*CCR 1360–64*, p. 243); occ. as proctor of Beauport abbey at West Ravendale 9 Oct. 1364 (Lincoln, Ep. Reg., X, f. 9r); 18 March 1366 (ibid., f. 13r); 9 June 1367 (ibid., f. 17v); 23 May 1367 (ibid., f. 18r); 3 Oct. 1367 (ibid., f. 20r); 10 June 1369 (ibid., f. 28r).

Nicholas Occ. 1377 (*Clerical Poll-Taxes*, p. 31, no. 418). Probably to be identified with the following.

Colin [? Nicholas] Jahnet (de Jaherenton) Occ. 12 Nov. 1377 (*CFR 1377–83*, p. 44). Received permission to stay in England Feb. 1378 (Matthew, *Norman Monasteries*, p. 160). A **Nicholas Johann** also described as pr. of West Ravendale was given the same permission on the same date (ibid.), presumably a version of Jahnet's name.

8 Feb. 1378 royal gt of the keeping of the priory during the French war to br. **Richard Ludelowe** (*CFR 1377–83*, p. 71); repeated 28 Apr. 1382 (ibid., p. 291).

THE GILBERTINE CANONS
AND NUNS

ALVINGHAM (Lincs), St Mary and St Aethelwold f. 1148 x 54
Lists in *VCH Lincs*, II, 194; *Heads*, I, 201.
William of Frisby Occ. 1213 (Bodl., ms. Laud Misc. 642, ff. 130v–131r).; n.d. (early 13th cent.)
(pal. *Gilbertine Chts.*, p. 113).
Thomas Occ. 13 Oct. 1218 (*Lincs F.*, I, 116).
Roger Occ. Easter Term 1229 (*CRR*, XIII, no.2062); 23 May 1229 (Bodl., ms. Laud. Misc. 642,
f. 146v); from 23 May 1229 to 21 Oct. 1234 (*Lincs F.*, I, pp. 223, 282).
William Occ. 5 May 1240 (ibid., 329); 6 May 1240 (Bodl., ms. Laud Misc. 642, f. 128r).
Richard Occ. 1247 (ibid., f. 142v).
Alexander Occ. 6 Oct. 1256 (ibid., f. 142v); 6 Oct. 1256, 20 Jan. 1257 (*Lincs F.*, II, 120, 148).
Ralph Occ.(R.) 10 May 1267 (Bodl., ms. Laud Misc.. 642, f. 41v); (Ranulph) 25 June 1269
(ibid., f. 161v); 14 June 1278 (ibid., f. 38r); 1281 (Ranulf) (PRO, Lincs. F., CP25/1/133/55,
no. 93); 1280, 1281 (Bodl., ms. Laud Misc. 642, ff. 162r, 121r); 1282 (Ranulph) (ibid., f. 57v);
(Ranulph) 9 & 13 Apr. 1283 (*Reg. Sutton*, I, 41, 43).
Thomas Occ. 9 Apr. 1307 (Bodl., ms. Laud Misc. 642, f. 121r).
Gilbert Occ. 23 Oct. 1309 (ibid., f. 41v).
William Occ. 24 Aug. 1317 (ibid., f. 85r).
John Occ. 9 May 1333 (*Reg. Burghersh*, I, no. 380).
William de Nesse William of Nesse mentioned 26 Sept. 1360 as former pr. who had been alle-
gedly threatened by Sir Robert Darcy, knight (*CPR 1358–61*, p. 464). G. (?Guillelmus) occ.
1340 (Bodl., ms. Laud Misc. 642, f. 137v); 18 May 1341 (*Reg. Burghersh*, I, no. 683).
Thomas of Brompton (Bromton) Occ. 16 May 1376 (Lincoln, Ep. Reg., XII, f. 146v); 1377
(*Clerical Poll-Taxes*, p. 56, no. 772).
John of Cockerington (Cokeryngton) Occ. 1381 (ibid., p. 134, no. 1695 & p. 154, no. 1904).

PRIORESSES
None known before 1538.

BRIDGE END (Lincs), St Saviour *or* **HOLLAND BRIDGE** (Pons Aslaci) f. -1200
List in *VCH Lincs*, II, 199 begins in 1445.
William Occ. 9 Feb. 1231 (*Lincs F.*, I, 226).
John Occ. 23 June 1337 (*Royal Inquest 1341*, p. 9, no. 91).
John Occ. 1377 (*Clerical Poll-Taxes*, p. 48, no. 692).
John de Scarhowe/Scarbowgh Occ. 1381 (Scarhowe) (ibid., p. 111, no. 1345); 1381
(Scarbowgh) (ibid., p. 156, no. 1936).

BULLINGTON (Lincs), St Mary f. 1148 x 1154
Lists in *VCH Lincs*, II, 192; *Heads*, I, 201; Thompson, *Women Religious*, p. 235 (to *c.* 1270).
Gamel Occ. 4 July 1209 (*Lincs F. 1199–1216*, no. 304).
G. Occ. Dec. 1217 x Dec. 1218 (*Reg. Wells*, I, 103; cf. *BIHR*, XLV (1972), 157–70), but could of
course be either Gamel or William (*G[ulielmus]*).

William Occ. in *Lincs F.*, I, ten times from 25 Nov. 1218 to 12 May 1240 (pp. 144, 306); Oct. 1225 x Oct.1226 (BL, Add. ms. 6118, f. 432r); 1229 (*CPR 1225–32*, p. 279); Mich. 1232 x 1235 (*Gilbertine Chts.*, p. 27); 1235 (BL, Add. ms. 6118, f. 407v); 1236 (*Medieval Lindsey Marsh*, no. 37); 21 May 1245 (*Lincs F.*, II, 7).

Simon Occ. 1231 x 1257, *temp.* Robert de Bolsover, can. of Lincoln, effectively 1245 x 1254 (BL, Add. ms. 6118, f. 414v); *temp.* Henry III (BL, Harl. Chts. 44 A 40, 41; 47 I 21).

Walter Occ. Oct. 1253 x Oct. 1254 (BL, Add. ms. 6118, f. 409r); 26 Apr. 1254 (PRO, Leics F., CP25/1/122/23, no. 415); June 1254 (BL, Harl Cht. 55 A 11); 13 Oct. 1254, 30 Apr. 1256, 3 Feb. 1259 (*Lincs F.*, II, 106, 126, 169); 23 Apr. 1262 (PRO, Leics. F., CP25/1/122/25, no. 472). Seal (*BM Seals*, nos. 2759–65).

William Occ. 23 Dec. 1263 (BL, Harl. Cht. 44 I 17).

Patrick Occ. n.d. [1263 x 1271] (Bodl., ms. Top. Yorks c. 8, f. 49v); *c.* 1270 (BL, Harl. Cht. 44 A 36); Feb. 1272 (BL, Cotton ms. Vespasian E XX, f. 58v). Possibly moved to Watton. q.v.

Geoffrey Occ. Hil. term 1284 (BL, Harl. Cht. 47 D 54).

William Occ. 14 May 1287 (Bodl., Douce ms. 136, f. 94v); 11 Apr. 1288 (PRO, Leics F., CP25/1/123/36, no. 171); 21 Apr. 1288 (BL, Harl. Cht. 58 G 9); 25 Jan. 1292 (BL, Harl. Cht. 44 I 18). Mentd 28 Dec. 1300 as former pr., when indulgence of 40 days issued (Lincoln, Ep. Reg., III, f. 22v).

Gilbert Occ. 29 Sept. 1299 (BL, Harl. Cht. 44 B 4); 1305 (PRO, E101/568/55, no. 3); 2 July 1309 (BL, Harl. Cht. 44 B 5). Seal (*Mon. Seals*, p. 14).

William Occ. 13 Feb. 1334 (*Reg. Burghersh*, I, no. 410).

Roger de Houton Occ. 18 May 1341 (ibid., no. 683); 30 Sept. 1343 (BL, Harl. Cht. 51 B 35).

William de Boneye Occ. 26 May 1348 (*CPR 1348–50*, p. 157).

Robert of Rampton (Rempton) Occ. 1377 (*Clerical Poll-Taxes*, p. 53, no. 759); 12 July 1378, *c.* Sept. 1378 (*CPR 1377–81*, pp. 302, 306); 30 July 1378, 29 Aug. 1378 (*CCR 1377–81*, pp. 209, 211). Pardon for Robert of Rampton, can. of Bullington, recently appealed as Robert, pr. of Bullington, 24 Nov. 1379 (*CPR 1377–81*, p. 405).

Roger of Beckering (Bekering) Occ. 1381 (*Clerical Poll-Taxes*, p. 126, no. 1577).

PRIORESSES

Katherine Pigot ? prs, occ. 1377 (ibid., p. 53, no. 759). Otherwise none known before the 16th cent.

CAMBRIDGE, St Edmund f. 1291

List in *VCH Cambs*, II, 256.

Philip of Barton –1298 El. Master of Sempringham, eln pres. to bp 23 July and eln conf. 31 July 1298 (*Reg. Sutton*, I, 230–4).

Osbert Occ. 27 July 1305 (Gray, *St Radegund*, p. 138; checked with original cht. Jesus Coll., Cambridge).[1]

John of Letchworth (Leccheworth) Occ. 28 Oct. 1355 (Trinity Coll., Cambridge, Michaelhouse muns. 109). One of the same name pr. of Chicksands 1355.

The next recorded pr, **John Burton**, occ. 30 Aug. 1429 (Trinity Coll. Cambridge, King's Hall muns. no. 69).

CATLEY (Lincs), St Mary f. 1148 x 54

Lists in *VCH Lincs*, II, 197 (from 1245); *Heads*, I, 201–2.

B. Occ. 1197 x 9 (*Reg. Ant. Lincoln*, II, no. 637); *c.* 1200 (*Gilbertine Chts.*, p. 75).

John Occ. 10 May 1229 (*Lincs F.*, I, 221).

[1] The *VCH* ref. to Henry de Gretford as pr. in 1341 (citing *CPR 1340–43*, p.84) is an error.

Henry Occ. 26 July 1231 (ibid., 233).

Thomas Occ. 17 Apr. 1244 (ibid., 345); 1245, 29 May 1250, 12 June 1250 (*Lincs F.*, II, 16, 59, 64); 1245 (*Lincs N. & Q.*,VI (1900–1), p. 239); 1250 x 61 (*Chicksands Chts.*, p. 116, no. 4).

William Occ. 18 Nov. 1271 (*Lincs F.*, II, 259).

John Occ. 1377 (*Clerical Poll-Taxes*, p. 57, no. 775).

PRIORESSES

Joan Occ. 1377 (*Clerical Poll-Taxes*, p. 58, no. 775).

No further prs known until 1538.

CHICKSANDS (Beds), St Mary f. *c.* 1150 (*KH*); 1147 x 1153 (Thompson)

Lists in *VCH Beds*, I, 393; *Heads*, I, 202; Thompson, *Women Religious*, p. 237 (to 1262).

Walter Last recorded occ. 18 Nov. 1211 (*Beds F.*, I, no. 173).

Simon Occ. 29 Oct. 1223 (ibid., no. 67); 5 Sept. 1224 (*CPR 1216–25*, p. 468); 1227 (*Beds Eyre*, no. 151).

Thomas Occ. 30 Sept. 1232 (*Beds F.*, I, no. 349); 1 July 1239 (*Cambs F.*, p. 21; PRO, Cambs F., CP25/1/24/18, no. 16); 18 Nov. 1240 (*Beds F.*, I, no. 436); 1240 (*Ctl. Wardon*, p. 187, no. 240).

Hugh of Leadenham (Ledenham) Occ. 25 June 1244, 13 Oct. 1247 (*Beds F.*, I, nos. 467, 490); 26 Nov. 1245 (*Bucks F.*, I, 86); (H.) June 1247 x June 1248 (*Reg. Grosseteste*, p. 331).

Richard le Blunt de Haulee Occ. 21 Feb. 1262 (*Reg. R. Gravesend*, p. 9).

Alan Occ. 29 May 1272 (*Cambs F.*, p. 46; PRO Cambs F., CP25/1/25/35, no. 45); 9 and 13 Apr. 1283 (*Reg. Sutton*, I, 41, 43).

Walter Occ. 23 July 1298 (ibid., 230–1).

William of Huggate (Hugate) Occ. 14 Feb. 1310 (*Ctl. Newnham*, no. 160).

John de Camelton Occ. July 1316 x July 1317 (*HMC Var. Coll.*, IV, p. 154); 10 June 1317 (Hants R.O. M69/C257, f. 44r); 1320 (*CCR 1318–23*, p. 233); 16 Mar., 8 Nov. 1324 (*CCR 1323–27*, pp. 164, 326).

Simon Occ. 12 June, 25 June 1325 (ibid., p.293); Trin. 1327–Mich. 1328 (*Index to Placita de Banco*, p. 3); 21 Dec. 1327, 4 June 1334 (Lincoln, Ep. Reg., IV, ff. 316r, 307v).

Roger Predecessor of John, mentioned Dec. 1355 (*Beds Sessions of the Peace*, p. 37, no. 12; Putnam, *Justices*, p. 45).

John of Letchworth (Lechworth) Occ. Dec. 1355 (*Beds Sessions of the Peace*, p. 37, no. 12; Putnam, *Justices*, p. 44).

The next recorded pr., **John Bretoun** (Bruton), occ. 18 July 1388 (*CCR 1385–89*, p. 510). Papal chaplain 5 Aug. 1388 (*CPL*, IV, 273).

PRIORESSES

The first recorded prs after 1201, **Joan Chawman**, occ. 21 June 1435 (*Reg. Langley*, IV, no. 1161).

CLATTERCOTE (Oxon), St Leonard f. 1148 x 66 (as hospital); 1251 x 1262 (priory) (*KH*); 1258 x 79 (priory) (Binns, p. 170).

List in *VCH Oxon*, II, 105

Robert Occ. as pr. 8 July 1232, 25 June 1236 (*Warws F.*, I, nos. 477, 511); 27 Mar. 1246 (*Reg. Ant. Lincoln*, III, no. 938).

Ingram (Engeramus) Occ. n.d. (mid-13th cent.; pal.) (PRO, E42/265). His precise place in the sequence of priors is uncertain.

N. Occ. 1251 x 1261 (*Chicksands Chts.*, p.116).

Walter Occ. 5 June 1262 (*Warws F.*, I, no. 804); 9 Apr. 1283 (*Reg. Sutton*, I, 41). Presumably the pr. Walter ment. as former pr. in 1317 (*Cal. Misc. Inq.*, II, 80).

Walter of Stotfold Occ. Easter 1287 (PRO, CP40/67, m. 67). ? the same as above.
Geoffrey Occ. 14 May 1287 (Bodl., Douce ms. 136, f. 94v).
Gerbald Occ. Mich. 1310 (PRO, CP40/183, attorneys mm. 4, 17d).
John Occ. 10 Nov. 1344 (BL, Add. Cht. 46914).
John Possibly the same, occ. 5 June 1388 (*CPR 1385–89*, p. 473).

ELLERTON ON SPALDING MOOR, St. Mary and St Laurence (St Mary – Binns, p. 170). f. 1199 x 1207.
   Lists in *VCH Yorks*, III, 252; *Heads*, I, 202.
Ranulf Occ. *c.* 1210 x 19 (*EYC*, II, no. 1263, see *Heads*, I, 202, n.3).
John Occ. from 9 Feb. 1219 to 30 June 1231 (*Yorks F., 1218–31*, pp. 21, 149); n.d. (*ante* 1225) (York, Reg. 12, ff. 105v, 110r); *temp.* Henry III (*Reg. Greenfield*, III, p. 119, n.1).
Yvo Occ. 22 July 1240 (*Yorks F.,1232–46*, pp. 80–1).
Geoffrey Occ. 6 May 1246 (*Yorks F.,1232–46*, p. 132); 25 Nov. 1247 (*Yorks F., 1246–72*, p. 5).
Henry Occ. 3 Feb. 1252 (*Yorks F., 1246–72*, p. 76); 1265 (Baildon, I, 53); n.d. (1262 x 1269) (Bodl., ms. Top. Yorks e. 8, f. 119r). To be identified with **Henry of Flixton**, immediate predecessor of Pr. Adam, mentd 1279 (PRO, Just.1/1055, m. 11).
Adam of Scarborough (Scardeburg(h)) Occ. 1279 (ibid.); 1282 (Baildon, I, 54); 9 Apr. 1283 (*Reg. Sutton*, I, 41).
Martin Occ. 14 May 1287 (Bodl., Douce ms. 136, f. 94v).
Robert Occ. 16 May 1294 (*Yorks F., 1272–1300*, p. 103).
Ralph Occ. Hilary 1305 (Baildon, I, 54); Epiphany 1307 (PRO, Just.1/1107, m. 31d).
Alan Occ. 1335, 1336 (*VCH* citing Baildon, ms. notes).
William of Howsham (Housom) Occ. 1348 (ibid.); 1353 (PRO, Just.1/1129, m. 2); 23 Oct. 1354 (*CCR 1354–60*, p. 91); 1371 (Baildon, I, 55).
Richard of Londesborough (Lounesburgh) Occ. 21 Dec. 1351 (York, Reg. 10, f. 212r).
William Hesill Occ. 8 Mar. 1372 (PRO, C81/1791/9)
The next recorded pr., **Giles**, occ. 7 Henry IV (Sept. 1402 x Sept. 1403) (PRO, 179/66/411).

FORDHAM (Cambs), St Peter and St Mary Magdalen f. -1227
   List in *VCH Cambs*, II, 258.
William Occ. 20 Oct. 1247, 27 Jan. 1258 (PRO, Cambs F., CP25/1/24/22, no. 5; CP25/1/25/29, no. 1).
Robert Occ. 20 May 1321 (*CCR 1318–23*, p.375); 19 Mar. 1325 (PRO, Just.1/98, m. 9).
William Occ. Jan. 1365 x Jan. 1366 (CUL, Add. ms. 3824, f. 153r).[2]

HAVERHOLME (Lincs), St Mary f. 1137 (Cist.); 1139 (Gilbertine)
   Lists in *VCH Lincs.*, II, 188; *Heads*, I, 202; Thompson, *Women Religious*, p. 242 (to 1272).
Vivian Occ. 7 Dec. 1213 (*Lincs F. 1199–1216*, p. 170, no. 330).
R. Occ. 1205 x 29 (*Reg. Ant. Lincoln*, III, no. 1093).
Simon Occ. 15 Sept. 1226 (*Lincs. F.*, I, 214); 27 Oct. 1226 (PRO, Notts F., CP25/ 1/182/4, no. 97); Trin. term 1229, Hil. term 1230 (*CRR*, XIII, nos. 2233, 2577); 2 Oct. 1234, 25 Oct. 1234 (*Lincs F.*, I, 260, 256).
Ralph Occ. 25 June 1236 (PRO, Leics F., CP25/1/121/15, no. 207); 13 Oct. 1236 (PRO, Notts F., CP25/1/182/7, no. 233).

---

[2] CUL., Add. ms. 3824 comprises transcripts ascribed to Thomas Tanner from the Public Records. Pr. William's occ. on f. 153r claims to be from the Close rolls for 39 Edward III. The published *CCR* for 39 Edward III yields no pr. William of Fordham.

Hugh Mentioned Easter Term 1242 as former pr., no clue as to place in sequence of priors (*CRR*, XVI, no. 2235).

Odo (Eudo) Occ. 1 Dec. 1241 (*Lincs F.*, I, 341); 6 May 1246 (*Yorks F., 1232–46*, p. 128; *Ctl. Kirkstall*, p. 222, no. 322); 1 May 1250 (*Yorks. F., 1246–72*, p. 14); 9 June 1252, 27 Jan. 1255; 13 June 1255, 3 Feb. 1257, 7 Apr. 1258 (*Lincs F.*, II, 93, 111, 112, 128, 165).

Martin Occ. (M.) 7 Apr. 1267 (*Reg. Ant. Lincoln*, II, no. 462); June 1267 (ibid., II, nos. 461, 463; VII, no. 2182); (M.) 9 Aug. 1268, 19 Oct. 1268 (*Reg. W. Giffard*, pp. 85, 87).

Alan Occ. 13 Oct. 1271, 1 Mar. 1272 (*Lincs F.*, II, 240, 264). Referred to as former pr. Easter 1275 (PRO, CP40/9, m. 17d).

Roger Occ. Easter 1275 (ibid.). 1281 ment. as former pr. (*Yorks F., 1272–1300*, p. 36).

Simon of Pickworth (Pykworthe) For name see *YB 19 Edward III*, p. 359. Occ. 16 Feb. 1281 (ibid.; *Ctl. Kirkstall*, p. 232., no. 330); 22 July 1281 (PRO, Lincs F., CP25/1/132/53, no. 30); 14 May 1287 (Bodl., Douce ms. 136, f. 94v).

Henry mentd 1345 as pr. *temp.* Edward I (*YB 19 Edward III*, p. 351). His position in the sequence of priors is unclear).

William de Walden Occ. 24 Nov. 1329 (*Reg. Burghersh*, I, no. 242); 7 Dec. 1330 (*CPR 1330–34*, p. 60).

Thomas Occ. 25 Apr. 1332 (*CPR 1343–45*, p. 248); 20 June 1334 (*CPR 1330–34*, p. 580).

William Occ. 22 Oct. 1334 (*CPR 1334–38*, pp. 67–8); 26 Oct. 1334 (*CPR 1343–45*, p. 249); Mich. 1345 (*YB 19 Edward III*, p. 351).

John of Malton Occ. 28 May 1348 (*CPR 1348–50*, p. 106).

Thomas of Welbourn (Welburne) Occ. 1381 (*Clerical Poll-Taxes*, pp. 109, 155, nos. 1321, 1910).

PRIORESSES

No prs recorded after **Alice**, occ. 26 Sept. 1201 (Foreville and Keir, *Book of St Gilbert*, pp. 280–3), until 1538.

HITCHIN (Herts), St Saviour f. 1361 x 1362
No list in *VCH Herts*, IV, 443.
No priors recorded for this period.

HOLLAND BRIDGE, *see* BRIDGE END

LINCOLN, St Katharine f. 1148+
Lists in *VCH Lincs*, II, 190–1; *Heads*, I, 203.

William Occ. *temp.* John (pal.; *HMC Rutland*, IV, 70); 1216 (BL, Add. Cht. 20512); 25 Nov. 1218 (*Lincs. F.*, I, 133, 144). Seal (*BM Seals*, no. 3476).

Vivian Occ. 25 Nov. 1225 (*Lincs F.*, I, 180). Cf. Haverholme, North Ormsby, York, St Andrew.

Hugh Occ. (H.) Dec. 1228 x Dec. 1229 (*Reg. Wells*, III, 168); 5 May 1229 (*CPR 1225–32*, p. 289); 8 May 1232 (*Lincs F.*, I, 248).

Roger Occ. 21 June 1236 (ibid., I, 293); 4 Oct. 1240 (PRO, Notts F. CP25/1/182/8, no. 280); (R.) 2 Apr. 1241 (*Reg. Gray*, p. 90 – could possibly be Ralph below).

Ralph Occ. 18 June 1245 (*Lincs F.*, II, 28; *Lincs N. and Q.*, VII, p. 41, no. 88); 27 Oct 1252 (*Lincs F.*, II, 98).

Henry Occ. from 22 Sept. 1256 to 28 May 1263 (ibid., 117, 207); 3 Nov. 1260 (PRO, Notts F. CP25/1/183/12, no. 475); 20 Jan. 1263 (*Lincs F.*, II, 217); 24 May 1263 (BL, Cotton ms. Faustina B I, f. 169v).

John of Malton Occ. n.d. (*temp.* Patrick, master of Sempringham 1262 x 1276) (LAO, D. & C., Dij/81/2/15); (J.) 10 May 1268 (*CPR 1266–72*, p. 227).

William Occ. 26 Apr. 1282 (PRO, Lincs F., CP25/1/133/54, no. 40); 9 Apr. 1283 (*Reg. Sutton*, I, 41); n.d. (BL, Harl. Cht. 44 A 36).

Gilbert Occ. 14 May 1287 (Bodl., Douce ms. 136, f. 94v); 25 Jan. 1292 (BL, Harl Ch. 44 I 18); (G.) 1293 (DCD, misc. cht. 4331); 1297 (*Coram Rege Roll*, p. 135); 1298 (*Reg. Sutton*, I, 230–1); recommendation from Archbp Henry Newark of York to the priors of O. Semp. to el. the unnamed pr. of St Katharine's as their master n.d. [1298] (*Reg. Newark*, II, pp. 295–6, no. 294); 1303 (PRO, Lincs F. CP25/1/134/69, no. 36); 1306 (ibid., 135/73, no. 63); 21 July 1314 (Lincoln, Ep. Reg., II, f. 51r); 27 Mar. 1315 (Lincoln, Ep. Reg., III, f. 317r); (G.) 13 Oct. 1319 (WAM no. 29410); 15 May 1326 (York, Reg. 9B, f. 445v).

William de Shireburn Occ. 6 May 1333, 26 Feb. 1334 (*CCR 1333–37*, pp. 109, 297); 6 May 1333, 20 Nov. 1333 (York, Reg. 9A, ff. 59v, 62r); 30 Sept. 1334 (*Reg. Burghersh*, I, no. 429); 8 Mar. 1335 (Lincoln, Ep. Reg., V, f. 493r).

Robert of Navenby Occ. 24 July 1336 (Lincoln, Ep. Reg., IV, f. 65r); 23 May 1339 (Lincoln, Ep. Reg., VI, f. 126r; *CPR 1340–43*, p. 50). El. Master of Sempringham 1340 (Lincoln, Ep. Reg., IV, ff. 92r–93r).

William Occ. 6 Oct. 1340 (*CCR 1339–41*, p. 633); 20 Sept. 1343, 12 June 1344, 6 July 1344 (*CPR 1343–45*, pp. 169, 298, 389); 23 Apr. 1344 (Lincoln, Ep. Reg., V, f. 137v); 1344 (*AASRP*, XXVII, 297).

Roger de Houton Occ. 25 July 1348 (*CPR 1317–21*, p. 357, later entry added to 1319 doc.).

Roger de Bankesfeld (Bankfeld) Occ. 1351 (*Lincoln Sessions 1351–54*, pp. 14, 26).

John (de) Whatton (Watton) Occ. 30 Apr. 1376 (PRO, C241/158/33); 1377 (*Clerical Poll-Taxes*, p. 38, no. 531); 1381 (ibid., p. 111, no. 1346).

The next recorded pr., **Hamo of Sutton**, occ. 18 July 1388 (*CCR 1385–89*, p. 510); 23 Feb. 1393 (PRO, C241/181/35).

MALTON (Yorks N.), St Mary f. 1150

Lists in *VCH Yorks*, III, 253–4; *Heads*, I, 203.

Adam Occ. 26 May 1214 (*Yorks F., John*, p. 174); 7 Dec. 1218 (*Yorks F., 1218–31*, p. 10); 25 June 1219 (*Lincs F.*, I, 133).

William of Ancaster –1256 Occ. 20 Dec. 1224, 1 July 1225 (BL, Cotton ms. Nero D III, f. 51r–v); 1226 (BL, Cotton ms. Claudius D XI, f. 120r); from 10 Dec. 1234 to 22 July 1240 (*Yorks F., 1232–46*, pp. 28, 77); 18 May 1246 (ibid., p. 177; *Lincs F.*, II, 280; PRO, F. Divers Cos CP25/1/283/12, no. 207); 27 Jan. 1249 (*Yorks F., 1246–72*, p. 9). D. 1256 (BL, Cotton ms. Claudius D XI, f. 3v).

John de Homerton –1276 Occ. n.d. (1251 × 1261) (*Chicksands Chts.*, p. 116 no. 4); (J.) 10 June 1257 (BL, Cotton ms. Claudius D XI, f. 67v); 13 Oct. 1259 (PRO, Herts F., CP25/1/85/28, no. 514); n.d. (1258 × 1262) (*Lincoln Reg. Ant.*, II, no. 449); Mich. 1265 – Hil. 1266 (Baildon, I, 53); 10 June 1268 (*Yorks F., 1246–72*, p. 146); 23 Feb. 1272 (PRO, Leics F., CP25/1/122/30, no. 583). El. master of Sempringham 1276 (*Reg. R. Gravesend*, p. 69).

Roger Occ. 15 Apr. 1265 (*CR 1264–68*, p. 111). ? error, see above, or else two priors named John.

Robert Occ. July 1278 (BL, Cotton ms. Claudius D XI, f. 247v); 1279 (PRO, Just.1/1056, m. 45d); 25 Apr. 1280 (*Yorks F., 1272–1300*, p. 31); 1282, 1284 (Baildon, I, 120); 9 Apr. 1283 (*Reg. Sutton*, I, 41). Mentioned 1288 as former pr. (Baildon, I, 121).

Geoffrey Occ. 14 May 1287 (Bodl., Douce ms. 136, f. 94v); Easter 1288 (Baildon, I, 121).

Ranulf of Richmond (Rich', Richemunde) Occ. n.d. (BL, Cotton ms. Claudius D XI, f. 117r); as former pr. 30 June 1289; res. to become Cistercian at Fountains mand. to receive surety for his delivery; he was in prison at York (*Reg. Romeyn*, II, 62–3); mand. to examine his vow since he wished to enter a stricter order (ibid., 63).

William Baudewyn *alias* **of Scarborough** (Baldewyn, Scarburg') Occ. 1290, 4 Feb. 1293, 3

Feb. 1297 (BL, Cotton ms. Claudius D XI, ff. 141v, 117r, 51r); 20 Apr. 1292 (PRO, C241/25/137, C241/36/307); 1294 (*Yorks F., 1272–1300*, p. 109); 1295 (BL, Harl. ms. 3897, ff. 8r, 12r, 13r); 16 June 1295 (*CPR 1334–38*, p. 177); Easter 1298 (PRO, CP40/123, m. 177d); Hil. – Mich. 1300 (Baildon, I, 122); 1305 (*Yorks F., 1300–1314*, p. 54); Epiphany 1306 (PRO, Just.1/1107, m. 27d); 1 July 1308 (*Yorks F., 1300–1314*, p. 66).

Thomas of Pocklington (Pokelyngton) Occ. 13 Apr. 1323 (BL, Cotton ms. Claudius D XI, ff. 142v–143r).

William Occ. 13 Sept. 1331 (*Reg. Burghersh*, I, no. 310).

Robert of Newton (Neuton) Occ. 31 May 1333 (*CCR 1333–37*, p. 112).

William Occ. 17 Dec. 1333, 1 June 1334, 14, 28 Aug. 1335, 14 Dec. 1336 (ibid., pp. 186, 314, 518, 526, 728); 1336 (BL, Cotton ms. Claudius D XI, f. 129r).

John of Winterton (Wyntrington, Wyntryngton) Occ. 1337, 28 Sept. 1340 (ibid., ff. 136r, 142r). Mentioned 3 Nov. 1342 and Mich. 1343 as former pr. (ibid., f. 142r; Baildon, I, 123).

John of Wintringham (Wyntringham) Occ. Occ. 26 Sept. 1343, 22 July 1344 (Lincoln, Ep. Reg. VI, ff. 129v, 138v); Mich. 1343 – Hil. 1344 (Baildon, I, 123); 10 Apr. 1350 (*Test. Ebor.*, I, 63).

Robert of Scagglethorpe (Skakelthorp) Occ. [Jan. x Nov.] 1360 (*temp.* Thomas of Woodstock as *custos* of England), 24 Feb. 1365 (BL, Cotton ms. Claudius D XI, ff. 294r, 154v). Despite the chronological discrepancy is prob. the pr. Robert Skakilthorp mentd in 1439 as having been pr. *temp.* Henry III, rather than the pr. Robert *temp.* Edward I above (Baildon, I, 125).

William de Beneth[am] (?Bentham) Occ. Mich. 1368, Easter 1370, Mich. 1372 (ibid., 124).

William Occ. 5 July 1377 (*CPR 1377–81*, p. 37), presumably William of Beverley, below.

William of Beverley (Beverlaco) –1391 Occ. 1377 (PRO, E179/63/10); 18 July 1388 (*CCR 1385–89*, p. 510). El. master of Sempringham 1391 (Lincoln, Ep. Reg., XI, f. 55r).

MARLBOROUGH (Wilts), St Margaret f. –1199

List in *VCH Wilts*, III, 318

Alexander Occ. 1249 (*Wilts F.*, I, 37); (A.) 1252 (*DKR 9*, p. 357); (A.) 1253 (BL, Campbell Cht. XXII. 11).

Richard Occ. 1260 (*Wilts F.*, I, 53).

Robert Occ. 13 Oct. 1281 (*Wilts F.*, II, 15–16).

[**Nicholas de Insula** Occ. 1331 (T. Phillipps, ex Reg. Epis. Sar., but this has not been found in Bp Wyvill's register).]

Thomas Occ. 24 July 1337 (*CPR 1334–38*, p. 510).

Walter Occ. Mich. 1351 (PRO, KB27/365, m. 41).

The next recorded pr, **Walter**, occ. 6 Nov. 1389 (Wilts RO, Brudenell-Bruce (Ailesbury) mss., no. 30); 26 Feb. 1403 (*Cal. Misc. Inq.*, VII, no. 244). It is uncertain whether he is the same as the 1351 pr.

MARMONT (Cambs), St Mary f. – c. 1203

Nicholas Occ. n.d. (BL, Add. ms. 46353, f. 83v – ctl. compiled 1315).

MATTERSEY (Notts), St Helen f. c. 1185

List in *VCH Notts*, II, 141.

Herbert Occ. 7 June 1232 (PRO, Notts F., CP25/1/182/5, no. 124); 29 Aug. 1233 (PRO, Notts F., 182/6, no. 176); 27 Apr. 1236 (*Lancs F.*, I, p. 75, no. 64).

Henry Ment. in case of 1303 as having been a predecessor of pr. Adam (see below), *temp.* Henry III. He was said to have pres. Walter de Donyngton to the church of Gamston (*Reg. Greenfield*, IV, p. 59, n.2); this dates the event to 1235 when Walter was inst. (*Reg. Gray*, p. 69).

Walter Occ. Nov. 1246 x Nov. 1247 (ibid., p. 257).

Robert Occ. 25 Nov. 1257 (PRO, Notts F., CP25/1/183/1, no. 438).

Adam Occ. (A.) 27 Jan. 1267 (*Reg. W. Giffard*, p. 93). To be identified with pr. Adam referred to in a case of 1303 as having been pr. *temp.* Henry III (*Reg. Greenfield*, IV, p. 59, n.2) and having pres. Roger of Doncaster to the rectory of Gamston – the latter was adm. 27 Jan. 1267 (*Reg. W. Giffard*, p. 62). Poss. Adam of Newmarket (de Novo Mercato), pr. of Mattersey, occ. Mar. 1265 among named executors of will (*CR 1264–68*, p. 104). It is just possible, however, that two people are being referred to, rather than the pr. actually being named.

Reginald Occ. 14 May 1287 (Bodl., Douce ms. 136, f. 94v).

John Occ. 26 Jan. 1303 (*CPR 1303–7*, p. 108).

Richard Occ. 13 Dec. 1349 (York, Reg. 10, f. 140v).

The next recorded pr., **Robert Beele**, occ. n.d. [between entries of Mar. 1394] (*CPL*, IV, 487).

NEWSTEAD-ON-ANCHOLME (Lincs), Holy Trinity f. -1173

Lists in *VCH Lincs*, II, 198 (16th cent.); *Heads*, I, 203–4.

Henry Occ. as 'pr. of Holy Trinity of the Order of Sempringham' 12th-13th cents. (BL, Add. ms. 6118, f. 420r).

Osbert Occ. 1215 (Soc. of Ant. ms. 38, f. 126r).

William Occ. 7 Jan. 1219 (*Lincs F.*, I, 131–2).

Alan Occ. 13 Oct. 1226 (ibid., I, 195); (A.). Dec. 1227 x Dec. 1228 (*Reg. Wells*, III, 160).

Simon Occ. n.d. (*c.* 1240 x 1245) (*Reg. Ant. Lincoln*, IV, no. 1267); *c.* 1265 (ibid., II, no. 455); 28 Oct. 1279 (*CPR 1272–81*, p. 348).

William Occ. 14 May 1287 (Bodl., Douce ms. 136, f. 94v).

Walter Occ. Nov. 1296 x Nov. 1297 (PRO, E210/8470).

Richard Occ. Mich. 1305 (PRO, CP40/153, mm. 259, 458).

John de Wylton Occ. 1377 (*Clerical Poll-Taxes*, p. 45, no. 634).

Robert of Staunton Occ. 1381 (ibid., p. 135, no. 1699, cf. p. 145, no. 1833).

NORTH ORMSBY (Nun Ormsby) (Lincs), St Mary f. 1148 x 54

Lists in *VCH Lincs*, II, 196; *Heads*, I, 204; Thompson, *Women Religious*, pp. 247–8 (to 1263).

Robert Latest record occ. May 1212 x May 1213 (*Lincs F.*, II, 316).

Thomas Occ. 24 Feb. 1219 but 2 Henry III [i.e. *recte* 1218] (Bodl., Dodsworth ms. 135, f. 142r).

Vivian Occ. 13 Oct. 1222 (*Lincs F.*, I, 163). ?Transferred to Lincoln, St Katharine before 1225 (ibid., 180).

William Occ. 13 Oct. 1224, 22 Feb. 1226 (ibid., 170, 177); Dec. 1225 x Dec. 1226 (*Reg. Wells*, III, 143).

Robert Occ. 20 Apr. 1231, 16 Oct. 1234 (*Lincs F.*, I, 226, 282).

Adam Occ. 22 Feb. 1240 (ibid., 311).

Thomas Occ. Oct. 1245 x Oct. 1246 (Bodl., Dodsworth ms. 135, f. 157v); 27 Jan. 1246, 10 Apr. 1250 (*Lincs F.*, II, 34, 75).

Robert Occ. from 30 May 1255 to 22 Sept. 1263 (ibid., 111, 203); Oct. 1262 x Oct. 1263 (Bodl., Dodsworth ms. 135, f. 158r).

Richard Occ. Jan. 1273 (PRO, E40/13,412); 25 Nov. 1281 (PRO, Lincs F., CP25/1/135/55, no. 96).

Peter Occ. 14 May 1287 (Bodl., Douce ms. 136, f. 94v).

William Occ. Trin. 1309 (PRO, CP40/178, m. 67), ? the same as below.

William Occ. Mich. 1320 (PRO, KB27/242, m. 24d; attorneys m. 5d).

Simon of Humbleton (Humbilton, Humbulton) Occ. 1377, 1381 (*Clerical Poll-Taxes*, p. 57, no. 773 and p. 154, no. 1903).

POULTON (Glos. formerly Wilts), St Mary f. 1348 x 1350
List in *VCH Wilts*, III, 319.
The earliest known pr., **John**, occ. 17 Feb. 1397 (Salisbury, Reg. Mitford, f. 117v).

RAVENSTONEDALE (Westd)

It is uncertain if Ravenstonedale, given to the order in the mid-12th cent., ever enjoyed status as an independent priory (Golding, *Gilbert of Sempringham and the Gilbertine Order*, p. 250). By 1200 it was a grange of Watton priory under a master. No names of masters have been found. See C.R. Irwin and M. Irwin, *The Gilbertines and Ravenstonedale* (Kirkby Stephen, 1990).

SEMPRINGHAM (Lincs), St Mary f. 1131

Lists in *VCH Lincs*, II, 186–7; basis to 1364 in *Ch. Sempringham* (PRO 31/9/16, pp. 2–4, transcript from Rome, Vatican, Barberini ms. xliii, 74 (2689), flyleaf); *Heads*, I, 204–5.

MASTERS OF THE ORDER OF SEMPRINGHAM

Gilbert II 1205–1225 4th master, succ. 1205, ruled 20 years (*Ch.*, p. 2). Occ. -1207 (BL, Cotton ms. Claudius D. XI, f. 227r); 27 Apr. 1208 (*Lincs F. 1199–1216*, no. 236); 1209 x 1223 (*Reg. Ant. Lincoln*, II, no. 638). D. 26 June 1225 (*Ch.*, p. 2).

Robert (of Stainby) 1225–1251 5th master, succ. 1225, ruled 25 years (ibid.). Occ. 10 May 1226 (*CPR 1225–32*, p. 31); 1227 (*EYC*, XII, no. 43); (R.) June 1235 x June 1236, June 1236 x June 1237, June 1238 x June 1239 (*Reg. Grosseteste*, pp. 134, 9, 34); *c.* summer 1237 (*Reg. Gray*, p. 77); 14 Apr. 1242 (Bodl., Norfolk Roll 83). Robert, pr. of Sempringham occ. 8 Feb. 1245 (*CPL*, I, 213), but since Thomas occ. as pr. at this time (see below) it is possible that Robert should have been desc. as master. BL, Harl. Cht. 44 I 23 ref. to him as former master and suggests that his name was Stainby (de Stighandby). He occ. as Sthyandby (Southwell Minster ms. 1, p. 421). D. 4 May 1251 (*Ch.*, p. 2). ? Seal (*BM Seals*, no. 3998).

William 1251–1262 6th master, succ. 1251, ruled 10 years (*Ch.*, p. 2). Occ. (W.) 18 Oct. 1252 (*Magnum Reg. Album Lichfield*, p. 314). D. 22 Jan. 1262 (*Ch.*, p. 2). Seal (*BM Seals*, no. 3993).

Patrick (of Middleton) 1262–1276 7th master, pr. of Watton, el. 2 Feb. 1262 and ruled 15 years and 12 weeks (*Ch.*, p. 2). Pres. to bp for bl. 7 Feb. 1262; eln conf. and prof. obed. 19 Feb. 1262; bl. by bp of Connor 21 Feb. 1262 (*Reg. R. Gravesend*, pp. 7–9). D. 27 Apr. 1276 (*Ch.*, pp. 2–3; cf. *Reg. R. Gravesend*, p. 69). BL, Harl. Cht. 44 I 23 ref. to him as former master and gives his name as Midelton. Seal (*BM Seals*, no. 3995).

John (II) of Hamerton 1276–1283 8th master, pr. of Malton, el. 8 May 1276 and ruled 5 (*sic*) years, 45 weeks and 3 days (*Ch.*, pp. 2–3); bl. 13 May 1276 (*Reg. R. Gravesend*, pp. 69, 283). D. 23 Mar. 1283 (*Ch.*, p. 3; cf. *Reg. Sutton*, I, 40).

Roger (II) of Bolingbroke (Bolingbrocke, Bolingbrok, Bulingbrok) **1283–1298** 9th master, pr. of Sempringham, el. 9 Apr. 1283 and ruled 15 years, 12 weeks and 4 days (*Ch.*, p. 3); letter of pres. by general chapter 9 Apr. 1283; eln conf. 13 Apr. 1283 (*Reg. Sutton*, I, 40–3). D. 4 July 1298 (*Ch.*, p. 3).

Philip of Barton 1298–1332 10th master, *inceptor theologie*, el. 23 July 1298 and ruled 34 years less a day (ibid.). Pr. of Cambridge, St Edmund, eln pres. to bp by general chapter 23 July 1298; eln conf. 31 July 1298 (*Reg. Sutton*, I, 230–4). D. 22 July 1332 (*Ch.*, p. 3). Seal (*BM Seals*, no. 3999).[3]

John of Glinton (Glynton(e)) **1332–1341** 11th master, *sac. pag. prof.*, pr. of Sempringham, el. 8 Aug. 1332 and ruled 8 years and 47 weeks (*Ch.*, p. 3); eln pres. to bp by general chapter 7

---

[3] At the 1298 vacancy Archbp Newark of York recommended the priors of the order to el [Gilbert], pr. of St Katharine, Lincoln, as master (*Reg. Newark*, II, pp. 295–6, no. 294).

(*sic*) Aug. 1332; eln conf. 14 July [*recte* Aug.] 1332 (*Reg. Burghersh*, I, no. 347). Cess. by 18 May 1341 (ibid., no. 683). Cess. office at the general chapter of Sempringham at the rogation days 1341, ?14–16 May, if stated tenure of office is correct (*Ch.*, p. 3). His cess. was without papal leave (cf. *CPP*, p. 188).

Robert of Navenby (Naveniby) **1341–1364** Pr. of Lincoln, St Katharine, el. 17 May 1341 and ruled 24 years, 13 weeks and 6 days (*Ch.*, p. 3); eln pres. to bp by general chapter 18 May 1341; eln conf. 26 May 1341 (*Reg. Burghersh*, I, no. 683). Inquiry instituted by pope 8 Dec. 1349 on ground that Robert has been apptd by certain people in derogation of the papal right (*CPP*, p. 188). D. 22 Aug. 1364 (*Ch.*, pp. 3–4).

William of Prestwold 1364–1391 Can. and pr. of Sempringham, el. 6 Sept. 1364 and ruled 25 years, 11 months and 3 weeks (ibid.). Occ. 17 Nov. 1366 (PRO, C81/1791/2); 12 Dec. 1366 (*CPR 1364–67*, p. 369); 1379 (BL, Add. Cht. 20620); 1380 (PRO, C81/1791/3); 1383 (PRO, C81/1791/4);1389 (PRO, C81/1791/5); 1390 (PRO, C81/1791/6). D. 3 Aug. 1391 (*Ch.*, pp. 3–4; cf. Lincoln, Ep. Reg., XI, f. 55r–v).

PRIORS OF SEMPRINGHAM

Adam Occ. 27 Apr. 1208 (*Lincs F. 1199–1216*, no. 236).

Richard Occ. 16 Feb. 1219 (*Lincs F.*, I, 141). Possibly the Richard of Beverley who occ. late12th – early 13th cents (*Sempringham Chts.*, pp. 34–5) and mentd without date in an inspeximus of 2 May 1363 (*CPR 1361–64*, p. 340).

Reginald Occ. 13 May 1222 (*Lincs F.*, I, 163).

Alan Occ. 29 Oct. 1223 (ibid.,167).

Thomas Occ. from 15 Sept. 1226 to 5 May 1240 (ibid., 192, 313); 18 Nov. 1226, 3 Aug. 1231 (*Yorks F., 1218–31*, pp. 78, 165); Mich. term 1228, Easter term 1229, Hil. term 1230 (*CRR*, XIII, nos. 913, 1944, 2576); Dec. 1230 x Dec. 1231 (*Reg. Wells*, III, 186–7); 14 Apr. 1242 (Bodl., Norfolk Roll 83); 20 Jan. 1245, 30 Apr. 1245, 26 May 1245 (*Lincs F.*, II, 3, 11, 24).

Robert Occ. from 3 May 1250 to 17 June 1263 (ibid., 61, 223).

Roger of Bolingbroke –**1283** Occ. 2 May 1271, 16 Feb. 1272 (ibid., 232, 275); 25 Nov. 1281 (PRO, Lincs F., CP25/1/133/55, no. 103); 9 Dec. 1281 (ibid., no. 88). El. master of Sempringham 1283 (*Reg. Sutton*, I, 40–3).

William Occ. 7 May 1284 (PRO, Lincs F., CP25/1/133/58, no. 62); 19 June 1286 (PRO, Cambs F., CP25/1/24/42, no. 1); 1287 (Bodl., Douce ms. 136, f. 94v); 1288 (PRO, CP40/72, m. 24); 31 May 1293 (PRO, Lincs F., CP25/1/135/63, no. 28); 12 Nov. 1293 (PRO, Lincs F., CP25/1/133/63, no. 53).

John de Hamilton Name in *Le Livere de Rois de Brittanie*, pp. 327, 329. Occ. 15 June 1298 (PRO, Lincs F., CP25/1/134/65, no. 48); 23 July 1298 (*Reg. Sutton*, I, 230–1); 1301 (PRO, Lincs F., CP25/1/134/67, no. 27); 1303 (PRO, Lincs F., CP25/1/134/69, no. 26); 1304 (PRO, F. Divers Cos., CP25/1/285/26, no. 330); (J.) 7 Sept. 1312 (*CPR 1307–13*, p. 533); order for arrest stayed 17 Sept. 1317 (*CCR 1313–18*, p. 498); 20 Jan. 1321 (*CPR 1317–21*, p. 602); 18 Oct. 1324 (*CCR 1323–27*, p. 321).

John of Glinton (Glenton, Glynton) –**1332** Occ. 18 Oct. 1325 (ibid., p. 513); 18 July 1326, 21 July 1326 (ibid., pp. 634, 635); 4 Feb. 1327 (PRO, E328/141); 1328 (*Index to Placita de Banco*, p. 343); 2 Nov. 1329 (*CCR 1327–30*, p. 580); 1330, 1331 (*Reg. Burghersh*, I, nos. 265, 302); 19 July 1331 (*CCR 330–33*, p. 328). El. master of Sempringham 1332 (q.v.).

William (of) Prestwold (Prestwell) Occ. 22 Mar. 1336 (*CCR 1333–37*, p. 654); Mich. 1337 (PRO, CP40/213, m. 21); 18 May 1341, 26 May 1341 (*Reg. Burghersh*, I, no. 683); 1343 (*CCR 1343–46*, pp. 243, 246); 25 June 1356, 17 Dec. 1358 (Lincoln, Ep. Reg., VIII, ff. 65r, 109v); 30 Nov. 1363 (*CCR 1360–64*, p. 559). El. master of Sempringham 1364 (q.v.).

William Ouson 1364– El. pr. 1364 (ibid). Occ. 14 June 1366 (Lincoln, Ep. Reg., XII, f. 49r).

The next recorded pr., **Adam Clowe of Leverington** *alias* **of Leverington** (Leveryngton), occ. 1381 (*Clerical Poll-Taxes*, p. 111, no. 1344 and p. 156, no. 1933); manumission by bp of Ely of *nativus noster* Adam Clowe de Leverington, pr. of Sempringham 15 Apr. 1387 (Ely, G/1/2, f. 58v); 18 July 1388 (*CCR 1385–89*, p. 510).

PRIORESSES
Edusia de Peynton, Elizabeth de Ardene, Matilda de Wiluby occ. 14 June 1366 (Lincoln, Ep. Reg., XII, f. 48v).

SHOULDHAM (Norfolk), Holy Cross and St Mary f. +1193 (*KH*); *c.* 1197 x 1198 (Thompson)

Lists in *VCH Norfolk*, II, 414 (from 1250); *Heads*, I, 205; Thompson, *Women Religious*, p. 252 (to *c.* 1270).

Jocelin Last recorded occ. 6 Oct. 1204 (*Norfolk F. 1201–1215*, no. 55).

Thomas Occ. Oct. 1233 x Oct. 1234 (*Norfolk F., (Rye)*, p. 50).

William Occ. Oct. 1237 x Oct. 1238 (ibid., p. 59); 18 May 1251 (BL, Add. ms. 46353, f. 35r). 1251 x 1261 (*Chicksands Chts.*, p. 117).[4]

Benedict Occ. from Nov. 1275 x Nov. 1276 to Nov. 1285 x Nov. 1286 (*Norfolk F. (Rye)*, pp. 115, 136); 1278 (PRO, KB27/41, mm. 13d, 21d, 55); 7 July 1281, 13 July 1281 (*CPR 1272–81*, pp. 446, 473); 9 Apr. 1283 (*Reg. Sutton*, I, 41); Mich. 1290–Hil. 1291 (*State Trials*, p. 12).

Thomas Occ. 6 May 1292 (*CPR 1281–92*, p. 489).

Nicholas Occ. 17 Aug. 1294 (*CPR 1292–1301*, p. 115).

Thomas de Carmirton *alias* **Carmelton** –1305 Occ. Trin. 1297 (PRO, CP40/119, m. 71). Res. before 1305 (PRO, Just.1/1235, mm. 38d, 45).

Robert Occ. 4 Oct. 1325 (*CPR 1324–27*, p. 191).

John de Eton Occ. Easter 1354 (*King's Bench, Edward III*, VI, 98).

John Jan. 1365 x Jan. 1366 (PRO, LR14/99; LR14/557).[5]

Thomas of Shropham (Schropham) Occ. 1373 (PRO, C85/135/5).

The next recorded pr., **Nicholas Feryby**, occ. 9 Mar. 1417 (PRO, C85/137/1); 17 May 1417 (PRO, C202/C/103/1).

PRIORESSES
None recorded for this period.

SIXHILLS (Lincs), St Mary f. 1148 x 54

Lists in *VCH Lincs*, II, 195; *Heads*, I, 205; Thompson, *Religious Women*, p. 252 (priors to 1279).

R. Occ. 1206 x *c.*1209 (*Reg. Ant. Lincoln*, V, no. 1572).

T. Occ. early 13th cent. (BL, Harl. Cht. 45 C 31, cited Thompson, p. 252).

Simon Occ. 25 June 1220 (*Lincs F.*, I, 153).

Nicholas Occ. from 29 Oct. 1224 to 19 May 1240 (ibid., 173, 330); 1230 (*CPR 1225–32*, p. 349); 1235 (*Medieval Lindsey Marsh*, no. 36); (N.) June 1236 x June 1237 (*Reg. Grosseteste*, p. 6); 6 Jan. 1243 (BL, Harl. Cht. 44 A 9); 20 Mar. 1243 (*Medieval Lindsey Marsh*, no. 39).

Reginald Occ. 12 Nov. 1252, 30 Sept. 1256, 9 Dec. 1271 (*Lincs F.*, II, 100, 118, 270); n.d. (*temp.* Archbp Ludham 1258 x 1265) (BL, Lansdowne ms. 402, f. 130r). Pr. R. occ. n.d. (*temp.* Edward I) is prob. to be identified with Reginald (BL, Harl. Cht. 56 A 12).

---

[4] Blomefield, *Norfolk*, VII, 424 has pr. Richard occ. late Henry III, but no source.

[5] According to *VCH* the next recorded pr. was Richard de Syvington who occ. 1387, citing patent roll 10 Richard II, m. 23. That entry is now calendared in *CPR 1385–89*, p. 223 (entry of 15 Oct. 1386), but refers to the pr. and convent without naming the pr.

William Occ. 19 June 1278 (*Yorks F., 1272–1300*, p. 13); Mich. 1279 (*Cal. Misc. Inq.*, I, 442).

Simon Occ. 9 Apr. 1283 (*Reg. Sutton*, I, 41); 1284 (PRO, Lincs F., CP25/1/133/58 no. 56); 1287 (Bodl., Douce ms. 136, f. 94v); 1292 (*Cal. Misc. Inq.*, I, 442); 25 Nov. 1293 (PRO, Lincs F., CP25/1/134/64 no. 11).

John de Henton Occ. 1302 (PRO, E101/568/63 no. 7). Mentd 1 July 1462 as occ. *c.* 31 Edward I (Nov. 1302 x Nov. 1303) (*CPR 1461–7*, p. 196). Seal (*Mon. Seals*, p. 82).

Alan Occ. 29 Feb. 1332 (*Reg. Burghersh*, I, no. 328).

William Occ. 26 Nov. 1343 (*CPR 1343–45*, p. 150).

Alexander of Beesby (Beseby) Occ. 1377 (*Clerical Poll-Taxes*, p. 57, no. 774).

Thomas Occ. 10 Sept. 1382 (*Lincs Sessions of the Peace 1381–96*, II, p. 74, no. 218).

PRIORESSES
None known before 1538.

WATTON (Yorks E.), St Mary f. 1150
Lists in *VCH Yorks*, III, 255; *Heads*, I, 205.

Peter Last recorded occ. 11 Nov. 1208 (*Yorks F. John*, p. 144).

Richard Occ. 27 Jan. 1219, 20 Apr. 1225 (*Yorks F., 1218–31*, pp. 15,59); 27 Jan., 19 Oct. 1224 (PRO, Westmd F., CP25/1/249/3, nos. 2–3). Prob. the **Richard de Morewych** mentd as former pr. in 1279, *temp.* the father of the party in the 1279 case (PRO, Just.1/1055, m. 60).

William Occ. (W.) 1 Apr. 1226 (BL, Cotton ms. Nero. D. III, f. 53v); 1228 (Baildon, I, 215); 6 May 1229 (*Yorks F. 1218–31*, p. 121).

Reginald Mentd in 1278 as former pr. disseised of some property by Adam de Novo Mercato 'after the first crossing over of King Henry [III] into Gascony', i.e. 1230 (Baildon, I, 216; F.M. Powicke, *The Thirteenth Century* (2nd edn, Oxford, 1962), pp. 94–5).

Roger Occ. 29 July 1240 (*Yorks F., 1232–46*, p. 85).; 8 Nov. 1241 (PRO, Westmd F., CP25/1/249/4, no. 2); n.d. (*temp.* Robert, master O. Semp. 1225 x 1252 (*Yorks Deeds*, VI, no. 325).

Patrick of Dalton –1262 Occ. n.d. (1251 x 1261) (*Chicksands Chts.*, p. 116); 20 Jan. 1252, 13 Oct. 1260 (*Yorks F.,1246–72*, pp. 64, 119). El. Master of Sempringham 1262 (*Reg. R. Gravesend*, p. 7). Mentd in 1279 as former pr. Patrick of Dalton (PRO, Just.1/1055, m. 75).

Roger of Cave Occ. 1265 (Baildon, I, 53); 14 Jan. 1272 (*Yorks F.,1246–72*, p. 180). Mentd 1279 as former pr., immediate predecessor of Patrick (PRO, Just.1/1055, m. 75, cf. m. 52d; Baildon, II, 48).

Patrick of Middleton (Middelton, Midelton) Occ. 8 May 1277 (*CCR 1272–79*, p. 385); Mich. 1278 (PRO, KB27/41, m. 17d); 1279 (PRO, Just.1/1055, mm. 52d, 60, 75; Just.1/1056, m. 49d); 9 Feb. 1280 (*Yorks F., 1272–1300*, p. 39); 20 June 1285 (*CPR 1317–21*, p. 263); 1285,1286 (Baildon, I, 217).

John de Heton (Hoton) –1304 Occ. 1300 (Baildon, I, 218); 7 Feb. 1301 (*Cal. Inq. PM*, VI, 264); Hil. 1304 (Baildon, II, 49). Res. 1304 (Baildon, I, 215).

John Occ. 2 Dec. 1311 (*CPR 1307–13*, p. 425).

Richard of Watton Occ. 25 May 1316 (*CPR 1313–17*, p. 467); 7 Sept. 1316 (PRO, C81/1791/11); Easter 1327 – Mich. 1328 (*Index to Placita de Banco*, II, 775); 10 Apr. 1350 (*Test. Ebor.*, I, 63); 8 Nov. 1351 (*CPR 1350–54*, p. 164).

John Occ. 9 June 1333 (*CCR 1333–37*, p. 116).

Richard Sparowe Predecessor of John of Etton, mentioned 6 Nov. 1355 (*CPR 1354–58*, p. 330).

John of Etton (Ecton) Occ. 6 Nov. 1355 (ibid.); 22 Mar. 1358 (*Yorks Deeds*, VI, no. 454); 1368,1372 (Baildon, I, 219); 13 Apr. 1357 (*CPL*, III, 588); 1362 (Baildon, II, 50); 1371 (ibid., I, 77); 8 Feb. 1371 (PRO, C81/1791/12).

William of Sheffield (Sh[efeld]) Occ. 1377 (PRO, E179/63/10); Easter 1378 (Baildon, I, 220).

PRIORESSES

The three prioresses, **Joan de Langdale, Joan Harncaster** and **Alice of Nafferton** (Naferton) occ. 1377 (PRO, E179/63/11).

YORK, St Andrew f. *c.* 1200 or earlier; (-1202 *Mon. Angl.*, VI, 962).

Lists in *VCH Yorks*, III, 256, *Heads*, I, 205–6; R.L. Kemp & C.P. Graves, *The Church and Gilbertine Priory of St Andrew, Fishergate* (York Archaeological Trust, AY 11/2, 1996), p. 66.

John Occ. 14 Aug. 1214 (*Ctl. Furness*, II, ii, p. 313; PRO, DL27/133); occ. (J.) n.d. (*c.* 1217) (*York Vicars Choral Chts.*, no. 370).

Baldwin Occ. 27 Jan. 1219 (*Yorks F. 1218–31*, p. 12); judge delegate (B.) 9 Oct. 1220 (*Ctl. St Bees*, p. 142, no. 104 – papal mand. of 10 Oct. 1218).

V. Occ. judge delegate *c.* 1220 (papal mand. of 5 Mar. 1220) (*Ctl. Bridlington*, p. 270), ? for Vivian (see *Heads*, I, 201, 206).

William Occ. (W.) 13 July 1222 (YMA, ms. XVI.A.1 (Ctl. St Mary's, York) f. 157r–v); judge delegate +20 Dec. 1224 (BL, Egerton ms. 2823, f. 93r); 1 July 1225 (*Ctl. Kirkstall*, no. 368); 25 Nov. 1226, 21 Apr. 1230 (*Yorks F., 1218–31*, pp. 82, 126; BL, Egerton ms. 2827, f. 261v); 25 June 1240 (*Yorks F., 1232–46*, p. 62); (W.) Mich. 1254 (*Ctl. Whitby*, II, 468).

Robert of Scalby (Scalleby) Occ. 1258 (Bodl., ms. Top. Yorks e. 7, f. 63r); n.d. (1259 x 1260 *or* 1270) (Bodl. ms. Top. Yorks e. 9, f. 19r); 19 May 1262 (*Yorks F. 1246–72*, p. 125); 15 July 1280 (*Yorks F., 1272–1300*, p. 49). Mentd 1293–4 as former pr. about 40 years previously (PRO, Just.1/1101, m. 81).

Adam Occ. 14 May 1287 (Bodl., Douce ms. 136, f. 94v). Presumably the **Adam of Aughton** (Aghton) mentd 1293–4 as former pr. about 14 years previously (PRO, Just.1/1098, m. 62d; Just.1/1101, m. 81).

Geoffrey ref. to him in Mich. 1303 as the predecessor of the present pr. (*YB 30–31 Edward I*, pp. 378–81).[6]

Ralph Occ. 8 Feb. 1335 (*CCR 1333–37*, p. 465).

Robert of Middlesbrough (Midelesburgh) Occ. 28 Feb. 1354 (*CPL*, III, 532); 21 Dec. 1351 (York, Reg. 10, f. 212r); 5 July 1377 (*CPR 1377–81*, p. 37).

The next recorded pr., **John**, occ. 12 Oct. 1415 (Baildon, II, 72).

---

[6] A royal confirmation of 28 June 1332 to Rievaulx abbey mentions a gift to the monks from Rand[ulf], pr. of St Andrew's, York, of land in Layerthorpe, York (*Ctl. Rievaulx*, p. 298). There is no clue as to the date of the original grant.

THE TRINITARIAN HOUSES

EASTON (Wilts). Holy Trinity (Easton Royal) f. 1245 (hospital); 1251 (Trinitarian) (*KH*).
List in *VCH Wilts*. III, 327; H.F. Chettle, 'The Trinitarian friars and Easton Royal', *Wilts AM*, 51 (1945–7), 365–77, at 376.

Nicholas O. Trin., occ. as warden of the hospital 1246 (Wilts RO, 9/15/15).

William Occ. 18 and 20 Apr. 1287, desc. as minister of Easton and of St Mary Magdalen by Hertford, going overseas (*CPR 1281–92*, p. 267).

John of Titchfield (Tycchefeld) Occ. n.d. (*c*. 1308) (Wilts RO, 9/15/3, 12); 7 July 1314, 25 July 1316, 9 May 1322, 10 Mar. 1326, 2 Oct. 1328 (ibid., 9/15, 22, 29, 24, 26–7); 9 May 1322 (*Reg. Martival*, II, ii, 521).

William Becclys (Bekkes) 1329– Br. of Easton, adm. as master and rector 14 July 1329, no reason given for vacancy (ibid., I, 397).

Edmund de Pollesden Pres. by patron and adm. by Robert, bp of Salisbury n.d. (Bodl., Rawlinson ms. B 444, ff. 3v–4r). Occ. 18 Feb. 1344, 23 Apr. 1349 (Wilts RO, 9/15/22, 32–3). Sometime pr., departed, allegedly, with embezzled revenues – went to Hertford *c*. 1360 (Logan, *Runaway Religious*, p. 240; cf. Bodl., Rawlinson ms. B 444, ff. 5r–8r). Formal res. 20 June 1364 (ibid., f. 8r).

[**Robert (of) England** (Engeland(e), Engelond, Ingeland) A secular priest, nominated by the patron; after inquiry res. Feb.–Mar. 1364 (ibid., ff. 2r, 11r). Bp's commn in case of Henry Estormy, the patron, presenting Robert, a secular priest, to rule the hospital by reason of the non-residence of Edmund the warden 8 June 1364 (Wilts RO, 9/15/38).]

Robert (de) Newynton(e) 1364– Pres. by patron and adm. by bp of Salisbury [1364] (Bodl., Rawlinson ms. B 444, f. 11r–v). In that year stated to be aged 30 *et amplius* (ibid., f. 4v). Occ. 12 May 1381, 6 Nov. 1389 (Wilts RO, 9/15/18, 30); n.d. (*c*. 1388) (ibid., 9/15/17).

The next recorded pr., **John Hakkleston** (Hakelston), occ. 16 Mar. 1392 (Wilts RO, 9/15/49); 17 Feb. 1397 (Salisbury, Reg. Mitford, f. 117v); 28 July 1412 (Wilts RO, 9/15/50).

HERTFORD, Holy Trinity and St Thomas the Martyr (but see below) f. -1199 (as hospital of St Mary Magdalen); *c*.1261
List in *VCH Herts*, IV, 453.

William Peverel Occ.as former *custos* 1255 (PRO, Just.1/320, m. 15).

Walter Occ. as *custos* of hosp. of St Mary Magdalen 1255 (ibid.).

MINISTERS

Robert Occ. 1263 (PRO, Herts. F., CP25/1/85/30, no. 571).

William Occ. as minister of the house of Easton and of the house of St Mary Magdalen by Hertford – going overseas Apr. 1287 (*CPR 1281–92*, p. 267).

HOUNSLOW (Middlesex), Holy Trinity f. 1224 x 1252
List in *VCH Middlesex*, I, 192. See also G.E. Bate, *A history of the priory and church of Holy Trinity, Hounslow* (Hounslow, 1924).

Nicholas Occ. Oct. 1256 x Oct. 1257 (*London and Middlesex F.*, I, 38).

Robert of Watford Occ. Mich. 1296 x Mich. 1297 (*Earldom of Cornwall Accounts*, I, 112); Easter 1298 (PRO, CP40/123, m. 135).

Ralph Occ. Mich. 1305 (PRO, CP40/153, m. 455d).

John of Staines (Stanes) Occ. 7 Oct. 1320 (*CCR 1318–23*, p.329).

Bartholomew Occ. 7 Oct. 1363 (*Reg. Sudbury*, I, 238).

William Occ. 25 Jan. 1369 (ibid., I, 264); 31 Oct. 1375 (*Reg. Brantingham*, I, 41); 1381 (McHardy, *Church in London*, no. 375).

The next minister, **Walter**, occ. 6 May 1401 (*CPR 1399–1401*, p. 478).

INGHAM (Norfolk), Holy Trinity and All Saints f. 1360

List in *VCH Norfolk*, II, 412.

Richard (of) Marlborough (Marleberge, Marlebergh) **1360–1383** Ordination of the house and Richard apptd pr. 12 July 1360 (Norwich, Reg/2/5, ff. 2v–3v). D. by 23 Sept. 1383 (Norwich, Reg/3/6, f. 93r–v).

KNARESBOROUGH (Yorks W.) f. *c.*1252

List in *VCH Yorks*, III, 300.

Robert Occ. 1253 (PRO, DL36/1/193).

John Aungle Occ. as minister *temp.* Richard, earl of Cornwall (d. 1272) (PRO, Just.1/1056, m. 46).

Ralph de Reddynges Occ. 1272 x 1280, *temp.* Edmund, earl of Cornwall (*CChR 1257–1300*, p. 240; PRO, DL36/1/59(ii)); 1284, 1286 (Baildon, I, 116).

John *dictus* **Sperry** (Sperri) Occ. 1290 (PRO, Just.1/1082, m. 11 and 1083, mm. 5, 1d, cited in *Reg. Greenfield*, II, p. 30, n. 2); 1301 (Baildon, II, 22–3); 6 June 1307 (*Reg. Greenfield*, II, p. 30, no. 727).

Henry of Knaresborough (Knaresburgh) Occ. 24 Aug. 1315 (ibid., V, no. 2483; W. Wheater, *Knaresburgh and its rulers* (Leeds, 1907), p. 311).

John (Spofford) Occ. 1343 (Baildon, I, 117); Trin. 1344 (*CPR 1343–5*, p. 348).

William de Donyngton Occ. 24 Apr. 1347 (York, Reg. 10, f. 245v); 20 May 1348 (*CPR 1348–50*, p. 97); 1349 (PRO, C143/296/14); desc. as former pr. 1360 (*CPR 1358–61*, p. 467).

Alan of Scarborough (Scardeburgh) Occ. 1360 (*CPR 1358–61*, pp. 467–9); 1 Dec. 1366 (York, Reg. 11, f. 292r; Baildon, I, 117).

William (of) Pudsey (Puddesey) Occ. 1372–4 (Baildon, I, 116, citing Knaresborough court rolls); desc. as former minister 5 Jan. 1388, by which time he had become provincial of the Order in England; occ. as provincial 1402–1403 (*CPL*, V, 551–2, 573).

The next recorded minister was William's immediate successor, **John Kyllyngwyk**, who occ. 5 Jan. 1388 (ibid., 551).

MOATENDEN (Kent), Holy Trinity f. *c.* 1224

List in *VCH Kent*, II, 208.

[**Robert** desc. as of the Trin. house of Moatenden (?minister) and *maior minister* of the order in England, Wales and Ireland 1253 (PRO, DL36/1/193).]

Ralph Occ. Mich. 1250 (*Essex F.*, I, 187).

William Occ. 27 Jan. 1289 (*Reg. Pecham*, I, 84).

John le Bray Occ. as warden of chapel of Holy Trinity, 'Totynton', 15 May 1325 (*CPR 1324–27*, p. 118), identified as Moatenden (*VCH Kent*).

Henry of Leeds (Ledes) Occ. as minister of Moatenden and provincial of the order in England 26 Feb. 1327 (Oxford, Merton Coll. mun. 2661).

Robert Occ. 2 May 1373 (*King's Bench, Edward III*, VI, 167).

The next minister, **William de Hortune**, occ. *c.* 1400 (*VCH*, citing PRO, CP40/572, m. 103).

NEWCASTLE UPON TYNE (Northumberland), Holy Trinity (or St Michael) (Acton's Hospital) (Wallknoll) f. 1360
No list.
William of Wakefield (Wackefeld, Wakefeld) **1360–** Apptd as first warden, mentd in Acton's cht. of 20 May 1360 (Bourne, *Hist. Newcastle*, (unpaginated) app., ref. to p. 142). Presumably he is the same as William of Wakefield, warden of the Trinitarian house of Berwick, occ. 23 Mar. 1360 (Durham, Reg. Hatfield, f. 40r). Occ. as minister 30 Nov. 1369 (*CPR 1367–70*, p. 333).

OXFORD, Holy Trinity f. (-1286) 1293; sold to New College, Oxford 1379 (*VCH Oxford*, II, 151)
William de Parys Occ. July 1314 x July 1315 (Wood, *City of Oxford*, II, 485).
William de Allerton Occ. 24–26 Feb. 1327 (Oxford, Merton Coll. muns. 2660–1).

THELSFORD (Warws), St John the Baptist and St Radegund f. +1170 (Aug.); ?1224 x 1240 (passed to Trinitarians).
List in *VCH Warws*, II, 106. See L. Watts and P. Rahtz eds., M. Gray, *The Trinitarian Order in England: excavations at Thelsford priory* (BAR, British ser., 226, 1993), pp. 15–20.
Geoffrey Occ. 6 Oct. 1221, Mich. 1221 (*Warws F.*, I, nos. 243, 267); Oct. 1231 x Oct. 1232 (PRO, E326/767).

TRINITARIAN
Elias Occ. Oct. 1246 x Oct. 1247 (*Mon. Angl.*, VIII, 1565); n.d. (Bodl., Phillipps Robinson ms. e. 77, f. 2v).
Robert Occ. 20 Apr. 1284 (*Reg. G. Giffard*, p. 231); n.d. (*Mon. Angl.*, VIII, 1564).
John Occ. Easter 1288 (PRO, CP40/72, m. 52); n. d. (late 13th cent., pal.) (PRO, E315/42/244).
Henry Occ. 25 Jan. 1298 (PRO, E326/802); 28 July 1308 (PRO, E315/51/75).
Simon of Charlecote (Churlecote) Absolution of Simon 23 Nov. 1312 (*Reg. Reynolds*, p. 56).
Thomas of Offington (Offyngton) Occ. 17 Apr. 1329 (Bodl., Phillipps Robinson ms. e. 77, f. 4r–v); 26 Nov. 1329 (*CPR 1327–30*, p. 464); 22 Aug. 1333 (PRO, E315/42/121). Occ. as master of hospital (? same as minister) n.d. and 10 Aug. 1332 (BL, Add. Chts. 21409–10).
Geoffrey Occ. 16 Sept. 1334, 10 July 1335, but see below (*Reg. Montacute*, pp. 146, 158).
John Occ. 2 Feb. 1335 (PRO, E315/38/81).
Thomas of Charlecote (Scherlecote) Occ. 1353 (*VCH*, following *Mon. Angl.*, no source); 4 Sept. 1354 (Bodl., Phillipps Robinson ms. e. 77, f. 9r); Jan. 1357 x Jan. 1358 (ibid., f. 4r); Nov. 1361 (PRO, E326/132); 21 May 1365 (PRO, E315/39/237)
The next recorded minister, **William**, occ. 1379 (PRO, E179/58/11, m. 2d), prob. the same as **William de Glaydon**, mentd in 1388 (*Cal. Misc. Inq.*, IV, 222), and to be identified with William de Clarindon occ. *temp*. Richard II (*VCH*).

TOTNES (Devon), Holy Trinity f. 1271 (Little Totnes *or* Werland)
No names of ministers found for this period, but **Thomas Parson** is found as warden of the chapel of Holy Trinity at 'la Warland' 4 Aug. 1380 (Exeter D. & C., vicars choral deed 3163).

MONASTERIES OF
BONHOMMES

No names have been found for Ruthin.

ASHRIDGE (Herts, formerly Bucks), The Precious Blood f. 1283
  Lists in *VCH Bucks*, II, 386–9; *VCH Herts*, IV, 386. Rectors mentioned in H.F. Chettle, 'The
  Boni Homines of Ashridge and Edington', *Downside Review* 62 (1944), 40–55.
Richard of Watford –1297 Edmund, earl of Cornwall mentd as patron and founder of the
  house in Bp Sutton's 7th year (19 May 1286–18 May 1287) ? on the occasion of an admis-
  sion (Bodl., Dodsworth ms. 107, f. 148r from the lost Huntingdon archdeaconry roll of Bp
  Sutton 1280–90). First rector, occ. with Joan, prs of Flamstead *c.*1285 x 1297 (Ctl.
  Flamstead, f. 28v). Res. by 24 May 1297 (*Reg. Sutton*, VIII, 164).
[William of Harrold (Harewold) Commn to examine eln 24 May 1297; eln quashed 27 May
  1297 (ibid., pp. 164–5; cf. ibid., VI, 2).]
Ralph of Aston 1297–1336 Br. of Ashridge, apptd by bp of Lincoln 4 June 1297 (ibid.,VIII,
  165–6). Comm. to receive res. 15 Nov. 1336 (Lincoln, Ep. Reg.,V, f. 542r–v).[1]
Richard de Sarecta –1346 Occ. 5 Jan 1337 (Lincoln, Ep. Reg., VI, f. 124v). D. by 30 Mar. 1346
  (ibid., f. 102r).
Gilbert Boweles 1346– Br. of Ashridge, eln conf. 30 Mar. 1346 (ibid.). Lic. to choose a confessor same day (Lincoln, Ep. Reg.,VII, f. 98r).
William Occ. 31 Oct. 1353 (*Reg. Black Prince*, IV, 105); 1358 (*Ctl. Edington*, no. 25). Commn to
  appt a coadjutor for William, aged and infirm, 2 Nov. 1368 (Lincoln, Ep. Reg., XII, f. 60v).
Ralph of Aston 1369–1396 Br. of Ashridge, commn to examine his eln 20 Feb.1369 (ibid., f.
  64v). D. 28 Sept. 1396 (Lincoln, Ep. Reg., XI, f. 420r).

EDINGTON (Wilts), St. Mary, St Katherine, and All Saints f. 1351 (chantry of secular
chaplains); 1358 (Bonhommes). See H.F. Chettle, 'The *Boni Homines* of Ashridge and
Edington', *Downside Review* 62 (1944), 40–55.
  List in *VCH Wilts*, III, 324.
John of Aylesbury (Ailesbury, Aillesbury, Ayllesbury) 1358–1382 Prev. br. of Ashridge. Lic.
  of bp of Lincoln 17 Dec. 1357 to transfer to Edington to rule the house (*Ctl. Edington*, no.
  24); similar lic. from the rector of Ashridge 25 Feb. 1358 (ibid., no. 25); inst. 12 Apr. 1358
  (ibid., no. 26), inducted 14 Apr. 1358 (ibid., no. 27). D. 24 or 25 Mar. 1382 (ibid., nos. 38,
  42); d. 24 Mar. 1382 (*Cal. Misc. Inq.*, IV, no. 214).

---

[1] A William de Friston occurs as rector of Ashridge on 15 Dec. 1326 (*CPR 1324–7*, p.343). Either this is a
mistake or Ralph of Aston's tenure was not continuous.

UNIDENTIFIED ORDER

WILKESWOOD (Dorset), St Leonard Unknown order (see *KH*, p. 462)
    List in *VCH Dorset*, II, 98.
Adam of Watercombe (Watcumb, Watercumb) Occ. as *custos* of house of St Leonard n.d.
    (Hutchins, III, 729, referring to Coker family records, not located).
Ralph de Sayr Occ. July 1315 x July 1317 (9–10 Edward II) (ibid., referring to Coker lease).
John Heryng Occ. 28 Dec. 1348 (*CPR 1348–50*, p. 223).
Henry Attechapelle 1373– Pres. 1373 (Hutchins, I, 641; III, 729).

HOUSE OF UNCERTAIN STATUS

KINLEY (in Nympsfield, Glos.), St Mary
KH, p. 428, states that the lands of the ancient 'priory' of Kinley were seized by William I but
    restored by William II in 1093 and soon became a secular college or free chapel. However,
    for comments on this foundation tradition see J. H. Denton, *English Royal Free Chapels
    1100–1300: a constitutional history* (Manchester, 1970), p. 10 and n. 3. In *Reg. G. Giffard*, p.
    115, it is recorded that on 24 Sept. 1279 **William**, can. of the priory of Kinley was adm. by
    the bp as pr. of Kinley (checked with f. 185r of the original register). *Reg. Bransford*, p. 29,
    also refers to the chapel of the *house* of Kinley in 1340. The references to a prior and a priory
    suggest some confusion about the status of this ecclesiastical institution.

THE NUNS

No names have been found in this period for Guyzance, Llanllugan, and Seton.

ACONBURY (Hereford), Holy Cross (*alias* St John the Baptist) f. *temp.* John (Hospitallers); 1237 (Augustinian priory) (*KH*); 1216 (Thompson). See H.J. Nicholson, 'Margaret de Lacy and the hospital of St John at Aconbury, Herefordshire' in *JEH*, 50 (1999), 629–51.

List in Thompson, *Women Religious*, p. 232 (to late 13th cent.).

A. Occ. as prs n.d. (first half of 13th cent.: pal.) (PRO, C115/58/4011). The precise sequence of prioresses at this point is unclear.

Constance Occ. *c.* 1232, styled *magistra* of Aconbury (PRO, E315/55, f. 42v).

Apr. 1236 Dispute between sub-prs and convent of Aconbury and the Knights Hospitallers over the el. of a prs, which had now been delayed for 6 years (*CPL*, I, 152–3, cf. pp. 136, 141 for earlier (1233–4) stages of the dispute. See also Nicholson article *supra*.

H. Occ. 1258 (PRO, E326/8696).

Margery Occ. 10 Aug. 1262 (PRO, E326/9770); late Hen. III (BL, Harl. Cht. 38 C 32); 1268 (PRO, E315/48/192); 25 Nov. 1269 (PRO, E315/51/1; Shrops.F., CP25/1/193/4 no. 116).

Beatrice de Gamages 1281– N. of Aconbury, eln quashed and apptd by bp of Hereford 17 Dec.1281 (*Reg. Cantilupe*, p. 292).

Petronilla Extranea Occ. n.d. (E315/55, f. 19r); (late 13th cent.: pal.) (BL, Harl. Cht. 48 C 33), possibly earlier than Beatrice.

Katherine de Geynville (Genevill, Genvyle, Genevyle, Geynvill, Geynvyle) 1287– N. of Aconbury, eln conf. 11 Oct. 1287, no reason given for vacancy (*Reg. Swinfield*, p. 195 – *marg. says 1288*); Occ. 29 Sept. 1289 (PRO, E326/4079); 12 May 1300 (Hereford Cath. mun. 478); 1301 (PRO, E326/8847=BL, Harl. Cht. 45 G13); 1303 (PRO, E315/33/240); 1306 (PRO, E213/427); 1308 (PRO, E326/8846); 1309 (PRO, E315/48/129); 1317 (Hereford Cath. mun. 1046, 1015); 1322 (PRO, E326/8704; E315/49/287, 294); 5 Sept. 1325 (PRO, E315/40/173); July 1325 x July 1326 (PRO, E326/8707).

Matilda de Geynville (Genevile, Genevylle, Geynvill) Occ. Jan. 1330 x Jan. 1331 (PRO, E326/8702); 1333 (PRO, E326/8697); Jan. 1333 x Jan. 1334 (PRO, E326/8693).

Matilda de Grandisson (Grandisone, Grandissono, Graunson) Occ. 1 May 1344 (PRO, E326/2618); 2 Sept. 1350 (PRO, E326/159); 25 May 1351 (PRO, E210/1220); 12 Mar. 1357 (PRO, E315/46/44).

Joan le Blount Occ. 24 Sept. 1363 (PRO, E326/2904).

Joan of Ledbury (Ledeburi, Ledebury) Occ. 6 Dec. 1374 (PRO, E315/36/23); 1 Mar. 1378 (PRO, E326/4396); 1 May 1379 (Hereford Cath. mun. no. 479); 23 Apr. 1385 (*Reg. J. Gilbert*, p. 119); 25 Oct. 1405 (Madox, *Form.*, p. 125, no. 213).

AMESBURY (Wilts), St Mary and St Mellor (Fontevraud) f. *c.*979 (Ben. abbey); ref. 1177 (priory of Fontevraud); nuns installed 1186.

Lists in *VCH Wilts*, III, 258; *Heads*, I, 207; Thompson, *Women Religious*, p. 233 (to 1273). Further details in Berenice Kerr, *Religious life for Women*, pp. 240–3, 246–7.

Emeline Occ. 1208 (*Ped. Fin.*, I, 145); *c.*1215 x 20 (*Ctl. Oseney*, I, 246); 1221 (BL, Stowe ms. 882, f. 39r).

Felicia Occ. 1227, 13 Oct. 1237 (*Wilts F.*, I, pp. 18, 29; *Downside Review*, 60 (1942), p. 37); Aug. 1228 (*CChR 1226–57*, p. 80); Oct. 1237 x Oct. 1238 (*Surrey F.*, p. 21).

Ida Occ. 1256 (Arch. Dép. de Maine et Loire, 243 H1 13); 20 Oct. 1272 (*Wilts F.*, I, p. 61); 25 Dec. 1273 (WCM no. 12128). Seal (*Proc. Soc. Antiq.*, 2nd Series, IX, 366).

Alice Occ. 18 Dec.1290 when attorneys apptd before she went overseas with Blanche, Queen of Navarre (*CPR 1281–92*, p. 409, cf. p.393 unnamed prs 30 Oct. 1290); 1290 (*Downside Review*, 60 (1942), p. 41); (A.) 28 May 1293 (*Reg. Sutton*, IV, pp. 87–8), when the bps of Lincoln and Durham apptd Ida de Gorges, sub-prs of Amesbury, as temporary custodian of the priory during the dispute between the abbess of Fontevraud and prs A. of Amesbury. Abb. of Stoneleigh apptd to custody of the priory, taken into the king's hands on account of its impoverishment 3 June 1293 (*CPR 1292–1301*, pp. 18–19).

Margaret Occ. Trin. 1293 (*Wilts F.*, II, p. 42n; *Downside Review*, 60 (1942) p. 41). Mentioned 10 June 1294 as former prs in contention with the abbess of Fontevraud (*CPR 1292–1301*, p. 71).

Joan de Jenes (Genes, Gennes, Genues, Jaynes) **1294–** N. of Amesbury, temps. 10 June 1294 (ibid.). 6 Mar. 1297 royal inspeximus of letters of abbess of Fontevraud dated 16 May 1294 praying the king to command the convent of Amesbury to receive Joan de Jenes, n. of Fontevraud, whom she has sent to be prs 'fame sage et viguereuse' (ibid., pp. 241–2). King asks abb. of Fontevraud to exhibit her goodwill to the prs and not to ordain anything regarding the temps. over the prs's head 1297 (*CCR 1296–1302*, p. 45). Occ. *c.* 27 May 1296 (*Wilts F.*, II., p. 42); 11 Dec.1306, 4 Jan.1309 (*Reg. Gandavo*, II, 683, 705).

Isabel de Geinville (Jeonevill) **1309–** Request of the king's sister, Mary, for the appt of a prs who is not an alien 9 May [1309] (PRO, SC1/34/128). Royal ass. sought 27 May 1309 (*Cal. Chanc. Warr.*, pp. 286–7). Occ. 1336 (Winchester, Reg. Orleton, I, f. 34r; PRO, C241/110/224); 1337 (PRO, DL41/9/6, m. 7).

Isabel of Lancaster (Lancastria) **–?1349** Sister of Henry, duke of Lancaster, cousin of the king. Still desc. as n. of Amesbury 5 Apr. 1340 (*CPR 1338–40*, p. 449). Occ. as prs 20 Aug. 1343 (*CChR 1341–1417*, p. 20); 1344 (*CPL*, III, 145,175; *CPP*, p. 78; *CPR 1343–45*, p. 225); 1345 (*CPP*, p. 98); 1345, 1347 (Salisbury, Reg. Wyvil, I, ff. 171r–172v). House void by 4 Feb. 1349 (*CCR 1349–54*, p. 5).

Margery (of) Purbrook (Pirebrok, Purebrok, Pyrebrok) **1349–1379** Occ. 17 Aug. 1349 (Salisbury, Reg. Wyvil II, f. 216r); 1356 (*CPR 1354–58*, p. 533). D., lic. to el. 28 Oct. 1379 (*CPR 1377–81*, p. 396).

PRIORS

John de Vinci Occ. *c.* 1215 x 20 (*Ctl. Oseney*, I, 246–7); 7 Oct. 1221 (*Sarum Chts.*, p. 114); 1221 (*Downside Review*, 60 (1942), p. 54); 1222 (*Ctl. Oseney*, II, 436); 29 Sept. 1229 (T.F. Kirby in *Archaeologia*, LIX (1904), 77).

Th[omas] Occ. (Th.) 1255 (Arch. Dép. de Maine et Loire, 243 H1 13).

Peter Occ. May 1293 (*CCR 1288–96*, p. 317); 28 May 1293 (*Reg. Sutton*, IV, 87).

John of Figheldean Occ. as former pr. 1315–16 (Arch. Dép. de Maine et Loire, 244 H1 3).

Richard de Greenborough Occ. as pr. and receiver 1316–1319 (ibid.).

?William Occ. as pr. of 'Aumbr' (? Amesbury) Mich. 1338 x Mich. 1339 (PRO, E372/184, rot. 15d).

John de Holt Occ. 1 Oct. 1356 (*CFR 1356–59*, p. 17); 20 Oct. 1357 (*CPR 1354–58*, p. 622).

William of Amesbury **1361–** Adm. 1361 (Arch. Dép. de Maine et Loire, cited in *VCH Wilts*, III, 258).

John Wynterborn Occ. 1381 (Kirby, 'Clerical Poll-Taxes', p. 166).

ANKERWYKE (Bucks), St. Mary Magdalen f. *c.*1160 (*KH*); –1163 (Thompson) (Benedictine priory)

> Lists in *VCH Bucks*, I, 357; Turner, 'Ankerwyke', p. 74; *Heads*, I, 207; Thompson, *Women Religious*, p. 233 (to 1270).

Lettice Last recorded occ. 1203 (*Essex F.*, I, 33).

[Emma D. ?1236 (*Mon. Angl.*, IV, 230) but see Thompson, p. 233 who suggests this ref. is a poss. error for a later prs, Emma of Kimberley.]

[Christina of London (Lond') Eln quashed by bp of Lincoln June 1237 x June 1238 (*Reg. Grosseteste*, p. 345).]

Celestria 1237/8 (1238/9)– N. of Little Marlow, apptd by bp of Lincoln June 1237 x June 1238 (ibid.). El. by convent; eln quashed and bp apptd her on the d. of unnamed prs June 1238 x June 1239 (ibid., p. 346). Occ. 1239 x 1241 (*Reg. Ant. Lincoln*, III, no. 656).

Juliana 1243/4– Sacrist of Ankerwyke, eln conf. June 1243 x June 1244, no reason given for vacancy (*Reg. Grosseteste*, p. 369).

Joan of Rouen (Rothomago) 1250/1– N. of Ankerwyke, el. and adm. June 1250 x June 1251, no reason given for vacancy (ibid., p. 381).

Margery of Hedsor (Heddeshovere) –1305 Occ. Oct. 1262 x Oct. 1263 (*Surrey F.*, p. 42); Oct. 1265 x Oct. 1266 (Margaret), Oct. 1270 x Oct. 1271 (Margery) (*London and Middlesex F.*, pp. 44, 47); occ. in cht. n.d., inspected 1267 (*CCR 1264–68*, p. 359); Oct. 1269 x Oct. 1270 (PRO, E42/323); 1270 (PRO, E40/7320); 20 Jan. 1270, 2 Aug. 1271 (PRO, E40/1590; 7297); 27 Oct. 1280 (*CCR 1279–88*, p. 54). Cess. by 14 Mar. 1305 (Lincoln, Ep. Reg., II, f. 177r.).

Alice de Saunford 1305 N. of Ankerwyke, eln quashed but apptd by bp 14 Mar. 1305 (ibid.). House vacant 16 Oct. 1316 (Lincoln, Ep. Reg., III, f. 356r).

Emma of Kimberley (Kymberle) 1316–1327 N. of Ankerwyke, commn to examine eln 9 Nov. 1316 (ibid., f. 357r–v). Occ. 5 July 1317 (ECR, 11/412). D. by 13 Feb. 1328 (Lincoln, Ep. Reg., IV, f. 333v), presumably by 20 June 1327 when commn to examine eln of unnamed prs issued (Lincoln, Ep. Reg., V, f. 393r).

Joan of Oxford (Oxon') 1328–?1349 N. of Ankerwyke, eln conf. 13 Feb. 1328 (Lincoln, Ep. Reg., IV, f. 333v). Lic. to el. (no reason given) 21 Apr. 1349 (Lincoln, Ep. Reg., IX, f. 21r).

Katherine Occ. n.d. (with abb. John of Chertsey) (*Ctl. Chertsey*, II, no. 686). From lay witnesses to this doct who occ. in other dated material it is likely that Abb. John is either John de Rutherwyk (1307–47) or John de Benham (1347–61), prob. the latter.

Alice Occ. 10 July 1375 (*Hustings Wills*, II, 182; Guildhall, ms. 9171/1, f. 311r).

The next recorded prs, **Letia**, occ. 17 Aug. 1381 (Bodl., Rawlinson ms. B.461, f. 29r).

ARDEN (Yorks N.), St Andrew f. -1147(?) (*KH*); *c.* 1147 x 1169 (Burton; Thompson) (Benedictine priory)

Lists in *VCH Yorks*, III, 115–16; *Heads*, I, 207; Thompson, *Women Religious*, p. 233 (to 1262).

Muriel Last recorded occ. Whitsun 1212 (*Ctl. Fountains*, II, 626).

Agatha Occ. 11 June 1262 (*Yorks F., 1246–72*, p. 125; *Mon. Angl.*, IV, 286).

[Alice Occ. 1273 (*VCH*, without source).]

Margaret Occ. 25 June 1290 (*Mon. Angl.*, IV, 285; Baildon, I, 2).

Juliana –1304 Res. on 29 Oct. 1304; letter of cess. issued 9 Nov. (*Reg. Corbridge*, II, 178). Mand. to install an unnamed prs 21 Nov. 1304 (ibid., 178, n.1; Baildon, I, 2).

Beatrice of Colton 1315– Eln conf. 25 Jan. 1315, no reason given for vacancy (*Reg. Greenfield*, III, p. 97, no. 1346).

Isabel Couvel(l) (Coule) 1324–1329 N. of Arthington, mand. to obey 25 Apr. 1324, whom the archbp of York had apptd on the res. of the previous (unnamed) prs (*Reg. Melton*, II, p. 102, nos. 243–4). Res. by 7 Feb. 1329 (ibid., pp. 135–6, no. 328). Mand. to re-admit her to Arthington 2 July 1329 (York, Reg. 9A, f. 220v).

Beatrice de Holm 1329– Eln quashed but apptd by archbp; mand. to install 27 Apr. 1329 (*Reg. Melton*, II, p. 136, no. 331).

Commn to adm. cess. of unnamed prs and to examine and conf. eln of a new prs 6 Oct. 1393 (York, Reg.14, f. 43v).

The next recorded prs, **Eleanor**, occ. 24 Feb. 1397 (York, Reg. 5A, f. 228r).

MASTERS

Br. Robert de Colevile 1302– Can. of Newburgh. Request to pr. of Newburgh to allow Robert to manage the nunnery's affairs 4 Oct. 1301 (*sic*) (*Reg. Corbridge*, I, 168); apptd as master 10 Oct. 1302 (ibid., 134).

Robert of Fulstow (Foulestowe) **1323–** Rector of Kirby Knowle, apptd as *custos* 11 Apr. 1323, no reason given for vacancy (*Reg. Melton*, II, pp. 86–7, no. 222).

Thomas Fox, rector of Gilling East, and **John of Speeton** (Speton) apptd as custodians of the priory 20 Jan. 1324, no reason given for vacancy (ibid., p. 102, no. 242).

ARMATHWAITE (Cumberland), St Mary f. -1200 (Benedictine priory)
List in *VCH Cumberland*, II, 192.

Isabel –1362 D. by 25 Aug. 1362 (*Reg. Welton*, no. 487).

Katharine of Lancaster (Lancastre) **1362–** N. of Armathwaite, el. 25 Aug.1362. eln conf. and mand. to install 2 Sept.1362 (ibid.).

The next recorded prs, **Isabel**, occ. 20 June 1480 (*CPR 1476–85*, p.203).

ARTHINGTON (Yorks W.), St Mary f. *c.*1154 x 5 (*KH*); *c.* 1150 x 1160 (Burton); *c.* 1150 x 1158 (Thompson) (Cluniac priory)
Lists in *VCH Yorks*, III, 190; Thompson, *Women Religious*, p. 233 (to 1241).

Sarah Occ. 14 Jan. 1242 (PRO, DL25/477).

Eleanor Mentioned 1299 as former prs (Baildon, I, 3).

Matilda of Keswick (Kesewike) **–1300** D. by 20 Jan. 1300 when commissaries apptd to conf. eln of a new prs (*Reg. Newark*, pp. 321–2, nos. 351, 357).

Agnes of Scriven (Skrevin) **–1302** Notif. of res. & lic. to el. 12 Nov. 1302 (*Reg. Corbridge*, I, 76).

Agnes of Pontefract 1302– N. of Arthington, notif. of appt 4 Dec. 1302 (ibid., 78).

Isabel of Barrowby (Berghby) **1312** Lic. to el. a new prs, no reason given for vacancy 26 Feb. 1312 (*Reg. Greenfield*, II, no. 945); custody gtd to Isabel, lately el. prs, with whom the vicar-general had associated Isabel Couvel, n. of Arthington (ibid., no. 948; cf. Arden above). Commn of inquiry to find out why she left and where she is now (ibid., no. 957; Logan, *Runaway Religious*, pp. 261–2); mand. to priory to receive Isabel, apostate nun 21 Sept.1312 (*Reg. Greenfield*, II, no.960); on 28 Sept. 1312 sent to Yedingham priory (ibid., p. 124, n.1 and III, no. 1289). Penance, as n. of Arthington, 9 Jan. 1316 (ibid., V, no. 2781).

Matilda of Batley (Batheley) **1312–** N. of Arthington, eln conf. 18 Sept. 1312 (ibid., II, no. 960).

Isabel la Dautry –1349 D. by 14 Sept. 1349 (York, Reg. 10, f. 37r).

Isabel of Barrowby (Berughby) **1349–** N. of Arthington, eln conf. 14 Sept. 1349 (ibid.).

The next recorded prs, **Isabel of Eccup** (Eccope), occ. Mich. 1413 (Baildon, I, 3).

CUSTODIANS

Adam de Potrington 1293– Rector of Kippax, apptd as guardian or curator 16 June 1293 (*Reg. Romeyn*, I, p. 125, no. 345).

Thomas of Stonegrave (Stayngreve) **1316–** Rector of Rossington, apptd to superintend the affairs of the priory 12 June 1316 (*Reg. Greenfield*, V, no. 2797).

Robert de Tang 1328– Apptd custodian 22 Feb. 1328 (York, Reg. 9A, f. 211v).

BARKING (Essex), St Mary and St Ethelburga f. -975 (Benedictine abbey)
Lists in *VCH Essex*, II, 120–2; (medieval lists, of no value, in *Mon. Angl.*, I, 441–2); *Heads*, I, 208.

Mabel of Bosham 1215–1247 Royal ass. 31 Aug. 1215 (*Rot. Lit. Pat.*, p.154, repeated 2 Sept. 1215; *Rot. Lit. Claus.* I, 227). Occ. Trin. 1220 to Easter 1243 (*Essex F.*, I, 57, 144). D. 1247 (cf. *CPR 1232–47*, pp. 505–7, void by 26 July 1247).

Matilda 1247–1252 N. of Barking, daughter of King John, royal ass. 5 Aug. 1247, temps. 19 Aug. 1247 (ibid., pp. 506, 507). D., lic. to el. 6 Feb. 1252 (*CPR 1247–58*, p. 128; PRO, C84/1/25).

Christiana of Bosham (Boseham) **1252–1258** El. 9 Feb. 1252 (PRO, C84/1/25). Royal ass. 14 Feb. 1252 (*CPR 1247–58*, p. 129). King took fealty and mand. for seisin 22 Feb. 1252; similar mand. 25 Feb. 1252 (*CCR 1251–53*, pp. 55–6). Res. 2 Dec. 1258 (PRO, C84/2/39, 3). Cess., lic. to el. 8 Dec. 1258 (*CPR 1258–66*, p. 7).

Matilda de Levelande (Levelaunde, Lovelaunde) **1258–1275** N. of Barking, eln pres. to king for royal ass. 14 Dec. 1258 (PRO, C84/2/6); royal ass. 15 Dec. 1258, temps. 19 Dec. 1258 (*CPR 1258–66*, p. 7). Res. by 13 Aug. 1275 (PRO, C84/5/40). Lic. to el. 18 Aug. 1275 (*CPR 1272–81*, p. 100).

Alice of Merton 1275/6–1291 Eln pres. to king for royal ass. 19 Oct. 1275 (PRO, C84/5/50). Letter re taking oath from abbess-el. 16 Jan. 1276 (PRO, SC1/16/34). Writ *de intendendo* 21 Jan. 1276 (*CPR 1272–81*, p. 131). D., lic. to el. 28 Nov. 1291 (*CPR 1281–92*, p. 461).

Isabel de Basinges (Basynge) **1291–1294** Prs of Barking, el. 30 Nov. 1291 (PRO, C84/10/26). Temps. 3 Dec. 1291 (*CPR 1281–92*, p. 462). Cert. conf. eln by bp of London 7 Dec. 1291 (PRO, C84/10/30). D. by 13 June 1294 (PRO, C84/12/7). D., lic. to el. 15 June 1294 (*CPR 1292–1301*, p. 72).

Matilda de Grey 1294–1295 Prs of Barking, el. 17 June 1294 (PRO, C84/12/9); royal ass. 17 June 1294, temps. 20 June 1294 (*CPR 1292–1301*, pp. 74, 76). Cert. conf. eln by bp of London 21 June 1294 (PRO, C84/12/10). Mand. to order restitution of temps. 22 June 1294 (*Cal. Chanc. Warr.*, p. 43). D., lic. to el. 5 May 1295 (*CPR 1292–1301*, p. 134).

Anne de Veer –1318 Occ. Easter 1308 (*Essex F.*, II, 118); 21 Feb. 1315 (*CCR 1313–18*, p. 337); 1316 (PRO, CP40/213, m. 1d). D., lic. to el. 17 Jan. 1318 (*CPR 1317–21*, p. 70).

Eleanor of Weston (Westone) **1318–1329** N. of Barking, royal ass. 26 Jan. 1318, temps. 17 Feb. 1318 (ibid., pp. 80, 102). Cert. conf. eln by bp of London 15 Feb. 1318 (PRO, C84/19/28). D. by 28 Apr. 1329 (*CFR 1327–37*, p. 131). D., lic. to el. 2 May 1329 (*CPR 1327–30*, p. 385).

Jolenta (Jolanda) of Sutton 1329–1341 N. of Barking, royal ass. 12 May 1329, temps. 15 June 1329 (ibid., pp. 387, 400). Cert. conf. eln by bp of London 3 June 1329 (PRO, C84/22/24). D., lic to el. 19 Mar. 1341 (*CPR 1340–43*, p. 163).

Matilda de Monte Acuto (Montague) **1341–1352** N. of Barking, royal ass. 28 Mar. 1341, temps. 30 Apr. 1341 (ibid., pp. 162, 179–80). D., lic. to el. 22 Nov. 1352 (*CPR 1350–54*, p. 375, cf. *CFR 1347–56*, p. 343).

Isabel de Monte Acuto (Montague) **1352–1358** N. of Barking, royal ass. 30 Nov. 1352, temps. 25 Dec. 1352 (*CPR 1350–54*, pp. 367, 379; PRO, C84/27/5). D. by 5 Feb. 1358 (PRO, C84/27/38). Lic. to el. 26 Feb. 1358 (*CPR 1358–61*, p. 14).

Katharine (of) Sutton 1358–1377 N. of Barking, eln pres. to king for royal ass. 7 Mar. 1358 (PRO, C84/27/39); royal ass. 15 Mar. 1358, temps. 29 Mar 1358 (*CPR 1358–61*, p. 62). D. by 14 Apr. 1377 (PRO, C84/31/47). Lic. to el. 16 Apr. 1377 (*CPR 1374–77*, p. 445). Seal (*Mon. Seals*, p. 5).

Matilda de Monte Acuto (Montague, Mountagu) **1377–1393** N. of Barking, eln pres. to king for royal ass. 19 Apr. 1377 (PRO, C84/31/48); royal ass. 20 Apr. 1377, temps. 23 Apr. 1377 (*CPR 1374–77*, p. 449–50); cert. of eln having been conf. by bp of London 20 Apr. 1377

(PRO, C84/31/49). Occ. 28 Jan. 1393 (PRO, C146/2426). D. by 2 Oct. 1393 (PRO, C84/35/51). D., lic. to el. 5 Oct. 1393 (*CPR 1391–96*, p. 317; London, Reg. Braybrooke, f. 339r).

BARROW GURNEY (Soms), St Mary and St Edward, king and martyr (Minchin Barrow) f. ?-1200 (*KH*); – *c.* 1201 (Thompson) (Benedictine priory)

List in *VCH Soms*, II, 109.

Alice Occ. 27 Dec. 1300 (PRO, Just.1/1318, m. 20).

Mand. to unnamed prs. to leave the management of secular matters to a *custos* apptd by the bp 26 June 1315 (*Reg. Droxford*, p. 92).

Joan de Gurnay 1316–1325 Commn to examine eln 4 Oct.1316, profession of her as a nun 20 July 1317 (ibid., pp. 115, 167). To be inducted *c.* Nov. 1317 (ibid., p. 173). Eln invalid since Joan was not professed. She is now fully professed but nomination lapsed to bp, who ordered her induction (ibid.). Guardians of mismanaged priory apptd by bp 6 Sept. 1323 and prs. to be restrained from wandering (ibid., p. 221). Official commissioned to remove her 18 Jan. 1325 (ibid., p. 238). Res. in visitation *c.* May 1325 and lic. to el. (ibid., p. 245). Warned (as a n. of Barrow Gurney) to obey new prs. on pain of excommunication 19 Feb. 1326 (ibid., p. 257).

Agnes de Sancta Cruce 1325–1328 Sub-prs. of Barrow Gurney, commn to examine eln 4 June 1325; further commn 5 Oct. 1325; previous commn revoked and new commn to complete the process of Agnes's eln 26 Nov. 1325 (ibid., pp. 246, 248–9, 252). Mand. to induct 9 Feb. 1326 (ibid., p. 250). D. by 11 Nov. 1328 (ibid., p. 294).

Basilia of Sutton 1328–1340 Eln pres. to bp 11 Nov. 1328 (ibid.). Prof. obed. n.d. (ibid., p. 295). D. 17 June 1340 (*Reg. R. Shrewsbury*, I, no. 1398). Lic. to el. 9 Aug. 1340 (ibid.).

Julian Gro(u)ndy 1340– El. 12 Aug. 1340, commn to conf. eln 20 Aug., eln conf. by commissary 20 Aug. 1340 (ibid.).

Agnes Balun 1348– N. of Barrow Gurney, eln conf. 20 Oct. 1348, no reason given for vacancy (ibid., II, no. 2048).

Joan Panys Occ. 1377 (PRO, E179/4/2, m. 1).

CUSTOS

William 1325– Rector of Backwell, apptd as *custos* by bp, to act with the advice of the sub-prs and Basilia of Sutton 13 Feb. 1325 (*Reg. Droxford*, p. 240).

BAYSDALE (Yorks N.), St Mary (Basedale) f. *c.*1162 (at Hutton Rudby); *c.*1167 (at Nunthorpe); *c.*1189 (at Baysdale) (*KH*); earlier sites *c.* 1139 x *c.* 1159; Baysdale *c.* 1190 x 1211 (Thompson) (Cistercian priory)

Lists in *VCH Yorks*, III,160; *Heads*, I, 208; Thompson, *Women Religious*, p. 233 (to 1268).

Isabel Occ. 1197 x 1211 (*EYC*, I, no. 564, dated by the abb. of St Mary's, York and the pr. of Guisborough).

Susanna Occ. 1229 x 1245 (*Ctl. Whitby*, I, no. 292).

Alice of Yarm (Jarum) n.d. (?1268 x 1283) (*Yorks Deeds*, V, no. 290).

Ellen Occ. 27 Jan. 1283 (*Yorks F., 1272–1300*, p. 66).

Joan Percy 1301– N. of Baysdale, eln conf. 10 May 1301, no reason given for vacancy (*Reg. Corbridge*, I, 124). Occ. 1302 (Baildon, I, 4); 29 Sept. 1305 (*Reg. Greenfield*, V, p. 263, no. 2846). Commn to dismiss unnamed prs on account of her dilapidations of the goods of the house and other offences and to conf. another to be el. in her place 16 May 1307 (prob. error for 15 June) (ibid., III, p.17, no. 1164 and n.3). Lic. to unnamed prs to eat meat 3 days a week on account of infirmity 11 Sept. 1307 (ibid., pp. 18–19, no. 1166). Order to prs and conv. of Sinningthwaite to receive her 13 July 1308 – she is desc. as n. of Baysdale, not prs (ibid., pp. 23–5, no. 1180). Order to Sinningthwaite to return her to Baysdale 15 Aug. 1309; her penance set out (ibid., pp. 48–9, no. 1233).

Emma Occ. 27 July 1323 (PRO, E210/5245).

Katherine Moubray Commn dated 18 Mar. 1344 to inquire into her conduct and depose her if necessary (York, Reg. 10, f. 155r).

Commn to adm. cess. of an unnamed prs and lic. to proceed with the eln of a successor 21 June 1359 (York, Reg. 11, f. 177v).

Alice Page −1377 Commn dated 9 June 1377 to adm. cess. of Alice and to proceed to eln (York, Reg. 12, f. 41r).

Eln of next recorded prs, **Elizabeth Cothom**, pres. to archbp 9 Mar. 1461 and eln conf. 8 May 1461 (York, Reg. 20, f. 67Ar).

CUSTODIANS/MASTERS

William of Bardney 1268– M. of Whitby, apptd as *custos*, during pleasure, 16 Mar. 1268 (*Reg. W. Giffard*, p. 54). See also Handale.

Peter Vicar of [Hutton] Rudby in Cleveland Occ. as master n.d. (? 1268 x 1283) (*Yorks Deeds*, V, no. 290)

Mag. Roger of Kelsey (Kelleshey) Rector of Crathorne, goods of priory committed to his care 18 May 1304 (*Reg. Corbridge*, I, 146).

BLACKBOROUGH (Norfolk), St Mary and St Katherine (Shiplade) f. *c.* 1150 (monks); *c.* 1200 (nuns). (Benedictine priory)

Lists in *VCH Norfolk*, II, 351; *Heads*, I, 208–9; Thompson, *Women Religious*, p. 234 (to 1262).

?Avelina Occ. n.d., possibly early 13th cent. (BL, Egerton ms. 3137, ff. 33v, 41v, 74v; *Heads*, I, 209).

Margaret Occ. Oct. 1221 x Oct. 1222 (*Norfolk F. (Rye)*, p. 38); 15 Sept. 1222, 26 Nov. 1223, 8 July 1228 (BL, Egerton ms. 3137, ff. 65r, 117v, 190r, 49v); *c.* 1222–23, 1222 x 1228 (Owen, *King's Lynn*, nos. 19, 29).

Katherine de Scalis Occ. 1238 (BL, Egerton ms. 3137, f. 62r).

Alice Occ. n.d. (? 13th cent.) (ibid., ff. 95v, 165r, 171v; Owen, *King's Lynn*, no. 28). The sequence of prioresses is uncertain.

Mary Occ. Oct. 1258 x Oct. 1259 (*Norfolk F. (Rye)*, p. 97); 3 Feb. 1259, 5 Jan. 1260 (BL, Egerton ms. 3137, ff. 177r, 197v, 213r, 61v); Christmas 1261 (Owen, *King's Lynn*, no. 23). Possibly Mary of London mentd n.d. (BL, Egerton ms. 3137, f. 167v).

Ida of Middleton (Middelton) 1304– N. of Blackborough, eln quashed, but apptd by bp 27 Apr. 1304, no reason given for vacancy (Norwich, Reg/1/1, f. 5v).

Katherine de Fitton (Fittone) 1310– Nun. of Blackborough, eln conf. 24 July 1310, no reason given for vacancy (ibid., f. 37r). Occ. 28 Oct. 1311 (BL, Egerton ms. 3137, f. 50r).

Lettice −1342 Occ. 8 Jan. 1333 (ibid., f. 179v). Res. by 30 Oct. 1342 (Norwich, Reg/1/3, f. 63r–v).

Winnesia of Boyton 1342– N. of Blackborough, commn to examine eln 30 Oct. 1342; eln conf. 17 Nov. 1342 (ibid.).

Isabel de Stanton 1349– N. of Blackborough, eln quashed, but apptd by bp 10 Sept 1349 (Norwich, Reg/2/4, f. 108r).

House vacant by 20 Apr. 1352 by res. of unnamed prs. (ibid., f. 140v).

Isabel of Hinton (Hynton) 1352–1384 N. of Blackborough, eln quashed, but apptd by bp 20 Apr. 1352 (ibid.). Cess. by 17 Oct. 1384 (Norwich, Reg/3/6, f. 103r), but cf. letter of sub-prs and convent to Roger de Scalis notifying him of the d. of Isabel de Hynton and asking for his lic. el el a new prs., n.d.; his lic. to el. n.d. (BL, Egerton ms. 3137, f. 207v).

BLITHBURY (Staffs), St Giles f. 1129+ (nuns 1158 x 1165); 1120 x 1147, eremitical origins (Thompson). ? in existence 1315; merged with Brewood Black Ladies by the 14th century (Benedictine priory)
Details (no list) in *VCH Staffs*, III, 220.
Alice Occ. n.d. [*c.* 1273 x 1281] (*Brewood Chts.*, pp. 201–2, 204).

BREWOOD BLACK LADIES (Staffs), St Mary f. -1150 (Benedictine priory)
  Lists in *VCH Staffs*, III, 222; *Brewood Chts.*, p. 220; Thompson, *Women Religious*, p. 234 (to 1295).
Amabel Occ. 15 July 1236 (*Staffs F. 2*, p. 230).
Isabel Occ. *c.*1258 x 95 (*temp.* Bp Roger de Meuland) (*Magnum Reg. Album Lichfield*, p. 292, no. 608); *c.*1260 x 1270 (*Brewood Chts.*, p. 205).
Amabel Occ. 17 July 1272 (ibid., p. 204); 8 July 1272, 17 July 1272 (*Staffs F. 2*, pp. 258, 256); *temp.* Edward I (*Brewood Chts.*, p. 201).
Emma Occ. 6 July 1301 (ibid., p. 186).
Alice of Swynnerton –1332 Occ. Trin. 1324 (*Staffs Plea Rolls 1307–27*, p. 104). Res. [? May x July] 1332 (Lichfield, B/A/1/2, f. 151r).
Helewise of Leicester (Leycestr') 1332– N. of Brewood, eln quashed but apptd by bp 1332 [between entries of May and July] (ibid.). Occ. 21 Nov. 1339 (*Brewood Chts.*, p. 188); 28 Apr. 1373 (ibid., p. 198).
The next recorded prs, **Petronilla**, occ. 29 Sept.1394 (*Brewood Chts.*, p. 208; Staffs RO, D3764/17).

BREWOOD WHITE LADIES (Shropshire), St Leonard (Boscobel) f. ? *c.*1199 (*KH*); -1186 (Thompson) (Augustinian priory)
  Lists in *VCH Shropshire*, II, 84; *Heads*, I, 209; Thompson, *Women Religious*, p. 234 (to 1256).
Aldith Occ. *c.* 1225 x 1233 (*Ctl. Shrewsbury*, II, no. 376b).
Cecily Occ. *c.* 1225 x 1233 (ibid., no. 376c).
Agnes Occ. 6 Oct. 1254 (PRO, Shrops F., CP25/1/193/4, no. 43); 3 Feb. 1256 (ibid. 193/4, no. 51); 9 Feb. 1266 (*Derbys F. (1889)*, p. 97).
Amice Occ. 15 Sept. 1273 acc. to 1295 plea roll (PRO, CP40/107, m. 129d).
Sarah Occ. 1292 (*YB 20–1 Edward I*, pp. 242–3).
Joan Occ. 1315 (Coughton Court, Throckmorton muniments, box 56, lease 1331).
Joan de Hugford (Huggeford) –1332 Possibly the same as above. Occ. 6 July 1331 (Lichfield, B/A/1/3, f. 26r); 5 Aug.1331 (ibid.). Res. by 29 May 1332 (Lichfield, B/A/1/2, f. 210r–v).
Alice of Harley (Harelegh, Harlee, Harleye) 1332–1349 N. of Brewood, eln quashed but apptd by bp 29 May 1332 (ibid.). Occ. 14 July 1348 (*CPL*, III, 271). D. by 29 July 1349 (Lichfield, B/A/1/2, f. 224r).
Beatrice de Dene 1349– N. of Brewood, apptd by bp 29 July 1349 (ibid.).
Margaret Corbet Occ. 1377 (PRO, E179/15/3, m. 1); 1380 x 1381 (PRO, E179/15/8A, m. 1).
The next recorded prs, **Joan Fillilode**, occ. 15 Jan. 1409 (*Reg. R. Mascall*, p. 174).

BRISTOL (Glos), St Mary Magdalen f. *c.*1173 (Augustinian priory)
  Lists in *VCH Glos*, II, 93; *Heads*, I, 209; Thompson, *Women Religious*, p. 234 (master only).
Commn to receive res. of unnamed prs, if she freely wishes to do so, 25 July 1285 (*Reg. G. Giffard*, p. 263).
Agnes Occ. 24 Mar. 1308 (*Worcs Reg. Sede Vacante*, p. 96).
Agnes of Gloucester (Glouc') Occ. 5 Feb.1347, 7 Feb.1347, 8 Feb.1347 (*Ctl. Bristol, St Mark's*, pp. 206–7, nos. 329–31).

Matilda of Littleton (Luttelton) **1349–1356** Apptd 27 Mar. 1349, no reason given for vacancy (*Reg. Bransford*, no. 997). Res. on 21 July 1356, and custody of the spiritualities and temps. committed to Sr Juliana, n. of the house, during the vacancy, 24 July (Worcester, Reg. Brian I, p. 38).

Margery Longe 1363– N. of Bristol, apptd by bp 2 Aug. 1363, no reason given for vacancy (Worcester, Reg. Barnet, p. 55).

Elizabeth Wodecroft 1369– N. of Bristol, apptd by bp 29 Oct. 1369, no reason given for vacancy (Worcester, Reg. Lenn, p. 46). Occ. 26 July 1386 (*CPR 1385–89*, p. 207).

The next recorded prs, **Alice Clayvile**, d. by 4 Dec. 1421 (Worcester, Reg. Morgan, p. 88).

MASTER

John Occ. 18 Nov. 1240, 1233 x 1240 (master of hospital of St Mary Magdalen) (*Ctl. Bristol, St Mark's*, p. 33, no. 32 and pp. 205–6, no. 328; *EEA*, 13, no. 47).

BROADHOLME (Notts), St Mary f. -1154 (*KH*); perhaps originally part of Newhouse abbey, separated by 1167 (Thompson) (Premonstratensian priory)

Lists in *VCH Notts*, II, 140; Colvin, p. 42, *Heads*, I, 209. See also R.E.G. Cole, 'The priory, or house of nuns, of St Mary of Brodholme, of the order of Prémontré', *AASRP*, XXVIII (1905), 48–86.

Avice of Grimsby n.d. Obit 17 Apr. (Newhouse obit, *HMC Ancaster*, p. 483).

Thomasina occ. 1201 x 1202 (Notts F., PRO transcripts V). Poss. earlier than Avice.

Matilda Mentioned 2 May 1326 as former prs (*CCR 1323–27*, p. 472); similarly desc. as 'long since' prs, 18 Feb. 1326 (*Cal. Misc. Inq.*, II, 223).

Joan de Riel Occ. 12 Mar. 1354 (*CPL*, VI, 159; *AASRP*, XXVIII, 64–5).

Agnes de Beckerham Occ. 1 Apr. 1371 (Norwich Consistory Court Will Register Heydon 1370–83, f. 6v); 15 Aug. 1373 (*CPR 1370–74*, p. 374); 1403 (*AASRP*, XXVIII, 65).

BROOMHALL (Berks), St Margaret f. -1200 (*KH*); -1157 x 1158 (Thompson) (Benedictine priory)

List in *VCH Berks*, II, 81; Thompson, *Women Religious*, p. 234 (to 1268).

Juliana Desc. as predecessor of Agnes (Cambridge, St John's Coll. ms. D14:167).

Agnes of St Edmund Occ. 1256 (*Ctl. Chertsey*, II, no. 809); 1268 (BL, Add. ms. 5829, f. 66v, no source); Nov. 1277 x Nov. 1278 (*Surrey F.*, p. 52).

Margaret (Margery) of Wycumbe 1281–1291 El. 9 Nov. 1281 (*Mon. Angl.*, IV, 506). Cess. by 21 May 1291 (PRO, C84/10/15A).

Isabel of Sonning (Sonnyngg, Sunnynge) **1291–1310** N. of Broomhall, petition for royal ass. 29 May 1311; cert. conf. eln by bp of Salisbury 3 June 1291 (PRO, E135/21/4). Occ. 3 Feb. 1298 (*Reg. Gandavo*, II, 568). Application for permission to res. 4 Apr. 1310 (ibid., 728). Cess. by 5 Apr. 1310 (PRO, C84/16/36). Cess., lic. to el. 8 Apr.1310 (*CPR 1307–13*, p. 223).

[**Matilda de Broghton** (Bergheton, Bor(o)ughton, Burghton) N. of Broomhall, citation for opposers of eln to appear on the next law day after Quasimodo Sunday [no year – between entries of 1302 and 1304 but may relate to 1310 unless Matilda had an earlier period of office] (*Reg. Gandavo*, I, 152–3). Royal ass. 10 Apr. 1310 (*CPR 1307–13*, p. 223; *Reg. Gandavo*, II, 729). Bp's commn to examine eln 13 Apr. 1310; cert. that there had been a disputed eln between Matilda and Clarice de Cotes. The nuns gave the bp the right of appt and he appts Clarice, dated 30 Apr. 1310 (ibid., 728–34; cf. *CPR 1307–13*, pp. 227–8). See below under 1317.]

Clarice de Cotes 1310–1317 N. of Broomhall, apptd by bp in place of Matilda, whose eln he had quashed 30 Apr. 1310 (*Reg. Gandavo*, II, 728–34). Temps. 22 May 1310 (*CPR 1307–13*, pp. 227–8; cf. PRO, C84/16/41). Mand. to install 31 May 1310 (*Reg. Gandavo*, II, 733–4).

Cess. by 16 Nov. 1317 (PRO, C84/19/16). Cess., lic. to el. 21 Nov. 1317 (*CPR 1317–21*, p. 52).

Matilda de Broghton (Boroughton, Burton) **1317–1326** Sacrist of Broomhall, royal ass. 11 Dec. 1317, temps. 7 Jan. 1318 (ibid., pp. 63, 71). Eln pres. to bp 9 Dec. 1317, conf. 23 Dec.1317 (*Reg. Martival*, I, 414–15; cf. PRO, C84/19/17). D., lic. to el. 15 Apr. 1326 (*CPR 1324–27*, p. 260).

Margery de Fouleston(e) 1326–1327 Sub-prs of Broomhall, eln quashed, but apptd by bp 8 May 1326 (*Reg. Martival*, I, 427–8; cf. PRO, C84/21/6). Temps. 9 May 1326 (*CPR 1324–27*, p. 265). D. by 15 Nov. 1327 (PRO, C84/21/43). D., lic. to el. 7 Dec. 1327 (*CPR 1327–30*, p. 193)

Gunnora (Gunnilda) of Bookham (Bokham) **1327–1349** Petition for royal ass. 18 Dec. 1327; royal lic. to give ass. 26 Dec. 1327; eln conf. 11 Jan. 1328 (PRO, SC1/37/166; cf. PRO, C84/21/45; *CPR 1327–30*, p. 198). Temps. 14 Jan. 1328 (*CPR 1327–30*, p. 208). D., lic. to el. 27 June 1349 (*CPR 1348–50*, p. 332).

Isabel de Hautford (Hartford) **1349–1357** N. of Broomhall, apptd by bp 1 Nov. 1349, no reason given for vacancy (Salisbury, Reg. Wyvil, II, f. 220v). Cess., lic. to el. 5 Sept. 1357 (*CPR 1354–58*, p. 602).

Alice de Falle Occ. 26 Nov. 1371 (*CCR 1368–74*, p. 260). Said to occ. 1358, 1363 (Willis, II, [addenda] p. 3, citing 'Mr Baker's collections');

The next recorded prs, **Eleanor**, occ. 1379 (Turner, 'Broomhall', p. 93); 30 Dec. 1392 (*Mon. Angl.*, IV, 507, also noted, with no source, in BL, Add. ms. 5829, f. 66v); June 1393 x June 1394 (PRO, E42/401); 21 Dec. 1396 (Lincoln, Ep. Reg., XII, f. 446v).

BUCKLAND (Soms), St John the Baptist (Minchin Buckland) f. *c.* 1166 (Aug. cans.); *c.*1180 (Sisters of the Order of St John of Jerusalem: Hospitallers) (*KH*); *c.* 1186 (Thompson).
   Lists in *VCH Soms*, II, 150; *Ctl. Buckland*, p. xxvii; *Heads*, I, 209 (preceptors are noted *VCH Soms*, II, 150; *Ctl. Buckland*, p. xxix; Thompson, *Women Religious*, p. 234).

Fina Said to be first prs., in office for 60 yrs, in 15th-cent. list in BL, Cotton ms. Nero E VI, f. 467v, not of much authority or precise accuracy (see *Heads*, I, 209).

Hawise Occ. 24 July 1279 (*Soms Pleas*, III, 205).

Eleanor de Actune Occ. 1280 (*Ctl. Buckland*, list, p. xxvii, no source).

Isabel la Louwe Occ. 15 July 1292 (Hugo, *Nunneries*, p. 33, citing quo warranto proceedings); 9 Oct. 1301 (ibid., pp. 34, 223, cf. *Reg. Droxford*, p. 294).

Isabel de Berkeleye Occ. 24 Sept. 1330 (Hugo, *Nunneries*, p. 44, citing PRO, CP40/283, m. 205d); 6 Feb. 1335, 3 Feb. 1337 (ibid., pp. 49–50, citing quo warranto proceedings).

Katherine (daughter of John de Erlegh) Occ. 1337 (ibid., p. 50, citing escheators' roll 28 Edward III, m. 71).

Mary Occ. 5 Aug. 1371 (ibid., p. 65, citing quo warranto proceedings).

The next recorded prs, **Alice**, occ. Easter 1389 (*YB 12 Richard II*, p. 151); 28 Apr. 1405 (*CPR 1405–08*, p. 8).

BUNGAY (Suffolk), St Mary and Holy Cross f. 1183. (1175 x 76, nuns installed 1183 – Thompson) (Benedictine priory)
   Lists in *VCH Suffolk*, II, 82; *Heads*, I, 209; Thompson, *Women Religious*, p. 235 (to 1270).

Mary of Huntingfield (Huntingefeud) Occ. early 13th cent. (BL, Topham Cht. no. 13). Seal (*BM Seals*, no. 2770).

A. Occ. *c.*1212 x 1221 (Suffolk RO, Ipswich, HD1538/345/1/15), possibly the same as Alice below.

Alice Occ. Oct. 1227 x Oct. 1228 (*Suffolk F. (Rye)*, p. 25).

Sarah de Straforde Occ. Oct. 1268 x Oct. 1269 (*Suffolk F. (Rye)*, p. 68); 7 Jan. 1269 (Suffolk RO, Ipswich, HD1538/345/1/23).

[**Mary** Occ. 1270 (BL, Add. ms. 19111, f. 160r, list – no source).]

Joan Occ. Trin.Term 1297 (*Coram Rege Roll*, pp. 93, 173; PRO, CP40/119, m. 94d); Trin. 1298 (PRO, KB27/155, mm. 7d, 55d); 9 May 1303 (*CPR 1301–07*, p.191). Possibly the prs Joan who occ. n.d. (Suffolk RO, Ipswich, HD1538/345/1/22). Seal matrix *c.* 1300 (C.H. Blair, 'Some medieval seal matrices' in *Antiquaries Journal*, 4 (1924), 243–4 & pl. no. 2; *Arch. J.*, XCIII (1936), pp. 35–6, no. 70; *BM Seals*, no. 2771).

Elizabeth Folioth 1306– N. of Bungay, eln conf. 1 Oct. 1306, no reason given for vacancy (Norwich, Reg/1/1, f. 211r).

Margery de Thebrygge 1309– N. of Bungay, apptd by bp 21 Mar. 1309, no reason given for vacancy (ibid., f. 31v). Occ. 28 Sept. 1323 (Suffolk RO, Ipswich, HD1538/345/1/28).

Mary de Castello –1335 D. by 21 Oct. 1335 (Norwich, Reg/1/2, f. 76v)

Katharine Fastolf 1335– N. of Bungay, eln conf. 21 Oct. 1335 (ibid.).

Ellen de Tytelesworth (Teclesworth) **1349–1380** N. of Bungay, eln quashed but apptd by bp 13 June 1349, no reason given for vacancy (*Reg. Bateman*, I, no. 605). Occ. 1359 (BL, Add. Cht. 37406); 1377 (Suffolk RO, Ipswich, HD1538/345/2/4). Res. by 26 Sept. 1380 (Norwich, Reg/3/6, f. 73r).

BURNHAM (Bucks), St Mary f. 1266 (Augustinian abbey)

Lists in *VCH Bucks*, I, 384; Thompson, *Women Religious*, p. 235 (to 1274).

Margery of Aston (Eston) **1266–1274** Sub-prs of Goring, eln conf. 20 June 1266 (*Reg. R. Gravesend*, pp. 240–1, 341). Res. by 22 Apr. 1274 (ibid., p. 251).

Matilda of Dorchester (Dorkecestr') **1274** Eln conf. 22 Apr. 1274 (ibid.). D. by 23 Sept. 1274 (ibid., p. 252).

Joan of Ridware (Redeware, Rideware) **1274–1314** Prs of Burnham, eln conf. 23 Sept. 1274 (ibid., pp. 252, 344). D. by 18 Oct. 1314 (Lincoln, Ep. Reg., II, f. 186v).

Idonea of Audley (Audele, Daudelegh(e)) **1314–1324** N. of Burnham, eln quashed but apptd by bp 18 Oct. 1314 (ibid.). House mentioned as void 6 June 1324 (*CCR 1323–27*, p. 113). Mon. stone (*Earliest English Brasses*, p. 182 & fig. 144). D. by 8 July 1324 (Lincoln, Ep. Reg., IV, f. 331r).

Joan de Somervill 1324– N. of Burnham, eln quashed but apptd by bp 8 July 1324 (ibid.).

Margery de Louches 1335– Commn to examine eln 28 Jan. 1335; same day lic. gtd that if eln conf. she may seek bl. from any Catholic bp (Lincoln, Ep. Reg., V, ff. 489v–490r). Bl. 22 Feb. 1335 (Salisbury, Reg. Wyvil II, f. 35v). Occ. 15 Nov. 1337 (*CPR 1334–38*, p. 559); 8 Mar. 1338 (*YB 18 Edward III*, p. 257, n. 5).

Joan of Dorney (Dorneye) **1340–1344** N. of Burnham, eln conf. 18 Feb. 1340, vacant by d. (*sic*) of Joan (*sic*) de Louches (Lincoln, Ep. Reg., IV, f. 355r). Lic. to receive bl. from Benedict, bp. *Cardicensis* 18 Feb. 1340 (Lincoln, Ep. Reg., V, f. 576r). **Margery de Louches**, former abbs., sent to Goring priory for the peace and quiet of the abbey, 11 Mar. 1340 (ibid., f. 576v). Conclusion of the dispute between Joan of Dorney, n. of Burham, and Margery de Louches, abbs of Burnham over the cure and rule of the monastery 1 May 1344. Joan renounced all rights and provision made for her (Lincoln, Ep. Reg.,VIIB, ff. 75v–76r).

Margery de Louches Occ. 8 Aug. 1350, 8 Jan. 1351 (Lambeth, Reg. Islip, ff. 22v, 105r).

Agnes Frankelyn 1367–1393 N. of Burnham, commn to cite any opposers to eln, no reason given for vacancy 20 Sept. 1367; eln conf. 9 Oct. 1367, certificate of commissary dated 11 Oct. 1367 (Lincoln, Ep. Reg., X, ff. 413r–414r). Res. accepted 8 Sept. 1393 (Lincoln, Ep. Reg., XI, f. 409r).

CAMBRIDGE, St Mary and St Radegund f. *c.* 1133 x 8 (*KH*); *c.* 1147 x 1154 (Thompson) (Benedictine priory)

Lists in *VCH Cambs*, II, 219; Gray, *St Radegund*, pp. 30–1, *Heads*, I, 209; Thompson, *Women Religious*, p. 235 (to 1274).

Lettice Occ. 1198 x *c.* 1202 (Cambridge, St John's Coll., ms. D.98.49); Oct. 1217 x Oct. 1218 (*Norfolk F. (Rye)*, p. 32); 29 Apr. 1229 (PRO, Cambs F., CP25/1/24/13, no. 4).

Millicent Occ. 27 Oct. 1247, 18 Nov. 1249 (PRO, Cambs F., CP25/1/24/22, nos. 7, 9; ibid. 24/25, no. 12); Oct. 1253 x Oct. 1254 (*Norfolk F. (Rye)*, p. 87).

Dera Occ. 6 Apr. 1258 (Cambridge, Jesus Coll., St Michael deeds Caryl W.2(a); *St Radegund*, no. 231a); n.d. (*St Radegund*, nos. 230g, 382).

Agnes (le) Burgulun (Burgeylun) Occ. n.d. (?1274 x 1275, dated by mayoralty) (ibid., no. 219f; cf. *VCH Cambs*, III, 39); n.d. (late 13th cent.) (*temp.* Bartholomew Goggyng, mayor of Cambridge) (*St Radegund*, no. 224).

Amice of Driffield Occ. late 13th cent. (*temp.* Bartholomew Goggyng, mayor of Cambridge) (ibid., no. 98).

Constance Occ. late 13th cent. (pal.) (Cambridge, Jesus Coll., St Andrew the Great deeds, Caryl F.3; *St Radegund*, no. 123).

[**Alice le Chamberlain** D. of Sir Walter le Chamberlain, said to occ. *c.* 1278 (Clay, *Hist. of Landbeach*, p. 15, but no precise ref.).]

Ellen Occ. 5 July 1285 (Cambridge, Jesus Coll., All Saints in the Jewry deeds, Caryl D.14(b); *St Radegund*, no. 96); 1286 (PRO, Just.1/86, mm. 12, 24d, 32, 36d); Easter 1288 (PRO, CP40/72, m. 94d); 12 Nov. 1296 (Cambridge, Jesus Coll., Cambridge and Barnwell Fields deeds, Caryl A.10(a)); 1299 (*St Radegund*, no. 167).

Christi(a)na of Braybrooke (Braybrok) Occ. Trin. 1309 (PRO, CP40/178, m. 298d); Mich. 1310 (PRO, CP40/183, attorneys m. 9); 1311 (Gray, list, p. 30, but without source).

Cecily of Cressingham Occ. 24 Sept. 1315 (Cambridge, Jesus Coll., All Saints by the Castle deeds, Caryl O.7; *St Radegund*, no. 272b); 24 June, 20 Dec. 1316 (Cambridge, Jesus Coll., St Michael deeds, Caryl A.33, W.1(f); *St Radegund*, nos. 238, 230e).

Mabel Martin Occ. 4 June 1325 (PRO, Just.1/98, mm. 5d, 10d); 1 Apr. 1330 (Cambridge, Jesus Coll., St Radegund deeds, Caryl C.15; *St Radegund*, no. 58); 25 June 1330 (Cambridge, Jesus Coll., Cambridge and Barnwell Fields deeds, Caryl Q.36; *St Radegund*, no. 346); 7 Apr. 1331 (Cambridge, Jesus Coll., Trippelowe's Benefaction 2, Caryl B.22(b); *St Radegund*, no. 49b); 7 Nov. 1332 (Cambridge, Jesus Coll., St Radegund deeds, Caryl B.17(b); *St Radegund*, no. 44b).

Alice Occ. 24 Nov. 1347 (Cambridge, Jesus Coll., Trippelowe's Benefaction 2, Caryl B.16(b); *St Radegund*, no. 43b).

Eve Wasteneys Occ. 26 Aug. 1356 (Cambridge, Jesus Coll., St Radegund deeds, Caryl C.16(a–b); *St Radegund*, nos. 59a–b). ? Prs.of Swaffham in 1373 (q.v.).

Margaret Clavyle (Clavile) –1378 Occ. 9 Apr., 21 Nov. 1363 (Cambridge, Jesus Coll., St Andrew the Less deeds, Caryl P.24–5; *St Radegund*, nos. 294, 296). Commn to receive res. 29 Jan 1378; res. adm. 1 Feb. 1378 (Ely, G/1/2, ff. 24v–25r). Lic. to el. 6 Feb. 1378 (ibid., f. 25r).

CAMPSEY ASH (Suffolk), St Mary f. *c.* 1195 (Augustinian priory)

Lists in *VCH Suffolk*, II, 115; *Heads*, I, 209–10; Thompson, *Women Religious*, p. 235 (to 1256)

Joan de Valognes Sister of founder and first prs. Occ. 18 Oct. 1211 (*Norfolk F. 1201–15*, no. 259); Oct. 1220 x Oct. 1221; Oct. 1228 x Oct. 1229; Oct. 1231 x Oct. 1232 (*Suffolk F. (Rye)*), pp. 21, 29, 32).

Agnes de Valognes Sister of Joan, occ. Mich. term 1232 (*CRR*, XIV, no. 2248); Oct. 1234 x

Oct. 1235 (*Suffolk F. (Rye)*, p. 33); Easter term 1236 (*CRR*, XV, no. 1805); 3 Nov. 1240, Trin. 1242 (*Essex F.*, I, 137, 141–2). Mentd 1248 as former prs (PRO, Just.1/231, m. 28).

Basilia Occ. 20 Jan. 1254, 20 Oct. 1256 (*Lincs F.*, II, 106, 122); Oct. 1257 x Oct. 1258 (*Suffolk F. (Rye)*, p. 60).

Alice of Boltby (Boltebi) Occ. 3 Nov. 1280 (PRO, CP40/41, m. 50); Nov. 1296 x Nov. 1297 (PRO, E210/8476).

Margery Occ. 15 Sept. 1316 (BL, Harl. Cht. 45 C 35).[1]

Mary of Wingfield (Wyngefeld) 1334– N. of Campsey Ash, commn to examine eln 22 Apr. 1334; eln quashed but apptd by bp 7 May 1334, no reason given for vacancy (Norwich, Reg/1/2, f. 65r). Occ. n.d. (Bodl., Norfolk Cht. 46).

Alice (Alesia) Occ. 6 Feb. 1352 (PRO, DL27/18).

Mary of Felton –1394 Occ. 23 and 25 Feb. 1365 (BL, Harl. ms. 3697, f. 151v); June 1380 x June 1381 (PRO, E179/45/5B, m. 2); 2 Nov. 1389 (Norwich, Reg/3/6, f. 349r). D. by 28 Sept. 1394 (ibid., f. 195v).

CANNINGTON (Soms), St Mary f. *c.* 1138 (KH); ? *c.* 1129 x *c.* 1153 (Thompson) (Benedictine priory)

List in *VCH Soms*, II, 111.

Commn to act in cause against violators of ecclesiastical liberties in the priory 13 July 1316 (*Reg. Droxford*, p. 129).

Emma of Bittiscombe (Bytelscomb) –1317 Commn apptd 24 Apr. 1317 to inquire into disorders following her res. (ibid., p. 126).

Matilda of Morton 1317 Eln pres. to bp 4 May 1317 (*Reg. Droxford*, pp. 6–7); commn to examine eln 28 May 1317 (ibid., p. 130); bp's commissaries quash eln 18 June 1317 (ibid., pp. 6–7); commn to acc. res. of prs-el. 15 Aug. 1317 (ibid., p. 167).

Joan de Bere 1317 Apptd by bp's commissaries 18 June 1317 (ibid., pp. 6–7). In July and Aug. further disorders led on 15 Aug. 1317 to commn to acc. both res. and to nominate a nun as prs (ibid., p. 167). See Hugo, *Nunneries*, pp. 15–21.

Matilda of Morton 1317–1334 Coll. by bp by lapse 5 Aug. 1317 (ibid., pp. 6–7). Res. by 12 Jan. 1334; lic. to el. (*Reg. R. Shrewsbury*, I, no. 636).

Willelma de Blachyngdon –1336 D. 4 May 1336 (*Reg. R. Shrewsbury*, I, no. 1071; Hugo, *Nunneries*, pp. 24–5).

Joan de Beare 1336– N. of Cannington, el. 17 May 1336 and eln conf. 3 June 1336 (*Reg. R. Shrewsbury*, I, no. 1071; Hugo, *Nunneries*, pp. 25–8).

Avice (de) Reigners (Reyner) 1343–1395 Eln conf. and mand. to install 12 Aug. 1343, no reason given for vacancy; further mand. to install 14 Sept., since archdn or his official could not be found (*Reg. R. Shrewsbury*, II, no. 1733). D., lic. to el. 28 Mar 1395 (*CPR 1391–96*, p. 562).

CANONSLEIGH (Devon), St Mary, St John the Evangelist and St Etheldreda
Augustinian Abbey refounded 1284, prev. priory of Aug. canons (q.v.)

List in *Ctl. Canonsleigh*, p. 117.

Matilda la Tablere (le Tablers) 1284– First abbs., prof. obed. 28 Oct. 1284 (*Reg. Quivil*, p. 340). Occ. in *Ctl. Canonsleigh* from 6 Dec. 1292 to 9 Oct. 1306 (nos. 226, 59).

Petronilla de Clare Occ. several times in *Ctl. Canonsleigh*, from 4 Apr. 1309 to 4 Aug. 1314 (nos. 236, 277); 1315 (PRO, E40/3601); 1318 (*Reg. Stapeldon*, p. 272). Joan de Radyngtone, canoness of Canonsleigh, apptd coadjutor for her 12 Jan. 1320 (ibid., p. 96).

---

[1] BL, Add. ms. 19096 (Davy's Suffolk collections), f. 66v gives Margery as occ. 11 Edward II (July 1317 x July 1318), but without source.

Margaret Aunger (Aucher) **1320–1345** Bl. 24 Aug. 1320 (ibid., p. 199). D. by 8 Oct. 1345, when the prs and canonesses transferred right of appt to bp (*Reg. Grandisson*, II, 998–9).

Juliana Lampre(y) 1345– Canoness of Canonsleigh, bp chose her 10 Oct.; letter asking her to consent 13 Oct.; consent 14 Oct.; letter to conv. to obey 20 Oct. 1345; bl. and prof. obed. 21 Dec. 1345; mand. to induct 4 Jan. 1346; certificate of induction 5 Jan. 1346 (ibid., 999–1002).

Lucy Warre 1370–1410[2] Commn to examine eln 7 June 1370, no reason given for vacancy; commn to bp of Hereford to bl. 8 June 1370 (*Reg. Brantingham*, II, 140). D. 11 Oct. 1410 (*Reg. Stafford*, p. 49).

CANTERBURY(Kent), **Holy Sepulchre** f. *c.* 1100 (*KH*); ? –1087 (Thompson)
(Benedictine priory)
  Lists in *VCH Kent*, II, 143; *Heads*, I, 210; Thompson, *Women Religious*, p. 236 (to 1280).

Juliana –1258 Occ. ? 1227 (*Mon. Angl.*, IV, 413, no source given); 27 Apr. 1236, 3 Feb. 1244 (*Kent F.*, pp. 132, 181); 1255 (BL, Harl. Cht. 75 F 60). D. 1258 (*Gervase*, II, 208).

Lettice 1258– Succ. 1258 (ibid.).

Benedicta of Sandwich Occ. n.d. (before 1275) (Canterbury D. & C., SVSB.III/74); 1272 x 1280 (BL, Harl. Cht. 76 G 34; *Mon. Angl.*, IV, 414, dated by Thompson); (B.) 29 Dec. 1293 (Canterbury D. & C., Ch. Ant. C.92).

Commn to appt coadjutors for unnamed prs 20 Apr. 1284 (*Reg. Peckham*, II, 708–9). Lic. to el. a new prs, no reason given for vacancy 20 Dec. 1295 (*Reg. Winchelsey*, I, 57).

Margery de Brunnesford Occ. Nov. 1296 x Nov. 1297 (PRO, E210/8478).

Sarah de Pecham 1323/4–1349 Commn to examine eln 17 Dec. 1323; commn to install 17 Feb. 1324; installed 18 Feb. 1324 (Lambeth, Reg. Reynolds, f. 131v). D. by 12 June 1349 (*Canterbury Sede Vacante Institutions*, p. 28).

Margaret Terry 1349–1356 El. on d. of Sarah; eln quashed as she was not yet professed but later conf. (Margery) as prs and made prof. obed. 12 June 1349 (ibid.). D. by 31 Dec. 1356 when lic. to el. gtd (Lambeth, Reg. Islip, f. 130r).

Cecily (de) Tonford (Tunford) **1357–1366** Sub-prs of Holy Sepulchre, eln conf. by commissaries, and installed 14 Jan. 1357 (ibid., f. 130v). Res. by 19 Feb. 1366 (ibid., f. 213r).

Joan (de) Chiryton (Chirynton) **1366–1368** Right of appt transferred to archbp 19 Feb. 1366. N. of Holy Sepulchre, apptd by commissary 3 Mar. 1366 and installed. Cert. to archbp dated 11 Mar. 1366 (ibid.). Res. 3 Mar. 1368 (*Reg. Langham*, pp. 232–3).

Agnes Broman (Bourghman) **1368–1369** N. of Holy Sepulchre, apptd by archbp 3 Mar. 1368 (ibid.). D. by 24 July 1369 (Lambeth, Reg. Whittlesey, f. 15r–v).

Alice Guston 1369–1376 N. of Holy Sepulchre, apptd by vicar-general 24 July 1369 (ibid.). Dep. by archbp 14 Apr. 1376 (Lambeth, Reg. Sudbury, f. 13r).

Margery Child 1376– N. of Holy Sepulchre, apptd 14 Apr. 1376 (ibid.). Occ. 16 July 1377 (ibid., f. 124v).

The next recorded prs, **Joan Whitfelde**, d. by 15 Dec. 1427 (*Reg. Chichele*, I, 108).

CUSTODIANS

John Flemyng 1358– Rector of Whitstable, apptd *custos* 30 Oct. 1358 (Lambeth, Reg. Islip, f. 144r); apptd for life 9 July 1359 (ibid., ff. 149v–150r).

Robert Flemyngg 1366– Rector of Harbledown, apptd 27 Feb. 1366 (ibid., f. 213r).

---

[2] Oliver, p. 225 states that Christina Edewis was el. 1371 but this is likely to be an error; Christina Edewik, prs of Canonsleigh petitioned the patron of the house for lic. to el. 1471 (*Ctl. Canonsleigh*, app. II, p. 114, no. D).

CARROW, *see* **NORWICH, ST MARY**

CASTLE HEDINGHAM (Essex), Holy Cross, St Mary, and St James f. -1191
(Benedictine priory)

    Lists in *VCH Essex*, II, 123; *Heads*, I, 210; Thompson, *Women Religious*, p. 236 (to mid-13th cent.).

Agnes 2nd prs, occ. *c.* 1230 (BL, Egerton ms. 2849 in bede roll of first prs Lucy). Possibly the same as prs who occ. Easter 1243, 27 Jan. 1248 (*Essex F.*, I, 145, 161).

Christiana Occ. n.d., 12th-13th cents. (BL, Cotton ms. Claudius D XI, f. 171r).

Juliana de Chepford Occ. n.d., ? 13th cent. (BL, Cotton ms. Nero E VI, f. 401r–v).

Dyamanda Mentd as former prs Trin. 1280 as grantor of a corrody in the case (PRO, CP40/34, m. 40d).

Amice Occ. Trin. 1280 (ibid.).

Joan de Clovill 1331– Apptd 13 Apr. 1331, no reason given for vacancy (*Reg. S. Gravesend*, p. 250).

Agnes Occ. 17 July 1340 (BL, Harl. Cht. 51 D 6).

Joan Occ. 20 Apr. 1353 (*CPL*, III, 507).

Agnes Occ. 1381 (McHardy, *Church in London*, no. 254).

CATESBY (Northants), St Mary and St Edmund (and ? St Thomas) f. *c.* 1175 (*KH*); *c.* 1150 x 1176 (Thompson) (Cistercian priory)

    Lists in *VCH Northants*, II, 125; Thompson, *Women Religious*, p. 236 (to 1276).

Amice Occ. 13 Oct. 1226 (PRO, Notts F., CP25/1/182/4, no. 88); prob. (A.) n.d. (*temp.* Bp Hugh II of Lincoln, d. 1235, after 1228) (PRO, E326/10338).

[**Math'** Sub-prs of Catesby, eln quashed by bp of Lincoln, no reason given for vacancy June 1244 x June 1245 (*Reg. Grosseteste*, p. 222).]

Margery of Abingdon (Abindon) N. of Catesby, apptd by bp of Lincoln June 1244 x June 1245 (ibid.). Sister of Edmund of Abingdon *alias* Rich, archbp of Canterbury (*Mon. Angl.*, IV, 635–6).[3] Occ. 10 May 1252 (PRO, E315/46/135); 14 Jan. 1253 (PRO, Northants F. CP25/1/173/38, nos. 611, 614); 3 Apr. 1253, sister of St Edmund, given exemption for life from suit of court on account of debility (*CPR 1247–58*, p. 186). D. 1257 (*MPCM*, V, 621), so presumably res. if following entry is correct.

Felicia –1276 Occ. 26 Apr. 1254 (PRO, Northants F., CP25/1/173/41, no. 688); 28 Nov. 1259 to 27 Oct. 1274 (PRO, Northants F., CP25/1/174/43, no. 729; CP25/1/174/51, no. 20). D. by 13 Sept. 1276 (*Reg. R. Gravesend*, p. 129).

Amabilia (Mabel) 1276–1285 Sub-prs of Catesby, eln conf. 13 Sept. 1276 (ibid., pp. 129, 304–5). Res. on 18 Jan. 1285 (*Reg. Sutton*, II, 42–3).

Isolda (Isoda) **Hasteng'** 1285–1291 Eln quashed but apptd by bp of Lincoln 21 Jan. 1285 (ibid.). Res. by 16 Mar. 1291 (ibid., 86–7).

Biblisia (Bibles) 1291–1292 Sub-prs of Catesby, el quashed but apptd by bp 16 Mar. 1291 (ibid.). D. by 30 Mar. 1292 (ibid., 99).

Joan of Northampton (Norhamt') 1292–1311 Cellaress of Catesby, eln pres. to bp of Lincoln 30 Mar. 1292; eln quashed but apptd by bp 31 Mar. 1292 (ibid.). D. by 1 Mar. 1311 (Lincoln, Ep. Reg. II, f. 121r).

Comm. to official of archdn of Northampton to examine eln of unnamed prs 22 Feb. 1311

---

[3] *MPCM*, V, 642 states that Alice, sister of St Edmund of Abingdon, also became prs. Presumably this is a mistake for Margery (see Thompson, p. 236).

(Lincoln, Ep. Reg., III, f. 207v). Similar comm. to Bp's Official 24 Feb. 1311, the former commn being revoked (ibid.).

Joan of Ludham (Loudham) **1311–1338** N. of Catesby, eln quashed but apptd by bp 1 Mar. 1311 (Lincoln, Ep. Reg., II, f. 121r). Res. by 23 Oct. 1338 (Lincoln, Ep. Reg., IV, f. 224r).

Alice of Rolleston 1338–1344 N. of Catesby, eln conf. 23 Oct 1338 (ibid.). D. by 3 Nov. 1344 (Lincoln, Ep. Reg., VI, f. 59v).

Katherine de Boyden 1344–1349 N. of Catesby, commn to examine eln 3 Nov. 1344 and on same day eln quashed and apptd by bp (ibid.). D. by 22 June 1349 (Lincoln, Ep. Reg., IX, f. 190v).

Orabilis (Orabilia) of Raunds (Raundes) **1349–1361** N. of Catesby, eln quashed but apptd by bp 22 June 1349 (ibid.). D. by 21 Aug. 1361 (ibid., f. 235r).

Joan Fabian *alias* **of Banbury** (Banneberi, Bannebury, Bauneby) **1361–1370** N. of Catesby, eln quashed but apptd by bp 21 Aug. 1361 (ibid.). D. by 28 June 1370 (Lincoln, Ep. Reg., X, f. 181r).

Joan (of) Ashby (Assheby, Ayscheby, Hasscheby) **1370–** Eln quashed but apptd by bp 28 June 1370 (ibid.). Occ. June 1379 x June 1380 (PRO, E326/11,496); June 1389 x June 1390 (PRO, E326/ 11,393); 1394 (PRO, E326/4598); 29 Sept. 1401 (PRO, E326/848).

The next recorded prs, **Elizabeth Swynford**, commn to examine eln, no reason given for vacancy, 27 Feb. 1405 (Lincoln, Ep. Reg., XIII, f. 244v).

PRIORS

Hugh 1266–1280 Adm. master, no reason given for vacancy 10 Dec. 1266 (*Reg. R. Gravesend*, pp. 108, 296–7). D. *c*. Sept./Oct. 1280 (*Reg. Sutton*, II, 5).

John of Catesby 1280– Can. of Catesby, eln quashed but apptd by bp *c*. Sept./Oct. 1280 on d. of Hugh (ibid.).

Robert of Wardon Can. of Canons Ashby, master of Catesby, had abandoned his duties and he was ordered to resume them 18 Oct. 1293 (ibid., IV, 123–4). ? the same as below.

Robert of Wardington 1294 Can. of Canons Ashby, apptd as master 20 Mar. 1294, no reason given for vacancy (ibid., IV, 179); El. pr. of Canons Ashby Aug. 1294 (q.v.)

William of Greatworth (Gruttewurth) **1294–** Can. of Catesby, adm. 23 Aug. 1294 until further notice, no reason given for vacancy (ibid., V, 23).

Roger of Daventry 1297– Can. of Catesby, apptd 22 Sept. 1297, no reason given for vacancy (ibid., VI, 31).

Richard of Staverton 1316– Can. of Catesby, apptd master 20 Aug. 1316, no reason given for vacancy (Lincoln, Ep. Reg., III, f. 351r).

Roger Clement Former master, bur. in the conventual church, indulgence for, issued 30 July 1319 (ibid., f. 421v).

Thomas of Greatworth (Grutteworth) **1320–** Can. of Catesby, apptd master by the Official *sede vacante* 25 Mar. 1320, no reason given for vacancy (Lincoln, Ep. Reg., II, f. 363r).

John of Yaxley (Jakesle) Occ. as master 30 June 1323 (Lincoln, Ep. Reg., V, f. 344v).

Thomas of Hellidon (Heliden) **1328–** Can. of Kenilworth, apptd as *custos* for 3 years 16 June 1328 (ibid., f. 412v).

Robert 1338– Rector of Stainby, apptd during pleasure 22 Dec. 1338, no reason given for vacancy (ibid., f. 566r).

Edmund of Watford Commn to hear account of Edmund, former master, 15 Mar. 1339 (ibid., f. 568v).

Roger of Woodhouse (Wodehous) **1339–** Rector of Harpole, apptd during pleasure 5 Apr. 1339, no reason given for vacancy (ibid., ff. 569v–570r).

John of Aylesbury (Aillesbury) **1349–** Vicar of Norton by Daventry, apptd 4 Jan. 1349, no reason given for vacancy (Lincoln, Ep. Reg., IX, f. 20r).

William Houles 1370– Can. of Catesby, apptd as *yconomus* during pleasure of bp of Lincoln and prs of Catesby 19 Apr. 1370 (Lincoln, Ep. Reg. X, f. 180r).

CHATTERIS (Cambs), St Mary (and All Saints) f. 1006 x 1016 (Benedictine abbey)

List in *VCH Cambs*, II, 222; *Ctl. Chatteris*, pp. 391–414; *Heads*, I, 210. I am most grateful to Dr Breay for making her notes on abbesses of Chatteris available to me in advance of the publication of her edition. With very few dated documents it is difficult to establish the precise sequence of abbesses.

Albreda Occ. n.d. (late 12th-early 13th cents.) (BL, Cotton ms. Julius A I, f. 137r: *Ctl.* no. 169).

I. *or* J. Occ. before 14 June 1216 (ibid., f. 135v: *Ctl.* no. 164).

Agnes Occ. *c.* 1200 x 1233 (Cambridge, St John's College, D.25.22: *Ctl.* no. 281); n.d. (late 12th-early 13th cents.) (BL, Cotton ms. Julius A I, f. 127r: *Ctl.* no. 146).

A. of Rouen Occ. n.d. (first half of 13th cent.) (ibid., f. 103r: *Ctl.* no. 93). Could be Albreda or Agnes.

Mabel de Bancis Occ. 13th cent., before *c.* 29 Oct. 1247 (BL, Cotton ms. Julius A I, f. 124r: *Ctl.* no. 139); similarly n.d., 13th cent., before 1265 (ibid., ff. 97v, 121r, 126r, 160r, 161r: *Ctl.* nos. 74, 132, 144, 226, 228).

Mary de Sancto Claro predecessor of Amice, occ. Whitsun 1259 (BL, Harl. ms. 3697, f. 229v); n.d. [13th cent. x 28 Sept. 1265] (BL, Cotton ms. Julius A I, ff. 89r, 95v, 106r, 117v, 124v, 126v, 162r: *Ctl.* nos. 51, 69, 100, 123, 141, 145, 231). See M. D. Legge, *Anglo-Norman Literature and its background* (Oxford, 1963), p. 264.

Emma of Somersham (Someresham) Occ. Mich. 1265 (BL, Cotton ms. Julius A I, f. 134v: *Ctl.* no. 163); 8 July 1268 (ibid., f. 141r: *Ctl.* no. 178; PRO, Herts F., CP25/1/85/30, no. 594, cf. *Colchester Leger Book*, p. 116).

Amice Occ. 16 Nov. 1275 (BL, Cotton ms. Julius A I, f. 118r: *Ctl.* no. 124); 1268 x 1280 (ibid., ff. 106r, 115r: *Ctl.* nos. 101, 119).

Agnes of Ely Occ. n.d., shortly before 17 Jan. 1280 (ibid., f. 138v: *Ctl.* no. 172); 1275 x 1290 (ibid., f. 115v: *Ctl.* no. 120); 1275 x 1293 (ibid., f. 140r: *Ctl.* no. 176).

Agnes of Burwell Occ. 14 May 1293 (Cambridge, Trinity College, Foxton manorial court rolls 2, m. 2).

Mand. to examine eln of prs of Chatteris as abb. (no names, no reason given for vacancy) n.d. [*c.* July 1298] (*Reg. Winchelsey*, I, 262–3), possibly Amice of Cambridge.

Amice of Cambridge Occ. shortly after 29 Sept. 1300, *c.* 1298 x 1306 (BL, Cotton ms. Julius A I, ff. 157r, 86r, 93v, 115r: *Ctl.* nos. 219, 38, 63, 119).

Mary of Shouldham Occ. 28 Mar. 1306, shortly after 29 Sept. 1317 (BL, Cotton ms. Julius A I, ff. 161v, 159v: *Ctl.* nos. 230, 225); also n.d. (ibid., ff. 94v, 96v, 161r: *Ctl.* nos. 66, 71, 229).

Batill' de Woveton Only known occ. n.d. (BL, Cotton ms. Julius A I, f. 171v: *Ctl.* no. 254). Her position in the sequence of abbesses is uncertain. She may have occ. 1329 x 1347 or 1347 x 1359 (*Ctl.*).

Alice of Shropham –1347 Occ. Mich. 1337 (PRO, CP40/312, m. 288); n.d. [1331 x 1347] (BL, Cotton ms. Julius A I, f. 148r: *Ctl.* no. 194). Res. by 13 Oct. 1347 (Ely, G/1/1, part 2, ff. 51r–52r). As a n. of Chatteris gtd papal indult to choose a confessor 29 Jan. 1355 (*CPL*, III, 553).

Matilda Bernard 1347– N. of Chatteris, el. 13 Oct. 1347, eln conf. 4th law day after St Luke (18 Oct.) (Ely, G/1/1, part 2, ff. 51r–52r).

Margaret Hotot Occ. 30 Sept. x 5 Dec. 1368 (BL, Cotton ms. Julius A I, f. 147v: *Ctl.* no. 192); 26 July 1373 (Lambeth, Reg. Whittlesey, f. 152v); 1379 (PRO, E179/23/1, m. 3; *East Anglian*, new ser., XIII (1909–10), 121).

Agnes Ashfield Occ. 21 July 1398 x 8 June 1413 (BL, Cotton ms. Julius A I, f. 149r: *Ctl.* no.

198); Sept. 1415 (ibid., f. 175r: *Ctl.* no. 259); shortly after 29 Sept. 1425 (ibid., f. 157v: *Ctl.* no. 220); 9 May 1428 (ibid., f. 150v: *Ctl.* no. 203); 20 July 1427 (ibid., f. 185r: *Ctl.* no. 276). D. before Apr. 1456 when prayers requested for her soul and that of Henry Buckworth, vicar of Chatteris, by whose industry and expense the cartulary was compiled (ibid., f. 72v: *Ctl.* no.1).

CHESHUNT (Herts), St Mary f. -1183 (KH); -1165 x 1166 (Thompson) (Benedictine priory)
Lists in *VCH Herts*, IV, 428; Thompson, *Women Religious*, pp. 236–7 (to 1257).
Clemencia Occ. ?1185 x 1193 (*Waltham Chts.*, no. 340; Thompson, p. 236)
Alice Occ. 1202 x 1223 (*Waltham Chts.* no. 346; *HMC 9th Rept.* App. I, 26a; Thompson, p. 236).
Isabel Occ. 1236 x 1240 (PRO, DL25/20; *Mon. Angl.*, IV, 329, no. ii).
Cassandra Occ. 30 Sept. 1250 (PRO, Norfolk F. CP25/1/157/75, no. 1037).
Denise Occ. Oct. 1256 x Oct. 1257 (*London & Middlesex. F.*, I, p. 37); Oct. 1257 x Oct. 1258 (*Surrey F.*, p. 37); n.d. (PRO, E326/11596).
Agnes Mentioned 20 Feb. 1298 as predecessor of Mary (*CPR 1292–1301*, p. 376).
Mary Occ. 20 Feb. 1298 (ibid.).
Ellen -1309 Res. by 27 Apr. 1309 (*Reg. Baldock*, p. 106).
[Emma of Hadstock (Haddestoke) N. of Cheshunt, eln quashed and new lic. to el. issued 27 Apr. 1309 (ibid., pp. 106–7).]
Alice de Sumery (Someri) Occ. 24 Aug. 1311 (PRO, C146/2433); 28 May 1315 (*CPR 1313–17*, p. 292).
Tiphania Chaumberleyn -1400/1 Occ. 30 May 1352 (*CPL*, III, 472). D. n.d. [between entries Nov. 1400 x Sept. 1401] (London, Reg. Braybrooke, f. 354v).

CHESTER, St Mary f. 1066; ref. *c.* 1140 (*KH*); *c.* 1141 x 1153 (Thompson) (Benedictine priory)
List in *VCH Cheshire*, III, 150; Thompson, *Women Religious*, p. 237 (to 1283); *Church in Chester 1300–1540*, pp. 179–80.
Alice Occ. 1202 x 1229 (BL, Harl. ms. 2063, f. 61r; *Cheshire Sheaf*, XLVI, 15, 22).
Lic to el. 22 June 1246, no reason given for vacancy, with power to John de Grey, justiciar of Chester, to give royal ass. to save the nuns labour and expense (*CPR 1232–47*, p. 482).
Alice of Stockport -1253 D. 1253 (PRO, SC1/11/58; Wood, *Letters of . . . Royal Ladies*, I, 34–6).
Alice de la Haye 1253–1283 Letter from nuns to Queen Eleanor asking for conf. of eln of Alice de la Haye [10 x 20 Aug. 1253] (PRO, SC1/11/58). Sub-prs of Chester, royal ass. 20 Aug. 1253, writ *de intendendo* 9 Sept. 1253 (*CPR 1247–58*, pp. 221–2). Res. by 20 Oct. 1283 (PRO, C84/8/16). Cess., lic. to el. 28 Oct. 1283 (*CPR 1281–92*, p. 84).
Alice de Pierrepont Occ. Nov. 1289 x Nov. 1290 (*Cheshire Sheaf*, XIX, 61); n.d. (BL, Harl. ms. 7568, f.190r, no source); n.d. (Madox, *Form.*, p. 163, no. cclxxiii).
Anota Occ. Nov. 1299 x Nov. 1300 (BL, Harl. ms. 7568, f. 190r, no source).
Agatha of Dutton (*alias* Sutton) 1307–1312 Eln conf. 24 Jan. 1307 (Lichfield, B/A/1/l, f. 10v). D. 28 Aug. 1312 (PRO, C84/17/9). D. (A.), lic. to el. 11 Sept. 1312 although king not been told of voidance (*CPR 1307–13*, p. 492).
Alice of Alderley (Alderlegh, Alderdelegh(e), Alderdeleych) 1312– N. of Chester, eln pres. to king for royal ass. 30 Aug. 1312 (PRO, C84/17/24); royal ass. 15 Oct. 1312, temps. 3 Oct. 1312 (*CPR 1307–13*, pp. 503, 507). Eln conf. 16 Oct. 1312 (Lichfield, B/A/1/1, f. 32v; cf. PRO, C84/17/11). Occ. 23 July, 9 Sept. 1313 (BL, Harl. ms. 2162, ff. 18v, 19r); 15 Apr. 1314 (Chester City RO, MR/20, m. 3d); 15 Mar. 1315 (ibid., MR/22, m. 2(b)).
Emma de Vernon 1316– Eln conf. 29 Nov. 1316, no reason given for vacancy (Lichfield, B/A/1/1, f. 62v). Occ. 1318 (*Vale Royal Ledger*, p. 117).

Mary of Chester (Cestr') –1349 Occ. from 14 Mar. 1328 to 5 Nov. 1330 (Chester City RO, MR/30, mm. 3, 5, 7, 8–8d); 25 Nov. 1335, 15 Oct. 1336 (*Reg. Burghersh*, I, nos. 483, 512); 7 Feb. 1344 (Lichfield, B/A/1/3, f. 146r). D. by 5 July 1349 (ibid., B/A/1/2, f. 123v).

Helewise of Mottershead (Mottromsheved) 1349– N. of Chester, apptd by bp 5 July 1349 (ibid.). Occ. 12 May 1352 (*CPL*, III, 442); Jan. 1355 x Jan. 1356 (*DKR 28*, pp. 56–7).

Mary Occ. 26 June 1373 (*HMC Var. Coll.*, II, 9).

Agnes of Dutton –1386 Occ. 1 Mar. 1375 (BL, Harl. ms. 2101, f. 35v); (Eleanor) 15 Nov. 1376 (Lambeth, Reg. Sudbury, f. 83v); 1379 (Bennett, 'Lancs and Cheshire Clergy', pp. 22–3). Request for lic. to el. 18 June 1386, granted 3 July 1386 (*DKR 36*, p. 94, app. II, no. 1).

CLEMENTHORPE, *see* YORK, ST CLEMENT

CLERKENWELL, *see* LONDON, CLERKENWELL

COOK HILL (Worcs), St Mary f. -1155 x 1156 (Cistercian priory)

Lists in *VCH Worcs*, II, 158; Thompson, *Women Religious*, p. 237 (to 1227). Thanks are due to Mrs M. Goodrich for help with this list.

Sarah Occ. 29 Sept. 1221 (*Warws F.*, I, no. 248); 11 Nov. 1226 (ibid., no. 359); 15 Oct. 1227 (*CPR 1225–32*, p. 167).

Alice de Frenes Occ n.d. (1270s) (Worcester Cath. Lib., mun. B225).

Agnes of Alcester (Alyncestr') –1288 Occ. n. d (late 13th cent.) (Worcester Cath. Lib., mun. B998). Res. by 15 June 1288 (*Reg. G. Giffard*, p. 342).

Cecilia de Sarnefeud 1288– Installed 15 June 1288 (ibid). Occ. 5 Dec. 1331 (Worcester Cath., Liber Albus, f. 140v).

Sarah –1349 Occ. *c*. 1335 (*Liber Elemosinarii*, p. 44, no. 180). D. by 29 May 1349 (*Reg. Bransford*, p. 428).

Christina Durvassal (Durnassal) 1349– Eln quashed but apptd by bp 29 May 1349 (ibid). Occ. 28 Oct. 1353 (*CCR 1349–54*, p. 621); 26 Mar. 1355 (*CCR 1354–60*, p. 186); 16 Sept. 1355 (Worcester, Reg. Brian I, p. 153).

Alice Rous 1361– N. of Cook Hill, apptd by bp 11 Nov. 1361, no reason given for vacancy (ibid., p. 79).

Alice Occ. 1379 (PRO, E179/58/11, m. 3); 31 May 1382 (*Reg. Wakefield*, p. 185, no. 895b), possibly the same as the above.

No further prs known before the 15th cent.

CORNWORTHY (Devon) St Mary f. 1205 x 38 (*KH*); -1238 (Thompson) (Augustinian priory)

Lists in Watkin, *Devon and Cornwall N. & Q.*, XI, (1921), pp. 6–7; Thompson, *Women Religious*, p. 237 (to 1242).

Hawise Occ. 13 July 1238, 13 Oct. 1242 (*Devon F.*, I, pp. 158, 183, nos. 318, 368).

Anastasia Occ. 6 Jan. 1277 (Devon RO, Hole of Parke 312M/TY91).

Joan de Fysshacre –1334 D. by 24 Mar. 1334 (*Reg. Grandisson*, II, 737, 742).

Mabel de Bradeforde 1334– N. of Cornworthy, eln quashed, but apptd by bp of Exeter 29 Apr. 1334 (ibid., 742).

Emma Occ. n.d. (?1377) (PRO, E179/24/10B).

Annuna (?) **Heynton** Occ. June 1379 x June 1380 (PRO, E179/24/9, m. 1). Watkin calls her 'Annima'.

The next prs, **Joan Lucy**, was d. by 3 Oct. 1411 (*Reg. Stafford*, p. 71).

CRABHOUSE (Norfolk), St Mary and St John the Evangelist (St Mary, St John and St Thomas) (Crabb's Abbey in Wigenhall) f. *c.* 1181 (Augustinian priory)

Lists in *VCH Norfolk*, II, 410; *Heads*, I, 210; Thompson, *Women Religious*, p. 237 (to 1271).

Katherine Occ. n.d., ?early 13th cent. (*Norfolk Arch.*, XI (1892), p. 16, no. 9).

Cecily Occ. 1250 (PRO, Just.1/560, m. 31d).

Christiana of Tilney Occ. *c.* 1271 (*Norfolk Arch.*, V (1859), 257); n.d. (ibid., XI (1892), p. 30, no. 48).

Agnes Occ. Trin. 1309 (PRO, CP40/178, m. 259d).

Agnes of Methwold (Metholwolde, Methelwold) **1315–1342** N. of Crabhouse, eln quashed but apptd by bp 2 May 1315, no reason given for vacancy (Norwich, Reg/1/1, f. 61r). D. by 9 Sept. 1342 (Norwich, Reg/1/3, f. 61v).

Margaret Costyn of Lynn (Lenn) **1342–** N. of Crabhouse, commn to examine eln 9 Sept. 1342, eln conf. 27 Sept. 1342 (ibid.).

Olive of Swaffham (Swafham) **1349–1351** N. of Crabhouse, apptd 31 July 1349, no reason given for vacancy (*Reg. Bateman*, I, no. 907). Res. by 28 Sept. 1351 (Norwich, Reg/2/4, f. 133v).

Cecily de Well **1351–** N. of Crabhouse, eln conf. 28 Sept. 1351 (ibid.).

Cecily Beupre **–1396** D. by 26 Dec. 1396 (Norwich, Reg/3/6, f. 219r–v). ? the same as above.

DAVINGTON (Kent) St. Mary Magdalen f. 1153 (*KH*); ? 1153, 1150 x 1161 (Thompson) (Benedictine priory)

Lists in *VCH Kent*, II, 145; *Heads*, I, 210; Thompson, *Women Religious*, p. 238 (to 1263).

Matilda Occ. 1216 x 1227 (Thompson, p. 238 citing Lambeth, Reg. Warham I, f. 157r); 9 May 1232 (*Kent F.*, p. 117).

Joan Occ. 8 July 1259, 20 Jan. 1263 (ibid., pp. 305, 332).

Alice Occ. 17 Aug. 1346 (PRO, C241/121/181).

Lucy de Appelderfeld **–1350** Res., lic. to el. dated 30 Oct. 1350 (Lambeth, Reg. Islip, f. 32v).

Margaret Borstall **1350–** N. of Davington, apptd by archbp (*hac vice*) 4 Nov. 1350 (ibid. f. 36v).

The next recorded prs, **Isabel Northhoo**, n. of Davington, commn to examine eln dated 26 Sept. 1383, no reason given for vacancy (Lambeth, Reg. Courtenay, f. 54v).

The obit in BL, Cotton ms. Faustina B. VI (i) is cited in Thompson, *Women Religious*, p. 238. The following she considers may refer to the 12th and 13th centuries: **Beatrice, Gunnora, Sarah**, f. 102v.; **Denise**, f. 103v; **Matilda**, twice, ff. 103v, 106v; **Constance**, f. 104r; **Joan**, f. 106v).

CUSTOS

10 Oct. 1279 the unnamed vicar of Faversham apptd to the custody of the priory (*Reg. Peckham*, I, 72–3).

DERBY, KINGSMEAD (Derbys), St Mary (de Pratis) f. 1149 x 1159 (*KH*); –1154 x 1159 (Thompson) (Benedictine priory)

Lists in *VCH Derbys*, III, 44–5; *Heads*, I, 211; Thompson, *Women Religious*, p. 238 (to 1261).

Emma Occ. –1210 (*Derby Chts.*, no. 2382); *c.* 1220 (*Ctl. Darley*, I, 121); 4 Sept. 1230 (*Derbys F.*, (1886), p. 27).

Rametta Occ. 6 Oct. 1236 (ibid., p. 35); n.d. early 13th cent. (Raimon) (*Derbys Chts.*, no. 2385).

Sibyl Occ. *c.* 1248 x 1261 (*Ctl. Darley*, I, pp. 178–9, no. D.16); 25 Apr. 1255 (PRO, Leics F., CP25/1/122/23, no. 420).

Ellen de Beresford **–1334** Occ. *c.* June 1330 (PRO, Just.1/167, m. 3). Res. by 29 Nov. 1334 (Lichfield, B/A/1/2, f. 73r).

Joan Touchet (Tuchet) **1334–1349** N. of Derby, apptd by bp to whom right of appt had been transferred, 29 Nov. 1334 (ibid.). D. by. 8 Sept. 1349 (ibid., f. 87r).

Alice de Irland 1349– N. of Derby, apptd by bp to whom the right of appt had been transferred 8 Sept. 1349 (ibid.).

The next recorded prs, **Elizabeth Stanley**, occ. 19 Dec. 1431 (*FA*, I, 277).

PRIOR OR CUSTOS

R. Occ. as pr. 1217 x 1229 Mar. 1218 (*EEA*, 19, no. 309 = BL, Woolley Chts. XI 25; *Derbys. Chts.*, no. 969).

William de Russell Occ. as *custos c.* 1220 (*Ctl. Darley*, I, 120–1, no. B27).

EASEBOURNE (Sussex), St Mary f. -1248 (Benedictine/Augustinian, *see KH*, pp. 258, 280).

List in *VCH Sussex*, II, 85.

Alice Mentd in 1339 as former abbs. (*sic*) who had acquired lands before the Statute of Mortmain (1279). Presumably also the same as prs Alice who occ. in an undated cht. mentd in 1313 (*Reg. Stapeldon*, p. 387).

Isabel de Perci Occ. Nov. 1296 x Nov. 1297 (PRO, E210/5558).

Edith 1313– Did homage to bp of Exeter Jan. 1313 (*Reg. Stapeldon*, p. 387). Occ. n.d. (early 14th cent.) (*Cowdray Archives*, I, ms. 4).

Beatrice Occ. Jan. 1327 x Jan. 1328 (*Sussex Arch. Coll.*, IX, 4).

Mary Occ. 14 Jan. 1339 (*CPR 1338–40*, p. 177).

Margaret Wyvile (Wyvele) Occ. 19 Jan. 1353 (*Cowdray Archives*, II, ms. 5129/2); 9 June 1362 (*Sussex Arch. Coll.*, IX, 5–6).

The next recorded prs, **Margery**, occ. 28 Oct. 1379 (*CFR 1377–83*, p. 168); 11 June 1405, 26 Aug. 1414 (*Reg. Rede*, II, 280; I, 165).

ELLERTON-IN-SWALEDALE (Yorks N.), St Mary f. *temp.* Henry II ? (*KH*); *c.* 1189 x 1204 (Thompson); *ante* 1227, prob. *ante* 1200 (Burton) (Cistercian priory)

List in *VCH Yorks*, III, 161; Thompson, *Women Religious*, p. 238 (to 1268).

Alice Occ. 13 Dec. 1227 (*CPR 1225–32*, p. 207).

Aubrey Occ. 22 May 1228 (*Yorks F., 1218–31*, p. 116).

Petronilla Occ. 6 Oct. 1251 (*Yorks F., 1246–72*, p. 18); n. d., ment. in royal conf. of 1348 (*CChR 1341–1417*, p. 75). Occ. as former prs in case of 1268 (PRO, Just.1/1050, m. 28).

Ellen Oc. 15 Apr. 1263, 22 July 1268 (*Yorks F., 1246–72*, pp. 199, 157–8; PRO, F.Var.Cos. CP25/1/284/19, no. 136).

Sibyl Occ. Easter 1299 x Trinity 1300 (Baildon, I, 56).

Margaret Occ. 17 Oct. 1342 (*CPR 1345–48*, p. 453); Clarkson, *Hist. of Richmond*, p. 325 gives occ. in 1347 but without source.

[**Mary Gray** Date uncertain (Burton, *Mon. Ebor.*, p. 263, no source).]

The next recorded prs, **Alice Sherwood**, occ. 6 Aug. 1429 (Burton, *Mon. Ebor.*, p. 263, citing D. and C., York, Parchment Book E, f. 44, not now locatable in York Minster Archives).

ELSTOW (Beds), [Holy Trinity,] St Mary and St Helen f. *c.*1078 (*KH*); 1076 x 1086 (Thompson) (Benedictine abbey)

Lists in *VCH Beds*, I, 357–8; *Heads*, I, 211; Thompson, *Women Religious*, pp. 238–9 (to 1281).

Mabel II 1213–1232/3 A successor's eln noted *s. a.* 1213 (*Ann. Dunstable*, p. 42). D., lic. to el. 6 Jan. 1233 (*CPR 1232–47*, p. 7).

Wymarca 1233–1241 Prs of Elstow, royal ass. 27 Jan. 1233, writ *de intendendo* 4 Mar. 1233 (ibid., pp. 8, 13). D. June x July 1241 (*Reg. Grosseteste*, p. 318, pontifical year and see next entry). D., lic. to el. (no name) 5 July 1241 (*CPR 1232–47*, p. 254). Presumably d. by 29 June 1241 when Simon of Norwich apptd to the custody of the vacant abbey (ibid.).

Agnes of Westbury (Westbir', Westbiry) **1241–?1249/50 (1251)** Sub-prs of Elstow, el. and adm. June 1241 x June 1242 (*Reg. Grosseteste*, p. 318). Royal ass. 13 July 1241, writ *de intendendo* 22 July 1241 (*CPR 1232–47*, pp. 254–5). Res. June 1249 x June 1250 (*Reg. Grosseteste*, pp. 335–6), presumably an error, since she res. 17 Feb. 1251 (PRO, C84/1/22).

Aubrey of Fécamp (Fiscampo) **?1249/50 (1251)–1251** N. of Elstow, el. on res. of Agnes, eln quashed but apptd by bp June 1249 x June 1250 (*Reg. Grosseteste*, p. 336, *sic*, see above). Res. (of Agnes of Westbury), lic. to el. 25 Feb. 1251 (*CPR 1247–58*, p. 88).

Aubrey de Saunford 1251–?1258 N. of Elstow, royal ass. 8 Mar. 1251 (ibid., p. 90). Lic. to el. (no reason given for vacancy) 12 Apr. 1258 (ibid., p. 622). As Thompson suggests (p. 238) it is prob. that Albreda of Fécamp and Albreda de Saunford are the same person; presumably there may have been some unknown delay in the choice of a new abbs. after Agnes of Westbury's res.

Annora de Baskervill 1258–1281 N. of Elstow, royal ass. 16 Apr. 1258, temps. 14 May 1258 (*CPR 1247–58*, pp. 623, 630). Mand. to restore vacancy revenues to her 4 July 1259 (*CCR 1256–59*, p. 402). D., lic. to el. 10 June 1281 (*CPR 1272–81*, p. 443).

Beatrice of Scotney (Scotenay, Scoteneye, Scoteny) **1281–1294** N. of Elstow, eln held 15 Aug. 1281. Bp quashed eln and apptd her 4 Nov. 1281. Eln had been divided and the prs, Agatha Gifford has received 20 votes (*Reg. Sutton*, VIII, 95–6). Royal ass. 8 Nov. 1281, temps. 10 Nov. 1281 (*CPR 1272–81*, p. 463). D. by 26 Aug. 1294 (PRO, C84/12/19). D., lic. to el. 31 Aug. 1294 (*CPR 1292–1301*, p. 86). Indulgence offered 4 July 1301 for her soul (Lincoln, Ep. Reg., III, f. 33r).

Clemencia de Balliol (Balliolo) **1294–1314** Precentrix of Elstow, el. 6 Sept. 1294 (PRO, C84/12/20); royal ass. 13 Sept. 1294, temps. 22 Sept. 1294 (*CPR 1292–1301*, pp. 86–7). Eln conf. 19 Sept. 1294, bl. 23 Sept. 1294 (*Reg. Sutton*, VIII, 113; PRO, C84/12/21). Res. accepted by bp 19 Nov. 1314 (Lincoln, Ep. Reg., III, f. 308v). Cess., lic. to el. 27 Nov. 1314 (*CPR 1313–17*, p. 200).

At an eln held following Clemencia's d. the votes were divided between Joan of Walton (Wauton), prs of Elstow, and Elizabeth of Beauchamp, n. of Elstow and the king ordered the bp to investigate 7 Feb. 1315 (ibid., p. 218). Elizabeth de Beauchamp pres. to the king by a number of named nuns 10 Jan. 1315; eln of Joan pres. to king for royal ass. by sub-prs and convent 11 Jan. 1315 (PRO, C84/18/3–4, 8). Bp acknowledges receipt of royal writ ordering enquiry (PRO, C270/33/3). On account of the vacancy the king presented to a living on 21 Mar. 1315 (Lincoln, Ep. Reg., II, f. 270r).

Joan of Walton (Wauton) **1315–1318** Abbs-el. presented. to bp the letters of Archbp Walter of Canterbury, dated 15 May 1315, confirming the eln which had lawfully devolved to him; prof. obed. to bp of Lincoln 7 July 1315 (ibid.; PRO, C84/18/19). Prs of Elstow, temps. restored 14 May 1315 (*CPR 1313–17*, p. 290). D. by 15 Sept. 1318 (PRO, C84/19/40). D., lic. to el. 22 Sept. 1318 (*CPR 1317–21*, p. 210). Indulgence of 40 days for the soul of Joan of Walton, buried in the chapter house, 30 June 1323 (Lincoln, Ep. Reg., V, f. 345v).

Elizabeth de Beauchamp (Bello Campo) **1318–1331** N. of Elstow, eln pres. to king for royal ass. 4 Oct. 1318 (PRO, C84/19/41); royal ass. 14 Oct. 1318, temps. 5 Dec. 1318 (*CPR 1317–21*, pp. 218, 260). Royal commn to take fealty 14 Nov. 1318 (PRO, C84/19/45). Eln conf. 18 Nov. 1318 (Lincoln, Ep. Reg., f. 273r–v; PRO, CP84/19/46); bl. by ex-archbp of Armagh 19 Nov. 1318 and prof. obed. (Lincoln, Ep. Reg., III, f. 401r). D., lic. to el. 17 Sept. 1331 (*CPR 1330–34*, p. 166).

Juliana Basset 1331–1333 Prs of Elstow, eln pres. to king for royal ass. 23 Sept. 1331 (PRO, C84/22/49); royal ass. 3 Oct. 1331, temps. 10 Oct. 1331 (*CPR 1330–34*, pp. 171, 182). Eln pres. to bp's commissary 11 Oct. 1331, eln quashed but apptd 13 Oct. 1331 (Lincoln, Ep. Reg., IV, f. 304r; cf. PRO, C84/22/50). D., lic. to el. 28 Aug. 1333 (*CPR 1330–34*, p. 466).

Elizabeth (de) Morteyn 1333–1371 N. of Elstow, royal ass. 14 Sept. 1333, temps. 10 Oct. 1333 (ibid., pp. 467, 471). Eln pres. to bp 1 Oct. 1333, quashed but apptd 2 Oct. 1333 (Lincoln, Ep. Reg., IV, f. 306v). D. by 6 Mar. 1371 (PRO, C84/25/1). D., lic to el. 8 Mar. 1371 (*CPR 1370–74*, p. 56).

Anastasia Dune (Duyn, Den) **1371–1392** N. of Elstow, eln pres. to king for royal ass. 12 Mar. 1371 (PRO, C84/30/33); royal ass. 20 Mar. 1371, temps. 7 Apr. 1371 (*CPR 1370–74*, pp. 57, 61). Cert. conf. eln by bp of Lincoln 3 Apr. 1371 (PRO, C84/30/36). Res. by 23 Nov. 1392 (PRO, C84/35/30). Cess., lic. to el. 26 Nov. 1392 (*CPR 1391–96*, p. 201).

ESHOLT (Yorks W.) St Mary and St Leonard f. -1184 (Cistercian priory)

Lists in *VCH Yorks*, III, 162–3; Thompson, *Women Religious*, p. 239 (to 1231); A.C. Macdonald, 'Women and the monastic life in late medieval Yorkshire' (Oxford D.Phil. thesis, 1997), app.1.

Agnes Occ. 22 Feb. 1219 (*Yorks F., 1218–31*, p. 30); 1231 (PRO, Just.1/1042, m. 16d); n.d. (*Yorks Deeds*, II, no. 143).

Alice Occ. Easter 1299 (PRO, CP40/127, m. 181).

Juliana de la Wodehall 1300– N. of Esholt, eln conf. 6 Dec. 1300, no reason given for vacancy (*Reg. Corbridge*, I, 40). Mandate that the archbp has not accepted her res. and she is to continue in office 5 Aug. 1303 (ibid., 92–3).

Joan of Hartlington (Hertlington) **–1315** Res., lic. to el. 18 Sept. 1315 (*Reg. Greenfield*, II, no. 1133).

Isabel of Calverley 1315–1353 N. of Esholt, eln conf. 21 Sept. 1315 (ibid.: the pd edn gives the name as Joan but the original ms., York, Reg. 8, f. 112r confirms that Isabel is written). Occ. 29 Sept. 1327 (*Calverley Chts.*, p. 105); 24 May 1349 (ibid., p. 174). D. by 26 July 1353 (*BIB*, 3, p. 37, no. 45).

Commn to el. and conf. eln of unnamed prs in succession to Isabel, who had died, 26 July 1353 (ibid).

Joan de Mohaut 1360– El. 25 June 1360 (Leeds, Stansfield ms. 795, m. 9d); occ. accounts 1360–65 (ibid.).[4]

The next recorded prs, **Matilda Ward(e)**, occ. 13 Apr. 1392 (BL, Add. Cht. 17,105); occ. 1401–7 (Leeds, Stansfield C/1/1, Esholt court rolls 779/1–2).

MASTER

Richard Vicar of Bradford, apptd as master 7 July 1301 (*Reg. Corbridge*, I, 53).

FAREWELL (Staffs), St Mary f. *c.* 1140 (originally an abbey but by 1210 was described as a priory) (*KH*); *c.* 1139 x 1147 (Thompson) (Benedictine priory)

Lists in *VCH Staffs*, III, 224–5; Thompson, *Women Religious*, p. 239.

Serena Occ. 1248 (*Mon. Angl.*, IV, 112, no. vi).

Julia Occ. *temp.* Henry III (*Staffs Plea Rolls 1272–94*, p. 94).

Matilda Occ. -1275, prob. early 1270s (*Magnum Reg. Album Lichfield*, no. 553).

Sibyl Contemporary of William de Asshewell, pr. of Llanthony Secunda (*c.* 1265 x 1283) (*Staffs Plea Rolls 1360–87*, p. 13).

Christina of Winchester (Wynton') **–1281/2** Prob. the prs of Farewell who was el. prs of Langley 19 May 1281 x 18 May 1282 (Bodl., Dodsworth ms. 107, f. 138r).

Margery Occ. 1293 (PRO, Just.1/805, m. 12).

---

[4] *VCH* entry citing Isabel of Calverley el. 1363 is an error.

Buabilla –1313 D. by 2 Aug. 1313; lic. to el. (Lichfield, B/A/1/1, f. 46r)

Isolda de Pype (Pipa) 1313–1321 Commn to examine eln 16 Apr. 1313 (ibid.); res. by 9 Nov. 1321 (Bp Langton's death) (ibid., f. 1r, and see below).

Margaret de Muneworth 1321– Sub-prs of Farewell. Disputed eln. A minority el. Margaret de Muneworth and a majority postulated Joan de Freford *in minori etate.* Bp Langton quashed Margaret's eln and refused Joan's postulation. He then died on 9 Nov. 1321. Subsequently the archbp of Canterbury commnd the Official *sede vacante* of Coventry and Lichfield to provide a prs 23 Nov. 1321, and he apptd Margaret 2 Dec. 1321 (ibid., f. 1r; Lambeth, Reg. Reynolds, f. 128v). Occ. Easter 1353 (*Staffs Plea Rolls 16–33 Edward III*, p. 118).

Agnes Foljambe Occ. 27 Apr. 1366 (*Anglesey Chts.*, no. 1599); Mich. term 1367 (*Staffs Plea Rolls 1360–87*, p. 62).

Agnes Turville –1398 Res. by 10 May 1398 (Lichfield, B/A/1/6, f. 50v).

FLAMSTEAD(Herts), St Giles (St Giles in the Wood, Woodchurch) f. ?*c.* 1150 (Benedictine priory)

 Lists in *VCH Herts*, IV, 433–4; *Heads*, I, 211; C.A. Butterill 'The Cartulary of Flamstead Priory – St Giles in the Wood' (University of Manitoba MA thesis, 1988), pp. 295–7; Thompson, *Women Religious*, p. 239 (to 1268).

Alice Occ. early 13th cent. (pal.: Guildhall, D. & C. of St Paul's, ms. 25121/1109; *HMC 9th Rept*, p. 27).

Agnes –1255/6 Occ. Oct. 1235 x Oct. 1236 (Ctl. Flamstead, f. 1r); 1243 (PRO Herts F., CP25/1/85/20 no. 307; Ctl. Flamstead, f. 28v); 1244 (*Bucks F.*, I, 83); 27 Jan. 1252, 3 Feb. 1254 (*Beds F.*, pp. 147, 154). D. by May 1255 x May 1256 (*Reg. Lexington*, p. 512).[5]

Petronilla de Lucy 1255/6– N. of Flamstead, eln quashed but apptd by bp May 1255 x May 1256 (ibid., pp. 511–12). Occ. 20 Oct. 1256 (*Bucks F.*, I, 105). For a poss. identification of this prs. see Butterill, pp. 195–7.

Sibyl –1268 D. by 13 Aug. 1268 (*Reg. R. Gravesend*, p. 173).

Loretta (Laurota) 1268– N. of Flamstead, eln conf. 13 Aug. 1268 (ibid., pp. 173, 317). Occ. 25 Nov. 1270 (*Bucks F.*, II, 23). Possibly the same as Lora below

Lora –1291 (poss. the same as Loretta above). Occ. n.d. (Ctl. Flamstead, f. 1v). D. by 25 Mar. 1291 (*Reg. Sutton*, VIII, 77).

Joan of Wheathampstead 1291–?1308 N. of Flamstead, eln conf. 25 Mar. 1291 (ibid.). Occ. 1296 (PRO E210/1423); 1291 x 1297 (Ctl. Flamstead, f. 28v). An unnamed prs (poss. Joan) d. by 22 July 1308 (Lincoln, Ep. Reg., II, f. 239r). Seal (*Mon. Seals*, p. 35).

Cecily de Morteyn (Mortein) 1308–1316 N. of Flamstead, commn to examine eln 22 July 1308 and subsequent conf. n.d. (Lincoln, Ep. Reg., II, f. 238v; ibid., III, f. 138v); mand. to install 9 Aug. 1308 (Lincoln, Ep. Reg., III, f. 140r). Cess. by 17 June 1316 (ibid., f. 348r).

Ellen of Dunstable (Dunstaple) 1316– N. of Flamstead, commn to conf. eln 17 June 1316 (ibid.).

Letitia of St Albans (de Sancto Albano) 1329– N. of Flamstead, commn to examine eln 21 Nov. 1329 (Lincoln, Ep. Reg., V, f. 398v).

The next recorded prs, **Matilda Lucy**, el. on d. of unnamed prs; commn to examine eln 6 Sept. 1415 (Lincoln, Ep. Reg., XIV, f. 361v).

A prs **Lucy** also occ. n.d. in the 13th cent. Ctl. (f. 22r).

[5] Prs Joan, said to occ. 1228, is in fact to be identified with Joan of Wheathampstead, prs from 1291. Ctl. Flamstead, f. 28v, in which Joan features is to be dated to 1291 x 1297 (the latter being the death date of Richard, rector of Ashridge, who also occ.). Prs Agatha can also be removed from the list.

MASTER

Roger of Crowle (Croule) **1337–** priest, apptd during pleasure 17 Mar. 1337 (Lincoln, Ep. Reg., V, f. 546v).

FLIXTON (Suffolk), St Mary and St Katherine f. 1258 (*KH*); 1258 x 1259 (Thompson) (Augustinian priory)

Lists in *VCH Suffolk*, II, 117; Thompson, *Women Religious*, p. 239 (to 1293).

Eleanor Occ. Oct. 1259 x Oct. 1260 (*Suffolk F. (Rye)*, p. 62). Cf. Thompson, *Women Religious*, p. 239 on Eleanor and Beatrice.

Beatrice of Rattlesden (Ratlesden, Ratlisden) Occ. 23 Mar. 1263 (BL, Stowe Cht. 294); 1266 (*Starrs and Jewish Chts.*, I, pp. 124–7, no. xxxi); Oct. 1268 x Oct. 1269, Nov. 1288 x Nov. 1289, Nov. 1291 x Nov. 1292 (*Suffolk F. (Rye)*, pp. 67, 92, 95); 1289 (PRO, F. Divers Cos. CP25/1/285/23, no. 197); 6 June 1293 (BL, Campbell Cht. III 116).

Emma de Welholm 1301– Eln conf. 21 Nov. 1301, no reason given for vacancy (Norwich, Reg/1/1, f. 7r). Occ. Mich. 1310 (PRO, C40/183, attorneys m. 13); 19 Dec. 1311, 13 July 1321, 30 Oct. 1321 (Norwich, Reg/1/1, ff. 44v, 90v, 92v).

Margery of Stonham –1345 Occ. 27 Oct. 1333 (BL, Stowe Cht. 333). D. by 9 Apr. 1345 (*Reg. Bateman*, I, no. 149).

Isabel de Welham 1345– N. of Flixton, eln conf. 9 Apr. 1345 (ibid.). Occ. 1 Dec. 1349 (BL, Stowe ms. 1083, no. 61).

Joan of Hempnall (Hemynhalle) Occ. 8 June 1356 (ibid., no. 62).

Joan Mareshal (Mareschal) Occ. 5 Oct. 1366 (ibid., no. 64); 14 July 1367 (ibid., no. 63).

Margery Hovel(l) 1376–1392 N. of Flixton, eln quashed, but apptd by bp 3 Apr. 1376, no reason given for vacancy (Norwich, Reg/3/6, f. 43v). D. by 16 Oct. 1392 (ibid., f. 170r).

FOSSE (Lincs), St Mary *alias* St Nicholas (Fosse under Torksey) f. –1184 (Cistercian priory)

Lists in *VCH Lincs*, II, 157; *Heads*, I, 211; Thompson, *Women Religious*, p. 239 (to 1278).

Beatrice Occ. Oct. 1225 x Oct. 1226 (*Rot. Lit. Claus.*, II, 149).

Katherine de [blank] 1236/7– N. of Fosse, el. and adm. June 1236 x June 1237 on d. of unnamed prs (*Reg. Grosseteste*, p. 137). Occ. 30 Apr. 1251 (*Lincs F.*, II, 90).

Hawise –1272 D. by 2 Dec. 1272 (*Reg. R. Gravesend*, p. 93).

Goda (Guna) 1272–1278 Eln conf. 2 Dec. 1272 (ibid., pp. 93, 291). Cess. by 20 Oct. 1278 (ibid., p. 97).

Ala of Canterbury (Cantuar') **1278–1283** N. of Fosse, eln quashed but apptd by bp, on cess. of Guna, 20 Oct. 1278 (ibid., pp. 97, 292). Removed from office about the time of St Gregory's mass (12 March) 1283 (*Reg. Sutton*, VIII, 4).

Alice of Rye 1283–1284 Eln quashed but bp apptd her 1 Apr. 1283 (ibid.). Res. by 16 May 1284, when in great distress and against the bp's efforts she had insisted on resigning (ibid., 5–6).

Agnes de Lexington (Laxinton) **1284–1297** Sub-prs of Fosse, eln conf. 16 May 1284 (ibid.). Res. by 22 Nov. 1297 (ibid., p. 29 – Alice given in summary but Agnes in ms.).

Agnes of Scothern (Schothorn, Schotethorn) **1297–1312** Sub-prs of Fosse, eln quashed but apptd by bp 22 Nov. 1297 (ibid.). D. by 29 Dec. 1312 (Lincoln, Ep. Reg., II, f. 96r–v).

Joan of Kettlethorpe (Ketelesthorp, Ketilthorp) **1313–1349** N. of Fosse, el. 29 Dec. 1312, bp's commn to examine eln 2 Jan. 1313, eln quashed 13 Jan. 1313 but Joan apptd by commissaries (ibid.; Lincoln, Ep. Reg., III, f. 267r). D. by 7 Nov. 1349 (Lincoln, Ep. Reg., IX, f. 159v).

Beatrice of Luddington (Ludington) **1349–1380** N. of Fosse, eln quashed but apptd by bp 7 Nov. 1349 (ibid.). D. by 8 Jan. 1381 (Lincoln, Ep. Reg., X, ff. 146v–147r), but cf. commn to examine eln of successor, Agnes of Grantham, 15 Dec. 1380 (Lincoln, Ep. Reg., XII, f. 216v).

MASTER

Philip Rector of Nettleham, apptd 26 Jan. 1305 (Lincoln, Ep. Reg., III, f. 78v). [The rectory of Nettleham was collated to Philip of Swayfield (Swafeld) on 15 Oct. 1300 (Lincoln, Ep. Reg., II, f. 83r)]

FOUKEHOLME (Yorks N.), St Stephen (Thimbleby) f. -1203 x 4; diss. 1350+ (*see* W. Brown, 'The nunnery of St Stephen's of Thimbleby', *YAJ*, IX (1886), 334–7). (Benedictine priory)

Lists in *VCH Yorks*, III, 116; Thompson, *Women Religious*, p. 239.

Acilla Occ. n.d. (13th cent.) (NYCRO, ZFL.8, Ingleby Arncliffe deeds: *YAJ*, IX (1886), 335). (For the different views about the dating of this charter see Thompson, *Women Religious*, p. 186, n.179).

Alice Gower 1350– Apptd by archbp 12 Apr. 1350 (York, Reg. 10, f. 168r).

GODSTOW (Oxon), St Mary and St John the Evangelist f. *c.* Easter 1133 (*KH*); -1133 (Thompson) (Benedictine abbey)

Lists in *VCH Oxon*, II, 74–5; *Heads*, I, 211–12; Thompson, *Women Religious*, p. 240 (to 1269).

Juliana Latest recorded occ. 1213 x 1219 (*Reg. Ant. Lincoln*, III, no. 657).

Felicia Occ. 6 Oct. 1220 (*Ctl. Godstow*, no. 784; cf. (Alice) *Soms F.*, I, 41); 3 Feb. 1223 (*Bucks F.*, I, 49); 27 Apr. 1225 (*Ctl. Godstow*, no. 152; PRO, Glos F., CP25/1/73/7, no. 80). Prob. vacated 1225, lic. to el. (no reason given) 30 May 1225 (*CPR 1216–25*, p. 530).

Amphelisa de Bade 1225–1241 Sub-prs of Godstow, royal ass. 8 July 1225 (ibid., p. 533). Occ. 15 July 1241 (PRO Glos F., CP25/1/73/14, no. 259). Lic. to el. (no reason given) 11 Dec. 1241 (*CPR 1232–47*, p. 268).

Flandrina (Flandria) de Braos(e) (Brewes) **1241–1248** Prs of Godstow, royal ass. 18 Dec. 1241 (ibid.). Mand. for seisin 30 Jan. 1242 (*CR 1237–42*, p. 388). Eln quashed but apptd by bp of Lincoln 15 Jan. 1242, no reason given for vacancy (*Reg. Grosseteste*, p. 471). Deposition reported to king 5 Apr. 1248 (ibid., p. 504; PRO, SC1/3/165). Dep., lic. to el. 15 Apr. 1248 (*CPR 1247–58*, p. 12).

Emma Bluet (Bloet) **1248–1269** N. of Godstow, royal ass. 23 Apr. 1248 (ibid., p. 12); mand. for seisin 16 May 1248 (*CCR 1247–51*, p. 48). El. and adm. on dep. of Flandrina and afterwards bl. by W., late bp of Carlisle June 1247 x June 1248, ? Jan. x June (*Reg. Grosseteste*, p. 491). Fine paid for custody in next coming vacancy 4 July 1269 (*CPR 1266–72*, p. 349); vacant by 10 July 1269 (ibid., p. 352). Res. 8 July 1269 (PRO, C84/3/47). Cess. by 12 July 1269 (*Reg. R. Gravesend*, p. 221).

Isolda (Isabel) de Durham (Derham, Duram) **1269–1278** Sub-prs of Godstow, royal ass. 15 July 1269 (*CPR 1266–72*, p. 353). Eln conf. 12 July 1269; bl. 14 July 1269 (*Reg. R. Gravesend*, pp. 221, 332). Notif. to king of bps' conf. 14 July 1269 (*DKR 5*, app. II, pp. 68–9, no. 553). Res. of unnamed abbs (prob. Isolda) 1278 on account of grave and incurable illness (ibid., p. 234).

Rose de Oxhaye (Oxeye) **1278–1283** Prs of Godstow, eln conf. 10 July 1278 on res. of previous abbs (ibid., pp. 234, 337). Royal ass. and temps. 10 July 1278 (*CRR 1272–81*, pp. 273–4). Cess., lic. to el. 15 Nov. 1283 (*CPR 1281–92*, p. 89).

Mabel la Wafre (? Annabel) **1283–1295** Temps. 16 Dec. 1283 (ibid., p. 108). Cess., lic. to el. 13 Oct. 1295 (*CPR 1292–1301*, p. 153). Occ. as former abbs. 1297 (PRO, E164/20, f. 114v).

Alice de Gorges 1295–1304 N. of Godstow, eln conf. 22 Oct. 1295 on res. of Annabel (? for Amabel) (*Reg. Sutton*, VIII, 189); temps. 28 Oct. 1295 (*CPR 1292–1301*, p. 156). D. (A.), lic. to el. 12 Nov. 1304 (*CPR 1301–7*, p. 267).

Matilda of Upton (Opton) **1304–1316** Sub-prs of Amesbury, prev. prs of Godstow, royal ass.

27 Nov. 1304, temps. 23 Dec. 1304 (ibid., pp. 291, 304). Eln conf. 12 Dec. 1304 and bl. 13 Dec. 1304 (Lincoln, Ep. Reg., II, f. 148r). D. by 22 Dec. 1316 (ibid., f. 167v).[6]

Margery (de) Dyve 1316–1335 N. of Godstow, eln quashed but apptd by bp of Lincoln 22 Dec. 1316 (ibid.). Bl. by ex-archbp of Armagh, prof. obed. 24 Dec. 1316 (Lincoln, Ep. Reg., III, f. 360r). D. by 11 Sept. 1335 (PRO, C84/23/36). D., lic. to el. 17 Sept. 1335 (*CPR 1334–38*, p. 166).

Matilda de Beauchamp (de Bello Campo) **1335–1349** N. of Godstow, eln pres. to king for royal ass. 24 Sept. 1335 (PRO, C84/23/37); temps. 24 Nov. 1335 (*CPR 1334–38*, p. 180). 26 Oct. 1335 commn to examine eln (Lincoln, Ep. Reg., V, f. 515r). Certificate of bp's Official that he has apptd Matilda (prev. eln quashed) 14 Nov. 1335 (Lincoln, Ep. Reg., IV, f. 273r–v). Letter giving permission, if her eln is conf., to receive bl. by any Catholic bp 30 Oct. 1335 (Lincoln, Ep. Reg., V, f. 516r). D., lic. to el. 20 May 1349 (*CPR 1348–50*, p. 293).

Agnes of Streatley (Stretele, Stretelegh, Stretle, Stretlee, Stretlie) **1349–1375** N. of Godstow, royal ass. 6 June 1349, temps. 10 July 1349 (ibid., pp. 325, 328, 345). Commn to examine eln 17 June 1349, eln conf. 4 July 1349 (Lincoln, Ep. Reg., IX, f. 224r). Permission from bp of Lincoln to receive bl. from any bp 17 June 1349 (PRO, SC1/42/47). Gt of all the issues and temps. of the vacancy 29 July 1349 (*CPR 1348–50*, p. 361). D. 11 Aug. 1375 (PRO, C84/32/14). D., lic. to el. 14 Aug. 1375 (*CPR 1374–77*, p. 130).

Margery Tracy 1375–1384 N. of Godstow, royal ass. 28 Aug. 1375, temps. 9 Sept. 1375 (ibid., pp. 164, 167). Cert. conf. eln by bp of Lincoln 8 Sept. 1375 (PRO, C84/31/36). D. by 11 Sept. 1384 (PRO, C84/33/22). D. (Margaret), lic. to el. 15 Sept. 1384 (*CPR 1381–85*, p. 455; cf. Lincoln., Ep. Reg., XI, f. 300r).

MASTERS OR WARDENS

Herbert formerly Vicar of St Giles, Oxford, provision made for his support June 1235 x June 1236 (*Reg. Grosseteste*, p. 448); (the chaplain) n.d. (*c.* 1225 x 1241) (PRO, E164/20, f. 92v).

William Dean of Woodstock occ. n.d. (1248 x 1269) (PRO, E164/20, f. 144r)

William Vicar of Cassington, n.d. (*c.*1250 x 61) (PRO, E164/20, ff. 24r, 94v).

William Vicar of 'Duninton' (? Dinton) occ. as master n.d. (dead by May 1270) (PRO, E164/20, ff. 37v, 123r; *Reg. R. Gravesend*, p. 245). The three Williams mentioned above could be all one person.

Robert 1270– Vicar of Donington, appt. as master 6 July 1270 (ibid., p. 222).

Robert Maynard Vicar of St Mary Magdalen, Oxford, from 1268 (*Reg. R. Gravesend*, pp. 221, 225). Occ. as *custos c.*1276 (PRO, E164/20, f. 106r).

Roger of Upton Occ. as *custos* Jan. 1277 (PRO, E164/20, f. 69v).

Nicholas de Clenefield 1308– Rector of Wescot Barton apptd 29 Nov. 1308 (Lincoln, Ep. Reg., III, f. 144v).

19 May 1316 the abb. of Eynsham and pr. of Bicester apptd masters (Lincoln, Ep. Reg., III, f. 343v) but cf. note 16.

Ivo of Edenham 1337– Priest, apptd during pleasure 9 Mar. 1337 (Lincoln, Ep. Reg., V, f. 546r).

GOKEWELL (Lincs), St Mary f. -1148 (?) (*KH*); 1147 x 1175 (Thompson) (Cistercian priory)

Lists in *VCH Lincs*, II, 156–7; Thompson, *Women Religious*, p. 240 (to 1279).

Juliana Occ. n.d. (Soc. of Ant. ms. 38, f. 126v – no indication of date, positioned with other chts. of early 13th cent.: ms. mid-14th cent.). Her precise place in the sequence of prioresses is uncertain.

---

[6] 10 Feb. 1316 appt during pleasure of the abb. of Eynsham and pr. of Bicester to be keepers of the abbey on account of its poverty and miserable state (*CPR 1313–17*, p. 391).

Avice Occ. 16 Oct. 1234 (*Lincs F.*, I, 257).

Isabel of Thornton 1279– N. of Gokewell, el. on res. of previous (unnamed) prs (*Reg. R..Gravesend*, pp. 84, 87, 288–9). Eln quashed but apptd by bp 22 Apr. 1279 (ibid., pp. 87, 288). Res. on account of ill-health 30 Jan. 1298 but restored 6 Feb. 1298 at request of sub-prs and convent (*Reg. Sutton*, VI, 57–9). Possibly d. by 31 Oct. 1300 (Lincoln, Ep. Reg., II, f. 83r – entry gives Matilda as prev. prs but the name is half-erased and may poss. have been a scribal error confusing the name of the new prs).

Matilda of Sapperton (Saperton) 1300– N. of Gokewell, eln quashed but apptd by bp 31 Oct. 1300 (Lincoln, Ep. Reg., II, f. 83r).

Olive n.d. mentioned as prs in an earlier gt confirmed on 18 Feb. 1314 (*CChR 1300–26*, p. 262). No clue as to sequence in the list.

Matilda de Newode –1349 Vacant by cess. by 5 July 1349 (Lincoln, Ep. Reg., IX, f. 156v).

Elizabeth Dautry 1349– N. of Gokewell. Right of appt transferred to bp who apptd Elizabeth 5 July 1349 (ibid.). Occ. Easter 1361 (PRO, CP40/406, mm. 221d, 238).

Alice de la Feld –1365 Res. on 14 Sept. 1365, right of appt transferred to bp (Lincoln, Ep. Reg., X, f. 130r).[7]

Alice of Egmanton (Egminton) 1365–1396 N. of Gokewell, apptd by bp 15 Sept. 1365 (ibid.). Occ. 1377 (*Clerical Poll-Taxes*, p. 65, no. 873). Cess. by 20 Feb. 1396 (Lincoln, Ep. Reg., XI, f. 116v).

MASTERS

Geoffrey 1312– Vicar of Hibaldstow, apptd master 16 Feb. 1312 (Lincoln, Ep. Reg., III, f. 246v).

Nicholas of Ousefleet (Usflet) 1343– Rector of Flixborough, apptd master 21 Nov. 1343 (Lincoln, Ep. Reg., VII, f. 47v).

GORING (Oxon), St Mary f. *temp.* Henry I (*KH*); –1135 (Thompson) (Augustinian priory) Lists in *VCH Oxon*, II, 104; *Goring Chts.*, I, p. xix; *Heads*, I, 212; Thompson, *Women Religious*, p. 240 (to 1271). See also J. Blair, 'The foundation of Goring Priory', *Oxoniensia*, LI (1986), 194–7.

Margaret (Margery) Occ. June 1200, Apr. 1203 (*Bucks F.*, I, 19, 22); n.d. (after May 1202) (*Newington Longville Chts.*, no. 60); 1205 x 1221 (*Ctl. Oseney*, IV, pp. 391–2, no. 349).

Alice Occ. 6 Oct. 1218 (PRO, Berks F., CP25/1/7/6, no. 5; *EEA*, 19, no. 290a).

Matilda Occ. 1227 (*Goring Chts.*, I, p. xix); Hil. term 1229 (*CRR*, XIII, no. 1567); 20 May 1229 (*Oxford F.*, p. 85, no. 51). Is most prob. the same as **Matilda Mortimer** who occ. n.d. (early 13th cent.: pal.) (PRO, E210/3001).

Matilda ? same as above. Occ. 15 July 1248 (PRO, Berks F., CP25/1/8/16, no. 26; *EEA*, 19, no. 290a).

Eularia –1268 Occ. 27 Jan. 1261 (*Oxford F.*, p. 180, no. 26); 20 June 1266 (*Reg. R. Gravesend*, p. 241). Res. by 23 Feb. 1268 (ibid., p. 220).

Christiana de Marisco (Marsh) 1268–1271 Eln conf. 23 Feb. 1268 (ibid.). Occ. 17 June 1268 (PRO, Berks F., CP25/1/8/27, no. 6). Res. by 8 July 1271 (*Reg. R. Gravesend*, p. 222).

Eularia 1271–1277 Eln conf. 8 July 1271 (ibid., pp. 222, 333). Cess. by 24 Nov. 1277 (ibid., p. 233).

Christiana of Wallingford 1277– Eln conf. 24 Nov. 1277 (ibid., pp. 233, 337).

Sarah of Oxford (Oxon', but also on one occasion Excester *sic*) 1282/3–1298 El. (Excester)19 May 1282 x 18 May 1283 (3rd year of Bp Sutton), lic. to el. having been obtained from the earl of Cornwall, patron (Bodl., Dodsworth ms. 107, f. 145r). D. by 13 Jan. 1298 (*Reg. Sutton*, VIII, 197–8).

---

[7] The year 1375 given in *VCH* for this entry is incorrect.

Agatha of Oxford (Oxon', Oxonia) **1298–1300** N. of Goring, eln quashed but apptd by bp 13 Jan. 1298 (ibid.). Res. 26 Oct. 1300 (Lincoln, Ep. Reg., III, f. 20r). Cess., lic to el. 29 Dec. 1300 (*CPR 1292–1301*, p. 561).

Margery Neel (Nel) **1301–1305** On the cess. of Agatha of Oxford, an eln resulted in 14 votes for Margery Neel, cellaress of Goring, 13 votes for Agnes of Ludgershall, 5 for Isabel of Westwell, and 1 for Petronilla of Hedsor (Hadesaghe). Account of eln exhibited before bp of Lincoln 1 Feb. 1301. The bp deprived the nuns of their right of eln and apptd Margery Neel on 4 Feb. 1301 (Lincoln, Ep. Reg., II, f. 143r). Temps. 9 Feb. 1301 (*CPR 1292–1301*, p. 569). Cess. by 26 Apr. 1305 (PRO, C84/15/30). Res., lic. to el. 2 May 1305 (*CPR 1301–07*, p. 336).

Agnes of Ludgershall (Lotegareshal, Lotegereshale, Lutegarshale) **1305–1313** Sub-prs of Goring, eln conf. 29 May 1305 (Lincoln, Ep. Reg., II, f. 148v). Royal ass. 12 May 1305, writ *de intendendo* 10 June 1305 (*CPR 1301–07*, pp. 337, 364). Cess., lic. to el. 13 Sept. 1313 (*CPR 1313–17*, p. 15).

Clarice of Morton 1313–1345 N. of Goring, eln pres. to king for royal ass. 21 Sept. 1313 (PRO, C84/17/26); royal ass. 28 Sept. 1313 (*CPR 1313–17*, p. 19). Eln quashed but apptd by bp 3 Oct. 1313 (Lincoln, Ep. Reg., II, f. 163v). D. by 20 Apr. 1345 (Lincoln, Ep. Reg., VI, f. 85v). Seal (*BM Seals*, no. 3184).

Margaret de Bale 1345–1361 N. of Goring, eln quashed but apptd by bp 20 Apr. 1345 (ibid.). D., lic. to el. 31 May 1361 (*Reg. Black Prince*, IV, 385).

Lucy of Tidmarsh (Tidemerssh) **1361–1394** Commn to take her fealty 30 June 1361 (ibid.. 387). D. by 10 Aug. 1394 (Lincoln, Ep. Reg., XI, ff. 324v, 430v).

MASTERS

Robert Rector of Glendon, apptd 12 June 1308 (Lincoln, Ep. Reg., III, f. 137r).

Nicholas Rector of Checkendon, apptd administrator 5 Dec. 1309 (ibid., f.165r)

GRACE DIEU (Leics), Holy Trinity and St Mary (Belton, Parc Grace Dieu) (Augustinian priory)

f. *c.* 1239 (*KH*); –1236 x 1242 (Thompson)

Lists in *VCH Leics*, II, 28; Thompson, *Women Religious*, p. 240 (to 1269).

Mary of Stretton 1242/3– N. of Grace Dieu, el. and adm. June 1242 x June 1243, no reason given for vacancy (*Reg. Grosseteste*, p. 420).

Agnes of Gresley (Greseley, Greseleye, Grisle) **–1286** Occ. May 1262 (PRO, Leics F., CP25/1/122/24, no. 450; *Gresley Chts.* no. 99); 28 May 1263 (PRO, Leics F., CP25/1/122/26, no. 500); Oct. 1268 x Oct. 1269 (*Derbys Chts.*, no. 399; *Kniveton Leiger*, no. 47); 20 Oct. 1279 (*Warws F.*, I, no. 940); 4 May 1281 (*Derbys F. (1890)*, p. 39). D. by 29 Sept. 1286 (*Reg. Sutton*, VIII, 36). Seal (*BM Seals*, no. 3220).

Agnes Gurdoun (Gordon, Gurdon) **?1286–1318** Presumably the unnamed prs, el. 29 Sept. 1286, on patron's lic., eln quashed but apptd by bp. 3 Oct. 1286 (ibid.). Occ. *temp.* Edward I (*HMC R.R. Hastings*, I, 29). D. 3 Apr. 1318 (PRO, C84/19/31). D., lic. to el. 12 Apr. 1318 (*CPR 1317–21*, p. 134). Indulgence of 30 days for late prs. 15 Apr. 1319 (Lincoln, Ep. Reg., III, f. 415r).

Joan de Hastinges (Hastyngges) **1318–1330** Sub-prs of Grace Dieu, commn to abb. of Leicester to grant royal ass. 16 Apr. 1318; royal ass. 26 Apr.; commn to take fealty 27 Apr. 1318; temps. 20 May 1318 (*CPR 1317–21*, pp. 134, 136, 139, 142; cf. PRO, C84/19/32). Eln quashed but apptd by bp 15 May 1318 (Lincoln, Ep. Reg., II, f. 215r; PRO, C84/19/35). Fealty given 16 May 1318 (PRO, C84/19/36). D., lic. to el. 7 Dec. 1330 (*CPR 1330–34*, p. 19). 12 Dec. 1330 power given to abb. of Leicester to give the royal ass. to the eln of a prs. in place of Joan de Hastinges, deceased, and to receive fealty. This power granted out of pity for the poverty of the sub-prs and convent (ibid., p. 30).

Joan de Meinwaryng (Mewaryn, Meyngwaryng) **1331–1349** N. of Grace Dieu, eln quashed but apptd by bp 11 Jan. 1331 (Lincoln, Ep. Reg., IV, f. 131r). Temps. 12 Jan. 1331 (*CPR 1330–34*, p. 33). D. by 3 Dec. 1349 (Lincoln, Ep. Reg., IX, f. 347r).

Cecily de Straule 1349– N. of Grace Dieu, eln quashed but apptd by bp. 3 Dec. 1349 (ibid.). Occ. 1377 (*Clerical Poll-Taxes*, p. 28, no. 372).

The next recorded prs, **Margaret of Twyford**, res. by 3 May 1401 (Lincoln, Ep. Reg., XIII, f. 193r).

GREENFIELD (Lincs), St Mary f. -1153 (*KH*); 1148 x 1166, ? -1153 (Thompson) (Cistercian priory)

Lists in *VCH Lincs*, II, 155–6; *Heads*, I, 212; Thompson, *Women Religious*, p. 240 (to 1275).

Matilda Occ. 1195 x 1223 (BL, Lansdowne ms. 207A, f. 16r); early 13th cent. (BL, Harl. Cht. 44 D 59).

Agnes Occ. 1230 (*CPR 1225–32*, p. 353); *temp.* Henry III (BL, Harl. Cht. 44 D 56).

Mabel (Amabilia) Occ. 29 Sept. 1237 (BL, Harl. Cht. 44 D 57); 12 May 1240 (*Lincs F.*, I, 320).

Alice of Lincoln (Lincolnia) **1250/1–** N. of Greenfield, eln conf. June 1250 x June 1251, no reason given for vacancy (*Reg. Grosseteste*, p. 122); n.d. (1250/1 x 1259/60, *temp.* pr. John of Markby). (BL, Harl. Cht. 44 G 5).

Matilda Occ. 1 May 1260 (BL, Harl. Cht. 44 D 60).

Joan de Heyw[o]rth (Eyeworth) **1275–1285** N. of Greenfield, eln conf. 29 Sept. 1275 on res. of unnamed prs (*Reg. R. Gravesend*, p. 66). Res. by 5 Oct. 1285 (*Reg. Sutton*, I, 68).

Sarah of Willoughby (Wyluby, Wylugby) **1285–1289** N. of Greenfield, eln quashed but apptd by bp 5 Oct. 1285 (ibid., 68–9). Res. by 30 July 1289 (ibid., 124).

Christiana of Owmby (Ouneby) **1289–1293** N. of Greenfield, eln conf. 30 July 1289 (ibid., 124–5). Mand. to receive her res. issued 26 Sept. 1293 or to absolve her from office if she would not res. Commn to examine and conf. future eln of a new prs 27 Sept. 1293 (ibid., 118–19).

Isabel (Elizabeth) of Harrington (Harington) **1293–1301** Eln conf. 21 Oct. 1293, no reason given for vacancy (ibid., I, 199–200). Res. by 28 Mar. 1301 (Lincoln, Ep. Reg., II, ff. 3v–4r).

Cecily de Parys 1301–1305 Commn to examine eln n.d. but prob. 20 Mar. 1301 (Lincoln, Ep. Reg., III, f. 27v). Eln conf. 28 Mar. 1301 (Lincoln, Ep. Reg., II, ff. 3v–4r). Res. by 29 May 1305 (ibid., f. 13v).

Agnes de Langholm 1305–1313 N. of Greenfield, eln quashed & apptd by bp 29 May 1305 (ibid.). Res. by 8 Aug. 1313 (ibid., f. 48r).

Ivetta of Ormsby (Ormesby) 1313– N. of Greenfield, eln quashed but apptd by bp 8 Aug. 1313 (ibid.). Occ. 9 Apr. 1325 (BL, Harl. Cht. 44 E 1); 13 June 1325 (BL, Harl. Cht. 44 E 3); 15 Oct. 1328 (*Medieval Lindsey Marsh*, p. 90, no. 51).

Margaret de Well' (Welle) 1331–1349 N. of Greenfield, commn to examine eln 18 June 1330, no reason given for vacancy (Lincoln, Ep. Reg., V, f. 432r). Occ. as godmother 1334 (Owen, *Church and Society in Medieval Lincolnshire*, p. 103). D. 1349 (see below), lic. to el. 22 Feb. 1350 (*CPR 1348–50*, p. 473). Priory vacant over 3 months, so that the right of appt devolves to the bp, who commns pr. of Markby and the rectors of Willoughby and Withern to go to the priory and choose and appt a prs 27 Feb. 1350 (Lincoln, Ep. Reg., IX, f. 42v).

Isabel Occ. 13 Mar. 1366 (BL, Harl. Cht 44 E 9).

Joan Fouler Occ. 1377, 1381 (*Clerical Poll-Taxes*, p. 42, no. 597 & pp. 121, 168, nos. 1487, 2088); 22 July 1397 (BL, Harl Cht. 44 E 10).

MASTERS

Roger Occ. *c.* 1227 x 1229 (BL, Cotton Cht. XXIX 72), *temp.* W. pr. of Hagnaby and John, vicar of Alford.

Benedict Occ. 29 Sept. 1237 (BL, Harl. Cht. 44 D 57).

Robert Occ. 21 July 1268 (BL, Harl. Cht. 48 A 12).

Henry of Langton ment. as former master, d. at Stamford 26 Apr. 1279 and bur. in the Franciscan friary at Stamford (*Medieval Lindsey Marsh*, p. 71, no. 31).

Richard Rector of Withern, apptd during pleasure 20 May 1335 (Lincoln, Ep. Reg., V, f. 498r).

GRIMSBY (Lincs), St Leonard f. -1184 (*KH*); -1171 x 1180 (Thompson) (Augustinian priory)

Lists in *VCH Lincs*, II, 179; *Heads*, I, 212; Thompson, *Women Religious*, p. 241.

Alice and **Emma** Occ. n.d., possibly late 12th cent. or 13th cent. (BL, Lansdowne ms. 207A, ff. 204r, 216v).

Philippa Occ. 27 Oct. 1256 (*Lincs F.*, II, 119).

Agnes of Bradley (Bradele) −1298 D. by 30 Mar. 1298 (*Reg. Sutton*, I, 226).

Matilda de Grafham 1298−1309 Sub-prs of Grimsby, eln conf. 30 Mar 1298 (ibid., 226−7). D. by 17 June 1309 (Lincoln, Ep. Reg., II, f. 29r).

Avice Frauncks 1309− N. of Grimsby, eln quashed but apptd by bp 17 June 1309 (ibid.). Occ. 1 Oct. 1313 (ibid., f. 48v); 1321 (BL, Lansdowne ms. 207A, f. 204r).

Alice of Aylesby (Alysby) −1370/1 Vacant by cess. n.d. but between entries for 28 Dec. 1370 and 8 Mar. 1371 (Lincoln, Ep. Reg., X, f. 44r).

Agnes de Humbilton (also Humberston) 1370/1− N. of Grimsby, eln quashed but apptd by bp n.d. (28 Dec. 1370 x 8 Mar. 1371) (ibid.). Occ. 1377, 1381 (*Clerical Poll-Taxes*, p. 54, no. 762; pp. 122, 169, nos. 1491, 2092). Occ. June 1392 x June 1393 (BL, Lansdowne ms. 207A, f. 204r).

The next recorded prs, **Eleanor Byllesby**, el. 1409, commn to examine eln 27 June 1409, no reason given for vacancy (Lincoln, Ep. Reg., XIV, f. 35v).

MASTERS

Robert Occ. n.d (BL, Lansdowne ms. 207A, ff. 203r, 205r) with no indication as to date, or place in the sequence of masters.

John of Lincoln 1231/2− Can. of Wellow, el. Dec. 1231 x Dec. 1232 (*Reg. Wells*, III, 202).

Philip Occ. 12 May 1265 (*Reg. R. Gravesend*, p. 19)

William of North Coates (Northcotes) Can. of Wellow, apptd 29 May 1303 (Lincoln, Ep. Reg., III, f. 56v).

Richard 1318− Vicar of Little Coates, apptd 30 Aug. 1318 (ibid., f. 395r). Commn to hear accounts of vicar of Little Coates as custodian of the goods of Grimsby 2 Sept. 1324 (Lincoln, Ep. Reg., V, f. 368r).

Geoffrey of Wyham (Wyhum) 1325− Can. of Wellow, apptd during pleasure 24 Nov. 1325 (ibid., f. 386v).

HALIWELL, *see* **LONDON, HALIWELL**

HAMPOLE (Yorks W.) St Mary. f. -1156 (Cistercian priory)

Lists in *VCH Yorks*, III, 165; Thompson, *Women Religious*, p. 241 (to mid-13th cent.).

Cecily Occ. 22 May 1204 (BI, CP.E.195). ? the same as occ. n. d. (*Ctl. Whalley*, III, 652).

Alice Occ. 1230 (*EYC*, II, 166).

Joan de Crescy Occ. 26 July 1259 (*Ctl. Whalley*, III, 696); n.d. (poss. 13th cent.) (*EYC*, III, 166).

Denise Occ. 3 Sept. 1285 (BL, Cotton ms. Nero D III, f. 58v).

Christina Occ. 24 June 1294 (*YB XXIII*, 55).

At a visitation in 1312 the unnamed prs was stated to be the sister of Hugh de Cressy (*Reg. Greenfield*, II, no. 962). She is almost certainly to be identified with **Constance (Custance) de Crescy**, n. of Hampole, sent to Swine priory to do penance 7 Mar. 1313 and allowed to return to Hampole in the same month (ibid., nos. 984, 987).

Agnes of Pontefract (Pontefracto) 1313–1320 Eln conf. 28 Feb. 1313, no reason given for vacancy (*Reg. Greenfield*, II, p. 139, no. 980). D., lic. to el. 29 Feb. 1320 (York, Reg. 9A, f. 167r)

Margaret of Heck (Hecke) 1320– N. of Hampole, eln quashed but apptd by archbp 14 Mar. 1320 (ibid., f. 167v). Occ. 23 Dec. 1321, 16 Jan. 1322 (*Ctl. Whalley*, III, 710, 713); Trinity 1335 (Baildon, I, 84).

Matilda Occ. 1346 (*VCH*, citing Baildon, ms. notes, no other source given)

Idonea Occ. 30 Nov. 1369 (Sheffield City Arch., Wentworth Woodhouse muns. D. 122).

Elizabeth Fairfax Occ. 1380 x 1389 (Burton, *Mon. Ebor.*, p. 265, citing Metham's register: doct of 138–). Occ. 1414 (Baildon, I, 85).

MASTERS

Ralph Vicar of Adwick le Street, occ. 1241 x 1247, prob. *c.* 1241 (*Ctl. Fountains*, I, 259; *Fasti Parochiales*, I, 1).

Richard (or Ralph) Vicar of Wath upon Dearne, apptd as *custos* 14 July 1280 (*Reg. Wickwane*, p. 28, no. 89 – duplicate registers give different Christian names).

John Vicar of Conisbrough, apptd as *custos* 9 Sept. 1281 (ibid., p. 37, no. 119). *Fasti Parochiales*, II, 71 names the vicar as John de Connesburc'.

HANDALE (Yorks N), St Mary. (Grendale) f. 1133 (*KH*); ? 1133, *c.* 1150 x 1170 (Thompson) (Cistercian priory)

Lists in *VCH Yorks*, III, 166; *Heads*, I, 212; Thompson, *Women Religious*, p. 241 (to 1269).

Rohays Occ. n.d. in earlier gt confirmed on 7 June 1336 (*CChR 1327–41*, p. 367), no clue as to place in the sequence of prioresses.

Beleisur Occ. 12 Nov. 1208 (*Yorks F. John*, p. 148).

Bella Occ. 17 June 1240 (*Yorks F., 1232–46*, pp. 58–9).

Avice Occ. 18 Oct. 1262, 11 Nov. 1269 (*Ctl. Guisborough*, II, 201, 223).

Ivetta Occ. 22 Apr. 1287 (ibid., II, 154); 1300, 1301, 1305 (Baildon, I, 86–7); Mich. 1305 (PRO, CP40/153, m. 189); 1305–6 case regarding assault on prs (Smith, *Court of York 1301–1399*, p. 2).

Cecily de Irton 1313–1315 N. of Handale, eln conf. 7 June 1313, no reason given for vacancy (*Reg. Greenfield*, III, p. 76, no. 1304). Commn to receive res. 12 May 1315 (ibid., pp. 106–7, no. 1363).

Mariota of Harlsey (Herlesey) –1318 Res. by 9 Aug. 1318 (*Reg. Melton*, II, p. 27, no. 54).

Alice of Hutton (Hoton) 1318–1320 N. of Handale, eln quashed but apptd by archbp 9 Aug. 1318 (ibid., pp. 27–8, nos. 54–5). Res., lic. to el. 15 Oct. 1320 (ibid., p. 62, no. 130).

Agnes 1320– Eln conf. & bl. 26 Oct. 1320 (ibid., p. 63, no. 134)

Commn to visit priory and to receive the cession of unnamed prs. 13 May 1335 (*Reg. Melton*, II, p. 169, no. 439).

The next recorded prs, **Katherine of Gilling** (Gillyng), occ. Michaelmas 1413 (Baildon, I, 87).

MASTERS

William of Bardney (Bardenay), m. of Whitby, apptd during pleasure 16 Mar. 1268 (*Reg. W. Giffard*, p. 54), see also Baysdale.

Thomas of Middlesbrough (Midlesburgh), Rector of Loftus, apptd as keeper of temps. of the priory 31 May 1318 (*Reg. Melton*, II, pp. 15–16, no. 35).

HARROLD (Beds), St Peter f. *c.* 1136 x 1138 (Arrouaisian); *c.* 1188 (independent) (Augustinian priory)

    Lists in *VCH Beds*, I, 389–90; *Ctl. Harrold*, pp. 13–14; *Heads*, I, 212–13; Thompson, *Women Religious*, pp. 241–2 (to 1268).

Agnes –1245/6 Occ. 1227 (*Beds Eyre*, nos. 97, 99); 10 May 1237 (*Beds F.*, I, no. 397; *Ctl. Harrold*, no. 40); 25 Nov. 1240 (*Beds F.*, I, no. 452). D. June 1245 x June 1246 (*Reg. Grosseteste*, p. 325).

Basilia de la Lee N. of Harrold, el. and adm. June 1245 x June 1246 (ibid.). Occ. 1251 (*Ctl. Harrold*, no. 10; BL, Harl. Cht. 84 F 34); 11 Nov. 1254 (*Beds F.*, I, no. 567; *Ctl. Harrold*, no. 149). Called **Maudut** (? for Mauduit) n.d. (*Ctl. Harrold*, no. 130).

Amice[8] Occ. 7 May 1262 (*Beds F.*, I, no. 627); 18 Apr. 1264 (*Ctl. Harrold*, no. 41); 14 Apr. 1268 (ibid., no. 17).

Margery of Hereford (Hereforde, Herford) –1304 Occ. n.d. (1270 x 1273) (ibid., no. 29); 1302 (ibid., no. 138*); 6 Feb. 1304 (ibid., no. 19). Res. by 29 June 1304 (Lincoln, Ep. Reg., II, f. 258r–v)

Cecily of Kent (Cant') 1304– N. of Harrold, eln quashed but apptd by bp 29 June 1304 (ibid.). Occ. 1 Sept. 1311 (*Ctl. Harrold*, no. 100). For Kent surname see ibid., p. 13.

Agnes Occ. 22 Sep. 1334 (Lincoln, Ep. Reg., V, f. 307v)

Petronilla de Ridewale (Rydewar) 1336–1354 N. of Harrold, commn to examine eln 27 Apr. 1336, no reason given for vacancy (ibid., ff. 527v–528r). Cess. by 29 Mar. 1354 (Lincoln, Ep. Reg., IX, f. 432r).

Christiana Murdak 1354–1357 N. of Harrold, eln quashed but apptd by bp 29 Mar. 1354 (ibid.). Cess. by 3 Aug. 1357 (ibid., f. 436r–v).

Matilda of Titchmarsh (Tichemersh) 1357– N. of Harrold, eln quashed but apptd by bp 3 Aug. 1357 (ibid., f. 436v). Occ. 13 Dec. 1362 (*Ctl. Harrold*, no. 173).

Katherine Occ. 1 Aug. 1367 (ibid., no. 145).

Commn to grant admin. of priory to Katherine of Tutbury, n. of Harrold during vacancy 11 Dec. 1369 (Lincoln, Ep. Reg., XII, f. 93r).

Commn to appt a prs in bp's name, the priory having been vacant over 6 months and to certify the bp 6 May 1370 (ibid., f. 94r).

Katherine of Tutbury (Tudbery, Tudbury, Tuttebury) –1394 Prob. the prs apptd. Occ. 1375 (*Ctl. Harrold*, no. 167); 1381 (ibid., no. 141); 1392 (ibid., no. 261). D. by 21 Mar. 1394 when commn ordered to examine eln of successor (Lincoln, Ep. Reg., XI, f. 430v).

MASTER

Mag. Robert de Wutton 1292– Apptd as master 23 Oct. 1292, no reason given for vacancy (*Reg. Sutton*, IV, 42).

HEDINGHAM, *see* **CASTLE HEDINGHAM**

HENWOOD (Warws), St Margaret f. 1154 x 1159 (*KH*); 1149 x 1157 (Thompson) (Benedictine priory)

    List in VCH *Warws*, II, 66; Thompson, *Women Religious*, p. 242 (to late Henry III).

Ellen Occ. 15 June 1252 (*Warws. F.*, I, no. 713).

Juliana Occ. n.d. (?13th cent.) (PRO, E326/11034; Madox, *Form.*, p. 377, no. dclxxxiii). The precise sequence of prioresses is uncertain.

Matilda Occ. ? 2nd half of 13th cent. (pal.) (BL, Cotton Cht. XXI 18).

---

[8] Juliana who occ. *VCH*, *Ctl. Harrold*, no. 14, is a miscopying for prs Jelita (*c.* 1200 x 1210); *Ctl. Harrold*, no. 117 is likewise a scribal error, copying the name of the grantor's wife.

Avice de Flateebiry Occ. n.d. (after 1268) (*Magnum Reg. Album Lichfield*, p. 346, no. 725).

Katherine Boydin –1310 Res. 8 Apr. 1310 and retired to Polesworth (Lichfield, B/A/1/1, ff. 35v–36r).

Margaret le Corzon 1310– Eln quashed, but apptd by bp 15 Apr. 1310 (ibid.). Occ. 4 July 1334 (PRO, E40/4438).

A prs (not named) was infirm and commn to to adm. cession and to proceed to eln issued 30 Mar. 1339. Prob. Margaret le Corzon (Lichfield, B/A/1/2, f. 34v).

Millicent (Milisanda) de Fokerham 1339– El. 30 Apr. 1337; eln quashed, but apptd by bp's commissary 15 May 1339 (ibid.). Occ. 9 Apr. 1344 (PRO, C146/5232).

A long time vacant as only 3 of its 15 nuns survived. Commn to supervise eln 19 Aug. 1349. The 3 nuns transferred right of appt to bp (Lichfield, B/A/1/2, f. 52r).

Joan (de) Fokerham 1349–1351 N. of Henwood, apptd by bp 22 Aug. 1349 (ibid.). Commn dated 2 Aug. 1351 to receive res. and appt new prs. (Lichfield, B/A/1/3, f. 128v).

Joan Blount 1351– N. of Henwood, appt by bp 13 Aug. 1351 (ibid.).

The next recorded prs, **Joan de Pickeford**, had d. by 12 Apr. 1392 (Lichfield, B/A/1/6, f. 7v).

HEYNINGS (Lincs), St Mary (Knaith) f.1135+ (*KH*); *c.* 1147 x 1152 (Thompson) (Cistercian priory)

   Lists in *VCH Lincs*, II, 151; Thompson, *Women Religious*, p. 242 (to 1272).

An unnamed n. of Heynings was apptd prs by bp June 1236 x June 1237, no reason given for vacancy (*Reg. Grosseteste*, p. 137).

Alice of the Bail of Lincoln (de Ballivo Lincolnie) 1241– N. of Heynings, apptd by bp by authority of the Council, 25 May 1241, no reason given for vacancy (ibid., pp. 143–4).

Isolda 1263/4– N. of Heynings, eln conf. 12 Apr. 1264, no reason given for vacancy (*Reg. R. Gravesend*, p. 90).

Margery of Pocklington –1299 Occ. 23 Feb. 1272 (*Lincs. F.*, II, 257); 12 Nov. 1284 (PRO, Lincs. F., CP/25/1/123/35, nos. 102, 123). Res. by 12 Oct. 1299 (*Reg. Sutton*, VIII, 30–1).

Margaret of Marton 1299– Eln pres. to bp 12 Oct. 1299, eln conf. 13 Oct. 1299 (ibid.).

Margaret de Swaleclif –1315 Res. by 12 June 1315 (Lincoln, Ep. Reg., II, f. 97v).

Joan of Collingham (Colingham) 1315–1319 Sub-prs of Heynings, eln conf. 12 June 1315 (ibid.). Res. by 12 Nov. 1319 (ibid., f. 101r).

Margaret Cause 1319–1348 N. of Heynings, eln quashed & apptd by bp 12 Nov. 1319 (ibid.). Res. by 3 Jan. 1348 (Lincoln, Ep. Reg., IX, f. 154r).

Eleanor Jorce 1348–1352 Sub-prs. of Heynings, apptd by bp, to whom the right of appt was transferred by the convent, 3 Jan. 1348 (ibid.). Res. by 31 Dec. 1352 (ibid., f.165r–v).

Alice of Coxwold (Cokeswald) 1353– N. of Heynings, eln pres. to bp 31 Dec. 1352, eln conf. 11 Jan. 1353 (ibid.).

Commn to examine eln of an unnamed prs, the previous prs (also unnamed) having died, dated 30 June 1369 (Lincoln, Ep. Reg., XII, f. 75r).

Commn 21 Jan. 1375 to receive the cess. of an unnamed prs and supervise el. of a successor (ibid., f. 136v).

Cecily of Watton Occ. 1377 (*Clerical Poll-Taxes*, p. 65, no. 871) and 1381 (ibid., p. 171, no. 2129).

The next prs, **Richilda de Scupholme**, had res. by 3 Aug. 1390, when eln of successor pres. to bp (Lincoln, Ep. Reg., XI, f. 105v).

MASTERS

Walter Occ. early 13th cent. (BL Harl. Cht. 45 D 12, with John, pr. of Torksey, res. 1236/7); mentioned in an inspeximus of 16 Aug. 1268 (*CChR 1257–1300*, p. 110).

Thomas de Perrariis (Perariis) 1290– Canon of Lincoln, apptd 4 June 1290 (*Reg. Sutton*, III,

96). Occ. 20 June 1291, when lic. was given to the vicar of Upton to take charge of their affairs, while T. de P. was unavoidably burdened with other business (ibid., 104).[9]

Henry 1294– Rector of Blankney, apptd 25 Apr. 1294 (ibid., IV, 184).[10]

William de Fynchesden 1340– Clerk, apptd 27 Oct. 1340 during pleasure (Lincoln, Ep. Reg., V, f. 586v).

HIGHAM (Kent), St Mary (Lillechurch) f. ?1148 (dependent on S. Sulpice, Rennes); 1227+ (independent) (*KH*); *c.* 1150 x 1152 (Thompson) (Benedictine priory)

Lists in *VCH Kent*, II, 146; *Heads*, I, 213; Thompson, *Women Religious*, p. 242 (to 1255).

Amphelisa Occ. 1185 x 1214 (Cambridge, St John's Coll., ms. D.10.22B, D.46. 41).

Alice Occ. 1243 x 1244 (ibid., D.46.93), possibly the prs Alice mentd n.d. (*Mon. Angl.*, IV, 378). Lic. to el. issued (no name) 21 Nov. 1247 (*CPR 1247–58*, p. 2).

Joan de Meriston 1247– N. of Higham, royal ass. 24 Nov. 1247 (ibid.); mand. to take fealty and for seisin 12 Dec. 1247 (*CCR 1247–51*, p. 16). Occ. 8 July 1255 (*Kent F.*, p. 268).

A badly faded doct among the series of ecclesiastical petitions (PRO, C84/3/52) relates to Higham *c.* 1265 or 1266. It possibly relates to a vacancy.

Acelina of Rochester (Roff') **–1275** Occ. 2 Mar. 1266 (*CPR 1258–66*, p.563). Cess., lic. to el. 27 Mar. 1275 (*CPR 1272–81*, p. 84; PRO, C84/5/27).

Amfelisia de Dunlegh(e) 1275–1295 N. of Higham, royal ass. 10 Apr. 1275 (ibid.). D. (Enfelise), lic. to el. 8 June 1295 (*CPR 1292–1301*, p. 136).

Matilda of London 1295–1301 N. of Higham, order to bp to execute his office in respect of the eln 14 July 1295 (*Cal. Chanc. Warr.*, p. 64). Temps. 6 Aug. 1295, having been conf. by bp of Rochester (*CPR 1292–1301*, p. 138). D. 19 Jan. 1301 (PRO, C84/14/7). D., lic. to el. 28 Jan. 1301 (*CPR 1292–1301*, p. 563).

Joan de Handlo (Hadlee) **1301–1329** N. of Higham, el. 13 Feb. 1301 (PRO, C84/14/5); royal ass. 22 Feb. 1301, temps. 11 Mar. 1301, eln having been conf. by Thomas, bp of Rochester (*CPR 1292–1301*, pp. 573, 579). D. 11 Jan. 1329 (PRO, C84/22/16). D., lic, to el. 25 Jan. 1329 (*CPR 1327–30*, p. 357). Said to have been bur. 3 Feb. 1329 (*Ang. Sac.*, I, 369).

Matilda de Greenestede (Grensted) **1329–1340** Called Colchester (Colecestre) according to *Ang. Sac.*, I, 369. N. of Higham, eln pres. to king for royal ass. 1 Feb. 1329 (PRO, C84/22/17); royal ass. 4 Feb. 1329, temps. 9 Feb. 1329 (*CPR 1327–30*, pp. 359–60). Eln pres. to bp, no reason given for vacancy 6 or 7 Feb. 1329, conf. 9 Feb. 1329 (*Reg. Hethe*, I, 240–1, 509–11; PRO, C84/22/18). D., lic. to el. 5 July 1340 (*CPR 1338–1340*, p. 550). Inq. *post mortem* 13 July 1340 (Cambridge, St John's Coll., D46.12).

Elizabeth de Delham 1340–1361 Sub-prs of Higham, eln pres. to king for royal ass. 8 July 1340 (PRO, C84/24/15A); royal ass. 10 July 1340, temps. 18 July 1340 (*CPR 1340–43*, pp. 4, 9; *Reg. Hethe*, II, 630). El. 7 July 1340; appt of proctor to seek conf. of eln 11 July; eln pres. to bp 13 July; bp conf. eln 17 July 1340 (ibid., 618–30; PRO, C84/24/16). Presumably the unnamed prs assaulted 1354 (*CPR 1354–58*, p. 98). Vacant by d. of Isabel (*sic*) de Delham, D. 22 Aug. 1361 (Maidstone, Centre for Kentish Studies, DRb/Ar1/2, f. 36v). D. (Elizabeth), lic. to el. 15 Sept. 1361 (ibid., f. 37v).

Cecily (de) Leyham 1361–1386 N. and cellarer of Higham, el. 23 Sept. 1361 (ibid., ff. 36v–37). Royal ass. 29 Sept. 1361 (ibid., f. 37v; *CPR 1361–64*, p. 78). Temps. 11 Nov. 1361 (ibid., p. 95). Commn of archbp of Canterbury to examine eln 2 Oct. 1361 (Rochester, DRb/Ar1/2, f. 37v). Eln conf. by commissary 14 Oct. 1361 (ibid.). Letter to king asking for release of temps. 25 Oct. 1361 (Lambeth, Reg, Islip, f. 226r). D. 26 Sept. 1386 (PRO, C84/34/7). D., lic. to el. 28 Sept. 1386 (*CPR 1385–89*, p. 216).

---

[9] Preb. of Dunham and Newport *c.* 1280 x 86 – 1305 (*Fasti 1066–1300*, III, 67; *Fasti 1300–1541*, I, 61).

[10] Henry de Alveleye instd to Blankney 1286 and re-instd 1287 (*Reg. Sutton*, I, 80, 95).

HINCHINGBROOKE (Hunts), St James (St James without Huntingdon) f. -1087 (*KH*); ?*temp.* William I (Papley); by 1186 x 1190 (Hinchingbrooke) (Thompson) (Benedictine priory) Lists in *VCH Hunts*, I, 390; *Heads*, I, 238; Thompson, *Women Religious*, p. 242 (to 1274).

Cecily Occ. Easter term 1228 (*CCR*, XIII, no. 687).

Agnes of Bottisham (Botheksham) **1245/6–** N. of Hinchingbrooke, el. and adm. June 1245 x June 1246, no reason given for vacancy (*Reg. Grosseteste*, p. 289).

Lucy de Sibtoft **–1258/9** Res. Nov. 1258 x Nov. 1259 (*Reg. R. Gravesend*, p. 167).

[**Cecily of Huntingdon** (Hunt') El. but not accepted (ibid.).]

Emma of Bedford **1258/9–1274** N. of Hinchingbrooke, apptd by bp on res. of Lucy Nov. 1258 x Nov. 1259 (ibid.). Occ. 2 June 1272 (PRO, Cambs F., CP25/1/25/35, no. 52). D. by 17 Mar. 1274 (*Reg. R. Gravesend*, p. 180).

Ellen la Waleys (Walensis) **1274–1293** N. of Hinchingbrooke, eln conf. 17 Mar. 1274 (ibid.). D. by 15 Mar. 1293 (*Reg. Sutton*, VIII, 80).

Alice of Barwick (Berewyk) **1293–1315** Sub-prs of Hinchingbrooke, eln conf. 15 Mar. 1293 (ibid.). D. by 28 Mar. 1315 (Lincoln, Ep. Reg., II, f. 248r).

Joan of Raunds (Raundes) **1315–** N. of Hinchingbrooke, eln quashed but apptd by bp 28 Mar. 1315 (ibid.). Occ. 29 Sept. and 17 Dec. 1318 (BL, Add. Cht. 34256).

Amice de Ardern **1334–** N. of Hinchingbrooke, commn to examine eln 23 Nov. 1334, no reason given for vacancy (Lincoln, Ep. Reg., V, f. 487v).

Isabel de Ulleswik **1337–** N. of Hinchingbrooke, commn to examine eln 9 Jan. 1337, no reason given for vacancy (Lincoln, Ep. Reg., V, ff. 544v–545r). Occ. 26 July 1339 (BL, Add. Cht. 34094).

Amice de Ardern Occ. 21 June 1346 (BL, Add. Cht. 33069). Presumably she had a second term as prs.

Isabel de Blythe (Blithe) **1349** N. of Hinchingbrooke, eln quashed but apptd by bp on d. of last (unnamed) prs 26 Feb. 1349 (Lincoln, Ep. Reg., IX, f. 386r). D. by 3 May 1349 (ibid., ff. 21v, 385v–386r).

Joan of Titchmarsh (Tychemersh, Tychmersh) **1349–** N. of Hinchingbrooke, commn to examine eln dated 3 May 1349 (ibid., f. 21v); eln quashed on account of irregularity but Joan apptd by commissary 7 May 1349 (ibid., ff. 385v–386r).

Anne Occ. 1 Sept. 1353 (BL, Add. Cht. 33489).

Joan of Titchmarsh (Tichemerssh, Tychmersh) **1358–1392** Commn to examine eln dated 14 Mar. 1358 (Lincoln, Ep. Reg., VIII, f. 99v). D. by 1 Aug. 1392 (Lincoln, Ep. Reg., IX, f. 268r–v).

HOLYSTONE (Northumberland), St Mary f. -1124, 1124 x 1152 (Thompson) (Ben.); 13th cent. (Augustinian). List in K.G. Hall, 'A note on the Benedictine nunnery at Holystone', *Proc. Soc. Ant. Newcastle*, 4th ser., 6 (1933–5), pp. 155–8, at 158.

Beatrice Occ. ? *c.* 1230 (*Early Newcastle Deeds*, p. 122, no. 196; *Hist. Northumberland*, XV, 460); 1240 (*Ctl. Brinkburn*, pp. 126–7, no. 151).

Agnes Occ. ? *c.* 1261 x 1262 (ibid., p. 128, no. 153, witn. Adam de Gesemwe, sheriff of Northumberland); Whitsun 1272 (*Ctl. Newminster*, p. 141).

Sibyl Bataille N. of Holystone, eln conf. by archbp, Durham *sede vacante* 5 Aug. 1283, no reason given for vacancy (*Reg. Wickwane*, pp. 223–4, no. 544).

Margery Paid homage to Edward I on 28 Aug. 1296 (*Cal. Docs. Scotland*, II, 213).

Margery of Horsley (Horseley, Horslay) **–1342** Possibly the same as above. Occ. July 1322 x July 1323 (PRO, E213/76). D. 1342 (*Reg. Pal. Dun.*, III, 496). Seal (*Northumberland and Durham Seals*, p. 165, no. 413).

Elizabeth of Sussex 1342– El. 1342 on d. of Margery de Horslay, commn to examine eln n.d. (ibid., 496–7). Occ. 1348 (PRO, Just.1/1435, m. 1d).

Joan Occ. 13 Mar. 1379 (Durham, Reg. Hatfield, f. 159r).

Katharine Conyers Occ. c. June x Aug. 1379 (PRO, E179/60/4, m. 1d – collection period for subsidy).

MASTER

William Prob. master, occ. ? c. 1230 (*Early Newcastle Deeds*, p. 123, no. 196).

HUNTINGDON, ST JAMES, *see* HINCHINGBROOKE

ICKLETON (Cambs), St Mary Magdalen f. -1154 (*KH*); -1158 (Thompson) (Benedictine priory)

Lists in *VCH Cambs*, II, 226; Goddard, *Ickleton Church and Priory*, pp. 186–7; *Heads*, I, 213; Thompson, *Women Religious*, p. 243 (to 1272).

Euphemia Occ. 1206 x 15 (p. j. d. decision +24 Apr. 1206; BL, Add. ms. 46353, f. 294r; cf. Cheney, *Inn. III*, no. 705).

Ellen Occ. 1232 (PRO, E326/11,550).

Lettice Occ. 13 Oct. 1257 (PRO, Cambs. F., CP25/1/25/28 no. 20).

Margaret of St Andrew (de Sancta Andrea) Occ. 1272 (*Mon. Angl.*, IV, 439 and n.; BL, Add ms. 5823, f. 52v).

Cecily Occ. Easter 1276 (PRO, CP40/14, m. 24d); 24 Apr. 1289 (PRO, Cambs. F., CP25/1/26/43 no. 17/1).

Mary –1338 D. by 8 Aug. 1338 (*CCR 1337–39*, p. 455).

Alice Lacy –1352 Dep. by Bp Lisle of Ely (PRO, CP40/378, m. 46).

Christiana Coleman Occ. Easter 1361 (PRO, CP40/406, m. 146d).

Avice Kersen' (Cressener) Occ. 8 Aug. 1373 (Lambeth, Reg. Whittlesey, f. 154v); 1379 (PRO, E179/23/1, m.3; *East Anglian*, XIII, 123); (Cressener) 10 Jan. 1389 (PRO, E315/44/275). 26 July 1402 (*Mon. Angl.*, IV, 439).

ILCHESTER (Soms), Holy Trinity (Whitehall) f. 1217 x 20 (as hospital); -1281 (as priory). ? Augustinian, not certain (*KH*, p. 288).

Archdn of Wells to hold enquiry touching the vacancy of the custody of the priory 1 Dec. 1313 (*Reg. Droxford*, p. 160).

Alice de la Yerde (Atteyerd) **–1315** Bp of Bath and Wells appts 2 incumbents to administer priory July 1315 (ibid., p. 93); further grant of custody 17 Aug. 1315 (ibid., p. 96). Commn to deprive the prs Nov. 1315 (ibid., p. 100). Alms begged for the expelled prs by the nuns; bp of Bath and Wells asks the archbp of Canterbury to make some provision, since an appeal is going on in the Court of Canterbury and the bp cannot act, 5 Sept. 1316 (ibid., p. 115).

Alice of Chilthorne (Chilterne, Chilthorn) **–1325** 2 custodians to take charge of priory through mismanagement of unnamed prs 18 Sept. 1323 (ibid., p. 228). Commn to enquire into offences imputed to the prs 29 Jan. 1324 (ibid.). Deprived after visitation; notification to patron on 3 Apr. 1325 (ibid., p. 245).

Cecily of Draycott (Draycote) Occ. 7 Aug. 1335 (*Reg. R. Shrewsbury*, I, no. 920).

Matilda Occ. Easter 1361 (PRO, CP40/406, m. 266); 1377 (PRO, E179/4/1, m. 6).

IVINGHOE (Herts, formerly Bucks), St Margaret (St Margaret-iuxta-Markyate) (Benedictine priory) f. 1107 x 1129.

Lists in *VCH Bucks*, I, 354–5; Thompson, *Women Religious*, p. 243 (to 1275).

Alice Occ. 8 Feb. 1237 (*CChR 1226–57*, p. 26).

Isolda –1261/2 Occ. *c.*1250 (*Mon. Angl.*, IV, 269 – no source). D. Nov. 1261 x Nov. 1262 (*Reg. R. Gravesend*, p. 237).

Cecily 1262–1275 N. of Ivinghoe, el. & adm. Nov. 1261 x Nov. 1262 (ibid., pp. 237, 339). Royal ass. 10 Apr. 1262 and order to grant her temps. if she is conf. by diocesan (*CCR 1261–64*, p. 41). Res. by 22 Jan. 1275 (*Reg. R. Gravesend*, p. 252).

Matilda of Hockliffe (Hocclive) 1275–1295 N. of Ivinghoe, eln conf. 22 Jan. 1275 (ibid.). D. by 17 Aug. 1295 (*Reg. Sutton*, VIII, 162).

Isabel de Beauchamp (Bello Campo) 1295– N. of Ivinghoe, eln conf. 17 Aug. 1295 (ibid.).

Isolda Occ. 14 Feb. 1326 (BL, Harl. Cht. 84 F 54; BL, Harl. ms. 4714, f. 109v).

Lic. from Bp Stratford of Winchester, as patron, to nuns for election of new prs, no reason for vacancy, 2 Sept. 1332 (Winchester, Reg. Stratford, f. 74r).

Sibyl of Flamstead (Flamsted) –1340 Commn to adm. cess. of Sibyl and supervise eln of successor 23 Nov. 1340 (Lincoln, Ep. Reg., V, f. 253v).

Sibyl Golde –1341 D. 22 Sept. 1341 (Winchester, Reg. Orleton, II, f. 90r). ? same as Sibyl of Flamstead and had not in fact ceded the priory.

Letter of sub-prs and convent to bp of Winchester as patron asking for lic. to el. 2 Oct. 1341 as prev. prs. Sibyl Golde had died 22 Sept. 1341. Lic. to el. dated 4 Oct. 1341 (ibid).

Matilda Cheynduyt (de Cheverdich) 1341–1355 N. of Ivinghoe, notification of eln dated 14 Oct. 1341, ass. of bp of Winchester 17 Oct. 1341 (ibid.). D. by 9 June 1355 when lic. to el. granted (*Reg. Edington*, I, no. 1033).

Emma de la Hay –1381 Occ. 6 Mar. 1366 (Lincoln, Ep. Reg., XII, f. 28r). At some point she appears to have given up office and then presumably resumed it, for there is a commn to administer goods of priory given to sr. Emma de la Hay, *former* prs, at the request of John de la Hay, knt, 25 June 1367 (Lincoln, Ep. Reg., XII, f. 41v). Cess., lic. to el. issued 30 Jan. 1381 (*Reg. Wykeham*, I, 112).

KELDHOLME (Yorks N.), St Mary f. -1135?, -1142–3 (*KH*); 1154 x 1166 (Burton; Thompson) (Cistercian priory)

Lists in *VCH Yorks*, III, 169–70; *Heads*, I, 213; Thompson, *Women Religious*, p. 243 (to late 13th cent.).

Basilia Occ. 19 Nov. 1208 (*Yorks F., John*, p. 152).

Sibyl Occ. 1224 x 1269 (*EYC*, IX, 93, correcting Burton, *Mon. Ebor.*, p. 380n. and other authorities).

Ellen Occ. second half of 13th cent. (BL, Cotton ms. Claudius D. XI, f. 4r).

Juliana Occ. 1279 (PRO, Just.1/1056, m. 66).

Beatrice of Grendale (Crend(ale)) –1294 Res. by 29 Jan. 1294, when lic. to el. (*Reg. Romeyn*, I, p. 179, no. 507).

Emma of Stapelton 1294–1301 N. of Keldholme, eln conf. 3 Feb. 1294 (ibid.). Res., lic. to el. 13 July 1301 (*Reg. Corbridge*, I, 128).

Archbp of York's mandate to enquire how long there had been no prs of Keldholme. If for more than 6 months to inform the archbp of the name of a suitable person as prs; if less, to warn the subprs and convent to el. one within a month 17 Apr. 1308. The commissaries reported that the right of appt had lapsed to the archbp and he, on 20 Apr. 1308, commissioned mag. John de Neuwerke and the official of the archdn of Cleveland to appoint Emma of York, nun of Keldholme, as prs (*Reg. Greenfield*, III, p. 20, no. 1169 and n.2).

Emma of York (Eboraco) 1308 Apptd soon after 20 April 1308 (see above). Cess. by 30 July 1308 in visitation (ibid., p. 27 no. 1188 and p. 29, no. 1192).

Joan of Pickering (Pykering) 1308–1309 N. of the Ben. house of Rosedale, apptd by archbp

30 July 1308 (ibid., III, p. 27, no. 1188 & n.1). Her installation was opposed by the nuns of Keldholme and the house placed under interdict until she could be peaceably received as prs 5 Aug. 1308 (ibid., pp. 29–31, no. 1192). On 3 Sept. 1308 4 rebel nuns were sent to other nunneries for opposing Joan (ibid., pp. 33–5, no. 1198). Occ. 4 Jan. 1309 (ibid., p. 38, no. 1213). By 1 Feb. 1309 patroness of nunnery, Joan de Wake, was to be informed that Joan had been adm. & to be requested to restore the temporalities (ibid., p. 39, no. 1216). 17 Feb. 1309 archbp's commission to receive res. of Joan (ibid., p. 40, no. 1218, n.1). Joan returned to Rosedale where she was conf. prs 12 Jan. 1311 (ibid., p. 58, no. 1266 & n.).

Emma of Stapelton 1309–1316 N. of Keldholme, eln conf. 7 Mar. 1309 (ibid. III, pp. 44–5, no. 1224). [as N. of Keldholme, reconciled for apostasy 1309 (Logan, *Runaway Religious*, p. 263)]. Res. on account of her age and ill-health by 13 Feb. 1316, lic. to el. (*Reg. Greenfield*, V, p. 258, no. 2830).

Emma of York 1316– Eln conf. 17 Mar. 1316 (ibid., V, p. 258, n.3).

Alice Occ. 14 Aug. 1352 (*CPR 1350–1354*, p. 340).

The next recorded prs, **Margaret Aslaby**, res. 25 June 1406 (York, Reg. 5A, f. 288v).

CUSTOS

Mag. Richard del (de le, dil) Clay Appt as *custos* of temps. of priory 7 Apr. 1310 (*Reg. Greenfield*, III, p. 54, no. 1247). On 20 March 1313 referred to as 'coadjutor' of prs (ibid., p. 74, no. 1295); occ. as *custos* (& vicar of Lastingham) 27 Oct. 1315 (ibid., p. 111, no. 1377).

KILBURN (Middlesex), St John the Baptist f. 1139 (*KH*); -1128 x 1134 (Thompson)
(Benedictine priory)

Lists in *VCH Middlesex*, I, 181–2; *Heads*, I, 213; Thompson, *Women Religious*, p. 243 (to 1269).

Adelina occ. n.d. (Oxford, New Coll., Reg. Secundum, f. 2v). There is no clue as to her position in the sequence of prioresses.

Margery (Margaret) Occ. early to mid. 13th cent. (Glasgow UL, Hunterian ms. U 2 6, ff. 25v–26r with Thomas of Durham, alderman of Fenchurch ward, cf. *Ctl. Clerkenwell*, no. 355); 1232 (*VCH Surrey*, III, 147); from Oct. 1242 x Oct. 1243 to Oct. 1246 x Oct. 1247 (*London and Middlesex F.*, pp. 27, 31); *c*. 1242 x 1248 (*Ctl. Holy Trinity, Aldgate*, no. 115); 1244 x 1248 (BL, Harl. ms. 4015, f. 94v); Oct. 1247 x Oct. 1248 (*Surrey F.*, p. 31); n.d. (PRO, E42/428).

Joan Occ. Oct. 1248 x Oct. 1249 (*London and Middlesex F.*, p. 32); *c*. 1254 x 1257 (*Mon. Angl.*, III, 424); 1258 x 1259 (*Ctl. St Bartholomew's, London*, no. 516); n.d. (PRO, E42/429); mentd as former prs 18 Apr. 1276 (*Sussex F.*, II, no. 862).

Matilda Oct. 1268 x Oct. 1269 (*Surrey F.*, p. 44).

Sabina Occ. n.d. (mid-13th cent. according to ed.) (*Ctl. St Bartholomew's, London*, no. 513).

Cecily Occ. 3 Feb. 1290 (WAM no. 4848); 16 Oct. 1290 (ibid., no. 4860); 23 Dec. 1290 (ibid., no. 4853).

Agnes Occ. Trin. 1301, 26 Mar. 1302 (*YB IX*, 45–7).

Matilda Occ. Trin. 1311 (ibid., 45).

Alice de Pommesbourne Occ. 28 Oct. 1339 (*Cal. London Letter Books F*, p. 53).

Agnes Occ. 31 Aug. 1345 (*CCR 1343–46*, p. 646).

Alice Pigoin Occ. 14 Aug. 1352 (*CPR 1350–54*, p. 340); 13 Feb. 1357 (*CPL*, III, 587); 1381 (McHardy, *Church in London*, no. 388).

The next recorded prs, **Emma de S. Omero**, occ. 14 Feb. 1403 (BL, Add. Cht. 5313).

KINGTON ST MICHAEL (Wilts) f. -1155 (*KH*); -1142 x 1156, ? *c*. 1142 (Thompson)
(Benedictine priory)

Lists in *VCH Wilts*, III, 261; *Heads*, I, 213–14; Thompson, *Women Religious*, pp. 243–4 (to 1243); obit book, CUL, ms. Dd. 8. 2, ff. 11r–20v, cf. *Wilts AM*, IV (1858), 54–6.

Mary Occ. 3 Aug. 1228 (PRO, F. Divers Cos. CP25/1/283/9, no. 65); 7 Aug. 1228 (*Devon F.*, I, pp. 378–9, no. 731; Seymour, *Torre Abbey*, p. 194, no. 187); 8 July 1241 (PRO, Glos F., CP25/1/73/16, no. 306); 11 Nov. 1243 (*Sarum Chts.*, pp. 288–9, no. ccxlvi).

Alice Occ. *temp.* Hen. III (*Berkeley Chts*, no. 382). Her correct place in the sequence of prioresses is uncertain.

Isabel Occ. 24 June 1268 (PRO, Berks F., CP25/1/8/27, no. 11); 8 July 1268 (ibid., no. 10); 3 Feb. 1272 (PRO, Hants F., CP25/1/204/11, no. 52).

Clarice Occ. 4 June 1291 (*HMC Wells*, I, 151). Mentioned 16 Sept. 1291 in inspeximus of cht. n.d. (1275 x 1291, *temp.* Robert Burnell, bp of Bath and Wells 1275–92 (*CChR 1257–1300*, p. 405; *Wilts AM*, IV, pp. 70–1, charter no. xi)).

Amice –1298 D. by 11 June 1298 (*Reg. Gandavo*, II, 582).

Amice of Wallingford (Walyngford) 1298– N. of Kington, mand. to install n.d. [1298] (ibid., 582–3). ?Obit 10 Nov. (CUL, ms. Dd. 8. 2, f. 19r).

Cecily –1319 Res. by 13 Dec. 1319 (*Reg. Martival*, I, 415–16) when convent asked lic. to el. Mentd 11 Jan. 1320 as former prs. (ibid., II, 322).

Joan (de) Durdent (Duredent) 1319–1326 N. of Kington, eln pres. to bp, quashed but apptd by him 20 Dec. 1319 (*Reg. Martival*, I, 415–6). Conf. by bp of his commissary's appt 10 Jan. 1320 (ibid., II, 322–3). Res. 8 Mar. 1326 (Lambeth, Reg. Reynolds, ff. 194v, 262r–v). Obit 28 Feb. (CUL, ms. Dd. 8. 2, f. 10v).

Denise de Horsulle (?Horsell) 1326– N. of Bromhall, apptd by archbp 20 July 1326 (Lambeth, Reg. Reynolds, f. 262r). Letter from bp of Salisbury to archbp about Denise de Horsulle whom he wishes to appt as prs, the right having devolved to the archbp *per lapsum temporis* 26 July 1326 (ibid., f. 194v).

Isabel Huse (Husye) Occ. 17 Nov. 1327 (*HMC Wells*, I, 397). Obit 27 Mar. (CUL, ms. Dd. 8. 2, f. 11v).

Lucy Paas N. of Kington, renounced eln but bp apptd her 14 Apr. 1349, no reason given for vacancy (Salisbury, Reg. Wyvill II, f. 205r). Occ. 21 Apr. 1365 (Suffolk RO, Bury, 449/2/688).

An unnamed prs d. 3 Jan. when the sub-prs, Alice More, sought episcopal lic. to el. a new prs (no year, between entries of Dec. 1430 and Mar. 1432) (Salisbury, Reg. Neville, part 2, f. 10r).

The late 15th-cent obit book also contains a ref. to a prs, **Christina Charlton** (CUL, ms. Dd. 8. 2, f. 9r, obit 4 Jan.) who has not been found in other sources. It could be that she fits somewhere into the 1216–1377 sequence.

KIRKLEES (Yorks W.), St Mary and St James f. ?–1138 (*KH*); *c.* 1135 x 1140 *or* 1166 x *c.* 1190 (Thompson, Burton) (Cistercian priory)

   Lists in *VCH Yorks*, III, 170, from *YAJ*, XVI, 321; Thompson, *Women Religious*, p. 244 (to 1240/1).

Lecia Occ. *c.* 1190 x 1210 (*EYC*, III, no. 1765; Thompson, *Women Religious*, p. 244).

Sibyl Occ. 1234 (*Yorks Deeds*, I, no. 218, cf. app. I, p. 224, no. V); 1240 (*YAJ*, VII, 404); Feb. 1241 (*YAJ*, XVI, 321 and n.1).

Alice le Mousters Occ. Epiphany 1306 (PRO, Just.1/1107, m. 24).

Margaret of Clayworth (Claworth) 1306– N. of Kirklees, eln conf. 28 Sept. 1306, no reason given for vacancy (*Reg. Greenfield*, II, p. 8, no. 687).

Alice of Scriven (Screvyn) 1308– N. of Kirklees, eln conf. 10 Jan. 1308, no reason given for vacancy (ibid., pp. 46–7, no. 770). Occ. Hilary 1328 (Baildon, I, 106).

Margaret de Seyvill 1350– Apptd by archbp 10 May 1350, no reason given for vacancy (York, Reg. 10, f. 48r). Occ. 19 Nov. 1353 (BL, Harl Cht. 55 G 26).

The next recorded prs, **Alice Mountenay**, is said to occ. 1403 at the time of the appropriation of Mirfield church to the priory (*YAJ*, XVI, p. 321, n. 3, citing BL, Harl. ms. 797, f. 39, copies of Dodsworth notes), but she does not feature by name in the appropriation and ordination of the vicarage 1403 (*Reg. Scrope*, I, nos. 50, 246).

Prs of unknown date:
YAJ, XVI, 321 and Baildon, I, 106 both cite **Elizabeth de Staynton** without date or source. I have not been able to find such a source so far.

LACOCK (Wilts), St Bernard f. 1230 x 1232 (as priory), 1239 (as abbey); 1229, 1231 x 1232 (first nuns) (Thompson) (Augustinian abbey)
Lists in *VCH Wilts*, III, 315–16; *Wilts AM*, XXVI, 43–4; Thompson, *Women Religious*, p. 244 (to 1280).

PRIORESS

Wymarka (Wymarca) Occ. n.d. (1232 x 1239) (*Lacock Chts.*, nos. 80, 415); 24 Apr. 1233 (PRO, Glos F., CP25/1/73/9, no.139; *Lacock Chts.*, no. 375).

ABBESSES

Ela Longespée 1239–1257 Countess Ela, widow of William Longespée, earl of Salisbury, founded the priory, subsequently entered the community and became the first abbess (*KH*, p. 281; Thompson, *Women Religious*, pp. 170–1; *Lacock Chts.*, no. 254). Occ. (E.) abb.-el. 15 Aug. 1239 (*Sarum Chts.*, pp. 251–2); occ. from 19 May 1241 to 30 Sept. 1249 (*Lacock Chts.*, nos. 236, 416); 6 May 1242, 12 July 1248 (*CChR 1226–57*, pp. 274, 332). Res. 21 Dec. 1257, d. 24 Aug. 1261 (*Wilts AM*, LI, (1951), p. 3; *Complete Peerage*, XI, 382; Bowles, *Ann. Lacock*, p. 275). Ledger-stone (possible post-medieval forgery) (*Earliest English Brasses*, p. 212, cf. *TMBS*, XIII, 35–40).

Beatrice of Kent 1257– Apptd 31 Dec. 1257, citing 'Book of Lacock' (Bowles, *Ann. Lacock*, pp. 273–4 & n.). Occ. from 10 Aug. 1259 to 1 Aug. 1280 (*Lacock Chts.*, nos. 225, 412); 1261 (*Wilts F.*, I, 54); Mich. 1278 (PRO, KB27/41, m. 43d); Trin. 1280 (PRO, CP40/34, m. 11); 1 Aug. 1280 (PRO, Wards 2/94B/59). *VCH* says she d. in or after 1280. See Sharpe, *Latin Writers*, p. 70.

Alice Occ. 4 June 1283 (*Lacock Chts.*, no. 177); 1284 (*Earliest English Law Reports*, I, 183); 28 Apr. 1286 (*Wilts F.*, II, 28; *Lacock Chts.*, no. 316); Easter term 1286 (ibid., no. 457); 12 May 1286 (PRO, Hants F., CP25/1/204/13, no. 78).

Juliana Occ. 7 July 1288, 20 Feb. 1289 (*Lacock Chts.*, nos. 435, 287–9); 20 Mar. 1291 (ibid., no. 31). Unnamed abbs. d. 1291 (BL, Cotton ms. Cleopatra D III, f. 49r).

Agnes Occ. 25 Mar. 1298, 29 Sept. 1298, 4 Oct. 1299 (*Lacock Chts.*, nos. 458, 436, 89).

Joan de Montfort (Mounfort, Mountfort) **–1332** Occ. frequently as abbs. in *Lacock Chts.* from Easter term 1304 to 11 June 1332 (nos. 117, 193); 26 Apr. 1304 (*Wilts F.*, II, 49).

Katherine (la) Cras 1332– Eln conf. 31 Aug. 1332, bl. 18 Oct. 1332, no reason given for vacancy (Salisbury, Reg. Wyvil, II, f. 18r). Occ. 9 Sept. 1332 (*Lacock Chts.*, no. 413); 26 Jan. 1333 (ibid., no. 191).

Sibyl de Sancta Cruce 1334–1349 N. of Lacock, eln conf. 28 May 1334, bl. 29 May 1334 (Salisbury, Reg. Wyvil, II, f. 29r). Occ. many times in *Lacock Chts.* from 7 June 1334 to 4 Sept. 1349 (nos. 47, 202).

Matilda de Montfort (Mountfort) **1349–1356** N. of Lacock, eln conf. 10 Oct. 1349, bl. 11 Oct. 1349 (Salisbury, Reg. Wyvil, II, f. 219r). D., lic. to el. 8 Feb. 1356 (*Reg. Black Prince*, IV, 180).

Agnes de Brymesden (Brymmesden) **1356–1361** N. of Lacock, prince's ass. 18 Feb. 1356 (ibid., 183). Commn to take fealty 1 Mar. 1356, as Agnes too feeble and ill to go to the prince's council in London (ibid., 184). D., lic. to el. 28 Oct. 1361 (ibid., 400).

Faith Selyman 1361–?1380 N. of Lacock, eln conf. 7 Nov. 1361, bl. 8 Dec. 1361 (Salisbury, Reg. Wyvil, II, f. 294r). Prince's ass. 20 Nov. 1361 (*Reg. Black Prince*, IV, 405). Occ. 1 Apr. 1363, 8 Nov. 1366 (*Lacock Chts.*, nos. 207, 208); 25 June 1371 (ibid., no. 209); 20 Dec. 1377 (ibid., no. 428). Lic. to el. (no reason given for vacancy) 9 May 1380 (*Reg. John of Gaunt 1379–83*, no. 924).

LAMBLEY (Northumberland), St Mary and St Patrick f. -1190 (*KH*); -1187 x 1188 (Thompson) (Benedictine priory)
A. Occ. n.d. (*c.* 1239) (*Northumberland and Durham Deeds*, p. 45).
Margery Occ. n.d. (*?c.* 1260 x 1263) (ibid., p. 74).
Joan of Sweethope (Swethop) Occ. 5 July 1323 (PRO, E213/71).
Isabel Munteny Occ. 1379 (PRO, E179/62/4, m.3d).

LANGLEY (Leics), St Mary f. *c.* 1150 (?) (*KH*); 1148 x 1166 (Thompson) (Benedictine priory)
   List in *VCH Leics*, II, 4–5; Thompson, *Women Religious*, p. 244 (to 1269); cf. S.P. Douglass, 'Langley Priory', *Trans. Leics. AHS*, 62 (1988), 16–30, list at 16–17.
Isabel de Adelwoldestona Occ. n.d. (early 13th cent.: pal.) (PRO, E326/1229).
Rose Occ. n.d. (1229, see *VCH Leics*, II, 3, n. 17 for date) (*Mon. Angl.*, IV, 222–3, no.5; Nichols, *Leics*, III, ii, 866); n.d. (*c.* 1229) ('Ctl. Breedon', nos. 137–8); (R.) n.d. (PRO, E315/40/199).
Burgia 1229/30– N. of Langley, el. and adm. Dec. 1229 x Dec. 1230, no reason given for vacancy (*Reg. Wells*, II, 312); (B.) n.d. (PRO, E326/8501(b)).
Isabel of Leicester (Leircestria, Leyrc') **1236/7–** N. of Langley, el. and adm. June 1236 x June 1237, no reason given for vacancy (*Reg. Grosseteste*, p. 393). Occ. 1248 (PRO, E326/894); *c.* 1251 (Nichols, *Leics*, III, ii, 867); 1261 (PRO, E326/8792); 1265 (PRO, E326/212).
Juliana of Winchester (Wynton) **1269–** Eln quashed, but apptd by bp 28 May 1269, no reason given for vacancy (*Reg. R. Gravesend*, pp. 149, 311). Occ. (Giliana) n.d. (PRO, E326/389); n.d. (PRO, E326/4059).
Alice de Tatyrsal (Tatishale, Tottishale) **–1276** Occ. 3 May 1275 (PRO, E326/1288); *c.* 1275 (PRO, E326/5135). D. (*blank* de Tatishale) by 19 Jan. 1276 (*Reg. R. Gravesend*, p. 158).
Margaret of Leicester (Leycestr') **1276–** Eln conf. 19 Jan. 1276 (ibid.). Occ. 8 Sept. 1276 (PRO, E326/418); 1278 x 1279 (PRO, E326/3496).
Christine of Winchester (Wynchestre, Wynton') **?1281/2–1296** In Dodsworth's abstract of Bp Sutton's now lost Leicester archdeaconry roll, it is noted that an unnamed prs of Farewell was el. as prs of Langley in his 2nd pontifical year (19 May 1281 x 18 May 1282) (Bodl., Dodsworth ms. 107, f. 138r). This was probably Christine of Winchester. Occ. *c.* 1280s (PRO, E326/205); 1284 (PRO, E329/144); 25 Mar. 1287 (PRO, E326/1314); *c.* 6 Oct. 1289 (PRO, E315/47/106). Res. by 19 Jan. 1296 (*Reg. Sutton*, VIII, p. 58). Seal (*Mon. Seals*, p. 49).
Amice de Burgo (also Boron) **1296–1302** N. of Langley, eln pres. to bp 19 Jan. 1296; eln quashed but apptd by bp 20 Jan. 1296 (*Reg. Sutton*, VIII, p. 58). Occ. (Boron) Nov. 1295 x Nov. 1296 (PRO, LR14/875); 10 Nov. 1298 (Burgo) (PRO, E40/7429). D. by 21 Oct. 1302 (Lincoln, Ep. Reg., II, f. 198v).
Alice Giffard 1302–1306 N. of Langley, eln quashed, but apptd by bp 21 Oct. 1302 (ibid.). D. by 5 July 1306 (ibid., f. 202r).
Elizabeth of Caldwell (Caldewell) **1306–1333** N. of Langley, royal ass. 25 June 1306 (*CPR 1301–07*, p. 445). Eln quashed, but apptd by bp 5 July 1306 (Lincoln, Ep. Reg., II, f. 202r; PRO, C84/15/43). Order to escheator not to intermeddle further with custody of the priory – the bp had conf. her, 2 July 1306 (*CCR 1302–07*, p. 401). D. by 14 May 1333 (Lincoln, Ep. Reg., IV, f. 138r).

Joan of Oadby (Oudeby, Out(h)eby) **1333–** N. of Langley, eln quashed, but apptd by bp 14 May 1333 (ibid.). Occ. 8 June 1333 (PRO, E326/1258); 1335 (PRO, E326/1857); 14 Feb. 1336 (PRO, E315/39/35); 1336 (PRO, E326/8202, 12547). Mention as former prs in connection with provision being made, 3 May 1349, 13 Oct. 1349 (Lincoln, Ep. Reg., IX, ff. 21v–22v).

The priory was presumably vacant on 14 Aug. 1349 when the sub-prs and convent are recorded as patrons of a living (ibid., f. 345r).

Matanye (Mathania) of Quarrington (Querington) **1349–** Commn to induct and install 9 Dec. 1349, the right of appt having devolved to the bp (ibid., f. 6r). Occ. 2 Aug. 1350 (PRO, E326/887); 9 May 1363 (Mathania/Mathama) stated that she had carried on a suit for her priory for 7 years (*CPP*, p. 419).

Margaret Sully (Solvy) **1355–** N. of Langley, commn to examine eln 8 Aug. 1355, no reason being given for vacancy (Lincoln, Ep. Reg., VIII, f. 70v). Occ. 14 Dec. 1355 (Matilda, ? error) (PRO, E326/478); Jan. 1358 x Jan. 1359 (E326/11,601); 29 Nov. 1368 (PRO, E315/40/269); Jan. 1371 x Jan. 1372 (PRO, E326/9176); 18 Oct. 1374 (PRO, E326/423); 10 Oct. 1376 (PRO, E315/42/7); 1376 (PRO, E326/9027); 1377 (*Clerical Poll-Taxes*, p. 28, no. 374).

LEGBOURNE (Lincs), St Mary f. *c.* 1150+ (*KH*); -1148 x 1166, ? 1150 (Thompson) (Cistercian priory)

Lists in *VCH Lincs*, II, 155; *Heads*, I, 214; *Women Religious*, p. 244 (to 1275); *Medieval Lindsey Marsh*, p. 85 (1275–1326).

Mabel Occ. 25 June 1219 (*Lincs F.*, I, 133).

Beatrice **–1247** Occ. 30 Apr. 1226 (ibid., I, 216–17). Res. June 1246 x June 1247 (*Reg. Grosseteste*, p. 88).

Alice of Holland (Hoyland) **1247–** N. of Legbourne, eln quashed but apptd by bp June 1246 x June 1247 (ibid.). Occ. 24 Apr. 1250 (*Lincs F.*, II, 87).

Joan Occ. 12 Nov. 1256 (ibid., 158); 19 May 1260 with Pr. Robert (*Reg. Ant. Lincoln*, II, no. 400).

Alice of Conisholme (Coninghisholm) **1275–** Eln conf. 16 Sept. 1275 on d. of unnamed prs (*Reg. R. Gravesend*, pp. 65, 282). Occ. Easter 1276 (PRO, CP40/14, m. 46d).

Isolda of Lincoln **–1285** Res. on 11 Sept. 1285 (*Reg. Sutton*, I, 67–8).

Petronilla of Saltfleetby (Salfletby) **1285–1296** Eln examined and quashed on 17 Sept. but bp apptd her on 25 Sept. 1285 (ibid.). Res. by 5 June 1296 (ibid., 207).

Joan Chaumberlayn **1296–** N. of Legbourne, eln quashed but appted by bp 5 June 1296 (ibid., 207–8). Occ. 1304 (Bodl., Dodsworth ms. 75, f. 26v).

Commn to examine a disputed eln 13 Mar. 1309 (Lincoln, Ep. Reg., III, f. 150v); his report dated 15 Mar. 1309 stated that Ellen of Theddlethorpe (Thedelthorp) had 19 votes but refused nomination; Ellen of Somercotes received 14 votes, Agatha de Jarwell 2 votes and three others (unnamed) with 1 vote each. Commissary quashed eln and apptd Ellen of Somercotes (Lincoln, Ep. Reg., II, ff. 24v–25r).

Ellen of Somercotes **1309** Apptd by commissary by 15 Mar. 1309 (ibid.). D. by 3 June 1309 (ibid., f. 28r).

Margaret le Vavas[s]our **1309–1313** N. of Legbourne, eln quashed but apptd by bp 3 June 1309 (ibid.). Cess. by 7 Aug. 1313 (ibid., f. 48r).

Matilda de Wythale **1313–1316** N. of Legbourne, eln quashed but apptd by bp 7 Aug. 1313 (ibid.). Res. acc. 15 Mar. 1316 (Lincoln, Ep. Reg., III, f. 343r).

Beatrice de Dunham **1316–** N. of Legbourne, commn to examine eln 20 Mar. 1316 (ibid., f. 343v). Eln quashed by bp's commissary who apptd her 23 Mar. 1316 (Lincoln, Ep. Reg., II, f. 58v).

Denise of Selby 1319–1326 N. of Legbourne, commn to examine eln 19 Mar. 1319, no reason given for vacancy (Lincoln, Ep. Reg., III, f. 412v). Eln quashed but apptd by bp's commissary 28 Mar. 1319 (Lincoln, Ep. Reg., II, f. 77r–v). Res. by 28 Apr. 1326 (*Reg. Burghersh*, I, no. 45).

Juliana de Askeby 1326–1338 N. of Legbourne, eln quashed but apptd by bp 28 Apr. 1326 (ibid.). Res. (called Joan de Askeby) *oretenus factam* by 6 July 1338 (ibid., no. 584).

[**Denise of Selby** N. of Legbourne, eln quashed by vicar-general 6 July 1338 (ibid.).]

Margaret of Withern (Wythern) **1338–** N. of Legbourne, apptd by vicar-general 12 July 1338 (ibid.).

The priory was presumably vacant in 1349 when presentation to Halloughton vicarage was made by the sub-prs and convent (Lincoln, Ep. Reg., IX, f. 59v).

Elizabeth Chaumberleyn –1368 Res. by [ ] Dec. 1368 (Lincoln, Ep. Reg., X, f. 26v).

Juliana de Redford 1368– N. of Legbourne, eln conf. [ ] Dec. 1368 (ibid.).

Joan Dawtre (Dautre, Dawe) **–1397** Occ. 1381 (*Clerical Poll-Taxes*, p. 121, no. 1488; p. 168, no. 2089). D. by 3 Apr. 1397 when commn issued to examine eln of a successor (Lincoln, Ep. Reg., XI, f. 87v).

MASTERS

Robert Occ. ? late 12th cent. (BL, Harl. Cht. 47 F 49 = *DC*, no. 478). 1205 to 1208 (*Lincs. F.*, I, 61, 69, 87); 13 Jan. 1228 (*CPR 1225–32*, p. 209); Hil. term 1230 (*CRR*, XIII, no. 2650); (prior) 12 July 1231 (*Lincs F.*, I, 245); n.d. (1220 x 1240) (PRO, DL36/2/195).

Robert Occ. 19 May 1260 (*Reg. Ant. Lincoln*, II, no. 400).

Thomas of Louth (Luda) Mentd Easter 1276 in a lawsuit. He had been chosen as master by the nuns and had been pres. to bp of Lincoln, without lic. of the patron of the priory (PRO, CP40/14, m. 46d).

Thomas of Grainthorpe (Germelthorp) **1295–** Chaplain, apptd 5 Jan. 1295 (*Reg. Sutton*, V, 51).

John 1307– Rector of Authorpe, apptd 7 Jan. 1307 (Lincoln, Ep. Reg., III, f. 109r).

Robert 1309– Vicar of Hainton, apptd 6 Apr. 1309 (ibid., f. 152r).

Ralph 1313– Rector of Ruckland, apptd 9 Aug. 1313 (ibid., f. 279r). Occ. 15 Mar. 1316 (ibid., f. 343r).

Mag. Hugh de Walmesford 1332– Can. of Lincoln Cathedral, apptd during pleasure 20 Aug. 1332 (Lincoln, Ep. Reg., V, f. 463v).

Richard of Goxhill (Gouxill) **1343–** Rector of Withern, apptd 26 June 1343 (Lincoln, Ep. Reg., VII, f. 36v). **Adam** vicar of Hallington associated with him when Richard busy with other business 3 Sept. 1343 (ibid., f. 43v).

Roger of Frieston (Freston) **1349–** Rector of Mavis Enderby, apptd 23 July 1349 (Lincoln, Ep. Reg., IX, f. 35r).

Robert 1366– Vicar of Skidbrook, apptd 29 July 1366 (Lincoln, Ep. Reg., XII, f. 33v).

LILLECHURCH, *see* HIGHAM

LIMEBROOK (Hereford), St Thomas of Canterbury f. -1221 (see Thompson, pp. 33–5, cf. J.W. Tonkin, 'The nunnery of Limebrook and its property', *Trans. Woolhope Nat. Field Club*, 41, part 1 (1974), 149–64); S.P. Thomas, 'Limebrook priory', *Trans. Radnorshire Soc.*, 56 (1986), 23–5. (Augustinian priory)

No prs has been found before **Matilda Whyteney**. Commn to receive her res. 13 Aug. 1429, res. 16 Aug. (*Reg. Spofford*, pp. 119–20).

LITTLE MARLOW (Bucks), St Mary f. -1218 (*KH*); -1194 x 1195 (Thompson)
(Benedictine priory)

Lists in *VCH Bucks*, I, 360; *Heads*, I, 214; Thompson, *Women Religious*, p. 245 (to 1273).

Margaret Occ. *c.* 1194 x 1195 (*Waltham Chts.*, pp. 390–1); *c.* -1220, ? -1217 (BL, Harl. ms. 391, ff. 103v–104v).

A. Occ. 1217 (*Ctl. Missenden*, II, no. 427). Prob. the same as below.

Alice -1229/30 Occ. 1227 (*Bucks Eyre*, p. 8, no. 125). (A.) d. Dec. 1229 x Dec. 1230 (*Reg. Wells*, II, 33).

Matilda de Anvers (d'Auvers) 1229/30– El. [*blank*] de Anvers, sub-prs of Little Marlow, el. and adm. Dec. 1229 x Dec. 1230 (ibid.). Occ. 22 Oct. 1232 (*Bucks F.*, I, 63).

Admiranda 1236/7– N. of Little Marlow, el. and adm. June 1236 x June 1237, no reason given for vacancy (*Reg. Grosseteste*, p. 344). Occ. Nov. 1251 (WAM, no. 13795).

Cecily de Turvill –1258/9 Occ. 3 Nov. 1257 (*Bucks F.*, I, 109). Res. Nov. 1258 x Nov. 1259 (*Reg. R. Gravesend*, p. 236).

Christiana de Whitmers 1258/9– N. of Little Marlow, eln conf. Nov. 1258 x Nov. 1259 (ibid., pp. 236, 338–9).

Felicia of Kimble (Kinebelle) 1264–1265 El. [?conf.] 26 June 1264, on d. of last (unnamed) prs. (ibid., pp. 239, 340). Res. by 19 Mar. 1265 (ibid., p. 239).

Gunnora (Gonnora) 1265–1274 N. of Little Marlow, el. and adm. 19 Mar. 1265 (ibid., pp. 239, 340). Res. by 13 Feb. 1274 (ibid., p. 250).

Margery of Waltham (Wautham) 1274– El. conf. 13 Feb. 1274 (ibid.).

Matilda Neyrnuyt (Neyrnut) El. during Bp Sutton's 4th pontifical year (i.e. 19 May 1283 x 18 May 1284), lic. to el. having been obtained from the countess of Gloucester and William de Cressy, knight (Bodl., Dodsworth ms. 107, f. 141r). Occ. 19 May 1286 (*Bucks F.*, II, 60).

Agnes of London –1290 Note of res. and lic. to el. on 1 June 1290 (*Reg. Sutton*, III, 5; VIII, 126).

Agnes of Cliveden (Clivedon) 1290–1298 Sub-prs of Little Marlow, eln quashed, and a second eln held which was conf. by bp 4 Dec. 1290 (ibid., VIII, 126). Res. on. 19 Sept. 1298, lic. to el. s.d. (ibid., VI, 110; VIII, 170).

Juliana of Hampton 1298–1305 Precentrix of Little Marlow, eln conf. 4 Oct. 1298 (ibid., VIII, 170). Cess. by 10 June 1305 (Lincoln, Ep. Reg., II, f. 178v).

Rose of Weston 1305– N. of Little Marlow, eln quashed, but apptd by bp 10 June 1305 (ibid.). Commn to examine eln of unnamed prs 18 May 1322 (Lincoln, Ep. Reg., V, f. 318r).

Cecily of St John (Seynt Johan) Occ. Mich. 1337 (PRO, CP40/312, m. 119).

Joan of Stonor (Stonore) 1338–1353 Commn to examine eln 3 June 1338 (Lincoln, Ep. Reg., V, f. 561r). Occ. 16 Oct. 1338 (*CPR 1338–40*, p. 336). D. by 15 Jan. 1353 (Lincoln, Ep. Reg., IX, f. 290r–v).

Margery Jerounde (Geround) 1353– Commn to examine eln 15 Jan. 1353; eln quashed, but bp's commissary apptd her 13 Feb. 1353 (ibid.). Occ. 26 Feb. 1361 (*CCR 1360–64*, p. 166).

The next recorded prs, **Susanna of Hampton**, is stated to have res. 1395 (*Mon. Angl.*, IV, 419).

MASTER

Robert de Fayrmere Rector of Rotherfield, apptd master 19 Apr. 1293 (*Reg. Sutton*, IV, 76–7).

LITTLEMORE (Oxon), St Mary, St Nicholas and St Edmund (Sandford) f. 1135 x 54 (*KH*); -1156 (Thompson) (Benedictine priory)

Lists in *VCH Oxon*, II, 77; *Heads*, I, 214; Thompson, *Women Religious*, p. 245 (to 1276/7).

Amice Occ. 9 June 1219 (*Cambs F.*, p. 10; PRO, Cambs F., CP25/1/23/9, no. 14); n.d. (early 13th cent.) (Bodl., Oxon Chts. 18, 38).

Isabel of Hendred 1229/30– N. of Littlemore, el. and adm. Dec. 1229 x Dec. 1230 (*Reg. Wells*, II, 32). Occ. Mich. term 1230 (*CRR*, XIV, nos. 963, 974); 13 Apr. 1231 (PRO, Berks F., CP25/1/7/10, no. 12; *Basset Chts.*, no. 136); 2 July 1235 (*Oxon F.*, p. 96).

Isabel Possibly as above or below. Occ. 21 Apr. 1241, 20 Jan. 1261 (ibid., pp. 116, 184).

Isabel de Stures (de Turribus) –1265 Occ. Easter 1265 (Bodl., Oxon Cht. 36). D. by 28 Oct. 1265 (*Reg. R. Gravesend*, p. 219).

Amibilia de Saunford 1265–1274/5 El. and adm. 28 Oct. 1265 (ibid., pp. 219, 331). D. Nov. 1274 x Nov. 1275 (ibid., p. 226).

Amice de Saunford 1274/5–1276/7 Eln conf. Nov. 1274 x Nov. 1275 (ibid., pp. 226, 335). D. Nov. 1276 x Nov. 1277 (ibid., p. 231).

Matilda of Gloucester (Glovernia) 1276/7–1293 El. [?conf.] Nov. 1276 x Nov. 1277 (ibid.). D. by 1 July 1293 (*Reg. Sutton*, VIII, 180).

Emma of Wantage (Waneting) 1293– Eln quashed but apptd by bp 1 July 1293 (ibid.). Occ. 1296 (PRO, E210/8488); Easter 1298 (PRO, CP40/123, m. 178); Easter 1299 (PRO, CP40/127, m. 80).

Alice of Abingdon (Abindone, Abynton) –1327 Occ. 20 Oct. 1303 (*Ctl. Oseney*, I, 223). D. by 15 Nov. 1327 (Lincoln, Ep. Reg., V, f. 393r).

Agatha of Oxford (Oxon') 1327–1340 Commn to examine eln 15 Nov. 1327 (ibid.). Commn to grant benediction 20 Nov. 1327 (ibid.). D. by 6 Apr. 1340 (Lincoln, Ep. Reg., IV, f. 284r).

Matilda de la Rye 1340– N. of Littlemore, eln voluntarily renounced and apptd by bp 6 Apr. 1340 (ibid.). Occ. 29 Mar. 1342 (Bodl., Oxon Cht. 42). Prob. the unnamed prs who d. by 13 Apr. 1349 (Lincoln, Ep. Reg., IX, f. 245r).

Ascelina Bulbek 1349– N. of Littlemore, eln quashed but apptd by bp 27 Apr. 1349 (ibid., f. 241v), but cf. similar entry, eln quashed for irregularity and bp apptd her 13 Apr. 1349 (ibid., f. 245r).

Christiana Occ. 28 Apr. 1356 (Bodl., Oxon Cht. 44).

Matilda Paunesfot –1391 Occ. 3 Dec. 1374 (*Ctl. St John the Baptist, Oxford*, I, 164); 13 Nov. 1379 (*Ctl. Oseney*, I, 307). D. by 20 Feb. 1391 (Lincoln, Ep. Reg., XI, f. 428v).

LLANLLYR (Cardigan) f. *c.* 1180 (daughter house of Strata Florida) (Cistercian priory) E. Occ. [1284] (*Litt. Wallie*, p. 89, no. 176).

LONDON, CLERKENWELL, St Mary de Fonte f. *c.* 1144 (cf. J.H. Round in *Archaeologia*, LVI, ii (1899), 223–8); *c.* 1141 x 1144 (Thompson) (Augustinian priory)
Lists in *Ctl. Clerkenwell*, pp. 281–3, based on medieval list, ibid., pp. 270–1; *VCH Middlesex*, I, 174; *Heads*, I, 214; Thompson, *Women Religious*, p. 245 (to 1265).

Alice Occ. 1216 x 1220 (*Ctl. Clerkenwell*, no. 286); 29 June 1220 (ibid., no. 287); 1221 (Altisia) (Stenton, *Eyre 1221–2*, no. 78); 1221 (*CRR*, X, 2); (Aleisia) Mich. term 1225 (ibid., XII, no. 1457).

Eleanor Occ. n.d. (1221 x 1223) (*Ctl. Clerkenwell*, no. 278).

Hawise Occ. 1231 x 1232 (ibid., no. 321); 12 May 1232 (*CR 1231–34*, p. 139); 13 Jan. 1238 (*ECSP*, no. 102); 1 July 1240 (*Essex F.*, I, 125); 5 July 1242 (PRO, Hants F., CP25/1/203/7, no. 601); Easter 1244 (*Essex F.*, I, 146).

Cecily Occ. 25 Nov. 1245 (Guildhall, D. & C. of St Paul's, 25151/178); 20 Jan. 1248 (PRO, Cambs F., CP25/1/24/24, no. 2); 17 May 1248 (*Oxford F.*, p. 152); n.d. (1244 x 1248) (BL, Harl. ms. 4015, f. 94v).

Margery Whatvyll (Watewyle, Watevile) Occ. Oct. 1251 x Oct. 1252 (Kingsford, *Grey Friars of London*, p. 149); 13 Jan. 1252 (PRO, E40/2121); 25 Nov. 1254 (*Essex F.*, I, 210); 1264 x 1265 (*Ctl. Clerkenwell*, app., p. 248, no. C).

Alice Oxeney Occ. Oct. 1270 x Oct. 1271, Nov. 1274 x Nov. 1275 (*London and Middlesex F.*, pp. 47, 52); Oct. x Nov. 1272 (*Ctl. Clerkenwell*, p. 271); Easter 1276 (*Essex F.*, II, 10).

Agnes de Marcy (Marci) −1305 Occ. 14 Feb. 1283 (*Cal. London Letter Books, A.*, p. 63); 22 Oct. 1285 (*Ctl. Clerkenwell*, app. p. 246); Mich. term 1285 (*Essex F.*, II, 52; *Ctl. Clerkenwell*, app. p. 247); 1295 x 1296 (*Ctl. Holy Trinity, Aldgate*, no. 665); 3 Dec. 1298 (*Cal. London Letter Books, B*, p. 82). D. shortly before 1 May 1305 (*Ctl. Clerkenwell*, app. pp. 266–7).

Denise Bras and **Margery Bray** occ. n.d. in list between Agnes de Marcy and Joan (of) Lewknor: no docs. survive in the ctl. relating to them (ibid., pp. 271, 282).

Joan (of) Lewknor (Leukenore, Lewkenore) Occ. July 1306 x July 1307 (Kingsford, *Grey Friars of London*, pp. 155–6); 1 July 1310 (*Ctl. Clerkenwell*, app. p. 271); Trinity 1313 (*YB XV*, pp. xxxii, 16–18); 24 June 1328 (*Ctl. Clerkenwell*, app. p. 258).

Joan (of) Fulham (Fullam) Occ. 29 May 1340 (*CPR 1340–43*, p. 69); 8 Mar. 1343 (*Ctl. Clerkenwell*, app. p. 257); 7 Aug. 1344 (*CCR 1343–46*, p. 453); 9 May 1345 (*Ctl. Clerkenwell*, p. 282, n. 9); Mich. 1345 (*YB 19 Edward III*, p. 411).

Idonea Let (Lewtier, Litier, Lutier, Lutiers, Lyter, Lyters, Lytier) Occ. 2 Sept. 1356 (*Assize of Nuisance*, p. 479); 24 Mar. 1357 (PRO, C241/136/149); 20 July 1357 (PRO, E326/3657); Easter 1361 (PRO, CP40/406, m. 5); 9 Apr. 1368 (*Ctl. Clerkenwell*, p. 282; *Cal. Misc. Inq.*, IV, no. 275). By 1379 Idonea was still alive but now just desc. as a n. of Clerkenwell (McHardy, *Church in London*, no. 14).

Katherine Braybrok −1384 Prob. successor of Idonea, she is assumed to have been prs in 1379 (ibid.); occ. 27 May 1381 (*Ctl. Clerkenwell*, p. 283). D. 27 Jan. 1384 (London, Reg. Braybrooke, f. 309r).

The position of **Lucy atte Wod** is uncertain (*Ctl. Clerkenwell*, p. 283); in the list she is mentd 5 Richard II, i.e. June 1381 x June 1382, which coincides with the priorate of Katherine Braybrok. She is desc. as a n. of Clerkenwell in 1379 (McHardy, *Church in London*, no. 14).

MASTERS

Matthew de Walenscin(i)s Occ. as *procurator*, 1230 x 1231, *c.* 1231 x 1245, 1234 x 1235, 1236 x 1237 (*Ctl. Clerkenwell*, pp. 218, 224, 231, 213, 221, 131). Also occ. as rector of St Magnus, London (ibid., p. 235).

Martin Occ. as *procurator* of the house, ? Easter 1244 x 25 Nov. 1245 (ibid., p. 219).

Richard de Purle Occ. as master and as *procurator c.* 1248 x *c.* 1265 (ibid., pp. 243–4).

LONDON, HALIWELL, St John the Baptist f. -1127 (*KH*); -1158 x 1162 (Thompson)
(Augustinian priory)

Lists in *VCH Middlesex*, I, 178; *Heads*, I, 215; Thompson, *Women Religious*, p. 246 (to 1284).

PRIORESSES

Matilda Occ. Oct. 1223 x Oct. 1224 (*Surrey F.*, p. 12); 1224 (*Ctl. Holy Trinity, Aldgate*, no. 811); (M.) 1224 (PRO, E42/352(ii)); Oct. 1224 x Oct. 1225 (*London and Middlesex F.*, p. 16); 1225 (PRO, E42/419(i)). Seal (*BM Seals*, no. 3247; *Mon. Seals*, p. 81).

Agnes Occ. 1237 (Spencer muns. II/1/83); 18 Nov. 1240, 25 Nov. 1240 (*Beds F.*, I, pp. 119, 122, nos. 439, 452); n.d. (1244 x 1248, *temp.* prs. Cecily of Clerkenwell and prs. Margaret of Kilburn) (BL, Harl. ms. 4015, f. 94v); 1246 (Spencer muns. II/1/84).

Juliana Occ. 20 Jan. 1248 (*Essex F.*, I, 168); 30 Sept. 1248, 27 Jan. 1254 (*Kent F.*, pp. 206, 410); 27 Jan. 1254 (PRO, F. Var. Cos. CP25/1/284/19, no. 110); Trinity 1256 (*Essex F.*, I, 213); 13 June 1260 (PRO, Herts F. CP25/1/85/28, no. 524); 25 Nov. 1261 (PRO, Herts F., 85/29, no. 538); 1 July 1262 (PRO, F. Unknown Cos. CP25/1/282/7, no. 150).

Avice Occ. 6 May 1268 (PRO, Herts F., CP25/1/85/31, no. 597); n.d. (mid 13th cent.) (Spencer muns. II/1/116).

Christi(a)na Occ. 1 July 1269 (*Kent F.*, p. 357); 27 Apr. 1270 (PRO, Herts F., CP25/1/86/33, no. 626); Nov. 1281 x Nov. 1282 (*London and Middlesex F.*, p. 58); Nov. 1282 x Nov. 1283, Nov. 1283 x Nov. 1284 (*Suffolk F. (Rye)*, pp. 83, 84); 1286 (PRO, Just.1/86, m. 4); 9 Dec. 1292 (*Reg. Sutton*, VIII, 80).

Alice Occ. 1293 (*HMC 9th Rept*, app., p. 19). Prob. to be identified with **Alice de Troockinge**, indulgence for her soul gtd by L., bp of St Asaph, 3 Dec. 1295 (Spencer muns. II/1/699).

Anastasia Occ. Trin. 1309 (PRO, CP40/178, attorneys m. 9d).

Christina Occ. 13 Apr. 1314 (*CPR 1313–17*, p. 146; PRO, Just.1/1367, m. 9); 3 Sept. 1314 (PRO, C81/1786/18).

Aubrey (Albreda) Mentioned 10 May 1329 as former prs (*CPR 1327–30*, p. 388).

Lucy of Colney (Colneye) Occ. 10 May 1329, 12 Feb. 1330 (ibid., pp. 388, 489, see below).

Mary of Stortford (Storteford) Occ. 1 Oct. 1329 (Lincoln, Ep. Reg., IV, f. 301r); 16 Mar. 1330 (*London IPM (Fry)*, p. 68); 21 May 1333 (Lincoln, Ep. Reg., IV, f. 305v); 4 Nov. 1334 (*CPR 1334–38*, pp. 92–3).

Tiffany (Theophania) la Blounde Occ. 5 Feb. 1336 (*YB 19 Edward III*, pp. 16–17); Mar. 1339 (Spencer muns. II/1/252).

Elizabeth de Montagu (Montacute, Monte Acuto) Occ. 30 Nov. 1340 (WAM no. 5747); Easter 1345 (*YB 19 Edward III*, p. 17); 15 Sept. 1346 (*Reg. Edington*, II, no. 32); 16 Feb. 1348 (*Ctl. St Frideswide's*, I, 9); 18 June 1349 (*CPL*, III, 360; *CPP*, p. 167); 25 July 1353, 20 May 1356, 22 July 1356 (*Assize of Nuisance*, nos. 446, 471, 434); 6 Dec. 1354 (*CCR 1354–60*, p. 99); 26 Jan. 1356 (*CPR 1354–58*, p. 383). Masses in St Frideswide's, Oxford, for the soul of prs Elizabeth mentd 1 Mar. 1379, presumably Montagu (*Ctl. St Frideswide's*, II, 15; *CPR 1377–81*, p. 479).

Ellen Gossham (Goshalm) Occ. 10 Mar. 1363 (*Cal. London Letter Books G.*, p. 152); 1 Oct. 1363, 23 Nov. 1366 (Spencer muns. II/1/279, 282). Mentd 14 Jan. 1376 as former prs having gtd 60-year lease to testator, who died 31 Jan. 1375 (*Cal. Plea Rolls 1364–81*, p. 213).

Anne Occ. 1381 (McHardy, *Church in London*, no. 197).

PRIORS

Richard Occ. 1224 (*Ctl. Holy Trinity, Aldgate*, no. 811).

Nicholas *dictus* **Existens** Occ. as master of Haliwell n.d. (1244 x 1248, *temp.* prs Cecily of Clerkenwell and prs. Margaret of Kilburn) (BL, Harl. ms. 4015, f. 94v).

NOTE

Mon. Angl., IV, 392, citing a ms. of E.R. Mores (not now located) names prs **Isabel** ?1261 and prs **Benigna** *temp.* Henry III. Juliana was prs in 1261 and it is uncertain where Isabel and Benigna fit into the sequence of prioresses. A prs Isabel is found in 1393 (Spencer muns. II/1/308).

LONDON, St Helen's and Holy Cross (St Helen's, Bishopgate) f. -1216 (*KH*); 1212 x c. 1214 (Thompson) (Benedictine priory)

Lists in *VCH London*, I, 460–1; *Heads*, I, 215; Thompson, *Women Religious*, p. 246 (to 1269).

Matilda Occ. before 1225 (PRO, E40/2213); early 13th cent., c. 1215 x 1229 (*Ctl. Holy Trinity, Aldgate*, no. 336).

Helen (Ellen) –1255 Occ. Oct. 1229 x Oct. 1230 (*London and Middlesex F.*, p. 18); 10 Feb. 1232 (*Kent F.*, p. 117); Oct. 1235 x Oct. 1236, Oct. 1243 x Oct. 1244, Oct. 1248 x Oct. 1249 (*London and Middlesex F.*, pp. 22, 28, 32); 1244 x 1248 (BL, Harl. ms. 4015, f. 94v); 3 Feb. 1254 (*Beds F.*, I, no. 547). D. (H.) by 8 May 1255 (Guildhall Lib., St Paul's D. & C., ms. 25,121/1108).

Scholastica –1269 Prob. unnamed prs el. by 8 May 1255 (ibid.). Occ. from 14 May 1256 to 4

May 1259 (*Beds F.*, I, nos. 571, 597); 1 July 1262 (*Essex F.*, I, 249); 1265 (PRO, E40/791). D. by 23 July 1269 (Guildhall, St Paul's D. & C., ms. 25,121/2039; *HMC 9th Rept.*, app. I, p. 57).

Felicia de Basinges 1269– Eln notif. 23 July 1269 (ibid.). Occ. 1285 (PRO, Just.1/242, m. 38).

Orabella Occ. Hil. 1295 (PRO, CP40/107, m. 96).

Joan of Winchester (Wynton') **–1324** D. by 30 July 1324 when lic. sought for eln of a successor (Guildhall, St Paul's D. & C., ms. 25,121/1107).

Beatrice le Boteler –1332 D. 3 Nov. 1332, bur. 5 Nov. (ibid., 25,121/1105).

Eleanor of Winchester (Wyncestre, Wynton') **1332–** Sub-prs of St Helen's, lic. for eln 9 Nov. 1332, el. 10 Nov. 1332 (ibid.); occ. Jan. 1333 x Jan. 1334 (PRO, E329/155); 11 June 1333 (Lincoln, Ep. Reg., IV, f. 311r); 2 July 1344 (BL, Harl. Ch. 44 F. 45); 24 July 1348 (*Ctl. Pyel*, p. 101, no. 1).

Margery de Honilane (Honylane) Occ. 10 Dec. 1349 (ibid., p. 101, no. 3); 6 Dec. 1354 (*CPL*, III, 528); 30 June 1363 (*Assize of Nuisance*, nos. 519–20); 16 June 1368 (ibid., no. 542).

Isabel Gloucestre Mentd 5 May 1374 as former prs (ibid., no. 599).

Mary Occ. 5 Dec. 1376 (ibid., no. 613).

The next recorded prs, **Constance Somersete**, is poss. the unnamed prs mentd in 1379 poll tax, since Constance does not feature among the nuns listed (McHardy, *Church in London*, p. 2, no. 5). D. 15 Apr. 1398 (Guildhall, St Paul's D. & C., ms. 25,121/1106).

LYMINSTER (Sussex), St Mary (S. Pierre d'Almenèches) f. *c.* 1082? (*KH*); late 11th cent. tradition; – *c.* 1201 (Thompson) (Benedictine priory)
List in *VCH Sussex*, II, 121; Thompson, *Women Religious*, p. 246 (to 1262/3).

Mabel Mentd 1262 x 1263 as predecessor of the then (unnamed) prs (PRO, Just.1/912A, m. 4d).

Agatha de la Poynte Occ. 6 Oct. 1271 (*Sussex F.*, II, no. 760); Nov.1295 x Nov. 1296 (PRO, E106/3/19, m. 16); royal protection, an alien, 7 Feb. 1296 (*CPR 1292–1301*, p. 177); Nov. 1296 x Nov. 1297 (PRO, E106/4/2, m. 1); Nov. 1297 x Nov. 1298 (PRO, E106/4/8, m. 1); Nov. 1298 x Nov. 1299 (PRO, E106/4/9, m. 1; E106/4/10, m. 1d); Easter 1300 (PRO, E106/4/14, m. 1d); Nov. 1302 x Nov. 1303 (PRO, E106/4/18, m. 1d).

Agnes Occ. 26 Feb. 1304 (ECR 56/55).

Agatha Occ. 8 Mar. 1309 (ECR 56/57).

Emelina (Omelina) Occ. 19 Feb. 1319 (ECR. 56/62); 16 Mar. 1320 (*CCR 1318–23*, p. 225); *c.* Mich. 1324 (PRO, E106/5/2, m. 4); July 1325 x July 1326 (PRO, E106/5/4, m. [2d]); 8 Oct. 1326 (*Memo. Roll 1326–7*, p. 271).

Joan del Isle (de Isle) **1346–1350** Occ. Jan. 1345 x Jan. 1346 (PRO, E106/9/21); 27 June 1346 (*CPR 1345–48*, p. 126). D. before 24 Mar. 1350 (*CFR 1347–56*, p. 235).

Joan de Ferraris Occ. 24 Mar. 1350 (ibid.); 30 Apr. 1360 (*CCR 1360–64*, p. 28).

Katherine de Lisle (del Isle, Lyle, Lysle) Occ. 1370 (PRO, E106/10/11); 6 Apr. 1374 (*Cal. Misc. Inq.*, III, 351); 1377 (PRO, E179/11/1A); 16 Nov. 1379 (*CFR 1377–83*, p. 170); Jan. 1381 (PRO, E179/11/9); 11 Sept. 1383 (*CFR 1383–91*, p. 4, cf. Matthew, *Norman Monasteries*, p. 156).

MALLING (Kent), St Mary and St Andrew f. *c.* 1090 (*KH*); *c.* 1095 (Thompson) (Benedictine abbey)
Lists in *VCH Kent*, II, 148; *Heads*, I, 215.

Berta Occ. late 12th cent. or early 13th cent. (Lambeth, Ch. Ant. V/98).

Regina Occ. 13 Oct. 1227 (*Kent F.*, p. 96); n.d. (*CChR 1341–1417*, p. 63); *c.* 1233, *c.* Mich. 1233 (Lambeth, Ch. Ant. V/101; V/99).

Isabel Occ. *c.* 1270 (ibid., V/103); n. d. (*CChR 1341–1417*, p. 62); Easter 1288 (PRO, CP40/72, m. 92).

Sarra de Plumbergh Occ. 7 Nov. 1310 (Lambeth, Ch. Ant. V/106); 21 Feb. 1311 (Norwich, Reg/1/1, f. 39v); n.d. (*CChR 1341–1417*, p. 62).

Elizabeth de Badlesmere (Badelesmer') –1321 Suspended from admin. of temps. on suspicion of dilapidation 13 Nov. 1321 following bp's visitation; fails to appear on account of ill health 16 Nov. 1321 (*Reg. Hethe*, I, 217–20). In 1322 Bp Cobham wrote to Bp Hethe asking him to continue his kindness to Isabel, formerly abbs. of Malling, who is insane (*Reg. Cobham*, p. 131).

Agnes of Leybourne –1324 D. 20 Sept. 1324 (*Reg. Hethe*, I, 140).

Lora of Ratling (Retlyng) 1324–1345 Prs. of Malling, el. and eln conf. 22 Sept 1324; bl. 23 Sept. 1324 (ibid., 140–4). Occ. 13 Oct. 1344 (ibid., II, 735). D. by 8 Sept. 1345 (ibid., 770).

Isabel de Pecham 1345–1349 Apptd by bp 8 Sept. 1345 on d. of Lora (ibid.). D. 5 May 1349 (ibid., 869).

Benedicta de Grey 1349 N. of Malling, el. 7 May 1349 on d. of Isabel, but abbs.-el. was sick and could not be carried to the high altar as usual. She died the following night 8 May; lic. to el. 8 May (ibid, 868–73).

Alice de Tendring 1349 N. of Malling, el. 9 May 1349; eln conf., bl. & prof. obed. 9 May 1349. 10 May 1349 letters to convent to obey (ibid, 873–5). Presumably d. soon after.

Margaret of Pattishall (Pateshull) 1349–1369 N. of Malling, el. 23 July 1349 after house had been directed to el. an abbess; eln conf. by commissary 23 July; bl. 24 July, no reason given for vacancy (ibid., 890–4). D. 6 Aug. 1369; lic. to el. sent to prs and convent [unfinished entry] (Rochester, Reg. Trillek, Drb/Ar.1/4, f. 19r–v).

The next recorded abbs, **Joan Baude**, mentd Trin. 1414 as former abbs (PRO, CP40/614, m. 354).

MARHAM (Norfolk), St Mary, St Barbara and St Edmund (cf. f. 2r of ctl.; *St Richard of Chichester*, p. 50, no. 87). f. 1249 (Cistercian abbey)

    List in *VCH Norfolk*, II, 370. See also A. Nichols, 'The history and cartulary of the Cistercian nuns of Marham Abbey, 1249–1536' (Kent State Univ., Ph. D. thesis, 1974).

Mary I Occ. n.d. (*c.* 1251) (Norfolk RO, Hare 1/232X, Ctl. Marham, ff. 20v, 22r, 22v); n.d. (*c.* 1274) (ibid., f. 24v); Nov. 1275 x Nov. 1276 (*Norfolk F (Rye)*, p. 116); n.d. (Norfolk RO, DN/SUN.8, f. 15r).

Mary II Occ. 26 Sept. 1306 (PRO, Just.1/591, m. 16).

Sarah Occ. Mich. 1309, July 1315 (PRO, Just.1/593, mm. 12, 34); Easter 1310 (PRO, CP40/183, n. 69, attorneys m. 1d); 1324 (Ctl. Marham, f. 9v).

[**Agatha Howard** Occ. Jan. 1342 x Jan. 1343 and as late abbess Jan. 1365 x Jan. 1366 (Blomefield, VII, 390, without source).]

Mary (Marroia) of Ingham 1365– Bl. and prof. obed. 7 July 1365, no reason having been given for vacancy (Norwich, Reg/2/5, f. 65r).

The next recorded abbess, **Egidia Howard**, occ. June 1379 x June 1380 (Blomefield, VII, 391, without source).

MARKYATE (Herts, formerly Beds), Holy Trinity (Caddendon; Cella; La Celle; De Bosco) f. 1145 (Benedictine priory)

    Lists in *VCH Beds*, I, 360–1; *Heads*, I, 215; Thompson, *Women Religious*, p. 246.

Isabel I and II Occ. early 13th cent. (BL, Cotton Cht. XXI 5); 29 Sept. 1221, 13 Oct. 1231 (*Warms F.*, I, nos. 290, 438); Trin. term. 1230 (*CRR*, XIV, no. 242). Isabel II sub-prs of Markyate succ. Isabel, deceased (*ECSP*, no. 155). It is not clear when Isabel I died.

Joan de Syret' (de la Sarette) **1238/9–** N. of Markyate, el. and adm. June 1238 x June 1239 (*Reg. Grosseteste*, p. 312). Occ. 15 July 1252, 22 July 1252 (*Warws F.*, I, nos. 719, 725).

Agnes Gobion (Cobyoun, Gobyon) **–1274** Occ. *c.* 1259–60 (*GASA*, I, 387); 3 Nov. 1271 (*Bucks F.*, II, 25). D. by 20 Nov. 1274 (*Reg. R. Gravesend*, p. 200).

Isabel Gobion (Gobiun) **1274–1281** El. (?conf.) 20 Nov. 1274 by lic. of D. and C. of St Paul's, (ibid.). Res. by 13 May 1281 (*Reg. Sutton*, VIII, 94).

Alice de Basevile (Baswill') **1281–1284** Sub-prs of Markyate, eln conf. 13 May 1281 (ibid.). Res. by 11 Sept. 1284 (ibid., 98).

Loretta (Lora) of Kent (Kantia) **1284–1291** Eln quashed, but apptd by bp 11 Sept. 1284 (ibid.). D. by 24 Aug. 1291 (ibid., 108).

Matilda of Luton 1291– Eln quashed, but apptd by bp 24 Apr. 1291 (ibid., 108–9). Occ. Trin. 1309 (PRO, CP40/178, m. 24); Trin.–Mich. 1328 (*Index to Placita de Banco*, p. 215).

Benedicta de Whitacr(e) 1332– N. of Markyate, commn to examine eln 13 May 1332 (Lincoln, Ep. Reg., V, ff. 459v–460r).

Joan Power –1348 House vacant by her death by [2] Apr. 1348 (Lincoln, Ep. Reg., IX, f. 421r, cf. f. 416v).

Alice Spigurnel (Spygurnell) **1348–1349** N. of Markyate, eln quashed, but apptd by bp 2 Apr. 1348 (ibid.). House vacant by 12 Aug. 1349 (Linc. Ep. Reg., IX, f. 420r).

Isabel de Assheby –1350 House vacant by her cess. by 1 Dec. 1350 (Lincoln, Ep. Reg., IX, f. 424r–v).

Joan (de) Stanebrigg (Stanbrigg) **1350–1386** N. of Markyate, eln quashed, but apptd by bp 1 Dec. 1350 (ibid.). D. by 2 Feb. 1386 (Lincoln, Ep. Reg. XII, f. 319r).

NOTE

In a 1311 case (*YB XI*, p. 97) several predecessors of the present prs of Markyate are named, without indication of dates. Three are not accounted for by other sources, viz: **Isoud** (? possibly Isabel), **M.**(? possibly Matilda) and **S**.

CUSTOS

William Occ. 14 Jan. 1324 (Lincoln, Ep. Reg., V, f. 356r).

MARLOW, *see* **LITTLE MARLOW**

MARRICK (Yorks N.), St Mary and St Andrew f. 1154 x 58 (Benedictine priory)

Lists in *VCH Yorks*, III, 118; *Heads*, I, 215; Thompson, *Women Religious*, pp. 246–7 (to 1263).

Alice occ. n.d. (1217 x 1236) (BL, Add. ms. 38816, f. 11v); n.d. (early 13th century, before 1243) (ibid., f. 11r).

Isabel Occ. 29 July 1240 (*Yorks F., 1232–46*, p. 86); 11 Nov. 1257 (Hull, Carlton Towers, DDCA(2)/29/77; *CTG*, V, 222); 15 May 1263 (Hull, Carlton Towers, DDCA(2)/29/86; *CTG*, V, 236). A note of a 1250 cht. gives her surname as Surrais (*CTG*, V, 239, but no source can now be found).

Ellen Occ. 1279 (PRO, Just.1/1056, m. 23d). ? the same as Alina.

Alina of Aske (Ask) Occ. n.d. *c.* 1280 (PRO, E326/3682); n.d. (PRO, E315/53/188).

Margaret Occ. 11 Nov. 1282 (Hull, Carlton Towers, DDCA(2)/29/94; *CTG*, V, 108).

Alice of Helperby Occ. 21 Dec. 1293 (*CTG*, V, 229); n.d. (late 13th cent.) (Ctl. Scrope of Bolton, f. 63r).

Juliana Occ. 11 Nov. 1298 (Hull, Carlton Towers, DDCA(2)/29/97; *CTG*, V, 238); n.d. (? early 14th cent.) (*Yorks Deeds*, X, no. 312).

Margaret of Hartlepool (Hertelpole) Occ. 26 Dec. 1319 (Ctl. Scrope of Bolton, f. 146r); 5 Apr. 1321 (Hull, Carlton Towers, DDCA(2)/29/99; *CTG*, V, 123; Ctl. Scrope of Bolton,

f. 34r); Hil. – Trin. 1328 (*Index to Placita de Banco*, p. 785; Baildon, I, 127). Mentd as late prs 1332 (ibid., 127).

Elizabeth de Verdon Occ. 13 May 1326; 11 Nov. 1333 (Hull, Carlton Towers, DDCA(2)/29/102; *CTG*, V, 108, 120); Trin. 1332 (Baildon, I, 127).

Elizabeth Occ. 1351 (PRO, Just.1/1129, m. 17). ? the same as above.

Matilda Melsonby (Melsinby) Occ. 6 May 1376 (Hull, Carlton Towers, DDCA(2)/29/104; *CTG*, V, 234–5).

The next recorded prs, **Sibyl of Aislaby** (Aslaby) occ. June 1379 x June 1380 (Plantagenet-Harrison, *Gilling West*, p. 219, citing plea of trespass).

MINSTER IN SHEPPEY (Kent), St Mary and St Sexburga f. *c.* 670; ref. ?1130 (for the confusion over the order (Augustinian/Benedictine), see Thompson, pp. 201–2).

    Lists in *VCH Kent*, II, 150; *Heads*, I, 215–16; Thompson, *Women Religious*, p. 247 (from obits); obits in the Davington obituary, *Mon. Angl.*, II, 49 from BL, Cotton ms. Faustina B VI, f. 101vff.; cf. *Heads*, I, 210n.

Agnes Last recorded occ. (A.) 1187 (Urry, p. 427, cf. p. 429). ? the prs Agnes whose obit was 4 Oct. (BL, Cotton ms. Faustina B VI, f. 106v).

Joan de Badlesmere (Badelismere) Obit 14 Mar. (*Mon. Angl.*, II, 49). On 24 May 1343 an unnamed prs is mentioned as being the sister of Bartholomew de Burghersh (*CChR 1341–1417*, p. 20). Probably this was Joan de Badlesmere – Bartholomew Burghersh, Lord Burghersh (d. 1355) was the son of Robert Burghersh and Maud, sister of Bartholomew, Lord Badlesmere (*Complete Peerage*, II, 425–6).

Joan Cobham –1368 D. 10 July 1368; lic. to el. 12 July 1368 (*Reg. Langham*, pp. 199, 195).

Isabel Honyton 1368– Cellaress of Minster, el. 17 Aug. 1368 and conf. by commissary s.d.; prof. obed. 17 Aug. 1368 (ibid., pp. 199–202); eln conf. by archbp 21 Aug. 1368 (ibid., pp. 203–4). Occ. 18 Jan. 1380 (*Cal. Misc. Inq.*, IV, no. 117).

Prs **Eustachia** (obit 20 Apr.) and prs **Christina** (obit 19 Sept.) (BL, Cotton ms. Faustina B VI, f. 104r, 106v) may possibly date from this period.

MOXBY (Yorks N.), St John the Evangelist f. -1167 (*KH*); -1158 (Burton; Thompson) (Benedictine/Augustinian priory)

    Lists in *VCH Yorks*, III, 240; Thompson, *Women Religious*, p. 247 (master only, 1225).

Alice of Farlington (Ferlyngton) Mentd as former prs in 1279 (PRO, Just.1/1056, m. 54d).

Beatrice de Laton Mentd as former prs in 1279 (ibid., m. 52d).

Eleanor Occ. 1279 (ibid., mm. 52d, 54d).

Euphemia –1310 Occ. 24 Dec. 1290 (PRO, C241/14/6); 16 Jan. 1304 (*CPR 1301–7*, p. 206). Res. 1 Dec. 1310 on account of ill health (*Reg. Greenfield*, III, p. 58, no. 1263).

Alice of Barton 1310– N. of Moxby, el. 4 Dec. 1310; eln conf. 12 Dec. 1310 (ibid.). Occ. as prs 17 Nov. 1322, when sent to Swine priory because Moxby had been wasted by the Scots (*Reg. Melton*, II, p. 84, no. 211, cf. p. 86, no. 220; *Letters from Northern Regs.*, p. 321).

Joan of Barton –1325 Res. 24 Jan. 1325; lic. to el. 24 Jan. 1325 (*Reg. Melton*, II, p. 103, no. 255). Penance for fornication with Laurence de Dysceford, chaplain, 3 Sept. 1325 (ibid., p. 105, no. 263, cf. pp. 127–8, no. 313).

Commn to visit priory with powers to replace prs 7 Mar. 1328 (ibid., pp. 125–6, no. 303).

Sabina of Applegarth (Appelgarth) –1328[11] Res. by 26 Mar. 1328 (ibid., p. 126, no. 305). [Prob. the Sabina of Applegarth, n. of Moxby, who was removed from various offices at the

---

[11] Baildon, I, 138 has a prs surnamed 'Salini' between Joan of Barton and Joan de Toucotes. I have assumed it is an error for Sabina.

1318 visitation and sent to Nun Monkton after the the Scots incursion in 1322 (ibid., p. 14, no. 31; p. 84, no. 211). Earlier as a n. of Moxby, she had returned penitent from apostasy, archbp's mand. to reconcile 24 Apr. 1312 (Logan, *Runaway Religious*, p. 258).]

Joan de Toucotes (Tucotes) **1328–1331** N. of Moxby, mand. to obey on res. of Sabina 26 Mar. 1328 (ibid., p. 126, no. 305). D. by 10 Feb. 1331, lic. to el. (York, Reg. 9B, f. 723v).

Elizabeth de Nevyll **–1398** D. by 31 Jan. 1398 (York, Reg. 5A, f. 235r).

MASTERS

Peter Occ. Mich. Term 1225 (*CRR*, XII, no. 827).

William 1282– Vicar of Thirkleby, apptd as master 14 Dec. 1282 (*Reg. Romeyn*, I, pp. 157–8, no. 436) – presumably had given up office by 1286 when a certain Peter was vicar of Thirkleby (ibid., p. 160).

Mag. Adam Irnepurse 1294– Vicar of Bossall, apptd as master 8 May 1294 (ibid., p. 180, no. 513).

NEASHAM (Durham) f. -1156/7 (Benedictine priory)

List in *VCH Durham*, II, 108.

Margaret Occ. Aug. 1349 x Aug. 1350 (*PRO DKR*, 31 (1870), p. 117).

Cecily de Doneham (Donham) Occ. 1360 (PRO, E210/8913); n.d. (PRO, E210/8071).

Joan of Coniscliffe (Conisclift) **1366–** N. of Neasham, commn to conf. eln and install 26 July 1366, cert. of conf. 3 Aug. 1366 (Durham, Reg. Hatfield, f. 62r).

Margaret (?de Eversalle *virtually illegible*) Occ. 1379 (PRO, E179/62/4, m. 3).

The next recorded prs, **Joan of Eggleston**, res. by 29 Nov. 1428 (*Reg. Langley*, III, no. 770).

NEWCASTLE-UPON-TYNE (Northumberland), St Bartholomew f. -1086; ref. ? c. 1135 (*KH*); 1143 x 1149, ? 1144 – tradition of earlier foundation (Thompson) (Benedictine priory)

Lists in A.M. Oliver, 'List of the prioresses of the Benedictine nunnery of St Bartholomew of Newcastle', *Proc. Soc. Ant. Newcastle*, 4th ser., 6 (1933–5), pp. 65–6; M. Hope Dodds, 'Prioresses of St Bartholomew's nunnery: supplementary note', ibid., p. 122; Thompson, *Women Religious*, p. 247 (to mid- 13th cent.).

Christiana Occ. 11 Feb. 1227 (*Northumberland and Durham F.*, I, p. 38, no. 83); 1233 (Madox, *Form.*, p. 132, no. 224).

Agnes Occ. n.d. (first half of 13th cent., before 1242/3 (PRO, E315/31/14; E315/41/10).

Emma Occ. n.d. (*temp.* Henry III, ? c. 1250) (*Northumberland and Durham Deeds*, pp. 135–6; BL, Add. Cht. 20529); 30 Apr. 1256 (*Northumberland and Durham F.*, p. 91, no. 220); 18 Nov. 1257 (ibid., p. 98, no. 239).

Christiana Occ. 20 May 1274 (*HMC Middleton*, p. 75).

Philippa of Boltby (Bolteby) Occ. 1292 x 1293 (*Northumberland and Durham Deeds*, p. 136); 1293 (*Hist. Northumberland*, XII, 475–6); n.d. (PRO, E315/35/194, E315/41/125; E326/8822); (one prob. 1303 or 1304 on acct of chief bailiff of Newcastle a witness) (Brand, *Hist. of Newcastle*, p. 215; cf. *Early Newcastle Deeds*, p. 209).

Margery Occ. 9 Dec. 1324 (*Northumberland and Durham Deeds*, p. 140); July 1322 x July 1323 (PRO, E213/86). Seal (*Mon. Seals*, p. 64).

Sibyl Gategang Occ. 1331 (*Mon. Angl.*, IV, 487); 1332 x 1333 (*Early Newcastle Deeds*, no. 339); n.d. (*temp.* John de Lilbourne, sheriff of Northumberland, 1327 x 1330 *or* 1339 (PRO, E326/9848).

Agnes Occ. n.d. (dated by *List of Sheriffs*, p. 97 – 1334 x 1340) (PRO, E326/6624; cf. *Early Newcastle Deeds*, p. 177, no. 339n.).

Christiana Occ. 1351 (PRO, E329/149).

Alice Davill 1355– Eln quashed but apptd by bp 9 May 1355 (Durham, Reg. Hatfield, f. 38v).

Isabel Russell Occ. 1360 (PRO, E326/8672). Mentd n.d. (R. Welford, *Hist. of Newcastle and Gateshead*, p. 157). D. by Mich. 1361 (*Hist. Northumberland*, XIII, 273; Dodds, p. 122).

Margery Mich. 1361 convent desolate by d. of prs Isabel – only 2 nuns left – a n. of Lambley called Margery, became prs. (poss. to be identified with Margaret of York below) (ibid.).

Margaret of York (Ebor') Occ. 11 July 1363 (PRO, E326/21386; *Proc. Soc. Ant. Newcastle*, 3rd ser., VIII (1917–8), p. 156, no. 11).

Amice of Belford (but once Bedford) Occ. 19 Mar. 1364 (Brand, *Hist. of Newcastle*, p. 217; Welford, *Hist. of Newcastle and Gateshead*, p. 163). Intruded: proceedings ordered 10 June 1367 (Durham, Reg. Hatfield, f. 47r). Prob. to be identified with prs. **Anne** occ. 24 June 1367 (*CCR 1364–68*, p. 390); 21 Apr. 1367 (Amya) *asserentem se priorissam* (Durham, Reg. Hatfield, f. 47r).

Katherine Occ. 30 Sept. 1367 in case against Amice of Bedford, n. of Newcastle, who asserted herself to be prs without eln or just title. Amice was dep. by the bp of Durham and is now a vagrant with the common seal and many goods of the house in her possession (*CPR 1367–70*, p. 50). Occ. 21 Sept. 1403 (Brand, *Hist. of Newcastle*, I, 222 & note g).

Whether she is the same as the next recorded prs, **Katherine of Langton**, who res. 30 Aug. 1413 (*Reg. Langley*, II, no. 319, cf. no. 306) is uncertain.

CUSTOS

Hugh of Arncliffe (Arnecliff, Ernecliff) Chaplain of St Nicholas, Newcastle, app. *custos* of house 18 Apr. 1367 (Reg. Hatfield, f. 47r); 10 June 1367 to proceed against Amice of Belford, intruded (ibid.).

NORTHAMPTON, St Mary de la Pré (Delapre) f. *c.* 1141 ? (at Fotheringay); 1145 (at Northampton) (*KH*); *c.* 1145 x 1153 (Thompson) (Cluniac abbey)

Lists in *VCH Northants.*, II, 115–16; *Heads*, I, 216; Thompson, *Women Religious*, p. 247 (to 1275).

Cecilia of Daventry 1220–1242 N. of Northampton, royal ass. 7 Nov. 1220 (*CPR 1216–25*, p. 270). D., lic. to el. 4 June 1242 (*CPR 1232–47*, p. 299).

Agatha of Navesby 1242–1275 Royal ass. 15 June 1242 (ibid.). D. by 7 Jan. 1275 (PRO, C84/5/16). D., lic. to el. 10 Jan. 1275 (*CPR 1272–81*, p. 75). Seal (*BM Seals*, no. 3751).

Emma Mallore (Malore) **1275–1282** N. of Northampton, eln pres. to king for royal ass. 14 Jan. 1275 (PRO, C84/5/18); royal ass. 19 Jan. 1275, writ *de intendendo* 29 Jan. 1275 (*CPR 1272–81*, pp. 76, 78). Eln pres. to bp 23 Jan. 1275, bl. 25 Jan. 1275 (*Reg. R. Gravesend*, pp. 124, 302; PRO, C84/5/22). D. 25 Apr. 1282 (*Reg. Sutton*, II, 18). D., lic. to el. 1 May 1282 (*CPR 1281–92*, p. 18).

Margery of Wollaston (Wolaston, Wolaveston, Wulaston) **1282–1297** Sub-prs of Northampton, eln pres. to king for royal ass. 10 May 1282 (PRO, C84/5/53); royal ass. 17 May 1282, temps. 7 June 1282 (*CPR 1281–92*, pp. 19, 25). Eln quashed but apptd by bp 22 May 1282; bl. 31 May 1282 (*Reg. Sutton*, II, 18–19). D., lic. to el. 25 Mar. 1297 (*CPR 1292–1301*, p. 244).

Margery of Brooke (Brok') **1297–1319** N. of Northampton, eln pres. to king for royal ass. 4 Apr. 1297 (PRO, C84/12/43); royal ass. 11 Apr. 1297, temps. 20 May 1297 (*CPR 1292–1301*, pp. 246, 249). Eln conf. 28 Apr. 1297; bl. 1 May 1297 (*Reg. Sutton*, II, 139; PRO, C81/12/1175). Cess. by 16 May 1319 (PRO, C84/8/24). Cess., lic. to el. 21 May 1319 (*CPR 1317–21*, p. 334).

Agnes (de) Pavely 1319–1327 N. of Northampton, eln pres. to king for royal ass. 28 May 1319 (PRO, C84/24/6); royal ass. 1 June 1319, temps. 5 July 1319 (*CPR 1317–21*, pp. 338, 356). Eln quashed but apptd by bp 28 June 1319 (Lincoln, Ep. Reg., II, f. 140r; PRO, C84/19/48).

Prof. obed. and bl. by ex-archbp of Armagh 29 June 1319 (Lincoln, Ep. Reg., III, f. 420r). D., lic. to el. 1 Jan. 1328 (*CPR 1327–30*, p. 196).

Margaret de Grey 1328–1334 N. of Northampton, eln pres. to king for royal ass. 6 Jan. 1328 (PRO, C84/21/29); royal ass. 11 Jan. 1338, temps. 22 Feb. 1338 (*CPR 1327–30*, pp. 201, 238). Comm to examine eln 14 Jan. 1328 (Lincoln, Ep. Reg., V, f. 410r); certificate of commissaries that they have conf. eln 15 Feb. 1328, bl. 25 Feb. 1328 (ibid., f. 411r). D., lic. to el. 12 Jan. 1334 (*CPR 1330–34*, p. 488).

The d. of Margaret was followed by the disputed eln of **Katherine Knyvet** and **Isabel de Cotesbrok**, nuns of Northampton (Lincoln, Ep. Reg., IV, f. 204r–v). Isabel gained royal ass. 30 Jan. 1334 (*CPR 1330–34*, p. 507). The elns pres. to bp 11 Feb. 1334 who quashed both on grounds of irregularity and apptd Katherine Knyvet 12 Feb. 1334 (Lincoln, Ep. Reg., IV, f. 204r–v).

Katharine Knyvet 1334–1349 Apptd by bp 12 Feb. 1334, lic. to receive bl. from the bp of Coventry and Lichfield (ibid.). Temps. 25 Feb. 1334 (*CPR 1330–34*, p. 516). Bl. by bp of Coventry and Lichfield 27 Feb. 1334 (Lichfield, B/A/1/3, f. 71r). D. by 5 Aug. 1349 (Lincoln, Ep. Reg., IX, f. 191r).

Isabel de Thorpe 1349–1366 N. of Northampton, royal ass. 23 July 1349, temps. 11 Aug. 1349 (*CPR 1348–50*, pp. 355, 354). Eln quashed but apptd by bp 5 Aug. 1349; bl. 8 Aug. 1349 (Lincoln, Ep. Reg., IX, f. 191r). Res. acc. 14 Jan. 1366 (Lincoln, Ep. Reg., XII, f. 26v). Res., lic. to el. 4 Feb. 1366 (*CPR 1364–67*, p. 219).

Joan Mallore (Mallor', Mallorre, Mallory) **1366–1394** N. of Northampton, eln pres. to king for royal ass. 3 Mar. 1366 (PRO, C84/29/53); royal ass. 12 Mar. 1366, temps. 2 Apr. 1366 (*CPR 1364–67*, pp. 227, 228). Commn to examine eln 10 Mar. 1366 (Lincoln, Ep. Reg., XII, f. 28v). Eln conf. by commissary 26 Mar. 1366; bl. 29 Mar. 1366 (Lincoln, Ep. Reg., IX, f. 170r–v). D., lic. to el. 26 June 1394 (*CPR 1391–96*, p. 447, cf. Lincoln, Ep. Reg. XI, f. 172v).

MASTERS

Simon vicar of 'Throp', apptd n.d. (between items of 23 July and 20 Aug 1316) (Lincoln, Ep. Reg., III, f. 349v).

Simon vicar of Fotheringay, apptd as master during pleasure 24 Nov. 1320 (Lincoln, Ep. Reg., V, f. 266v).

NORWICH, St Mary (Carrow) f. *temp.* Henry I (site 1); *c.* 1146 (site 2) (*KH*); *c.* 1136 (site 1); *c.* 1145 x 1147 (site 2) (Thompson) (Benedictine priory)

    Lists in *VCH Norfolk*, II, 354; Rye, *Carrow Abbey*, pp. 38–9; *Heads*, I, 216; Thompson, *Women Religious*, p. 248 (to 1264).

Matilda Called Le Strange by Blomefield (*Norfolk*, IV, 525, no source). Occ. 26 Oct. 1198 (*Norfolk F. 1198–1202*, no. 189); 6 Aug. 1206 (*Norfolk F. 1201–15*, no. 92); Oct. 1221 x Oct. 1222 (*Norfolk F. (Rye)*, p. 37).

Agnes de Montchensy (Monte Caenesi, Montecaniso) Occ. n.d. (early 13th cent.) (*Norfolk Arch. Misc.*, II, 496); 1224 (Blomefield, *Norfolk*, IV, 525, no source); *c.* 1230 x 1247/49 (*Norwich Cath. Chts.*, II, no. 370); from Oct. 1233 x Oct. 1234 to Oct. 1256 x Oct. 1257 (*Norfolk F. (Rye)*, pp. 52, 93); 1250 (PRO, Just.1/560, m. 7).

Magdalen Occ. 1264 (Blomefield, *Norfolk*, IV, 525, no source); Oct. 1265 x Oct. 1266, Oct. 1267 x Oct. 1268 (*Norfolk F. (Rye)*, pp. 99, 102); n.d. *temp.* Bp Roger Skerning of Norwich (1266–78) (*HMC 9th Rept.*, app. p. 351).

Petronilla −1289 D. 1289 (Blomefield, *Norfolk*, IV, 525, no source).

Amabilia of Ufford −1294 Occ. from 1290. Bur. 18 Mar. 1294 (*Mon. Angl.*, IV, 69; Rye, *Carrow*, p. 39).

Katharine of Wendling 1294– El. 22 Mar. 1294 (ibid.). Occ. Nov. 1296 x Nov. 1297 (PRO, E210/8432).

Beatrice of Hulme (Hulmo) **1310–** Sacrist of Carrow, eln conf. 8 Jan. 1311, no reason given for vacancy (Norwich, Reg/1/1, f. 39r). Occ. 15 Sept. 1315 (PRO, Just.1/593, m. 37d).

Agnes of Carlton (Carletone) **1324–** N. of Carrow, eln conf. 6 Oct. 1324, no reason given for vacancy (Norwich, Reg/1/1, f. 111r).

Agnes of Lynn (Lenn) **–1341** Occ. 21 Aug. 1338 (Norwich, Reg/1/3, f. 16r). Res. 10 Apr. 1341, res. adm. 12 Apr. 1341 (ibid., f. 45r).[12]

Cecily of Plumstead (Plumsted(e)) **1341–** Commn to examine eln 18 Apr. 1341 and eln conf. 19 Apr. 1341, installed same day (ibid., f. 44v). Occ. 21 Jan. 1349 (*CPL*, III, 310).

Alice of Hethersett (Hedersete) **1349–** N. of Carrow, eln conf. and apptd 4 July 1349, no reason given for vacanacy (*Reg. Bateman*, I, no. 734).

Margery Cat 1366–1369 N. of Carrow, eln conf. 28 Jan. 1366 (Norwich, Reg/2/5, ff. 67v–68r). D. by 15 Sept. 1369 (Lambeth, Reg. Whittlesey, ff. 143v–144r).

Margery de Inges (Enges) **1369–1396** N. of Carrow, eln conf. 15 Sept. 1369 (ibid.). D. by 8 Jan. 1396 (Norwich, Reg/3/6, f. 205v).

NUN APPLETON (Yorks W.), St Mary and St John the Evangelist f. *c.* 1150 (*KH*); *c.* 1148 x 1154 (Thompson) (Cistercian priory)

Lists in *VCH Yorks*, II, 173–4; Thompson, *Women Religious*, p. 248 (to 1262).

Alice Occ. Whitsun 1227 (Bodl., Dodsworth ms. 95, f. 45Av); 8 Nov. 1234 (*Yorks F., 1232–46*, p. 9); 1235 (Baildon, I, 159); 8 July 1256 (*Lincs F.*, II, 293; PRO, F., Var. Cos. CP25/1/284/19 no. 127).

Mabel Occ. 1262 (Bodl., Dodsworth ms. 76, f. 62v; *Cal. Bodl. Chts.*, 697).

Hawise –1294 Occ. 1277 (*VCH*, citing Baildon, ms. notes); 1279 x 83 (Bodl., ms. Top. Yorks e. 9, f. 50v); 1290 (Baildon, I, 160). Commn to accept res. and to conf. eln of a successor 12 Nov. 1294 (*Reg. Romeyn*, I, 145).

Isolda Occ. Hil. 1300 – Trin. 1302 (Baildon, I, 160).

Joan de Normanvile 1303– Eln conf. 29 Apr. 1303, no reason given for vacancy (*Reg. Corbridge*, I, 82). Occ. 1306 (*VCH*, citing Baildon, ms. notes).

Elizabeth of Holbeck (Holbech, Holbek(e)) **1316–1320** N. of Nun Appleton, eln conf. 23 Oct. 1316, no reason given for vacancy (*Reg. Greenfield*, V, no. 2806). Res. by 5 Nov. 1320 (York, Reg. 9A, f. 173r) when lic. to el. granted.

Isabel de Normanvill 1320– Comm. to exam. eln of Isabel, n. of Nun Appleton, and to conf. if canonical 16 Nov. 1320 (ibid., f. 173v).

Sibyl de Normanvilla Occ. 21 June 1322 (*CCR 1318–23*, p. 563). ? the same as Isabel above.

Margaret de Nevill –1334 Excused from office on account of infirmity 8 Nov. 1334 (York, Reg. 9A, f. 244r). Lic. to el. 10 Nov. 1334 (ibid., f. 244v).

An unnamed prs, possibly **Idonia**, was in office by 30 Apr. 1335 (ibid., f. 247r).

Idonia Occ. Mich. 1342 (Baildon, I, 160). Perhaps to be identified with **Idonea of Gainsborough** (Gainesburgh), whose tombstone in Ryther church is described in H. Speight, *Lower Wharfedale* (London, 1902), p. 82.

Lucy of Gainsborough (Gaynesburgh) **–1367** D. by 25 May 1367 (York, Reg. 11, f. 142v).

Agnes of Egmanton 1367– N. of Nun Appleton, eln conf. 25 May 1367 (ibid). Occ. Hil. 1368 (Baildon, I, 160).

The next recorded prs, **Emma of Langton**, occ. 18 July 1387 (BI, CP.E.148); Hil. 1388 (Baildon, I, 161).

---

[12] Rye, *Carrow*, p. 39 gives Margaret of St Edmund as prs between Agnes of Lynn and Cecily of Plumstead, but there is no source and she does not seem to fit into the sequence.

CUSTOS

Roger of Saxton, rector of Aberford, apptd as *custos* 9 May 1306 (*Reg. Greenfield*, II, no. 664); commn to audit his accounts as *custos* 21 Sept. 1307 (ibid., no. 758).

NUN COTHAM (Lincs), St Mary (Coton) f. 1147 x 53 (*KH*), 1148 x 1153, prob. -1149 (Thompson) (Cistercian priory)

Lists in *VCH Lincs*, II, 153; *Heads*, I, 216; *Women Religious*, p. 248 (to 1268).

Alice Occ. 25 Nov. 1218, 7 Jan. 1219 (*Lincs F.*, I, 144, 131).

Emma 1230/1– N. of Nun Cotham, el. and adm. Dec. 1230 x Dec. 1231, no reason given for vacancy (*Reg. Wells*, III, 195). Occ. 1 Oct. 1234 (Bodl., ms. Top. Lincs d. 1, f. 21v); 7 Oct. 1234 (*Lincs F.*, I, 277).

Joan de Thorne 1265– Eln examined 12 May 1265, vacant by cess. of last prs. (unnamed) (*Reg. R. Gravesend*, pp. 19, 269). Adm. by bp since eln not canonical, mandate to install 19 May 1265 (Bodl., ms. Top. Lincs d. 1, f. 47v). Occ. (J.) 7 Mar. 1269 (ibid., f. 50r).

Lucy of Mabelthorpe (Malbertorp) **1271–1282** El. 30 Nov. 1271 (ibid., f. 42r). Res. by 28 Sept. 1282 (*Reg. Sutton*, I, 31).

Anne/Amy of Barrow (Barwe, Barna) **1282–1310** El. 28 Sept. 1282 but eln quashed and apptd by bp 29 Sept. 1282 (ibid., 31–2). D. by 16 Mar. 1310 (Lincoln, Ep. Reg., II, f. 32v).

Christine *dicta* Cotty de Lincoln 1310–1320 N. of Nun Cotham, eln quashed but apptd by bp 16 Mar. 1310 (ibid.). D. by 28 Jan. 1320 (ibid., f. 349r).

Isabel de Bonyngton (Boynton) **1320–1332** N. of Nun Cotham, eln quashed on account of irregularity; but apptd by the Official *sede vacante* 28 Jan. 1320 (ibid.). D. by 4 Oct. 1332 (*Reg. Burghersh*, I, no. 364).

Amabilia of Stainton (Staynton) **1332–** N. of Nun Cotham, eln quashed but apptd by bp 4 Oct. 1332 (ibid.).

Cecily de Hanley (?Hauley, Hauly) **–1381** Occ. 30 Sept. [ ] Edward III (date incomplete, must be 1376 or earlier) (Bodl., ms. Top. Lincs d. 1, f. 73v); n.d. but related to entry of 25 Nov. 1377 (Lincoln, Ep. Reg., XII, f. 151v); 1377 (*Clerical Poll-taxes*, p. 45, no. 635); 1381 (ibid., p.145, no. 1834). D. by 12 Sept. 1381 (Lincoln, Ep. Reg., X, f. 115r).

MASTERS

Samson occ. several times in Ctl. without date. Prob. late 12th or early 13th cent. (Bodl., ms. Top. Lincs d. 1, ff. 8v, 9r, 24v, 94v). Possible predecessor of William of Winceby (ibid., f. 24v, incl. Walter son of Segram of Croxton who also occ. in William's charter of 1219 (ibid., f. 25r)).

William of Winceby (Wincebi) Occ. 26 Mar. 1218 (Bodl., ms. Top. Lincs d. 1, f. 39Br); (prior) 7 Jan. 1219 (*Rolls of Lincolnshire Justices*, no. 226); Easter 1219 (Bodl., ms. Top. Lincs d. 1, f. 25r).

Walter Occ. Easter 1224 (ibid., f. 25v); 1233 (ibid., f. 37v); Easter 1235 (ibid.).

Adam Occ. Easter 1239 (ibid., ff. 28v, 37r); 8 Oct. 1241 (ibid., f. 40v).

John of Barton (Bart') Occ. 24 Sept. 1246 (ibid., f. 47v); 22 July 1258 (ibid., f. 46v); 11 Feb. 1261 (ibid., f. 46v).

Robert Cause Occ. n.d. (mid 13th cent) (ibid., ff. 39Br, 41v).

Adam Can. of house, apptd master 8 Mar. 1269, no reason given for vacancy (*Reg. R. Gravesend*, p. 35). Occ. n.d. (1271 x 1282) (Bodl., ms. Top. Lincs d. 1, f. 51r, also f. 48r–v).

Walter –1293 Occ. n.d. (*c.* 1280 x 1293) (ibid., f.55v). D. by 9 Aug. 1293 (*Reg. Sutton*, IV, 101–102).

Walter of Skegness (Skegenes, Skegnes) **1293–** Can. of Nun Cotham, apptd as master 9 Aug. 1293 (ibid). Occ. 1314 (*CPR 1313–17*, p. 237); 11–12 May 1317 (ibid., pp. 696, 698).

Roger Malecak 1318–1319 Rector of a mediety of Keelby, apptd master 24 Dec. 1318, no reason given for vacancy (Lincoln, Ep. Reg., III, f. 404r). Appt. revoked 26 Feb. 1319 (ibid., f. 410r).

Hugh 1319– Vicar of Kirmington, apptd master 26 Feb. 1319 (ibid).

William of Brocklesby (Brockelesby, Broclesby, Broclosby) 1333– Priest, apptd during pleasure 4 Nov. 1333 (Lincoln, Ep. Reg., V, f. 468r). Occ. as *custos* 4 Aug. 1336 (ibid., f. 535v); (master) 6 Apr. 1343, 20 Sept. 1345 (Lincoln, Ep. Reg., VII, ff. 94v, 97r).

NUN KEELING (Yorks E.), St Mary and St Helen f. 1152 (*KH*); 1143 x 1153 (Burton); 1143 x 1147 *or* 1153 x 1154 (Thompson) (Benedictine priory)
 List in *VCH Yorks*, III, 121–2; Thompson, *Women Religious*, p. 249 (to 1267).

Agnes of Mappleton[13] Occ. early Henry III (*Hatton's Book of Seals*, p. 107, no. 151; BL Harl Cht. 44 E 56).

Avice Occ. 1235 (i.e. 25 Mar. 1235 x 24 Mar. 1236) (Bodl., Dodsworth ms. 7, f. 258r); 1252 (PRO, Just.1/1046 m. 62); 2 Feb. 1252 ('Ctl. Meaux' no. 308, pp. 499–501).

Sibyl Occ. *ante* 21 Nov. 1251, when ref. to a toft that prs Sibyl once held (*Yorks F., 1246–72*, p. 45).

Agnes of Beverley (Beverle) 1268–1304 Eln quashed but apptd by archbp 2? Feb. 1268 (*Reg. W. Giffard*, p. 50 – 'ij. Feb.' in ms. but Giffard's clerks use the Roman calendar and presumably calends/nones/ides have been omitted in the register copy). Occ. 1273 (BL, Add. ms. 26736, f. 174r, cf. f. 95v – Agnes la Ruisse). Commn to receive her res. (Agnes of Beverley) 25 Feb. 1304 (*Reg. Corbridge*, I, 196).

Avice de Mora (de la More) 1304–1316 Sub-prs of Nunkeeling, eln conf. 12 Mar. 1304 (ibid., 197). Cess. 11 Aug. 1316 (*Reg. Greenfield*, V, p. 267, no. 2856). Provision for pension 20 Sept. 1316 (ibid., pp. 268–9, no. 2858).

Isabel of St Quintin (de Sancto Quintino) 1316– N. of Nun Keeling, apptd 20 Aug. 1316 by Dean and Chapter of York *sede vacante* (ibid., p. 267, no. 2856). Occ. 1329 (Baildon, I, 163).

The next recorded prs, **Isabel of Burton**, eln conf. 31 Mar. 1400, no reason given for vacancy (*Reg. Scrope*, I, no. 392).

MASTER/CUSTOS

Yvo Occ. as master early Henry III (*Hatton's Book of Seals*, p. 107, no. 151).

Gregory of Lissett (Lesset) 1267– Can. of Newburgh, mand. to pr. of Newburgh to appt him as *custos* 6 Nov. 1267 (*Reg. W. Giffard*, pp. 108–9). Pr. of Marton 1280 (q.v.).

Robert of Lissett (Leset) 1322– Priest, apptd 14 Oct. 1322 (York, Reg. 9A, f. 349v).

NUN MONKTON (Yorks W.), St Mary f. -1147 x 53 (*KH*); 1151 x 1153 (*EEA*, 5, nos. 125–6; Thompson) (Benedictine priory)
 Lists in *VCH Yorks*, III, 123; *Heads*, I, 217–18; Thompson, *Women Religious*, pp. 249–50 (to 1278).

Agnes Occ. 28 Apr. 1224, 1 Dec. 1226 (*Yorks F., 1218–31*, pp. 55, 86); 1227 (Baildon, I, 165 – a fine, without source, ? the 1226 fine cited previously).

Amabel Occ. 3 July 1240 (*Yorks F., 1232–46*, p. 72).

Avice Occ. 30 Sept. 1251 (*Yorks F., 1246–72*, p. 17); Oct. 1257 x Oct. 1258 (PRO, C260/69, no. 14); Nov. 1267 (*Ctl. Fountains*, I, 433); 9 Oct. 1268 (*Reg. W. Giffard*, p. 27). Prob. the **Avice de Cotam** former prs, mentd in 1279 (PRO, Just.1/1056, m. 46).

Mary (Mariota) Occ. 12 Aug. 1278 (BL, Add. Cht. 17962[A]); 1279 (PRO, Just.1/1056, m. 46); 29 Sept. 1281 (Yorke records, Halton Place, Hellifield, Skipton, 5); Whitsun 1284 (Sheffield Archives, Wentworth Woodhouse mun., Add. drawer E1/7); 1293 (Burghley House, Exeter mss. 202/132); *c.* 1300 (ibid., 203/133).

---

[13] The sequence of the first three prioresses is not entirely clear.

Hilary Occ. 4 July 1319 (Sheffield Archives, Wentworth Woodhouse mun., Add. drawer E1/12).

Alice de Thorp −1346 Occ. before 1346 (Baildon, I, 165).

Amabel (Amabilla) Occ. 21 July 1351 (PRO, Just.1/1129, m. 19).

Margaret of Wilsthorpe (Willesthorp, Wilthorp) 1365–1376 Letters conf. eln 13 Nov. 1365 (Thompson, *YAJ*, XXV, p. 171, no. 35). D. 17 Aug. 1376 (ibid., p. 183, no. 114).

Isabel Nevill 1376– El. 23 Aug. 1376 (ibid., p. 183, no. 114).

The next recorded prs, **Margaret Fayrfax** (Fayrefax), occ. 7 June 1393 (BI, Prob. Reg. 1, f. 61v); 30 Apr. 1397 (*YAJ*, XXV, p. 196, no. 209).

NUNBURNHOLME (Yorks E.), St Mary f. *temp.* Henry II (*KH*), − 1199 (Thompson) (Benedictine priory)

> Lists in *VCH Yorks*, III, 119; M.C.F. Morris, *Nunburnholme and its history and antiquities* (London, 1907), p. 306; *Heads*, I, 216.

Millicent Occ. 25 July 1206 (*Yorks F., John*, p. 101).

Alice Occ. 10 Mar. 1282 (*Reg. Wickwane*, p. 53, no. 181).

Joan de Holm −1306 D. by 1 July 1306 (*Reg. Greenfield*, III, no. 1391).

Avice of Beverley 1306–1310 N. of Nunkeeling, commn to conf. eln 1 July 1306 (ibid.). D. by 27 Oct. 1310 (ibid., no. 1530), when commn to conf. eln of a successor issued.

Idonia of Pocklington (Pokelyngton) −1316 Res. by 4 Dec. 1316 when provision made for her (*Reg. Greenfield*, V, no. 2858).

The next recorded prs, **Isabel Thweng**, conf. 1523 (Baildon, I, 162).

CUSTOS

William, rector of Londesborough. Apptd to supervise the business of Nunburnholme priory 23 June 1314 (*Reg. Greenfield*, III, no.1610A). He is probably to be identified with William Dar[r]eyns, rector of Londesborough, who occ. as sequestrator in the archdeaconries of the East Riding and Cleveland (ibid., pp. xv–xvi, xxxvi, nos. 1162, 1403, 1530).

NUNEATON (Warws), St Mary (Fontevrault) f. *c.* 1153 (at Kintbury); *c.* 1195 (at Nuneaton) (*KH*); *c.* 1147 x 1153 (Kintbury); *c.* 1153 x 1157 (Nuneaton) (Thompson)

> Lists in *VCH Warws*, II, 69–70; *Heads*, I, 216–17; Thompson, *Women Religious*, pp. 248–9 (to *c.* 1272). Further details in Berenice M. Kerr, *Religious life for Women*, pp. 243–5, 247–8.

PRIORESSES

Ida Occ. 6 Oct. 1214, 1221, 18 Nov. 1226 (BL, Add. Chts. 47958, 49121, 49068; *Warws F.*, I, no. 421).

Sibyl Occ. 23 Sept. 1227 (*CPR 1225–32*, p. 165); 7 Dec. 1227 (BL, Add. Cht. 47742; PRO, Northants F., CP25/1/171/23, no. 228); 1227 x 1228 (PRO, E40/5785); Hil. term 1230 (*CRR*, XIII, no. 2524); Easter 1232 (BL, Add. Cht. 48152); 16 May 1232 (*Warws F.*, I, no. 446).

Ida II Occ. 6 Oct. 1238 (PRO, Bucks F., CP25/1/15/23, no. 14, cf. *Bucks F.*, I, 73–4); 16 June 1247 (PRO, Rutland F., CP25/1/192/3, no. 27); Mich. 1240, Mich. 1247 (BL, Add. Chts. 47997, 48497).

Cecily de Lexinton (Lexynton) Occ. Oct. 1256 x Oct. 1257 (*Suffolk F. (Rye)*, p. 58; BL, Add. Cht. 47594); 3 Nov. 1256 (BL, Add. Chts. 47961–2); 1260 (BL, Add. Cht. 48501); 7 Jan. 1260 (*Select Cases of Procedure*, no. 105, pp. 110–11 – allegedly had been prs 8 years previously).

Cecily of Sutton Occ. n.d. (*c.* 1272) (BL, Add. Cht. 48335). Indulgence for those praying for her soul 7 June 1288, repeated 21 May 1292 (*Reg. Sutton*, IV, 2). Seal (*BM Seals*, no. 3792).

Possibly the same as Cecily of Lexington. The Lexington and Sutton families were closely connected (cf. *Rufford Chts.*, I, xcviii, cviii–cxvi; *Reg. Sutton*, III, xiv–xvi).

Agnes of Sutton Occ. 12 Nov. 1284, 6 Dec. 1287 (BL, Add Chts. 47550, 48509); 12 Nov. 1284 (PRO, Leics F.,CP25/1/123/34, no. 97); 6 Oct. 1285 (*Warws F.*, II, no. 1031); 1286 (BL, Add. Cht. 47964A,C). Indulgence for those praying for her soul 21 May 1292 (*Reg. Sutton*, IV, 2).

Agatha of Sutton Occ. 11 Nov. 1290 (BL, Add. Cht. 48097); 1291 (ibid., 48514); 1294 (ibid., 48515); 16 Jan. 1297 (ibid., 48005); 30 June 1297 (ibid., 47858).

Hawise de Sancto Mauro Occ. from 7 Apr. 1298 and 7 May 1300 (BL, Add. Chts. 48519A–B, 48521).

Joan of Bristol (Bristoll(ia)) Moved from Westwood in 1300 to become prs (Kerr, citing Arch. dép. de Maine et Loire, 246 H2 5). Occ. from 27 Sept. 1303 to 9 May 1318 (BL Add. Chts. 48357, 48534).

House void by 25 Feb. 1320 and again 11 Apr. 1320 (BL, Add. Chts. 47861, 47860).

Isabel de Sudlee (Sudley, Sullee) Occ. 1318, el. locally supported by earl of Lancaster and the bp of Coventry and Lichfield (Kerr, p. 133, citing Arch. dép. de Maine et Loire, 246 H2 6–10). 1 Dec. 1320, mentd as being intruded by bp of Coventry and Lichfield (*CPL*, II, 209); 21 Jan. 1321 (BL, Add. Cht. 48535). Dep. and forced to recant (Kerr, p. 133 & n. 33).

Katherine of Stafford Originally apptd by abbs of Fontevraud in or before 1 Dec. 1320 but ousted by bp's nominee, Isabel (*CPL*, II, 209; Kerr, p. 134). Occ. 1 Mar. 1322 (*CPR 1321–24*, p. 147); 1322, 29 Sept. 1323 (BL, Add. Chts. 47861C–E, 49145).

Theophania la Fourriere apptd prs after an investigation into the expulsion of Katharine of Stafford ?1320; also expelled (Kerr, p. 134, citing Arch. dép. de Maine et Loire, 246 H2 11 3).

Agatha of Averham Occ. from 14 Feb. 1329 to 14 Sept. 1332 (BL, Add. Chts. 47398(21), 48542).

Margery de Shirford (Schireford) Occ. from 25 Sept. 1342 to 29 May 1345 (BL, Add. Chts. 48422, 48554).

Agatha (de) Bruys Occ. from 13 Jan. 1351 to 31 Mar. 1365 (BL, Add. Chts 48559, 48578).

Margaret Seliman (Celiman) Occ. from 1 Aug. 1366 to 4 Oct. 1386 (BL, Add. Chts. 49711, 48611).

The next prs, **Rose Everyngham**, occ. from 6 Oct. 1387 (BL, Add. Cht. 49074).

PRIORS

G. Occ. early 13th cent. (BL, Add. Cht. 47484).

Nicholas Occ. 17 Nov. 1221 (*CRR*, X, 247). ? the same as pr. N. occ. c. 1213 x 1214 (*Heads*, I, 217).

Robert Occ. 1227 x 1228 (PRO, E40/5785 – styled Richard in later copy of doct, BL, Add. Cht. 48490; *Heads*, I, 217, n. 6); 29 Sept. 1240 (BL, Add. Cht. 47997); May 1243 (ibid., 47998).

Gilbert Romanus –1249 Occ. Mich. 1247 (BL, Add. Cht. 48497). 31 May 1249 took habit of Dominican at Oxford (*Ann. Osney*, p. 98).

Peter de Palerne Occ. n.d. *temp.* Henry III (?c. 1250) (BL, Add. Cht. 48151). His position in the sequence of priors is not certain.

William de Verny (Verni) Occ. Oct. 1256 x Oct. 1257 (BL, Add. Cht. 47594); 7 Jan. 1260 and allegedly 8 years previously; also pr. temp. Ida (II) (*Select Cases of Procedure*, no. 105, pp. 110–11). Occ. with prs. Cecily de Lexinton (BL, Add. Chts. 48498–9) and Cecily de Sutton (Bodl., Douce Cht. a. 1. 4; BL, Add. Chts. 48500, 48506–7). Seal (*Mon. Seals*, p. 69). Also pr. of Grovebury (q.v.).

Henry Occ. n.d. (c. 1272) (BL, Add. Chts. 48335, 48506).

William Occ. 20 May 1280 (*CPR 1272–81*, p. 409).

Roger de Verny Occ. 6 Dec. 1287, 10 May 1291 (BL, Add. Chts. 48509, 48514). Occ. n.d. with prs Cecily de Sutton (BL, Add. Cht. 48508).

Walter Occ. *c.* 24 June 1294 (BL, Add. Cht. 48515).

Hugh Occ. 7 Apr. 1298, 7 May 1300 (BL, Add. Chts. 48519A–B, 48521).

Robert Occ. 2 Feb. 1308, 1316, 1317, 9 May 1318 (BL, Add. Chts. 48051, 48533, 47656, 48534). ? same as below.

Robert de Rodbourn(e) (Rodburne) Occ. 29 Sept. 1323 (BL, Add. Cht. 49145); 14 Feb. 1329, accounted for receipts and expenditure from 2 Mar. 1322 to 2 Feb. 1329 (BL, Add. Cht. 47398(21)).

Richard de Greneburgh (Grennebourgh) Occ. Mar. 1329 (BL, Add. Chts. 48538, 48539); Nov. 1329–Nov. 1330 (BL, Add. Cht. 49726). Occ. as proctor of abbs. of Fontevrault 28 July 1337 (*CPR 1334–38*, p. 483).

[**Roger de Lalleford** Occ. as receiver of the house 28 Sept. 1331 – 25 Apr. 1332 (BL, Add. Roll 49727).]

Richard Overton Occ. Apr. 1332–Apr. 1334 (BL, Add. Cht. 49709).

John de Wappenbur(i) Occ. 5 Oct. 1336, 1342, 1343 (BL Add. Chts. 49339, 48425, 48548–9); 16 May 1344 (*CCR 1343–46*, p. 383).

John Rodene Occ. from 29 May 1345 to 28 Mar. 1362 (BL, Add. Chts. 48554, 48572).

Henry de Eton Occ. from 30 June 1364 to 1 Nov. 1364 (BL, Add. Chts. 48575–77).

Baldwin Occ. from 1 Aug. 1366 (BL, Add. Cht. 49715).

William Ledbury Occ. Mich. 1372–Mich. 1373 to 24 Nov. 1377 (BL, Add. Chts. 49715, 49226).

The next recorded pr., **Roger Appelby** (Appulby), occ. from 29 Sept. 1392 (BL, Add. Cht. 47438). He became Bp of Ossory; provision 26 Sept. 1400 (*Orig. Papal Letters*, p. 236, no. 465; cf. *CPR 1399–1401*, p. 401).

OLDBURY (Warws), *see* Polesworth (Benedictine)

In Trin. 1309 a case involved **Albreda**, prs. of Oldbury, but it was claimed that Albreda was '*commonialis abbatisse de Polesworth et non priorissa perpetua sed ad voluntatem eiusdem abbatisse sue removenda*' (PRO, CP40/178, m. 283). Was there a cell of Polesworth here?

ORFORD or IRFORD (Lincs), St Mary f. *c.* 1155 x 1160 (*KH*); 1153 x *c.* 1156, ? 1189 as separate establishment (Thompson) (Premonstratensian priory)

Lists in *VCH Lincs*, II, 209; Colvin, p. 422; *Heads*, I, 218; Thompson, *Women Religious*, p. 250 (to mid.- 13th cent.).

PRIORESSES

Eda Occ. early 13th cent. (*Reg. Ant. Lincoln*, VIII, no. 2277).

Julian de Redemere Occ. 15 June 1341 (*CCR 1341–43*, p. 242).

Matilda of Burwell (Borwell) Occ. n.d. (Newhouse obit, *HMC Ancaster*, p. 483. D. 17 Apr.).

The next recorded prs, **Joan T(h)ompson**, occ. 8 July 1539 (*DKR 8*, app. II, p. 24).

PRIORS

Thomas Occ. 1228 x 32 (*Gilbertine Chts.*, p. 11).

Robert Occ. 9 Oct. 1251 (*CChR 1226–57*, p. 367); *temp.* Henry III (BL, Cotton Cht. V, 71), Hugh 'dean of Scarthoe' a witness: Hugh was inst. to Scarthoe 1230 x 1231 (*Reg. Wells*, III, 191) and prob. died in 1289 (*Reg. Sutton*, I, 125).

PINLEY (Warws), St Mary f. -1135 (*KH*); -1125 x 1150 (Thompson) (Cistercian priory)

List in *VCH Warws*, II, 83; Thompson, *Women Religious*, p. 250 (to 1269).

Margery Occ. 25 Nov. 1226 (*Warws F.*, I, no. 395).

Amice Occ. 8 June 1236, 27 Oct. 1240 (ibid. nos. 528, 564); 1 July 1248 (PRO, Berks F., CP25/1/8/16, no. 4).

Lucy de Sapy (Sapie) **1269–** Eln conf. 6 Nov. 1269, no reason given for vacancy (*Reg. G. Giffard*, p. 27). Mentd 14 Apr. 1326 as former prs in conf. of an earlier n.d. cht. (*CChR 1300–26*, p. 485).

Margery Occ. 9 Feb. 1285 (*Warws F.*, II, no. 1023).

Helewise of Langley (Langelegh) **1321–1325** Eln conf. & prof. obed. 7 Oct. 1321 (*Reg. Cobham*, pp. 31–2). Res. acc. 6 Mar. 1325 on account of infirmity and lic. to el. (ibid., p. 177).

Elizabeth de Loteryntone 1325– Commn to examine eln 12 Mar. 1325 (ibid.).

Amice de Hynton 1342–1352 Eln conf. 21 Aug. 1342, no reason given for vacancy (*Reg. Bransford*, no. 485). Occ. n.d. (PRO, E315/34/213). Commn to adm. cess. and to supervise the eln of a successor 24 Feb. 1352 (Worcester, Reg. Thoresby, p. 84).

NOTE: A problem arises with this nunnery at the 1352 vacancy. The *VCH* list gives references to the succession of **Matilda le Bret** in 1352 and her res. in 1358. The Worcester episcopal register references (Reg. Thoresby, f. 32v and Reg. Brian, f. 25) have been checked – the registers are now paginated but the old foliation is clear – and I can find no references to Matilda le Bret and Pinley on these folios. The res. of Amice de Hynton in 1363 (see below) seems to link with Amice elected in 1342. On the other hand she apparently res. in 1352 unless that particular Thoresby entry was not effective upon the commissary's investigation. Is Matilda le Bret confused with Matilda Bryt who occ. in 1379 (see below)?

Amice de Hynton (Hyneton) **–1363** Res. by 20 Aug. 1363 (Worcester, Reg. Barnet, p. 55).

Emma of Chadderton (Chaderton, Chathurton) **1363–1366** Apptd by bp of Worcester 20 Aug. 1363 (ibid.). Res. by 6 Feb. 1366 (Worcester, Reg. Whittlesey, p. 26).

Joan Holkene (Iwyne) **1366–** N. of Cook Hill, apptd 6 Feb. 1366 (ibid.). Occ. 30 Nov. 1367 (BL, Cotton Cht. XX. 29).

The next recorded prs, **Matilda Bryt**, occ. 1379 (PRO, E179/58/11, m. 2d).

POLESWORTH (Warws), St Edith ref. *c.* 980 (?) (at Polesworth); 1066 x 1070 (priory at Oldbury); *c.* 1130 (abb. at Polesworth) (Benedictine priory)

Lists in *VCH Warws*, II, 64; *Heads*, I, 218; Thompson, *Women Religious*, p. 250 (to 1277).

Ossana Occ. prob. 1171 x 1174 (*MB*, I, 287)

Muriel Occ. 20 Oct. 1221 (*Warws F.*, I, no. 242); 24 Apr. 1222 (PRO, Leics F., CP25/1/121/10, no. 77); (M.) 1231 x 1234 (*Ctl. Burscough*, p. 67, no. 58).

Cecily 1234–1237 Prs of Polesworth, royal ass. 8 May 1234 (*CPR 1232–47*, p. 45). D., lic. to el. 3 June 1237 (ibid., p. 184).

Margery of Appleby (Appelby) **1237–?1262** N. of Polesworth, royal ass. (Margaret) 21 June 1237, writ *de intendendo* 16 Sept. 1237 (ibid., pp. 188, 196). Occ. 3 Nov. 1240 (PRO, Leics F., CP25/1/131/17, no. 262); 1242 (*CChR 1226–57*, p. 269); 1247 (PRO, Leics F., CP25/1/122/18, no. 294); 1249, 1254 (*Warws F.*, I, nos. 685, 749); 1258 (*Derbys F. (1888)*, p. 152); 12 Nov. 1261 (*Staffs F. 2*, p. 250). Unnamed abbs d. by 1 May 1262 (PRO, C84/2/28).

Joan de Saucheverel (Sauchaveral) **1262–** Royal ass. 9 May 1262 (*CPR 1258–66*, p. 213).

Sarah de Mamecestre 1269–1276 N. of Polesworth, royal ass. 5 Dec. 1269 (*CPR 1266–72*, p. 398). D., lic. to el. 20 Dec. 1276 (*CPR 1272–81*, p. 186).

Albreda (Albra) **de Canvill** (Canvile) **1277–1291** N. of Polesworth, royal ass. 3 Jan. 1277 (ibid., p. 188); order to sheriff to take fealty and restore temps. 27 Feb. 1277, eln having been conf. by R., bp of Coventry and Lichfield (*CFR 1272–1307*, p. 77). D. by 5 Aug. 1291 (PRO, C84/10/16). D., lic. to el. 8 Aug. 1291 (*CPR 1281–92*, p. 442).

Katherine of Appleby (Appelby, Appilby) **1291–1301** N. of Polesworth, eln pres. to king for royal ass. 23 Aug. 1291 (PRO, C84/10/17); royal ass. 30 Aug. 1291 (*CPR 1281–92*, p. 442). D. 15 Apr. 1301 (PRO, C84/14/14). D., lic. to el.16 Apr. 1301 (*CPR 1292–1301*, p. 588).

Erneburga of Hartshill (Hardishull, Hardreshull, Herdeshull) **1301–1322** N. of Polesworth, eln pres. to king for royal ass. 19 Apr. 1301 (PRO, C84/14/15); royal ass. 21 Apr.1301, temps. 21 May 1301 (*CPR 1292–1301*, pp. 588, 595). Cert. conf. eln by bp of Coventry and Lichfield 2 May 1301 (PRO, C84/14/17). Order to restore any issues of abbey received during voidance 21 May 1301 (*CCR 1296–1302*, p. 446). D., lic. to el. 4 Mar. 1322 (*CPR 1321–24*, p. 79; cf. Lichfield, B/A/1/2, f. 2r).

Matilda de Pype (Pipa, Pipe) **1322–1348** N. of Polesworth, royal ass. 9 Mar. 1322, temps. 20 Apr.1322 (*CPR 1321–24*, pp. 81, 102). Commn to examine eln 22 Jan. x 22 Mar. 1322 (Lambeth, Reg. Reynolds, f. 129v). Eln conf. by archbp of Canterbury *sede vacante* 5 Apr. 1322 (Lichfield, B/A/1/2, f. 2r). D., lic. to el. 24 Aug. 1348 (*CPR 1348–50*, p. 140).

Letitia de Hexstal (Hoxstal(l)) **1348–1349** N. of Polesworth, royal ass. 11 Sept. 1348, temps. 14 Oct. 1348 (ibid., pp. 149, 192). Eln conf. 1 Oct. 1348 (Lichfield, B/A/1/2, ff. 46v–47r). D., lic. to el. 30 July 1349 (*CPR 1348–50*, p. 352; cf. Lichfield, B/A/1/2, f. 50v).

Agnes de Somervill (Somervyll) **1349–1361** N. of Polesworth, royal ass. 23 Aug. 1349, temps. 13 Oct. 1349 (*CPR 1348–50*, pp. 370, 405). El. but renounced eln. Convent submitted to bp and he apptd Agnes 3 Sept. 1349 (Lichfield, B/A/1/2, f. 50v). Occ. 5 July 1361 (*Reg. Stretton*, I, 14); 26 Aug. 1361 (Worcester, Reg. Brian I, p. 73). D. by 30 Dec. 1361 (PRO, C84/28/34).

Matilda de Bottourd (Botourd, Botturd, Butword) **1361/2–1400** N. of Polesworth, postn notified to king for royal ass. 31 Dec. 1361 (PRO, C84/28/34); royal ass. 28 Jan. 1362, temps. 8 Mar. 1362 (*CPR 1361–64*, pp. 157, 171). El. 1361 while only 20 years of age, so special dispensation had to be arranged; commn to examine eln 22 Feb. 1362, eln conf. 5 Mar. 1362 (*Reg. Stretton*, I, 28; PRO, C84/28/38). Res., lic. to el. 13 Nov. 1400 (*CPR 1399–1401*, p. 370).

POLSLOE (Devon), St Catherine f. -1160 (Benedictine priory)

Lists in Watkin, *Devon and Cornwall N. & Q.*, XI, (1921), 6–7; E. Lega-Weekes, 'History of St Katherine's priory, Polsloe, part I', *TDA*, 66 (1934), 195–6; Thompson, *Women Religious*, p. 250 (to 1267).

Avelina Occ. n.d. (?1218) (*TDA*, 66, 195, citing Devon RO, ED/M.15, erroneously dated to 1266 by Oliver, *Mon. Exon.*, p. 163).

Isabel de Brente Occ. 1256 (? 31 Dec. 1255 x 21 Oct. 1256) (*EEA*, 12, no. 326; *Reg. Bronescombe*, p. 7).

Margaret (Margery) de Morchad 1267– Adm. 24 Dec. 1267, having been dispensed on acct of illegitimacy (*Reg. Bronescombe*, p. 163). Occ. (Margery) 22 Apr. 1268 (*Devon F.*, I, p. 341, no. 669); (Margery) Nov. 1272 x Nov. 1273 (*Ctl. St Nicholas Exeter*; p. 375, no. 228); (Margery) 16 May 1278 (*Reg. Bronescombe*, p. 121; *Reg. W. Bronescombe*, II, no. 1276); 1295 x 1307 (*Beauchamp Reg.*, p. 62). Poss. the unnamed prs, for whom attorneys were apptd because of her debility 13 May 1297 (*CPR 1292–1301*, p. 248).

Margery de Swyndone (Swingdone) **1308–1321** Sub-prs. of Polsloe, commn for an eln 6 May 1308, eln conf. 15 June, mand. for installation 26 June 1308 (*Reg. Stapeldon*, pp. 243, 316). D. 27 June 1321, bur. 30 June 1321, lic. for eln requested 2 July 1321, lic. gtd 7 July (ibid., p. 243).

Matilda de Bloyhou 1321– Eln conf. 28 Sept. 1321 (ibid.). Occ. 1326 (Oliver, *Supplement*, p. 17, said to be mentd in deed, but no source).

Margery de Wydepole –1347 D. 15 Apr. 1347, bur. 17 Apr. 1347 (*Reg. Grandisson*, II, 1016). Gt of custody of vacant house 16 Apr. 1347 (ibid., 1014–15); lic. to el. 18 Apr. (ibid., 1015–16).

Juliana of Bruton (Brutone) **1347–** Sacrist of Polsloe, el. 20 Apr. 1347, consent of el. 22 Apr., cert. of no opposers to eln 30 Apr.; eln conf. n.d. (ibid., 1014–20).

The next recorded prs, **Joan**, occ. 4 Nov. 1388 (*Reg. Brantingham*, II, 675). She was d. by 6 Apr. 1394 (PRO, C84/36/12).

REDLINGFIELD (Suffolk), St Mary and St Andrew f. 1120 (Benedictine priory)

Lists in *VCH Suffolk*, II, 85; *Heads*, I, 218; Thompson, *Women Religious*, p. 251 (13th cent.).

Emma Occ. early 13th cent. (pal.) (BL, Add. Cht. 10640; Thompson, *Women Religious*, p. 251)

Alice Davolers (Davelers) Occ. *temp.* Henry III (BL, Add. ms. 19090, f. 70v); n.d. (early/mid-13th cent.: pal.) (Suffolk RO, Ipswich, HD1538/327/1–2).

Margery of Bedingfield (Bedingfeld) **1303–1314** N. of Redlingfield, eln conf. 14 Dec. 1303, no reason given for vacancy (Norwich, Reg/1/1, f. 4v). D. by 8 Mar. 1314 (PRO, C84/17/33–4). D., lic. to el. 23 Mar. 1314 (*CPR 1313–17*, p. 94).

Agnes of Stuston (Stustone) **1314–1331** N. of Redlingfield, royal ass. 1 Apr. 1314 (ibid., p. 97); eln conf. 13 Apr. 1314, no reason given for vacancy (Norwich, Reg/1/1, f. 57r). D. by 11 Sept. 1331 (Norwich, Reg/1/2, f. 43r).

Juliana de Weylond 1331– N. of Redlingfield, eln conf. 11 Sept. 1331 (ibid.).

Alice Wynter (Wenter) **of Orford 1349–1394** N. of Redlingfield, eln quashed but apptd by bp of Norwich 10 July 1349, no reason given for vacancy (*Reg. Bateman*, I, no. 767). Occ. 29 Dec. 1353 (*CPL*, III, 510). D. by 1 Sept. 1394 (Norwich, Reg/3/6, f. 195r).

ROMSEY (Hants), St Mary and St Aethelfleda ref. 967 (Benedictine abbey)

Lists in *VCH Hants*, II, 132; *Heads*, I, 218–19; D.K. Coldicott, *Hampshire Nunneries*, App. I, pp. 161–2.

Matilda Patriz (Patric) **1199–1230** Sister of Walter Walerand, el. 3 June 1199 (*Ann. Winchester*, p. 72). Occ. 30 Mar. 1219 (PRO, Hants F. CP25/1/203/4, no. 18); Mich. term 1228 (*CRR*, XIII, no. 1222). Presumably the Matilda who died by 14 Dec. 1230 when lic. was given to elect (*CPR 1225–32*, p. 418).

Matilda de Barbefle 1231–1237 N. of Romsey, royal ass. 19 Jan. 1231 (ibid., p. 420). D., lic. to el. 28 Apr. 1237 (*CPR 1232–47*, p. 180).

Isabel de Nevill 1237– N. of Romsey, royal ass. 5 May 1237, writ *de intendendo* 15 May 1237 (ibid., pp. 180, 182). Mand. for seisin 15 May 1237 (*CR 1234–37*, p. 443).

Cecily Liveing suggests she may have become abbs. 1238, but there is no real evidence (Liveing, *Records of Romsey Abbey*, pp. 64–5). Occ. 25 June 1241 (*Wilts F.*, I, 32); 8 July 1244 (PRO, Hants F., CP25/1/203/7 no. 75).

Constance de la Rochelle 1247–?1261 Prs of Romsey, royal ass. 6 Sept. 1247 (*CPR 1232–47*, p. 509); mand. for seisin 26 Sept. 1247 (*CR 1242–47*, p. 537). Occ. 12 Apr. 1249 (PRO, Hants F., CP25/1/203/8, no. 38); 15 July 1250 (*CR 1247–51*, p. 359); 1251 (PRO, E315/42/122); 24 Sept. 1256 (CPR, 1247–58, p. 153). Prob. d. 1260 as house void for 6 months before the el. of Amice (Liveing, *Records of Romsey Abbey*, p. 64). Lic. to el. (no reason given for vacancy) 17 May 1261 (*CPR 1258–66*, p. 153). Seal (Liveing, *Records of Romsey Abbey*, facing p. 64).

Amice de Sulleye 1261–1268 Prs of Romsey, royal ass. 27 May 1261, temps. 6 June 1261 (*CPR 1258–66*, pp. 156–7). Cert. conf. eln by archbp of Canterbury 3 June 1261 (PRO, C84/2/21). D., lic. to el. 10 July 1268 (*CPR 1266–72*, p. 244).

Alice Waleraund (Walraund, Warlerond) **1268–1298** N. of Romsey, royal ass. 28 July 1268, too ill to come to the king to make fealty (ibid., p. 249). Coadjutrices apptd for unnamed abbs *c.* 1284 (*Reg. Peckham*, II, 658–61). D. 10 Apr. 1298 (PRO, SC6/983/34). D., lic. to el. 13 Apr. 1298 (*CPR 1292–1301*, p. 342).

Philippa de Stokes 1298–1307 N. of Romsey, eln pres. to king for royal ass. 18 Apr. 1298 (PRO, C84/13/12); royal ass. 21 Apr. 1298, temps. 28 Apr. 1298, eln having been conf. by mag. Philip de Barton, vicegerent of Bp. J. of Winchester (*CPR 1292–1301*, pp. 345, 347; PRO, C84/13/14). Attorneys apptd for unnamed abbs on account of infirmity 19 Feb. 1305 (*CPR 1301–7*, p. 314). Occ. 8 June 1307 (ibid., p. 527). D., lic. to el. 23 Sept. 1307 (*CPR 1307–13*, p. 5).

Clementia of Guildford (Gildeford, Guldeford(e)) **1307–1314** N. of Romsey, royal ass. 15 Oct. 1307, writ *de intendendo* 27 Oct. 1307 (ibid., pp. 8, 12). Eln conf. n.d. (Oct. 1307) (*Reg. Woodlock*, I, 216–17); mand. to obey new abbs and mand. to induct 24 Nov. 1307 (ibid., 224). On account of illness she is unable to attend to business and attorneys are apptd 3 Sept. 1311 (*CPR 1307–13*, p. 387). Occ. 24 Mar. 1314 (*CPR 1313–17*, p. 191). D. by 26 Dec. 1314 (PRO, C84/18/2). D., lic. to el. 30 Dec. 1314 (*CPR 1313–17*, p. 206).

Alice de Wynter(e)shulle (Wyntreshull(e)) **1315** N. of Romsey, eln pres. to king for royal ass. 16 Jan. 1315 (PRO, C84/18/5–6); royal ass. 23 Jan. 1315, temps. 5 Feb. 1315 (*CPR 1313–17*, pp. 210, 216). Cert. conf. eln by bp of Winchester 4 Feb. 1315 (PRO, C84/18/11). D. by 4 May 1315 (*CFR 1307–19*, p. 247, but cf. PRO, C84/18/17 – d. 5 May 1315). D., lic. to el. 11 May 1315 (*CPR 1313–17*, p. 281). The commission of inquiry 28 May, 11 July 1315 to investigate persons who had made her intoxicated and then killed her (ibid., pp. 327, 403).

Sibyl Carbonel 1315–1333 N. of Romsey, eln pres. to king for royal ass. 4 July 1315 (PRO, C84/6/43); royal ass. 10 July 1315, temps. 8 Aug. 1315 (*CPR 1313–17*, pp. 333, 340). Cert. conf. eln by bp of Winchester 5 Aug. 1315 (PRO, C84/18/22). D. 1 June 1333 (Winchester, Reg. Stratford, f. 81v). D., lic. to el. 11 June 1333 (*CPR 1330–34*, p. 452, cf. *CFR 1327–37*, p. 361).

Joan Icche (Icthe, de Lethe) **1333–1349** Cellaress of Romsey, el. 25 June 1333 and notif. to bp 9 July (Winchester, Reg. Stratford, ff. 81v–82r). Royal ass. 2 July 1333, temps 7 Aug. 1333 (*CPR 1330–34*, pp. 453, 460, cf. *CCR 1333–37*, pp. 70–1). Eln pres. to bp 12 July and conf. 23 July 1333; mand. to install 3 Sept. (Winchester, Reg. Stratford, ff. 134v–136r). D. by 25 Apr. 1349 (PRO, C84/25/32). D., lic. to el. 28 Apr. 1349 (*CPR 1348–50*, p. 278). Mon. stone in Romsey abbey (Liveing, *Records of Romsey Abbey*, p. 121 and facsimile opp. p. 120).

Joan Gerveys (Gervays, Gerveise, Jerveis, Jerveys) **1349–1352** N. of Romsey, proclamation of eln 6 May 1349 (*Reg. Edington*, I, no. 514). Eln pres. to king for royal ass. 5 May 1349 (PRO, C84/25/36); royal ass. 7 May 1349, temps. 22 May 1349 (*CPR 1348–50*, pp. 285, 296). Commn to examine eln 8 May and eln conf. 15 May 1349 (*Reg. Edington*, I, no. 544). Bl. 24 May 1349 (ibid., II, no. 214). D., lic. to el. 27 Oct. 1352 (*CPR 1350–54*, p. 348).

Isabel (de) Camoys 1352–1396 N. of Romsey, eln pres. to king for royal ass. 7 Nov. 1352 (PRO, C84/27/4); royal ass. 10 Nov. 1352, temps. 26 Nov. 1352 (*CPR 1350–54*, pp. 360–1). Commn to examine eln 24 Nov; eln conf. 25 Nov. 1352 (*Reg. Edington*, I, nos. 916–21). D. by 12 Apr. 1396 (PRO, C84/36/26). D., lic. to el. 17 Apr. 1396 (*CPR 1391–96*, p. 686; *Reg. Wykeham*, I, 202).

ROSEDALE (Yorks N.), St Mary f. -1158 (KH); c.1130 x c.1160 (Thompson); -1160 (Burton) (Cistercian priory)

Lists in *VCH Yorks*, III, 176; Thompson, *Women Religious*, p. 251 (to 1251).

Aubrey Occ. Oct. 1242 x Oct. 1243 (*Cumbd F.*, p. 223); 10 June 1246 (*Yorks F., 1232–46*, p. 148).

Juliana Occ. 18 Nov. 1251 (*Yorks F., 1246–72*, p. 43).

Isabel Walone (Waloue) Occ. n.d. (1280 x 1292) (*temp.* Ralph, bp of Carlisle) (York, Reg. 11, f. 134v).

Mary de Ros −1310 Pres. unnamed prs, the dau. of Sir William de Ros of Ingmanthorpe, to whom she had lic. to visit twice a year 30 Dec. 1306 (*Reg. Greenfield*, III, no. 1158). Commn to enquire about certain articles against the prs 25 Aug. 1310; res. by 28 Sept. 1310, when lic. to el. (ibid., no. 1259). Eln delayed until after her death, lic. to el. issued 1 Jan. 1311 (*CPR 1307–13*, p. 301).

Joan of Pickering (Pykering) **1311–** N. of Rosedale, [for a brief period prs of Keldholme but not accepted by nuns]. Eln conf. by archbp. on d. of Mary de Ros 12 Jan. 1311 (*Reg. Greenfield*, III, no. 1266). Royal ass. 18 Jan. 1311 (*CPR 1307–13*, p. 302).

Isabel of Whitby (Whiteby) **–1336** Cess. by 19 Dec. 1336 (*Reg. Melton*, II, no. 473).

Elizabeth of Kirkby Moorside (Moresheved) **1336–** Mand. to Rosedale to obey Elizabeth, nun of Rosedale, whose eln conf. by the archbp 19 Dec. 1336 (ibid., nos. 473–4).

Joan Colvyle Occ. 1377 (PRO, E179/63/11, m. 1).

The next recorded prs, **Isabel de Lomley**, occ. June 1387 x June 1388 (PRO, E210/2465); 30 Nov. 1399 (*CPR 1399–1401*, p. 155).

ROTHWELL (Northants), St John the Baptist f. -1262 (*KH*); -1249 (Thompson) (Augustinian priory)

 List in *VCH Northants*, II, 138.

Agnes –1305 D. by [20 Sept. x 7 Nov.] 1305 (Lincoln, Ep. Reg., II, f. 110r).

Alice de Cravenho (Cravenhou, Crawenho) **1305–1313** Appt. by bp [20 Sept. x 7 Nov.] 1305; letters of ass. of patron 5 Oct. 1305 (ibid.). Res. by 30 Mar. 1313 (ibid., f. 124r).

Amice of Naseby (Navesby) **1313–** N. of Rothwell, nominated by sisters, apptd by bp 30 Mar. 1313 (ibid.).

Katherine of Isham 1349– N. of Rothwell, apptd by bp 'Nones 1349' (*sic*), no reason being given for vacancy. Appears between entries of 3 nones and 8 ides Aug., ?5 Aug. 1349 (Lincoln, Ep. Reg., IX, f. 190v).

Katherine del Grene –1381 D. by 13 July 1381 (Lincoln, Ep. Reg., X, f. 224r–v). ? same as above.

ROWNEY (Herts), St John the Baptist f. *c.* 1164 (*KH*); *c.* 1146 x *c.* 1160 (Thompson) (Benedictine priory)

 List in *VCH Herts*, IV, 435; Thompson, *Women Religious*, p. 251 (to 1277); H.C. Andrews, 'Rowney Priory', *Trans. East Herts Arch. Soc.* 6 (1915), 1–29, list at 29.

Rose –1257/8 Occ. n.d. (13th cent.) (BL, Campbell Cht. IV 2); Res. May 1257 x May 1258 (*Reg. Lexington*, p. 513).

Nicholaa 1257/8–1277 N. of Rowney, el. and inst. May 1257 x May 1258 (ibid., pp. 513–14). Res. by 14 Jan. 1277 (*Reg. R. Gravesend*, p. 183).

Acelina of Brockhall (Brochole) **1277–** Eln conf. 14 Jan. 1277 (ibid., pp. 183, 320).

Unnamed sub-prs el. as prs year 7 of Bp Sutton (19 May 1286 x 18 May 1287), lic. to el. having been given by John de Kirkeby, patron (Bodl., Dodsworth ms. 107, f. 148r). Prob. Agnes of London.

Agnes of London (Lond') **–1291** Res. 29 Aug. 1291 (*Reg. Sutton*, III, 143; ibid., VIII, 77).

Alice of Chingford (Chinchelford) **1291–1318** Sub-prs of Rowney, eln conf. 19 Sept. 1291 (ibid., VIII, 77). D. by 2 May 1318 (Lincoln, Ep. Reg., II, f. 252r).

Joan of London (Lond') **1318–** N. of Rowney, eln quashed, but apptd by bp 2 May 1318 (ibid.). See also below under 1338.

Joan (le) Spenser 1328– N. of Rowney, commn to examine eln 16 Dec. 1327 (Lincoln, Ep. Reg., V, f. 409v). Commissary quashed eln, but apptd her on bp's behalf 19 Jan. 1328 (ibid., ff. 410v–411r).

Joan of London Occ. 10 Sept. 1338 (*CPR 1338–40*, p. 154). See above under 1318.

Margaret Beauchamp 1348– N. of Rowney, commn to examine eln 14 Feb. 1348 (Lincoln,

Ep. Reg., IX, f. 9r).

Margaret Costance –1371 D. by 5 Mar. 1371 (Lincoln, Ep. Reg., X, f. 301r–v). ? the same as above.

Katherine de Hemsted (Hempstede) 1371– N. of Rowney, commn to examine eln 5 Mar. 1371; eln conf. 22 Apr. 1371 (ibid.). Occ. 1387 (*HMC Var. Coll.*, VII, 307); 1397 and 1399 (PRO, SC2/178/11). Poss. the same as **Katherine Grenefeld** who occ. as former prs on 31 Oct. 1418 when commn issued to investigate the procedure by which she had been removed from office (*Reg. Repingdon*, III, no. 492).

MASTERS

Richard Punchard de Wyly 1318– Chaplain, apptd 2 May 1318 (Lincoln, Ep. Reg., III, f. 388r).

Ralph 1328– Rector of Great Munden, apptd during pleasure 10 Feb. 1328 (Lincoln, Ep. Reg., V, f. 411r).

Robert Martyn 1389– Rector of Great Munden, apptd 20 July 1389 (Lincoln, Ep. Reg., XII, f. 360v).

NOTE

Christina occ. as prs n.d. in a charter copied into a 15th-cent. roll (PRO, E211/303F). The document could be of any date and there is no clue as to her place in the sequence of prioresses.

RUSPER (Sussex), St Mary Magdalen f. -1200 (*KH*); ? -1174 (Thompson) (Benedictine priory)

List in *VCH Sussex*, II, 64; Thompson, *Women Religious*, p. 251 (to 1256).

Katherine Occ. Oct. 1229 x Oct. 1230 (*Surrey F.*, p. 17); 1232 (*Ctl. Sele*, no. 39).

Alice of Bishopstone (Bissepeston) Occ. 1239 x 1247 (*Ctl. Chichester*, no. 596); 28 Sept. 1247 (BL, Cotton ms. Nero E VI, f. 149v); 3 Nov. 1255 (*Sussex F.*, II, no. 555).

Isabel Occ. Mich. 1325 (PRO, Just.1/938/1, m. 14). Is this the **Isabel Croyroys**, prs. of Rusper, whose obit was 31 July (*Guildford Obits*, p. 95)?

Agnes de Littlyngton –1353 Occ. 1343 (PRO, Just.1/631, m. 71). D. by 22 Apr. 1353 (*CPL*, III, 482). Ment. as former prs 9 Oct. 1353 (*CPR 1350–54*, p. 495).

Juliana Young 1353 Bp of Chichester had made her prs., although under age: mand. to summon her by pope (*CPL*, III, 482). Occ. 9 Oct. 1353 (*CPR 1350–54*, p. 495); 19 Nov. 1356 (*CPR 1354–58*, p. 477); 7 May 1367 (*CPR 1364–67*, p. 388).

[**Joan de Kingesfolde** N. of Rusper, mand. to appt Joan, since the priory had been vacant so long it had lapsed to the pope 22 Apr. 1353 (*CPL*, III, 482) – ineffective – Joan occ. as n. of Rusper on 23 May 1353 (ibid., 493).]

Lucy Occ. as daughter of the testator, Nicholas de Carren, mentd in father's will of 13 Oct. 1387 (Lambeth, Reg. Courtenay I, f. 232v).

ST MARY DE PRE (Herts) f. 1194 (as hospital for leprous women); 1328+ (as priory); 1328 x 1336 adopted Ben. rule (Thompson) (Benedictine priory)

List in *VCH Herts*, IV, 431; Thompson, *Women Religious*, p. 251 (to 1278).

MASTERS/WARDENS

John de Walden Occ. 1194 x 1195 (*GASA*, I, 201).

William Occ. as *custos* Mich. 1228 (*CRR*, XIII, no. 853).

Richard Occ. 1235 (*GASA*, I, 305).

William Occ. 17 May 1248 (PRO, Herts F., CP25/1/85/21, no. 344).

Richard Occ. 14 Dec. 1278 (PRO, Herts F. CP25/1/86/37, no. 97).

Roger Occ. c. July 1318 x July 1319 (PRO, SC12/8/38).

Richard of Bovingdon (Bovyndon) Occ. Sept. 1341 x Sept. 1342 (PRO, SC6/867/21).
Nicholas Redhod Occ. Mar. 1352 x Mar. 1353 (PRO, SC8/867/25).
John de Kirkely Occ. 13 Aug. 1356 x 25 Mar. 1357 (PRO, SC8/867/26).

PRIORESSES
None recorded by name before unnamed sister of **John de la Moot**, abb. of St Albans, who was
prs at the time of his d. in 1401 (*GASA*, III, 452).

ST RADEGUND, *see* CAMBRIDGE

SEWARDSLEY (Northants), St Mary Magdalen (St Mary) f. *temp.* Henry II (*KH*); 1148 x
1166 (Thompson) (Cistercian priory)
   List in *VCH Northants*, II, 127; Thompson, *Women Religious*, p. 252 (to 1261).
Felicia Occ. 1218 (PRO, E326/5827); n.d. (BL, Egerton ms. 3033, f. 6v).
Ivetta de Pavely (Paveli(e)) Occ. 20 Oct. 1240 (PRO, Northants F. CP25/1/173/31, no. 450);
   n.d. (first half of 13th cent. pal.) (PRO, E315/36/50; E315/49/158; E326/1191;
   E326/2919).
Alice –1247/8 Occ. n.d. (PRO, E326/4644). D. June 1247 x June 1248 (*Reg. Grosseteste*, p. 234).
Juliana of Sywell 1247/8–1261 N. of Sewardsley, eln conf. June 1247 x June 1248 (ibid.). Occ.
   Oct. 1255 x Oct. 1256 (PRO, E315/50/175); 22 July 1261 (*Bucks F.*, II, 5; PRO, F. Divers
   Counties CP25/1/283/15, no. 396). Res. Nov. 1260 x Nov. 1261, but presumably July x
   Nov. 1261 (*Reg. R. Gravesend*, p. 100 and see previous entry).
Florence 1261– N. of Sewardsley, eln quashed but apptd by bp Nov. 1260 x Nov. 1261 (pre-
   sumably July x Nov. 1261) (ibid., pp. 100, 293).
Beatrice de Bosevile (Beseville, Besewyle, Bosewyle, le Besevile) Occ. Easter 1269 (PRO,
   E315/37/61); Dec. 1271 (PRO, E315/45/148); 1282 (PRO, E326/3761); 1286 (PRO,
   E315/44/241); 1289 (PRO, E315/33/163); 1293 (PRO, E315/48/216); 1298 (PRO,
   E315/40/30); 9 Dec. 1299 (PRO, E315/47/199); n.d. (PRO, E315/36/22; E315/39/159;
   E315/42/97, 101; E326/2467; E326/10373).
Lucy of Wheathampstead (Wetamsted(e)) Occ. 14 June 1304 (PRO, E315/45/41); 1305
   (PRO, E326/2770); 1307 (PRO, E315/47/123); 1315 (PRO, E210/11027); 1316 (PRO,
   E315/46/87); July 1317 x July 1318 (PRO, E210/8986); 16 June 1325 (PRO, E315/37/74).
Denise de Boseville 1325–1349 N. of Sewardsley, commn to examine eln 17 Sept. 1325
   (Lincoln, Ep. Reg., V, f. 383r). D., lic. to el. 5 Aug. 1349 (*CPR 1348–50*, p. 353).
Margaret (de) Lodebrok (Lodbroc, Lodbrok, Ladbrok) **1349**– N. of Sewardsley, royal ass.
   11 Aug. 1349 (ibid., p. 365). Eln quashed, but apptd by bp of Lincoln 25 Aug. 1349 (Lincoln,
   Ep. Reg., IX, f. 191r). Occ. from 22 Oct. 1349 to 20 Feb. 1361 (PRO, E315/37/21,
   E315/34/235);
Matilda Kut (Cut, Cutes, Kutes) Sub-prs of Sewardsley, given care and adm. of spiritual and
   temporal goods as the bp of Lincoln had discovered at recent visitation that the prs been
   absent 3 years without cause (n.d. but between items of 27 Feb. 1367 and 28 Feb. 1367, cf.
   however date of first occ. below) (Lincoln, Ep. Reg., XII, f. 38r–v). Occ. 17 May 1366 (PRO,
   E315/36/234); 1371 (PRO, E326/3226); 1378 (PRO, E326/11863); 1384 (PRO,
   E315/34/176); and 28 Apr. 1386 (PRO, E315/31/237).

MASTER
John Rector of a mediety of Collingtree, apptd 9 July 1303 (Lincoln, Ep. Reg., III, f. 58v).

SHAFTESBURY (Dorset), St Mary and St Edward f. *c.* 888 (Benedictine abbey)
   Lists in *VCH Dorset*, II, 79; *Heads*, I, 219.

Joan 1216–?1223 (J.) sub-prs, el. -29 Nov. 1216 (*CPR 1216–25*, p. 7).[14] Occ. (J.) 18 Jan. 1219 (*CPL*, I, 61); 6 Oct. 1221 (*Sussex F.*, I, no. 171). Lic. to el. (no reason given for vacancy) 23 June 1223 (*CPR 1216–25*, p. 376).

Amice Russell 1223–1242 N. of Shaftesbury, royal ass. 3 July 1223 (ibid.). Occ. 16 June 1241, 23 June 1241 (*Wilts F.*, I, 33, 34). Lic. to el. (no reason given for vacancy), commn to archbp of York and William de Cantilupe to give royal ass. 11 Sept. 1242 (*CPR 1232–47*, p. 324); 13 Oct. 1242, lic. to el. and commn to Ralph de Eston and Thurstan de Middelton, notwithstanding previous gt (ibid., pp. 329–30). Mand. to deliver to Robert Passelewe the jewels of Amice, late abbs of Shaftesbury 10 Jan. 1244 (ibid., p. 416).

[Agnes de Ferrariis]

[Constance Saunzaver] Prs seeks new lic. to el. 30 July 1243 (PRO, C84/1/14). House vacant 30 Sept. 1243 as Agnes de Ferrariis had renounced eln and the eln of Constance Saunzaver had been quashed by the bp's commissaries; further lic. to el. (*CPR 1232–47*, p. 396).

Agnes Longespee (Lungespe(e)) **1243–?1246** N. of Wherwell, royal ass. and writ *de intendendo* 9 Oct. 1243 (ibid., p. 397). Lic. to el. (no reason given for vacancy) 14 May 1246 (ibid., p. 480).

Agnes de Ferrariis (de la Ferere) **1247–?1258** N. of Shaftesbury. King to the bp of Salisbury. It was agreed between them to remove all suspicion about Agnes's eln as abbs (since she was said to be a blood relative of W. de Mariscis, the traitor), that the king's clerks, Roger de Cantilupe and A. le Seculer should take part in the examination of the election and person of the el. The king has now apptd W. de Poywic as his proctor in the matter and is sending him to the bp 17 Oct. 1246 (*CPR 1232–47*, p. 489). N. of Shaftesbury, royal ass. 9 Jan. 1247; writ *de intendendo* 29 Jan. 1247 (ibid., pp. 495, 497). Occ. 24 July 1247 (Wilts RO, Acc.192/54); 31 May 1249, 6 June 1249, 12 June 1256, 25 June 1256 (*Wilts F.*, I, pp. 38, 47); 1256 (*Devon F.*, I, no. 566). Abbey void by 13 May 1258 (*CPR 1247–58*, p. 629). Lic. to el. (no reason given for vacancy) 18 May 1258 (ibid., p. 630).

Juliana de Bauzeyn (Bauzan) **1258–1279** N. of Shaftesbury, royal ass. 23 May 1258, temps. 30 May 1258 (ibid., pp. 630, 631). Cert. of conf. eln by bp of Salisbury 29 May 1258 (PRO, C84/1/50). D. 14 Apr. 1279 (PRO, C84/6/37). D., lic. to el. 22 Apr. 1279 (*CPR 1272–81*, p. 307).

Laurentia de Muscegros (Mucegros) **1279–1290** N. of Shaftesbury, eln pres. to king for royal ass. 30 Apr. 1279 (PRO, C84/6/19); royal ass. 8 May 1279, temps. 5 July 1279 (*CPR 1272–81*, pp. 314, 318). Cert. of conf. eln by bp of Salisbury 14 June 1279 (PRO, C84/6/22). Advance fine paid for custody 25 Jan. 1290 (*CPR 1281–92*, p. 338; *CFR 1272–1307*, p. 269). D. by 23 Jan. 1290 (PRO, C84/9/44). D., lic. to el. 30 Jan. 1290 (*CPR 1281–92*, p. 339).

Joan of Bridport (Brideport) **1290–1291** Prs. of Shaftesbury, royal ass. 25 Feb. 1290, writ *de intendendo* 27 Mar. 1290 (ibid., pp. 347, 348). Cert. of conf. eln by *locum tenens* of bp of Salisbury 24 Mar. 1290 (PRO, C84/9/46). Unnamed abbs d. 1291 (BL, Cotton ms. Cleopatra D III, f. 49r). D. by 4 Oct. 1291 (PRO, C84/10/20). D., lic. to el. 5 Oct. 1291 (*CPR 1281–92*, p. 447).

Mabel Giffard 1291–1302 Sister of Bps Godfrey and Walter Giffard, mentd in Bp Godfrey's will (*Reg. Gainsborough*, pp. 51–2). N. of Shaftesbury, royal ass. 22 Oct. 1291, temps. 10 Nov. 1291 (*CPR 1282–91*, pp. 448, 450). D. 9 Sept. 1302 (PRO, C84/14/35). D. (M.), lic. to el. 20 Sept. 1302 (*CPR 1301–07*, p. 63).

---

[14] On 31 Aug. 1217 Pope Honorius III commissioned the abb. of Warden, the pr. of Dunstable and William Scot to examine and adjudicate in the case of A., n. of Shaftesbury who, having been el. as abbs, was, as she complains, forced by the electors to renounce, they electing another (*CPL*, I, 49). In 1219 it was noted that she was sacrist of Shaftesbury. The pope imposed silence on A. and dismissed her claim (ibid., 61–2).

Alice of Lavington (Lavyngton, Lavynton) *alias* **of Winchester** (Wyntonia) **1302–1315** Prs of Shaftesbury. Eln pres. to king for royal ass. 1 Oct. 1302 (PRO, C84/14/36); royal ass. 12 Oct. 1302, temps. 9 Nov. 1302 (*CPR 1301–07*, pp. 64, 70). Eln pres. to bp 16 Oct. 1302, conf. 5 Nov. 1302 (*Reg. Gandavo*, I, 97; II, 619). Bl. 2 Dec. 1302 (ibid., II, 619). Occ. (Wyntonia) 1314 (*CFR 1307–19*, p. 191). D., lic. to el. 14 Sept. 1315 (*CPR 1313–17*, p. 349).

Margaret Aucher (Auchier) **1315–1329** Sub-prs of Shaftesbury, eln pres. to king for royal ass. 9 Oct. 1315 (PRO, C84/17/42); royal ass. 2 Dec. 1315, temps. 1 Feb. 1316 (*CPR 1313–17*, pp. 371, 382). Eln pres. to bp 24 Dec. 1315, conf. 8 Jan. 1316, bl. 8 Feb. 1316 in Lincoln cathedral (*Reg. Martival*, I, 412–13, cf. ibid., II, 164; Lincoln, Ep. Reg., III, f. 338v). Occ. 31 Jan. 1329 (*Reg. Martival*, I, 388). D. by 16 June 1329 (PRO, C84/22/25). D., lic. to el. 26 June 1329 (*CPR 1327–30*, p. 400).

Denise la Bl(o)unde 1329–1345 N. of Shaftesbury, eln pres. to king for royal ass. 3 July 1329 (PRO, C84/22/27). Eln presented to bp 6 July 1329, conf. 15 July, bl. 23 July 1328 (*Reg. Martival*, I, 398; PRO, C84/22/28). D. by 20 Aug. 1345 (*CCR 1343–46*, pp. 599–600). D., lic. to el. 25 Aug. 1345 (*CPR 1343–45*, p. 539).

Joan Duket 1345–1350 Prs of Shaftesbury, eln pres. to king for royal ass. 2 Sept. 1345 (PRO, C84/24/48); temps. 28 Sept. 1345 (*CPR 1343–45*, p. 551). Cert. of conf. eln by bp of Salisbury 24 Sept. 1345 (PRO, C84/24/49). D. by 20 June 1350 (*CCR 1349–54*, p. 190). D., lic. to el. 24 June 1350 (*CPR 1348–50*, p. 548).

Margaret (of) Lewknor (Leukenore) **1350–1362** N. of Shaftesbury, eln pres. to king for royal ass. 1 July 1350 (PRO, C84/26/38); royal ass. 5 July 1350, temps. 19 July 1350 (*CPR 1348–50*, pp. 548, 550). Cert. of conf. eln by bp of Salisbury 17 July 1350 (PRO, C84/26/39). D. 29 June 1362 (PRO, C84/28/43). D., lic. to el. 5 July 1362 (*CPR 1361–64*, p. 224).

Joan Formage (Furmage) **1362–1394** N. of Shaftesbury, eln pres. to king for royal ass. 11 July 1362 (PRO, C84/28/44); royal ass. 16 July 1362, temps. 3 Aug. 1362 (*CPR 1361–64*, pp. 232, 241). Eln conf. 30 July 1362 (Salisbury, Reg. Wyvil, II, f. 297v; PRO, C84/28/45). Will dated 4 May 1393, annulled 2 Sept. 1394 (*Reg. Waltham*, nos. 118–19, 121). D. 13 Aug. 1394 (*CPR 1391–96*, p. 565). Lic. to el. 26 Aug. 1394 (ibid., p. 479).

SINNINGTHWAITE (Yorks W.), St Mary f. *c.* 1160 (*KH*); –1155 (Burton) (Cistercian priory)

Lists in *VCH Yorks*, III, 178; *Heads*, I, 219; Thompson, *Women Religious*, p. 252 (to 1267).

Sapiencia Ment. as predecessor of Eufemia *temp.* John 'in the time of peace in the time of King John' (*Yorks Assize Rolls*, p. 85).

Eufemia (Euferia) Haget Occ. 18 Feb. 1219; 20 Jan. 1220 (*Yorks F., 1218–31*, pp. 26, 35); 11 Nov. 1229 (*Yorks Deeds*, VI, no. 544); 1251 (*Yorks Assize Rolls*, p. 85). Occ. as Euphemia Haget in *Ctl. Healaugh Park*, p. 1.

Isabel Occ. 18 Nov. 1276 (*Mon. Angl.*, V, pp. 264–5, no. v).

Commn to adm. cess. of unnamed prs and to conf. eln of a successor 18 Aug. 1294 (*Reg. Romeyn*, I, p. 142, no. 390).

Margery –1313 Occ. 22 Feb. 1297 (Baildon, I, 204). Commn to receive res. on account of age and ill-health 30 Jan. 1313 (*Reg. Greenfield*, II, no. 974).

Commn to receive cess. of unnamed prs if she wishes to res. on account of age and bodily infirmities 27 Apr. 1318 (York, Reg. 9A, f. 155r).

Elizabeth le Walleys –1320 Commn to receive her cess. and give lic. to el. 3 Nov. 1320 (ibid., f. 172v).

Margaret Occ. Trin. 1322 (Baildon, II, 42).

Commn to el. new prs on d. of unnamed prs 4 July 1323 (York, Reg. 9A, f. 194v).

Sibyl of Ripon 1323– N. of Sinningthwaite, eln conf. 12 July 1323 (ibid., f. 194v). Occ. Mich. 1328 (*Index to Placita de Banco*, p. 803).

Margery FitzSimon Occ. Trin. 1344 (Baildon, I, 205).

Commn ordered 28 Aug. 1356 to enquire into proposed cess. of unnamed prs who is infirm and old, and to accept cess. if the reasons are good and to el. successor (York, Reg. 11, f. 86r).

Joan Dayvell Occ. 26 Feb. 1379 (YMA, M2/1h, f. 16r). Presumably the prs Joan who occ. 21 Sept. 1382 (BI, Ph. 104).

The next recorded prs, **Margaret**, occ. 1397 (Baildon, II, 42).

CUSTOS

Walter of Stoke Appt to the custody of the priory on account of the grave dissensions which had arisen there 28 Nov. 1276 (*CPR 1272–81*, p. 166).

SOPWELL (Herts), St Mary f. c. 1140 (Benedictine priory)
Lists in *VCH Herts*, IV, 425 (from 1233); *Heads*, I, 220; Thompson, *Women Religious*, pp. 252–3 (to 1233).

Amice occ. 1173 x Sept. 1174 (*PUE* III, no. 214); n.d. (late 12th/early 13th cent.; pal.) (PRO, E210/7715). ? same as Avice (*Heads*, I, 220).

Cecily Occ. n.d. (early 13th cent.; pal.) (PRO, E42/380); n.d. (PRO, E42/380(i); E210/5358; E210/7331).

Extranea Occ. n.d. (early 13th cent.) (PRO, E210/3272); 8 July 1233 (PRO, Herts F., CP25/1/84/14, no. 163); (E.) 19 Mar. 1234 (PRO, E210/285).

Margery Occ. 1271 (PRO, E326/6184); 8 May 1272 (PRO, Herts F. CP25/1/86/33, no. 641).

Alice de Yrlaunde Occ. Nov. 1288 x Nov. 1289 (PRO, E210/7571).

Philippa Occ. 1 Oct. 1310 (PRO, E210/611); 1313 (PRO, E210/8918); Easter–Trinity 1327 (*Index to Placita de Banco*, p. 219); Jan. 1332 x Jan. 1333 (PRO, E210/6580). D. c. Mich. [no year, *temp.* abb. Richard of St Albans 1326–35] (*GASA*, II, 212).

[**Alice de Hakeneye** El. on d. of Philippa but without knowledge of St Albans (ibid.).]

Alice of Pegsdon (Pekesdene) Sub-prs of Sopwell, apptd on d. of Philippa by Richard, abb. of St Albans no year, [1326–35] (ibid., 212–13). Occ. Jan. 1335 x Jan. 1336 (PRO, E210/2324).

Margaret Fermeland (Fremban') Occ. 21 Feb. 1341 (PRO, E210/1286); 1348 (PRO, E210/11202); n.d. (PRO, E210/8888).

Joan Occ. Jan. 1356 x Jan. 1357 (PRO, E210/6345); Jan. 1369 x Jan. 1370 (PRO, E210/9347); 6 Jan. 1371 (PRO, E40/5443); Mar. 1384 (PRO, E210/419).

The next recorded prs., **Matilda Flamstede**, occ. 28 Sept. 1388 (PRO, E210/463); June 1395 x June 1396 (PRO, E210/2546); 20 March 1396 (PRO, E40/6725).

STAINFIELD (Lincs), St Mary and St Andrew (St Mary) f. c. 1154 (*KH*); –1168 (Thompson) (Benedictine priory)
Lists in *VCH Lincs*, II, 132; *Heads*, I, 220; Thompson, *Women Religious*, p. 253 (to 1272).

Petronilla El. 24 Aug. 1203 x 10 May 1206 (*EEA*, 4, no. 291). D. 16 x 17 Apr. 1209 x 25 (*Mon. Angl.*, IV, 308; cf. obit 17 Apr. Newhouse obit, *HMC Ancaster*, p. 483; *Heads*, I, 220 and n.2).

Constance Letter to bp of Lincoln asking to adm. the prs-elect *post* 16 Apr. 1223 (*Mon. Angl.*, IV, 309–10; BL, Harl Cht 44 I 28). Occ. 20 Aug. 1226 (*Mon. Angl.*, IV, 309; *Reg. Gray*, p. 111); 23 Nov. 1226 (*CPR 1225–32*, p. 72).

An unnamed prs, formerly n. of Stainfield, el. and adm. June 1236 x June 1237, no reason given for vacancy (*Reg. Grosseteste*, p. 11).

Agnes of Torrington (Thorinton) 1243/4– N. of Stainfield, eln quashed but bp apptd her June 1243 x June 1244, no reason given for vacancy (ibid., p. 72). Occ. 24 Apr. 1245, 14 May

1245 (*Lincs F.*, II, 33, 36); 4 June 1246 (*Yorks F., 1232–46*, p. 142 = *Ctl. Sallay*, I, p, 26); 1 May 1250, 12 June 1250 (*Lincs F.*, II, 51, 78).

Matilda –1258/9 D. Nov. 1258 x Nov. 1259 (*Reg. R. Gravesend*, p. 2).

Euphemia Constable (Constabular') **1258/9** N. of Stainfield, eln conf. Nov. 1258 x Nov. 1259 and d. same pontifical year (ibid.).

Katherine of Durham (Dunelmo, Dunham) **1258/9–1283** N. of Stainfield, eln conf. Nov. 1258 x Nov. 1259 (ibid.). D. 27 Oct. 1283 and bur. 30 Oct. (*Reg. Sutton*, I, 49).

Isolda of Beelsby (Belesby) **1283–1296** Sub-prs of Stainfield, el. 15 Nov. 1283, eln quashed and apptd by bp 25 Nov. 1283 (ibid., 49–50). Res. 2 July 1296 (ibid., V, 164). Indulgence offered for prayers for soul of Isolda late prs 28 Dec. 1300 (Lincoln, Ep. Reg., III, f. 22v).

Christine la Vavassour (Vavasur) **1296–1310** N. of Stainfield, eln quashed but apptd by bp 9 Sept. 1296 (*Reg. Sutton*, I, 208–9). D. by 28 Feb. 1310 (Lincoln, Ep. Reg., II, f. 32r).

Agnes Longvilers 1310– N. of Stainfield, eln quashed but apptd by bp 28 Feb. 1310 (ibid.). Occ. 3 Mar. 1317 (*Reg. Greenfield*, V, no. 2817); 28 Oct. 1329, 22 May 1330, 13 Dec. 1334 (*Reg. Burghersh*, I, nos. 240, 275, 441).

Elizabeth de Nevill 1343– N. of Stainfield, commn to examine eln 18 Dec. 1343, no reason for vacancy (Lincoln, Ep. Reg., VII, f. 186v).

Margaret Lisours (Liseux, Lyseux, Lyshures) **–1394** Occ. 1377 (*Clerical Poll-Taxes*, p. 53, no. 760); 5 May 1378 (Lincoln, Ep. Reg., XII, f. 169v); 1381 (*Clerical Poll-Taxes*, p. 126, no. 1576). D. by 25 Jan. 1394 (Lincoln, Ep. Reg., XI, f. 69v).

MASTERS

William of Appleby (Appelby) Mentioned 23 Nov. 1226 as former master (*CPR 1225–32*, p. 72).

Robert de Sammar' 1223– M. of Whitby, adm. as master 4 Apr. 1223 (*Reg. Wells*, III, 126–7). Occ. Easter 1226 (*CRR*, XII, no. 2611); (R.) 20 Aug. 1226 (*Reg. Gray*, p. 11n.; *Mon. Angl.*, IV, 309).

Gilbert of Kingston (Kingeston) M. of Whitby, apptd June 1238 x June 1239 (*Reg. Grosseteste*, p. 35). Occ. n.d. (*c.* 1243 x *c.* 1250) (*Reg.Gray*, p. 11n., *temp.* prs Agnes).

Gilbert of Panton (Paunton) **1258/9–** M. of Bardney, eln conf. and inst. master Nov. 1258 x Nov. 1259, no reason given for vacancy (*Reg. R. Gravesend*, p. 2).

John of Barton 1263– M. of Bardney, el. and adm. master 7 Nov. 1263, no reason given for vacancy (ibid., p. 14).

Benedict of Billingborough (Biligburg') **1270–** M. of Whitby, apptd master 9 May 1270, no reason given for vacancy (ibid., p. 41).

STAMFORD (Northants), St Mary and St Michael f. *c.* 1155 (*KH*); ? 1135 x 1154 (Thompson) (Benedictine priory)

Lists in *VCH Northants*, II, 100–1; *Heads*, I, 220; Thompson, *Women Religious*, pp. 253–4 (to 1272).

Amabilia Occ. 1214 x 1222 (*temp.* abb. Robert of Peterborough) (Madox, *Form.*, p. 371, no. 666); *ante* 1217 (Bucks RO, D42/B1/2, *ex inf.* Professor B.R. Kemp).

Agnes de Boby 1220– N. of Stamford, adm. 5 June 1220 (*Reg. Wells*, III, 107; *Acta Wells*, no. 141; Peterborough D. & C. ms. 1, f. 116v).

Alice de Nevill(a) –?1238/9 Occ. 1225 x 1229 (*Ctl. Peterborough*, no. 391; PRO, E326/4740, with Henry of Fiskerton, pr. of Stamford); 1230 (*Bucks F.*, I, 59; *Reg. Wells*, II, 79); 1235 x 1236 (PRO, E326/8785); *c.* Easter 1237 with pr. Serlo (PRO, E315/48/273). D. after 1235 (Soc. of Ant. ms. 60, f. 208r). Occ. (A.) June 1238 x June 1239 (*Reg. Grosseteste*, p. 32). The priory was vacant and in the hands of the abb. of Peterborough on 28 May 1239 (ibid., pp. 39–40).

Denise 1238/9– Eln quashed but apptd by bp by authority of the [Lateran] Council June 1238 x June 1239, no reason given for vacancy (ibid., pp. 32–3).

Petronilla of Stamford El. *c*. 1240 (Soc. of Ant. ms. 60, f. 208r), said to be successor of Alice. Occ. n.d. (PRO, E315/41/138; E315/42/84).

[Auricia N. of Stamford, eln quashed June 1247 x June 1248, no reason given for vacancy (*Reg. Grosseteste*, p. 104).]

Sibyl 1247/8– Sub-prs of Stamford, apptd by bp by authority of the Council, June 1247 x June 1248 (ibid.). Occ. *c*. 1247 x 1250/1, with Henry of Caversham, pr. of Stamford (PRO, E326/4790); n.d. mid-13th cent. (PRO, E210/193; E315/35/1; E315/47/4). But cf. PRO, E210/165 dated 1246.

Amice de Stoke (Stokes) –1272 Occ. 16 Feb. 1253 (PRO, Rutland F., CP25/1/192/3 no. 45); 1257, with John Keten, pr. of Stamford (PRO, E210/195); Oct. 1258 x Oct. 1259 (PRO, E210/5288); 1260, with Hugh of Leicester, pr. of Stamford (PRO, E210/186); 1271 (*Reg. Ant. Lincoln*, X, no. 2823); 23 Feb. 1272 (PRO, Leics F., CP25/1/122/30, no. 583). Res. by 13 July 1272 (*Reg. R. Gravesend*, p. 52).

Elizabeth 1272–1286 Eln conf. 13 July 1272 (ibid.). Res. on 3 Jan. 1286 (*Reg. Sutton*, I, 74).

Matilda de Lenn (Len, Lenna, Lenne) 1286–1306 El. on 10 Jan. 1286, eln quashed but apptd by bp 14 Jan. 1286 (ibid., 74–5). D. by 22 Nov. 1306 (Lincoln, Ep. Reg., II, f. 18v).

Mabel le Venur (Venour) **1306–1337** N. of Stamford, eln quashed but apptd by bp 22 Nov. 1306 (ibid.). Res. 1 Apr. 1337 (BL, Cotton ms. Vespasian E. XXII, f. 50r).

Margaret of Riby (Ryby) **1337–** N. of Stamford, commn to examine eln 10 Apr. 1337, no reason given for vacancy (Lincoln, Ep. Reg., V, f. 548r). Occ. 7 Nov. 1340 (PRO, E315/44/47).

Margaret atte (del, de la) See Occ. 13 Nov. 1350 (PRO, E326/4684); 1353 (PRO, E315/42/124); 2 Oct. 1356 (PRO, E315/46/256; E326/1208).

Agnes of Brackenborough (Brakenbergh, Brakynberugh) **1359–1363** N. of Stamford, commn to examine eln 11 June 1359, no reason given for vacancy (Lincoln, Ep. Reg., VIII, f. 111v). Occ. 27 Dec. 1359 (PRO, E315/38/44); Jan. 1361 x Jan. 1362 (PRO, E210/7784); 1361 (PRO, E329/435). Conf. of provision made for her 29 June 1363 (Lincoln, Ep. Reg., XII, ff. 2v–3r).

Katherine Russell Occ. 13 May 1364 (PRO, E315/37/207).

Isabel of Maltby (Malteby) Occ. 7 Feb. 1367 (PRO, E210/893); Jan. 1367 x Jan. 1368 (PRO, E315/89); Jan. 1368 x Jan. 1369 (PRO, E118/1/3); 8 Dec. 1372 (PRO, E315/34/22). Occ. as former prs, when lic. gtd dispensing her from attendance at divine service in the choir on account of age and health 28 Sept. 1377 (Lincoln, Ep. Reg., XII, f. 157r).

Alice Coupledyk (Cobildik, Copildyk, Copuldik, Copuldyn, Coupeldyk, Cuppeldik, Cupuldik) **–1391** Occ. 31 May 1376 (PRO, E326/1234); Jan. 1376 x Jan. 1377 (PRO, E210/8117); 1377 (*Clerical Poll-Taxes*, p. 13, no. 166); 1379 (PRO, E326/4770); 1382 (PRO, E326/1196); 1385 (PRO, E326/4774); 1387 (PRO, E326/1366); 1388 (PRO, E315/35/50). Res. by 5 Oct. 1391 (Lincoln, Ep. Reg., XI, f. 56r).

PRIORS/MASTERS

Peter occ. as pr. n.d. (late 12th/early 13th cents.: pal.) ((PRO, E326/200).

William de Hoyland Occ. n.d. (early 13th cent.; pal.) (PRO, E210/2070).

Richard of Scotter (Scoter) **1223–** M. of Peterborough, apptd *custos* 24 Mar. 1223 (*Reg. Wells*, III, 126).

Henry of Fiskerton 1224/5–1228/9 Adm. Dec. 1224 x Dec. 1225 (ibid., III, 142). Res. Dec. 1228 x Dec. 1229 (ibid., 173).

Serlo of Peterborough (de Burgo) **1228/9–** M. of Peterborough, adm. Dec. 1228 x Dec. 1229 (ibid.). Occ. 29 Sept. 1235 (PRO, E40/172; E210/172); *c.* Easter 1237 (PRO, E315/48/273); *c.* 1238 x 40 (PRO, E210/3614).

Roger of Ketton (Keten) **1243–1247/8** Precentor of Peterborough, adm. 4 Jan. 1243, no reason given for vacancy (*Reg. Grosseteste*, p. 69). Res. June 1247 x June 1248 (ibid., p. 97).

Henry of Caversham (Kaveresham) **1247/8–1250/1** M. of Peterborough, adm. *custos* June 1247 x June 1248 (ibid.). Res. by June 1250 x June 1251 (ibid., pp. 121–2).

Thomas of Grimsby (Grimesby) **1250/1–** M. of Peterborough, inst. as *custos* June 1250 x June 1251 (ibid., pp. 121–2).

John of Ketton (Keten(e)) **–1259/60** Occ. 1257 (PRO, E210/195). Res. Nov. 1259 x Nov. 1260 (*Reg. R. Gravesend*, p. 4).

Hugh of Leicester (Leyc', Leycester, Leycestr') **1259/60–1266** M. of Peterborough, adm. Nov. 1259 x Nov. 1260 (ibid.). Occ. 29 Sept. 1260 (PRO, E210/186). D. by 23 Sept. 1266 (*Reg. R. Gravesend*, p. 22).

William of Weston 1266– M. of Peterborough, adm. master 23 Sept. 1266 (ibid.). Occ. 28 July 1270 x 27 Sept. 1271 (*Reg. Ant. Lincoln*, X, no. 2823).

Henry of Overton 1271– M. of Peterborough, adm. as *custos* 29 Sept. 1271, no reason given for vacancy (*Reg. R. Gravesend*, pp. 118, 299).

John Rouland 1275–1282 M. of Peterborough, adm. as *custos* 4 Jan. 1275, no reason given for vacancy (ibid., p. 61). Res. by 26 Aug. 1282, presumably 16 May 1282 (*Reg. Sutton*, I, 29).

William de Stokes (Stok', Stokys) **1282–1302** M. of Peterborough, letter of pres. 16 May 1282; adm. on res. of John 26 Aug. 1282 (ibid., 29–30). Res. by 10 May 1302 (Lincoln, Ep. Reg., II, f. 5v).

Stephen of Peterborough (de Burgo) **1302–1315** M. of Peterborough, adm. 10 May 1302 (ibid.). Res. by 27 Oct. 1315 (ibid., f. 57v).

Thomas of Salisbury (Sarum) **1315–1316** M. of Peterborough, adm. 27 Oct. 1315 (ibid.). Res. by 24 Nov. 1316 (ibid., f. 63v).

Thomas of Stamford (Staunford) **1316–** M. of Peterborough, adm. 24 Nov. 1316 (ibid.).

William of Weston –1333 D. by 27 Dec. 1333 (*Reg. Burghersh*, I, no. 402).

Thomas of Stamford (Staunford) **1333–** M. of Peterborough, adm. 27 Dec. 1333 (ibid.).

William of Greatford (Gretford) **1335–1345** M. of Peterborough, commn to enquire into pres. by Adam abb. of Peterborough 11 Jan. 1335 (Lincoln, Ep. Reg., V, ff. 221v–222r). Res. by 3 Mar. 1345 (Lincoln, Ep. Reg., VI, f. 16r–v).

Richard of Offord (Dufford) **1345–** M. of Peterborough, adm. 3 Mar. 1345 (ibid.). Occ. (Dufford) 1 Aug. 1345 (PRO, E326/1368).

William de Wykenesthorp 1349– M. of Peterborough, apptd 22 Dec. 1349 (Lincoln, Ep. Reg., IX, f. 82r).

John of Ramsey (Rameseye) **1380–** M. of Peterborough, adm. *custos* 20 Jan. 1380 (Lambeth, Reg. Sudbury, f. 130v).

STIXWOULD (Lincs), St Mary f. *c.* 1135 (*KH*); 1139 x 1142 (Thompson) (Cistercian priory)

 Lists in *VCH Lincs*, II, 149; *Heads*, I, 220–1; Thompson, *Women Religious*, p. 254 (to 1265).

PRIORESSES

Beatrice Latest occ. 1206 (*CRR*, IV, 87). See Thompson, p. 254.

Matilda –1236 Occ. 1209 x 1235, prob. –1227 (*Reg. Ant. Lincoln*, VI, no. 1943).

An unnamed n. el. and adm. June 1236 x June 1237, no reason being given for vacancy (*Reg. Grosseteste*, p. 11).

Iveta de Chauret 1244/5– N. of Stixwould, eln quashed but apptd by bp, no reason being given for vacancy June 1244 x June 1245 (ibid., p. 74).

Lucy of Pinchbeck (Pincebek) **1248/9–** N. of Stixwould, eln quashed but apptd by bp, no reason being given for vacancy June 1248 x June 1249 (ibid., p. 111).

Isabel de Brus –1265 Occ. Nov. 1262 x Nov. 1263 (*Reg. R. Gravesend*, p. 89). D. by 1 Oct. 1265 (ibid., p. 19).

Isabel of Lavington (Lavyngton) **1265–** Eln conf. 1 Oct. 1265 (ibid.).

Margery Gobaud (Gobaut, Goubude, Gubaud(e), Guboud) **1275–1287** N. of Stixwould, eln conf. 8 May 1275, no reason being given for vacancy (ibid., p. 63). Occ. in five n.d. chts. (*HMC 11th Rept*, app. vii (Waterford), pp. 60–2, nos. 9, 1618, 26). Res. by 11 Sept. 1287 (*Reg. Sutton*, I, 99–100). Indulgence of 20 days for her soul 27 July 1313 (Lincoln, Ep. Reg., III, f. 278v).

Eva de Hertepole 1287–1304 N. of Stixwould, eln quashed but apptd by bp 11 Sept. 1287 (*Reg. Sutton*, I, 99–100). D. by 3 Aug. 1304 (Lincoln, Ep. Reg., II, f. 10v). Indulgence of 30 days for her soul 20 Sept. 1322 (she was bur. in the conventual ch.) (Lincoln, Ep. Reg., V, f. 321r).

Isabel of Driby 1304–?1326 N. of Stixwould, eln quashed but apptd by bp 3 Aug. 1304 (Lincoln, Ep. Reg., II, f. 10v). Occ. 25 Jan. 1317 (*CPR 1313–17*, p. 682); July 1320 x July 1321 (PRO, DL36/2/166). A prs. (unnamed) d. by 9 Sept. 1326 (*Reg. Burghersh*, I, no. 152). Indulgence of 40 days for her soul 14 May 1332 (she was bur. in the conventual ch.) (Lincoln, Ep. Reg., V, f. 460r).

Elizabeth of Swillington (Swylington) **1326–1336** N. of Stixwould, eln quashed but apptd by bp 9 Sept. 1326 (*Reg. Burghersh*, I, no. 152). Commn to admit cess. 30 Apr. 1336 and supervise eln of a successor (Lincoln, Ep. Reg., V, f. 528r).

Isabel Malet –1376 Commn to supervise eln on d. of Isabel 21 May 1376 (Lincoln, Ep. Reg., XII, f. 143v).

Eustachia de Ravenser –1403 Occ. 1377 (*Clerical Poll-Taxes*, p. 56, no. 768). Occ. 15 May 1385, 1 Apr. 1390, 7 Sept. 1395 (Lincoln, Ep. Reg., XII, ff. 326v, 364v, 441v). D. by 30 Apr. 1403 (Lincoln, Ep. Reg., XIII, f. 160r). Seal (*BM Seals*, no. 4122). Sister of John de Ravenser, keeper of the hanaper of chancery (*CPR 1396–99*, p. 377).

MASTERS

Hugh Occ. 1205 (*Lincs F. 1199–1216*, no. 198); 1195 x 1223, *temp.* Roger, dean of Lincoln (BL, Lansdowne ms. 207A, f. 116r).

Matthew Occ. 1209 x 1235, ? –1227 (*Reg. Ant. Lincoln*, IV, no. 1943).

Geoffrey ? [Geoffrey] of Stixwould (Stikeswauda), el. as master Dec. 1217 x Dec. 1218 (*Reg. Wells*, I, 117, for dating *BIHR*, XLV, 157–70). Occ. Dec. 1225 x Dec. 1226 (*Reg. Wells*, III, 148); 29 Sept. 1227 (*CPR 1225–32*, p. 165); 18 Jan. 1228 (*CPR 1225–32*, p. 209); 1235 (*Medieval Lindsey Marsh*, no. 36); 1247 (*Lincs N & Q*, VII, 116); 12 Nov. 1247, 29 May 1250, 25 June 1250, 8 July 1251 (*Lincs F.*, II, 45, 70, 55, 90).[15]

Roger Occ. Nov. 1262 x Nov. 1263 (*Reg. R. Gravesend*, p. 89); 6 Oct. 1273 (PRO, F.Various Cos. CP25/1/285/27, no. 2).

Robert of Benniworth (Beningwrth') **1296–** Rector of South Willingham, apptd 28 May 1296 (*Reg. Sutton*, V, 155).

Nicholas de Redingg 1313– Rector of Waddingham, apptd 6 Sept. 1313 (Lincoln, Ep. Reg., III, f. 282r).

John 1314– Rector of Stainby, apptd during pleasure 14 Aug. 1314 (ibid., f. 303r); apptd again 11 Mar. 1315 (ibid., f. 316r).

Master Henry 1319– Rector of Stenigot, apptd 18 Sept. 1319 (ibid., f. 424v).

William Occ. 26 Feb. 1323 (Lincoln, Ep. Reg., V, f. 333v).

---

[15] Pr. Roger (*sic*) occ. 1247 (*HMC Leeds*, p. 61).

STRATFORD-AT-BOW (Middlesex), St Leonard f. -1122 (Benedictine priory)
Lists in *VCH Middlesex*, I, 159 (from 1264); *Heads*, I, 221; Thompson, *Women Religious*, p. 254 (to *c.* 1284).

Lettice Occ. *c.* 15 June 1203 (*CRR*, II, 277).

Alice Occ. Oct. 1226 x Oct. 1227 (*Rot. Lit. Claus.*, II, 206b).

Katherine Occ. Hil. term 1245, 20 Jan. 1248 (*Essex F.*, I, 151, 160, 178); *c.* 1250 (*Hornchurch Priory*, p. 79, no. 341).

Lucy Occ. n.d. (1265 x 1284, *temp.* pr. Eustace of Holy Trinity, London) (*Mon. Angl.*, IV, 121; PRO, E42/471); 8 May 1272 (PRO, Cambs F., CP25/1/25/34, no. 44).

Le[ti]cia de Markam Mentd as former prs in case of 1344 (*YB 19 Edward III*, p. 487). Presumably the prs Lettice who occ. in a case of 1321 (*YB XXVI*, pp. 136, 267).

Isabel la Blunt (Blounde) Occ. 20 Sept. 1341 (*CCR 1341–43*, p. 272); 24 Oct. 1344 (*YB 19 Edward III*, p. 487).

Matilda Occ. 23 Sept. 1368 (*Reg. Sudbury*, II, 60); 25 Apr. 1371 (*Ctl. Tutbury*, no. 102).

Mary Suharde Occ. 23 Sept. 1375 (Guildhall, ms. 9171/1, f. 16v); 1381 (McHardy, *Church in London*, no. 366); 19 May 1396 (BL, Add. ms. 5843, f. 174r); 8 July 1397 (London, Reg. Braybrooke, f. 388v).

STUDLEY (Oxon), St Mary f. *c.* 1176 (*KH*); -1175 x 1179 *or* 1187 x 1189 (Thompson) (Benedictine priory)
Lists in *VCH Oxon*, II, 79; *Heads*, I, 221; Thompson, *Women Religious*, p. 255 (to 1276).

Petronilla Occ. 27 Jan. 1200, 7 Mar. 1227 (*Oxford F.*, pp. 15, 82).[16]

Juliana Occ. 14 Oct. 1230 (*Bucks F.*, I, 60); Mich. term 1230 (*CRR*, XIV, no. 864); 30 July 1232 (PRO, Northants F. CP25/1/172/25, no. 293); n.d. (1242 x 1243, dated by mayoralty) (*Ctl. St John the Baptist, Oxford*, I, 425).

Alice of Crowcombe (Craucumb) **1251–** N. of Studley, el. and apptd June 1250 x June 1251, no reason given for vacancy (*Reg. Grosseteste*, p. 499).

Elizabeth –**1276** Occ. 7 Apr. 1258 (*Oxford F.*, p. 175); Oct. 1271 x Oct. 1272 (*CCR 1323–27*, p. 428: inspeximus). D. by 26 Oct. 1276 (*Reg. R. Gravesend*, p. 228).

Margery Clement 1276– Eln conf. 26 Oct. 1276 (ibid., pp. 228, 336). Occ. Trin. 1283 (PRO, CP40/50, m. 17d).

Mabel ?1287/8–1292 Note of vacancy and pres. by Edmund, earl of Cornwall 19 May 1287 x 18 May 1288, no name of prs ment., presumably Mabel (Bodl., Dodsworth ms. 107, f. 146r). Occ. 9 Feb. 1289 (*Wilts F.*, II, 31). D. by 8 Apr. 1292 (*Reg. Sutton*, VIII, 177).

Clemencia Sweyn 1292–1322 Apptd by bp 8 Apr. 1292 after nuns' attempt to el. a successor had been a failure (ibid.). Res. by 16 May 1322 (Lincoln, Ep. Reg., IV, f. 247v).

Agnes Husee (Huse) **1322–** N. of Studley, pres. 18 [*sic*] May, eln quashed but apptd by bp 16 May 1322 (ibid.). Occ. 22 June 1337 (*Beauchamp Reg.*, p. 88; *DKR 8*, p. 149).

Margery of Berkesdon (Berchesdone, Bergesdon, Berkesdon) **1339–1378** N. of Studley, commn to examine eln 17 June 1339, no reason given for vacancy (Lincoln, Ep. Reg., V, f. 572v). D., lic. to el. 3 Apr. 1378 (*CPR 1377–81*, p. 169; lic. repeated 10 Apr., ibid., p. 177).

MASTER

Warner 1292– Vicar of Hanslope, apptd as master 11 Nov. 1292 (*Reg. Sutton*, IV, 44–5); apptd as above as general adviser to the nunnery 13 Dec. 1292 (ibid., 54); similar appt 9 July 1293 (ibid., 94).

---

[16] Petronilla also occ. as prs in a fine of 25 May 1231 (*Bucks F.*, I, 60). It is difficult to fit this prs in the sequence unless Petronilla and Juliana alternated for a short period, or the fine is wrongly dated.

SWAFFHAM BULBECK (Cambs), St Mary f. (*KH*) *c.* 1150 x 63; (Thompson) – 1199 (esp. p. 223, n. 10) (Benedictine priory)

Lists in *VCH Cambs*, II, 228–9 from W.M. Palmer, 'The Benedictine Nunnery of Swaffham Bulbeck'; in *CAS*, XXXI, (1928), 30–65, at 38–9; Thompson, *Women Religious*, p. 255 (to 1272).

Agnes Occ. *temp.* John (BL, Add. ms. 5819, f. 139r); 15 June 1235 (PRO, Cambs F. CP25/1/24/17, no. 42).

Sibyl ? succeeded Agnes (unpublished proofs of E. Hailstone's work, *History of Swaffham Bulbeck*, now CUL, ms. Bb. 892. 1, cited by Thompson). Mentd in 1375 case as occ. *temp.* Henry III as successor of Agnes (*VCH*, citing BL, Add. ms. 5819, f. 139r).

Matilda Occ. 17 May 1243, 10 May 1248, 4 May 1253 (PRO, Cambs F., CP25/1/24/21, no. 15; 24/24, no. 3; 24/27, no. 4).

Alice Occ. Oct. 1268 x Oct. 1269 (*Suffolk F. (Rye)*, p. 68) 6 Oct. 1270 (PRO, Cambs F., CP25/1/25/32, no. 14); 1272 (PRO, Just. 1/84, m. 2d); 22 July 1286 (PRO, Cambs F., CP25/1/26/42, no. 15); 1286 (PRO, Just.1/86, mm. 17d, 18, 25, 26d).

Cecily Occ. July 1315 (PRO, Just.1/593, m. 36d).

Agnes of Ely –1340 D. by 17 Nov. 1340 (Ely, G/1/1, part 1, ff. 22v–23r).

Isabel of Abbotsley (Aboteslee, Albotesle) **1340–** N. of Swaffham, eln held 17 Nov. 1340 (ibid.). Bp quashed eln 4 Dec. 1340 but apptd her prs. Letters patent about the appt 8 Dec. 1340 (ibid.).

Eve Wasteneys (Wastoneys) Occ. 4 Aug. 1373 (Lambeth, Reg. Whittelsey, f. 154r); 27 Apr. 1375 (BL, Add. ms. 5819, f. 138r); 1379 (PRO, E179/23/1, m. 3). ? the same as the prs of St Radegund, Cambridge, in 1356 (q.v.).

SWINE (Yorks E.), St Mary f. -1153 (*KH*); *c.* 1143 x 1153 (Burton; Thompson) (Cistercian priory)

Lists in *VCH Yorks*, III, 182; *Heads*, I, 221; Thompson, *Women Religious*, p. 255 (to 1251).

Helewise Occ. 14 Dec. 1226 (*Yorks F., 1218–31*, p. 97); 1227 (Baildon, I, 207).

Sibyl Occ. 4 May 1236 (*Yorks F., 1232–46*, p. 43); n.d. (*Yorks Deeds*, VIII, 4–5 with Peter rector of Swine, i.e. earlier than 1251 – hence could be second prs Sibyl below).

Matilda Occ. 29 July 1240, 14 Jan. 1241 (*Yorks F., 1232–46*, pp. 86, 94).

Sibyl Occ. 10 June 1246 (ibid., p. 151); 25 Nov. 1251, 20 Oct. 1252 (*Yorks F., 1246–72*, pp. 48, 88).

Isabel of Haisthorpe (Hasthorp) Mentd as former prs in 1279 (PRO, Just.1/1056, m. 59d).

Mabel Occ. 1279 (PRO, Just.1/1056, m. 59d); 20 Jan. 1280 (*Yorks F., 1272–1300*, p. 37).

Gundreda –1288 Res. 29 Nov. 1288 (*Reg. Romeyn*, II, p. 207, no. 578). Lic. to el. in her place s.d. (ibid.).

Cecily of Walkingham 1288–1290 N. of Swine, eln conf. 30 Dec. 1288 (ibid). Cess. by 28 Sept. 1290 (ibid., p. 213, no. 603).

Josiana of Anlaby (Analaghby, Anelacby, Anlaghby) **1290–1303** Eln conf. 28 Sept. 1290 (ibid). Res. by 24 Jan. 1303 when permission given for her to leave priory for a time for reasons of health (*Reg. Corbridge*, I, 181).

Joan de Moubray –1309 Occ. Trin. 1306 (*YB 33–35 Edward I*, pp. 274–5); 2 Feb. 1309 (*Reg. Greenfield*, III, p. 150, no. 1469). Ex-prs., provision made for her on her retirement *c.* Aug. – Sept. 1309 (ibid., pp. 162–3, no. 1492).

Josiana of Anlaby –1320 Cess. acc. and lic. to el. 4 Sept. 1320 (York, Reg. 9A, f. 336v). Provision for her as ex-prs 4 Sept. 1320 (ibid.).

Commn to examine eln of unnamed prs 4 Sept. 1320 (ibid.); unnamed prs referred to 13 Jan. 1321 (ibid., f. 339r).[17]

---

[17] Baildon, I, 207 lists Matilda Wade as succ. Josiana but with no dates or source. In fact Matilda Wade was prs in the 15th cent. and res. by 4 Mar. 1483 (*Reg. Rotherham*, I, no. 236).

Cecily Occ. Hil. 1338 (Baildon, I, 207).

Denise Occ. Easter 1361 (PRO, CP40/406, m. 192).

Joan Skirlaw Occ. 10 July 1389 (*CPR Supplement*, no. 434); 6 Aug. 1389 (*CCR 1389–93*, p. 16). 1 Aug. 1404 mentd as sister of Walter Skirlaw, bp of Durham (*Test. Ebor.*, I, 314); 24 Jan. 1405 (BI, Prob. Reg. 3, f. 231v).

MASTERS

Peter Occ. as master n.d. (?1221 x 1235) ('Ctl. Meaux', p. 463, no. 279).

Hamo Can. of Healaugh Park, occ. n.d. (1235 x 1249) (*Ch. Meaux*, II, 13).

Robert of Spalding 1287–1290 Can. of Croxton, apptd as master 15 Apr. 1287 (*Reg. Romeyn*, I, p. 203, no. 565). Letter to the General Chapter of Prémontré to allow him to be master 3 Sept. 1287 (ibid., p. 204, no. 567). Request to the abb. of Croxton to allow him to continue as master 4 Jan. 1290 (ibid., pp. 209–10, no. 591). Letters testimonial of his good behaviour 30 Jan. 1290 (ibid., p. 211, no. 596) Res. by 3 Apr. 1290 (ibid. p. 217, no. 615).

John Bustard (Burtard) 1290– Can. of St Robert, Knaresborough, apptd master of Swine, in place of Robert of Spalding 3 Apr. 1290 (ibid.). Request to the minister of Knaresborough to allow him to be master 3 Apr. 1290 (ibid., p. 344, no. 986). 22 June 1291 letter to master of Knaresborough to recall him (ibid., pp. 219–20, no. 625).

Robert of Spalding 1295– Apptd master 8 Sept. 1295, no reason given for vacancy (ibid., p. 239, no. 689).

William Darains (Darreins) 1298– Rector of Londesborough, apptd as master 15 Sept. 1298, no reason given for vacancy (*Reg. Newark*, II, p. 222, no. 63); apptd again 11 Apr. 1301 (*Reg. Corbridge*, I, 163).

[**Walter of Kelk** apptd by archbp to take charge of the *maiora negotia* of the priory n.d. [1312], surrounded by entries of Aug.–Sept. 1312] (*Reg. Greenfield*, III, p. 203, no. 1561).]

Hugh 1315– Rector of the chapel of Nuthill, apptd to look after the temporal goods of the priory 8 Sept. 1315 (ibid., pp. 263–4, no. 1665).

Richard of Bielby (Beleby) 1319– Vicar of Wawne, apptd *custos* 1 June 1319 (York, Reg. 9A, f. 333v); occ. 14 July 1319 (ibid., f. 334r).

Richard of Melton 1335– Rector of Brandsburton, apptd custos 5 May 1335 (ibid., f. 392v).

John Vicar of Swine, apptd as 'coadjutor' of the prs and convent of Swine 13 July 1344 '*ad curandum, custodiendum et administrandum sub priorissa monasterii de Swyna dicte diocesis in bonis temporalibus priorisse et conventus eiusdem*' (York, Reg. 10, f. 177r).

TARRANT KAINES (Dorset), St Mary and All Saints *c.* 1186(?) (cell); -1228 (Cist.); - 1169 x 1176 (Thompson) (Cistercian abbey)

List in *VCH Dorset*, II, p. 90; Thompson, *Women Religious*, p. 255 (to 1280).

ABBESSES

Clarice Prof. made to Bp Poore (who was transferred to Durham in 1228) (Salisbury D. & C., press 2, box 1).

Evelina Prof. n.d. (?early 13th cent.) (ibid.).

Cecily occ. n.d. (early 13th cent.) (PRO, E315/45/306). The precise sequence of abbesses at this point is unclear.

Matilda de Brione (Brydone, Bryene) Occ. several times from 26 Feb. 1240 to 8 Dec. 1252 (*CChR 1226–57*, pp. 250, 411); 23 Feb. 1240 (PRO, F. Var. Cos. CP25/1/284/18, no. 54); 14 May 1242 (PRO, F. Divers Cos. CP25/1/ 283/11, no. 175); 14 May 1249 (PRO, F. Var. Cos., CP25/1/284/19, no. 87); 23 Oct. 1270 (*CChR 1257–1300*, p. 227, cf. 160, 229–30);. n.d. (late 13th cent.) (*HMC Middleton*, p. 76; PRO, E315/31/39, 212; E326/4451).

Isolda Occ. n.d. *temp.* William de Brione, *ante* 1280 (*CChR 1257–1300*, p. 229); 20 Apr. 1281 (PRO, Hants. F. CP25/1 /204/13, no. 14).[18]

Emelina Occ. Hil. 1286 (PRO, Just.1/1273, mm. 28d, 34).

Ellen 1298– Bl. 19 Oct. 1298 (*Reg. Gandavo*, II, 581).

Anne Occ. 26 Jan. 1351 (*CPL*, III, 407).

Clemence de Cernyngton Occ. 25 Apr. 1377 (*CPR 1381–85*, p. 29).

The next recorded abbs, **Joan**, occ. 30 May 1382 (*CCR 1381–85*, p. 425); 11 Mar. 1388 (*Cal. Misc. Inq.*, IV, no. 398), poss. the same as **Joan Kyngeston**, who occ. 3 Sept. 1389 (BL, Harl. ms. 61, f. 121r).

PROCTOR
William Occ. 1237 (*Lib. Rolls 1226–40*, p. 280).

THETFORD (Norfolk), St George and St Gregory (St George) f. (? at Ling); *c.* 1160 (at Thetford) (*KH*); *c.* 1163 x 1180 (Thompson) (Benedictine priory)

Lists in *VCH Norfolk*, II, 355–6; *VCH Suffolk*, II, 86; *Heads*, I, 221; Thompson, *Women Religious*, p. 255 (to 1254).

Agnes Occ. Oct. 1253 x Oct. 1254 (*Suffolk F., (Rye)*, p. 56).

Ellen of Bardwell (Berdewell(e)) **1311–** N. of Thetford, eln defective but apptd by bp 22 Feb. 1311 (Norwich, Reg/1/1, ff. 39v–40r). Occ. 16 Nov. 1312 (ibid., f. 49r); Mich. 1328 (*Index to Placita de Banco*, p. 458).

Margaret (de) Bretoun 1330 N. of Thetford, eln conf. 8 Jan. 1330 (Norwich, Reg/1/2, f. 33v); D. by 13 June 1330 (ibid., ff. 36v–37r).

Beatrice of Liston (Lyston(e)) **1330–1339** N. of Thetford, eln conf. 13 June 1330 (ibid.). D. by 13 Apr. 1339 (Norwich, Reg/1/3, f. 24v).

Dametta of Bagthorpe (Bakethorp) **1339–** N. of Thetford, eln conf. 13 Apr. 1339 (ibid.). Occ. 1377 x 1381 (PRO, E179/45/7C).

Margaret Campleon 1397– N. of Thetford, eln conf. 8 April 1397, on cess of unnamed prs (Norwich, Reg/3/6, f. 222v).

THICKET (Yorks E.), St Mary (Ben.) f. – 1180 (Benedictine priory)

Lists in *VCH Yorks*, III, 125; *Heads*, I, 221; Thompson, *Women Religious*, p. 256 (to 1260s).

Sibyl Occ. 1214 (Baildon, I, 208, without source); 16 Feb. 1219 (*Yorks F. 1218–31*, p. 24).

Eva Occ. 12 June 1231 (ibid., p. 135).

Alice mentd 1279 and 1282 as late prs, occurring *temp.* Henry, pr. of Ellerton, i.e. 1250s x 1260s (PRO, Just.1/1056, m. 41; Baildon, II, 44).

Joan Occ. 1279 (PRO, Just.1/1056, m. 41); 30 Sept. 1280 (*Yorks F., 1272–1300*, p. 45); 1282 (Baildon, II, 44); Trin. 1283 (PRO, CP40/50, m. 39); 1290 (*Ctl. Fountains*, II, 814); Hil. 1300–Hil. 1301 (Baildon, I, 208–9); Nov. 1303 x Nov. 1304 (PRO, C260/161, no. 41); 18 Nov. 1305 (*Yorks F., 1300–14*, p. 51); 1306 (Baildon, II, 44).

Alice of Alverthorpe (Alverthorp) **1309–1335** N. of Thicket, eln conf. 12 Aug. 1309, no reason given for vacancy (*Reg. Greenfield*, III, p. 162, no. 1491). Res., lic. to el. 20 Apr. 1335 (York, Reg. 9A, f. 392r).

Elizabeth del Haye 1335– N. of Thicket, eln quashed but apptd by archbp 2 May 1335 (ibid.). Occ. Trin. 1337 (Baildon, II, 45).

The next recorded prs, **Hawise**, occ. 1412 (Baildon, II, 45).

---

[18] Hutchins, III, 121, gives her occ. Nov. 1279 x Nov. 1280, but with no source.

USK (Monmouth). St Mary f. -1236 (Benedictine priory)
The nuns of Usk have lic. to el. 25 June 1246 (*CPR 1232–47*, p. 483; *Welsh Episcopal Acts*, II, p. 726, no. L.436)
B. Occ. as prs n.d. (between entries of Dec. 1269 and Jan. 1270) (*Reg. G. Giffard*, p. 33).

WALLINGWELLS (Notts), St Mary. f. *c.* 1140 x 1144 (*KH*); *c.* 1144 (Thompson) (Benedictine priory)
  Lists in *VCH Notts*, II, 90; Thompson, *Women Religious*, p. 256 (to late 13th cent.).
Isolda Occ. 9 Feb. 1240 (PRO, Notts F., CP25/1/182/8, no. 257); 25 June 1240 (*Yorks F., 1232–46*, p. 61); 6 July 1245 (PRO, Notts F., CP25/1/182/9, no. 335).
Agnes Occ. 23 July 1262 (*Reg. W. Giffard*, p. 327,).
Alice de Montenay Occ. n.d. ? 2nd half of 13th cent. (BL, Harl. Cht. 112 F 30).
Margaret Occ. 23 Oct. 1289 (*Reg. Romeyn*, I, p. 90, no. 236); 8 June 1292 (*Lancs F.*, I, pp. 169–70, no. 42).
Emma of Stockwell (Stocwell, Stockewell) **1295–** Apptd 18 Oct. 1295, no reason given for vacancy (*Reg. Romeyn*, I, p. 332, no. 951). Occ. 21 Apr. 1297 (*Ctl. Monk Bretton*, p. 180, no. 574).
Denise –1326 Cess., lic. to el. 27 Mar. 1326 (York, Reg. 9B, f. 428v).
Commn to examine eln of unnamed prs 27 Aug. 1326 (ibid., f. 431r).
Alice of Sheffield (Sheffeld) **–1354** Commn to adm. cess. and to hold an eln 3 Feb. 1354 (York, Reg. 11, f. 25r).
The next recorded prs, **Ellen of Bolsover** (Bollesovere), commn to receive res. 7 Jan. 1403 (*Reg. Scrope*, I, no. 565).

MASTERS
Matthew the chaplain, occ. as master of the nuns 'de Parco' 1228 x 1244 (*Rufford Chts.*, III, no. 855). For the identification of Wallingwells and the nunnery of St Mary 'of the Park' see *VCH Notts*, II, 89.
William 1301/2– Vicar of Mattersey, apptd as master 28 Dec. 1301 (cancelled and repeated 1 Jan. 1302) (*Reg. Corbridge*, I, 224 & n.).

WESTWOOD (Worcs.), St Mary Fontevraud f. +1154 (*KH*); 1155 x 1158 (Thompson); *c.* 1158 (Goodrich)
  Lists in *VCH Worcs.*, II, 151; *Heads*, I, 221; Thompson, *Women Religious*, p. 256 (priors to - 1260); cf. M. Goodrich, 'Westwood, a rural English nunnery with its local and French connections' in J. Greatrex ed., *The Vocation of Service to God and Neighbour: essays on the interests, involvements and problems of religious communities and their members in medieval society* (International Medieval Research 5, Turnhout, Brepols, 1998), pp. 43–57. For further details see B. Kerr, *Religious life for Women*, pp. 245–6, 249.
Sibyl Occ. 7 June 1221 (PRO, Worcs F., CP25/1/258/2, no. 34).
Amice Occ. 23 July 1236 (PRO, Hereford F., CP25/1/80/8, no. 133). Possibly the same as prs. Avice occ. *c.* 29 Sept. 1239 (BCL, Hampton 473641).
Benedicta de Clifford (Cliffort) Occ. *c.* 25 Mar. 1270, 24 June 1272 (BCL, Hampton 474346, 474345); n.d. (ibid., 474350, 473646).
Beatrice Occ. 29 Sept. 1301, 29 Sept. 1310, 18 Feb. 1313, 22 Sept. 1314 (ibid., 474352, 474355, 474353).
B. (prob. the same as Beatrice) Occ. 23 Aug. 1319 (ibid., 474356).
Joyce Occ. 17 June 1342, 23 June 1342 (ibid., 474359, 474362).
Alice Occ. 16 Apr. 1351 (ibid., 474364).
Isabel Occ. 7 May 1365, 25–26 June 1365 (ibid., 475220, 474365, 474358); (Bella) 21 Sept. 1368 (ibid., 173).

Isabel Gros –1384 Prob. the same as the above. Occ. 1379 (PRO, E179/58/11, m. 3). D. by 8 June 1384 (Worcester Cath. Lib., B.823).

PRIORS

Helias Occ. *c.* 27 Oct. 1207 (*CRR*, V, 58); n.d. (late 12th/early 13th cents.) (PRO, E315/43/292).

Nicholas Occ. *c.* 29 Sept. 1239 (BCL, Hampton 473641). Occ. as former pr. 1 Oct. 1260 (*CCR 1259–61*, p. 212).

Robert Douet Occ. *c.* 25 Mar. 1270, 24 June 1272 (BCL, Hampton 474346, 474345).

Richard *dictus* **Normaund** Occ. n.d. (late 13th cent., with prs Benedicta de Clifford) (ibid., 473646).

Richard Occ. 18 Feb. 1313, 22 Sept. 1314, 23 Aug. 1319 (ibid., 474354, 474353, 474356).

Richard de Greneburgh Occ. 17 June 1342, 23 June 1342 (ibid., 474359, 474362).

Robert Occ. 16 May 1344 (*CCR 1343–46*, p. 383), possibly the br. Robert de Westwode mentd 6 Sept. 1343 (ibid., p. 232).

Robert de Sotherey Occ. 12 May – 30 Sept. 1350 (BCL, Hampton 473423).

Robert Prob. the same as above. Occ. 16 Apr. 1351 (BCL, Hampton 474364).

William Occ. 22 June 1371 (*CPR 1370–74*, p. 113); 1379 (PRO, E179/58/11, m. 3).

WHERWELL (Hants) Holy Cross and St Peter f. *c.* 960 or before (Benedictine abbey)
Lists in *VCH Hants*, II, 137; *Heads*, I, 222; D. K. Coldicott, *Hampshire Nunneries*, App. I, pp. 163–4; *Hampshire Notes and Queries*, IV (1889), pp. 93–4.

Euphemia –1257 Occ. 9 May 1219 (PRO, Berks F. CP25/1/7/7, no. 46); 1234 (BL, Egerton ms. 2104A, f. 34v); 14 Jan. 1241 (PRO, Hants F., CP25/1/203/7, no. 36); 28 Apr. 1245 (*CPR 1232–47*, p. 452); 1254 (BL, Egerton ms. 2104A, ff. 45r, 65r); Oct. 1255 (ibid., f. 31v). Gt to prs. and nuns of Wherwell of the keeping of the abbey on its next voidance by the cess. or d. of abb. Euphemia 25 Apr. 1257 (*CPR 1247–58*, p. 551). D. 26 Apr. 1257 after forty years as a n. at Wherwell (BL, Egerton ms. 2104A, f. 43v). Lic. to el. 30 Apr. 1257 (*CPR 1247–58*, p. 552).

Mary 1257–1259 Prs. of Wherwell, royal ass. 20 May 1257 (*CPR 1247–58*, p. 555); mand. for seisin, having been conf. by Robert de Karvile, treasurer of Salisbury and official of A., bp-el. of Winchester 30 May 1257 (*CR 1256–59*, p. 59). D., lic. to el. 22 Feb. 1259 (*CPR 1258–66*, p. 13; cf. PRO, C84/2/7).

Constance 1259–1262 Sacrist of Wherwell, royal ass. 7 Mar. 1259, temps. (Christiana) 12 Mar. 1259, after eln conf. by Boniface, archbp of Canterbury *sede vacante* (*CPR 1258–66*, pp. 14, 15). D. 1 Oct. 1262 (PRO, C84/2/34). D., lic. to el. 26 Oct. 1262 (*CPR 1266–72*, p. 738; PRO, SC1/7/135; *CR 1261–64*, p. 162).

Mabel of Tichborne (Tichbourne, Ticheburn, Tycheburne) 1262–1281 N. of Wherwell, eln pres. to king for royal ass. 15 Nov. 1262 (PRO, C84/2/36); cert. conf. eln by bp of Winchester 29 Nov. 1262 (PRO, C84/2/38); temps. 4 Dec. 1262 (*CPR 1258–66*, p. 237). D. (unnamed abbs.) by 13 Dec. 1281 (PRO, C84/7/41). Lic. to el. 14 Dec. 1281 (*CPR 1281–92*, p. 6). Obit 12 Dec. (Coldicott, p. 163; Thomson, *MSS. from St Albans*, I, 59).

Ellen de Percy (Perci) 1282–1297 N. of Wherwell, eln pres. to king for royal ass. 7 Jan. 1282 (PRO, C84/7/45); royal ass. 13 Jan. 1282, temps. 2 Feb. 1282 (*CPR 1281–92*, p. 9). Cert. conf. eln by archbp of Canterbury 22 Jan. 1282 (PRO, C84/7/46). Bl. 15 Feb. 1282 (*Reg. Pontissara*, I, 181). Appt of J. de Ver, prs of Wherwell, as coadjutrix for unnamed abbs. [27 Jan.] 1284 (*Reg. Peckham*, II, 654–5). D. 2 Dec. 1297 (PRO, SC6/983/34, but cf. PRO, C84/13/7, d. by 1 Dec. 1297). D., lic. to el. 17 Jan. 1298 (*CPR 1292–1301*, p. 326; BL, Egerton ms. 2104A, f. 118r–v).

Isabel (de) Wynt(e)reshull(e) 1298–1333 N. of Wherwell, el. 23 Jan. 1298 (BL, Egerton ms. 2104A, ff. 184r–185v); eln pres. to king for royal ass. 24 Jan. 1298 (PRO, C84/13/9); royal ass. 28 Jan. 1298, temps. 8 Feb. 1298 (*CPR 1292–1301*, pp. 328–9; BL, Egerton ms. 2104A, f. 118r). Episcopal conf. of eln sought 25 Jan 1298, eln conf. by Official of Winchester 2 Feb. 1298 (BL, Egerton ms. 2104A, ff. 118v–119r). Cess., lic. to el. 22 Oct. 1333 (*CPR 1330–34*, p. 478). Temps. to be returned to prs. and convent 26 Oct. 1333 after cess. of Isabel (*CCR 1335–37*, p. 149).

Matilda of Littleton (Litleton(e)) **1333–1340** N. of Wherwell, royal ass. 26 Nov. 1333. temps. 27 Dec. 1333 (*CPR 1330–34*, pp. 483, 488). Eln quashed, but apptd by bp 17 Dec. 1333; mand. to convent to obey 19 Dec. (Winchester, Reg. Stratford, f. 139r). Obit 14 Mar. (Coldicott, p. 163, citing Cambridge, Fitzwilliam Museum, McLean ms. 45). D., lic. to el. 18 Mar. 1340 (*CPR 1338–40*, p. 442).

Amice Ladde 1340–1361 N. of Wherwell, royal ass. 5 Apr. 1340, temps. 14 Apr. 1340 (ibid., pp. 449, 461; BL, Egerton ms. 2104A, f. 69r–v). Eln conf. 13 Apr. 1340 (Winchester, Reg. Orleton, I, f. 87r–v). Petition of prs. and convent asking for lic. to el. on d. of Amice 15 Sept. 1361 (BL, Egerton ms. 2104A, f. 129v). D., lic. to el. 21 Sept 1361 (*CPR 1361–64*, p. 74).

Constance (de) Wyntreshull 1361 N. of Wherwell, eln pres. to king for royal ass. 1 Oct. 1361 (BL, Egerton ms. 2104A, ff. 129v–130r); royal ass. 4 Oct. 1361, temps. 25 Oct. 1361 (ibid., f. 151v; *CPR 1361–64*, pp. 87, 91). Examination of eln 23 Oct. 1361; eln conf. and bl. 24 Oct. 1361 (*Reg. Edington*, I, nos. 1464–70; BL, Egerton ms. 2104A, f. 130r). D. by 27 Nov. 1361 (PRO, C84/28/22); prob. d. 26 Nov., as vacancy dated from then (BL, Egerton ms. 2104A, f. 215v). D., lic. to el. 29 Nov. 1361 (*CPR 1361–64*, p.125).

Joan Cokerel(l) (Kokerel) **1361–1375** N. of Wherwell, royal ass. 22 Dec. 1361, temps. 27 Dec. 1361 (ibid., pp. 134, 136; BL, Egerton ms. 2104A, f. 151v). Eln conf. 24 Dec. 1361; bl. 25 Dec. 1361 (*Reg. Edington*, I, nos. 1480–3). Prob. d. 17 Sept. 1375, as vacancy dated from then (BL, Egerton ms. 2104A, f. 216r). D., lic. to el. 22 Sept. 1375 (*CPR 1374–77*, p. 168).

Cecily (of) Lavington (Lavyngton, Lavynton(e)) **1375–1412** N. of Wherwell, royal ass. 8 Oct. 1375, temps. 22 Oct. 1375 (ibid., pp. 172, 183). Eln conf. by bp's commissary 20 Oct. 1375; bl. and prof. obed. 21 Oct. 1375 (*Reg. Wykeham*, I, 69–74). Prob. d. 23 May 1412, as vacancy dated from then (BL, Egerton ms. 2104A, f. 216v). D., lic. to el. 25 May 1412 (*CPR 1408–13*, p. 400).

WHISTONES (Worcs), St Mary Magdalen f. 1237 x 1240 (*KH*); –1241 (Thompson). See also M. Goodrich, 'The White Ladies of Worcester: their place in contemporary medieval life', *Trans. Worcs Archaeol. Soc.*, 3rd series, 14 (1994), 129–47. (Cistercian priory)

List in *VCH Worcs.*, II, 156.

Juliana Occ. 1262 (*VCH*, citing Worcester Cath., Liber Albus, f. 67).

Anneys Occ. 11 July 1297 (Worcester Cath. Lib., B1222). ? same as Agnes below.

Agnes of Bromwich (Bromwych) **–1308** Occ. 17 Mar 1302 (*Worcs. Lib. Albus*, I, no. 82). D. by 24 May 1308, although the register entry subsequently states she died on the Monday before St Bartholomew and buried the next day (i.e. d. 19 Aug.) – clearly some clerical error (*Worc. Reg. Sede Vacante*, pp. 112, 114).

Alice de la (atte) Flagge 1308–1328 N. of Whistones, lic. to el. issued 24 May 1308; el. 1 July 1308, eln proclaimed 3 July 1308, commn to examine 17 July, eln conf. 12 Aug. 1308. (ibid., pp. 111–15). D. by 10 Apr. 1328 (*Reg. Orleton (Worcs)*, no. 34).

Juliana de Power 1328–1349 N. of Whistones, apptd 10 Apr. 1328 (ibid., nos. 34, 643). D. by 3 July 1349 (*Reg. Bransford*, p. 430).

Agnes de Monynton 1349– Apptd 3 July 1349 (ibid.).

The next recorded prs, **Elizabeth**, occ. 2 Nov. 1407 (Worcester Cath. Lib., Liber Pensionum, p. 43, no. 135); 3 Jan. 1409 (ibid., p. 25, no. 89). Possibly the same as prs **Elizabeth Hembury**, d. 5 Jan. 1428 (Worcester, Reg. Poulton, p. 86 (f. 41v).

WILBERFOSS (Yorks E.), St Mary f. -1153 (*KH*); 1147 x 1153 (Burton; Thompson) (Benedictine priory)

Lists in *VCH Yorks.*, III, 126; Thompson, *Women Religious*, p. 256 (to 1276).

Christiana Occ. 21 June 1231 (*Yorks F., 1218–31*, p. 144); 7 Nov. 1234, 20 Jan. 1235 (*Yorks F., 1232–46*, pp. 9, 37–8).

Lettice Occ. 17 June 1240 (ibid., p. 58). D. in office and succ. by Agnes (PRO, KB27/155, m. 26).

Agnes Occ. 1260 (J. Foster ed., *Visitations of Yorkshire* (1875), p. 84; BL, Harl. ms. 2101, f. 86v).

Isabel Succ. Agnes (PRO, KB27/155, m. 26). Occ. 1276 (Baildon, I, 226). Mentioned as former prs. 1290 (ibid.).

Emma of Walkeringham (Walcryngham) –1310 Occ. Trin. 1298 (PRO, KB27/155, m. 26). Mand. to receive cession and to conf. eln of a successor 2 Aug. 1310 (*Reg. Greenfield*, III, p. 177, no. 1514). Res. 3 Aug. 1310 (ibid., pp. 177–9, no. 1514).

Margaret de Alta Ripa (Dawtry) El. 3 Aug. 1310 and eln conf. same day (ibid.).

Commn to examine and conf. eln of an unnamed prs 27 Mar. 1319 (York, Reg. 9A, f. 333r).

Isabel (de) Spynys (Spynes) Occ. 16 Dec. 1348 (York, Reg. 10, f. 193r). Letter to Archbp Thoresby asking to resign on account of illness 8 June (?1356) (*BIHR*, 27 (1954), 190–2).

The next recorded prs, **Agnes**, occ. 1396 (Baildon, II, 53).

CUSTOS

Robert (de Apeltone), rector of Sutton upon Derwent Apptd as *custos* 9 May 1294 (*Reg. Romeyn*, I, p. 234, no. 672; for surname cf. *Reg. Wickwane*, p. 86, no. 300).

WILTON (Wilts), St Mary, St Bartholomew, and St Edith f. 890 (Benedictine abbey)

Lists in *VCH Wilts*, III, 241; J. E. Nightingale, *Memorials of Wilton*, pp. 14ff.; *Heads*, I, 222–3.

Ascelina May have been el. 1203 (cf. *EEA*, 3, no. 603). Latest recorded occ. *c.* 15 July 1208 (*Wilts F.*, I, 10).

Margaret –1222 Occ. 30 June 1216 (*Rot. Chart.*, p. 223). D., lic. to el. 12 Feb. 1222 (*CPR 1216–25*, p. 326).

Isabel de Warenne (Warenna) 1222–1228 N. of Wilton, royal ass. 27 Feb. 1222 (ibid., p. 327). D., lic. to el. 1 Apr. 1228 (*CPR 1225–32*, p. 181).

Alice 1228–?1237 Prs of Wilton, royal ass. 11 Apr. 1228 (ibid.); mand. for seisin 11 Apr. 1228 (*CR 1227–31*, p. 33). Lic. to el. (no reason given for vacancy) 7 May 1237 (*CPR 1232–47*, p. 181).

Alice 1237–?1252 Prs of Wilton, royal ass. 20 May 1237, writ *de intendendo* 29 May 1237 (ibid., pp. 182–3). Occ. 9 July 1241 (*Cornwall F.*, I, p. 37, no. 76); 31 May 1249 (*Wilts F.*, I, 38). Abbey vacant by 25 Aug. 1252 (*CPR 1247–58*, p. 148). Lic. to el. (no reason given for vacancy) 29 Aug. 1252 (ibid., p. 149).

Matilda de la Mare 1252–1271 Prs of Wilton, royal ass. 23 Sept. 1252 writ *de intendendo* 30 Sept. 1252 (ibid., p. 150); mand. for seisin 30 Sept. 1252 (*CCR 1251–53*, p. 162). Abbey vacant by 27 Oct. 1271 (*CR 1268–72*, p. 384). D., lic. to el. 2 Nov. 1271 (*CPR 1266–72*, p. 602).

27 Dec. 1271. The king for a fine made previously had granted keeping to the nuns, but such disputes had arisen over the eln that the king had committed the house to Walter Scammel, treasurer of Salisbury, jointly with the nuns (ibid., p. 612).

Alice de Witefeld –1272 D. by 28 Oct. 1272 when sub-prs and convent asked king for lic. to el. (PRO, C84/4/17).

Juliana Giffard 1272–1296 N. of Wilton, el. 11 Nov. 1272 (PRO, C84/4/18); bp of Salisbury asks for temps. to be restored 23 Nov. 1272 (PRO, SC1/8/36); writ *de intendendo* 29 Nov.

1272, the royal ass. having been given by Henry III and eln conf. by R., bp of Salisbury (*CPR 1272–81*, p. 1). Mentd as bp of Worcester's sister (*Reg. G. Giffard*, p. 72). D., lic. to el. 6 July 1296 (*CPR 1292–1301*, p. 190).

Petronilla de Vallibus (Waux) **1296–1299** N. of Wilton, power given to Edward the king's son to give royal ass. to an eln at Wilton, to save the labour of the nuns 6 July 1296 (ibid.); temps. 15 Aug. 1296 (ibid., p. 191). Cert. conf. eln by bp of Salisbury 4 Aug. 1296 (PRO, C84/12/28). D. 30 Apr. 1299 (PRO, C84/13/30). D., lic. to el. 8 May 1299 (*CPR 1292–1301*, p. 412).

Emma la Blounde (Blonda, Blund(e)) **1299–1321** N. of Wilton, eln pres. to king for royal ass. 13 May 1299 (PRO, C84/34/31); royal ass. 16 May 1299, temps. 24 May 1299 (*CPR 1292–1301*, pp. 415, 417). Eln conf. 21 May and bl. 23 May 1299 (*Reg. Gandavo*, II, 583–4). Installation feast 13 Sept.1299 (Wilts Rec. Soc., XII, pp. 143, 145, 154). Occ. 8 Feb. 1321 (*CFR 1319–27*, p. 46). D., lic. to el. 20 Nov. 1321 (*CPR 1321–24*, p. 36).

Constance de Percy 1321–1344 N. of Wilton, royal ass. 12 Dec. 1321, temps. 14 Feb. 1322 (ibid., pp. 43, 70). Eln pres. to bp 18 Dec. 1322 (*Reg. Martival*, I, 417); eln conf. 12 Jan. 1322 (ibid.; PRO, C84/20/10). D., lic. to el. 14 Aug. 1344 (*CPR 1343–45*, p. 331).

Robergia of Popham 1344–1346 N. of Wilton, eln pres. to king for royal ass. 27 Aug. 1344 (PRO, C84/25/33); royal ass. 31 Aug. 1344, temps. 24 Nov. 1344 (*CPR 1343–45*, pp. 343, 367). D. by 1 May 1346 (PRO, C84/25/2). D., lic. to el. 4/6 May 1346 (*CPR 1345–48*, pp. 79, 81).

Lucy (de) Loveny (Loveneye) **1346–1361** N. of Wilton, royal ass. 14 May 1346, temps. 17 June 1346 (ibid., pp. 83, 123). Cert. conf. eln by bp of Salisbury 15 June 1346 (PRO, C84/25/3). D., lic. to el. 30 Oct. 1361 (*CPR 1361–64*, p. 97).

Sibyl Aucher (Auchier) **1361–1374** Prs of Wilton, eln pres. to king for royal ass. 8 Nov. 1361 (PRO, C84/28/16); royal ass. 10 Nov. 1361, temps. 27 Nov. 1361 (*CPR 1361–64*, pp. 107, 128). Eln conf. 27 Nov. 1361 (Salisbury, Reg. Wyvil II, f. 294r; PRO, C84/28/23). D., lic. to el. 20 June 1374 (*CPR 1370–74*, p. 457).

Matilda (of) Buckland (Boclaunde, Bok(e)land) **1374–1395** N. of Wilton, eln pres. to king for royal ass. 28 June 1374 (PRO, C84/31/13); royal ass. 3 July 1374, temps. 24 July 1374 (*CPR 1370–74*, pp. 458, 467). Cert. conf. eln by bp of Salisbury 21 July 1374 (PRO, C84/31/14). Occ.(Margaret Bokland) 1380 x 1381 (Kirby, 'Clerical Poll-taxes', p. 166). D. by 6 Oct. 1395 (PRO, C84/36/18). D., lic. to el. 12 Oct. 1395 (*CPR 1388–92*, p. 632). Seal (*BM Seals*, no. 4337).

WINCHESTER (Hants), **St Mary** (Nunminster) ref. 963 (Benedictine abbey)
Lists in *VCH Hants*, II, 126; *Heads*, I, 223; D. K. Coldicott, *Hampshire Nunneries*, App. I, pp. 159–60.

Clarice 1174– N. of Wilton, app. 1174 (*Diceto*, I, 396); Occ. 20 July 1207 (BL, Add. ms. 39977, f. 251r – Baigent collection, cited Coldicott, p. 159; *Rot. Chart.*, p. 167b).

Isabel –1236 Occ. 21 Mar. 1219 (PRO, Berks F., CP25/1/7/6, no. 2); 20 Jan. 1223 (ibid., 7/8, no. 10);. *c.* 20 Jan. 1223 (*Ctl. Edington*, no. 468); 18 Mar. 1229 (*CR 1227–31*, p. 161); Mich. term 1230 (*CRR*, XIV, no. 546). D., lic. to el. 22 Feb. 1236 (*CPR 1232–47*, p. 137).

[**Natalia** Mand. to escheator to take custody of the abbey 21 Mar 1236. Natalia, whom a part of the nuns have el. is not permitted to have temp. administration (*CR 1234–37*, p. 251). Lic. to el. (no reason given for vacancy) 22 May 1236 (*CPR 1232–47*, p. 148).]

Agnes 1236–1265 (A.) prs of Wherwell, writ *de intendendo* 13 June 1236 (ibid., p. 149). D. 30 Aug. 1265 (*Ann. Winchester*, p. 102). Gt to Thomas de Rowell, king's clerk, of custody of the vacant abbey 3 Sept. 1265 (*CPR 1258–66*, p. 447).

Euphemia (Eufemia) 1265–1270 N. of Winchester, el. 11 Sept. 1265 and received by king s.d.

(*Ann. Winchester*, p. 102). Royal ass. 12 Sept. 1265 (*CPR 1258–66*, p. 449). D. 20 Nov. 1270 (*Ann. Winchester*, p. 109; *Ann. Worcs.*, p. 460).

Lucy 1270– Prs. of Winchester, royal ass. 6 Dec. 1270 (*CPR 1266–72*, p. 496). Succ. 1270 and received by king in Winchester castle 5 Dec. 1270 (*Ann. Worcs.*, p. 460; *Ann. Winchester*, p. 109). Occ. Easter 1278 (PRO, CP40/24, m. 56d).

Matilda Occ. 23 Nov. 1281 which was her 5th year of office (BL, Add. Cht. 17519). Occ. 20 May 1284, very aged *quam centenariam credimus, et adeo debilem quod raro poterit ire de camera sua ad ecclesiam* (*HMC Var. Coll.*, IV, 153). D. 14 Dec. (obit in Winchester Psalter, now at Romsey Abbey parish church, cited by Coldicott, p. 251).

Lucy Occ. 17 June 1285 (PRO, E42/481; *Mon. Seals*, p. 99).

Christi(a)na of Winchester 1288–1299 Sacrist of Winchester, royal ass. 3 Feb. 1288, temps. 12 Feb. 1288 (*CPR 1281–92*, pp. 290, 291). D. by 19 Jan. 1299 (PRO, C84/13/24). D., lic. to el. 26 Jan. 1299 (*CPR 1292–1301*, p. 393, cf. *Reg. Pontissara*, I, 182).

Agnes of Ashley (Assele, Assheley(e)) **1299–1313** N. of Winchester, eln pres. to king for royal ass. 6 Feb. 1299 (PRO, C84/13/27); royal ass. 14 Feb. 1299, temps. 16 Feb. 1299 (*CPR 1292–1301*, pp. 394, 395). D. by 31 Mar. 1313 (PRO, C84/17/15). D. (A.), lic. to el. 1 Apr. 1313 (*CPR 1307–13*, p. 559).

Matilda de Peccham (Pechham) **1313–1337** N. of Winchester, eln pres. to king for royal ass. 6 Apr. 1313 (PRO, C84/17/16); royal ass. 18 Apr. 1313, temps. 1 May 1313 (*CPR 1307–13*, pp. 561, 567). 20 Apr. citation of objectors to eln – to appear 24 Apr. Eln quashed, but bp apptd her 24 Apr. 1313; mand. for induction 8 May 1313 (*Reg. Woodlock*, I, 606–7, 610–11; PRO, C84/17/17). Complaints against abbs Matilda – cited to appear before vicar-general – citation dated 12 June 1331 (Winchester, Reg. Stratford, f. 56r); commn to examine and deal with the *comperta* against abbs Matilda in the recent visitation 4 July 1331 (ibid., f. 57v). D. by 3 Nov. 1337 (*CFR 1337–47*, p. 57). D., lic. to el. 5 Nov. 1337 (*CPR 1334–38*, p. 546).

Matilda (de) Spine (Spyne) **1337–1349** Sacrist of Winchester, royal ass. 23 Nov. 1337, temps. 12 Dec. 1337 (ibid., pp. 555, 557). Eln conf. 11 Dec. 1337 (Winchester, Reg. Orleton I, ff. 66v–67r). D. 19 May 1349 (PRO, C84/25/41). D., lic. to el. 28 May 1349 (*CPR 1348–50*, p. 297).

Margaret de Molyns (Moleyns, Molyneux) **1349–1361** N. of Winchester, eln pres. to king for royal ass. 6 June 1349 (PRO, C84/26/1); royal ass. 7 June 1349, temps. 14 June 1349 (*CPR 1348–50*, pp. 302, 304). Proclamation of eln 7 June 1349 (*Reg. Edington*, I, no. 577); eln conf. by commissaries 12 June; conf. by bp 14 June and bl. s.d. (ibid., nos. 588–93; PRO, C84/26/4). D., lic. to el. 16 Oct. 1361 (*CPR 1361–64*, p. 83).

Christiana la Wayte 1361–1365 N. of Winchester, eln pres. to king for royal ass. 29 Oct. 1361 (PRO, C84/28/14); royal ass. 3 Nov. 1361, temps. 25 Nov. 1361 (*CPR 1361–64*, pp. 100, 106). Eln examined 13 Nov.; eln. conf. and bl. 14 Nov. 1361 (*Reg. Edington*, I, nos. 1471–4). D., lic. to el. 21 July 1365 (*CPR 1364–67*, p. 160).

Alice de la Mare 1365–1385 N. of Winchester, royal ass. 28 July 1365, temps. 25 Aug. 1365 (ibid., pp. 160, 161). Commn to examine eln 28 July; eln conf. 11 Aug. 1365; bl. 17 Aug.; mand. to install 19 Aug. (*Reg. Edington*, I, nos. 1694–1701). Occ. 22 Jan. 1385 (*CPR 1385–89*, p. 113). D. 9 Feb. 1385 (PRO, C84/33/25). D., lic. to el. 12 Feb. 1385 (*CPR 1381–85*, p. 525).

WINTNEY (Hants). St Mary, St Mary Magdalene, and St John the Baptist. f. -1200 (*KH*); -1154 x 1161 (Thompson) (Cistercian priory)

Lists in *VCH Hants*, II, 151; *Heads*, I, 223–4; D. K. Coldicott, *Hampshire Nunneries*, App. I, pp. 165–6; Thompson, *Women Religious*, pp. 256–7 (to c. 1250). Obits from BL, Cotton ms. Claudius D. VIII, ff. 140v–159r).

Rose (Roisa) Occ. 26 Apr. 1219 (PRO, Hants F., CP25/1/203/4, no. 55). Obit 29 Sept. (f. 158r).

Lucy Occ. Oct. 1223 x Oct. 1224 (*London and Middlesex F.*, p. 215); 25 Oct. 1224 (PRO, F. Divers Cos. CP25/1/282/8, no. 35). Obit 20 June (f. 151v).

Sabina Occ. 16 Apr. 1228 (PRO, Hants F., CP25/1/203/5, no. 42). Obit 14 Apr. (f. 147r).

Hawisia (Avice) Occ. 14 Jan. 1236, 25 June 1248, 3 Feb. 1249 (PRO, Hants F., CP25/1/203/6, no. 32; 203/8, no. 14; 203/8, no. 65); 1248 (*Berks Eyre*, no. 576). Obit 2 Sept. (f. 156v).

Lucy Said to occ. 1254 (*VCH* without source). Occ. 24 Apr 1256, 1 July 1258 (PRO, Hants F. CP25/1/204/9, no. 88; 204/10, no. 9); 29 Apr. 1263 (*HMC Var. Coll.*, IV, 148); 6 May 1263 (Hants RO, 44M69/C2). Obit 23 Aug. (f. 155v).

Cecily (de) Banastre –1294 Occ. n.d. *c.* 1270 x 1280 (*HMC Var. Coll.*, IV, 150); 9 Feb. 1280 (PRO, Hants F., CP25/1/204/12, no. 56). Res. acc. 28 Oct. 1294 (*Reg. Pontissara*, I, 67). Obit 10 Sept. (f. 157r).

Royal mand. to constable of Odiham to relax sequestration imposed in vacancy 12 Apr. 1295 (*Reg. Pontissara*, II, 509).

Clarice de Meleburne –1301 D. before 13 May 1301 (Coldicott, p. 165, citing PRO, E368/72, m. 44). Obit 5 May (f. 148v).

Alice of Dummer (Dummere) 1301–1309 Eln conf. 30 May 1301 (*Reg. Pontissara*, I, 98). Res. by *c.* Feb./Mar. 1309 (*Reg. Woodlock*, I, 343). Appt of commissaries to aid and advise nuns on the choice of a new prs n.d. [Feb/Mar. 1309] (ibid., 343–4). Obit 21 Aug. (f. 155v).

Christina –1329 D. by 3 June 1329 (Winchester, Reg. Stratford, f. 115r). No obit but memorandum, f. 18r of martyrology (Coldicott, p. 165).

Alice of Westcot (Westcote, Wescote) 1329–1336 N. of Wintney, el. and bl. 3 June 1329 (Winchester, Reg. Stratford, f. 115r). Adm. of cess. 20 Nov. 1336 (Winchester, Reg. Orleton, I, f. 46v).

Covina de Mareys (Coumia Gervaise *sic*) 1336–1349 N. of Wintney, el. 20 Nov. 1336, bl. and install. same day (ibid.). House vacant by 7 June 1349 (*Reg. Edington*, I, no. 578, cf. ibid., no. 632 for d. of Coumia Gervaise; see also Coldicott, p. 96 and n. 21 scribal error).

Emma de Winterburn 1349– N. of Wintney, commn to examine eln 17 July 1349, eln conf. 18 July (*Reg. Edington*, I, no. 632). ? Obit 7 Jan. (f. 140v).

Alice Fyfhide (Fyshide) –1415 Had been prs about 20 years in 1405 (*CPL*, VI, 55). Res. by Mar. 1415 (Winchester, Reg. Beaufort, I, f. 50+r).

Isilia (?) and **Juliana** mentioned on the obit roll (respectively 30 Apr. (f. 148r) and 15 Aug. (f. 155r)) have not been found.

WIX (Essex), St Mary (Sopwick) f. ?1123 x 1133 (*KH*); ?1132 (Thompson) (Benedictine priory) Lists in *VCH Essex*, II, 124–5; *Heads*, I, 224; Thompson, *Women Religious*, p. 257 (to 1295).

Christina Occ. *c.* Mich. 1226 (PRO, E40/13989); early 13th cent. (PRO, E40/3357; /3529; /3706; /8897; /10767; /13686; /13702; /13705; /13717; /13745–9; /13763–5; /13833–5; /13977; /13979; /13990; /14541c–d; PRO, E42/478).

Constance Occ. Oct. 1234 x Oct. 1235 (PRO, E40/14039); 20 Jan. 1235, Trin. term 1247 (*Essex F.*, I, 98,156); Oct. 1246 x Oct. 1247 (PRO, E40/13956).

Idonea de Ruly Occ. Oct. 1250 x Oct. 1251 (PRO, E40/13673, 13676, 13682).

Basilia of Wilbraham (Welbraham) Occ. 29 Dec. 1257 (PRO, E40/3563); full name (PRO, E40/13692); n.d. (PRO, E40/13708, 13711, 13981).

Isabel of Braham Occ. Oct. 1261 x Oct. 1262 (PRO, E40/13800); 28 Oct. 1262 (PRO, E40/3350); Oct. 1268 x Oct. 1269 (*Suffolk F. (Rye)*, p. 66); (I.) Nov. 1277 x Nov. 1278 (PRO, E40/13945); 29 May 1278 (PRO, E40/3388); Nov. 1279 x Nov. 1280 (PRO, E40/13784); Nov. 1284 x Nov. 1285 (PRO, E40/13955, 13957); 1286 (PRO, E40/3374; /3547); Nov. 1290 x Nov. 1291 (PRO, E40/13952); 5 June 1295 (PRO, E40/3353).

Agnes Carbonel Occ. 8 Sept. 1303 (PRO, E40/3670); 29 Sept. 1303 (PRO, E40/3467); Nov. 1303 x Nov. 1304 (PRO, E40/13953); Nov. 1304 x Nov. 1305 (PRO, E40/13733); 23 Apr. 1306 (PRO, E40/3835).

Sarah de Bourchelle (Burghille, Burghull) Occ. 9 Jan. 1317 (PRO, E40/3544); July 1317 x July 1318 (PRO, E40/13734–5); July 1319 x July 1320 (PRO, E40/13699); 1331 (PRO, E40/3373); Jan. 1333 x Jan. 1334 (PRO, E40/13819, 13822, 13824).

Alice Marmyoun (Marmioun, Marmyon) **1338–1361** Mand. to install 10 Sept. 1338 (PRO, E40/14866). Occ. Jan. 1338 x Jan.1339 (PRO, E40/13723–4, 13727); Jan. 1351 x Jan. 1352 (PRO, E40/13804); 1356 (PRO, E40/3779); 1357 (PRO, E40/517); Jan. 1357 x Jan. 1358 (E49/13756). D. by 10 Feb. 1361 (PRO, E40/14877).

Matilda of Whelnetham 1362–1370 King's pardon for trespass for convent having sought lic. to el. from heir of earl of Northampton instead of the king 27 Jan. 1362 (*CPR 1361–64*, p. 154). N. of Wix, el. conf. 10 Feb. 1362 (PRO, E40/14877). Absolution of prs from suspension and excommunication 1368 (PRO, E40/14997). D. 12 May and bur. 13 May 1370 (*Reg. Sudbury*, I, 138).

Matilda (de) Cornerth(e) (Cornherde) **1370–** N. of Wix, patron's lic. to el. 15 May 1370; el. 20 May 1370; ass. by earl of Hereford, Essex and Northampton to her eln 21 May 1370; commn to examine eln 27 May, certif. 1 June; eln conf. by commissary 1 June 1370 (ibid., 134–42). Occ. Jan. 1373 x Jan. 1374 (PRO, E40/13920); June 1381 x June 1382 (PRO, E40/13919); 1383 (*HMC 9th Rept*, p. 38); June 1388 x June 1389 (PRO, E40/13918); 4 Feb. 1393 (PRO, E40/10232); 5 Nov. 1396 (PRO, E40/5515); 27 Nov. 1401 (PRO, E40/3941); Sept. 1410 x Sept. 1411 (PRO, E40/13806, 13810); Mar. 1413 x Mar. 1414 (PRO, E40/13913).

WORCESTER, *see* WHISTONES

WOTHORPE (Northants), St Mary (Worthorpe, Wyrethorp) f. *c.* 1160 (?), diss. 1354 (Benedictine priory)

    Lists in *VCH Northants*, II, 101; *Women Religious*, p. 257 (to 1257).

Denise de Col[. . .]ll 1224– N. of Stamford, postulated and eln. conf. 29 May 1224, no reason given for vacancy (*Reg. Wells*, II, 120).

Clarice 1244/5– N. of Wothorpe, inst. June 1244 x June 1245, no reason given for vacancy (*Reg. Grosseteste*, p. 221).

Isabel Occ. 1257 (PRO, E210/195).

Marjorie (Margery) Occ. n.d. (mid-13th cent.) (PRO, E315/42/146; E315/44/59; cf. E315/44/101, 114). Precise sequence uncertain.

Matilda de Glinton –1290 D. by 19 Apr. 1290 (*Reg. Sutton*, II, 81–2).

Isolda of Wothorpe (Wirthorp') **1290–1312** N. of Wothorpe, eln quashed but apptd by bp 19 Apr. 1290 (ibid.). D. by 15 Jan. 1313 (Lincoln, Ep. Reg., II, f. 123v).

Emma of Pinchbeck (Pyncebek) **1313–** N. of Wothorpe, eln quashed but apptd by bp 15 Jan. 1313 (ibid.).

Katherine le Chaumberleyn 1321– N. of Wothorpe, commn to examine eln 13 Oct. 1321, no reason given for vacancy (Lincoln, Ep. Reg., V, f. 296r).

Katherine of Corby –1327 Commn to receive her res. 28 July 1327 (ibid., f. 394r). ? Same as above.

Isabel of Wakerley (Wakerle) Occ. 15 Apr. 1335 (PRO, E210/1633); Jan. 1344 x Jan. 1345 (PRO, E210/6481).

Agnes (de) Bowes 1349–1354 Apptd by bp 6 Aug. 1349 on the death of the last prs (unnamed), only Agnes left, all her fellows having died (Lincoln, Ep. Reg., IX, ff. 190v–191r). Occ.

Mich. 1351 (PRO, KB27/365, m. 31); Jan. 1353 x Jan. 1354 (PRO E210/6477). Mandate to prs of Stamford, St Michael to enquire after her (described as former prs of Wothorpe), now wandering in apostasy in secular habit, and when found to punish her for her apostasy 30 July 1359 (Lincoln, Ep. Reg., VIII, f. 116r; Logan, *Runaway Religious*, pp. 72, 259).

Lic. for union of Wothorpe priory with the priory of St Michael, Stamford, 11 March 1354 (*CPR 1354–58*, pp. 27–8). Bishop's decree uniting the priories 11 June 1354 (*Reg. Ant. Lincoln*, I, no. 200). Cf. Lincoln, Ep. Reg., IX, f. 95v dated 13 July 1354 [the first version being dated the 3 ides of June, the second the 3 ides of July]

MASTERS OR WARDENS

Walter Rector of Nettleham, occ. 1257 (PRO, E210/195).

Robert 1308– Rector of Pilton, apptd 12 June 1308 (Lincoln, Ep. Reg., III, f. 137r).

Rector of Stamford, St John (unnamed) apptd as master during pleasure 15 June 1325 (Lincoln, Ep. Reg., V, f. 378r).

William de Sancto Mauro 1325– Rector of Thornhaugh, apptd as master during pleasure 25 Aug. 1325 (ibid., f. 350r)

WROXALL (Warws), St Leonard f. *c.* 1135 (?) (*KH*); ?1141 (1123 x 1153) (Thompson) (Benedictine priory)

    Lists in *VCH Warws*, II, 72–3, based on a list cited in Dugdale, *Warwickshire*, II, 649; *Records of Wroxall*, p. xxiii, *Heads*, I, 224; Thompson, *Women Religious*, p. 257 (to *c.* 1270). For an early antiquarian list see *Mon. Angl.*, IV, 89.

Matilda (Maud) Referred to as predecessor of Helen in 1221 (Stenton, *Eyre 1221–2*, no. 417).

Helen (Ellen) Occ. 1221 (ibid.); Hil. term 1229, Easter term 1229 (*CRR*, XIII, nos. 1540, 2025); 8 June 1236 (*Warws. F.*, I, no. 518).

Ida Occ. 27 Oct. 1241 (ibid., no. 593).

Avice/Amice Occ. (Avice) n. d. (late 13th cent.: pal.) (PRO, E210/216, dated *c.* 1270 *Records of Wroxall*, no. 395); (Amiscia) n.d. (late 13th cent.: pal.) (PRO, E315/35/250). Possibly there were two prioresses.

Agnes of Kinwarton (Kynewarton) –**1285** Occ. 1285 (PRO, Just.1/956, m. 4d; *Records of Wroxall*, no. 23).

Sibyl Dabetot 1285–1311 Inst. 5 Apr. 1285, no reason given for vacancy (*Reg. G. Giffard*, p. 256). Occ. 26 July 1286 (*Records of Wroxall*, no. 26; PRO, E315/46/167). Commn to receive res. 8 Nov. 1311– to res. on account of infirmity. Gt of lic. to el. (*Reg. Reynolds*, p. 27). Bur. 25 Nov. 1311 (ibid., p. 30).

Agnes of Aylesbury 1311– N. of Wroxall, Lic. to el. from Official of Worcester on d. of Sibyl; commn to conf. eln 5 Dec. 1311; eln conf. 6 Dec. 1311; mand. to install s.d. (ibid., pp. 29–30). Occ. n.d. (but after 1312 since petition mentions the suppression of the Templars) (PRO, SC8/68/3357).

Isabel de Fokeram Occ. 13 Mar. 1328 (*Records of Wroxall*, no. 44); 2 Oct. 1328 (PRO, E326/5500).

Agnes de Broy (Broi) –**1339** Occ. *c.* Feb. 1339 (*Worcs Reg. Sede Vacante*, pp. 275, 277). Res. by 25 Oct. 1339 (*Reg. Bransford*, no. 279).

Isabel de Fokerham (Fokeram) **1339–1352** N. of Wroxall, appt by bp and mand. to install 25 Oct. 1339 (ibid., nos. 279–81). 13 May 1352 Isabel begs permission to res. on account of age and infirmity; res. acc. and lic. to supervise the eln of a successor (Worcester, Reg. Thoresby, pp. 90, 105).

Alice de Clynton –**1356** Res. 2 July 1356 (Worcester, Reg. Brian I, p. 37).

Joan Russell 1356– N. of Wroxall, apptd 2 July 1356 (ibid.).

Horabilis (Orabilla) of Aylesbury (Aillesbury, Ayllesbury) **1361–** N. of Wroxall, eln quashed, but apptd by bp 19 Aug. 1361, no reason given for vacancy (Worcester, Reg. Brian I, p. 72). Occ. 17 Feb. 1365 (PRO, E315/35/250; *Records of Wroxall*, no. 72).

Katherine Beauchamp Occ. 5 June 1375 (*Records of Wroxall*, no. 78).

The next recorded prs, **Katherine Eymore**, occ. 1379 (PRO, E179/58/11, m. 1d) and **Beatrice**, occ. 11 Apr. 1398 (PRO, E315/47/109; *Records of Wroxall*, no. 89).

WYKEHAM (Yorks. N.) St Mary and St Michael f. *c.* 1153 (Cistercian priory)

Lists in *VCH Yorks*, III, 184; *Heads*, I, 224; Thompson, *Women Religious*, p. 257 (to 1234).

Eva Occ. 18 Nov. 1234, 7 Dec. 1234 (*Yorks F., 1232–46*, pp. 14, 27); 1235 fine (Baildon, I, 228, but prob. 1234).

Alice Occ. n.d. (? mid-13th cent., ment. of Peter de Percy and Alan Buscell) (Bodl., Dodsworth ms. 7, f. 293r).

Emma of Dunston (Duffeld) **1286–1300** Eln conf. 8 Aug. 1286 (*Reg. Romeyn*, I, p. 158, no. 438). Commn to admit cess. (Duffeld) 3 Dec. 1300 (*Reg. Corbridge*, I, 120).

Isabel Occ. 12 Nov. 1307 (Bodl., ms. Top. Yorks e 7, ff. 168v–169r, but cf. ibid. f. 127r–v, where dated 12 Nov. 1337); 20 June 1321 (York, Reg. 9A, f. 242r); n.d. (1st half of 14th cent.) (Bodl., Dodsworth ms. 7, f. 297r).

Isabel Occ. Hil. 1388 (Baildon, I, 228).[19]

MASTERS

Simon Occ. 1203 x 1214 (*HMC 10th Report*, app. IV, 321–2).

H. n. d. (Bodl., ms. Top. Yorks e 7, f. 166v).

T. n. d. (Bodl., ms. Top. Yorks e 9, f. 47v).

Walter of Harpham Occ. as rector of the house 1233 (i.e. 25 Mar. 1234 to 24 Mar. 1235) (Bodl., Dodsworth ms. 7, f. 293r). Occ. as rector of the house of Yedingham 1239 (Bodl., ms. Top. Yorks e 9, f. 44r).

YEDINGHAM (Little Mareis) (Yorks E.), St Mary f. –1163 (*KH*); –1158 (Thompson) (Benedictine priory)

Lists in *VCH Yorks*, III, 128–9; *Heads*, I, 224; Thompson, *Religious Women*, pp. 257–8 (to 1241).

Christina Occ. 12th or 13th cent. (BL, Cotton ms. Claudius D XI, f. 171r – mid-13th cent. ctl.; Bodl., Dodsworth ms. 95, f. 33r).

Sibyl Occ. 3 Feb. 1219 (*Yorks F. 1218–31*, p. 18).

Emma of Humbleton Occ. 1238 (Bodl., Dodsworth ms. 95, f. 33v); Apr. 1239 (Bodl., ms. Top. Yorks e. 9, f. 44r); 1241 (*Reg. Gray*, p. 90n citing Burton, *Mon. Ebor.*, 286; Bodl., ms. Top. Yorks e. 9, f. 76v); 1251 (Bodl., Dodsworth ms. 7, f. 183r).

Gundreda Occ. 8 July 1280 (*Yorks F. 1272–1300*, p. 48); n.d. (Bodl., ms. Top. Yorks e. 8, f. 171r and e. 9, f. 44r).

Margaret de Scard' (? Scarborough) Occ. Mich. 1290 – Mich. 1292 (Baildon, I, 229); n.d. (after 1291) (Bodl., ms. Top. Yorks e. 7, f. 131r).

Alice of Pickering (Pykeringe) Occ. Hil. 1300 – Easter 1301 (Baildon, I, 229–30). 1 Feb. 1322 (Bodl., ms. Top. Yorks e. 7, f. 116v); 2 June 1325 (Bodl., Dodsworth ms. 7, f. 189r – the only source to give her surname, but cf. below). Said to have died 1331 (*Mon. Angl.*, IV, 274 – based on Burton, *Mon. Ebor.*, p. 287, no source given).

Alice Occ. Mar. 1336 (PRO, E303/26/1063); if the 1331 date is unsubstantiated, ? the same as the above.

Margaret of Lutton –1345 Occ. 3 Feb. 1344 (PRO, E303/26/1073). Lic. to el. 12 May 1345, priory vacant by her death (York, Reg. 10, f. 157v).

---

[19] Elizabeth Edmundson is listed as prs by Baildon, I, 228 without date or reference.

On 21 Jan. 1349 the unnamed prs was identified as the daughter of Agnes de Percy (Percehay), widow of Sir Walter Percy, knight (*Test. Ebor.*, I, 53–4).

Alice of Pickering (Pykering, Pykeryng) Occ. 12 May 1352 (PRO, E303/26/1075); n.d. (between entries for 17 and 22 Sept. 1352) (*BIB*, I, p.80, no.33); 13 Nov. 1352 (PRO, E303/26/1064); 1353 (Bodl., Dodsworth ms. 95, f. 38r); 1358 (PRO, E303/26/1080); 1367 (Baildon, I, 230); 1368 (Bodl., ms. Top. Yorks e. 7, f. 117r–v; Dodsworth ms. 94, f. 128r; Dodsworth ms. 95, f. 33r); 24 June 1372 (PRO, E303/26/11076); 17 Jan. 1373 (PRO, E303/26/1067).

The next recorded prs, **Margaret of Ulrome** (Ulram, Wlram), occ. 13 June 1392 (PRO, E303/26/1092); commn to receive res. 4 Feb. 1406 (York, Reg. 5A, ff. 276v–277r).

MASTERS

Andrew Pr. of Kirkham (cf. *Heads*, I, 168), master of Yedingham, occ. *c.*1200 x 1219 (*EYC*, I, no. 390); early 13th cent. (Bodl., ms. Top. Yorks e. 7, f. 118v).

Walter of Harpham Occ. as rector of the house with prs Emma of Humbleton April 1239 (Bodl., ms. Top. Yorks e. 9, f. 44r). Master of Wykeham priory (q.v.).

Robert de Brus of Pickering Apptd as *custos* 1 Mar. 1280 (*Reg. Wickwane*, p. 58, no. 188).

YORK, St Clement (Clementhorpe) f. *c.* 1125 x 1133 (R.B. Dobson & S. Donaghey, *The History of Clementhorpe Nunnery* (York, 1984), pp. 9–11; *EEA*, 5, no. 74). (Benedictine priory) Lists in *VCH Yorks*, III, 130–1; *Heads*, I, 224; Thompson, *Women Religious*, p. 258 (to 1268).

Alice Occ. 1192 (*Gesta Henrici II*, II, 240).

Ascelina Occ. 20 Oct. 1221 (*Yorks F., 1218–31*, p. 40)

A. Occ. *c.* 1230 x 1235 (*Ctl. Healaugh Park*, p. 179, cf. p. 195). Could be either Ascelina or Agnes.

Agnes Occ. 26 Nov. 1234 (*Yorks F., 1232–46*, pp. 16–17); 1235, possibly 1234 (Baildon, I, 235); n.d. (1233 x 1239) (Bodl. ms. Top. Yorks e. 8, f. 146r); 1246 (PRO, Just.1/1045, m. 44d).

Margaret Occ. 10 June 1268 (*Yorks F., 1246–72*, p. 146); Dec. 1272 (*York Vicars Choral Chts.*, no. 9); Easter 1278 (Baildon, I, 235); n.d. (*temp.* Archbp Giffard 1266 x 1279) (BL, Lansdowne ms. 402, f. 100v).

Agnes de Wyten Occ. 3 Nov. 1279 (*Yorks F., 1272–1300*, p. 18); 1280 (*Mon. Angl.*, IV, 324); 10 Aug. 1284 (Bodl., ms. Top. Yorks e. 7, ff. 44v–45r).

Alice Occ. Mich. 1299 (Baildon, I, 235).

Constance Basy 1315– Eln conf. and apptd 28 Aug. 1315, no reason given for vacancy (*Reg. Greenfield*, II, p. 222, no. 1131).

Agnes of Methley (Methelay, Metheley) **1316–1324** Double election of Agnes of Methley and Beatrice of Brandsby, nuns of St Clement; elns quashed and archbp of York apptd Agnes, no reason given for vacancy 26 July 1316 (ibid., V, p. 249, no. 2802). Cess. by 23 July 1324, lic. to el. a new prs (York, Reg. 9A, f. 199v).

Alice of Pakenham (Pakenam) D. by 26 Oct. 1396 (York, Reg. 14, f. 60r).

INDEX OF HEADS

This index is solely a list of heads, the information being kept to a minimum for convenience in use. Where possible the heads are indexed by surname. When this is not possible the order within Christian names places abbots and abbesses before priors and prioresses. Individuals who held more than one office are brought together in one entry, but where there is no precise evidence for identifying persons of the same name as a single individual the entries are kept separate.

A., abb. Abbey Cwmhir, 258
A., abb. Bardsey, 329
A., abb. Basingwerk, 259
A., abb. Grace Dieu, 283
A., abb. Hulton, 285
A., abbs-el. Shaftesbury, 605 n.14
A., pr. Canons Ashby, 356
A., pr. Cockerham, 369
A. (Alan?) pr. Exeter, St Nicholas, 101
A., pr. Gloucester, St Oswald, 381
A., pr. Ware, 205
A., prs Aconbury, 537
A., prs Bungay, 546
A., prs Lambley, 578
A., prs Little Marlow, 581
A., prs York, St Clement, 626
Abbeville, Peter de, pr. Lenton, 233
Abbot, Robert, pr. Upavon, 205
Abbotsley, Isabel of, prs Swaffham Bulbeck, 613
Abbotsley, William of, abb. Bourne, 341
Abell, John, master Farne, 102; master Jarrow, 115
Aberford, Henry of, pr. Nostell, 439
Abifago, Hugh de, pr. Avebury, 144
Abingdon, Alice of, prs Littlemore, 582
Abingdon, John of, abb. Missenden, 425
Abingdon, John of, pr. Christchurch (Twynham), 366
Abingdon, Margery of, prs Catesby, 551
Abraham, abb. Neath, 295
Abraham, pr. Kidwelly, 115
Absalom, pr. Torksey, 473
Absolom, abb. Walden, 77
Absolon, pr. Cartmel, 361
Acaster, John of, pr. Rumburgh, 125
Acclome, Laurence de [Furness], 281
Acey(o), John de, pr. Lapley, 172
Acharius, pr. Norton, 437
Acholt, William de, abb. Ramsey, 59
Acilla, prs Foukeholme, 562
Acius, abb. Beaulieu, 260
Acle, William of, pr. Hoxne, 112

Acle, William of, pr. Weybridge, 484
Acra, Robert, pr. Tickhill, 131
Acre, Henry of, pr. Westacre, 483
Acre, John of, pr. Castle Acre, 224
Acre, John of, pr. Westacre, 483
Acre, Roger of, pr. Wymondham, 136
Acton, John (de), abb. Bordesley, 265
Actune, Eleanor de, prs Buckland, 546
Acum, Thomas de, pr. Breedon, 345
Adam II, abb. Abbey Dore, 258
Adam, abb. Bardsey, 329
Adam, abb. Blanchland, 480
Adam, abb. Buildwas, 269
Adam, abb. Byland, 270
Adam, abb. Chertsey, 32
Adam, abb. Combermere, 274
Adam, abb. Croxton Kerrial, 498
Adam, abb. Dieulacres, 276
Adam, abb. Eynsham, 43
Adam, abb. Forde (1240–), 278
Adam, abb. Forde (1354–), 279
Adam, abb. Fountains, 280
Adam, abb. Garendon, 282
Adam, abb. Hailes, 284
Adam, abb. Keynsham, 400
Adam, abb. Kirkstall, 288
Adam, abb. Medmenham, 294
Adam, abb. Missenden, 424
Adam, abb. Newminster, 298
Adam, abb. Robertsbridge, 304
Adam, abb. Roche, 305
Adam, abb. Sallay, 307
Adam, abb. Sawtry, 307
Adam II, abb. Shrewsbury, 70
Adam III, abb.-el. Shrewsbury, 70
Adam, abb. Tilty, 316
Adam, abb. Titchfield, 511
Adam, abb. Valle Crucis, 318
Adam, abb. Warden, 320
Adam, abb. Waverley, 320
Adam II, abb. Waverley, 320

Adam, abb. Wigmore, 485
Adam, master Legbourne, 580
Adam, master Nun Cotham (occ. 1239 x 41), 593
Adam, master Nun Cotham (1269–), 593
Adam, pr. Arbury, 328
Adam, pr. Bentley, 333
Adam, pr. Binham, 93
Adam, pr. Blythburgh, 338
Adam, pr. Bolton, 340
Adam, pr. Burwell, 149
Adam, pr. Butley, 353
Adam, pr. Canons Ashby, 357
Adam, pr. Castle Acre, 224
Adam, pr. Chipley, 364
Adam, pr. Clifford, 225
Adam, pr. Cold Norton, 370
Adam, pr. Drax, 376
Adam, pr. Ewyas Harold, 100
Adam, pr. Hastings, 386
Adam, pr. Hatfield Peverel, 107
Adam, pr. Haugham, 166
Adam, pr. Hinton, 325
Adam, pr. Holme East, 229
Adam, pr. Hurley, 113
Adam, pr. Ixworth, 397
Adam, pr. Kings Lynn, 116
Adam, pr. Llanthony Prima, 413
Adam, pr. Malton, 524
Adam, pr. Mattersey, 526
Adam, pr. Monk Bretton, 236
Adam, pr. Monks Horton, 236
Adam, pr. Much Wenlock, 242 n.5
Adam, pr. North Ormsby, 526
Adam, pr. Reigate, 451
Adam, pr. Sempringham, 528
Adam, pr. Studley, 465
Adam, pr. Tandridge, 466
Adam, pr. York, St Andrew, 531
Adderbury, William of, pr. Wroxton, 489
Adelina, prs Kilburn, 575
Adelwoldestona, Isabel de, prs Langley, 578
Admiranda, prs Little Marlow, 581
Aette, Gilbert de, pr. Merton, 422
Agatha, prs Arden, 539
Agatha, prs Lyminster, 585
Agnes, abbs Chatteris, 553
Agnes, abbs Lacock, 577
Agnes, abbs Winchester, 620
Agnes, prs Brewood White Ladies, 544
Agnes, prs Bristol, St Mary Magdalen, 544
Agnes, prs Castle Hedingham (occ. c. 1230 x 48), 551

Agnes, prs Castle Hedingham (occ. 1340), 551
Agnes, prs Castle Hedingham (occ. 1381), 551
Agnes, prs Cheshunt, 554
Agnes, prs Crabhouse, 556
Agnes, prs Esholt, 559
Agnes, prs Flamstead, 560
Agnes, prs Greenfield, 566
Agnes, prs Handale, 568
Agnes, prs Harrold (–1245/6), 569
Agnes, prs Harrold (occ. 1334), 569
Agnes, prs Holystone, 572
Agnes, prs Kilburn (occ. 1301 x 2), 575
Agnes, prs Kilburn (occ. 1345), 575
Agnes, prs London, Haliwell, 583
Agnes, prs Lyminster, 585
Agnes, prs Minster in Sheppey, 588
Agnes, prs Newcastle-upon-Tyne (occ. ante 1242/3), 589
Agnes, prs Newcastle-upon-Tyne (occ. 1334 x 40), 589
Agnes, prs Nun Monkton, 594
Agnes, prs Rothwell, 602
Agnes, prs Swaffham Bulbeck, 613
Agnes, prs Thetford, St George, 615
Agnes, prs Wallingwells, 616
Agnes, prs Wilberfoss (occ. 1260), 619
Agnes, prs Wilberfoss (occ. 1396), 619
Agnes, prs York, St Clement, 626
Aiguel, William, pr. London, Holy Trinity, Aldgate, 416
Airaines, William de, pr. St Clears, 249
Aislaby, Sibyl of, prs Marrick, 588
Ake, Alan de, abb. Louth Park, 291
Akeden, Roger de, abb. Newminster, 298
Akenham, Robert of, pr. Kersey, 400
Alan, abb. Boxley, 265
Alan, abb. Chertsey, 32
Alan, abb. Hagnaby, 503
Alan, abb. Leiston, 507
Alan, abb. Lessness, 409
Alan, abb. Lilleshall, 410
Alan, abb. Newhouse, 508
Alan, abb. Robertsbridge, 303
Alan, abb. Roche, 304
Alan, pr. Brinkburn (occ. c. 1243 x 57), 347
Alan, pr. Carlisle, 360
Alan, pr. Chicksands, 521
Alan, pr. Drax, 375
Alan, pr. Ecclesfield, 157
Alan, pr. Ellerton on Spalding Moor, 522
Alan, pr. Exeter, St Nicholas, 101
Alan, pr. Felixstowe, 102

Alan, pr. Hamble, 164
Alan, pr. Haverholme, 523
Alan, pr. Hickling, 392
Alan, pr. Linton and Isleham, 174
Alan, pr. Markby, 419
Alan, pr. Newstead-on-Ancholme, 526
Alan, pr. Nocton Park (occ. 1205 x 6), 433
Alan, pr. Sempringham, 528
Alan, pr. Sixhills, 530
Alan, pr. Southwark, 460
Alan, pr. Stansgate, 251
Alan, pr. Trentham, 475
Alan, pr. Walsingham, 477
Alard, abb. Sawtry, 307
Alard, pr. St Denys, 454
Alba Malla, Stephen de, pr. Cogges, 152
Albert, pr. Lewes, 233
Albigneye, William de, pr. Ellingham, 159
Albin, pr. Arbury, 328
Albo Dyoto, Richard de, pr. Otterton, 186
Albreda, abbs Chatteris, 553
Albreda, prs Oldbury, 597
Albricus, ?pr. Livers Ocle, 175
Albrighton, Robert of, abb. Alcester, 19
Alcester, Agnes of, prs Cook Hill, 555
Alconbury, Geoffrey of, pr. Merton, 423
Aldborough, Robert of, pr. Kirkham, 401
Aldborough, William of, abb. Coverham, 497
Aldeburg, Ralph de, abb. Jervaulx, 286
Aldeby, John of, abb. Sibton, 309
Alderley, Alice of, prs Chester, 554
Aldewod(e), Robert de, pr. Brinkburn, 347
Aldgate, Nicholas of, alias of London, pr. London,
    Holy Trinity, Aldgate, 416
Aldham, John of, pr. Bilsington, 337
Aldinge, Peter de, pr. Monks Horton, 236
Aldith, prs Brewood White Ladies, 544
Alelm, pr. Daventry, 226
Alench', John de, pr. Lancaster, 171
Alencon, John of, ?pr. Atherington, 143
Alencon, Robert d', pr. Castle Acre, 223
Alenzun, Robert de, pr. Westacre, 483
Alexander, abb. Beeleigh, 480
Alexander, abb. Boxley, 265
Alexander, abb. Canterbury, St Augustine, 28
Alexander, abb. Fountains, 280
Alexander, abb. Haughmond, 387
Alexander, abb. Selby (1214–21), 66
Alexander, abb. Selby (1237–45), 67
Alexander, abb. Sibton, 308
Alexander, abb-el. Wardon, 320
Alexander, pr. Alvingham, 519

Alexander, pr. Arbury, 328
Alexander, pr. Bromfield, 94
Alexander, pr. Caldwell, 354
Alexander, pr. Freiston, 105
Alexander, pr. Hastings, 387
Alexander, pr. Kings Lynn, 116
Alexander, pr. Marlborough, 525
Alexander, pr. Southwark, 460
Alexander, pr. Stansgate, 251
Alexander, pr. Stonely, 464
Alexander, pr. Wolston, 214
Alfred, abb. Tavistock, 72
Alfred, pr. Gloucester, St Oswald, 381
Alfred, pr. Ranton, 450
Algarkirk, Robert of, abb. Louth Park, 291
Algia, Geoffrey de, pr. Tregoney, 475
Alice, abbs Lacock, 577
Alice, abbs Wilton (1228–?37), 619
Alice, abbs Wilton (1237–?52), 619
Alice, prs Amesbury, 538
Alice, prs Ankerwyke, 539
Alice, ?prs Arden, 539
Alice, prs Barrow Gurney, 542
Alice, prs Blackborough, 543
Alice, prs Blithbury, 544
Alice, prs Buckland, 546
Alice, prs Bungay, 546
Alice, prs Cambridge, St Mary and St Radegund,
    548
Alice, prs Campsey Ash, 549
Alice, prs Cheshunt, 554
Alice, prs Chester, 554
Alice, prs Cook Hill, 555
Alice, prs Davington, 556
Alice, prs Easebourne, 557
Alice, prs Ellerton-in-Swaledale, 557
Alice, prs Esholt, 559
Alice, prs Flamstead, 560
Alice, prs Goring, 564
Alice, prs Grimsby, 567
Alice, prs Hampole, 567
Alice, prs Haverholme, 523
Alice, prs Higham, 571
Alice, prs Ivinghoe, 574
Alice, prs Keldholme, 575
Alice, prs Kington St Michael, 576
Alice, prs Little Marlow, 581
Alice, prs London, Clerkenwell, 582
Alice, prs London, Haliwell, 584
Alice, prs Marrick, 587
Alice, prs Nun Appleton, 592
Alice, prs Nun Cotham, 593

Alice, prs Nunburnholme, 595
Alice, prs Sewardsley, 604
Alice, prs Stratford-at-Bow, 612
Alice, prs Swaffham Bulbeck, 613
Alice, prs Thicket, 615
Alice, prs Westwood, 616
Alice, prs Wykeham, 625
Alice, prs Yedingham, 625
Alice, prs York, St Clement (occ. 1192), 626
Alice, prs York, St Clement (occ. 1299), 626
Aling, Peter, abb. Fountains, 280
Alkmundbury, John, pr. St Ives, 128
Alkrington, Richard de, abb. Stoneleigh, 311
Allerton, Adam of, master Bamburgh, 329
Allerton, William of, abb. Fountains, 280
Allerton, William of, minister Oxford, Holy
    Trinity, 534
Allerton, William of, pr. Newstead (in Sherwood),
    432
Allington, Henry of, abb. Wellow, 482
Almoner, John the, pr. Spalding, 193
Alnele (?Alvele), John, pr. Blythburgh, 338
Alneto, Henry (Hervey) de, pr. Hinckley, 168
Alneto, William de, pr. Tickford, 200
Alneyo, John de, pr. Pembroke, 187
Alnmouth, William of, abb. Alnwick, 491
Alnwick, John of, abb. Alnwick, 491
Alresford, Nicholas of, archpriest or pr. Barton, 331
Alsop, William de, abb. Darley, 373
Alston, Henry of, abb. Shrewsbury, 70
Alta Ripa, Margaret de, prs Wilberfoss, 619
Altaribus, Peter de, pr. Wootton Warren, 214
Aluinus, pr. St Michael's Mount, 189
Alverthorpe, Alice of, prs Thicket, 615
Alverton, Robert de, abb. Kirkstead, 290
Alverton, Thomas de, abb. Jervaulx, 286
Alvred, pr. St Germans, 455; see also Alfred
Alwinton, Simon of, ?master Farne, 102
Amabel, prs Brewood Black Ladies (occ. 1236), 544
Amabel, prs Brewood Black Ladies (occ. 1272), 544
Amabel, prs Catesby, 551
Amabel, prs Nun Monkton (occ. 1240), 594
Amabel, prs Nun Monkton (occ. 1351), 595
Amabel, prs Stamford, St Mary and St Michael,
    608
Amabilia, see Amabel
Ambr', Nicholas de, pr. Grovebury, 163
Ambrose, pr. Hamble, 164
Ambrose, pr. Nostell, 438
Amcotes, Nicholas, abb. Notley, 441
Amersham, John of, pr. Newnham, 430
Amesbury, Michael of, abb. Glastonbury, 46

Amesbury, William of, pr. Amesbury, 538
Amfred, pr. Burwell, 149
Amice, abbs Chatteris, 553
Amice, prs Brewood White Ladies, 544
Amice, prs Castle Hedingham, 551
Amice, prs Catesby, 551
Amice, prs Harrold, 569
Amice, prs Kington St Michael, 576
Amice, prs Littlemore, 581
Amice, prs Pinley, 598
Amice, prs Sopwell, 607
Amice, prs Westwood, 616
Amice, prs Wroxall, 624
Amisus, pr. Woodbridge, 486
Amphelisa, prs Higham, 571
Ampney, Nicholas (of), abb. Cirencester, 368
Amwell, Henry of, abb. Waltham, 478
Amys, Richard, pr. Stogursey, 195
Anais son of Goroun, pr. Penmon, 446
Anastasia, prs Cornworthy, 555
Anastasia, prs London Haliwell, 584
Ancaster, William of, pr. Malton, 524
Andreas, Miletus, pr. Minster, 176
Andrew, abb. Beeleigh (occ. 1265), 494
Andrew, abb. Beeleigh (occ. 1272 x 80), 495
Andrew, abb. Garendon, 282
Andrew, abb. Kingswood, 287
Andrew, abb. Quarr, 300
Andrew, abb. St Dogmells, 189
Andrew, abb. Walden, 77
Andrew, master Yedingham (pr. Kirkham), 626
Andrew, pr. Bicknacre, 335
Andrew, pr. Carisbrooke, 150
Andrew, pr. Deerhurst, 155
Andrew, pr. Holy Island, 110
Andrew, pr. Kirkham, 401, 626
Andrew, pr. Maiden Bradley, 418
Andrew, pr. Mullicourt, 55
Andrew, pr. Newent, 182
Andrew, pr. Norton, 437
Andrew, pr. Thornholme, 468
Andrew, pr. Tywardreath, 204
Andrew, pr. Winchester, St Swithun, 83
Aneslevilla, Peter de, see Textor, Peter
Angele, William le, pr. St Denys, 455
Angers, John of, pr. Monks Kirby, 181
Angerus, abb. West Dereham, 516
Anglica Villa, John de, pr. Steventon, 194
Anglicus, Nicholas, pr. Blyth, 146
Anian, abb. Conway, 274
Anian, abb. Llantarnam, 290
Anian ap Meredith, abb. Valle Crucis, 318

Anketil, Richard, pr. Stratfield Saye, 197

Anlaby, Josiana of, prs Swine, 613

Anne, abbs Tarrant Kaines, 615

Anne, prs Hinchingbrooke, 572

Anne, prs London, Haliwell, 584

Anne, prs Newcastle-upon-Tyne, 590

Anneys, prs Whistones, 618

Anno, Walter de, pr. Bath, 21

Anota, prs Chester, 554

Ansketil, pr. Boxgrove, 146

Anthony, pr. Plympton, 447

Anvers, Matilda de, prs Little Marlow, 581

Apeltone, Robert de, *custos* Wilberfoss, 619

Appelby, Roger, pr. Hereford, 109

Appelby, Roger, pr. Nuneaton, 597
    see also Appleby

Appelderfeld, Lucy de, prs Davington, 556

Appeleigh, Walter de, pr. Cranborne, 96

Appleby (Appelby):

    Appleby, Adam of, pr. Chacombe, 362

    Appleby, Katherine of, abbs Polesworth, 598

    Appleby, Margery of, abbs Polesworth, 598

    Appleby, Peter of, pr. Bridlington, 346

    Appleby, William of, master Stainfield, 608

    Appleby, William of, pr. Monk Bretton, 53
        see also Appelby

Appleford, Henry of, abb. Reading, 61

Appleford, John of, abb. Reading, 61

Appleford, William, pr. Poughley, 449

Applegarth, Sabina of, prs Moxby, 588

Appleton, Richard of, pr. Rumburgh, 126

Appleton, Thomas of, pr. Hexham, 391

Appletree, Richard II of, abb. Osney, 441

Aqua Partita, John de, pr. Stoke by Clare, 196

Aquila, John de, pr. Wilsford, 213

Aquila, William de, pr. Hinckley, 168

Aquitaine, *see* Monte Ardito, Peter de

Archebaud, Laurence, pr. Monkton Farleigh, 238

Arcubus, Robert de, pr. Dover, 97

Arcubus, Robert de, pr. Leominster, 117

Arcy, Robert d', pr. Northampton, St Andrew, 244

Ardembourgh, Giles de, pr. Throwley, 199

Ardene, Elizabeth de, prs Sempringham, 529

Ardern, Amice de, prs Hinchingbrooke, 572

Arena, William de, pr. Hinckley, 168

Arenis, William de, pr. Exeter, St James, 228

Argenciis, Roger de, pr. Brimpsfield, 147

Argenteles, Emery de, pr. Lancaster, 171

Arlato, Guy de, pr. Lenton, 232

Arleston, John of, abb. Wigmore, 485

A(r)miger *alias* Le Squyer, Gervase, bailiff of
    Atherington, 144

Arnauld de Calhauet, William, pr. Burwell, 149

Arncliffe, Hugh of, *custos* Newcastle-upon-Tyne,
    590

Arniburgh, John (de), pr. Royston, 454

Arnold, pr. Derby, St James, 226

Arnold, pr. Kyme, 402

Arnold, pr. Lewisham, 173

Arnold, pr.-el. Nocton Park, 434

Arnold, pr. Titley, 201

Arnulf, pr. Northampton, St Andrew, 244

Arnulphi, Philip, pr. Warminghurst, 208

Arundel, Adam of, abb. Quarr, 300

Ascelin, pr. Blyth, 145

Ascelina, abbs Wilton, 619

Ascelina, prs York, St Clement, 626

Ascellis, Simon de, pr. Barnwell, 330

Ashbourne, William of, abb. Croxden, 275

Ashby, Joan (of), prs Catesby, 552

Ashby, Peter of, pr. Daventry, 226

Ashby, Richard of, abb. Croxden, 276

Ashby, Robert of, abb. Lilleshall, 411

Ashby, Robert of, pr. Canons Ashby, 357
    see also Assheby

Ashfield, Agnes, abbs Chatteris, 553

Ashley, Agnes of, abbs Winchester, 621

Ashwell, John of, pr. Gloucester, St Oswald, 382

Ashwell, William of, pr. Llanthony Secunda, 414

Aske, Alina of, prs Marrick, 587

Askeby, Juliana de, prs Legbourne, 580

Aslaby, Margaret, prs Keldholme, 575

Aslackby, Richard of, pr. Finchale, 103

Aslackby, Roger of, pr. Rumburgh, 126

Aslackby I, William of, abb. Selby, 67

Aslackby II, William of, abb. Selby, 67

Aslackby, William of, pr. Lytham, 120

Aslockton, William of, abb. Welbeck, 515

Aspley, Nicholas of, pr. Stafford, 462–3

Assh, John de, abb. North Creake, 435

Asshe, Ralph de, abb. Bristol, St Augustine, 349

Assheby, Isabel de, prs Markyate, 587
    see also Ashby

Astley, Henry of, abb. Haughmond, 387

Astley, Robert of, pr. Kenilworth, 398

Aston, John of, abb. Roche, 305

Aston, Margery of, abbs Burnham, 547

Aston, Ralph of, rector Ashridge, 535

Aston, Ralph of (another), rector Ashridge, 535

Aston, Roger of, pr. Church Gresley, 367

Aston, Walter of, abb. Rocester, 453

Aston, William (of), abb. Stoneleigh, 312

Aston, William of, pr. Dodford, 374

Astwick, John of, pr. Newnham, 430

Aswardby, Adam of, abb. Bardney, 20

Athelyngton(e), John de, pr. Woodbridge, 486

Atherstone, Robert of, abb. Combe, 273; abb. Stoneleigh, 311

Atrio, William de, pr. Astley, 143

Atteberge, John de, pr. Stone, 464

Attechapelle, Henry, pr. Wilkeswood, 536

Attewell, John, pr. Charley, 363

Aubel, William, pr. Ravenstone, 451

Aubery, Maurice, pr. Monks Kirby, 181

Aubrey, prs Ellerton-in-Swaledale, 557

Aubrey, prs London, Haliwell, 584

Aubrey, prs Rosedale, 601

Aubry, William, pr. Ipswich, Holy Trinity, 395

Aubyn, Hugh, pr. York, Holy Trinity, 217

Aubyn, Philip de (Obyn), *alias* of Worcester, pr. Worcester, 85

Aucher, Margaret, abbs Shaftesbury, 606

Aucher, Sibyl, abbs Wilton, 620

Audley, Idonea of, abbs Burnham, 547

Audreia, Richard de, pr. Hinckley, 168

Aufri, Michael, pr. Hinckley, 169

Augens, Walter de, abb.-el. Notley, 440

Auger, abb. North Creake, 434

Auger, pr. Exeter, St James, 228

Auger, pr. St Germans, 455

Auger, William, pr. Chepstow, 151

Aughton, Adam of, pr. York, St Andrew, 531

Augo, Richard de, pr. Llangennith, 175

Augustine, abb. Lavendon, 506

Augustine, abb. Quarr, 300

Augustine, pr. Conishead, 371

Augustine, pr. Great Bricett, 383

Augustine, pr.-el. Newstead (in Sherwood), 431

Aumeney, Simon de, abb. Malmesbury, 51

Auncel(le), Richard, pr. Scilly, 128

Auncel(l), Thomas, pr. Wilmington, 211

Aunger, Margaret, abbs Canonsleigh, 550

Aungle, John, minister Knaresborough, 533

Auricia, prs-el. Stamford, St Mary and St Michael, 609

Austwick, Stephen of, pr. Lincoln, St Mary Magdalen, 118

Austwick, Stephen of, pr. Rumburgh, 126

Austwick, Stephen of, pr. St Bees, 127

Avalon, Robert de, pr. Wilmington, 211

Avelina, ?prs Blackborough, 543

Avelina, prs Polsloe, 599

Aveneye, Simon de, pr. Pilton, 124

Avenis, Nicholas, pr. Creeting, 154

Avenis, Nicholas, pr. Everdon, 159

Averham, Agatha of, prs Nuneaton, 596

Avernaz, William de (le), pr. Prittlewell, 248

Avice, prs Gokewell, 564

Avice, prs Handale, 568

Avice, prs London, Haliwell, 583

Avice, prs Nun Keeling, 594

Avice, prs Nun Monkton, 594

Avice, prs Wroxall, 624

Avignon, John of, pr. Lewes, 234; *see also* Chartres; Thifford; Tickford

Avyroun, John de, pr. Wootton Wawen, 215

Axebrugge, Richard, pr. Longleat, 418

Aycliffe, John of, master Monkwearmouth, 122; pr. Oxford, Durham cell, 123

Aylesbury, Agnes of, prs Wroxall, 624

Aylesbury, Horabilis (Orabilla) of, prs Wroxall, 624

Aylesbury, John of, *custos* Catesby, 552

Aylesbury, John of, rector Edington, 535

Aylesbury, Roger of, abb. Missenden, 424

Aylesby, Alice of, prs Grimsby, 567

Aylesford, Henry of, abb. Battle, 22

Aylsham, John of, abb. St Benet of Hulme, 65

Aylsham, Robert of, abb. St Benet of Hulme, 65

Aymo, pr. St Helen's, 250

see also Hamo

Aymo (Hamo), pr. Thetford, St Mary, 251

Aystun, Walter de, abb. Winchester, Hyde, 81

B., abb. Netley, 296 n.17

B., ?abb. Sallay, 306 n.32

B., pr. Catley, 520

B., prs Usk, 616

B., prs Westwood, 616

Babraham, John of, abb. Waltham, 479

Bacon, John, pr. Fineshade, 380

Bacun, John, pr. London, St Bartholomew, 417

Bade, Amphelisa de, abbs Godstow, 562

Baderum, Richard, pr. Titley, 201

Badlesmere, Elizabeth de, abbs Malling, 586

Badlesmere, Joan de, prs Minster in Sheppey, 588

Badminton, William of, abb. Malmesbury, 51

Bages, Oliver de, pr. York, Holy Trinity, 217

Bagthorpe, Dametta of, prs Thetford, St George, 615

Baillif, Henry le [Weedon Beck], 208

Bakewell, Robert, pr. Church Gresley, 367

Bakewell, Simon of, abb. Roche, 305

Balderstone, Simon of, pr. Pontefract, 247

Baldock, Nicholas of, pr. Newnham, 431

Baldwin, abb. Bourne, 340

Baldwin, pr. Axmouth, 144

Baldwin, pr. Barnstaple, 219

Baldwin, pr. Bodmin, 339

Baldwin, pr. Newent, 183

Baldwin, pr. Nuneaton, 597

Baldwin, pr. Peterstone, 448

Baldwin, pr. Thetford, Holy Sepulchure, 468

Baldwin, pr. Weedon Lois, 209

Baldwin, pr. Wombridge, 485

Baldwin, pr. York, St Andrew, 531

Bale, Margaret de, prs Goring, 565

Balliol, Clemencia de, abbs Elstow, 558

Bally, John, pr. Much Wenlock, 242

Bally, William (de), pr. Wareham, 207

Balne, Robert (of), pr. Warter, 480

Balsham, William de, pr. Monkton Farleigh, 238

Baltonsborough, Robert of, pr. Burtle, 352

Balun, Agnes, prs Barrow Gurney, 542

Bamburgh, Ambrose of, pr. Lytham, 120

Bamburgh, Henry of, abb. Alnwick, 491

Bamburgh, Thomas of, master Farne, 102

Bamburgh, William of, pr. Holy Island, 111

Bampton, Hugh of, abb. Cirencester, 367

Bampton, John of, pr. Kyme, 402

Banastre, Cecily (de), prs Wintney, 622

Banastre, Richard, see Reading, Richard of

Banbury, Godfrey of, pr. Llanthony Secunda, 414

Banbury, Joan of, see Fabian, Joan

Banbury, Nicholas of, abb. Dieulacres, 277

Bancis, Mabel de, abbs Chatteris, 553

Bancs, Henry de, pr. Ely, 40

Bandeworth, William, pr. Butley, 354

Banhaco, Humbert de, pr. Montacute, 240

Bankesfeld, Roger de, pr. Lincoln, St Katharine, 524

Bant, Auger, pr. Bodmin, 339

Banville, William de, pr. Wilmington, 211

Barbarot(e), Nicholas, pr. Folkestone, 161

Barbe, Nicholas la, alias de Seint Piere, pr. Modbury, 179

Barbefle, Matilda de, abbs Ramsey, 600

Barbeyn, William dictus, pr. Cogges, 152

Bardney, William of, custos Baysdale, 543

Bardney, William of, master Handale, 568

Bardsey, John of, abb. Kirkstall, 289

Bardwell, Ellen of, prs Thetford, St George, 615

Barford, William of, pr. Warwick, 481

Bark, William de la, [Wilsford], 213

Barkby, Roger of, abb. Owston, 443

Barking, Alan of, pr. Bicknacre, 335

Barking, Richard of, abb. Westminster, 78

Barly, William de, pr. Wareham (?same as Bally), 207

Barnack, Thomas (of), abb. Crowland, 37

Barnard Castle, John of, pr. Stamford, St Leonard, 130

Barnby, John of, pr. Finchale, 104; pr. Lytham, 120

Barnby, John of, pr. Upholland, 76

Barnby, Richard of, pr. Holy Island, 111

Barnevill, John de, abb. Muchelney, 54

Barningham, Richard of, abb. Easby 501

Baron, John, pr. Hardham, 386

Barqueto, John de, pr. Wootton Wawen, 215

Barra, Stephen de, pr. Wareham, 207

Barre, Richard de la, pr. Sandwell, 66

Barre, Walter, pr. Avebury, 144

Barri, Ralph, pr. Carlisle, 359

Barrow, Anne (Amy) of, prs Nun Cotham, 593

Barrow, John of, abb. Hagnaby, 503

Barrow, Roger (of), abb. Bardney, 21

Barrowby, Isabel of, prs Arthington, 540

Barrowby, Isabel of (?another), prs Arthington, 540

Barry, James, abb. Bristol, St Augustine, 348

Barsham, Eustace of, pr. Peterstone, 447

Bartholomew, [Takeley] 198

Bartholomew, abb. Alcester, 18

Bartholomew, abb. Alnwick, 491

Bartholomew, abb. Halesowen, 503

Bartholomew, minister Hounslow, 533

Bartholomew, pr. Bradwell, 24

Bartholomew, pr. Carlisle, 359

Bartholomew, pr. Great Bricett, 383

Bartholomew, pr. Kerswell, 230

Bartholomew, pr. Llanthony Prima, 413

Bartholomew, pr. Throwley, 199

Bartholomew, pr. Tickford, 199

Bartholomew, pr. Tutbury, 203

Bartholomew, pr. York, Holy Trinity, 217

Bartholomew, warden Scarborough, 308

Barton, Alice of, prs Moxby, 588

Barton, Geoffrey of, pr. Dunstable, 376

Barton, Joan of, prs Moxby, 588

Barton, John of, master Nun Cotham, 593

Barton, John of, master Stainfield, 608

Barton, John of, pr. Newark, 428

Barton, Peter of, abb. Bardney, 20

Barton, Philip of, master Sempringham, 527; pr. Cambridge, St Edmund, 520

Barton, Richard of, abb. Meaux, 293

Barton(e), Richard, abb. Thame, 315

Barton, Simon of, abb. Hulton, 286

Barton, William of, pr. Elsham, 378

Barwick, Alice of, prs Hinchingbrooke, 572

Basevile, Alice de, prs Markyate, 587

Basford, Robert of, pr. Thurgarton, 471

Basilia, prs Campsey Ash, 549

Basilia, prs Keldholme, 574

Basing, William de, pr. Winchester, St Swithun, 84
  see also Basyng(e)
Basinges, Felicia de, prs London, St Helen's and
  Holy Cross, 585
Basinges, Henry de, pr. Merton, 422
Basinges, Isabel de, abbs Barking, 541
Baskervill, Annora de, abbs Elstow, 558
Basset, Juliana, abbs Elstow, 558
Bassingbourne, Stephen of, pr. Shelford, 459
Bast, William, ?pr. Woodbridge, 486 n. 50
Basy, Constance, prs York, St Clement, 626
Basyng, Hugh (de), pr. Winchester, St Swithun, 84
Basyng(e), William de, pr. Selbourne, 458
  see also Basing(es)
Bataille, Sibyl, prs Holystone, 572
Batelay, Roger de, pr.-el. Thurgarton, 471
Bath, Adam of, abb. Biddlesden, 261
Bath, Robert of, pr. Bath, 21
Bathampton, Richard of, pr. Gloucester, St
  Oswald, 381
Batley, Matilda of, prs Arthington, 540
Battersby, Henry of, abb. Byland, 269
Battle, Robert of, abb. Battle, 23
Battle, Robert of, abb. Canterbury, St Augustine,
  29
Bath, Robert of, abb. Glastonbury, 46
Baude, Joan, abbs Malling, 586
Baudewyn, William, alias of Scarborough, pr.
  Malton, 524
Baugiaco, Francis de, pr. Montacute, 240; pr.
  Prittlewell, 249
Baukwell, John(de), abb. Welbeck, 515
Baunevilla, John de, pr. Haugham, 167
Bauzeyn, Juliana de, abbs Shaftesbury, 605
Bawtry, John of, pr. Charley, 362
Bawtry, John of (?another), pr. Charley, 363
Baxstere, John, pr. Ipswich, Holy Trinity, 396
Baxter, John, pr. Butley, 354
Beachampton, Richard of, pr. Bolton, 340
Beaminster, Ralph of, pr. Kidwelly, 115
Beatrice, prs Davington, 556
Beatrice, prs Easebourne, 557
Beatrice, prs Fosse, 561
Beatrice, prs Holystone, 572
Beatrice, prs Legbourne, 579
Beatrice, prs Stixwould, 610
Beatrice, prs Westwood, 616
Beatrice, prs Wroxall, 625
Beauchamp, Elias de, pr. Earls Colne, 99
Beauchamp, Elizabeth de, abbs Elstow, 558
Beauchamp, Hugh de, pr. Caldwell, 355
Beauchamp, Isabel de, prs Ivinghoe, 574

Beauchamp, John de, pr. Royston, 454
Beauchamp, Katherine, prs Wroxall, 625
Beauchamp, Margaret, prs Rowney, 602
Beauchamp, Matilda de, abbs Godstow, 563
Beauchamp, Thomas de, pr. Leighs, 409
Beaulieu, Hugh of, see Cardeville, Hugh of
Beaulieu, William of, pr. Haugham, 166
Beaumond, William, abb. Hartland, 386
Beaumont, Geoffrey de, pr. York, Holy Trinity, 217
Beaumont, Richard de, pr. Andwell, 140
Beaumont, Richard de, pr. Hamble, 164
Beaumont, William de, pr. St Neots, 191
Beaumont-le-Roger, Richard of, pr. Titley, 201
Beausevall, Richard de, pr. Ogbourne St George,
  184
Beauver, Jakes de, pr. Newent, 183
Beauver, William de, pr. Belvoir, 91
  see also Belvoir
Beauvey, William de, pr. Edith Weston, 158
Beauveys, Thomas, pr. Dover, 98
Beauvill, William de, pr. Wilmington, 211
Bebington, William of, abb. Chester, 33
Bec, Peter of, pr. St Neots, 191
Bec, William of, alias dictus Lecaron, pr. St Neots,
  190
Beccles, Edmund of, abb. Sibton, 309
Becclys, William, minister Easton, 532
Bechington, Henry de, pr. Birkenhead, 23
Bechington, Robert de, pr. Birkenhead, 23
Beck, Robert de, pr. Malpas, 235
Beckerham, Agnes de, prs Broadholme, 545
Beckering, Geoffrey of, pr. Torksey, 474
Beckering, Roger of, pr. Bullington, 520
Beckingham, Richard of, master Monkwearmouth,
  121
Beckingham, Richard of, pr. Holy Island, 111
Bedford, Emma of, prs Hinchingbrooke, 572
Bedford, John of, pr. Newnham, 430
Bedford, Matthew of, pr. Caldwell, 355
Bedford, Philip of, pr. Fineshade, 379
Bedford, William of, pr. Tynemouth, 131
Bedford, William of, pr. Worcester, 85
Bedingfield, John of, pr. Aldeby, 89
Bedlingfield, Margery of, prs Redlingfield, 600
Bedwyn, Philip of, abb. Waverley, 321
Beeding, Robert of, pr. Sele, 192
Beele, Robert, pr. Mattersey, 526
Beelsby, Isolda of, prs Stainfield, 608
Beelsby, John of, abb. Tupholme, 513
Beesby, Alexander of, pr. Sixhills, 530
Beeston, Walter (William) of, pr. Beeston, 333
Behall, Robert de, pr. Nostell, 438

Belay, Michael, pr. Ellingham, 159
Beleisur, prs Handale, 568
Beley, Hugh de, pr. Calwich, 356
Belfeld, John, abb. Whalley, 322
Belford, Amice of, prs Newcastle-upon-Tyne, 590
Belgrave, Walter of, abb. Sulby, 510
Bella, prs Handale, 568
Bella Aqua, Robert de, pr. Upavon, 205
Bello Campo, Robert de, pr. Harmondsworth, 165
Bello Ramo, John de, *custos* York, Holy Trinity, 217
Bello Ramo, John de, pr. Montacute, 239
Bellocier, John, pr. Tutbury, 204
Bellomonte, William de, pr. Stoke by Clare, 196
Beloc, William, pr. Tutbury, 204
Belsted, John de, ?pr. Burstall, 148
Belton, John of, pr. Rumburgh, 125
Belton, Roger of, pr. Thornholme, 469
Belvoir, Richard of, pr. Belvoir, 92
Belvoir, William of, pr. Belvoir, 91
Benacre, Henry of, pr. Dodnash, 374
Benart, William, pr. Monk Sherborne, 180
Benedict, abb. Alnwick, 491
Benedict II, abb. Athelney, 19
Benedict, abb. Bayham, 493
Benedict, abb. Stratford Langthorne, 313
Benedict, master Greenfield, 567
Benedict, pr. Burscough, 352
Benedict, pr. Deerhurst, 155
Benedict, pr. Herringfleet, 390
Benedict, pr. St Ives, 128
Benedict, pr. Shouldham, 529
Benedict, pr. Tiptree, 472
Beneth(am), William de, pr. Malton, 525
Beneton, John de, pr. Ravenstone, 451
Benham, John of, abb. Chertsey, 32
Benigna, prs London, Haliwell, 584
Bennington, Robert of, abb. Newbo, 507
Benniworth, Robert of, master Stixwould, 611
Benniworth, Walter of, abb. Bardney, 20
Bense, William, [Upchurch], 514
Benseval, Thomas de, pr. St Neots, 190
Bercheston, Simon de, abb. Westminster, 79
Berd(e)feld, Alexander de, pr. Hatfield Regis, 166
Bere, Joan de, prs Cannington, 549
Bere, John de, pr. Bentley, 333
Beresford, Ellen de, prs Derby, Kingsmead, 556
Berewyk, John (de), pr. Bath, 22
Bergham, Roger de, pr. Ely, 40
Berham, John de, abb. Vaudey, 319
Berham, Peter de, pr. Newstead by Stamford, 433
Berkadone, John (de), abb. Torre, 513
Berkeleye, Isabel de, prs Buckland, 546

Berkesdon, Margery of, prs Studley, 612
Berkhamstead, John of, abb. St Albans, 63
Berlegh, Henry de, pr. Mendham, 235
Bermondsey, William of, pr. Deerhurst, 155
Bernaio, Walter de, pr. St Neots, 190
Bernard, abb. Coverham, 497
Bernard, pr. Great Bricett, 383
Bernard, pr. Hexham, 390
Bernard, Matilda, abbs Chatteris, 553
Bernard, Robert, pr. Norton, 438
Bernard, William, pr. Tynemouth, 132
Bernerii, John, pr. St Cross, 188
Berners, Adam de, abb. Osney, 441
Bernevalle, Reginald de, *see* Cossam, Reginald de
Bernham, Peter de, pr. Bromehill, 349
Bernham, William de, abb. Bury St Edmunds, 27
Berrington, John of, pr. Finchale, 104
Berrington, Nicholas of, abb. Haughmond, 388
Berrington, Robert, of Walworth, pr. Durham, 40
Berta, abbs Malling, 585
Bertholt, Thomas, pr. Horsham St Faith, 170
Berton, John de, pr. Weybridge, 484
Berton(e), Thomas de, pr. Mottisfont, 426
Berton, William de, pr.-el. Cold Norton, 370
Berton(e), William (de), pr. Wormsley, 489
    see also Burton
Beschu, Peter le, pr. Covenham, 153
Besiles, Geoffrey de, pr. Bradenstoke, 342
Beston, Roger de, pr. Wymondley, 490
Beteslegh(e), Adam de, pr. Pilton, 124
Beton, Richard, keeper Upchurch, 514
Betts, Richard, pr. Buckenham, 351
Beulu, William de, pr. Alvecote, 89
Beumes, Geoffrey de, pr. Tutbury, 203
Beupre, Cecily, prs Crabhouse, 556
Beverley, Agnes of, prs Nun Keeling, 594
Beverley, Avice of, prs Nunburnholme, 595
Beverley, Hugh of, pr. Kirkham, 401
Beverley, John of [keeper of Holy Island], 111
Beverley, John of, senior, master Jarrow, 114; ?pr.
    Finchale, 104; pr. Oxford, Durham cell, 122
Beverley, John of, pr. North Ferriby, 436
Beverley, Robert of, abb. Meaux, 294
Beverley, William of, pr. Malton, 525
Beville, Ralph de, abb. Sawtry, 308
Bevyle, John, pr. Exeter, St James, 229
Bewcastle, John of, pr. Lanercost, 403
Biblisia (Bibles), prs Catesby, 551
Bibury, John of, abb. Osney, 442
Bibury, Richard of, pr. Ewyas Harold, 100
Bickerton, Richard of, master Jarrow, 115
Bickton, William of, abb. Titchfield, 511

Biddenham, John of, pr. Newnham, 431

Biddenham, William of, pr. Newnham, 430

Biddlesden, Ralph of, abb. Bordesley, 264

Bidford, Henry of, abb. Pershore, 56

Bielby, Richard of, master Swine, 614

Bigod, Thomas (le), pr. Thetford, St Mary, 252

Billesdon, John of, abb. Croxden, 275

Billesfield, John of, pr. Holy Island, 111; pr.
    Stamford, St Leonard, 131

Billeslye, Martin de, abb. Hailes, 284

Billeyo, Gilbert de, pr. Modbury, 179

Billing, John of, pr. Bradwell, 24

Billing, John of, pr. Fineshade, 379

Billingborough, Benedict of, master Stainfield, 608

Billingsley, Richard of, pr. St Helen's, 250

Billockby, Laurence of, pr. Weybridge, 484

Bilney, Richard of, pr. Hoxne, 113

Bilton, Adam of, pr. Breedon, 345; pr. Nostell, 439

Binbrook, Henry of, abb. Humberston, 49

Bingham, Ralph of, pr. Charley, 363

Bingham, Walter of, pr. Gloucester, St Oswald, 382

Birdsall, John of, abb. Kirkstall, 289

Birmingham, Roger of, keeper Calwich, 356

Birmingham, Thomas of, abb. Halesowen, 504

Birne, John de, pr. Henes and Sandtoft, 108; pr.
    Lincoln, St Mary Magdalen, 118

Birne, John (de), pr. Rumburgh, 125–6

Birstall, William of, pr. Nostell, 439

Birthwaite, John of, pr. Monk Bretton, 53

Birtley, Richard of, pr. Finchale, 104; pr. Lytham,
    120

Birtley, Robert of, master Farne, 102

Bishops Cleeve, Richard of, abb. Abingdon, 17

Bishopstone, Alice of, prs Rusper, 603

Bishopton, John of, master Monkwearmouth, 121

Bishopton, Robert, abb. Fountains, 280

Bisley, Simon of, pr. Great Malvern, 107

Bittedene, Richard de, pr. Frithelstock, 381

Bitteden(e), William de, pr. Exeter, St James, 228

Bittiscombe, Emma of, prs Cannington, 549

Biwelle, John de, pr. Hexham, 390

Blachyngdon, Willelma de, prs Cannington, 549

Blacklaw, Robert of, pr. Oxford, Durham cell, 123

Blagrave, Nicholas of, keeper Calwich, 356

Blak, Adam le, abb. Cockersand, 496

Blakeney, Richard of, pr. Norwich, St Leonard,
    122

Blakenham, Robert of, pr. Bicknacre, 335

Blaket, Robert, pr. Bicester, 334

Blanchevile, Geoffrey de, abb. Newenham, 296

Blankney, Roger of, abb. Tupholme, 513

Blebury, Henry de, see Shalyngforde, Henry de

Blevill, Hugh de, pr. Brimpsfield, 147

Blewyn, John, pr. Monmouth, 182

Bloc, Walter dictus, pr. Throwley, 199

Blockley, Thomas of, pr. Penwortham, 123

Blont, Henry, abb. Gloucester, 47
    see also Blount; Blunt

Blosmeville, John de, abb. Abingdon, 16

Blossevill, William de, pr. Hayling, 167

Bl(o)unde, Denise la, abbs Shaftesbury, 606

Blounde, Emma la, abbs Wilton, 620

Blounde, Tiffany la, prs London, Haliwell, 584

Blount, Joan, prs Henwood, 570

Blount, Joan le, prs Aconbury, 537

Blount, Walter (le), pr. Mottisfont, 426
    see also Blont; Blunt

Bloxham, William of, pr. Arbury, 329

Bloxworth, Philip of, abb. Cerne, 31

Bloyhou, Matilda de, prs Polsloe, 599

Bluet, Emma, abbs Godstow, 562

Bluet, Hugh, pr. Lenton, 231

Blund, Robert dictus, pr. Plympton, 448

Blunt, Isabel la, prs Stratford-at-Bow, 612

Blunt, Richard le, de Haulee, pr. Chicksands, 521
    see also Blont; Blount

Bluntisham, Reginald (Robert) of, pr. Huntingdon,
    394

Blyth, Adam of, pr. Healaugh Park, 389

Blythe, Isabel de, pr Hinchingbrooke, 572

Blyton, Simon of, abb. Colchester, 34–5; pr. Snape,
    129

Boby, Agnes de, prs Stamford, St Mary and St
    Michael, 608

Bocton(e), Geoffrey de, abb. Faversham, 45

Bodekesham, Martin de, pr. Belvoir, 90

Bodeketon, Robert de, see Glottyng', Robert de

Bodiers, John de, pr. Wareham, 207

Bodman, John, pr. Stavordale, 463

Bokelow, Robert de, ?abb. St Osyth, 457 n. 40

Boldon, Uthred of, pr. Finchale, 104; [Oxford,
    Durham cell], 123

Bolewyk, John de, pr.-el. Launde, 406

Bolingbroke, Roger (II) of, master Sempringham,
    527; pr. Sempringham, 528

Bolsover, Ellen of, prs Wallingwells, 616

Boltby, Alice of, prs Campsey Ash, 549

Boltby, Philippa of, prs Newcastle-upon-Tyne, 589

Bolton, John, abb. Furness, 282

Bolton, John of, master Jarrow, 115

Bolton, Richard of, pr. Conishead, 372

Bonay, William de, abb. Dale, 499

Boneboz, Richard de, pr. Wilsford, 212

Bonehomme, Richard, pr. Boxgrove, 147

Bonesboz, William de, pr. St Neots, 190
Boneye, William de, pr. Bullington, 520
Bonndaye, W., pr. Wootton Wawen, 214
Bonnet, John, pr. Astley, 143
Bonus, abb. Tavistock, 73
Bonvillars, Henry de, pr. Much Wenlock, 241
Bonville, Henry de, *alias* Normanus, pr.
    Bermondsey, 221
Bonyn, William de, pr. Beckford and Colsterworth,
    332
Bonyngton, Isabel de, prs Nun Cotham, 593
Bookham, Gunnora (Gunnilda) of, prs Broomhall,
    546
Bool, Meredith, abb. Strata Florida, 312
Boothby, Adam of, abb. Peterborough, 58
Boothby, John of, pr. Lanercost, 403
Borden, William of, *alias* Verduno, pr. Leeds, 407
Bordene, John de, pr. Exeter, St Nicholas, 101
Borel, Alan, pr. Great Bricett, 383
Borne, Ralph de, abb. Canterbury, St Augustine,
    29
Boroughbridge, Gilbert of, pr. Hexham, 391; pr.
    Thurgarton, 472
Borrenco, Richard de, pr. Burstall, 148
Borstall, Margaret, prs Davington, 556
Bosco, Bartholomew de, pr. Northampton, St
    Andrews, 245
Bosco, Gilbert de, abb. Rocester, 453
Bosco, Guy de, pr. St Helen's, 250
Bosco, Peter de, pr. Kerswell, 231
Bosco, Peter de, pr. Monmouth, 182
Bosco, Peter de, pr. Thetford, St Mary, 252
Bosco, Robert de, pr. Ecclesfield, 157
Bosco, Thomas de, pr. Newent, 183
Bosco, William de, *alias* de Yvelont, pr.
    Harmondsworth 165
Bosco Reynaldi, John de, pr. St Neots, 190
Bosden, Jordan of, abb. Cockersand, 497
Bosden, William of, abb. Cockersand, 497
Bosevile, Beatrice de, prs Sewardsley, 604
Boseville, Denise de, prs Sewardsley, 604
Bosham, Christiana of, abbs Barking, 541
Bosham, Mabel of, abbs Barking, 541
Bosse, Robert, abb. Tavistock, 72
Boston, Geoffrey of, pr. Stamford, St Leonard, 130
Boston, John (de), pr. Torksey, 474
Botayl, Richard, pr. Avebury, 144
Boteham, Henry de, pr. Ivychurch, 397
Boteler, Beatrice le, prs London, St Helen's and
    Holy Cross, 585
    see also Botiller
Boterwell, Richard, pr. Bradenstoke, 342

Botile, Gilbert de, pr. Wetheral, 135
Botiller, Simon le, pr. Worcester, 86
    see also Boteler
Botone, Geoffrey de, pr. Beeston, 333
Bottevile, William de, pr. Ware, 206
Bottisham, Agnes of, prs Hinchingbrooke, 572
Bottisham, John of, pr. Anglesey, 328
Bottourd, Matilda de, abbs Polesworth, 599
Botwell, John of, pr. Bradenstoke, 342
Bouch, Michael de la, pr. Wootton Wawen, 215
Bouers, John (de/le), pr. Totnes, 202
Bouges, Michael (de), pr. Totnes, 202
Bouges, William (de) pr. Minster, 176
Bouges, William, pr. Tywardreath, 204
Bougevilla, William de, pr. St Neots, 190
Bourchelle, Sarah de, prs Wix, 623
Bourdet, William, pr. Linton and Isleham, 174
Bourdigny, Richard de, pr. Monk Sherbourne, 180
Boutyn, Stephen, pr. Wolston, 214
Bovingdon, Luke of, pr. Hatfield Peverel, 107
Bovingdon, Richard of, master St Mary de Pre,
    604
Boweles, Gilbert, rector Ashridge, 535
Boweles, Thomas de, keeper Calwich, 355
Bowes, Agnes (de), prs Wothorpe, 623
Boxworth, Richard of, abb. Owston, 443
Boyden, Katherine de, prs Catesby, 552
Boydin, Katherine, prs Henwood, 570
Boydyn, William, keeper Calwich, 356
Boyfeld, John (de), abb. Gloucester, 49
Boyfeld, Roger de, pr. Cardiff, 95
Boyland, John of, pr. Wormegay, 488
Boyn(e), Giles, pr. Beckford and Colsterworth, 332
Boys, William (du/de), abb. Evesham, 42
Boys, William de, pr. Horkesley, 230
Boys Brimol, John de, pr. York, Holy Trinity, 217
Boyton, Winnesia of, prs Blackborough, 543
Boyville, Adam de, master Jarrow, 114
Bozoun, Robert de, pr. Castle Acre, 223
Bozoun, Simon, pr. Norwich cath., 56; pr.
    Norwich, St Leonard, 122
Brabantia, Gobert de, pr. Lapley, 172
Brackenborough, Agnes of, prs Stamford, St Mary
    and St Michael, 609
Brackley, Alexander of, abb. Eynsham, 43
Brackley, Robert of, pr. Chetwode, 364
Brackley, William of, abb. Croxton Kerrial, 498
Brackley, William of, pr. Luffield (1231–63), 49
Brackley, William of, pr. Luffield (1285), 50
Brackley, William of, pr. Luffield (1294–1316), 50
Bracton, William de, pr. Henes and Sandtoft, 107;
    pr. Lincoln, St Mary Magdalen, 118

Bradeforde, Mabel de, prs Cornworthy, 555
Bradeleye, Thomas of, pr. Hatfield Regis, 166
Bradenham, Ralph of, abb. Sibton, 309
Braderugge, John, abb. Bordesley, 265
Bradewell, Wiliam, pr. Tortington, 475
Bradewey, Henry de, keeper Calwich, 356
Bradewey, Henry de, pr. Kenilworth, 399
Bradeweye, John (de), abb. Alcester, 19
Bradewey(e), Peter (de), abb. Pershore, 57
Bradford, John of, abb. Keynsham, 400
Bradford, John of, pr. Horton, 112
Bradford, Laurence of, abb. Sherborne, 68
Bradley, Agnes of, prs Grimsby, 567
Bradley, Robert of, pr. Ranton, 450
Bradley, William of, abb. Missenden, 425
Bradstone, William of, alias of Berkeley, abb.
    Bristol, St Augustine, 347
Braham, Isabel of, prs Wix, 622
Braham, John of, master Bamburgh, 329
Braintree, Richard of, pr. Thremhall, 471
Bramertone, Nicholas de, pr. Norwich cath., 55
Bramfield, Richard of, pr. Hatfield Peverel, 107
Brampton, William of, abb. Blanchland, 495
Brampton, William of, pr. Stonely, 465
Brandon, John of Weasenham, pr. Great
    Massingham, 384
Brandon, Thomas of, abb. North Creake, 435
Branewyk, Henry de, abb. Halesowen, 503; abb.
    Titchfield, 511
Branscombe alias Exeter, Richard of, abb.
    Newenham, 298
Bransford, Wulstan of, pr. Worcester, 86
Branvilla, Geoffrey de, pr. St Neots, 191
Braos(e), Flandrina de, abbs Godstow, 562
Bras, Denise, prs London, Clerkenwell, 583
Bratoft, John of, abb. Humberston, 49
Bratoft, Roger of, pr. Markby, 419
Braughing, Edmund of, pr. London, St
    Bartholomew, 417
Braunforde, William de, pr. Ipswich, Holy Trinity,
    396
Braunston, Henry of, pr. Launde, 406
Braunstone, William of, abb. Owston, 443
Braunvill, Geoffrey de, pr. Stoke by Clare, 196
Brawby, Simon of, pr. Marton, 420
Bray, John le, minister Moatenden, 533
Bray, Margery, prs London, Clerkenwell, 583
Bray, Matthew de, abb. Leicester, 407
Braybrok, Katherine, prs London, Clerkenwell, 583
Braybrok, William, see Calne, William of
Braybrooke, Christi(a)na of, prs Cambridge, St
    Mary and St Radegund, 548

Breamore, Robert of, pr. Mottisfont, 426
Brecles, William de, pr. Ipswich, Holy Trinity,
    395
Brecon, John of, pr. Exeter, St Nicholas, 101
Bredon, Thomas of, abb. Gloucester, 47
Bredon, Thomas of, pr. Great Malvern, 105
Breedon, Nicholas of, pr. Brooke, 349
Breedon, William of, procurator of Breedon, 329
Brek, Gervase le, pr. Pembroke, 187
Brenchesle(s), Thomas, pr. Bilsington, 337
Brent, Isabel de, prs Polsloe, 599
Bret, Matilda le, ?prs Pinley, 598
Bret, Richard le, abb. Cleeve, 271
Bretby, Nicholas of, abb. Calder, 271
Bretford, William of, abb. Combe, 273
Breth(e), John atte, pr. Reigate, 451
Brethenham, Robert, pr. Alnesbourn, 327
Breton, Drogo, pr. Kyme, 402
Breton, William (le), pr. Shelford, 459
Bretoun, Fulk, pr. Flitcham, 380
Bretoun, John, pr. Chicksands, 521
Bretoun, Margaret (de), prs Thetford, St George,
    615
Brettevill, William de, [Long Bennington], 291
Bret(t)eville, Nicholas de, pr. Blyth, 145
Bretun, William le, pr. Dunstable, 377
Breyles, Robert de, pr. Warwick, 480
Breyntone(e), John de, abb. Glastonbury, 47
Brian, abb. Torre, 512
Brian, pr. Sudbury, 131
Brice, pr. Freiston, 104
Brice, pr. Letheringham, 410
Brid, John, abb. Cambe, 273
Bridekirk, John of, pr. Hexham, 391
Brideton, Roger de, abb. Abbotsbury, 15
Bridford, William de, pr. Wetheral, 135
Bridgnorth, Stephen of, [Northampton, St
    Andrews], 245
Bridgnorth, William of, abb. Lilleshall, 411
Bridlington, John of, pr. Kirkham, 402
Bridport, Joan of, abbs Shaftesbury, 605
Brierley, Hugh of, pr. Monk Bretton, 53
Brigge, Robert of, abb. Dieulacres, 277
Brigges, William de, pr. Pontefract, 246
Brightwalton, William of, pr. Coventry, 35
Brignall, Thomas of, pr. St Bees, 127
Brineston, William de, abb. Whitby, 79
Brinkley, John of, abb. Bury St Edmunds, 27
Brione, Matilda de, abbs Tarant Kaines, 614
Brioto, Laurence de, pr. Frampton, 161
Brisley, Roger of, pr. Great Massingham, 384
Brissele, John (de), abb.. Wendling, 516

Bristol, Gervase of, pr. Penman, 446

Bristol, Joan of, prs Nuneaton, 596

Bristow, William, pr. Dunster, 99

Britenis, Oliver, see Faugeriis, Oliver Britenis de

Brito, Ran(n)ulf, abb. Ramsey, 59

Brixworth, William of, pr. Chetwode, 363

Broadway, Peter of, pr. Cranborne, 96

Broadway, William of, pr. Little Malvern, 119

Brocia, John de, pr. Wootton Wawen, 215

Brockhall, Acelinia of, prs Rowney, 602

Brockhampton, John of, abb. Evesham, 42

Brockhampton, Richard of, pr. Wormsley, 489

Brocklesby, William of, master Nun Cotham, 594

Brockworth, Simon of, pr. Llanthony Secunda, 415

Broghton, Matilda de, prs Broomhall, 545–6

Brok, Henry de, abb. St Benet of Hulme, 65

Brok, Hugh de, pr. Warwick, 481

Brokenborough, Adam of, abb. Cirencester, 368

Brokeneborwe, Thomas, pr. Pilton, 124

Brom, Henry, pr. Woodbridge, 486

Brom, Hugh de, pr. Buckenham, 351

Bromall, Henry, pr. Cranborne, 96

Broman, Agnes, prs Canterbury, Holy Sepulchure, 550

Bromden, Richard of, pr. Southwick, 462

Bromholm, John of, pr. Kings Lynn, 116

Bromley, William of, abb. Burton, 25

Bromley, William (de), pr. Hurley, 114

Bromleye, John (of), pr. Ivychurch, 397

Brompton, Henry of, see London, Henry of

Brompton, Richard of, abb. Wigmore, 485

Brompton, Thomas of, pr. Alvingham, 519

Brompton, William of, pr. Launde, 405

Bromsgrove, Richard of, pr. Brooke, 349

Bromsgrove, William of, abb. Halesowen, 504

Bromwich, Agnes of, prs Whistones, 618

Bromwich, Reginald of, pr. Maxstoke, 421

Bromwich, Richard of, pr. Abergavenny, 138

Brooke, Margery of, abbs Northampton, De La Pré, 590

Brooke, Richard of, abb. Haughmond, 388

Broome, John de, pr. Royston, 454

Broughton, John of, abb. Eynsham, 43

Brounyng, James (John), pr. Lewisham, 173

Brownknave, Richard, alias Chanon, pr. Bradley, 343

Broxbourne, William of, pr. Merton, 422–3

Broxolio, Gilbert de, pr. Montacute, 239

Broy, Agnes de, prs Wroxall, 624

Bruer', Roger de la, pr. Eye, 159

Bruges, Francis de, pr. Northampton, St Andrews, 245

Bruges, John de, abb. Colchester, 34

Bruges, John de, pr. Wormsley, 489

Bruges, William, see Tyrry, William

Brugge, Richard de, abb. Haughmond, 388

Brugis, Richard de, pr. Plympton, 447

Brun, Hugh le, abb. Furness, 282

Brun, Richard le, Colchester, St Botolph, 369

Brune, Robert de, pr. Rumburgh, 126

Brunne, John de, pr. Barnwell, 331

Brunnesford, Margery de, prs Canterbury, Holy Sepulchre, 550

Bruno, Michael de, abb. Meaux, 293

Brus, Isabel de, prs Stixwould, 611

Brus, Robert de, of Pickering, custos Yedingham, 626

see also Bruys

Bruton, Juliana of, prs Polsloe, 600

Bruys, Agatha (de), prs Nuneaton, 596

see also Brus

Brycoo, Laurence de, pr. Panfield and Well, 186

Brygge, Richard, abb. St Radegund, 509

Bryght, William, de Wyghton, pr. Peterstone, 447

Brykebek, Thomas de, pr. Brimpsfield, 147

Brykenyle (or Brykevyle), John, pr. Mottisfont, 426

Brykevile, Richard de, pr. Launceston, 404

Brykhull, Robert de, abb. Burton, 26

Brymesden, Agnes de, abbs Lacock, 577

Brynkeleye, Geoffrey de, pr. Swavesey, 197

Bryt, Matilda, prs Pinley, 598

Brytone, John, abb. Buckland, 268

Bu, Godfrey de, pr. Stogursey, 195

Buabilla, prs Farewell, 560

Buckden, John of, pr. Wymondley, 490

Buckebroc, John de, pr. Sandwell, 66

Buckenham, Peter of, see Bysshop, Peter

Buckenham, Richard of, abb. St Benet of Hulme, 65

Buckingham, Adam of, pr. Canons Ashby, 357

Buckingham, Henry of, abb. Missenden, 425

Buckingham, Henry of, pr. Torksey, 474

Buckingham, Thomas of, abb. Biddlesden, 262

Buckland, John (of), abb. Osney, 442

Buckland, Matilda (of), abbs Wilton, 620

Buckland, Peter of, abb. Owston, 442

Buckland, Robert of, abb. Beaulieu, 260

Buckwell, William of, pr. Dover, 97

Budworth, Roger of, pr. Norton, 437

Bueys, Oger de, alias Cordon alias de Monte, pr. Otterton, 186

Buket, John, pr. Hayling, 167

Bukton, John (de), pr. Ely, 41

Buiyns, Roger de, pr. Sudbury, 131

Bulbek, Ascelina, prs Littlemore, 582
Bulmer, William of, pr.-el. Marton, 420
Bulmere, Richard de, *see* Dulverne, Richard de
Bulun, Walter de, pr. Tynemouth, 132
Bumsted, Walter, pr. Blackmore, 338
Bungay, Roger of, pr. Butley, 354
Bungy, William, abb. Buildwas, 269
Burbach(e), Robert (de), abb. Milton, 53
Burbage, John of, pr. Arbury, 329
Burchelles, Thomas de, abb. Chester, 33
Burdet, John, pr. Ecclesfield, 158
Burdon, Geoffrey of, pr. Durham, 39; pr.
    Finchale, 103; pr. Lytham, 120;
    [Monkwearmouth], 121; pr. Oxford, Durham
    cell, 122
Burdon, Peter, pr. Warmington, 208
Burdon(e), Thomas de, pr. Launceston, 405
Burdon, William, pr. Blyth, 145
Bures, Robert de, pr. Wing, 213
Burford, John of, pr. Stamford, St Leonard, 129
Burgate, Bartholomew de, ?abb. North Creake, 435
    n. 31
Burgate, Robert of, abb. Reading, 61
Burgensis, Richard, pr. Swavesey, 197
Burgeys, Geoffrey of Isle of Wight, *alias* de Lille,
    pr. Andwell, 140
Burgh, Henry de, pr. Lanercost, 403
Burgh, Thomas de, abb. Cockersand, 497
Burghill, Thomas, pr. Hereford, 109 n.13
Burgia, prs Langley, 578
Burgiloun, Robert le, abb. Dieulacres, 277
Burgo, Alexander de, pr. Hatfield Peverel, 107
Burgo, Amice de, prs Langley, 578
Burgo, John de, pr. Launde, 406
Burgulun, Agnes (le), prs Cambridge, St Mary and
    St Radegund, 548
Burgundiensis, Hugh, pr. Lenton, 231
Buris, Adam de, pr. Cowick, 153
Burn(e), Giles de, pr. Merton, 421
Burnedissh, John de, pr. Woodbridge, 486
Burnell, Henry, abb. Buildwas, 269
Burnell, William, pr. Loders, 176
Burneville, John de, pr. Wilsford, 212
Burnham, William of, pr. Norwich cath., 55
Burrill, William of, abb. Easby, 501
Burstall, Henry of, pr. Ipswich, St Peter and St
    Paul, 396
Burstallis, John de, abb. Boxley, 265
Burstoke, Walter, abb. Forde, 279
Burtle, Stephen of, pr. Burtle, 352
Burton, Adam of, abb. Combermere, 274
Burton, Gerard of, pr. Bridlington, 346

Burton, Isabel of, prs Nun Keeling, 594
Burton, John of (*alias* Fisher *alias* Stapenhulle),
    abb. Burton, 25
Burton, John, pr. Cambridge, St Edmund, 520
Burton, Laurence of, abb. Darley, 374
Burton, Peter of, pr. Rumburgh, 126
Burton, Richard of, abb. Sulby, 511
Burton, Richard of, pr. Rumburgh, 126
Burton, William (of), abb. Whitby, 80
Burton, William of, pr. Kenilworth, 398
Burum, William de, pr. Exeter, St Nicholas, 101
Burwell, Agnes of, abbs Chatteris, 553
Burwell, John of, pr. Spinney, 462
Burwell, Matilda of, prs Orford, 597
Bury, Richard of, pr. Snape, 129
Busot(is), John, pr. Harmondsworth, 165
Busquet, William, pr. Astley, 143
Bussa, Gilbert de, pr. Bermondsey, 220
Busse, Robert, pr. Montacute, 240
Busseria, Guy de, pr. Northampton, St Andrew,
    244
Bustard, John, master Swine, 614
Bustethorn, Richard de, pr. Christchurch
    (Twynham), 366
Butley, Nicholas (of), pr. Westacre, 483
Buttrebuske, William, pr. Breedon, 345
Bydenham, William, pr. Wymondley, 490
Byham, William de, *alias* Wiham, abb. Biddlesden,
    262
Byllesby, Eleanor, prs Grimsby, 567
Bylyngton, Roger de, abb.-el. Burton, 25
Bynet, Nicholas *dictus*, pr. Hinckley, 168
Bynet, Nicholas, pr. Wareham, 207
Bynham, William (de), pr. Wallingford, 134
Byrton, Elias de, pr. Drax, 376
Bysshop, Peter, *alias* of Buckenham, pr. Pentney,
    447

C., abb. Strata Marcella, 313
C., pr. Tynemouth, 131
C., John de, pr. Dudley, 227
Cabourne, William of, abb. Wellow, 482
Cabulone, John de, pr. Monks Horton, 237
Caddington, Walter of, pr. Caldwell, 355
Cadecote, Robert de, pr. Burtle, 352
Cadwgan, abb. Abbey Cwmhir, 258
Cadwgan, abb. Cymmer, 276
Cadwgan ap Yeva, abb. Abbey Cwmhir, 258
Caen, Reginald of, pr. Monk Sherborne, 180
Caistor, Alexander of, pr. Hoxne, 113
Calceya, Robert de, pr. Weedon Lois, 210
Caldecote, Vincent of, pr. Pentney, 447

Caldewelle, Henry de, abb. Pershore, 56

Caldun, Michael de, abb. Cleeve, 271

Caldwell, Elizabeth of, prs Langley, 578

Caldwell, John of, pr. Beadlow, 90

Caldwell, John of, pr. Binham, 93

Caldwell, William of, pr. Wroxton, 489

Caleto, John de, pr. Carisbrooke, 150

Calhauet, *see* Arnauld de Calhauet, William

Calida, William de, pr. Steventon, 194

Call(e), John, pr. Kersey, 400

Calne, William of, *alias* Braybrok, pr. Ivychurch, 397

Calstone, Thomas of, abb. Stanley, 309

Calthorp, Simon de, pr. Beeston, 333

Calverley, Isabel of, prs Esholt, 559

Calvicuria, John de, pr. Newent, 182

Cambois, Robert of, pr. Lytham, 120; pr. Stamford, St Leonard, 130

Cambremer, Theobald de, pr. Ogbourne, St George, 184

Cambridge, -, pr. Church Preen, 225

Cambridge, Amice of, abbs Chatteris, 553

Cambridge, Henry of, pr. Spinney, 462

Cambridge, John of, pr. Huntingdon, 394

Camelton, John de, pr. Chicksands, 521

Camera, John de, pr. Rumburgh, 125

Camme, Roger de, abb. Tintern, 317

Camme, Walter (de), abb. Malmesbury, 52

Camon, William, pr. Monks Kirby, 181

Camoys, Isabel (de), abbs Romsey, 601

Campden, Gilbert of, abb. Haughmond, 387

Campden, William of, pr. Bristol, St James, 94

Campeden, John de, pr. Earls Colne, 99

Campeney, Nicholas de, pr. Warmington, 208

Campes, Adam de, abb. Colchester, 34

Campesete, William de, pr. Bilsington, 336

Campleon, Margaret, prs Thetford, St George, 615

Campsall, Thomas of, pr. Drax, 376

Cancelot, William, pr. Ellingham, 158

Candover, Roger of, abb. Titchfield, 511

Can(e)ford, Robert de, pr. Mottisfont, 426

Caningges, Simon de, abb. Winchester, Hyde, 82

Canoun, Denis, pr. Andover, 140

Cant, Warisius de, abb. St Radegund, 509

Cantelo, John de, abb. Margam, 292

Canterbury, Ala of, prs Fosse, 561

Canterbury, Edmund of, *alias* Roper *alias* Westgate, pr. Bilsington, 337

Canterbury, John of, pr. Witham, 326

Canterbury, Ralph of, pr. London, Holy Trinity, Aldgate, 416

Canterbury, Richard of, *see* Kent, Richard of

Canterbury, William of, pr. Stansgate, 251

Cantley, John of, pr. Wormegay, 488

Canvill, Albreda (Albra) de, abbs Polesworth, 598

Canyng, John de, abb. Abingdon, 17

Capella, John de, pr. Hinckley, 168

Capella, Richard de, pr. Hinckley, 168

Capenhurst, Thomas of, abb. Chester, 33

Capiago, Roger Hayn, *dictus* de, pr. Barnstaple, 220

Carbonel, Agnes, prs Wix, 623

Carbonel, Sibyl, abbs Romsey, 601

Carbunel, Berengar, pr. Horsham St Faith, 169

Carcutt, Gilbert of, pr. Upavon, 205

Cardeville, Hugh of (of Beaulieu), abb. Beaulieu, 260 & n. 2

Cardington, Thomas of, pr.-el. Caldwell, 354

Carentonio, William de, *alias dictus* le Condu, pr. Loders, 175

Carevyle, Stephen de, pr. Bruton, 351

Cariloco, *see* Caroloco

Carlemle (?Carlevile) de Swenington, Thomas de, pr. Mountjoy, 427

Carleville, Thomas, pr. Mountjoy, 427

Carlton, Agnes of, prs Norwich (Carrow), 592

Carlton, John of, pr. London, St Bartholomew, 417

Carlton, Robert of, abb. Cockersand, 497

Carlton, Robert of, pr. Worksop, 487

Carlton, William of, pr. Bentley, 333

Carmarthen, Adam of, abb. Neath, 295

Carmarthen, Robert of, pr. Carmarthen, 360

Carmelton, Thomas de, *see* Carmirton, Thomas de

Carmirton, Thomas de, *alias* Carmelton, pr. Shouldham, 529

Carnarii, Drogo, pr. Deerhurst, 157

Carnellow, William, pr. Bodmin, 339

Caroloco, Bernard de, pr. Northampton, St Andrew, 244

Caroloco (Charlieu), Guichard de, pr. Much Wenlock, 242; pr. Northampton, St Andrew, 245; pr. Pontefract, 246; [Prittlewell], 248

Caroloco (Cariloco), John de, pr. Bermondsey, 222; pr. Lewes, 235

Caroloco, Peter de, pr. Clifford, 225

Carpenter, Peter, pr. York, Holy Trinity, 218

Carr, Henry, abb. Kirkstall, 288

Cartaret, Ralph de, pr. St Michael's Mount, 189

Carville, Peter de, pr. St Michael's Mount, 189

Cary, Henry, pr. Horsley, 170, 393

Cary, Richard, pr. Horsley, 170, 393

Cary, William, pr. Horsley, 170, 393

Casewick, Henry of, abb. Crowland, 37

Cassandra, prs Cheshunt, 554

Castell, John de, pr. Puffin Island, 449
Castell, John, *alias* Eschall, pr. York, Holy Trinity, 218
Castello, Mary de, prs Bungay, 547
Castello Kyver, Thomas de, pr. Breadsall, 343
Casterton, Thomas of, abb. Croxden, 276
Castleford, Simon of, pr. Pontefract, 246
Castone, Roger de, pr. Standon, 194
Castor, Thomas of, abb. Thorney, 75
Castro Novo, John de, pr. Monkton Farleigh, 238
Castro Novo, Peter de, *custos* Scarborough, 308
Cat, Margery, prs Norwich (Carrow), 592
Caterford, William de, pr. Flitcham, 380
Catesby, John of, pr. Catesby, 552
Catherington, Richard of, pr. Ivychurch, 397
Catterick, John of, pr. Newburgh, 429
Catton, John of, pr. Mountjoy, 427
Caunton, John of, pr. Thurgarton, 472 n. 46
Caus, Stephen de, pr. West Mersea, 210
Cause, Margaret, prs Heynings, 570
Cause, Robert, master Nun Cotham, 593
Caux, John de, abb. Peterborough, 58
Caux, John de, pr. Winchester, St Swithun, 83
Cave, John of, abb. Newhouse, 507
Cave, Roger of, pr. Watton, 530
Cavendish, John of, pr. Chipley, 364
Caversfield, Adam of, pr. Grafton Regis, 382
Caversham, Henry of, pr. Stamford, St Mary and St Michael, 610
Caversham, John of, abb. Dorchester, 375
Cawood, David of, abb. Selby, 67
Cawood, Robert of, pr. Lincoln, St Mary Magdalen, 118
Cecilia, *see* Cecily
Cecily, abbs Polesworth, 598
Cecily, abbs Romsey, 600
Cecily, abbs Tarrant Kaines, 614
Cecily, prs Brewood White Ladies, 544
Cecily, prs Crabhouse, 556
Cecily, prs Hampole, 567
Cecily, prs Hinchingbrooke, 572
Cecily, prs Ickleton, 573
Cecily, prs Ivinghoe, 574
Cecily, prs Kilburn, 575
Cecily, prs Kington St Michael, 576
Cecily, prs London, Clerkenwell, 582
Cecily, prs Sopwell, 607
Cecily, prs Swaffham Bulbeck, 613
Cecily, prs Swine, 614
Cedifor, abb. Strata Florida, 312
Celestria, prs Ankerwyke, 539
Cerboneur(?), *see* Tubonour

Cerne, Ralph of, abb. Cerne, 31
Cerne, Walter of, abb. Muchelney, 54
Cerne, William, abb. Abbotsbury, 16
Cernecote, Richard de, pr. Bradenstoke, 342
Cerney, Nicholas de, pr. Wroxton, 489
Cernoun, John de, pr. Sporle, 193
Cernyngton, Clemence de, abbs Tarant Kaines, 615
Chacombe, Elias of, pr. Canons Ashby, 357
Chacombe, Richard of, pr. St Denys, 455
Chacombe, Walter of, abb. Croxden, 275
Chadderton, Emma of, prs Pinley, 598
Chaddesley, Geoffrey de, pr. Merton, 423
Chagford, William of, pr.-el. Canonsleigh, 357
Chalons, John de, pr. Monkton Farleigh, 238
Chaluns, John, pr. Prittlewell, 249
Chamberlain, Alice de, ?prs Cambridge, St Mary and St Radegund, 548
Chamberlain, Simon the, abb. Reading, 60
Champagne, Fulk of, pr. Tickford, 200
Champeaux, Robert, abb. Tavistock, 72
Champene, Nicholas, pr. Ware, 207
Champneys, John, abb. Vale Royal (Darnhall), 317
Chanbard, Robert, master Carham, 358
Chanon, Richard, *see* Brownknave, Richard
Chaperon, John, pr. Minting, 178
Chapmannesford, Walter de, pr. Newark, 427
Charite, Matthew, pr. Weedon Lois, 209
Charité, La, William of, *alias* Kant, pr. Bermondsey, 221
Charlecote, Simon of, minister Thelsford, 534
Charlecote, Thomas of, minister Thelsford, 534
Charles, abb. Whalley (Stanlow), 322
Charlieu, *see* Caroloco
Charlton, Christina, prs Kington St Michael, 576
Charlton, Richard of, abb. Cirencester, 368
Charlton, Robert of, pr. Stavordale, 463
Charlton, Walter of, pr. Kenilworth, 399
Charrins, Guy de, pr. Castle Acre, 224
Chart, William of, pr. Combwell, 371
Chartham, William of, pr. Dover, 98
Chartres (= Avignon = Thifford = Tickford, q.v.), John de, pr. Bermondsey, 221
Charwelton, Peter Devias of, abb. Biddlesden, 262
Chatet, John, pr. Wolston, 214
Chatteris, John of, pr. Deeping, 96
Chatton, Ingram of, pr. Stamford, St Leonard, 130
Chaumberlayn, Elizabeth, prs Legbourne, 580
Chaumberlayn, Joan, prs Legbourne, 579
Chaumberlayn, John (le), abb. Owston, 442
Chaumberlayn, Katherine le, prs Wothorpe, 623
Chaumberlayn, Tiphania, prs Cheshunt, 554

Chaumes, Aymo de, pr. Thetford, St Mary, 252

Chaundes, John, pr. Carmarthen, 361

Chaundes, John (de), pr. Llanthony Secunda, 414

Chauret, Iveta de, prs Stixwould, 610

Chauvertune, Walter de, pr. Newnham, 430

Chawman, Joan, prs Chicksands, 521

Chay, Henry de, see Miouns, Henry de

Cheadle, Robert of, pr. Stafford, 463

Cheadle, William of, abb. Rocester, 453

Cheam, Peter of, pr. Southwark, 460

Cheddar, Adam of, pr. Dunster, 99

Cheddington, John of, pr. Dunstable, 377

Chelfham, Ralph (de), pr. Exeter, St James, 229;
    pr. Kerswell, 231
    see also Chelpham

Chelmesho, Thomas de, pr. Leighs, 409

Chelpham, Ralph (? same as Chelfham), pr.
    Barnstaple, 220

Cheltenham, John of, abb. Eynsham, 43

Chentriaco, Guichard de, pr. Prittlewell, 249
    see also Cheyntriaco; Chintriaco

Chepford, Juliana de, prs Castle Hedingham, 551

Chepstow, Roger of, abb. Grace Dieu, 284

Cherdesle(y), John de, abb. Notley, 440

Cheriton, Nicholas of, pr. Southwick, 462

Cherobles, Stephen de, pr. Pontefract, 246

Cherring, John de, pr. Brecon, 93

Cheryton, Nicholas, pr. Folkestone, 161

Chesham, Alan of, abb. Leicester, 407

Chesledene, Walter de, abb. Netley, 296

Chesnayo, William de, pr. Wootton Wawen, 216

Chester, John of, abb. Combermere, 274

Chester, Mary of, prs. Chester, 555

Chester, Philip of, pr. Ranton, 450

Chester, Richard of, abb. Combermere, 274

Chester, William of, abb. Combe, 273

Chesterfield, John of, abb. Welbeck, 515

Chesterton, Thomas of, abb. Tewkesbury, 74

Cheswardine, John of, abb. Rocester, 453

Chetham, John de, pr. Canterbury, Christ Church,
    27

Chetwynd, John of, abb. Lilleshall, 411

Cheuen, John, pr. Minting, 178

Cheverer, John, pr. Montacute, 239

Chevre, John (le), alias of Creake, abb. North
    Creake, 435

Cheynduyt, Matilda, prs Ivinghoe, 574

Cheyne, Michael, [Wootton Wawen], 215

Cheyneston, Robert (de), abb. Vale Royal, 318

Cheyntriaco, Philip de, pr. Kerswell, 231; pr.
    Montacute, 240
    see also Chentriaco; Chintriaco

Chichele, Richard de, pr. York, Holy Trinity, 218

Chichester, Peter of, abb. Beaulieu, 260

Chichester, Richard of, abb. Newenham, 297

Chichester, Richard of, abb. Reading, 61

Chichester, Roger of, abb. Canterbury, St
    Augustine, 29

Chichester, William of, pr. Monkton Farleigh, 237

Child, Margery, prs Canterbury, Holy Sepulchre,
    550

Child, Walter, pr. Grafton Regis, 383

Childeston, Richard de, pr. Dunster, 99

Childhay, John (of), abb. Forde, 279

Chill, Nicholas, pr. Woodspring, 487

Chillenden, Adam of, pr. Canterbury, Christ
    Church, 28

Chilthorne, Alice of, prs Ilchester, 573

Chilton, Michael of, see Gunnerton, Michael of

Chilwell, Thomas of, pr. Shelford, 459

Chingford, Alice of, prs Rowney, 602

Chinnoc(k), William, abb. Stanley, 310

Chintriaco, Geoffrey de, pr. Lenton, 232; Geoffrey
    de, pr. Montacute, 240

Chintriaco, Hugh de, pr. Lewes, 235
    see also Chentriaco; Cheyntriaco

Chirbury, Thomas of, pr. Chirbury, 365

Chiriton, William de, abb. Evesham, 42

Chiriton, William de, pr. Llanthony Secunda, 415

Chiryton, Joan (de), prs Canterbury, Holy
    Sepulchre, 550

Chiseldon, Roger of, pr. Ivychurch, 397

Chishall, Ralph of, pr. Bicknacre, 335

Chishull, Richard, abb. Tilty, 316

Chiveny(?), Geoffrey de, pr. York, Holy Trinity,
    217

Chosiaco, John de, pr. York, Holy Trinity, 218

Christiana, prs Castle Hedingham, 551

Christiana, prs Littlemore, 582

Christi(a)na, prs London, Haliwell (occ. 1269 x
    86), 584

Christiana, prs Newcastle-upon-Tyne (occ. 1227 x
    33), 589

Christiana, prs Newcastle-upon-Tyne (occ. 1274),
    589

Christiana, prs Newcastle-upon-Tyne (occ. 1351),
    589

Christiana, prs Wilberfoss, 619

Christina, prs Hampole, 567

Christina, prs London, Haliwell (occ. 1314), 584

Christina, prs Minster in Sheppey, 588

Christina, prs Rowney, 603

Christina, prs Wintney, 622

Christina, prs Wix, 622

Christina, prs Yedingham, 625

Chubb(e), John, abb. Tavistock, 72; pr. Scilly, 128

Churchstow, John of, abb. Buckfast, 267

Chyerbitz, Peter de, pr. St Helen's, 250

Chylheglys, John, abb. Forde, 279

Chynnock, *alias* Wynchestre, John, abb. Glastonbury, 47

Cibe, John, pr. Harmondsworth, 165

Cillardy, William, [West Ravendale], 518

Cirencester, William of, pr. Leonard Stanley, 117

Cirencester, William of, pr. Worcester, 85

Claines, *alias* Worcester, John of, pr. Great Malvern, 105

Clare, Petronilla de, abbs Canonsleigh, 549

Clare, Robert de, abb. Netley, 295

Clare, Thomas de, pr. Walsingham, 478

Clare, William de, pr. Ely, 41

Clarel, Michael, pr. Clatford, 151

Clarell, Stephen, pr. Healaugh Park, 389

Clarice, abbs Tarrant Kaines, 614

Clarice, abbs Winchester, 620

Clarice, prs Kington St Michael, 576

Clarice, prs Wothorpe, 623

Clarus, pr. Steventon, 194

Clavyle, Margaret, prs Cambridge, St Mary and St Radegund, 548
   see also Clayvile

Claxton, Richard of, pr. Durham, 38; pr. Holy Island, 110

Claxton, Robert of, pr. Stamford, St Leonard, 130

Claxton, Robert of, pr. Thurgarton, 472

Claxton, William of, pr. Norwich cath., 56; pr. Yarmouth, 137

Clay, Richard del, *custos* Keldholme, 575

Clay, William del, pr. Hexham, 390

Clayvile, Alice, prs Bristol, St Mary Magdalen, 545
   see also Clavyle

Clayworth, Margaret of, prs Kirklees, 576

Clayworth, Robert of, pr. Haltemprice, 385

Cleeve, Robert of, abb. Cleeve, 271

Clehonger, John of, abb. Wigmore, 485; pr. Wormsley, 489

Clemencia, prs Cheshunt, 554

Clement, abb. Barlings, 492

Clement, abb. Conway, 275

Clement, abb. Neath, 295

Clement, abb. Osney, 441

Clement, abb. St Radegund, 509

Clement, pr. Bromholm, 223

Clement, pr. Finchale, 103

Clement, pr. Lytham, 119

Clement, Margery, prs Studley, 612

Clement, Roger, pr. Catesby, 552

Clement ap Richart, abb. Strata Florida, 313

Clenefeld, Nicholas de, master Godstow, 563

Cleobury, Adam of, [Much Wenlock], 242

Cleobury, Adam of, abb. Shrewsbury, 70

Clepenville, Roger de, pr. Lenton, 231

Clerbaud, Henry, abb. Cirencester, 368 n.14

Clere, John de, pr. Southwick, 461

Clere, Roger de, pr. Ravenstone, 451

Cley, John de le, ?pr. Hexham, 391

Cley, Peter of, pr. Mountjoy, 427

Cleydon, John de, [Wootton Wawen], 214

Clifford, Benedicta de, prs Westwood, 616

Clifford, Nicholas of, pr. Derby, St James, 227

Clifford, Simon of, pr. Craswell, 256

Clifford, William of, master Bamburgh, 329

Clifford, William of, pr. Nostell (*? same as above*), 439

Clifton, Robert of, pr. Elsham, 378

Clifton, Walter of, abb. Wardon, 320

Clifton, William of, abb. Darley, 374

Cliponvill, Roger de, pr. Montacute, 239

Clitheroe, Richard of, abb. Sallay, 307

Cliveden, Agnes of, prs Little Marlow, 581

Clivilla, Robert de, pr. Blyth, 145

Clopcote, Robert de, pr. Bath, 22

Clopton, William of, abb. Thorney, 75

Cloune, William, abb. Leicester, 408

Clovill, Joan de, prs Castle Hedingham, 551

Clowe, Adam, of Leverington, *alias* of Leverington, pr. Sempringham, 528

Cluny, Benedict of, pr. Castle Acre, 224

Clynton, Alice de, prs Wroxall, 624

Clyve, Robert de, abb. Lessness, 410

Clyve, Simon de, pr. Rochester, 62

Clyve, William (de), abb. Chertsey, 32

Coates, William of, pr. Elsham, 378

Cobham, Joan, prs Minster in Sheppey, 588

Cobham, John de, pr. Little Dunmow, 412

Coch, Philip, abb. Strata Florida, 312

Coci, John, pr. Deerhurst, 156

Cockerham, John of, abb. Furness, 282

Cockerham, William of, abb. Furness, 282

Cockerington, John of, pr. Alvingham, 519

Cockyng, Richard, pr. Bruton, 351

Coddenham, Alan of, pr. Great Bricett, 383

Codham, John de, pr. Tandridge, 466

Coggeshall, William of, abb. Stratford Langthorne, 314

Cokayn, John de, abb. Furness, 282

Cok(e), William, abb. Bristol, St Augustine, 348

Coker, Geoffrey of, pr. Kidwelly, 115

Coker, Richard of, pr. Kidwelly, 115
Coker, Robert, pr. Bruton, 351
Cokerel(l), Joan, abbs Wherwell, 618
Cokiswell, Hugh de, abb. Newenham, 296
Cokiswell, John de, abb. Newenham, 297
Cokkyng, William de, pr. Witham, 326
Col(...)ll, Denise de, prs Wothorpe, 623
Colbern, Robert, abb. Tavistock, 72
Colby, John de, pr. Hertford, St Mary, 110
Colchester, John of, pr. Blythburgh, 338
Colchester, John of, pr. Hatfield Regis, 166
Coleman, Christiana, prs Ickleton, 573
Coleman, William, of Hatfield, abb. Walden, 77
Colepitte, Peter de, abb. Buckfast, 267
Colerne, William of, abb. Malmesbury, 51
Colesden(e), Simon de, pr. Bushmead, 353
Coleville, David de, pr. Monmouth, 182
Coleville, Robert de, master Arden, 540
Coleville, Walter de, pr. Monmouth, 182
Coleville, Walter de, pr. Sele, 191
Colewell, John de, pr. Little Malvern, 119
Coleworth(e), Richard de, pr. Hurley, 113
Colle, John, pr. Alberbury, 256
Colle, John, pr. Tickford, 201
Collingbourne, Henry of, pr. Southwark, 461
Collingham, Hugh of, pr. Newstead (in Sherwood), 432
Collingham, Joan of, prs Heynings, 570
Collingham, John of, abb. Waverley, 321
Collingham, William of, pr. Chacombe, 362
Colman, Thomas, of Lichfield, pr. Launde, 406
Colne, John of, pr. Snape, 129
Colne, John of, pr. Tickford, 199
Colne, Richard of, abb. Colchester, 35
Colne, Richard of, pr. Snape, 129
Colney, Lucy of, prs London, Haliwell, 584
Colneys, William de, pr. Ipswich, St Peter and St Paul, 396
Colsterworth, Thomas of, abb. Bourne, 341
Colton, Beatrice of, prs Arden, 539
Colton, John de, pr. Norton, 438
Colton, Nicholas of, pr. Buckenham, 351
Colum, John de, pr. Colchester, St Botolph, 369
Columbers (blank) de, pr. Cowick, 153
Columbers, Miles de, pr. Lewes, 234
Colvyle, Joan, prs Rosedale, 602
Colwell, Thomas de, abb. Canterbury, St Augustine, 30
Colyn, Richard, master Carham, 359
Combe, John of, abb. Titchfield, 511
Combe, William of, abb. Dunkeswell, 277
Combe, William of, abb. Stanley, 310

Comberton, Thomas of, pr. Spinney, 462
Combes, Gerard de, abb. Northampton, St James, 437
Combor, Helias de, pr. Andover, 139–40
Combor(e), Ralph de, pr. Andover, 140
Combo(u)r, Robert de, pr. Andover, 139
Combornio, Ralph de, pr. Monmouth, 182
Compendio, Thomas de, pr. Weedon Lois, 209
Comp(e)ton, Hugh de, pr. Lincoln, St Mary Magdalen, 118; pr. St Bees, 127
Compton, John of, abb. Sherborne, 69
Compton, John of, pr. Gloucester, St Oswald, 382
Compton, John of, pr. Horton, 112
Compton, Nicholas of, pr. Sandwell, 66
Compton, William of, abb. Beeleigh, 480
Comyn, Nicholas, pr. Sele, 192
Conan, abb. Coverham, 497
Conan, pr. Northampton, St Andrew, 245
Conchis, Roger de, pr. Wootton Wawen, 214
Condreto, John de, pr. Lancaster, 171
Condu, William, dictus le, see Carentonio, William de
Coniscliffe, Joan of, prs Neasham, 589
Conisholme, Alice of, prs Legbourne, 579
Conka, Robert de, pr. Totnes, 202
Conon, pr. Monks Horton, 236
Conqueterre, William, pr. Tickford, 200
Constable, Euphemia, prs Stainfield, 608
Constance, abbs Wherwell, 617
Constance, prs Aconbury, 537
Constance, prs Cambridge, St Mary and St Radegund, 548
Constance, prs Davington, 556
Constance, prs Stainfield, 607
Constance, prs Wix, 622
Constantine, abb. Sibton, 308
Constantine, abb. West Dereham, 517
Constantine, pr. Fineshade, 379
Contepoyntour, Humphrey, dictus le, pr. Harmondsworth, 165
Conyers, Katherine, prs Holystone, 573
Conyngston, John de, pr. Trentham, 476
Cook, Thomas, pr. Taunton, 467
Copgrave, Robert, abb. Fountains, 281
Copley, Thomas of, pr. Bolton, 340
Coppingford, Joseph of, pr. Bushmead, 353
Corbel, Robert, pr. Monk Sherborne, 180
Corbet, Margaret, prs Brewood White Ladies, 544
Corbet, Simon, pr. Arbury, 328
Corby, Katherine of, prs Wothorpe, 623
Corby, Robert, abb.-el. Thorney, 75
Corcellis, Peter de, corrector Alberbury, 255

Corciis, Astorgius de, pr. Lenton, 232
Corden, Oger de, *see* Bueys, Oger de
Cordwayner, Gerard le, pr. Winghale, 213
Corfe, Walter of, abb. Milton, 52
Cormelis, Jerome de, pr. Everdon, 159
Cormellan, John le Fevre de, [Stratfield Saye], 196
Cormellis, Jerome de, pr. Creeting, 154
Corner, Nicholas (le), pr. Arundel, 142
Cornerth(e), Matilda (de), prs Wix, 623
Corneville, Richard de, pr. Newent, 183
Cornu, Andrew de, pr. Carisbrooke, 150
Cornu, Ralph le, pr. Hinckley, 169
Cornwall, Alan of, abb. Tavistock, 72; pr. Scilly, 128
Cornwall, Alan of, pr. Cardiff, 95
Cornwall, Peter of, pr. London, Holy Trinity, Aldgate, 415
Cornwall, Stephen of, abb. Buckfast, 268
Cornwall, William of, abb. Newenham, 297
Corp, Peter, pr. Minster Lovell, 177
Corzon, Margaret le, prs Henwood, 570
Cosby, Ivo of, abb. Owston, 442–3
Cosgrove, John of, pr. Snelshall, 71
Cossam, Reginald de, *alias* Bernevalle, pr. Tickford, 200
Costance, Margaret, prs Rowney, 603
Costyn, Margaret, of Lynn, prs Crabhouse, 556
Cosyn, John, pr. Flanesford, 380
Cotam, Avice de, prs Nun Monkton, 594
Cotelford, Richard de, abb. Torre, 512
Cotes, Clarice de, prs Broomhall, 545
Cotes, Gilbert of, abb. Kirkstall, 288
Cotes, John de, abb. Tewkesbury, 74
Cotes, Peter de(l), pr. Bridlington, 346
Cotes, Roger of, pr. Kirby Bellars, 400
Cotesbrok, Isabel de, abbs-el. Northampton, De La Pré, 591
Cotheridge, William of, pr. Warwick, 481
Cothom, Elizabeth, prs Baysdale, 543
Cotrodes, Raymond de, pr. Horsham St Faith, 169
Cottesmore, William of, abb. Owston, 443
Cottingham, Thomas of, pr. St Bees, 127
Cottisford, Roger of, pr. Bicester, 334
Cotty, Christine *dictus*, of Lincoln, prs Nun Cotham, 593
Coucham, R. de, pr. Warwick, 481
Coudray, Ralph *dictus*, pr. Wareham, 207
Coupledyk, Alice, prs Stamford, St Mary and St Michael, 609
Courait, Ralph, pr. Lancaster, 171
Courour, Vincent le, pr. Minster Lovell, 177
Courtenay, John de, (Lewes), 234

Courtenay, John (de), abb. Tavistock, 72–3
Couvel(l), Isabel, prs Arden, 539
Coveley, William, pr. Kilpeck, 115
Coventry, John of, abb. Halesowen, 503
Coventry, Ralph of, abb. Battle, 22
Coventry, Ralph of, pr. Wolston, 214
Coventry, Roger of, abb. Osney, 441
Cowton, William of, pr. Durham, 39
Coxwold, Alice of, prs Heynings, 570
Coxwold, Walter (of), abb. Fountains, 281
Coxwold, William of, abb. Humberston, 49
Cramlington, Nicholas of, pr. Brinkburn, 347
Cranworth, Robert of, pr. Wormegay, 488
Cras, Katherine (la), abbs Lacock, 577
Craswell, Roger of, corrector Grosmont, 257
Cratfield, John of, abb. Sibton, 309
Crauden, John de, pr. Ely, 41
Craven, *alias* Giggleswick, Walter of, pr. Lytham, 120
Craven, William of, pr. Marton, 420
Cravenho, Alice de, prs Rothwell, 602
Craveton, Richard de, pr. Henes and Sandtoft, 108
Creeting, Walter of, pr. Alnesbourn, 327
Creeting, William of, pr. Letheringham, 410
Crek, Walter de, pr. Newstead by Stamford, 432
Crendon, Richard of, abb. Notley, 440
Crescy, Constance de, prs Hampole, 568
Crescy, Joan de, prs Hampole, 567
Crespy, Reginald de, pr. Lenton, 232
Cressi, Nicholas, pr. Mendham, 235
Cressingham, Cecily of, prs Cambridge, St Mary and St Radegund, 548
Crewkerne, William of, *alias* le Fria *alias* Fry, abb. Forde, 279
Crich, Thomas, pr. Kerswell, 231
Criche, Wiliam, pr. Kerswell, 231
Criencis, Peter de, pr. Loders, 175
Crispyn, Peter, pr. Wilmington, 211
Crist, Thomas, pr. Bath, 22
Cristeshale, Roger de, pr. Hatfield Regis, 166
Crohadas, Robert, pr. Newent, 183
Crokesby, Walter de, pr.-el. Oxford, St Frideswide, 444
Crokesle(y), Richard de, abb. Westminster, 78
Crompe, Simon, pr. Worcester, 86
Cromus, Hugh, abb. Abbey Dore, 259
Croquet, John de, pr. Winghale, 213
Crosby, Gilbert of, pr. Carlisle, 359
Crosse, John, pr. Leonard Stanley, 117
Crossholm, Ralph de, pr. Elsham, 378
Crowcombe, Alice of, prs Studley, 612

Crowland, Godfrey of, abb. Peterborough, 58
Crowland, Henry of, pr. Torksey, 474
Crowland, Richard of, abb. Crowland, 37
Crowle, Roger of, master Flamstead, 561
Croxby, William of, abb. Wellow, 482
Croxton, Richard of, master Hornby, 504
Croxton, William of, abb. Welbeck, 514
Croyroys, Isabel, prs Rusper, 603
Cubley, Alexander of, abb. Croxden, 276
Cublington, John of, pr. Alberbury, 255; pr.
   Craswell, 257
Cuddeworth, Roger de, pr. Norton, 438
Cudoe, Peter, pr. Deerhurst, 156
Cudworth, John of, abb. Muchelney, 54
Cuhelyn, pr. Beddgelert, 332
Cukefeld, Nicholas de, pr. Prittlewell, 247
Culchief, John de, pr. Breedon, 345
Culham, Nicholas of, abb. Abingdon, 16
Culmeston, Alexander, pr. Newark, 428
Culmstock, Ralph of, pr. Taunton, 467
Cumbrok, Thomas de, pr. Hurley, 114
Cumbwelle, Robert de, pr. Exeter, St Nicholas, 101
Cumnor, William (of), abb. Abingdon, 17
Cumnor, William of, abb. Bindon, 263; abb. Forde,
   279
Cunebaud, Robert, pr. Edith Weston, 158
Curcy, William de, pr. Madbury, 179
Curle, Nicholas, pr. Hempton, 389
Curry, Peter de, pr. Minster Lovell, 177
Curteys, William, pr. Leighs, 409
Curtipalacio, Theobald de, pr. Barnstaple, 219
Curtlyngton, William de, abb. Westminster, 78
Cury, Robert de, pr. Modbury, 179
Cusancia, James de, pr. Prittlewell, 234, 248–9; pr.
   Thetford, St Mary, 252
Cusancia, John de, pr. Bermondsey, 222, 234
Cut, Everard, abb. Bourne, 340
   see also Kut
Cymy, Thomas, of Wales, pr. Cardigan, 95
Cynfrig, abb. Conway, 275

Dabetot, Sibyl, prs Wroxall, 624
Dadington, William de, pr. Chetwode, 363
Dadyngtone, Hugh de, abb. Bristol, St Augustine,
   348
Dagworth, Nicholas of, pr. Blythburgh, 338
Dalling, Adam of, pr. Coxford, 372
Dalling, John of, abb. Wardon, 320
Dalmatius, pr. Lenton, 231
Dalmatius, pr. Pontefract, 246
Dalton, Adam of, senior, pr. Richmond, 125
Dalton, Adam of, pr. Wetheral, 135

Dalton, Patrick of, pr. Watton, 530
Dalton, Stephen of, pr. Lytham, 119
Dalton, Thomas of, pr. Lincoln, St Mary
   Magdalen, 118
Dalton, William of, pr. Finchale, 104
Daniel, pr. Rumburgh, 125
Daniel, pr. St Bees, 127
Dannanchiis, Imbert de, pr. Barnstaple, 220
Darains, William, master Swine, 614
Darcy, John, pr. Stansgate, 251
Darenth, Richard of, pr. Darenth, 96; pr.
   Rochester, 62
Darfield, Thomas of, pr. Nostell, 439
Darley, John of, abb. Beauchief, 494
Darlington, Hugh of, pr. Durham, 38
Darlington, John of, pr. Guisborough, 385
Darlington, Robert of, abb. Thornton Curtis, 470
Darlington, Simon of, pr. Lytham, 120
Darlington, William of, abb. Kirkstall, 288
Darsham, Adam of, pr. Great Bricett, 383
Dartford, Roger of, abb. Lessness, 409
Dautry, Elizabeth, prs Gokewell, 564
Dautry, Isabel la, prs Arthington, 540
Daventry, Cecilia of, abbs Northampton de la Pré,
   590
Daventry, Roger of, pr. Catesby, 552
David, abb. Conway, 275
David, abb. Llantarnam, 290
David, abb. Neath, 295
David, abb. St Dogmells, 189
David, abb. St Osyth (occ. c. 1207/21 x 47), 456
David, abb. St Osyth (occ. 1305 x 16), 457
David, abb. Strata Marcella (occ. 1215), 313
David, abb. Strata Marcella (occ. 1377 x 96), 313
David, abb. Thorney, 75
David, pr. Ewenny, 100
David, pr. Ivychurch, 397
David, pr. Kenilworth, 398
David, pr. Llanthony Prima, 413
David, pr. Sele, 192
David, pr. Tonbridge, 473
David ap Rice, abb. Margam, 292
Davill, Alice, prs Newcastle-upon-Tyne, 590
   see also Dayvell; Deyville
Daviston, Robert de, pr. Carmarthen, 360
Davolers, Alice, prs Redlingfield, 600
Davy, James, pr. St Anthony in Roseland, 454
Dawtre, Joan, prs Legbourne, 580
Dayleford, William de, pr. Wroxton, 489
Dayvell, Joan, prs Sinningthwaite, 607
   see also Davill; Deyville
Decimarii, William, pr. Minster, 176

Dedham, John (of), abb. Colchester, 35
Deen, Richard de, pr. Wroxton, 489
Deeping, Geoffrey of, abb. Bourne, 341
Deeping, John (of), abb. Thorney, 76
Deeping, Thomas of, pr. Newstead by Stamford, 433
Deerhurst, William of, pr. Cardiff, 95
Defensor, pr. Monks Kirby, 181
Delham, Elizabeth de, prs Higham, 571
Dene, Beatrice de, prs Brewood White Ladies, 544
Dene, Richard de, archpriest or pr. Barton, 331
Dene, William de, pr. Hastings, 387
Deneys, Robert, pr. Scilly, 128
Denis, abb. Beaulieu, 260
Denis, abb. Cerne, 31
Denis, abb. Hulton, 286
Denis, pr. Arundel, 141
Denis, pr. Ellingham, 158
Denis, pr. Holme East, 229
Denise, prs Cheshunt, 554
Denise, prs Davington, 556
Denise, prs Hampole, 567
Denise, prs Stamford, St Mary and St Michael, 609
Denise, prs Swine, 614
Denise, prs Wallingwells, 616
Denise, prs Wothorpe, 623
Denton, Robert of, ?abb. Swineshead, 314
Dera, prs Cambridge, St Mary and St Radegund, 548
Derby, Ralph of, pr. Caldwell, 355
Derby, Ralph of, pr. Repton, 452
Derby, Richard of, pr. Cardiff, 95
Derby, William of, pr. St Bees, 127
Dereham, David of, pr. Mullicourt, 55
Dereham, John of, pr. Mullicourt, 55
Derham, Richard de, abb. Athelney, 19
Dermor, Henry de, master Bamburgh, 329
Desertis, Oliver de, pr. Monks Kirby, 181
Deserto, Peter de, pr. Wareham, 207
Devenys, John (de), abb. Canterbury, St Augustine, 30
Deverel, William, abb. Netley, 296
Deverell, Thomas de, pr. Bruton, 351
Devias, Peter, of Charwelton, abb. Biddlesden, 262
Devizes, Richard of, pr. Bristol, St James, 94
Dew, Lewis, abb. Whitland, 323
Dewsbury, John of, pr. Nostell, 439
Dewsbury, Richard of, master Bamburgh, 329
Deyville, John, pr. Maxstoke, 421
    see also Davill; Dayvell
Didcot, Ralph of, abb. Dorchester, 375

Difford, John de, abb. Byland, 270
Digepet, William de, abb. Langdon, 504
Digun/?im, Richard dictus, [Throwley], 199
Diluiz, Walter de, pr. Bermondsey, 222
Dinanno, Nicholas de, pr. West Ravendale, 517–18
Disenhurste, Peter de, pr. Selborne, 458
Dishforth, Walter of, alias of Yarm, abb. Byland, 270
Disny, Alexander, pr. Elsham, 378
Ditchburn, Robert of, pr. Lytham, 120
Divisis, William de, pr. Ravenstone, 450
Docking, Robert of, abb. North Creake, 435
Dodford, John of, pr. Canons Ashby, 357
Dodford, John (of), pr. Oxford, St Frideswide, 445
Dodlegh, Walter de, abb. Rocester, 453
Dokesworth, John, pr. Northampton, St Andrew, 245
Dokynfeld, Richard de, see Kokenfeld, Richard de
Dol, Richard de, [Sudbury], 131
Dolerti, William, see St Neots, William of
Dolyna, William de, pr. Lenton, 232
Doncaster, Adam of, pr. Hertford, St Mary, 110
Doncaster, Thomas of, abb. Beauchief, 494
Doncaster, Thomas of, pr. Upholland, 76
Doneham, Cecily de, prs Neasham, 589
Donington, Hugh of, pr. Norton, 437
Donyngton, John de, pr. Burscough, 352
Donyngton, William of, minister Knaresborough, 533
Dorchester, Matilda of, abbs Burnham, 547
Dorchester, Richard of, abb. Notley, 440
Dore, Robert, pr. Loders, 176
Dorleg, William de, abb. Lilleshall, 410
Dorney, Joan of, abbs Burnham, 547
Dosa, Geoffrey de, pr. Montacute, 239
Doublel, Blase dictus, pr. Carisbrooke, 150
Douet, Robert, pr. Westwood, 617
Doul, Thomas, pr. Dodford, 374
Doulyssh, Thomas, pr.-el. Plympton, 448
Dounton, Richard de, pr. Bermondsey, 222
Dountone, Thomas de, pr. Breamore, 344
Dover, John of, abb. Eynsham, 43
Dover, William of, alias Staunford, pr. Dover, 96
Dover, William (of), pr. Dover, 98
Dovra, James de, pr. Lewisham, 173
Downham, Robert de, abb. Louth Park, 292
Drake, Nicholas, pr. Burtle, 352
Draughton, Richard of, abb. Bury St Edmunds, 27
Draycott, Cecily of, prs Ilchester, 573
Drayton, Hugh of, abb. Selby, 67
Drayton, John of, abb. Shrewsbury, 70
Drayton, Walter of, pr. Bradley, 343

Driby, Isabel of, prs Stixwould, 611
Drieu, John, pr. Tickford, 200
Driffield, Amice of, prs Cambridge, St Mary and
    St Radegund, 548
Driffield, Roger of, abb. Meaux, 293
Driffield, Simon of, pr. Elsham, 378
Driffield, Simon of, pr. Lanercost, 403
Driffield, Thomas of, abb. Sallay, 306
Driffield, William of, abb. Kirkstall, 289
Driffield, William of, abb. Meaux, 293
Driffield, William of, pr. Kirkham, 402
Dringhoe, William of, abb. Meaux, 293–4
Drinkstone, Alexander of, pr. Butley, 354
Dryffeld, Thomas, ?pr. St Cross, 188
Drynyngham, Roger de, pr. Peterstone, 447
Duckmanton, John of, abb. Welbeck, 515
Dudley, Benedict of, master Hirst, 392
Dugas, John, pr. Allerton Mauleverer, 139
Duk, Thomas, pr. Gloucester, St Oswald, 382
Duket, Joan, abbs Shaftesbury, 606
Dulverne, Richard de, pr. Trentham, 476
Dumbleton, Hugh of, abb. Hailes, 284
Dumbleton, John of, pr. Little Malvern, 119
Dumbleton, Richard of, pr. Worcester, 85
Dumbleton, William of, abb. Reading, 61
Dumbleton, William of, pr. Leominster, 117
Dummer, Alice of, prs Wintney, 622
Dumo, Ralph de, pr. Boxgrove, 146
Dune, Anastasia, abbs Elstow, 559
Dunham, Beatrice de, prs Legbourne, 579
Dunham, Ralph de, pr. Bicknacre, 335
Dunham, Ralph de, pr. Tynemouth, 132
Dunham, Richard de, abb. Louth Park, 291
Dunlegh(e), Amfelisia de, prs Higham, 571
Dunstable, Ellen of, prs Flamstead, 560
Dunstable, Hugh of, pr. Snelshall, 71
Dunstable, William of, pr. Coventry, 36
Dunster, John of, abb. Bruern, 266
Dunster, John of, pr. Bath, 22
Dunston, Emma of, prs Wykeham, 625
Dunston, Hugh of, pr. Nocton Park, 434
Dunstone, Thomas of, abb. Buckland, 268
Dunton, John of, pr. Peterstone, 447
Dunton, Osbert of, abb. Leicester, 407
Dunton, Walter of, abb. West Dereham, 516
Dunwith, Alexander of, pr. Blythburgh, 338
Dupont, Matthew, pr. Cogges, 152
Durand, abb. Buckfast, 267
Durand, pr. Little Dunmow, 412
Durand, pr. Modbury, 178
Durand, pr. Montacute, 238
Duraunte, John, pr. Scilly, 128

Durdent, Joan (de), prs Kington St Michael, 576
Durevill(e), John de, pr. Winchester, St Swithun,
    84
Durham, Isolda (Isabel) de, abbs Godstow, 562
Durham, John of, abb. Roche, 305
Durham, John of, pr. Warter, 480
Durham, Katherine of, prs Stainfield, 608
Durham, Peter of, pr. Brinkburn, 347
Durham, Robert of, master Jarrow, 114; master
    Monkwearmouth, 121
Durham, Stephen of, pr. Lytham, 119
Durham, Thomas of, abb. Egglestone, 502
Durham, Walter of, pr. Durham, 37
Durnford, John of, pr. Mottisfont, 426
Duro Sensu, Peter de, pr. Newent, 183
Durvassal, Christina, prs Cook Hill, 555
Duston, Alan of, abb. Northampton, St James, 436
Dutot, Robert, pr. Boxgrove, 147
Dutton, Agatha of, alias Sutton, prs Chester, 554
Dutton, Agnes of, prs. Chester, 555
Duvone, Peter de, abb. Rewley, 301
Dwyt, Robert, pr. Alnesbourn, 327
Dyamanda, prs Castle Hedingham, 551
Dygon, Peter de, pr. Weedon Lois, 209
Dyioun, Peter de, pr. Weedon Lois, 209
Dyva, Henry de, pr. Stoke by Clare, 196
Dyve, Margery (de), abbs Godstow, 536

E., abb. Talley, 511
E., abb. Welbeck, 515 n. 23
E., pr. Gloucester, St Oswald, 381
E., prs Llanllyr, 582
Easby, Alexander of, abb. Egglestone, 502
Easby, John of, abb. Egglestone, 502
Easby, Peter of, abb. Egglestone, 502
Easingwold, Peter of, pr. Rumburgh, 125
Eastcott (?), Ralph of, abb. Cirencester, 368
Eastfield, John (of), pr. Spalding, 193
Easton Neston, William of, pr. Luffield, 50
Eastry, Anselm of, pr. Dover, 97
Eastry, Henry of, pr. Canterbury, Christ Church,
    28
Eastry, Oswald of, abb. Faversham, 45
Eastry, Robert of, abb. Langdon, 505
Eaton, Simon of, pr. Dunstable, 377
Ebblosbury, Thomas de, abb. Cerne, 31
Ebolo, John de, [Wootton Wawen], 214
Eboracum, see York
Eccleshall, John of, pr. Ranton, 450
Eccup, Isabel of, prs Arthington, 540
Echyndenn, John, pr. Brecon, 94
Eda, prs Orford, 597

Edbert, pr. Hinton, 325

Edeneweyn, abb. Strata Marcella, 313

Edenham, Ivo of, master Godstow, 563

Edenham, Thomas of, abb. Barlings, 492

Edith, prs Easebourne, 557

Edlington, John of, pr. Markby, 419

Edmund, abb. Tilty, 316

Edmund, pr. Bodmin, 339

Edmund, pr. Little Dunmow, 412

Edmundsbury, William of, ?abb. Newminster, 298 n. 20

Edmundson, Elizabeth, prs Wykeham, 625 n. 19

Edoreston, John de, abb. Bordesley, 264

Edoreston, William de, abb. Bordesley, 265

Edrich, John, pr. Carmarthen, 360

Edward, abb. Notley, 440

Edward, pr. Mullicourt, 54

Edwyne, Robert, pr. Thetford, Holy Sepulchre, 468

Efreno, John de, pr. Wilsford, 212

Eggleston, Joan of, prs Neasham, 589

Eglewyskadell, Gregory de, abb. Bardsey, 329

Egmanton, Agnes of, prs Nun Appleton, 592

Egmanton, Alice of, prs Gokewell, 564

Eisneille, William, pr. Monks Kirby, 181

Eketone, Geoffrey de, pr. Canons Ashby, 357

Eldesfelde, John de, pr. Bromfield, 95

Eleanor, prs Arden, 540

Eleanor, prs Arthington, 540

Eleanor, prs Broomhall, 546

Eleanor, prs Flixton, 561

Eleanor, prs London, Clerkenwell, 582

Eleanor, prs Moxby, 588

Elemosina, Peter de, pr. Wareham, 207

Elerius, abb. Pershore, 56; pr. Cogges, 151

Elias, abb. Calder, 271

Elias, abb. Coverham, 497

Elias, abb. Croxton Kerrial, 498

Elias, abb. Dieulacres, 277

Elias, abb. Easby, 500 n.14

Elias, abb. Lessness, 409

Elias, abb. Quarr, 300

Elias, abb. Revesby, 301

Elias, abb. Swineshead, 314

Elias, abb. Wardon, 320

Elias, minister Thelsford, 534

Elias, pr. Barlinch, 330

Elias, pr. Bridlington, 345

Elias, pr. Bromfield, 94

Elias, pr. Healaugh Park, 388

Elias, pr. Lamanna, 116

Elias, pr. Rochester, 61

Elias, pr. Thurgarton, 471

see also Helias

Elizabeth, prs Marrick, 588

Elizabeth, prs Stamford, St Mary and St Michael, 609

Elizabeth, prs Studley, 612

Elizabeth, prs Whistones, 618

Elkeley, Alan de, pr. Felley, 379

Ella, Thomas of, pr. Haltemprice, 385

Elleboef, Robert de, pr. Deerhurst, 155

Ellen, abbs Tarrant Kaines, 615

Ellen, prs Baysdale, 542

Ellen, prs Cambridge, St Mary and St Radegund, 548

Ellen, prs Cheshunt, 554

Ellen, prs Ellerton-in-Swaledale, 557

Ellen, prs Henwood, 569

Ellen, prs Ickleton, 573

Ellen, prs Keldholme, 574

Ellen, prs Marrick, 587

Ellerbeck, William of, abb. Rievaulx, 302

Ellingham, John of, pr. Weybourne, 484

Ellingham, Ralph of, pr. Yarmouth, 136

Ellington, John (of), pr. Stonely, 465

Ellington, Robert of, abb. Waltham, 479

Elm, Nicholas of, pr. Wormegay, 488

Elm, Robert of, abb.-el. Thorney, 74; pr. Deeping, 96

Elmdon, William of, abb. Alcester, 18

Elmham, H. of, pr. Hoxne, 112

Elmham, Henry of, pr. Coxford, 373

Elmham, Hugh of, pr. Coxford, 372

Elmham, Simon of, pr. Norwich cath., 55

Elstow, Simon of, pr. Bradwell, 24

Elveden, John of, pr. Mountjoy, 427

Elvet, Ralph of, pr. Finchale, 103

Elvet, William of, pr. Stamford, St Leonard, 129

Elwick, Gilbert of, pr. Holy Island, 111; pr. Oxford, Durham cell, 122

Elwick, John of, [keeper of Holy Island], 111; master Jarrow, 115

Ely, Agnes of, abbs Chatteris, 553

Ely, Agnes of, prs Swaffham Bulbeck, 613

Ely, John of, see Salmon, John

Ely, Nicholas of, pr. Daventry, 226

Ely, Ralph of, pr. Bicknacre, 335

Ely, Richard of, abb. Sibton, 309

Emelina, abbs Tarrant Kaines, 615

Emelina, prs Amesbury, 537

Emelina, prs Lyminster, 585

Emeric, bailiff of Atherington, 144

Emerton, Richard de, abb. Lavendon, 506

Emma, ?prs Ankerwyke, 539
Emma, prs Baysdale, 543
Emma, prs Brewood Black Ladies, 544
Emma, prs Cornworthy, 555
Emma, prs Derby, Kingsmead, 556
Emma, prs Grimsby, 567
Emma, prs Newcastle-upon-Tyne, 589
Emma, prs Nun Cotham, 593
Emma, prs Redlingfield, 600
Empingham, William of, pr. Newburgh, 428
Enerardemeville, Walter de, pr. Newton Longville, 242
Enford, John, abb. Waverley, 321
Enford, Richard of, pr. Winchester, St Swithun, 84
Engaine, William, pr. Fineshade, 379
Engayne, Robert, pr. Haltemprice, 385
Engelard, abb. Haughmond, 387
England, Robert (of), [Easton], 532
Englebourne, John of, pr. Plympton, 448
Enstone, Robert (of), pr. Cold Norton, 370
Ercall, John of, pr. Stafford, 462
Ercall, Robert of, abb. Lilleshall, 411
Erdeslose, Peter de, abb. Faversham, 44
Erlegh, Katherine daughter of John de, prs Buckland, 546
Ermenovill(a), Ralph de, pr. Deerhurst, 156
Eryholme, William of, abb. Easby, 501
Esau, abb. Cymmer, 276
Escayo, John de, [Long Bennington], 291
Eschall, John, see Castell, John
Escrick, Richard of, pr. Finchale, 103
Escrop, William, pr. Elsham, 377
Eselberg, Richard de, pr. Sandwell, 66
Esingdon, John de, abb. Thame, 315
Esmerville, William de, pr. Cogges, 152
Esse, Richard de, abb. Tavistock, 73
Essesden, John de, abb. Notley, 440
Essex, John of, pr. Great Bricett, 383
Essintun, H. de, pr. Earls Colne, 99
Estal, Robert de, abb. Bruern, 266
Eston, Richard of, pr. Pontefract, 247
Eston, Stephen of, abb. Fountains, 280; abb. Newminster, 298; abb. Sallay, 306
Eston(e), Richard de, pr. Great Malvern, 106
Estrepanacho, John de, pr. Hamble, 164
Estrepany, William de, pr. Steventon, 194
Eswelle, Samson de, pr. Hurley, 113
Eton, Henry de, pr. Nuneaton, 597
Eton, John de, pr. Shouldham, 529
Eton, Walter de, pr. Stavordale, 463
Etton, John of, pr. Watton, 530
Eudo, pr. Caldwell, 354

Eudo, pr. Hatfield Regis, 165
Eudo, pr. Markby, 419
Eudo, pr. Sandwell, 65
Eularia, prs Goring, 564
Euphemia, abbs Wherwell, 617
Euphemia, abbs Winchester, 620
Euphemia, prs Ilchester, 573
Euphemia, prs Moxby, 588
Eustace, abb. Garendon, 283
Eustace, abb. Jervaulx, 286
Eustace, abb. Milton, 52
Eustace, abb. Sibton, 309
Eustace, pr. Cardiff, 95
Eustace, pr. Cowick, 153
Eustace, pr. London, Holy Trinity, Aldgate, 416
Eustace, pr. Merton, 422
Eustace, pr. Newnham, 429
Eustace, pr. Newstead (in Sherwood), 431
Eustace, pr. Southwark, 460
Eustachia, prs Minster in Sheppey, 588
Eustorgius, pr. Horsham St Faith, 169
Eva, prs Thicket, 615
Eva, prs Wykeham, 625
Evelina, abbs Tarrant Kaines, 614
Evenley, Walter of, pr. Huntingdon, 394
Everard, pr. Llanthony Secunda, 414
Everard, pr. Longleat, 418
Eversalle (?), Margaret de, prs Neasham, 589
Eversden, Hugh of, abb. St Albans, 63
Eversdon, William, pr. Hatfield Peverel, 107
Everyngham, Rose, prs Nuneaton, 596
Evesham, Alexander of, abb. Stoneleigh, 312
Evesham (?), John of, abb. Whitby, 79
Evesham, John of, pr. Studley, 466
Evesham, John of, pr. Worcester, 86
Evesham, Richard of, abb. Vale Royal, 317
Evesham, Silvester of, pr. Worcester, 85
Evesham, Thomas of, pr. Charley, 362
Evesham, Thomas of, pr. Ranton, 450
Evesham, Walter of, pr. Ulverscroft, 477
Evesham, William of, pr. Kenilworth, 398
Ewelme, Robert of, pr. Oxford, St Frideswide, 444
Ewys, Richard, pr. Felley, 379
Exeter, John of, abb. Hartland, 386
Exeter, Matthew of, pr. Exeter, St Nicholas, 101
Exeter, Richard of, see Branscombe, Richard of
Exeter, Roger of, alias Pope, archpriest or pr. Barton, 331
Exeter, W. of, pr. Brecon, 93
Existens, Nicholas dictus, pr. London, Haliwell, 584
Extranea, prs Sopwell, 607

Extranea, Petronilla, prs Aconbury, 537
Eye, Henry of, pr. Barnwell, 330
Eye, Reginald of, *alias* de Montargi, pr. Thetford, St Mary, 252
Eye, Richard of, pr. Snelshall, 71
Eye, Simon of, abb. Ramsey, 60
Eymore, Katherine, prs Wroxall, 625
Eynham, Roger de, pr. Newark, 428
Eynsham, John of, pr.-el. Wymondley, 490
Eyr, Henry, pr. Christchurch (Twynham), 366
Eyr, William le, pr. Breamore, 344

F., pr. Leeds, 407
Faber, Roger, pr. Creeting, 154
Faber, Roger, pr. Everdon, 159
Fabian, Joan, *alias* of Banbury, prs Catesby, 552
Fabri, John, [Beckford and Colsterworth], 332; [Chepstow], 151; pr. Newent, 183
Fabri, John, pr. Brimpsfield, 148
Fabri, John, pr. Newton Longville, 243
Faceby, Henry of, pr. Lytham, 120
Faceby, Robert of, master Farne, 102
Fadir, Philip, pr. Caldy, 149
Fae, Geoffrey *dictus*, pr. St Neots, 191
Fagerlon, Hugh de, pr. St Neots, 190
Fairfax, Elizabeth, prs Hampole, 568
Fakenham, Geoffrey of, pr. Great Massingham, 383
Falco (Falk), Peter de, *alias* of St Stephen, pr. Ogbourne, St George, 185; pr. St Neots, 191
Falle, Alice de, prs Broomhall, 546
Faloniis, Hugh de, pr. Monks Horton, 237
Fangfoss, Henry of, *dictus* Scot, pr. Lincoln, St Mary Magdalen, 118
Fangnellon, Richard de, pr. Wilsford, 212
Faningho, Robert de, pr. Wroxton, 489
Farbourn, Richard de, pr. Breedon, 345
Faringdon, John of, abb. Forde, 279
Faringdon, Roger Harnhull of, *see* Harnhull, Roger
Farlington, Alice of, prs Moxby, 588
Farnecote, Thomas de, pr. Brooke, 350
Farnham, Adam of, pr. Winchester, St Swithun, 84
Farsey, Arnulph, pr. Burwell, 149
Fastolf, Katherine, prs Bungay, 547
Fauconer, Robert le, abb. Milton, 52
Fauconer, William le, abb. Abbotsbury, 15
Faugeriis, Oliver Britenis de, pr. Swavesey, 197
Fautrariis, Henry de, pr. Prittlewell, 248
Fauvel, John *dictus*, pr. Ecclesfield, 157
Favers, William de, pr. Tutbury, 203
Faversham, Eustace of, [pr. Dover], 97
Faversham, Robert of, abb. Faversham, 45

Fawsley, John of, pr. Daventry, 226
Fayrfax, Margaret, prs Nun Monkton, 595
Fayrfax, William, pr. Holy Island, 112
Fayrmere, Robert de, master Little Marlow, 581
Fécamp, Aubrey of, abbs Elstow, 558
Fécamp, John of, pr. Monkton Farleigh, 238
Fécamp, John of, pr. St Helen's, 250
Fécamp, William of, pr. Wymondham, 135
Feckenham, Richard of, pr. Worcester, 85
Feering, John (of), abb. Walden, 77
Feering, Robert (of), pr. Little Dunmow, 412
Feld, Alice de la, prs Gokewell, 564
Felda, John de, abb. Gloucester, 48
Felicia, abbs Godstow, 562
Felicia, prs Amesbury, 537
Felicia, prs Catesby, 551
Felicia, prs Sewardsley, 604
Felton, Mary of, prs Campsey Ash, 549
Fenwick, Thomas of, pr. Hexham, 391
Feringges, Geoffrey de, abb. Winchester, Hyde, 82
Fermeland, Margaret, prs Sopwell, 607
Ferrariis, Agnes de, abbs Shaftesbury, 605
Ferraris, Joan de, prs Lyminster, 585
Ferret, Guy, pr. Hempton, 389
Ferriby, William of, pr. Worcester, 480
Ferrybridge, Hugh of, abb. Jervaulx, 287
Ferthyng, Thomas, pr. Poughley, 449
Fertrer, Gehelius (Joel) le, pr. Minster, 176
Feryby, Nicholas, pr. Shouldham, 529
Fessinis, John de, pr. Wing, 213
Feverer, John, *alias* Smyth, pr. Hough, 394
Fevre, John le, *see* Cormellan, John le Fevre de
Fifehead, Walter (of), abb. Winchester, Hyde, 82
    see also Fyfhide
Figheldean, John of, pr. Amesbury, 538
Fikeys, Hugh, abb. Buildwas, 269
Fillilode, Joan, prs Brewood White Ladies, 544
Fina, prs Buckland, 546
Finchampstead, William of, pr. Leominster, 117
Finningham, John of, abb. Walden, 77
Finningham, John of, pr. Alnesbourn, 327
Fisher, John, *see* Burton, John of
Fiskerton, Henry of, pr. Stamford, St Mary and St Michael, 609
Fissacre, Robert de, pr. Launceston, 404
Fissheburn, Peter de, pr. *Castri Richmond*, 125 n.17
Fitton, Katherine de, prs Blackborough, 543
FitzSimon, Margery, prs Sinninghthwaite, 607
Flagge, Alice de la (atte), prs Whitstones, 618
Flagge, Walter de la, abb. Halesowen, 503
Flammaville, Richard de, pr. Ogbourne St George, 184

Flamstead, Nicholas of, pr. Binham, 93; pr. Hertford, St Mary, 110

Flamstead, Sibyl of, prs Ivinghoe, 574

Flamstead, William of, abb. Owston, 442

Flamstead, William of, pr. Redbourn, 124

Flamstede, Matilda, prs Sopwell, 607

Flateebiry, Avice de, prs Henwood, 570

Flecknoe, Peter of, pr. Coxford, 373

Fleg, Simon de, pr. Mountjoy, 427

Flegly, Henry de, pr. Monkton Farleigh, 237

Flemyng, John, custos Canterbury, Holy Sepulchre, 550

Flemyng, William, pr. Conishead, 372

Flemyngg, Robert, custos Canterbury, Holy Sepulchre, 550

Flete, Thomas, pr. Sudbury, 131

Fleury, Otto de, pr. Much Wenlock, 242

Flitcham, John of, pr. Flitcham (1349–), 380

Flitcham, John of, pr. Flitcham (1404–), 380

Flitcham, Vincent of, pr. Flitcham, 380

Flixton, Henry of, pr. Ellerton on Spalding Moor, 522

Flore, John of, pr. Brooke, 349

Flore, Nicholas of, abb. Northampton, St James, 437

Florence, pr. Monmouth, 182

Florence, prs Sewardsley, 604

Floriaco, Otto de, pr. St Helen's, 250

Florie, Richard de, pr. Hamble, 164

Fokeram, Isabel de, prs Wroxall, 624

Fokerham, Joan (de), prs Henwood, 570

Fokerham, Millicent of, prs Henwood, 570

Folcard, pr. Throwley, 199

Foliot, Henry, abb. Gloucester, 48; pr. Bromfield, 94

Foliot, Hugh, abb. Ramsey, 59

Foliot, Richard, pr. Bushmead, 353

Foliot(h), William, pr. Bristol, St James, 94

Folioth, Elizabeth, prs Bungay, 547
    see also Folyot

Foljambe, Agnes, prs Farewell, 560

Folkingham, William of, abb. Beauchief, 494

Folon, Hugh dictus, see Lorriaco, Hugh dictus Folon de

Folyot, Robert, pr. Bradwell, 24
    see also Foliot

Fonte, John de, pr. Hinckley, 169

Fonte, Richard de, pr. Llangennith, 175

Fontibus, Roger de, pr. Tywardreath, 204

Forde, John de la, pr. Hereford, 109

Forde, Robert (of), pr. Plympton, 448

Forde, Roger of, abb. Glastonbury, 46

Fordham, John of, pr. Thetford, St Mary, 253

Fordham, Robert of, pr. Wormegay, 488

Fordham, William of, pr. Anglesey, 327

Fordington, John of, abb. Hagnaby, 503

Forest, Ralph, pr. Hereford, 108

Formage, Joan, abbs Shaftesbury, 606

Formby, Robert of, abb. Cockersand, 496

Fornham, David de, alias Thornham, pr. Chipley, 364

Forsett, Ralph of, pr. Rumburgh, 125

Fosse, Stephen, pr. Avebury, 144

Fossor (Fossour), John, pr. Durham, 39; master Monkwearmouth, 121; pr. Stamford, St Leonard, 130

Fotheringay, Simon of, abb. Lilleshall, 411

Foukes, Stephen, pr. West Mersea, 210

Foulbrook, William of (I), pr. Burtle, 352

Foulbrook, William of (II), pr. Burtle, 352

Fouler, Joan, prs Greenfield, 566

Fouleston(e), Margery de, prs Broomhall, 546

Founteynes, Firmin de, pr. Takeley, 198

Fourriere, Theophania la, prs Nuneaton, 596

Fouville, William de, pr. Lewes, 233

Fouville, William de, pr. Northampton, St Andrew, 244

Fovea, John de, pr. Modbury, 179

Fovet/Fouet, Nicholas, pr. Cammeringham, 496

Fox, Thomas, master Arden, 540

Foxholes, John of, pr. Newburgh, 428

Foxley, William of, pr. Hamble, 164

Foy, Geoffrey, pr. Poughley, 449

Fraccinis, Robert de, pr. Creeting, 154; pr. Everdon, 159

Framlingham, Henry of, pr. Dodnash, 374

Framlingham, Ralph of, pr. Letheringham, 410; pr. Pentney, 447

Franceys, William le, pr. Newnham, 430
    see also Fraunceys

Franciscus, Peter, pr. Monks Kirby, 181

Frankelyn, Agnes, abbs Burnham, 547

Frasebii, Roger de, pr. Huntingdon, 394

Fraunceys, Walter le, pr. Castle Acre, 224
    see also Franceys

Frauncks, Avice, prs Grimsby, 567

Fraunkevyle, John de, pr. Harmondsworth, 165

Fraunkevylle, Thomas de, pr. Norton, 438

Freauvill, William de, pr. Upavon, 205

Frechevyl, John, abb. Alnwick, 491

Frend, Roger, abb. Chester, 33

Frendesbury, William, pr. Tonbridge, 473

Frenes, Alice de, prs Cook Hill, 555

Frenze, John of, pr. Weybourne, 484

Fresnay, John de, ?pr. Tickford, 200
Fressingfield, John of, pr. Ely, 41
Fria, William le, abb. Forde, 279; abb. Newenham, 297
Fria, William le, *see* Crewkerne, William of
Frieston, Roger of, master Legbourne, 580
Frigideo Monte, Richard de [Wareham], 207
Frilford, Henry of, abb. Abingdon, 16
Fring, Henry of, abb. Rufford, 305
Frisby, William of, pr. Alvingham, 519
Frison, Ralph le, pr. Cogges, 152
Friston, William de, pr. Merton, 423
Friston, William de, ?rector Ashridge, 535 n.1
Frith, John (de), abb. Sherborne, 69
Frollesham, Simon de, pr. Cold Norton, 370
Frome, Edward (of), pr. Maiden Bradley, 419
Frome, Henry of, pr. Maiden Bradley, 418
Frome, William of, pr. Maiden Bradley, 419
Fromond, Geoffrey, abb. Glastonbury, 46
Frond, William, pr. Dudley, 227
Froste, Peter, pr. Lanercost, 403
Frowe, Durand, pr. Eye, 160
Froyle, Richard of, pr. Reigate, 451
Frumund, pr. Derby, St James, 226
Frusselu, Walter, pr. Grafton Regis, 382
Fry, William, *see* Crewkerne, William of
Frye, John le, pr. Maiden Bradley, 418
Fryket, Odo, pr. York, Holy Trinity, 218
Frysby, Robert, pr. Nocton Park, 434
Fulcher, pr. Lancaster, 171
Fulchis, Vincent de, pr. Modbury, 179
Fulham, Joan (of), prs London, Clerkenwell, 583
Fulk, abb. Lessness, 409
Fulk, pr. Bicknacre, 334
Fulk, pr. Leeds, 406
Fulk, pr. Pontefract, 246
Fulk, pr. Tutbury, 203
Fulk, pr. Ware, 206
Fulstow, R. of, abb. Beauchief, 494
Fulstow, Robert of, master Arden, 540
Fultorp, William de, *provisor et custos* Hagnaby, 502
Furmentin, Robert, abb. Leicester, 408
Furnarii, Philip, pr. Modbury, 179
Fyfhide, Alice, prs Wintney, 622
    see also Fifehead
Fynch, John, pr. Canterbury, Christ Church, 28
Fynchesden, William de, master Heynings, 571
Fynden, Thomas de, abb. Canterbury, St Augustine, 29
Fysshacre, Joan de, prs Cornworthy, 555

G., abb. Calder, 270

G., abb. Sibton, 308
G., abb. Talley, 511
G., pr. Breedon, 345
G., pr. Bullington, 519
G., pr. London, St Bartholomew, 417
G., pr. Nuneaton, 596
G., pr. Stogursey, 194
Gabriel(e), William, pr. Llangennith, 175
Gacius, pr. Minster Lovell, 177
Gaddesby, Geoffrey de, abb. Selby, 68
Gaddesby, Robert of, pr. Hornby, 504
Gaddesby, Robert of, pr. Ulverscroft, 476
Gainsborough, Idonea of, prs Nun Appleton, 592
Gainsborough, Lucy of, prs Nun Appleton, 592
Gainsborough, Richard of, abb. Bardney, 21
Gainsborough, Richard of, pr. Thornholme, 469
Galeard, Ralph *dictus*, pr. West Ravendale, 517
Galeys, Philip le, abb. Wigmore, 485
Galganus, pr. Winghale, 213
Gallard(i), John, pr. Stogursey, 195
Galle, William, abb. Barlings, 492
Galloway, John of, pr. Lanercost, 403
Galner, Walter de, pr. Newnham, 430
Galouber, Thomas, pr. Monk Sherborne, 180
Gamages, Beatrice de, prs Aconbury, 537
Gamages, John de, abb. Gloucester, 48; pr. Ewenny, 100; pr. Hereford, 108
Gamel, pr. Bullington, 519
Gamelay, Nicholas de, pr.-el. Thurgarton, 471
Gamston, George of, abb. Welbeck, 515
Gardino, William de, pr. Hough, 394
Garford, Robert of, abb. Abingdon, 17
Garriz, John de, pr. Tickford, 200
Garner, pr. Lancaster, 171
Garton, John of, pr. Rumburgh, 126
Garton, Thomas of, pr. Henes and Sandtoft, 108
Garyn, Simon, pr. Otterton, 186
Gascoing, Geoffrey le, pr. Beckford and Colsterworth, 332
Gascur, Robert de, pr. Wareham, 207
Gastard, Fulk, pr. Abergavenny, 138
Gasturia, Robert de, pr. Carisbrooke, 150
Gategang, Sibyl, prs Newcastle-upon-Tyne, 589
Gateley, William of, pr. Beeston, 333
Gaugire, Nicholas, pr. Carisbrooke, 150
Gawcott, Robert of, pr. Canons Ashby, 357
Gaydenzar, Peter, pr. Montacute, 239
Gaynaire, Nicholas de, pr. Hinckley, 168
Gayniaco, Michael de, pr. Hinckley, 168
Gayterigg, John de, pr. Rumburgh, 126
Gayton, Richard de, abb. Lessness, 410
Gedding, William of, pr. Binham, 92

Gedling, Alexander of, pr. Thurgarton, 471–2

Geinville, Isabel de, prs Amesbury, 538
   see also Gineville; Guineville

Gelham, John de, pr. Little Dunmow, 412

Gelyn, Oliver, pr. West Ravendale, 518

Geninero, Peter de, pr. Lapley, 172

Geoffrey, abb. Basingwerk, 259

Geoffrey, abb. Bruern, 266

Geoffrey, abb. Buckland, 268

Geoffrey, abb. Coggeshall, 272

Geoffrey, abb. Combe (occ. 1332), 273

Geoffrey, abb. Combe (–1345), 273

Geoffrey, abb. Croxton Kerrial, 498

Geoffrey, abb. Easby, 500

Geoffrey, abb. Humberston, 49

Geoffrey, abb. Langley (–1340), 505

Geoffrey, abb. Langley (1368–), 505

Geoffrey, abb. Leiston, 506

Geoffrey, abb. Malmesbury, 51

Geoffrey, abb. Meaux, 293

Geoffrey, abb. Medmenham, 294

Geoffrey, abb. Newbo, 507

Geoffrey, abb. Newhouse, 507

Geoffrey, abb. North Creake, 435

Geoffrey, abb. Quarr, 300

Geoffrey, abb. Rufford, 305

Geoffrey, abb. Sallay, 307

Geoffrey, abb. Sibton, 309

Geoffrey, abb. Swineshead, 314

Geoffrey, abb. Tupholme, 513

Geoffrey, abb. Warden, 320

Geoffrey, *custos* of Alberbury, 255

Geoffrey, master Gokewell, 564

Geoffrey, master Stixwould, 611

Geoffrey, minister Thelsford, 534

Geoffrey, pr. Allerton Mauleverer,139

Geoffrey, pr. Blythburgh, 338

Geoffrey, pr. Bradenstoke, 342

Geoffrey, pr. Bromehill, 349

Geoffrey, pr. Bullington, 520

Geoffrey, pr. Burscough, 352

Geoffrey, pr. Carlisle, 360

Geoffrey, pr. Clattercote, 522

Geoffrey, pr. Covenham, 153

Geoffrey, pr. Coventry, 35

Geoffrey, pr. Craswell, 256

Geoffrey, pr. Dudley, 227

Geoffrey, pr. Ellerton on Spalding Moor, 522

Geoffrey, pr. Ellingham, 158

Geoffrey, pr. Finchale, 103

Geoffrey, pr. Great Bricett, 383

Geoffrey, pr. Hatfield Peverel, 107 n.12

Geoffrey, pr. Haverford West, 388

Geoffrey, pr. Hickling, 392

Geoffrey, pr. Holme East, 229

Geoffrey, pr. Hurley, 113

Geoffrey, pr. Ipplepen, 295

Geoffrey, pr. Lancaster, 171

Geoffrey, pr. Latton, 404

Geoffrey, pr. Little Dunmow, 412

Geoffrey, pr. Maiden Bradley, 418

Geoffrey, pr. Malton, 524

Geoffrey, pr. Minster Lovell, 177

Geoffrey, pr. Modbury, 179

Geoffrey, pr. Monks Horton, 236

Geoffrey, pr. Monks Kirby, 181

Geoffrey, pr. Newstead by Stamford, 433

Geoffrey, ?pr. Pentney, 446 n. 36

Geoffrey, pr. Peterstone, 447

Geoffrey, pr. Pontefract, *see* Godfrey

Geoffrey, pr. Rumburgh, 126

Geoffrey, pr. St Cross, 188

Geoffrey, pr. St Germans, 456

Geoffrey, pr. Thelsford, 467, 534

Geoffrey, pr. Thornholme, 469

Geoffrey, pr. Titley, 201

Geoffrey, pr. Totnes, 202

Geoffrey, pr. Trentham, 475

Geoffrey, pr. Tywardreath, 204

Geoffrey, pr. Wallingford, 133

Geoffrey, pr. Wareham, 207

Geoffrey, pr. Wing, 213

Geoffrey, pr. Wroxton, 489

Geoffrey, pr. York, St Andrew, 531

George, ?abb. Barlings, 492

Gerard, abb. Furness, 281

Gerard, pr. Alberbury, 255

Gerard, pr. London, St Bartholomew, 417

Gerard, pr. Wootton Wawen, 214

Gerard, John, pr. Leominster, 117

Gerard, Lawrence, pr. Beckford and Colsterworth, 332

Gerbald, pr. Clattercote, 522

German, abb. Basingwerk, 260

German, pr. Bodmin, 339

German, pr. Tynemouth, 131

German, pr. Wallingford, 133

Gerond, John, pr. Ware, 206

Gervaganus, pr. Drax, 376

Gervaise, Coumia, prs Wintney, 622

Gervase, abb. Holm Cultram, 285

Gervase, abb. Neath, 295

Gervase, abb. Pershare, 56

Gervase (Iorwerth), abb. Valle Crucis, 318

Gervase, pr. Andwell, 140
Gervase, pr. Arundel, 142
Gervase, pr. Breedon, 344
Gervase, pr. Cogges, 152
Gervase, pr. Kidwelly, 115
Gervase, pr. Modbury, 178
Gervase, pr. Norman's Burrow, 243
Gervase, pr. Sandaleford, 457
Gervase ap David, abb. Bardsey, 330
Gerveys, Joan, abbs Romsey, 601
Gery, John de, pr. Exeter, St James, 228
Gevelston, John de, pr. Nocton Park, 434
Geynville, Katherine de, prs Aconbury, 537
Geynville, Matilda de, prs Aconbury, 537
Geystwayth, Roger de, pr. Weybourne, 484
Geyton(e), William de, pr. Butley, 354
Geytyngton, John, abb. Newenham, 297
Gidding, Walter of, [Stonely], 465
Giffard, abb. Biddlesden, 261
Giffard, Alice, prs Langley, 578
Giffard, Juliana, abbs Wilton, 619
Giffard, Mabel, abbs Shaftesbury, 605
Giffard, Walter, abb. Waverley, 321
Giffard, William, abb. Buckfast, 267
Giggleswick, Adam of, abb. Roche, 305
Giggleswick, Walter of, see Craven, Walter of
Gilbert, abb. Beauchief, 493
Gilbert, abb. Boxley, 265
Gilbert, abb. Cleeve, 271
Gilbert, abb. Coverham, 497
Gilbert, abb. Haughmond, 387
Gilbert, abb. Holm Cultram, 285
Gilbert, abb. Langley, 505
Gilbert, abb. Leiston, 506
Gilbert, abb. Margam, 292
Gilbert, ?abb. St Radegund, 509 n. 20
Gilbert, abb. Tintern, 317
Gilbert II, master Sempringham, 527
Gilbert, pr. Allerton Mauleverer, 138
Gilbert, pr. Alvingham, 519
Gilbert, pr. Berden, 333
Gilbert, pr. Blyth (occ. 1224 x ?28), 145
Gilbert, pr. Blyth (occ. 1365), 146
Gilbert, pr. Brimpsfield, 147
Gilbert, pr. Bullington, 520
Gilbert, pr. Burstall, 148
Gilbert, pr. Corsham, 152
Gilbert, pr. Exeter, St James, 228
Gilbert, pr. Finchale, 103
Gilbert, pr. Hinckley, 168
Gilbert, pr. Horsley, 170, 392
Gilbert, pr. Ipswich, St Peter and St Paul, 396

Gilbert, pr. Ixworth, 398
Gilbert, pr. Lincoln, St Katharine, 524, 527 n. 3
Gilbert, pr. Llanthony Secunda, 414
Gilbert, pr. Monmouth, 182
Gilbert, pr.-el. Oxford, St Frideswide, 444
Gilbert, pr. Ranton, 450
Gilbert, pr. Stansgate, 251
Gilbert, pr. Stone, 464
Gilbert, pr. Sudbury, 131
Gilbert, pr. Tickford, 199
Gilbert, pr. West Mersea, 210
Gilbert, pr. Wilsford, 212
Gilbert, Robert, pr. Sandaleford, 457
Giles, abb. Robertsbridge, 303
Giles, pr. Ellerton on Spalding Moor, 522
Giles, pr. Hempton, 389
Giles, pr. Hough, 394
Giles, pr. Lewisham, 173
Giles, pr. Stogursey, 194
Giles, pr. Witham, 326
Gilling, John of, abb. York, St Mary, 87; pr.
    Wetheral, 134
Gilling, Katherine of, prs Handale, 568
Gilling, Stephen of, senior, pr. Rumburgh, 125
Gilling, Stephen of, pr. St Bees, 127
Gillyngham, Richard, pr. Canterbury, Christ
    Church, 28
Gineville, John de, pr. Stoke by Clare, 195
    see also Geinville; Guineville
Ginneux, William, pr. Newton Longville, 242
Gir', pr. St Cross, 188
Gisburn, John of, abb. Sallay, 307
Gisburn(e), Robert de, dictus Twentiman
    (Twentyman), pr. Henes and Sandtoft, 108;
    pr. Wetheral, 135
Gisors, William de, abb. of Beaulieu, 260
Glanford Brigg, Thomas of, abb. Thornton Curtis,
    470
Glanvill, Alexander de, pr. Rochester, 62
Glanvilla, Robert de, pr. Cowick, 154
Glanvilla, Robert de, pr. St Neots, 191
Glaydon, William de, minister Thelsford, 534
Glemham, John of, abb. Leiston, 506
Glemham, William of, abb. Colchester, 34
Glen, Roger of, pr. Charley, 363
Glen, Roger of, pr. Ulverscroft, 477
Gleyne, Walter dictus, pr. Weedon Lois, 209
Glinton, John of, master Sempringham, 527; pr.
    Sempringham, 528
Glinton, Matilda de, prs Wothorpe, 623
Glottyng', Robert de, alias de Bodeketon, pr.
    Hardham, 385; pr. Shulbred, 459

Gloucester, Agnes of, prs Bristol, St Mary Magdalen, 544

Gloucester, Gilbert of, abb. Eynsham, 43

Gloucester, John of, abb. Hailes (1305–), 284

Gloucester, John of, abb. Hailes (1368–97/9), 284

Gloucester, John of, abb. London, St Mary Graces, 290

Gloucester, John of, abb. Notley, 440

Gloucester, John of, pr. Leominster, 117

Gloucester, John of, pr. Llanthony Prima, 413

Gloucester, John of, pr. Southwick, 462

Gloucester, Laurence of, pr. Boxgrove, 147

Gloucester, Matilda of, prs Littlemore, 582

Gloucester, Robert of, pr. Llanthony Secunda, 415

Gloucester, Thomas of, abb. Evesham, 42

Gloucester, Thomas of, pr. Llanthony Prima, 413

Gloucester, Thomas of, pr. Penwortham, 123

Gloucester, Walter of, abb. Cirencester, 367

Gloucester, William of, pr. Oxford, St Frideswide, 444

(Gloucestre), Isabel, prs London, St Helen's and Holy Cross, 585

Gloz, William de, pr. Carisbrooke, 149

Goathurst, Richard of, abb. Athelney, 19

Gobaud, Margery, prs Stixwould, 611

Gobion, Agnes, prs Markyate, 587

Gobion, Isabel, prs Markyate, 587

Goch, Matthew (Martin), pr. Penmon, 446

Goda (Guna), prs Fosse, 561

God(d)ard, John, abb. Cleeve, 271; abb. Newenham, 296

Godelli, John, pr. Deerhurst, 156

Goderinggus, pr. Brecon, 93

Godes, John, pr. Sporle, 194

Godfrey, abb. Abbey Dore, 258

Godfrey, abb. Vaudey, 319

Godfrey, pr. Combwell, 371

Godfrey, pr. Launceston, 404

Godfrey, pr. Llanthony Prima, 414

Godfrey (Geoffrey), pr. Pontefract, 246

Godfrey, pr. Rumburgh, 125

Godfrey, pr. St Germans (occ. 1230), 455

Godfrey, pr. St Germans (occ. 1245), 455

Godin, William, [Wootton Wawen], 214

Godmanchester, William of, abb. Ramsey, 60

Goldale, John, pr. Swavesey, 198

Goldcliff, John of, abb. Margam, 292

Golde, Sibyl, prs Ivinghoe, 574

Goldington, Michael of, pr. Newnham, 430

Goldsborough, John of, [Monkwearmouth], 121; master Jarrow, 114; pr. Holy Island, 111

Goldsborough, William of, pr. Finchale, 104; pr. Holy Island, 111

Gomervill, Robert de, pr. Wilsford, 212

Gorecote, John de, pr. Studley, 466

Gorges, Alice de, abbs Godstow, 562

Gorney, Simon de, pr. Barnstaple, 219

Goronwy, abb. Strata Marcella, 313

Gosberton, John of, pr. Kyme, 403

Gosberton, Thomas of, pr. Deeping, 96

Gossham, Ellen, prs London, Haliwell, 584

Got, Raymond de, [Ogbourne St George], 184

Gotham, Roger of, abb. Biddlesden, 262

Goude, Edward, abb. Sherborne, 69

Goue, Andrew de (la), pr. Takeley, 198

Goulaffre, Lewis, pr. Wareham, 207

Goupillariis, Philip de, pr. Goldcliff, 162–3

Goupilleriis, Simon de, pr. Newent, 183

Gower, Alice, prs Foukeholme, 562

Gower, William, abb. Fountains, 281

Goxhill, Laurence of, pr. Thornholme, 469

Goxhill, Richard of, master Legbourne, 580

Goyer, William, pr. Hamble, 164

Goyn, Nicholas, pr. Cogges, 152

Gracius, pr. Minster Lovell, 177

Graculi, Thomas, pr. Deerhurst, 156

Grafham, Matilda de, prs Grimsby, 567

Grafton, Matthew of, pr. Bicknacre, 335

Grafton, Thomas of, abb. Pipewell, 299

Grainthorpe, Thomas of, master Legbourne, 580

Grana, Peter de, pr. Stogursey, 195

Grandisson, Matilda de, prs Aconbury, 537

Grangia, Richard de, pr. Newstead (in Sherwood), 432

Grangiis, John de, pr. Castle Acre, 224

Grantesdon, Simon de, pr. Bushmead, 353

Grantham, John of, abb. Croxton Kerrial, 498

Grantham, Thomas of, abb. Bourne, 341

Grantham, William of, abb. Croxton Kerrial, 498

Gras, John dictus, abb. Torre, 512

Gras, Richard le, abb. Evesham, 41; pr. Hurley, 113

Grasby, William of, abb. Thornton Curtis, 470

Gratel(e)y, Walter, pr. Taunton, 467

Grauleriis, William de, pr. Monks Kirby, 181

Grauncourt, John, abb. Dale, 499

Graunt, Ralph le, pr. Ware, 206

Grave, Richard de la, pr. Bruton, 351

Grave, Richard de la, pr. Horsley, 170, 393

Graveley, Robert of, abb. Thorney, 74

Gravenhurst, Roger of, pr. Dunstable, 377

Gray, Mary, ?prs Ellerton-in-Swaledale, 557

Gray, Richard de, abb. Osney, 441

Graystanes, Thomas of, master Jarrow, 114; pr. Finchale, 104

Greatford, Hamo, pr. Newstead by Stamford, 432

Greatford, William of, pr. Stamford, St Mary and St Michael, 610

Greatworth, Thomas of, master Catesby, 552

Greatworth, William of, pr. Catesby, 552

Greenborough, Richard de, pr. Amesbury, 538

Greene, Robert, pr. Bolton, 340

Greensted, Robert of, abb. Colchester, 34

Greenstede, Matilda de, prs Higham, 571

Greenstreet, John de, pr. Rochester, 62

Greetham, Thomas (of), abb. Thornton Curtis, 470 & n. 43

Gregi, Richard le, pr. Ware, 206

Gregory, abb. Leiston, 506

Gregory, abb. Strata Marcella, 313

Gregory, pr. Mottisfont, 425

Gregory, pr. Sudbury, 131

Gregory, pr. Wallingford, 133

Grendale, Beatrice of, prs Keldholme, 574

Grendon, John of, abb. Notley, 440

Grendon, William (of), pr. Daventry, 226

Grene, Katherine del, prs Rothwell, 602

Greneburgh, Richard de, pr. Grovebury, 164; pr. Nuneaton, 597; pr. Westwood, 617

Greneburgh, William de, pr. Coventry, 36

Grenefeld, Katherine, prs Rowney, 603

Gresley, Agnes of, prs Grace Dieu, 565

Gresteno, Roger de, pr. Toft Monks, 201

Grete, Peter de, pr. Bicester, 334

Grey, Benedicta de, abbs Malling, 586

Grey, Margaret de, abbs Northampton, De La Pré, 591

Grey, Matilda de, abbs Barking, 541

Greystoke, Roger of, pr. Shelford, 459

Griffin, abb. Abbey Cwmhir, 258

Griffin, abb. Biddlesden, 262

Griffin, abb. Llantarnam, 290

Griffin, Thomas, pr. Ivychurch, 397

Grilli, Adam, abb. Northampton, St James, 436

Grimoaldi, Peter, pr. Craswell, 256

Grimsby, Avice of, prs Broadholme, 545

Grimsby, John of, pr. Nocton Park, 434

Grimsby, Robert of, pr. Charley, 362

Grimsby, Thomas of, pr. Stamford, St Mary and St Michael, 610

Grimsby, William of, pr. Elsham, 378

Grimsby, William of, pr. Nocton Park, 434

Grimston, Hugh of, abb. Kirkstall, 288

Grimston, Robert of, pr. Henes and Sandtoft, 107

Grimston, William of, pr. Healaugh Park, 389

Grindham, John de, pr. Bruton, 351

Gristhwaite, Thomas of, abb. Jervaulx, 287

Gritton, William de, abb. Colchester, 35

Gros, Isabel, prs Westwood, 617

Gros, Peter le, pr. St Cross, 188

Grosmont, John de, abb. Abbey Dore, 259

Groundewell, James de, pr. Ivychurch, 397

Gro(u)ndy, Julian, prs Barrow Gurney, 542

Grove, Thomas de la, pr. Wroxton, 489

Gruffud, abb. Strata Florida, 312

Gruffudd, abb. Strata Marcella, 313

Gruffudd, abb. Talley, 511

Grutelyngthon, Roger de, pr. Dunster, 99

Grylle, Hugh, abb. Chester, 33

Grym, John, pr. Kings Lynn, 116

Grytton, William de, pr. Snape, 129

Gubion, Ralph, pr. Tynemouth, 131

Guernsey, Geoffrey of, see Rocherio, Geoffrey de

Guichard, pr. Bermondsey, 220

Guichard, pr. Kerswell, 230

Guildford, Clementia of, abbs Romsey, 601

Guilemore, Roger de, pr. Wilsford, 212

Guilliam, Robert, pr. Ecclesfield, 157

Guineville, William de, pr. Ogbourne St George, 184

  see also Geinville; Gineville

Guisborough, William of, pr. Durham, 39

Guist, William of, pr. North Creake, 434

Gummes, Philip de, abb.-el. Wellow, 481

Gundicote, Richard de, pr. Worcester, 85

Gundreda, prs Swine, 613

Gundreda, prs Yedingham, 625

Gunnerton, Michael of, alias Chilton, pr. Holy Island, 111

Gunness, Philip of, pr. Nocton Park, 433

Gunnora, prs Davington, 556

Gunnora, prs Little Marlow, 581

Gunston, William (of), abb. Croxden, 276

Gurdoun, Agnes, prs Grace Dieu, 565

Gurnay, Joan de, prs Barrow Gurney, 542

Gusford, John of, pr. Dodnash, 374

Guston, Alice, prs Canterbury, Holy Sepulchre, 550

Guy, pr. Blythburgh, 338

Guy, pr. Canterbury, St Gregory, 358

Guy, pr. Gloucester, St Oswald, 382

Guy, pr. Kings Lynn, 116

Guy, pr. St Bees, 127

Guy, pr. Southwick, 461

Guy, pr. Sporle, 193

Guymond, pr. Frampton, 161

Guyngis, Robert de, see Laurencz de Guyngis, Robert dictus

Guyntran(d), Stephen, pr. Swavesey, 197
Guyser, Peter, pr. Stratfield Saye, 197
G(wrgeneu), abb. Abbey Cwmhir, 258
Gyleforde, William de, abb. Stoneleigh, 311
Gylly, Adam, abb. Northampton, St James, 436
Gymeges, William de, pr. Wilmington, 211
Gyot, John, pr. Kerswell, 231
Gysburgh, William de, abb. Sulby, 511
Gyvele, William de, abb. Muchelney, 54

H., abb. Croxton Kerrial, 498
H., abb. Egglestone, 501
H., abb. Quarr, 300
H., abb. Strata Marcella, 313
H., master Wykeham, 625
H., pr. Bridlington, 345
H., pr. Canwell, 30
H., pr. Hornby, 504
H., pr. Rumburgh, 125
H., pr. Thoby, 468
H., prs Aconbury, 537
Habitu, Stephen de, *see* Ivry, Stephen de Habitu of
Haceby, Robert of, abb. Bourne, 341
Hackington, John of, abb. Langdon, 505
Hacleston, William, abb. Rewley, 301
Haddiscoe, Roger de, pr. Herringfleet, 390
Haddiscoe, William of, abb. St Benet of Hulme, 65
Haddon, William of, abb. Thorney, 75
Hadleigh, John of, pr. Woodbridge, 486
Hadstock, Emma of, prs-el. Cheshunt, 554
Haget, Eufemia, prs Sinningthwaite, 606
Hagworthingham, Thomas of, pr. Markby, 419
Hailes, Richard of, abb. Bindon, 263
Haisthorpe, Isabel of, prs Swine, 613
Haitlee, Richard de, pr. Charley, 363
Hakebeach, Robert de, pr. Castle Acre, 224
Hakeleston, William, abb. Waverley, 321
Hakeneye, Alice de, prs-el. Sopwell, 607
Haketo, Roger de, pr. Brimpsfield, 148
Hakeville, William de, pr. Newent, 183
Hakkleston, John, minister Easton, 532
Hakoun, Geoffrey, pr. Royston, 454
Hales, John de, abb. Bindon, 264
Hales, William de, abb. Lilleshall, 411
Halesworth, William of, pr. Butley, 354
Halgton, Richard de, pr. Monk Bretton, 53
Haliburn, William de, abb. Bindon, 263
Hallam, Richard of, pr. Newstead (in Sherwood), 432
Halley, Simon, pr. Brimpsfield, 148
Hallington, Robert of, pr. Oxford, Durham cell, 122; pr. Stamford, St Leonard, 130

Haltham, Ranulph of, abb. Humberston, 49
Halton, Walter of, pr. Spalding, 193
Halton, William of, pr. Chetwode, 364
Haltone, Thomas, abb. Stoneleigh, 312
Haltwhistle, Simon of, pr. Carlisle, 360
Haltwhistle, William of, pr. Carlisle, 359
Hamars, Nicholas de, pr. Haugham, 167
Hambeya, Galvan de, pr. Ellingham, 159
Hambury, Adam de, pr. Studley, 466
Hameldon, William of, abb. Beaulieu, 260
Hamelech, William de, pr. Healaugh Park, 388
Hamelin, Robert, pr. Tickford, 199
Hamelton, Henry de, pr. St Denys, 455
  see also Hamilton
Hamelyn, John, pr. Castle Acre, 224
Hamerton (Homerton), John (II) of, master
  Sempringham, 527; pr. Malton, 524
Hamilton, John de, pr. Sempringham, 528
  see also Hamelton
Hamme, Robert de, abb. Bourne, 341
Hamo, abb. Dieulacres, 277
Hamo, abb. Egglestone, 502
Hamo, master Swine, 614
Hamo, pr. York, Holy Trinity, 216
  see also Aymo
Hamonis, *alias* Hamon, William, pr. Cogges, 152
Hampnett, Henry of, abb. Cirencester, 368
Hampton, Geoffrey of, keeper Calwich, 356
Hampton, John, abb. Halesowen, 504
Hampton, Juliana of, prs Little Marlow, 581
Hampton, Nicholas of, pr. St Denys, 455
Hampton, Richard of [Astley], 143
Hampton, Richard of, abb. Halesowen, 504
Hampton, Susanna of, prs Little Marlow, 581
Han...rd, Robert, pr. Leominster, 117
Hancrisham, Walter de, pr. Bentley, 333
Handlo, Joan de, prs Higham, 571
Hanewell, John de, pr. Herringfleet, 390
Hanifield, Adam de, abb. Lessness, 409
Hanley, Cecily de, prs Nun Cotham, 593
Hanney, Peter of, abb. Abingdon, 18
Hansard, John, pr. Tandridge, 466
Hanslope, Nicholas of, pr. Snelshall, 71
Hanworth, Philip of, pr.-el. Nocton Park, 434
Hanworth, Richard of, abb. Barlings, 492
Hanworth, Thomas of, pr. Chetwode, 363
Hanworth, William of, pr. Thetford, Holy
  Sepulchre, 468
Happisburgh, John of, pr. Norwich, St Leonard, 122
Harby, Walter of, pr. Kyme, 402
Hardingham, John of, pr. Bromholm, 223

Hardwick, Richard of, pr. Caldwell, 355

Hardwick, Thomas of, pr. Holy Island, 111

Hardy, John, pr. St Michael's Mount, 189

Hardy, Roger *dictus*, pr. Cogges, 152

Harecourt, John, pr. Ranton, 450

Harell, William, pr. Sandwell, 66

Harepathe, Richard, pr. St Michael's Mount, 189

Harescombe, John de, pr. Gloucester, St Oswald, 382

Harethorn, William, pr. Shulbred, 459

Harewes, Richard de, abb. Waltham, 478

Hariel, Roger (Oger) *dictus*, pr. Loders, 175
  see also Haryel

Harlestone, Richard of, pr. Grafton Regis, 382

Harley, Alice of, prs Brewood White Ladies, 544

Harlsey, John of, abb. Rufford, 306

Harlsey, Mariota of, prs Handale, 568

Harncaster, Joan, prs Watton, 531

Harnhull, Roger, of Faringdon, abb. Bindon, 263

Harold, Philip, pr. Haverford West, 388

Harome, John of, pr. St Bees, 127

Harpham, Peter of, pr. Haltemprice, 385

Harpham, Walter of, master Wykeham, 625

Harpham, Walter of, pr. Rumburgh, 125

Harpham, Walter of, rector Yedingham, 626

Harpley, John of, abb. North Creake, 435

Harpole, Peter of, pr. Daventry, 226

Harrietsham, John of, abb. Boxley, 265

Harrington, Isabel (Elizabeth) of, prs Greenfield, 566

Harrold, Ralph of, abb. Wardon, 320

Harrold, William of, rector-el. Ashridge, 535

Hartlepool, John of, pr. Kirkham, 402

Hartlepool, Margaret of, prs Marrick, 587

Hartlington, Joan of, prs Esholt, 559

Hartlip, John of, pr. Felixstowe, 102; pr. Rochester, 63

Harton, Robert of, pr. Bolton, 340

Hartshill, Erneburga of, abbs Polesworth, 599

Harvington, William of, abb. Pershore, 57

Haryel, Roger, pr. Appuldurcombe, 141
  see also Hariel

Hascule, pr. Colchester, St Botolph, 369

Haseyo, John de, pr. Beckford and Colsterworth, 332

Hasleton, Robert of, abb. Winchombe, 80

Hassok, John, pr. Hastings, 387

Hasteng', Isolda, prs Catesby, 551

Hastings, Joan de, prs Grace Dieu, 565

Hatch, Robert of, abb. Athelney, 20

Hatfield, Clement of, pr. Spalding, 193

Hatfield, Peter of, abb. Walden, 77

Hatfield, Walter, *see* Pedeleshurst, Walter de

Hatfield, William Coleman of, abb. Walden, 77

Hatford, Richard de, pr. Redbourn, 124

Hathbrand, Robert de, of Ringwould, pr. Dover, 98

Hathbrande, Robert, pr. Canterbury, Christ Church, 28

Hathern, Robert of, pr. Thurgarton, 472

Hathfield, William (de), pr. Ely, 41

Hatton, Richard of, pr. Alberbury, 256

Hatton, William of, abb. Bardney, 20

Haugh *or* Haugham, James of, pr.-el. Spalding, 193

Haughley, Henry of, pr. Alnesbourn, 327

Haukesgarth, Thomas de, abb. Whitby, 80

Haukesgarth, Thomas de, pr. Middlesbrough, 121

Haulee, Richard le Blunt de, *see* Blunt, Richard le

Haunsard, John, abb. Lessness, 410

Haustede, Laurence de, pr. Horsley, 170, 393

Hautford, Isabel de, prs Broomhall, 546

Hauton, Simon de, pr. Spalding, 192

Havage, John, pr. Newent, 183

Havelers, John de, pr. Stoke by Clare, 195

Haverford, Walter of, pr. Carmarthen, 360

Hawe, John de, pr. Combwell, 371

Hawise, prs Buckland, 546

Hawise, prs Cornworthy, 555

Hawise, prs Fosse, 561

Hawise, prs London, Clerkenwell, 582

Hawise, prs Nun Appleton, 592

Hawise, prs Thicket, 615

Hawise (Avice), prs Wintney, 622

Hawkeswell, Simon of, pr. Bilsington, 336

Haworth, Robert (of), abb. Whalley (Stanlow), 322

Haxby, Geoffrey of, master Jarrow, 114

Haxley, Thomas de, abb. Easby, 501

Hay, Emma de la, prs Ivinghoe, 574

Haya, Peter de, pr. Beckford and Colsterworth, 332

Haye, Alice de la, prs Chester, 554

Haye, Elizabeth del, prs Thicket, 615

Haye, John de la, pr. Avebury, 144

Hay(e), William de la, pr. Tywardreath, 205

Hayl, Nicholas, abb. Kingswood, 287

Hayn, Roger, *dictus* de Capiago, *see* Capiago

Heck, Margaret of, prs Hampole, 568

Hedon, John of, pr. Markby, 419

Hedon, John of, pr. North Ferriby, 436

Hedon, Thomas of, abb. Newhouse, 508

Hedon, Thomas of, pr. Thornholme, 469

Hedsor, Margery of, prs Ankerwyke, 539

Hegan, John, pr. Abergavenny, 138

Hegsete, Henry de, pr. Leighs, 409

Heigham, Thomas of, pr. Canons Ashby, 357

Hele, John de (la), abb. Sherborne, 68

Helen, prs London, St Helen's and Holy Cross, 584

Helen, prs Wroxall, 624

Helewise, prs Swine, 613

Helgeye, Thomas de, pr. Pentney, 447

Helghton, Roger de, abb. Sibton, 309

Helias, pr. Monmouth, 182

Helias, pr. Westwood, 617
    see also Elias

Hellidon, Robert of, pr. Daventry, 226

Hellidon, Thomas of, *custos* Catesby, 552

Hellidon, Thomas of, keeper Calwich, 356

Helmenden, Nicholas de, pr. Little Dunmow, 412

Helmsley, Robert of, abb. Byland, 270

Helmsley, William of, abb. Byland, 270

Helmsley, William of, abb. Wardon, 320

Helperby, Alice of, prs Marrick, 587

Helpeston, Robert de, pr. Carlisle, 359

Helyes, William, pr. Stratfield Saye, 197

Helyon, John de, pr. Ewenny, 100

Helyon(e), Henry de, pr. Oxford, Gloucester coll, 123

Hembury, Elizabeth, prs Whistones, 618

Hemingbrough, John of, pr. Stamford, St Leonard, 131

Hemingstone, John of, pr. Ely, 40

Hempnall, Joan of, prs Flixton, 561

Hempstead I and II, John of, pr. Llanthony Secunda, 414

Hempton, Robert of, pr. Southwick, 461

Hempton, William of, pr. Coxford, 373

Hemsby I, Richard of, pr. Hickling, 392

Hemsby II, Richard of, pr. Hickling, 392

Hemsted, Katherine de, prs Rowney, 603

Henditot, John (de), pr. Stoke by Clare, 196

Hendred, Adam of, pr. Luffield, 50

Hendred, Isabel of, prs Littlemore, 582

Hendred, Richard of, abb. Abingdon, 16

Hendred, Robert of, abb. Abingdon, 16

Hendred, Roger of, pr. Belvoir, 91

Henle(e), Thomas de, abb. Westminster, 79

Henlegh, Simon de, pr. Sudbury, 131

Henley, Robert of, pr. Cardigan, 95

Henry, abb. Abbey Dore, 258

Henry, abb. Basingwerk, 260

Henry, abb. Beeleigh, 494

Henry, abb. Bindon (–1212), 262

Henry, abb. Bindon (occ. 1303), 263

Henry, abb. Bordesley, 264

Henry, abb. Boxley, 265

Henry, abb. Buckfast, 267

Henry, abb. Buildwas (occ. 1303 x 15), 269

Henry, abb. Buildwas (occ. 1337), 269

Henry, abb. Byland, 270

Henry, abb. Cleeve (occ. 1275 x 97), 271

Henry, abb. Cleeve (occ. 1318 x 19), 271

Henry, abb. Cockersand, 496

Henry, abb. Combe, 273

Henry, abb., then pr. Combwell, 371

Henry, abb. Durford, 500

Henry, abb. Easby, 500

Henry, abb. Forde, 279

Henry, abb. Garendon (occ. 1246 x 7), 282

Henry, abb. Garendon (1303–), 283

Henry, abb. Holm Cultram, 285

Henry, abb. Hulton (occ. *c.* 1288 x 1302), 286

Henry, abb. Hulton (occ. 1317), 286

Henry, abb. Hulton (occ. 1369 x 74), 286

Henry, abb. Kirkstead, 289

Henry, abb. Margam, 292

Henry, abb. Medmenham, 294

Henry, abb. Merevale, 294

Henry, abb. Newhouse, 508

Henry, abb. Newminster, 298

Henry, abb. Quarr, 300

Henry, abb. Revesby (occ. 1286 x 91), 301

Henry, abb. Revesby (1302–), 301

Henry, abb. Revesby (occ. 1381 x 85), 301

Henry, abb. Rievaulx (1215–16), 302

Henry, abb. Rievaulx (–1302), 302

Henry, abb. Rievaulx (occ. 1308 x 11), 302

Henry, abb. Rufford, 305

Henry, abb. St Osyth, 456

Henry, abb. St Radegund, 508

Henry, (*another*), abb. St Radegund, 508 n. 19

Henry, abb. Sherborne, 68

Henry, abb. Shrewsbury (1223–?44), 69

Henry, abb. Shrewsbury (1251–8), 70

Henry, abb. Sibton (occ. 1244 x 45), 308

Henry, abb. Sibton (occ. 1267), 309

Henry, abb. Stratford Langthorne, 314

Henry, abb. Sulby (occ. 1262), 510

Henry, abb. Sulby (occ. 1286 x 1310), 510

Henry, abb. Swineshead, 314

Henry, abb. Vale Royal (Darnhall), 317

Henry, abb. Vaudey, 319

Henry, abb. Woburn, 324

Henry, keeper Calwich, 355

Henry, master Heynings, 571

Henry, master Stixwould, 611

Henry, minister Thelsford, 534

Henry, pr. Anglesey, 328

Henry, pr. Bermondsey, 221

Henry, ?pr. Bicester, 334

Henry, pr. Bolton, 340
Henry, pr. Bradley, 342
Henry, pr. Bristol, St James, 94
Henry, pr. Bromehill, 349
Henry, pr. Canonsleigh, 357
Henry, pr. Canterbury, St Gregory, 358
Henry, pr. Castle Acre, 223
Henry, pr. Catley, 521
Henry, pr. Church Gresley, 367
Henry, pr. Cockerham, 369
Henry, pr. Colchester, St Botolph, 369
Henry, pr. Deerhurst, 155
Henry, pr. Derby, St James, 227
Henry, pr. Earls Colne, 99
Henry, pr. Ellerton on Spalding Moor, 522
Henry, pr. Elsham, 377
Henry, pr. Felley, 378
Henry, pr. Goldcliff, 162
Henry, pr. Hardham, 385
Henry, pr. Hastings, 387
Henry, pr. Hatfield Peverel, 107 n.12
Henry, ?pr. Haugham, 166
Henry, pr. Haverholme, 523
Henry, pr. Hempton, 389
Henry, pr. Hereford, 108
Henry, pr. Herringfleet, 390
Henry, pr. Horkesley, 230
Henry, pr. Hurley, 113
Henry, pr. Kenilworth, 398
Henry, pr. Kersey (occ. 1218/19 x 45), 399
Henry, pr. Kersey (occ. 1301 x 2), 399
Henry, pr. Kyme, 402
Henry, pr. Launceston (occ. 1244), 404
Henry, pr. Launceston (occ. 1277 x 79), 404
Henry, pr. Launceston (occ. 1285), 404
Henry, pr. Leighs, 409
Henry, pr. Lincoln, St Katharine, 523
Henry, pr. Longleat, 418
Henry, pr. Marton, 419
Henry, pr. Mattersey, 525
Henry, pr. Newstead-on-Ancholme, 526
Henry, pr. Nuneaton, 596
Henry, pr. Otterton, 185
Henry, pr. Pill, 187
Henry, pr. Pynham by Arundel, 449
Henry, pr. Rumburgh, 125
Henry, pr. St Germans (occ. 1244), 455
Henry, pr. St Germans (occ. 1293 x 1315), 456
Henry, pr. St Helen's, 250
Henry, pr. Shulbred, 459
Henry, pr. Thoby, 468
Henry, pr. Thurgarton, 471

Henry, pr. Torksey, 473
Henry, pr. Tortington, 475
Henry, ?pr. Tynemouth, 132
Henry, pr. Wangford, 253
Henry, pr. Wombridge, 485
Henry, pr. Woodspring, 487
Henry de S., abb. St Radegund, 509
Henry dictus Medicus, abb. Notley, 440
Henton, John de, abb. Muchelney, 54
Henton, John de, pr. Montacute, 240
Henton, John de, pr. Sixhills, 530
Henton, John of, abb. Sherborne, 69
Henton, Thomas de, pr. Shulbred, 459
Henycie, John, pr. Frithelstock, 381
Hepscott, Walter of, abb. Alnwick, 491
Hepworth, Thomas of, pr. Chipley, 364
Herberd(e), William, pr. Ware, 206
Herbert, master Godstow, 563
Herbert, pr. Coxford, 372
Herbert, pr. Mattersey, 525
Herbert, pr. Rumburgh, 125
Herbert, pr. Ware, 205
Herbert/Hubert, pr. Westacre, 483
Herefeld, Adam de, master Newstead by Stamford, 432
Hereford, Hugh of, pr. Chirbury, 365
Hereford, Margery of, prs Harrold, 569
Hereford, Walter of, abb. Tintern, 317
Hereford, Walter of, abb. Vale Royal, 317
Hereford, William of, abb. Abbey Dore, 259
Hereford, Little, Roger of, pr. Church Preen, 225
Heremite, Ralph le, pr. Titley, 201
  see also Hermite
Hereward, abb. Cockersand, 496
Hereward, William, abb. Cirencester, 368
Herford, Roger de, abb. Sawtry, 307
Herforton (Hersinton), Guy de, pr. Dodford, 374; pr. Warwick, 481
Heribel, John, pr. Astley, 143
Herierd, Alexander, pr. Winchester, St Swithun, 84
  see also Herriard
Herlyngg, Thomas, pr. Bromholm, 233
Hermita, Nicholas, pr. Andover, 139
Hermite, Ralph, pr. Andwell, 140
  see also Heremite
Heron, William, pr. Wallingford, 133
Herriard, Edmund of, pr. Merton, 422
  see also Herierd
Herrington, John of, master Farne, 102
Hersinton, Guy de, see Herforton, Guy de
Hertepole, Eva de, prs Stixwould, 611

Hertford, John of, abb. St Albans, 63
Hertford, Richard of, abb. Waltham, 479
Hertford, Richard of, pr. Beadlow, 90; pr. Hertford, St Mary, 109
Hertford, William of, pr. Hertford, St Mary, 109
Hervey, abb. Haughmond, 387
Hervey, pr. Bicester, 334
Hervey, pr. Hatfield Regis, 165
Hervey, pr. Hoxne, 112
Hervey, pr. Newnham, 429
Hervey, pr. Spinney, 462
Hervey, John, pr. Dunster, 99
Heryng, John, pr. Wilkeswood, 536
Heryng(e), Walter, abb. Beaulieu, 261
Hesill, William, pr. Ellerton on Spalding Moor, 522
Heslington, John of, abb. Selby, 68
Hessle, Walter of, pr. North Ferriby, 436
Hetham, Richard de, pr. Letheringham, 410
Hethcote, John, pr. Church Gresley, 367
Hethe, Hamo de, pr. Rochester, 62
Hethe, William de, abb. Lessness, 410
Hethersett, Alice of, prs Norwich (Carrow), 592
Hethersett, John of, pr. Norwich, St Leonard, 122
Hethersett, Richard of, pr. Wymondham, 136
Heton, John de, abb. Sallay, 307
Heton, John de, pr. Watton, 530
Hette, Richard, pr. Brimpsfield, 147
Hetton, Richard of, pr. Pontefract, 247
Heuerwyk, John, abb. Durford, 500
Heved, William, pr. Gloucester, St Oswald, 382
Hexham, Robert of, pr. Holy Island, 111; pr. Stamford, St Leonard, 130
Hexham, Thomas of, pr. Lanercost, 403
Hexham, William of, master Farne, 102
Hexham, William of, pr. Cockerham, 369
Hextal, Letitia de, abbs Polesworth, 599
Heyford(e), William of, abb. Bordesley, 264; abb. Stoneleigh, 311
Heyham, Richard de, abb. Pipewell, 299
Heyham, Robert de, pr. Merton, 422
Heynfre, Thomas, pr. Toft Monks, 201
Heynton, Annuna (?), prs Cornworthy, 555
Heyron, Thomas, pr. London, Holy Trinity, Aldgate, 416
Heytesbury, John of, pr. Maiden Bradley, 418
Heyw(o)rth, Joan de, prs Greenfield, 566
Hickling, Adam of, pr. Weybridge, 484
Hickling, John of, pr. Haltemprice, 385
Hickling, John of, pr. Thurgarton, 472
Hickling, Robert of, pr. Haltemprice, 385
Hickling, Robert of, pr. Thurgarton, 472

Higham, Ralph of, abb. Northampton, St James, 437
Hilary, abb. Thame, 315
Hilary, prs Nun Monkton, 595
Hilderstone, Richard of, pr. Stafford, 463
Hilderstone, Robert of, pr.-el. Stafford, 463
Hillington, John of, pr. Flitcham, 380
Hillum, John de, abb. Pipewell, 299
Hilton, John of, abb. Abbotsbury, 15
Hingham, John, pr. Norwich, St Leonard, 122
Hingham, William of, pr. Blythburgh, 338
Hinton, Isabel of, prs Blackborough, 543
   see also Hynton
Hockliffe, Matilda of, prs Ivinghoe, 574
Hockwold, Adam of, pr. Thetford, Holy Sepulchre, 468
Hocthorp, Robert de, abb. Merevale, 295
Hoddesdon, John of, abb. Lessness, 409
Hodenco, Robert de, pr. Minster Lovell, 177
Hodierne, William (de), pr. Stogursey, 195
Hoedlew, abb. Whitland, 323
Hog, William, pr. Bolton, 340
Hok(e), Adam de la, abb. Malmesbury, 51
Holbeck, Elizabeth of, prs Nun Appleton, 592
Holbrook, John of, pr. Felley, 379
Holderness, Alexander of, abb. Peterborough, 57
Holkene, Joan, prs Pinley, 598
Holland, Alice of, prs Legbourne, 579
Holm, Beatrice de, prs Arden, 539
Holm(e), Geoffrey de, pr. Markby, 419; abb. Thornton Curtis, 469
Holm, Joan de, prs Nunburnholme, 595
Holt, John de, pr. Amesbury, 538
Holt, Richard de, pr. Fineshade, 380
Holt, William (of), abb. West Dereham, 517
Holte, Richard de, pr. Horsley, 170, 393
Hoton, William of, pr. Woodbridge, 486
Holy Cross, Walter of, abb. Garendon, 283
Holy Cross, William (?Walter) of, abb. London, St Mary Graces, 290
Holy Island, Robert of, pr. Finchale, 103
Holy Island, William of, master Farne, 102
Homerton, John de, *see* Hamerton, John of
Homme, Reginald de, abb. Gloucester, 48
Hommet, William du, abb. Westminster, 78; pr. Frampton, 161
Honilane, Margery de, prs London, St Helen's and Holy Cross, 585
Honnburne, Adam de, pr. Studley, 465
Honyburgh, Richard de, pr. Haverford West, 388
Honyngburgh, John de, pr. Haverford West, 388
Honyton, Isabel, prs Minster in Sheppey, 588

663

Hoo, John of, abb. Vale Royal, 317
Hoo, John of, pr. Yarmouth, 137
Hoo, Nicholas de, pr. Norwich cath., 56
Hoo, Simon of, *see* Luton, Simon of
Hoo, William de, pr. Rochester, 62
Hook Norton, William of, pr. Cold Norton, 370
Hopton, Adam de, pr. Chirbury, 365
Hopton, Denis de, [Monks Horton], 237
Hopton, Henry of, abb. Rocester, 453
Horapeldre, John de, abb. Faversham, 44
Horkeleye, Robert de, abb. Stoneleigh, 311
Horkstow, John of, abb. Humberston, 49
Horncastle, John of, pr. Carlisle, 360
Horninghold, Robert of, pr. Bradley, 343
Hornyk, Nicholas, [Montacute], 241
Horsage, Peter de, pr. Thetford, Holy Sepulchre, 468
Horsey, Matthew of, pr. Weybridge, 484
Horsley, John of, abb. Dale, 499
Horsley, Margery of, prs Holystone, 572
Horsley, William of, abb. Dale, 499
Horsulle, Denise de, prs Kington St Michael, 576
Horton, Henry of, abb. Kingswood, 287
Horton(e), Roger of, pr. Launceston, 404
Horton, Thomas de, abb. Gloucester, 48
Horton, William of, pr. Tynemouth, 132; pr. Wymondham, 136
Hortune, William de, minister Moatenden, 533
Horwod, R. de, pr. Brecon, 93
Horwode, Richard, pr. Exeter, St Nicholas, 101
Horwode, Walter de, pr. Horsley, 170, 393
Horwood, John of, pr. Bradwell, 25
Horwood, William (of), pr. Luffield, 51
Hoton, Richard de, pr. Durham, 38; pr. Lytham, 120
Hotot, Jordan de, pr. Wilsford, 212
Hotot, Margaret, abbs Chatteris, 553
Hotot, William de, abb. Peterborough, 57
Houe, Walter de la, abb. Newenham, 297
Hough, John of, pr. Nocton Park, 434
Hougham, Richard of, pr. Dover, 98
Houghton, William de, ?abb. Croxton Kerrial, 498 n.10
Houles, William, *yconomus* Catesby, 553
Hourgulhulle, Thomas de, pr. Bromfield, 95
Houteville, William de, pr. West Ravendale, 517
Houton, John de, abb. Wellow, 482
Houton, John de, pr. Luffield, 50
Houton, Roger de, pr. Bullington, 520
Houton, Roger de, pr. Lincoln, St Katharine, 524
Houwhel, Henry *dictus*, pr. Coventry, 36
Hovel(l), Margery, prs Flixton, 561

Hoveton, Roger, abb. Thame, 315
Hovingham, Robert of, pr. Newburgh, 428
Howard, Agatha, ?abbs Marham, 586
Howard, Egidia, ?abbs Marham, 586
Howden, John of, abb. Sallay, 307
Howden, John of, abb. Vaudey, 319
Howden, John of, master Monkwearmouth, 121
Howden, Stephen of, junior, pr. Holy Island, 111
Howell, abb. Buckfast, 267
Howham, John de, pr. Peterstone, 447
Howsham, William of, pr. Ellerton on Spalding Moor, 522
Howton, William of, abb. Croxden, 275
Hoxne, Richard of, pr. Butley, 354
Hoxne, Richard of, pr. Hoxne, 112
Hoxne, Roger of, pr. Weybourne, 484
Hoyland, Robert de, pr. Studley, 465
Hoyland, William de, pr. Stamford, St Mary and St Michael, 609
Hubert, pr. Bridlington, 345
Hubert, pr. Hickling, 392
Hubert, pr. Leominster, 117
Hubert/Herbert, pr. Westacre, 483
Huctred, abb. Buildwas, 268
Hudicot, John, pr. Steventon, 194
Hugford, Joan de, prs Brewood White Ladies, 544
Huggate, William of, pr. Chicksands, 521
Hugh (II), abb. Abbotsbury, 15
Hugh, abb. Abingdon, 16
Hugh, abb. Alcester (1252–), 18
Hugh, abb. Alcester (1266–75), 18
Hugh, abb. Basingwerk, 259
Hugh (II), abb. Beaulieu, 260 & n. 2
Hugh, abb. Bruern, 266
Hugh, abb. Buildwas, 269
Hugh, abb. Canterbury, St Augustine, 29
Hugh, abb. Cleeve, 271
Hugh, abb. Flaxley (occ. 1276), 278
Hugh, abb. Flaxley (occ. 1338), 278
Hugh, abb. Hartland, 386
Hugh, abb. Kirkstead, 287
Hugh, abb. Langley, 505
Hugh, abb. Leiston, 506
Hugh, abb. Lessness, 409
Hugh, abb. Meaux, 292
Hugh, abb. Quarr, 300
Hugh, abb. St Radegund, 508
Hugh, abb. Stratford Langthorne, 314
Hugh, abb. Sulby (occ. 1273), 510
Hugh, abb. Sulby (1276–), 510
Hugh, abb. Welbeck, 515
Hugh, corrector Craswell, 256

Hugh, *custos* Begare, 261
Hugh, *custos* Upchurch, 514
Hugh, keeper Calwich, 355
Hugh, master Nun Cotham, 594
Hugh, master Stixwould, 611
Hugh, master Swine, 614
Hugh, pr. Alkborough, 89
Hugh, pr. Anglesey, 328
Hugh, pr. Arbury, 328
Hugh, pr. Barlinch (occ. 1283 x 4), 330
Hugh, pr. Barlinch (–1321), 330
Hugh, pr. Bermondsey, 220
Hugh, pr. Bodmin, 339
Hugh, pr. Bradenstoke, 342
Hugh, pr. Buckenham, 351
Hugh, ?pr. Burstall, 148
Hugh, pr. Butley, 354
Hugh, pr. Canons Ashby, 356
Hugh, pr. Canterbury, St Gregory, 358
Hugh, pr. Carisbrooke, 149
Hugh, pr. Catesby, 552
Hugh, pr. Cathale, 361
Hugh, pr. Cogges (1225/6–1226/7), 151
Hugh, pr. Cogges (–1262), 152
Hugh, pr. Cogges (1277–), 152
Hugh, pr. Cold Norton, 370
Hugh, pr. Edith Weston, 158
Hugh, pr. Exeter, St Nicholas, 100
Hugh, pr. Haverholme, 523
Hugh, pr. Hayling, 167
Hugh, pr. Ipswich, Holy Trinity (occ. *c.* 1280), 395
Hugh, pr. Ipswich, Holy Trinity (occ. 1309 x 10), 395
Hugh, pr. Launde, 405
Hugh, pr. Leighs (occ. 1246 x 51), 409
Hugh, pr. Leighs (occ. 1351 x 55), 409
Hugh, pr. Lewes, 233
Hugh, pr. Lincoln, St Katharine, 523
Hugh, pr. Lincoln, St Mary Magdalen, 118
Hugh, pr. London, St Bartholomew, 417
Hugh, pr. Maiden Bradley, 418
Hugh, pr. Monks Horton, 236
Hugh, pr. Nuneaton, 597
Hugh, pr. Pontefract, 246
Hugh, pr. Snelshall, 71
Hugh, pr. Takeley, 198
Hugh, pr. Throwley, 199
Hugh, pr. Tickford, 199
Hugh, pr. Weybridge, 484
Hugh, pr. Winterborn Monkton, 254
Hugh, pr. Wormsley, 488
Hugh, pr. Wroxton, 489

Hugh, pr. Wymondley, 490
Hugolini, Thomas, pr. Haugham, 166
Hugonis, Peter, 'rector' Upchurch, 514
Hull, John of, [Meaux], 294
Hulme, Beatrice of, prs Norwich (Carrow), 592
Hulyn, Clement, pr. Toft Monks, 202
Humberston, Robert of, pr. Tickhill, 131
Humbert, pr. Lewes, 233
Humbert (Imbert), pr. Much Wenlock, 241
Humbilton, Agnes de, prs Grimsby, 567
Humbleton, Emma of, prs Yedingham, 625
Humbleton, Simon of, pr. North Ormsby, 526
Humphrey, [Barlinch], 330
Humphrey, pr. Kenilworth, 398
Humphrey, pr. Southwark, 460
Humphrey, pr. Stone, 464
Humphrey, pr. Tandridge, 466
Humphrey, pr. Weybridge, 484
Hundered, David, abb. Bristol, St Augustine, 347
Hune, William de la, pr. Minster, 176
Hungerford, Nicholas, pr. Oxford, St Frideswide, 445
Hungerford, William of, abb. Cerne, 31
Hungerford, William of, abb. Waverley, 321
Hunnyfeld, Herman, abb. Stratford Longthorne, 314
Hunstanton, Henry of, abb. Bury St Edmunds, 27
Huntingdon, Cecily of, pr.-el. Hinchingbrooke, 572
Huntingdon, William of, abb. Croxton Kerrial, 498
Huntingdon, William of, pr. Belvoir, 91
Huntingdon, William of, pr. Hatfield Peverel, 107
Huntingfield, Mary of, prs Bungay, 546
Huntingfield, Roger of, pr. Letheringham, 410
Huntingfield, Walter of, abb. Colchester, 34
Hur', pr. Mountjoy, 427
Hurle(e), John de, pr. Wymondham, 136
Hurworth, John of, pr. Guisborough, 385
Huscen', John (de), pr. Folkestone, 161
Huse, Isabel, prs Kington St Michael, 576
Husee, Agnes, prs Studley, 612
Husthwaite, Adam of, abb. Byland, 270
Husthwaite, Thomas of, pr. Newburgh, 429
Huttoft, Walter of, abb. Thornton Curtis, 470
Hutton, Alice of, prs Handale, 568
Hutton, John of, pr. Newburgh, 429
Hutton, Robert of, pr. Marton, 421
Huxton, Nicholas de, pr. Stafford, 463
Hynton, Amice de, prs Pinley, 598
    see also Hinton
Hywel, abb. Valle Crucis, 318

I./J., abbs Chatteris, 553
see also J.
Ibelound, John de, pr. Harmondsworth, 165
Ibstock, John of, abb. Burton, 26
Icche, Joan, abbs Romsey, 601
Ida, prs Amesbury, 538
Ida I, prs Nuneaton, 595
Ida II, prs Nuneaton, 595
Ida, prs Wroxall, 624
Idbury, Richard of, abb. Winchcombe, 81
Idonea, prs Hampole, 568
Idonia, prs Nun Appleton, 592
Ieuaf (Joab), abb. Strata Marcella, 313
Ieuan, ?abb. Valle Crucis, 318 n. 37
Ieuan ap Rhys, abb. Conway, 275
Iford, John of, pr. Bath, 22
Ile, Robert de, abb. Athelney, 19
Île-Dieu, Richard of l', pr. Upchurch, 514
Illegh, John Parker de, see Parker, John
Imbert, pr. Bermondsey, 220
Inganus, pr. Lapley, 172
Inges, Margery de, prs Norwich (Carrow), 592
Ingham, Mary (Marroia) of, abbs Marham, 586
Ingleby, John of, pr. Kersal, 230
Ingleby, William of, abb. Rievaulx, 302
Inglesham, Henry (of), abb. Netley, 296
Inglys, John, abb. Egglestone, 502
Ing(e)ram, abb. Barlings, 492
Ingram, abb. Blanchland, 495
Ingram, pr. Clattercote, 521
Ingram, pr. Newburgh, 428
Inguerand, pr. Monk Sherborne, 180
Innocent, John, pr. Lancaster, 172
Insula, Alexander de, pr.-el. Shelford, 459
Insula, Geoffrey de, pr. Titley, 201
Insula, John de, pr. Breedon, 345
Insula, John de, pr. Carisbrooke, 150
Insula, John de, pr. Nostell, 439
Insula, John de, pr. York, Holy Trinity, 217
Insula, Nicholas de, ?pr. Marlborough, 525
Insula, Peter de, pr. Throwley, 199
Insula, Richard de, abb. Burton, 25
Insula, Richard, abb. Bury St Edmunds, 26
Insula, W. de, pr. Livers Ocle, 174
Insula, Walter de, pr. Selborne, 458
Insula Bona, John de, pr. Wilsford, 212
Insulis, John de, pr. Hough, 393
Iorwerth, see Gervase
Iorwerth, abb. Talley, 511
Iou, Guichard de, pr. Montacute, 239
Ipsley, John of, abb. Alcester, 18
Ipswich, Clement of, pr. Ipswich, St Peter and St Paul, 396

Ipswich, Nicholas of, pr. Ipswich, St Peter and St Paul, 396
Ipswich, William of, pr. Hurley, 114
Ipswich, William of, pr. Ipswich, St Peter and St Paul, 396
Ipwell, Robert of, abb. Winchcombe, 81
Irby, Nigel of, abb. Easby, 501
Ireby, William (de), pr. Hereford, 108
Ireland, Nicholas of, pr. Stamford, St Leonard, 129
Irland, Alice de, prs Derby, Kingsmead, 557
see also Yrlaunde
Irnepurse, Adam, master Moxby, 589
Irreys, Geoffrey, keeper of Calwich, 356
Irreys, Henry, pr. Coventry, 36
Irreys, William, pr. Coventry, 36
Irton, Cecily de, prs Handale, 568
Irton, Ralph of, pr. Guisborough, 384
Isaac, abb. Titchfield, 511
Isaac, William, ?abb. Easby, 501
Isaac, William, pr. Bristol, St James, 94
Isabel, abbs Malling, 586
Isabel, abbs Winchester, 620
Isabel, prs Armathwaite (–1362), 540
Isabel, prs Armathwaite (occ. 1480), 540
Isabel, prs Baysdale, 542
Isabel, prs Brewood Black Ladies, 544
Isabel, prs Cheshunt, 554
Isabel, prs Greenfield, 566
Isabel, prs Kington St Michael, 576
Isabel, prs Littlemore, 582
Isabel, prs London, Haliwell, 584
Isabel I, prs Markyate, 586
Isabel II, prs Markyate, 586
Isabel, prs Marrick, 587
Isabel, prs Rusper, 603
Isabel, prs Sinningthwaite, 606
Isabel, prs Westwood, 616
Isabel, prs Wilberfoss, 619
Isabel, prs Wothorpe, 623
Isabel, prs Wykeham (occ. 1307 x 21), 625
Isabel, prs Wykeham (occ. 1388), 625
Isabella, Nicholas, pr. St Michael's Mount, 189
Isembert, pr. York, Holy Trinity, 216
Isham, Katherine of, prs Rothwell, 602
Isilia(?), prs Wintney, 622
Isle, Joan del, prs Lyminster, 585
Isleham, Robert of, pr. Spinney, 462
Isolda, abbs Tarrant Kaines, 615
Isolda, prs Heynings, 570
Isolda, prs Ivinghoe (–1261/2), 574
Isolda, prs Ivinghoe (occ. 1326), 574
Isolda, prs Nun Appleton, 592
Isolda, prs Wallingwells, 616

Isoud, prs Markyate, 587
Ive, John *dictus*, abb. Faversham, 45
Ivelyn, Nicholas, pr. Eye, 160
Ivetta, prs Handale, 568
Ivo, abb. Beauchief, 494
Ivo, abb. Titchfield, 511
Ivo, pr. Exeter, St James, 228
Ivo, pr. Poughley, 449
Ivo, pr. Pynham by Arundel, 449
Ivo, pr. Torksey, 473
    see also Yvo
Ivry, Ralph de Montfort of, pr. Minster Lovell, 177
Ivry, Stephen de Habitu of, pr. Minster Lovell, 177
Iweleghe, Richard de, pr. Pilton, 124
Ixworth, William of, pr. Ixworth, 398

J., abb. Cleeve, 271
J., abb. Flaxley, 278
J., abb. Newbo, 507
J., abb. St Dogmells, 189
J., abb. Tintern, 316
J., pr. Carisbrooke, 149
J., pr. Haugham, 166
J., pr. Ixworth, 398
J., pr. Penman, 446
J., pr. Pilton, 124
J., pr. Spalding, 192
J., pr. Witham, 326
Jacob, Richard, pr. Eye, 160
Jahnet, Colin (?Nicholas), pr. West Ravendale, 518
James, abb. Cleeve, 271
James, abb. Strata Marcella, 313
James, abb. Vaudey, 319
James, abb. Whitland, 323
James, pr. Blackmore, 338
James, pr. Covenham, 153
James, pr. Daventry, 226
James, pr. Grosmont, 257
James, pr. Minster Lovell, 177
James, pr. Monk Sherborne, 180
James, pr. Monks Horton (occ. 1295/6 x 1310), 236
James, pr. Monks Horton (occ. 1327), 237
James, pr. Poughley, 449
James, pr. Thetford, St Mary, 253
James, pr. Tywardreath, 204
James, pr. Wangford, 253
James, pr. West Mersea, 210
Janicuria, John de, pr. Lewes, 235
Jargolio, William de, pr. Minting, 178
Jarieta, Reyner de, pr. Hinckley, 168
Jenes, Joan de, prs Amesbury, 538
Jerdale, John, pr. Ravenstone, 451
Jernon, Geoffrey de, pr. St Michael's Mount, 189

Jerounde, Margery, prs Little Marlow, 581
Jevan ap Bled, pr. Beddgelert, 333
Joab, abb. Strata Florida, 312
Joab, *see* Ieuaf
Joan, abbs Shaftesbury, 605
Joan, abbs Tarrant Kaines, 615
Joan, prs Brewood White Ladies, 544
Joan, prs Bungay, 547
Joan, prs Castle Hedingham, 551
Joan, prs Catley, 521
Joan, prs Davington, 556
Joan, prs Holystone, 573
Joan, prs Kilburn, 575
Joan, prs Legbourne, 579
Joan, prs Polsloe, 600
Joan, prs Sopwell, 607
Joan, prs Thicket, 615
Jocelin, pr. Hereford, 108
Jocelin, pr. Shouldham, 529
Jocelin, pr. Totnes, 202
Jocellis, Peter de, pr. Castle Acre, 224; pr. Lewes, 235
Johann, Nicholas, pr. West Ravendale, 518
Johel, pr. Frithelstock, 381
John, [Swine], 614
John, abb. Abbey Cwmhir, 258
John, abb. Abbey Dore, 259
John, abb. Bardsey, 329
John, abb. Basingwerk, 259
John, abb. Bayham (occ. 1251 x 7), 493
John, abb. Bayham (?1272), 493 n. 2
John, abb. Beauchief, 494 n. 6
John, abb. Beeleigh, 494
John, abb. Biddlesden (1317–), 262
John, abb. Biddlesden (occ. 1360), 262
John, abb. Biddlesden (1397–), 262
John, abb. Bindon (occ. 1232), 262
John, abb. Bindon (occ. 1359), 263
John, abb. Bordesley, 264
John, abb. Boxley (?1216–), 265
John, abb. Boxley (–1236), 265
John, abb. Bruern (occ.1246 x 55), 266
John, abb. Bruern (occ.1303 x 15), 266
John, abb. Buckland, 268
John, abb. Buildwas, 269
John, abb. Byland (1287–), 270
John, abb. Byland (1318–), 270
John, abb. Byland (1349–), 270
John, abb. Cleeve, 271
John, abb. Coggeshall (occ. *c* .1299), 272
John, abb. Coggeshall (occ. 1318), 272
John, abb. Coggeshall (1387–), 272
John, abb. Combe (occ. 1351), 273

John, abb. Combe (occ. 1361), 273
John, abb. Combermere, 274
John, abb. Conway, 275
John, abb. Coverham, 497
John, abb. Coverham (occ.1387 x 1404/5), 497
John, abb. Croxton Kerrial (occ. 1241), 498 n. 9
John, ?abb. Croxton Kerrial (occ. 1310), 498 n. 12
John, abb. Dunkeswell (occ. 1219), 277
John, abb. Dunkeswell (occ. 1238), 277
John, abb. Dunkeswell (occ. 1260 x 75), 277
John, abb. Dunkeswell (1311–), 277
John, abb. Dunkeswell (occ. 1340), 278
John, abb. Durford (occ. 1257 x 96/7), 500
John, abb. Durford (occ. 1321), 500
John, abb. Durford (occ. 1361), 500
John, abb. Easby, 501
John, abb. Egglestone, 502
John II, abb. Fountains, 279
John, abb. Garendon (1295–), 283
John, abb. Garendon (occ. 1310 x 30), 283
John, abb. Garendon (occ. 1360), 283
John, abb. Garendon (occ. 1406), 283
John, abb. Grace Dieu, 283
John, abb. Hagnaby (1290–), 503
John, abb. Hagnaby (occ. 1377), 503
John, abb. Hartland, 386
John, abb. Holm Cultram, 285
John, abb. Jervaulx, 286
John, abb. Kingswood (occ. 1236 x 44), 287
John, abb. Kingswood (occ. 1309 x 17), 287
John, abb. Kingswood (occ. 1328), 287
John, abb. Kirkstead (occ. 1263 x 6), 289
John, abb. Kirkstead (1336–), 290
John, abb. Langdon, 504
John, abb. Leiston, 507
John, abb. Llantarnam, 290
John, abb. Margam (occ. 1366), 292
John, abb. Margam (occ. 1385), 292
John, abb. Merevale (occ. 1216 x 22), 294
John, abb. Merevale (1294–), 295
John, abb. Neath, 295
John, abb. Netley (1348–), 296
John, abb. Netley (–1372), 296
John, abb. Newhouse, 508
John, abb. Newminster, 299
John, abb. Pipewell, 300
John, abb. Quarr, 300
John, abb. Rievaulx, 303
John, abb. Robertsbridge (occ. 1223 x 31), 303
John, abb. Robertsbridge (occ. 1369 x 73), 304
John, abb. Roche (1300), 304
John, abb. Roche (occ. 1341 x 4), 305

John, abb. Rufford, 305
John, abb. St Dogmells (occ. 1302), 189
John, abb. St Dogmells (occ. 1364 x 76), 189
John, abb. St Osyth (1280–), 456
John, abb. St Osyth (occ. 1385 x 6), 457
John, abb. St Radegund, 508
John, abb. Sallay, 307
John, abb. Sawtry (1303–), 307
John, abb. Sawtry (1314–), 307
John, abb. Shap, 509
John, abb. Sibton, 309
John, abb. Stanley (occ. 1324 x 30), 310
John, abb. Stanley (occ. 1363 x 4), 311
John, abb. Strata Florida (occ. 1299), 312
John, abb. Strata Florida (occ. 1385), 313
John, abb. Strata Marcella, 313
John, abb. Stratford Langthorne, 314
John, abb. Sulby (early 13th cent.), 510
John, abb. Sulby (occ. 1377 x 80), 511
John, abb. Swineshead (1309–), 314
John, abb. Swineshead (occ. 1351), 314
John, abb. Swineshead (occ. 1411), 315
John, abb. Tintern (–1277), 316
John, abb. Tintern (occ. 1349 x 75), 317
John, abb. Valle Crucis, 318
John, abb. Vaudey (occ. 1225), 319
John, abb. Vaudey (occ. 1331 x 49), 319
John, abb. Vaudey (occ. 1377), 319
John, abb. Wardon, 320
John III, abb. Waverley, 320
John, abb. Waverley (1349–), 321
John, abb. Wellow, 482
John, abb. Wendling, 516
John, abb. Whitby, 79
John, corrector Alberbury, 255
John, custos Hampole, 568
John, custos Hayling, 167
John, custos Spalding, 192
John, master Bristol, St Mary Magdalen, 545
John, master Legbourne, 580
John, master Sewardsley, 604
John, master Stixwould, 611
John, minister Knaresborough, 533
John, minister Thelsford (occ. 1288), 534
John, minister Thelsford (occ. 1335), 534
John, pr. Alnesbourn, 327
John, pr. Alvingham, 519
John, pr. Andover, 139
John, pr. Astley, 143
John, pr. Barlinch, 330
John, pr. Barnstaple (occ. 1308), 219
John, pr. Barnstaple (occ. 1319 x 27), 219

John, pr. Bath, 22
John, pr. Beauvale, 325
John, pr. Beddgelert, 332
John, pr. Berden, 333
John, pr. Bermondsey, 221
John, pr. Blackmore, 338
John, pr. Bodmin, 339
John, pr. Bolton, 339
John, pr. Boxgrove, 147
John, pr. Bradwell (early 13th cent.), 24
John, pr. Bradwell (mid 13th cent.), 24
John, pr. Bradwell (d.1320), 24
John, pr. Brecon (occ. 1203 x 26), 93
John, pr. Brecon (occ. 1375 x 80/1), 94
John, pr. Bridge End (occ. 1337), 519
John, pr. Bridge End (occ. 1377), 519
John, pr. Bridlington, 346
John, pr. Bristol, St James, 94
John, pr. Bromholm, 223
John, ?pr. Burstall, 148 n. 3
John, pr. Burwell, 149
John, pr. Butley, 354
John, pr. Cammeringham, 496
John, pr. Canterbury, St Gregory, 358
John, pr. Canwell, 31
John, pr. Cardigan, 95
John, pr. Carlisle, 359
John, pr. Cartmel, 361
John, pr. Castle Acre, 224 n. 2
John, pr. Catley (occ. 1229), 520
John, pr. Catley (occ. 1377), 521
John, pr. Clattercote (occ. 1344), 522
John, pr. Clattercote (occ. 1388), 522
John, pr. Clifford, 225
John, pr. Colchester, St Botolph (–1279/80), 369
John, ?pr. Colchester, St Botolph (occ. 1312), 369
John, pr. Colchester, St Botolph (occ. 1326 x 38), 369
John, pr. Conishead (occ. 1230 x 61), 371
John, pr. Conishead (occ. 1280 x 81), 372
John, pr. Conishead (occ. c.1340 x 54), 372
John, pr. Coxford, 372
John, pr. Dodford, 374
John, pr. Dodnash (occ. 1279), 374
John, pr. Dodnash (occ. 1304 x 16), 374
John, pr. Dudley, 227
John, pr. Edith Weston (occ. 1295/6 x 1302/3), 158
John, pr. Edith Weston (occ. 1375 x 7), 158
John, pr. Ellerton on Spalding Moor, 522
John, pr. Exeter, St James, 228
John, pr. Exeter, St Nicholas, 100
John, pr. Felixstowe, 102

John, pr. Flitcham, 380
John, pr. Folkestone, 160
John, pr. Frithelstock (occ. 1224 x 28), 380
John, pr. Frithelstock (occ. 1365), 381
John, pr. Great Bricett, 383
John, pr. Hamble, 164
John, pr. Hardham (occ. 1328), 385
John, pr. Hardham (occ. 1336), 385
John, pr. Harmondsworth, 165
John, pr. Hastings (occ. 1215 x 17), 386
John, pr. Hastings (–1300), 387
John, pr. Hastings (occ. 1382 x 85), 387
John, pr. Hatfield Peverel, 107
John, pr. Haugham, 166
John, pr. Haverford West, 388
John, pr. Herringfleet, 390
John, pr. Hertford, St Mary (1223–35), 109
John, pr. Hertford, St Mary (occ. 1378 x 9), 110
John, pr. Hickling, 392
John, ?pr. Horkesley, 230
John, pr. Hoxne, 113
John, pr. Huntingdon, 394
John, pr. Ipswich, Holy Trinity, 295
John, pr. Kilpeck, 115
John, pr. Kings Lynn, 116
John, pr. Kingston upon Hull, 325
John, pr. Lanercost (occ. late 12th/early 13th cent.), 403
John, pr. Lanercost (occ. 1380), 403
John, pr. Lapley, 172
John, pr. Latton (occ. 1357), 404
John, pr. Latton (occ. 1375), 404
John, pr. Lewisham, 173
John, pr. Linton and Isleham, 174
John, pr. London, St Bartholomew, 417
John, pr. Marton, 420
John, pr. Mattersey, 526
John, pr. Mendham (occ. 1239 x 40), 235
John, pr. Mendham (occ. 1295/6 x 1328), 235
John, pr. Michelham, 424
John, pr. Minster Lovell, 177
John, pr. Minting, 178
John, pr. Monks Horton (occ. c. 1324 x 26), 237
John, pr. Monks Horton (occ. 1369), 237
John, pr. Monks Kirby, 181
John, pr. Monmouth, 182
John, pr. Morville, 122
John, pr. Mottisfont, 426
John, pr. Mountjoy, 427
John, pr. Newark, 427
John, pr. Newburgh, 428
John, pr. Newent, 183

John, pr. Nostell, 438
John, pr. Panfield and Well, 186
John, pr. Pembroke, 187
John, pr. Penmon, 446
John, pr. Penwortham, 123
John, pr. Pilton, 124
John, pr. Pontefract, 246
John, pr. Poughley, 449
John, pr. Poulton, 527
John, pr. Puffin Island, 449
John, pr. Pynham by Arundel, 450
John, pr. Ranton, 450
John, pr. Repton, 452
John, pr. St Bees, 127
John, pr. St Carrok, 249
John, pr. St Michael's Mount (pre-1226), 189
John, pr. St Michael's Mount (occ. 1282), 189
John, pr. Sandaleford (occ. 1235 x 52), 457
John, pr. Sandaleford (occ. 1354), 457
John, pr. Sandaleford (occ. 1384), 457
John, pr. Sandwell (occ. 1195 x 1222), 65
John, pr. Sandwell (occ. 1269), 66
John, pr. Sandwell (occ. 1360), 66
John, pr. Scilly, 128
John, pr. Shouldham, 529
John, pr. Shulbred (occ. 1242), 459
John, pr. Shulbred (occ. 1265), 459
John, pr. Shulbred (occ. 1354 x 58), 459
John, pr. Snape, 128
John, pr. Snelshall, 71
John, pr. Sporle, 193
John, pr. Stansgate, 251
John, pr. Stratfield Saye, 196
John, pr. Swavesey, 197
John, pr. Takeley, 198
John, pr. Taunton (occ. 1197/1205 x 1228), 466
John, pr. Taunton (occ. 1276 x 1313), 467
John, pr. Thetford, St Mary, 252
John, pr. Thremhall (occ. 1231 x 61), 471
John, pr. Thremhall (occ. 1306), 471
John, pr. Thurgarton, 471
John, pr. Tiptree, 472
John, pr. Tonbridge (occ. 1202), 473
John, pr. Tonbridge (occ. 1242/3 x 48), 473
John, pr. Tonbridge (1279–), 473
John, pr. Torksey (–1236/7), 473
John, pr. Torksey (–1262/3), 473
John, pr. Tortington, 475
John, pr. Totnes, 202
John, pr. Tywardreath, 204
John, pr. Upavon, 205
John, pr. Wallingford (occ. 1229), 133

John, pr. Wallingford (occ. 1268), 133
John, pr. Wallingford (occ. 1300), 133
John, pr. Walsingham, 477
John, pr. Wangford (occ. 1217/18), 253
John, pr. Wangford (occ. 1324), 253
John, pr. Ware, 206
John, pr. Watton (occ. 1311), 530
John, pr. Watton (occ. 1333), 530
John, pr. Weedon Lois, 209
John, pr. West Mersea, 210
John, pr. Westacre, 483
John, pr. Wilmington, 211
John, pr. Winterborn Monkton, 253
John, pr. Witham, 326
John, pr. Wombridge, 486
John, pr. Woodspring (occ. 1223), 487
John, pr. Woodspring (occ. 1255/6 x 77), 487
John, pr. Worksop (occ. mid 13th cent), 487
John, pr. Worksop (occ. 1396), 488
John, pr. Wormsley, 488
John, pr. Wymondham (occ. 1229), 136
John, pr. Wymondham (occ. c. 1381), 136
John, pr. York, St Andrew (occ. 1214 x c. 1217), 531
John, pr. York, St Andrew (occ. 1415), 531
John ap Rees, abb. Conway, 275
John de C., pr. Dudley, 227
John R., abb. St Radegund, 509
John the Almoner, pr. Spalding, 193
Joldayn, William, abb. Coggeshall, 272
Jol(l)an, abb. Calder, 271
Jora, Reginald de, pr. Lenton, 232
Jorce, Eleanor, prs Heynings, 570
Jordan, abb. Beauchief, 493
Jordan, abb. Durford, 500
Jordan, abb. Hailes, 284
Jordan, abb. Lavendon, 506
Jordan, abb. Roche, 304
Jordan, abb. Swineshead, 314
Jordan, abb. Tavistock, 71
Jordan, pr. Bristol, St James, 94
Jordan, pr. Dodnash, 374
Jordan, pr. Kyme, 402
Jordan, Richard dictus, pr. Otterton, 185
Jori, Bernard, pr. Horsham St Faith, 169
Josbert (Joybert), pr. Much Wenlock, 241
Joseph, abb. Bristol, St Augustine, 347
Joseph, abb. Dieulacres, 276
Joseph, pr. Mottisfont, 426
Jou, Guichard de, [Lenton], 232
Joyce, prs Westwood, 616
Julia, prs Farewell, 559

Julian [Cammeringham], 495
Juliana, abbs Godstow, 562
Juliana, abbs Lacock, 577
Juliana, prs Ankerwyke, 539
Juliana, prs Arden, 539
Juliana, prs Broomhall, 545
Juliana, prs Canterbury, Holy Sepulchre, 550
Juliana, prs Gokewell, 563
Juliana, prs Henwood, 569
Juliana, prs Keldholme, 574
Juliana, prs London, Haliwell, 583
Juliana, prs Marrick, 587
Juliana, prs Rosedale, 601
Juliana, prs Studley, 612
Juliana, prs Whistones, 618
Juliana, prs Wintney, 622
Jumièges, William of, pr. Carisbrooke, 150
Jussell, John, pr. Carmarthen, 361

Kambreis, Peter de, pr. Wilsford, 211
Kankale, Ralph de, pr. St Michael's Mount, 189
Kant, William, see Charité, La, William of
Kari, Stephen de, pr. Brooke, 350
Katherine, prs Ankerwyke, 539
Katherine, prs Buckland, 546
Katherine, prs Crabhouse, 556
Katherine, prs Fosse, 561
Katherine, prs Harrold, 569
Katherine, prs Newcastle-upon-Tyne, 590
Katherine, prs Rusper, 603
Katherine, prs Stratford-at-Bow, 612
Kay, William, pr. Mottisfont, 426
Kaynnes, Henry, pr. Frithelstock, 380
Kaysthorp, Alexander de, pr. Chacombe, 362
Keal, Walter of, abb. Revesby, 301
Kedleston, Henry of, abb. Darley, 373
Kedyngton, Richard de, alias de Sudburia, abb.
     Westminster, 78
Keelby, Stephen of, pr. Elsham, 378
Keelby, William of, pr.-el. Torksey, 474
Kegworth, Henry of, pr. Chacombe, 362
Keinton, Robert de, [Chetwode], 363
Kele, Walter de, pr. Kingston upon Hull, 325
Kelfield, Nicholas of, pr. Rumburgh, 126
Kelfield, Robert of, pr.-el. Torksey, 474
Kelk, Walter of, [Swine], 614
Kellawe, Richard, pr. Holy Island, 111
Kellet, Richard of, pr. Cartmel, 361
Kelloe, Robert of, pr. Lytham, 120
Kelmarsh, Adam of, abb. Northampton, St James,
     436
Kelsey, Roger of, custodian Baysdale, 543

Kelsick, Robert of, abb. Holm Cultram, 285
Kempsey, Thomas of, abb. Tewkesbury, 74
Kendal, Adam of, abb. Holm Cultram, 284
Kendal, John of, pr. Belvoir, 91
Kendal, William of, abb. Welbeck, 515
Kendal, William of, pr. Cartmel, 361
Kendal, William of, pr. Hexham, 391
Kenric, abb. Bardsey, 329
Kensington, John of, pr. London, St Bartholomew,
     417
Kent, Beatrice of, abbs Lacock, 577
Kent, Cecily of, prs Harrold, 569
Kent, John of, abb. Fountains, 279
Kent, John of, abb. Glastonbury, 46
Kent, John of, pr. Hardham, 385
Kent(e), John, pr. Reigate, 451
Kent, Loretta (Lora) of, prs Markyate, 587
Kent, Richard of, pr. Binham, 92
Kent, Richard of, alias Canterbury, pr. Selborne,
     458
Kent, Simon of, pr. Bradwell, 24
Kent, Thomas of, pr. Merton, 423
Kent, William of, pr. Castle Acre, 224
Kentford, John of, pr. Ipswich, Holy Trinity, 395
Kenting, Richard, pr. Clifford, 225
Kenweryc, abb. Llantarnam, 290
Kenyngton, William de, abb.-el. Canterbury, St
     Augustine, 30
Kernet, William de, abb. Tavistock, 72; pr.
     Otterton, 185
Kerneth, Ralph, pr. Durham, 38
Kernic, Oger de, abb. Hartland, 386
Kersen', Avice, prs Ickleton, 573
Kersey, Henry of, pr. Ipswich, St Peter and St
     Paul, 396
Kersey, Roger of, pr. Thetford, Holy Sepulchre,
     468
Kesburgh, Robert de, abb. Roche, 305
Kesteven, Nicholas, see also Thokeby, Nicholas de
Kesteven, Nicholas of, abb. Hulton, 286
Keswick, Matilda of, prs Arthington, 540
Kettlestone, Nicholas of, pr. Hempton, 389
Kettlethorpe, Joan of, prs Fosse, 561
Ketton, John of, pr. Stamford, St Mary and St
     Michael, 610
Ketton, Richard of, keeper of Calwich, 355; pr.
     Brooke, 349–50
Ketton, Roger of, pr. Stamford, St Mary and St
     Michael, 610
Ketton, Stephen of, pr. Brooke, 349
Keyford, Richard II of, pr. Witham, 326
Keyham, Stephen of, pr. Charley, 362

Keynsham, Thomas of, pr. Bristol, St James, 94
Keynsham, William of, abb. Bindon, 263
Kibworth, John of, abb. Owston, 443
Kidderminster, Henry of, pr. Sandwell, 66
Kidderminster, Robert of, pr. Gloucester, St Oswald, 382
Kidknowle, Robert of, abb. Tavistock, 72
Kidlington, Thomas of, abb. Osney, 442
Kilham, John of, pr. North Ferriby, 436
Kilkhampton, John of, pr. Bodmin, 339
Killingworth, Robert of, pr. Stamford, St Leonard, 130
Kilvington, Robert of, master Farne, 102
Kimberley, Emma of, prs Ankerwyke, 539
Kimble, Felicia of, prs Little Marlow, 581
Kimble, Robert of, abb. Missenden, 424
Kinoulton, William of, pr. Shelford, 459
King (?), Henry, abb. Abbey Dore, 258
Kingesfolde, Joan de, [Rusper], 603
Kingsbury, John of, pr. Taunton, 467
Kingston, Gilbert of, master Stainfield, 608
Kingston, John of, pr. Canwell, 31
Kingston, John of, pr. Derby, St James, 227
Kingston, John of, pr. Llanthony Prima, 413
Kingston, John of, pr. Sandwell, 66
Kingston, William of, abb.-el. Abbotsbury, 15
Kinton, William of, pr. Leominster, 117
Kinwarton, Agnes of, prs Wroxall, 624
Kirkby, John of, pr. Aldeby, 89
Kirkby, John of, pr. Carlisle, 360
Kirkby, John of, pr. Felley, 379
Kirkby, John of, pr. Launde, 406
Kirkby, Reginald of, pr. Launde, 405
Kirkby, Thomas of, abb. Alnwick, 491
Kirkby, William of, pr. Norwich cath., 55
Kirkby Moorside, Elizabeth of, prs Rosedale, 602
Kirkeby, John of, pr. Bradley, 343 & n. 4
Kirkeby, William de, pr. Beadlow, 90; pr. Belvoir, 91; pr. Hertford, St Mary, 110
Kirkeby, William de, pr. Wallingford, 133
Kirkella, John of, pr. Kirkham, 401
Kirkely, John de, master St Mary de Pré, 604
Kirkham, William of, abb. Whitby, 80
Kirkstead, Roger of, pr. Ixworth, 398
Kirtlington, Robert of, pr. Bicester, 334
Kirton, John of, abb. Barlings, 492
Knaresborough, Adam of, master Farne, 102
Knaresborough, Henry of, minister Knaresborough, 533
Knaresborough, John of, abb. Coverham, 497
Knoll(e), Adam (de), pr. Launceston, 405
Knulle, Edmund of, abb. Bristol, St Augustine, 348

Knyvet, Katharine, abbs Northampton, De La Pré, 591
Kokenfeld, Richard de, alias Dokynfeld, abb. Basingwerk, 260
Kut, Matilda, prs Sewardsley, 604
see also Cut
Kylington, John de, ?pr. Newburgh, 429
Kyllyngwyk, John, minister Knaresborough, 533
Kylyngworthe, William de, pr. Wymondham, 136
Kyneford, John de, pr. Wormsley, 489
Kyngeston, Joan, abbs Tarant Kaines, 615
Kynton, William de, abb. Pipewell, 299
Kyrketon, Roger de, abb. Dale, 499
Kyrkholm, Roger de, pr. Kirkham, 401
Kyver, see Castello Kyver, Thomas de

Lacmers, John de, pr. Wilsford, 212
Lacu, John de, pr. Caldwell, 355
Lacy, Alice, prs Ickleton, 573
Lacy, Hugh de, abb. Shrewsbury, 69
Ladde, Amice, abbs Wherwell, 618
Lakenham, Henry of, pr. Norwich cath., 55
Lakinton, Thomas de, pr. Leonard Stanley, 117
Lalleford, Roger de, [Nuneaton], 597
Lalleford, William de, abb. Pipewell, 299
Laloyer, Nicholas, pr. Clatford, 151
Lamberhurst, John of, abb. Robertsbridge, 303
Lambert, abb. Swineshead, 315
Lambert, custos of Alberbury, 255
Lambert, pr. Carisbrooke, 150
Lambourn, Adam (of), abb. Eynsham, 43
Lambourn, Geoffrey of, abb. Eynsham, 44
Lambourn, John of, pr. Poughley, 449
Lamesley, Alexander of, master Jarrow, 114
Lamley, Isabel de, prs Rosedale, 602
Lampre(y), Juliana, abbs Canonsleigh, 550
Lancaster, Isabel of, prs Amesbury, 538
Lancaster, Katharine of, prs Armathwaite, 540
Langdale, Joan de, prs Watton, 531
Langdon, Robert of, abb. Burton, 25
Langdon, Robert of, pr. Studley, 466
Langdon, Stephen (of), abb. Tavistock, 73
Langford, John of, pr. Ivychurch, 397
Langham, Simon de, abb. Westminster, 79
Langholm, Agnes de, prs Greenfield, 566
Langley, Alexander of, pr. Wymondham, 135
Langley, Helewise of, prs Pinley, 598
Langley, Hugh of, abb. Welbeck, 515
Langley, Robert of, pr. Norwich cath., 56
Langryche, John, pr. Witham, 326
Langtoft, Robert of, abb. Whitby, 79
Langtoft, Simon of, pr. Freiston, 105

Langton, Bernard of, abb. Egglestone, 502
Langton, Emma of, prs Nun Appleton, 592
Langton, Henry of, master Greenfield, 567
Langton, John of, pr. Stamford, St Leonard, 130
Langton, Katherine of, prs Newcastle-upon-Tyne, 590
Langton, Nicholas of, pr. St Bees, 127
Langton, William of, abb. Rievaulx, 303
Lanuci, Arnald, pr. Newton Longville, 243
Larriens, Stephen de, pr. Horkesley, 230
Las, David, abb. Abbey Cwmhir, 258
Lascels, Thomas (de), pr. Rumburgh, 126
Lassy, William, pr. Brinkburn, 347
Lastingham, John of, pr. St Bees, 127
Lastingham, John (of), pr. Warter, 479
Lathbury, Adam of, abb. Reading, 60; pr. Leominster, 116
Lathbury, John de, abb. Lavendon, 506
Laton, Beatrice de, prs Moxby, 588
Laughton, William of, pr. Markby, 419
Launcel, William (de), pr. Tortington, 475
Laund, John of, pr. Bolton, 340
Launde, Simon de la, pr. Appuldurcombe, 141
Laurence, abb. Bayham, 493
Laurence, abb. Coverham, 497
Laurence, abb. Robertsbridge, 303
Laurence, abb. Sawtry, 307
Laurence, abb. Thame, 315
Laurence, abb. Torre, 512
Laurence, abb. Wardon, 320
Laurence, pr. Alberbury, 255
Laurence, pr. Appuldurcombe, 141
Laurence, pr. Guisborough, 384
Laurence, pr. Hereford, 108
Laurence, pr.-el. Launceston, 404
Laurence, pr. Royston, 454
Laurence, pr. Shelford, 458
Laurencz de Guyngis, Robert dictus, pr. Exeter, St Nicholas, 101
Lavercoyo, William de, pr. Wootton Wawen, 215
Lavinden, Richard de, pr. Trentham, 476
Lavington, Alice of, abbs Shaftesbury, 606
Lavington, Cecily (of), abbs Wherwell, 618
Lavington, Humphrey of, pr. Gloucester, St Oswald, 382
Lavington, Isabel of, prs Stixwould, 611
Lawley, John of, pr. Wombridge, 486
Layton, John of, pr. Finchale, 103; pr. Holy Island, 111
Lazenby, John of, pr. Hexham, 390
Leadenham, Hugh of, pr. Chicksands, 521
Leamington, William of, pr. Daventry, 226

Leaute, Thomas, pr. Frithelstock, 381
Leavington, Richard of, pr. Healaugh Park, 389
Leavington, Stephen of, pr. Healaugh Park, 389
Lecaron, William dictus, see Bec, William of
Leccinton, Richard de, pr. Royston, 454
Lech, Thomas de, abb. Halesowen, 504
Leche, John de, abb. Osney, 441
Leche, Philip de, pr. Cardiff, 95
Lecia, prs Kirklees, 576
Leckhampstead, Hugh of, pr. Snelshall, 71
Ledbury, Joan of, prs Aconbury, 537
Ledbury, Robert of, pr. Brooke, 349
Ledbury, Robert of, pr. Hereford, 108
Ledbury, William of, pr. Great Malvern, 105
Ledbury, William, pr. Nuneaton, 597
Lee, Basilia de la, prs Harrold, 569
Lee, Roger de la, pr. Canterbury, Christ Church, 27
Lee, William de, abb. Combermere, 274
Lee, William de la, pr. Sandwell, 66
Lecebourne, Roger de, abb. Bruern, 266
Leeds, Geoffrey of, pr. Breedon, 345
Leeds, Henry of, minister Moatenden, 533
Leeds, John of, master Hirst, 392
Leeds, Roger of, abb. Kirkstall, 289
Leeds, William (of), abb. Kirkstall, 288
Leek, Richard de, pr. Markby, 419
Leek(e), Laurence de, pr. Norwich cath., 56
Lega, Gerard de, abb. Pipewell, 299
Legat, Geoffrey dictus, pr. Otterton, 185
Legat, Thomas, master Jarrow, 115
Legat, William, of Preston, pr. Wymondley, 490
Legga, John, abb. Newenham, 298
Legh, Walter de, pr. Worcester, 86
Leghe, Ralph (de), pr. Exeter, St James, 229
Legh(e), Robert de, pr. Christchurch (Twynham), 366
Leghe, Thomas de, abb. Tewkesbury, 74
Legh(e), Thomas de, pr. Great Malvern, 106
Legh(e), Walter de, pr. Bruton, 351
Leghe, William de, abb. Pershore, 56
Leicester, Helewise of, prs Brewood Black Ladies, 544
Leicester, Henry of, pr. Coventry, 36
Leicester, Hugh of, pr. Stamford, St Mary and St Michael, 610
Leicester, Isabel of, prs Langley, 578
Leicester, John of, keeper Calwich, 355
Leicester, John of, pr. Launde, 406
Leicester, Margaret of, prs Langley, 578
Leicester, Peter of, abb. Owston, 442
Leicester, Peter of, pr.-el. Launde, 406

Leicester, Ralph of, abb. Darley, 373
Leicester, Robert of, pr. Brooke, 350
Leicester, Walter of, pr. Lincoln, St Mary Magdalen, 118
Leicester, William of, abb. Merevale, 295
Leicester, William of, pr. Charley, 363
Leicester, William of, pr. Shelford, 459
Leme, John, pr. Michelham, 424
Len', William de, pr. Kersey, 399
Lenn, Matilda de, prs Stamford, St Mary and St Michael, 609
Lenton, Peter of, abb. Bardney, 20
Lenton, Walter of, pr. Worksop, 487
Leone, Henry de, pr. Stoke by Clare, 196
Leone (Merial), Robert de, [Ogbourne St George], 184
Leonibus, Thomas de, pr. Cowick, 154
Leonibus, Thomas de, pr. Goldcliff (*possibly same as above*), 163
Leonius, abb. Rievaulx, 302
Lespard, John, pr. Exeter, St James, 228
Lespicer, William, pr. Minting, 178
Let, Idonea, prs London, Clerkenwell, 583
Letchworth, John of, pr. Cambridge, St Edmund, 520
Letchworth, John of, pr. Chicksands, 521
Letia, prs Ankerwyke, 539
Letour, John, pr. Frampton, 161
Lettice, prs Ankerwyke, 539
Lettice, prs Blackborough, 543
Lettice, prs Cambridge, St Mary and St Radegund, 548
Lettice, prs Canterbury, Holy Sepulchre, 550
Lettice, prs Ickleton, 573
Lettice, prs Stratford-at-Bow, 612
Lettice, prs Wilberfoss, 619
Levelande, Matilda de, abbs Barking, 541
Leven, Hugh of, abb. Meaux, 293
Leverington, Adam de, pr. Bushmead, 353
Leverington, Adam of, *see* Clowe, Adam
Leverington, Robert of, pr. Ely, 40
Leverington, Simon of, pr. Wormegay, 488
Leverton, Gilbert of, pr. Lincoln, St Mary Magdalen, 118
Levesham, Philip (de), abb. Westminster, 78
Lewes, Roger of, pr. Clifford, 225
Lewes, Thomas (of), pr. Breadsall, 344
Lewes, William, abb. Robertsbridge, 304
Lewknor, Hugh of, abb. Waverley, 321
Lewknor, Joan (of), prs London, Clerkenwell, 583
Lewknor, John of, pr. Oxford, St Frideswide, 444
Lewknor, Margaret (of), abbs Shaftesbury, 606

Lexington, Alice de, prs Fosse, 561
Lexin(g)ton, Cecily de, prs Nuneaton, 595
Lexington, John de, pr. Newstead (in Sherwood), 431
Lexington, Stephen of, abb. Stanley, 310
Lexington, Thomas of, pr. Shelford, 458
Leybourne, Agnes of, abbs Malling, 586
Leye, Roger, pr. Launceston, 405
Leyham, Cecily (de), prs Higham, 571
Leyn, John de, pr. Beddgelert, 332
Lichfield, John of, pr. Repton, 452
Lichfield, Richard of, pr. Brooke, 349
Lichfield, Thomas Colman of, *see* Colman, Thomas
Lichfield, William of, abb. Dieulacres, 277
Lilebon, John de, pr. Wilsford, 212
Lilford, Roger de, pr. Leominster, 117
Lilford, Walter of, pr. St Ives, 128
Lille, Geoffrey de, *see* Burgeys, Geoffrey
Limpevilla, William de, pr. Cogges, 152
Linby, Elias of, pr. Felley, 379
Lincoln, Alice of, prs Greenfield, 566
Lincoln, Alice of the Bail of, prs Heynings, 570
Lincoln, Christine of, *see* Cotty, Christine *dictus*
Lincoln, Hugh of, abb. Dale, 499
Lincoln, Isolda of, prs Legbourne, 579
Lincoln, Joel of, pr. Torksey, 474
Lincoln, John of, abb. Dale, 499
Lincoln, John of, master Grimsby, 567
Lincoln, John of, pr. Drax, 376
Lincoln, John of, pr. Torksey, 474
Lincoln, Peter of, pr. Kyme, 402
Lincoln, Ralph of, abb. Croxton Kerrial, 498
Lincoln, Richard of, abb. Louth Park, 292
Lincoln, Robert of, abb. Owston, 443
Lincoln, Robert of, pr. Kyme, 402
Lincoln, Roger of, pr. Norton, 437
Lincoln, Simon of, abb. Tupholme, 513
Lincoln, William of, abb. Thornton Curtis, 470
Lincoln, William of, pr. Newton Longville, 242
Lindley, John of, abb. Whalley, 322
Lindsey, Gilbert (of), pr. Exeter, St Nicholas, 101
Lindsey, John of, pr. Mendham, 235
Lindsey, Robert of, abb. Peterborough, 57
Lineya, Thomas de, [Steventon], 194
Lisle, Henry de, pr. Horsley, 170, 393
Lisle, Katherine de, prs Lyminster, 585
   see also Insula
Lisours, Margaret, prs Stainfield, 608
Lissett, Gregory of, *custos* Nun Keeling, 594
Lissett, Gregory of, pr. Marton, 420
Lissett, Robert of, master Nun Keeling, 594

Liston, Beatrice of, prs Thetford, St George, 615
Litherland, Thomas of, pr. Burscough, 352
Litlington, Nicholas de, abb. Westminster, 79
  see also Lytlynton
Little Hereford, Roger of, *see* Hereford, Little,
  Roger of
Littlemore, John of, pr. Oxford, St Frideswide, 445
Littleport, William of, pr. Spalding, 193
Littleton, Matilda of, abbs Wherwell, 618
Littleton, Matilda of, prs Bristol, St Mary
  Magdalen, 545
Littlyngton, Agnes de, prs Rusper, 603
Llandyfai, Cadwgan of, abb. Whitland, 323
Llangiwen, Hilary de, pr. Llangua, 175
Llewelyn, abb. Whitland, 323
Llewelyn, pr. Beddgelert, 332
Llywelyn, abb. Cymmer, 276
Lobenham, William de, abb. Calder, 271
Lockington, Thomas of, pr. Ulverscroft, 477
Loddon, John of, pr. Great Bricett, 383
Loddon, Roger of, abb. Sibton, 309
Lodebrok, Margaret (de), prs Sewardsley, 604
Lodelowe, Richard, pr. St Clears, 250
Lodenne, Clement de, abb. Faversham, 45
Loders, Benedict of, abb. Abbotsbury, 15
Lokyngham, John de, pr. Pilton, 124
Lombard, Peter, pr. Hinckley, 168
Lonboul, William de, pr. Abergavenny, 138
Loncastell, John, abb. Cymmer, 276
Londa, Richard de, pr. Hough, 394
Londa, Simon de, pr. Loders, 175
Londesborough, Richard of, pr. Ellerton on
  Spalding Moor, 522
London, Agnes of, prs Little Marlow, 581
London, Agnes of, prs Rowney, 602
London, Alan of, pr. Worksop, 487
London, Andrew of, *alias* of St Martin, pr.
  Winchester, St Swithun, 83
London, Christina of, prs-el. Ankerwyke, 539
London, Geoffrey of, pr. Newark, 427
London, Henry of, *alias* Brompton, pr. Leighs, 409
London, Henry of, pr. Sudbury, 131
London, Joan of, prs Rowney, 602
London, John of, pr. Cogges, 151
London, John of, pr. Dunstable, 377
London, Matilda of, prs Higham, 571
London, Nicholas of, *see* Aldgate, Nicholas of
London, Peter, corrector Alberbury, 255
London, Richard of, abb. Peterborough, 58
London, Simon of, abb. Missenden, 424
London, Thomas of, pr. Breadsall, 343
London, Thomas of, pr. Dudley, 227

London, Thomas of, pr. Nocton Park, 433
London, Walter of, abb. Croxden, 275
London, Walter of, pr. Hurley, 113
London, William of, abb. Missenden, 424
London, William of, abb. Waverley, 321
London, William of, pr. Ewyas Harold, 100
Longavilla, Thomas de, pr. Northampton, St
  Andrew, 243
Longchamp, *see* Longo Campo
Longden, Robert de, pr. Tutbury, 203
Longe, Margery, prs Bristol, St Mary Magdalen,
  545
Longe, William, abb. Bristol, St Augustine, 348
Longen', John de, pr. Kilpeck, 115
Longeney, Walter of [Llanthony Secunda], 415
Longford, Giles of, pr.-el. Tutbury, 203
Longney, John of, pr. Hereford, 109
Longnor, Nicholas of, abb. Haughmond, 388
Longo Campo, Henry de, abb. Crowland, 36
Longo Campo, Robert II de, abb. York, St Mary, 86
Longespée, Agnes, abbs Shaftesbury, 605
Longespée, Ela, abbs Lacock, 577
Longvilers, Agnes, prs Stainfield, 608
Lora, prs Flamstead, 560
Loretta, prs Flamstead, 560
Loring, Walter, abb. Malmesbury, 51
Lorriaco, Hugh *dictus* Folon de, pr. Minting, 178
Lose, John (de), pr. Brecon, 93
Lose, John de, pr. Combwell, 371
Loteryntone, Elizabeth de, prs Pinley, 598
Louches, Margery de, abbs Burnham, 547
Louers, Robert de, pr. Astley, 143
Loughborough, Roger of, abb. Rocester, 453
Loughborough, Thomas of, abb. Croxton Kerrial,
  498
Loughborough, Thomas of, abb. Garendon, 283
Loughborough, William of, abb. Biddlesden, 262
Loughton, William of, pr. Bradwell, 24
Louth, Adam of, abb. Louth Park, 291
Louth, John of, abb. Kirkstead, 290
Louth, John of, abb. Louth Park, 291
Louth, John of, pr. Burwell, 149
Louth, Thomas of, master Legbourne, 580
Louth, Thomas of, pr. Nocton Park, 434
Louth, Thomas of (?another), pr. Nocton Park, 434
Louth, Walter of, abb. Louth Park, 292
Louwe, Isabel la, prs Buckland, 546
Lovel, Robert, pr. Canons Ashby, 357
Lovel, Robert, pr. Otterton, 186
Lovel, William, pr. Haugham, 166
Loveny, Lucy (de), abbs Wilton, 620
Lovers, John de, pr. Wootton Wawen, 215

Lovetot, William de, pr. Felley, 378
Lowthorpe, William of, pr. Newburgh, 428
Lu, John *dictus*, abb. Northampton, St James, 436
Lubbenham, Robert of, pr. Bushmead, 353
Lucian, William, pr. Thurgarton, 471
Lucy, abbs Winchester (1270–), 621
Lucy, abbs Winchester (occ. 1285), 621
Lucy, prs Flamstead, 560
Lucy, prs Rusper, 603
Lucy, prs Stratford-at-Bow, 612
Lucy, prs Wintney (occ. 1223 x 24), 622
Lucy, prs Wintney (occ. 1256 x 63), 622
Lucy, Joan, prs Cornworthy, 555
Lucy, Matilda, prs Flamstead, 560
Lucy, Petronilla de, prs Flamstead, 560
Lucy, Stephen de, pr. Winchester, St Swithun, 82
Luddington, Beatrice of, prs Fosse, 561
Luddington, Richard of, pr. Brooke, 349
Ludelowe, Richard, [West Ravendale], 518
Ludgershall, Agnes of, prs Goring, 565
Ludham, Joan of, prs Catesby, 552
Ludlow, John of, pr. Weedon Lois, 210
Ludlow, Thomas of, pr. Clifford, 226
Ludlow, Walter of, abb.-el. Wigmore, 485
Luffenham, Osbert of, abb. Northampton, St James, 436
Luffenham, Simon of, abb. Crowland, 37
Luffield, Ralph of, *see* Silverstone, Ralph of
Lufwyk, Robert de, pr. Caldwell, 355
Luke, abb. Abingdon, 16
Luke, abb. Newbo, 507
Luke, pr. Ipplepen, 295
Luke, pr. Southwick, 461
Luke, pr. Witham, 326
Lumley, Emery of, master Jarrow, 114; pr. Finchale, 104; pr. Lytham, 120
Lumley, John of, master Jarrow, 115
Lummier', Giles de, pr. Abergavenny, 138
Lund, John of, pr. Bolton, 340; pr. Marton, 420
Lund, Robert of, pr. Warter, 480
Lund, Thomas (of), pr. Finchale, 103
Lunda, John de, pr. Boxgrove, 147
Lunde, Michael de la, ?pr. Clatford, 151
Lupynyaco, John de [Long Bennington], 291
Lusby, Henry of, pr. Durham, 38; pr. Holy Island, 111
Lusby, Nicholas of, pr. Finchale, 104
Lusby, Nigel of, pr. Stamford, St Leonard, 130
Luscote, John, pr. Hinton, 325; pr. London, Charterhouse, 326
Lutehale, John, pr. Cammeringham, 496
Lutlynton, Robert de, abb.-el. Pershore, 57

Luton, Adam of, abb. Woburn, 323
Luton, Matilda of, prs Markyate, 587
Luton, Simon of, *alias* of Hoo, abb. Bury St Edmunds, 26
Lutterell, John, master Farne, 102
Lutterell, William, pr. Stamford, St Leonard, 129
Lutton, Margaret of, prs Yedingham, 625
Lydgate, Simon de, pr. Spinney, 462
Lyencourt, William de, pr. Grovebury, 164
Lymbiri, Humphrey de, pr. Barlinch, 330
Lyndestede, William de, pr. Canterbury, St Gregory, 358
Lyndley, Roger, abb. Combermere, 274
Lyneham, Roger of, pr. Chetwode, 363
Lyneham, William of, abb. Cirencester, 368
Lynham, William, abb. Bruern, 266
Lynn, Agnes of, prs Norwich (Carrow), 592
Lynn, Alexander of, pr. Hempton, 389
Lynn, John of, pr. Alnesbourn, 327
Lynn, John of, pr. Great Massingham, 383
Lynn, Margaret of, *see* Costyn, Margaret
Lynn, William of, pr. Hoxne, 112
Lyra, John de, pr. Hurley, 113
Lytlynton, John de, pr. Merton, 423
  see also Litlington
Lyvet, Elias, abb. Rufford, 306

M., abb. Valle Crucis, 318
M., pr. Finchale, 103
M., pr. Monks Kirby, 181
M., prs Markyate, 587
Mabel II, abbs Elstow, 557
Mabel, prs Greenfield, 566
Mabel, prs Legbourne, 579
Mabel, prs Lyminster, 585
Mabel, prs Nun Appleton, 592
Mabel, prs Studley, 612
Mabel, prs Swine, 613
  see also Amabel
Mabere, John, pr. Wareham, 207
Mablethorpe, Lucy of, prs Nun Cotham, 593
Mackworth, Hugh of, pr. Breadsall, 343
Macrell, John, pr. Tynemouth, 133
Madeley, Richard of, *alias* Straddel, abb. Abbey Dore, 259
Madoc, abb. Valle Crucis (–1254), 318
Madoc, abb. Valle Crucis (occ. 1275 x 84), 318
Madoc, pr. Beddgelert, 332
Magdalen, prs Norwich (Carrow), 591
Magnavilla, Robert de, pr. Toft Monks, 201
Mahe, Alan, pr. Sporle, 193
Maheil, Betrand, pr. Goldcliff, 163

Maidford, Peter of, pr. Beadlow, 90; pr. Belvoir, 91

Maidstone, Adam of, pr. Leeds, 407

Maidstone, Robert of, pr. Leeds, 407

Maidstone, William of, abb. Faversham, 45

Maigre, John, [Wilmington], 211

Mainard, abb. Robertsbridge, 303

Mainer, pr. Monkton Farleigh, 237

Maisiulio, John de, pr. Takeley, 198

Maldon, Thomas of, pr. Earls Colne, 99

Malebisse, Henry, pr. Spinney, 462

Malecak, Roger, master Nun Cotham, 593

Malcherbe, Ralph *dictus*, pr. West Ravendale, 517

Malengiene, John de, pr. Weedon Lois, 210

Malet, Isabel, prs Stixwould, 611

Malet, Nicholas, [Wootton Wawen], 215

Malet, Nicholas, pr. Beckford and Colsterworth, 332

Malherbe, William, pr. Sele, 191 n.10

Malitote, James de, pr. Stogursey, 194

Malleya, Robert de, pr. Dudley, 227

Malling, South, Ralph of, pr. Bilsington, 336

Malling, Nicholas of, pr. Clifford, 226

Malling, William of, pr. Tonbridge, 473

Mallore, Emma, abbs Northampton, De La Pré, 590

Mallore, Henry, abb. Biddlesden, 261

Mallore, Joan, abbs Northampton, De La Pré, 591

Mallyng, Robert, pr. Tonbridge, 473

Malmesbury, Richard of, abb. Bristol, St Augustine, 348

Maltby, Isabel of, prs Stamford, St Mary and St Michael, 609

Malteby, John de, pr. Mullicourt, 55

Malton, Benedict of, abb. York, St Mary, 87

Malton, Benedict of, pr. St Bees, 127

Malton, John de, pr. Buckenham, 351

Malton, John of, pr. Haverholme, 523

Malton, John of, pr. Lincoln, St Katharine, 523

Malton, Thomas of, abb. Whitby, 80

Malvern, Richard *dictus* of, pr. Alvecote, 89

Malvern, William of, abb. Leicester, 408

Mamecestre, Roger of, pr. Norton, 437

Mamecestre, Sarah de, abbs Polesworth, 598

Man, Richard, pr. Chipley, 364

Manepeny, William, abb. Woburn, 324

Maners, Richard de, abb. Bindon, 263

Mangeaunt, John, pr. Hereford, 109

Mansel, Ralph le, pr. Spalding, 192

Mansfield, Robert of, pr. Shelford, 459

Maplebeck, Robert of, abb. Rufford, 306

Mappleton, Agnes of, prs Nun Keeling, 594

Marcham, Roger (of), abb. Thame, 315

Marchant, Guy de, pr. Montacute, 239

Marcheford, William de, pr. Freiston, 105

Marchia, John de, pr. Berden, 334

Marcy, Agnes de, prs London, Clerkenwell, 583

Marden, John of, pr. Combwell, 371

Mare, Alice de la, abbs Winchester, 621

Mare, Matilda de la, abbs Wilton, 619

Mare, Thomas de la, abb. St Albans, 64

Mare, Thomas de la, pr. Tynemouth, 133

Mare, William de la, abb. Missenden, 425

Maredwt, abb. Conway, 275

Mareis, Henry de, pr. Carlisle, 359

Marescall, Thomas (le), pr. Dunstable, 377

Mareschal, Ralph, abb. Missenden, 425

Mareschal, Richard le, abb. Missenden, 424

Mareschal, Robert, abb. Shap, 510

Mareshal, Joan, prs Flixton, 561

Mareskallo, John de, [Takeley], 198

  see also Marschall

Mareys, Covina de, prs Wintney, 622

Margaret, abbs Wilton, 619

Margaret, prs Amesbury, 538

Margaret, prs Arden, 539

Margaret, prs Blackborough, 543

Margaret, prs Ellerton-in-Swaledale, 557

Margaret, prs Goring, 564

Margaret, prs Little Marlow, 581

Margaret, prs Marrick, 587

Margaret, prs Neasham (occ. 1349 x 50), 589

Margaret, prs Neasham (occ. 1379), 589

Margaret, prs Sinningthwaite (occ. 1322), 606

Margaret, prs Sinningthwaite (occ. 1397), 607

Margaret, prs Wallingwells, 616

Margaret, prs York, St Clement, 626

Margery, prs Aconbury, 537

Margery, prs Campsey Ash, 549

Margery, prs Easebourne, 557

Margery, prs Farewell, 559

Margery, prs Holystone, 572

Margery, prs Kilburn, 575

Margery, prs Lambley, 578

Margery, prs Pinley (occ. 1226) 597

Margery, prs Pinley (occ. 1285) 598

Margery, prs Newcastle-upon-Tyne (occ. 1322/3 x 24), 589

Margery, prs Newcastle-upon-Tyne (occ. 1361), 590

Margery, prs Sinningthwaite, 606

Margery, prs Sopwell, 607

  see also Marjorie

Marham, Richard of, pr. Pentney, 446

Mari, John de, pr. Kings Lynn, 116

Marigneio, Thomas de, pr. Titley, 201
Marina, John de, abb. Bristol, St Augustine, 348
Marisco, Christiana de, prs Goring, 564
Marisco, Jordan de, archpriest or pr. Barton, 331
Marjorie (Margery), prs Wothorpe, 623
  see also Margery
Mark, abb. Lessness, 409
Mark, pr. Montacute, 238
Markam, Le[ti]cia de, prs Stratford-at-Bow, 612
Marlborough, Richard of, pr. Bisham, 337
Marlborough, Richard (of), pr. Ingham, 533
Marlborough, Thomas of, abb. Evesham, 41
Marlborough, William of, abb. Evesham, 42
Marmion, William, abb. Chester, 33
Marmyoun, Alice, prs Wix, 623
Marreys, William (de), abb. York, St Mary, 88
Marschall, Walter, pr. Exeter, St James, 229
  see also Mareschal, etc.
Martel, Thomas, pr. Hertford, St Mary, 109
Martel, William, pr. Goldcliff, 163
Martham, Ralph of, pr. Kings Lynn, 116
Martham, Robert of, pr. Weybridge, 484
Martin, abb. Halesowen, 503
Martin, abb. Missenden, 424
Martin, master London, Clerkenwell, 583
Martin, pr. Bentley, 333
Martin, ?pr. Dunster, 99
Martin, pr. Ellerton on Spalding Moor, 522
Martin, pr. Frampton, 161
Martin, pr. Haverholme, 523
Martin, pr. Redbourn, 124
Martin, pr. St Ives, 128
Martin, pr. Southwark, 460
Martin, pr. West Ravendale, 517
Martin, pr. Wymondley, 490
Martin, Mabel, prs Cambridge, St Mary and St
  Radegund, 548
Martini, Peter, pr. Lancaster, 172
Martival, Richard (de), pr. Launde, 405
Martival, Robert (de), pr. Launde, 405
Martley, Walter of, pr. Llanthony Secunda, 414
Martley, William of, abb. Cirencester, 368
Marton, Alan of, pr. Monkwearmouth, 121
Marton, Alexander of, pr. Hexham, 391
Marton, John of, pr. Rumburgh, 126
Marton, Margaret of, prs Heynings, 570
Martyn, Robert, master Rowney, 603
Mary I, abbs Marham, 586
Mary II, abbs Marham, 586
Mary, abbs Wherwell, 617
Mary, prs Blackborough, 543
Mary, prs Buckland, 546

Mary, ?prs Bungay, 547
Mary, prs Cheshunt, 554
Mary, prs Chester, 555
Mary, prs Easebourne, 557
Mary, prs Ickleton, 573
Mary, prs Kington St Michael, 576
Mary, prs London, St Helen's and Holy Cross, 585
Mary (Mariota), prs Nun Monkton, 594
Maryn, Michael (*dictus*), pr. West Ravendale, 517
Maryns, John de, abb. St Albans, 63
Masham, William of, pr. Stamford, St Leonard,
  129
Masiner, Robert le, pr. Brimpsfield, 147
Mason, John, abb. Cleeve, 271
Massingham, John of, pr. Peterstone, 447
Massingham, Richard (Richer) of, abb. Langley,
  505
Math', prs-el. Catesby, 551
Matheu, Philip, pr. Andover, 140
Matilda, abbs Barking, 541
Matilda, abbs Winchester, 621
Matilda, prs Broadholme, 545
Matilda, prs Davington, 556
Matilda (?another), prs Davington, 556
Matilda, prs Farewell, 559
Matilda, prs Goring, 564
Matilda (?another), prs Goring, 564
Matilda, prs Greenfield (occ. early 13th cent.), 566
Matilda, prs Greenfield (occ. 1260), 566
Matilda, prs Hampole, 568
Matilda, prs Henwood, 569
Matilda, prs Ilchester, 573
Matilda, prs Kilburn (occ. 1268 x 9), 575
Matilda, prs Kilburn (occ. 1311), 575
Matilda, prs London, Haliwell, 583
Matilda, prs London, St Helen's and Holy Cross,
  584
Matilda, prs Norwich (Carrow), 591
Matilda, prs Stainfield, 608
Matilda, prs Stixwould, 610
Matilda, prs Stratford-at-Bow, 612
Matilda, prs Swaffham Bulbeck, 613
Matilda, prs Swine, 613
Matilda, prs Wroxall, 624
Matthew, abb. Alcester, 18
Matthew, abb. Bardney, 20
Matthew, abb. Leiston, 506
Matthew, abb. Newbo, 507
Matthew, abb. Strata Marcella, 313
Matthew, master Stixwould, 611
Matthew, master Wallingswells, 616
Matthew, pr. Clatford, 151

Matthew, pr. Hatfield Peverel, 107
Matthew, pr. Lenton, 232
Mat(t)hew, pr. Monks Kirby, 181
Matthew, pr. Monmouth, 182
Matthew (Martin) Goch, pr. Penmon, 446
Matthew, pr. Southwick, 461
Matthew, pr. Stamford, St Leonard, 129
Matthew, pr. Tortington, 475
Matthew, pr. Weedon Lois (1266–76), 209
Matthew, pr. Weedon Lois (1277–82), 209
Maubert, John, pr. Wootton Wawen, 216
Maudut, Basilia, prs Harrold, 569
Maunby, John of, pr. Rumburgh, 126
Maunby, John of (?the same), pr. Rumburgh, 126
Maunsel, Robert, see Yardley, Robert of
Maunsell, Peter, pr. Llangua, 175
Maunvill, Richard de, pr. Wilsford, 212
Maupol, Peter (de), pr. Southwick, 461
Maurice, abb. Biddlesden, 261
Maurice, abb. Kirkstall, 288
Maurice, custos Scarborough, 308
Maurice, pr. Cowick, 153
Maurice, pr. Goldcliff, 162
Maury, Richard, abb. Milton, 52
Maury, Richard, pr. Christchurch (Twynham), 366
Maydenethe, Reginald de, abb. Waltham, 478
Maydenford, Peter de, pr. Hatfield Peverel, 107
Mayel, Richard, pr. Calwich, 356
Maylock, Ralph, pr. Livers Ocle, 174
Maynard, Robert, custos Godstow, 563
Maynard, Robert, pr. Avebury, 144
Meaburn, Robert of, pr. Lanercost, 403
Measham, Henry of, abb. Croxden, 275
Meders, Walter de, pr. Leominster, 117
Medici, William, pr. Folkestone, 160
Medicus, Henry dictus, abb. Notley, 440
Medicus, Thomas, pr. Wymondham, 135
Medmenham, John of, abb. Chertsey, 32
Medmenham, John of, abb. Medmenham, 294
Medunta, John de, pr. Deerhurst, 156
Medunta, John de, pr. Otterton, 185
Meiaco, William de, pr. Weedon Lois, 210
Meinwaryng, Joan de, prs Grace Dieu, 566
Meisiaco, Stephen de, pr. Astley, 142
Melbourn, Peter de, alias Le Norreis, pr.
    Gloucester, St Oswald, 382
Meleburne, Clarice de, prs Wintney, 622
Melkinthorpe, Henry of, pr.-el. Bridlington, 346
Melkinthorpe, Henry of, pr. Marton, 420
Melsonby, Matilda, prs Marrick, 588
Melsonby, Thomas of, pr. Durham, 38
Melton, Richard of, master Swine, 614

Melton, Richard of, pr. Wombridge, 486
Melton, Walter of, abb. Northampton, St James,
    436
Menedep, Geoffrey de, pr. Chirbury, 365
Menere, William de la, ?pr. Corsham, 152
Meneria, William de, pr. Tickford, 200
Menfrey, Nicholas, pr. Linton and Isleham, 174
Menillo, William, pr. Pembroke, 187
Mentmore, Michael of, abb. St Albans, 64
Meopham, John of, pr. Felixstowe, 102
Meppershall, Adam of, pr. Tynemouth, 132
Mercer, John, pr. Arundel, 142
Merdene, Henry de, pr. Hexham, 390
Mere, Richard de, pr. Stafford, 463
Mere, William de, pr. Nocton Park, 434
Meret, Amfrid, pr. Aston Priors, 143
Merewell, Henry de, see Woodlock, Henry
Meriston, Joan de, prs Higham, 571
Merk, Ralph, abb. Crowland, 37
Merlawe, John de, pr. Winchester, St Swithun, 84
Merse, Gilbert de, pr. Luffield, 50
Merschton, William de, pr. Penwortham, 124
Merser/Messer, John (le), bailiff of Atherington,
    144
Merstham, John of, pr. Tandridge, 466
Merston, Hamund de, pr. Breadsall, 343
Merston, John de, pr. Bentley, 333
Merston, Robert de, pr. Arbury, 329
Merstone, William de, pr. Mullicourt, 55
Merton, Alice of, abbs Barking, 541
Meslier, Peter, pr. Blyth, 146
Mesnill, Henry de, pr. St Neots, 190
Mesnillo, William de, pr. Arundel, 142
Messyngham, Robert de, pr. Taunton, 467
Methley, Agnes of, prs York, St Clement, 626
Methley, John of [Pontefract], 247
Methley, Roger of, pr. Holy Island, 111
Methwold, Agnes of, prs Crabhouse, 556
Methwold, William (of), abb. St Benet of Hulme,
    65
Michael, abb. Buckfast, 267
Michael, abb. Combe, 272
Michael, bailiff of Atherington, 144
Michael, pr. Brecon, 93
Michael, pr. Cogges, 151
Michael, pr. Ellingham, 158
Michael, pr. Frampton, 161
Michael, pr. Guisborough, 384
Michael, pr. Hatfield Regis, 166
Michael, pr. Ipswich, St Peter and St Paul, 396
Michael, pr. Monk Sherborne, 180
Michael (?another), pr. Monk Sherborne, 180

Michael, pr. Ruislip, 188

Michael, pr. Tywardreath, 204

Michael, Richard, pr. St Germans, 456

Michel, John, pr. Modbury, 179

Micheldever, Adam of, pr. Bilsington, 336

Middleham, Ralph of, master Jarrow, 114

Middleham, Robert of, master Farne, 102

Middlesbrough, Robert of, pr. York, St Andrew, 531

Middlesbrough, Thomas of, master Handale, 568

Middlesbrough, William of, pr. Guisborough, 384

Middleton, Bertram of, pr. Durham, 38

Middleton, Ida of, prs Blackborough, 543

Middleton, Patrick of, master Sempringham, 527; pr. Watton, 530

Middleton, William of, abb. Furness, 282

Middleton, William of, pr. Holy Island, 111

Mideforth, Robert de, pr. Henes and Sandtoft, 107

Miggele, Simon de, abb. Jervaulx, 286

Mikelay, Hugh, abb. Kirkstall, 288

Milham, Simon de, abb. Langley, 505

Millevill, John de, pr. Upavon, 205

Millicent, prs Cambridge, St Mary and St Radegund, 548

Millicent, prs Nunburnholme, 595

Milo, pr. Binham, 92

Milverton, William of, pr. Horsley, 170, 393

Minguet, William, pr. Wareham, 207

Minsterworth, Maurice of, abb. Alcester, 19; pr. Leonard Stanley, 117

Minterne, Gilbert of, abb. Cerne, 31

Miouns, Henry de, *alias* de Chay, pr. Much Wenlock, 242

Moerges, Stephen de, pr. Lenton, 232

Mohaut, Joan de, prs Esholt, 559

Molendinis, William de, pr. Little Malvern, 119

Molesia, G. de, ?pr. Totnes, 202

Molesworth, Gilbert of, pr. Ravenstone 451

Molis, Michael de, pr. Wareham, 207

Molton, John, pr. Canwell, 31

Molton, Robert de, pr. Plympton, 447

Molyns, Margaret de, abbs Winchester, 621

Monasteriis, William de, pr. Hamble, 164

Mondrevilla, Bertaud (Berthold), de, pr. Minster Lovell, 177

Mondrevilla, Richard de, pr. Frampton, 161

Monesle, Nicholas de, pr. Ixworth, 398

Mongeham, Stephen, pr. Canterbury, Christ Church, 28

Monkton, Geoffrey of, pr. Richmond, 125

Monkton, Robert (of), abb. Fountains, 281

Monmouth, Walter of, pr. Ewyas Harold, 100

Mont St Vincent, Peter of, pr. Bermondsey, 221

Montagu, Elizabeth de, prs London, Haliwell, 584

Montargi, Reginald de, *see* Eye, Reginald of

Montargis, Thomas de, pr. Monkton Farleigh, 238

Montchensy, Agnes de, prs Norwich (Carrow), 591

Monte, Oger de, *see* Bueys, Oger de

Monte Alto, Hugh de [keeper of Holy Island], 111

Monte Acuto, Isabel de, abbs Barking, 541

Monte Acuto, John de, abb. Bindon, 263

Monte Acuto, Matilda de, abbs Barking, 541

Monte Ardito, Peter de, of Aquitaine, pr. Burwell, 149

Monte Ardito, Peter de, pr. Wing, 213

Monte Calvet, John de, pr. Minster Lovell, 177

Monte Martini, John de, pr. Lewes, 234; pr. Prittlewell, 247

Montellier, Peter de, pr. Prittlewell, 247

Montemauri, Henry de, pr. Bermondsey, 221

Montenay, Alice de, prs Wallingwells, 616

Montfort, Joan de, abbs Lacock, 577

Montfort, Matilda de, abbs Lacock, 577

Montfort, Ralph de, of Ivry, *see* Ivry, Ralph de Montfort of

Montgomeri, Philip de, pr. Chirbury, 365

Montibus, Aymo de, pr. Bermondsey, 220; pr. Much Wenlock, 241

Montigneyo, Nicholas (Richard) de, pr. Frampton, 161

Montimato, John de, pr. Sporle, 193

Monyngeham, Robert de, abb. St Radegund, 509

Monynton, Agnes de, prs Whistones, 618

Monyron, Thomas, pr. Snape, 129

Monyton(e), Walter de, abb. Glastonbury, 47

Moot, John de la, abb. St Albans, 604

Mora, Avice de, prs Nun Keeling, 594

Mora, John de, [Longleat], 417

Morchad, Margaret (Margery) de, prs Polsloe, 599

Morcott, Henry of, abb. Peterborough, 59

Mordon, John de, pr. Wymondley, 490

Mordon, John de (*another*), pr. Wymondley, 490

Moredon, Stephen of, pr. Ivychurch, 397

Morel, John, pr. Felixstowe, 103

Morel, John, pr. West Mersea, 210

Morel, Ralph, [Toft Monks], 201

Morelli, John, pr. Hinckley, 168

Mores, Richard de, pr. Dunstable, 376

Moreteau, Geoffrey, pr. Monmouth, 182

Morevyle, Philip, pr. Kidwelly, 115

Morewych, Richard de, pr. Watton, 530

Morice, Nicholas, abb. Waltham, 479

Morland, Lambert of, abb. Shap, 510

Morlande, James de, pr. Rumburgh, 126

Morpayn, Robert, pr. Eye, 160
Morteyn, Cecily de, prs Flamstead, 560
Morteyn, Elizabeth (de), abbs Elstow, 559
Morthyng, Thomas (occ. 1270 x 71), pr. Conishead, 372
Morthyng, Thomas de (occ. 1339), pr. Conishead, 372
Mortimer, Matilda, prs Goring, 564
Mortimer, Philip de, pr. Castle Acre, 223
Mortmart, Peter de, pr. Montacute, 240
Morton, Alan of, pr. Marton, 420
Morton, Clarice of, prs Goring, 565
Morton, John of, abb. Haughmond, 387
Morton, Matilda of, prs Cannington, 549
Morton, Walter of, abb. Dieulacres, 277
Moryn, John, pr. Panfield and Well, 187
Mota, Adam de, pr. Binham, 92
Mota, Gervase de, pr. Arundel, 141
Mottershead, Helewise of, prs Chester, 555
Mottisfont, William of, pr. Newstead (in Sherwood), 431
Moubray, Joan de, prs Swine, 613
Moubray, Katherine, prs Baysdale, 543
Moulton, Lambert of, pr. Lincoln, St Mary Magdalen, 118
Moulton, Thomas of, abb. York, St Mary, 87
Mouner, Walter ?le, pr. Tutbury, 203
Mountenay, Alice, prs Kirklees, 577
Moussores, Ralph (de), pr. Burstall, 148
Mouster, Peter de, pr. Appuldurcombe, 141
Mousters, Alice le, prs Kirklees, 576
Moveron, Thomas, abb. Colchester, 35
Moyaz, John (de), pr. Newent, 183
Moyaz, Simon, pr. Newent, 182
Moyne, Isaak le, see Pontefract, Isaak le Moyne of
Moysiaco, Stephen de alias de Sorfrato, pr. Deerhurst, 155
Muchelney, Ralph of, abb. Muchelney, 54
Mucklestone, Nicholas of, pr. Trentham, 476
Muckley, William of, abb. Shrewsbury, 70
Mul(e)wych, Richard de, pr. Ranton, 450
Multon, Lambert de, pr. Rumburgh, 125
Multon, Thomas (de), pr. Tiptree, 473
Mulwych, Thomas de, pr. Stone, 464
Mundene, Henry de, abb. Cirencester, 368
Mundesley, Ralph of, pr. Kings Lynn, 116
Muneworth, Margaret de, prs Farewell, 560
Mungumbray, Roger de, pr. Eye, 159
Munteny, Isabel, prs Lambley, 578
Murdak, Christiana, prs Harrold, 569
Muriel, abbs Polesworth, 598
Muriel, prs Arden, 539

Muscegros, Laurentia de, abbs Shaftesbury, 605
Muschamp, William de, pr. Kirkham, 401
Mymmelonde, Mathias (Matthew) de, pr. Plympton, 448
Myouns, Ralph de, pr. Prittlewell, 249
Myrel, John, pr. Exeter, St James 228
Myton, John of, abb. Byland, 270
Myton, William of, pr. Rumburgh, 125

N., abb. Welbeck, 515
N., pr. Clattercote, 521
N., pr. Repton, 452
N., procurator of Bamburgh, 329
Nabynaux, Peter de, pr. Sele, 192
Nafferton, Alice of, prs Watton, 531
Nafferton, Geoffrey of, pr. Bridlington, 346
Nafferton, Thomas of, abb. Kirkstead, 290
Naget, William, pr. Panfield and Well, 186
Nag(u)et, William, pr. Frampton, 161
Nanchal, Michael, bailiff of Atherington, 144
Nanchal, Michael de (probably same as above), pr. Arundel, 142
Nantolio, John de, pr. Barnstaple, 219; pr. Exeter, St James, 228
Naples, Berard of, pr. Andover, 139
Narborough, Hugh of, pr. Pentney, 446
Naseby, Amice of, prs Rothwell, 602
Nassaundres, William de, pr. Wilsford, 212
Nassington, Robert of, abb. Ramsey, 60
Nassington, Robert of, pr. Deeping, 96
Nassington, Robert of, pr. St Ives, 128
Nassington, Thomas of, pr. Huntingdon, 395
Nassington, Thomas of, alias of Spalding, pr. Spalding, 193
Natalia, abbs-el. Winchester, 620
Natas, Berengar, pr. Horsham St Faith, 170
Natyngton, Guy de, pr.-el. Combwell, 371
Naudaria, Simon de, pr. Minting, 178
Navenby, Robert of, master Sempringham, 528; pr. Lincoln, St Katharine, 524
Navenby, Thomas of, pr. Nocton Park, 433
Navenby, Walter of, pr. Nocton Park, 434
Navesby, Agatha of, abbs Northampton, De La Pré, 590
Nayland, John of, pr. Colchester, St Botolph, 369
Neasham, A. of, pr. Holy Island, 110
Neatishead, Adam of, abb. St Benet of Hulme, 65
Neel, Margery, prs Goring, 565
Neldesle, Philip de, pr. Penwortham, 123
Nequam, Alexander, abb. Cirencester, 367
Ness, Alan of, abb. York, St Mary, 87; pr. St Bees, 127

Nesse, William de, pr. Alvingham, 519

Neston, James of, pr.-el. Birkenhead, 23

Netheravene, John, pr. Mottisfont, 426

Netheravon, William of, pr. Christchurch (Twynham), 366

Netisherde, John, pr. Hickling, 392

Neubold, Defensor de, pr. Monks Kirby, 181
  see also Newbold

Neuman, Adam (le), pr. Dodnash, 374

Neuport, Alexander de, pr. Hurley, 113

Nevill(a), Alice de, prs Stamford, St Mary and St Michael, 608

Nevill (Nevyll), Elizabeth de, prs Moxby, 589

Nevill, Elizabeth de, prs Stainfield, 608

Nevill, Isabel de, abbs Romsey, 600

Nevill, Isabel, prs Nun Monkton, 595

Nevill, Margaret de, prs Nun Appleton, 592

Newark, Adam of, pr. Beadlow, 90

Newbold, Robert of, abb. Pipewell, 299
  see also Neubold

Newbury, William of, abb. Abingdon, 16

Newby, John of, abb. Jervaulx, 287

Newcastle, Geoffrey of, pr. Stamford, St Leonard, 129

Newcastle, Henry of, pr. Finchale, 103

Newcastle, John of, abb. Easby, 501

Newcastle, John of, pr. Lewes, 234

Newcastle, Ralph of, abb. Kirkstall, 288

Newcastle, Thomas of, [Jarrow], 114

Newebury, Richard, pr. St Helen's, 250

Newenham, John, pr. Dover, 98

Newland, Adam of, pr. Guisborough, 384

Newode, Matilda de, prs Gokewell, 564

Newport, John de, see Pratt(e), John

Newport, Thomas of, abb. Chester, 34

Newsham, Robert of, pr. Elsham, 378

Newton, John of, [Meaux], 294

Newton, John of, master Monkwearmouth, 121; pr. Finchale, 104

Newton, Peter of, pr. Rumburgh, 126

Newton, Robert of, pr. Alberbury, 256; pr. Grosmont, 257

Newton, Robert of, pr. Malton, 525

Newton, Thomas of, pr. St Denys, 455

Newton, William, pr. Alvecote, 89

Newton, William of, pr. Rumburgh, 126

Newynton(e), Robert (de), minister Easton, 532

Neyland, Thomas of, pr. Snape, 129

Neyrnuyt, Matilda, prs Little Marlow, 581

Neyrnuyt, Walter, pr. Canons Ashby, 357

Nibley, Ralph (Richard) of, pr. Snelshall, 71

Nicholaa, prs Rowney, 602

Nicholas, abb. Buckfast, 267

Nicholas, abb. Buildwas (occ.1236 x 56), 268

Nicholas, abb. Buildwas (occ.1347 x 8), 269

Nicholas, abb. Calder, 271

Nicholas, abb. Coverham, 497

Nicholas, abb. Durford, 500

Nicholas, abb. Eynsham, 43

Nicholas, abb. Faversham, 44

Nicholas, abb. Flaxley, 278

Nicholas, abb. Forde (1284–), 279

Nicholas, abb. Forde (occ.? 1338 x 40), 279

Nicholas, abb. Fountains, 280

Nicholas, abb. Furness, 281

Nicholas, abb. Halesowen, 503

Nicholas, abb. Haughmond, 387

Nicholas, abb. Keynsham, 400

Nicholas, abb. Kingswood (occ. 1376 x 9), 288

Nicholas, abb. Langdon, 504

Nicholas, abb. Leiston, 506

Nicholas, abb. Medmenham, 294

Nicholas, abb. Pipewell, 299

Nicholas, abb. Robertsbridge (occ. 1222), 303

Nicholas, abb. Robertsbridge (occ. 1320), 303

Nicholas, abb. Stanley, 310

Nicholas, abb. Stratford Longthorne, 314

Nicholas, abb. Tilty, 316

Nicholas, abb. Vaudey, 319

Nicholas, abb. Welbeck, 515

Nicholas, abb. Wendling, 515

Nicholas, abb West Dereham, 517

Nicholas, abb. Woburn, 323

Nicholas, keeper Calwich, 355

Nicholas, master Goring, 565

Nicholas, minister Hounslow, 532

Nicholas, pr. Andwell, 140

Nicholas, pr. Arbury, 328

Nicholas, pr. Arundel, 141

Nicholas, pr. Berden, 333

Nicholas, pr. Blackmore, 338

Nicholas, pr. Blyth, 145

Nicholas, pr. Blythburgh, 338

Nicholas, pr. Brecon (temp. Henry III), 93

Nicholas, pr. Brecon (occ. 1309), 93

Nicholas, pr. Burscough, 352

Nicholas, pr. Chepstow (occ. 1213), 151

Nicholas, pr. Chepstow (occ. 1254), 151

Nicholas, pr. Creeting, 154

Nicholas, pr. Deerhurst, 155

Nicholas, pr. Freiston, 104

Nicholas, pr. Gloucester, St Oswald, 381

Nicholas, pr. Hastings, 386

Nicholas, pr. Haugham, 166

Nicholas, pr. Hempton, 389
Nicholas, pr. Hickling, 392
Nicholas, pr. Holy Island, 110
Nicholas, pr. Horkesley, 230
Nicholas, pr. Hough, 393
Nicholas, pr. Ivychurch, 396
Nicholas, pr. Kenilworth, 398
Nicholas, pr. Kerswell, 230
Nicholas, pr. Kings Lynn (occ. c. 1200), 116
Nicholas, pr. Kings Lynn (occ. 1372 x 74), 116
Nicholas, pr. Leeds, 407 n. 27
Nicholas, pr. Llanthony Prima, 413
Nicholas, pr. Marmont, 525
Nicholas, pr. Minster, 176
Nicholas, pr. Monk Sherborne, 180
Nicholas, pr. Monks Kirby, 180
Nicholas, pr. Nuneaton, 596
Nicholas, pr. Otterton, 185
Nicholas, pr. Shouldham, 529
Nicholas, pr. Sixhills, 529
Nicholas, pr. Snape, 128
Nicholas, pr. Spinney, 462
Nicholas, pr. Stafford, 462
Nicholas, pr. Stansgate, 252
Nicholas, pr. Stogursey, 194
Nicholas, pr. Studley, 465
Nicholas, pr. Tandridge, 466
Nicholas, pr. Thetford, Holy Sepulchre, 468
Nicholas, pr. Thoby, 468
Nicholas, pr. Toft Monks, 201
Nicholas, pr. Tortington, 475
Nicholas, pr. Totnes, 202
Nicholas, pr. Tutbury, 203
Nicholas, pr. Ware, 206
Nicholas, pr. Weedon Lois, 208
Nicholas, pr. West Ravendale (occ. 1245/6 x 48/9), 517
Nicholas, pr. West Ravendale (occ. 1295/6 x 1300), 517
Nicholas, pr. West Ravendale (occ. 1377), 518
Nicholas, pr. Westwood, 617
Nicholas, pr. Weybridge, 484
Nicholas, pr. Woodkirk, 486
Nicholas, pr. Wormegay, 488
Nicholas, warden Easton, 532
Nigel, pr. Lancaster, 171
Noble, Stephen de, pr. Little Dunmow, 412
Nocton, Adam of, pr. Felley, 378
Nocus, John, pr. Healaugh Park, 388
Noiale, Gerard de, pr. Holme East, 229
Nony, Robert, pr. Hertford, St Mary, 110
Norbury, Gregory of, abb. Whalley, 322

Norham, A(?dam) of, pr. Stamford, St Leonard, 129
Norman, Geoffrey, pr. York, Holy Trinity, 216
Norman, Richard le, pr. Ewyas Harold, 100
Norman, William, pr. Little Malvern, 118; pr. Worcester, 85
Normanby, John of, pr. Finchale, 104; pr. Lytham, 120
Normand, John, abb. Stratford Langthorne, 314
Normanton, John of, pr. Ulverscroft, 477
Normanton, Richard of, abb. Dale, 499
Normanton, Roger of, pr. Lenton, 232
Normanus, Henry, see Bonville, Henry de
Normanvile, Joan de, prs Nun Appleton, 592
Normanvill, Isabel de, prs Nun Appleton, 592
Normanvilla, Sibyl de, prs Nun Appleton, 592
Normaund, Richard dictus, pr. Westwood, 617
Norreis, le, Peter, see Melbourn, Peter de
Norreis, Roger, pr. Penwortham, 123
Norreys, Roger, abb. Lilleshall, 411
North Coates, William of, master Grimsby, 567
Northampton, Adam of, pr. Monk Bretton, 236
Northampton, Henry of, abb. Tavistock, 72
Northampton, Joan of, prs Catesby, 551
Northampton, John of, abb. Newenham, 297
Northampton, John of, pr. Freiston, 104
Northampton, John of, pr. Prittlewell, 247
Northampton, Richard of, pr. Beadlow, 90
Northburn, Richard, abb. Whalley (Stanlow), 322
Northburne, John de, abb. Battle, 23
Northfleet, John of, pr. Dover, 97
Northhoo, Isabel, prs Davington, 556
Northstreet, Matthew of, see York, Matthew of
Northwold, Hugh of, abb. Bury St Edmunds, 26
Northwold, John of, abb. Bury St Edmunds, 26
Norton, John of [Monkwearmouth], 121
Norton, John of, master Jarrow, 114
Norton, John (of), pr. Blythburgh, 338
Norton, John of, pr. Finchale, 104
Norton, Ralph of, pr. Barnwell, 331
Norton, Richard of, abb. Tewkesbury, 74
Norton(e), Roger of, abb. St Albans, 63
Norton, Roger of, pr. Tynemouth, 132
Norton, Thomas of, pr. Bristol, St James, 94
Norton, Walter of, pr. Lytham, 120
Norton, William of, abb. Blanchland, 495
Norton, William of, pr. Hatfield Peverel, 107
Nortune, William, abb. Torre, 513
Norwich, John of, abb. Langley, 505
Norwich, John of, abb. Wendling, 516
Norwich, John of, pr.-el. Herringfleet, 390
Norwich, Richard of, pr. Chipley, 364

Norwich, Thomas of, pr. Herringfleet, 390
Norwich, William son of Odo of, pr. Norwich cath., 55
Nottingham, John of, abb. Welbeck, 515
Nottingham, John of, pr. Shelford, 458
Nova Mansione, William de, pr. Modbury, 179
Nova Villa, Thomas de, pr. Weedon Lois (?same as Villa Nova), 209
Novavilla, Robert de, pr. Weedon Lois, 210
Noyers, Hugh de, pr. Montacute, 239
Noys, William de, pr. Wareham, 207
Nubibus, Ralph de, pr. Frampton, 161
Nympsfield, Henry of, pr. Stavordale, 463
Nympsfield, Walter of, pr. Stavordale, 463

Oadby, Joan of, prs Langley, 579
Oakley, Henry of, pr. Woodbridge, 486
Obyn, see Aubyn
Odiham, William of, abb. Winchester, Hyde, 82
Odo, pr. Haverholme, 523
Odo, pr. Newton Longville, 242
Odo, pr. Northampton, St Andrew, 244
Odo, pr. Rumburgh, 125
Offington, Hamo of, abb. Battle, 23
Offington, Thomas of, minister Thelsford, 534
  see also Offynton
Offord, Richard, pr. Stamford, St Mary and St Michael, 610
Offynton, Richard de, abb. St Radegund, 509
  see also Offington
Ogerii, John, pr. Astley, 143
Ogier, see Auger
Oissencourt, Gerard de, pr. Takeley, 198
Olive, prs Gokewell, 564
Oliver, pr. Birkenhead, 23
Oliver, pr. Frithelstock, 381
Oliver, pr. Tickford, 199
Oliver, William, bailiff of Atherington, 143
Olney, Robert of, pr.Oxford, St Frideswide, 444
Olney, Simon of, pr. Grafton Regis, 383
Ombersley, John of, abb. Evesham, 42
Orabella, prs London, St Helen's and Holy Cross, 585
Orcharde, Robert, abb. Dunkeswell, 278
Ore, Roger de, abb. Langdon, 504
Orford, Alice Wynter of, see Wynter, Alice
Orford, Robert of, pr. Ely, 40
Orfreiser, John (le), abb. Faversham, 45
Orgericiis, Peter de, bailiff of Atherington, 143
Orlescote, Thomas de, abb. Bordesley, 264
Orlescote, Thomas de, abb. Stoneleigh, 311
Ormesby, Robert of, pr. Hoxne, 112

Ormesby, Stephen of, pr. Middlesbrough, 121
Ormsby, Ivetta of, prs Greenfield, 566
Osanne, John (de), [Loders], 175
Osanne, John (de), pr. Appuldurcombe, 141
Osays, Guichard de, pr. Lewes, 233
Osbert, abb. Durford, 500
Osbert, abb. Haughmond, 387
Osbert, abb. Newhouse, 507
Osbert, pr. Blythburgh, 338
Osbert, pr. Cambridge, St Edmund, 520
Osbert, pr. Canons Ashby, 356
Osbert, pr. Chirbury, 364
Osbert, pr. Goldcliff, 162
Osbert, pr. Launde, 405
Osbert, pr. Newstead-on-Ancholme, 526
Osbert, pr. Royston, 454
Osmington, Richard of, abb. Cerne, 31
Osmondi, Robert, pr. Loders, 175
Osmund, abb. Athelney, 19
Osmund, abb. Flaxley, 278
Osney, John of, abb. Osney, 442
Osney, Robert of, pr. Canterbury, St Gregory, 358
Osney, Robert of, pr. Southwark, 460
Osprengge, John, pr. Tonbridge, 473
Ossana, abbs Polesworth, 598
Ostborth, John de, pr. Lewisham, 173
Oteringeber, Stephen de, pr. Brecon, 93
Otley, Henry, abb. Fountains, 280
Otley, John of, abb. Alnwick, 491
Otley, Richard of, pr. Buckenham, 351
Otley, Robert of, pr. Bolton, 340
Ottringham, Richard of, abb. Meaux, 293
Ottringham, Simon of, pr. Markby, 419
Oudeby, Robert de, abb. Alcester, 18
Oumayo, Geoffrey de, pr. Winghale, 213
Oundle, John de, pr. Freiston, 105
Ounesby, Gilbert de, alias of York, pr. Drax, 376
Ousefleet, Nicholas of, master Gokewell, 564
Ouson, William, pr. Sempringham, 528
Ouston, William, pr. Blyth, 146
Over, William of, abb. Croxden, 275
Overton, Henry of, abb. Peterborough, 59
Overton, Henry of, pr. Newstead by Stamford, 433
Overton, Henry of, pr. Stamford, St Mary and St Michael, 610
Overton, John of, pr. Guisborough, 384
Overton, Richard, pr. Nuneaton, 597
Overton, Thomas of, abb. Muchelney, 54
Overton, Thomas of, pr. Haltemprice, 385
Oving, Roger (of), pr. Snelshall, 71
Ovyngge, Thomas, pr. Exeter, St Nicholas, 101
Owmby, Christiana of, prs Greenfield, 566

Owmby, John of, pr. Torksey, 474
Oxenden, Richard de, pr. Christ Church, Canterbury, 28
Oxendon, Richard of, pr. Brooke, 350
Oxeney, Alice, prs London, Clerkenwell, 583
Oxford, Agatha of, prs Goring, 565
Oxford, Agatha of, prs Littlemore, 582
Oxford, Joan of, prs Ankerwyke, 539
Oxford, John of, abb. Eynsham, 43
Oxford, Robert of, pr. Frithelstock, 381
Oxford, Sarah of, prs Goring, 564
Oxhaye, Rose de, abbs Gostow, 562
Oxnead, John of, pr. Kings Lynn, 116
Oxney, James of, *see* Ston(e) James de
Oysel, John *dictus*, pr. Pembroke, 187

P., abb. Strata Florida, 312
P., pr. Finchale, 103
Paas, Lucy, prs Kington St Michael, 576
Paceio, Richard de, pr. Hinckley, 168
Paceyo, Hilderic de, pr. Wareham, 207
Packington, Thomas of, abb. Burton, 25
Pacok, Gilbert, abb. Louth Park, 291–2
Paderstow, William, abb. Buckfast, 268
Pagam, Thomas, pr. Otterton, 186
Page, Alice, prs Baysdale, 543
Pagham, Thomas of, abb. Talley, 511
Painpare, Robert, pr. Hough, 393
Painswick, John of, pr. Alvecote, 89; pr. Great Malvern, 107
Pakenham, Alice of, prs York, St Clement, 626
Pakenham, Matthew of, pr. Butley, 354
Palerne, Peter de, pr. Nuneaton, 596
Palmer, John, pr. Warminghurst, 208
Palmer(e), John, pr. Tortington, 475
Palmere, Robert *dictus* le, pr. Prittlewell, 249
Panfield, Richard of, abb. Coggeshall, 272
Panton, Gilbert of, master Stainfield, 608
Panys, Joan, prs Barrow Gurney, 542
Pape, John, abb. Newminster, 299
Parco, Richard de, *alias* Rufus de Winchelcumbe, pr. Binham, 92; pr. Tynemouth, 132
Parco, Robert de, pr. Blythburgh, 338
Parco, Thomas de, pr. Thoby, 468
Pardines, Hugh de, pr. Horsham St Faith, 169
Parell, Gerard de, pr. Sele, 192
Paris, Simon of, pr. Minster Lovell, 177
Paris, Stephen of, pr. Deerhurst, 155
    see also Parys
Parker, John, de Illegh, pr. Kersey, 400
Parmenter, William, pr. Stratfield Saye, 196
Parnys, William de, pr. Ware, 206

Parson, Thomas, warden Totnes, Holy Trinity, 534
Parys, Cecily de, prs Greenfield, 566
Parys, John *dictus* de, pr. Barnstaple, 219
Parys, William de, minister Oxford, Holy Trinity, 534
Parys, William de, pr. Beadlow, 90
    see also Paris
Pascasius, pr. Barnstaple, 219
Pasquerii (Pasquier), James, pr. Andwell, 141; pr. Hamble, 164
Passiaco, Peter de, pr. Lapley, 172
Passu, John de, pr. Allerton Mauleverer, 139
Patay, Hugh de, pr. Weedon Lois, 209
Patrick, pr. Bridlington, 520
Patriz, Matilda, abbs Romsey, 600
Pattishall, Robert of, abb. Pipewell, 299
Paul, pr. Sleves Holm, 251
Paul, pr. West Ravendale, 517
Paumiflet, Henry, pr. Rumburgh, 125
Paunesfot, Matilda, prs Littlemore, 582
Pattishall, Margaret of, abbs Malling, 586
Pavely, Agnes (de), abbs Northampton, De La Pré, 590
Pavely, Ivetta de, prs Sewardsley, 604
Pavilliaco, Roger de, pr. Wootton Wawen, 215
Pavy, Thomas (de), pr. Coventry, 36
Peatling, John of, pr. Launde, 406
Pecham, Henry (de), pr. Tandridge, 466
Pecham, Isabel de, abbs Malling, 586
Pecham, John (de), pr. Southwark, 460–1
Pecham, John, pr. Tonbridge, 473
Pec(c)ham, Matilda de, abbs Winchester, 621
Pecham, Michael de, abb. Canterbury, St Augustine, 30
Pecham, Sarah de, prs Canterbury, Holy Sepulchre, 550
Pedeleshurst, Walter de, *alias* Hatfield, pr. Tandridge, 466
Pegsdon, Alice of, prs Sopwell, 607
Pegsdon, John of, pr. London, St Bartholomew, 417
Pekynghulle, Henry de, pr. Pilton, 124
Pelagay, John, pr. Llangennith, 175
Pelata, Peter, pr. Burwell, 149
Peleter, John le, pr. Abergavenny, 138
Pellene, Michael, pr. Ellingham, 158
Pelliparius, William, pr. Abergavenny, 138
Pembridge, John of, pr. Wormsley, 488
Penbury, William of, pr. Llanthony Secunda, 415
Pendock, Peter of, abb. Pershore, 57
Pennavilla, John de, pr. Newton Longville, 242
Penrith, John (of), pr. Carlisle, 360

Pentelowe, John, abb. Walden, 77
Penyord, Thomas, pr. Bromfield, 95
Peplow, William of, abb. Lilleshall, 411
Pepyn, John, pr. Carisbrooke, 150; pr. Hinckley, 168
Pepyn, Roger, pr. York, Holy Trinity, 216
Pepyn, William, abb. Leicester, 407
Pepyn, William, pr. Monmouth, 182
Perci, Isabel de, prs Easebourne, 557
Perci, Thomas, pr. Leeds, 407
Percy, Constance de, abbs Wilton, 620
Percy, Ellen de, abbs Wherwell, 617
Percy, Joan, prs Baysdale, 542
Perer, Richard, pr. St Michael's Mount, 189
Perle, John, pr. Morville, 122
Perpelun (?), Richard, pr. Wilsford, 212
Perrariis, Thomas de, master Heynings, 570
Perrouse, Gervase de, pr. Puffin Island, 449
Pershore, Robert of, pr. Brooke, 350
Person, Ralph, pr. Plympton, 448
Peschon, William, abb. Keynsham, 400
Pesmere, Ralph de, pr. Poughley, 449
Pestlamore, William de, pr. Harmondsworth, 165
Peter, abb. Alnwick, 491
Peter, abb. Buckfast, 267
Peter, abb. Dieulacres, 277
Peter, abb. Faversham, 44
Peter, abb. Langdon, 504
Peter, abb. Langley, 505
Peter, abb. Leiston, 506
Peter, abb. Medmenham, 294
Peter, abb. Rievaulx, 302
Peter, abb. Shap, 509
Peter, abb. Stanley, 310
Peter, abb. Vale Royal, 317
Peter, abb. Whalley (Stanlow), 322
Peter, master Baysdale, 543
Peter, master Moxby, 589
Peter, master Swine, 614
Peter, pr. Amesbury, 538
Peter, pr. Barnstaple, 219
Peter, pr. Bermondsey, 220
Peter, pr. Brinkburn, 347
Peter, pr. Butley, 354
Peter, pr. Canons Ashby, 356
Peter, pr. Canterbury, St Gregory, 358
Peter, pr. Daventry, 226
Peter, pr. Derby, St James, 227
Peter, pr. Ewenny, 99
Peter, pr. Exeter, St Nicholas, 100
Peter, pr. Finchale, 103
Peter, pr. Folkestone, 160

Peter, pr. Hagnaby, 502
Peter, pr. Haltemprice, 385
Peter, pr. Hinton, 325
Peter, pr. Horkseley, 230
Peter, pr. Horsham St Faith, 169
Peter, pr. Latton (occ. 1361), 404
Peter, pr. Latton (occ. 1381), 404
Peter, pr. Leonard Stanley, 117
Peter, pr. Livers Ocle, 174
Peter, pr. London, St Bartholomew, 417
Peter, pr. Longleat, 418
Peter, pr. Michelham, 423
Peter, pr. North Ormsby, 526
Peter, pr. Panfield and Well, 186
Peter, pr. Pontefract (c. 1238–9), 246
Peter, pr. Pontefract (1260–), 246
Peter, pr. Prittlewell, 247
Peter, pr. Repton, 452
Peter, pr. Stamford, St Mary and St Michael, 609
Peter, pr. Stansgate, 251
Peter, pr. Thetford, Holy Sepulchre, 468
Peter, pr. Tonbridge, 473
Peter, pr. Totnes, 202
Peter, pr. Walsingham, 477
Peter, pr. Ware, 206
Peter, pr. Watton, 530
Peter, pr. Winterborn Monkton, 254
Peterborough, Serlo of, pr. Stamford, St Mary and St Michael, 609
Peterborough, Stephen of, pr. Stamford, St Mary and St Michael, 610
Peterborough, Walter of, abb. Dorchester, 375
Petersfield, William of, pr. Stansgate, 251
Petherton, Richard of, abb. Newenham, 297
Petherton, Robert of, abb. Glastonbury, 46
Petherton, Thomas of, pr. Taunton, 467
Pethy, Thomas (de), abb. Winchester, Hyde, 82
Petit, Thomas dictus le, pr. Ellingham, 158
Petra Ficta, John de, pr. Cowick, 154
Petronilla, prs Brewood Black Ladies, 544
Petronilla, prs Ellerton-in-Swaledale, 557
Petronilla, prs Norwich (Carrow), 591
Petronilla, prs Stainfield, 607
Petronilla, prs Studley, 612 & n.17
Petrowe, William, pr. Abergavenny, 138
Petrus, John, abb. Beaulieu, 261
Pevensey, John of, pr. Witham, 326
Pevensey, Roger of, abb. Battle, 23; pr. Exeter, St Nicholas, 101
Peverel, William, custos Hertford, 532
Peynton, Edusia de, prs Sempringham, 529

Peynton, William (de), abb. Lilleshall, 412

Peyt, Richard, abb. Flaxley, 278

Peyton, John de, pr. Kenilworth, 399

Phileby, Adam de, abb. Langley, 505

Philip, abb. Abbey Cwmhir, 258

Philip, abb. Biddlesden, 261

Philip, abb. Bindon, 263

Philip, abb. Bordesley, 264

Philip, abb. Buckfast, 268

Philip, abb. Combe, 273

Philip, abb. Cymmer, 276

Philip, abb. Hartland, 386

Philip, abb. Jervaulx, 286

Philip, abb. Lavendon, 506

Philip, abb. Leiston, 506

Philip, abb. Quarr (–1238), 300

Philip, abb. Quarr (occ. 1262 x c. 1268), 300

Philip, abb. Rocester, 453

Philip, abb. Roche, 304

Philip, abb. Sherborne, 68

Philip Coch, abb. Strata Florida, 312

Philip, abb. Tupholme, 513

Philip, master Fosse, 562

Philip, master Grimsby, 567

Philip, pr. Beddgelert, 332

Philip II, pr. Beddgelert, 332

Philip, pr. Chirbury, 364

Philip, pr. Flitcham, 380

Philip, pr. Hastings, 387

Philip, pr. Horkesley, 230

Philip, pr. Ixworth, 398

Philip, pr. Llanthony Prima, 413

Philip, pr. Minster, 176

Philip, pr. Newburgh, 428

Philip, pr. Nocton Park, 433

Philip, pr. Peterstone, 447

Philip, pr. Pill, 187

Philip, pr. Stafford, 462

Philip, pr. Tywardreath, 204

Philip, pr. Walsingham, 477

Philip, pr. Weedon Lois, 208

Philip, pr. Winghale, 213

Philip, pr. Witham, 326

Philip, pr. Wombridge, 486

Philip, pr. Wootton Wawen, 214

Philippa, prs Grimsby, 567

Philippa, prs Sopwell, 607

Pickard, Robert de, pr. Wilmington, 211

Pickburn, Robert of, pr. Worksop, 487

Pickeford, Joan de, prs Henwood, 570

Pickering, Alice of, prs Yedingham (occ. 1300/1 x
?1331), 625

Pickering, Alice of, prs Yedingham (occ. 1352 x 73),
626

Pickering, Geoffrey of, abb. Byland, 270

Pickering, Joan of, prs Keldholme, 574; prs
Rosedale, 602

Pickering, John of, custos Wetheral, 135

Pickering, John of, senior, pr. Richmond, 125

Pickering, Robert de Brus, see Brus, Robert de

Pickworth, Simon of, pr. Haverholme, 523

Picot, John, pr. Wilmington, 211

Picot, Walter, pr. Castle Acre, 225

Piel, Warin (dictus), pr. Carisbrooke, 150

Piercebridge, John of, abb. Easby, 501

Pierrepont, Alice de, prs Chester, 554

Pig, William, pr. Canterbury, St Gregory, 358

Pigoin, Alice, prs Kilburn, 575

Pigot, Katherine, prs Bullington, 520

Pile, Simon, pr. Barlinch, 330

Pimme, Simon, pr. Worcester, 85

Pimperne, Thomas of, pr. Breamore, 344

Pinchart, William (Guillerinus) dictus, pr. Wootton
Wawen, 215

Pinchbeck, Emma of, prs Wothorpe, 623

Pinchbeck, Lucy of, prs Stixwould, 611

Pinchbeck, Walter of, abb. Chester, 33

Pinneaus, Mathew de, pr. Covenham, 153

Pinnebury, William de, [Lenton], 232 n.4

Pinoliis, Arnold de, [Clifford], 225

Pire, William de, [Llangennith], 175

Pirton, Thomas of, abb. Pershore, 57

Piry, John de, pr. Fineshade, 380

Piscarius, Livinus, pr. Lewisham, 173

Pizdoe, Reginald, pr. Barnstaple, 220

Pleasley, Ralph of, pr. Felley, 379

Plescy, Richard de, pr. Little Dunmow, 412

Plessae, John de, [Ogbourne St George], 184

Plesseto, John de, abb. Walden, 77

Pleyces, John de, pr. Thoby, 468

Plumbergh, Sarra de, abbs Malling, 586

Plumstead, Cecily of, prs Norwich (Carrow), 592

Plunket, Thomas, pr. Henes and Sandtoft, 107

Plympton, Simon of, abb. Torre, 512

Pocklington, Idonia of, prs Nunburnholme, 595

Pocklington, Margery of, prs Heynings, 570

Pocklington, Thomas of, pr. Malton, 525

Podmore, Walter (of), pr. Stone, 464

Poflington, Hugh de, pr. Little Dunmow, 412

Pogier, (Pougier), William, pr. Panfield and Well,
186

Poignant, John, pr. Torksey, 474

Pole, William at, pr. Dodford, 374

Polgover, Richard (de), pr. St Germans, 456

Polhey, William de, abb. Walden, 77

Pollesden, Edmund de, minister Easton, 532

Polstead, Gilbert of, pr. Snape, 128

Poly, Roger (de), pr. London, Holy Trinity, Aldgate, 416

Pomariis, John de, pr. Andover, 140; pr. Sele, 192

Pommesbourne, Alice de, prs Kilburn, 575

Poncius, pr. St Clears, 250

Ponfichet, Peter (de), pr. Deerhurst, 156

Ponhier, William, pr. Upavon, 205

Pont-Audemer, Bertrand of, pr. Steventon, 194

Pont-Audemer, Walter of, pr. Wilsford, 212

Ponte, John de, pr. Burwell, 149

Ponte, Ralph de, pr. Weedon Lois, 210

Ponte, Robert de, pr. Creeting, 154

Ponte, Robert de, pr. Everdon, 159

Ponte Antonis, Michael de, pr. Wilsford, 212

Ponte Episcopi, Elias de, pr. St Neots, 190

Ponte Episcopi, Eustace de, pr. Cowick, 153

Ponte Episcopi, John de, pr. Cowick, 154

Ponte Episcopi, William de, pr. Cowick, 153

Ponte Episcopi, William de, pr. Ogbourne St George, 184

Pontefract, Adam of, pr. Stamford, St Leonard, 130

Pontefract, Agnes of, prs Arthington, 540

Pontefract, Agnes de, prs Hampole, 568

Pontefract, Isaak le Moyne of, pr. Monk Bretton, 236

Pontefract, Robert of, pr. Breedon, 345

Pontefract, William of, pr. Dudley, 227

Pontefract, William of, pr. Much Wenlock, 242

Ponteseye, John de, pr. Swavesey, 197

Pope, Roger, see Exeter, Roger of

Poperinghes, William de, pr. Throwley, 199

Popham, Edmund of, pr. Selborne, 458

Popham, Robergia of, abbs Wilton, 620

Popham, Robert of, abb. Winchester, Hyde, 82

Poppleton, Clement of, pr. Rumburgh, 125

Poppleton, John of, pr. Richmond, 124

Poringland Magna, Philip of, pr. Herringfleet, 390

Porta I, John (de) la, pr. Montacute, 240

Porta II, John (de) la, pr. Montacute, 240

Porta, William de, pr. Cowick, 153

Port(e), Roger, abb. Coggeshall, 272

Portel, Richard, pr. Minister, 176

Porter, Robert, pr. Castle Acre, 224

Portes, Ralph de, pr. Astley, 142

Portskewit, Thomas of, abb. Margam, 292

Portu, Alexander de, pr. Tutbury, 204

Portu, James de, warden Scarborough, 308

Porty, R./John, pr. Linton and Isleham, 174

Poterel, Richard, pr. Kirkham, 401

Potrington, Adam de, custodian Arthington, 540

Potterne, William of, pr. Ewyas Harold, 100

Poucyn, John, pr. Carisbrooke, 150

Poucyn, Thomas, abb. Canterbury, St Augustine, 30

Power, Joan, prs Markyate, 587

Power, Juliana de, prs Whistones, 618

Poynte, Agatha de la, prs Lyminster, 585

Pratellis, William de, pr. Otterton, 185

Pratis, Peter de, abb. Keynsham, 400

Pratt(e), alias de Newport, John, pr. Allerton Mauleverer, 139

Preaus, Richard de, pr. Carisbrooke, 150

Prechour, John, pr. St Germans, 456

Pressour, Mathew dictus, pr. Weedon Lois, 209

Preston, Adam of, pr. Cranborne, 95

Preston, John of, pr. North Ferriby, 436

Preston, Ralph of, pr. Brinkburn, 347

Preston, William of, abb. St Radegund, 509

Preston, William, pr. Monkton Farleigh, 238

Preston, William Legat of, see Legat, William

Prestwold, William of, master Sempringham, 528

Prestwold, William of, pr. Newstead by Stamford, 433

Prestwold, William (of), pr. Sempringham, 528

Prevot, William, pr. Astley, 143

Price, Hugh, ? pr. Barlinch, 330 n.1

Provost, Ralph (le), see Valmont, Ralph (le) Provost of

Provost, Richard le, pr. Upavon, 205

Provost, Thomas le, pr. Folkestone, 160

Provost, Thomas (le), pr. Stogursey, 195

Pruet, John, pr. Colchester, St Botolph, 369

Puckleworth, Walter of, abb. Stanley, 310

Pudsey, William (of), minister Knaresborough, 533

Pugnenay, Almaric (Emery) de, pr. Carisbrooke, 150

Pulein, Peter, pr. St Cross, 188

Puleyn, William, pr. Eye, 159

Pulleyn, Adam, pr. Wymondham, 136

Punchard, Richard, de Wyly, master Rowney, 603

Pupplisbury, Robert of, abb. Newenham, 297

Purbrook, Margery (of), prs Amesbury, 538

Purle, Richard de, master London, Clerkenwell, 583

Purle(e), William de, pr. Bicknacre, 335

Purleigh, Richard of, abb. Beeleigh, 495

Puryton, William de, pr. Dover, 98

Puteo, Mathew de, pr. Hinckley, 168

Puteolis, John de, pr. Exeter, St James, 228

Putley, William of, pr. Cranborne, 96

Putt, John, pr. Wilmington, 211
Puttok, Gilbert *dictus*, pr. Norton, 438
Pychervill, John de, pr. Patrixbourne, 446
Pykouteston, Stephen de, pr. Taunton, 467
Pylath, Walter, of Welton, abb. Louth Park, 291
Pynart, Simon, pr. Winghale, 213
Pynnok(e), John, pr. Frithelstock, 381
Pype, Isolda de, prs Farewell, 560
Pype, Matilda de, abbs Polesworth, 599
Pype, Thomas (de), *alias* Weston(e), abb. Stoneleigh, 311–12
Pyribroke, Hugh de, pr. Little Malvern, 119
Pyribroke, Roger de, pr. Little Malvern, 119
Pyrie, John de (la), pr. Reigate, 451

Quarrington, Matanye (Mathania) of, prs Langley, 579
Quatersoule, Francis, pr. Tickford, 200
Quatresout, Francis (? *same as above*), pr. Allerton Mauleverer, 139
Quenton, Walter de, pr. Bicester, 334
Quercii, Robert de, [Wootton Wawen], 215
Quintin, William, pr. Christchurch (Twynham), 366
Quintyn, Thomas, abb. Coggeshall, 272
Quisse, John de, pr. Pembroke, 187
Quorndon, John of, pr. Bradley, 343
Quy, John of, pr. Barnwell, 331
Quy, William (of), pr. Anglesey, 328

R., pr. Axmouth, 144
R., pr. Canonsleigh, 357
R., pr. Derby, Kingsmead, 557
R., pr. Dunster, 99
R., pr. Hatfield Regis, 165
R., pr. Haverholme, 522
R., pr. Leeds, 407
R., pr. Lenton, 231
R., pr. Loders, 175
R., pr. Monk Bretton, 236
R., pr. St Michael's Mount, 189
R., pr. Sixhills, 529
R., pr. Thornholme, 469
R., pr. Tortington, 475
R., pr. Witham, 326
R., pr. Wymondham, 135
R., John, abb. St Radegund, 509
Rabarus, Denis, pr. Allerton Mauleverer, 139
Rachel, Ralph, pr. Henes and Sandtoft, 107
Radclif, Nicholas de, pr. Wymondham, 136
Radcliff, Roger, master Bamburgh, 329
Radcliffe, Robert of, abb. Beauchief, 494

Radeclive, Robert de, pr.-el. Charley, 363
Radford, William of, pr. Grafton Regis, 383
Radnor, Elias of, pr. Cardiff, 95
Radnor, Hugh of, pr. Hereford, 108
Radnor, Reginald of, pr. Bromfield, 95
Radouno, John de, pr. Winghale, 213
Ragon, Thomas, abb. Vale Royal, 318
Rainham, John of, pr. Rochester, 62
Raithby, Robert of, abb. Revesby, 301
Rale, John de, abb. Swineshead, 314
Ralighe, John (Roger) de, abb. Hartland, 386
Ralph, abb. Bardsey (?), 329
Ralph, abb. Barlings, 492
Ralph, abb. Basingwerk, 260
Ralph, abb. Beauchief, 494
Ralph, abb. Bindon, 262
Ralph, abb. Calder, 271
Ralph, abb. Coggeshall, 272
Ralph, abb. Dieulacres, 277
Ralph, abb. Dunkeswell, 277
Ralph, abb. Haughmond (early 13th cent.), 387
Ralph, abb. Haughmond (occ. *c.* 1227 x 36), 387
Ralph, abb. Holm Cultram, 284
Ralph, abb. Langley, 505
Ralph, abb. Lavendon, 506
Ralph, abb. Lilleshall, 410
Ralph, abb. Louth Park, 291
Ralph, abb. Merevale (occ. 1241/2 x 47), 294
Ralph, abb. Merevale (occ. 1302/3 x 17), 295
Ralph, abb. Newbo (occ. 1227), 507
Ralph, abb. Newbo (occ. 1318), 507
Ralph, abb. Newhouse, 508
Ralph, abb. Revesby, 301
Ralph, abb. Sawtry, 307
Ralph, abb. Sibton, 309
Ralph, abb. Stanley, 309
Ralph, abb. Stoneleigh, 311
Ralph, abb. Tintern (–1245), 316
Ralph, abb. Tintern (occ. 1280s x 1304), 316
Ralph, abb. Tupholme, 513
Ralph, abb. Waverley, 321
Ralph (II), abb. West Dereham, 516
Ralph, abb. Wigmore, 485
Ralph, master Hampole, 568
Ralph, master Legbourne, 580
Ralph, master Rowney, 603
Ralph, minister Hounslow, 532
Ralph, minister Moatenden, 533
Ralph, pr. Alvingham, 519
Ralph (?), pr. Blyth, 145
Ralph, pr. Breamore, 344
Ralph, pr. Brecon, 93

Ralph, pr. Brinkburn (occ. late 12th cent.), 347
Ralph, pr. Brinkburn (occ. 1305), 347
Ralph, pr. Brooke, 349
Ralph, pr. Bruton, 350
Ralph, pr. Cammeringham, 495
Ralph, pr. Chepstow, 151
Ralph, pr. Cold Norton, 369
Ralph, pr. Darenth, 96
Ralph, pr. Debden, 154
Ralph, pr. Ellerton on Spalding Moor, 522
Ralph, pr. Ely, 40
Ralph, pr. Finchale, 103
Ralph, pr. Haverholme, 522
Ralph, pr. Hinton, 325
Ralph, pr. Holy Island, 110
Ralph, pr. Lincoln, St Katharine, 523
Ralph, pr. Maiden Bradley, 418
Ralph, pr. Minister, 176
Ralph, pr. Modbury, 178
Ralph, pr. Monks Kirby, 180
Ralph, pr. Newton Longville, 242
Ralph, pr. North Ferriby, 435
Ralph, pr. Northampton, St Andrew, 243
Ralph (junior), pr. Nostell, 438
Ralph, pr. Ogbourne St George, 184
Ralph, pr. Pembroke, 187
Ralph, pr. Ruislip, 188
Ralph, pr. St Bees, 127
Ralph, pr. St Cross, 188
Ralph, pr. Studley, 465
Ralph, pr. Thoby, 468
Ralph, pr. Wallingford, 133
Ralph, pr. Warmington, 208
Ralph, pr. West Mersea, 210
Ralph, pr. Wootton Wawen, 214
Ralph, pr. Worksop, 487
Ralph, pr. Wormegay, 488
Ralph, pr. Wormsley, 488
Ralph, pr. Yarmouth, 136
Ralph, pr. York, St Andrew, 531
Ramesden(e), Robert de, pr. Bicknacre, 335
Rametta, prs Derby, Kingsmead, 556
Rampton, Robert of, abb. Barlings, 492
Rampton, Robert of, pr. Bullington, 520
Ramsbury, Edmund of, pr. Christchurch
    (Twynham), 336
Ramsbury, Robert of, abb. Sherborne, 69
Ramsey, Alexander of, abb. Barlings, 492
Ramsey, John (of), abb. Titchfield, 512
Ramsey, John of, pr. Stamford, St Mary and St
    Michael, 610
Ramsey, John, [West Mersea], 210

Ramsey, Martin of, abb. Peterborough, 57
Ramsey, Robert of, abb. Peterborough, 59
Ramsey, Robert of, pr. Bradwell, 24
Ramsey, William of, abb. Sawtry, 308
Randolph, corrector Alberbury, 255
Randulf, abb. Evesham, 41
Rand[ulf], pr. York, St Andrew, 531 n.6
Randulf, William, pr. Great Bricett, 383
Ranulf (Ranulph), abb. Dieulacres, 277
Ranulf, pr. Ellerton on Spalding Moor, 522
Ranulf, pr. Hickling, 392
Ranulf, pr. Norton, 437
Ranulf, pr. Ogbourne St George, 184
Ranulf, pr. Warter, 479
Ranulf, pr. York, Holy Trinity, 216
Rasen, John of, pr. Drax, 376
Rasen, William of, pr. Torksey, 474
Ratlesden, Peter, pr.-el. Bushmead, 353
    see also Rattlesden
Ratling, Lora of, abbs Malling, 586
Rattlesden, Beatrice of, prs Flixton, 561
Rattlesden, Nicholas of, pr. Kings Lynn, 116
    see also Ratlesden
Raulun, Stephen, pr. Montacute, 239
Raunds, Joan of, prs Hinchingbrooke, 572
Raunds, Orabilis (Orabilia) of, prs Catesby, 552
Raveley, Richard of, pr. St Ives, 128
Ravensden, Robert of, pr. Cold Norton, 370
Ravenser, Eustachia de, prs Stixwould, 611
Ravenstone, Ralph of, pr. Ravenstone, 451
Ravenswath, Adam, abb. Fountains, 280
Rawbankes, Robert de, abb. Holm Cultram, 285
Raymbaut, William, pr. Lancaster, 172
Raymond, pr. Burwell, 149
Raymond, pr. Minting, 178
Raynham, John of, pr. Great Massingham, 384
Re, John atte, abb. Durford, 500
Reading, John of, abb. Osney, 441
Reading, Richard of alias Banastre, abb. Reading,
    61
Rearsby, John of, pr. Launde, 406
Reda, Simon de, pr. Tickford, 200; pr. York, Holy
    Trinity, 217
Redborn, Richard, pr. Bradenstoke, 342
Redbourn(e), Simon de, pr. Bushmead, 353
Reddynges, Ralph de, minister Knaresborough,
    533
Rede, John le, abb. St Dogmells, 189
Rede, Thomas, pr. Frithelstock, 381
Redemere, Julian de, prs Orford, 597
Redford, Juliana de, prs Legbourne, 580
Redham, Thomas of, abb. North Creake, 435

Redhod, Nicholas, master St Mary de Pré, 604
Redingg, Nicholas de, master Stixwould, 611
Ree, William del, pr. Sandwell, 66
Reel, William de, pr. West Mersea, 210
Rees ap David, abb. Talley, 511
Rees ap Jevan, abb. Talley, 511
Regina, abbs Malling, 585
Reginald, abb. Abbey Dore, 258
Reginald, abb. Alnwick, 491
Reginald, abb. Battle, 22
Reginald, abb. Bayham (occ. 1222 x 44), 493
Reginald, abb. Bayham (occ. 1246 x 9), 493
Reginald, abb. Beeleigh, 494
Reginald, abb. Bindon, 262
Reginald, abb. Fountains, 280
Reginald, abb. Garendon, 282
Reginald, abb. Pipewell, 299
Reginald, abb. Roche, 304
Reginald, abb. St Benet of Hulme, 64
Reginald, abb. Walden, 76
Reginald, abb. Wellow, 481
Reginald, corrector Craswell, 256
Reginald, pr. Bicester, 334
Reginald, pr. Brecon, 93
Reginald, pr. Covenham, 152
Reginald, pr. Grosmont, 257
Reginald, pr. Horkesley, 230
Reginald, pr. Ixworth, 398
Reginald, pr. Kersey, 399
Reginald, pr. Lapley, 172
Reginald, pr. Mattersey, 526
Reginald, pr. Repton, 452
Reginald, pr. St Neots, 190
Reginald, pr. Sempringham, 528
Reginald, pr. Sixhills, 529
Reginald, pr. Stone, 464
Reginald, pr. Wangford, 253
Reginald, pr. Watton, 530
Reginald, pr. Wilmington, 211
Reginald, pr. Woodspring (–1243), 487
Reginald, pr. Woodspring (occ. 1318), 487
Reginald, pr. Wooton Wawen, 214
Regney, Osmund, abb. Athelney, 19
Reigners, Alice (de), prs Cannington, 549
Renard, Henry, pr. Hayling, 167
Renard, Robert, pr. Andwell, 140
Renaut, Robert, pr. Linton and Isleham, 174
Repps, Warin of, pr. Peterstone, 447
Repton, Henry of, abb. Darley, 373
Repton, William of, pr. Breadsall, 343
Retford, Roger of, abb. Hagnaby, 503
Retlyng, Alan de, abb. Battle, 23

Rex, John dictus, pr. Lancaster, 171
Reynard, Michael, pr. Eye, 160
Reynard, Robert, pr. St Cross, 188
Rey(n)bod, Philip, pr. Pill, 187
Reyner, pr. Beadlow, 89
Reyner, pr. Belvoir, 91
Reyner, pr. Coxford, 372
Reyner, pr. Daventry, 226
Reyner, pr. Tortington, 475
Reynes, Alexander de, abb. Wardon, 320
Reynold, ? pr. Burstall, 148
Reyo, William de, pr. Lancaster, 171
Riby, Margaret of, prs Stamford, St Mary and St
    Michael, 609
Riccall, Hugh of, pr. Marton, 420
Richard, abb. Abbey Dore, 259
Richard, abb. Basingwerk, 260
Richard, abb. Battle, 22
Richard, abb. Bayham, 493
Richard, abb. Bordesley, 264
Richard, abb. Boxley, 265
Richard, abb. Bruern, 266
Richard, abb. Calder (1322–), 271
Richard, abb. Calder (occ. 1432), 271
Richard, abb. Cerne, 31
Richard, abb. Cockersand, 496
Richard, abb. Coggeshall, 272
Richard, abb. Combe, 273
Richard, abb. Combermere (occ. c. 1237 x 40), 273
Richard, abb. Combermere (–?1281), 274
Richard, abb. Crowland, 37
Richard, abb. Dieulacres (occ. 1214), 276
Richard, abb. Dieulacres (occ. 1292), 277
Richard, abb. Dieulacres (occ. 1293), 277
Richard, abb. Dorchester, 375 n.17
Richard, abb. Dunkeswell (occ. 1218 x 33), 277
Richard, abb. Dunkeswell (occ. 1378), 278
Richard I, abb. Halesowen, 503, 514 n.21
Richard II, abb. Halesowen, 503
Richard, abb. Hulton, 286
Richard, abb. Keynsham, 400
Richard, abb. Kingswood (occ. 1318), 287
Richard, abb. Kingswood (1319–), 287
Richard, abb. Kingswood (occ. 1335), 287
Richard, abb. Langdon, 504
Richard, abb. Lessness, 409
Richard, abb. Merevale, 295
Richard I, abb. Muchelney, 53
Richard II, abb. Muchelney, 53
Richard, abb. Netley, 296
Richard, abb. North Creake, 434
Richard, abb. Ramsey, 59

Richard, abb. Rewley (occ. 1284 x 5), 301
Richard, abb. Rewley (occ. 1291 x 97), 301
Richard, abb. Rewley (1302–), 301
Richard, abb. Rievaulx (occ. 1317), 302
Richard, abb. Rievaulx (1349–), 303
Richard, abb. Rocester, 453
Richard, abb. Roche, 304
Richard, abb. Rufford, 306
Richard, abb. St Radegund, 508
Richard, abb. Sallay, 306
Richard, abb. Sawtry, 307
Richard, abb. Selby (1221–3), 66
Richard, abb. Selby (1223–37), 66
Richard, abb. Shap, 509
Richard, abb. Stanley, 310
Richard, abb. Stratford Langthorne, 313
Richard, abb. Titchfield, 511
Richard, abb. Torre, 512
Richard, abb. Vaudey, 319
Richard, abb. Walden, 77
Richard, abb. Waltham, 478
Richard I, abb. Wellow, 481
Richard II, abb. Wellow, 481
Richard, abb. West Dereham, 517
Richard, abb. Woburn (–1234), 323
Richard, abb. Woburn (occ. 1241), 323
Richard, bailiff of Atherington, 144
Richard, keeper Long Bennington, 291
Richard, master Esholt, 559
Richard, master Greenfield, 567
Richard, master Grimsby, 567
Richard (or Ralph), master Hampole, 568
Richard, master St Mary de Pré (occ. 1235), 603
Richard, master St Mary de Pré (occ. 1278), 603
Richard, pr. Abergavenny, 138
Richard, pr. Allerton Mauleverer, 139
Richard, pr. Alvingham, 519
Richard, pr. Andwell, 140
Richard, pr. Anglesey, 327
Richard, pr. Appuldurcombe, 141
Richard, pr. Barnstaple, 219
Richard, pr. Binham (occ. 1215 x 20), 92
Richard, pr. Binham (occ. c. 1378 x 81), 93
Richard, pr. Blackmore, 337
Richard, pr. Blyth, 145
Richard, pr. Bodmin, 339
Richard, pr. Bolton, 340
Richard, pr. Bradwell (occ. 1201), 24
Richard, pr. Bradwell (–1236/7), 24
Richard, pr. Bruton, 350
Richard, pr. Burscough, 352
Richard, pr. Cartmel, 361

Richard, pr. Chirbury, 364
Richard, pr. Christchurch (Twynham), 365
Richard, pr. Church Gresley (occ. 1245), 367
Richard, pr. Church Gresley (–1281), 367
Richard, pr. Colchester, St Botolph, 369
Richard, pr. Creeting, 154
Richard, pr. Deeping, 96
Richard, pr. Dodnash, 374
Richard, pr. Earls Colne, 99
Richard, pr. Exeter, St Nicholas, 101
Richard, pr. Finchale (occ. 1280 x 83), 103
Richard, pr. Finchale (occ. 1289), 103
Richard, pr. Frampton, 161
Richard, pr. Gloucester, St Oswald, 381
Richard, pr. Great Massingham, 383
Richard, pr. Hardham, 385
Richard, pr. Harmondsworth, 165
Richard, pr. Hempton, 389
Richard, pr. Hertford, St Mary (1237/8–), 109
Richard, pr. Hertford, St Mary (–1253), 109
Richard, pr. Huntingdon, 394
Richard, pr. Kerswell, 230
Richard, pr. Kilpeck, 115
Richard, pr. Kirkham, 401
Richard, pr. Launceston, 404
Richard, pr. Leeds, 407
Richard, pr. Leonard Stanley, 117
Richard, pr. Little Malvern, 118
Richard, pr. London, Haliwell, 584
Richard, pr. Longleat, 418
Richard, pr. Marlborough, 525
Richard, pr. Marton, 420
Richard, pr. Mattersey, 526
Richard, pr. Modbury, 179
Richard, pr. Newark, 427
Richard, pr. Newburgh, 428
Richard, pr. Newstead-on-Ancholme, 526
Richard, pr. Newton Longville, 243
Richard, pr. North Ormsby, 526
Richard, pr. Norton, 437
Richard, pr. Repton, 452
Richard, pr. St Germans (–1279), 455
Richard, pr. St Germans (occ. 1332 x 3), 456
Richard, pr. Selborne, 458
Richard, pr. Sempringham, 528
Richard, pr. Shouldham, 529 n.4
Richard, pr. Stafford (occ. 1248), 462
Richard, pr. Stafford (occ. 1277), 463
Richard, pr. Stoke by Clare, 195
Richard, pr. Stone, 464
Richard, pr. Studley, 465
Richard, pr. Taunton, 467

Richard, pr. Thetford, Holy Sepulchre (occ. 1202), 467
Richard, pr. Thetford, Holy Sepulchre (occ. 1242 x 3), 467
Richard, pr. Thetford, St Mary, 251
Richard, pr. Thurgarton, 471
Richard, pr. Trentham (occ. 1224 x 38), 475
Richard, pr. Trentham (occ. c. 1272), 475
Richard, pr. Wallingford, 133
Richard, pr. Ware, 206
Richard, pr. Warter, 479
Richard, pr. Warwick, 480
Richard, pr. Wath, 208
Richard, pr. Watton, 530
Richard, pr. West Ravendale, 517
Richard, pr. Westacre (occ. 1229), 483
Richard, pr. Westacre (occ. 1288 x 97), 483
Richard, pr. Westwood, 617
Richard, pr. Witham, 326
Richard, pr. Woodspring, 487
Richard, pr. Wormsley, 489
Richard, pr. Wroxton (1231/2–), 489
Richard, pr. Wroxton (occ. 1410), 490
Richere, Peter, pr. Cammeringham, 496
Richmond, John of, abb. Whitby, 80
Richmond, Ranulf of, pr. Malton, 524
Rickinghall, William of, pr. Norwich, St Leonard, 122
Rickmansworth, John of, pr. Redbourn, 124
Rickmansworth, John of, pr. Sudbury, 131
Ridale, Richard of, pr. Lanercost, 403
Ridewale, Petronilla de, prs Harrold, 569
Ridware, Joan of, abbs Burnham, 547
Rie, Henry de, pr. Hinckley, 168
Riel, Joan de, prs Broadholme, 545
Rihale, William de, pr. Monk Bretton, 53, 236
Ringefeude, William de, abb. St Benet of Hulme, 65
Ringmer, Thomas of, pr. Canterbury, Christ Church, 28
Ringwould, Robert of, see Hathbrand, Robert de
Rinhaco, Martin de, pr. Wangford, 253
Ripariis, Peter de, pr. Clifford, 225
Ripon, Osbert of, pr. Richmond, 125
Ripon, Sibyl of, prs Sinningthwaite, 607
Ripon, William of, master Farne, 102
Ripton, John of, pr. Stonely, 465
Ripton, Walter of, abb. Bourne, 341
Rise, Simon de, abb. Rufford, 305
Rissa, Arnold, corrector Alberbury, 255
Risyng(g), William (de), pr. London, Holy Trinity, Aldgate, 416
Riym, Gossewin, pr. Lewisham, 173

Roald, pr. West Ravendale, 517
Robert, [Scarborough], 308
Robert, abb. Athelney, 19
Robert, abb. Barlings, 492
Robert, abb. Basingwerk, 259
Robert, abb. Bayham (occ. 1366 x 7), 493
Robert, abb. Bayham (occ. 1395), 493
Robert, abb. Beauchief, 494
Robert, abb. Bindon, 262
Robert, abb. Bordesley, 265
Robert, abb. Boxley, 265
Robert, abb. Bruern (occ. 1284 x 5), 266
Robert, abb. Bruern (occ. 1290), 266
Robert, abb. Bruern (1330–), 266
Robert, abb. Buckfast (1280–), 267
Robert, abb. Buckfast (1316–), 267
Robert, abb. Buckland, 268
Robert, abb. Byland, 269
Robert, abb. Calder, 271
Robert, abb. Coggeshall (mid 13th cent.), 272
Robert, abb. Coggeshall (occ. 1364 x 80), 272
Robert, abb. Combe, 272
Robert, abb. Combermere (occ. 1228 x 36), 273
Robert, abb. Combermere (occ. 1310), 274
Robert, abb. Coverham (?13th cent.), 497
Robert, abb. Coverham (occ. 1351), 497
Robert, abb. Dieulacres, 276
Robert, abb. Durford, 500
Robert, abb. Egglestone (occ. 1216), 501 n.17
Robert, abb. Egglestone (occ. 1251 x 4), 502
Robert, abb. Flaxley, 278
Robert, abb. Forde, 279
Robert, abb. Furness, 281
Robert, abb. Grace Dieu, 283
Robert, abb. Hailes, 284
Robert, abb. Hulton (occ. 1237 x 40), 285
Robert, abb. Hulton (occ. 1340), 286
Robert, abb. Keynsham, 400
Robert, abb. Langdon, 504
Robert, abb. Leiston, 506
Robert, abb. Lessness, 409
Robert, abb. Merevale (occ. 1230 x 36), 294
Robert, abb. Merevale (occ. 1254 x 62), 295
Robert, abb. Merevale (occ. 1276 x 78), 295
Robert, abb. Merevale (occ. 1351), 295
Robert, abb. Missenden, 424
Robert, abb. Neath, 295
Robert, abb. Newhouse, 507
Robert, abb. Newminster, 298
Robert, abb. North Creake, 434
Robert, abb. Pipewell, 299
Robert, abb. Quarr, 300

Robert, abb. Revesby, 301
Robert, abb. Rewley, 301
Robert, abb. Rievaulx, 302
Robert, ?abb. Robertsbridge, 303 n.27
Robert, abb. Rocester, 453
Robert, abb. Roche (occ. 1279/80 x 82), 304
Robert, abb. Roche (1300–), 304
Robert, abb. Rufford (occ. 1219 x 28), 305
Robert, abb. Rufford (1318–), 305
Robert, abb. Shap, 509
Robert, abb. Stanley (–1248), 310
Robert, abb. Stanley (occ. 1320 x 30), 310
Robert, abb. Stanley (occ. 1377), 311
Robert, abb. Stratford Langthorne, 314
Robert, abb. Sulby, 510
Robert III, abb. Tewkesbury, 74
Robert, abb. Thornton Curtis, 469
Robert, abb. Tilty, 316
Robert, abb. Torre, 512
Robert I, abb. Walden, 76
Robert II, abb. Walden, 76
Robert, abb. Wardon, 320
Robert, abb. Waverley, 321
Robert, abb. Wendling, 515
Robert, abb. Woburn, 324
Robert, *custos* Catesby, 552
Robert, *custos* Wilberfoss, 619
Robert, keeper Long Bennington, 291
Robert, master Godstow, 563
Robert, master Goring, 565
Robert, master Greenfield, 567
Robert, master Grimsby, 567
Robert, master Legbourne (early 13th cent.), 580
Robert, master Legbourne (occ. 1260), 580
Robert, master Legbourne (1309–), 580
Robert, master Legbourne (1366–), 580
Robert, master Wothorpe, 624
Robert, minister Hertford, 532
Robert, minister Knaresborough, 533
Robert, ? minister Moatenden (occ. 1253), 533
Robert, minister Moatenden (occ. 1373), 533
Robert, minister Thelsford, 534
Robert, pr. Alnesbourn, 327
Robert, pr. Andwell, 140
Robert, pr. Anglesey, 328
Robert, pr. Barlinch, 330
Robert, pr. Bentley, 333
Robert, pr. Bermondsey, 221
Robert, pr. Bicester (late 12th / early 13th cent.), 334
Robert, pr. Bicester (–1239/40), 334
Robert, pr. Birkenhead, 23

Robert, pr. Bisham, 337
Robert, pr. Bolton, 339
Robert, pr. Boxgrove (occ. 1215 x 16), 146
Robert, pr. Boxgrove (occ. 1278 x 81), 146
Robert, pr. Boxgrove (? 1328), 147
Robert, pr. Boxgrove (1363–), 147
Robert, pr. Bradley, 342
Robert, pr. Butley (occ. 1213), 353
Robert, pr. Butley (occ. 1268/9 x 71), 354
Robert, pr. Cammeringham, 495
Robert, pr. Canterbury, St Gregory, 358
Robert, pr. Carlisle, 359
Robert II, pr. Carlisle, 359
Robert, pr. Castle Acre, 223
Robert, pr. Chepstow, 151
Robert, pr. Church Gresley (–1286), 367
Robert, pr. Church Gresley (occ. 1309), 367
Robert, pr. Clattercote, 521
Robert, pr. Colchester, St Botolph, 369
Robert, pr. Combwell, 371
Robert, pr. Conishead, 372
Robert, ? pr. Coxford, 372
Robert, pr. Coxford (1289–), 373
Robert, pr. Creeting, 154
Robert, pr. Dodnash, 374
Robert, pr. Drax (occ. 1227 x 43), 376
Robert, pr. Drax (occ. 1250 x 52), 376
Robert, pr. Ecclesfield, 157
Robert, pr. Edith Weston, 158
Robert, pr. Ellerton on Spalding Moor, 522
Robert, pr. Finchale, 103
Robert, pr. Fineshade, 380
Robert, pr. Fordham, 522
Robert, pr. Frampton, 161
Robert, pr. Great Bricett, 383
Robert, pr. Great Massingham, 383
Robert, pr. Hardham (occ. *ante* 1225), 385
Robert, pr. Hardham (occ. 1279), 385
Robert, pr. Hayling, 167
Robert, pr. Hinton, 325
Robert, pr. Horkesley (occ. ? 1229), 230
Robert, pr. Horkesley (occ. 1261), 230
Robert, pr. Hornby, 504
Robert, pr. London, St Bartholomew, 417
Robert, pr. Malton, 524
Robert, pr. Marlborough, 525
Robert, pr. Marton, 421
Robert, pr. Mattersey, 526
Robert, pr. Minster, 176
Robert, pr. Minster Lovell, 177
Robert, pr. Minting, 178
Robert, pr. Modbury, 179

Robert, pr. Mullicourt, 54
Robert, pr. Newstead (in Sherwood), 431
Robert, pr. North Creake, 434
Robert, pr. North Ferriby (occ. 1234), 435
Robert, pr. North Ferriby (occ. 1284), 435
Robert, pr. North Ormsby (occ. 1212 x 13), 526
Robert, pr. North Ormsby (occ. 1231 x 4), 526
Robert, pr. North Ormsby (occ. 1255 x 63), 526
Robert, pr. Nuneaton (occ. 1227/8 x 43), 596
Robert, pr. Nuneaton (occ. 1308 x 18), 597
Robert, pr. Orford, 597
Robert, pr. Pill, 187
Robert, pr. Pontefract, 246
Robert, pr. Poughley (occ. *c.* 1214 x 22), 449
Robert, pr. Poughley (occ. 1252 x 68), 449
Robert, pr. St Carrok, 249
Robert, pr. St Helen's, 250
Robert, pr. Sandaleford, 457
Robert, pr. Sele, 191
Robert, pr. Sempringham, 528
Robert, pr. Shelford, 458
Robert, pr. Shouldham, 529
Robert, pr. Stavordale (occ. 1254 x 63), 463
Robert, pr. Stavordale (occ. 1382), 464
Robert, pr. Stogursey, 194
Robert, pr. Taunton, 467
Robert, pr. Thremhall, 470
Robert, pr. Tiptree, 472
Robert, pr. Tortington, 475
Robert, pr. Totnes, 202
Robert, pr. Tutbury, 203
Robert, pr. Wallingford, 134
Robert, pr. Warmington, 208
Robert, pr. Weedon Lois, 209 n.14
Robert, pr. West Ravendale, 517
Robert, pr. Westwood (occ. 1344), 617
Robert, pr. Westwood (occ. 1351), 617
Robert, pr. Weybridge, 484
Robert, pr. Worksop, 487
Robert, pr. Wormsley, 488
Robert, pr. York, Holy Trinity, 216
Robertsbridge, John of, abb. Newenham, 296
Rocester, Thomas of, abb. Rocester, 453
Rochario, Geoffrey de, *see* Rocherio, Geoffrey de
Roche, Gerald (William), pr. Montacute, 240
Rochelle, Constance de la, abbs Romsey, 600
Rocherio (Rochario), Geoffrey de, *alias* of
    Guernsey, pr. Lenton, 233; pr. Thetford, St
    Mary, 253
Rochester, Acelina of, prs Higham, 571
Rochester, Benedict of, *alias* Woldham, pr.
    Bicknacre, 335

Rochester, John of, abb. Tavistock, 72
Rochester, Thomas of, pr. Leeds, 407
Rockland, William of, abb. Beeleigh, 495
Rodbourne, John of, pr. Pilton, 124
Rodbourn(e), Robert de, pr. Nuneaton, 597
Rodene, John, pr. Nuneaton, 597
Rodeyerd, Richard (de), abb. Combermere, 274
Rodmarton, Roger of, abb. Cirencester, 367
Rodmersham, Peter of, abb. Faversham, 44
Roger, abb. Abbey Dore, 259
Roger, abb. Athelney, 19
Roger, abb. Beauchief, 494
Roger, abb. Beeleigh, 494
Roger, abb. Biddlesden, 261
Roger, abb. Bindon, 262
Roger, abb. Bruern, 266
Roger, abb. Buildwas, 269
Roger, abb. Cockersand (early 13th cent.), 496
Roger, ? abb. Cockersand (occ. 1300), 496 n.7
Roger, abb. Cockersand (1311–), 496
Roger I, abb. Combe, 273
Roger II, abb. Combe, 273
Roger, abb. Dorchester, 375
Roger, abb. Easby, 500
Roger, abb. Egglestone, 501
Roger, abb. Flaxley, 278
Roger, abb. Forde, 278
Roger, abb. Garendon, 283
Roger, abb. Grace Dieu, 283
Roger, abb. Halesowen, 503
Roger, abb. Margam (occ. 1267 x 8), 292
Roger, abb. Margam (occ. *c.* 1305), 292
Roger, abb. Medmenham, 294
Roger, abb. Pipewell, 300
Roger, abb. Rievaulx, 302
Roger, abb. Robertsbridge, 303
Roger, ?abb. Roche, 304 n.28
Roger, abb. St Radegund, 508
Roger, abb. Sallay, 306
Roger, abb. Shap, 509
Roger, abb. Vaudey, 319
Roger, abb. Walden (3rd abb.), 76
Roger, abb. Walden (6th abb.), 77
Roger II, abb. Wardon, 319
Roger, abb. Wellow, 481
Roger, abb. West Dereham, 516
Roger, abb. Woburn (1234–), 323
Roger, abb. Woburn (–1281), 323
Roger, master Greenfield, 566
Roger, master St Mary de Pré, 603
Roger, master Stixwould, 611
Roger, pr. Alberbury, 255

Roger, pr. Alnesbourn, 327

Roger, pr. Alvingham, 519

Roger, pr. Arbury, 328

Roger, pr. Beadlow, 89

Roger, pr. Beeston, 333

Roger, pr. Blackmore (*temp.* King John), 337

Roger, pr. Blackmore (occ. 1270), 338

Roger, pr. Bromholm, 223

Roger, pr. Canonsleigh, 357

Roger, pr. Chicksands, 521

Roger, pr. Christchurch (Twynham), 365

Roger, pr. Cogges, 151

Roger, pr. Cold Norton (occ. 1229), 369

Roger, pr. Cold Norton (occ. 1261 x 2), 370

Roger, pr. Craswell, 256

Roger, pr. Dodnash, 374

Roger, pr. Dudley (occ. 1278), 227

Roger, pr. Dudley (occ. 1380), 227

Roger, pr. Earls Colne, 99

Roger, pr. Exeter, St Nicholas (early 13th cent.), 100

Roger, pr. Exeter, St Nicholas (occ. 1294/5 x 1306), 101

Roger, pr. Frampton, 161

Roger, pr. Hastings, 386

Roger, pr. Haverholme, 523

Roger, pr. Hereford, 109

Roger, pr. Hickling, 391

Roger, pr. Holy Island, 111

Roger, pr. Horkesley, 230

Roger, pr. Hoxne, 112

Roger, pr. Kersey, 399

Roger, pr. Kirkham, 401

Roger, pr. Kyme, 402

Roger, pr. Lapley, 172

Roger, pr. Launceston, 404

Roger, pr. Leeds, 407

Roger, pr. Lenton, 231

Roger, pr. Lincoln, St Katharine, 523

Roger, pr. Little Malvern, 118

Roger, pr. Luffield, 49

Roger, pr. Malton, 524

Roger I, pr. Michelham, 423

Roger II, pr. Michelham, 423

Roger III, pr. Michelham, 423

Roger, pr. Monk Bretton, 236

Roger, pr. Monk Sherborne, 180

Roger, pr. Penwortham, 123

Roger, pr. Peterstone, 447

Roger, pr. Ratlinghope, 450

Roger, pr. St Neots, 190

Roger, pr. Shulbred, 459

Roger, pr. Stratfield Saye, 196

Roger, pr. Swavesey, 197

Roger, pr. Thoby, 468

Roger, pr. Thornholme, 469

Roger, pr. Tonbridge, 473

Roger, pr. Tortington, 475

Roger, pr. Totnes, 202

Roger, pr. Trentham (occ. 1242 x 55), 475

Roger, pr. Trentham (occ. 1267), 475

Roger, pr. Watton, 530

Roger, pr. Weedon Lois, 208

Roger, pr. West Ravendale, 517

Roger, pr. Wilsford, 211

Roger, pr. Wombridge, 485

Roger, pr. Wroxton, 489

Roger, pr. Wymondham, 136

Roger, pr. Wymondley, 490

Roger(s), Michael, pr. Long Bennington, 291

Rohays, prs Handale, 568

Roland, [Ipplepen], 395 n.24

Roland, pr. Isleham, 171

Roland, pr. Linton and Isleham, 174

　see also Rowland

Rolleston, Alice of, prs Catesby, 552

Romanus, Gilbert, pr. Nuneaton, 596

Romelot, Peter de, pr. Lapley, 172

Romenhale, John de, abb.-el. Faversham, 45

Romilly, Ralph de, pr. Carisbrooke, 150

Romney, John of, pr. Bilsington, 336

Romney, John of (II), pr. Bilsington, 336

Romney, John of (III), pr. Bilsington, 337

Romney, Robert, pr. Winghale, 213

Romney, William of, abb. Boxley, 265

Romsey, William of, pr. Hertford, St Mary, 109

Roncevill(e), Ralph de, pr. Goldcliff, 162

Ronetone, William de, pr. Canonsleigh, 358

Rookwith, John of, abb. Jervaulx, 287

Roper, Edmund, *see* Canterbury, Edmund of

Rorrington, Roger of, *alias* Rufin, pr. Chirbury, 365

Ros, John (de), pr. Wormsley, 489

Ros, Mary de, prs Rosedale, 601

Rose, prs Langley, 578

Rose, prs Rowney, 602

Rose (Roisa), prs Wintney, 622

Rosee, Giles, pr. Stogursey, 195

Rotes, Robert de, pr. Beckford and Colsterworth, 332

Rothbury, Robert of, abb. Alnwick, 491

Rothbury, Simon of, master Farne, 102

Rotherham, Robert of, abb. Beauchief, 494

Rotherwick, John of, abb. Chertsey, 32

Rothis, Alexander de, pr. Cowick, 154

Rothley, Henry of, abb. Leicester, 408
Rothonis, Gerald, pr. Lewes, 235
Rothwell, William of, pr. Lincoln, St Mary
    Magdalen, 118; pr. St Bees, 127
Rouen, A. of, abbs Chatteris, 553
Rouen, Joan of, prs Ankerwyke, 539
Rouen, Richard of, pr. Wetheral, 134
Rouge, William (de), pr. Minster Lovell, 177
Rougecok(e), John de, pr. Pembroke, 187
Rouland, John, pr. Stamford, St Mary and St
    Michael, 610
Roundel, Michael *dictus*, pr. Richmond, 125
Roundell, William, abb. York, St Mary, 86; pr.
    Wetheral, 134
Rous, Alice, prs Cook Hill, 555
Rous, John le, abb. Titchfield, 512
Rowland, pr. St Denys, 454
    see also Roland
Rowley, Henry of, pr. Canwell, 31
Rowsham, Robert of, pr. Bradwell, 24
Roxby, Walter of, pr. Thornholme, 469
Roxton, Henry of, pr. Huntingdon, 395
Royewelle, Andrew de, abb. Pipewell, 299
Rualend, pr. Wallingford, 133
Rucof, William *dictus*, [West Ravendale], 517
Rudeby, Roger de, abb. Pershore, 56
Rudston, Geoffrey of, pr. Rumburgh, 126
Rudston, John of, pr. Thurgarton, 472
Ruffeto, Geoffrey de, pr. Minister Lovell, 177
Rufford, John de, pr. Llanthony Prima, 413
Rufford, William of, abb. Dorchester, 375
Ruffus, Walter, pr. Winchester, St Swithun, 83
Rufin, Roger, *see* Rorrington, Roger of
Rufus, Richard, de Winchelcombe, *see* Parco,
    Richard de
Ruihiaco, Martin de, pr. Thetford, St Mary, 252
Ruly, Idonea de, prs Wix, 622
Rupe, William de, pr. Winghale, 213
Rus, William le, pr. Newnham, 430
Ruscavilla, William de, pr. Frampton, 161
Rushbrooke, Henry of, abb. Bury St Edmunds, 26
Rushford, Reginald of, pr. Chipley, 364
Russell, Amice, abbs Shaftesbury, 605
Russell, Isabel, prs Newcastle-upon-Tyne, 590
Russell, Joan, prs Wroxall, 624
Russell, Katherine, prs Stamford, St Mary and St
    Michael, 609
Russell, Laurence, pr. Swavesey, 198
Russell, Ralph, pr. Winchester, St Swithun, 83
Russell, William de, *custos* Derby, Kingsmead, 557
Russelun, Martin (de), pr. Lewes, 233
Rutham, John de, abb. West Dereham, 516

Rya, Robert de, pr. Exeter, St Nicholas, 101
Rya, William de, abb. Flaxley, 278
    see also Rye
Rybus, William de, pr. Stamford, St Leonard, 129
Rye, Alice of, prs Fosse, 561
Rye, Matilda de la, prs Littlemore, 582
Rye, Walter of, pr. Bilsington, 336
    see also Rya
Rygton, William, abb. Fountains, 280
Ryslay, John de, abb. Meaux, 293
Rysle, John de, pr. Bushmead, 353
Ryvere, Thomas de la, [Totnes], 202

S., abb. Buildwas, 268
S., Henry de, abb. St Radegund, 509
S., abb. Sibton, 308
S., pr. Berden, 333
S., pr. Chepstow, 151
S., pr. Hereford, 108
S., pr. Lanercost, 403
S., prs Markyate, 587
S., pr. Pontefract, 246
S., pr. Wombridge, 486
Sabina, prs Kilburn, 575
Sabina, prs Wintney, 622
Sacro Fonte, Andrew de, abb. Athelney, 19
Sagio, William de, pr. Modbury, 179
Saham, Simon of, abb. Waltham, 478
Saham, Thomas of, pr. Bromhill, 349
St Albans, Geoffrey of, pr. Hertford, St Mary, 110;
    pr. Redbourn, 124
St Albans, Gregory of, pr. Beadlow, 90
St Albans, Letitia of, prs Flamstead, 560
St Albans, Thomas of, pr. Tandridge, 466
St Albans, William of, abb. Bourne, 341
St Albans, William of, pr. Wymondham, 136
St Alphege, Roger of, pr. Canterbury, Christ
    Church, 28
St Andrew, Margaret of, prs Ickleton, 573
St Bees, Thomas of, pr. Wetheral, 134
St Clement, William of, pr. Monks Kirby, 181
St Clement, William of, pr. Wing, 213
St Edmund, Agnes of, prs Broomhall, 545
St Edmund, Hugh of, pr. Cowick, 153
St Edmund, John of, pr. Bicknacre, 335
St Edmund, Luke of, pr. Letheringham, 410
St Edmund, Martin of, pr. Hertford, St Mary, 109
St Edmund, Walter of, abb. Peterborough, 57
St Edmund, Walter of, pr. North Ferriby, 435
St Edward, Laurence of, abb. Burton, 25
St Edward, William of, *dictus* of Shaftesbury, pr.
    Bruton, 350

St Fromund, William of, pr. Monk Sherbourne, 180

St John, Cecily of, prs Little Marlow, 581

St John, John of, pr. Andover, 139

St John, Richard of, pr. Wootton Wawen, 214

St John, Walter of, abb. Gloucester, 48

St Laurence, Peter of, pr. Bermondsey, 221

St Martin, Andrew of, *see* London, Andrew of

St Neots, Henry of, pr. Beadlow, 90

St Neots, Henry of, pr. St Neots, 190

St Neots, Henry of, pr. Wilsford, 212

St Neots, William of, *alias* Dolerti, pr. Fineshade, 379

St Neots, William of, abb. Robertsbridge, 303

St Nicholas, John of, pr. Ipswich, St Peter and St Paul, 396

S. Omero, Emma de, prs Kilburn, 575

St Peter, William of, pr. Eye, 159

S. Pierre sur Dives, Robert of, pr. Carisbrooke, 150

St Quintin, Isabel of, prs Nunkeeling, 594

St Quintin, Jordan of, abb. Bayham, 492

St Stephen, Clement of, pr. St Neots, 191

St Stephen, Durand of, pr. Cowick, 154; pr. Wilsford, 212

St Stephen, Peter of, *see* Falco (Falk), Peter de

St Stephen, Stephen of, [Steventon], 194

St Valery, Roger of, abb. Winchester, Hyde, 81

St Vigor, William of, abb. Glastonbury, 46

Sais, Anian, abb. Strata Florida, 312

Sakkot, Thomas, pr. Colchester, St Botolph, 369

Salburn, John of, pr. Standon, 194

Sale, John de la, abb. Stoneleigh, 311

Sales, Peter de, pr. Newton Longville, 243

Saling, Simon of, pr. Leighs, 409

Salisbury, John of, abb. Biddlesden, 262

Salisbury, Thomas of, pr. Stamford, St Mary and St Michael, 610

Salle, Robert de, pr. Kenilworth, 399

Sallerii, William, pr. Titley, 201

Salmon, John *alias* of Ely, pr. Ely, 40

Salmonby, Gilbert of, abb. Beauchief, 494

Saltfleetby, Petronilla of, prs Legbourne, 579

Sammar', Robert de, master Stainfield, 608

Sampson, abb. Kingswood, 287

Sampson, abb. St Benet of Hulme, 64

Sam(p)son, master Nun Cotham, 593

Sampson, pr. Beckford and Colsterworth, 332

Sampson, pr. Brecon, 93

Sampson, pr. Bromfield, 94

Sampson *senex*, pr. Folkestone, 161

Sampson, pr. West Ravendale, 517

Sampson, pr. Wolston, 214

Samuel, pr. Cold Norton, 369

Sanarvill, Robert de, pr. Astley, 142

Sancta Cruce, Agnes de, prs Barrow Gurney, 542

Sancta Cruce, Sibyl de, abbs Lacock, 577

Sancta Eugenia, William de, pr. Ware, 205

Sancta Fide, Henry de, abb. Notley, 440

Sancta Gemma, John de, pr. Barnstaple, 219

Sancta Genoveva, William de, pr. Upavon, 205

Sancto Albino, John de, pr. Tutbury, 203

Sancto Albino, John de, pr. Wolston, 213

Sancto Albino, William de, pr. Goldcliff, 162–3

Sancto Albino, William de, pr. Wilsford, 212

Sancto Antonio, Peter de, pr. Plympton, 448

Sancto Botulpho, Adam de, pr. Rumburgh, 126

Sancto Claro, Mary de, abbs Chatteris, 553

Sancto Johanne, William *dictus* de, pr. Warwick, 480

Sancto Landulo, Henry de, pr. Haugham, 167

Sancto Lupo, Hugh de, *custos* Scarborough, 308

Sancto Marcello, Thomas de, *alias* de Villa Nova, pr. Weedon Lois, 209

Sancto Mauro, Hawise de, prs Nuneaton, 596

Sancto Mauro, William de, master Wothorpe, 624

Sancto Paterno, William de, [Ogbourne St George], 184

Sancto Remigio, Nicholas de, pr. Tregoney, 475

Sancto Romano, Peter de, pr. Ecclesfield, 157

Sancto Romano, Stephen de, pr. Lewes, 234

Sancto Simphoriano, Peter de, pr. Bermondsey, 221

Sancto Vedasto, German de, pr. Goldcliff, 163

Sancto Vedasto, William de, pr. Goldcliff, 163; pr. Ogbourne St George, 185; pr. St Neots, 191

Sandale, Robert de, pr. Torksey, 474

Sandon, [John] of, pr.-el. Oxford, St Frideswide, 444

Sandruge, William de, pr. Hertford, St Mary, 109

Sandwich, Benedicta of, prs Canterbury, Holy Sepulchre, 550

Sandwich, Elias of, pr. Canterbury, St Gregory, 358

Sandwich, John of, pr. Bilsington, 336

Sandwich, Nicholas of, pr. Canterbury, Christ Church, 27

Sandwich, Thomas of, abb. Lessness, 409

Sapiencia, prs Sinningthwaite, 606

Sapperton, Matilda of, prs Gokewell, 564

Sapy, Lucy de, prs Pinley, 598

Sarah, abbs Marham, 586

Sarah, prs Arthington, 540

Sarah, prs Brewood White Ladies, 544

Sarah, prs Cook Hill (occ. 1221 x 7), 555

Sarah, prs Cook Hill (–1349), 555

Sarah, prs Davington, 556

Sarecta, Richard de, rector Ashridge, 535

Sarnay, Philip de, pr. Deerhurst, 155

Sarnefeud, Cecilia de, prs Cook Hill, 555

Sateforde, John de, pr. Little Dunmow, 412

Saucheveral, Joan de, abbs Polesworth, 598

Saunde, John de, abb. Sherborne, 68

Saunford, Alice de, prs Ankerwyke, 539

Saunford, Amibilia de, prs Littlemore, 582

Saunford, Amice de, prs Littlemore, 582

Saunford, Aubrey de, abbs Elstow, 558

Saunford, Walter de, abb. Abbotsbury, 15

Saunzaver, Constance, abbs-el., Shaftesbury, 605

Sauston, Baldwin de, pr. Kersey, 400

Sauvage, John *dictus,* pr. Pembroke, 187

Sauvalle, Nicholas, pr. Everdon, 159

Sauvarvilla, John de, pr. Wilsford, 212

Saver, John, pr. Prittlewell, 249

Sawbridge, Walter of, pr. Daventry, 226

Sawtry, John of, abb. Ramsey, 60

Saxilby, Thomas of, pr. Torksey, 474

Saxlingham, William of, abb. Wendling, 516

Saxton, John of, pr. Drax, 376

Saxton, Roger of, *custos* Nun Appleton, 593

Saxton, Thomas of, pr. Chacombe, 362

Sayer, John, pr. Barnstaple, 219

Sayr, Ralph de, pr. Wilkeswood, 536

Scagglethorpe, Robert of, pr. Malton, 525

Scalby, Robert of, pr. Watton, 531

Scalis, Katherine de, prs Blackborough, 543

Scarborough, Adam of, pr. Ellerton on Spalding Moor, 522

Scarborough, Alan of, minister Knaresborough, 533

Scarborough, Robert of, pr. Bridlington, 346

Scarborough, Roger of, abb. Whitby, 79

Scarborough, Simon of, abb. Selby, 67

Scarborough, William of, *see* Baudewyn, William

Scarborough, William of, abb. Meaux, 294

Scard', Margaret de, prs Yedingham, 625

Scarhowe/Scarbowgh, John de, pr. Bridge End, 519

Scarisbrick, Walter of, [Jarrow], 114

Scarle, Ivo of, pr. Nocton Park, 433

Scheynton, Thomas de, abb. Merevale, 295

Schireborn, Adam de, pr.-el. Newnham, 430

Scholastica, prs London, St Helen's and Holy Cross, 584

School Aycliffe, Richard of, master Monkwearmouth, 121

Schorham, William de, pr. Castle Acre, 224

Scopulo, Arnulph de, pr. Titley, 201

Scot, Henry, *see* Fangfoss, Henry of

Scot, Richard, pr. St Ives, 128

Scotelare, James, pr. Throwley, 199

Scothern, Agnes of, prs Fosse, 561

Scotney, Beatrice of, abbs Elstow, 558

Scotney, Robert of, pr. Reigate, 451

Scotter, Richard of, pr. Stamford, St Mary and St Michael, 609

Scotton, Peter of, pr. Markby, 419

Scotus, Elias, pr. Oxford, St Frideswide, 444

Scriven, Agnes of, prs Arthington, 540

Scriven, Alice of, prs Kirklees, 576

Scupholme, Richilda de, prs Heynings, 570

Seagrave, William of, pr. Charley, 363

Seagrave, William of, pr. Thornholme, 469

Seddyngton, Robert de, pr. Bristol, St James, 94

Sedgebrook, Richard of, master Farne, 102; master Jarrow, 115

Sedgefield, Peter of, pr. Stamford, St Leonard, 130

Sedgeford, William of, pr. Ipswich, St Peter and St Paul, 396

Sedile, Thomas, pr. Otterton, 186

Seduno, Giles de, pr. Prittlewell, 248

See, Margaret atte, prs Stamford, St Mary and St Michael, 609

Sées, Simon of, [Barnwell], 331

Sées, Thomas of, pr. Burstall, 148

Seger, William, pr. Hurley, 113

Seint Piere, Nicholas de, *see* Barbe, Nicholas la

Seintoill, Ber(n)ard de, pr. Horsham St Faith, 170

Seintpere, Robert de, pr. Trentham, 475

Selby, Denise of, prs Legbourne, 580

Selby, Richard of, *custos* Woodkirk, 486

Selby, William, abb. Whalley, 323

Selford, Richard de, pr. Binham, 92

Seliman, Margaret, prs Nuneaton, 596

Selyman, Faith, abbs Lacock, 578

Seman, pr. Stonely, 464

Senex, Sampson, pr. Folkestone, 161

Sens, Stephen de, pr. Sele, 192

Sentelleys, William de, pr. Tutbury, 203

Senteney, Walter de, *alias* de Todeni, abb. Dale, 499

Septennent, Richard, pr. Patrixbourne, 446

Serena, prs Farewell, 559

Sergotz, William (de), pr. Lewisham, 173

Serveria, Pontius de, pr. Horsham St Faith, 169

Sewale, Thomas, abb. Cerne, 31

Sewoldby, Thomas de, abb. Rufford, 306

Sewstern, Roger of, pr. Kirby Bellars, 401

Sexdecim Vallibus, William de, pr. Henes and Sandtoft, 108

Seyer, John, pr. St Clears, 249
Seyer, Peter, pr. St Clears, 249
Seynesbury, Richard de, abb. Chester, 33
Seynesbury, William de, pr. St Bees, 127
Seynt Moys, Peter de, pr. Exeter, St James, 228
Seyntliz, John de, pr. Wootton Wawen, 215
Seys, Howel, abb. Whitland, 323
Seys, John, pr. Penmon, 446
Seyvill, Margaret de, prs Kirklees, 576
Shackerstone, Robert of, pr. Brooke, 350; keeper Calwich, 356
Shaftesbury, William of, *see* St Edward, William of
Shaftoe, John of, master Farne, 102; master Monkwearmouth, 121
Shalstone, Peter of, pr. Luffield, 50
Shalyngforde, Henry de, *alias* Blebury, abb. Bristol, St Augustine, 348
Shamelisford, John de, pr. Hoxne, 112
Shapwick, Ralph of, abb. Newenham, 297
Sheffield, Alice of, prs Wallingwells, 616
Sheffield, William of, pr. Watton, 531
Shelden, William of, keeper Calwich, 355
Shelevestrode, Thomas de, pr. Prittlewell, 248
Shelford, Thomas de, pr. Rochester, 62
Shelvestrode, William de, pr. Michelham, 424
Shenington, Richard of, abb. Ramsey, 60
Shenington, Thomas of, pr. Huntingdon, 395
Shepey, Richard, abb. Boxley, 266
Sheppey, John de, pr. Rochester, 62
Sheppey, Reginald of, pr. Dover, 96
Shepreth, John of, pr. Ely, 40
Shepshed, Richard of, abb. Croxden, 276
Shepshed, Roger of, pr. Ulverscroft, 477
Shepshed, William of, abb. Leicester, 408
Shepton, William (of), abb. Muchelney, 54
Sherborne, Ralph of, abb. Abbotsbury, 15
Sherborne, Thomas of, abb. Winchcombe, 81
Sherborne, William of, abb. Winchcombe, 81
Sherbourne, Peter of, abb. Abbotsbury, 15
Sherbourne, Philip of, abb. Abbotsbury, 15
Sherburn, Alan of, pr.-el. Marton, 420
Sherburn, Gilbert of, ?pr. Holy Island, 111; pr. Stamford, St Leonard, 130
Sherburn, John of, abb. Selby, 68
Sherburn, Thomas of, pr. Drax, 376
Shereford, William of, pr. Thremhall, 471
Sheringham, William of, abb. Notley, 440
Sherrard, Stephen, abb. Cerne, 31
Sherwood, Alice, prs Ellerton-in-Swaledale, 557
Sherwood, Henry of, pr. Drax, 376
Shipdham, Adam of, pr. Kings Lynn, 116
Shipton, John of, pr. Gloucester, St Oswald, 382

Shirebrook, Richard of, pr. Felley, 379
Shireburn, William de, pr. Lincoln, St Katharine, 524
Shirford, Margery de, prs Nuneaton, 596
Shobindon, Nicholas de, pr. Bicester, 334
Shockeleg', John de, pr. Little Malvern, 119
Sholdon, John of (senior), pr. Dover, 98
Sholdon, Luke of, abb. Bayham, 493
Shoreham, Walter of, pr. Boxgrove, 146
Shottenden, Nicholas of, pr. Canterbury, St Gregory, 358
Shouldham, Mary of, abbs Chatteris, 553
Shrewsbury, Alan of, abb. Haughmond, 387
Shrewsbury, Luke of, abb. Lilleshall, 411
Shrewsbury, Ralph of, abb. Lilleshall, 411
Shrewsbury, Richard of, abb. Lilleshall, 411
Shrivenham, William of, pr. Kilpeck, 115
Shropham, Alice of, abbs Chatteris, 553
Shropham, Roger of, pr. Wangford, 253
Shropham, Thomas of, pr. Shouldham, 529
Sibtoft, Lucy de, prs Hinchingbrooke, 572
Sibton, John of, abb. Sibton, 309
Sibyl, prs Derby, Kingsmead, 556
Sibyl, prs Ellerton-in-Swaledale, 557
Sibyl, prs Farewell, 559
Sibyl, prs Flamstead, 560
Sibyl, prs Keldholme, 574
Sibyl, prs Kirklees, 576
Sibyl, prs Nun Keeling, 594
Sibyl, prs Nuneaton, 595
Sibyl, prs Stamford, St Mary and St Michael, 609
Sibyl, prs Swaffham Bulbeck, 613
Sibyl, prs Swine (occ. 1236), 613
Sibyl, prs Swine (occ. 1246 x 52), 613
Sibyl, prs Thicket, 615
Sibyl, prs Westwood, 616
Sibyl, prs Yedingham, 625
Siccavalle, John de, pr. St Neots, 190
Sideling, Walter de, abb. Milton, 52
Sigor, pr. Lewisham, 173
Sigston, Philip of, abb. Easby, 501
Sileby, Roger of, pr. Chacombe, 362
Silesiis, William de, pr. Titley, 201
Silvaneto, John de, pr. Wootton Wawen, 215
Silverstone, *alias* of Luffield, Ralph of, pr. Luffield, 50
Silverstone, Richard of, pr. Luffield, 50
Silvestr(e), William, pr. Edith Weston, 158
Simon, abb. Basingwerk, 259
Simon, abb. Bayham, 493
Simon, abb. Biddlesden, 261
Simon, abb. Boxley, 265

Simon, abb. Buckfast, 267
Simon, abb. Buildwas, 268
Simon, abb. Cleeve, 271
Simon, abb. Combe, 273
Simon, abb. Combermere, 273
Simon, abb. Dale, 499
Simon, abb. Dunkeswell, 278
Simon, abb. Garendon, 283
Simon, abb. Hulton, 285
Simon, abb. Humberston, 49
Simon, abb. Kirkstall, 288
Simon, abb. Kirkstead (occ. 1249 x 51), 289
Simon, abb. Kirkstead (occ. 1277 x 81), 289
Simon, abb. Leiston, 507
Simon, abb. Netley, 296
Simon the chamberlain, abb. Reading, 60
Simon, abb. Rewley, 301
Simon, abb. Robertsbridge, 304
Simon, abb. St Radegund, 508
Simon, abb. Sulby, 510
Simon, abb. Talley, 511
Simon, abb. Thame, 315
Simon, abb. Tilty (–1214), 316
Simon, abb. Tilty (occ. 1328), 316
Simon, abb. Torre, 512
Simon, abb. Vaudey, 319
Simon, abb. West Dereham, 516
Simon, abb. Whalley (Stanlow), 322
Simon, archpriest or pr. Barton, 331
Simon, master Northampton, De La Pré (occ. 1316), 591
Simon, master Northampton, De La Pré (occ. 1320), 591
Simon, master Wykeham, 625
Simon, pr. Bradenstoke, 342
Simon, pr. Breamore, 344
Simon, pr. Bullington, 520
Simon, pr. Cardiff, 95
Simon, pr. Cartmel, 361
Simon, pr. Charley, 362
Simon, pr. Chicksands (occ. 1233 x 7), 521
Simon, pr. Chicksands (occ. 1325 x 34), 521
Simon, pr. Colchester, St Botolph, 369
Simon, pr. Conishead, 372
Simon, pr. Dodford, 374
Simon, pr. Haverholme, 522
Simon, pr. Hayling, 167
Simon, ?pr Hertford, St Mary, 109
Simon, pr. Holy Island, 110
Simon, pr. Horkesley, 230
Simon, pr. Llanthony Prima, 413
Simon, pr. Markby, 419

Simon, pr. Marton, 420
Simon, pr. Mendham, 235
Simon, pr. Monkton Farleigh, 237
Simon, pr. Mullicourt, 54
Simon, pr. Newburgh, 428
Simon, pr. Newstead-on-Ancholme, 526
Simon, pr. Norman's Burrow, 243
Simon, pr. North Ferriby, 435
Simon, pr. Oxford, St Frideswide, 443
Simon, pr. Pentney (occ. 1200), 446
Simon (?another), pr. Pentney (occ. 1227/8 x 1254/5), 446
Simon, pr. Peterstone, 447
Simon, pr. St Ives, 128
Simon, pr. Sixhills (occ. 1220), 529
Simon, pr. Sixhills (occ. 1283 x 93), 530
Simon, pr. Stonely, 465
Simon, pr. Sudbury, 131
Simon, pr.-el. Thornholme, 469
Simon, pr. Tywardreath, 204
Simon, ?pr. Westacre, 483 n.48
Simon, Robert, abb. Buckfast, 268
Simplex, Ralph, abb. Thorney, 74
Simplex, Ralph, pr. Belvoir, 90
Siriniaco, Peter de, pr. Lenton, 232
Sisserfens, Gilbert of, pr. Redbourn, 124
Sittingbourne, John of, pr. Canterbury, Christ Church, 27
Sixhills, John of, pr. Thornholme, 469
Skegness, Walter of, master Nun Cotham, 593
Skelton, William of, pr. Luffield, 51
Skerne, Adam of, abb. Meaux, 293
Skerne, Robert of, abb. Meaux, 293
Skerning, Roger de, pr. Norwich cath., 55
Skilhare, Hugh, abb. Furness, 282
Skipton, John of, pr. Newburgh, 428
Skirlaw, Joan, prs Swine, 614
Skynnere, Peter le, see Warwick, Peter of
Slade, William atte, abb. Buckfast, 267
Slawston, Arnold of, abb. Owston, 443; pr. Fineshade, 378
Smethcote, John of, abb. Haughmond, 388
Smethe, William, pr. St Carrok, 249
Smyth, John, see Feverer, John
Smytherby, Richard de, pr. Repton, 452
Snoring, John of, pr. Walsingham, 478
Snotbrame, Roger de, pr. Tonbridge, 473
Snow(e), John, abb. Bristol, St Augustine, 348
Snytton, John de, abb. Wendling, 516
Sodbury, Adam of, abb. Glastonbury, 47
Sola, John de, pr. West Ravendale, 517
Soliaco, Peter de, pr. Minting, 178

Somborne, Robert of, archpriest or pr. Barton, 332
Somerby, William of, pr. Launde, 405
Somercotes, Ellen of, prs Legbourne, 579
Somersete, Constance, prs London, St Helen's and Holy Cross, 585
Somersham, Emma of, abbs Chatteris, 553
Somerton, John of, abb. Muchelney, 54
Somerton, Walter of, pr. Binham, 92
Somervill, Agnes de, abbs Polesworth, 599
Somervill, Joan de, abbs Burnham, 547
Sonning, Isabel of, prs Broomhall, 545
Sorel, Roger, pr. Harmondsworth, 165
Sorfrato, Stephen de, see Moysiaco, Stephen de
Sothayk, Robert de, abb. Holm Cultram, 285
Sotherey, Robert de, pr. Westwood, 617
Souef', Robert de, pr. Wootton Wawen, 215
Soulbury, Hugh of, abb. Woburn, 323
Souldrop, William of, pr. Caldwell, 355
South Creake, Thomas of, abb. North Creake, 435
South Malling, Ralph of, pr. Bilsington, 336
Southam, John de, pr. Arbury, 329
Southam, Thomas (of), abb. Burton, 26
Southber, John de, abb. Stanley, 310
Southfleet, Robert of, pr. Felixstowe, 102; pr. Rochester, 62
Southfleet, Thomas of, see Wouldham, Thomas de
Southwark, Thomas of, pr. Southwark, 460
Southwell, Richard of, abb. Welbeck, 514
Spalding, Robert of, abb. Welbeck, 515
Spalding, Robert of, master Swine, 614
Spalding, Thomas of, see Nassington, Thomas of
Spalding, Thomas of, abb. Sawtry, 308
Spalding, Thomas of, pr. Kyme, 402
Spalding, Thomas of (?another), pr. Kyme, 402
Spalding, William of, abb. Bourne, 341
Spalding, William of, pr. Fineshade, 380
Spalding, William of, pr. Kyme, 402
Spaldwick, William of, abb. Colchester, 34
Sparsholt, Henry of, abb. Newenham, 296
Sparsholt, Henry of, abb. Titchfield, 511
Sparowe, Richard, pr. Watton, 530
Speeton, John of, master Arden, 540
Speldhurst, John of, pr. Rochester, 62
Spenser, Joan (le), prs Rowney, 602
Sperry, John dictus, minister Knaresborough, 533
Spicer, Thomas, pr. Bradenstoke, 342
Spigurnel, Alice, prs Markyate, 587
Spilsby, Simon of, abb. Revesby, 301
Spinallo, Baldwin de, pr. Lapley, 172
Spine, Matilda (de), abbs Winchester, 621
Spixworth, William of, pr. Buckenham, 351
Spofford, John, minister Knaresborough, 533

Spofforth, Robert of, pr. Healaugh Park, 389
Spondon, William of, pr. Ulverscroft, 476
Sporle, John de, [Sporle], 193
Spynys, Isabel (de), prs Wilberfoss, 619
Squyer, Le, Gervase, see A(r)miger, Gervase
Stafford, Gregory of, [Breadsall], 343
Stafford, John of, abb. Burton, 25
Stafford, Katherine of, prs Nuneaton, 596
Stainby, Robert of, master Sempringham, 527
Staines, John of, minister Hounslow, 533
Stainton, Amabilia of, prs Nun Cotham, 593
Stainton, John of, abb. Blanchland, 495
Stainton, Stephen of, abb. Roche, 304
Stainton, William of, pr. Monk Bretton, 53
    see also Staynton; Steynton
Stakedern (Stakedorn), John de, pr. Beadlow, 90; pr. Belvoir, 91
Stakes, Richard de, pr. Southwark, 461
Stalbridge, Hugh of, abb. Sherbourne, 68
Stallington, John of, pr. Stone, 464
Stamford, Geoffrey of, abb. Wardon, 320
Stamford, Henry of, pr. Finchale, 103
Stamford, Petronilla of, prs Stamford, St Mary and St Michael, 609
Stamford, Richard of, abb. Thorney, 74; pr. Deeping, 96
Stamford, Robert of, abb. Owston, 443
Stamford, Robert of, pr. Huntingdon, 394
Stamford, Robert of, pr. Newstead by Stamford, 433
Stamford, Thomas of, pr. Stamford, St Mary and St Michael, 610
Stamford, Thomas of (?the same), pr. Stamford, St Mary and St Michael, 610
Stamford, William of, abb. Eynsham, 44
Standish, Reginald of, pr. Ewenny, 100
Standon, Walter of, pr. Beadlow, 89
Stanebrigg, Joan (de), prs Markyate, 587
Stanford, Stephen de, pr. Fineshade, 378
Stanford, William de, pr. Hurley, 113
Stangrief, Thomas, ? abb. Rievaulx, 302 n.25
Stanham, alias of Whitby, Ralph de, pr. Wymondham, 135
Stanhope, Roger of, pr. Lytham, 120
Stanlake, William of, abb. Dunkeswell, 277
Stanle, Nicholas de, pr. Boxgrove, 147
Stanlegh(e), Adam de, abb. Rewley, 301
Stanleghe, John de, pr. Pilton, 124
Stanley, Elizabeth, prs Derby, Kingsmead, 557
Stanleye, Paul de, pr. Warwick, 481
Stanmer, Walter de, pr. Castle Acre, 224
Stansfield, Laurence of, pr. Barnwell, 330

Stansted, Walter of, pr. Blythburgh, 338

Stanton, Fulk de, pr. Barnwell, 331

Stanton, Isabel de, prs Blackborough, 543

Stanton, John de, abb. Blanchland, 495

Stapenhulle, John de, *see* Burton, John of

Stapleton (Stapelton), Emma of, prs Keldholme, 574–5

Stapleton, John of, abb. Wigmore, 485

Stapleton, Thomas of, abb. Bardney, 21

Stapleton, William of, pr. Newburgh, 428

Staunford(e), Alan de, abb. Alnwick, 491

Staunford, Richard (de), pr. St Denys, 455

Staunford, Walter de, pr.-el. Launde, 406

Staunford, William of, *see* Dover, William of

Staunton, Adam of, abb. Gloucester, 48

Staunton, Henry of, pr. Little Malvern, 119

Staunton, Robert of, pr. Newstead-on-Ancholme, 526

Staunton, Robert of, pr. Repton, 452

Staverton, John of, pr. Daventry, 226

Staverton, Richard of, pr. Catesby, 552

Staynton, Elizabeth de, ?prs Kirklees, 577
  see also Stainton; Steynton

Stelharde, John, abb. Netley, 296

Stephen, abb. Beauchief, 493

Stephen, abb. Buckfast, 267

Stephen, abb. Buildwas, 268

Stephen, abb. Coggeshall, 272

Stephen, abb. Dieulacres, 276

Stephen, abb. Hulton, 286

Stephen, abb. Langdon, 505

Stephen, abb. Netley, 296

Stephen, abb. Vale Royal, 318

Stephen, pr. Alberbury, 255

Stephen, pr. Appuldurcombe, 141

Stephen, pr. Berden, 333

Stephen, pr. Brimpsfield, 148

Stephen, pr. Burtle, 352

Stephen, pr. Combwell, 371

Stephen, pr. Derby, St James, 227

Stephen, pr. Exeter, St James, 228

Stephen, pr. Great Bricett, 383

Stephen, pr. Grosmont, 257

Stephen, pr. Hatfield Regis, 165

Stephen, pr. Hayling, 167

Stephen, pr. Horsley, 170, 392

Stephen, pr. Leeds, 407

Stephen, pr. Lewes, 233

Stephen, pr. Llanthony Prima, 413

Stephen, pr. Lytham (occ. *c.* 1259 x 62), 119

Stephen, pr. Lytham (occ. 1272), 119

Stephen, pr. Minting, 178

Stephen, pr. Modbury, 179

Stephen, pr. Monkton Farleigh, 237

Stephen, pr. Mottisfont, 425

Stephen, pr. Newnham, 430

Stephen, pr. Nostell, 438

Stephen, pr. Pontefract, 246

Stephen, pr. Pynham by Arundel, 449

Stephen, pr. Sandaleford, 457

Stephen, pr. Southwark, 460

Stephen, pr. Sporle, 193

Stephen, pr. Thetford, St Mary, 251

Stephen, pr. Winchester, St Swithun, 82

Stephen, pr. York, Holy Trinity, 216

Sterteforde, William, ? pr. Thremhall, 471 n.44

Steveinheth, Hugh de, pr. Little Dunmow, 412

Stevenage, John of, pr. Wymondham, 136

Stevens, Nicholas, abb. Shrewsbury, 70

Steventon, William of, pr. Wallingford, 134

Stevington, William de, ? pr. Belvoir, 91

Steynton, William de, abb. Thame, 315

Stichill, Robert of, pr. Finchale, 103

Stillington, Robert of, pr. Marton, 421

Stixwould, Geoffrey of, master Stixwould, 611

Stockingford, Thomas of, pr. Daventry, 226

Stockport, Alice of, prs Chester, 554

Stockton, Jocelin of, pr.-el. Bushmead, 353

Stockton, Richard of, pr. Bushmead, 353

Stockton, Walter of, pr. Norwich, St Leonard, 122
  see also Stocton

Stockwell, Emma of, prs Wallingwells, 616

Stocton, J. de, pr. Kings Lynn, 116

Stocton, Thomas de, pr. Bath, 21
  see also Stockton

Stok', Robert de, abb. Woburn, 323

Stoke, Amice de, prs Stamford, St Mary and St Michael, 609

Stoke, John of, pr. Alnesbourn, 327

Stoke, Henry de, abb. Lilleshall, 411

Stok(e), Stephen de, pr. Wilsford, 212

Stoke, Thomas de, abb. Tewkesbury, 74

Stoke, Walter of, *custos* Sinningthwaite, 607

Stoke(s), William de, abb. Milton, 52

Stokes, Philippa de, abbs Romsey, 601

Stokes, Richard, pr. Bradley, 343

Stokes, Thomas de, pr. Bristol, St James, 94

Stokes, Walter de, abb. Abbotsbury, 16

Stokes, Walter de, pr. Breedon, 345

Stokes, William de, pr. Stamford, St Mary and St Michael, 610

Stokeys, Robert de, pr. Folkestone, 160

Ston(e), James de, of Oxney, pr. Dover, 98

Stone, John de la, abb. Stanley, 310

Stonegrave, John of, abb. Whitby, 79
Stonegrave, Thomas of, abb. Rufford, 305
Stonegrave, Thomas of, custodian Arthington, 540
Stonegrave, Thomas of, pr. Richmond, 125
Stoneham, Robert of, pr. St Denys, 455
Stonham, Margery of, prs Flixton, 561
Stonor, Joan of, prs Little Marlow, 581
Stopsley, John of, pr. Beadlow, 90
Storey, John, abb. St Osyth, 457
Storm, Simon, see Wyneton, Simon de
Stormy, Nicholas, pr. Flanesford, 380
Stortford, John of, pr. Thremhall, 471
Stortford, Mary of, prs London, Haliwell, 584
Stotfold, Walter of, pr. Clattercote, 522
Stour, John of, abb. Athelney, 19
Stowe, Edmund de, pr.-el. Dodnash, 374
Stowe, John de, pr. Stonely, 465
Stowe, John de, pr. Westacre, 483
Stowell, John, pr. Ewenny, 100
Straddel, Richard, see Madeley, Richard of
Stradull, John de, pr. Cranborne, 96
Straforde, Sarah de, prs Bungay, 547
Stratford, Alexander of, pr. Butley, 354
Stratford, Benedict of, abb. Coggeshall, 272
Stratford, Thomas (of), pr. Caldwell, 355
Stratford, William de, abb. Egglestone, 502
Stratton, John of, pr. Kings Lynn, 116
Stratton, John de, pr. Minster, 177
Stratton, Walter de, pr. Cold Norton, 370
Stratton, William, abb. Thame, 315
Straule, Cecily de, prs Grace Dieu, 566
Streatley, Agnes of, abbs Godstow, 563
Strenes, John de, pr. Deerhurst, 155
Strete, John, abb. St Radegund, 509
Strete, Robert de, pr. Monkton Farleigh, 238
Stretehende, Nicholas atte, pr. Stafford, 463
Stretford, Henry de, pr. Charley, 363
Stretton, Mary of, prs Grace Dieu, 565
Stretton, Richard of, pr. Alberbury, 255
Strumpeshagh, John de, abb. Langley, 505
Stukele(e), Thomas, abb. Colchester, 35
Stukeley, Henry of, pr. Wymondham, 136
Stukeley, Hugh of, abb.-el. St Albans, 64
Stures, Isabel de, prs Littlemore, 582
Sturminster, Nicholas of, pr. Christchurch (Twynham), 365–6
Sturmy, Robert, [Minster], 176
Sturte, John de la, pr. Plympton, 448
Stuston, Agnes of, prs Redlingfield, 600
Suberi, William, ? de, pr. Blythburgh, 338
Subiria, Adam de, pr. Wilsford, 211
Suche, John la, pr. Studley, 466

Sudburia, Richard de, see Kedyngton, Richard de
Sudbury, Richard of, pr. Earls Colne, 99
Sudlee, Isabel de, prs Nuneaton, 596
Suessione, James de, pr. Folkestone, 160
Suffred, pr. Wetheral, 134
Suham, W. de, abb. Combe, 272
Suharde, Mary, prs Stratford-at-Bow, 612
Sulgrave, Hugh of, abb. Ramsey, 59; pr. St Ives, 128
Sulleye, Amice de, abbs Romsey, 600
Sully, Margaret, prs Langley, 579
Sumery, Alice de, prs Cheshunt, 554
Surlingham, John of, pr. Herringfleet, 390
Susanna, prs Baysdale, 542
Susanne, Richard, pr. Alnesbourn, 327
Sussebury, John de, see Tyssebury, John de
Sussex, Elizabeth of, prs Holystone, 573
Suthayk, William de, pr. Lanercost, 403
Suthil, John, abb. Winchester, Hyde, 81
Suthrey, Stephen de, pr. Belvoir, 92
Sutterby, Thomas of, abb. Humberston, 49
Sutterby, William of, abb. Humberston, 49
Sutton, Adam of, alias Winton, pr. Thurgarton, 471
Sutton, Agatha of, see Dutton, Agatha of
Sutton, Agatha of, prs Nuneaton, 596
Sutton, Agnes of, prs Nuneaton, 596
Sutton, Alexander of, pr. Oxford, St Frideswide, 444
Sutton, Basilia of, prs Barrow Gurney, 542
Sutton, Cecily of, prs Nuneaton, 595
Sutton, Hamo of, pr. Lincoln, St Katharine, 524
Sutton, Henry, pr. Fineshade, 380
Sutton, John of, abb. Abingdon, 17
Sutton, John of, abb. Dorchester, 375
Sutton, John of, abb. Reading, 61
Sutton, Jolenta (Jolenda) of, abbs Barking, 541
Sutton, Katharine (of), abbs Barking, 541
Sutton, Richard of, abb. Barlings, 492
Sutton, Robert of, abb. Peterborough, 58
Sutton, Robert of, pr. Bath, 22
Sutton, Robert of, pr. Dunster, 99
Sutton, Simon of, pr. Repton, 452
Sutton, Thomas of, abb. Welbeck, 515
Sutton, Thomas of, pr. St Bees, 127
Sutton, William of, abb. Osney, 441
Sutton, William of, abb. Reading, 61
Suwell, Richard de, abb. Cerne, 31
Swaffham, John of, pr. Ixworth, 398
Swaffham, John, pr. Little Dunmow, 413
Swaffham, John of, pr. Westacre, 483
Swaffham, Olive of, prs Crabhouse, 556

Swaleclif, Margaret de, prs Heynings, 570
Swarby, Nicholas of, pr.-el. Kyme, 402
Swavesey, Geoffrey de, pr. Minster, 176
Sweethope, Joan of, prs Lambley, 578
Swenington, Thomas de, *see* Carlemle, Thomas de
Sweyn, Clemencia, prs Studley, 612
Swillington, Elizabeth of, prs Stixwould, 611
Swineshead, John of, abb. Keynsham, 400
Swineshead, John of, abb. Wigmore, 485
Swineshead, William of, abb. Swineshead, 315
Swinstead, William, abb.-el. Bourne, 341
Swyndone, Margery de, prs Polsloe, 599
Swynford, Elizabeth, prs Catesby, 552
Swynnerton, Alice of, prs Brewood Black Ladies, 544
Sydemanton, John, abb. Titchfield, 511
Symunds, William, pr. Carmarthen, 361
Synartcleus, Thomas de, pr. Northampton, St Andrew, 245
Syret', Joan de, prs Markyate, 587
Syvington, Richard de, ?pr. Shouldham, 529 n.5
Sywell, Juliana of, prs Sewardsley, 604

T., abb. Hartland, 386
T., master Wykeham, 625
T., pr. Breedon, 345
T., pr. Conishead, 371
T., pr. Sixhills, 529
T., pr. York, Holy Trinity, 216
Tablere, Matilda la, abbs Canonsleigh, 549
Tachbrook, Thomas of, pr. Fineshade, 378
Tadeshale, Philip de, pr. Mountjoy, 427
Takeley, John of, pr. Thremhall, 471
Talaya, William de, pr. Newton Longville, 243
Talbot, John, pr. Combwell, 371
Taleboth, John, pr. Bentley, 333
Talkan, Thomas de, abb. Holm Cultram, 285
Tanfield, William of, master Jarrow, 114; pr. Durham, 39
Tanfield, William of, pr. Bolton, 340
Tanfield, William of, pr. Rumburgh, 126
Tanfield, William of, junior, pr. Richmond, 125
Tanfield I, William of, pr. Wetheral, 134
Tanfield II, William of, pr. Wetheral, 135
Tang, Robert de, custodian Arthington, 540
Tannere, William, pr. Burtle, 352
Tannione, John de, pr. Lapley, 172
Tarente, Nicholas de, pr. Winchester, St Swithun, 84
Targe, Hugh, pr. Horsham St Faith, 169
Tatyrsal, Alice de, prs Langley, 578
Taunton, John of, abb. Glastonbury, 46

Taunton, John, pr. Barlinch, 330
Taunton, Simon of, pr. Tynemouth, 132
Taunton, Thomas of, pr. Little Dunmow, 412
Taunton, Walter of, abb. Glastonbury, 47
Taunton, William of, abb. Milton, 52
Taunton, William of, pr. Winchester, St Swithun, 83
Taurin, pr. Wootton Wawen, 214
Taymer, Walter, pr. Carmarthen, 361
Tealby, William of, abb. Newhouse, 508
Teesdale, Henry of, pr. Finchale, 103
Teingterer, William, pr. Launceston, 404
Telonio, Peter de, *see* Tenolio, Peter de
Templo, Richard de, pr. London, Holy Trinity, Aldgate, 415
Temvile, Richard, pr. Stratfield Saye, 196
Tendring, Alice de, abbs Malling, 586
Tenhaer, abb. Valle Crucis, 318
Tenolio (Telonio, Tenoleo, Tevolio), Peter de, pr. Bermondsey, 222; pr. Monks Horton, 237; pr. Pontefract, 247; [Prittlewell], 249
Terrington, John of, pr. Anglesey, 328
Terry, Margaret, prs Canterbury, Holy Sepulchre, 550
Tetbury, Robert of, abb. Kingswood, 287
Tetsworth, Robert of, abb. Thame, 315
Teuren, Laurence, abb. Dale, 499
Tevolio, Peter de, *see* Tenolio, Peter de
Tewing, Adam of, pr. Tynemouth, 132
Tewing, Richard of, pr. Tynemouth, 132
Tewkesbury, John of, pr. Ewenny, 100
Tewkesbury, William of, pr. Cold Norton, 370
Textor, Peter, *alias* Aneslevilla, pr. Blyth, 146
Teyngiis, John de, pr. Lewes, 234
Thame, John of, abb. Notley, 440
Thame, John of, abb. Thame, 315
Thame, Roger of, abb. Abingdon, 17
Thame, Stephen of, abb. Medmenham, 294
Thanet, John of, abb. Battle, 23
Thanington, Simon de, pr. Wallingford, 133
Thaxted, John (of), pr. Bicknacre, 336
Theakston, John of, abb. Egglestone, 502
Thebregg', Roger de, pr. Beadlow, 89
Thebrygge, Margery de, prs Bungay, 547
Thelsford, Richard of, pr. Kenilworth, 399
Thenford, John of, pr. Cold Norton, 370
Thenford, William (de), abb. Missenden, 425
Theobald, pr. Blyth, 145
Theobald, pr. Exeter, St James, 228
Theobald, pr. Hurley, 113
Theobald, pr. Stansgate, 251
Theobald, pr. Tywardreath, 204

Theobald, pr. York, Holy Trinity, 217

Theodore, pr. St Cross, 188

Theodoric, *procurator* Lewisham, 173

Theovill, Thomas de, pr. Northampton, St Andrew, 243

Thetford, John of, pr. Thetford, Holy Sepulchre, 468

Thetford, Robert of, pr. Thetford, Holy Sepulchre, 468

Thetford, Thomas of, pr. St Clears, 250

Theydon, Reginald of, pr. Bicknacre, 335

Thifford, John de, pr. Much Wenlock, 241; pr. Northampton, St Andrew, 244; *see also* Avignon; Chartres; Tickford

Thirkleby, John Topcliff of, *see* Topcliff, John

Thirsk, John of, pr. Marton, 420

Thirsk, John of, pr. Newburgh, 429

Thockrington, Thomas of, abb. Pipewell, 299

Thokeby, Nicholas de, *alias* Kesteven, abb. Combermere, 274

Thoky, John, abb. Gloucester, 48

Thomas, abb. Alnwick, 491

Thomas, abb. Bayham, 493

Thomas, abb. Biddlesden, 261

Thomas, abb. Bordesley, 265

Thomas, abb. Bruern (occ. 1230 x 43), 266

Thomas, abb. Bruern (occ. 1320 x 28), 266

Thomas, abb. Buckland, 268

Thomas, abb. Byland, 270

Thomas, abb. Cockersand (occ. 1286 x 8), 496

Thomas, abb. Cockersand (occ. 1305 x 7), 496

Thomas, abb. Coggeshall, 272

Thomas, abb. Combermere, 273

Thomas, abb. Coverham, 497

Thomas, ?abb. Croxton Kerrial, 498 nn. 10–11

Thomas, abb. Dorchester, 375

Thomas, abb. Dunkeswell, 277

Thomas, abb. Durford, 500

Thomas, abb. Easby, 501

Thomas, abb. Egglestone, 502

Thomas, abb. Forde (occ. 1258), 278

Thomas, abb. Forde (occ. 1301), 279

Thomas, abb. Hailes (occ. 1345 x 6), 284

Thomas, abb. Hailes (1354–), 284

Thomas, abb. Hartland, 386

Thomas, abb. Jervaulx (occ. 1218 x 21), 286

Thomas, abb. Jervaulx (occ. 1258 x 66), 286

Thomas, abb. Jervaulx (occ. 1279 x 80), 286

Thomas, abb. Keynsham, 400

Thomas, abb. Kingswood, 287

Thomas, abb. Kirkstead (1313–), 290

Thomas, abb. Kirkstead (occ. 1354), 290

Thomas, abb. Kirkstead (occ. 1404), 290

Thomas, abb. Langley, 505

Thomas, abb. Margam, 292

Thomas, abb. Merevale, 295

Thomas, abb. Neath, 295

Thomas, abb. Newhouse (occ. 1242), 507

Thomas, abb. Newhouse (occ. 1267 x 75), 507

Thomas, abb. Northampton, St James, 436

Thomas, abb. Pipewell, 300

Thomas, abb. Rewley, 301

Thomas, abb. Rievaulx (1286/7–), 302

Thomas, abb. Rievaulx (occ. 1314 x 15), 302

Thomas, abb. Robertsbridge, 303

Thomas, abb. Rufford (occ. 1350), 306

Thomas, abb. Rufford (1366–), 306

Thomas, abb. St Osyth, 457

Thomas, abb. Shrewsbury, 70

Thomas, abb. Swineshead, 314

Thomas, abb. Tupholme (occ. 1276 x 89), 513

Thomas, abb. Tupholme (occ. 1354), 513

Thomas, abb. Valle Crucis, 318

Thomas, abb. Vaudey, 319

Thomas, abb. Walden (occ. 1236), 77

Thomas, abb. Walden (–1270), 77

Thomas, abb. Wardon, 320

Thomas, abb. Winchcombe, 80

Thomas, pr. Alvecote, 89

Thomas, pr. Alvingham (occ. 1218), 519

Thomas, pr. Alvingham (occ. 1307), 519

Tho(mas), pr. Amesbury, 538

Thomas, pr. Arbury, 329

Thomas, pr. Beadlow, 90

Thomas, pr. Beeston, 333

Thomas, pr. Blackmore, 338

Thomas, pr. Blythburgh, 338

Thomas, pr. Bolton, 339

Thomas, pr. Boxgrove, 146

Thomas, pr. Breamore, 344

Thomas, pr. Bridlington, 346

Thomas, pr. Butley, 354

Thomas, pr. Canterbury, St Gregory (–?1241), 358

Thomas, pr. Canterbury, St Gregory (occ. 1340), 358

Thomas, pr. Canwell, 30

Thomas, pr. Carmarthen, 360

Thomas, pr. Castle Acre, 225

Thomas, pr. Catley, 521

Thomas, pr. Chacombe, 362

Thomas, pr. Chicksands, 521

Thomas, pr. Clatford, 151

Thomas, pr. Cowick, 153

Thomas, pr. Coxford, 372
Thomas, pr. Ewyas Harold, 100
Thomas, pr. Gloucester, St Oswald, 382
Thomas, pr. Hagnaby, 502
Thomas, pr. Hastings, 386
Thomas, pr. Hatfield Regis, 166
Thomas, pr. Haverholme, 523
Thomas, pr. Hinton (occ. mid/late 13th cent.), 325
Thomas, pr. Hinton (occ. 1343), 325
Thomas, pr. Holy Island, 110
Thomas, pr. Hurley, 113
Thomas, pr. Ipplepen, 395
Thomas, pr. Ipswich, Holy Trinity, 396
Thomas, pr. Ivychurch, 397
Thomas, pr. Kilpeck, 115
Thomas, pr. Lanercost, 403
Thomas, pr. Llangennith, 175
Thomas, pr. Llanthony Prima, 413
Thomas, pr. Leominster, 116
Thomas, pr. Lytham, 119
Thomas, pr. Marlborough, 525
Thomas, pr. Monkton Farleigh (occ. 1248), 237
Thomas, pr. Monkton Farleigh (occ. 1318), 238
Thomas, pr. Mountjoy, 427
Thomas, pr. Newark, 427
Thomas, pr. North Ormsby (occ. 1218/19), 526
Thomas, pr. North Ormsby (occ. 1245/6 x 50), 526
Thomas, pr. Northampton, St Andrew, 245
Thomas, pr. Orford, 597
Thomas, pr. Peterstone, 447
Thomas, pr. Poughley, 449
Thomas, pr. Pynham by Arundel, 449
Thomas, pr. Ranton, 450
Thomas, pr. Royston (occ. 1302 x 5), 454
Thomas, pr. Royston (occ. 1346), 454
Thomas, pr. Sandaleford, 457
Thomas, pr. Sandwell, 66
Thomas, pr. Sempringham, 528
Thomas, pr. Shouldham (occ. 1233 x 4), 529
Thomas, pr. Shouldham (occ. 1292), 529
Thomas, pr. Sixhills, 530
Thomas, pr. Snape, 128
Thomas, pr. Stafford, 463
Thomas, pr. Tandridge, 466
Thomas, pr. Thetford, St Mary, 251
Thomas, pr. Thoby, 468
Thomas, pr. Ulverscroft, 476
Thomas, pr. Wallingford, 133
Thomas, pr. Warter, 479
Thomas, pr. Warwick, 480
Thomas, pr. Wetheral (occ. 1203 x 14), 134
Thomas, pr. Wetheral (occ. 1241), 134

Thomas, pr. Weybourne, 484
Thomas, pr. Winterborn Monkton, 254
Thomas, pr. Witham, 326
Thomas, ?pr. Woodbridge, 486 n. 50
Thomas, pr. Woodspring, 487
Thomas, pr. Worcester, 85
Thomas *medicus*, pr. Wymondham, 135
Thomasina, prs Broadholme, 545
T(h)ompson, Joan, prs Orford, 597
Thompson, John of, pr. Mendham, 236
Thonoile, William de, [Northampton, St Andrew], 245
Thoralby, William of, pr. Carham, 359
Thoriaco, Thomas de, pr. Minting, 178
Thorley, Jolan of, pr. Barnwell, 330
Thornber, John de, abb. Biddlesden, 262
Thornberg(e), William de, pr. Bicester, 334
Thornbergh, John de, abb. Kirkstall, 289
Thornborough, William of, abb. Biddlesden, 262
Thorne, Joan de, prs Nun Cotham, 593
Thorne, Nicholas, abb. Canterbury, St Augustine, 29
Thorne, William atte, pr. Canterbury, St Gregory, 358
Thorney, John (de), abb. Titchfield, 512
Thornford, John of, abb. Sherborne, 69
Thornham, David de, *see* Fornham, David de
Thornham, John of, pr. Coxford, 373
Thornham, Michael of, pr. Wormegay, 488
Thornham, Thomas of, pr. Dodnash, 375
Thornham, William of, pr. Letheringham, 410
Thornhaugh, Henry de, pr. Torksey, 474
Thornton, Isabel of, prs Gokewell, 564
Thornton, J. of, abb. Newminster, 298
Thornton, Richard of, abb. Meaux, 293
Thornton, Richard, abb. Whalley (Stanlow), 322
Thornton, Richard of, pr. Elsham, 378
Thornton, Robert, abb. Fountains, 280
Thornton, Robert of, abb. Newhouse, 508
Thornton, Thomas of, abb. Woburn, 324
Thornton, William de, [Scarborough], 308 n. 33
Thornton, William of, pr. Henes and Sandtoft, 107
Thorp, Alice de, prs Nun Monkton, 595
Thorp, Robert de, abb. Garendon, 283
Thorpe, Edmund (of), pr. Chacombe, 362
Thorpe, Isabel de, abbs Northampton, De La Pré, 591
Thorpe, John de, abb. Wellow, 483
Thorpe, John of, pr. Coxford, 373
Thorpe, John of, pr. Warter, 480
Thorpe, John of, pr. Wetheral, 134

Thorpe, William of, abb. Northampton, St James, 437

Thorpe, William of, abb. Tupholme, 513

Thorpe, William of, pr. Newnham, 430

Thorveston, Robert de, pr. Oxford, St Frideswide, 444

Threxton, Ralph of, pr. Bromehill, 349

Throuncton, Robert de, pr. Brinkburn, 347

Throwley, William of, abb. Canterbury, St Augustine, 30

Thudden, William de, pr.-el. Winchester, St Swithun, 84

Thurgarton, Alexander of, [Thurgarton], 472 n. 45

Thurgarton, Richard of, pr. Thurgarton, 472

Thurgarton, William of, pr. Newstead (in Sherwood), 432

Thurlaston, Ralph of, pr. Mottisfont, 426

Thurlby, Peter of, pr. Nocton Park, 433

Thurston, Roger of, pr. Hoxne, 112

Thurverton, Roger de, abb. Newbo, 507

Thweng, Isabel, prs Nunburnholme, 595

Thwing, Adam of, pr. Lincoln, St Mary Magdalen, 118

Thwing, John of, pr. Bridlington (afterwards St John of Bridlington), 346

Tibenham, John of, pr. Herringfleet, 390

Tichborne, Mabel of, abbs Wherwell, 617

Tickford, John of, see Chartres, John de

Tickhill, John of, master Jarrow, 115; pr. Finchale, 104

Tickhill, John of, pr. Worksop, 487

Tickhill, Roger of, pr. Marton, 420

Ticknall, Ralph of, pr. Repton, 452

Tidcombe, Thomas of, pr. Maiden Bradley, 419

Tidmarsh, Lucy of, prs Goring, 565

Tierry, Michael, [Cammeringham], 495

Tilletai, Adam de, abb. Rievaulx, 302

Tilney, Christiana of, prs Crabhouse, 556

Tilney, Paul of, abb. West Dereham, 516

Tilshead, John of, pr. Maiden Bradley, 418

Tilton, John of, abb. Croxden, 275

Timberdene, Walter de, pr. Reigate, 451

Timberland, John of, pr. Kyme, 402

Tiney, John, pr. Stone, 464

Tintern, John of, abb. Malmesbury, 51

Titchfield, John of, minister Easton, 532

Titchmarsh, Joan of, prs Hinchingbrooke, 572

Titchmarsh, Matilda of, prs Harrold, 569

Tittleshall, Thomas of, abb. Wendling, 516

Todeni, Walter de, see Senteney, Walter de

Toft, Roger of, pr. Kyme, 402

Tofts, John of, pr. Weybridge, 484

Toky, John, pr. Bromfield, 95

Toky, Richard, pr. Hereford, 109

Tolberton, William de, pr. Rumburgh, 126

Toller, Henry (of), abb. Abbotsbury, 16

Tolleshunt, William of, abb. Coggeshall, 272

Tondre, William, pr. Dunster, 99

Tonford, Cecily (de), prs Canterbury, Holy Sepulchre, 550

Tonge, Richard, master Woodkirk, 486

Tonnelier, John le, pr. Wootton Wawen, 215

Tonolio, William de, pr. Newton Longville, 243

Tooting, John of, pr. London, Holy Trinity, Aldgate, 415

Topcliff, John, of Thirkleby, abb. Kirkstall, 287

Topcliffe, Robert of, abb. Whalley, 322

Tordousta (?), William de, pr. Otterton, 185

Torksey, John of, pr. Elsham, 378

Torksey, Robert of, abb. St Benet of Hulme, 65

Torksey, William of, abb. Bardney, 20

Torniaco, Peter de, pr. Deerhurst, 155

Torrington, Agnes of, prs Stainfield, 607

Tothale, John de, pr. Hurley, 114

Toto, Ralph de, pr. Blyth, 146

Toton, William of, pr. Felley, 379
   see also Totton

Tottington, Thomas of, abb. Bury St Edmunds, 27

Totton, Richard, pr. Pilton, 124
   see also Toton

Touchet, Joan, prs Derby, Kingsmead, 557

Toucotes, Joan de, prs Moxby, 589

Tour, William de, [Frampton], 161

Tours, Richard (de), abb. Leicester, 408

Toursey, Henry, abb. Thame, 315

Towcester, Ralph of, pr. Brooke, 350

Towthorpe, William of, pr. Lincoln, St Mary Magdalen, 118; pr. Rumburgh, 126

Tracy, Margery, abbs Godstow, 563

Trawers, Thomas, pr. Conishead, 372

Trediddan, Stephen, pr. Launceston, 405

Tregony, Nicholas (of), pr. Merton, 422

Tregony, Richard of, pr. Plympton, 448

Trembliaco, Robert de, pr. Deerhurst, 155

Trenchfoil, Philip, abb. Tavistock, 72

Treskelly, William (de), pr. St Germans, 456

Trewvineke, Henry de, pr. Canonsleigh, 357

Tribus Montibus, William de, pr. Wilsford, 212

Triffour, Hugh, pr. Nocton Park, 434

Trilley, Nicholas, pr. Llanthony Prima, 413

Tring, Matthew of, abb. Missenden, 424

Troarn, Christian of, pr. St Neots, 191

Troarn, James de, pr. Frampton, 161

Troies, William, pr. St Clears, 250

Tronolio, William de, pr. Newton Longville, 243

Troston, Thomas of, pr. Woodbridge, 486

Truard, William de, pr. Tutbury, 203

Trumpington, William of, abb. St Albans, 63

Trungey, Adam de, pr. Hinckley, 168

Truno, Ralph de, pr. Lancaster, 171

Truwerd, Robert, pr. Modbury, 179

Trygal, Sam(p)son, pr. Appuldurcombe, 141; pr. Loders, 176

Tryquet, Thomas, [West Ravendale], 518

Tubonour/Cerboneur, Peter le, pr. Brimpsfield, 148

Tud(d)enham, Richard, pr. Stratfield Saye, 197

Tuddington, Henry of, abb. Winchcombe, 80
    see also Tudyngton

Tudor, abb. Conway, 275

Tudyngton, John de, pr. Hickling, 392
    see also Tuddington

Tunstall, John, pr. Pontefract, 247

Tunstall, Laurence of, pr. Kings Lynn, 116; pr. Yarmouth, 137

Turpitone, Richard de, abb. Wigmore, 485

Turre, Iterus dictus de, pr. Minting, 178

Turvill, Cecily de, prs Little Marlow, 581

Turville, Agnes de, prs Farewell, 560

Tutbury, Henry of, pr. Rumburgh, 125; pr. Wetheral, 134

Tutbury, Katherine of, prs Harrold, 569

Tuttington, William of, pr. Bromholm, 223

Tuyn, pr. Exeter, St James, 228

Twangham, Jordan of, abb. Combe, 273

Twentiman (Twentyman), Robert, see Gisburn(e), Robert de

Twye, William de, pr. Cold Norton, 370

Twyford, John of, abb. Bordesley, 264

Twyford, Margaret of, prs Grace Dieu, 566

Twyford, Richard of, abb. Croxden, 275

Tybout, Vincent, pr. Stogursey, 194

Tycehurst, Roger of, pr. Combwell, 371

Tyddesbury, Roger de, pr. Birkenhead, 24

Tyddesbury, Thomas de, pr. Birkenhead, 23

Tydnesouere, Thomas de, pr. Stafford, 463

Tydolveshyde, William de, pr. Christchurch (Twynham), 366

Tyenloy, Hugh de, pr. Weedon Lois, 209

Tymy, Thomas, pr. Cogges, 152

Tymy, Thomas, pr. Monmouth, 182

Tynemouth, Roger of, pr. Lytham, 120; pr. Stamford, St Leonard, 130

Tynghurst, William de, abb. Stanley, 310

Tyntenhull, Thomas, pr. Holme East, 229

Tynton, William de, abb. Tupholme, 514

Tyrewache, William (de), pr. Christchurch (Twynham), 366

Tyringham, Thomas de, pr. Leonard Stanley, 117

Tyrry, William, alias Bruges, abb. Buildwas, 269

Tysoe, William of, abb. Stoneleigh, 311

Tyssebury, John de, alias Sussebury, pr. Breamore, 344

Tytelesworth, Ellen de, prs Bungay, 547

Tythby, Richard of, pr. Shelford, 459

Tywe, Henry de, pr. Ranton, 450

Uddewin, Ralph, pr. Otterton, 185

Ufford, Amabilia of, prs Norwich (Carrow), 591

Ulcombe, Robert of, pr. Dover, 97

Ulleswik, Isabel de, prs Hinchingbrooke, 572

Ulrome, Margaret of, prs Yedingham, 626

Ulrome, Roger of, pr. Richmond, 125

Ultra Aquam (Ultra Aqua), Peter de, pr. Carisbrooke, 150; pr. Wareham, 207

Upton, John of, abb. Woburn, 324

Upton, Matilda of, abbs Godstow, 562

Upton, Nicholas of, abb. Eynsham, 44

Upton, Richard of, abb. Kirkstead, 290

Upton, Richard of, pr. Launceston, 404

Upton, Roger of, custos Godstow, 563

Upton, Roger of, pr. Breadsall, 344

Upton, Roger of, pr. Worksop, 488

Upton, William of, abb. Shrewsbury, 70

Usk, John (of), abb. Chertsey, 32

Utterby, John of, abb. Wellow, 482

Utterby, Richard of, abb. Wellow, 482

Utterby, William of, abb.-el. Wellow, 482

V., pr. York, St Andrew, 531

Val Oscul, Thomas de, pr. Carisbrooke, 150

Valentine, abb. Durford, 500

Valentine, pr. Winchester, St Swithun, 83

Valeran, William, pr. Stratfield Saye, 196

Valibus, Hugh de, pr. Burwell, 149
    see also Vallibus

Valle, Hugh de, pr. Astley, 143

Valle, Peter de, pr. Stoke by Clare, 196

Valle, Ralph de, pr. Astley, 143

Valle, Ralph de, pr. Patrixbourne, 446

Valle, Thomas de, pr. Clatford, 151

Vallibus, Bertrand de, pr. Winterborn Monkton, 254

Vallibus, Petronilla de, abbs Wilton, 620
    see also Valibus

Valmont, Ralph (le) Provost of, pr. Stratfield Saye, 196

Valognes, Agnes de, prs Campsey Ash, 548

Valognes, Joan de, prs Campsey Ash, 548
Vanceye, Denis de, pr. Monk Sherborne, 180
Vassal, Alberic, [Beckford and Colsterworth], 332
Vasseur, Peter, pr. Tutbury, 204
Vateman, Richard, pr. Toft Monks, 201; pr.
    Warmington, 208
Vaughan, Llewelyn, abb. Strata Florida, 312
Vaux, John de, pr. Wilmington, 211
Vavasour, William, master Jarrow, 115
Vavassour, Christine la, prs Stainfield, 608
Vavas[s]our, Margaret le, prs Legbourne, 579
Vavasur, William le, pr. Haugham, 167
Veer, Anne de, abbs Barking, 541
Vendagio, John de, pr. Totnes, 202
Ventadour, William of, pr. Thetford, St Mary, 252
Venur, Mabel le, prs Stamford, St Mary and St
    Michael, 609
Verdon, Elizabeth de, prs Marrick, 588
Verduno, William de, see Borden, William of
Veretot, Hugh, pr. Warminghurst, 208
    see also Verretot
Verge, William de, pr. Prittlewell, 247
Verney, William de, pr. Grovebury, 163
Vernon, Emma de, prs Chester, 554
Verny, Roger de, pr. Nuneaton, 597
Verny, William de, pr. Nuneaton, 596
Verrer, Richard le, [Pembroke], 187
Verrer, Richard le (possibly the same as above), pr.
    Winghale, 213
Verretot, Robert de, pr. Avebury, 144
    see also Veretot
Vetolio, John de, pr. Deerhurst, 156
Veulys, Peter de, pr. Hayling, 167
Vignorosi, John, pr. Exeter, St James, 229
Vigor, pr. Cogges, 152
Villa, Jordan de, abb. Thornton Curtis, 469
Villa, Richard de, abb. Thornton Curtis, 469
Villa Nova, Matthew de, pr. Minster Lovell, 177
Villa Nova, Thomas de, see Sancto Marcello,
    Thomas de
Villaribus, Guy de, pr. Astley, 142
Villaribus, Peter de, pr. St Neots, 191
Villiaco, Peter de, pr. Lewes, 234
Villicus, Geoffrey, pr. Tickford, 200
Vincent, pr. Bromholm, 223
Vincent, pr. Goldcliff, 162
Vincent, pr. Redbourn, 124
Vincent, pr. Stogursey, 194
Vincent, pr. Thetford, St Mary, 251
Vinci, John de, pr. Amesbury, 538
Virgo, Roger, pr. Ivychurch, 397
Virgulto, William de, pr. Allerton Mauleverer, 139

Vitalis, pr. Grovebury, 163
Vivacio, John de, pr. Pembroke, 187
Vivian, pr. Haverholme, 522
Vivian, pr. Lincoln, St Katharine, 523
Vivian, pr. North Ormsby, 526
Volant, John (le), pr. St Michael's Mount, 189
Volet, Peter, [Ecclesfield], 157
Vyel, Ralph dictus, pr. St Michael's Mount, 189
Vyoun, John le, pr. Ellingham, 158

W., abb. Basingwerk, 259
W., abb. Boxley, 265
W., abb. Bruern, 266
W., abb. Lessness, 409
W., abb. Rocester, 452
W., abb. Torre, 512
W., abb. Whalley (Stanlow), 322
W., pr. Astley, 142
W., pr. Bradenstoke, 342
W., pr. Bromholm, 223
W., pr. Buckenham, 351
W., pr. Combwell, 371
W., pr. Hagnaby, 502
W., pr. Holy Island, 110
W., pr. Kenilworth, 398
W., pr. Lanercost, 403
W., pr. Stamford, St Leonard, 129
W., pr. Stratfield Saye, 196
W., pr. Swavesey, 197
W(?), pr. Thetford, St Mary, 251
W., pr. Wareham, 207
Wabeton, Stephen de, pr. Leominster, 117
Wackerfield, Robert of, pr. Stamford, St Leonard,
    130
Wade, John, abb. Strata Marcella, 313
Wadington, Peter de, pr. Cold Norton, 370
Wadsworth, Walter of, abb. Roche, 304
Wafre, Mabel la, abbs Godstow, 562
Wainfleet, Robert of, abb. Bardney, 20
Wainfleet, Simon of, abb. Wellow, 482
Wakefield, William of, minister Newcastle upon
    Tyne, 534
Wakerley, Isabel of, prs Wothorpe, 623
Walcher, pr. Lapley, 172
Walda, Guy de, pr. Dover, 97
Walda, Roger de, abb. Easby, 501
Walden, Gilbert of, pr. London, St Bartholomew,
    417
Walden, John de, master St Mary de Pré, 603
Walden, Simon of, pr. Tynemouth, 132
Walden, Simon of (?another), pr. Tynemouth,
    132

Walden, William de, pr. Haverholme, 523
 see also Waleden(e)
Waldia, Richard de, pr. Wymondley, 490
Walecote, Walter de, pr. Penwortham, 123
Waleden(e), Richard de, pr. Hurley, 113
 see also Walden
Waleis, Richard *dictus* le, pr. Kersey, 399
Walenscin(is), Matthew de, master London,
 Clerkenwell, 583
Walensis, John, abb. Malmesbury, 51
 see also Wallensis
Waleran, pr. Allerton Mauleverer, 138
Waleraund, Alice, abbs Romsey, 600
Wales, Thomas of, *see* Cymy, Thomas
Waleys, Ellen de, prs Hinchingbrooke, 572
Waleys, Henry, pr. Brooke, 350
Waleys, William le, pr. Southwark, 460
Walkelin, pr. St Denys, 454
Walkelin, pr. Southwick, 461
Walkelyn, John, pr. Deerhurst, 157
Walkelyn, John, ? pr. Linton and Isleham, 174 n.6
Walk(e)lyn, John, pr. Swavesey, 197
Walker, John, pr. Flanesford, 380
Walkeringham, Emma of, prs Wilberfoss, 619
Walkeringham, Cecily of, prs Swine, 613
Wallensis, John, pr. Morville, 122
 see also Walensis
Walleys, Elizabeth le, prs Sinningthwaite, 606
Wallingford, Amice of, prs Kington St Michael, 576
Wallingford, Christiana of, prs Goring, 564
Wallingford, John (of), pr. Oxford, St Frideswide,
 445
Wallingford, Nicholas of, abb. Burton, 25
Wallingford, Richard of, abb. St Albans, 64
Wallop, Benedict of, pr. Mottisfont, 426
Wallop, John of, pr. Breamore, 344
Wallop, Walter of, pr. Mottisfont, 426
Wallop, William of, abb. Titchfield, 512
Wallyngfeld, John de, abb. Robertsbridge, 303
Walmesford, Hugh de, master Legbourne, 580
Walmsgate, Roger of, pr. Markby, 419
Walone, Isabel, prs Rosedale, 601
Walpole, Alexander of, abb. Sibton, 309
Walpole, Edmund of, abb. Bury St Edmunds, 26
Walrand, abb. Hartland, 386
Walrant, John, pr. Church Gresley, 367
Walsham, Nicholas of, abb. St Benet of Hulme, 65
Walsham, William of, pr. Norwich cath., 55
Walsingham, Alan of, pr. Ely, 41
Walsingham, John of, pr. Hertford, St Mary, 110
Walsingham, Thomas of, pr. Binham, 93
Walter, [Burtle], 352

Walter, ? abb. Abingdon, 17 n.1
Walter, abb. Alnwick (occ. 1245 x 6), 491
Walter, abb. Alnwick (–1362), 491
Walter, abb. Beeleigh, 494
Walter, abb. Biddlesden, 261
Walter, abb. Bindon, 263
Walter, abb. Bordesley, 264
Walter, abb.-el. Bristol, St Augustine, 348
Walter, abb. Bruern, 267
Walter, abb. Buckland, 268
Walter, abb. Byland (occ. 1212 x 17), 269
Walter, abb. Byland (1334–), 270
Walter, abb. Calder, 271
Walter, abb. Durford, 500
Walter, abb. Grace Dieu, 283
Walter, abb. Hagnaby, 503
Walter, abb. Hailes, 284
Walter, abb. Kirkstall (*temp.* Henry III), 288
Walter, abb. Kirkstall (1314–), 289
Walter, abb. Llantarnam, 290
Walter, abb. Newminster (–1217), 298
Walter, abb. Newminster (occ. 1328), 298
Walter, abb. Newminster (occ. 1335 x 37), 298
Walter, abb. Newminster (occ. 1358), 299
Walter, abb. Quarr, 300
Walter, abb. Revesby (occ. 1256 x 73), 301
Walter, abb. Revesby (occ. 1284), 301
Walter, abb. Robertsbridge, 303
Walter, abb. Rocester, 453
Walter, abb. Roche, 304
Walter, abb. Rufford, 305
Walter, abb. St Dogmells, 188
Walter, abb. Salley, 306
Walter, abb. Shap, 509
Walter, abb. Shrewsbury, 69
Walter, abb. Sibton (occ. 1280 x 88), 309
Walter, abb. Sibton (1375–), 309
Walter, abb. Sulby (–1231/2), 510
Walter, abb. Sulby (occ. 1323 x 28), 510
Walter, abb. Sulby (occ. 1348 x 55/6), 510
Walter, abb. Tilty, 316
Walter, abb. Tintern, 317
Walter, abb. Vale Royal (Darnhall), 317
Walter, abb. Vaudey, 319
Walter, abb. West Dereham, 516
Walter, abb. Wigmore, 485
Walter, *custos* Hertford, 532
Walter, master Heynings, 570
Walter, master Newstead by Stamford (1224/5–),
 432
Walter, master Newstead by Stamford (1231/2–),
 432

Walter, master Nun Cotham (occ. 1224 x 35), 593
Walter, master Nun Cotham (−1293), 593
Walter, master Studley, 612
Walter, master Wothorpe, 624
Walter, minister Hounslow, 533
Walter, pr. Beauvale, 325
Walter, pr. Bedemans Berg, 90
Walter, pr. Breamore, 344
Walter, pr. Brecon, 93
Walter, pr. Bristol, St James, 94
Walter, pr. Buckenham, 351
Walter, pr. Bullington, 520
Walter, pr. Burscough, 352
Walter, pr. Butley, 354
Walter, pr. Canterbury, Christ Church, 27
Walter, pr. Canwell, 31
Walter, pr. Chicksands (occ. 1211), 521
Walter, pr. Chicksands (occ. 1298), 521
Walter, pr. Chirbury (? 13th cent.), 364
Walter, pr. Chirbury (occ. 1406), 365
Walter, pr. Church Gresley, 367
Walter, pr. Clattercote, 521
Walter, pr. Cold Norton, 370
Walter, pr. Combwell, 371
Walter, pr. Dudley (occ. early 13th cent.), 227
Walter, pr. Dudley (occ. 1276), 227
Walter, pr. Dunster, 99
Walter, pr. Ely, 40
Walter, pr. Felley, 378
Walter, pr. Gloucester, St Oswald, 381
Walter, pr. Goldcliff, 162
Walter, pr. Great Malvern, 105
Walter, pr. Hamble, 164
Walter, pr. Holme East, 229
Walter, pr. Leighs, 409
Walter, pr. Leominster, 116
Walter, pr. Llanthony Prima (occ. c. 1217 x 27), 413
Walter, pr. Llanthony Prima (occ. 1266 x 67), 413
Walter, pr. Llanthony Prima (occ. 1305 x 14), 413
Walter, pr. Marlborough (occ. 1351), 525
Walter, pr. Marlborough (occ. 1389 x 1403), 525
Walter, pr. Marton, 420
Walter, pr. Mattersey, 526
Walter, pr. Merton, 421
Walter, pr. Mobberley, 425
Walter, pr. Morville, 122
Walter, pr. Newburgh, 428
Walter, pr. Newnham, 430
Walter, pr. Newstead-on-Ancholme, 526
Walter, pr. Northampton, St Andrew, 243
Walter, pr. Nuneaton, 597
Walter, pr. Patrixbourne, 446

Walter, pr. Pontefract (occ. 1219), 246
Walter, pr. Pontefract (occ. 1372), 247
Walter, pr. St Cross, 188
Walter, pr. Sandaleford, 457
Walter, pr. Shelford, 458
Walter, pr. Stamford, St Leonard, 129
Walter, pr. Stavordale, 463
Walter, pr. Throwley, 199
Walter, pr. Tiptree, 472
Walter, pr. Tortington, 475
Walter (? le Mouner), pr. Tutbury, 203
Walter, pr. Ulverscroft, 476
Walter, pr. Wangford, 253
Walter, pr. West Mersea, 210
Walter, pr. Westacre, 483
Walter II, pr. Winchester, St Swithun, 82
Walter III, pr. Winchester, St Swithun, 83
Walter, pr. Winterburn Monkton, 254
Walter, pr. Witham, 326
Walter, pr. Wombridge, 486
Walter, pr. Wroxton, 489
Walteri, John, pr. Modbury, 179
Waltham, Alexander of, abb. Dorchester, 375
Waltham, Margery of, prs Little Marlow, 581
Waltham, Robert of, pr. Binham, 92
Waltham, Simon de, pr. Prittlewell, 247
Waltham, William of, pr. Wymondham, 136
Walton, Alexander of, abb. Furness, 282
Walton, Geoffrey of, pr. Monkton Farleigh, 238
Walton, Geoffrey of, pr. Pontefract, 247
Walton, Joan of, abbs Elstow, 558
Walton, John of, pr. Gloucester, St Oswald, 382
Walton, John of, pr. Mendham, 235
Walton, Simon of, abb. Bourne, 341
Walton, Walter of, abb. Darley, 373
Walton, William of, pr. Cartmel, 361
Walworth, John of, pr. Hexham, 391
Walworth, Nicholas of, pr. Holy Island, 111
Walworth, Robert Berrington of, pr. Durham, 40
Wande, William de, abb. Colchester, 34
Wandesleye, Thomas de, abb. Jervaulx, 286
Wantage, Emma of, prs Littlemore, 582
Wappenbur(i), John de, pr. Nuneaton, 597
Wappesleghe, Thomas de, abb. Buckland, 268
Ward(e), Matilda, prs Esholt, 559
Warde, Richard le, pr. Sandwell, 66
Warde, Roger, pr. Bicester, 334
Wardeden, Nicholas, pr. Brecon, 93
Wardington, Robert of, pr. Canons Ashby, 357
Wardington, Robert of, pr. Catesby, 552
Wardon, John of, abb. Tilty, 316
Wardon, Robert of, pr. Catesby, 552

Wardon, Robert of, pr. Chacombe, 362

Wardon, William (of), abb. London, St Mary
Graces, 290

Ware, Nicholas of, pr. Sudbury, 131

Ware, Richard of, abb. Westminster, 78

Ware, Roger (de), pr. Horkesley, 230

Wareham, Ranulph of, pr. Norwich cath., 55
see also Warham

Wareng(e), John de, pr. Boxgrove, 147

Warenne, Isabel de, abbs Wilton, 619

Warenne, William de, pr. Castle Acre, 224; pr.
Monks Horton, 237

Waresley, William de, abb. Combermere, 273

Warham, Geoffrey de, pr. Westacre, 483

Warham, Nicholas de, pr. Christchurch
(Twynham), 365

Warham, Thomas (of), pr. Peterstone, 447

Warham, Thomas of (?another), pr. Peterstone, 447

Warham, William de, St Denys, 455
see also Wareham

Warin, abb. Calder, 271

Warin, abb. Combe, 273

Warin, abb. Grace Dieu, 283

Warin, abb. Louth Park, 291

Warin, abb. Rewley, 301

Warin, abb. Sallay, 306

Warin, pr. Snelshall, 71

Warin, Nicholas, pr. Hough, 394

Warmington, John of, pr. Chetwode, 363

Warmington, Thomas of, pr. Kenilworth, 399

Warneford, Thomas (de), pr. Snaith, 128

Warner, pr. Arundel, 141

Warnham, Richard, pr. Reigate, 452

Warram, John, pr. Beadlow, 90

War(r)e, John de la, abb. Margam, 292

Warre, Lucy, abbs Canonsleigh, 550

Warter, Adam of, pr. Kirkham, 402

Warter, Richard of, pr. Nostell, 439

Warthill, Thomas of, abb. York, St Mary, 87

Warwick, Adam of, pr. Carlisle, 359

Warwick, John of, abb. Dorchester, 375

Warwick, John of, abb. Forde, 278

Warwick, Peter of, alias le Skynnere, pr. Warwick,
481

Warwick, Simon of, abb. York, St Mary, 87

Warwickshire, Hamo of, pr. Bilsington, 336

Was(c)elyn, John de, pr. Thornholme, 469

Washbourne, Henry of, pr. Bristol, St James, 94

Wasoun, William de, pr. Horsley, 170, 393

Wastel, William, pr. Blyth, 145

Wasteneys, Eve, prs Cambridge, St Mary and St
Radegund, 548

Wasteneys, Eve (? the same), prs Swaffham
Bulbeck, 613

Watercombe, Adam of, custos Wilkeswood, 536

Waterham, William, pr. Folkestone, 160

Waternewton, Reginald of, abb. Thorney, 75

Watford, Edmund of, master Catesby, 552

Watford, John (de), pr. Wombridge, 486

Watford, Richard of, rector Ashridge, 535

Watford, Robert of, minister Hounslow, 532

Watford, Robert of, pr. Maxstoke, 421

Watford, Thomas of, pr. London, St Bartholomew,
417

Wath, Alexander of, pr. Rumburgh, 126

Wath, (?same as Watlyngton), Richard de, abb.
Thame, 315

Watlington, Ralph of, pr. Belvoir, 91; pr.
Wallingford, 133

Watlington, Richard of, abb. Owston, 442

Watlyngton, Richard, abb. Thame, 315

Watnall, Thomas of, pr. Felley, 379

Watton, Cecily of, prs Heynings, 570

Watton, Richard of, pr. Watton, 530

Watton, Roger of, pr. Coventry, 35

Watton(e), Stephen de, pr. Leominster, 117

Watton, Stephen de, pr. London, Holy Trinity,
Aldgate, 416

Wauville, Richard de, pr. Ellingham, 158

Wauz, Alan de, abb. Bourne, 341

Wavere, William de, abb. Merevale, 295

Wayte, Christiana le, abbs Winchester, 621

Wearmouth, Adam of, [Jarrow], 114

Wearmouth, William of, pr. Stamford, St Leonard,
129

Weasenham, John Brandon of, see Brandon, John

Weasenham, Ralph of, pr. Castle Acre, 224

Weasenham, William of, pr. Westacre, 483

Weaverham, Walter of, pr. Norton, 438

Weaverthorpe, Peter of, pr. Bridlington, 346

Wederhore, William de, pr. Dunstable, 377

Wedmore, William of, abb. Dunkeswell, 278

Weeting, John of, abb. West Dereham, 517

Weeting, John of, pr. Mountjoy, 427

Welbourn, Thomas of, pr. Haverholme, 523

Welewe, William de, pr. Maiden Bradley, 418

Welford, John of, abb. Sulby, 510

Welham, Isabel de, prs Flixton, 561

Welham, Walter de, pr. Holme East, 229

Welholm, Emma de, prs Flixton, 561

Well, Cecily de, prs Crabhouse, 556

Welle, John de, pr. Bromehill, 349

Well(e), Margaret de, prs Greenfield, 566

Welle, Thomas de, abb. Crowland, 37

Well(e), Thomas de, abb. Eynsham, 43
Welles, John de, pr. Maiden Bradley, 418
Welles, Robert (de), pr. Southwark, 460
Well(e)s, William de, pr. Blyth, 145
Wellingore, Thomas of, abb. Wellow, 482
Wellis, John de, abb. Dunkeswell, 278
Wells, Jocelin of, abb. Glastonbury, 46
Welton(e), Benedict of, pr. Barnwell, 331
Welton, Walter Pylath of, see Pylath, Walter
Welwick, Richard of, pr. Warter, 480
Welynton, John, pr. Llanthony Prima, 414
Wencheape, Richard de, pr. Dover, 97
Wenchepe, Robert de, pr. Canterbury, St Gregory, 358
Wendene, Richard de, pr. Hertford, St Mary, 109
Wendling, Katharine of, prs Norwich (Carrow), 592
Wendover, Roger of, pr. Belvoir, 90
Wenge, William, pr. York, Holy Trinity, 216
Wenlock, Luke of, abb. Shrewsbury, 70
Wenlock, Richard of, pr. Little Malvern, 119
Wenlock, Walter of, abb. Westminster, 78
Wennington, Roger of, pr. Caldwell, 355
Wensley, Thomas of, abb. Swineshead, 314
Wentbridge, William of, pr. Monk Bretton, 53
Were, William de la, pr. Alvecote, 89
Wersleg, William de, abb. Hulton, 285
West, John, pr. Royston, 454
West Dereham, David of, pr. Mullicourt, 55
Westacre, Richard of, pr. Hempton, 389
Westbrom, Richard de, pr. Colchester, St Botolph, 369
Westbury, Agnes of, abbs Elstow, 558
Westbury, John of, pr. Chetwode, 364
Westbury, John of, pr. Luffield, 51
Westcot, Alice of, prs Wintney, 622
Westerham, John of, pr. Rochester, 62
Westgate, Edmund of, see Canterbury, Edmund of
Weston, Eleanor of, abbs Barking, 541
Weston, John of, pr. Huntingdon, 395
Weston, Laurence of, pr. Flitcham, 380
Weston, Roger of, pr. Anglesey, 328
Weston, Roger (of), pr. Oxford, St Frideswide, 444
Weston, Rose of, prs Little Marlow, 581
Weston, Walter of, abb.-el. Crowland, 37
Weston, William of, pr. Stamford, St Mary and St Michael (1266–), 610
Weston, William of, pr. Stamford, St Mary and St Michael (–1333), 610
Westone, Thomas, see Pype, Thomas (de)
Westwelle, Osbert de, abb. Stoneleigh, 311
Wetacre, Robert de, pr. Dover, 97

Wetwang, William of, pr. Kirkham, 401
Weylond, Juliana de, prs Redlingfield, 600
Whaddon, Ralph of, pr. Newton Longville, 242
Whaddon, Richard of, pr. Newton Longville, 242
Whaley, William of, pr. Birkenhead, 23
Whalley, Thomas of, abb. Selby, 67
Whaplode, Gilbert of, pr. Westacre, 483
Whaplode, Henry of, pr. Kyme, 402
Whaplode, Nicholas of, abb. Reading, 61
Whateley, Ralph de, pr. Penwortham, 123
Whatlington, John of, abb. Battle, 23
Whatton, John (de), pr. Lincoln, St Katharine, 524
Whatton, Richard de, pr. Trentham, 476
Whatvyll, Margery, prs London, Clerkenwell, 582
Wheathampstead, Clement of, pr. Tynemouth, 133
Wheathampstead, Elias of, pr. Wymondley, 490
Wheathampstead, Joan of, prs Flamstead, 560
Wheathampstead, Lucy of, prs Sewardsley, 604
Wheathampstead, Richard of, pr. Hertford, St Mary, 110
Wheatley, Henry of, pr. Healaugh Park, 388
Wheldrake, John of, pr. Warter, 480
Wheldrake, William (of), abb. Woburn, 324
Whelnetham, Matilda of, prs Wix, 623
Whelpington, John of, abb. Newminster, 298
Whelpington, Robert of, pr. Hexham, 391
Whelpley, Geoffrey of, abb. Missenden, 424
Whichchirche, Ralph, pr. Hatfield Peverel, 107
Whichchirche, Ralph, pr. Hatfield Peverel; pr. Wallingford, 134
see also Whitchurch
Whitacr(e), Benedicta de, prs Markgate, 587
Whitby, Isabel of, prs Rosedale, 602
Whitby, Ralph of, see Stanham, Ralph de
Whitchurch, Simon of, abb. Chester, 33
Whitchurch, William of, abb. Alcester, 18
Whitchurch, William of, abb. Evesham, 42
see also Whichchirche
Whitele, John de, pr. Cardigan, 95
Whitfelde, Joan, prs Canterbury, Holy Sepulchre, 550
see also Witefeld
Whitmers, Christiana de, prs Little Marlow, 581
Whitsand, Peter de, pr. Horton, 112
Whittlesey, John of, pr. Linton and Isleham, 174
Whittlesey, Odo of, abb. Thorney, 75
Whittone, John de, abb. Wigmore, 485
Whitwell, Geoffrey of, keeper Calwich, 356
Whitwell, Giles of, pr. Pentney, 446
Whyteney, Matilda, prs Limebrook, 580
Wich, John de, pr. Selborne, 457
Wicham, Richard de, pr. Little Dunmow, 412

Wichio, Thomas de, pr. Great Malvern, 105
Wickwane, Walter de, abb. Winchcombe, 81
Wickwane, William of, pr. Alvecote, 89
Wickwane, William of, pr. Great Malvern, 105
Wiggenhall, Thomas of, pr. Castle Acre, 225
Wighale, Hugh de, abb. Sallay, 306
Wigmore, Henry of, pr. Ewenny, 100
Wigmore, John of, abb. Gloucester, 48
Wigton, John of, pr. Drax, 376
Wiham, William de, *see* Byham, William de
Wilbraham, Basilia of, prs Wix, 62
Wilbraham, William of, pr. Bicknacre, 335
Wildbof, John de, pr. Bushmead, 353
Wilecote (Wylecote), Ralph de, pr. Penwortham, 123
Willeys, William (de), pr. Breedon, 345
William, [Headley], 167
William, [Long Bennington], 291
William, abb.-el. of Alcester, 18
William, abb. Barlings, 492
William, abb. Basingwerk, 259
William, abb. Bayham, 493
William, abb. Beauchief, 493
William, abb. Beeleigh, 480
William, abb. Biddlesden (occ. 1239), 261
William, abb. Biddlesden (occ. 1254 x 5), 261
William, abb. Bindon (occ. 1331), 263
William, abb. Bindon (1361–), 264
William, abb. Bindon (occ. 1386), 264
William, abb. Blanchland, 495
William, abb. Bordesley (occ. 1250), 264
William, abb. Bordesley (–1270/1), 264
William, abb. Bordesley (occ. 1316 x 22), 264
William, abb. Bruern, 267
William, abb. Buckfast, 267
William, abb. Buckland (occ. 1288 x 9), 268
William, abb. Buckland (occ. *c.* 1335), 268
William, abb. Buildwas (occ. 1215 x 23), 268
William, abb. Buildwas (occ. 1258 x *c.* 1263), 269
William, abb. Byland, 270
William, abb. Calder, 271
William, abb. Cleeve, 271
William, abb. Coggeshall (occ. 1227 x 30), 272
William, abb. Coggeshall (occ. 1310), 272
William II, abb. Combe, 272
William, abb. Combe (1234–), 272
William, abb. Combe (occ. 1288 x 98), 273
William, abb. Combwell, 371
William, abb. Coverham, 497
William, abb. Croxton Kerrial (1294–), 498
William, abb. Croxton Kerrial (occ. 1338 x 48), 498
William, abb. Dale, 499

William, abb. Dieulacres (occ. 1237 x 40), 276
William, abb. Dieulacres (occ. 1251), 276
William, abb. Dunkeswell (occ. 1202 x 19), 277
William, abb. Dunkeswell (1318–), 277
William, abb. Dunkeswell (occ. 1328 x 9), 277
William, abb. Durford (early 13th cent.), 500
William, abb. Durford (occ. 1231 x 44), 500
William, abb. Easby, 501
William, abb. Egglestone (occ. 1226), 501
William, abb. Egglestone (1309–), 502
William, abb. Flaxley (occ. 1221), 278
William, abb. Flaxley (occ. 1253 x 57), 278
William, abb. Flaxley (1277–), 278
William, abb. Flaxley (occ. 1307), 278
William, abb. Flaxley (occ. 1361), 278
William, abb. Forde (–1262), 278
William, abb. Forde (1319–), 279
William, abb. Furness, 281
William, abb. Garenden, 282
William, abb. Grace Dieu, 283
William, abb. Hagnaby (occ. 1310), 503
William, abb. Hagnaby (occ. *c.* 1336 x 46), 503
William, abb. Halesowen, 503
William, abb. Hartland, 386
William, abb. Haughmond, 387
William, abb. Holm Cultram, 285
William, abb. Hulton (occ. 1242 x 4), 285
William, abb. Hulton (occ. 1332 x 6), 286
William, abb. Jervaulx, 286
William, abb. Kingswood, 287
William, abb. Kirkstall, 288
William, abb. Kirkstead (occ. 1210), 289
William, abb. Kirkstead (occ. 1253 x 9), 289
William, abb. Kirkstead (occ. 1271), 289
William, abb. Kirkstead (occ. 1348), 290
William, abb. Langdon (occ. *c.* 1258), 504
William, abb. Langdon (occ. 1284), 504
William, abb. Langley (occ. 1277 x 8), 505
William, abb. Langley (occ. 1350), 505
William, abb. Lavendon (? early 13th cent.), 506
William, abb. Lavendon (occ. 1310), 506
William, abb. Leiston, 507
William, abb. Merevale, 294
William, abb. Neath, 295
William, abb. Netley, 296
William, abb. Newbo (occ. 1257), 507
William, abb. Newbo (1277–), 507
William, abb. Newbo (occ. *temp.* Edward I), 507
William, abb. Newminster, 298
William, abb. North Creake, 434
William, abb. Pipewell, 299
William, abb. Quarr, 300

William, abb. Revesby (occ. mid 13th cent.), 301
William, abb. Revesby (occ. 1271), 301
William, abb. Revesby (1294–), 301
William, abb. Revesby (occ. 1362), 301
William III, abb. Rievaulx, 302
William, abb. Rievaulx (occ. 1268), 302
William, abb. Rievaulx (1275–), 302
William, abb. Rievaulx (1318–), 302
William, abb. Rievaulx (?1361–), 303
William, abb. Robertsbridge (occ. 1194 x 1222), 303
William, abb. Robertsbridge (occ. 1235 x 52), 303
William, abb. Roche, 305
William, abb. Rufford, 305
William, abb. St Osyth, 457
William, abb. St Radegund, 509
William, abb. Sallay, 306
William, abb. Sawtry (occ. 1285/6 x 93), 307
William, abb. Sawtry (1316–), 307
William, abb. Sawtry (occ. 1351 x 9), 308
William, abb. Shap, 509
William, abb. Shrewsbury, 70
William, abb. Stanley (occ. 1229), 310
William, abb. Stanley (occ. 1272), 310
William, abb. Stanley (occ. 1321 x 3), 310
William, abb. Strata Marcella, 313
William, abb. Stratford Langthorne (occ. 1350), 314
William, abb. Stratford Langthorne (occ. 1358 x 9), 314
William, abb. Sulby (occ. 1222), 510
William, abb. Sulby (1231/2–), 510
William, abb. Tilty, 316
William, abb. Tupholme (occ. 1247 x 73), 513
William, abb. Tupholme (1310–), 513
William, abb. Vaudey (occ. 1214/15 x 1219), 319
William, abb. Vaudey (occ. 1271), 319
William, abb. Vaudey (occ. 1305 x 10), 319
William, abb. Wardon, 320
William, abb. Waverley (occ. 1313 x 28), 321
William, ?abb. Waverley (1341), 321 n. 38
William, abb. Waverley (occ. 1397), 321
William, abb. Welbeck, 514
William, abb. Woburn, 323
William, archpriest or pr. Barton, 331
William, bailiff of Atherington, 143
William, custos Barrow Gurney, 542
William, custos Charlton, 496
William, custos Markyate, 587
William, custos Nunburnholme, 595
William, custos St Mary de Pré, 603
William, custos Upchurch, 514

William, master Godstow (dean of Woodstock), 563
William, master Godstow (vicar of Cassington), 563
William, master Godstow (vicar of 'Duninton'), 563
William, ?master Holystone, 573
William, master Moxby, 589
William, master St Mary de Pré, 603
William, master Sempringham, 527
William, master Stixwould, 611
William, master Wallingwells, 616
William, minister Easton and Hertford, 532
William, minister Hertford, 532
William, minister Hounslow, 533
William, minister Moatenden, 533
William, minister Thelsford, 534
William pelliparius, pr. Abergavenny, 138
William, pr. Alvingham (occ. 1240), 519
William, pr. Alvingham (occ. 1317), 519
William, ?pr. Amesbury, 538
William, pr. Andwell, 140
William, pr. Anglesey, 328
William, pr. Arundel, 141
William, pr. Avebury (occ. 1249), 144
William, pr. Avebury (late 13th cent.), 144
William, pr. Barlinch, 330
William, pr. Beauvale, 325
William, pr. Berden, 333
William, pr. Bicester, 334
William, pr. Binham (occ. 1332), 93
William, pr. Binham (temp. Richard II), 93
William, pr. Blackmore (occ. 1232 x 44), 337
William, pr. Blackmore (occ. 1327), 338
William, pr. Blyth (early 13th cent.), 145
William, pr. Blyth (occ. 1231), 145
William, pr. Blyth (late 13th cent.), 145
William, pr. Blythburgh (early 13th cent.), 338
William, pr. Blythburgh (occ. c. 1237 x 64/5), 338
William, pr. Boxgrove, 146
William, pr. Bradenstoke, 342
William, pr. Brecon, 93
William, pr. Bridge End, 519
William, ? pr. Bridlington, 346 n.6
William, pr. Brinkburn (occ. c. 1243 x 57), 347
William, pr. Brinkburn (occ. 1279), 347
William, pr. Bromehill, 349
William, pr. Bruton (early 13th cent.), 350
William, pr. Bruton (occ. 1271), 351
William, pr. Bullington (occ. 1218 x 45), 520
William, pr. Bullington (occ. 1263), 520
William, pr. Bullington (occ. 1287 x 92), 520

William, pr. Bullington (occ. 1334), 520
William, pr. Burscough, 352
William, pr. Butley, 353
William, pr. Caldwell, 354
William, pr. Cammeringham, 495
William, pr. Carlisle, 360
William, pr. Cartmel, 361
William, pr. Catley, 521
William, pr. Charley, 362
William, pr. Church Gresley, 367
William, pr. Clifford (first half of 13th cent.), 225
William, pr. Clifford (occ. 1349 x 51), 226
William, pr. Covenham, 153
William, pr. Cowick, 153
William, pr. Coxford (–?1233/4), 372
William, pr. Coxford (occ. 1255 x 8), 372
William, pr. Creeting, 154
William, pr. Deerhurst, 155
William, pr. Dudley (occ. 1301 x 2), 227
William, pr. Dudley (occ. 1352 x 61), 227
William, pr. Earls Colne, 99
William, pr. Everdon, 159
William, pr. Fordham (occ. 1247 x 58), 522
William, pr. Fordham (occ. 1365 x 6), 522
William, pr. Frithelstock (occ. 1249), 380
William, pr. Frithelstock (occ. 1373), 381
William, pr. Gloucester, St Oswald (occ. 1218 x 31), 381
William, pr. Gloucester, St Oswald (occ. 1260), 381
William, pr. Goldcliff, 162
William, pr. Great Massingham, 383
William, pr. Grovebury, 163
William, pr. Hamble (pre-1263), 164
William, pr. Hamble (occ. c. 1295 x 8), 164
William, pr. Hamble (occ. 1300), 164
William, pr. Harmondsworth, 165
William, pr. Hatfield Regis, 166
William, pr. Haverholme, 523
William, pr. Herringfleet, 390
William, pr. Hexham, 390
William, pr. Holme East (occ. 1302), 229
William, pr. Holme East (occ. 1361), 229
William, pr. Holy Island, 110
William, pr. Horsham St Faith, 169
William, pr. Horsley, 170, 393
William, pr. Horton, 112
William, pr. Hough, 393
William, pr. Ipswich, Holy Trinity (occ. 1226 x 1250/1), 395
William, pr. Ipswich, Holy Trinity (occ. 1269), 395

William, pr. Ipswich, Holy Trinity (occ. 1286/7 x 89), 395
William, pr. Isleham, 171
William, pr. Ixworth, 398
William, pr. Kenilworth, 398
William, pr. Kersey (occ. 1245 x 7), 399
William, pr. Kersey (occ. 1268 x 9), 399
William, pr. Kinley, 536
William, pr. Launceston, 404
William, pr. Leeds, 407
William, pr. Leighs, 408
William, pr. Lincoln, St Katharine (occ. 1216 x 18), 523
William, pr. Lincoln, St Katharine (occ. 1282 x 3), 524
William, pr. Lincoln, St Katharine (occ. 1340 x 4), 524
William, pr. Linton and Isleham, 174
William, pr. Little Dunmow, 412
William, pr. Livers Ocle, 174
William, pr. Longleat, 418
William, pr. Lytham, 119
William, pr. Maiden Bradley, 418
William, pr. Malpas, 235
William, pr. Malton (occ. 1331), 525
William, pr. Malton (occ. 1333 x 36), 525
William, pr. Malton (occ. 1377), 525
William, pr. Marton (occ. 1262 x 3), 420
William, pr. Marton (occ. 1370 x 1), 421
William, pr. Mendham, 236
William, pr. Michelham, 423
William, pr. Monk Bretton (occ. c. 1185 x 1211), 53
William, pr. Monk Bretton (occ. 1385), 236
William, pr. Monk Sherborne, 179
William, pr. Monks Horton, 236
William, pr. Newburgh, 429
William, pr. Newstead-on-Ancholme (occ. 1219), 526
William, pr. Newstead-on-Ancholme (occ. 1287), 526
William, pr. Newton Longville, 242
William, pr. Nocton Park (early 13th cent.), 433
William, pr. Nocton Park (occ. 1256), 433
William, pr. North Ferriby, 436
William, pr. North Ormsby (occ. 1224 x 6), 526
William, pr. North Ormsby (occ. 1309), 526
William, pr. North Ormsby (occ. 1320), 526
William, pr. Nuneaton, 596
William, pr. Ogbourne St George, 184
William, pr. Pentney, 446
William, pr. Pilton, 124
William, pr. Pontefract, 246

William, pr. Poughley, 449
William, pr. Prittlewell, 247
William, pr. Pynham by Arundel, 449
William, pr. Rochester, 61
William, pr. Royston, 454
William, pr. Ruislip, 188
William, pr. Runcton, 188
William, pr. St Helen's, 250
William, pr. St Neots, 190
William, pr. Sandwell, 65
William, pr. Sempringham, 528
William, pr. Shelford, 458
William, pr. Shouldham, 529
William, pr. Sixhills (occ. 1278 x 9), 530
William, pr. Sixhills (occ. 1343), 530
William, pr. Snelshall, 71
William, pr. Stavordale, 463
William, pr. Steep Holme, 464
William, pr. Steventon, 194
William, pr. Stoke by Clare, 195
William, pr. Studley, 465
William, pr. Thetford, Holy Sepulchre (occ. 1218 x 1234/5), 467
William, pr. Thetford, Holy Sepulchre (occ. 1272 x 5), 468
William, pr. Thetford, St Mary, 251
William, pr. Thoby (occ. 1227), 468
William, pr. Thoby (occ. 1324), 468
William, pr. Thremhall, 470
William, pr. Thurgarton, 471
William, pr. Tickford (1220–31), 199
William, pr. Tickford (occ. 1295/6 x 1298/9), 200
William, pr. Tortington, 475
William, pr. Trentham, 475
William, pr. Tutbury (occ. 1248 x c. 1260), 203
William, pr. Tutbury (occ. 1285), 203
William, pr. Upholland, 76
William, pr. Wallingford, 133
William, pr. Walsingham (c. 1207 – c. 1254), 477
William, pr. Walsingham (occ. 1275/6 x 8), 477
William, pr. Wangford, 253
William, pr. Ware, 205
William, pr. Warwick, 480
William, pr. Watton, 530
William, pr. Weedon Lois, 209
William, pr. West Ravendale, 518
William, pr. Westacre (occ. 1200), 483
William, pr. Westacre (occ. 1227/8), 483
William, pr. Westwood, 617
William, pr. Wilmington (occ. 1299), 211
William, pr. Wilmington (occ. 1370), 211

William, pr. Winghale (occ. 1324), 213
William, pr. Winghale (occ. 1369), 213
William, pr. Witham (? 13th cent), 326
William, pr. Witham (occ. 1363), 326
William, pr. Wormsley (occ. 1225 x 31), 488
William, pr. Wormsley (occ. 1395 x 1407), 489
William, pr. Wymondley, 490
William, pr. York, Holy Trinity (occ. c. 1207/14 x 28/9), 216
William, pr. York, Holy Trinity (1248–), 216
William, pr. York, St Andrew, 531
William, proctor Tarrant Kaines, 615
William, rector Ashridge, 535
William, Robert, [Upavon], 205
William son of Alan, pr. Ewyas Harold, 100
Willingham, Robert of, pr. Torksey, 474
Willoughby, Robert of, abb. Calder, 271
Willoughby, Sarah of, prs Greenfield, 566
  see also Wiluby
Wilsthorpe, John of, pr. Newstead (in Sherwood), 432
Wilsthorpe, Margaret of, prs Nun Monkton, 595
Wilton, John of, pr. Markby, 420
Wilton, Robert of, pr. Guisborough, 384
Wilton, Walter of, pr. Cold Norton, 370
Wilton, William de, pr. Warwick, 481
Wiltshire, Thomas (de), pr. Bisham, 337
Wiluby, Matilda de, prs Sempringham, 529
  see also Willoughby
Wimborne, Gilbert of, pr. Sele, 192
Wincanton, John (of), pr. Stavordale, 463
Winceby, William of, master Nun Cotham, 593
Winchendon, Robert of, abb. Dorchester, 375
Winchester, Adam of, pr. Lewes, 234
Winchester, Andrew of, pr. Southwick, 461
Winchester, Bartholomew of, abb. Chertsey, 32
Winchester, Christi(a)na of, abbs Winchester, 621
Winchester, Christina of, prs Farewell, 559
Winchester, Christine of, prs Langley, 578
Winchester, Eleanor of, prs London, St Helen's and Holy Cross, 585
Winchester, Henry of, pr. Mottisfont, 426
Winchester, Hugh of, pr. Hinckley, 168
Winchester, Joan of, prs London, St Helen's and Holy Cross, 585
Winchester, John of, pr. Boxgrove, 146
Winchester, Juliana of, prs Langley, 578
Winchester, Nicholas of, pr. Selborne, 458
Winchester, Peter of, abb. Titchfield, 512
Winchester, Robert of, pr. Sandaleford, 457
Winchester, Thomas of, pr. Bath, 22
Winchester, Thomas of, pr. Selborne, 458

Winchester, William of, pr. Southwick, 461
see also Wynchestre
Windsor, Robert of, pr. Merton, 423
Winferton, Walter of, abb. Winchcombe, 81
Wingfield, Mary of, prs Campsey Ash, 549
Wingham, Thomas of, abb. Faversham, 45
Winkburn, John of, abb. Byland, 270
Winslow, William (of), pr. Beadlow, 90
Winterburn, Emma de, prs Wintney, 622
Winterton, John of, pr. Malton, 525
Winton, Adam of, see Sutton, Adam of
Wintringham, John of, pr. Malton, 525
Wintringham, Richard of, pr. Thetford, Holy
    Sepulchre, 468
Winwick, Robert of, pr.-el. of Daventry, 226
Wircestre, Roger, pr. Bristol, St James, 94
Wircestre, Simon de, see Wyre, Simon de
see also Worcester
Wirsop, John de, abb. Welbeck, 515
Wistanstow, Richard of, pr. Church Preen, 225
Wistow I, John of, abb. Selby, 67
Wistow II, John of, abb. Selby, 67
Witefeld, Alice de, abbs Wilton, 619
see also Whitfelde
Witeville, Ralph de, pr. Axmouth, 144
Withcall, Robert of, abb. Kirkstead, 289
Withenham, Stephen de, pr. Hertford, St Mary,
    110
Witherley, Thomas of, abb. Bordesley, 264
Witherley, Thomas of (possibly the same as above),
    abb. Merevale, 295
Withern, Margaret of, prs Legbourne, 580
Withersfield, Walter of, pr. Anglesey, 328
Witlesey, John, pr. Swavesey, 197
Witsand, Peter (de), pr. Monks Horton, 237
Wittelesham, Nicholas de, pr. Butley, 354
Wittenham, Stephen of, pr. Wallingford, 133
Witton, William of, pr. Bromholm, 223
Wiz, Adam de, abb. Waltham, 478
Wlfe, Nicholas, pr. Skewkirk, 459
Wl'icus (?Wulfric), abb. Hartland, 386
Wllst, Thomas de, pr. Merton, 421
Wlricus, pr. Bromholm, 223
Wod, Lucy atte, prs London, Clerkenwell, 583
Wodecroft, Elizabeth, prs Bristol, St Mary
    Magdalen, 545
Wodehall, Juliana de la, prs Esholt, 559
Wodehouse, Robert de, pr. Little Dunmow, 412
see also Wodhous(e); Woodhouse
Wodenham, John, pr. Christchurch (Twynham),
    367
Woderove, J., pr. Redbourne, 124

Wodewale, Simon, pr.-el. Hickling, 392
Wodhous(e), John (de), abb. Dale, 499
see also Wodehouse; Woodhouse
Wodhulle, Robert, abb. Wardon, 320
Wokingham, Philip of, pr. Tandridge, 466
Woldham, Benedict, see Rochester, Benedict of
Wolfreton, William de, pr. Haltemprice, 385
Wollaston, Margery of, abbs Northampton, De La
    Pré, 590
Wolmersty, Thomas of, abb. Waltham, 479
Wolterton, Roger de, pr. Yarmouth, 137
Wombwell, Richard of, pr. Nostell, 439
Woodburn, Hugh of, master Monkwearmouth,
    121; pr. Lytham, 120
Woodford, Adam of, pr. Cold Norton, 370
Woodford, Henry of, pr. Merton, 431
Woodford, William of, abb. Peterborough, 58
Woodford, William of, pr. Newnham, 431
Woodhouse, Roger of, custos Catesby, 552
see also Wodehouse; Wodhous(e)
Woodlock, Henry, de Merewell, pr. Winchester, St
    Swithun, 84
Woodstock, John of, pr. Chetwode, 363
Woodstock, Thomas of, abb. Croxden, 275
Woolley, Simon of, pr. Stonely, 465
Wootton, John of, pr. Brooke, 349
Wootton, John of, pr. Cold Norton, 370
Worcester, Henry of, abb. Evesham, 42
Worcester, John of, pr. Little Malvern (1287-99),
    119
Worcester, John of, pr. Little Malvern (1369-),
    119
Worcester, John of, see Claines, John of
Worcester, Peter of, abb. Tewkesbury, 73
Worcester, Philip of, see Aubyn, Philip de
Worcester, Roger of, pr. Stone, 464
Worcester, Stephen of, abb. Abbey Dore, 258
Worcester, Walter of, abb. Alcester, 18; pr.
    Alvecote, 89
Worcester, William of, abb. Winchester, Hyde, 82
see also Wirecestre
Workesle, Elias de, abb. Whalley, 322
Worme, John de, pr. Bromfield, 95
Wormedale, John de, abb. Robertsbridge, 304
Wormleighton, Stephen of, pr. Brooke, 350
Wormsley, Thomas of, pr. Wormsley, 489
Worstead, Adam of, pr. Thetford, Holy Sepulchre,
    468
Worstead, John of, pr. Hoxne, 112
Worterleigh, John de, see Worton, John de
Worth, John of, pr. Michelham, 424
Worth, Richard, abb. Bayham, 493

Worton, John de, *alias* Worterleigh, abb. Forde, 279

Wothorpe, Isolda of, prs Wothorpe, 623

Wouldham, Thomas de, *alias* Southfleet, pr. Rochester, 62

Woveton, Batill' de, abbs Chatteris, 553

Wrockeshale, William de, pr. Pilton, 124
   see also Wrokkeshale; Wroxhale

Wrohz, William, abb. Abbey Dore, 259

Wrokkeshale, William, pr. Barlinch, 330
   see also Wrockeshale; Wroxhale

Wroth, Robert, abb. Abbey Dore, 259 & n. 1

Wrotting, Gilbert de, pr. London, Holy Trinity, Aldgate, 416

Wrottinge, Richard de, pr. Anglesey, 328

Wroxhale, William, ? pr. Barlinch, 330 n. 2
   see also Wrockeshale; Wrokkeshale

Wroxham, William (of), pr. Hickling, 392

Wrthe, Richard de, abb. Dorchester, 375

Wutton, Robert de, master Harrold, 569

Wybbebire, Thomas de, abb. Hertford, 386

Wybunbury, Ralph de, pr. Morville, 122

Wyche, Peter, abb. Stoneleigh, 311

Wyche, Richard (del), pr., then abb. Norton, 438

Wychenden, John, abb. Notley, 440

Wycheton, John de, abb. Bourne, 341

Wycombe, William of, abb. Hartland, 386

Wycumbe, Margaret (Margery) of, prs Broomhill, 545

Wycumbe, William of, pr. Carmarthen, 360

Wydepole, Margery de, prs Polsloe, 599

Wye, John of, pr. Bilsington, 336

Wye, John of, pr. Exeter, St Nicholas, 101

Wygepole, James, pr. Prittlewell, 249

Wyght, Richard de, abb. Stratford Longthorne, 314

Wyghton, William de, *see* Bryght, William

Wyghtone, Walter de, pr. Walsingham, 477

Wyham, Adam de, abb. St Osyth, 456

Wyham, Geoffrey of, master Grimsby, 567

Wyk, Robert de, pr. Tynemouth, 133

Wyke, Hugh de, abb. Tintern, 316

Wyke, Hugh de, pr. Great Malvern, 106

Wyke, John de, pr. Worcester, 86

Wykenesthorp, William de, pr. Stamford, St Mary and St Michael, 610

Wykham, Henry de, pr. Chetwode, 364

Wykham, William, pr. Blythburgh, 338

Wylecote, *see* Wilecote

Wylmyn, Henry, pr. Spinney, 462

Wylton, John de, *custos* Montacute, 239

Wylton, John de, pr. Newstead-on-Ancholme, 526

Wyly, Richard Punchard de, *see* Punchard, Richard

Wymarca, abbs Elstow, 557

Wymarka, prs Lacock, 577

Wymbyssh(e), Richard (de), pr. London, Holy Trinity, Aldgate, 416

Wymond, Thomas, pr. Blyth, 146

Wymondham, John of, abb. Colchester, 34

Wymondham, Thomas of, pr. Wetheral, 134

Wymondham, William of, abb. Darley, 373

Wymondley, [*blank*] of, pr.-el. Wymondley, 490

Wymondley, Adam of, pr. Ravenstone, 450

Wymondley, John of, pr. Wymondley, 490

Wymonville, John de, pr. Avebury, 144

Wynchestre, John, abb. Quarr, 300

Wynchestre, John, *see* Chynnok, John
   see also Winchester

Wynel *or* Wyvel, Roger, pr. Dudley, 227

Wyneton, Simon de, *alias* Storm, pr. Walsingham, 478

Wyneyerde, John, pr. Gloucester, St Oswald, 382

Wynnegod, Richard, pr. St Cross, 188

Wynscote, David de, abb. Hartland, 386

Wynter, Alice, of Orford, prs Redlingfield, 600

Wynter, John, pr. Carmarthen, 361

Wynterborn, John, pr. Amesbury, 538

Wynter(e)shulle, Alice de, abbs Romsey, 601

Wynt(e)reshulle, Isabel de, abbs Wherwell, 617

Wyntreshull, Constance (de), abbs Wherwell, 618

Wyre, Simon de, *alias* de Wircestre, pr. Worcester, 85

Wysbech(e), John, abb. Grace Dieu, 284; abb. Tintern, 317

Wysdon, John, abb. Robertsbridge, 304

Wyten, Agnes de, prs York, St Clement, 626

Wytenhull, John de, pr. Studley, 465

Wythale, Matilda de, prs Legbourne, 579

Wytherington, John de, pr. Launde, 406

Wythyford, John de, pr. St Helen's, 250

Wyttenham, James de, pr. Breamore, 344

Wyvel, Roger, pr. Much Wenlock, 242

Wyvel, *see* Wynel

Wyvile, Margaret, prs Easebourne, 557

Yanworth, John of, abb. Winchcombe, 80

Yardley, Robert of, *alias* Maunsel, pr. Ravenstone, 451

Yarm, Alice of, prs Baysdale, 542

Yarm, John of, pr. Kirkham, 401

Yarm, Thomas of, pr. Healaugh Park, 389

Yarm, Walter of, *see* Dishforth, Walter of

Yarwell, Richard of, pr. Nocton Park, 433

Yatton, John (de), pr. Llanthony Prima, 414

Yaxham, William of, pr. Norwich, St Leonard, 122

Yaxley, John of, master Catesby, 552

Yaxley, Richard of, pr. Butley, 354

Yaxley, William of, pr. Deeping, 96; abb. Thorney, 75

Yelveden(e), Walter de, pr. Anglesey, 328

Yerde, Alice de la, prs Ilchester, 573

Yllesiis, William de, pr. Titley, 201

York, Emma of, prs Keldholme, 574–5

York, Gilbert of, see Ounesby, Gilbert de

York, Hamo of, pr. Healaugh Park, 388

York, John of, abb. Newminster, 298

York, Margaret of, prs Newcastle-upon-Tyne, 590

York, alias Northstreet, Matthew of, pr. Rumburgh, 126

York, Richard of, pr.-el. Hexham, 390

York, Thomas of, pr. Richmond, 125

York, William of, pr. Monk Bretton, 53

York, William of, pr. St Helen's, 250

Young, Juliana, prs Rusper, 603

Ypre, John de, pr. Caldwell, 355

Yrlaunde, Alice de, prs Sopwell, 607
  see also Ireland; Irland

Ysewode, Richard, pr. Prittlewell, 249

Yvelont, William de, see Bosco, William de

Yvo, master Nun Keeling, 594

Yvo, pr. Ellerton on Spalding Moor, 522
  see also Ivo

INDEX OF RELIGIOUS HOUSES

Abbreviations for Orders, etc.

A	Augustinian canons
AB	Bonhommes
B	Benedictine monks
BC	Cluniac monks
BF	Order of Fontevraud
BG	Order of Grandmont
BT	Order of Tiron
C	Cistercian monks
CA	Carthusian monks
G	Gilbertine canons
NA	Augustinian canonesses
NB	Benedictine nuns
NBC	Cluniac nuns
NBF	Fontevraud (Double Order)
NC	Cistercian nuns
NG	Gilbertine (Double Order)
NK	Sisters of St John of Jerusalem
NP	Premonstratensian canonesses
P	Premonstratensian canons
T	Trinitarian Houses
a (as suffix)	Alien
(a) (as suffix)	Alien, but later Denizen

Abbey Cwmhir C 258
Abbey Dore C 258–9
Abbotsbury B 15–16
Abergavenny B(a) 138
Abingdon B 16–18
Aconbury NA 537
Acre, *see* Castle Acre
Alberbury BG 255–6
Alcester B 18–19
Aldeby B 89
Aldermanshaw BC 219
Alkborough B 89
Allerton Mauleverer Ba 138–9
Alnesbourn A 327
Alnwick P 491
Alvecote B 89
Alvingham NG 519
Amesbury NBF 537–8
Andover Ba 139–40
Andwell BTa 140–1
Anglesey A 327–8

Ankerwyke NB 538–9
Appuldurcombe Ba 141
Arbury A 328–9
Arden NB 539–40
Armathwaite NB 540
Arthington NBC 540
Arundel Ba 141–2
Arundel, *see* Pynham by Arundel
Ashby, *see* Canons Ashby
Ashridge AB 535
Astley Ba 142–3
Aston Priors ?Ba 143
Athelney B 19–20
Atherington Ba 143–4
Avebury Ba 144
Axmouth Ba 144

Bamburgh A 329
Bardney B 20–1
Bardsey A 329–30
Barking NB 541–2

Barlinch A 330
Barlings P 492
Barnstaple BC 219–20
Barnwell A 330–1
Barrow Gurney NB 542
Barton A 331–2
Basingwerk C 259–60
Bath B 21–2
Battle B 22–3
Bayham P 492–3
Baysdale NC 542–3
Beadlow B 89–90
Beauchief P 493–4
Beaulieu C 260–1
Beauvale CA 325
Beckford A 332
Beddgelert A 332–3
Bedeman's Berg B 90
Beeleigh P 494–5
Beeston A 333
Begare C 261
Belvoir B 90–2
Bennington, see Long Bennington
Bentley A 333
Berden A 333–4
Bermondsey BC 220–3
Bicester A 334
Bicknacre A 334–6
Biddlesden C 261–2
Bilsington A 336–7
Bindon C 262–4
Binham B 92–3
Birkenhead B 23–4
Bisham A 337
Blackborough NB 543
Blackmore A 337–8
Blanchland P 495
Blithbury NB 544
Blyth B(a) 144–6
Blythburgh A 338
Bodmin A 339
Bolton A 339–40
Bordesley C 264–5
Bourne A 340–1
Boxgrove B(a) 146–7
Boxley C 265–6
Bradenstoke A 342
Bradley A 342–3
Bradley, see Maiden Bradley
Bradsole, see St Radegund
Bradwell B 24–5
Breadsall A 343–4

Breamore A 344
Brecon B 93–4
Breedon A 344–5
Bretton, see Monk Bretton
Brewood Black Ladies NB 544
Brewood White Ladies NA 544
Bricett, see Great Bricett
Bridge End G 519
Bridlington A 345–6
Brimpsfield Ba 147–8
Brinkburn A 347
Bristol, St Augustine A 347–8
Bristol, St James B 94
Bristol, St Mary Magdalen NA 544–5
Broadholme NP 545
Bromehill A 349
Bromfield B 94–5
Bromholm BC 223
Brooke A 349–50
Broomhall NB 545–6
Bruern C 266–7
Bruton A 350–1
Buckenham A 351
Buckfast C 267–8
Buckland C 268
Buckland NK 546
Buildwas C 268–9
Bullington NG 519–20
Bungay NB 546–7
Burnham NA 547–8
Burscough A 352
Burstall Ba 148–9
Burtle A 352
Burton B 25–6
Burwell Ba 149
Bury St Edmunds B 26–7
Bushmead A 352–3
Butley A 353–4
Byland C 269–70

Calder II C 270–1
Caldwell A 354–5
Caldy BTa 149
Calwich A 355–6
Cambridge, St Edmund G 520
Cambridge, St Radegund NB 548
Cammeringham P 495–6
Campsey Ash NA 548–9
Cannington NB 549
Canons Ashby A 356–7
Canonsleigh A 357–8
Canonsleigh NA 549–50

Canterbury, Christ Church cathedral priory B 27–8
Canterbury, Holy Sepulchre NB 550
Canterbury, St Augustine B 28–30
Canterbury, St Gregory A 358
Canwell B 30–1
Cardiff B 95
Cardigan B 95
Carham A 358–9
Carisbrooke Ba 149–50
Carlisle A 359–60
Carmarthen A 360–1
Carrow, see Norwich, St Mary
Cartmel A 361
Castle Acre BC 223–5
Castle Hedingham NB 551
Catesby NC 551–3
Cathale A 361
Catley NG 520–1
Cerne B 31–2
Chacombe A 362
Charley A 362–3
Charlton P 496
Chatteris NB 553–4
Chepstow B(a) 151
Chertsey B 32
Cheshunt NB 554
Chester, St Mary NB 554–5
Chester, St Werburgh B 32–4
Chetwode A 363–4
Chicksands NG 521
Chipley A 364
Chirbury A 364–5
Christchurch (Twynham) A 365–7
Church Gresley A 367
Church Preen BC 225
Cirencester A 367–8
Clatford Ba 151
Clattercote G 521–2
Cleeve C 271–2
Clementhorpe, see York, St Clement
Clerkenwell, see London, Clerkenwell
Clifford BC 225–6
Cockerham A 369
Cockersand P 496–7
Cogges Ba 151–2
Coggeshall C 272
Colchester, St Botolph A 369
Colchester, St John B 34–5
Cold Norton A 369–70
Colne, see Earls Colne

Colsterworth A 332
Combe C 272–3
Combermere C 273–4
Combwell A 370–1
Conishead A 371–2
Conway C 274–5
Cook Hill NC 555
Cornworthy NA 555
Corsham Ba 152
Cottingham, see Haltemprice
Covenham Ba 152–3
Coventry cathedral priory B 35–6
Coverham P 497–8
Cowick B(a) 153–4
Coxford A 372–3
Crabhouse NA 556
Cranborne B 95–6
Cranwell NA 556
Craswell BG 256–7
Creake, see North Creake
Creeting Ba 154
Crowland B 36–7
Croxden C 275–6
Croxton Kerrial P 498
Cwmhir, see Abbey Cwmhir
Cymmer C 276

Dale P 499
Darenth B 96
Darington NB 556
Darley A 373–4
Darnhall C 276, 317
Daventry BC 226
Debden ?Ba 154
Deeping B 96
Deerhurst B(a) 155–7
Derby, Kingsmead NB 556–7
Derby, St James BC 226–7
Dereham, West, see West Dereham
Dieulacres C 276–7
Dodford A 374
Dodlinch, see Woodspring
Dodnash A 374–5
Dorchester A 375
Dore, see Abbey Dore
Dover B 96–8
Drax A 375–6
Dudley BC 227
Dunkeswell C 277–8
Dunmow, see Little Dunmow
Dunstable A 376–7
Dunster B 98–9

Dunwich Ba 157
Durford P 500
Durham cathedral priory B 37–40

Earls Colne B 99
Easby P 500–1
Easebourne NB/NA 557
Easton T 532
Ecclesfield Ba 157–8
Edington AB 535
Edith Weston Ba 158
Egglestone P 501–2
Ellerton-in-Swaledale NC 557
Ellerton on Spalding Moor G 522
Ellingham Ba 158–9
Elsham A 377–8
Elstow NB 557–9
Ely cathedral priory B 40–1
Esholt NC 559
Everdon Ba 159
Evesham B 41–3
Ewenny B 99–100
Ewyas Harold B 100
Exeter, St James BC 228–9
Exeter, St Nicholas B 100–1
Eye B(a) 159–60
Eynsham B 43–4

Farewell NB 559–60
Farleigh, see Monkton Farleigh
Farne B 101–2
Faversham B 44–5
Felixstowe B 102–3
Felley A 378–9
Ferriby, see North Ferriby
Field Dalling C 291
Finchale B 103–4
Fineshade A 379–80
Flamstead NB 560–1
Flanesford A 380
Flaxley C 278
Flitcham A 380
Flixton NA 561
Folkestone B(a) 160–1
Forde C 278–9
Fordham G 522
Fosse NC 561–2
Foukeholme NB 562
Fountains C 279–81
Frampton Ba 161
Freiston B 104–5

Frithelstock A 380–1
Furness C 281–2

Garendon C 282–3
Glastonbury B 46–7
Gloucester, St Oswald A 381–2
Gloucester, St Peter B 47–9
Godstow NB 562–3
Gokewell NC 563–4
Goldcliff B(a) 162–3
Goring NA 564–5
Grace Dieu C 283–4
Grace Dieu NA 565–6
Grafton Regis A 382–3
Great Bricett A 383
Great Malvern B 105–7
Great Massingham A 383–4
Greenfield NC 566–7
Gresley, see Church Gresley
Grimsby, St Leonard NA 567
Grosmont BG 257
Grovebury BFa 163–4
Guisborough A 384–5
Guyzance NP 537

Hagnaby P 502–3
Hailes C 284
Haliwell, see London, Haliwell
Haltemprice A 385
Halywell A 327
Hamble BTa 164–5
Hampole NC 567–8
Handale NC 568
Hardham A 385–6
Harmondsworth Ba 165
Harrold NA 569
Hartland A 386
Hastings A 386–7
Hatfield Peverel B 107
Hatfield Regis B(a) 165–6
Haugham Ba 166–7
Haughmond A 387–8
Haverford West A 388
Haverholme NG 522–3
Hayling Ba 167
Headley Ba 167
Healaugh Park A 388–9
Hedingham, see Castle Hedingham
Hempton A 389
Henes B 107–8

Henwood NB 569–70
Hereford B 108–9
Herringfleet A 390
Hertford, Holy Trinity T 532
Hertford, St Mary B 109–10
Hexham A 390–1
Heynings NC 570–1
Hickling A 391–2
Higham NB 571
Hinchingbrooke NB 572
Hinckley Ba 168–9
Hinton CA 325
Hirst A 392
Hitchin G 523
Holbeck Ba 169
Holland Bridge, see Bridge End
Holm, see Sleves Holm
Holm Cultram C 284–5
Holme, see Steep Holme
Holme East BC 229
Holy Island B 110–12
Holystone NA 572–3
Hood A 327
Horkesley BC 229–30
Hornby P 504
Horsham St Faith B(a) 169–70
Horsley Ba 170–1
Horsley A 392–3
Horton B 112
Horton, see Monks Horton
Hough A 393–4
Hounslow T 532–3
Hoxne B 112–13
Hull, see Kingston upon Hull
Hulme, see St Benet of Hulme
Hulton C 285–6
Humberston B 49
Huntingdon A 394–5
Huntingdon, St James, see Hinchingbrooke
Hurley B 113–14

Ickleton NB 573
Ilchester ?NA 573
Ingham T 533
Ipplepen A 395
Ipswich, Holy Trinity A 395–6
Ipswich, St Peter and St Paul A 396
Irford, see Orford
Isleham Ba 171, and see Linton
Ivinghoe NB 573–4
Ivychurch A 396–7
Ixworth A 397–8

Jarrow B 114–15
Jervaulx C 286–7

Keldholme NC 574–5
Kenilworth A 398–9
Kersal BC 230
Kersey A 399–400
Kerswell BC 230–1
Keynsham A 400
Kidwelly B 115
Kilburn NB 575
Kilpeck B 115
King's Lynn B 116
Kingston upon Hull CA 325
Kingswood C 287–8
Kington St Michael NB 575–6
Kinley 536
Kirby, see Monks Kirby
Kirkby Bellars A 400–1
Kirkham A 401–2
Kirklees NC 576–7
Kirkstall C 288–9
Kirkstead C 289–90
Knaresborough T 533
Kyme A 402–3

Lacock NA 577–8
Lamanna B 116
Lambley NB 578
Lancaster Ba 171–2
Lanercost A 403
Langdon P 504–5
Langley NB 578–9
Langley P 505
Lanthony, see Llanthony
Lapley Ba 172–3
Latton A 404
Launceston A 404–5
Launde A 405–6
Lavendon P 506
Leeds A 406–7
Legbourne NC 579–80
Leicester A 407–8
Leighs A 408–9
Leiston P 506–7
Lenton BC 231–3
Leominster B 116–17
Leonard Stanley B 117
Lessness A 409–10
Letheringham A 410
Lewes BC 233–5
Lewisham Ba 173

Lillechurch, *see* Higham
Lilleshall A 410–12
Limebrook NA 580
Lincoln, St Katherine G 523–4
Lincoln, St Mary Magdalen B 118
Lindisfarne, *see* Holy Island
Linton Ba 173–4
Little Dunmow A 412–13
Little Malvern B 118–19
Little Marlow NB 581
Littlemore NB 581–2
Livers Ocle Ba 174–5
Llangennith Ba 175
Llangua Ba 175
Llanllugan NC 537
Llanllyr NC 582
Llantarnam C 290
Llanthony Prima A 413–14
Llanthony Secunda A 414–15
Loders Ba 175–6
London, Charterhouse CA 325–6
London, Clerkenwell NA 582–3
London, Haliwell NA 583–4
London, Holy Trinity Aldgate A 415–16
London, St Bartholomew A 417
London, St Helen's and Holy Cross NB 584–5
London, St Mary Graces C 290–1
Long Bennington C 291
Longleat A 417–18
Louth Park C 291–2
Luffield B 49–51
Lyminster NB 585
Lynn, *see* King's Lynn
Lytham B 119–20

Maiden Bradley A 418–19
Malling NB 585–6
Malmesbury B 51–2
Malpas BC 235
Malton G 524–5
Malvern, *see* Great Malvern, Little Malvern
Margam C 292
Marham NC 586
Markby A 419
Markyate NB 586–7
Marlborough G 525
Marlow, *see* Little Marlow
Marmont G 525
Marrick NB 587–8
Marsh Barton A 327
Marton A 419–21
Massingham, Great, *see* Great Massingham

Mattersey G 525–6
Maxstoke A 421
Meaux C 292–4
Medmenham C 294
Mendham BC 235–6
Merevale C 294–5
Mersea, *see* West Mersea
Merton A 421–3
Michelham A 423–4
Middlesborough B 121
Milton B 52–3
Minster Ba 176–7
Minster in Sheppey NB/NA? 588
Minster Lovell Ba 177
Minting Ba 178
Missenden A 424–5
Moatenden T 533
Mobberley A 425
Modbury B(a) 178–9
Monk Bretton B 53
Monk Bretton BC 236
Monk Sherborne Ba 179–80
Monks Horton BC 236–7
Monks Kirby Ba 180–2
Monkton, *see* Winterborn Monkton
Monkton Farleigh BC 237–8
Monkwearmouth B 121–2
Monmouth B(a) 182
Montacute BC 238–41
Morville B 122
Mottisfont A 425–6
Mountjoy A 426–7
Moxby NB/NA 588–9
Much Wenlock BC 241–2
Muchelney B 53–4
Mullicourt B 54–5

Neasham NB 589
Neath C 295
Netley C 295–6
Newark A 427–8
Newbo P 507
Newburgh A 428–9
Newcastle-upon-Tyne (Holy Trinity) T 534
Newcastle-upon-Tyne, St Bartholomew NB 589–90
Newenham C 296–8
Newent Ba 182–3
Newhouse P 507–8
Newminster C 298–9
Newnham A 429–31
Newstead (in Sherwood) A 431–2

Newstead by Stamford A 432-3
Newstead-on-Ancholme G 526
Newton Longville BC 242-3
Nocton Park A 433-4
Norman's Burrow BC 243
North Creake A 434-5
North Ferriby A 435-6
North Ormsby NG 526
Northampton, St Andrew BC 243-5
Northampton, St James A 436-7
Northampton, St Mary de la Pré NBC 590-1
Norton A 437-8
Norton, see also Cold Norton
Norwich, Holy Trinity cathedral priory B 55-6
Norwich, St Leonard B 122
Norwich, St Mary (Carrow) NB 591-2
Nostell A 438-9
Notley A 440-1
Nottingham (Basford) BC 219
Nun Appleton NC 592-3
Nun Cotham NC 593-4
Nun Keeling NB 594
Nun Monkton NB 594-5
Nunburnholme NB 595
Nuneaton NBF 595-7

Ogbourne St George Ba 183-5
Oldbury NB 597
Orford (or Irford) NP 597
Osney A 441-2
Otterton Ba 185-6
Owston A 442-3
Oxford (Durham cell, later College) B 122-3
Oxford (Gloucester cell, later College) B 123
Oxford, Holy Trinity T 534
Oxford, St Frideswide A 443-5

Panfield Ba 186-7
Patrixbourne A 446
Pembroke B(a) 187
Penmon A 446
Pentney A 446-7
Penwortham B 123-4
Pershore B 56-7
Peterborough B 57-9
Peterstone A 447
Pill BTa 187
Pilton B 124
Pinley NC 597-8
Pipewell C 299-300
Plympton A 447-8
Polesworth NB 598-9
Polsloe NB 599-600

Pontefract BC 246-7
Poughley A 448-9
Poulton G 527
Preen, see Church Preen
Prittlewell BC 247-9
Puffin Island A 449
Pynham by Arundel A 449-50

Quarr C 300

Ramsey B 59-60
Ranton A 450
Ratlinghope A 450
Ravendale, West, see West Ravendale
Ravenstone A 450-1
Ravenstonedale G 527
Reading B 60-1
Redbourn B 124
Redlingfield NB 600
Reigate A 451-2
Repton A 452
Revesby C 301
Rewley C 301
Richmond B 124-5
Rievaulx C 302-3
Robertsbridge C 303-4
Rocester A 452-3
Roche C 304-5
Rochester B 61-3
Romsey NB 600-1
Rosedale NC 601-2
Roseland, see St Anthony in Roseland
Rothwell NA 602
Rowney NB 602-3
Royston A 454
Rufford C 305-6
Ruislip Ba 188
Rumburgh B 125-6
Runcton Ba 188
Rusper NB 603
Ruthin AB 535

St Albans B 63-4
St Anthony in Roseland A 454
St Bees B 127
St Benet of Hulme B 64-5
St Carrok BC 249
St Clears BC 249-50
St Cross BTa 188
St Denys A 454-5
St Dogmells BTa 188-9
St Frideswide, see Oxford, St Frideswide
St German's A 455-6

St Helen's BC 250
St Ives B 128
St Mary de Pré NB 603–4
St Michael's Mount Ba 189
St Neots B(a) 190–1
St Olave's, see Herringfleet
St Osyth A 456–7
St Radegund P 508–9
St Radegund, see Cambridge
Sallay C 306–7
Sandaleford A 457
Sandtoft B 107–8
Sandwell B 65–6
Sawtry C 307–8
Scarborough C 308
Scilly B 128
Selborne A 457–8
Selby B 66–8
Sele Ba 191–2
Sempringham NG 527–8
Seton NB 537
Sewardsley NC 604
Shaftesbury NB 604–6
Shap P 509–10
Shelford A 458–9
Sherborne B 68–9
Sherborne, see Monk Sherborne
Shouldham NG 529
Shrewsbury B 69–71
Shulbred A 459
Sibton C 308–9
Sinningthwaite NC 606–7
Sixhills NG 529–30
Skewkirk A 459
Sleves Holm BC 251
Snaith B 128
Snape B 128–9
Snelshall B 71
Sopwell NB 607
Southwark A 460–1
Southwick A 461–2
Spalding B(a) 192–3
Spinney A 462
Sporle Ba 193–4
Stafford A 462–3
Stainfield NB 607–8
Stamford, St Leonard B 129–31
Stamford, St Mary and St Michael NB 608–10
Standon Ba 194
Stanley C 309–11
Stanley, see Leonard Stanley
Stanlow, see Whalley
Stansgate BC 251

Stavordale A 463–4
Steep Holme A 464
Steventon Ba 194
Stixwould NC 610–11
Stogursey Ba 194–5
Stoke by Clare Ba 195–6
Stone A 464
Stoneleigh C 311–12
Stonely A 464–5
Strata Florida C 312–13
Strata Marcella C 313
Stratfield Saye Ba 196–7
Stratford-at-Bow NB 612
Stratford Langthorne C 313–14
Studley A 465–6
Studley NB 612
Sudbury B 131
Sulby P 510–11
Swaffham Bulbeck NB 613
Swavesey Ba 197–8
Swine NC 613–14
Swineshead C 314–15

Takeley Ba 198
Talley P 511
Tandridge A 466
Tarrant Kaines NC 614–15
Taunton A 466–7
Tavistock B 71–3
Tewkesbury B 73–4
Thame C 315
Thelsford A 467
Thelsford T 534
Thetford, Holy Sepulchre A 467–8
Thetford, St George and St Gregory NB 615
Thetford, St Mary BC 251–3
Thicket NB 615–16
Thoby A 468
Thorney B 74–6
Thornholme A 468–9
Thornton Curtis A 469–70
Thremhall A 470–1
Throwley Ba 198–9
Thurgarton A 471–2
Tickford B(a) 199–201
Tickhill B 131
Tilty C 315–16
Tintern C 316–17
Tiptree A 472–3
Titchfield P 511–12
Titley BTa 201
Tockwith, see Skewkirk
Toft Monks Ba 201–2

Tonbridge A 473
Torksey A 473-4
Torre P 512-13
Tortington A 475
Totnes B(a) 202-3
Totnes T 534
Tregoney A 475
Trentham A 475-6
Tupholme P 513-14
Tutbury B(a) 203-4
Twynham, *see* Christchurch
Tynemouth B 131-3
Tywardreath B(a) 204-5

Ulverscroft A 476-7
Upavon Ba 205
Upchurch P 514
Upholland B 76
Usk NB 616

Vale Royal C 317-18
Valle Crucis C 318
Vaudey C 319

Walden B 76-7
Wallingford B 133-4
Wallingwells NB 616
Wallknoll, *see* Newcastle-upon-Tyne
Walsingham A 477-8
Waltham A 478-9
Wangford BC 253
Wardon C 319-20
Ware Ba 205-7
Wareham Ba 207
Warminghurst Ba 208
Warmington Ba 208
Warter A 479-80
Warwick A 480-1
Wath Ba 208
Watton NG 530-1
Waverley C 320-1
Wearmouth, *see* Monkwearmouth
Weedon Beck Ba 208
Weedon Lois Ba 208-10
Welbeck P 514-15
Well Ba 186-7
Wellow A 481-3
Wendling P 515-16
Wenlock, *see* Much Wenlock
West Dereham P 516-17
West Mersea Ba 210
West Ravendale P 517-18

Westacre A 483
Westminster B 77-9
Westwood NBF 616-17
Wetheral B 134-5
Weybourne A 484
Weybridge A 484
Whalley C 321-3
Wherwell NB 617-18
Whistones NC 618
Whitby B 79-80
Whitland C 323
Wigmore A 484-5
Wilberfoss NB 619
Wilkeswood 536
Wilmington Ba 211
Wilsford Ba 211-13
Wilton NB 619-20
Winchcombe B 80-1
Winchester, Hyde B 81-2
Winchester, St Mary NB 620-1
Winchester cathedral priory B 82-4
Wing Ba 213
Winghale Ba 213
Winterborn Monkton BC 253-4
Wintney NC 621-2
Witham CA 326
Wix NB 622-3
Woburn C 323-4
Wolston Ba 213-14
Wombridge A 485-6
Woodbridge A 486
Woodkirk A 486
Woodspring A 487
Wootton Wawen Ba 214-16
Worcester cathedral priory B 84-6
Worcester, *see also* Whistones
Worksop A 487-8
Wormegay A 488
Wormsley A 488-9
Wothorpe NB 623-4
Wroxall NB 624-5
Wroxton A 489-90
Wykeham NC 625
Wymondham B 135-6
Wymondley A 490

Yarmouth B 136-7
Yedingham NB 625-6
York, Holy Trinity B(a) 216-18
York, St Andrew G 531
York, St Clement NB 626
York, St Mary B 86-8

Printed in the United Kingdom
by Lightning Source UK Ltd.
113371UKS00001B/1-15

9 780521 028486